Koren Talmud Bavli
THE NOÉ EDITION

MENAḤOT · PART ONE

Shefa

KOREN

תלמוד בבלי

KOREN TALMUD BAVLI

THE NOÉ EDITION

מנחות א

MENAḤOT · PART ONE

COMMENTARY BY

Rabbi Adin Even-Israel
Steinsaltz

EDITOR-IN-CHIEF

Rabbi Dr Tzvi Hersh Weinreb

EXECUTIVE EDITOR

Rabbi Joshua Schreier

SHEFA FOUNDATION
KOREN PUBLISHERS JERUSALEM

MATANEL
FOUNDATION
GRANTED TO GIVE

Supported by the Matanel Foundation

Koren Talmud Bavli, The Noé Edition
Volume 35: Tractate Menaḥot, Part One

Standard Size Color Edition, ISBN 978 965 301 596 8

First Hebrew/English Edition, 2018

Koren Publishers Jerusalem Ltd.
PO Box 4044, Jerusalem 9104001, ISRAEL
PO Box 8531, New Milford, CT 06776, USA
www.korenpub.com

Shefa Foundation

Shefa Foundation is the parent organization of institutions established by Rabbi Adin Even-Israel Steinsaltz

PO Box 45187, Jerusalem 91450 ISRAEL
Telephone: +972 2 646 0900, Fax +972 2 624 9454
www.hashefa.co.il

Hardcover design by Ben Gasner
Cover image courtesy of The Temple Institute

הִנֵּה יָמִים בָּאִים, נְאֻם אֲדֹנָי יֱהוִה, וְהִשְׁלַחְתִּי רָעָב בָּאָרֶץ,
לֹא־רָעָב לַלֶּחֶם וְלֹא־צָמָא לַמַּיִם, כִּי אִם־לִשְׁמֹעַ אֵת דִּבְרֵי יהוה.

Behold, days are coming – says the Lord God –
I will send a hunger to the land, not a hunger for bread
nor a thirst for water, but to hear the words of the Lord.

(Amos 8:11)

The Noé edition of the Koren Talmud Bavli
with the commentary of Rabbi Adin Even-Israel Steinsaltz
is dedicated to all those who open its cover
to quench their thirst for Jewish knowledge,
in our generation of Torah renaissance.

This beautiful edition is for the young, the aged,
the novice and the savant alike,
as it unites the depth of Torah knowledge
with the best of academic scholarship.

Within its exquisite and vibrant pages,
words become worlds.

It will claim its place in the library of classics,
in the bookcases of the Beit Midrash,
the classrooms of our schools,
and in the offices of professionals and businesspeople
who carve out precious time to grapple with its timeless wisdom.

For the Student and the Scholar

DEDICATED BY LEO AND SUE NOÉ

Shefa

Managing Editor

Rabbi Jason Rappoport

Senior Content Editor

Rabbi Dr. Shalom Z. Berger

Editors

Rabbi Dr. Joshua Amaru, *Coordinating Editor*
Rabbi Yehoshua Duker, *Final Editor*
Rabbi Yedidya Naveh, *Content Curator*
Rabbi Avishai Magence, *Content Curator*
Menucha Chwat
Rabbi Dov Foxbrunner
Rabbi Yonatan Shai Freedman
Raphael Friedman
Rabbi Ayal Geffon
Nechama Greenberg
Rabbi Alan Haber
Noam Harris
Yisrael Kalker
Rabbi Tzvi Chaim Kaye
Rabbi Yonatan Kohn
Rabbi Adin Krohn
Elisha Loewenstern
Rabbi Eli Ozarowski
Rabbi David Sedley
Rabbi Michael Siev
Avi Steinhart
Rabbi Yitzchak Twersky

Hebrew Edition Editors

Rabbi Yehonatan Eliav
Rabbi Avraham Gelbstein
Rabbi Gershon Kitsis

Copy Editors

Aliza Israel, *Coordinator*
Ita Olesker
Debbie Ismailoff
Shira Finson
Ilana Sobel
Deena Nataf
Eliana Kurlantzick Yorav
Erica Hirsch Edvi
Sara Henna Dahan
Oritt Sinclair

Language Consultants

Dr. Stéphanie E. Binder, *Greek & Latin*
Rabbi Yaakov Hoffman, *Arabic*
Dr. Shai Secunda, *Persian*
Shira Shmidman, *Aramaic*

KOREN

Design & Typesetting

Dena Landowne Bailey, *Typesetting*
Tomi Mager, *Typesetting*
Tani Bayer, *Jacket Design*
Raphaël Freeman, *Design & Typography*

Images

Rabbi Eliahu Misgav, *Illustration & Image Acquisition*
Daniel Gdalevich, *Illustration & Image Acquisition*

He who honors his past receives blessings for the future

In memory of my parents:

Wolff Kadischevitz Klabin (זאב בן ישראל)
Rose Haas Klabin (רחל בת אברהם)

With blessings for my children:

Alberto Klabin (אברהם בן ישראל)
Mauricio Klabin (משה בן ישראל ז״ל)
Leonardo Klabin (אריה בן ישראל)
Stela Klabin (אסתר בת ישראל)
Maria Klabin (מרים בת ישראל)
Dan Klabin (דן בן ישראל)
Gabriel Klabin (גבריאל זאב בן ישראל)

Israel Klabin

Contents

For the vocalized Vilna Shas layout, please open as a Hebrew book.

Haskama

Rabbi Moshe Feinstein

RABBI MOSES FEINSTEIN
455 F. D. R. DRIVE
New York N. Y. 10002
OREgon 7-1222

משה פיינשטיין
ר"ם תפארת ירושלים
בנוא יארק

ב"ה

הנה ראיתי הפירוש החשוב של הרב הגאון מוהר"ר עדין שטיינזלץ שליט"א מעיה"ק ירושלים, על מסכתות ביצה ור"ה. באמת כבר ידוע לי פירושו של הרה"ג הנ"ל על מסכתות מתלמוד בבלי, וכבר כתבתי מכתב הסכמה עליהם. ובאתי בזה רק להדגיש מחדש איך שהפירושים של הרה"ג הנ"ל, שכולל פירוש חדש על הגמרא עצמו וגם פירוש שיש בו סיכום להלכה מהנידונים שבגמרא, נוסף לעוד כמה חלקים, הם באמת עבודה גדולה, שיכולים להיות לתועלת לא רק לאלו שכבר מורגלים בלמוד הגמרא, ורוצים להעמק יותר, אלא גם לאלו שמתחילים ללמוד, להדריכם בדרכי התורה איך להבין ולהעמיק בים התלמוד.

והריני מברך להרה"ג הנ"ל שיצליחהו השי"ת בספריו אלו ושיזכה לחבר עוד ספרים, להגדיל תורה ולהאדירה, לתפארת השם ותורתו.

ועל זה באתי על החתום לכבוד התורה ביום ז' לחודש אייר תשמ"ג.

משה פיינשטיין

משה פיינשטיין

…These new commentaries – which include a new interpretation of the Talmud, a halakhic summary of the debated issues, and various other sections – are a truly outstanding work; they can be of great benefit not only to those familiar with talmudic study who seek to deepen their understanding, but also to those who are just beginning to learn, guiding them through the pathways of the Torah and teaching them how to delve into the sea of the Talmud.

I would like to offer my blessing to this learned scholar. May the Holy One grant him success with these volumes and may he merit to write many more, to enhance the greatness of Torah, and bring glory to God and His word…

Rabbi Moshe Feinstein
New York, 7 Adar 5743

ר' משה פיינשטיין שליט"א

הנה ראיתי את מסכת אחת מהש"ס שנקד אותה וגם צייר צורות הצמחים וכדומה מדברים שלא ידוע לכמה אנשים הרה"ג ר' עדין שטיינזלץ מירושלים שליט"א וגם הוסיף שם בגליון פירושים וחידושים וניכר שהוא ת"ח וראויין לעיין בהם ת"ח ובני הישיבה וטוב גם לקנותם בבתי כנסיות ובבתי מדרשות שיש שיהיו להם לתועלת. — ועל זה באתי עה"ח ג' אדר ב' תש"ל.

נאם משה פיינשטיין
ר"מ תפארת ירושלים, ניו־יורק, ארה"ב

I have seen one tractate from the Talmud to which the great scholar Rabbi Adin Steinsaltz שליט"א has added *nikkud* (vowels) and illustrations to explain that which is unknown to many people; he has also added interpretations and innovations, and is evidently a *talmid ḥakham*. *Talmidei ḥakhamim* and yeshiva students ought to study these volumes, and synagogues and *batei midrash* would do well to purchase them, as they may find them useful.

Rabbi Moshe Feinstein
New York, Adar 5730

Haskama

Rabbi Menachem Mendel Schneerson

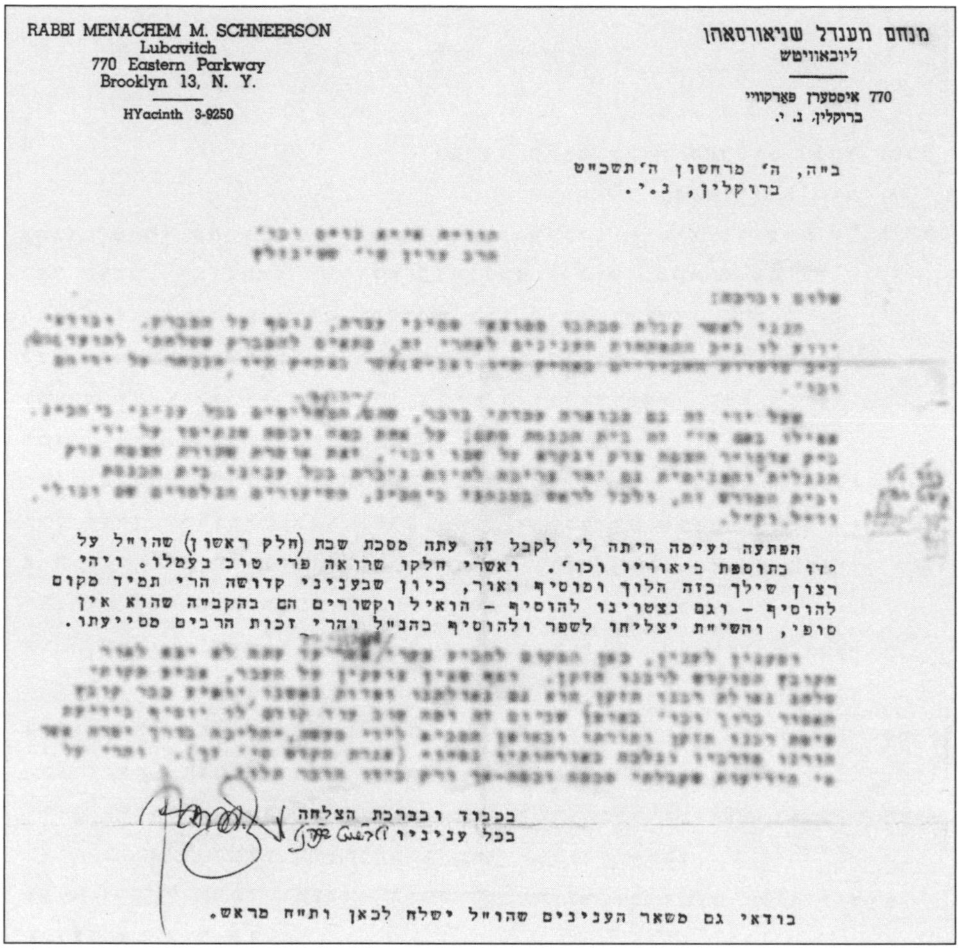

RABBI MENACHEM M. SCHNEERSON
Lubavitch
770 Eastern Parkway
Brooklyn 13, N. Y.
HYacinth 3-9250

מנחם מענדל שניאורסאהן
ליובאוויטש
770 איסטערן פארקוויי
ברוקלין, נ. י.

ב"ה, ה' מרחשון ה'תשכ"ט
ברוקלין, נ.י.

הפתעה נעימה היתה לי לקבל זה עתה מסכת שבת (חלק ראשון) שהו"ל על ידו בתוספת ביאוריו וכו'. ואשרי חלקו שרואה פרי טוב בעמלו. ויהי רצון שילך בזה הלוך ומוסיף ואור, כיון שבעניני קדושה הרי תמיד מקום להוסיף - וגם נצטוינו להוסיף - הואיל וקשורים הם בהקב"ה שהוא אין סופי, והשי"ת יצליחו לשפר ולהוסיף בהנ"ל והרי זכות הרבים מסייעתו.

בכבוד ובברכת הצלחה
בכל עניניו

בודאי גם משאר הענינים שהו"ל ישלח לכאן ות"ח מראש.

…I have just had the pleasant surprise of receiving tractate *Shabbat* (part one), which has been published by [Rabbi Steinsaltz] along with his explanations, etc. Happy is the man who sees good fruits from his labors. May he continue in this path and increase light, for in the matters of holiness there is always room to add – and we have been commanded to add – for they are linked to the Holy One, Blessed be He, Who is infinite. And may the Holy One grant him success to improve and enhance this work, since the greater good strengthens his hand…

Rabbi Menachem Mendel Schneerson
The Lubavitcher Rebbe
Brooklyn, 5 Marḥeshvan 5729

Haskama

Rabbi Moshe Zvi Neria

הסכמה של הרב משה צבי נריה

ב"ה

"ושמעו ביום ההוא החרשים דברי ספר"

(ישעי' כט' יח')

תרגום ספרי קדמונים לשפת דורות אחרונים – היא משימתם של חכמי דור ודור. ובישראל שמצוות "ושננתם לבניך" מקיפה את כל חלקי האומה, ודאי שהיתה זאת המשימה בכל עידן ועידן.

בכל דור כך, ובדורנו אשר רבים בו הקרובים שנתרחקו וחוזרים ומתקרבים – לא כל שכן. כי רבים היום האומרים "מי ישקנו מים מבאר" התלמוד, ומועטים הם הדולים ומשקים.

ראוי אפוא להערכה מיוחדת נסיונו המבורך של הצעיר המופלא, הרב עדין שטינזלץ, לפרש פרקי-תלמוד בהסברה מורחבת-תמציתית, אשר נוסף על הפרוש המלולי והעניני הוא מעלה גם את ההגיון של הדברים ומתרגמת אותם לשפת-המושגים של בן-דורנו.

דומה שכל הנגשים אל חומר למודי מתוך רצון להבינו – התלמיד החרוץ והמבוגר המשכיל – לא יתקלו בשום קושי בבואם ללמוד סוגיא תלמודית לפי פרוש זה. ולא עוד אלא שיש לקוות כי ההסברה הגיונית תעמידם מיד על טוב-הטעם [redacted] של דף-הגמרא, והם ימשכו יותר ויותר אל הלמוד העיוני הזה אשר טובי המוחות בישראל לנו בעומקו, ואשר ממנו פינה, ממנו יתד לבנין חיינו.

נועם ד' על המפרש הנמרץ להמשיך במפעלו, וברוכים כל העוזרים להוצאתו לאור-עולם.

ביקר אורייתא

(חתימה)

The translation of the books of our past into the language of the present – this was the task of the sages of every generation. And in Israel, where the command to "teach them repeatedly to your children" applies to all parts of the nation, it was certainly the task of every era. This is true for every generation, and in our time – when many of those who have strayed far are once again drawing near – all the more so. For many today say, "Who will let us drink from the well" of Talmud, and few are those who offer up the waters to drink.

We must, therefore, particularly commend the blessed endeavor of Rabbi Adin Steinsaltz to explain the chapters of the Talmud in this extensive yet succinct commentary, which, in addition to its literal interpretation of the text, also explicates the latter's underlying logic and translates it into the language of our generation.

It appears that all those who seek to study Talmud – the diligent student and the learned adult – will have no difficulty understanding when using this commentary. Moreover, we may hope that the logical explanation will reveal to them the beauty of the talmudic page, and they will be drawn deeper and deeper into the intellectual pursuit which has engaged the best Jewish minds, and which serves as the cornerstone of our very lives…

Rabbi Moshe Zvi Neria

 THIS HASKAMA REFERS TO THE ORIGINAL HEBREW EDITION OF THE STEINSALTZ TALMUD, UPON WHICH THIS VOLUME IS BASED

Haskama

Rabbi Mordechai Eliyahu

ב"ה

MORDECHAI ELIAHU
FORMER CHIEF RABBI OF ISRAEL & RICHON LEZION

מרדכי אליהו
ראשון לציון והרב הראשי לישראל לשעבר

ז' בתשרי תשנ"ד
נד.5-137

מכתב ברכה

הגמרא בעירובין כ"א: אומרת: דרש רבא מאי דכתיב ויותר שהיה קהלת חכם, עוד לימד דעת את העם - ואזן וחקר תקן משלים הרבה". לימד דעת את העם - קבע כיצד לקרוא פסוק וסימנים בין תיבות המקרא וממשיכה הגמרא ואומרת: אמר עולא אמר ר' אליעזר בתחילה היתה תורה דומה לכפיפה שאין לה אזנים עד שבא שלמה ועשה לה אזנים". וכדברי רש"י שם: "וע"י כך אוחזין ישראל במצוות שנתרחקו מן העבירה כדרך שנוח לאחוז בכלי שיש לו בית יד וכו' (ערובין כ"א, י').

דברים מעין אלו אפשר לאמר על האי גברא יקירא, על איש מורם מעם, משכמו ומעלה בתורה ובמידות. ויותר ממה שעשה בתורה שבע"פ עושה בתורה שבכתב - מלמד דעת את העם. ולא זו בלבד אלא גם עושה אזנים לתורה, היא תורת התלמוד שהוא חתום וסתום בפני רבים. ורק מעט מזער מבני עליה שהם מועטים ומי שלומד בישיבה יכל כיום ללמוד בש"ס ולהבין מה שלפניו, ואף שיש לנו פירוש רש"י, עדין לא הכל ממשמשין בו. עד שקם הרב הגדול מעוז ומגדול הרה"ג ר' **עדין שטיינזלץ** שליט"א ועשה אזנים לתורה, שאפשר לאחוז גמרא ביד וללמוד, ואפי' לפשוטי העם ועשה פרושים ושם אותם בצד הארון, פרושים נאים בשפה ברורה ונעימה דבר דבור על אופניו. ועם הסברים וציורים להבין ולהשכיל, כדי שמי שרוצה לקרבה אל מלאכת ה' ללמוד יכל לעשות זאת.

ועיני ראו ולא זר שבשיעורי תורה בגמרא הרבה באים עם גמרות בידם ואלה שבאים עם "פירוש הרב שטיינזלץ לתלמוד הבבלי" הם מוכנים ומבינים טוב יותר. כי כבר יש להם הקדמה מפרושיו ומבאוריו.
ואמינא לפועלו יישר ומן שמיא זכו ליה ללמד דעת את העם .

ויהי רצון שחפץ בידו יצלח, וכל אשר יפנה ישכיל ויצליח, ויזכה להגדיל תורה ולהאדירה, ויוסיף לנו עוד גמרות מבוארות כהנה וכהנה עד לסיומו , "וישראל עושה חיל".

ובזכות לימוד תורה ואני זאת בריתי וכו', ובא לציון גואל, בב"א.

מרדכי אליהו
ראשון לציון הרב הראשי לישראל לשעבר

The Talmud in *Eruvin* 21b states: Rava continued to interpret verses homiletically. What is the meaning of the verse: "And besides being wise, Kohelet also taught the people knowledge; and he weighed, and sought out, and set in order many proverbs" (Ecclesiastes 12:9)? He explains: He taught the people knowledge; he taught it with the accentuation marks in the Torah, and explained each matter by means of another matter similar to it. And he weighed [*izen*], and sought out, and set in order many proverbs; Ulla said that Rabbi Eliezer said: At first the Torah was like a basket without handles [*oznayim*] until Solomon came and made handles for it. And as Rashi there explains: And thus were Israel able to grasp the mitzvot and distance themselves from transgressions – just as a vessel with handles is easily held, etc.

Such things may be said of this beloved and eminent man, a great sage of Torah and of virtue. And far more than he has done with the Oral Torah, he does with the Written Torah – teaching the people knowledge. And beyond that, he also affixes handles to the Torah, i.e., to the Talmud, which is obscure and difficult for many. Only the intellectual elite, which are a precious few, and those who study in yeshiva, can today learn the Talmud and understand what it says – and even though we have Rashi, still not everyone uses him. But now the great scholar Rabbi Adin Steinsaltz שליט"א has come and affixed handles to the Torah, allowing the Talmud to be held and studied, even by simple men. And he has composed a commentary alongside the text, a fine commentary in clear, comprehensible language, "a word fitly spoken" with explanations and illustrations, so that all those who seek to study the work of God can do so.

Rabbi Mordechai Eliyahu
Former Chief Rabbi of Israel, 7 Tishrei 5754

Message from Rabbi Adin Even-Israel Steinsaltz

The Talmud is the cornerstone of Jewish culture. True, our culture originated in the Bible and has branched out in directions besides the Talmud, yet the latter's influence on Jewish culture is fundamental. Perhaps because it was composed not by a single individual, but rather by hundreds and thousands of Sages in *batei midrash* in an ongoing, millennium-long process, the Talmud expresses the deepest themes and values not only of the Jewish people, but also of the Jewish spirit. As the basic study text for young and old, laymen and learned, the Talmud may be said to embody the historical trajectory of the Jewish soul. It is, therefore, best studied interactively, its subject matter coming together with the student's questions, perplexities, and innovations to form a single intricate weave. In the entire scope of Jewish culture, there is not one area that does not draw from or converse with the Talmud. The study of Talmud is thus the gate through which a Jew enters his life's path.

The *Koren Talmud Bavli* seeks to render the Talmud accessible to the millions of Jews whose mother tongue is English, allowing them to study it, approach it, and perhaps even become one with it.

This project has been carried out and assisted by several people, all of whom have worked tirelessly to turn this vision into an actual set of books to be studied. It is a joyful duty to thank the many partners in this enterprise for their various contributions. Thanks to Koren Publishers Jerusalem, both for the publication of this set and for the design of its very complex graphic layout. Thanks of a different sort are owed to the Shefa Foundation and its director, Rabbi Menachem Even-Israel, for their determination and persistence in setting this goal and reaching it. Many thanks to the translators, editors, and proofreaders for their hard and meticulous work. Thanks to the individuals and organizations that supported this project, chief among them the Matanel Foundation and the Noé family of London. And thanks in advance to all those who will invest their time, hearts, and minds in studying these volumes – to learn, to teach, and to practice.

Rabbi Adin Even-Israel Steinsaltz
Jerusalem 5773

Acknowledgments

We are indeed privileged to dedicate this edition of the *Koren Talmud Bavli* in honor of the generous support of Leo and Sue Noé of London.

The name Noé is synonymous with philanthropy. The family's charitable endeavors span a vast range of educational projects, welfare institutions, and outreach organizations across the globe, with a particular emphasis on the "nurturing of each individual." Among so many other charitable activities, the Noés have been deeply involved with Kisharon, which provides the British Jewish community with vital support for hundreds of people with learning difficulties and their families; they provide steadfast support of SEED, which stands at the forefront of adult Jewish education in the UK, and Kemach, an organization in Israel that "helps Haredi students sustain themselves in dignity," providing both professional and vocational training for the Haredi community in Israel.

The Noés are not simply donors to institutions. They are partners. Donors think of a sum. Partners think of a cause, becoming rigorously and keenly involved, and giving of their time and energy. We are honored that they have chosen to partner with our two organizations, Shefa and Koren Publishers Jerusalem, enabling us to further and deepen learning among all Jews.

Leo and Sue are the proud parents and grandparents of five children and their families. The next generation has been taught by example that with life's gifts come the responsibilities to be active within and contribute to society – both Jewish and non-Jewish – as is consistent with the noblest of Jewish values.

Rabbi Adin Even-Israel Steinsaltz
Matthew Miller, Publisher
Jerusalem 5773

Introduction by the Editor-in-Chief

The publication of tractate *Menaḥot* is another noteworthy achievement for the Koren Talmud Bavli project. With this, the second tractate of *Seder Kodashim*, the Order of Consecrated Items, we take yet another step toward our goal, the completion of a new and unique translation of the Babylonian Talmud.

Presenting the English-speaking world with a translation that possesses all the merits of the original Hebrew work by Rabbi Steinsaltz, the text provides assistance for the beginner of any age who seeks to obtain the necessary skills to become an adept talmudist. Beginning with *Berakhot* and continuing through *Menaḥot*, the team has brought excellence to every aspect of the daunting task of translating Rabbi Adin Even-Israel Steinsaltz's masterful Hebrew translation of the Talmud into English.

Rabbi Steinsaltz's work is much more than a mere translation. It includes a coherent interpretation of the Mishna and the Gemara, and an expansion of the text that provides an array of intriguing marginal notes. Rendering this masterpiece into English called for talents that include biblical and talmudic scholarship, literary skills, linguistic expertise, editorial acumen, graphic and visual creativity, and most of all, teamwork and diligence. Congratulations to every member of the team are in order, and celebration of our achievement is well deserved.

I'd like to take this opportunity to express our gratitude to the Almighty for giving us the strength to persevere at this sacred task for the past several years. These years have been difficult ones for the Jewish people, and especially for those of us who dwell in Eretz Yisrael. But the difficulties have not diminished our ability to succeed in our goals. For that we thank the Master of the Universe.

Students of tractate *Menaḥot* will be both informed and inspired. They will be informed of the centrality of the Holy Temple in our faith tradition, and will learn in detail about the sacrificial rites performed there. They will be inspired by the meticulous care with which those rites were performed and by the attention given to the requirement that the sacrifices be offered with the proper intentions. Although sacrifices are no longer offered in the absence of the Holy Temple, the reader will find contemporary relevance in the passages which discuss the mitzvot of *tzitzit* and *tefilin*, and the rules of priorities in mitzva performance. As always, we consider our efforts successful if the reader comes away from the text a better person, and not just a better-informed person. For it is our contention that Talmud study fosters lifelong ethical development and a profound sensitivity to the needs and concerns of other human beings.

We have now had the opportunity to survey hundreds of responses submitted by our readers. Naturally, these include constructive criticism and reports of errors that are inevitable in such an undertaking. We have systematically preserved such responses so that we can correct them in future editions. Indeed, we have already begun to do so for the initial tractates in our series.

The most exciting result of our survey has been our discovery that "consumers" of Koren Talmud Bavli are a remarkably diverse group. They range from beginners who have never before been exposed to a *blatt gemara*, to accomplished scholars who have completed the study of the entire Talmud more than once. Beginners find our work not only a helpful introduction to Talmud study, but an impetus to the further study of rabbinic texts. Experienced scholars report that our work provides them with unexpected insights and fresh perspectives that enhance their appreciation of texts with which they have long been acquainted.

Tractate *Menaḥot*, part I, is the thirty-fifth volume of the project. Like the preceding volumes, it includes the entire original text, in the traditional configuration and pagination of the famed Vilna edition of the Talmud. This enables the student to follow the core text with the commentaries of Rashi, *Tosafot*, and the customary marginalia. It also provides a clear English translation in contemporary idiom, faithfully based upon the modern Hebrew edition.

At least equal to the linguistic virtues of this edition are the qualities of its graphic design. Rather than intimidate students by confronting them with a page-size block of text, we have divided the page into smaller thematic units. Thus, readers can focus their attention and absorb each discrete discussion before proceeding to the next unit. The design of each page allows for sufficient white space to ease the visual task of reading. The illustrations, one of the most innovative features of the Hebrew edition, have been substantially enhanced and reproduced in color.

The end result is a literary and artistic masterpiece. This has been achieved through the dedicated work of a large team of translators, headed by Rabbi Joshua Schreier; the unparalleled creative efforts of the gifted staff at Koren; and the inspired and impressive administrative skills of Rabbi Jason Rappoport, managing editor of the Koren Talmud Bavli project.

It is an honor for me to acknowledge the role of Matthew Miller of Koren Publishers Jerusalem in this historic achievement. Without him this work would never have begun. Its success is attributable to his vision and supervision. I owe a great personal debt to him for selecting me as editor-in-chief, and I am continually astounded by his commitment to Jewish learning, the Jewish people, and the Jewish homeland.

The group of individuals who surround Rabbi Steinsaltz and support his work deserve our thanks as well. I have come to appreciate their energy, initiative, and persistence. And I thank the indefatigable Rabbi Menachem Even-Israel, whom I cannot praise highly enough. The quality of his guidance and good counsel is surpassed only by his commitment to the dissemination and perpetuation of his father's precious teachings.

Finally, in humility, awe, and great respect, I acknowledge Rabbi Adin Even-Israel Steinsaltz. I thank him for the inspirational opportunity he has granted me to work with one of the outstanding sages of our time.

Rabbi Tzvi Hersh Weinreb
Jerusalem 5778

Preface by the Executive Editor

The *Koren Talmud Bavli* is in the midst of its treatment of the fifth order of the Talmud, *Kodashim*, the Order of Consecrated Items, an order that deals primarily with the sublime and the spiritual. As the Rambam wrote in his *Guide of the Perplexed*, it is the spiritual that constitutes the ultimate form of worshipping God.

In the previous order, *Nezikin*, the Order of Damages, the primary focus is on actions and the ramifications of those actions, as they are manifest in the laws of damages, labor relations, transactions, and the like. One's intent is less significant, as, for example, with regard to damages, the Sages stated (*Sanhedrin* 72a): One is liable whether the damage was unintentional or intentional, whether by unavoidable accident, or whether willingly.

In *Kodashim*, the primary focus is on intent. Clearly, there are actions that must be performed; however, the effectiveness of those actions is dictated by the accompanying intent. This is exemplified by the laws governing the sacrifice of animal offerings. There are four sacrificial rites, which constitute the essence of the offering. They are: Slaughter, collection of the blood, conveying the blood to the altar, and sprinkling the blood on the altar. If during the performance of these rites one's intent was to consume the offering after its designated time, the offering is disqualified.

My involvement in the production of the *Koren Talmud Bavli* has been both a privilege and a pleasure. The Shefa Foundation, headed by Rabbi Menachem Even-Israel and devoted to the dissemination of the wide-ranging, monumental works of Rabbi Adin Even-Israel Steinsaltz, constitutes the Steinsaltz side of this partnership; Koren Publishers Jerusalem, headed by Matthew Miller, constitutes the publishing side of this partnership. The combination of the inspiration, which is the hallmark of Shefa, with the creativity and professionalism for which Koren is renowned and which I experience on a daily basis, has lent the *Koren Talmud Bavli* its outstanding quality in terms of both content and form.

I would be remiss if I failed to mention the contribution of Raphaël Freeman, who guided this project from its inception and is largely responsible for transforming the content of the Steinsaltz Talmud into the aesthetic *Koren Talmud Bavli* that is before you. He was succeeded by Dena Landowne Bailey, who facilitated a seamless transition and continued to ensure that the *Koren Talmud Bavli* lives up to the lofty standards that are the hallmark of Koren Publishers. Tomi Mager has assumed responsibility for the layout beginning with tractate *Menaḥot*. I would like to welcome her aboard, and wish her much success in her new undertaking.

I would like to express my appreciation for Rabbi Dr. Tzvi Hersh Weinreb, the editor-in-chief, whose insight and guidance have been invaluable. Rabbi Jason Rappoport, the managing editor, has added professionalism to this project, systematizing the work of the large staff, and it is thanks to him that the project is proceeding with efficiency and excellence. Rabbi Dr. Joshua Amaru, the coordinating editor, oversees the work of the translators and editors, and is largely responsible for ensuring the consistently high quality of their work. The contribution of my friend and colleague, Rabbi Dr. Shalom Z. Berger, the senior content editor, cannot be overstated; his title does not begin to convey the excellent direction he has provided in all aspects of this project.

The staff of copy editors, headed by Aliza Israel, with Ita Olesker as production coordinator, pleasantly but firmly ensures that the finished product conforms to standards and is consistently excellent. The erudite and articulate men and women who serve as translators, editors, and copy editors generate the content that is ultimately the *raison d'etre* of the *Koren Talmud Bavli*.

I would also like to express appreciation for the invaluable contribution of the technical staff. Without them, the jobs of the entire staff of translators and editors would be much more difficult. Thanks to Tani Bednarsh, Adena Frazer, Yaakov Shmidman, Shaltiel Shmidman, and Nava Wieder.

Thanks to my former and present fellow occupants of the Koren *beit midrash*: Rabbi David Fuchs, Rabbi Yinon Chen, Efrat Gross, and others. Their mere presence creates an atmosphere conducive to the serious endeavor that we have undertaken and their assistance in all matters, large and small, is appreciated.

At the risk of being repetitious, I would like to thank Rabbi Dr. Berger for introducing me to the world of Steinsaltz. Finally, I would like to thank Rabbi Menachem Even-Israel, with whom it continues to be a pleasure to move forward in this great enterprise.

Rabbi Joshua Schreier
Jerusalem 5778

Introduction by the Publisher

The Talmud has sustained and inspired Jews for thousands of years. Throughout Jewish history, an elite cadre of scholars has absorbed its learning and passed it on to succeeding generations. The Talmud has been the fundamental text of our people.

Beginning in the 1960s, Rabbi Adin Even-Israel Steinsaltz שליט״א created a revolution in the history of Talmud study. His translation of the Talmud, first into modern Hebrew and then into other languages, as well the practical learning aids he added to the text, have enabled millions of people around the world to access and master the complexity and context of the world of Talmud.

It is thus a privilege to present the *Koren Talmud Bavli*, an English translation of the talmudic text with the brilliant elucidation of Rabbi Steinsaltz. The depth and breadth of his knowledge are unique in our time. His rootedness in the tradition and his reach into the world beyond it are inspirational.

Working with Rabbi Steinsaltz on this remarkable project has been not only an honor, but a great pleasure. Never shy to express an opinion, with wisdom and humor, Rabbi Steinsaltz sparkles in conversation, demonstrating his knowledge (both sacred and worldly), sharing his wide-ranging interests, and, above all, radiating his passion. I am grateful for the unique opportunity to work closely with him, and I wish him many more years of writing and teaching.

Our intentions in publishing this new edition of the Talmud are threefold. First, we seek to fully clarify the talmudic page to the reader – textually, intellectually, and graphically. Second, we seek to utilize today's most sophisticated technologies, both in print and electronic formats, to provide the reader with a comprehensive set of study tools. And third, we seek to help readers advance in their process of Talmud study.

To achieve these goals, the *Koren Talmud Bavli* is unique in a number of ways:

- The classic *tzurat hadaf* of Vilna, used by scholars since the 1800s, has been reset for greater clarity, and opens from the Hebrew "front" of the book. Full *nikkud* has been added to both the talmudic text and Rashi's commentary, allowing for a more fluent reading with the correct pronunciation; the commentaries of *Tosafot* have been punctuated. Upon the advice of many English-speaking teachers of Talmud, we have separated these core pages from the translation, thereby enabling the advanced student to approach the text without the distraction of the translation. This also reduces the number of volumes in the set. At the bottom of each *daf*, there is a reference to the corresponding English pages. In addition, the Vilna edition was read against other manuscripts and older print editions, so that texts which had been removed by non-Jewish censors have been restored to their rightful place.

- The English translation, which starts on the English "front" of the book, reproduces the *menukad* Talmud text alongside the English translation (in bold) and commentary and explanation (in a lighter font). The Hebrew and Aramaic text is presented in logical paragraphs. This allows for a fluent reading of the text for the non-Hebrew or non-Aramaic reader. It also allows for the Hebrew reader to refer easily to the text alongside. Where the original text features dialogue or poetry, the English text is laid out in a manner appropriate to the genre. Each page refers to the relevant *daf*.
- Critical contextual tools surround the text and translation: personality notes, providing short biographies of the Sages; language notes, explaining foreign terms borrowed from Greek, Latin, Persian, or Arabic; and background notes, giving information essential to the understanding of the text, including history, geography, botany, archaeology, zoology, astronomy, and aspects of daily life in the talmudic era.
- Halakhic summaries provide references to the authoritative legal decisions made over the centuries by the rabbis. They explain the reasons behind each halakhic decision as well as the ruling's close connection to the Talmud and its various interpreters.
- Photographs, drawings, and other illustrations have been added throughout the text – in full color in the Standard and Electronic editions, and in black and white in the Daf Yomi edition – to visually elucidate the text.

This is not an exhaustive list of features of this edition; it merely presents an overview for the English-speaking reader who may not be familiar with the "total approach" to Talmud pioneered by Rabbi Steinsaltz.

Several professionals have helped bring this vast collaborative project to fruition. My many colleagues are noted on the Acknowledgments page, and the leadership of this project has been exceptional.

RABBI MENACHEM EVEN-ISRAEL, DIRECTOR OF THE SHEFA FOUNDATION, was the driving force behind this enterprise. With enthusiasm and energy, he formed the happy alliance with Koren and established close relationships among all involved in the work.

RABBI DR. TZVI HERSH WEINREB שליט״א, EDITOR-IN-CHIEF, brought to this project his profound knowledge of Torah, intellectual literacy of Talmud, and erudition of Western literature. It is to him that the text owes its very high standard, both in form and content, and the logical manner in which the beauty of the Talmud is presented.

RABBI JOSHUA SCHREIER, EXECUTIVE EDITOR, assembled an outstanding group of scholars, translators, editors, and copy editors, whose standards and discipline enabled this project to proceed in a timely and highly professional manner.

RABBI MEIR HANEGBI, EDITOR OF THE HEBREW EDITION OF THE STEINSALTZ TALMUD, lent his invaluable assistance throughout the work process, supervising the reproduction of the Vilna pages.

RAPHAËL FREEMAN created this Talmud's unique typographic design which, true to the Koren approach, is both elegant and user-friendly.

It has been an enriching experience for all of us at Koren Publishers Jerusalem to work with the Shefa Foundation and the Steinsaltz Center to develop and produce the *Koren Talmud Bavli*. We pray that this publication will be a source of great learning and, ultimately, greater *avodat Hashem* for all Jews.

Matthew Miller, Publisher
Koren Publishers Jerusalem
Jerusalem 5773

Introduction to **Menaḥot**

Tractate *Menaḥot* discusses the *halakhot* of various offerings, specifically those that are brought from grain, i.e., wheat or barley, as well as the libations of oil and wine sacrificed in the Temple. *Menaḥot* therefore complements tractate *Zevaḥim*, which examines the *halakhot* of offerings brought from livestock or birds, and there are many parallels between the two tractates.

Just as there are various types of animal and bird offerings, so too, there are several types of meal offerings: Voluntary meal offerings, obligatory meal offerings, meal offerings brought as atonement for a transgression, individual meal offerings, and communal meal offerings. Similarly, just like animal offerings, there are portions of the meal offerings that are burned on the altar and other portions consumed by the priests. But whereas animal offerings are divided into two categories: Offerings of lesser sanctity and offerings of the most sacred order, all meal offerings are classified as offerings of the most sacred order. Accordingly, their consumption is permitted only to male members of the priesthood, and they may be eaten only inside the Temple courtyard.

Perhaps most importantly, the four sacrificial rites performed during the service of a meal offering parallel the four rites performed with an animal offering. In other words, the removal of a handful from the meal offering, the sanctification of that handful in a service vessel, its conveyance to the altar, and the burning of the handful on the altar parallel, respectively, the slaughter of an animal offering, the collection of its blood, the conveyance of that blood to the altar, and the presentation of the blood on the altar. Additionally, just as the presentation of the blood of an offering renders the remainder of that offering permitted for consumption by the priests or for sacrifice on the altar, so too, the burning of the handful on the altar renders the remainder of the meal offering permitted to the priests for consumption. Furthermore, just as the improper performance of one of the rites of an animal offering, or improper intent during one of these rites, disqualifies the offering, so too, meal offerings are disqualified through improper performance of one of their rites or improper intent during one of them.

There are also certain differences between meal offerings and animal offerings. Whereas an animal offering is fit for slaughter in its natural state, a meal offering must be prepared before it can be brought as an offering. Additionally, an animal offering is a single body, i.e., the animal itself, whereas a meal offering comprises several elements, namely, the flour, oil, and frankincense.

Together, tractates *Zevaḥim* and *Menaḥot* provide an extensive analysis of the sacrificial rites of all offerings sacrificed in the Temple. It is worth noting that the latter part of *Menaḥot* deals with *halakhot* applying to all sacrificial offerings. The tractate also concludes with a celebrated general statement: It is written with regard to an animal burnt offering: "An offering made by fire, of a pleasing aroma" (Leviticus 1:9), and with regard to a bird burnt offering: "An offering made by fire, of a pleasing aroma" (Leviticus 1:17), and also with regard to a meal offering: "An offering made by fire, of a pleasing aroma" (Leviticus 2:2). This teaches that one who brings an expensive offering and one who brings a less expensive offering are equal before God, provided that they direct their hearts toward Heaven.

There are many ways to categorize the various types of meal offerings. One can distinguish between meal offerings that are voluntary, those that are obligatory, and those that are brought as atonement for a transgression. One can also differentiate between individual meal offerings and communal ones, or between meal offerings that are brought as independent offerings and those that are brought in conjunction with slaughtered offerings. Furthermore, one can distinguish between meal offerings based on their contents, as some are brought from wheat while others are brought from barley, and some contain oil and frankincense, whereas others contain only one of these ingredients or even neither.

Meal offerings can also be classified by the manner of their preparation: Some are sacrificed as a raw mixture of flour and oil, while others are baked or fried before they are sacrificed. Of these, most meal offerings are baked or fried to form unleavened bread, while a minority of them are prepared as leavened bread. Additionally, most meal offerings undergo the sacrificial rite of the removal of a handful, which is the only part of the offering that is sacrificed upon the altar. Some meal offerings are burned in their entirety upon the altar without the removal of a handful.

In total, there are fifteen different types of meal offerings: Eleven are meal offerings brought by an individual, three are communal offerings, and the last includes all meal offerings that accompany the libations brought with slaughtered offerings. With regard to this last type, there is no distinction between the individual and the community.

Of the eleven types of individual meal offerings, five are voluntary offerings, described in the Torah according to their manner of preparation (see Leviticus 2:1–10): A meal offering of flour, a meal offering of loaves, a meal offering of wafers, a meal offering prepared in a pan, and a meal offering prepared in a deep pan. The remaining six are the meal offering of a sinner, brought by one who is obligated to bring a sliding-scale offering and cannot afford to bring an animal or bird (see Leviticus 5:11–13); the meal offering of jealousy, brought by a *sota* (see Numbers 5:25); the inaugural meal offering, brought by all priests when they begin their service in the Temple (see Leviticus 6:13); the griddle-cake offering of the High Priest, brought daily by the High Priest, half of which is sacrificed in the morning and the other half of which is sacrificed in the afternoon (see Leviticus 6:15); the loaves brought with a thanks offering (see Leviticus 7:12–14); and the loaves of a nazirite, sacrificed by a nazirite together with the offerings he must bring at the completion of his naziriteship (see Numbers 6:14).

There are three types of communal meal offerings: The *omer* meal offering (see Leviticus 23:10–11), the two loaves of bread brought on *Shavuot* (see Leviticus 23:17), and the shewbread, placed every Shabbat on the Table inside the Sanctuary (see Leviticus 24:5–8). The *halakhot* of the bread sacrificed with the inaugural ram offerings brought by Aaron and his sons when they were anointed as priests (see Leviticus, chapter 8) are also discussed in this tractate.

Tractate *Menaḥot* also contains halakhic deliberations concerning topics not directly related to meal offerings, which are nevertheless examined at length due to their mention in the *mishnayot*. In fact, the overwhelming majority of *halakhot* and aggadic literature pertaining to the mitzvot of ritual fringes, phylacteries, and *mezuza* are found in *Menaḥot*. There are additional discussions relating to these topics dispersed throughout the rest of the Talmud, but the main analyses of the commentaries and rabbinic authorities on these topics are based on the passages in this tractate.

In all, tractate *Menaḥot* has thirteen chapters, the first four of which appear in this volume. Some chapters focus on a single topic, while others deal with multiple issues.

Chapter One discusses the *halakhot* of meal offerings that are disqualified through improper intent, e.g., an offering that was sacrificed not for its own sake, or that was sacrificed with the intent to partake of it outside its proper place or beyond its proper time. It also addresses the sacrificial rites during which improper intent disqualifies the offering, as well as which individuals disqualify it when they perform its rites.

Chapter Two focuses on those instances where improper intent with regard to one part of a meal offering disqualifies the entire offering.

Chapter Three deals with multiple topics. The beginning of the chapter mentions those instances where improper intent with regard to a meal offering does not disqualify it. The chapter also discusses the parts of meal offerings that are indispensable to the whole, i.e., their absence or invalidation disqualifies the entire offering. In line with this last topic, the *mishnayot* cite various instances where the individual parts of an item are indispensable. It is in this context that the Gemara expands upon the *halakhot* of *mezuza* and phylacteries.

Chapter Four lists various items whose individual parts are not indispensable to the whole despite the fact that it would have been logical to suggest otherwise. An extensive analysis of the *halakhot* of ritual fringes is found in this chapter.

Introduction to **Perek I**

And when one brings a meal offering unto the Lord, his offering shall be of fine flour; and he shall pour oil upon it, and put frankincense upon it. And he shall bring it to Aaron's sons, the priests; and he shall remove his handful of its fine flour, and of its oil, together with all its frankincense; and the priest shall make its memorial part smoke upon the altar, an offering made by fire, of a pleasing aroma to the Lord.

(Leviticus 2:1–2)

This is the law of the burnt offering, of the meal offering, and of the sin offering, and of the guilt offering, and of the consecration offering, and of the sacrifice of peace offerings.

(Leviticus 7:37)

Although meal offerings differ greatly from slaughtered offerings, e.g., meal offerings are brought from flour whereas slaughtered offerings are brought from livestock, and meal offerings require preparation before their sacrifice whereas slaughtered offerings are fit for sacrifice in their natural state, nevertheless, the Torah teaches that the same basic *halakhot* apply to both meal offerings and slaughtered offerings, as indicated by the verse: "This is the law of the burnt offering, of the meal offering, and of the sin offering" (Leviticus 7:37). Accordingly, many comparisons can be drawn between the *halakhot* of meal offerings and those of slaughtered offerings, particularly with regard to what does and does not disqualify an offering.

The first chapter of *Menaḥot* in many aspects parallels the first chapter of *Zevaḥim*, as both address the various ways in which an offering can be disqualified through improper intent. This chapter will deal extensively with comparisons between meal offerings and slaughtered offerings. For example, certain slaughtered offerings are not rendered unfit when they are slaughtered not for their sake, despite the fact that the owner does not fulfill his obligation through that offering. Other slaughtered offerings are disqualified entirely through such intent. This chapter will discuss the *halakha* of meal offerings whose sacrificial rites are performed not for their sake, and will address the question of which meal offerings are fit and which are disqualified. Furthermore, slaughtered offerings are disqualified when their sacrificial rites are performed with the intent to sacrifice them or to partake of them beyond their designated time or outside their designated area [*piggul*]. If the improper intent concerns their designated time, the offerings are rendered *piggul* as well. This chapter will discuss which meal offerings are disqualified on account of such intent and which are rendered *piggul*. Since an offering is disqualified due to this intent only if one had such intent during the performance of one of the offering's four sacrificial rites, this chapter will also clarify the details of the four sacrificial rites of meal offerings, which parallel those of slaughtered offerings.

Additionally, just as slaughtered offerings are disqualified when their sacrificial rites are performed by one unfit to perform the rites or in a manner unfit for those rites, so too, meal offerings are disqualified as a result of these factors. The sacrifice of a meal offering involves procedures different from those of a slaughtered offering, and this chapter will analyze which procedures disqualify a meal offering when not performed in their proper manner, and which do not disqualify it after the fact.

As already noted, slaughtered offerings require no preparation before their slaughter. By contrast, with regard to meal offerings, one must first mix oil into the flour and then place frankincense upon the mixture before the priest may begin the sacrificial process by removing a handful from the flour. As this process differs significantly from that of a slaughtered offering, this chapter will deal extensively with various questions that arise with regard to the mixture of flour, oil, and frankincense, and the removal of the handful, as well as its proper measure.

These are the main issues addressed in this chapter, although other *halakhot* involving meal offerings will also be examined.

מתני׳ כָּל הַמְּנָחוֹת שֶׁנִּקְמְצוּ שֶׁלֹּא לִשְׁמָן – כְּשֵׁירוֹת, אֶלָּא שֶׁלֹּא עָלוּ לַבְּעָלִים לְשֵׁם חוֹבָה, חוּץ מִמִּנְחַת חוֹטֵא וּמִנְחַת קְנָאוֹת.

MISHNA When one brings a meal offering to the Temple, the priest removes a handful from it, places the handful into a service vessel, conveys it to the altar, and burns it. At that point, the remainder is permitted to the priests for consumption and the owner has fulfilled his obligation. In this context, the mishna teaches: **All the meal offerings**[N] from **which a handful was removed not for their sake**[NH] but for the sake of another meal offering **are fit**[N] for sacrifice. **But** these offerings **did not satisfy the obligation of the owner,** who must therefore bring another offering. This is the *halakha* with regard to all meal offerings **except for the meal offering of a sinner**[NH] **and the meal offering of jealousy,** which is brought as part of the rite of a woman suspected by her husband of having been unfaithful [*sota*]. In those cases, if the priest removed the handful not for its own sake, the offering is disqualified.

מִנְחַת חוֹטֵא וּמִנְחַת קְנָאוֹת שֶׁקְּמָצָן שֶׁלֹּא לִשְׁמָן, נָתַן בִּכְלִי וְהִלֵּךְ וְהִקְטִיר שֶׁלֹּא לִשְׁמָן, אוֹ לִשְׁמָן וְשֶׁלֹּא לִשְׁמָן, אוֹ שֶׁלֹּא לִשְׁמָן וְלִשְׁמָן – פְּסוּלוֹת.

With regard to **the meal offering of a sinner and the meal offering of jealousy** from **which** the priest **removed a handful not for their sake,** or where **he placed** a handful from them **in a vessel, or conveyed** the handful to the altar, **or burned** the handful on the altar, **not for their sake, or for their sake and not for their sake, or not for their sake and for their sake,** they **are disqualified.**

כֵּיצַד לִשְׁמָן וְשֶׁלֹּא לִשְׁמָן – לְשֵׁם מִנְחַת חוֹטֵא וּלְשֵׁם מִנְחַת נְדָבָה, שֶׁלֹּא לִשְׁמָן וְלִשְׁמָן – לְשֵׁם מִנְחַת נְדָבָה וּלְשֵׁם מִנְחַת חוֹטֵא.

The mishna elaborates: **How** are these rites performed **for their sake and not for their sake?** It is in a case where one removed the handful with two intentions: **For the sake of the meal offering of a sinner and for the sake of a voluntary meal offering.** How are these rites performed **not for their sake and for their sake?** It is in a case where one removed the handful with two intentions: **For the sake of a voluntary meal offering and for the sake of the meal offering of a sinner.**

גמ׳ לָמָּה לִי לְמִיתְנָא ״אֶלָּא״? לִיתְנֵי: וְלֹא עָלוּ לַבְּעָלִים לְשֵׁם חוֹבָה!

GEMARA The mishna teaches: All the meal offerings from which a handful was removed not for their sake but for the sake of another meal offering are fit for sacrifice, but these offerings did not satisfy the obligation of the owner. The Gemara asks: **Why do I need the mishna to teach: But** these offerings did not [***ella shelo***][N] satisfy the obligation of the owner? **Let it teach** simply: **And they did not** [***velo***] **satisfy the obligation of the owner.** What does the word *ella* add?

NOTES

All the meal offerings, etc. – **כָּל הַמְּנָחוֹת וכו׳:** There are eight types of meal offerings whose sacrifice requires the removal of a handful, which is then burned upon the altar. For these meal offerings, the removal of the handful and its subsequent sacrifice upon the altar renders permitted the remainder of the meal offering to the priests for consumption. Five of these meal offerings are brought as gift offerings: A meal offering of flour, a meal offering of loaves, a meal offering of wafers, a meal offering prepared in a pan, and a meal offering prepared in a deep pan (see Leviticus 2:1–10). The three remaining meal offerings are the meal offering of a sinner (see Leviticus 5:11–13); the meal offering of jealousy brought by a *sota* (see Numbers 5:25); and the *omer* meal offering (see Leviticus 23:10–11), which is not mentioned in this mishna but is the subject of a dispute between *amora'im* on 4a.

Not for their sake – **שֶׁלֹּא לִשְׁמָן:** The Gemara (*Zevaḥim* 2b) establishes that this refers specifically to an instance where a priest sacrifices an offering explicitly for the sake of a different offering, e.g., he sacrifices a burnt offering with the intent that it be a peace offering. But if a priest sacrifices an offering without specific intent, the offering is valid and it fulfills the obligation of the owner. Even the meal offering of a sinner and a meal offering of jealousy are valid when sacrificed without any specific intent (*Likkutei Halakhot*).

The Gemara does not cite a source for the *halakha* that meal offerings must be sacrificed for their own sake. *Tosafot* explain that it is based on the *halakha* of peace offerings, as the verse equates the different offerings: "This is the law of the burnt offering, of the meal offering, and of the sin offering, and of the guilt offering, and of the consecration offering, and of the sacrifice of peace offerings" (Leviticus 7:37). The Sages derive from this verse that the obligation to sacrifice an offering for its own sake applies to all types of offerings (*Zevaḥim* 4a).

Fit – **כְּשֵׁירוֹת:** The remainder of the sacrificial rites of these offerings must be performed in the appropriate manner (Rambam's Commentary on the Mishna). Accordingly, the handful of this meal offering must be burned upon the altar, after which the remainder is eaten by the priests (Rashi).

The meal offering of a sinner – **מִנְחַת חוֹטֵא:** There are several sins for which one must bring a sliding-scale offering in order to achieve atonement. In these cases, a wealthy individual sacrifices a lamb or a goat as a sin offering. If one cannot afford this, he sacrifices doves or pigeons instead. If he is too poor to afford even that, he brings a meal offering (Rashi).

Why do I need the mishna to teach: But [*ella*] – **לָמָּה לִי לְמִיתְנָא אֶלָּא:** The Gemara's question is based on the assumption that the *tanna* of a mishna invariably uses concise and efficient language. Accordingly, the term *ella* indicates that an offering that was slaughtered not for its own sake is considered valid in multiple aspects, and its only deficiency as an offering is that it does not fulfill the obligation of the owner. In light of this, the Gemara asks the following question: Aside from the fact that its remainder may be consumed by the priests, in what other respect is this offering considered valid, as indicated by the word *ella*? (*Shita Mekubbetzet*).

HALAKHA

All the meal offerings from which a handful was removed not for their sake – **כָּל הַמְּנָחוֹת שֶׁנִּקְמְצוּ שֶׁלֹּא לִשְׁמָן:** A meal offering can be disqualified through certain improper intentions during the performance of any of its four sacrificial rites, i.e., the removal of the handful, the placement of the handful in a service vessel, its conveyance to the altar, and its placement on the fire upon the altar. With regard to meal offerings whose sacrificial rites were not performed for their own sake, e.g., if a handful was removed from a voluntary meal offering for the sake of the meal offering of a sinner, or a handful was removed from a deep-pan meal offering for the sake of a pan meal offering, or if a rite was performed not for the sake of its owner, e.g., the meal offering of one person was sacrificed for the sake of another person, these offerings are valid, but they do not satisfy the obligations of their owners (Rambam *Sefer Avoda, Hilkhot Pesulei HaMukdashin* 13:1, 6, 15:2).

Except for the meal offering of a sinner, etc. – **חוּץ מִמִּנְחַת חוֹטֵא וכו׳:** In the case of the meal offering of a sinner and the meal offering of jealousy, if any of the four sacrificial rites of meal offerings were performed not for their sake, the meal offering is entirely disqualified (Rambam *Sefer Avoda, Hilkhot Pesulei HaMukdashin* 15:2).

HALAKHA

And it is prohibited to deviate – וְאָסוּר לְשַׁנּוֹיֵי: It is prohibited to perform the sacrificial rites of offerings with improper intentions. Therefore, if a sacrificial animal was slaughtered not for its own sake, or if a handful was taken from a meal offering not for its own sake, the subsequent sacrificial rites of the offering must be performed for their own sake, whether the initial deviation was intentional or unwitting (Rambam *Sefer Avoda, Hilkhot Pesulei HaMukdashin* 15:3).

הָא קָא מַשְׁמַע לָן: לַבְּעָלִים הוּא דְּלָא עָלוּ לְשׁוּם חוֹבָה, הָא מִנְחָה גּוּפָהּ כְּשֵׁרָה וְאָסוּר לְשַׁנּוֹיֵי. כִּדְרָבָא, דְּאָמַר רָבָא: עוֹלָה שֶׁשְּׁחָטָהּ שֶׁלֹּא לִשְׁמָהּ – אָסוּר לִזְרוֹק דָּמָהּ שֶׁלֹּא לִשְׁמָהּ;

The Gemara responds: By adding this word, the mishna **teaches us** that the only deficiency of these offerings is that **they did not satisfy the obligation of the owner; but the meal offering itself** is **valid and** it is still **prohibited to deviate**[NH] from the protocol of its sacrificial process. For example, if a handful was removed from a meal offering not for its own sake, it is prohibited to also burn it not for its own sake. This *halakha* is **in accordance with** the statement **of Rava, as Rava says:** With regard to **a burnt offering that one slaughtered not for its own sake,** it is still **prohibited to sprinkle its blood** on the altar **not for its own sake.**

אִיבָּעֵית אֵימָא סְבָרָא, וְאִיבָּעֵית אֵימָא קְרָא. אִיבָּעֵית אֵימָא סְבָרָא: מִשּׁוּם דְּמְשַׁנֵּי בָּהּ, כָּל הָנֵי לִישַׁנֵּי בָּהּ וְנֵיזִיל?!

The Gemara adds: **If you wish, propose a logical argument** to support this statement; **and if you wish, cite a verse**[N] as proof. The Gemara elaborates: **If you wish, propose a logical argument:** Just **because one deviated** from protocol **in its** sacrifice once, by removing the handful, could it be that **he should continue to deviate** from protocol **in all** the rest of the sacrificial rites? One deviation does not justify additional deviations.

וְאִיבָּעֵית אֵימָא קְרָא: ״מוֹצָא שְׂפָתֶיךָ תִּשְׁמֹר וְעָשִׂיתָ כַּאֲשֶׁר נָדַרְתָּ לַה׳ אֱלֹהֶיךָ נְדָבָה״; נְדָבָה? נֶדֶר הוּא! קָרֵי לֵיהּ נֶדֶר וְקָרֵי לֵיהּ נְדָבָה? אֶלָּא, אִם כְּמָה שֶׁנָּדַרְתָּ עָשִׂיתָ – יְהֵא נֶדֶר, וְאִם לָאו – יְהֵא נְדָבָה;

And if you wish, cite a verse: "That which has gone out of your lips you shall observe and do; according to what you have vowed as a gift offering to the Lord your God, that which you have promised with your mouth" (Deuteronomy 23:24). The Gemara analyzes the verse: Is it **a gift** offering? **It is a vow** offering.[N] Why does the verse first **call it a vow** offering **and** subsequently **call it a gift** offering? **Rather,** the verse teaches that **if you acted in accordance with how you vowed,** i.e., if you sacrificed the offering for its own sake, your obligation to fulfill your **vow will be** fulfilled; **but if** you did **not** act in accordance with your vow, it does not fulfill the obligation incurred by the vow, and **will be** considered **a gift** offering.[N]

NOTES

And it is prohibited to deviate – וְאָסוּר לְשַׁנּוֹיֵי: Some commentaries infer from Rashi's explanation that it is prohibited to deviate from protocol only with regard to subsequent rites. There is no prohibition against deviating further with regard to the same rite that was already performed not for its own sake (commentary attributed to Rashba).

And if you wish cite a verse, etc. – וְאִיבָּעֵית אֵימָא קְרָא וכו׳: Why it is necessary to provide a verse as a source for the prohibition against deviating if there is a logical basis for this prohibition? The answer is that based on logic alone one can suggest the opposite, that if one has already deviated from protocol and removed a handful not for its own sake, perhaps no prohibition is violated with further deviating. In light of the verse, this reasoning cannot be accepted, as the verse teaches that the animal is now considered an entirely different offering, i.e., a gift offering. Consequently, any previous errors have no bearing on future deviations from the protocol of this new offering (see *Ḥiddushim UVeurim*).

Is it a gift offering, it is a vow offering – נְדָבָה נֶדֶר הוּא: Although both vow offerings and gift offerings are designated by means of a vow, the relationship between the individual bringing the offering and the animal differs in each case. A vow offering is an obligation imposed upon the person, i.e., one takes a vow by saying: It is incumbent upon me to bring such and such an offering. Therefore, if the designated animal is lost or becomes disqualified, the donor is obligated to bring a different one in its place. By contrast, a gift offering relates to a specific item, where one says: This item or animal is a gift offering. Accordingly, if it is lost or becomes disqualified, the donor is not required to replace it (see *Kinnim* 1:1).

But if you did not it will be considered a gift offering – וְאִם לָאו יְהֵא נְדָבָה: In other words, this animal is now considered as though it is a different offering from the one the owner was obligated to bring, and therefore it does not serve to fulfill his obligation. With regard to the *halakhot* of its sacrifice and consumption it is not actually a gift offering; it must be treated as though it were the offering brought to fulfill the initial obligation, and it must still be sacrificed for its own sake (*Netivot HaKodesh*; see *Likkutei Halakhot* on *Zevaḥim* 2a).

וּנְדָבָה מִי שָׁרֵי לְשַׁנּוֹיֵי בָּהּ?

The Gemara concludes the proof from the verse: **And** with regard to **a gift offering, is it permitted to deviate** from **its** protocol *ab initio*?[N] Clearly one may not do so. Accordingly, if one of the sacrificial rites of a meal offering was performed for the sake of a different meal offering, it is still prohibited to perform any of its other sacrificial rites improperly.

לֵימָא, מַתְנִיתִין דְּלָא כְּרַבִּי שִׁמְעוֹן? דְּתַנְיָא, רַבִּי שִׁמְעוֹן אוֹמֵר: כׇּל הַמְּנָחוֹת שֶׁנִּקְמְצוּ שֶׁלֹּא לִשְׁמָן – כְּשֵׁירוֹת וְעָלוּ לַבְּעָלִים לְשֵׁם חוֹבָה.

§ The mishna teaches that all the meal offerings from which a handful was removed not for their sake are fit for sacrifice but they do not fulfill the obligation of the owner. The Gemara suggests: **Let us say that the mishna is not in accordance with** the opinion of **Rabbi Shimon, as it is taught** in a *baraita* that **Rabbi Shimon says: All the meal offerings** from **which a handful was removed not for their sake are fit** for sacrifice **and they** even **satisfy the obligation of the owner.**

שֶׁאֵין הַמְּנָחוֹת דּוֹמוֹת לַזְּבָחִים, שֶׁהַקּוֹמֵץ מַחֲבַת לְשׁוּם מַרְחֶשֶׁת – מַעֲשֶׂיהָ מוֹכִיחִין עָלֶיהָ לְשׁוּם מַחֲבַת, חֲרֵיבָה לְשׁוּם בְּלוּלָה – מַעֲשֶׂיהָ מוֹכִיחִין עָלֶיהָ לְשׁוּם חֲרֵיבָה;

The *baraita* continues: Conversely, consecrated animals that were sacrificed not for their sake do not fulfill the obligation of the owner, **as** in this regard **meal offerings are not similar to slaughtered offerings.** The difference is **that** when **one removes a handful** from **a pan** meal offering **for the sake of a deep-pan** meal offering,[N] **its mode of preparation proves** that **it** is in fact **for the sake of a pan** meal offering, as the two offerings differ in appearance. Similarly, with regard to a **dry** meal offering, e.g., the meal offering of a sinner, which contains no oil, whose handful is removed **for the sake of** a meal offering that is **mixed** with oil, **its mode of preparation proves** that **it** is **for the sake of a dry** meal offering, and one's improper intent is therefore disregarded.

אֲבָל בִּזְבָחִים אֵינוֹ כֵּן, שְׁחִיטָה אַחַת לְכוּלָּן, וּזְרִיקָה אַחַת לְכוּלָּן, וְקַבָּלָה אַחַת לְכוּלָּן.

But with regard to slaughtered offerings it is not so, as there is **one** manner of **slaughter for all** offerings, **and one** manner of **sprinkling** the blood **for all** offerings, **and one** manner of **collection** of the blood **for all** offerings. Since the differentiation between slaughtered offerings is established only through intention, one who sacrifices an animal offering not for its own sake does not fulfill the obligation of the owner. Rabbi Shimon apparently disagrees with the *tanna* of the mishna on two counts: First, he claims that if the handful of a meal offering was removed not for its own sake it satisfies the obligation of the owner, whereas the mishna teaches that the obligation is not fulfilled. Second, Rabbi Shimon does not differentiate between the meal offering of a sinner or the meal offering of jealousy, and the other types of meal offerings.

הָנִיחָא לְרַב אַשִׁי, דְּאָמַר: כָּאן בְּקוֹמֵץ מַחֲבַת לְשׁוּם מַרְחֶשֶׁת, כָּאן בְּקוֹמֵץ מִנְחַת מַחֲבַת לְשׁוּם מִנְחַת מַרְחֶשֶׁת,

The Gemara comments: **This works out well,** i.e., the mishna can be explained in accordance with the opinion of Rabbi Shimon, **according to Rav Ashi, who says** (3b), in a resolution of two apparently contradictory statements of Rabbi Shimon: **Here,** where Rabbi Shimon says that the meal offering is fit and fulfills the owner's obligation, he is referring to a case **where** one states that he is **removing a handful** from **a pan** meal offering **for the sake of a deep pan,** i.e., he mentions only the vessel, not the type of meal offering. Conversely, **there,** where Rabbi Shimon says that the meal offering does not satisfy the owner's obligation, he is referring to a case **where** one states that he is **removing a handful** from **a pan meal offering for the sake of a deep-pan meal offering.**

מַתְנִיתִין – מִנְחָה לְשׁוּם מִנְחָה הִיא. אֶלָּא לְרַבָּה וְרָבָא מַאי אִיכָּא לְמֵימַר?

Accordingly, it can be explained that **the mishna is** referring to a case where one removes a handful from **a meal offering for the sake of** another **meal offering,** which is why it does not satisfy the obligation of the owner. **But according to** the statements of **Rabba and Rava,** who resolved that contradiction in a different manner, **what can be said?**

NOTES

And with regard to a gift offering is it permitted to deviate from its protocol *ab initio* – וּנְדָבָה מִי שָׁרֵי לְשַׁנּוֹיֵי בָּהּ: According to Rashi (*Zevaḥim* 2b), the source for the prohibition against deviating from the sacrificial process of any offering is the phrase: "Neither shall it be attributed [*lo yeḥashev*]" (Leviticus 7:18), which may also be translated as: He shall not intend, i.e., it is prohibited for one to have improper intentions with regard to offerings (see *Zevaḥim* 29b). See also the Rambam (*Sefer Avoda, Hilkhot Pesulei HaMukdashin* 18:2), who writes that having improper intentions with regard to an offering is tantamount to blemishing it. Many commentaries maintain that the Rambam is referring only to those intentions that disqualify an offering entirely, e.g., the intent to sacrifice it outside its designated time (see also Ramban's addendum to *Sefer HaMitzvot*, prohibition 4).

A pan meal offering for the sake of a deep-pan meal offering – מַחֲבַת לְשׁוּם מַרְחֶשֶׁת: The pan used for a pan meal offering was shallow, and a minimal amount of oil was added to the flour, which rendered the meal offering relatively hard. In contrast, the pan used for a deep-pan meal offering was deeper, as indicated by its name, and there was a significant amount of oil added to the flour, which rendered the meal offering soft (63a). According to some commentaries, the pan was an entirely flat surface with no rim, whereas the deep pan had a surrounding rim (Rambam).

BACKGROUND

Sin offering – חַטָּאת: If a Jew commits a transgression punishable by *karet*, i.e., excision from the World-to-Come, if performed intentionally, he is obligated to bring a sin offering if he did so unwittingly. A sin offering brought by an individual is either a female lamb or a goat, and it must be in its first year. It must be slaughtered in the northern section of the Temple courtyard, and its blood is collected there and sprinkled on each of the four corners of the altar. The fat of the sin offering is burned on the altar, and its meat is eaten by the priests. Other sin offerings are brought in certain cases as part of the purification rites at the conclusion of a period of ritual impurity, e.g., that of a woman who has given birth, that of a leper, and that of a nazirite. There are yet other sin offerings that serve to atone for the community, as well as special sin offerings brought by the leaders of the people to atone for transgression.

וְכִי תֵּימָא, כִּדְקָא מְשַׁנֵּי רַבָּה: כָּאן בְּשִׁינּוּי קֹדֶשׁ, כָּאן בְּשִׁינּוּי בְּעָלִים;

The Gemara elaborates: **And if you would say** that the contradiction addressed by Rav Ashi is resolved **as Rabba answers,** this is problematic. Rabba resolved the contradiction as follows: **Here,** where Rabbi Shimon says that the meal offering satisfies the owner's obligation, he is referring **to a change of sanctity,** i.e., it was sacrificed for the sake of another type of meal offering, whereas **there,** where Rabbi Shimon says that it does not fulfill the owner's obligation, he is referring **to a change of owner,** e.g., the meal offering of Reuven was sacrificed for the sake of Shimon.

הָא מַתְנִיתִין שִׁינּוּי קוֹדֶשׁ הוּא, דְּקָתָנֵי: כֵּיצַד לִשְׁמָן וְשֶׁלֹּא לִשְׁמָן – לְשׁוּם מִנְחַת חוֹטֵא וּלְשׁוּם מִנְחַת נְדָבָה!

The Gemara explains that the reason this is problematic is that if one accepts Rabba's resolution, how can the mishna be explained in accordance with the opinion of Rabbi Shimon? **The mishna is** clearly discussing the case of **a change of sanctity, as it teaches: How** are these rites performed **for their sake and** then **not for their sake,** whereby the offering does not satisfy the owner's obligation? It is in a case where one initially removed the handful **for the sake of the meal offering of a sinner and** then **for the sake of a voluntary meal offering.** This is a change involving a different type of meal offering.

וְאִי נַמִי כִּדְקָא מְשַׁנֵּי רָבָא: כָּאן בְּקוֹמֵץ מִנְחָה לְשׁוּם מִנְחָה, כָּאן בְּקוֹמֵץ מִנְחָה לְשׁוּם זֶבַח;

And alternatively, if you would say that the contradiction addressed by Rav Ashi is resolved **as Rava answers,** this is equally problematic. Rava resolved the contradiction as follows: **Here,** where Rabbi Shimon says that the meal offering satisfies the owner's obligation, he is referring to a case **where one removes a handful** from **a meal offering for the sake of** another **meal offering,** whereas **there,** where Rabbi Shimon says that it does not satisfy the owner's obligation, he is referring to a case **where one removes a handful** from **a meal offering for the sake of a slaughtered offering.**

הָא מַתְנִיתִין מִנְחָה לְשׁוּם מִנְחָה הִיא, דְּקָתָנֵי: שֶׁלֹּא לִשְׁמָן וְלִשְׁמָן – לְשֵׁם מִנְחַת נְדָבָה לְשֵׁם מִנְחַת חוֹטֵא! אֶלָּא לְרַבָּה וְרָבָא מְחַוַּורְתָּא, מַתְנִיתִין דְּלָא כְּרַבִּי שִׁמְעוֹן.

The Gemara explains that if one accepts Rava's resolution, the mishna cannot be in accordance with the opinion of Rabbi Shimon: **The mishna is** discussing a case where one removes a handful from **a meal offering for the sake of** another **meal offering, as it teaches:** How are these rites performed **not for their sake and for their sake?** It is a case where one removed the handful **for the sake of a voluntary meal offering** and then **for the sake of the meal offering of a sinner.** The Gemara concludes: **Rather, according to** the resolutions offered by **Rabba and Rava, it is clear** that **the mishna is not in accordance with** the opinion of **Rabbi Shimon.**

וְרָמֵי דְּרַבִּי שִׁמְעוֹן אַדְּרַבִּי שִׁמְעוֹן. דְּתַנְיָא, רַבִּי שִׁמְעוֹן אוֹמֵר: ״קֹדֶשׁ קָדָשִׁים הִיא כַּחַטָּאת וְכָאָשָׁם״ – יֵשׁ מֵהֶן כַּחַטָּאת וְיֵשׁ מֵהֶן כָּאָשָׁם;

§ The Gemara cites the *baraita* that is the basis for the apparent contradiction between the statements of Rabbi Shimon, which was mentioned in the previous discussion: **And** a Sage **raises a contradiction** from one statement **of Rabbi Shimon and** another statement **of Rabbi Shimon, as it is taught** in a *baraita*: **Rabbi Shimon says** that the verse written concerning the meal offering: **"It is most sacred, as the sin offering, and as the guilt offering"** (Leviticus 6:10), indicates that **there are some** meal offerings whose *halakha* is **like** that of **a sin offering,**[B] **and there are some** whose *halakha* is **like** that of **a guilt offering.**

מִנְחַת חוֹטֵא הֲרֵי הִיא כַּחַטָּאת, לְפִיכָךְ קְמָצָהּ שֶׁלֹּא לִשְׁמָהּ – פְּסוּלָה כַּחַטָּאת, מִנְחַת נְדָבָה הֲרֵי הִיא כָּאָשָׁם, לְפִיכָךְ קְמָצָהּ שֶׁלֹּא לִשְׁמָהּ – כְּשֵׁירָה;

Rabbi Shimon elaborates: The *halakha* with regard to **the meal offering of a sinner is like** that of **a sin offering. Therefore,** if one **removed a handful** from **it not for its own sake,** it is **disqualified,** just **like a sin offering** that was slaughtered not for its own sake. Conversely, the *halakha* with regard to **a voluntary meal offering is like** that of **a guilt offering. Therefore,** if one **removed a handful** from **it not for its own sake,** it is **valid,** like a guilt offering that was slaughtered not for its own sake.

וְכָאָשָׁם, מָה אָשָׁם כָּשֵׁר וְאֵינוֹ מְרַצֶּה – אַף מִנְחַת נְדָבָה כְּשֵׁירָה וְאֵינָהּ מְרַצָּה!

Rabbi Shimon adds: **And** a voluntary meal offering is **like a guilt offering** in another aspect as well: **Just as a guilt offering** is **valid but it does not effect acceptance,** i.e., it does not satisfy the owner's obligation, **so too, a voluntary meal offering** is **valid but it does not effect acceptance.** Rabbi Shimon here apparently contradicts his ruling that all meal offerings from which a handful was removed not for their sake satisfy the obligation of the owner.

אֲמַר רַבָּה, לָא קַשְׁיָא: כָּאן בְּשִׁינּוּי קוֹדֶשׁ, כָּאן בְּשִׁינּוּי בְּעָלִים.

Rabba said in resolution of this contradiction: This is **not difficult. Here,** where Rabbi Shimon says that the meal offering satisfies the owner's obligation, he is referring **to a change of sanctity,** i.e., it was sacrificed for the sake of another type of meal offering, whereas **there,** where he says that it does not fulfill the owner's obligation, he is referring **to a change of owner,** e.g., the meal offering of Reuven was sacrificed for the sake of Shimon.

אֲמַר לֵיהּ אַבָּיֵי: מִכְּדֵי מַחְשָׁבָה דְּפָסַל רַחֲמָנָא הֶקֵּישָׁא הִיא, מַה לִּי שִׁינּוּי קוֹדֶשׁ מַה לִּי שִׁינּוּי בְּעָלִים?

Abaye said to Rabba: **Now** consider, the fact **that the Merciful One disqualifies** a meal offering due to improper **intent is** derived from the Torah's **comparison**[N] of meal offerings to sin offerings and guilt offerings. If so, **what** difference is there **to me** if there was **a change of sanctity,** and **what** difference is there **to me** if there was **a change of owner?** In the case of a guilt offering either of these changes prevents it from satisfying the obligation of the owner.

אֲמַר לֵיהּ: ״מַעֲשֶׂיהָ מוֹכִיחִין״ דְּקָאָמַר רַבִּי שִׁמְעוֹן – סְבָרָא הִיא, דְּרַבִּי שִׁמְעוֹן דָּרֵישׁ טַעְמָא דִּקְרָא;

Rabba **said to** Abaye: The claim that **its mode of preparation proves** one's intent, **which Rabbi Shimon states** in explanation of why offerings are disqualified through improper intent, **is** based on **logical reasoning, as Rabbi Shimon interprets the reason** behind the mitzva **in the verse**[N] and draws halakhic conclusions based on that interpretation.

מַחְשָׁבָה דְּלָא מִינְכְּרָא – פָּסַל רַחֲמָנָא, מַחְשָׁבָה דְּמִינְכְּרָא – לָא פָּסַל רַחֲמָנָא.

Rabba continues: This is significant, as Rabbi Shimon holds that **the Merciful One disqualifies** improper **intent that is not recognizably** false,[N] i.e., when the intent is not in clear contradiction to the sacrificial rites performed. The intent to sacrifice an offering for the sake of another owner does not include a change in the sacrificial rites and it therefore disqualifies the offering. **The Merciful One does not disqualify** improper **intent that is recognizably** false and contradicts the sacrificial rites performed, e.g., if one removes a handful from a pan meal offering for the sake of a deep-pan meal offering, as the different substance itself indicates that it is a pan meal offering.

(סִימָן: עוֹלָה, עוֹלָה, מָלַק וּמִיצָּה, חַטַּאת הָעוֹף, קׇדְשֵׁי קָדָשִׁים, קָדָשִׁים קַלִּים).

The Gemara lists several questions with regard to Rabba's statement, for which it provides **a mnemonic:**[B] **Burnt offering, burnt offering, pinched and squeezed, bird sin offering, offerings of the most sacred order, offerings of lesser sanctity.**

BACKGROUND

Mnemonic – סִימָן: Because the Talmud was studied orally for many generations, mnemonic devices were used as memory aids for various series of statements and the order in which they were taught.

NOTES

The fact that the Merciful One disqualifies a meal offering due to improper intent is derived from the Torah's comparison, etc. – דְּפָסַל רַחֲמָנָא הֶקֵּישָׁא הִיא וכו׳: According to Rashi, the Gemara is referring to the comparison cited here, that of a meal offering to a sin offering or a guilt offering. *Tosafot* explain that the Gemara is referring to the conclusion in *Zevaḥim* 8a that the disqualification of all offerings sacrificed with improper intent is derived from the comparison of other types of offerings to a peace offering (Leviticus 7:37). The Sages derive from a verse that a peace offering must be sacrificed for its own sake (*Zevaḥim* 4a; see commentary attributed to Rashba).

As Rabbi Shimon interprets the reason behind the mitzva in the verse – דְּרַבִּי שִׁמְעוֹן דָּרֵישׁ טַעְמָא דִּקְרָא: Many Sages explained the rationales for particular mitzvot. Rabbi Shimon was unique in that he would draw halakhic conclusions from such interpretations. He claims that just as *halakhot* are learned through *a fortiori* inferences, paradigms, and other methods, they may be derived from the rationales for certain mitzvot, whether or not the Torah explicitly states these rationales. The significance of Rabbi Shimon's method in this context is as follows: Since the Torah juxtaposes meal offerings to animal offerings, one might have thought that there is no reason to differentiate between a change of sanctity and a change of owner, in accordance with the principle that when there is an analogy based on juxtaposition, all relevant conclusions are inferred from the analogy. Nevertheless, in light of the rationale of improper intent, according to which only intent that is not recognizably false disqualifies an offering, there is reason to differentiate between these two types of changes (see commentary attributed to Rashba).

Intent that is not recognizably false – מַחְשָׁבָה דְּלָא מִינְכְּרָא: There is a fundamental disagreement between the commentaries with regard to the nature of the disqualification of offerings through improper intent. According to some, improper intent alone disqualifies an offering, without any verbal articulation of such intent, and a priest is deemed credible if he claims that he sacrificed an offering with improper intent (Rambam; Ritva). By contrast, many commentaries maintain that improper intentions must be expressed verbally in order to disqualify an offering (Rashi; *Tosafot*; *Or Zarua*; *Sefer HaEshkol*). According to this opinion, the reason the Gemara refers to the intentions themselves, rather than their expression, is that it is ultimately the improper intention that disqualifies an offering; one's verbal articulation is merely an expression of his intent. Alternatively, in referring to intent the Gemara follows the language of the verse that discusses improper intentions, which states: "Neither shall it be attributed [*lo yeḥashev*]" (Leviticus 7:18), which has the root *ḥet*, *shin*, *beit*, which is also the root for thinking. Rabbi Shimon's distinction between intent that is not recognizably false and intent that is recognizably false apparently lends support to the second opinion, since if intent alone were sufficient to disqualify an offering without any verbal expression, then all improper intentions would be indiscernible.

BACKGROUND

Pinching – מְלִיקָה: Doves and pigeons brought as offerings in the Temple were not killed by ritual slaughter with a knife as other offerings were, but rather by pinching the napes of their necks. This was considered an especially difficult activity to perform. The priest would hold the bird in his left hand, with its legs and wings between his fingers and the nape of its neck stretched out and facing upward. With his right fingernail, which he grew especially long for this purpose, the priest would cut the bird's neck and spine from the back, until he reached and severed its windpipe and gullet. If the bird was to be sacrificed as a burnt offering, the priest would completely sever its head. If it was designated as a sin offering, he would leave the head attached. A bird killed by pinching that was not intended for sacrificial use was considered an unslaughtered carcass and was not permitted for consumption, whereas one killed by pinching and sacrificed as a sin offering was permitted for eating by the priests. It was permitted only for a priest to perform pinching, whereas animals intended as offerings in the Temple could be slaughtered by a non-priest.

NOTES

Bird burnt offering…bird sin offering – עוֹלַת הָעוֹף...חַטַּאת הָעוֹף: There are several differences between a bird burnt offering and a bird sin offering with regard to the presentation of their blood on the altar (see *Zevaḥim* 64b). In the case of a burnt offering, the priest stands on the ledge surrounding the altar and squeezes the remaining blood onto the altar (Rashi). By contrast, for a sin offering the priest stands beside the altar, on the floor of the Temple courtyard, and, while holding the bird in his hand, sprinkles its blood upon the altar. Afterward, he squeezes the remaining blood onto the altar (Rashi on *Zevaḥim* 64b). Additionally, the head of a bird burnt offering is severed entirely from its body by cutting the windpipe and gullet, whereas the head of a bird sin offering is not completely severed.

אֶלָּא מֵעַתָּה, עוֹלַת הָעוֹף שֶׁמְּלָקָהּ לְמַעְלָה מִשּׁוּם חַטַּאת הָעוֹף תֵּרָצֶה; מַעֲשֶׂיהָ מוֹכִיחִין עָלֶיהָ דְּעוֹלַת הָעוֹף הִיא, דְּאִי חַטַּאת הָעוֹף הִיא – לְמַטָּה הֲוֵי עָבֵיד לַהּ!

The Gemara first asks: But **if that is so,** that only intent that is not recognizably false disqualifies an offering, then in the case of **a bird burnt offering where one pinched**[B] the nape of **its** neck **above** the red line that divides the upper and lower halves of the altar **for the sake of a bird sin offering,**[N] it **should effect acceptance** according to Rabbi Shimon. The reason is **the actions** performed **on it prove that it is a bird burnt offering. Because if it is** in fact **a bird sin offering, he would have performed** the pinching **below** the red line while standing beside the altar. Nevertheless, Rabbi Shimon agrees with the ruling of the mishna (*Zevaḥim* 64b) that this bird offering does not satisfy its owner's obligation.

אַטּוּ חַטַּאת הָעוֹף לְמַעְלָה מִי לֵיתָא? הָאָמַר מָר: מְלִיקָה בְּכָל מָקוֹם בַּמִּזְבֵּחַ כְּשֵׁרָה!

The Gemara rejects this: **Is that to say** that a case of **a bird sin offering** that is pinched **above** the red line **is not** possible? **Didn't the Master say:** The **pinching** of a bird sin offering that is performed **in any place on the altar**[H] **is valid** after the fact? Accordingly, there is no discernible difference between the pinching of a bird burnt offering and the pinching of a bird sin offering, so the owner's obligation is not fulfilled.

עוֹלַת הָעוֹף שֶׁמִּיצָּה דָּמָהּ לְמַעְלָה לְשֵׁם חַטַּאת הָעוֹף תֵּרָצֶה; מַעֲשֶׂיהָ מוֹכִיחִין עָלֶיהָ דְּעוֹלַת הָעוֹף הִיא, דְּאִי חַטַּאת הָעוֹף הִיא – לְמַטָּה הֲוָה עָבֵיד לַהּ הַזָּאָה!

The Gemara raises another difficulty: If recognizably false intent does not disqualify an offering, then **a bird burnt offering where** a priest **squeezed its blood above** the red line **for the sake of a bird sin offering should effect acceptance,** as **the actions** performed **on it prove that it is a bird burnt offering. Because if it is** in fact **a bird sin offering, he would have performed** the required act of holding the body of the bird and **sprinkling** its blood **below** the red line, instead of squeezing out its blood above that line.

HALAKHA

The pinching of a bird sin offering that is performed in any place on the altar – מְלִיקָה בְּכָל מָקוֹם בַּמִּזְבֵּחַ: A bird sin offering may be pinched in any place upon the altar, but its blood must be sprinkled on the lower half of the altar. If the priest sprinkled from its blood on the upper half the offering is valid, provided that he places some of the first blood that comes from the slaughtered bird on the lower half of the altar (Rambam *Sefer Avoda, Hilkhot Ma'aseh HaKorbanot* 7:9).

Perek **I**
Daf **3** Amud **a**

NOTES

It is the squeezing that follows sprinkling – מִיצּוּי דְּבָתַר הַזָּאָה הוּא: Although in the case of a sin offering it is the sprinkling of the bird's blood, not its squeezing, which effects atonement, the blood must be squeezed on the lower half of the altar after the rite of sprinkling. Nevertheless, as this squeezing is not critical to the atonement, and it is not indispensable to the rite, it is valid even if performed in an improper place on the altar (Rabbeinu Gershom Meor HaGola).

אָמְרִי: דִּילְמָא מִיצּוּי דְּבָתַר הַזָּאָה הוּא, דְּאָמַר מָר: מִיצָּה דָּמָהּ בְּכָל מָקוֹם בַּמִּזְבֵּחַ – כְּשֵׁירָה.

The Gemara responds: This is not considered recognizably false intent, as people might **say: Perhaps** it is actually a sin offering and he has already sprinkled its blood below the red line. And as for the fact that he squeezed its blood above the red line, they will say: **It is the squeezing that follows sprinkling,**[N] which may be performed above the red line in the case of a sin offering. **As the Master said:** If one **squeezed the blood of** a bird sin offering **in any place on the altar,**[H] the offering is **valid.** Since people might erroneously think that this bird is actually a sin offering, this intent is not considered recognizably false, so the offering is disqualified.

HALAKHA

If one squeezed the blood of a bird sin offering in any place on the altar – מִיצָּה דָּמָהּ בְּכָל מָקוֹם בַּמִּזְבֵּחַ: The squeezing of the blood of a bird sin offering onto the altar is an indispensable part of its sacrificial process. This ruling is apparently in accordance with the Gemara in *Me'ila* (8b), which indicates that the squeezing of the blood of a bird sin offering is valid only over the base of the altar (*Likkutei Halakhot* on *Zevaḥim* 64a). Other early commentaries maintain that the squeezing of the blood of a bird sin offering is not an indispensable part of its sacrificial process. Accordingly, such a sin offering is valid even if its blood was squeezed anywhere on the altar (Rambam *Sefer Avoda, Hilkhot Ma'aseh HaKorbanot* 7:7).

חַטַּאת הָעוֹף שֶׁהִזָּה דָּמָהּ לְמַטָּה לְשֵׁם עוֹלַת הָעוֹף תְּרַצֶּה; דְּמַעֲשֶׂיהָ מוֹכִיחִין עָלֶיהָ דְּחַטַּאת עוֹף הִיא, דְּאִי עוֹלַת הָעוֹף הִיא – לְמַעְלָה הֲוָה עָבֵיד לָהּ, וּמִיצּוּי הֲוָה עָבֵיד לֵיהּ!

The Gemara asks another question: According to Rabba's resolution, **a bird sin offering whose blood** a priest **sprinkled below** the red line **for the sake of a bird burnt offering should effect acceptance,**[N] **as the actions** performed **on it prove that it is a bird sin offering. Because if it is** in fact **a bird burnt offering, he would have performed it above** the red line, **and he would have performed** the act of **squeezing** instead of sprinkling.

הָכִי נַמִי, אֶלָּא "לְפִי שֶׁאֵין הַמְּנָחוֹת דּוֹמוֹת לִזְבָחִים" קָאָמַר – לִזְבָחִים, וְלֹא לְעוֹפוֹת.

The Gemara responds: **Indeed,** according to Rabbi Shimon such a bird offering effects acceptance and fulfills the obligation of the owner. In fact, bird offerings were not discussed by Rabbi Shimon at all. **Rather, he said: Because meal offerings are not similar to slaughtered offerings,** which means that they are not similar **to slaughtered** animal **offerings, but** he did not say that they are **not** similar **to bird** offerings.

קָדְשֵׁי קָדָשִׁים שֶׁשְּׁחָטָן בַּצָּפוֹן לְשֵׁם קָדָשִׁים קַלִּים לִירַצּוּ; מַעֲשֵׂיהֶן מוֹכִיחִין עֲלֵיהֶן דְּקָדְשֵׁי קָדָשִׁים נִינְהוּ, דְּאִי קָדָשִׁים קַלִּים – בַּדָּרוֹם הֲוָה עָבֵיד לְהוּ!

The Gemara asks: But if so, then **offerings of the most sacred order that one slaughtered in the northern** part of the Temple courtyard, which is a requirement that applies only to offerings of the most sacred order, **for the sake of offerings of lesser sanctity,**[HB] **should effect acceptance** for their owners, as **the actions** performed **on them prove that they are offerings of the most sacred order. Because if** they are in fact **offerings of lesser sanctity, he would have performed their** slaughter **in the southern** part of the Temple courtyard.

אֵימוּר דְּאָמַר רַחֲמָנָא – אַף בַּדָּרוֹם, בַּדָּרוֹם וְלֹא בַּצָּפוֹן מִי אָמַר? דִּתְנַן: שְׁחִיטָתָן בְּכָל מָקוֹם בָּעֲזָרָה.

The Gemara answers: The slaughter of an offering in the northern part of the Temple courtyard is not indicative of the type of offering one intends it to be, as one can **say that the Merciful One states** that offerings of lesser sanctity may be slaughtered **even in the southern** part of the courtyard. **Did He say** that these offerings must be slaughtered specifically **in the southern** part **and not in the northern** part? This is **as we learned** in a mishna (*Zevaḥim* 55a), that **the slaughter of** offerings of lesser sanctity may be performed **in any place within the** Temple **courtyard.**

קָדָשִׁים קַלִּים שֶׁשְּׁחָטָן בַּדָּרוֹם לְשֵׁם קָדְשֵׁי קָדָשִׁים לִירַצּוּ; מַעֲשֵׂיהֶן מוֹכִיחִין עֲלֵיהֶן דְּקָדָשִׁים קַלִּים נִינְהוּ, דְּאִי קָדְשֵׁי קָדָשִׁים – בַּצָּפוֹן הֲוָה עָבֵיד לְהוּ!

The Gemara asks: If so, then **offerings of lesser sanctity that one slaughtered in the southern** part of the Temple courtyard **for the sake of offerings of the most sacred order should effect acceptance** for their owners, as **the actions** performed **on them prove that they are offerings of lesser sanctity. Because if** they are in fact **offerings of the most sacred order, he would have performed their** slaughter **in the northern** part of the Temple courtyard.

אָמְרִי: קָדְשֵׁי קָדָשִׁים נִינְהוּ, וּמִיעְבַּר הוּא דַּעֲבַר וְשָׁחַט לְהוּ בַּדָּרוֹם.

The Gemara responds: The fact that an offering was slaughtered in the southern part of the Temple courtyard is not a clear indication that it was intended as an offering of lesser sanctity, as people might **say: They are** in fact **offerings of the most sacred order, but** the priest **transgressed** the mitzva to slaughter them in the northern part of the courtyard **and slaughtered them in the southern** part.

אִי הָכִי, מַחֲבַת לְשֵׁם מַרְחֶשֶׁת נַמִי, הַאי דְּקָא קָמֵיץ לָהּ לְמַרְחֶשֶׁת – אָמַר: הַאי בְּמַרְחֶשֶׁת נָדַר, וְהָא דְּמַיְיתֵי לָהּ בְּמַחֲבַת – דְּמַרְחֶשֶׁת הִיא, וּמִעְבַּר הוּא דַּעֲבַר וְאַתְיָיהּ בְּמַחֲבַת!

The Gemara asks: **If so,** i.e., if people might suspect an individual of performing the rite of an offering in an improper manner, then if a priest removes a handful from **a pan** meal offering **for the sake of a deep-pan** meal offering **as well,** one who sees **that this** priest **removes a handful for** the sake of **a deep-pan** meal offering might **say: This** owner **took a vow** to bring a meal offering **in a deep pan, and** as for the fact **that he brings it in a pan, it is** actually the meal offering **of a deep pan and** the owner **transgressed** the mitzva to bring it in a deep pan, **and brought it in a pan.** Why, then, does Rabbi Shimon maintain that such a meal offering satisfies the obligation of its owner?

הָתָם כִּי נַמִי בְּמַרְחֶשֶׁת נָדַר, כִּי מַיְיתֵי לָהּ בְּמַחֲבַת – מַחֲבַת הָוְיָא,

The Gemara explains: **There,** where the priest removed the handful from a pan meal offering for the sake of a deep-pan meal offering, **even if** the owner **took a vow** to bring a meal offering **in a deep pan, when he brings it in a pan it is** considered a valid **pan** meal offering, and therefore the priest's intention is recognizably false.

NOTES

A bird sin offering whose blood he sprinkled below the red line for the sake of a bird burnt offering should effect acceptance – חַטַּאת הָעוֹף שֶׁהִזָּה דָּמָהּ לְמַטָּה לְשֵׁם עוֹלַת הָעוֹף תְּרַצֶּה: In such a case, one cannot mistake a sin offering for a burnt offering, as the blood of a burnt offering is squeezed onto the altar rather than sprinkled. Additionally, if the blood of a bird burnt offering was not squeezed above the red line, the offering is disqualified (see *Zevaḥim* 64b).

HALAKHA

Offerings of the most sacred order…offerings of lesser sanctity – קָדְשֵׁי קָדָשִׁים...קָדָשִׁים קַלִּים: Offerings of the most sacred order may be slaughtered and their blood collected only in the northern part of the Temple courtyard. Offerings of lesser sanctity may be slaughtered and their blood collected anywhere within the Temple courtyard (Rambam *Sefer Avoda, Hilkhot Ma'aseh HaKorbanot* 5:2).

BACKGROUND

Offerings of the most sacred order…offerings of lesser sanctity – קָדְשֵׁי קָדָשִׁים...קָדָשִׁים קַלִּים: The offerings sacrificed in the Temple are divided into two main categories: Offerings of the most sacred order and offerings of lesser sanctity. Offerings of the most sacred order include those sacrificed on Yom Kippur, communal sin offerings, burnt offerings, sin offerings, guilt offerings, and communal peace offerings. Offerings of lesser sanctity include peace offerings, animal tithe offerings, thanks offerings, firstborn offerings, and the Paschal offering. One of the primary differences between the two types of offerings is that those of the most sacred order are slaughtered only in the north of the Temple courtyard, while those of lesser sanctity may be slaughtered anywhere in the courtyard. Offerings of the most sacred order may be consumed on the day of their slaughter and the following night, while many offerings of lesser sanctity may be consumed on the subsequent day as well. Offerings of the most sacred order may be consumed only by male priests, while offerings of lesser sanctity may be consumed by ritually pure Jews.

כְּדִתְנַן: הָאוֹמֵר ״הֲרֵי עָלַי בְּמַחֲבַת״ וְהֵבִיא בְּמַרְחֶשֶׁת, ״בְּמַרְחֶשֶׁת״ וְהֵבִיא בְּמַחֲבַת – מַה שֶּׁהֵבִיא הֵבִיא וִידֵי נִדְרוֹ לֹא יָצָא.

This is as we learned in a mishna (102b): **One who says: It** is incumbent **upon me** to bring a meal offering prepared **in a pan,**[H] **and he brought** it **in a deep pan,** or if he says: It is incumbent upon me to bring a meal offering prepared **in a deep pan, and he brought** it **in a pan,** the meal offering **that he brought, he brought,** i.e., it is valid and the priest performs the rites of the meal offering that he actually brought, **but he did not fulfill** the obligation resulting from **his vow,** and he must bring another meal offering to fulfill that obligation.

וְדִילְמָא אָמַר ״זוֹ לְהָבִיא בְּמַחֲבַת״ וְהֵבִיא בְּמַרְחֶשֶׁת, כְּדִתְנַן: ״זוֹ לְהָבִיא בְּמַחֲבַת״ וְהֵבִיא בְּמַרְחֶשֶׁת, ״בְּמַרְחֶשֶׁת״ וְהֵבִיא בְּמַחֲבַת – הֲרֵי זוֹ פְּסוּלָה!

The Gemara asks: **But** even so, the priest's improper intent remains indiscernible, as people might think: **Perhaps** the owner **said: This** tenth of an ephah of flour is a meal offering that I must **bring in a pan, and** in spite of this **he brought** it **in a deep pan.** Such a meal offering is disqualified and is not considered a valid pan meal offering, **as we learned** in that same mishna: One who took a vow, saying: **This** tenth of an ephah of flour is a meal offering that I must **bring in a pan, and he brought** it **in a deep pan,** or if he vowed: This tenth of an ephah of flour is a meal offering that I must bring **in a deep pan, and he brought** it **in a pan, it is disqualified,** as he did not fulfill his vow. If so, how can Rabbi Shimon say that such a meal offering satisfies the owner's obligation, when the intent is not recognizably false?

לְרַבָּנַן הָכִי נַמִי; לְרַבִּי שִׁמְעוֹן, כֵּיוָן דְּאָמַר רַבִּי שִׁמְעוֹן: אַף יְדֵי נִדְרוֹ יָצָא, אַלְמָא קְבִיעוּתָא דְּמָנָא וְלָא כְלוּם הוּא, וְלָא שְׁנָא אֲמַר ״זוֹ״ וְלָא שְׁנָא אֲמַר ״עָלַי״.

The Gemara responds: **According to the Rabbis,** i.e., according to the opinion of the mishna just cited, there is **indeed** a difficulty. But **according to Rabbi Shimon** there is no difficulty, **since** with regard to a case where one took a vow, saying: It is incumbent upon me to bring a pan meal offering, and then he brought it in a deep pan, **Rabbi Shimon says: He has fulfilled even** the obligation resulting from **his vow. Evidently, the designation of the vessel** for a meal offering **is nothing** according to Rabbi Shimon, **and** there **is no difference** in this regard whether **he said: This** is for a particular type of meal offering, **and there is no difference** whether **he said:** It is incumbent **upon me** to bring a particular meal offering. In both instances the unique actions of each particular meal offering prove its identity, and therefore the owner fulfills his obligation regardless of the priest's improper intent.

אֶלָּא מֵעַתָּה, עוֹלָה שֶׁשְּׁחָטָהּ לְשֵׁם חַטָּאת תְּרַצֶּה, דְּהַאי זָכָר וְהַאי נְקֵבָה! כֵּיוָן דְּאִיכָּא שְׂעִיר נָשִׂיא דְּזָכָר הוּא, לָא יְדִיעַ.

The Gemara asks: **If that is so,** that in a case where the manner of its preparation proves the identity of an offering the owner fulfills his obligation, then **a burnt offering that one slaughtered for the sake of a sin offering should effect acceptance.** His actions prove that it is a burnt offering, **as this,** a burnt offering, is always **male, and that,** a sin offering, is **female.**[N] The Gemara answers: **Since there is** one sin offering, **the goat of the** ***Nasi*****,**[B] **which is male, it is unknown** whether this animal was a burnt offering or the sin offering of the *Nasi,* and its gender is not conclusive proof.

אֲמַר ״לְשֵׁם חַטַּאת יָחִיד״ מַאי אִיכָּא לְמֵימַר? וְתוּ, חַטַּאת יָחִיד שֶׁשְּׁחָטָהּ לְשֵׁם עוֹלָה תְּרַצֶּה, דְּחַטָּאת נְקֵבָה וְעוֹלָה זָכָר! מִיכַּסְיָא בְּאַלְיָה.

The Gemara continues to ask: But in a case where one **said:** I am hereby slaughtering this animal **for the sake of a sin offering of an individual,** which is always female, **what can be said?** Since a male animal cannot be mistaken for such a sin offering, why doesn't this burnt offering satisfy the obligation of the owner? **And furthermore, a sin offering of an individual that one slaughtered for the sake of a burnt offering should effect acceptance, as** such **a sin offering** is always **female, and a burnt offering** is always **male.** The Gemara responds: It is difficult to discern whether a lamb is male or female, as its genitals are **covered by** its **tail.**[B] Accordingly, its gender is not considered proof of the type of offering being sacrificed.

הָתֵינַח הֵיכָא דְּאַיְיתֵי כִּבְשָׂה, אַיְיתֵי שְׂעִירָה מַאי אִיכָּא לְמֵימַר? אֶלָּא, בֵּין זְכָרִים לִנְקֵבוֹת לָאו אַדַּעְתַּיְיהוּ דֶּאֱינָשֵׁי.

The Gemara asks: This **works out well** in a case **where one brought a female lamb** as his sin offering, as its tail makes it difficult to discern its sex. But in a case where he **brought a female goat, what can be said?** Its gender is easily recognized, as goats do not have tails that cover their genitals. The Gemara answers: **Rather,** discerning **between males and females is not on people's minds,** i.e., they do not take notice of the offering's gender and therefore this aspect of an animal is not considered discernible.

HALAKHA

One who says, it is incumbent upon me to bring it in a pan – הָאוֹמֵר הֲרֵי עָלַי בְּמַחֲבַת: In the case of one who says: It is incumbent upon me to bring a meal offering prepared in a pan, and he brought it in a deep pan, or if he says: It is incumbent upon me to bring a meal offering prepared in a deep pan, and he brought it in a pan, the meal offering is valid but he has not fulfilled his vow. Conversely, if one says: This meal offering is to be brought in a pan, and he brought it in a deep pan, or if he vowed: This meal offering is to be brought in a deep pan, and he brought it in a pan, the meal offering is disqualified (Rambam *Sefer Avoda, Hilkhot Ma'aseh HaKorbanot* 17:2).

NOTES

As this is always male and that is female – דְּהַאי זָכָר וְהַאי נְקֵבָה: In such a case, nobody would think that this individual brought a male animal as a sin offering in violation of his obligation to bring a female one, as a male animal brought as a sin offering has no sanctity at all (*Ḥazon Ish*, citing *Temura* 20a).

BACKGROUND

Goat of the *Nasi* – שְׂעִיר נָשִׂיא: If a king commits a transgression that results in the obligation of a sin offering, he does not bring a female goat or lamb like an ordinary individual does; rather, he brings a male goat. In all other respects, the procedure of this offering is identical to that of a regular sin offering (see Leviticus 4:22–26).

Tail – אַלְיָה: This refers to the tail of a certain breed of lamb that was commonly found in Eretz Yisrael and the surrounding area. The tail was long and fatty, and covered the lamb's backside to the point that its gender was virtually indiscernible. This was especially true with regard to young lambs.

Fat-tailed sheep

פֶּסַח שֶׁשְּׁחָטוֹ לְשֵׁם אָשָׁם לֵירַצֵּי, דְּהַאי בֶּן שָׁנָה וְהַאי בֶּן שְׁתַּיִם! כֵּיוָן דְּאִיכָּא אֲשַׁם נָזִיר וַאֲשַׁם מְצוֹרָע, לָא פְּסִיקָא לֵיהּ.

The Gemara continues to challenge the opinion of Rabba: **A Paschal offering that one slaughtered for the sake of a guilt offering should effect acceptance, as this,** the Paschal offering, is **in its** first **year, and that,** a guilt offering, is **in its second** year. The Gemara answers: **Since there are** two guilt offerings that are brought from lambs in their first year, i.e., **the guilt offering of a nazirite** (see Numbers 6:12) **and the guilt offering of a leper** (see Leviticus 14:10), **it is not definitively** clear **to** an onlooker what type of offering this lamb is.

אָמַר ״לְשׁוּם אֲשַׁם גְּזֵילוֹת וּלְשׁוּם אֲשַׁם מְעִילוֹת״, מַאי אִיכָּא לְמֵימַר? וְתוּ, אֲשַׁם גְּזֵילוֹת וַאֲשַׁם מְעִילוֹת שֶׁשְּׁחָטָן לְשׁוּם פֶּסַח לֵירַצוּ, דְּפֶסַח בֶּן שָׁנָה וְהָנֵי בְּנֵי שְׁתֵּי שָׁנִים!

The Gemara asks: But if one **said:** I am hereby slaughtering this lamb **for the sake of a guilt offering for robbery, or** if he said: I am slaughtering it **for the sake of a guilt offering for misuse** of consecrated property, **what can be said?** These guilt offerings must each be brought from an animal in its second year, and therefore they cannot be mistaken for a Paschal offering, which is in its first year. **And furthermore, a guilt offering for robbery or a guilt offering for misuse** of consecrated property[N] **that one slaughtered for the sake of a Paschal offering should effect acceptance, as a Paschal offering is** always **in its** first **year, and these are in their second year.**

אֶלָּא, בֵּין בֶּן שָׁנָה לְבֵין בֶּן שְׁתֵּי שָׁנִים לָאו אַדַּעְתַּיְיהוּ דְּאֶינָשֵׁי, דְּאִיכָּא בֶּן שָׁנָה דְּמִיחְזֵי כְּבֶן שְׁתַּיִם, וְאִיכָּא בֶּן שְׁתַּיִם דְּמִיחְזֵי כְּבֶן שָׁנָה.

The Gemara answers: **Rather,** the difference in appearance **between** an animal that is **in its first year and** one that is **in its second year is not on people's minds,** i.e., this is not a clearly recognizable difference, **as there** can **be** an animal **in its first year that appears as** though it is **in its second** year, **and there** can **be** an animal **in its second** year **that appears as** though it is **in its** first **year.**

שָׂעִיר שֶׁשְּׁחָטוֹ לְשׁוּם אָשָׁם לֵירַצֵּי, דְּהַאי צֶמֶר וְהַאי שֵׂיעָר! אָמְרִי: דִּיכְרָא אוּכָּמָא הוּא.

The Gemara challenges: **A goat** sin offering **that one slaughtered for the sake of a guilt offering should effect acceptance.** It is clearly not a guilt offering, **as this,** a guilt offering, is a ram, with white **wool, and that,** a goat, has black **hair.**[N] The Gemara responds: People will **say** that this goat **is** actually **a black ram,**[B] and they may indeed mistake it for a guilt offering.

עֵגֶל וּפַר שֶׁשְּׁחָטָן לְשׁוּם פֶּסַח וְאָשָׁם לֵירַצוּ, דְּעֵגֶל וּפַר בְּפֶסַח וְאָשָׁם לֵיכָּא! אִין הָכִי נַמִי,

The Gemara challenges: **A calf or a bull that one slaughtered for the sake of** either **a Paschal offering or a guilt offering should effect acceptance.** It is clear that such animals cannot be either offering, **as a calf or bull** offering **is not** sacrificed either **as a Paschal offering or** as **a guilt offering.** The Gemara responds: **Yes, it is indeed so,** as according to Rabbi Shimon such offerings effect acceptance for their owners.

Perek **I**
Daf **3** Amud **b**

וּמַאי זְבָחִים? רוֹב זְבָחִים.

And what does Rabbi Shimon mean when he says that meal offerings are not similar to **slaughtered offerings?** He means that they are not similar to **most slaughtered offerings.** There are, however, certain slaughtered offerings whose preparation, which is unique to that particular offering, is proof that it is that offering. In those instances, Rabbi Shimon maintains that the offerings fulfill the obligations of their respective owners despite the improper intent.

רָבָא אָמַר, לָא קַשְׁיָא: כָּאן בְּקוֹמֵץ מִנְחָה לְשׁוּם מִנְחָה, כָּאן בְּקוֹמֵץ מִנְחָה לְשׁוּם זֶבַח.

§ The Gemara cites another resolution of the apparent contradiction between the two *baraitot* that report conflicting opinions of Rabbi Shimon. **Rava said:** It is **not difficult. Here,** where Rabbi Shimon says that a meal offering that was sacrificed not for its own sake fulfills the owner's obligation, he is referring to a case **where one removes a handful** from **a meal offering for the sake of a meal offering. There,** where he says that it does not fulfill the owner's obligation, he is referring to a case **where one removes a handful** from **a meal offering for the sake of a slaughtered offering.**

NOTES

A guilt offering for robbery or a guilt offering for misuse of consecrated property – אֲשַׁם גְּזֵילוֹת וַאֲשַׁם מְעִילוֹת: Although the ages of the animal sacrificed as a guilt offering for robbery and as a guilt offering for misuse of consecrated property are not explicit in the Torah, Rashi explains that the word ram (see Leviticus 5:15, 25) means an animal in its second year, as opposed to the term lamb, which invariably refers to an animal in its first year.

As this is a ram with wool and that goat has hair – דְּהַאי צֶמֶר וְהַאי שֵׂיעָר: According to Rashi, the Gemara is pointing out that whereas wool is curly, the hair of goats is long and straight. Others explain that the Gemara is referring to the difference in their color, i.e., wool is generally white, whereas the hair of a goat is typically black. Accordingly, the Gemara answers that people might mistake a black goat for a black ram (*Tosafot*).

BACKGROUND

Black ram – דִּיכְרָא אוּכָּמָא: In talmudic times most goats were black whereas the majority of sheep were white or spotted. Nevertheless, there were sheep whose color was especially dark, even black. If one were to look from a distance, such a sheep could indeed be confused with a black goat.

מִנְחָה לְשׁוּם מִנְחָה – "וְזֹאת תּוֹרַת הַמִּנְחָה", תּוֹרָה אַחַת לְכָל הַמְּנָחוֹת; מִנְחָה לְשׁוּם זֶבַח – "וְזֹאת תּוֹרַת הַמִּנְחָה וְזֶבַח" לָא כְּתִיב.

Rava elaborates: If one removes a handful from **a meal offering for the sake of** a different **meal offering** he fulfills his obligation, as the verse states: **"And this is the law of the meal offering"** (Leviticus 6:7). This indicates that there is **one law for all the meal offerings,** i.e., they are all considered variations of the same offering, and are different only with regard to how they should be sacrificed *ab initio*. Conversely, if one sacrificed **a meal offering for the sake of a slaughtered offering,** since the phrase: **And this is the law of the meal offering and a slaughtered offering, is not written** anywhere, there is no reason to conclude that one fulfills his obligation under such circumstances.

וְהָא תַּנָּא "מִפְּנֵי שֶׁמַּעֲשֶׂיהָ מוֹכִיחִין עָלֶיהָ" קָאָמַר! הָכִי קָאָמַר: אַף עַל גַּב דְּמַחֲשָׁבָה דְּלָא מִינַּכְּרָא הִיא וְתִיפָּסֵל – "וְזֹאת תּוֹרַת הַמִּנְחָה", תּוֹרָה אַחַת לְכָל הַמְּנָחוֹת.

The Gemara questions how Rava can say that the verse "And this is the law of the meal offering" serves as the basis for the opinion of Rabbi Shimon: **But doesn't the *tanna*,** i.e., Rabbi Shimon, **say** that his reasoning is **that** for any particular meal offering, **its mode of preparation proves** what **it** is?[N] The Gemara explains that **this** is what Rabbi Shimon **is saying: Even though** sacrificing a meal offering for the sake of a different meal offering is a case **where it is not recognizable**[N] that the **intention** fits the offering,[N] i.e., the intent does not match the rites being performed, **and** the offering **should** therefore **be disqualified,** the verse states: **"And this is the law of the meal offering,"** which teaches that there is **one law for all the meal offerings.**

וּמַאי "אֲבָל בִּזְבָחִים אֵינוֹ כֵּן"?

And what does Rabbi Shimon mean when he says: **But with regard to slaughtered offerings it is not so?**[N] This clause indicates that the similarity between the rites of various slaughtered offerings is a reason why they should not be valid, whereas according to the above reasoning the opposite is so.

אַף עַל גַּב דִּשְׁחִיטָה אַחַת לְכוּלָּן – "וְזֹאת תּוֹרַת הַמִּנְחָה וְזֶבַח" לָא כְּתִיב.

The Gemara explains this part of Rabbi Shimon's statement: **Even though** there is **one** manner of **slaughter for all** animal offerings, and therefore one might think that the owner has fulfilled his obligation despite the improper intent, the phrase: **And this is the law of the meal offering and a slaughtered offering, is not written.** In other words, it is not stated: This is the law of a slaughtered offering, in the manner that a verse states: "This is the law of the meal offering." Therefore, the owner of a slaughtered offering does not fulfill his obligation if there is improper intent, notwithstanding the similarity between the acts of slaughter.

NOTES

Its mode of preparation proves what it is – מַעֲשֶׂיהָ מוֹכִיחִין עָלֶיהָ: Rava's resolution apparently conflicts with Rabbi Shimon's own statement. Rabbi Shimon indicates that if the rites demonstrate what type of offering it is, this is a reason that the offering should be accepted, whereas according to Rava this is a reason to disqualify the offering, as otherwise in a case where one sacrificed a meal offering for the sake of a slaughtered offering it would certainly be accepted (Rashi).

Even though it is a case where it is not recognizable, etc. – אַף עַל גַּב...דְּלָא מִינַּכְּרָא וכו׳: Rabba and Rava disagree with regard to the status of recognizably false intent. According to Rabba, if one's actions relating to an offering are in clear contradiction to his stated intent, then his intent is disregarded and the offering is valid, as intent that is recognizably false does not negate one's actions. By contrast, Rava holds that if one's actions demonstrate that his stated intent is false, then his intent is cause for disqualifying the offering, either in order to prevent people from concluding that it is permitted to deviate from protocol with regard to offerings (Rashi), or simply because the recognizable falseness of his intent should disqualify the offering more than intent that is not recognizably improper (*Keren Ora* on 4a).

Where it is not recognizable that the intention fits the offering, etc. – דְּמַחֲשָׁבָה דְּלָא מִינַּכְּרָא וכו׳: The commentaries are puzzled by this statement, since earlier, with regard to the opinion of Rabba, the Gemara used the terminology: Not recognizable, to mean that it is unclear that the intent is false, whereas here it uses the same terminology in reference to a case where the intent clearly does not match the offering in question, i.e., it is recognizable that the intent is false. How can the same terminology be used in opposing senses? Some suggest that with regard to a consideration that serves as a reason to disqualify the offering, in accordance with the different rationales of Rabba and Rava, the Gemara chooses to describe it on each occasion in the negative form as not recognizable (*Tosafot*). Others add that since Rabba stated: Not recognizable, with regard to the disqualified meal offering, Rava did the same, despite the fact that they employ this phrase in very different ways (*Shita Mekubbetzet*).

And what does Rabbi Shimon mean when he says, but with regard to slaughtered offerings it is not so – וּמַאי אֲבָל בִּזְבָחִים אֵינוֹ כֵּן: In the *baraita*, Rabbi Shimon apparently states that animal offerings do not fulfill their owner's obligations when sacrificed not for their sake because one's intent with regard to them is not recognizably false. The Gemara therefore asks: According to Rava, this should be a reason for animal offerings to be valid, as he holds that clearly false intent is worse than intent that is not recognizably improper.

אֶלָּא מֵעַתָּה, חַטַּאת חֵלֶב שֶׁשְּׁחָטָהּ לְשֵׁם חַטַּאת דָּם, לְשׁוּם חַטַּאת עֲבוֹדָה זָרָה, לְשׁוּם חַטַּאת נָזִיר, לְשׁוּם חַטַּאת מְצוֹרָע – תְּהֵא כְּשֵׁירָה וְתַרְצֶה, דְּאָמַר רַחֲמָנָא: "וְזֹאת תּוֹרַת הַחַטָּאת" – תּוֹרָה אַחַת לְכָל חַטָּאוֹת!

The Gemara asks: **If that is so,** that the phrase "And this is the law of the meal offering" teaches that a meal offering is not disqualified despite the improper intent for a different meal offering, then analogously, **a sin offering** brought to atone for eating forbidden **fat**[N] **that one slaughtered for the sake of a sin offering** to atone for drinking **blood,** or **for the sake of a sin offering** to atone for **idol worship,** or **for the sake of a sin offering of a nazirite,** or **for the sake of a sin offering of a leper should be valid and effect acceptance. As the Merciful One states: "And this is the law of the sin offering"** (Leviticus 6:18), from which it should be derived that there is **one law for all sin offerings.**

לְרַבִּי שִׁמְעוֹן הָכִי נָמֵי; לְרַבָּנַן, הָא אָמַר: חַטַּאת חֵלֶב שֶׁשְּׁחָטָהּ לְשֵׁם חַטַּאת דָּם, לְשׁוּם חַטַּאת עֲבוֹדָה זָרָה – כְּשֵׁירָה, לְשֵׁם חַטַּאת נָזִיר, מְצוֹרָע – פְּסוּלָה, דְּהָנֵי עוֹלוֹת בַּהֲדַיְיהוּ נִינְהוּ.

The Gemara responds: **According to** the opinion of **Rabbi Shimon,** such a sin offering is **indeed** valid and effects acceptance for its owner. The Gemara notes: **According to the Rabbis,** Rava **says: A sin offering** brought to atone for eating forbidden **fat that one slaughtered for the sake of a sin offering** to atone for drinking **blood**[H] or **for the sake of a sin offering** to atone for **idol worship is valid.** But if he slaughtered it **for the sake of a sin offering of a nazirite** or for the sake of a sin offering of **a leper** it is **disqualified,** as with regard to **these** offerings, **there are burnt offerings** brought together **with them.**

רַב אַחָא בְּרֵיהּ דְּרָבָא מַתְנֵי לֵיהּ לְכוּלְּהוּ לִפְסוּלָא: "וְשָׁחַט אוֹתָהּ לְחַטָּאת" – לְשֵׁם אוֹתוֹ חַטָּאת.

Rav Aḥa, son of Rava, teaches that Rava holds that the *halakha* in **all of these** cases is **disqualification** of the sin offering. The reason is that the verse states: **"And slaughter it for a sin offering"** (Leviticus 4:33). The word "it" indicates that it must be sacrificed **for the sake of that** particular **sin offering,** and it may not be slaughtered for the sake of a different one.

רַב אַשִׁי אֲמַר, לָא קַשְׁיָא: כָּאן בְּקוֹמֵץ מִנְחַת מַחֲבַת לְשׁוּם מַרְחֶשֶׁת, כָּאן בְּקוֹמֵץ מִנְחַת מַחֲבַת לְשׁוּם מִנְחַת מַרְחֶשֶׁת.

§ The Gemara cites a third resolution of the apparent contradiction between the two *baraitot* that report conflicting opinions of Rabbi Shimon. **Rav Ashi said** that it is **not difficult. Here,** where Rabbi Shimon says that the meal offering is fit and fulfills the obligation of the owner, he is referring to a case **where** one states that he is **removing a handful** from **a pan meal offering for the sake of a deep pan,** i.e., he mentions only the vessel and not the offering. **There, where** it does not fulfill the owner's obligation, **he** states that he is **removing a handful** from **a pan meal offering for the sake of a deep-pan meal offering.**

מִנְחַת מַחֲבַת לְשׁוּם מַרְחֶשֶׁת – בְּמָנָא קָא מְחַשֵּׁב, וּמַחֲשָׁבָה בְּמָנָא לָא פָּסְלָה; מִנְחַת מַחֲבַת לְשׁוּם מִנְחַת מַרְחֶשֶׁת – בְּמִנְחָה, דְּפָסְלָה בָּהּ מַחֲשָׁבָה, קָא מְחַשֵּׁב.

Rav Ashi elaborates: When one bringing a pan meal offering states that he is removing a handful from **a pan meal offering for the sake of a deep pan, he has intent** only **with regard to** the type of **vessel, and intention with regard to** the type of **vessel does not disqualify** offerings, as he is not sacrificing the vessel, and therefore the owner's obligation is fulfilled. By contrast, when he states that he is removing a handful from **a pan meal offering for the sake of a deep-pan meal offering, he has intent with regard to** the type of **meal offering, which** improper **intention does disqualify.** Consequently, the owner's obligation is not fulfilled.

HALAKHA

A sin offering for forbidden fat that one slaughtered for the sake a sin offering for blood – חַטַּאת חֵלֶב שֶׁשְּׁחָטָהּ לְשֵׁם חַטַּאת דָּם: Any sin offering that is slaughtered for the sake of another offering is disqualified, whether it is slaughtered for the sake of an entirely different offering, e.g., a burnt offering, or for the sake of another sin offering, e.g., a sin offering brought to atone for the consumption of forbidden fat that is slaughtered for the sake of a sin offering brought to atone for consuming blood (Rambam *Sefer Avoda, Hilkhot Pesulei HaMukdashin* 15:3, 6).

NOTES

A sin offering brought to atone for eating forbidden fat – חַטַּאת חֵלֶב: This refers to a standard sin offering brought for the unwitting transgression of any sin whose punishment is *karet* when transgressed intentionally. It is called a sin offering of forbidden fat because the prohibition against consuming forbidden fat is mentioned in the Torah in proximity to the passage concerning sin offerings (Rashi on *Karetot* 22b). Another reason why a standard sin offering is referred to as a sin offering of forbidden fat is that the prohibition against consuming forbidden fat is most relevant, as this fat is found in one's home and can be confused with permitted fat (Rosh on *Nedarim* 4a).

וְהָא תַּנָּא ״מִפְּנֵי שֶׁמַּעֲשֶׂיהָ מוֹכִיחִין עָלֶיהָ״ קָאָמַר! הָכִי קָאָמַר: אַף עַל גַּב דְּמַחֲשָׁבָה מִינְּכָר הִיא תִּיפָּסֵל.

The Gemara questions how Rav Ashi can maintain that this is the reasoning of Rabbi Shimon: **But doesn't the *tanna*,** i.e., Rabbi Shimon, **say** that his reasoning is **that** for any particular meal offering, **its mode of preparation proves** what **it** is? The Gemara explains that **this** is what Rabbi Shimon **is saying: Even though** when he removes a handful from a pan meal offering explicitly for the sake of a deep pan, it is a case where the falseness of the **intention is recognizable** and the offering **should** therefore **be disqualified,** it is nevertheless valid and fulfills the owner's obligation, as intentions with regard to the vessel are irrelevant.

וּמַאי ״אֲבָל בִּזְבָחִים אֵינוֹ כֵּן״? אַף עַל גַּב דִּשְׁחִיטָה אַחַת לְכוּלָּן, זְרִיקָה אַחַת לְכוּלָּן, קַבָּלָה אַחַת לְכוּלָּן – בִּזְבִיחָה דְּפָסְלָה בֵּיהּ מַחֲשָׁבָה קָא מְחַשֵּׁב.

The Gemara asks: **And what** does Rabbi Shimon mean when he says: **But with regard to slaughtered offerings it is not so?** He means that **even though** there is **one** manner of **slaughter for all** offerings, and **one** manner of **sprinkling** of the blood **for all** offerings, and **one** manner of **collection** of the blood **for all** offerings, i.e., if one performs any of these rites for the sake of a different offering it is not recognizable that his intent is false, and therefore it might have been thought that the owner does fulfill his obligation, nevertheless he **has** improper **intent with regard to** an aspect of **slaughtering,** such as slaughtering a burnt offering for the sake of a peace offering, **which** improper **intention does disqualify.**

אֲמַר לֵיהּ רַב אַחָא בְּרֵיהּ דְּרָבָא לְרַב אַשִׁי: חֲרֵבָה מִשּׁוּם בְּלוּלָה אַמַּאי אֲמַר רַבִּי שִׁמְעוֹן? אֲמַר לֵיהּ: לְשׁוּם בִּילָּה בְּעָלְמָא.

Rav Aḥa, son of Rava, said to Rav Ashi: If this is the reasoning of Rabbi Shimon, then with regard to a case where one removes a handful from **a dry** meal offering **for the sake of** a meal offering **mixed** with oil, **why did Rabbi Shimon say** that it fulfills the owner's obligation? Since his intent concerns the meal offering itself, it should disqualify the offering. Rav Ashi **said to him:** When Rabbi Shimon says that such a meal offering fulfills the owner's obligation he is referring to a case where one removes a handful **merely for the sake of mixing,** not for the sake of a meal offering mixed with oil.

אִי הָכִי, לְשׁוּם שְׁלָמִים נַמִי – לְשׁוּם שְׁלָמִים בְּעָלְמָא!

The Gemara challenges: **If so,** then when one slaughters a burnt offering **for the sake of a peace offering as well,** one can say that his intent is **merely for the sake of peace** [*shelamim*] between himself and God. Why then does Rabbi Shimon say that this burnt offering does not fulfill the obligation of the owner?

הָכִי הָשְׁתָּא? הָתָם זֶבַח גּוּפֵהּ אִיקְּרֵי שְׁלָמִים, דִּכְתִיב: ״הַמַּקְרִיב אֶת דַּם הַשְּׁלָמִים״ ״הַזּוֹרֵק אֶת דַּם הַשְּׁלָמִים״, הָכָא מִנְחָה גּוּפַהּ מִי אִיקְּרֵי בְּלוּלָה? ״וְכָל מִנְחָה בְּלוּלָה בַשֶּׁמֶן״ כְּתִיב, ״בְּלוּלָה בַשֶּׁמֶן״ אִיקְּרֵי, ״בְּלוּלָה״ סְתָמָא לָא אִיקְּרֵי.

The Gemara rejects this challenge: **How can** these cases **be compared? There,** the **offering itself is called** ***shelamim*****, as it is written: "Who sacrifices the blood of the peace offering [*shelamim*]"** (Leviticus 7:33), and it is also written: **"Who sprinkles the blood of the peace offering"** (Leviticus 7:14). **Here, by contrast, is a meal offering itself called mixed?** It is **written: "And every meal offering, mixed with oil"** (Leviticus 7:10), indicating that there is a meal offering that **is called: Mixed with oil,** but **it is not simply called: Mixed.** One's intent to sacrifice a dry meal offering for the sake of mixing is therefore not a reference to the offering itself.

כּוּלְּהוּ כְּרַבָּה לָא אָמְרִי – דְּאַדְּרַבָּה, מַחֲשָׁבָה דְּמִנְּכְרָא פָּסַל רַחֲמָנָא;

§ Three resolutions have been suggested for the apparent contradiction between the statements of Rabbi Shimon in two *baraitot* concerning whether or not a meal offering whose handful was removed not for its own sake fulfills the obligation of its owner. Rabba's answer was that there is a difference between intent for another meal offering, in which case the owner fulfills his obligation, as the intent is recognizably improper, and intent for someone else, which is not recognizably improper. The Gemara comments: **All** the other Sages, i.e., Rava and Rav Ashi, **do not say as Rabba** did in resolving the contradiction, as they do not accept his reasoning, claiming **that on the contrary, the Merciful One disqualifies recognizably** false **intent.**

כְּרָבָא לָא אָמְרִי – ״וְזֹאת תּוֹרַת״ לָא מַשְׁמַע לְהוּ;

The Gemara continues: Rava resolved the contradiction by saying that a meal offering from which a handful was removed for the sake of another meal offering effects acceptance for the owner, as the verse states: "And this is the law of the meal offering" (Leviticus 6:7), indicating that there is one law for all meal offerings, whereas a meal offering from which a handful was removed for the sake of an animal offering does not effect acceptance. Rabba and Rav Ashi **do not say as Rava** did in resolving the contradiction, as the verse that states: **"And this is the law** of the meal offering," **does not indicate to them** that there should be one law for all meal offerings.

כְּרַב אַשִׁי לָא אָמְרִי – מִשּׁוּם קוּשְׁיָא דְּרַב אַחָא בְּרֵיהּ דְּרָבָא.

The Gemara continues: Rav Ashi resolved the contradiction by saying that when one removes the handful from a meal offering for the sake of a vessel the meal offering effects acceptance for the owner, as intent concerning the vessel itself is inconsequential, whereas when one removes the handful for the sake of another meal offering, the meal offering does not fulfill the owner's obligation. Rabba and Rava **did not say as Rav Ashi** did in resolving the contradiction **because of the difficulty** posed **by Rav Aḥa, son of Rava,**[N] from a case where one removes the handful of a dry meal offering for the sake of a mixed one. Rabbi Shimon holds that such a meal offering fulfills the owner's obligation even though his intent concerns the meal offering itself, not the vessel.

מִילְּתָא דִּפְשִׁיטָא לֵיהּ לְרַבָּה לְהַאי גִּיסָא וּלְרָבָא לְהַאי גִּיסָא, מִיבַּעְיָא לֵיהּ לְרַב הוֹשַׁעְיָא; דְּבָעֵי רַב הוֹשַׁעְיָא, וְאָמְרִי לַהּ בְּעָא מִינֵּיהּ רַב הוֹשַׁעְיָא מֵרַבִּי אַסִּי: מִנְחָה לְשׁוּם זֶבַח

The Gemara notes: **The matter that is obvious to Rabba in one way,** i.e., that with regard to meal offerings recognizably false intention is disregarded, but when the false intention is not recognizable the offering does not fulfill the owner's obligation, **and** that is obvious **to Rava in the other way,** i.e., that in cases of recognizably false intention the offering should not fulfill the owner's obligation, **is a dilemma for Rav Hoshaya.**[P] **As Rav Hoshaya raises a dilemma, and some say** that **Rav Hoshaya raises** this **dilemma before Rav Asi:** In the case of one who sacrifices **a meal offering for the sake of a slaughtered offering,**

NOTES

Because of the difficulty posed by Rav Aḥa son of Rava – מִשּׁוּם קוּשְׁיָא דְּרַב אַחָא בְּרֵיהּ דְּרָבָא: Although Rav Ashi responded to this difficulty by saying that Rabbi Shimon is referring to a case where one removes a handful for the sake of mixing rather than for the sake of a meal offering mixed with oil, the other two Sages consider this an unreasonable answer, as such meal offerings are in fact referred to simply as mixed (Rashi).

PERSONALITIES

Rav Hoshaya – רַב הוֹשַׁעְיָא: There are several *amora'im* with the name Rav Hoshaya. The Rav Hoshaya mentioned here was a third-generation *amora* who was born in Babylonia and lived in Neharde'a. There he studied under Rav Yehuda and Rav Huna, who were the greatest Sages of the generation preceding his. Rav Hoshaya eventually moved to Eretz Yisrael, where he studied under Rabbi Yoḥanan, and as indicated by the Gemara here, under Rav Asi and others as well. Rav Hoshaya is often mentioned in the Gemara as discussing halakhic matters with Rav Ḥananya. The Gemara notes that Rabbi Yoḥanan wanted to ordain them but he was ultimately unsuccessful in this endeavor. It was said of Rav Hoshaya and Rav Ḥananya that they descended from the house of Eli the High Priest, and there are some who maintain that they were brothers, and that Rabba was their brother as well.

Perek **I**
Daf **4** Amud **a**

מַה לִּי אָמַר רַבִּי שִׁמְעוֹן? טַעְמָא דְּרַבִּי שִׁמְעוֹן מִשּׁוּם מַחֲשָׁבָה דְּמִינְכְּרָא לָא פָּסְלָה, וְהָא מַחֲשָׁבָה דְּמִינְכְּרָא הוּא,

what should **I** understand that **Rabbi Shimon says** with regard to such a case? Is **the reason of Rabbi Shimon,** who says that a meal offering from which a handful was removed for the sake of another meal offering is valid and effects acceptance, **that intent that is recognizably** false **does not disqualify** an offering? **And** if so, **this** meal offering from which a handful is removed for the sake of an animal offering **is** also a case of **intent that is recognizably** false, and therefore the meal offering should not be disqualified.

אוֹ דִּילְמָא טַעְמָא דְּרַבִּי שִׁמְעוֹן מִשּׁוּם דִּכְתִיב: ״וְזֹאת תּוֹרַת הַמִּנְחָה״, וְזֶבַח לָא כְּתִיב? אֲמַר לֵיהּ: כְּלוּם הִגַּעְנוּ לְסוֹף דַּעְתּוֹ שֶׁל רַבִּי שִׁמְעוֹן?

Or perhaps the reason of Rabbi Shimon is that it is written: "And this is the law of the meal offering" (Leviticus 6:7), which indicates that there is one law for all meal offerings. If so, then a meal offering from which a handful was removed for the sake of an animal offering should be disqualified, since it **is not written:** And this is the law of the meal offering **and a slaughtered offering.** Rav Asi **said to** Rav Hoshaya: **Have we ascertained the depth of the opinion of Rabbi Shimon** in this matter? In other words, Rabbi Shimon's reasoning is not known.

כְּרַבָּה לָא מְשַׁנֵּי לֵיהּ – מִשּׁוּם קוּשְׁיָא דְּאַבָּיֵי;

The Gemara explains why Rav Asi did not resolve this dilemma. Rav Asi **did not resolve** the dilemma of Rav Hoshaya in accordance **with** the resolution stated by **Rabba,** that there is a distinction between one who removes the handful of a meal offering for the sake of another meal offering and one who removes it for the sake of another owner, **because of the difficulty** posed by **Abaye** (2b), that the *halakha* of both these cases is derived from the same comparison in the Torah between meal offerings and animal offerings.

כְּרָבָא לָא מְשַׁנֵּי לֵיהּ – מִשּׁוּם קוּשְׁיָא ״וְזֹאת תּוֹרַת הַחַטָּאת״;

Likewise, Rav Asi **did not resolve** the dilemma **in accordance with** the resolution stated by **Rava,** that the verse "And this is the law of the meal offering" teaches that a meal offering from which a handful was removed for the sake of another meal offering is valid, whereas a meal offering from which a handful was removed for the sake of an animal offering is disqualified. This is **because of the difficulty** arising from the verse: **"And this is the law of the sin offering"** (Leviticus 6:18), i.e., despite this verse, the *halakha* is that a sin offering that was slaughtered for the sake of another sin offering is not valid.

כְּרַב אַשִׁי לָא מְשַׁנֵּי לֵיהּ – מִשּׁוּם קוּשְׁיָא דְּרַב אַחָא בְּרֵיהּ דְּרָבָא.

Finally, Rav Asi **did not resolve** the dilemma **in accordance with** the resolution stated by **Rav Ashi,** that there is a distinction between one who removes the handful of a meal offering prepared in one vessel for the sake of a different vessel, and one who removes it for the sake of a meal offering prepared in a different vessel, **because of the difficulty** posed by **Rav Aḥa, son of Rava.** This difficulty concerns a case where one removes the handful of a dry meal offering for the sake of one mixed with oil; Rabbi Shimon holds that such a meal offering is valid despite the fact that the person's intent referred to the meal offering itself, not the vessel.

״חוּץ מִמִּנְחַת חוֹטֵא וּמִנְחַת קְנָאוֹת״. בִּשְׁלָמָא מִנְחַת חוֹטֵא – חַטָּאת קָרְיֵיהּ רַחֲמָנָא: ״לֹא יָשִׂים עָלֶיהָ שֶׁמֶן וְלֹא יִתֵּן עָלֶיהָ לְבוֹנָה כִּי חַטָּאת הִיא״ וגו׳, אֶלָּא מִנְחַת קְנָאוֹת מְנָלַן?

§ The mishna teaches that all meal offerings from which a handful was removed not for their sake but for the sake of another meal offering are fit for sacrifice, **except for the meal offering of a sinner and the meal offering of jealousy.** The Gemara asks: **Granted, the meal offering of a sinner** is disqualified when a handful is removed from it not for its own sake, as **the Merciful One calls it a sin offering,** in the verse: **"He shall put no oil upon it, neither shall he put any frankincense upon it, for it is a sin offering.** And he shall bring it to the priest, and the priest shall take his handful" (Leviticus 5:11–12). This verse indicates that just as a sin offering is disqualified when sacrificed not for its own sake, so too, the meal offering of a sinner is disqualified when a handful is removed from it not for its own sake. **But** with regard to **the meal offering of jealousy, from where do we** derive that this is the *halakha*?

דְּתָנֵי תַּנָּא קַמֵּיהּ דְּרַב נַחְמָן: מִנְחַת קְנָאוֹת מוֹתָרָהּ נְדָבָה.

The Gemara answers that this *halakha* may be derived from a *baraita*, **as** a ***tanna*** **taught** a *baraita* **before Rav Naḥman:** With regard to money that was designated for **a meal offering of jealousy, its surplus,** i.e., the money remaining after the purchase of the meal offering, is used to purchase communal **gift** offerings.[NH]

אֲמַר לֵיהּ: שַׁפִּיר קָאָמְרַתְּ, ״מַזְכֶּרֶת עָוֹן״ כְּתִיב בָּהּ, וּבְחַטָּאת כְּתִיב: ״וְאֹתָהּ נָתַן לָכֶם לָשֵׂאת אֶת עֲוֹן הָעֵדָה״, מָה חַטָּאת מוֹתָרָהּ נְדָבָה – אַף מִנְחַת קְנָאוֹת מוֹתָרָהּ נְדָבָה; וְכַחַטָּאת, מָה חַטָּאת פְּסוּלָה שֶׁלֹּא לִשְׁמָהּ – אַף מִנְחַת קְנָאוֹת פְּסוּלָה שֶׁלֹּא לִשְׁמָהּ.

Rav Naḥman **said to him: You are saying well,** as **it is written with regard to** a meal offering of jealousy: **"Bringing iniquity to remembrance"** (Numbers 5:15), **and it is written with regard to a sin offering: "And He has given it you to bear the iniquity of the congregation"** (Leviticus 10:17). A verbal analogy is drawn between the two uses of the term "iniquity" in these verses. This teaches that **just as** in the case of **a sin offering, its surplus** is used to purchase communal **gift** offerings, **so too,** with regard to **a meal offering of jealousy, its surplus** is used to purchase communal **gift** offerings. **And** a meal offering of jealousy is also **like a sin offering** in another aspect: **Just as a sin offering is disqualified** when sacrificed **not for its own sake, so too, a meal offering of jealousy is disqualified** when a handful is removed from it **not for its own sake.**

אֶלָּא מֵעַתָּה, אָשָׁם יְהֵא פָּסוּל שֶׁלֹּא לִשְׁמוֹ, דְּגָמַר ״עָוֹן״ ״עָוֹן״ מֵחַטָּאת!

The Gemara asks: **If that is so,** that the *halakha* of a meal offering of jealousy is derived from a verbal analogy to a sin offering based on the word "iniquity," then **a guilt offering should** also **be disqualified** if it was sacrificed **not for its own sake, as** a similar verbal analogy may be **derived from** the verse that states: "The **iniquity** [*avon*] of the congregation" (Leviticus 10:17), with regard to **a sin offering,** and the verse that states: "And shall bear his **iniquity**" (Leviticus 5:17), in connection with a guilt offering.

דָּנִין ״עָוֹן״ מֵ״עָוֹן״ וְאֵין דָּנִין ״עֲוֹנוֹ״ מֵ״עָוֹן״.

The Gemara responds: **One derives** a verbal analogy based on the word **"iniquity" from** a verse that likewise uses the term **"iniquity," but one does not derive** a verbal analogy based on the term **"his iniquity [*avono*]" from** a verse that uses the term **"iniquity."**

מַאי נָפְקָא מִינַּהּ? וְהָא תָּנָא דְּבֵי רַבִּי יִשְׁמָעֵאל: ״וְשָׁב הַכֹּהֵן״ ״וּבָא הַכֹּהֵן״ – זוֹ הִיא שִׁיבָה, זוֹ הִיא בִּיאָה!

The Gemara asks: **What difference is** there? **Didn't the school of Rabbi Yishmael teach** the following verbal analogy with regard to leprosy of houses? The verse states: **"And the priest shall return [*veshav*]** on the seventh day" (Leviticus 14:39), and another verse concerning the priest's visit seven days later states: **"And the priest shall come [*uva*]** and look" (Leviticus 14:44). **This returning** and **this coming** have the same meaning, and one can therefore derive by verbal analogy that the *halakha* that applies if the leprosy had spread at the conclusion of the first week applies if it had spread again by the end of the following week. All the more so should a less pronounced difference of one letter between *avon* and *avono* not prevent the teaching of a verbal analogy.

NOTES

Its surplus is used to purchase communal gift offerings – מוֹתָרָהּ נְדָבָה: According to Rashi, the surplus was placed in collection horns that were located in the Temple, whose funds were used to purchase communal burnt offerings that were sacrificed upon the altar after the obligatory offerings of the day, so that the altar did not remain idle (see *Shekalim* 2:5, 6:1, 6:6). Conversely, the Rambam maintains that the surplus was used for the purchase of voluntary meal offerings, as the surplus from a meal offering is used toward another meal offering (see Meiri on *Shekalim* 2:5).

HALAKHA

A meal offering of jealousy, its surplus is used to purchase communal gift offerings – מִנְחַת קְנָאוֹת מוֹתָרָהּ נְדָבָה: If one designated money for the meal offering of a sinner or brought flour for it, the surplus flour or money is used to purchase voluntary meal offerings. This *halakha* applies even to a meal offering of jealousy, which is brought from barley, i.e., its surplus is sold and the money raised is used to purchase wheat flour (Rambam *Sefer Avoda, Hilkhot Pesulei HaMukdashin* 5:8, and see *Or Same'aḥ* there).

וְעוֹד, לִיגְמַר ״עֲוֹנוֹ״ ״עֲוֹנוֹ״ מֵעֲוֹן דִּשְׁמִיעַת הַקּוֹל, דִּכְתִיב: ״אִם לוֹא יַגִּיד וְנָשָׂא עֲוֹנוֹ״!

And furthermore, let one derive a verbal analogy through the term **"his iniquity"** stated with regard to a guilt offering, and the term **"his iniquity" from** the verse concerning the sin offering brought for the **iniquity for hearing the voice,** i.e., the sin offering of one who takes a false oath that he does not have any information relevant to a matter when another requests that he testify about it, **as it is written: "If he does not utter it, then he shall bear his iniquity"** (Leviticus 5:1).

אֶלָּא כִּי גָּמְרִי גְּזֵירָה שָׁוָה – לְמוֹתַר נְדָבָה הוּא דְּגָמְרִי.

Rather, it must be that **when the verbal analogy was derived, it was derived** only with regard **to** the *halakha* that the **surplus** from the money designated for a meal offering of jealousy is used to purchase communal **gift** offerings, and not with regard to the *halakha* that a meal offering of jealousy from which a handful was removed not for its own sake is disqualified.

וְכִי תֵּימָא: אֵין גְּזֵירָה שָׁוָה לְמֶחֱצָה – גַּלֵּי רַחֲמָנָא גַּבֵּי חַטָּאת: ״וְשָׁחַט אוֹתָהּ לְחַטָּאת״ – אוֹתָהּ לִשְׁמָהּ כְּשֵׁירָה, שֶׁלֹּא לִשְׁמָהּ פְּסוּלָה, אֲבָל כׇּל קׇדָשִׁים – בֵּין לִשְׁמָן בֵּין שֶׁלֹּא לִשְׁמָן כְּשֵׁרִים.

And if you would say that there is a principle that **there is no partial verbal analogy,**[N] that principle does not apply in this instance. As **the Merciful One revealed with regard to a sin offering** that the *halakha* of other offerings may not be derived from this case, as the verse states: **"And slaughter it for a sin offering"** (Leviticus 4:33). This verse indicates that **it,** i.e., a sin offering, when slaughtered **for its own sake** is **valid,** and when slaughtered **not for its own sake** is **disqualified. But all** other **sacrificial** animals, **whether** sacrificed **for their sake or not for their sake, are valid.**

אֶלָּא מִנְחַת חוֹטֵא וּמִנְחַת קְנָאוֹת דִּפְסוּלִין שֶׁלֹּא לִשְׁמָן, מְנָלַן?

The Gemara asks: **But** if the Merciful One revealed that one cannot derive the *halakha* of other offerings that were sacrificed not for their sake from a sin offering, then **from where do we** derive the *halakha* **that the meal offering of a sinner and the meal offering of jealousy are disqualified** when a handful is removed from them **not for their sake?**

חַטָּאת טַעְמָא מַאי – מִשּׁוּם דִּכְתִיב בָּהּ ״הִיא״, הָכִי נַמִי – הָא כְּתִיב בְּהוּ ״הִיא״.

The Gemara explains: With regard to **a sin offering, what is the reason** that it is disqualified when sacrificed not for its own sake? It is **because it is written with regard to** this offering: **"It,"** in a verse discussing the sin offering of the *Nasi*: "It is a sin offering" (Leviticus 4:24). This indicates that a sin offering is valid only when it is sacrificed for its own sake. **So too, it is written with regard to them,** i.e., the meal offering of a sinner and the meal offering of jealousy: **"It."** In the case of the meal offering of a sinner the verse states: "It is a sin offering" (Leviticus 5:11), and with regard to the meal offering of jealousy it is written: "It is a meal offering of jealousy" (Numbers 5:15).

אָשָׁם נַמִי, הָא כְּתִיב בֵּיהּ ״הוּא״! הַהוּא ״הוּא״ לְאַחַר הַקְטָרַת אֵימוּרִין הוּא דִּכְתִיב,

The Gemara challenges: But if so, concerning **a guilt offering as well, it is written about** this offering: **"It,"** as the verse states: "It is a guilt offering" (Leviticus 7:5). Accordingly, a guilt offering should likewise be disqualified if it is slaughtered not for its own sake. The Gemara responds: **That** term **"it" is written with regard to** the stage **after the burning of** the **sacrificial portions** [*eimurin*][L] of a guilt offering, which are intended for burning upon the altar.

כִּדְתַנְיָא: אֲבָל אָשָׁם לֹא נֶאֱמַר בּוֹ ״הוּא״ אֶלָּא לְאַחַר הַקְטָרַת אֵימוּרִין, הוּא עַצְמוֹ שֶׁלֹּא הוּקְטְרוּ אֵימוּרָיו – כָּשֵׁר.

As it is taught in a *baraita*: One derives from the word "it" that if the offering was slaughtered not for its own sake it is disqualified only in the case of a sin offering. **But** concerning **a guilt offering, it is stated about** this offering: **"It is a guilt offering," only** with regard to the stage **after the burning of** the **sacrificial portions.** The *baraita* adds: One cannot derive that if these portions were burned not for the sake of a guilt offering then the offering is disqualified, since the guilt offering **itself** is **valid** if **its sacrificial portions were not burned** upon the altar at all.[N]

NOTES

There is no partial verbal analogy – אֵין גְּזֵירָה שָׁוָה לְמֶחֱצָה: It is a Torah edict that *halakhot* may be derived by verbal analogy. Accordingly, one cannot decide based on logic which aspects of a *halakha* are derived from a particular verbal analogy and which are not. That said, when the Torah itself limits the application of a particular *halakha*, that limitation should be applied to the verbal analogy as well, and the limitation does not indicate that the verbal analogy is incorrect (see *Sefer HaKeritut* 1:2, 11).

It itself is valid if its sacrificial portions were not burned upon the altar at all – הוּא עַצְמוֹ שֶׁלֹּא הוּקְטְרוּ אֵימוּרָיו כָּשֵׁר: Improper intent disqualifies an offering only when it concerns one of the four sacrificial rites involving the blood of the offering, i.e., its slaughter, the collection of its blood, the conveying of its blood to the altar, and the presentation of its blood upon the altar. The sacrificial portions of an offering are burned upon the altar only after its blood has already been presented and atonement achieved. Accordingly, the burning of the sacrificial portions of an offering is not critical to its validity (Rashi on *Zevaḥim* 5b).

LANGUAGE

Sacrificial portions [*eimurin*] – אֵימוּרִין: There are various explanations of the source of the word *eimurin*, sacrificial portions, i.e., those portions sacrificed and consumed upon the altar. Based on the Gemara in *Sukka* (55b), its root is *alef, mem, reish,* which means: Say. According to this explanation, the name was given because these are the portions about which it is said to sacrifice them upon the altar (*Tosefot Yom Tov* on *Pesaḥim* 5:10). Some say that according to this interpretation the word should be pronounced *amurin*.

Alternatively, the word is based on the term *mar*, master (*Arukh*), and refers to the most important parts of an offering, or the master portions, which are sacrificed upon the altar. *Mishne LaMelekh* relates *eimurin* to the verse: "You have avouched [*he'emarta*] the Lord this day to be your God" (Deuteronomy 26:17). According to many linguists, *eimurin* comes from a Greek word, either μῆρα, *mēra*, or μηρία, *mēria*, both of which refer to thighbones and their flesh.

HALAKHA

A guilt offering that was consigned to grazing, etc. – אָשָׁם שֶׁנִּיתַּק לִרְעִיָּה וכו׳: With regard to a guilt offering that was consigned to grazing, if one proceeded to sacrifice it as a burnt offering, it is valid. This is in accordance with the conclusion of the Gemara in *Pesaḥim* (73a) that this guilt offering is valid as a burnt offering only when slaughtered explicitly for the sake of a burnt offering (Rambam *Sefer Avoda, Hilkhot Pesulei HaMukdashin* 4:15, and see *Kesef Mishne* and *Leḥem Mishne* there).

וְאֶלָּא ״הוּא״ לָמָּה לִי? לְכִדְרַב הוּנָא אָמַר רַב: אָשָׁם שֶׁנִּיתַּק לִרְעִיָּה וּשְׁחָטוֹ סְתָם – כָּשֵׁר לְשׁוּם עוֹלָה;

The Gemara asks: **But** if so, **why do I** need the word **"it"** stated with regard to a guilt offering? The Gemara answers: It is necessary **for that which Rav Huna** says that **Rav says:** With regard to **a guilt offering** whose owner died or whose transgression was otherwise atoned for, and **that was** therefore **consigned** by the court **to grazing**[NH] until it develops a blemish so that it can be sold and the proceeds used to purchase a burnt offering, if, before it developed a blemish, someone **slaughtered it without specification** of its purpose, it is **fit** if it was sacrificed **as a burnt offering.**[N]

נִיתַּק – אִין, לֹא נִיתַּק – לָא, אָמַר קְרָא: ״הוּא״ – בַּהֲוָיָיתוֹ יְהֵא.

The Gemara infers: If **it was consigned** to grazing, **yes,** it is fit if it was sacrificed as a burnt offering if slaughtered. By inference, if **it was not consigned** to grazing, it is **not** fit. What is the reason for this? **The verse states: "It** is a guilt offering," indicating that **it shall** remain **as it is,**[N] i.e., as a guilt offering, unless it is consigned by the court to another purpose.

אָמַר רַב: מִנְחַת הָעוֹמֶר שֶׁקְּמָצָהּ שֶׁלֹּא לִשְׁמָהּ – פְּסוּלָה, הוֹאִיל וּבָאת לְהַתִּיר וְלֹא הִתִּירָה. וְכֵן אַתָּה אוֹמֵר בַּאֲשַׁם נָזִיר

§ The mishna teaches that all the meal offerings from which a handful was removed not for their sake are fit for sacrifice but they do not fulfill the owner's obligation. Concerning this, **Rav says:** With regard to **the** ***omer*** **meal offering,** i.e., the measure of barley brought as a communal offering on the sixteenth of Nisan (see Leviticus 23:9–14), if the priest **removed a handful** from it **not for its own sake** it is **disqualified.** It is disqualified **since** an *omer* meal offering **came** for a specific purpose, namely, **to permit** the consumption of the new crop, **and** this meal offering **did not permit** the consumption of the new crop because its rites were performed not for its own sake. **And so you say with regard to the guilt offering of a nazirite** who became ritually impure, whose proper sacrifice enables the nazirite to restart his naziriteship afresh in purity,

NOTES

A guilt offering that was consigned to grazing – אָשָׁם שֶׁנִּיתַּק לִרְעִיָּה: The Sages learned by tradition that in any instance where a sin offering is left to die, e.g., if its owner died or atoned for his sin with another animal, a guilt offering in a similar situation is consigned to grazing until it becomes blemished, after which it is sold and the money used to purchase communal burnt offerings. As for what is considered consignment, Rashi explains that this is the transferal of the animal to the care of a shepherd (see also Rashi on *Pesaḥim* 73a and Meiri on *Nazir* 25b). Alternatively, the animal is consigned when the court or Temple treasurer declares that the guilt offering should be sent to graze (Rashi on *Zevaḥim* 5b). Elsewhere (*Pesaḥim* 73a), Rashi indicates that the owner himself consigns the animal to graze.

Someone slaughtered it without specification, it is fit as a burnt offering – וּשְׁחָטוֹ סְתָם כָּשֵׁר לְשׁוּם עוֹלָה: A guilt offering that was not yet consigned to grazing is fit for sacrifice as a burnt offering only if it is slaughtered explicitly for the sake of a burnt offering, as this explicit intent uproots the status of guilt offering from the animal (Rashi). Based on a variant text of the Gemara, which states: If he slaughtered it for the sake of a burnt offering it is valid, other commentaries maintain that only a guilt offering already consigned to grazing can be valid as a burnt offering, and this is the *halakha* only when it is slaughtered explicitly for the sake of a burnt offering. A guilt offering that has not been consigned to grazing will be disqualified even when slaughtered explicitly for the sake of a burnt offering (Rabbeinu Gershom Meor HaGola). According to this opinion, the Gemara derives this *halakha* from the word "it," which teaches that a guilt offering that was not consigned to grazing remains in its current state, so that even explicit intent to slaughter it for the sake of a burnt offering does not uproot its status as a guilt offering.

The verse states, it is a guilt offering, it shall remain as it is – אָמַר קְרָא הוּא בַּהֲוָיָיתוֹ יְהֵא: By citing a verse as the source for this distinction between an animal that was consigned to grazing and one that was not, the Gemara indicates that this *halakha* applies by Torah law, i.e., if this guilt offering was slaughtered before it was consigned to grazing it is disqualified. Other sources (see *Shevuot* 12b) indicate that by Torah law such a guilt offering is in fact valid as a burnt offering, and it is the Sages who disqualified it out of a concern that one might sacrifice it as a burnt offering before he achieves atonement with another animal. Some commentaries therefore suggest that the two discussions in the Gemara reflect a dispute with regard to the status of a guilt offering that was slaughtered before it was consigned to grazing, and each discussion in the Gemara is in accordance with a different opinion (Ramban on *Shevuot* 12b; see *Tosafot*, citing Rabbeinu Tam, and *Sefer HaYashar* 514, 777).

Perek **I**
Daf **4** Amud **b**

וַאֲשַׁם מְצוֹרָע שֶׁשְּׁחָטָן שֶׁלֹּא לִשְׁמָן – פְּסוּלִין, הוֹאִיל וּבָאוּ לְהַכְשִׁיר וְלֹא הִכְשִׁירוּ.

and so you say with regard to **the guilt offering of a leper,** whose proper sacrifice enables the leper to enter the Israelite camp and to partake of offerings of sanctity, **that** if one **slaughtered** these offerings **not for their sake, they are disqualified.** They are disqualified **since** their sacrifice **came to render** the nazirite and leper **fit, and** these guilt offerings **did not render** them **fit.**

תְּנַן: כׇּל הַמְּנָחוֹת שֶׁנִּקְמְצוּ שֶׁלֹּא לִשְׁמָן – כְּשֵׁירוֹת, אֶלָּא שֶׁלֹּא עָלוּ לַבְּעָלִים לְשׁוּם חוֹבָה, חוּץ מִמִּנְחַת חוֹטֵא וּמִנְחַת קְנָאוֹת; וְאִם אִיתָא, לִיתְנֵי נַמִּי: חוּץ מִמִּנְחַת הָעוֹמֶר!

The Gemara asks: **We learned** in the mishna that **all the meal offerings** from **which a handful was removed not for their sake are fit** for sacrifice **but they did not satisfy the obligation of the owner, except for the meal offering of a sinner and the meal offering of jealousy. And if it is so** that an *omer* meal offering from which a handful was removed not for its own sake is disqualified, then **let** the mishna **also teach: Except for the** ***omer*** **meal offering.**

כִּי קָתָנֵי – בָּאָה יָחִיד, בָּאָה צִבּוּר לָא קָתָנֵי; כִּי תָּנֵי – בָּאָה בִּגְלַל עַצְמָהּ, בָּאָה בִּגְלַל זֶבַח לָא קָתָנֵי;

The Gemara responds: **When** the mishna **teaches** this *halakha*, it teaches it only with regard to meal offerings that **come** on behalf of **an individual.** The mishna **does not teach** the *halakha* with regard to those meal offerings that **come** on behalf of the **community.** Additionally, **when** the mishna **teaches** this *halakha*, it is only with regard to a meal offering that **comes on account of itself,** i.e., as an independent offering. The mishna **does not teach** the *halakha* with regard to a meal offering that **comes on account of,** i.e., together with, **a slaughtered offering,** e.g., the *omer* meal offering, which is brought along with two sheep.

כִּי קָתָנֵי – הָנָךְ שֶׁאֵין קָבוּעַ לָהֶן זְמָן, הָא דִּקְבוּעַ לָהּ זְמָן לָא קָתָנֵי.

The Gemara adds: Furthermore, **when** the mishna **teaches** this *halakha*, it is only with regard to **those** meal offerings **whose time is not set,** i.e., they may be sacrificed on any date. The mishna **does not teach** the *halakha* with regard to **this** *omer* meal offering, **whose time** for offering **is set** on the sixteenth of Nisan.

אָמַר מָר: וְכֵן אַתָּה אוֹמֵר בַּאֲשַׁם נָזִיר וַאֲשַׁם מְצוֹרָע שֶׁשְּׁחָטָן שֶׁלֹּא לִשְׁמָן – פְּסוּלִין, הוֹאִיל וּבָאוּ לְהַכְשִׁיר וְלֹא הִכְשִׁירוּ.

§ The Gemara analyzes the statement of Rav. **The Master said: And so you say with regard to the guilt offering of a nazirite** who became ritually impure, **and** so you say with regard to **the guilt offering of a leper, that** if one **slaughtered** these offerings **not for their sake, they are disqualified.** They are disqualified **since** their proper sacrifice **came to render** the nazirite and leper **fit, and they did not render** them **fit.**

תְּנַן: כָּל הַזְּבָחִים שֶׁשְּׁחָטָן שֶׁלֹּא לִשְׁמָן – כְּשֵׁירִין, אֶלָּא שֶׁלֹּא עָלוּ לַבְּעָלִים לְשׁוּם חוֹבָה, חוּץ מִפֶּסַח וְחַטָּאת; וְאִם אִיתָא, לִיתְנֵי נַמִי: חוּץ מֵאֲשַׁם נָזִיר וַאֲשַׁם מְצוֹרָע, דְּבָאוּ לְהַכְשִׁיר וְלֹא הִכְשִׁירוּ!

The Gemara asks: **We learned** in a mishna (*Zevaḥim* 2a): **All slaughtered offerings that one slaughtered not for their sake**[H] **are fit, but they did not satisfy the obligation of the owner.** This is the *halakha* with regard to all offerings **except for the Paschal offering and the sin offering,** which are disqualified when slaughtered not for their sake. **And if it is so** that the *halakha* is in accordance with the statement of Rav, **let** the mishna **also teach: Except for the guilt offering of a nazirite and the guilt offering of a leper, since they came to render** one **fit and they did not render** one **fit.**

כֵּיוָן דְּאִיכָּא אֲשַׁם גְּזֵילוֹת וַאֲשַׁם מְעִילוֹת דִּלְכַפָּרָה אָתוּ, לָא פְּסִיקָא לֵיהּ.

The Gemara answers: **Since there** are other guilt offerings, i.e., **the guilt offering for robbery,** which one brings for taking a false oath denying an accusation of robbery, **and the guilt offering** brought **for misuse** of consecrated property, **that come for atonement,** which do not render one fit and are fit for sacrifice if they were slaughtered not for their sake, the *tanna* of the mishna could **not** state the *halakha* with regard to guilt offerings in **an absolute** manner, and therefore he refrains from mentioning guilt offerings at all.

מַאי שְׁנָא אֲשַׁם נָזִיר וַאֲשַׁם מְצוֹרָע דְּבָאוּ לְהַכְשִׁיר וְלֹא הִכְשִׁירוּ, הָנֵי נַמִי בָּאוּ לְכַפָּרָה וְלֹא כִּפְּרוּ!

The Gemara asks: **What is different** about **the guilt offering of a nazirite and the guilt offering of a leper?** Why are they disqualified when slaughtered not for their sake **since they came to render fit and they did not render fit? These,** i.e., the guilt offerings for robbery and for misuse of consecrated property, should **likewise** be disqualified when slaughtered not for their sake, since they **came for atonement and they did not atone.**

אֲמַר רַבִּי יִרְמְיָה: מָצִינוּ שֶׁחִלֵּק הַכָּתוּב בֵּין מְכַפְּרִים וּבֵין מַכְשִׁירִין, מְכַפְּרִין – אִית בְּהוּ דְּאָתוּ לְאַחַר מִיתָה, מַכְשִׁירִין – לֵית בְּהוּ דְּאָתוּ לְאַחַר מִיתָה. דִּתְנַן: הָאִשָּׁה שֶׁהֵבִיאָה חַטָּאתָהּ וּמֵתָה – יָבִיאוּ יוֹרְשִׁין עוֹלָתָהּ, עוֹלָתָהּ וּמֵתָה – לֹא יָבִיאוּ יוֹרְשִׁין חַטָּאתָהּ.

Rabbi Yirmeya said in response: **We find that the Torah differentiates between** those guilt offerings that **atone and** those that **render fit,** and the *halakha* is more stringent with regard to those that render fit. Rabbi Yirmeya elaborates: With regard to those guilt offerings that **atone, there are among them** offerings **that come after death,**[N] i.e., they are sacrificed after the death of their owners, whereas with regard to those that **render fit, there are none among them that come after death. As we learned** in a mishna (*Kinnim* 2:5): With regard to **a woman** after childbirth **who brought her sin offering**[H] for her ritual purification **and died,**[N] **the heirs shall bring her burnt offering,** which comes to atone. If she set aside **her burnt offering and died, the heirs shall not bring her sin offering,** as it comes to render her fit to partake of offerings.

HALAKHA

All slaughtered offerings that one slaughtered not for their sake – כָּל הַזְּבָחִים שֶׁשְּׁחָטָן שֶׁלֹּא לִשְׁמָן: All slaughtered offerings that one slaughtered not for their sake are fit but they did not fulfill the obligation of the owner. The exceptions are the Paschal offering and the sin offering, which are disqualified when slaughtered not for their sake. The guilt offering of a nazirite and the guilt offering of a leper are also fit when slaughtered not for their sake; see 5a (Rambam *Sefer Avoda, Hilkhot Pesulei HaMukdashin* 15:1).

A woman who brought her sin offering – הָאִשָּׁה שֶׁהֵבִיאָה חַטָּאתָהּ: With regard to a woman after childbirth or a woman who experienced a discharge of uterine blood after her menstrual period [*zava*], if she brought her sin offering and then died, her heirs bring her burnt offering. This is the case even if she had not yet designated money for its purchase (Rambam *Sefer Korbanot, Hilkhot Meḥusrei Kappara* 1:13).

NOTES

Guilt offerings that atone, there are among them offerings that come after death, etc. – מְכַפְּרִין אִית בְּהוּ דְּאָתוּ לְאַחַר מִיתָה וכו׳: Some commentaries explain the significance of this distinction as follows: The fact that offerings that atone may be sacrificed after death indicates that not only are they considered an atonement for their owners, but they are considered gift offerings as well. Accordingly, they are valid even when sacrificed not for their sake, like gift offerings (see 2a). Conversely, those offerings that render one fit may not be brought after death because their entire purpose is to render their owners fit, a purpose that becomes irrelevant once the owner dies. Consequently, this offering is disqualified when sacrificed not for its own sake, as it is not considered a gift offering (see *Ḥiddushei HaGriz* and *Netivot HaKodesh*).

A woman after childbirth who brought her sin offering and died, etc. – הָאִשָּׁה שֶׁהֵבִיאָה חַטָּאתָהּ וּמֵתָה וכו׳: Rashi explains that the burnt offering is brought as the atonement for a woman after childbirth, whereas the sin offering renders her fit to partake of offerings. The sin offering is not brought as an atonement, as she committed no sin (*Tosafot Ḥitzoniyyot*). Accordingly, the mishna is cited as proof of both aspects of Rabbi Yirmeya's statement, i.e., that an atonement offering is brought after the owner's death, and that an offering that renders one fit is not. Others maintain that the woman's sin offering is in fact brought as an atonement. Since her burnt offering accompanies her sin offering, the burnt offering is also considered an atonement offering. Her burnt offering is brought after her death because a burnt offering may be sacrificed as a gift offering. The mishna is therefore proof only of Rabbi Yirmeya's claim that some atonement offerings may be brought after death (Rabbeinu Gershom Meor HaGola).

מַתְקִיף לָהּ רַבִּי יְהוּדָה בְּרֵיהּ דְּרַבִּי שִׁמְעוֹן בֶּן פָּזִי: מַכְשִׁירִין נַמִי מִי לֵית בְּהוּ דְּאָתוּ לְאַחַר מִיתָה? וְהָתְנַן: הַמַּפְרִישׁ מָעוֹת לִנְזִירוּתוֹ – לֹא נֶהֱנִין וְלֹא מוֹעֲלִין, מִפְּנֵי שֶׁרְאוּיִין לָבֹא כּוּלָּן שְׁלָמִים.

Rabbi Yehuda, son of Rabbi Shimon ben Pazi,[P] **objects to this:** With regard to offerings that **render fit as well, are there not among them** offerings **that come after death? But didn't we learn** in a mishna (*Me'ila* 11a): In the case of **one who separates funds for** the offerings of **his naziriteship,**[H] i.e., his sin offering, burnt offering, and peace offering, a person **may not derive benefit** from them[N] *ab initio*, **but** if one benefited from them after the fact, he is **not** liable for **misuse** of consecrated property,[N] i.e., he is not required to bring a guilt offering and is not obligated to repay the principal and an additional fifth. This is **because** the coins **are all fit for bringing peace offerings,** and there is no misuse of consecrated property with regard to funds fit for a peace offering.

מֵת וְהָיוּ לוֹ מָעוֹת סְתוּמִין – יִפְּלוּ לִנְדָבָה. מְפוֹרָשִׁין, דְּמֵי חַטָּאת – יוֹלִיךְ לְיָם הַמֶּלַח, לֹא נֶהֱנִין וְלֹא מוֹעֲלִין; דְּמֵי עוֹלָה – יָבִיא בָּהֶן עוֹלָה וּמוֹעֲלִין בָּהֶן;

The mishna continues: If the nazirite **died and he had undesignated funds** that he set aside to pay for his nazirite offerings without specifying how much money should be allocated toward each offering, **they will be allocated for** communal **gift** offerings. If he left behind **allocated** funds, then with regard to **the money for a sin offering,** one must **take** it and cast it **into the Dead Sea;**[B] **one may not benefit** from it *ab initio*, **but** if one benefited from it after the fact, he is **not** liable for **misuse** of consecrated property. With regard to **the money for a burnt offering, one brings with it a burnt offering, and** one is liable for **misusing them.**

דְּמֵי שְׁלָמִים – יָבִיא בָּהֶן שְׁלָמִים, וְנֶאֱכָלִין לְיוֹם אֶחָד וְאֵין טְעוּנִין לֶחֶם. וְהָא עוֹלָה וּשְׁלָמִים דְּנָזִיר דְּמַכְשִׁירִים נִינְהוּ, וְקָא אָתוּ לְאַחַר מִיתָה!

The mishna concludes: With **the money for a peace offering, one brings a peace offering with it,**[N] **and** these offerings **are eaten for one day,** like the peace offering brought by a nazirite, **and do not require** the **loaves** that are normally bought with the peace offering of a nazirite. Rabbi Yehuda explains his question: **But** the **burnt offering and peace offering of a nazirite are** offerings **that render** the nazirite **fit** to drink wine, **and yet they come after death.**

אֲמַר רַב פַּפָּא, הָכִי קָא אָמַר רַבִּי יִרְמְיָה: לֹא מָצִינוּ הֶכְשֵׁר קָבוּעַ דְּבָא לְאַחַר מִיתָה; וּדְנָזִיר הֶכְשֵׁר שֶׁאֵינוֹ קָבוּעַ הוּא,

Rav Pappa said in response that **this is what Rabbi Yirmeya is saying: We do not find** an instance of **a fixed** manner of **rendering fit that comes after death,** i.e., there is no instance where the only offering that will render one fit to act in a manner previously prohibited to him may be sacrificed after death. **And** the offerings **of a nazirite** are examples of a means of **rendering fit that is not fixed,**

PERSONALITIES

Rabbi Yehuda son of Rabbi Shimon ben Pazi – רַבִּי יְהוּדָה בְּרֵיהּ דְּרַבִּי שִׁמְעוֹן בֶּן פָּזִי: Rabbi Yehuda, son of Rabbi Shimon ben Pazi, was a third-generation *amora* from Eretz Yisrael and a student of the disciples of Rabbi Yoḥanan. According to some commentaries, this Rabbi Yehuda is the same individual as the Rabbi Yehuda ben Pazi who is cited throughout the Talmud. Others hold that this *amora* is Rabbi Yehuda, son of Rabbi Simon, who appears mostly in midrashic literature.

HALAKHA

One who separates funds for the offerings of his naziriteship, etc. – הַמַּפְרִישׁ מָעוֹת לִנְזִירוּתוֹ וכו׳: One who designates money for his naziriteship offerings may not derive benefit from the money, but if he derives benefit from it he is not liable for misuse of consecrated property, as all the money is fit for the purchase of peace offerings. In a case where he died and money remained from those funds, if the money was undesignated it is allocated for communal gift offerings. If they were designated funds, the money for a sin offering is cast into the Dead Sea; one may not derive benefit from it but if he does so he is not liable for misuse of consecrated property. The money for a burnt offering is used to purchase burnt offerings, and one who derives benefit from it is liable for misuse of consecrated property. With the money for a peace offering one brings a peace offering that may be eaten for one day and does not require loaves (Rambam *Sefer Hafla'a*, *Hilkhot Nezirut* 9:10 and *Sefer Avoda*, *Hilkhot Me'ila* 4:3).

BACKGROUND

Dead Sea – יָם הַמֶּלַח: The term Dead Sea can sometimes refer to saltwater seas in general, as opposed to freshwater lakes, but it usually means specifically the Dead Sea, also referred to in talmudic sources as the Sea of Sodom. Any item from which it is prohibited to derive benefit is cast into the Dead Sea, as there are no fishermen or people who will retrieve items thrown into it. It is also possible that due to the high density of salt in the Dead Sea, items cast into it will become rusty and decay in a short period of time, thereby preventing their further use.

Rusty tire eroded by salt at the Dead Sea

NOTES

May not derive benefit from them – לֹא נֶהֱנִין: Rashi explains that the Sages prohibited deriving benefit from this money due to the portion of the money intended for a burnt offering and sin offering. Others maintain that it is prohibited by Torah law to derive benefit from this money (*Shita Mekubbetzet*, citing *Tosafot Ḥitzoniyyot*). It is even prohibited to derive benefit from the portion of the funds intended for a peace offering, despite the fact that this is an offering of lesser sanctity, as the verse states: "He shall not break his word; he shall do according to all that proceeds out of his mouth" (Numbers 30:3).

But he is not liable for misuse of consecrated property, etc. – וְלֹא מוֹעֲלִין וכו׳: The *halakhot* of the misuse of consecrated property apply to a peace offering only with regard to those portions that are intended for the altar, and only after its blood is sprinkled on the altar. Money used to purchase a peace offering belongs to the owner, and therefore the *halakhot* of misuse do not apply to it. Consequently, one who derives benefit from part of the undesignated money intended for the purchase of the offerings of a nazirite is not liable for misuse, as each portion of the money is fit to be used for purchasing a peace offering (Rashi on *Me'ila* 11a). By contrast, one who benefits from all of the money is liable for misuse of consecrated property and must bring a guilt offering for misuse, as a portion of the money was nevertheless intended for purchasing a burnt offering and a sin offering. Others maintain that all of the undesignated money may be used to purchase peace offerings, and therefore the *halakhot* of misuse do not apply (*Tosafot* on *Me'ila* 11a). Alternatively, the *halakhot* of the misuse of consecrated property are relevant only to items that have been clearly designated. They do not apply to undesignated funds (Rosh on *Nazir* 24b).

With the money for a peace offering one brings a peace offering with it, etc. – דְּמֵי שְׁלָמִים יָבִיא בָּהֶן שְׁלָמִים וכו׳: According to Rashi, loaves are not brought with the peace offering because the verse states in reference to the loaves: "And he shall put them upon the hands of the nazirite" (Numbers 6:19). Since the nazirite is dead this is not possible. Others explain that loaves are brought but they are not waved (Rosh on *Nazir* 24b, citing Rabbeinu Yitzḥak).

דְּאָמַר מָר: גִּילֵּחַ עַל אַחַת מִשְּׁלָשְׁתָּן – יָצָא.

as **the Master said** about the nazirite (*Nazir* 45a): And if he **shaved**[B] **after** the sacrifice of any **one of the three of them,**[H] i.e., after sacrificing his sin offering, burnt offering, or peace offering, **he has fulfilled** his obligation after the fact, i.e., he has successfully completed his term of naziriteship. Accordingly, there is no specific offering that renders him fit.

מֵיתִיבֵי: אֲשַׁם מְצוֹרָע שֶׁנִּשְׁחַט שֶׁלֹּא לִשְׁמוֹ, אוֹ שֶׁלֹּא נִיתַּן מִדָּמוֹ עַל גַּבֵּי בְּהוֹנוֹת – הֲרֵי זֶה עוֹלֶה לְגַבֵּי מִזְבֵּחַ, וְטָעוּן נְסָכִים, וְצָרִיךְ אָשָׁם אַחֵר לְהַכְשִׁירוֹ! תְּיוּבְתָּא דְּרַב.

The Gemara **raises an objection** from a *baraita*: With regard to **the guilt offering of a leper that was slaughtered not for its own sake,**[H] **or** if **none of its blood was placed on** the leper's right **thumb and big toe, this** guilt offering **is offered up upon the altar and it requires libations,** in accordance with the *halakha* of the guilt offering of a leper. **But** the leper **must** nevertheless bring **another guilt offering to render him fit** to partake of offerings. This *baraita* is **a conclusive refutation** of the statement **of Rav,** who said that the guilt offering of a leper that was slaughtered not for its own sake is entirely disqualified because it did not render the leper fit.

וְרַבִּי שִׁמְעוֹן בֶּן לָקִישׁ אָמַר: מִנְחַת הָעוֹמֶר שֶׁקְּמָצָהּ שֶׁלֹּא לִשְׁמָהּ – כְּשֵׁירָה, וּשְׁיָרֶיהָ אֵין נֶאֱכָלִין עַד שֶׁתָּבִיא מִנְחַת הָעוֹמֶר אַחֶרֶת וְתַתִּירֶנָּה.

§ The Gemara returns to its discussion concerning the *omer* meal offering. **And Rabbi Shimon ben Lakish says,** with regard to **an *omer* meal offering** from **which** a priest **removed a handful not for its own sake,** that it is **valid** and the handful is burned on the altar. **But its remainder may not be consumed** by the priests **until** a priest **brings another *omer* meal offering** on the same day **and** thereby **permits** the first offering for consumption, as the prohibition against consuming the new crop remains in effect.

שֶׁשְּׁיָרֶיהָ אֵין נֶאֱכָלִין עַד שֶׁתָּבִיא מִנְחַת הָעוֹמֶר אַחֶרֶת, מִקְרָב הֵיכִי קָרְבָה? ״מִמַּשְׁקֵה יִשְׂרָאֵל״ – מִן הַמּוּתָּר לְיִשְׂרָאֵל!

The Gemara asks: But if **its remainder may not** be **consumed** by the priests **until** they **bring another *omer* meal offering, how can** the handful removed from this *omer* meal offering **be sacrificed** upon the altar? Before the *omer* meal offering is sacrificed, the new crop is forbidden for consumption, and the verse states: **"From the well-watered pastures of Israel;** for a meal offering, and for a burnt offering, and for peace offerings" (Ezekiel 45:15), from which it is derived that one may sacrifice only **from that which is permitted to the Jewish people.**[H]

אֲמַר רַב אַדָּא בַּר אַהֲבָה, קָסָבַר רֵישׁ לָקִישׁ: אֵין מְחוּסַּר זְמָן לְבוֹ בַּיּוֹם.

Rav Adda bar Ahava said in response: **Reish Lakish holds** that an offering is **not** considered one **whose time has not yet** arrived if it is to be brought **on that day.**[N] Accordingly, since the new crop will be permitted for consumption on the same day that this handful was removed from the *omer* meal offering, it is already considered fit to be sacrificed upon the altar.

מְתִיב רַב אַדָּא בְּרֵיהּ דְּרַב יִצְחָק: יֵשׁ בָּעוֹפוֹת שֶׁאֵין בַּמְּנָחוֹת, יֵשׁ בַּמְּנָחוֹת שֶׁאֵין בָּעוֹפוֹת; יֵשׁ בָּעוֹפוֹת – שֶׁהָעוֹפוֹת בָּאִין בִּנְדָבַת שְׁנַיִם, אֲבָל מְנָחוֹת ״נֶפֶשׁ״ כְּתִיבָא;

Rav Adda, son of Rav Yitzḥak, raises an objection to Rav Adda bar Ahava's explanation from a *baraita*: **There is a** *halakha* that applies **to birds that** does **not** apply **to meal offerings,** and **there is a** *halakha* that applies **to meal offerings that** does **not** apply **to birds.** The *baraita* elaborates: **There is a** *halakha* that applies **to birds** that does not apply to meal offerings, **as birds** may be **brought as a gift** offering on behalf **of two** people, i.e., two people may take a vow to bring a single bird offering jointly. **But** with regard to **meal offerings** it **is written:** "And when **one** brings a meal offering" (Leviticus 2:1), indicating that only individuals may vow to bring a meal offering.

BACKGROUND

Shaved – גִּילֵּחַ: In the following instances, the Torah requires shaving one's head or one's entire body as part of a process of purification and the assumption of a different status: First is the case of a nazirite who completes his term of naziriteship (see Numbers 6:18–19). Upon the termination of the period of his vow, the nazirite shaves his head. This is performed in a special chamber within the women's courtyard in the Temple. Afterward, the nazirite's hair is placed in the fire upon which his peace offering is cooked. Another case is that of a nazirite who has become ritually impure due to contact with a corpse. He must shave his head on the day he purifies himself. On the following day, he brings the required offerings and begins his nazirite vow anew (see Numbers 6:9). Finally, a leper shaves his entire body twice as part of his process of purification (see Leviticus 14:8–9).

HALAKHA

If he shaved after the sacrifice of any one of the three of them – גִּילֵּחַ עַל אַחַת מִשְּׁלָשְׁתָּן: The order of the offerings that a nazirite must bring in order to be permitted to shave is as follows: First, he brings a sin offering, then he brings a burnt offering, and lastly he brings a peace offering. After he has sacrificed all three, he then shaves his hair. If he shaves after the slaughter of the sin offering or the burnt offering, he has fulfilled his obligation (Rambam *Sefer Hafla'a, Hilkhot Nezirut* 8:2).

The guilt offering of a leper that was slaughtered not for its own sake – אֲשַׁם מְצוֹרָע שֶׁנִּשְׁחַט שֶׁלֹּא לִשְׁמוֹ: With regard to the guilt offering of a leper that was slaughtered not for its own sake, or if the priest did not put any of its blood on the leper's right thumb and big toe, it is sacrificed on the altar and requires libations. Nevertheless, the leper must bring another guilt offering to render him fit, as stated in the *baraita* (Rambam *Sefer Avoda, Hilkhot Pesulei HaMukdashin* 15:17 and *Sefer Korbanot, Hilkhot Meḥusrei Kappara* 5:2).

From that which is permitted to the Jewish people – מִן הַמּוּתָּר לְיִשְׂרָאֵל: One may not bring a meal offering or libations from untithed produce, nor from the new crop before the sacrifice of the *omer* meal offering, nor from a mixture of the portion of the produce designated for the priest [*teruma*] with non-sacred produce. Needless to say, one may not bring meal offerings or libations from the fruit of a tree during the first three years after its planting [*orla*], nor from diverse kinds sown in a vineyard, as this would constitute a mitzva performed by means of a transgression (Rambam *Sefer Avoda, Hilkhot Issurei Mizbe'aḥ* 5:9, and see Radbaz there).

NOTES

An offering is not considered one whose time has not yet arrived if it is to be brought on that day – אֵין מְחוּסַּר זְמָן לְבוֹ בַּיּוֹם: In other words, an offering whose suitability for sacrifice depends on a particular time of day is already considered fit for sacrifice from the beginning of the day that it is to be sacrificed. Accordingly, despite the fact that the new crop is prohibited for consumption until another *omer* meal offering is brought, the first offering is not disqualified on account of the phrase in the verse "from the well-watered pastures of Israel," as the actual *omer* will be sacrificed that same day. This *halakha* applies only when the time that has not yet arrived is independent of the offering itself. If the offering itself has not yet reached the appropriate age for its intended sacrifice, even if it is too young by only one hour, then it is not valid if sacrificed (see *Zevaḥim* 25b).

וּמְחוּסְּרֵי כַּפָּרָה, זָב וְזָבָה יוֹלֶדֶת וּמְצוֹרָע;

The *baraita* continues: **And** another *halakha* that applies to birds but not meal offerings involves one who **has not yet** brought his **atonement** offering, i.e., **a man who experienced a gonorrhea-like discharge** [*zav*],[B] **or woman who experienced a discharge of uterine blood after her menstrual period** [*zava*],[B] **or a woman after childbirth, or a leper,** all of whom must bring an offering to complete their atonement process. They bring a bird offering, not a meal offering.

וְהוּתְּרוּ מִכְּלַל אִיסּוּרָן בַּקּוֹדֶשׁ, מַה שֶּׁאֵין כֵּן בַּמְּנָחוֹת.

And furthermore, with regard to birds, **their general prohibition was permitted when** they are **consecrated,** i.e., killing a non-sacred bird by pinching the nape of its neck renders it a carcass, whose consumption is prohibited, and yet pinching the nape of a bird offering enables it to be sacrificed upon the altar and permits it for consumption, **which is not so with regard to meal offerings,** i.e., there is no prohibition that applies to the non-consecrated ingredients of a meal offering that does not apply to actual meal offerings as well.

וְיֵשׁ בַּמְּנָחוֹת – שֶׁהַמְּנָחוֹת טְעוּנוֹת כְּלִי וּתְנוּפָה וְהַגָּשָׁה, וְיֶשְׁנָן בְּצִיבּוּר כְּבַיָּחִיד, מַה שֶּׁאֵין כֵּן בָּעוֹפוֹת;

The *baraita* continues: **And there is** a *halakha* that applies **to meal offerings** that does not apply to birds. **As meal offerings require** placement in a service **vessel, and** they require **waving and bringing,** i.e., they must be brought to the corner of the altar prior to removal of the handful. **And** lastly, **there are** meal offerings **of the community just as** there are meal offerings **of individuals,** e.g., the *omer* meal offering is a communal meal offering, **which is not so with regard to birds.** Bird offerings do not require the use of service vessels, they do not require waving or bringing, and there are no communal bird offerings.

וְאִם אִיתָא, בַּמְּנָחוֹת נַמִי מַשְׁכַּחַתְּ לָהּ דְּהוּתְּרוּ מִכְּלַל אִיסּוּרָן בַּקּוֹדֶשׁ, וּמַאי נִיהוּ? מִנְחַת הָעוֹמֶר!

Rav Adda, son of Rav Yitzḥak, explains his objection: **And if it is so** that a handful that was removed from an *omer* meal offering not for its own sake is fit for burning upon the altar, then **with regard to meal offerings as well, you find that their general prohibition was permitted when** they are **consecrated. And what is this** meal offering that was permitted? It is **the *omer* meal offering** from which a handful was removed not for its own sake, as although the new crop remains prohibited to the Jewish people until another *omer* meal offering is brought, the handful of this meal offering may be sacrificed upon the altar.

כֵּיוָן דְּאֵין מְחוּסַּר זְמָן לְבוֹ בַּיּוֹם, לָאו אִיסּוּרָא הוּא.

The Gemara answers: **Since** an offering is **not** considered one **whose time has not yet** arrived if it is to be brought **on that day,** the sacrificing of that handful **is not a prohibition** that was permitted. Instead, it was initially fit for sacrifice upon the altar, as though another *omer* meal offering had already been brought to permit it.

מְתִיב רַב שֵׁשֶׁת: הִקְדִּים מַתַּן שֶׁמֶן לְמַתַּן דָּם – יְמַלְּאֶנּוּ שֶׁמֶן וְיַחֲזוֹר וְיִתֵּן שֶׁמֶן אַחַר מַתַּן דָּם, מַתַּן בְּהוֹנוֹת לְמַתַּן שֶׁבַע – יְמַלְּאֶנּוּ שֶׁמֶן וְיַחֲזוֹר וְיִתֵּן מַתַּן בְּהוֹנוֹת אַחַר מַתַּן שֶׁבַע;

Rav Sheshet raises an objection from a *baraita* that discusses the ritual purification of a leper: If the priest **performed the placement of oil** on the leper's right thumb and big toe **before the placement of blood**[H] from the leper's guilt offering on the leper's right thumb and big toe, i.e., his actions were in the opposite order from those prescribed in the Torah (see Leviticus 14:14–17), **he fills** the vessel that holds a *log* of **oil and he** then **puts oil** on the leper's right thumb and big toe **again after the placement of blood.** If the priest **performed the placement of** oil on the leper's right **thumb and big toe before the placement of seven** sprinklings of oil before the Lord, **he fills** the vessel that holds a *log* of **oil and he again puts** oil on the leper's right **thumb and big toe after the placement of seven** sprinklings.

וְאִי אָמְרַתְּ אֵין מְחוּסַּר זְמָן לְבוֹ בַּיּוֹם, אַמַּאי יַחֲזוֹר וְיִתֵּן? מַאי דַּעֲבַד עֲבַד!

Rav Sheshet explains his objection: **And if you say** that an offering is **not** considered as one **whose time has not yet** arrived if it is to be brought **on that day,** then **why should** the priest **place** the oil on the leper's right thumb and big toe **again? What he performed, he** already **performed,** i.e., since the oil was going to be placed on the leper's right thumb and big toe on that day, the placement should be valid even when done out of order.

BACKGROUND

Zav – זָב: A *zav* is a man suffering from a gonorrhea-like discharge. The *halakhot* relating to the severe ritual impurity caused by this condition are detailed in the Torah (see Leviticus 15:1–15) and in tractate *Zavim*. The *zav* becomes ritually impure as a result of the secretion of a white, pus-like discharge from his penis. A man who experiences a discharge of this kind on one occasion becomes ritually impure as a *zav* for one day, like one who has discharged semen. If he experiences a second discharge on the same day or the following day, or a prolonged initial discharge, he contracts the more severe ritual impurity of a *zav*, which lasts until he counts seven clean days. If he experiences a third discharge within the next day, he is obligated to bring a pair of doves, one for a sin offering and one for a burnt offering, as part of his purification process.

Not only does the man himself become ritually impure, but he imparts ritual impurity by coming into contact with vessels or people; by being moved by them; by moving them; by lying or sitting on them; or through the medium of a large stone that he is lying on, if it is positioned over them. The fluids he secretes, i.e., his spittle, urine, and semen, impart ritual impurity, and any article upon which he sits or lies becomes a primary source of ritual impurity and itself imparts ritual impurity to other items.

Zava – זָבָה: This is a woman who experiences a flow resembling menstrual blood on three consecutive days during a time of the month when she is not due to experience menstrual bleeding. The first secretion renders her ritually impure, but until the third day her status is that of a woman who observes a clean day for each day she experiences a discharge. After experiencing bleeding on the third day, the woman is considered a *zava* and after counting seven clean days is obligated to bring an offering as part of her purification process. A *zava* imparts ritual impurity in the same manner as a *zav*. In addition, a man who engages in intercourse with her becomes a primary source of ritual impurity and imparts ritual impurity to others.

HALAKHA

If the priest preformed the placement of oil before the placement of blood – הִקְדִּים מַתַּן שֶׁמֶן לְמַתַּן דָּם: If the priest placed the oil on the leper's right thumb and big toe before placing the blood from the leper's guilt offering on the leper's right thumb and big toe, he should fill the vessel that holds a *log* of oil and then put oil on the leper's right thumb and big toe again after the placement of blood. If the placement of oil on the leper's right thumb and big toe was performed before the seven sprinklings of oil in the direction of the Holy of Holies, he should fill the vessel that holds a *log* of oil and put oil on the leper's right thumb and big toe again after performing the seven sprinklings (Rambam *Sefer Korbanot*, *Hilkhot Meḥusrei Kappara* 5:6).

אֲמַר רַב פַּפָּא: שָׁאנֵי הִלְכוֹת מְצוֹרָע, דִּכְתִיבָא בְּהוּ הֲוָיָה, דְּאָמַר הַכָּתוּב: ״זֹאת תִּהְיֶה תּוֹרַת הַמְּצוֹרָע״, ״תִּהְיֶה״ – בַּהֲוָיָיתָהּ תְּהֵא.

Rav Pappa said in response: **The *halakhot* of a leper are different,** as it is **written concerning them** an expression of **being, as the verse states: "This shall be the law of the leper"** (Leviticus 14:2). The term **"shall be"** indicates that **it shall be as it is,** i.e., the purification process of a leper must be performed in accordance with the precise order prescribed in the Torah.

מְתִיב רַב פַּפָּא: הִקְדִּים חַטָּאתוֹ לַאֲשָׁמוֹ – לֹא יְהֵא אַחֵר מְמָרֵס בְּדָמָהּ, אֶלָּא תְּעוּבַּר צוּרָתָהּ וְתֵצֵא לְבֵית הַשְּׂרֵיפָה!

Rav Pappa raises an objection from a *baraita*: If the priest **performed** the slaughter of a leper's **sin offering before** the slaughter of **his guilt offering,**[H] i.e., the priest's actions were in the opposite order from those prescribed in the Torah (see Leviticus 14:13–19), **there** should **not be another** priest **stirring the blood of** the leper's sin offering to prevent it from congealing in order that his guilt offering may be slaughtered and its blood sprinkled before the blood of his sin offering. **Rather,** the sin offering is left until **its form decays,** i.e., until the next morning, at which point it is definitively disqualified due to remaining in the Temple overnight **and** can be **taken out to the place** designated **for burning.** The objection is as follows: If an offering that is to be brought on that day is not considered one whose time has not yet arrived, why must this sin offering be left to decay? It should be considered as though it was slaughtered after the guilt offering.

אַמַּאי קָא מוֹתִיב רַב פַּפָּא? וְהָא רַב פַּפָּא הוּא דַּאֲמַר: שָׁאנֵי הִלְכוֹת מְצוֹרָע דִּכְתִיבָא בְּהוּ הֲוָיָה! אֶלָּא רַב פַּפָּא הָכִי קָא קַשְׁיָא לֵיהּ: אֵימָא הָנֵי מִילֵּי עֲבוֹדָה, שְׁחִיטָה לָאו עֲבוֹדָה הִיא; וְאִי אֵין מְחוּסַּר זְמַן לְבוֹ בַּיּוֹם – יְהֵא אַחֵר מְמָרֵס בְּדָמָהּ, וְלִקְרִיב אָשָׁם וַהֲדַר לִיקְרַב חַטָּאת!

The Gemara asks: **Why does Rav Pappa raise** this **objection? But isn't it Rav Pappa** himself **who said: The *halakhot* of a leper are different, as** it is **written concerning them** an expression of **being,** which indicates that the order of slaughter of a leper's offerings must be preserved? **Rather, this is what is difficult to Rav Pappa** from the *baraita*: You can **say** that **this statement,** the *halakha* that the order is indispensable to the purification process of a leper, applies only to a sacrificial **rite,** whereas the act of **slaughter is not** considered **a rite.**[N] **And if** an offering is **not** considered one **whose time has not yet** arrived if it is to be brought **on that day,** then **another** priest **should be stirring the blood of** the leper's sin offering to prevent it from congealing, **and** a priest **should sacrifice** the **guilt offering** and present its blood in the meantime, **and afterward he should sacrifice** the **sin offering.**

אֶלָּא אֲמַר רַב פַּפָּא: הַיְינוּ טַעְמָא דְּרֵישׁ לָקִישׁ, דְּקָסָבַר: הֵאִיר מִזְרָח מַתִּיר. דְּרַבִּי יוֹחָנָן וְרֵישׁ לָקִישׁ דְּאָמְרִי תַּרְוַיְיהוּ: אֲפִילּוּ בִּזְמַן שֶׁבֵּית הַמִּקְדָּשׁ קַיָּים,

Rather, Rav Pappa said: This is the reason of Reish Lakish, who said **that** the handful of an *omer* meal offering that was removed not for its own sake is valid and may be burned upon the altar: It is that **he holds that the illumination of** the **eastern** horizon on the morning of the sixteenth of Nisan **permits** the new crop[N] to the Jewish people even before the *omer* meal offering is sacrificed, **as Rabbi Yoḥanan and Reish Lakish both say: Even when the Temple is standing,**

HALAKHA

If the priest performed the slaughter of a leper's sin offering before the slaughter of his guilt offering – הִקְדִּים חַטָּאתוֹ לַאֲשָׁמוֹ: If the slaughter of a leper's sin offering was performed before the slaughter of his guilt offering, there should not be another priest stirring the blood of his sin offering until the guilt offering is slaughtered. Rather, the sin offering is left until its form decays, i.e., until the next morning, and is taken out to the place designated for burning, as stated in the *baraita* (Rambam *Sefer Korbanot, Hilkhot Meḥusrei Kappara* 5:3).

NOTES

The act of slaughter is not considered a rite – שְׁחִיטָה לָאו עֲבוֹדָה הִיא: According to Rashi, the slaughter of an offering is not considered a sacrificial rite because it may be performed by a non-priest. The *halakha* that slaughter is not considered a sacrificial rite is derived from the fact that the Torah mentions the priests' performance of the sacrificial rites only from the collection of the blood onward (*Zevaḥim* 32a). *Tosafot* cite Rabbi Ya'akov of Orleans, who explains that slaughter is not considered a sacrificial rite because its performance is not unique to offerings, as even non-sacred animals must be slaughtered in order to render them permitted for consumption. Regardless of the reason, slaughter is not considered a sacrificial rite and therefore is not considered a part of the sacrificial process of a leper (see *Ḥiddushei HaGriz*).

The illumination of the eastern horizon permits the new crop – הֵאִיר מִזְרָח מַתִּיר: The verse states: "And you shall eat neither bread, nor parched grain, nor fresh stalks, until this very day" (Leviticus 23:14). Accordingly, the new crop is permitted from the beginning of that very day, i.e., the sixteenth of Nisan. Nevertheless, Reish Lakish holds that the remainder of the *omer* meal offering may not be consumed by the priests at that point because the same verse also states: "Until you have brought the offering of your God," which indicates that it is a mitzva to delay the consumption of the new crop until after the sacrifice of the *omer* meal offering (Rashi on 5b, citing 68a).

הֵאִיר מִזְרָח מַתִּיר.

the illumination of the **eastern** horizon **permits** the new crop.

וְהָא דְּרֵישׁ לָקִישׁ לָאו בְּפֵירוּשׁ אִיתְּמַר אֶלָּא מִכְּלָלָא אִיתְּמַר, דִּתְנַן: אֵין מְבִיאִין מִנְחַת בִּכּוּרִים וּמִנְחַת בְּהֵמָה קוֹדֶם לָעוֹמֶר, דְּבָעֵינַן ״מִמַּשְׁקֵה יִשְׂרָאֵל״, וְאִם הֵבִיא – פָּסוּל;

The Gemara notes: **And this** statement **of Reish Lakish was not stated explicitly; rather, it was stated by inference,** i.e., it is evident from a different statement of Reish Lakish that this is his opinion. **As we learned** in a mishna (68b): **One may not bring a meal offering, the first fruits,**[HB] **or the meal offering** brought with the libations accompanying **an animal** offering, from the new crop, **prior to** the sacrifice of **the** ***omer*****.** The Gemara interrupts its citation of the mishna to add that the reason is **that we require** that an offering be **"from the well-watered pastures of Israel,"** i.e., it must be brought from that which is permitted to the Jewish people, and the new crop has not yet been permitted to them. The mishna concludes: **And if he brought** these offerings from the new crop they are **unfit.**

קוֹדֶם לִשְׁתֵּי הַלֶּחֶם לֹא יָבִיא, מִשּׁוּם דְּאִיקְּרוּ בִּכּוּרִים, וְאִם הֵבִיא – כָּשֵׁר.

The mishna continues: After the *omer* but **prior to the two loaves one may not bring**[N] those offerings from the new crop. The Gemara explains that this is **because** the two loaves **are called first fruits,** and therefore they should precede all other offerings from the new crop. The mishna adds: **But if he brought** those offerings from the new crop, they are **fit.**

וְאָמַר רַבִּי יִצְחָק אָמַר רֵישׁ לָקִישׁ: לֹא שָׁנוּ אֶלָּא בְּאַרְבָּעָה עָשָׂר וּבַחֲמִשָּׁה עָשָׂר, אֲבָל בְּשִׁשָּׁה עָשָׂר – אִם הֵבִיא כָּשֵׁר; וְקַשְׁיָא לִי: לֶיהֱווּ כִּמְחוּסַּר זְמַן! אַלְמָא קָסָבַר: הֵאִיר הַמִּזְרָח מַתִּיר.

And Rav Yitzḥak says that **Reish Lakish says:** The Sages **taught** that a meal offering that was brought from the new crop before the *omer* meal offering is disqualified **only** if it was brought **on the fourteenth or on the fifteenth** of Nisan. **But** if it was **on the sixteenth,** then even **if he brought** it prior to the *omer* meal offering, it is **valid.** He continues: **And** this statement poses **a difficulty for me:** Why should meal offerings be valid when sacrificed on the sixteenth if they were sacrificed before the *omer* meal offering? **Let them be** considered **like** offerings **whose time has not yet** arrived. The Gemara comments: **Apparently,** Reish Lakish **holds** that **the illumination of the eastern** horizon **permits** the new crop.

HALAKHA

One may not bring a meal offering, first fruits, etc. – אֵין מְבִיאִין מִנְחַת בִּכּוּרִים וכו׳: Standard meal offerings, meal offerings that accompany the libations of slaughtered offerings, and first fruits, may not be brought from the new crop before the offering of the *omer*. If one sacrificed any of these from the new crop, the offering is not valid. Furthermore, one may not bring an offering from the new crop before the sacrifice of the two loaves *ab initio*. If he did so, it is valid (Rambam *Sefer Zera'im, Hilkhot Bikkurim* 2:6 and *Sefer Avoda, Hilkhot Temidin UMusafin* 7:17).

BACKGROUND

First fruits – בִּכּוּרִים: The obligation to bring first fruits to the Temple is stated in the Torah (see Deuteronomy 26:1–11) and is discussed in great detail in tractate *Bikkurim*, in both the mishna and in the Jerusalem Talmud. This mitzva involves the bringing of a small amount of first fruits, one-sixtieth of the harvest, before *teruma* is separated from the crop. The first fruits must be brought from the seven types of fruit for which Eretz Yisrael is praised (see Deuteronomy 8:8), all the way to the Temple in Jerusalem. A large, festive ceremony accompanied the procession of the first fruits to the city. The owner of the fruit would bring his basket up to the altar, where he would wave it and recite the prayers of praise and thanksgiving that appear in the Torah. At this stage of the ritual, the status of the first fruits became like that of *teruma*, and the fruits became the property of the priest.

NOTES

After the *omer* but prior to the two loaves one may not bring, etc. – קוֹדֶם לִשְׁתֵּי הַלֶּחֶם לֹא יָבִיא וכו׳: Just as the *omer* meal offering permits the new crop for consumption, the two loaves sacrificed on *Shavuot* permit the sacrifice of offerings from the new crop, as the verse states: "And on the day of the first fruits, when you bring a new meal offering for the Lord" (Numbers 28:26), which indicates that the meal offering brought on *Shavuot* must be new, i.e., the first brought from the new crop. Alternatively, the verse: "As an offering of first fruits" (Leviticus 2:12), is the source for this *halakha* (Rashi; see commentary attributed to Rashba). In any event, a meal offering that was brought from the new crop before the two loaves were sacrificed is valid, as the new crop was already permitted to Jews for consumption (68b).

וְרָבָא אָמַר: מִנְחַת הָעוֹמֶר שֶׁקְּמָצָהּ שֶׁלֹּא לִשְׁמָהּ – כְּשֵׁירָה, וּשְׁיָרֶיהָ נֶאֱכָלִין, וְאֵינָהּ צְרִיכָה מִנְחַת הָעוֹמֶר אַחֶרֶת לְהַתִּירָהּ; שֶׁאֵין מַחְשָׁבָה מוֹעֶלֶת אֶלָּא בְּמִי שֶׁרָאוּי לַעֲבוֹדָה, וּבְדָבָר הָרָאוּי לַעֲבוֹדָה, וּבְמָקוֹם הָרָאוּי לַעֲבוֹדָה.

§ The Gemara previously cited the opinion of Rav that an *omer* meal offering from which a handful was removed not for its own sake is disqualified. The Gemara also cited the opinion of Reish Lakish that this meal offering is valid but another *omer* meal offering is necessary to permit the new crop for consumption. **And Rava says:** With regard to **an *omer* meal offering** from **which** the priest **removed a handful not for its own sake,**[H] it is **valid and its remainder is consumed, and it does not require another *omer* meal offering to permit it** for consumption. The reason is **that** improper **intent is effective** [*mo'elet*][L] to disqualify an offering **only**[N] when it is expressed **by one who is fit for the** Temple **service,**[HN] **and** with **regard to an item that is fit for the** Temple **service,**[H] **and in a place that is fit for the** Temple **service.**[H]

בְּמִי שֶׁרָאוּי לַעֲבוֹדָה – לְאַפּוֹקֵי כֹּהֵן בַּעַל מוּם; וּבְדָבָר הָרָאוּי לַעֲבוֹדָה – לְאַפּוֹקֵי מִנְחַת הָעוֹמֶר דְּלָא חֲזְיָא, דְּחִדּוּשׁ הוּא; וּבְמָקוֹם הָרָאוּי לַעֲבוֹדָה – לְאַפּוֹקֵי נִפְגַּם הַמִּזְבֵּחַ.

Rava elaborates: The condition that improper intent disqualifies only when expressed **by one who is fit for the** Temple **service** serves **to exclude** the intent of **a blemished priest,** who is disqualified from performing the Temple service. The condition that it disqualifies only when expressed **with regard to an item that is fit for the** Temple **service** serves **to exclude the *omer* meal offering, which** is generally **unfit** for the Temple service, **as it is a novelty,** in that it is brought from barley whereas most meal offerings are brought from wheat. **And** finally, the condition that it disqualifies only when expressed **in a place that is fit for the** Temple **service** serves **to exclude** sacrificial rites that were performed with improper intent while **the altar was damaged.** At such a time improper intent does not disqualify an offering, and therefore if the altar is repaired on the same day, the offering may be sacrificed upon the altar.

תָּנוּ רַבָּנַן: כְּשֶׁהוּא אוֹמֵר "מִן הַבָּקָר" לְמַטָּה, שֶׁאֵין תַּלְמוּד לוֹמַר! אֶלָּא לְהוֹצִיא אֶת הַטְּרֵפָה.

§ The Gemara discusses the prohibition against sacrificing an item that is prohibited to the Jewish people. **The Sages taught** in a *baraita*: It is derived from a passage in the Torah that discusses burnt offerings: "You shall bring your offering from the cattle, even from the herd or from the flock" (Leviticus 1:2), that certain animals are prohibited for sacrifice upon the altar (see *Temura* 28a). **When it states later,** in the next verse: "If his offering is a burnt offering **of the herd**" (Leviticus 1:3), this is difficult, **as** there is **no** need for **the verse to state** this, as it was already written earlier. **Rather,** this serves **to exclude an animal with a wound that will cause it to die within twelve months** [*tereifa*][HB] from being brought as an offering.

LANGUAGE

Effective [*mo'elet*] – מוֹעֶלֶת: Generally, this word refers to that which effects a positive result, and this root is used in such a manner throughout the Bible. In rabbinic literature it can refer to any act that effects halakhic consequences, even negative ones.

NOTES

That improper intent is effective only, etc. – שֶׁאֵין מַחְשָׁבָה מוֹעֶלֶת אֶלָּא וכו׳: In other words, improper intentions, e.g., the intention to sacrifice or consume an offering outside of its designated time, have halakhic significance with regard to an offering only when the offering itself was sacrificed in its proper manner and would otherwise have been fit. If the offering would have been disqualified regardless of the improper intention, e.g., if its rites were performed by one unfit for Temple service or if the altar was damaged at the time of its sacrifice, then the improper intention has no halakhic significance. Although the offering is disqualified either way, the fact that such improper intentions do not disqualify it in such a case is significant as it means that this offering will not be considered an offering that was sacrificed with the intent to consume it after its designated time [*piggul*], and therefore one who consumes it will not be punished with *karet*.

By one who is fit for the Temple service – בְּמִי שֶׁרָאוּי לַעֲבוֹדָה: According to Rashi on *Zevaḥim* 32a, this is derived from a verse discussing *piggul*: "Neither shall it be attributed to him that sacrifices it" (Leviticus 7:18). This indicates that only one who is fit to sacrifice the offering can render it unfit through improper intentions. Accordingly, the improper intentions of those listed in the mishna on 6a do not disqualify an offering.

BACKGROUND

Tereifa – טְרֵפָה: Generally speaking, a *tereifa* is an animal suffering from a condition that will cause it to die within twelve months. It is prohibited by Torah law to eat an animal that has been injured in this manner or stricken with a disease of this nature, although the source for this prohibition is a matter of dispute. Some authorities cite the verse: "You shall not eat any flesh that is torn of beasts in the field" (Exodus 22:30), while others suggest: "You shall not eat of anything that died of itself" (Deuteronomy 14:21). According some commentaries, both verses together serve as the source for the prohibition (*Minḥat Ḥinnukh*).

HALAKHA

An *omer* meal offering from which the priest removed a handful not for its own sake – מִנְחַת הָעוֹמֶר שֶׁקְּמָצָהּ שֶׁלֹּא לִשְׁמָהּ: An *omer* meal offering from which a priest removed a handful not for its own sake is valid, and its remainder is consumed, and it does not require another *omer* meal offering to render it permitted for consumption. The *halakha* is in accordance with the opinion of Rava, as he is the latest of the *amora'im* involved in the dispute (Rambam *Sefer Avoda*, *Hilkhot Pesulei HaMukdashin* 14:3, and see *Kesef Mishne* there).

Improper intent is effective [*mo'elet*] only by one who is fit for the Temple service – אֵין מַחְשָׁבָה מוֹעֶלֶת אֶלָּא בְּמִי שֶׁרָאוּי לַעֲבוֹדָה: Improper intent disqualifies an offering only if it was expressed by one fit for the Temple service. Therefore, if someone unfit for performing the Temple service collected the blood of an offering, conveyed it to the altar, or presented it upon the altar, while expressing intent to sacrifice or consume the offering outside of its designated place or time, the offering is not rendered *piggul* on account of his intention. The blood that he collected or presented must be poured into the Temple courtyard drain. If any of the blood that first squirted from the slaughtered animal remains, a priest fit for performing the Temple service should collect it and perform the sacrificial rites with proper intention (Rambam *Sefer Avoda*, *Hilkhot Pesulei HaMukdashin* 14:2).

With regard to an item that is fit for the Temple service – בְּדָבָר הָרָאוּי לַעֲבוֹדָה: Improper intent disqualifies an offering only when it was expressed with regard to an item that is fit for the Temple service. Accordingly, an *omer* meal offering from which a handful was removed not for its own sake is considered as though its handful were removed for its own sake, i.e., it is valid and its remainder is permitted for consumption. This is because the *omer* is brought from barley, and barley is not fit for use in other offerings. Similarly, improper intent in the case of a meal offering of jealousy with frankincense upon it does not disqualify the offering, as it is not fit for service until the frankincense is removed. The *halakha* is in accordance with the statement of Rava (Rambam *Sefer Avoda*, *Hilkhot Pesulei HaMukdashin* 14:3, and see Ra'avad there).

In a place that is fit for the Temple service – בְּמָקוֹם הָרָאוּי לַעֲבוֹדָה: Improper intent disqualifies an offering only if it was expressed in a place that is fit for the Temple service. Therefore, if while the altar was damaged one intended to sacrifice an offering outside of its designated place or time, the offering is not disqualified, as the damaged altar is unfit for the Temple service. Similarly, if one removed a handful from a meal offering outside of the Temple courtyard with the intention to sacrifice it outside of its designated place or time, his intention has no effect (Rambam *Sefer Avoda*, *Hilkhot Pesulei HaMukdashin* 14:4).

To exclude a *tereifa* – לְהוֹצִיא אֶת הַטְּרֵפָה: It is prohibited to sacrifice upon the altar an animal with a wound that will cause it to die within twelve months (Rambam *Sefer Avoda*, *Hilkhot Issurei Mizbe'aḥ* 2:10).

LANGUAGE

Ordinary person [*hedyot*] – הֶדְיוֹט: From the Greek ἰδιώτης, *idiotēs*, which refers to a common person who holds no position of authority. In the Gemara, it is used in several ways. It can mean an ordinary priest, as opposed to the High Priest, or a commoner, as opposed to a king, or it can refer to private property, as opposed to consecrated property.

וַהֲלֹא דִּין הוּא: וּמָה בַּעַל מוּם שֶׁמּוּתֶּרֶת לְהֶדְיוֹט – אֲסוּרָה לְגָבוֹהַּ, טְרֵיפָה שֶׁאֲסוּרָה לְהֶדְיוֹט – אֵין דִּין שֶׁאֲסוּרָה לְגָבוֹהַּ? חֵלֶב וְדָם יוֹכִיחוּ, שֶׁאֲסוּרִין לְהֶדְיוֹט וּמוּתָּרִין לְגָבוֹהַּ!

The *baraita* questions the need for this derivation: **But could this not** be derived through an *a fortiori* **inference? And if a blemished** animal, **which is permitted to an ordinary person [*lehedyot*]**[L] for consumption, is nevertheless **prohibited** as an offering **for the Most High** (see Leviticus 22:19), then certainly with regard to **a *tereifa*, which is forbidden to an ordinary person** for consumption (see Exodus 22:30), **is it not logical that it is prohibited for the Most High?** The *baraita* responds: **Fat [*ḥelev*] and blood prove** that this *a fortiori* inference is not valid, **as they are forbidden to an ordinary person and** yet **they are permitted for the Most High.**

מָה לְחֵלֶב וְדָם שֶׁכֵּן בָּאִין מִכְּלַל הֵיתֵּר, תֹּאמַר בִּטְרֵיפָה שֶׁכּוּלָּהּ אֲסוּרָה, וְלֹא תְּהֵא מוּתֶּרֶת לְגָבוֹהַּ!

The *baraita* rejects this suggestion: **What** is notable **about fat and blood?** They are notable **in that they come from** an item that is **generally permitted,** i.e., the animal from which they come is itself permitted for consumption. Will **you say** the same **with regard to a *tereifa*, which is entirely forbidden** for eating, **and** therefore **should not be permitted for the Most High?**

מְלִיקָה תּוֹכִיחַ, שֶׁכּוּלָּהּ אִיסּוּר, וַאֲסוּרָה לְהֶדְיוֹט וּמוּתֶּרֶת לְגָבוֹהַּ.

The *baraita* responds: The **pinching** of bird offerings **will prove** that one cannot derive by means of an *a fortiori* inference that a *tereifa* is disqualified. **As** a bird killed by the pinching of its nape is also **entirely forbidden, and** yet although it is **forbidden** for consumption **to an ordinary person,** as it is rendered a carcass, it is nevertheless **permitted for the Most High,** as bird offerings are killed by the pinching of their napes. The verse is therefore necessary to disqualify a *tereifa*.

מָה לִמְלִיקָה שֶׁכֵּן קְדוּשָּׁתָהּ אוֹסַרְתָּהּ; בִּשְׁעַת קְדוּשָּׁתָהּ לְמִזְבֵּחַ הִיא נֶאֶסְרָה לְהֶדְיוֹט, דְּהַיְינוּ מְלִיקָתָהּ, אֲבָל קוֹדֶם לָכֵן לֹא נֶאֶסְרָה לְהֶדְיוֹט; מָה שֶׁאֵין כֵּן בִּטְרֵיפָה שֶׁאֵין קְדוּשָּׁתָהּ אוֹסַרְתָּהּ!

The *baraita* rejects this suggestion as well: **What** is notable **about pinching?** It is notable **in that its sanctity prohibits it,** i.e., only **at the time** when **it** becomes **sanctified for the altar** does **it** become **prohibited** for consumption **to an ordinary person, which is** at the time of **its pinching. But before this** time it is **not** yet **prohibited to an ordinary person** for consumption. This **is not the case with regard to a *tereifa*, as its sanctity does not prohibit it** for consumption, since it is always prohibited to eat it. Accordingly, by logical inference alone one can arrive at the conclusion that a *tereifa* should not be permitted for the Most High.

וְאִם הֲשֵׁבוֹתָהּ, כְּשֶׁהוּא אוֹמֵר ״מִן הַבָּקָר״ לְמַטָּה – שֶׁאֵין תַּלְמוּד לוֹמַר, לְהוֹצִיא אֶת הַטְּרֵיפָה.

The *baraita* concludes with a statement that will soon be explained: **And if you have responded,** i.e., if you succeeded in rejecting the *a fortiori* inference, then **when** the verse **states later: "Of the herd"** (Leviticus 1:3), **as** there is **no** need for **the verse to state** this phrase, it serves **to exclude a *tereifa*.**

מָה ״אִם הֲשֵׁבוֹתָהּ״? (סִימָן: רְקִיחַ מָר אַדָּא לְשִׁישֵׁיהּ).

The Gemara asks: **What** response is alluded to by the statement: **If you have responded?** The conclusion of the *baraita* had indicated that the *a fortiori* inference must be accepted. The Gemara cites several suggestions, for which it provides the following **mnemonic: *Rekiaḥ, Mar, Adda, Leshisheih.*** These terms allude to the names of some of the Sages mentioned in the following discussion: Rav; Rabbi Akiva; Rav Aḥa; Mar, son of Ravina; Rav Adda; and Rav Sheisha, son of Rav Idi.

אָמַר רַב, מִשּׁוּם דְּאִיכָּא לְמֵימַר: מִנְחַת הָעוֹמֶר תּוֹכִיחַ, שֶׁאֲסוּרָה לְהֶדְיוֹט וּמוּתֶּרֶת לְגָבוֹהַּ. מָה לְמִנְחַת הָעוֹמֶר שֶׁכֵּן מַתֶּרֶת חָדָשׁ!

Rav said that this is the response: The *halakha* that a *tereifa* is unfit for sacrifice must be derived from a verse **because it may be said** that **the *omer* meal offering proves** that the *halakha* concerning a *tereifa* cannot be derived by the *a fortiori* inference, **as** the *omer* is **prohibited** for consumption **to an ordinary person,** since it comes from the new crop, **and** yet it is **permitted** as an offering **for the Most High.** The Gemara rejects this suggestion: **What** is notable **about the *omer* meal offering?** It is notable **in that** the *omer* **renders** the **new** crop **permitted**[N] for consumption, whereas a *tereifa* does not render anything permitted.

NOTES

In that it renders the new crop permitted – שֶׁכֵּן מַתֶּרֶת חָדָשׁ: The mitzva of the *omer* meal offering has a special feature in that it renders the new crop permitted for consumption. Accordingly, an item normally prohibited for eating, i.e., the new crop, is permitted for use as the *omer* meal offering. By contrast, a *tereifa* does not render anything permitted (*Shita Mekubbetzet*, citing Rashi). Others reject this explanation, suggesting instead that the *omer* meal offering is not considered a typical offering because it serves neither to appease nor to atone, but to render the new crop permitted for consumption. Accordingly, one cannot derive the *halakha* of a *tereifa* offering from the *omer* (*Sefat Emet*).

בַּשְּׁבִיעִית. שְׁבִיעִית נַמִי, שֶׁכֵּן מַתֶּרֶת סְפִיחִין בַּשְּׁבִיעִית! כְּרַבִּי עֲקִיבָא, דְּאָמַר: סְפִיחִין אֲסוּרִים בַּשְּׁבִיעִית.

The Gemara responds: Although the *omer* meal offering generally renders the new crop permitted, the *omer* brought **during a Sabbatical Year**[B] does not render the crop permitted, as it is prohibited to plant during the Sabbatical Year, and consequently there is no new crop for the *omer* offering to permit. The Gemara counters this suggestion: The *omer* meal offering brought during **a Sabbatical Year also** renders something permitted, **as it permits produce that grew without being purposely planted** [*sefiḥin*] **during the Sabbatical Year.**[H] The Gemara responds: Nevertheless, **in accordance with** the opinion of **Rabbi Akiva, who says** that *sefiḥin* **are prohibited during the Sabbatical Year,** the *omer* meal offering brought during a Sabbatical Year does not render the new crop permitted for consumption, and yet it is permitted for the Most High. A verse is therefore necessary to derive that a *tereifa* may not be sacrificed.

אֲמַר לֵיהּ רַב אַחָא בַּר אַבָּא לְרַב אַשִׁי, לְרַבִּי עֲקִיבָא נַמִי לִפְרוֹךְ: מַה לְּמִנְחַת הָעוֹמֶר שֶׁכֵּן מַתֶּרֶת חָדָשׁ בְּחוּצָה לָאָרֶץ!

Rav Aḥa bar Abba said to Rav Ashi: According to the opinion of **Rabbi Akiva as well, let us refute** the statement of Rav, as **what** is notable **about the *omer* meal offering?** It is notable **in that** the *omer* **permits** the **new** crop for consumption **outside of Eretz** Yisrael,[H] where the prohibitions of the Sabbatical Year do not apply.

וַאֲפִילּוּ לְמַאן דְּאָמַר: חָדָשׁ בְּחוּץ לָאָרֶץ לָאו דְּאוֹרַיְיתָא – שֶׁכֵּן בָּאָה לְהַתִּיר לָאו שֶׁבְּתוֹכָהּ!

And even according to the one who says that the consumption of produce from the **new** crop grown **outside of Eretz** Yisrael is **not** prohibited **by Torah law,** Rav's statement can be refuted in another manner: What is notable about the *omer* meal offering? It is notable **in that** the *omer* **comes to permit a prohibition** that applies to a substance **that** was previously **within it,** i.e., the burning upon the altar of a handful from the *omer* meal offering renders the remainder of the meal offering permitted to the priests, whereas a *tereifa* is entirely forbidden.

אֲמַר לֵיהּ רַב אַחָא מִדִּיפְתִּי לְרָבִינָא: אִי הָכִי, טְרֵיפָה נַמִי תַּקְרִיב וְתַתִּיר לָאו שֶׁבְּתוֹכָהּ! אֶלָּא פָּרֵיךְ הָכִי: מַה לְּמִנְחַת הָעוֹמֶר שֶׁכֵּן מִצְוָתָהּ בְּכָךְ.

Rav Aḥa of Difti said to Ravina: This is not a refutation, as, **if that is so,** then with regard to **a *tereifa* as well, you should sacrifice** it **and you will** thereby **permit a prohibition** that applies to a substance **that** was previously **within it,** and its meat will become permitted to the priests for consumption. Therefore, a verse is needed to exclude a *tereifa*. **Rather,** one can **refute** the statement of Rav **like this: What** is notable **about the *omer* meal offering?** It is notable **in that its mitzva is in this** manner, i.e., the Torah requires the *omer* meal offering to be brought from the new crop in order to permit the new crop for consumption. By contrast, there is no mitzva to sacrifice specifically a *tereifa*.

רֵישׁ לָקִישׁ אָמַר, מִשּׁוּם דְּאִיכָּא לְמֵימַר: מְפַטֵּם הַקְּטֹרֶת יוֹכִיחַ, שֶׁאָסוּר לְהֶדְיוֹט וּמוּתָּר לְגָבוֹהַּ. מְפַטֵּם גַּבְרָא הוּא!

Reish Lakish said that this is the response alluded to at the end of the *baraita*: The *halakha* that a *tereifa* is unfit for sacrifice must be derived from a verse **because it can be said** that **the one who prepares the incense proves** that the *halakha* concerning a *tereifa* may not be derived by the *a fortiori* inference, **as this is prohibited to an ordinary person, and** is nevertheless **permitted for the Most High.** The Gemara questions the terminology of Reish Lakish: But **the one who prepares** the incense **is a person.** How can it be said that a person is prohibited to an ordinary person?

אֶלָּא, פִּטּוּם הַקְּטֹרֶת יוֹכִיחַ, שֶׁאָסוּר לְהֶדְיוֹט וּמוּתָּר לְגָבוֹהַּ. מַה לְּפִטּוּם הַקְּטֹרֶת שֶׁכֵּן מִצְוָתוֹ בְּכָךְ!

Rather, Reish Lakish meant that **the preparation of the incense proves** it, **as** it is **prohibited** to prepare the incense mixture for use **by an ordinary person** (see Exodus 30:37), **and** yet it is **permitted** to do so **for the Most High.** The Gemara refutes this claim: **What** is notable **about preparation of the incense?** It is notable **in that its mitzva is in this** manner. By contrast, there is no mitzva to sacrifice specifically a *tereifa*.

מָר בְּרֵיהּ דְּרָבִינָא אָמַר, מִשּׁוּם דְּאִיכָּא לְמֵימַר: שַׁבָּת תּוֹכִיחַ, שֶׁאֲסוּרָה לְהֶדְיוֹט וּמוּתֶּרֶת לְגָבוֹהַּ.

Mar, son of Ravina, said that this is the response of the *baraita*: The *halakha* that a *tereifa* is unfit for sacrifice must be derived from a verse **because it can be said** that **Shabbat proves** that the *halakha* concerning a *tereifa* cannot be derived by the *a fortiori* inference, **as it is prohibited for an ordinary person** to perform labor on Shabbat, **and** yet the labor involved in the Temple service is **permitted** on Shabbat **for the Most High.** Without the verse, one might similarly conclude that a *tereifa* is permitted for the Most High despite the fact that it is prohibited for consumption.

BACKGROUND

Sabbatical Year – שְׁבִיעִית: The Sabbatical Year is the last year of the seven-year Sabbatical cycle. The first such cycle began after the conquest of Eretz Yisrael by Joshua. The *halakhot* of the Sabbatical Year are based on Torah law (see Leviticus 25:1–7), but most authorities maintain that the conditions enabling performance of the mitzva by Torah law do not currently exist. Consequently, present-day observance is based on rabbinic ordinance. The Hebrew term for the Sabbatical Year, *shemitta*, means abandonment or release, as during the Sabbatical Year all agricultural land must lie fallow. It is prohibited to work the land, except for doing that which is necessary to keep existing crops alive. All produce that does grow is ownerless and must be left unguarded in the fields so that any creature, including wild animals and birds, can have ready access to it. As long as produce can still be found in the fields it may be eaten, although it may not be bought and sold in the normal manner, nor used for purposes other than food. After the last remnants of a crop have been removed from the field, whatever remains of that crop in the house must be eradicated.

HALAKHA

***Sefiḥin* during the Sabbatical Year – סְפִיחִין בַּשְּׁבִיעִית:** Produce that grows during the Sabbatical Year without being purposely planted is called *sefiḥin*. By Torah law it is permitted to eat such produce, but the Sages prohibited its consumption (Rambam *Sefer Zera'im*, *Hilkhot Shemitta VeYovel* 4:2).

The new crop outside of Eretz Yisrael – חָדָשׁ בְּחוּצָה לָאָרֶץ: In accordance with the mishna in tractate *Orla* (3:9), most early commentaries maintain that the new crop is forbidden by Torah law both inside and outside of Eretz Yisrael. There is much discussion among the later commentaries with regard to possible justifications for the fact that Jews residing outside of Eretz Yisrael are lenient in this matter (Rambam *Sefer Kedusha*, *Hilkhot Ma'akhalot Assurot* 10:2; *Shulḥan Arukh*, *Oraḥ Ḥayyim* 489:10, and see *Mishna Berura* there; *Shulḥan Arukh*, *Yoreh De'a* 293:1).

מַה לְשַׁבָּת שֶׁכֵּן הוּתְּרָה מִכְּלָלָהּ אֵצֶל הֶדְיוֹט בְּמִילָה!

The Gemara rejects this: **What** is notable **about Shabbat?** It is notable **in that the general prohibition** against labor on Shabbat **was permitted with regard to an ordinary person in** the case of **circumcision,** as the mitzva of circumcision must be performed in its proper time, even on Shabbat, despite the fact that the act of circumcision is generally prohibited on Shabbat.

אַטּוּ מִילָה צוֹרֶךְ הֶדְיוֹט הוּא? מִילָה מִצְוָה הִיא! אֶלָּא, מַה לְשַׁבָּת שֶׁכֵּן מִצְוָתָהּ בְּכָךְ!

The Gemara asks: **Is that to say** that **circumcision is** considered **a requirement of an ordinary person,** whose performance was exempted from the general prohibition against labor on Shabbat for one's private needs? **Circumcision is a mitzva. Rather,** the statement of Mar, son of Ravina, can be refuted like this: **What** is notable **about Shabbat?** It is notable **in that its mitzva is in this** manner, i.e., the Torah requires that offerings be brought on Shabbat. By contrast, there is no mitzva to sacrifice specifically a *tereifa*.

רַב אַדָּא בַּר אַבָּא אָמַר, מִשּׁוּם דְּאִיכָּא לְמֵימַר: כִּלְאַיִם תּוֹכִיחַ, שֶׁאֲסוּרִין לְהֶדְיוֹט וּמוּתָּרִין לַגָּבוֹהַּ.

Rav Adda bar Abba said that this is the response mentioned in the *baraita*: The *halakha* that a *tereifa* is unfit for sacrifice must be derived from a verse **because it can be said** that the prohibition against **diverse kinds proves** that the *halakha* of a *tereifa* cannot be derived from the *a fortiori* inference, **as it is prohibited for an ordinary person** to wear garments sewn from a mixture of diverse kinds (Deuteronomy 22:11), **and** yet such garments are **permitted for the Most High,** as the belt of the priestly vestments was fashioned from a mixture of diverse kinds.

מַה לְכִלְאַיִם שֶׁכֵּן הוּתְּרוּ מִכְּלָלָן אֵצֶל הֶדְיוֹט בְּצִיצִית! אַטּוּ צִיצִית צוֹרֶךְ הֶדְיוֹט הִיא? מִצְוָה הִיא! אֶלָּא,

The Gemara rejects this: **What** is notable **about** the prohibition against **diverse kinds?** It is notable **in that** the **general prohibition** against wearing a garment sewn from diverse kinds **was permitted in** the case of **an ordinary person with regard to ritual fringes,** as a string of sky-blue wool must be placed on a four-cornered garment even if that garment is made from linen. The Gemara asks: **Is that to say** that **ritual fringes** are considered **a requirement of an ordinary person,** whose performance was exempted from the general prohibition concerning diverse kinds with regard to one's private needs? Placing ritual fringes on a garment **is a mitzva. Rather,** the claim of Rav Adda bar Abba can be refuted like this:

Perek **I**
Daf **6** Amud **a**

מַה לְכִלְאַיִם שֶׁמִּצְוָתוֹ בְּכָךְ!

What is notable **about diverse kinds?** It is notable **in that its mitzva is in this** manner, since the belt of the priestly vestments must be sewn from diverse kinds. By contrast, there is no mitzva to sacrifice specifically a *tereifa*.

רַב שִׁישָׁא בְּרֵיהּ דְּרַב אִידִי אָמַר: מִשּׁוּם דְּאִיכָּא לְמֵימַר, לִיהֲדַר דִּינָא וְתֵיתֵי בְּמָה הַצַּד: מַה לִמְלִיקָה שֶׁכֵּן קְדוּשָּׁתָהּ אוֹסַרְתָּהּ – חֵלֶב וָדָם יוֹכִיחוּ;

Rav Sheisha, son of Rav Idi, said: The *halakha* that a *tereifa* is unfit for sacrifice must be derived from the verse, **because it can be said: Let** this claim **be derived by** analogy from **the common element** of two sources, as follows: With regard to the question of the *baraita*: **What** is notable **about pinching?** It is notable **in that its sanctity prohibits it,** one can respond: **Fat and blood prove** that this consideration is not enough to reject the *a fortiori* inference, as these are prohibited before they are sanctified and are nevertheless permitted for the Most High.

מַה לְחֵלֶב וָדָם שֶׁכֵּן בָּאִים מִכְּלַל הֶיתֵּר – מְלִיקָה תּוֹכִיחַ;

Similarly, with regard to the question: **What** is notable **about fat and blood?** They are notable **in that they come from** an item that is **generally permitted,** i.e., the animal from which they come is itself permitted for consumption, one can reply: **Pinching proves** that this consideration is insufficient for a rejection of the *a fortiori* inference, as a bird that was killed by pinching is entirely prohibited for eating, and yet a pinched bird is permitted to the altar.

וְחָזַר הַדִּין, לֹא רְאִי זֶה כִּרְאִי זֶה וְלֹא רְאִי זֶה כִּרְאִי זֶה, הַצַּד הַשָּׁוֶה שֶׁבָּהֶן – שֶׁאֲסוּרִין לְהֶדְיוֹט וּמוּתָּרִין לַגָּבוֹהַּ, אַף אֲנִי אָבִיא טְרֵפָה, אַף עַל פִּי שֶׁאֲסוּרָה לְהֶדְיוֹט תְּהֵא מוּתֶּרֶת לַגָּבוֹהַּ. מַה לְּהַצַּד הַשָּׁוֶה שֶׁבָּהֶן שֶׁכֵּן מִצְוָתָהּ בְּכָךְ!

Rav Sheisha concludes: **And** accordingly, **the inference has reverted** to its starting point. **The aspect of this** case **is not like the aspect of that case and the aspect of that** case **is not like the aspect of this** case; **their common element** is **that they are prohibited** for consumption **to an ordinary person and are** nevertheless **permitted for the Most High.** Therefore, **I will also bring** the case of **a** ***tereifa*** and say: **Even though is it prohibited** for consumption **to an ordinary person, it should be permitted for the Most High.** It is therefore necessary to derive from a verse that a *tereifa* is unfit for sacrifice. The Gemara rejects this: **What** is notable **about their common element?** It is notable in **that** with regard to fat and blood, and pinching, in both cases **its mitzva** is performed **in this** manner.

אֶלָּא אָמַר רַב אַשִׁי, מִשּׁוּם דְּאִיכָּא לְמֵימַר: מֵעִיקָּרָא דְּדִינָא פִּרְכָא, מֵהֵיכָא קָא מַיְיתֵית לַהּ? מִבַּעַל מוּם;

Rather, Rav Ashi said: It is necessary to derive the *halakha* of a *tereifa* from a verse **because one can say** that the **refutation of the** *a fortiori* **inference** is present **from the outset.** Rav Ashi elaborates: **From where do you** wish to **derive** the *halakha* that a *tereifa* is unfit for sacrifice? You wish to derive it from an *a fortiori* inference **from** the case of **a blemished** animal, as a blemished animal is permitted for consumption and prohibited for sacrifice. This is problematic.

מַה לְּבַעַל מוּם שֶׁכֵּן עָשָׂה בּוֹ מַקְרִיבִין כִּקְרֵיבִין.

Rav Ashi explains: **What** is notable **about a blemished** animal? It is notable **in that with regard to** blemishes the Torah **rendered those who sacrifice like that which is sacrificed,** i.e., a blemished priest may not sacrifice an offering just as a blemished animal is unfit for sacrifice (see Leviticus, chapter 22). This cannot be said with regard to a *tereifa*, as a priest with a wound that will cause him to die within twelve months may perform the Temple service. It is therefore necessary to derive from the verse the fact that a *tereifa* is unfit for sacrifice.

אֲמַר לֵיהּ רַב אַחָא סָבָא לְרַב אַשִׁי: יוֹצֵא דוֹפֶן יוֹכִיחַ, שֶׁלֹּא עָשָׂה בּוֹ מַקְרִיבִין כִּקְרֵיבִין, וּמוּתָּר לְהֶדְיוֹט וְאָסוּר לַגָּבוֹהַּ!

Rav Aḥa Sava said to Rav Ashi: But an animal **born by caesarean section proves** that this *a fortiori* inference cannot be rejected based on that consideration, **as with regard to it** the Torah **did not render those who sacrifice like that which is sacrificed,** since an animal born by caesarean section is unfit for sacrifice whereas a priest born in such a manner may perform the Temple service. **And** yet an animal born by caesarean section is **permitted** for consumption **to an ordinary person and prohibited for the Most High.** If so, one cannot reject the *a fortiori* inference because with regard to blemishes the Torah rendered those who sacrifice like that which is sacrificed. Why then is a verse necessary in order to derive that a *tereifa* is unfit?

מַה לְּיוֹצֵא דוֹפֶן שֶׁכֵּן אֵינוֹ קָדוֹשׁ בִּבְכוֹרָה.

Rav Ashi responds: **What** is notable **about** an animal **born by caesarean section?** It is notable **in that** such an animal **is not sanctified with firstborn** status, whereas a firstborn animal that was born as a *tereifa* is sanctified. Accordingly, without the verse one might have concluded that a *tereifa* may be sacrificed.

בַּעַל מוּם יוֹכִיחַ! מַה לְּבַעַל מוּם שֶׁכֵּן עָשָׂה בּוֹ מַקְרִיבִין כִּקְרֵיבִין. יוֹצֵא דוֹפֶן יוֹכִיחַ!

Rav Aḥa Sava answers: **A blemished** animal **proves** that this is not the decisive consideration, as it does become sanctified with the sanctity of a firstborn, and it too is permitted for consumption and prohibited for the Most High. And if you say: **What** is notable **about a blemished** animal? It is notable **in that with regard to it** the Torah **rendered those who sacrifice like that which is sacrificed,** one can respond: An animal **born by caesarean section proves** that this consideration is not decisive, as a priest born by caesarean section may perform the Temple service.

וְחָזַר הַדִּין, לֹא רְאִי זֶה כִּרְאִי זֶה וְלֹא רְאִי זֶה כִּרְאִי זֶה, הַצַּד הַשָּׁוֶה שֶׁבָּהֶן – שֶׁמּוּתָּרִין לְהֶדְיוֹט וַאֲסוּרִים לַגָּבוֹהַּ, וְכׇל שֶׁכֵּן טְרֵפָה שֶׁאֲסוּרָה לְהֶדְיוֹט תְּהֵא אֲסוּרָה לַגָּבוֹהַּ!

Rav Aḥa Sava concludes: **And** therefore, **the inference has reverted** to its starting point. **The aspect of this** case **is not like the aspect of that** case **and the aspect of that** case **is not like the aspect of this** case; **their common element** is **that they are permitted** for consumption **to an ordinary person and prohibited for the Most High. And all the more so a** ***tereifa*****, which is prohibited to an ordinary person, should be prohibited for the Most High.** If so, the derivation from a verse is unnecessary.

מַה לְּהַצַּד הַשָּׁוֶה שֶׁבָּהֶן שֶׁכֵּן לֹא הוּתְּרוּ מִכְּלָלָן, תֹּאמַר בִּטְרֵיפָה שֶׁהוּתְּרָה מִכְּלָלָהּ!

Rav Ashi refutes the proof of Rav Aḥa Sava: **What** is notable **about their common element?** It is notable **in that their general prohibition was not permitted,** since blemished animals and those born by caesarean section are never permitted for sacrifice. **Will you say** that the same applies **to a *tereifa*, whose general prohibition was permitted,** as will be explained? Accordingly, it is necessary to derive from the verse that a *tereifa* is unfit for sacrifice.

אֲמַר לֵיהּ רַב אַחָא בְּרֵיהּ דְּרָבָא לְרַב אַשִׁי: טְרֵפָה שֶׁהוּתְּרָה מִכְּלָלָהּ מַאי הִיא? אִילֵימָא מְלִיקָה דְּעוֹלַת הָעוֹף לַגָּבוֹהַּ – בַּעַל מוּם נַמִּי בְּעוֹפוֹת אִשְׁתַּרוּיֵי אִשְׁתְּרֵי, תַּמּוּת וְזַכְרוּת בִּבְהֵמָה וְאֵין תַּמּוּת וְזַכְרוּת בְּעוֹפוֹת!

Rav Aḥa, son of Rava, said to Rav Ashi: This ***tereifa* whose general prohibition was permitted, what is it,** i.e., to what case is this referring? **If we say** that it is referring to the **pinching of a bird burnt offering**[N] **for the Most High,** whereby the bird is initially rendered a *tereifa* at the start of the pinching process, and nevertheless it is sacrificed upon the altar, then the same may be said of **a blemished** animal **as well.** As **with regard to birds** it is **permitted** to sacrifice a blemished bird. This is in accordance with the *halakha* that the requirement that an offering must be **unblemished and male** applies **to animal** offerings, **but there is no** requirement that an offering must be **unblemished and male in** the case of **bird** offerings.

אֶלָּא מְלִיקָה דְּחַטַּאת הָעוֹף לַכֹּהֲנִים – כֹּהֲנִים מִשּׁוּלְחַן גָּבוֹהַּ קָא זָכוּ!

Rather, this permitting the general prohibition found in the context of a *tereifa* is referring to the *halakha* that the **pinching of a bird sin offering** renders it permitted **to the priests** for consumption despite the fact that it was not slaughtered by cutting its neck with a knife. This claim can be refuted as well, as the **priests receive** their portion **from the table of the Most High,** i.e., they may partake of the sin offering only because it was permitted for sacrifice upon the altar. Accordingly, there is no difference between a *tereifa* due to pinching and a blemished bird, as both were released from their general prohibition in this regard, since both are permitted for sacrifice upon the altar and both are therefore permitted for consumption by the priests. Consequently, the *a fortiori* inference remains valid, and the verse is unnecessary.

וְאֶלָּא פָּרֵיךְ הָכִי: מַה לְּהַצַּד הַשָּׁוֶה שֶׁבָּהֶן שֶׁכֵּן מוּמָן נִיכָּר, תֹּאמַר בִּטְרֵיפָה שֶׁכֵּן אֵין מוּמָהּ נִיכָּר, מִשּׁוּם הָכִי אִיצְטְרִיךְ קְרָא.

Rather, refute the *a fortiori* inference **like this: What** is notable **about their common element?** It is notable **in that** with regard to both a blemished animal and one born by caesarean section **their blemish is noticeable,** as a blemished animal is visibly blemished and it is well known when an animal is born by caesarean section. **Will you say** that they can serve as the source of the *halakha* **of a *tereifa*, whose blemish is not** necessarily **noticeable? Due to that** reason, **the verse:** "Of the herd" (Leviticus 1:3), **was necessary,** to teach that a *tereifa* is unfit for sacrifice.

וּטְרֵיפָה מֵהָכָא נָפְקָא? מֵהָתָם נָפְקָא: "מִמַּשְׁקֵה יִשְׂרָאֵל" – מִן הַמּוּתָּר לְיִשְׂרָאֵל;

§ After trying to prove why a derivation from a verse is necessary, the Gemara questions the very source provided by the *baraita* on 5b for the disqualification of a *tereifa*, i.e., the verse: "Of the herd" (Leviticus 1:3). **But is** the *halakha* that **a *tereifa*** is unfit for sacrifice **derived from here? It is derived from there,** i.e., from the verse: **"From the well-watered pastures of Israel"** (Ezekiel 45:15), from which it is derived that an offering may be brought only **from** that **which is permitted to the Jewish people.**

מִ"כֹּל אֲשֶׁר יַעֲבוֹר תַּחַת הַשָּׁבֶט" נָפְקָא – פְּרָט לִטְרֵיפָה שֶׁאֵינָהּ עוֹבֶרֶת!

Alternatively, this *halakha* can be **derived from** a verse discussing animal tithe offerings: **"Whatever passes under the rod,** the tenth shall be holy for the Lord" (Leviticus 27:32). This teaches that all animals may be sacrificed as the animal tithe, **excluding a *tereifa*, as it does not pass** under the rod on account of its weakness, and the Sages derived from this the *halakha* that a *tereifa* is unfit for any type of offering.

NOTES

Pinching of a bird burnt offering – מְלִיקָה דְּעוֹלַת הָעוֹף: To ensure that the act of pinching, i.e., the severing of the bird's gullet and windpipe [*simanim*], occurs while the bird is still alive, the priest first cuts its spinal cord and neck bone, leaving most of the flesh of its neck intact. At this point, the bird becomes a *tereifa*, as the priest has inflicted a mortal wound upon it. The priest then severs one of the *simanim* of the bird in the case of a sin offering, or both of the *simanim* in the case of a burnt offering, severing a majority of the flesh surrounding its neck as well (see *Ḥullin* 21a). Only a bird offering, which is killed by means of pinching the back of its neck, is rendered a *tereifa* prior to its death. By contrast, a bird killed through ritual slaughter, which is performed on the front side of the neck, is not rendered a *tereifa*, as the *simanim* are severed already at the initial stage of slaughter (see Rashi on *Ḥullin* 20b).

צְרִיכִי, דְּאִי מִ״מַּשְׁקֵה יִשְׂרָאֵל״ הֲוָה אָמִינָא: לְמַעוּטֵי הֵיכָא דְּלָא הָיְתָה לָהּ שְׁעַת הַכּוֹשֶׁר, דּוּמְיָא דְּעׇרְלָה וְכִלְאֵי הַכֶּרֶם, אֲבָל הָיְתָה לָהּ שְׁעַת הַכּוֹשֶׁר אֵימָא תִּתַּכְשַׁר – כְּתַב רַחֲמָנָא: ״כֹּל אֲשֶׁר יַעֲבוֹר״;

The Gemara responds: All of these verses **are necessary, because if** the disqualification of a *tereifa* was derived **from** the verse **"the well-watered pastures of Israel," I would say** that this verse serves **to exclude** a *tereifa* only in a case **where it did not have a period of fitness**, e.g., if it was born a *tereifa* and was therefore never fit for sacrifice. This is **similar to** the case of **the fruit of a tree during the first three years after its planting** [*orla*][B] **and diverse kinds** planted **in a vineyard,**[B] whose disqualification is derived from this verse. **But** with regard to a *tereifa* that **had a period of fitness,** one might **say** that **it should be fit.** Therefore, **the Merciful One writes: "Whatever passes** under the rod," to teach that all animals that do not pass under the rod are unfit for sacrifice, even if they were once fit.

וְאִי כְּתַב רַחֲמָנָא ״כֹּל אֲשֶׁר יַעֲבוֹר״ הֲוָה אָמִינָא: לְמַעוּטֵי הֵיכָא דְּנִטְרְפָה וּלְבַסּוֹף הִקְדִּישָׁהּ, דּוּמְיָא דְּמַעֲשֵׂר, אֲבָל הִקְדִּישָׁהּ וּלְבַסּוֹף נִטְרְפָה, דְּבְעִידָּנָא דְּאַקְדְּשָׁהּ הֲוָה חֲזְיָא אֵימָא תִּתַּכְשַׁר – כְּתַב רַחֲמָנָא: ״מִן הַבָּקָר״, צְרִיכִי.

The Gemara continues: **And if the Merciful One had written** only: **"Whatever passes** under the rod," **I would say** that this verse serves **to exclude** a *tereifa* only **where it was rendered a *tereifa* and** its owner **subsequently sanctified it.** This is **similar to** the case of animal **tithes,** as this verse is teaching that a *tereifa* cannot be subsequently sanctified as a tithe. **But** if the owner **sanctified it and it was subsequently rendered a *tereifa*,** which means **that at the time when it was sanctified it was fit,** one might **say** that **it should be fit.** Therefore, **the Merciful One wrote: "Of the herd,"** to teach that even an animal that became a *tereifa* after it was already sanctified is unfit for sacrifice. Accordingly, all three verses **are necessary.**

מתני׳ אֶחָד מִנְחַת חוֹטֵא וְאֶחָד כׇּל הַמְּנָחוֹת שֶׁקְּמָצָן זָר, אוֹנֵן, טְבוּל יוֹם, מְחוּסַּר בְּגָדִים, מְחוּסַּר כִּיפּוּרִים, שֶׁלֹּא רָחַץ יָדָיו וְרַגְלָיו, עָרֵל, טָמֵא, יוֹשֵׁב, עוֹמֵד עַל גַּבֵּי כֵלִים, עַל גַּבֵּי בְהֵמָה, עַל גַּבֵּי רַגְלֵי חֲבֵירוֹ – פָּסוּל.

MISHNA **Both the meal offering of a sinner and** all other **meal offerings** with regard to which the one who **removed their handful**[H] was **a non-priest,**[H] or a priest who was **an acute mourner,**[H] i.e., whose relative died and was not yet buried, or a priest who was ritually impure **who immersed that day**[H] and was waiting for nightfall for the purification process to be completed, or a priest **lacking** the requisite priestly **vestments,**[H] or a priest **who had not yet** brought **an atonement** offering[H] to complete the purification process, or a priest **who did not wash his hands and feet**[H] from the water in the Basin prior to performing the Temple service, or **an uncircumcised**[H] priest, or **a ritually impure**[H] priest, or a priest who removed the handful while **sitting,** or while **standing** not on the floor of the Temple but **upon vessels,**[HN] or **upon an animal,** or **upon the feet of another** person; in all these cases the meal offerings are **unfit** for sacrifice.

קָמַץ בִּשְׂמֹאל – פָּסוּל, בֶּן בְּתֵירָא אוֹמֵר: יַחֲזִיר וְיַחֲזוֹר וְיִקְמוֹץ בְּיָמִין.

If the priest **removed the handful with** his **left** hand[H] the meal offering is **unfit. Ben Beteira says: He must return** the handful to the vessel that contains the meal offering **and again remove the handful,** this time **with** his **right** hand.

BACKGROUND

Orla – **עָרְלָה**: It is prohibited to eat or derive benefit from the fruit that grows on a tree during the first three years after the tree was planted (see Leviticus 19:23). This prohibition applies only to the fruit, not to the other parts of the tree. In addition, the prohibition does not apply to trees planted as a fence for property or as a wind buffer rather than for their fruit.

Diverse kinds planted in a vineyard – כִּלְאֵי הַכֶּרֶם: It is prohibited to plant or maintain other crops in a vineyard in addition to the grapes (see Deuteronomy 22:9). In contrast to the prohibition against a mixture of diverse kinds, the prohibited crop grown in a vineyard may not be eaten or used. It renders the entire vineyard prohibited, and all the produce must be burned.

NOTES

Upon vessels, etc. – עַל גַּבֵּי כֵלִים וכו׳: Just as a service vessel sanctifies items placed inside it, so too, the floor of the Temple sanctifies the service of a priest performing the Temple service upon it. Accordingly, just as a service vessel sanctifies only when there is no interposition between it and the item placed inside it, so too, the Temple floor sanctifies the service of a priest only when there is no interposition between it and the priest's feet. Therefore, the services performed by a priest standing upon vessels, animals, or the feet of others are disqualified (see *Zevaḥim* 24a).

HALAKHA

With regard to which the one who removed their handful, etc. – שֶׁקְּמָצָן וכו׳: With regard to any meal offering, if the one who removed its handful was unfit to perform the Temple service, the offering is disqualified (Rambam *Sefer Avoda, Hilkhot Pesulei HaMukdashin* 11:1).

Non-priest – זָר: A non-priest is defined as anyone who is not a male descendant of Aaron. Temple service performed by such a person is not valid (Rambam *Sefer Avoda, Hilkhot Biat HaMikdash* 9:1).

Acute mourner – אוֹנֵן: Temple service performed by an acute mourner is not valid (Rambam *Sefer Avoda, Hilkhot Biat HaMikdash* 2:6–7).

One who immersed that day – טְבוּל יוֹם: With regard to a ritually impure priest who immersed himself and performed the Temple service before sunset of the same day, his service is not valid (Rambam *Sefer Avoda, Hilkhot Biat HaMikdash* 4:4).

A priest lacking the requisite priestly vestments – מְחוּסַּר בְּגָדִים: Temple services performed by a High Priest while he is not wearing his eight priestly vestments, or by an ordinary priest without his four priestly vestments are not valid because they lack the requisite priestly vestments (Rambam *Sefer Avoda, Hilkhot Kelei HaMikdash* 10:4).

One who had not yet brought an atonement offering – מְחוּסַּר כִּיפּוּרִים: The services performed by one who lacks atonement, i.e., one who has not yet brought an atonement offering to complete his purification process, are not valid (Rambam *Sefer Avoda, Hilkhot Biat HaMikdash* 4:5).

One who did not wash his hands and feet – שֶׁלֹּא רָחַץ יָדָיו וְרַגְלָיו: The services performed by a priest who did not wash his hands and feet are not valid (Rambam *Sefer Avoda, Hilkhot Biat HaMikdash* 5:1).

Uncircumcised – עָרֵל: The services of an uncircumcised male are not valid, even if he is a descendant of Aaron (Rambam *Sefer Avoda, Hilkhot Biat HaMikdash* 6:8).

Ritually impure – טָמֵא: The service of a ritually impure priest is not valid (Rambam *Sefer Avoda, Hilkhot Biat HaMikdash* 4:1).

Sitting or standing upon vessels, etc. – יוֹשֵׁב עוֹמֵד עַל גַּבֵּי כֵלִים וכו׳: Temple service performed by a priest while he was sitting is not valid. A priest must stand on the floor of the Temple while performing the service. If something interposes between his feet and the Temple floor, e.g., if he performs the service while standing upon a vessel, upon an animal, or upon the feet of another, his service is not valid (Rambam *Sefer Avoda, Hilkhot Biat HaMikdash* 5:17).

Removed the handful with his left hand – קָמַץ בִּשְׂמֹאל: If a priest removed a handful from a meal offering with his left hand, it is not valid, as all sacrificial rites must be performed with the right hand (Rambam *Sefer Avoda, Hilkhot Biat HaMikdash* 5:18).

LANGUAGE

Pinch [*koret*] – קוֹרֶט: This refers to a small item or a fraction. The word is of unknown origin, although it is close to the Greek κεράτιον, *keration*, a unit of measurement or a small horn. The word carat comes from the same Greek source, although the Greek word itself might have a Semitic origin. Some sources assert that the word *koret* is a slight variation of the Hebrew term *keretz*, which means a slice or a small piece.

Overflowing [*mevoratz*] – מְבוֹרָץ: The root of this term, *beit*, *reish*, *tzadi*, denotes an item that has exceeded its boundaries. This root has the same meaning in ancient Syriac and it has the same meaning as the Greek word βράζω, *brazo*, which means to boil, froth up, or ferment.

BACKGROUND

Frankincense – לְבוֹנָה: Frankincense, included by the Torah among the ingredients that collectively form the incense, is commonly identified as a sap secreted from trees of the genus *Boswellia*. Some maintain that it is specifically the sap of the species *Boswellia sacra*, found in the southern Arabian Peninsula, while others suggest that it is the sap of the species *Boswellia frereana*, found in eastern Africa. A verse in Isaiah (60:6) states that frankincense comes from the kingdom of Sheba.

When one cuts the bark of these trees, a sap is secreted that eventually hardens and turns into beads of frankincense. In ancient times it was used in incense and as an ingredient in various medicines. Frankincense was burned as a part of a mixture and also by itself. There are various grades of quality of frankincense, ranked according to the various types and conditions of the trees that secrete the sap. Frankincense of the highest quality is referred to as pure frankincense.

Frankincense tree

קָמַץ וְעָלָה בְּיָדוֹ צְרוֹר אוֹ גַּרְגֵּר מֶלַח אוֹ קוֹרֶט שֶׁל לְבוֹנָה – פָּסוּל, מִפְּנֵי שֶׁאָמְרוּ: הַקּוֹמֶץ הַיָּתֵר וְהֶחָסֵר – פָּסוּל. וְאֵיזֶהוּ הַיָּתֵר – שֶׁקְּמָצוֹ מְבוֹרָץ, וְחָסֵר – שֶׁקְּמָצוֹ בְּרָאשֵׁי אֶצְבְּעוֹתָיו.

If a priest **removed the handful** of flour, **and a stone, a grain of salt, or a pinch** [*koret*][L] **of frankincense**[B] **emerged in his hand,** the meal offering is **unfit due to** the fact **that** the Sages **said: The handful that is outsized or that is lacking**[H] **is unfit.** The existence of one of these foreign items in the handful means that the requisite measure of flour is lacking. **And which is the outsized** handful? It is one **where he removed the handful overflowing** [*mevoratz*][L] in a manner in which his fingers do not hold the flour. **And** which is the **lacking** handful? It is one **where he removed the handful with the tips of his fingers.**

גמ׳ לָמָּה לִי לְמִתְנָא ״אֶחָד מִנְחַת חוֹטֵא וְאֶחָד כָּל הַמְּנָחוֹת״? לִיתְנֵי: כָּל הַמְּנָחוֹת שֶׁקְּמָצָן זָר וְאוֹנֵן!

GEMARA The Gemara asks: **Why do I** need the mishna **to teach: Both the meal offering of a sinner and all** other **meal offerings? Let it teach: All the meal offerings** with regard to **which** the one who **removed their handful** was **a non-priest or an acute mourner.** Why does the mishna single out the case of the meal offering of a sinner?

לְרַבִּי שִׁמְעוֹן אִיצְטְרִיךְ; דְּתַנְיָא, אָמַר רַבִּי שִׁמְעוֹן: בְּדִין הוּא שֶׁתְּהֵא מִנְחַת חוֹטֵא טְעוּנָה שֶׁמֶן וּלְבוֹנָה, שֶׁלֹּא יְהֵא חוֹטֵא נִשְׂכָּר, וּמִפְּנֵי מָה אֵינָהּ טְעוּנָה? שֶׁלֹּא יְהֵא קָרְבָּנוֹ מְהוּדָּר; וּבְדִין הוּא שֶׁתְּהֵא חַטַּאת חֵלֶב טְעוּנָה נְסָכִים,

The Gemara responds: **It was necessary** for the mishna to teach this *halakha* in this manner **in accordance with** the opinion of **Rabbi Shimon. As it is taught** in a *baraita* that **Rabbi Shimon says: By right the meal offering of a sinner should require oil and frankincense** like other meal offerings, **so that the sinner will not profit. And for what** reason does **it not require** oil and frankincense? So **that his offering will not be of superior quality. And** likewise, **by right** the **sin offering of** forbidden **fat,** i.e., the offering brought by one who unwittingly ate the forbidden fat of a domesticated animal, **should require libations**

שֶׁלֹּא יְהֵא חוֹטֵא נִשְׂכָּר, וּמִפְּנֵי מָה אֵינָהּ טְעוּנָה? שֶׁלֹּא יְהֵא קָרְבָּנוֹ מְהוּדָּר; סָלְקָא דַּעְתָּךְ אָמִינָא, הוֹאִיל וְאָמַר רַבִּי שִׁמְעוֹן: שֶׁלֹּא יְהֵא קָרְבָּנוֹ מְהוּדָּר, כִּי קָמְצִי לָהּ פְּסוּלִין נַמִי תִּתַּכְשַׁר, קָא מַשְׁמַע לָן.

so that the **sinner will not profit. And for what** reason **does** his offering **not require** libations? So **that his offering will not be of superior quality.** Accordingly, it might **enter your mind to say** that **since Rabbi Shimon says:** In order **that his offering will not be of superior quality, when the handful is removed** by one of those **unfit** for performing the Temple service, the offering **should also be valid,** as it too is of inferior quality. Therefore, the mishna **teaches us** the *halakha* in a manner that emphasizes that even according to the opinion of Rabbi Shimon the meal offering of a sinner is disqualified when the handful is removed by one who is unfit.

HALAKHA

The handful that is outsized or that is lacking – הַקּוֹמֶץ הַיָּתֵר וְהֶחָסֵר: How was a handful properly removed from a meal offering? The priest would extend his fingers over the palm of his hand and would thereby remove a handful. If he removed it with only his fingertips, or if he removed it from the sides of the vessel, he should not burn that handful upon the altar, but if he did, it effects acceptance. If he took more than a handful, e.g., if his fingers were spread apart while removing the handful, the handful is disqualified (Rambam *Sefer Avoda, Hilkhot Pesulei HaMukdashin* 11:3 and *Hilkhot Ma'aseh HaKorbanot* 13:13).

אִי הָכִי, הָתָם נַמִי לִיתְנֵי: "אֶחָד חַטַּאת חֵלֶב וְאֶחָד כׇּל הַזְּבָחִים שֶׁקִּבְּלוּ דָּמָן זָר וְאוֹנֵן", וְלֵימָא: לְרַבִּי שִׁמְעוֹן אִצְטְרִיךְ!

The Gemara asks: **If so,** then **there as well,** i.e., with regard to slaughtered offerings, **let** the mishna (*Zevaḥim* 15b) **teach: Both the sin offering of** forbidden **fat and all the slaughtered offerings** with regard to **which** the one who **collected their blood** was **a non-priest or** a priest who is **an acute mourner,** are disqualified. **And let us say** that **it was necessary** to teach the mishna in this manner **in accordance with** the opinion of **Rabbi Shimon,** to emphasize that although the sin offering is not of superior quality, in that it does not require that libations be brought with it, nevertheless it is disqualified if its blood was collected by one unfit for Temple service. Why then does that mishna teach simply: All the slaughtered offerings with regard to which the one who collected their blood was a non-priest are disqualified?

אַלְמָא, כֵּיוָן דִּתְנָא לֵיהּ "כׇּל" וְלָא קָתָנֵי "חוּץ" – כּוּלְּהוּ מַשְׁמַע; הָכָא נַמִי, כֵּיוָן דִּתְנָא "כׇּל" וְלָא קָתָנֵי "חוּץ" – כּוּלְּהוּ מַשְׁמַע!

The Gemara concludes its question: **Apparently, since** the *tanna* **teaches** that mishna with the term: **All, and he does not teach: Except, all** offerings **are indicated** by the general disqualification, and there is no need to emphasize the *halakha* with regard to a sin offering, even in accordance with the opinion of Rabbi Shimon. **Here too,** with regard to meal offerings, **since** the *tanna* **teaches** the mishna with the term: **All, and he does not teach: Except,** this means that **all of them are indicated,** even the meal offering of a sinner. Why then does the mishna specifically mention the meal offering of a sinner?

אִצְטְרִיךְ, סָלְקָא דַּעְתָּךְ אָמִינָא: הוֹאִיל וְאוֹקִימְנָא לְרֵישָׁא דְּלָא כְּרַבִּי שִׁמְעוֹן – סֵיפָא נַמִי דְּלָא כְּרַבִּי שִׁמְעוֹן, קָא מַשְׁמַע לַן.

The Gemara explains: **It was necessary** to teach the mishna in this manner as it might **enter your mind to say: Since I have established that the first clause,** i.e., the mishna on 2a, is **not in accordance with** the opinion of **Rabbi Shimon,** with regard to **the last clause as well,** i.e., the mishna here, it may be concluded **that** it is **not in accordance with** the opinion of **Rabbi Shimon.** Therefore, the mishna **teaches us** the *halakha* in this manner, to emphasize that it is in accordance with his opinion.

אָמַר רַב: זָר שֶׁקָּמַץ – יַחֲזִיר. וְהָא אֲנַן פָּסַל תְּנַן! מַאי פָּסַל? פָּסַל עַד שֶׁיַּחֲזִיר.

§ **Rav says:** In the case of **a non-priest who removed a handful, he should return** the handful to the meal offering. The Gemara challenges: **But we learned** in the mishna that a non-priest **disqualified** the meal offering by removing a handful from it. The Gemara responds: **What** does the mishna mean when it says: **Disqualified?** It means that the non-priest has **disqualified** the meal offering **until** such time as **he returns** the handful to the meal offering, whereupon a priest fit for the Temple service should again remove a handful from the meal offering and sacrifice it.

אִי הָכִי, הַיְינוּ בֶּן בְּתֵירָא! אִי דְּאִיתֵיהּ לְקוֹמֶץ בְּעֵינֵיהּ – לָא פְּלִיגִי רַבָּנַן עֲלֵיהּ דְּבֶן בְּתֵירָא; כִּי פְּלִיגִי – דְּחָסַר קוֹמֶץ, רַבָּנַן סָבְרִי: לֹא יָבִיא מִתּוֹךְ בֵּיתוֹ וִימַלְּאֶנּוּ, בֶּן בְּתֵירָא סָבַר: יָבִיא מִתּוֹךְ בֵּיתוֹ וִימַלְּאֶנּוּ.

The Gemara challenges: **If so,** then **this is** identical to the opinion of **ben Beteira** in the mishna, who says that if a priest removed a handful with his left hand it is returned to the meal offering whereupon the priest removes a handful from the offering with his right hand. What difference is there between the two opinions in the mishna? The Gemara explains: **If the handful** that was removed by one unfit for Temple service **is in its unadulterated form,** then **the Rabbis do not disagree with** the opinion of **ben Beteira,** and the handful is returned to the meal offering. **They disagree when** the **handful is lacking. The Rabbis hold: One does not bring** flour **from within his house and refill** the vessel containing the handful, whereas **ben Beteira holds** that **one brings** flour **from within his house and refills it.**

אִי הָכִי, בֶּן בְּתֵירָא אוֹמֵר: יַחֲזִיר וְיַחֲזוֹר וְיִקְמוֹץ בְּיָמִין? בֶּן בְּתֵירָא אוֹמֵר: יַחֲזִיר וְיָבִיא מִתּוֹךְ בֵּיתוֹ וִימַלְּאֶנּוּ וְיַחֲזוֹר וְיִקְמוֹץ בְּיָמִין, מִיבָּעֵי לֵיהּ!

The Gemara asks: **If so,** i.e., if the mishna is referring to a handful that is lacking, then the statement of the mishna: **Ben Beteira says he must return** the handful to the vessel with the meal offering **and again remove a handful with** his **right** hand, is imprecise, as the mishna **should have** taught: **Ben Beteira says he must return** the handful to the vessel with the meal offering **and bring** flour **from within his house and refill** the missing amount, **and again remove a handful with** his **right** hand.

כִּי קָא אָמַר רַב – לְבֶן בְּתֵירָא. פְּשִׁיטָא! מַהוּ דְּתֵימָא: עַד כָּאן לָא קָא מַכְשַׁר בֶּן בְּתֵירָא אֶלָּא בִּשְׂמֹאל, אֲבָל בִּשְׁאָר פְּסוּלִין לָא, קָא מַשְׁמַע לָן.

The Gemara therefore suggests a different answer: **When Rav said** that the handful is returned to the meal offering, he said this only **according to** the opinion of **ben Beteira.** The Gemara asks: But isn't it **obvious** that this is the opinion of ben Beteira? The Gemara responds: Rav's statement is necessary **lest you say** that **ben Beteira deems** the meal offering **fit only** when the handful was removed **with** one's **left** hand, **but with regard to other disqualifications,** he does **not** deem it fit. Therefore, Rav **teaches us** that with regard to all of the disqualifications cited in the mishna, ben Beteira holds that the handful is returned to the meal offering whereupon a new handful is removed from it and sacrificed upon the altar.

מַאי שְׁנָא שְׂמֹאל – דְּאַשְׁכַּחַן לָהּ הֶכְשֵׁירָא בְּיוֹם הַכִּפּוּרִים, זָר נַמִי – אַשְׁכַּחַן לָהּ הֶכְשֵׁירָא בִּשְׁחִיטָה!

The Gemara asks: **What is different** in the case of a handful removed with a priest's **left** hand that one might have thought that ben Beteira's opinion applies only in this case? Perhaps the reason is **that we find** that the Temple service performed with the priest's left hand is **fit on Yom Kippur,** i.e., when the High Priest would enter the Holy of Holies holding the vessel containing the incense in his left hand. But with regard to **a non-priest as well, we find** that the Temple service is **fit with regard to slaughter,** as an offering may be slaughtered by a non-priest. Why then is it necessary for Rav to teach that the opinion of ben Beteira applies to the case of a non-priest as well?

שְׁחִיטָה לָאו עֲבוֹדָה הִיא.

The Gemara responds: **Slaughter is not** considered a sacrificial **rite,** and it is for that reason that a non-priest may slaughter an offering. Accordingly, without the statement of Rav one would not have concluded that ben Beteira holds that a handful removed by a non-priest may be returned, as the Temple service is never fit when performed by a non-priest.

וְלָא? וְהָאָמַר רַבִּי זֵירָא אָמַר רַב: שְׁחִיטַת פָּרָה בְּזָר – פְּסוּלָה, וַאֲמַר רַב עֲלָהּ: אֶלְעָזָר וְחוּקָּה כְּתִיב בָּהּ! שָׁאנֵי פָּרָה, דְּקָדְשֵׁי בֶּדֶק הַבַּיִת הִיא.

The Gemara asks: **And** is slaughter really **not** considered a sacrificial rite? **But doesn't Rabbi Zeira say** that **Rav says: The slaughter of** a red **heifer by a non-priest**[H] is **not valid? And Rav said with regard to this** *halakha*: This is because both the term: **"Elazar** the priest" (Numbers 19:3), **and** the term: **"Statute"** (Numbers 19:2), **are written in** the Torah's description of the slaughter of the red heifer. The term "statute" indicates that if one deviates from any of the details of the service as delineated in the verses, the service is not valid. The Gemara answers: The *halakhot* of the red **heifer are different, as** the heifer **is** considered **sanctified for** the purpose of **Temple maintenance,**[HN] not for sacrifice upon the altar. Accordingly, one cannot derive from the case of the red heifer that the slaughter of an offering is considered a sacrificial rite.

וְלָאו כׇּל דְּכֵן הוּא? קׇדְשֵׁי בֶּדֶק הַבַּיִת בָּעוּ כְּהוּנָּה, קׇדְשֵׁי מִזְבֵּחַ לָא בָּעוּ כְּהוּנָּה? אֲמַר רַב שֵׁישָׁא בְּרֵיהּ דְּרַב אִידִי: מִידֵּי דַּהֲוָה אַמַּרְאוֹת נְגָעִים, דְּלָאו עֲבוֹדָה נִינְהוּ וּבָעֵי כְּהוּנָּה.

The Gemara asks: **But is it not all the more so?** If items **sanctified for** the purpose of **Temple maintenance require** that the performance of rites relevant to them be performed by a member of the **priesthood,** then with regard to items **sanctified for** sacrifice upon the **altar, shouldn't they** certainly **require** that their rites be performed by a member of the **priesthood? Rav Sheisha, son of Rav Idi, said** in response: The requirement that the red heifer be slaughtered by a priest is not proof that its slaughter is a sacrificial rite. Rather, that requirement is **just as it is in** the case of examination of the **shades of** leprous **marks, which is** obviously **not** considered a sacrificial **rite, and** yet the Torah **requires** that these marks be examined by a member of the **priesthood.**

HALAKHA

The slaughter of a red heifer by a non-priest – **שְׁחִיטַת פָּרָה בְּזָר**: The red heifer may be slaughtered by a non-priest, as a non-priest is always fit to perform the rite of slaughter. This *halakha* is in accordance with the opinion of Rabbi Yoḥanan cited in *Yoma* 42a (Rambam *Sefer Avoda, Hilkhot Pesulei HaMukdashin* 1:2, and see *Sefer Tahara, Hilkhot Para Aduma* 4:3 and *Kesef Mishne* there).

As the heifer is considered sanctified for the purpose of Temple maintenance – **דְּקָדְשֵׁי בֶּדֶק הַבַּיִת הִיא**: The red heifer is considered sanctified for the purpose of Temple maintenance. Nevertheless, as it is called a sin offering by the Torah, those disqualifications that render an animal unfit for sacrifice upon the altar disqualify a red heifer as well. Similarly, one who benefits from the red heifer before it has been reduced to ashes is liable for misuse of consecrated property, as one is liable for misuse of a sin offering from the moment of its consecration (Rambam *Sefer Avoda, Hilkhot Me'ila* 2:5 and *Sefer Tahara, Hilkhot Para* 1:7 and Mahari Kurkus there).

NOTES

As the heifer is considered sanctified for the purpose of Temple maintenance – **דְּקָדְשֵׁי בֶּדֶק הַבַּיִת הִיא**: Although the red heifer is called a sin offering by the Torah (see Numbers, chapter 19), and in many ways it resembles items sanctified for the altar (see *Avoda Zara* 23b), its preparation is nevertheless not considered like the sacrificial rites of an offering, because it is prepared outside the Temple and its purpose is to purify rather than to appease. Additionally, it is not sanctified as an item intended for the altar, concerning which the sanctity inheres in the item itself, but like an item intended for Temple maintenance.

וְנֵילַף מִבָּמָה!

The Gemara asks: Nevertheless, why was it necessary for Rav to teach that the removal of a handful by a non-priest does not disqualify the meal offering according to ben Beteira? **Let us derive** it **from** the fact that there was a period of fitness for rites performed by a non-priest, as before the construction of the Temple it was permitted for non-priests to sacrifice offerings upon a private **altar.**[N]

וְכִי תֵּימָא, מִבָּמָה לָא יָלְפִינַן, וְהָתַנְיָא: מִנַּיִן לַיּוֹצֵא שֶׁאִם עָלָה לֹא יֵרֵד – שֶׁהֲרֵי יוֹצֵא כָּשֵׁר בְּבָמָה!

And if you would say that **we do not derive** *halakhot* of the rites performed in the Temple **from** those performed on a private **altar,** one can respond: **But isn't it taught** in a *baraita*: **From where** is it derived with regard to an item, e.g., the limbs of an offering, **that emerged** from the Temple courtyard and was thereby rendered unfit for sacrifice upon the altar, **that if** it nevertheless **ascended** upon the altar **it shall not descend?**[H] It is derived from the fact **that** an item that **emerged is valid** for sacrifice **on** a private **altar.** This indicates that one can learn the *halakhot* of offerings in the Temple from the *halakhot* of a private altar.

תַּנָּא אַ״זֹאת תּוֹרַת הָעֹלָה״ סָמֵיךְ לֵיהּ.

The Gemara rejects this: The *tanna* of that *baraita* **relies on** the verse: **"This is the law of the burnt offering"** (Leviticus 6:2), from which it is derived that any item that ascends upon the altar shall not descend from it, even if it was disqualified. In other words, the verse is the source for the *halakha* of the *baraita*, whereas the case of a private altar is cited merely as a support for this ruling.

אֶלָּא טַעְמָא דְּאַשְׁמְעִינַן רַב, הָא לָאו הָכִי, הֲוָה אָמֵינָא: בִּשְׁאָר פְּסוּלִין פָּסַל בֶּן בְּתֵירָא? וְהָתַנְיָא, רַבִּי יוֹסֵי בְּרַבִּי יְהוּדָה וְרַבִּי אֶלְעָזָר בְּרַבִּי שִׁמְעוֹן אוֹמְרִים: מַכְשִׁיר הָיָה בֶּן בְּתֵירָא בְּכָל הַפְּסוּלִין כּוּלָּן.

The Gemara asks: **Rather, the reason** it is known that ben Beteira permits the return to the meal offering of a handful removed by a non-priest is **that Rav taught us** so. Were it **not** for **this, I would say** that **with regard to other disqualifications,** i.e., other than a handful removed with the left hand, **ben Beteira invalidates** the meal offering. **But isn't it taught** in a *baraita* that **Rabbi Yosei, son of Rabbi Yehuda, and Rabbi Elazar, son of Rabbi Shimon,** both **say: Ben Beteira would deem fit in** the case of **all the** other **disqualifications** listed in the mishna?

וְתַנְיָא: ״וְקָמַץ מִשָּׁם״ – מִמָּקוֹם שֶׁרַגְלֵי הַזָּר עוֹמְדוֹת;

The Gemara continues: **And it is taught** in a *baraita* with regard to the verse: "And he shall bring it to Aaron's sons the priests; **and he shall remove from there** his handful" (Leviticus 2:2), that this verse indicates that the removal of a handful from a meal offering may be performed **from the place where the feet of the non-priest stand,** i.e., anywhere within the Temple courtyard.

בֶּן בְּתֵירָא אוֹמֵר: מִנַּיִן שֶׁאִם קָמַץ בִּשְׂמֹאל שֶׁיַּחֲזִיר וְיַחֲזוֹר וְיִקְמוֹץ בְּיָמִין? תַּלְמוּד לוֹמַר: ״וְקָמַץ מִשָּׁם״ – מִמָּקוֹם שֶׁקָּמַץ כְּבָר;

The *baraita* continues: **Ben Beteira says** that the verse should be interpreted as follows: **From where** is it derived **that if** one **removed a handful with** his **left** hand, **that he must return** the handful to the vessel with the meal offering **and again remove the handful with** his **right** hand? It is derived from that which **the verse states: "And he shall remove from there,"** indicating that the handful is removed **from the place where he already removed** it, i.e., the handful is returned to the meal offering and thereupon removed from the same meal offering with the right hand. This concludes the *baraita*.

וְכֵיוָן דִּקְרָא סְתָמָא כְּתִיב בָּהּ, מַה לִּי שְׂמֹאל וּמַה לִּי שְׁאָר הַפְּסוּלִין?

The Gemara explains the difficulty from the *baraita*: **And since the verse is written** in an **unspecified** manner, i.e., it does not mention which handfuls are returned, **what** difference is it **to me** if the handful was removed with the **left** hand, **and what** difference is it **to me** if it was removed by means of one of **the other disqualifications?**

אֶלָּא הָא קָמַשְׁמַע לָן רַב: קָמַץ – וַאֲפִילּוּ קִידֵּשׁ; וּלְאַפּוּקֵי מֵהָנֵי תַּנָּאֵי, דְּתַנְיָא, רַבִּי יוֹסֵי בֶּן יוֹסֵי בֶּן יַאסִיַּין וְרַבִּי יְהוּדָה הַנַּחְתּוֹם אָמְרוּ: בַּמֶּה דְּבָרִים אֲמוּרִים – שֶׁקָּמַץ וְלֹא קִידֵּשׁ, אֲבָל קִידֵּשׁ – פָּסַל.

The Gemara therefore suggests an alternative explanation: **Rather, this** is what **Rav teaches us:** Ben Beteira holds that if one unfit for Temple service **removed a handful** it may be returned to the meal offering **even** if **he sanctified**[N] the handful by placing it in a service vessel. **And** the statement of Rav serves **to exclude** the opinion **of these *tanna'im*: As it is taught** in a *baraita*: **Rabbi Yosei ben Yosei ben Yasiyyan and Rabbi Yehuda the baker said: In what** case **is this statement** of ben Beteira **said,** i.e., in which case does he rule that the handful may be returned to the meal offering? It is in a case **where** the unfit individual **removed a handful and did not sanctify** it by placing it inside a service vessel. **But if he sanctified** it then **he** has **disqualified** it, even according to ben Beteira, and it may not be returned to the meal offering.

NOTES

Private altar – בָּמָה: A private altar is any altar that is not in the Tabernacle or Temple. Although it is generally prohibited to sacrifice an offering outside the Temple, there were periods when this practice was permitted, namely, before the Tabernacle was erected in the wilderness, from the time of the entrance of the Jews into Eretz Yisrael until the erection of the Tabernacle in Shiloh, and from the time of the destruction of the Tabernacle in Shiloh until the completion of the Temple in Jerusalem.

If one unfit for Temple service removed a handful it may be returned even if he sanctified – קָמַץ וַאֲפִילּוּ קִידֵּשׁ: According to Rabbi Yehuda HaNasi (*Tosefta* 1:9), the reason for this is that a service vessel does not sanctify a handful that was not removed in its proper fashion (see *Ḥasdei David*). Alternatively, it does not sanctify a handful that was never actually removed, i.e., the removal of a handful in this manner is considered an insignificant act (*Ḥazon Yeḥezkel*).

HALAKHA

An item that emerged from the Temple courtyard, that if it nevertheless ascended upon the altar it shall not descend – לַיּוֹצֵא שֶׁאִם עָלָה לֹא יֵרֵד: With regard to an offering that emerged from the Temple courtyard, if a portion of it that is otherwise fit for the altar ascended upon the altar, it shall not descend (Rambam *Sefer Avoda*, *Hilkhot Pesulei HaMukdashin* 3:7).

NOTES

Until he performs the stage of its placement in a vessel – עַד דְּעָבֵיד לָהּ מַתַּן כְּלִי: As long as the handful has not been placed in the service vessel, it has not been designated as the portion belonging to the Most High (Rashi on *Zevaḥim* 83a). Accordingly, if the priest has not yet placed it inside a service vessel it may be returned to the meal offering.

HALAKHA

Until he performs the stage of its placement in a vessel – עַד דְּעָבֵיד לָהּ מַתַּן כְּלִי: A handful of a meal offering that was sacrificed without having been placed inside a service vessel is disqualified. This *halakha* is in accordance with the mishna on 26a (Rambam *Sefer Avoda, Hilkhot Pesulei HaMukdashin* 11:6).

וְאִיכָּא דְּאָמְרִי: קָמַץ – אִין, קִידֵּשׁ – לָא; כְּמַאן? כְּהָנֵי תַּנָּאֵי, וּלְאַפּוֹקֵי מִתַּנָּא קַמָּא.

And there are those **who say** that Rav teaches the opposite, that if an unfit person merely **removed a handful, yes,** ben Beteira permits such a handful to be returned to the meal offering from which it was removed, but if he already **sanctified** the handful by placing it inside a service vessel, it may **not** be returned. **In accordance with whose** opinion is this explanation? It is **in accordance with** the opinion of **these *tanna'im*,** i.e., Rabbi Yosei ben Yosei ben Yasiyyan and Rabbi Yehuda the baker, **and** it is **to exclude** the opinion **of the first *tanna*** in that *baraita*, who disagrees with the ruling of Rabbi Yosei ben Yosei ben Yasiyyan and Rabbi Yehuda the baker and maintains that a handful may be returned even after it was sanctified by a service vessel.

מַתְקִיף לָהּ רַב נַחְמָן: מַאי קָא סָבְרִי הָנֵי תַּנָּאֵי? אִי קְמִיצַת פְּסוּלִין עֲבוֹדָה הִיא – אַף עַל גַּב דְּלָא עָבֵיד לֵיהּ מַתַּן כְּלִי! אִי קְמִיצַת פְּסוּלִין לָאו עֲבוֹדָה הִיא, כִּי עָבַד לָהּ מַתַּן כְּלִי מַאי הָוֵה?

Rav Naḥman objects to this: What do these *tanna'im* of the *baraita* **hold? If** they hold that **the removal of a handful by** one **unfit** for Temple service **is** considered the performance of a sacrificial **rite** to the extent that it disqualifies the offering, then the meal offering should be disqualified **even though he did not perform** the stage of the **placement** of the handful **in a vessel.** And **if** they hold that **the removal of a handful by an unfit** individual **is not** considered the performance of a **rite,** then **when he performed** the stage of **its placement in a vessel, what** significance **was** there to this action? He can still return the handful to the meal offering.

הֲדַר אָמַר רַב נַחְמָן: לְעוֹלָם עֲבוֹדָה הִיא, וְלָא גָּמְרָה עֲבוֹדָתָהּ עַד דְּעָבֵיד לָהּ מַתַּן כְּלִי.

Rav Naḥman reconsidered and **then said: Actually,** those *tanna'im* hold that the removal of a handful by one unfit for Temple service **is** considered the performance of a sacrificial **rite, but the rite of** the handful **is not complete until he performs** the stage of **its placement in a vessel.**[NH] Consequently, the meal offering is disqualified only after a person unfit for Temple service places the handful inside a service vessel.

אִי הָכִי, אֲפִילּוּ לֹא קִידֵּשׁ,

The Gemara challenges: **If so,** i.e., if the placement of the handful inside a service vessel completes the rite that begins with the handful's removal, then **even** if the handful was removed by an unfit individual who has **not** yet **sanctified** it in the service vessel designated for the handful,

Perek **I**
Daf **7** Amud **a**

וְכִי מַהֲדַר לֵיהּ לְקוֹמֶץ לְדוּכְתֵּיהּ תִּקְדּוֹשׁ וְלִפְסוֹל!

when he returns the handful to its former **place** in the service vessel that contains the meal offering **it should become sanctified,** as it is now placed inside a service vessel, **and it should** therefore **become disqualified.** It should not matter whether the handful was placed in the vessel designated for it, or back in the same vessel it was taken from.

אָמַר רַבִּי יוֹחָנָן, זֹאת אוֹמֶרֶת: כְּלֵי שָׁרֵת אֵין מְקַדְּשִׁין אֶלָּא מִדַּעַת.

Concerning this challenge, **Rabbi Yoḥanan said: That is to say** that **service vessels sanctify** items placed in them **only** when they are placed there **with** specific **intent**[H] that they be sanctified by that vessel. Since the priest does not return the handful to the vessel containing the meal offering with such intent, the handful is not disqualified, because the rite was not completed.

HALAKHA

Service vessels sanctify only with specific intent – כְּלֵי שָׁרֵת אֵין מְקַדְּשִׁין אֶלָּא מִדַּעַת: Service vessels sanctify items placed inside them only when they were placed there with the intent to sanctify them, in accordance with the opinion of Rabbi Yoḥanan (Rambam *Sefer Avoda, Hilkhot Pesulei HaMukdashin* 3:20).

הָא מִדַּעַת מְקַדְּשִׁין? וְהָא בְּעָא מִינֵּיהּ רֵישׁ לָקִישׁ מֵרַבִּי יוֹחָנָן: כְּלֵי שָׁרֵת מַהוּ שֶׁיְּקַדְּשׁוּ פְּסוּלִין לְכַתְּחִילָּה לִיקָּרֵב? וַאֲמַר לֵיהּ: אֵין מְקַדְּשִׁין! אֲמַר לֵיהּ: אֵין מְקַדְּשִׁין לִיקָּרֵב, אֲבָל מְקַדְּשִׁין לִיפָּסֵל.

The Gemara asks: It may be inferred from this statement that if items are placed into service vessels **with intent,** the service vessels **sanctify**[N] them. **But didn't Reish Lakish raise a dilemma before Rabbi Yoḥanan: What is** the *halakha* with regard to **service vessels,** i.e., do they **sanctify disqualified** items to the extent that they may be **sacrificed** upon the altar ***ab initio*? And** Rabbi Yoḥanan **said to him** that **they do not sanctify** the items. The Gemara responds: This is what Rabbi Yoḥanan **said to him: They do not sanctify** the disqualified items that are placed inside them **to** the extent that they may be **sacrificed, but they** do **sanctify** them **to** the extent **that** they **are disqualified.**[H]

רַב עַמְרָם אָמַר: כְּגוֹן שֶׁהֶחֱזִירוֹ לְבִיסָא גְּדוּשָׁה.

Rav Amram says: Even if service vessels sanctify items without specific intent, it is possible to return the handful to the meal offering without the vessel sanctifying the handful, **such as** in a case **where he returned it to a heaped bowl** [*levisa*],[L] i.e., he placed the handful upon the heap of flour in such a manner that the handful did not enter the airspace of the vessel containing the meal offering. Consequently, the handful is not sanctified by the vessel.

וּמִקְמָץ הֵיכִי קָמַץ? אֶלָּא, כְּגוֹן שֶׁהֶחֱזִירוֹ לְבִיסָא טְפוּפָה.

The Gemara asks: **But** if the meal offering was heaped, **how** was he initially able to **remove a handful** from it? The handful must initially be removed from within a vessel. **Rather,** it is possible to return the handful without sanctifying it in a case **where he returned it to a full** [*tefufa*] **bowl,** i.e., it was full to the brim but not heaped. When the priest initially removes a handful from such a vessel, he removes it from inside the vessel, but when it is returned, it does not enter the airspace of the vessel.

וְכֵיוָן דִּקְמַץ לֵיהּ עֲבַד לֵיהּ גּוּמָא, כִּי מַהֲדַר – לְגַוֵּיהּ דְּמָנָא קָא מַהֲדַר לֵיהּ! מִכִּי מַהֲדַר לֵיהּ מַנַּח לֵיהּ אַדִּפְנָא דְּמָנָא, וּמְנִיד לֵיהּ וְנָפַל מִמֵּילָא, דְּנַעֲשָׂה כְּמִי שֶׁהֶחֱזִירוֹ הַקּוֹף.

The Gemara asks: **But once he removed a handful, he formed a furrow** in the surface of the meal offering, and therefore **when he returns** the handful to its previous place inside the vessel, **he is** in fact **returning it to** a spot **within the vessel,** i.e., the furrow. If so, the handful should be sanctified to the extent that the vessel disqualifies it. The Gemara responds: **When he returns it** to the vessel containing the meal offering, he does not place it directly in the furrow. Rather, he **lays it on the wall of the vessel and moves** the vessel, **and** the handful **falls by itself** into the furrow. In this manner, **it is as though a monkey** rather than a person **returned** the handful to the furrow, and the handful is therefore not sanctified.

אֲמַר לֵיהּ רַבִּי יִרְמְיָה לְרַבִּי זֵירָא: וְלוֹקְמָהּ כְּגוֹן שֶׁהֶחֱזִירוֹ לִכְלִי הַמּוּנָּח עַל גַּבֵּי קַרְקַע! אֶלָּא שְׁמַע מִינָּהּ: קוֹמְצִין מִכְּלִי שֶׁעַל גַּבֵּי קַרְקַע? אֲמַר לֵיהּ: קָא נָגְעַתְּ בִּבְעָיָא דְּאִיבַּעְיָא לָן, דְּרַבִּי אֲבִימִי תָּנֵי מְנָחוֹת בֵּי רַב חִסְדָּא.

§ The Gemara returns to its discussion of the opinion of ben Beteira. **Rabbi Yirmeya said to Rabbi Zeira: And let** one **interpret** ben Beteira's ruling as speaking of a case in which the handful is not sanctified by the vessel containing the meal offering, **such as where he returned it to a vessel that is resting upon** the **ground. Rather,** the fact that this was not suggested indicates that service vessels sanctify items placed inside them even while resting on the ground. Is it correct to **conclude from** here that **one may remove a handful** of a meal offering **from** a service **vessel that** is resting **upon** the **ground?** Rabbi Zeira **said to him: You have touched upon a dilemma that was** already **raised before us, when Rabbi Avimi**[P] was **learning** tractate ***Menaḥot*** in the **study hall of Rav Ḥisda.**

וַאֲבִימִי בֵּי רַב חִסְדָּא תָּנֵי? וְהָאֲמַר רַב חִסְדָּא, קוּלְפֵי טָאבִי בָּלְעִי מֵאֲבִימִי עֲלָהּ דְּהָא שְׁמַעְתָּא: בָּא לְהַכְרִיז רְצוּפִין – שְׁלֹשִׁים יוֹם, שֵׁנִי וַחֲמִישִׁי וְשֵׁנִי – שִׁשִּׁים יוֹמֵי!

The Gemara interrupts this statement with a question: **And** did Rabbi **Avimi** really **learn** in the **study hall of Rav Ḥisda? But didn't Rav Ḥisda say: I absorbed many blows** [*kulfei*][L] **from Avimi** as a result **of that** ***halakha***, i.e., Avimi would mock me when I questioned his statements with regard to the sale of orphans' property by the courts, which were contradictory to the ruling of a particular *baraita*. Avimi explained to me that if the court **comes to announce** such a sale on **consecutive** days, then it is announced for **thirty days,** in accordance with that *baraita*. But if it will be announced only on **Monday, Thursday, and Monday,** then it is announced over the course of **sixty days.** If so, Rav Ḥisda was in fact the pupil while Rabbi Avimi was his teacher.

NOTES

Items are placed into service vessels with intent they sanctify, etc. – **הָא מִדַּעַת מְקַדְּשִׁין וכו׳**: This is not an incidental discussion, but relates to the main issue at hand. If, as Rabbi Yoḥanan apparently proceeds to claim, service vessels do not sanctify disqualified items at all, then this handful removed by a non-priest should likewise not be sanctified and he should be able to return the handful to the original vessel and the meal offering should not be disqualified (*Shita Mekubbetzet*).

HALAKHA

They sanctify to the extent that they are disqualified – **מְקַדְּשִׁין לִיפָּסֵל**: If an item that is fit to be placed inside a service vessel was placed inside one, even if the item was disqualified, it is sanctified to the extent that it may not be redeemed. But with regard to blood that was collected in a vessel, it is sanctified even to the extent that it may be sacrificed upon the altar (Rambam *Sefer Avoda, Hilkhot Pesulei HaMukdashin* 3:18, and see Mahari Kurkus, *Kesef Mishne*, and *Leḥem Mishne* there; see also 3:19–21).

LANGUAGE

Bowl [*bisa*] – **בִּיסָא**: From the Greek βῆσσα, *bēssa*, which refers to a large cup.

Blows [*kulfei*] – **קוּלְפֵי**: Apparently related to the Persian kūpāl, club. The *ge'onim* describe it as a stick, one side of which was thick, into which one could embed protruding nails or other sharp items.

PERSONALITIES

Rabbi Avimi – **רַבִּי אֲבִימִי**: Avimi was a Babylonian *amora* who lived during the time of the first and second generations of *amora'im*. He discussed *halakhot* with numerous other *amora'im*, and transmitted many of their opinions as well. As is evident here, Rav Ḥisda was a trusted student of his, and Avimi requested his help to recall the *halakhot* of this tractate.

אֲבִימִי מַסֶּכְתָּא אִיתְעַקְרָא אִיתְעֲקַר לֵיהּ, וַאֲתָא קַמֵּיהּ דְּרַב חִסְדָּא לְאַדְכּוּרֵי גְּמָרֵיהּ. וְלִישְׁלַח לֵיהּ וְלֵיתֵי לְגַבֵּיהּ! סָבַר: הָכִי מִסְתַּיְּיעָא מִילְּתָא טְפֵי.

The Gemara answers: **Avimi** was in fact the teacher, but **tractate** *Menaḥot* **was uprooted for him,** i.e., he forgot it, **and** Avimi **came before** his student **Rav Ḥisda to** help him **recall his learning.** The Gemara asks: If Rav Ḥisda was in fact Avimi's student, **let** Avimi **send for him and** Rav Ḥisda **come to** Avimi. The Gemara responds: Avimi **thought** that **this** would be **more helpful** in this **matter,**[N] i.e., that by exerting the effort to travel to his pupil in order to learn from him, he would better retain his studies.

פְּגַע בֵּיהּ רַב נַחְמָן, אֲמַר לֵיהּ: כֵּיצַד קוֹמְצִין? אֲמַר לֵיהּ: מִכְּלִי זֶה. אֲמַר לֵיהּ: וְכִי קוֹמְצִין מִכְּלִי שֶׁעַל גַּבֵּי קַרְקַע? אֲמַר לֵיהּ: דְּמַגְבַּהּ לֵיהּ כֹּהֵן.

The Gemara returns to the statement of Rabbi Zeira: **Rav Naḥman encountered** Avimi upon his return from the study hall of Rav Ḥisda. Rav Naḥman **said to him: How** does one properly **remove a handful** from a meal offering? Avimi pointed to a vessel that was resting on the ground and **said to him: From this vessel** one may properly remove a handful. Rav Naḥman **said to him: But may one remove a handful from a vessel that** is resting **upon** the **ground?** Avimi **said to him:** When I said that such a vessel may be used, I meant **that** one **priest** would first **raise it**[N] from the ground and then another priest would remove a handful from it.

כֵּיצַד מְקַדְּשִׁין אֶת הַמְּנָחוֹת? אֲמַר לֵיהּ: נוֹתְנָהּ לִכְלִי זֶה. וְכִי מְקַדְּשִׁין בִּכְלִי שֶׁעַל גַּבֵּי קַרְקַע? אֲמַר לֵיהּ: דְּמַגְבַּהּ לֵיהּ כֹּהֵן.

Rav Naḥman proceeded to ask Avimi another question: **How** does one properly **sanctify the meal offerings?** Avimi pointed to a vessel that was resting on the ground and **said to him:** The priest **places it into this vessel.** Rav Naḥman again said to him: **But can one sanctify** a meal offering **in a vessel that** is resting **upon** the **ground?** Avimi **said to him:** When I said that such a vessel may be used, I meant **that** another **priest** would initially **raise it** from the ground, and only then would the meal offering be placed inside it.

אֲמַר לֵיהּ: אִם כֵּן, הוּצְרַכְתָּה שְׁלֹשָׁה כֹּהֲנִים! אֲמַר לֵיהּ: וּתְהֵא צְרִיכָה שְׁלֹשָׁה עָשָׂר, כְּתָמִיד.

Rav Naḥman **said to** Avimi: **If so,** then **you require** the involvement of **three**[N] **priests,** i.e., one to raise the vessel, one to sanctify the meal offering, and one to remove the handful from the meal offering. Avimi **said to him: And let it require** even **thirteen** priests, **just as** the service of the **daily** burnt **offering** required the involvement of thirteen priests. The need for several priests presents no difficulty.

אֵיתִיבֵיהּ, זֶה הַכְּלָל: כָּל הַקּוֹמֵץ וְנוֹתֵן בִּכְלִי, הַמּוֹלִיךְ וְהַמַּקְטִיר לֶאֱכוֹל דָּבָר שֶׁדַּרְכּוֹ לֶאֱכוֹל וכו׳,

Rav Naḥman **raised** another **objection** to the statement of Avimi from a mishna (12a) that discusses the *halakha* that improper intentions during the service of a meal offering disqualify it. **This is the principle:** In the case of **anyone who removes the handful, or places** the handful **in the vessel,** or **who conveys** the vessel with the handful to the altar, **or who burns** the handful on the altar, with the intent **to partake of an item whose** typical **manner** is such that one **partakes** of it, or to burn an item whose typical manner is such that one burns it on the altar, e.g., the handful or the frankincense, outside its designated area, the meal offering is unfit but there is no liability for excision from the World-to-Come [*karet*].

וְאִילּוּ מַגְבִּיהַּ לָא קָתָנֵי! תַּנָּא סֵדֶר עֲבוֹדוֹת נָקֵיט, וְלָא סֵדֶר כֹּהֲנִים.

Rav Naḥman explained his objection: All the rites of a meal offering are taught in the mishna, **and yet raising** the vessel from the ground **is not taught.** This indicates that there is no requirement to raise a vessel from the ground in order to use it for the service of a meal offering. Avimi responded: The ***tanna*** **cited the order of** sacrificial **rites,** i.e., those rites concerning which improper intentions disqualify a meal offering, **but** he did **not** cite **the order of the priests,** i.e., he did not cite the total number of priests involved in the service.

NOTES

This would be more helpful in this matter – הָכִי מִסְתַּיְּיעָא מִילְּתָא טְפֵי: According to Rashi, Avimi was employing the principle of: I have labored and I have found (*Megilla* 6b), i.e., when one exiles himself from his dwelling and undertakes hardships to seek out the Torah, that effort itself aids him in his Torah study (*Or Zarua*). Others explain that he hoped the self-degradation of traveling to his pupil to learn from him would serve as a catalyst for recalling his learning (*Einei Shmuel*).

That one priest would first raise it – דְּמַגְבַּהּ לֵיהּ כֹּהֵן: The priest removing the handful from the vessel cannot be the one who raises the vessel from the ground, as the removal of the handful must be performed with the priest's right hand, and the vessel must also be raised with the right hand, as this is a requirement with regard to the Temple service in general. Therefore, an additional priest was required (*Tosafot Ḥitzoniyyot*).

You require the involvement of three – הוּצְרַכְתָּה שְׁלֹשָׁה: The commentary to the Gemara follows the opinion of Rabbeinu Gershom Meor HaGola, that Rav Naḥman is referring to the sanctification of the meal offering and the subsequent removal of a handful from that meal offering. According to the version of the Gemara that Rashi had, the Gemara is discussing a case where two priests are required to hold two service vessels while one priest performs both the removal of the handful from the vessel containing the meal offering as well as the sanctification of the handful by placing it into the second vessel. Some commentaries note a difficulty with regard to Rashi's explanation: It is not essential for two priests to raise the two service vessels, as it would suffice for one priest to lift up the first vessel containing the meal offering, at which point a second priest would remove a handful from it, after which the first priest would set down the first vessel and raise a second vessel into which the second priest could place the handful and sanctify it (*Tosafot Ḥitzoniyyot*).

בָּעוּ מִינֵּיהּ מִדְּרַב שֵׁשֶׁת: מַהוּ לִקְמוֹץ מִכְּלִי שֶׁעַל גַּבֵּי קַרְקַע? אֲמַר לֵיהּ, פּוּק חֲזֵי מָה עָבְדִין לְגָאו: אַרְבָּעָה כֹּהֲנִים נִכְנָסִין, שְׁנַיִם בְּיָדָם שְׁנֵי סְדָרִים וּשְׁנַיִם בְּיָדָם שְׁנֵי בָזִיכִין, וְאַרְבָּעָה מְקַדְּמִין לִפְנֵיהֶם, שְׁנַיִם לִיטּוֹל שְׁנֵי סְדָרִים וּשְׁנַיִם לִיטּוֹל שְׁנֵי בָזִיכִין;

On the same topic, the Sages **raised a dilemma before Rav Sheshet: What is** the *halakha* with regard to the permissibility of **removing a handful from a vessel that** is resting **upon the ground?** Is this removal valid? Rav Sheshet **said to** one of the Sages who raised the dilemma: **Go out** and **see what they do within** the Sanctuary when they remove the bowls containing the frankincense that were placed upon the Table of the shewbread[B] in order to burn the frankincense upon the altar. The mishna (99b) states: When the priests would replace the shewbread every Shabbat, **four priests** would **enter** the Sanctuary, **two** with the **two arrangements** of the new shewbread **in their hands and two** with the **two bowls**[B] of frankincense **in their hands. And four** priests would **precede** them and enter the Sanctuary **before them, two to remove** the **two arrangements** of the old shewbread **and two to remove** the **two bowls** of frankincense.[H]

BACKGROUND

Table of the shewbread – שׁוּלְחָן: The image shows the priests replacing the old arrangements of the shewbread with two new arrangements. Two bowls of frankincense were placed on the Table alongside the two arrangements.

Priests placing shewbread on the Table

Bowls [*bazikhin*] – בָּזִיכִין: Several commentaries explain that these were actually large spoons, i.e., bowls with handles. The basis for this interpretation is the Aramaic translation of the phrase: "One spoon" (Numbers 7:20), as: One *bazikh* (Rabbi Ovadya Bartenura; *Tosefot Yom Tov*).

HALAKHA

The arrangement of the shewbread – סִידּוּר לֶחֶם הַפָּנִים: How was the shewbread arranged upon the Table? Four priests would enter the Sanctuary, two with the two arrangements of the new shewbread in their hands and two with the two bowls of frankincense. Four other priests would enter the Sanctuary before them, two to remove the two arrangements of the old shewbread and two to remove the two old bowls of frankincense. The priests who were placing the new bread and bowls stood to the north, facing the south, while those who were removing the old stood to the south and faced north. The priests standing to the south would pull the shewbread toward them, while those standing to the north would simultaneously push the new shewbread into its position, so that it would immediately replace the old shewbread, in order that the Table would never be without shewbread (Rambam *Sefer Avoda*, *Hilkhot Temidin UMusafin* 5:4).

Perek **I**
Daf **7** Amud **b**

וְאִילּוּ מַגְבִּיהַּ אֶת הַשּׁוּלְחָן לָא קָתָנֵי!

Rav Sheshet notes: The entire process of the replacement of the shewbread is taught in the mishna, **and yet** the statement: A priest **raises the Table** above the ground so that the bowls of frankincense can be properly removed from them, **is not taught.** One can therefore conclude from the mishna that just as the bowls of frankincense are removed from a vessel that is resting upon the ground, i.e., the Table, so too, one may remove a handful of a meal offering from a vessel that is resting upon the ground.

לָאו אָמְרַתְּ הָתָם: סֵדֶר עֲבוֹדוֹת נָקַט? הָכָא נַמִּי סֵדֶר עֲבוֹדוֹת נָקַט.

The Gemara rejects this proof: **Didn't you** already **say there,** with regard to the mishna that discusses improper intentions expressed during the service of a meal offering (12a), that the *tanna* **cited** only **the order of** sacrificial **rites? Here too,** the *tanna* **cited** only **the order of** sacrificial **rites.** Therefore, one cannot prove from here that there is no requirement to raise the Table.

מִי דָּמֵי? הָתָם לָא נָחֵית לְמִנְיָינָא דְּכֹהֲנִים, הָכָא נָחֵית לְמִנְיָינָא דְּכֹהֲנִים, אִם אִיתָא – לִיתְנֵי מַגְבִּיהַּ! אֶלָּא שְׁמַע מִינָּהּ: קוֹמְצִין מִכְּלִי שֶׁעַל גַּבֵּי קַרְקַע, שְׁמַע מִינָּהּ.

The Gemara asks: **Are** these *mishnayot* **comparable? There,** on 12a, the *tanna* **did not delve into the number of priests** involved in the service of a meal offering. **Here,** on 99b, the *tanna* **does** in fact **delve into the number of priests** involved in the service of the shewbread. Therefore, **if it is so,** i.e., if the Table must be raised before the bowls of frankincense are removed, **let** the *tanna* **teach** that another priest **raises** the Table. **Rather, conclude from** the mishna that **one may remove a handful** of a meal offering **from a vessel that** is resting **upon** the **ground.** The Gemara affirms: **Conclude from** here that this is so.

אֲמַר רָבָא: פְּשִׁיטָא לִי, קוֹמֵץ מִכְּלִי שֶׁעַל גַּבֵּי קַרְקַע – שֶׁכֵּן מָצִינוּ בְּסִילּוּק בָּזִיכִין, מְקַדְּשִׁין מִנְחָה בִּכְלִי שֶׁעַל גַּבֵּי קַרְקַע – שֶׁכֵּן מָצִינוּ בְּסִידּוּר בָּזִיכִין.

§ **Rava said:** It is **obvious to me** that a priest may **remove a handful from a vessel that** is resting **upon** the **ground,**[H] **as we find** such an instance **in** the case of **the removal of** the **bowls** of frankincense from the Table of the shewbread, since the Table is resting upon the ground of the Sanctuary when they are removed. Similarly, **one can sanctify a meal offering in a vessel that** is resting **upon** the **ground, as we find** such an instance **in** the case of **the arrangement of** the **bowls** of frankincense upon the Table of the shewbread.

HALAKHA

Remove a handful from a vessel that is resting upon the ground, etc. – קוֹמֵץ מִכְּלִי שֶׁעַל גַּבֵּי קַרְקַע וכו׳: One may remove a handful from a service vessel that is resting upon the ground, and one may likewise sanctify a handful in such a vessel. The *halakha* is in accordance with the opinion of Rava, as he is a later *amora* (Rambam *Sefer Avoda*, *Hilkhot Ma'aseh HaKorbanot* 12:13).

בָּעֵי רָבָא: קִידּוּשׁ קוֹמֶץ מַאי? מִמִּנְחָה יָלְפִינַן לַהּ, אוֹ מִדָּם יָלְפִינַן לַהּ? הֲדַר פַּשְׁטַהּ: מִדָּם יָלְפִינַן לַהּ.

Rava raises a dilemma: With regard to the **sanctification of a handful** by placing it in a vessel that is resting upon the ground, **what** is the *halakha*? Do **we derive** this *halakha* **from** the sanctification of **a meal offering,** in which case one can sanctify a handful in this manner, just as he can do so with a meal offering? **Or** do **we derive it from** the collection of the **blood**[N] of an offering, in which case one cannot do so, just as the blood of an offering may not be collected in a vessel that is resting upon the ground? Rava **then resolves** the dilemma: **We derive it from** the collection of the **blood.**

וּמִי אָמַר רָבָא הָכִי? וְהָא אִתְּמַר: קוֹמֶץ שֶׁחִלְּקוֹ בִּשְׁנֵי כֵלִים – רַב נַחְמָן אָמַר: אֵינוֹ קָדוֹשׁ, וְרָבָא אָמַר: קָדוֹשׁ; וְאִם אִיתָא, לֵילַף מִדָּם! הֲדַר בֵּיהּ רָבָא מֵהַהִיא.

The Gemara asks: **And did Rava** really **say this,** that the *halakha* with regard to the sanctification of a handful is derived from the collection of the blood? **But it was stated:** With regard to a full measure of **a handful that** a priest **divided**[H] and placed **in two vessels, Rav Naḥman says** that **it is not sanctified, and Rava says** that it is **sanctified. And if it is so** that the *halakha* of the handful is derived from the collection of the blood, then **let** Rava **derive from blood** that the handful is not sanctified in this manner, just as the blood is not sanctified when divided into two. The Gemara responds: **Rava retracted that** statement and ruled that a handful is not sanctified when divided and placed into two vessels.

וְדָם מְנָלַן דְּלָא קָדוֹשׁ לַחֲצָאִין? דְּתָנֵי רַב תַּחְלִיפָא בֶּן שָׁאוּל: קִידֵּשׁ פָּחוֹת מִכְּדֵי הַזָּאָה בִּכְלִי זֶה, וּפָחוֹת מִכְּדֵי הַזָּאָה בִּכְלִי זֶה – לֹא קִידֵּשׁ.

The Gemara further discusses the *halakha* with regard to the collection of the blood. **And** with regard to **blood, from where do we** derive **that it is not sanctified in halves,** i.e., when collected in two vessels? It is derived from **that** which **Rav Taḥlifa ben Shaul teaches** with regard to the water of purification: If the priest **sanctified** the water in two vessels in such a manner that he sanctified **less than the amount of sprinkling**[H] **in this vessel,** i.e., there was not enough water into which he could dip a bundle of hyssop and sprinkle the water with it, **and** he sanctified **less than the amount of sprinkling in that vessel,** then **he has not sanctified** the water. Even if he subsequently combines the contents of both vessels into a single vessel, the water is not sanctified.

וְאִיבַּעְיָא לְהוּ: בְּדָם מַאי? הִלְכְתָא הִיא, וּמֵהִלְכְתָא לָא יָלְפִינַן;

The Gemara continues: **And a dilemma was raised before** the Sages: **With regard to** the collection of **blood** of a sin offering for the purpose of sprinkling it upon the altar, **what** is the *halakha*? **Is** the ruling with regard to the water of purification **a** ***halakha*** transmitted to Moses from Sinai, in which case the *halakha* with regard to blood may not be derived from it, as **we do not derive** other cases **from a** ***halakha*** transmitted to Moses from Sinai?

אוֹ דִּלְמָא הָתָם מַאי טַעְמָא – דִּכְתִיב: ״וְטָבַל בַּמַּיִם״, הָכָא נַמִי הָכְתִיב: ״וְטָבַל בַּדָּם״?

The Gemara explains the other side of the dilemma: **Or perhaps, there,** in the case of the water of purification, **what is the reason** that it is not sanctified? It is possible that the reason is **that it is written** in a verse that is referring to the water initially placed in the vessel: **"And dip it in the water"** (Numbers 19:18). If this verse is the source of the *halakha* that the hyssop may be dipped in the water of purification only when there was initially enough water in the vessel for sprinkling, then **here too,** in the case of the blood of a sin offering, **isn't it written: "And** the priest **shall dip** his finger **in the blood"** (Leviticus 4:6)?

וְאִיתְּמַר, אָמַר רַבִּי זְרִיקָא אָמַר רַבִּי אֶלְעָזָר: אַף בְּדָם לֹא קִידֵּשׁ. אָמַר רָבָא, תַּנְיָא נַמִי הָכִי בִּפְנֵי כֹּהֵן מַנִּיחַ: ״וְטָבַל״ – וְלֹא מְסַפֵּג,

The Gemara continues: **And it was stated** with regard to this dilemma: **Rabbi Zerika says** that **Rabbi Elazar says: Even in** the case of the **blood, one has not sanctified**[H] it if he collected less than a full measure of blood in a single vessel. **Rava said** that **this is also taught in** a *baraita* **with regard to** the bull of **the anointed priest.**[N] The verse states: "And the priest shall dip his finger in the blood, and sprinkle of the blood" (Leviticus 4:6). From the term **"And** the priest **shall dip"** it is derived that there must be enough blood inside the vessel in which to dip his finger, **and** there should **not** be so little blood that he must resort to **wiping** his finger along the walls of the vessel.

NOTES

We derive it from the collection of the blood – מִדָּם יָלְפִינַן לַהּ: The four sacrificial rites performed with a meal offering parallel the four rites performed with the blood of an animal offering, as the handful of a meal offering and the blood of an animal offering are both sacrificed upon the altar, and they both render permitted the remainder of their respective offerings for consumption. Accordingly, the removal of the handful corresponds to the slaughter of an offering, the sanctification of the handful by placing it into a service vessel parallels the collection of the blood, the conveying of the handful to the altar corresponds to the same act that is performed with the blood, and the burning of the handful upon the altar corresponds to the presentation of the blood upon the altar. Nevertheless, the commentaries note that the collection of the blood is not entirely analogous to the sanctification of the handful, as the vessel receives the flowing blood, whereas the handful is actively placed into its vessel.

With regard to the anointed priest [*kohen manniaḥ*] – בִּפְנֵי כֹּהֵן מַנִּיחַ: Although the standard version of the Gemara reads *kohen manniaḥ*, many commentaries note that this should read: *Kohen mashiaḥ*, literally, the anointed priest, which is a standard term for the High Priest. Other commentaries say that these words should be omitted entirely (see *Shita Mekubbetzet*).

HALAKHA

A handful that a priest divided – קוֹמֶץ שֶׁחִלְּקוֹ: A handful that was removed from a meal offering and divided between two service vessels is not sanctified. The *halakha* is in accordance with the statement of Rav Naḥman, as Rava agrees with his opinion (Rambam *Sefer Avoda*, *Hilkhot Ma'aseh HaKorbanot* 13:12).

Sanctified less than the amount of sprinkling – קִידֵּשׁ פָּחוֹת מִכְּדֵי הַזָּאָה: How was the water sanctified with the ashes of the red heifer? A priest would place the water in a vessel, after which he would place the ashes upon the water. If the priest sanctified, in one vessel, less than the amount of water required for sprinkling, and in a second vessel he also sanctified less than the amount of water required for sprinkling, none of the water is sanctified. The *halakha* is in accordance with the *baraita* cited by Rav Taḥlifa ben Shaul (Rambam *Sefer Tahara*, *Hilkhot Para Aduma* 9:1).

Even in the case of the blood one has not sanctified – אַף בְּדָם לֹא קִידֵּשׁ: If the blood of an offering was collected in a vessel but there was not enough blood with which to sprinkle, the blood has not been sanctified, in accordance with the opinion of Rabbi Elazar (Rambam *Sefer Avoda*, *Hilkhot Ma'aseh HaKorbanot* 4:8).

„בַּדָּם" – שֶׁיְּהֵא בַּדָּם שִׁיעוּר טְבִילָה מֵעִיקָּרוֹ, „מִן הַדָּם" – מִן הַדָּם שֶׁבָּעִנְיָן.

The *baraita* continues: Additionally, from the term **"in the blood"** it is derived **that there should initially be in** the vessel containing **the blood a measure** fit for **dipping** his finger. Furthermore, it is derived from the term **"of the blood"** that he must sprinkle **from the blood of the matter,** as will be explained.

וְאִיצְטְרִיךְ לְמִכְתַּב „וְטָבַל" וְאִיצְטְרִיךְ לְמִכְתַּב „בַּדָּם", דְּאִי כָּתַב רַחֲמָנָא „וְטָבַל", הֲוָה אָמִינָא אַף עַל גַּב דְּלָא קִיבֵּל שִׁיעוּר טְבִילוֹת, דְּהַיְינוּ הַזָּאָה שֶׁבַע פְּעָמִים, מֵעִיקָּרוֹ – כְּתַב רַחֲמָנָא „בַּדָּם";

And it was necessary for the Merciful One **to write: "And** the priest **shall dip," and it was necessary** for the Merciful One **to write: "In the blood,"** despite the fact that both terms are referring to the amount of blood that must be in the vessel. **Because if the Merciful One had written** only: "And the priest **shall dip," I would say** that it is enough if the vessel contains enough blood for even one sprinkling, **even though** the priest **did not initially collect a measure** fit for all of the **sprinklings, that is,** enough with which to **sprinkle seven times.** Therefore, **the Merciful One writes: "In the blood."**

וְאִי כָּתַב רַחֲמָנָא „בַּדָּם", הֲוָה אָמִינָא אֲפִילּוּ מְסַפֵּיג – כְּתַב רַחֲמָנָא „וְטָבַל".

And if the Merciful One had written only: **"In the blood," I would say** that if there was initially a full measure collected in the vessel then the sprinkling is valid **even** if now the priest must resort to **wiping** his finger. Therefore, **the Merciful One writes: "And** the priest **shall dip,"** indicating that the priest must be able to dip his finger into the blood and not have to wipe it on the walls of the vessel.

„מִן הַדָּם שֶׁבָּעִנְיָן" לְמַעוּטֵי מַאי? אֲמַר רָבָא: לְמַעוּטֵי שִׁירַיִם שֶׁבָּאֶצְבַּע. מְסַיַּיע לֵיהּ לְרַבִּי אֶלְעָזָר, דְּאָמַר: שִׁירַיִם שֶׁבָּאֶצְבַּע – פְּסוּלִין.

The Gemara returns to the last statement of the *baraita*, that the priest must sprinkle **from the blood of the matter.** This statement serves **to exclude what? Rava said:** It serves **to exclude** the **remainder** of blood **on** his **finger**[H] from the previous sprinkling, i.e., the priest must dip his finger into the blood before each sprinkling; he may not sprinkle with the blood that remains on his finger from the previous sprinkling. The Gemara notes: This **supports** the opinion **of Rabbi Elazar, who says** that the **remainder** of blood **that** remained **on** the priest's **finger is unfit** for sprinkling.

אֲמַר לֵיהּ רָבִין בַּר רַב אַדָּא לְרָבָא: אָמְרִי תַּלְמִידָךְ אָמַר רַב עַמְרָם, תַּנְיָא: הָיָה מַזֶּה וְנִתְּזָה הַזָּאָה מִיָּדוֹ, אִם עַד שֶׁלֹּא הִזָּה – טָעוּן כִּיבּוּס, מִשֶּׁהִזָּה – אֵין טָעוּן כִּיבּוּס;

Ravin bar Rav Adda said to Rava: Your students say that **Rav Amram**[P] **says** that **it is taught** in a *baraita*: In a case where a priest **was sprinkling** from the blood of a sin offering **and** the blood of the **sprinkling sprayed from his hand**[H] onto a garment, the *halakha* is as follows: **If** the blood sprayed onto the garment **before he sprinkled,** the garment **requires laundering,** as is the *halakha* when the blood of a sin offering that is fit for sprinkling fell on a garment. But if the blood sprayed onto the garment **after he** had already **sprinkled,** it **does not require laundering.**

מַאי לָאו עַד שֶׁלֹּא גָּמַר הַזָּאָתוֹ וּמִשֶּׁגָּמַר הַזָּאָתוֹ? שְׁמַע מִינָּהּ דְּשִׁירַיִם שֶׁבָּאֶצְבַּע – כְּשֵׁירִים!

Ravin bar Rav Adda asks: **What, is it not** correct to say that this means if the blood sprayed onto the garment **before he completed** all of **his sprinkling,** then the garment requires laundering, **and** if the blood sprayed onto the garment **after he completed his sprinkling,** then the garment does not require laundering? If so, one can **conclude from** the *baraita* **that** the **remainder** of blood **that** remained **on** his **finger** between each sprinkling is **fit** for sprinkling, as otherwise, it would not result in a requirement to launder a garment upon which it sprayed.

PERSONALITIES

Rav Amram – רַב עַמְרָם: There are two *amora'im* referred to in the Gemara as Rav Amram. The first, a second-generation *amora*, was a student of Rav. The second, the Rav Amram mentioned in the Gemara here, was a third- or fourth-generation Babylonian *amora*. He studied under Rav Sheshet and Rav Naḥman, and is mentioned in the Gemara as discussing *halakhot* with Abaye.

Out of respect for their teacher, Rava's pupils did not want to question his opinion from a statement that they heard from Rav Amram, who was a contemporary of Rava. Ravin bar Rav Adda therefore said that his own contemporaries, i.e., the students of Rava, heard that Rav Amram had said it.

HALAKHA

The remainder of blood on his finger – שִׁירַיִם שֶׁבָּאֶצְבַּע: When the priest sprinkles the blood of a sin offering, he must place blood on each corner of the altar. After placing the blood upon the first corner, he wipes his finger on the edge of the bowl containing the blood and then dips his finger again into the blood, as the blood that remains on his finger is unfit for sprinkling upon another corner (Rambam *Sefer Avoda, Hilkhot Ma'aseh HaKorbanot* 5:8).

A priest was sprinkling and the blood of the sprinkling sprayed from his hand – הָיָה מַזֶּה וְנִתְּזָה הַזָּאָה מִיָּדוֹ: With regard to the blood of a sin offering, only that which is fit for sprinkling causes garments to require laundering. Therefore, in a case where the blood of a sin offering sprayed from one's finger onto a garment, if this occurred after the blood of the sprinkling left his hand, the garment does not require laundering, as the remainder of blood on his finger is unfit for sprinkling (Rambam *Sefer Avoda, Hilkhot Ma'aseh HaKorbanot* 8:6, 8).

HALAKHA

When he completed all the sprinklings he wipes his hand, if he has not completed all of them he must wipe his finger – גָּמַר מְקַנֵּחַ יָדוֹ לֹא גָּמַר מְקַנֵּחַ אֶצְבָּעוֹ: The remainder of blood on the finger of the priest who performed the service of the red heifer is unfit for sprinkling. Therefore, between each sprinkling the priest wipes his finger on the body of the red heifer. Similarly, upon completion of the sprinklings, he wipes his hand on the body of the heifer. This ruling of the Rambam is apparently in direct contradiction to the conclusion of the Gemara here. Some maintain that the Rambam had a different version of the Gemara. Others explain that the Rambam rules in accordance with a *baraita* in *Torat Kohanim* (*Ma'aseh Roke'aḥ*). Yet others contend that the Rambam agrees that the priest wipes his finger between sprinklings on the edge of the bowl containing the blood (Rambam *Sefer Tahara*, *Hilkhot Para Aduma* 3:2 and *Sefer Avoda*, *Hilkhot Ma'aseh HaKorbanot* 5:8 and *Leḥem Mishne* there).

LANGUAGE

Atoning bowls [*keforei*] of gold – כְּפוֹרֵי זָהָב: The meaning of the root *kaf*, *peh*, *reish* is to wipe away. This is the basis for the notion of *kappara*, forgiveness, in the sense of wiping away one's sins. There is a similar root in Syriac that also refers to atonement as well as scrubbing.

לָא, עַד שֶׁלֹּא יָצְתָה מִיָּדוֹ הַזָּאָה – טָעוּן כִּיבּוּס, וּמִשֶּׁיָּצְאָה הַזָּאָה מִיָּדוֹ וְנִתְּזָה מִמַּה שֶּׁנִּשְׁאַר – אֵין טָעוּן כִּיבּוּס.

The Gemara rejects this suggestion: **No,** the *baraita* is saying that if the blood sprayed from his hand onto the garment **before** any particular **sprinkling left his hand,** the garment **requires laundering. But** if the blood was sprayed **after a sprinkling left his hand,** in which case the blood **sprayed from that which remained** on his finger following that sprinkling, then the garment **does not require laundering,** as the blood left on his finger was already rendered unfit for sprinkling.

אֵיתִיבֵיהּ אַבַּיֵּי: גָּמַר מִלְּהַזּוֹת, מְקַנֵּחַ יָדוֹ בְּגוּפָהּ שֶׁל פָּרָה; גָּמַר – אִין, לֹא גָּמַר – לָא!

Abaye raised an objection to Rava from a mishna discussing the red heifer (*Para* 3:9): When the priest has **completed sprinkling** the blood of the red heifer toward the entrance to the Sanctuary, **he wipes his hand** from the blood **on the body of the heifer.** Abaye explains his objection: The mishna states that when the priest **completed** all the sprinklings, then **yes,** he wipes his hand. It may be inferred that if he **did not complete** the sprinklings, he does **not** wipe his hand, even though blood remains on his finger from each preceding sprinkling. This proves that the blood that remains on his finger is fit for sprinkling.

אֲמַר לֵיהּ: גָּמַר – מְקַנֵּחַ יָדוֹ, לֹא גָּמַר – מְקַנֵּחַ אֶצְבָּעוֹ.

Rava **said to** Abaye: The mishna means that when the priest **completed** all of the sprinklings, **he wipes his hand.** If he has **not** yet **completed** all of them, then he does not wipe his hand but he must **wipe his finger**[H] to remove the blood after each sprinkling, as that blood is no longer fit for subsequent sprinklings.

בִּשְׁלָמָא גָּמַר מְקַנֵּחַ יָדוֹ בְּגוּפָהּ שֶׁל פָּרָה – דִּכְתִיב: ״וְשָׂרַף אֶת הַפָּרָה לְעֵינָיו״, אֶלָּא לֹא גָּמַר מְקַנֵּחַ אֶצְבָּעוֹ, בְּמַאי מְקַנֵּחַ? דְּאִי אָמְרַתְּ בְּגוּפָהּ שֶׁל פָּרָה, אִיבָּעֵי לֵיהּ לְמִיתְנֵי: מְקַנֵּחַ יָדוֹ וְאֶצְבָּעוֹ בְּגוּפָהּ שֶׁל פָּרָה; מִדְּלָא קָתָנֵי הָכִי, שְׁמַע מִינָּהּ דְּלָא בָּעֵי קִינּוּחַ.

The Gemara raises a difficulty: **Granted,** after **he completed** all the sprinklings **he wipes his hand on the body of the heifer, as it is written: "And the heifer shall be burned in his sight;** her skin, and her flesh, and her blood" (Numbers 19:5), which indicates that the blood of the red heifer must be burned together with its flesh. **But** if when the priest had **not** yet **completed** the sprinklings **he wipes his finger,** then **with what** does he **wipe?**[N] **Because if you say** that he wipes his finger **on the body of the heifer,** the mishna **should have taught:** He **wipes his hand and his finger on the body of the heifer.** Rather, **from** the fact **that** the mishna **does not teach this,** that he wipes his finger on the body of the heifer, one can **conclude from** this mishna **that** his finger **does not require wiping** between sprinklings.

אֲמַר אַבַּיֵּי: בִּשְׂפַת מִזְרָק, כִּדְכְתִיב: ״כְּפוֹרֵי זָהָב״ וגו׳.

Abaye said: He wipes his finger **on the edge of** the **bowl** containing the blood, **as it is written: "Atoning bowls [*keforei*]**[L] **of gold"** (Ezra 1:10), which is referring to the bowls containing the blood. The root *kafar* can also mean to wipe.

וּמִי אָמַר רַבִּי אֶלְעָזָר הָכִי? וְהָא אִיתְּמַר: חֲבִיתֵּי כֹּהֵן גָּדוֹל – רַבִּי יוֹחָנָן אָמַר: אֵינָהּ קְדוֹשָׁה לַחֲצָאִין, רַבִּי אֶלְעָזָר אָמַר: מִתּוֹךְ שֶׁקְּרֵבָה לַחֲצָאִין – קְדוֹשָׁה לַחֲצָאִין;

§ The Gemara returns to the issue of the sanctification of blood collected in two vessels: **And did Rabbi Elazar** really **say this,** that blood is sanctified only when a full measure is initially collected in a single vessel? **But it was stated** with regard to the **High Priest's griddle-cake** offering: **Rabbi Yoḥanan says** that **it is not sanctified in halves,** i.e., if half of a tenth of an ephah was placed in one vessel, and a second half in another vessel, neither is sanctified. **Rabbi Elazar says: Since it is sacrificed in halves,** as half of the meal offering is sacrificed in the morning and half in the afternoon, it may be **sanctified in halves.**

NOTES

His finger, with what does he wipe, etc. – אֶצְבָּעוֹ בְּמַאי מְקַנֵּחַ וכו׳: At the time of the sprinkling the priest stands atop the Mount of Olives opposite the entrance to the Sanctuary, while the body of the red heifer remains at a lower height, on the mountain where it was slaughtered. Obviously the priest cannot return to the body of the heifer between each sprinkling in order to wipe his finger (Rashi). Other commentaries reject this explanation, as they maintain that the sprinkling occurred in the same location as the slaughter and burning of the red heifer (*Tosafot* on *Zevaḥim* 93b; Rabbi Shimshon of Saens on *Torat Kohanim*; see *Tosafot* here). Rashi on *Zevaḥim* 93b explains that it would have been unbefitting for the priest to wipe his finger on the body of the heifer between each sprinkling, as this would have caused hairs from the heifer to become stuck to his finger, where they would have remained during subsequent sprinklings.

וְאִם אִיתָא, לֵילַף מִדָּם! וְכִי תֵּימָא, רַבִּי אֶלְעָזָר מִילְּתָא מִמִּילְּתָא לָא גָּמַר, וְהָא אָמַר רַבִּי אֶלְעָזָר: מִנְחָה שֶׁקְּמָצָהּ בַּהֵיכָל – כְּשֵׁרָה, שֶׁכֵּן מָצִינוּ בְּסִילּוּק בָּזִיכִין!

And if it is so that Rabbi Elazar holds that blood may not be sanctified in halves, **let him derive** the *halakha* of the High Priest's griddle-cake offering **from** that of **blood. And if you would say** that in this case **Rabbi Elazar does not derive** the *halakha* of the **matter** of a meal offering **from** that of another **matter,** that is difficult: **But doesn't Rabbi Elazar say: A meal offering** from **which** the priest **removed a handful** while **inside the Sanctuary**[H] is **valid,** despite the fact that the handful should be removed in the Temple courtyard; the reason is **that we find** a similar case in the Sanctuary, **with regard to the removal of** the **bowls** of frankincense from the Table of the shewbread? Just as the bowls permit the shewbread for consumption when removed in the Sanctuary, so too, the handful permits the remainder of the meal offering for consumption. This indicates that Rabbi Elazar does derive the *halakha* of a meal offering from that of another matter.

מִנְחָה מִמִּנְחָה יָלֵיף, מִנְחָה מִדָּם לָא יָלֵיף.

The Gemara responds: Rabbi Elazar does **derive** the *halakha* with regard to **a meal offering from** that of another **meal offering;** the shewbread is considered a meal offering. But **he does not derive** the *halakha* with regard to **a meal offering from** that of **blood.**

וּמִנְחָה מִמִּנְחָה מִי יָלֵיף? וְהָתַנְיָא: עַד שֶׁלֹּא פֵּירְקָהּ נִפְרַס לַחְמָהּ – הַלֶּחֶם פָּסוּל וְאֵין מַקְטִיר עָלָיו אֶת הַבָּזִיכִין, מִשֶּׁפֵּירְקָהּ נִפְרַס לַחְמָהּ – הַלֶּחֶם פָּסוּל וּמַקְטִיר עָלָיו אֶת הַבָּזִיכִין;

The Gemara asks: **And does** Rabbi Elazar **derive** the *halakha* of one **meal offering from** that of another **meal offering? But isn't it taught** in a *baraita*: If **before** the priest **detached** the arrangement of shewbread and the bowls of frankincense from upon the Table, the **bread broke**[HN] into pieces, **the bread** is **unfit** for consumption **and** the priest **does not burn the** frankincense contained in the **bowls on** account of **it.** If the **bread broke after** the priest **detached it, the bread is unfit**[N] **but** the priest **burns the** frankincense contained in the **bowls on** account of **it.**

וְאָמַר רַבִּי אֶלְעָזָר: לֹא פֵּירְקָהּ מַמָּשׁ, אֶלָּא כֵּיוָן שֶׁהִגִּיעַ זְמַנָּהּ לְפָרֵק, אַף עַל פִּי שֶׁלֹּא פֵּירְקָהּ – כְּמִי שֶׁפֵּירְקָהּ דָּמְיָא;

The Gemara continues: **And Rabbi Elazar says:** When the *baraita* refers to the detachment of the shewbread, it does **not** mean that the priest **actually detached it. Rather,** it means that **once** the **time to detach it has arrived, even though he has not** yet **detached it** and has not removed the bowls, **it is considered as though he has detached it.** Accordingly, if the shewbread broke after that time, the frankincense is burned.

וְאַמַּאי? תֶּיהֱוֵי כְּמִנְחָה שֶׁחָסְרָה קוֹדֶם קְמִיצָה!

The Gemara explains its question: **And** if Rabbi Elazar derives the *halakha* of one meal offering from another, **why** does he say that frankincense contained in the bowls are burned in a case where the shewbread broke when the time to detach the bread had arrived? **It should be like** the case of **a meal offering that became lacking** in its measure **before the removal of the handful.** Such a handful is not removed and is not sacrificed upon the altar. Likewise, the frankincense was still on the Table when the shewbread broke and should therefore be disqualified.

HALAKHA

From which the priest removed a handful while inside the Sanctuary – שֶׁקְּמָצָהּ בַּהֵיכָל: The removal of the handful from a meal offering is performed anywhere inside the Temple courtyard. If the handful was removed inside the Sanctuary, it is valid, as stated by Rabbi Elazar (Rambam *Sefer Avoda*, *Hilkhot Ma'aseh HaKorbanot* 12:12).

The bread broke – נִפְרַס לַחְמָהּ: In a case where a loaf of the shewbread broke, if this occurred before the shewbread was removed from the Table then the loaves are disqualified and the bowls of frankincense are not sacrificed upon the altar. If the loaf broke after the shewbread was removed from the Table, the loaves are disqualified but the bowls of frankincense are sacrificed upon the altar. If the time for removing the shewbread, i.e., after the sixth hour (Radbaz), had arrived, the bread is considered to have been removed, and therefore if a loaf broke after this time the bowls of frankincense are sacrificed even if the arrangement had not yet been removed from the Table (Rambam *Sefer Avoda*, *Hilkhot Temidin UMusafin* 5:15–16).

NOTES

The bread broke – נִפְרַס לַחְמָהּ: According to some commentaries, this disqualification is due to the fact that the shewbread now lacks a full measure (see Rabbeinu Gershom Meor HaGola and *Sefat Emet* on 9b). Based on other sources this is apparently a unique disqualification, as the verse states: "It is most holy" (Leviticus 24:9), from which the Sages derive that the shewbread must remain in the state of its initial preparation, i.e., whole (see *Sifrei* on Numbers 6:19). Consequently, if it breaks it is disqualified (see *Torat Kohanim* and the commentary of Rabbi Shimshon of Saens on Leviticus 24:9).

If the bread broke after the priest detached it the bread is unfit – מִשֶּׁפֵּירְקָהּ נִפְרַס לַחְמָהּ הַלֶּחֶם פָּסוּל: The shewbread may not be eaten if it is broken, because the priests may consume a meal offering only if it is whole. The Sages derived this from the *halakha* that the remainder of a meal offering that became lacking between the removal and burning of its handful upon the altar is prohibited for consumption (Rashi; see 9b).

הָא לָא קַשְׁיָא, מִנְחָה לָא בְּרִיר בְּרִירָה קוֹמֶץ דִּידֵיהּ, וְהָא בְּרִיר בְּרִירָה קוֹמֶץ דִּידָהּ, וְכֵיוָן שֶׁהִגִּיעַ זְמַנָּהּ לְפָרֵק – כְּמַאן דִּפְרְקָהּ דָּמְיָא.

The Gemara answers: **This is not difficult,** as there is a difference between these meal offerings. In the case of **a meal offering** that became lacking before the removal of a handful, **its handful was not clearly designated.** Consequently, if the meal offering became lacking before a handful was removed, one may no longer remove a handful from it. **But** in the case of the shewbread and the bowls of frankincense, **its handful,** i.e., the frankincense, **was clearly designated** at the time when the frankincense was placed in the bowls, since the frankincense is in a separate container from the bread. **And** therefore, **once the time to detach** the bread **has arrived, it is considered as though he has detached it.**

אֶלָּא מֵעַתָּה, תֶּיהֱוֵי כְּשִׁירַיִם שֶׁחָסְרוּ בֵּין קְמִיצָה לְהַקְטָרָה, דְּאֵין מַקְטִירִין קוֹמֶץ עֲלֵיהֶן! לָאו פְּלוּגְתָּא נִינְהוּ? רַבִּי אֶלְעָזָר סָבַר לָהּ כְּמַאן דְּאָמַר: שִׁירַיִם שֶׁחָסְרוּ בֵּין קְמִיצָה לְהַקְטָרָה, מַקְטִיר קוֹמֶץ עֲלֵיהֶן.

The Gemara asks: But **if that is so,** then even if the time to detach the shewbread arrived, why is the frankincense burned? **It should be like** a case where the **remainder** of a meal offering **became lacking**[H] **between** the **removal of the handful and** the **burning** upon the altar; the *halakha* in this case is **that** one **does not burn the handful on** account of such a meal offering. The Gemara responds: **Isn't it a dispute** among the *amora'im* (9a) whether or not the handful is burned in such a case? One can say that **Rabbi Elazar holds in accordance with** the opinion of **the one who says** that if the **remainder** of a meal offering became **lacking between** the **removal of the handful and** the **burning,** the priest **burns the handful on** account of such a meal offering.

גּוּפָא: חֲבִיתֵּי כֹּהֵן גָּדוֹל – רַבִּי יוֹחָנָן אָמַר: אֵינָהּ קְדוֹשָׁה לַחֲצָאִין, וְרַבִּי אֶלְעָזָר אָמַר: מִתּוֹךְ שֶׁקְּרֵבָה לַחֲצָאִין קְדוֹשָׁה לַחֲצָאִין. אֲמַר רַבִּי אַחָא: מַאי טַעְמָא דְּרַבִּי יוֹחָנָן? אָמַר קְרָא: ״מִנְחָה...מַחֲצִיתָהּ״ – הָבֵיא מִנְחָה וְאַחַר כָּךְ חוֹצֵיהוּ.

§ The Gemara discusses **the** matter **itself:** With regard to the **griddle-cake** offering **of** the **High Priest,**[H] **Rabbi Yoḥanan says** that **it is not sanctified in halves, and Rabbi Elazar says: Since it is sacrificed in halves,** as half of the meal offering is sacrificed in the morning and half in the afternoon, it may likewise be **sanctified in halves. Rav Aḥa said: What is the reasoning of Rabbi Yoḥanan? The verse states: "A meal offering** perpetually, **half of it** in the morning, and half of it in the evening" (Leviticus 6:13). This means: First **bring** a whole **meal offering, and** only **afterward divide it** into halves.

מֵיתִיבֵי: חֲבִיתֵּי כֹּהֵן גָּדוֹל לֹא הָיוּ בָּאוֹת חֲצָאִין, אֶלָּא מֵבִיא עִשָּׂרוֹן שָׁלֵם וְחוֹצֵהוּ; וְתַנְיָא: אִילּוּ נֶאֱמַר ״מִנְחָה מַחֲצִית״ הָיִיתִי אוֹמֵר: מֵבִיא חֲצִי עִשָּׂרוֹן מִבֵּיתוֹ שַׁחֲרִית וּמַקְרִיב, חֲצִי עִשָּׂרוֹן מִבֵּיתוֹ עַרְבִית וּמַקְרִיב – תַּלְמוּד לוֹמַר: ״מַחֲצִיתָהּ בַּבֹּקֶר״, מֶחֱצָה מִשָּׁלֵם הוּא מֵבִיא!

The Gemara **raises an objection** to the opinion of Rabbi Elazar. The mishna teaches (50b): The **griddle-cake** offering **of the High Priest did not come in halves. Rather,** the High Priest **brings a full tenth** of an ephah **and** then **divides it** into two. **And it is taught** in a *baraita* with regard to this mishna: **If it were stated: A meal offering, half** in the morning, and half in the evening, **I would say: He brings half of a tenth from his home** in the **morning and sacrifices** it, and another **half of a tenth from his home** in the **evening and sacrifices** it. Therefore, **the verse states: "Half of it in the morning,"** indicating that **he brings a half from a whole,** and he does not bring a half by itself.

לְמִצְוָה. אֲמַר לֵיהּ רַב גְּבִיהָא מִבֵּי כָּתִיל לְרַב אַשִׁי: וְהָא חוּקָּה כְּתִיב בָּהּ! אֲמַר לֵיהּ: לָא נִצְרְכָא אֶלָּא לַהֲבִיאָהּ שָׁלֵם מִבֵּיתוֹ.

The Gemara responds: Rabbi Elazar maintains that the verse requires that a whole meal offering be brought in the morning only **for a mitzva,** i.e., *ab initio*. Nevertheless, if half of a tenth was brought in the morning it is valid after the fact. **Rav Geviha from Bei Katil**[P] **said to Rav Ashi: But** the term **"statute" is written with regard to** the griddle-cake offering, as the verse states: "A statute forever" (Leviticus 6:15), and there is a principle that whenever the Torah calls a mitzva a statute, the details of its performance are indispensable. Rav Ashi **said to him: It was necessary** for the Torah to define this mitzva as a statute **only with regard to** the requirement that the High Priest **bring a full** tenth **from his home.**[N] With regard to its sanctification in a service vessel, it can be sanctified in halves.

וּמִי אֲמַר רַבִּי יוֹחָנָן הָכִי? וְהָא אִיתְּמַר: הִפְרִישׁ חֲצִי עִשָּׂרוֹן וְדַעְתּוֹ לְהוֹסִיף – רַב אָמַר: אֵינוֹ קָדוֹשׁ, וְרַבִּי יוֹחָנָן אָמַר: קָדוֹשׁ; וְאִם אִיתָא, לֵילַף מֵחֲבִיתִּין!

The Gemara asks: **And did Rabbi Yoḥanan** really **say this? But it was stated:** If one **set aside half a tenth** of an ephah for any meal offering, **and his intention** was **to add** to the half in order to reach a full tenth, **Rav says** that **it is not sanctified,** as he did not bring a full tenth, **and Rabbi Yoḥanan says** that it is **sanctified. And if it is so** that Rabbi Yoḥanan holds that the griddle-cake offering cannot be sanctified in halves, **let him derive from** the **griddle-cake** offering that no meal offering may be sanctified in halves.

HALAKHA

The remainder of a meal offering became lacking – שִׁירַיִם שֶׁחָסְרוּ: In a case where the remainder of a meal offering became lacking or was disqualified in some other manner between the removal of the handful and the burning of the handful upon the altar, if part of the meal offering remained fit then the handful is burned upon the altar. This is in accordance with the opinion of Rabbi Yehoshua in the mishna on 26a, as explained by Rav (Rambam *Sefer Avoda, Hilkhot Pesulei HaMukdashin* 11:20).

The griddle-cake offering of the High Priest – חֲבִיתֵּי כֹּהֵן גָּדוֹל: How is the griddle-cake offering of the High Priest prepared? The High Priest brings a full tenth of an ephah of flour and sanctifies it. He then divides it into two halves using the vessel that holds one-half of a tenth. The offering cannot be sanctified in halves despite the fact that it is sacrificed in that manner. The *halakha* is in accordance with the opinion of Rabbi Yoḥanan, as there is a principle that the *halakha* follows his opinion in his disputes with Rabbi Elazar (Rambam *Sefer Avoda, Hilkhot Ma'aseh HaKorbanot* 13:2 and Mahari Kurkus there).

PERSONALITIES

Rav Geviha from Bei Katil – רַב גְּבִיהָא מִבֵּי כָּתִיל: Rav Geviha was a fifth- to sixth-generation Babylonian *amora*. Apparently he lived an exceptionally long life, as he was a member of the generation of Sages that studied under Rava, but was considered a major Sage of the subsequent generation as well. He was also a contemporary of Rav Ashi, with whom he would discuss matters of *halakha*. He survived Rav Ashi, and it is recorded in the letter of Rav Sherira Gaon that Rav Geviha served as head of the rabbinic school in Pumbedita in the years 429–434 CE.

NOTES

A full tenth from his home – שָׁלֵם מִבֵּיתוֹ: This does not mean that the High Priest must bring a single vessel from his home containing a full tenth of an ephah. Rather, Rav Ashi means that when the High Priest brings his offering to the Temple, in whichever vessel or vessels he chooses, and then places it inside a service vessel, there must be a full tenth of an ephah inside the service vessel (*Zevaḥ Toda*).

וְכִי תֵּימָא, רַבִּי יוֹחָנָן מִילְּתָא מִמִּילְּתָא לָא יָלֵיף, וְהָאָמַר רַבִּי יוֹחָנָן: שְׁלָמִים שֶׁשְּׁחָטָן בַּהֵיכָל – כְּשֵׁירִין, דִּכְתִיב: ״וּשְׁחָטוֹ פֶּתַח אֹהֶל מוֹעֵד״, שֶׁלֹּא יְהֵא טָפֵל חָמוּר מֵעִיקָּר!

And if you would say that Rabbi Yoḥanan does not derive the *halakha* of one **matter** with regard to consecrated items **from** that of another **matter,** that is difficult: **But doesn't Rabbi Yoḥanan say: Peace offerings that** were **slaughtered in the Sanctuary**[H] **are valid, as it is written: "And slaughter it at the entrance of the Tent of Meeting"** (Leviticus 3:2), i.e., in the courtyard. Rabbi Yoḥanan explains: It is logical **that** the *halakha* with regard to the **minor** area, i.e., the courtyard, **should not be more stringent than** the *halakha* with regard to the **major** area, the Tent of Meeting. Evidently, Rabbi Yoḥanan derives a *halakha* with regard to the Sanctuary from the Temple courtyard.

דַּעְתּוֹ לְהוֹסִיף שָׁאנֵי, דְּתַנְיָא: ״מְלֵאִים״ – אֵין מְלֵאִים אֶלָּא שְׁלֵמִים, כְּלוֹמַר, שֶׁאֵינוֹ קָדוֹשׁ עַד שֶׁיְּהֵא עִשָּׂרוֹן שָׁלֵם; וְאָמַר רַבִּי יוֹסֵי: אֵימָתַי? בִּזְמַן שֶׁאֵין דַּעְתּוֹ לְהוֹסִיף, אֲבָל בִּזְמַן שֶׁדַּעְתּוֹ לְהוֹסִיף – רִאשׁוֹן רִאשׁוֹן קָדוֹשׁ.

The Gemara responds: Rabbi Yoḥanan does in fact derive the *halakha* of one matter from another, and therefore he learns the *halakha* with regard to all meal offerings from the griddle-cake offering, that in general they are not sanctified in halves. But a case where one expresses **his intention to add** to the half measure **is different, as it is taught** in a *baraita* with regard to the verse: "Both of them **full** of fine flour" (Numbers 7:13). **"Full"** is a reference **only** to **full** measurements; **that is to say,** the flour **is not sanctified until there is a full tenth** inside the vessel. **And Rabbi Yosei said: When** is it the *halakha* that the flour is sanctified only if a full tenth is inside the vessel? It is **at a time when his intention** was **not** initially **to add** to that which he placed inside the vessel. **But at a time when his intention** was initially **to add, each initial** bit of flour is **sanctified** by the vessel.

וְרַב בַּחֲבִיתִּין כְּמַאן סְבִירָא לֵיהּ? אִי כְּרַבִּי אֶלְעָזָר, לֵילַף מֵחֲבִיתִּין!

The Gemara asks: **And Rav,** who holds that standard meal offerings are not sanctified in halves even if one's initial intention was to add to the half measure, **with regard to a griddle-cake** offering, **in accordance with whose** opinion **does he hold? If** he holds **in accordance with** the opinion of **Rabbi Elazar,** who says that a griddle-cake offering can be sanctified in halves, then **let him derive from** the *halakha* of **griddle-cake** offerings that all meal offerings may be sanctified in halves.

וְכִי תֵּימָא, רַב מִילְּתָא מִמִּילְּתָא לָא יָלֵיף, וְהָאָמַר רַב: מִנְחָה קְדוֹשָׁה בְּלֹא שֶׁמֶן (וּבְלֹא לְבוֹנָה) – שֶׁכֵּן מָצִינוּ בְּלֶחֶם הַפָּנִים; בְּלֹא לְבוֹנָה – שֶׁכֵּן מָצִינוּ בְּמִנְחַת נְסָכִים;

And if you would say that **Rav does not derive** the *halakha* of one **matter from** that of another **matter,** that is difficult: **But doesn't Rav say:** A standard **meal offering,** which is brought with oil and frankincense, **is sanctified** by a service vessel even **without** its **oil**[HN] and without its frankincense. It is sanctified without its oil, **as we find** such a *halakha* **with regard to the shewbread,** which is sacrificed without oil and is nevertheless sanctified by a service vessel. Similarly, it is sanctified even **without** its **frankincense, as we find** such a *halakha* **with regard to the meal offering** accompanying the **libations** of an offering, which is sacrificed without frankincense and is nevertheless sanctified by a service vessel.

בְּלֹא שֶׁמֶן וּבְלֹא לְבוֹנָה – שֶׁכֵּן מָצִינוּ בְּמִנְחַת חוֹטֵא! עַל כָּרְחָיךְ רַב כְּרַבִּי יוֹחָנָן סְבִירָא לֵיהּ.

Finally, a standard meal offering is sanctified by a service vessel even **without** its **oil and without** its **frankincense, as we find with regard to the meal offering of a sinner,** which includes neither of these. This indicates that Rav does derive the *halakha* of a meal offering from other meal offerings. Rather, **perforce,** with regard to the griddle-cake offering, **Rav holds in accordance with** the opinion of **Rabbi Yoḥanan,** that this offering is not sanctified in halves, and it is derived from there that no meal offerings are sanctified in halves.

גּוּפָא, אָמַר רַב: מִנְחָה קְדוֹשָׁה בְּלֹא שֶׁמֶן, וְאֵין דִּינָהּ כְּעִשָּׂרוֹן חָסֵר – שֶׁכֵּן מָצִינוּ בְּלֶחֶם הַפָּנִים, בְּלֹא לְבוֹנָה – שֶׁכֵּן מָצִינוּ בְּמִנְחַת נְסָכִים, בְּלֹא שֶׁמֶן וּבְלֹא לְבוֹנָה – שֶׁכֵּן מָצִינוּ בְּמִנְחַת חוֹטֵא.

§ The Gemara discusses **the** matter **itself: Rav says** that **a meal offering is sanctified without** its **oil, and its *halakha* is not** the same **as** when **a tenth** of an ephah of flour is **lacking, as we find** such a *halakha* **with regard to the shewbread,** which is sacrificed without oil and is nevertheless sanctified by a service vessel. Similarly, it is sanctified even **without** its **frankincense, as we find** such a *halakha* **with regard to the meal offering** accompanying the **libations** of an offering, which is sacrificed without frankincense and is nevertheless sanctified. Additionally, a meal offering is sanctified even **without** its **oil and without** its **frankincense, as we find** such a *halakha* **with regard to the meal offering of a sinner,** which lacks both oil and frankincense and is nevertheless sanctified by a service vessel.

HALAKHA

Peace offerings that were slaughtered in the Sanctuary – שְׁלָמִים שֶׁשְּׁחָטָן בַּהֵיכָל: Peace offerings may be slaughtered anywhere inside the Temple courtyard. If they were slaughtered inside the Sanctuary, they are valid. The *halakha* is in accordance with the opinion of Rabbi Yoḥanan (Rambam *Sefer Avoda, Hilkhot Ma'aseh HaKorbanot* 5:4).

A standard meal offering is sanctified even without its oil – מִנְחָה קְדוֹשָׁה בְּלֹא שֶׁמֶן: The Rambam does not rule on this issue. *Likkutei Halakhot* rules that the *halakha* is in accordance with the opinion of Rav that a meal offering may be sanctified without its oil, as the Gemara (8b) establishes that Shmuel agrees with the opinion of Rav.

NOTES

A standard meal offering is sanctified even without its oil, etc. – מִנְחָה קְדוֹשָׁה בְּלֹא שֶׁמֶן וכו׳: This does not mean that a meal offering may be sacrificed without its oil, as it is explicitly taught in the mishna (27a) that the flour and oil are both indispensable. Rather, Rav means that the flour may become sanctified without its accompanying oil, i.e., the flour becomes consecrated and may no longer be redeemed. Subsequently, this flour would become disqualified through contact with one who immersed himself that day and is waiting for nightfall for the purification process to be completed, or with one who has not yet brought his atonement offering, and it would also become disqualified by being left overnight (*Me'ila* 9a).

BACKGROUND

Log – לוֹג: This is the basic liquid measure used by the Sages. It is equivalent to the volume of six eggs, one-quarter of a *kav*, or one twenty-fourth of a *se'a*. A range of modern opinions estimate that this volume is between 300 and 600 ml.

וְשֶׁמֶן וּלְבוֹנָה קָדְשִׁי הַאי בְּלָא הַאי וְהַאי בְּלָא הַאי; שֶׁמֶן – שֶׁכֵּן מָצִינוּ בְּלוֹג שֶׁמֶן שֶׁל מְצוֹרָע, לְבוֹנָה – שֶׁכֵּן מָצִינוּ בַּלְּבוֹנָה הַבָּאָה בַּבָּזִיכִין. וְרַבִּי חֲנִינָא אָמַר:

Rav continues: **And oil and frankincense are** each **sanctified** by service vessels, **this** substance **without that** one, **and that** substance **without this** one. **Oil** is sanctified on its own, **as we find** such a *halakha* **with regard to the** ***log***[B] **of oil of a leper,** which is sanctified on its own. **Frankincense** is sanctified on its own, **as we find** such a *halakha* **with regard to the frankincense that comes in the bowls** that are brought with the shewbread; there is no oil in that case and yet the frankincense is sanctified in the bowls. **And Rabbi Ḥanina says:**

Perek **I**
Daf **8** Amud **b**

HALAKHA

The vessels used for liquids, etc. – כְּלֵי הַלַּח וכו׳: The liquid measures sanctify the liquids placed in them, but they do not sanctify any dry items placed in them. Likewise, dry measures do not sanctify liquids placed in them (Rambam *Sefer Avoda, Hilkhot Pesulei HaMukdashin* 3:19).

Bowls – מִזְרָקוֹת: The bowls sanctify both liquids and dry items, as stated by Shmuel (Rambam *Sefer Avoda, Hilkhot Pesulei HaMukdashin* 3:19).

BACKGROUND

Bowls – מִזְרָקוֹת: *Mizrakot*, bowls or cups, were vessels used for holding liquids that could contain a fairly large volume. Apparently these vessels were referred to as *mizrakot* due to their use in the performance of the sprinkling of the blood, *zerika*. Based on descriptions throughout the rabbinic literature, they were round, and either rounded or pointed underneath, so that they could not be put down without a special stand to stabilize them. They could still be held with only one hand, and it is possible that they had a handle.

Replica of a cup used in the Temple

לֹא זוֹ קְדוֹשָׁה בְּלֹא זוֹ, וְלֹא זוֹ קְדוֹשָׁה בְּלֹא זוֹ.

Neither is **this** substance **sanctified**[N] **without that, nor is that sanctified without this.** Rather, any meal offering that requires oil and frankincense is sanctified by a service vessel only when the flour, oil, and frankincense are all placed in the same vessel at the same time.

וּלְרַבִּי חֲנִינָא, עִשָּׂרוֹן לָמָּה נִמְשַׁח? וַהֲלֹא אֵינוֹ עָשׂוּי אֶלָּא לִמְדִידַת קֶמַח בִּלְבָד, וְהַקֶּמַח אֵינוֹ קָדוֹשׁ בְּלֹא שֶׁמֶן! לְמִנְחַת חוֹטֵא.

The Gemara asks: **And according to** the opinion of **Rabbi Ḥanina, for what** purpose was the vessel that measured **a tenth** of an ephah **anointed,** making it possible for it to sanctify items placed inside it? This vessel **was fashioned only for measuring flour, and** according to Rabbi Ḥanina **the flour is not sanctified without oil.** What then does this vessel sanctify? The Gemara answers: The vessel was anointed **for** the purpose of sanctifying the **meal offering of a sinner,** which contains neither oil nor frankincense.

וְלוֹג לָמָּה נִמְשַׁח? לְלוֹג שֶׁל מְצוֹרָע.

The Gemara further asks: **And for what** purpose was the vessel that measured one ***log*** of oil **anointed?** After all, according to Rabbi Ḥanina oil for a meal offering cannot be sanctified by itself. The Gemara explains: It was anointed **for** the purpose of sanctifying the ***log*** of oil **of a leper,** which is not brought as part of a meal offering. This oil is sanctified without flour or frankincense.

וְאַף שְׁמוּאֵל סָבַר לָהּ לְהָא דְּרַב, דִּתְנַן: כְּלֵי הַלַּח מְקַדְּשִׁין אֶת הַלַּח, וּמִדּוֹת הַיָּבֵשׁ מְקַדְּשִׁין אֶת הַיָּבֵשׁ, וְאֵין כְּלֵי הַלַּח מְקַדְּשִׁין אֶת הַיָּבֵשׁ, וְלֹא מִדּוֹת הַיָּבֵשׁ מְקַדְּשִׁין אֶת הַלַּח;

The Gemara notes: **And Shmuel also holds in accordance with this** statement **of Rav,** that a service vessel sanctifies the flour of a meal offering even without its oil, **as we learned** in a mishna (*Zevaḥim* 88a): **The vessels** used for **liquids**[H] **sanctify** only **the liquids, and the** vessels that serve as **dry measures**[N] **sanctify** only **the dry** goods. **But the vessels** used for **liquids do not sanctify the dry** goods, **and the** vessels that serve as **dry measures do not sanctify the liquids.**

וְאָמַר שְׁמוּאֵל: לֹא שָׁנוּ אֶלָּא מִדּוֹת, אֲבָל מִזְרָקוֹת שֶׁל דָּם מְקַדְּשׁוֹת אֶת הַיָּבֵשׁ, שֶׁנֶּאֱמַר: ״שְׁנֵיהֶם מְלֵאִים סֹלֶת בְּלוּלָה בַשֶּׁמֶן לְמִנְחָה״.

And Shmuel says with regard to this mishna: **They taught** that vessels used for liquids do not sanctify dry goods **only** with regard to vessels used as **measures. But bowls**[HB] that are used for collecting and tossing the **blood** of offerings **sanctify the dry goods** as well, **as it is stated** with regard to the offerings of the princes brought during the inauguration of the Tabernacle: **"Both of them full of fine flour mixed with oil for a meal offering"** (Numbers 7:13), which indicates that the bowl sanctifies meal offerings, which are dry.

NOTES

Neither is this substance sanctified, etc. – לֹא זוֹ קְדוֹשָׁה וכו׳: According to Rabbi Ḥanina, the flour, oil, and frankincense of a meal offering are all considered like a single item. He further maintains in accordance with the opinion of Rabbi Yoḥanan that only a full measure may be sanctified, and not half measures (*Netivot HaKodesh*).

The vessels used for liquids…and the vessels that serve as dry measures – כְּלֵי הַלַּח...וּמִדּוֹת הַיָּבֵשׁ: Service vessels sanctify only those items that are fit to be placed inside them, as they were anointed and sanctified only to that end (see *Zevaḥim* 86a, 88a).

אָמַר לֵיהּ רַב אַחָא מִדִּפְתִּי לְרָבִינָא: מִנְחָה לַחָה הִיא! אֲמַר לֵיהּ: לָא נִצְרְכָא אֶלָּא לְיָבֵשׁ שֶׁבָּהּ, דְּהַיְינוּ לְבוֹנָה.

The Gemara continues its proof: And **Rav Aḥa of Difti said to Ravina,** with regard to this derivation of Shmuel: But the **meal offering** of the verse **is** also considered **a liquid,** as it is mingled with oil. How then can one derive from it the *halakha* with regard to items that are entirely dry? Ravina **said to him:** The verse cited by Shmuel **is necessary only to** teach that **the dry** part **of** a meal offering, **that is,** the **frankincense,**[N] which invariably does not come into contact with the oil, is sanctified by the bowls as well.

וְאִי סָלְקָא דַּעְתָּךְ קָסָבַר שְׁמוּאֵל אֵין מִנְחָה קְדוֹשָׁה עַד שֶׁיְּהוּ כּוּלָּן, יָבֵשׁ שֶׁבָּהּ הֵיכִי מַשְׁכַּחַתְּ לַהּ? וַהֲלֹא כּוּלָּן לַחִים הֵן, מִפְּנֵי הַשֶּׁמֶן! אֶלָּא שְׁמַע מִינַּהּ: קָסָבַר שְׁמוּאֵל הַאי בְּלָא הַאי.

The Gemara concludes its proof with regard to Shmuel's opinion: **And if it enters your mind** that **Shmuel holds** that **a meal offering is not sanctified** by a service vessel **until all** of its components **are** together in the vessel, then **how can you find** a case where the **dry** parts **of** a meal offering are by themselves? **Is it not** correct that when meal offerings are sanctified, **all of them are liquids, due to the oil** that is mixed with them? **Rather, conclude from** here that **Shmuel holds** that **this** substance may be sanctified **without that** one.

וְאִיבָּעֵית אֵימָא: מִנְחָה לְגַבֵּי דָּם כְּיָבֵשׁ דָּמְיָא.

And if you wish, say instead in answer to Rav Aḥa of Difti's question: **A meal offering,** even when it is mixed with oil, is, **relative to blood, considered as a dry** item. Accordingly, one may derive from the verse that the bowls sanctify dry items, and just as a bowl sanctifies a meal offering that contains oil, as it is considered dry in comparison to blood, so too, it sanctifies a meal offering that is entirely dry, i.e., that contains no oil, as claimed by Rav.

גּוּפָא, אָמַר רַבִּי אֶלְעָזָר: מִנְחָה שֶׁקְּמָצָהּ בַּהֵיכָל – כְּשֵׁרָה, שֶׁכֵּן מָצִינוּ בְּסִילּוּק בָּזִיכִין.

§ The Gemara discusses **the** matter **itself. Rabbi Elazar says: A meal offering** from **which** the priest **removed a handful** while **inside the Sanctuary** is **valid,** despite the fact that the handful should be removed in the Temple courtyard; the reason is **that we find** a similar case in the Sanctuary, **with regard to the removal of** the **bowls** of frankincense from the Table of the shewbread. Just as the bowls permit the shewbread for consumption, so too, the handful permits the remainder of the meal offering for consumption.

מְתִיב רַבִּי יִרְמְיָה: ״וְקָמַץ מִשָּׁם״ – מִמָּקוֹם שֶׁרַגְלֵי הַזָּר עוֹמְדוֹת;

Rabbi Yirmeya raises an objection to this opinion from a *baraita* discussing the verse: "And he shall bring it to Aaron's sons the priests; **and he shall remove from there** his handful" (Leviticus 2:2). The verse indicates that the removal of a handful from a meal offering may be performed **from the place where the feet of the non-priest** may **stand,**[N] i.e., anywhere within the Temple courtyard.

בֶּן בְּתֵירָא אוֹמֵר: מִנַּיִן שֶׁאִם קָמַץ בִּשְׂמֹאל שֶׁיַּחֲזִיר וְיִקְמוֹץ בְּיָמִין? תַּלְמוּד לוֹמַר: ״וְקָמַץ מִשָּׁם״ – מִמָּקוֹם שֶׁקָּמַץ כְּבָר!

The *baraita* continues: **Ben Beteira,** who holds that a handful is not disqualified when removed with the left hand, **says** that the verse should be interpreted as follows: **From where** is it derived **that if** one **removed a handful with** his **left** hand, **that he must return** the handful to the vessel that contains the meal offering **and** again **remove the handful with** his **right** hand? **The verse states: "And he shall remove from there."** This indicates that the handful is removed **from the place where he already removed** it, i.e., the handful is returned to the meal offering and thereupon removed from the same meal offering, this time with his right hand. It is clear from the statement of the first *tanna* that the handful of a meal offering may be removed only in the place where the feet of a non-priest may stand, but not in the Sanctuary.

אִיכָּא דְּאָמְרִי: הוּא מוֹתִיב לַהּ וְהוּא מְפָרֵק לַהּ; אִיכָּא דְּאָמְרִי, אֲמַר לֵיהּ רַבִּי יַעֲקֹב לְרַבִּי יִרְמְיָה בַּר תַּחְלִיפָא: אַסְבְּרָא לָךְ, לָא נִצְרְכָא אֶלָּא לְהַכְשִׁיר אֶת כָּל עֲזָרָה כּוּלָּהּ, שֶׁלֹּא תֹּאמַר: הוֹאִיל וְעוֹלָה קׇדְשֵׁי קׇדָשִׁים וּמִנְחָה קׇדְשֵׁי קׇדָשִׁים, מָה עוֹלָה טְעוּנָה צָפוֹן – אַף מִנְחָה טְעוּנָה צָפוֹן.

Some say that Rabbi Yirmeya **raises the objection and he resolves it** as well. And **some say** that **Rabbi Ya'akov said to Rabbi Yirmeya bar Taḥlifa: I will explain to you** the resolution of this objection: The verse **is necessary only to permit the entire** Temple **courtyard** for removing the handful there, not to prohibit the removal of a handful inside the Sanctuary. The reason is **that you should not say: Since a burnt offering** is **an offering of the most sacred order, and a meal offering** is likewise **an offering of the most sacred order,** then **just as a burnt offering requires** that its slaughter be performed in the **northern** part of the Temple courtyard, **so too, a meal offering requires** that the removal of its handful be in the **northern** part.

NOTES

Is necessary only to teach that the dry part of a meal offering, that is, the frankincense, etc. – לָא נִצְרְכָא אֶלָּא לְיָבֵשׁ שֶׁבָּהּ דְּהַיְינוּ לְבוֹנָה וכו׳: The section beginning with the phrase: That is, the frankincense, until the end of the next paragraph: Shmuel holds that this substance may be sanctified without that one, is missing from many versions of the Gemara. Certainly, the Gemara's reference to the frankincense is not easily understood in this context. Some commentaries explain that the Gemara is referring to those parts of the flour that remain dry even after the oil is mixed into it, as there will necessarily remain small granules of flour that did not come into contact with the oil (Rashi; Rabbeinu Gershom Meor HaGola). Accordingly, Shmuel is claiming that just as the bowl sanctifies the dry parts of a meal offering, so too, it sanctifies the flour that contains no oil at all (see Rashi, *Tosafot*, and *Shita Mekubbetzet*).

From the place where the feet of the non-priest may stand – מִמָּקוֹם שֶׁרַגְלֵי הַזָּר עוֹמְדוֹת: This is referring to the Israelite courtyard, the place where the owner brings his meal offering, in accordance with the verse "And he shall bring it to Aaron's sons the priests; and he shall remove from there his handful."

BACKGROUND

Enter the Sanctuary – נִכְנָסִין לַהֵיכָל: All the courtyards of the Temple, with the exception of several chambers, were enclosed areas without roofing. When Jerusalem was under siege and the gentiles fired projectiles into the courtyards, those standing inside the courtyards were exposed to their fire. In contrast, the Sanctuary was a roofed building, which provided protection from the gentiles' fire.

Temple courtyards and Sanctuary

מַה לְעוֹלָה שֶׁכֵּן כָּלִיל! מֵחַטָּאת.

The Gemara raises a difficulty with regard to this comparison: **What** is notable **about a burnt offering?** It is notable **in that** it is more sacred, as it is **consumed** in its entirety upon the altar. The Gemara responds: The same comparison may be drawn **from a sin offering,** which is also an offering of the most sacred order and is not sacrificed in its entirety upon the altar, and yet it must be slaughtered in the northern part of the Temple courtyard.

מַה לְחַטָּאת שֶׁכֵּן מְכַפֶּרֶת עַל חַיָּיבֵי כָרֵיתוֹת! מֵאָשָׁם.

The Gemara raises a difficulty with regard to this comparison as well: **What** is notable **about a sin offering?** It is notable **in that** the *halakhot* of a sin offering are more stringent, as its sacrifice **atones for** those sins whose transgression causes one to be **liable to** receive ***karet***. The Gemara responds: The comparison may be drawn **from a guilt offering,** as it too is an offering of the most sacred order, it is not sacrificed in its entirety upon the altar, it does not atone for such sins, and yet it must be slaughtered in the northern part of the Temple courtyard.

מַה לְאָשָׁם שֶׁכֵּן מִינֵי דָמִים! מִכּוּלְּהוּ נַמִי, שֶׁכֵּן מִינֵי דָמִים!

The Gemara rejects this suggestion as well: **What** is notable **about a guilt offering?** It is notable **in that** a guilt offering has a loftier status, as it is one of **the types of** offerings whose atonement is achieved through their **blood,** i.e., it is an animal offering. The Gemara adds: Once this claim has been accepted, **from all of them as well,** i.e., from a burnt offering and sin offering, one cannot draw a comparison to a meal offering either, **as** they are all of **the types of** offerings whose atonement is achieved through their **blood.**

אֶלָּא אִיצְטְרִיךְ, סָלְקָא דַעְתָּךְ אָמִינָא, הוֹאִיל וּכְתִיב: ״וְהִקְרִיבָהּ אֶל הַכֹּהֵן וְהִגִּישָׁהּ אֶל הַמִּזְבֵּחַ וְקָמַץ״, מָה הַגָּשָׁה בְּקֶרֶן דְּרוֹמִית מַעֲרָבִית – אַף קְמִיצָה נַמִי בְּקֶרֶן דְּרוֹמִית מַעֲרָבִית, קָא מַשְׁמַע לָן.

Rather, the verse **was necessary** in order to permit the removal of a handful anywhere in the Temple courtyard because it might **enter your mind to say** that **since it is written: "And it shall be presented to the priest, and he shall bring it to the altar"** (Leviticus 2:8), and it states: **"And he shall remove** from there his handful" (Leviticus 2:2), one could claim: **Just as** the **bringing** of the meal offering is **in the southwestern corner** of the altar, **so too,** the **removal of the handful** must **also** be performed **in the southwestern corner.** Therefore, the verse **teaches us** that the removal of the handful may be performed anywhere in the Temple courtyard, but this does not serve to exclude the Sanctuary.

גּוּפָא, אָמַר רַבִּי יוֹחָנָן: שְׁלָמִים שֶׁשְּׁחָטָן בַּהֵיכָל – כְּשֵׁרִין, שֶׁנֶּאֱמַר: ״וּשְׁחָטוֹ פֶּתַח אֹהֶל מוֹעֵד״, וְלֹא יְהֵא טָפֵל חָמוּר מִן הָעִיקָּר.

§ The Gemara discusses **the** matter **itself. Rabbi Yoḥanan says: Peace offerings that** were **slaughtered in the Sanctuary are valid, as it is stated: "And slaughter it at the entrance of the Tent of Meeting"** (Leviticus 3:2), i.e., in the courtyard. **And** it is logical that the *halakha* with regard to the **minor** area, i.e., the courtyard, **should not be more stringent than** the *halakha* with regard to **the major** one, the Tent of Meeting or the Sanctuary.

מֵיתִיבִי, רַבִּי יְהוּדָה בֶּן בְּתֵירָא אוֹמֵר: מִנַּיִן שֶׁאִם הִקִּיפוּ גּוֹיִם אֶת הָעֲזָרָה, שֶׁהַכֹּהֲנִים נִכְנָסִין לַהֵיכָל וְאוֹכְלִין בְּקָדְשֵׁי קָדָשִׁים וּשְׁיָרֵי מְנָחוֹת? תַּלְמוּד לוֹמַר:

The Gemara **raises an objection** to the opinion of Rabbi Yoḥanan from a *baraita*. **Rabbi Yehuda ben Beteira says: From where** is it derived **that if gentiles surrounded the** Temple **courtyard** and were firing projectiles inside to the point that it became impossible to remain in the courtyard on account of the threat, **that the priests enter the Sanctuary**[B] **and partake of the offerings of the most sacred order and the remainders of** the **meal offerings** while inside the Sanctuary? **The verse states:**

״בְּקֹדֶשׁ הַקֳּדָשִׁים תֹּאכְלֶנּוּ״.

"Every meal offering of theirs, and every sin offering of theirs, and every guilt offering of theirs, which they may render unto Me, shall be most holy for you and for your sons. **In the Sanctuary you shall eat them"** (Numbers 18:9–10). This indicates that although the mitzva is to consume offerings of the most sacred order in the courtyard, in certain instances the priests may consume these offerings inside the Sanctuary, the most holy place.

וְהָא לָמָּה לִי קְרָא? לֵימָא: ״בַּחֲצַר אֹהֶל מוֹעֵד יֹאכְלוּהָ״, וְלֹא יְהֵא טָפֵל חָמוּר מִן הָעִיקָּר!

The Gemara explains its objection: **But** according to the opinion of Rabbi Yoḥanan, **why do I need this verse? Let him say** here as well that as the verse states: **"In the court of the Tent of Meeting they shall eat it"** (Leviticus 6:9), i.e., in the Temple courtyard, it is logical that the *halakha* with regard to the **minor** area **should not be more stringent than** the *halakha* with regard to **the major** one, i.e., if one may consume a peace offering in the Temple courtyard then all the more so may he consume it in the Sanctuary.

עֲבוֹדָה, דְּאָדָם עוֹבֵד בִּמְקוֹם רַבּוֹ – אָמְרִינַן שֶׁלֹּא יְהֵא טָפֵל חָמוּר מִן הָעִיקָּר; אֲכִילָה, שֶׁאֵין אָדָם אוֹכֵל בִּמְקוֹם רַבּוֹ, טַעְמָא דִּכְתַב קְרָא, הָא לָא כְּתַב קְרָא – לֹא יְהֵא טָפֵל חָמוּר מִן הָעִיקָּר לָא אָמְרִינַן.

The Gemara explains: Consuming an offering is not the same as slaughtering it. The slaughter of an offering is part of the sacrificial **service,** and it is not considered disrespectful **for a person** to **serve** his master **in the place of his master,** i.e., within the Sanctuary as well as in the courtyard. Therefore, **we say that** the *halakha* with regard to the **minor** area **should not be more stringent than** the *halakha* with regard to **the major** one. By contrast, with regard to the **consumption** of an offering, **since a person may not eat in the place of his master, the** only **reason** that it is permitted to consume an offering inside the Sanctuary is **that** it is **written** in **the verse:** "In a most holy place you shall eat them." **Had** this **not** been **written** in **the verse** explicitly, **we** would **not say** that the *halakha* with regard to the **minor** area **should not be more stringent than** the *halakha* with regard to **the major** one.

אִיתְּמַר: בְּלָלָהּ חוּץ לְחוֹמַת עֲזָרָה – רַבִּי יוֹחָנָן אָמַר: פְּסוּלָה, רֵישׁ לָקִישׁ אָמַר: כְּשֵׁרָה. רֵישׁ לָקִישׁ אָמַר כְּשֵׁרָה – דִּכְתִיב: ״וְיָצַק עָלֶיהָ שֶׁמֶן וְנָתַן עָלֶיהָ לְבוֹנָה״, וַהֲדַר: ״וֶהֱבִיאָהּ אֶל בְּנֵי אַהֲרֹן הַכֹּהֲנִים וְקָמַץ״.

§ **It was stated:** If one **mixed** the oil of a meal offering into **it outside the wall of** the Temple **courtyard,**[H] **Rabbi Yoḥanan says** that it is **disqualified,** and **Reish Lakish says** that it is **valid. Reish Lakish says:** It is **valid, as it is written: "And he shall pour oil upon it, and put frankincense upon it"** (Leviticus 2:1), **and then** it is written: **"And he shall bring it to Aaron's sons the priests; and he shall remove"** (Leviticus 2:2).

מִקְּמִיצָה וָאֵילָךְ מִצְוַת כְּהוּנָּה, לִימֵּד עַל יְצִיקָה וּבְלִילָה שֶׁכְּשֵׁרִין בְּזָר; וּמִדִּכְהוּנָּה לָא בָּעֲיָא, פְּנִים נַמִּי לָא בָּעֲיָא.

Reish Lakish explains: The Sages derived from here that **from the removal of the handful onward**[H] the rites performed with the meal offering are solely **a mitzva** of the **priesthood.** Accordingly, the verse **taught about pouring and mixing that they are valid** when performed **by a non-priest. And from** the fact **that** the **priesthood is not required** for the mixing, it may be derived that it **is also not required** that its performance be **inside** the walls of the Temple courtyard.

וְרַבִּי יוֹחָנָן אָמַר: פְּסוּלָה, כֵּיוָן דַּעֲשִׂיָּיתָהּ בִּכְלִי הוּא, נְהִי דִּכְהוּנָּה לָא בָּעֲיָא, פְּנִים מִיהַת בָּעֲיָא. תַּנְיָא כְּווֹתֵיהּ דְּרַבִּי יוֹחָנָן: בְּלָלָהּ זָר – כְּשֵׁרָה, חוּץ לְחוֹמַת הָעֲזָרָה – פְּסוּלָה.

And Rabbi Yoḥanan says: This meal offering is **disqualified, since** a meal offering's **performance is in** a service **vessel.** Therefore, **granted that** the **priesthood is not required,** yet **in any event** its performance **inside** the Temple courtyard **is required.** The Gemara notes that **it is taught** in a *baraita* **in accordance with** the opinion **of Rabbi Yoḥanan:** If a meal offering was **mixed** by a **non-priest** it is **valid.** But if it was mixed **outside the wall of the** Temple **courtyard** it is **disqualified.**

אִיתְּמַר: מִנְחָה שֶׁחָסְרָה קוֹדֶם קְמִיצָה – רַבִּי יוֹחָנָן אָמַר: יָבִיא מִתּוֹךְ בֵּיתוֹ וִימַלְּאֶנָּה, רֵישׁ לָקִישׁ אָמַר: לֹא יָבִיא מִתּוֹךְ בֵּיתוֹ וִימַלְּאֶנָּה.

§ **It was stated:** With regard to a **meal offering that became lacking** in its full measure **before the removal of the handful, Rabbi Yoḥanan says** that the owner **shall bring** additional flour **from within his home**[H] **and shall fill** the missing part of the measure of the meal offering. **Reish Lakish says: He shall not bring** flour **from within his home and fill it.** Instead, he must bring a new meal offering.

רַבִּי יוֹחָנָן אָמַר מֵבִיא מִתּוֹךְ בֵּיתוֹ וִימַלְּאֶנָּה – קְמִיצָה קָבְעָה לֵיהּ; רֵישׁ לָקִישׁ אָמַר לֹא יָבִיא מִתּוֹךְ בֵּיתוֹ וִימַלְּאֶנָּה – קְדוּשַּׁת כְּלִי קָבְעָה לֵיהּ.

The Gemara explains: **Rabbi Yoḥanan says** that **he brings** flour **from within his home and he fills it,** as the **removal of the handful establishes it** as a meal offering to the extent that it may become disqualified. Before the removal, one may always add flour to the meal offering. **Reish Lakish says: He shall not bring** flour **from within his home and fill it,** as **the sanctity of** the service **vessel establishes it** as a meal offering. Therefore, once the meal offering was placed in a service vessel and sanctified, it is disqualified if it becomes lacking.

HALAKHA

If one mixed the oil of a meal offering into it outside the wall of the Temple courtyard – בְּלָלָהּ חוּץ לְחוֹמַת עֲזָרָה: A meal offering whose oil was mixed outside the walls of the Temple courtyard is not valid. In general, when there is a disagreement between Rabbi Yoḥanan and Reish Lakish, the *halakha* is in accordance with the opinion of Rabbi Yoḥanan, especially when the Gemara cites a *baraita* in support of his opinion, as is the case here (Rambam *Sefer Avoda, Hilkhot Pesulei HaMukdashin* 11:6, and see *Kesef Mishne* there).

From the removal of the handful onward – מִקְּמִיצָה וָאֵילָךְ: From the time of the removal of the handful from a meal offering onward, the rites performed with the offering are mitzvot of the priesthood. Accordingly, the pouring and mixing of the oil into the meal offering, which come before that stage, may be performed by a non-priest. This *halakha* is in accordance with the opinion of the Rabbis; see 18b (Rambam *Sefer Avoda, Hilkhot Pesulei HaMukdashin* 11:7).

He shall bring additional flour from within his home – יָבִיא מִתּוֹךְ בֵּיתוֹ: If one's meal offering became lacking before a handful was removed from it, he should bring additional flour from his home and refill it (Rambam *Sefer Avoda, Hilkhot Pesulei HaMukdashin* 11:16).

איתיביה רבי יוחנן לרבי שמעון בן לקיש: חסר הלוג, אם עד שלא יצק – ימלאנו! תיובתא.

Rabbi Yoḥanan raised an objection to Rabbi Shimon ben Lakish, Reish Lakish, from a mishna (*Nega'im* 14:10) discussing the *log* of oil brought by a leper: In a case where **the *log* lacked**[H] a full measure, **if** it became lacking **before** the priest **poured** from it into his palm in order to place it on the right thumb and big toe of the leper, **he shall fill it.** Clearly the service vessel containing the *log* does not sanctify the oil to the extent that it can become disqualified. The Gemara notes: Indeed, this is **a conclusive refutation** of the opinion of Reish Lakish.

איתמר: שירים שחסרו בין קמיצה להקטרה – רבי יוחנן אמר: מקטיר קומץ עליהן, וריש לקיש אמר: אין מקטיר קומץ עליהן. אליבא דרבי אליעזר כולי עלמא לא פליגי, כי פליגי – אליבא דרבי יהושע.

§ **It was stated:** With regard to the **remainder** of a meal offering **that became lacking**[H] **between** the **removal of the handful and** its **burning** upon the altar, **Rabbi Yoḥanan says** that one **burns the handful on** account of such a remainder, and that the remainder is then permitted for consumption. **And Reish Lakish says** that one does **not burn the handful on** account of the remainder. The Gemara notes: **According to** the opinion **of Rabbi Eliezer, everyone agrees** that the handful is burned on account of the remainder. In other words, both *amora'im*, Rabbi Yoḥanan and Reish Lakish, concur that this is the *halakha* according to the *tanna* Rabbi Eliezer. **When they disagree,** it is concerning the *halakha* **according to** the opinion **of Rabbi Yehoshua.**

דתנן: נטמאו שיריה, נשרפו שיריה, אבדו שיריה – כמדת רבי אליעזר כשרה, כמדת רבי יהושע פסולה;

The Gemara cites the dispute in question. **As we learned** in a mishna (26a): If, after the handful was removed, **the remainder of** the meal offering **became ritually impure,** or if **the remainder of** the meal offering **was burned,** or if **the remainder of** the meal offering **was lost, according to the principle of Rabbi Eliezer,** who says that with regard to an animal offering the blood is fit for sprinkling even if there is no meat that can be eaten, the meal offering is **fit,** and the priest burns the handful. **But according to the principle of Rabbi Yehoshua,** who says that with regard to an animal offering the blood is fit for sprinkling only if there is meat that can be eaten, it is **unfit**[H] and the priest does not burn the handful, as the handful serves to render the remainder permitted.

מאן דפסל – כרבי יהושע, ומאן דמכשר – עד כאן לא אמר רבי יהושע התם אלא דלא אישתייר, אבל היכא דאישתייר – אפילו רבי יהושע מודה ליה.

The one who disqualifies the remainder of a meal offering that became lacking between the removal of the handful and its burning upon the altar, i.e., Reish Lakish, holds **in accordance with** the plain meaning of the opinion of **Rabbi Yehoshua. And the one who deems** that remainder **fit,** i.e., Rabbi Yoḥanan, maintains that when **Rabbi Yehoshua says** that the remainder is unfit, he says so **only there,** in a case **where nothing remained** from the meal offering other than the remainder. Since the handful is intended to render permitted for consumption the remainder of the meal offering, if there is no remainder at all then the handful is not burned. **But** in a case **where there remained** a portion of the remainder, Rabbi Yoḥanan maintains that **even Rabbi Yehoshua concedes to** Rabbi Eliezer that the handful is fit to be burned.

דתניא, רבי יהושע אומר: כל הזבחים שבתורה שנשתייר מהם כזית בשר או כזית חלב – זורק הדם, כחצי זית בשר כחצי זית חלב – אינו זורק את הדם.

The Gemara cites a proof for Rabbi Yoḥanan: It is clear that this is Rabbi Yehoshua's opinion, **as it is taught** in a *baraita* that **Rabbi Yehoshua says:** With regard to **any of the offerings that** are mentioned **in the Torah from which there remains** either **an olive-bulk**[HB] **of meat or an olive-bulk of fat,** the *halakha* is that the priest **sprinkles the blood** of that offering and thereby permits either the remaining meat for consumption or the remaining fat for sacrifice upon the altar. But if there remains only **half an olive-bulk of meat** and **half an olive-bulk of fat, he does not sprinkle the blood,** as the consumption or burning of anything less than an olive-bulk is not significant enough to warrant the sprinkling of the blood. The volumes of the meat and the fat do not combine to form a whole olive-bulk.

ובעולה, אפילו כחצי זית בשר וכחצי זית חלב – זורק את הדם, מפני שבעולה כולה כליל. ובמנחה, אף על פי שכולה קיימת – לא יזרוק.

The *baraita* continues: **And in** the case of **a burnt offering, even** if there remains only **half an olive-bulk of flesh and half an olive-bulk of fat, he sprinkles the blood, because in** the case of **a burnt offering it is entirely consumed,** i.e., as the flesh and fat are both burned upon the altar, there is in fact an olive-bulk of the offering that is designated for burning upon the altar. **And with regard to a meal offering, even though it** remains **entirely intact, he shall not sprinkle.**

HALAKHA

The *log* lacked – חסר הלוג: If the *log* of oil of a leper became lacking before the priest poured from it, the priest should refill it (Rambam *Sefer Korbanot, Hilkhot Meḥusrei Kappara* 5:4).

The remainder of a meal offering that became lacking – שירים שחסרו: With regard to the remainder of a meal offering that became lacking between the removal and burning of the handful, if there still remains a small amount the priest should burn the handful (Rambam *Sefer Avoda, Hilkhot Pesulei HaMukdashin* 11:20).

The remainder of the meal offering became ritually impure…it is unfit – נטמאו שיריה...פסולה: If the entire remainder of a meal offering became ritually impure or if it was completely lost after the handful was removed but before it was burned, the priest should not burn the handful. If he burned it, the offering effects acceptance. This *halakha* is in accordance with the opinion of Rabbi Yehoshua (Rambam *Sefer Avoda, Hilkhot Pesulei HaMukdashin* 11:20, and see *Kesef Mishne* there).

From which there remains an olive-bulk – שנשתייר מהם כזית: In a case where part of any offering whose blood was collected but not sprinkled upon the altar became lacking, if there remained either an olive-bulk of meat or an olive-bulk of the sacrificial portions for burning upon the altar, the priest sprinkles the blood of that offering. If there remained only half an olive-bulk of meat and half an olive-bulk of fat, he does not sprinkle the blood. With regard to a burnt offering, even if there remained only half an olive-bulk of flesh and half an olive-bulk of fat, he sprinkles the blood. If there remained less than an olive-bulk and the priest nevertheless sprinkled the blood, it does not effect acceptance even after the fact. The commentaries discuss possible reasons as to the difference between the *halakha* of a meal offering whose remainder was entirely lost, which effects acceptance after the fact, and that of a burnt offering, where if there remains less than an olive-bulk from the offering then the sprinkling of its blood does not effect acceptance even after the fact (Rambam *Sefer Avoda, Hilkhot Pesulei HaMukdashin* 1:30–31).

BACKGROUND

Olive-bulk – כזית: An olive-bulk is one of the most significant halakhic units of volume. By Torah law, the act of eating is defined as consuming one olive-bulk, and virtually every Torah law that either requires or prohibits eating pertains to this measure. The measure is defined in terms of the water displacement of a particular strain of olive, and the precise size of this measurement is not clear. One talmudic passage indicates that it is almost half an egg-bulk in size, whereas it can be inferred from another passage that it is less than one-third of an egg-bulk. The different opinions with regard to the measure of an egg-bulk range from 7 to 50 cc.

מִנְחָה מַאי עֲבִידְתָּהּ? אֲמַר רַב פַּפָּא: מִנְחַת נְסָכִים;

Parenthetically, the Gemara asks: **What is** the mention of **a meal offering doing** here, in a *baraita* that discusses slaughtered offerings? There is no sprinkling in the case of a meal offering. **Rav Pappa said:** The *baraita* is referring to **a meal offering** that accompanies the **libations**[N] brought with a slaughtered offering.

סָלְקָא דַעְתָּךְ אָמִינָא: הוֹאִיל וּבַהֲדֵי זֶבַח אָתְיָא – כִּי גּוּפֵיהּ דְּזֶבַח דָּמְיָא, קָא מַשְׁמַע לָן.

Rav Pappa elaborates: It might **enter your mind to say** that **since** such a meal offering **comes with a** slaughtered **offering, it is considered like** the **offering itself.** Accordingly, if the only part remaining from an offering is the meal offering that is brought with it, perhaps it is considered as though part of the offering itself remains, and therefore the priest may sprinkle the offering's blood on account of it. Therefore, the *baraita* **teaches us** that this is not the *halakha*. In any event, Rabbi Yehoshua states in this *baraita* that the blood of an offering is sprinkled if a minimum amount remains from it. The same should apply to the remainder of a regular meal offering.

וּמַאן דְּפָסַל? שָׁאנֵי הָכָא, דְּאָמַר קְרָא: ״וְהֵרִים הַכֹּהֵן מִן הַמִּנְחָה אֶת אַזְכָּרָתָהּ וְהִקְטִיר הַמִּזְבֵּחָה״, ״הַמִּנְחָה״ – עַד דְּאִיתָא לְכוּלָּהּ מִנְחָה לֹא יַקְטִיר.

Rabbi Yoḥanan cited this *baraita* as proof that even according to Rabbi Yehoshua, if a portion of the remainder of a meal offering remains intact then the handful may be burned on account of it. The Gemara asks: **And** concerning **the one who disqualifies** the handful when the remainder is lacking, i.e., Reish Lakish, how does he explain the opinion of Rabbi Yehoshua? The Gemara responds: Reish Lakish would claim that it **is different here,** in the case of a meal offering, **as the verse states: "And the priest shall remove from the meal offering its memorial part, and shall make it smoke upon the altar"** (Leviticus 2:9). Since it is clear that the verse is discussing a meal offering, the apparently superfluous mention of **"the meal offering"** teaches that **unless the entire meal offering is** intact, the priest **shall not burn** the handful.

וְאִידָּךְ? ״מִן הַמִּנְחָה״ – מִנְחָה שֶׁהָיְתָה כְּבָר שְׁלֵימָה בִּשְׁעַת קְמִיצָה יַקְטִיר, אַף עַל גַּב דְּהָשְׁתָּא אֵינָהּ שְׁלֵימָה.

The Gemara continues: **And the other** *amora*, Rabbi Yoḥanan, how does he interpret that verse? Rabbi Yoḥanan claims that the phrase **"from the meal offering"** is referring to **a meal offering that was already whole at the time of the removal of** its **handful,** and the verse teaches that **he shall burn** its handful **even though it is currently not whole.**

אֵיתִיבֵיהּ רַבִּי יוֹחָנָן לְרֵישׁ לָקִישׁ: עַד שֶׁלֹּא פֵּירְקָהּ נִפְרַס הַלֶּחֶם – פָּסוּל, וְאֵין מַקְטִיר עָלָיו אֶת הַבָּזִיכִין, וְאִם מִשֶּׁפֵּירְקָהּ נִפְרַס לַחְמָהּ – הַלֶּחֶם פָּסוּל וּמַקְטִיר עָלָיו אֶת הַבָּזִיכִין; וְאָמַר רַבִּי אֶלְעָזָר: לֹא פֵּירְקָהּ מַמָּשׁ, אֶלָּא כֵּיוָן שֶׁהִגִּיעַ זְמַנָּהּ לְפָרֵק וְאַף עַל פִּי שֶׁלֹּא פֵּירְקָהּ!

Rabbi Yoḥanan raised an objection to Reish Lakish from a *baraita*: If **before** the priest **detached** the arrangement of shewbread and the bowls of frankincense from upon the Table, the **bread broke** into pieces, the bread is **unfit** for consumption **and** the priest **does not burn** the frankincense contained in **the bowls on** account **of it. And if** the **bread broke after** the priest **detached it, the bread is unfit but** the priest **burns the** frankincense contained in the **bowls on** account **of it. And Rabbi Elazar says:** The *baraita* does **not** mean that the priest **actually detached** the shewbread. **Rather,** it means that **once** the **time to detach it has arrived** the frankincense contained in the bowls may be burned, **even though he has not** yet **detached it.** Just as the frankincense contained in the bowls is burned despite the broken shewbread, likewise, the handful of a meal offering should be burned even when the remainder is lacking.

NOTES

A meal offering that accompanies the libations – מִנְחַת נְסָכִים: These meal offerings are prescribed by the Torah (see Numbers 15:1–15) to accompany the sacrifice of burnt offerings, peace offerings, and the sin offering and guilt offering of a leper. They are the only meal offerings that are not brought as independent offerings but in addition to slaughtered offerings. Furthermore, whereas other meal offerings consist of flour, oil, and frankincense, these meal offerings consist only of flour and oil. Lastly, in contrast to other meal offerings, these meal offerings are burned in their entirety upon the altar and no remainder is left for the priests.

אָמַר לֵיהּ: הָא מַנִּי? רַבִּי אֱלִיעֶזֶר הִיא. אֲמַר לֵיהּ: אֲנָא אָמֵינָא לָךְ מִשְׁנָה שְׁלֵימָה, וְאָמְרַתְּ לִי אַתְּ רַבִּי אֱלִיעֶזֶר?

Reish Lakish **said to** Rabbi Yoḥanan in response: In accordance with **whose** opinion **is this? It is** in accordance with the opinion of **Rabbi Eliezer,** who permits the burning of a handful even when the remainder has been entirely destroyed. And I hold in accordance with the opinion of Rabbi Yehoshua. Rabbi Yoḥanan **said to him: I am stating a complete *halakha* to you,** i.e., a *baraita* of an unspecified opinion, **and you say to me** that this *baraita* is in accordance with the opinion of **Rabbi Eliezer** alone?

אִי רַבִּי אֱלִיעֶזֶר, מַאי אִירְיָא נִפְרַס? אֲפִילּוּ שָׂרוּף וְאָבוּד נַמִּי מַכְשַׁר! אִישְׁתִּיק.

Rabbi Yoḥanan added: And furthermore, **if** the *baraita* is in accordance with the opinion of only **Rabbi Eliezer,** then **why** does the *baraita* mention **specifically** an instance where the bread **broke?** According to Rabbi Eliezer, **even** if the bread was **burned or lost** entirely, **he deems** the frankincense contained in the bowls **fit** for burning **as well.** The Gemara notes: Reish Lakish **was silent** and did not respond to the objections of Rabbi Yoḥanan.

וְאַמַּאי שָׁתַק? לֵימָא לֵיהּ: צִבּוּר שָׁאנֵי, הוֹאִיל וְאִישְׁתְּרֵי טוּמְאָה לְגַבַּיְיהוּ, אִישְׁתְּרֵי נַמִּי חֲסֵרוֹת! אָמַר רַב אַדָּא בַּר אַהֲבָה, זֹאת אוֹמֶרֶת: הַחִסָּרוֹן כְּבַעַל מוּם דָּמֵי, וְאֵין בַּעַל מוּם בְּצִבּוּר.

The Gemara asks: **But why was** Reish Lakish **silent? Let him say to** Rabbi Yoḥanan that one cannot cite a proof from a *baraita* that discusses the shewbread, a communal offering, because offerings of the **community are different, since ritual impurity was permitted for them,** i.e., communal offerings may be sacrificed even in a state of ritual impurity. Therefore, it **was also permitted** to sacrifice them when they **are lacking. Rav Adda bar Ahava said:** The fact **that** Reish Lakish did not respond in **this** manner **is to say** that a meal offering that is **lacking** in measure **is considered like a blemished** animal, not merely like an impure offering, **and there is no** instance of **a blemished** animal being permitted for use as an offering, even **in** the case of **a communal** offering.

יָתֵיב רַב פַּפָּא וְקָאָמַר לְהָא שְׁמַעְתָּא. אֲמַר לֵיהּ רַב יוֹסֵף בַּר שְׁמַעְיָה לְרַב פַּפָּא: מִי לָא עָסְקִינַן דְּרַבִּי יוֹחָנָן וְרֵישׁ לָקִישׁ בְּמִנְחַת הָעוֹמֶר דְּצִיבּוּר הִיא? וּפְלִיגִי.

The Gemara relates that **Rav Pappa** was once **sitting and saying this *halakha*,** and he noted that Reish Lakish was silent and did not respond to Rabbi Yoḥanan's objections by differentiating between a communal offering and that of an individual, and that Rav Adda bar Ahava derived from Reish Lakish's silence that a lack in the measure of a meal offering is tantamount to a blemish. **Rav Yosef bar Shemaya said to Rav Pappa: Are we not dealing** with a disagreement **that** exists between **Rabbi Yoḥanan and Reish Lakish** even **in** the case of **the *omer* meal offering, which is a communal** offering? **And** even so, they **disagree.** Accordingly, Reish Lakish could not have responded to the objections of Rabbi Yoḥanan by distinguishing between a communal and an individual offering, and therefore one cannot derive from his silence that a meal offering lacking in its measure is like a blemished animal.

אָמַר רַב מַלְכִּיּוּ, תָּנָא חֲדָא: ״מִסָּלְתָּהּ״ – שֶׁאִם חָסְרָה כׇּל שֶׁהוּא פְּסוּלָה, ״מִשַּׁמְנָהּ״ – שֶׁאִם חָסְרָה כׇּל שֶׁהוּא פָּסוּל;

The Gemara further discusses the disagreement between Rabbi Yoḥanan and Reish Lakish. **Rav Malkiyu says** that **one *baraita* taught:** The verse states: "And he shall remove… **of its fine flour"** (Leviticus 2:2). This indicates **that if** the meal offering **lacks any amount** of its flour, it is **disqualified** and the priest may not remove a handful from it. Similarly, the term: **"Of its oil"** (Leviticus 2:2), teaches **that if** the meal offering **lacks any amount** of its oil, it is **disqualified.**

וְתַנְיָא אִידָּךְ: ״וְהַנּוֹתֶרֶת מִן הַמִּנְחָה״ – פְּרָט לְמִנְחָה שֶׁחָסְרָה הִיא וְשֶׁחָסַר קוּמְצָהּ וְשֶׁלֹּא הִקְטִיר מִלְּבוֹנָתָהּ כְּלוּם;

And it is taught in **another *baraita*** that the verse that states: **"But that which is left of the meal offering** shall be Aaron's and his sons'" (Leviticus 2:3), teaches that the remainder of the meal offering is given to the priests only if there was initially a whole meal offering, **to the exclusion of a meal offering that was lacking, or whose handful was lacking, or from which** the priest **did not burn any frankincense.** In such cases, the meal offering is disqualified and its remainder may not be consumed by the priests.

תְּרֵי קְרָאֵי בַּחֲסֵרוֹת לָמָּה לִי? לָאו חַד לְמִנְחָה שֶׁחָסְרָה קוֹדֶם קְמִיצָה, וְחַד לְשִׁירַיִם שֶׁחָסְרוּ בֵּין קְמִיצָה לְהַקְטָרָה?

Rav Malkiyu asks: **Why do I** need **two verses to** disqualify meal offerings that are **lacking?** Is it **not** correct to say that **one** verse is referring **to a meal offering that became lacking before the removal of the handful,** i.e., that one may not refill it, **and one** verse is referring **to the remainder** of a meal offering **that became lacking between the removal of the handful and** its **burning** upon the altar, and it teaches that one may not burn a handful on account of such a remainder?

וּתְיוּבְתָּא דְּרַבִּי יוֹחָנָן בִּתְרְוַיְיהוּ!

Rav Malkiyu concludes: **And** if so, then this is **a conclusive refutation of** the opinion of **Rabbi Yoḥanan in both** instances where he disagrees with Reish Lakish, i.e., in the case of a meal offering that became lacking before the removal of the handful, as Rabbi Yoḥanan holds that one may refill it, and in the case of the remainder that became lacking between the removal of the handful and its burning, as he holds that the handful may be burned.

לָא, חַד לְמִנְחָה שֶׁחָסְרָה קוֹדֶם קְמִיצָה, דְּאִי מֵבִיא מִבֵּיתוֹ וִימַלְּאֶנָּה – אִין, וְאִי לָא – לָא; וְחַד לְשִׁירַיִם שֶׁחָסְרוּ בֵּין קְמִיצָה לְהַקְטָרָה, דְּאַף עַל גַּב דְּמַקְטִיר קוֹמֶץ עֲלֵיהֶן, אוֹתָן שִׁירַיִם אֲסוּרִים לַאֲכִילָה.

The Gemara rejects this suggestion: **No; one** verse is indeed referring **to a meal offering that became lacking before the removal of the handful,** but it is not teaching that this meal offering is disqualified. Rather, this verse indicates **that if he brings** flour **from his home and fills it** so that the meal offering is no longer lacking, then **yes,** it is fit, **but if** he does **not** bring more flour, it is **not** fit. **And one** verse is indeed referring **to** the **remainder** of a meal offering **that became lacking between the removal of the handful and** its **burning** upon the altar; nevertheless, it does not indicate that the handful may not be burned. Rather, it teaches **that even though** the priest **burns** the **handful on** account of such a remainder, **that remainder is prohibited**[H] **for consumption.**

דְּאִיבַּעְיָא לְהוּ: לְדִבְרֵי הָאוֹמֵר שִׁירַיִם שֶׁחָסְרוּ בֵּין קְמִיצָה לְהַקְטָרָה מַקְטִיר קוֹמֶץ עֲלֵיהֶן, אוֹתָן שִׁירַיִם מָה הֵן בַּאֲכִילָה?

The Gemara continues: This is indeed the appropriate explanation of the verses, **as a dilemma was raised before** the Sages: According **to the statement of** the one **who says that** in a case where the **remainder** of a meal offering **became lacking between the removal of the handful and** its **burning** upon the altar, the priest **burns** the **handful on** account of this remainder, concerning the **remainder itself, what** is its status **with regard to consumption,** i.e., may the remainder be eaten?

אָמַר זְעֵירִי, אָמַר קְרָא: ״וְהַנּוֹתֶרֶת״ – וְלֹא הַנּוֹתֶרֶת מִן הַנּוֹתֶרֶת; וְרַבִּי יַנַּאי אָמַר: ״מֵהַמִּנְחָה״ – מִנְחָה שֶׁהָיְתָה כְּבָר.

Ze'eiri said that **the verse states: "But that which is left** of the meal offering shall be Aaron's and his sons'," which teaches that the priests may consume the remainder of a meal offering, **but not the remainder of the remainder,** i.e., if the remainder became lacking before the handful was burned, the remaining part of the remainder may not be consumed. Alternatively, **Rabbi Yannai says** that **"of the meal offering** shall be Aaron's and his sons'" indicates that the priests may consume only the remainder of **a meal offering that was previously** whole[N] when the handful was burned, not the remainder of the remainder.

״קָמַץ בִּשְׂמֹאל״. מְנָא הָנֵי מִילֵּי? אָמַר רַבִּי זֵירָא, דְּאָמַר קְרָא: ״וַיַּקְרֵב אֶת הַמִּנְחָה וַיְמַלֵּא כַפּוֹ מִמֶּנָּה״, כַּף זֶה אֵינִי יוֹדֵעַ מַהוּ, כְּשֶׁהוּא אוֹמֵר: ״וְלָקַח הַכֹּהֵן מִלּוֹג הַשָּׁמֶן וְיָצַק עַל כַּף הַכֹּהֵן הַשְּׂמָאלִית״ – כָּאן שְׂמָאלִית, הָא כָּל מָקוֹם שֶׁנֶּאֱמַר כַּף אֵינוֹ אֶלָּא יָמִין.

§ The mishna teaches: If the priest **removed the handful with** his **left** hand the meal offering is unfit. The Gemara asks: **From where are these matters** derived? **Rabbi Zeira said** that it is derived from **that** which **the verse states: "And the meal offering was presented; and he filled his hand from it"** (Leviticus 9:17). Rabbi Zeira explains: **This hand, I do not know what it is,** i.e., the left hand or the right. **When** the verse **states** with regard to the atonement of a leper: **"And the priest shall take of the *log* of oil, and pour it into the palm of his own left hand"** (Leviticus 14:15), it mentions the left hand. One can therefore derive that **here,** where the verse specifies, the priest must use his **left** hand, whereas in **any place where it is stated** in a verse **"hand"** without specification, it is referring **only** to the **right** hand.

וְהָא מִיבְּעֵי לֵיהּ לְגוּפֵיהּ! שְׂמָאלִית אַחֲרִינָא כְּתִיב.

The Gemara asks: **But** how can this conclusion be derived from the verse discussing the atonement of a leper? This verse **is necessary for itself,** i.e., to teach that the oil must be poured on the priest's left hand, not his right. The Gemara answers that **another** mention of the **left** hand **is written** in the same passage (see Leviticus 14:16). From this additional mention of the left hand it may be derived that any unspecified reference to a hand is referring to the right hand.

וְאֵימָא: אֵין מִיעוּט אַחַר מִיעוּט אֶלָּא לְרַבּוֹת! שְׂמָאלִית אַחֲרִינָא כְּתִיב, כָּאן שְׂמָאלִית וְאֵין אַחֵר שְׂמָאלִית.

The Gemara challenges: **But say** that according to the hermeneutical principle that one **restriction after** another **restriction** serves **only to amplify,** it should be inferred from the additional specification of the left hand that the oil may be poured onto the priest's right hand. The Gemara responds: Yet **another** specification of the **left** hand **is written** in that passage (see Leviticus 14:26). Accordingly, the hermeneutical principle that one restriction after another serves only to amplify does not apply. Instead, the verse indicates that **here** the **left** hand is required, **and there is no other** instance where the Torah requires the **left** hand.

HALAKHA

That remainder is prohibited – אוֹתָן שִׁירַיִם אֲסוּרִים: In a case where the priest removed the handful from a meal offering and the remainder of the meal offering became ritually impure, was burned, became lost, or left the walls of the Temple courtyard, then if at least a small portion of the remainder was still intact and valid, the priest burns the handful but the remainder is prohibited for consumption. The *halakha* is in accordance with the opinion of Rabbi Yoḥanan (Rambam *Sefer Avoda, Hilkhot Pesulei HaMukdashin* 11:20).

NOTES

Rabbi Yannai says that "of the meal offering" indicates that the priests may consume only the remainder of a meal offering that was previously whole – רַבִּי יַנַּאי אָמַר מֵהַמִּנְחָה מִנְחָה שֶׁהָיְתָה כְּבָר: The commentary on the Gemara follows the opinion that there is no halakhic disagreement between Ze'eiri and Rabbi Yannai. Rather, they disagree only with regard to the source of this *halakha* (Rashi in his second interpretation; Rabbeinu Gershom Meor HaGola). According to Rashi's first interpretation, Rabbi Yannai does disagree with Ze'eiri, as he derives from the verse that provided that the meal offering was whole when the handful was removed from it, the handful is burned and the remainder may be consumed by the priests even if it later became lacking.

NOTES

Four mentions of the left hand are written, two with regard to a poor leper and two with regard to a wealthy one – אַרְבָּעָה שְׂמָאלִית כְּתִיבִי, תְּרֵי בְּעָנִי וּתְרֵי בְּעָשִׁיר: Although there are differences between the offerings brought by a wealthy leper and those brought by a poor one, these differences concern only the burnt offering and the sin offering. With regard to the lamb guilt offering and the *log* of oil through which the leper is purified, there is no difference between a wealthy and a poor leper. Nevertheless, the Torah repeats the details of the purification process for each of them (see Leviticus, chapter 14).

It should be noted that there are various explanations of the precise manner in which Rabbi Zeira interprets these four specifications (see Rashi and commentary attributed to Rashba).

וְאֵימָא: אַדְּרַבָּה, מָה כָּאן שְׂמָאלִית – אַף בְּעָלְמָא נַמִי שְׂמָאלִית! אַרְבָּעָה שְׂמָאלִית כְּתִיבִי, תְּרֵי בְּעָנִי וּתְרֵי בְּעָשִׁיר.

The Gemara challenges: **But** one can **say** that **on the contrary, just as here** the **left** hand is required, **so too generally,** the **left** hand is required **as well.** The Gemara responds: **Four** mentions of the **left** hand **are written** in the passage, **two with regard to a poor** leper (Leviticus 14:26–27), **and two with regard to a wealthy** one (Leviticus 14:15–16).[N] Accordingly, three of the specifications serve to indicate that the oil may be poured only onto the left hand, while the additional mention serves to restrict the use of the left hand to the case of a leper alone.

אֲמַר לֵיהּ רַבִּי יִרְמְיָה לְרַבִּי זֵירָא: ״עַל בֹּהֶן יָדוֹ הַיְמָנִית וְעַל בֹּהֶן רַגְלוֹ הַיְמָנִית״ דִּכְתִיב בְּשֶׁמֶן דִּמְצוֹרָע עָשִׁיר לָמָּה לִי?

Rabbi Yirmeya said to Rabbi Zeira: According to your opinion, one interprets homiletically the additional specifications in the passage discussing the purification of a leper. If so, there is another apparently superfluous verse: **"Upon the thumb of his right hand, and upon the big toe of his right foot"** (Leviticus 14:17), **which is written with regard to** the placement of the **oil** upon the right thumb and big toe **of a wealthy leper. Why do I** need the verse to specify that the oil is placed on the leper's right thumb and big toe?

Perek **I**
Daf **10** Amud **a**

דְּהָא כְּתַב: ״עַל דַּם הָאָשָׁם״! חַד לְהַכְשִׁיר צְדָדִין, וְחַד לִפְסוֹל צִידֵּי צְדָדִין.

After all, a verse already indicates that the oil must be placed on the right thumb and big toe, **as** it is **written: "Upon the blood of the guilt offering"** (Leviticus 14:17). Since the Torah has already specified that the blood is placed upon the right thumb and big toe (Leviticus 14:14), it is clear that the oil is placed there as well. Similarly, why must the verse specify with regard to a poor leper that the oil is placed on the right thumb and big toe? Isn't already clear from the verse where the oil must be placed, as it states: "Upon the place of the blood of the guilt offering" (Leviticus 14:28)? The Gemara responds: **One** specification, stated with regard to a wealthy leper, serves **to permit** the placement of the oil on the **sides** of the thumb and sides of the big toe in addition to the nail side of the thumb and big toe, **and one,** stated with regard to a poor leper, serves **to disqualify the sides of sides,** i.e., their undersides.

״עַל דַּם הָאָשָׁם״, ״עַל מְקוֹם דַּם הָאָשָׁם״ לְמַאי אָתוּ?

The Gemara inquires with regard to the verse: **"Upon the blood of the guilt offering"** (Leviticus 14:17), stated with regard to the purification of a wealthy leper, and the verse: **"Upon the place of the blood of the guilt offering"** (Leviticus 14:28), stated with regard to the purification of a poor leper. **For what** purpose **do they come,**[N] i.e., why are both verses necessary?

הָנֵי צְרִיכִי, אִי כְּתַב רַחֲמָנָא ״עַל דַּם הָאָשָׁם״, הֲוָה אָמֵינָא: אִיתֵיהּ – אִין, נִתְקַנֵּחַ – לָא, כְּתַב רַחֲמָנָא: ״עַל מְקוֹם״;

The Gemara responds: **These** verses **are necessary, because if the Merciful One had written** only: **"Upon the blood of the guilt offering," I would say:** If the blood **is** still on the right thumb and big toe of the leper, **yes,** the priest places the oil upon the blood. But if it **was wiped** from there, he does **not** place the oil. Therefore, **the Merciful One writes: "Upon the place** of the blood of the guilt offering," indicating that the oil is placed upon the location of the blood, not necessarily upon the blood itself.

NOTES

For what purpose do they come – לְמַאי אָתוּ: Rashi explains that the Gemara is questioning the need for both verses, as the phrase "upon the blood of the guilt offering" already indicates that the oil must be placed upon the blood rather than beside the blood. Apparently the version of the Gemara that Rashi possessed read: Why do I need, as opposed to: For what purpose do they come.

Alternatively, the Gemara's question focuses on the difference in terminology between the verses: For what purpose do they differ? Either both verses should state: Upon the blood of the guilt offering, or they should both state: Upon the place of the blood of the guilt offering (*Tosafot*).

וְאִי כָּתַב רַחֲמָנָא "עַל מְקוֹם", הֲוָה אָמִינָא: דַּוְקָא נִתְקַנֵּחַ, אֲבָל אִיתֵיהּ – אֵימָא הָוֵי חֲצִיצָה, קָא מַשְׁמַע לָן: "עַל דַּם הָאָשָׁם".

And conversely, **if the Merciful One had written** only: **"Upon the place** of the blood of the guilt offering," **I would say:** The oil is placed on his right thumb and big toe **specifically** when the blood **was wiped** from there. **But** if the blood **is** still there, I will **say** that the blood **is an interposition** between the oil and the thumb or toe. Therefore, the verse **teaches us** that the oil is placed **"upon the blood of the guilt offering,"** and the blood is not considered an interposition.

אֲמַר רָבָא: מֵאַחַר דִּכְתִיב "עַל דַּם הָאָשָׁם" וְ"עַל מְקוֹם הָאָשָׁם", וּכְתִיבָא יְמָנִית בַּדָּם, "עַל בֹּהֶן יָדוֹ הַיְמָנִית וְעַל בֹּהֶן רַגְלוֹ הַיְמָנִית", וּכְתִיבִי בְּשֶׁמֶן דִּמְצוֹרָע עָשִׁיר וְעָנִי, לָמָּה לִי?

Rava said: Since it is written that the priest places the oil **"upon the blood of the guilt offering,"** and: **"Upon the place of** the blood of **the guilt offering," and it is** also **written** with regard to a wealthy leper (see Leviticus 14:14) and a poor one (see Leviticus 14:25) that the **right** hand and foot are required **for** the placement of **the blood,** as the verses state: **"Upon the thumb of his right hand, and upon the big toe of his right foot," and** this **is** also **written with regard to** the **oil of a wealthy leper** (see Leviticus 14:17) **and a poor** one (see Leviticus 14:28), one can ask: **Why do I** need all of these verses?

אֶלָּא אֲמַר רָבָא: "יָד" "יָד" לִקְמִיצָה,

Rather, Rava said: The verses that specify that the oil must be placed on the right thumb and big toe do not teach a *halakha* with regard to a leper, as it is clear that the oil must be placed on the right thumb and big toe, as it states: "Upon the place of the blood of the guilt offering." Rather, these verses are the source of verbal analogies for other *halakhot*. When the verse states with regard to a wealthy leper: "Of his right hand" (Leviticus 14:17), this teaches a verbal analogy between the term **"hand"** written here and **"hand"** written **with regard to the removal of a handful,** as the verse states about the removal of a handful: "And he filled his hand from it" (Leviticus 9:17). The verbal analogy teaches that the removal of the handful must also be performed with the right hand.

"רֶגֶל" "רֶגֶל" לַחֲלִיצָה,

Similarly, when the verse states: "Of his right foot" (Leviticus 14:17), with regard to a wealthy leper, this teaches a verbal analogy between the term **"foot"** written here and **"foot"** written **with regard to the ritual through which the *yavam*, a man whose married brother died childless, frees his brother's widow, the *yevama*, of her levirate bonds [*ḥalitza*],** as the verse states with regard to *ḥalitza*: "And remove his shoe from upon his foot" (Deuteronomy 25:9). The verbal analogy teaches that the shoe is removed from his right foot.

"אוֹזֶן" "אוֹזֶן" לִרְצִיעָה.

Additionally, when the verse states: "Upon the tip of the right ear of him that is to be cleansed" (Leviticus 14:17), with regard to a wealthy leper, this teaches a verbal analogy between the term **"ear"** written here and **"ear"** written **with regard to** the **piercing** of a Hebrew slave's ear with an awl, as the verse states: "And his master shall bore his ear through with an awl" (Exodus 21:6). The verbal analogy teaches that the slave's right ear is pierced.

שְׂמָאלִית (הֶעָנִי) לְמַאי אֲתָא? אֲמַר רַב שִׁישָׁא בְּרֵיהּ דְּרַב אִידִי: לִיפְסוֹל יָמִין דְּכֹהֵן בִּמְצוֹרָע, שֶׁלֹּא תֹּאמַר: וּמַה בְּמָקוֹם שֶׁלֹּא נִתְרַבְּתָה שְׂמֹאל – נִתְרַבְּתָה יָמִין, בְּמָקוֹם שֶׁנִּתְרַבְּתָה שְׂמֹאל – אֵינוֹ דִּין שֶׁנִּתְרַבְּתָה יָמִין?

The Gemara asks: With regard to the additional mention of the **left** hand in the verse dealing **with the poor** leper, **for what** purpose **does** it **come?**[N] **Rav Sheisha, son of Rav Idi, said:** It comes **to disqualify** the **right** hand **of a priest for** the purification of **a leper.** This teaches **that you should not say: And if in a place where** the **left** side **is not included,** as sacrificial rites in general are disqualified when performed with the left hand, the **right** hand **is included,** i.e., those rites must be performed with the right hand, then **in a place where** the **left** hand **is included,** in the case of a leper, **isn't it logical that** the **right** hand should also be **included?** Therefore, the verse repeats that the oil is poured into the priest's left hand, in order to disqualify the right hand.

וְאִידָךְ שְׂמָאלִית, וְיָד וְרֶגֶל יְמָנִית דְּעָנִי, לְמַאי אֲתָא? לְכִדְתָנָא דְּבֵי רַבִּי יִשְׁמָעֵאל: כָּל פָּרָשָׁה שֶׁנֶּאֶמְרָה וְנִשְׁנֵית, לֹא נִשְׁנֵית אֶלָּא בִּשְׁבִיל דָּבָר שֶׁנִּתְחַדֵּשׁ בָּהּ.

The Gemara asks: **And** concerning **the other** verses that specify the **left** hand of a poor leper (Leviticus 14:26–27) as well as the **right hand and foot of a poor** leper (Leviticus 14:25–28), **for what** purpose do they **come?** The Gemara responds: These verses come **for that which the school of Rabbi Yishmael taught: Any passage that was stated** in the Torah **and was** then **repeated, was repeated only for** the sake of **a matter that was introduced** for the first time **in** the repeated passage. That is, sometimes the Torah repeats an entire passage just to teach a single new detail. In this case, the verses that discuss the purification of a poor leper were repeated only for the sake of the differences in the offerings between a wealthy leper and a poor one. No additional *halakha* should be derived from them.

NOTES

The left hand in the verse dealing with the poor leper, for what purpose does it come – שְׂמָאלִית (הֶעָנִי) לְמַאי אֲתָא: All of the commentaries agree that the text of the Gemara is corrupt, as it is not discussing a verse that deals with the poor leper; rather, it is discussing the second mention of the left hand in the verses discussing a wealthy leper. Furthermore, it cannot be referring to the first mention of the left hand in the case of a wealthy leper, as that verse is necessary to teach that *halakha* itself, that the oil is in fact poured into the priest's left hand.

HALAKHA

The foot of the right side, etc. – **הָרֶגֶל שֶׁל יָמִין וכו׳**: When the priests would bring up the limbs of a burnt offering to the altar, one priest would carry the head and the right leg of the offering, holding the head in his right hand and the leg in his left. This teaches that any action that is not indispensable to the atonement may be performed with the left hand (Rambam *Sefer Avoda*, *Hilkhot Ma'aseh HaKorbanot* 6:11; see also *Hilkhot Avodat Yom HaKippurim* 4:1 and Mahari Kurkus there).

If one collected the blood with his left hand it is disqualified – **קִבֵּל בִּשְׂמֹאל פָּסַל**: Any sacrificial rite performed in the Temple must be performed with the right hand. If a priest used his left hand to perform a rite, it is not valid (Rambam *Sefer Avoda*, *Hilkhot Biat HaMikdash* 5:18; see also *Hilkhot Pesulei HaMukdashin* 2:24).

אָמַר רַבָּה בַּר בַּר חָנָה אָמַר רַבִּי שִׁמְעוֹן בֶּן לָקִישׁ: כׇּל מָקוֹם שֶׁנֶּאֶמְרָה אֶצְבַּע וּכְהוּנָּה – אֵינָהּ אֶלָּא יָמִין.

§ **Rabba bar bar Ḥana says** that **Rabbi Shimon ben Lakish says: Any place** in the Torah **in which** it **is stated** that an action is performed with **a finger or** by the **priesthood,** i.e., that one uses his finger to perform the action or that a priest performs it, this teaches that it is performed **only** with the **right** hand.

קָא סָלְקָא דַּעְתִּין: אֶצְבַּע וּכְהוּנָּה בָּעֵינַן, כְּדִכְתִיב: ״וְלָקַח הַכֹּהֵן מִדַּם הַחַטָּאת בְּאֶצְבָּעוֹ״, וְגָמַר מִמְּצוֹרָע, דִּכְתִיב: ״וְטָבַל הַכֹּהֵן אֶת אֶצְבָּעוֹ הַיְמָנִית״; הֲרֵי קְמִיצָה דְּלָא כְּתִיבָא בָּהּ אֶלָּא כְּהוּנָּה, וּתְנַן: קָמַץ בִּשְׂמֹאל פָּסוּל!

The Gemara comments: It might **enter our mind** to say that this means that **we require both a finger and the priesthood** to be stated together in the verse in order to mandate use of the right hand, e.g., **as it is written: "And the priest shall take of the blood of the sin offering with his finger"** (Leviticus 4:25). **And** the fact that this verse is referring to a finger from his right hand **is derived from a leper, as it is written: "And the priest shall dip his right finger"** (Leviticus 14:16). This cannot be correct, **as** there is the verse that addresses **the removal of a handful** from a meal offering, **in which only** the **priesthood is written, and** yet **we learned** in a mishna (6a): If the priest **removed the handful with** his **left** hand the meal offering is **unfit.**

אֲמַר רָבָא: אוֹ אֶצְבַּע אוֹ כְּהוּנָּה.

Therefore, **Rava said:** This statement means that if the verse mentions **either a finger or** the **priesthood,** only the right hand may be used.

אֲמַר לֵיהּ אַבָּיֵי: הֲרֵי הוֹלָכַת אֵבָרִים לַכֶּבֶשׁ דִּכְתִיב בְּהוּ כְּהוּנָּה, דִּכְתִיב: ״וְהִקְרִיב הַכֹּהֵן אֶת הַכֹּל הַמִּזְבֵּחָה״, וְאָמַר מָר: זוֹ הוֹלָכַת אֵבָרִים לַכֶּבֶשׁ; וּתְנַן: הָרֶגֶל שֶׁל יָמִין בִּשְׂמֹאל וּבֵית עוֹרָהּ לַחוּץ!

Abaye said to Rava: But this is contradicted by the verse discussing **the conveyance of** the **limbs** of the daily burnt offering **to the ramp** of the altar, **as priesthood is written with regard to it, as it is written: "And the priest shall sacrifice the whole** and make it smoke **upon the altar"** (Leviticus 1:13), **and the Master said** that **this** verse is referring to **the conveyance of** the **limbs to the ramp. And** yet **we learned** in a mishna (*Tamid* 31b): When the priest conveys the limbs to the ramp, **the foot of** the **right** side[H] of the offering is carried **in** the **left** hand of the priest, **and the place of its skin,** i.e., the side of the limb covered in skin, is held facing **outward.** Clearly, use of the left hand does not disqualify the conveyance of the limbs.

כִּי אָמְרִינַן אוֹ אֶצְבַּע אוֹ כְּהוּנָּה – בְּדָבָר הַמְעַכֵּב כַּפָּרָה.

The Gemara responds: **When we say** that if the verse states **either finger or priesthood** then the left hand is disqualified, this is only **with regard to a matter that precludes atonement,** i.e., a rite whose performance is indispensable to the atonement, similar to the sprinkling of the oil on the leper (see Leviticus 14:16). The conveyance of the limbs, by contrast, is not indispensable to atonement.

וַהֲרֵי קַבָּלָה דָּבָר הַמְעַכֵּב כַּפָּרָה הוּא, וְכָתַב בָּהּ כְּהוּנָּה, דִּכְתִיב: ״וְהִקְרִיבוּ בְּנֵי אַהֲרֹן הַכֹּהֲנִים אֶת הַדָּם״ – זוֹ קַבָּלַת הַדָּם; וּתְנַן: קִבֵּל בִּשְׂמֹאל – פָּסַל, וְרַבִּי שִׁמְעוֹן מַכְשִׁיר!

The Gemara asks: **But** isn't there the **collection** of the blood in a service vessel, **which is a matter indispensable to atonement, and about which priesthood is written? As it is written: "And Aaron's sons, the priests, shall present the blood"** (Leviticus 1:5), and **this** is referring to **the collection of the blood. And** yet **we learned** in a mishna (*Zevaḥim* 15b): If **one collected** the blood **with** his **left** hand, the blood is **disqualified**[H] for offering, **and Rabbi Shimon deems** it **fit,** despite the fact that priesthood is mentioned in the verse.

לְרַבִּי שִׁמְעוֹן קָאָמְרַתְּ? רַבִּי שִׁמְעוֹן תַּרְתֵּי בָּעֵי.

The Gemara responds: **You are saying** that there is a difficulty **according to** the opinion of **Rabbi Shimon? Rabbi Shimon requires** that **both** matters appear in the verse, i.e., both finger and priesthood.

וּמִי בָּעֵי רַבִּי שִׁמְעוֹן תַּרְתֵּי? וְהָתַנְיָא, רַבִּי שִׁמְעוֹן אוֹמֵר: כׇּל מָקוֹם שֶׁנֶּאֶמְרָה יָד – אֵינָהּ אֶלָּא יָמִין, אֶצְבַּע – אֵינָהּ אֶלָּא יָמִין! אֶצְבַּע לָא בָּעֲיָא כְּהוּנָּה, כְּהוּנָּה בָּעֲיָא אֶצְבַּע.

The Gemara asks: **And does Rabbi Shimon** really **require both? But isn't it taught** in a *baraita*: **Rabbi Shimon says:** In **any place** in the Torah in **which** the word **hand is stated,** the verse **is** referring **only** to the **right** hand, and whenever a verse mentions the word **finger,** it **is** referring **only** to a finger of the **right** hand? The Gemara responds: According to Rabbi Shimon, if the verse mentions only the word **finger,** it **does not require** a mention of the **priesthood** as well for the limitation to apply. But if the verse mentions only the **priesthood,** it **requires** mention of the term **finger** for the limitation to apply.

אלא כהן למה לי? בכהונו.

The Gemara asks: **But** according to Rabbi Shimon, if the mention of the priesthood alone does not suffice to disqualify the right hand, then **why do I** need the superfluous reference to **a priest** with regard to the collection of the blood? After all, the verse already states that the collection must be performed by the sons of Aaron. The Gemara responds: The additional mention of the priesthood indicates that a priest must perform the collection of the blood **in his priestly state,** i.e., while wearing the priestly vestments.

והרי זריקה דלא כתב ביה אלא כהונה, ותנן: זרק בשמאל – פסול, ולא פליג רבי שמעון! אמר אביי: פליג בברייתא, דתניא: קבל בשמאל – פסול, ורבי שמעון מכשיר; זרק בשמאל – פסול, ורבי שמעון מכשיר.

The Gemara asks: But isn't there the **sprinkling** of the blood, **concerning which only** the **priesthood is written** in the verse, **and we learned:** If **one sprinkled** the blood **with** his **left** hand it is **disqualified; and Rabbi Shimon does not disagree** with this ruling, indicating that Rabbi Shimon holds that a mention of the priesthood does not require a mention of the word finger? **Abaye says: He disagrees** with this ruling **in a *baraita*,**[B] **as it is taught** in a *baraita*: If **one collected** the blood **with** his **left** hand it is **disqualified, and Rabbi Shimon deems** it **fit.** Additionally, if **one sprinkled** the blood **with** his **left** hand it is **disqualified, and Rabbi Shimon deems** it **fit.**

ואלא הא דאמר רבא: "יד" "יד" לקמיצה, למה לי? מכהונה נפקא!

The Gemara asks: **But that which Rava says** with regard to the superfluous terms in the passage discussing a leper: One derives a verbal analogy between the word **"hand"** written in that passage and the word **"hand"** written **with regard to the removal of a handful** from a meal offering, to indicate that the latter must also be performed with the right hand, **why do I** need this verbal analogy? One can **derive** that the handful must be removed with the right hand **from** the verse's mention of the **priesthood,** as it is stated: "And the priest shall remove his handful" (Leviticus 5:12).

חד לקומץ, וחד לקידוש קומץ.

The Gemara responds: Both derivations are necessary, **one for** the removal of the **handful** from a meal offering, **and one for the sanctification of** the **handful,** i.e., placing it into a second service vessel. Both must be performed with the right hand.

לרבי שמעון דלא בעי קידוש קומץ, ולמאן דאמר נמי דבעי קידוש קומץ לרבי שמעון, ובשמאל אכשורי מכשר, "יד" "יד" דרבא למה לי?

The Gemara asks: **And according to Rabbi Shimon, who does not require sanctification of** the **handful, or according to the one who says that Rabbi Shimon also requires the sanctification of** the **handful but** that **he deems** the sanctification **fit** when performed **with the left** hand (see 26a), **why do I** need the verbal analogy **of** Rava between **"hand"** and **"hand"?**

אי לקמיצה גופה אליבא דרבי שמעון – מדרבי יהודה בריה דרבי חייא נפקא, דאמר רבי יהודה בריה דרבי חייא: מאי טעמא דרבי שמעון? דאמר קרא: "קדש קדשים היא כחטאת וכאשם",

If one suggests that it is necessary **to** indicate that the **removal of the handful itself** must be performed with the right hand, this cannot be, since this is **derived from** the verse cited by **Rabbi Yehuda, son of Rabbi Ḥiyya.**[P] **As Rabbi Yehuda, son of Rabbi Ḥiyya, says: What is the reason that Rabbi Shimon** does not require that the handful be sanctified in a service vessel? **As the verse states** with regard to the meal offering: **"It is most holy, as the sin offering, and as the guilt offering"** (Leviticus 6:10).

BACKGROUND

Baraita – **ברייתא:** Literally, the word *baraita* means external, and it is used to refer to tannaitic material that was not included in the final compilation of the Mishna. When Rabbi Yehuda HaNasi redacted the canon of tannaitic material it was necessary to exclude much of it from the Mishna. The *baraitot*, some of which comprise other collections, contain variant texts and other important material.

PERSONALITIES

Rabbi Yehuda son of Rabbi Ḥiyya – רבי יהודה בריה דרבי חייא: Rabbi Yehuda was one of the twin sons of Rabbi Ḥiyya the Great, who was himself a contemporary and disciple-colleague of Rabbi Yehuda HaNasi. Rabbi Yehuda, together with his twin brother Ḥizkiyya, studied under his father as well as under Rabbi Yehuda HaNasi and his disciples. Rabbi Yehuda and Ḥizkiyya are sometimes cited together in the Gemara as Yehuda and Ḥizkiyya, the sons of Rabbi Ḥiyya.

Rabbi Yehuda was famous in his own right, not only for his Torah knowledge but also for his righteousness, to the extent that his father-in-law, Rabbi Yannai, who was himself an important scholar, would accord Rabbi Yehuda great respect. Rabbi Yehuda died at a young age, and it is for this reason that he is not often cited in the Gemara.

בָּא לַעֲבוֹדָה בַּיָּד – עֲבוֹדָה בְּיָמִין כְּחַטָּאת, בָּא לַעֲבוֹדָה בִּכְלִי – עֲבוֹדָה בִּשְׂמֹאל כְּאָשָׁם!

Rabbi Yehuda, son of Rabbi Ḥiyya, elaborates: The verse compares the meal offering to a sin offering and a guilt offering. Therefore, if the priest **comes to perform** the burning of the handful **with** his **hand, he performs it with** his **right** hand, **like** in the case of **a sin offering,** whose blood is sprinkled with the hand. And if he **comes to perform it with a vessel,** i.e., if he first sanctifies the handful in a service vessel, then **he** may **perform it with** his **left** hand, **like** in the case of **a guilt offering,** whose blood is sprinkled from a vessel. Since the removal of the handful is performed with the hand, the verse indicates that it must be performed with the right hand, and the verbal analogy is unnecessary.

לָא נִצְרְכָא אֶלָּא לְקוֹמֶץ דְּמִנְחַת חוֹטֵא, סָלְקָא דַּעְתָּךְ אָמִינָא: הוֹאִיל וְאָמַר רַבִּי שִׁמְעוֹן שֶׁלֹּא יְהֵא קׇרְבָּנוֹ מְהוּדָּר, כִּי קָמֵיץ לַהּ נָמֵי בִּשְׂמֹאל תִּתַכְשַׁר, קָמַשְׁמַע לַן.

The Gemara responds: The verbal analogy **is necessary only for the handful of the meal offering of a sinner,** to teach that it must be removed with the right hand. It might **enter your mind to say: Since Rabbi Shimon says** that this offering does not require oil and frankincense **so that** a sinner's **offering will not be of superior quality,** perhaps **when** the priest **removed the handful with** his **left** hand, which is a manner of inferior quality, **it should be fit as well.** The verbal analogy therefore **teaches us** that the handful must always be removed with the right hand, even in the case of the meal offering of a sinner.

״קָמַץ וְעָלָה בְּיָדוֹ צְרוֹר אוֹ גַּרְגִּר מֶלַח

§ The mishna teaches: If a priest **removed the handful** of flour, **and a stone or a grain of salt emerged in his hand,**

אוֹ קוֹרֶט לְבוֹנָה – פָּסוּל״. כׇּל הָנֵי לָמָּה לִי?

or a pinch of frankincense emerged in his hand, the meal offering is **unfit,** as the handful lacks a full measure on account of these items. The Gemara asks: **Why do I** need **all these** examples? Any one of them would convey the fact that the handful must contain a full measure.

צְרִיכָא, דְּאִי תְּנָא צְרוֹר – מִשּׁוּם דְּלָאו בַּת הַקְרָבָה הִיא, אֲבָל מֶלַח דְּבַת הַקְרָבָה הִיא – אֵימָא תִּתַכְשַׁר;

The Gemara explains: All of the cases are **necessary. Because if** the mishna had **taught** only the example of **a stone,** it might have been thought that only a stone diminishes the measure of the handful, **because it is not fit for sacrifice. But** with regard to **salt, which is fit for sacrifice,** as the priest places salt on the handful before burning it upon the altar, one might **say** that the handful **should be fit,** as the salt should not subtract from the handful's measure.

וְאִי תְּנָא מֶלַח – דְּלָא אִיקְּבַע בַּהֲדֵי מִנְחָה מֵעִיקָּרָא, שֶׁאֵינוֹ מוֹלֵחַ אֶלָּא הַקּוֹמֶץ בִּלְבַד, אֲבָל לְבוֹנָה דְּאִיקְּבַע בַּהֲדֵי מִנְחָה מֵעִיקָּרָא – אֵימָא תִּתַכְשַׁר, קָא מַשְׁמַע לַן.

And if the mishna had **taught** only the example of **salt,** it might have been thought that the salt diminishes the handful's measure **as it was not initially fixed** together **with** the entire **meal offering.** The reason is **that** the priest **salts the handful alone. But** with regard to the **frankincense, which was initially fixed** together **with** the entire **meal offering,** i.e., it is placed upon the meal offering before the priest removes a handful from it, one might **say** that the handful **should be fit** and the frankincense should not diminish from the handful's measure. Therefore, the mishna **teaches us** that in any of these instances the meal offering is unfit.

״מִפְּנֵי שֶׁאָמְרוּ: הַקּוֹמֶץ הֶחָסֵר אוֹ הַיָּתֵר – פָּסוּל״. מַאי אִירְיָא מִשּׁוּם חָסֵר וְיָתֵר? וְתִיפּוֹק לֵיהּ מִשּׁוּם חֲצִיצָה! אָמַר רַבִּי יִרְמְיָה: מִן הַצַּד.

§ The mishna teaches that if a stone, or a grain of salt, or a pinch of frankincense emerged in the priest's hand together with the handful, the meal offering is unfit **due to** the fact **that** the Sages **said: The handful that is lacking or that is outsized** is **unfit.** The Gemara asks: **Why** does the *tanna* explain that the offering is not valid **specifically because** it is **lacking or outsized? But let** the *tanna* **derive** that such a handful is not valid **due to** the fact that there is **an interposition** between the priest's hand and the handful. **Rabbi Yirmeya says:** Since there are certain instances where these items do not interpose between one's hand and the handful, e.g., when they are located **on the side** of the handful, the mishna teaches that they disqualify the handful due to the fact that they reduce its measure.

אֲמַר לֵיהּ אַבַּיֵי לְרָבָא: כֵּיצַד קוֹמְצִין? אֲמַר לֵיהּ: כִּדְקָמְצִי אֱינָשֵׁי. אֵיתִיבֵיהּ: זוֹ זֶרֶת, זוֹ קְמִיצָה,

§ **Abaye said to Rava: How do** the priests properly **remove the handful**[H] from a meal offering? Rava **said to him:** They remove it **as people** normally **remove handfuls,** by folding all of their fingers over the palm of the hand. Abaye **raised an objection to** Rava from a *baraita* discussing the mitzva function of each of the fingers: **This** small finger is for measuring **a span** (see Exodus 28:16), i.e., the distance between the thumb and the little finger. **This** fourth finger is used for **removal of a handful** from the meal offering, i.e., the measurement of a handful begins from this finger, as the priest removes a handful by folding the middle three fingers over his palm.

זוֹ אַמָּה, זוֹ אֶצְבַּע, זוֹ גּוּדָל!

Furthermore, **this** middle finger is used for measuring **a cubit,** the distance from the elbow to the tip of the middle finger. **This** forefinger, next to the thumb, is the **finger** used to sprinkle the blood of offerings on the altar. And finally, **this thumb** is the one on which the blood and oil is placed during the purification ritual of a leper (see Leviticus 14:17). Evidently, the little finger is not used in the removal of a handful.

אֶלָּא לְהַשְׁווֹת. כְּלוֹמַר, קוֹמֵץ מְלֹא הַיָּד כְּדֵי שֶׁלֹּא יְהֵא חָסֵר, וְאַחַר כָּךְ מוֹחֵק בְּאֶצְבַּע קְטַנָּה מִלְּמַטָּה.

The Gemara responds: The little finger is used **only for** the purposes of **leveling** the handful, **that is to say,** the priest first **removes a handful** with **a full hand,**[N] i.e., all of his fingers, **so that it should not be lacking** in measure, **and then he wipes** away the protruding flour **with** his **little finger from the bottom,** and with his thumb from the top.

הֵיכִי עָבֵיד? אָמַר רַב זוּטְרָא בַּר טוֹבִיָּה אָמַר רַב: חוֹפֶה שָׁלֹשׁ אֶצְבְּעוֹתָיו עַד שֶׁמַּגִּיעַ עַל פַּס יָדוֹ וְקוֹמֵץ.

The Gemara asks: **How** is the removal of the handful **performed? Rav Zutra bar Toviyya says that Rav says:** When the priest places his hand in the meal offering, **he bends his** middle **three fingers until** the tips of his fingers **reach over the palm of his hand, and** he then **removes the handful.**

NOTES

The little finger is used only for leveling…he first removes a handful with a full hand, etc. – אֶלָּא לְהַשְׁווֹת...קוֹמֵץ מְלֹא הַיָּד וכו׳: According to this explanation, Rava holds that the priest initially removes a handful with all of his fingers and only then does he wipe away from the bottom with his little finger. If so, Rava's opinion contradicts the *baraita* cited later on, as well as the opinion of Rav, according to which the priest initially removes the flour with only his middle three fingers. It should be noted that this explanation, introduced by the term: That is to say, does not appear in certain versions of the Gemara. Rashi states that when Rava said that handfuls are removed as people normally remove handfuls, he meant that all five fingers are used in the process of the removal. Nevertheless, Rava concurs that the flour is actually removed with only the middle three fingers. According to this opinion, Rava is saying that the wiping of the handful with the priest's thumb and little finger is part of the rite of the removal, and must therefore be performed with the right hand (see *Tosafot* on *Ketubot* 5b). Similarly, it cannot be performed by a second priest (*Ḥazon Ish*).

Position of priest's hand after smoothing out the handful

HALAKHA

How do the priests properly remove the handful – כֵּיצַד קוֹמְצִין: The handful of a meal offering is removed as anyone would remove a handful, i.e., the priest extends all of his fingers across the palm of his hand until the flour is secured in his hand, whereupon he removes it from the rest of the meal offering. This ruling of the Rambam is in accordance with the opinion of Rav Pappa rather than that of the *baraita*, and therefore the opinion that the rite of the removal of the handful is considered a particularly difficult rite is rejected (Rambam's Commentary on the Mishna). Other early commentaries maintain that the priest extends only his middle three fingers over his palm, and that in the case of pan and deep-pan meal offerings, he uses his thumb and little finger to wipe away the protruding pieces from his hand, as stated in the *baraita* (see *Likkutei Halakhot*). The Radbaz writes that even the Rambam agrees that in the case of pan and deep-pan meal offerings the priest removes the flour with his middle three fingers (Rambam *Sefer Avoda*, *Hilkhot Ma'aseh HaKorbanot* 13:13).

תַּנְיָא נַמִּי הָכִי: ״מְלֹא קֻמְצוֹ״ – יָכוֹל מְבוֹרָץ? תַּלְמוּד לוֹמַר: ״בְּקֻמְצוֹ״;

The Gemara notes **that** this **is also taught** in a *baraita*. From the verse that states: "And he shall remove from there **his handful**" (Leviticus 2:2), one **might** have thought that the handful should be **overflowing. Therefore,** another **verse states:** "And he shall take up from it **with his handful** [***bekumtzo***]" (Leviticus 6:8). The prefix that means "with" can also mean: In, indicating that the proper measure of a handful is that which is contained within one's fingers alone.

אִי ״בְּקֻמְצוֹ״, יָכוֹל בְּרָאשֵׁי אֶצְבְּעוֹתָיו? תַּלְמוּד לוֹמַר: ״מְלֹא קֻמְצוֹ״; הָא כֵּיצַד? חוֹפֶה שָׁלֹשׁ אֶצְבְּעוֹתָיו עַל פַּס יָדוֹ וְקוֹמֵץ;

The *baraita* continues: **If** the measurement of a handful is determined by the term **"with his handful,"** one **might** have thought that the priest removes a handful **with his fingertips,**[N] i.e., that a handful consists of that which the priest removes by folding his fingers onto themselves. Therefore, **the verse states: "His handful,"** indicating that the handful must be full and not merely that which is contained within his fingers. **How so? He scoops** by closing **his three fingers over the palm of his hand, and** in this way **takes a handful** from the flour of the meal offering.

בְּמַחֲבַת וּבְמַרְחֶשֶׁת מוֹחֵק בְּגוּדָלוֹ מִלְּמַעְלָה וּבְאֶצְבָּעוֹ קְטַנָּה מִלְּמַטָּה, וְזוֹ הִיא עֲבוֹדָה קָשָׁה שֶׁבַּמִּקְדָּשׁ.

The *baraita* continues: **In** the case of **a pan** meal offering **and** that **of a deep-pan** meal offering,[N] when the flour was fried before being scooped and was therefore hard, the priest **wipes** away **with his thumb** any flour that was overflowing **above** his handful, **and with his little finger** he wipes away the flour that was pushing out **below. And this** precise taking of the handful of a meal offering **is** the most **difficult** sacrificial **rite in the Temple,** as the priest must wipe away any protruding elements without removing any flour from the handful itself.

זֶהוּ וְתוּ לָא? וְהָאִיכָּא מְלִיקָה, וְהָאִיכָּא חֲפִינָה! אֶלָּא, זוֹ הִיא אַחַת מֵעֲבוֹדוֹת קָשׁוֹת שֶׁבַּמִּקְדָּשׁ.

The Gemara asks: **This one** is the hardest sacrificial rite, **and no other? But isn't there pinching**[N] the nape of the neck of a bird offering, which is also considered extremely difficult to perform, **and isn't there** the **scooping** of the handful of incense[N] by the High Priest on Yom Kippur, another rite that is extremely difficult to perform? **Rather,** the *baraita* means that **this** taking of the handful of a meal offering **is one of** the most **difficult** sacrificial **rites in the Temple.**

NOTES

With his fingertips – בְּרָאשֵׁי אֶצְבְּעוֹתָיו: According to Rashi, this means that the priest does not spread his fingers across his palm, but folds his fingers onto themselves in such a manner that none of the flour is contained in the palm. Others explain that the priest removes flour with the tips of his fingers and his thumb (Ra'avad in his commentary on *Torat Kohanim*).

In the case of a pan meal offering and that of a deep-pan meal offering – בְּמַחֲבַת וּבְמַרְחֶשֶׁת: These meal offerings are fried and then broken into pieces before their handfuls are removed (see 75b). Consequently, when the priest removes a handful, there will certainly be pieces protruding from his fingers that must be wiped away. Such a procedure is exceptionally difficult, as the priest must ensure that he does not add to or detract from the proper amount of the handful, all while using only his thumb and little finger (see *Tosafot* and *Mevoei HaKodashim*). Likewise, the Gemara (54a) says that the removal of the handful from the meal offering of a sinner is also exceptionally difficult, as the flour falls easily from the priest's hand, because there is no oil mixed with it. By contrast, other meal offerings of flour have oil mixed into them, which renders the removal of their handfuls easier (see *Tosafot* on *Yoma* 49b).

But isn't there pinching – וְהָאִיכָּא מְלִיקָה: The difficulty in the performance of this act stems from the fact that the priest must hold the bird steady in a particular manner with only one hand. Others explain that the difficulty is that the priest pinches its nape using the thumbnail of the same hand with which he is holding the bird (see *Zevaḥim* 64b).

And isn't there the scooping of the handful of incense – וְהָאִיכָּא חֲפִינָה: According to Rashi, the Gemara is not referring to the stage when the incense is initially taken and placed into a bowl, as this is no more difficult than any other act of scooping. Rather, it is referring to later in the rite, after the High Priest lowers the coal pan onto the floor of the Holy of Holies. At this point the High Priest scoops the incense from inside the bowl into his hands in order to place it upon the coals (see *Yoma* 49b and Rambam's Commentary on the Mishna, *Yoma* 1:5).

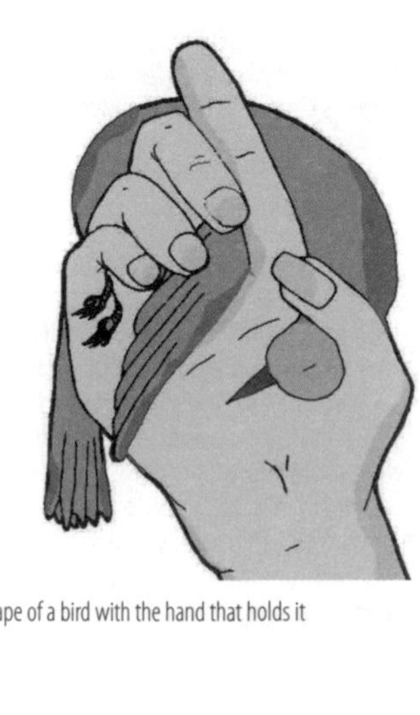

Pinching the nape of a bird with the hand that holds it

אֲמַר רַב פַּפָּא: פְּשִׁיטָא לִי, ״מְלֹא קֻמְצוֹ״ – כִּדְקָמְצִי אֱינָשֵׁי. בָּעֵי רַב פַּפָּא: קָמַץ בְּרָאשֵׁי אֶצְבְּעוֹתָיו, מַאי?

Rav Pappa said: It is **obvious to me** that the term **"his handful"** means that the removal of the handful from a meal offering should be performed *ab initio* **in the manner that people** usually **remove a handful,**[N] with their fingertips angled to the side. **Rav Pappa raises a dilemma: What** is the *halakha* if the priest **removed a handful with his fingertips,**[NH] i.e., if he placed his hand horizontally over the meal offering and filled his palm with flour by closing his fingers to his palm? Does this disqualify the taking of the handful or not?

מִן הַצְּדָדִין, מַאי? מִמַּטָּה לְמַעְלָה, מַאי? תֵּיקוּ.

Similarly, if the priest took a handful **from the sides,**[N] by passing the back of his hand back and forth over the flour in the vessel so that the flour collected in his palm by way of the side of his palm, **what** is the *halakha*? Furthermore, if he took the handful with the back of his hand placed **downward** in the vessel, and with his fingers he collected the flour **upward** into his palm, **what** is the *halakha*? Are the handfuls removed in this manner fit for sacrifice? The Gemara states: These dilemmas **shall stand** unresolved.[B]

אֲמַר רַב פַּפָּא: פְּשִׁיטָא לִי, ״מְלֹא חָפְנָיו״ – כִּדְחָפְנִי אֱינָשֵׁי. בָּעֵי רַב פַּפָּא: חָפַן בְּרָאשֵׁי אֶצְבְּעוֹתָיו, מַהוּ? מִן הַצְּדָדִין, מַהוּ? חָפַן בְּזוֹ וּבְזוֹ וְקֵירְבָן זוֹ אֵצֶל זוֹ, מַהוּ? תֵּיקוּ.

Rav Pappa said: It is **obvious to me** that when the Torah states: **"His handful"** (Leviticus 16:12), in the context of the scooping of handfuls of incense by the High Priest on Yom Kippur, it means **in the manner that people** usually **scoop a handful,** by placing the backs of their hands into the vessel and bringing their hands together. **Rav Pappa raises a dilemma: What is** the *halakha* if the High Priest **scooped a handful with his fingertips? What is** the *halakha* if he took a handful **from the sides? What is** the *halakha* **if he scooped a handful with this** hand **and with that** hand separately **and** then **brought them together?** The Gemara states: These dilemmas **shall stand** unresolved.

בָּעֵי רַב פַּפָּא: דַּבְּקֵיהּ לַקּוֹמֶץ בְּדָפְנֵיהּ דְּמָנָא, מַאי? תּוֹךְ כְּלִי בָּעֵינַן וְהָאִיכָּא, אוֹ דִּלְמָא הַנָּחָה בְּתוֹכוֹ בָּעֵינַן וְלֵיכָּא? תֵּיקוּ.

Rav Pappa raises yet another **dilemma:** If the priest took the handful from the vessel containing the meal offering and **stuck the handful**[H] **onto the side of** the second **vessel** in order to sanctify it, i.e., the handful was not placed directly into the vessel, **what** is the *halakha*? Do **we require** that the handful be **inside** the **vessel, and** that **is** the case here? **Or perhaps we require** that the handful be **placed** properly **inside** the vessel, **and** that **is not** the case in this instance. No answer is found, and the Gemara concludes: The dilemma **shall stand** unresolved.

בָּעֵי מָר בַּר רַב אַשִׁי: הַפְּכֵיהּ לְמָנָא וְדַבְּקֵיהּ לַקּוֹמֶץ בְּאַרְעִיתָא דְּמָנָא, מַאי? הַנָּחָה בְּתוֹכוֹ בָּעֵינַן וְהָאִיכָּא, אוֹ דִּלְמָא כְּתִיקְנוֹ בָּעֵינַן וְלֵיכָּא? תֵּיקוּ.

Mar bar Rav Ashi raises a similar **dilemma:** If the priest **overturned the vessel and stuck the handful to the underside of the vessel,** in a case where there was an indentation on the underside, **what** is the *halakha*? Do **we require** that the handful be **placed inside** the vessel, **and that** requirement **is** fulfilled here, as the handful is within the indentation? **Or perhaps we require** that it be placed **properly** in the vessel, **and that is not** the case here. The Gemara states: The dilemma **shall stand** unresolved.

NOTES

Rav Pappa said, it is obvious to me that the term his handful means in the manner that people usually remove a handful – אֲמַר רַב פַּפָּא פְּשִׁיטָא לִי מְלֹא קֻמְצוֹ כִּדְקָמְצִי אֱינָשֵׁי: The commentaries explain that Rav Pappa is not referring to the number of fingers used for removing the flour from the meal offering, but to the manner in which the priest places his hand into the flour. According to Rashi, one normally removes a handful by placing his hand into the flour so that the sides of his fingers are facing downward, before folding those fingers onto his palm. Others explain that the normal manner of removing a handful is by placing one's palm onto the flour and then pressing one's fingers through the flour until his fingertips are folded onto the palm of his hand (Rabbeinu Elyakim on *Yoma* 47b).

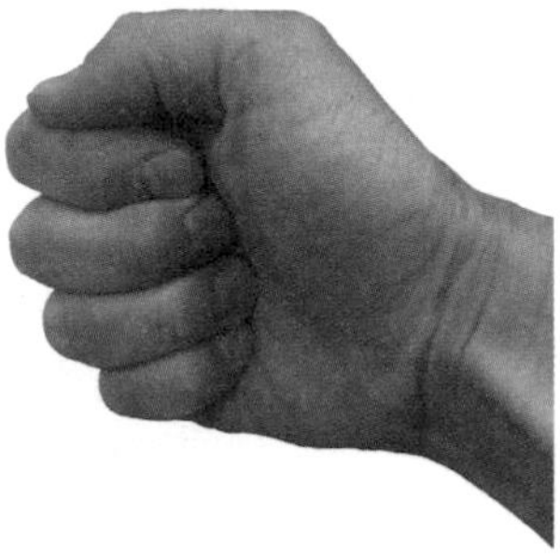

Position of hand in taking a common handful

With his fingertips – בְּרָאשֵׁי אֶצְבְּעוֹתָיו: According to Rashi and *Tosafot*, Rav Pappa is not referring to the same situation as the *baraita* cited earlier in the Gemara, where one takes only the flour contained within his fingers. Rather, he is referring to a case where one inserts his fingers into the flour with his palm resting upon the surface of the flour, using his fingers to raise the flour into his palm. Some commentaries explain that the problem with removing a handful in such a manner is that the flour is not taken with the priest's palm, but is elevated into it with his fingers (Meiri on *Yoma* 47b).

From the sides – מִן הַצְּדָדִין: Rashi here states that the priest passes the back of his hand over the flour until the flour collects in the palm of his hand from the sides. Rashi on *Yoma* 47b explains that this motion caused the flour to collect in his palm from between his extended fingers. Accordingly, the phrase: From the sides, means that the flour collected in his hand in an unusual manner. Rashi here also suggests that Rav Pappa may be referring to a case where the priest removed the handful from the sides of the vessel rather than from the middle, which would have been the typical manner (see also Rabbeinu Gershom Meor HaGola and Rabbeinu Elyakim on *Yoma* 47b). Others suggest that the priest tilted the vessel containing the meal offering onto its side until a handful fell into his palm (Meiri).

BACKGROUND

Shall stand unresolved [*teiku*] – תֵּיקוּ: Various explanations have been suggested with regard to the etymology of this term. One explanation is that it is an abbreviated version of *tikom*, let it stand. Another is that its source is the word *tik*, a case or pouch, whose contents are unknown, just like the resolution of the dilemma is unknown to us, as though it were hidden inside a case (*Arukh*). Although not the literal meaning, some interpret the term as an acrostic for the Hebrew phrase: *Tishbi yetaretz kushyot uve'ayot*, or: The Tishbite, i.e., Elijah the prophet, will resolve questions and dilemmas (*Tosefot Yom Tov*). This idea refers to the tradition that when Elijah returns to announce the coming of the Messiah, he will also reveal the solutions to outstanding halakhic difficulties.

HALAKHA

What is the *halakha*…with his fingertips, etc. – בְּרָאשֵׁי אֶצְבְּעוֹתָיו מַאי וכו׳: If one removed the handful with his fingertips or from the sides, he should not burn it upon the altar. If he burns it, it effects acceptance. Since the dilemmas of Rav Pappa were left unresolved, the *halakha* is lenient after the fact (Rambam *Sefer Avoda*, *Hilkhot Ma'aseh HaKorbanot* 13:13 and *Kesef Mishne* there).

Stuck the handful, etc. – דַּבְּקֵיהּ לַקּוֹמֶץ וכו׳: If the priest stuck the handful onto the side of the vessel and then removed it, or if he flipped the vessel onto his hand and then removed a handful from it while the vessel remained upside down, he should not burn the handful upon the altar *ab initio*. If he burns it, it effects acceptance. The *halakha* is lenient, as the dilemmas of Rav Pappa were left unresolved (Rambam *Sefer Avoda*, *Hilkhot Pesulei HaMukdashin* 11:25 and *Kesef Mishne* there).

מתני׳ כיצד הוא עושה? פושט את אצבעותיו על פס ידו. ריבה שמנה, חסר שמנה, חיסר לבונתה – פסולה.

MISHNA **How does** the priest **perform**[H] the removal of a handful? **He extends his fingers onto the palm of his hand.** If **one increased its oil,**[N] **decreased its oil,**[H] or **decreased its frankincense,** beyond the appropriate measures, the meal offering is **unfit.**

גמ׳ היכי דמי ריבה שמנה? אמר רבי אליעזר: כגון שהפריש לה שני לוגין. ולוקמה כגון דעריב בה שמן דחולין ושמן דחבירתה!

GEMARA **What are the circumstances** of a case where the meal offering is disqualified due to the fact that one **increased its oil? Rabbi Eliezer says:** The circumstances are a case **where he separated two** ***log*** of oil **for** the meal offering[H] instead of one *log*, and mixed them into a tenth of an ephah of flour. The Gemara raises a difficulty: **And let** Rabbi Eliezer **interpret** the mishna as referring to a case **where he mixed non-sacred oil or the oil of another** meal offering[H] **into** the meal offering.

וכי תימא, שמן דחולין ושמן דחבירתה לא פסל, מתקיף לה רב זוטרא בר טוביה: אלא מעתה, מנחת חוטא דפסל בה שמן היכי משכחת לה?

And if you would say that **non-sacred oil and the oil of another** meal offering **do not disqualify** a meal offering, **Rav Zutra bar Toviyya objects to this** claim: **If that is so,** then with regard to the **meal offering of a sinner,** of which it is stated (59b) **that oil disqualifies it, how can you find** the circumstances where it is in fact disqualified?

אי דידה – הא לית לה, אי דחולין ודחבירתה – הא אמרת: לא פסל! ואי אמרת דאפריש לה שמן, כיון דלית לה שמן כלל – חולין נינהו!

Rav Zutra bar Toviyya elaborates: **If** you suggest that he mixed **its own** oil into the flour, such a case does not exist, as the meal offering of a sinner **does not have** any oil. **If** he mixed **non-sacred** oil **or** that **of another** meal offering into the flour, the meal offering should not be disqualified, as **you said** that such oil **does not disqualify** a meal offering. **And if you would say that he designated oil for** his meal offering and mixed it into the flour despite the Torah prohibition against mixing oil into it, I say that **since** the meal offering of a sinner **does not have oil at all,** any oil that he separates and mixes into it **is** considered **non-sacred,** and you have already said that non-sacred oil does not disqualify a meal offering.

ורבי אליעזר: לא מיבעיא קאמר; לא מיבעיא דחולין ודחבירתה דפסיל, אבל הפריש לה שני לוגין, הואיל והאי חזי ליה והאי חזי ליה – אימא לא ליפסיל, קא משמע לן.

The Gemara responds: In fact, non-sacred oil and the oil of another meal offering do disqualify a meal offering, **and Rabbi Eliezer is speaking** utilizing the style of: **It is not necessary,** as follows: **It is not necessary** to say **that non-sacred** oil **and the** oil **of another** meal offering **disqualify** a meal offering. **But** in a case where one **separated two** ***log*** **for** his meal offering, **since this** first *log* **is fit for** the meal offering, **and that** second *log* **is** also **fit for it,** one might **say** that even when he mixes both *log* into the meal offering, **it should not disqualify** the meal offering. Therefore, Rabbi Eliezer **teaches us** that the meal offering is disqualified in this case as well.

ומנא ליה לרבי אליעזר הא? אמר רבא: מתניתין קשיתיה, מאי איריא דתני ״ריבה שמנה״? ליתני: ריבה לה שמן! אלא הא קא משמע לן, דאף על גב דהפריש לה שני לוגין.

The Gemara asks: **And from where does Rabbi Eliezer** derive **this** conclusion? **Rava said:** The terminology of **the mishna posed a difficulty for him,** as one can ask: **Why does** the *tanna* **specifically teach** that the meal offering is disqualified if **he increased its oil,** which indicates that he increased it with oil belonging to the offering itself? **Let** the mishna **teach** simply: **He increased the oil. Rather, this** is what the mishna **teaches us: That even though he** initially **separated two** ***log*** of oil **for** the meal offering, its own oil disqualifies the offering when there is too much.

״חיסר לבונתה״. תנו רבנן: חסרה ועמדה על קורט אחד – פסולה, על שני קרטין – כשרה, דברי רבי יהודה. רבי שמעון אומר: על קורט אחד – כשרה, פחות מכאן – פסולה.

§ The mishna teaches that if one **decreased its frankincense** beyond its appropriate measure, the meal offering is unfit. Concerning this, **the Sages taught** in a *baraita*: If one **decreased** its frankincense to the point that the amount **stood at** only **one pinch,** it is **disqualified,** but if the decreased amount stood **at two pinches,** it is **fit;** this is **the statement of Rabbi Yehuda. Rabbi Shimon says:** If the decreased amount stood **at one pinch,** it is **fit; less than that,** it is **disqualified.**

HALAKHA

How does he perform – כֵּיצַד הוּא עוֹשֶׂה: The High Priest scoops the incense on Yom Kippur as anyone would scoop it, i.e., by placing both of his hands into the bowl of incense and then bringing them together. If he scooped the handful with the tips of his fingers, or from the sides, or by placing his hand above the incense and scooping the incense into his palm using his fingers, or if he scooped with each hand separately, the *halakha* in all of these cases is uncertain, and therefore he should not sacrifice the incense *ab initio*. If he sacrifices it, it effects acceptance (Rambam *Sefer Avoda, Hilkhot Avodat Yom HaKippurim* 4:1, 5:28).

Decreased its oil – חִסֵּר שַׁמְנָהּ: If one decreased the oil of a meal offering to less than its appropriate measure, the offering is disqualified (Rambam *Sefer Avoda, Hilkhot Pesulei HaMukdashin* 11:8).

Increased its oil…where he separated two *log* of oil for the meal offering – רִיבָּה שַׁמְנָהּ...כְּגוֹן שֶׁהִפְרִישׁ לָהּ שְׁנֵי לוּגִּין: All meal offerings that are sacrificed upon the altar require one *log* of oil for every tenth of an ephah of flour. If one increased the oil but there was still less than two *log* of oil for every tenth of an ephah, the meal offering remains fit. If he placed more than this, it is disqualified. This ruling of the Rambam is in accordance with Rabbi Eliezer's interpretation of the mishna, as the Rambam maintains that according to Rabbi Eliezer any amount less than two *log* of oil per tenth of an ephah does not disqualify an offering (Rambam *Sefer Avoda, Hilkhot Ma'aseh HaKorbanot* 12:7 and *Hilkhot Pesulei HaMukdashin* 11:9).

Non-sacred oil or the oil of another offering – שֶׁמֶן דְּחוּלִּין וְשֶׁמֶן דַּחֲבֵירְתָּהּ: If any amount of oil from another meal offering or any non-sacred oil fell into a meal offering, the meal offering is disqualified (Rambam *Sefer Avoda, Hilkhot Pesulei HaMukdashin* 11:8).

NOTES

Increased its oil, etc. – רִיבָּה שַׁמְנָהּ וכו׳: With regard to those meal offerings that require oil, the ratio of oil to flour is one *log* of oil for every tenth of an ephah of flour, in accordance with the verse: "And one tenth part of an ephah of fine flour mingled with oil for a meal offering, and a *log* of oil" (Leviticus 14:21). The proper amount of frankincense for meal offerings is one handful (106a; see also *Torat Kohanim* on Leviticus 2:1). Although the mishna does not explicitly mention the *halakha* of an increase or decrease in the amount of flour, it is clear from the *Tosefta* (1:17) that such a change does disqualify the meal offering.

וְהָתַנְיָא, רַבִּי שִׁמְעוֹן אוֹמֵר: קוֹמֶץ וּלְבוֹנָה שֶׁחָסַר כָּל שֶׁהוּא – פָּסוּל! תְּנֵי: קוֹרֶט לְבוֹנָה שֶׁחָסַר כָּל שֶׁהוּא – פָּסוּל. וְאִיבָּעֵית אֵימָא: כָּאן בִּלְבוֹנָה הַבָּאָה עִם הַמִּנְחָה, כָּאן בִּלְבוֹנָה הַבָּאָה בִּפְנֵי עַצְמָהּ.

The Gemara asks: **But isn't it taught** in a *baraita* that **Rabbi Shimon says: A handful** of flour **or frankincense that was decreased** by **any amount** from its full measure **is disqualified?** The Gemara answers that one should **teach** the *baraita* as follows: **A pinch of frankincense** that was **decreased** by **any amount is disqualified. And if you wish, say** instead that **here,** the first cited statement of Rabbi Shimon, is referring to the case **of frankincense that comes with a meal offering,** and this frankincense is disqualified only when there is less than a pinch, whereas **there,** the second statement of Rabbi Shimon, is referring to the case **of frankincense that comes by itself.**[N] Such frankincense is disqualified if it comprises any less than its full measure.

אָמַר רַבִּי יִצְחָק בַּר יוֹסֵף אָמַר רַבִּי יוֹחָנָן: שָׁלֹשׁ מַחְלוֹקוֹת בַּדָּבָר, רַבִּי מֵאִיר סָבַר: קוֹמֶץ בַּתְּחִילָּה וְקוֹמֶץ בַּסּוֹף, וְרַבִּי יְהוּדָה סָבַר: קוֹמֶץ בַּתְּחִילָּה וּשְׁנֵי קְרָטִין בַּסּוֹף, וְרַבִּי שִׁמְעוֹן סָבַר: קוֹמֶץ בַּתְּחִילָּה וְקוֹרֶט אֶחָד בַּסּוֹף.

Rabbi Yitzḥak bar Yosef says that **Rabbi Yoḥanan says:** There are **three disputes** of *tanna'im* **with regard to the matter. Rabbi Meir holds**[N] that the priest must remove **a handful at the beginning, and ultimately** the entire **handful** must be burned upon the altar. **And Rabbi Yehuda holds** that the priest must remove **a handful at the beginning, and ultimately** at least **two pinches**[H] from it must be burned upon the altar. **And Rabbi Shimon holds** that the priest must remove **a handful at the beginning and ultimately** at least **one pinch** from it must be burned upon the altar.

וּשְׁלָשְׁתָּן מִקְרָא אֶחָד דָּרְשׁוּ: ״וְאֵת כָּל הַלְּבוֹנָה אֲשֶׁר עַל הַמִּנְחָה״, רַבִּי מֵאִיר סָבַר: עַד דְּאִיתָא לִלְבוֹנָה דְּאִיקְּבַעָה בַּהֲדֵי מִנְחָה מֵעִיקָּרָא; וְרַבִּי יְהוּדָה סָבַר: ״כָּל״ – וַאֲפִילּוּ חַד קוֹרֶט, ״אֵת״ – לְרַבּוֹת קוֹרֶט אַחֵר; וְרַבִּי שִׁמְעוֹן ״אֵת״ לָא דָּרֵישׁ.

And all **three of them interpret a single verse** differently. The verse states: "And he shall take up from there his handful, of the fine flour of the meal offering, and of the oil of it, **and** [*ve'et*] **all the frankincense that is upon the meal offering,** and shall make it smoke upon the altar" (Leviticus 6:8). **Rabbi Meir holds** that one may not make the offering smoke upon the altar **unless there** remains **the** entire measure of **frankincense that was initially fixed together with the meal offering. And Rabbi Yehuda holds** that when the verse states: **"All** [*kol*]," it is referring to any part of the frankincense, **even a single pinch,** as *kol* can mean any amount (see II Kings 2:4). And when the verse states: **"*Et*,"** this serves **to include another pinch.** Accordingly, at least two pinches must remain to be burned upon the altar. **And Rabbi Shimon** interprets the word "all" in the same manner as does Rabbi Yehuda, but he **does not interpret** and derive a *halakha* from the term **"*et*,"** and he therefore holds that only one pinch must remain to be burned.

וְאָמַר רַבִּי יִצְחָק בַּר יוֹסֵף אָמַר רַבִּי יוֹחָנָן: מַחְלוֹקֶת בִּלְבוֹנָה הַבָּאָה עִם הַמִּנְחָה, אֲבָל בִּלְבוֹנָה הַבָּאָה בִּפְנֵי עַצְמָהּ – דִּבְרֵי הַכֹּל קוֹמֶץ בַּתְּחִילָּה וְקוֹמֶץ בַּסּוֹף; לְהָכִי אִיצְטְרִיךְ ״אֲשֶׁר עַל הַמִּנְחָה״, דְּבַהֲדֵי מִנְחָה – אִין, בִּפְנֵי עַצְמָהּ – לָא.

And Rabbi Yitzḥak bar Yosef further **says** that **Rabbi Yoḥanan says:** The **dispute** between these *tanna'im* **is with regard to frankincense that comes with a meal offering. But with regard to frankincense that comes by itself,**[H] **everyone,** even Rabbi Yehuda and Rabbi Shimon, **agrees** that the priest must bring **a handful at the beginning, and ultimately** the entire **handful** must be burned upon the altar. **For this** reason it **was necessary** for the verse to state: **"That is upon the meal offering,"** as this indicates **that together with a meal offering, yes,** one may burn the frankincense even if there remains only a pinch or two, but with regard to frankincense that comes **by itself,** one may **not** burn it if it is in that state.

HALAKHA

A handful at the beginning and ultimately at least two pinches – קוֹמֶץ בַּתְּחִילָּה וּשְׁנֵי קְרָטִין בַּסּוֹף: All meal offerings that are sacrificed upon the altar require a handful of frankincense. If one used less than this, the offering is valid provided that there are at least two pinches of frankincense. If there is less than that the offering is disqualified. Although the mishna is in accordance with the opinion of Rabbi Meir, Rabbi Yehuda and Rabbi Shimon disagree with him, and the *halakha* follows the majority. The *Kesef Mishne* adds that the *halakha* is in accordance with the opinion of Rabbi Yehuda in a dispute between him and Rabbi Shimon (Rambam *Sefer Avoda, Hilkhot Ma'aseh HaKorbanot* 12:7 and *Hilkhot Pesulei HaMukdashin* 11:8).

Frankincense that comes by itself – לְבוֹנָה הַבָּאָה בִּפְנֵי עַצְמָהּ: If one took a vow to sacrifice a handful of frankincense by itself, it must be a complete handful from the beginning of its sacrificial process until the end. If it was decreased by any amount it is disqualified (Rambam *Sefer Avoda, Hilkhot Pesulei HaMukdashin* 11:17).

NOTES

Frankincense that comes by itself – לְבוֹנָה הַבָּאָה בִּפְנֵי עַצְמָהּ: An individual may take a vow to bring an offering of frankincense by itself, and its measure is one handful (see 106b). Since in this case the frankincense is the entire offering, it must contain a full measure.

Rabbi Meir holds – רַבִּי מֵאִיר סָבַר: Rabbi Meir's opinion is not cited explicitly either in the mishna or in the *baraita*. Rashi explains that the mishna itself is in accordance with the opinion of Rabbi Meir. This is in accordance with the principle (see *Megilla* 2a) that any unattributed mishna represents the opinion of Rabbi Meir. Consequently, when the mishna states: If he decreased its frankincense the meal offering is unfit, this means that it is unfit if he decreased it by any amount. Other commentaries claim that the mishna can be interpreted in accordance with the opinions of any of these *tanna'im* (*Likkutei Halakhot*).

NOTES

A case where he separated two handfuls for the meal offering – כְּגוֹן שֶׁהִפְרִישׁ לָהּ שְׁנֵי קְמָצִין: If he separated more than one handful but less than two, it is not disqualified (Rashi). The reason is that the measure of a handful is itself somewhat subjective, as a larger hand will remove a larger handful (commentary attributed to Rashba). Alternatively, as there are *tanna'im* who consider a handful that was diminished to less than its full measure fit for sacrifice, it is evident that the requirement to sacrifice specifically a handful is not absolute, and consequently, if one increased its measure slightly, it likewise remains valid (*Keren Ora*).

וְאָמַר רַבִּי יִצְחָק בַּר יוֹסֵף אָמַר רַבִּי יוֹחָנָן: מַחֲלוֹקֶת בִּלְבוֹנָה הַבָּאָה עִם הַמִּנְחָה, אֲבָל בִּלְבוֹנָה הַבָּאָה בְּבָזִיכִין – דִּבְרֵי הַכֹּל שְׁנֵי קְמָצִין בַּתְּחִילָּה וּשְׁנֵי קְמָצִין בַּסּוֹף.

And Rabbi Yitzḥak bar Yosef says that **Rabbi Yoḥanan says:** The **dispute** between these *tanna'im* is **with regard to frankincense that comes with a meal offering. But with regard to frankincense that comes in bowls**[H] together with the shewbread, **everyone,** even Rabbi Yehuda and Rabbi Shimon, **agrees** that there must be **two handfuls in the beginning,** one handful for each bowl, **and ultimately** there must also be **two handfuls.**

פְּשִׁיטָא! מַהוּ דְּתֵימָא: כֵּיוָן דְּבַהֲדֵי לֶחֶם אָתְיָא, כַּ״אֲשֶׁר עַל הַמִּנְחָה״ דָּמְיָא, קָא מַשְׁמַע לַן.

The Gemara asks: Isn't it **obvious** that this is the case, as with regard to this *halakha* the verse does not state the term: All, from which one might derive that it is referring to any part of the frankincense? The Gemara explains: This ruling is necessary, **lest you say** that **since** the frankincense in the bowls **comes together with bread,** i.e., the shewbread, it should be **considered as:** "Frankincense **that is upon the meal offering**" (Leviticus 6:8), and therefore Rabbi Yehuda and Rabbi Shimon claim that one may sacrifice it even if less than two handfuls remain. Rabbi Yitzḥak bar Yosef **teaches us** that this is not the case.

פְּלִיגִי בָּהּ רַבִּי אַמִי וְרַבִּי יִצְחָק נַפָּחָא, חַד אָמַר: מַחֲלוֹקֶת בִּלְבוֹנָה הַבָּאָה עִם הַמִּנְחָה, אֲבָל בִּלְבוֹנָה הַבָּאָה בִּפְנֵי עַצְמָהּ – דִּבְרֵי הַכֹּל קוֹמֶץ בַּתְּחִילָּה וְקוֹמֶץ בַּסּוֹף; וְחַד אָמַר: כְּמַחֲלוֹקֶת בְּזוֹ כָּךְ מַחֲלוֹקֶת בְּזוֹ.

The Gemara notes: **Rabbi Ami and Rabbi Yitzḥak Nappaḥa disagree with regard to** the case of frankincense that comes by itself. **One says** that the **dispute** between the *tanna'im* with regard to whether or not a handful of frankincense that became lacking may be sacrificed upon the altar applies only **with regard to frankincense that comes with a meal offering, but with regard to frankincense that comes by itself, everyone agrees** that the priest must remove **a handful at the beginning and ultimately** the entire **handful** must be burned upon the altar. **And one says: Just as** there is **a dispute in this** case, **so too,** there is **a dispute in that** case.

״חִיסֵּר לְבוֹנָתָהּ״. הָא יָתֵיר – כְּשֵׁרָה; וְהָתַנְיָא: יָתֵיר – פְּסוּלָה! אָמַר רָמִי בַּר חָמָא: כְּגוֹן שֶׁהִפְרִישׁ לָהּ שְׁנֵי קְמָצִין.

§ The mishna teaches that if the priest **decreased its frankincense** beyond its appropriate measure, the meal offering is unfit. The Gemara infers from this statement that if **he increased** its frankincense, it is **fit.** The Gemara asks: **But isn't it taught** in a *baraita* that if he **increased** its frankincense the meal offering is **disqualified? Rami bar Ḥama said:** The *baraita* rules that the meal offering is disqualified in a case **where he separated two handfuls** of frankincense **for** the meal offering[NH] and placed both of them onto the meal offering.

וְאָמַר רָמִי בַּר חָמָא: הִפְרִישׁ לָהּ שְׁנֵי קְמָצִין וְאָבַד אֶחָד מֵהֶן, קוֹדֶם קְמִיצָה – לֹא הוּקְבְּעוּ, אַחַר קְמִיצָה – הוּקְבְּעוּ.

And Rami bar Ḥama says: In a case where **one separated two handfuls** of frankincense **for** the meal offering **and** subsequently **lost one of them,**[H] if it was lost **before the removal of the handful** of the meal offering, the additional frankincense **was not fixed** with the meal offering, and therefore it does not disqualify the meal offering. But if this occurred **after the removal of the handful** of the meal offering, since both handfuls **were** already **fixed** with the meal offering, it is disqualified, as he increased its frankincense by a large amount.

HALAKHA

Frankincense that comes in bowls – לְבוֹנָה הַבָּאָה בְּבָזִיכִין: The two bowls of frankincense that accompany the shewbread must each contain one handful, from the time of the initial placement of the frankincense inside the bowls until their sacrifice upon the altar. If the frankincense in either bowl was decreased by any amount, they are both disqualified (Rambam *Sefer Avoda, Hilkhot Pesulei HaMukdashin* 11:17).

A case where he separated two handfuls for the meal offering – כְּגוֹן שֶׁהִפְרִישׁ לָהּ שְׁנֵי קְמָצִין: In a case where one increased the amount of frankincense in a meal offering, if the amount stood at less than two handfuls the offering remains valid. If he increased it to the point that there were two handfuls or more, it is disqualified, as stated by Rami bar Ḥama (Rambam *Sefer Avoda, Hilkhot Pesulei HaMukdashin* 11:9).

One separated two handfuls of frankincense for it and subsequently lost one of them – הִפְרִישׁ לָהּ שְׁנֵי קְמָצִין וְאָבַד אֶחָד מֵהֶן: In a case where one separated two handfuls of frankincense for a single meal offering and one of those handfuls was lost, if it was lost before the removal of the handful of the meal offering, the offering is valid, as the additional handful of frankincense was not fixed together with the meal offering. If it was lost after the removal of the handful, then the additional frankincense was already fixed with the meal offering and therefore disqualified the offering (Rambam *Sefer Avoda, Hilkhot Pesulei HaMukdashin* 11:18).

וְאָמַר רָמִי בַּר חָמָא: הִפְרִישׁ אַרְבָּעָה קְמָצִין לִשְׁנֵי בָזִיכִין וְאָבְדוּ שְׁנַיִם מֵהֶן, קוֹדֶם סִילּוּק בָּזִיכִין – לֹא הוּקְבְּעוּ, לְאַחַר סִילּוּק בָּזִיכִין – הוּקְבְּעוּ.

And Rami bar Ḥama says: In a case where **one separated four handfuls** of frankincense **for** placement in the **two bowls**[H] that accompany the shewbread, **and two of them** were subsequently **lost,** the *halakha* depends on when they were lost. If they were lost **before the removal of** the **bowls** from the Table of the shewbread, then the additional frankincense **was not** yet **fixed** with the shewbread, and the frankincense remains fit for sacrifice. But if they were lost **after the removal of** the **bowls,** then all four handfuls **were** already **fixed** with the shewbread, and therefore the frankincense is disqualified.

הָא תּוּ לָמָּה לִי? הַיְינוּ הָךְ!

The Gemara asks: **Why do I also** need **this? This** statement of Rami bar Ḥama is identical to **that** previous statement, as the burning of the frankincense permits the shewbread for consumption just as the frankincense permits the meal offering for consumption. Consequently, the removal of the bowls of frankincense is comparable to the removal of the handful from a meal offering.

מַהוּ דְּתֵימָא: כֵּיוָן דְּבָרִיר קוֹמֶץ דִּידֵהּ, כֵּיוָן שֶׁהִגִּיעַ זְמַנָּהּ לְפוֹרְקָהּ – כְּמַאן דִּפְרִיקָה דָּמְיָא, קָא מַשְׁמַע לַן.

The Gemara explains: The last statement of Rami bar Ḥama is necessary, **lest you say** that **since** the **handful of** frankincense of the shewbread **is** already considered **designated** for burning, as it is placed in a separate bowl and burned in its entirety, then **once the time arrives for removing** the bowls from upon the Table of the shewbread, **it is considered as though** the bowls were already **removed,** and the shewbread should therefore be disqualified on account of the additional frankincense. Therefore, Rami bar Ḥama **teaches us** that the additional handfuls disqualify the shewbread only if they were inside the bowls at the time of their actual removal from the Table.

מתני׳ הַקּוֹמֵץ אֶת הַמִּנְחָה לֶאֱכוֹל שְׁיָרֶיהָ בַּחוּץ אוֹ כַּזַּיִת מִשְּׁיָרֶיהָ בַּחוּץ, לְהַקְטִיר קוּמְצָהּ בַּחוּץ אוֹ כַּזַּיִת קוּמְצָהּ בַּחוּץ, אוֹ לְהַקְטִיר לְבוֹנָתָהּ בַּחוּץ – פָּסוּל וְאֵין בּוֹ כָּרֵת. לֶאֱכוֹל שְׁיָרֶיהָ לְמָחָר אוֹ כַּזַּיִת מִשְּׁיָרֶיהָ לְמָחָר, לְהַקְטִיר קוּמְצָהּ לְמָחָר אוֹ כַּזַּיִת מִקּוּמְצָהּ לְמָחָר, אוֹ לְהַקְטִיר לְבוֹנָהּ לְמָחָר

MISHNA With regard to **one who removes a handful from the meal offering** with the intent **to partake of its remainder outside**[HN] the Temple courtyard **or** to partake of **an olive-bulk of its remainder outside** the Temple courtyard, **to burn its handful outside** the Temple courtyard **or** to burn **an olive-bulk of its handful outside** the Temple courtyard, **or to burn its frankincense outside** the Temple courtyard, in all these cases the offering is **unfit, but there is no** liability for ***karet*** for one who partakes **of it.** If one had the intent **to partake of its remainder on the next day**[HN] or to partake of **an olive-bulk of its remainder on the next day, to burn its handful on the next day or** to burn **an olive-bulk of its handful on the next day, or to burn** its **frankincense on the next day,**

HALAKHA

Four handfuls of frankincense for placement in the two bowls – אַרְבָּעָה קְמָצִין לִשְׁנֵי בָזִיכִין: If one separated four handfuls of frankincense for the two bowls of frankincense that accompany the shewbread, and two of those handfuls were lost before the bowls were removed from the Table, the additional frankincense is not considered fixed with the shewbread, and the other frankincense is fit for offering. If they were lost after the bowls were already removed, they are considered fixed to the shewbread and the frankincense is disqualified on account of the increase in its measure (Rambam *Sefer Avoda, Hilkhot Pesulei HaMukdashin* 11:18).

To partake of its remainder outside, etc. – לֶאֱכוֹל שְׁיָרֶיהָ בַּחוּץ וכו׳: In a case where one removes the handful from a meal offering with the intent to partake of its remainder, or an olive-bulk of it outside the Temple courtyard; or to burn its handful or an olive-bulk of it outside the Temple courtyard; or to burn an olive-bulk of its frankincense outside the Temple courtyard, the offering is unfit, but one who partakes of it is not liable to receive *karet* (Rambam *Sefer Avoda, Hilkhot Pesulei HaMukdashin* 13:1, 14:10).

To partake of its remainder on the next day, etc. – לֶאֱכוֹל שְׁיָרֶיהָ לְמָחָר וכו׳: If one removes the handful of a meal offering with the intent to partake of its remainder, or an olive-bulk of it, on the next day; or to burn its handful, or an olive-bulk of it, the next day; or to burn an olive bulk of its frankincense the next day, the offering is rendered *piqqul* and one who partakes of it is liable to receive *karet* (Rambam *Sefer Avoda, Hilkhot Pesulei HaMukdashin* 13:1, 14:10).

NOTES

One who removes a handful from the meal offering with intent to partake of its remainder outside, etc. – הַקּוֹמֵץ אֶת הַמִּנְחָה לֶאֱכוֹל שְׁיָרֶיהָ בַּחוּץ וכו׳: This mishna is similar to a mishna in *Zevaḥim* (27b) that discusses the same *halakhot* with regard to the sacrificial rites of a slaughtered offering. The Gemara there analyzes each *halakha* at length and derives their sources, which are summarized by Rashi here. See also the Gemara at the beginning of this tractate (2b), where the commentaries disagree with regard to the definition of intent, i.e., whether this refers to mental intention alone (Rambam), or whether a verbal expression of such intent is necessary in order to disqualify an offering (Rashi).

Outside…on the next day – בַּחוּץ...לְמָחָר: The parts of any offering that are burned upon the altar must be sacrificed on the day of the slaughter of the offerings or that night. Additionally, these parts may not be sacrificed outside the Temple courtyard. With regard to the consumption of an offering, different *halakhot* apply to the various types of offerings. A meal offering, which is an offering of the most sacred order, may be consumed only by priests, and only within the walls of the Temple courtyard, and it must be eaten on the day or the night following the sacrifice of its handful. Any part remaining from the meal offering by the following morning is rendered *notar*, leftover, and is prohibited for consumption.

פיגול וחייבין עליו כרת.

the offering is ***piggul***,[B] **and one is liable** to receive ***karet*** **for** partaking of the remainder of that meal offering.[N]

זה הכלל: כל הקומץ, [או] נותן בכלי, המוליך, המקטיר, לאכול דבר שדרכו לאכול ולהקטיר דבר שדרכו להקטיר, חוץ למקומו – פסול ואין בו כרת, חוץ לזמנו – פיגול וחייבין עליו כרת, ובלבד שיקריב המתיר כמצותו.

This is the principle: In the case of **anyone who removes the handful,**[HN] **or places** the handful **in the vessel,** or **who conveys** the vessel with the handful to the altar, or **who burns** the handful on the altar, with the intent **to partake of an item whose** typical **manner** is such that one **partakes** of it, e.g., the remainder, **or to burn an item whose** typical **manner** is such that one **burns** it on the altar, e.g., the handful or the frankincense, **outside its** designated **area,** the meal offering is **unfit but there is no** liability for ***karet.*** If his intent was to do so **beyond its** designated **time,** the offering is ***piggul*** **and one is liable** to receive ***karet*** **on account of it, provided that the permitting** factor, i.e., the handful, **was sacrificed in accordance with its mitzva.**[H] If the permitting factor was not sacrificed in accordance with its mitzva, although the meal offering is unfit, the prohibition of *piggul* does not apply to it.

כיצד קרב המתיר כמצותו? קמץ בשתיקה, נתן בכלי והוליך והקטיר חוץ לזמנו; או שקמץ חוץ לזמנו, נתן בכלי והוליך והקטיר בשתיקה; או שקמץ ונתן בכלי והוליך והקטיר חוץ לזמנו – זהו שקרב המתיר כמצותו.

How is **the permitting factor** considered to have been **sacrificed in accordance with its mitzva?** If one **removed the handful in silence,** i.e., with no specific intent, and **placed** it **in the vessel, conveyed** it, **and burned** the handful on the altar, with the intent to partake of the remainder **beyond its** designated **time; or** if one **removed the handful** with the intent to partake of the or burn the handful or frankincense **beyond its** designated **time,** and **placed** it **in the vessel, and conveyed** it, **and burned** the handful on the altar **in silence,** with no specific intent; **or** if one **removed the handful** and **placed** it **in the vessel, conveyed** it, **and burned** the handful on the altar, with the intent to partake of the remainder **beyond its** designated **time, that is** the case of an offering **whose permitting factor was sacrificed in accordance with its mitzva,** and one is liable to receive *karet* for partaking of it due to *piggul.*

כיצד לא קרב המתיר כמצותו? קמץ חוץ למקומו, נתן בכלי והוליך והקטיר חוץ לזמנו; או שקמץ חוץ לזמנו, נתן בכלי והוליך והקטיר חוץ למקומו; או שקמץ נתן בכלי והוליך והקטיר חוץ למקומו – זהו שלא קרב המתיר כמצותו.

How is **the permitting factor not sacrificed in accordance with its mitzva?** If one **removed the handful** with the intent to partake of the remainder or burn the handful or frankincense **outside its** designated **area,**[N] or **placed** it **in the vessel, conveyed** it, **and burned** the handful on the altar, with the intent to partake of the remainder **beyond its** designated **time; or** if one **removed the handful** with the intent to partake of the remainder or burn the handful or frankincense **beyond its** designated **time,** and **placed** it **in the vessel, conveyed** it, **and burned** the handful on the altar, with the intent to partake of the remainder **outside its** designated **area; or** if one **removed the handful** and **placed** it **in the vessel, and conveyed** it, **and burned** the handful on the altar, with the intent to partake of the remainder **outside its** designated **area, that is** the case of an offering **whose permitting factor was not sacrificed in accordance with its mitzva.**

NOTES

The offering is *piggul* and one is liable to receive *karet* for partaking of the remainder of that meal offering – פיגול וחייבין עליו כרת: *Piggul* status applies only to the remainder of the meal offering, not to the handful. Although it is certainly prohibited to consume the handful, *piggul* applies only to those items whose consumption or sacrifice is permitted through another item, and not to that which permits another item. Since the burning of the handful permits the remainder for consumption, the handful cannot be rendered *piggul* (see *Zevaḥim* 42b).

Who removes the handful, etc. – הקומץ וכו׳: The fact that a meal offering is disqualified through improper intent is derived from the *halakha* of slaughtered offerings, either by the Torah's comparison of a meal offering to a sin offering and a guilt offering (Rashi), or by the more general comparison of all offerings to peace offerings (*Tosafot* on 2b). The Sages teach that the four sacrificial rites performed with the handful of a meal offering parallel the four rites performed with the blood of a slaughtered offering. The removal of the handful is equivalent to the slaughter of an offering, the placement of the handful in a service vessel parallels the collection of the blood in a vessel, they are both conveyed to the altar, and the burning of the handful on the altar corresponds to the presentation of the blood upon the altar (see *Zevaḥim* 13b). Accordingly, improper intent does not disqualify a meal offering before the removal of the handful, just as it does not disqualify an animal offering before its slaughter (see *Tosafot* on *Zevaḥim* 13b).

Removed the handful outside its designated area, etc. – קמץ חוץ למקומו וכו׳: In other words, if any one of these rites were performed with the intent to consume its remainder outside its designated area and the remaining rites were performed with intent to consume the remainder outside its designated time, the offering is considered to have been sacrificed not in accordance with its mitzva (Rashi).

BACKGROUND

Piggul – **פיגול:** The *halakha* of *piggul* is based on the verse: "And if any of the meat of the sacrifice of his peace offerings be at all eaten on the third day, it shall not be accepted, neither shall it be attributed to him that sacrifices it; it shall be *piggul*" (Leviticus 7:18). The Sages interpreted this verse as referring to one who had the intent, during the performance of one of the sacrificial rites in the Temple, to eat from the offering after its designated time or to sacrifice it after its designated time. That intent disqualifies the offering, and one who eats from it is liable to receive *karet*. Some Sages hold that it is *piggul* only if one expresses this intent aloud.

HALAKHA

Anyone who removes the handful, etc. – כל הקומץ וכו׳: In the case of one who removes the handful, or places the handful in a service vessel, or conveys it to the altar, or burns the handful on the altar, with the intention to consume its remainder or an olive-bulk of it, or to burn its handful or an olive-bulk of it, or to burn an olive-bulk of its frankincense, outside the Temple courtyard, the meal offering is disqualified but the person is not liable to receive *karet* on account of it. If his intention was to consume the remainder or to burn the handful or the frankincense on the next day, the offering is *piggul* and one who eats from its remainder is liable to receive *karet* (Rambam *Sefer Avoda, Hilkhot Pesulei HaMukdashin* 13:1, 6).

Provided that the permitting factor was sacrificed in accordance with its mitzva – ובלבד שיקריב המתיר כמצותו: A meal offering is rendered *piggul* on account of the intent to consume it or sacrifice it beyond its designated time only if there was no other disqualifying intent during its sacrificial rites. If in addition to the intent that renders it *piggul*, one intended to consume it or burn it outside its designated area, or one performed one of its rites for the sake of another offering in the specific cases of the meal offering of a sinner or a meal offering of jealousy, the offering is disqualified but it is not rendered *piggul*. How is a meal offering rendered *piggul*? If one removed the handful and placed it in a vessel and conveyed it to the altar and burned it upon the altar, all while intending to consume its remainder or burn its handful outside its designated time; or if this was his intention during the performance of any one of these rites, while he had proper intention during the others; or if he had no intention at all during the performance of the other rites, the offering is *piggul*. If he removed the handful with intention to consume its remainder outside its designated time, and placed it in the vessel, conveyed it to the altar, and burned it on the altar, with the intention to consume its remainder outside its designated area; or if he removed the handful with the intention to consume its remainder outside its designated area, and placed it in the vessel, conveyed it, and burned it upon the altar, with the intention to consume its remainder outside its designated time, the meal offering is disqualified but is not rendered *piggul* (Rambam *Sefer Avoda, Hilkhot Pesulei HaMukdashin* 16:1).

מִנְחַת חוֹטֵא וּמִנְחַת קְנָאוֹת שֶׁקְּמָצָן שֶׁלֹּא לִשְׁמָן, נָתַן בִּכְלִי וְהוֹלִיךְ וְהִקְטִיר חוּץ לִזְמַנּוֹ; אוֹ שֶׁקָּמַץ חוּץ לִזְמַנּוֹ, נָתַן בִּכְלִי וְהוֹלִיךְ וְהִקְטִיר שֶׁלֹּא לִשְׁמָן; אוֹ שֶׁקָּמַץ וְנָתַן בִּכְלִי וְהוֹלִיךְ וְהִקְטִיר שֶׁלֹּא לִשְׁמָן – זֶהוּ שֶׁלֹּא קָרַב הַמַּתִּיר כְּמִצְוָתוֹ.

The meal offering of a sinner and the meal offering of jealousy brought by a *sota* **that one removed their handful not for their sake** and **placed** it **in the vessel, conveyed** it, **and burned** the handful on the altar, with the intent to partake of the remainder or burn the handful **beyond its** designated **time; or that one removed the handful** with the intent to partake of the remainder or burn the handful **beyond its** designated **time** or **placed** it **in the vessel, conveyed** it, **and burned** the handful on the altar, **not for their sake; or that one removed the handful, and placed** it **in the vessel, and conveyed** it, **and burned** the handful on the altar, **not for their sake, that is** the case of an offering **whose permitting factor was not sacrificed in accordance with its mitzva.**

לֶאֱכוֹל כְּזַיִת בַּחוּץ כְּזַיִת לְמָחָר, כְּזַיִת לְמָחָר כְּזַיִת בַּחוּץ, כַּחֲצִי זַיִת בַּחוּץ כַּחֲצִי זַיִת לְמָחָר, כַּחֲצִי זַיִת לְמָחָר כַּחֲצִי זַיִת בַּחוּץ – פָּסוּל וְאֵין בּוֹ כָּרֵת.

If one performed one of these rites with the intent **to partake of an olive-bulk outside** its designated area and **an olive-bulk the next day,**[HN] or **an olive-bulk the next day** and **an olive-bulk outside** its designated area, or **half an olive-bulk outside** its designated area and **half an olive-bulk the next day,**[N] or **half an olive-bulk the next day** and **half an olive-bulk outside** its designated area, the offering is **unfit but there is no** liability for ***karet***.

אָמַר רַבִּי יְהוּדָה, זֶה הַכְּלָל: אִם מַחְשֶׁבֶת הַזְּמַן קָדְמָה לְמַחְשֶׁבֶת הַמָּקוֹם – פִּיגּוּל וְחַיָּיבִין עָלָיו כָּרֵת, אִם מַחְשֶׁבֶת הַמָּקוֹם קָדְמָה לְמַחְשֶׁבֶת הַזְּמַן – פָּסוּל וְאֵין בּוֹ כָּרֵת. וַחֲכָמִים אוֹמְרִים: זֶה וָזֶה פָּסוּל וְאֵין בּוֹ כָּרֵת.

Rabbi Yehuda says that **this is the principle: If the intent** with regard to **the time preceded the intent** with regard to **the area,** the offering is ***piggul*** **and one is liable** to receive ***karet*** **on account of it. If the intent** with regard to **the area preceded the intent** with regard to **the time,** the offering is **unfit but there is no** liability for ***karet***. **And the Rabbis say:** In both **this** case, where the intent with regard to time was first, **and that** case, where the intent with regard to area came first, the offering is **unfit**[N] **but there is no** liability for ***karet***.

גמ׳ אִיבַּעְיָא לְהוּ: לְדִבְרֵי הָאוֹמֵר שִׁירַיִם שֶׁחָסְרוּ בֵּין קְמִיצָה לְהַקְטָרָה – מַקְטִיר קוֹמֶץ עֲלֵיהֶן, וְקַיְימָא לַן דְּאוֹתָן שִׁירַיִם אֲסוּרִים בַּאֲכִילָה, מַהוּ דְּתֵיהַנֵּי לְהוּ הַקְטָרָה לְמִיקְבְּעִינְהוּ בְּפִיגּוּל

GEMARA **A dilemma was raised before** the Sages: **According to the statement of the one who says** that if the **remainder** of a meal offering became **lacking**[H] **between the removal of the handful and the burning** of the handful on the altar the priest nevertheless **burns the handful on** account of such a meal offering, **and** as **we maintain that** despite the fact that the handful is burned on account of it **that remainder is prohibited for consumption, what is** the *halakha* with regard to *piggul*? Should the **burning** of the handful **be effective in establishing** such a remainder as ***piggul*** when the handful was burned with the intent to partake of the remainder the next day?

וּלְפַקְּינְהוּ מִידֵי מְעִילָה?

And similarly, is the burning of the handful effective **in removing** such a remainder **from** being subject to **misuse**[H] of consecrated property, just as a complete remainder is removed being subject to this prohibition after the burning of the handful, when it becomes permitted to the priests for consumption?

HALAKHA

An olive-bulk outside and an olive-bulk the next day – כְּזַיִת בַּחוּץ כְּזַיִת לְמָחָר: If one's intention with regard to any of the four sacrificial rites, or with regard to all of them, was to consume an olive-bulk of an item fit for consumption outside its designated area and also an olive-bulk the next day, or an olive-bulk the next day and also an olive-bulk outside, or half an olive-bulk outside and also half an olive-bulk the next day, or half an olive-bulk the next day and also half an olive-bulk outside, the offering is disqualified but is not rendered *piggul*. The *halakha* is in accordance with the opinion of the Rabbis (Rambam *Sefer Avoda, Hilkhot Pesulei HaMukdashin* 16:2).

The remainder became lacking, etc. – שִׁירַיִם שֶׁחָסְרוּ וכו׳: In a case where the remainder of a meal offering became lacking between the removal of the handful and its burning upon the altar, if the priest burned the handful with the intention to consume the remainder outside its designated time it is uncertain whether or not this intention renders it *piggul* (Rambam *Sefer Avoda, Hilkhot Pesulei HaMukdashin* 16:11).

And to remove such a remainder from misuse – וּלְפַקְּינְהוּ מִידֵי מְעִילָה: In a case where the remainder of a meal offering was disqualified or became lacking between the removal of the handful and its burning upon the altar, and the handful was subsequently burned upon the altar, it is uncertain whether or not the remainder is subject to misuse of consecrated property (Rambam *Sefer Avoda, Hilkhot Me'ila* 2:7).

NOTES

To partake of an olive-bulk outside its designated area and an olive-bulk the next day, etc. – לֶאֱכוֹל כְּזַיִת בַּחוּץ כְּזַיִת לְמָחָר וכו׳: This *halakha* is apparently a repetition of the previous statement of the mishna, that if the permitting factor was not sacrificed in accordance with its mitzva the offering is disqualified and one is not liable to receive *karet*. Rashi explains that the mishna is introducing a new facet to the *halakha*, that if both of his disqualifying intentions occurred during the performance of the same rite, the offering is not rendered *piggul*. Although it can be claimed that this ruling is obvious, as here the intention that would render the offering *piggul* is mixed with another disqualifying intention, the mishna teaches it in order to convey that according to Rabbi Yehuda even in such a case the offering is *piggul*, provided that the intention to consume it outside its designated time preceded the intention to consume it outside its designated area.

Half an olive-bulk outside its designated area and half an olive-bulk the next day – כַּחֲצִי זַיִת בַּחוּץ כַּחֲצִי זַיִת לְמָחָר: The mishna is teaching that although neither intention on its own disqualifies an offering as each one refers to less than an olive-bulk, the intentions combine to disqualify it.

And the Rabbis say, in both this case and that case the offering is unfit – וַחֲכָמִים אוֹמְרִים זֶה וָזֶה פָּסוּל: Although the opinion of the Rabbis is essentially the same as that of the first *tanna*, it is common in the Mishna that the authoritative opinion is reiterated in the name of the Rabbis in order to emphasize that this is the *halakha*. This is in accordance with the principle that in a disagreement between an individual Sage and the majority of Sages, the *halakha* follows the majority opinion (*Tosafot*). Others explain that the Rabbis in fact disagree with the first *tanna*, as they maintain that improper intention negates the intention capable of rendering an offering *piggul* only when they both occur in the same rite; if they occur during the performance of separate rites the offering is *piggul* (*Ḥok Natan*).

אֲמַר רַב הוּנָא, אֲפִילּוּ לְרַבִּי עֲקִיבָא דְּאָמַר: זְרִיקָה מוֹעֶלֶת לְיוֹצֵא – הָנֵי מִילֵּי יוֹצֵא,

Rav Huna said: Even according to the opinion of **Rabbi Akiva, who says** that the **sprinkling** of the blood of an offering, which renders its meat permitted for consumption and removes it from being subject to misuse of consecrated property, **is effective in** removing the meat of an offering that **left** the Temple courtyard from being subject to misuse of consecrated property despite the fact that such meat is prohibited for consumption, **that statement** applies only when the meat was disqualified by means of **leaving.**

דְּאִיתֵיהּ בְּעֵינֵיהּ וּפָסוּל מֵחֲמַת דָּבָר אַחֵר הוּא, אֲבָל חִסָּרוֹן, דִּפְסוּלָא דְּגוּפֵיהּ הוּא – לָא מְהַנֵּי לֵיהּ הַקְטָרָה.

Rav Huna explains: The reason is **that** the meat remains **as is, and** the **disqualification** of the meat by means of leaving is **on account of something else,** i.e., a factor external to the meat itself. **But** in the case of **a lack** in the measure of the remainder of a meal offering, **which is a disqualification** on account **of itself,** the **burning** of the handful **is not effective in** removing the remainder from being subject to misuse of consecrated property, nor to establish it as *piggul.*

אֲמַר לֵיהּ רָבָא: אַדְּרַבָּה, אֲפִילּוּ לְרַבִּי אֱלִיעֶזֶר דְּאָמַר: אֵין זְרִיקָה מוֹעֶלֶת לְיוֹצֵא – הָנֵי מִילֵּי יוֹצֵא, דְּלֵיתֵיהּ בִּפְנִים, אֲבָל חִסָּרוֹן דְּאִיתֵיהּ בִּפְנִים – מְהַנְּיָא לֵיהּ הַקְטָרָה.

Rava said to Rav Huna: **On the contrary; even according to** the opinion of **Rabbi Eliezer, who says** that **sprinkling is not effective in** removing the meat that **left** the Temple courtyard from being subject to misuse of consecrated property, **that statement** applies only when the meat was disqualified by means of **leaving, as** the meat **is not inside** the Temple courtyard where the sprinkling could be effective for it. **But** with regard to **a lack** in the measure of the remainder of a meal offering **that is inside** the Temple courtyard, the **burning** of the handful **is effective** in removing the remainder from being subject to misuse of consecrated property as well as in establishing it as *piggul.*

אֲמַר רָבָא: מְנָא אָמִינָא לַהּ? דִּתְנַן: הַקּוֹמֵץ אֶת הַמִּנְחָה לֶאֱכוֹל שְׁיָרֶיהָ בַּחוּץ אוֹ כַּזַּיִת מִשְּׁיָרֶיהָ בַּחוּץ, וְתָנֵי רַבִּי חִיָּיא: הַקּוֹמֵץ אֶת הַמִּנְחָה, וְלָא תָּנֵי "אוֹ כַּזַּיִת";

Rava said: From where do I say[N] that even remainders that lack a full measure can be rendered *piggul*? This can be inferred from that **which we learned** in the mishna: With regard to **one who removes a handful from the meal offering** with the intent **to partake** of its **remainder outside** the Temple courtyard **or** to partake of **an olive-bulk of its remainder outside** the Temple courtyard, the meal offering is unfit but there is no liability for *karet*, and if he removes a handful from the meal offering with the intent to partake of its remainder beyond the designated time or to partake of an olive-bulk of its remainder beyond the designated time the offering is *piggul* and one is liable to receive *karet* for partaking of the remainder of that meal offering. **And Rabbi Ḥiyya teaches**[B] in his version of the mishna: **One who removes a handful from the meal offering** with the intent to partake of its remainder, **and he does not teach: Or an olive-bulk** of its remainder.

מַאי טַעְמָא לָא תָּנֵי "אוֹ כַּזַּיִת", לָאו כְּגוֹן שֶׁחָסְרוּ שִׁירַיִם וְקָמוּ לְהוּ אַכַּזַּיִת? וְכֵיוָן דִּבְמַתַּן כְּלִי בְּהִילּוּךְ וּבְהַקְטָרָה לָא מִתְנֵי לֵיהּ:

Rava continues: **What is the reason** that Rabbi Ḥiyya diverged from the standard text of the mishna and **did not teach: Or an olive-bulk?** Is it **not** because his mishna is discussing a case **where** the **remainder** later **became lacking and** its measure **stood at an olive-bulk? And** therefore Rabbi Ḥiyya did not include the clause: Or an olive-bulk, **since** later in the mishna, **with regard to the placement** of the handful **in a vessel,** and **with regard to** the **conveyance** of the vessel to the altar, **and with regard to** the **burning** of the handful, **he** could **not teach** the phrase:

NOTES

From where do I say, etc. – מְנָא אָמִינָא לַהּ וכו׳: Rava's underlying assumption is that Rabbi Ḥiyya agrees with the *halakha* stated in the mishna, and rephrases the mishna in order to explain it. Accordingly, one can infer the circumstances of the case Rabbi Ḥiyya is discussing from the change in terminology in his mishna.

BACKGROUND

Rabbi Ḥiyya teaches – תָּנֵי רַבִּי חִיָּיא: During the period of the *tanna'im*, many Sages would teach their own collection of *mishnayot*, which were either received through tradition from their teachers or were of their own composition. Consequently, by the generation of Rabbi Yehuda HaNasi, who redacted the Mishna, and the subsequent generations, there were many collections of *mishnayot* among the Sages. In the same manner that Rabbi Yehuda HaNasi selected particular *mishnayot* from the vast collection of statements accumulated until his time and arranged them into the body of the Mishna, Rabbi Ḥiyya, a disciple-colleague of Rabbi Yehuda HaNasi, also arranged *mishnayot* in an organized body, which included many *halakhot* that are not found in the Mishna. It is certain that the Mishna of Rabbi Yehuda HaNasi was also available to him.

It is clear from the Gemara that Rava assumes that the Mishna of Rabbi Yehuda HaNasi serves as the foundation for the collection of *mishnayot* of Rabbi Ḥiyya. Accordingly, the terminologies of the *mishnayot* of Rabbi Ḥiyya can serve to shed light on the proper interpretation of the Mishna of Rabbi Yehuda HaNasi. By contrast, on the following *amud* Abaye claims that the *mishnayot* of Rabbi Ḥiyya are not necessarily modeled after the Mishna of Rabbi Yehuda HaNasi but are a compilation of other sources.

״אוֹ כַּזַּיִת״ אַשִּׁירַיִם – בִּקְמִיצָה נַמִּי לֶאֱכוֹל שִׁירַיִם לָא תָּנֵי ״אוֹ כַּזַּיִת״; וְקָתָנֵי סֵיפָא: פִּיגּוּל וְחַיָּיבִין עָלָיו כָּרֵת, אַלְמָא מְהַנְיָא לְהוּ הַקְטָרָה.

Or an olive-bulk, in the case of one's intent with regard to the consumption of the **remainder,** because the remainder is already the size of an olive-bulk. Therefore, **in** the case of the **removal of the handful as well,** i.e., when he teaches: One who removes a handful **to partake of its remainder,** Rabbi Ḥiyya **did not teach:**[N] **Or** to consume **an olive-bulk** of its remainder, despite the fact that he could have done so in that clause. Rava concludes his proof: **And** yet **the latter clause teaches** that if one burned the handful with the intent to consume the remainder after its designated time, the offering is ***piggul*** **and one is liable** to receive ***karet*** **on** account of **it. Evidently, burning is effective in** rendering a lacking remainder as *piggul.*

אֲמַר לֵיהּ אַבַּיֵי: לָא, הָא מַנִּי? רַבִּי אֶלְעָזָר הִיא, דִּתְנַן: הַקּוֹמֶץ, וְהַלְּבוֹנָה, וְהַקְּטֹרֶת, וּמִנְחַת כֹּהֲנִים, וּמִנְחַת כֹּהֵן מָשִׁיחַ, וּמִנְחַת נְסָכִים, שֶׁהִקְרִיב מֵאַחַת מֵהֶן כַּזַּיִת בַּחוּץ – חַיָּיב, וְרַבִּי אֶלְעָזָר פּוֹטֵר עַד שֶׁיַּקְרִיב אֶת כּוּלּוֹ;

Abaye said to Rava: **No,** one cannot prove from here that the mishna is discussing the case of a remainder that became lacking. The reason for this is: In accordance with **whose** opinion **is this** mishna of Rabbi Ḥiyya? **It is** in accordance with the opinion of **Rabbi Elazar, as we learned** in a mishna (*Zevaḥim* 109b): With regard to **the handful** of flour, **and the frankincense,**[NH] **and the incense, and the meal offering of priests** (see Leviticus 6:16), **and the meal offering of the anointed priest** (see Leviticus 6:12–15), **and the meal offering** that accompanies the **libations** brought with animal offerings (see Numbers 15:1–16), **where one sacrificed an olive-bulk from one of them outside** the Temple courtyard, he is **liable** for sacrificing outside the courtyard. **And Rabbi Elazar exempts** one from liability **until he sacrifices** them in their **entirety** rather than just an olive-bulk from them.

כֵּיוָן דִּבְהַקְטָרַת קְמִיצָה לָא מִתְנֵי לֵיהּ ״אוֹ כַּזַּיִת מִקּוּמְצָהּ בַּחוּץ״ – בְּשִׁירַיִם נַמִּי לָא מִתְנֵי לֵיהּ ״אוֹ כַּזַּיִת״.

Abaye concludes: **Since with regard to the burning of the handful he** could **not teach: Or** burn **an olive-bulk of its handful outside** the Temple, as according to Rabbi Elazar one is not liable for burning anything less than the full handful and therefore intent to burn only an olive-bulk does not render the offering *piggul*, **with regard to** the **remainder as well, he did not teach: Or an olive-bulk.**

אִי רַבִּי אֶלְעָזָר, הַאי ״לְהַקְטִיר קוּמְצָהּ״, ״לְהַקְטִיר קוּמְצָהּ וּלְבוֹנָתָהּ״ מִיבְּעֵי לֵיהּ! דִּתְנַן: הַקּוֹמֶץ וְהַלְּבוֹנָה שֶׁהִקְרִיב אֶת אֶחָד מֵהֶן בַּחוּץ – חַיָּיב, וְרַבִּי אֶלְעָזָר פּוֹטֵר עַד שֶׁיַּקְרִיב אֶת שְׁנֵיהֶם!

The Gemara asks: **If** the mishna of Rabbi Ḥiyya is really in accordance with the opinion of **Rabbi Elazar,** then **this** statement: **To burn its handful** outside the Temple courtyard, **should have** been phrased: **To burn its handful and its frankincense** outside the Temple courtyard, **as we learned** in a mishna (*Zevaḥim* 110a): With regard to **the handful and the frankincense,** in a case **where one sacrificed** only **one of them outside** the Temple courtyard, he is **liable. Rabbi Eliezer exempts** from liability one who burns only one of them **until he sacrifices both of them** together.

לָא נִצְרְכָא אֶלָּא לְקוֹמֶץ דְּמִנְחַת חוֹטֵא.

The Gemara responds: The mishna of Rabbi Ḥiyya **is necessary only for the handful of the meal offering of a sinner,**[N] which has no frankincense. Since only the burning of the handful permits the remainder of the sinner's meal offering for consumption, one's intent to burn it the next day renders the offering *piggul.* With regard to this meal offering, one is not liable for burning anything less than the full handful, according to Rabbi Elazar, and therefore it does not teach: Or an olive-bulk.

וְאִיכְּפַל תַּנָּא לְאַשְׁמוּעִינַן קוֹמֶץ דְּמִנְחַת חוֹטֵא? אִין. וְכֵן כִּי אֲתָא רַב דִּימִי אֲמַר רַבִּי אֶלְעָזָר: קוֹמֶץ דְּמִנְחַת חוֹטֵא הוּא, וְרַבִּי אֶלְעָזָר הִיא.

The Gemara asks: **And did the** ***tanna*** **go to all that trouble** [*ve'ikhpal*][NL] just **to teach us** a *halakha* that is applicable only in the case of **the handful of the meal offering of a sinner?** The Gemara responds: **Yes,** he did. **And similarly, when Rav Dimi came** to Babylonia from Eretz Yisrael, he said that **Rabbi Elazar** ben Pedat **said:** When the mishna discusses an instance where one has intent to sacrifice the handful of a meal offering outside, **it is** referring to the **handful of the meal offering of a sinner, and it is** in accordance with the opinion of **Rabbi Elazar.**

NOTES

In the case of the removal of the handful as well… Rabbi Ḥiyya did not teach, etc. – בִּקְמִיצָה נַמִּי...לָא תָּנֵי וכו׳: Rashi explains that the statement of the mishna: One who removes a handful with the intent to partake of its remainder or to burn an olive-bulk of its handful, cannot be referring to an instance where one removed a handful from a meal offering that was actually lacking in measure, as one does not remove a handful from a meal offering that is already unfit. Instead, the mishna is referring to a case where one removed the handful with the intent to consume an olive-bulk from the remainder in the event that it becomes lacking after the removal of the handful. Accordingly, Rabbi Ḥiyya's mishna can teach: Or to burn an olive-bulk of its handful the next day, as the handful itself is not currently lacking in measure. Nevertheless, with regard to the other rites, i.e., the placing of the handful in a service vessel, its conveyance to the altar, and the burning of the handful, Rabbi Ḥiyya did not teach: Or an olive-bulk, for the reason explained in the Gemara; therefore, he did not teach it in the context of the rite of the removal of the handful either.

The handful and the frankincense, etc. – הַקּוֹמֶץ וְהַלְּבוֹנָה וכו׳: The common element of these items is that they are all sacrificed in their entirety upon the altar. Some of them, i.e., the handful and the frankincense, permit the consumption of the remainder of the meal offering by the priests, while others are simply sacrificed in their entirety and do not permit other items for consumption.

For the handful of the meal offering of a sinner – לְקוֹמֶץ דְּמִנְחַת חוֹטֵא: According to this explanation, when the mishna of Rabbi Ḥiyya states: To burn its frankincense the next day, it is not referring to the frankincense of a meal offering, but to the frankincense of the shewbread, which is burned by itself. Since the frankincense is the only permitting factor, one renders the shewbread *piggul* with the intention to burn the frankincense the next day (see *Sefat Emet*).

Did the *tanna* go to all that trouble – אִיכְּפַל תַּנָּא: The Gemara sometimes poses such a question when a mishna or *baraita* is interpreted as referring to a particular instance or a specific combination of conditions. Essentially, the Gemara is asking: Would the *tanna* go to all the trouble of teaching an entire mishna or *baraita* in a general manner to have it apply only in a particular instance?

HALAKHA

The handful and the frankincense, etc. – הַקּוֹמֶץ וְהַלְּבוֹנָה וכו׳: With regard to the handful of flour, the frankincense, the incense, the meal offering of priests, and the meal offering of the anointed priest, if one sacrificed an olive-bulk from one of them outside the Temple courtyard, he is liable for sacrificing outside the courtyard (Rambam *Sefer Avoda, Hilkhot Ma'aseh HaKorbanot* 19:8).

LANGUAGE

Go to all that trouble [*ikhpal*] – אִיכְּפַל: Elsewhere Rashi indicates that the term *ikhpal* is derived from the root *alef, kaf, peh,* meaning to make a strenuous effort (see *Shabbat* 5a). According to this interpretation, the *lamed* appearing at the end of the word is an addition to the root. Some explain that the word *ikhpat,* care, is from the same root.

הָדַר אָמַר רָבָא: לָאו מִילְּתָא הִיא דַּאֲמַרִי, דְּתַנְיָא: "קֹדֶשׁ קָדָשִׁים הוּא", שֶׁאִם נִפְרְסָה אַחַת מֵהֶן – חַלּוֹתֶיהָ כּוּלָּן פְּסוּלוֹת;

Rava then said: That which **I said,** that the burning of the handful with the intent to consume the remainder the next day is effective in rendering even a remainder that became lacking in measure as *piggul* and to remove it from being subject to misuse of consecrated property **is nothing, as it is taught** in a *baraita*: The verse states with regard to the shewbread: **"It is most holy"** (Leviticus 24:9). The restrictive term "it" teaches that the shewbread must remain whole, so **that if one of** the loaves of the shewbread **broke**[HN] and consequently became lacking in measure, then **all of its loaves are disqualified,** and the burning of the bowls of frankincense do not render them permitted for consumption.

הָא יָצְאת – הָנֵי דְּאִיכָּא גַּוַּואי כְּשֵׁרוֹת. מַאן שָׁמְעַתְּ לֵיהּ דְּאָמַר: זְרִיקָה מוֹעֶלֶת לַיּוֹצֵא? רַבִּי עֲקִיבָא הִיא, וְקָאָמַר: נִפְרְסָה – לָא.

Rava continues: It can be inferred from the *baraita* that if the loaves remained whole **but** one of them **left** the Temple, **those that are inside** the Temple are still **fit.** And **whom have you heard who says:** The **sprinkling** of the blood **is effective in** rendering *piggul* an item that **left** the Temple? **It is Rabbi Akiva. And** yet **he says** in this *baraita* that if one of the loaves **broke,** the burning of the frankincense is **not** effective for them. Similarly, with regard to the remainder of a meal offering that became lacking in measure, even Rabbi Akiva agrees that the burning of the handful is ineffective in rendering it *piggul*.

אֲמַר לֵיהּ אַבָּיֵי: מִי קָתָנֵי "הָא יָצְאת"? דִּלְמָא, הָא נִטְמֵאת – הָנָךְ כְּשֵׁרוֹת,

Abaye said to Rava: How can you cite a proof from this *baraita*? **Is** it **taught** in this *baraita*: But if a loaf of shewbread **left,** those loaves that remain inside are fit? **Perhaps** all of the loaves are disqualified if even one of them left, and one should infer a different *halakha* from the *baraita*, that **if** one of the loaves **became ritually impure, these** that remain pure **are fit.**

מַאי טַעְמָא? דִּמְרַצֶּה צִיץ, אֲבָל יָצְאת – לָא, וְרַבִּי אֱלִיעֶזֶר הִיא, דְּאָמַר: אֵין זְרִיקָה מוֹעֶלֶת לַיּוֹצֵא;

Abaye explains: **What is the reason** for such a distinction? The reason is **that the frontplate**[B] of the High Priest **effects acceptance** for ritually impure offerings. **But** in a case where a loaf of shewbread **left,** the frontplate does **not** effect acceptance, and therefore all of the loaves are disqualified, as in a case where one loaf breaks. **And** if so, the *baraita* **is** in accordance with the opinion of **Rabbi Eliezer, who says** that **sprinkling is not effective** with regard **to** an item **that left** the Temple courtyard.

וּבְדִין הוּא דְּאִיבָּעֵי לֵיהּ לְמִיתְנֵי נַמִי יָצְאת, וְהַאי דְּקָתָנֵי נִפְרְסָה – הָא קָא מַשְׁמַע לַן, דַּאֲפִילּוּ נִפְרְסָה, דְּאִיתֵיהּ בִּפְנִים – לָא מְהַנְּיָא לֵיהּ הַקְטָרָה. אֲבָל לְרַבִּי עֲקִיבָא דְּאָמַר: זְרִיקָה מוֹעֶלֶת לַיּוֹצֵא, אֲפִילּוּ חִסָּרוֹן נַמִי מְהַנְּיָא לֵיהּ הַקְטָרָה.

Abaye continues: **And by right** the *baraita* **should have also taught** that if one of the loaves of shewbread **left,** all the loaves are disqualified. **And** as for the fact **that it teaches** the *halakha* specifically with regard to a loaf that **broke, this** is what the *baraita* **teaches us: That even** if the loaf **broke,** in **which** case the loaf **is** still **inside** the Temple, **burning is not effective** with regard **to it. But according to Rabbi Akiva, who says** that **sprinkling is effective** with regard **to** an item that **left** the Temple, **even** in the case of **a lacking** measure, **burning is effective** with regard **to it.**

מתני׳ לֶאֱכוֹל כַּחֲצִי זַיִת וּלְהַקְטִיר כַּחֲצִי זַיִת – כָּשֵׁר, שֶׁאֵין אֲכִילָה וְהַקְטָרָה מִצְטָרְפִין.

MISHNA If one's intent was **to partake of half an olive-bulk**[H] of the remainder **and to burn half an olive-bulk** of it not at the appropriate time or not in the appropriate area, the offering is **fit,**[N] **because eating and burning do not join together.**

HALAKHA

One of the loaves broke – נִפְרְסָה אַחַת מֵהֶן: If one of the loaves of a thanks offering, or one of the loaves of the shewbread, broke before the completion of its sacrificial rites, all of the loaves are disqualified (Rambam *Sefer Avoda, Hilkhot Temidin UMusafin* 5:15 and *Hilkhot Pesulei HaMukdashin* 12:14).

To partake of half an olive-bulk, etc. – לֶאֱכוֹל כַּחֲצִי זַיִת וכו׳: If one's intent with regard to a meal offering was to eat half an olive-bulk outside its designated area and to burn half an olive-bulk outside its designated area, his intentions do not combine and the offering is not disqualified (Rambam *Sefer Avoda, Hilkhot Pesulei HaMukdashin* 14:10).

BACKGROUND

Frontplate – צִיץ: The frontplate of the High Priest was a plate of gold on which the words: "Sacred to the Lord" (Exodus 28:36), were engraved. This plate was tied to the forehead of the High Priest, adjacent to where his hairline began. The frontplate was one of the eight priestly vestments that made up the raiment of the High Priest. It was one of the four that were called the golden vestments. The High Priest would wear all eight vestments year round, except during part of the Yom Kippur service, when he would wear only the four white vestments that all priests wore.

Frontplate

NOTES

That if one of the loaves broke – שֶׁאִם נִפְרְסָה אַחַת מֵהֶן: If a loaf breaks, a piece will certainly fall from it and the loaf will thereby become lacking in measure (*Sefat Emet*). Alternatively, a broken loaf itself is considered deficient (*Or HaYashar*; see 8a).

According to Rashi, the *baraita* is referring to the loaves of the shewbread. Others reject this interpretation, as Rava is seeking to prove that the *baraita* is in accordance with the opinion that the sprinkling of the blood is effective with regard to an item that left the Temple, and there is no sprinkling of the blood in the case of the shewbread (Rabbeinu Meir; Rashbam). They therefore explain that the *baraita* is referring to the loaves that accompanied the offerings brought during the inauguration of the Tabernacle (see Exodus 29:23). Alternatively, the *baraita* is referring to the loaves of a thanks offering (Rambam).

To partake of half an olive-bulk and to burn half an olive-bulk, the offering is fit – לֶאֱכוֹל כַּחֲצִי זַיִת וּלְהַקְטִיר כַּחֲצִי זַיִת כָּשֵׁר: In other words, the offering is entirely valid whether the intent with regard to both halves concerned their designated time or their designated area, and certainly if the intent with regard to one half concerned the time and the intent with regard to the other half concerned its area.

NOTES

And Rabbi Eliezer deems it unfit – וְרַבִּי אֱלִיעֶזֶר פּוֹסֵל: Even Rabbi Eliezer concedes that the offering is not rendered *piggul*; see 17a.

גמ׳ טַעְמָא דְּלֶאֱכוֹל וּלְהַקְטִיר, הָא לֶאֱכוֹל וְלֶאֱכוֹל דָּבָר שֶׁאֵין דַּרְכּוֹ לֶאֱכוֹל – מִצְטָרֵף.

GEMARA The Gemara infers from the mishna: **The reason that** the two halves of an olive-bulk do not join together is because his intent was **to partake of** half an olive-bulk **and to burn** half an olive-bulk, which indicates that if his intent was **to partake** of half an olive-bulk of the remainder **and to partake of** half an olive-bulk of **an item whose** typical **manner** is such that one does **not consume** it, i.e., the handful, then the halves do **join together** to the amount of an olive-bulk and disqualify the offering.

וְהָקְתָנֵי רֵישָׁא: לֶאֱכוֹל דָּבָר שֶׁדַּרְכּוֹ לֶאֱכוֹל וּלְהַקְטִיר דָּבָר שֶׁדַּרְכּוֹ לְהַקְטִיר; דָּבָר שֶׁדַּרְכּוֹ לֶאֱכוֹל – אִין, שֶׁאֵין דַּרְכּוֹ לֶאֱכוֹל – לָא! מַאן תַּנָּא?

The Gemara notes an apparent contradiction: **But the first clause teaches,** in the earlier mishna: If one's intent was **to partake of an item whose** typical **manner** is such that one **partakes** of it, **or to burn an item whose** typical **manner** is such that one **burns** it on the altar, beyond its designated time, the offering is *piggul*. One can infer from this mishna that if his intent was to partake of **an item whose** typical **manner** is such that one **partakes** of it, **yes,** such intent disqualifies an offering. But if his intent was to partake of an item **whose** typical **manner is** such that one does **not partake** of it, this intent does **not** disqualify the offering, and likewise such intent does not join together with another to this end. If so, **who** is the *tanna* who **taught** the latter clause?

אָמַר רַבִּי יִרְמְיָה: הָא מַנִּי? רַבִּי אֱלִיעֶזֶר הִיא, דְּאָמַר: מְחַשְּׁבִין מֵאֲכִילַת אָדָם לְמִזְבֵּחַ וּמֵאֲכִילַת מִזְבֵּחַ לְאָדָם,

Rabbi Yirmeya said: In accordance with **whose** opinion **is this** mishna? **It is** in accordance with the opinion of **Rabbi Eliezer, who says** that **one can** have improper **intent from the consumption** performed by **a person to** the consumption performed by **the altar, and from the consumption** performed by the **altar to** the consumption performed by **a person.** In other words, if one's intent was to burn the remainder the next day or to consume the handful the next day, such intent disqualifies an offering even though the remainder is intended for consumption by the priests and the handful is intended for burning upon the altar.

דִּתְנַן: הַקּוֹמֵץ אֶת הַמִּנְחָה לֶאֱכוֹל דָּבָר שֶׁאֵין דַּרְכּוֹ לֶאֱכוֹל וּלְהַקְטִיר דָּבָר שֶׁאֵין דַּרְכּוֹ לְהַקְטִיר – כָּשֵׁר, וְרַבִּי אֱלִיעֶזֶר פּוֹסֵל.

The Gemara cites the relevant ruling of Rabbi Eliezer. **As we learned** in a mishna (17a): In the case of **one who removes a handful from the meal offering** with the intent **to consume** after its designated time **an item whose** typical **manner is** such that one does **not consume** it, i.e., the handful, **or to burn** beyond its designated time **an item whose** typical **manner is** such that one does **not burn** it on the altar, i.e., the remainder of the meal offering, the meal offering is **fit. And Rabbi Eliezer deems** it **unfit,**[N] although it is not *piggul* and consuming it is not punishable by *karet*.

אַבַּיֵּי אָמַר: אֲפִילּוּ תֵּימָא רַבָּנַן, לָא תֵּימָא: הָא לֶאֱכוֹל וְלֶאֱכוֹל דָּבָר שֶׁאֵין דַּרְכּוֹ לֶאֱכוֹל, אֶלָּא אֵימָא: הָא לֶאֱכוֹל וְלֶאֱכוֹל דָּבָר שֶׁדַּרְכּוֹ לֶאֱכוֹל.

Abaye said: You may **even say** that the mishna here is in accordance with the opinion of **the Rabbis.** And **do not say that** one should infer from the mishna that if his intent was **to partake** of half an olive-bulk of an item whose typical manner is such that one consumes it **and to partake of** half an olive-bulk of **an item whose** typical **manner is** such that one does **not partake** of it, the offering is disqualified. **Rather, say** that if his intent was **to partake** of half an olive-bulk on the next day **and to partake** of half an olive-bulk outside the Temple, and each of these halves is from **an item whose** typical **manner** is such that one **partakes** of it, then the halves are joined together and disqualify the offering.

וּמַאי קָא מַשְׁמַע לַן? הָא בְּהֶדְיָא קָתָנֵי לַהּ: לֶאֱכוֹל כַּזַּיִת בַּחוּץ וְכַזַּיִת לְמָחָר, כַּזַּיִת לְמָחָר וְכַזַּיִת בַּחוּץ, כַּחֲצִי זַיִת בַּחוּץ וְכַחֲצִי זַיִת לְמָחָר, כַּחֲצִי זַיִת לְמָחָר וְכַחֲצִי זַיִת בַּחוּץ – פָּסוּל וְאֵין בּוֹ כָּרֵת;

The Gemara asks: **And what is** this **teaching us?** The previous mishna already **teaches** that principle **explicitly:** If one performed one of these rites with the intent **to partake of an olive-bulk outside** its designated area **and an olive-bulk the next day,** or **an olive-bulk the next day and an olive-bulk outside** its designated area, or **half an olive-bulk outside** its designated area **and half an olive-bulk the next day,** or **half an olive-bulk the next day and half an olive-bulk outside** its designated area, the offering is **unfit but there is no** liability for *karet*.

NOTES

Why do I also need this – **הָא תּוּ לָמָּה לִי**: The section beginning: But you already learn the *halakha* in this case from the first clause of the latter clause of the previous mishna, until the end of the paragraph, does not appear in certain versions of the Gemara. If it is included, then earlier it should read: Both from an item whose typical manner is such that one partakes of it, as the proof refers to a case where the meal offering is rendered *piggul*. The version of the Gemara that Rashi possessed apparently omitted that section, and instead read as follows: From an item whose typical manner is such that one does not partake of it, and the mishna teaches us that they do not join together, but you learn the *halakha* in such a case from the first clause of the previous mishna. Rashi explains that this first clause is the start of the earlier mishna: With the intent to partake of an item whose typical manner is such that one partakes of it. This indicates that the *halakha* of the mishna does not apply to an item whose typical manner is such that one does not consume it. See the parallel discussion in *Zevaḥim* 31b. Either way, the thrust of the discussion is essentially the same: If Abaye is correct in his claim that the mishna is in accordance even with the opinion of the Rabbis, it is apparently unnecessary, as the *halakha* taught in this mishna can be inferred from the previous one. According to the Gemara's conclusion, Abaye's claim is not rejected, and therefore the mishna can be understood in accordance with the opinion of the Rabbis.

הָא תּוּ לָמָּה לִי? אִי לֶאֱכוֹל וְלֶאֱכוֹל דָּבָר שֶׁ(אֵין) דַּרְכּוֹ לֶאֱכוֹל קָא מַשְׁמַע לָן דְּמִצְטָרֵף – מֵרֵישָׁא דְּסֵיפָא שָׁמְעַתְּ מִינָּהּ, דְּקָתָנֵי: כַּחֲצִי זַיִת בַּחוּץ כַּחֲצִי זַיִת לְמָחָר – פָּסוּל, הָא כַּחֲצִי זַיִת לְמָחָר וְכַחֲצִי זַיִת לְמָחָר – פִּיגּוּל!

According to Abaye, **why do I also** need **this**[N] mishna here? **If** you will suggest that this mishna is necessary, as one can infer from it that if one intended **to partake** of half an olive-bulk the next day **and** then intended **to partake of** another half an olive-bulk the next day, both from **an item whose** typical **manner** is such that one **partakes** of it, the mishna **teaches us that** they **join together** in order to render the offering *piggul*, this suggestion can be rejected: But **you** already **learn** the *halakha* in this case **from the first clause of the latter clause** of the previous mishna, **as it teaches: Half an olive-bulk outside and half an olive-bulk the next day,** the offering is **unfit.** One can infer from this **that** if his intent was to consume **half an olive-bulk the next day and half an olive-bulk the next day,** it is ***piggul*****.**

אִי לֶאֱכוֹל וּלְהַקְטִיר, דְּהִיא גּוּפָא קָא מַשְׁמַע לָן – מִדִּיּוּקָא דְּרֵישָׁא שָׁמְעַתְּ מִינָּהּ,

If you suggest that the mishna is necessary for a case where one intended **to consume and to burn,** i.e., **that** the mishna **teaches us the** matter **itself,** that intent to consume does not join together with intent to burn, this too cannot be. The reason is that **from the inference of the first clause** of the mishna **you** can already **learn** the *halakha* in this case, as it teaches: If one intended to partake of an item whose typical manner is such that one partakes of it, the offering is rendered *piggul*. This indicates that if his intent was to consume an item whose typical manner is such that one does not consume it, the offering is not rendered *piggul*.

דְּהַשְׁתָּא מַה לֶאֱכוֹל וְלֶאֱכוֹל דָּבָר שֶׁאֵין דַּרְכּוֹ לֶאֱכוֹל, אָמְרַתְּ: לָא מִצְטָרֵף, לֶאֱכוֹל וּלְהַקְטִיר מִיבַּעְיָא?

The Gemara explains how the *halakha* **that** intent to consume and burn do not combine can be inferred from the mishna: **Now** consider, **if** when one intended **to partake** of an item whose typical manner is such that one partakes of it **and to partake of an item whose** typical **manner is** such that one does **not partake of** it, **you say** that his intentions **do not join together,** despite the fact that both of his intentions referred to consumption, **is it necessary** for the mishna to teach that intentions **to consume and to burn** do not join together?

אִין, לֶאֱכוֹל וּלְהַקְטִיר אִיצְטְרִיכָא לֵיהּ; סָלְקָא דַעְתָּךְ אָמִינָא: הָתָם הוּא דְּלָא כִּי אוֹרְחֵיהּ קָמְחַשֵּׁב,

The Gemara responds: **Yes;** although the mishna teaches the *halakha* of a case where one intended to consume an item typically consumed and to consume an item typically not consumed, **it was necessary for** the mishna to teach the *halakha* of a case where one intended **to eat and to burn.** As it might **enter your mind to say** that **there,** where one's intentions referred solely to consumption, the *halakha* **is** that his intentions do not join together, **as he intended** to act **not in accordance with its** typical **manner,** since he intended to consume that which is not meant to be consumed.

אֲבָל הָכָא דְּבְהַאי כִּי אוֹרְחֵיהּ קָמְחַשֵּׁב, וּבְהַאי כִּי אוֹרְחֵיהּ קָא מְחַשֵּׁב אֵימָא לִיצְטָרֵף, קָא מַשְׁמַע לָן.

The Gemara continues: **But here,** where his intent was to consume half an olive-bulk and to burn half an olive-bulk, **where with regard to this** half **he intends** in **accordance with its** typical **manner, and with regard to this** half **he intends in accordance with its** typical **manner,** one might **say** that **they should join together,** despite the fact that each intention concerns only half an olive-bulk. Therefore, the mishna **teaches us** that such intentions do not join together, and the mishna can be explained even in accordance with the opinion of the Rabbis.

הדרן עלך כל המנחות

Summary of **Perek I**

In this chapter it was concluded that meal offerings must be sacrificed for their own sake, i.e., the removal of the handful from the meal offering, the placement of the handful in a service vessel, the conveyance of that vessel to the altar, and the burning of the handful on the altar must all be performed for the sake of the appropriate offering. Meal offerings that were sacrificed not for their sake remain valid but they do not fulfill the obligation of their owners. There are three exceptions: The meal offering of a sinner, the meal offering of jealousy, and, according the conclusion of the Gemara, the *omer* meal offering, all of which are disqualified entirely when sacrificed not for their sake.

In more general terms, there are significant similarities between meal offerings and slaughtered offerings in terms of their respective sacrificial rites: The removal of the handful from a meal offering is the equivalent of the slaughter of an animal, the placement of the handful in a vessel parallels the collection of the blood of a slaughtered offering, and the conveyance of the handful and its burning upon the altar are analogous to the conveyance and presentation of the blood of a slaughtered offering upon the altar, respectively. Just as the intent to partake of a slaughtered offering, or to sacrifice it, in an improper manner, disqualifies the offering, so too, such intent disqualifies a meal offering. Consequently, one's intention to partake of the remainder of a meal offering beyond its designated time, i.e., the next day, renders the offering *piggul*, and one who partakes of it is liable to receive *karet*.

Similar to a slaughtered offering, if one intended to sacrifice a meal offering or to partake of it outside its designated area, the offering is disqualified, although one who partakes of it is not liable to receive *karet*. This is the *halakha* only when the improper intention concerned at least an olive-bulk of the offering; otherwise, the offering is not disqualified. Additionally, an offering is rendered *piggul* only when the sole disqualifying intent concerning the offering was the one that can render it *piggul*. If one had two separate improper intentions with regard to the same offering, the offering is disqualified but is not rendered *piggul*.

With regard to the performance of the rites of a meal offering, if any of the rites were performed by one unfit to perform them, e.g., a non-priest or a ritually impure priest, or if any of them were performed in an improper manner, e.g., if the priest performing the rite was sitting down or if he was standing on a vessel, the meal offering is disqualified, as is the *halakha* with regard to slaughtered offerings.

Meal offerings may also become disqualified in ways unique to their particular rites, e.g., if the handful was removed in an improper manner, or if the measure of the handful was greater than or less than the proper amount, or if the measure contained a foreign substance. Essentially, a meal offering is valid only if the proper measure of a handful was removed in the appropriate manner by a priest fit for performing the removal.

In this chapter, the *halakhot* pertaining to the removal of the handful were discussed at length. This includes the manner of removal; the instances in which the handful becomes sanctified by a service vessel, e.g., whether or not it may be sanctified in halves and whether the handful becomes sanctified when placed in a vessel that rests on the floor or only in a vessel held by a priest; the ramifications of the removal of a handful in an improper manner, e.g., whether there is a way to restore the meal offering or whether it is disqualified entirely; the status of the remainder of a meal offering that became lacking in its measure, i.e., whether or not the entire meal offering is disqualified on account of it; and several other halakhic issues with regard to the removal of the handful.

Introduction to **Perek II**

The second chapter of *Menaḥot* continues the discussion concerning *piggul*, i.e., the intent to sacrifice or partake of a meal offering outside its designated time or place. Like slaughtered offerings, a meal offering is rendered *piggul* when a priest performs one of its sacrificial rites that is a permitting factor with the intent to sacrifice on the next day the portions designated for burning on the altar, or to partake on the next day of the portion meant for consumption. While there is only one permitting factor in the case of slaughtered offerings, i.e., the blood, there are two permitting factors for meal offerings, namely the handful and the frankincense. Both of these must be burned properly in order to render the remainder of a meal offering permitted, i.e., fit for consumption.

Accordingly, two fundamental questions arise which are addressed in this chapter: If one burns the handful with the intent to burn the frankincense the next day, is the offering rendered *piggul*? In more abstract terms, does *piggul* intent with regard to one permitting factor while sacrificing another permitting factor render an offering *piggul*? Second, in a case where there are two permitting factors, is *piggul* intent during the sacrifice of one of them, concerning that factor alone, sufficient to render the entire meal offering *piggul*?

There are certain scenarios in which these questions become even more complicated. For example, in a case of two permitting factors that permit two items, e.g., the two bowls of frankincense, whose burning on the altar permits the two arrangements of shewbread for priestly consumption, the question arises: Does improper intent to partake of only one of the arrangements of shewbread render that arrangement *piggul*? If so, is the second arrangement rendered *piggul* as well? Furthermore, what is the *halakha* if the priest burned only one of the bowls of frankincense with the intent to partake of one arrangement of shewbread the next day?

Additionally, one can ask: If the various parts of an offering are rendered *piggul* on account of one another, is there a distinction between offerings whose permitted items are of equal importance and those that are composed of principal and secondary parts, e.g., a thanks offering and its accompanying loaves, or a slaughtered offering and its accompanying libations. In other words, are the principal and secondary parts of such offerings always disqualified together, or is the secondary part disqualified when the principal part is disqualified, but not vice versa?

This chapter discusses the various opinions with regard to these questions.

מתני׳ הַקּוֹמֵץ אֶת הַמִּנְחָה לֶאֱכוֹל שְׁיָרֶיהָ אוֹ לְהַקְטִיר קוּמְצָהּ לְמָחָר – מוֹדֶה רַבִּי יוֹסֵי בָּזֶה שֶׁהוּא פִּיגּוּל וְחַיָּיבִין עָלָיו כָּרֵת. לְהַקְטִיר לְבוֹנָתָהּ לְמָחָר – רַבִּי יוֹסֵי אוֹמֵר: פָּסוּל וְאֵין בּוֹ כָּרֵת, וַחֲכָמִים אוֹמְרִים: פִּיגּוּל וְחַיָּיבִין עָלָיו כָּרֵת.

MISHNA In the case of a priest **who removes a handful from the meal offering**[NH] with the intent **to partake of its remainder or to burn its handful** on **the next day, Rabbi Yosei concedes in this** instance **that it is** a case of ***piggul* and he is liable** to receive ***karet* for** partaking of **it.**[N] But if the priest's intent was **to burn its frankincense the next day, Rabbi Yosei says:** The meal offering is **unfit but** partaking of it **does not include** liability to receive ***karet.* And the Rabbis say:** It is a case of ***piggul* and he is liable** to receive ***karet* for** partaking of the meal offering.

אָמְרוּ לוֹ: מַה שִּׁינָּה זֶה מִן הַזֶּבַח? אָמַר לָהֶן: שֶׁהַזֶּבַח דָּמוֹ וּבְשָׂרוֹ וְאֵימוּרָיו אֶחָד, וּלְבוֹנָה אֵינָהּ מִן הַמִּנְחָה.

The Rabbis **said to** Rabbi Yosei: In **what** manner does **this differ from** an animal **offering,** where if one slaughtered it with the intent to sacrifice the portions consumed on the altar the next day, it is *piggul*? Rabbi Yosei **said to** the Rabbis: There is a difference, **as** in **the** case of an animal **offering, its blood, and its flesh, and its portions** consumed on the altar are all **one** entity. Consequently, intent with regard to any one of them renders the entire offering *piggul.* **But the frankincense is not** part **of the meal offering.**

גמ׳ לָמָּה לִי לְמִיתְנָא: מוֹדֶה רַבִּי יוֹסֵי בָּזוֹ?

GEMARA The Gemara questions the terminology of the mishna: **Why do I** need the *tanna* **to teach** that **Rabbi Yosei concedes in this** instance? Let the *tanna* simply state: If one removes the handful from a meal offering with the intent to partake of its remainder or to burn the handful on the next day, Rabbi Yosei says that the offering is *piggul* and one is liable to receive *karet* for partaking of the remainder.

מִשּׁוּם דְּקָא בָּעֵי לְמִיתְנָא סֵיפָא: לְהַקְטִיר לְבוֹנָתָהּ לְמָחָר – רַבִּי יוֹסֵי אוֹמֵר: פָּסוּל וְאֵין בּוֹ כָּרֵת;

The Gemara responds: It was necessary for the *tanna* to teach that Rabbi Yosei concedes, **because he wants to teach the latter clause** of the mishna, that if his intent was **to burn its frankincense the next day, Rabbi Yosei says** that the meal offering is **unfit, but** partaking of it **does not include** liability to receive ***karet.***

מַהוּ דְּתֵימָא, טַעְמָא דְּרַבִּי יוֹסֵי מִשּׁוּם דְּקָסָבַר: אֵין מְפַגְּלִין בַּחֲצִי מַתִּיר, וַאֲפִילּוּ רֵישָׁא נָמֵי,

The Gemara elaborates: The reason the *tanna* links the two cases of the mishna is **lest you say** that **the reason that Rabbi Yosei** does not render the meal offering *piggul* is **because he holds** that **one cannot render** an offering ***piggul* with** intent that concerns only **half of** its **permitting factors. And** consequently, since the burning of the handful and the frankincense render the remainder of a meal offering permitted for consumption, then **even** in **the first clause** of the mishna, where one intends to burn the handful the next day, Rabbi Yosei should hold that the offering is not rendered *piggul,* as the intent does not refer to the frankincense as well.

NOTES

A priest who removes a handful from the meal offering, etc. – **הַקּוֹמֵץ אֶת הַמִּנְחָה וכו׳:** Although this case was already taught in the mishna on 11b, the *tanna* repeats it as an introduction to the dispute between Rabbi Yosei and the Rabbis; the mishna in the previous chapter cites only the opinion of the Rabbis without attribution (see also *Tosafot*).

That it is a case of *piggul* and he is liable to receive *karet* for partaking of it – **שֶׁהוּא פִּיגּוּל וְחַיָּיבִין עָלָיו כָּרֵת:** One who partakes of the remainder of the meal offering is liable to receive *karet*. One is not liable to receive *karet* for consuming either the handful or the frankincense, as they are both permitting factors, but are not themselves rendered permitted by another item, and the status of *piggul* takes effect only on those items that become permitted either for consumption on the altar, e.g., the portions burned on the altar, or for human consumption, and not on items which are themselves permitting factors, i.e., they themselves render other items permitted (see *Zevaḥim* 42b).

HALAKHA

A priest who removes a handful from the meal offering, etc. – **הַקּוֹמֵץ אֶת הַמִּנְחָה וכו׳:** If one removes the handful from a meal offering with the intent to partake of its remainder on the next day, or to burn its handful on the next day, the offering is *piggul*. This is also the *halakha* if he intended to burn the frankincense on the next day. According to the Rambam, the offering is *piggul* only if he has improper intent during the removal of the handful and during the collection of the frankincense, as both are considered permitting factors with regard to the rite of removal, and one must have the improper intent during the sacrifice of all of the permitting factors in order to render the offering *piggul*. Otherwise, the offering is disqualified, but it is not *piggul* (Rambam *Sefer Avoda, Hilkhot Pesulei HaMukdashin* 14:10 and 16:7; see *Likkutei Halakhot*).

קָא מַשְׁמַע לָן דִּבְהָא מוֹדֶה.

Therefore, the *tanna* **teaches us that in this** case Rabbi Yosei **concedes** that if the handful is removed with the intent to burn only the handful on the next day, the offering is rendered *piggul*. Accordingly, Rabbi Yosei holds that one renders an offering *piggul* with intent that concerns only half of its permitting factors, and the offering is not rendered *piggul* in the case of the latter clause for a different reason, as the Gemara will discuss later.

״לְהַקְטִיר לְבוֹנָתָהּ לְמָחָר – רַבִּי יוֹסֵי אוֹמֵר: פָּסוּל וְאֵין בּוֹ כָּרֵת״. אָמַר רֵישׁ לָקִישׁ, אוֹמֵר הָיָה רַבִּי יוֹסֵי: אֵין מַתִּיר מְפַגֵּל אֶת הַמַּתִּיר,

§ The mishna teaches that if one removed the handful from a meal offering with the intent **to burn its frankincense** on **the next day, Rabbi Yosei says** that the meal offering is **unfit but** partaking of it **does not include** liability to receive ***karet***. Concerning this, **Reish Lakish says: Rabbi Yosei would say,** i.e., this is Rabbi Yosei's reasoning: **A permitting factor does not render** another **permitting factor *piggul*.**[N] In other words, if, while performing the rites of a permitting factor, one had intent to perform the rites of a different permitting factor outside its designated time, the offering is not rendered *piggul* on account of this intent.

וְכֵן אַתָּה אוֹמֵר בִּשְׁנֵי בָּזִיכֵי לְבוֹנָה שֶׁל לֶחֶם הַפָּנִים, שֶׁאֵין מַתִּיר מְפַגֵּל אֶת הַמַּתִּיר.

Reish Lakish adds: **And you** would **say the same with regard to** the **two bowls of frankincense of the shewbread, that a permitting factor does not render** another **permitting factor *piggul*,** and therefore if the priest burned one of the bowls with the intent to burn the other bowl the next day, the shewbread is not rendered *piggul*.

מַאי ״וְכֵן אַתָּה אוֹמֵר״? מַהוּ דְּתֵימָא, טַעְמָא דְּרַבִּי יוֹסֵי בִּלְבוֹנָה – מִשּׁוּם דְּלָאו מִינָהּ דְּמִנְחָה הִיא, אֲבָל בִּשְׁנֵי בָזִיכֵי לְבוֹנָה דְּמִינָהּ דַּהֲדָדֵי נִינְהוּ – אֵימָא מְפַגְּלִי אַהֲדָדֵי, קָא מַשְׁמַע לָן.

The Gemara asks: **What** is the purpose of the apparently superfluous statement: **And you** would **say the same** with regard to the two bowls of frankincense? Is there reason to assume that Rabbi Yosei would hold that the shewbread is rendered *piggul* in such a case? The Gemara responds that it is necessary, **lest you say** that **the reason that Rabbi Yosei** holds that there is no *piggul* **in** the case of the **frankincense** is **because it is not** of the same **type as a meal offering. But with regard to** the **two bowls of frankincense, which are of the same type as each other,** one might **say** that **they do render one another *piggul*.** Therefore, Reish Lakish **teaches us** that in both instances one permitting factor does not render another permitting factor *piggul*.

וּמִי מָצֵית אָמְרַתְּ טַעְמָא דְּרַבִּי יוֹסֵי בִּלְבוֹנָה לָאו מִשּׁוּם דְּלָאו מִינָהּ דְּמִנְחָה הִיא? וְהָא קָתָנֵי סֵיפָא, אָמְרוּ לוֹ: מַה שִּׁינְּתָה מִן הַזֶּבַח? אָמַר לָהֶן: הַזֶּבַח דָּמוֹ וּבְשָׂרוֹ וְאֵימוּרָיו אֶחָד, וּלְבוֹנָה אֵינָהּ מִן הַמִּנְחָה!

The Gemara asks: **And can you say** that **the reason** for the opinion **of Rabbi Yosei in** the case of the **frankincense** in the mishna **is not due to** the fact **that** the frankincense **is not** of the same **type as a meal offering? But isn't it taught** in **the latter clause** of the mishna that the Rabbis **said to** Rabbi Yosei: In **what** manner does the frankincense **differ from** an animal **offering,** where if one slaughtered it with the intent to sacrifice the portions consumed on the altar the next day it is *piggul*; and Rabbi Yosei **said to** the Rabbis: There is a difference, as in **the** case of an animal **offering, its blood, and its flesh, and its portions** consumed on the altar are all **one** entity, **but** the **frankincense is not** part **of the meal offering?** The mishna indicates that according to Rabbi Yosei the reason the meal offering is not *piggul* is because the frankincense is not of the same type as the meal offering.

מַאי ״אֵינָהּ מִן הַמִּנְחָה״ – אֵינָהּ בְּעִיכּוּב מִנְחָה, דְּלָאו כִּי הֵיכִי דִּמְעַכֵּב לְהוּ קוֹמֶץ לַשִּׁירַיִם, דְּכַמָּה דְּלָאו מִתְקַטַּר קוֹמֶץ לָא מִיתְאַכְלִי שִׁירַיִם – הָכִי נַמִּי מְעַכֵּב לָהּ לַלְּבוֹנָה; אֶלָּא אִי בָּעֵי הַאי מַקְטַר בְּרֵישָׁא, וְאִי בָּעֵי הַאי מַקְטַר בְּרֵישָׁא.

The Gemara explains: **What** does Rabbi Yosei mean when he says that the frankincense **is not** part **of the meal offering?** He means that **it is not** part **of** the **preclusion** of the **meal offering.**[N] The Gemara elaborates: This means **that** the *halakha* is **not** that **just as** the **handful precludes** the **remainder,** i.e., **that as long as** the **handful is not burned** the **remainder may not be consumed, so too** the handful **precludes the frankincense** from being burned upon the altar. **Rather, if** the priest **wants, he burns this first, and if he wants, he burns that first,** i.e., he may burn the frankincense before or after the burning of the handful. Accordingly, the frankincense is an independent permitting factor. For this reason, intent with regard to the frankincense that occurred during the removal of the handful does not render a meal offering *piggul*.

NOTES

A permitting factor does not render another permitting factor *piggul* – אֵין מַתִּיר מְפַגֵּל אֶת הַמַּתִּיר: Since the remainder of a meal offering is permitted for consumption through the sacrifice of the handful and frankincense, it becomes *piggul* due to intent occurring during those rites. By contrast, the handful and frankincense are independent of one another and neither permits the other. Accordingly, intent during the sacrifice of one cannot render the other *piggul* (*Nezer HaKodesh*).

It is not part of the preclusion of the meal offering – אֵינָהּ בְּעִיכּוּב מִנְחָה: Rabbi Yosei holds that the frankincense is not *piggul* because one permitting factor cannot render another permitting factor *piggul*. When Rabbi Yosei says that the frankincense is not part of the meal offering, he means that it is independent of the handful because it is not permitted by the handful, as it itself is a permitting factor. This is the meaning of Rabbi Yosei's response in the mishna to the claim of the Rabbis that the frankincense is equivalent to the portions of a slaughtered offering that are burned on the altar: Rabbi Yosei explains that both the portions and the flesh are permitted through the sprinkling of the blood, whereas the frankincense may be burned on the altar independent of the handful.

וְרַבָּנַן? כִּי אָמְרִינַן אֵין מַתִּיר מְפַגֵּל אֶת הַמַּתִּיר, גַּבֵּי שָׁחַט אֶחָד מִן הַכְּבָשִׂים לֶאֱכוֹל מֵחֲבֵירוֹ לְמָחָר, דְּאָמְרַתְּ שְׁנֵיהֶם כְּשֵׁרִים – הָנֵי מִילֵּי הֵיכָא דְּלָא אִיקְּבַעוּ בְּחַד מָנָא, אֲבָל הֵיכָא דְּאִיקְּבַעוּ בְּחַד מָנָא – כְּחַד דָּמֵי.

The Gemara asks: **And the Rabbis,** who say that the meal offering is rendered *piggul* in such a case, what is their opinion? The Gemara responds: They hold that **when we say** that **a permitting factor does not render** another **permitting factor *piggul*,** this is **with regard to** the case taught in a mishna (16a) concerning one who **slaughtered one of the lambs**[H] whose sacrifice permits the consumption of the two loaves meal offering brought on *Shavuot*, with the intent **to partake of the other** lamb **the next day.** The Gemara elaborates: **When you said** in the mishna that **both** permitting factors **are fit, this statement** applies only **where they were not fixed in one vessel. But** in a situation **where they were fixed in one vessel,** as is the case with regard to the handful and the frankincense, they are **considered like one** unit, and therefore they render one another *piggul*.

אָמַר רַבִּי יַנַּאי: לִיקּוּט לְבוֹנָה בְּזָר – פָּסוּל. מַאי טַעְמָא? אָמַר רַבִּי יִרְמְיָה: מִשּׁוּם הוֹלָכָה נָגְעוּ בָּהּ; קָסָבַר: הוֹלָכָה שֶׁלֹּא בָּרֶגֶל שְׁמָהּ הוֹלָכָה, וְהוֹלָכָה בְּזָר – פְּסוּלָה.

§ With regard to the frankincense, **Rabbi Yannai says:** The **collection** of the **frankincense** from a meal offering, when performed **by a non-priest,**[HN] **is not valid** and disqualifies the meal offering. The Gemara asks: **What is the reason? Rabbi Yirmeya said:** It is **because** the rite of **conveying**[N] **has touched it,** i.e., the collection of the frankincense is considered part of the rite of the conveying of the frankincense to the altar for the purpose of burning. Even if the non-priest simply collected the frankincense and thereafter transferred it to a priest, Rabbi Yannai **holds** that **conveying** even **without** moving one's **leg**[H] **is called conveying, and** the *halakha* is that the performance of the rite of **conveying by a non-priest**[H] is **not valid.**

אָמַר רַב מָרִי: אַף אֲנַן נָמֵי תְּנֵינָא, זֶה הַכְּלָל: כׇּל הַקּוֹמֵץ וְנוֹתֵן בִּכְלִי וְהַמּוֹלִיךְ וְהַמַּקְטִיר;

Rav Mari said: We learn this *halakha* in the mishna on 12a, which discusses those sacrificial rites of a meal offering during which improper intent renders an offering *piggul*, **as well.** The mishna teaches: **This is the principle:** In the case of **anyone who removes the handful, or places** the handful **in the vessel,** or **who conveys** the vessel with the handful to the altar, or **who burns** the handful on the altar, with the intent to partake of an item whose typical manner is such that one partakes of it, or to burn an item whose typical manner is such that one burns it on the altar, outside its designated area, the meal offering is unfit but there is no liability for *karet*. If his intent was to perform any of these actions beyond their designated time, the offering is *piggul* and one is liable to receive *karet* on account of it, provided that the permitting factor, i.e., the handful, was sacrificed in accordance with its mitzva.

בִּשְׁלָמָא קוֹמֵץ – הַיְינוּ שׁוֹחֵט, מוֹלִיךְ נָמֵי – הַיְינוּ מוֹלִיךְ, מַקְטִיר – הַיְינוּ זוֹרֵק, אֶלָּא נוֹתֵן בִּכְלִי מַאי קָא עָבֵיד?

Rav Mari analyzes the first part of this mishna: **Granted,** the **removal of the handful** from a meal offering **is** the same as, i.e., equivalent to, the **slaughter**[N] of animal offerings. The **conveying** of the handful to the altar in order to burn it **is also** the same as the **conveying** of the blood of a slaughtered offering to the altar in order to sprinkle it. Similarly, the **burning** of the handful and frankincense of a meal offering **is** comparable to the **sprinkling** of the blood of a slaughtered offering upon the altar. **But** as for **placing** the handful **in the** service **vessel, what** rite **is he performing** that is comparable to a rite of slaughtered offerings?

HALAKHA

One who slaughtered one of the lambs – שָׁחַט אֶחָד מִן הַכְּבָשִׂים: If one slaughtered one of the two lambs brought on *Shavuot* together with the two loaves, with the intent to partake of the second lamb the next day, both lambs are valid, as intent with regard to one does not disqualify the other (see 16a). With regard to the two bowls of frankincense that accompany the shewbread, since they both rest upon the table of the shewbread and are both sanctified by it, it is considered as though their contents are in the same vessel. Accordingly, if the priest removed one of the bowls with the intent to burn the second bowl the next day, it is *piggul*, in accordance with the opinion of the Rabbis in the mishna (Rambam *Sefer Avoda, Hilkhot Pesulei HaMukdashin* 17:17; see *Likkutei Halakhot*).

The collection of the frankincense by a non-priest – לִיקּוּט לְבוֹנָה בְּזָר: If a non-priest, or anyone else who is unfit to perform the Temple service, collected the frankincense from upon the meal offering, the offering is disqualified, in accordance with the opinion of Rabbi Yannai (Rambam *Sefer Avoda, Hilkhot Pesulei HaMukdashin* 11:1).

Conveying without moving one's leg – הוֹלָכָה שֶׁלֹּא בָּרֶגֶל: Conveying without moving one's leg is not considered a valid performance of the rite of conveying. Accordingly, if a priest collected and sprinkled the blood of a slaughtered offering while standing in the same place, the offering is disqualified. This *halakha* is in accordance with the opinion of Rabbi Yoḥanan on *Zevaḥim* 14b (Rambam *Sefer Avoda, Hilkhot Pesulei HaMukdashin* 1:23).

Conveying by a non-priest – הוֹלָכָה בְּזָר: All of the rites of meal offerings that precede the removal of the handful may be performed by non-priests. From the removal onward, its rites must be performed by priests (Rambam *Sefer Avoda, Hilkhot Ma'aseh HaKorbanot* 12:23 and *Hilkhot Pesulei HaMukdashin* 1:22, 11:7).

NOTES

The collection of the frankincense by a non-priest – לִיקּוּט לְבוֹנָה בְּזָר: Meal offerings were sacrificed in the following manner: After the flour of the offering was mixed with its oil, frankincense was placed upon the meal offering, and then the priest would present the vessel containing the entire offering before the altar. The priest would subsequently remove a handful from the flour and sanctify it in a second service vessel. Next, he would collect the frankincense from the meal offering and place it upon the handful in the second vessel, after which he would burn the handful and frankincense on the altar (*Tosefta, Sota* 14:2). The later commentaries note that this description, in which the priest burns the handful at the end of the process, apparently contradicts the assumption of the Gemara here that the frankincense may be sacrificed before the handful; see *Ḥok Natan*; *Yad David*, and *Minḥat Avraham*, who discuss this at length.

Because the rite of conveying – מִשּׁוּם הוֹלָכָה: According to Rashi, Rabbi Yirmeya claims that if the collection is performed by a non-priest, then the priest will not be performing the mitzva of conveying in its entirety. Consequently, if the non-priest merely collected the frankincense but the priest took it from the non-priest's hand, the offering is valid. According to Rav Mari, who maintains that the collection of the frankincense is considered a significant rite because it is an indispensable part of the preparation of the frankincense for sacrifice on the altar, even if they performed such an exchange the meal offering would be disqualified (*Zevaḥ Toda*).

The removal of the handful is the same as slaughter – קוֹמֵץ הַיְינוּ שׁוֹחֵט: The parallels drawn by Rav Mari are based on the fact that the *halakhot* of *piggul* are derived from verses discussing peace offerings, which are subsequently applied to all slaughtered offerings and meal offerings (see *Zevaḥim* 4b and 13b). It is therefore logical that meal offerings are rendered *piggul* only when the intent occurs during the performance of a sacrificial rite that is equivalent to one of the rites of slaughtered offerings. The removal of the handful is equated to the slaughter of an animal because the permitting factor of a slaughtered offering, i.e., the blood, is removed from the animal through its slaughter, just as the handful, which permits the remainder of the meal offering, is removed from the meal offering.

אִילֵימָא מִשּׁוּם דְּדָמֵי לְקַבָּלָה, מִי דָּמֵי? הָתָם מִמֵּילָא, הָכָא קָא שָׁקֵיל וְרָמֵי!

If we say that the meal offering is *piggul* **because** the placing of the handful into a vessel **is comparable to** the **collection** of the blood of a slaughtered offering into a service vessel, one can ask: **Are** these rites in fact **comparable? There,** in the case of animal offerings, the blood enters the vessel **by itself,** whereas **here,** the priest **takes** the handful from the meal offering **and casts** it into the vessel.

אֶלָּא מִשּׁוּם דְּכֵיוָן דְּלָא סַגְיָא לֵיהּ דְּלָא עָבֵד לַהּ – עֲבוֹדָה חֲשׁוּבָה הִיא, עַל כָּרְחֵיךְ מְשַׁוֵּי לַהּ כְּקַבָּלָה; הָכָא נַמִי, כֵּיוָן דְּלָא סַגְיָא לַהּ דְּלָא עָבֵד לַהּ – עֲבוֹדָה חֲשׁוּבָה הִיא, עַל כָּרְחֵיךְ מְשַׁוֵּי לַהּ כִּי הוֹלָכָה!

Rather, it must be **due to** the following reason: **Since it is not possible** to sacrifice the handful **without** first **performing** the act of placing it in a vessel, the placement of the handful in a vessel **is** considered **a significant rite,** and **perforce** this factor causes it to be **considered like** the **collection** of the blood. **Here too,** with regard to the collection of the frankincense, **since it is not possible** to sacrifice the frankincense **without** first **performing** the act of collecting it from the vessel, the collection of the frankincense **is a significant rite** that **perforce** causes it to be **considered like** the rite of **conveying.**

לָא, לְעוֹלָם דְּדָמֵי לְקַבָּלָה. וּדְקָא קַשְׁיָא לָךְ: הָתָם מִמֵּילָא, הָכָא קָא שָׁקֵיל וְרָמֵי!

The Gemara rejects this suggestion: **No,** this is not the reason, and one cannot prove from the mishna that the collection of the frankincense from a meal offering performed by a non-priest is not valid. **Actually,** the reason why intent during the placement of the handful renders the offering *piggul* is in fact **because it is comparable to** the **collection**[N] of the blood of a slaughtered offering. **And as for** the **difficulty you** raised, that **there** the blood enters the vessel **by itself,** whereas **here he takes** the handful from the meal offering **and casts** it into the vessel, this is not a true difficulty.

מִכְּדֵי תַּרְוַיְיהוּ קְדוּשַּׁת כְּלִי הוּא, מַה לִּי מִמֵּילָא, מַה לִּי קָא שָׁקֵיל וְרָמֵי.

The Gemara explains: **Now** consider, **both of them,** i.e., the collection of the blood and the placing of the handful, involve the **sanctity of a vessel,** in which a service vessel sanctifies a permitting factor to the altar, either the handful or the blood. **What** difference is it **to me** if the permitting factor enters the vessel **by itself or** whether one **takes** the item **and casts** it into the vessel?

מתני׳ שָׁחַט שְׁנֵי כְּבָשִׂים לֶאֱכוֹל אַחַת מִן הַחַלּוֹת לְמָחָר, הִקְטִיר שְׁנֵי בָּזִיכִין לֶאֱכוֹל אֶחָד מִן הַסְּדָרִים לְמָחָר, רַבִּי יוֹסֵי אוֹמֵר: אוֹתוֹ הַחַלָּה וְאוֹתוֹ הַסֵּדֶר שֶׁחִישֵּׁב עָלָיו – פִּיגּוּל וְחַיָּיבִין עָלָיו כָּרֵת, וְהַשֵּׁנִי פָּסוּל וְאֵין בּוֹ כָּרֵת; וַחֲכָמִים אוֹמְרִים: זֶה וָזֶה פִּיגּוּל וְחַיָּיבִין עָלָיו כָּרֵת.

MISHNA If **one slaughtered** the **two lambs**[N] that accompany the two meal offering loaves sacrificed on *Shavuot* with the intent **to partake of one of the** two **loaves the next day,** or if **one burned** the **two bowls** of frankincense accompanying the shewbread with the intent **to partake of one of the arrangements** of the shewbread **the next day, Rabbi Yosei says: That loaf and that arrangement of which he intended** to partake the next day are ***piggul* and one is liable** to receive ***karet* for** their consumption, **and the second** loaf and arrangement are **unfit, but there is no** liability to receive ***karet* for** their consumption. **And the Rabbis say: This** loaf and arrangement **and that** loaf and arrangement are both ***piggul***[H] **and one is liable** to receive ***karet* for** their consumption.

גמ׳ אָמַר רַב הוּנָא, אוֹמֵר הָיָה רַבִּי יוֹסֵי: פִּיגֵּל בְּיָרֵךְ שֶׁל יָמִין – לֹא נִתְפַּגֵּל הַיָּרֵךְ שֶׁל שְׂמֹאל; מַאי טַעְמָא? אִיבָּעֵית אֵימָא: סְבָרָא, וְאִיבָּעֵית אֵימָא: קְרָא.

GEMARA **Rav Huna says: Rabbi Yosei would say,** in accordance with his opinion that intent of *piggul* with regard to one loaf or one arrangement does not render the second loaf or arrangement *piggul,* that if one **had intent of *piggul* with regard to the right thigh,** i.e., he slaughtered an offering with the intent to partake of the right thigh the next day, then **the left thigh has not become *piggul*** and one is not liable to receive *karet* for its consumption. **What is the reason** for this? **If you wish, propose a logical argument, and if you wish, cite a verse.**

אִיבָּעֵית אֵימָא סְבָרָא: לָא עֲדִיפָא מַחֲשָׁבָה מִמַּעֲשֵׂה הַטּוּמְאָה, אִילּוּ אִיטַּמֵּי חַד אֵבֶר, מִי אִיטַּמֵּי לֵיהּ כּוּלֵּיהּ? וְאִיבָּעֵית אֵימָא קְרָא: ״וְהַנֶּפֶשׁ הָאֹכֶלֶת מִמֶּנּוּ עֲוֹנָהּ תִּשָּׂא״, מִמֶּנּוּ – וְלֹא מֵחֲבֵירוֹ.

Rav Huna elaborates: **If you wish, propose a logical argument:** Disqualifying **intent is no stronger than an incident of ritual impurity,** and **if one limb** of an offering **became impure, did the entire** offering then **become impure?** Accordingly, one limb can be rendered *piggul* without the other. **And if you wish, cite a verse** that addresses *piggul*: **"And the soul that eats of it shall bear his iniquity"** (Leviticus 7:18). The verse indicates that one who eats specifically **"of it,"** i.e., from one part, shall bear his iniquity, **and not** one who eats **from the other** part of the offering.

NOTES

It is because it is comparable to the collection – דְּדָמֵי לְקַבָּלָה: In other words, one cannot prove from the placement of the handful in a service vessel that any action that is indispensable to the sacrifice of an offering is similar to the rite of conveying. Accordingly, the collection of the frankincense may in fact not be considered a rite at all. Rather, only the placement of the handful in a vessel is comparable to the collection of the blood of an offering, and the collection of the frankincense is considered an entirely different action, despite the fact that it too is indispensable (Rashi).

If one slaughtered the two lambs, etc. – שָׁחַט שְׁנֵי כְּבָשִׂים וכו׳: In addition to the seven lambs that were sacrificed as burnt offerings as part of the additional offerings brought on *Shavuot*, the Torah commands that two lambs must be brought as peace offerings to accompany the public offering of two loaves from the new wheat. When the priest would wave the two loaves, he would wave the limbs of these two lambs as well (see Leviticus 23:18–20).

Although there is a dispute in the mishna on 45b as to whether the loaves are indispensable for the sacrifice of the lambs or vice versa, and the primary offering appears to consist of the two loaves, nevertheless the *halakha* is that the lambs render the loaves permitted, i.e., the slaughter of the lambs sanctifies the loaves for sacrifice, and the sprinkling of the lambs' blood renders the loaves permitted for consumption by the priests (see *Me'ila* 9a).

HALAKHA

This and that are *piggul* – זֶה וָזֶה פִּיגּוּל: If one slaughtered the two lambs of *Shavuot* with the intent to partake of one of the loaves the next day, the loaves are *piggul*. Similarly, if a priest burned the two bowls of frankincense with the intent to partake of one of the loaves of shewbread the next day, all the loaves are *piggul* (Rambam *Sefer Avoda*, *Hilkhot Pesulei HaMukdashin* 17:10–11).

אֵיתִיבֵיהּ רַב נַחְמָן לְרַב הוּנָא: וַחֲכָמִים אוֹמְרִים: לְעוֹלָם אֵין בּוֹ כָּרֵת עַד שֶׁיְּפַגֵּל בִּשְׁתֵּיהֶן בִּכְזַיִת; בִּשְׁתֵּיהֶן – אִין, בְּאַחַת מֵהֶן – לָא.

Rav Naḥman raised an objection to Rav **Huna** from a *baraita*: **And the Rabbis say** that **there is never** liability to receive ***karet*** for partaking of the two loaves **unless one has intent of *piggul* with regard to an olive-bulk of both of them,** i.e., one's intent renders both loaves *piggul* only if he slaughters the lambs with the intent to consume an amount equal to an olive-bulk from both loaves combined outside their proper time. One can infer from this that if he had intent **with regard to both of them, yes,** both loaves are *piggul*. But if his intent was **with regard to** only **one of them, no,** the other loaf is not *piggul*.

מַנִּי? אִילֵימָא רַבָּנַן, אֲפִילּוּ בְּאַחַת מֵהֶן נַמִי! אֶלָּא פְּשִׁיטָא רַבִּי יוֹסֵי; אִי אָמְרַתְּ בִּשְׁלָמָא חַד גּוּפָא הוּא – מִשּׁוּם הָכִי מִצְטָרֵף,

Rav Naḥman continues: In accordance with **whose** opinion is the *baraita*? **If we say** that it is in accordance with the opinion of **the Rabbis** of the mishna, then **even** if his intent was **with regard to** only **one of them,** both loaves are rendered *piggul*. **Rather,** it is **obvious** that the *baraita* is in accordance with the opinion of **Rabbi Yosei.** Now, **granted, if you say** that according to Rabbi Yosei the left and right thighs of an offering are considered **one body,** and consequently *piggul* intent with regard to one thigh renders the other thigh *piggul* as well, then **due to that** reason it is understandable that if the *piggul* intent was for an amount equal to one total olive-bulk from both of the loaves, then the intent with regard to each loaf is **combined** with the other.

אֶלָּא אִי אָמְרַתְּ תְּרֵי גּוּפֵי נִינְהוּ, מִי מִיצְטָרְפִי?

But if you say that Rabbi Yosei holds that the right and left thighs of an offering **are** considered **two** distinct **bodies,** and therefore *piggul* intent with regard to one does not render the other *piggul*, then in the case of the two loaves, **would** the intentions concerning both loaves **combine** to render them both *piggul*?

הָא מַנִּי? רַבִּי הִיא, דְּתַנְיָא: הַשּׁוֹחֵט אֶת הַכֶּבֶשׂ לֶאֱכוֹל חֲצִי זַיִת מֵחַלָּה זוֹ וְכֵן חֲבֵירוֹ לֶאֱכוֹל חֲצִי זַיִת מֵחַלָּה זוֹ, רַבִּי אוֹמֵר: אוֹמֵר אֲנִי שֶׁזֶּה כָּשֵׁר;

Rav Huna responds: One cannot infer anything from this *baraita* with regard to the opinion of Rabbi Yosei, as in accordance with **whose opinion is this** *baraita*? **It is** in accordance with the opinion of **Rabbi** Yehuda HaNasi, **as it is taught** in another *baraita*: With regard to **one who slaughters** one of **the lambs** brought as peace offerings on *Shavuot* with the intent **to consume half an olive-bulk from this loaf**[H] the next day, **and similarly,** he slaughtered **the other** lamb with the intent **to consume half an olive-bulk from that** second **loaf** the next day, **Rabbi** Yehuda HaNasi **says: I say that this** offering **is valid,** as his intentions do not combine.

טַעְמָא דְּאָמַר חֲצִי חֲצִי, אֲבָל אָמַר כַּזַּיִת מִשְּׁתֵּיהֶן – מִצְטָרֵף.

Rav Huna continues: It may be inferred that **the reason** why the priest's intentions do not combine is **that** his intent was **said** with regard to **a half** and **a half,**[N] i.e., he slaughtered each lamb with the intent to consume half an olive-bulk from one loaf the next day. **But** if he **said** during the slaughter of each of the lambs that he is slaughtering it with the intent to consume **an olive-bulk from both of them,** then the halves **combine** to render the offering *piggul*.

וְרַבִּי אַלִּיבָּא דְּמַאן? אִי אַלִּיבָּא דְּרַבָּנַן, אֲפִילּוּ בְּאַחַת מֵהֶן נַמִי! אִי אַלִּיבָּא דְּרַבִּי יוֹסֵי, הֲדַרָא קוּשְׁיַין לְדוּכְתֵּיהּ!

The Gemara asks: **And** as for **Rabbi** Yehuda HaNasi, who says that the two loaves are *piggul* only if he has intent with regard to an amount equal to an olive-bulk from both of them combined, **in accordance with whose** opinion[N] is his statement? **If** it is **in accordance with** the opinion **of the Rabbis** of the mishna, who hold that *piggul* intent with regard to one loaf renders both loaves *piggul*, then **even** if his intent was **with regard to** only **one of them,** both loaves should be *piggul*. And **if** it is **in accordance with** the opinion **of Rabbi Yosei,** who holds that *piggul* intent with regard to one loaf does not render the second loaf *piggul*, then **our difficulty returns to its place:** If Rabbi Yosei holds that the right and left thighs are considered two distinct bodies, how can intentions with regard to two halves of an olive-bulk combine to render both loaves *piggul*?

HALAKHA

To consume half an olive-bulk from this loaf – לֶאֱכוֹל חֲצִי זַיִת מֵחַלָּה זוֹ: With regard to one who slaughters one of the two lambs that accompany the two loaves brought on *Shavuot* with the intent to consume half an olive-bulk from one loaf the next day, and then slaughters the second lamb with the intent to consume half an olive-bulk from the second loaf the next day, these intentions combine to render the offering *piggul*. The *halakha* is in accordance with the opinion of the Rabbis, who disagree with Rabbi Yehuda HaNasi; see 14b and16b (Rambam *Sefer Avoda, Hilkhot Pesulei HaMukdashin* 17:15).

NOTES

His intent was said with regard to a half and a half, etc. – אָמַר חֲצִי חֲצִי וכו׳: During the slaughter of each lamb, it is not necessary for one to have intent to consume an olive-bulk from both loaves collectively in order for his intentions to be combined. Rather, even if he intended each time to consume half an olive-bulk from each loaf, his intentions combine to render the offering *piggul* (*Yashar VaTov*). One can further infer from Rabbi Yehuda HaNasi's statement that if, during the slaughter of each lamb, he had intent with regard to an olive-bulk from a different loaf, his intentions combine, despite the fact that each time he had a different loaf in mind. The reason is that according to this opinion the two loaves are considered like a single body (commentary attributed to Rashba).

In accordance with whose opinion – אַלִּיבָּא דְּמַאן: In other words, even if this *baraita* is in accordance with the opinion of Rabbi Yehuda HaNasi, this does not resolve the difficulty against the opinion of Rabbi Yosei. One cannot simply say that Rabbi Yehuda HaNasi's opinion is unconnected to the dispute between Rabbi Yosei and the Rabbis. The reason is that the dispute between Rabbi Yosei and the Rabbis is a fundamental disagreement with regard to whether *piggul* in one part of an offering renders another part of it *piggul*. Rabbi Yehuda HaNasi must hold in accordance with one of these two opinions; there is no room for a third opinion in this situation.

לְעוֹלָם אַלִּיבָּא דְּרַבָּנַן, וְלָא תֵּימָא: עַד שֶׁיְּפַגֵּל בִּשְׁתֵּיהֶן, אֶלָּא: בִּשְׁנֵיהֶן, וַאֲפִילּוּ בְּאַחַת מֵהֶן;

The Gemara responds: **Actually,** Rabbi Yehuda HaNasi's statement is **in accordance** with the opinion **of the Rabbis. And do not say** that the *baraita* states: It is not *piggul* **unless one has the intent of** ***piggul*** **with regard to both of them** [*bishteihen*], in the feminine form, whereby the *baraita* would be referring to the loaves. **Rather,** the *baraita* states: **With regard to both of them** [***bishneihen***], in the masculine form, i.e., unless he slaughters both lambs with *piggul* intent, **and** in such a case, **even** if his intent was with regard to only **one of the** loaves, the offering is *piggul*.

וּלְאַפּוּקֵי מִדְּרַבִּי מֵאִיר דְּאָמַר: מְפַגְּלִין בַּחֲצִי מַתִּיר, קָא מַשְׁמַע לַן דְּלָא.

The Gemara adds: **And** this *baraita* serves **to exclude** the opinion **of Rabbi Meir, who says** in the mishna on 16a: **One renders** an offering ***piggul*** by means of intent during the sacrifice **of half a permitting factor,** e.g., if one slaughtered one of the lambs with the intent to consume the two loaves the next day, the loaves are *piggul*. This *baraita* **teaches us that** this is **not** the *halakha*.

אִי הָכִי, מַאי ״לְעוֹלָם״? אִי אָמְרַתְּ בִּשְׁלָמָא בִּשְׁתֵּיהֶן וּבִשְׁנֵיהֶן וְרַבִּי יוֹסֵי הִיא, וּלְאַפּוּקֵי מִדְּרַבִּי מֵאִיר וּמִדְּרַבָּנַן קָאָתֵי – הַיְינוּ דְּקָאָמַר ״לְעוֹלָם״;

The Gemara asks: **If so,** then **what** is the meaning of the emphasis in the *baraita*: There is **never** liability? **Granted,** this phrase is understandable **if you say** that the *baraita* means that the loaves are not *piggul* unless he has intent **with regard to both of the** loaves **and both of the** lambs, i.e., they are *piggul* only if he slaughters both lambs with the intention to partake of both loaves the next day. In that case the *baraita* **is** in accordance with the opinion of **Rabbi Yosei, and it comes to exclude** the statements **of** both **Rabbi Meir and the Rabbis,** and **this is** the reason **that** the *baraita* **states:** There is **never** liability, to emphasize that Rabbi Yosei disagrees with both of these opinions.

אֶלָּא אִי אָמְרַתְּ רַבָּנַן וּלְאַפּוּקֵי מִדְּרַבִּי מֵאִיר, מַאי ״לְעוֹלָם״?

But if you say that the *baraita* is in accordance with the opinion of **the Rabbis and** that it serves **to exclude** only the opinion **of Rabbi Meir,** for **what** reason does the *baraita* stress: There is **never** liability? The *tanna* would not use such a word to exclude merely one opinion. Rather, it must be that the *baraita* is in accordance with the opinion of Rabbi Yosei. If so, then the difficulty raised against Rav Huna, who says that *piggul* intent concerning the right thigh does not render the left one *piggul*, remains unresolved.

וְעוֹד, הָא אָמַר רַב אָשֵׁי: תָּא שְׁמַע, רַבִּי אוֹמֵר מִשּׁוּם רַבִּי יוֹסֵי: פִּיגֵּל בְּדָבָר הַנַּעֲשֶׂה בַּחוּץ – פִּיגֵּל, בְּדָבָר הַנַּעֲשֶׂה בִּפְנִים – לֹא פִּיגֵּל,

And furthermore, didn't Rav Ashi say: Come and **hear** a refutation of the opinion of Rav Huna from a *baraita*: **Rabbi** Yehuda HaNasi **says in the name of Rabbi Yosei** that if, while performing the sacrificial rites for the bulls or goats which are burned as an offering, the priest had an intention that can **render** the offering ***piggul*** **with regard to a matter that is performed outside** the Sanctuary, i.e., in the Temple courtyard, **he has rendered** the offering ***piggul***. If his intention was **with regard to a matter that is performed inside**[HN] the Sanctuary or the Holy of Holies, **he has not rendered** the offering ***piggul***.

HALAKHA

He had an intention that can render it *piggul*, with regard to a matter that is performed outside…with regard to a matter that is performed inside – פִּיגֵּל בְּדָבָר הַנַּעֲשֶׂה בַּחוּץ...בְּדָבָר הַנַּעֲשֶׂה בִּפְנִים: With regard to a sin offering whose blood is placed inside the Sanctuary, if a priest who was standing in the Temple courtyard had intent concerning an action performed inside the Sanctuary, the offering is not *piggul*. If he had intent concerning an action performed outside the Sanctuary, the offering is *piggul*. How so? If he said in the courtyard: I am hereby slaughtering this animal with the intent to sprinkle its blood the next day, the offering is not *piggul*, as the sprinkling of its blood is performed inside the Sanctuary. If he said in the Sanctuary: I am sprinkling the blood with the intent to pour the remaining blood the next day, the offering is not *piggul*, since while standing in the Sanctuary he had intent concerning an action performed in the courtyard, as the blood is poured onto the base of the external altar. But if he slaughtered the animal in the courtyard with the intent to pour the remaining blood on the next day, or to burn the portions on the next day, the offering is *piggul*, as while standing outside he had intent with regard to an action performed outside (Rambam *Sefer Avoda, Hilkhot Pesulei HaMukdashin* 17:4–6).

NOTES

He has rendered the offering *piggul*, if his intention was with regard to a matter that is performed inside – פִּיגֵּל בְּדָבָר הַנַּעֲשֶׂה בִּפְנִים: The *baraita* discusses the offerings of bulls and goats that were burned outside Jerusalem. Like all other offerings, these animals were slaughtered in the Temple courtyard and their portions were burned on the outer altar. In contrast to other offerings, their blood was sprinkled inside the Sanctuary toward the Curtain separating the Sanctuary and the Holy of Holies, and was also placed upon the golden altar.

The *halakhot* taught in the *baraita* are derived from the Torah's juxtaposition of the bull of the High Priest, which is one of the offerings burned outside Jerusalem, to a peace offering, which is the source for the *halakhot* of *piggul*. Accordingly, just as peace offerings are rendered *piggul* only when one's actions and intentions of *piggul* concern a rite performed on the external altar, so too, in the case of the bull of the High Priest, the offering is rendered *piggul* only when the actions and intentions of *piggul* involve a rite performed on the external altar (see *Zevaḥim* 44b).

כֵּיצַד? הָיָה עוֹמֵד בַּחוּץ, וְאָמַר: ״הֲרֵינִי שׁוֹחֵט עַל מְנָת לְהַזּוֹת מִדָּמוֹ לְמָחָר״ – לֹא פִּיגֵּל, שֶׁמַּחֲשָׁבָה בַּחוּץ בְּדָבָר הַנַּעֲשֶׂה בִּפְנִים; הָיָה עוֹמֵד בִּפְנִים, וְאָמַר: ״הֲרֵינִי מַזֶּה עַל מְנָת לְהַקְטִיר אֵימוּרִין לְמָחָר וְלִשְׁפּוֹךְ שִׁירַיִים לְמָחָר״ – לֹא פִּיגֵּל, שֶׁמַּחֲשָׁבָה בִּפְנִים בְּדָבָר הַנַּעֲשֶׂה בַּחוּץ;

The *baraita* elaborates: **How so? If he was standing outside** when slaughtering the animal **and said: I hereby slaughter** the animal **with the intention of sprinkling its blood tomorrow** inside the Sanctuary, **he has not rendered** the offering ***piggul*****.** The reason is **that** when one has **an intention outside with regard to a matter that is performed inside,** he has not rendered the offering *piggul*. Likewise, if he **was standing inside** when sprinkling, **and said: I hereby sprinkle** the blood of the sin offering **in order to burn** its **sacrificial portions** on the external altar **tomorrow and to pour out** its **remainder** on the base of the altar **tomorrow, he has not rendered** the offering ***piggul*****,** as he had **an intention inside with regard to a matter that is performed outside.**

הָיָה עוֹמֵד בַּחוּץ, וְאָמַר: ״הֲרֵינִי שׁוֹחֵט עַל מְנָת לִשְׁפּוֹךְ שִׁירַיִים לְמָחָר וּלְהַקְטִיר אֵימוּרִין לְמָחָר״ – פִּיגֵּל, שֶׁמַּחֲשָׁבָה בַּחוּץ בְּדָבָר הַנַּעֲשֶׂה בַּחוּץ.

But if **he was standing outside and said: I hereby slaughter** the animal **with the intention to pour out** the **remainder** of its blood **tomorrow, or to burn** its **sacrificial portions tomorrow, he has rendered** the offering ***piggul*****,** as he had **an intention outside with regard to a matter that is performed outside.**

לִשְׁפּוֹךְ שִׁירַיִים לְאִיפַּגּוּלֵי מַאי? אִילֵימָא לְאִיפַּגּוּלֵי דָּם, דָּם מִי מִיפַּגַּל? וְהָתְנַן, אֵלּוּ דְּבָרִים שֶׁאֵין חַיָּיבִין עֲלֵיהֶן מִשּׁוּם פִּיגּוּל: הַקּוֹמֶץ, וְהַלְּבוֹנָה, וְהַקְּטוֹרֶת, וּמִנְחַת כֹּהֲנִים, וּמִנְחַת נְסָכִים, וּמִנְחַת כֹּהֵן מָשִׁיחַ, וְהַדָּם!

The Gemara analyzes this *baraita*: With regard to the case where one slaughtered the offering with the intent **to pour the remaining** blood the next day, **what could be rendered *piggul*? If we say** the **blood could be rendered *piggul*****,**[N] one can ask: **Does blood become *piggul*? But didn't we learn** in a mishna (*Zevaḥim* 42b): **These are** the **items for which one is not liable** to receive *karet* **due to** the prohibition of ***piggul*****:**[H] **The handful; the frankincense;**[N] **the incense; the meal offering of priests; the meal offering** accompanying the **libations** brought with an animal offering; **the meal offering of** the **anointed priest; and the blood?**

אֶלָּא פְּשִׁיטָא, לְאִפַּגּוּלֵי בָּשָׂר. הָשְׁתָּא, וּמָה הָתָם דְּלָא חָשֵׁיב בֵּיהּ בְּבָשָׂר גּוּפֵיהּ, אֲמַר רַבִּי יוֹסֵי: מִיפַּגַּל, הָכָא דְּחָשֵׁיב בֵּיהּ בְּזֶבַח גּוּפֵיהּ, לֹא כׇּל שֶׁכֵּן דְּפִיגֵּל בְּיָרֵךְ יָמִין פִּיגֵּל בְּיָרֵךְ שְׂמֹאל?

Rather, it is **obvious** that the *baraita* means that it is the **meat** of the offering that **could be rendered *piggul*****. Now** consider: **And if there,** in the *baraita*, **where he did not have intent with regard to the meat itself,** as his intention was not to partake of the meat the next day but to pour the remaining blood the next day, and yet **Rabbi Yosei said** that the meat **is rendered *piggul***; then **here, where he has intent** to partake of the right thigh the next day, which is part **of the offering itself,** is it **not all the more so that** if **he had intent of *piggul* with regard to the right thigh, he has rendered the left thigh *piggul*** as well?

וְעוֹד, הָאָמַר רָבִינָא: תָּא שְׁמַע, הַקּוֹמֵץ אֶת הַמִּנְחָה לֶאֱכוֹל שְׁיָרֶיהָ אוֹ לְהַקְטִיר קוּמְצָהּ לְמָחָר, מוֹדֶה רַבִּי יוֹסֵי בָּזוֹ שֶׁפִּיגֵּל וְחַיָּיבִין עָלָיו כָּרֵת;

And furthermore, doesn't Ravina say: Come and **hear** a refutation of the statement of Rav Huna from the mishna (13a): In the case of **one who removes a handful from the meal offering** with the intent **to partake of its remainder or to burn its handful** on **the next day, Rabbi Yosei concedes in this** instance **that he has rendered** the offering ***piggul*** **and he is liable** to receive ***karet*** **for** partaking **of it.**

לְהַקְטִיר קוּמְצָהּ לְאִיפַּגּוּלֵי מַאי? אִילֵימָא לְאִיפַּגּוּלֵי קוֹמֶץ, קוֹמֶץ מִי מִיפַּגַּל? וְהָתְנַן, אֵלּוּ דְּבָרִים שֶׁאֵין חַיָּיבִין עֲלֵיהֶן מִשּׁוּם פִּיגּוּל: הַקּוֹמֶץ כו׳! אֶלָּא פְּשִׁיטָא, לְאִיפַּגּוּלֵי שִׁירַיִים. הָשְׁתָּא, וּמָה הָתָם דְּלָא חָשֵׁיב בְּהוּ בְּשִׁירַיִים גּוּפַיְהוּ,

Ravina continues: When one removes the handful with the intent **to burn its handful, what could be rendered *piggul*? If we say that the handful could be rendered *piggul*, does the handful become *piggul*? But didn't we learn** in a mishna (*Zevaḥim* 42b): **These are** the **items for which one is not liable** to receive *karet* **due to** the prohibition of ***piggul*****: The handful, etc. Rather,** it is **obvious** that the **remainder could be rendered *piggul*****. Now** consider: **And if there,** in the mishna, **where he did not have intent with regard to** the **remainder itself,** i.e., to partake of the remainder the next day,

HALAKHA

Items for which one is not liable due to the prohibition of *piggul* – דְּבָרִים שֶׁאֵין חַיָּיבִין עֲלֵיהֶן מִשּׁוּם פִּיגּוּל: The following items can never become *piggul*: The handful; the frankincense; the incense; the blood; and any meal offering that is burned in its entirety on the altar, e.g., the meal offering of priests and the meal offering accompanying the libations of a slaughtered offering. This *halakha* is in accordance with the mishna on *Zevaḥim* 42b (Rambam *Sefer Avoda, Hilkhot Pesulei HaMukdashin* 18:8).

NOTES

If we say the blood could be rendered *piggul* – אִילֵימָא לְאִיפַּגּוּלֵי דָּם: Although one is already liable to receive *karet* for consuming the blood on account of the prohibition against the consumption of blood, perhaps one might be further liable to receive *karet* for consuming *piggul*. Some commentaries explain that the *baraita* is referring to a case where one consumed the blood unintentionally. Accordingly, the Gemara is suggesting that one who consumes the blood might be obligated to bring two sin offerings, one for each transgression whose intentional violation renders him liable to receive *karet* (Rabbeinu Gershom Meor HaGola).

The handful, the frankincense – הַקּוֹמֶץ וְהַלְּבוֹנָה: Rashi explains that the same reasoning applies to all the items listed in the mishna: *Piggul* takes effect only on items that become permitted through their respective permitting factors, whether for consumption or for sacrifice upon the altar. The mishna lists items that are themselves permitting factors, e.g., the blood, handful, and frankincense, as well as items that have no permitting factors, such as the incense and certain meal offerings, which are burned in their entirety on the altar.

NOTES

The verse renders them one body, etc. – הַכָּתוּב עֲשָׂאָן גּוּף אֶחָד וכו׳: The early commentaries disagree as to the meaning of Rabbi Yoḥanan's statement. According to Rashi, the fact that the loaves preclude one another indicates that they are considered a single entity. At the same time, they are considered separate entities with regard to the fact that each loaf must be prepared separately. Others explain that Rabbi Yoḥanan's statement is based on a specific verse in the Torah, and not based on the *halakhot* pertaining to the loaves. The verse in question states: "You shall bring a wave-loaf" (Leviticus 23:17), which indicates that the loaves are considered one body. As the same verse also states: "Two of two tenths of an ephah," it indicates that the loaves are distinct from one another (*Tosafot*).

If one had intent of *piggul* with regard to the loaves of a thanks offering – פִּיגֵּל בְּלַחְמֵי תוֹדָה: The Torah states that there are four parts to the loaves of a thanks offering: Three parts, which are unleavened, are called loaves, wafers, and loaves soaked in oil, and one part is leavened loaves (see Leviticus 7:12 and 77a). With regard to baked meal offerings as well, the Torah states that they consist of both loaves and wafers (see Leviticus 2:4).

מִיפַּגְּלִי, הָכָא דְּחָשֵׁיב בְּהוּ בִּזְבִיחָה גּוּפָהּ לֹא כׇּל שֶׁכֵּן?

and yet Rabbi Yosei said that the remainder **is rendered *piggul*;** then **here, where he has intent** to partake of the right thigh the next day, which is part **of the offering itself,** is it **not all the more so** that both thighs should become *piggul*?

אֶלָּא אָמַר רַבִּי יוֹחָנָן, הַיְינוּ טַעְמָא דְּרַבִּי יוֹסֵי: הַכָּתוּב עֲשָׂאָן גּוּף אֶחָד וְהַכָּתוּב עֲשָׂאָן שְׁנֵי גוּפִין, גּוּף אֶחָד – דִּמְעַכְּבִי אַהֲדָדֵי, שְׁנֵי גוּפִין – דְּאָמַר רַחֲמָנָא: הָא לְחוֹדַהּ עֲבִידָא וְהָא לְחוֹדַהּ עֲבִידָא;

Rather, Rabbi Yoḥanan said: Rabbi Yosei holds that intent of *piggul* with regard to one thigh renders the other thigh *piggul* as well, as they are of one body. Similarly, with regard to two loaves, Rabbi Yosei is of the opinion that if one intends to consume an amount equal to an olive-bulk from both loaves, both loaves are rendered *piggul*. And as for his statement that intent of *piggul* with regard to one loaf does not render the other loaf *piggul*, **this is the reasoning of Rabbi Yosei: The verse renders** the two loaves **one body,**[N] **and the verse** also **renders them two bodies.** The verse renders them **one body** in the sense **that they preclude one another,** i.e., neither loaf is valid without the other. The verse also renders them **two bodies, as the Merciful One states: This** loaf **is prepared alone and that is prepared alone,** i.e., the kneading and arrangement of each loaf must be performed separately.

עָרְבִינְהוּ – מִתְעָרְבִין, דְּהַכָּתוּב עֲשָׂאָן גּוּף אֶחָד, פַּלְגִינְהוּ – מִיפַּלְגִי, דְּהַכָּתוּב עֲשָׂאָן שְׁנֵי גוּפִין.

Therefore, if the priest **mixed them** together by intending to consume an olive-bulk from both of them, then **they are mixed** and they are both *piggul*, **as the verse renders them one body.** But **if he separated them** by having intent with regard to only one loaf, in that case **they are separated** and only that loaf is *piggul*, **as the verse renders them two bodies.**

בָּעֵי רַבִּי יוֹחָנָן: פִּיגֵּל בְּלַחְמֵי תוֹדָה, מַהוּ? בְּמִנְחַת מַאֲפֶה, מַהוּ? תְּנָא לֵיהּ רַב תַּחְלִיפָא מִמַּעַרְבָא: וְכֵן אַתָּה אוֹמֵר בְּלַחְמֵי תוֹדָה, וְכֵן אַתָּה אוֹמֵר בְּמִנְחַת מַאֲפֶה.

Rabbi Yoḥanan raises a dilemma: If one **had intent of *piggul* with regard to** one type of loaf from the **loaves of a thanks offering,**[NH] **what is** the *halakha* concerning the remaining types of loaves, i.e., are they rendered *piggul* as well? Similarly, if one had intent of *piggul* **with regard to** either the loaves or the wafers of **baked meal offerings, what is** the *halakha* with regard to the remaining type? **Rav Taḥlifa from the West,** i.e., Eretz Yisrael, **taught him** a *baraita* that states: **And likewise you say with regard to the bread of a thanks offering, and likewise you say with regard to a baked meal offering,** that the *halakha* is a matter of dispute between Rabbi Yosei and the Rabbis.

תָּנוּ רַבָּנַן: בִּשְׁעַת שְׁחִיטָה חִישֵּׁב לֶאֱכוֹל חֲצִי זַיִת וּבִשְׁעַת זְרִיקָה חִישֵּׁב לֶאֱכוֹל חֲצִי זַיִת – פִּיגּוּל, מִפְּנֵי שֶׁשְּׁחִיטָה וּזְרִיקָה מִצְטָרְפִין.

§ **The Sages taught** in a *baraita*: If **at the time of** the **slaughter** of an offering one **had intent to consume half an olive-bulk**[H] of its meat the next day, **and at the time of** the **sprinkling** of the blood **he had intent to consume half** of another **olive-bulk** of meat the next day, the offering is ***piggul*,** as intentions that occur during the **slaughter and sprinkling combine** to render an offering *piggul*.

HALAKHA

If one had intent of *piggul* with regard to the loaves of a thanks offering – פִּיגֵּל בְּלַחְמֵי תוֹדָה: If one has intent of *piggul* concerning one of the loaves of the bread of a thanks offering, or one of the loaves of a baked meal offering, all of the loaves are rendered *piggul* (Rambam *Sefer Avoda, Hilkhot Pesulei HaMukdashin* 17:12).

At the time of the slaughter one had intent to consume half an olive-bulk, etc. – בִּשְׁעַת שְׁחִיטָה חִישֵּׁב לֶאֱכוֹל חֲצִי זַיִת וכו׳: If one had intent during the slaughter of an offering to consume half an olive-bulk in an improper manner, and then had intent during the sprinkling of the blood to consume half an olive-bulk in an improper manner; or if one had such intent with regard to half an olive-bulk during the collection of the blood and similar intent during the conveying of the blood, these intentions combine to disqualify the offering in a case where his intentions were to consume the halves outside their designated area, or they combine to render the offering *piggul* in a case where his intentions were to consume the halves outside their designated time. This is because the four sacrificial rites of an offering are considered one rite. The Rambam rules in accordance with the stringent interpretation of the *baraita* because the Gemara indicates that the *baraita* is in accordance with the opinion of the Rabbis. Additionally, the *halakha* generally follows the second interpretation of a *baraita* (Rambam *Sefer Avoda, Hilkhot Pesulei HaMukdashin* 14:10, and see *Kesef Mishne* there; see *Likkutei Halakhot*).

אִיכָּא דְּאָמְרִי: שְׁחִיטָה וּזְרִיקָה דְּתַרְוַיְיהוּ מַתִּירִין – אִין, קַבָּלָה וְהוֹלָכָה – לָא; וְאִיכָּא דְּאָמְרִי: הָנָךְ דִּמְרַחֲקָן, וְכׇל שֶׁכֵּן הָנֵי דִּמְקַרְבָן.

There is a dispute between *amora'im* with regard to the *halakha* of this *baraita*: **Some say** that in the case of intentions that occur specifically during the **slaughter**[N] **and sprinkling, as both of them are permitting factors** of the offering, **yes,** the intentions combine. But intentions that occur during the **collection** of the blood in a service vessel **and the conveying** of the blood to the altar do **not** combine, as neither rite is a permitting factor. **And some say** that if intentions during **those** rites **that are distant** from one another, i.e., the slaughter and sprinkling, combine, **all the more so** intentions during **these** rites **that are close** to one another, i.e., collection and conveying, certainly combine.

אִינִי? וְהָא תָּנֵי לֵוִי, אַרְבַּע עֲבוֹדוֹת אֵין מִצְטָרְפוֹת לְפִיגּוּל: שְׁחִיטָה וּזְרִיקָה, קַבָּלָה וְהוֹלָכָה! אֲמַר רָבָא, לָא קַשְׁיָא: הָא רַבִּי, הָא רַבָּנַן;

The Gemara asks: **Is that so,** i.e., that intentions during the slaughter and sprinkling combine? **But Levi teaches** in a *baraita*: Intentions that occur during the **four** sacrificial **rites do not combine to** render an offering ***piggul***, and those rites are: **Slaughter and sprinkling, collection and conveying. Rava said:** It is **not difficult; this** statement of Levi is in accordance with the opinion of **Rabbi** Yehuda HaNasi, whereas **that** *baraita* is in accordance with the opinion of **the Rabbis.**

דְּתַנְיָא: הַשּׁוֹחֵט אֶת הַכֶּבֶשׂ לֶאֱכוֹל חֲצִי זַיִת מֵחַלָּה זוֹ, וְכֵן חֲבֵירוֹ לֶאֱכוֹל חֲצִי זַיִת מֵחַלָּה זוֹ – רַבִּי אוֹמֵר: אוֹמֵר אֲנִי שֶׁזֶּה כָּשֵׁר.

As it is taught in a *baraita* with regard to the two loaves and two lambs sacrificed on *Shavuot*: With regard to **one who slaughters** one of **the lambs** brought as peace offerings on *Shavuot* with the intent **to consume half an olive-bulk from this loaf** the next day, **and similarly,** he slaughtered **the other** lamb with the intent **to consume half an olive-bulk from that** second **loaf** the next day, **Rabbi** Yehuda HaNasi **says:**[N] **I say that this** offering **is valid.** Clearly, Rabbi Yehuda HaNasi holds that intentions that occur during the performance of two permitting factors do not combine to render an offering *piggul*.

אֲמַר לֵיהּ אַבָּיֵי: אֵימַר דְּשָׁמְעַתְּ לֵיהּ לְרַבִּי חֲצִי מַתִּיר וַחֲצִי אֲכִילָה, כּוּלּוֹ מַתִּיר וַחֲצִי אֲכִילָה מִי שָׁמְעַתְּ לֵיהּ?

Abaye said to Rava: You can **say that you have heard that Rabbi** Yehuda HaNasi holds that intentions do not combine to render an offering *piggul* when each intention is concerning **half a permitting factor and half** a measure of **consumption,** i.e., one lamb and half an olive-bulk. But in a case where one had intentions during the performance of **an entire permitting factor,** i.e., during the slaughter and sprinkling, **and** concerning **half** a measure of **consumption, did you hear him** say that such intentions do not combine?

אֲמַר לֵיהּ רָבָא בַּר רַב חָנָן לְאַבָּיֵי: וְאִי אִית לֵיהּ לְרַבִּי כּוּלּוֹ מַתִּיר וַחֲצִי אֲכִילָה, לִגְזוֹר חֲצִי מַתִּיר וַחֲצִי אֲכִילָה אַטּוּ כּוּלּוֹ מַתִּיר וַחֲצִי אֲכִילָה, דְּהָא רַבִּי יוֹסֵי גָּזַר וְרַבָּנַן גָּזְרִי;

Rava bar Rav Ḥanan[P] **said to Abaye: But if Rabbi** Yehuda HaNasi **is of** the opinion that intentions during the performance of **an entire permitting factor and** concerning **half** a measure of **consumption** combine to render an offering *piggul*, why does he rule that when one slaughters each lamb with the intent to consume half an olive-bulk from one loaf the next day the offering is entirely valid? **Let him decree** that intentions during **half a permitting factor and** concerning **half** a measure of **consumption** disqualify an offering, **due to** the fact that intentions during **an entire permitting factor and** concerning **half** a measure of **consumption** render the offering *piggul*, **as** one finds in similar instances that **Rabbi Yosei decreed and the Rabbis decreed** in this manner.

רַבִּי יוֹסֵי גָּזַר, דִּתְנַן: לְהַקְטִיר לְבוֹנָתָהּ לְמָחָר – רַבִּי יוֹסֵי אוֹמֵר: פָּסוּל וְאֵין בּוֹ כָּרֵת, וַחֲכָמִים אוֹמְרִים: פִּיגּוּל וְחַיָּיבִין עָלֶיהָ כָּרֵת;

Rava bar Rav Ḥanan elaborates: **Rabbi Yosei decreed**[N] in such a case, **as we learned** in a mishna (13a): With regard to one who removes a handful from the meal offering with the intent to burn its handful on the next day, everyone agrees that the meal offering is *piggul*. But if his intent was **to burn its frankincense** on **the next day, Rabbi Yosei says:** The meal offering is **unfit, but** partaking of it **does not include** liability to receive ***karet*****. And the Rabbis say:** It is a case of ***piggul*** **and one is liable** to receive ***karet*** **for** partaking of the meal offering. Since one is not liable to receive *karet*, Rabbi Yosei evidently disqualifies the meal offering as a rabbinic decree due to concern over a case where his intention was to burn the handful the next day.

NOTES

Slaughter – שְׁחִיטָה: Rashi explains that the slaughter of an offering is considered a permitting factor because it sanctifies the blood for sacrifice upon the altar (see *Tosafot*).

Rabbi Yehuda HaNasi says, etc. – רַבִּי אוֹמֵר וכו׳: Although the *baraita* makes no explicit mention of any opinion of the Rabbis, it can be inferred from Rabbi Yehuda HaNasi's statement: I say, that the Rabbis disagree and maintain that the offering is in fact *piggul* (*Piskei HaRid*; see 16b).

Rabbi Yosei decreed, etc. – רַבִּי יוֹסֵי גָּזַר וכו׳: It is clear from the Gemara that in any situation involving *piggul* where the offering is disqualified but one is not liable to receive *karet* for partaking of it, it is a rabbinic decree, unless there is another reason for the offering to be disqualified, e.g., if one intended to partake of it outside its designated place, or sacrificed it not for its sake. With regard to the opinion of Rabbi Yosei in the mishna (13b) that if one slaughtered both lambs with the intent to partake of one loaf on the next day, the second loaf is disqualified and there is no liability to receive *karet*, the commentaries disagree whether this too is a rabbinic decree, or whether the second loaf is disqualified by Torah law.

PERSONALITIES

Rava bar Rav Ḥanan – רָבָא בַּר רַב חָנָן: Rava bar Rav Ḥanan was a fourth-generation Babylonian *amora*, a contemporary of Abaye and Rava, also known as Rava bar Rav Yosef bar Ḥama. It is mentioned several times in the Gemara that Rava bar Rav Ḥanan was a disciple of Rabba, and he, along with Abaye, learned from Rabba in Pumbedita, Rava bar Rav Ḥanan's hometown. Rava bar Rav Ḥanan and Abaye were considered faithful students of Rabba, since he assumed that they would properly eulogize him upon his death. Rava bar Rav Ḥanan is often mentioned in the Gemara as disagreeing with Abaye, posing difficulties to Abaye's opinions, or raising halakhic inquiries to him. Apparently Rav Yosef, the second teacher of Abaye, was a neighbor of Rava bar Rav Ḥanan, and Rava bar Rav Ḥanan refused to accept his opinion in a dispute between neighbors.

וְרַבָּנַן נַמִּי גָּזְרִי, דִּתְנַן: פִּיגֵּל בַּקּוֹמֶץ וְלֹא בַּלְּבוֹנָה, בַּלְּבוֹנָה וְלֹא בַּקּוֹמֶץ – רַבִּי מֵאִיר אוֹמֵר: פִּיגּוּל וְחַיָּיבִין עָלָיו כָּרֵת, וַחֲכָמִים אוֹמְרִים: אֵין בּוֹ כָּרֵת עַד שֶׁיְּפַגֵּל בְּכָל הַמַּתִּיר!

And the Rabbis decreed as well, as we learned in a mishna (16a): If one had **intent of *piggul* during** the burning of **the handful but not during** the burning of **the frankincense,** or if he had such intent **during** the burning of **the frankincense but not during** the burning of **the handful, Rabbi Meir says:** The meal offering is ***piggul* and one is liable** to receive ***karet* for** its consumption, **and the Rabbis say: There is no** liability to receive ***karet* for** its consumption **unless he has intent of *piggul* during** the burning of **the entire permitting factor,** i.e., both the handful and the frankincense. Since the Rabbis state that there is no liability to receive *karet*, but they do not rule that the offering is valid, evidently they maintain that the offering is disqualified by rabbinic law, due to concern over a case of *piggul* intent during the burning of the entire permitting factor.

אֲמַר לֵיהּ: הָכִי הַשְׁתָּא? בִּשְׁלָמָא הָתָם גָּזַר רַבִּי יוֹסֵי קוֹמֶץ דִּלְבוֹנָה – אַטּוּ קוֹמֶץ דְּמִנְחָה,

Abaye **said to** Rava bar Rav Ḥanan: **How can** these cases **be compared? Granted there, Rabbi Yosei decreed** that the offering is disqualified in a case of intent involving **the handful of frankincense due to** the concern of intent involving **the handful of the meal offering,** as the two cases are similar.

רַבָּנַן גָּזְרִי קוֹמֶץ – אַטּוּ קוֹמֶץ דְּמִנְחַת חוֹטֵא, וּלְבוֹנָה – אַטּוּ לְבוֹנָה הַבָּאָה בְּבָזִיכִין,

Similarly, **the Rabbis decreed** that the offering is disqualified in a case of intent involving the **handful due to** a similar case of intent concerning **the handful of the meal offering of a sinner.** There is no frankincense in the case of a meal offering of a sinner, and consequently the priest's intent with regard to the handful alone renders the offering *piggul*, as it is the sole permitting factor. **And** the Rabbis also decreed in a case of intent with regard to the **frankincense due to** a similar case of intent concerning the **frankincense that comes in** the **bowls** that accompany the shewbread. Here there is no handful, and consequently intent with regard to the frankincense alone renders the shewbread *piggul*.

כְּבָשִׂים נַמִּי – כֶּבֶשׂ אַטּוּ כֶּבֶשׂ חֲבֵירוֹ,

In the case of the two **lambs** that accompany the two loaves brought on *Shavuot* **as well** (16a), the Rabbis rule that if one slaughters one of the lambs with the intent to consume both loaves the next day the offering is disqualified, but one is not liable to receive *karet* for partaking of it. This is a rabbinic decree in a case of intent during the slaughter of one **lamb due to the other lamb,** as were one to slaughter both lambs with intent of *piggul*, the loaves would be rendered *piggul*, since his intent occurred during the slaughter of the entire permitting factor.

בָּזָךְ – אַטּוּ בָּזָךְ חֲבֵירוֹ.

Similarly, when one burns a single **bowl** of frankincense from those that accompany the shewbread with the intent to consume both arrangements of shewbread the next day, the Rabbis disqualify the shewbread by rabbinic decree **due to the other bowl,** i.e., due to the concern over *piggul* intent during the burning of both bowls, as this intent involves the burning of the entire permitting factor.

אֶלָּא הָכָא, מִי אִיכָּא חֲצִי מַתִּיר וַחֲצִי אֲכִילָה בְּעָלְמָא, דְּלֵיקוּם וְלִיגְזַר?

Abaye concludes: **But here,** in the case of the *baraita* where one slaughtered each of the two lambs with the intent to consume half an olive-bulk from a different loaf, **is there** another instance **in general** where intent during the performance of a rite concerning **half a permitting factor and** with regard to **half** a measure **of consumption** renders an offering *piggul*, **that** Rabbi Yehuda HaNasi **will arise and decree** that the lambs in this instance are disqualified?

הָכִי נַמִּי מִסְתַּבְּרָא דְּטַעְמָא דְּרַבָּנַן מִשּׁוּם הָכִי הוּא, דְּקָתָנֵי סֵיפָא: מוֹדִים חֲכָמִים לְרַבִּי מֵאִיר בְּמִנְחַת חוֹטֵא וּמִנְחַת קְנָאוֹת, שֶׁאִם פִּיגֵּל בַּקּוֹמֶץ – שֶׁפִּיגּוּל וְחַיָּיבִין עָלֶיהָ כָּרֵת, שֶׁהַקּוֹמֶץ הוּא הַמַּתִּיר;

The Gemara notes: **So too, it is reasonable that the reasoning of the Rabbis is due to that** explanation, i.e., they disqualified the offerings in the aforementioned cases due to the fact that in similar instances the offering is *piggul*. This is evident from the fact **that** it **is taught** in **the latter clause** of the mishna (16a): **The Rabbis concede to Rabbi Meir in** the case of **the meal offering of a sinner and the meal offering of jealousy that if one had intent of *piggul* during** the burning of **the handful,** the meal offering is ***piggul* and one is liable** to receive ***karet* for** its consumption, **as the handful is the** sole **permitting factor.**

הא למה לי למיתנא כלל? פשיטא, מי איכא מתיר אחרינא? אלא לאו הא קא משמע לן, דטעמא דקומץ – משום דאיכא קומץ דמנחת חוטא דדמי ליה.

The Gemara explains this proof: **Why do I** need the mishna **to teach** this last statement **at all?** Isn't it **obvious** that these meal offerings are *piggul*, as **is there another permitting factor** aside from the handful? **Rather, is it not** correct to say that **this** is what the mishna **teaches us, that the reason that** the Rabbis disqualified a standard meal offering when only the **handful** was removed with the intent of *piggul* is **because there is** the case of **the handful of the meal offering of a sinner, which is similar to it** and is rendered *piggul* due to intent involving the handful alone?

מתני׳ נטמאת אחת מן החלות או אחד מן הסדרים – רבי יהודה אומר: שניהם יצאו לבית השריפה, שאין קרבן ציבור חלוק. וחכמים אומרים: הטמא בטומאתו, והטהור יאכל.

MISHNA If **one of the** two **loaves** of *Shavuot* **or one of the** two **arrangements** of the shewbread **became ritually impure,**[HN] **Rabbi Yehuda says: Both must be taken to the place of burning**[B] like any other disqualified offering, **as no communal offering is divided.** That is, it is either fit in its entirety or unfit in its entirety. **And the Rabbis say: The impure one** remains **in its** state of **impurity and the pure one shall be eaten.**

גמ׳ אמר רבי אלעזר: מחלוקת לפני זריקה, אבל לאחר זריקה – דברי הכל הטמא בטומאתו והטהור יאכל.

GEMARA **Rabbi Elazar says:** The **dispute** between Rabbi Yehuda and the Rabbis applies only to a case where one loaf became ritually impure **before the sprinkling**[N] of the blood of the lambs, as this is the act that renders the loaves permitted for consumption. Accordingly, they disagree whether the sprinkling is effective in permitting the remaining pure loaf for consumption. **But** in a case where one loaf was rendered impure **after the sprinkling,** meaning that both loaves were initially permitted for consumption, **everyone agrees** that **the impure one** remains **in its** state of **impurity and the pure one shall be eaten.**

ולפני זריקה במאי פליגי? אמר רב פפא: בציץ מרצה על אכילות קא מיפלגי,

The Gemara asks: **And** in the case where the loaves become impure **before** the **sprinkling** of the blood, **with regard to what** principle **do they disagree? Rav Pappa said: They disagree with regard to** the **frontplate** of the High Priest, i.e., whether it **effects acceptance**[N] only for the impurity of items sacrificed on the altar, or even **for** the impurity of items that would normally be **consumed** by the priests.

HALAKHA

One of the two loaves or one of the two arrangements became ritually impure – נטמאת אחת מן החלות או אחד מן הסדרים: If one of the two loaves, or one of the arrangements of shewbread, or one of the loaves of bread from a thanks offering became ritually impure, regardless of whether they became impure before or after the sprinkling of the blood, the impure loaves or arrangements are prohibited for consumption, while the remaining loaves or arrangements are consumed in a state of ritual purity (Rambam *Sefer Avoda, Hilkhot Pesulei HaMukdashin* 17:13; see also *Sefer Avoda, Hilkhot Temidin UMusafin* 5:16).

BACKGROUND

The place of burning – בית השריפה: This term is used in the Talmud to refer to three different places. One was in the Temple courtyard, where offerings that became disqualified within the Temple would be burned. The second was outside the Temple, on the Temple Mount, where sacrificial bulls and goats that had become disqualified due to leaving the Temple courtyard were burned. The third was outside Jerusalem, where the priests would burn those sacrificial bulls and goats whose ritual entailed burning them outside the Temple.

The bull and the goat of Yom Kippur being brought to the place of burning

NOTES

One of the two loaves or one of the two arrangements became ritually impure – נטמאת אחת מן החלות או אחד מן הסדרים: This mishna is cited here because it contrasts with the previous mishna, i.e., whereas the previous mishna taught that when one loaf becomes *piggul* the other loaf becomes *piggul* as well, this mishna teaches that when one loaf becomes ritually impure, the impure one remains in its state of impurity while the pure one is consumed (see Rambam *Sefer Avoda, Hilkhot Pesulei HaMukdashin* 17:13).

The dispute applies only before the sprinkling – מחלוקת לפני זריקה: This refers specifically to the case of the two loaves, as the sprinkling of the blood of the lambs renders the loaves permitted for consumption. With regard to the shewbread, Rabbi Elazar would say that the dispute between Rabbi Yehuda and the Rabbis applies only in a case where the arrangement became impure before the bowls of frankincense were burned, as that act renders the shewbread permitted for consumption.

With regard to the frontplate, whether it effects acceptance – בציץ מרצה: The verse states with regard to the frontplate: "And it shall be upon Aaron's forehead, and Aaron shall bear the iniquity committed in the holy items, which the children of Israel shall sanctify, even in all their holy gifts; and it shall be always upon his forehead, that they may be accepted before the Lord" (Exodus 28:38). The Sages teach that the iniquity borne by the frontplate is that of ritual impurity in the Temple, i.e., an offering that becomes impure is "accepted before the Lord" on account of the frontplate (see 25a–b).

Modern reconstruction of the frontplate

רַבָּנַן סָבְרִי: הַצִּיץ מְרַצֶּה עַל אֲכִילוֹת, וְרַבִּי יְהוּדָה סָבַר: אֵין הַצִּיץ מְרַצֶּה עַל אֲכִילוֹת.

The Rabbis hold that **the frontplate effects acceptance**[H] **for** items that are normally **consumed** by the priests but have become ritually impure. Consequently, the sprinkling of the blood in this case is an entirely valid act that is capable of rendering the remaining pure loaf permitted for consumption. **And Rabbi Yehuda holds** that **the frontplate does not effect acceptance for** items that are **consumed** by the priests and have become impure. Accordingly, the sprinkling of the blood is ineffective in rendering the remaining pure loaf permitted for consumption.

אֲמַר לֵיהּ רַב הוּנָא בְּרֵיהּ דְּרַב נָתָן לְרַב פַּפָּא: וְהָא עוֹלִין, דְּהַצִּיץ מְרַצֶּה עַל הָעוֹלִין, וּפְלִיגִי!

Rav Huna, son of Rav Natan, said to Rav Pappa: Can this be the dispute between Rabbi Yehuda and the Rabbis? **But** what about items that normally **ascend** upon the altar? Even Rabbi Yehuda concedes **that the frontplate effects acceptance for** impure items **that** normally **ascend** the altar, **and** Rabbi Yehuda and the Rabbis nevertheless **disagree** with regard to the remaining item in a case of this kind.

דְּתַנְיָא: נִטְמָא אֶחָד מִן הַבָּזִיכִין – רַבִּי יְהוּדָה אוֹמֵר: שְׁנֵיהֶם יֵעָשׂוּ בְּטוּמְאָה, לְפִי שֶׁאֵין קָרְבַּן צִיבּוּר חָלוּק; וַחֲכָמִים אוֹמְרִים: הַטָּמֵא בְּטוּמְאָתוֹ וְהַטָּהוֹר בְּטָהֳרָתוֹ!

The Gemara provides the source for this claim. **As it is taught** in a *baraita*: If **one of the bowls** of frankincense accompanying the shewbread, which are meant to be burned upon the altar, **became impure,**[H] **Rabbi Yehuda says** that the rites of **both of them may be performed in impurity,** i.e., the priest may even render the second bowl impure and burn both of them together, **as no communal offering is divided,** and the mitzva to sacrifice communal offerings overrides the prohibition against rendering them impure. **And the Rabbis say: The impure one** remains **in its** state of **impurity and the pure one** remains **in its** state of **purity.** Evidently, their dispute does not depend on whether the frontplate effects acceptance.

וְעוֹד אֲמַר רַב אַשִׁי: תָּא שְׁמַע, רַבִּי יְהוּדָה אוֹמֵר: אֲפִילּוּ שֵׁבֶט אֶחָד טָמֵא וְכָל הַשְּׁבָטִים טְהוֹרִין – יֵעָשׂוּ בְּטוּמְאָה, לְפִי שֶׁאֵין קָרְבְּנוֹת צִיבּוּר חָלוּק; וְהָכָא מַאי הַצִּיץ מְרַצֶּה אִיכָּא?

And furthermore, Rav Ashi said: Come and **hear** an additional proof that the dispute between Rabbi Yehuda and the Rabbis does not concern the frontplate, as we learn in a mishna (*Pesaḥim* 80a) with regard to the consumption of the Paschal offering in a state of impurity, that **Rabbi Yehuda says: Even** if **one tribe is ritually impure**[N] **and all** the rest of **the tribes are pure,** all the tribes **may perform** the rite of the Paschal offering **in** a state of **impurity, as no communal offerings are divided.** Rav Ashi explains: **But here, what** relevance **is there** to the question of whether **the frontplate effects acceptance?** The frontplate effects acceptance for offerings that have become impure; but it does not render it permitted for one who is ritually impure to sacrifice an offering.

וְעוֹד הָאָמַר רָבִינָא: תָּא שְׁמַע, נִטְמֵאת אַחַת מִן הַחַלּוֹת אוֹ אַחַת מִן הַסְּדָרִין – רַבִּי יְהוּדָה אוֹמֵר: שְׁנֵיהֶם יֵצְאוּ לְבֵית הַשְּׂרֵיפָה, לְפִי שֶׁאֵין קָרְבַּן צִיבּוּר חָלוּק, וַחֲכָמִים אוֹמְרִים: הַטָּמֵא בְּטוּמְאָתוֹ וְהַטָּהוֹר יֵאָכֵל;

And furthermore, doesn't Ravina say: Come and **hear** a proof that the matter of the frontplate cannot be the subject of the dispute between Rabbi Yehuda and the Rabbis, as the mishna teaches: If **one of the** two **loaves** brought on *Shavuot* **or one of the** two **arrangements** of shewbread **became ritually impure, Rabbi Yehuda says: Both must be taken to the place of burning, as no communal offering is divided. And the Rabbis say: The impure one** remains **in its impurity and the pure one may be eaten.**

HALAKHA

The frontplate effects acceptance – הַצִּיץ מְרַצֶּה: The frontplate effects acceptance for impure sacrificed items, but it does not effect acceptance for items that are consumed, nor for a person who is impure from a known source of impurity. The exception is with regard to instances where impurity is overridden in cases involving the public, as the frontplate effects acceptance for such impurities (Rambam *Sefer Avoda, Hilkhot Biat HaMikdash* 4:7).

If one of the bowls of frankincense became impure – נִטְמָא אֶחָד מִן הַבָּזִיכִין: If one of the bowls of frankincense accompanying the shewbread was rendered impure, the impure frankincense remains in its impure state and the pure frankincense remains in its pure state (Rambam *Sefer Avoda, Hilkhot Temidin UMusafin* 5:16).

NOTES

Even if one tribe is ritually impure – אֲפִילּוּ שֵׁבֶט אֶחָד טָמֵא: In contrast to other communal offerings, which may be sacrificed even in a state of ritual impurity but may not be consumed, the Paschal offering may also be consumed in a state of impurity, provided that the majority of the congregation or the priests are ritually impure, as the entire purpose of the Paschal offering is its consumption. But if only a minority of the congregation are ritually impure, then those in a state of purity sacrifice the Paschal offering in purity, while the impure minority purify themselves and bring their Paschal offerings on the second *Pesaḥ*. According to Rashi, Rabbi Yehuda holds that a single tribe is tantamount to a congregation, and consequently if one tribe was ritually impure, all of the tribes may bring their Paschal offerings in a state of impurity. By contrast, the Rabbis, i.e., Rabbi Shimon (see *Pesaḥim* 79b), maintain that when one tribe is impure, that tribe sacrifices the Paschal offering in a state of impurity, while the remaining tribes must sacrifice theirs in a state of purity.

וְאִם אִיתָא, ״לְפִי שֶׁאֵין הַצִּיץ מְרַצֶּה עַל אֲכִילוֹת״ מִיבְּעֵי לֵיהּ! אֶלָּא אָמַר רַבִּי יוֹחָנָן: תַּלְמוּד עָרוּךְ הוּא בְּפִיו שֶׁל רַבִּי יְהוּדָה, שֶׁאֵין קׇרְבַּן צִיבּוּר חָלוּק.

The Gemara explains the difficulty: **And if it is so,** i.e., that the dispute between them concerns the frontplate, then Rabbi Yehuda **should have** said: They are both burned, **because the frontplate does not effect acceptance for** impure items that are **consumed** by the priests. **Rather, Rabbi Yoḥanan says: It is a settled tradition**[N] **in the mouth of Rabbi Yehuda that no communal offering is divided,** and if one part of an offering becomes impure, the entire offering is disqualified.

מתני׳ הַתּוֹדָה מְפַגֶּלֶת אֶת הַלֶּחֶם, וְהַלֶּחֶם אֵינוֹ מְפַגֵּל אֶת הַתּוֹדָה. כֵּיצַד? שָׁחַט אֶת הַתּוֹדָה לֶאֱכוֹל מִמֶּנָּה לְמָחָר – הִיא וְהַלֶּחֶם מְפוּגָּלִין; לֶאֱכוֹל מִן הַלֶּחֶם לְמָחָר – הַלֶּחֶם מְפוּגָּל וְהַתּוֹדָה אֵינָהּ מְפוּגֶּלֶת.

MISHNA **The thanks offering renders the** accompanying **loaves** ***piggul***[H] **but the loaves do not render the thanks offering** ***piggul*****. How so? If one slaughtered the thanks offering,** which may be consumed only during the day it is slaughtered and the night thereafter, with the intent **to partake of it the next day,** the offering **and the** accompanying **loaves are rendered** ***piggul*****.** If he slaughtered it with the intent **to partake of the loaves the next day, the loaves are rendered** ***piggul*** **and the thanks offering is not** ***piggul*****.**

הַכְּבָשִׂים מְפַגְּלִין אֶת הַלֶּחֶם, וְהַלֶּחֶם אֵינוֹ מְפַגֵּל אֶת הַכְּבָשִׂים. כֵּיצַד? הַשּׁוֹחֵט אֶת הַכְּבָשִׂים לֶאֱכוֹל מֵהֶן לְמָחָר – הֵם וְהַלֶּחֶם מְפוּגָּלִין, לֶאֱכוֹל אֶת הַלֶּחֶם לְמָחָר – הַלֶּחֶם מְפוּגָּל וְהַכְּבָשִׂים אֵינָן מְפוּגָּלִין.

Likewise, **the lambs** sacrificed with the two loaves meal offering on *Shavuot* **render the** accompanying **loaves** ***piggul*****,**[H] **but the loaves do not render the lambs** ***piggul*****. How so? If one slaughtered the lambs,** which may be consumed only during the day they are slaughtered and the night thereafter, with the intent **to partake of them the next day,** the lambs **and the** accompanying **loaves are rendered** ***piggul*****.** If he did so with the intent **to partake of the loaves the next day, the loaves are rendered** ***piggul*** **and the lambs are not** ***piggul*****.**

גמ׳ מַאי טַעְמָא? אִילֵימָא מִשּׁוּם דְּרַב כָּהֲנָא, דְּאָמַר רַב כָּהֲנָא: מִנַּיִן לְלַחְמֵי תוֹדָה שֶׁנִּקְרְאוּ תוֹדָה? שֶׁנֶּאֱמַר: ״וְהִקְרִיב עַל זֶבַח הַתּוֹדָה חַלּוֹת״,

GEMARA The Gemara asks: **What is the reason** that a thanks offering renders its accompanying loaves *piggul*? **If we say** that it is **due to that** which **Rav Kahana** says, this is problematic. **As Rav Kahana says: From where** is it derived that **the loaves of a thanks offering are** themselves **called a thanks offering?** It is derived from **that** which **is stated** in the verse: **"Then he shall offer with the sacrifice of thanks offering loaves"** (Leviticus 7:12). The juxtaposition of the words "thanks offering" and "loaves" indicates that the loaves are themselves called a thanks offering.

אִי הָכִי אִיפְּכָא נַמִי! הָא לָא קַשְׁיָא, לֶחֶם אִיקְּרֵי תוֹדָה, תוֹדָה לָא אִיקְּרֵי לֶחֶם.

The Gemara explains why the *halakha* of the mishna cannot be derived from Rav Kahana's exposition. **If so,** then **the opposite** should be the *halakha* **as well,** that intent of *piggul* with regard to the loaves should likewise render the thanks offering *piggul*. The Gemara rejects this suggestion: **This is not difficult,** as the **loaves are called a thanks offering,** but **a thanks offering is not called loaves.**

אֶלָּא הָא דְּקָתָנֵי: הַכְּבָשִׂים מְפַגְּלִין אֶת הַלֶּחֶם וְהַלֶּחֶם אֵינוֹ מְפַגֵּל אֶת הַכְּבָשִׂים, לֶחֶם הֵיכָא אַשְׁכַּחַן דְּאִיקְּרֵי כְּבָשִׂים? אֶלָּא לָאו הַיְינוּ טַעְמָא: לֶחֶם גְּלָל תּוֹדָה וְאֵין תּוֹדָה גְּלָל דְּלֶחֶם, לֶחֶם גְּלָל דִּכְבָשִׂים וְאֵין כְּבָשִׂים גְּלָל דְּלֶחֶם.

The Gemara asks: **But** with regard to **that which** the mishna **teaches: The lambs** sacrificed with the two loaves meal offering on *Shavuot* **render the** accompanying **loaves** ***piggul*** **but the loaves do not render the lambs** ***piggul*****, where do we find that** the two **loaves are called lambs? Rather, is it not** correct that **this is the reason** why the thanks offering renders the loaves *piggul* but not vice versa: The **bread** is brought **on account of** **[*gelal*]**[L] the **thanks offering, but** the **thanks offering is not** brought **on account of** the **bread,** i.e., the thanks offering is the primary element of the sacrifice. Similarly, the two loaves of **bread are** brought **on account of** the **lambs,**[N] **and** the **lambs are not** brought **on account of** the **bread.**

NOTES

It is a settled tradition – תַּלְמוּד עָרוּךְ: In other words, Rabbi Yehuda learned this *halakha* from his teachers (Rashi). The Rambam's Commentary on the Mishna explains that Rabbi Yehuda received a tradition, not based on any particular verse or logical reasoning, that whenever even part of a communal offering may not be properly sacrificed due to ritual impurity, the entire offering is considered impure. There are stringent and lenient ramifications of this tradition. For example, if one of the loaves or arrangements becomes impure, then all of the other loaves or arrangements are rendered impure and must be burned, even if the frontplate effects acceptance of the ritual impurity of items normally consumed by the priests. Conversely, with regard to items that may be sacrificed in a state of impurity, or in the case of the Paschal offering, which may be consumed in impurity, this tradition results in a leniency, as these items may be consumed or sacrificed.

Some commentaries maintain that according to Rabbi Yoḥanan there is no difference whether the loaf became impure before or after the sprinkling of the blood; in all instances Rabbi Yehuda maintains that both loaves are burned. By contrast, the Rambam's Commentary on the Mishna indicates that Rabbi Yoḥanan's statement was meant only as a refutation of the assumption of Rav Pappa that the dispute between the Rabbis and Rabbi Yehuda concerns the frontplate. But if the loaf became impure after the sprinkling of the blood, even Rabbi Yehuda rules that the other loaf remains pure (see Rashash and *Tohorat HaKodesh*).

The bread is brought on account of the thanks offering…the two loaves of bread are brought on account of the lambs – לֶחֶם גְּלָל תּוֹדָה...לֶחֶם גְּלָל דִּכְבָשִׂים: The Gemara does not mean that the two loaves are brought because of the lambs, as the loaves are the principal offering brought on *Shavuot*, while the lambs are brought to accompany them (see *Horayot* 13a). Rather, the Gemara is referring to the fact that the loaves are permitted for consumption to the priests only through the proper slaughter of the lambs (*Mitzpe Eitan*). The mishna (45b) records a dispute as to whether the loaves preclude the lambs or vice versa. The commentaries discuss whether the mishna here is only in accordance with the opinion that the lambs preclude the loaves (see *Keren Ora* on 45b and *Tosefta*, *Menaḥot* 3:8).

LANGUAGE

On account of [*gelal*] – גְּלָל: This word, which more often appears in the Gemara in the form *biglal*, is used in many different senses, all of which denote some connection between two matters. Sometimes it refers to the reason for a matter, or to express that one factor is the cause of the other. It can also signify which item is primary and which is secondary. Occasionally it means that one item is dependent on the existence of the other, as is the case in the Gemara here. Finally, it sometimes merely expresses a physical connection between two items, i.e., that they come together (see 4b).

HALAKHA

The thanks offering renders the loaves ***piggul*****, etc. – הַתּוֹדָה מְפַגֶּלֶת אֶת הַלֶּחֶם וכו׳:** The thanks offering renders the loaves *piggul*. Accordingly, if one slaughtered the thanks offering and had intention to sprinkle its blood, or to partake of its meat, or to burn its sacrificial portions, the next day, both the animal and the loaves are *piggul*. If his intention was to partake of the loaves the next day, the loaves are *piggul* but the animal is not *piggul* (Rambam *Sefer Avoda, Hilkhot Pesulei HaMukdashin* 17:7).

The lambs render the loaves ***piggul*****, etc. – הַכְּבָשִׂים מְפַגְּלִין אֶת הַלֶּחֶם וכו׳:** With regard to the two lambs brought on *Shavuot*, if one slaughtered them with the intention to partake of one of them the next day, the lambs and loaves are rendered *piggul*. But if one slaughtered them with the intention to partake of the loaves the next day, the loaves are *piggul* but the lambs are not *piggul* (Rambam *Sefer Avoda, Hilkhot Pesulei HaMukdashin* 17:8).

וצריכי, דאי אשמעינן תודה – התם הוא דכי מפגל בלחם לא מפגלא תודה, משום דלא הוזקקו זה לזה בתנופה, אבל כבשים דהוזקקו זה לזה בתנופה, אימא כי מפגל בלחם ליפגלי נמי כבשים, צריכא.

The Gemara notes: **And** both of these *halakhot* **are necessary, as, had** the mishna **taught us** the *halakha* only in the case of **a thanks offering,** then one might say: **It is** only **there,** with regard to a thanks offering, **that when one renders the loaves *piggul* the thanks offering is not rendered *piggul,* because they were not bound to one another by waving,** i.e., the mitzva of waving the thanks offering may be fulfilled without the bread. **But** with regard to the **lambs,** in **which** the two items **were bound to one another by waving,** as the two loaves are waved together with the lambs, one might **say** that **when he renders the bread *piggul,*** the **lambs should be rendered *piggul* as well.** Therefore, it was **necessary** for the mishna to teach this *halakha* also with regard to the case of the lambs.

NOTES

Which serves to render *piggul*…which come to render another item *piggul* but do not render *piggul* – המפגל...הבא לפגל ולא פיגל: That is to say, since the loaves are rendered *piggul* only because they are subordinate to an animal offering that is rendered *piggul,* then in a case where the offering is not rendered *piggul,* the loaves should not be rendered *piggul* either (*Sefat Emet*).

בעא מיניה רבי אלעזר מרב: השוחט את התודה לאכול כזית ממנה ומלחמה למחר, מהו? לאיפגולי תודה לא מיבעיא לי; השתא כולו מלחמה לא מיפגלא, ממנה ומלחמה מיבעיא?

§ **Rabbi Elazar raised a dilemma before Rav:** If one slaughters **the thanks offering** with the intent **to consume an olive-bulk from it and from its loaves the next day, what is** the *halakha*? Rabbi Elazar elaborates: **I do not raise the dilemma with regard to rendering** the **thanks offering *piggul,*** for the following reason: **Now** that in a case where his intent was to consume **the entire** olive-bulk **from its loaves** alone, the thanks offering **is not rendered *piggul,*** in accordance with the mishna's ruling that *piggul* intent with regard to the loaves does not render the thanks offering *piggul,* then in a case where his intent is to consume half an olive-bulk **from** the thanks offering **and** half an olive-bulk **from its loaves,** in which case the offering is rendered *piggul* only if the two intentions of less than a full measure are combined, is it **necessary** to teach that the thanks offering is not *piggul*?

כי קא מיבעיא לי – לאיפגולי לחם, מי מצטרפה תודה לאיפגולי ללחם או לא?

Rather, **when I raise the dilemma,** it is with regard **to rendering the loaves *piggul,*** which can be rendered *piggul* via intent concerning the loaves alone. In this case, **does** the intention of the priest with regard to the **thanks offering combine** with his intention concerning the loaves **to render the loaves *piggul,* or not?**

אמר ליה: אף בזו, הלחם מפוגל והתודה אינה מפוגלת. ואמאי? לימא קל וחומר: ומה תודה המפגל – אין מתפגל, הבא לפגל ולא פיגל – אינו דין שלא יתפגל?

Rav **said to** Rabbi Elazar: **Even in this** case, **the loaves are rendered *piggul* and the thanks offering is not rendered *piggul.*** The Gemara asks: **But why** should the loaves be rendered *piggul*? **Let us say** the following ***a fortiori*** inference: **And if** the **thanks offering, which** in this case serves to **render** the loaves ***piggul,*** is itself **not rendered *piggul,*** then the loaves, **which come to render** the thanks offering ***piggul,* but do not render** it ***piggul,***[N] as the intent to consume half an olive-bulk from the loaves does not combine with the intent to consume half an olive-bulk from the thanks offering to render the thanks offering *piggul,* **is it not logical that the** loaves themselves **should not be rendered *piggul*?**

ומי אמרינן קל וחומר כי האי גוונא? והתניא: מעשה באחד

The Gemara asks: **And do we say an *a fortiori*** inference **in this way? But isn't it taught** in a *baraita*: There was **an incident involving one**

Perek **II**
Daf **15** Amud **b**

שזרע כרמו של חבירו סמדר, ובא מעשה לפני חכמים, ואסרו את הזרעים והתירו את הגפנים; ואמאי? לימא קל וחומר הוא: ומה האוסר אינו נאסר, הבא לאסור ולא אסר אינו דין שלא יתאסר!

who planted seeds in **the vineyard of an another** when the grapes on the vines were **budding,**[H] **and the incident came before the Sages and they deemed the seeds prohibited** due to the prohibition against planting diverse kinds in a vineyard, **but they deemed the vines permitted.** The Gemara continues: **But why** did they deem the seeds prohibited? **Let** the Sages **say** through an analogous ***a fortiori*** inference that the seeds should be permitted: **And if that which renders** an item **prohibited,** i.e., the vine, which causes the seeds to be prohibited, **is** itself **not prohibited,** then with regard to the seeds, **which come to render** the vines **prohibited but did not render** the vines **prohibited, is it not logical that they should not be rendered prohibited?**

HALAKHA

Who planted seeds in the vineyard of another when the grapes were budding – שזרע כרמו של חבירו סמדר: One cannot render prohibited an item that does not belong to him. Accordingly, in a case where one causes his grapevines to overhang the grain of another, the vines are prohibited while the grain remains permitted (Rambam *Sefer Zera'im, Hilkhot Kilayim* 5:8).

הָכִי הָשְׁתָּא? הָתָם קַנְבּוֹס וְלוּף אָסְרָה תּוֹרָה, דִּתְנַן: הָיְתָה שָׂדֵהוּ זְרוּעָה קַנְבּוֹס וְלוּף – לֹא יְהֵא זוֹרֵעַ עַל גַּבֵּיהֶם, שֶׁהֵן עוֹשׂוֹת לְשָׁלֹשׁ שָׁנִים; שְׁאָר זְרָעִים מִדְּרַבָּנַן הוּא דַּאֲסִירִי, הַאי דְּעָבֵיד אִיסּוּרָא קַנְסוּהּ רַבָּנַן, הַאי דְּלָא עָבֵיד אִיסּוּרָא לָא קַנְסוּהּ רַבָּנַן, אֲבָל הָכָא לֵימָא קַל וָחוֹמֶר!

The Gemara rejects the comparison: **How can these cases be compared?**[N] **There,** in the *baraita*, only **hemp**[B] **and arum**[B] **are prohibited by Torah law**[H] to be sown in a vineyard, **as we learned** in a mishna (*Kilayim* 2:5): **If one's field was sown with hemp and arum, he should not sow above them, as they produce** a yield only once every **three years.**[N] **Other seeds are prohibited by rabbinic law.** Therefore, with regard to **this** person **who committed a transgression** by planting the seeds in the vineyard of another, **the Sages penalized him** and deemed his seeds prohibited, but as for **that** person **who did not commit a transgression,** i.e., the owner of the vineyard, **the Sages did not penalize him. But here,** in the case of *piggul*, which is a biblical prohibition, **let us say** such **an *a fortiori*** inference.

וְאִיכָּא דְּמַתְנֵי לַהּ אַכְּבָשִׂים. בְּעָא מִינֵּיהּ רַבִּי אֶלְעָזָר מֵרַב: הַשּׁוֹחֵט אֶת הַכְּבָשִׂים לֶאֱכוֹל כְּזַיִת מֵהֶן וּמִלַּחְמָן, מַהוּ?

And there are those who teach the dilemma of Rabbi Elazar **with regard to the lambs** brought with the two loaves, and not with regard to a thanks offering. **Rabbi Elazar raised a dilemma before Rav:** In a case where **one slaughters the lambs** with the intent **to consume an olive-bulk from them and from their loaves**[H] the next day, **what is** the *halakha*?

לְאִיפַּגּוּלֵי כְּבָשִׂים לָא קָא מִיבַּעְיָא לִי, הָשְׁתָּא כּוּלּוֹ מִלֶּחֶם לָא מְפַגֵּל, מֵהֶן וּמִלַּחְמָן מִיבַּעְיָא? כִּי קָא מִיבַּעְיָא לִי – לְאִיפַּגּוּלֵי לֶחֶם, מִי מִצְטָרְפִי כְּבָשִׂים לְאִיפַּגּוּלֵי לֶחֶם אוֹ לָא?

Rabbi Elazar elaborated: **I do not raise the dilemma with regard to rendering** the **lambs** ***piggul*** for the following reason: **Now** that in a case where his intent was to consume **an entire** olive-bulk **from the loaves** alone, the lambs **are not rendered *piggul*,** as the mishna teaches that *piggul* intent with regard to the loaves does not render the lambs *piggul*, then in a case where his intent is to consume half an olive-bulk **from them and** half an olive-bulk **from their loaves, is it necessary** to teach that the lambs are not *piggul*? Rather, **when I raised the dilemma,** it was **with regard to rendering the loaves *piggul*. Does** his intention with regard to the **lambs combine** with his intention with regard to the loaves **to render the loaves *piggul* or not?**

HALAKHA

Hemp and arum are prohibited by Torah law – קַנְבּוֹס וְלוּף אָסְרָה תּוֹרָה: By Torah law, one is liable for sowing diverse kinds in a vineyard only for sowing grains, or for sowing any vegetable crop that ripens at the same time as the grapes of the vineyard, such as hemp or arum. With regard to other seeds, some are prohibited by rabbinic decree, while others are entirely permitted (Rambam *Sefer Zera'im, Hilkhot Kilayim* 5:3, 6, 19; and see Radbaz, *Kesef Mishne*, and Mahari Kurkus there).

To consume an olive-bulk from them and from their loaves, etc. – לֶאֱכוֹל כְּזַיִת מֵהֶן וּמִלַּחְמָן וכו׳: If, during the performance of one of the four sacrificial rites, whether in the case of a thanks offering or the communal lamb offering brought on *Shavuot*, one had intent to consume a collective olive-bulk the next day from the meat of the animal and the loaves, the loaves are *piggul*, while the animal is not. The Rambam rules in accordance with the first presentation of the dilemma of Rabbi Elazar, that the loaves accompanying both a thanks offering and the lambs brought on *Shavuot* are rendered *piggul*. Although the Rambam generally rules in accordance with the second presentation of a dilemma, here he rules in accordance with the first presentation, as according to the first presentation, it is certain that the loaves accompanying the lambs sacrificed on *Shavuot* are rendered *piggul*, while according to the second presentation, there is an uncertainty with regard to the case of the lambs (Rambam *Sefer Avoda, Hilkhot Pesulei HaMukdashin* 17:8, and see *Kesef Mishne* and Mahari Kurkus there).

NOTES

How can these cases be compared, etc. – הָכִי הָשְׁתָּא וכו׳: There is a close link between a thanks offering and its loaves, as the loaves are rendered *piggul* on account of the thanks offering. Accordingly, it is reasonable to say that if the thanks offering is not rendered *piggul*, neither are the loaves. By contrast, the seeds planted in a vineyard are not rendered prohibited on account of the vines, but as the consequence of a penalty imposed by the Sages upon one who transgresses a rabbinic prohibition. Therefore, it is not reasonable to suggest that the seeds should be permitted due to the fact that the vines were not rendered prohibited, as the vines are owned by one who did not do anything to warrant a penalty (commentary attributed to Rashba).

If one's field was sown with hemp and arum…as they produce a yield only once every three years – הָיְתָה שָׂדֵהוּ זְרוּעָה קַנְבּוֹס וְלוּף...שֶׁהֵן עוֹשׂוֹת לְשָׁלֹשׁ שָׁנִים: Although that mishna discusses the prohibition against sowing diverse kinds and not the prohibition of planting diverse kinds in a vineyard, it may be inferred from the mishna that there is a particular reason why only hemp and arum were prohibited from being planted in a vineyard, namely, that they are considered significant because their seeds endure (see Rashi and Rabbeinu Gershom Meor HaGola).

BACKGROUND

Hemp – קַנְבּוֹס: This apparently refers to the *Cannabis sativa* plant, an annual herb with loose branches that can grow to a height of nearly 3 m. Hemp has many commercial applications. Already in ancient times its fibers were used in the textile industry, and oil was produced from its seeds for industrial use. It is also known for the use of its flowers in the production of the drug hashish, and it is possible that it was used in talmudic times as a sleep aid. The early commentaries discuss the difficulty posed by the mishna's statement that hemp produces a yield only once every three years, which appears to contradict experience. Among the suggested resolutions is that the mishna is referring to the fact that hempseeds may regerminate multiple times over several years while remaining in the ground.

Cannabis plant

Arum – לוּף: This plant is generally identified as the arum of Eretz Yisrael, *Arum palaestinum*, from the Araceae family. This plant has a bulb in the ground from which large leaves sprout. The arum plant's flowers have has a unique structure and are covered with a special type of leaf called a spathe. All parts of the plant contain calcium oxalate, $Ca(COO)_2$, which is poisonous and causes extreme itching to any skin that comes in contact with it. Consequently, arum is not eaten by people in its raw state, and few animals draw sustenance from it. The bulb and leaves are cooked or roasted to make them fit for human consumption. The plant grows in the wild in all regions of Eretz Yisrael.

Arum plant

אֲמַר לֵיהּ: אַף בָּזוֹ, הַלֶּחֶם מְפוּגָּל וְהַכְּבָשִׂים אֵינָן מְפוּגָּלִין. וְאַמַּאי? לֵימָא קַל וָחוֹמֶר: וּמָה הַמְפַגֵּל אֵינוֹ מִתְפַּגֵּל, הַבָּא לְפַגֵּל וְלֹא פִּיגֵּל – אֵינוֹ דִּין שֶׁלֹּא יִתְפַּגֵּל!

Rav **said to** Rabbi Elazar: **Even in this** case, **the loaves are rendered *piggul* and the lambs are not rendered *piggul*.** The Gemara asks: **But why** should the loaves be rendered *piggul*? **Let us say** the following ***a fortiori*** inference: **And if that which renders** an item ***piggul***, i.e., the lambs, since it is maintained that intent to consume half an olive-bulk from the lambs assists to render the loaves *piggul*, **is** itself **not rendered *piggul*,** then with regard to the loaves, **which come to render** the lambs ***piggul*, but do not render** them ***piggul***, as the intent to consume half an olive-bulk from the loaves does not combine with the intent to consume half an olive-bulk from the lambs to render them *piggul*, **is it not logical that** the loaves themselves **should not be rendered *piggul*?**

וּמִי אָמְרִינַן קַל וָחוֹמֶר כִּי הַאי גַּוְונָא? וְהָתַנְיָא: מַעֲשֶׂה בְּאֶחָד שֶׁזָּרַע כַּרְמוֹ שֶׁל חֲבֵירוֹ סְמָדַר וכו׳, וְאַמַּאי? לֵימָא קַל וָחוֹמֶר: מָה הָאוֹסֵר אֵינוֹ נֶאֱסָר, הַבָּא לֶאֱסוֹר וְלֹא אָסַר אֵינוֹ דִּין שֶׁלֹּא יִתְאַסֵּר!

The Gemara asks: **And do we say an *a fortiori*** inference **of this kind? But isn't it taught** in a *baraita* that there was **an incident involving one who planted** seeds in **the vineyard of his friend** when the grapes on the vines were **budding,** and the incident came before the Sages and they deemed the seeds prohibited due to the prohibition against planting diverse kinds in a vineyard, but they deemed the vines permitted. The Gemara continues: **But why** did they deem the seeds prohibited? **Let** the Sages **say** through an analogous ***a fortiori*** inference that the seeds should be permitted: **And** if **that which renders** an item **prohibited,** i.e., the vine, which causes the seeds to be prohibited, **is** itself **not prohibited,** then with regard to the seeds, **which come to render** the vines **prohibited but did not render** the vines **prohibited, is it not logical that** they **should not be rendered prohibited?**

הָכִי הָשְׁתָּא? הָתָם קַנַּבּוֹס וְלוּף אָסְרָה תּוֹרָה, שְׁאָר זְרָעִים מִדְּרַבָּנַן הוּא דַּאֲסִירִי, הַאי דְּעָבַד אִיסּוּרָא קַנְסוּהּ רַבָּנַן, דְּלָא עֲבַד אִיסּוּרָא לָא קַנְסוּהּ רַבָּנַן; אֲבָל הָכָא לֵימָא קַל וָחוֹמֶר!

The Gemara rejects the comparison: **How can** these cases **be compared? There,** in the *baraita*, only **hemp and arum** are **prohibited** by **Torah** law to be sown in a vineyard. **Other seeds are prohibited by rabbinic** law. Therefore, with regard to **this** person **who committed a transgression** by planting the seeds in the vineyard of another, **the Sages penalized him** and deemed his seeds prohibited, but as for **this** person **who did not commit a transgression,** i.e., the owner of the vineyard, **the Sages did not penalize him. But here,** in the case of *piggul*, which is a biblical prohibition, **let us say** such **an *a fortiori*** inference.

מַאן דְּמַתְנֵי לָהּ אַתּוֹדָה – כׇּל שֶׁכֵּן אַכְּבָשִׂים, וּמַאן דְּמַתְנֵי לָהּ אַכְּבָשִׂים – כְּבָשִׂים הוּא דְּהוּזְקְקוּ זֶה לָזֶה לִתְנוּפָה, אֲבָל תּוֹדָה דְּלֹא הוּזְקְקָה זֶה לָזֶה בִּתְנוּפָה – לָא.

The Gemara notes: **The one who teaches** that the dilemma of Rabbi Elazar was raised **with regard to the thanks offering** and the accompanying loaves, **all the more so** will hold that the dilemma may be raised **with regard to** the case of **the lambs** brought with the two loaves on *Shavuot*. **But the one who teaches** that Rabbi Elazar's dilemma was raised **with regard to the lambs** and the two loaves, it is possible that he holds that the dilemma **was** raised only with regard to the **lambs** and the two loaves, **as they were bound to one another by waving,** since the priest waves the lambs and loaves together (see Leviticus 23:20). **But** with regard to **a thanks offering** and its loaves, **as they were not bound to one another by waving,** the dilemma was **not** raised, since it is obvious in this case that his intentions do not combine.

רַבִּי אַבָּא זוּטִי בָּעֵי לָהּ הָכִי, בְּעָא מִינֵּיהּ רַבִּי אֶלְעָזָר מֵרַב: הַשּׁוֹחֵט אֶת הַכֶּבֶשׂ לֶאֱכוֹל כְּזַיִת מֵחֲבֵירוֹ לְמָחָר, מַהוּ? ״חֲבֵירוֹ״ כֶּבֶשׂ מַשְׁמַע וְלָא מְפַגֵּל, אוֹ דִּלְמָא לֶחֶם מַשְׁמַע וּמְפַגֵּל לֵיהּ?

Rabbi Abba the small taught that Rabbi Elazar **raises the dilemma** in **this** manner: **Rabbi Elazar raised a dilemma before Rav:** If **one slaughters** one of **the lambs** brought on *Shavuot* with the two loaves intending **to consume an olive-bulk from the other**[NH] **the next day, what is the** *halakha*? When this individual thinks of **the other,** does he **mean** the other **lamb, and** if so, the lamb **is not rendered *piggul*,** as one permitting factor does not render another permitting factor *piggul*? **Or perhaps** when this individual thinks of the other he **means** the other part of the offering, i.e., the two **loaves,**[N] **and** if so his intention **renders it *piggul*,** as taught in the mishna.

NOTES

An olive-bulk from the other – כְּזַיִת מֵחֲבֵירוֹ: Some commentaries explain that when someone in this situation thinks of: The other, he is generally understood to be referring to the other lamb. The Gemara is referring to a case where the priest later stated that his intention was actually concerning the loaves. The Gemara is asking whether it is a reasonable claim that one referred to the loaves as the other (*Sefat Emet*).

He means the loaves, etc. – לֶחֶם מַשְׁמַע וכו׳: This dilemma is raised only with regard to the opinion of Rabbi Meir (16a), who holds that one can render an item *piggul* by having *piggul* intent during the sacrifice of part of its permitting factors, e.g., during the slaughter of one lamb. Some commentaries suggest that the dilemma is raised even according to the opinion of the Rabbis on 16a, provided that it is accepted that the Gemara here is not using the word *piggul* literally, but is simply referring to the disqualification of the loaves (*Shita Mekubbetzet*; see *Keren Ora*).

HALAKHA

To consume an olive-bulk from the other, etc. – לֶאֱכוֹל כְּזַיִת מֵחֲבֵירוֹ וכו׳: If one slaughters one of the lambs that accompanies the two loaves brought on *Shavuot* with the intention to consume an olive-bulk from the other the next day, both of the lambs are fit, as stated in the mishna on 16a (Rambam *Sefer Avoda*, *Hilkhot Pesulei HaMukdashin* 17:17).

אֲמַר לֵיהּ, תְּנִיתוּהָ: שָׁחַט אֶחָד מִן הַכְּבָשִׂים לֶאֱכוֹל מִמֶּנּוּ לְמָחָר – הוּא פִּיגּוּל וַחֲבֵירוֹ כָּשֵׁר, לֶאֱכוֹל מֵחֲבֵירוֹ לְמָחָר – שְׁנֵיהֶם כְּשֵׁרִים; אַלְמָא "חֲבֵירוֹ" כֶּבֶשׂ מַשְׁמַע! דִּלְמָא דְּפָרֵישׁ וְאָמַר: "חֲבֵירוֹ כֶּבֶשׂ".

Rav **said to** Rabbi Elazar: **You learned** in a mishna (16a): If **one slaughtered one of the lambs** with the intent **to partake of it the next day, that** lamb **is *piggul* and the other is fit.** If he slaughtered one lamb with the intent **to partake of the other the next day, both** lambs **are fit,** as one permitting factor does not render another permitting factor *piggul.* Rav concludes: **Evidently,** in this context the term: **The other, means** the other **lamb.** The Gemara rejects this proof: **Perhaps** the mishna is discussing a case **where he clarifies and says: The other lamb,** but the mishna is not referring to a case where he merely thought: The other.

מתני׳ הַזֶּבַח מְפַגֵּל אֶת הַנְּסָכִים מִשֶּׁקָּדְשׁוּ בִּכְלִי, דִּבְרֵי רַבִּי מֵאִיר. הַנְּסָכִים אֵינָן מְפַגְּלִים אֶת הַזֶּבַח. כֵּיצַד? הַשּׁוֹחֵט אֶת הַזֶּבַח לֶאֱכוֹל מִמֶּנּוּ לְמָחָר – הוּא וּנְסָכָיו מְפוּגָּלִין, לְהַקְרִיב נְסָכָיו לְמָחָר – הַנְּסָכִים מְפוּגָּלִין, הַזֶּבַח אֵינוֹ מְפוּגָּל.

MISHNA The animal **offering renders the** accompanying **libations**[N] and meal offerings ***piggul*** **from** the moment **that they were consecrated in the vessel,** but not before; this is **the statement of Rabbi Meir. The libations do not render the** animal **offering *piggul.* How so?** In the case of **one who slaughters the offering** with the intent **to partake of it the next day,** the offering **and its libations are rendered *piggul.*** But if one slaughters the offering with the intent **to sacrifice its libations the next day, the libations are rendered *piggul,*** while **the offering is not *piggul.***

גמ׳ תָּנוּ רַבָּנַן: נִסְכֵּי בְהֵמָה חַיָּיבִין עֲלֵיהֶן מִשּׁוּם פִּיגּוּל, מִפְּנֵי שֶׁדַּם הַזֶּבַח מַתִּירָן לִקְרֵב, דִּבְרֵי רַבִּי מֵאִיר.

GEMARA **The Sages taught** in a *baraita*: With regard to the **libations of an animal** offering, **one is liable for** eating **them due to** violation of the prohibition of ***piggul,***[H] **as the blood of the offering permits them to be offered** on the altar, and any item that becomes permitted for consumption or for sacrifice through a permitting factor can be rendered *piggul,* and one who partakes of such an item after its permitting factors were sacrificed is liable to receive *karet.* This is **the statement of Rabbi Meir.**

אָמְרוּ לוֹ לְרַבִּי מֵאִיר: וַהֲלֹא אָדָם מֵבִיא זִבְחוֹ הַיּוֹם וּנְסָכָיו עַד עֲשָׂרָה יָמִים! אָמַר לָהֶן: אַף אֲנִי לֹא אָמַרְתִּי אֶלָּא בַּבָּאִין עִם הַזֶּבַח. אָמְרוּ לוֹ: אֶפְשָׁר לְשַׁנּוֹתוֹ לְזֶבַח אַחֵר.

The Rabbis **said to Rabbi Meir: But a person may bring his offering today**[H] **and** the accompanying **libations from now until** even **ten days** later. Evidently, then, the blood of the offering does render the libations permitted. Rabbi Meir **said to them: I, too, spoke only about** libations that **come** to be sacrificed together **with the offering** and were already sanctified in a service vessel for that purpose. The Rabbis **said to him:** But **it is possible to switch** the libations **for** use with **another offering.** Clearly, then, they are not considered an indispensable part of that offering.

אֲמַר רָבָא, קָסָבַר רַבִּי מֵאִיר: הוּקְבְּעוּ בִּשְׁחִיטָה, כְּלַחְמֵי תוֹדָה.

Rava said: Rabbi Meir holds that the libations **are fixed** to this particular offering **at** the time of its **slaughter,** and one may not use them with another offering. Accordingly, these libations are rendered *piggul* on account of intent during the slaughter of the offering, just **like the loaves of a thanks offering,** which are fixed to a particular thanks offering upon its slaughter and become *piggul* on account of intent during the slaughter of that particular thanks offering.

תָּנוּ רַבָּנַן: לוֹג שֶׁמֶן שֶׁל מְצוֹרָע חַיָּיבִין עָלָיו מִשּׁוּם פִּיגּוּל, מִפְּנֵי שֶׁדַּם אָשָׁם מַתִּירוֹ לִבְהוֹנוֹת, דִּבְרֵי רַבִּי מֵאִיר. אָמְרוּ לוֹ לְרַבִּי מֵאִיר: וַהֲלֹא אָדָם מֵבִיא אֲשָׁמוֹ הַיּוֹם וְלוּגּוֹ מִיכָּן וְעַד עֲשָׂרָה יָמִים!

In a similar vein, **the Sages taught:** With regard to the ***log* of oil of the leper** (see Leviticus 14:10–20),[H] **one is liable for** eating **it due to** violation of the prohibition of ***piggul*** if the guilt offering that this oil accompanied became *piggul,* **as the blood** of the offering **permits it to** be placed on **the** right **thumb and big toe** of the leper. This is **the statement of Rabbi Meir.** The Rabbis **said to Rabbi Meir: But a person may bring his guilt offering today and** the accompanying ***log*** of oil **from now until** even **ten days** later. Evidently, the *log* of oil is not considered part of the guilt offering, and therefore it should not be rendered *piggul* on account of it.

אָמַר לָהֶן: אַף אֲנִי לֹא אָמַרְתִּי אֶלָּא בַּבָּא עִם הָאָשָׁם. אֶפְשָׁר לְשַׁנּוֹתוֹ לְאָשָׁם אַחֵר. אֲמַר רָבָא, קָסָבַר רַבִּי מֵאִיר: הוּקְבְּעוּ בִּשְׁחִיטָה, כְּלַחְמֵי תוֹדָה.

Rabbi Meir **said to them: I, too, spoke only about** a *log* of oil that **comes with the guilt** offering. The Rabbis said to him: But even in this case, the oil should not be considered part of the offering, as **it is possible to switch** the oil **for** use with **another guilt offering. Rava said: Rabbi Meir holds** that the *log* of oil **is fixed** to this particular guilt offering **at** the time of its **slaughter** and is therefore rendered *piggul* on account of it, just **like the loaves of a thanks offering,** as the slaughter of the thanks offering fixes the accompanying loaves to that particular offering.

NOTES

Libations – נְסָכִים: Any individual who brings a burnt offering or peace offering must also bring a meal offering of flour mixed with oil, which is offered in its entirety upon the altar, as well as wine for pouring upon the altar (see Numbers, chapter 15). The meal offerings, oil, and wine accompanying these offerings are all collectively referred to by the Sages as libations. The mishna's statement that the libations of an offering do not render the animal *piggul* is unanimous. In addition, the Rabbis maintain that the animal cannot render its libations *piggul* either, as it is not considered a permitting factor of the libations. Accordingly, libations can never be rendered *piggul,* as there is no factor that permits them for sacrifice or consumption (see *Zevaḥim* 43a).

HALAKHA

With regard to the libations of an animal, one is liable for them due to *piggul* – נִסְכֵּי בְהֵמָה חַיָּיבִין עֲלֵיהֶן מִשּׁוּם פִּיגּוּל: One is never liable for the consumption of *piggul* by partaking of libations, whether he partakes of a meal offering or wine that accompanies an offering, or the wine that is poured upon the altar as an independent offering. The *halakha* is in accordance with the opinion of the Rabbis on *Zevaḥim* 43a, and not Rabbi Meir (Rambam *Sefer Avoda, Hilkhot Pesulei HaMukdashin* 18:8).

Bring his offering today – מֵבִיא זִבְחוֹ הַיּוֹם: One may sacrifice an animal offering on one day and its accompanying libations ten days later (Rambam *Sefer Avoda, Hilkhot Ma'aseh HaKorbanot* 2:12).

The *log* of oil of the leper – לוֹג שֶׁמֶן שֶׁל מְצוֹרָע: One is not liable for the consumption of *piggul* on account of partaking of the *log* of oil of a leper. Although the blood of the guilt offering renders the oil permitted for placement on the right thumb and big toe of the leper, it is not dependent on the guilt offering, as one may bring his guilt offering on one day and the *log* of oil ten days later (Rambam *Sefer Avoda, Hilkhot Pesulei HaMukdashin* 18:8 and *Sefer Korbanot, Hilkhot Meḥusrei Kappara* 5:4).

מתני׳ פִּיגֵּל בְּקוֹמֶץ וְלֹא בַלְּבוֹנָה, בַּלְּבוֹנָה וְלֹא בַקּוֹמֶץ – רַבִּי מֵאִיר אוֹמֵר: פִּיגּוּל וְחַיָּיבִין עָלָיו כָּרֵת, וַחֲכָמִים אוֹמְרִים: אֵין בּוֹ כָּרֵת עַד שֶׁיְּפַגֵּל בְּכָל הַמַּתִּיר.

MISHNA With regard to the burning of the handful of a meal offering and the frankincense, both of which render the meal offering permitted for consumption: If the priest had an intention that can **render** the offering ***piggul*** **during** the burning of **the handful but not during** the burning of **the frankincense,**[N] or **during** the burning of **the frankincense but not during** the burning of **the handful,** i.e., he burned one of them with the intention to eat the remainder of the offering beyond its designated time, **Rabbi Meir says:** The offering is ***piggul*** **and one** who eats it is **liable** to receive ***karet*** for its consumption. **And the Rabbis say: There is no** liability to receive ***karet*** **in this** case **unless he renders** the offering ***piggul*** **during** the sacrifice of **the entire permitting factor,**[H] i.e., the burning of both the handful and the frankincense.

וּמוֹדִים חֲכָמִים לְרַבִּי מֵאִיר בְּמִנְחַת חוֹטֵא וּבְמִנְחַת קְנָאוֹת, שֶׁאִם פִּיגֵּל בְּקוֹמֶץ – שֶׁהוּא פִּיגּוּל וְחַיָּיבִין עָלָיו כָּרֵת, שֶׁהַקּוֹמֶץ הוּא הַמַּתִּיר.

And the Rabbis concede to Rabbi Meir in the case of **a meal offering of a sinner and in** the case of **a meal offering of jealousy** of a *sota* **that if one had intent of *piggul* during** the burning of **the handful, that** the meal offering is ***piggul*** **and one is liable** to receive ***karet*** for its consumption, **as** here **the handful is the** sole **permitting factor.**

שָׁחַט אֶחָד מִן הַכְּבָשִׂים לֶאֱכוֹל שְׁתֵּי חַלּוֹת לְמָחָר, הִקְטִיר אֶחָד מִן הַבָּזִיכִין לֶאֱכוֹל שְׁנֵי סְדָרִים לְמָחָר – רַבִּי מֵאִיר אוֹמֵר: פִּיגּוּל וְחַיָּיבִין עָלָיו כָּרֵת, וַחֲכָמִים אוֹמְרִים: אֵין בּוֹ כָּרֵת עַד שֶׁיְּפַגֵּל בְּכָל הַמַּתִּיר.

If **one slaughtered one of the** two **lambs**[H] sacrificed with the two loaves on *Shavuot* with the intent **to partake of** the **two loaves the next day,** or if **one burned one of the bowls** of frankincense with the intent **to partake of two arrangements** of shewbread **the next day, Rabbi Meir says:** The meal offering is ***piggul*** **and one is liable** to receive ***karet*** for its consumption, **and the Rabbis say: There is no** liability to receive ***karet*** **unless he has intent of *piggul* during** the sacrifice of **the entire permitting factor.**

שָׁחַט אֶחָד מִן הַכְּבָשִׂים לֶאֱכוֹל מִמֶּנּוּ לְמָחָר – הוּא פִּיגּוּל וַחֲבֵירוֹ כָּשֵׁר, לֶאֱכוֹל מֵחֲבֵירוֹ לְמָחָר – שְׁנֵיהֶם כְּשֵׁרִים.

If **one slaughtered one of the lambs** with the intent **to partake of it the next day,**[H] **that** lamb **is *piggul***[N] **and the other is a fit** offering. If he slaughtered one lamb with the intent **to partake of the other the next day,**[H] **both** lambs **are fit** offerings, as one permitting factor does not render another permitting factor *piggul*.

NOTES

He had an intention that can render it *piggul* during the burning of the handful but not during the burning of the frankincense – פִּיגֵּל בְּקוֹמֶץ וְלֹא בַלְּבוֹנָה: The mishna (13a) cited a dispute between the Rabbis and Rabbi Yosei as to whether intent of *piggul* with regard to one permitting factor during the sacrifice of another renders an offering *piggul*, e.g., if one removes the handful with the intent to burn the frankincense the next day. In such a case, the Rabbis deem the offering *piggul*. This mishna discusses an altogether different case, where one has intent, during the burning of the handful but not during the burning of the frankincense, to partake of the remainder the next day. In this case, Rabbi Meir deems the offering *piggul*, as he maintains that intent with regard to part of the permitting factors is enough to render the offering *piggul*, whereas the Rabbis do not deem the offering *piggul* unless there is intent during the sacrifice of all of the permitting factors, as the remainder is permitted through the burning of both the handful and the frankincense.

If one slaughtered one of the lambs with the intent to partake of it the next day, that lamb is *piggul*, etc. – שָׁחַט אֶחָד מִן הַכְּבָשִׂים לֶאֱכוֹל מִמֶּנּוּ לְמָחָר הוּא פִּיגּוּל וכו׳: In the previous case, the Rabbis ruled that intent during the slaughter of one of the lambs to partake of the loaves the next day does not render the offering *piggul*, because with regard to the loaves, each lamb is considered part of the permitting factor. With regard to the lambs themselves, the slaughter of each of the lambs is its sole permitting factor (see 15b). The other lamb remains fit because intent of *piggul* with regard to one permitting factor is ineffective with regard to another permitting factor, except in a case where both permitting factors are in one vessel, e.g., the handful and frankincense of a meal offering (see 17a).

HALAKHA

Unless he renders it *piggul* during the sacrifice of the entire permitting factor – עַד שֶׁיְּפַגֵּל בְּכָל הַמַּתִּיר: If one had intent to perform a rite or partake of a meal offering outside its designated time during the removal of the handful but not during the collection of the frankincense; or if one had such intent during the collection of the frankincense but not during the removal of the handful; or if one burned only the frankincense or the handful with the intent to partake of the remainder the next day, then the offering is disqualified, but it is not *piggul*. It is rendered *piggul* only if one has intent of *piggul* during the sacrifice of the entire permitting factor, i.e., during the removal of the handful and the collection of the frankincense; or during their placement into a service vessel; or during their conveying to the altar; or during their placement upon the altar. The *Ḥok Natan* notes that this ruling is not in accordance with the Gemara here, but rather is in accordance with a *baraita* cited on *Sota* 14b (Rambam *Sefer Avoda, Hilkhot Pesulei HaMukdashin* 16:7–8).

If one slaughtered one of the two lambs, etc. – שָׁחַט אֶחָד מִן הַכְּבָשִׂים וכו׳: If one slaughtered one of the two lambs that are brought with the two loaves on *Shavuot* with the intent to consume an olive-bulk from the loaves the next day; or if one had intent while burning one of the bowls of frankincense accompanying the shewbread to partake of the shewbread the next day, the offering is disqualified, but it is not *piggul*. It is rendered *piggul* only if he has such intent while slaughtering both lambs, or while burning both bowls of frankincense (Rambam *Sefer Avoda, Hilkhot Pesulei HaMukdashin* 17:14).

To partake of it the next day – לֶאֱכוֹל מִמֶּנּוּ לְמָחָר: If one had intent while slaughtering one of the two lambs brought on *Shavuot* to partake of it the next day, and sacrificed the other lamb in its proper manner, the first lamb is *piggul* but the second one is not *piggul* (Rambam *Sefer Avoda, Hilkhot Pesulei HaMukdashin* 17:16).

To partake of the other the next day – לֶאֱכוֹל מֵחֲבֵירוֹ לְמָחָר: If one had intent during the slaughter of one of the lambs brought on *Shavuot* to partake of the other lamb the next day, both lambs are fit, as during the sacrifice of one lamb one cannot have *piggul* intent with regard to the other (Rambam *Sefer Avoda, Hilkhot Pesulei HaMukdashin* 17:17).

גמ׳ אָמַר רַב: מַחֲלוֹקֶת – שֶׁנָּתַן אֶת הַקּוֹמֶץ בִּשְׁתִיקָה וְאֶת הַלְּבוֹנָה בְּמַחֲשָׁבָה,

GEMARA **Rav says:** The **dispute**[N] between Rabbi Meir and the Rabbis with regard to a case where one has intent of *piggul* by either the handful or the frankincense applies only, for instance, **when he placed the handful** upon the altar **in silence,** i.e., without specific intent, **and** thereafter placed **the frankincense with intent** to partake of the remainder the next day. In such a case, it is evident that his intent relates only to the frankincense.

אֲבָל נָתַן הַקּוֹמֶץ בְּמַחֲשָׁבָה וְאֶת הַלְּבוֹנָה בִּשְׁתִיקָה – דִּבְרֵי הַכֹּל פִּיגּוּל, שֶׁכׇּל הָעוֹשֶׂה – עַל דַּעַת רִאשׁוֹנָה הוּא עוֹשֶׂה. וּשְׁמוּאֵל אָמַר: עֲדַיִין הוּא מַחֲלוֹקֶת.

But if **he placed the handful with** the **intent** to partake of the remainder the next day **and** then placed **the frankincense in silence,**[H] **all agree** that the meal offering is ***piggul*****, as anyone who performs** the rites in such a manner **performs** them **in accordance with** his **initial intent. And Shmuel says:** Even in such a case, there **is still a dispute**[N] between the Rabbis and Rabbi Meir.

יָתֵיב רָבָא וְקָאָמַר לָהּ לְהָא שְׁמַעְתָּא. אֵיתִיבֵיהּ רַב אַחָא בַּר רַב הוּנָא לְרָבָא: בַּמֶּה דְּבָרִים אֲמוּרִים – בִּקְמִיצָה וּבְמַתַּן כְּלִי וּבְהִילּוּךְ;

Rava sat and stated this *halakha* in accordance with the opinion of Rav. **Rav Aḥa bar Rav Huna raised an objection to Rava** from a *baraita*: **In what** case **is this statement,** that intent of *piggul* concerning only the handful renders the meal offering *piggul*, **said?** It is stated in a case where one had such intent **during the removal of the handful, or during the placement of** the handful in a service **vessel, or during the conveying** of the vessel to the altar. Since these rites are not performed with the frankincense, during these stages the handful is the only relevant permitting factor.

בָּא לוֹ לְהַקְטָרָה, נָתַן אֶת הַקּוֹמֶץ בִּשְׁתִיקָה וְאֶת הַלְּבוֹנָה בְּמַחֲשָׁבָה, אֶת הַקּוֹמֶץ בְּמַחֲשָׁבָה וְאֶת הַלְּבוֹנָה בִּשְׁתִיקָה – רַבִּי מֵאִיר אוֹמֵר: פִּיגּוּל וְחַיָּיבִין עָלָיו כָּרֵת, וַחֲכָמִים אוֹמְרִים: אֵין בּוֹ כָּרֵת עַד שֶׁיְּפַגֵּל בְּכׇל הַמַּתִּיר.

The *baraita* continues: But once the priest **comes to** perform **the burning** of the handful, then if he **placed the handful** on the fire of the altar **in silence and** he placed **the frankincense with intent** of *piggul*, or if he placed **the handful with intent and the frankincense in silence, Rabbi Meir says:** It is ***piggul* and one is liable** to receive ***karet*** **for** its consumption, **and the Rabbis say: There is no** liability to receive ***karet*** **unless he has intent of *piggul* during** the sacrifice of **the entire permitting factor.**

קָתָנֵי מִיהָא: נָתַן אֶת הַקּוֹמֶץ בְּמַחֲשָׁבָה וְאֶת הַלְּבוֹנָה בִּשְׁתִיקָה, וּפְלִיגִי!

Rav Aḥa bar Rav Huna explains his objection: **In any event,** the *baraita* **teaches** a case where he **placed the handful with intent and the frankincense in silence, and** yet the Rabbis **disagree** with Rabbi Meir and they do not say that one performs the rite of the frankincense with one's initial intent.

אֵימָא: וּכְבָר נָתַן אֶת הַלְּבוֹנָה בִּשְׁתִיקָה מֵעִיקָּרָא. שְׁתֵּי תְשׁוּבוֹת בַּדָּבָר: חֲדָא, דְּהַיְינוּ קַמַּיְיתָא. וְעוֹד, הָתַנְיָא: אַחַר כָּךְ!

Rava answered: **Say** that this is what the *baraita* means: If he placed the handful with intent, **and he had already placed the frankincense in silence from the outset,** then Rabbi Meir and the Rabbis disagree. The Gemara rejects this statement: **There are two** possible **refutations of** this **statement. One is that** if Rava's answer is accepted, then **this** case **is** identical to **the first** case of the *baraita*, which already taught that there is a dispute if the initial permitting factor was sacrificed in silence. **And furthermore, isn't it taught** explicitly in another *baraita*: **After** placing the handful he burned the frankincense.

תִּרְגְּמָא רַב חֲנִינָא: בִּשְׁתֵּי דֵיעוֹת.

Rabbi Ḥanina interpreted this *baraita* in accordance with the opinion of Rav: This *baraita* is referring to a case **of two intentions,** i.e., there were two priests, the first one of whom burned the handful with intent of *piggul*, and the second burned the frankincense in silence. Since the intent of one priest is entirely independent of the other, it cannot be said that the second priest burns the frankincense in accordance with the intent of the first priest.

תָּא שְׁמַע: בַּמֶּה דְּבָרִים אֲמוּרִים – בְּדָמִים הַנִּיתָּנִין עַל מִזְבֵּחַ הַחִיצוֹן,

The Gemara continues: **Come** and **hear** a proof for the opinion of Shmuel from a *baraita* that addresses *piggul* during the sprinkling of the blood. **In what** case **is this statement,** that the offering is rendered *piggul* even when he intends only while performing the first placement to eat it beyond its designated time, **said?** It is rendered *piggul* **in** the case of **blood that is placed on the external altar,**[H] where one placement renders the offering permitted.

NOTES

Rav says the dispute – **אָמַר רַב מַחֲלוֹקֶת**: According to Rav, Rabbi Meir holds that intent of *piggul* during the sacrifice of half of the permitting factors always renders an offering *piggul*. By contrast, Reish Lakish (*Zevaḥim* 41b) explains that even Rabbi Meir agrees that generally an offering is not rendered *piggul* through intent during the sacrifice of half of its permitting factors. Rather, Rabbi Meir holds that such intent renders an offering *piggul* only when one burned the handful with intent of *piggul* and burned the frankincense in silence, as it is assumed that one performs a rite in accordance with one's initial intent.

There is still a dispute – **עֲדַיִין הוּא מַחֲלוֹקֶת**: Rashi (*Zevaḥim* 41b) explains that this is because intention alone, in this case demonstrated by the priest's silence, is ineffective without verbal expression of such intent. See 2b, where this assumption, which Rashi applies to offerings in general, is disputed by other early commentaries.

HALAKHA

He placed the handful with intent and the frankincense in silence – **נָתַן הַקּוֹמֶץ בְּמַחֲשָׁבָה וְאֶת הַלְּבוֹנָה בִּשְׁתִיקָה**: The Rambam does not provide an explicit ruling with regard to this dispute between Rav and Shmuel. Nevertheless, it may be inferred from the Rambam's ruling with regard to the blood presented on the golden altar that intent of *piggul* during the sacrifice of half of a permitting factor does not render an offering *piggul* even when it can be maintained that he acted in accordance with his initial intent, as stated by Shmuel (Rambam *Sefer Avoda, Hilkhot Pesulei HaMukdashin* 16:8; see also *Likkutei Halakhot*).

In the case of blood that is placed on the external altar – **בְּדָמִים הַנִּיתָּנִין עַל מִזְבֵּחַ הַחִיצוֹן**: With regard to any blood that is presented on the external altar, if one placed the first placement with the intent to consume the offering outside its designated time and the remaining placements with the intent to consume the offering outside its designated location, the offering is *piggul*, as the first placement is the principal one. Conversely, with regard to blood that is presented on the inner altar, since all the placements are indispensable and are therefore considered like one placement, if one had intent to consume the offering outside its designated time during one of the placements, even if the intent occurred during the first placement and he remained silent for the remaining placements; or if he placed all of the blood properly except for the final placement, which he performed with intent to consume the offering outside its designated time, the offering is disqualified but it is not *piggul*. It is rendered *piggul* only if he had such intent during the sacrifice of the entire permitting factor (Rambam *Sefer Avoda, Hilkhot Pesulei HaMukdashin* 17:1–2).

אבל דמים הניתנין על מזבח הפנימי, כגון ארבעים ושלש של יום הכיפורים, ואחת עשרה של פר כהן משוח, ואחת עשרה של פר העלם דבר של ציבור, פיגל בין בראשונה בין בשניה ובין בשלישית – רבי מאיר אומר: פיגול וחייבין עליו כרת, וחכמים אומרים: אין בו כרת עד שיפגל בכל המתיר.

But with regard to the **blood placed** inside, in the Holy of Holies, on the Curtain, and **on the inner altar,**[N] **for example,** the **forty-three** presentations of the blood **of** the bull and goat **of Yom Kippur, and the eleven** presentations of the blood **of the bull for** an unwitting sin of the **anointed priest, and the eleven** presentations of the blood **of the bull for an unwitting communal sin,** if the priest had an intention that can **render** the offering ***piggul,* whether in the first** set of presentations, **whether in the second** set, **or whether in the third** set, i.e., in any of the requisite sets of presentations, e.g., in the case of the Yom Kippur bull in the Holy of Holies, on the Curtain, and on the inner altar, **Rabbi Meir says:** The offering is ***piggul* and one is liable** to receive ***karet* for** its consumption. **And the Rabbis say: There is no** liability to receive ***karet* unless he** had an intention that can **render** the offering ***piggul* during** the performance of **the entire permitting factor.**

קתני מיהא: פיגל בין בראשונה בין בשניה ובין בשלישית, ופליגי!

The Gemara explains the proof: **In any event,** this *baraita* **teaches:** If the priest had an intention that can **render** the offering ***piggul,* whether in the first** set of presentations, **whether in the second** set, **or whether in the third** set; **and** Rabbi Meir and the Rabbis **disagree** in this case as well. Evidently, the Rabbis are not of the opinion that anyone who performs a rite performs it in accordance with his initial intent.

וכי תימא: הכא נמי בשתי דעות – הניחא למאן דאמר: "בפר" ואפילו בדמו של פר, אלא למאן דאמר: "בפר" ולא בדמו של פר, מאי איכא למימר?

And if you would say that **here too,** the *baraita* is referring to a case **of two intentions,** e.g., one High Priest performed the initial presentation and was thereafter disqualified from performing the other presentations, and a second priest replaced him and performed the remaining presentations, there is still a difficulty: **This works out well according to the one who says** that the verse: "With this shall Aaron come into the sacred place: **With** a young **bull"** (Leviticus 16:3), indicates that a High Priest may enter the Sanctuary **even with the blood of a bull,** i.e., he may continue the presentations with the blood of the offerings slaughtered by another High Priest. **But according to the one who says** that the verse indicates that a High Priest may enter **"with** a young **bull," but not with the blood of a bull,** i.e., a replacement High Priest must slaughter another bull and begin the presentations again, **what can be said?** If so, it is impossible for these presentations to be performed by two priests.

אמר רבא: הכא במאי עסקינן – כגון שפיגל בראשונה ושתק בשניה ופיגל בשלישית, דאמרינן: אי סלקא דעתך כל העושה על דעת ראשונה הוא עושה, מיהדר פיגולי בשלישית למה לי?

Rava said: According to Rav, **here,** in the *baraita,* **we are dealing with** a case **where** the High Priest **had intent of *piggul* during the first** set of presentations **and was silent during the second** set, **and** again **had intent of *piggul* during the third** set. In such a case, **we say: If** it **enters your mind** to say that **anyone who performs** a rite **performs** it **in accordance with his initial intention,** then **why do I** need the High Priest to **repeat** his intent of ***piggul* during the third** set? The fact that he repeats his intention during the third set indicates that he did not perform the second set in accordance with his initial intent. Accordingly, the Rabbis hold that the offering is not *piggul,* as he did not have intent of *piggul* during the presentation of the entire permitting factor.

מתקיף לה רב אשי: מידי שתק קתני? אלא אמר רב אשי: הכא במאי עסקינן – כגון שפיגל בראשונה ובשניה ובשלישית, דאמרינן: אי סלקא דעתך כל העושה על דעת ראשונה הוא עושה, מיהדר פגולי בשניה ובשלישית למה לי?

Rav Ashi objects to this explanation: **Does** the *baraita* **teach** that the High Priest was **silent? Rather, Rav Ashi said: Here we are dealing with** a case **where he had** explicit **intent of *piggul* during the first, second, and third** presentations, and was silent during the subsequent presentations. In such a case, **we say: If it enters your mind** to say that **anyone who performs** a rite **performs** it **in accordance with his initial intention, why do I** need the High Priest to **repeat** his intent of ***piggul* during the second and third** presentations?

HALAKHA

In the case of blood that is placed on the external altar – בדמים הניתנין על מזבח החיצון: With regard to any blood that is presented on the external altar, if one placed the first placement with the intent to consume the offering outside its designated time and the remaining placements with the intent to consume the offering outside its designated location, the offering is *piggul*, as the first placement is the principal one. Conversely, with regard to blood that is presented on the inner altar, since all the placements are indispensable and are therefore considered like one placement, if one had intent to consume the offering outside its designated time during one of the placements, even if the intent occurred during the first placement and he remained silent for the remaining placements; or if he placed all of the blood properly except for the final placement, which he performed with intent to consume the offering outside its designated time, the offering is disqualified but it is not *piggul*. It is rendered *piggul* only if he had such intent during the sacrifice of the entire permitting factor (Rambam *Sefer Avoda*, *Hilkhot Pesulei HaMukdashin* 17:1–2).

NOTES

Blood placed on the inner altar – דמים הניתנין על מזבח הפנימי: The difference between the blood presented on the external altar and blood presented inside the Sanctuary lies in the fact that the Torah utilizes restrictive expressions such as: Law, or: In this manner, with regard to blood presented inside. These expressions indicate that each presentation inside the Sanctuary is indispensable.

וְהָא "בֵּין" "בֵּין" קָתָנֵי! קַשְׁיָא.

The Gemara raises a difficulty against Rav Ashi's interpretation: **But the** *baraita* **teaches: Whether** during the first presentation or **whether** during the second, which indicates that the Rabbis disagree with Rabbi Meir even with regard to a case where the priest had intent of *piggul* during any one of the presentations. The Gemara notes: Indeed, this poses **a difficulty.**

אָמַר מָר, רַבִּי מֵאִיר אוֹמֵר: פִּגּוּל וְחַיָּיבִין עָלָיו כָּרֵת. מִכְּדֵי כָּרֵת לָא מִיחַיֵּיב עַד שֶׁיִּקְרְבוּ כָּל הַמַּתִּירִין,

§ The Gemara returns to the discussion of the *baraita* itself. **The Master said** above: If the priest had intent of *piggul*, whether in the first set of presentations, whether in the second set, or whether in the third set, **Rabbi Meir says:** The offering is ***piggul*** **and one is liable** to receive ***karet*** **for** its consumption, despite the fact that he performed the rest of the rite silently. The Gemara asks: **Now** consider, **one is not liable** to receive ***karet*** **unless all the permitting factors** of the offering **have been sacrificed,**[H] i.e., if the whole service is completed, including the presentation of the blood.

דְּאָמַר מָר: "יֵרָצֶה" – כְּהַרְצָאַת כָּשֵׁר כָּךְ הַרְצָאַת פָּסוּל, מָה הַרְצָאַת כָּשֵׁר עַד שֶׁיִּקְרְבוּ כָּל הַמַּתִּירִין – אַף הַרְצָאַת פָּסוּל עַד שֶׁיִּקְרְבוּ כָּל הַמַּתִּירִין;

The Gemara provides the source for this claim. **As the Master said** that the verse states with regard to *piggul*: **"It shall** not **be accepted"** (Leviticus 7:18), which indicates that **the acceptance of a disqualified** offering is **like the acceptance of a valid** offering, of which the verse states: "It shall be accepted" (Leviticus 22:27), and **just as** there is no **acceptance of a valid** offering **unless all** its **permitting factors have been sacrificed, so too** there is no lack of **acceptance of a disqualified** offering, i.e., it is not rendered *piggul*, **unless all** its **permitting factors have been sacrificed.** That is to say, in the absence of one of its permitting factors it does not become *piggul*.

וְהַאי כֵּיוָן דַּחֲשִׁיב בָּהּ בִּפְנִים – פַּסְלֵיהּ, כִּי מַדֵּי בַּהֵיכָל – מַיָּא בְּעָלְמָא הוּא דְּקָא מַדֵּי!

Accordingly, the Gemara challenges: **And** with regard to **this** case, of the blood of the bull and goat brought on Yom Kippur, **since he had intent** of *piggul* **with regard to it** when he was presenting the blood **inside** the Holy of Holies, **he has disqualified it.**[N] If so, **when he sprinkles** the blood again later **in the Sanctuary,** on the Curtain and the inner altar, it is as though **he is merely sprinkling water,** and not the blood of the offering. Consequently, the permitting factors of the offering have not been sacrificed, and therefore the offering should not be rendered *piggul*.

אָמַר רַבָּה: מַשְׁכַּחַתְּ לָהּ בְּאַרְבָּעָה פָּרִים וְאַרְבָּעָה שְׂעִירִים.

Rabba said: You find it possible **in** a case where there were **four bulls**[N] **and four goats,** i.e., in a case where after the High Priest presented the blood inside the Holy of Holies with *piggul* intent, the remaining blood spilled. Consequently, he was required to bring another bull and goat in order to present their blood on the Curtain separating the Sanctuary and Holy of Holies. During that presentation he had intent of *piggul*, after which the remaining blood spilled, requiring him to bring another bull and goat in order to present their blood on the corners of the golden altar. He again had intent of *piggul* during that presentation, and then the blood spilled, which meant he had to bring yet another bull and goat in order to present their blood upon the golden altar itself.

HALAKHA

Unless all the permitting factors have been sacrificed – עַד שֶׁיִּקְרְבוּ כָּל הַמַּתִּירִין: With regard to any part of an offering that has permitting factors, one is not liable for consuming *piggul*, or *notar*, or a ritually impure offering, unless its permitting factors were sacrificed properly (Rambam *Sefer Avoda, Hilkhot Pesulei HaMukdashin* 18:16).

NOTES

Since he had intent with regard to it inside the Holy of Holies he has disqualified it – כֵּיוָן דַּחֲשִׁיב בָּהּ בִּפְנִים פַּסְלֵיהּ: The Gemara's question applies only according to the opinion of Rabbi Meir, who holds that an offering is rendered *piggul* through intent during the first presentation. The Rabbis hold that the offering is not rendered *piggul* on account of such intent. The Gemara's question is as follows: If the offering is rendered *piggul* due to one's intent during the first presentation, this means that the remaining presentations are performed in a manner that is not valid, which should prevent the offering from becoming *piggul* (*Shita Mekubbetzet*).

Rashi asks: If the remaining rites are considered to have been performed in a manner that it not valid when they follow a rite performed with intent of *piggul*, then how is it ever possible to render an offering *piggul* through intent occurring during slaughter or during the removal of the handful of a meal offering? Rashi explains that since the slaughter of an offering is a complete rite in and of itself, then if it was performed with intent of *piggul*, that entire permitting factor was sacrificed with such intent. By contrast, all the presentations inside the Sanctuary are considered one continuous rite. Therefore, unless all of them were performed in their proper manner, the permitting factor is not considered to have been performed properly.

Four bulls, etc. – אַרְבָּעָה פָּרִים וכו׳: Each group of presentations, e.g., those in the Holy of Holies and those in the Sanctuary, is considered an independent atonement. Accordingly, if the blood is spilled after the completion of the presentations inside the Holy of Holies, the High Priest does not need to return to the Holy of Holies to present the new blood (Rashi). The commentaries note that the Gemara could also have referred to a situation where only one additional bull and goat were necessary to complete the remaining presentations, as in this case too, the entire permitting factor was performed in its proper manner. Rabba refers to a situation involving four bulls and four goats merely to teach that such a case is possible (*Tosafot* on *Zevaḥim* 42b).

רָבָא אֲמַר: אֲפִילּוּ תֵּימָא פָּר אֶחָד וְשָׂעִיר אֶחָד, לְפַגּוּלֵי מְרַצֵּי.

Rava said: You may **even say** that the *baraita* is referring to a case of only **one bull and one goat,** and the remaining blood was in fact disqualified. Nevertheless, **with regard to rendering** an offering ***piggul,*** the presentations performed with the disqualified blood **effect acceptance,** as though the entire permitting factor was performed in its proper manner. In other words, even though the High Priest sprinkled the blood inside the Holy of Holies with improper intent, and thereby disqualified the offering, nevertheless, since he completed the service he is considered as having sacrificed all the permitting factors with regard to *piggul.*

״אַרְבָּעִים וְשָׁלֹשׁ״. וְהָתַנְיָא: אַרְבָּעִים וְשֶׁבַע! לָא קַשְׁיָא: הָא כְּמַאן דְּאָמַר מְעָרְבִין לַקְּרָנוֹת, וְהָא כְּמַאן דְּאָמַר אֵין מְעָרְבִין.

§ The *baraita* mentioned that there are **forty-three** presentations of the blood of the bull and the goat sacrificed on Yom Kippur. The Gemara asks: **But isn't it taught** otherwise in a different *baraita,* which states that there are **forty-seven** presentations of that blood? The Gemara answers: This is **not difficult. This** statement, that there are forty-three presentations, is **in accordance with** the opinion of **the one who says** that the High Priest **mixes** the blood of the bull and the goat before placing it **on the corners**[HN] of the inner altar, rather than placing the blood of each one separately. **And that** statement, that there are forty-seven presentations, is **in accordance with** the opinion of **the one who says** that the High Priest **does not mix** the two types of blood before placing them on the corners, but sprinkles four times from the blood of the bull and another four times from the blood of the goat, and only afterward mixes the blood of the two animals for placement on the top of the altar.

וְהָתַנְיָא: אַרְבָּעִים וּשְׁמוֹנֶה! לָא קַשְׁיָא: הָא כְּמַאן דְּאָמַר שִׁירַיִם מְעַכְּבִין, הָא כְּמַאן דְּאָמַר שִׁירַיִם לֹא מְעַכְּבִין.

The Gemara raises another difficulty: **But isn't it taught** in yet another *baraita* that there are **forty-eight** presentations? The Gemara answers: This is **not difficult. This** statement, that there are forty-eight presentations, is **in accordance with** the opinion of **the one who says** that the pouring of the **remainder** of the blood on the base of the external altar **is indispensable,** and therefore this act is added to the total. **That** statement, that there are only forty-seven presentations, is **in accordance with** the opinion of **the one who says** that the pouring of the **remainder** of the blood **is not indispensable.**[H]

אִיבַּעְיָא לְהוּ: פִּיגֵּל בְּהוֹלָכָה, מַהוּ?

§ The mishna teaches: If one had intent of *piggul* during the sacrifice of only part of the permitting factors, e.g., during the burning of the handful but not during the burning of the frankincense, the Rabbis rule that the offering is not *piggul.* Concerning this, **a dilemma was raised before** the Sages: If one **had intent of *piggul* during** the **conveying**[H] of the handful to the altar but not during the conveying of the frankincense, **what is** the *halakha*?[N]

אָמַר רַבִּי יוֹחָנָן: הוֹלָכָה כִּקְמִיצָה, וְרֵישׁ לָקִישׁ אָמַר: הוֹלָכָה כְּהַקְטָרָה.

Rabbi Yoḥanan says: The *halakha* with regard to **conveying** the handful is **like** that of the **removing of the handful.** Just as intent of *piggul* with regard to removing only the handful renders the offering *piggul,* as it is the sole permitting factor with which the rite of removal is performed, the same applies to conveying the handful. **And Reish Lakish says:** The **conveying** of the handful is **like** its **burning.** Just as intent of *piggul* is required during the burning of both the handful and the frankincense for the offering to be rendered *piggul,* as both of them are burned on the altar, the same *halakha* applies to conveying.

HALAKHA

Mixes the blood of the bull and the goat before placing it on the corners – מְעָרְבִין לַקְּרָנוֹת: After the High Priest sprinkled from the blood of the bull and goat of Yom Kippur on the Curtain separating the Sanctuary and Holy of Holies, he would mix their blood and sprinkle it on each of the four corners of the inner altar. He would then sprinkle the blood mixture an additional seven times on the center of the altar, in accordance with the unattributed mishna on *Yoma* 53b (Rambam *Sefer Avoda, Hilkhot Yom HaKippurim* 3:5).

The remainder is not indispensable – שִׁירַיִם לֹא מְעַכְּבִין: If after the High Priest completed the sprinklings performed inside the Sanctuary the remaining blood was spilled, he does not need to bring other blood to pour on the base of the external altar, as the pouring is not an indispensable rite (Rambam *Sefer Avoda, Hilkhot Yom HaKippurim* 5:8).

If one had intent of *piggul* during the conveying – פִּיגֵּל בְּהוֹלָכָה: The Rambam rules that *piggul* intent during the conveying of the handful to the altar does not render the offering *piggul* unless one has such intent during the conveying of the entire permitting factor, i.e., the handful and the frankincense. Similarly, intent during the removal of the handful does not render the offering *piggul* unless one has such intent during the collection of the frankincense. This ruling is not in accordance with the Gemara here, but in accordance with a *baraita* cited on *Sota* 14b (*Ḥok Natan*). If one were to rule in accordance with the Gemara here, then intent of *piggul* during the conveying of the handful should render the offering *piggul*, in accordance with the opinion of Rabbi Yoḥanan, as the difficulty raised against the opinion of Reish Lakish remains unresolved, and the *halakha* generally follows the opinion of Rabbi Yoḥanan in a dispute with Reish Lakish (Rambam *Sefer Avoda, Hilkhot Pesulei HaMukdashin* 16:7, and see *Likkutei Halakhot*).

NOTES

Mixes the blood of the bull and the goat before placing it on the corners – מְעָרְבִין לַקְּרָנוֹת: The forty-three presentations are as follows: Sixteen inside the Holy of Holies, eight from the blood of the bull and eight from the goat; sixteen on the Curtain separating the Sanctuary and Holy of Holies, eight from the blood of each animal; four on the corners of the inner altar with the mixed blood of the bull and goat; and seven upon the altar with the mixture of blood. According to the opinion that the blood of the two animals is not mixed before the presentation on the corners of the altar, there were an additional four presentations, as the blood of the bull was first presented on the corners, followed by four presentations with the blood of the goat, only after which were the two types of blood mixed.

If one had intent of *piggul* during the conveying, what is the *halakha* – פִּיגֵּל בְּהוֹלָכָה מַהוּ: There is no dispute with regard to intent of *piggul* during the removal of the handful or during its placement in a service vessel. In such cases everyone agrees that the offering is *piggul*, as these rites are performed with only the handful, not the frankincense. The dilemma raised in the Gemara applies only to the conveying of the handful to the altar: Is the conveying of the frankincense to the altar also considered the performance of a permitting factor?

בִּשְׁלָמָא לְרֵישׁ לָקִישׁ – אִיכָּא נַמִי הוֹלָכָה דִּלְבוֹנָה, אֶלָּא לְרַבִּי יוֹחָנָן מַאי טַעְמָא?

The Gemara asks: **Granted,** one can understand the ruling of **Reish Lakish,** as the conveying of the handful is only part of the permitting factors, since **there is also the conveying of** the **frankincense. But** as for the ruling of **Rabbi Yoḥanan, what is the reason** that intent of *piggul* during the conveying of only the handful renders the offering *piggul*? After all, he has not had intent of *piggul* during the conveying of all of the permitting factors.

אֲמַר רָבָא, קָסָבַר רַבִּי יוֹחָנָן: כָּל עֲבוֹדָה שֶׁאֵינָהּ מַתֶּרֶת, עֲבוֹדָה חֲשׁוּבָה הִיא לְפַגֵּל עָלֶיהָ בִּפְנֵי עַצְמָהּ.

Rava said: Rabbi Yoḥanan holds that if one performed **any** sacrificial **rite that does not permit** the offering, e.g., conveying, even if he performed it with only one of the permitting factors, such as with the handful and not with the frankincense, **it is considered a significant rite with regard to rendering** the offering ***piggul***[N] **on account of it, by itself.** It is not comparable to a case of intent of *piggul* during the sacrifice of only part of the permitting factors, as this rite of conveying does not render the offering permitted.

אֲמַר לֵיהּ אַבַּיֵי: הֲרֵי שְׁחִיטַת אֶחָד מִן הַכְּבָשִׂים, דַּעֲבוֹדָה שֶׁאֵינָהּ מַתִּירָתָהּ, וּפְלִיגִי!

Abaye said to Rava: **But** what about **the slaughter of one of the lambs** brought with the two loaves on *Shavuot*, **which** is **a rite that does not permit** the offering, as neither the sacrifice of its portions designated for burning upon the altar nor the consumption of the meat of the offering and the two loaves is permitted by this slaughter, **and** yet the Rabbis **disagree** with Rabbi Meir in this case?

דִּתְנַן: שָׁחַט אֶחָד מִן הַכְּבָשִׂים לֶאֱכוֹל שְׁתֵּי חַלּוֹת לְמָחָר, הִקְטִיר אֶחָד מִן הַבָּזִיכִין לֶאֱכוֹל שְׁנֵי סְדָרִים לְמָחָר – רַבִּי מֵאִיר אוֹמֵר: פִּגּוּל וְחַיָּיבִין עָלָיו כָּרֵת, וַחֲכָמִים אוֹמְרִים: אֵין בּוֹ כָּרֵת עַד שֶׁיְּפַגֵּל בְּכָל הַמַּתִּיר!

As we learned in the mishna: If **one slaughtered one of the** two **lambs** with the intent **to partake of two loaves the next day,** or if **one burned one of the bowls** of frankincense with the intent **to partake of two arrangements** of shewbread **the next day, Rabbi Meir says:** The meal offering is ***piggul*** **and one is liable** to receive ***karet*** **for** its consumption, **and the Rabbis say: There is no** liability to receive ***karet*** **unless he has intent of *piggul* during** the sacrifice of **the entire permitting factor.** Although the slaughter of one of the lambs is a rite that does not render an offering permitted, nevertheless the Rabbis maintain that it is not considered a significant rite with regard to rendering the offering *piggul* by itself.

אֲמַר לֵיהּ: מִי סָבְרַתְּ לֶחֶם בַּתַּנּוּר קָדוֹשׁ? שְׁחִיטַת כְּבָשִׂים מְקַדְּשָׁא לֵיהּ, וְהַבָּא לְקַדֵּשׁ – כְּבָא לְהַתִּיר דָּמֵי.

Rava **said to** Abaye: **Do you maintain** that the two loaves of **bread** are already **sanctified** from when they are **in the oven,** and require only the sprinkling of the blood to render them permitted for consumption? In fact, **the slaughter of the lambs sanctifies** the loaves, **and** an act **that comes to sanctify is considered like** that which **comes to permit.** Since the slaughter of the two lambs sanctifies the loaves, the slaughter of each lamb is considered half a permitting factor; the slaughter of each lamb independently cannot render the loaves *piggul.*

מְתִיב רַב שִׁימִי בַּר אַשִׁי, אֲחֵרִים אוֹמְרִים: הִקְדִּים מוּלִים לַעֲרֵלִים – כָּשֵׁר, הִקְדִּים עֲרֵלִים לְמוּלִים – פָּסוּל;

Rav Shimi bar Ashi raises an objection from a *baraita* that discusses the slaughter of the Paschal offering. The first *tanna* rules that if one slaughtering the Paschal offering intended for it to be consumed by both disqualified individuals, e.g., uncircumcised males, and fit individuals, e.g., circumcised males, the offering is not disqualified. ***Aḥerim*** **say:** In a case where one slaughtered a Paschal offering and severed one of the two organs of ritual slaughter with a disqualifying intention, and severed the other organ with a valid intention, then if one's intent with regard to **circumcised** males **preceded the** intent with regard to the **uncircumcised** males, the offering is **valid.** But if the intent with regard to the **uncircumcised** males **preceded** the intent with regard to the **circumcised** males, it is **disqualified.**

וְקַיְימָא לָן דִּבַחֲצִי מַתִּיר פְּלִיגִי! אֲמַר לֵיהּ: מִי סָבְרַתְּ דָּם בְּצַוַּאר בְּהֵמָה קָדוֹשׁ? דָּם – סַכִּין מְקַדְּשָׁא לֵיהּ, וְהַבָּא לְקַדֵּשׁ – כְּבָא לְהַתִּיר דָּמֵי.

Rav Shimi bar Ashi continues: **And we maintain that** the first *tanna* and *Aḥerim* **disagree with regard to** whether the sacrifice of **half a permitting factor** with disqualifying intent disqualifies the entire offering. In this case, although this slaughter does not sanctify anything, the severing of one of the organs is considered half of a permitting factor. Rava **said to** Rav Shimi bar Ashi: **Do you maintain** that the **blood** is already **sanctified** while **inside the neck of** the **animal?** In fact, the **knife sanctifies** the **blood, and that which comes to sanctify is considered like** that which **comes to permit.** Consequently, the slaughter of the animal is a permitting factor, and the severing of one of its organs is half a permitting factor.

NOTES

It is a significant rite with regard to rendering the offering *piggul*, etc. – **עֲבוֹדָה חֲשׁוּבָה הִיא לְפַגֵּל וכו׳**: This principle applies only to the performance of certain rites that the Sages determined are significant enough to render the offering *piggul*. Since these rites do not permit any part of the offering, Rabbi Yoḥanan holds that they render the offering *piggul* even if they were performed with improper intent only with regard to a single permitting factor. As for the reason for Rabbi Yoḥanan's opinion, Rashi explains that with regard to rites that permit the offering, e.g., burning, each permitting factor is dependent upon the proper sacrifice of the others in order to collectively permit the meal offering. Accordingly, in each case the *piggul* status of the offering depends on the other permitting factors. By contrast, since conveying does not serve to permit, here the *piggul* status is unaffected by the performance of permitting factors of the offering.

תָּא שְׁמַע: בַּמֶּה דְּבָרִים אֲמוּרִים – בִּקְמִיצָה וּבְמַתַּן כְּלִי וּבְהִילּוּךְ;

The Gemara suggests: **Come and hear** a proof from a *baraita*: **In what** case **is this statement,** that intent of *piggul* with regard to only the handful renders the meal offering *piggul,* **said?** It is said in a case where one had such intent **during the removal of the handful, or during the placement** of the handful in a service **vessel, or during the conveying.**

מַאי לָאו הִילּוּךְ דְּהַקְטָרָה? לָא, הִילּוּךְ דְּמַתַּן כְּלִי.

The Gemara clarifies the proof: **What, is it not** correct to say that the *baraita* is referring to the **conveying** of the handful **for burning** upon the altar, in which case it is teaching that intent of *piggul* with regard to the handful during its conveying renders the offering *piggul*? The Gemara responds: **No;** the *baraita* is referring to the **conveying of** the handful before its **placement** into the service **vessel** that sanctifies it. Since the frankincense is not placed into a vessel, in this case the conveying of the handful alone is considered the performance of the entire rite.

אִי הָכִי, בְּמַתַּן כְּלִי וּבְהִילּוּךְ – בְּהִילּוּךְ וּבְמַתַּן כְּלִי מִיבָּעֵי לֵיהּ! הָא לָא קַשְׁיָא, תְּנֵי הָכִי.

The Gemara asks: **If so,** why does the *baraita* state: **During the placement** of the handful in **a vessel or during the conveying?** This indicates that it is referring to an act of conveying that occurs after the placement. **It should have** stated: **During the conveying or during the placement** of the handful in **a vessel.** The Gemara responds: **This** is **not difficult,** as one should emend the *baraita* and **teach** it in **that** order, i.e., with the conveying before the placement.

בָּא לוֹ לְהַקְטָרָה – בָּא לוֹ לַהוֹלָכָה מִיבָּעֵי לֵיהּ! הָא לָא קַשְׁיָא, כֵּיוָן דְּהוֹלָכָה צוֹרֶךְ דְּהַקְטָרָה הִיא, קָרֵי לָהּ הַקְטָרָה.

The Gemara raises another objection from the next clause of the same *baraita*: Once **he comes to** perform **the burning** of the handful, there is no liability to receive *karet* unless he has intent of *piggul* during the sacrifice of the frankincense as well. The Gemara asks: According to Reish Lakish, the *baraita* **should have** stated: Once **he comes to** perform **the conveying** and to perform the burning. Reish Lakish maintains that the conveying mentioned previously in the *baraita* occurs earlier, before its placement into a service vessel, which means that there is another act of conveying. The Gemara responds: **This** is **not difficult; since** this **conveying is for the purpose of burning, it is called burning** in the *baraita.*

אֶלָּא, נָתַן אֶת הַקּוֹמֶץ בִּשְׁתִיקָה – הוֹלִיךְ מִיבָּעֵי לֵיהּ! קַשְׁיָא.

The Gemara further challenges: **But** the *baraita* also states: If he **placed the handful** on the altar **in silence,** and he placed the frankincense with intent of *piggul.* According to Reish Lakish, **it should have** also stated: If **he carried** the handful in silence, and the frankincense with intent of *piggul,* as according to Reish Lakish it is the act of conveying that he is performing at this stage. The Gemara responds: Indeed, this is **a difficulty.**

הִקְטִיר שׁוּמְשׁוּם לֶאֱכוֹל שׁוּמְשׁוּם, עַד שֶׁכָּלָה קוֹמֶץ כּוּלּוֹ – רַב חִסְדָּא וְרַב הַמְנוּנָא וְרַב שֵׁשֶׁת, חַד אָמַר: פִּיגּוּל, וְחַד אָמַר: פָּסוּל, וְחַד אָמַר: כָּשֵׁר.

§ The Gemara continues its discussion of *piggul* intent that occurred during the sacrifice of part of a permitting factor. If one **burned** an amount the size of **a sesame** seed of the handful and frankincense with the intent **to consume** an amount the size of **a sesame** seed[H] from the remainder the next day, and he repeated the same action with the accompanying intent **until** he burned **the entire** measure of the **handful** and frankincense, the *halakha* in this case is a matter of dispute between **Rav Ḥisda, Rav Hamnuna, and Rav Sheshet. One says** that the entire meal offering is ***piggul,* and one says** that the offering is **disqualified** but is not *piggul,* **and one says** that the offering remains **fit.**

לֵימָא, מַאן דְּאָמַר פִּיגּוּל – כְּרַבִּי מֵאִיר, וּמַאן דְּאָמַר פָּסוּל – כְּרַבָּנַן, וּמַאן דְּאָמַר כָּשֵׁר – כְּרַבִּי?

The Gemara suggests: **Let us say** that **the one who says** that the meal offering is ***piggul*** holds **in accordance with** the opinion of **Rabbi Meir,** who says that one renders an offering *piggul* on account of *piggul* intent during the sacrifice of even part of its permitting factors. **And the one who says** that the offering is **disqualified** holds **in accordance with** the opinion of **the Rabbis,** who say that such intent disqualifies an offering but does not render it *piggul.* **And** finally, **the one who says** that the offering is **fit** holds **in accordance with** the opinion of **Rabbi** Yehuda HaNasi, who says (14a) that if one slaughters each of the two lambs brought on *Shavuot* with the two loaves, each time intending to consume half an olive-bulk from a different loaf the next day, the offering is fit, as the halves do not combine to render the offering *piggul.*

HALAKHA

If one burned the size of a sesame seed with the intent to consume the size of a sesame seed – הִקְטִיר שׁוּמְשׁוּם לֶאֱכוֹל שׁוּמְשׁוּם: If one burned an amount the size of a sesame seed of the handful and frankincense with the intent to consume an amount the size of a sesame seed of the remainder the next day, and repeated this process until he had burned the entire measure of the handful and frankincense in this manner, the offering is disqualified but it is not *piggul.* The reason is that although this is its manner of consumption, it is not its manner of burning. The Rambam deems this offering unfit because there is an uncertainty with regard to the *halakha* here, and there is a principle that one is stringent in cases of uncertainty involving Torah law. The offering is not *piggul,* as in a case of uncertainty with regard to punishments the *halakha* is lenient. Alternatively, the Rambam does not deem the offering *piggul* because two Sages hold that it is not *piggul,* as opposed to one Sage who says that it is *piggul.* Likewise, he does not deem the offering fit, as the majority hold that the offering is nevertheless disqualified (Rambam *Sefer Avoda, Hilkhot Pesulei HaMukdashin* 16:9, and see *Kesef Mishne* there).

מִמַּאי? דִּלְמָא עַד כָּאן לָא קָאָמַר רַבִּי מֵאִיר הָתָם אֶלָּא דְּחִישֵּׁב בְּשִׁיעוּרוֹ, אֲבָל הָכָא דְּלָא חִישֵּׁב בְּשִׁיעוּרוֹ – לָא!

The Gemara rejects this suggestion: **From where** is this conclusion drawn? **Perhaps Rabbi Meir states** that one renders an offering *piggul* on account of *piggul* intent during the sacrifice of part of the permitting factors **only there, where he had intent with regard to its** entire **measure. But here, where he did not have intent with regard to its** entire **measure,** but instead had a series of intentions with regard to a measure equivalent to a sesame seed, it is possible that Rabbi Meir does **not** render the offering *piggul*.

וְעַד כָּאן לָא קָא אָמְרִי רַבָּנַן הָתָם אֶלָּא דְּלָא חִישֵּׁב בֵּיהּ בְּכוּלֵּיהּ מַתִּיר, אֲבָל הָכָא דְּחִישֵּׁב בֵּיהּ בְּכוּלֵּיהּ מַתִּיר – הָכִי נַמִי דְּפַגֵּיל!

And furthermore, perhaps **the Rabbis state** that one does not render an offering *piggul* unless he has *piggul* intent during the sacrifice of the entire permitting factor **only there, where he did not have intent concerning it during the entire permitting factor,** but only during the burning of the handful. **But here, where he had intent during the entire permitting factor,** i.e., during the burning of both the handful and the frankincense, **he has indeed rendered** the offering ***piggul*,** despite the fact that each intention referred only to a small portion of the entire measure.

וְעַד כָּאן לָא קָא אָמַר רַבִּי הָתָם אֶלָּא דְּלָא הֲדַר מַלְיֵיהּ מֵאוֹתָהּ עֲבוֹדָה, אֲבָל הָכָא דַּהֲדַר מַלְיֵיהּ מֵאוֹתָהּ עֲבוֹדָה – הָכִי נַמִי דְּפָסֵיל!

And perhaps **Rabbi** Yehuda HaNasi **states** that the offering is valid if one had intent of *piggul* with regard to half an olive-bulk from each loaf **only there, where he did not subsequently complete** his intention with regard to a full measure **from the same** sacrificial **rite,** as he had *piggul* intent with regard to half an olive-bulk during the slaughter of each lamb independently. **But here, where he subsequently completed** his intention with regard to a full measure **from the same rite,** perhaps **he has indeed disqualified** the offering.

אֶלָּא מַאן דְּאָמַר פִּיגּוּל – דִּבְרֵי הַכֹּל, מַאן דְּאָמַר פָּסוּל – דִּבְרֵי הַכֹּל, מַאן דְּאָמַר כָּשֵׁר – דִּבְרֵי הַכֹּל;

Rather, the one who says that an offering is ***piggul*** when one repeatedly burns an amount the size of a sesame seed from the handful and frankincense with the intent to consume an amount the size of a sesame seed from the remainder the next day, would claim that **all** of the *tanna'im* **agree** that it is *piggul*. Similarly, **the one who says** that it is **disqualified** would contend that **all agree** that it is disqualified, and **the one who says** that it is **fit** would maintain that **all agree** that it is fit.

מַאן דְּאָמַר פִּיגּוּל דִּבְרֵי הַכֹּל – קָסָבַר: דֶּרֶךְ אֲכִילָה בְּכָךְ וְדֶרֶךְ הַקְטָרָה בְּכָךְ; וּמַאן דְּאָמַר פָּסוּל דִּבְרֵי הַכֹּל – קָסָבַר: אֵין דֶּרֶךְ אֲכִילָה בְּכָךְ וְאֵין דֶּרֶךְ הַקְטָרָה בְּכָךְ, וַהֲוַאי לָהּ כְּמִנְחָה שֶׁלֹּא הוּקְטְרָה; וּמַאן דְּאָמַר כָּשֵׁר דִּבְרֵי הַכֹּל – קָסָבַר: דֶּרֶךְ הַקְטָרָה בְּכָךְ וְאֵין דֶּרֶךְ אֲכִילָה בְּכָךְ.

The Gemara elaborates: **The one who says** that **all agree** it is ***piggul*** **maintains** that **the manner of** its **consumption is in such** a manner, i.e., in small portions, **and** likewise **the manner of** its **burning is** also **in such** a manner. **And the one who says** that **all agree** it is **disqualified holds** that **the manner of** its **consumption** is **not in such** a manner. Accordingly, this type of *piggul* intent does not render the offering *piggul*. **And the manner of** its **burning** is also **not in such** a manner,[N] **and** consequently **it is like a meal offering** whose handful **was not burned** properly, and is therefore disqualified. **And** finally, **the one who says** that **all agree** it is **fit holds** that **the manner of** its **burning** is **in such** a manner, and therefore the burning was performed properly, **but the manner of** its **consumption** is **not in such** a manner, which means that the *piggul* intent is inconsequential.

אָמְרִי

§ So **say**

NOTES

And the manner of its burning is also not in such a manner – וְאֵין דֶּרֶךְ הַקְטָרָה בְּכָךְ: According to this explanation, it makes no difference whether this is the manner in which the remainder is consumed. The fact that the meal offering is not burned in this manner means that the offering was not sacrificed properly, and consequently it cannot be rendered *piggul* but is instead disqualified. In fact, some commentaries maintain that according to Rashi the Gemara should read: The manner of its consumption is in such a manner (*Shita Mekubbetzet*).

חריפי דפומבדיתא: הקטרה מפגלת הקטרה. ואפילו לרבנן דאמרי: אין מפגלין בחצי מתיר – הני מילי היכא דחישב ביה בשירים, ולבונה במילתא קיימא, אבל הכא דחישב לה בלבונה – כמה דחישב ביה בכוליה מתיר דמי.

the sharp people in the city **of Pumbedita:**[P] **Burning renders burning *piggul*,** e.g., burning the handful with the intent to burn the frankincense the next day renders the meal offering *piggul*. **And** this is the *halakha* **even according to the Rabbis, who say** that **one does not render** an offering ***piggul* with** intent occurring during the sacrifice of **half of a permitting factor,**[N] e.g., when sacrificing the handful alone with intent of *piggul*. The reason is that **this statement** applies only **where he had intent during** the sacrifice of the handful to consume **the remainder** the next day, **and** the **frankincense stands intact,** i.e., he had no intent with regard to it. **But here, when he had intent with regard to the frankincense** while burning the handful, **it is considered as though he had intent with regard to the entire permitting factor.**

אמר רבא: אף אנן נמי תנינא, זה הכלל: כל הקומץ ונותן בכלי, והמוליך והמקטיר, לאכול דבר שדרכו לאכול ולהקטיר דבר שדרכו להקטיר, חוץ למקומו – פסול ואין בו כרת, חוץ לזמנו – פגול וחייבין עליו כרת;

Rava said: We learn this *halakha* in a mishna, **as well** (12a): **This is the principle:** In the case of **anyone who removes the handful, or places** the handful **in the vessel,** or **who conveys** the vessel with the handful to the altar, or **who burns** the handful on the altar, with the intent **to partake of an item whose** typical **manner** is such that one **partakes** of it, **or to burn an item whose** typical **manner** is such that one **burns** it on the altar, **outside its** designated **area,** the meal offering is **unfit but there is no** liability **for *karet*.** If his intent was to do so **beyond its** designated **time,** the offering **is *piggul* and one is liable** to receive ***karet* on account of it.**

מאי לאו הקטרה דומיא דהנך? מה הנך – בין לאכול בין להקטיר, אף הקטרה – בין לאכול בין להקטיר?

Rava explains: **What, is it not** correct to say that the *halakha* with regard to **burning** is **similar to these,** i.e., the removal of the handful, its placement in a vessel, and the conveying? Accordingly, **just as** with regard to **these, whether** one's intent was **to partake** of the remainder the next day **or to burn** the frankincense the next day, the *halakha* is that the offering is *piggul*, **so too** with regard to **burning, whether** one's intent was **to partake** of the remainder **or to burn**[N] the frankincense the next day, the offering is *piggul*.

לא, הנך – בין לאכול בין להקטיר; הקטרה, לאכול – אין, להקטיר – לא.

The Gemara rejects this comparison: **No,** with regard to **these, whether** one's intent was **to partake** of the remainder **or to burn** the frankincense the next day, the offering is in fact *piggul*. But with regard to **burning,** if one's intent was **to partake** of the remainder the next day, **yes,** it is *piggul*, but if one's intent was **to burn** the frankincense the next day, it is **not** *piggul*.

יתיב רב מנשיא בר גדא קמיה דאביי, ויתיב וקא אמר משמיה דרב חסדא: אין הקטרה מפגלת הקטרה. ואפילו לרבי מאיר דאמר: מפגלין בחצי מתיר,

The Gemara relates that **Rav Menashya bar Gadda sat before Abaye, and** while he was **sitting he said in the name of Rav Ḥisda: Burning does not render burning *piggul*,**[H] e.g., burning the handful with the intent to burn the frankincense the next day does not render the offering *piggul*. **And** this is the *halakha* **even according to** the opinion of **Rabbi Meir, who says** in the mishna that one **renders** an offering ***piggul*** through intent **during** the sacrifice of **half of a permitting factor,** e.g., when sacrificing the handful but not the frankincense with intent of *piggul*.

PERSONALITIES

The sharp people in the city of Pumbedita – חריפי דפומבדיתא: According to the Gemara on *Sanhedrin* 17b, this refers to the brothers Eifa and Avimi, sons of the Sage Raḥava of Pumbedita, who was a preeminent disciple of Rav Yehuda, the founder of the yeshiva in Pumbedita. Rav Yehuda himself was a second generation Babylonian *amora*. Eifa and Avimi are cited several times throughout the Gemara as raising difficulties with regard to the opinions of other *amora'im*, as well as questioning each other's statements. The Gemara relates that Eifa studied tractate *Shevuot* under Rabba, and Avimi tested his knowledge of the tractate. Eifa and Avimi are also cited in the Jerusalem Talmud, where their opinions are discussed by the Sages of Eretz Yisrael, although there Eifa is referred to as Ḥeifa.

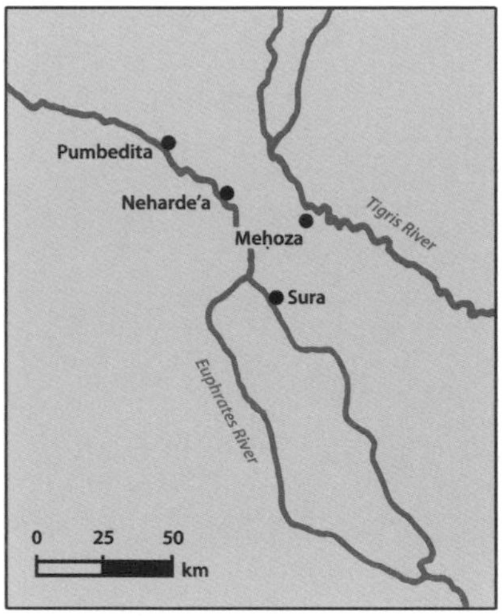

Location of Pumbedita

HALAKHA

Burning does not render burning *piggul* – אין הקטרה מפגלת הקטרה: If one had intent during the burning of the handful to burn the frankincense the next day, the meal offering is not *piggul*, as burning does not render burning *piggul* (Rambam *Sefer Avoda*, *Hilkhot Pesulei HaMukdashin* 16:8).

NOTES

Even according to the Rabbis, who say that one does not render an offering *piggul* with intent occurring during the sacrifice of half of a permitting factor, etc. – אפילו לרבנן דאמרי אין מפגלין בחצי מתיר וכו׳: Rabbi Meir also maintains that the offering is *piggul*, as he holds that one renders an offering *piggul* with improper intent during the sacrifice of half of a permitting factor. According to Rabbi Yosei, who holds that one permitting factor cannot render another permitting factor *piggul* (13b), the offering is not rendered *piggul* with such intent. There is an opinion that even Rabbi Yosei concedes that the offering is *piggul* in this case, as the handful and frankincense were fixed in one vessel, and the *piggul* action as well as the *piggul* intent both refer to the rite of burning. Therefore, the intent of *piggul* extends over the entire meal offering (*Shita Mekubbetzet* on 13b, citing *Tosafot Ḥitzoniyyot*).

We learn in a mishna as well…so too with regard to burning, whether one's intent was to partake of the remainder or to burn it – אף אנן נמי תנינא...אף הקטרה בין לאכול בין להקטיר: The mishna cannot be referring to a case where one burns the handful with the intent to burn the handful itself the next day, as he is in fact burning it now. Rather, the mishna must be referring to a priest who intends to burn the frankincense the next day (Rabbeinu Gershom Meor HaGola).

הָנֵי מִילֵּי הֵיכָא דְּחִישֵּׁב בְּהוּ בַּשִּׁירַיִם, דְּקוֹמֶץ מַתִּיר דִּידְהוּ, אֲבָל הָכָא דְּקוֹמֶץ לָאו מַתִּיר דִּלְבוֹנָה הוּא – לָא מָצֵי מְפַגֵּל בֵּיהּ.

Rav Menashya bar Gadda explains that the reason is that **this statement** of Rabbi Meir applies only **where he had intent during** the sacrifice of the handful to consume **the remainder** the next day, **as the handful** is **their permitting factor. But here, as the handful is not a permitting factor of the frankincense,** the offering **cannot be rendered *piggul* through it.**

אֲמַר לֵיהּ אַבַּיֵי: עֲנֵי מָרִי, מִשְּׁמֵיהּ דְּרַב? אֲמַר לֵיהּ: אִין. אִיתְּמַר נַמִּי, אָמַר רַב חִסְדָּא אָמַר רַב: אֵין הַקְטָרָה מְפַגֶּלֶת הַקְטָרָה.

Abaye said to Rav Menashya: **Answer me, my Master,** did Rav Ḥisda state this *halakha* **in the name of Rav?** Rav Menashya **said to** Abaye: **Yes.** The Gemara notes that it **was also stated** explicitly that **Rav Ḥisda says** that **Rav says: Burning does not render burning *piggul*.**

אֲמַר רַב יַעֲקֹב בַּר אִידִי מִשְּׁמֵיהּ דְּאַבַּיֵי, אַף אֲנַן נַמִּי תְּנֵינָא: שָׁחַט אֶחָד מִן הַכְּבָשִׂים לֶאֱכוֹל מִמֶּנּוּ לְמָחָר – הוּא פִּיגּוּל וַחֲבֵירוֹ כָּשֵׁר, לֶאֱכוֹל מֵחֲבֵירוֹ לְמָחָר – שְׁנֵיהֶם כְּשֵׁרִין; מַאי טַעְמָא? לָאו מִשּׁוּם דְּכֵיוָן דְּלָאו מַתִּיר דִּידֵיהּ הוּא, לָא מָצֵי מְפַגֵּל בֵּיהּ?

Rav Ya'akov bar Idi said in the name of Abaye: We learn in the mishna **as well** that the *halakha* is in accordance with the opinion of Rav: If **one slaughtered one of the lambs** with the intent **to partake of it the next day, that** lamb **is *piggul* and the other** lamb **is fit.** If he slaughtered one lamb with the intent **to partake of the other the next day, both** lambs **are fit. What is the reason?** Is it **not due to the fact that since** the first lamb **is not a permitting factor of** the second lamb, **it cannot render** the second lamb ***piggul*?** The same reasoning should apply to the case of the handful and frankincense.

לָא, הָתָם הוּא דְּלָא אִיקְּבַע בְּחַד מָנָא, אֲבָל הָכָא דְּאִיקְּבַע בְּחַד מָנָא – כִּי חַד דָּמוּ.

The Gemara rejects this suggestion: **No;** there is a difference between these cases. **It is** only **there,** in the mishna, that one lamb cannot render the other *piggul*, **as it was not fixed in one vessel** with the other lamb, and therefore each animal stands independent of the other. **But here, as** the handful and frankincense **were fixed in one vessel** for the purpose of offering them, **they are considered like one** item and one of them therefore renders the other *piggul*.

אֲמַר רַב הַמְנוּנָא: הָא מִילְּתָא אַבְלַע לִי רַבִּי חֲנִינָא, וּתְקִילָא לִי כְּכוּלֵּיהּ תַּלְמוּדַאי: הִקְטִיר קוֹמֶץ לְהַקְטִיר לְבוֹנָה, וּלְבוֹנָה לֶאֱכוֹל שִׁירַיִם לְמָחָר – פִּגּוּל.

§ **Rav Hamnuna said: Rabbi Ḥanina helped me internalize this** following **matter, and to me it is equivalent to all** the rest of **my learning,** as it contains a significant novelty: If **one burned** the **handful** with the intent **to burn** the **frankincense** the next day, **and** burned the **frankincense** with the intent **to partake of** the **remainder**[N] **the next day,**[H] the meal offering **is *piggul*.**

מַאי קָא מַשְׁמַע לָן? אִי הַקְטָרָה מְפַגֶּלֶת הַקְטָרָה קָא מַשְׁמַע לָן – לֵימָא: הִקְטִיר קוֹמֶץ לְהַקְטִיר לְבוֹנָה! אִי מְפַגְּלִין בַּחֲצִי מַתִּיר קָא מַשְׁמַע לָן – לֵימָא: הִקְטִיר קוֹמֶץ לֶאֱכוֹל שִׁירַיִם לְמָחָר! אִי תַּרְוַיְיהוּ אֲתָא קָא מַשְׁמַע לָן – לֵימָא: הִקְטִיר קוֹמֶץ לְהַקְטִיר לְבוֹנָה וְלֶאֱכוֹל שִׁירַיִם לְמָחָר!

The Gemara asks: **What is** Rabbi Ḥanina **teaching us? If** he **is teaching us** that **burning renders burning *piggul*,** then **let him** simply **say:** If one **burned the handful** with the intent **to burn** the **frankincense,** the offering is *piggul*. **If** he **is teaching us** that one **renders** an offering ***piggul*** through intent **during** the sacrifice of **half of a permitting factor,** then **let him say:** If one **burned** the **handful** with the intent **to partake of** the **remainder the next day,** the offering is *piggul*. **If** he **is coming** to teach us **both of** these *halakhot*, **let him say:** If one **burned** the **handful** with the intent **to burn** the **frankincense or to partake of** the **remainder the next day,** the offering is *piggul*.

HALAKHA

Burned the handful with the intent to burn the frankincense the next day and burned the frankincense with the intent to partake of the remainder the next day – **הִקְטִיר קוֹמֶץ לְהַקְטִיר לְבוֹנָה וּלְבוֹנָה לֶאֱכוֹל שִׁירַיִם לְמָחָר**: If one burned the handful with the intent to burn the frankincense the next day, and subsequently burned the frankincense with the intent to partake of the remainder the next day, the offering is *piggul*, since *piggul* intent has extended over the entire meal offering. The Rambam rules in accordance with this version of the Gemara. According to Rashi's version, even if one had intent during the burning of the handful to burn the frankincense and to partake of the remainder the next day, the offering is *piggul* (Rambam *Sefer Avoda*, *Hilkhot Pesulei HaMukdashin* 16:8, and see *Likkutei Halakhot*).

NOTES

To burn the frankincense the next day, and burned the frankincense with the intent to partake of the remainder – **לְהַקְטִיר לְבוֹנָה וּלְבוֹנָה לֶאֱכוֹל שִׁירַיִם**: According to this version of the Gemara, which is apparently the same text used by the Rambam, the Gemara's question is as follows: Why does Rabbi Ḥanina teach a case where one burned the frankincense with the intent to partake of the remainder the next day, when he could have referred to a case where one burned the handful with the intent both to burn the frankincense and to partake of the remainder the next day? Rashi omits the term: And the frankincense, which means that the case involves one who burned the handful with the intent to burn the frankincense and to partake of the remainder. According to Rashi, the Gemara's question is as follows: If Rabbi Ḥanina intends to teach that this offering is *piggul*, why does he cite a case where there are two viable reasons for rendering the offering *piggul*? Why doesn't Rabbi Ḥanina teach a case where only one of the reasons applies, i.e., either he burned the handful with the intent to burn the frankincense the next day or he did so with the intent to partake of the remainder the next day. This would indicate that either reason is sufficient to render an offering *piggul*.

אָמַר רַב אַדָּא בַּר אַהֲבָה: לְעוֹלָם קָסָבַר אֵין הַקְטָרָה מְפַגֶּלֶת הַקְטָרָה, וְאֵין מְפַגְּלִין בַּחֲצִי מַתִּיר, וְשָׁאנֵי הָכָא, דִּפְשָׁטָא לֵיהּ מַחֲשָׁבָה בְּכוּלָּהּ מִנְחָה.

Rav Adda bar Ahava said: Actually, Rabbi Ḥanina **holds** that **burning does not render burning *piggul*,** and therefore if one burned only the handful with the intent to burn the frankincense the next day, the offering is not *piggul*. **And** he also holds that one **does not render** an offering *piggul* through intent **during** the sacrifice of **half of a permitting factor,** and consequently if one burned only the handful with the intent to partake of the remainder the next day, the offering is not *piggul* either. **But** it **is different here, as intent** of *piggul* has **extended**[N] **over the entire meal offering,** as he had intent of *piggul* during the burning of the handful with regard to the frankincense and during the burning of the frankincense with regard to the remainder.

תָּנֵי תַּנָּא קַמֵּיהּ דְּרַב יִצְחָק בַּר אַבָּא: הִקְטִיר קוֹמֶץ לֶאֱכוֹל שִׁירַיִם – לְדִבְרֵי הַכֹּל פִּגּוּל. וְהָא מִיפְלַג פְּלִיגִי! אֶלָּא אֵימָא: לְדִבְרֵי הַכֹּל פָּסוּל.

The Gemara relates that **a *tanna* taught** a *baraita* **before Rav Yitzḥak bar Abba: If one burned** the **handful** with the intent **to partake of** the **remainder** the next day,[H] **everyone agrees** that the meal offering is ***piggul*.** The Gemara raises a difficulty: **But don't** Rabbi Meir and the Rabbis **disagree** in the mishna with regard to this very case? **Rather, say** that the *baraita* states: **Everyone agrees** that the offering is **disqualified,** as although the Rabbis hold that such intent does not render an offering *piggul*, they concede that it disqualifies the offering.

וְלֵימָא: הֲרֵי זֶה פִּגּוּל, וְרַבִּי מֵאִיר הִיא! תַּנָּא "דִּבְרֵי הַכֹּל" אַתְנְיוּהּ, "פִּיגּוּל" בְּ"פָסוּל" מִיחְלַף לֵיהּ, "הֲרֵי זֶה" בְּ"דִבְרֵי הַכֹּל" לָא מִיחְלַף לֵיהּ.

The Gemara challenges: **But** if one must emend the *baraita*, **let him say** that the *baraita* states: **It is *piggul*, and** that **it is** in accordance with the opinion of **Rabbi Meir.** The Gemara responds: It is reasonable that the ***tanna* taught** that **everyone agrees,** and that he accidentally **exchanged** the word ***piggul* for disqualified.** But **he would not confuse** the phrase:[N] **This is** the opinion of Rabbi Meir, **with** the phrase: **Everyone agrees.**

הדרן עלך הקומץ את המנחה

NOTES

As intent of *piggul* has extended – דִּפְשָׁטָא לֵיהּ מַחֲשָׁבָה: According to Rashi's version of the Gemara, in which the case involves one who burned the handful with the intent to burn the frankincense and partake of the remainder the next day, burning does not render burning *piggul* because intent is lacking with regard to the remainder. Similarly, this is considered half of a permitting factor, which cannot render the offering *piggul*, as intent is lacking during the sacrifice of the remaining permitting factor, i.e., the frankincense. Nevertheless, the combination of these intentions, which refer to the remainder and the frankincense, is sufficient to render the offering *piggul*. According to the Rambam's version of the Gemara, such intent is insufficient, as it occurs during the sacrifice of only half of the permitting factor. He maintains that an offering is rendered *piggul* only when one has *piggul* intent during the sacrifice of all of the permitting factors, regardless of the combination of intentions.

He would not confuse the phrase – לָא מִיחְלַף לֵיהּ: Most *baraitot* were not committed to writing, but rather, were memorized by the *tanna'im*. It is therefore understandable that some *tanna'im* might err in the recitation of a *baraita*. It is generally assumed that such mistakes were limited and did not constitute dramatic deviations from the authentic language of the *baraita*. Consequently, while it is probable that the *tanna* would confuse disqualified with *piggul*, it is unlikely that he might interchange: This is the opinion of Rabbi Meir, with the term: Everyone agrees.

HALAKHA

If one burned the handful with the intent to partake of the remainder the next day, etc. – הִקְטִיר קוֹמֶץ לֶאֱכוֹל שִׁירַיִם וכו׳: If one burned only the frankincense or only the handful with the intent to partake of the remainder the next day, the meal offering is disqualified. The *halakha* is in accordance with the opinion of the Rabbis in the mishna, not Rabbi Meir (Rambam *Sefer Avoda*, *Hilkhot Pesulei HaMukdashin* 16:8).

Summary of **Perek II**

The second chapter of *Menaḥot* deals primarily with the relationship between the various parts of a meal offering, specifically with regard to the *halakhot* of *piggul* and the disqualification of a meal offering.

One conclusion is that if a priest burns the handful of a meal offering with the intent to burn the frankincense the next day, the meal offering is rendered *piggul*. Although everyone accepts the principle that improper intent with one permitting factor does not render another permitting factor *piggul*, this principle applies only when each permitting factor remains independent, e.g., in the case of the communal peace offering of two lambs that accompanies the two loaves on *Shavuot*. By contrast, in a case such as that of the handful and frankincense of a meal offering, since the handful and frankincense are fixed in one vessel, they are considered a single permitting factor with regard to rendering one another *piggul*. Similarly, each of the bowls of frankincense that accompany the shewbread renders the other *piggul*, as both bowls are fixed in a single vessel, i.e., on the table of the shewbread.

Additionally, the Gemara concludes that if one sacrifices the handful of a meal offering with the intent to partake of the remainder the next day, but has no such intent during the sacrifice of the frankincense, or vice versa, the offering is not rendered *piggul*, in accordance with the principle that *piggul* is effected only when one has improper intent during the sacrifice of all the permitting factors of an offering. Similarly, the shewbread is rendered *piggul* only if one burns both bowls with intent of *piggul*. If all of the permitting factors of an offering are sacrificed with intent of *piggul*, then even if one's intent referred to only part of the offering, e.g., one arrangement of shewbread, the entire offering is *piggul*.

In light of the discussion concerning intent of *piggul* while sacrificing an element of an offering, some *halakhot* involving the ritual impurity of part of an offering are discussed in this chapter as well. The Gemara concludes that if one part of an offering becomes impure, e.g., one arrangement of shewbread or one of the loaves from the meal offering brought on *Shavuot*, the remaining part is not rendered impure on account of it, and it must be consumed in a state of ritual purity.

The Gemara's conclusion that the status of *piggul* extends from one part of an offering to another is relevant only to offerings whose parts are of equal importance, e.g., the two arrangements of shewbread. This is not the *halakha* when an offering comprises a principal element and a secondary one, e.g., a thanks offering and its accompanying loaves. Instead, the Gemara concludes that *piggul* intent with regard to the principal element renders the secondary element *piggul* as well, but not vice versa. Accordingly, *piggul* intent with regard to the two lambs that accompany the two loaves on *Shavuot* renders both the lambs and the loaves *piggul*, whereas improper intent with regard to the loaves renders the loaves *piggul* but not the lambs. This is because the loaves are sanctified on account of the slaughter of the lambs, and since the loaves are the secondary element, they do not render the lambs *piggul*.

These *halakhot* are applicable only to offerings whose parts are sanctified and sacrificed together. With regard to the libations that accompany an animal offering, these do not render the animal *piggul*, as they are secondary to the animal. They are not even rendered *piggul* on account of the animal, since they may be brought even several days after the sacrifice of the animal.

Introduction to **Perek III**

And when one brings a meal offering unto the Lord, his offering shall be of fine flour; and he shall pour oil upon it, and put frankincense upon it. And he shall bring it to Aaron's sons, the priests; and he shall remove his handful of its fine flour, and of its oil, together with all its frankincense; and the priest shall make its memorial part smoke upon the altar, an offering made by fire, of a pleasing aroma to the Lord. But that which is left of the meal offering shall be Aaron's and his sons'; it is most holy of the offerings of the Lord made by fire. And when you bring a meal offering baked in the oven, it shall be unleavened cakes of fine flour mingled with oil, or unleavened wafers spread with oil. And if your offering is a meal offering baked on a griddle, it shall be of fine flour unleavened, mingled with oil. You shall break it in pieces, and pour oil on it; it is a meal offering.

(Leviticus 2:1–6)

And every meal offering of yours you shall season with salt; neither shall you suffer the salt of the covenant of your God to be lacking from your meal offering; you shall sacrifice salt with all your offerings.

(Leviticus 2:13)

And this is the law of the meal offering: The sons of Aaron shall sacrifice it before the Lord, in front of the altar.

(Leviticus 6:7)

And you shall make a Candelabrum of pure gold; of beaten work will the Cundelabrum be made, even its base, and its shaft; its goblets, its knobs, and its flowers shall be of one piece with it. And there shall be six branches going out of its sides: Three branches of the Candelabrum out of its one side, and three branches of the Candelabrum out of its other side; three goblets made like almond blossoms in one branch, a knob and a flower; and three goblets made like almond blossoms in the other branch, a knob and a flower; so for the six branches going out of the Candelabrum. And in the Candelabrum four goblets made like almond blossoms, its knobs, and its flowers. And a knob under two branches of one piece with it, and a knob under two branches of one piece with it, and a knob under two branches of one piece with it, for the six branches going out of the Candelabrum. Their knobs and their branches shall be of one piece with it; the whole of it one beaten work of pure gold. And you shall make its lamps, seven; and they shall light its lamps, to give light over against it. And its tongs, and its pans, shall be of pure gold. Of a talent of pure gold it will be made, with all these vessels. And see that you make them after their pattern, which is being shown you in the mount.

(Exodus 25:31–40)

This chapter discusses two main topics. The first is meal offerings whose rites were performed improperly, or where various problems arose prior to their being burned on the altar. The chapter examines when these meal offerings are fit and when they are unfit.

The chapter begins with the case of meal offerings that were sacrificed with the improper intent in a situation where this intent does not disqualify the offering. Next, the chapter discusses the various rites of the meal offering prescribed by the Torah and addresses which of these are indispensable to its sacrifice.

Another topic is mixtures of meal offerings, a broad category that includes the case of two meal offerings that became intermingled, a meal offering that became intermingled with a handful removed from a meal offering, and a remainder of a meal offering that became intermingled with its handful or that of another meal offering.

The chapter also explores the case of a meal offering that contracted ritual impurity. It discusses the *halakha* of a handful that became impure and the *halakha* of a meal offering whose remainder, which is designated to be eaten by a priest, became impure or was lost or burned. Is it sufficient to burn the handful of this meal offering in order to fulfill one's obligation, or is there no halakhic significance to the burning of the handful when there is nothing left of the meal offering from which it was taken?

The chapter then examines the last part of the service of a meal offering, which is the burning of the handful. It discusses how this burning is performed, e.g., whether the handful must be placed in a vessel, and when exactly the remainder is permitted to be eaten by the priests.

The details of these *halakhot*, which address mainly the issue of when meal offerings whose rites were improperly performed are entirely fit and when they are unfit, form the subject matter of the first section of the chapter.

The second section of the chapter begins with a discussion of the two parts of the meal offering: The handful and the remainder. Although they differ from one another, the absence of one prevents fulfillment of the mitzva with the other, and a meal offering is fit only if both parts are intact. From here the chapter provides a lengthy list of mitzvot that have various elements, or different aspects to their performance, each of which is indispensable to their fulfillment. This list includes the Candelabrum in the Temple and its parts, which are subject to detailed examination in this chapter, and the passages from the Torah written in a *mezuza* and on the parchment of phylacteries. In all of these cases, the Gemara analyzes the sources in the verses and discusses the details of the performance of these mitzvot.

מתני׳ הַקּוֹמֵץ אֶת הַמִּנְחָה, לֶאֱכוֹל דָּבָר שֶׁאֵין דַּרְכּוֹ לֶאֱכוֹל וּלְהַקְטִיר דָּבָר שֶׁאֵין דַּרְכּוֹ לְהַקְטִיר – כָּשֵׁר, רַבִּי אֱלִיעֶזֶר פּוֹסֵל.

MISHNA In the case of **one who removes a handful**[B] **from the meal offering** with the intent **to consume,** beyond its designated time, **an item whose** typical **manner**[H] is such that one does **not consume** it, i.e., the handful, **or to burn,** beyond its designated time, **an item whose** typical **manner** is such that one does **not burn** it on the altar, i.e., the remainder of the meal offering, the meal offering is **fit. Rabbi Eliezer deems** it **unfit,** although it is not *piggul*, and consuming it is therefore not punishable by excision from the World-to-Come [*karet*].

לֶאֱכוֹל דָּבָר שֶׁדַּרְכּוֹ לֶאֱכוֹל וּלְהַקְטִיר דָּבָר שֶׁדַּרְכּוֹ לְהַקְטִיר פָּחוֹת מִכַּזַּיִת – כָּשֵׁר. לֶאֱכוֹל כַּחֲצִי זַיִת וּלְהַקְטִיר כַּחֲצִי זַיִת – כָּשֵׁר, שֶׁאֵין אֲכִילָה וְהַקְטָרָה מִצְטָרְפִין.

In the case of one who removes a handful from the meal offering with the intent **to consume,** beyond its designated time, **an item whose** typical **manner** is such that one does **consume** it, **or to burn,** beyond its designated time, **an item whose** typical **manner** is such that one does **burn** it on the altar, but his intent was to consume or burn improperly **less than an olive-bulk,**[H] the offering is **fit.** If his intent was both **to consume half an olive-bulk and to burn half an olive-bulk**[H] beyond its designated time, the meal offering is nevertheless **fit, because eating and burning do not join together.**

גמ׳ אָמַר רַבִּי אַסִי אָמַר רַבִּי יוֹחָנָן: מַאי טַעְמָא דְּרַבִּי אֱלִיעֶזֶר? אָמַר קְרָא: ״וְאִם הֵאָכֹל יֵאָכֵל מִבְּשַׂר זֶבַח שְׁלָמָיו״ – בִּשְׁתֵּי אֲכִילוֹת הַכָּתוּב מְדַבֵּר, אֶחָד אֲכִילַת אָדָם וְאֶחָד אֲכִילַת מִזְבֵּחַ, לוֹמַר לָךְ: כְּשֵׁם שֶׁמְּחַשְּׁבִין בַּאֲכִילַת אָדָם – כָּךְ מְחַשְּׁבִין בַּאֲכִילַת מִזְבֵּחַ,

GEMARA **Rabbi Asi says** that **Rabbi Yoḥanan says: What is the reason** for the ruling **of Rabbi Eliezer** that the intention to consume, beyond its designated time, an item that is not usually consumed renders the meal offering unfit? **The verse states** with regard to consuming an offering after its designated time: **"And if any of the flesh of the sacrifice of his peace offerings is at all consumed [*he'akhol ye'akhel*]"** (Leviticus 7:18), repeating for emphasis the term for consumption. He derives from the repeated term that **the verse is speaking of two** types of **consumption: One** is **the consumption** of the offering **by a person,** e.g., by the priests or the owner of the offering, **and** the other **one is the consumption** of the sacrificial portions **by** their being burned on the **altar.** This serves **to tell you** that **just as** one's improper **intention with regard to the consumption of a person** renders the offering unfit, **so too,** one's improper **intention with regard to the consumption of** the **altar** renders the offering unfit.

וּכְשֵׁם שֶׁמְּחַשְּׁבִין מֵאֲכִילַת אָדָם לַאֲכִילַת אָדָם וּמֵאֲכִילַת מִזְבֵּחַ לַאֲכִילַת מִזְבֵּחַ – כָּךְ מְחַשְּׁבִין מֵאֲכִילַת אָדָם לְמִזְבֵּחַ וּמֵאֲכִילַת מִזְבֵּחַ לְאָדָם;

And furthermore, this serves to tell you that **just as** one's improper **intention** that a portion of the offering designated for **consumption by a person** will be **consumed** on the following day **by a person** renders the offering unfit, **and** one's improper **intention** that a portion of the offering designated for **consumption of** the **altar** will be **consumed** on the following day **by** the **altar** renders the offering unfit, **so too,** one's improper **intention** that a portion of the offering designated for **consumption by a person** will be **consumed on** the **altar** renders the offering unfit, **and** one's improper intention that a portion of the offering designated for **consumption of** the **altar** will be **consumed** on the following day **by a person** renders the offering unfit.

מַאי טַעְמָא? מִדְּאַפְּקִינְהוּ רַחֲמָנָא לְהַקְטָרָה בִּלְשׁוֹן אֲכִילָה.

What is the reason for this derivation? It is derived **from** the fact **that the Merciful One expresses** the **burning** of the offering **using the language of consumption.**

וְרַבָּנַן? הַאי דְּאַפְּקִינְהוּ רַחֲמָנָא בִּלְשׁוֹן אֲכִילָה,

And the Rabbis, who disagree with Rabbi Eliezer, maintain the following: **This** fact **that the Merciful One expresses** the burning of the offering **using the language of consumption**

HALAKHA

One who removes a handful from the meal offering with the intent to consume an item whose typical manner, etc. – הַקּוֹמֵץ אֶת הַמִּנְחָה לֶאֱכוֹל דָּבָר שֶׁאֵין דַּרְכּוֹ וכו׳: In the case of one who removes a handful from the meal offering with the intent to consume on the following day an item that is not typically consumed, or to burn on the following day an item that is not typically burned on the altar, the meal offering is fit, in accordance with the opinion of the Rabbis (Rambam *Sefer Avoda, Hilkhot Pesulei HaMukdashin* 14:8).

Less than an olive-bulk – פָּחוֹת מִכַּזַּיִת: If one's intent while performing the sacrificial rites of an offering is to burn on the following day less than an olive-bulk of an item that is typically burned on the altar, or to consume less than an olive-bulk of an item that is typically consumed, the offering is fit (Rambam *Sefer Avoda, Hilkhot Pesulei HaMukdashin* 14:10).

If his intent was to consume half an olive-bulk and to burn half an olive-bulk – לֶאֱכוֹל כַּחֲצִי זַיִת וּלְהַקְטִיר כַּחֲצִי זַיִת: If one's intent while performing the sacrificial rites of an offering is to consume less than an olive-bulk and to burn less than an olive-bulk beyond the offering's designated time or outside of its designated area, the offering is fit, as consumption and burning do not join together (Rambam *Sefer Avoda, Hilkhot Pesulei HaMukdashin* 14:10).

BACKGROUND

Handful – קְמִיצָה: Most meal offerings require that a handful be taken by a priest and burned on the altar. Although this service parallels the service of slaughtering performed on an animal sacrifice, which does not require a priest, the removal of the handful could be performed only by a priest. According to many authorities, the priest would scoop the flour out with the three middle fingers of his right hand, using his thumb and little finger to remove any surplus flour. He would then place the flour in a sacred vessel used for the Temple service to consecrate it. Since the priest had to scoop out a precise handful of flour, no more and no less, the scooping of the handful was one of the more difficult services performed in the Temple (see 11a).

דְּלָא שְׁנָא כִּי מְחַשֵּׁב בִּלְשׁוֹן אֲכִילָה לַמִּזְבֵּחַ וְלָא שְׁנָא כִּי מְחַשֵּׁב בִּלְשׁוֹן הַקְטָרָה לַמִּזְבֵּחַ;

demonstrates **that there is no difference if one expresses his intention using the language of: Consumption on** the **altar,**[H] **and there is no difference if one expresses his intention using the language of: Burning on** the **altar.** Therefore, if the priest removed the handful from the meal offering while expressing the intention that it should be burned on the altar on the following day, whether this intention was phrased as: Consumed on the altar, or: Burned on the altar, the offering is *piggul*.

אִי נָמֵי, מָה אֲכִילָה בִּכְזַיִת אַף הַקְטָרָה בִּכְזַיִת; וּלְעוֹלָם אֲכִילָה דְּאוֹרְחָא מַשְׁמַע.

Alternatively, the doubled expression serves to teach that **just as** one renders the offering *piggul* only when one's intention involves the **consumption of an olive-bulk,** as this is the minimal measure for an act to be considered eating, **so too,** one renders the offering *piggul* only when one's intention involves the **burning of an olive-bulk.**[H] **But actually,** the expression for **consumption** found in the verse **indicates** consuming it **in the usual manner,** and therefore an offering is rendered unfit only if one's improper intention involved consuming an item that is usually consumed, or burning an item that is usually burned.

וְרַבִּי אֱלִיעֶזֶר? אִם כֵּן, לִכְתּוֹב רַחֲמָנָא: ״אִם הֵאָכֹל הֵאָכֵל״, אִי נָמֵי ״אִם יֵאָכֵל יֵאָכֵל״, מַאי ״הֵאָכֹל יֵאָכֵל״? שְׁמַעַתְּ מִינַּהּ תַּרְתֵּי.

And what would **Rabbi Eliezer** respond? He would say that **if that were so,** that the verse intends to teach only that *halakha*, **let the Merciful One write** either: **If** ***he'akhol he'akhol*****, or: If** ***ye'akhel ye'akhel***, repeating the same form of the word twice. **What** is the reason that the verse states ***"he'akhol ye'akhel,"*** employing both repetition and variation? **Learn from** this formulation **two** ***halakhot***. One, as the Rabbis explain, is that the offering is rendered unfit whether one uses an expression of consumption or an expression of burning, provided that one's intention is with regard to at least an olive-bulk. The second is that the offering is rendered unfit if one intends to burn on the altar an item that is usually consumed by a person, or to consume an item that is usually burned on the altar.

אֲמַר לֵיהּ רַבִּי זֵירָא לְרַב אַסִי: וְאִי טַעְמָא דְּרַבִּי אֱלִיעֶזֶר מִשּׁוּם הָכִי הוּא, כָּרֵת נָמֵי לִיחַיַּיב! וְכִי תֵּימָא הָכִי נָמֵי, וְהָא אַתְּ הוּא דַּאֲמַרְתְּ מִשְּׁמֵיהּ דְּרַבִּי יוֹחָנָן: מוֹדֶה רַבִּי אֱלִיעֶזֶר שֶׁאֵין עָנוּשׁ כָּרֵת!

Rabbi Zeira said to Rav Asi: But if the reasoning of Rabbi Eliezer is due to that derivation, and he understands that the verse equates the improper intent to consume an item that is usually consumed with the improper intent to consume an item that is usually burned, then **let one also be liable to** receive ***karet*** for consuming an offering brought with intention to consume, after its designated time, the part of the offering that is burned, or for intention to burn, after its designated time, an item that is usually consumed. Why does Rabbi Eliezer state only that the offering is rendered unfit? **And if you would say** that **indeed,** Rabbi Eliezer does hold that one who consumes such an offering is liable to receive *karet*, that is difficult: **But aren't you the one who said in the name of Rabbi Yoḥanan: Rabbi Eliezer concedes that** doing so is **not punishable by** ***karet*****?**

HALAKHA

Using the language of consumption on the altar – בִּלְשׁוֹן אֲכִילָה לַמִּזְבֵּחַ: If one performed one of the sacrificial rites with the intention of consuming half an olive-bulk after the time designated for eating the offering, and the intention that another half olive-bulk would be consumed on the altar after the designated time for burning the offering, the two half olive-bulks combine and the offering is *piggul*, because both utilize the same expression of consumption. This is in accordance with the Gemara's statement in tractate *Zevaḥim* (31a), and in accordance with the opinion of the Rabbis here (Rambam *Sefer Avoda*, *Hilkhot Pesulei HaMukdashin* 14:10).

Burning of an olive-bulk – הַקְטָרָה בִּכְזַיִת: The smallest measure of eating is an olive-bulk, and the smallest measure of burning an offering is an olive-bulk. Therefore, if one intends to eat after its designated time or outside of its designated location less than an olive-bulk of an item that is usually eaten, or to burn less than an olive-bulk of an item that is usually burned, the offering remains fit (Rambam *Sefer Avoda*, *Hilkhot Pesulei HaMukdashin* 14:10, and see *Hilkhot Biat HaMikdash* 9:4).

אֲמַר לֵיהּ: תַּנָּאֵי הִיא אַלִּיבָּא דְּרַבִּי אֱלִיעֶזֶר, אִיכָּא לְמַאן דְּאָמַר: פְּסוּלָה דְּאוֹרָיְיתָא, וְאִיכָּא לְמַאן דְּאָמַר: פְּסוּלָה דְּרַבָּנַן.

Rav Asi **said to him: It is a dispute between** ***tanna'im*** **as to the** opinion **of Rabbi Eliezer. There is one who says** that Rabbi Eliezer deems the offering to be **unfit by Torah law** and one is liable to receive *karet*. It was in accordance with this opinion that Rabbi Yoḥanan cited the proof from the verse. **And there is one who says** that Rabbi Eliezer deems the offering to be **unfit by rabbinic law,** and it was in accordance with this opinion that Rabbi Yoḥanan said that according to Rabbi Eliezer there is no punishment of *karet* for this transgression.

דְּתַנְיָא: הַשּׁוֹחֵט אֶת הַזֶּבַח לִשְׁתּוֹת מִדָּמוֹ לְמָחָר, לְהַקְטִיר מִבְּשָׂרוֹ לְמָחָר, לֶאֱכוֹל מֵאֵימוּרָיו לְמָחָר – כָּשֵׁר, וְרַבִּי אֱלִיעֶזֶר פּוֹסֵל. לְהַנִּיחַ מִדָּמוֹ לְמָחָר – רַבִּי יְהוּדָה פּוֹסֵל. אָמַר רַבִּי אֶלְעָזָר: אַף בָּזוֹ רַבִּי אֱלִיעֶזֶר פּוֹסֵל וַחֲכָמִים מַכְשִׁירִין.

As it is taught in a *baraita*: In the case of **one who slaughters the offering**[H] with the intention **to drink** some **of its blood,** which is designated to be presented on the altar, **on the next day,** or **to burn** some **of its meat,** which is meant to be eaten, **on the next day,** or **to eat** some **of its sacrificial portions,** which are designated to be burned on the altar, **on the next day,** the offering is **fit,** as his intention is either to eat an item that is usually sacrificed on the altar, or to burn on the altar an item that is usually eaten. **But Rabbi Eliezer deems** the offering **unfit.** If one slaughters the offering with the intention **to leave** some **of its blood for the next day,**[H] but not to present it or consume it, **Rabbi Yehuda deems** the offering **unfit. Rabbi Elazar said: Even in this** case **Rabbi Eliezer deems** the offering **unfit, and the Rabbis deem** it **fit.**

רַבִּי יְהוּדָה אַלִּיבָּא דְּמַאן? אִילֵימָא אַלִּיבָּא דְּרַבָּנַן, הָשְׁתָּא וּמַה הָתָם דְּקָא מְחַשֵּׁב בִּלְשׁוֹן אֲכִילָה מַכְשְׁרִי רַבָּנַן, הָכָא לֹא כׇּל שֶׁכֵּן?

The Gemara clarifies: **In accordance with whose** opinion is the statement of **Rabbi Yehuda** that the offering is unfit even if he intends only to leave the blood for the next day, but not present it or consume it? **If we say** it is **in accordance with** the opinion **of the Rabbis, now** consider: **And if there, where** the priest **expresses his intention using the language of consumption, the Rabbis** nevertheless **deem** the offering **fit,** despite the fact that if he had used this expression with regard to the portion burned on the altar, the offering would be *piggul*, is it **not all the more so** the case that **here,** when he intends only to leave the blood until the next day, the offering should be fit?

אֶלָּא אַלִּיבָּא דְּרַבִּי אֱלִיעֶזֶר; וְאָמַר רַבִּי אֶלְעָזָר: אַף בָּזוֹ רַבִּי אֱלִיעֶזֶר פּוֹסֵל וַחֲכָמִים מַכְשִׁירִין; רַבִּי אֶלְעָזָר הַיְינוּ רַבִּי יְהוּדָה!

Rather, it must be that Rabbi Yehuda's statement is **in accordance with** the opinion **of Rabbi Eliezer. And** yet the *baraita* continues: **Rabbi Elazar said: Even in this** case **Rabbi Eliezer deems** the offering **unfit, and the Rabbis deem** it **fit.** If Rabbi Yehuda's statement is in accordance with the opinion of Rabbi Eliezer, then the explanation of **Rabbi Elazar** of Rabbi Eliezer's opinion **is** identical to that of **Rabbi Yehuda,** and there does not appear to be any disagreement between the two.

אֶלָּא לָאו כָּרֵת אִיכָּא בֵּינַיְיהוּ, דְּרַבִּי יְהוּדָה (דְּתַנָּא קַמָּא) סָבַר: לְהַנִּיחַ – פְּסוּלָא בְּעָלְמָא, בְּהָנָךְ – כָּרֵת נַמִי מִיחַיַּיב, וַאֲתָא רַבִּי אֶלְעָזָר לְמֵימַר: אִידִי וְאִידִי פָּסוּל וְאֵין בּוֹ כָּרֵת!

Rather, is it not so that the difference **between** Rabbi Elazar and Rabbi Yehuda is with regard to liability for *karet*? The difference lies in **that Rabbi Yehuda holds** that if one's intention is **to leave** the blood for the next day, then according to Rabbi Eliezer the offering is **only** rendered **unfit,** whereas **in those** cases listed in the mishna, such as where one's intention is to eat the sacrificial portions on the next day, he would be **liable** to receive ***karet*** **as well. And Rabbi Elazar comes to say** that according to Rabbi Eliezer, both in **this** case **and** in **that** case, the offering is **unfit but there is no** liability to receive ***karet*** **for it.**

לָא, דְּכוּלֵּי עָלְמָא כָּרֵת לֵיכָּא, וְהָכָא שָׁלֹשׁ מַחְלוֹקוֹת בַּדָּבָר, תַּנָּא קַמָּא סָבַר: בְּהָנָךְ פְּלִיגִי, לְהַנִּיחַ – דִּבְרֵי הַכֹּל כָּשֵׁר;

The Gemara rejects this suggestion: **No,** it may be **that everyone agrees** that according to Rabbi Eliezer in a case where one's intention is to eat, after its designated time, an item that is usually burned, or to burn an item that is usually eaten, **there is no** liability to receive ***karet*****. And here** there are **three disputes with regard to the matter. The first** ***tanna*** **holds** that the Rabbis and Rabbi Eliezer **disagree** only **in those** cases, with regard to whether the offering is rendered unfit due to the intention to eat an item that is usually burned or to burn an item that is usually eaten. But with regard **to leaving** of its blood until the next day, **everyone agrees** that the offering is **fit.**

HALAKHA

One who slaughters the offering, etc. – הַשּׁוֹחֵט אֶת הַזֶּבַח וכו׳: If one slaughters an offering with the intention of drinking of its blood, eating its sacrificial portions, or burning its meat on the next day or outside of its designated location, the offering is fit, as he intended either to eat of an item that is usually burned on the altar, or to burn on the altar an item that is usually eaten (Rambam *Sefer Avoda, Hilkhot Pesulei HaMukdashin* 14:8).

The intention to leave of its blood for the next day – לְהַנִּיחַ מִדָּמוֹ לְמָחָר: If while performing one of the sacrificial rites, i.e., slaughter, collection of the blood, conveying the blood to the altar, and presentation of the blood, one's intention is to leave the blood or sacrificial portions for the next day, the offering is fit. This is in accordance with the opinion of the Rabbis on *Zevaḥim* 35b (Rambam *Sefer Avoda, Hilkhot Pesulei HaMukdashin* 13:8).

NOTES

Was especially dear to him until one [*ad le'aḥat*] – והיה חביב לו ביותר עד לאחת: Rashi offers two explanations for the phrase: Until one. According to the first explanation, the statement means that Yosef the Babylonian was especially dear to Rabbi Elazar, and the two were engaged in learning together until they reached one *halakha*. According to the second explanation, the Gemara is stating that every ruling Rabbi Elazar taught was especially dear to Yosef the Babylonian, until they began discussing one *halakha* that he did not immediately accept, as described in the continuation of the story.

In contrast to Rashi, who explains that *ad le'aḥat* means until [*ad*] one [*aḥat*], *Megillat Setarim* explains that the term means very much [*leḥada*], and therefore the Gemara is stating that Yosef the Babylonian was very dear to Rabbi Elazar. He also suggests, while noting that this is not the straightforward meaning, that *ad le'aḥat* means: To a soul, as the soul is called a unit [*yeḥida*].

LANGUAGE

Face lit up [*tzahavu panav*] – צהבו פניו: The root *tzadi, heh, beit* can have two contradictory meanings in rabbinic usage. It can mean, as it does here, to light up [*tzahov*] with joy. In contrast, it can have a negative meaning, as the Aramaic translation of the Prophets translates the phrase: "And her rival vexed her" (I Samuel 1:6), as: And her rival taunted [*metzahava*] her.

ורבי יהודה סבר: בהנך פליגי, להניח – דברי הכל פסול, מאי טעמא? גזירה מקצת דמו אטו כל דמו; וכל דמו פסולא דאורייתא,

And Rabbi Yehuda holds that the Rabbis and Rabbi Eliezer **disagree** only **in those** cases, where one's intention is to drink the blood or burn the meat of the offering. In those cases, the Rabbis deem the offering fit, since the improper intention involves making use of the item in an unusual manner. But if one's intention is **to leave** of its blood until the next day, **everyone agrees** that the offering is **unfit. What is the reason** for this? It is a rabbinic **decree** disqualifying the offering when **some of its blood** is left over until the next day **due to** the concern that a priest may intend to leave over **all of its blood, and** if one's intention is to leave **all of its blood** until the next day, the offering is rendered **unfit by Torah law.**

דתניא, אמר להם רבי יהודה: אי אתם מודים לי שאם הניחו למחר שפסול? חישב להניחו למחר נמי פסול.

As it is taught in a *baraita*: **Rabbi Yehuda said to** the Rabbis: **Do you not concede to me that if he left** the blood **until the next day** without presenting it, **that** the offering is **unfit?** Therefore, **if he intended to leave** the blood **until the next day,** it is **also unfit.**

ואתא רבי אלעזר למימר: אף בזו רבי אליעזר פוסל וחכמים מכשירין.

And Rabbi Elazar comes to say that **even in this** case **Rabbi Eliezer deems** the offering **unfit and the Rabbis deem** it **fit,** as there is no distinction between a case where one intended to drink of the blood on the next day and where one intended to merely leave the blood until the next day.

וסבר רבי יהודה: להניח מדמו למחר דברי הכל פסול? והתניא, אמר רבי: כשהלכתי למצות מדותי אצל רבי אלעזר בן שמוע, ואמרי לה: למצות מדותיו של רבי אלעזר בן שמוע, מצאתי יוסף הבבלי יושב לפניו, והיה חביב לו ביותר עד לאחת, אמר לו: רבי, השוחט את הזבח להניח מדמו למחר, מהו?

The Gemara asks: **And** does **Rabbi Yehuda** in fact **hold** that if one's intention is **to leave** some **of the blood until the next day, everyone agrees** that the offering is **unfit? But isn't it taught** in a *baraita*: **Rabbi** Yehuda HaNasi **said: When I went to Rabbi Elazar ben Shammua**[P] **to clarify my knowledge, and some say** that Rabbi Yehuda HaNasi said: When I went **to clarify the knowledge of,** i.e., study under, **Rabbi Elazar ben Shammua, I found Yosef the Babylonian**[P] **sitting before** Rabbi Elazar ben Shammua. **And** every ruling that Rabbi Elazar ben Shammua taught **was especially dear to him, until** they began discussing **one**[N] *halakha*, when Yosef the Babylonian **said to him: My teacher,** with regard to **one who slaughters the offering** with the intention **to leave** some **of its blood for the next day, what is** the *halakha*?

אמר לו: כשר; ערבית – אמר לו: כשר; שחרית – אמר לו: כשר; צהרים – אמר לו: כשר; מנחה – אמר לו: כשר, אלא שרבי אליעזר פוסל. צהבו פניו של יוסף הבבלי.

Rabbi Elazar ben Shammua **said to him:** The offering is **fit.** Yosef the Babylonian repeated this question that **evening,** and Rabbi Elazar ben Shammua **said to him** that the offering is **fit.** He asked again the following **morning,** and Rabbi Elazar ben Shammua **said to him** that the offering is **fit.** Once again, he asked this question at **noon,** and Rabbi Elazar ben Shammua **said to him** that the offering is **fit.** When he asked the question a further time that late **afternoon,** Rabbi Elazar ben Shammua **said to him:** I hold that the offering is **fit, but Rabbi Eliezer deems** it **unfit. Yosef the Babylonian's face lit up [*tzahavu panav*]**[L] with joy.

PERSONALITIES

Rabbi Elazar ben Shammua – רבי אלעזר בן שמוע: Rabbi Elazar ben Shammua was a *tanna* in the generation prior to the redaction of the Mishna. He was a priest and was among the greatest of Rabbi Akiva's students. Rabbi Elazar ben Shammua was among the leaders of the Jewish people in the years of persecution in the wake of the failure of the bar Kokheva rebellion. Despite the dire situation, many students studied with him. One of his primary students was Rabbi Yehuda HaNasi, the redactor of the Mishna. Not many of Rabbi Elazar ben Shammua's statements are cited in the Mishna, but he was held in high esteem by the Sages of the following generations. Rav, an *amora*, referred to him as the happiest of the Sages, and Rabbi Yoḥanan said of him: The hearts of the early Sages were like the Entrance Hall to the Sanctuary. In the Mishna and in *baraitot*, he is called simply Rabbi Elazar.

Rabbi Elazar ben Shammua lived a long life, and according to one tradition he was 105 years old when he was executed. He is listed among the ten martyrs executed by the Romans.

Yosef the Babylonian – יוסף הבבלי: Yosef the Babylonian was a *tanna* in the generation before Rabbi Yehuda HaNasi. As his name suggests, Yosef the Babylonian was a native of Babylonia, specifically from the Jewish settlement and great learning center of Huzal. Apparently his father's name was Yehuda, and he was therefore also called Gur Arye, lion cub (see Genesis 49:9). Upon arriving in Eretz Yisrael, he studied with several of Rabbi Akiva's students and became adept at describing the various philosophies and teaching techniques of different Sages. According to the Jerusalem Talmud, he was also called Rabbi Yosef Katnuta, and he is praised in the Mishna for his pious character. Halakhic and aggadic statements in his name are recorded in the Babylonian Talmud.

אָמַר לוֹ: יוֹסֵף, כִּמְדוּמֶּה אֲנִי שֶׁלֹּא כִּיוַּונְנוּ שְׁמוּעָתֵינוּ עַד עַתָּה! אָמַר לוֹ: רַבִּי, הֵן! אֶלָּא שֶׁרַבִּי יְהוּדָה פָּסוּל שָׁנָה לִי, וְחָזַרְתִּי עַל כָּל תַּלְמִידָיו וּבִקַּשְׁתִּי לִי חָבֵר וְלֹא מָצָאתִי, עַכְשָׁיו שֶׁשָּׁנִיתָ לִי פָּסוּל הֶחֱזַרְתָּ לִי אֲבֵידָתִי.

Rabbi Elazar ben Shammua **said to him: Yosef, it seems to me that our,** i.e., my, ***halakhot* were not accurate until now,** when I said that the offering is fit. Yosef the Babylonian **said to him: My teacher, yes,** I agree that the offering is fit, as you said. **But** my reluctance to accept your statement was due to the fact **that Rabbi Yehuda taught me** that the offering is **unfit, and I went around to all of** Rabbi Yehuda's **disciples, seeking another** disciple who had also heard this from him, **but I could not find** one, and thought that I must have been mistaken. **Now that you have taught me** that Rabbi Eliezer deems it **unfit, you have returned to me that which I had lost.**

זָלְגוּ עֵינָיו דְּמָעוֹת שֶׁל רַבִּי אֶלְעָזָר בֶּן שַׁמּוּעַ, אָמַר: אַשְׁרֵיכֶם תַּלְמִידֵי חֲכָמִים שֶׁדִּבְרֵי תוֹרָה חֲבִיבִין עֲלֵיכֶם בְּיוֹתֵר! קָרָא עָלָיו הַמִּקְרָא הַזֶּה: "מָה אָהַבְתִּי תוֹרָתֶךָ כָּל הַיּוֹם הִיא שִׂיחָתִי" וגו', הָא מִפְּנֵי שֶׁרַבִּי יְהוּדָה בְּנוֹ שֶׁל רַבִּי אֶלְעַאי וְרַבִּי אֶלְעַאי תַּלְמִידוֹ שֶׁל רַבִּי אֱלִיעֶזֶר, לְפִיכָךְ שָׁנָה לְךָ מִשְׁנַת רַבִּי אֱלִיעֶזֶר.

The *baraita* continues: Upon hearing this, **Rabbi Elazar ben Shammua's eyes streamed with tears,** and **he said: Happy are you, Torah scholars, for whom matters of Torah are exceedingly dear.** Rabbi Elazar ben Shammua **recited this verse about** Yosef the Babylonian: **"O how I love Your Torah; it is my meditation all the day"** (Psalms 119:97). He continued: **Because Rabbi Yehuda** is **the son of Rabbi Elai, and Rabbi Elai** is **the student of Rabbi Eliezer, therefore** Rabbi Yehuda **taught you the mishna of Rabbi Eliezer** that the offering is unfit.

וְאִי סָלְקָא דַּעְתָּךְ דִּבְרֵי הַכֹּל פָּסוּל אַתְנְיֵיהּ, מַאי "הֶחֱזַרְתָּ לִי אֲבֵידָתִי"? אִיהוּ פְּלוּגְתָּא קָאָמַר לֵיהּ!

The Gemara explains its objection: **And if it enters your mind** that Rabbi Yehuda **taught** Yosef the Babylonian that **all agree** that the offering is **unfit, what** did Yosef the Babylonian mean when he said to Rabbi Elazar ben Shammua: **You have returned to me that which I had lost?** Rabbi Elazar ben Shammua **had said to him** only that whether the offering is rendered unfit is subject to **a dispute,** and Yosef the Babylonian would have been taught that all agree that it is unfit.

אֶלָּא מַאי? כָּשֵׁר, וְרַבִּי אֱלִיעֶזֶר (פָּסוּל) פּוֹסֵל אַתְנְיֵיהּ? אִי הָכִי, מַאי "הָא מִפְּנֵי" פְּלוּגְתָּא? אֲנַן נַמִי פְּלוּגְתָּא קָא מַתְנֵינַן!

Rather, what is it that Rabbi Yehuda taught Yosef the Babylonian? Did he **teach him** that the Rabbis deem the offering **fit and Rabbi Eliezer deems** it **unfit? If that is so, what** did Rabbi Elazar ben Shammua mean when he said **that** it was only **because** Rabbi Yehuda was the son of Rabbi Elai, who was the student of Rabbi Eliezer, that Rabbi Yehuda taught this **dispute?** According to Rabbi Elazar ben Shammua, **we too teach** this **dispute.** The fact that Rabbi Yehuda taught both opinions in a dispute does not require justification.

אֶלָּא, לְעוֹלָם דִּבְרֵי הַכֹּל פָּסוּל אַתְנְיֵיהּ, וּמַאי "הֶחֱזַרְתָּ לִי אֲבֵידָתִי" – דַּהֲדַר לֵיהּ מִיהָא שׁוּם פְּסָלוּת בָּעוֹלָם.

Rather, it must be that **actually,** Rabbi Yehuda **taught** Yosef the Babylonian that **all agree** that the offering is **unfit; and what** did Yosef the Babylonian mean when he said: **You have returned to me that which I had lost?** He meant **that** Rabbi Elazar ben Shammua **had in any event returned to him** that there is **some** opinion **in the world** concerning the **unfitness** of the offering if one's intention was to leave over the blood until the next day. His answer reassured Yosef the Babylonian that there is in fact such an opinion.

מתני' לֹא יָצַק, לֹא בָּלַל, וְלֹא פָּתַת, וְלֹא מָלַח, וְלֹא הֵנִיף, לֹא הִגִּישׁ, אוֹ שֶׁפְּתָתָן פִּתִּים מְרוּבּוֹת וְלֹא מְשָׁחָן – כְּשֵׁירָה.

MISHNA If one **did not pour** the oil[N] onto the meal offering, or **did not mix**[H] the oil into the meal offering, **or did not break** the loaves into pieces,[N] **or did not** add **salt, or did not wave** the *omer* meal offering or the meal offering of a *sota*, or **did not bring** the meal offering to the altar, **or** if it happened **that** the priest **broke** the meal offerings that require breaking into **greater pieces** than appropriate, **or did not smear** oil on the wafers requiring this (see Leviticus 2:4), in all these cases the meal offering is **fit.**

NOTES

If one did not pour oil – לֹא יָצַק: Most meal offerings require the addition of oil. As explained in a subsequent mishna (74b), meal offerings that are prepared in a vessel, as opposed to oven-baked meal offerings, require three applications of oil. Oil is added to the vessel before flour is added, then oil is poured upon the flour and mixed together with the flour. Afterward, in the case of shallow-pan meal offerings and deep-pan meal offerings, after kneading with water and crumbling it, the priest pours the remainder of the oil on the meal offering. After this final addition, he brings the meal offering to the altar, separates a handful, and burns that handful on the altar. Rashi comments that when the mishna states that the offering is fit even if the oil was not poured on the offering, it is referring to a case where not all three applications of oil were performed, as all of the requisite amount of oil was poured on the offering at an earlier stage. But if some of the requisite amount of oil was never poured on the offering, the meal offering is unfit.

Did not break the loaves into pieces – לֹא פָּתַת: The mishna is referring to meal offerings that are baked after being kneaded, i.e., the shallow-pan meal offering, the deep-pan meal offering, and oven-baked meal offerings of loaves and wafers. After they were baked, each loaf was broken into two equal pieces, and each piece was broken into another set of two equal pieces, so that each piece was the measure of an olive-bulk. The pieces were then returned to the vessel, and the handful was taken. Some understand the mishna to be stating that even if the meal offering was never broken up, it is fit (*Tosefot Yom Tov* and *Tiferet Yisrael*, explaining the Rambam). By contrast, Rashi explains based on a subsequent mishna (75b) that the case here is one where only an amount sufficient for taking a handful was broken, but if the entire offering remained unbroken, the offering is unfit (*Ḥok Natan*; *Sefat Emet*).

HALAKHA

Did not mix, etc. – לֹא בָּלַל וכו': If one did not mix the oil into the meal offering, break the loaves into pieces, bring the offering to the altar, or wave the meal offerings that are to be waved, in all of these cases the meal offering is considered fit, as these actions are required *ab initio*, but their absence does not disqualify the offering. If one did not pour oil onto the meal offering, it is unfit (Rambam *Sefer Avoda*, *Hilkhot Ma'aseh HaKorbanot* 13:11 and *Hilkhot Pesulei HaMukdashin* 11:7).

HALAKHA

A priest did not pour oil but a non-priest did – לֹא יָצַק כֹּהֵן אֶלָּא זָר: If the one who poured oil onto a meal offering was unfit for performing the sacrificial rites, e.g., a non-priest, the meal offering is fit. This is also the *halakha* with regard to mixing the oil, breaking the loaves, or adding salt, as only from the stage of removal of a handful does the service require priests alone (Rambam *Sefer Avoda, Hilkhot Pesulei HaMukdashin* 11:7, and see *Hilkhot Biat HaMikdash* 9:5).

גמ׳ מַאי לֹא יָצַק? אִילֵימָא לֹא יָצַק כְּלָל – עִיכּוּבָא כְּתַב בַּהּ! אֶלָּא, לֹא יָצַק כֹּהֵן אֶלָּא זָר; אִי הָכִי, לֹא בָּלַל נַמִי – לֹא בָּלַל כֹּהֵן אֶלָּא זָר, הָא לֹא בָּלַל כְּלָל – פְּסוּלָה.

GEMARA The Gemara asks: **What** does the mishna mean when it states that if one **did not pour** the oil onto the meal offering, the meal offering is fit? **If we say** that it means that **he did not pour** oil **at all,** that is difficult: Doesn't the verse **write with regard to** the pouring of the oil that doing so is **indispensable? Rather,** the mishna must be referring to a case where **a priest did not pour** the oil onto the meal offering, **but a non-priest** did[H] pour it. The Gemara notes: **If so,** that the first clause of the mishna is understood in this manner, then the next *halakha* in the mishna: If one **did not mix** the oil into the meal offering, should **also** be understood as referring to a case where **a priest did not mix** the oil into the meal offering, **but a non-priest** did mix it, so it is fit. **This** would indicate that if one **did not mix** the oil into the meal offering **at all,** the meal offering is **unfit.**

Perek **III**
Daf **18** Amud **b**

HALAKHA

Sixty tenths of flour can be mixed with a *log* of oil, etc. – שִׁשִּׁים נִבְלָלִין וכו׳: One may not bring a meal offering of more than sixty tenths of flour in one vessel. If one does bring a larger amount, one must place the extraneous part in another vessel, since more than sixty tenths of flour cannot be mixed properly with the oil. This is the *halakha* despite the fact that mixing is not indispensable, as the meal offering must be fit for mixing, in accordance with the statement of Rabbi Zeira (Rambam *Sefer Avoda, Hilkhot Ma'aseh HaKorbanot* 17:6).

וְהָתְנַן: שִׁשִּׁים נִבְלָלִין, שִׁשִּׁים וְאֶחָד אֵין נִבְלָלִין; וְהָוֵינַן בָּהּ: כִּי אֵינָם נִבְלָלִין מַאי הָוֵי? וְהָתְנַן: לֹא בָּלַל – כְּשֵׁרָה!

The Gemara asks: **But didn't we learn** in a mishna (103b): One who volunteers to bring a meal offering of sixty-one tenths of an ephah of flour must bring a meal offering of sixty tenths of an ephah in one vessel and a meal offering of a tenth of an ephah in a second vessel, because **sixty** tenths of an ephah of flour **can be** properly **mixed** with a *log* of oil[H] but **sixty-one** tenths **cannot be** properly **mixed** with the oil. **And we discussed it** and asked: Even **if** sixty-one tenths of an ephah **do not mix** with one *log* of oil, **what of it? But didn't we learn** in the mishna here that although there is a mitzva to mix the oil into the meal offering, if **one did not mix** the oil into it, the meal offering is still **fit?**

וַאֲמַר רַבִּי זֵירָא: כׇּל הָרָאוּי לְבִילָּה – אֵין בִּילָּה מְעַכֶּבֶת בּוֹ, וְכׇל שֶׁאֵינוֹ רָאוּי לְבִילָּה – בִּילָּה מְעַכֶּבֶת בּוֹ!

And Rabbi Zeira said the following explanation: For **any** measure of flour **that is suitable for mixing** with oil in a meal offering, the lack of **mixing does not invalidate** the meal offering. Even though there is a mitzva to mix the oil and the flour *ab initio*, the meal offering is fit for sacrifice even if the oil and the flour are not mixed. **And** for **any** measure of flour **that is not suitable for mixing** with oil in a meal offering, the lack of **mixing invalidates** the meal offering. This discussion demonstrates that when the mishna here says that the oil was not mixed into the meal offering, it means that it was not mixed at all. Therefore, the mishna's statement that the meal offering is fit even if the oil was not poured should be understood as referring to a case where the oil was never poured, and not, as the Gemara inferred, as referring to a case where a non-priest poured it.

מִידֵּי אִירְיָא? הָא כִּדְאִיתָא וְהָא כִּדְאִיתָא, לֹא יָצַק – לֹא יָצַק כֹּהֵן אֶלָּא זָר, לֹא בָּלַל – לֹא בָּלַל כְּלָל.

The Gemara refutes this proof: **Are the cases comparable? This** case is **as it is, and that** case is **as it is.** When the mishna states: If one **did not pour** the oil onto the meal offering, it is referring to a case where **a priest did not pour** oil onto the meal offering **but a non-priest** did pour it. When it states: If one **did not mix** the oil into the meal offering, it means **he did not mix** the oil **at all.**

״אוֹ שֶׁפְּתָתָן פִּתִּים מְרוּבּוֹת – כְּשֵׁרָה״. הַשְׁתָּא לֹא פָּתַת כְּלָל כְּשֵׁרָה, פִּתִּין מְרוּבּוֹת מִיבַּעְיָא? מַאי ״פִּתִּין מְרוּבּוֹת״ – שֶׁרִיבָּה בִּפְתִיתִין.

§ The mishna teaches: **Or** if it happened **that** the priest **broke** the meal offerings that require breaking into **greater pieces** [*pittim merubbot*] than appropriate, the meal offering is **fit.** The Gemara asks: **Now** that it has already been stated in the mishna that if one **did not break** the loaves into pieces **at all** the meal offering is **fit, is** it **necessary** to state that if one broke the meal offering into **greater pieces** than appropriate the meal offering is fit? The Gemara answers: **What** does the expression ***pittin merubbot*** mean? It means **that he increased** [*ribba*] the amount of the meal offering's **pieces** by breaking the loaves into many pieces that were each smaller than an olive-bulk.

וְאִיבָּעֵית אֵימָא: לְעוֹלָם פִּתִּים מְרוּבּוֹת מַמָּשׁ, וּמַהוּ דְּתֵימָא: הָתָם הוּא דְּאִיכָּא תּוֹרַת חַלּוֹת עֲלֵיהֶן, אֲבָל הָכָא, דְּלָא תּוֹרַת חַלּוֹת אִיכָּא, וְלָא תּוֹרַת פְּתִיתִין אִיכָּא, קָא מַשְׁמַע לָן.

And if you wish, say instead that the mishna is **actually** referring **literally to large pieces** [*pittim merubbot*],[H] **and** it was necessary to teach this explicitly, **lest you say** that the meal offering is fit **there,** when the loaves are not broken, **since they have the status of loaves, but here, when** the loaves are broken into excessively large pieces and **no** longer **have the status of loaves,** as they have been broken up, **but** still **do not have the status of pieces,** as they are not the correct size, the offering is not fit. Therefore, it is necessary for the mishna to **teach us** this *halakha* explicitly.

לֵימָא, מַתְנִיתִין דְּלָא כְּרַבִּי שִׁמְעוֹן; דְּתַנְיָא, רַבִּי שִׁמְעוֹן אוֹמֵר: כׇּל כֹּהֵן שֶׁאֵינוֹ מוֹדֶה בַּעֲבוֹדָה – אֵין לוֹ חֵלֶק בַּכְּהוּנָּה, שֶׁנֶּאֱמַר: ״הַמַּקְרִיב אֶת דַּם הַשְּׁלָמִים וְאֶת הַחֵלֶב מִבְּנֵי אַהֲרֹן לוֹ תִהְיֶה שׁוֹק הַיָּמִין לְמָנָה״, מוֹדֶה בַּעֲבוֹדָה – יֵשׁ לוֹ חֵלֶק בַּכְּהוּנָּה, שֶׁאֵינוֹ מוֹדֶה בַּעֲבוֹדָה – אֵין לוֹ חֵלֶק בַּכְּהוּנָּה.

§ Based on the Gemara's earlier inference that when the mishna states that the meal offering is valid even if the priest did not pour the oil it is referring to a case where a non-priest did perform this action, the Gemara suggests: **Let us say that the mishna is not in accordance with** the opinion of **Rabbi Shimon. As it is taught** in a *baraita* that **Rabbi Shimon says: Any priest who does not admit**[H] **to** the validity **of the** sacrificial **rites**[N] **has no portion in** the gifts of **the priesthood. As it is stated: "He among the sons of Aaron, that offers the blood of the peace offerings, and the fat, shall have the right thigh for a portion"** (Leviticus 7:33). This teaches that one who **admits to** the validity of **the** sacrificial **rites** and accepts responsibility for them **has a portion in the priestly** gifts, but one **who does not admit to** the validity of **the** sacrificial **rites does not have a portion in the priestly** gifts.

וְאֵין לִי אֶלָּא זוֹ בִּלְבָד, מִנַּיִן לְרַבּוֹת חֲמֵשׁ עֶשְׂרֵה עֲבוֹדוֹת.

The *baraita* continues: **And I have** derived **only** that a priest does not have a share in the priestly gifts if he does not admit to the validity of **these** rites of the presenting of the blood or the burning of the fats **alone,** which are the sacrificial rites of a slaughtered offering, as those rites are enumerated in the verse. **From where** is it derived that this *halakha* also **includes** one who does not admit to the validity of the **fifteen** sacrificial **rites** performed by the priests?

הַיְּצִיקוֹת, וְהַבְּלִילוֹת, וְהַפְּתִיתוֹת, וְהַמְּלִיחוֹת, וְהַתְּנוּפוֹת, וְהַהַגָּשׁוֹת, וְהַקְּמִיצוֹת, וְהַקְטָרוֹת, וְהַמְּלִיקוֹת, וְהַקַּבָּלוֹת, וְהַזָּאוֹת, וְהַשְׁקָאַת סוֹטָה, וַעֲרִיפַת עֶגְלָה, וְטׇהֳרַת מְצוֹרָע, וּנְשִׂיאוּת כַּפַּיִם בֵּין מִבִּפְנִים בֵּין מִבַּחוּץ, מִנַּיִן?

The *baraita* clarifies: These are the rites of a meal offering, i.e., **the pouring** of oil, **the mixing, the breaking, the salting, the waving, the bringing** of the offering to the altar, **the removal of the handful, and the burning** of the handful on the altar. **And** it includes other rites as well: **The pinching** of the nape of the neck of a bird offering, **and the receiving** of the blood in a vessel, **and the sprinkling** of the blood, **and the giving of water to a woman suspected by her husband of having been unfaithful** [*sota*], **and the** ritual of **breaking a heifer's neck, and the purification of a leper, and lifting of the hands** for the Priestly Benediction, **whether inside or outside** the Temple. **From where** is it derived that this *halakha* also includes one who does not admit to the validity of these rites?

תַּלְמוּד לוֹמַר: ״מִבְּנֵי אַהֲרֹן״, עֲבוֹדָה הַמְּסוּרָה לִבְנֵי אַהֲרֹן, כׇּל כֹּהֵן שֶׁאֵינוֹ מוֹדֶה בָּהּ – אֵין לוֹ חֵלֶק בַּכְּהוּנָּה!

The *baraita* continues: **The verse states: "Among the sons of Aaron,"** teaching that with regard to any sacrificial **rite that is entrusted to the sons of Aaron, any priest who does not admit to its** validity **does not have a portion in the priestly** gifts. Since the pouring of the oil is included in the list of sacrificial rites entrusted to the priests, according to Rabbi Shimon the offering should not be fit if this service was performed by a non-priest.

אֲמַר רַב נַחְמָן, לָא קַשְׁיָא: כָּאן בְּמִנְחַת כֹּהֲנִים, כָּאן בְּמִנְחַת יִשְׂרָאֵל; מִנְחַת יִשְׂרָאֵל דְּבַת קְמִיצָה הִיא – מִקְּמִיצָה וָאֵילָךְ מִצְוַת כְּהוּנָּה, לִימֵּד עַל יְצִיקָה וּבְלִילָה שֶׁכְּשֵׁירָה בְּזָר; מִנְחַת כֹּהֲנִים דְּלָאו בַּת קְמִיצָה הִיא – מֵעִיקָּרָא בָּעֲיָא כְּהוּנָּה.

Rav Naḥman said: This is **not difficult. There,** in the *baraita*, Rabbi Shimon is referring to **the meal offering of priests,** whereas **here,** in the mishna, the context is **a meal offering of an Israelite.** In the case of a **meal offering of an Israelite, which is** one that **requires the removal of a handful** to be burned on the altar, a verse teaches that **from** the stage of **the removal of the handful onward,** the rites performed with the meal offering are solely **the mitzva of** the members of the **priesthood.** Therefore, this verse also **teaches that** the **pouring** of the oil **and** the **mixing,** rites performed before the removal of the handful, **are valid** even if they are performed **by a non-priest.** By contrast, **the meal offering of priests, which is** one that **does not require the removal of a handful,** as the entire meal offering is burned on the altar, **requires** that **from the outset** the rites must be performed by a member of the **priesthood;** otherwise it is unfit.

HALAKHA

Large pieces – פִּתִּים מְרוּבּוֹת: In the case of all four baked meal offerings, after they are baked the loaves should be broken in half, and each half should then be broken into two pieces and separated. Each piece should be the measure of an olive-bulk, but if the loaves are broken into smaller or larger pieces, the meal offering is fit. This is in accordance with both of the Gemara's explanations of the mishna (Rambam *Sefer Avoda, Hilkhot Ma'aseh HaKorbanot* 13:10).

Any priest who does not admit, etc. – כׇּל כֹּהֵן שֶׁאֵינוֹ מוֹדֶה וכו׳: There are twenty-four gifts that were designated for the priests, as a covenant with Aaron, all of which are listed explicitly in the Torah. Any priest who does not admit to the validity of the rites has no share in the priesthood and receives no share in the priestly gifts (Rambam *Sefer Zera'im, Hilkhot Bikkurim* 1:1).

NOTES

Any priest who does not admit to the rites – כׇּל כֹּהֵן שֶׁאֵינוֹ מוֹדֶה בַּעֲבוֹדָה: This refers to a priest who believes that these mitzvot are meaningless and invented by Moses, rather than commanded by God (Rashi on *Ḥullin* 133a). Others disagree, explaining that in the case of a true heretic there is no need to state that he has no share in the priestly gifts; rather, it refers to a priest who makes light of the sacrificial rites, saying that they are not obligatory and indispensable (Ritva). Alternatively, there are those who explain that this priest denies that the sacrificial rites are a true form of Divine worship, claiming that their purpose is only to reform idol worshippers (*Ḥatam Sofer*). Others suggest that this priest believes the sacrificial rites to be valid when performed by non-priests (*Mizbaḥ Kappara*).

HALAKHA

From the removal of the handful onward, etc. – **מִקְּמִיצָה וְאֵילָךְ וכו׳**: All of the sacrificial rites of the meal offering that precede the removal of the handful are valid when performed by a non-priest, from the grinding that takes place outside of the Temple courtyard to the baking that takes place inside of it. From the removal of the handful onward, the rites must be performed by a priest (Rambam *Sefer Avoda*, *Hilkhot Ma'aseh HaKorbanot* 12:23 and *Hilkhot Pesulei HaMukdashin* 11:7, and see *Hilkhot Biat HaMikdash* 9:5).

אֲמַר לֵיהּ רָבָא: מִכְּדִי מִנְחַת כֹּהֲנִים מֵהֵיכָא אִיתְרַבֵּי לִיצִיקָה? מִמִּנְחַת יִשְׂרָאֵל, מַה הָתָם כְּשֵׁירָה בְּזָר – אַף הָכָא נַמִי כְּשֵׁירָה בְּזָר!

Rava said to him: After all, in the case of **the meal offering of priests, from where** was it **included** that there is an obligation **to pour** the oil? It is derived **from the** *halakha* of **the meal offering of an Israelite,** where this *halakha* is stated explicitly. Therefore, **just as there** the rite is **valid** when performed **by a non-priest, so too here,** the rite is **also valid** when performed **by a non-priest.**

אִיכָּא דְּאָמְרִי: אֲמַר רַב נַחְמָן, לָא קַשְׁיָא: כָּאן בְּנִקְמָצוֹת, כָּאן בְּשֶׁאֵין נִקְמָצוֹת.

There are those **who say** the discussion took place as follows: **Rav Naḥman said:** This is **not difficult. Here,** when the mishna teaches that a meal offering is fit if the oil was poured by a non-priest, it is referring to meal offerings **from which a handful is removed,** whereas **there,** in the *baraita* that lists the pouring of the oil as one of the rites performed by the priests, it is referring to meal offerings **from which a handful is not removed.**

אֲמַר לֵיהּ רָבָא: מִכְּדִי שֶׁאֵין נִקְמָצוֹת מֵהֵיכָא אִיתְרַבֵּי לִיצִיקָה? מִנִּקְמָצוֹת; כְּנִקְמָצוֹת, מַה הָתָם כְּשֵׁירָה בְּזָר – אַף הָכָא נַמִי כְּשֵׁירָה בְּזָר! אֶלָּא מְחַוַּורְתָּא, מַתְנִיתִין דְּלָא כְּרַבִּי שִׁמְעוֹן.

Rava said to him: After all, in the case of meal offerings **from which a handful is not removed, from where was it included** that there is also an obligation **to pour** the oil? It is derived **from** meal offerings **from which a handful is removed,** where this *halakha* is stated explicitly. Therefore, the *halakha* with regard to meal offerings from which a handful is not removed **is like** the *halakha* with regard to those **from which a handful is removed; just as there,** the rite is **valid** when performed **by a non-priest, so too here,** the rite is **also valid** when performed **by a non-priest. Rather,** since Rava deflected Rav Naḥman's explanation of the opinion of Rabbi Shimon in the *baraita,* **it is clear** that **the mishna is not in accordance with** the opinion of **Rabbi Shimon.**

מַאי טַעְמָא דְּרַבָּנַן? אָמַר קְרָא: ״וְיָצַק עָלֶיהָ שֶׁמֶן וְנָתַן עָלֶיהָ לְבוֹנָה וֶהֱבִיאָהּ אֶל בְּנֵי אַהֲרֹן הַכֹּהֲנִים וְקָמַץ״, מִקְּמִיצָה וְאֵילָךְ מִצְוַת כְּהוּנָּה, לִימֵּד עַל יְצִיקָה וּבְלִילָה שֶׁכְּשֵׁירָה בְּזָר.

The Gemara asks: **What is the reasoning of the Rabbis,** who hold that the offering is fit even if the oil was poured by a non-priest? **The verse states: "And he shall pour oil upon it and put frankincense upon it. And he shall bring it to Aaron's sons, the priests; and he shall remove** his handful" (Leviticus 2:1–2). From here it is derived that **from the removal of the handful onward,**[H] the rites of the meal offering are solely **the mitzva** of the members **of the priesthood.** Therefore, this verse also **teaches** that the **pouring** of the oil **and** the **mixing,** rites performed before the removal of the handful, **are valid** even if they are performed **by a non-priest.**

וְרַבִּי שִׁמְעוֹן? ״בְּנֵי אַהֲרֹן

The Gemara asks: **And** what would **Rabbi Shimon** say in response? He would say that when it states: **"Aaron's sons,**

Perek **III**
Daf **19** Amud **a**

HALAKHA

Collection shall be only with the right hand… placing shall be only with the right hand – **שֶׁלֹּא תְּהֵא קַבָּלָה אֶלָּא בְּיָמִין...שֶׁלֹּא תְּהֵא נְתִינָה אֶלָּא בְּיָמִין**: The Temple rites must be performed with one's right hand. If one performed a rite with his left hand, that rite is not valid, but he is not flogged. This is in accordance with the opinion of the Rabbis, who disagree with Rabbi Shimon in a mishna on *Zevaḥim* 15b (Rambam *Sefer Avoda*, *Hilkhot Biat HaMikdash* 5:18).

הַכֹּהֲנִים״ – מִקְרָא נִדְרָשׁ לְפָנָיו וּלְאַחֲרָיו.

the priests," the **verse is interpreted** as referring **to** the matter that **precedes it and to** the matter that **succeeds it.** Before mentioning the priests, the verse states the *halakha* of pouring the oil on the meal offering, and after mentioning the priests, it states the *halakha* of the removal of the handful. Therefore, a priest is required for each of these rites.

וְסָבַר רַבִּי שִׁמְעוֹן מִקְרָא נִדְרָשׁ לְפָנָיו וּלְאַחֲרָיו? וְהָתַנְיָא: ״וְלָקַח הַכֹּהֵן מִדַּם הַחַטָּאת בְּאֶצְבָּעוֹ וְנָתַן עַל קַרְנֹת הַמִּזְבֵּחַ״, ״בְּאֶצְבָּעוֹ וְלָקַח״ – מְלַמֵּד שֶׁלֹּא תְּהֵא קַבָּלָה אֶלָּא בְּיָמִין, ״בְּאֶצְבָּעוֹ וְנָתַן״ – מְלַמֵּד שֶׁלֹּא תְּהֵא נְתִינָה אֶלָּא בְּיָמִין.

The Gemara questions this explanation: **And does Rabbi Shimon hold** that **a verse is interpreted** as referring **to** the matter that **precedes it and to** the matter that **succeeds it? But isn't it taught** in a *baraita*: The verse states: **"And the priest shall take of the blood of the sin offering with his finger and put it upon the corners of the altar"** (Leviticus 4:34). The term **"with his finger"** is interpreted as referring to the term **"and the priest shall take."** This **teaches that** the **collection** of the blood **shall be** performed **only with the right** hand, since the term "finger," when stated in the context of the sacrificial rites, always is referring to the finger of the right hand. The term **"with his finger"** is also interpreted as referring to the term **"and put it."** This **teaches that the placing** of the blood on the altar **shall be** performed **only with the right** hand.[H]

אָמַר רַבִּי שִׁמְעוֹן: וְכִי נֶאֱמַר יָד בְּקַבָּלָה? הוֹאִיל וְלֹא נֶאֱמַר יָד בְּקַבָּלָה, קִיבֵּל בִּשְׂמֹאל – כָּשֵׁר;

The *baraita* continues: **Rabbi Shimon said: But is** the term **hand stated with regard to** the **collection** of the blood? **Since** the term **hand is not stated with regard to** the **collection** of the blood, only with regard to the placement of the blood, then even if the priest **collected** the blood **with** his **left** hand, the offering is **fit.**

וְאָמַר אַבַּיֵי: בְּמִקְרָא נִדְרָשׁ לְפָנָיו וּלְאַחֲרָיו קָא מִיפַּלְגִי, וְרַבִּי שִׁמְעוֹן סָבַר: לְאַחֲרָיו נִדְרָשׁ וּלְפָנָיו אֵין נִדְרָשׁ!

And Abaye said: Rabbi Shimon and the Rabbis **disagree with regard to** whether **a verse is interpreted** as referring **to** the matter that **precedes it and to** the matter that **succeeds it.** The Rabbis hold that the term "with his finger" is referring to both to the term "and the priest shall take" that precedes it, and the term "and put it" that succeeds it. **And Rabbi Shimon holds** that a verse **is interpreted** as referring **to** the matter that **succeeds it, but is not interpreted** as referring **to** the matter that **precedes it.** In that case, Rabbi Shimon's opinion that the pouring of oil must be performed by a priest can no longer be ascribed to the opinion that the phrase "Aaron's sons, the priests" should be interpreted as referring to the description of pouring the oil that precedes it.

אֶלָּא הַיְינוּ טַעְמָא דְּרַבִּי שִׁמְעוֹן: ״וֶהֱבִיאָהּ״ – וָי״ו מוֹסִיף עַל עִנְיָן רִאשׁוֹן.

Rather, this is the reasoning of Rabbi Shimon: The verse states: "And he shall pour oil upon it and put frankincense upon it. **And he shall bring it** to Aaron's sons, the priests" (Leviticus 2:1–2). He therefore employs the principle that the conjunction "and," represented by the letter ***vav*****, adds to the previous matter,** demonstrating that the rite of the pouring of the oil is to be performed by Aaron's sons, the priests.

וְסָבַר רַבִּי שִׁמְעוֹן וָי״ו מוֹסִיף עַל עִנְיָן רִאשׁוֹן? אֶלָּא מֵעַתָּה, דִּכְתִיב: ״וְשָׁחַט אֶת בֶּן הַבָּקָר... וְהִקְרִיבוּ בְּנֵי אַהֲרֹן הַכֹּהֲנִים אֶת הַדָּם וְזָרְקוּ אֶת הַדָּם״ – מִקַּבָּלָה וָאֵילָךְ מִצְוַת כְּהוּנָּה, מְלַמֵּד עַל שְׁחִיטָה שֶׁכְּשֵׁירָה בְּזָר; אִי לְרַבִּי שִׁמְעוֹן וָי״ו מוֹסִיף עַל עִנְיָן רִאשׁוֹן, שְׁחִיטָה הָכִי נַמִי בְּזָר תְּהֵא פְּסוּלָה!

The Gemara asks: **But does Rabbi Shimon hold** that the letter ***vav*** **adds to the previous matter? If that is so,** then this would pose a problem with regard to that **which is written: "And he shall slaughter the bull** before the Lord, **and Aaron's sons, the priests, shall sacrifice the blood and sprinkle the blood"** (Leviticus 1:5). The Sages infer from here that **from** the stage of the sacrificing of the blood, which begins with the **collection** of the blood, **and onward, it is the mitzva** exclusively of members **of the priesthood.** By inference, this **teaches that** the **slaughter** of the offering, which is performed earlier, is **valid** when performed **by a non-priest.**[H] **If according to** the opinion of **Rabbi Shimon** the letter ***vav*** **adds to the previous matter,** if the **slaughter** of the offering is performed **by a non-priest,** it **should also be unfit.**

שָׁאנֵי הָתָם, דְּאָמַר קְרָא: ״וְסָמַךְ...וְשָׁחַט״, מַה סְמִיכָה בְּזָרִים – אַף שְׁחִיטָה בְּזָרִים.

The Gemara answers: **There,** with regard to the slaughter of an offering, it **is different,** as earlier **the verse states: "And he shall place** his hands upon the head of the burnt offering; and it shall be accepted for him to make atonement for him. **And he shall slaughter** the bull before the Lord" (Leviticus 1:4–5), associating the placing of the hands on the head of an offering, which is performed by the owner of the animal, with the slaughter of the offering. Therefore, **just as the placing of the hands**[H] on the offering is performed **by non-priests, so too,** the **slaughter** of the offering is performed **by non-priests.**

אִי מַה סְמִיכָה בִּבְעָלִים, אַף שְׁחִיטָה בִּבְעָלִים! הַהוּא לָא מָצֵית אָמְרַתְּ, קַל וָחוֹמֶר: וּמַה זְרִיקָה דְּעִיקַּר כַּפָּרָה לָא בָּעְיָא בְּעָלִים, שְׁחִיטָה דְּלָאו עִיקַּר כַּפָּרָה לֹא כׇּל שֶׁכֵּן?

The Gemara asks: **If** there is a juxtaposition of the placing of the hands and the slaughter of the animals, why not also say that **just as the placing of the hands** on the offering is performed only **by the owner** of the animal, **so too,** the **slaughter** of the offering may be performed only **by the owner** of the animal? The Gemara answers: **You cannot say that,** due to an ***a fortiori*** inference from the *halakha* of the sprinkling of the blood: **And just as the sprinkling** of the blood, **which is the essential** rite that enables the one who brings the offering to achieve **atonement, does not require** the **owner** to perform it, as the priests perform this rite on his behalf, with regard to the **slaughter** of the offering, **which is not the essential** rite that enables the one who brings the offering to achieve **atonement,** is it **not all the more so** clear that it does not need to be performed by the owner?

HALAKHA

The slaughter of an offering is valid when performed by a non-priest – שְׁחִיטָה כְּשֵׁירָה בְּזָר: The slaughter of an offering, even an offering of the most sacred order, may be performed *ab initio* by those disqualified to perform the sacrificial rites (Rambam *Sefer Avoda, Hilkhot Pesulei HaMukdashin* 1:1–2).

The placing of the hands – סְמִיכָה: Anyone may perform the placing of the hands on his offering, except for a deaf-mute, an imbecile, a minor, a Canaanite slave, a woman, a blind person, or a gentile. The owner must perform the act himself, and not by means of an agent (Rambam *Sefer Avoda, Hilkhot Ma'aseh HaKorbanot* 3:8).

וְכִי תֵּימָא, אֵין דָּנִין אֶפְשָׁר מִשֶּׁאִי אֶפְשָׁר – גַּלֵּי רַחֲמָנָא בְּיוֹם הַכִּפּוּרִים: ״וְשָׁחַט אֶת פַּר הַחַטָּאת אֲשֶׁר לוֹ״ – מִכְּלָל דִּשְׁחִיטָה בְּעָלְמָא לָא בָּעֵינַן בְּעָלִים.

And if you would say that **one cannot derive** the **possible from** the **impossible,** and the owner may not sprinkle the blood as he is not a priest, but he may still be obligated to slaughter the animal, as this rite may be performed by a non-priest, **the Merciful One revealed** in the Torah **in** the context of the **Yom Kippur** service with regard to the High Priest: **"And he shall slaughter the bull of the sin offering which is for himself"** (Leviticus 16:11).[H] **By inference,** from the fact that the verse specifies that here the High Priest, who is the owner of the offering, must perform the slaughter, it is clear **that usually** the **slaughter does not require** the participation of the **owner.**

אָמַר רַב: כׇּל מָקוֹם שֶׁנֶּאֱמַר תּוֹרָה וְחוּקָּה – אֵינוֹ אֶלָּא לְעַכֵּב. קָא סָלְקָא דַּעְתִּין תַּרְתֵּי בָּעֲיָא, כְּדִכְתִיב: ״זֹאת חֻקַּת הַתּוֹרָה״;

§ Apropos the mishna's list of rites that are not indispensable for the meal offering, the Gemara explains that **Rav says:** With regard to **any** sacrificial rite **where** the term **law and statute are stated,** they are stated **only to** teach that the absence of the performance of that rite **invalidates** the offering. The Gemara comments: **It enters our mind** to say that the **two** terms are both **required** for this principle to be in effect, **as it is written** with regard to a red heifer: **"This is the statute of the law"** (Numbers 19:2).

(סִימָן: נת״ץ יקמ״ל).

Before continuing its discussion of this principle, the Gemara presents **a mnemonic**[B] for the questions that follow: ***Nun, tav, tzadi; yod, kuf, mem, lamed.*** They represent: Nazirite; thanks offering [*toda*]; leper [*metzora*]; Yom Kippur; offerings [*korbanot*]; meal offering [*minḥa*]; shewbread [*leḥem hapanim*].

וַהֲרֵי נָזִיר דְּלָא כְּתִיבָא בֵּיהּ אֶלָּא תּוֹרָה, וְאָמַר רַב: תְּנוּפָה בְּנָזִיר מְעַכְּבָא! שָׁאנֵי הָתָם, כֵּיוָן דִּכְתִיב: ״כֵּן יַעֲשֶׂה״ כְּמַאן דִּכְתִיבָא בְּהוּ חוּקָּה דָּמֵי.

The Gemara asks: **But** what of the offering of **a nazirite, about which it is written only "law,"** as the verse states: "This is the law of the nazirite who vows, and of his offering to the Lord for his naziriteship, beside that for which his means suffice; according to his vow which he vows, so he must do after the law of his naziriteship" (Numbers 6:21), **and** yet **Rav says** that the lack of **waving of** the offering by **a nazirite**[H] **invalidates** the offering? The Gemara answers: **There it is different, since it is written** in the continuation of the verse: **"So he must do,"** and therefore **it is considered as if** the term **statute were written with regard to it.**

הֲרֵי תּוֹדָה דְּלָא כְּתִיבָא בֵּיהּ אֶלָּא תּוֹרָה, וּתְנַן: אַרְבָּעָה שֶׁבַּתּוֹדָה מְעַכְּבִין זֶה אֶת זֶה! שָׁאנֵי תּוֹדָה דְּאִיתְקַשׁ לְנָזִיר, דִּכְתִיב: ״עַל זֶבַח תּוֹדַת שְׁלָמָיו״, וְאָמַר מָר: ״שְׁלָמָיו״ – לְרַבּוֹת שַׁלְמֵי נָזִיר.

The Gemara asks: **But** what of the **thanks offering, about which it is written only "law,"** as the verse states: "This is the law of the sacrifice of peace offerings" (Leviticus 7:11), **and we learn** in a mishna (27a) that with regard to the **four** types of loaves **that** accompany **the thanks offering,**[H] failure to bring **each** of them **prevents fulfillment of the mitzva with the others?** The Gemara answers: The **thanks offering is different, since it is juxtaposed** in the Torah **to** the offering of **a nazirite; as it is written** in a verse describing the thanks offering: **"With the sacrifice of his peace offerings for thanksgiving"** (Leviticus 7:13), instead of simply stating: The sacrifice of his thanks offering. **And the Master says:** The term **"his peace offerings"** serves **to include** the loaves of **the peace offering of** the **nazirite,** to teach that the same *halakhot* apply to both.

וַהֲרֵי מְצוֹרָע דְּלָא כְּתִיב בֵּיהּ אֶלָּא תּוֹרָה, וּתְנַן: אַרְבָּעָה מִינִין שֶׁבִּמְצוֹרָע מְעַכְּבִין זֶה אֶת זֶה! שָׁאנֵי הָתָם, כֵּיוָן דִּכְתִיב: ״זֹאת תִּהְיֶה תּוֹרַת הַמְּצֹרָע״ כְּמַאן דִּכְתִיב בֵּיהּ חוּקָּה דָּמֵי.

The Gemara asks: **But** what of the offering of **a leper, about which it is written only "law,"** as the verse states: "This shall be the law of the leper" (Numbers 14:2), **and we learn** in a mishna (27a) that with regard to the **four species that** are used **in** the purification process of **the leper,**[H] i.e., cedar, hyssop, scarlet wool, and birds, failure to bring **each** of them **prevents fulfillment of the mitzva with the others?** The Gemara answers: **There it is different, since it is written: "This shall be the law of the leper."** Due to the added emphasis of the term "shall be," it is **considered as if** the term **statute were written with regard to it.**

וַהֲרֵי יוֹם הַכִּפּוּרִים דְּלָא כְּתִיב בֵּיהּ אֶלָּא חוּקָּה, וּתְנַן: שְׁנֵי שְׂעִירֵי יוֹם הַכִּפּוּרִים מְעַכְּבִין זֶה אֶת זֶה! אֶלָּא אוֹ תּוֹרָה אוֹ חוּקָּה.

The Gemara asks: **But** what of **Yom Kippur, about which it is written only "statute,"** as the verse states: "And it shall be a statute for you forever" (Leviticus 16:29), **and we learn** in a mishna (27a) that with regard to **the two goats of Yom Kippur,** the absence of **each** goat **prevents fulfillment of the mitzva with the other? Rather,** it must be that Rav meant that wherever **either** the term **law or** the term **statute** is employed, this signifies that the rite is an indispensable requirement.

HALAKHA

And he shall slaughter the bull of the sin offering which is for himself – וְשָׁחַט אֶת פַּר הַחַטָּאת אֲשֶׁר לוֹ: With regard to the bull of the High Priest that is sacrificed on Yom Kippur, if it is slaughtered by a non-priest, the offering is fit, despite the fact that the verse states explicitly that it is to be slaughtered by Aaron. This is in accordance with the opinion of Rav and Rabbi Yoḥanan on *Yoma* 42a and 43b (Rambam *Sefer Avoda, Hilkhot Pesulei HaMukdashin* 1:2).

The waving of a nazirite – תְּנוּפָה בְּנָזִיר: If a nazirite does not perform the rite of waving this does not preclude him from partaking of wine or becoming impure due to a corpse. This is because the statement of Rav is presented in accordance with the opinion of Rabbi Eliezer in tractate *Nazir* (46a), whereas the *halakha* is actually in accordance with the opinion of the Rabbis who disagree with him there. According to the opinion of the Rabbis, once blood is sprinkled upon the nazirite from one of his offerings, it is permitted for him to partake of wine (Rambam *Sefer Hafla'a, Hilkhot Nezirut* 8:5, and see *Kesef Mishne* there).

The four types of loaves that accompany the thanks offering – אַרְבָּעָה שֶׁבַּתּוֹדָה: With regard to the four types of loaves that accompany the thanks offering, failure to bring any of the types prevents fulfillment of the mitzva with the others (Rambam *Sefer Avoda, Hilkhot Ma'aseh HaKorbanot* 9:24).

The four species that are used in the purification process of the leper – אַרְבָּעָה מִינִין שֶׁבִּמְצוֹרָע: With regard to the four species that are used in the purification process of the leper, failure to bring any of the species prevents fulfillment of the mitzva with the others (Rambam *Sefer Tahara, Hilkhot Tumat Tzara'at* 11:1).

BACKGROUND

Mnemonic – סִימָן: Because the Talmud was studied orally for many generations, mnemonic devices were necessary to remember the order in which a series of *halakhot* were taught.

וַהֲרֵי שְׁאָר קׇרְבָּנוֹת דִּכְתִיב בְּהוּ תּוֹרָה, וְלָא מְעַכְּבִי! תּוֹרָה בָּעֲיָא חוּקָּה, וְחוּקָּה לָא בָּעֲיָא תּוֹרָה.

The Gemara questions this understanding of Rav's statement: **But** what of **the rest of the offerings, as** the term **"law" is written with regard to them, and** yet failure to perform all of their different rites **does not invalidate** those offerings? The verse states: "This is the law of the burnt offering, of the meal offering, and of the sin offering, and of the guilt offering, and of the consecration offering, and of the sacrifice of peace offerings" (Leviticus 7:37). The Gemara answers: When the term **law** appears, it is still **necessary** for the term **statute** to appear, in order to teach that failure to perform the rites invalidates the offering. **But** when the term **statute** appears, it is **not necessary** for the term **law** to appear as well. The term statute is sufficient.

וְהָא תּוֹרָה וְחוּקָּה קָא אָמַר! הָכִי קָאָמַר: אַף עַל גַּב דִּכְתִיב תּוֹרָה, אִי כְּתִיבָא חוּקָּה – אִין, וְאִי לָא – לָא.

The Gemara questions this explanation: **But doesn't** Rav **say:** Wherever the terms **law and statute** appear? Apparently, both are necessary for his principle to apply. The Gemara answers: **This** is what Rav **is saying: Even** in a context **where** the term **law is written, if** the term **statute is written** as well, then **yes,** failure to perform the rites invalidates the offering; **but if** the term statute does **not** accompany the term law, then failure to perform the rites does **not** invalidate the offering.

וַהֲרֵי מִנְחָה דִּכְתִיב בָּהּ חוּקָּה, וְאָמַר רַב: כׇּל מָקוֹם שֶׁהֶחֱזִיר הַכָּתוּב בְּתוֹרַת מִנְחָה אֵינוֹ אֶלָּא לְעַכֵּב; הֶחֱזִיר – אִין, לֹא הֶחֱזִיר – לָא!

The Gemara questions this explanation: **But** what of the **meal offering, as** the term **"statute" is written with regard to it,** as the verse states: "Every male among the children of Aaron may eat of it, as a statute forever" (Leviticus 6:11), **and** yet **Rav says:** With regard to **every** sacrificial rite of **the law of the meal offering that the verse repeats,** as the details of the meal offering are discussed in Leviticus, chapter 2, and again in Leviticus, chapter 6, it is repeated **only to** teach that the failure to perform that rite **invalidates** the offering? Doesn't this demonstrate that where the verse **repeated** the command, then **yes,** failure to perform the rite invalidates the offering; but if the verse **did not repeat** it, then failure to perform the rite does **not** invalidate the offering, whether or not the term statute appears?

שָׁאנֵי הָתָם, דְּכִי כְּתִיבָא חוּקָּה – אַאֲכִילָה כְּתִיבָא.

The Gemara answers: **There it is different, as when** the term **statute is written, it is written with regard to the eating** of the meal offering rather than with regard to the sacrificial rites.

וַהֲרֵי לֶחֶם הַפָּנִים, דְּכִי כְּתִיבָא חוּקָּה אַאֲכִילָה כְּתִיבָא, וּתְנַן: שְׁנֵי סְדָרִים מְעַכְּבִין זֶה אֶת זֶה, שְׁנֵי בָזִיכִין מְעַכְּבִין זֶה אֶת זֶה, הַסְּדָרִין וְהַבָּזִיכִין מְעַכְּבִין זֶה אֶת זֶה!

The Gemara asks: **But** what of **the shewbread, where when** the term **statute is written, it is written with regard to the eating** of the shewbread, as the verse states: "And they shall eat it in a holy place, for it is most holy to him of the offerings of the Lord made by fire, a perpetual statute" (Leviticus 24:9), **and we learn** in the mishna (27a): With regard to **the two arrangements** of the shewbread, failure to place **each** of the arrangements **prevents fulfillment of the mitzva with the other.** With regard to the **two bowls** of frankincense that accompany the shewbread, failure to place **each** of the arrangements **prevents fulfillment of the mitzva with the other.** With regard to **the arrangements** of the shewbread **and the bowls** of frankincense, failure to bring **each** of them **prevents fulfillment of the mitzva with the other.**[H]

אֶלָּא, כׇּל הֵיכָא דִּכְתִיבָא אַאֲכִילָה – אַכּוּלָּא מִילְּתָא כְּתִיבָא;

Rather, it must be that **anywhere that** the term statute **is written with regard to eating, it is written with regard to the entire matter,** i.e., all the *halakhot* of the offering, and teaches that failure to perform the rites invalidates the offering.

שָׁאנֵי הָתָם, דְּאָמַר קְרָא: "מִגִּרְשָׂהּ וּמִשַּׁמְנָהּ",

The Gemara answers: **There,** with regard to the meal offering, it **is different,** and it is only the rites that are repeated that are indispensable, **as the verse states: "Of its groats, and of its oil"** (Leviticus 2:16), rather than simply: Of the groats and oil,

HALAKHA

With regard to the arrangements and the bowls, failure to bring each of them prevents fulfillment of the mitzva with the other – הַסְּדָרִין וְהַבָּזִיכִין מְעַכְּבִין זֶה אֶת זֶה: With regard to the two arrangements of the shewbread, failure to place each of the arrangements prevents fulfillment of the mitzva with the other. With regard to the two bowls of frankincense that accompany the shewbread, failure to place each of the bowls prevents fulfillment of the mitzva with the other. With regard to the arrangements of the shewbread and the bowls of frankincense, failure to bring each of them prevents fulfillment of the mitzva with the other. This is in accordance with the mishna on 27a (Rambam *Sefer Avoda, Hilkhot Temidin UMusafin* 5:3).

HALAKHA

Service vessels used for liquids sanctify only the liquids – כְּלֵי הַלַּח מְקַדְּשִׁין אֶת הַלַּח: Service vessels used for liquids do not sanctify dry substances placed in them, and service vessels used to measure dry substances do not sanctify liquids placed in them. This is stated with regard to the vessels for liquids and dry substances that were found in the Temple, in accordance with the mishna in tractate *Zevaḥim* (88a). Cups sanctify dry substances as well as liquids, in accordance with the statement of Shmuel (Rambam *Sefer Avoda, Hilkhot Pesulei HaMukdashin* 3:19).

גֶּרֶשׂ וְשֶׁמֶן מְעַכְּבִין, וְאֵין דָּבָר אַחֵר מְעַכֵּב.

teaching that the **groats and oil are indispensable, and nothing else is indispensable,** despite the fact that the term statute appears.

גּוּפָא, אָמַר רַב: כׇּל מָקוֹם שֶׁהֶחֱזִיר לְךָ הַכָּתוּב בַּתּוֹרָה מִנְחָה אֵינוֹ אֶלָּא לְעַכֵּב. וּשְׁמוּאֵל אָמַר: גֶּרֶשׂ וְשֶׁמֶן מְעַכְּבִין, וְאֵין דָּבָר אַחֵר מְעַכֵּב. וְלִשְׁמוּאֵל, אַף עַל גַּב דִּתְנָא בֵּיהּ קְרָא לָא מְעַכְּבָא לֵיהּ?!

§ The Gemara discusses **the** matter **itself: Rav says:** With regard to **every** sacrificial **rite of the meal offering that the verse in the Torah repeats,** it is repeated **only to** teach that the failure to perform that rite **invalidates** the offering. **And Shmuel says:** Only the **groats and oil are indispensable, and nothing else is indispensable.** The Gemara asks: **And according to Shmuel,** is it true that **even though** a rite of the meal offering is **repeated** in another **verse he does not deem it indispensable?**

אֶלָּא, כׇּל הֵיכָא דִּתְנָא בֵּיהּ קְרָא וַדַּאי מְעַכְּבָא, וְהָכָא בִּ״מְלֹא קוּמְצוֹ״ ״בְּקוּמְצוֹ״ קָא מִיפַּלְגִי. דְּתַנְיָא: ״מְלֹא קֻמְצוֹ״ ״בְּקֻמְצוֹ״ – שֶׁלֹּא יַעֲשֶׂה מִדָּה לַקּוֹמֶץ;

Rather, Shmuel must agree that **wherever the verse repeats** a rite it is **certainly** understood to be **indispensable; and here,** Rav and Shmuel **disagree with regard to** the expressions **"his handful"** (Leviticus 2:2) and **"with his hand"** (Leviticus 6:8). **As it is taught** in a *baraita*: The verse states: "And he shall remove **his handful,**" and elsewhere it states: "And he shall take up from it **with his hand.**" The change in terminology between the two verses teaches **that** the priest **should not** use a utensil to **measure an amount for the handful** of a meal offering, but should use his hand.

רַב סָבַר: הָא נַמִי תְּנָא בֵּיהּ קְרָא, דִּכְתִיב: ״וַיַּקְרֵב אֶת הַמִּנְחָה וַיְמַלֵּא כַפּוֹ מִמֶּנָּה״, וּשְׁמוּאֵל: דּוֹרוֹת מִשָּׁעָה לָא יָלְפִינַן.

Rav holds that **this** *halakha* of using one's hand and not a utensil is **also repeated** in another **verse, as it is written** in the context of Aaron's service on the eighth day of the consecration of the Tabernacle: **"And he presented the meal offering; and he filled his hand from it"** (Leviticus 9:17), demonstrating that the handful is removed by hand and not with a utensil. **And Shmuel** holds that **we do not derive** the *halakha* for all **generations from a temporary** situation. Therefore, using one's hand is not indispensable, as the general requirements of the rites of the meal offering cannot be derived from a verse referring to the meal offering that was sacrificed during the consecration of the Tabernacle.

וְלָא יָלֵיף שְׁמוּאֵל דּוֹרוֹת מִשָּׁעָה? וְהָתְנַן: כְּלֵי הַלַּח מְקַדְּשִׁין אֶת הַלַּח, וּמִדּוֹת יָבֵשׁ מְקַדְּשִׁין אֶת הַיָּבֵשׁ, וְאֵין כְּלֵי הַלַּח מְקַדְּשִׁין אֶת הַיָּבֵשׁ, וְלֹא מִדּוֹת יָבֵשׁ מְקַדְּשִׁין אֶת הַלַּח;

The Gemara asks: **And does Shmuel not derive** the *halakha* for all **generations from a temporary** situation? **But didn't we learn** in a mishna (*Zevaḥim* 88a): Service **vessels** used for **the liquids sanctify** only **the liquids**[H] placed in them, **and** service vessels used to **measure dry** substances **sanctify** only **the dry** substances that are placed in them. **But** service **vessels** used for **the liquids do not sanctify the dry** substances placed in them, **and** service vessels used to **measure dry** substances **do not sanctify the liquids** placed in them.

וְאָמַר שְׁמוּאֵל: לֹא שָׁנוּ אֶלָּא מִדּוֹת, אֲבָל מִזְרָקוֹת מְקַדְּשִׁין, דִּכְתִיב: ״שְׁנֵיהֶם מְלֵאִים סֹלֶת״!

And Shmuel says concerning this mishna: **They taught** that *halakha* **only** with regard to service vessels used to **measure** liquids, e.g., wine or oil. **But cups,** which are used for collecting the blood of offerings, **sanctify** dry substances placed in them as well, **as it is written** with regard to the offerings of the princes during the inauguration of the Tabernacle: "One silver cup of seventy shekels, after the shekel of the Sanctuary; **both of them full of fine flour** mingled with oil for a meal offering" (Numbers 7:13), indicating that the cups were also fashioned for use with flour, a dry substance. In this case, Shmuel does derive the general *halakha* from a temporary situation, in this case the offerings of the princes.

שָׁאנֵי הָתָם, דִּתְנָא בַּהּ קְרָא תְּרֵיסַר זִימְנִין.

The Gemara answers: **There,** with regard to the offering of the princes, it **is different, as the verse is repeated twelve times,** once with regard to each and every prince. Therefore, Shmuel derives a *halakha* for all generations from it. Nevertheless, generally speaking, the *halakha* for all generations cannot be derived from a temporary situation.

אָמְרוּ לֵיהּ רַב כָּהֲנָא וְרַב אַסִּי לְרַב: וַהֲרֵי הַגָּשָׁה דִּתְנָא בַּהּ קְרָא, וְלָא מְעַכְּבָא! מַאן תְּנָא בֵּיהּ? דִּכְתִיב: ״וְזֹאת תּוֹרַת הַמִּנְחָה הַקְרֵב אוֹתָהּ בְּנֵי אַהֲרֹן לִפְנֵי ה׳״!

The Gemara returns to discussing Rav's statement that a rite is deemed indispensable if it is repeated in the verses. **Rav Kahana and Rav Asi said to Rav: But** what of **bringing** the meal offering to the corner of the altar, **which is repeated** in **the verse,** as it is stated: "And he shall bring it to the altar" (Leviticus 2:8); **and** it is **not indispensable,** as stated in the mishna (18a)? The Gemara elaborates: **Where is it repeated? As it is written: "And this is the law of the meal offering: The sons of Aaron shall sacrifice it before the Lord,** in front of the altar" (Leviticus 6:7).

הַהוּא לִקְבּוֹעַ לָהּ מָקוֹם הוּא דְּאָתָא. דְּתַנְיָא: "לִפְנֵי ה'" – יָכוֹל בַּמַּעֲרָב? תַּלְמוּד לוֹמַר: "אֶל פְּנֵי הַמִּזְבֵּחַ";

The Gemara answers: **That** verse is not a repetition of the mitzva for the priest to bring the meal offering to the corner of the altar; rather, it **comes** only **to establish the place for** the meal offering and describe where it should be brought. **As it is taught** in a *baraita*: The verse states: "And this is the law of the meal offering. The sons of Aaron shall sacrifice it before the Lord, in front of the altar" (Leviticus 6:7). From the phrase: **"Before the Lord,"** one **might** have thought that the meal offering must be brought **on the western** side of the altar, which faces the Sanctuary and is therefore "before the Lord." Therefore, **the verse states: "In front of the altar,"** which is its southern side, where the priests ascend the ramp.

אִי אֶל פְּנֵי הַמִּזְבֵּחַ, יָכוֹל בַּדָּרוֹם? תַּלְמוּד לוֹמַר: "לִפְנֵי ה'"; הָא כֵּיצַד? מַגִּישָׁהּ בְּקֶרֶן דְּרוֹמִית מַעֲרָבִית כְּנֶגֶד חוּדָּהּ שֶׁל קֶרֶן וְדַיּוֹ.

The *baraita* continues: **If** the verse had merely stated: **In front of the altar,** one **might** have thought that the meal offering is brought only **on the southern** side of the altar, as just mentioned. Therefore, **the verse states: "Before the Lord,"** which indicates the western side. **How can these** texts be reconciled? The *baraita* answers: The priest **brings it** near **on the southwest corner** of the altar,[H] **opposite the edge of the corner** of the altar, **and** that will **suffice for him.**

רַבִּי אֱלִיעֶזֶר אוֹמֵר: יָכוֹל יַגִּישֶׁנָּה לְמַעֲרָבָהּ שֶׁל קֶרֶן אוֹ לִדְרוֹמָהּ שֶׁל קֶרֶן? אָמַרְתָּ: כׇּל מָקוֹם שֶׁאַתָּה מוֹצֵא שְׁתֵּי מִקְרָאוֹת, אֶחָד מְקַיֵּים עַצְמוֹ וּמְקַיֵּים חֲבֵירוֹ, וְאֶחָד מְקַיֵּים עַצְמוֹ וּמְבַטֵּל אֶת חֲבֵירוֹ – מַנִּיחִין אֶת שֶׁמְּקַיֵּים עַצְמוֹ וּמְבַטֵּל חֲבֵירוֹ, וְתוֹפְשִׂין אֶת שֶׁמְּקַיֵּים עַצְמוֹ וּמְקַיֵּים חֲבֵירוֹ;

The *baraita* continues: **Rabbi Eliezer says:** One **might** have thought that the verse presents the priest with the option that **he may bring it on the western side of** the **corner or on the southern side of** the **corner. You say** the following principle: Any time **you find two verses, one** of which **fulfills itself and fulfills the other, and one** of which **fulfills itself and negates the other, we set aside** the verse **that fulfills itself and negates the other, and we seize** the verse **that fulfills itself and fulfills the other.**

שֶׁכְּשֶׁאַתָּה אוֹמֵר "לִפְנֵי ה'" בַּמַּעֲרָב – בִּטַּלְתָּה "אֶל פְּנֵי הַמִּזְבֵּחַ" בַּדָּרוֹם, וּכְשֶׁאַתָּה אוֹמֵר "אֶל פְּנֵי הַמִּזְבֵּחַ" בַּדָּרוֹם – קִיַּימְתָּה "לִפְנֵי ה'".

He explains: **As, when you say** to bring the meal offering **"before the Lord,"** which indicates that it shall be brought **on the western** side, **you have nullified** the other part of the verse, which states to bring it **"in front of the altar,"** which is **on the southern** side. **But when you say** to bring the meal offering **"in front of the altar"** and offer it **on the southern** side, **you have** also **fulfilled** the other part of the verse, which states to bring it **"before the Lord."**

וְהֵיכָא קִיַּימְתָּה? אֲמַר רַב אַשִׁי: קָסָבַר הַאי תַּנָּא כּוּלֵּיהּ מִזְבֵּחַ בַּצָּפוֹן קָאֵי.

The Gemara asks: **But** if one brought the meal offering on the southern side, **where have you fulfilled:** "Before the Lord"? **Rav Ashi said: This *tanna*,** i.e., Rabbi Eliezer, **holds** that **the entire altar stood in the northern** part[B] of the Temple courtyard. The southern side of the altar was aligned with the midpoint of the Temple courtyard, opposite the Holy of Holies, directly before the Lord. In any event, it can be seen in this *baraita* that the purpose of the verse: "The sons of Aaron shall offer it before the Lord, in front of the altar" is to establish the precise location where the meal offering is brought, and it does not serve as a repetition.

מַתְקִיף לַהּ רַב הוּנָא: הֲרֵי מֶלַח דְּלָא תְּנָא בֵּיהּ קְרָא, וּמְעַכְּבָא בֵּיהּ! דְּתַנְיָא: "בְּרִית מֶלַח עוֹלָם הוּא" – שֶׁתְּהֵא

The Gemara cites another objection to Rav's statement that a rite of the meal offering is deemed indispensable if it is repeated in the verses. **Rav Huna objects to this: But** what of the placement of the **salt** on the handful of the meal offering before it is burned, **which is not repeated** in **the verse, and** yet it is still **indispensable in its** sacrifice? **As it is taught** in a *baraita*: The verse states: **"It is an everlasting covenant of salt"** (Numbers 18:19), teaching **that there will be**

BACKGROUND

The entire altar stood in the northern part – כּוּלֵּיהּ מִזְבֵּחַ בַּצָּפוֹן: This diagram shows the position of the altar if it were situated entirely in the north of the courtyard. If so, its southern edge would have been positioned directly in front of the entrance to the Sanctuary.

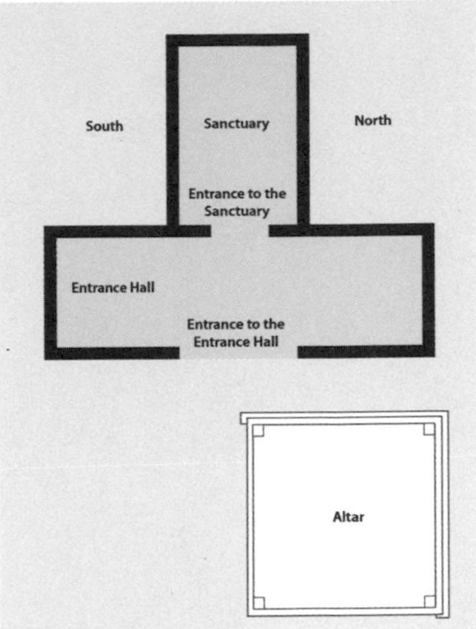

Altar situated entirely in the north

HALAKHA

The priest brings it near on the southwest corner of the altar – מַגִּישָׁהּ בְּקֶרֶן דְּרוֹמִית מַעֲרָבִית: All meal offerings that are burned on the altar must be brought near the western side of the altar, opposite the southwest edge of the corner of the altar. This is in accordance with the opinion of the first *tanna* (Rambam *Sefer Avoda, Hilkhot Ma'aseh HaKorbanot* 13:12).

בְּרִית אֲמוּרָה בְּמֶלַח, דִּבְרֵי רַבִּי יְהוּדָה. רַבִּי שִׁמְעוֹן אוֹמֵר: נֶאֱמַר כָּאן ״בְּרִית מֶלַח עוֹלָם הוּא״, וְנֶאֱמַר לְהַלָּן ״בְּרִית כְּהֻנַּת עוֹלָם״, כְּשֵׁם שֶׁאִי אֶפְשָׁר לַקָּרְבָּנוֹת בְּלֹא כְּהוּנָּה – כָּךְ אִי אֶפְשָׁר לַקָּרְבָּנוֹת בְּלֹא מֶלַח!

a covenant stated with regard to salt,[H] ensuring that the offerings should always be salted; this is **the statement of Rabbi Yehuda. Rabbi Shimon says: It is stated here: "It is an everlasting covenant of salt"** (Numbers 18:19), **and it is stated there,** with regard to the reward given to Pinehas: **"The covenant of an everlasting priesthood"** (Numbers 25:13). This teaches that **just as it is impossible for the offerings** to be sacrificed **without** the involvement of the **priesthood, so too, it is impossible for the offerings** to be sacrificed **without salt.** The *baraita* demonstrates that the rite of salting is an indispensable requirement, despite the fact that the rite is not repeated in the verses.

אֲמַר רַב יוֹסֵף: רַב כְּתַנָּא דִּידָן סְבִירָא לֵיהּ, דְּאָמַר: לֹא מָלַח – כָּשֵׁר. אֲמַר לֵיהּ אַבַּיֵי: אִי הָכִי, לֹא יָצַק נַמִּי – לֹא יָצַק כְּלָל? אֶלָּא, לֹא יָצַק כֹּהֵן אֶלָּא זָר; הָכָא נַמִּי – לֹא מָלַח כֹּהֵן אֶלָּא זָר!

Rav Yosef said: Rav, who holds that the only sacrificial rites that are indispensable are the ones repeated in the verses, **holds in accordance with the *tanna* of our** mishna, **who says:** If one **did not** add **salt,** the meal offering is still **fit.** According to this *tanna*, adding salt is not indispensable. **Abaye said to him: If that is so** and you understand the mishna to be referring to a case where no salt is added at all, then you should **also** understand the mishna's statement: If one **did not pour** the oil, as referring to a case where he **did not pour** oil **at all.** This cannot be, as the rite of pouring oil is repeated in the verses and is clearly indispensable. **Rather,** the mishna must be referring to a case where **a priest did not pour** oil onto the meal offering, **but a non-priest** did pour the oil. **Here too,** the *tanna* of the mishna means only that **a priest did not** add **salt, but a non-priest** did[H] add salt. If no salt is added, even this *tanna* holds that the meal offering is unfit.

אֲמַר לֵיהּ: וְכִי תַּעֲלֶה עַל דַּעְתְּךָ שֶׁזָּר קָרֵב לְגַבֵּי מִזְבֵּחַ?

Rav Yosef **said to** Abaye: **But could it enter your mind that a non-priest would approach** the **altar** to salt the handful of the meal offering? A non-priest may not enter the area near the altar. Since it is not conceivable that this would take place, it must be that when ruling that the meal offering is fit, the *tanna* of the mishna is referring to a case where the salt was never added.

וְאִי בָּעֵית אֵימָא: כֵּיוָן דִּכְתִיבָא בֵּיהּ בְּרִית, כְּמַאן דִּתְנָא בֵּיהּ קְרָא דָּמְיָא.

And if you wish, say instead that Rav holds that **since** with regard to the application of salt, the term **"covenant" is written about it, it is considered as though it were repeated in** another **verse,** as the term "covenant" teaches that it is an indispensable rite.

וְלָא תְּנָא בֵּיהּ קְרָא? וְהָכְתִיב: ״וְכָל קָרְבַּן מִנְחָתְךָ בַּמֶּלַח תִּמְלָח״! הַהוּא מִיבָּעֵי לֵיהּ לְכִדְתַנְיָא: אִילּוּ נֶאֱמַר קָרְבָּן בְּמֶלַח, שׁוֹמֵעַ אֲנִי אֲפִילּוּ עֵצִים וְדָם שֶׁנִּקְרְאוּ קָרְבָּן?

With regard to the question that was raised to challenge the statement of Rav, the Gemara asks: **And** is it correct that the application of salt **is not repeated in the verse? But isn't it written: "And every meal offering of yours you shall season with salt"** (Leviticus 2:13)? The Gemara answers: **That** verse does not function as a repetition, since it is **necessary for that which is taught** in a *baraita*: **Had** the verse **stated** only: And every **offering** you shall season **with salt,**[H] **I** would **derive** that this applies to even the **wood and** the **blood, which are** also **termed: An offering.**

HALAKHA

A covenant stated with regard to salt – בְּרִית אֲמוּרָה בְּמֶלַח: There is a positive mitzva to apply salt to all offerings before sacrificing them on the altar. One who sacrifices an offering that has not been salted is punished with lashes, although the offering is still fit. In the case of a meal offering, if the handful that is burned on the altar is not salted, the offering is unfit. This is in accordance with the opinion of Rabbi Yehuda that a covenant was made with regard to salt in the case of the meal offerings, rendering it indispensable, and in accordance with the Gemara's explanation (Mahari Kurkus; *Kesef Mishne*). Alternatively, this is the *halakha* because the Rambam rules in accordance with the opinion of Abaye that the mishna, which rules that the meal offering is fit even if salt was not applied, is referring to a case where the salt was applied by a non-priest (*Likkutei Halakhot*, citing Rambam's Commentary on the Mishna). Other early commentaries rule that in the case of the meal offering, salt is not indispensable (*Sefer Yere'im*), in accordance with the straightforward understanding of the mishna on 18b (Rambam *Sefer Avoda, Hilkhot Issurei Mizbe'aḥ* 5:12 and *Hilkhot Pesulei HaMukdashin* 11:16).

A priest did not add salt, but a non-priest did – לֹא מָלַח כֹּהֵן אֶלָּא זָר: Any offering that was salted by a non-priest is fit, in accordance with the mishna and the explanation of Abaye (Rambam *Sefer Avoda, Hilkhot Pesulei HaMukdashin* 11:7).

Every offering you shall season with salt, etc. – קָרְבָּן בְּמֶלַח וכו׳: Although there is a mitzva to apply salt to all offerings before offering them on the altar, the wine libations, blood, and wood do not require salt; see 20b (Rambam *Sefer Avoda, Hilkhot Issurei Mizbe'aḥ* 5:11; see *Hilkhot Ma'aseh HaKorbanot* 16:11).

תַּלְמוּד לוֹמַר: מִנְחָה, מַה מִּנְחָה מְיוּחֶדֶת שֶׁאֲחֵרִים בָּאִין חוֹבָה לָהּ – אַף כׇּל שֶׁאֲחֵרִים בָּאִין חוֹבָה לָהּ.

To counter this, **the verse states:** "And every **meal offering** of yours," to teach that **just as the meal offering is unique** in **that other** items **come as a requirement for it,** as the wood is required for the burning of the handful of the meal offering, **so too any** item that is unique in **that other** items **come as a requirement for it** requires the application of salt. By contrast, the wood and the blood do not require salting, as the wood itself requires no wood, and the blood is presented on the altar and does not require wood.

אִי מַה מִּנְחָה מְיוּחֶדֶת שֶׁמַּתֶּרֶת – אַף כׇּל שֶׁמַּתִּיר, אָבִיא דָּם שֶׁמַּתִּיר! תַּלְמוּד לוֹמַר: "מֵעַל מִנְחָתֶךָ", וְלֹא מֵעַל דָּמְךָ.

The *baraita* continues: **If** that logic is employed, one could say: **Just as** the handful of the **meal offering** that is burned **is unique** in **that it permits** the remainder of the meal offering to be eaten by the priests, and it requires salting, **so too, any** item that is unique in **that it permits** other items requires the application of salt. Accordingly, **I will include blood** in the obligation to be salted, **as** its presentation **permits** the offering to be sacrificed and eaten. To counter this, the continuation of **the verse states:** "Neither shall you suffer the salt of the covenant of your God to be lacking **from your meal offering,**" demonstrating that it cannot be lacking from the meal offering, **but not from your blood.**

יָכוֹל תְּהֵא מִנְחָה כּוּלָּהּ טְעוּנָה מֶלַח? תַּלְמוּד לוֹמַר: "קׇרְבָּן" – קׇרְבָּן טָעוּן מֶלַח, וְאֵין מִנְחָה כּוּלָּהּ טְעוּנָה מֶלַח.

The *baraita* continues: One **might** have thought that **the entire meal offering requires salting,** including the remainder of the offering that is eaten by the priests. To counter this, **the verse states:** "And every meal **offering** [***korban***] of yours you shall season with salt" (Leviticus 2:13), teaching that the handful, which is burned as **an offering** [***korban***] on the altar, **requires salting, but the entire meal offering** [***minḥa***] **does not require salting.**

וְאֵין לִי אֶלָּא קוֹמֶץ מִנְחָה, מִנַּיִן לְרַבּוֹת אֶת הַלְּבוֹנָה? מְרַבֶּה אֲנִי אֶת הַלְּבוֹנָה שֶׁכֵּן בָּאָה עִמָּהּ בִּכְלִי אֶחָד.

And I have derived **only** that **the handful of a meal offering** requires salting. **From where** is it derived **to include the frankincense,** which is also burned on the altar, in the requirement to be salted? **I include the frankincense due to** the fact **that it comes along with** the handful **in one vessel** and is therefore included in the expression "offering."

מִנַּיִן לְרַבּוֹת אֶת הַלְּבוֹנָה הַבָּאָה בִּפְנֵי עַצְמָהּ, וּלְבוֹנָה הַבָּאָה בְּבָזִיכִין, וְהַקְּטֹרֶת,

From where is it derived **to include** in the requirement to be salted **the frankincense that comes by itself** as a separate offering? One may accept the obligation to bring an offering of frankincense to be burned on the altar. From where is it derived that this frankincense requires salting? Moreover, from where is it derived to include in the requirement to be salted the **frankincense that comes in bowls** together with the shewbread, **and the incense?**

מִנְחַת כֹּהֲנִים, וּמִנְחַת כֹּהֵן מָשִׁיחַ, וּמִנְחַת נְסָכִים, אֵימוּרֵי חַטָּאת, וְאֵימוּרֵי אָשָׁם, וְאֵימוּרֵי קׇדְשֵׁי קׇדָשִׁים, וְאֵימוּרֵי קׇדָשִׁים קַלִּים, וְאֵבְרֵי עוֹלָה, וְעוֹלַת הָעוֹף, מִנַּיִן?

Moreover, from where is it derived in the requirement of salting in the case of the meal offerings from which a handful is not removed, i.e., **the meal offering of priests,**[H] **and the meal offering of the anointed priest** that is brought every day by the High Priest, **and the meal offering** that accompanies the **libations** brought with burnt offerings and peace offerings? From where is it derived in the requirement of salting with regard to **the sacrificial portions of the sin offering** consumed on the altar, **and the sacrificial portions of the guilt offering, and the sacrificial portions of the offerings of the most sacred order, and the sacrificial portions of the offerings of lesser sanctity, and the limbs of the burnt offering, and the bird burnt offering? From where** is it derived that all these require salting?

HALAKHA

The meal offering of priests, etc. – **מִנְחַת כֹּהֲנִים וכו׳:** After removing the handful from the meal offering and sanctifying it by placing it in a service vessel, the priest adds frankincense and brings it to the altar, where he applies salt and burns it on the fire of the altar. In the case of a meal offering of priests, he does not remove a handful. Rather, he salts and burns the entire offering on the fire of the altar (Rambam *Sefer Avoda, Hilkhot Ma'aseh HaKorbanot* 13:12).

תַּלְמוּד לוֹמַר: ״עַל כׇּל קׇרְבָּנְךָ תַּקְרִיב מֶלַח״.

The *baraita* continues: Therefore, **the verse states: "You shall sacrifice salt with all your offerings"** (Leviticus 2:13), demonstrating that everything burned on the altar requires salting. From this *baraita*, it is apparent that the mitzva to apply salt is necessary in order to teach about the circumstances where salt is added, and therefore it cannot be used as an instance where the mitzva is repeated in order to teach that the rite is indispensable.

אָמַר מָר: אֵין לִי אֶלָּא קוֹמֶץ מִנְחָה, מִנַּיִן לְרַבּוֹת אֶת הַלְּבוֹנָה? מְרַבֶּה אֲנִי אֶת הַלְּבוֹנָה שֶׁכֵּן בָּאָה עִמָּהּ בִּכְלִי אֶחָד. וְהָא אֲמַרְתְּ: מַה מִּנְחָה מְיוּחֶדֶת שֶׁאֲחֵרִים בָּאִין חוֹבָה לָהּ!

§ The Gemara discusses the *baraita* cited above: **The Master said: I have** derived **only** that **the handful of a meal offering** requires salting. **From where** is it derived **to include the frankincense,**[H] which is also burned on the altar, in the requirement to be salted? **I include the frankincense, due to** the fact **that it comes along with** the handful **in one vessel** and therefore is included in the expression "offering." The Gemara asks: Why is this verse needed? **But didn't you state** earlier that **just as a meal offering is unique** in **that other** items **come as a requirement for it,** as the wood is required for the burning of the handful of the meal offering, so too, anything that is unique in that other items come as a requirement requires the application of salt? Therefore, it is already known that the frankincense and all the other items require salting, since wood is required for their burning.

הָכִי קָאָמַר, אֵימָא: קׇרְבָּן – כְּלָל, וּמִנְחָה – פְּרָט; כְּלָל וּפְרָט – אֵין בִּכְלָל אֶלָּא מַה שֶּׁבַּפְּרָט, מִנְחָה – אִין, מִידֵּי אַחֲרִינָא – לָא!

The Gemara answers: When the *tanna* says: I have derived only that the handful of the meal offering requires salting, **this** is what **he is saying:** One might understand the verse "And every meal offering of yours you shall season with salt" (Leviticus 2:13) differently and **say** the following exposition: The term **"offering"** that appears here is **a generalization,** while **"meal offering"** is **a detail.** According to the hermeneutical principles, in the case of **a generalization and a detail, there is nothing in the generalization other than what is in the detail.** Therefore, in the case of **a meal offering, yes,** it requires salting, but **anything else** does **not** require salting. From where, then, is the *halakha* of salting in all other cases derived?

הֲדַר אָמַר: ״עַל כׇּל קׇרְבָּנְךָ״ – חָזַר וְכָלַל; כְּלָל וּפְרָט וּכְלָל – אִי אַתָּה דָן אֶלָּא כְּעֵין הַפְּרָט, מַה הַפְּרָט מְפוֹרָשׁ שֶׁאֲחֵרִים בָּאִין חוֹבָה לָהּ, אַף כֹּל שֶׁאֲחֵרִים בָּאִין חוֹבָה לָהּ.

Therefore, the verse **then states:** "You shall sacrifice salt **with all your offerings"** (Leviticus 2:13), and **it then generalized** again, so that the verse includes **a generalization, and a detail, and a generalization,** in which case according to the hermeneutical principles **you may deduce** that the verse is referring **only** to items **similar to the detail. Just as the specified detail,** i.e., the meal offering, is unique in **that other** items **come as a requirement for it, so too, anything** that is unique in **that other** items **come as a requirement for it** requires the application of salt. That is why the latter part of the verse is needed.

אֲחֵרִים דְּבָאִין חוֹבָה לָהּ מַאי נִיהוּ? עֵצִים, אַף כֹּל – עֵצִים.

The Gemara elaborates: **What are** the **other** items **that come as a requirement for** the meal offering? This is referring to the **wood,** as the wood is required for the burning of the handful of the meal offering. **So too,** the expression: **Anything** that is unique in that other items come as a requirement for it, is referring to anything that requires **wood** so that it may be burned on the altar.

אֵימָא: אֲחֵרִים דְּבָאִין חוֹבָה לָהּ נִיהוּ – לְבוֹנָה, וְאַיְיתֵי דָּם, דְּאִיכָּא נְסָכִים! נְסָכִים בַּהֲדֵי אֵימוּרִין הוּא דְּאָתוּ, מַאי טַעְמָא? אֲכִילָה וּשְׁתִיָּה. אַדְּרַבָּה, כַּפָּרָה וְשִׂמְחָה!

The Gemara asks: Why not **say** that the **other** items **that come as a requirement for** the meal offering **is** referring to the **frankincense,** which accompanies the meal offering, **and** therefore by means of the hermeneutical principle applying to a generalization, and a detail, and a generalization, **include blood, which is** accompanied by **libations?** The Gemara answers: The **libations** are not considered to accompany the sprinkling of the blood; rather, **they accompany the sacrificial portions** that are burned on the altar. **What is the reason?** It is because the burning of the sacrificial parts and the pouring of the libations are the **eating and drinking** of the altar. The Gemara counters: **On the contrary,** the libations are considered to accompany the blood, since the **atonement** that is effected by the presentation of the blood is followed by the **joy** that is displayed in the libation of wine.

HALAKHA

From where is it derived to include the frankincense – מִנַּיִן לְרַבּוֹת אֶת הַלְּבוֹנָה: Frankincense that is sacrificed by itself as a voluntary offering as well as the frankincense that comes in bowls together with the shewbread must be salted (Rambam *Sefer Avoda, Hilkhot Ma'aseh HaKorbanot* 16:14 and *Hilkhot Temidin UMusafin* 4:10).

אֶלָּא לְבוֹנָה בָּאָה עִמָּהּ בִּכְלִי אֶחָד, אֲבָל עֵצִים, כִּי הֵיכִי דְּמִתַּכְשְׁרָא בְּהוּ מִנְחָה – הָכִי מִתַּכְשְׁרָא בְּהוּ כּוּלְּהוּ קָרְבָּנוֹת.

Rather, one must say that since the **frankincense comes** together **with** the meal offering **in one vessel,** while the blood is not brought together with the libations in one vessel, the blood is not comparable to the meal offering. **But** when it is explained that the expression: The other items that come as a requirement for the meal offering, is referring to the **wood,** this means that **just as the meal offering is rendered fit by** means of the wood, **so too, all offerings are rendered fit by** means of the wood.

וְאֵימָא: מָה הַפְּרָט מְפוֹרָשׁ שֶׁאֲחֵרִים בָּאִין חוֹבָה לָהּ וּמַתֶּרֶת, אַף כָּל שֶׁאֲחֵרִים בָּאִין חוֹבָה לָהּ וּמַתֶּרֶת, וּמַאי נִיהוּ? לְבוֹנָה הַבָּאָה בְּבָזִיכִין, דְּשַׁרְיָא לֶחֶם, אֲבָל מִידֵּי אַחֲרִינָא לָא!

The Gemara asks: **But** why not **say: Just as** the item mentioned in **the detail,** i.e., the handful of the meal offering, is clearly **defined as** an item **for which other** items **come as a requirement, and** in addition it **renders** other items **permitted, so too, anything** that is unique in **that other** items **come as a requirement for it and renders** other items **permitted** requires the application of salt. **And what is** included due to this derivation? **Frankincense that comes in** the **bowls** that are placed upon the shewbread, **as it renders** the bread **permitted** to be eaten. **But** every **other item** should **not** be included.

מִדְּאִיצְטְרִיךְ ״מֵעַל מִנְחָתֶךָ״ – וְלֹא מֵעַל דָּמְךָ, מִכְּלָל דְּהָנָךְ כּוּלְּהוּ אָתוּ בְּחַד צַד.

The Gemara answers: It is apparent that all other items require only the factor of having other items come as a requirement for them to be considered similar to the meal offering. This is clear **from** the fact **that** in the case of blood, which is similar to the meal offering only in that it renders the offering permitted, it **was necessary** to teach that salt is not placed on blood, by means of the phrase: "Neither shall you suffer the salt of the covenant of your God to be lacking **from your meal offering,"** from which it is derived: **But not from your blood.** Had it been necessary for all items to have both aspects in common with the meal offering, there would be no need for a derivation to exclude blood. **By inference, these** other items **derived** from a meal offering are similar to it **in one respect.**

אָמַר מָר: ״מֵעַל מִנְחָתֶךָ״ – וְלֹא מֵעַל דָּמְךָ. וְאֵימָא: ״מֵעַל מִנְחָתֶךָ״ – וְלֹא מֵעַל אֵיבָרֶיךָ!

§ The Gemara continues its discussion of the *baraita*: **The Master said** above: The verse states: "Neither shall you suffer the salt of the covenant of your God to be lacking **from your meal offering,"** demonstrating that salt cannot be lacking from the meal offering, **but not from your blood.** The Gemara asks: **But** since the verse does not allude to blood explicitly, why not **say** that the verse teaches that salt cannot be lacking **from your meal offering, but not from your limbs** of the burnt offering that are sacrificed on the altar?

מִסְתַּבְּרָא אֵבָרִים הֲוָה לֵיהּ לְרַבּוֹיֵי, שֶׁכֵּן (אשב״נ טמ״א סימן)

The Gemara answers: **It stands to reason** that the **limbs** of a burnt offering **should be included** in the requirement to have salt applied, **since** they share many characteristics with a meal offering that blood does not. The Gemara presents **a mnemonic** for the characteristics that they share: ***Alef, shin, beit, nun; tet, mem, alef.***[N] These are a reference to others [*aḥerim*], fire [*ishim*], external [*baḥutz*], *notar*; ritual impurity [*tuma*], and misuse of consecrated property [*me'ila*].

אֲחֵרִים בָּאִין חוֹבָה לָהּ כְּמוֹתָהּ, אִישִּׁים כְּמוֹתָהּ, בַּחוּץ כְּמוֹתָהּ, נוֹתָר כְּמוֹתָהּ,

In the case of the limbs of a burnt offering, **other** items **come as a requirement for it, as** is the *halakha* with regard to a meal offering. The burnt offering requires require wood in order to be burned on the altar, which is not the case with regard to the blood. The limbs of the burnt offering are burned in the **fire** of the altar, **as** is the *halakha* with regard to a meal offering, whereas the blood is presented on the corners of the altar. The burnt offering is sacrificed **on the external** altar, **as** is the *halakha* with regard to a meal offering, as opposed to the blood, which is presented inside the Sanctuary in the cases of the bull and goat of Yom Kippur. It is prohibited to partake of its **leftover** [***notar***][B] parts, **as** is the *halakha* with regard to a meal offering, which is not relevant to blood.

טוּמְאָה כְּמוֹתָהּ, מְעִילָה כְּמוֹתָהּ.

It is prohibited to partake of a burnt offering while in a state of **ritual impurity, as** is the *halakha* with regard to a meal offering, which is not relevant to blood. It is subject to the *halakhot* of **misuse** of consecrated property,[B] **as** is the *halakha* with regard to a meal offering, which is not so with regard to the blood.

NOTES

***Alef, shin, beit, nun; tet, mem, alef* – אשב״נ טמ״א:** *Tosafot* point out that the last letter of the mnemonic, *alef*, does not appear to stand for any point of comparison between the limbs of the burnt offering and the meal offering. They cite Rabbeinu Tam's explanation that the letter *alef* represents the first letter of the term food [*okhel*], since in contrast to blood, both the flour of the meal offering and the meat of the burnt offering are types of food (*Shita Mekubbetzet*). This serves as a point of comparison, despite the fact that the sacrificial limbs and the handful of the meal offering are burned and not eaten, as it is customary to salt food that is to be eaten.

BACKGROUND

***Notar* – נוֹתָר:** Any offering whose meat is eaten has a set time in the Torah for its consumption. For a thanks offering and a sin offering, for example, the meat may be eaten until the morning after its sacrifice; a peace offering may be eaten for two days. After the deadline has passed, the leftover meat is called *notar*, and it may not be eaten, nor may any benefit be derived from it. One who eats *notar* incurs the punishment of *karet*.

Misuse of consecrated property – מְעִילָה: The *halakhot* of misuse of consecrated property are stated in the Torah (see Leviticus 5:14–16) and discussed in greater detail in tractate *Me'ila*. The basic principle is that one who derives benefit from consecrated property unwittingly, i.e., without the knowledge that it was consecrated property, transgresses this prohibition. One who does so is obligated to bring an offering and to pay to the Temple the value of the item from which he derived benefit. In addition, he must pay an extra one-fifth of the value as a fine. In most cases, after one uses such an item it loses its consecrated status, which is transferred to the money that he pays to the Temple. The Torah does not discuss one who derives benefit from consecrated property intentionally. Therefore, such a person cannot atone for deriving benefit by sacrificing an offering or by paying the additional one-fifth of the value as a fine.

NOTES

According to the statement of Rabbi Yehuda HaNasi, wood requires the removal of a handful – לְדִבְרֵי רַבִּי עֵצִים טְעוּנִין קְמִיצָה: The priest must first remove a handful of splinters from the logs and place them on the arrangement of wood on the altar (commentary attributed to Rashba, citing Rashi). Alternatively, he grinds up the wood into splinters and then removes a handful (Rashi on 106b; *Shita Mekubbetzet*).

אַדְּרַבָּה, דָּם הֲוָה לֵיהּ לְרַבּוּיֵי, שֶׁכֵּן מַתִּיר כְּמוֹתָהּ, נִפְסָל בִּשְׁקִיעַת הַחַמָּה כְּמוֹתָהּ! הָנָךְ נְפִישָׁן.

The Gemara rejects this proof: **On the contrary, blood should be included** in the requirement to have salt applied, **since it renders** the offering **permitted** to be sacrificed and eaten, **as** is so with regard to the handful, which renders the remainder of the meal offering permitted to be eaten. In addition, blood **becomes invalid at sunset** and can no longer be sprinkled on the altar, **as** is the *halakha* with regard to the handful of a meal offering, whereas the limbs of the burnt offering may be sacrificed at any point during the night. The Gemara responds: **These** characteristics shared by the meal offering and the limbs of the burnt offering are **more** than those shared by the blood and the meal offering.

אָמַר מָר: שׁוֹמֵעַ אֲנִי אֲפִילּוּ עֵצִים וָדָם שֶׁנִּקְרְאוּ קָרְבָּן. מַאן שָׁמְעַתְּ לֵיהּ דְּאָמַר: עֵצִים אִיקְּרִי קָרְבָּן – רַבִּי, לְרַבִּי מִבָּעֲיָא בָּעוּ מֶלַח!

§ The Gemara continues discussing the *baraita*: **The Master said** above: Had the verse stated only: And every offering you shall season with salt, **I** would **derive** that this applies to **even** the **wood** and the **blood, which are** also **termed: An offering.** Therefore, the verse states "and every meal offering of yours" (Leviticus 2:13), to teach that just as the meal offering is unique in that other items come as a requirement for it, so too, anything that is unique in that other items come as a requirement for it requires the application of salt. Therefore, the wood and the blood do not require salting, as in their case no other item is needed. The Gemara asks: **Whom did you hear who says** that the **wood is termed an offering?** It is **Rabbi** Yehuda HaNasi. But **according to Rabbi** Yehuda HaNasi, doesn't the wood in fact **require salting?**

דְּתַנְיָא: "קָרְבַּן מִנְחָה" – מְלַמֵּד שֶׁמִּתְנַדְּבִין עֵצִים, וְכַמָּה? שְׁנֵי גְּזָרִין, וְכֵן הוּא אוֹמֵר: "וְהַגּוֹרָלוֹת הִפַּלְנוּ עַל קָרְבַּן הָעֵצִים". רַבִּי אָמַר: עֵצִים קָרְבַּן מִנְחָה הֵן, וּטְעוּנִין מֶלַח וּטְעוּנִין הַגָּשָׁה.

This is **as it is taught** in a *baraita*: The verse states: "And when one brings **a meal offering** [***korban minḥa***]" (Leviticus 2:1). The superfluous word *korban* **teaches that one can voluntarily give wood**[H] as an offering for the altar. **And how much** wood must one bring if he does not specify an amount? **Two logs. And** the support for the fact that wood can be brought as a voluntary offering is from a verse, **as** the verse **states: "And we cast lots for the wood offering"** (Nehemiah 10:35). **Rabbi** Yehuda HaNasi **says:** This voluntary donation of **wood is** an offering like **a meal offering, and** therefore it **requires salt and requires bringing** to the corner of the altar, like a meal offering.

וְאָמַר רָבָא: לְדִבְרֵי רַבִּי – עֵצִים טְעוּנִין קְמִיצָה; וְאָמַר רַב פַּפָּא: לְדִבְרֵי רַבִּי – עֵצִים צְרִיכִין עֵצִים!

And Rava says: According to the statement of Rabbi Yehuda HaNasi, **wood** donated in this manner **requires** the **removal of a handful,**[N] just as in the case of a meal offering, a portion of the wood must be removed and sacrificed separately. **And Rav Pappa says** that **according to the statement of Rabbi** Yehuda HaNasi, since it is an offering for the altar, the **wood** that is brought as an offering **needs** to be placed on other **wood** to burn, like any other offering that is burned on wood on the altar. Apparently, this means that Rabbi Yehuda HaNasi, who holds that the wood is termed an offering, also holds that it requires the application of salt, in contrast to the ruling in the *baraita*.

סְמֵי מִיכָּן עֵצִים. וְאֶלָּא קְרָא לְמַעוּטֵי מַאי? אִי לְמַעוּטֵי דָּם, מֵ"עַל מִנְחָתֶךָ" נָפְקָא!

The Gemara responds: **Remove wood from** the *baraita* **here,** as it is not excluded by the term "and every meal offering of yours." The Gemara asks: **But** then, the phrase in **the verse** "and every meal offering of yours" is **to exclude what? If** it serves **to exclude blood,** this is **derived from** the continuation of the verse, which states: **"From your meal offering,"** as explained in the continuation of the *baraita*.

HALAKHA

That one can voluntarily give wood – שֶׁמִּתְנַדְּבִין עֵצִים: One who says: It is incumbent upon me to bring wood to the altar, must bring no less than two logs of wood that are at least one cubit long and have the thickness of a level used for leveling a mound of grain. If he said: It is incumbent upon me to bring a log of wood, he should bring one log. If he prefers, he may instead donate the value of the wood. This is in accordance with the opinion of the Rabbis, and not that of Rabbi Yehuda HaNasi (Rambam *Sefer Avoda*, *Hilkhot Ma'aseh HaKorbanot* 16:13, and see Mahari Kurkus and Radbaz there).

אַפֵּיק עֵצִים וְעַיֵּיל נְסָכִים, דְּתַנְיָא: אֲבָל הַיַּיִן וְהַדָּם, וְהָעֵצִים וְהַקְּטֹרֶת – אֵין טְעוּנִין מֶלַח.

The Gemara responds: **Wood** is **removed** from the *baraita*, **and insert** in its place wine **libations,**[N] teaching that they do not require the addition of salt. **As it is taught** in a *baraita*: **But the wine** libations **and the blood,**[H] **and the wood and the incense, do not require salt.**

מַנִּי? אִי רַבִּי – קַשְׁיָא עֵצִים, אִי רַבָּנַן – קַשְׁיָא קְטֹרֶת!

The Gemara asks: In accordance with **whose** opinion is this *baraita*? **If** you say it is in accordance with the opinion of **Rabbi** Yehuda HaNasi, the ruling of the *baraita* concerning **wood** is **difficult,** as the *baraita* rules that wood does not require salt, whereas Rabbi Yehuda HaNasi holds that wood does require salt. **If** you say it is the opinion of **the Rabbis,** the ruling of the *baraita* concerning **incense** is **difficult,** as they taught in the *baraita* on 20a that any item for which another item is necessary requires salt, and this includes the incense, which is burned with wood.

הַאי תַּנָּא הוּא, דְּתַנְיָא, רַבִּי יִשְׁמָעֵאל בְּנוֹ שֶׁל רַבִּי יוֹחָנָן בֶּן בְּרוֹקָה אוֹמֵר: מָה הַפְּרָט מְפוֹרָשׁ – דָּבָר שֶׁמְּקַבֵּל טוּמְאָה וְעוֹלֶה לָאִשִּׁים וְיֶשְׁנוֹ עַל מִזְבֵּחַ הַחִיצוֹן, אַף כָּל דָּבָר הַמְקַבֵּל טוּמְאָה וְעוֹלֶה לָאִשִּׁים וְיֶשְׁנוֹ עַל מִזְבֵּחַ הַחִיצוֹן;

The Gemara suggests: The *baraita* **is** in accordance with **this** following ***tanna***, who explains the verse that was interpreted in the *baraita* in a different manner. **As it is taught** in a *baraita*: **Rabbi Yishmael, son of Rabbi Yoḥanan ben Beroka, says:** The verse states: "And every meal offering of yours you shall season with salt" (Leviticus 2:13). **Just as the specified detail,** i.e., the meal offering, is **an item that is susceptible to ritual impurity, and is brought on the fire** of the altar, **and** is sacrificed **on the external altar, so too, any item that is susceptible to ritual impurity, and is brought on the fire** of the altar, **and is** sacrificed **on the external altar** requires salting.

יָצְאוּ עֵצִים – שֶׁאֵין מְקַבְּלִין טוּמְאָה, יָצְאוּ דָּם וְיַיִן – שֶׁאֵין עוֹלִים לָאִשִּׁים, יָצְאָה קְטֹרֶת – שֶׁאֵינָהּ עַל מִזְבֵּחַ הַחִיצוֹן.

Therefore, **wood is excluded,** as it is **not susceptible to ritual impurity. Wine and blood are excluded,** as **they are not brought on the fire** of the altar but rather are sprinkled on the corner of the altar. The **incense** is **excluded,** as it is sacrificed **not on the external altar** but rather on the inner altar.

אֶלָּא טַעְמָא דְּמַעֲטֵיהּ קְרָא לְדָם, הָא לָאו הָכִי – הֲוָה אָמֵינָא: דָּם לִיבְעֵי מֶלַח? כֵּיוָן דִּמְלָחֵיהּ נָפֵיק לֵיהּ מִתּוֹרַת דָּם! דְּאָמַר זְעֵירִי אָמַר רַבִּי חֲנִינָא: דָּם שֶׁבִּישְּׁלוֹ – אֵינוֹ עוֹבֵר עָלָיו, וְרַב יְהוּדָה אָמַר זְעֵירִי: דָּם שֶׁמְּלָחוֹ – אֵינוֹ עוֹבֵר עָלָיו,

The Gemara asks: **But** how can it be that according to all opinions, **the reason that** blood does not require salting is that **the verse excluded blood,** indicating **that if not for that, I would say** that **blood requires salt? Once** one **salts** the blood, **it exits the category of blood, as Ze'eiri says** that **Rabbi Ḥanina says:** With regard to **blood that one cooked,**[H] **one does not transgress** the prohibition against consuming blood **by** drinking **it,** since it no longer has the status of blood that is fit to be presented on the altar. **And Rav Yehuda says** that **Ze'eiri** says: With regard to **blood that one salted, one does not transgress** a prohibition **by** drinking **it,** since salted blood has the status of cooked blood.

וְרַב יְהוּדָה דִּידֵיהּ אָמַר: אֵבָרִים שֶׁצְּלָאָן וְהֶעֱלָן – אֵין בָּהֶם מִשּׁוּם לְרֵיחַ נִיחוֹחַ!

And similarly, **Rav Yehuda himself says:** With regard to the **limbs** of a burnt offering **that** one first **roasted**[H] **and** afterward **brought them up** to the altar, **they do not constitute** fulfillment of the requirement of the verse that an offering be **"an aroma pleasing** to the Lord" (Exodus 29:25).

מַהוּ דְּתֵימָא, מִשְׁדָּא בָּהּ מַשֶּׁהוּ לְמִצְוָה בְּעָלְמָא, קָא מַשְׁמַע לַן.

The Gemara answers: It is still necessary to derive that blood does not require salt, **lest you say** that the priest should **sprinkle any amount** of salt, even a minute quantity, **on** the blood, **merely for** the fulfillment of the **mitzva,** as such an amount would not render the blood as cooked. To counter this, the verse **teaches us** that blood requires no application of salt.

גּוּפָא, אָמַר זְעֵירִי אָמַר רַבִּי חֲנִינָא: דָּם שֶׁבִּישְּׁלוֹ אֵינוֹ עוֹבֵר עָלָיו. יָתֵיב רָבָא וְקָא אָמַר לָהּ לְהָא שְׁמַעְתָּא. אֵיתִיבֵיהּ אַבָּיֵי: הִקְפָּה אֶת הַדָּם וַאֲכָלוֹ, אוֹ שֶׁהִמְחָה אֶת הַחֵלֶב וּגְמָעוֹ – חַיָּיב!

§ The Gemara discusses **the** matter **itself: Ze'eiri says** that **Rabbi Ḥanina says:** With regard to **blood that one cooked, one does not transgress** a prohibition **by** drinking **it. Rava was sitting and saying this *halakha*. Abaye raised an objection to** him from a *baraita* (*Tosefta, Karetot* 2:19): If **one curdled blood and consumed it, or** in a case **where one melted** forbidden **fat and swallowed it,**[H] even though he changed its form, he is **liable.** This demonstrates that even after its form is changed, the blood's status remains unchanged.

NOTES

And insert in its place libations – **וְעַיֵּיל נְסָכִים**: The libations are also considered an offering, and they do not require any other item as a prerequisite since they are not poured on the flames of the altar but rather on the corner of the altar, from which they would descend into the drainpipes (see the mishna on *Sukka* 48a and the discussion on *Sukka* 49a).

HALAKHA

But the wine libations and the blood, etc. – **אֲבָל הַיַּיִן וְהַדָּם וכו׳**: There is a positive mitzva to apply salt to all offerings, and nothing may be sacrificed on the altar without salt except for the wine libations, the blood, and the wood. One quarter-*kav* of salt of Sodom is added to the incense after its spices are crushed. This is in accordance with the opinion of the Rabbis, and not in accordance with the *baraita* here (Rambam *Sefer Avoda, Hilkhot Issurei Mizbe'aḥ* 5:11, and see *Hilkhot Kelei HaMikdash* 2:3).

Blood that one cooked – **דָּם שֶׁבִּישְּׁלוֹ**: According to the majority of the authorities, the consumption of cooked or salted blood is not prohibited by Torah law, in accordance with the statement of Ze'eiri according to the explanation of *Tosafot* here. According to Rashi in tractate *Ḥullin* (109a) and the Rambam, it is prohibited by Torah law and is even punishable by *karet* (Rambam *Sefer Kedusha, Hilkhot Ma'akhalot Assurot* 6:6; *Tur, Yoreh De'a* 76; *Arukh HaShulḥan, Yoreh De'a* 67:5–6).

The limbs of a burnt offering that one first roasted – **אֵבָרִים שֶׁצְּלָאָן**: With regard to limbs that one first roasted and afterward took up to the altar, this does not constitute fulfillment of the requirement that the offering must be sacrificed for a pleasing aroma (Rambam *Sefer Avoda, Hilkhot Ma'aseh HaKorbanot* 6:4).

Where one melted forbidden fat and swallowed it – **שֶׁהִמְחָה אֶת הַחֵלֶב וּגְמָעוֹ**: With the exception of meat cooked in milk and prohibited mixtures of diverse kinds planted in a vineyard, one is liable for partaking of prohibited foods only if one eats them in a pleasurable manner. Therefore, if one melted forbidden fat and then swallowed it while it was still hot, thereby burning his throat, he is not liable for consuming it (Rambam *Sefer Kedusha, Hilkhot Ma'akhalot Assurot* 14:11).

לָא קַשְׁיָא: כָּאן שֶׁהִקְפָּה בָּאוּר, כָּאן שֶׁהִקְפָּה בַּחַמָּה; בָּאוּר – לָא הָדַר, בַּחַמָּה – הָדַר.

Rava responded: This is **not difficult,** as **here,** Ze'eiri's statement relates to a case **where he curdled** the blood **by** means of **the fire,** whereas **there,** in the case of the *baraita*, **he curdled** the blood **by** means of **the sun.** Blood curdled **by** means of **a fire cannot return** to its former state, so one is not liable, whereas blood curdled **by** means of **the sun can return**[N] to its former state, so one is liable.

בַּחַמָּה נַמִי, לֵימָא: הוֹאִיל וְאִידְּחֵי אִידְּחֵי, דְּהָא בְּעָא מִינֵּיהּ רַבִּי מָנִי מֵרַבִּי יוֹחָנָן: דָּם שֶׁקָּרַשׁ וַאֲכָלוֹ, מַהוּ? אֲמַר לֵיהּ: הוֹאִיל וְנִדְחָה יִדָּחֶה! אִישְׁתִּיק.

Abaye objected: But **even** when blood is curdled **by** means of **the sun, let us say** that **since it was disqualified** from being presented on the altar, **it was disqualified,** i.e., excluded, from the prohibition against consuming blood; **as Rabbi Mani inquired of Rabbi Yoḥanan:** With regard to **blood that was congealed and one ate it, what is** the *halakha*? Rabbi Yoḥanan responded: He is not liable; **since it was disqualified** from being presented on the altar, **it shall be disqualified** from the prohibition against consuming blood. Rava **was silent** and had no answer.

אֲמַר לֵיהּ: דִּלְמָא וַדַּאי כָּאן בַּחַטָּאוֹת הַחִיצוֹנִיּוֹת, כָּאן בַּחַטָּאוֹת הַפְּנִימִיּוֹת!

Abaye **said to him: Perhaps here** the *baraita* **is certainly** referring **to** the blood of **the external sin offerings,**[N] which is sprinkled on the external altar in the Temple courtyard, whereas **there** Ze'eiri is referring **to** the blood of **the inner sin offerings,** which is sprinkled inside the Sanctuary.

אֲמַר: אַדְכַּרְתָּן מִילְּתָא, דְּאָמַר רַב חִסְדָּא: דָּם שֶׁקָּרַשׁ בַּחַטָּאוֹת וַאֲכָלוֹ – חַיָּיב, ״וְלָקַח... וְנָתַן״ אָמַר רַחֲמָנָא, בַּר לְקִיחָה וּנְתִינָה הוּא; בַּחַטָּאוֹת הַפְּנִימִיּוֹת וַאֲכָלוֹ – פָּטוּר, ״וְטָבַל... וְהִזָּה״ אָמַר רַחֲמָנָא, וְהַאי לָאו בַּר טְבִילָה וְהַזָּאָה הוּא.

Rava **said** to him: **You have reminded me of a matter, as Rabbi Ḥisda says:** With regard to **blood that became congealed,** if it is blood **of the** external **sin offerings and one ate it,** he is **liable,** as **the Merciful One states** in the Torah: **"And** the priest **shall take** of the blood of the sin offering with his finger, **and place it** upon the corners of the altar of burnt offering" (Leviticus 4:25), and congealed blood **is suitable for taking and placing,** as one can take the congealed blood and place it upon the altar. By contrast, if it is blood **of the inner sin offerings and one ate it,** he is **exempt,** as **the Merciful One states** in the Torah: **"And** the priest **shall dip** his finger in the blood, **and sprinkle** of the blood" (Leviticus 4:6), **and this** congealed blood **is not suitable for dipping and sprinkling.**

וְרָבָא דִּידֵיהּ אָמַר: אֲפִילּוּ בַּחַטָּאוֹת הַפְּנִימִיּוֹת וַאֲכָלוֹ – חַיָּיב, הוֹאִיל וּכְנֶגְדּוֹ רָאוּי בַּחַטָּאוֹת הַחִיצוֹנוֹת. אָמַר רַב פַּפָּא: הִלְכָּךְ, דַּם חֲמוֹר שֶׁקָּרַשׁ וַאֲכָלוֹ – חַיָּיב, הוֹאִיל וּכְנֶגְדּוֹ רָאוּי בַּחַטָּאוֹת הַחִיצוֹנוֹת.

And Rava himself says: Even if there was blood **of the inner sin offerings and one ate it,** he is **liable, since** blood **corresponding to** this blood is **suitable** to be placed on the altar **in** the case of **the external sin offerings. Rav Pappa says: Therefore,** according to the same reasoning, in the case of **the blood of a donkey that became congealed and one ate it,** he is **liable,** despite the fact that a donkey's blood is not fit to be brought as an offering, **since** blood **corresponding to** this blood **is suitable** to be placed on the altar **in** the case of **the external sin offerings.**

אָמַר רַב גִּידֵּל אָמַר זְעֵירִי: דָּם, בֵּין לַח בֵּין יָבֵשׁ – חוֹצֵץ. מֵיתִיבֵי: הַדָּם וְהַדְּיוֹ, וְהַדְּבַשׁ וְהֶחָלָב – יְבֵשִׁין חוֹצְצִין, לַחִין אֵינָן חוֹצְצִין! לָא קַשְׁיָא: הָא דִּסְרִיךְ, הָא דְּלָא סְרִיךְ.

In the context of the *halakhot* of blood, **Rav Giddel says** that **Ze'eiri says: Blood, whether moist or dry, interposes** during ritual immersion. The Gemara **raises an objection** from a *baraita* (*Tosefta, Mikvaot* 6:9): With regard to **blood, ink,**[H] **honey, or milk** on a person's skin, when **they are dry, they interpose** during immersion; but when **they are moist, they do not interpose.** The Gemara explains: This is **not difficult; this** statement of Rav Giddel is referring to a case **where** the blood **adheres** to the skin, as it has begun to congeal and therefore interposes. **That** *baraita* is referring to a case **where** the blood **did not adhere** and therefore does not interpose.

״תִּמְלָח״ לְמַאי אֲתָא? לְכִדְתַנְיָא: ״בַּמֶּלַח״ – יָכוֹל תְּבוֹנֵהוּ? תַּלְמוּד לוֹמַר: ״תִּמְלָח״; אִי ״תִּמְלָח״, יָכוֹל בְּמֵי מֶלַח? תַּלְמוּד לוֹמַר: ״בַּמֶּלַח״.

§ The Gemara returns to its interpretation of the verse: "And every meal offering of yours you shall season with salt" (Leviticus 2:13), and asks: **For what** purpose does the expression **"you shall season" come?** The Gemara answers: It is written **for that which is taught** in a *baraita*: Had the verse stated only: And every meal offering of yours shall be **with salt,** one **might** have thought that the *halakha* is ***tevonehu***,[L] a term that will be explained in the Gemara. Therefore, **the verse states: "You shall season."** Conversely, **had** the verse stated only: **"You shall season,"** one **might** have thought that this obligation can be fulfilled **by** means of adding **salt water.** Therefore, **the verse states "with salt."**

NOTES

By means of a fire cannot return, by means of the sun can return – בָּאוּר לָא הָדַר בַּחַמָּה הָדַר: Rashi explains that when congealed in the sun, blood can later become liquid again. By contrast, *Tosafot Ḥitzoniyyot* explain that Rava's primary point is that the act of cooking the blood is what changes its status, and this does not apply when it is merely left in the sun and congeals. The *Ḥazon Ish* explains similarly.

Perhaps here the *baraita* is certainly referring to the external sin offerings, etc. – דִּלְמָא וַדַּאי כָּאן בַּחַטָּאוֹת הַחִיצוֹנִיּוֹת וכו׳: According to Rashi, Abaye is suggesting abandoning the distinction between blood that was congealed by means of fire and blood that was congealed by means of the sun. Ze'eiri's statement that one is not liable if the blood is cooked is then understood as referring to congealed blood of sin offerings that is sprinkled inside the Sanctuary. One is liable in the case of congealed blood of sin offerings brought on the external altar, since the blood is fit for effecting atonement. Similarly, one is liable in the case of congealed non-sacred blood.

By contrast, *Tosafot* explain that Ze'eiri's statement is not rejected, and according to all opinions cooked blood does not retain the status of blood. The distinction made by Rava and Rav Ḥisda between sin offerings brought on the external altar and sin offerings whose blood is sprinkled inside the Sanctuary applies only with regard to blood that was congealed by the heat of the sun.

The early commentaries disagree with regard to the *halakha*, with the majority agreeing with *Tosafot* that everyone agrees with Ze'eiri, and cooked blood is prohibited only by rabbinic law (*Yad David*; see *Encyclopedia Talmudit*, under the entry: Blood).

HALAKHA

Blood, ink, etc. – הַדָּם וְהַדְּיוֹ וכו׳: With regard to blood, ink, milk, honey, and sap, when they are dry they constitute an interposition, but while they are moist they do not. Blood that adheres to the skin, or to any surface, constitutes an interposition even when moist (Rambam *Sefer Tahara, Hilkhot Mikvaot* 2:2; *Shulḥan Arukh, Yoreh De'a* 198:15–16 and *Shakh* there).

LANGUAGE

Tevonehu – תְּבוֹנֵהוּ: The root *tav, beit, nun* in its various conjugations appears rarely in the language of the *tanna'im*, and therefore its origin and meaning is a matter of dispute in the Talmud.

"וְלֹא תַשְׁבִּית מֶלַח" – הָבֵא מֶלַח שֶׁאֵינָהּ שׁוֹבֶתֶת, וְאֵיזוֹ? זוֹ מֶלַח סְדוֹמִית. וּמִנַּיִן שֶׁאִם לֹא מָצָא מֶלַח סְדוֹמִית שֶׁמֵּבִיא מֶלַח אִיסְתְּרוֹקָנִית? תַּלְמוּד לוֹמַר: "תַּקְרִיב" – תַּקְרִיב כָּל שֶׁהוּא, תַּקְרִיב מִכָּל מָקוֹם, תַּקְרִיב וַאֲפִילּוּ בְּשַׁבָּת, תַּקְרִיב וַאֲפִילּוּ בְּטוּמְאָה.

The continuation of the verse: **"And you shall not omit** [*tashbit*] **salt** from your meal offering," teaches that **one should bring salt that never rests** [*shovetet*], i.e., it is found continuously. **And what** type of salt **is this? This** is referring to **salt of Sodom. And from where** is it derived **that if one did not find salt of Sodom that he should bring salt of *istrokanit*,**[LB] which is quarried from rock? **The verse states** immediately afterward: "With all your offerings **you shall sacrifice** salt" (Leviticus 2:13), in order to emphasize that **you should sacrifice any** type of salt; **you should sacrifice** salt **from any place,** even from a location outside of Eretz Yisrael; **you should sacrifice** salt **even on Shabbat;** and **you should sacrifice** salt **even** in a state of **ritual impurity.**

מַאי "תְּבוּנֵהוּ"? אֲמַר רַבָּה בַּר עוּלָּא, הָכִי קָאָמַר: יָכוֹל יִתְבּוֹנְנוּ כְּתֶבֶן בְּטִיט. אֲמַר לֵיהּ אַבַּיֵּי: אִי הָכִי, "יִתְבּוֹנְנוּ" מִיבְּעֵי לֵיהּ! אֶלָּא אֲמַר אַבַּיֵּי: יָכוֹל יַעֲשֶׂנּוּ כְּבִנְיָן. אֲמַר לֵיהּ רָבָא: אִי הָכִי, "יִבְנֶנּוּ" מִיבְּעֵי לֵיהּ! אֶלָּא אֲמַר רָבָא: יָכוֹל תְּבוּנֵהוּ.

The Gemara clarifies: **What** is the meaning of the term ***tevonehu*? Rabba bar Ulla said: This** is what the *baraita* **is saying:** One **might** have thought that **one should mix into it** [*yitabonenu*] large quantities of salt, **just as** one mixes **straw** [*teven*] **into clay. Abaye said to him: If so,** the *baraita* **should have said: *Yitabonenu*,** and not *tevonehu*. **Rather, Abaye said:** The *baraita* is saying that one **might** have thought **one should form** the addition of salt **just as** one builds **a building** [*binyan*], by adding layer upon layer. **Rava said to him: If so,** the *baraita* **should have said: He should build it** [*yivnenu*] and not *tevonehu*. **Rather, Rava said:** The *baraita* states: One **might** have thought ***tevonehu*.**

מַאי "תְּבוּנֵהוּ"? אֲמַר רַב אַשִׁי: יָכוֹל יִתֵּן בּוֹ טַעַם כְּבִינָה? תַּלְמוּד לוֹמַר: "תִּמְלָח", כֵּיצַד הוּא עוֹשֶׂה? מֵבִיא הָאֵבֶר וְנוֹתֵן עָלָיו מֶלַח, וְחוֹזֵר וְהוֹפְכוֹ וְנוֹתֵן עָלָיו מֶלַח וּמַעֲלֵהוּ.

The Gemara asks: **What** is meant by ***tevonehu*? Rav Ashi said:** One **might** have thought that **one should infuse** the entire offering with the **taste** of salt, **just as understanding** [*bina*][N] infuses a person with wisdom. To counter this, **the verse states: "You shall season." How does he act? He brings the limb** that is to be sacrificed on the altar **and applies salt,**[H] **and then turns it over and again applies salt, and brings it up** to the altar.

אָמַר אַבַּיֵּי: וְכֵן לִקְדֵירָה.

Abaye says: And one acts **similarly** before placing meat **into a pot.**[H] If one wishes to cook meat and needs to salt it in order to extract its blood, it is sufficient to apply salt to both sides and let it sit until the blood drains. Then, after it is washed, the meat is ready to be cooked and eaten.

LANGUAGE

Istrokanit – **אִיסְתְּרוֹקָנִית**: The *Arukh* explains that Istrokan is the name of a town. It apparently refers to the town Ostrakine, located on the border between Eretz Yisrael and Egypt. In the time of the Talmud it was a center for the production of salt; salt was harvested from the sea brine there by means of evaporation of the water using the sun's heat. Others explain that this refers to salt that comes from the region of Astrakhan, which is situated near the Caspian Sea. The sea itself is a saline lake, and many minerals are found there, including salt.

BACKGROUND

Salt of Sodom and salt of *istrokanit* – מֶלַח סְדוֹמִית וְאִיסְתְּרוֹקָנִית: The *ge'onim* explain the word Sodom literally, as meaning salt extracted from Mount Sodom, near the Dead Sea, a mountain made almost entirely of rock salt. This salt, which is crystallized and hard as stone, remains noticeable when added to food. *Istrokanit* salt is produced by drawing seawater into ponds and then evaporating the water in the sun. In ancient times such salt was moist and far more brittle than salt extracted from stone.

Rock salt formation at the peak of Mount Sodom

Salt cave at Mount Sodom

HALAKHA

He brings the limb and applies salt – מֵבִיא הָאֵבֶר וְנוֹתֵן עָלָיו מֶלַח: It is a mitzva to salt sacrificial meat properly, as one salts meat that is to be roasted, by applying salt to the underside of the limb. If one applied any minimal amount of salt, the meat is fit. This is in accordance with the *baraita* (Rambam *Sefer Avoda*, *Hilkhot Issurei Mizbe'a* 5:11).

And one acts similarly before placing meat into a pot – וְכֵן לִקְדֵירָה: Before cooking meat it is necessary to apply salt to it. One must scatter salt over the entire surface of the meat, on both sides. One must apply enough salt that one is unable to consume the meat, and there is no need to apply a greater amount of salt. This is in accordance with the statement of Abaye (Rambam *Sefer Kedusha*, *Hilkhot Ma'akhalot Assurot* 6:10; *Shulḥan Arukh*, *Yoreh De'a* 69:4, and see 76:1–2).

NOTES

Taste, just as understanding – טַעַם כְּבִינָה: According to Rashi and *Tosafot*, Rav Ashi explains that one might have thought that it is necessary to salt the meat heavily. Therefore, the verse states: "You shall season," teaching that it is not necessary to salt it heavily, as it is sufficient to simply apply salt to both sides. The majority of the commentaries maintain the opposite, that one might have thought that one had to apply only a small taste of salt, and the term "you shall season" teaches that it is necessary to apply salt generously (Rabbeinu Gershom Meor HaGola; *Arukh*; Rabbeinu Tam). According to the second explanation, the continuation of the *baraita*, which states: One might have thought that this obligation can be fulfilled by means of salt water, is not meant as a leniency but rather as a stringency, i.e., that the salt must cover every part of the meat (Ritva on *Ḥullin* 112a).

HALAKHA

Salt that is on the limb of an offering – מֶלַח שֶׁעַל גַּבֵּי הָאֵבֶר: With regard to salt that is on the limb of an offering, one who derives benefit from it is liable for misuse of consecrated property, but in the case of salt that is on the ramp or at the top of the altar, one who benefits from it is not liable for misuse of consecrated property. This is in accordance with the *baraita* (Rambam *Sefer Avoda*, *Hilkhot Me'ila* 8:7).

About the salt and about the wood – עַל הַמֶּלַח וְעַל הָעֵצִים: The court instituted an ordinance concerning the salt and wood in the Temple that the priests may use them in eating their portions of the offerings (Rambam *Sefer Avoda*, *Hilkhot Me'ila* 8:6).

In three locations, etc. – בִּשְׁלֹשָׁה מְקוֹמוֹת וכו׳: Salt was found in three locations in the Temple: In the Chamber of the Salt, where the hides of sacrificial animals were salted; on the ramp, where the sacrificial limbs were salted; and at the top of the altar, where the handful of the meal offering, the frankincense, the meal offerings that are entirely burned, and the bird burnt offering were salted. This is in accordance with the *baraita*. The Rambam does not mention the salting of the incense, since this was performed when the incense was prepared (Rambam *Sefer Avoda*, *Hilkhot Issurei Mizbe'aḥ* 5:13, and see Radbaz there).

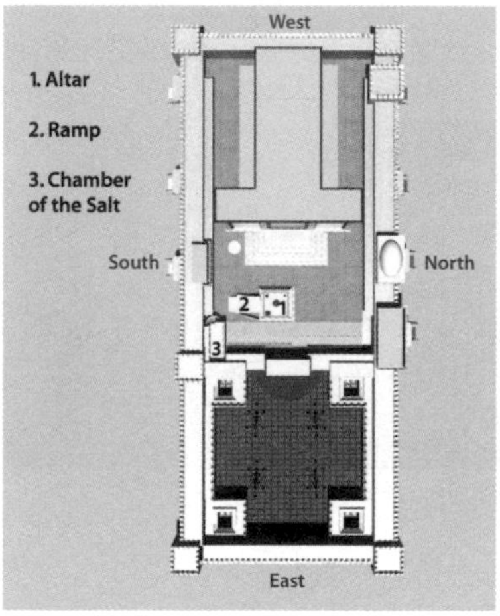

Locations of salt

תָּנוּ רַבָּנַן: מֶלַח שֶׁעַל גַּבֵּי הָאֵבֶר – מוֹעֲלִין בּוֹ, שֶׁעַל גַּבֵּי הַכֶּבֶשׁ וְשֶׁבְּרֹאשׁוֹ שֶׁל מִזְבֵּחַ – אֵין מוֹעֲלִין בּוֹ. וַאֲמַר רַב מַתָּנָה: מַאי קְרָאָה? ״וְהִקְרַבְתָּם לִפְנֵי ה׳ וְהִשְׁלִיכוּ הַכֹּהֲנִים עֲלֵיהֶם מֶלַח וְהֶעֱלוּ אוֹתָם עֹלָה לַה׳״.

The Sages taught in a *baraita* (*Tosefta* 6:4): With regard to **salt that is on the limb** of an offering,[H] one who derives benefit **from it** is liable for **misuse** of consecrated property,[N] but in the case of salt **that is on the ramp or that is on top of the altar,**[N] one who derives benefit **from it is not** liable for **misuse** of consecrated property. **And Rav Mattana said: What is the verse** from which it is derived that the salt found upon a sacrificial limb is subject to the *halakhot* of misuse of consecrated property? The verse states: **"And you shall sacrifice them before the Lord, and the priests shall cast salt upon them, and they shall offer them up for a burnt offering to the Lord"** (Ezekiel 43:24). In this verse, the limbs, together with the salt, are termed a burnt offering, and therefore the salt on the limb is also subject to the *halakhot* of misuse of consecrated property.

תְּנַן הָתָם: עַל הַמֶּלַח וְעַל הָעֵצִים, שֶׁיְּהוּ הַכֹּהֲנִים נֵאוֹתִין בָּהֶן. אָמַר שְׁמוּאֵל: לֹא שָׁנוּ אֶלָּא לְקָרְבָּנָם, אֲבָל לַאֲכִילָה – לֹא.

With regard to the *halakha* that salt is not subject to the *halakhot* of misuse of consecrated property, **we learned** in a mishna **elsewhere** (*Shekalim* 7:7): The court instituted an ordinance **about the salt and about the wood**[H] in the Temple to the effect **that the priests may derive benefit from them. Shmuel says: They taught only** that the priests may derive benefit from the salt **for** use on **their offerings, but not for eating** it.

קָא סָלְקָא דַעְתִּין: מַאי ״לְקָרְבָּנָם״ – לִמְלוֹחַ קָרְבָּנָם, ״לֶאֱכוֹל״ – אֲכִילַת קָדָשִׁים; הָשְׁתָּא לִמְלוֹחַ עוֹרוֹת קָדָשִׁים יָהֲבִינַן, לַאֲכִילַת קָדָשִׁים לָא יָהֲבִינַן?

The Gemara comments: **It enters our mind** to say: **What** did Shmuel mean by the expression: **For** use on **their offerings?** He meant that the priests were permitted **to salt their** personal **offerings.** And when Shmuel states that **for** the purpose of **eating** it is not permitted for the priests to derive benefit from the salt, he is referring to adding salt when **eating** the meat **of sacrificial** animals, e.g., the portions of the sin offering and guilt offering that are given to the priests. The Gemara challenges this explanation: **Now,** if **we give** the priests salt in order **to salt the hides of sacrificial** animals that are given to the priests to keep, so that they can process them, is it reasonable to rule that **we do not give them** salt in order **to** add it when they **eat** the meat of **sacrificial** animals?

דְּתַנְיָא: נִמְצֵאתָ אַתָּה אוֹמֵר, בִּשְׁלֹשָׁה מְקוֹמוֹת הַמֶּלַח נְתוּנָה: בְּלִשְׁכַּת הַמֶּלַח, וְעַל גַּבֵּי הַכֶּבֶשׁ, וּבְרֹאשׁוֹ שֶׁל מִזְבֵּחַ; בְּלִשְׁכַּת הַמֶּלַח – שֶׁשָּׁם מוֹלְחִין עוֹרוֹת קָדָשִׁים, עַל גַּבֵּי הַכֶּבֶשׁ – שֶׁשָּׁם מוֹלְחִים אֶת הָאֵבָרִים, בְּרֹאשׁוֹ שֶׁל מִזְבֵּחַ – שֶׁשָּׁם מוֹלְחִין הַקּוֹמֶץ וְהַלְּבוֹנָה, וְהַקְּטוֹרֶת, וּמִנְחַת כֹּהֲנִים, וּמִנְחַת כֹּהֵן מָשִׁיחַ, וּמִנְחַת נְסָכִים, וְעוֹלַת הָעוֹף!

The Gemara explains its challenge: **As it is taught** in a *baraita* (*Tosefta* 6:2): **You are found** to be **saying** that **the salt is placed in three locations**[H] in the Temple: **In the Chamber of the Salt, and on the ramp, and on top of** the **altar.** It is placed **in the Chamber of the Salt, since** the priests **salted there the hides of sacrificial** animals that are given to them. It is placed **on the ramp, since** the priests **salted there the** sacrificial **limbs.** It is placed **on top of** the **altar, since** the priests **salted there the handful** of the meal offering, **the frankincense, the incense, the meal offering of priests, the meal offering of** the **anointed priest, the meal offering** that accompanies the **libations, and the bird burnt offering.** Evidently, it was permitted for the priests to add salt to their portions of sacrificial meat.

NOTES

Liable for misuse of consecrated property – מוֹעֲלִין: If one accidentally derives benefit from consecrated property, he must return the value of his benefit, along with an additional one-fifth of its value. He also must bring a guilt offering for unwitting misuse of consecrated property.

Salt that is on the ramp or that is on top of the altar – שֶׁעַל גַּבֵּי הַכֶּבֶשׁ וְשֶׁבְּרֹאשׁוֹ שֶׁל מִזְבֵּחַ: As the Gemara explains, these are locations where the offerings were salted. Rashi explains that the *baraita* is referring to salt that was applied to sacrificial limbs and fell off after the salting. Since it is no longer fit to salt with, it is not returned to the altar, and one who derives benefit from it is not liable for misuse of consecrated property. By contrast, if the limbs of a burnt offering fall from the altar they are returned to it, and one who derives benefit from them is liable for misuse of consecrated property (see *Zevaḥim* 108a).

Some commentaries raise objections to Rashi's explanation, and explain that the *baraita* is referring to salt that is left at these locations for the purpose of being used for salting. Although this salt belongs to the Temple treasury and ostensibly one who benefits from it should be liable for misuse of consecrated property, the court instituted an ordinance permitting the priests to make use of salt, as the Gemara explains later (*Keren Ora*; *Sefat Emet*).

אלא מאי "לקרבנם" – לאכילת קרבנם, ומאי "לאכילה" – אכילה דחולין.

The Gemara suggests a different explanation of Shmuel's statement: **Rather, what** did Shmuel mean by the expression: **For** use on **their offerings?** He meant that it is permitted for the priests **to** add salt when they **eat** the meat of **their offerings,** e.g., the portions of the guilt offerings and sin offerings that are given to the priests, as well as when they eat the remainder of the meal offering. **And what** is meant when Shmuel states that **for** the purpose of **eating** it is not permitted for the priests to derive benefit from the salt? He is referring to using the salt for the purpose of **eating non-sacred** food.

חולין, פשיטא! מאי בעו התם? אף על גב דאמר מר: "יאכלו" – שיאכלו עמה חולין ותרומה כדי שתהא נאכלת על השובע, אפילו הכי מלח דקדשים לא יהבינן להו.

The Gemara objects: Isn't it **obvious** that the salt is not to be eaten with **non-sacred** food? **What** would non-sacred food be **doing there** in the Temple courtyard? The Gemara answers: **Even though the Master says** in the *baraita* that the verse stated with regard to the meal offering: "And that which is left of it Aaron and his sons **shall eat**" (Leviticus 6:9), teaching **that** the priests **shall eat non-sacred** food **and *teruma* along with** the remainder of the meal offering[H] **so that** the remainder of the meal offering **will be eaten in** a manner that the priest will be **satiated** when he finishes eating it, demonstrating that non-sacred food may be brought to the Temple courtyard, **even so we do not give them consecrated salt.**[H]

אמר ליה רבינא לרב אשי: הכי נמי מסתברא, דאי סלקא דעתך מאי "לקרבנם" – למלוח, טעמא דאתני בית דין, הא לא אתני בית דין – לא; השתא לישראל יהבינן, לכהנים לא יהבינן?

Ravina said to Rav Ashi: So too, it is reasonable to explain that Shmuel's explanation of the mishna in *Shekalim* is that the ordinance of the court permitted the priests to eat the salt with sacrificial foods. **As, if it enters your mind** to say: **What** did Shmuel mean by the expression: **For** use on **their offerings?** He meant that the priests were permitted **to salt** their personal offerings; then one must extrapolate from the mishna that **the reason** this is permitted is **that the court stipulated** that it should be, **but had the court not stipulated** this, it would **not** be permitted. That cannot be, as **now** that **we give** salt **to Israelites** to salt their offerings, will **we not give** salt **to priests** for the same purpose?

דתניא: יכול האומר "הרי עלי מנחה" יביא מלח מתוך ביתו, כדרך שמביא לבונה מתוך ביתו? ודין הוא: נאמר הביא מנחה והביא מלח, ונאמר הביא מנחה והביא לבונה, מה לבונה מתוך ביתו – אף מלח מתוך ביתו.

As it is taught in a *baraita* that we provide salt for the offerings of Israelites: One **might** have thought that **one who says:** It is incumbent **upon me** to bring a **meal offering, must bring salt from his home,** i.e., his own salt, to salt the handful that is burned on the altar, **just as he brings frankincense from his home** for his meal offering. **And** this would seem to be **a logical inference:** It **is stated** in the Torah that one shall **bring a meal offering, and** it is stated that one shall **bring salt,** as it is written: "And every meal offering of yours you shall season with salt" (Leviticus 2:13); **and it is stated** that one shall **bring a meal offering, and** it is stated that one shall **bring frankincense.** Therefore, **just as** one brings **frankincense from his home,** as it is written: "And put frankincense on it. And he shall bring it to Aaron's sons the priests" (Leviticus 2:1–2), **so too,** one must bring **salt from his home.**

או כלך לדרך זו: נאמר הביא מנחה והביא מלח, ונאמר הביא מנחה והביא עצים, מה עצים משל ציבור – אף מלח משל ציבור?

Or perhaps, **go this way:** It **is stated** in the Torah that one shall **bring a meal offering and** that one shall **bring salt, and it is stated** that one shall **bring a meal offering and** that one shall **bring wood,** as the meal offering cannot be burned on the altar without the wood. Therefore, **just as the wood** comes **from communal** supplies, **so too,** the **salt** shall come **from communal** supplies.[H]

נראה למי דומה, דנין דבר הנוהג בכל הזבחים מדבר הנוהג בכל הזבחים, ואל תוכיח לבונה שאינה נוהגת בכל הזבחים.

The *baraita* continues: **Let us see to which** salt **is** more **similar,** i.e., which comparison seems more reasonable: **We derive** the *halakha* of salt, which is **a matter that applies to all offerings, from** the *halakha* of wood, which is also **a matter that applies to all offerings. And** do **not** let the *halakha* of **frankincense prove** otherwise, **as it does not apply to all offerings,** only to the meal offerings.

או כלך לדרך זו: דנין דבר הבא עמה בכלי אחד מדבר הבא עמה בכלי אחד, ואל יוכיחו עצים שאינן באין עמה בכלי אחד?

Or perhaps, **go this way: We derive** the *halakha* of salt, which is **a matter that accompanies** the meal offering **in one vessel, from** the *halakha* of frankincense, which is also **a matter that accompanies** the meal offering **in one vessel. And** do **not** let the *halakha* of **wood prove** otherwise, **as it does not accompany** the meal offering **in one vessel.**

HALAKHA

The priests shall eat non-sacred food and *teruma* along with it – יֹאכְלוּ עִמָּהּ חוּלִּין וּתְרוּמָה: If the portion of the offering given to the priests contains only a small amount of meat, the priests should eat non-sacred food and *teruma* with it so that they will be satiated. The *halakha* is the same with regard to the remainder of the meal offering. This is in accordance with the *baraita* (Rambam *Sefer Korbanot, Hilkhot Ma'aseh HaKorbanot* 10:11).

We do not give them consecrated salt – מֶלַח דְּקָדָשִׁים לָא יָהֲבִינַן לְהוּ: It is prohibited for the priests to use consecrated salt when eating non-consecrated food, in accordance with Gemara's interpretation of Shmuel's statement (Rambam *Sefer Avoda, Hilkhot Me'ila* 8:6).

Salt shall come from communal supplies – מֶלַח מִשֶּׁל צִיבּוּר: The salt that is used on offerings comes from communal supplies, and an individual does not bring his own salt, in accordance with the *baraita* (Rambam *Sefer Avoda, Hilkhot Issurei Mizbe'aḥ* 5:13).

HALAKHA

Any priest who does not contribute his shekel, etc. – **כָּל כֹּהֵן שֶׁאֵינוֹ שׁוֹקֵל וכו׳**: The priests are obligated to give the half-shekel like all Jews, in accordance with the opinion of Rabban Yoḥanan ben Zakkai (Rambam *Sefer Zemanim, Hilkhot Shekalim* 1:7).

תַּלְמוּד לוֹמַר: ״בְּרִית מֶלַח עוֹלָם הוּא״, וּלְהַלָּן הוּא אוֹמֵר: ״מֵאֵת בְּנֵי יִשְׂרָאֵל בְּרִית עוֹלָם״, מַה לְהַלָּן מִשֶּׁל צִיבּוּר – אַף כָּאן מִשֶּׁל צִיבּוּר!

The *baraita* continues: **The verse states: "It is an everlasting covenant of salt"** (Numbers 18:19), **and there,** with regard to the shewbread, **it states: "It is from the children of Israel, an everlasting covenant"** (Leviticus 24:8); Therefore, **just as** the phrase written **there:** "From the children of Israel, an everlasting covenant," means that it is brought **from communal** supplies, as the shewbread is a communal offering, **so too here,** the verse that speaks of the everlasting covenant of salt means that the salt is brought **from communal** supplies. Evidently, salt is provided for offerings of Israelites, and should likewise be provided for the offerings of priests. Accordingly, there would have been no need for the court to permit the priests to salt their offerings, and it must be that the ordinance of the court permitted the priests to use salt when eating sacrificial foods.

אֲמַר לֵיהּ רַב מָרְדֳּכַי לְרַב אַשִׁי, הָכִי קָאָמַר רַב שֵׁישָׁא בְּרֵיהּ דְּרַב אִידִי: לָא נִצְרְכָא אֶלָּא לְבֶן בּוּכְרִי,

Rav Mordekhai said to Rav Ashi: This is what **Rav Sheisha, son of Rav Idi, says:** The initial understanding of Shmuel's interpretation of the mishna is correct, i.e., that the ordinance of the court permitted the priests to salt their offerings; and the ruling of the mishna **is necessary only according to** the opinion of **ben Bukhri,** who holds that priests are not obligated to contribute a yearly half-shekel to purchase the communal supplies.

דִּתְנַן: אָמַר רַבִּי יְהוּדָה, הֵעִיד בֶּן בּוּכְרִי בְּיַבְנֶה: כׇּל כֹּהֵן שֶׁשּׁוֹקֵל אֵינוֹ חוֹטֵא; אָמַר לוֹ רַבָּן יוֹחָנָן בֶּן זַכַּאי: לֹא כִּי, אֶלָּא כׇּל כֹּהֵן שֶׁאֵינוֹ שׁוֹקֵל חוֹטֵא, אֶלָּא שֶׁהַכֹּהֲנִים דּוֹרְשִׁין מִקְרָא זֶה לְעַצְמָן.

As we learned in a mishna (*Shekalim* 1:4): **Rabbi Yehuda said** that **ben Bukhri testified in Yavne: Any priest who contributes his shekel is not** considered **a sinner,** despite the fact that he is not obligated to do so. Rabbi Yehuda added that **Rabban Yoḥanan ben Zakkai said to** ben Bukhri: **That is not** the case; **rather, any priest who does not contribute his shekel**[H] is considered **a sinner,** as they are obligated in this mitzva like all other Jews. **But the priests** who do not contribute the shekel **interpret this** following **verse to their own** advantage in order to excuse themselves from the mitzva.

״וְכׇל מִנְחַת כֹּהֵן כָּלִיל תִּהְיֶה לֹא תֵאָכֵל״, הוֹאִיל וְעוֹמֶר וּשְׁתֵּי הַלֶּחֶם וְלֶחֶם הַפָּנִים שֶׁלָּנוּ הִיא, הֵיאַךְ נֶאֱכָלִין?

The verse states: **"And every meal offering of the priest shall be wholly made to smoke; it shall not be eaten"** (Leviticus 6:16). Those priests claim as follows: **Since the** ***omer*** **offering and the two loaves,**[N] i.e., the public offering of two loaves from the new wheat, brought on the festival of *Shavuot*, **and the shewbread** placed on the Table in the Sanctuary each Shabbat, which are all meal offerings, are **ours,** then if we contribute shekels we will have partial ownership of these communal offerings, as they are purchased with the shekels. **How,** then, **can they be eaten?** They would then be regarded as priests' meal offerings, which must be wholly burned.

וּלְבֶן בּוּכְרִי, כֵּיוָן דִּלְכַתְּחִילָּה לָא מִיחַיַּיב לְאֵיתוּיֵי, כִּי מַיְיתֵי נַמִי – חוֹטֵא הוּא, דְּקָא מְעַיֵּיל חוּלִּין לָעֲזָרָה! דְּמַיְיתֵי וּמָסַר לְהוּן לְצִיבּוּר.

The Gemara clarifies: **But according to** the opinion of **ben Bukhri,** why is a priest who contributes a half-shekel not considered a sinner? **Since he is not obligated to bring** it ***ab initio***, **when he brings** the half-shekel **he is also a sinner, since he is** causing the **bringing** of **a non-sacred** item **into the** Temple **courtyard.** He is not contributing the half-shekel as part of the communal offering, as he is exempt from this obligation. Therefore, his donation is the donation of an individual, and a communal offering cannot be brought on behalf of an individual. His donation should disqualify all offerings brought from the communal funds. The Gemara answers: The priest **brings and transfers** the half-shekel **to the community,** so it is considered part of the communal funds.

סָלְקָא דַעְתָּךְ אָמִינָא,

The Gemara states the relevance of the opinion of ben Bukhri to the statement of Shmuel: According to the opinion of ben Bukhri it might **enter your mind to say** that

NOTES

Since the *omer* offering and the two loaves, etc. – **הוֹאִיל וְעוֹמֶר וּשְׁתֵּי הַלֶּחֶם וכו׳**: The Rabbis hold that there is a distinction between the meal offering of an individual priest, which may not be eaten, and a communal meal offering of which the priest is one contributor, which may be eaten (Jerusalem Talmud, *Shekalim* 1:3). Rashi in tractate *Arakhin* (4a) explains that in the case of communal offerings the majority of the contributors are Israelites, and therefore it is not considered a meal offering of priests.

כִּי זָכֵי לְהוּ רַחֲמָנָא – לְיִשְׂרָאֵל, דְּאִית לְהוּ לִשְׁכָּה, לַכֹּהֲנִים דְּלֵית לְהוּ לִשְׁכָּה – לָא זָכֵי לְהוּ רַחֲמָנָא, קָא מַשְׁמַע לַן.

when the Merciful One granted the Jewish people the right to use the salt when eating their offerings, he granted this **to Israelites, who have** an obligation to donate their half-shekels to the **chamber,** as this fund supplies the salt that is applied to the offerings. With regard **to the priests, who do not have** an obligation to donate their half-shekels to the **chamber, the Merciful One did not grant them** the right to make use of the salt. To counter this, the mishna in tractate *Shekalim* **teaches us** that the court granted to the priests the right to use the salt when eating their offerings.

וְעֵצִים דִּפְשִׁיטָא לֵיהּ לְתַנָּא דְּמִשֶּׁל צִיבּוּר, מְנָלַן? דְּתַנְיָא: יָכוֹל הָאוֹמֵר "הֲרֵי עָלַי עוֹלָה" יָבִיא עֵצִים מִתּוֹךְ בֵּיתוֹ, כְּדֶרֶךְ שֶׁמֵּבִיא נְסָכִים מִתּוֹךְ בֵּיתוֹ? תַּלְמוּד לוֹמַר: "עַל הָעֵצִים אֲשֶׁר עַל הָאֵשׁ אֲשֶׁר עַל הַמִּזְבֵּחַ", מָה מִזְבֵּחַ מִשֶּׁל צִיבּוּר – אַף עֵצִים וְאֵשׁ מִשֶּׁל צִיבּוּר, דִּבְרֵי רַבִּי אֶלְעָזָר בַּר רַבִּי שִׁמְעוֹן;

The Gemara asks: **And** with regard to the **wood,** concerning **which** it is **obvious to the *tanna*** of the *baraita* **that** it is brought **from communal** supplies, **from where do we** derive this *halakha*? The Gemara answers: **As it is taught** in a *baraita*: One **might** have thought that **one who says:** It is incumbent **upon me** to bring **a burnt offering, must bring wood from his home** on which the burnt offering will be sacrificed, **just as he brings libations from his home** along with a burnt offering (see Numbers, chapter 15). Therefore, **the verse states** with regard to the burnt offering: **"On the wood that is on the fire which is upon the altar"** (Leviticus 1:12); the Torah juxtaposes the wood to the altar, teaching that **just as** the **altar** was built **from communal** funds, **so too,** the **wood and fire** are brought **from communal** supplies.[H] This is **the statement of Rabbi Elazar bar Rabbi Shimon.**

רַבִּי אֶלְעָזָר בֶּן שַׁמּוּעַ אוֹמֵר: מָה מִזְבֵּחַ שֶׁלֹּא נִשְׁתַּמֵּשׁ בּוֹ הֶדְיוֹט – אַף עֵצִים וְאֵשׁ שֶׁלֹּא נִשְׁתַּמֵּשׁ בָּהֶן הֶדְיוֹט. מַאי בֵּינַיְיהוּ? אִיכָּא בֵּינַיְיהוּ: חַדְתִּי.

The *baraita* continues: **Rabbi Elazar ben Shammua says: Just as** the **altar was not used by an ordinary** person, as it was built for the purpose of serving as an altar for God, **so too,** the **wood and fire** should **not have been used** previously **by an ordinary** person,[H] so one does not bring the wood from his home. The Gemara asks: **What** is the difference **between** the two opinions? The Gemara answers: The difference **between** the two **is whether** there is a requirement that the wood be **new,**[H] i.e., that it had never been used. According to the opinion of Rabbi Elazar bar Rabbi Shimon, the wood is fit provided that it comes from communal supplies, even if it is not new wood, whereas according to Rabbi Elazar ben Shammua it must be new wood.

וְעַתִּיקֵי לָא? וְהָכְתִיב: "וַיֹּאמֶר אֲרַוְנָה אֶל דָּוִד יִקַּח וְיַעַל אֲדֹנִי הַמֶּלֶךְ הַטּוֹב בְּעֵינָיו רְאֵה הַבָּקָר לָעֹלָה וְהַמֹּרִגִּים וּכְלֵי הַבָּקָר לָעֵצִים"! הָכָא נַמִי בְּחַדְתִּי.

The Gemara asks: **And** is it in fact the *halakha* that **old,** i.e., previously used, wood is **not** fit to be burned on the altar? **But isn't it written: "And Araunah said to David: Let my lord the king take and offer up what seems good to him; behold the oxen for the burnt offering, and the threshing instruments [*morigim*] and the equipment of the oxen for the wood"** (II Samuel 24:22)? Despite the fact that the threshing instruments and equipment of the oxen have been used previously, apparently they are fit to be used when offering a burnt offering. The Gemara answers: **Here too,** the verse is speaking **of new** instruments and equipment that had not been previously used.

HALAKHA

The wood and fire are brought from communal supplies – עֵצִים וְאֵשׁ מִשֶּׁל צִיבּוּר: An individual does not bring his own wood when bringing an offering. This is in accordance with the *baraita* and the statement of Rabbi Elazar bar Rabbi Shimon, as even Rabbi Elazar ben Shammua does not disagree with him (Rambam *Sefer Avoda, Hilkhot Issurei Mizbe'aḥ* 5:13).

Should not have been used previously by an ordinary person – שֶׁלֹּא נִשְׁתַּמֵּשׁ בָּהֶן הֶדְיוֹט: The Temple service vessels should be built for the express purpose of serving as consecrated vessels. If they were built for an ordinary purpose, they may not be used as sacred vessels. This is based on the *Tosefta, Megilla* 2:16 (Rambam *Sefer Avoda, Hilkhot Beit HaBeḥira* 1:20).

Whether there is a requirement that the wood be new – חַדְתִּי: Wood salvaged from a demolished building is permanently unfit; only new wood, i.e., wood that had never been used for any other purpose, is fit for arrangement upon the altar. This is in accordance with the *Tosefta* (9:14) and the opinion of Rabbi Elazar ben Shammua (Rambam *Sefer Avoda, Hilkhot Issurei Mizbe'aḥ* 6:2, and see *Leḥem Mishne* there).

LANGUAGE

Turbal – טֻרְבָּל: Apparently from the Greek τρίβολος, *tribolos*, which can mean sledge or threshing board, i.e., a heavy wooden board with notches or spikes on its underside. When this board is dragged by an animal over grain on the threshing floor, the grain kernels are separated from the stalks.

Threshing board

Serrated [*kurkesa*] – דְּקוּרְקְסָא: The word *kurkesa* apparently originates in the Greek κίρκος, *kirkos*, or κρίκος, *krikos*, meaning circle, circular object, or ring. Among its meanings is a wheel used for threshing.

Illustration of wheeled threshing sledge from the mishnaic period

מַאי "מוֹרִיגִים"? אָמַר עוּלָּא: מִטָּה שֶׁל טֻרְבָּל. מַאי מִטָּה שֶׁל טֻרְבָּל? אָמַר רַב יְהוּדָה: עִיזָּא דְקוּרְקְסָא דְּדָשׁוּ בַּהּ דִּשְׁתָּאֵי. אָמַר רַב יוֹסֵף: מַאי קְרָאָה? "הִנֵּה שַׂמְתִּיךְ לְמוֹרַג חָרוּץ חָדָשׁ בַּעַל פִּיפִיּוֹת תָּדוּשׁ הָרִים".

Tangentially, the Gemara asks: **What is the meaning of the term** ***morigim*** mentioned in this verse? **Ulla said:** It is **a** ***turbal***[L] **bed.** This was not a known expression in Babylonia, so the Gemara asks: **What is a** ***turbal*** **bed? Rav Yehuda said:** It is referring to **a serrated** [*dekurkesa*][L] **board that the threshers use for threshing,** which is dragged over the grain by an animal in order to separate the kernels from the stalks. **Rav Yosef said: What is the verse** from which the meaning of *morigim* is derived? It is the verse that states: **"Behold, I have made you a new threshing sledge** [*morag*] **having sharp teeth; you shall thresh the mountains"** (Isaiah 41:15).

מתני׳ נִתְעָרֵב קוּמְצָהּ בְּקוֹמֶץ חֲבֵירְתָּהּ, בְּמִנְחַת כֹּהֲנִים, בְּמִנְחַת כֹּהֵן מָשִׁיחַ, בְּמִנְחַת נְסָכִים – כְּשֵׁרָה.

MISHNA If **a handful** of one meal offering, which is to be burned on the altar, **was intermingled**[H] **with a handful of another** meal offering, or **with the meal offering of priests,** or **with the meal offering of** the **anointed priest,** i.e., the High Priest, or **with the meal offering of libations** accompanying burnt offerings and peace offerings, all of which are burned in their entirety on the altar, it is **fit** for sacrifice, and the mixture is burned on the altar.

רַבִּי יְהוּדָה אוֹמֵר: בְּמִנְחַת כֹּהֵן מָשִׁיחַ, בְּמִנְחַת נְסָכִים – פְּסוּלָה, שֶׁזּוֹ בְּלִילָתָהּ עָבָה וְזוֹ בְּלִילָתָהּ רַכָּה, וְהֵן בּוֹלְעוֹת זוֹ מִזּוֹ.

Rabbi Yehuda says: If the handful was intermingled **with the meal offering of** the **anointed priest,** or **with the meal offering of libations,** the mixture is **unfit because** with regard to **this,** the handful from the standard meal offering, **its mixture is thick,** one *log* of oil mixed with a tenth of an ephah of flour, **and** with regard to **that,** the meal offering of the anointed priest and the meal offering of libations, **its mixture is loose,** three *log* of oil mixed with a tenth of an ephah of flour. **And** the mixtures, which are not identical, **absorb from each other,** increasing the amount of oil in the handful and decreasing the amount of oil in the meal offering of the anointed priest or the meal offering of libations, thereby invalidating both.

גמ׳ תְּנַן הָתָם: דָּם שֶׁנִּתְעָרֵב בְּמַיִם, אִם יֵשׁ בּוֹ מַרְאִית דָּם – כָּשֵׁר. נִתְעָרֵב בְּיַיִן – רוֹאִין אוֹתוֹ כְּאִילּוּ הוּא מַיִם. נִתְעָרֵב בְּדַם בְּהֵמָה אוֹ בְּדַם חַיָּה – רוֹאִין אוֹתוֹ כְּאִילּוּ הוּא מַיִם. רַבִּי יְהוּדָה אוֹמֵר: אֵין דָּם מְבַטֵּל דָּם.

GEMARA We learned in a mishna **there** (*Zevaḥim* 77b): In the case of **blood** of an offering fit for sacrifice **that was mixed**[H] **with water, if** the mixture **has the appearance of blood,** it is **fit** for presenting on the altar, even though the majority of the mixture is water. If the blood **was mixed with** red **wine, one views** the wine **as though it were water.** If that amount of water would leave the mixture with the appearance of blood, it is fit for presentation. Likewise, if the blood **was mixed with the blood of** a non-sacred **domesticated animal or the blood of** a non-sacred **undomesticated animal, one considers** the blood **as though it were water. Rabbi Yehuda says: Blood does not nullify blood.** Therefore, the priest presents the blood of the mixture on the altar regardless of the ratio of sacred to non-sacred blood.

אָמַר רַבִּי יוֹחָנָן, וּשְׁנֵיהֶם מִקְרָא אֶחָד דָּרְשׁוּ: "וְלָקַח מִדַּם הַפָּר וּמִדַּם הַשָּׂעִיר" – הַדָּבָר יָדוּעַ שֶׁדָּמוֹ שֶׁל פָּר מְרוּבֶּה מִדָּמוֹ שֶׁל שָׂעִיר; רַבָּנַן סָבְרִי:

Rabbi Yoḥanan says: And both the the first *tanna* and Rabbi Yehuda **derived** their opinions **from one verse.** With regard to the sacrificial rites performed by the High Priest on Yom Kippur, the Torah teaches that after sprinkling of the blood of the bull and of the goat separately between the staves of the Ark and on the Curtain, the blood of the two animals is mixed together and presented on the golden altar inside the Sanctuary. The verse states: **"And he shall take of the blood of the bull and of the blood of the goat** and put it on the corners of the altar" (Leviticus 16:18). **It is a known matter that the blood of the bull is more than the blood of a goat.** Why then is the blood of the goat not nullified? Rabbi Yoḥanan explains: **The Rabbis,** i.e, the first *tanna*, **hold:**

HALAKHA

If a handful of one meal offering was intermingled – נִתְעָרֵב קוּמְצָהּ: If the handful of one meal offering was intermingled with a handful of another meal offering, the two are burned together and the meal offerings are fit. Similarly, if the handful of one meal offering was intermingled with the meal offering of priests, the meal offering of the anointed priest, or with the meal offering of libations accompanying burnt offerings and peace offerings, the mixture is fit for sacrifice, because all of these offerings are burned in their entirety on the altar. This is in accordance with the opinion of the Rabbis (Rambam *Sefer Avoda, Hilkhot Pesulei HaMukdashin* 11:28).

Blood of an offering that was mixed – דָּם שֶׁנִּתְעָרֵב: In a case where water fell into a cup of the blood of an offering, if the mixture retains the appearance of blood, it is fit. If wine or non-sacred blood fell into a cup of the blood, the wine or non-sacred blood is viewed as though it were water. If that amount of water would cause the mixture to not have the appearance of blood, then the mixture is unfit for presentation. If that amount of water would leave the mixture with the appearance of blood, it is fit for presentation. This is in accordance with the opinion of the Rabbis in the mishna in tractate *Zevaḥim* (77b) and with the statement of Rabbi Yoḥanan there (Rambam *Sefer Avoda, Hilkhot Pesulei HaMukdashin* 2:22).

מִכָּאן לָעוֹלִין שֶׁאֵין מְבַטְּלִין זֶה אֶת זֶה, וְרַבִּי יְהוּדָה סָבַר: מִכָּאן לְמִין בְּמִינוֹ שֶׁאֵינוֹ בָּטֵל.

From here it is learned **that** with regard to a mixture of items that **ascend** to the altar, e.g., the blood of the bull and the goat, the different components of the mixture **do not nullify one another. And Rabbi Yehuda holds: From here** it is learned **that** any **substance** in contact **with** the **same** type of **substance is not nullified.**

רַבָּנַן סָבְרִי: מִכָּאן לָעוֹלִין שֶׁאֵין מְבַטְּלִין זֶה אֶת זֶה. וְדִלְמָא מִשּׁוּם דְּמִין בְּמִינוֹ הוּא!

The Gemara examines Rabbi Yoḥanan's explanation of the dispute between the Rabbis and Rabbi Yehuda. With regard to the first part of his explanation, that **the Rabbis hold: From here** it is learned **that** with regard to a mixture of items that **ascend** to the altar the different components of the mixture **do not nullify one another,** the Gemara suggests: **But perhaps** the blood of the goat is not nullified when mixed with the blood of the bull **due to** the fact **that it is a substance** in contact **with** the **same** type of **substance.**

אִי אַשְׁמְעִינַן מִין בְּמִינוֹ וְלָא אַשְׁמְעִינַן עוֹלִין – כִּדְקָא אָמְרַתְּ; הָשְׁתָּא דְּאַשְׁמְעִינַן עוֹלִין – מִשּׁוּם דְּעוֹלִין.

The Gemara answers: **Had** the verse **taught us** this *halakha* by using an example of **a substance** in contact **with** the **same** type of **substance, and not taught us** a case of a mixture of items that **ascend** to the altar, the verse would be interpreted **as you said.** But **now that** the verse **taught us** this *halakha* through a case of a mixture of items that **ascend** to the altar, it is understood that the reason it is not nullified is **due to** the fact **that** it is part of a mixture of items that **ascend** to the altar, not because the substances are of the same type.

וְדִלְמָא עַד דְּאִיכָּא מִין בְּמִינוֹ וְעוֹלִין! קַשְׁיָא.

The Gemara suggests: **But perhaps** it is not nullified **until** both criteria **are** met, and unless the mixture is both **a substance** in contact **with** the **same** type of **substance and** a mixture of items that **ascend** to the altar, one nullifies the other. The Gemara concedes: This is **difficult.**

וְרַבִּי יְהוּדָה סָבַר: מִכָּאן לְמִין בְּמִינוֹ שֶׁאֵינוֹ בָּטֵל. וְדִלְמָא מִשּׁוּם דְּעוֹלִין הוּא!

With regard to the second part of Rabbi Yoḥanan's explanation: **And Rabbi Yehuda holds: From here** it is learned **that** any **substance** in contact **with** the **same** type of **substance is not nullified,** the Gemara suggests: **But perhaps** the blood of the goat is not nullified when mixed with the blood of the bull **due to** the fact **that it is** a mixture of items that **ascend** to the altar.

אִי אַשְׁמְעִינַן עוֹלִין מִין בְּשֶׁאֵינוֹ מִינוֹ – כִּדְקָאָמְרַתְּ; הָשְׁתָּא דְּאַשְׁמְעִינַן מִין בְּמִינוֹ – מִשּׁוּם דְּמִין בְּמִינוֹ הוּא.

The Gemara answers: **Had** the verse **taught us** this *halakha* by using an example of a mixture of items that **ascend** to the altar where the **substance** is in contact **with a different** type of **substance,** the verse would be interpreted **as you say.** But **now that** the verse **taught us** this *halakha* in a case of **a substance** in contact **with** the **same** type of **substance,** it is understood that the reason it is not nullified is **due to** the fact **that it is a substance** in contact **with** the **same** type of **substance.**

וְדִילְמָא עַד דְּאִיכָּא מִין בְּמִינוֹ וְעוֹלִין! קַשְׁיָא.

The Gemara suggests: **But perhaps** it is not nullified **until** both criteria **are** met, and unless the mixture is both **a substance** in contact **with** the **same** type of **substance and** a mixture of items that **ascend** to the altar, one nullifies the other. The Gemara concedes: This is **difficult.**

תְּנַן, רַבִּי יְהוּדָה אוֹמֵר: בְּמִנְחַת כֹּהֲנִים בְּמִנְחַת כֹּהֵן מָשִׁיחַ וּבְמִנְחַת נְסָכִים – פְּסוּלָה, שֶׁזּוֹ בְּלִילָתָהּ עָבָה וְזוֹ בְּלִילָתָהּ רַכָּה, וְהֵן בּוֹלְעוֹת זוֹ מִזּוֹ. וְכִי בּוֹלְעוֹת זוֹ מִזּוֹ מַה הֲוֵי? מִין בְּמִינוֹ הוּא!

The Gemara raises another objection to the explanation of Rabbi Yoḥanan: **We learned** in the mishna here that **Rabbi Yehuda says:** If the handful was intermingled **with the meal offering of priests, with the meal offering of** the **anointed priest, or with the meal offering of libations,** the mixture is **unfit because** with regard to **this,** the handful from the standard meal offering, **its mixture is thick, and** with regard to **that,** the meal offering of the anointed priest and the meal offering of libations, **its mixture is loose. And** the mixtures, which are not identical, **absorb from each other,** invalidating both. The Gemara asks: **But when** the mixtures **absorb**[N] **from each other, what of it?** This **is** a case of **a substance** in contact **with** the **same** type of **substance,**[H] and therefore neither oil nullifies the other and both should be sacrificed on the altar.

NOTES

We learned in the mishna here that Rabbi Yehuda says…but when the mixtures absorb, etc. – תְּנַן רַבִּי יְהוּדָה אוֹמֵר...וְכִי בּוֹלְעוֹת וכו׳: Despite the fact that the handful absorbs some of the oil of the meal offering of libations or the meal offering of the priests, since this oil is not nullified it is viewed as though it were still a part of the meal offering of libations (Commentary attributed to Rashba; *Ḥok Natan*; Rabbi Akiva Eiger; Rashash).

HALAKHA

A substance in contact with the same type of substance – מִין בְּמִינוֹ: If a prohibited substance was mixed with a permitted substance of the same type, and its taste is indiscernible, by Torah law it is nullified in a simple majority, in accordance with the opinion of the Rabbis. By rabbinic law a mixture of liquids or a mixture of dry goods that were ground or cooked together requires a proportion such that the prohibited substance can no longer be considered an item of significance in its own right. The Sages distinguished between different prohibitions: In some cases a ratio of one to sixty is required, in some the required ratio is one to one hundred, while in others it is one to two hundred (Rambam *Sefer Kedusha*, *Hilkhot Ma'akhalot Assurot* 15:1, 4–5; *Shulḥan Arukh*, *Yoreh De'a* 98:1, 109:1).

HALAKHA

Where one added oil to the handful that is removed from the meal offering of a sinner – קוֹמֶץ דְּמִנְחַת חוֹטֵא שֶׁשְּׁמָנוֹ: If oil was added to the handful that is removed from the meal offering of a sinner, it is unfit. This is in accordance with the opinion of Rabbi Yoḥanan, since in a disagreements between Rabbi Yoḥanan and Reish Lakish, the *halakha* is in accordance with the opinion of Rabbi Yoḥanan (Rambam *Sefer Avoda, Hilkhot Pesulei HaMukdashin* 11:10).

NOTES

That one should not designate oil for it – שֶׁלֹּא יִקְבַּע לָהּ שֶׁמֶן: Rashi explains that this means one may not apply oil to the sinner's meal offering before the handful is removed, but it is permitted to add oil to the handful itself; this is in keeping with the continuation of the Gemara. Others explain, in keeping with the straightforward meaning of the text, that this means one should not bring oil specially to accompany the sinner's meal offering, but it is permitted to add oil that is left over from another meal offering or unconsecrated oil (Rabbeinu Gershom Meor HaGola; Griz). Alternatively, the Gemara means that one may not add an entire *log* of oil, as this is the amount added to other meal offerings, but there is no prohibition against adding a small amount of oil (*Sefat Emet*, explaining Rashi). In any event, according to Rabbi Yoḥanan, it is prohibited to apply even a smaller quantity of oil, although it is uncertain whether the prohibition applies only to the addition of at least an olive-bulk of oil or any quantity (see 60a).

Shall not sacrifice it – לֹא יַקְרִיב: The objection is not clear, as the opinion of Reish Lakish seems to accord with that of the first *tanna* in the *baraita*. Rashi explains that the first *tanna* holds that the meal offering shall be sacrificed only because items that ascend to the altar do not nullify one another, so the oil in the mixture is ascribed only to the meal offering into which it was initially mixed. But in the case discussed by Reish Lakish, where the oil was added directly to the meal offering of the sinner, the first *tanna* would hold that the meal offering should not be sacrificed (see Rabbeinu Gershom Meor HaGola).

אֲמַר רָבָא, קָסָבַר רַבִּי יְהוּדָה: כָּל שֶׁהוּא מִין בְּמִינוֹ וְדָבָר אַחֵר – סַלֵּק אֶת מִינוֹ כְּמִי שֶׁאֵינוֹ, וְשֶׁאֵינוֹ מִינוֹ רָבֶה עָלָיו וּמְבַטְּלוֹ.

Rava said: Rabbi Yehuda holds that in the case of **any** mixture **that consists of a substance** in contact **with the same** type of **substance as well as another** type of **substance,** the *halakha* is to **disregard** the **same substance,** considering it **as though it were not** there, **and** in the event that the **different** type of **substance is more than** the first substance, the different substance **nullifies** the first substance. In the case of the mishna here, the handful of the meal offering is mixed with other types of meal offerings that comprise greater quantities of oil. The oil of the handful is disregarded, and the flour of the handful, which is present in greater quantities than the oil of the other meal offering that is absorbed in it, nullifies this oil of the other meal offering. That oil is now considered to be one with the oil of the handful, and therefore the oil of the handful is increased, and the handful is unfit.

אִיתְּמַר: קוֹמֶץ דְּמִנְחַת חוֹטֵא שֶׁשְּׁמָנוֹ – רַבִּי יוֹחָנָן אוֹמֵר: פָּסוּל, וְרֵישׁ לָקִישׁ אָמַר: הוּא עַצְמוֹ מְשַׁכְשְׁכוֹ בְּשִׁירֵי הַלּוֹג וּמַעֲלֵהוּ.

§ **It was stated** that the *amora'im* disagreed with regard to the *halakha* **where one added oil to the handful** that is removed from **the meal offering of a sinner,**[H] which does not include oil. **Rabbi Yoḥanan says:** It is **unfit, and Reish Lakish says:** The *halakha* of the meal offering **itself** is to **wipe it,** *ab initio*, **in the remainder of the** ***log*** of oil that remains in the vessels that were used previously for other meal offerings, **and** the priest then **brings it up** and burns it on the altar. This is done so that the meal offering will not be completely dry.

וְהָכְתִיב: "לֹא יָשִׂים עָלֶיהָ שֶׁמֶן וְלֹא יִתֵּן עָלֶיהָ לְבוֹנָה"! הַהוּא שֶׁלֹּא יִקְבַּע לָהּ שֶׁמֶן כַּחֲבֵרוֹתֶיהָ.

The Gemara asks: **But isn't it written** with regard to the meal offering of a sinner: **"He shall put no oil upon it, neither shall he put any frankincense on it"** (Leviticus 5:11)? How, then, can any oil be added? The Gemara answers: **That** verse teaches **that one should not designate oil for it**[N] as one designates oil for the **other** meal offerings, but the meal offering of a sinner is not rendered unfit by the addition of a small amount of oil.

אֵיתִיבֵיהּ רַבִּי יוֹחָנָן לְרֵישׁ לָקִישׁ: חָרֵב שֶׁנִּתְעָרֵב בְּבָלוּל – יַקְרִיב, רַבִּי יְהוּדָה אוֹמֵר: לֹא יַקְרִיב; מַאי לָאו קוֹמֶץ דְּמִנְחַת חוֹטֵא דְּאִיעֲרַב בְּקוֹמֶץ דְּמִנְחַת נְדָבָה?

Rabbi Yoḥanan raised an objection to Reish Lakish from a *baraita* (*Tosefta* 4:4): In the case of **a dry** meal offering **that was intermingled with** a meal offering that was **mixed** with oil, the priest **shall sacrifice** it. **Rabbi Yehuda says:** The priest **shall not sacrifice** it.[N] **What, is** the *baraita* **not** referring to **a handful of the meal offering of a sinner that was intermingled with a handful of a voluntary meal offering,** demonstrating that the oil invalidates the handful of a meal offering of a sinner?

לָא, מִנְחַת פָּרִים וְאֵילִים בְּמִנְחַת כְּבָשִׂים.

Reish Lakish responded: **No,** the *baraita* is referring to **the meal offering** that accompanies the libations brought with the offerings **of bulls or rams,** for which two *log* of oil is mixed with a tenth of an ephah of flour, that became intermingled **with the meal offering** that accompanies the libations brought with the offering **of sheep,** for which three *log* of oil is mixed with a tenth of an ephah of flour, as the former is considered dry relative to the latter.

וְהָא בְּהֶדְיָא קָתָנֵי לָהּ: מִנְחַת פָּרִים וְאֵילִים בְּמִנְחַת כְּבָשִׂים, וְחָרֵב שֶׁנִּתְעָרֵב בְּבָלוּל – יִקְרַב, רַבִּי יְהוּדָה אוֹמֵר: לֹא יִקְרַב! פֵּירוּשֵׁי קָמְפָרֵשׁ לָהּ.

Rabbi Yoḥanan objected: **But** another *baraita* **teaches this explicitly** as a separate *halakha*: With regard to **the meal offering** that accompanies the offerings **of bulls or rams** that became intermingled **with the meal offering** that accompanies the offering **of sheep, and a dry** meal offering **that was intermingled with** a meal offering that was **mixed** with oil, the meal offering **shall be sacrificed. Rabbi Yehuda says: It shall not be sacrificed.** Therefore, the latter case must be referring to other meal offerings. Reish Lakish responded: The latter clause **is explaining** the first clause of the *baraita*, teaching that the reason one may not offer a meal offering that accompanies bulls and rams that was intermingled with the meal offering that accompanies sheep is because one may not offer a dry offering that was intermingled with one that is mixed with oil.

בָּעֵי רָבָא: קוֹמֶץ שֶׁמִּיצָּה שַׁמְנוֹ עַל גַּבֵּי עֵצִים, מַהוּ? חִיבּוּרֵי עוֹלִין כְּעוֹלִין דָּמוּ, אוֹ לָאו כְּעוֹלִין דָּמוּ? אֲמַר לֵיהּ רָבִינָא לְרַב אַשִׁי: לָאו הַיְינוּ דְּרַבִּי יוֹחָנָן וְרֵישׁ לָקִישׁ?

§ **Rava raises a dilemma:** In the case of **a handful whose oil** the priest **squeezed onto the wood**[H] and only afterward he placed the handful on the wood to be burned, **what is the** *halakha*? Are substances that are **contiguous to** items that **ascend** upon the altar **considered** to be **as** part of the items that **ascend** upon the altar,[N] in which case the oil that was absorbed into the wood and is contiguous to the handful of the meal offering is considered part of the handful? **Or** are they **not considered** to be **as** part of the items that **ascend** upon the altar, and the oil is not viewed as part of the handful, and therefore the handful is missing oil? **Ravina said to Rav Ashi: Is this not** the same disagreement **as** the dispute between **Rabbi Yoḥanan and Reish Lakish?**

דְּאִיתְּמַר: הַמַּעֲלֶה אֵבֶר שֶׁאֵין בּוֹ כַּזַּיִת וְעֶצֶם מַשְׁלִימוֹ לְכַזַּיִת – רַבִּי יוֹחָנָן אָמַר: חַיָּיב, רֵישׁ לָקִישׁ אָמַר: פָּטוּר;

As it was stated: With regard to **one who offers up,** outside the Temple courtyard, **a limb that contains less than an olive-bulk** of meat,[H] **but** the offering's **bone completes** the measure of the offering **to an olive-bulk, Rabbi Yoḥanan says:** He is **liable,** and **Reish Lakish says:** He is **exempt.**

רַבִּי יוֹחָנָן אָמַר חַיָּיב – חִיבּוּרֵי עוֹלִין כְּעוֹלִין דָּמוּ, וְרֵישׁ לָקִישׁ אָמַר פָּטוּר – חִיבּוּרֵי עוֹלִין לָאו כְּעוֹלִין דָּמוּ?

Rabbi Yoḥanan says that one is **liable** because he holds that substances that are **contiguous to** items that **ascend** upon the altar are **considered** to be **as** part of the items that **ascend** upon the altar. Therefore, the measure of the bone is added to the measure of the meat, resulting in a total measure of an olive-bulk, which is the measure that determines liability. **And Reish Lakish says** that one is **exempt** because he holds that substances that are **contiguous to** items that **ascend** upon the altar **are not considered** to be **as** part of the items that **ascend** upon the altar. Since less than an olive-bulk of meat was sacrificed, he is not liable.

תִּיבָּעֵי לְרַבִּי יוֹחָנָן, וְתִיבָּעֵי לְרֵישׁ לָקִישׁ; תִּיבָּעֵי לְרַבִּי יוֹחָנָן, עַד כָּאן לֹא קָא אָמַר רַבִּי יוֹחָנָן הָתָם אֶלָּא בְּעֶצֶם, דְּמִינָא דְּבָשָׂר הוּא, אֲבָל הַאי דְּלָאו דְּמִינָא דְּקוֹמֶץ הוּא – לָא.

Rav Ashi responded: Rava's **dilemma can be raised according to Rabbi Yoḥanan, and** Rava's **dilemma can be raised according to Reish Lakish.** The circumstances in their dispute are not the same as in Rava's dilemma, so their opinions in that case may not be applicable to this one. Rav Ashi elaborates: The **dilemma can be raised according to Rabbi Yoḥanan,** even though he holds that the bone is considered to be part of the meat to complete the measure of an olive-bulk. Perhaps **Rabbi Yoḥanan says** his opinion **only there, in** the case of **a bone, because** the bone **is** the same **type as** the **meat,** i.e., it is from the same animal, and is therefore considered to be part of the sacrificial meat. **But in this** case of oil, **which is not** the same **type as** the **handful,** it is **not** considered to be a part of the handful even if it is contiguous to it.

HALAKHA

Handful whose oil the priest squeezed onto the wood [*etzim*] – קוֹמֶץ שֶׁמִּיצָּה שַׁמְנוֹ עַל גַּבֵּי עֵצִים: If the oil from a handful of the meal offering was squeezed out onto a bone and the bone subsequently descended from the altar, it should be returned to the altar, since it is uncertain whether items that are contiguous to offerings are considered to be part of the offering. The Rambam's ruling here is based on his version of the text, in which the Gemara is discussing oil that was squeezed out onto a bone [*etzem*] and not onto the wood [*etzim*]. According to the Rambam, the Gemara's question is whether oil that descended from the altar must be returned to it, since the *halakha* is that a bone that descended from the altar is not returned to it (see *Zevaḥim* 85b). Due to the uncertainty he ruled that it should be returned, since consecrated property should not be denigrated by not being returned to the altar (see *Kesef Mishne* and Mahari Kurkus). Rashi and the Ra'avad have the standard version of the text, in which the Gemara is discussing oil that was squeezed onto the wood (Rambam *Sefer Avoda, Hilkhot Pesulei HaMukdashin* 3:17).

One who offers up a limb that contains less than an olive-bulk of meat – הַמַּעֲלֶה אֵבֶר שֶׁאֵין בּוֹ כַּזַּיִת: If one sacrifices outside of the Temple courtyard the limb of an offering that contains less than an olive-bulk of meat, but the offering's bone completes the measure of the offering to an olive-bulk, he is liable. This is in accordance with the opinion of Rabbi Yoḥanan, since in a disagreement between Rabbi Yoḥanan and Reish Lakish, the *halakha* is in accordance with the opinion of Rabbi Yoḥanan (Rambam *Sefer Avoda, Hilkhot Ma'aseh HaKorbanot* 19:10).

NOTES

Are substances that are contiguous to items that ascend upon the altar [*ḥibburei olin*] considered as part of the items that ascend upon the altar – חִיבּוּרֵי עוֹלִין כְּעוֹלִין דָּמוּ: According to Rashi's first explanation, the Gemara's question is whether the oil is still considered to be part of the handful if it was squeezed from the handful onto the wood, and then the handful was placed on the wood. Does the fact that the two are contiguous suffice, or does the fact that the oil is no longer absorbed within the handful mean that the handful is missing its oil? Similarly, *Tosafot* explain that the question is whether the oil is considered to be part of the offering since it is not extant but absorbed into the wood. Others explain that the question here is not whether the oil is attached to the handful, but whether the wood is attached to it (Ra'avad). According to all of these explanations, it is clear that if there is no attachment to the handful, then the handful is lacking and unfit.

According to Rashi's second explanation, this itself is the subject of the Gemara's question. The Gemara is not discussing oil that is contiguous to the handful, but rather the oil that should have been put on the handful. This is also the opinion of the Rambam. According to this explanation, the term *ḥibburei olin* does not mean substances that are contiguous to items that ascend upon the altar. Rather, it means a substance that is a secondary component of an offering. The Gemara asks: Is the oil, which is a secondary component of the offering and not the primary component, indispensable, or can it be lacking when the handful is burned? This explanation presumes that the oil was squeezed onto regular wood and not the wood that is burned on the altar. Explaining that the Gemara is referring to secondary components of the handful fits well with the continuation of the Gemara, where the term *ḥibburei olin* is used to describe bones that are attached to the meat of the offering (see *Zevaḥim* 107b).

HALAKHA

Two meal offerings from which a handful was not removed and that were intermingled – שְׁתֵּי מְנָחוֹת שֶׁלֹּא נִקְמְצוּ וְנִתְעָרְבוּ: In the case of two meal offerings from which a handful was not removed that became intermingled with each other, if one is able to remove a handful from each separately, they are fit, and if not, they are unfit (Rambam *Sefer Avoda, Hilkhot Pesulei HaMukdashin* 11:29).

A handful that was intermingled with a meal offering from which a handful was not removed – קוֹמֶץ שֶׁנִּתְעָרֵב בְּמִנְחָה שֶׁלֹּא נִקְמְצָה: In the case of a handful that was intermingled with a meal offering from which a handful was not removed, one should not burn the mixture on the altar. If the mixture was burned, the meal offering from which the handful was taken satisfies the obligation of the owner, and the meal offering from which the handful was not taken does not satisfy the obligation of the owner (Rambam *Sefer Avoda, Hilkhot Pesulei HaMukdashin* 11:30).

Its handful was intermingled with its remainder, etc. – נִתְעָרֵב קוּמְצָהּ בִּשְׁיָרֶיהָ וכו׳: If after the handful was removed it was intermingled with the remainder of the meal offering or if the remainder was intermingled with the remainder of another meal offering, it should not be burned on the altar. If it was burned, it satisfies the obligation of the owner (Rambam *Sefer Avoda, Hilkhot Pesulei HaMukdashin* 11:31).

The meat of an unslaughtered animal carcass is nullified in a larger quantity of meat of a slaughtered animal – נְבֵילָה בְּטֵילָה בִּשְׁחוּטָה: If the meat of an unslaughtered animal carcass is intermingled with a larger quantity of meat of a slaughtered animal, the meat of the animal carcass is nullified in the meat of the slaughtered animal and does not impart impurity through contact, although it does impart impurity by carrying, in accordance with the opinion of Rabbi Yosei bar Ḥanina in tractate *Bekhorot* (23a). The reason for this *halakha* is that meat from a slaughtered animal cannot attain the status of a carcass. The animal carcass meat can attain the status of a slaughtered animal, since when a carcass rots to the extent that it is no longer edible, it loses its impure status. Therefore, it is nullified in a larger quantity of meat of a slaughtered animal. This is in accordance with the opinion of Rav Ḥisda.

The Ra'avad explains that the entire discussion here is in accordance with the opinion of Rabbi Yehuda, but according to the Rabbis a substance in contact with the same type of substance is nullified in all cases (Rambam *Sefer Tahara, Hilkhot She'ar Avot HaTumot* 1:17).

אוֹ דִּלְמָא אֲפִילּוּ לְרֵישׁ לָקִישׁ, לָא קָא אָמַר אֶלָּא בְּעֶצֶם, דָּבָר מִפְרָשׁ הוּא, וְאִי פָּרֵישׁ – לָאו מִצְוָה לְאַהֲדוּרֵי, אֲבָל שֶׁמֶן דְּלָאו בַּר מִפְרָשׁ הוּא – לָא. אוֹ דִּלְמָא לָא שְׁנָא? תֵּיקוּ.

Or perhaps, even according to Reish Lakish, he says his ruling **only in** the case of the **bone,** teaching that it does not add to the quantity of the meat. The reason is **that** the bone **is able to be separated** from the meat, **and if it separated,** there is **no mitzva to return it** to the fire. Therefore, he views it as distinct from the meat. **But** in this case of **oil, which is not able to be separated** from the handful of the meal offering, as it must be burned together with the handful, he will **not** hold that the oil is viewed as separate from the handful. **Or perhaps there is no difference** between the case of the bone and the case of the oil, and Rabbi Yoḥanan and Reish Lakish would have the same opinions, respectively, in both cases. The Gemara comments: The dilemma **shall stand** unresolved.

מתני׳ שְׁתֵּי מְנָחוֹת שֶׁלֹּא נִקְמְצוּ וְנִתְעָרְבוּ זוֹ בָּזוֹ, אִם יָכוֹל לִקְמוֹץ מִזּוֹ בִּפְנֵי עַצְמָהּ וּמִזּוֹ בִּפְנֵי עַצְמָהּ – כְּשֵׁירוֹת, וְאִם לָאו – פְּסוּלוֹת.

MISHNA In the case of **two meal offerings from which a handful was not removed and** that **were intermingled**[H] **with each other, if** the priest **can remove a handful from this** meal offering **by itself and from that** meal offering **by itself, they are fit** meal offerings, **but if not, they are unfit,** as the handful of each meal offering must be taken from its original source.

קוֹמֶץ שֶׁנִּתְעָרֵב בְּמִנְחָה שֶׁלֹּא נִקְמְצָה – לֹא יַקְטִיר, וְאִם הִקְטִיר – זוֹ שֶׁנִּקְמְצָה עוֹלָה לַבְּעָלִים, וְזוֹ שֶׁלֹּא נִקְמְצָה לֹא עוֹלָה לַבְּעָלִים.

In the case of **a handful that was intermingled with a meal offering from which a handful was not removed,**[H] the priest **should not burn** the mixture on the altar. **And if he burned** it, **this** meal offering **from which the handful was taken satisfies the obligation of the owner and that** meal offering **from which the handful was not taken does not satisfy the obligation of the owner.**

נִתְעָרֵב קוּמְצָהּ בִּשְׁיָרֶיהָ אוֹ בִּשְׁיָרֶיהָ שֶׁל חֲבֵירְתָּהּ – לֹא יַקְטִיר, וְאִם הִקְטִיר – עוֹלָה לַבְּעָלִים.

If, after it was removed, **its handful was intermingled with its remainder**[H] **or with the remainder of another** meal offering, the priest **should not burn** the mixture on the altar, **but if he burned** it, **it satisfies the obligation of the owner.**

גמ׳ אָמַר רַב חִסְדָּא: נְבֵילָה בְּטֵילָה בִּשְׁחוּטָה, שֶׁאִי אֶפְשָׁר לִשְׁחוּטָה שֶׁתֵּעָשֶׂה נְבֵילָה;

GEMARA **Rav Ḥisda says:** The meat of an unslaughtered **animal carcass** is **nullified in** a larger quantity of meat of **a slaughtered** animal.[H] Although meat from a carcass generally imparts impurity, if one touches the mixture of the two meats he does not become ritually impure, as the carcass meat is considered a different type of substance from the slaughtered animal and is therefore nullified. This is not considered a mixture that comprises a substance in contact with the same type of substance, **because** meat from **a slaughtered** animal **cannot attain the status of a carcass,** and it is therefore viewed as a different type of substance.

וּשְׁחוּטָה אֵינָהּ בְּטֵילָה בִּנְבֵילָה, שֶׁאֶפְשָׁר לִנְבֵילָה שֶׁתֵּעָשֶׂה שְׁחוּטָה, דִּלְכִי מַסְרְחָה פָּרְחָה טוּמְאָתָהּ.

By contrast, if meat of a slaughtered animal became intermingled with a larger quantity of meat of animal carcass, the meat of the **slaughtered** animal **is not nullified in** the larger quantity of meat of the **carcass, as it is possible for a carcass to attain the status of a slaughtered** animal with regard to the *halakhot* of ritual impurity, as it can lose its ability to transmit ritual impurity. This is **because when** a carcass **rots** to the extent that it is no longer edible, **it loses its impure** status. The *halakha* that the carcass meat has the ability to attain the ritually pure status of meat of a slaughtered animal renders the two meats as the same type of substance, and the mixture retains its status of intermingled carcass meat and meat of a slaughtered animal.

וְרַבִּי חֲנִינָא אָמַר: כָּל שֶׁאֶפְשָׁר לוֹ לִהְיוֹת כָּמוֹהוּ – אֵינוֹ בָּטֵל, וְכָל שֶׁאִי אֶפְשָׁר לוֹ לִהְיוֹת כָּמוֹהוּ – בָּטֵל.

And Rabbi Ḥanina says the opposite: **Any** small quantity of an item **that can possibly become like** the item that is present in larger quantities is **not nullified** when the two are intermingled, **but any** small quantity of an item **that cannot possibly become like** the item that is present in larger quantities is **nullified** in the larger quantity. Accordingly, a small quantity of meat of a slaughtered animal is nullified in a larger quantity of unslaughtered animal carcass meat, since the meat of a slaughtered animal cannot become like the animal carcass meat; but a small quantity of animal carcass meat is not nullified in a larger quantity of meat of a slaughtered animal, since it can lose its impure status and become akin to the meat of a slaughtered animal.

אַלִּיבָּא דְּמַאן? אִי אַלִּיבָּא דְּרַבָּנַן – הָא אָמְרִי: עוֹלִין הוּא דְּלָא מְבַטְּלִי אַהֲדָדֵי, אֲבָל מִין בְּמִינוֹ בָּטֵל!

The Gemara asks: **In accordance with whose** opinion do Rabbi Ḥanina and Rav Ḥisda state their opinions? **If** their opinions are **in accordance with** the opinion **of the Rabbis,** this is difficult: **Didn't** the Rabbis **say** that **it is** in the case of a mixture of items that **ascend** to the altar **that** the different components of the mixture **do not nullify one another, but** otherwise, **a substance** in contact **with** the **same** type of **substance** is **nullified?** Therefore, in any case where meat of a slaughtered animal becomes intermingled with unslaughtered animal carcass meat, the smaller quantity is nullified in the larger quantity.

אִי אַלִּיבָּא דְּרַבִּי יְהוּדָה – וְהָא

If their opinions are **in accordance with** the opinion **of Rabbi Yehuda,** who holds that the blood of an offering is not nullified in the blood of a non-sacred animal because the two are the same type of substance, this is difficult: **But**

Perek **III**
Daf **23** Amud **b**

רַבִּי יְהוּדָה בָּתַר חֲזוּתָא אָזֵיל, וְאִידֵי וְאִידֵי מִין בְּמִינוֹ הוּא!

Rabbi Yehuda follows the appearance[N] of the item in determining whether the two items are the same type of substance. **And** therefore, **this** meat of a slaughtered animal **and that** meat of an unslaughtered carcass are viewed as **a substance** in contact **with** the **same** type of **substance,** since their appearances are identical, and neither one nullifies the other.

אֶלָּא אַלִּיבָּא דְּרַבִּי חִיָּיא, דְּתָנֵי רַבִּי חִיָּיא: נְבֵילָה וּשְׁחוּטָה בְּטֵילוֹת זוֹ בָּזוֹ.

Rather, it must be explained that the opinions of Rav Ḥisda and Rabbi Ḥanina are **in accordance with** the opinion **of Rabbi Ḥiyya. As Rabbi Ḥiyya teaches:** The meat of an unslaughtered **animal carcass and** the meat of **a slaughtered** animal **are nullified one in the other.** Rav Ḥisda understands this statement to mean that the meat of an animal carcass is nullified in a larger quantity of meat of a slaughtered animal, whereas Rabbi Ḥanina understands the statement to be referring to meat of a slaughtered animal that is nullified in a larger quantity of meat of an unslaughtered animal carcass.

רַבִּי חִיָּיא אַלִּיבָּא דְּמַאן? אִי אַלִּיבָּא דְּרַבָּנַן – הָא אָמְרִי: עוֹלִין הוּא דְּלָא מְבַטְּלִי אַהֲדָדֵי, הָא מִין בְּמִינוֹ בָּטֵיל! וְאִי אַלִּיבָּא דְּרַבִּי יְהוּדָה – כָּל מִין בְּמִינוֹ לְרַבִּי יְהוּדָה לָא בָּטֵיל!

The Gemara asks: But then **in accordance with whose** opinion did **Rabbi Ḥiyya** himself state his opinion? **If** his opinion is **in accordance with** the opinion **of the Rabbis,** that is difficult: **Didn't** the Rabbis **say** that **it is** in the case of a mixture of items that **ascend** to the altar **that** the different components of the mixture **do not nullify one another, but** in general, **a substance** in contact **with** the **same** type of **substance** is **nullified? And if** his statement is **in accordance with** the opinion **of Rabbi Yehuda,** that is difficult: **According to** the opinion of **Rabbi Yehuda any substance** in contact **with** the **same** type of **substance** is **not nullified.**

לְעוֹלָם אַלִּיבָּא דְּרַבִּי יְהוּדָה, וְכִי קָא אָמַר רַבִּי יְהוּדָה מִין בְּמִינוֹ לָא בָּטֵל – הָנֵי מִילֵּי הֵיכָא דְּאֶפְשָׁר לֵיהּ לְמֶיהֱוֵי כְּווֹתֵיהּ, אֲבָל הֵיכָא דְּלָא אֶפְשָׁר לֵיהּ לְמֶיהֱוֵי כְּווֹתֵיהּ – בָּטֵל;

The Gemara answers: **Actually,** the statement of Rabbi Ḥiyya is **in accordance with** the opinion **of Rabbi Yehuda, and** Rabbi Ḥiyya holds that **when Rabbi Yehuda says** that **a substance** in contact **with** the **same** type of **substance** is **not nullified, this statement** applies only **where it is possible for one to become like** the other. **But where it is not possible for one to become like** the other, it is **nullified,** since the two are not considered the same substance.

וּבְהָא קָא מִיפַּלְגִי, דְּרַב חִסְדָּא סָבַר: בָּתַר מְבַטֵּל אָזְלִינַן,

And Rav Ḥisda and Rabbi Ḥanina **disagree with regard to this, as Rav Ḥisda holds** that **we follow the** potentially **nullifying** substance, i.e., the larger quantity, and if it can attain the status of the smaller quantity, the two are considered identical substances and the smaller quantity is not nullified in the larger quantity. Therefore, if meat of a slaughtered animal became mingled with a larger quantity of meat of an animal carcass, the meat of the slaughtered animal is not nullified, as it is possible for a carcass to attain the status of a slaughtered animal with regard to ritual impurity, as when a carcass rots it loses its impure status.

NOTES

Follows the appearance – בָּתַר חֲזוּתָא אָזֵיל: According to Rabbi Yehuda, in the context of nullifying minority components of a mixture, the halakhic status of the components is not relevant. Therefore, meat of an animal carcass and meat of a slaughtered animal are considered to be identical substances. This is because according to Rabbi Yehuda, the reason that the blood of the bull that is sacrificed on Yom Kippur does not nullify the blood of the goat when the two are mixed is not because both are offerings, but because both are identical substances of identical appearance.

NOTES

And this remainder does not nullify, etc. – **וְלָא קָא מְבַטְּלִי שִׁירַיִם וכו׳**: Why does the Gemara assume that the volume of the remainder of the first meal offering will be greater than the meal offering from which a handful has not yet been removed? It is explained in the *Shita Mekubbetzet* that although the total volume of the second meal offering is greater, it is inevitable that at some point where the two meal offerings meet, there will be a greater volume of the remainder of the first meal offering, which should nullify the part of the second meal offering that is in that spot. Once that part is nullified, the second meal offering will be lacking the requisite measure and should be disqualified (see *Hazon Ish*).

וְרַבִּי חֲנִינָא סָבַר: בָּתַר בָּטֵל אָזְלִינַן.

And Rabbi Ḥanina holds that **we follow** the potentially **nullified** substance, i.e., the smaller quantity, and only if it can attain the status of the larger quantity, e.g., in the case of meat of an animal carcass that was intermingled with a larger quantity of meat of a slaughtered animal, the two are considered identical substances and the smaller quantity is not nullified in the larger quantity.

תְּנַן: שְׁתֵּי מְנָחוֹת שֶׁלֹּא נִקְמְצוּ וְנִתְעָרְבוּ זוֹ בְּזוֹ, אִם יָכוֹל לִקְמוֹץ מִזּוֹ בִּפְנֵי עַצְמָהּ וּמִזּוֹ בִּפְנֵי עַצְמָהּ – כְּשֵׁרוֹת, וְאִם לָאו – פְּסוּלוֹת. וְהָא הָכָא, כֵּיוָן דְּקָמֵיץ לֵיהּ מֵחֲדָא – אִידָּךְ הֲוָה לֵיהּ שִׁירַיִם, וְלָא קָא מְבַטְּלִי שִׁירַיִם לְטִיבְלָא;

The Gemara offers support for the opinion of Rabbi Ḥanina: **We learned** in the mishna: In the case of **two meal offerings from which a handful was not removed and** which **were intermingled with each other, if** the priest **can remove a handful from this** meal offering **by itself and from that** meal offering **by itself, they are fit** meal offerings, **but if not, they are unfit,** as the handful of each meal offering must be taken from its original source. **And here, once he removes a handful from one, the rest** of it **becomes** the **remainder,** which is designated for the priests, **and this remainder does not nullify**[N] the other **meal offering from which a handful has not yet been removed.**

מַנִּי? אִי רַבָּנַן – הָא אָמְרִי: עוֹלִין הוּא דְּלָא מְבַטְּלִי הֲדָדֵי, הָא מִין בְּמִינוֹ בָּטֵל! אֶלָּא פְּשִׁיטָא רַבִּי יְהוּדָה;

In accordance with **whose** opinion is the mishna? **If** it is in accordance with the opinion of **the Rabbis,** that is difficult: **Didn't** the Rabbis **say** that **it is** in the case of a mixture of items that **ascend** to the altar **that** the different components of the mixture **do not nullify one another, but** in general, **a substance** in contact **with** the **same** type of **substance** is **nullified?** Therefore, the remainder of the first meal offering should nullify the second meal offering, as both consist of the same substances, flour and oil. **Rather,** it is **obvious** that the mishna is in accordance with the opinion of **Rabbi Yehuda,** who holds that the meal offering is not nullified in the remainder, as any substance in contact with the same type of substance is not nullified.

בִּשְׁלָמָא לְמַאן דְּאָמַר: בָּתַר בָּטֵל אָזְלִינַן – בָּטֵל הָוֵי כִּמְבַטֵּל, דִּלְכִי קָמֵיץ מֵאִידָּךְ – הָווּ לְהוּ שִׁירַיִם כִּי הָנֵי.

Now, **granted, according to** Rabbi Ḥanina, who is **the one who says** that **we follow** the potentially **nullified** substance, in the mishna's case the potentially **nullified** substance can **become like** the potentially **nullifying** substance, **as when** the priest **removes the handful from the other** meal offering, the intermingled offering **will become a remainder** that is designated for the priests, just **like that** of the first meal offering. Therefore, the intermingled second meal offering is not nullified in the remainder of the first meal offering.

אֶלָּא לְמַאן דְּאָמַר: בָּתַר מְבַטֵּל אָזְלִינַן, שִׁירַיִם מִי קָא הָווּ טִיבְלָא? לֵימָא אַלִּיבָּא דְּרַב חִסְדָּא דְּלָא כְּרַבִּי חִיָּיא?

But according to Rav Ḥisda, who is **the one who says** that **we follow** the potentially **nullifying** substance, **can** the **remainder** of the first meal offering **become a meal offering from which a handful has not yet been removed?** Therefore, **shall we say** that **according to Rav Ḥisda** the mishna here **is not in accordance with** the opinion of **Rabbi Ḥiyya** with regard to Rabbi Yehuda's opinion?

הָתָם כִּדְרַבִּי זֵירָא, דְּאָמַר רַבִּי זֵירָא: נֶאֶמְרָה הַקְטָרָה בְּקוֹמֶץ וְנֶאֶמְרָה הַקְטָרָה בְּשִׁירַיִם,

The Gemara answers: **There,** the *halakha* of the mishna is **in accordance with** the opinion **of Rabbi Zeira, as Rabbi Zeira says** that the verse teaches that nullification does not take place when remainders are intermingled with handfuls. He explains: The term **burning is stated with regard to** the **handful** removed from the meal offering (see Leviticus 2:2), as it is a mitzva to burn the handful, **and** the term **burning is stated with regard to** the **remainder** of the meal offering (see Leviticus 2:11), as it is taught that it is prohibited to burn the remainder.

מַה הַקְטָרָה הָאֲמוּרָה בְּקוֹמֶץ – אֵין הַקּוֹמֶץ מְבַטֵּל אֶת חֲבֵירוֹ, אַף הַקְטָרָה הָאֲמוּרָה בְּשִׁירַיִם – אֵין שִׁירַיִם מְבַטְּלִין אֶת הַקּוֹמֶץ.

This verbal analogy teaches that **just as** in the case of the **burning that is stated with regard to** the **handful,** if two handfuls are mixed together **one handful does not nullify the other** and all agree that the two are burned on the altar, **so too,** in the case of the **burning that is stated with regard to** the **remainder** of the meal offering, if the remainder of one offering is intermingled with another meal offering, the **remainder** of the meal offering **does not nullify** the **handful** or the remainder of the second meal offering.

תָּא שְׁמַע: הַקּוֹמֶץ שֶׁנִּתְעָרֵב בְּמִנְחָה שֶׁלֹּא נִקְמְצָה – לֹא יַקְטִיר, וְאִם הִקְטִיר – זוֹ שֶׁנִּקְמְצָה עָלְתָה לַבְּעָלִים, וְזוֹ שֶׁלֹּא נִקְמְצָה לֹא עָלְתָה לַבְּעָלִים, וְלָא קָא מְבַטֵּיל לֵיהּ טִיבְלָא לְקוֹמֶץ;

The Gemara suggests: **Come** and **hear** a proof from the mishna here: In the case of **the handful that was intermingled with a meal offering from which a handful was not removed,** the priest **should not burn** the mixture on the altar, **and if he burned** it, **this** meal offering **from which the handful was taken satisfied the obligation of the owner and that** meal offering **from which the handful was not taken did not satisfy the obligation of the owner.** This is a case of a mixture of identical substances, **and the meal offering from which a handful has not yet been removed does not nullify** the **handful,** since after the fact if the mixture is burned on the altar the meal offering from which the handful was taken satisfies the obligation of the owner.

מַנִּי? אִי רַבָּנַן – הָא אָמְרִי: עוֹלִין הוּא דְּלָא מְבַטְּלִי הֲדָדֵי, הָא מִין בְּמִינוֹ בָּטֵיל! אֶלָּא פְּשִׁיטָא רַבִּי יְהוּדָה;

The Gemara explains the proof: In accordance with **whose** opinion is the mishna? **If** it is in accordance with the opinion of **the Rabbis,** that is difficult: **Didn't** the Rabbis **say** that **it is** in the case of a mixture of items that **ascend** to the altar **that** the different components of the mixture **do not nullify one another, but** in general, **a substance** in contact **with** the **same** type of **substance** is **nullified? Rather,** it is **obvious** that the mishna is in accordance with the opinion of **Rabbi Yehuda,** who holds that any substance in contact with the same type of substance is not nullified.

בִּשְׁלָמָא לְמַאן דְּאָמַר: בָּתַר מְבַטֵּל אָזְלִינַן – מְבַטֵּל הָוֵי כְּבָטֵל, דְּכָל פּוּרְתָּא חֲזֵי לְמִקְמַץ מִינֵּיהּ, וְהָוֵי לֵיהּ מִין וּמִינוֹ, וּמִין בְּמִינוֹ לֹא בָּטֵל;

Now, **granted, according to** Rav Ḥisda, who is **the one who says** that **we follow** the potentially **nullifying** substance, in the mishna's case the potentially **nullifying** substance can **become like** the potentially **nullified** substance, **since every bit** of the meal offering **is fit to have the handful taken from it. And** therefore, the mixture **is** considered to be one that consists of **a substance** in contact **with** the **same** type of **substance, and a substance** in contact **with** the **same** type of **substance** is **not nullified.**

אֶלָּא לְמַאן דְּאָמַר: בָּתַר בָּטֵל אָזְלִינַן, קוֹמֶץ מִי קָא הָוֵי טִיבְלָא? לֵימָא, דְּלָא כְּרַבִּי חִיָּיא? הָא נַמִי כִּדְרַבִּי זֵירָא.

But according to Rabbi Ḥanina, who is **the one who says** that **we follow** the potentially **nullified** substance, **can** the **handful become a meal offering from which a handful has not yet been removed,** so that it would not be nullified by the other meal offering whose handful was not removed? Therefore, **shall we say that** according to Rabbi Ḥanina the mishna here is **not in accordance with** the opinion of **Rabbi Ḥiyya** with regard to Rabbi Yehuda's opinion? The Gemara answers: **This** mishna **as well** is **in accordance with** the opinion **of Rabbi Zeira,** who explains that a Torah edict establishes that the remainder does not nullify the handful, and similarly, a meal offering from which a handful has not yet been removed does not nullify the handful.

תָּא שְׁמַע: נִתְעָרֵב קוּמְצָהּ בְּשִׁירַיִם שֶׁל חֲבֶרְתָּהּ – לֹא יַקְטִיר, וְאִם הִקְטִיר – עָלְתָה לַבְּעָלִים; וְהָא הָכָא דְּלָא הָוֵי מְבַטֵּל כְּבָטֵיל, וְלָא קָא מְבַטְּלִי לֵיהּ שִׁירַיִם לְקוֹמֶץ,

The Gemara suggests: **Come** and **hear** a proof from the mishna here: If, after it was removed, **its handful was intermingled with the remainder of another** meal offering, the priest **should not burn** the mixture on the altar, **and if he burned** it, **it satisfied the obligation of the owner.** The Gemara explains the proof: **But here,** the potentially **nullifying** substance **cannot become like** the potentially **nullified** substance, since the remainder of the meal offering cannot become like the handful, and the potentially nullified substance cannot become like the potentially nullifying substance, since the handful cannot become like the remainder of the meal offering; **and** the mishna teaches that the **remainder** of the meal offering **does not nullify** the **handful.**

מַנִּי? אִי רַבָּנַן וכו׳!

In accordance with **whose** opinion is the mishna? **If** it is in accordance with the opinion of **the Rabbis,** that is difficult: Didn't the Rabbis say that it is in the case of a mixture of items that ascend to the altar that the different components of the mixture do not nullify one another, but in general, a substance in contact with the same type of substance is nullified? Rather, it is obvious that the mishna is in accordance with the opinion of Rabbi Yehuda, who holds that any substance in contact with the same type of substance is not nullified. But in contrast to Rabbi Ḥiyya's statement, Rabbi Yehuda apparently holds that nullification takes place even if the nullifying substance cannot become like the nullified substance, or if the nullified substance cannot become like the nullifying substance.

BACKGROUND

Black cumin – קֶצַח: Black cumin, *Nigella sativa*, from the Ranunculaceae family, is an annual herb that grows to a height of 30 cm and beyond. The leaves of the black cumin plant are divided into short lobes. The plant has blue flowers that grow to a circumference of 3 cm and bloom in early spring. Its black, nearly triangular seeds, which are found in a five-sectioned sheath, are only 2–3 mm in both width and length, with up to five hundred seeds weighing a single gram. Used today as a spice, black cumin was also used in the past for medicinal purposes, and appears already in the Bible as a cultivated plant (see Isaiah 28:25–27).

Black cumin flower

אֲמַר רַבִּי זֵירָא: נֶאֶמְרָה הַקְטָרָה בְּקוֹמֶץ וְנֶאֶמְרָה הַקְטָרָה בְּשִׁירַיִם, מַה הַקְטָרָה הָאֲמוּרָה בְּקוֹמֶץ – אֵין קוֹמֶץ מְבַטֵּל אֶת חֲבֵירוֹ, אַף הַקְטָרָה הָאֲמוּרָה בְּשִׁירַיִם – אֵין שִׁירַיִם מְבַטְּלִין אֶת הַקּוֹמֶץ.

Rabbi Zeira said: This mishna is an independent *halakha*, based on a Torah edict that nullification does not take place when remainders are intermingled with handfuls. He explains: The term **burning is stated with regard to** the **handful** removed from the meal offering, **and** the term **burning is stated with regard to** the **remainder** of the meal offering. This verbal analogy teaches that **just as** in the case of the **burning that is stated with regard to** the **handful,** if two handfuls are mixed together **one handful does not nullify the other** and all agree that the two are burned on the altar, **so too,** in the case of the **burning that is stated with regard to** the **remainder** of the meal offering, if the remainder of one offering is intermingled with another meal offering, the **remainder** of the meal offering **does not nullify the handful** or the remainder of the second meal offering.

תָּא שְׁמַע: תִּיבְּלָהּ בְּקֶצַח, בְּשׁוּמְשְׁמִין, וּבְכָל מִינֵי תַבְלִין – כְּשֵׁרָה, מַצָּה הִיא אֶלָּא שֶׁנִּקְרֵאת מַצָּה מְתוּבֶּלֶת. קָא סָלְקָא דַעְתָּךְ דְּאַפֵּישׁ לָהּ תַּבְלִין טְפֵי מִמַּצָּה;

The Gemara suggests another proof from a *baraita* (*Tosefta, Pesaḥim* 2:21): **Come** and **hear:** In the case of *matza* that one **seasoned with black cumin,**[BH] **with sesame, or with any type of spice,** it is **fit** to be eaten during the festival of Passover, as **it is** considered ***matza*****, but it is called seasoned *matza*.** The Gemara comments: **It enters your mind** to explain that this is a case **where** there were **more spices than** the ***matza*** itself.

בִּשְׁלָמָא לְמַאן דְּאָמַר: בָּתַר בָּטֵל אָזְלִינַן – בָּטֵיל הָוֵי כִּמְבַטֵּל, דִּלְכִי מִעַפְּשָׁא – הָוֵי לָהּ כְּתַבְלִין; אֶלָּא לְמַאן דְּאָמַר: בָּתַר מְבַטֵּל אָזְלִינַן, תַּבְלִין מִי קָא הָווּ מַצָּה?

Now, **granted, according to** Rabbi Ḥanina, who is **the one who says** that **we follow** the potentially **nullified** substance, in the case here the potentially **nullified** substance can **become like** the potentially **nullifying** substance, **as when** the *matza* **becomes moldy it becomes like** the **spices,** as it is no longer fit to be used to fulfill the mitzva of eating *matza*. Therefore, the smaller quantity of *matza* is not nullified by the larger quantity of spices. **But according to** Rav Ḥisda, who is **the one who says** that **we follow** the potentially **nullifying** substance, **can** the **spices become** like the ***matza*****?**

הָכָא בְּמַאי עָסְקִינַן – דְּלָא אַפֵּישׁ לָהּ תַּבְלִין, דְּרוּבָּהּ מַצָּה הִיא וְלָא בָּטְלָה. דַּיְקָא נַמִי, דְּקָתָנֵי: מַצָּה הִיא אֶלָּא שֶׁנִּקְרֵאת מַצָּה מְתוּבֶּלֶת, שְׁמַע מִינָּהּ.

The Gemara answers: **What are we dealing with here?** We are dealing with a case **where** there are **not more spices** than *matza,* but rather **the majority is *matza*** **and** therefore the *matza* is **not nullified.** The Gemara notes: According to this explanation, the language of the *baraita* **is also precise, as it teaches:** **It is** considered ***matza*****, but it is called seasoned *matza*. Learn from** here that the *baraita* is referring to an entity whose majority is *matza,* and therefore it is referred to as seasoned *matza*.

HALAKHA

***Matza* that one seasoned with black cumin, etc. – תִּיבְּלָהּ בְּקֶצַח וכו׳:** If one seasoned the remainder of the meal offering with different types of oils or spices, it is fit and is still considered to be *matza*, although it is called seasoned *matza*. This is in accordance with the *baraita*, which the Rambam interprets as referring to meal offerings that are brought as *matza*, as well as the *matza* that is eaten on Passover. According to the Ra'avad, it is permitted to add these ingredients only after the *matza* is baked. One may not add these items to the dough, lest they cause the *matza* to become leavened. The same dispute exists with regard to *matza* on Passover, with the Rambam ruling that it is permitted to add these ingredients to the dough, and the Ra'avad ruling that one may add them only to the already baked *matza*. The *Shulḥan Arukh* rules, citing the *Roke'aḥ*, that one should not add spices to the dough *ab initio*, but after the fact the *matza* is still considered permitted for eating on Passover, provided that there is an olive-bulk of dough aside from the additions. In any event, some say that one cannot fulfill the mitzva of eating *matza* on the first night of Passover with this *matza*, since it is not considered bread of affliction (Rambam *Sefer Avoda, Hilkhot Ma'aseh HaKorbanot* 12:17 and *Sefer Zemanim, Hilkhot Ḥametz UMatza* 5:20; *Shulḥan Arukh, Oraḥ Ḥayyim* 455:6, and see *Magen Avraham* and *Mishna Berura* there).

כִּי סָלֵיק רַב כָּהֲנָא, אַשְׁכַּחִינְהוּ לִבְנֵי רַבִּי חִיָּיא דְּיָתְבִי וְקָאָמְרִי: עִשָּׂרוֹן שֶׁחִלְּקוֹ

§ The Gemara relates: **When Rav Kahana**[P] **ascended** from Babylonia to Eretz Yisrael, **he found the sons of Rabbi Ḥiyya,**[P] **who were sitting and saying** the following: In the case of **a tenth** of an ephah of a meal offering **that one divided**

PERSONALITIES

Rav Kahana – רַב כָּהֲנָא: There were several *amora'im* named Rav Kahana who appear in the Talmud. Here, apparently, the reference is to the earliest Rav Kahana. As his name suggests, Rav Kahana was a priest [*kohen*], and he was a disciple-colleague of Rav in Babylonia. It is related that Rav Kahana and his colleague Rav Asi learned halakhic traditions from Rav, but were independent in their analysis of those traditions. It is related in several places that they did not refrain from challenging Rav's opinion, forcing Rav to explain his opinion, and on more than one occasion Rav's response was to remain silent rather than to attempt to resolve their difficult questions. Nevertheless, the two always treated Rav with the utmost esteem, and in turn were treated by Rav with great respect.

As related here, Rav Kahana moved to Eretz Yisrael and met the sons of Rabbi Ḥiyya, who had moved at a young age to Eretz Yisrael with their father. He met Rabbi Shimon, son of Rabbi Yehuda HaNasi, and taught Rabbi Yoḥanan and Reish Lakish.

Both the Jerusalem Talmud and the Babylonian Talmud relate events that transpired when Rav Kahana moved to Eretz Yisrael as a young man, which was in Rabbi Yoḥanan's old age. Based on the chronological implications of that fact, some understand the Gemara here to be referring to a different student of Rav named Rav Kahana.

The sons of Rabbi Ḥiyya – בְּנֵי רַבִּי חִיָּיא: Yehuda and Ḥizkiyya were the twin sons of Rabbi Ḥiyya. One was born at the beginning of their seventh month of gestation, while the other was born at the end of the ninth month, so that they were born three months apart. They moved from Babylonia with their father in their youth and at this point were already considered to be great Sages. This is seen by the declaration of the Sages that when Rabbi Ḥiyya and his sons moved to Eretz Yisrael they revived and established the Torah in Eretz Yisrael.

In several places it is related that they were extremely righteous people, whose prayers were answered. Like their father, the sons of Rabbi Ḥiyya did not support themselves through their Torah study, but rather engaged in agriculture.

The sons of Rabbi Ḥiyya appear in sources together, as well as separately. Yehuda, who was nicknamed: The esteemed one, married the daughter of one of the greatest Torah Sages of his generation, Rabbi Yannai, who thought very highly of him. He passed away during the lifetime of his father-in-law. Ḥizkiyya, like his father, Rabbi Ḥiyya, redacted *baraitot*, and many of his statements are found in the Jerusalem Talmud as well as the Babylonian Talmud.

It appears that the sons of Rabbi Ḥiyya lived in Tiberias, where they were later buried along with their father.

Perek **III**
Daf **24** Amud **a**

וְהִנִּיחוֹ בְּבִיסָא, וְנָגַע טְבוּל יוֹם בְּאֶחָד מֵהֶן, מַהוּ? כִּי תְּנַן כְּלִי מְצָרֵף מַה שֶּׁבְּתוֹכוֹ לַקֹּדֶשׁ – הָנֵי מִילֵּי הֵיכָא דְּנָגְעִי בַּהֲדָדֵי, אֲבָל הֵיכָא דְּלָא נָגְעִי בַּהֲדָדֵי לָא, אוֹ דִּילְמָא לָא שְׁנָא?

and placed in a receptacle such that the flour of the measure was in two places, not in contact with each other, **and one** who was ritually impure **who immersed that day** and is waiting for nightfall for the purification process to be completed **touched**[N] **one of** the portions of the meal offering, **what is the *halakha*?** Does he disqualify only the part of the meal offering that he touched, or the other part as well? **When we learned** in a mishna (*Ḥagiga* 20b) that **a vessel joins** all the food **that is in it**[H] **with regard to sacrificial** food, meaning that if some of the contents become impure all the contents become impure as well, does **this matter** apply only **where** the contents **are touching each other, but where** the contents **are not touching each other** the ritual impurity is **not** imparted to the other contents? **Or perhaps** there is **no difference.**

NOTES

One who immersed that day touched – וְנָגַע טְבוּל יוֹם: When one becomes ritually impure by Torah law, even after immersing himself he is prohibited from partaking of sacrificial meat or *teruma* until sunset, as derived by the Sages from the verse: "And when the sun is down, he shall be clean; and afterward he may eat of the sacred items" (Leviticus 22:7). During this interval he renders sacrificial items with which he comes into contact ritually impure. There is a dispute as to whether these items render other items impure; the final ruling, as well as the premise of the Gemara here, is that these items do not render other items impure. Rashi explains that it is for this reason that the Gemara specifically addresses the case where the ritual impurity is imparted by one who immersed that day, because if the impurity had been imparted by one whose impurity was of a more severe nature, there would be no need for the vessel to combine the different components within it. The vessel itself would become impure due to the oil of the meal offering (*Olat Shlomo*), and then impart impurity to the remaining contents.

HALAKHA

A vessel joins all the food that is in it – כְּלִי מְצָרֵף מַה שֶּׁבְּתוֹכוֹ: If a vessel is filled with different, separated items, and an impure item touches one of them, all of the contents of the vessel become ritually impure. This is the *halakha* in the case of sacrificial food, but not in the case of *teruma*. The *halakha* here is in accordance with the mishna in tractate *Ḥagiga* (20b) and the statement of Rav Kahana (Rambam *Sefer Tahara*, *Hilkhot She'ar Avot HaTumot* 12:7).

אֲמַר לְהוּ אִיהוּ: מִי תְּנַן "כְּלִי מְחַבֵּר"? "כְּלִי מְצָרֵף" תְּנַן, כָּל דְּהוּ. הוֹשִׁיט אֶחָד לְבֵינֵיהֶן, מַהוּ?

Rav Kahana **said to** the sons of Rabbi Ḥiyya: **Did we learn** in the mishna that **a vessel connects** the contents within it? **We learned** that **a vessel joins** the contents within it, indicating that it does so in **any** case, whether or not the contents are in contact with one another. The sons of Rabbi Ḥiyya then asked Rav Kahana: If one **inserted** another **one** half-tenth of an ephah **between them,**[HN] and one who was ritually impure who immersed that day touched it, **what is** the *halakha*? Are the first two half-tenths rendered impure?

אֲמַר לְהוּ: צָרִיךְ לַכְּלִי – כְּלִי מְצָרְפוֹ, אֵין צָרִיךְ לַכְּלִי – אֵין כְּלִי מְצָרְפוֹ.

Rav Kahana **said to them:** Only when an item **requires a vessel** in order for it to be sanctified, e.g., in the case of the two half-tenths of an ephah of a meal offering, does the **vessel join it** together. In the case of an item that **does not require a vessel,** such as this half-tenth that was placed between them, the **vessel does not join it.**

הוֹשִׁיט טְבוּל יוֹם אֶת אֶצְבָּעוֹ בֵּינֵיהֶן, מַהוּ? אֲמַר לְהוּ: אֵין לְךָ דָּבָר שֶׁמְּטַמֵּא מֵאֲוִירוֹ אֶלָּא כְּלִי חֶרֶס בִּלְבַד.

The sons of Rabbi Ḥiyya then asked: If **one who immersed that day inserted his finger between** the two half-tenths of the ephah that were placed in the receptacle, without touching either one, **what is** the *halakha*? Are the two half-tenths rendered impure? Rav Kahana **said to them** in response: The **only item you have that transmits impurity through its airspace**[H] is **an earthenware vessel alone.**

הֲדַר אִיהוּ בְּעָא מִינַּיְיהוּ: מַהוּ לִקְמוֹץ מִזֶּה עַל זֶה? צֵירוּף דְּאוֹרַיְיתָא אוֹ דְּרַבָּנַן?

Rav Kahana **himself then asked** the sons of Rabbi Ḥiyya: If two half-tenths of an ephah of a meal offering are placed in one vessel but are not in contact with each other, **what is** the *halakha*? Can one **remove a handful from this** half-tenth of an ephah **on** behalf of **that** half-tenth of an ephah?[H] Is the **joining** of the contents of the vessel effective **by Torah law or by rabbinic law?** If it is effective by Torah law, then the removal of the handful is valid. If it is effective by rabbinic law, then the removal of the handful was not performed correctly, since it was not taken from the entire tenth of an ephah of the meal offering.

אָמְרוּ לוֹ: זוֹ לֹא שָׁמַעְנוּ, כַּיּוֹצֵא בּוֹ שָׁמַעְנוּ, דִּתְנַן: שְׁנֵי מְנָחוֹת שֶׁלֹּא נִקְמְצוּ וְנִתְעָרְבוּ זוֹ בְּזוֹ, אִם יָכוֹל לִקְמוֹץ מִזּוֹ בִּפְנֵי עַצְמָהּ וּמִזּוֹ בִּפְנֵי עַצְמָהּ – כְּשֵׁירוֹת, וְאִם לָאו – פְּסוּלוֹת;

They said to Rav Kahana: **We did not hear** the *halakha* with regard to **this** case explicitly, but **we heard** the *halakha* with regard to a case **similar to this. As we learned** in the mishna: In the case of **two meal offerings from which a handful was not removed and** which **were intermingled with each other, if** the priest **can remove a handful from this** meal offering **by itself and from that** meal offering **by itself, they are fit** meal offerings, **but if not, they are unfit,** as the handful of each meal offering must be taken from its original source.

כִּי יָכוֹל לִקְמוֹץ מִיהָא כְּשֵׁירוֹת, אַמַּאי? הָךְ דִּמְעָרַב הָא לָא נָגַע!

They explain: **In any event,** the mishna teaches that in a case **when he can remove a handful** from each meal offering, the meal offerings **are fit. Why** is this considered a valid removal of the handful? **But this** part of the meal offering **that is intermingled** with the other meal offering **does not touch** the part of the meal offering from which the handful is removed. Evidently, the vessel joins the different parts of the meal offering together, and one can remove the handful from any part of its contents, even if they are not touching.

HALAKHA

If one inserted another one between them, etc. – הוֹשִׁיט אֶחָד לְבֵינֵיהֶן וכו׳: In a case where there were two piles within one vessel and another item between them, and one of the piles became impure, if the item requires the vessel, the vessel joins all of them together and all are rendered impure. If the item does not require the vessel, then only the pile that was touched by the source of impurity is rendered impure. This is in accordance with the opinion of Rav Kahana (Rambam *Sefer Tahara, Hilkhot She'ar Avot HaTumot* 12:8, and see Ra'avad there).

Transmits impurity through its airspace – מְטַמֵּא מֵאֲוִירוֹ: The only vessel that transmits impurity through its airspace without direct contact is an earthenware vessel (Rambam *Sefer Tahara, Hilkhot Kelim* 13:1).

Can one remove a handful from this half-tenth of an ephah on behalf of that half-tenth of an ephah – לִקְמוֹץ מִזֶּה עַל זֶה: If a tenth of an ephah of a meal offering was placed in a vessel and divided into two parts that were not touching each other, and there was no partition between them, it is uncertain whether the vessel joins them together so that the handful can be removed from one on behalf of both. Therefore, one should not remove a handful from one, and if one did so, it should not be burned on the altar. If it was burned, the meal offering is accepted, but the remainder may not be eaten. This is entirely because the dilemma remained unresolved in the Gemara (Rambam *Sefer Avoda, Hilkhot Pesulei HaMukdashin* 11:23, and see *Kesef Mishne* there).

NOTES

If one inserted another one half-tenth between them – הוֹשִׁיט אֶחָד לְבֵינֵיהֶן: According to Rashi, the question here is whether the original two half-tenths are rendered impure if one added another half-tenth between them and then one who immersed that day touched it. The Ra'avad offers a similar explanation, maintaining that the question is whether the new half-tenth is rendered impure if one who immersed that day touched one of the original half-tenths.

According to the Rambam, the Gemara is asking another question entirely: Whether the placement of another item that is not a part of the meal offering (*Kesef Mishne*) between the two half-tenths of an ephah prevents the spread of the impurity from one to the other. A parallel discussion in the Jerusalem Talmud (*Hagiga* 3:2) supports an interpretation in this vein. There, the Gemara begins by asking whether the impurity is transferred from one side of the vessel to the other, and then asks whether it is transferred even when there is an item in the middle (see *Kesef Mishne* and *Keren Ora*).

אֲמַר רָבָא: דִּלְמָא בְּגוּשִׁין הַמְחוּלָּקִין הָעֲשׂוּיִין כְּמַסְרֵק.

Rava said: This cannot be inferred from the mishna, as **perhaps** the ruling of the mishna is stated **with regard to** a case where the **clumps** of the meal offering **are divided like** the teeth of **a comb,**[B] so that although the handful is removed from a clump of the meal offering that is separate from the clump that is intermingled with the other offering, all parts of the meal offering are still in contact with one another. It may still be that in the case presented by Rav Kahana, where the parts are truly separated from one another, it is possible that one cannot remove the handful from one part on behalf of the other.

מַאי הָוֵי עֲלַהּ? אֲמַר רָבָא: תָּא שְׁמַע, דְּתַנְיָא: "וְהֵרִים מִמֶּנּוּ" – מִן הַמְחוּבָּר, שֶׁלֹּא יָבִיא עִשָּׂרוֹן בִּשְׁנֵי כֵלִים וְיִקְמוֹץ; הָא בִּכְלִי אֶחָד דּוּמְיָא דִּשְׁנֵי כֵלִים – קָמֵיץ.

The Gemara asks: Since this question was not resolved, **what** halakhic conclusion **was** reached **about** this matter? **Rava said: Come** and **hear** a proof, **as it is taught** in a *baraita*: The verse states: **"And he shall take up from it** his handful" (Leviticus 6:8), meaning that he shall take the handful **from** the meal offering **that is connected.** This teaches **that one shall not bring a tenth** of an ephah divided **in two vessels and remove the handful** from one on behalf of the other. It can therefore be inferred that **in** the case of **one vessel** that is **similar to two vessels,** as the entirety of the meal offering is brought in one vessel although the different parts are not touching, one may **remove the handful** from one part on behalf of the other part.

אֲמַר לֵיהּ אַבָּיֵי: דִּילְמָא שְׁנֵי כֵלִים הֵיכִי דָּמֵי? כְּגוֹן קְפִיזָא בְּקַבָּא, דְּאַף עַל גַּב דַּעֲרִיבִי מֵעֵילַּאי, כֵּיוָן דְּמִיפְסַק מְחִיצְתָא דִּקְפִיזָא מִתַּתָּא;

Abaye said to Rava: **Perhaps** one could say: **What are the circumstances** when the *baraita* states that one may not bring a tenth of an ephah in **two vessels?** The circumstances are, **for example,** if one hollowed out the area of a smaller ***kefiza***[L] measure **within** the area of a larger ***kav***[L] measure,[N] so that within the one receptacle there were two cavities divided by a partition that did not reach the top of the receptacle. In this case, **even though** the two **are intermingled on top,** above the partition, **since the partition of the *kefiza* measure divides** them **below,** they are still separated and not joined together.

הָא כְּלִי אֶחָד דּוּמְיָא דִּשְׁנֵי כֵלִים הֵיכִי דָּמֵי? כְּגוֹן עֲרֵיבָתָהּ שֶׁל תַּרְנְגוֹלִין, וְאַף עַל גַּב דְּמִיפְסְקָן מְחִיצָתָא – הָא נָגְעַ; אֲבָל הָכָא דְּלָא נָגְעַ כְּלָל תִּיבָּעֵי לָךְ!

Abaye continues: **What are the circumstances** of **one vessel** that is **similar to two vessels,** with regard to which you inferred that one may remove the handful from one part on behalf of the other part? The circumstances are, **for example, a hen trough**[HN] that is filled with water or fodder, **and even though a partition divides** the top of the trough, the contents are **touching** below. **But here,** in the case of two half-tenths of an ephah that are placed in a receptacle **that are not touching** each other **at all, you should raise the dilemma** as to whether the handful may be removed from one part on behalf of the other.

בָּעֵי רַבִּי יִרְמְיָה: צֵירוּף כְּלִי וְחִיבּוּר מַיִם, מַהוּ?

Rabbi Yirmeya raises a dilemma: In a scenario where **a vessel joins** the two half-tenths of an ephah that are inside the vessel but not touching, **and** there is **a connection** by means of **water**[H] between one of the half-tenths of the ephah inside the vessel and another half-tenth of an ephah that is outside the vessel, and one who immersed that day touched the other half-tenth of an ephah that is inside the vessel, **what is** the *halakha*? Does he also disqualify the half-tenth of an ephah that is outside the vessel?

BACKGROUND

Like the teeth of a comb – הָעֲשׂוּיִין כְּמַסְרֵק:

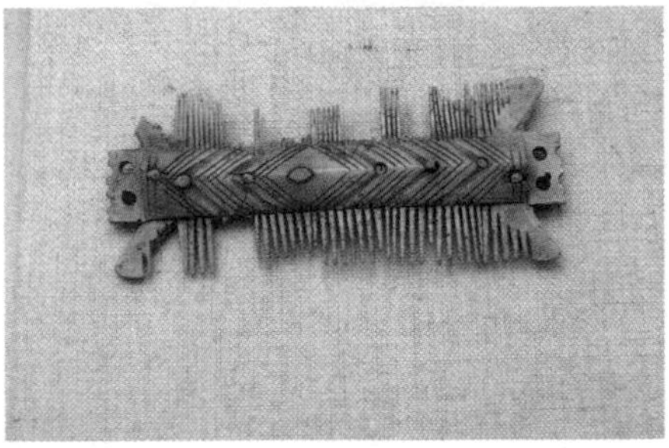

Roman comb

LANGUAGE

Kefiza – קְפִיזָא: The origin of this word is from Iranian languages. In Middle Persian, the form is kabīz, which refers to a measurement of volume. The Talmud does not explain the exact volume of a *kefiza* measure, but from the description here and in other places, it is clear that it is a smaller measure than a *kav*, which is equal to four *log*. Some hold that a *kefiza* measure is the volume of three *log*. Others hold that it is the equivalent of half a *kav*, or two *log*, while others explain that it is equal to one *log*. One *log* is equal to 345 cc according to Rabbi Ḥayyim Na'e, and 600 cc according to the *Ḥazon Ish*.

Kav – קַבָּא: The *kav* measure is mentioned in the Bible (II Kings 6:25) and refers to a dry measure that is also used as a liquid measure. A *kav* is equivalent to twenty-four egg-bulks, which is the equivalent of four *log*. A *kav* is one-sixth of a *se'a* and one-eighteenth of an ephah. One *kav* is equal to 1.38 ℓ according to Rabbi Ḥayyim Na'e, and 2.4 ℓ according to the *Ḥazon Ish*.

HALAKHA

For example a *kefiza* measure within a *kav* measure… For example a hen trough – כְּגוֹן קְפִיזָא בְּקַבָּא...כְּגוֹן עֲרֵיבָתָהּ שֶׁל תַּרְנְגוֹלִין: If a partition divides the bottom of a vessel in two, then even if the parts of the tenth of an ephah in the vessel are intermingled above the partition, one may not remove the handful from the vessel. If one did remove the handful, then the meal offering is disqualified. One may remove the handful from a vessel that is divided by a partition at the top but the contents still are touching below. This is in accordance with the statement of Abaye (Rambam *Sefer Avoda, Hilkhot Pesulei HaMukdashin* 11:21–22).

A vessel joins the two half-tenths inside the vessel, and there is a connection by means of water – צֵירוּף כְּלִי וְחִיבּוּר מַיִם: If there were two distinct piles in a vessel, with one connected to a source of water outside the vessel, and a ritually impure person touched the other pile, the first pile as well as the water that it is connected to are rendered impure. This ruling is in accordance with the principle that when the Gemara raises a dilemma, and then states: If you say, concerning one of the sides of the dilemma, the *halakha* is in accordance with that side. If an impure person touched the water, the pile that is connected to it is rendered impure, but it is uncertain whether the other pile is also included, since the Gemara's question remains unresolved (Rambam *Sefer Tahara, Hilkhot She'ar Avot HaTumot* 12:9, see 11:6).

NOTES

A *kefiza* measure within a *kav* measure – קְפִיזָא בְּקַבָּא: Since measuring vessels were made from wood, at times the vessel was thick enough to allow for another, smaller measure to be carved into the sides of the vessel, with the side of the smaller measure serving as a partition between the two cavities. The explanation here that the partition did not reach the top of the vessel is in accordance with the understanding of the Rambam. According to the understanding of Rashi, the case here is one where the partition does reach the top, so that the contents of each measure could be intermingled only if they were heaped up above the sides.

For example a hen trough, etc. – כְּגוֹן עֲרֵיבָתָהּ שֶׁל תַּרְנְגוֹלִין וכו׳: Just as in the previous example of a *kefiza* measure within a *kav* measure, this example is subject to dispute between Rashi and the Rambam. According to Rashi, the trough is divided by a partition to separate the water from the fodder, which does not reach the top of the trough. According to the Rambam, this is a trough that has a small partition that divides the top to keep the hens separate as they come to eat, but the contents of the trough themselves are touching below.

HALAKHA

A tenth that one divided, etc. – **עִשָּׂרוֹן שֶׁחִלְּקוֹ וכו׳**: In a case where consecrated food had become impure and was placed in a vessel along with pure consecrated food, if the two are not touching, the latter remains pure. If one who immersed that day touched the impure food, it is uncertain whether the pure food is then considered to be joined with the impure food and rendered impure, or whether the impure food was already saturated with impurity and therefore no change occurs (Rambam *Sefer Tahara, Hilkhot She'ar Avot HaTumot* 12:10).

כִּי תְּנַן כְּלִי מְצָרֵף מַה שֶּׁבְּתוֹכוֹ לַקֹּדֶשׁ – הָנֵי מִילֵּי דְּגַוַּאי, אֲבָל דְּבָרַאי – לָא, אוֹ דִּילְמָא כֵּיוָן דִּמְחַבַּר מְחַבַּר?

When we learned in a mishna (*Ḥagiga* 20b) that **a vessel joins** all the food **that is in it with regard to sacrificial** food, meaning that if some of the contents become impure all the contents become impure as well, does **this matter** apply only to **that** which is **inside** the vessel, **but not** to **that** which is **outside** of it, despite the fact that the outer item is connected to an item inside the vessel? **Or perhaps, since** the half-tenth of an ephah found outside the vessel **is connected** to an impure item, it **is connected** and becomes impure.

וְאִם תִּימְצֵי לוֹמַר כֵּיוָן דִּמְחַבַּר מְחַבַּר, חִיבּוּר מַיִם וְצֵירוּף כְּלִי וְנָגַע טְבוּל יוֹם מִבַּחוּץ, מַהוּ?

Rabbi Yirmeya continues: **And if you say** that **since** the half-tenth of an ephah found outside the vessel **is connected** to an impure item, it **is connected** and becomes impure, one can raise another dilemma. In a case where there is **a connection** by means of **water** between a half-tenth of an ephah outside a vessel and another half-tenth of an ephah that is inside the vessel, **and** the **vessel joins** two half-tenths of an ephah that are inside the vessel, **and one who immersed that day touched** the half-tenth of an ephah **that is outside** the vessel, **what is** the *halakha*?

כִּי תְּנַן כְּלִי מְצָרֵף – הָנֵי מִילֵּי דְּנָגַע מִגַּוַּאי, אֲבָל מִבָּרַאי – לָא, אוֹ דִּילְמָא לָא שְׁנָא? תֵּיקוּ.

When we learned in a mishna that **a vessel joins** all the food that is in it with regard to sacrificial food, meaning that if some of the contents become impure all the contents become impure as well, does **this matter** apply only in a case **where** the one who immersed that day **touched** that **which is inside** the vessel, thereby transmitting impurity to all of the contents of the vessel, and due to the connection by means of water the impurity is then transmitted to that which is outside the vessel, **but** it does **not** apply in a case **where** the one who immersed that day touched that **which is outside** of the vessel, and only the half-tenth of an ephah that is connected to the outer item becomes impure? **Or perhaps** this case **is no different,** and the vessel joins all of its contents with regard to ritual impurity. The Gemara comments: The dilemma **shall stand** unresolved.

בָּעֵי רָבָא: עִשָּׂרוֹן שֶׁחִלְּקוֹ, וְנִטְמָא אֶחָד מֵהֶן וְהִנִּיחוֹ בְּבִיסָא, וְחָזַר טְבוּל יוֹם וְנָגַע בְּאוֹתוֹ טָמֵא, מַהוּ? מִי אָמְרִינַן שָׂבַע לוֹ טוּמְאָה, אוֹ לָא?

§ It has been demonstrated that a vessel joins the contents that are found in it, even if they are not touching one another, with regard to ritual impurity, such that if some of the contents become impure, all of the contents are rendered impure. **Rava raised a dilemma:** With regard to **a tenth** of an ephah of a meal offering **that one divided**[H] and then placed the two halves in different vessels, **and one of them became impure and** afterward **he placed it in a receptacle** along with the second half-tenth of an ephah, **and then one who immersed that day touched that one** that was already rendered **impure, what is** the *halakha*? **Do we say** that the item is already **saturated with impurity** and cannot be rendered impure a second time, and therefore the second half-tenth of the ephah is not rendered impure even though it is joined in the same receptacle, **or not?**

אֲמַר לֵיהּ אַבַּיֵי: וּמִי אָמְרִינַן שָׂבַע לֵיהּ טוּמְאָה? וְהָתְנַן: סָדִין טָמֵא

Abaye said to him: And do we say that an item that is already **saturated with impurity** cannot be rendered impure a second time? **But didn't we learn** in a mishna (*Kelim* 27:9): With regard to **a sheet**[B] that is impure due to **ritual impurity**

BACKGROUND

Sheet [*sadin*] – **סָדִין**: The term *sadin* is found in the Bible (see Judges 14:12), where it refers to a linen sheet. From statements of the Sages, it appears that the sheet was not used as a garment, possibly because it is not comfortable to wear clothing made of linen. Rather, it was used for a variety of purposes: It was slept upon, used as a curtain, and served an aesthetic purpose. It was also used for shade, for wrapping coins, and for other purposes. Although it is mentioned several times that people would clothe themselves in a sheet, the sheet was not their primary garment but an addition to their standard garment or a substitute for it, for example, in the summer.

מִדְרָס וַעֲשָׂאוֹ וִילוֹן – טָהוֹר מִן הַמִּדְרָס, אֲבָל טָמֵא מַגַּע מִדְרָס.

imparted by **treading,** e.g., if a man who experiences a gonorrhea-like discharge [*zav*] lay down on it and transferred to it this severe impurity, **and** afterward **one made a curtain** [***villon***][L] **of it,**[H] it is **pure** with regard to ritual impurity **imparted by treading,** as it is no longer fit for sitting or lying down. **But** it is **impure** due to having been in **contact** with an item that became ritually impure with impurity imparted by **treading,** as it is viewed as having been in contact with itself, and therefore it can impart impurity to food and drink.

אָמַר רַבִּי יוֹסֵי: בְּאֵיזֶה מִדְרָס נָגַע זֶה? אֶלָּא, שֶׁאִם נָגַע בּוֹ הַזָּב – טָמֵא מַגַּע הַזָּב.

The mishna continues: **Rabbi Yosei said: What** source of impurity imparted by **treading did this** curtain **touch? Rather,** the *halakha* is **that if a** ***zav***[B] **touched** the sheet itself before it was made into a curtain, and did not only lie on it without touching it directly, then although the curtain is pure with regard to ritual impurity imparted by treading, it is nevertheless **impure** due to **contact** with **a** ***zav.*** This is because the impurity transmitted by contact with a *zav* applies in the case of a curtain, which is not the *halakha* with regard to impurity imparted by treading.

כִּי נָגַע בּוֹ הַזָּב מִיהָא טָמֵא, וַאֲפִילּוּ לְבַסּוֹף, כְּטָמֵא מִדְרָס וְאַחַר כָּךְ מַגַּע הַזָּב. אַמַּאי? לֵימָא: שָׂבַע לֵיהּ טוּמְאָה!

Abaye comments: **When a** ***zav*** **touched** the sheet, **in any event** it was rendered **impure, even** if he touched it **after** he lay on the sheet, thereby rendering it impure with impurity imparted by treading. In this manner, it was rendered impure with the **ritual impurity** imparted by **treading, and afterward** it was again rendered impure due to **contact** with **a** ***zav.*** According to the statement of Rava, **why** would this be the *halakha*? **Let us say** that the item is already **saturated with impurity** and cannot be rendered impure a second time.

אָמַר לֵיהּ: וּמִמַּאי דְּהַאי ״שֶׁאִם נָגַע בּוֹ הַזָּב״ לְבָתַר מִדְרָס? דִּילְמָא מִקַּמֵּי מִדְרָס, דְּהָוְיָא טוּמְאָה חֲמוּרָה עַל טוּמְאָה קַלָּה,

Rava **said to him** in response: **And from where** do you know **that this** statement of Rabbi Yosei: **That if a** ***zav*** **touched** the sheet it is nevertheless impure due to contact with a *zav*, is referring **to** a case where a *zav* touched the sheet **after** it was rendered impure with the ritual impurity imparted by **treading? Perhaps** he was referring to a case where a *zav* touched the sheet, rendering it impure due to contact with a *zav*, **before** he lay on it and rendered it impure with the ritual impurity imparted by **treading.** In that case, the **severe** form of ritual **impurity** imparted by the treading of the *zav*, which is a primary source of ritual impurity that imparts impurity to all people and items, **takes effect in addition to** the **lesser** form of **impurity** imparted by contact with a *zav*, which imparts impurity only to food and drink.

אֲבָל הָכָא דְּאִידִי וְאִידִי טוּמְאָה קַלָּה – לָא!

But here, in the case of part of a meal offering that was touched by one who immersed that day after having already become impure due to the touch of one who immersed that day, **where** both **this and that** are **lesser** forms of **impurity,** perhaps the impurity does **not** take effect a second time, as it is already impure.

LANGUAGE

Curtain [*villon*] – וִילוֹן: From the Latin velum, which can mean curtain or screen.

HALAKHA

One made a curtain of it – עֲשָׂאוֹ וִילוֹן: If one converted a sheet that was impure with ritual impurity imparted by treading into a curtain, it is rendered pure with regard to ritual impurity imparted by treading from the time that one ties the loops from which it is to be hung as a curtain. In his Commentary on the Mishna, the Rambam rules in accordance with the opinion of Rabbi Yosei that the curtain is also pure in every respect. In contrast to the Gemara's explanation here that the curtain is impure with the impurity imparted through contact with a *zav* if the impurity was incurred while the curtain was still a sheet, the Rambam explains that it is impure in this respect only if it was touched by a *zav* after having been made into a curtain (Rambam *Sefer Tahara, Hilkhot Kelim* 23:10, and see *Mishne LaMelekh* there).

BACKGROUND

Zav – **זָב:** This refers to a man who experienced a gonorrhea-like discharge. The *halakhot* relating to the severe ritual impurity caused by this condition are detailed in the Torah (Leviticus 15:1–15) and in tractate *Zavim*. The *zav* becomes ritually impure as a result of the secretion of a white, pus-like discharge from his penis. A man who experiences a discharge of that kind on one occasion becomes ritually impure for one day, like a man who has discharged semen. If he experiences a second discharge on the same day or the following day, or a prolonged initial discharge, he contracts the more severe ritual impurity of a *zav*, which lasts until he counts seven clean days. If he experiences a third discharge within the day after the second discharge, he is obligated to bring a pair of doves, one for a sin offering and one for a burnt offering, as part of his purification process. Not only does the man himself become ritually impure, but he imparts ritual impurity by coming into contact with vessels or people, by being moved by them, by moving them, by lying or sitting on them, or through the medium of a large stone that the *zav* is lying on, if it is positioned over them. The fluids he secretes, i.e., his spittle, urine, and semen, impart ritual impurity, and any item on which he sits or lies becomes a primary source of ritual impurity and can itself impart ritual impurity to other objects.

אֶלָּא מִסֵּיפָא: מוֹדֶה רַבִּי יוֹסֵי בִּשְׁנֵי סְדִינִין הַמְקוּפָּלִין וּמוּנָּחִין זֶה עַל זֶה, וְיָשַׁב זָב עֲלֵיהֶן – שֶׁהָעֶלְיוֹן טָמֵא מִדְרָס, וְהַתַּחְתּוֹן טָמֵא מִדְרָס וּמַגַּע מִדְרָס; וְאַמַּאי? לֵימָא: שָׂבַע לֵיהּ טוּמְאָה!

The Gemara suggests: **Rather,** the proof against the existence of a principle that an item can be saturated with impurity and not susceptible to becoming impure a second time is **from the last clause** of a *baraita* that corresponds to the mishna: **Rabbi Yosei concedes that in** a case of **two sheets that are folded and placed on** top of **one another, and a** *zav* **sat upon them, the top** sheet is rendered impure with the **ritual impurity** imparted by **treading, and the bottom** sheet is rendered impure with the **ritual impurity** imparted by **treading and** due to **contact** with the top sheet that has become ritually impure with impurity imparted by **treading.** The Gemara explains: **But** according to the opinion advanced in Rava's dilemma, **why** would this be the case? **Let us say** that the bottom sheet is already **saturated with impurity** and cannot be rendered impure a second time.

הָתָם בְּבַת אַחַת, הָכָא בָּזֶה אַחַר זֶה.

The Gemara rejects this proof: **There,** with regard to the bottom sheet, the two types of impurity take effect **simultaneously,** whereas **here,** with regard to the impure meal offering, the two forms of impurity take effect **one after the other.** It is only in the latter case that Rava suggests that the second type of impurity does not take effect. Therefore, there is no conclusive proof, and the question raised by Rava remains unresolved.

אָמַר רָבָא: עִשָּׂרוֹן שֶׁחִלְּקוֹ, וְאָבַד אֶחָד מֵהֶן וְהִפְרִישׁ אַחֵר תַּחְתָּיו, וְנִמְצָא הָרִאשׁוֹן, וַהֲרֵי שְׁלָשְׁתָּן מוּנָּחִין בְּבִיסָא; נִטְמָא אָבוּד – אָבוּד וְרִאשׁוֹן מִצְטָרְפִין, מוּפְרָשׁ אֵין מִצְטָרֵף;

§ **Rava says:** In a case where one **divided a tenth** of an ephah[H] of a meal offering into two halves, **and one** half was **lost and he separated another** half **in its stead, and** afterward **the first** lost half **was found, and all three are placed in a receptacle** together, if the one that had been **lost became impure, the** previously **lost** half-tenth of an ephah **and** the **first** half-tenth of an ephah **join together** and become impure, in accordance with the mishna cited earlier (*Ḥagiga* 20b) that a vessel joins the two together with regard to ritual impurity. But the half-tenth of an ephah that was **separated** to replace the lost half-tenth **does not join together** with the other half-tenths, and it remains pure.

נִטְמָא מוּפְרָשׁ – מוּפְרָשׁ וְרִאשׁוֹן מִצְטָרְפִין, אָבוּד אֵין מִצְטָרֵף; נִטְמָא רִאשׁוֹן – שְׁנֵיהֶם מִצְטָרְפִין.

If the one that had been **separated** to replace the lost half-tenth **became impure,** then the **separated** half-tenth **and** the **first** half-tenth **join together** and become impure, since the former was separated in order to complete the tenth together with the first half-tenth, while the previously **lost** half-tenth **does not join together** with them. If the **first** half-tenth **became impure,** then **both** the previously lost half-tenth as well as the half-tenth that was separated as its replacement **join together** and become ritually impure, as each of them had at one point been part of the same tenth as the first half-tenth.

HALAKHA

One divided a tenth of an ephah, etc. – **עִשָּׂרוֹן שֶׁחִלְּקוֹ וכו׳**: In a case where one divided a tenth of an ephah of a meal offering into two halves and one half was lost, and one separated another half in its stead, and afterward the first lost half was found, and all three half-tenths were placed in one vessel together without touching one another, if the one that had been lost became impure, the previously lost half-tenth of an ephah and the first half-tenth of an ephah join together and become impure. The replacement half-tenth does not join together with the other half-tenths, and with the addition of a new half-tenth, it should be sacrificed as a meal offering. If the replacement half-tenth became impure, then the replacement half-tenth and the first half-tenth join together and become impure, while the previously lost half-tenth does not join together with them. If the first half-tenth became impure, then both the previously lost half-tenth as well as the replacement half-tenth join together and are rendered impure. This is in accordance with the opinion of Rava (Rambam *Sefer Avoda, Hilkhot Pesulei HaMukdashin* 11:26).

אַבַּיֵי אָמַר: אֲפִילּוּ נִטְמָא אֶחָד מֵהֶן נַמִּי – שְׁנֵיהֶם מִצְטָרְפִין, מַאי טַעְמָא? כּוּלְּהוּ בְּנֵי בִיקְתָא דַּהֲדָדֵי נִינְהוּ.

Abaye says: Even if any **one of** the half-tenths **became impure, both** remaining half-tenths **join together** and become impure as well. **What is the reason? They are all residents of one cabin,** i.e., they were meant to be part of the same meal offering.

וְכֵן לְעִנְיַן קְמִיצָה, קָמַץ מִן הָאָבוּד – שְׁיָרָיו וְרִאשׁוֹן נֶאֱכָלִין, מוּפְרָשׁ אֵינוֹ נֶאֱכָל; קָמַץ מִן הַמּוּפְרָשׁ – שְׁיָרָיו וְרִאשׁוֹן נֶאֱכָלִין, אָבוּד אֵינוֹ נֶאֱכָל;

And similarly, according to Rava, **with regard to the removal of the handful,**[H] if one **removed the handful from** the previously **lost** half-tenth, **its remainder and** the remainder of the **first** half-tenth of an ephah **are eaten** by the priests, while the half-tenth of an ephah that was **separated** in its stead **is not eaten.** Since it was not meant to join together with this other half-tenth, the removal of the handful does not permit its consumption. If one **removed the handful from** the one that had been **separated** in place of the lost half-tenth, then **its remainder and** the **first** half-tenth of an ephah **are eaten,** while the previously **lost** half-tenth **is not eaten.**

קָמַץ מִן רִאשׁוֹן – שְׁנֵיהֶם אֵינָן נֶאֱכָלִין.

If one **removed the handful from** the **first** half-tenth, then **both** the previously lost half-tenth as well as the half-tenth that had been separated in its stead **are not eaten.** This is because the removal of the handful allows the remainder of only one tenth to be eaten, and it is not known whether the consumption of the previously lost half-tenth or the replacement half-tenth has now been permitted.

אַבַּיֵי אָמַר: אֲפִילּוּ קָמַץ מֵאֶחָד מֵהֶן – שְׁנֵיהֶן אֵינָן נֶאֱכָלִין, מַאי טַעְמָא? כּוּלְּהוּ נַמִּי בְּנֵי בִיקְתָא דַּהֲדָדֵי נִינְהוּ.

Abaye says: Even if one **removed the handful from** any **one of them, both** remaining half-tenths **are not eaten. What is the reason? They are all residents of one cabin,** and it is not possible to know whether the consumption of one or of the other has been permitted.

מַתְקִיף לַהּ רַב פַּפָּא: וְשִׁירַיִם דִּידֵיהּ מִיהָא נֶאֱכָלִין? הָא אִיכָּא דַּנְקָא דְּקוֹמֶץ דְּלָא קָרֵיב!

Rav Pappa objects to this ruling of Abaye: **And** is that to say that **in any event** the **remainder of** the half-tenth itself from which the handful was taken **is eaten? But one-sixth** [*danka*][L] **of the handful** that was removed **was not sacrificed** to permit this remainder. The handful was removed to permit the consumption of the remainders of all three half-tenths of an ephah in the receptacle. Since the handful included one-third that was removed to account for the half-tenth that is not needed, it turns out that each of the two actual half-tenths should have had an additional one-sixth removed to render them permitted.

מַתְקִיף לַהּ רַב יִצְחָק בְּרֵיהּ דְּרַב מְשַׁרְשִׁיָּא: וְקוֹמֶץ גּוּפֵיהּ הֵיכִי קָרֵיב? הָא אִיכָּא תִּילְתָּא חוּלִּין!

Rav Yitzḥak, son of Rav Mesharshiyya, also **objects to this** ruling of Abaye: **And** with regard to **the handful itself, how can it be sacrificed? But one-third** of it, i.e., the portion separated to permit the extraneous half-tenth of an ephah, **is non-sacred.**

רַב אָשֵׁי אָמַר: קוֹמֶץ בְּדַעְתָּא דְּכֹהֵן תַּלְיָא מִילְּתָא, וְכֹהֵן כִּי קָמֵיץ – אַעִשָּׂרוֹן קָא קָמֵיץ.

Rav Ashi said: These questions present no difficulty, since with regard to the removal of the **handful, the matter is dependent on the intention of** the **priest. And when** the **priest removes the handful, he removes it to** permit the remainder of **the tenth** of an ephah, and not the remainder of the extraneous half-tenth. Still, the other two halves may not be eaten because it is not possible to know whether the consumption of one or of the other has been permitted.

LANGUAGE

One-sixth [*danka*] – דַּנְקָא: *Danka* is a Persian monetary unit that appears in Middle Persian sources as dāng. Like the Aramaic *ma'a*, it constituted one-sixth of a dinar. The term was also used to mean one-sixth of anything, as in this passage.

HALAKHA

And similarly with regard to the removal of the handful – וְכֵן לְעִנְיַן קְמִיצָה: The *halakha* with regard to being joined in a case of impurity is identical to the *halakha* with regard to the removal of the handful. If one removed the handful from the previously lost half-tenth, its remainder and the first half-tenth of an ephah are eaten, while the replacement half-tenth is not eaten. If one removed the handful from the replacement half-tenth, then its remainder and the first half-tenth of an ephah are eaten, while the previously lost half-tenth is not eaten. If one removed the handful from the first half-tenth, then both the previously lost half-tenth as well as the replacement half-tenth are not eaten, since the removal of the handful allows only a tenth of an ephah to be eaten, and since the two together are a tenth of an ephah, it is as though a handful were never removed from them, and therefore it is prohibited to consume them. The reason that a handful can be removed in cases such as these, where it is seemingly removed from three half-tenths of an ephah, is that the removal of the handful is dependent on the intention of the priest, and here he removes it for the tenth of an ephah and not the extraneous half-tenth, which can be accomplished as the half-tenths are not in contact with each other. This is in accordance with the opinion of Rava and the explanation of Rav Ashi (Rambam *Sefer Avoda, Hilkhot Pesulei HaMukdashin* 11:27).

HALAKHA

If the handful became ritually impure and despite this the priest sacrificed it, etc. – **נִטְמָא הַקּוֹמֶץ וְהִקְרִיבוֹ וכו׳**: If the handful became ritually impure and nevertheless the priest sacrificed it, the frontplate effects acceptance of the meal offering. If the handful went out of its designated area, and the priest then returned it and sacrificed it, the frontplate does not effect acceptance of it (Rambam *Sefer Avoda, Hilkhot Pesulei HaMukdashin* 11:19).

NOTES

If you say he atones for the sin of *piggul*, etc. – **אִם תֹּאמַר עֲוֹן פִּיגּוּל וכו׳**: Although the Sages use the term *piggul* to refer to the intention to sacrifice or eat the offering after the permitted time, in this context the term refers to the intention to sacrifice or eat the offering outside of its designated location, corresponding to the authoritative interpretation of *piggul* in the Bible. So too, when the *baraita* states that *notar* is not accepted, here the term *notar* does not refer to sacrificial meat that was left after the time that one was permitted to eat it, since the offering was already accepted at the time of the sprinkling of the blood. Rather, it refers to what is usually known as *piggul*, meaning that at the time of the sacrificial rites the priest intended to sacrifice or eat the offering after the permitted time (*Tosafot*, citing *Zevaḥim* 29a).

מתני׳ נִטְמָא הַקּוֹמֶץ וְהִקְרִיבוֹ – הַצִּיץ מְרַצֶּה, יָצָא וְהִקְרִיבוֹ – אֵין הַצִּיץ מְרַצֶּה, שֶׁהַצִּיץ מְרַצֶּה עַל הַטָּמֵא וְאֵינוֹ מְרַצֶּה עַל הַיּוֹצֵא.

MISHNA **If the handful became ritually impure and** despite this the priest **sacrificed it,**[H] **the frontplate** worn by the High Priest **effects acceptance** of the meal offering, and the remainder is eaten by the priests. If the handful **left** its designated area **and** despite this the priest then **sacrificed it, the frontplate does not effect acceptance.** The reason is **that the frontplate effects acceptance for** offerings sacrificed when **ritually impure and does not effect acceptance for** offerings **that leave** their designated areas.

גמ׳ תָּנוּ רַבָּנַן: ״וְנָשָׂא אַהֲרֹן אֶת עֲוֹן הַקֳּדָשִׁים״ – וְכִי אֵיזֶה עָוֹן הוּא נוֹשֵׂא? אִם תֹּאמַר: עֲוֹן פִּיגּוּל – הֲרֵי כְּבָר נֶאֱמַר ״לֹא יֵחָשֵׁב״! אִם תֹּאמַר: עֲוֹן נוֹתָר – הֲרֵי כְּבָר נֶאֱמַר ״לֹא יֵרָצֶה״!

GEMARA **The Sages taught** in a *baraita*: It is written with regard to the frontplate: "And it shall be upon Aaron's forehead, **and Aaron shall bear the sin committed with the sacred items,** which the children of Israel shall hallow, even all their sacred gifts; and it shall be always upon his forehead, that they may be accepted before the Lord" (Exodus 28:38). The Sages expounded: **But which sin does he bear? If you say** he atones for **the sin of *piggul*,**[N] **it is already stated: "It shall not be credited** to him" (Leviticus 7:18). **If you say** he atones for **the sin of *notar*,** it **is already stated** in the same verse: **"It shall not be accepted."**

הָא אֵינוֹ נוֹשֵׂא אֶלָּא עֲוֹן טוּמְאָה, שֶׁהוּתְּרָה מִכְּלָלָהּ בְּצִיבּוּר.

Evidently, the High Priest wearing the frontplate **bears only the sin of impurity** in the offering of an individual. The frontplate is understood to atone for the sin of sacrificing an impure offering, **as its general prohibition was permitted** in certain circumstances, specifically **in** the case of the **community,** since in a situation where the entire community is impure it is permitted to sacrifice impure communal offerings *ab initio*.

מַתְקִיף לַהּ רַבִּי זֵירָא, אֵימָא: עֲוֹן יוֹצֵא, שֶׁהוּתַּר מִכְּלָלוֹ בְּבָמָה!

Rabbi Zeira objects to this: Why not **say** that the frontplate atones for the **sin** of sacrificing offerings that **leave** the courtyard and are thereby disqualified, **as its general prohibition was permitted** in certain circumstances, specifically **in** the case of an offering sacrificed on a private **altar** during the period after the Jewish people had entered Eretz Yisrael and before there was an established location for the Tabernacle?

אֲמַר לֵיהּ אַבָּיֵי, אָמַר קְרָא: ״לְרָצוֹן לָהֶם לִפְנֵי ה׳״, עָוֹן דִּלִפְנֵי ה׳ – אִין, עֲוֹן דְּיוֹצֵא – לָא.

Abaye said to him: The verse states with regard to the frontplate: "And it shall be always upon his forehead, **that they may be accepted before the Lord"** (Exodus 28:38), teaching that in the case of **a sin** whose general prohibition is permitted **before the Lord,** i.e., in the Temple, **yes,** the frontplate atones for it. But in the case of the **sin** of offerings **that leave** the courtyard, whose general prohibition is not permitted before the Lord, the frontplate does **not** atone for it.

מַתְקִיף לַהּ רַבִּי אִילְעָא, אֵימָא: עֲוֹן שְׂמֹאל, שֶׁהוּתַּר מִכְּלָלוֹ בְּיוֹם הַכִּפּוּרִים!

Rabbi Ile'a objects to this: Why not **say** that the frontplate atones for the **sin** of performing the service using one's **left** hand instead of one's right, **as its general prohibition was permitted** in certain circumstances, specifically **in** the case of **Yom Kippur,** when the High Priest carries the spoon bearing the incense into the Holy of Holies with his left hand?

אֲמַר לֵיהּ אַבָּיֵי, אָמַר קְרָא: ״עָוֹן״ – עָוֹן שֶׁהָיָה בּוֹ וּדְחִיתִיו, לְאַפּוֹקֵי יוֹם הַכִּפּוּרִים דְּהֶכְשֵׁירוֹ בִּשְׂמֹאל הוּא.

Abaye said to him: The verse states: "And Aaron shall bear **the sin** committed with the sacred items" (Exodus 28:38), to say that the frontplate atones for **a sin that was** committed **with** the offering **and I deferred it.** This serves **to exclude** the spoon bearing the incense of **Yom Kippur,** where there is no sin that was deferred, **since its proper** performance **is** for the High Priest to hold it **with** his **left** hand, as he must hold both the coal pan and the spoon of incense.

רַב אַשִׁי אָמַר: ״עֲוֹן הַקֳּדָשִׁים״ – וְלֹא עֲוֹן הַמַּקְדִּישִׁין.

Rav Ashi said: The frontplate does not atone for the sin of sacrificing an offering with the left hand for a different reason: The verse states: "And Aaron shall bear **the sin committed with the sacred items** [*hakodashim*]," demonstrating that the frontplate atones for a sin inherent in the offering itself, **and not** for **a sin** committed by **those who bring the offering** [*hamakdishin*].

אֲמַר לֵיהּ רַב סִימָא בְּרֵיהּ דְּרַב אִידִי לְרַב אַשִׁי, וְאָמְרִי לָהּ רַב סִימָא בְּרֵיהּ דְּרַב אַשִׁי לְרַב אַשִׁי: וְאֵימָא עֲוֹן בַּעַל מוּם, שֶׁהוּתַּר מִכְּלָלוֹ בְּעוֹפוֹת, דְּאָמַר מָר: תַּמּוּת וְזַכְרוּת בִּבְהֵמָה, וְאֵין תַּמּוּת וְזַכְרוּת בְּעוֹפוֹת!

Rav Sima, son of Rav Idi, said to Rav Ashi; and some say that it was **Rav Sima, son of Rav Ashi,** who said **to Rav Ashi: But** why not **say** that the frontplate atones for **the sin of a blemished animal** that is sacrificed, **as its general prohibition was permitted** in certain circumstances, specifically **in the case of birds? As the Master says:** The *halakha* that an offering must be **unblemished and** the *halakha* that a burnt offering must be **male** are taught **with regard to animal** offerings, **but** there is **no** requirement that an offering must be **unblemished and male with regard to birds.**[H]

אֲמַר לֵיהּ, עָלֶיךָ אָמַר קְרָא: "לֹא יֵרָצֶה", "כִּי לֹא לְרָצוֹן יִהְיֶה לָכֶם".

Rav Ashi **said to him: With regard to your** claim, **the verse states** about blemished animals: **"It shall not be accepted"** (Leviticus 22:23), and: "But whatsoever has a blemish that you shall not bring; **for it shall not be acceptable for you"** (Leviticus 22:20), teaching that in no case are blemished animals accepted as offerings, even due to the frontplate.

תָּנוּ רַבָּנַן: דָּם שֶׁנִּטְמָא וּזְרָקוֹ, בְּשׁוֹגֵג – הוּרְצָה, בְּמֵזִיד – לֹא הוּרְצָה; בַּמֶּה דְּבָרִים אֲמוּרִים – בְּיָחִיד, אֲבָל בְּצִיבּוּר, בֵּין בְּשׁוֹגֵג בֵּין בְּמֵזִיד – הוּרְצָה; וּבְגוֹי, בֵּין בְּשׁוֹגֵג בֵּין בְּמֵזִיד, בֵּין בְּאוֹנֶס בֵּין בְּרָצוֹן

§ **The Sages taught** in a *baraita*: In the case of **blood** of an offering **that became impure**[H] **and** a priest **sprinkled it** on the altar, if he did so **unwittingly,** the offering is **accepted** and effects atonement for the owner of the offering. If he sprinkled the blood **intentionally,** the offering is **not accepted. In what** case **is this statement said? In** the case of the offering of **an individual. But in** the case of **a communal** offering, **whether** he sprinkled the blood **unwittingly** or **whether** he did so **intentionally,** the offering is **accepted. And in** the case of an offering of **a gentile** where the blood of the offering became impure, **whether** the priest sprinkled the blood **unwittingly** or **whether** he did so **intentionally, whether** he did so **due to circumstances beyond his control** or **whether** he did so **willingly,**

HALAKHA

There is no requirement that an offering must be unblemished and male with regard to birds – אֵין תַּמּוּת וְזַכְרוּת בְּעוֹפוֹת: It is not necessary for a bird offering to be male; female birds may be used for any bird offering. Likewise, there is no requirement for a bird offering to be unblemished. This applies only to minor blemishes, but if the bird's wing dried out or it was missing an eye or leg, it is disqualified from being used as an offering (Rambam *Sefer Avoda, Hilkhot Issurei Mizbe'aḥ* 3:1).

Blood that became impure – דָּם שֶׁנִּטְמָא: According to the Rambam, the blood of consecrated animals is not susceptible to ritual impurity. This ruling does not accord with the *baraita* cited here, as well as other sources, but is consistent with the ruling of Rabbi Yosei ben Yo'ezer of Tzereida (see *Eduyyot* 8:4) and the statement of Rav Pappa in tractate *Pesaḥim* (17b). According to Rashi, Rav Pappa retracted his statement, and the blood of consecrated animals is susceptible to ritual impurity (Rambam *Sefer Avoda, Hilkhot Pesulei HaMukdashin* 1:36).

לֹא הוּרְצָה.

the offering is **not accepted,** as the verse states with regard to the frontplate: "That it may be accepted for them before the Lord" (Exodus 28:38), with the term "for them" teaching that this applies only for Jews, not for gentiles.

וּרְמִינְהִי: עַל מָה הַצִּיץ מְרַצֶּה? עַל הַדָּם וְעַל הַבָּשָׂר וְעַל הַחֵלֶב שֶׁנִּטְמָא, בֵּין בְּשׁוֹגֵג בֵּין בְּמֵזִיד, בֵּין בְּאוֹנֶס בֵּין בְּרָצוֹן, בֵּין בְּיָחִיד בֵּין בְּצִיבּוּר!

And the Gemara **raises a contradiction** from another *baraita*: **For what does the frontplate** worn by the High Priest **effect acceptance?** It effects acceptance **for the blood, for the flesh, and for the fat** of an offering **that became impure** in the Temple, **whether** they were rendered impure **unwittingly or intentionally, whether due to circumstances beyond one's control or willfully, whether in** the case of the offering of **an individual or in** the case of **a communal** offering. In contrast to the statement of the previous *baraita*, this *baraita* teaches that the frontplate does effect acceptance in the case of an individual offering for blood that became impure and was sprinkled intentionally.

אָמַר רַב יוֹסֵף, לָא קַשְׁיָא: הָא רַבִּי יוֹסֵי, הָא רַבָּנַן; דְּתַנְיָא: אֵין תּוֹרְמִין מִן הַטָּמֵא עַל הַטָּהוֹר, וְאִם תָּרַם, בְּשׁוֹגֵג – תְּרוּמָתוֹ תְּרוּמָה, בְּמֵזִיד – אֵין תְּרוּמָתוֹ תְּרוּמָה. רַבִּי יוֹסֵי אוֹמֵר: בֵּין בְּשׁוֹגֵג בֵּין בְּמֵזִיד – תְּרוּמָתוֹ תְּרוּמָה.

Rav Yosef said: This is **not difficult. This** *baraita*, which teaches that the frontplate effects acceptance for impure blood of an individual offering that was sprinkled intentionally, is in accordance with the opinion of **Rabbi Yosei,** whereas **that** *baraita*, which teaches that the frontplate does not effect acceptance, is in accordance with the opinion of **the Rabbis. As it is taught** in a *baraita*: **One may not separate** ***teruma*[B] from ritually impure** produce **for ritually pure** produce. **And if he separated** ***teruma*** from impure produce **unwittingly,[H] his** ***teruma*** **is** considered ***teruma,*** but if he did so **intentionally,** the Sages penalize him and **his** ***teruma*** **is not** ***teruma.*** **Rabbi Yosei says: Whether** he did so **unwittingly or intentionally, his** ***teruma*** **is** ***teruma.*** Like the ruling found in the second *baraita*, Rabbi Yosei does not distinguish between a case where one acted unwittingly and where one acted intentionally.

אֵימַר דְּשָׁמְעַתְּ לֵיהּ לְרַבִּי יוֹסֵי – דְּלָא קָנֵיס, דִּמְרַצֶּה צִיץ עַל אֲכִילוֹת מִי שָׁמְעַתְּ לֵיהּ? וְהָתַנְיָא, רַבִּי אֱלִיעֶזֶר אוֹמֵר: הַצִּיץ מְרַצֶּה עַל אֲכִילוֹת, רַבִּי יוֹסֵי אוֹמֵר: אֵין הַצִּיץ מְרַצֶּה עַל אֲכִילוֹת!

The Gemara objects to the comparison: You can **say that you heard** that **Rabbi Yosei** holds **that** the Sages **do not penalize** him. **Did you hear him** say, as the *baraita* teaches, **that the frontplate effects acceptance for** the impurity of the portions of offerings that are to be **eaten? But isn't it taught** in a *baraita* that **Rabbi Eliezer says: The frontplate effects acceptance for** the impurity of the portions of offerings that are to be **eaten,** and **Rabbi Yosei says: The frontplate does not effect acceptance for** the impurity of portions of offerings that are to be **eaten?[H]**

אֵיפוּךְ, רַבִּי אֱלִיעֶזֶר אוֹמֵר: אֵין הַצִּיץ מְרַצֶּה עַל אֲכִילוֹת, רַבִּי יוֹסֵי אוֹמֵר: הַצִּיץ מְרַצֶּה עַל אֲכִילוֹת.

The Gemara answers: **Reverse** the opinions, so that **Rabbi Eliezer says: The frontplate does not effect acceptance for** the impurity of the portions of offerings that are to be **eaten,** and **Rabbi Yosei says: The frontplate does effect acceptance for** the impurity of portions of offerings that are to be **eaten.**

מַתְקִיף לָהּ רַב שֵׁשֶׁת: וּמִי מָצֵית אָפְכַתְּ לָהּ? וְהָתַנְיָא: יָכוֹל בָּשָׂר שֶׁנִּטְמָא לִפְנֵי זְרִיקַת דָּמִים יְהוּ חַיָּיבִין עֲלֵיהֶן מִשּׁוּם טוּמְאָה?

Rav Sheshet objects to this: And are you able to reverse the opinions and say that according to Rabbi Eliezer the frontplate does not effect acceptance for the impurity of portions that are to be eaten? **But isn't it taught** in a *baraita*: One **might** have thought **that** one who partakes of **impure sacrificial meat,** i.e., one who partakes of the meat while in a state of ritual impurity, **before the sprinkling of the blood** takes place, **is liable for** eating **it due to** violation of the prohibition against partaking of the meat while **ritually impure.**

תַּלְמוּד לוֹמַר: ״כָּל טָהוֹר יֹאכַל בָּשָׂר. וְהַנֶּפֶשׁ אֲשֶׁר תֹּאכַל בָּשָׂר מִזֶּבַח הַשְּׁלָמִים אֲשֶׁר לַה׳ וְטֻמְאָתוֹ עָלָיו וְנִכְרְתָה״ – הַנִּיתָּר לַטְּהוֹרִין חַיָּיבִין עָלָיו מִשּׁוּם טוּמְאָה,

To counter this, **the verse states: "Every one that is ritually pure may eat of it"** (Leviticus 7:19), and immediately afterward the verse states: **"But the soul that eats of the meat of the sacrifice of peace offerings, that belong to the Lord, having his impurity upon him,** that soul **shall be cut off** from his people" (Leviticus 7:20). The juxtaposition of these verses teaches that if one who is impure partakes of **that which has become permitted to those who are ritually pure,** he is **liable for** eating **it due to** violation of the prohibition against partaking of the meat while **ritually impure.**

BACKGROUND

Teruma – תְּרוּמָה: Whenever this term appears without qualification, it is referring to *teruma gedola*, the great *teruma*. The Torah commands that "the first fruit of your oil, your wine, and your grain" (Numbers 18:12) must be given to the priest. The Sages extended the scope of this mitzva to include all produce. This mitzva applies only in Eretz Yisrael. After the first fruits have been set aside from the new crop, a certain portion of the remaining produce must be given to the priests. While the Torah does not specify the amount of *teruma* that must be donated, and one can fulfill his obligation by Torah law by separating a single kernel of grain from an entire heap, the Sages established fixed measures for *teruma*: One-fortieth of the produce for a generous gift, one-fiftieth for an average gift, and one-sixtieth for a miserly gift. One may not set aside the other tithes until he has set aside *teruma*.

Teruma is considered sanctified and may be eaten only by a priest and his household while they are in a state of ritual purity (see Leviticus 22:9–15). To emphasize this requisite state of ritual purity, the Sages obligated the priests to wash their hands before partaking of *teruma*. This is the source for the practice of washing one's hands prior to eating bread. A ritually impure priest or a non-priest who eats *teruma* is subject to the penalty of death at the hand of Heaven. If *teruma* contracts ritual impurity, it may no longer be eaten and must be destroyed. Nevertheless, it remains the property of the priest and he may derive benefit from its destruction. Nowadays, *teruma* is not given to priests because they have no definite proof of their priestly lineage. The obligation to separate *teruma* remains in force, although only a small portion of the produce is separated and then disposed of.

HALAKHA

If he separated ***teruma*** **from impure produce unwittingly, etc.** – אִם תָּרַם בְּשׁוֹגֵג וכו׳: It is prohibited to separate *teruma* from ritually impure produce to render pure produce permitted. If one did so unwittingly, his *teruma* is considered *teruma*, but if he acted intentionally the produce remains untithed, and he must separate *teruma* again. The impure produce he set aside as *teruma* is also *teruma*. The *halakha* is in accordance with the mishna in tractate *Terumot* (2:2) and the explanation of Rav Natan, son of Rabbi Oshaya, on *Yevamot* 89a (Rambam *Sefer Zera'im*, *Hilkhot Terumot* 5:8).

The frontplate does not effect acceptance for the impurity of portions of offerings that are to be eaten – אֵין הַצִּיץ מְרַצֶּה עַל אֲכִילוֹת: The frontplate effects acceptance for the ritual impurity of several components of the offerings in the Temple, including the fat, the portions of the offering that are consumed on the altar, and the sacrificial limbs of the burnt offering. It does not effect acceptance for the ritual impurity of the portions of offerings that are consumed by the priests. This is in accordance with the opinion of Rabbi Yosei because there is no other *tanna* who agrees with Rabbi Eliezer that the frontplate effects acceptance for the impurity of portions of offerings that are consumed by the priests (Rambam *Sefer Avoda*, *Hilkhot Biat HaMikdash* 4:7, and see *Hilkhot Pesulei HaMukdashin* 1:34).

וְשֶׁאֵינוֹ נִיתָּר לַטְּהוֹרִין אֵין חַיָּיבִין עָלָיו מִשּׁוּם טוּמְאָה.

But if one who is impure partakes of **that which is not permitted to those who are pure,**[H] he is **not liable for** eating **it due to** violation of the prohibition against partaking of the meat while **ritually impure.** Since it is not permitted to eat the sacrificial meat before the sprinkling of the blood, one who partakes of it at that point is not liable to receive *karet* for eating it while ritually impure.

אוֹ אֵינוֹ, אֶלָּא: נֶאֱכָל לַטְּהוֹרִין חַיָּיבִין עָלָיו מִשּׁוּם טוּמְאָה, וְשֶׁאֵינוֹ נֶאֱכָל לַטְּהוֹרִין אֵין חַיָּיבִין עָלָיו מִשּׁוּם טוּמְאָה; אוֹצִיא אֲנִי אֶת הַלָּן וְאֶת הַיּוֹצֵא שֶׁאֵינָן נֶאֱכָלִין לַטְּהוֹרִים!

The *baraita* continues: **Or** perhaps, **is** the verse teaching **only** that if one who is impure partakes of that which **is eaten by those who are ritually pure,** he is **liable for** eating **it due to** violation of the prohibition against partaking of the meat while **ritually impure; but** in a case **where** he partakes of **that which is not eaten by those who are ritually pure,** he is **not liable for** eating **it due to** violation of the prohibition against partaking of the meat while **ritually impure** despite the fact that its blood has already been sprinkled? **I would** then **exclude** sacrificial meat **that** was **left overnight and** meat **that leaves** the Temple courtyard, **which are not** permitted to be **eaten by those who are ritually pure,** and I would derive that one who is impure who partakes of them is not liable for eating them.

תַּלְמוּד לוֹמַר: ״אֲשֶׁר לַה׳״ – רִיבָּה.

Therefore, **the verse states: "That belong to the Lord,"** which teaches that the verse **included** leftover meat and meat that leaves the Temple courtyard in the prohibition, and one who partakes of them while impure is liable for partaking of them.

יָכוֹל שֶׁאֲנִי מְרַבֶּה אֶת הַפִּיגּוּלִין וְאֶת הַנּוֹתָרוֹת?

One **might** have thought **that I include** in the prohibition **the** meat that was rendered ***piggul*** through one's intention of consuming it after its designated time **and the** meat that was rendered ***notar.***

נוֹתָרוֹת הַיְינוּ לָן! אֶלָּא: אַף הַפִּיגּוּלִין כַּנּוֹתָרוֹת? תַּלְמוּד לוֹמַר: ״מִזֶּבַח הַשְּׁלָמִים״ – מִיעֵט.

The *baraita* interjects: **Isn't *notar*** identical to meat that was **left overnight,** and it has already been established that one is liable for partaking of leftover meat while in an impure state? **Rather,** what is meant is as follows: One might have thought to include in the prohibition **even the** meats that were rendered ***piggul,*** just **as *notar*** is included. Therefore, **the verse states: "Of the meat of the sacrifice of peace offerings,"** and the term "of the meat" **excluded** one who is impure who partakes of *piggul.*

וּמָה רָאִיתָ לְרַבּוֹת אֶת אֵלּוּ וּלְהוֹצִיא אֶת אֵלּוּ? אַחַר שֶׁרִיבָּה הַכָּתוּב וּמִיעֵט, אָמַרְתָּ: מְרַבֶּה אֲנִי אֶת אֵלּוּ שֶׁהָיְתָה לָהֶן שְׁעַת הַכּוֹשֶׁר, וּמוֹצִיא אֲנִי אֶת אֵלּוּ שֶׁלֹּא הָיְתָה לָהֶן שְׁעַת הַכּוֹשֶׁר;

The *baraita* asks: **And what did you see to include these,** i.e., leftover meat and meat that leaves the courtyard, **and to exclude those,** i.e., *piggul*? It answers: **After the verse included** some offerings **and excluded** others, **you** should **say** the following: **I include these,** the leftover meat and the meat that leaves the Temple courtyard, **as they had a period of fitness** after their blood was sprinkled, before they were rendered unfit by being left over or by leaving the Temple courtyard. **And I exclude those,** *piggul,* **as they never had a period of fitness,** as they were already unfit when the blood was sprinkled.

וְאִם תֹּאמַר: בָּשָׂר שֶׁנִּטְמָא לִפְנֵי זְרִיקַת דָּמִים וַאֲכָלוֹ לְאַחַר זְרִיקַת דָּמִים, מִפְּנֵי מָה חַיָּיבִין עָלָיו מִשּׁוּם טוּמְאָה? מִפְּנֵי שֶׁהַצִּיץ מְרַצֶּה.

The *baraita* concludes: **And if you say** that if that is the case, then with regard to sacrificial **meat that became impure before the sprinkling of the blood, and** one who was impure **ate it after the sprinkling of the blood, for what** reason is he **liable for** eating **it due to** violation of the prohibition against partaking of the meat while **ritually impure** if it never had a period of fitness? The answer is that he is liable **because the frontplate effects acceptance** and the sprinkling is valid.

נִטְמָא – אִין, יוֹצֵא – לָא;

It arises from this *baraita* that if the offering **became impure,** then **yes,** the frontplate effects acceptance; but in the case of sacrificial meat that **leaves** the Temple courtyard, the frontplate **does not** effect acceptance, and therefore it was never considered to have a period of fitness.

מַאן שָׁמְעַתְּ לֵיהּ דְּאָמַר: אֵין זְרִיקָה מוֹעֶלֶת לַיּוֹצֵא – רַבִּי אֱלִיעֶזֶר, וְקָתָנֵי דִּמְרַצֶּה צִיץ עַל אֲכִילוֹת!

Rav Sheshet now states his question: **Who did you hear who says** that the **sprinkling** of the blood is **not effective** in the case of sacrificial meat that **leaves** the Temple courtyard? This is the opinion of **Rabbi Eliezer,** as seen in tractate *Me'ila* (6b), **and** yet although this *baraita* is then clearly in accordance with his opinion, it **teaches that** the **frontplate effects acceptance for** the impurity of the portions of offerings that are to be **eaten.** Therefore, this too is the opinion of Rabbi Eliezer, and the opinions in the *baraita* cited above should not be reversed.

HALAKHA

But if one who is impure partakes of that which is not permitted to those who are pure – וְשֶׁאֵינוֹ נִיתָּר לַטְּהוֹרִין: If one who is ritually impure partakes of the sacrificial meat before its blood is sprinkled, he is not liable for eating it due to violation of the prohibition against partaking of sacrificial meat while ritually impure. This is because in the case of any item that has permitting factors, one is not liable for the prohibitions of *piggul*, *notar*, or impurity until the permitting factors were sacrificed properly (Rambam *Sefer Avoda*, *Hilkhot Pesulei HaMukdashin* 18:16).

אֶלָּא אֲמַר רַב חִסְדָּא, לָא קַשְׁיָא: הָא רַבִּי אֱלִיעֶזֶר, הָא רַבָּנַן.

Rather, Rav Ḥisda said: It is **not difficult. This** *baraita*, which teaches that the frontplate effects acceptance for the impurity of the portions of offerings that are to be eaten, is in accordance with the opinion of **Rabbi Eliezer,** whereas **that** *baraita*, which teaches that the frontplate does not effect acceptance, is in accordance with the opinion of **the Rabbis.**

אֵימַר דְּשָׁמְעַתְּ לֵיהּ לְרַבִּי אֱלִיעֶזֶר – דִּמְרַצֶּה צִיץ עַל אֲכִילוֹת, דְּלָא קָנֵיס מִי שָׁמְעַתְּ לֵיהּ? אִין, כִּי הֵיכִי דְּשָׁמְעַתְּ לֵיהּ לְרַבִּי יוֹסֵי – שָׁמְעַתְּ לֵיהּ לְרַבִּי אֱלִיעֶזֶר; דְּתַנְיָא, רַבִּי אֱלִיעֶזֶר אוֹמֵר: בֵּין בְּשׁוֹגֵג בֵּין בְּמֵזִיד – תְּרוּמָתוֹ תְּרוּמָה.

The Gemara asks: You can **say that you heard** that **Rabbi Eliezer** holds **that** the **frontplate effects acceptance for** the impurity of the portions of offerings that are to be **eaten,** but **did you hear him** say **that** the Sages **did not penalize** one who acted willfully? The Gemara answers: **Yes. Just as you heard** that **Rabbi Yosei** holds with regard to *teruma* that one who separated impure produce on behalf of pure produce is not penalized, **you heard** that **Rabbi Eliezer** holds the same. This is **as it is taught** in a *baraita*: **Rabbi Eliezer says: Whether** one acted **unwittingly or intentionally, his** ***teruma*** **is** ***teruma.***

אֵימַר דְּשָׁמְעַתְּ לֵיהּ לְרַבִּי אֱלִיעֶזֶר – בִּתְרוּמָה דְּקִילָּא, בְּקָדָשִׁים דַּחֲמִירִי מִי שָׁמְעַתְּ לֵיהּ? אִם כֵּן, הָא אַמַּאן תִּרְמְיֵיהּ?

The Gemara objects: You can **say that you heard Rabbi Eliezer** state this *halakha* **with regard to** ***teruma,*** **which** is **lenient,** but **did you hear him** say this **with regard to consecrated** items, **which** are more **severe?** The Gemara answers: **If** it is **so** that Rabbi Eliezer does not hold the same opinion with regard to consecrated items, **to whom will you attribute this** *baraita* that rules that the Sages did not penalize one who acted willfully? Rather, it must be that this is the opinion of Rabbi Eliezer.

רָבִינָא אֲמַר: טוּמְאָתוֹ, בֵּין בְּשׁוֹגֵג בֵּין בְּמֵזִיד – הוּרְצָה; זְרִיקָתוֹ, בְּשׁוֹגֵג – הוּרְצָה, בְּמֵזִיד – לֹא הוּרְצָה.

Ravina said that the contradiction between the two *baraitot* should be resolved as follows: With regard to the circumstances of the contraction of **its ritual impurity,** regardless of whether the blood was rendered impure **unwittingly or intentionally,** the frontplate effects acceptance for the impurity and the offering is **accepted,** as the second *baraita* teaches. By contrast, with regard to **the sprinkling of** the blood, if it was **unwittingly** sprinkled after becoming ritually impure, meaning that the priest was unaware that it was impure, then the offering is **accepted,** but if it was **intentionally** sprinkled after becoming impure, it is **not accepted,**[H] as the first *baraita* teaches.

וְרַב שֵׁילָא אֲמַר: זְרִיקָתוֹ, בֵּין בְּשׁוֹגֵג בֵּין בְּמֵזִיד – הוּרְצָה; טוּמְאָתוֹ, בְּשׁוֹגֵג – הוּרְצָה, בְּמֵזִיד – לֹא הוּרְצָה.

And Rabbi Sheila said the opposite resolution: With regard to **the sprinkling of** the blood, **whether** it was performed **unwittingly or intentionally,** the offering is **accepted.** By contrast, with regard to the circumstances of the contraction of **its ritual impurity,** if it was rendered impure **unwittingly** the offering is **accepted,** and if it was rendered impure **intentionally** it is **not accepted.**

וּלְרַב שֵׁילָא, דְּקָתָנֵי: שֶׁנִּטְמָא בֵּין בְּשׁוֹגֵג בֵּין בְּמֵזִיד! הָכִי קָאָמַר: נִטְמָא בְּשׁוֹגֵג, וּזְרָקוֹ בֵּין בְּשׁוֹגֵג בֵּין בְּמֵזִיד.

The Gemara explains: **And according to Rav Sheila,** concerning that **which is taught** in the second *baraita*, that the frontplate effects acceptance for blood **that was rendered impure** regardless of **whether** it happened **unwittingly or intentionally, this** is what **it is saying:** If the blood **was rendered impure unwittingly and one sprinkled** its blood, **whether** it was sprinkled **unwittingly or intentionally,** it is accepted.

HALAKHA

If it was unwittingly sprinkled the offering is accepted but if it was intentionally sprinkled it is not accepted – בְּשׁוֹגֵג הוּרְצָה בְּמֵזִיד לֹא הוּרְצָה: If it was discovered before the blood was sprinkled that the meat of a Paschal offering had become ritually impure, even though the portions that are consumed on the altar remain pure, its blood should not be sprinkled on the altar. If the blood is sprinkled, it is not valid even after the fact. If the impurity was not discovered until after the blood was sprinkled, the offering is accepted, because the frontplate effects acceptance in cases where the blood is unwittingly sprinkled while the meat is impure, but not in cases where the blood is intentionally sprinkled while the meat is impure. This is in accordance with the opinion of Ravina, since he is a later *amora*, and this ruling is in accordance with the inference of the mishna in tractate *Pesaḥim* (80b). It also accords with the wording of the *baraita*. Although the Rambam rules that the frontplate does not effect acceptance for the ritual impurity of the portions of offerings that are eaten, this is not the *halakha* with regard to the Paschal offering, whose primary purpose is to be eaten (Rambam *Sefer Korbanot, Hilkhot Korban Pesaḥ* 4:2 and Mahari Kurkus there, and see *Sefer Avoda, Hilkhot Biat HaMikdash* 4:6).

תָּא שְׁמַע: דָּם שֶׁנִּטְמָא וּזְרָקוֹ, בְּשׁוֹגֵג – הוּרְצָה, בְּמֵזִיד – לֹא הוּרְצָה! הָכִי קָאָמַר: דָּם שֶׁנִּטְמָא וּזְרָקוֹ בֵּין בְּשׁוֹגֵג בֵּין בְּמֵזִיד, נִטְמָא בְּשׁוֹגֵג – הוּרְצָה, בְּמֵזִיד – לֹא הוּרְצָה.

The Gemara suggests a refutation of Rav Sheila's opinion based on the first *baraita*: **Come and hear:** In the case of **blood** of an offering **that became impure and** a priest **sprinkled it** on the altar, if he did so **unwittingly,** the offering is **accepted** and achieves atonement for the owner of the offering. If he sprinkled the blood **intentionally,** the offering is **not accepted.** This contradicts Rav Sheila's statement that even if the priest sprinkled the blood intentionally, it is accepted. The Gemara rejects this proof: According to Rav Sheila, **this** is what the *baraita* **is saying:** In the case of **blood that became impure and** a priest **sprinkled it, whether** it was sprinkled **unwittingly or intentionally,** if it was **rendered impure unwittingly** it is **accepted,** but if it was rendered impure **intentionally** then it is **not accepted.**

מתני׳ נִטְמְאוּ שְׁיָרֶיהָ, נִשְׂרְפוּ שְׁיָרֶיהָ, אָבְדוּ שְׁיָרֶיהָ – כְּמִדַּת רַבִּי אֱלִיעֶזֶר כְּשֵׁירָה, וּכְמִדַּת רַבִּי יְהוֹשֻׁעַ פְּסוּלָה.

MISHNA If after the handful was removed **the remainder of** the meal offering **became ritually impure,** or if **the remainder of** the meal offering **was burned,**[H] or if **the remainder of** the meal offering **was lost, according to the principle of Rabbi Eliezer,** who says that with regard to an animal offering the blood is fit for sprinkling even if there is no meat that can be eaten, the meal offering is **fit,** and the priest burns the handful. **But according to the principle of Rabbi Yehoshua,** who says that with regard to an animal offering the blood is fit for sprinkling only if there is meat that can be eaten, it is **unfit** and the priest does not burn the handful, as the handful serves to render permitted the remainder.

גמ׳ אָמַר רַב: וְהוּא שֶׁנִּטְמְאוּ כׇּל שְׁיָרֶיהָ, אֲבָל מִקְצָת שְׁיָרֶיהָ – לֹא.

GEMARA With regard to the mishna's statement that according to Rabbi Yehoshua the meal offering is unfit if its remainder is rendered impure, **Rav says: And this is** the *halakha* only **when all of its remainder became impure.**[H] **But** if only **a part of its remainder** became impure, the meal offering is **not** unfit.

קָא סָלְקָא דַעְתָּךְ: נִטְמָא – אִין, אָבוּד וְשָׂרוּף – לָא. מַאי קָסָבַר? אִי קָסָבַר: שִׁיּוּרָא מִילְּתָא הִיא, אֲפִילּוּ אָבוּד וְשָׂרוּף נָמֵי! אִי קָסָבַר: שִׁיּוּרָא לָאו מִילְּתָא הִיא, וְנִטְמָא מַאי טַעְמָא – דִּמְרַצֶּה צִיץ, אִי הָכִי, כׇּל שְׁיָרֶיהָ נָמֵי!

The Gemara comments: It **enters your mind** that Rav holds that only if a part of the remainder **became impure,** then **yes,** the meal offering is fit; but if part of the remainder **was lost or burned,** then the meal offering is **not** fit. The Gemara asks: **What does** Rav **hold? If he holds** that **what remains is significant,** so that even if a portion of the remainder cannot be eaten the handful is still sacrificed to render the rest permitted, then why would this not also be the *halakha* **even** if part of the remainder **was lost or burned?** Alternatively, **if he holds** that **what remains is not significant,** and the Gemara interjects: **And** accordingly, **what is the reason** that the handful is sacrificed if a part of the remainder **became impure?** It is **because** the **frontplate effects acceptance** for the impurity; **if that is so,** then **even** if **all of the remainder** became impure, the handful should still be sacrificed.

HALAKHA

If the remainder of it became ritually impure or if the remainder of it was burned – **נִטְמְאוּ שְׁיָרֶיהָ נִשְׂרְפוּ שְׁיָרֶיהָ:** If the priest removed the handful from the meal offering and then all of the remainder became ritually impure, was burned, left the Temple courtyard, or was lost, the handful should not be sacrificed. If it was nevertheless sacrificed, it is accepted after the fact. Other commentaries object, as this ruling is not stated in a case where the remainder was lost or burned (see *Zevaḥ Toda*). Some explain that the Rambam rules in accordance with Rabbi Yosei in tractate *Pesaḥim* (78b), and not in accordance with Rabbi Yehoshua (Rambam *Sefer Avoda, Hilkhot Pesulei HaMukdashin* 11:20, and see *Kesef Mishne* and *Leḥem Mishne* there).

And this is when all of its remainder became impure – **וְהוּא שֶׁנִּטְמְאוּ כׇּל שְׁיָרֶיהָ:** If a part of the remainder is still fit, then the priest should burn the handful and the remainder is not permitted to be eaten. This is in accordance with the opinion of Rav and the Gemara's conclusion on 9b (Rambam *Sefer Avoda, Hilkhot Pesulei HaMukdashin* 11:20).

לְעוֹלָם קָסָבַר: שִׁיּוּרָא מִילְּתָא הִיא, וְנִטְמָא – וְהוּא הַדִּין לְאָבוּד וְשָׂרוּף, וְהַאי דְּקָאָמַר נִטְמָא – רֵישַׁיְיהוּ נָקַט.

The Gemara explains: **Actually, he holds** that **what remains is significant,**[N] **and** just as when a part of the remainder **became impure** but the offering is still fit, the rest of the remainder is sacrificed, **the same is true** with regard **to** a case where a part of the remainder **was lost or burned. And** the reason **that he stated** this *halakha* specifically in a case where it **became impure** is that **he employed** the terminology of **the beginning of** the mishna, which discusses a case where the remainder became impure.

כִּדְתַנְיָא, רַבִּי יְהוֹשֻׁעַ אוֹמֵר: כׇּל הַזְּבָחִים שֶׁבַּתּוֹרָה שֶׁנִּשְׁתַּיֵּיר מֵהֶן כַּזַּיִת בָּשָׂר אוֹ כַּזַּיִת חֵלֶב – זוֹרֵק אֶת הַדָּם,

Rava's statement accords with the opinion of Rabbi Yehoshua, **as it is taught** in a *baraita*: **Rabbi Yehoshua says:** With regard to **all the offerings in the Torah from which there remains an olive-bulk**[H] **of meat** that is fit to be eaten **or an olive-bulk of fat** that is fit to be sacrificed on the altar, the priest **sprinkles the blood.** Similarly, if a part of the remainder can be eaten the handful is still sacrificed, as the status of the remainder relative to the handful corresponds to the status of the meat relative to the blood.

כַּחֲצִי זַיִת בָּשָׂר וְכַחֲצִי זַיִת חֵלֶב – אֵינוֹ זוֹרֵק אֶת הַדָּם. וּבָעוֹלָה אֲפִילּוּ כַּחֲצִי זַיִת בָּשָׂר וְכַחֲצִי זַיִת חֵלֶב – זוֹרֵק אֶת הַדָּם, מִפְּנֵי שֶׁכּוּלָּהּ כָּלִיל. וּבַמִּנְחָה אֲפִילּוּ כּוּלָּהּ קַיֶּימֶת – לֹא יִזְרוֹק.

The Gemara cites the continuation of the *baraita*: If all that remains is **half an olive-bulk of meat and half an olive-bulk of fat,** the priest **does not sprinkle the blood.** This is because the half olive-bulk of meat and the half olive-bulk of fat do not combine to form one olive-bulk, since the former is eaten and the latter is sacrificed on the altar. **And with regard to a burnt offering, even** if all that was left was **half an olive-bulk of meat and half an olive-bulk of fat,** the priest **sprinkles the blood, because it is consumed** on the altar **in its entirety.** Since both the meat and the fat are sacrificed on the altar, they combine to form one olive-bulk. **And with regard to a meal offering, although all of it remains** pure, the priest **shall not sprinkle** the blood.

מִנְחָה מַאי עֲבִידְתָּהּ? אָמַר רַב פַּפָּא: מִנְחַת נְסָכִים, סָלְקָא דַּעְתָּךְ: הוֹאִיל וּבַהֲדֵי זֶבַח קָא אָתְיָא – כְּגוּפֵיהּ דְּזִיבְחָא דָּמְיָא, קָא מַשְׁמַע לַן.

The Gemara questions the last ruling of the *baraita*: **What is** the mention of **a meal offering doing** here? The discussion is about sprinkling blood, which is not relevant in the case of a meal offering. **Rav Pappa said:** The meal offering mentioned is **the meal offering** that accompanies the **libations** that accompany animal offerings. It could **enter your mind** to say: **Since** this meal offering **accompanies** the animal **offering,** it is **comparable to the offering itself,** and therefore if the offering became impure but the meal offering remained pure, the blood of the offering is sprinkled due to the remaining meal offering. To counter this, the *baraita* **teaches us** that this is not the *halakha*.

מְנָהָנֵי מִילֵּי? אָמַר רַבִּי יוֹחָנָן מִשּׁוּם רַבִּי יִשְׁמָעֵאל, וּמָטוּ בָּהּ מִשּׁוּם רַבִּי יְהוֹשֻׁעַ בֶּן חֲנַנְיָא, אָמַר קְרָא: ״וְהִקְטִיר הַחֵלֶב לְרֵיחַ נִיחֹחַ לַה׳״, חֵלֶב – וְאַף עַל פִּי שֶׁאֵין בָּשָׂר.

The Gemara returns to its discussion of the *halakha* that if only an olive-bulk of the fat remains, the priest sprinkles the blood of the offering. **From where is this matter** derived? **Rabbi Yoḥanan says in the name of Rabbi Yishmael, and** there are those who **determined** that it was stated **in the name of Rabbi Yehoshua ben Ḥananya: The verse states:** "And the priest shall sprinkle the blood against the altar of the Lord at the door of the Tent of Meeting, **and he shall make the fat smoke for a pleasing aroma to the Lord"** (Leviticus 17:6). This verse never mentions the meat, but only the **fat,** indicating that the blood is sprinkled **even if there is no** ritually pure **meat,** but only fat.

וְאַשְׁכַּחַן חֵלֶב, יוֹתֶרֶת וּשְׁתֵּי כְלָיוֹת מְנָלַן? דְּקָתָנֵי: וּבַמִּנְחָה אֲפִילּוּ כּוּלָּהּ קַיֶּימֶת – לֹא יִזְרוֹק; מִנְחָה הוּא דְּלֹא יִזְרוֹק, הָא יוֹתֶרֶת וּשְׁתֵּי כְלָיוֹת – יִזְרוֹק.

The Gemara asks: **And we found** a source for the *halakha* that the priest sprinkles the blood if only **fat** remains. **From where do we** derive that the priest sprinkles the blood if all that is left is the **lobe** of the liver **or** the **two kidneys,** which are also sacrificed on the altar? The Gemara answers: The *halakha* that the priest sprinkles the blood in that case is derived from **that** which **is taught** at the end of the *baraita*: **And with regard to a meal offering, although all of it remains** pure, the priest **shall not sprinkle** the blood. This teaches that **it is** in the case of **a meal offering that** the priest **shall not sprinkle** the blood, as the meal offering is not part of the animal; **but** if the **lobe** of the liver **or** the **two kidneys** remain, the priest **sprinkles** the blood.

NOTES

What remains is significant – שִׁיּוּרָא מִילְּתָא הִיא: This question is discussed by Rabbi Yoḥanan and Reish Lakish (9a). According to Rabbi Yoḥanan, if the meal offering was missing but a part of the remainder was left, then according to Rabbi Yehoshua the handful is still burned. Rabbi Yoḥanan agrees with Reish Lakish that the remainder may not be eaten.

HALAKHA

All the offerings in the Torah from which there remains an olive-bulk – כׇּל הַזְּבָחִים שֶׁבַּתּוֹרָה שֶׁנִּשְׁתַּיֵּיר מֵהֶן כַּזַּיִת: With regard to all offerings that were lost or burned after their blood was collected, if there remains an olive-bulk of their meat or of the sacrificial portions, the blood is presented on the altar, and if not then the blood is not presented. In the case of a burnt offering, even if there remains only half an olive-bulk of meat and half an olive-bulk from the sacrificial portions, the blood is presented, since the entire offering is burned on the altar. This is in accordance with the opinion of Rabbi Yehoshua (Rambam *Sefer Avoda, Hilkhot Pesulei HaMukdashin* 1:30).

HALAKHA

A handful that was not sanctified in a service vessel – שֶׁלֹּא בִּכְלִי שָׁרֵת: If the meal offering or handful was not sanctified in a service vessel, or if the handful was not sacrificed on the altar in a service vessel, it is unfit, in accordance with the opinion of the Rabbis (Rambam *Sefer Avoda*, *Hilkhot Pesulei HaMukdashin* 11:6).

BACKGROUND

Vessel [*makeida*] – מְקֵידָה: This is a vessel generally made of clay. According to the *ge'onim*, it is identical to a vessel known as a *kod*, which is made of either clay or wood. It was used primarily for drinking, and some say that it was made in such a manner that it could easily be disassembled into two parts, so that each part could be used separately.

מְנָלַן? רַבִּי יוֹחָנָן דִּידֵיהּ אָמַר: ״לְרֵיחַ נִיחֹחַ״ – כׇּל שֶׁאַתָּה מַעֲלֶה לְרֵיחַ נִיחוֹחַ.

The Gemara asks: **From where do we** derive this *halakha*? The Gemara answers that **Rabbi Yoḥanan himself says:** The verse states: **"For a pleasing aroma** to the Lord" (Leviticus 17:6). This teaches that the blood is sprinkled whenever **anything that you offer up** on the altar **for a pleasing aroma** remains. This includes anything burned on the altar.

וְאִיצְטְרִיךְ לְמִכְתַּב ״חֵלֶב״ וְאִיצְטְרִיךְ לְמִיכְתַּב ״לְרֵיחַ נִיחֹחַ״, דְּאִי כְּתַב ״חֵלֶב״, הֲוָה אָמֵינָא: חֵלֶב – אִין, יוֹתֶרֶת וּשְׁתֵּי כְלָיוֹת – לָא, כְּתַב רַחֲמָנָא: ״רֵיחַ נִיחֹחַ״; וְאִי כְּתַב רַחֲמָנָא ״לְרֵיחַ נִיחֹחַ״, הֲוָה אָמֵינָא אֲפִילּוּ מִנְחָה, כְּתַב רַחֲמָנָא: ״חֵלֶב״.

The Gemara notes: **And** it **was necessary to write "fat"** in that verse, **and** it **was necessary to write "for a pleasing aroma." As, if** the Merciful One **had written** only **"fat," I would say** that if **fat** remains, **yes,** the priest sprinkles the blood, but if only the **lobe** of the liver **or the two kidneys** remain, since they are not as significant as the fat, the blood is **not** sprinkled. Therefore, **the Merciful One wrote "for a pleasing aroma." And if the Merciful One had written** only **"for a pleasing aroma," I would say** that it includes **even a meal offering** brought with the libations that accompany animal offerings. Therefore, **the Merciful One wrote "fat,"** to teach that this *halakha* applies only to sacrificial parts of the animal, but not to accompanying libations and meal offerings.

מתני׳ שֶׁלֹּא בִּכְלִי שָׁרֵת – פָּסוּל, וְרַבִּי שִׁמְעוֹן מַכְשִׁיר. הִקְטִיר קוּמְצָהּ פַּעֲמַיִם – כְּשֵׁרָה.

MISHNA A handful of a meal offering **that was not** sanctified **in a service vessel**[H] **is unfit, and Rabbi Shimon deems** it **fit.** If the priest **burned the handful of** a meal offering **twice,** i.e., in two increments, it is **fit.**

גמ׳ אָמַר רַבִּי יְהוּדָה בְּרֵיהּ דְּרַבִּי חִיָּיא: מַאי טַעְמָא דְּרַבִּי שִׁמְעוֹן? אָמַר קְרָא: ״קֹדֶשׁ קָדָשִׁים הִיא כַּחַטָּאת וְכָאָשָׁם״, בָּא לְעוֹבְדָהּ בַּיָּד כְּחַטָּאת – עוֹבְדָהּ בְּיָמִין כַּחַטָּאת, בִּכְלִי – עוֹבְדָהּ בִּשְׂמֹאל כָּאָשָׁם.

GEMARA **Rabbi Yehuda, son of Rabbi Ḥiyya, says: What is the reasoning of Rabbi Shimon? The verse states** with regard to a meal offering: **"It is most holy, as the sin offering, and as the guilt offering"** (Leviticus 6:10). Rabbi Shimon derives from here that the handful of the meal offering may be placed on the altar in the manner of the blood of either a sin offering or a guilt offering. If a priest **comes to perform the** sacrificial **rites of** a meal offering **with** his **hand, as** one performs the sprinkling of the blood of **a sin offering,** which is performed with the priest's right index finger, **he must perform its rites with** his **right** hand, **like the sin offering.** If he performs the sacrificial rites **with a vessel,** as one performs the sprinkling of the blood of a guilt offering, whose blood is sprinkled from a vessel on the altar and whose sprinkling may be performed with the priest's left hand, **he may perform its rites with** his **left** hand, **like the guilt offering.**[N]

וְרַבִּי יַנַּאי אָמַר: כֵּיוָן שֶׁקְּמָצוֹ מִכְּלִי שָׁרֵת, מַעֲלֵהוּ וּמַקְטִירוֹ אֲפִילּוּ בְּהֶמְיָינוֹ, וַאֲפִילּוּ בִּמְקֵידָה שֶׁל חֶרֶשׂ. רַב נַחְמָן בַּר יִצְחָק אָמַר: הַכֹּל מוֹדִים בְּקוֹמֶץ שֶׁטָּעוּן קִידּוּשׁ.

And Rabbi Yannai says: According to Rabbi Shimon there are no restrictions on the manner in which the handful is sacrificed, as **once** the priest has **removed the handful from a service vessel, he may bring it up and burn it even** if he placed it **in his belt, or even in an earthenware vessel.**[B] **Rav Naḥman bar Yitzḥak says: All concede that** the **handful requires sanctification**[N] in a service vessel before it is sacrificed.

NOTES

If he performs the sacrificial rites with a vessel he may perform its rites with his left hand like the guilt offering – בִּכְלִי עוֹבְדָהּ בִּשְׂמֹאל כָּאָשָׁם: It is permitted for the priest to perform these rites even with his left hand, as Rabbi Shimon holds that the rites of the guilt offering, as well as any other offering whose blood is presented on the altar from a vessel and not with a finger, may be performed with the left hand as well as with the right.

Rav Naḥman bar Yitzḥak says: All concede that the handful requires sanctification – רַב נַחְמָן בַּר יִצְחָק אָמַר הַכֹּל מוֹדִים בְּקוֹמֶץ שֶׁטָּעוּן קִידּוּשׁ: According to Rav Naḥman bar Yitzḥak, when the mishna states that Rabbi Shimon deems the handful fit even without sanctification in a service vessel, it means that once the handful is sanctified in a service vessel, it does not need to be brought to the altar and sacrificed in a service vessel.

HALAKHA

The burning of the fats and the limbs, etc. – **הֶקְטֵר חֲלָבִים וְאֵבָרִים וכו׳**: With regard to the portions of offerings that are burned on the altar, the limbs of burnt offerings, the handful of the meal offering, the frankincense, and the meal offerings that are burned after being sanctified in a service vessel, if any of these were placed on the altar's fire, either by hand or in a vessel, using either one's right or left hand, they are fit, in accordance with the *baraita*. The *Arukh HaShulḥan HeAtid* adds that in any event they must be brought up to the altar in a service vessel (Rambam *Sefer Avoda, Hilkhot Pesulei HaMukdashin* 2:24, and see Mahari Kurkus there).

מֵיתִיבֵי: הֶקְטֵר חֲלָבִים וְאֵבָרִים וְעֵצִים שֶׁהֶעֱלָן בֵּין בַּיָּד בֵּין בִּכְלִי, בֵּין בְּיָמִין וּבֵין בִּשְׂמֹאל – כְּשֵׁרִין; הַקּוֹמֶץ וְהַקְּטוֹרֶת וְהַלְּבוֹנָה שֶׁהֶעֱלָן בֵּין בַּיָּד בֵּין בִּכְלִי, בֵּין בְּיָמִין בֵּין בִּשְׂמֹאל – כְּשֵׁרִין; תְּיוּבְתָּא דְּרַבִּי יְהוּדָה בְּרֵיהּ דְּרַבִּי חִיָּיא!

The Gemara **raises an objection** to the statement of Rabbi Yehuda, son of Rabbi Ḥiyya, from a *baraita* (*Tosefta, Zevaḥim* 1:11): With regard to **the burning of the fats, and the limbs,**[H] **and the wood** that were brought up to the altar, **that** the priest **brought them up** to the altar, **whether by hand or with a vessel, whether with the right** hand **or with the left** hand, **they are fit.** With regard to **the handful, and the incense, and the frankincense, that** the priest **brought them up** to the altar, **whether by hand or with a vessel, whether with the right** hand **or with the left** hand, **they are fit.** The Gemara suggests: This is **a conclusive refutation**[B] of the opinion **of Rabbi Yehuda, son of Rabbi Ḥiyya,** who stated that if the handful is sacrificed by hand, it must be sacrificed only with the right hand.

אָמַר לָךְ רַבִּי יְהוּדָה בְּרֵיהּ דְּרַבִּי חִיָּיא: לִצְדָדִין קָתָנֵי, בַּיָּד – בְּיָמִין, בִּכְלִי – בֵּין בְּיָמִין בֵּין בִּשְׂמֹאל.

The Gemara responds: **Rabbi Yehuda, son of Rabbi Ḥiyya,** could **say to you** that the *tanna* of the *baraita* **teaches** it **disjunctively,** and the statement should be understood as follows: If these items are brought up **by hand, with the right** hand, or **with a vessel, whether with the right** hand **or with the left,** they are fit.

תָּא שְׁמַע: קְמָצוֹ שֶׁלֹּא מִכְּלִי שָׁרֵת, וְקִידְּשׁוֹ שֶׁלֹּא בִּכְלִי שָׁרֵת, וְהֶעֱלוֹ וְהִקְטִירוֹ שֶׁלֹּא בִּכְלִי שָׁרֵת – פָּסוּל; רַבִּי אֶלְעָזָר וְרַבִּי שִׁמְעוֹן מַכְשִׁירִין בְּמַתַּן כְּלִי!

The Gemara attempts to refute the opinion of Rav Naḥman bar Yitzḥak that all concede that the handful requires sanctification in a service vessel before it is sacrificed. **Come** and **hear** that which is taught in a *baraita*: If the priest **removed the handful,** but **not from a service vessel, and sanctified it,** but **not in a service vessel, and brought it up and burned it,** but **not in a service vessel,** then it is **unfit. Rabbi Elazar and Rabbi Shimon deem** it **fit in** a case where the handful had been **placed** in any type of **vessel.** This contradicts Rav Naḥman bar Yitzḥak's claim that all concede that the handful must be sanctified in a service vessel.

אֵימָא: מִמַּתַּן כְּלִי וְאֵילָךְ.

The Gemara responds: **Say** that according to Rabbi Elazar and Rabbi Shimon, **from** the point when the handful has been **placed** in a service **vessel** and sanctified **and onward,** it is no longer necessary to take it in a service vessel to the altar to sacrifice it. Therefore, the *baraita* does not contradict Rav Naḥman bar Yitzḥak's statement.

תָּא שְׁמַע, וַחֲכָמִים אוֹמְרִים: קוֹמֶץ טָעוּן כְּלִי שָׁרֵת, כֵּיצַד? קוֹמְצוֹ מִכְּלִי שָׁרֵת, וּמְקַדְּשׁוֹ בִּכְלִי שָׁרֵת, וּמַעֲלוֹ וּמַקְטִירוֹ בִּכְלִי שָׁרֵת. רַבִּי שִׁמְעוֹן אוֹמֵר: כֵּיוָן שֶׁקְּמָצוֹ מִכְּלִי שָׁרֵת, מַעֲלוֹ וּמַקְטִירוֹ שֶׁלֹּא בִּכְלִי שָׁרֵת וְדַיּוֹ!

The Gemara suggests another refutation of Rav Naḥman bar Yitzḥak's opinion from a *baraita* (*Tosefta* 4:15). **Come** and **hear: And the Rabbis say:** The **handful requires** sanctification in **a service vessel. How** is this sanctification performed? The priest **removes the handful from a service vessel, and sanctifies it in a service vessel, and brings it up and burns it in a service vessel. Rabbi Shimon says: Once the handful is removed from a service vessel,** the priest may **bring it up and burn it** even if it is **not in a service vessel, and** this **is sufficient for it.** This *baraita* demonstrates that, in contrast to Rav Naḥman bar Yitzḥak's statement, Rabbi Shimon does not hold that the handful must be sanctified in a service vessel.

אֵימָא: כֵּיוָן שֶׁקְּמָצוֹ וְקִדְּשׁוֹ בִּכְלִי שָׁרֵת, מַעֲלוֹ וּמַקְטִירוֹ וְדַיּוֹ.

The Gemara answers: **Say** that according to Rabbi Shimon, **once** the priest **removes the handful and sanctifies it in a service vessel,** he may **bring it up and burn it, and** this **is sufficient for it.**

תָּא שְׁמַע: קָמַץ בִּימִינוֹ וְנָתַן בִּשְׂמֹאלוֹ – יַחֲזִיר לִימִינוֹ; בִּשְׂמֹאלוֹ

The Gemara suggests another proof. **Come** and **hear:** If the priest **removed the handful with his right** hand **and put** it **in his left** hand, **he shall return it to his right** hand. If the handful was **in his left** hand

BACKGROUND

Conclusive refutation [*teyuvta*] – **תְּיוּבְתָּא**: This term is usually used when the Gemara presents a conclusive refutation of an amoraic statement on the basis of a tannaitic source that contradicts the statement of the *amora*. This is one of several expressions based on the Aramaic root *tav, vav, beit* that have the connotation of refutation. When an *amora* objects to the opinion of another *amora*, citing a tannaitic source, the expression used is *eitivei*, meaning: He raised an objection to him. When an *amora* raises an objection against an unattributed amoraic opinion, citing a tannaitic source, the expression employed is *meitiv*, meaning: He raised an objection. When the Gemara itself raises an objection citing a tannaitic source, the term is *meitivei*, meaning that the Gemara raises an objection. When the refutation is conclusive, the expression *teyuvta* is often used, bringing the discussion to a close.

וְחִישֵּׁב עָלֶיהָ, בֵּין חוּץ לִמְקוֹמוֹ בֵּין חוּץ לִזְמַנּוֹ – פָּסוּל וְאֵין בּוֹ כָּרֵת.

and he intended[N] to partake **of** the meal offering in an improper manner, **whether outside its** designated **area or beyond its** designated **time,** the offering is **not valid, but there is no** liability to receive ***karet*** if one partakes **of it.**

(ל״א) חִישֵּׁב עָלֶיהָ חוּץ לִמְקוֹמוֹ – פָּסוּל וְאֵין בּוֹ כָּרֵת, חוּץ לִזְמַנּוֹ – פִּיגּוּל וְחַיָּיבִין עָלָיו כָּרֵת, דִּבְרֵי רַבִּי אֶלְעָזָר וְרַבִּי שִׁמְעוֹן.

The Gemara presents an alternative version of this *baraita*: If, while the handful was in his right hand, **he intended** to partake **of** the meal offering **outside its** designated **area,** the offering is **not valid, but there is no** liability to receive ***karet*** if one partakes **of it.** If he intended to partake of it **beyond its** designated **time,** then the offering is ***piggul*** **and** one who partakes of it **is liable** to receive ***karet.*** This is **the statement of Rabbi Elazar and Rabbi Shimon.**

וַחֲכָמִים אוֹמְרִים: כֵּיוָן שֶׁנְּתָנוֹ לִשְׂמֹאל – פְּסָלַתּוּ מַתְּנָתוֹ; מַאי טַעְמָא? מִשּׁוּם דְּבָעֵי קְדוּשָּׁה בִּכְלִי, וְכֵיוָן שֶׁנְּתָנוֹ לִשְׂמֹאל – נַעֲשָׂה כְּדָם שֶׁנִּשְׁפַּךְ מִצַּוַּאר בְּהֵמָה עַל הָרִצְפָּה וַאֲסָפוֹ, שֶׁפָּסוּל;

And the Rabbis say: Once he put the handful **in his left** hand,[H] the **placing** of it in his left hand **renders it unfit** and it cannot be rendered fit by returning it to his right hand. **What is the reason?** It is **because it requires sanctification in** a service **vessel, and once he put it in** his **left** hand, **it is considered like blood that spilled from an animal's neck**[H] **onto the floor** before being collected in a service vessel **and one** then **gathered it, which** is **unfit** and cannot be rendered fit by then being placed in a service vessel.

מִכְּלָל דְּרַבִּי אֶלְעָזָר וְרַבִּי שִׁמְעוֹן לָא בָּעוּ מַתַּן כְּלִי, תְּיוּבְתָּא דְּרַב נַחְמָן! תְּיוּבְתָּא.

The Gemara notes: **By inference,** one can conclude **that Rabbi Elazar and Rabbi Shimon do not require** sanctification of the handful by **placing** it in a service **vessel.** Accordingly, this serves as **a conclusive refutation** of the opinion **of Rav Naḥman** bar Yitzḥak, who stated that even Rabbi Shimon requires sanctification in a service vessel. The Gemara affirms: This is **a conclusive refutation** of his opinion.

לְרַבִּי יְהוּדָה בְּרֵיהּ דְּרַבִּי חִיָּיא מְסַיְּיעָא לֵיהּ, לְרַבִּי יַנַּאי לֵימָא תֶּיהֱוֵי תְּיוּבְתָּא?

The *baraita* teaches that according to Rabbi Shimon, if the priest transferred the handful to his left hand he should return the handful to his right hand. The Gemara comments: This **supports** the statement of **Rabbi Yehuda, son of Rabbi Ḥiyya,** as he said that according to the opinion of Rabbi Shimon the rites of the meal offering must be performed with the priest's right hand. The Gemara asks: **Shall we say** that this *baraita* **is a conclusive refutation** of the opinion **of Rabbi Yannai,** as it teaches that the handful must be transferred back to his right hand, whereas he states that once the handful has been removed from a service vessel it may be sacrificed in any manner?

אָמַר לָךְ רַבִּי יַנַּאי: אֲנָא דַּאֲמַרִי כְּתַנָּא דְּהֶקְטֵר, וְלָאו לִצְדָדִים קָתָנֵי.

The Gemara answers: **Rabbi Yannai** could **say to you: I stated** my ruling **in accordance with** the opinion of **the *tanna*** who taught **that** the **burning** of the fats and the limbs and the sacrifice of the meal offering can all take place with either the right or left hand. **And** I hold that he **does not teach** it **disjunctively,** as it was explained in order to reconcile the *baraita* with the statement of Rabbi Yehuda, son of Rabbi Ḥiyya. Rather, it is to be understood according to its straightforward meaning.

HALAKHA

Once he put the handful in his left hand – כֵּיוָן שֶׁנְּתָנוֹ לִשְׂמֹאל: If the priest removed the handful with his right hand, then transferred it to his left hand, and afterward placed it in a vessel, it is unfit, in accordance with the opinion of the Rabbis (Rambam *Sefer Avoda, Hilkhot Pesulei HaMukdashin* 11:2).

Blood that spilled from an animal's neck – דָּם שֶׁנִּשְׁפַּךְ מִצַּוַּאר בְּהֵמָה: If one slaughtered an animal, collected the blood in a vessel, and then the blood spilled on the floor and was gathered up, it is fit to be presented. If the blood spilled directly from the slaughtered animal's neck onto the floor and was then gathered up and placed in a service vessel, the offering is disqualified. This is based on *Zevaḥim* 25a and 32a (Rambam *Sefer Avoda, Hilkhot Pesulei HaMukdashin* 1:25).

NOTES

And he intended, etc. – וְחִישֵּׁב עָלֶיהָ וכו׳: Even if the priest intended to partake of the offering after its designated time, there is no punishment of *karet* since the improper intent disqualifies only an offering whose rites were otherwise performed properly (see 5b), and if the rites of the meal offering were performed with the priest's left hand then Rabbi Shimon does not hold that they were performed properly.

Rashi explains that this is a case where the priest first removed the handful with his right hand and then transferred it to his left hand, at which point the improper intention took place. By contrast, it is explained in *Tosafot Ḥitzoniyyot* that the *baraita* is referring to a case where the handful was removed with the priest's left hand, and it is therefore rendered unfit even according to Rabbi Shimon, and not because of the improper intention. Alternatively, it is a case where the priest used his left hand when burning the handful.

"הִקְטִיר קוּמְצָהּ פַּעֲמַיִם – כְּשֵׁרָה". אָמַר רַבִּי יְהוֹשֻׁעַ בֶּן לֵוִי: פַּעֲמַיִם – וְלֹא פַּעֲמֵי פְּעָמִים, וְרַבִּי יוֹחָנָן אָמַר: פַּעֲמַיִם – וַאֲפִילּוּ פַּעֲמֵי פְּעָמִים.

§ The mishna teaches: If the priest **burned the handful of** a meal offering **twice**, i.e., in two increments, it is **fit.** The Gemara comments: **Rabbi Yehoshua ben Levi says:** The handful is fit if it is burned **twice,** where half of the handful is burned each time, **but not** if it is burned **several times,** in smaller increments. **And Rabbi Yoḥanan says:** It is fit if it is burned **twice, and** it is fit **even** if it is burned **several times.**

מַאי בֵּינַיְיהוּ? אָמַר רַבִּי זֵירָא: יֵשׁ קוֹמֶץ פָּחוֹת מִשְּׁנֵי זֵיתִים וְיֵשׁ הַקְטָרָה פְּחוּתָה מִכַּזַּיִת אִיכָּא בֵּינַיְיהוּ;

The Gemara asks: **What** is the basis for the dispute **between** the two opinions? **Rabbi Zeira said:** The dispute **between** the two **is** with regard to whether **there is** significance to **a handful** that is **less than** the size of **two olives and whether there is** significance to the **burning** of **less than an olive-bulk** on the altar.

רַבִּי יְהוֹשֻׁעַ בֶּן לֵוִי סָבַר: אֵין קוֹמֶץ פָּחוֹת מִשְּׁנֵי זֵיתִים, וְאֵין הַקְטָרָה פְּחוּתָה מִכַּזַּיִת; וְרַבִּי יוֹחָנָן סָבַר: יֵשׁ קוֹמֶץ פָּחוֹת מִשְּׁנֵי זֵיתִים, וְיֵשׁ הַקְטָרָה פְּחוּתָה מִכַּזַּיִת.

Rabbi Yehoshua ben Levi holds that **there is no** significance to **a handful** that is **less than** the size of **two olives**[H] **and there is no** significance to the **burning** of **less than an olive-bulk**[H] on the altar. Therefore, the mishna's statement that the handful may be burned in two increments is meant literally, and the handful may be divided into only two equal portions, where each one contains exactly one olive-bulk. It may not be divided further, since doing so would result in the burning of less than an olive-bulk on the altar. **And Rabbi Yoḥanan holds** that **there is** significance to **a handful** that is **less than** the size of **two olives and there is** significance to the **burning** of **less than an olive-bulk**[N] on the altar. Therefore, if the handful was divided into several small portions and each portion was burned separately, it is fit.

אִיתְּמַר: קוֹמֶץ מֵאֵימָתַי מַתִּיר שִׁירַיִם בַּאֲכִילָה? רַבִּי חֲנִינָא אוֹמֵר: מִשֶּׁמָּשְׁלָה בּוֹ אֶת הָאוּר, רַבִּי יוֹחָנָן אָמַר: מִשֶּׁתַּצִּית בּוֹ אֶת הָאוּר בְּרוּבּוֹ.

§ **It was stated: From when** precisely **does** the sacrifice of the **handful render permitted** the **remainder** of the meal offering **for consumption** by the priests? **Rabbi Ḥanina says: From when the fire takes hold of it,** i.e., when it ignites. **Rabbi Yoḥanan says: From when the fire consumes most of** the handful.[H]

אֲמַר לֵיהּ רַב יְהוּדָה לְרַבָּה בַּר רַב יִצְחָק: אַסְבְּרָהּ לָךְ טַעְמָא דְּרַבִּי יוֹחָנָן, אָמַר קְרָא: "וְהִנֵּה עָלָה קִיטֹר הָאָרֶץ כְּקִיטֹר הַכִּבְשָׁן", אֵין כִּבְשָׁן מַעֲלֶה קִיטוֹר עַד שֶׁתַּצִּית הָאוּר בְּרוּבּוֹ.

Rav Yehuda said to Rabba bar Rav Yitzḥak: I will explain to you the reasoning of Rabbi Yoḥanan. The verse states: "And behold, the smoke of the land went up as the smoke of a furnace" (Genesis 19:28), and **a furnace does not release smoke until the fire takes hold of the majority of** the fuel. Rabbi Yoḥanan derived from this verse that the majority of the handful must be consumed by the fire, since the priests are instructed to make the handful smoke, as it is written: "And the priest shall make the memorial part thereof smoke upon the altar" (Leviticus 2:2).

אֲמַר לֵיהּ רָבִין בַּר רַב אַדָּא לְרָבָא: אָמְרִי תַּלְמִידָיךְ אָמַר רַב עַמְרָם, תַּנְיָא: אֵין לִי אֶלָּא דְּבָרִים שֶׁדַּרְכָּן לִיקְרַב בַּלַּיְלָה, כְּגוֹן אֵבָרִים וּפְדָרִים – שֶׁמַּעֲלָן וּמַקְטִירָן מִבּוֹא הַשֶּׁמֶשׁ וּמִתְעַכְּלִין וְהוֹלְכִין כָּל הַלַּיְלָה כּוּלָּהּ;

Ravin bar Rav Adda said to Rava: Your students say that **Rav Amram said** that **it is taught** in a *baraita*: **I have** derived **only** with regard to **items whose** usual **manner**[N] **is to be sacrificed at night, for example,** the **limbs** of the burnt offering **and the fats** [***pedarim***][HL] of the burnt offering, **that** the priest **may bring them up and burn them after sunset and they are consumed throughout the entire night.** This is derived from the verse: "This is the law of the burnt offering: It is that which goes up on its firewood upon the altar all night unto the morning" (Leviticus 6:2).

NOTES

There is significance to a handful that is less than two olives and there is significance to burning less than an olive-bulk – יֵשׁ קוֹמֶץ פָּחוֹת מִשְּׁנֵי זֵיתִים וְיֵשׁ הַקְטָרָה פְּחוּתָה מִכַּזַּיִת: Rabbi Yoḥanan's reasoning is as follows: Since a handful can consist of less than two olive-bulks, as a priest's hand could be smaller than the average hand, resulting in a smaller handful (see Jerusalem Talmud, *Yoma* 2:1), and yet the mishna here still teaches that if the handful is burned in two increments it is fit, it must be that less than an olive-bulk may be burned on the altar. Once this is established, there is no difference between the sacrifice of a handful in two increments and the sacrifice of a handful in many increments (*Shita Mekubbetzet*, citing Rashi).

Items whose usual manner, etc. – דְּבָרִים שֶׁדַּרְכָּן וכו׳: The *baraita* does not mean that these items must be burned after sunset. Rather, they may be burned at night, although they are ideally sacrificed and burned during the day. For this reason, the fat is burned on Shabbat day, despite the fact that it could be burned after the conclusion of Shabbat, since it is preferable to perform the mitzva at its designated time (*Pesaḥim* 68b).

HALAKHA

There is no significance to a handful that is less than the size of two olives – אֵין קוֹמֶץ פָּחוֹת מִשְּׁנֵי זֵיתִים: The handful of a meal offering may not be less than two olive-bulks. The *halakha* is in accordance with the opinion of Rabbi Yehoshua ben Levi because the *halakha* is normally in accordance with his opinion in his disputes with Rabbi Yoḥanan, and furthermore, it is also the opinion of Rava on 58b (Rambam *Sefer Avoda*, *Hilkhot Ma'aseh HaKorbanot* 13:14, and see *Kesef Mishne* there).

There is no significance to burning less than an olive-bulk – אֵין הַקְטָרָה פְּחוּתָה מִכַּזַּיִת: The Rambam writes that a handful that was removed in two increments is fit. According to the *Mishne LaMelekh*, the correct version of the text of the Rambam refers to a handful that was burned in two increments. This is the *halakha* even if it was burned in many increments, provided that an entire olive-bulk is burned at once, since there is no significance to burning less than an olive-bulk on the altar. The *halakha* is in accordance with the opinion of Rabbi Yehoshua ben Levi because the *halakha* is normally in accordance with his opinion in his disputes with Rabbi Yoḥanan. Furthermore, it is also the opinion of Rava on 58b (Rambam *Sefer Avoda*, *Hilkhot Pesulei HaMukdashin* 11:15, and see *Kesef Mishne* and *Or Same'aḥ* there).

From when the fire consumes most of the handful – מִשֶּׁתַּצִּית בּוֹ אֶת הָאוּר בְּרוּבּוֹ: The remainder of the meal offering may be eaten once the fire consumes most of the handful. This is in accordance with the opinion of Rabbi Yoḥanan, since the discussion of the *amora'im* focuses on his opinion (Rambam *Sefer Avoda*, *Hilkhot Ma'aseh HaKorbanot* 12:13, and see *Kesef Mishne* there).

The limbs and the fats – אֵבָרִים וּפְדָרִים: Any sacrificial item whose permitting factor was burned during the day may be sacrificed on the altar at night. Similarly, the limbs of the burnt offering may burned at any point during the night, until dawn. Nevertheless, in order to ensure that the priests would not forget to burn these sacrificial items, the Sages decreed that they could be burned only until midnight. Some early commentaries do not hold that the Sages prohibited burning them after midnight (Rambam *Sefer Avoda*, *Hilkhot Ma'aseh HaKorbanot* 4:2, and see *Mishne LaMelekh* there).

LANGUAGE

Fats [*pedarim*] – פְּדָרִים: This is the plural form of the biblical term *peder* (Leviticus 1:8), meaning fat. Some understand that it is related to the Akkadian term *pitru*, meaning oil. The Rambam explains based on the mishna in tractate *Yoma* (26a) that it refers to a specific thin layer of fat that separates the upper and lower gastrointestinal tracts.

דְּבָרִים שֶׁדַּרְכָּן לִיקָרֵב בַּיּוֹם, כְּגוֹן הַקּוֹמֶץ וְהַלְּבוֹנָה וְהַקְּטֹרֶת, וּמִנְחַת כֹּהֲנִים וּמִנְחַת כֹּהֵן מָשׁוּחַ וּמִנְחַת נְסָכִים, שֶׁמַּעֲלָן וּמַקְטִירָן מִבּוֹא הַשֶּׁמֶשׁ.

The *baraita* continues: With regard to **items whose** usual **manner is to be sacrificed during the day,**[H] **for example, the handful** of the meal offering, **the frankincense, the incense, the meal offering of priests, the meal offering of** the **anointed priest,** i.e., the High Priest, **and the meal offering** that accompanies the **libations,** from where is it derived **that** the priest **may bring them up and burn them after sunset?**

וְהָא אָמְרַתְּ: דַּרְכָּן לִיקָרֵב בַּיּוֹם! אֶלָּא: עִם בֹּא הַשֶּׁמֶשׁ, שֶׁמִּתְעַכְּלִין וְהוֹלְכִין כָּל הַלַּיְלָה מִנַּיִן? תַּלְמוּד לוֹמַר: ״זֹאת תּוֹרַת הָעֹלָה״ – רִיבָּה;

The Gemara interjects: Why would they be allowed to be burned after sunset? **But didn't you say** that these are items **whose** usual **manner is to be sacrificed during the day?** The Gemara clarifies: **Rather,** the question of the *baraita* is as follows: **From where** is it derived that these items may be brought up and burned concurrent **with the setting of the sun,** in **which** case **they are consumed throughout the entire night** and not during the day? **The verse states: "This is the law of the burnt offering"** (Leviticus 6:2), which **included** everything that is sacrificed on the altar.

וְהָא עִם בֹּא הַשֶּׁמֶשׁ לָא מַשְׁכַּחַתְּ לָהּ שֶׁתַּצִּית הָאוּר בְּרוּבּוֹ! לָא קַשְׁיָא: כָּאן לְקָלוֹט, כָּאן לְהַתִּיר.

Ravin bar Rav Adda challenges: **But** if the handful is brought up and burned concurrent **with the setting of the sun, you do not find that the majority of it is consumed by the fire** before sunset. How does this *baraita* accord with Rabbi Yoḥanan's statement that the majority of the handful must be consumed by the fire in order to render permitted the consumption of the remainder by the priests? The Gemara answers: This is **not difficult. Here,** where the *baraita* does not require the consumption by fire of the majority of the handful, it is referring only to that which is required in order for the altar **to receive** the handful, so that it is considered the food of the altar and may continue to burn all night long. **There,** Rabbi Yoḥanan states that in order **to render permitted** the consumption of the remainder by the priests, the majority of the handful must be consumed by the fire.

רַבִּי אֶלְעָזָר מַתְנֵי לַהּ ״מִבּוֹא הַשֶּׁמֶשׁ״, וּמוֹקֵים לַהּ בְּפוֹקְעִין. וְכֵן כִּי אֲתָא רַב דִּימִי אֲמַר רַבִּי יַנַּאי: בְּפוֹקְעִין.

The Gemara notes: **Rabbi Elazar teaches** the *baraita* the way it was initially presented, as asking how it is known that items that are usually sacrificed during the day may be burned **after sunset. And he interprets** the *baraita* as referring **to** parts of the offering that were **dislodged** from the fire after sunset, which may be returned to the fire throughout the night. **And similarly, when Rav Dimi came** from Eretz Yisrael to Babylonia he said that **Rabbi Yannai said** the *baraita* is referring **to** parts that were **dislodged** from the fire after sunset.

וּמִי אֲמַר רַבִּי יַנַּאי הָכִי? וְהָא אָמַר רַבִּי יַנַּאי: קְטֹרֶת שֶׁפָּקְעָה מֵעַל גַּבֵּי הַמִּזְבֵּחַ, אֲפִילּוּ קָרְטִין שֶׁבָּהּ אֵין מַחֲזִירִין אוֹתָן; וְתָנֵי רַב חֲנִינָא בַּר מִנְיוּמִי בִּדְבֵי רַבִּי אֱלִיעֶזֶר בֶּן יַעֲקֹב: ״אֲשֶׁר תֹּאכַל הָאֵשׁ אֶת הָעֹלָה עַל הַמִּזְבֵּחַ״ – עִיכּוּלֵי עוֹלָה אַתָּה מַחֲזִיר, וְאִי אַתָּה מַחֲזִיר עִיכּוּלֵי קְטֹרֶת! סְמֵי מִיכָּן קְטֹרֶת.

The Gemara asks: **And did Rabbi Yannai** in fact **say this? But doesn't Rabbi Yannai say:** In the case of **incense that was dislodged**[H] **from on top of the altar,** the priests **may not return even small lumps of it**[N] to the fire? **And** similarly, **Rav Ḥanina bar Minyumi from the school of Rabbi Eliezer ben Ya'akov taught** in a *baraita*: The verse states: **"That which the fire will consume of the burnt offering on the altar"** (Leviticus 6:3).[N] This teaches that if parts **of a burnt offering** that were partially **consumed** were dislodged from the external altar **you shall return** them, **but you do not return incense** that was partially **consumed** and was dislodged from the internal altar. The Gemara answers: **Remove from** the *baraita* **here**[B] the word **incense,** so that it is not included in the list of items that may be burned throughout the night.

HALAKHA

Whose usual manner is to be sacrificed during the day – שֶׁדַּרְכָּן לִיקָרֵב בַּיּוֹם: All items that are burned only during the day must be sacrificed and burned before sunset (*Or Same'aḥ*). They may be consumed by the fire during the night. Such items include the handful of the meal offering, the frankincense, the incense, the meal offerings that are burned on the altar, and the libations that accompany the sacrifice of an offering, but not the libations that are sacrificed alone (Rambam *Sefer Avoda, Hilkhot Ma'aseh HaKorbanot* 4:4–5).

Incense that was dislodged – קְטֹרֶת שֶׁפָּקְעָה: In the case of incense that is dislodged from the altar, even significant pieces are not returned to the altar, in accordance with the opinion of Rabbi Yannai (Rambam *Sefer Avoda, Hilkhot Temidin UMusafin* 3:2).

BACKGROUND

Remove from here – סְמֵי מִיכָּן: This expression and others like it are used only in connection with *baraitot* lacking a reliable amoraic tradition. Each Sage received different anthologies of *baraitot*, which he would review and transmit to others. Sometimes, prominent contemporaneous Sages would teach that a certain *halakha* should be removed from the anthology because it was not sufficiently reliable. This was generally done based on a more authoritative variant reading or by comparison with other accredited statements of those same Sages.

NOTES

Even small lumps of it – אֲפִילּוּ קָרְטִין שֶׁבָּהּ: Not only are tiny crumbs of incense not returned to the fire, just as tendons and bones of offerings are not returned (*Zevaḥim* 86a), but even small lumps that have some importance are not returned (Rashi; commentary attributed to Rashba).

That which the fire will consume of the burnt offering on the altar – אֲשֶׁר תֹּאכַל הָאֵשׁ אֶת הָעֹלָה עַל הַמִּזְבֵּחַ: This phrase is seemingly superfluous, since the verse already states "and he shall remove the ashes." Therefore, the verse is understood as teaching that parts of the burnt offering that have already been consumed by the fire but were dislodged should be returned to the fire (Rashi on *Zevaḥim* 83b).

אָמַר רַבִּי אַסִּי: כִּי פָּשֵׁיט רַבִּי אֶלְעָזָר בִּמְנָחוֹת בָּעֵי הָכִי, בָּעֵי רַבִּי אֶלְעָזָר: קוֹמֶץ שֶׁסִּידְּרוֹ וְסִידֵּר עָלָיו אֶת הַמַּעֲרָכָה, מַהוּ? דֶּרֶךְ הַקְטָרָה בְּכָךְ, אוֹ אֵין דֶּרֶךְ הַקְטָרָה בְּכָךְ? תֵּיקוּ.

Rabbi Asi said: When Rabbi Elazar would explain the *halakhot* **of the meal offerings,** he would **raise this dilemma: Rabbi Elazar raises a dilemma:** With regard to **a handful that** a priest **arranged** on the altar, **and he arranged the arrangement** of wood on the altar **on top of it, what is** the *halakha*? Is **this** considered a proper **manner of burning, or is this not** considered a proper **manner of burning,** since the handful is not arranged on top of the wood? The Gemara comments: No answer was found, and the dilemma **shall stand** unresolved.[B]

בָּעֵי חִזְקִיָּה: אֵבָרִין שֶׁסִּידְּרָן וְסִידֵּר עֲלֵיהֶן אֶת הַמַּעֲרָכָה, מַהוּ? ״עַל הָעֵצִים״ אָמַר רַחֲמָנָא – דַּוְקָא עַל הָעֵצִים. אוֹ דִּלְמָא, כֵּיוָן דִּכְתִיב קְרָא אַחֲרִינָא: ״אֲשֶׁר תֹּאכַל הָאֵשׁ אֶת הָעֹלָה עַל הַמִּזְבֵּחַ״ – אִי בָּעֵי הָכִי עָבֵיד, אִי בָּעֵי הָכִי עָבֵיד? תֵּיקוּ.

Ḥizkiyya raises a dilemma: With regard to the **limbs** of the burnt offering **that** a priest **arranged**[H] on the altar **and arrangedthe arrangement** of wood on the altar **on top of them, what is** the *halakha*? Do we say that **the Merciful One states:** "And Aaron's sons, the priests, shall lay the pieces and the head, and the fat, in order **upon the wood** that is on the fire upon the altar" (Leviticus 1:8), teaching that they must be placed **specifically upon the wood? Or perhaps, since it is written** in **another verse: "That which the fire will consume of the burnt offering on the altar"** (Leviticus 6:3), indicating that the burnt offering may be arranged directly on the altar, **if** the priest **desires** to arrange the limbs in **this** manner he may **do** so, **and if** he **desires** to arrange them in **that** manner he may also **do** so. The Gemara comments: No answer was found, and the dilemma **shall stand** unresolved.

בָּעֵי רַבִּי יִצְחָק נַפָּחָא: אֵבָרִין שֶׁסִּידְּרָן בְּצִידֵּי הַמַּעֲרָכָה, מַהוּ? אַלִּיבָּא דְּמַאן דְּאָמַר: ״עַל״ מַמָּשׁ – לָא תִּיבָּעֵי לָךְ,

Rabbi Yitzḥak Nappaḥa raises a dilemma: With regard to the **limbs** of an offering **that** a priest **arranged adjacent to the arrangement** of wood on the altar, **what is** the *halakha*?[N] The Gemara explains: **Do not raise the dilemma according to** the opinion **of the one who says** that the phrase **"upon [*al*]** the wood" is meant **literally,**

BACKGROUND

Shall stand unresolved [*teiku*] – תֵּיקוּ: Various explanations have been offered with regard to the etymology of this term. One explanation is that the word is an abbreviated form of the word *tikom*, meaning: Let it stand. Another explanation is that its source is the word *tik*, meaning case or pouch. Just as upon seeing a case or pouch one is unsure of its contents, so too, the word *teiku* is used in a situation where a resolution is unknown as though it were hidden inside a case (*Arukh*). Although not the literal meaning, some suggest that the term *teiku* is an acrostic for the Hebrew phrase: *Tishbi yetaretz kushyot uve'ayot*, or: The Tishbite, i.e., Elijah the prophet, will resolve questions and dilemmas (*Tosefot Yom Tov*). This is a reference to the tradition that when Elijah returns to announce the advent of the Messiah, he will also reveal the solutions to outstanding halakhic difficulties.

HALAKHA

Handful that a priest arranged…limbs that a priest arranged, etc. – קוֹמֶץ שֶׁסִּידְּרוֹ...אֵבָרִין שֶׁסִּידְּרָן וכו׳: If one placed the limbs or handful on the altar and then placed the arrangement of wood on top, or if one placed them adjacent to the wood, it is uncertain whether this is considered a proper manner of burning or not. Therefore, one should not burn them in this manner *ab initio*, but after the fact it is accepted, as these three dilemmas are not resolved in the Gemara (Rambam *Sefer Avoda*, *Hilkhot Pesulei HaMukdashin* 2:26).

NOTES

With regard to limbs that he arranged adjacent to the arrangement of wood on the altar, what is the *halakha* – אֵבָרִין שֶׁסִּידְּרָן בְּצִידֵּי הַמַּעֲרָכָה מַהוּ: This dilemma is relevant only according to the opinion that the limbs may not be placed under the wood. According to this opinion, even though it is decided that the limbs must be placed "upon [*al*] the wood" specifically, it can still be explained that "*al*" in fact means adjacent to the wood. According to the opinion that "upon the wood" is not meant literally and the limbs may also be placed directly on the altar, there is no distinction between placement under the arrangement of wood or adjacent to it (*Zevaḥ Toda*; see *Or HaYashar*).

Perek **III**
Daf **27** Amud **a**

דְּ״עַל הָעֵצִים״ כְּתִיב.

as **"upon [*al*]** the wood" **is written,** and not: Next to the wood.

כִּי תִּיבָּעֵי לָךְ – אַלִּיבָּא דְּמַאן דְּאָמַר: ״עַל״ – בְּסָמוּךְ, מַאי? הָכָא נַמִי ״עַל״ – בְּסָמוּךְ, אוֹ דִּלְמָא: ״עַל הָעֵצִים״ דּוּמְיָא דְּ״עַל הַמִּזְבֵּחַ״, מַה הָתָם ״עַל״ – מַמָּשׁ, אַף הָכָא נַמִי ״עַל״ – מַמָּשׁ? תֵּיקוּ.

When should you raise the dilemma? Raise it **according to** the opinion **of the one who says** in the mishna (96a) that the term **"upon [*al*]"** (see Numbers 2:20) means **adjacent to.** According to that *tanna*, **what** is the *halakha* in this case? Is it explained that **here, too,** the phrase **"upon [*al*]** the wood" can mean **adjacent to** the wood? **Or perhaps,** the phrase "upon [*al*] the wood that is on the fire upon the altar" teaches that **"upon the wood"** is to be understood as **similar to "upon the altar": Just as there "upon** the altar" is meant **literally, so too here,** the phrase **"upon** the wood" is meant **literally.** The Gemara comments: No answer was found, and the dilemma **shall stand** unresolved.

מתני׳ הַקּוֹמֶץ, מִיעוּטוֹ מְעַכֵּב אֶת רוּבּוֹ. עִשָּׂרוֹן, מִיעוּטוֹ מְעַכֵּב אֶת רוּבּוֹ. הַיַּיִן, מִיעוּטוֹ מְעַכֵּב אֶת רוּבּוֹ. הַשֶּׁמֶן, מִיעוּטוֹ מְעַכֵּב אֶת רוּבּוֹ.

MISHNA With regard to **the handful,** failure to sacrifice **the minority of it**[H] **prevents the majority of it,** which was sacrificed, from rendering it permitted for the priests to consume the remainder of the meal offering. With regard to **a tenth** of an ephah of flour[H] brought as a meal offering, failure to sacrifice **the minority of it prevents the majority of it,** which was sacrificed, from qualifying as a proper meal offering. With regard to **the wine**[H] poured as a libation, failure to pour **the minority of it prevents the majority of it,** which was poured, from qualifying as a proper libation. With regard to **the** *log* of **oil** that is required for the meal offering, failure to add **the minority of it prevents the majority of it,** which was added, from being a sufficient measure of oil.

הַסּוֹלֶת וְהַשֶּׁמֶן מְעַכְּבִין זֶה אֶת זֶה. הַקּוֹמֶץ וְהַלְּבוֹנָה מְעַכְּבִין זֶה אֶת זֶה.

With regard to **the fine flour and the oil,** failure to bring **each prevents fulfillment of the mitzva with the other.** With regard to **the handful and the frankincense,** failure to burn **each prevents fulfillment of the mitzva with the other.**

גמ׳ מַאי טַעְמָא? אָמַר קְרָא: ״מְלֹא קֻמְצוֹ״ תְּרֵי זִימְנֵי.

GEMARA **What is the reason** that the failure to sacrifice the minority of the handful disqualifies the entire offering? This is derived from the fact that **the verse states "his handful" twice,** once with regard to the voluntary meal offering (Leviticus 2:2) and once with regard to the meal offering of a sinner (Leviticus 5:12), and any *halakha* repeated in the verses is deemed indispensable.

עִשָּׂרוֹן מִיעוּטוֹ מְעַכֵּב אֶת רוּבּוֹ, מַאי טַעְמָא? אָמַר קְרָא: ״מִסָּלְתָּהּ״ – שֶׁאִם חָסְרָה כָּל שֶׁהוּא פְּסוּלָה.

The mishna teaches: With regard to **a tenth** of an ephah of flour brought as a meal offering, failure to sacrifice **the minority of it prevents the majority of it** from qualifying as a proper meal offering. **What is the reason? The verse states:** "The priest shall remove of it a handful **of its fine flour**" (Leviticus 2:2). The usage of the term "of its fine flour" instead of: Of the fine flour, teaches **that if any amount** of its flour **was missing,** it is **not valid.**

הַיַּיִן מִיעוּטוֹ מְעַכֵּב אֶת רוּבּוֹ – ״כָּכָה״.

The mishna teaches: With regard to **the wine** poured as a libation, failure to pour **the minority of it prevents the majority of it** from qualifying as a proper libation. What is the reason? The verse states concerning the libations: **"So** shall it be done" (Numbers 15:11). The term "so" indicates that the libations must be sacrificed exactly in the manner described, without any deviation.

הַשֶּׁמֶן מִיעוּטוֹ מְעַכֵּב אֶת רוּבּוֹ; דְּמִנְחַת נְסָכִים – ״כָּכָה״, וּמִנְחַת נְדָבָה – אָמַר קְרָא ״וּמִשַּׁמְנָהּ״ – שֶׁאִם חָסֵר כָּל שֶׁהוּא – פְּסוּלָה.

The mishna teaches: With regard to **the** *log* of **oil** that is required for the meal offering, failure to add **the minority of it prevents the majority of it** from being a sufficient measure of oil. In the case of the oil **of the meal offering** that accompanies the **libations,** this *halakha* is learned from the term: **"So"** (Numbers 15:11), stated with regard to the libations. **And** in the case of the *log* of oil that accompanies **a voluntary meal offering, the verse states: "And of its oil"** (Leviticus 2:2), demonstrating **that if any amount** of its oil was **missing,** it is **not valid.**

הַשֶּׁמֶן וְהַסּוֹלֶת מְעַכְּבִין זֶה אֶת זֶה – ״מִסָּלְתָּהּ וּמִשַּׁמְנָהּ״, ״מִגִּרְשָׂהּ וּמִשַּׁמְנָהּ״.

The mishna teaches: With regard to **the fine flour and the oil,** failure to bring **each prevents fulfillment of the mitzva with the other.** The *halakha* that each is indispensable is derived from the fact that the two are juxtaposed in the verse: "The priest shall remove of it a handful **of its fine flour and of its oil"** (Leviticus 2:2), and the fact that this requirement is repeated in the verse: **"Of its groats, and of its oil"** (Leviticus 2:16), teaches that each is indispensable.

הַקּוֹמֶץ וְהַלְּבוֹנָה מְעַכְּבִין זֶה אֶת זֶה – ״עַל כָּל לְבוֹנָתָהּ״, ״וְאֵת כָּל הַלְּבוֹנָה אֲשֶׁר עַל הַמִּנְחָה״.

The mishna teaches: With regard to **the handful and the frankincense,** failure to burn **each prevents fulfillment of the mitzva with the other.** The *halakha* that each is indispensable is derived from the repetition of the mention of the two together in the verse, as it is written: "The priest shall remove of it a handful of its fine flour and of its oil, **as well as all of its frankincense"** (Leviticus 2:2), and again with regard to the meal offering of a sinner it is stated: **"And all the frankincense which is upon the meal offering"** (Leviticus 6:8).

HALAKHA

With regard to the handful, failure to sacrifice the minority of it, etc. – הַקּוֹמֶץ מִיעוּטוֹ וכו׳: If a part of the handful is lacking, the entire handful is invalidated. If part of the oil is lacking, the entire *log* is invalidated. With regard to the fine flour and the oil, failure to bring each prevents fulfillment of the mitzva with the other. So too with the handful and the frankincense: Failure to burn each prevents fulfillment of the mitzva with the other (Rambam *Sefer Avoda, Hilkhot Ma'aseh HaKorbanot* 13:14).

A tenth of an ephah of flour – עִשָּׂרוֹן: All meal offerings that are sacrificed on the altar must be made up of at least a tenth of an ephah of flour, and if a part is missing the entire meal offering is invalid (Rambam *Sefer Avoda, Hilkhot Ma'aseh HaKorbanot* 12:5).

The wine – הַיַּיִן: If any amount is added to or missing from the wine libations, the libations are not valid (Rambam *Sefer Avoda, Hilkhot Ma'aseh HaKorbanot* 2:5).

מתני׳ שְׁנֵי שְׂעִירֵי יוֹם הַכִּפּוּרִים מְעַכְּבִין זֶה אֶת זֶה. שְׁנֵי כִּבְשֵׂי עֲצֶרֶת מְעַכְּבִין זֶה אֶת זֶה. שְׁתֵּי חַלּוֹת מְעַכְּבוֹת זוֹ אֶת זוֹ.

MISHNA With regard to **the two goats of Yom Kippur,** the absence of **each** goat **prevents fulfillment of the mitzva with the other.** With regard to **the two sheep** brought together with the meal offering of the two loaves on ***Shavuot,*** failure to bring **each** of the sheep **prevents fulfillment of the mitzva with the other.** With regard to the **two loaves**[H] brought on *Shavuot,* failure to bring **each** of the loaves **prevents fulfillment of the mitzva with the other.**

שְׁנֵי סְדָרִין מְעַכְּבִין זֶה אֶת זֶה. שְׁנֵי בָּזִיכִין מְעַכְּבִין זֶה אֶת זֶה. הַסְּדָרִין וְהַבָּזִיכִין מְעַכְּבִין זֶה אֶת זֶה.

With regard to the **two arrangements** of the shewbread,[H] failure to place **each** of the arrangements **prevents fulfillment of the mitzva with the other.** With regard to the **two bowls** of frankincense that accompany the shewbread, failure to place **each** of the bowls **prevents fulfillment of the mitzva with the other.** With regard to **the arrangements** of the shewbread **and the bowls** of frankincense, failure to bring **each** of them **prevents fulfillment of the mitzva with the other.**

שְׁנֵי מִינִים שֶׁבַּנָּזִיר, שְׁלֹשָׁה שֶׁבַּפָּרָה, וְאַרְבָּעָה שֶׁבַּתּוֹדָה, וְאַרְבָּעָה שֶׁבַּלּוּלָב, וְאַרְבַּע שֶׁבַּמְּצוֹרָע – מְעַכְּבִין זֶה אֶת זֶה.

With regard to the **two types** of loaves **that** accompany the offerings **of a nazirite:**[H] The bread and wafers (see Numbers 6:15); the **three** species **that** are part of the rite **of the red heifer:**[H] The cedar, hyssop, and scarlet wool (see Numbers 19:6); **and** the **four** types of loaves **that** accompany **the thanks offering:**[H] The loaves, wafers, loaves soaked in hot water, and leavened bread (see Leviticus 7:12); **and** the **four** species **of the *lulav*:**[H] The *lulav, etrog,* myrtle, and willow (see Leviticus 23:40); **and** the **four** species **that are** used **in** the purification process of **the leper:**[H] The cedar, hyssop, scarlet wool, and birds (see Leviticus 14:4), failure to bring **each** of the components **prevents fulfillment of the mitzva with the others.**

שִׁבְעָה הַזָּאוֹת שֶׁבַּפָּרָה מְעַכְּבוֹת זוֹ אֶת זוֹ. שֶׁבַע הַזָּיוֹת שֶׁעַל בֵּין הַבַּדִּים, שֶׁעַל הַפָּרֹכֶת, שֶׁעַל מִזְבַּח הַזָּהָב – מְעַכְּבוֹת זוֹ אֶת זוֹ.

With regard to the **seven sprinklings** of the blood **of the** red **heifer**[H] that the priest sprinkles opposite the entrance to the Sanctuary (see Numbers 19:4), failure to sprinkle **each prevents fulfillment of the mitzva with the others.** With regard to the **seven sprinklings** of the blood of the bull and goat of Yom Kippur **that** are sprinkled **on** the Ark **between the staves** (see Leviticus 16:14–15), the seven sprinklings **that** are sprinkled **on the Curtain** separating the Sanctuary and Holy of Holies, and the sprinklings **that** are sprinkled **on the golden altar**[H] on Yom Kippur, and from all other inner sin offerings, failure to sprinkle **each prevents fulfillment of the mitzva with the others.**

HALAKHA

Two sheep brought on *Shavuot*…two loaves – שְׁנֵי כִּבְשֵׂי עֲצֶרֶת...שְׁתֵּי חַלּוֹת: With regard to the two sheep brought together with the meal offering of the two loaves on *Shavuot,* failure to bring each of the sheep prevents fulfillment of the mitzva with the other. With regard to the two loaves brought on *Shavuot,* failure to bring each of the loaves prevents fulfillment of the mitzva with the other (Rambam *Sefer Avoda, Hilkhot Temidin UMusafin* 8:14).

Two arrangements of the shewbread, etc. – שְׁנֵי סְדָרִין וכו׳: With regard to the two arrangements of the shewbread, failure to place each of the arrangements prevents fulfillment of the mitzva with the other. With regard to the two bowls of frankincense that accompany the shewbread, failure to place each of the bowls prevents fulfillment of the mitzva with the other. With regard to the arrangements of the shewbread and the bowls of frankincense, failure to bring each of them prevents fulfillment of the mitzva with the other (Rambam *Sefer Avoda, Hilkhot Temidin UMusafin* 5:3).

Two types of loaves that accompany the offerings of a nazirite – שְׁנֵי מִינִים שֶׁבַּנָּזִיר: With regard to the two types of loaves that accompany the offerings of a nazirite, failure to bring each prevents fulfillment of the mitzva with the other (Rambam *Sefer Avoda, Hilkhot Ma'aseh HaKorbanot* 9:24).

Three species that are part of the rite of the red heifer – שְׁלֹשָׁה שֶׁבַּפָּרָה: The cedar, hyssop, and scarlet wool that are part of the rite of the red heifer are all indispensable, so that failure to bring one component prevents fulfillment of the mitzva with the others (Rambam *Sefer Tahara, Hilkhot Para Aduma* 3:2).

Four types of loaves that accompany the thanks offering – אַרְבָּעָה שֶׁבַּתּוֹדָה: The four types of loaves that accompany the thanks offering are all indispensable, so that failure to bring one prevents fulfillment of the mitzva with the others (Rambam *Sefer Avoda, Hilkhot Ma'aseh HaKorbanot* 9:24).

Four species of the *lulav* – אַרְבָּעָה שֶׁבַּלּוּלָב: The four species of the *lulav* constitute one mitzva, and the absence of one prevents fulfillment of the mitzva with the others. Therefore, if one species is absent, one should not recite a blessing over the others, but instead take them only as a remembrance. When taking them as a remembrance, one must take care not to intend to fulfill a mitzva, as this would constitute a violation of the prohibition against subtracting from the performance of a mitzva (Rambam *Sefer Zemanim, Hilkhot Shofar VeSukka VeLulav* 7:5; *Shulḥan Arukh, Oraḥ Ḥayyim* 651:12, and see *Beur Halakha* there).

Four species that are in the purification process of the leper – אַרְבַּע שֶׁבַּמְּצוֹרָע: The four species that are used in the purification process of the leper are all indispensable, so that failure to bring each of the components prevents fulfillment of the mitzva with the others (Rambam *Sefer Tahara, Hilkhot Tumat Tzara'at* 11:1).

Seven sprinklings of the red heifer – שִׁבְעָה הַזָּאוֹת שֶׁבַּפָּרָה: If one of the sprinklings of the blood of the red heifer was not performed, the rite is not valid (Rambam *Sefer Tahara, Hilkhot Para Aduma* 4:7).

That are on the golden altar – שֶׁעַל מִזְבַּח הַזָּהָב: With regard to the sprinklings of blood on the inner golden altar, if one is not performed, atonement is not effected (Rambam *Sefer Avoda, Hilkhot Pesulei HaMukdashin* 2:3).

גמ׳ שְׁנֵי שְׂעִירֵי יוֹם הַכִּפּוּרִים מְעַכְּבִין זֶה אֶת זֶה – חוּקָּה.

GEMARA The mishna teaches: With regard to **the two goats of Yom Kippur,** the absence of **each** goat **prevents fulfillment of the mitzva with the other.** This is derived from the verse that states with regard to the Yom Kippur service: "And it shall be **a statute** forever" (Leviticus 16:29), since wherever the term "statute" appears concerning a sacrificial rite, it signifies that the rite is an indispensable requirement.

שְׁנֵי כִבְשֵׂי עֲצֶרֶת מְעַכְּבִין זֶה אֶת זֶה – הֲוָיָה. שְׁתֵּי חַלּוֹת – הֲוָיָה.

The mishna teaches: With regard to **the two sheep** brought together with the meal offering of the two loaves on *Shavuot*, failure to bring **each** of the sheep **prevents fulfillment of the mitzva with the other.** This is derived from the verse: "They shall be holy" (Leviticus 23:20), since the employment of a term of **being** indicates an indispensable requirement. Similarly, with regard to the **two loaves** brought on *Shavuot*, the reason failure to bring each of the loaves prevents fulfillment of the mitzva with the other is that the verse states: "They shall be of fine flour" (Leviticus 23:17), employing a term of **being.**

שְׁנֵי סְדָרִין – חוּקָּה. שְׁנֵי בָזִיכִין – חוּקָּה. הַסְּדָרִין וְהַבָּזִיכִין – חוּקָּה.

With regard to the **two arrangements** of the shewbread, the reason failure to place each of the arrangements prevents fulfillment of the mitzva with the other is that the verse employs the term **statute** concerning them (see Leviticus 24:9). With regard to the **two bowls** of frankincense that accompany the shewbread, the reason failure to place each of the bowls prevents fulfillment of the mitzva with the other is that the verse employs the term **statute** concerning them (see Leviticus 24:9). With regard to **the arrangements** of the shewbread **and the bowls** of frankincense, the reason failure to bring each of them prevents fulfillment of the mitzva with the other is that the verse employs the term **statute** concerning them, as that verse addresses each of these two components.

שְׁנֵי מִינִים שֶׁבְּנָזִיר – דִּכְתִיב: "כֵּן יַעֲשֶׂה". שְׁלֹשָׁה שֶׁבְּפָרָה – חוּקָּה.

With regard to the **two types** of loaves **that** accompany the offerings **of a nazirite,** each prevents fulfillment of the mitzva with the others, **as it is written** with regard to the nazirite: **"So he must do** after the law of his naziriteship" (Numbers 6:21), demonstrating that must bring his offerings precisely as detailed in the verse. With regard to the **three** species **that** are part of the rite **of the** red **heifer,** each prevents fulfillment of the mitzva with the others, since the term **statute** is written about them: "This is the statute of the law" (Numbers 19:2).

אַרְבָּעָה שֶׁבְּתוֹדָה – דְּאִיתְקַשׁ לְנָזִיר, דִּכְתִיב: "עַל זֶבַח תּוֹדַת שְׁלָמָיו", וְאָמַר מָר: "שְׁלָמָיו" – לְרַבּוֹת שַׁלְמֵי נָזִיר.

With regard to the **four** types of loaves **that** accompany **the thanks offering,** each prevents fulfillment of the mitzva with the others, **since** the thanks offering **is juxtaposed to** the offerings of **a nazirite, as it is written** with regard to the thanks offering: **"With the sacrifice of his peace offerings for thanksgiving"** (Leviticus 7:13). **And the Master said:** The term **"his peace offerings"** serves **to include** the loaves of **the peace offering of a nazirite,** and it has already been demonstrated that with regard to the loaves that accompany the offerings of a nazirite, each prevents fulfillment of the mitzva with the others.

וְאַרְבָּעָה שֶׁבִּמְצוֹרָע – דִּכְתִיב: "זֹאת תִּהְיֶה תּוֹרַת הַמְּצֹרָע". וְאַרְבָּעָה שֶׁבְּלוּלָב – "וּלְקַחְתֶּם" – לְקִיחָה תַּמָּה.

And with regard to the **four** species **that are in** the purification process of **the leper,** each prevents fulfillment of the mitzva with the others, **as it is written: "This shall be the law of the leper"** (Leviticus 14:2), and the term "shall be" indicates an indispensable requirement. **And** with regard to the **four** species **of the *lulav*,** each prevents fulfillment of the mitzva with the others, as the verse states: **"And you shall take"** [***ulkaḥtem***]" (Leviticus 23:40), which alludes to: **A complete taking** [***lekiḥa tamma***], comprising all four species.

אָמַר רַב חָנָן בַּר רָבָא: לֹא שָׁנוּ אֶלָּא שֶׁאֵין לוֹ, אֲבָל יֵשׁ לוֹ – אֵין מְעַכְּבִין.

§ **Rav Ḥanan bar Rava says:** The mishna **taught** that the four species of the *lulav* are necessary for the fulfillment of the mitzva **only** in a case **where one did not have** all four species; **but if one has** all four species, failure to take each of the components **does not prevent** fulfillment of the mitzva[NH] with the others, and he fulfills the mitzva by taking each species individually.

NOTES

But if one has all four species failure to take each does not prevent fulfillment of the mitzva – אֲבָל יֵשׁ לוֹ אֵין מְעַכְּבִין: The majority of the early commentaries explain that even if one did not lift all of the species together, he has fulfilled the mitzva of taking the *lulav* (*Halakhot Gedolot*; Rif). The Rambam explains that the specification: If one has all four species, means that they are all present before him. The Ramban disagrees, understanding that: Where one does not have, means that he does not possess all four species and takes only some of the species, and: If he has all of them, means that at a later point he acquires the missing species; in this case, he is retroactively deemed to have fulfilled his obligation, despite the fact that the remaining species came into his possession only at a later point (see Meiri on *Sukka* 31a).

Rabbeinu Tam objects to the majority opinion that if one did not lift all the species together he has fulfilled the mitzva, explaining that since all four constitute one mitzva, it is not reasonable to suggest that one can fulfill the mitzva by taking each component separately (Rosh). He therefore explains that what is meant is that one can fulfill one's obligation even if the different species are not bound together. This also appears to be the opinion of Rashi (*Tosafot*). With regard to the significance of Rabbeinu Tam's emendation of the text of the Gemara, see *Arukh LaNer* on *Sukka* 34b.

HALAKHA

If one has all four species failure to take each does not prevent fulfillment of the mitzva – יֵשׁ לוֹ אֵין מְעַכְּבִין: If all four species of the *lulav* were in one's presence and one took each one of them separately, he has fulfilled his obligation, in accordance with the statement of Rav Ḥanan bar Rava, provided that they are all before him (Rambam *Sefer Zemanim, Hilkhot Shofar VeSukka VeLulav* 7:6; *Shulḥan Arukh, Oraḥ Ḥayyim* 651:12).

מֵיתִיבִי: אַרְבָּעָה מִינִין שֶׁבְּלוּלָב, שְׁנַיִם מֵהֶן עוֹשִׂין פֵּירוֹת וּשְׁנַיִם מֵהֶם אֵין עוֹשִׂין פֵּירוֹת; הָעוֹשִׂין פֵּירוֹת יְהִיוּ זְקוּקִין לְשֶׁאֵין עוֹשִׂין, וְשֶׁאֵין עוֹשִׂין פֵּירוֹת יְהִיוּ זְקוּקִין לָעוֹשִׂין פֵּירוֹת, וְאֵין אָדָם יוֹצֵא יְדֵי חוֹבָתוֹ בָּהֶן עַד שֶׁיְּהוּ כּוּלָּן בַּאֲגוּדָּה אַחַת;

The Gemara **raises an objection** from a *baraita*: With regard to the **four species of the *lulav*, two of them,** the *lulav* and *etrog*, **produce fruit, and two of them,** the myrtle and willow, **do not produce fruit. Those that produce fruit have a bond with those that do not produce fruit, and those that do not produce fruit have a bond with those that produce fruit. And a person does not fulfill his obligation** of taking the *lulav* **until they are all** bound together **in a single bundle.**

וְכֵן יִשְׂרָאֵל בְּהַרְצָאָה – עַד שֶׁיְּהוּ כּוּלָּן בַּאֲגוּדָּה אַחַת, שֶׁנֶּאֱמַר: ״הַבּוֹנֶה בַשָּׁמַיִם מַעֲלוֹתָיו וַאֲגֻדָּתוֹ עַל אֶרֶץ יְסָדָהּ״!

And so too, when **the Jewish people** fast and pray **for acceptance** of their repentance, this is not accomplished **until they are all** bound together **in a single bundle, as it is stated: "It is He that builds His upper chambers in the Heaven, and has established His bundle upon the earth"** (Amos 9:6), which is interpreted as stating that only when the Jewish people are bound together are they established upon the earth. This *baraita* contradicts Rav Ḥanan bar Rava's statement, since it teaches that the four species of the *lulav* must be taken together in order for one to fulfill his obligation of taking the *lulav*.

תַּנָּאֵי הִיא, דְּתַנְיָא: לוּלָב בֵּין אָגוּד בֵּין שֶׁאֵינוֹ אָגוּד – כָּשֵׁר; רַבִּי יְהוּדָה אוֹמֵר: אָגוּד – כָּשֵׁר, שֶׁאֵינוֹ אָגוּד – פָּסוּל.

The Gemara answers: Whether the different species must be taken together **is** a dispute between ***tanna'im*; as it is taught** in a *baraita*: **A *lulav*, whether** it is **bound** with the myrtle and willow or **whether** it is **not bound,** is **fit. Rabbi Yehuda says:** If it is **bound,** it is **fit**; if it is **not bound,** it is **unfit.**

מַאי טַעְמָא דְּרַבִּי יְהוּדָה? גָּמַר קִיחָה קִיחָה מֵאֲגוּדַּת אֵזוֹב,

The Gemara asks: **What is the reasoning of Rabbi Yehuda?** The Gemara answers: By means of a verbal analogy, he **derives** the term **taking,** written with regard to the four species, **from** the term **taking** written with regard to **the bundle of hyssop.** It is written there, in the context of the sacrifice of the Paschal offering in Egypt: "Take a bundle of hyssop" (Exodus 12:22), and it is written here, with regard to the four species: "And you shall take for you on the first day the fruit of a beautiful tree, branches of a date palm, boughs of dense-leaved trees, and willows of the brook" (Leviticus 23:40).

מַה לְּהַלָּן בַּאֲגוּדָּה – אַף כָּאן בַּאֲגוּדָּה. וְרַבָּנַן? לָא גָּמְרִי קִיחָה קִיחָה.

Just as there, with regard to the Paschal offering, the mitzva to take the hyssop is specifically **in a bundle, so too here,** the mitzva to take the four species is specifically **in a bundle.** The Gemara asks: **And** what is the reasoning of **the Rabbis?** The Gemara answers: **They do not derive** the meaning of the term **taking** from the meaning of the term **taking** by means of the verbal analogy.

כְּמַאן אָזְלָא הָא דְּתַנְיָא: לוּלָב מִצְוָה לְאוֹגְדוֹ, וְאִם לֹא אֲגָדוֹ – כָּשֵׁר, כְּמַאן? אִי כְּרַבִּי יְהוּדָה, לֹא אֲגָדוֹ אַמַּאי כָּשֵׁר? אִי רַבָּנַן, מַאי מִצְוָה?

The Gemara asks: **In accordance with whose** opinion **is that which is taught** in a *baraita*: There is **a mitzva to bind** the myrtle and the willow together with the ***lulav*,**[H] **but if one did not bind it,** it is **fit? In accordance with whose** opinion is the *baraita*? **If** it is **in accordance with** the opinion of **Rabbi Yehuda, if one did not bind it, why** is it **fit? If** it is in accordance with the opinion of **the Rabbis, what mitzva** is one fulfilling by binding it?

לְעוֹלָם רַבָּנַן, וּמַאי מִצְוָה? מִשּׁוּם ״זֶה אֵלִי וְאַנְוֵהוּ״.

The Gemara answers: **Actually,** it is in accordance with the opinion of **the Rabbis. And what mitzva** is one fulfilling? The mitzva is **due to** the fact that it is stated: **"This is my God and I will beautify Him"** (Exodus 15:2), which is interpreted to mean that one should beautify himself before God in the performance of the mitzvot. The Rabbis agree that although failure to bind the three species does not render them unfit for performing the mitzva, the performance of the mitzva is more beautiful when the *lulav* is bound.

HALAKHA

There is a mitzva to bind the myrtle and the willow with the *lulav* – לוּלָב מִצְוָה לְאוֹגְדוֹ: In order for the mitzva to be performed in the best possible manner, it is preferable to bind the *lulav*, myrtle, and willow together, as one should perform mitzvot in a manner that is most aesthetically pleasing. If one did not bind them together, he has still fulfilled his obligation, in accordance with the opinion of Rabbis (Rambam *Sefer Zemanim*, *Hilkhot Shofar VeSukka VeLulav* 7:6; *Shulḥan Arukh*, *Oraḥ Ḥayyim* 651:1).

שֶׁבַע הַזָּאוֹת שֶׁבַּפָּרָה מְעַכְּבוֹת זוֹ אֶת זוֹ – חוּקָּה.

§ The mishna teaches: With regard to the **seven sprinklings** of the blood **of the heifer** that the priest sprinkles opposite the entrance to the Sanctuary, failure to sprinkle **each prevents fulfillment of the mitzva with the others,** since the term **statute** is written about them (see Numbers 19:2).

שֶׁבַע הַזָּאוֹת שֶׁעַל בֵּין הַבַּדִּים וְשֶׁעַל מִזְבַּח הַזָּהָב וְשֶׁעַל הַפָּרוֹכֶת מְעַכְּבוֹת זוֹ אֶת זוֹ; דְּיוֹם הַכִּפּוּרִים – כְּתִיב חוּקָּה,

The mishna further teaches: With regard to the **seven sprinklings** of the blood of the bull and goat of Yom Kippur **that** are sprinkled **on** the Ark **between the staves, and** the sprinklings **that** are sprinkled **on the golden altar** on Yom Kippur, and the sprinklings from all other inner sin offerings that are sprinkled on the golden altar, **and** the seven sprinklings **that** are sprinkled **on the Curtain** separating the Sanctuary and Holy of Holies, failure to sprinkle **each prevents fulfillment of the mitzva with the others.** With regard to the sprinklings **of Yom Kippur,** the reason that each prevents fulfillment of the mitzva with the others is that the term **"statute" is written** about the Yom Kippur service (see Leviticus 16:29).

דְּפַר כֹּהֵן מָשׁוּחַ וּדְפַר הֶעְלֵם דָּבָר שֶׁל צִיבּוּר וְדִשְׂעִירֵי עֲבוֹדָה זָרָה – כְּדִתַנְיָא: "וְעָשָׂה לַפָּר כַּאֲשֶׁר עָשָׂה לְפַר" מַה תַּלְמוּד לוֹמַר? לִכְפּוֹל בַּהַזָּאוֹת,

With regard to the sprinklings **of the bull of** the **anointed priest,** i.e., the High Priest, **and of the bull for an unwitting communal sin, and** those **of the goats of idol worship,** which are sprinkled on the Curtain and on the golden altar, the reason that each prevents fulfillment of the mitzva with the others is **as it is taught** in a *baraita*: The verse states with regard to the bull for an unwitting communal sin: **"So shall he do with the bull; as he did with the bull** of the sin offering" of the anointed priest (Leviticus 4:20). **Why must the verse state** that the bull offering for an unwitting communal sin is sacrificed in the same manner as the bull of the anointed priest, when the Torah has already explicitly specified the manner in which the service should take place? The reason it states it is in order **to repeat** the command **of the sprinklings,**

Perek **III**
Daf **27** Amud **b**

שֶׁאִם חִיסֵּר אַחַת מִן הַמַּתָּנוֹת – לֹא עָשָׂה כְּלוּם.

to teach **that if one omitted one of the placements** of blood, **he has done nothing.**

תָּנוּ רַבָּנַן: שֶׁבַע הַזָּאוֹת שֶׁבַּפָּרָה שֶׁעֲשָׂאָן, בֵּין שֶׁלֹּא לִשְׁמָן, בֵּין שֶׁלֹּא מְכוּוָּנוֹת אֶל נֹכַח פְּנֵי אוֹהֶל מוֹעֵד – פְּסוּלוֹת;

§ **The Sages taught** in a *baraita*: If the priest **performed the seven sprinklings of** the blood of **the red heifer**[HN] improperly, **either** by performing them **not for their** own **sake or** performing them **not precisely toward the entrance of the Tent of Meeting** of the Tabernacle (Numbers 19:4), which corresponds to the Sanctuary in the Temple,[B] **they are not valid.**

NOTES

Seven sprinklings of the blood of the red heifer, etc. – שֶׁבַע הַזָּאוֹת שֶׁבַּפָּרָה וכו׳: The rites of the red heifer would take place in the wilderness outside of the camp to the east, and in Jerusalem on the Mount of Olives. Before the heifer's flesh was burned, the priest was required to sprinkle of its blood seven times "toward the front of the Tent of Meeting" (Numbers 19:4), i.e., westward, as he faced the front of the Sanctuary, which was to the east. The reason that if the sprinkling was not done for its own sake it was not valid is that despite not actually being an offering, the red heifer is called a sin offering (see Numbers 19:9), and sin offerings are disqualified when they are sacrificed not for their own sake. With regard to the fact that the sprinkling is not valid when performed not precisely toward the entrance of the Tent of Meeting, Rashi explains that this is because the term "statute" is used with regard to the red heifer.

HALAKHA

Seven sprinklings of the blood of the red heifer – שֶׁבַע הַזָּאוֹת שֶׁבַּפָּרָה: If the blood of the red heifer is sprinkled not for its own sake, or is sprinkled not toward the Sanctuary, it is not valid, in accordance with the *baraita* (Rambam *Sefer Tahara, Hilkhot Para Aduma* 4:3, 5).

BACKGROUND

The Temple – מִקְדָּשׁ:

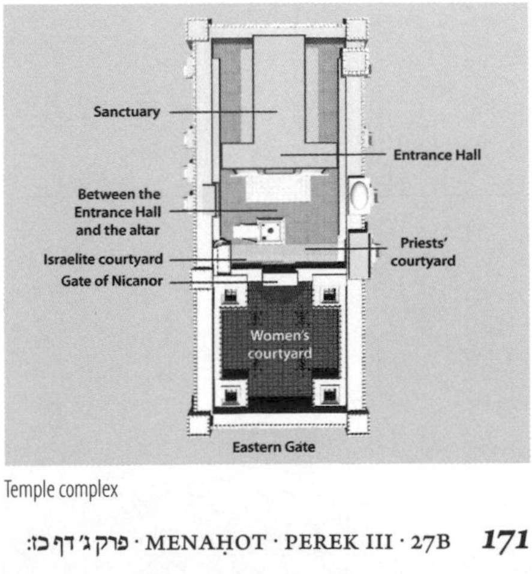

Temple complex

וְשֶׁבִּפְנִים וְשֶׁבִּמְצוֹרָע, שֶׁלֹּא לִשְׁמָן – פְּסוּלוֹת, שֶׁלֹּא מְכוּוָּנוֹת – כְּשֵׁרוֹת.

But with regard to the sprinkling of the blood **that** takes place **inside** the Sanctuary, of inner sin offerings, the blood of the bull and goat of Yom Kippur, the blood of the bull of the anointed priest, the blood of the bull for an unwitting communal sin, and the blood of the goats of idol worship, which are to be sprinkled "before the Lord, in front of the Curtain of the Sanctuary" (Leviticus 4:6), **and** the sprinkling of the oil **that** takes place during the purification **of the leper,**[H] which is done "seven times before the Lord" (Leviticus 14:16), if these are performed **not for their** own **sake,**[H] then **they are not valid.** But if they are performed **not precisely**[H] toward the direction where they should be sprinkled, **they are valid.**

וְהָתַנְיָא גַּבֵּי פָּרָה: שֶׁלֹּא לִשְׁמָן – פְּסוּלוֹת, שֶׁלֹּא מְכוּוָּנוֹת – כְּשֵׁרוֹת! אָמַר רַב חִסְדָּא, לָא קַשְׁיָא: הָא רַבִּי יְהוּדָה, הָא רַבָּנַן.

The Gemara asks: **But isn't it taught** in a *baraita* **concerning** the sprinklings of the blood of the red **heifer** that if they were performed **not for their** own **sake, they are not valid,** but if they were performed **not precisely** toward the entrance of the Tent of Meeting or Sanctuary, **they are valid? Rav Ḥisda said:** This is **not difficult; this** second *baraita* is in accordance with the opinion of **Rabbi Yehuda,** whereas **that** first *baraita* is in accordance with the opinion of **the Rabbis.**

דְּתַנְיָא: מְחוּסְּרֵי כַפָּרָה שֶׁנִּכְנְסוּ לָעֲזָרָה בְּשׁוֹגֵג – חַיָּיב חַטָּאת, בְּמֵזִיד – עָנוּשׁ כָּרֵת, וְאֵין צָרִיךְ לוֹמַר טְבוּל יוֹם וּשְׁאָר כָּל הַטְּמֵאִים.

As it is taught in a *baraita* (*Tosefta, Kelim* 1:10): With regard to **those who have not yet** brought **an atonement** offering to complete the purification process, and therefore are not permitted to enter the Temple or partake of sacrificial meat, **who entered the** Temple **courtyard**[H] **unwittingly,** they are **liable** to bring **a sin offering.** If they entered **intentionally,** then this is **punishable by *karet*. And needless to say,** the same applies to **one** who was ritually impure **who immersed that day** and is waiting for nightfall for the purification process to be completed **and all the others who are ritually impure**[H] and have not yet immersed.

HALAKHA

Sprinkling that takes place during the purification of the leper – הַזָּאוֹת שֶׁבִּמְצוֹרָע: When the priest sprinkles oil on the leper from the *log* of oil, he must sprinkle in the direction of the Holy of Holies, and if he performed the sprinklings not for their sake, they are not valid. If he did not sprinkle in the correct direction, they are valid (Rambam *Sefer Korbanot, Hilkhot Meḥusrei Kappara* 4:2, 5:7).

Sprinkling of the blood that takes place inside the Sanctuary …not for their own sake – שֶׁבִּפְנִים...שֶׁלֹּא לִשְׁמָן: Any sin offering, including inner sin offerings, whose blood is sprinkled not for its own sake is unfit (Rambam *Sefer Tahara, Hilkhot Pesulei HaMukdashin* 15:1).

Sprinkling of the blood that takes place inside the Sanctuary …not precisely – שֶׁבִּפְנִים...שֶׁלֹּא מְכוּוָּנוֹת: The blood of the bull and the blood of the goat of Yom Kippur were each sprinkled separately eight times between the staves of the Ark and eight times on the Curtain. The blood of the two of them was then mixed together and sprinkled four times on the four corners of the golden altar and seven times on the middle of the golden altar in the Sanctuary. If the inner sprinklings are not directed correctly, they are still valid (Rambam *Sefer Avoda, Hilkhot Ma'aseh HaKorbanot* 5:12).

Those who have not yet brought an atonement offering who entered the Temple courtyard – מְחוּסְּרֵי כַפָּרָה שֶׁנִּכְנְסוּ לָעֲזָרָה: The Rambam rules that those who have not yet brought an atonement offering and enter the Israelite courtyard, inside the gate of Nicanor, are punished with lashes for rebelliousness. According to his opinion, they have violated a prohibition by rabbinic law; this does not accord with the *baraita* cited here, which rules that they are liable to receive *karet*, indicating that the prohibition is by Torah law. The Ra'avad rules that just like any other impure person, if one who has not yet brought an atonement offering enters intentionally he is liable to receive *karet*, and if he does so unwittingly he is liable to bring a sliding-scale sin offering, in accordance with the *Tosefta* and the *baraita* here (Rambam *Sefer Avoda, Hilkhot Biat HaMikdash* 3:9 and *Kesef Mishne* there, and *Hilkhot Beit HaBeḥira* 7:18).

One who immersed that day and all the others who are ritually impure – טְבוּל יוֹם וּשְׁאָר כָּל הַטְּמֵאִים: Any impure person, including one who immersed that day and is waiting for nightfall for the purification process to be completed, who entered the Temple courtyard inside the gate of Nicanor, is liable to receive *karet* if he entered there intentionally, and must bring a sliding-scale sin offering if he entered there unwittingly. This is in accordance with the *baraita* (Rambam *Sefer Avoda, Hilkhot Biat HaMikdash* 3:12, 14).

וּטְהוֹרִים שֶׁנִּכְנְסוּ לִפְנִים מִמְּחִיצָּתָן, לַהֵיכָל כּוּלּוֹ – בְּאַרְבָּעִים, מִבֵּית לַפָּרֹכֶת אֶל פְּנֵי הַכַּפֹּרֶת – בְּמִיתָה. רַבִּי יְהוּדָה אוֹמֵר: כָּל הֵיכָל כּוּלּוֹ וּמִבֵּית לַפָּרֹכֶת – בְּאַרְבָּעִים, וְאֶל פְּנֵי הַכַּפֹּרֶת – בְּמִיתָה.

And with regard to those who are **pure who entered**[H] **beyond their boundaries,** i.e., beyond where it is permitted for them to enter, such as a priest who enters the Sanctuary for a purpose other than performing the Temple service, if one entered **any part of the Sanctuary,** he is liable **to** receive **forty** lashes. If he entered **within the Curtain** separating the Sanctuary and Holy of Holies, i.e., into the Holy of Holies, or he entered the Holy of Holies all the way until he was **before the Ark Cover,** he is liable **to** receive **death** at the hand of Heaven. **Rabbi Yehuda says:** If he entered **any part of the Sanctuary or within the Curtain** separating the Sanctuary and Holy of Holies, he is liable **to** receive **forty** lashes; **but** if he entered the Holy of Holies all the way until he was **before the Ark Cover,** he is liable **to** receive **death** at the hand of Heaven.

בְּמַאי קָא מִיפַּלְגִי? בְּהַאי קְרָא: "וַיֹּאמֶר ה׳ אֶל מֹשֶׁה דַּבֵּר אֶל אַהֲרֹן אָחִיךָ וְאַל יָבוֹא בְכָל עֵת אֶל הַקֹּדֶשׁ מִבֵּית לַפָּרֹכֶת אֶל פְּנֵי הַכַּפֹּרֶת אֲשֶׁר עַל הָאָרֹן וְלֹא יָמוּת", רַבָּנַן סָבְרִי: אֶל הַקּוֹדֶשׁ – בְּלֹא יָבֹא, מִבֵּית לַפָּרֹכֶת וְאֶל פְּנֵי הַכַּפֹּרֶת – בְּלֹא יָמוּת;

With regard to what issue **do** the Rabbis and Rabbi Yehuda **disagree?** They disagree **with regard to** the proper understanding of **this verse: "And the Lord said to Moses: Speak to Aaron your brother, that he not come at all times into the holy place, within the Curtain, before the Ark Cover which is upon the Ark, that he not die"** (Leviticus 16:2). **The Rabbis hold** that entering **into the holy place,** i.e., the Sanctuary, is **subject to** the prohibition of: **He shall not come,** and one who violates it is punished with lashes, whereas entering **within the Curtain** separating the Sanctuary and Holy of Holies **and before the Ark Cover** is **subject to** the warning of: **He shall not die,** and entering there is punished by death at the hand of Heaven.

וְרַבִּי יְהוּדָה סָבַר: אֶל הַקּוֹדֶשׁ וּמִבֵּית לַפָּרֹכֶת – בְּלֹא יָבֹא, וְאֶל פְּנֵי הַכַּפֹּרֶת – בְּלֹא יָמוּת.

And Rabbi Yehuda holds that entering **into the holy place,** i.e., the Sanctuary, **and within the Curtain** separating the Sanctuary and Holy of Holies is **subject to** the prohibition of: **He shall not come,** and one who violates it is punished with lashes, whereas entering **before the Ark Cover** is **subject to** the warning of: **He shall not die,** and entering there is punished by death at the of Heaven.

מַאי טַעְמָא דְּרַבָּנַן? אִי סָלְקָא דַּעְתָּךְ כִּדְקָאָמַר רַבִּי יְהוּדָה – לִכְתּוֹב רַחֲמָנָא אֶל הַקּוֹדֶשׁ וְאֶל פְּנֵי הַכַּפֹּרֶת, וְלָא בָּעֵי מִבֵּית לַפָּרֹכֶת, וַאֲנָא אָמֵינָא: הֵיכָל מִיחַיֵּיב, מִבֵּית לַפָּרֹכֶת מִבַּעְיָא?! מִבֵּית הַפָּרֹכֶת דִּכְתַב רַחֲמָנָא לָמָּה לִי? שְׁמַע מִינָּהּ בְּמִיתָה.

The Gemara asks: **What is the reason** for the interpretation **of the Rabbis?** The Gemara answers: **If** it should **enter your mind** to explain the verse **as Rabbi Yehuda says,** then **let the Merciful One write:** That he not come at all times **into the holy place and before the Ark Cover** that he not die, **and there is no need** to write **"within the Curtain," and I would say:** If one **becomes liable** to receive lashes for even entering the **Sanctuary, is** it **necessary** to teach that one incurs this punishment for entering **within the Curtain? Why do I** need the phrase **"within the Curtain" that the Merciful One wrote? Learn from** that seemingly extraneous term that entering the Holy of Holies is punishable **by death** at the hand of Heaven.

וְרַבִּי יְהוּדָה: אִי כָּתַב רַחֲמָנָא אֶל הַקּוֹדֶשׁ וְלֹא כָּתַב מִבֵּית לַפָּרֹכֶת, הֲוָה אָמֵינָא: מַאי קוֹדֶשׁ – מִבֵּית לַפָּרֹכֶת, אֲבָל הֵיכָל – לָאו נַמִי לָא. וְרַבָּנַן: הַהוּא לָא מָצֵית אָמְרַתְּ, דְּהֵיכָל כּוּלּוֹ אִיקְּרִי "קוֹדֶשׁ", שֶׁנֶּאֱמַר: "וְהִבְדִּילָה הַפָּרֹכֶת לָכֶם בֵּין הַקֹּדֶשׁ וּבֵין קֹדֶשׁ הַקֳּדָשִׁים".

And Rabbi Yehuda understands: **If the Merciful One had written** only that it is prohibited to come **"into the holy place"** and **did not write "within the Curtain," I would say: What is the holy place?** It is **within the Curtain,** i.e., the Holy of Holies, and one who enters it violates a prohibition, **but** if one enters the **Sanctuary** he does **not even** violate **a prohibition. And the Rabbis** respond to this claim: **You cannot say that, as the entire Sanctuary is called** "the **holy place,"** as it is stated: **"And the Curtain shall divide for you between the holy place and the Holy of Holies"** (Exodus 26:33).

HALAKHA

And those who are pure who entered – וּטְהוֹרִים שֶׁנִּכְנְסוּ: If an ordinary priest or the High Priest entered the Holy of Holies on any day except for Yom Kippur, or if the High Priest entered on Yom Kippur for a purpose other than performing the sacrificial rites of the day, he is liable to receive death at the hand of Heaven. If an ordinary priest or the High Priest entered the Sanctuary outside of the Holy of Holies for a purpose other than performing the sacrificial rites or to prostrate himself, he receives lashes. This is in accordance with the opinion of the Rabbis (Rambam *Sefer Avoda, Hilkhot Biat HaMikdash* 2:3–4).

וְרַבִּי יְהוּדָה מַאי טַעְמָא? אִי סָלְקָא דַּעְתָּךְ כִּדְקָא אָמְרִי רַבָּנַן – לִכְתּוֹב רַחֲמָנָא אֶל הַקּוֹדֶשׁ וּמִבֵּית לַפָּרֹכֶת, וְלָא בָּעֵי אֶל פְּנֵי הַכַּפֹּרֶת, וַאֲנָא אָמִינָא: מִבֵּית לַפָּרוֹכֶת בְּמִיתָה, אֶל פְּנֵי הַכַּפֹּרֶת מִיבַּעְיָא?! אֶל פְּנֵי הַכַּפֹּרֶת דִּכְתַב רַחֲמָנָא לָמָּה לִי? שְׁמַע מִינָּהּ: אֶל פְּנֵי הַכַּפֹּרֶת – בְּמִיתָה, מִבֵּית לַפָּרֹכֶת – בְּאַזְהָרָה.

And what is the reason for the interpretation **of Rabbi Yehuda?** Why does he hold that one who enters the Holy of Holies violates a prohibition but is not punished with death at the hand of Heaven? The Gemara answers: Rabbi Yehuda holds that **if** it should **enter your mind** to explain **as the Rabbis say,** that entering the Holy of Holies is punishable by death at the hand of Heaven, **let the Merciful One write:** That he not come at all times **into the holy place and within the Curtain** that he not die, **and there is no need** to write **"before the Ark Cover." And I would say:** If entering **within the Curtain,** i.e., the Holy of Holies, is punished **with death** at the hand of Heaven, **is** it **necessary** to teach that one incurs this punishment for entering **before the Ark Cover? Why do I** need the phrase **"before the Ark Cover" that the Merciful One wrote? Learn from** that seemingly extraneous term that entering **before the Ark Cover** is punishable **by death** at the hand of Heaven, but entering **within the Curtain** merely violates **a prohibition.**

וְרַבָּנַן: הָכִי נַמִי דְּלָא צְרִיךְ, וְהַאי דִּכְתַב רַחֲמָנָא אֶל פְּנֵי הַכַּפֹּרֶת – לְמַעוּטֵי דֶּרֶךְ מְשׁוּפָּשׁ,

And the Rabbis understand: **Indeed,** it is so **that** in order to teach the punishment of death at the hand of Heaven it **is not necessary** for the verse to also state "before the Ark Cover." **And** the reason **that the Merciful One wrote "before [*el penei*] the Ark Cover"** was in order **to exclude** one who entered the Holy of Holies through **a roundabout path,** as one who did not enter facing the Ark Cover, i.e., from the east, is not punished with death at the hand of Heaven.

כִּדְתָנָא דְּבֵי רַבִּי אֱלִיעֶזֶר בֶּן יַעֲקֹב: "אֶל פְּנֵי הַכַּפֹּרֶת קֵדְמָה" – זֶה בָּנָה אָב, כָּל מָקוֹם שֶׁנֶּאֱמַר "פְּנֵי" אֵינוֹ אֶלָּא פְּנֵי קָדִים.

This is **as the school of Rabbi Eliezer ben Ya'akov taught:** With regard to the verse: "And he shall sprinkle it with his finger **before [*el penei*] the Ark Cover to the east"** (Leviticus 16:14), **this established a paradigm**[B] that **any place** in the Torah **where it is stated: "Before [*penei*],"** it is referring to **nothing other than before** the **eastern** side.

וְרַבִּי יְהוּדָה: לֵימָא קְרָא: "פְּנֵי", מַאי "אֶל"? שְׁמַע מִינָּהּ: "אֶל" דַּוְקָא. וְרַבָּנַן: "אֶל" לָאו דַּוְקָא.

The Gemara asks: **And** how does **Rabbi Yehuda** respond to this, as it is clear that the term "before [*el penei*] the Ark Cover" is necessary to exclude one who entered the Holy of Holies through a roundabout path? The Gemara answers: According to Rabbi Yehuda, if the purpose was for that reason, **let the verse say: Before [*penei*]** the Ark Cover. **What** is the purpose of the word ***el*? Learn from** that seemingly extraneous term that one is punished with death at the hand of Heaven **specifically** if he entered directly **before** the Ark, but not if he merely entered the Holy of Holies. **And the Rabbis** hold that the term ***"el"*** does **not** mean **specifically** one who enters directly before the Ark Cover.

וְרַבִּי יְהוּדָה דְּאָמַר: "אֶל פְּנֵי הַכַּפֹּרֶת" דַּוְקָא – "וְהִזָּה אֶל נֹכַח" נַמִי דַּוְקָא.

The Gemara now returns to its suggestion that the contradiction between the two *baraitot* with regard to whether the sprinklings of the red heifer are valid or not when performed not precisely toward the entrance of the Tent of Meeting can be resolved by explaining that one *baraita* is in accordance with the opinion of Rabbi Yehuda and the other is in accordance with the opinion of the Rabbis. **And Rabbi Yehuda, who says** that the expression **"before [*el penei*] the Ark Cover"** teaches that the punishment is limited to one who **specifically** entered directly before the Ark Cover, holds that the expression: **"And sprinkle** of its blood **toward [*el*] the front"** (Numbers 19:4), **also** means that the sprinklings must be performed **specifically** toward the front of the Sanctuary.

BACKGROUND

Established a paradigm – בָּנָה אָב: This is a form of interpretation based on induction. Three types of inductive analogies are found in rabbinic literature: (1) An analogy based on the question: What do we find with regard to…? (2) An analogy based on one verse. (3) An analogy based on two verses. The simplest form of the analogy is the question: What do we find with regard to…? Just as in case A, *halakha* X applies, so too it may be inferred that in case B, which is similar to case A, *halakha* X should apply. It is an extrapolation from one case or verse, where certain details are specified, to a similar case or series of cases where those details are not specified.

וְרַבָּנַן, מִדְּהָתָם לָאו דַּוְקָא – הָכָא נַמִי לָאו דַּוְקָא.

And the Rabbis are of the opinion that **from** the fact **that there** the term *el* does **not** mean **specifically** that one is liable to be punished with death at the hand of Heaven only if he enters directly before the Ark Cover, **here too** they hold that it is **not** meant **specifically,** and therefore the sprinklings are valid even when performed not precisely toward the entrance of the Tent of Meeting.

מַתְקִיף לַהּ רַב יוֹסֵף: לְרַבִּי יְהוּדָה מִדְּ״אֶל״ דַּוְקָא – (״אֶל נֹכַח״) [״עַל״] נַמִי דַּוְקָא; אֶלָּא דְּמִקְדָּשׁ שֵׁנִי דְּלָא הָווּ אָרוֹן וְכַפּוֹרֶת, הָכִי נַמִי דְּלָא עָבֵיד הַזָּאוֹת?

Rav Yosef objects to this explanation: **According to Rabbi Yehuda, from** the fact **that** there the term *el* is used **specifically,** the verse: "And he shall sprinkle of the blood **before** [*al penei*] the Ark Cover" (Leviticus 16:14) should **also** mean that the sprinkling must be performed **specifically** upon the Ark Cover. **But** in the time **of the Second Temple, where there was no Ark or Ark Cover,** would Rabbi Yehuda then say that **indeed** the **sprinklings were not performed?** This is clearly not correct, as all agree that the sprinklings were performed in the Second Temple (see *Yoma* 53b).

אֲמַר רַבָּה בַּר עוּלָּא, אָמַר קְרָא: ״וְכִפֶּר אֶת מִקְדַּשׁ הַקֹּדֶשׁ״ – מָקוֹם הַמְקוּדָּשׁ לַקּוֹדֶשׁ.

Rabba bar Ulla said in response: **The verse states** with regard to the Yom Kippur service: **"And he shall make atonement for the most holy place [*mikdash hakodesh*]"** (Leviticus 16:33), which is interpreted as follows: He will sprinkle the blood to make atonement not specifically on the Ark [*hakodesh*], but even on **the place that is dedicated [*hamkudash*] for the Ark [*lakodesh*].**

רָבָא אֲמַר: הָא וְהָא רַבָּנַן,

The Gemara offers another resolution of the contradiction between the *baraitot* concerning whether the sprinklings of the red heifer are valid or invalid when performed not precisely toward the entrance of the Tent of Meeting. **Rava said:** Both **this** *baraita* **and that** *baraita* are in accordance with the opinion of **the Rabbis:**

Perek **III**
Daf **28** Amud **a**

הָא דְּקָאֵי מִזְרָח וּמַעֲרָב וְאַדֵּי, הָא דְּקָאֵי צָפוֹן וְדָרוֹם וְאַדֵּי.

This *baraita,* which teaches that the sprinklings are valid only when performed precisely toward the entrance of the Tent of Meeting, is referring to a case **where** the priest is **standing** with his back to the **east and** his front facing **west and he sprinkles** the blood. In this case, although the priest does not direct the sprinklings precisely toward the entrance of the Sanctuary, they are valid since he himself is facing the Sanctuary. **That** *baraita,* which teaches that the sprinklings are not valid when performed not precisely toward the entrance of the Tent of Meeting, is referring to a case **where** the priest is **standing** facing **north or south and he sprinkles** the blood. In this case, since he is facing the wrong direction they are not valid.

אָמַר מָר: וְשֶׁבִּפְנִים וְשֶׁבַּמְּצוֹרָע, שֶׁלֹּא לִשְׁמָן – פְּסוּלוֹת, שֶׁלֹּא מְכוּוָּנוֹת – כְּשֵׁירוֹת. וְהָתַנְיָא: בֵּין שֶׁלֹּא לִשְׁמָן בֵּין שֶׁלֹּא מְכוּוָּנוֹת – כְּשֵׁירוֹת!

§ **The Master says** in the *baraita*: **But** with regard to the sprinkling of the blood **that** takes place **inside** the Sanctuary **and** the sprinkling of the oil **that** takes place during the purification **of the leper,** if these are performed **not for their** own **sake,** then **they are not valid.** But if they were performed **not precisely** toward the Holy of Holies, **they are valid.** The Gemara asks: **But isn't it taught** in a *baraita* that with regard to the sprinklings of oil during the purification of the leper, **whether** they were performed **not for their** own **sake or** whether they were performed **not precisely** toward the Holy of Holies, **they are valid?**

BACKGROUND

Candelabrum – **מְנוֹרָה:** This is a diagram of the Candelabrum as drawn by the Rambam. He writes that his intention was not to draw a precise image of the Candelabrum but to illustrate the form of the Candelabrum. It is worth noting two points that are subject to much discussion. The first is that in the diagram the branches of the Candelabrum are straight and rise up diagonally, as opposed to the rounded branches that appear on coins and reliefs from the time of the Temple. The second noteworthy point is that the conical goblets appear to be upside down, with the narrow base on top and the wide brim on the bottom.

Rambam's sketch of the Candelabrum

אָמַר רַב יוֹסֵף, לָא קַשְׁיָא: הָא רַבִּי אֱלִיעֶזֶר וְהָא רַבָּנַן, רַבִּי אֱלִיעֶזֶר דְּמַקִּישׁ אָשָׁם לְחַטָּאת – מַקִּישׁ נַמִּי לוֹג לְאָשָׁם, רַבָּנַן לָא מַקְשִׁי.

Rav Yosef said: This is **not difficult. This** first *baraita* is in accordance with the opinion of **Rabbi Eliezer, and that** second *baraita* is in accordance with the opinion of **the Rabbis.** He explains: **Rabbi Eliezer** is the *tanna* **who juxtaposes** the **guilt offering to a sin offering,** teaching that just as a sin offering is disqualified when sacrificed not for its sake, so too, the guilt offering, such as the leper's guilt offering, is disqualified when sacrificed not for its sake, as it is written: "As is the sin offering, so is the guilt offering; there is one law for them" (Leviticus 7:7). He **also juxtaposes** the ***log*** of oil of the leper **to** the **guilt offering** of the leper in the same verse, teaching that if the sprinkling from the *log* of oil was performed not for its own sake, it is not valid. In contrast, **the Rabbis do not juxtapose** the guilt offering to the sin offering, and therefore they have no reason to invalidate the sprinkling from the leper's *log* of oil that is performed not for its own sake.

וּלְרַבִּי אֱלִיעֶזֶר, וְכִי דָּבָר הַלָּמֵד בְּהֶיקֵּשׁ חוֹזֵר וּמְלַמֵּד בְּהֶיקֵּשׁ?

The Gemara asks: **But according to Rabbi Eliezer, is it so that a matter derived via juxtaposition then teaches** a *halakha* to another case **via juxtaposition?** There is a principle that with regard to consecrated matters, a *halakha* derived via juxtaposition cannot subsequently teach a *halakha* via juxtaposition. Therefore, the necessity for the sprinklings of the *log* of oil to be performed for its own sake cannot be derived from juxtaposition between the guilt offering of the leper and the sprinkling of the oil.

אֶלָּא אֲמַר רָבָא: הָא וְהָא רַבָּנַן, כָּאן – לְהַכְשִׁיר הַקָּרְבָּן, כָּאן – לְהַרְצוֹת, שֶׁלֹּא עָלוּ לַבְּעָלִים לְשׁוּם חוֹבָה.

Rather, Rava said: Both **this** *baraita* **and that** *baraita* are in accordance with the opinion of **the Rabbis. Here,** where the *baraita* teaches that the sprinklings are valid, it means that they were effective **in rendering the offering valid** and allowing the priests to partake of the remainder of the *log,* whereas **there,** where the *baraita* teaches that the sprinklings are not valid, it means that they do not **effect acceptance, as they do not satisfy the obligation of the owner,** and therefore the leper is still prohibited from partaking of sacrificial meat.

מתני׳ שִׁבְעָה קְנֵי מְנוֹרָה מְעַכְּבִין זֶה אֶת זֶה. שִׁבְעָה נֵרוֹתֶיהָ מְעַכְּבִין זֶה אֶת זֶה. שְׁתֵּי פָּרָשִׁיּוֹת שֶׁבַּמְּזוּזָה מְעַכְּבוֹת זוֹ אֶת זוֹ, אֲפִילּוּ כְּתָב אֶחָד מְעַכְּבָן.

MISHNA With regard to the **seven branches of the Candelabrum** (see Exodus 25:32),[BH] the absence of **each prevents fulfillment of the mitzva with the others.** With regard to **its seven lamps** atop the branches, the absence of **each prevents fulfillment of the mitzva with the others.** With regard to the **two passages that are in the *mezuza*,**[H] which are the first (Deuteronomy 6:1–9) and second (Deuteronomy 11:13–21) paragraphs of *Shema*, the absence of **each prevents fulfillment of the mitzva with the other.** Furthermore, the absence of **even one letter prevents fulfillment of the mitzva with** the rest of **them.**

HALAKHA

Seven branches of the Candelabrum, etc. – **שִׁבְעָה קְנֵי מְנוֹרָה וכו׳:** With regard to the seven branches of the Candelabrum, the absence of each prevents fulfillment of the mitzva with the others. With regard to its seven lamps atop the branches, the absence of each prevents fulfillment of the mitzva with the others (Rambam *Sefer Avoda, Hilkhot Beit HaBeḥira* 3:7).

Passages that are in the *mezuza* – **פָּרָשִׁיּוֹת שֶׁבַּמְּזוּזָה:** With regard to the two passages that are in the *mezuza*, which are the first (Deuteronomy 6:1–9) and second (Deuteronomy 11:13–21) paragraphs of *Shema*, the absence of each prevents fulfillment of the mitzva with the others. Furthermore, if even one stroke is missing from one letter, the mitzva cannot be fulfilled by Torah law until every letter is complete (Rambam *Sefer Ahava, Hilkhot Tefillin UMezuza VeSefer Torah* 1:2; *Shulḥan Arukh, Yoreh De'a* 288:3).

אַרְבַּע פָּרָשִׁיּוֹת שֶׁבַּתְּפִילִּין מְעַכְּבִין זוֹ אֶת זוֹ, אֲפִילּוּ כְּתָב אֶחָד מְעַכְּבָן. אַרְבַּע צִיצִיּוֹת מְעַכְּבוֹת זוֹ אֶת זוֹ, שֶׁאַרְבַּעְתָּן מִצְוָה אַחַת; רַבִּי יִשְׁמָעֵאל אוֹמֵר: אַרְבַּעְתָּן אַרְבַּע מִצְוֹת.

With regard to the **four passages that are in the phylacteries,**[H] which are the two passages in the *mezuza* and two additional passages (Exodus 13:1–10, 11–16), the absence of **each prevents fulfillment of the mitzva with the others.** Furthermore, the absence of **even one letter prevents fulfillment of the mitzva with** the rest of **them.** With regard to the **four ritual fringes**[H] on a garment, the absence of **each prevents fulfillment of the mitzva with the others, as the four of them** constitute **one mitzva. Rabbi Yishmael says: The four of them are four** discrete **mitzvot,** and the absence of one does not prevent fulfillment of the mitzva with the rest.

גמ׳ מַאי טַעְמָא? הֲוָיָה כְּתִיב בְּהוּ.

GEMARA **What is the reason** that the absence of any of the seven branches of the Candelabrum prevents fulfillment of the mitzva with the others? The Gemara answers: **It is written concerning them** a term of **being:** "Their knobs and their branches shall be of one piece with it" (Exodus 25:36), and a term of being indicates an indispensable requirement.

תָּנוּ רַבָּנַן: מְנוֹרָה הָיְתָה בָּאָה מִן הָעֶשֶׁת וּמִן הַזָּהָב; עֲשָׂאָהּ מִן הַגְּרוּטָאוֹת – פְּסוּלָה, מִשְּׁאָר מִינֵי מַתָּכוֹת – כְּשֵׁרָה. מַאי שְׁנָא מִן הַגְּרוּטָאוֹת פְּסוּלָה – דִּכְתִיב מִקְשָׁה וַהֲוָיָה, שְׁאָר מִינֵי מַתָּכוֹת נַמִי – זָהָב וַהֲוָיָה!

The Sages taught (*Tosefta*, *Ḥullin* 1:18): The **Candelabrum was fashioned from** a complete **block** [*ha'eshet*][L] **and from gold.**[H] If they **fashioned it from fragments** [*hagerutaot*][L] of gold then it is **unfit,** but if they fashioned it **from other types of metal** rather than gold, it is **fit.** The Gemara asks: **What is different** about a Candelabrum made **from fragments** of gold, that it is rendered **unfit? As it is written** with regard to it: "Their knobs and their branches shall be of one piece with it, the whole of it one beaten work of pure gold" (Exodus 25:36), employing the term **"beaten** [*miksha*]"[L] **and** a term of **being,** indicating that it is an indispensable requirement. But accordingly, a Candelabrum fashioned from **other types of metal** should be rendered unfit **as well,** since the verse states that it is made from **gold and** uses a term of **being.**

אָמַר קְרָא: "תֵּיעָשֶׂה" – לְרַבּוֹת שְׁאָר מִינֵי מַתָּכוֹת. וְאֵימָא: לְרַבּוֹת גְּרוּטָאוֹת! לָא סָלְקָא דַּעְתָּךְ, דְּאַמִּקְשָׁה כְּתִיבָה הֲוָיָה.

The Gemara answers: **The verse states:** "And you shall make a Candelabrum of pure gold; of beaten work **will** the Candelabrum **be made"** (Exodus 25:31), **to include other types of metal.** The Gemara asks: **But** why not **say** that the expression "will be made" serves **to include** a Candelabrum fashioned from **fragments** of gold? The Gemara answers: **It cannot enter your mind** to say this, **as** the term of **being,** which indicates an indispensable requirement, **is written with regard to** the command that the Candelabrum be **a beaten work,** i.e., fashioned from a single block and not from different fragments, as it is stated: "Shall be of one beaten work" (Exodus 25:36).

"תֵּיעָשֶׂה" נַמִי אַמִּקְשָׁה כְּתִיב! "מִקְשָׁה" "מִקְשָׁה" לְעַכֵּב.

The Gemara challenges: But the term **"will be made" is also written with regard to** the command that the Candelabrum be **a beaten work,** as it is written: "Of beaten work will the Candelabrum be made" (Exodus 25:31). The Gemara answers: The term **"beaten work"** appears in Exodus 25:31, and the term **"beaten work"** appears again in Exodus 25:36, **to** demonstrate that this requirement is **indispensable.**

"זָהָב" "זָהָב" נַמִי לְעַכֵּב!

The Gemara challenges: But the term **"gold"** appears in Exodus 25:31, and the term **"gold"** appears again in Exodus 25:36. Why not also say that this **as well** is **to** demonstrate that this requirement is **indispensable?**

הַאי מַאי? אִי אָמְרַתְּ בִּשְׁלָמָא: מִן הַגְּרוּטָאוֹת פְּסוּלָה, מִשְּׁאָר מִינֵי מַתָּכוֹת כְּשֵׁרָה – הַיְינוּ "זָהָב" "זָהָב" "מִקְשָׁה" "מִקְשָׁה" לִדְרָשָׁא; אֶלָּא אִי אָמְרַתְּ: מִן הַגְּרוּטָאוֹת כְּשֵׁרָה, מִשְּׁאָר מִינֵי מַתָּכוֹת פְּסוּלָה – "זָהָב" "זָהָב" "מִקְשָׁה" "מִקְשָׁה" מַאי דָּרְשַׁתְּ בֵּיהּ?

The Gemara answers: **What is this** comparison? **Granted, if you say** that when the Candelabrum is fashioned **from fragments** of gold it is **unfit** but when fashioned **from other types of metal** it is **fit,** then **this is** the reason that it was necessary for the verse to state **"gold," "gold"** twice, and **"a beaten work," "a beaten work"** twice, **to** teach **an interpretation,** which is explained shortly. **But if you say** that when the Candelabrum is fashioned **from fragments** of gold it is **fit** but when fashioned **from other types of metal** it is **unfit, what do you interpret from** the repeated terms **"gold," "gold"** and **"a beaten work," "a beaten work"?**

HALAKHA

Four passages that are in the phylacteries – אַרְבַּע פָּרָשִׁיּוֹת שֶׁבַּתְּפִילִּין: With regard to the four passages that are in the phylacteries, if even one stroke is missing from one letter the mitzva cannot be fulfilled (Rambam *Sefer Ahava, Hilkhot Tefillin UMezuza VeSefer Torah* 1:1; *Shulḥan Arukh, Oraḥ Ḥayyim* 32:4).

Four ritual fringes – אַרְבַּע צִיצִיּוֹת: With regard to the four ritual fringes on a garment, the absence of each prevents fulfillment of the mitzva with the others, as the four of them constitute one mitzva. If even one fringe is missing, it is as though one were not wearing ritual fringes and has neglected a positive mitzva (Rambam *Sefer Ahava, Hilkhot Tzitzit* 1:5; *Shulḥan Arukh, Oraḥ Ḥayyim* 13:1, and see *Mishna Berura* there).

From a complete block and from gold, etc. – מִן הָעֶשֶׁת וּמִן הַזָּהָב וכו׳: If the Candelabrum is made of gold, it must be made from a solid mass, but if it is made from other types of metal it may be hollow (*Kesef Mishne*). Others explain that according to the Rambam it may be hollow even when made from gold. It may never be formed from fragments, irrespective of whether it is made from gold or other types of metal (Rambam *Sefer Avoda, Hilkhot Beit HaBeḥira* 3:4–5).

LANGUAGE

Block [*eshet*] – עֶשֶׁת: Derived from the identical biblical term (see Song of Songs 5:14), this means a block or large piece of cast material. The plural form of the word, *ashashiyyot*, is found elsewhere in the Talmud, for example, in tractate *Yoma* (34b).

Fragments [*gerutaot*] – גְּרוּטָאוֹת: From the Greek γρύτη, *grutē*, meaning a case or tool bag.

Beaten [*miksha*] – מִקְשָׁה: All agree that this refers to the requirement that the Candelabrum be hammered from a single mass of metal rather than by connecting different parts together. There is a dispute with regard to the meaning of the word itself. According to the *Sifrei*, *miksha* is a form of the word hard [*kashe*], and means that it comes from hard matter; perhaps this means that the metal mass is solid and not hollow (see Rambam). Other sources explain that the source is the word stretched [*mashukh*] and refers to the fact that the craftsman pulls the branches of the Candelabrum in either direction when hammering, as opposed to casting the metal in a mold (*Sifrei Zuta*; *Targum Onkelos*; *Lekaḥ Tov*). Rashi explains that it is a form of the word hitting [*hiksheh*], since the sculptor strikes the gold with a hammer. According to the Ibn Ezra, *miksha* refers to a matter performed with precision.

BACKGROUND

Talent – כִּכָּר: The talent is a measure of weight mentioned many times in the Bible. Each talent consisted of fifteen hundred shekels, which is equivalent to sixty *maneh*. In modern measurements it is the equivalent of 21.25 kg. According to the Gemara elsewhere (*Bekhorot* 5a) the sacred *maneh* used in the Tabernacle was double the value of a standard *maneh*; therefore, the weight of the talent should be doubled, to 42.5 kg.

LANGUAGE

Candlestick [*pamot*] – פָּמוֹט: The origin of this word is unclear. There are those who believe that it is a corruption of the Greek φωτισμός, *fotismos*, meaning illumination or light. An alternative opinion is that the word is from the Latin pavimentum, meaning a base, since a *pamot* is a base for a candle.

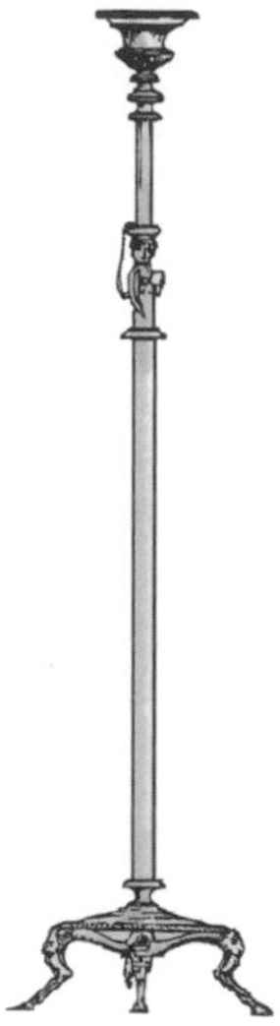

Depiction of a large candlestick from Pompeii, from the mishnaic period

מַאי דְּרָשָׁא? דְּתַנְיָא: "כִּכָּר זָהָב טָהוֹר יַעֲשֶׂה אֹתָהּ אֵת כׇּל הַכֵּלִים הָאֵלֶּה", בָּאָה זָהָב – בָּאָה כִּכָּר, אֵינָהּ בָּאָה זָהָב – אֵינָהּ בָּאָה כִּכָּר; "גְּבִיעֶיהָ כַּפְתּוֹרֶיהָ וּפְרָחֶיהָ", בָּאָה זָהָב – בָּאָה גְּבִיעִים כַּפְתּוֹרִים וּפְרָחִים, אֵינָהּ בָּאָה זָהָב – אֵינָהּ בָּאָה גְּבִיעִים כַּפְתּוֹרִים וּפְרָחִים.

The Gemara elaborates: **What interpretation** is referenced above? **As it is taught** in a *baraita*: The verse states: **"Of a talent of pure gold will it be made, with all these vessels"** (Exodus 25:39); this verse teaches that if the Candelabrum is **fashioned of gold,** it must be **fashioned** with the precise weight of **a talent;**[B] and if it is **not fashioned** of **gold** but of other types of metal, then it does **not** need to be **fashioned** with the precise weight of **a talent.** Similarly, the verse: "And you will make a Candelabrum of pure gold; of beaten work shall the Candelabrum be made, even its base, its shaft, **its goblets, its knobs, and its flowers**" (Exodus 25:31), teaches that if the Candelabrum is **fashioned** of **gold** it must be **fashioned** with **goblets, knobs, and flowers,**[H] and if it is **not fashioned** of **gold** but of other types of metal, then it does **not** need to be **fashioned** with **goblets, knobs, and flowers.**

וְאֵימָא נַמִי: בָּאָה זָהָב – בָּאָה קָנִים, אֵינָהּ בָּאָה זָהָב – אֵינָהּ בָּאָה קָנִים! הַהוּא פָּמוֹט מִיקְּרֵי.

The Gemara asks: **But** then why not **also say** with regard to the branches of the Candelabrum, which are described in Exodus 25:31 along with the term "gold," that if the Candelabrum is **fashioned** of **gold** it must be **fashioned** with **branches,** but if it is **not fashioned** of **gold** but of other types of metal, then it does **not** need to be **fashioned** with **branches?** The Gemara answers: A vessel like **that is called a candlestick** [***pamot***],[L] not a candelabrum.

"וְזֶה מַעֲשֵׂה הַמְּנֹרָה מִקְשָׁה זָהָב", בָּאָה זָהָב – בָּאָה מִקְשָׁה, אֵינָהּ בָּאָה זָהָב – אֵינָהּ בָּאָה מִקְשָׁה.

With regard to the second derivation mentioned, the Gemara elaborates: The verse states: **"And this was the work of the Candelabrum, beaten work of gold,** to the base thereof, and to the flowers thereof, it was beaten work" (Numbers 8:4). This teaches that if the Candelabrum is **fashioned** of **gold** it must be **fashioned** as **a beaten work,** but if it is **not fashioned** of **gold** but of other types of metal, then it does **not** need to be **fashioned** as **a beaten work** and may be made from fragments.

"מִקְשָׁה" דְּסֵיפָא לְמַאי אֲתָא? לְמַעוֹטֵי חֲצוֹצְרוֹת, דְּתַנְיָא: חֲצוֹצְרוֹת הָיוּ בָּאִים מִן הָעֶשֶׁת מִן הַכֶּסֶף; עֲשָׂאָם מִן הַגְּרוּטָאוֹת – כְּשֵׁרִים, מִשְּׁאָר מִינֵי מַתָּכוֹת – פְּסוּלִים.

The Gemara asks: **For what** purpose does the term **"beaten work"** that is repeated again **in the latter clause** of the verse **come?** The Gemara answers: It comes **to exclude** the **trumpets,**[H] teaching that they are fit even if they were not fashioned from a single block. **As it is taught** in a *baraita*: The silver **trumpets** that Moses was commanded to fashion in the wilderness **were** to be **fashioned from** a complete **block** and **from silver.** If one **fashioned them from fragments they are fit,** but if he fashioned them **from other types of metal** then **they are unfit.**

וּמַאי שְׁנָא מִשְּׁאָר מִינֵי מַתָּכוֹת פְּסוּלִים – דִּכְתִיב כֶּסֶף וְהָוְיָה, מִן הַגְּרוּטָאוֹת נַמִי – מִקְשָׁה וְהָוְיָה! מִיעֵט רַחֲמָנָא גַּבֵּי מְנוֹרָה: "מִקְשָׁה הִיא", הִיא – וְלֹא חֲצוֹצְרוֹת.

The Gemara asks: **And what** is **different** about trumpets made **from other types of metal** that **they are** rendered **unfit? As it is written** with regard to the trumpets: "Make for yourself two trumpets of silver; of beaten work you shall make them; and they shall be for you for the calling of the congregation" (Numbers 10:2). The verse employs the terms **silver and being,** indicating that it is an indispensable requirement. But accordingly, trumpets fashioned **from fragments** should be rendered unfit **as well,** since the verse employs the terms **beaten work and being.** The Gemara answers: **The Merciful One excludes** the trumpets when it states **with regard to** the **Candelabrum: "It was beaten work"** (Numbers 8:4), indicating that **it** alone, **but not** the **trumpets,** was beaten work.

§ תָּנוּ רַבָּנַן: כׇּל הַכֵּלִים

§ **The Sages taught** in a *baraita*: **All of the vessels**

HALAKHA

If it is fashioned of gold it must be fashioned with the weight of a talent…it must be fashioned with goblets, knobs, and flowers – בָּאָה זָהָב בָּאָה כִּכָּר...בָּאָה גְּבִיעִים כַּפְתּוֹרִים וּפְרָחִים: If the Candelabrum is made from gold, then all of it, including its goblets, must be the precise weight of a talent. If it is made from another type of metal then its weight is not required to be the weight of a talent. Similarly, if it is made from other types of metal, then it is not required to be made with goblets, knobs, and flowers. This is in accordance with the *baraita* (Rambam *Sefer Avoda, Hilkhot Beit HaBeḥira* 3:4).

Trumpets – חֲצוֹצְרוֹת: The priests would sound trumpets on Festivals and New Moons during the service of the offering. The trumpets were made from a solid mass of silver. If they were made from fragments of silver they are fit, but not if they were made from other types of metal. This is in accordance with the *baraita* (Rambam *Sefer Avoda, Hilkhot Kelei HaMikdash* 3:5).

שֶׁעָשָׂה מֹשֶׁה – כְּשֵׁרִים לוֹ וּכְשֵׁרִים לְדוֹרוֹת, חֲצוֹצְרוֹת – כְּשֵׁרוֹת לוֹ וּפְסוּלוֹת לְדוֹרוֹת.

that Moses fashioned were **fit for his** generation **and** were **fit for** future **generations.** Yet the **trumpets** that Moses fashioned were **fit for his** generation **but** were **unfit for** future **generations.**

חֲצוֹצְרוֹת מַאי טַעְמָא? אִילֵימָא דְּאָמַר קְרָא: ״עֲשֵׂה לְךָ״ – לְךָ וְלֹא לְדוֹרוֹת, אֶלָּא מֵעַתָּה, ״וְעָשִׂיתָ לְּךָ אֲרוֹן עֵץ״, הָכִי נַמִי דִּלְךָ – וְלֹא לְדוֹרוֹת?!

The Gemara asks: **What is the reason** that the **trumpets** were unfit for future generations? **If we say that** it is because **the verse states: "Make for you** two silver trumpets" (Numbers 10:2), meaning that they are fit **for you, but not for** future **generations,** that is difficult; **if that is so,** then the verse: **"Make for you an Ark of wood"** (Deuteronomy 10:1), should **also** teach **that** the Ark is fit only **for you, but not for** future **generations.** This cannot be the *halakha*, as the *baraita* stated explicitly that all vessels, other than the trumpets, that were fashioned by Moses were fit for future generations.

אֶלָּא, אִי לְמַאן דְּאָמַר: ״לְךָ״ – מִשֶּׁלְּךָ, אִי לְמַאן דְּאָמַר: כִּבְיָכוֹל, בְּשֶׁלְּךָ אֲנִי רוֹצֶה יוֹתֵר מִשֶּׁלָּהֶם; הָאִי נַמִי מִיבְּעֵי לֵיהּ לְהָכִי! שָׁאנֵי הָתָם, דְּאָמַר קְרָא ״לְךָ״ ״לְךָ״ תְּרֵי זִימְנֵי: ״עֲשֵׂה לְךָ״ ״וְהָיוּ לְךָ״.

Rather, the term "for you" that is written with regard to the fashioning of the Ark should be understood **either according to the one who says** that **"for you"** means **from your own** property, **or according to the one who says** that God said to Moses: **I desire, as it were,** that the Ark be fashioned **from your** property **more than** I desire that it be fashioned **from** the property **of** the rest of the nation (see *Yoma* 3b). Accordingly, **here too,** with regard to the trumpets, the term "for you" **should be** understood in **this** manner. The Gemara responds: **There,** with regard to the trumpets, **it is different, as the verse states "for you" twice: "Make for you** two trumpets of silver, of beaten work you shall make them, **and they shall be for you** for the calling of the congregation" (Numbers 10:2).

תָּנֵי רַב פָּפָּא בְּרֵיהּ דְּרַב חָנִין קַמֵּיהּ דְּרַב יוֹסֵף: מְנוֹרָה הָיְתָה בָּאָה מִן הָעֶשֶׁת מִן הַזָּהָב, עֲשָׂאָהּ שֶׁל כֶּסֶף – כְּשֵׁרָה; שֶׁל בַּעַץ וְשֶׁל אֵבֶר וְשֶׁל גִּיסְטְרוֹן – רַבִּי פּוֹסֵל, וְרַבִּי יוֹסֵי בְּרַבִּי יְהוּדָה מַכְשִׁיר; שֶׁל עֵץ וְשֶׁל עֶצֶם וְשֶׁל זְכוּכִית – דִּבְרֵי הַכֹּל פְּסוּלָה.

§ The Gemara relates: **Rav Pappa, son of Rav Ḥanin, taught** a *baraita* **before Rav Yosef:** The **Candelabrum** could be **fashioned from** a complete **block** and **from gold.** If one **fashioned it from silver,** it is **fit.** If one fashioned it **from tin, or from lead, or from other types of metal** [*gisteron*],[L] **Rabbi** Yehuda HaNasi **deems** it **unfit, and Rabbi Yosei, son of Rabbi Yehuda, deems** it **fit.** If one fashioned it **from wood, or from bone, or from glass, everyone agrees** that it is **unfit.**

אֲמַר לֵיהּ: מַאי דַּעְתָּךְ? אֲמַר לֵיהּ: בֵּין מָר וּבֵין מָר כְּלָלֵי וּפְרָטֵי דָּרְשִׁי,

Rav Yosef **said to him: What,** in **your opinion,** is the explanation of the dispute between Rabbi Yehuda HaNasi and Rabbi Yosei, son of Rabbi Yehuda? Rav Pappa, son of Rav Ḥanin, **said to him: Both** this **Sage and** that **Sage interpret** the verse: "And you will make a Candelabrum of pure gold; of beaten work will the Candelabrum be made" (Exodus 25:31), by means of the principle of **generalizations and details.** The verse begins with a generalization: "And you will make a Candelabrum," followed by a detail: "Of pure gold," which is then followed by a generalization: "Will the Candelabrum be made." According to the hermeneutic principle of generalizations and details, this teaches that any item that is similar to the detail is also deemed fit.

מִיהוּ מָר סָבַר: מָה הַפְּרָט מְפוֹרָשׁ – שֶׁל מַתֶּכֶת, אַף כֹּל – שֶׁל מַתֶּכֶת, וּמָר סָבַר: מָה הַפְּרָט מְפוֹרָשׁ – דָּבָר חָשׁוּב, אַף כֹּל – דָּבָר חָשׁוּב. אֲמַר לֵיהּ: סְמִי דִּידָךְ מִקַּמֵּי דִּידִי,

But one **Sage,** Rabbi Yosei, son of Rabbi Yehuda, **holds** that **just as** the item mentioned in **the detail** is clearly **defined** as a type **of metal, so too, all** other types **of metal** may be used in fashioning the Candelabrum. **And** one **Sage,** Rabbi Yehuda HaNasi, **holds** that **just as** the item mentioned in **the detail** is clearly **defined** as **an item of substantial value, so too, all items of substantial value** may be used in fashioning the Candelabrum. Rav Yosef **said to him: Remove your** *baraita* **in light of my** *baraita*.

דְּתַנְיָא: כְּלֵי שָׁרֵת שֶׁעֲשָׂאָן שֶׁל עֵץ – רַבִּי פּוֹסֵל, וְרַבִּי יוֹסֵי בְּרַבִּי יְהוּדָה מַכְשִׁיר. בְּמַאי קָא מִיפַּלְגִי? רַבִּי דָּרֵישׁ כְּלָלֵי וּפְרָטֵי, וְרַבִּי יוֹסֵי בְּרַבִּי יְהוּדָה דָּרֵישׁ רִיבּוּיֵי וּמִיעוּטֵי;

Rav Yosef continued: **As it is taught** in a *baraita*: With regard to Temple **service vessels**[H] **that** one **fashioned from wood, Rabbi** Yehuda HaNasi **deems** them **unfit and Rabbi Yosei, son of Rabbi Yehuda, deems** them **fit.** According to this *baraita*, their dispute was with regard to a Candelabrum fashioned from wood, not from metal. Rav Yosef explains: **With regard to what** principle **do they disagree? Rabbi** Yehuda HaNasi **interprets** verses by means of the principle of **generalizations and details, and Rabbi Yosei, son of Rabbi Yehuda, interprets** verses by means of the principle of **amplifications and restrictions.**[N]

LANGUAGE

Other types of metal [*gisteron*] – גִּיסְטְרוֹן: From the Greek κασσίτερος, *kassiteros*, meaning tin. This was possibly the name of a tin and lead alloy, and some commentaries define it as a metal alloy (*Arukh*).

HALAKHA

Service vessels – כְּלֵי שָׁרֵת: The Candelabrum and its vessels, the Table and its vessels, the incense altar, and all other service vessels must be fashioned from some form of metal, and may be fashioned even from tin. If they were made of wood, bone, stone, or glass, they are unfit. This is in accordance with the opinion of Rabbi Yehuda HaNasi, since in a disagreement between Rabbi Yehuda HaNasi and a colleague of his, the *halakha* is in accordance with his opinion. It is also in accordance with the *baraita* taught by Rav Yosef (Rambam *Sefer Avoda, Hilkhot Beit HaBeḥira* 1:18–19, and see Mahari Kurkus and *Kesef Mishne* there).

NOTES

Generalizations and details…amplifications and restrictions – כְּלָלֵי וּפְרָטֵי...רִיבּוּיֵי וּמִיעוּטֵי: These are two distinct methodologies of interpreting verses that speak in general terms and also provide specific details. In the method of generalizations and details, the detail is seen as a clarification of the scope of the generalization. When there is only one generalization followed by a detail, the *halakha* is restricted to the specific instance of the detail; when the detail is followed by a second generalization, the *halakha* is restricted to the type of item specified in the detail. In the method of amplifications and restrictions, the first amplification broadens the application of the *halakha*, and the restriction then restricts the *halakha* to the specific item or scenario mentioned. The second amplification would in principle broaden the application of the *halakha* to what it had been, but the restriction still serves a function in that it limits one specific item or scenario, one deemed least similar to the detail mentioned in the restriction.

LANGUAGE

Portico [*akhsadra*] – אַכְסַדְרָה: From the Greek ἐξέδρα, *exedra*, or the Latin exedra, meaning entrance room or sitting room.

רַבִּי דָּרֵישׁ כְּלָלֵי וּפְרָטֵי: ״וְעָשִׂיתָ מְנֹרַת״ – כְּלָל, ״זָהָב טָהוֹר״ – פְּרָט, ״מִקְשָׁה תֵּיעָשֶׂה הַמְּנוֹרָה״ – חָזַר וְכָלַל; כְּלָל וּפְרָט וּכְלָל – אִי אַתָּה דָּן אֶלָּא כְּעֵין הַפְּרָט, מַה הַפְּרָט מְפוֹרָשׁ – שֶׁל מַתֶּכֶת, אַף כֹּל – שֶׁל מַתֶּכֶת.

Rabbi Yehuda HaNasi **interprets** the verse: "And you will make a Candelabrum of pure gold; of beaten work will the Candelabrum be made" (Exodus 25:31), by means of the principle of **generalizations and details. "And you will make a Candelabrum of"** is a **generalization,** as the material of the Candelabrum is not specified; **"pure gold"** is a **detail,** limiting the material exclusively to gold; and by then stating: **"Of beaten work will the Candelabrum be made,"** the verse **then makes a generalization.** The result is **a generalization and a detail and a generalization,** from which **you may deduce** that the verse is referring **only** to items **similar to the detail,** leading to this conclusion: **Just as** the item mentioned in **the detail** is clearly **defined** as a type **of metal, so too, all** other types **of metal** may be used in fashioning the Candelabrum.

רַבִּי יוֹסֵי בְּרַבִּי יְהוּדָה דָּרֵישׁ רִיבּוּיֵי וּמִיעוּטֵי: ״וְעָשִׂיתָ מְנוֹרַת״ – רִיבָּה, ״זָהָב טָהוֹר״ – מִיעֵט, ״מִקְשָׁה תֵּיעָשֶׂה הַמְּנוֹרָה״ – חָזַר וְרִיבָּה; רִיבָּה וּמִיעֵט וְרִיבָּה – רִיבָּה הַכֹּל, וּמַאי רַבֵּי? רַבֵּי כָּל מִילֵּי, וּמַאי מִיעֵט? מִיעֵט שֶׁל חֶרֶס.

By contrast, **Rabbi Yosei, son of Rabbi Yehuda, interprets** the verse by means of the principle of **amplifications and restrictions. "And you will make a Candelabrum of"** is **an amplification,** as the material of the Candelabrum is not specified; **"pure gold"** is **a restriction,** limiting the material exclusively to gold; and by then stating: **"Of beaten work will the Candelabrum be made,"** the verse **repeated and amplified.** There is a hermeneutical principle that when a verse **amplified and** then **restricted and** then **amplified, it amplified** the relevant category to include **everything** except the specific matter excluded in the restriction. **And what did** the verse **include? It includes all materials,** even wood. **And what did** the verse **exclude** with this restriction? **It excluded** a Candelabrum fashioned **from earthenware,** which is furthest in quality from gold.

אַדְּרַבָּה, סְמֵי דִּידָךְ מִקַּמֵּי דִּידִי! לָא סָלְקָא דַּעְתָּךְ, דְּתַנְיָא: אֵין לוֹ זָהָב – מֵבִיא אַף שֶׁל כֶּסֶף, שֶׁל נְחֹשֶׁת, שֶׁל בַּרְזֶל, וְשֶׁל בְּדִיל, וְשֶׁל עוֹפֶרֶת; רַבִּי יוֹסֵי בְּרַבִּי יְהוּדָה מַכְשִׁיר אַף בְּשֶׁל עֵץ.

Rav Pappa, son of Rav Ḥanin, said to him: **On the contrary, remove your** *baraita* **in light of my** *baraita*. Rav Yosef responded: That **cannot enter your mind, as it is taught** in another *baraita*: If the one who is fashioning the Candelabrum **has no gold, he may bring even** a Candelabrum made **of silver, of copper, of iron, of tin, or of lead. Rabbi Yosei, son of Rabbi Yehuda, deems** it **fit even** if it was fashioned **from wood.** It is evident from this *baraita* that the dispute pertains only to a Candelabrum fashioned from wood, and Rabbi Yehuda HaNasi agrees that it may be fashioned from other types of metal.

וְתַנְיָא אִידָּךְ: לֹא יַעֲשֶׂה אָדָם בַּיִת תַּבְנִית הֵיכָל, אַכְסַדְרָה כְּנֶגֶד אוּלָם, חָצֵר כְּנֶגֶד עֲזָרָה, שֻׁלְחָן כְּנֶגֶד שֻׁלְחָן, מְנוֹרָה כְּנֶגֶד מְנוֹרָה, אֲבָל עוֹשֶׂה הוּא שֶׁל חֲמִשָּׁה וְשֶׁל שִׁשָּׁה וְשֶׁל שְׁמֹנָה; וְשֶׁל שִׁבְעָה לֹא יַעֲשֶׂה וַאֲפִילּוּ מִשְּׁאָר מִינֵי מַתָּכוֹת.

And it is taught in **another** *baraita*: **A person may not construct**[H] **a house** in the exact **form of** the **Sanctuary,** nor **a portico** [*akhsadra*][L] **corresponding to** the **Entrance Hall** of the Sanctuary, nor a **courtyard corresponding to** the Temple **courtyard,** nor **a table corresponding to** the **Table** in the Temple, nor **a candelabrum corresponding to** the **Candelabrum** in the Temple. **But one may fashion** a candelabrum **of five or of six or of eight** branches. **And** one **may not fashion** a candelabrum **of seven** branches, **and** this is the *halakha* **even** if he constructs it **from other kinds of metal** rather than gold, since the Candelabrum used in the Temple may be fashioned from other metals.

HALAKHA

A person may not construct – לֹא יַעֲשֶׂה אָדָם: One may not construct a house in the form of the Sanctuary, nor may one build a portico like the Entrance Hall of the Temple, nor a courtyard like the courtyard of the Temple, nor a table in the shape of the Table in the Temple. One may not construct a metal candelabrum with seven branches, even if it is a different height than that of the Candelabrum in the Temple, and even if it is not made with goblets, knobs, and flowers, as these details are not indispensable (see *Shakh* and *Pitḥei Teshuva*). One may construct a candelabrum with five or eight branches, or a wooden candelabrum with seven branches (*Shakh*). This is in accordance with the *baraita* (*Shulḥan Arukh*, *Yoreh De'a* 141:8).

רַבִּי יוֹסֵי בַּר רַבִּי יְהוּדָה אוֹמֵר: אַף שֶׁל עֵץ לֹא יַעֲשֶׂה, כְּדֶרֶךְ שֶׁעָשׂוּ מַלְכֵי בֵּית חַשְׁמוֹנַאי. אָמְרוּ לוֹ: מִשָּׁם רְאָיָה? שַׁפּוּדִים שֶׁל בַּרְזֶל הָיוּ וְחִיפּוּם בְּבַעַץ, הֶעֱשִׁירוּ – עֲשָׂאוּם שֶׁל כֶּסֶף, חָזְרוּ וְהֶעֱשִׁירוּ – עֲשָׂאוּם שֶׁל זָהָב.

The *baraita* continues: **Rabbi Yosei, son of Rabbi Yehuda, says:** One **may not even fashion** a candelabrum **from wood, in the manner that the kings of the Hasmonean monarchy**[B] **did** in the Temple. The Candelabrum used in the Temple in the time of the Hasmonean kings was fashioned from wood. The Rabbis **said to** Rabbi Yosei, son of Rabbi Yehuda: You seek to bring **a proof from there?** In the time of the Hasmoneans the Candelabrum was not fashioned from wood but from **spits** [***shappudim***][L] **of iron, and they covered them with tin.**[B] Later, when **they grew richer** and could afford to fashion a Candelabrum of higher-quality material, **they fashioned** the Candelabrum **from silver.**[H] When **they again grew richer, they fashioned** the Candelabrum **from gold.**

אָמַר שְׁמוּאֵל מִשְּׁמֵיהּ דְּסָבָא: גּוֹבְהָהּ שֶׁל מְנוֹרָה שְׁמֹנָה עָשָׂר טְפָחִים; הָרַגְלַיִם וְהַפֶּרַח שְׁלֹשָׁה טְפָחִים, וּטְפָחַיִים חָלָק, וְטֶפַח שֶׁבּוֹ גָּבִיעַ וְכַפְתּוֹר וָפֶרַח, וּטְפָחַיִים חָלָק, וְטֶפַח כַּפְתּוֹר,

§ **Shmuel says in the name of** a certain **elder: The height of the Candelabrum**[H] was **eighteen handbreadths. The base and the flower** that was upon the base were a height of **three handbreadths; and two handbreadths** above that were **bare; and** there was above that **one handbreadth, which** had **a goblet, knob, and flower**[N] **on it. And two handbreadths** above that were **bare, and** there was above that **one handbreadth** that had **a knob.**

וּשְׁנֵי קָנִים יוֹצְאִין מִמֶּנּוּ אֶחָד אֵילָךְ וְאֶחָד אֵילָךְ וְנִמְשָׁכִין וְעוֹלִין כְּנֶגֶד גּוֹבְהָהּ שֶׁל מְנוֹרָה, וְטֶפַח חָלָק, וְטֶפַח כַּפְתּוֹר, וּשְׁנֵי קָנִים יוֹצְאִין מִמֶּנּוּ אֶחָד אֵילָךְ וְאֶחָד אֵילָךְ נִמְשָׁכִין וְעוֹלִין כְּנֶגֶד גּוֹבְהָהּ שֶׁל מְנוֹרָה, וְטֶפַח חָלָק, וְטֶפַח כַּפְתּוֹר, וּשְׁנֵי קָנִים יוֹצְאִין מִמֶּנּוּ אֶחָד אֵילָךְ וְאֶחָד אֵילָךְ וְנִמְשָׁכִין וְעוֹלִין כְּנֶגֶד גּוֹבְהָהּ שֶׁל מְנוֹרָה, וּטְפָחַיִים חָלָק, נִשְׁתַּיְּירוּ שָׁם שְׁלֹשָׁה טְפָחִים שֶׁבָּהֶן שְׁלֹשָׁה גְּבִיעִין וְכַפְתּוֹר וָפֶרַח.

And two branches emerge from the knob, **one toward this** direction **and one toward that** direction, **and they extend and rise up to the height of the Candelabrum. And one handbreadth** above that was **bare, and** there was above that **one handbreadth** that had **a knob. And two branches emerge from** the knob, **one toward this** direction **and one toward that** direction, **and they extend and rise up to the height of** the **Candelabrum. And one handbreadth** above that was **bare, and** there was above that one **handbreadth** that had **a knob. And two branches emerge from** the knob, **one toward this direction and one toward that** direction, **and they extend and rise up to the height of** the **Candelabrum. And two handbreadths** above that were **bare.** There then **remained there three handbreadths in which** there were **three goblets, and a knob, and a flower.**

וּגְבִיעִין לְמָה הֵן דּוֹמִין? כְּמִין כּוֹסוֹת אֲלֶכְּסַנְדְּרִיִּים, כַּפְתּוֹרִים לְמָה הֵן דּוֹמִין? כְּמִין תַּפּוּחֵי הַכַּרְתִּיִּים, פְּרָחִים לְמָה הֵן דּוֹמִין? כְּמִין פִּרְחֵי הָעַמּוּדִין. וְנִמְצְאוּ גְּבִיעִין – עֶשְׂרִים וּשְׁנַיִם, כַּפְתּוֹרִים – אַחַד עָשָׂר, פְּרָחִים – תִּשְׁעָה.

And the **goblets** of the Candelabrum, **to what are they similar?**[H] They were **like Alexandrian goblets,**[N] which are long and narrow. The **knobs, to what are they similar?** They were **like** the shape of **the apples of the Cherethites.**[N] The **flowers, to what are they similar?** They were **like the ornaments** that are etched in **columns.**[BN] **And** there **are found to be** a total of **twenty-two goblets, eleven knobs,** and **nine flowers** on the Candelabrum.

HALAKHA

When they grew richer they fashioned the Candelabrum from silver, etc. – **הֶעֱשִׁירוּ עֲשָׂאוּם שֶׁל כֶּסֶף וכו׳:** If the nation is poor, the service vessels may be fashioned even from tin, and if they become affluent then new vessels are fashioned from gold. If the nation is able and willing, then even the bowls, the rakes of the external altar, the spits, and the measuring vessels are fashioned of gold. If they are able to afford it, then even the gates of the courtyard are covered with gold (Rambam *Sefer Avoda, Hilkhot Beit HaBeḥira* 1:19).

The height of the Candelabrum – **גּוֹבְהָהּ שֶׁל מְנוֹרָה:** The height of the Candelabrum was eighteen handbreadths: The base and the flower were three handbreadths; two handbreadths were then bare. There was then one handbreadth containing the goblet, knob, and flower; two handbreadths were then bare, and there was one handbreadth for the knob. Two branches emerged from the knob, one on each side, which extended and reached the height of the Candelabrum. Then there was another bare handbreadth, and one handbreadth for the knob. Two more branches emerged from that knob, one on each side, which extended and reached the height of the Candelabrum. Then there was one bare handbreadth, and one handbreadth for the next knob. Two more branches emerged from that knob, one on each side, which extended and reached the height of the Candelabrum. There were then two bare handbreadths, and there remained three handbreadths in which there were three goblets, a knob, and a flower (Rambam *Sefer Avoda, Hilkhot Beit HaBeḥira* 3:10).

The goblets of the Candelabrum, to what are they similar, etc. – **וּגְבִיעִין לְמָה הֵן דּוֹמִין וכו׳:** The goblets of the Candelabrum resembled Alexandrian goblets, whose edges were wide and bottoms narrow. The knobs were like Cherethite apples, which are slightly elongated like an egg. The flowers were like the tops of columns, which resembled a bowl with its edges bent outward. This is in accordance with the *baraita* (Rambam *Sefer Avoda, Hilkhot Beit HaBeḥira* 3:9).

BACKGROUND

Kings of the Hasmonean monarchy – **מַלְכֵי בֵּית חַשְׁמוֹנַאי:** The Hasmonean dynasty was begun by Mattathias and his sons, who led the revolt against the Seleucid king Antioch in 168 BCE. They achieved sovereignty for the residents of Judea and rededicated the Temple, commemorated by the festival of Hanukkah. The dynasty lasted approximately 130 years.

Tin [*ba'atz*] – **בַּעַץ:** *Ba'atza* is Aramaic for tin. Tin is an easy metal to work with, and it was used and is still used today for soldering and coating different metals because it has an appearance similar to silver, although it is darker, and because it is not easily oxidized and therefore prevents rusting.

The ornaments in columns – **פִּרְחֵי הָעַמּוּדִין:** The Rambam describes ornaments similar to the curls on the capital of the column pictured below. In between the curls, one can also see geometric decorations similar to flowers. These resemble Rashi's interpretation of the ornaments mentioned here.

Capital from an Ionic column

LANGUAGE

Spits [*shappudim*] – **שַׁפּוּדִים:** Apparently from the Greek σποδός, *spodos*, meaning ashes. Others believe it to be of Semitic origin, as it resembles other similar words in Syriac.

NOTES

Goblet, knob, and flower – **גָּבִיעַ וְכַפְתּוֹר וָפֶרַח:** According to the Rambam, these were formed one on top of the other, with the flower formed above the knob, which was formed above the goblet. According to Rashi, each was formed on a different side of the Candelabrum, possibly because it is hard to assume that all three would fit within one handbreadth. There are those who explain as Rashi does even with regard to other parts of the Candelabrum, even though those parts have room for all three to be formed one on top of the other (*Ma'aseh Ḥoshev*).

Like Alexandrian goblets – **כְּמִין כּוֹסוֹת אֲלֶכְּסַנְדְּרִיִּים:** According to Rashi, they were long and narrow. According to the Rambam, they were similar to goblets that are wide on top and narrow toward the base. From the image that the Rambam added to his commentary on the mishna, it appears that they were like overturned goblets, with the wide top at the bottom and the narrow part above.

The apples of the Cherethites [*Kartiyyim*] – **תַּפּוּחֵי הַכַּרְתִּיִּים:** According to Rashi, the Gemara is referring to apples that came from the country or island of the Cherethites (see Zephaniah 2:5). Other early commentaries have other versions of this word, which appears as *beratim* or *berutim*. It is explained in the *Arukh* that it refers to an apple whose length is greater than its width. Similarly, the Ramban explains that they are not perfectly round, but rather elongated like an egg. Another explanation is that it refers to a type of pomegranate (*Sefer Kadmoniyyot HaYehudim*).

The ornaments in columns – **פִּרְחֵי הָעַמּוּדִין:** Rashi explains that there are designs that are etched on the body of the Candelabrum, like the etchings that are made in columns. The Rambam, citing the *ge'onim*, explains that it refers to a flower border that is made around each branch of the Candelabrum, like the blossoms on the tops of columns of earlier time periods.

HALAKHA

The goblets, the absence of each prevents fulfillment of the mitzva with the others – **גְּבִיעִים מְעַכְּבִין וכו׳**: The Candelabrum contained twenty-two goblets, nine flowers, and eleven knobs. If even one of these was absent, the Candelabrum was unfit; this is in accordance with the *baraita*. This is the *halakha* with regard to a gold Candelabrum. If the Candelabrum was fashioned from another type of metal, then it did not contain goblets, knobs, and flowers, in accordance with the *baraita* on 28a (Rambam *Sefer Avoda, Hilkhot Beit HaBeḥira* 3:3–4).

גְּבִיעִים מְעַכְּבִין זֶה אֶת זֶה, כַּפְתּוֹרִים מְעַכְּבִין זֶה אֶת זֶה, פְּרָחִים מְעַכְּבִין זֶה אֶת זֶה, גְּבִיעִים כַּפְתּוֹרִים וּפְרָחִים – מְעַכְּבִין זֶה אֶת זֶה.

With regard to the **goblets,** the absence of **each prevents fulfillment of the mitzva with the others;**[H] with regard to the **knobs,** the absence of **each prevents fulfillment of the mitzva with the others;** with regard to the **flowers,** the absence of **each prevents fulfillment of the mitzva with the others.** With regard to the **goblets, knobs, and flowers,** the absence of **each prevents fulfillment of the mitzva with the others.**

בִּשְׁלָמָא גְּבִיעִים עֶשְׂרִים וּשְׁנַיִם – דִּכְתִיב: ״וּבַמְּנֹרָה אַרְבָּעָה גְבִעִים״ וגו׳, וּכְתִיב: ״שְׁלֹשָׁה גְבִעִים מְשֻׁקָּדִים בַּקָּנֶה הָאֶחָד כַּפְתֹּר וָפֶרַח״ וגו׳, אַרְבָּעָה דִּידָהּ

The Gemara asks: **Granted,** there were **twenty-two goblets** on the Candelabrum, **as it is written: "And in the Candelabrum four goblets** made like almond blossoms" (Exodus 25:34), **and it is written: "Three goblets made like almond blossoms in one branch, a knob, and a flower;** and three goblets made like almond blossoms in the other branch, a knob, and a flower; so for the six branches going out of the Candelabrum" (Exodus 25:33). Therefore, the Candelabrum contains the **four** goblets **of its** main shaft,

Perek **III**
Daf **29** Amud **a**

NOTES

Shimi, is it you – **שִׁימִי אַתְּ**: According to Rashi, Rav asks in bewilderment: Can it be that you, the great Sage Shimi, do not know the answer to this question on your own? (Rashi on *Bekhorot* 43b). Alternatively, in tractate *Nidda* (24a), Rashi explains that Rav addressed his grandson Rav Shimi bar Ḥiyya in such a manner out of fondness for him, as if to say: Shimi, you know the answer.

וּתְמָנֵי סְרֵי דְּקָנִים – הָא עֶשְׂרִין וְתַרְתֵּין; כַּפְתּוֹרִין נַמִי אַחַד עָשָׂר: כַּפְתּוֹרִין תְּרֵי דִּידָהּ, וְשִׁשָּׁה דְּקָנִים, וְכַפְתֹּר וְכַפְתֹּר וְכַפְתֹּר – הָא חַד סָר;

and the **eighteen of the** six **branches; this** equals **twenty-two** goblets. Concerning the **knobs as well,** it is clear how the number **eleven** was reached. The Candelabrum contains the **two knobs of its** main shaft, as the verse states: "Its knobs" (Exodus 25:34), with the plural "knobs" indicating that there were two, **and the six of** the six **branches,** as it is written: "In one branch, a knob and a flower" (Exodus 25:33). In addition to these eight knobs, the verse states: "**And a knob** under two branches of one piece with it, **and a knob** under two branches of one piece with it, **and a knob** under two branches of one piece with it" (Exodus 25:35); **this** equals **eleven** knobs.

אֶלָּא פְּרָחִים תִּשְׁעָה מְנָלַן? פְּרָחִים תְּרֵי דִּידָהּ וְשִׁשָּׁה דְּקָנִים – תְּמָנְיָא הָווּ! אֲמַר רַב שַׁלְמָן, כְּתִיב: ״עַד יְרֵכָהּ עַד פִּרְחָהּ מִקְשָׁה הִיא״.

But from where do we derive that the Candelabrum contained **nine flowers?** According to the verse there are the **two flowers of its** main shaft, as it is written: "And its flowers" (Exodus 25:34), **and the six of** the six **branches,** as it is written: "In one branch, a knob and a flower" (Exodus 25:33), meaning that **there are eight,** not nine, flowers on the Candelabrum. **Rav Shalman said** in response: **It is written: "It was a beaten work, from the base to the flower"** (Numbers 8:4), which teaches that there was a ninth flower near the base.

אָמַר רַב: גּוֹבְהָהּ שֶׁל מְנוֹרָה תִּשְׁעָה טְפָחִים. אֵיתִיבֵיהּ רַב שִׁימִי בַּר חִיָּיא לְרַב: אֶבֶן הָיְתָה לִפְנֵי מְנוֹרָה וּבָהּ שָׁלֹשׁ מַעֲלוֹת, שֶׁעָלֶיהָ הַכֹּהֵן עוֹמֵד וּמֵטִיב אֶת הַנֵּרוֹת!

Rav says: The height of the **Candelabrum** is **nine handbreadths. Rav Shimi bar Ḥiyya raised an objection to** the statement of **Rav:** We learned in a mishna (*Tamid* 30b): **There was a stone before** the **Candelabrum**[H] **and it had three steps, upon which the priest** would **stand and prepare the lamps** for kindling. If the Candelabrum was only nine handbreadths high, why would it be necessary for the priest to stand on an elevated surface to reach the lamps?

אֲמַר לֵיהּ: שִׁימִי, אַתְּ? כִּי קָאָמִינָא מִשְּׁפַת קָנִים וּלְמַעְלָה.

Rav **said to him: Shimi,** is it **you**[N] who is asking me such a question? **When I said** that the height of the Candelabrum is nine handbreadths, I was referring not to the total height, which is eighteen handbreadths; rather, I meant that the Candelabrum is nine handbreadths **from the point** at which the **branches** extend from the main shaft **and above.**

HALAKHA

There was a stone before the Candelabrum – **אֶבֶן הָיְתָה לִפְנֵי מְנוֹרָה**: A stone with three steps stood before the Candelabrum in the Temple. It is upon this stone that the priest would stand to prepare the lamps. In addition, the priest would rest the utensils holding the oil, the tongs, and the pans upon this stone while he prepared the lamps (Rambam *Sefer Avoda, Hilkhot Beit HaBeḥira* 3:11).

כְּתִיב: ״וְהַפֶּרַח וְהַנֵּרוֹת וְהַמֶּלְקָחַיִם זָהָב הוּא מִכְלוֹת זָהָב״, מַאי ״מִיכְלוֹת זָהָב״? אָמַר רַב אַמִי: שֶׁכִּילַּתּוּ לְכָל זָהָב סָגוּר שֶׁל שְׁלֹמֹה; דְּאָמַר רַב יְהוּדָה אָמַר רַב: עֶשֶׂר מְנוֹרוֹת עָשָׂה שְׁלֹמֹה, וְכָל אַחַת וְאַחַת הֵבִיא לָהּ אֶלֶף כִּכַּר זָהָב, וְהִכְנִיסוּהוּ אֶלֶף פְּעָמִים לַכּוּר וְהֶעֱמִידוּהוּ עַל כִּכָּר.

§ **It is written: "And the flowers, and the lamps, and the tongs, of gold, and that perfect gold [*mikhlot zahav*]"** (II Chronicles 4:21). The Gemara asks: **What is** meant by ***mikhlot zahav*****? Rav Ami says:** It is a reference to the fact **that** the Candelabrum and its vessels **exhausted [*kilattu*] all of Solomon's pure [*sagur*]**[L] **gold [*zahav*],**[N] which was used in its fashioning in such great quantities. **As Rav Yehuda says** that **Rav said: Solomon made ten Candelabrums, and for each and every one he brought one thousand talents of gold, and they placed** the gold **in the furnace** to refine it **one thousand times, until they reduced** the gold **to** one **talent** for each Candelabrum, as it is stated: "Of a talent of pure gold shall it be made" (Exodus 25:39).

אִינִי? וְהָכְתִיב: ״וְכָל כְּלֵי מַשְׁקֵה הַמֶּלֶךְ שְׁלֹמֹה זָהָב וְכָל כְּלֵי בֵּית יַעַר הַלְּבָנוֹן זָהָב סָגוּר אֵין כֶּסֶף נֶחְשָׁב בִּימֵי שְׁלֹמֹה לִמְאוּמָה״! זָהָב סָגוּר קָא אָמְרִינַן.

The Gemara asks: **Is that so** that all of Solomon's gold was exhausted for the fashioning of the Candelabrum and its vessels? **But isn't it written: "And all King Solomon's drinking vessels were of gold, and all the vessels of the house of the forest of Lebanon were of pure gold; silver was nothing accounted of in the days of Solomon"** (II Chronicles 9:20)? The Gemara answers: **We are saying** that Solomon's **pure gold** was exhausted for the fashioning of the Candelabrum, but not all of his gold.

וּמִי חָסֵר כּוּלֵּי הַאי? וְהָתַנְיָא, רַבִּי יוֹסֵי בְּרַבִּי יְהוּדָה אוֹמֵר: מַעֲשֶׂה וְהָיְתָה [מְנוֹרַת] בֵּית הַמִּקְדָּשׁ יְתֵירָה עַל שֶׁל מֹשֶׁה בְּדִינָר זָהָב קוֹרְדִּיקִינִי, וְהִכְנִיסוּהָ שְׁמוֹנִים פְּעָמִים לַכּוּר וְהֶעֱמִידוּהָ עַל כִּכָּר! כֵּיוָן דְּקָאֵי קָאֵי.

The Gemara asks: **And would** refining the gold **reduce** it **to this extent,** that one thousand talents of gold would be reduced to one talent? **But isn't it taught** in a *baraita*: **Rabbi Yosei, son of Rabbi Yehuda, says: An incident** occurred where the weight of **the Candelabrum of the Temple was** found to be **greater than** the weight of the Candelabrum **of Moses by** one ***Kordikini* gold dinar, and they placed it in the furnace eighty times until** the weight of the Candelabrum **stood at** precisely one **talent.** Evidently, putting the Candelabrum into a furnace reduces its weight by very little. The Gemara answers: **Once it is standing, it is standing,** i.e., since the gold was refined to such a degree in the time of Solomon, later when it was refined eighty times it was reduced by the weight of only one dinar.

אָמַר רַבִּי שְׁמוּאֵל בַּר נַחְמָנִי אָמַר רַבִּי יוֹנָתָן, מַאי דִּכְתִיב: ״עַל הַמְּנֹרָה הַטְּהֹרָה״? שֶׁיָּרְדוּ מַעֲשֶׂיהָ מִמְּקוֹם טָהֳרָה. אֶלָּא מֵעַתָּה, ״עַל הַשֻּׁלְחָן הַטָּהוֹר״ – שֶׁיָּרְדוּ מַעֲשָׂיו מִמָּקוֹם טָהוֹר? אֶלָּא, טָהוֹר מִכְּלָל שֶׁהוּא טָמֵא, הָכָא נַמִי – טְהוֹרָה מִכְּלָל שֶׁהִיא טְמֵאָה!

§ **Rabbi Shmuel bar Naḥmani says** that **Rabbi Yonatan says: What is** the meaning of that **which is written: "Upon the pure Candelabrum"** (Leviticus 24:4)? It teaches **that** the procedure for **fashioning it descended,** i.e., was shown to Moses, **from the place of purity,** i.e., by God, who showed Moses a model of the Candelabrum. The Gemara asks: **If that is so,** is that to say that phrase **"upon the pure Table"** (Leviticus 24:6)[NH] also teaches **that** the procedure for **fashioning it** was shown to Moses **from the place of purity? Rather,** the expression "the **pure** Table" teaches, **by inference, that it is** susceptible to becoming **ritually impure. Here too,** the expression "the **pure** Candelabrum" teaches, **by inference, that it is** susceptible to becoming **ritually impure.**

בִּשְׁלָמָא הָתָם כִּדְרֵישׁ לָקִישׁ, דְּאָמַר רֵישׁ לָקִישׁ, מַאי דִּכְתִיב: ״עַל הַשֻּׁלְחָן הַטָּהוֹר״, מִכְּלָל שֶׁהוּא טָמֵא? כְּלִי עֵץ הֶעָשׂוּי לְנַחַת הוּא, וְכָל כְּלִי עֵץ הֶעָשׂוּי לְנַחַת אֵינוֹ מְקַבֵּל טוּמְאָה! אֶלָּא, מְלַמֵּד שֶׁמַּגְבִּיהִין אוֹתוֹ לְעוֹלֵי רְגָלִים וּמַרְאִים לָהֶם לֶחֶם הַפָּנִים, וְאוֹמֵר לָהֶם: רְאוּ חִיבַּתְכֶם לִפְנֵי הַמָּקוֹם.

The Gemara rejects this: **Granted,** the inference drawn **there** with regard to the Table is **in accordance with** that **which Reish Lakish** says; **as Reish Lakish says: What** is the meaning of that **which is written: "Upon the pure Table"** (Leviticus 24:6)? The expression "pure Table" teaches, **by inference, that it is** susceptible to becoming **ritually impure,** but why? Isn't the Table **a wooden vessel designated to rest**[H] in a fixed place, **and any wooden vessel that is designated to rest** in a fixed place **is not susceptible to** becoming **ritually impure? Rather,** this **teaches that** the Table was not always left in a fixed place; the priests would **lift** the Table with its shewbread **to display the shewbread to the pilgrims**[N] standing in the Temple courtyard, **and** a priest would **say to them: See your affection before the Omnipresent.** For this reason, the Table is susceptible to becoming ritually impure.

NOTES

Pure gold [*zahav sagur*] – זָהָב סָגוּר: Rashi explains in accordance with the Gemara in tractate *Yoma* (45a) that it is called *zahav sagur*, which literally means closed gold, because when a shop opens to sell it, all the other shops close [*nisgarot*], as no one is interested in purchasing any other type of gold. The Ralbag explains that it means pure gold, and it is called *zahav sagur* because it is closed in a forge to remove its imperfections (see I Kings 7:49).

Upon the pure Table, etc. – עַל הַשֻּׁלְחָן הַטָּהוֹר וכו׳: The Rashba explains that the reason the Gemara assumes that the form of the Table was not shown to Moses, as was the form of the Candelabrum, is that it is only with regard to the Candelabrum that the verse states: "According to the pattern which the Lord had shown Moses, so he made the Candelabrum" (Numbers 8:4). Alternatively, the design of the Table was relatively straightforward, so there would be no need for it to be shown to Moses.

That they would lift the Table to display the shewbread to the pilgrims – שֶׁמַּגְבִּיהִין אוֹתוֹ לְעוֹלֵי רְגָלִים וּמַרְאִים לָהֶם לֶחֶם הַפָּנִים: According to the Rambam, the Table was taken out of the Sanctuary (Rambam *Sefer Tahara, Hilkhot Metamei Mishkav UMoshav* 11:11). *Tosafot* in tractate *Ḥagiga* (26b) explain that the Table was not taken out of the Sanctuary; it was simply shown through the entrance of the Sanctuary.

HALAKHA

The pure Table, etc. – הַשֻּׁלְחָן הַטָּהוֹר וכו׳: At the conclusion of each Festival, all of the vessels in the Temple would be immersed in a ritual bath, since they were touched over the course of the Festival by those who are unreliable with regard to ritual purity. Therefore, all were told: Do not touch the Table in the Temple when it is shown to the pilgrims during the Festival, as this will cause it to be ritually impure after the Festival, and it will then require immersion in a ritual bath and the arrival of nightfall (Rambam *Sefer Tahara, Hilkhot Metamei Mishkav UMoshav* 11:11).

Wooden vessel designated to rest – כְּלִי עֵץ הֶעָשׂוּי לְנַחַת: A wooden utensil designated to remain fixed in its place and never moved is not susceptible to contracting ritual impurity, either by Torah or rabbinic law, even if it is small (Rambam *Sefer Tahara, Hilkhot Kelim* 3:1).

LANGUAGE

Pure [*sagur*] – סָגוּר: It is clear that this describes high-quality gold, but it is difficult to determine the literal meaning of the term *sagur* in terms of other known meanings of the word. In any event, there is a similar term in Akkadian, *skaru*, meaning a type of pure gold.

מַאי חִיבַּתְכֶם? כִּדְרַבִּי יְהוֹשֻׁעַ בֶּן לֵוִי, דְּאָמַר רַבִּי יְהוֹשֻׁעַ בֶּן לֵוִי: נֵס גָּדוֹל נַעֲשָׂה בְּלֶחֶם הַפָּנִים, סִילּוּקוֹ כְּסִידּוּרוֹ, שֶׁנֶּאֱמַר: ״לָשׂוּם לֶחֶם חֹם בְּיוֹם הִלָּקְחוֹ״.

Parenthetically, the Gemara asks: **What** is meant by: See **your affection** before God? It is **in accordance with** that which **Rabbi Yehoshua ben Levi** says, **as Rabbi Yehoshua ben Levi says: A great miracle was performed with the shewbread:** Its condition at the time of **its removal** from the Table, after having been left there for a week, was **like** its condition at the time of **its arrangement** on the Table, **as it is stated: "To place hot bread on the day when it was taken away"** (I Samuel 21:7), indicating that it was as hot on the day of its removal as it was on the day when it was placed on the Table.

אֶלָּא הָכָא טְהוֹרָה מִכְּלָל שֶׁהִיא טְמֵאָה – פְּשִׁיטָא, כְּלֵי מַתָּכוֹת נִינְהוּ, וּכְלֵי מַתָּכוֹת מְקַבְּלִין טוּמְאָה! אֶלָּא שֶׁיָּרְדוּ מַעֲשֶׂיהָ מִמְּקוֹם טׇהֳרָה.

The Gemara resumes stating its objection: **But here,** with regard to the Candelabrum, there is no reason to explain that the expression "the **pure** Candelabrum" teaches, **by inference, that it is** susceptible to becoming **ritually impure;** this is **obvious,** as the Candelabrums **are metal vessels, and metal vessels are susceptible to** becoming **ritually impure** whether or not they remain in a fixed location. **Rather,** it must be that the expression "the pure Candelabrum" teaches **that** the procedure for **fashioning it descended,** i.e., was shown to Moses, **from the place of purity.**

תַּנְיָא, רַבִּי יוֹסֵי בְּרַבִּי יְהוּדָה אוֹמֵר: אֲרוֹן שֶׁל אֵשׁ וְשֻׁלְחָן שֶׁל אֵשׁ וּמְנוֹרָה שֶׁל אֵשׁ יָרְדוּ מִן הַשָּׁמַיִם, וְרָאָה מֹשֶׁה וְעָשָׂה כְּמוֹתָם, שֶׁנֶּאֱמַר: ״וּרְאֵה וַעֲשֵׂה בְּתַבְנִיתָם אֲשֶׁר אַתָּה מׇרְאֶה בָּהָר״.

§ **It is taught** in a *baraita*: **Rabbi Yosei, son of Rabbi Yehuda, says: An Ark of fire and a Table of fire and a Candelabrum of fire descended from the Heavens, and Moses saw** their format **and fashioned** the vessels for the Tabernacle **in their likeness. As it is stated** after the command to fashion these items: **"And see that you make them after their pattern, which is being shown to you in the mount"** (Exodus 25:40).

אֶלָּא מֵעַתָּה, ״וַהֲקֵמֹתָ אֶת הַמִּשְׁכָּן כְּמִשְׁפָּטוֹ אֲשֶׁר הׇרְאֵיתָ בָּהָר״ הָכִי נָמֵי? הָכָא כְּתִיב: ״כְּמִשְׁפָּטוֹ״, הָתָם כְּתִיב: ״כְּתַבְנִיתָם״.

The Gemara asks: **If that is so,** is that to say that the verse: **"And you shall set up the Tabernacle according to its fashion which has been shown to you in the mount"** (Exodus 26:30), **also** indicates that God showed Moses a Tabernacle of fire? The Gemara answers: **Here,** with regard to the Tabernacle, **it is written: "According to its fashion,"** meaning that it should be built according to the instructions given to Moses, whereas **there,** with regard to the Ark, Table, and Candelabrum, **it is written: "After their pattern,"** indicating that an actual model of the items was shown to Moses.

אָמַר רַבִּי חִיָּיא בַּר אַבָּא אָמַר רַבִּי יוֹחָנָן: גַּבְרִיאֵל חָגוּר כְּמִין פְּסִיקְיָא הָיָה, וְהֶרְאָה לוֹ לְמֹשֶׁה מַעֲשֵׂה מְנוֹרָה, דִּכְתִיב: ״וְזֶה מַעֲשֵׂה הַמְּנֹרָה״.

Apropos this discussion the Gemara relates: **Rabbi Ḥiyya bar Abba says** that **Rabbi Yoḥanan says:** The angel **Gabriel** was **girded with a type of** wide **belt** [*pesikiyya*][L] in the manner of artisans who tie up their clothes to prevent these clothes from hindering them in their work. **And he showed** the precise **way to fashion the Candelabrum to Moses, as it is written: "And this is the work of the Candelabrum"** (Numbers 8:4), and the term "this" indicates that an exact replica was shown to him.

תָּנָא דְּבֵי רַבִּי יִשְׁמָעֵאל: שְׁלֹשָׁה דְּבָרִים הָיוּ קָשִׁין לוֹ לְמֹשֶׁה, עַד שֶׁהֶרְאָה לוֹ הַקָּדוֹשׁ בָּרוּךְ הוּא בְּאֶצְבָּעוֹ, וְאֵלּוּ הֵן: מְנוֹרָה, וְרֹאשׁ חֹדֶשׁ, וּשְׁרָצִים; מְנוֹרָה – דִּכְתִיב: ״וְזֶה מַעֲשֵׂה הַמְּנֹרָה״; רֹאשׁ חוֹדֶשׁ – דִּכְתִיב: ״הַחֹדֶשׁ הַזֶּה לָכֶם רֹאשׁ חֳדָשִׁים״; שְׁרָצִים – דִּכְתִיב: ״וְזֶה לָכֶם הַטָּמֵא״; וְיֵשׁ אוֹמְרִים: אַף הִלְכוֹת שְׁחִיטָה, שֶׁנֶּאֱמַר: ״וְזֶה אֲשֶׁר תַּעֲשֶׂה עַל הַמִּזְבֵּחַ״.

The school of Rabbi Yishmael taught: Three matters were difficult for Moses to comprehend precisely, **until the Holy One, Blessed be He, showed** them to **him with His finger, and these are** the three matters: The form of the **Candelabrum, and** the exact size of the **new moon, and** the impure **creeping animals.** The **Candelabrum** was shown to him, **as it is written: "And this is the work of the Candelabrum"** (Numbers 8:4). The **new moon** was shown to him, **as it is written: "This month shall be for you the beginning of months"** (Exodus 12:2). The **creeping animals** were shown to him, **as it is written: "And these are they which are unclean for you** among the swarming things" (Leviticus 11:29). **And there are** those **who say** that God **also** showed Moses **the *halakhot* of slaughtering, as it is stated: "Now this is that which you shall sacrifice upon the altar"** (Exodus 29:38), and slaughtering is the first ritual of sacrifice.

״שְׁתֵּי פָּרָשִׁיּוֹת שֶׁבַּמְּזוּזָה מְעַכְּבוֹת זוֹ אֶת זוֹ, וַאֲפִילּוּ כְּתָב אֶחָד מְעַכְּבָן״. פְּשִׁיטָא!

§ The mishna teaches: With regard to the **two passages that are in the *mezuza*,**[H] the absence of **each prevents fulfillment of the mitzva with the others. And** furthermore, the absence of **even one letter prevents fulfillment of the mitzva with** the rest of **them.** The Gemara asks: Isn't it **obvious** that the absence of even one letter prevents fulfillment of the mitzva, since it is written: "And you shall write them [*ukhtavtam*]" (Deuteronomy 6:9), which teaches that the writing [*ketav*] must be complete [*tam*]?

LANGUAGE

Belt [*pesikiyya*] – **פְּסִיקְיָא:** From the Latin fascia, meaning wide belt or girdle.

HALAKHA

Two passages that are in the *mezuza* – שְׁתֵּי פָּרָשִׁיּוֹת שֶׁבַּמְּזוּזָה: With regard to the two passages that are in the *mezuza*, i.e., the first and second paragraphs of *Shema*, the absence of even one letter prevents fulfillment of the mitzva by Torah law (Rambam *Sefer Ahava*, *Hilkhot Tefillin UMezuza VeSefer Torah* 1:2; *Shulḥan Arukh*, *Oraḥ Ḥayyim* 32:4 and *Yoreh De'a* 288:7).

אָמַר רַב יְהוּדָה אָמַר רַב: לֹא נִצְרְכָה אֶלָּא לְקוֹצָהּ שֶׁל יוֹד. וְהָא נַמִּי פְּשִׁיטָא! אֶלָּא לְכִאידָךְ דְּרַב יְהוּדָה אָמַר רַב, דְּאָמַר רַב יְהוּדָה אָמַר רַב: כׇּל אוֹת שֶׁאֵין גְּוִיל מוּקָּף לָהּ מֵאַרְבַּע רוּחוֹתֶיהָ – פְּסוּלָה.

Rav Yehuda says that **Rav says:** It was **necessary** to state that **only** to teach that even the absence of **the thorn,** i.e., the small stroke, **of** a letter ***yod***[N] prevents fulfillment of the mitzva. The Gemara asks: **But** isn't **this also obvious,** since the letter is not formed properly? **Rather,** it is necessary **according to another** statement **that Rav Yehuda says** that Rav says, **as Rav Yehuda says** that **Rav says: Any letter that is not encircled with** blank **parchment**[H] **on** all **four of its sides,** i.e., where its ink connects to the letter above it, below it, preceding it, or succeeding it, is **unfit.** When the mishna makes reference to one letter preventing fulfillment of the mitzva, it is referring to a letter that touches an adjacent letter.

אָמַר אֲשִׁיָּאן בַּר נַדְבָּךְ מִשְּׁמֵיהּ דְּרַב יְהוּדָה: נִיקַּב תּוֹכוֹ שֶׁל הֵ״י – כָּשֵׁר, יְרֵיכוֹ – פָּסוּל. אָמַר רַבִּי זֵירָא: לְדִידִי מְפָרְשָׁה לִי מִינֵּיהּ דְּרַב הוּנָא; וְרַבִּי יַעֲקֹב אָמַר, לְדִידִי מְפָרְשָׁה לִי מִינֵּיהּ דְּרַב יְהוּדָה: נִיקַּב תּוֹכוֹ שֶׁל הֵ״י – כָּשֵׁר; יְרֵיכוֹ, אִם נִשְׁתַּיֵּיר בּוֹ כְּשִׁיעוּר אוֹת קְטַנָּה – כָּשֵׁר, וְאִם לָאו – פָּסוּל.

Ashiyan bar Nadbakh says in the name of Rav Yehuda: If the inner part **of the letter *heh* was perforated**[H] it is **fit,**[N] but if the perforation was in **the leg of** the letter *heh*[BH] it is **unfit. Rabbi Zeira says:** This matter was **explained to me by Rav Huna, and Rabbi Ya'akov says:** This matter was **explained to me by Rav Yehuda: If the inner** part **of the letter *heh* was perforated** it is **fit.** In a case where the perforation was in **the leg of** the letter *heh,* then **if there remained in** the leg that is attached to the roof of the letter **the equivalent of the measure of a small letter,**[BN] i.e., the letter *yod,* then it is **fit. But if not,** it is **unfit.**

אַגְרָא חֲמוּהּ דְּרַבִּי אַבָּא

The Gemara relates: **Agra, the father-in-law of Rabbi Abba,**

BACKGROUND

Inner part of the letter *heh*…leg of the letter *heh* – תּוֹכוֹ שֶׁל הֵ״י...יְרֵיכוֹ:

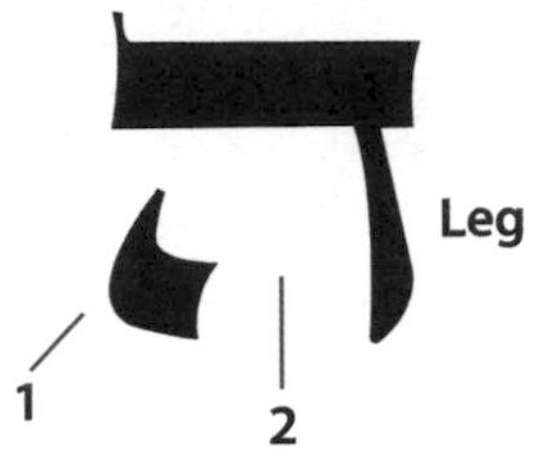

Inner part of the letter *heh* according to two explanations of Rashi

If there remained in the leg the equivalent of the measure of a small letter – אִם נִשְׁתַּיֵּיר בּוֹ כְּשִׁיעוּר אוֹת קְטַנָּה:

Letter *heh* with the minimal portion of its leg intact according to Rashi

NOTES

The thorn of a letter *yod* – קוֹצָהּ שֶׁל יוֹד: According to Rashi, this refers to the right leg of the letter *yod*. Rabbeinu Tam objects to this, explaining that this is obvious, as without the right leg there remains no letter *yod*. He explains the Gemara to be referring to the portion of the roof of the letter *yod* that is bent down on the left side. According to the Rosh (*Hilkhot Sefer Torah* 12) it refers to the stroke that extends upward from the left edge of the letter *yod*; see *Piskei HaRid* for a refutation of this opinion.

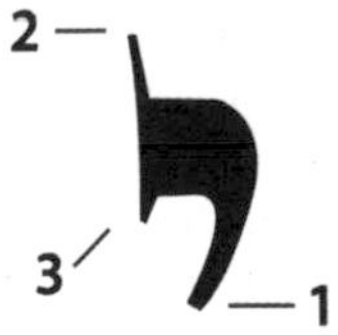

Thorn of the *yod* according to Rashi (1), the Rosh (2), and Rabbeinu Tam (3)

If the inner part of the letter *heh* was perforated it is fit – נִיקַּב תּוֹכוֹ שֶׁל הֵ״י כָּשֵׁר: According to Rashi's first explanation, this refers to the left leg of the letter *heh*. Other early commentaries object to this, claiming that it does not fit with the language of the Gemara, which is speaking of the inner part of the letter, and that there is no reason to call the left leg and not the right leg the inside of the letter (*Sefer HaTeruma* 204). The Rambam and others agree with Rashi's second explanation, that it refers to the space within the letter. It is stated in the Jerusalem Talmud in the name of Ashiyan that the letter is fit only if the inside, as well as the outside, is encircled on all four sides with parchment.

In the leg of the letter *heh* if there remained in it the equivalent of the measure of a small letter – יְרֵיכוֹ אִם נִשְׁתַּיֵּיר בּוֹ כְּשִׁיעוּר אוֹת קְטַנָּה: According to Rashi, this refers to the right leg of the letter *heh*, as the left leg is referred to as the inside of the letter. Therefore, the requirement that the equivalent of a letter *yod* remain applies only to the right leg, but in the case of the left leg if any amount remains it is fit (Rosh). Others disagree, and hold that the requirement that the equivalent of a letter *yod* remain applies to both the left and the right leg (*Nimmukei Yosef*). Rashi's explanation is difficult, since if all that remains of the right leg is the equivalent of the letter *yod* that is attached to the roof of the letter, then the left leg is not parallel to it but rather below it, and the form of the letter *heh* does not remain. For this reason, some explain the opposite, that it is in the case of the left leg that the letter is still fit if the equivalent of a letter *yod* remains (Rabbi David Luria).

HALAKHA

Encircled with blank parchment – גְּוִיל מוּקָּף לָהּ: Every letter must be surrounded by blank parchment on all four sides, rather than being connected to an adjacent letter. If it is not surrounded by parchment then it is not fit (Rambam *Sefer Ahava, Hilkhot Tefillin UMezuza VeSefer Torah* 1:19; *Shulḥan Arukh, Oraḥ Ḥayyim* 32:4 and *Yoreh De'a* 274:4).

If the inner part of the letter *heh* was perforated – נִיקַּב תּוֹכוֹ שֶׁל הֵ״י: If, after the letter *heh* or *mem* was written, its inner space was perforated, it is fit, even if the perforation filled the entire space. This is in accordance with the second explanation of Rashi. It appears that according to the Jerusalem Talmud it is necessary for the inside of the letter and not only the outside to be surrounded by parchment. One should act in accordance with the opinion of the Jerusalem Talmud *ab initio* (Rambam *Sefer Ahava, Hilkhot Tefillin UMezuza VeSefer Torah* 1:20; *Shulḥan Arukh, Oraḥ Ḥayyim* 32:15, and see *Mishna Berura* there).

If the perforation was in the leg of the letter *heh* – נִיקַּב...יְרֵיכוֹ: If the perforation was in the right leg of the letter *heh*, then if there remains of the leg the equivalent of the letter *yod*, then it is fit; if not, it is unfit. If the left leg was perforated, as long as some small amount remained of it, it is fit according to the Rosh and the first explanation of Rashi. According to other authorities it is fit only if there remains the equivalent of the letter *yod*, and this is the *halakha* in practice (Rambam *Sefer Ahava, Hilkhot Tefillin UMezuza VeSefer Torah* 1:20; *Shulḥan Arukh, Oraḥ Ḥayyim* 32:15, and in the comment of Rema).

אִיפְּסִיקָא לֵיהּ כַּרְעָא דְּהֵ״י דְּ״הָעָם״ בְּנִיקְבָא, אֲתָא לְקַמֵּיהּ דְּרַבִּי אַבָּא, אֲמַר לֵיהּ: אִם מִשְׁתַּיֵּיר בּוֹ כְּשִׁיעוּר אוֹת קְטַנָּה – כָּשֵׁר, וְאִם לָאו – פָּסוּל.

had the **leg of** the letter ***heh*** **in** the term: "**The nation** [***ha'am***]" (Exodus 13:3), written in his phylacteries, **severed by a perforation. He came before** his son-in-law **Rabbi Abba** to clarify the *halakha*. Rabbi Abba **said to him: If there remains in** the leg that is attached to the roof of the letter **the equivalent of the measure of a small letter**, i.e., the letter *yod*, it is **fit. But if not,** it is **unfit.**

רָאמִי בַּר תַּמְרֵי, דְּהוּא חֲמוּהּ דְּרָמִי בַּר דִּיקוּלֵי, אִיפְּסִיקָא לֵיהּ כַּרְעָא דְּוָי״ו דְּ״וַיַּהֲרֹג״ בְּנִיקְבָא, אֲתָא לְקַמֵּיהּ דְּרַבִּי זֵירָא, אֲמַר לֵיהּ: זִיל אַיְיתֵי יְנוּקָא דְּלָא חַכִּים וְלָא טִפֵּשׁ, אִי קָרֵי לֵיהּ ״וַיַּהֲרֹג״ – כָּשֵׁר, אִי לָא – ״יֵהָרֵג״ הוּא, וּפָסוּל.

The Gemara relates: **Rami bar Tamrei, who was the father-in-law of Rami bar Dikkulei,** had the **leg of** the letter ***vav*** **in** the term: "**And** the Lord **slew** [***vayaharog***] all the firstborn" (Exodus 13:15), written in his phylacteries, **severed by a perforation. He came before Rabbi Zeira** to clarify the *halakha*. Rabbi Zeira **said to him: Go bring a child who is neither wise nor stupid,**[HN] but of average intelligence; **if he reads** the term as "**And the Lord slew** [***vayaharog***]" then it is **fit,** as despite the perforation the letter is still seen as a *vav*. But **if not,** then it is as though the term **were: Will be slain** [***yehareg***], written without the letter *vav*, **and** it is **unfit.**

אָמַר רַב יְהוּדָה אָמַר רַב: בְּשָׁעָה שֶׁעָלָה מֹשֶׁה לַמָּרוֹם, מְצָאוֹ לְהַקָּדוֹשׁ בָּרוּךְ הוּא שֶׁיּוֹשֵׁב וְקוֹשֵׁר כְּתָרִים לָאוֹתִיּוֹת, אָמַר לְפָנָיו: רִבּוֹנוֹ שֶׁל עוֹלָם, מִי מְעַכֵּב עַל יָדֶךָ? אָמַר לוֹ: אָדָם אֶחָד יֵשׁ שֶׁעָתִיד לִהְיוֹת בְּסוֹף כַּמָּה דּוֹרוֹת וַעֲקִיבָא בֶּן יוֹסֵף שְׁמוֹ, שֶׁעָתִיד לִדְרוֹשׁ עַל כָּל קוֹץ וְקוֹץ תִּילִּין תִּילִּין שֶׁל הֲלָכוֹת.

§ **Rav Yehuda says** that **Rav says: When Moses ascended on High, he found the Holy One, Blessed be He, sitting and tying crowns**[B] **on the letters**[N] of the Torah. Moses **said before** God: **Master of the Universe, who is preventing You** from giving the Torah without these additions? God **said to him: There is a man who is destined** to be born **after several generations, and Akiva ben Yosef**[P] **is his name; he is destined to derive from each and every thorn** of these crowns **mounds** upon **mounds of *halakhot*.** It is for his sake that the crowns must be added to the letters of the Torah.

אָמַר לְפָנָיו: רִבּוֹנוֹ שֶׁל עוֹלָם, הַרְאֵהוּ לִי. אָמַר לוֹ: חֲזוֹר לַאֲחוֹרֶךָ. הָלַךְ וְיָשַׁב בְּסוֹף שְׁמוֹנֶה שׁוּרוֹת, וְלֹא הָיָה יוֹדֵעַ מָה הֵן אוֹמְרִים, תָּשַׁשׁ כֹּחוֹ; כֵּיוָן שֶׁהִגִּיעַ לְדָבָר אֶחָד, אָמְרוּ לוֹ תַּלְמִידָיו: רַבִּי, מִנַּיִן לְךָ? אָמַר לָהֶן: הֲלָכָה לְמֹשֶׁה מִסִּינַי. נִתְיַישְּׁבָה דַּעְתּוֹ.

Moses **said before** God: **Master of the Universe, show him to me.** God **said to him: Return behind you.**[B] Moses **went and sat at the end of the eighth row** in Rabbi Akiva's study hall **and did not understand what they were saying.** Moses' **strength waned,** as he thought his Torah knowledge was deficient. **When** Rabbi Akiva **arrived at** the discussion of **one matter, his students said to him: My teacher, from where do you** derive this? Rabbi Akiva **said to them:** It is a ***halakha*** transmitted **to Moses from Sinai.** When Moses heard this, **his mind was put at ease,** as this too was part of the Torah that he was to receive.

חָזַר וּבָא לִפְנֵי הַקָּדוֹשׁ בָּרוּךְ הוּא, אָמַר לְפָנָיו: רִבּוֹנוֹ שֶׁל עוֹלָם, יֵשׁ לְךָ אָדָם כָּזֶה וְאַתָּה נוֹתֵן תּוֹרָה עַל יָדִי? אָמַר לוֹ: שְׁתוֹק, כָּךְ עָלָה בְּמַחֲשָׁבָה לְפָנַי. אָמַר לְפָנָיו: רִבּוֹנוֹ שֶׁל עוֹלָם, הֶרְאִיתַנִי תּוֹרָתוֹ, הַרְאֵנִי שְׂכָרוֹ. אָמַר לוֹ: חֲזוֹר. חָזַר לַאֲחוֹרָיו, רָאָה שֶׁשּׁוֹקְלִין בְּשָׂרוֹ בְּמַקּוּלִין, אָמַר לְפָנָיו: רִבּוֹנוֹ שֶׁל עוֹלָם, זוֹ תּוֹרָה וְזוֹ שְׂכָרָהּ? אָמַר לוֹ: שְׁתוֹק, כָּךְ עָלָה בְּמַחֲשָׁבָה לְפָנַי.

Moses **returned and came before the Holy One, Blessed be He,** and **said before Him: Master of the Universe, You have a man** as great **as this and** yet **You** still choose to **give the Torah through me.** Why? God **said to him: Be silent; this intention arose before Me.** Moses **said before** God: **Master of the Universe, You have shown me** Rabbi Akiva's **Torah,** now **show me his reward.** God **said to him: Return** to where you were. Moses **went back** and **saw that they were weighing** Rabbi Akiva's **flesh in a butcher shop** [***bemakkulin***],[L] as Rabbi Akiva was tortured to death by the Romans. Moses **said before Him: Master of the Universe, this is Torah and this is its reward?** God **said to him: Be silent; this intention arose before Me.**

NOTES

Who is neither wise nor stupid – דְּלָא חַכִּים וְלָא טִפֵּשׁ: If the child is wise, then he will understand from the context what the word should be and will read it correctly even if it is no longer written correctly. If the child is foolish then he will be unable to identify the letter unless it is written perfectly (Rashi).

He found the Holy One Blessed be He sitting and tying crowns on the letters – מְצָאוֹ לְהַקָּדוֹשׁ בָּרוּךְ הוּא שֶׁיּוֹשֵׁב וְקוֹשֵׁר כְּתָרִים לָאוֹתִיּוֹת: These crowns are the decorative strokes that are added to the letters. Some are strokes that extend from the edge of the letters (see Rashi and *Tosafot*), while others appear as though they were a thin letter *zayin* that is written upon the roof of the letter. The early commentaries also document different types of decorative ornamentation, including unique forms of letters that were passed down as a tradition. These are all found in *Sefer Tagei*, part of which can still be found in the *Maḥzor Vitri*; this work contains detailed instructions with regard to the writing of a Torah scroll, including lists of the ornamentation and unique letters. It is attributed to Eli the High Priest, who is thought to have copied the information from the stones in Gilgal upon which Joshua inscribed the Torah (see Rav Se'adya Gaon's commentary on *Sefer Yetzira* and the introduction to the Ramban's commentary on the Torah). Many relevant sources can be found in *Torah Shelema*, volume 29.

HALAKHA

Severed…bring a child who is neither wise nor stupid – אִיפְּסִיקָא...אַיְיתֵי יְנוּקָא דְּלָא חַכִּים וְלָא טִפֵּשׁ: Any letter that cannot be read correctly by a child of average intelligence is not fit. Therefore, one must be careful to ensure that the letter *yod* does not appear to be a *vav*, that the letter *vav* not appear to be a *yod*, that the letter *kaf* not resemble a letter *beit* and vice versa, and that the letter *dalet* does not resemble the letter *reish* and vice versa. If a straight letter, such as the letters *vav* or *zayin*, was severed, or if the leg of the final form of the letter *nun* or *kaf* was severed, if a child of average intelligence can identify it, then it is fit, and if not then it is unfit. The Rema writes that if it is apparent that the letter is no longer written correctly, even if it can be identified by a child it is unfit (Rambam *Sefer Ahava, Hilkhot Tefillin UMezuza VeSefer Torah* 1:19; *Shulḥan Arukh, Oraḥ Ḥayyim* 32:16).

BACKGROUND

Tying crowns – קוֹשֵׁר כְּתָרִים: Though the expression tying crowns is meant figuratively, i.e., attaching crowns to the letters, there is significance to the literal meaning, as many crown-like items, e.g., garlands, are formed by tying smaller items to one another.

Return behind you – חֲזוֹר לַאֲחוֹרֶךָ: This expression, which means: Turn to that which is after you, refers to that which will be in the future. In the Bible, the term after can refer to that which is to come in the future (see Isaiah 41:23), and stands in contrast to that which is before you, which refers to events that have already transpired (see Deuteronomy 4:32). Similarly, in rabbinic usage the terms: That which is before, and: What will be after, refer to past and future events, respectively (see *Ḥagiga* 11b and *Tosefta*, *Ḥagiga* 2:7).

PERSONALITIES

Akiva ben Yosef – עֲקִיבָא בֶּן יוֹסֵף: Akiva ben Yosef, known as Rabbi Akiva, was one of the greatest of the *tanna'im* from just after the destruction of the Second Temple until the bar Kokheva revolt.

According to tradition, Rabbi Akiva began his studies at the age of forty, when Rachel, the daughter of the wealthy Kalba Savua, agreed to marry him on condition that he would go and study Torah. Rabbi Akiva became the student of Rabbi Eliezer ben Hyrcanus and Rabbi Yehoshua ben Ḥananya. Ultimately, he became a great scholar, with 24,000 students of his own.

Rabbi Akiva's foremost students included Shimon ben Azzai and Shimon ben Zoma, with whom he studied esoteric elements of the Torah. Later, he taught Rabbi Meir and Rabbi Shimon bar Yoḥai, among others. He supported bar Kokheva's revolt against the Roman authorities, declaring him the Messiah. Even when the Roman emperor Hadrian banned the study of Torah, Rabbi Akiva continued gathering Jews and teaching Torah. Ultimately, he was captured and executed. He is listed as one of the ten martyrs whose execution by the Romans is described in liturgy.

Rabbi Akiva collected early rabbinic statements and worked to organize the Oral Torah systematically. The work done by Rabbi Akiva and his students served as the basis for the Mishna, which was later redacted by Rabbi Yehuda HaNasi and his disciples.

LANGUAGE

Butcher shop [*makkulin*] – מַקּוּלִין: From the Latin macellum, meaning butcher shop.

אָמַר רָבָא: שִׁבְעָה אוֹתִיּוֹת צְרִיכוֹת שְׁלֹשָׁה זִיּוּנִין, וְאֵלּוּ הֵן: שעטנ״ז ג״ץ. אָמַר רַב אַשִׁי: חֲזֵינָא לְהוּ לְסָפְרֵי דַּוְוקָנֵי דְּבֵי רַב, דְּחָטְרִי לְהוּ לְגַגֵּיהּ דְּחֵי״ת וְתָלוּ לֵיהּ לְכַרְעֵיהּ דְּהֵ״י;

§ The Gemara continues its discussion of the crowns on letters of the Torah: **Rava says: Seven letters require three crowns [*ziyyunin*],**[LN] **and they are the letters *shin, ayin, tet, nun, zayin; gimmel* and *tzadi*.**[HBN] **Rav Ashi says: I have seen that the exacting scribes of the study hall of Rav would put a hump-like stroke on the roof of** the letter ***het***[BN] **and they would suspend the left leg of** the letter ***heh*,**[BN] i.e., they would ensure that it is not joined to the roof of the letter.

חָטְרִי לְהוּ לְגַגֵּיהּ דְּחֵי״ת – כְּלוֹמַר: חַי הוּא בְּרוּמוֹ שֶׁל עוֹלָם; וְתָלוּ לֵיהּ לְכַרְעֵיהּ דְּהֵ״י – כִּדְבָעָא מִינֵּיהּ רַבִּי יְהוּדָה נְשִׂיאָה מֵרַבִּי אַמִי: מַאי דִּכְתִיב ״בִּטְחוּ בַיי׳ עֲדֵי עַד כִּי בְּיָהּ יי׳ צוּר עוֹלָמִים״? אֲמַר לֵיהּ: כָּל הַתּוֹלֶה בִּטְחוֹנוֹ בְּהַקָּדוֹשׁ בָּרוּךְ הוּא – הֲרֵי לוֹ מַחֲסֶה בָּעוֹלָם הַזֶּה וְלָעוֹלָם הַבָּא.

Rava explains: **They would put a hump-like stroke on the roof of** the letter ***het* as if to** thereby **say:** The Holy One, Blessed be **He, lives [*hai*] in the heights of the universe. And they would suspend the** left **leg of the letter *heh*, as Rabbi Yehuda Nesia asked Rabbi Ami: What** is the meaning of that **which is written: "Trust in the Lord forever, for in the Lord [*beYah*] is God, an everlasting [*olamim*] Rock"** (Isaiah 26:4)? Rabbi Ami **said to him: Anyone who puts their trust in the Holy One, Blessed be He,** will have Him as **his refuge in this world and in the World-to-Come.** This is alluded to in the word "*olamim*," which can also mean: Worlds.

אֲמַר לֵיהּ: אֲנָא הָכִי קָא קַשְׁיָא לִי, מַאי שְׁנָא דִּכְתִיב ״בְּיָהּ״ וְלָא כְּתִיב ״יָהּ״?

Rabbi Yehuda Nesia **said to** Rabbi Ami: I was not asking about the literal meaning of the verse; **this is what poses a difficulty for me: What is different** about that **which is written:** "For in the Lord **[*beYah*]," and it is not written:** For **the Lord [*Yah*]?**

NOTES

Three crowns [*ziyyunin*] – שְׁלֹשָׁה זִיּוּנִין: A *ziyyun* is an small ornamental stroke that extends from the roof of the letter. In the case of letters that have several roofs, the stroke extends from the left roof (see *Nimmukei Yosef*). The Rambam explains that it refers to a hair-thin line that has a thick stroke on top, and therefore has an appearance similar to the letter *zayin*. Other early commentaries explain that the *ziyyun* is not a crown on top of the letter, but rather an instruction with regard to the writing of the letters themselves, specifically that their roofs should not be rounded but rather formed from three angles (*Sefer Yere'im*; Rid, citing Rabbeinu Gershom Meor HaGola).

***Shin, ayin, tet, nun, zayin; gimmel* and *tzadi* – שעטנ״ז ג״ץ:** These are the only letters that can be written with this type of crown, since they are the only letters that contain a straight and not diagonal or rounded roof (*Or Zarua, Hilkhot Tefillin* 554). See other explanations in the commentary attributed to Rashba, and esoteric explanations cited by the *Mishna Berura* (36:15) in the name of the *Sefer HaTiyyul*. According to most of the early commentaries, the Gemara is referring to all instances where these letters appear in the Torah. According to the Rambam and Rabbi Yehuda of Barcelona, the context is the mishna's discussion of the passages in the *mezuza*, and therefore Rava means that there is one instance in these passages where each of these letters requires three crowns. See the discussion in the *Tur* and *Beit Yosef* (*Orah Hayyim* 36) for the opinions of other early commentaries who suggest that all instances of these letters require crowns, but these seven instances require larger strokes.

Would put a hump-like stroke [*hatrei*] on the roof of the letter *het* – דְּחָטְרִי לְהוּ לְגַגֵּיהּ דְּחֵי״ת: Rashi explains that the term *hatrei* is derived from the word stick [*hutra*] and therefore refers to a leftward stroke from the roof of the letter *het* (*Tosafot*; Rosh). Rabbeinu Tam explains that it refers to a hump-like mark, in accordance with the mishna in tractate *Shabbat* (104b), where it is explained that the letter *het* is made up of two instances of the letter *zayin* joined together.

And they would suspend the left leg of the letter *heh* – וְתָלוּ לֵיהּ לְכַרְעֵיהּ דְּהֵ״י: Just as the scribes would extend the leg of the letter *het* upward above the roof, so too they would take care to ensure that the left leg of the letter *heh* would not touch the roof of the letter. The early commentaries ask why this is described as the behavior of exacting scribes and not simply the basic halakhic requirement, as otherwise the letter *heh* appears to be the letter *het* (see *Shabbat* 103b). Some explain that while the basic requirement calls only for a tiny space to be left between the roof and the left leg of the *heh*, these exacting scribes would take care to place the leg at a greater distance from the roof (Rivash). Others explain that the letter *heh* is also closed on three sides but is distinguishable from the letter *het* as its left leg is closer to the middle of the roof and not all the way to its side (commentary attributed to Rashba), or because the upper edge of the *het* is thick, whereas that of the *heh* is thin (*Tashbetz*). It is explained in the Jerusalem Talmud (*Megilla* 1:9) that during certain periods the letter *heh* was written as closed on three sides; this can be seen in different manuscripts throughout many generations.

Het made up of two letters *zayin*

LANGUAGE

Crowns [*ziyyunin*] – זִיּוּנִין: Some explain that this word refers to a decoration, akin to the crowns mentioned before. There is a similar expression in Arabic meaning decoration, زينة, *zīnah*. Others explain that it refers to the letter *zayin*, which is written in small print upon the roof of the words.

HALAKHA

***Shin, ayin, tet, nun, zayin; gimmel* and *tzadi* – שעטנ״ז ג״ץ:** When writing a Torah scroll, phylacteries, or *mezuza*, it is necessary to add crowns to the letters *shin, ayin, tet, nun, zayin, gimmel*, and *tzadi*. The scribes customarily add crowns to other letters as well. Even if crowns were not added to the letters *shin, ayin, tet, nun, zayin, gimmel*, and *tzadi*, the item is fit (Rambam *Sefer Ahava, Hilkhot Tefillin UMezuza VeSefer Torah* 2:9, 5:3, 7:9–10; *Shulhan Arukh, Orah Hayyim* 36:3 and *Yoreh De'a* 274:6, 288:7).

BACKGROUND

***Shin, ayin, tet, nun, zayin; gimmel* and *tzadi* – שעטנ״ז ג״ץ:**

Letters with three crowns

Would put a hump-like stroke on the roof of the letter *het* – חָטְרִי לְהוּ לְגַגֵּיהּ דְּחֵי״ת: These samples from the Dead Sea Scrolls show strokes on both sides of the roof of the letter *het*.

Samples of the letter *het* from the Dead Sea Scrolls excavated at Qumran

They would suspend the left leg of the letter *heh* – תָּלוּ לֵיהּ לְכַרְעֵיהּ דְּהֵ״י: The samples from the Dead Sea Scrolls in the image show that scribes would customarily inscribe the letter *heh* so that it was closed on three sides, without the left leg of the letter suspended in the air. Therefore, the primary difference between a letter *heh* and a letter *het*, aside from the strokes on the roof of the *het*, was the placement of the leg of the letter *heh* near the center of the letter. Similarly, the distinction between the two can be seen in the image of the excerpt from the Aleppo Codex, which was written in Tiberias in the tenth century. Here, another difference is apparent, as the upper edge of the left leg of the *heh* is narrower than that of the *het*.

Samples of the letter *heh* from the Dead Sea Scrolls excavated at Qumran

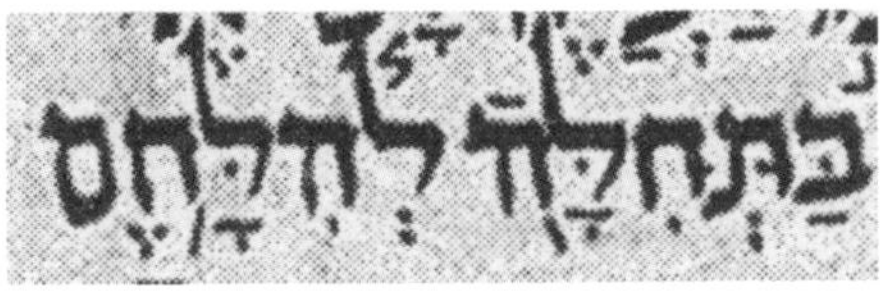

Excerpt from the Aleppo Codex

HALAKHA

Three may be corrected, etc. – **שלש יתקן וכו׳**: It is prohibited to retain a Torah scroll in one's possession for more than thirty days if it has mistakes that have not been corrected. Instead it must be corrected or buried. A Torah scroll that has three mistakes in every column should be corrected, but if there were four mistakes in every column it should be buried. If the majority of the scroll was corrected and the remaining portion had four mistakes in every column, but there remained even one column from the corrupted part without four mistakes, it should be corrected. This is in accordance with the *baraita*, and with the statement of Rabbi Yitzḥak bar Shmuel bar Marta in the name of Rav. This is the *halakha* only when the mistakes pertain to missing letters, since it is improper for the Torah scroll to contain so many insertions above the lines. If the errors pertained to words containing too many letters, they should be corrected, since erasing the letters is not denigrating for the Torah scroll. This is in accordance with the statement of Rav Yosef and the explanation of Rav Kahana (Rambam *Sefer Ahava, Hilkhot Tefillin UMezuza VeSefer Torah* 7:12; *Shulḥan Arukh, Yoreh De'a* 279:4).

כדדרש רבי יהודה בר רבי אילעאי: אלו שני עולמות שברא הקדוש ברוך הוא, אחד בה״י ואחד ביו״ד, ואיני יודע אם העולם הבא ביו״ד והעולם הזה בה״י, אם העולם הזה ביו״ד והעולם הבא בה״י;

Rav Ashi responded: It is **as Rabbi Yehuda bar Rabbi Elai taught:** The verse "For in the Lord [*beYah*] is God, an everlasting Rock [*Tzur olamim*]" is understood as follows: The term "*Tzur olamim*" can also mean Creator of worlds. **These** letters *yod* and *heh* that constitute the word *yah* are referring to the **two worlds that the Holy One, Blessed be He, created; one with** [*be*] the letter ***heh*** **and one with** [*be*] the letter ***yod*****. And I do not know whether the World-to-Come** was created **with** the letter ***yod*** **and this world** was created **with** the letter ***heh*****,** or **whether this world** was created **with the** letter ***yod*** **and the World-to-Come** was created **with** the letter ***heh*****.**

כשהוא אומר: ״אלה תולדות השמים והארץ בהבראם״ – אל תקרי ״בהבראם״ אלא: בה״י בראם.

When the verse **states: "These are the generations of the heaven and of the earth when they were created [*behibare'am*]"** (Genesis 2:4), **do not read** it as ***behibare'am***, meaning: When they were created; **rather,** read it as ***beheh bera'am***, meaning: He created them with the letter *heh*. This verse demonstrates that the heaven and the earth, i.e., this world, were created with the letter *heh*, and therefore the World-to-Come must have been created with the letter *yod*.

ומפני מה נברא העולם הזה בה״י? מפני שדומה לאכסדרה, שכל הרוצה לצאת יצא. ומאי טעמא תליא כרעיה? דאי הדר בתשובה מעיילי ליה.

And for what reason **was this world created** specifically **with the** letter ***heh***? It is **because** the letter *heh*, **which** is open on its bottom, has **a similar** appearance **to a portico,** which is open on one side. And it alludes to this world, **where anyone who wishes to leave may leave,** i.e., every person has the ability to choose to do evil. **And what is the reason** that the left **leg of** the letter *heh* **is suspended,** i.e., is not joined to the roof of the letter? It is **because if one repents, he is brought** back **in** through the opening at the top.

וליעייל בהך! לא מסתייעא מילתא; כדריש לקיש, דאמר ריש לקיש, מאי דכתיב: ״אם ללצים הוא יליץ ולענוים יתן חן״? בא לטהר – מסייעין אותו, בא לטמא – פותחין לו. ומאי טעמא אית ליה תאגא? אמר הקדוש ברוך הוא: אם חוזר – אני קושר לו קשר.

The Gemara asks: **But** why not **let him enter through that** same way that he left? The Gemara answers: That would **not be effective,** since one requires assistance from Heaven in order to repent, **in accordance with** the statement **of Reish Lakish. As Reish Lakish says: What** is the meaning of that **which is written: "If it concerns the scorners, He scorns them, but to the humble He gives grace"** (Proverbs 3:34)? Concerning one who **comes** in order **to become pure, he is assisted** from Heaven, as it is written: "But to the humble He gives grace." Concerning one who **comes to become impure, he is provided with an opening** to do so. The Gemara asks: **And what is the reason** that the letter *heh* **has a crown** on its roof? The Gemara answers: **The Holy One, Blessed be He, says: If** a sinner **returns,** repenting for his sin, **I tie** a crown **for him** from above.

מפני מה נברא העולם הבא ביו״ד? מפני שצדיקים שבו מועטים. ומפני מה כפוף ראשו? מפני שצדיקים שבו כפוף ראשיהם, מפני מעשיהן שאינן דומין זה לזה.

The Gemara asks: **For what** reason **was the World-to-Come created** specifically **with** the letter ***yod***, the smallest letter in the Hebrew alphabet? The Gemara answers: It is **because the righteous** of the world **are so few. And for what** reason is the left side of **the top of** the letter *yod* **bent** downward? It is **because the righteous who are in** the World-to-Come **hang their heads** in shame, **since the actions of one are not similar to those of another.** In the World-to-Come some of the righteous will be shown to be of greater stature than others.

אמר רב יוסף: הני תרתי מילי אמר רב בספרים, ותניא תיובתיה; חדא, הא דאמר רב: ספר תורה שיש בו שתי טעיות בכל דף ודף – יתקן, שלש – יגנז;

§ **Rav Yosef says: Rav states these two matters with regard to scrolls, and** in each case a statement **is taught** in a *baraita* that constitutes **a refutation of his** ruling. **One** is **that which Rav says: A Torah scroll that contains two errors on each and every column may be corrected,** but if there are **three** errors on each and every column then it **shall be interred.**

ותניא תיובתיה: שלש – יתקן, ארבע – יגנז. תנא: אם יש בו דף אחת שלימה – מצלת על כולו. אמר רבי יצחק בר שמואל בר מרתא משמיה דרב: והוא דכתיב רוביה דספרא שפיר.

And a statement **is taught** in a *baraita* that constitutes **a refutation of his** ruling: A Torah scroll that contains **three** errors on every column **may be corrected,**[H] but if there are **four** errors on every column then it **shall be interred.** A *tanna* **taught** in a *baraita*: **If** the Torah scroll **contains one complete column** with no errors, **it saves the entire** Torah scroll, and it is permitted to correct the scroll rather than interring it. **Rabbi Yitzḥak bar Shmuel bar Marta says in the name of Rav: And this** is the *halakha* only **when the majority of the scroll is written properly** and is not full of errors.

אֲמַר לֵיהּ אַבַּיֵי לְרַב יוֹסֵף: אִי אִית בְּהַהוּא דַּף שָׁלֹשׁ טָעֻיּוֹת, מַאי? אֲמַר לֵיהּ: הוֹאִיל וְאִיתְיְהִיב לְאִיתַּקּוּנֵי, מִיתַּקַּן. וְהָנֵי מִילֵּי חֲסֵירוֹת, אֲבָל יְתֵירוֹת לֵית לָן בַּהּ. חֲסֵירוֹת מַאי טַעְמָא לָא? אֲמַר רַב כָּהֲנָא: מִשּׁוּם דְּמֶיחֱזֵי כִּמְנוּמָּר.

Abaye said to Rav Yosef: If that column contained three errors, what is the *halakha*? Rav Yosef **said to him: Since** the column itself **may be corrected,** it **enables the correction** of the entire scroll. The Gemara adds: **And** with regard to the *halakha* that a Torah scroll may not be fixed if it is full of errors, **this statement** applies when letters **are missing** and must be added in the space between the lines. **But** if there were **extraneous** letters, **we have no** problem **with it,** since they can easily be erased. The Gemara asks: **What is the reason** that a scroll with letters **missing** may **not** be corrected? **Rav Kahana said: Because it would look speckled** if one adds all of the missing letters in the spaces between the lines.

אַגְרָא חֲמוּהּ דְּרַבִּי אַבָּא הֲוָה לֵיהּ יְתֵירוֹת בְּסִיפְרֵיהּ, אֲתָא לְקַמֵּיהּ דְּרַבִּי אַבָּא, אֲמַר לֵיהּ: לָא אֲמָרָן אֶלָּא בַּחֲסֵירוֹת,

The Gemara relates: **Agra, the father-in-law of Rabbi Abba, had** many **extraneous** letters **in his scroll. He came before Rabbi Abba** to clarify the *halakha*. Rabbi Abba **said to him: We said** that one may not correct the scroll **only in** a case where the letters are **missing.**

Perek **III**
Daf **30** Amud **a**

אֲבָל יְתֵרוֹת לֵית לָן בַּהּ.

But if there are **extraneous** letters, **we have no** problem **with it,** and one may erase them. This is the first *halakha* that Rav stated, which is refuted in a *baraita*.

אִידָךְ, דְּאָמַר רַב: הַכּוֹתֵב סֵפֶר תּוֹרָה וּבָא לִגְמוֹר, גּוֹמֵר וַאֲפִילּוּ בְּאֶמְצַע הַדַּף. מֵיתִיבֵי: הַכּוֹתֵב סֵפֶר תּוֹרָה, בָּא לוֹ לִגְמוֹר – לֹא יִגְמוֹר בְּאֶמְצַע הַדַּף כְּדֶרֶךְ שֶׁגּוֹמֵר בְּחוּמָּשִׁין, אֶלָּא מְקַצֵּר וְהוֹלֵךְ עַד סוֹף הַדַּף! כִּי קָא אָמַר רַב – בְּחוּמָּשִׁין.

The other is that **which Rav says: One who writes a Torah scroll and comes to finish** writing it **may finish** writing it anywhere in the column, **and** this is the *halakha* **even** with regard to finishing it **in the middle of the column.** The Gemara **raises an objection** from a *baraita*: **One who writes a Torah scroll** and **comes to finish** writing it **may not finish** writing it **in the middle of the column in the manner that one finishes** writing one of the **five** books of the Torah written as an independent scroll. **Rather,** he should **progressively shorten** the width of the lines **until** he finishes the scroll at the **end of the column.** The Gemara answers: **When Rav says** that one may finish writing even in the middle of a column, he was referring **to** one of the **five** books of the Torah.

וְהָא סֵפֶר תּוֹרָה קָאָמַר! בְּחוּמָּשִׁין שֶׁל סֵפֶר תּוֹרָה. אִינִי? וְהָאָמַר רַבִּי יְהוֹשֻׁעַ בַּר אַבָּא אָמַר רַב גִּידֵּל אָמַר רַב: "לְעֵינֵי כָּל יִשְׂרָאֵל" בְּאֶמְצַע הַדַּף! הַהִיא בְּאֶמְצַע שִׁיטָה אִיתְּמַר.

The Gemara asks: **But doesn't** Rav **say** his statement with regard to **a Torah scroll?** The Gemara answers: He was referring **to** one of the **five** books **that** constitute **a Torah scroll.** Rav meant that when writing a Torah scroll, one may finish writing any of the first four books in the middle of a column. The Gemara asks: **Is that so? But doesn't Rabbi Yehoshua bar Abba say** that **Rav Giddel says** that **Rav says:** The words: **"In the sight of all Israel"** (Deuteronomy 34:12), which conclude the Torah, may be written even **in the middle of the column?** The Gemara answers: **That** ruling that **was stated** is **with regard to** finishing the Torah scroll **in the middle of the line,** i.e., in the middle of the width of the column.

רַבָּנַן אָמְרִי: אַף בְּאֶמְצַע שִׁיטָה. רַב אַשִׁי אָמַר: בְּאֶמְצַע שִׁיטָה דַּוְקָא. וְהִלְכְתָא: בְּאֶמְצַע שִׁיטָה דַּוְקָא.

The Gemara cites another opinion: **The Rabbis say** that one may finish writing a Torah scroll **even in the middle of** the **line,**[N] but one may finish writing it at the end of the line as well. **Rav Ashi says** that one must finish writing the Torah scroll **specifically in the middle of the line. And the *halakha*** is that it must be ended **specifically in the middle** of the **line.**[H]

NOTES

The Rabbis say one may finish writing a Torah scroll even in the middle of the line – **רַבָּנַן אָמְרִי אַף בְּאֶמְצַע שִׁיטָה**: The straightforward understanding of the Gemara here is that the Rabbis and Rav Ashi disagree as to the meaning of the term: In the middle of the line. According to the Rabbis, it means that one may conclude writing the Torah scroll even in the middle of the line, whereas according to Rav Ashi it means that one must conclude writing the Torah scroll in the middle of the line, to demonstrate that this is the conclusion of the Torah (Rabbi David Luria; *Tosafot Ḥitzoniyyot*; *Nimmukei Yosef*).

According to Rashi, the Rabbis and Rav Ashi are continuing the dispute as to whether or not one may conclude writing the Torah scroll in the middle of a sheet of parchment. According to the Rabbis, one may conclude writing the Torah scroll in the middle of a line, and similarly in the middle of a sheet of parchment, in accordance with the straightforward meaning of Rav's statement. According to Rav Ashi, one may conclude writing the Torah scroll in the middle of a line but not in the middle of a sheet of parchment, in accordance with the Gemara's explanation of Rav's statement in light of the difficulty posed by the *baraita*. The commentaries discuss extensively the reason that Rashi felt the need to explain the Gemara in this manner (see commentary attributed to Rashba, *Tzon Kodashim*, and Rashash).

HALAKHA

In the middle of the line – **בְּאֶמְצַע שִׁיטָה**: When writing a Torah scroll, one must end in the middle of the last line of the column. If there are many lines of the column remaining, one should write using tall letters, so that one word will occupy the space usually occupied by four or five lines (*Tur*). One should begin at the beginning of the line but should not finish the line. In this way, one ensures that the words "in the sight of all Israel" (Deuteronomy 34:12) appear in the middle of the line at the end of the column (Rambam *Sefer Ahava*, *Hilkhot Tefillin UMezuza VeSefer Torah* 7:7; *Shulḥan Arukh*, *Yoreh De'a* 272:4).

אָמַר רַבִּי יְהוֹשֻׁעַ בַּר אַבָּא אָמַר רַב גִּידֵּל אָמַר רַב: שְׁמוֹנָה פְּסוּקִים שֶׁבַּתּוֹרָה, יָחִיד קוֹרֵא אוֹתָן בְּבֵית הַכְּנֶסֶת. כְּמַאן? דְּלָא כְּרַבִּי שִׁמְעוֹן;

§ **Rabbi Yehoshua bar Abba says** that **Rav Giddel says** that **Rav says:** With regard to the last **eight verses of the Torah** (Deuteronomy 32:5–12),[H] a single **individual reads them**[N] **in the synagogue,** as that section may not be divided between two readers. The Gemara asks: **In accordance with whose** opinion is this said? It is **not in accordance with** the opinion of **Rabbi Shimon.**

דְּתַנְיָא: "וַיָּמָת שָׁם מֹשֶׁה עֶבֶד ה׳". אֶפְשָׁר מֹשֶׁה חַי, וְכָתַב: "וַיָּמָת שָׁם מֹשֶׁה"? אֶלָּא עַד כָּאן כָּתַב מֹשֶׁה, מִכָּאן וָאֵילָךְ כָּתַב יְהוֹשֻׁעַ בִּן נוּן, דִּבְרֵי רַבִּי יְהוּדָה, וְאָמְרִי לָהּ רַבִּי נְחֶמְיָה.

As it is taught in a *baraita*: The verse states: **"And Moses the servant of the Lord died there"** (Deuteronomy 34:5). **Is it possible** that after **Moses died, he** himself **wrote: "And Moses died there"? Rather, Moses wrote** the entire Torah **until this** point, and **Joshua bin Nun wrote from this** point **forward;** this is **the statement of Rabbi Yehuda. And some say** that **Rabbi Neḥemya** stated this opinion.

אָמַר לוֹ רַבִּי שִׁמְעוֹן: אֶפְשָׁר סֵפֶר תּוֹרָה חָסֵר אוֹת אַחַת? וּכְתִיב: "לָקֹחַ אֵת סֵפֶר הַתּוֹרָה הַזֶּה וְשַׂמְתֶּם אֹתוֹ" וגו׳!

Rabbi Shimon said to him: Is it possible that the **Torah scroll** was **missing a single letter? But it is written** that God instructed Moses: **"Take this Torah scroll and put it** by the side of the Ark of the Covenant" (Deuteronomy 31:26), indicating that the Torah was complete as is and that nothing further would be added to it.

אֶלָּא, עַד כָּאן הַקָּדוֹשׁ בָּרוּךְ הוּא אוֹמֵר וּמֹשֶׁה כּוֹתֵב וְאוֹמֵר, מִכָּאן וָאֵילָךְ הַקָּדוֹשׁ בָּרוּךְ הוּא אוֹמֵר וּמֹשֶׁה כּוֹתֵב בְּדֶמַע, כְּמָה שֶׁנֶּאֱמַר לְהַלָּן: "וַיֹּאמֶר לָהֶם בָּרוּךְ מִפִּיו יִקְרָא אֵלַי אֵת כָּל הַדְּבָרִים הָאֵלֶּה וַאֲנִי כֹּתֵב עַל הַסֵּפֶר בַּדְּיוֹ";

Rabbi Shimon explains: **Rather, until this** point, i.e., the verse describing the death of Moses, **the Holy One, Blessed be He, dictated and Moses wrote** the text **and repeated** after Him. **From this** point **forward,** with regard to Moses' death, **the Holy One, Blessed be He, dictated and Moses wrote with tears** without repeating the words, due to his great sorrow. **As it is stated there** with regard to Jeremiah's dictation of the prophecy of the destruction of the Temple to Baruch ben Neriah: **"And Baruch said to them: He dictated all these words to me, and I wrote them with ink in the scroll"** (Jeremiah 36:18), but he did not repeat the words after Jeremiah.

לֵימָא, דְּלָא כְּרַבִּי שִׁמְעוֹן? אֲפִילּוּ תֵּימָא רַבִּי שִׁמְעוֹן, הוֹאִיל וְאִישְׁתַּנֵּי אִישְׁתַּנֵּי.

The Gemara now states its inference: **Shall we say that** the ruling of Rav that the last verses of the Torah are read by only one reader is **not in accordance with** the opinion of **Rabbi Shimon,** since according to Rabbi Shimon these verses are similar to all other verses of the Torah, as they were all written by Moses? The Gemara answers: **You** may **even say** that Rav's ruling was stated in accordance with the opinion of **Rabbi Shimon; since they differ** from the rest of the Torah in one way, as Moses wrote them without repeating the words, **they differ** from the rest of the Torah in this way as well, and they may not be divided between two readers.

וְאָמַר רַבִּי יְהוֹשֻׁעַ בַּר אַבָּא אָמַר רַב גִּידֵּל אָמַר רַב: הַלּוֹקֵחַ סֵפֶר תּוֹרָה מִן הַשּׁוּק – כְּחוֹטֵף מִצְוָה מִן הַשּׁוּק; כְּתָבוֹ – מַעֲלֶה עָלָיו הַכָּתוּב כְּאִילּוּ קִיבְּלוֹ מֵהַר סִינַי. אָמַר רַב שֵׁשֶׁת: אִם הִגִּיהַּ אֲפִילּוּ אוֹת אַחַת – מַעֲלֶה עָלָיו כְּאִילּוּ כְּתָבוֹ.

And Rabbi Yehoshua bar Abba says that **Rav Giddel says** that **Rav says: One who purchases a Torah scroll in the marketplace**[HN] **is akin to one who snatches a mitzva in the marketplace,** as the proper manner in which to perform the mitzva of writing a Torah scroll is to write one for himself. And if he himself **writes** a Torah scroll, **the verse ascribes him** credit **as though he received it at Mount Sinai. Rav Sheshet says: If he emended even a single letter** of the Torah scroll, thereby completing it, the verse **ascribes him** credit **as though he had written it** in its entirety.

HALAKHA

Eight verses of the Torah – שְׁמוֹנָה פְּסוּקִים שֶׁבַּתּוֹרָה: According to the Rambam, the last eight verses of the Torah may be read even in the absence of a quorum of ten men. Despite the fact that they are an integral part of the Torah and were said to Moses by God, because they are presented as being after Moses' death they differ from the rest of the Torah. Most authorities hold that the meaning of the Gemara is that the eight verses may not be divided into two sections when read in the synagogue, but must be read all together by one individual (Rambam *Sefer Ahava, Hilkhot Tefilla* 13:6; *Shulḥan Arukh, Oraḥ Ḥayyim* 428:7).

One who purchases a Torah scroll in the marketplace, etc. – הַלּוֹקֵחַ סֵפֶר תּוֹרָה מִן הַשּׁוּק וכו׳: There is a positive mitzva that every Jewish man write a Torah scroll for himself, as it is stated: "Now therefore write this song for you" (Deuteronomy 31:19), which is interpreted as meaning that every person should write a Torah scroll that contains the song referred to in that verse. The Rema, citing *Nimmukei Yosef*, writes that if one hires a scribe to write a Torah scroll on his behalf, or if one purchases a scroll that contains errors and fixes them, it is as though he wrote the Torah scroll himself. If one purchased a Torah scroll in the market without emending any part of it, it is as though he seized the mitzva from the market and did not fulfill his obligation. Others hold that he has fulfilled the positive mitzva (Gra, citing Rashi). The *Shulḥan Arukh* writes that nowadays it is a mitzva to write individual books of the Torah, Mishna, Gemara, and their commentaries. Halakhic authorities disagree whether this is in place of the mitzva to write a Torah scroll or in addition to it (Rambam *Sefer Ahava, Hilkhot Tefillin UMezuza VeSefer Torah* 7:1; *Shulḥan Arukh, Yoreh De'a* 270:1–2, and see *Be'er Heitev* and *Pitḥei Teshuva* there).

NOTES

A single individual reads them – יָחִיד קוֹרֵא אוֹתָן: Rashi understands that a single individual reads these verses without interruption. Another suggestion is that these verses must be read as a distinct passage without the previous text, so as not to mix this section with the rest of the Torah (Ri Migash on *Bava Batra* 15a). According to the Rambam, an individual may read these verses in the synagogue even in the absence of a quorum of ten men. Some claim that the term: An individual, means an important person, and therefore these verses must be read by a Torah scholar (Mordekhai). *Tosafot* cite Rabbeinu Meshullam as ruling that one person reads the verses rather than having one person recite the blessings and another person read, which is the custom in most places today concerning the rest of the Torah.

One who purchases a Torah scroll in the marketplace, etc. – הַלּוֹקֵחַ סֵפֶר תּוֹרָה מִן הַשּׁוּק וכו׳: There is a mitzva for every Jewish man to write a Torah scroll, as it is stated: "Now therefore write this song for you" (Deuteronomy 31:19). According to the Rambam, if one did not write the Torah scroll himself or by means of an agent, then he did not fulfill this mitzva. According to Rashi he did not fulfill the mitzva in the optimal manner, but he nevertheless fulfilled the mitzva. According to this opinion, it appears that the principle purpose of the mitzva is not to have written a Torah scroll but rather to own a Torah scroll in order to study from it.

(סימן סגל״ם) תָּנוּ רַבָּנַן: עוֹשֶׂה אָדָם יְרִיעָה מִבַּת שָׁלֹשׁ דַּפִּין וְעַד בַּת שְׁמֹנָה דַּפִּין, פָּחוֹת מִיכָּן וְיָתֵר עַל כֵּן לֹא יַעֲשֶׂה.

§ Before continuing its discussion of the *halakhot* of writing a Torah scroll, the Gemara presents **a mnemonic** for the upcoming *halakhot*: ***Samekh*, *gimmel*, *lamed*, *mem*. The Sages taught: A person may prepare** for a Torah scroll **a sheet** of parchment of any size **from three columns**[H] **and until eight columns, but one may not prepare** a sheet of parchment that has **less than** three **or more than** eight columns.[N]

וְלֹא יַרְבֶּה בְּדַפִּין – מִפְּנֵי שֶׁנִּרְאָה אִגֶּרֶת, וְלֹא יְמַעֵט בְּדַפִּין – מִפְּנֵי שֶׁעֵינָיו מְשׁוֹטְטוֹת, אֶלָּא כְּגוֹן: ״לְמִשְׁפְּחוֹתֵיכֶם לְמִשְׁפְּחוֹתֵיכֶם לְמִשְׁפְּחוֹתֵיכֶם״ שָׁלֹשׁ פְּעָמִים.

And he may not increase the number **of columns,**[H] e.g., by writing eight columns on a narrow sheet of parchment, **since** then each column **has the appearance of a missive** due to its narrow lines. **And he may not decrease** the number **of columns,** e.g., by writing three columns on a wide sheet of parchment, **since** then the lines will be so wide that the reader's **eyes will wander,** as it will be difficult to find the beginning of a line. **Rather,** the ideal width of a line is, **for example,** where one can write **"*lemishpeḥoteikhem*," "*lemishpeḥoteikhem*," "*lemishpeḥoteikhem*,"** for a total of **three times.**

נִזְדַּמְּנָה לוֹ יְרִיעָה בַּת תֵּשַׁע דַּפִּים – לֹא יַחֲלוֹק שָׁלֹשׁ לְכָאן וְשֵׁשׁ לְכָאן, אֶלָּא אַרְבַּע לְכָאן וְחָמֵשׁ לְכָאן.

If one **happened** to acquire **a sheet** of parchment that **has** space for **nine columns,** exceeding the eight-column limit, **he should not divide** it into two sheets of parchment with **three** columns **here and six** columns **there; rather,** he should divide it into two sheets of parchment with **four** columns **here and five** columns **there,** so that the two sheets will be similar in width.

בַּמֶּה דְּבָרִים אֲמוּרִים – בִּתְחִלַּת הַסֵּפֶר, אֲבָל בְּסוֹף הַסֵּפֶר – אֲפִילּוּ פָּסוּק אֶחָד וַאֲפִילּוּ דַּף אֶחָד. פָּסוּק אֶחָד סָלְקָא דַּעְתָּךְ? אֶלָּא אֵימָא: פָּסוּק אֶחָד בְּדַף אֶחָד.

In what case **is this statement** that the sheet must contain a minimum of three columns **said?** It is said with regard to sheets **at the beginning** and middle **of the scroll. But at the end of the scroll,** a sheet may consist of **even one verse, and even one column.** The Gemara asks: Can it **enter your mind** to say that a sheet may contain **one verse?**[N] **Rather, say** that it may consist of even **one verse on one column.**

שִׁיעוּר גִּלָּיוֹן: מִלְּמַטָּה – טֶפַח, מִלְמַעְלָה – שָׁלֹשׁ אֶצְבָּעוֹת, וּבֵין דַּף לְדַף – כִּמְלֹא רֶיוַח רוֹחַב שְׁתֵּי אֶצְבָּעוֹת; וּבְחוּמָּשִׁין, מִלְּמַטָּה – שָׁלֹשׁ אֶצְבָּעוֹת, מִלְמַעְלָה – שְׁתֵּי אֶצְבָּעוֹת, וּבֵין דַּף לְדַף – כִּמְלֹא רֶיוַח רוֹחַב גּוּדָל;

The measure of the **margin**[H] of a Torah scroll is as follows: The size of the **lower** margin is **one handbreadth** [*tefaḥ*].[L] There is a requirement for a large margin there, so that a reader not inadvertently rest his arm on the writing. The size of the **upper** margin, which is less susceptible to that occurrence, is **three fingerbreadths** [*etzba'ot*], **and** the space **between each column is equal to the full width of two fingerbreadths. And with regard to** one of **the five** books of the Torah that is written as an independent scroll, the size of the **lower** margin is **three fingerbreadths,** the size of the **upper** margin is **two fingerbreadths, and** the space **between each column is equal to the full width of a thumb-breadth** [*gudal*].[B]

NOTES

One may not prepare a sheet of parchment that has less than three or more than eight columns – פָּחוֹת מִיכָּן וְיָתֵר עַל כֵּן לֹא יַעֲשֶׂה: The sheets of parchment may not contain fewer than three columns of writing. This is because the sheets are sewn together, and if each sheet is too narrow then the seams will be too close together (Rashi). They may not be made up of more than eight columns, since it is explained in tractate *Megilla* (32a) that when furling a Torah scroll, one must ensure that it closes on the seam, and if the seams are too far apart this will be difficult to accomplish (*Nimmukei Yosef*).

Open Torah scroll with seams and columns visible

Can it enter your mind that a sheet may contain one verse – פָּסוּק אֶחָד סָלְקָא דַּעְתָּךְ: The *halakha* is that it is necessary to end the Torah scroll at the bottom of a column. Therefore, it is not possible for one to write a single verse on an entire sheet of parchment. The Gemara answers that the *baraita* meant that if only one verse remained, one could write the verse on a narrow column, writing only one word in each line, to ensure that he ends the Torah scroll at the bottom of a column (*Shita Mekubbetzet*, citing Rashi). *Tosafot* explain that one should write each word using extremely wide letters. The Rosh adds that if there are not enough words in the verse to write one word on every line of the column, then one should write using extremely tall letters so that each word will take up the space normally occupied by several lines.

LANGUAGE

Handbreadth [*tefaḥ*] – טֶפַח: The handbreadth is a measurement that is mentioned in the Torah (Exodus 25:25). It refers to the width of four fingers, excluding the thumb, when they are side by side. By contrast, an expansive handbreadth is measured with the fingers spread apart. There are those who understand the term to relate to the palm. Radak explains the rabbinic usage *metapeḥin* for clapping based on this assumption, as it means to bang the palms against each other. Others hold that a *tefaḥ* is equivalent to a fist. Calculations for the measurement of the handbreadth range between 8 cm (Rabbi Ḥayyim Na'e) and 9.6 cm (*Ḥazon Ish*).

BACKGROUND

Fingerbreadth [*etzba*] and thumb-breadth [*gudal*] – אֶצְבַּע וְגוּדָל: The rabbinic term *etzba*, when used to signify a measure of size, usually refers to the width of the thumb at its widest point (see 41b), and calculations of this measurement range between 2 and 2.4 cm. In some contexts the term *etzba* refers to the index finger and not the thumb. Some explain that here the measure referred to as an *etzba* must be the index finger, since the thumb is also mentioned as a separate measure of size (see *Beit Yosef*, *Yoreh De'a* 283).

HALAKHA

A sheet of parchment from three columns, etc. – יְרִיעָה מִבַּת שָׁלֹשׁ דַּפִּין וכו׳: A sheet of parchment for a Torah scroll must be prepared for the writing of at least three columns and no more than eight columns. If one happened to acquire a sheet of parchment large enough for the writing of nine columns, he should not divide it into a sheet of three columns and a sheet of six columns; rather, he should divide it into a sheet of four columns and a sheet of five columns. This is the *halakha* with regard to the beginning and middle of the Torah scroll. At the end of the scroll, one may write a single column with one verse on a sheet and sew it to the rest of the sheets of parchment (Rambam *Sefer Ahava, Hilkhot Tefillin UMezuza VeSefer Torah* 9:12; *Shulḥan Arukh, Yoreh De'a* 272:3).

And he may not increase the number of columns – וְלֹא יַרְבֶּה בְּדַפִּין: The length of a line in a Torah scroll is the equivalent of thirty letters, i.e., one handbreadth. It should not be narrower than this, because then the column has the appearance of a missive, and it should not be wider than this, because it will cause the reader's eyes to wander and not be able to find the correct beginning of the following line. This is said specifically when the writing is small, but if the letters are very large then it is simply a question of what is aesthetically pleasing, since one would not have difficulty finding the beginning of the line if the letters were large enough (Rambam *Sefer Ahava, Hilkhot Tefillin UMezuza VeSefer Torah* 7:4; *Shulḥan Arukh, Yoreh De'a* 272:2, and see *Shakh* there).

The measure of the margin, etc. – שִׁיעוּר גִּלָּיוֹן וכו׳: The measure of the margins of a Torah scroll is as follows: The size of the lower margin is four thumb-breadths, the size of the upper margin is three thumb-breadths, and the space between each column is two thumb-breadths. Therefore, one should leave enough space at the beginning of every sheet of parchment to allow for both a thumb-breadth and the space needed to sew the parchment together with the other sheets, to ensure that after the sheets are sewn together there remains a space of two thumb-breadths. Between each line there should also be the space of a line. All of these measurements are necessary to fulfill the mitzva in the optimal fashion, but if they are not followed the Torah scroll is fit (Rambam *Sefer Ahava, Hilkhot Tefillin UMezuza VeSefer Torah* 7:4–5, 9:2; *Shulḥan Arukh, Yoreh De'a* 273:1, 5).

וּבֵין שִׁיטָה לְשִׁיטָה – כִּמְלֹא שִׁיטָה, וּבֵין תֵּיבָה לְתֵיבָה – כִּמְלֹא אוֹת קְטַנָּה, וּבֵין אוֹת לְאוֹת – כִּמְלֹא חוּט הַשַּׂעֲרָה.

And the space **between** one **line** of a Torah scroll **and** the following **line** must be **equal to** the space of **a full line, and** the space **between** one **word and** the following **word**[H] must be **equal to a full small letter,** and as for the space **between** one **letter and** the following **letter,** it is sufficient for it to be **equal to a full hairbreadth.**

אַל יְמַעֵט אָדָם אֶת הַכְּתָב, לֹא מִפְּנֵי רֶיוַח שֶׁל מַטָּה וְלֹא מִפְּנֵי רֶיוַח שֶׁל מַעְלָה, וְלֹא מִפְּנֵי רֶיוַח שֶׁבֵּין שִׁיטָה לְשִׁיטָה, וְלֹא מִפְּנֵי רֶיוַח שֶׁבֵּין פָּרָשָׁה לְפָרָשָׁה.

The *halakhot* of the margins notwithstanding, **a person may not reduce**[H] the size of **the writing** in a manner that the size of the writing is not consistent, **not in order to** ensure the correct amount of **space for the lower** margin, **nor in order to** ensure the correct amount of **space for the upper** margin, **nor in order to** ensure the correct amount of **space between** one **line and** the following **line, nor in order to** ensure the correct amount of **space between** one **passage and** the following **passage,** as this is not aesthetically pleasing.

נִזְדַּמְּנָה לוֹ תֵּיבָה בַּת חָמֵשׁ אוֹתִיּוֹת – לֹא יִכְתּוֹב שְׁתַּיִם בְּתוֹךְ הַדַּף וְשָׁלֹשׁ חוּץ לַדַּף,

If one happens upon a word[H] **that comprises five letters** and cannot be written in its entirety within the column, **he may not write two** letters **within the column and three outside of the column,** in the margin.

HALAKHA

And the space between one word and the following word, etc. – **וּבֵין תֵּיבָה לְתֵיבָה וכו׳**: Every letter must be surrounded on all four sides by blank parchment and not be joined to another letter. The space between each letter may be as small as a hairbreadth, and should not be much larger than that, to prevent one word from appearing as though it were two separate words. There should be a space between each word equal to the size of a small letter; two words may not be written closer together, lest they appear to be one word. If the scribe did not follow these instructions and left a larger space between two letters so that a child of average intelligence reads the one word as two words, then the scroll is unfit (Rambam *Sefer Ahava, Hilkhot Tefillin UMezuza VeSefer Torah* 8:4; *Shulḥan Arukh, Yoreh De'a* 274:4).

A person may not reduce, etc. – **אַל יְמַעֵט אָדָם וכו׳**: One may not reduce the size of the letters in order to preserve the correct amount of space for the upper or lower margins, or in order to preserve the correct amount of space between different passages (Rambam *Sefer Ahava, Hilkhot Tefillin UMezuza VeSefer Torah* 7:5; *Shulḥan Arukh, Yoreh De'a* 273:2).

If one happens upon a word – **נִזְדַּמְּנָה לוֹ תֵּיבָה**: In a case where one is almost at the end of a line and must now write a word containing five letters, he may not write two letters inside the column and then write the remaining three in the margin of the column. Rather, he should write three letters in the column, and then write two in the margin of the column. If there is not enough room to write three letters, he should not stretch out the letters of the final word on the line in an attempt to fill the line, but rather should leave the space blank and continue writing on the following line (Rambam *Sefer Ahava, Hilkhot Tefillin UMezuza VeSefer Torah* 7:5; *Shulḥan Arukh, Yoreh De'a* 273:3).

Perek **III**
Daf **30** Amud **b**

NOTES

One may even wipe away – **אַף מוֹחֵק**: Although the new writing will not be as clear, one may even wipe away the word while the ink is still wet rather than scraping away the dried ink. Alternatively, according to Rabbeinu Gershom Meor HaGola this means that one may use water to erase the ink even after it has dried.

אֶלָּא שָׁלֹשׁ בְּתוֹךְ הַדַּף וּשְׁתַּיִם חוּץ לַדַּף. נִזְדַּמְּנָה לוֹ תֵּיבָה בַּת שְׁתֵּי אוֹתִיּוֹת – לֹא יִזְרְקֶנָּה לְבֵין הַדַּפִּין, אֶלָּא חוֹזֵר וְכוֹתֵב בִּתְחִילַּת הַשִּׁיטָה.

Rather, he should write **three** letters **in the column and two outside of the column. If he happens** upon **a word that comprises two letters**[H] and cannot be written in its entirety within the column, **he may not cast it** in the margin **between the** two **columns; rather, he should return and write** the word **at the beginning of the** following **line.**

הַטּוֹעֶה בַּשֵּׁם – גּוֹרֵר אֶת מַה שֶּׁכָּתַב, וְתוֹלֶה אֶת מַה שֶּׁגָּרַר, וְכוֹתֵב אֶת הַשֵּׁם עַל מְקוֹם הַגְּרָר, דִּבְרֵי רַבִּי יְהוּדָה. רַבִּי יוֹסֵי אוֹמֵר: אַף תּוֹלִין אֶת הַשֵּׁם. רַבִּי יִצְחָק אוֹמֵר: אַף מוֹחֵק וְכוֹתֵב.

§ **One who mistakenly** omitted **the name** of God and wrote the next word before discovering his error should **scrape off that which he wrote, and suspend** the words **that he scraped off** above the line, **and write the name** of God **upon the place that had been scraped;** this is **the statement of Rabbi Yehuda. Rabbi Yosei says: One may even suspend the name** of God above the line,[H] without scraping off the word that was written in its place. **Rabbi Yitzḥak says:** Not only may one scrape off the dry ink of the next word, but one may **even wipe away**[N] the word while the ink is still wet **and write** the name of God in its place.

HALAKHA

A word that comprises two letters – **תֵּיבָה בַּת שְׁתֵּי אוֹתִיּוֹת**: If one is at the end of a line and must now write a word containing two letters, he should not write it outside of the column but instead should write it on the next line (Rambam *Sefer Ahava, Hilkhot Tefillin UMezuza VeSefer Torah* 7:6; *Shulḥan Arukh, Yoreh De'a* 273:3, and in the comment of Rema).

One may even suspend the name of God above the line – **אַף תּוֹלִין אֶת הַשֵּׁם**: If one forgot to write the name of God, he may suspend it above the line. If part of the name is written in the line and part of it above the line, it is unfit. This is in accordance with the opinion of Rabbi Shimon Shezuri. It is permitted to write the name of God on the place that had been scraped or wiped away, in accordance with the opinion of Rabbi Yosei and Rabbi Yitzḥak. If possible, one should scrape or wipe off the word that was accidentally written in its place rather than writing the name of God above the line (Rambam *Sefer Ahava, Hilkhot Tefillin UMezuza VeSefer Torah* 1:16; *Shulḥan Arukh, Yoreh De'a* 273:6, 276:6–7, and see *Oraḥ Ḥayyim* 32:24).

רַבִּי שִׁמְעוֹן שְׁזוּרִי אוֹמֵר: כָּל הַשֵּׁם כּוּלּוֹ תּוֹלִין, מִקְצָתוֹ אֵין תּוֹלִין. רַבִּי שִׁמְעוֹן בֶּן אֶלְעָזָר אוֹמֵר מִשּׁוּם רַבִּי מֵאִיר: אֵין כּוֹתְבִין אֶת הַשֵּׁם לֹא עַל מְקוֹם הַגְּרָר וְלֹא עַל מְקוֹם הַמְּחָק וְאֵין תּוֹלִין אוֹתוֹ, כֵּיצַד עוֹשֶׂה? מְסַלֵּק אֶת הַיְרִיעָה כּוּלָּהּ וְגוֹנְזָהּ.

Rabbi Shimon Shezuri[P] **says:** A scribe **may suspend the entire name** of God above the line, but he **may not suspend part of** the name of God above the line. **Rabbi Shimon ben Elazar says in the name of Rabbi Meir:** A scribe **may not write the name** of God **either upon the place that had been scraped or upon the place that had been wiped away, and** he **may not suspend it** above the line, as none of these options exhibit sufficient respect for the name of God. **What should** the scribe **do? He should remove the entire sheet** of parchment **and inter it.**

אִיתְּמַר: רַב חֲנַנְאֵל אָמַר רַב, הֲלָכָה: תּוֹלִין אֶת הַשֵּׁם. רַבָּה בַּר בַּר חָנָה אָמַר רַבִּי יִצְחָק בַּר שְׁמוּאֵל, הֲלָכָה: מוֹחֵק וְכוֹתֵב.

It was stated that the *amora'im* disagreed with regard to the final halakhic ruling: **Rav Ḥananel says** that **Rav** says: The ***halakha*** is that one **suspends the name** of God above the line. **Rabba bar bar Ḥana says** that **Rabbi Yitzḥak bar Shmuel** says: The ***halakha*** is that one may even **wipe away** the word while the ink is still wet **and write** the name of God in its place.

וְלֵימָא מָר הֲלָכָה כְּמָר, וּמָר הֲלָכָה כְּמָר! מִשּׁוּם דְּאַפְכִי לְהוּ.

The Gemara asks: **And** why is it necessary to state the actual opinions? **Let this Sage**, Rav Ḥananel in the name of Rav, **say** that the ***halakha*** **is in accordance with** the opinion of **this Sage**, Rabbi Yosei; **and** let **this Sage**, Rabba bar bar Ḥana in the name of Rabbi Yitzḥak bar Shmuel, say that the ***halakha*** is **in accordance with** the opinion of that **Sage**, Rabbi Yitzḥak. The Gemara answers: **Since** there are those **who reverse** the opinions of the *tanna'im*, they needed to state the opinions explicitly.

אָמַר רָבִין בַּר חִינָּנָא אָמַר עוּלָּא אָמַר רַבִּי חֲנִינָא: הֲלָכָה כְּרַבִּי שִׁמְעוֹן שְׁזוּרִי; וְלֹא עוֹד, אֶלָּא כָּל מָקוֹם שֶׁשָּׁנָה רַבִּי שִׁמְעוֹן שְׁזוּרִי – הֲלָכָה כְּמוֹתוֹ.

Ravin bar Ḥinnana says that **Ulla says** that **Rabbi Ḥanina says:** The ***halakha*** is **in accordance with** the opinion of **Rabbi Shimon Shezuri; and moreover,** not only is the *halakha* in accordance with his opinion with regard to this matter, but in **any place where Rabbi Shimon Shezuri taught** a *halakha*, the ***halakha*** is **in accordance with his** opinion.

אַהַיָּיא? אִילֵימָא אַהָא, רַבִּי שִׁמְעוֹן שְׁזוּרִי אוֹמֵר: כָּל הַשֵּׁם כּוּלּוֹ תּוֹלִין, מִקְצָתוֹ אֵין תּוֹלִין; וְהָא אִיתְּמַר עֲלָהּ: אָמַר רַב חֲנַנְאֵל אָמַר רַב, הֲלָכָה: תּוֹלִין אֶת הַשֵּׁם, וְרַבָּה בַּר בַּר חָנָה אָמַר רַב יִצְחָק בַּר שְׁמוּאֵל, הֲלָכָה: מוֹחֵק וְכוֹתֵב;

The Gemara asks: **To which** statement of Rabbi Shimon Shezuri is this referring? **If we say** that it is referring **to** the statement **here,** where **Rabbi Shimon Shezuri says:** A scribe **may suspend the entire name** of God above the line, but he **may not suspend part of** the name of God above the line, that is difficult: **But wasn't it stated with regard to that** *baraita* that **Rav Ḥananel says** that **Rav says:** The ***halakha*** is that one **suspends the name** of God above the line, **and Rabba bar bar Ḥana says** that **Rabbi Yitzḥak bar Shmuel** says: The ***halakha*** is that one may even **wipe away** the word while the ink is still wet **and write** the name of God in its place?

וְאִם אִיתָא, הוּא נַמִּי לֵימָא!

And if it is so that when Rabbi Ḥanina said that the *halakha* is in accordance with the opinion of Rabbi Shimon Shezuri he was referring to this matter, then **let** Ravin bar Ḥinnana **also say** along with those *amora'im* that the *halakha* is that one suspends the entire name of God above the line, but not a part of the name.

אֶלָּא אַהָא, רַבִּי שִׁמְעוֹן שְׁזוּרִי אוֹמֵר: אֲפִילּוּ בֶּן חָמֵשׁ שָׁנִים וְחוֹרֵשׁ בַּשָּׂדֶה – שְׁחִיטַת אִמּוֹ מְטַהֲרַתּוּ;

Rather, say that Rabbi Ḥanina's statement that the *halakha* is in accordance with the opinion of Rabbi Shimon Shezuri was referring not to the discussion here, but was stated **with regard to this** mishna (*Ḥullin* 74b): **Rabbi Shimon Shezuri says:** If one ritually slaughtered a pregnant cow and the calf was then removed alive, the ritual slaughter of the mother is effective with regard to the calf as well. And **even** if the calf is **five years old and plowing the field** when one wants to eat it, **the** earlier **slaughter of its mother renders it permitted,**[H] and it does not require ritual slaughter before it is eaten.

הָא אִיתְּמַר עֲלָהּ, זְעֵירִי אָמַר רַבִּי חֲנִינָא: הֲלָכָה כְּרַבִּי שִׁמְעוֹן שְׁזוּרִי, וְאִם אִיתָא, הוּא נַמִּי לֵימָא!

The Gemara asks: **But wasn't it** already **stated with regard to that** mishna that **Ze'eiri says** that **Rabbi Ḥanina** says: The ***halakha*** is **in accordance with** the opinion of **Rabbi Shimon Shezuri? And if it is so** that when Rabbi Ḥanina said that the *halakha* is in accordance with the opinion of Rabbi Shimon Shezuri he was referring to this matter, then **let** Ravin bar Ḥinnana **also say** along with Ze'eiri that the *halakha* is in accordance with the opinion of Rabbi Shimon Shezuri.

PERSONALITIES

Rabbi Shimon Shezuri – רַבִּי שִׁמְעוֹן שְׁזוּרִי: A fourth-generation *tanna*, Rabbi Shimon Shezuri is called by the name of the place where he lived, Shezur. He was a disciple of Rabbi Tarfon, and from the Gemara it appears that he was the teacher of Rabbi Yosei ben Keifar.

HALAKHA

The slaughter of its mother renders it permitted – שְׁחִיטַת אִמּוֹ מְטַהֲרַתּוּ: If one ritually slaughters an animal and discovers a live fetus inside, although it is fully formed and can live on its own, slaughter is not required in order to eat it, as the slaughter of its mother renders it permitted. If after the slaughter of the mother the fetus then emerged and stood upon the ground, then it must be slaughtered before it is eaten, lest people come to permit the consumption of animals that have not been slaughtered. This is in accordance with the opinion of the Rabbis, who disagree with Rabbi Shimon Shezuri, and according to Rav Ashi's ruling in *Ḥullin* 75b (Rambam *Sefer Kedusha, Hilkhot Ma'akhalot Assurot* 5:14; *Shulḥan Arukh, Yoreh De'a* 13:2).

אֶלָּא אַהָא, בָּרִאשׁוֹנָה הָיוּ אוֹמְרִים: הַיּוֹצֵא בְּקוֹלָר וְאָמַר ״כִּתְבוּ גֵּט לְאִשְׁתִּי״ – הֲרֵי אֵלּוּ יִכְתְּבוּ וְיִתְּנוּ, חָזְרוּ לוֹמַר: אַף הַמְפָרֵשׂ וְהַיּוֹצֵא בְּשַׁיָּירָא, רַבִּי שִׁמְעוֹן שְׁזוּרִי אוֹמֵר: אַף הַמְסוּכָּן.

Rather, say that Rabbi Ḥanina's statement was **with regard to this** mishna (*Gittin* 65b): **Initially** the Sages **would say:** With regard to **one who was taken out in a collar** [*kolar*][HL] to be executed **and said: Write a bill of divorce for my wife, these** people **should write and give** her the document. Although he did not explicitly say the word give, this is understood to have been his intention, in order to release her from the obligation to perform levirate marriage or *ḥalitza*. **They then said** that this *halakha* applies **even to one who sets sail and one who departs with a caravan** to a distant place. A bill of divorce is given to his wife under these circumstances even if her husband said only: Write a bill of divorce for my wife. **Rabbi Shimon Shezuri says: Even** in the case of **one who is dangerously ill** who gives that instruction, they write the bill of divorce and give it to his wife.

אִי נַמִי, אַהָא: תְּרוּמַת מַעֲשֵׂר שֶׁל דְּמַאי שֶׁחָזְרָה לִמְקוֹמָהּ – רַבִּי שִׁמְעוֹן שְׁזוּרִי אוֹמֵר: אַף בַּחוֹל שׁוֹאֲלוֹ וְאוֹכְלוֹ עַל פִּיו;

Alternatively, Rabbi Ḥanina's statement was **with regard to this** *halakha*: In the case of ***teruma* of the tithe**[B] **of *demai*,**[B] which is separated from the produce received from an *am ha'aretz*, who is suspected of not separating tithes properly, **that returned to its** original **place,**[H] i.e., it became mixed with the produce from which it had been separated, **Rabbi Shimon Shezuri says:** In this situation, not only did the Sages permit one to ask the *am ha'aretz* whether he had set aside his tithes in the proper manner and to rely on his response on Shabbat, a day when it is not permitted to separate tithes, but **one may ask him and eat based on his** statement **even on a weekday.**[N]

וְהָא אִיתְּמַר עֲלָהּ, אָמַר רַבִּי יוֹחָנָן: הֲלָכָה כְּרַבִּי שִׁמְעוֹן שְׁזוּרִי בִּמְסוּכָּן וּבִתְרוּמַת מַעֲשֵׂר שֶׁל דְּמַאי, וְאִם אִיתָא, הוּא נַמִי לֵימָא!

The Gemara asks: **But wasn't it** already **stated with regard to** those *mishnayot* that **Rabbi Yoḥanan says:** The ***halakha* is in accordance with** the opinion of **Rabbi Shimon Shezuri in** the case of one who is **dangerously ill, and in** the case of ***teruma* of the tithe of *demai*? And if it is so** that when Rabbi Ḥanina said that the *halakha* is in accordance with the opinion of Rabbi Shimon Shezuri he was referring to these *mishnayot*, then **let** Ravin bar Ḥinnana **also say** along with Rabbi Yoḥanan that the *halakha* is in accordance with the opinion of Rabbi Shimon Shezuri.

NOTES

One may ask him and eat based on his statement even on a weekday – אַף בַּחוֹל שׁוֹאֲלוֹ וְאוֹכְלוֹ עַל פִּיו: *Demai* is produce received from an *am ha'aretz*, who is not trusted with regard to the separation of tithes. The Sages decreed that tithes and *teruma* of the tithe must be set aside from this produce, but not *teruma*, as even *amei ha'aretz* were careful with regard to its separation. The Sages ruled that on Shabbat one may ask an *am ha'aretz* whether he had separated his tithes and may eat the produce if he affirms that he did so. At the conclusion of Shabbat one may no longer eat from that produce until he himself has separated the tithes. Rabbi Shimon Shezuri maintains that just as the Sages ruled that it is permitted for one to rely on an *am ha'aretz* on Shabbat because it is not permitted to separate the tithes on Shabbat, the same applies in this case, in which the situation also cannot be rectified: Since the *teruma* of the tithe of *demai* fell back into its original place, where it renders forbidden non-sacred produce of up to ninety-nine times its volume, the Sages allowed one to rely on the statement of an *am ha'aretz* (Rashi). In the Jerusalem Talmud a different reason is stated: The Sages rendered it permitted for one to rely on an *am ha'aretz* on Shabbat because he is afraid to lie on that holy day (see *Tosafot*). Similarly, in this case, where there is *teruma* of the tithe within his produce, he becomes fearful with regard to this prohibition and would not lie when questioned about it (Rashi on *Ḥullin* 75a). The Rambam explains that this is a case where the *am ha'aretz* was seen initially separating the *teruma* of the tithe. Therefore, once it fell back in, he is deemed credible when he says that he rectified the produce after the *teruma* of the tithe fell back inside.

BACKGROUND

***Teruma* of the tithe – תְּרוּמַת מַעֲשֵׂר:** The Levites are commanded to separate one-tenth of the tithe given to them and to give it to the priests. The Torah calls this: "A tithe from the tithe" (Numbers 18:26), and the Sages refer to it as the *teruma* of the tithe. All of the *halakhot* applying to *teruma* also apply to *teruma* of the tithe. Even today, *teruma* of the tithe must be separated from produce, though it is ritually impure and therefore may not be eaten.

***Demai* – דְּמַאי:** *Demai* is produce, or food made from produce, that was purchased from one who may not have separated the various tithes as required by *halakha*. The literal meaning of the word *demai* is suspicion, i.e., produce about which there is a suspicion that tithes were not properly taken from it. In the Second Temple period, the Sages decreed that this produce should be considered as having uncertain status, even if the owner claims that he separated the tithes. Therefore, the buyer of this produce must tithe it himself. Nevertheless, since it was probable that the produce was in fact tithed, certain leniencies were permitted with regard to eating and using *demai*.

HALAKHA

One who was taken out in a collar, etc. – הַיּוֹצֵא בְּקוֹלָר וכו׳: With regard to one who is dangerously ill; one who is taken out with a collar around his neck to be executed, even if his execution is due to a monetary matter; and one who sets sail in a boat or departs in a caravan to a distant place; if he said: Write a bill of divorce for my wife, the witnesses should write, sign, and give her the document, as it is clear that his intention was for them to write and give it to her. The *halakha* is in accordance with the opinion of Rabbi Shimon Shezuri, as Rabbi Yoḥanan ruled in accordance with his opinion (Rambam *Sefer Nashim, Hilkhot Geirushin* 2:12; *Shulḥan Arukh, Even HaEzer* 141:16).

***Teruma* of the tithe of *demai* that returned to its original place – תְּרוּמַת מַעֲשֵׂר שֶׁל דְּמַאי שֶׁחָזְרָה לִמְקוֹמָהּ:** In a case where one who is unreliable with regard to tithes was seen separating *teruma* of the tithe from his produce, if this *teruma* fell back into the produce or into other produce and that person claims that he set aside the *teruma* of the tithe again from that produce, his statement is accepted, and one may eat the produce even on a weekday. This is because even those who are unreliable with regard to tithes are not suspected of feeding others a mixture of non-sacred produce and *teruma*. The *halakha* is in accordance with the opinion of Rabbi Shimon Shezuri, as Rabbi Yoḥanan ruled in accordance with his opinion (Rambam *Sefer Zera'im, Hilkhot Ma'aser* 12:4, and see Ra'avad and Mahari Kurkus there).

LANGUAGE

Collar [*kolar*] – קוֹלָר: From the Latin collare, referring to a neck band or chain collar worn by captives and others.

Roman prisoner's neck chain or collar

אֶלָּא אַהָא, רַבִּי יוֹסֵי בֶּן כֵּיפַר אוֹמֵר מִשּׁוּם רַבִּי שִׁמְעוֹן שְׁזוּרִי: פּוֹל הַמִּצְרִי שֶׁזְּרָעוֹ לְזֶרַע, מִקְצָתוֹ הִשְׁרִישׁ לִפְנֵי רֹאשׁ הַשָּׁנָה וּמִקְצָתוֹ אַחַר רֹאשׁ הַשָּׁנָה – אֵין תּוֹרְמִין מִזֶּה עַל זֶה, לְפִי שֶׁאֵין תּוֹרְמִין וּמְעַשְּׂרִין לֹא מִן הֶחָדָשׁ עַל הַיָּשָׁן וְלֹא מִן הַיָּשָׁן עַל הֶחָדָשׁ,

Rather, say that Rabbi Ḥanina's statement was made **with regard to this** *halakha*: **Rabbi Yosei ben Keifar**[P] **says in the name of Rabbi Shimon Shezuri:** If one **planted a cowpea**[BH] plant **for its seed,**[N] i.e., not to be eaten as a vegetable but for one to either eat or plant its seeds, and **some of** the plants **took root before Rosh HaShana, while some of** them took root only **after Rosh HaShana, one may not separate** *teruma* or tithes **from this for that, as one may not separate** *teruma* **or tithes from the new** crop **for the old**[H] **or from the old** crop **for the new.**

כֵּיצַד יַעֲשֶׂה? צוֹבֵר גָּרְנוֹ לְתוֹכוֹ, וְנִמְצָא תּוֹרֵם וּמְעַשֵּׂר מִן הֶחָדָשׁ שֶׁבּוֹ עַל הֶחָדָשׁ שֶׁבּוֹ, וּמִן הַיָּשָׁן שֶׁבּוֹ עַל הַיָּשָׁן שֶׁבּוֹ;

How, then, **shall one act** so that he not err and set aside *teruma* and tithes incorrectly? It is difficult to know when the plants took root. He shall **pile** the entire stock onto **his threshing floor, into the** middle **of it,** mix the stock together, and then separate *teruma* and tithes; **and** consequently **it will turn out** that he has **separated** *teruma* **and tithes from the new** crop in the mixture **for the new** crop **in it, and from the old** crop **in** the mixture **for the old** crop **in it.**

הָא אִיתְּמַר עֲלָהּ, אָמַר רַבִּי שְׁמוּאֵל בַּר נַחְמָנִי אָמַר רַבִּי יוֹחָנָן: הֲלָכָה כְּרַבִּי שִׁמְעוֹן שְׁזוּרִי, וְאִם אִיתָא, הוּא נַמִּי לֵימָא!

The Gemara asks: **Wasn't it** already **stated with regard to that** *baraita* that **Rabbi Shmuel bar Naḥmani says that Rabbi Yoḥanan says:** The *halakha* **is in accordance with** the opinion of **Rabbi Shimon Shezuri? And if it is so** that when Rabbi Ḥanina said that the *halakha* is in accordance with the opinion of Rabbi Shimon Shezuri he was referring to this *baraita*, then **let** Ravin bar Ḥinnana **also say** along with Rabbi Shmuel bar Naḥmani that the *halakha* is in accordance with the opinion of Rabbi Shimon Shezuri.

אֶלָּא אֲמַר רַב פַּפָּא: אַשִּׁידָּה, רַב נַחְמָן בַּר יִצְחָק אָמַר: אַיַּיִן. רַב פַּפָּא אֲמַר:

Rather, Rav Pappa said: Rabbi Ḥanina's statement was **with regard to a chest. Rav Naḥman bar Yitzḥak said** that it was **with regard to wine.** The Gemara elaborates: **Rav Pappa said**

BACKGROUND

Cowpea – פּוֹל הַמִּצְרִי: According to the Jerusalem Talmud, it appears that this plant, whose name in Aramaic literally means Egyptian bean, is *Vigna luteola* of the Faboideae family.

It appears that the reference here is to one of the climbing varieties of this plant. The stems climb or spread out a considerable distance. The pods are 7–13 cm long, and the seeds are small. The plant is edible fresh or dry. Today it is grown as animal fodder, but apparently in ancient times it was also grown for its seeds.

Cowpea seeds

Cowpea stalks

Cowpea flower

HALAKHA

Cowpea – פּוֹל הַמִּצְרִי: In the case of the cowpea, even if part of it took root before Rosh HaShana and part took root only after Rosh HaShana, one should pile the entire stock onto his threshing floor, mix the stock together, and then set aside *teruma* and tithes, because the tithe year follows the time of the full ripening of the produce. This is in accordance with the opinion of Rabbi Shimon Shezuri and the explanation of Shmuel, who rules in accordance with this opinion on *Rosh HaShana* 13b (Rambam *Sefer Zera'im*, *Hilkhot Ma'aser Sheni* 1:8).

One may not separate *teruma* or tithes from the new crop for the old – אֵין תּוֹרְמִין וּמְעַשְּׂרִין לֹא מִן הֶחָדָשׁ עַל הַיָּשָׁן: One may not set aside *teruma* or tithes from this year's crop on behalf of last year's crop, or from last year's crop on behalf of this year's crop. If he separated them in this manner, his *teruma* is not considered *teruma*, as it is stated: "You shall tithe…that which is brought forth in the field year by year" (Deuteronomy 14:22). This is in accordance with the mishna in *Terumot* 1:5 (Rambam *Sefer Zera'im*, *Hilkhot Terumot* 5:11).

PERSONALITIES

Rabbi Yosei ben Keifar – רַבִּי יוֹסֵי בֶּן כֵּיפַר: This Sage, who was from the last generation of *tanna'im*, is mentioned in the *Tosefta* and in *baraitot*, but not in the Mishna. He was apparently a primary disciple of Rabbi Elazar ben Shammua, and most of the statements he cites are in his teacher's name. It is related that he was one of the emissaries sent to Babylonia to raise funds for the scholars of Eretz Yisrael. He is grouped together with Rabbi Dostai, son of Rabbi Yehuda, and Rabbi Dostai, son of Rabbi Yannai, who were also among the last of the *tanna'im*.

A Rabbi Yosei ben Keifar is also mentioned in the context of an important mission of the Sages of Eretz Yisrael to quash the attempts of Ḥananya to determine the calendar outside Eretz Yisrael. Based on the chronology, this was apparently a different Sage with the same name.

NOTES

If one planted a cowpea plant for its seed – פּוֹל הַמִּצְרִי שֶׁזְּרָעוֹ לְזֶרַע: Had it been planted to be eaten as a vegetable, it would have the same status as all other vegetables, which are subject to *teruma* and tithes from the time that they are harvested and not from when they take root. Therefore, there would be no uncertainty, since they are all picked during the course of the same year.

אַשִּׁידָּה, דִּתְנַן: בֵּית שַׁמַּאי אוֹמְרִים: נִמְדֶּדֶת מִבִּפְנִים, וּבֵית הִלֵּל אוֹמְרִים: מִבַּחוּץ, וּמוֹדִים אֵלּוּ וְאֵלּוּ שֶׁאֵין עוֹבִי הָרַגְלַיִם וְעוֹבִי הַלִּבְזְבָזִין נִמְדָּד;

that Rabbi Ḥanina's statement was **with regard to a chest,**[H] **as we learned** in a mishna (*Kelim* 18:1): A wooden chest that is large enough to contain forty *se'a* is not susceptible to contracting ritual impurity, since it is no longer considered a vessel. In determining its capacity, **Beit Shammai say** that **it is measured on the inside, and Beit Hillel say** that **it is measured on the outside** so that the volume of the walls of the chest itself is included in the measurement. **And** both Beit Shammai **and** Beit Hillel **concede that the volume of the legs and the volume of the rims** [***halevazbazin***][L] **are not measured.**

רַבִּי יוֹסֵי אוֹמֵר: מוֹדִים שֶׁעוֹבִי הָרַגְלַיִם וְעוֹבִי הַלִּבְזְבָזִין נִמְדָּד, וּבֵינֵיהֶן אֵין נִמְדָּד; רַבִּי שִׁמְעוֹן שְׁזוּרִי אוֹמֵר: אִם הָיוּ רַגְלַיִם גְּבוֹהוֹת טֶפַח – אֵין בֵּינֵיהֶן נִמְדָּד, וְאִם לָאו – בֵּינֵיהֶן נִמְדָּד.

Rabbi Yosei says: They concede that the volume of the legs and the volume of the rims are **measured,**[N] **but** the space enclosed **between** the rims and the legs **is not measured. Rabbi Shimon Shezuri says: If** the **legs were** one **handbreadth high** then the space **between** the legs **is not measured,** since the area has an independent significance, **but if** the space is **not** one handbreadth high, the space **between** the legs **is measured** as part of the chest. It is with regard to this statement that Rabbi Ḥanina said the *halakha* is in accordance with the opinion of Rabbi Shimon Shezuri.

רַב נַחְמָן בַּר יִצְחָק אָמַר: אַיַּיִן, דִּתְנַן, רַבִּי מֵאִיר אוֹמֵר: שֶׁמֶן תְּחִלָּה לְעוֹלָם, וַחֲכָמִים אוֹמְרִים: אַף הַדְּבַשׁ, רַבִּי שִׁמְעוֹן שְׁזוּרִי אוֹמֵר: אַף הַיַּיִן. מִכְּלָל דְּתַנָּא קַמָּא סָבַר: יַיִן לָא? אֵימָא, רַבִּי שִׁמְעוֹן שְׁזוּרִי אוֹמֵר: יַיִן.

Rav Naḥman bar Yitzḥak said that Rabbi Ḥanina's statement was **with regard to wine, as we learned** in a mishna (*Teharot* 3:2): **Rabbi Meir says: Oil,** an example of a liquid, that contracted impurity, is **always** considered to have **first**-degree ritual impurity,[H] even if it came into contact with an item that was impure with second-degree ritual impurity, which, according to the standard *halakhot* of ritual impurity, should result in it having third-degree ritual impurity. **And the Rabbis say** that this is the *halakha* **even** with regard to **honey. Rabbi Shimon Shezuri says:** This is the *halakha* **even** with regard to **wine.** The Gemara asks: **By inference,** is that to say **that the first *tanna*** holds that **wine** is **not** considered a liquid? Rather, **say** as follows: **Rabbi Shimon Shezuri says: Wine** is considered a liquid, but oil and honey are not.

תַּנְיָא, אָמַר רַבִּי שִׁמְעוֹן שְׁזוּרִי: פַּעַם אַחַת נִתְעָרֵב לִי טֶבֶל בְּחוּלִּין, וּבָאתִי וְשָׁאַלְתִּי אֶת רַבִּי טַרְפוֹן, וְאָמַר לִי: לֵךְ קַח לָךְ מִן הַשּׁוּק וְעַשֵּׂר עָלָיו;

§ The Gemara relates another statement of Rabbi Shimon Shezuri: **It is taught** in a *baraita* that **Rabbi Shimon Shezuri said: Once, my untithed produce**[B] **became mixed together with** a greater quantity of **non-sacred,** i.e., tithed, **produce, and I came and asked Rabbi Tarfon** how I should separate tithes from the untithed produce that was mixed with the tithed produce. **And he said to me: Go and take from the market** doubtfully tithed produce, which requires the removal of tithes by rabbinic law, **and separate tithes from it on behalf of** the untithed produce that is mixed with the tithed produce.

LANGUAGE

Rims [*levazbazin*] – לִבְזְבָזִין: From the Greek λαβίς, *labis*, meaning a handle. The Talmud uses this term in reference to the part of a vessel added for decoration or for some other purpose.

NOTES

They concede that the volume of the legs and the volume of the rims are measured – מוֹדִים שֶׁעוֹבִי הָרַגְלַיִם וְעוֹבִי הַלִּבְזְבָזִין נִמְדָּד: Rabbi Yosei's opinion is ostensibly difficult, as he explains that Beit Shammai agree that the volume of the legs is included in the measurement, whereas it is stated explicitly in the mishna that Beit Shammai do not include the volume of the walls of the chest itself. The commentaries explain that in fact according to Rabbi Yosei, Beit Shammai and Beit Hillel do not disagree about whether the volume of the walls of the chest is included in the measurement (*Shita Mekubbetzet*).

BACKGROUND

Untithed produce – טֶבֶל: This is produce from which *teruma* and tithes have not been separated. The Torah prohibits the consumption of untithed produce. One who eats untithed produce is punished with death at the hand of Heaven. Once the tithes are separated, even if they have not yet been given to those for whom they are designated, the produce no longer has the status of untithed produce and may be eaten.

HALAKHA

Chest – שִׁידָּה: A vessel that is designated to rest in a fixed place, such as a chest, is not susceptible to ritual impurity provided that it has a capacity of forty *se'a*, i.e., it measures at least one cubit by one cubit by three cubits. In determining the holding capacity, the item is measured on its outside, and if it meets this criterion, even though the interior holds less than forty *se'a*, it is not susceptible to ritual impurity. This is in accordance with the opinion of Beit Hillel. The thickness of the rims and legs are not included in the measurement, which is not in accordance with the opinion of Rabbi Shimon Shezuri. Despite the fact that Rav Pappa rules in accordance with his opinion, the Rambam rules in accordance with the opinion of Rav Ashi in tractate *Ḥullin* (75a), who states that the *halakha* is in accordance with the opinion of Rabbi Shimon Shezuri only in the case of one who is dangerously ill and in the case of *teruma* of the tithe (Rambam *Sefer Tahara, Hilkhot Kelim* 3:4).

Oil is always considered to have first-degree ritual impurity, etc. – שֶׁמֶן תְּחִלָּה לְעוֹלָם וכו׳: Oil or honey that became impure, then congealed, and afterward returned to a liquid state is always considered to be impure with first-degree ritual impurity, since it is considered liquid despite the fact that it became congealed after contracting ritual impurity. This is in accordance with the opinion of Rabbis, and not that of Rabbi Shimon Shezuri, who ruled this way in the case of wine, in accordance with the ruling of Rav Ashi in tractate *Ḥullin* (75a). According to the Rambam, oil is not susceptible to contracting ritual impurity when it is in a congealed state, since it is not a liquid or a food. According to the Ra'avad, oil can contract first-degree ritual impurity even when it is congealed (Rambam *Sefer Tahara, Hilkhot Tumat Okhalin* 1:19 and see *Kesef Mishne* there, 9:1).

קָסָבַר: דְּאוֹרַיְיתָא בְּרוּבָּא בָּטֵל, וְרוֹב עַמֵּי הָאָרֶץ מְעַשְּׂרִים הֵן, וַהֲוָה לֵיהּ כְּתוֹרֵם מִן הַפְּטוּר עַל הַפְּטוּר.

The Gemara explains: Rabbi Tarfon **holds** that **by Torah law** the minority of untithed produce is **nullified in the majority** of tithed produce and is therefore exempt from tithes; it is by rabbinic law that it is not nullified and one is obligated to separate tithes from it. **And** additionally, he holds that **the majority of those who are unreliable with regard to tithes** [*amei ha'aretz*] **do separate tithes,** in which case by Torah law one is not obligated to separate tithes from produce purchased from the market. **And** therefore, if Rabbi Shimon Shezuri receives produce from an *am ha'aretz*, **he is considered** by Torah law **to be separating tithes from exempt** produce **on behalf of exempt** produce,[N] while all of it is obligated in tithes by rabbinic law.

וְלֵימָא לֵיהּ: לֵךְ קַח מִן הַגּוֹי! קָסָבַר: אֵין קִנְיָן לְגוֹי בְּאֶרֶץ יִשְׂרָאֵל לְהַפְקִיעַ מִיַּד מַעֲשֵׂר, וַהֲוָה לֵיהּ מִן הַחִיּוּב עַל הַפְּטוּר.

The Gemara suggests: **But let** Rabbi Tarfon **say to him: Go and take** produce **from a gentile.** Since it is exempt from tithes by Torah law but requires tithing by rabbinic law, he could then separate tithes from this produce on behalf of the untithed produce that is nullified by the tithed produce. The Gemara explains: Rabbi Tarfon **holds** that **a gentile has no acquisition** of land **in Eretz Yisrael**[H] **to abrogate** the sanctity of the land, thereby removing it **from** the obligation to **tithe** its produce. **And** therefore, if Rabbi Shimon Shezuri were to take produce from a gentile, he would be **considered to be** separating tithes **from** produce **that is obligated** in tithes by Torah law **on behalf of exempt** produce, which one may not do.

אִיכָּא דְּאָמְרִי, אֲמַר לֵיהּ: לֵךְ קַח מִן הַגּוֹי; קָסָבַר: יֵשׁ קִנְיָן לְגוֹי בְּאֶרֶץ יִשְׂרָאֵל לְהַפְקִיעַ מִיַּד מַעֲשֵׂר, וַהֲוָה לֵיהּ מִן הַפְּטוּר עַל הַפְּטוּר.

There are those **who say** that Rabbi Tarfon **said to him: Go and take** produce **from a gentile** and separate tithes from it on behalf of the untithed produce that is intermingled in the majority of tithed produce. Accordingly, Rabbi Tarfon **holds** that **a gentile has acquisition** of land **in Eretz Yisrael to abrogate** the sanctity of the land, thereby removing it **from** the obligation to **tithe** its produce. **And** therefore, if Rabbi Shimon Shezuri takes produce from a gentile, **he is considered,** by Torah law, **to be** separating tithes **from exempt** produce **on behalf of exempt** produce, while all of it is obligated in tithes by rabbinic law.

וְלֵימָא לֵיהּ: קַח מֵהַשּׁוּק! קָסָבַר: אֵין רוֹב עַמֵּי הָאָרֶץ מְעַשְּׂרִין.

The Gemara suggests: **But let** Rabbi Tarfon **say to him:** Go and **take** produce **from** an *am ha'aretz* in **the market** and separate tithes from it on behalf of the mixed untithed produce. The Gemara explains: Rabbi Tarfon **holds** that **the majority of** ***amei ha'aretz*** **do not separate tithes,** in which case he is considered to be separating tithes from produce that is obligated in tithes by Torah law on behalf of exempt produce.

שְׁלַח לֵיהּ רַב יֵימָר בַּר שֶׁלֶמְיָא לְרַב פַּפָּא, הָא דַּאֲמַר רָבִין בַּר חִינָּנָא אָמַר עוּלָּא אָמַר רַבִּי חֲנִינָא: הֲלָכָה כְּרַבִּי שִׁמְעוֹן שְׁזוּרִי, וְלֹא עוֹד, אֶלָּא כָּל מָקוֹם שֶׁשָּׁנָה רַבִּי שִׁמְעוֹן שְׁזוּרִי הֲלָכָה כְּמוֹתוֹ, אַף בְּנִתְעָרֵב לֵיהּ טֶבֶל בְּחוּלִּין?

Rav Yeimar bar Shelamya sent the following question **to Rav Pappa: That which Ravin bar Ḥinnana said** that **Ulla says** that **Rabbi Ḥanina says:** The ***halakha*** **is in accordance with** the opinion of **Rabbi Shimon Shezuri, and moreover, any place where Rabbi Shimon Shezuri taught** a *halakha*, the ***halakha*** **is in accordance with his** opinion, was that said **even with regard to** the case of **one whose untithed produce became mixed together with non-sacred,** i.e., tithed, **produce,** or was Rabbi Ḥanina referring only to cases where Rabbi Shimon Shezuri stated his opinion in the Mishna, but not in a *baraita*?

אֲמַר לֵיהּ: אִין. אֲמַר רַב אַשִׁי: אֲמַר לִי מָר זוּטְרָא, קָשֵׁי בָּהּ רַבִּי חֲנִינָא מִסּוּרָא: פְּשִׁיטָא!

Rav Pappa **said to him: Yes,** the *halakha* is in accordance with the opinion of Rabbi Shimon Shezuri even with regard to untithed produce that was mixed together with tithed produce. **Rav Ashi said: Mar Zutra**[P] **said to me: Rabbi Ḥanina of Sura raised a difficulty with this:** Isn't it **obvious?**

NOTES

He is considered to be separating tithes from exempt produce on behalf of exempt produce – הֲוָה לֵיהּ כְּתוֹרֵם מִן הַפְּטוּר עַל הַפְּטוּר: He would be separating tithes from produce that is exempt by Torah law and requires tithing by rabbinic law, on behalf of produce that is exempt by Torah law and requires tithing by rabbinic law. One may not separate tithes from produce that requires tithing by Torah law on behalf of produce that requires tithing only by rabbinic law, or vice versa (*Terumot* 1:5).

PERSONALITIES

Mar Zutra – מָר זוּטְרָא: A colleague of Rav Ashi, Mar Zutra was one of the most prominent Sages of his generation and was a disciple-colleague of Rav Pappa and Rav Naḥman bar Yitzḥak. Beyond his greatness in *halakha* and *aggada*, Mar Zutra was a noted orator, and his homiletic interpretations are cited throughout the Talmud. The title Mar is indicative of his affiliation with the house of the Exilarch, where he apparently held an official position as scholar and orator. Late in his life, he was appointed head of the yeshiva of Pumbedita. Some believe Mar Zutra to be the Sage known as Mar Zutra Ḥasida, who was renowned for his piety and humility.

HALAKHA

A gentile has no acquisition of land in Eretz Yisrael – אֵין קִנְיָן לְגוֹי בְּאֶרֶץ יִשְׂרָאֵל: A gentile has no acquisition of land in Eretz Yisrael to abrogate the sanctity of the land. Therefore, if a Jew purchases land from a gentile, he is obligated to separate *terumot*, tithes, and first fruits from the produce of that land, as though the land were never owned by a gentile. The *halakhot* of the Sabbatical Year apply to this land as well. The *Pe'at HaShulḥan* (16:40) discusses whether this is also the *halakha* while the land is in the possession of the gentile, and whether this is the *halakha* nowadays, when the *halakhot* of *terumot*, tithes, and the Sabbatical Year apply only by rabbinic law (Rambam *Sefer Zera'im*, *Hilkhot Terumot* 1:10; *Shulḥan Arukh*, *Yoreh De'a* 331:3).

מִי קָאָמַר "בְּמִשְׁנָתֵינוּ"? "כׇּל מָקוֹם שֶׁשָּׁנָה" קָאָמַר.

Does Rabbi Ḥanina **say** that wherever Rabbi Shimon Shezuri taught a *halakha* **in our Mishna** the *halakha* is in accordance with his opinion? Rather, **he says** that **any place where he taught** a *halakha* the *halakha* is in accordance with his opinion, and this applies even to *baraitot*.

אָמַר רַב זְעֵירָא אָמַר רַב חֲנַנְאֵל אָמַר רַב: קֶרַע הַבָּא בִּשְׁנֵי שִׁיטִּין – יִתְפּוֹר, בְּשָׁלֹשׁ – אַל יִתְפּוֹר. אֲמַר לֵיהּ רַבָּה זוּטִי לְרַב אָשֵׁי, הָכִי אָמַר רַבִּי יִרְמְיָה מִדִּיפְתִּי מִשְּׁמֵיהּ דְּרָבָא: הָא דְּאָמְרִינַן בְּשָׁלֹשׁ אַל יִתְפּוֹר – לָא אֲמָרַן אֶלָּא בְּעַתִּיקָתָא, אֲבָל חֲדַתָּתָא לֵית לַן בַּהּ;

§ **Rav Ze'eira says** that **Rav Ḥananel says** that **Rav says: If a tear** in the parchment of a Torah scroll **extends into two lines,**[H] **one can sew** the parchment to render the scroll fit, but if it extends **into three** lines then **one cannot sew** it to render it fit. **Rabba Zuti said to Rav Ashi: This** is what **Rabbi Yirmeya of Difti said in the name of Rava: That which we say,** that if the tear extends **into three** lines **one cannot sew** it to render it fit, **we say only with regard to old** sheets of parchment. **But** in the case of **new** sheets of parchment, **we have no** problem **with it.**

וְלָא עַתִּיקָתָא – עַתִּיקָתָא מַמָּשׁ, וְלָא חֲדַתָּתָא – חֲדַתָּתָא מַמָּשׁ, אֶלָּא הָא דְּלָא אֲפִיצָן, הָא דַּאֲפִיצָן; וְהָנֵי מִילֵּי בְּגִידִין, אֲבָל בִּגְרָדִין לָא.

The Gemara adds: **And old** does **not** mean **literally old, and new** does **not** mean **literally new. Rather, those** sheets of parchment **that are not processed with gall**[B] are labeled as old and cannot be sewn, whereas **those** sheets of parchment **that are processed with gall** are labeled as new and can be sewn. **And this statement,** that one can sew the parchment and render it fit, applies to sewing it **with sinew;**[H] **but** if one sews the parchment **with thread** [*bigradin*],[L] it is **not** rendered fit.[N]

בָּעֵי רַב יְהוּדָה בַּר אַבָּא: בֵּין דַּף לְדַף, בֵּין שִׁיטָה לְשִׁיטָה, מַאי? תֵּיקוּ.

Rav Yehuda bar Abba asks: If the tear occurred in the space **between** one **column and** another **column** but it was of the length that had it occurred inside a column it would have extended more than three lines, and similarly, if the tear occurred **between** one **line and** another **line**[H] horizontally, but not tearing through any letters, **what** is the *halakha*? No answer was found, and therefore the dilemma **shall stand** unresolved.

אָמַר רַבִּי זְעֵירִי אָמַר רַב חֲנַנְאֵל אָמַר רַב: מְזוּזָה שֶׁכְּתָבָהּ שְׁתַּיִם שְׁתַּיִם – כְּשֵׁרָה. אִיבַּעְיָא לְהוּ: שְׁתַּיִם וְשָׁלֹשׁ וְאַחַת, מַהוּ? אָמַר רַב נַחְמָן בַּר יִצְחָק: כׇּל שֶׁכֵּן, שֶׁעֲשָׂאָהּ כְּשִׁירָה. מֵיתִיבִי: עֲשָׂאָהּ כְּשִׁירָה, אוֹ שִׁירָה כְּמוֹתָהּ – פְּסוּלָה! כִּי תַּנְיָא הַהִיא בְּסֵפֶר תּוֹרָה.

§ **Rabbi Ze'eiri says** that **Rav Ḥananel says** that **Rav says: A** *mezuza* **that one wrote two by two,** i.e., two words on each line, **is fit.**[N] **A dilemma was raised before** the Sages: If one wrote **two** words on one line, **and three** words on the following line, **and one** word on the line after that, **what is the** *halakha*? **Rav Naḥman bar Yitzḥak said: All the more so** that it is fit, **as he prepared it** as one writes **a poem**[B] in the Torah scroll. The song sung by the Jewish people at the sea after the Exodus is written in lines whose length is not uniform. The Gemara **raises an objection** from a *baraita*: **If one wrote it as** one writes **a poem** in the Torah, **or if one wrote a poem** in the Torah **as** one writes it, it is **unfit.** The Gemara answers: **When that** *baraita* **is taught,** it is referring **to a Torah scroll,**[H] not a *mezuza*.

HALAKHA

If a tear in the parchment of a Torah scroll extends into two lines – קֶרַע הַבָּא בִּשְׁנֵי שִׁיטִּין וכו׳: If there is a tear in the parchment of a Torah scroll that extends into two lines, one may repair it by sewing it, but if it extends into three lines one may not repair it by sewing it. This applies in the case of a scroll whose gall is not noticeable. If it is recognizable that the sheet had been processed with gall, one may repair it by sewing a tear that extends even into three lines, but no more than that (Rema, citing Rivash). Some say that one may repair it by sewing it even if it extends into more than three lines (see *Pitḥei Teshuva*). The *halakha* is in accordance with the statement of Rava, as explained by the Rambam. The parchment used nowadays has the status of parchment that was processed with gall (*Shakh*). With regard to all tears, one must take care not to remove a letter or alter its shape, and likewise one must make sure that the needle does not pierce the writing. If a single letter was divided by the tear, that letter is unfit, and there is no way to correct this flaw (Rambam *Sefer Ahava, Hilkhot Tefillin UMezuza VeSefer Torah* 9:15; *Shulḥan Arukh, Yoreh De'a* 280:1).

And this statement applies to sewing with sinew – וְהָנֵי מִילֵּי בְּגִידִין: One may sew a tear in the parchment of a Torah scroll only with sinew *ab initio*. The Rema writes that the custom is to sew with silk threads, and this too is fit, although preferably one should use sinew. The Rosh, citing the Jerusalem Talmud, rules that it is permitted to glue parchment behind the place of the tear (Rambam *Sefer Ahava, Hilkhot Tefillin UMezuza VeSefer Torah* 9:15; *Shulḥan Arukh, Yoreh De'a* 280:1).

Between one column and another column, between one line and another line – בֵּין דַּף לְדַף בֵּין שִׁיטָה לְשִׁיטָה: If the parchment of a Torah scroll was torn between one column and another, or between one word and another, one may repair it by sewing it. The reason for this ruling is that the dilemma is left unresolved by the Gemara, and in such instances the *halakha* is lenient in matters of rabbinic law. This is in accordance with the version of the text in the Rambam's possession, which reads: Between one word and another (*Beit Yosef*). The *Tur* is stringent in this regard, and in practice one should be stringent and not sew between one word and another if the tear extends into three lines (Rambam *Sefer Ahava, Hilkhot Tefillin UMezuza VeSefer Torah* 9:15; *Shulḥan Arukh, Yoreh De'a* 280:1, and see *Taz* there).

When that *baraita* is taught, it is referring to a Torah scroll – כִּי תַּנְיָא הַהִיא בְּסֵפֶר תּוֹרָה: If one wrote a prose passage of the Torah in the format of a poem written in the Torah, or a poem written in the Torah in the prose format, the Torah scroll is unfit. Some authorities permit its use provided that the song was written differently from the rest of the text, in the special format of a half-brick arranged upon a whole brick, even if not in the customary manner (Rambam *Sefer Ahava, Hilkhot Tefillin UMezuza VeSefer Torah* 7:11; *Shulḥan Arukh, Yoreh De'a* 275:3).

BACKGROUND

Processed with gall – אֲפִיצָן: Gall is a growth found on various kinds of trees, such as oak, sumac, and others, as a result of an infestation from certain species of insects. Gall contains a large amount of tannin, which is used in both leather tanning and the manufacture of ink.

Soaking animal skins in a solution including tannin serves to stabilize them and prepare them for use. Nowadays, most ink is made from a solution of gall with added iron salts. However, in talmudic times ink was usually manufactured from soot and oils.

He prepared it as one writes a poem – עֲשָׂאָהּ כְּשִׁירָה:

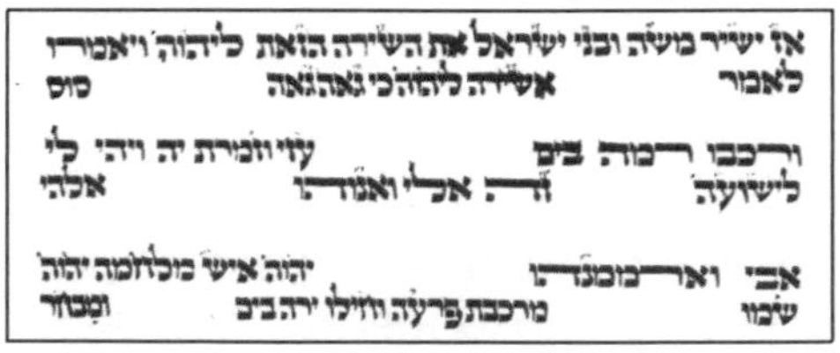

Excerpt from Song at the Sea as it appears in a Torah scroll

LANGUAGE

Thread [*geradin*] – גְּרָדִין: Apparently from the Greek γέρδιος, *gerdios*, meaning weaver. Several terms involving weaving and the loom are derived from this root.

NOTES

But with thread it is not rendered fit – אֲבָל בִּגְרָדִין לָא: This is due to the principle that one may sew a Torah scroll only with threads made of sinew, which is a *halakha* transmitted to Moses at Sinai (Rid; see *Megilla* 19a). Other early commentaries write that there is a difference between the sewing of sheets together, for which sinews are required, and the correction of a sheet, which may be performed with another material (Rosh, in a responsum). According to this opinion, the reason one may not use thread is that it impairs the appearance of the Torah scroll, or because these threads are not as strong as sinews. The commentaries add that following this reasoning, if one were to use silk threads it would be fit (*Sefer HaTeruma*; see *Kiryat Sefer*).

A *mezuza* that one wrote two by two is fit – מְזוּזָה שֶׁכְּתָבָהּ שְׁתַּיִם שְׁתַּיִם כְּשֵׁרָה: This is not the case with regard to a Torah scroll, in which each line must be long enough to contain the word *lemishpeḥoteikhem* at least three times (*Tohorat HaKodesh*, citing 30a; see *Kesef Mishne* on Rambam *Sefer Ahava, Hilkhot Tefillin UMezuza VeSefer Torah* 5:1).

אִתְּמַר נַמִּי: אָמַר רַבָּה בַּר בַּר חָנָה אָמַר רַבִּי יוֹחָנָן, וְאָמְרִי לַהּ אָמַר רַב אַחָא בַּר בַּר חָנָה אָמַר רַבִּי יוֹחָנָן: מְזוּזָה שֶׁעֲשָׂאָהּ שְׁתַּיִם וְשָׁלֹשׁ וְאַחַת – כְּשֵׁרָה, וּבִלְבַד שֶׁלֹּא יַעֲשֶׂנָּה כְּקוּבָּה, וּבִלְבַד שֶׁלֹּא יַעֲשֶׂנָּה כְּזָנָב.

It was stated by *amora'im* **as well: Rabba bar bar Ḥana says** that **Rabbi Yoḥanan says, and some say** it was **Rav Aḥa bar bar Ḥana** who **says** that **Rabbi Yoḥanan says:** With regard to **a** ***mezuza*** **that one prepared** with **two** words on one line, **and three** words on the following line, **and one** word on the line after that,[H] it is **fit, provided that he does not prepare it like** the shape of **a tent,** i.e., progressively widening the lines, starting with a line of one word, then a line of two words and a line of three, **and provided that he does not prepare it like** the shape of **a tail,** progressively shortening the lines, from three words to two to one.

אָמַר רַב חִסְדָּא: ״עַל הָאָרֶץ״ – בְּשִׁיטָה אַחֲרוֹנָה; אִיכָּא דְּאָמְרִי: בְּסוֹף שִׁיטָה, וְאִיכָּא דְּאָמְרִי: בִּתְחִילַּת שִׁיטָה.

§ **Rav Ḥisda says:** One writes the last two words of a *mezuza*, ***al ha'aretz***,[H] meaning "above the earth" (Deuteronomy 11:21), by themselves **on the final line,** without the preceding word. The Sages disagreed as to how this is done. **Some say** that one writes this phrase **at the end of** the final **line, and some say** that one writes it **at the beginning of** the final **line.**

מַאן דְּאָמַר בְּסוֹף שִׁיטָה – ״כִּגְבֹהַּ שָׁמַיִם עַל הָאָרֶץ״, וּמַאן דְּאָמַר בִּתְחִילַּת שִׁיטָה – כִּי הֵיכִי דְּמַרְחַקָא שָׁמַיִם מֵאָרֶץ.

The Gemara explains their dispute: **The one who says** that one writes it **at the end of** the final **line** interprets the verse: "That your days may be multiplied, and the days of your children, upon the land which the Lord swore unto your fathers to give them, as the days of the heaven above the earth," in a similar manner to the verse: **"For as the heaven is high above the earth"** (Psalms 103:11). Consequently, if one writes "above the earth" at the end of the final line, it will appropriately be below the term "the heaven" at the end of the previous line. **And the one who says** that one writes it **at the beginning of** the final **line** explains the phrase "as the days of the heaven above the earth" as meaning: **Just as the heaven is far from the earth.** Consequently, if one writes "above the earth" at the beginning of the final line, it is far from the term "the heaven" at the end of the previous line.

אָמַר רַבִּי חֶלְבּוֹ: חֲזֵינָא לֵיהּ לְרַב הוּנָא דְּכָרֵיךְ לַהּ מֵ״אֶחָד״ כְּלַפֵּי ״שְׁמַע״, וְעוֹשֶׂה פָּרְשִׁיּוֹתֶיהָ סְתוּמוֹת.

Rabbi Ḥelbo said: I saw Rav Huna wrap a written *mezuza* **from** the word ***eḥad*** **to** the word ***shema***,[H] i.e., rolling it from left to right, as the first verse written in a *mezuza* is: "Listen [*Shema*], O Israel, the Lord our God, the Lord is one [*eḥad*]" (Deuteronomy 6:4). **And he prepared** the two **passages of** the *mezuza* **in the closed**[B] manner, i.e., starting the second passage (Deuteronomy 11:13–21) on the same line that he finished writing the first passage (Deuteronomy 6:4–9).

מֵיתִיבִי, אָמַר רַבִּי שִׁמְעוֹן בֶּן אֶלְעָזָר: רַבִּי מֵאִיר הָיָה כּוֹתְבָהּ עַל דּוּכְסוּסְטוּס כְּמִין דַּף,

The Gemara **raises an objection** from a *baraita*: **Rabbi Shimon ben Elazar said: Rabbi Meir would write** a *mezuza* **on** ***dokhsostos***,[L] the inner layer of animal hide, not on parchment, which is from the outer layer, and he would prepare it **like a column**[N] of a Torah scroll, i.e., long and narrow.

BACKGROUND

He prepared the two passages of the ***mezuza*** **closed – עוֹשֶׂה פָּרְשִׁיּוֹתֶיהָ סְתוּמוֹת:** For many hundreds of years the custom of scribes has been to write the *mezuza* in a fixed format of twenty-two lines, with each line beginning with a designated word. According to this ancient custom, the seventh line opens with second passage of the *mezuza*. This custom does not allow the scribe to render the passages closed, following the standard definition of a closed passage, i.e., with the new passage starting on the same line on which the previous passage ended. The custom is in accordance with the opinion of the Rambam that the first passage concludes before the end of a line, and the second passage begins a little after the start of the next line. One can further see in this image that the words *al ha'aretz* are written at the beginning of the last line.

שמע ישראל יהוה אלהינו יהוה אחד ואהבת את
יהוה אלהיך בכל לבבך ובכל נפשך ובכל מאדך והיו
הדברים האלה אשר אנכי מצוך היום על לבבך ושננתם
לבניך ודברת בם בשבתך בביתך ובלכתך בדרך
ובשכבך ובקומך וקשרתם לאות על ידך והיו לטטפת
בין עיניך וכתבתם על מזזות ביתך ובשעריך
והיה אם שמע תשמעו אל מצותי אשר אנכי
מצוה אתכם היום לאהבה את יהוה אלהיכם ולעבדו
בכל לבבכם ובכל נפשכם ונתתי מטר ארצכם בעתו
יורה ומלקוש ואספת דגנך ותירשך ויצהרך ונתתי
עשב בשדך לבהמתך ואכלת ושבעת השמרו לכם
פן יפתה לבבכם וסרתם ועבדתם אלהים אחרים
והשתחויתם להם וחרה אף יהוה בכם ועצר את
השמים ולא יהיה מטר והאדמה לא תתן את יבולה
ואבדתם מהרה מעל הארץ הטבה אשר יהוה נתן לכם
ושמתם את דברי אלה על לבבכם ועל נפשכם וקשרתם
אתם לאות על ידכם והיו לטוטפת בין עיניכם ולמדתם
אתם את בניכם לדבר בם בשבתך בביתך ובלכתך
בדרך ובשכבך ובקומך וכתבתם על מזוזות ביתך
ובשעריך למען ירבו ימיכם וימי בניכם על האדמה
אשר נשבע יהוה לאבתיכם לתת להם כימי השמים
על הארץ

Text of a *mezuza*

LANGUAGE

Dokhsostos **– דּוּכְסוּסְטוּס:** From the Greek δίσχιστος, *diskhistos*, meaning cut in half or divided. Alternatively, it might be related to the Greek δίξοος, *dixoos*, meaning separated into two or forked. This term was applied to one of the parts of a hide that was split in two.

NOTES

Like a column – כְּמִין דַּף: Some commentaries explain that Rabbi Meir would write the two chapters of *Shema* in a single column rather than in two (Rid; see 33a). Others say that he wrote it like a column, which has a base and a capital, i.e., some of the lines were of equal length, whereas in other areas their length differed (*Nimmukei Yosef*).

HALAKHA

That one prepared with two words and three words and one word, etc. – שֶׁעֲשָׂאָהּ שְׁתַּיִם וְשָׁלֹשׁ וְאַחַת וכו׳: All the lines of a *mezuza* should be equal in length. If a line was longer than the preceding line, and the next line was shorter than the two preceding lines, the *mezuza* is fit, but if it is in the form of a tail, a tent, or a circle, the *mezuza* is unfit (Rambam *Sefer Ahava, Hilkhot Tefillin UMezuza VeSefer Torah* 5:1, 5; *Shulḥan Arukh, Yoreh De'a* 288:9, 11).

Al ha'aretz **– עַל הָאָרֶץ:** It is proper to write the words *al ha'aretz* on the final line of the *mezuza*, either at the start or in the middle of the line. The custom is to write them at the start of the last line (Rambam *Sefer Ahava, Hilkhot Tefillin UMezuza VeSefer Torah* 5:5; *Shulḥan Arukh, Yoreh De'a* 288:12).

From the word ***eḥad*** **to the word** ***shema*** **– מֵאֶחָד כְּלַפֵּי שְׁמַע:** A *mezuza* should be rolled up from the end of its lines to the beginning, so that one can read it as it is unrolled, as indicated by the incident involving Rav Huna (Rambam *Sefer Ahava, Hilkhot Tefillin UMezuza VeSefer Torah* 5:6; *Shulḥan Arukh, Yoreh De'a* 288:14).

וְעוֹשֶׂה רֶיוַח מִלְמַעְלָה וְרֶיוַח מִלְּמַטָּה, וְעוֹשֶׂה פָּרָשִׁיּוֹתֶיהָ פְּתוּחוֹת. אָמַרְתִּי לוֹ: רַבִּי, מַה טַּעַם? אָמַר לִי: הוֹאִיל וְאֵין סְמוּכוֹת מִן הַתּוֹרָה;

And he would make a space above and a space below the text **and would prepare the passages of** the *mezuza* in the **open** manner, i.e., he would begin the second passage on the line following the end of the first passage. **I said to him: My teacher,** for **what reason** do you prepare the passages in the open manner, when in a Torah scroll those same passages are written in the closed manner? **He said to me: Since** the passages **are not adjacent** to one another **in the Torah,**[N] as the first passage is Deuteronomy 6:4–9 and the second is Deuteronomy 11:13–21, I prepare them as open passages.

וְאָמַר רַב חֲנַנְאֵל אָמַר רַב: הֲלָכָה כְּרַבִּי שִׁמְעוֹן בֶּן אֶלְעָזָר, מַאי לָאו אַפְּתוּחוֹת?

The Gemara continues: **And Rav Ḥananel says** that **Rav says:** The ***halakha*** **is in accordance with** the opinion of **Rabbi Shimon ben Elazar. What, is it not** correct that Rav stated this **with regard to** Rabbi Shimon ben Elazar's opinion that one prepares the passages in the **open** manner? This would present a difficulty to the opinion of Rav Huna, Rav's student, who wrote them in the closed manner.

לָא, אַרֶיוַח. וְכַמָּה רֶיוַח? אָמַר רַב מְנַשְּׁיָא בַּר יַעֲקֹב, וְאָמְרִי לַהּ אָמַר רַב שְׁמוּאֵל בַּר יַעֲקֹב: כִּמְלֹא אַטְבָּא דְּסִיפְרֵי.

The Gemara answers: **No;** he meant that the *halakha* is in accordance with the opinion of Rabbi Shimon ben Elazar **with regard to** the **space** that one must leave above and below the text. The Gemara asks: **And how much space** must one leave? **Rav Menashya bar Ya'akov says, and some say** it is **Rav Shmuel bar Ya'akov** who **says:** The space **of a full scribe's clip** [*atba*],[LN] with which the sheets of parchment are held.

אֲמַר לֵיהּ אַבַּיֵי לְרַב יוֹסֵף: וְאַתְּ לָא תִּסְבְּרָא דְּכִי אֲמַר רַב אַרֶיוַח? וְהָא רַב אִית לֵיהּ מִנְהָגָא, וְהָאִידָּנָא נְהוּג עָלְמָא בִּסְתוּמוֹת;

Abaye said to Rav Yosef: And you, do you not hold that when Rav said that the *halakha* is in accordance with the opinion of Rabbi Shimon ben Elazar he was referring **to the space,** not the manner of writing the passages? **But Rav is of** the opinion that an established **custom** must be observed, **and nowadays the general custom** is to write the passages of the *mezuza* **in the closed** manner.

דְּאָמַר רַבָּה אָמַר רַב כָּהֲנָא אָמַר רַב: אִם יָבֹא אֵלִיָּהוּ וְיֹאמַר חוֹלְצִין בְּמִנְעָל – שׁוֹמְעִין לוֹ, אֵין חוֹלְצִין בְּסַנְדָּל – אֵין שׁוֹמְעִין לוֹ, שֶׁכְּבָר נָהֲגוּ הָעָם בְּסַנְדָּל.

The Gemara provides the source that according to Rav one must observe established customs. *Ḥalitza* is the ritual that frees the widow of a childless man from the obligation to enter into levirate marriage with her late husband's brother. This ceremony involves the widow removing her brother-in-law's sandal from his foot. Rabba spoke of the importance of observing customs in that context, **as Rabba says** that **Rav Kahana says** that **Rav says: If Elijah comes and says** that **one performs *ḥalitza***[B] **with a shoe,**[H] the Sages **listen to him.** But if he says that **one may not perform *ḥalitza* with a sandal, they do not listen to him, as the people are already accustomed** to performing *ḥalitza* **with a sandal.**

וְרַב יוֹסֵף אָמַר רַב כָּהֲנָא אָמַר רַב: אִם יָבֹא אֵלִיָּהוּ וְיֹאמַר אֵין חוֹלְצִין בְּמִנְעָל – שׁוֹמְעִין לוֹ, אֵין חוֹלְצִין בְּסַנְדָּל – אֵין שׁוֹמְעִין לוֹ, שֶׁכְּבָר נָהֲגוּ הָעָם בְּסַנְדָּל;

The Gemara presents another version of Rav's statement: **And Rav Yosef says** that **Rav Kahana says** that **Rav says: If Elijah comes and says** that **one may not perform *ḥalitza* with a shoe,** the Sages **listen to him;** if he says that **one may not perform *ḥalitza* with a sandal, they do not listen to him, as the people are already accustomed** to performing *ḥalitza* **with a sandal.**

LANGUAGE

Clip [*atba*] – אַטְבָּא: The term is *etev* in Hebrew, and it is of uncertain origin. Some maintain that it is a shortened version of *atba'a*, from the root *tet, beit, ayin,* meaning degraded or lowered, as the *etev* lowers a sheet and brings it near another sheet.

BACKGROUND

One performs *ḥalitza* – חוֹלְצִין: *Ḥalitza* is the ceremony that frees the widow of a man who died childless from the obligation to marry one of her deceased husband's brothers and allows her to remarry someone else (see Deuteronomy 25:7–10). The term *ḥalitza* is derived from the central element of this ceremony, which involves the removal [*ḥilutz*] by the widow of a special sandal from the foot of one of her deceased husband's brothers. *Ḥalitza* must be performed before a rabbinical court. The *halakhot* governing this ceremony are discussed in detail in tractate *Yevamot*.

HALAKHA

One performs *ḥalitza* with a shoe – חוֹלְצִין בְּמִנְעָל: The Rambam maintains that one may perform *ḥalitza* with a shoe *ab initio*. Most halakhic authorities contend that the *halakha* is in accordance with the opinion of Rabba that one may not use a shoe *ab initio*. Nevertheless, since this form of sandal is not available nowadays, they write that one should use a shoe that is at least somewhat similar to a sandal, which they define in various ways (Rambam *Sefer Nashim, Hilkhot Yibbum VaḤalitza* 4:6; *Shulḥan Arukh, Even HaEzer* 169:16, and in the comment of Rema).

NOTES

Since the passages are not adjacent to one another in the Torah – הוֹאִיל וְאֵין סְמוּכוֹת מִן הַתּוֹרָה: The purpose of a closed passage is to link two passages of the Torah, i.e., it is an indication that the second passage completes the previous one. Since the passages of the *mezuza* do not appear adjacent to one another in the Torah, this is not necessary (Responsa of the Maharshal, 37).

The space of a full scribe's clip – כִּמְלֹא אַטְבָּא דְּסִיפְרֵי: This refers to a piece of wood with a crack in the middle, into which the upper edge of a sheet of parchment, or several sheets, are inserted to ensure that they do not fold over while the scribe is writing (see Rashi and Rid). This itself is the reason for the space at the top, so that the clip does not touch the writing (*Nimmukei Yosef*). The *ge'onim* write that its measure is half a nail. Others explain that this refers to an iron implement, a kind of etcher with two heads with a fixed distance between them. This tool is used for scoring the lines on parchment, so that the space between the lines will be equal (*Sefer HaIttur*, citing Rav Amram Gaon).

וְאָמְרִינַן: מַאי בֵּינַיְיהוּ? מִנְעָל לְכַתְּחִילָּה אִיכָּא בֵּינַיְיהוּ! אֶלָּא לָאו שְׁמַע מִינָּהּ אֲוֵירוֹת, שְׁמַע מִינָּהּ.

Abaye continues: **And we say,** when discussing these versions of his statement: **What is the** difference **between** these two versions of his statement? The **difference is** whether one may use **a shoe *ab initio*.**[N] In any case, according to both statements Rav maintains that a custom must be observed, and the custom in this case is to write the passages in a closed manner. **Rather,** must one **not conclude from it** that when Rav says that the *halakha* is in accordance with the opinion of Rabbi Shimon ben Elazar he was speaking **of the space,** not the manner of preparing the passages? The Gemara affirms: **Conclude from it** that this is correct.

רַב נַחְמָן בַּר יִצְחָק אָמַר: מִצְוָה לַעֲשׂוֹתָן סְתוּמוֹת, וְאִי עָבְדִינְהוּ פְּתוּחוֹת – שַׁפִּיר דָּמֵי, וּמַאי פְּתוּחוֹת דְּקָאָמַר רַבִּי שִׁמְעוֹן בֶּן אֶלְעָזָר – אַף פְּתוּחוֹת.

§ **Rav Naḥman bar Yitzḥak said:** It is **a mitzva** *ab initio* **to prepare** the passages of a *mezuza* in the **closed**[H] manner, **but if one prepared them** in the **open** manner, it is **permitted** to use the *mezuza*. **And what is Rabbi Shimon ben Elazar saying** when he says that Rabbi Meir would prepare the passages in the **open** manner? He means that one may prepare them **even** in the **open** manner.

לֵימָא מְסַיֵּיעַ לֵיהּ: כַּיּוֹצֵא בּוֹ, סֵפֶר תּוֹרָה שֶׁבָּלָה וּתְפִילִּין שֶׁבָּלוּ אֵין עוֹשִׂין מֵהֶן מְזוּזָה, לְפִי שֶׁאֵין מוֹרִידִין מִקְּדוּשָּׁה חֲמוּרָה לִקְדוּשָּׁה קַלָּה; הָא מוֹרִידִין – עוֹשִׂין,

The Gemara suggests: **Let us say** that a *baraita* **supports his** opinion: **Similarly,** just as one may not convert phylacteries of the head into phylacteries of the arm, with regard to **a Torah scroll that became worn**[H] **and** parchment of **phylacteries that became worn, one may not fashion them into a *mezuza*** by excising the relevant passages, despite the fact that the Torah passages of a *mezuza* appear in them. This is prohibited **because one does not reduce** the sanctity of an item **from** a level of **greater sanctity,** that of a Torah scroll or phylacteries, **to** a level of **lesser sanctity,** that of a *mezuza*. The Gemara infers from this *baraita*: If it were permitted to **reduce** the sanctity of an item from a level of greater sanctity to a level of lesser sanctity, one could **fashion** a *mezuza* from a Torah scroll.

אַמַּאי? הָכָא סְתוּמוֹת וְהָכָא פְּתוּחוֹת! דִּלְמָא לְהַשְׁלִים.

The Gemara explains the proof: But **why** is that the *halakha*, when **here,** in a Torah scroll, the passages are prepared in the **closed** manner, **but there,** in a *mezuza*, the passages are prepared in the **open** manner? Evidently, it is permitted to write a *mezuza* with the passages prepared in the closed manner. The Gemara refutes this proof: **Perhaps** one should infer from the *baraita* that were it not for the fact that it is prohibited to reduce the sanctity of an item from a level of greater sanctity to a level of lesser sanctity, one would be allowed **to complete** a line or two of a *mezuza* by sewing to it those lines from a Torah scroll or parchment of phylacteries that became worn, but one may not fashion an entire *mezuza* from a sheet of a Torah scroll or parchment of phylacteries, as the passages in a Torah scroll and phylacteries are prepared in the closed manner.

הָא מוֹרִידִין – עוֹשִׂין? וְהָתַנְיָא: הֲלָכָה לְמֹשֶׁה מִסִּינַי – תְּפִילִּין עַל הַקְּלָף וּמְזוּזָה עַל דּוּכְסוּסְטוּס; קְלָף בִּמְקוֹם בָּשָׂר, דּוּכְסוּסְטוּס בִּמְקוֹם שֵׂעָר! לְמִצְוָה.

The Gemara asks another question: The *baraita* indicates **that** if it were permitted to **reduce** the sanctity of an item from a level of greater sanctity to a level of lesser sanctity, one could **fashion** a *mezuza* from phylacteries. **But isn't it taught** in a *baraita* that it is **a *halakha*** transmitted **to Moses from Sinai**[B] that the passages of **phylacteries** are written **on parchment,** the outer layer of an animal's hide, **and** the passages of **a *mezuza*** are written **on *dokhsostos*,**[HB] the inner layer, and when writing on **parchment,** one writes **on the side of** the hide that faced the **flesh;** when writing on ***dokhsostos*,** one writes **on the side of** the hide on which there was **hair?** How, then, can one use the other side of the hide for a *mezuza*? The Gemara answers that this requirement is of *dokhsostos* for a *mezuza* is stated **as a mitzva,** but it is not indispensable.

HALAKHA

It is a mitzva to prepare the passages of a *mezuza* closed – מִצְוָה לַעֲשׂוֹתָן סְתוּמוֹת: It is a mitzva to render closed the space between the two chapters of *Shema* in a *mezuza*; the *Shakh* describes how one should do so in practice. If one rendered them open, the *mezuza* is fit, as the chapters are not adjacent in the Torah. The *halakha* is in accordance with the opinion of Rav Naḥman bar Yitzḥak (Rambam *Sefer Ahava, Hilkhot Tefillin UMezuza VeSefer Torah* 5:2; *Shulḥan Arukh, Yoreh De'a* 288:13).

A Torah scroll that became worn, etc. – סֵפֶר תּוֹרָה שֶׁבָּלָה וכו׳: The appropriate passages from phylacteries or a Torah scroll that became worn may not be used in a *mezuza*, because one does not reduce the sanctity of an item from a level of greater sanctity to a level of lesser sanctity (Rambam *Sefer Ahava, Hilkhot Tefillin UMezuza VeSefer Torah* 5:1; *Shulḥan Arukh, Yoreh De'a* 290:1).

Phylacteries are written on parchment and a *mezuza* is written on *dokhsostos* – תְּפִילִּין עַל הַקְּלָף וּמְזוּזָה עַל דּוּכְסוּסְטוּס וכו׳: It is a *halakha* transmitted to Moses from Sinai that the passages of the phylacteries must be written on parchment, on the side of the flesh, whereas a *mezuza* is written on *dokhsostos*, on the side of the hair. If one wrote phylacteries on *dokhsostos*, they are unfit; if one wrote a *mezuza* on parchment or on hide that was processed with gall, it is fit, as the requirement of *dokhsostos* is only a mitzva *ab initio*. Nowadays, parchment is not prepared in precisely the same way as in the talmudic era, as the hide is not split into two. Rather, the side of the flesh is scrubbed heavily until only parchment remains, and the outer layer where there is hair is smoothed and processed. This has the halakhic status of talmudic-era parchment, and one should write on the side of the flesh. If one wrote on the side of the hair, some authorities rule leniently that it is fit after the fact (Rambam *Sefer Ahava, Hilkhot Tefillin UMezuza VeSefer Torah* 1:8; *Shulḥan Arukh, Oraḥ Ḥayyim* 32:7 and *Beur Halakha* there, and *Yoreh De'a* 271:3 and in the comment of Rema, 288:6).

BACKGROUND

***Halakha* transmitted to Moses from Sinai – הֲלָכָה לְמֹשֶׁה מִסִּינַי:** This refers to a *halakha* with no biblical basis, but which, according to tradition, was transmitted by God to Moses orally together with the Written Torah. These *halakhot* have the status of Torah law.

Parchment and *dokhsostos* – קְלָף וְדוּכְסוּסְטוּס: Torah scrolls and *megillot* were usually written on *gevil*, which is animal hide that has been processed through salting, flouring, and soaking in gallnut water in order to shrink and strengthen the hide. The process includes the removal of hair and the thin layer with the hair, as well as the removal of mucus and fat on the inner side. One would write on the outer side, which was smoother and more processed, not on the inner, greasier, and looser side.

The desire to make optimal use of the hide and the goal of minimizing the thickness of books led to the manufacture of parchment that was especially thin. For that reason, the thickness of the hide was split into two layers, parchment and *dokhsostos*, as is the case with scrolls found in the Judean Desert. From the period of the early commentaries, in most places hide that has been thoroughly processed on both sides has been used for books as well as for phylacteries and *mezuzot*. Although it is not identical to the parchment described by the Sages, it has the same halakhic status.

NOTES

The difference is whether one may use a shoe *ab initio* – מִנְעָל לְכַתְּחִילָּה אִיכָּא בֵּינַיְיהוּ: By Torah law both a sandal and a shoe are fit for *ḥalitza*. The Sages dispute whether one may use a shoe *ab initio*. Some say one may not do so, lest he use a shoe that is not whole. This concern does not apply to a sandal, which is made from a single piece of material (see *Yevamot* 102b). It can be inferred from Rabba's statement that one should not use a shoe *ab initio*, and therefore he says that only if Elijah comes and permits one to use it, the Sages listen to him. Conversely, Rav Yosef maintains that one may use a shoe *ab initio*, and for this reason he states that if Elijah comes and declares that one should not use it, the Sages listen to him (Rashi).

וְהָתַנְיָא: שִׁינָּה – פָּסוּל! בִּתְפִילִּין. וְהָתַנְיָא: שִׁינָּה בֵּין בָּזֶה וּבֵין בָּזֶה – פָּסוּל! אִידִי וְאִידִי בִּתְפִילִּין, וְהָא דְּכַתְבִינְהוּ אַקְלָף בִּמְקוֹם שֵׂעָר, וְהָא

The Gemara asks: **But isn't it taught** in a *baraita* that if one **changed** between parchment and *dokhsostos*, the item is **unfit?** The Gemara responds that this *baraita* is referring **to phylacteries** that one wrote on *dokhsostos* in the manner of a *mezuza*, not to a *mezuza* which one wrote on parchment. The Gemara raises a further difficulty: **But isn't it taught** in a *baraita* that if one **changed whether in this** manner **or in that** manner, it is **unfit?** The Gemara explains that this *baraita* does not mean that one changed either in the case of phylacteries or a *mezuza*. Rather, both **this** manner **and that** manner are referring **to phylacteries, and this** case is **where one wrote them on parchment** but **on the side of** the hide on which there was **hair,** not on the side that faced the flesh, **and that**

Perek **III**
Daf **32** Amud **b**

דְּכָתְבִינְהוּ אַדּוּכְסוּסְטוּס בִּמְקוֹם בָּשָׂר.

case is **where one wrote them on *dokhsostos* on the side** that faced the **flesh.**[N] In both of these situations the phylacteries are unfit, but a *mezuza* that one wrote on parchment is fit.

וְאִיבָּעֵית אֵימָא: שִׁינָּה בָּזֶה וּבָזֶה תַּנָּאֵי הִיא, דְּתַנְיָא: שִׁינָּה בָּזֶה וּבָזֶה – פָּסוּל, רַבִּי [אַחָא מַכְשִׁיר מִשּׁוּם רַבִּי] אַחַאי בְּרַבִּי חֲנִינָא, וְאָמְרִי לָהּ: מִשְּׁמֵיהּ דְּרַבִּי עֲקִיבָא בְּרַבִּי חֲנִינָא.

And if you wish, say instead that the ruling of the *baraita* that if one **changed whether in this** manner **or in that** manner it is unfit is in fact referring to a *mezuza* that one wrote on parchment, and this **is** a dispute between ***tanna'im*****, as it is taught** in a *baraita*: If one **changed in this** manner **or in that** manner it is **unfit. Rabbi Aḥa, in the name of Rabbi Aḥai, son of Rabbi Ḥanina, deems** it **fit; and some say** he said this ruling **in the name of Rabbi Akiva, son of Rabbi Ḥanina.**

הָא מוֹרִידִין – עוֹשִׂין? וְהָא בָּעֲיָא שִׂרְטוּט! דְּאָמַר רַב מִנְיוּמִי בַּר חִלְקִיָּה אָמַר רַב חָמָא בַּר גּוּרְיָא אָמַר רַב: כָּל מְזוּזָה שֶׁאֵינָהּ מְשׁוּרְטֶטֶת – פְּסוּלָה, וְרַב מִנְיָמִין בַּר חִלְקִיָּה דִּידֵיהּ אָמַר: שִׂרְטוּט שֶׁל מְזוּזָה – הֲלָכָה לְמֹשֶׁה מִסִּינַי!

§ The *baraita* indicates **that** if it were permitted to **reduce** the sanctity of an item from a level of greater sanctity to a level of lesser sanctity, one could **make** a *mezuza* from phylacteries that became worn. The Gemara raises a difficulty: **But** a *mezuza* **requires scoring,** i.e., the parchment must have lines etched in it before writing, **as Rav Minyumi bar Ḥilkiya says** that **Rav Ḥama bar Gurya says** that **Rav says:** **Any *mezuza* that is not scored** is **unfit, and Rav Minyumi bar Ḥilkiya himself says** concerning this: **The scoring of a *mezuza*** is **a *halakha*** transmitted **to Moses from Sinai.** With regard to phylacteries, by contrast, he does not teach that their parchment requires scoring.

תַּנָּאֵי הִיא; דְּתַנְיָא, רַבִּי יִרְמְיָה אוֹמֵר מִשּׁוּם רַבֵּינוּ: תְּפִילִּין וּמְזוּזוֹת נִכְתָּבוֹת שֶׁלֹּא מִן הַכְּתָב, וְאֵין צְרִיכוֹת שִׂירְטוּט.

The Gemara answers that this **is** a dispute between ***tanna'im*****, as it is taught** in a *baraita* that **Rabbi Yirmeya says in the name of our teacher,** Rav: **Phylacteries and *mezuzot* may be written** when the scribe is **not** copying **from a written** text, **and** their parchment **does not require scoring.**

NOTES

Where one wrote them on *dokhsostos* on the side that faced the flesh – דְּכָתְבִינְהוּ אַדּוּכְסוּסְטוּס בִּמְקוֹם בָּשָׂר: In other words, if one wrote phylacteries on *dokhsostos* they are unfit even if he wrote them on the side that faced the flesh, despite the fact that they are fit if written on parchment on the side that faced the flesh. All the more so are the phylacteries unfit if they are written on *dokhsostos* on the side on which there was hair, as in such a case they are unfit even if written on parchment (*Tosafot* on 32a).

וְהִילְכְתָא: תְּפִילִּין לָא בָּעֵי שִׂרְטוּט, וּמְזוּזָה בָּעֲיָא שִׂירְטוּט, וְאִידִי וְאִידִי נִכְתָּבוֹת שֶׁלֹּא מִן הַכְּתָב; מַאי טַעְמָא? מִיגְרַס גְּרִיסִין.

The Gemara concludes: **And the *halakha* is that the parchment of phylacteries does not require scoring,**[NH] **but** the parchment of **a *mezuza* requires scoring.**[H] And unlike a Torah scroll, both **these and those,** phylacteries and *mezuzot,* **may be written** when the scribe is **not** copying **from a written text.**[H] **What is the reason** for this leniency? These short texts **are well known** to all scribes, and therefore it is permitted to write them by heart.

אָמַר רַב חֶלְבּוֹ: אֲנָא חֲזֵיתֵיהּ לְרַב הוּנָא דַּהֲוָה יָתֵיב אַפּוּרְיָא דְּסֵפֶר תּוֹרָה עֲלֵיהּ, וְכַף לְכַדָּא אַאַרְעָא וְאַנַּח עֲלֵיהּ סֵפֶר תּוֹרָה, וַהֲדַר יָתֵיב בְּמִיטָּה; קָסָבַר: אָסוּר לֵישֵׁב עַל גַּבֵּי מִיטָּה שֶׁסֵּפֶר תּוֹרָה מוּנָּח עָלֶיהָ.

In connection to Rav Ḥelbo relating the customs of Rav Huna, the Gemara cites that **Rav Ḥelbo says: I myself saw Rav Huna as** he wished **to sit on his bed, which had a Torah scroll** placed **on it. And he overturned a jug on the ground and placed the Torah scroll on it, and only then sat on the bed.** The reason he did so is that **he holds** that it is **prohibited to sit on a bed upon which a Torah scroll is placed.**[H]

וּפְלִיגָא דְּרַבָּה בַּר בַּר חָנָה, דְּאָמַר רַבָּה בַּר בַּר חָנָה אָמַר רַבִּי יוֹחָנָן: מוּתָּר לֵישֵׁב עַל גַּבֵּי מִיטָּה שֶׁסֵּפֶר תּוֹרָה מוּנָּח עָלֶיהָ, וְאִם לְחָשְׁךָ אָדָם לוֹמַר: מַעֲשֶׂה בְּרַבִּי אֶלְעָזָר שֶׁהָיָה יוֹשֵׁב עַל הַמִּיטָּה וְנִזְכַּר שֶׁסֵּפֶר תּוֹרָה מוּנָּח עָלֶיהָ, וְנִשְׁמַט וְיָשַׁב עַל גַּבֵּי קַרְקַע, וְדוֹמֶה כְּמִי שֶׁהִכִּישׁוֹ נָחָשׁ – הָתָם סֵפֶר תּוֹרָה עַל גַּבֵּי קַרְקַע הֲוָה.

The Gemara notes: **And this *halakha* disagrees** with a ruling **of Rabba bar bar Ḥana, as Rabba bar bar Ḥana says** that **Rabbi Yoḥanan says: It is permitted to sit on a bed upon which a Torah scroll is placed. And if a person whispers to you, saying:** There was **an incident involving Rabbi Elazar, who was sitting on a bed and realized that a Torah scroll was placed on it, and** he immediately **slipped off** the bed **and sat upon the ground, and** in doing so he looked **like one who had been bitten by a snake,** i.e., he jumped up in a panic, that incident is no proof. **There,** the **Torah scroll was** placed **on the ground.**[NH] It is certainly disgraceful for one to sit on a bed while a Torah scroll is on the ground.

אָמַר רַב יְהוּדָה אָמַר שְׁמוּאֵל: כְּתָבָהּ אִגֶּרֶת – פְּסוּלָה; מַאי טַעְמָא? אָתְיָא כְּתִיבָה כְּתִיבָה מִסֵּפֶר.

The Gemara returns to the discussion about the *halakhot* of writing a *mezuza.* **Rav Yehuda says** that **Shmuel says:** If one **wrote** a *mezuza* in the manner of **a missive**[H] that one composes to a friend, i.e., without being exact about the lettering of each word, it is **unfit.**[N] **What is the reason?** This is **derived** by a verbal analogy between **"writing,"** and **"writing," from a scroll,**[N] which must be written in precisely the correct manner.

HALAKHA

The parchment of phylacteries does not require scoring – תְּפִילִּין לָא בָּעֵי שִׂרְטוּט: The parchment for the passages in the phylacteries does not require scoring, but scoring the top line is required. If a scribe must score each line in order to be able to write in straight lines he should do so in order to beautify the mitzva, but even if the lines are written crookedly it is fit after the fact (*Mishna Berura*). Some say that the parchment should be scored above the writing, below it, and at the two margins, even if one knows how to write without scoring, and this opinion is accepted in practice. The universal practice nowadays is to score each line of the parchment (Rambam *Sefer Ahava, Hilkhot Tefillin UMezuza VeSefer Torah* 1:12; *Shulḥan Arukh, Oraḥ Ḥayyim* 32:6, and in the comment of Rema).

The parchment of a *mezuza* requires scoring – וּמְזוּזָה בָּעֲיָא שִׂירְטוּט: It is a *halakha* transmitted to Moses from Sinai that the parchment of a *mezuza*, like that of a Torah scroll, requires scoring on each and every line. A *mezuza* written without scoring is unfit. One should not score with lead or any similar substance that colors the parchment (Rambam *Sefer Ahava, Hilkhot Tefillin UMezuza VeSefer Torah* 1:12; *Shulḥan Arukh, Yoreh De'a* 271:5, 288:8).

Written when the scribe is not copying from a written text – נִכְתָּבוֹת שֶׁלֹּא מִן הַכְּתָב: It is permitted to write phylacteries and a *mezuza* without copying from a written text, as their passages are well known. If one is not familiar enough with them, he should use a text or have someone else read them to him. The optimal manner of performing the mitzva is always to copy from a written text (Rambam *Sefer Ahava, Hilkhot Tefillin UMezuza VeSefer Torah* 1:12; *Shulḥan Arukh, Oraḥ Ḥayyim* 32:29, and see *Mishna Berura* there).

A bed upon which a Torah scroll is placed – מִיטָּה שֶׁסֵּפֶר תּוֹרָה מוּנָּח עָלֶיהָ: It is prohibited to sit on a bed, chair, or bench on which a Torah scroll is resting, as indicated by the incident involving Rav Huna. Some say that if the Torah scroll was placed at a location that is one handbreadth higher than where he sits, it is permitted (Ra'avad, citing the Jerusalem Talmud). It is a pious custom to be stringent and to raise the Torah scroll ten handbreadths from where one is sitting, or at least three handbreadths (Rambam *Sefer Ahava, Hilkhot Tefillin UMezuza VeSefer Torah* 10:6; *Shulḥan Arukh, Yoreh De'a* 282:7, and see *Shakh* there).

On the ground – עַל גַּבֵּי קַרְקַע: It is prohibited to place a Torah scroll on the ground, including the stairs before the Holy Ark in a synagogue. The same applies to other sacred books (*Shulḥan Arukh, Yoreh De'a* 282:7 in the comment of Rema).

If one wrote a *mezuza* in the manner of a missive – כְּתָבָהּ אִגֶּרֶת: If one wrote a *mezuza* and did not score the parchment or was not careful with regard to which words are plene or deficient, i.e., spelled with or without the letters *vav* and *yod*, or if he added even one superfluous letter, it is unfit. The *halakha* is in accordance with the opinion of Rav Yehuda, citing Shmuel (Rambam *Sefer Ahava, Hilkhot Tefillin UMezuza VeSefer Torah* 5:3, and see *Kesef Mishne* there).

NOTES

The parchment of phylacteries does not require scoring – תְּפִילִּין לָא בָּעֵי שִׂרְטוּט: The reason is that the purpose of scoring is to straighten the writing, to preserve its beauty. Since phylacteries are not designed to be read, as they are covered with hide and sewn up, this act is unnecessary. A *mezuza*, by contrast, can be opened and read at any time (Meiri, citing Rambam). Others suggest that the reason is that a *mezuza* is examined and read carefully every seven years, whereas phylacteries are checked only once every fifty years (Ran on *Megilla* 18b). Yet others say that the difference is due to the fact that phylacteries are written on very thin parchment, which might be torn by scoring (*Nimmukei Yosef*). The Meiri says that in fact this is the effect, not the cause: Since phylacteries do not require scoring, they are written on thin parchment.

Mezuza parchment with scoring visible at the tops of the letters

There the Torah scroll was placed on the ground – הָתָם סֵפֶר תּוֹרָה עַל גַּבֵּי קַרְקַע הֲוָה: This does not mean that the Torah scroll was literally on the ground, as the Gemara had stated that it was placed upon the bed. Rather, it was resting on the lower part of the bed, while Rabbi Elazar was sitting above it (commentary attributed to Rashba). Others explain that part of the Torah scroll was on the ground (see Rashi).

If one wrote a *mezuza* in the manner of a missive it is unfit, etc. – כְּתָבָהּ אִגֶּרֶת פְּסוּלָה וכו׳: Rashi provides two interpretations of this statement. First, that one wrote it without scoring; second, that one wrote it without being precise with regard to whether the words were written plene or deficient, i.e., without being particular about the letters *vav* and *yod*, which are sometimes included in a word and at other times omitted.

Writing and writing from a scroll – כְּתִיבָה כְּתִיבָה מִסֵּפֶר: While all agree that the verse employing a term of writing in the context of a *mezuza* is: "And you shall write them upon the doorposts of your house" (Deuteronomy 6:9), there is a disagreement among the early authorities as to the identity of the other verse in the verbal analogy. Rashi cites two opinions, either that it is referring to a verse stated with regard to the writing of a bill of divorce: "And he writes her a bill of divorce, and gives it in her hand" (Deuteronomy 24:1), or a verse stated with regard to the mitzva to eradicate the tribe of Amalek: "Write this for a memorial in the book, and rehearse it in the ears of Joshua: For I will utterly blot out the remembrance of Amalek from under the heaven" (Exodus 17:14). *Sefer HaEshkol* cites the verse stated with regard to the mitzva for a king to write a Torah scroll: "That he shall write him a copy of this law in a book" (Deuteronomy 17:18). The meaning of the term scroll in the Gemara will vary accordingly.

וְאָמַר רַב יְהוּדָה אָמַר שְׁמוּאֵל: תְּלָאָהּ בְּמַקֵּל – פְּסוּלָה; מַאי טַעְמָא? "בִּשְׁעָרֶיךָ" בָּעֵינַן. תַּנְיָא נַמִי הָכִי: תְּלָאָהּ בְּמַקֵּל אוֹ שֶׁהִנִּיחָהּ אַחַר הַדֶּלֶת – סַכָּנָה וְאֵין בָּהּ מִצְוָה.

And Rav Yehuda says that **Shmuel says:** If **one hung** a *mezuza* **on a stick**[H] in the entranceway, without affixing it to the doorpost, it is **unfit. What is the reason? We require** the fulfillment of the verse: "And you shall write them upon the doorposts of your house, and **upon your gates**" (Deuteronomy 6:9). **This** ruling **is also taught** in a *baraita*: If **one hung** a *mezuza* **on a stick, or placed it** so that it was affixed **behind the door**[BHN] within the house, he exposes himself to **danger, and it** does **not** enable him to fulfill the **mitzva.**[N]

שֶׁל בֵּית מוּנְבַּז הַמֶּלֶךְ הָיוּ עוֹשִׂין בְּפוּנְדְּקוֹתֵיהֶן כֵּן, זֵכֶר לִמְזוּזָה.

The Gemara relates: The members **of the household of King Munbaz**[P] **would do so,** i.e., hang *mezuzot* on sticks, **in their inns,** i.e., when they would sleep in an inn. They would not do this in order to fulfill the mitzva, as one who sleeps in an inn is exempt from placing a *mezuza,* but **in remembrance of** the ***mezuza.*** Since they would travel frequently, they wanted to remember the mitzva of *mezuza,* which they did not fulfill often.

וְאָמַר רַב יְהוּדָה אָמַר שְׁמוּאֵל: מִצְוָה לְהַנִּיחָהּ בְּתוֹךְ חֲלָלוֹ שֶׁל פֶּתַח. פְּשִׁיטָא, "בִּשְׁעָרֶיךָ" אָמַר רַחֲמָנָא! סָלְקָא דַּעְתָּךְ אָמִינָא, הוֹאִיל וְאָמַר רָבָא: מִצְוָה לְהַנִּיחָהּ

And Rav Yehuda says that **Shmuel says:** It is **a mitzva to place** the *mezuza* **within the airspace of the entrance,**[H] not on the outside. The Gemara asks: Isn't this **obvious?** After all, **the Merciful One states:** "And **upon your gates,**" which indicates that it must be within the area of the gate, rather than the outside. The Gemara explains that it might **enter your mind to say** that **since Rava says:** It is **a mitzva to place** the *mezuza*

BACKGROUND

Placed it so that it was affixed behind the door – הִנִּיחָהּ אַחַר הַדֶּלֶת: The proper placement of a *mezuza* is on the doorpost outside the door.

Unfit placement of the *mezuza* behind the door according to Rashi (1) and Rabbeinu Tam (2).

PERSONALITIES

Munbaz – מוּנְבַּז: Munbaz was the king of Adiabene at the end of the Second Temple period. This tiny principality was an independent kingdom in the Parthian empire located in northern Aram Naharaim, in the area of modern-day Kirkuk and Mosul. Members of the royal family of Adiabene and some of the military joined the rebels against Rome during the great rebellion before the destruction of the Temple. Munbaz's mother, Queen Helene, and her two sons Munbaz and Izitus, called Zutus in the talmudic sources, converted to Judaism and scrupulously kept the mitzvot (see Genesis *Rabba*, chapter 46, and *Nidda* 17a). Initially, Munbaz abdicated the throne in favor of his brother, but he later assumed the throne upon his brother's death.

This family is praised for its good deeds on many occasions in the Talmud, and Josephus describes its history and conversion in detail.

Like the rest of his family, Munbaz was apparently buried in the Tombs of the Kings in Jerusalem.

Sarcophagus of Queen Helene, mother of Munbaz

HALAKHA

If one hung a *mezuza* on a stick – תְּלָאָהּ בְּמַקֵּל: A *mezuza* hung by a stick is unfit, even if it is positioned in the correct place. The reason is that the *mezuza* is not affixed to the doorpost (Rambam *Sefer Ahava, Hilkhot Tefillin UMezuza VeSefer Torah* 5:8; *Tur, Yoreh De'a* 289).

Placed it so that it was affixed behind the door – הִנִּיחָהּ אַחַר הַדֶּלֶת: The Rambam writes that if one placed a *mezuza* behind the door, his action is of no consequence. Others rule that it is fit, provided that he places it on the doorpost itself (Rema, citing *Tur*). The later commentaries maintain that the *halakha* is in accordance with the opinion of the Rambam, but those who live in houses that open out into areas frequented by gentiles may rely on the lenient opinion (*Shakh*). The custom is to be lenient whenever there is a concern about theft or that the *mezuza* might become soiled (Rambam *Sefer Ahava, Hilkhot Tefillin UMezuza VeSefer Torah* 5:8; *Shulḥan Arukh, Yoreh De'a* 289:2 in the comment of Rema, and see *Arukh HaShulḥan* there).

It is a mitzva to place the *mezuza* within the airspace of the entrance – מִצְוָה לְהַנִּיחָהּ בְּתוֹךְ חֲלָלוֹ שֶׁל פֶּתַח: The correct place to affix a *mezuza* is within the airspace of the entrance, in the handbreadth closest to the outside. The *halakha* is in accordance with the opinions of Shmuel and Rava. The Rema writes, citing the *Tur*, that the *mezuza* is fit provided that he places it on the doorpost itself. Some understand this to mean that it must be somewhere within the airspace of the entrance, while others say that it may even be on the outside of the entrance (Rambam *Sefer Ahava, Hilkhot Tefillin UMezuza VeSefer Torah* 6:12; *Shulḥan Arukh, Yoreh De'a* 289:2, and in the comment of Rema).

NOTES

Placed it so that it was affixed behind the door – הִנִּיחָהּ אַחַר הַדֶּלֶת: Some explain that he affixed it in the airspace of the entrance itself, but on the inside of the door, not on the part near the public domain (see Rabbeinu Tam and Rambam). Rashi indicates that the problem is that he affixed it in the wall of the house on the inside, not on the doorframe itself. According to this interpretation, the same applies if he affixed it to the wall of the house on the outside (*Nimmukei Yosef*).

He exposes himself to danger and it does not enable him to fulfill the mitzva – סַכָּנָה וְאֵין בָּהּ מִצְוָה: Rashi and Rabbeinu Gershom Meor HaGola explain that he does not fulfill the mitzva of *mezuza*, and thereby he exposes himself to danger. The danger mentioned here is that this *mezuza* does not protect the inhabitants of the house from harmful spirits (see 33b). A different explanation is suggested by Rabbeinu Tam: The danger is not that of harmful spirits, as if it were, the same could be said of all unfit *mezuzot*. Rather, the danger is that one who enters the door might hit his head on the *mezuza* hanging there or placed wrongly behind the door where he will not notice it. Yet others maintain that this is referring to a time of persecution, when the gentiles have banned *mezuzot*, and the Gemara is saying that one who places a *mezuza* behind the door exposes himself to discovery for no purpose, as he does not fulfill the mitzva (*Sefer Yere'im*).

בַּטֶּפַח הַסָּמוּךְ לִרְשׁוּת הָרַבִּים, כַּמָּה דִּמְרַחַק מְעַלֵּי, קָא מַשְׁמַע לַן.

in the handbreadth adjacent to the public domain, perhaps **the further** the *mezuza* is from the inside of the house the **better,** and one may affix it even fully outside the airspace of the entrance. To counter this, Shmuel **teaches us** that the *mezuza* must be within the airspace of the entrance itself.

וְאָמַר רַב יְהוּדָה אָמַר שְׁמוּאֵל: כְּתָבָהּ עַל שְׁנֵי דַפִּין – פְּסוּלָה. מֵיתִיבֵי: כְּתָבָהּ עַל שְׁנֵי דַפִּין וְהִנִּיחָהּ בִּשְׁנֵי סִיפִּין – פְּסוּלָה; הָא בְּסַף אֶחָד – כְּשֵׁרָה! רְאוּיָה לִשְׁנֵי סִיפִּין קָאָמַר.

And Rav Yehuda says that **Shmuel says:** If one **wrote** a *mezuza* **on two sheets**[HN] it is **unfit.** The Gemara **raises an objection** from a *baraita* that teaches: If one **wrote** a *mezuza* **on two sheets and placed it on** the **two doorposts** of the entrance, it is **unfit.** The Gemara states the objection: By inference, if the *mezuza* was affixed **on one doorpost,** it is **fit,** despite the fact that it is written on two sheets. The Gemara answers: The *baraita* is not referring to a case where one affixed the *mezuza* on two doorposts. Rather, the *baraita* **is saying** that if it was written on two sheets in such a manner that it is **fit to** be affixed to **two doorposts,** i.e., there is a space between the writing of the first and second passages, so that one can separate the two sheets for different doorposts, it is unfit. This is in accordance with the statement of Rav Yehuda, citing Shmuel.

וְאָמַר רַב יְהוּדָה אָמַר שְׁמוּאֵל: בִּמְזוּזָה הַלֵּךְ אַחַר הֶיכֵּר צִיר. מַאי הֶיכֵּר צִיר? אָמַר רַב אַדָּא: אַבַקְתָּא. הֵיכִי דָּמֵי? כְּגוֹן פִּיתְחָא דְּבֵין תְּרֵי בָתֵּי, בֵּין בֵּי גַבְרֵי לְבֵי נָשֵׁי.

And Rav Yehuda says that **Shmuel says:** The *halakha* is that a *mezuza* must be affixed to the doorpost on its right side, and the right side is determined by the direction from which one enters the room. **With regard to a *mezuza*,** when deciding which side is the right side, one should **follow the indication of** the **hinge.**[H] The Gemara asks: **What is the indication of** the **hinge? Rav Adda said: The socket**[N] into which the hinge is inserted. The room with the socket is considered the inside room, and the *mezuza* is affixed to the side which is on one's right when entering that room. The Gemara asks: **What are the circumstances,** i.e., in what kind of case was this guideline to follow the indication of the hinge necessary? The Gemara answers: This indication is necessary in a case **where** there is **an entrance that is between two houses,** e.g., **between a room for men and a room for women,** as in such a situation the direction of the entrance is unclear.

רֵישׁ גָּלוּתָא בְּנָא בֵּיתָא, אֲמַר לֵיהּ לְרַב נַחְמָן: קְבַע לִי מְזוּזָתָא, אֲמַר רַב נַחְמָן: תְּלֵי דָשֵׁי בְּרֵישָׁא.

The Gemara relates: **The Exilarch built** a new **house. He said to Rav Naḥman: Affix *mezuzot* for me** in the house. **Rav Naḥman said: First erect the doors,**[HN] so that I can affix the *mezuzot* in the appropriate places, according to the placement of the hinges.

HALAKHA

If one wrote a *mezuza* on two sheets – כְּתָבָהּ עַל שְׁנֵי דַפִּין: The two chapters of a *mezuza* are written in a single column on one sheet of parchment. If one wrote it in two or three columns, it is fit. If he wrote it on two sheets of parchment it is unfit, even if he sewed them together. This ruling is in accordance with the explanation of the majority of the early commentaries, not that of Rashi (Rambam *Sefer Ahava, Hilkhot Tefillin UMezuza VeSefer Torah* 5:1; *Shulḥan Arukh, Yoreh De'a* 288:2, 4).

Follow the indication of the hinge – הַלֵּךְ אַחַר הֶיכֵּר צִיר: With regard to an entrance between two houses, e.g., if one divided his home into two sections, each of which has an entrance to the public domain, and in the partition between them there is an entrance from one to another, the side in which the socket for the door hinge is found is considered the inside room, and therefore one affixes the *mezuza* to the right side entering that room. The *halakha* is in accordance with the opinion of Shmuel. One does not follow the indication of the hinges in a place where the direction of the entrance is established, or if it is clear that one of the rooms is the main one (Rambam *Sefer Ahava, Hilkhot Tefillin UMezuza VeSefer Torah* 6:11; *Shulḥan Arukh, Yoreh De'a* 289:3, and see *Pitḥei Teshuva* there).

First erect the doors – תְּלֵי דָשֵׁי בְּרֵישָׁא: If one affixed the *mezuza* to the doorpost while it was still detached from the framework of the house, and then he attached the doorpost to the entrance, it is unfit, as indicated by the incident involving Rav Naḥman. The Rambam maintains that one should fix the doors in place before affixing the *mezuzot* (Rambam *Sefer Ahava, Hilkhot Tefillin UMezuza VeSefer Torah* 5:8; *Shulḥan Arukh, Yoreh De'a* 289:5).

NOTES

If one wrote a *mezuza* on two sheets [*dappin*] – כְּתָבָהּ עַל שְׁנֵי דַפִּין: According to Rashi, this does not mean that he wrote the *mezuza* on two separate pieces of parchment. Rather, he wrote it on two different columns, which is generally what is meant by *dappin*. Most of the early commentaries maintain that this is referring to two separate pieces of parchment (Rambam; *Tosafot*; Rosh).

Socket [*avakta*] – אַבַקְתָּא: Some commentaries explain that the term *avakta* refers to holes in the threshold and in the lintel into which the hinge of the door is inserted (Rashi). Some say, based on the usage of this term elsewhere, that it is a strap with which the door is tied (*Sefer HaEshkol*; Meiri). In any case, the idea is that the main entranceway determines the direction into which the door will open, and that dictates where the hinge or closing mechanism is placed.

First erect the doors – תְּלֵי דָשֵׁי בְּרֵישָׁא: The commentary follows the explanation of the *Halakhot Gedolot*, which maintains that this incident continues the discussion with regard to the indication of hinges. By contrast, Rashi explains that the Exilarch sought to affix the *mezuzot* to the framework of the doorposts before the doorposts were put in place. Rav Naḥman therefore informed him that this would violate the principle concerning mitzvot: Prepare it and not from that which has already been prepared, i.e., one must perform the mitzva when the obligation is in force, rather than arrange matters so that when the obligation applies, i.e., when the doorposts are erected, the mitzva is fulfilled by default. The Rambam apparently explains it in a similar manner, only with regard to the doors rather than the posts, i.e., he maintains that the obligation of a *mezuza* is not in effect before one places the doors in the entrance (see *Kesef Mishne*).

אָמַר רַב יְהוּדָה אָמַר רַב: עֲשָׂאָהּ כְּמִין נֶגֶר – פְּסוּלָה. אִינִי? וְהָא כִּי אֲתָא רַב יִצְחָק בַּר יוֹסֵף אֲמַר: כּוּלְּהוּ מְזוּזָתָא דְּבֵי רַבִּי כְּמִין נֶגֶר הֲווּ עֲבִידָן, וְהַהִיא פִּיתְחָא דְּעָיֵיל בֵּיהּ רַבִּי לְבֵי מִדְרְשָׁא לָא הֲוָה לַהּ מְזוּזָה! לָא קַשְׁיָא: הָא דַּעֲבִידָא כְּסִיכְתָּא, הָא דַּעֲבִידָא כְּאִיסְתְּוִירָא.

Rav Yehuda says that **Rav says:** If one **fashioned** a *mezuza* **like a bolt,**[BH] i.e., he wedged it into a hole in the doorpost of a gate, or affixed it to the doorpost horizontally, it is **unfit.** The Gemara raises a difficulty: **Is that so? But when Rav Yitzḥak bar Yosef came** from Eretz Yisrael to Babylonia, **he said: All the *mezuzot* in the house of Rabbi** Yehuda HaNasi **were fashioned like a bolt, and** he also said: **That entrance by which Rabbi** Yehuda HaNasi **entered the study hall did not have a *mezuza*.** The Gemara answers: This is **not difficult. This** ruling, that it is unfit, is referring to a case **where it is prepared like a peg,** i.e., he inserted it deep into the doorpost while it was lying horizontally. **That** ruling, that it is fit, is referring to a case **where it is prepared like an ankle** [***ke'istevira***],[BLN] i.e., it is vertical.

אִינִי? וְהָא הַהוּא פִּיתְחָא דַּהֲוָה עָיֵיל בֵּהּ רַב הוּנָא לְבֵי מִדְרְשָׁא וַהֲוָיא לַהּ מְזוּזָה! הַהוּא רָגִיל הֲוָה, דְּאָמַר רַב יְהוּדָה אָמַר רַב: בִּמְזוּזָה הַלֵּךְ אַחַר הָרָגִיל.

With regard to the second element of Rav Yitzḥak bar Yosef's statement, that the entrance by which Rabbi Yehuda HaNasi entered the study hall did not have a *mezuza*, the Gemara asks: **Is that so? But** what of **that entrance by which Rav Huna would enter the study hall,**[H] **which had a *mezuza*?** The Gemara answers: **That** entrance **was** the one through which all were **accustomed** to enter the study hall.[N] By contrast, the entrance that Rabbi Yehuda HaNasi used was a side entrance, which was designated for him alone. Consequently, it was exempt from the obligation to affix a *mezuza*, **as Rav Yehuda says** that **Rav says: With regard to a *mezuza*, follow the** entrance that people are **accustomed** to using.

BACKGROUND

Like a bolt – כְּמִין נֶגֶר: This refers to a metal rod that was inserted into a socket cut into a doorpost in order to prevent the opening of the door. Some bolts were placed along the width of the entrance, from one doorpost to the other, but there were also bolts placed vertically, i.e., inserted into the top of the doorframe.

Mezuza positioned like a bolt

Where it is prepared like an ankle [*istevira*] – דַּעֲבִידָא כְּאִיסְתְּוִירָא: The *istevira* is probably the ankle, which comprises three bones: First, the tibia (1), which is the larger of the two bones beneath the knee. This bone protrudes at the inner part of the ankle. Second, the fibula (2), which is a thinner bone on the outer side. These two bones meet at the talus (3), which is positioned in a way that creates the angle between the lower leg and the foot. The early commentaries engage in a dispute whether the comparison of the placement of a *mezuza* to an *istevira* refers to the tibia alone, or to the angled appearance of the ankle. Both of these interpretations are cited by Rashi. Others apparently explain that the reference is to the horizontal line formed by the side protrusions at the bottom of the tibia and the fibula (Rabbeinu Tam). Yet others indicate that the Gemara is speaking of the talus and the adjacent bones on the top of the foot, the navicular (4) and cuneiform (5) bones, which form a kind of slope toward the toes.

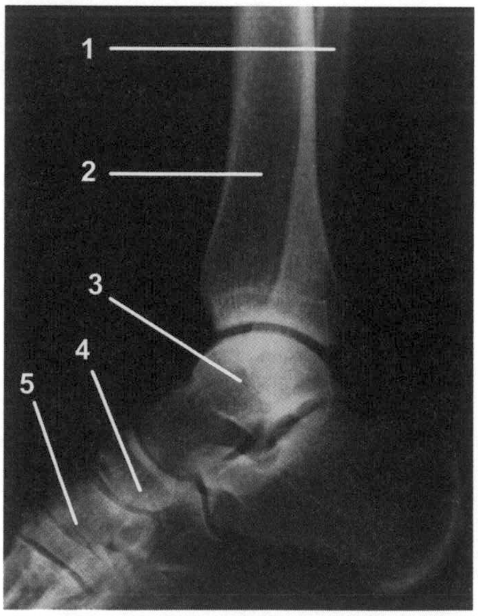

Bones of the ankle

LANGUAGE

Ankle [*istevira*] – אִיסְתְּוִירָא: The etymology of this word is unclear, but it may be a compound from the Middle Persian ast-bara, meaning bone carrier. It is also notable that the word astuxwān in Persian means bone.

HALAKHA

If one fashioned a *mezuza* like a bolt, etc. – עֲשָׂאָהּ כְּמִין נֶגֶר וכו׳: The *mezuza* must be affixed upright, in accordance with the opinion of Rashi. This is the Sephardic custom. The Rema writes: Some say that a *mezuza* which is upright is unfit, as it must be affixed horizontally. Those who are particular fulfill both opinions by affixing it at a diagonal, and this is the Ashkenazic custom. The top of the *mezuza* should be toward the inside, and the bottom toward the outside. Some Ashkenazim have the custom of affixing it vertically, as maintained by Rashi (Rambam *Sefer Ahava*, *Hilkhot Tefillin UMezuza VeSefer Torah* 5:8; *Shulḥan Arukh*, *Yoreh De'a* 289:6, and see *Beur HaGra* there).

Study hall – בֵּי מִדְרְשָׁא: A study hall is exempt from the requirement of a *mezuza*. If it has an entrance through which one usually exits to his house, one must affix a *mezuza* to that entrance. This ruling is in accordance with the explanation of the Rambam. Some say, citing the Jerusalem Talmud, that the obligation of a *mezuza* applies to a study hall, and it is correct to act in accordance with this opinion, but one should not recite a blessing when affixing this *mezuza* (Rambam *Sefer Ahava*, *Hilkhot Tefillin UMezuza VeSefer Torah* 6:11, and see 6:6; *Shulḥan Arukh*, *Yoreh De'a* 286:10, and see 286:3).

NOTES

Where it is prepared like a peg…like an ankle – דַּעֲבִידָא כְּסִיכְתָּא...כְּאִיסְתְּוִירָא: The commentary follows Rashi's explanation, that a *mezuza* must be affixed vertically. Rav Amram Gaon likewise writes that the *mezuza* should be placed upright, like a book is placed on a shelf (*Sha'arei Teshuva*). As for the reason for this requirement, some say that its shape must follow that of the doorpost itself (Rid), while others claim that this is the most respectful way of placing the parchment (*Nimmukei Yosef*). Therefore, if one affixed it in a crack in the doorpost, like a bolt, when it is upright like an ankle, it is fit. If it is prepared like a peg, i.e., inserted deep into the doorpost, it is unfit. According to most commentaries, the problem here is that it is lying horizontally rather than vertically. Rashi cites another explanation, according to which the comparison to an ankle means that it is half lying and half standing, like the link between the calf and the foot. It was necessary to affix the *mezuzot* in this manner in the house of Rabbi Yehuda HaNasi because his *mezuzot* were very long (Rid).

Others contend, based on the Gemara elsewhere, that it is disrespectful to affix a *mezuza* upright. They explain in the opposite manner, that when the Gemara refers to a *mezuza* affixed like a peg, it means like a peg inserted vertically into the ground, whereas the mention of an ankle is referring to the protruding bone on the two sides of the ankle, which is horizontal (Rabbeinu Tam). Therefore, according to this opinion one should affix the *mezuza* lying horizontally in relation to the doorpost. The commentaries suggest that the Ashkenazic custom of placing the *mezuza* diagonally is a compromise between the two opinions, as this is considered like an ankle according to both of them (*Tosafot*). Others state that the mention of an ankle is referring to the tilted bone between the bone of the ankle and the toes, and this is another source for the Ashkenazic practice, according to which it is the proper custom *ab initio* (*Sefer HaEshkol*, citing Rav Hai Gaon).

That entrance was the one through which all were accustomed to enter the study hall – הַהוּא רָגִיל הֲוָה: The commentaries note that although entrances to study halls are generally exempt from the requirement of a *mezuza*, in Rav Huna's case the door also served as the entrance to his house (*Shita Mekubbetzet*, citing *Tosafot*). The Rambam indicates that this entrance was between the study hall and Rav Huna's house (*Sefer Ahava*, *Hilkhot Tefillin UMezuza VeSefer Torah* 6:11), and the statement: That entrance was the one through which all were accustomed to enter, means that Rav Huna himself was accustomed to entering and exiting that way, and therefore one was obligated to affix a *mezuza*, as it was considered an entrance to his house (*Mishna Sedura*). Others cite a different version of the text, according to which it was not the entrance to the study hall but the door of his house, via which he would leave for the study hall (*Tosafot*).

אָמַר רַבִּי זֵירָא אָמַר רַב מַתָּנָא אָמַר שְׁמוּאֵל: מִצְוָה לְהַנִּיחָהּ בִּתְחִלַּת שְׁלִישׁ הָעֶלְיוֹן, וְרַב הוּנָא אָמַר: מַגְבִּיהַּ מִן הַקַּרְקַע טֶפַח, וּמַרְחִיק מִן הַקּוֹרָה טֶפַח, וְכָל הַפֶּתַח כּוּלּוֹ כָּשֵׁר לִמְזוּזָה.

§ **Rabbi Zeira says** that **Rav Mattana says** that **Shmuel says:** It **is a mitzva to place** the *mezuza* **at the beginning of the upper third** of the doorpost.[H] **And Rav Huna says:** One **raises** the *mezuza* **a handbreadth from the ground, or** one **distances** it **from the** cross **beam,** i.e., the lintel, **a handbreadth, and the entire entrance** between those two handbreadths is **fit for** the placement of the ***mezuza.***

מֵיתִיבֵי: מַגְבִּיהַּ מִן הַקַּרְקַע טֶפַח, וּמַרְחִיק מִן הַקּוֹרָה טֶפַח, וְכָל הַפֶּתַח כּוּלּוֹ כָּשֵׁר לִמְזוּזָה, דִּבְרֵי רַבִּי יְהוּדָה; רַבִּי יוֹסֵי אוֹמֵר: ״וּקְשַׁרְתָּם...וּכְתַבְתָּם״, מָה קְשִׁירָה בְּגוֹבַהּ – אַף כְּתִיבָה בְּגוֹבַהּ.

The Gemara **raises an objection** from a *baraita*: One **raises** the *mezuza* **a handbreadth from the ground, or** one **distances** it **from the** cross **beam a handbreadth, and the entire entrance** between those two handbreadths is **fit for** the placement of the ***mezuza***; this is **the statement of Rabbi Yehuda. Rabbi Yosei says:** The verse states: **"And you shall bind them** for a sign upon your arm" (Deuteronomy 6:8), and then it states: **"And you shall write them** upon the doorposts of your house" (Deuteronomy 6:9). **Just as** the **binding** of the phylacteries is performed **on the upper** part of the arm, **so too,** the **writing,** i.e., the placement, of a *mezuza* must be specifically **on the upper** part of the entrance.

בִּשְׁלָמָא לְרַב הוּנָא – הוּא דְּאָמַר כְּרַבִּי יְהוּדָה, אֶלָּא לִשְׁמוּאֵל דְּאָמַר כְּמַאן? לָא כְּרַבִּי יְהוּדָה וְלָא כְּרַבִּי יוֹסֵי!

The Gemara explains the objection: **Granted, according to Rav Huna, he states** his ruling **in accordance with** the opinion of **Rabbi Yehuda; but according to Shmuel, in accordance with whose** opinion **does he state** his ruling? It is **not in accordance with** the opinion of **Rabbi Yehuda, and** it is **not in accordance with** the opinion of **Rabbi Yosei.**

אֲמַר רַב הוּנָא בְּרֵיהּ דְּרַב נָתָן: לְעוֹלָם כְּרַבִּי יוֹסֵי,

Rav Huna, son of Rav Natan, said: Actually, Shmuel's ruling is **in accordance with** the opinion of **Rabbi Yosei,**

HALAKHA

At the beginning of the upper third of the doorpost – בִּתְחִלַּת שְׁלִישׁ הָעֶלְיוֹן: The *mezuza* should be affixed at the beginning of the upper third of the height of the entrance. If one affixed it higher than that, it is fit, provided that he kept it one handbreadth from the lintel. The *halakha* is in accordance with the opinion of Shmuel and Rav Huna. If one affixed the *mezuza* below the upper third, it is unfit (*Shakh*), as stated in the *baraita* and in accordance with the Gemara's explanation of the opinion of Rav Huna (Rambam *Sefer Ahava, Hilkhot Tefillin UMezuza VeSefer Torah* 6:12; *Shulḥan Arukh, Yoreh De'a* 289:2).

Perek **III**
Daf **33** Amud **b**

וּמַאי תְּחִילַּת שְׁלִישׁ הָעֶלְיוֹן דְּקָא אָמַר – לְהַרְחִיקָהּ, שֶׁלֹּא לְהַרְחִיקָהּ מִן הַקּוֹרָה שֶׁל מַעְלָה יוֹתֵר מִשְּׁלִישׁ.

and what is the meaning of the phrase: **The beginning of the upper third** of the entrance, **that** Shmuel **says?** This is referring **to** the maximum **distancing** of the *mezuza* from the doorframe, i.e., **that one should not distance it from the upper** cross **beam more than one-third** of the height of the entrance.

אָמַר רָבָא: מִצְוָה לְהַנִּיחָהּ בְּטֶפַח הַסָּמוּךְ לִרְשׁוּת הָרַבִּים. מַאי טַעְמָא? רַבָּנַן אָמְרִי: כְּדֵי שֶׁיִּפְגַּע בַּמְּזוּזָה מִיָּד, רַב חֲנִינָא מִסּוּרָא אוֹמֵר: כִּי הֵיכִי דְּתִינַטְרֵיהּ.

§ **Rava says:** It is **a mitzva to place** the *mezuza* **in the handbreadth adjacent to the public domain.**[H] The Gemara asks: **What is the reason** for this? **The Rabbis say** that it is **in order that one encounter the *mezuza* immediately** upon one's entrance to the house. **Rav Ḥanina from Sura says:** It is **in order that** the *mezuza* **protect**[N] the entire house, by placing it as far outside as one can.

אָמַר רַבִּי חֲנִינָא: בּוֹא וּרְאֵה שֶׁלֹּא כְּמִדַּת הַקָּדוֹשׁ בָּרוּךְ הוּא מִדַּת בָּשָׂר וָדָם, מִדַּת בָּשָׂר וָדָם – מֶלֶךְ יוֹשֵׁב מִבִּפְנִים וְעַם מְשַׁמְּרִין אוֹתוֹ מִבַּחוּץ, מִדַּת הַקָּדוֹשׁ בָּרוּךְ הוּא אֵינוֹ כֵּן, עֲבָדָיו יוֹשְׁבִין מִבִּפְנִים וְהוּא מְשַׁמְּרָן מִבַּחוּץ, שֶׁנֶּאֱמַר: ״ה׳ שׁוֹמְרֶךָ ה׳ צִלְּךָ עַל יַד יְמִינֶךָ״.

The Gemara adds: **Rabbi Ḥanina says: Come and see that the attribute of flesh and blood is not like the attribute of the Holy One, Blessed be He. The attribute of flesh and blood** is that **a king sits inside** his palace, **and** the **people protect him from the outside,** whereas with regard to **the attribute of the Holy One, Blessed be He,** it is **not so.** Rather, **His servants,** the Jewish people, **sit inside** their homes, **and He protects them from the outside. As it is stated: "The Lord is your keeper, the Lord is your shade upon your right hand"** (Psalms 121:5).[N]

HALAKHA

In the handbreadth adjacent to the public domain – בְּטֶפַח הַסָּמוּךְ לִרְשׁוּת הָרַבִּים: One places the *mezuza* in the space of the doorway, in the handbreadth adjacent to the outside. This requirement is not indispensable. The *halakha* is in accordance with the opinion of Rava (Rambam *Sefer Ahava, Hilkhot Tefillin UMezuza VeSefer Torah* 6:12; *Shulḥan Arukh, Yoreh De'a* 285:2, 289:2).

NOTES

In order that the *mezuza* protect – כִּי הֵיכִי דְּתִינַטְרֵיהּ: That is, so that the *mezuza* will protect one from harmful spirits (Rashi) by ensuring that the entire house is within the area protected by the *mezuza* (*Tur, Yoreh De'a* 285). Some commentaries maintain that the *mezuza* does not protect one from harmful spirits. Rather, its protection lies in the fact that it reminds one of the unity of God and the requirement to fear Him, which protects one from sin (Rambam *Sefer Ahava, Hilkhot Tefillin UMezuza VeSefer Torah* 5:4, 6:13).

The Lord is your shade upon your right hand – ה׳ צִלְּךָ עַל יַד יְמִינֶךָ: This is a reference to the *mezuza*, which is found on the right side of the entrance (Rashi; see *She'iltot deRav Aḥai Gaon* 145).

דָּרַשׁ רַב יוֹסֵף בְּרֵיהּ דְּרָבָא מִשְּׁמֵיהּ דְּרָבָא: הֶעֱמִיק לָהּ טֶפַח – פְּסוּלָה. לֵימָא מְסַיְּיעָא לֵיהּ: הִנִּיחָהּ בְּפַצִּין אוֹ שֶׁטָּלָה עָלֶיהָ מַלְבֵּן, אִם יֵשׁ שָׁם טֶפַח – צָרִיךְ מְזוּזָה אַחֶרֶת, אִם לָאו – אֵינוֹ צָרִיךְ מְזוּזָה אַחֶרֶת!

Rav Yosef, son of Rava, taught in the name of Rava: If one **dug one handbreadth deep** into the doorpost[H] and placed a *mezuza* there, it is **unfit.** The Gemara suggests: **Let us say** that the following *baraita* **supports his** ruling: In a case where one **affixed** a *mezuza* deep **in the wooden doorpost** of an entrance, **or** after placing it in the entrance one **added** [*tala*][L] an inner **framework** [*malben*][L] **to** it that covers the doorpost, **if there is** a depth of **one handbreadth there,** one **requires another** *mezuza,* but **if not,** one **does not require another** *mezuza.*

כִּי תַּנְיָא הַהִיא, בְּפֶתַח שֶׁאֲחוֹרֵי הַדֶּלֶת.

The Gemara deflects the support: **When that** *baraita* **is taught,** it is referring **to an entrance that is behind the door,**[B] i.e., there is another entrance on the other side of the framework, which serves for both entrances. The *baraita* is teaching that if the framework is one handbreadth thick, then each side is considered a separate entrance, and each requires its own *mezuza.*

הָא בְּהֶדְיָא קָתָנֵי לָהּ: פֶּתַח שֶׁאֲחוֹרֵי הַדֶּלֶת, אִם יֵשׁ שָׁם טֶפַח – צָרִיךְ מְזוּזָה אַחֶרֶת, וְאִם לָאו – אֵינוֹ צָרִיךְ מְזוּזָה אַחֶרֶת! כֵּיצַד קָתָנֵי.

The Gemara raises a difficulty: But the same *baraita* **teaches explicitly** this ruling of the case of another entrance: With regard to **an entrance that is behind the door, if there is** a depth of **one handbreadth there,** one **requires another** *mezuza,* **but if not,** one **does not require another** *mezuza.* The Gemara explains: This clause of the *baraita* is **teaching which** case is the subject of the previous clause, i.e., the *baraita* does not state two *halakhot* but only one, which it explains as it proceeds: In what case is it taught that if there is a depth of a handbreadth there, one requires another *mezuza*? It is taught in the case of an entrance that is behind the door.

תָּנָא: הֶעֱמִיד לָהּ מַלְבֵּן שֶׁל קָנִים, חוֹתֵךְ שְׁפוֹפֶרֶת וּמַנִּיחָהּ. אָמַר רַב אַחָא בְּרֵיהּ דְּרָבָא: לֹא שָׁנוּ אֶלָּא שֶׁהֶעֱמִיד וּלְבַסּוֹף חָתַךְ וְהִנִּיחָהּ, אֲבָל חָתַךְ וְהִנִּיחַ וּלְבַסּוֹף הֶעֱמִיד – פְּסוּלָה, ״תַּעֲשֶׂה״ – וְלֹא מִן הֶעָשׂוּי.

§ It is **taught** in a *baraita* with regard to the affixing of a *mezuza:* If one **positions** a *mezuza* in an entrance which was **a framework of reeds,** to which one cannot affix the *mezuza* with nails, he **carves** a kind of **tube** from the reed on the right side **and places** the *mezuza* in that tube. **Rav Aḥa, son of Rava, says: They taught** that one may affix the *mezuza* in this manner **only** in a case **where one positioned** the framework in its place first, **and ultimately carved** a tube **and** then **placed** the *mezuza* in **it. But** if before positioning the framework one **carved** a tube **and placed** the *mezuza* in it, **and ultimately positioned** the framework,[H] the *mezuza* **is unfit.** This in accordance with the principle stated with regard to objects used for mitzvot: **Prepare it, and not from what has already been prepared.**[N] In this case he affixed the *mezuza* before the obligation took effect with regard to the framework.

HALAKHA

If one dug a handbreadth deep into the doorpost – הֶעֱמִיק לָהּ טֶפַח: If one dug a handbreadth deep into the wall and placed the *mezuza* there, it is unfit, as maintained by Rava (Rambam *Sefer Ahava, Hilkhot Tefillin UMezuza VeSefer Torah* 5:8; *Shulḥan Arukh, Yoreh De'a* 289:4).

One carved a tube and placed the *mezuza* in it and ultimately positioned the framework – חָתַךְ וְהִנִּיחַ וּלְבַסּוֹף הֶעֱמִיד: If one carved a reed and inserted a *mezuza* into it, and then attached that reed to other reeds and formed a doorpost with them, the *mezuza* is unfit, because the affixing of the *mezuza* was performed before the post was established as the doorpost of the entrance (Rambam *Sefer Ahava, Hilkhot Tefillin UMezuza VeSefer Torah* 5:8; *Shulḥan Arukh, Yoreh De'a* 289:5).

NOTES

Prepare it and not from what has already been prepared – תַּעֲשֶׂה וְלֹא מִן הֶעָשׂוּי: The term prepare does not appear in the verse with regard to a *mezuza.* Rather, this principle is derived from the *halakha* of a *sukka,* where it is stated: "You shall prepare the feast of *Sukkot*" (Deuteronomy 16:13). The Sages interpreted this as teaching that one must prepare the mitzva and not perform it using that which has already been prepared, as is similarly derived with regard to a *lulav* (see *Sukka* 11b). Some commentaries maintain that in the case of a *mezuza* this *halakha* applies by rabbinic law (*Kiryat Sefer*).

BACKGROUND

Entrance that is behind the door – פֶּתַח שֶׁאֲחוֹרֵי הַדֶּלֶת:

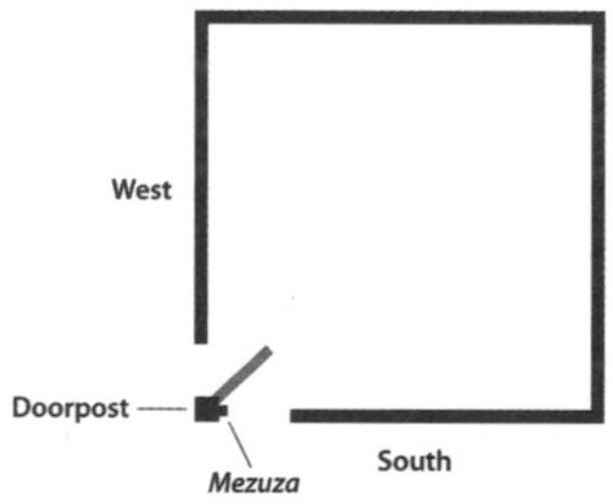

Location of *mezuza* according to Rashi. Some say the *mezuza* is located on the right side of the southern entrance.

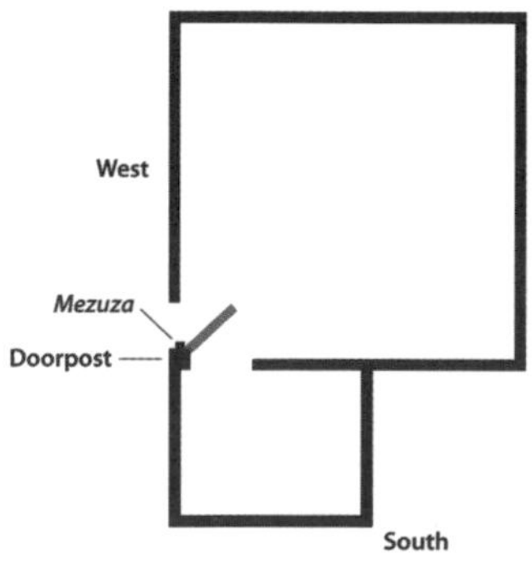

Location of *mezuza* according to the Mordekhai

LANGUAGE

Added [*tala*] – טָלָה: The verb *tala* is typically used by the Sages in reference to the stitching of patches [*telai*] on clothes and the like. This is possibly also the meaning of *talu* in the verse: "Every speckled and *talu* sheep" (Genesis 30:32), i.e., a sheep that appears to have patches. It bears a similar meaning here, as one places a kind of patch to cover an entrance that is not properly formed. It is also possible that the letter *tet* appears instead of the letter *tav* in *tala,* as *tala* spelled with a *tav* has a virtually identical pronunciation and means to hang.

Framework [*malben*] – מַלְבֵּן: The term *malben* appears in the Bible in reference to a mold for fashioning bricks: "Draw you water for the siege, strengthen your fortresses; go into the clay, and tread the mortar, lay hold of the brick mold [*malben*]" (Nahum 3:14). In rabbinic usage it appears in reference to a square framework, e.g., the *malben* of a chair, or even for square pieces of earth. Here, as in many places, *malben* means the inner framework of a window or entrance, generally made of wood.

Brick mold

וְאָמַר רָבָא: הָנֵי פִּיתְחֵי שִׁימָאֵי פְּטוּרִין מִן הַמְּזוּזָה. מַאי פִּיתְחֵי שִׁימָאֵי? פְּלִיגִי בָּהּ רַב רִיחוּמִי וְאַבָּא יוֹסֵי, חַד אָמַר: דְּלֵית לְהוּ תִּקְרָה, וְחַד אָמַר: דְּלֵית לְהוּ שְׁקוֹפֵי.

And Rava says: With regard to **these broken entrances** [***pitḥei shima'ei***],[L] which lack the proper form of doorways, one is **exempt from the** obligation of placing a *mezuza*. The Gemara asks: **What are broken entrances? Rav Riḥumi and Abba Yosei disagree with regard to this. One says that they do not have** a proper **ceiling,**[H] **and one says that they do not have lintels** [***shakofei***][HN] above the openings.

אָמַר רַבָּה בַּר שֵׁילָא אָמַר רַב חִסְדָּא: אַכְסַדְרָה פְּטוּרָה מִן הַמְּזוּזָה, לְפִי שֶׁאֵין לָהּ פַּצִּימִין. הָא יֵשׁ לָהּ פַּצִּימִין – חַיֶּיבֶת? לְחִיזּוּק תִּקְרָה הוּא דַּעֲבִידִי!

Rabba bar Sheila says that **Rav Ḥisda says:** With regard to **a portico,**[B] i.e., a structure at the entrance to a house that is entirely open on its front side, one is **exempt from the** obligation of placing **a *mezuza*, because it does not have doorposts** [***patzimin***][L] on its sides. The Gemara questions this reason: This indicates **that if it has doorposts,** one would be **obligated** to place a *mezuza*. But that is not logical, as these doorposts are not there to serve as an entrance; rather, **they are made to strengthen the ceiling.** In that case, why should one be obligated?

הָכִי קָאָמַר: אַף עַל פִּי שֶׁיֵּשׁ לָהּ פַּצִּימִין – פְּטוּרָה, שֶׁאֵין עֲשׂוּיִין אֶלָּא לְחִיזּוּק לַתִּקְרָה. אָמַר אַבָּיֵי: חֲזֵינָא לְהוּ לְאִיסְפְּלִידֵי דְּבֵי מָר דְּאִית לְהוּ פַּצִּימֵי וְלֵית לְהוּ מְזוּזָתָא, קָסָבַר: לְחִיזּוּק תִּקְרָה הוּא דַּעֲבִידִי.

The Gemara answers: **This is what** Rav Ḥisda **is saying: Even if it has doorposts,** one is **exempt** from the obligation to place a *mezuza* there, **because they are made only to strengthen the ceiling,** not as an entrance. Similarly, **Abaye said: I saw the porticos** [***le'ispelidei***][L] **of the house of the Master,** Rabba, **that they had doorposts but they did not have *mezuzot*.** Rabba evidently **holds** that its doorposts **are made to strengthen the ceiling.**

BACKGROUND

Portico – אַכְסַדְרָה:

Portico of a building in Doubs, France

Portico of the school of Rav according to Rashi

Roman portico according to Rashi

LANGUAGE

Broken entrances [*pitḥei shima'ei*] – פִּיתְחֵי שִׁימָאֵי: Rashi explains that the gates are broken, similar to the term *ashmai*, meaning crooked. Elsewhere he associates *shima'ei* with *shemama*, desolation. The *Arukh* cites Rabbeinu Ḥananel's interpretation that it means entrances of Eretz Yisrael. Rabbeinu Ḥananel's statement is based on the Arabic الشام, *al-shām*, which is the traditional name for Syria and Eretz Yisrael.

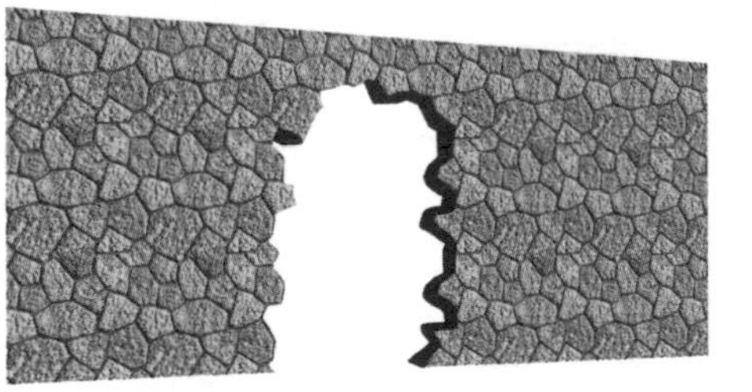

Broken entrance according to Rashi's explanation

Doorpost [*patzim*] – פַּצִּים: The meaning of the word *patzim* or *patzin* is a post or a board. It is generally used in reference to doorposts of entrances. The root is probably *peh, tzadi, mem*, which means breaking or cleaving; see the verse: "You have made the land to shake, You have cleft it [*petzamta*]; heal its breaches, for it totters" (Psalms 60:4). Accordingly, *patzimin* refers to boards or pieces of wood.

Porticos [*ispelidei*] – אִיסְפְּלִידֵי: Some suggest that this term is derived from the Greek σπηλάδιον, *spēladion*, meaning cave, cave-like, or curved. Others suggest that it is derived from the word ψαλίδος, *psalidos*, the genitive form of ψαλίς, *psalis*, meaning a vault.

HALAKHA

That they do not have a proper ceiling – דְּלֵית לְהוּ תִּקְרָה: A house that does not have a ceiling is exempt from a *mezuza*. In a case where it is partly covered with a ceiling and partly uncovered, if the ceiling is over the entrance and measures at least four by four cubits, one is obligated to affix a *mezuza* to that entrance (Rambam *Sefer Ahava, Hilkhot Tefillin UMezuza VeSefer Torah* 6:5; *Shulḥan Arukh, Yoreh De'a* 286:14).

That they do not have lintels – דְּלֵית לְהוּ שְׁקוֹפֵי: An entrance that does not have a lintel and two doorposts is exempt from the obligation to affix a *mezuza*. The *Taz*, citing the *Tur*, comments that the same applies if the lintel or the doorpost is not straight but is built of uneven stones (Rambam *Sefer Ahava, Hilkhot Tefillin UMezuza VeSefer Torah* 6:1; *Shulḥan Arukh, Yoreh De'a* 287:1).

NOTES

That they do not have a proper ceiling [*tikra*]…that they do not have lintels [*shakofei*] – דְּלֵית לְהוּ תִּקְרָה...דְּלֵית לְהוּ שְׁקוֹפֵי: In his first explanation, Rashi states that a case where there is no *tikra* refers to a case where there is no upper lintel to the doorframe. Alternatively, it means that the lintel is not constructed in a straight manner over the door, as the stones are uneven (*Tosafot*). According to this opinion, the term *shakofei* is a reference to doorposts, not lintels, and it is stating that the doorposts are not straight, as their stones are uneven (*Eiruvin* 11a). According to Rashi's second explanation, a case where there is no *tikra* refers to a house that does not have a ceiling at all.

BACKGROUND

Gatehouse – בֵּית שַׁעַר: A gatehouse is a small structure built at the gate of a courtyard to prevent people from entering directly into the courtyard. It is generally small and open at the front, as the gate of the courtyard serves as its back wall. If the courtyard is guarded, the guard might sit in the gatehouse.

Gatehouse at the entrance of an ancient palace in Amman, Jordan

Bei harziki – בֵּי הַרְזִיקֵי:

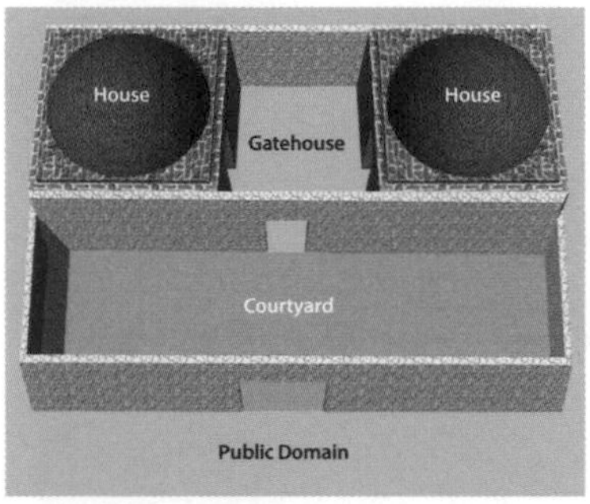

Bei harziki according to Rashi

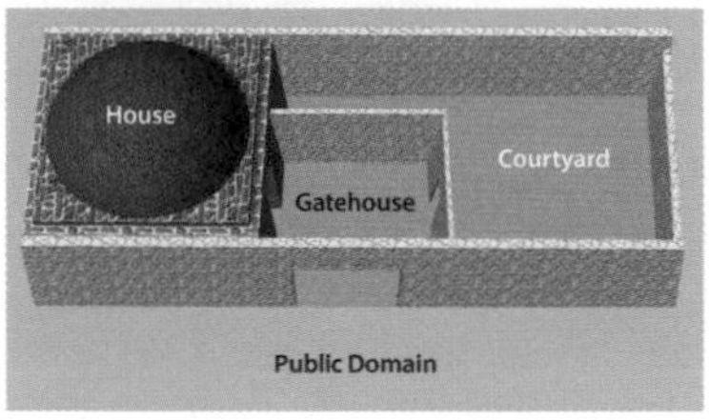

Bei harziki according to the Ramban and the Ran

מֵיתִיבֵי: בֵּית שַׁעַר, אַכְסַדְרָה, וּמִרְפֶּסֶת – חַיָּיבִין בִּמְזוּזָה! בְּאַכְסַדְרָה דְּבֵי רַב. אַכְסַדְרָה דְּבֵי רַב כְּאִינְדְּרוֹנָא מְעַלְּיְיתָא הוּא! בְּאַכְסַדְרָה רוֹמִיתָא.

The Gemara **raises an objection** from a *baraita*: With regard to a **gatehouse,**[B] **a portico, and a balcony,**[H] one is **obligated to** place a *mezuza*. The Gemara answers: The *halakha* of the *baraita* is stated **with regard to** a specific type of portico, **the portico of a study hall,**[H] which is closed on all sides, but its walls do not reach the ceiling. The Gemara raises a difficulty: **A portico of a study hall is like a full-fledged room** [*inderona*],[L] and therefore it should not be labeled a portico with regard to the *halakhot* of *mezuza*. The Gemara answers: The *halakha* of the *baraita* is stated **with regard to a Roman portico,**[N] which is more open than the portico of a study hall, as it is built with many windows instead of proper walls. The *baraita* is teaching that one is obligated to place a *mezuza* on this type of portico.

אָמַר רַחֲבָה אָמַר רַב יְהוּדָה: בֵּי הַרְזִיקֵי חַיָּיב בִּשְׁתֵּי מְזוּזוֹת. מַאי בֵּי הַרְזִיקֵי? אָמַר רַב פַּפָּא סָבָא מִשְּׁמֵיהּ דְּרַב: בֵּית שַׁעַר הַפָּתוּחַ לְחָצֵר, וּבָתִּים פְּתוּחִין לְבֵית שַׁעַר.

§ **Raḥava says** that **Rav Yehuda says:** With regard to a ***bei harziki***,[BL] one is **obligated to** place **two *mezuzot*.** The Gemara asks: **What is** a ***bei harziki***? **Rav Pappa the Elder says in the name of Rav:** It is a **gatehouse that opens to a courtyard, and houses** also **open** directly **to the gatehouse.**[H] It requires two *mezuzot*, one for the entrance from the courtyard to the gatehouse, and one for the entrance from the gatehouse to the houses.

תָּנוּ רַבָּנַן: בֵּית שַׁעַר הַפָּתוּחַ לְגִינָּה וּלְקִיטוֹנִית – רַבִּי יוֹסֵי אוֹמֵר: נִידּוֹן כְּקִיטוֹנִית, וַחֲכָמִים אוֹמְרִים: נִידּוֹן כְּבֵית שַׁעַר. רַב וּשְׁמוּאֵל דְּאָמְרִי תַּרְוַיְיהוּ: מִגִּינָּה לַבַּיִת כּוּלֵּי עָלְמָא לָא פְּלִיגִי דְּחַיָּיב, מַאי טַעְמָא? בִּיאָה דְּבַיִת הִיא,

The Sages taught in a *baraita*: With regard to **a gatehouse that** has two entrances, as it **opens** both **to a garden,** which is exempt from a *mezuza*, **and to a small room** [***ulekitonit***],[NL] **Rabbi Yosei says: Its** halakhic **status is like** that of **a small room,** and it requires a *mezuza*, **and the Rabbis say:** Its halakhic status **is like** that of **a gatehouse,** and it does not require a *mezuza*. There is a difference of opinion among *amora'im* with regard to this dispute. **Rav and Shmuel both say:** With regard to the entrance through which one enters **from the garden to the house,** i.e., the entrance of the gatehouse to the small room, **everyone agrees** that one is **obligated** to place a *mezuza*. **What is the reason? It is** the way of **entering** the **house,** and the house requires a *mezuza*.

כִּי פְּלִיגִי – מִבַּיִת לַגִּינָּה, מָר סָבַר: קִיטוֹנִית עִיקָּר, וּמָר סָבַר: גִּינָּה עִיקָּר.

Rav and Shmuel continue: **When they disagree** it is with regard to the entrance through which one enters **from** the **house to the garden,** i.e., the entrance of the gatehouse to the garden. One **Sage,** Rabbi Yosei, **holds** that the **small room** into which the gatehouse opens is the **main** area, and therefore the gatehouse, which is used for entering the small room, is considered like a regular gatehouse to a house, and all its entrances require a *mezuza*. **And** one **Sage,** the Rabbis, **hold** that the **garden** is the **main** area, and therefore this entrance does not require a *mezuza*.

NOTES

Roman portico – אַכְסַדְרָה רוֹמִיתָא: There are several explanations with regard to the structure of these buildings. Rashi here states that the portico of a study hall has walls, but they are low and do not reach the ceiling, whereas a Roman portico is one whose walls are made entirely of windows. In tractate *Bava Batra* (11b) he explains in the opposite manner. Most commentaries maintain that the portico of a study hall has very wide doorposts and is similar to a house, while a Roman portico has three walls and two posts about a cubit in width on the fourth side (*Arukh*). Others state that the portico of a study hall is not open at all, but is like a narrow corridor (*Sefer HaEshkol*, citing Rav Sherira Gaon). The Rid claims that a Roman portico consists entirely of entrances, each of which requires a *mezuza*.

A gatehouse that opens to a garden and to a small room – בֵּית שַׁעַר הַפָּתוּחַ לְגִינָּה וּלְקִיטוֹנִית: The *halakha* of a garden differs from that of a courtyard, which was dealt with by the Gemara in the case of a *bei harziki*. A courtyard serves residential purposes, as the inhabitants of the house use it for certain household functions, such as washing clothing, and therefore one is obligated to affix a *mezuza* there. Conversely, a garden is used for planting vegetation or for ornamental purposes, and for that reason one is exempt from affixing a *mezuza* there.

HALAKHA

A gatehouse, a portico, and a balcony – בֵּית שַׁעַר אַכְסַדְרָה וּמִרְפֶּסֶת: A gatehouse, a portico, a balcony, a garden, and a stable are exempt from the obligation of *mezuza*, because they do not serve as a residence. If these open directly into a house, a *mezuza* is required (Rif; Rambam). The *Tur*, citing Rabbeinu Yitzḥak, says that a gatehouse requires a *mezuza* even if it does not lead directly to a house, but this requirement applies by rabbinic law (Rambam *Sefer Ahava*, *Hilkhot Tefillin UMezuza VeSefer Torah* 6:7; *Shulḥan Arukh*, *Yoreh De'a* 286:7).

The portico of a study hall – אַכְסַדְרָה דְּבֵי רַב: With regard to a portico, which is a place with three walls and a ceiling, even if it has two doorposts on its fourth side it is exempt from the obligation to affix a *mezuza*. The reason is that its doorposts are there to support the ceiling, not to serve as actual doorposts for the entrance. If it has a partition on the fourth side, even a low one, or if it consists entirely of windows, one is obligated to place a *mezuza* there (Rambam *Sefer Ahava*, *Hilkhot Tefillin UMezuza VeSefer Torah* 6:3; *Shulḥan Arukh*, *Yoreh De'a* 286:6).

A gatehouse that opens to a courtyard and houses open to the gatehouse – בֵּית שַׁעַר הַפָּתוּחַ לְחָצֵר וּבָתִּים פְּתוּחִין לְבֵית שַׁעַר: A gatehouse that opens to a house and a courtyard requires two *mezuzot*, in addition to the entrance through which one comes in from the public domain (*Shakh*, based on *Tur*). One of these two *mezuzot* is placed where it opens to the house, and the other where it opens to the courtyard (*Shulḥan Arukh*, *Yoreh De'a* 286:8).

LANGUAGE

Room [*inderona*] – אִינְדְּרוֹנָא: Apparently from the Greek ἀνδρών, *andron*, meaning a house for men or a parlor in the house. The Romans used it in reference to a corridor, a room which joins two houses or courtyards.

Bei harziki – בֵּי הַרְזִיקֵי: Probably from the Middle Persian fra-zēk, meaning prison or punishment, this term is found in Arabic and Mandaic, and it means jailhouse. It can have the same meaning in the Talmud.

Small room [*kitonit*] – קִיטוֹנִית: From the Greek κοιτών, *koiton*, meaning a bedroom. The Sages use it in reference to other small rooms as well.

רַבָּה וְרַב יוֹסֵף דְּאָמְרִי תַּרְוַויְהוּ: מִבַּיִת לְגִינָּה דְּכוּלֵּי עָלְמָא לָא פְּלִיגִי דְּפָטוּר, מַאי טַעְמָא? פִּיתְחָא דְּגִינָּה הוּא, כִּי פְּלִיגִי – מִגִּינָּה לְבַיִת, מָר סָבַר: בִּיאָה דְּבַיִת הוּא, וּמָר סָבַר: כּוּלָּהּ

Conversely, **Rabba and Rav Yosef both say:** With regard to the entrance through which one enters **from the house to the garden,** i.e., the entrance between the gatehouse and the garden, **everyone agrees** that one is **exempt** from placing a *mezuza.* **What is the reason? It is the entrance to the garden,** and the garden does not require a *mezuza.* **When they disagree** it is with regard to the entrance **from** the **garden to the house,** i.e., the entrance between the gatehouse and the small room. One **Sage,** Rabbi Yosei, **holds** that **it is** the way of **entering the house,** and the house requires a *mezuza,* **and** one **Sage,** the Rabbis, **holds** that **the entire**

Perek **III**
Daf **34** Amud **a**

אַדַּעְתָּא דְּגִינָּה הוּא דַּעֲבִידָא.

area **is made for the purpose of** reaching the **garden,** not for entering the house, and therefore even with regard to the entrance between the gatehouse and small room, one is exempt from placing a *mezuza* at the entrance of the small room.

אַבָּיֵי וְרָבָא עָבְדִי כְּרַבָּה וְרַב יוֹסֵף, וְרַב אָשֵׁי עָבֵיד כְּרַב וּשְׁמוּאֵל לְחוּמְרָא. וְהִילְכְתָא כְּרַב וּשְׁמוּאֵל לְחוּמְרָא.

The Gemara relates that **Abaye and Rava would act in accordance with** the explanation of **Rabba and Rav Yosef,** i.e., they would not place a *mezuza* on the two entrances of a gatehouse, neither to the garden nor to the small room, in accordance with the ruling of the Rabbis. **And Rav Ashi would act in accordance with** the explanation of **Rav and Shmuel, stringently,**[H] i.e., following the ruling of Rabbi Yosei that both entrances require a *mezuza.* The Gemara concludes: **And the *halakha* is in accordance with** the explanation of **Rav and Shmuel, stringently.**

אִיתְּמַר: לוּל פָּתוּחַ מִן הַבַּיִת לַעֲלִיָּיה, אָמַר רַב הוּנָא: אִם יֵשׁ לוֹ פֶּתַח אֶחָד – חַיָּיב בִּמְזוּזָה אַחַת, אִם יֵשׁ לוֹ שְׁנֵי פְתָחִין – חַיָּיב בִּשְׁתֵּי מְזוּזוֹת. אָמַר רַב פָּפָּא: שְׁמַע מִינָּהּ מִדְּרַב הוּנָא, הַאי אִינְדְּרוֹנָא דְּאִית לֵיהּ אַרְבָּעָה בָּאבֵי – חַיָּיב בְּאַרְבַּע מְזוּזוֹת. פְּשִׁיטָא! לָא צְרִיכָא, אַף עַל גַּב דְּרָגִיל בְּחַד.

§ **It was stated:** With regard to **an aperture that opens from** the ceiling of **a house** occupied by one person **to a loft**[H] occupied by another, with a walled staircase leading from the lower floor to the loft, **Rav Huna says: If** the staircase **has one entrance,** i.e., one doorway, either from the house or from the upper story, one is **obligated** to affix **one *mezuza*; if it has two entrances,** both from below and above, one is **obligated to** affix **two *mezuzot.* Rav Pappa says:** One can **learn from that** statement **of Rav Huna** that with regard to **this** type of **room that has four gates,** one is **obligated to** affix **four *mezuzot.*** The Gemara asks: Isn't it **obvious?** The Gemara explains: **No,** it is **necessary** to teach that **even though one is accustomed to** using **one** particular gate,[H] nevertheless, all four require a *mezuza.*

HALAKHA

In accordance with the explanation of Rav and Shmuel, stringently – כְּרַב וּשְׁמוּאֵל לְחוּמְרָא: A gatehouse between a garden and a house requires two *mezuzot,* one in the entrance that opens to the house and the other in the entrance that opens to the garden. According to the Rambam, the same applies to a gatehouse between a garden and a courtyard. The *halakha* is in accordance with the opinion of Rav Ashi (Rambam *Sefer Ahava, Hilkhot Tefillin UMezuza VeSefer Torah* 6:8; *Shulḥan Arukh, Yoreh De'a* 286:9).

From a house to a loft – מִן הַבַּיִת לַעֲלִיָּיה: With regard to an aperture between a house and a loft, through which one ascends by stairs, if partitions are placed around the stairs, either at the bottom of the stairs or at the top, and the partitions form the shape of an entrance, that entrance requires a *mezuza.* If it has the shape of an entrance both above and below, it requires two *mezuzot,* as maintained by Rav Huna (Rambam *Sefer Ahava, Hilkhot Tefillin UMezuza VeSefer Torah* 6:10; *Shulḥan Arukh, Yoreh De'a* 286:19).

Even though one is accustomed to using one particular gate – אַף עַל גַּב דְּרָגִיל בְּחַד: If a house has many entrances that open to a courtyard or a public domain, and from the outset all of them were designed for the entry and exit of the members of the household, then all the entrances require a *mezuza,* even if the number of residents decreased so that only one of the entrances is currently used. The *halakha* is in accordance with Rashi's second explanation of Rav Pappa's statement. Likewise, if a house has many doors, even if one usually uses only one of them he must place a *mezuza* on each entrance. This is in accordance with Rashi's first interpretation and that of the Rambam (Rambam *Sefer Ahava, Hilkhot Tefillin UMezuza VeSefer Torah* 6:10; *Shulḥan Arukh, Yoreh De'a* 286:18, and see the comment of Rema and *Beur HaGra* there).

LANGUAGE

These [*adei*] – עֲדֵי: This word occurs rarely in the Talmud. It is the plural form of *ada*, which means: This, similar to *hada*, or the shortened form *da*.

HALAKHA

To the right of the entrance – מִיָּמִין: The *mezuza* should be affixed to the right of a doorway, as one enters the house. Placement of a *mezuza* on the left side is not valid, whether or not the owner is left-handed (Rambam *Sefer Ahava, Hilkhot Tefillin UMezuza VeSefer Torah* 6:12; *Shulḥan Arukh, Yoreh De'a* 289:2, and in the comment of Rema).

אֲמַר אַמֵימָר: הַאי פִּיתְחָא דְּאַקַּרְנָא חַיָּיב בִּמְזוּזָה. אֲמַר לֵיהּ רַב אַשִׁי לְאַמֵימָר: וְהָא לֵית לֵיהּ פַּצִּימִין! אֲמַר לֵיהּ: עֲדֵי פַּצִּימֵי.

Ameimar said: With regard to **this entrance which** is located **at the corner** of a house,[N] one is **obligated to** affix **a** ***mezuza*****. Rav Ashi said to Ameimar: But it does not have doorposts.** Ameimar **said to him: These** [*adei*][L] **are its doorposts,** i.e., the end of the walls serve as its doorposts.

רַב פַּפָּא אִיקְלַע לְבֵי מָר שְׁמוּאֵל, חֲזָא הַהוּא פִּיתְחָא דְּלָא הֲוָה לֵיהּ אֶלָּא פַּצִּים אֶחָד מִשְּׂמָאלָא וַעֲבִידָא לֵיהּ מְזוּזָה, אֲמַר לֵיהּ: כְּמַאן, כְּרַבִּי מֵאִיר? אֵימַר דְּאָמַר רַבִּי מֵאִיר – מִיָּמִין, מִשְּׂמֹאל מִי אָמַר?

The Gemara relates: **Rav Pappa happened** to come **to the house of Mar Shmuel, where he saw a certain entrance that had only one doorpost to the left** of the entrance,[N] **and** yet Mar Shmuel **had affixed a** ***mezuza*** **to** that doorpost. Rav Pappa **said to him: In accordance with whose** opinion did you do this? Did you act **in accordance with** the opinion of **Rabbi Meir,** who deems one obligated to affix a *mezuza* to an entrance that has only one doorpost? But one can **say that Rabbi Meir says** that one must do so only in a case where the doorpost is **to the right** of the entrance.[H] **Does he say** that it requires a *mezuza* if the entrance is **to the left?**

מַאי הִיא? דְּתַנְיָא: ״בֵּיתֶךָ״ – בִּיאָתְךָ מִן הַיָּמִין; אַתָּה אוֹמֵר: מִן הַיָּמִין, אוֹ אֵינוֹ אֶלָּא מִשְּׂמֹאל! תַּלְמוּד לוֹמַר: ״בֵּיתֶךָ״. מַאי תַּלְמוּדָא? אָמַר רַבָּה: דֶּרֶךְ בִּיאָתְךָ מִן הַיָּמִין, דְּכִי עָקַר אִינִישׁ כַּרְעֵיהּ – דִּימִינָא עָקַר.

The Gemara asks: **What** is the source for **this** requirement that the *mezuza* be affixed to the right side? **As it is taught** in a *baraita*: When the verse states: "And you shall write them upon the doorposts of **your house** [***beitekha***]" (Deuteronomy 6:9), the word *beitekha* is interpreted as ***biatekha***, your entry, i.e., the *mezuza* must be affixed to the side by which you enter, which is **from the right. Do you say** it is **from the right, or** is it **only from the left?** Therefore, **the verse states: Your house** [***beitekha***]. The Gemara asks: **What is the** biblical **derivation** here? **Rabba says:** The *mezuza* is affixed in **the way that you enter** the house, which is **from the right, as when a person lifts his foot** to begin walking, **he lifts his right** foot first. Therefore, the *mezuza* is affixed to the right side of the doorway.

NOTES

This entrance which is located at the corner of a house – הַאי פִּיתְחָא דְּאַקַּרְנָא: In other words, it is as though the corner were clipped, i.e., parts of the adjoining walls were removed, so that there is a diagonal entrance to the room between the two ends of the walls (Rashi; see *Ḥazon Ish*). Others explain that one of the walls does not reach the corner (Rid). Yet others contend that this refers to a house which has one side that is entirely open, so that the two walls on its sides can be seen as doorposts (Rosh). Although one is exempt from affixing a *mezuza* to a portico, as stated on 33b, this refers to a case where there is a door along the entire width of the side (*Derisha*). Alternatively, one is exempt from affixing a *mezuza* to a portico because it is used solely as a passageway, whereas this is referring to a proper room (*Yad HaKetanna*).

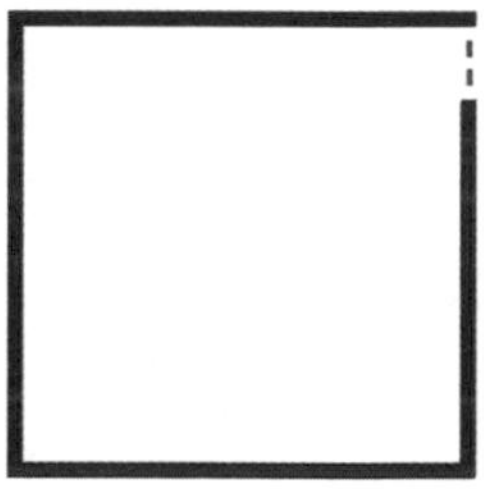

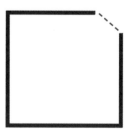

Rid's explanation

Rashi's explanation

Rosh's explanation

That had only one doorpost to the left of the entrance – דְּלָא הֲוָה לֵיהּ אֶלָּא פַּצִּים אֶחָד מִשְּׂמָאלָא: For example, the right side of the entrance is a wall that continues onward, and there is a doorpost only on the left side (Rosh). Some understand Rashi's explanation in the same manner.

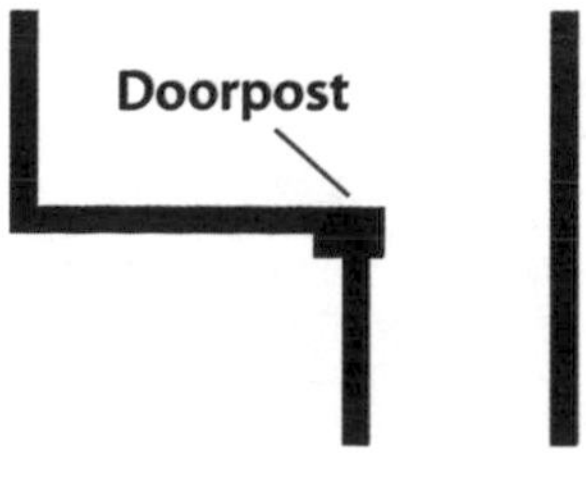

Doorpost to the left of the entrance, according to the Rosh's explanation

רַב שְׁמוּאֵל בַּר אַחָא קַמֵּיהּ דְּרַב פַּפָּא מִשְּׁמֵיהּ דְּרָבָא בַּר עוּלָּא אָמַר, מֵהָכָא: ״וַיִּקַּח יְהוֹיָדָע הַכֹּהֵן אֲרוֹן אֶחָד וַיִּקֹּב חֹר בְּדַלְתּוֹ וַיִּתֵּן אוֹתוֹ אֵצֶל הַמִּזְבֵּחַ מִיָּמִין בְּבוֹא אִישׁ בֵּית ה׳ וְנָתְנוּ שָׁמָּה הַכֹּהֲנִים שׁוֹמְרֵי הַסַּף אֶת כָּל הַכֶּסֶף הַמּוּבָא בֵּית ה׳״.

Rav Shmuel bar Aḥa said before Rav Pappa in the name of Rava bar Ulla that the requirement that the *mezuza* be affixed to the right of the entrance is derived **from here: "And Jehoiada the priest took a chest, and bored a hole in the lid of it, and set it beside the altar, on the right side as one comes into the House of the Lord; and the priests that kept the threshold put in there all the money that was brought into the House of the Lord"** (II Kings 12:10). This indicates that an object designed for those entering a house is placed to the right of the one entering.

מַאי רַבִּי מֵאִיר? דְּתַנְיָא: בַּיִת שֶׁאֵין לוֹ אֶלָּא פַּצִּים אֶחָד – רַבִּי מֵאִיר מְחַיֵּיב בִּמְזוּזָה, וַחֲכָמִים פּוֹטְרִין. מַאי טַעְמָא דְּרַבָּנַן? ״מְזוּזֹת״ כְּתִיב.

The Gemara further inquires: **What is** this statement of **Rabbi Meir**, referred to by Rav Pappa, that he deems one obligated to place a *mezuza* on an entrance that has only one doorpost? **As it is taught** in a *baraita*: With regard to **a house that has only one doorpost,**[H] **Rabbi Meir deems** one **obligated to** affix **a** ***mezuza*****, and the Rabbis deem** him **exempt** from affixing a *mezuza*. The Gemara asks: **What is the reasoning of the Rabbis? It is written:** "And you shall write them upon the **doorposts** of your house" (Deuteronomy 6:9), in the plural, which indicates that there must be two doorposts.

מַאי טַעְמָא דְּרַבִּי מֵאִיר? דְּתַנְיָא: ״מְזוּזֹת״ – שׁוֹמֵעַ אֲנִי מִיעוּט מְזוּזוֹת שְׁתַּיִם, כְּשֶׁהוּא אוֹמֵר ״מְזוּזֹת״ בְּפָרָשָׁה שְׁנִיָּה – שֶׁאֵין תַּלְמוּד לוֹמַר, הֲוֵי רִיבּוּי אַחַר רִיבּוּי, וְאֵין רִיבּוּי אַחַר רִיבּוּי אֶלָּא לְמַעֵט, מִעֲטוֹ הַכָּתוּב לִמְזוּזָה אַחַת, דִּבְרֵי רַבִּי יִשְׁמָעֵאל.

The Gemara asks: **What is the reason of Rabbi Meir,** that one doorpost suffices to obligate one to affix a *mezuza*? **As it is taught** in a *baraita*: When it states **"doorposts"** (Deuteronomy 6:9), **I** would **derive the minimum** number **of doorposts,** which is **two. When it says "doorposts" in the second passage** (Deuteronomy 11:20), this also serves to teach a *halakha*, **as** otherwise there is **no** need for **the verse to state** this. This **is** one **amplification following** another **amplification, and** the principle is that **an amplification following an amplification is** stated **only** in order **to restrict** its extent. In this manner **the verse restricted** the minimum number **to one doorpost.**[N] This is **the statement of Rabbi Yishmael.**

רַבִּי עֲקִיבָא אוֹמֵר: אֵינוֹ צָרִיךְ, כְּשֶׁהוּא אוֹמֵר: ״עַל הַמַּשְׁקוֹף וְעַל שְׁתֵּי הַמְּזוּזֹת״ – שֶׁאֵין תַּלְמוּד לוֹמַר ״שְׁתֵּי״, מַה תַּלְמוּד לוֹמַר ״שְׁתֵּי״? זֶה בָּנָה אָב, כׇּל מָקוֹם שֶׁנֶּאֱמַר ״מְזוּזוֹת״ אֵינוֹ אֶלָּא אַחַת, עַד שֶׁיְּפָרֵט לְךָ הַכָּתוּב שְׁתַּיִם.

Rabbi Akiva says: This proof **is not necessary.** Rather, **when the** verse **states: "**And strike **the lintel and the two doorposts"** (Exodus 12:22), one can claim that there is a superfluous word in this verse, **as** there is **no** need for **the verse to state "two,"** since the minimum of doorposts is two. **What is** the meaning when **the verse states "two"? This established a paradigm** that **anywhere where it is stated "doorposts,"** it means **only one** doorpost, **unless the verse specifies** that it is referring to **two** doorposts.

תָּנוּ רַבָּנַן: ״וּכְתַבְתָּם״ – יָכוֹל יִכְתְּבֶנָּה עַל הָאֲבָנִים? נֶאֱמַר כָּאן כְּתִיבָה וְנֶאֱמַר לְהַלָּן כְּתִיבָה, מַה לְּהַלָּן עַל הַסֵּפֶר – אַף כָּאן עַל הַסֵּפֶר.

The Sages taught in a *baraita*: The verse states: **"And you shall write them** upon the doorposts of your house, and upon your gates" (Deuteronomy 6:9). One **might** have thought that **one writes** a *mezuza* **on the stones** of the entrance. To counter this, an expression of **writing is stated here,** with regard to a *mezuza*, **and** an expression of **writing is stated there.**[N] **Just as there** the mitzva of writing means **on a book,** i.e., parchment, **so too,** a *mezuza* must be written **on a book.**

אוֹ כַּלֵּךְ לְדֶרֶךְ זוֹ: נֶאֱמַר כָּאן כְּתִיבָה וְנֶאֱמַר לְהַלָּן כְּתִיבָה, מַה לְּהַלָּן עַל הָאֲבָנִים – אַף כָּאן עַל הָאֲבָנִים!

The *baraita* suggests: **Or** perhaps, **go [*****kalekh*****]**[L] **this way,** i.e., one can suggest a different interpretation: An expression of **writing is stated here,** with regard to a *mezuza*, **and writing is stated there,** with regard to the mitzva of writing the words of the Torah on stones upon the entry to Eretz Yisrael (Deuteronomy 27:3). **Just as there,** the words are written **on the stones** themselves, **so too here,** the *mezuza* should be written **on the stones.**

נִרְאֶה לְמִי דּוֹמֶה, דָּנִין כְּתִיבָה הַנּוֹהֶגֶת לְדוֹרוֹת מִכְּתִיבָה הַנּוֹהֶגֶת לְדוֹרוֹת, וְאֵין דָּנִין כְּתִיבָה הַנּוֹהֶגֶת לְדוֹרוֹת מִכְּתִיבָה שֶׁאֵינָהּ נוֹהֶגֶת לְדוֹרוֹת, וּכְמוֹ שֶׁנֶּאֱמַר לְהַלָּן: ״וַיֹּאמֶר לָהֶם בָּרוּךְ מִפִּיו יִקְרָא אֵלַי אֶת הַדְּבָרִים הָאֵלֶּה וַאֲנִי כֹּתֵב עַל הַסֵּפֶר בַּדְּיוֹ״.

The *baraita* continues: **Let us see to which it is similar,** i.e., which comparison appears more apt. **We derive writing that is performed in** all **generations,** i.e., that of a *mezuza*, **from** another **writing that is performed in** all **generations, but we do not derive writing that is performed in** all **generations from writing that is not performed in** all **generations. And** furthermore, a *mezuza* must be written with ink, **as it is stated below: "And Baruch said to them: He dictated all these words to me, and I wrote them with ink in the scroll"** (Jeremiah 36:18).

HALAKHA

A house that has only one doorpost – בַּיִת שֶׁאֵין לוֹ אֶלָּא פַּצִּים אֶחָד: An entrance requires a *mezuza* only if it has two doorposts, in accordance with the opinion of the Rabbis, who disagree with Rabbi Meir (*Beur HaGra*), and following the statement of Rava on 33a (*Be'er HaGola*). Others maintain that even in a case where it has only one doorpost, e.g., on the side opposite the one doorpost the wall extends beyond the entrance, if the doorpost is on the right side then it requires a *mezuza*, which one should affix without reciting a blessing (Rosh; *Tur*; *Shakh*). If the doorpost is on the left side, it is exempt from a *mezuza*, in accordance with the opinion of Rabbi Meir, as Rabbi Yishmael and Rabbi Akiva agree with his ruling, and as indicated by the incident involving Rav Pappa in Mar Shmuel's house (Rambam *Sefer Ahava, Hilkhot Tefillin UMezuza VeSefer Torah* 6:1; *Shulḥan Arukh, Yoreh De'a* 287:1).

NOTES

The verse restricted the minimum number to one doorpost [***mezuza*****], etc. – מִעֲטוֹ הַכָּתוּב לִמְזוּזָה אַחַת וכו׳:** The word *mezuza* can be used to refer both to a doorpost and to the scroll that one affixes to the doorpost. Rashi explains that Rabbi Yishmael and Rabbi Akiva, like Rabbi Meir, are discussing an entrance that has one doorpost [*mezuza*], and this is the source for his opinion that one is obligated to affix a *mezuza* to such an entrance. Others maintain that this *baraita*, as its straightforward reading indicates, is referring to the number of *mezuzot* that one must place at the entrance to the house, not the *halakha* stated by Rabbi Meir (*Smag*). The later commentaries explain that according to this interpretation, the Gemara is saying that Rabbi Meir expounds the verse in the same manner as does Rabbi Yishmael and Rabbi Akiva, but he derives an additional *halakha* from here, i.e., that it is enough if the entrance has one doorpost (*Yad David*; see *Sefat Emet*).

And an expression of writing is stated there – וְנֶאֱמַר לְהַלָּן כְּתִיבָה: Rashi explains that this refers to the writing of a bill of divorce, concerning which the verse states: "That he writes her a bill of divorce, and gives it in her hand" (Deuteronomy 24:1). *Tosafot* suggest that this refers to either the verse: "That he shall write him a copy of this law in a book" (Deuteronomy 17:18), written with regard to the mitzva for a king to write a Torah scroll, or the verse: "And the priest shall write these curses in a scroll" (Numbers 5:23), written with regard to the *sota* rite.

LANGUAGE

Go [***kalekh*****] – כַּלֵּךְ:** This term is found in rabbinic usage and in halakhic midrash, at times appearing as *lekha lekh* or *holekha lekh*. The word *kalekh* is variously interpreted as a shortened form of *lekha lekh* (*Ḥokhmat Manoaḥ*) or a shortened form of *kaleh velekh* (Ya'avetz), all of which bear the same basic meaning of go out or go forth.

HALAKHA

Complete writing, and then should one place them upon the doorposts – כְּתִיבָה תַּמָּה וְהָדָר עַל הַמְּזוּזוֹת: There is a positive mitzva to write down the first two passages of *Shema*, Deuteronomy 6:4–9 and 11:13–21, and place them on the doorpost of the entrance to one's house (*Shulḥan Arukh, Yoreh De'a* 285:1).

That even the absence of the thorn of a letter *yod* – לְקוֹצוֹ שֶׁל יוֹ״ד: The absence of even one letter in any one of the four passages of the phylacteries prevents fulfillment of the mitzva by Torah law. They must all be written completely (Rambam *Sefer Ahava, Hilkhot Tefillin UMezuza VeSefer Torah* 1:1; *Shulḥan Arukh, Oraḥ Ḥayyim* 32:4).

Any letter that is not encircled with blank parchment, etc. – כָּל אוֹת שֶׁאֵין גְּוִיל מוּקָף לָהּ וכו׳: Every letter must be surrounded by blank parchment on all four sides. If it is not surrounded by parchment, it is unfit (Rambam *Sefer Ahava, Hilkhot Tefillin UMezuza VeSefer Torah* 1:19; *Shulḥan Arukh, Oraḥ Ḥayyim* 32:4).

NOTES

And the absence of even one letter prevents fulfillment of the mitzva with the rest of them, etc. – וַאֲפִילּוּ כְּתָב אֶחָד מְעַכְּבָן וכו׳: This discussion already appeared on 29a with regard to the passages of a *mezuza*, where it is elucidated in detail.

אֲמַר לֵיהּ רַב אַחָא בְּרֵיהּ דְּרָבָא לְרַב אָשֵׁי, רַחֲמָנָא אָמַר ״עַל מְזוּזוֹת״, וְאַתְּ אָמְרַתְּ: נֵילַף כְּתִיבָה כְּתִיבָה?! אֲמַר קְרָא: ״וּכְתַבְתָּם״ – כְּתִיבָה תַּמָּה, וַהֲדַר ״עַל הַמְּזוּזוֹת״.

Rav Aḥa, son of Rava, said to Rav Ashi: The Merciful One states: "Upon the doorposts," which indicates that a *mezuza* should be written on the doorposts themselves, **and** yet **you say: Let us derive** a verbal analogy between **"writing"** and **"writing,"** to teach that one writes it on parchment. Why isn't the verse interpreted in accordance with its straightforward meaning? Rav Ashi said to him: **The verse states: "And you shall write them [*ukhtavtam*],"** which means that it should first be **complete writing [*ketiva tamma*]**, i.e., the full passages written down, **and** only **then** should one place them **"upon the doorposts"**[H] of the house.

וּמֵאַחַר דִּכְתִיב, הַאי גְּזֵירָה שָׁוָה לָמָּה לִי? אִי לָאו גְּזֵירָה שָׁוָה, הֲוָה אָמֵינָא לִיכְתְּבָא אַאַבְנָא וְלִיקְבְּעָה אַסֵּיפָא, קָא מַשְׁמַע לַן.

The Gemara asks: **And since it is written:** "And you shall write them," from which it is derived that the *mezuza* should be written first and then placed on the doorpost, **why do I need this verbal analogy** between "writing" and "writing"? The Gemara explains that **were it not** for the **verbal analogy, I would say** that one **should write** the passages of a *mezuza* **on a stone, and** afterward **affix** the stone **to the doorpost.** To counter this, the verbal analogy **teaches us** that a *mezuza* must be written on a scroll.

״אַרְבַּע פָּרָשִׁיּוֹת שֶׁבַּתְּפִילִּין מְעַכְּבוֹת זוֹ אֶת זוֹ, וַאֲפִילּוּ כְּתָב אֶחָד מְעַכְּבָן״. פְּשִׁיטָא!

§ The mishna teaches: With regard to **the four passages that are in the phylacteries,** i.e., the two passages that are written in the *mezuza* and two additional passages (Exodus 13:1–9, 11–16), the absence of **each prevents fulfillment of the mitzva with the others, and** the absence of **even one letter prevents fulfillment of the mitzva with** the rest of **them.**[N] The Gemara asks: Isn't it **obvious** that the inclusion of every letter is necessary?

אָמַר רַב יְהוּדָה אָמַר רַב: לָא נִצְרְכָא אֶלָּא לְקוֹצוֹ שֶׁל יוֹ״ד. וְהָא נַמִי פְּשִׁיטָא! לָא נִצְרְכָא אֶלָּא לְאִידָךְ דְּרַב יְהוּדָה, דְּאָמַר רַב יְהוּדָה אָמַר רַב: כׇּל אוֹת שֶׁאֵין גְּוִיל מוּקָף לָהּ מֵאַרְבַּע רוּחוֹתֶיהָ – פְּסוּלָה.

Rav Yehuda says that **Rav says:** It is **necessary** to state this ruling **only** to teach **that** even the absence of **the thorn,** i.e., a small stroke, **of a** letter ***yod***[H] prevents fulfillment of the mitzva. The Gemara asks: **But** isn't **this also obvious,** since the letter is not formed properly? **Rather, it is necessary only according to another** statement **that Rav Yehuda** says. **As Rav Yehuda says** that **Rav says: Any letter that is not encircled with** blank **parchment**[H] **on** all **four of its sides,** as its ink connects to the letter above it, below it, preceding it, or succeeding it, is **unfit.**

Perek **III**
Daf **34** Amud **b**

תָּנוּ רַבָּנַן: ״לְטֹטָפֹת״ ״לְטֹטָפֹת״ ״לְטוֹטָפֹת״ – הֲרֵי כָּאן אַרְבַּע, דִּבְרֵי רַבִּי יִשְׁמָעֵאל.

§ **The Sages taught** in a *baraita*: With regard to the number of compartments in the phylacteries of the head, the verse states: "It shall be for a sign upon your hand, and **for *totafot*** between your eyes" (Exodus 13:16), with the word *totafot* spelled deficient, without a *vav* before the final letter, in a way that can be read as singular; and again: "They shall be **for *totafot*** between your eyes" (Deuteronomy 6:8), spelled as a singular word; and again: "They shall be **for *totafot***[N] between your eyes" (Deuteronomy 11:18), this time spelled plene, with a *vav* before the final letter, in a manner that must be plural. **There are four** mentions of *totafot* **here,** as the third one is written in the plural and therefore counts as two. Consequently, it is derived that the phylacteries of the head must have four compartments. This is **the statement of Rabbi Yishmael.**

NOTES

For *totafot*, for *totafot*, for *totafot* – לְטֹטָפֹת לְטֹטָפֹת לְטוֹטָפֹת: According to the traditional text of the Torah in use today, the word *totafot* is spelled without a second *vav* in all three instances. The only difference is that the *totafot* in Deuteronomy 6:8 has no *vav* at all, whereas the other two have one *vav* near the beginning of the word. It is clear from the *baraita* that the *tanna'im* possessed a different version of the biblical text in which one of the three instances was spelled with a second *vav*. This is not the only example of this phenomenon; there are other cases where it is clear that the biblical text possessed by the *tanna'im* or *amora'im* differs from contemporary texts with regard to the spelling of certain words with or without a *vav* or *yod*. In these instances, the Ran is of the opinion that the spelling of Torah scrolls should be corrected to match the Gemara's version. Normative *halakha* follows the Responsa of the Rashba and the Radbaz, who say that the traditional texts should be maintained, as is indicated in tractate *Soferim*.

In *Sanhedrin* 4b, Rashi states that in Exodus 13:16 and Deuteronomy 6:8 the word *totafot* lacks a *vav* entirely, whereas in Deuteronomy 11:18 it has two instances of the letter *vav*. According to this explanation, the *baraita* follows the order of the verses. The Rid explains similarly, although in his version the word *totafot* in Deuteronomy 11:18 has one *vav*.

רַבִּי עֲקִיבָא אוֹמֵר: אֵינוֹ צָרִיךְ, "טֹט" בְּכַתְפֵּי שְׁתַּיִם, "פַּת" בְּאַפְרִיקִי שְׁתַּיִם.

Rabbi Akiva says: There is no need for this proof, as the requirement of four compartments can be derived from the word *totafot* itself: The word ***tot*** **in** the language of **Katfei** means **two,** and the word ***pat*** **in** the language of **Afriki** also means **two,** and therefore *totafot* can be understood as a compound word meaning four.

תָּנוּ רַבָּנַן: יָכוֹל יִכְתְּבֵם עַל אַרְבָּעָה עוֹרוֹת, וְיַנִּיחֵם בְּאַרְבָּעָה בָּתִּים בְּאַרְבָּעָה עוֹרוֹת? תַּלְמוּד לוֹמַר: "וּלְזִכָּרוֹן בֵּין עֵינֶיךָ" – זִכָּרוֹן אֶחָד אָמַרְתִּי לְךָ, וְלֹא שְׁנַיִם וּשְׁלֹשָׁה זִכְרוֹנוֹת, הָא כֵּיצַד? כּוֹתְבָן עַל אַרְבָּעָה עוֹרוֹת, וּמַנִּיחָן בְּאַרְבָּעָה בָּתִּים בְּעוֹר אֶחָד.

The Sages taught in a *baraita*: One **might** have thought that a scribe **should write** the passages of the phylacteries of the head **on four** separate **hides,** i.e., parchments, **and place them in four compartments of four hides,** one passage in each compartment. Therefore, **the verse states: "And for a memorial between your eyes"** (Exodus 13:9). This teaches: **I said to you** that the phylacteries are **one memorial, but not** that they are **two or three memorials,** i.e., the phylacteries themselves must be one unit. **How so?** One **writes** the passages **on four hides and places them in four compartments** fashioned **of one hide.**[HN]

וְאִם כְּתָבָן בְּעוֹר אֶחָד וְהִנִּיחָן בְּאַרְבָּעָה בָּתִּים – יָצָא. וְצָרִיךְ שֶׁיְּהֵא רֶיוַח בֵּינֵיהֶן, דִּבְרֵי רַבִּי, וַחֲכָמִים אוֹמְרִים: אֵינוֹ צָרִיךְ; וְשָׁוִין, שֶׁנּוֹתֵן חוּט אוֹ מְשִׁיחָה בֵּין כָּל אַחַת וְאַחַת. וְאִם אֵין חֲרִיצָן נִיכָּר – פְּסוּלוֹת.

And if a scribe **wrote** all four of **them on one hide and placed them in four compartments** by slitting the parchment between each of the passages, one who dons these phylacteries has **fulfilled** his obligation. **And** in such a case it is **necessary for there to be a space between** each of the passages,[N] so that each can be placed in a separate compartment; this is **the statement of** Rabbi Yehuda HaNasi. **And the Rabbis say: It is not necessary** for there to be a space between them. **And** Rabbi Yehuda HaNasi and the Rabbis **agree that one places a string or** a thicker **band between each and every one** of the four compartments.[N] The *baraita* adds: **And if their furrows,** i.e., the lines marking the separation between the compartments, **are not noticeable**[H] from the outside, the phylacteries **are unfit.**

NOTES

And places them in four compartments of one hide – וּמַנִּיחָן בְּאַרְבָּעָה בָּתִּים בְּעוֹר אֶחָד: Rashi explains the process of preparing phylacteries of the head: One takes soft hide and places it on a mold that has four protrusions one alongside the other. After wetting and drying the hide, four compartments are formed.

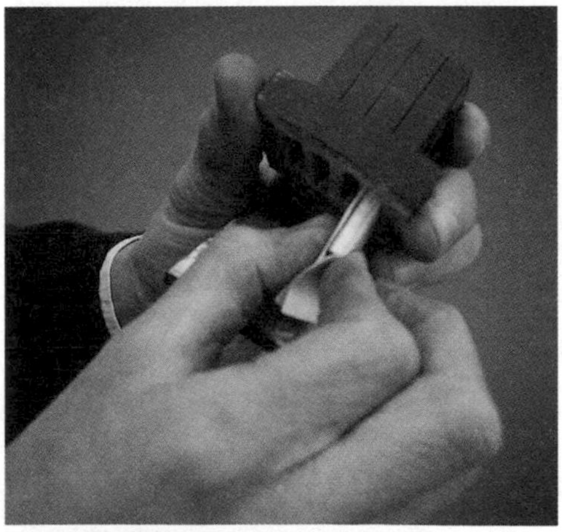

Inserting the parchment into the phylacteries of the head

And in such a case it is necessary for there to be a space between the passages – וְצָרִיךְ שֶׁיְּהֵא רֶיוַח בֵּינֵיהֶן: The commentaries disagree as to the meaning of this statement, and they also disagree with regard to how Rashi explains this statement. Most of the commentaries maintain that this refers to the writing of the passages on one parchment: According to Rabbi Yehuda HaNasi there must be a space between the passages so that each of them can be inserted fully into its own compartment, whereas the Rabbis hold that this is not necessary, as in any case one will place a single hide over all of them (Rid). Others contend that the Rabbis agree that there must be a space, but the difference is that Rabbi Yehuda HaNasi rules that a large space is required between them, as though each of them were rolled up separately (*Derisha*; *Baḥ*). Yet others are of the opinion that this refers to the space between the compartments, i.e., Rabbi Yehuda HaNasi says that there must be enough space between them so that each is clearly a separate compartment (Rabbeinu Simḥa, cited in *Or Zarua*; *Nimmukei Yosef*; *Beit Yosef*).

And they agree that one places a string or thicker band between each and every one of the four compartments – וְשָׁוִין שֶׁנּוֹתֵן חוּט אוֹ מְשִׁיחָה בֵּין כָּל אַחַת וְאַחַת: Although the Rabbis do not require a space between the passages or between the compartments, they concede that one must at least place a string or a thread in the furrow between the compartments in order to separate them from one another. This thread is sewn onto the hide of the *titora*, the base of phylacteries, upon which the compartments rest (*Sefer HaTeruma*).

HALAKHA

In four compartments of one hide – בְּאַרְבָּעָה בָּתִּים בְּעוֹר אֶחָד: The mitzva of phylacteries requires that the four passages be written on four parchments, which are rolled up separately and inserted into four compartments fashioned of one hide. If one wrote all four passages on a single parchment it is fit, even if there is no space between them, provided that there is a string or thread between the compartments, in accordance with the opinion of the Rabbis. One should place this thread even if the passages were written on different parchments, as stated by *Tosafot*, although this is not an indispensable requirement (Rambam *Sefer Ahava*, *Hilkhot Tefillin UMezuza VeSefer Torah* 2:1, 3:11; *Shulḥan Arukh*, *Oraḥ Ḥayyim* 32:2, 38, 47, 51, and see *Mishna Berura* there).

Their furrows marking the separation between the compartment are not noticeable – אֵין חֲרִיצָן נִיכָּר: The furrow between each of the compartments of the phylacteries of the head must reach the sewn line between the compartments and the *titora*, the base of the phylacteries (see 35a). If it does not reach that far down, the phylacteries are fit, provided that the four compartments are clearly marked as separate from one another. If the furrow is not noticeable at all, the phylacteries are unfit, as stated in the *baraita* (Rambam *Sefer Ahava*, *Hilkhot Tefillin UMezuza VeSefer Torah* 3:11; *Shulḥan Arukh*, *Oraḥ Ḥayyim* 32:40).

LANGUAGE

The Distinguished [*Beribbi*] – בריבי: This honorific title for a great person was added to the names of several Sages. The word is probably a contraction of the two words *bar* and rabbi, which together mean son of a Sage. It was first used as an honorific for Sages who were sons of Sages, but its meaning was later broadened to refer even to great scholars who did not have distinguished fathers.

תנו רבנן: כיצד כותבן? תפלה של יד – כותבה על עור אחד, ואם כתבה בארבע עורות והניחה בבית אחד – יצא. וצריך לדבק, שנאמר: "והיה לך לאות על ידך", כשם שאות אחת מבחוץ – כך אות אחת מבפנים, דברי רבי יהודה. רבי יוסי אומר: אינו צריך.

The Sages taught in a *baraita*: **How does** a scribe **write them?** With regard to **the phylacteries of the arm,**[H] **he writes it on one hide. But if he wrote it on four** separate **hides and placed it in one compartment,** one who wears it has **fulfilled** his obligation. **And** in such a case **it is necessary to attach** the four parchments, **as it is stated: "And it shall be for a sign for you upon your arm"** (Exodus 13:9). This teaches that **just as** the phylacteries of the arm are **one sign on the outside,** as the compartment is fashioned from a single hide, **so too,** they must be **one sign on the inside,** i.e., the four passages must be on a single parchment. This is **the statement of Rabbi Yehuda. Rabbi Yosei says: It is not necessary** to attach the passages.

אמר רבי יוסי: ומודה לי רבי יהודה בריבי, שאם אין לו תפילין של יד ויש לו שתי תפילין של ראש, שטולה עור על אחת מהן ומניחה. מודה? היינו פלוגתייהו! אמר רבא: מדבריו של רבי יוסי, חזר בו רבי יהודה.

Rabbi Yosei says: And Rabbi Yehuda the Distinguished [*Beribbi*][L] **concedes to me that if one does not have phylacteries of the arm**[H] **but has two phylacteries of the head, that he covers one of them with patches of hide,** to render it like one compartment, **and places it** on his arm. The Gemara asks: How can Rabbi Yosei say that Rabbi Yehuda **concedes** to him in this case? **This is** the very situation in which **their dispute** applies, as they disagree over whether or not the passages of the phylacteries of the arm may be written on separate parchments. **Rava said: From Rabbi Yosei's statement** one can infer that **Rabbi Yehuda retracted** his opinion and accepted Rabbi Yosei's ruling.

איני? והא שלח רב חנניה משמיה דרבי יוחנן: תפלה של יד עושין אותה של ראש, ושל ראש אין עושין אותה של יד, לפי שאין מורידין מקדושה חמורה לקדושה קלה!

Rabbi Yosei said that all agree that one can convert phylacteries of the head into phylacteries of the arm. The Gemara asks: **Is that so? But Rav Ḥananya sent** the following ruling **in the name of Rabbi Yoḥanan:** If one has **phylacteries of the arm, he can convert it to** phylacteries **of the head, but** if one has phylacteries **of the head,** he **cannot convert it to** phylacteries **of the arm, because one does not reduce** the sanctity of an item **from** a level of **greater sanctity** of phylacteries of the head **to** a level of **lesser sanctity**[N] of phylacteries of the arm.

HALAKHA

The phylacteries of the arm – תפלה של יד: The phylacteries of the arm have one compartment. One writes the four passages on one parchment, in four separate columns, and rolls it up in the manner of a Torah scroll from the end to the beginning, and then places it in the compartment. If one writes the passages on four parchments and places them in a single compartment, it is fit. The *halakha* is in accordance with the opinion of Rabbi Yosei, as Rabbi Yehuda concedes to his opinion. The Rema writes that the custom in such a case is to attach the parchments so that they appear as a single parchment, and one should be careful to use glue that is fit, i.e., from a kosher animal. After the fact, the phylacteries are fit even if one does not attach the pieces of parchment (Rambam *Sefer Ahava, Hilkhot Tefillin UMezuza VeSefer Torah* 2:1, 3:6; *Shulḥan Arukh, Oraḥ Ḥayyim* 32:2, 38, 47, and see *Mishna Berura* there).

If one does not have phylacteries of the arm, etc. – אין לו תפילין של יד וכו׳: It is prohibited to convert phylacteries of the head into phylacteries of the arm. One may not even take a strap from phylacteries of the head and use it for phylacteries of the arm, because one does not downgrade an item from a level of greater sanctity to a level of lesser sanctity. The phylacteries of the head are considered to have greater sanctity than those of the arm because the majority of the letters *shin*, *dalet*, and *yod*, are on the phylacteries of the head. By contrast, one may convert phylacteries of the arm into phylacteries of the head. If the phylacteries were new and had not yet been worn, one may even convert phylacteries of the head into phylacteries of the arm, by covering them with a single hide so that they appear to have one compartment (Rambam *Sefer Ahava, Hilkhot Tefillin UMezuza VeSefer Torah* 3:17; *Shulḥan Arukh, Oraḥ Ḥayyim* 42:1).

NOTES

From a level of greater sanctity to a level of lesser sanctity – מקדושה חמורה לקדושה קלה: Rashi explains that the sanctity referred to here is the name of God, as the majority of the letters *shin*, *dalet*, and *yod*, which spell a name of God, are found on the phylacteries of the head: The *shin* protrudes from the side of the compartment itself, and the *dalet* is on the knot at the lower back of the head. The phylacteries of the arm, by contrast, has only the letter *yod* on its knot. Others commentaries are puzzled by this interpretation, as these letters, which are not joined together, do not constitute an actual name of God (*Tosafot* on 35b). It is perhaps for this reason that Rashi suggests a different explanation: The main praise of God through phylacteries is the phylacteries of the head, with regard to which it is stated: "And all the nations of the land shall see that the name of the Lord is called upon you, and they will fear you" (Deuteronomy 28:10; see 35b). Others state that the very fact that the phylacteries of the head are placed on one's head, which is a more dignified place on the body than one's arm, accords them a greater level of sanctity (*Piskei HaRid*).

לָא קַשְׁיָא: הָא בְּעַתִּיקָתָא, הָא בַּחֲדַתְתָּא. וּלְמַאן דְּאָמַר הַזְמָנָה מִילְּתָא הִיא – דְּאַתְנֵי עֲלַיְיהוּ מֵעִיקָּרָא.

The Gemara answers: This is **not difficult,** as **this** ruling is stated **with regard to old** phylacteries, which have already been worn on one's head and therefore have a greater level of sanctity, whereas **that** ruling is stated **with regard to new** phylacteries, which have not yet been used. The Gemara adds: **And according to the one who says** that **designation is significant,** i.e., once one designates an item for use in fulfilling a particular mitzva, it assumes the sanctity of an item used for mitzvot, this ruling is stated with regard to a case **where he stipulated with regard to them from the outset** that he may convert it from phylacteries of the head to phylacteries of the arm, and only in this circumstance it is permitted to convert them.

תָּנוּ רַבָּנַן: כֵּיצַד סִדְרָן? "קַדֶּשׁ לִי" "וְהָיָה כִּי יְבִיאֲךָ" מִיָּמִין, "שְׁמַע" "וְהָיָה אִם שָׁמוֹעַ" מִשְּׂמֹאל.

§ **The Sages taught** in a *baraita*: **How does one arrange** the four passages inside the phylacteries?[BHN] The passage of: **"Sanctify unto Me"** (Exodus 13:1–10), and the passage of: **"And it shall be when He shall bring you"** (Exodus 13:11–16), are placed **on the right;** the passage of: **"Listen, O Israel"** (Deuteronomy 6:4–9), and the passage of: **"And it shall come to pass, if you shall hearken diligently"** (Deuteronomy 11:13–21), are placed **on the left.**

וְהָתַנְיָא אִיפְכָא! אֲמַר אַבַּיֵי, לָא קַשְׁיָא: כָּאן מִימִינוֹ שֶׁל קוֹרֵא, כָּאן מִימִינוֹ שֶׁל מַנִּיחַ, וְהַקּוֹרֵא קוֹרֵא כְּסִדְרָן.

The Gemara asks: **But isn't it taught** in a *baraita* that one places them in the **opposite** manner, with the first two passages on the left and the latter two on the right? **Abaye said** that it is **not difficult: Here** it means **to the right of** the **reader,** i.e., one who is standing opposite the one donning the phylacteries, whereas **there** it means **to the right of** the **one who is donning** the phylacteries. **And** in this manner **the reader reads** the passages **in their order,** as they appear in the Torah, starting with Exodus 13:1–10 to his right.

אָמַר רַב חֲנַנְאֵל אָמַר רַב: הֶחֱלִיף פָּרָשִׁיּוֹתֶיהָ – פְּסוּלוֹת. אֲמַר אַבַּיֵי: לָא אֲמָרָן

Rav Ḥananel says that **Rav says: If one exchanged its passages,** i.e., placed them in a different order within the compartment, the phylacteries **are unfit. Abaye said: We did not say** this

HALAKHA

How does one arrange the four passages inside the phylacteries – כֵּיצַד סִדְרָן: The order of the passages in phylacteries of the head, according to Rashi and the Rambam, is as follows: Exodus 13:1–10, in the leftmost compartment relative to the one donning the phylacteries; then Exodus 13:11–16; followed by Deuteronomy 6:4–9; and finally Deuteronomy 11:13–21, in the fourth compartment, which is the one farthest to his right. According to Rabbeinu Tam, one places Deuteronomy 11:13–21 in the third compartment and Deuteronomy 6:4–9 in the fourth. The accepted custom is in accordance with the opinion of Rashi and the Rambam. A God-fearing person should wear both types, but only if he is renowned and famous for his piety. In recent generations many have adopted the custom to wear both types, and various practices are observed by different communities (Rambam *Sefer Ahava, Hilkhot Tefillin UMezuza VeSefer Torah* 3:5; *Shulḥan Arukh, Oraḥ Ḥayyim* 34:1–2).

NOTES

How does one arrange the four passages inside the phylacteries, etc. – כֵּיצַד סִדְרָן וכו׳: The *ge'onim* and the early commentaries disagree with regard to the meaning of this passage. According to Rashi and the Rambam, this order follows the order in the Torah, as indicated by the statement of the *baraita*: And in this manner the reader reads the passages in their order. Therefore, when the reader stands opposite the one donning the phylacteries he reads from right to left: Exodus 13:1–10, Exodus 13:11–16, Deuteronomy 6:4–9, and Deuteronomy 11:13–21. Other commentaries reject this interpretation, claiming that if that were so, there would be no need for the *baraita* to say that these two passages are to the right and those two to the left, when it could simply have listed them in order (Rabbeinu Tam). One resolution of this difficulty is that the *baraita* seeks to refer to the four passages as two sets of two, those from Exodus and those from Deuteronomy (Ya'avetz).

According to Rabbeinu Tam and other *ge'onim* and early commentaries, the order is: Exodus 13:1–10, Exodus 13:11–16, Deuteronomy 11:13–21, and Deuteronomy 6:4–9. Rav Hai Gaon provides a mnemonic to remember this order: The *havayot*, i.e., the passages beginning with the word *vehaya*, are adjacent to each other. The Rambam, in his responsum to the Sages of Lunel, writes that even those who accept this order maintain their opinion only with regard to the phylacteries of the head, but everyone agrees that the phylacteries of the arm must be in the order that the passages appear in the Torah (see *Kesef Mishne* on Rambam *Sefer Ahava, Hilkhot Tefillin UMezuza VeSefer Torah* 3:6). Other early commentaries disagree with the Rambam's conclusion. In addition to these two opinions, there are two other opinions among the early commentaries. According to one, the two *havayot* passages are in fact in the middle, but their order is from the right to the left of the one wearing the phylacteries, not the reader opposite him (Ra'avad, citing Rav Hai Gaon). Finally, there is the opinion of the *Shimusha Rabba*, an ancient text on scribal writing, which follows the opinion of Rashi with regard to the order of the passages, but holds that they are inserted from the right to the left of the one donning the phylacteries.

BACKGROUND

How does one arrange the four passages inside the phylacteries – כֵּיצַד סִדְרָן: The images illustrate the order of the passages in the phylacteries of the head according to the various opinions, shown from the side of the one donning the phylacteries.

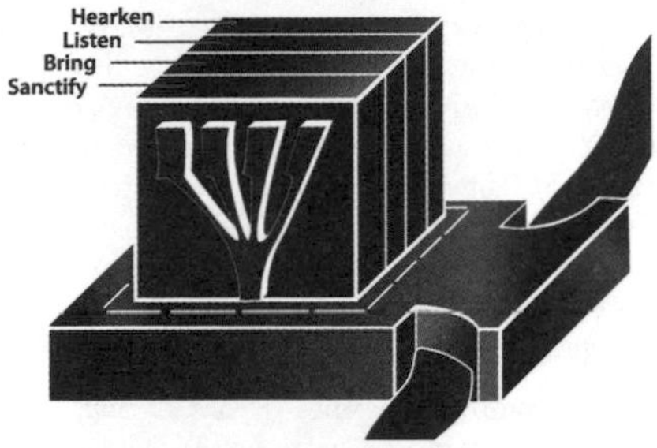

Opinion of Rashi

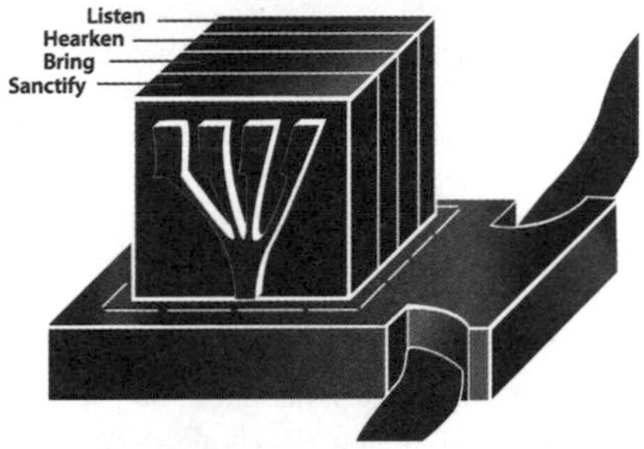

Opinion of Rabbeinu Tam

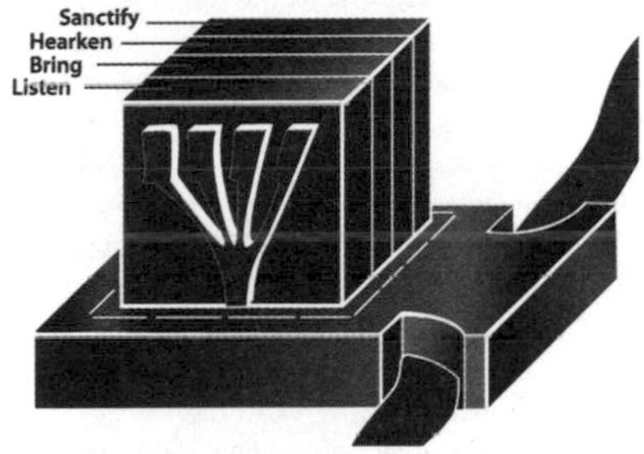

Opinion of the Ra'avad, citing Rav Hai Gaon

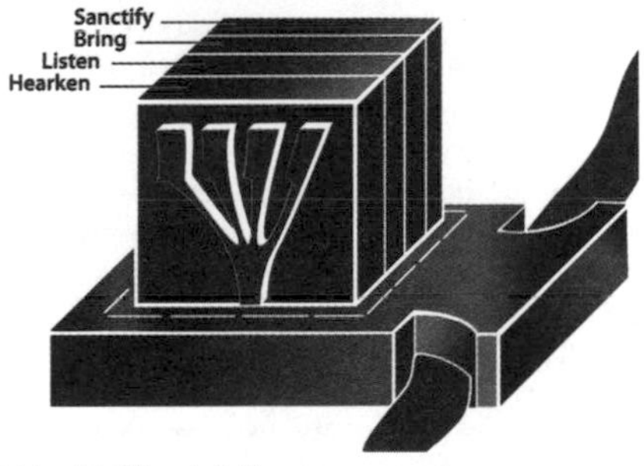

Opinion of the *Shimusha Rabba*

אֶלָּא גַּוַּויְיתָא לְבָרַיְיתָא וּבָרַיְיתָא לְגַוַּויְיתָא, אֲבָל גַּוַּויְיתָא לְגַוַּויְיתָא וּבָרַיְיתָא לְבָרַיְיתָא – לֵית לָן בָּהּ.

unless it is a case where one exchanges **an inner** passage **for an outer** one, e.g., he placed the passage of Exodus 13:11–16 to the right of Exodus 13:1–10, **or an outer** passage **for an inner one,** e.g., he placed the passage of Deuteronomy 11:13–21 to the right of Deuteronomy 6:4–9. **But** if one exchanges **an inner** passage **for** the other **inner** one, i.e., he exchanges Exodus 13:11–16 with Deuteronomy 6:4–9, **or an outer** passage **for** the other **outer** one, i.e., he exchanges Exodus 13:1–10 with Deuteronomy 11:13–21, **we have no** problem **with it.**

אֲמַר לֵיהּ רָבָא: מַאי שְׁנָא גַּוַּויְיתָא לְבָרַיְיתָא וּבָרַיְיתָא לְגַוַּויְיתָא דְּלָא – דְּהָךְ דְּבָעֵי לְמֶיחֱזֵי אֲוִירָא לָא קָא חַזְיָא, וְהָא דְּלָא קָא בָּעֵי לְמֶיחֱזֵי אֲוִירָא קָא חַזְיָא; בָּרַיְיתָא לְבָרַיְיתָא וְגַוַּויְיתָא לְגַוַּויְיתָא נַמִי – הָךְ דְּבָעֲיָא לְמֶיחֱזֵי אֲוִירָא דְּיָמִין קָא חַזְיָא אֲוִירָא דִּשְׂמֹאל, וְדִשְׂמֹאל קָא חַזְיָא אֲוִירָא דְּיָמִין! אֶלָּא לָא שְׁנָא.

Rava said to Abaye: **What is different** about the cases of exchanging **an inner** passage **for an outer** one, **and an outer** passage **for an inner** one, such **that** the phylacteries are **not** fit? The reason is **that this** passage, **which needs to see the air,** i.e., to be placed on the outer side, **does not see** it, **and that** passage, **which does not need to see the air, does see it.** But in a case where one exchanges **an outer** passage **for** the other **outer** one **or an inner** passage **for** the other **inner** one, it should be unfit **as well,** as **this** passage, **which needs to see the air of** the **right** side, **sees the air of** the **left** side, **and** that passage, which requires to see the air **of** the **left** side, **sees the air of** the **right** side. **Rather,** there **is no difference** between any of these cases, and any change in the order renders the phylacteries unfit.

וְאָמַר רַב חֲנַנְאֵל אָמַר רַב: תִּיתּוֹרָא דִּתְפִילִּין – הֲלָכָה לְמֹשֶׁה מִסִּינַי. אֲמַר אַבַּיֵי: מַעְבַּרְתָּא דִּתְפִילִּין – הֲלָכָה לְמֹשֶׁה מִסִּינַי. וְאָמַר אַבַּיֵי: שִׁי״ן שֶׁל תְּפִילִּין – הֲלָכָה לְמֹשֶׁה מִסִּינַי,

§ **And Rav Ḥananel says** that **Rav says:** The requirement to have **the *titora*[N] of phylacteries,[H]** i.e., the base of phylacteries upon which the compartments rest, is **a *halakha*** transmitted **to Moses from Sinai. Abaye said:** The requirement to have **the *ma'ebarta* of phylacteries,[H]** i.e., the passageway through which the straps are inserted, is **a *halakha*** transmitted **to Moses from Sinai. And Abaye says:** The requirement to have a letter ***shin*** protruding **on the phylacteries[H]** of one's head, which is achieved by pressing the hide into the shape of that letter, is **a *halakha*** transmitted **to Moses from Sinai.**

וְצָרִיךְ שֶׁיַּגִּיעַ חָרִיץ לִמְקוֹם הַתֶּפֶר; רַב דִּימִי מִנְּהַרְדְּעָא אָמַר: כֵּיוָן דְּמִנְכַּר לָא צְרִיךְ.

Abaye further says: **And there is a requirement that** the **furrow** between each of the compartments of phylacteries of the head **reach the place of the stitches,[HN]** i.e., the *titora*, to which the compartments are sewn. **Rav Dimi of Neharde'a says: Once it is noticeable** that there is a furrow between each of the compartments, **it is not necessary** for them to reach all the way to the *titora*.

וְאָמַר אַבַּיֵי: הַאי קִילְפָא דִּתְפִילִּין צָרִיךְ לְמִיבְדְּקֵיהּ, דְּדִילְמָא אִית בָּהּ רֵיעוּתָא, וּבָעֵינָא כְּתִיבָה תַּמָּה וְלֵיכָּא. רַב דִּימִי מִנְּהַרְדְּעָא אָמַר: לָא צְרִיךְ, קוּלְמוֹסָא בָּדֵיק לָהּ.

And Abaye says: With regard to **this parchment** upon which one writes the passages **of phylacteries,** the scribe **must examine it** before writing, **as perhaps it has a flaw,** i.e., a perforation, **and complete writing is required,[N] and** that requirement would **not** be fulfilled if a letter were perforated. **Rav Dimi of Neharde'a says: No** prior examination is **required;** rather, **the quill examines it** as one writes, as any perforation which the ink covers is disregarded.

HALAKHA

The *titora* of phylacteries – תִּיתּוֹרָא דִּתְפִילִּין: The requirement of a *titora* in phylacteries is a *halakha* transmitted to Moses from Sinai. This means that one must cover the openings below the compartments with hide, as maintained by Rav. Some authorities rule that the compartments and the *titora* must be fashioned from a single hide (Rambam *Sefer Ahava, Hilkhot Tefillin UMezuza VeSefer Torah* 3:1; *Shulḥan Arukh, Oraḥ Ḥayyim* 32:44, and see *Beur Halakha* there).

The *ma'ebarta* of phylacteries – מַעְבַּרְתָּא דִּתְפִילִּין: The requirement of a *ma'ebarta* in phylacteries is a *halakha* transmitted to Moses from Sinai. This means that the *titora* must be long on one side, where it contains a passageway, a *ma'ebarta*, through which the strap passes. One should cut off some of the hide of the *ma'ebarta* slightly on both sides so that it is not as wide as the *titora*, in order that the square of the *titora* will be conspicuous (Rambam *Sefer Ahava, Hilkhot Tefillin UMezuza VeSefer Torah* 3:1; *Shulḥan Arukh, Oraḥ Ḥayyim* 32:44).

***Shin* protruding on the phylacteries – שִׁי״ן שֶׁל תְּפִילִּין:** It is a *halakha* transmitted to Moses from Sinai that the box of the phylacteries of the head must have an embossed letter *shin* on either side. If one forms the *shin* using a mold, one must push out the letter itself. In other words, one may not form it indirectly by forming the area around a letter, e.g., by lowering the area around its shape, leaving the letter raised. The *shin* on the right side of the box has three branches, like the standard letter *shin*, while the one on the left side has four branches. The *Shimusha Rabba* rules that if one reversed which letter is on which side, the phylacteries are fit (Rambam *Sefer Ahava, Hilkhot Tefillin UMezuza VeSefer Torah* 3:1; *Shulḥan Arukh, Oraḥ Ḥayyim* 32:42).

That the furrow reach the place of the stitches – שֶׁיַּגִּיעַ חָרִיץ לִמְקוֹם הַתֶּפֶר: The furrow between each of the compartments of phylacteries of the head must reach the place of the stitches. If they do not reach all the way down, the phylacteries are fit, provided that it is clear from the furrow that there are four compartments. Likewise, the point of the letter *shin* must reach the place of the stitches below. The *halakha* is in accordance with the opinion of Abaye, as elucidated in both explanations of the Rosh (Rambam *Sefer Ahava, Hilkhot Tefillin UMezuza VeSefer Torah* 3:11; *Shulḥan Arukh, Oraḥ Ḥayyim* 32:40, 43).

NOTES

***Titora* – תִּיתּוֹרָא:** According to Rashi, this refers to the lower part of the box of phylacteries, which looks like a wide board and serves as the base of the compartment in which the passages are placed. Rashi writes that after the parchment is folded into the compartments, which are like the fingers of a glove, one then folds over the hide beneath them to seal them from below. Others maintain that one does not use the same hide for this purpose; rather, one takes a thicker hide, which is folded in two and has a hole in the top half into which the compartments holding the passages are inserted (Rabbeinu Yitzḥak).

And there is a requirement that the furrow reach the place of the stitches – וְצָרִיךְ שֶׁיַּגִּיעַ חָרִיץ לִמְקוֹם הַתֶּפֶר: Some commentaries maintain that this refers not to the furrow between the compartments but to the *shin*, and is teaching that the lowest part of the *shin* must reach the stitches of the *titora*. The custom is to follow both opinions (Rosh).

And complete writing is required – וּבָעֵינָא כְּתִיבָה תַּמָּה: As stated on 34a, this is derived from: "And you shall write them [*ukhtavtam*]" (Deuteronomy 6:9), which means that it should be complete writing [*ketiva tamma*]. This verse teaches that any letter that is not encircled with blank parchment on all four sides is not valid, and that there may not be a perforation in any letter (see 29a).

אָמַר רַבִּי יִצְחָק: רְצוּעוֹת שְׁחוֹרוֹת – הֲלָכָה לְמֹשֶׁה מִסִּינַי. מֵיתִיבֵי: תְּפִילִּין אֵין קוֹשְׁרִין אוֹתָן אֶלָּא בְּמִינָן, בֵּין יְרוּקוֹת בֵּין שְׁחוֹרוֹת בֵּין לְבָנוֹת; אֲדוּמּוֹת לֹא יַעֲשֶׂה, מִפְּנֵי גְּנַאי וְדָבָר אַחֵר.

Rabbi Yitzḥak says: The requirement that the **straps** of the phylacteries be **black**[H] is **a *halakha*** transmitted **to Moses from Sinai.** The Gemara **raises an objection** from a *baraita*: **One may tie phylacteries only** with straps **of their same type,** i.e., the straps must be made from hide, and it does not matter **whether** they are **green, or black, or white.** Nevertheless, **one should not make red** straps, **because** this is **deprecatory** to him, as it looks like he has wounds on his head, **and** also due to **something else,** i.e., lest people suspect him of engaging in sexual intercourse with a menstruating woman and getting blood on the straps.

אָמַר רַבִּי יְהוּדָה: מַעֲשֶׂה בְּתַלְמִידוֹ שֶׁל רַבִּי עֲקִיבָא שֶׁהָיָה קוֹשֵׁר תְּפִילָּיו בִּלְשׁוֹנוֹת שֶׁל תְּכֵלֶת וְלֹא אָמַר לוֹ דָּבָר, אֶיפְשָׁר אוֹתוֹ צַדִּיק רָאָה תַּלְמִידוֹ וְלֹא מִיחָה בּוֹ? אָמַר לוֹ: הֵן! לֹא רָאָה אוֹתוֹ, וְאִם רָאָה אוֹתוֹ – לֹא הָיָה מַנִּיחוֹ.

The Gemara cites the continuation of that *baraita.* **Rabbi Yehuda said:** There was **an incident involving Rabbi Akiva's student, who would tie his phylacteries with strips of sky-blue wool** rather than hide, **and** Rabbi Akiva **did not say anything to him.** Is it **possible** that **that righteous man saw his student** doing something improper **and he did not object to his** conduct? Another Sage **said to** Rabbi Yehuda: **Yes,** it is possible that the student acted improperly, as Rabbi Akiva **did not see him, and if he had seen him, he would not have allowed him** to do so.

מַעֲשֶׂה בְּהוּרְקָנוֹס בְּנוֹ שֶׁל רַבִּי אֱלִיעֶזֶר בֶּן הוּרְקָנוֹס שֶׁהָיָה קוֹשֵׁר תְּפִילָּיו בִּלְשׁוֹנוֹת שֶׁל אַרְגָּמָן וְלֹא אָמַר לוֹ דָּבָר, אֶיפְשָׁר אוֹתוֹ צַדִּיק רָאָה בְּנוֹ וְלֹא מִיחָה בּוֹ? אָמְרוּ לוֹ: הֵן, לֹא רָאָה אוֹתוֹ, וְאִם רָאָה אוֹתוֹ – לֹא הָיָה מַנִּיחוֹ.

The *baraita* continues: There was **an incident involving Hyrcanus, the son of Rabbi Eliezer ben Hyrcanus,**[P] **who would tie his phylacteries with strips of purple wool, and** his father **did not say anything to him.** Is it **possible** that **that righteous man saw his son** doing something improper **and he did not object to his** conduct? The Sages **said to him: Yes,** it is possible that his son acted improperly, as Rabbi Eliezer **did not see him, and if he had seen him, he would not have allowed him** to do so. This concludes the *baraita.*

קָתָנֵי מִיהָא: בֵּין יְרוּקוֹת בֵּין שְׁחוֹרוֹת וּבֵין לְבָנוֹת! לָא קַשְׁיָא: כָּאן מִבִּפְנִים, כָּאן מִבַּחוּץ.

The Gemara explains the objection from the *baraita*: **In any event,** the *baraita* **teaches** that it does not matter **whether** the straps are **green, or black, or white,** whereas Rabbi Yitzḥak maintains that it is a *halakha* transmitted to Moses from Sinai that the straps of the phylacteries must be black. The Gemara answers that it is **not difficult. Here,** the *baraita* is referring to **the inside** of the straps, which touch the body. These may be any color other than red. Conversely, **there,** when Rabbi Yitzḥak says that the straps of the phylacteries must be black, he is speaking of **the outside** of the straps.

אִי מִבִּפְנִים, מַאי גְּנַאי וְדָבָר אַחֵר אִיכָּא? זִימְנִין דְּמִתְהַפְּכִין לֵיהּ.

The Gemara raises a difficulty: **If** the *baraita* is discussing **the inside** of the straps, **what deprecatory** matter **or** problem of **something else is there** with straps that are red on the inside? After all, this side is not seen. The Gemara answers: **Sometimes his** straps **become reversed,** and therefore these concerns are applicable.

HALAKHA

The requirement that the straps of the phylacteries be black, etc. – רְצוּעוֹת שְׁחוֹרוֹת וכו׳: It is a *halakha* transmitted to Moses from Sinai that the straps of phylacteries must be painted black on the side facing outward. On the side facing inward they may be any color one chooses, except for red, lest the straps be turned around, in which case people might say that they were stained from the blood of a wound. Likewise, the hide of the compartments should be black. Some say this is based on the general requirement that items used for a mitzva must be beautiful, as derived from the verse: "This is my God and I will beautify Him" (Exodus 15:2), which is interpreted to mean that one should beautify himself before God in the performance of mitzvot. Others maintain that there is a specific *halakha* that the compartments must be black (Rambam *Sefer Ahava, Hilkhot Tefillin UMezuza VeSefer Torah* 3:14; *Shulḥan Arukh, Oraḥ Ḥayyim* 33:3, and see *Mishna Berura* there).

PERSONALITIES

Rabbi Eliezer ben Hyrcanus – רַבִּי אֱלִיעֶזֶר בֶּן הוּרְקָנוֹס: Also called Rabbi Eliezer the Great, Rabbi Eliezer ben Hyrcanus lived during the period of the destruction of the Second Temple. Rabbi Eliezer was the son of a wealthy family that traced its lineage to Moses. He began to study Torah only at the age of twenty, when he went to Jerusalem to study under Rabban Yoḥanan ben Zakkai. Rabban Yoḥanan ben Zakkai had great esteem for Rabbi Eliezer and considered him the greatest of his disciples, so much so that he claimed he was equal to all the Sages of the Jewish people. Rabban Yoḥanan ben Zakkai further described him as a plastered well that does not lose a drop, as his learning was based mostly on the traditions he received from his teacher. His approach differed from his teacher in that he tended to agree with the opinions of Beit Shammai. Rabbi Eliezer began to teach Torah before the destruction of the Temple and was among Rabban Yoḥanan's students who joined him in founding the great yeshiva in Yavne after that tragedy. He married Ima Shalom, the sister of the *Nasi*, Rabban Gamliel of Yavne. In the wake of a fundamental dispute between Rabbi Eliezer and the other Sages with regard to the process of halakhic decision-making, Rabban Gamliel excommunicated Rabbi Eliezer (see *Bava Metzia* 59 a–b).

תָּנָא: תְּפִילִּין מְרוּבָּעוֹת – הֲלָכָה לְמֹשֶׁה מִסִּינַי. אָמַר רַב פָּפָּא: בְּתִפְרָן וּבַאֲלַכְסוֹנָן.

It is **taught** in a *baraita*: The requirement that **phylacteries be square**[BH] is a ***halakha*** transmitted **to Moses from Sinai.**[N] **Rav Pappa says** about this *halakha*: Square means **along their seams and their diagonals,** i.e., they must be perfectly square where the compartments are sewn to the *titora*.

לֵימָא מְסַיֵּיעַ לֵיהּ: הָעוֹשֶׂה תְּפִילָּתוֹ עֲגוּלָּה – סַכָּנָה וְאֵין בָּהּ מִצְוָה! אָמַר רַב פָּפָּא: מַתְנִיתִין – דַּעֲבִידָא כִּי אַמְגּוּזָא.

The Gemara suggests: **Let us say** that a mishna **supports** this opinion (*Megilla* 24b): **One who fashions his phylacteries in a round** shape[BH] exposes himself to **danger, and it** does **not** enable him to fulfill the **mitzva** of phylacteries. **Rav Pappa said:** This is no support, as one can say that **the mishna** is referring to phylacteries **that are fashioned like a nut,** i.e., their underside is rounded, and therefore there is a danger that if he strikes his head on a wall the underside will press into his head and injure him. By contrast, if the underside is flat one might have thought that it is fit despite the fact that it is not square. Therefore, the *baraita* teaches that phylacteries must be square.

אָמַר רַב הוּנָא: תְּפִילִּין, כָּל זְמַן שֶׁפְּנֵי טַבְלָא קַיֶּימֶת – כְּשֵׁירוֹת. רַב חִסְדָּא אָמַר: נִפְסְקוּ שְׁתַּיִם – כְּשֵׁירוֹת, שָׁלֹשׁ – פְּסוּלוֹת.

§ **Rav Huna says:** With regard to **phylacteries** of the head, **as long as the surface of outer hide is intact,**[H] i.e., it is not torn, **they are fit,** even if the hide between the compartments has torn. **Rav Ḥisda says:** If **two** of the walls between the compartments **tore,** such phylacteries **are fit,** but if **three** of these inner walls tore, **they are unfit.**

BACKGROUND

The requirement that phylacteries be square – תְּפִילִּין מְרוּבָּעוֹת: This image shows the square shape of the compartments, stitching, and *titora*, apart from the *ma'ebarta*.

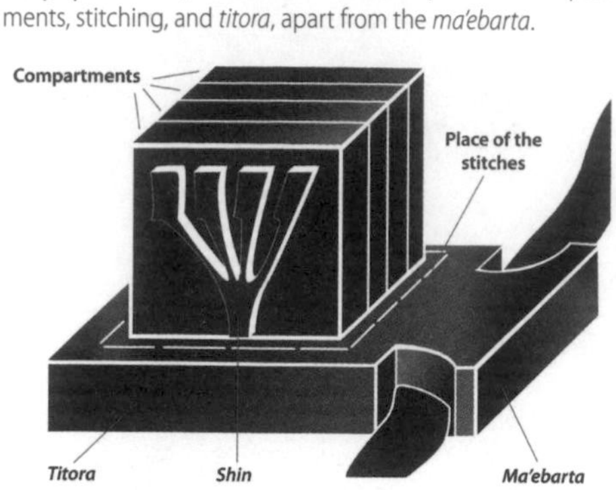

Phylacteries of the head

One who fashions his phylacteries in a round shape – הָעוֹשֶׂה תְּפִילָּתוֹ עֲגוּלָּה: As indicated by the statements of the early commentaries, the requirement that phylacteries be square was not observed in all places with regard to the phylacteries of the arm (see *Tosafot* with regard to the phylacteries of the head). Proof of this can be seen from this rendition of phylacteries found in the Cairo Geniza.

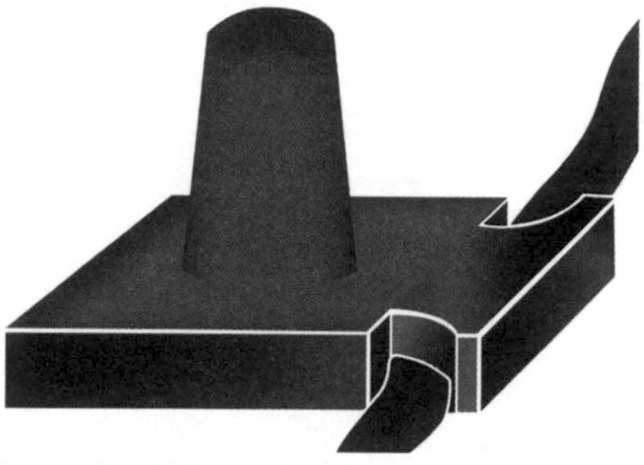

Depiction of rounded phylacteries found in the Cairo Geniza

HALAKHA

The requirement that phylacteries be square – תְּפִילִּין מְרוּבָּעוֹת: It is a *halakha* transmitted to Moses from Sinai that both the phylacteries of the arm and the phylacteries of the head must be square. This means along their seams and their diagonals, as stated by Rav Pappa, i.e., the ratio between all the sides and the diagonal should be constant. This *halakha* applies both to the base of the phylacteries as well as to the box that sits on the base. They do not need to be a perfect cube, and therefore the height of the box need not be the same dimension as its length and width (Rema, citing Rambam). Some say that in a case where the phylacteries were originally square, if they become damaged and are no longer square, they must be repaired (Rambam *Sefer Ahava, Hilkhot Tefillin UMezuza VeSefer Torah* 3:1; *Shulḥan Arukh, Oraḥ Ḥayyim* 33:3).

One who fashions his phylacteries in a round shape – הָעוֹשֶׂה תְּפִילָּתוֹ עֲגוּלָּה: One who fashions his phylacteries in a round shape like a nut does not fulfill the mitzva at all (Rambam *Sefer Ahava, Hilkhot Tefillin UMezuza VeSefer Torah* 4:3).

As long as the surface of outer hide is intact – כָּל זְמַן שֶׁפְּנֵי טַבְלָא קַיֶּימֶת: In a case where the hide of two adjacent compartments of the phylacteries of the head became torn, if the compartments are old then the phylacteries are unfit. If they are new, then they remain fit provided that the hide of the seat of the compartments, and the external hide (Rema), are intact. What are considered new phylacteries? They are considered new in any case where if one were to pull them by the straps the compartment would stretch and open; if it does not open, the phylacteries are classified as old. The Rema adds that there is an opinion that disqualifies the phylacteries in the case of new ones and deems old ones fit (Rashi; Rosh), and therefore one should act stringently in accordance with both opinions. If two compartments that are not adjacent to another become torn, the phylacteries are fit even if they are old. If three compartments become torn, then the phylacteries are unfit.

The *Shulḥan Arukh* further writes: In a case where the stitches of phylacteries opened, if these are two stitches alongside one another, or three stitches even if they are not alongside one another, the phylacteries are unfit. In what case is this statement said? In a case of old phylacteries. New ones remain fit, provided that the base of the phylacteries is intact, in accordance with the opinion of the Rif and the Rambam. With regard to the definition of new and old in this context, if one were to hold part of the hide whose stitches tore and hang the phylacteries on it and it is strong enough to bear the weight, these phylacteries are considered new. If one cannot hang the phylacteries in this manner, as the hide would split, the phylacteries are old. Some authorities maintain the opposite, that new phylacteries are unfit whereas old ones are fit (Rashi; Rosh), in accordance with the standard version of the text of the Gemara. One should therefore be stringent in accordance with both opinions (Rambam *Sefer Ahava, Hilkhot Tefillin UMezuza VeSefer Torah* 3:18; *Shulḥan Arukh, Oraḥ Ḥayyim* 33:1–2).

NOTES

That phylacteries be square is a *halakha* transmitted to Moses from Sinai – תְּפִילִּין מְרוּבָּעוֹת הֲלָכָה לְמֹשֶׁה מִסִּינַי: Some commentaries explain that Rav Pappa's statement, that square means along their seams and their diagonals, serves to explain the *baraita*, i.e., the square that is a *halakha* transmitted to Moses from Sinai is the one along the seams and diagonals. Accordingly, the compartments themselves need not be square. See *Tosafot* and the Mordekhai, who cite a custom to fashion the tops of phylacteries of the arm circular. Others maintain that the *tanna* of the *baraita* is referring to the compartments themselves, and Rav Pappa is adding that the stitching which links the compartments to the *titora* must also be square, e.g., one must not stretch the threads so tight that the hide on one side shrinks (Rashi; see Rosh and *Shita Mekubbetzet*, citing Rashi). The Rosh further states that the *titora* itself must be square, and for that reason one cuts some of the hide on the sides of the *ma'ebarta*.

אֲמַר רָבָא: הָא דְּאָמְרַתְּ שְׁתַּיִם כְּשֵׁירוֹת, לָא אֲמָרַן אֶלָּא זֶה שֶׁלֹּא כְּנֶגֶד זֶה, אֲבָל זֶה כְּנֶגֶד זֶה – פְּסוּלוֹת; וְזֶה כְּנֶגֶד זֶה נַמִי לָא אֲמָרַן אֶלָּא בְּחַדְתָּתָא, אֲבָל בְּעַתִּיקָתָא לֵית לָן בַּהּ.

Rava said: Concerning **that which you said,** that if **two** of the walls between the compartments tore **they are fit, we said** this **only** if the inner walls that tore are **not aligned with each other,**[N] i.e., they are not adjacent to one another. **But** if the torn walls are **aligned with each other,** the phylacteries **are unfit. And** furthermore, **even** in a case where the torn walls are **aligned with each other, we said** that they are unfit **only with regard to new** phylacteries,[N] as the hide is certainly defective. **But with regard to old** phylacteries, **we have no** problem **with it,** as they tore due to aging.

אֲמַר לֵיהּ אַבָּיֵי לְרַב יוֹסֵף: הֵיכִי דָּמְיָין חַדְתָּתָא, וְהֵיכִי דָּמְיָין עַתִּיקָתָא? אֲמַר לֵיהּ: כָּל הֵיכָא כִּי מִיתְלֵי בֵּיהּ בְּשַׁלְחָא וְהָדַר חָלֵים – עַתִּיקָתָא, וְאִידָּךְ חַדְתָּתָא;

Abaye said to Rav Yosef: What are the circumstances of new phylacteries, **and what are the circumstances** of **old** phylacteries? Rav Yosef **said to him:** In **any** case **where if one holds the hide and pulls it, it returns to its place** [*ḥaleim*],[L] these phylacteries are considered **old; and** in **the other** case, where hide that was pulled does not return to its place, they are considered **new.**

NOTES

If the inner walls that tore are not aligned with each other – זֶה שֶׁלֹּא כְּנֶגֶד זֶה: An example of this is if there is a tear in the first and third compartments while the second remains intact. The case where the torn walls are aligned with each other is when the tear is found in adjacent walls, such as the first and second compartments. Rashi cites an alternative, far more lenient interpretation, that the phrase: Not aligned with each other, applies even if the walls are adjacent, but the perforations are not exactly opposite one another.

We said that they are unfit only with regard to new phylacteries – לָא אֲמָרַן אֶלָּא בְּחַדְתָּתָא וכו׳: Some commentaries explain that it is only in the case of new phylacteries that it is unseemly for them to be torn or have holes, whereas this is expected in old ones due to regular wear and tear (*Shita Mekubbetzet*). Others explain that in new ones, where the shape of the hide has not yet settled, there is more of a concern that they might come apart and the parchments might fall out, whereas in old ones the compartments have already strengthened (Rid). There is an alternative version of the text, according to which old phylacteries are unfit, as the tear is likely to extend (Rif; *Nimmukei Yosef*), which is less likely in the case of new ones (see Rambam).

LANGUAGE

To its place [*ḥaleim*] – חָלֵים: The meaning of this Aramaic term, both here and elsewhere, is attachment, i.e., an object that is attached or adhered to another. This word is ascribed by some linguists to the root *heh*, *lamed*, *mem*, which is found in rabbinic usage, as well as in Arabic, Mandaic, and modern Hebrew, e.g., when one says that the crown suits [*holem*] the man.

Perek **III**
Daf **35** Amud **b**

וְאִי נַמִי, כָּל הֵיכִי דְּכִי מִיתְלֵי בֵּיהּ בְּמִתְנָא אָתְיָיה אַבַּתְרֵיהּ – חַדְתָּתָא, וְאִידָּךְ עַתִּיקָתָא.

Alternatively, in **any** case **where if** the phylacteries are **hanging by the strap** the compartment **follows** the strap, i.e., it remains attached, these phylacteries are considered **new; and** in **the other** case, where the phylacteries would fall off, they are considered **old.**

אַבָּיֵי הֲוָה יָתֵיב קַמֵּיהּ דְּרַב יוֹסֵף, אִיפְסִיק לֵיהּ רְצוּעָה דִּתְפִילֵּי, אֲמַר לֵיהּ: מַהוּ לְמִיקְטְרֵיהּ? אֲמַר לֵיהּ: ״וּקְשַׁרְתָּם״ כְּתִיב, שֶׁתְּהֵא קְשִׁירָה תַּמָּה.

§ The Gemara relates: **Abaye was sitting before Rav Yosef** when the **strap of his phylacteries tore.**[H] Abaye **said to** Rav Yosef: **What is** the *halakha* as **to** whether one may **tie** the strap? Rav Yosef **said to him: It is written** with regard to phylacteries: **"And you shall bind them** [*ukshartam*] for a sign upon your arm" (Deuteronomy 6:8), which teaches **that** the **binding must be complete** [***keshira tamma***], whole and beautiful, and that would not be the case with a makeshift knot.

HALAKHA

The strap of his phylacteries tore, etc. – אִיפְסִיק לֵיהּ רְצוּעָה דִּתְפִילֵּי וכו׳: If the strap of one's phylacteries tore within the requisite measure, one should not tie it. If one did tie it, it is unfit. Likewise, one should not sew the strap, and if one did so, it is unfit. The *halakha* is in accordance with the opinion of Rav Yosef and Rav Ashi, following Rashi's explanation that Rav Ashi's answer was meant as a stringency. Some permit one to sew the strap on the inside in such a manner that the stitches cannot be seen, but only with sinews, not threads (based on the opinion of Rabbeinu Tam). The *Beit Yosef* rules that in exigent circumstances one may rely on the lenient opinion, in order to avoid neglecting the mitzva of phylacteries (Rambam *Sefer Ahava, Hilkhot Tefillin UMezuza VeSefer Torah* 3:19; *Shulḥan Arukh, Oraḥ Ḥayyim* 33:5).

אֲמַר לֵיהּ רַב אַחָא בְּרֵיהּ דְּרַב יוֹסֵף לְרַב אַשִׁי: מַהוּ לְמִיתְפְּרֵיהּ וְעַיְּילֵיהּ לַתְּפִירָה לְגָאו? אֲמַר: פּוֹק חֲזִי מַה עַמָּא דָּבַר.

Rav Aḥa, son of Rav Yosef, said to Rav Ashi: What is the *halakha* as **to** whether one may **sew** a strap that tore **and insert the stitching inside,** so that it is not visible from the outside? Rav Ashi **said** to him: **Go out and see what the people are doing.**[N] If the common custom is to do this, it is permitted.

אָמַר רַב פַּפָּא: גַּרְדּוּמֵי רְצוּעוֹת כְּשֵׁירוֹת. וְלָאו מִילְּתָא הִיא, מִדְּאָמְרִי בְּנֵי רַבִּי חִיָּיא: גַּרְדּוּמֵי תְּכֵלֶת וְגַרְדּוּמֵי אֵזוֹב כְּשֵׁירִין – הָתָם הוּא דְּתַשְׁמִישֵׁי מִצְוָה נִינְהוּ, אֲבָל הָכָא דְּתַשְׁמִישֵׁי קְדוּשָּׁה נִינְהוּ – לָא.

Rav Pappa says: The remnants of straps,[H] i.e., what remains when part of the strap has been cut off, **are fit.** The Gemara comments: **And it is not so,** as can be derived **from** the fact **that the sons of Rabbi Ḥiyya say: The remnants of** the **sky-blue wool** of ritual fringes, when only a small thread remains, **and** likewise **the remnants of** the **hyssop,** used for the sprinkling of the purification water of the red heifer, **are fit.** They did not include the remnants of straps of phylacteries in this *halakha*. The reason for this difference is that **it is there** that the remnants are fit, **as they are** mere **articles** used in the performance **of a mitzva; but here,** phylacteries **are articles of sanctity,**[N] which are of greater sanctity, and therefore their remnants are **not** fit.

מִכְּלָל דְּאִית לְהוּ שִׁיעוּרָא, וְכַמָּה שִׁיעוּרַיְיהוּ? אָמַר רָמִי בַּר חָמָא אָמַר רֵישׁ לָקִישׁ: עַד אֶצְבַּע צְרֵדָה. רַב כָּהֲנָא מַחֲוֵי כָּפוּף. רַב אַשִׁי מַחֲוֵי פָּשׁוּט.

The Gemara states: From this line of inquiry one can conclude **by inference that** the straps of phylacteries **have** a minimum requisite **measure. And how much is their measure?**[H] **Rami bar Ḥama says** that **Reish Lakish says:** It is **until the index finger.**[N] In explanation of this size, **Rav Kahana** would **demonstrate a bowed** measure, i.e., from the tip of the middle finger until the tip of the index finger, with the fingers spread. **Rav Ashi** would **demonstrate a straight** measure, from the tip of the thumb until the tip of the index finger, with the fingers spread.

רַבָּה קָטַר לְהוּ וּפָשֵׁיט וְשָׁדֵי לְהוּ. רַב אַחָא בַּר יַעֲקֹב קָטַר לְהוּ וּמְתַלֵּית לְהוּ. מָר בְּרֵיהּ דְּרַבָּנָא עָבֵיד כְּדִידַן.

The Gemara relates: **Rabba** would **tie** the straps **and release** them **and let them fall** behind him. **Rav Aḥa bar Ya'akov** would **tie them and plait them** together[N] like a braid. **Mar, son of Rabbana,** would **act like we** do, i.e., he would let the straps fall and hang over the front of his body.

HALAKHA

The remnants of straps – גַּרְדּוּמֵי רְצוּעוֹת: The remnants of straps that have been reduced to less than the requisite measure are unfit. The *halakha* is not in accordance with the opinion of Rav Pappa (*Kesef Mishne*). Nevertheless, if one does not have other phylacteries, he should don these without reciting a blessing (Rambam *Sefer Ahava, Hilkhot Tefillin UMezuza VeSefer Torah* 3:19; *Shulḥan Arukh, Oraḥ Ḥayyim* 33:5).

How much is their measure – כַּמָּה שִׁיעוּרַיְיהוּ: The length of the straps of phylacteries of the arm must be enough for one to wrap and bind them around one's arm and to stretch them to the middle finger so that they can be wrapped around that finger three times and then tied. The universal custom is to wrap the straps six or seven times around one's arm. This ruling follows the interpretation of the majority of the commentaries that the Gemara is referring to the phylacteries of the arm, that the *tzereda* is the middle finger, and that the mention of plaiting the straps together is referring to the wrapping around the finger. If needed, one may recite a blessing even if the strap is only two handbreadths long, in accordance with Rashi's explanation, following the opinion of the *Sefer Yere'im* that according to Rashi the Gemara is referring to the phylacteries of the arm as well (*Artzot HaḤayyim*).

The straps of the phylacteries of the head must be long enough for them to hang down in front of the wearer and reach his navel, or slightly higher. Some say that the strap on one's right side should reach his navel while the strap on his left should reach his heart. These lengths are not indispensable, although some claim that they must hang down in front of him at least a little (*Magen Avraham*). Some maintain that they must hang down at least two handbreadths, which is until the index finger in accordance with the straight measure, as explained by Rashi (*Artzot HaḤayyim*). If they do not reach that far, one should don the phylacteries without reciting a blessing.

The width of the straps should be at least the length of a barley kernel. If the straps are wider or narrower than that, they are fit, but if they are narrower than the length of a wheat kernel one may not recite the blessing when donning them (Rambam *Sefer Ahava, Hilkhot Tefillin UMezuza VeSefer Torah* 3:12; *Shulḥan Arukh, Oraḥ Ḥayyim* 27:8, 11).

NOTES

Go out and see what the people are doing – פּוֹק חֲזִי מַה עַמָּא דָּבַר: Rashi explains that it is not customary for people to sew the straps. Others maintain, based on other instances where the Sages use this expression, that it indicates a leniency, i.e., people have the custom to sew them (Rabbeinu Tam). Some early commentaries note that it can be inferred from the Jerusalem Talmud (*Megilla* 1:11) that it is permitted to sew the straps.

Articles used in the performance of a mitzva…articles of sanctity – תַּשְׁמִישֵׁי מִצְוָה...תַּשְׁמִישֵׁי קְדוּשָּׁה: Examples of articles used in the performance of a mitzva include a *shofar* and a *lulav*. Examples of articles of sanctity include the cases used for storing Torah scrolls and the straps of phylacteries. These are considered sacred due to the words of Torah or the name of God they contain. The main difference between articles used in the performance of a mitzva and articles of sanctity is that once the mitzva for which an article used for the performance of a mitzva has been completed, e.g., a *lulav* after *Sukkot*, they do not retain any sanctity, whereas articles of sanctity possess inherent sanctity, which does not lapse even after use. Consequently, such articles must be stored away or interred in a respectful manner (see *Megilla* 26b).

How much is their measure…until the index finger [*tzereda*] – כַּמָּה שִׁיעוּרַיְיהוּ...עַד אֶצְבַּע צְרֵדָה: Rashi explains that the Gemara here is referring to the length of the straps of the phylacteries of the head after the knot has been tied. Some maintain that the same applies to the phylacteries of the arm (*Sefer Yere'im*). According to this explanation, *tzerada* is referring to the finger closest to the thumb. If so, when the Gemara proceeds to refer to a straight measure, it means the distance between the tip of the thumb and the tip of the index finger, whereas the bowed measure, which is shorter than the straight measure, is the distance between the tip of the middle finger and the tip of the index finger. Alternatively, bowed means from the base of the thumb to the tip of the index finger when they are adjacent to one another, while a straight measure means from the base of the thumb to the tip of the index finger when they are spread (*Arukh*).

Most commentaries contend that the Gemara is referring to the phylacteries of the arm, and that the *tzereda* finger is the middle finger, which is called by this name because it is the main rival [*tzara*] of the thumb, i.e., the one used with the thumb to snap one's fingers (see *Yoma* 19b). According to this interpretation, the Gemara is saying that the length of the strap of the phylacteries of the arm must reach the tip of that finger, and the matter discussed immediately afterward is whether it must reach the tip of the middle finger when it is bent or straight (see *Tosafot*, citing *Arukh* and Rabbi Elazar HaKalir).

Would tie them and plait them together – קָטַר לְהוּ וּמְתַלֵּית לְהוּ: According to some commentaries, this is referring to the straps of the phylacteries of the head. After binding them, Rav Aḥa bar Ya'akov would plait them like a braid, rather than placing them behind him like Rabba (Rashi). Others explain that he would wrap them two or three times around his head (*Sefer HaIttur*), and yet others add that this was necessary due to the great length of the straps (*Nimmukei Yosef*). According to other early commentaries, who interpret this discussion in reference to the phylacteries of the arm, Rav Aḥa bar Ya'akov would tie the strap on his finger, and the reference to plaiting means that he would wrap it around his finger three times (see Rambam and Rosh).

אָמַר רַב יְהוּדָה בְּרֵיהּ דְּרַב שְׁמוּאֵל בַּר שֵׁילַת מִשְּׁמֵיהּ דְּרַב: קֶשֶׁר שֶׁל תְּפִלִּין – הֲלָכָה לְמֹשֶׁה מִסִּינַי. אָמַר רַב נַחְמָן: וְנוֹיֵיהֶן לְבַר. רַב אַשִׁי הֲוָה יָתֵיב קַמֵּיהּ דְּמָר זוּטְרָא, אִיתְהַפְכָא לֵיהּ רְצוּעָה דִּתְפִילִּין, אֲמַר לֵיהּ: לָא סָבַר לָהּ מָר וְנוֹיֵיהֶן לְבַר? אֲמַר לֵיהּ: לָאו אַדַּעְתַּאי.

Rav Yehuda, son of Rav Shmuel bar Sheilat, says in the name of Rav: The form of the knot of phylacteries,[BH] i.e., that there must be the form of a letter *dalet* in the knot of the phylacteries of the head and the letter *yod* in the knot of the phylacteries of the arm, **is a** *halakha* **transmitted to Moses from Sinai. Rav Naḥman says: And their decorative** side, the black side of the knot where the shape of the letter is visible, must face **outward.**[HN] The Gemara relates: **Rav Ashi was sitting before Mar Zutra** when the **strap of** his **phylacteries became reversed.** Mar Zutra **said to him: Doesn't the Master hold** in accordance with the ruling that **their decorative** side must face **outward?** Rav Ashi **said to him:** It did **not** enter **my mind,** i.e., I did not notice.

"וְרָאוּ כׇּל עַמֵּי הָאָרֶץ כִּי שֵׁם ה׳ נִקְרָא עָלֶיךָ וְיָרְאוּ מִמֶּךָּ" – תַּנְיָא, רַבִּי אֱלִיעֶזֶר הַגָּדוֹל אוֹמֵר: אֵלּוּ תְּפִילִּין שֶׁבָּרֹאשׁ. "וַהֲסִרֹתִי אֶת כַּפִּי וְרָאִיתָ אֶת אֲחֹרָי" – אָמַר רַב חָנָא בַּר בִּיזְנָא אָמַר רַבִּי שִׁמְעוֹן חֲסִידָא: מְלַמֵּד שֶׁהֶרְאָה לוֹ הַקָּדוֹשׁ בָּרוּךְ הוּא לְמֹשֶׁה קֶשֶׁר שֶׁל תְּפִילִּין.

With regard to the verse: **"And all the nations of the land shall see that the name of the Lord is called upon you, and they shall be afraid of you"** (Deuteronomy 28:10), **it is taught** in a *baraita* that **Rabbi Eliezer the Great says: This** is a reference to **the phylacteries of the head,**[N] upon which the name of God is written, as they demonstrate to all that the name of God is called upon the Jewish people. With regard to the statement of God to Moses: **"And I will remove My hand, and you will see My back"** (Exodus 33:23), **Rav Ḥana bar Bizna says** that **Rabbi Shimon Ḥasida says:** This **teaches that the Holy One, Blessed be He, showed Moses the knot of** the **phylacteries** of the head.[N]

אָמַר רַב יְהוּדָה: קֶשֶׁר שֶׁל תְּפִילִּין צָרִיךְ שֶׁיְּהֵא לְמַעְלָה, כְּדֵי שֶׁיִּהְיוּ יִשְׂרָאֵל לְמַעְלָה וְלֹא לְמַטָּה; וְצָרִיךְ שֶׁיְּהֵא כְּלַפֵּי פָּנִים, כְּדֵי שֶׁיִּהְיוּ יִשְׂרָאֵל לְפָנִים וְלֹא לְאָחוֹר.

Rav Yehuda says: The knot of phylacteries must be above, i.e., it must rest on the head rather than on the neck, **in order that the Jewish people should be above and not below. And likewise it must be placed toward the front [*panim*],**[HN] i.e., not on the sides of the head, **in order that the Jewish people should be in front [*lefanim*] and not behind.**

BACKGROUND

Knot of phylacteries – קֶשֶׁר שֶׁל תְּפִילִּין:

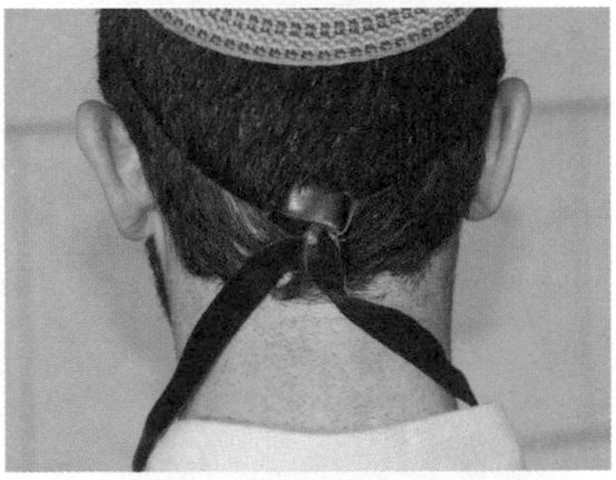

Phylacteries of the head, with knot in the shape of a *dalet*

Phylacteries of the arm, with knot in the shape of a *yod*

HALAKHA

Knot of phylacteries – קֶשֶׁר שֶׁל תְּפִילִּין: It is a *halakha* transmitted to Moses from Sinai that one must tie the strap of the phylacteries of the head in a square manner so that it has the appearance of the letter *dalet*. Some tie it in the form of a letter *mem*, but this is not the correct manner (*Mishna Berura*). The knot of the phylacteries of the arm should be tied like a letter *yod*, so that together with the two letters on the phylacteries of the head it spells *Shaddai*, which is a name of God. The *halakha* is in accordance with the opinion of Rav (Rambam *Sefer Ahava, Hilkhot Tefillin UMezuza VeSefer Torah* 3:1, 13; *Shulḥan Arukh, Oraḥ Ḥayyim* 32:52).

And their decorative side must face outward – וְנוֹיֵיהֶן לְבַר: The part of the knot of the phylacteries of the head that has the appearance of the letter *dalet* should face outward. Likewise, one should take care that the knot of the phylacteries of the arm not be turned around (Mordekhai). The black side of the straps should face outward, in both the phylacteries of the head and the phylacteries of the arm. This ruling follows both explanations of Rashi. This *halakha* applies only to the parts of the strap that encircle the head and the bicep; nonetheless, for ornamental reasons all areas of the strap that face outward should be black (*Shulḥan Arukh, Oraḥ Ḥayyim* 27:10–11 and *Mishna Berura* there).

Toward the front – כְּלַפֵּי פָּנִים: The knot behind one's head should be placed at the end of the back of the skull. It should be above the indentation in the neck *ab initio*, but in any case not below the bottom of the hairline. Furthermore, the knot should be positioned in the middle of the head, not to either side (Rambam *Sefer Ahava, Hilkhot Tefillin UMezuza VeSefer Torah* 4:1; *Shulḥan Arukh, Oraḥ Ḥayyim* 27:10).

NOTES

And their decorative side must face outward – וְנוֹיֵיהֶן לְבַר: The context indicates that this is referring to the decorative side of the knot, i.e., the side on which the letter *dalet* is visible, as on the other side one sees the knot itself (Rashi's first explanation). In tractate *Eiruvin* (97a) Rashi states that this also refers to the *shin* on the phylacteries of the head. Other commentaries maintain that the term: Their decorative side, indicates that the Gemara is referring to the straps in general, the topic of the discussion from the outset. If so, the reference is to the smooth, black side of the straps (Rashi's second explanation). This can also be inferred from the incident involving Rav Ashi, which is recorded immediately afterward (Rosh).

This is a reference to the phylacteries of the head – אֵלּוּ תְּפִילִּין שֶׁבָּרֹאשׁ: Two of the three letters of one of the names of God, *Shaddai*, is found on the phylacteries of the head: The *shin* is on the compartments, and the *dalet* is in the form of the knot (Rashi). Others explain that this derivation is based on the phrase "And all the nations of the land shall see," as the phylacteries of the head are clearly visible to all (*Tosafot*).

This teaches that the Holy One Blessed be He showed Moses the knot of the phylacteries of the head – מְלַמֵּד שֶׁהֶרְאָה לוֹ הַקָּדוֹשׁ בָּרוּךְ הוּא לְמֹשֶׁה קֶשֶׁר שֶׁל תְּפִילִּין: Some commentaries explain that God showed Moses how to tie the knot of the phylacteries, just as He showed him the plan of the Tabernacle and its vessels (Rav Hai Gaon). According to the Rambam in the *Guide of the Perplexed*, the knot of the phylacteries represents the nature of God's connection with the world and His guidance of it, and that is what was revealed to Moses (*Midrash Shlomo*).

Toward the front [*panim*] – כְּלַפֵּי פָּנִים: According to Rashi's second interpretation, this should be read as *penim*, i.e., inward, and the letter *dalet* should be toward the outside. Others maintain that this refers to the knot of the phylacteries of the arm, which, like the phylacteries themselves (see 37b), must be on the upper arm and directed inward toward the heart (Rosh; see *Beit Yosef*).

אָמַר רַב שְׁמוּאֵל בַּר בִּידְרִי אָמַר רַב, וְאָמְרִי לַהּ אָמַר רַבִּי אַחָא אֲרִיכָא אָמַר רַב הוּנָא, וְאָמְרִי לַהּ אָמַר רַב מְנַשְּׁיָא אָמַר שְׁמוּאֵל: תְּפִילִּין מֵאֵימָתַי מְבָרֵךְ עֲלֵיהֶן? מִשְּׁעַת הַנָּחָתָן. אִינִי? וְהָא אָמַר רַב יְהוּדָה אָמַר שְׁמוּאֵל: כׇּל הַמִּצְוֹת כּוּלָּן מְבָרֵךְ עֲלֵיהֶן עוֹבֵר לַעֲשִׂיָּיתָן! אַבַּיֵּי וְרָבָא דְּאָמְרִי תַּרְוַיְיהוּ: מִשְּׁעַת הַנָּחָה וְעַד שְׁעַת קְשִׁירָה.

§ **Rav Shmuel bar Bideri says** that **Rav says, and some say** that **Rabbi Aḥa Arikha,** i.e., Rabbi Aḥa the Tall, **says** that **Rav Huna says, and some say** that **Rav Menashya says** that **Shmuel says:** With regard to **phylacteries, from when does one recite a blessing over them? From the time when one dons them** on the arm and onward. The Gemara raises a difficulty: **Is that so? But doesn't Rav Yehuda say** that **Shmuel says:** With regard to **all the mitzvot, one recites a blessing over them prior to their performance?** How, then, can one recite a blessing over phylacteries after donning them? **Abaye and Rava both say:** One recites the blessing **from the time of donning** the phylacteries[H] **until the time of binding** them, as the binding constitutes the performance of the mitzva.

HALAKHA

From the time of donning the phylacteries – מִשְּׁעַת הַנָּחָה: In general, one should recite the blessing over the performance of a mitzva prior to, but as close as possible to, its performance. Consequently, one should recite the blessing over the phylacteries of the arm after placing them on the bicep but before binding them, as the binding is considered the performance of the mitzva. Likewise with regard to the phylacteries of the head, one should recite the blessing after donning them but before tightening them on his head (Rambam *Sefer Ahava, Hilkhot Tefillin UMezuza VeSefer Torah* 4:7; *Shulḥan Arukh, Oraḥ Ḥayyim* 25:8, and in the comment of Rema).

Perek **III**
Daf **36** Amud **a**

אָמַר רַב חִסְדָּא: סָח בֵּין תְּפִילָּה לִתְפִילָּה – חוֹזֵר וּמְבָרֵךְ.

§ **Rav Ḥisda says:** If one **spoke between** donning the **phylacteries** of the arm **and** the **phylacteries** of the head, he must **recite the blessing again** when donning the phylacteries of the head.

סָח – אִין, לֹא סָח – לָא? וְהָא שְׁלַח רַב חִיָּיא בְּרֵיהּ דְּרַב הוּנָא מִשְּׁמֵיהּ דְּרַבִּי יוֹחָנָן: עַל תְּפִילָּה שֶׁל יָד אוֹמֵר: "בָּרוּךְ אֲשֶׁר קִדְּשָׁנוּ בְּמִצְוֹתָיו וְצִוָּנוּ לְהַנִּיחַ תְּפִילִּין", עַל תְּפִילִּין שֶׁל רֹאשׁ אוֹמֵר: "בָּרוּךְ אֲשֶׁר קִדְּשָׁנוּ בְּמִצְוֹתָיו וְצִוָּנוּ עַל מִצְוַת תְּפִילִּין"!

The Gemara notes: One can infer that if he **spoke, yes,** he must recite a blessing when donning the phylacteries of the head, but if he **did not speak,** he does **not** recite a blessing. The Gemara challenges this: **But Rav Ḥiyya, son of Rav Huna, sent** a ruling **in the name of Rabbi Yoḥanan: On the phylacteries of the arm** one **says** the blessing: **Blessed** are You, Lord our God, King of the Universe, **Who has sanctified us through His mitzvot and commanded us to don phylacteries. On the phylacteries of the head**[H] one **says** the blessing: **Blessed** are You, Lord our God, King of the Universe, **Who has sanctified us through His mitzvot and commanded us concerning the mitzva of phylacteries.** This indicates that one always recites a blessing when donning the phylacteries of the head.

אַבַּיֵּי וְרָבָא דְּאָמְרִי תַּרְוַיְיהוּ: לֹא סָח – מְבָרֵךְ אַחַת, סָח – מְבָרֵךְ שְׁתַּיִם.

Abaye and Rava both say, to resolve this apparent contradiction: Rabbi Yoḥanan meant that if one **did not speak,** he **recites one** blessing; if he **spoke,** he **recites two** blessings,[N] when donning the phylacteries of the head as well as when donning the phylacteries of the arm.

תָּנָא: סָח בֵּין תְּפִילָּה לִתְפִילָּה – עֲבֵירָה הִיא בְּיָדוֹ, וְחוֹזֵר עָלֶיהָ מֵעֶרְכֵי הַמִּלְחָמָה.

Concerning this, it is **taught** in a *baraita*: If one **spoke between** donning the **phylacteries** of the arm **and** the **phylacteries** of the head,[H] **he has a sin,**[N] **and due to** that sin **he returns from the ranks of** soldiers waging **war.** This is referring to the preparation for war, when the officers announce: "What man is there who is fearful and fainthearted? Let him go and return to his house" (Deuteronomy 20:8). The Sages explained that this is referring to one who is fearful due to his transgressions.

NOTES

If one did not speak he recites one blessing, if he spoke he recites two blessings – לֹא סָח מְבָרֵךְ אַחַת, סָח מְבָרֵךְ שְׁתַּיִם: Rashi explains that if one did not speak, he fulfills his obligation through the blessing he recited when donning the phylacteries of the arm, which concludes: To don phylacteries. When Rabbi Yoḥanan says that one recites the blessing that concludes: Concerning the mitzva of phylacteries, when donning the phylacteries of the head, he was referring to one who spoke after donning the phylacteries of the arm (see *She'iltot deRav Aḥai Gaon* and Rif). Other early commentaries raise many difficulties with this interpretation, including the problematic idea that the Sages instituted a blessing for one who committed a sin (see Mordekhai and commentary attributed to Rashba). Another explanation is that if one did not speak, he recites only one extra blessing when donning the phylacteries of the head, as stated by Rabbi Yoḥanan, and if he spoke, then he recites two blessings when donning the phylacteries of the head, both the blessing that concludes with: To don phylacteries, and the blessing that concludes with: Concerning the mitzva of phylacteries (*Halakhot Gedolot*; Rav Amram; Rabbeinu Tam).

He has a sin – עֲבֵירָה הִיא בְּיָדוֹ: According to Rashi, this refers to one who spoke between donning the phylacteries of the arm and those of the head; he is considered to have sinned if he does not subsequently recite a blessing for the phylacteries of the head. Many commentaries challenge Rashi's interpretation. One commentary contends that the sin is the unnecessary extra blessing he must recite, since had he not spoken he would have had to recite only one blessing (*Tosefot HaRosh* on *Sota* 47b). The Rambam indicates that the act of speaking between the donning of the two phylacteries is itself a sin. This is in accordance with the explanation of the Ran, which is as follows: Since the verse connects the two phylacteries, as it states: "And it shall be for a sign upon your hand and for frontlets between your eyes" (Exodus 13:16), the phylacteries of the head must be donned immediately after those of the arm without any interruption (Meiri on *Rosh HaShana* 35a).

HALAKHA

On the phylacteries of the arm…on the phylacteries of the head – עַל תְּפִילָּה שֶׁל יָד...עַל תְּפִילִּין שֶׁל רֹאשׁ: When donning phylacteries of the arm one recites the blessing: Blessed are you, the Lord, our God, King of the Universe, Who has sanctified us through His mitzvot and commanded us to don phylacteries. One does not recite a blessing when donning phylacteries of the head. The Rema writes: There is an opinion that when donning phylacteries of the head one recites the blessing that concludes with: Concerning the mitzva of phylacteries (Rabbeinu Tam; Rosh), and this is the accepted custom in the lands of Ashkenaz. Since there is a concern here of possibly reciting an unnecessary blessing, one should recite following the second blessing, after tightening the phylacteries, the formula: Blessed be the name of His glorious kingdom forever and all time (Rambam *Sefer Ahava, Hilkhot Tefillin UMezuza VeSefer Torah* 4:4; *Shulḥan Arukh, Oraḥ Ḥayyim* 25:5, and in the comment of Rema).

If one spoke between donning the phylacteries of the arm and the phylacteries of the head – סָח בֵּין תְּפִילָּה לִתְפִילָּה: It is prohibited for one to speak between donning the phylacteries of the arm and the phylacteries of the head. One may not even reply to a greeting from his teacher, or say the responses during the communal prayers of *kaddish* or *kedusha*. Rather, he should be silent during these parts of the prayer and listen with the appropriate intention. If he did speak, he has sinned, and he must recite a second blessing, which concludes with: Concerning the mitzva of phylacteries, and then don the phylacteries of the head. According to the Ashkenazic custom that one always recites two blessings, if one did speak he is required to recite two blessings when donning the phylacteries of the head (Rambam *Sefer Ahava, Hilkhot Tefillin UMezuza VeSefer Torah* 4:6; *Shulḥan Arukh, Oraḥ Ḥayyim* 25:9–10, and in the comment of Rema).

תָּנָא: כְּשֶׁהוּא מַנִּיחַ – מַנִּיחַ שֶׁל יָד וְאַחַר כָּךְ מַנִּיחַ שֶׁל רֹאשׁ, וּכְשֶׁהוּא חוֹלֵץ – חוֹלֵץ שֶׁל רֹאשׁ וְאַחַר כָּךְ חוֹלֵץ שֶׁל יָד. בִּשְׁלָמָא כְּשֶׁהוּא מַנִּיחַ, מַנִּיחַ שֶׁל יָד וְאַחַר כָּךְ מַנִּיחַ שֶׁל רֹאשׁ – דִּכְתִיב: ״וּקְשַׁרְתָּם לְאוֹת עַל יָדֶךָ״ וַהֲדַר: ״וְהָיוּ לְטוֹטָפֹת בֵּין עֵינֶיךָ״,

It is further **taught** in a *baraita*: **When one dons** phylacteries, he first **dons** the phylacteries **of the arm and afterward dons** the phylacteries **of the head. And when he removes** his phylacteries,[H] he first **removes** the phylacteries **of the head and afterward removes** the phylacteries **of the arm.** The Gemara asks: **Granted,** the ruling that **when one dons** phylacteries he first **dons** the phylacteries **of the arm and afterward dons** the phylacteries **of the head** is understood, **as it is** first **written: "And you shall bind them for a sign upon your arm,"** and then it is written: **"And they shall be for frontlets between your eyes"** (Deuteronomy 6:8).

אֶלָּא כְּשֶׁהוּא חוֹלֵץ, חוֹלֵץ שֶׁל רֹאשׁ וְאַחַר כָּךְ חוֹלֵץ שֶׁל יָד, מְנָלַן? אֲמַר רַבָּה: רַב הוּנָא אַסְבְּרָא לִי, אָמַר קְרָא: ״וְהָיוּ לְטוֹטָפֹת בֵּין עֵינֶיךָ״, כָּל זְמַן שֶׁבֵּין עֵינֶיךָ יְהוּ שְׁתַּיִם.

But from where do we derive the *halakha* that **when he removes** his phylacteries, he first **removes** the phylacteries **of the head and afterward he removes** the phylacteries **of the arm? Rabba said** in explanation: **Rav Huna explained to me** the source of this *halakha*. **The verse states:** "And you shall bind them for a sign upon your arm **and they shall be for frontlets between your eyes,"** and it is derived from here: **As long as** the phylacteries of the head are **between your eyes,** the number of phylacteries you are wearing **shall be two.**

תָּנוּ רַבָּנַן: תְּפִילִּין מֵאֵימָתַי מְבָרֵךְ עֲלֵיהֶן? מִשְּׁעַת הַנָּחָתָן. כֵּיצַד? הָיָה מַשְׁכִּים לָצֵאת לַדֶּרֶךְ וּמִתְיָירֵא שֶׁמָּא יֹאבְדוּ – מַנִּיחָן, וּכְשֶׁיַּגִּיעַ זְמַנָּן מְמַשְׁמֵשׁ בָּהֶן וּמְבָרֵךְ עֲלֵיהֶן.

The Sages taught in a *baraita*: With regard to **phylacteries, from when does one recite a blessing over them? From** when **the time** arrives to **don them. How so? If one is rising early to leave** his home **to** travel on **the road**[H] **and is afraid lest** his phylacteries **become lost** during the journey, he **dons them** even at night, despite the fact that this is not the proper time for the mitzva of phylacteries. **And when** the **time** for **their** mitzva **arrives,** in the morning, **he touches them and recites a blessing over them.**

וְעַד מָתַי מַנִּיחָן? עַד שֶׁתִּשְׁקַע הַחַמָּה, רַבִּי יַעֲקֹב אוֹמֵר: עַד שֶׁתִּכְלֶה רֶגֶל מִן הַשּׁוּק, וַחֲכָמִים אוֹמְרִים: עַד זְמַן שֵׁינָה; וּמוֹדִים חֲכָמִים לְרַבִּי יַעֲקֹב, שֶׁאִם חֲלָצָן לָצֵאת לְבֵית הַכִּסֵּא אוֹ לִיכָּנֵס לְבֵית הַמֶּרְחָץ וְשָׁקְעָה חַמָּה, שׁוּב אֵינוֹ חוֹזֵר וּמַנִּיחָן.

And until when does one wear them?[H] **Until the sun sets. Rabbi Ya'akov says: Until traffic in the marketplace ceases. And the Rabbis say: Until the time of sleep. And the Rabbis concede to Rabbi Ya'akov that if one removed them to go out to the bathroom or to enter the bathhouse and the sun set, one does not don them again.**

אָמַר רַב נַחְמָן: הֲלָכָה כְּרַבִּי יַעֲקֹב. רַב חִסְדָּא וְרַבָּה בַּר רַב הוּנָא מְצַלּוּ בְּהוּ בְּאוּרְתָּא. אִיכָּא דְּאָמְרִי: אֵין הֲלָכָה כְּרַבִּי יַעֲקֹב.

Rav Naḥman says: The *halakha* **is in accordance with** the opinion of **Rabbi Ya'akov.** The Gemara likewise relates that **Rav Ḥisda and Rabba bar Rav Huna would pray in the evening,** i.e., the evening service, **with** phylacteries. **Some say** that Rav Naḥman ruled that the *halakha* **is not in accordance with** the opinion of **Rabbi Ya'akov** but in accordance with the opinion of the first *tanna* that the mitzva of phylacteries ends at sunset.

HALAKHA

And when he removes his phylacteries – וּכְשֶׁהוּא חוֹלֵץ: When one dons phylacteries, he first dons the phylacteries of the arm and then the phylacteries of the head. When removing his phylacteries, he removes the phylacteries of the head and then removes the phylacteries of the arm, as stated in the *baraita* (Rambam *Sefer Ahava, Hilkhot Tefillin UMezuza VeSefer Torah* 4:5; *Shulḥan Arukh, Oraḥ Ḥayyim* 25:5, 28:2).

If one is rising early to leave his home to travel on the road – הָיָה מַשְׁכִּים לָצֵאת לַדֶּרֶךְ: The time for donning phylacteries in the morning is from when one can discern an individual with whom he is somewhat familiar at a distance of four cubits (see *Berakhot* 9b). If one wishes to set out on a journey before this time, he may don his phylacteries, and when the time for the mitzva arrives he should touch them and recite the blessing (Rambam *Sefer Ahava, Hilkhot Tefillin UMezuza VeSefer Torah* 4:10; *Shulḥan Arukh, Oraḥ Ḥayyim* 30:1, 3).

And until when does one wear them – וְעַד מָתַי מַנִּיחָן: It is prohibited to don phylacteries at night, from sunset onward. Some rule that this applies from the emergence of the stars (*Magen Avraham*). If one had not donned phylacteries that day, he should don them at twilight, which is after sunset and before the emergence of three stars, without reciting a blessing (Rambam *Sefer Ahava, Hilkhot Tefillin UMezuza VeSefer Torah* 4:10; *Shulḥan Arukh, Oraḥ Ḥayyim* 30:2, and see *Mishna Berura* there).

Perek **III**
Daf **36** Amud **b**

וְהָא רַב חִסְדָּא וְרַבָּה בַּר רַב הוּנָא מְצַלּוּ בְּהוּ בְּאוּרְתָּא! הַהוּא פְּלִיגָא.

The Gemara raises a difficulty: **But Rav Ḥisda and Rabba bar Rav Huna would pray in the evening with** phylacteries. The Gemara explains: **That** opinion represented in this incident **disagrees** with the ruling of Rav Naḥman.

וּמִי אֲמַר רַבָּה בַּר רַב הוּנָא הָכִי? וְהָא אָמַר רַבָּה בַּר רַב הוּנָא: סָפֵק חֲשֵׁיכָה סָפֵק לֹא חֲשֵׁיכָה – לֹא חוֹלֵץ וְלֹא מַנִּיחַ; הָא וַדַּאי חֲשֵׁיכָה – חוֹלֵץ! הָתָם בְּעֶרֶב שַׁבָּת אִיתְּמַר.

The Gemara asks: **And did Rabba bar Rav Huna** actually **say this,** that the mitzva of phylacteries applies at night? **But doesn't Rabba bar Rav Huna say:** If it is **uncertain** whether it is **nightfall** or whether it is **not nightfall,** one **neither removes** his phylacteries, as it is not yet definitely night, **nor dons** them *ab initio*. **This** indicates that if it is **definitely nightfall,** one **removes** his phylacteries. The Gemara answers: Rabba bar Rav Huna's ruling **there was stated with regard to Shabbat eve,** as one may not don phylacteries on Shabbat, when the mitzva does not apply.

מַאי קָסָבַר? אִי קָסָבַר: לַיְלָה זְמַן תְּפִילִּין – שַׁבָּת נַמִּי זְמַן תְּפִילִּין! אִי קָסָבַר: שַׁבָּת לָאו זְמַן תְּפִילִּין – לַיְלָה נַמִּי לָאו זְמַן תְּפִילִּין, דְּמֵהֵיכָא דִּמְמַעֵט שַׁבָּת מֵהָתָם מְמַעֵט לֵילוֹת!

The Gemara raises a difficulty with regard to this answer: **What does** Rabba bar Rav Huna **hold? If he holds** that **night** is **a time** when one performs the mitzva of wearing **phylacteries,** then **Shabbat** is **also a time** when one performs the mitzva of wearing **phylacteries. If he holds** that **Shabbat** is **not a time** when one performs the mitzva of wearing **phylacteries,** then **night** is **also not a time** when one performs the mitzva of wearing **phylacteries.** The reason for this statement is **that from** the source **where Shabbat is excluded** from the mitzva of phylacteries, **nights are excluded from there** as well.

דְּתַנְיָא: ״וְשָׁמַרְתָּ אֶת הַחֻקָּה הַזֹּאת לְמוֹעֲדָהּ מִיָּמִים יָמִימָה״, ״יָמִים״ – וְלֹא לֵילוֹת, ״מִיָּמִים״ – וְלֹא כׇּל יָמִים, פְּרָט לְשַׁבָּתוֹת וְיָמִים טוֹבִים, דִּבְרֵי רַבִּי יוֹסֵי הַגְּלִילִי; רַבִּי עֲקִיבָא אוֹמֵר: לֹא נֶאֱמַר חוּקָּה זוֹ אֶלָּא לְפֶסַח בִּלְבָד!

As it is taught in a *baraita* with regard to the end of the passage of the Torah that discusses both the mitzvot of the Paschal offering and phylacteries: **"And you shall observe this ordinance in its season from year [*miyamim*] to year"** (Exodus 13:10). This indicates that these mitzvot apply during the **days [*yamim*] but not** during the **nights.** Furthermore, the letter *mem*, meaning from, in the term: **"From year [*miyamim*],"** teaches: These mitzvot apply on some days, **but not on all days.** This **excludes *Shabbatot* and Festivals,**[H] on which phylacteries are not worn. This is **the statement of Rabbi Yosei HaGelili. Rabbi Akiva says: This** verse, mentioning **an ordinance, is stated only with regard to the Paschal** offering, and it is not referring to phylacteries at all. Evidently, Rabbi Yosei HaGelili, who says that at night one is exempt from the obligation of donning phylacteries, says that on Shabbat one is exempt as well.

נָפְקָא לֵיהּ מֵהֵיכָא דְּנָפְקָא לֵיהּ לְרַבִּי עֲקִיבָא; דְּתַנְיָא, רַבִּי עֲקִיבָא אוֹמֵר: יָכוֹל יַנִּיחַ אָדָם תְּפִילִּין בְּשַׁבָּתוֹת וּבְיָמִים טוֹבִים? תַּלְמוּד לוֹמַר: ״וְהָיָה לְאוֹת עַל יָדְךָ וּלְטוֹטָפֹת בֵּין עֵינֶיךָ״ – מִי שֶׁצְּרִיכִין אוֹת, יָצְאוּ שַׁבָּתוֹת וְיָמִים טוֹבִים שֶׁהֵן גּוּפָן אוֹת.

The Gemara answers: Rabba bar Rav Huna **derives** the exemption from the obligation to don phylacteries on Shabbat **from** a different source, the source **where Rabbi Akiva derives it from, as it is taught** in a *baraita* that **Rabbi Akiva says:** One **might** have thought that **a person should don phylacteries on *Shabbatot* and Festivals.** To counter this, **the verse states: "And it shall be for a sign for you on your arm, and for a remembrance between your eyes,** so that God's law shall be in your mouth; for with a strong arm God brought you out of Egypt" (Exodus 13:9). This teaches that the obligation to don phylacteries applies when the Jewish people **require a sign** to assert their status as God's nation, i.e., during the week. This serves to **exclude *Shabbatot* and Festivals, as they themselves are signs** of the Jewish people's status as God's nation and a remembrance of the exodus from Egypt. Consequently, no further sign is required on these days.

אָמַר רַבִּי אֶלְעָזָר: כׇּל הַמַּנִּיחַ תְּפִילִּין אַחַר שְׁקִיעַת הַחַמָּה – עוֹבֵר בַּעֲשֵׂה, וְרַבִּי יוֹחָנָן אָמַר: עוֹבֵר בְּלָאו. לֵימָא, בְּרַבִּי אָבִין אָמַר רַבִּי אֶילְעָא קָא מִיפַּלְגִי, דְּאָמַר רַבִּי אָבִין אָמַר רַבִּי אֶילְעָא: כׇּל מָקוֹם שֶׁנֶּאֱמַר ״הִשָּׁמֵר״ ״פֶּן״ וְ״אַל״ – אֵינוֹ אֶלָּא לֹא תַעֲשֶׂה,

Rabbi Elazar says: Anyone who dons phylacteries after sunset[H] **violates a positive mitzva. And Rabbi Yoḥanan says: He violates a prohibition.** The Gemara suggests: **Let us say** that these Sages **disagree with regard to** the principle that **Rabbi Avin says** that **Rabbi Ile'a says. As Rabbi Avin says** that **Rabbi Ile'a says: Any place where it is stated** in the Torah any of the terms: **Observe,** or: **Lest,** or: **Do not,** this means **nothing other than a prohibition,** as these are negative terms.

HALAKHA

Excludes *Shabbatot* and Festivals – פְּרָט לְשַׁבָּתוֹת וְיָמִים טוֹבִים: The mitzva of wearing phylacteries does not apply on *Shabbatot* and Festivals, as it states: "And it shall be for a sign" (Exodus 13:16). and *Shabbatot* and Festivals themselves are signs of the Jewish people's status as God's nation. Therefore, if one were to add another sign this would be a disparagement of their signs. Not only is there no obligation to wear phylacteries on Shabbat and Festivals, it is actually prohibited to wear them, as this is a mark of disrespect of the sacred day. The early commentaries dispute whether one wears phylacteries on the intermediate days of a Festival. Since the kabbalistic tradition is not to wear phylacteries on the intermediate days of a Festival, all Sephardic and Hassidic communities follow suit. This is also the prevailing custom in Eretz Yisrael (Rambam *Sefer Ahava, Hilkhot Tefillin UMezuza VeSefer Torah* 4:10; *Shulḥan Arukh, Oraḥ Ḥayyim* 31:1–2).

Who dons phylacteries after sunset – הַמַּנִּיחַ תְּפִילִּין אַחַר שְׁקִיעַת הַחַמָּה: One does not wear phylacteries at night, as he might fall asleep while wearing them and treat them disrespectfully. This prohibition applies by rabbinic law, as the *halakha* is in accordance with Rabbi Akiva, who maintains that the mitzva of phylacteries applies at night. The Rambam holds that the prohibition against wearing phylacteries at night applies by Torah law, as indicated by the discussion here. Nevertheless, all authorities agree that if one donned phylacteries during the day he need not remove them after nightfall; but a public ruling is not issued to that effect (Rambam *Sefer Ahava, Hilkhot Tefillin UMezuza VeSefer Torah* 4:11; *Shulḥan Arukh, Oraḥ Ḥayyim* 30:2).

דְּמַר אִית לֵיהּ דְּרַבִּי אָבִין, וּמַר לֵית לֵיהּ דְּרַבִּי אָבִין?

The Gemara explains this suggestion: **As this Sage,** Rabbi Yoḥanan, **is of** the opinion that the ruling is in accordance with the opinion **of Rabbi Avin,** and therefore the verse: "And you shall observe this ordinance in its season from year to year," from which the exclusion of nights is derived, is a prohibition, as it employs the term "observe." **And that Sage,** Rabbi Elazar, **is of** the opinion that the ruling **is not** in accordance with the opinion **of Rabbi Avin,** and therefore the term: "And you shall observe," is a positive mitzva.

לָא, דְּכוּלֵּי עָלְמָא אִית לְהוּ דְּרַבִּי אָבִין אָמַר רַבִּי אִילְעָא, וְהָכָא בְּהָא קָא מִיפַּלְגִי, מַר סָבַר: ״הִשָּׁמֶר״ דְּלָאו – לָאו, וְ״הִשָּׁמֶר״ דַּעֲשֵׂה – עֲשֵׂה, וּמָר סָבַר: ״הִשָּׁמֶר״ דַּעֲשֵׂה נָמֵי לָאו.

The Gemara counters: **No, everyone is of** the opinion that the ruling is in accordance with the opinion **that Rabbi Avin** says that **Rabbi Ile'a says, and here they disagree with regard to this:** One **Sage,** Rabbi Elazar, **holds** that the term **"observe"** written **with regard to a prohibition** has the status of **a prohibition,** whereas that same term **"observe"** written **with regard to a positive** mitzva has the status of **a positive** mitzva, as the Torah is issuing a warning to take special care in the observance of a mitzva. Accordingly, the command with regard to the positive mitzva of phylacteries is a positive mitzva. **And** one **Sage,** Rabbi Yoḥanan, **holds** that the term **"observe"** written **with regard to a positive** mitzva is **also a prohibition.**

וְאָמַר רַבִּי אֶלְעָזָר: וְאִם לְשָׁמְרָן – מוּתָּר. וְאָמַר רָבִינָא: הֲוָה יָתֵיבְנָא קַמֵּיהּ דְּרַב אַשִׁי וְחָשַׁךְ וְהִנִּיחַ תְּפִילִּין, וַאֲמַרִי לֵיהּ: לְשָׁמְרָן קָא בָּעֵי לְהוּ מָר? וַאֲמַר לִי: אִין, וַחֲזֵיתֵיהּ לְדַעְתֵּיהּ דְּלָאו לְשָׁמְרָן הוּא בָּעֵי, קָסָבַר: הֲלָכָה וְאֵין מוֹרִין כֵּן.

And Rabbi Elazar says: And although it is prohibited to don phylacteries at night, **if** one does so in order **to safeguard them**[H] from theft and the like, it is **permitted. And Ravina said: I was sitting before Rav Ashi and it grew dark, and he donned phylacteries.**[N] **And I said to him: Does the Master need to safeguard them? And he said to me: Yes. But I saw that his intention** in donning them was **not** that he **needed to safeguard them;** rather, Rav Ashi **holds:** This is the ***halakha,*** that night is an appropriate time for phylacteries, **but** a public **ruling is not issued to that effect.**[HN]

אָמַר רַבָּה בַּר רַב הוּנָא: חַיָּיב אָדָם לְמַשְׁמֵשׁ בִּתְפִילִּין בְּכָל שָׁעָה, קַל וָחוֹמֶר מִצִּיץ: וּמָה צִיץ שֶׁאֵין בּוֹ אֶלָּא אַזְכָּרָה אַחַת – אָמְרָה תּוֹרָה: ״וְהָיָה עַל מִצְחוֹ תָּמִיד״ שֶׁלֹּא תַּסִּיחַ דַּעְתּוֹ מִמֶּנּוּ, תְּפִילִּין שֶׁיֵּשׁ בָּהֶן אַזְכָּרוֹת הַרְבֵּה, עַל אַחַת כַּמָּה וְכַמָּה!

Rabba bar Rav Huna says: A person is obligated to touch his **phylacteries** regularly for **the entire time**[H] that he is wearing them. This is derived from **an *a fortiori*** inference **from** the **frontplate** of the High Priest, as follows: **And if** with regard to the **frontplate, which has only one mention** of God's name, **the Torah states: "And it should be always upon his forehead"** (Exodus 28:38), which means that the High Priest must always be aware that the frontplate is placed on his head and **that he should not be distracted from it,** then with regard to **phylacteries, which have numerous mentions** of God's name, **all the more so** one must always be aware of them.

תָּנוּ רַבָּנַן: ״יָדְךָ״ – זוֹ שְׂמֹאל; אַתָּה אוֹמֵר: שְׂמֹאל, אוֹ אֵינוֹ אֶלָּא יָמִין? תַּלְמוּד לוֹמַר: ״אַף יָדִי יָסְדָה אֶרֶץ וִימִינִי טִפְּחָה שָׁמַיִם״, וְאוֹמֵר: ״יָדָהּ לַיָּתֵד תִּשְׁלַחְנָה וִימִינָהּ לְהַלְמוּת עֲמֵלִים״, וְאוֹמֵר: ״לָמָּה תָשִׁיב יָדְךָ וִימִינְךָ מִקֶּרֶב חֵיקְךָ כַלֵּה״.

§ **The Sages taught** with regard to the verse: "And it shall be for a sign for you on **your arm** [***yadkha***]" (Exodus 13:9), that **this** is referring to the **left** arm.[H] **Do you say** it means the **left** arm, **or is it** only the **right** arm? **The verse states: "Even My hand** [***yadi***] **has laid the foundation of the earth, and My right hand** [***vimini***] **has spread out the heavens"** (Isaiah 48:13). **And** another verse **states: "Her hand** [***yadah***] **she put to the tent pin, and her right hand** [***viminah***] **to the workmen's hammer"** (Judges 5:26), **and** another verse **states: "Why do You withdraw Your hand** [***yadkha***], **even Your right hand** [***viminekha***]? **Draw it out of Your bosom and consume them"** (Psalms 74:11). All these verses employ the term *yad* with regard to the left hand, and use the term *yamin,* literally, right, without the term *yad,* to indicate the right hand.

HALAKHA

And if one does so in order to safeguard them, etc. – **וְאִם לְשָׁמְרָן וכו׳:** If one did not remove his phylacteries at sunset, as he had nowhere safe to place them and he sought to safeguard them from theft and the like, this is permitted. A public ruling is issued to this effect, in accordance with the opinion of Rabbi Elazar and Rav Ashi, based on the version of the text accepted by the Rif. The *Beit Yosef* rules that one may not don them in order to guard them *ab initio*, but the *Beur HaGra* and *Olat Tamid* permit even this (Rambam *Sefer Ahava, Hilkhot Tefillin UMezuza VeSefer Torah* 4:12; *Shulḥan Arukh, Oraḥ Ḥayyim* 30:2).

This is the *halakha* but a public ruling is not issued to that effect – **הֲלָכָה וְאֵין מוֹרִין כֵּן:** It is prohibited to don phylacteries after sunset, but if one donned them before sunset he is not obligated to remove them and may wear them all night, provided that he does not sleep while wearing them. A public ruling is not issued to this effect, and a Sage should not act in this manner in public (*Magen Avraham*). This ruling is inferred from the incident involving Rav Ashi, in accordance with the version of the text accepted by the Rif (Rambam *Sefer Ahava, Hilkhot Tefillin UMezuza VeSefer Torah* 4:11; *Shulḥan Arukh, Oraḥ Ḥayyim* 30:2).

A person is obligated to touch his phylacteries regularly the entire time – **חַיָּיב אָדָם לְמַשְׁמֵשׁ בִּתְפִילִּין בְּכָל שָׁעָה:** One is obligated to touch his phylacteries regularly the entire time he is wearing them, so he will not be distracted from them even for a moment. It is not necessary to touch them while praying or studying Torah (*Mishna Berura*, citing *Magen Avraham*; see *Beur Halakha*). *Tosafot* rule that when one touches them, he should touch the phylacteries of the arm first, followed by the phylacteries of the head (Rambam *Sefer Ahava, Hilkhot Tefillin UMezuza VeSefer Torah* 4:14; *Shulḥan Arukh, Oraḥ Ḥayyim* 28:1).

Your arm, this is referring to the left arm – **יָדְךָ זוֹ שְׂמֹאל:** One binds the phylacteries of the arm on his left arm (Rambam *Sefer Ahava, Hilkhot Tefillin UMezuza VeSefer Torah* 4:2; *Shulḥan Arukh, Oraḥ Ḥayyim* 27:1).

NOTES

And it grew dark and he donned phylacteries – **וְחָשַׁךְ וְהִנִּיחַ תְּפִילִּין:** The standard version of the text indicates that Rav Ashi donned the phylacteries after nightfall. An alternative version reads: And he did not remove phylacteries, i.e., he was wearing them before nightfall and did not remove them (Rif; Rambam).

This is the *halakha* but a public ruling is not issued to that effect – **הֲלָכָה וְאֵין מוֹרִין כֵּן:** In other words, Rav Ashi maintains, in opposition to the opinion of Rabbi Elazar, that phylacteries are worn at night and that one may don them *ab initio*. He did not wish to issue this ruling publicly, so that people would not fall asleep while wearing phylacteries, which is unbecoming. Some explain that Rav Ashi is of the opinion that night is not an appropriate time for phylacteries, but he rules that although it is prohibited to don them at night, and one who dons them at night violates a positive mitzva from the Torah, if he is wearing them at nightfall he is not obligated to remove them. A public ruling is not issued to this effect; rather, people are instructed to remove them (*Beit Yosef*, citing Rambam; Rif).

LANGUAGE

HaḤorem – הַחוֹרֵם: Rashi explains this appellation as similar to *ḥarum* (see Leviticus 21:18), one with a sunken nose (see *Bekhorot* 43b). Other commentaries are puzzled by the suggestion that the Sages would give someone a nickname based on a blemish. They therefore associate HaḤorem with *ḥerem*, a fisherman's net, due to his occupation.

HALAKHA

One without a complete arm – גִּידֵּם: One whose left arm has been amputated up to the elbow but still has an upper arm should don phylacteries on that arm, even if only his bicep remains intact (*Mishna Berura*). This ruling is in accordance with the explanation of *Tosafot* that the *tanna'im* cited in the second *baraita* are not in disagreement with each other. One who dons phylacteries in this manner should not recite a blessing, in light of the opinion of the *Or Zarua* that the arm mentioned here is the arm below the elbow and that the first *tanna* deems him exempt in such a case. If his left arm including his bicep is missing, he is entirely exempt from donning phylacteries, even on his right arm. One who is missing his right arm is nevertheless obligated to don phylacteries on his left, and he should do so with the help of others (*Shulḥan Arukh*, *Oraḥ Ḥayyim* 27:1, and see *Mishna Berura* there).

רַבִּי יוֹסֵי הַחוֹרֵם אוֹמֵר: מָצִינוּ יָמִין שֶׁנִּקְרָא יָד, שֶׁנֶּאֱמַר: ״וַיַּרְא יוֹסֵף כִּי יָשִׁית אָבִיו יַד יְמִינוֹ״. וְאִידָךְ? יַד יְמִינוֹ אִיקְרִי, יָד סְתָמָא לָא אִיקְרִי.

Rabbi Yosei HaḤorem[L] **says:** This is no proof, as **we have found that** the **right** hand is also **called** ***yad*****, as it is stated: "And when Joseph saw that his father was laying his right hand [*yad yemino*]"** (Genesis 48:17). The Gemara asks: **And the other** ***tanna*****,** who maintains that the right hand is not called *yad*, how does he respond to this proof? He maintains that the right hand **is called "his right hand [*yad yemino*],"** but it **is not called a** ***yad*** **without** further **specification.**

רַבִּי נָתָן אוֹמֵר: אֵינוֹ צָרִיךְ, הֲרֵי הוּא אוֹמֵר: ״וּקְשַׁרְתָּם...וּכְתַבְתָּם״, מַה כְּתִיבָה בְּיָמִין – אַף קְשִׁירָה בְּיָמִין, וְכֵיוָן דִּקְשִׁירָה בְּיָמִין – הַנָּחָה בִּשְׂמֹאל הִיא. וְרַבִּי יוֹסֵי הַחוֹרֵם, הַנָּחָה דִּבִשְׂמֹאל מְנָא לֵיהּ? נָפְקָא לֵיהּ מֵהֵיכָא דְּנָפְקָא לֵיהּ לְרַבִּי נָתָן.

Rabbi Natan says: This proof is **not necessary,** as **it says: "And you shall bind them** for a sign upon your arm" (Deuteronomy 6:8), and then it states: **"And you shall write them** upon the doorposts of your house" (Deuteronomy 6:9). This teaches that **just as writing is with** the **right** hand, as most people write with their right hands, **so too,** the **binding** of phylacteries must be performed **with** the **right** hand. **And since binding is with** the **right** hand, this means that **donning is on** the **left** arm, as one cannot bind the phylacteries with the same hand upon which he is donning them. The Gemara asks: **And from where does Rabbi Yosei HaḤorem,** who holds that the right hand is also called *yad* in the Torah, **derive that donning** phylacteries is **on the left** arm? The Gemara answers: **He derives it from where Rabbi Natan derives it.**

רַב אַשִׁי אָמַר: מִ״יָּדְכָה״ כְּתִיב בְּהֵ״י – כֵּהָה. אֲמַר לֵיהּ רַבִּי אַבָּא לְרַב אַשִׁי, וְאֵימָא: יָדְךָ שֶׁבְּכֹחַ! אֲמַר לֵיהּ: מִי כְּתִיב בְּחֵי״ת?

Rav Ashi said: The requirement that phylacteries be donned on the left arm is derived **from** the verse: "It shall be for a sign upon **your arm [*yadkha*]**" (Exodus 13:16), which **is written with** a letter ***heh*** at the end. This is expounded as though it stated: Your **weak [*keha*]** arm.[N] **Rabbi Abba said to Rav Ashi: But** one can **say** that *yadkha* should be interpreted as *yadko'aḥ*, with a letter *ḥet* at the end instead of a *heh*. If so, this would mean: **Your arm that is of strength [*shebeko'aḥ*],** which is the right arm. Rav Ashi **said to** Rabbi Abba: **Is** this word **written with a** ***ḥet*****?**

כְּתַנָּאֵי: ״יָדְכָה״ בְּהֵ״י – זוֹ שְׂמֹאל; אֲחֵרִים אוֹמְרִים: ״יָדְךָ״ – לְרַבּוֹת אֶת הַגִּידֵּם. תַּנְיָא אִידָךְ: אֵין לוֹ זְרוֹעַ – פָּטוּר מִן הַתְּפִילִּין; אֲחֵרִים אוֹמְרִים: ״יָדְכָה״ – לְרַבּוֹת אֶת הַגִּידֵּם.

The Gemara notes that Rav Ashi's opinion, that the *halakha* that phylacteries are donned on the left arm is derived from the term *yadkha*, is **subject to** a dispute between ***tanna'im*****,** as it is taught in a *baraita*: ***Yadkha*** is written **with a** ***heh*****,** indicating weakness, and **this** is referring to the **left** arm. **Others say: "Your arm,"** i.e., *yadkha,* serves **to include one without** a complete **arm,**[HN] i.e., one whose arm ends at the elbow, in the obligation to don phylacteries, as the remaining part is also categorized as a weak arm. **It is taught** in **another** *baraita*: If one **does not have** a left **arm,**[N] i.e., not even above the elbow, he is **exempt from the** mitzva of **phylacteries. Others say:** ***Yadkha*** serves **to include one without** a left **arm** even above the elbow, teaching that he must don phylacteries on his right arm.

NOTES

From your arm [*yadkha*] which is written with a *heh* as though it stated: Your weak [*keha*] arm – מִיָּדְכָה כְּתִיב בְּהֵ״י כֵּהָה: According to the alternative interpretation cited by Rashi, the letter *heh* at the end of the word, which is generally indicative of the feminine form, teaches that one must don phylacteries on the weaker hand. If so, Rav Ashi mentions weak in order to explain the result of this derivation, that the feminine *heh* is referring to the weaker hand. For a similar example of a word derived as in the feminine form, see *Berakhot* 32a.

Your arm [*yadkha*] serves to include one without a complete arm – יָדְךָ לְרַבּוֹת אֶת הַגִּידֵּם: Although the standard version of the text has *yadkha* without the letter *heh*, virtually all the commentaries concur that the correct reading is *yadkha* with a *heh*. Accordingly, the opinion cited in the name of: Others say, also expounds *yadkha* as weak [*keha*]. Yet, since that opinion derives the requirement to don phylacteries on the left arm from one of the other sources stated earlier, e.g., from the verses that state: "And you shall bind them…and you shall write them," it explains that *yadkha* refers to one without hands, i.e., his left hand is crushed and atrophied, but his upper arm, upon which the phylacteries are placed, is intact (*Or Zarua*, citing Rabbeinu Elyakim; see Rashi).

If one does not have a left arm, etc. – אֵין לוֹ זְרוֹעַ וכו׳: It would appear that both opinions are discussing the same case, that of one who does not have a left arm. If so, the first *tanna* holds that one who is missing his arm above the elbow, the bicep, is entirely exempt from donning phylacteries of the arm, whereas the opinion cited in the name of: Others say, is that he dons the phylacteries on his right arm or on his left shoulder (Rid). Other early commentaries contend that when the first *tanna* mentions a left arm, he is referring to the lower arm. According to this interpretation, this *tanna* is of the opinion that even one who has a bicep is exempt from phylacteries, as he does not have a whole arm, whereas the opinion cited in the name of: Others say, is that one dons it on the bicep (*Or Zarua*, citing Rabbeinu Elyakim).

תָּנוּ רַבָּנַן: אִטֵּר מַנִּיחַ תְּפִילִּין בִּימִינוֹ שֶׁהוּא שְׂמֹאלוֹ. וְהָתַנְיָא: מַנִּיחַ בִּשְׂמֹאלוֹ שֶׁהוּא שְׂמֹאלוֹ שֶׁל כׇּל אָדָם! אָמַר אַבָּיֵי: כִּי תַּנְיָא הַהִיא – בְּשׁוֹלֵט בִּשְׁתֵּי יָדָיו.

The Sages taught in a *baraita*: **A left-handed person**[H] **dons phylacteries on his right** arm, **which is** equivalent to **his left** arm, i.e., his weaker arm. The Gemara raises a difficulty: **But isn't it taught** in a *baraita* that a left-handed person **dons** phylacteries **on his left** arm, **which is the left** arm **of every** other **person? Abaye said: When that** *baraita* **is taught,** it is referring **to one who has** equal **control with both his hands,**[H] i.e., an ambidextrous person. Since such an individual also uses his right hand, he dons phylacteries on his left arm.

תָּנָא דְּבֵי מְנַשֶּׁה: "עַל יָדֶךָ" – זוֹ קִיבּוֹרֶת, "בֵּין עֵינֶיךָ" – זוֹ קׇדְקֹד. הֵיכָא? אָמְרִי דְּבֵי רַבִּי יַנַּאי: מְקוֹם שֶׁמּוֹחוֹ שֶׁל תִּינוֹק רוֹפֵס.

The school of Menashe taught with regard to the verse: "And you shall bind them for a sign on your arm, and they shall be as frontlets between your eyes" (Deuteronomy 6:8): **"On your arm"; this** is the **bicep.**[BH] **"Between your eyes"; this** is the **crown** of the head.[H] The Gemara asks: **Where** exactly on the crown of the head are the phylacteries placed? **The school of Rabbi Yannai say:** Phylacteries are placed on the **place where** the bone above **the baby's brain is soft** after birth.[BN]

בְּעָא מִינֵּיהּ פְּלִימוֹ מֵרַבִּי: מִי שֶׁיֵּשׁ לוֹ שְׁנֵי רָאשִׁים, בְּאֵיזֶה מֵהֶן מַנִּיחַ תְּפִילִּין? אֲמַר לֵיהּ: אוֹ קוּם גְּלֵי אוֹ קַבֵּל עֲלָךְ שַׁמְתָּא. אַדְּהָכִי אֲתָא הָהוּא גַּבְרָא, אֲמַר לֵיהּ: אִיתְיְלִיד לִי יָנוּקָא דְּאִית לֵיהּ תְּרֵי רֵישֵׁי, כַּמָּה בָּעֵינַן לְמֵיתַב לְכֹהֵן? אֲתָא הָהוּא סָבָא תְּנָא לֵיהּ: חַיָּיב לִיתֵּן לוֹ עֲשָׂרָה סְלָעִים.

§ The Sage **Peleimu**[LP] **raised a dilemma before Rabbi** Yehuda HaNasi: In the case of **one who has two heads, on which of them does he don phylacteries?** Rabbi Yehuda HaNasi **said to him: Either get up** and **exile** yourself[N] from here **or accept upon yourself excommunication** for asking such a ridiculous question. **In the meantime, a certain man arrived** and said to Rabbi Yehuda HaNasi: A firstborn **child has been born to me who has two heads.**[BH] **How much** money **must I give to the priest** for the redemption of the firstborn? **A certain elder came** and **taught him: You are obligated to give him ten** ***sela*****,** the requisite five for each head.

HALAKHA

Left-handed person – אִטֵּר: If a left-handed person performs all activities primarily with his left hand, he should don phylacteries on his right arm. If he writes with his right hand but performs all other activities with his left, or writes with his left but performs all other activities with his right, some say that he should don phylacteries on his physically weaker arm, in accordance with the derivation of Rav Ashi. Others maintain that the hand with which he writes is considered his right hand for the purposes of this *halakha*, in accordance with Rabbi Natan's derivation based on the comparison of writing to binding, and therefore he dons phylacteries on the other arm (Rambam *Sefer Ahava, Hilkhot Tefillin UMezuza VeSefer Torah* 4:3; *Shulḥan Arukh, Oraḥ Ḥayyim* 27:6).

To one who has equal control with both his hands – בְּשׁוֹלֵט בִּשְׁתֵּי יָדָיו: An ambidextrous person dons phylacteries on the left arm, like most people. The *halakha* is in accordance with the ruling of the *baraita*, as explained by Abaye (Rambam *Sefer Ahava, Hilkhot Tefillin UMezuza VeSefer Torah* 4:3; *Shulḥan Arukh, Oraḥ Ḥayyim* 27:6).

This is the bicep – זוֹ קִיבּוֹרֶת: The proper place for the donning of the phylacteries of the arm is the bicep of the left arm. The *halakha* is in accordance with the ruling of the school of Menashe. The commentaries write that one should don the phylacteries on the half of the bicep nearer to the elbow, not on the half nearer to the armpit (Rambam *Sefer Ahava, Hilkhot Tefillin UMezuza VeSefer Torah* 4:2; *Shulḥan Arukh, Oraḥ Ḥayyim* 27:1, and see the comment of Rema and *Beur Halakha* there).

This is the crown of the head – זוֹ קׇדְקֹד: The proper place for the phylacteries of the head is the crown, i.e., from the beginning of one's original hairline on the forehead to the end of the place where a baby's head is soft after birth. The *halakha* is in accordance with the ruling of the school of Menashe and the school of Rabbi Yannai (Rambam *Sefer Ahava, Hilkhot Tefillin UMezuza VeSefer Torah* 4:1; *Shulḥan Arukh, Oraḥ Ḥayyim* 27:9).

A child has been born to me who has two heads – אִיתְיְלִיד לִי יָנוּקָא דְּאִית לֵיהּ תְּרֵי רֵישֵׁי: For a firstborn male who has two heads, one must give ten *sela* to a priest for the redemption of the firstborn. This *halakha* is in accordance with the answer of the elder in the story in the Gemara. The Rambam and the *Shulḥan Arukh* do not cite this *halakha*, as they maintain that this child is a *tereifa* (*Tur, Yoreh De'a* 305, and see *Arukh HaShulḥan* there).

NOTES

The place where the baby's brain is soft after birth – מְקוֹם שֶׁמּוֹחוֹ שֶׁל תִּינוֹק רוֹפֵס: This does not mean that one must put the phylacteries on that specific place. Rather, one can position them from his original hairline, as explained on the following *amud*, until the spot where a baby's head is soft after birth. It is likewise stated in tractate *Eiruvin* (95b) that there is enough space on the head for two phylacteries. From that point to behind the head is not considered "between your eyes," nor is it the upper part of the head (*Sefer HaTeruma*).

Get up and exile yourself – קוּם גְּלֵי: In other words, find a place where such creatures exist and ask your question there (*Keren Ora*; see *Tosafot* and *Tzon Kodashim*). Elsewhere the Talmud teaches that if a Torah scholar is accused of belittling Sages or their statements he would not be fully excommunicated or ostracized, as these penalties have defined and severe halakhic ramifications. The Sages would refrain from excommunicating Torah scholars (*Moed Katan* 17a). Instead, they would remove the offending scholar from the study hall (see, e.g., *Horayot* 13b with regard to Rabbi Yehuda HaNasi's father, and *Bava Batra* 23b). Accordingly, Rabbi Yehuda HaNasi is telling Peleimu that he must either exile himself from the study hall or accept excommunication.

BACKGROUND

Bicep – קִיבּוֹרֶת:

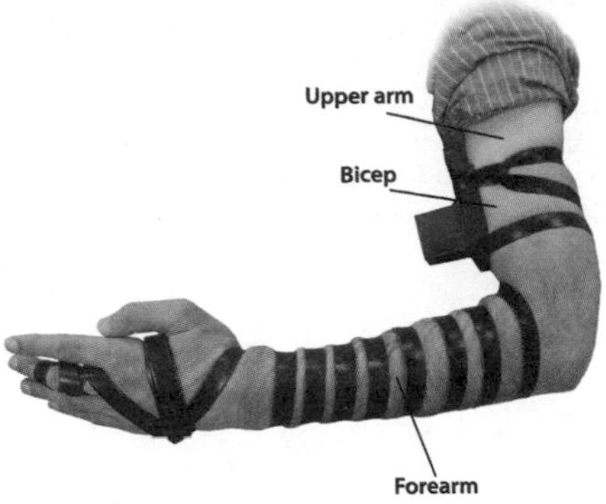

Placement of the phylacteries on the arm

The place where the baby's brain is soft after birth – מְקוֹם שֶׁמּוֹחוֹ שֶׁל תִּינוֹק רוֹפֵס: The skull consists of several bones, joined by sutures. The two meeting points of these sutures, called fontanels or soft spots, are open during the early stages of life, which means that the brain is not covered by bone. This enables quicker growth of the skull. The place mentioned here as where a baby's head is soft refers to the anterior fontanel, which closes when the child is roughly one and a half years old.

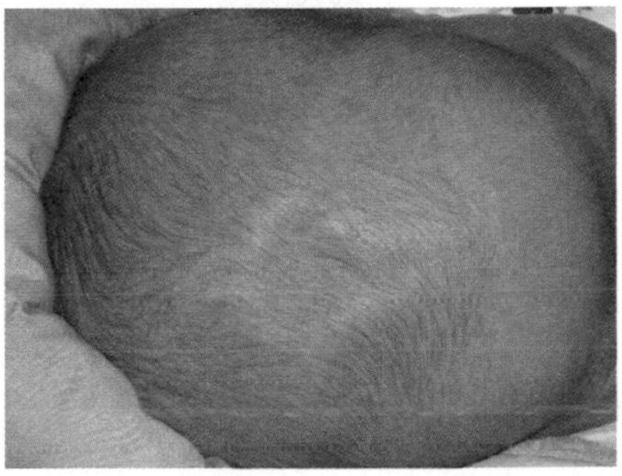

Soft impression at the anterior fontanel

One who has two heads – מִי שֶׁיֵּשׁ לוֹ שְׁנֵי רָאשִׁים: This rare phenomenon of one who is born with two heads, both in the case of humans and animals, has been attested to throughout history from ancient times. In most, though not all, cases, these beings die shortly after birth.

One with two heads can be a set of conjoined twins, one of whom lacks many body parts. Alternatively, it can be an instance of recorded cases of double limbs found in one body; this is how the commentaries in the main treat the case described here.

LANGUAGE

Peleimu – פְּלִימוֹ: Apparently from the Greek Παλαίμων, *palaimon*, from the root παλαιός, *palaios*, meaning old in years. Similar names are used in various Jewish ethnicities as a sign for good luck. In the Jerusalem Talmud, this Sage is called Panimon.

PERSONALITIES

Peleimu – פְּלִימוֹ: The Sage Peleimu was one of the foremost students of Rabbi Yehuda HaNasi. He is frequently cited as asking Rabbi Yehuda HaNasi sharp questions related to *halakha*. Some of his *halakhot* are mentioned in *baraitot*, where he often disagrees with Rabbi Yehuda HaNasi's colleague, Rabbi Elazar, son of Rabbi Shimon. There are also several incidents related about his righteousness.

אינִי? והתני רמי בר חמא: מתוך שנאמר "פדה תפדה את בכור האדם", שומע אני אפילו נטרף בתוך שלשים? תלמוד לומר:

The Gemara asks: **Is that so? But Rami bar Ḥama teaches: Since it is stated** with regard to the redemption of the firstborn: **"The firstborn of man you shall redeem"** (Numbers 18:15), **I would derive** that **even if he was ravaged,**[N] e.g., by an animal, **within thirty** days of his birth,[H] one should redeem him. To counter this, **the verse states:**

HALAKHA

Ravaged by an animal within thirty days of his birth – **נטרף בתוך שלשים**: A father is not required to redeem his male firstborn child if he died or was mortally wounded within thirty days of his birth, including on the thirtieth day itself. Even if the father had already given the redemption money to a priest, the priest should return it to him (Rambam *Sefer Zera'im, Hilkhot Bikkurim* 11:7; *Shulḥan Arukh, Yoreh De'a* 305:12).

NOTES

I would derive that even if he was ravaged [*nitraf*] – **שומע אני אפילו נטרף**: Rashi explains that the baby died during the first thirty days of its life even though it was considered to be fully viable. Other early commentaries explain that the Gemara's term *nitraf* means: Became a *tereifa*, i.e., it developed a fatal condition during its first thirty days that will certainly lead to its eventual death. In such a case, even if the child lives beyond thirty days there is no obligation to redeem it, as it is not considered to be viable (Rabbeinu Tam; see *Tosafot*).

Perek **III**
Daf **37** Amud **b**

"אך" חלק! שאני הכא, דבגולגולת תלא רחמנא.

"Yet the firstborn of man you shall redeem"; the addition of the word "yet" serves to **differentiate** and teach that there is a firstborn who is not redeemed, namely, one that was ravaged. A child with two heads is like one that was ravaged, as he will certainly not live. The Gemara answers: **Here it is different, as the Merciful One makes** the redemption of the firstborn **dependent on** his **skull,**[N] as it is stated: "You shall take five shekels apiece, by the skull" (Numbers 3:47), which indicates that there is a case in which a firstborn with more than one skull must be redeemed.

אמר מר: "ידך" – זו קיבורת. מנלן? דתנו רבנן: "על ידך" – זו גובה שביד; אתה אומר: זו גובה שביד, או אינו אלא על ידך ממש? אמרה תורה: הנח תפילין ביד והנח תפילין בראש, מה להלן בגובה שבראש – אף כאן בגובה שביד.

The Gemara returns to its discussion of the *baraita*: **The Master says: "On your arm"; this** is the **bicep.** The term *yad* can mean either hand or arm. Therefore, the Gemara asks: **From where do** we derive this? **As the Sages taught: "On your arm [*yadkha*]"; this** is the **upper** part **of the arm. Do you say** that **this** is the **upper** part **of the arm, or is it only literally on your** actual **hand,**[B] i.e., on the palm of the hand? **The Torah says: Don phylacteries on the** ***yad*** **and don phylacteries on the head; just as there,** with regard to the head, it means **on the upper** part **of the head,** as will be explained, **so too here,** it means **on the upper** part **of the arm.**

רבי אליעזר אומר: אינו צריך, הרי הוא אומר: "והיה לך לאות" – לך לאות, ולא לאחרים לאות. רבי יצחק אומר: אינו צריך, הרי הוא אומר: "ושמתם את דברי אלה על לבבכם...וקשרתם" – שתהא שימה כנגד הלב.

Rabbi Eliezer says: This proof is **not necessary, as** the verse **states: "And it shall be for a sign for you** upon your arm" (Exodus 13:9), which teaches: It shall be **a sign for you, but not a sign for others,**[H] i.e., one must don the phylacteries of the arm in a place where they are not seen by others. This is the arm, which is usually covered, whereas the hand is usually visible. **Rabbi Yitzḥak says:** This proof is **not necessary, as** the verse **states: "Therefore you shall place these words in your heart** and in your soul, **and you shall bind them"** (Deuteronomy 11:18). This teaches **that placing** the words, i.e., donning the phylacteries, **shall be opposite the heart,**[H] on the bicep.

רבי חייא ורב אחא בריה דרב אויא מכוין ומנח ליה להדי ליביה. רב אשי הוה יתיב קמיה דאמימר, הוה צירייא בידיה וקא מתחזיין תפילין, אמר ליה, לא סבר לה מר: לך לאות – ולא לאחרים לאות? אמר ליה: במקום לך לאות איתמר.

The Gemara relates: **Rabbi Ḥiyya and Rav Aḥa, son of Rav Avya,** would **direct** the placement of his phylacteries of the arm **and don** them **opposite his heart. Rav Ashi was sitting before Ameimar,** and **there was a cut in** the sleeve covering Ameimar's **arm, and** as a result his **phylacteries were visible,** as they were not covered by a garment. Rav Ashi **said to** Ameimar: **Doesn't the Master hold** that the phylacteries shall be **a sign for you but not a sign for others?** Ameimar **said to him:** This does not mean that phylacteries must be hidden; rather, this **was stated** in order to teach that they must be donned **in a place** that is **a sign for you,** i.e., the bicep, which is generally not seen, but it does not matter if in practice the phylacteries are visible.

NOTES

Here it is different as the Merciful One makes the redemption of the firstborn dependent on his skull – **שאני הכא דבגולגולת תלא רחמנא**: In other words, the verse: "You shall take five shekels apiece, by the skull" (Numbers 3:47), indicates that it is possible for a child to have more than one skull that requires redemption. As for the exclusion of the term "yet," this does not apply to a child with two heads, as he is currently living (Rashi). According to the opinion of Rabbeinu Tam that a child with two heads is a *tereifa*, the commentaries explain that it is a Torah edict that the obligation of redemption applies to this child despite the fact that it is a *tereifa* (*Tohorat HaKodesh*).

BACKGROUND

Or is it only literally on your actual hand – **או אינו אלא על ידך ממש**: The mishna in tractate *Megilla* (24b) indicates that this is not a mere theoretical suggestion, as there was a known custom of donning the phylacteries of the head on the forehead and the phylacteries of the arm on the palm of the hand. The mishna calls this practice the way of the heretics, in reference to the practices of certain sects at the end of the Second Temple period and onward. These sects, whose customs diverged to varying extents from the ways of the Sages, may have included the early Christians.

HALAKHA

A sign for you but not a sign for others – **לך לאות ולא לאחרים לאות**: One does not need to be particular about whether the phylacteries of the arm are visible or covered, in accordance with the opinion of Ameimar. Nevertheless, one should cover them *ab initio*. By contrast, the phylacteries of the head should be clearly visible, although one who covers them has fulfilled the mitzva after the fact (*Mishna Berura*). The Ari maintains that it is proper to cover the phylacteries of the head as well (*Shulḥan Arukh, Oraḥ Ḥayyim* 27:11, and in the comment of Rema).

Placing the words shall be opposite the heart – **שימה כנגד הלב**: When donning the phylacteries of the arm, one tilts them slightly inward toward the body, so that when he bends his arm downward the phylacteries are opposite his heart, in fulfillment of the verse (Deuteronomy 6:6): "And these words, which I command you this day, shall be upon your heart" (Rambam *Sefer Ahava, Hilkhot Tefillin UMezuza VeSefer Torah* 4:2; *Shulḥan Arukh, Oraḥ Ḥayyim* 27:1).

גּוֹבַהּ שֶׁבָּרֹאשׁ מְנָלַן? דְּתָנוּ רַבָּנַן: "בֵּין עֵינֶיךָ" – זוֹ גּוֹבַהּ שֶׁבָּרֹאשׁ; אַתָּה אוֹמֵר: זוֹ גּוֹבַהּ שֶׁבָּרֹאשׁ, אוֹ אֵינוֹ אֶלָּא בֵּין עֵינֶיךָ מַמָּשׁ? נֶאֱמַר כָּאן "בֵּין עֵינֶיךָ", וְנֶאֱמַר לְהַלָּן "לֹא תָשִׂימוּ קָרְחָה בֵּין עֵינֵיכֶם לָמֵת", מַה לְהַלָּן בְּגוֹבַהּ שֶׁבָּרֹאשׁ, מָקוֹם שֶׁעוֹשֶׂה קָרְחָה – אַף כָּאן בְּגוֹבַהּ שֶׁל רֹאשׁ, מָקוֹם שֶׁעוֹשֶׂה קָרְחָה.

With regard to the statement of the *baraita* that the phylacteries of the head are donned on the **upper** part **of the head,**[B] the Gemara asks: **From where do we** derive this? **As the Sages taught: "Between your eyes"** (Exodus 13:9); **this is the upper** part **of the head. Do you say** that **this is the upper** part **of the head, or is it only literally between your eyes? It is stated here: "Between your eyes," and it is stated there:** "You shall not cut yourselves, **nor make any baldness between your eyes for the dead"** (Deuteronomy 14:1), **Just as there,** the phrase "between your eyes" is referring to a place **on the upper** part **of the head,** as that is **a place where** one can **render** himself **bald** by removing his hair, **so too,** the place where phylacteries are donned is **on the upper** part **of the head, a place where** one can **render** himself **bald.**

רַבִּי יְהוּדָה אוֹמֵר: אֵינוֹ צָרִיךְ, אָמְרָה תּוֹרָה: הַנַּח תְּפִילִּין בַּיָּד הַנַּח תְּפִילִּין בָּרֹאשׁ, מַה לְהַלָּן בְּמָקוֹם הָרָאוּי לִיטַּמֵּא בְּנֶגַע אֶחָד – אַף כָּאן בְּמָקוֹם הָרָאוּי לִיטַּמֵּא בְּנֶגַע אֶחָד;

Rabbi Yehuda says: This proof is **not necessary,** as **the Torah says: Don phylacteries on the arm** and **don phylacteries on the head. Just as there,** with regard to the phylacteries of the arm, it is referring **to a place which is fit to become ritually impure with** only **one** type of leprous **mark,** that of the skin, **so too here,** with regard to the phylacteries of the head, it is referring **to a place which is fit to become ritually impure with** only **one** type of leprous **mark,** that of a place of hair (see Leviticus 13:29–37).

לְאַפּוּקֵי "בֵּין עֵינֶיךָ", דְּאִיכָּא בָּשָׂר וְשֵׂעָר, דְּאִיכָּא שֵׂעָר לָבָן וְאִיכָּא נָמֵי שֵׂעָר צָהוֹב.

Rabbi Yehuda continues: This serves **to exclude** the area which is literally **"between your eyes," as there is flesh and the hair** of the eyebrows present there, and therefore **there is** a possibility of leprosy through the growth of **a white hair,** which is impure according to the *halakhot* of leprosy of the skin (see Leviticus 13:3), **and there is also** a possibility of leprosy through the growth of **a yellow hair,** which is impure according to the *halakhot* of leprosy of the head or the beard (see Leviticus 13:30).

"אַרְבַּע צִיצִיּוֹת מְעַכְּבוֹת זוֹ אֶת זוֹ, שֶׁאַרְבַּעְתָּן מִצְוָה אַחַת". מַאי בֵּינַיְיהוּ? אֲמַר רַב יוֹסֵף: סָדִין בְּצִיצִית אִיכָּא בֵּינַיְיהוּ.

§ The mishna teaches: With regard to the **four ritual fringes** on a garment, the absence of **each prevents fulfillment of the mitzva with the others, as the four of them** constitute **one mitzva.** Rabbi Yishmael says: The four of them are four discrete mitzvot, and the absence of one does not prevent fulfillment of the rest. The Gemara asks: **What** is the difference **between** the opinions of the first *tanna* and Rabbi Yishmael? **Rav Yosef said:** The difference **between** their opinions **is** with regard to a linen **sheet with** woolen **ritual fringes** that has fewer than four ritual fringes. The first *tanna* maintains that since one is not performing a mitzva, he may not wrap himself in the sheet, due to the prohibition of diverse kinds, i.e., the prohibition against wearing clothing made from a mixture of wool and linen threads. Conversely, Rabbi Yishmael permits one to wrap himself in it, as each ritual fringe is a separate mitzva, and the mitzva of ritual fringes overrides the prohibition against wearing diverse kinds.

רָבָא בַּר אָהִינָא אֲמַר: טַלִּית בַּעֲלַת חָמֵשׁ אִיכָּא בֵּינַיְיהוּ.

Rava bar Ahina said: The difference **between** their opinions **is** with regard to **a cloak with five** corners.[H] It is derived that a cloak of this kind requires ritual fringes (see 43b), but it is unclear whether ritual fringes must be placed on each corner. If each fringe is a discrete mitzva, then the obligation applies to the fifth corner as well, but if it is one mitzva then it applies only to four of the corners of this garment.

רָבִינָא אֲמַר: דְּרַב הוּנָא אִיכָּא בֵּינַיְיהוּ, דְּאָמַר רַב הוּנָא: הַיּוֹצֵא בְּטַלִּית שֶׁאֵינָה מְצוּיֶּיצֶת כְּהִלְכָתָהּ בְּשַׁבָּת – חַיָּיב חַטָּאת.

Ravina said: The difference **between** their opinions **is** with regard to the opinion **of Rav Huna,**[H] **as Rav Huna says: One who goes out** unwittingly to the public domain **on Shabbat with** a four-cornered **cloak that does not have** all of **the requisite ritual fringes** attached to its corners is **liable** to bring **a sin offering,** because the remaining fringes are not an integral part of the garment. Since they do not enable the wearer to fulfill the mitzva, they are considered a burden, which may not be carried into the public domain on Shabbat. The first *tanna* agrees with this ruling, whereas Rabbi Yishmael maintains that since each corner with ritual fringes is the fulfillment of a mitzva, one is not liable to bring a sin offering due to carrying on Shabbat for wearing it into the public domain.

BACKGROUND

On the upper part of the head – גּוֹבַהּ שֶׁבָּרֹאשׁ:

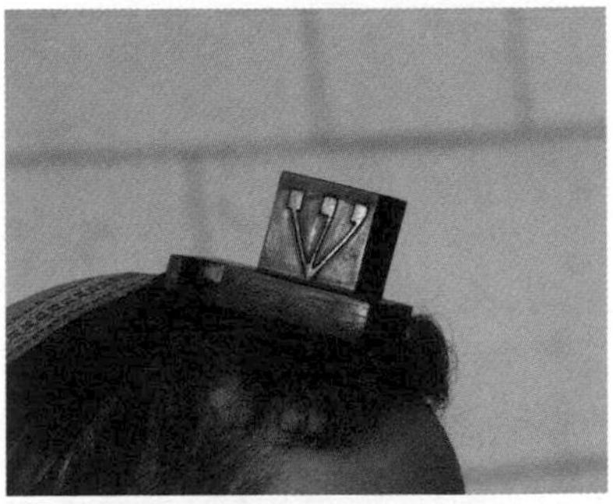

Placement of the phylacteries on the head

HALAKHA

The difference between their opinions is with regard to a cloak with five corners – טַלִּית בַּעֲלַת חָמֵשׁ אִיכָּא בֵּינַיְיהוּ: The obligation of ritual fringes applies to a garment that has more than four corners, and one should place four ritual fringes on the four most distant corners. The *halakha* is in accordance with the opinion of the first *tanna*, as explained by Rava bar Ahina (Rambam *Sefer Ahava*, *Hilkhot Tzitzit* 3:3, and see *Kesef Mishne* there; *Shulḥan Arukh*, *Oraḥ Ḥayyim* 10:1, and see *Beur HaGra* there).

The difference between their opinions is with regard to the opinion of Rav Huna – דְּרַב הוּנָא אִיכָּא בֵּינַיְיהוּ: The absence of any of the four ritual fringes on a garment prevents fulfillment of the mitzva with the others. Therefore, one who wears a garment with fewer than four ritual fringes and walks into the public domain on Shabbat is liable to bring a sin offering for carrying a burden into the public domain on Shabbat. The reason for this ruling is that the fringes are not considered part of the garment because they were not affixed in accordance with *halakha*, and the owner does not intend to discard them as he wishes to complete the number of ritual fringes in order to fulfill the mitzva. This ruling is in accordance with the opinion of the first *tanna*, as explained by Rava (Rambam *Sefer Zemanim*, *Hilkhot Shabbat* 19:20; *Shulḥan Arukh*, *Oraḥ Ḥayyim* 13:1; 301:38).

HALAKHA

Who cuts the corner of his garment – דְּבַצְרֵיהּ לִגְלִימֵיהּ: If one had a garment of four corners and he cut one of them diagonally so that it formed two corners, it is considered a garment with five corners, to which the obligation of ritual fringes applies. This *halakha* is in accordance with the opinion of Rav Sheisha, son of Rav Idi (Rambam *Sefer Ahava, Hilkhot Tzitzit* 3:3; *Shulḥan Arukh, Oraḥ Ḥayyim* 10:2).

Who ties his garment…who sews his garment – דְּצַיְירֵיהּ לִגְלִימֵיהּ...דְּחַיְיטֵיהּ לִגְלִימֵיהּ: If one folded the corners of his robe and then tied or sewed them, so that it appears as though he cut them off and it has no corners, the obligation of ritual fringes nevertheless applies to this garment, in accordance with the opinions of Rav Mesharshiyya and Rav Dimi of Neharde'a (*Shulḥan Arukh, Oraḥ Ḥayyim* 10:3).

NOTES

Who cuts the corner of his garment – דְּבַצְרֵיהּ לִגְלִימֵיהּ: Rashi explains that he damaged the corner of the garment so that it appeared to have two corners. Alternatively, he cut the corner diagonally (*Shita Mekubbetzet*, citing Rashi), in an effort to have a garment of only three corners, which would be exempt from ritual fringes (Rid).

Who ties his garment – דְּצַיְירֵיהּ לִגְלִימֵיהּ: Rashi explains that one folded his garment in two and tied the ends, thereby creating two corners at the fold. Rav Mesharshiyya is saying that if he places ritual fringes on the place of the folds he has not fulfilled the mitzva, as these are not considered the corners of the garment, because the knot will be untied. On the following *amud*, Rashi suggests an alternative interpretation: One made a knot in each of the corners of the garment so that it would not have corners at all and would therefore be exempt from the mitzva of ritual fringes.

Who sews his garment – דְּחַיְיטֵיהּ לִגְלִימֵיהּ: As in the previous case, here too Rashi explains that one folded his robe and sewed it up. If so, the novelty of the statement of Rav Dimi of Neharde'a is that the same *halakha* applies to sewing as to tying a knot. Nevertheless, as a *baraita* cited on 41a explicitly states that this is not the *halakha*, Rashi on the following *amud* rejects this interpretation. Instead, he states that this man folded over the four corners and sewed them up, in order to exempt the garment from the mitzva of ritual fringes.

אָמַר רַב שֵׁישָׁא בְּרֵיהּ דְּרַב אִידִי: הַאי מַאן דְּבַצְרֵיהּ לִגְלִימֵיהּ – לָא עֲבֵיד וְלָא כְלוּם, שַׁוְיֵיהּ טַלִּית בַּעֲלַת חָמֵשׁ.

Rav Sheisha, son of Rav Idi, said: One who cuts the corner of **his garment**[HNB] **has not done anything** of consequence with regard to exempting the garment from the obligation of ritual fringes, as **he has rendered it a cloak with five** corners, to which the obligation of ritual fringes applies.

אָמַר רַב מְשַׁרְשְׁיָא: הַאי מַאן דְּצַיְירֵיהּ לִגְלִימֵיהּ – לָא עֲבַד וְלָא כְלוּם; מַאי טַעְמָא? דִּכְמַאן דְּשַׁרְיֵיהּ דָּמֵי, וּתְנַן נַמִי: כׇּל חֵמָתוֹת הַצְּרוּרוֹת טְהוֹרוֹת, חוּץ מִשֶּׁל עַרְבִיִּים.

Rav Mesharshiyya similarly **says: One who ties his garment**[NB] **has not done anything** of consequence with regard to exempting the garment from the obligation of ritual fringes. **What is the reason? It is considered as though** the garment is **untied,** since the knot can be loosened at any time. **And we learned likewise** in a mishna (*Kelim* 26:4): **All bound** leather **jugs,**[B] i.e., those whose bottoms are not sewn but tied, **are ritually pure,** i.e., they are not susceptible to ritual impurity. This is because they are not considered receptacles, as these knots will be untied, **except for** leather **jugs of Arabs,** who would tie them with a permanent knot.

אָמַר רַב דִּימִי מִנְּהַרְדְּעָא: הַאי מַאן דְּחַיְיטֵיהּ לִגְלִימֵיהּ – לָא עֲבַד וְלָא כְלוּם, אִם אִיתָא דְּלָא מִיבְּעֵי לֵיהּ, לִיפְסוֹק וְלִישְׁדְּיֵיהּ.

Rav Dimi of Neharde'a similarly **says: One who sews his garment,**[HNB] i.e., he folded over a long garment and sewed the edges together, **has not done anything** of consequence with regard to the obligation of ritual fringes, and he must place ritual fringes on the original corners. The reason is that **if it is so that he does not need** the folded part, which is why he is sewing it, **let him cut** it **and throw it** away.

BACKGROUND

Who cuts the corner of his garment – דְּבַצְרֵיהּ לִגְלִימֵיהּ:

Cut on the corner of the garment according to Rashi's explanation

Cut on the corner of the garment according to the *Shita Mekubbetzet*, citing Rashi

Jugs – חֵמָתוֹת:

Man carrying jug made from a whole hide

Who ties his garment – דְּצַיְירֵיהּ לִגְלִימֵיהּ:

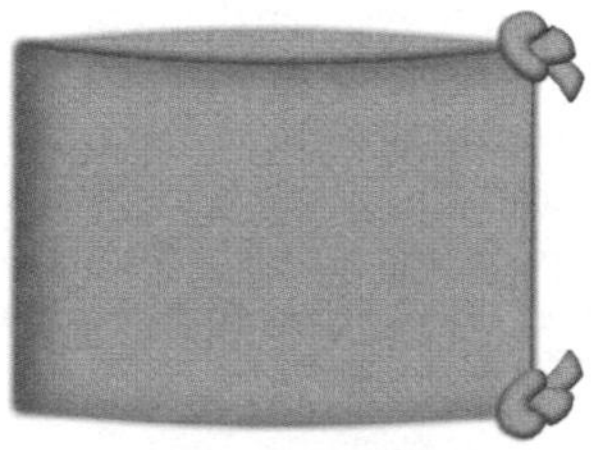

Tying the garment according to Rashi's first explanation

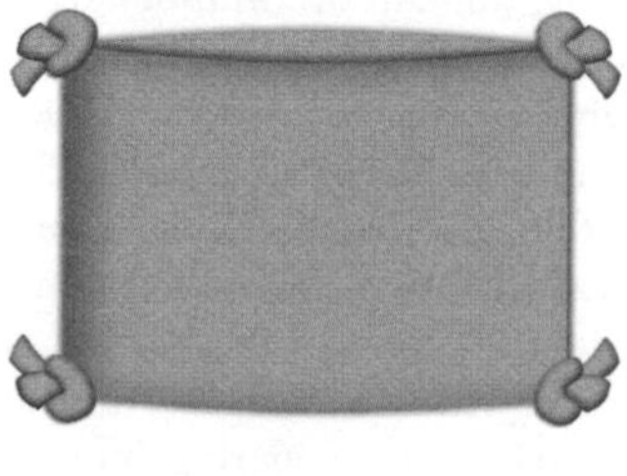

Tying the garment according to Rashi's second explanation

Who sews his garment – דְּחַיְיטֵיהּ לִגְלִימֵיהּ:

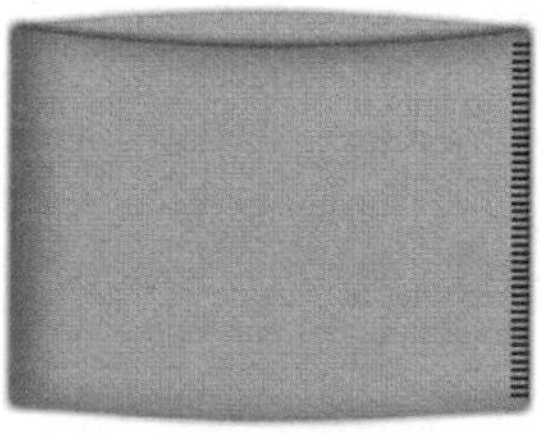

Sewing the garment according to Rashi's first explanation

Sewing the garment according to Rashi's second explanation

"רַבִּי יִשְׁמָעֵאל אוֹמֵר: אַרְבַּעְתָּן אַרְבַּע מִצְוֹת". אָמַר רַב יְהוּדָה אָמַר שְׁמוּאֵל: הֲלָכָה כְּרַבִּי יִשְׁמָעֵאל. וְלֵית הִלְכְתָא כְּוָתֵיהּ.

§ The mishna teaches that **Rabbi Yishmael says: The four of them are four** discrete **mitzvot,** and the absence of one does not prevent fulfillment of the rest. **Rav Yehuda says that Shmuel says:** The ***halakha*** **is in accordance with** the opinion of **Rabbi Yishmael.** The Gemara states: **But the *halakha* is not in accordance with his** opinion.

רָבִינָא הֲוָה קָא אָזֵיל אֲבַתְרֵיהּ דְּמָר בַּר רַב אַשִׁי בְּשַׁבַּתָּא דְּרִיגְלָא, אִיפְסִיק קַרְנָא דְּחוּטֵיהּ וְלָא אֲמַר לֵיהּ וְלָא מִידֵּי; כִּד מְטָא לְבֵיתֵיהּ, אֲמַר לֵיהּ: מֵהָתָם אִיפְסִיק. אֲמַר לֵיהּ: אִי אֲמַרְתְּ לִי, מֵהָתָם שְׁדִיתֵיהּ.

The Gemara relates: **Ravina was walking behind Mar bar Rav Ashi on the Shabbat of the Festival**[B] when **the corner** of Mar bar Rav Ashi's garment **on which his ritual fringes** were hanging **tore, and** yet Ravina **did not say anything to him. When he arrived at** Mar bar Rav Ashi's **house,** Ravina **said to him: Back there,** along the way, the corner **tore.** Mar bar Rav Ashi **said to him: If you would have told me** then, **I would have thrown off** the garment **there,** as once one of the ritual fringes is torn no mitzva is performed with the rest, and it is prohibited to walk in the public domain on Shabbat wearing such a garment. This is in accordance with the opinion of the first *tanna*, who disagrees with the ruling of Rabbi Yishmael.

וְהָא אָמַר מָר: גָּדוֹל כְּבוֹד הַבְּרִיּוֹת שֶׁדּוֹחֶה אֶת לֹא תַעֲשֶׂה שֶׁבַּתּוֹרָה!

The Gemara raises a difficulty: **But didn't the Master say: Great is human dignity, as it overrides a prohibition in the Torah?** This includes the prohibition against carrying on Shabbat in the public domain. That being the case, why would he remove his garment in public?

תַּרְגּוּמָה רַב בַּר שַׁבָּא קַמֵּיהּ דְּרַב כָּהֲנָא:

The Gemara answers: **Rav bar Shabba interpreted** that statement **before Rav Kahana:**

BACKGROUND

Shabbat of the Festival – שַׁבַּתָּא דְּרִיגְלָא: Normally, the Sages would lecture only before the students of their academies. The public lectures during the months of Adar and Elul, called the *yarḥei kalla*, were designed for Torah scholars who had come from afar. *Shabbatot* of Festivals were different, as the entire community would gather to hear lectures about the *halakhot* of the Festival from the foremost scholars of the academies, or from the Exilarch. Therefore, a great mass of people assembled on these special *Shabbatot*, and the lectures were exceptionally crowded. These *Shabbatot* were the Shabbat before the Festival or the Shabbat during Festival (see *Sukka* 26a). Several incidents are related in the Talmud with regard to the behavior of the Sages during these events.

בְּלָאו דְּ"לֹא תָסוּר".

He stated this **with regard to the prohibition of:** "**You shall not deviate** to the left or the right of that which they tell you" (Deuteronomy 17:11). A prohibition by rabbinic law is overridden by human dignity, but not a prohibition by Torah law. Therefore, Mar bar Rav Ashi would have removed his garment had he known about the tear.

וְאִיכָּא דְּאָמְרִי: מֵהָתָם אֲמַר לֵיהּ, וַאֲמַר לֵיהּ: מַאי דַּעְתִּיךְ, לְמִישְׁדְּיֵיהּ? וְהָאָמַר מָר: גָּדוֹל כְּבוֹד הַבְּרִיּוֹת שֶׁדּוֹחֶה אֶת לֹא תַעֲשֶׂה שֶׁבַּתּוֹרָה! וְהָא תַּרְגּוּמָה רַב בַּר שַׁבָּא קַמֵּיהּ דְּרַב כָּהֲנָא: בְּלָאו דְּ"לֹא תָסוּר"! הָכָא נַמִי כַּרְמְלִית דְּרַבָּנַן הִיא.

And there are those **who say** there is a different version of this discussion: It was **when** they were **there,** in the place where the corner of Mar bar Rav Ashi's garment tore, that Ravina **said to him** that it had torn, **and** Mar bar Rav Ashi **said to him** in response: **What is your opinion?** Do you think **that I should throw** the garment off? **But doesn't the Master say: Great is human dignity, as it overrides a prohibition in the Torah?** The Gemara raises a difficulty: **But Rav bar Shabba interpreted** that statement **before Rav Kahana:** He stated this **with regard to the prohibition of: "You shall not deviate,"** not the prohibition against carrying in the public domain, which applies by Torah law. The Gemara answers that **here too,** it is not a prohibition by Torah law, as the place where they were walking was not a full-fledged public domain but **a *karmelit*,** in which carrying **is** prohibited **by rabbinic law.**[NH]

הדרן עלך הקומץ

NOTES

Here too it was a *karmelit*, in which carrying is prohibited by rabbinic law – הָכָא נַמִי כַּרְמְלִית דְּרַבָּנַן הִיא: By Torah law, there are two domains with regard to which one may not move items from one to the other on Shabbat: The public domain and the private domain. Likewise, it is prohibited to carry an item four cubits in the public domain. Both of these domains are precisely defined. The Sages established that any place which is not traversed by the public and yet is not a private domain either is considered a separate domain, called a *karmelit*. It is prohibited by rabbinic law to move articles to or from a public or private domain to this domain, nor may one carry in this domain itself.

HALAKHA

A *karmelit*, in which carrying is prohibited by rabbinic law – כַּרְמְלִית דְּרַבָּנַן הִיא: One who is walking in the public domain on Shabbat and becomes aware that the ritual fringes of the garment he is wearing have become unfit must remove the garment even if he would be left naked. The reason is that human dignity does not override a prohibition that is by Torah law. With regard to the definition of a public domain, see *Shulḥan Arukh, Oraḥ Ḥayyim* 345:7. If he is in a *karmelit* when he discovers that it has become unfit, he need not remove the garment until he reaches his house, as human dignity overrides a prohibition that is by rabbinic law. The Rema writes that this applies only on Shabbat, when it is prohibited to prepare ritual fringes, and therefore he is not considered to be neglecting the positive mitzva of ritual fringes. On a weekday, by contrast, it is prohibited to continue wearing the garment, as he would thereby be neglecting the performance of a positive mitzva (*Shulḥan Arukh, Oraḥ Ḥayyim* 13:3, and see *Mishna Berura* there).

Summary of **Perek III**

The first and main section of this chapter addressed a number of issues concerning the validity of a meal offering whose rites were not performed in the proper manner and the actions that are indispensable to its sacrifice.

Continuing the discussion of the previous chapters with regard to *piggul*, the Gemara stated that intent to eat or burn a meal offering beyond its designated time disqualifies the offering only if the intent to eat referred to an item whose typical manner is such that one does partake of it, e.g., the remainder of the meal offering, or if the intent to burn referred to an item whose typical manner is such that one does burn it on the altar, e.g., the handful or the frankincense. This intent has no effect if it was intent to burn an item fit for consumption or to eat that which is supposed to be burned, despite the fact that burning on the altar is also called consumption. Furthermore, intentions with regard to quantities one intends to eat and burn improperly do not combine to equal an olive-bulk, the minimum volume to incur liability.

The chapter then addressed the question of which rites of a meal offering are indispensable to its sacrifice. With regard to the mixing of the flour in oil, the breaking into pieces, in the case of those meal offerings which require breaking into pieces, and bringing of the offering to the altar, all these are not indispensable. Conversely, the pouring of oil on the meal offering and its salting before burning, in addition to the rites of the handful itself, i.e., removing the handful, placing the handful in a vessel, conveying the handful to the altar, and burning the handful, are all indispensable. In sum, if a requirement is repeated in the Torah, or if a term of emphasis was stated with regard to it, e.g., the word "statute," it is indispensable to the sacrifice.

In relation to the above, the chapter discussed at length the issue of salting offerings. This includes the question of which offerings require salting, how they are salted, and when it is permitted for priests to use the salt in the Temple for the purpose of eating the offerings.

With regard to the case of mixtures of meal offerings, the Gemara states some novel *halakhot* that apply to mixtures in general, particularly with regard to the definition of the concept of a substance in contact with the same type of substance and a substance in contact with a different type of substance. As far as meal offerings are concerned, the conclusion is that in the case of a mixture of items that are sacrificed on the altar, the different components of the mixture do not nullify one another. Consequently, if handfuls of meal offerings became intermingled, or intermingled with meal offerings that are entirely burned, the whole mixture should be sacrificed upon the altar. Furthermore, if a handful became intermingled with the remainder of a meal offering, which is not sacrificed on the altar, it is not permitted to burn this mixture, but if one nevertheless sacrificed it, the owner has fulfilled his obligation.

In a case of two meal offerings that became intermingled, if one can remove a separate handful from each, they are fit; if not, they are unfit. One may not consecrate a meal offering in two separate vessels; rather, the meal offering must be joined together. Apropos this ruling, the Gemara discussed at length the *halakha* of a vessel that combines all its contents with regard to sacrificial matters despite the fact that the various parts are not in contact with one another.

On the topic of ritual impurity, the Gemara stated that if a handful contracted ritual impurity, it is not permitted to sacrifice it, but if one nevertheless sacrificed it, the owner of the meal offering has fulfilled his obligation. The reason is that the frontplate worn by the High Priest effects acceptance of the meal offering. Despite this, if one intentionally rendered the handful impure, the Sages prohibited the remainder in consumption. If the entire remainder contracted ritual impurity, or if it was burned or lost, one may not sacrifice the handful, as the rite of the handful depends on the existence of the remainder. Some say that in a case where the remainder became impure, the frontplate effects acceptance after the fact. If part of the remainder remains and is valid, one sacrifices the handful *ab initio*.

Another *halakha* established in this chapter is that a meal offering must first be placed in a vessel before the handful is removed, and likewise the handful must be placed in a service vessel and one must sacrifice it in a service vessel. All these requirements are indispensable. It is permitted for the priests to eat the remainder of a meal offering from the time the fire of the altar takes holds of the majority of the handful.

In the second section of the chapter it is stated that the various portions of a meal offering, i.e., the tenth of an ephah of flour, the handful, and the frankincense, invalidate the meal offering if part of one of the elements is lacking, even if most of it is present. Likewise, the absence of any of them prevents fulfillment of the mitzva with the others. Incidental to this *halakha*, the Gemara listed several cases involving offerings and other mitzvot that consist of different parts, either various items or multiple actions, where each of these parts is indispensable to the fulfillment of the mitzva as a whole. In this context, the Candelabrum in the Temple was discussed at length, with regard to both the matters that are indispensable for its construction as well as its form and its various components.

The mitzvot of *mezuza* and phylacteries were also analyzed in this chapter. This is the most comprehensive discussion of these *halakhot* in the Talmud, as there is no tractate devoted to the details of these mitzvot except for minor tractates that are not part of the Mishna and for which there is no Gemara. The issues discussed in this context were the *halakhot* of the Torah passages included in a *mezuza* and phylacteries, the manner of their writing, and the appropriate method for preparing them.

Introduction to **Perek IV**

And the Lord spoke to Moses, saying: Speak to the children of Israel, and command them that they prepare for themselves throughout their generations strings on the corners of their garments, and they shall put on the fringe of the corner a sky-blue thread. And it shall be to you for a fringe, that you may look upon it, and remember all the commandments of the Lord, and do them; and that you go not about after your own heart and your own eyes, after which you use to go astray; that you may remember and do all My mitzvot, and be holy to your God. I am the Lord your God, who brought you out of the land of Egypt, to be your God: I am the Lord your God.

(Numbers 15:37–41)

You shall not wear diverse kinds, wool and linen together. You shall prepare for yourself twisted cords upon the four corners of your covering, with which you cover yourself.

(Deuteronomy 22:11–12)

This is the offering of Aaron and of his sons, which they shall offer to the Lord in the day when he is anointed: The tenth-part of an ephah of fine flour for a meal offering perpetually, half of it in the morning, and half of it in the evening. On a griddle it shall be made with oil; when it is soaked, you shall bring it in; in broken pieces shall you offer the meal offering for a pleasing aroma to the Lord. And the anointed priest that shall be in his stead from among his sons shall offer it, it is a statute forever; it shall be wholly made to smoke to the Lord.

(Leviticus 6:13–15)

This chapter, like the one that precedes it, includes a compilation of *halakhot* pertaining to mitzvot that have multiple components. Chapter Four focuses on components of mitzvot that can function independently, such that the lack of one component does not prevent the fulfillment of the mitzva with another component.

The beginning of the chapter deals with the white and sky-blue strings of ritual fringes, and the phylacteries worn on the arm and head. It goes on to discuss the relationship between offerings sacrificed on the same day, such as the daily offering and the additional offerings. Similarly, it discusses the relationship between the various additional offerings themselves. It also addresses the two loaves, i.e., the communal offering on *Shavuot* of two loaves from the new wheat, and the communal peace offering of two sheep that accompanies the two loaves on *Shavuot*. These loaves and sheep are separate from the additional offering sacrificed on *Shavuot* as on other Festivals.

There is also a similar discussion concerning offerings that are sacrificed in two halves, split between the morning and the afternoon, such as the daily offerings and the incense. Are the two halves considered two components of one mitzva or two independent mitzvot? This leads into a tangential in-depth discussion of the griddle-cake offering of the High Priest, which is also sacrificed half in the morning and half in the afternoon.

מתני׳ הַתְּכֵלֶת אֵינָהּ מְעַכֶּבֶת אֶת הַלָּבָן, וְהַלָּבָן אֵינוֹ מְעַכֵּב אֶת הַתְּכֵלֶת. תְּפִלָּה שֶׁל יָד אֵינָהּ מְעַכֶּבֶת אֶת שֶׁל רֹאשׁ, וְשֶׁל רֹאשׁ אֵינָהּ מְעַכֶּבֶת אֶת שֶׁל יָד.

MISHNA The absence of **the sky-blue [*tekhelet*]**[B] strings **does not prevent** fulfillment of the mitzva[N] of ritual fringes with **the white** strings,[NH] **and the** absence of **white** strings **does not prevent** fulfillment of the mitzva with **the sky-blue** strings. If one has only one, he wears it without the other. Absence of the **phylacteries of** the **arm does not prevent** fulfillment of the mitzva of the phylacteries **of the head,**[NH] **and** absence of the phylacteries **of the head does not prevent** fulfillment of the mitzva of the phylacteries **of the arm.** If one has only one, he dons it without the other.

גמ׳ לֵימָא מַתְנִיתִין דְּלָא כְּרַבִּי; דְּתַנְיָא: "וּרְאִיתֶם אֹתוֹ" – מְלַמֵּד שֶׁמְּעַכְּבִין זֶה אֶת זֶה, דִּבְרֵי רַבִּי, וַחֲכָמִים אוֹמְרִים: אֵין מְעַכְּבִין.

GEMARA The Gemara suggests: **Let us say** that **the mishna is not in accordance with** the opinion of **Rabbi** Yehuda HaNasi. **As it is taught** in a *baraita*: When the verse requires one to place white and sky-blue strings upon the corners of his garments and then states: **"That you may look upon it"** (Numbers 15:39), it **teaches** that the lack of either **one prevents** fulfillment of the mitzva **with the other;** this is **the statement of Rabbi** Yehuda HaNasi. **But the Rabbis say:** The lack of one **does not prevent the** fulfillment of the mitzva with the other.

מַאי טַעְמָא דְּרַבִּי? דִּכְתִיב: "הַכָּנָף" – מִין כָּנָף, וּכְתִיב: "פְּתִיל תְּכֵלֶת", וְאָמַר רַחֲמָנָא: "וּרְאִיתֶם אוֹתוֹ" – עַד דְּאִיכָּא תַּרְוַיְיהוּ בְּחַד.

The Gemara inquires: **What is the reasoning of Rabbi** Yehuda HaNasi, i.e., how does he derive his ruling from this verse? The Gemara explains: **As it is written:** "And they shall put on the fringe of the corner a sky-blue thread" (Numbers 15:38). "The fringe of **the corner"** is a reference to strings that are of the same **type** as the **corner** of the garment. Since garments are usually white, this phrase is referring to white strings. **And it is written** in this same verse: **"A sky-blue thread." And the Merciful One states** in the following verse, referring to both types of strings: "And it shall be to you for a fringe **that you may look upon it"** (Numbers 15:39), in the singular. This teaches that one does not fulfill his obligation **until both** types **are present together.**

NOTES

Does not prevent fulfillment of the mitzva – אֵינָהּ מְעַכֶּבֶת: According to Rashi, this case of ritual fringes is not parallel to the case in the mishna with regard to phylacteries. In the case of phylacteries, one simply dons whichever one of the phylacteries he has and does not don the one he does not have. In the case of ritual fringes, one is always required to insert four strings into the garment. Consequently, if one does not have white or sky-blue strings, one does not insert fewer strings but rather adds to the number of strings of the color that he does have. The language of the Rambam seems to indicate otherwise (see Rambam *Sefer Ahava*, *Hilkhot Tzitzit* 1:4, and *Kesef Mishne* there and on 1:18).

The absence of the sky-blue strings does not prevent fulfillment of the mitzva of ritual fringes with the white strings – הַתְּכֵלֶת אֵינָהּ מְעַכֶּבֶת אֶת הַלָּבָן: The Gemara (41b) concludes that four strings are inserted into a hole near the corner of the garment, so that the strings are doubled over to form eight strings, with which the windings and knots are formed.

Absence of the phylacteries of the arm does not prevent fulfillment of the mitzva of the phylacteries of the head – תְּפִלָּה שֶׁל יָד אֵינָהּ מְעַכֶּבֶת אֶת שֶׁל רֹאשׁ: Despite the implicit comparison between phylacteries and ritual fringes in the mishna, there is a fundamental difference between them. The phylacteries of the head and the arm are donned in two distinct acts and constitute two independent mitzvot. Consequently, a separate blessing is recited for each (see 36b), and the Rambam, in his *Sefer HaMitzvot*, enumerates these obligations as two of the 613 mitzvot. By contrast, although the white and sky-blue strings are not dependent on each other, they are actually two components of the same mitzva, and one fulfills both components simultaneously when he dons the garment (Responsa of the Rivash 137).

HALAKHA

The absence of the sky-blue strings does not prevent fulfillment of the mitzva of ritual fringes with the white strings – הַתְּכֵלֶת אֵינָהּ מְעַכֶּבֶת אֶת הַלָּבָן: The absence of the sky-blue strings in the ritual fringes does not prevent fulfillment of the mitzva with the white strings, and the absence of the white strings does not prevent fulfillment of the mitzva with the sky-blue strings. Consequently, if one does not have sky-blue strings, he fashions his ritual fringes using four white strings. Similarly, if he does not have any white strings, he fashions his ritual fringes using four sky-blue strings. So too, if one had both white and sky-blue strings, but the white strings broke off and only the sky-blue strings remained, they are still fit. This is in accordance with the mishna as interpreted by Rava (Rambam *Sefer Ahava*, *Hilkhot Tzitzit* 1:4; *Arukh HaShulḥan*, *Oraḥ Ḥayyim* 9:3).

Absence of the phylacteries of the arm does not prevent fulfillment of the mitzva of the phylacteries of the head – תְּפִלָּה שֶׁל יָד אֵינָהּ מְעַכֶּבֶת אֶת שֶׁל רֹאשׁ: Absence of the phylacteries of the head does not prevent fulfillment of the mitzva of the phylacteries of the arm, and absence of the phylacteries of the arm does not prevent fulfillment of the mitzva of the phylacteries of the head, since they are two independent mitzvot. Therefore, if an individual has only one of the phylacteries, he wears the one that he has and recites the appropriate blessing (Rambam *Sefer Ahava*, *Hilkhot Tefillin UMezuza VeSefer Torah* 4:4; *Shulḥan Arukh*, *Oraḥ Ḥayyim* 26:1).

BACKGROUND

Sky-blue [*tekhelet*] – תְּכֵלֶת: *Tekhelet* is mentioned numerous times in the Bible and by the Sages. It is not the name of a particular color, as in modern Hebrew usage, but rather refers to wool dyed with a particular substance. Based upon references in the Bible, statements of the Sages, and other sources, it is clear that *tekhelet* was a rare commodity, used primarily as a dye for the clothing of royalty and other extremely prominent individuals.

This dye was prepared from a species known as *ḥilazon* (see 44b). It was produced mostly in the tribal territory of Zebulun, along the northern coast of Eretz Yisrael and up to Tyre, in areas where the *ḥilazon* could be caught. It is known from various sources that the ancient Phoenicians, who lived on the coast of what is today Lebanon, were also involved in the production and sale of *tekhelet*. Archeological discoveries along the coast of Eretz Yisrael have confirmed the existence of the dye industry, including the production of *tekhelet* and the purple dye known as *argaman*.

Over time the production of *tekhelet* dwindled, due both to the lower cost and greater availability of plant-derived alternatives and to various limitations that the Romans and Byzantines attached to the production of *tekhelet*. It continued to be used in ritual fringes during the talmudic era, but by the era of the *ge'onim tekhelet* was no longer available, and the tradition of *tekhelet* was lost.

In recent generations, there has been a renewed effort to identify the *ḥilazon* used for *tekhelet* and to prepare dye for use in ritual fringes. The most widely accepted identification is the *Murex trunculus* snail, and this identification is corroborated by archeological evidence and chemical analysis.

Wool dyed with the secretions of the *Murex trunculus*

וְרַבָּנַן? "וּרְאִיתֶם אוֹתוֹ", כָּל חַד לְחוּדֵיהּ מַשְׁמַע.

The Gemara asks: **And** how do **the Rabbis,** who hold that the one can fulfill one obligation without the other, understand this verse? The Gemara answers: They hold that the phrase **"that you may look upon it" indicates** that one fulfills a mitzva with **each one individually.**

לֵימָא דְּלָא כְּרַבִּי? אֲמַר רַב יְהוּדָה אֲמַר רַב: אֲפִילּוּ תֵּימָא רַבִּי, לָא נִצְרְכָא אֶלָּא לְקַדֵּם;

The Gemara concludes its initial suggestion: **Shall we say that** the mishna, which states that one can fulfill the mitzva with either white or sky-blue strings even in the absence of the other, is **not in accordance with** the opinion of **Rabbi** Yehuda HaNasi? The Gemara responds: **Rav Yehuda said** that **Rav said: You** may **even say** that the mishna is in accordance with the opinion of **Rabbi** Yehuda HaNasi, and the ruling of the mishna **is necessary only with regard to granting precedence.**[NH] The white strings should precede the blue strings, but if the order is reversed, one still fulfills the mitzva.

דְּתַנְיָא: מִצְוָה לְהַקְדִּים לָבָן לַתְּכֵלֶת, וְאִם הִקְדִּים תְּכֵלֶת לַלָּבָן – יָצָא, אֶלָּא שֶׁחִיסֵּר מִצְוָה. מַאי חִיסֵּר מִצְוָה?

This is **as it is taught** in a *baraita*: It is **a mitzva to** insert the **white** strings into the garment **before** inserting **the sky-blue** strings, **but if** one inserted the **sky-blue** strings **before the white** strings, he **fulfilled** his obligation **but omitted** the **mitzva.** The Gemara asks: **What** does the *baraita* mean by the phrase: **Omitted** the **mitzva?**

NOTES

Necessary only with regard to granting precedence – לָא נִצְרְכָא אֶלָּא לְקַדֵּם: Rashi interprets this to mean that one is supposed to insert the white strings into the hole in the garment before inserting the blue string, yet if he inserts the blue string first, he still fulfills the mitzva. *Tosafot* challenge this explanation on the grounds that the order in which the strings were inserted is not evident when looking at the final product. They therefore interpret this Gemara as stating that it is proper to begin the windings with a white string and then to perform some windings with the sky-blue string (*Shita Mekubbetzet*). This also seems to be the interpretation of the Rambam (see Rambam *Sefer Ahava*, *Hilkhot Tzitzit* 1:7).

HALAKHA

Necessary only with regard to granting precedence – לָא נִצְרְכָא אֶלָּא לְקַדֵּם: After inserting the four strings into the corner of the garment, one takes a white string and wraps it once around the other strings. He then takes the sky-blue string and wraps it around the other strings (Rambam *Sefer Ahava*, *Hilkhot Tzitzit* 1:7).

Perek **IV**
Daf **38** Amud **b**

אִילֵימָא חִיסֵּר מִצְוָה דְּלָבָן, וְקִיֵּים מִצְוָה דִּתְכֵלֶת – לְרַבִּי עִכּוּבֵי מְעַכֵּב אַהֲדָדֵי!

If we say that the individual **omitted** the **mitzva of white** strings **and fulfilled** only the **mitzva of sky-blue** strings, how is this possible? **According to** the opinion of **Rabbi** Yehuda HaNasi, the absence of either one **prevents**[N] fulfillment of the mitzva **with the other,** and therefore in this case one would not fulfill any mitzva at all.

אֲמַר רַב יְהוּדָה אֲמַר רַב: שֶׁחִיסֵּר מִצְוָה וְעָשָׂה מִצְוָה, וּמַאי חִיסֵּר מִצְוָה? דְּלָא עֲבַד מִצְוָה מִן הַמּוּבְחָר.

The Gemara answers that **Rav Yehuda said** that **Rav said:** It means **that he omitted a mitzva but** nevertheless **performed a mitzva. And what** does it mean that he **omitted a mitzva?** It means **that he did not perform** the **mitzva in the optimal manner** because he did not insert the white strings first, but he did fulfill the mitzva of ritual fringes.

הָתֵינַח לָבָן דְּאֵינוֹ מְעַכֵּב אֶת הַתְּכֵלֶת, תְּכֵלֶת דְּאֵינָהּ מְעַכֶּבֶת אֶת הַלָּבָן מַאי הִיא?

The Gemara asks: **This works out well** with regard to the mishna's statement that absence of the **white** strings **does not prevent** fulfillment of the mitzva with **the sky-blue** strings, which has been interpreted to mean that failing to insert the white strings before the sky-blue strings does not invalidate the ritual fringes. But **what is** the meaning of the mishna's statement **that** the absence of **sky-blue** strings **does not prevent** fulfillment of the mitzva with **the white** strings?

אֲמַר רָמִי בַּר חָמָא: לָא נִצְרְכָא אֶלָּא לְטַלִּית שֶׁכּוּלָּהּ תְּכֵלֶת.

Rami bar Ḥama said: That statement of the mishna **is necessary only** in the case of **a garment that** consists **entirely** of **sky-blue wool.**[N] In such a case, one is supposed to insert the sky-blue strings before the white strings.

אִיתְּמַר נַמִי, אֲמַר לֵיהּ לֵוִי לִשְׁמוּאֵל: אַרְיוֹךְ, לָא תֵּיתִיב אַכַּרְעָךְ עַד דִּמְפָרְשַׁתְּ לִי לְהָא מִילְּתָא: הַתְּכֵלֶת אֵינָהּ מְעַכֶּבֶת אֶת הַלָּבָן, וְהַלָּבָן אֵינוֹ מְעַכֵּב אֶת הַתְּכֵלֶת, מַאי הִיא? אֲמַר לֵיהּ: לָא נִצְרְכָא אֶלָּא לְסָדִין בְּצִיצִית, דְּמִצְוָה לְאַקְדּוּמֵי לָבָן בְּרֵישָׁא,

The Gemara notes that this **was also stated** by *amora'im*: **Levi said to Shmuel: Aryokh,**[L] **do not sit on your feet until you explain to me this matter:** When the mishna states that the absence of **the sky-blue** strings **does not prevent** fulfillment of the mitzva of ritual fringes **with the white** strings, **and the** absence of **white** strings **does not prevent** fulfillment of the mitzva **with the sky-blue** strings, **what does it mean?** Shmuel **said to** Levi: That statement **is necessary only** in the case of a linen **cloak** on which one places **ritual fringes, where** there is **a mitzva to** insert the **white** strings **first.**

NOTES

According to the opinion of Rabbi Yehuda HaNasi the absence of one prevents, etc. – לְרַבִּי עִכּוּבֵי מְעַכֵּב וכו׳: Since the Gemara is interpreting the mishna as referring to the issue discussed in this *baraita* and in accordance with the opinion of Rabbi Yehuda HaNasi, the *baraita* needs to be understood in accordance with his opinion. *Tosafot* add that the *baraita* is even more difficult according to the opinion of the Rabbis: Since they hold that even if one does not have one of the types of strings at all he can fulfill the mitzva with the other, it would be difficult to understand why one has omitted the mitzva if he merely inserted the sky-blue strings before inserting the white ones.

That statement of the mishna is necessary only in the case of a garment that consists entirely of sky-blue wool – לָא נִצְרְכָא אֶלָּא לְטַלִּית שֶׁכּוּלָּהּ תְּכֵלֶת: It appears that the citation of Rami bar Ḥama's interpretation was placed here erroneously and was transposed from later in the text, where this same statement appears (see *Shita Mekubbetzet*). When the Gemara states: This was also stated, it means to say that *amora'im* interpreted the mishna as referring to the order in which the white and sky-blue strings are inserted into the garment. The Gemara then asks how the mishna's second statement can be understood according to this interpretation, and then quotes the explanation of Rami bar Ḥama. Rashi also interprets the Gemara in this manner.

LANGUAGE

Aryokh – אַרְיוֹךְ: Aryokh is the ancient name of one of the powerful kings who invaded Eretz Yisrael in the time of Abraham (see Genesis 14:1). It is also the name of one of Nebuchadnezzar's officers (see Daniel 2:15). This nickname was given to Shmuel because he was treated as a king or ruler, due to the fact that his rulings are accepted in monetary law (*Bekhorot* 49b), just as the edicts of a ruler are binding. Rashi here explains that Aryokh refers to a king, as in the verse describing Judah, the tribe of kingship: "Judah is a lion [*aryeh*] cub" (Genesis 49:9). In tractate *Shabbat* (53a) Rashi explains that it derives from the word *reikha*, meaning king (*Bava Batra* 4a). *Reikha* is derived in turn from the Latin word for king, rex.

מַאי טַעְמָא? "הַכָּנָף" – מִין כָּנָף, וְאִי אַקְדֵּים תְּכֵלֶת לַלָּבָן לֵית לָן בָּהּ.

What is the reason for this? The verse states: "And they shall put on the fringe of the corner a sky-blue thread" (Numbers 15:38). "The fringe of **the corner**" is a reference to the string that is the same **type** as the **corner** of the garment. In the case of a linen cloak, which is generally white, this is a reference to the white strings, and since the verse mentions "the fringe of the corner" before the sky-blue thread, the white strings must be inserted before the sky-blue strings. The mishna therefore teaches that **if** one inserted the **sky-blue** strings **before the white** strings, **we have no** problem **with it** after the fact, and the ritual fringes are valid.

תֵּינַח לָבָן דְּאֵינוֹ מְעַכֵּב אֶת הַתְּכֵלֶת, תְּכֵלֶת דְּאֵינָהּ מְעַכֶּבֶת אֶת הַלָּבָן מַאי הִיא?

The Gemara asks: This **works out well** with regard to the mishna's statement **that** absence of the **white** strings **does not prevent** fulfillment of the mitzva **with the sky-blue** strings. But **what is** the meaning of the mishna's statement **that** the absence of **sky-blue** strings **does not prevent** fulfillment of the mitzva **with the white** strings?

אֲמַר לֵיהּ רָמִי בַּר חָמָא: לָא נִצְרְכָא אֶלָּא לְטַלִּית שֶׁכּוּלָּהּ תְּכֵלֶת, דְּמִצְוָה לְאַקְדּוֹמֵי תְּכֵלֶת בְּרֵישָׁא, דְּ"הַכָּנָף" – מִין כָּנָף, וְאִי אַקְדֵּים לָבָן בְּרֵישָׁא לֵית לָן בָּהּ.

Rami bar Ḥama said to him:[N] That statement of the mishna **is necessary only** in the case of a **garment that** consists **entirely** of **sky-blue wool, where** it is **a mitzva to** insert the **sky-blue** strings **first,** as the phrase: "The fringe of **the corner**" indicates that the first strings one inserts into the garment are those that are the same **type** as the **corner** of the garment. The mishna therefore teaches that **if** one inserted the **white strings first, we have no** problem **with it** after the fact, and the ritual fringes are fit.

אֲמַר רָבָא: מִידֵּי צִיבְעָא קָא גָּרֵים? אֶלָּא אָמַר רָבָא: לָא נִצְרְכָא אֶלָּא לְגַרְדּוּמִין, דְּאִי אִיגַּרְדַּם תְּכֵלֶת וְקָאֵי לָבָן, וְאִי אִיגַּרְדַּם לָבָן וְקָאֵי תְּכֵלֶת – לֵית לָן בָּהּ.

Rava said: Is it actually the **color** of the garment that **determines** the proper order[N] in which one should insert the strings? **Rather, Rava said:** The ruling of the mishna **is necessary only for** a case of **severed** strings. The mishna teaches **that if** the **sky-blue** strings **were severed and** the **white** ones **remain, or if** the **white** strings **were severed and** the **sky-blue** strings **remain,**[H] **we have no** problem **with it,** and the ritual fringes are fit.

דְּאָמְרִי בְּנֵי רַבִּי חִיָּיא: גַּרְדּוּמֵי תְּכֵלֶת כְּשֵׁרִין, וְגַרְדּוּמֵי אֵזוֹב כְּשֵׁרִין. וְכַמָּה שִׁיעוּר גַּרְדּוּמִין? אָמַר בַּר הַמְדּוּרִי אָמַר שְׁמוּאֵל: כְּדֵי לְעָנְבָן.

As the sons of Rabbi Ḥiyya say: Severed white or **sky-blue** strings **are fit,**[HN] **and** similarly, **severed hyssop** branches[H] **are fit** for sprinkling the water of purification mixed with the ashes of a red heifer. The Gemara asks: **What measure** do **severed** strings need to be[N] in order to remain fit? **Bar Hamduri says** that **Shmuel says:** The strings must remain long **enough to tie them in a slipknot.**

HALAKHA

If the white strings were severed and the sky-blue strings remain – אִי אִיגַּרְדַּם לָבָן וְקָאֵי תְּכֵלֶת: If the white strings were severed and only the sky-blue strings remain, the ritual fringes are still fit. This is in accordance with the mishna as interpreted by Rava (Rambam *Sefer Ahava*, *Hilkhot Tzitzit* 1:4).

Severed white or sky-blue strings are fit – גַּרְדּוּמֵי תְּכֵלֶת כְּשֵׁרִין: Even if all of the ritual fringes on one corner of a garment are severed, as long as each one is still long enough to be wrapped around the other strings and tied in a slipknot, the ritual fringes are fit. If any one of the four strings that are initially inserted into the garment is severed on both sides to the point that it cannot be wrapped around the other strings and tied in a slipknot, it is unfit. According to Rabbeinu Tam, the ritual fringes remain fit only if two of the original four strings are fully intact, and there is enough of the severed strings left to wind around the other strings and tie in a slipknot. If three of the eight loose hanging strings become severed, one must be concerned that they are from three of the four original strings. Consequently, even if they are long enough to wrap around the other strings and tie in a slipknot, one must be concerned that the ritual fringes are unfit. It is preferable to act in accordance with this stringent opinion.

According to Rashi, in order for a severed string to remain fit, there must be enough of the loose hanging part of the string remaining to wrap around the other strings and tie in a slipknot. According to Rabbeinu Yitzḥak, even if the entire loose hanging part of the string is severed but part of the string remains in the section of the windings, the string remains fit. The custom is in accordance with the opinion of Rashi, and therefore one may rely on the opinion of Rabbeinu Yitzḥak only when there is no other option (Rambam *Sefer Ahava*, *Hilkhot Tzitzit* 1:18; *Shulḥan Arukh*, *Oraḥ Ḥayyim* 12:1, 3).

Severed hyssop branches – גַּרְדּוּמֵי אֵזוֹב: Even if the stems of the hyssop separate and the leaves fall off, as long as any amount remains, the hyssop is still fit for use with the water of purification (Rambam *Sefer Tahara*, *Hilkhot Para Aduma* 11:4).

NOTES

Rami bar Ḥama said to him – אֲמַר לֵיהּ רָמִי בַּר חָמָא: It is noted in the *Shita Mekubbetzet* that the term: To him, appears to have been added in error in this sentence.

Is it actually the color of the garment that determines the proper order – מִידֵּי צִיבְעָא קָא גָּרֵים: Some commentaries hold that Rava disagrees with the assertion that the strings that are the same type as the corner of the garment are those that are the same color; Rava holds that this is determined based on the material from which the garment and the strings are made (Responsa of the Rashba 3:280; see *Tosafot* on 41b). Conversely, Rashi holds that Rava agrees that the strings that are the same type as the corner of the garment are those that are the same color, but Rava holds that since most garments were white when the verse was written, the Torah's intention in stating that one should first insert the strings that are the color of the garment and then insert the sky-blue strings is that one should always insert the white strings and then the sky-blue ones, regardless of whether or not the garment is actually white (see *Shita Mekubbetzet* and Rambam *Sefer Ahava*, *Hilkhot Tzitzit* 2:8 in the comment of the Ra'avad). There are also those who suggest that Rava disagrees with the basic premise that ritual fringes must include two different colors. The Torah requires strings that are the same color as the garment and strings that are sky-blue. If the garment is sky-blue, then all of the ritual fringes would be sky-blue (*Sefat Emet*).

Severed white or sky-blue strings are fit – גַּרְדּוּמֵי תְּכֵלֶת כְּשֵׁרִין: This is because by Torah law even a string of minimal length is fit; it was the Sages who required longer strings in order to fulfill the mitzva in a more honorable fashion. In a case where one affixed strings of the proper length and then they became severed, the Sages did not require one to take the trouble to replace them (*Levush*).

What measure do severed strings need to be – וְכַמָּה שִׁיעוּר גַּרְדּוּמִין: According to Rashi, as cited in *Tosafot* and *Shita Mekubbetzet*, this is referring to the strings that hang loose after the windings and knots. *Tosafot*, citing Rabbeinu Yitzḥak, and many other commentaries hold that this is referring to the section of the strings that includes the windings and knots. These commentaries adduce proof to their opinion from the *Sifrei*.

אִיבַּעְיָא לְהוּ: כְּדֵי לְעָנְבָן – לְעָנְבָן כּוּלְּהוּ בַּהֲדָדֵי, אוֹ דִּלְמָא כָּל חַד וְחַד לְחוּדֵיהּ? תֵּיקוּ.

A dilemma was raised before the Sages: When Shmuel says that severed strings must still be long **enough to tie them in a slipknot,** does that mean **to tie all of the** strings **together in a slipknot? Or perhaps** the strings may be even shorter, provided that they are long enough to tie **each one individually.** The Gemara concludes: The dilemma **shall stand** unresolved.

בָּעֵי רַב אַשִׁי: אַלִּימֵי דְּלָא מִיעַנְבִי וְאִי הָווּ קְטִינֵי מִיעַנְבִי, מַאי? אֲמַר לֵיהּ רַב אַחָא בְּרֵיהּ דְּרָבָא לְרַב אַשִׁי: כָּל שֶׁכֵּן דְּמִינְכַּר מִצְוָתַיְיהוּ.

Rav Ashi asks: If the strings are **thick** and **cannot be tied in a slipknot, but if they were** the same length but **thin** they **could be tied in a slipknot, what** is their status? **Rav Aḥa, son of Rava, said to Rav Ashi:** If the strings are long enough to be fit if they are thin, **all the more so** they are fit if they are thick, **as the mitzva** one fulfills **with them is** more **recognizable**[H] with thicker strings.

וּמַאן תַּנָּא דִּפְלִיג עֲלֵיהּ דְּרַבִּי? הַאי תַּנָּא הוּא, דְּתַנְיָא: רַבִּי יִצְחָק אוֹמֵר מִשּׁוּם רַבִּי נָתָן, שֶׁאָמַר מִשּׁוּם רַבִּי יוֹסֵי הַגְּלִילִי, שֶׁאָמַר מִשּׁוּם רַבִּי יוֹחָנָן בֶּן נוּרִי: אֵין לוֹ תְּכֵלֶת – מַטִּיל לָבָן.

The Gemara cited the opinion of Rabbi Yehuda HaNasi, who holds that one cannot fulfill the mitzva of ritual fringes without both white and sky-blue strings, and the Gemara explained that the mishna can be interpreted in accordance with his opinion. The Gemara now asks: **Who is the *tanna* who disagrees with Rabbi** Yehuda HaNasi and holds that the sky-blue strings and the white strings are not interdependent? The Gemara answers: **It is this** following ***tanna*****, as it is taught** in a *baraita*: **Rabbi Yitzḥak says in the name of Rabbi Natan, who said in the name of Rabbi Yosei HaGelili, who said in the name of Rabbi Yoḥanan ben Nuri: If one does not have sky-blue** strings, he nevertheless **affixes white** strings.[NH]

אֲמַר רָבָא, שְׁמַע מִינַּהּ: צָרִיךְ לְקְשׁוֹר עַל כָּל חוּלְיָא וְחוּלְיָא, דְּאִי סָלְקָא דַּעְתָּךְ לָא צָרִיךְ, הָא דְּאָמְרִי בְּנֵי רַבִּי חִיָּיא: גַּרְדּוּמֵי תְּכֵלֶת כְּשֵׁרִין וְגַרְדּוּמֵי אֵזוֹב כְּשֵׁרִין, כֵּיוָן דְּאִישְׁתְּרֵי לֵיהּ עִילָּאֵי – אִישְׁתְּרֵי לֵיהּ כּוּלָּהּ!

Rava said: Learn from the sons of Rabbi Ḥiyya that one is **required to tie** a knot **after each and every set** of windings,[N] and one cannot suffice with only one knot at the end of all the windings. **As, if it enters your mind** to say that one is **not required** to tie a knot after each set of windings, then **that which the sons of Rabbi Ḥiyya say: Severed** white or **sky-blue** strings **are fit, and** similarly, **severed hyssop** branches **are fit,** is difficult: **Once the uppermost** knot **is undone,**[N] all of the windings on **the entire** corner will **come undone,** as there are no other knots holding the windings in place, and in that case the garment will not have valid ritual fringes.

NOTES

If one does not have sky-blue strings he affixes white strings – אֵין לוֹ תְּכֵלֶת מַטִּיל לָבָן: The *baraita* (38a) states: But the Rabbis say: The lack of one does not prevent the fulfillment of the mitzva with the other. This indicates that even if one lacks white strings, he nevertheless affixes sky-blue strings. The Rambam holds that although one can affix white strings in the absence of sky-blue strings, he cannot affix sky-blue strings in the absence of white strings. The reason for this is that the verse states: "And they shall put on the fringe of the corner a sky-blue thread" (Numbers 15:38). This indicates that the "sky-blue thread" is affixed to a garment only if it also contains "the fringe of the corner," i.e., white strings (*Sefat Emet*).

To tie a knot after each and every set of windings – לְקְשׁוֹר עַל כָּל חוּלְיָא וְחוּלְיָא: The ritual fringes are prepared by inserting four strings into a hole near the corner of the garment, thereby in effect creating eight strings that hang down from the hole. Then one ties a double knot, takes one of the strings, and wraps it several times around the others, thereby creating a set of windings. Several sets of windings are formed in this fashion; the precise number will be discussed in the Gemara (39b). One then ties a double knot, or, according to the *Halakhot Gedolot*, a triple knot, and the remainder of the strings are left to hang loose. Rava teaches that one must place a double knot between each set of windings, and he may not merely distinguish between the sets by leaving space between them (*Beit Yosef*, based on Rambam) or by means of a single knot (*Hazon Ish*) or by alternating the colors of the strings used for the sets of windings (*Kelil Tekhelet*).

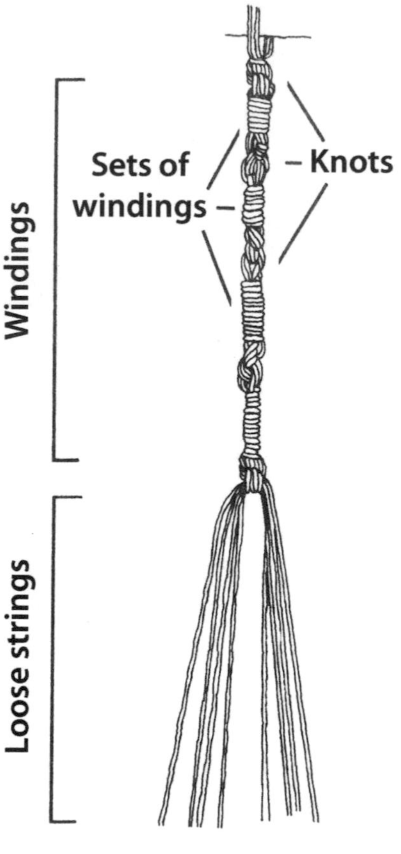

Tied fringes

Once the uppermost knot is undone – כֵּיוָן דְּאִישְׁתְּרֵי לֵיהּ עִילָּאֵי: This is referring to the final knot, which separates the windings and the free-hanging strings. It is referred to as the uppermost knot because it is the top of the portion containing the windings when one gathers the ritual fringes by the ends and lifts them (*Shita Mekubbetzet*). Others suggest that it is called uppermost because it is above the parts of the strings that hang loose (Mordekhai). Rava's point is that if the strings are severed up to the last knot, the knot will become undone, and then the windings will also become undone (Rashi; and see *Tosafot*).

HALAKHA

As the mitzva one fulfills with them is more recognizable – דְּמִינְכַּר מִצְוָתַיְיהוּ: If the ritual fringes that became severed are thick and cannot be wound around the other strings and tied in a slipknot, but they are long enough that one could do so if the severed strings were thinner, they remain fit. The determination of whether the severed strings are long enough is calculated based upon whether strings of average thickness could be wound around the other strings and tied in a slipknot (*Shulḥan Arukh, Oraḥ Ḥayyim* 12:2, and in the comment of Rema).

If one does not have sky-blue strings he affixes white strings – אֵין לוֹ תְּכֵלֶת מַטִּיל לָבָן: The absence of the sky-blue string in the ritual fringes does not prevent fulfillment of the mitzva with the white strings. Consequently, if one does not have sky-blue strings, he ties four white strings to his garment. According to Rashi, if he has no white strings, he ties four sky-blue strings to his garment. The *halakha* is in accordance with the opinion of the Rabbis who disagree with Rabbi Yehuda HaNasi; although the *halakha* is in accordance with Rabbi Yehuda HaNasi when he disagrees with one of his colleagues, that is not the case when he disagrees with multiple colleagues (Rambam *Sefer Ahava, Hilkhot Tzitzit* 1:4; *Arukh HaShulḥan, Oraḥ Ḥayyim* 9:3).

דִּלְמָא דְּאִיקְטַר.

The Gemara rejects this proof: **Perhaps** the sons of Rabbi Ḥiyya were referring to a case **where** one **tied knots** between the sets of windings even though there is no obligation to do so.

וְאָמַר רַבָּה, שְׁמַע מִינָּהּ: קֶשֶׁר עֶלְיוֹן דְּאוֹרָיְיתָא, דְּאִי סָלְקָא דַּעְתָּךְ דְּרַבָּנַן, מַאי אִיצְטְרִיךְ לְמִישְׁרֵי סָדִין בְּצִיצִית? פְּשִׁיטָא, הַתּוֹכֵף תְּכִיפָה אַחַת אֵינוֹ חִיבּוּר! אֶלָּא שְׁמַע מִינָּהּ: דְּאוֹרָיְיתָא.

And Rabba says: Learn from it[N] that **the uppermost knot**[N] in the ritual fringes is required **by Torah** law.[H] **As, if it enters your mind** to say that it is **by rabbinic** law, whereas by Torah law it is sufficient to merely insert the strings into the hole without tying any knots, for **what** reason **was it necessary** for the Torah **to permit** placing wool **ritual fringes** on a linen **cloak?**[N] It is **obvious** that it is permitted, since if **one attaches** a swatch of wool and a swatch of linen **with a single connection, it is not** considered **a connection**[H] with regard to the prohibition against wearing a garment that includes both wool and linen. **Rather, learn from** it that the uppermost knot is required **by Torah law.**

HALAKHA

The uppermost knot in the ritual fringes is required by Torah law – קֶשֶׁר עֶלְיוֹן דְּאוֹרָיְיתָא: If one forms one set of windings and then ties a knot, his ritual fringes are fit for the mitzva according to Torah law. Therefore, it is permitted to wear such a garment in the public domain on Shabbat and to recite the blessing on it. Some authorities say that the knot that is tied before the windings is required by Torah law, and it is appropriate to take their opinion into account *ab initio* (*Shulḥan Arukh, Oraḥ Ḥayyim* 11:13, and see *Magen Avraham* and *Mishna Berura* there).

A single connection, it is not considered a connection – תְּכִיפָה אַחַת אֵינוֹ חִיבּוּר: If one attaches a swatch of wool and a swatch of linen with a single connection, it is not deemed a violation of the prohibition of diverse kinds of wool and linen (Rambam *Sefer Zera'im, Hilkhot Kilayim* 10:24; *Shulḥan Arukh, Yoreh De'a* 300:2).

NOTES

Learn from it – שְׁמַע מִינָּהּ: Although this expression is generally used to draw a conclusion from a previously cited statement or ruling, in this instance it refers to the upcoming statement that it was necessary for the Torah to permit one to affix wool strings to a linen garment, which is an exception to the general prohibition against wearing garments containing both wool and linen.

The uppermost knot – קֶשֶׁר עֶלְיוֹן: Rashi explains that that this refers to the knot that is tied after the windings (B). Rabba's point is that Torah law requires one to tie a knot with the ritual fringes. If one is going to tie only one knot, it makes sense to tie it after the windings so that the knot will keep the windings from unraveling. Another version of Rashi's opinion (*Sanhedrin* 88b, cited by *Tosafot* here) is that Rabba is referring to the knot that is tied immediately after one inserts the strings into the garment (A). This explanation also appears in the Responsa of the *Ge'onim*.

The knot is formed by tying the four strings that are on one side of the garment with the four strings that are on the other side in a single knot, double knot, or triple knot. Many early commentaries hold that the knot is formed differently: One winds one of the strings around the others, then tucks that same string underneath the windings and pulls it taut (Rabbeinu Yehonatan of Lunel; see also *Kelil Tekhelet*).

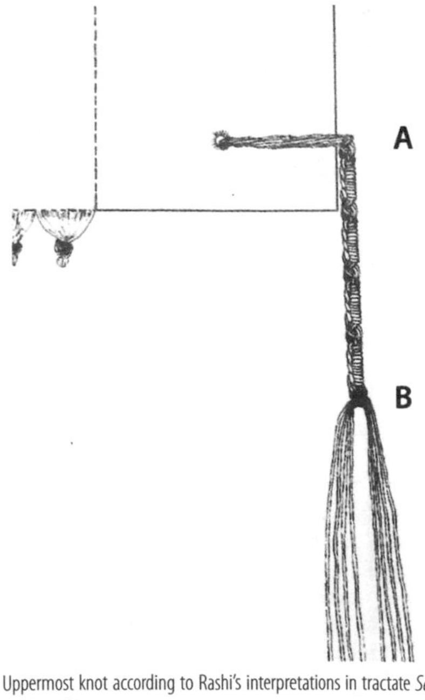

Uppermost knot according to Rashi's interpretations in tractate *Sanhedrin* (A) and here (B)

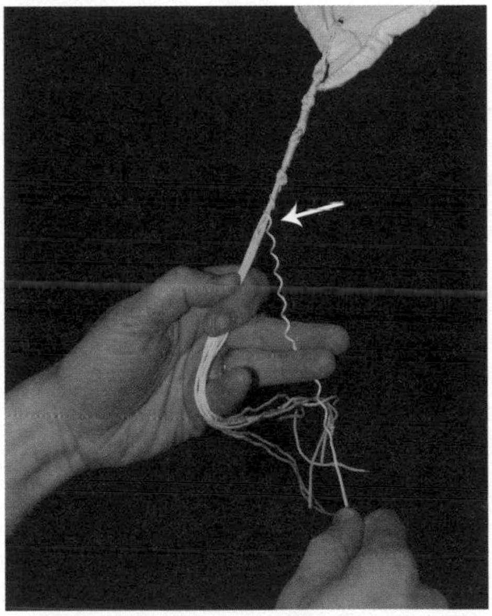
Untied strings of the ritual fringes

For what reason was it necessary for the Torah to permit placing wool ritual fringes on a linen cloak – מַאי אִיצְטְרִיךְ לְמִישְׁרֵי סָדִין בְּצִיצִית: Rashi explains that this is indicated by the Torah's juxtaposition of the verse: "You shall not wear diverse kinds, wool and linen together" (Deuteronomy 22:11) to: "You shall prepare yourself twisted cords upon the four corners of your covering, with which you cover yourself" (Deuteronomy 22:12). This juxtaposition indicates that the prohibition against wearing wool and linen in the same garment is suspended, when necessary, for the purpose of affixing ritual fringes. Others hold that Rabba is not referring to the juxtaposition of the verses themselves but to the fact that the Sages found it necessary to call attention to the permissibility of affixing wool strings to a linen garment (*Shita Mekubbetzet*). If Torah law did not require any knots in the ritual fringes, it would be possible to fulfill the mitzva without tying any knots, in which case no dispensation from the prohibition against wearing wool and linen would be necessary.

אָמַר רַבָּה בַּר רַב אַדָּא אָמַר רַב אַדָּא אָמַר רַב: אִם נִפְסַק הַחוּט מֵעִיקָּרוֹ – פְּסוּלָה. יָתֵיב רַב נַחְמָן וְקָא אָמַר לְהָא שְׁמַעְתָּא. אֵיתִיבֵיהּ רָבָא לְרַב נַחְמָן: בַּמֶּה דְּבָרִים אֲמוּרִים – בִּתְחִילָּתוֹ, אֲבָל סוֹפוֹ – שְׁיָרָיו וְגַרְדּוּמָיו כָּל שֶׁהוּא;

§ **Rabba bar Rav Adda says** that **Rav Adda says** that **Rav says: If a string was severed at its base,**[H] i.e., where it is connected to the garment, the ritual fringes are **unfit. Rav Naḥman sat** in the study hall **and stated this *halakha*. Rava raised an objection to Rav Naḥman** from a *baraita*: **In what** case **is this statement said,** i.e., that there is a minimum length required for the strings? That is only when the strings are **initially** affixed to the garment. **But** in the **end,** i.e., after the strings are affixed in an acceptable manner, **its remainder and its severed** strings are fit at **any** length.

מַאי שְׁיָרָיו וּמַאי גַּרְדּוּמָיו? מַאי לָאו שְׁיָרָיו – דְּאִיפְּסִיק מִינַּיְיהוּ וְאִישְׁתַּיַּיר מִינַּיְיהוּ, גַּרְדּוּמָיו – דְּאִיגַּרְדּוּם אִיגַּרְדּוּמֵי!

The Gemara clarifies: **What is its remainder and what** are **its severed** strings? **What, is it not** that when the *baraita* mentions **its remainder**[N] it is referring to a case **where** parts **of the** strings **were severed and** parts **of them remain, and** when the *baraita* mentions **its severed** strings it is referring to a case **where** the strings **were completely severed,** and nevertheless the strings are fit for the mitzva?

לָא, חֲדָא קָתָנֵי, שִׁיּוּרֵי גַּרְדּוּמָיו כָּל שֶׁהוּא. וְלֵימָא גַּרְדּוּמָיו, שְׁיָרָיו לָמָּה לִי? הָא קָא מַשְׁמַע לַן, דְּבָעֵינַן שִׁיּוּרָא לְגַרְדּוּמָיו כְּדֵי לְעָנְבָן.

The Gemara responds to Rava's objection: **No,** the *tanna* of the *baraita* **is teaching one** *halakha*, and the *baraita* should be understood as follows: **The remainder of its severed** strings are fit at **any length.** The Gemara asks: If so, **let** the *baraita* simply **say: Its severed** strings are fit at any length; **why do I** need the mention of **its remainder? This teaches us that we require a remainder of its severed** strings long **enough to** wrap them around the other strings and **tie them in a slipknot.**

יָתֵיב רַבָּה וְקָאָמַר מִשְּׁמֵיהּ דְּרַב: חוּט שֶׁל כֶּרֶךְ עוֹלֶה מִן הַמִּנְיָן. אֲמַר לֵיהּ רַב יוֹסֵף: שְׁמוּאֵל אֲמַרַהּ וְלָא רַב. אִיתְּמַר נַמִי: אָמַר רַבָּה בַּר בַּר חָנָה, סָח לִי רַבִּי יֹאשִׁיָּה דְּמִן אוּשָׁא: חוּט שֶׁל כֶּרֶךְ עוֹלֶה לָהּ מִן הַמִּנְיָן.

§ **Rabba sat** in the study hall **and said in the name of Rav:** The **string** used **for winding** around the other strings **is counted in the quota** of ritual fringes,[H] i.e., it is one of the eight strings on each corner, and there is no need to have an additional string for winding. **Rav Yosef said to** Rabba: **Shmuel said it, and not Rav.** This **was also stated** by another *amora*: **Rabba bar bar Ḥana says: Rabbi Yoshiya of Usha told me** that the **string** used **for winding** around the other strings **is counted in the quota** of ritual fringes.

יָתֵיב רָבָא וְקָא אָמַר מִשְּׁמֵיהּ דִּשְׁמוּאֵל: תְּכֵלֶת שֶׁכְּרָךְ רוּבָּהּ – כְּשֵׁרָה. אֲמַר לֵיהּ רַב יוֹסֵף: רַב אֲמַרַהּ וְלָא שְׁמוּאֵל. אִיתְּמַר נַמִי, אָמַר רַב הוּנָא בַּר יְהוּדָה אָמַר רַב שֵׁשֶׁת אָמַר רַב יִרְמְיָה בַּר אַבָּא אָמַר רַב: תְּכֵלֶת שֶׁכְּרָךְ רוּבָּהּ – כְּשֵׁרָה.

Rava sat in the study hall **and said in the name of Shmuel:** If one **wound the majority of** the white and the **sky-blue** strings[N] instead of leaving the larger portion of the strings hanging loose beyond the windings, the ritual fringes are nevertheless **fit. Rav Yosef said to** Rava: **Rav said it, and not Shmuel.** The Gemara supports Rav Yosef's version from that which **was also stated: Rav Huna bar Yehuda says** that **Rav Sheshet says** that **Rav Yirmeya bar Abba says** that **Rav says:** If one **wound the majority of** the white and the **sky-blue** strings, the ritual fringes are nevertheless **fit.**

רַב חִיָּיא בְּרֵיהּ דְּרַב נָתָן מַתְנֵי הָכִי, אָמַר רַב הוּנָא אָמַר רַב שֵׁשֶׁת אָמַר רַב יִרְמְיָה בַּר אַבָּא אָמַר רַב: תְּכֵלֶת שֶׁכְּרָךְ רוּבָּהּ – כְּשֵׁרָה, וַאֲפִילּוּ לֹא כְּרָךְ בָּהּ אֶלָּא חוּלְיָא אַחַת – כְּשֵׁרָה. וְנוֹיֵי תְכֵלֶת – שְׁלִישׁ גְּדִיל וּשְׁנֵי שְׁלִישֵׁי עָנָף.

Rav Ḥiyya, son of Rav Natan, teaches this discussion **like this: Rav Huna says** that **Rav Sheshet says** that **Rav Yirmeya bar Abba says** that **Rav says:** If one **wound the majority of** the white and the **sky-blue** strings, the ritual fringes are nevertheless **fit. And even** if **he wound only one set of** windings,[H] the ritual fringes are **fit. But** the **finest** way to affix the white and **sky-blue** strings[H] is to ensure that **one-third** of the length of the strings is **windings and two-thirds** are **loose** hanging strings.

HALAKHA

If a string was severed at its base – אִם נִפְסַק הַחוּט מֵעִיקָּרוֹ: If even one of the ritual fringes was severed at its base, i.e., where the strings are inserted into the garment, the ritual fringes are unfit (Rambam *Sefer Ahava, Hilkhot Tzitzit* 1:18; *Shulḥan Arukh, Oraḥ Ḥayyim* 12:3).

The string used for winding is counted in the quota of ritual fringes – חוּט שֶׁל כֶּרֶךְ עוֹלֶה מִן הַמִּנְיָן: The strings used for the windings around the ritual fringes are counted in the quota of eight strings (Rambam *Sefer Ahava, Hilkhot Tzitzit* 1:7).

And even if he wound only one set of windings – וַאֲפִילּוּ לֹא כָּרַךְ בָּהּ אֶלָּא חוּלְיָא אַחַת: Even if one formed only a single set of windings, the ritual fringes are fit (Rambam *Sefer Ahava, Hilkhot Tzitzit* 1:8; *Shulḥan Arukh, Oraḥ Ḥayyim* 11:13).

The finest way to affix the white and sky-blue strings – נוֹיֵי תְכֵלֶת: The finest way to affix the ritual fringes is to ensure that the windings and knots compose one-third of the length of the strings and to let the strings hang loose for two-thirds of their total length. If the majority of the length of the strings consists of windings and knots, the ritual fringes remain fit. If the entire length of the strings is taken up with windings and knots, the ritual fringes are unfit (Rambam *Sefer Ahava, Hilkhot Tzitzit* 1:8; *Shulḥan Arukh, Oraḥ Ḥayyim* 11:14; *Magen Avraham* 11:20).

NOTES

What, is it not that when the *baraita* mentions its remainder, etc. – מַאי לָאו שְׁיָרָיו וכו׳: Rashi explains that the Gemara is saying that when the *baraita* mentions a remainder it means that part of each fringe still remains, and when the *baraita* mentions strings that were severed it is referring to strings that were completely severed. *Tosafot* claim that both terms mean that the string was completely severed, but in the case of the remainder there are other strings that still remain.

If one wound the majority of the white and the sky-blue strings – תְּכֵלֶת שֶׁכְּרָךְ רוּבָּהּ: Rashi points out that here, as is often the case, the Gemara explicitly mentions the sky-blue strings, but is actually referring to the white strings as well. The Rambam holds that the Gemara is referring specifically to the sky-blue string, as he maintains that this is the only string that one winds around the others. The case is where one used the sky-blue string to create windings around the other strings for the majority of the length of those strings.

וְכַמָּה שִׁיעוּר חוּלְיָא? תַּנְיָא, רַבִּי אוֹמֵר: כְּדֵי שֶׁיִּכְרוֹךְ וְיִשְׁנֶה וִישַׁלֵּשׁ. תָּאנָא: הַפּוֹחֵת לֹא יִפְחוֹת מִשֶּׁבַע, וְהַמּוֹסִיף לֹא יוֹסִיף עַל שְׁלֹשׁ עֶשְׂרֵה;

The Gemara asks: **And what** is the **measure** of a **set** of windings? It **is taught** in a *baraita* that **Rabbi** Yehuda HaNasi **says:** It is **such that one winds** once **and** winds **a second and third** time, i.e., each set must contain at least three windings. It was **taught: One who minimizes** the sets of windings **may not** have **fewer than seven** sets,[H] **and one who adds** to this number of sets **may not** have **more than thirteen** sets of windings.

הַפּוֹחֵת לֹא יִפְחוֹת מִשֶּׁבַע – כְּנֶגֶד שִׁבְעָה רְקִיעִים, וְהַמּוֹסִיף לֹא יוֹסִיף עַל שְׁלֹשׁ עֶשְׂרֵה – כְּנֶגֶד שִׁבְעָה רְקִיעִין וְשִׁשָּׁה אֲוִירִין שֶׁבֵּינֵיהֶם.

The Gemara provides explanations for these guidelines: **One who minimizes** the sets of windings **may not** wind **fewer than seven** sets, **corresponding to the seven firmaments.**[N] **And one who adds** to this number of sets **may not** wind **more than thirteen** sets of windings, **corresponding to** the **seven firmaments and** the **six air** spaces **between them.**

תָּנָא: כְּשֶׁהוּא מַתְחִיל – מַתְחִיל בַּלָּבָן, "הַכָּנָף" – מִין כָּנָף, וּכְשֶׁהוּא מְסַיֵּים – מְסַיֵּים בַּלָּבָן, מַעֲלִין בַּקּוֹדֶשׁ וְלֹא מוֹרִידִין.

It was **taught: When one begins** to form the windings, he **begins** winding **with a white** string.[N] This is because the verse indicates that one first inserts "the fringe of **the corner**" (Numbers 15:38), i.e., the white strings, which are of the same **type** as the **corner** of the garment. **And when he concludes** the windings, **he concludes with a white** string, in accordance with the principle: **One elevates** to a higher level **in** matters of **sanctity and does not downgrade.**[N]

רַב וְרַבָּה בַּר בַּר חָנָה הָווּ יָתְבִי, הֲוָה קָא חָלֵיף וְאָזֵיל הַהוּא גַּבְרָא דְּמִיכַּסֵּי גְּלִימָא דְּכוּלָּהּ תְּכֶלְתָּא, וְרָמֵי לֵיהּ תְּכֶלְתָּא,

§ The Gemara relates: **Rav and Rabba bar bar Ḥana were sitting** together. **A certain man was passing by wearing a cloak that** was made **entirely of sky-blue** wool, **on which he had affixed** white and **sky-blue** strings,

HALAKHA

May not have fewer than seven sets – לֹא יִפְחוֹת מִשֶּׁבַע: There must be at least three windings in each set of windings. One does not do less than seven windings on each corner of the garment, nor more than thirteen. Nowadays, in the absence of sky-blue wool, there is no obligation to have sets of windings, and there is no specific number of windings that one must have. It is customary to have four sets of windings on each corner. The first set consists of seven windings; the second contains nine, or eight according to the Ari, which is the common practice (*Magen Avraham*). The third set consists of eleven windings. The fourth set consists of thirteen. *Magen Avraham* notes that others wrap ten in the first set, five in the second, six in the third and five in the fourth set. These numbers correspond to the numerical values of the letters in the Tetragrammaton (Rambam *Sefer Ahava, Hilkhot Tzitzit* 1:8; *Shulḥan Arukh, Oraḥ Ḥayyim* 11:14).

NOTES

May not wind fewer than seven sets, corresponding to the seven firmaments – לֹא יִפְחוֹת מִשֶּׁבַע כְּנֶגֶד שִׁבְעָה רְקִיעִים: The seven firmaments are enumerated in tractate *Ḥagiga* (12b). The relationship between the ritual fringes and the firmaments can be understood based on the Gemara (43b) that states that sky-blue wool is placed in ritual fringes because its color resembles that of the sea, which in turn resembles the firmament, which resembles the Throne of Glory.

Early commentaries write that in times when sky-blue wool is not available, there is no need for seven sets of windings. Instead, it became customary to tie five double knots and four sets of windings between the knots (Rashi; Rosh).

Tosafot maintain that even when there were sky-blue strings there were only five knots: A knot after the strings are inserted into the garment, then two sets of windings and another knot, two more sets of windings and a knot, two more sets of windings and a knot, followed by one set of windings and one final knot. According to this interpretation, when Rava said (38a) that one is required to tie a knot after each and every set of windings, he meant every double set of white and sky-blue windings.

The Ra'avad cites an entirely different understanding of this Gemara in the name of Rav Natronai Gaon. He understands the range of seven to thirteen as referring to the number of windings in each set, rather than to the total number of sets of windings. This is the basis for the common practice to have seven windings in the first set of windings, followed by sets of eight and eleven windings, and culminating with thirteen windings in the last set (see *Beit Yosef* and *Darkhei Moshe*).

When one begins to form the windings he begins with a white string – כְּשֶׁהוּא מַתְחִיל מַתְחִיל בַּלָּבָן: According to Rav Amram Gaon, this means that one uses a white string to form the first set of windings, a sky-blue string to form the next set, and continues alternating in this manner. Since there may be either seven or thirteen sets, the final set will also be formed with a white string. Conversely, the Rambam holds that all of the windings are done with the sky-blue string, except for the first winding of the first set and the last winding in the final set, which are done with a white string (Rambam *Sefer Ahava, Hilkhot Tzitzit* 1:7). The Ra'avad cites Rav Natronai Gaon, who maintains that each set of windings comprises one winding with a white string, followed by three windings with a sky-blue string, and an additional winding with a white string.

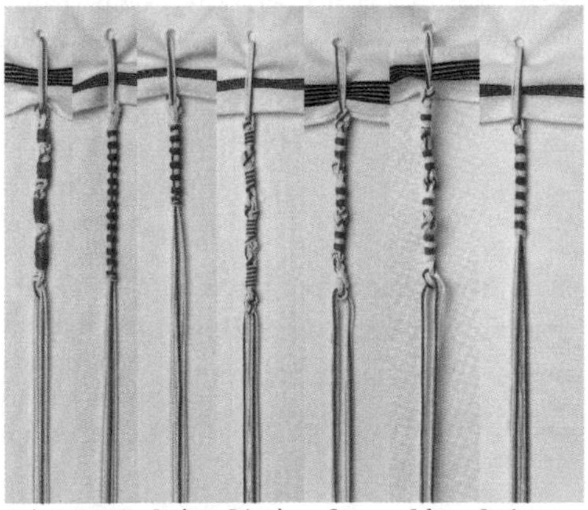

Various methods for tying sky-blue strings

One elevates to a higher level in matters of sanctity and does not downgrade – מַעֲלִין בַּקּוֹדֶשׁ וְלֹא מוֹרִידִין: If one were to conclude with a sky-blue string it would be a downgrade from the white string with which he began (Rashi). Some explain that the white strings are primary, as seen from the fact that the verse mentions them before the sky-blue strings (*Sefer HaIttur*). Others claim that this is not true, maintaining that the sky-blue wool certainly has greater importance, as it resembles the Throne of Glory (see 43b). They explain that since the white string was used to begin the windings, it is improper to downgrade it from its status (*Nimmukei Yosef*).

וּגְדִילָא מִיגְדִיל, אָמַר רַב: יָאֵי גְּלִימָא וְלָא יָאֵי תְּכֶלְתָּא, רַבָּה בַּר בַּר חָנָה אָמַר: יָאֵי גְּלִימָא וְיָאֵי תְּכֶלְתָּא.

and the ritual fringes were composed **entirely** of **windings**,[N] without any portion of the strings hanging loose. **Rav said: The cloak is beautiful, but the** white and **sky-blue** strings are **not beautiful. Rabba bar bar Ḥana said: The cloak is beautiful, and the** white and **sky-blue** strings are also **beautiful.**

בְּמַאי קָא מִיפַּלְגִי? רַבָּה בַּר בַּר חָנָה סָבַר: כְּתִיב ״גְּדִיל״ וּכְתִיב ״פְּתִיל״, אוֹ גָּדִיל אוֹ פְּתִיל;

The Gemara asks: **With regard to what** principle **do they disagree?** The Gemara answers: **Rabba bar bar Ḥana holds** that since **it is written** in one verse: "You shall prepare yourself **twisted cords**" (Deuteronomy 22:12), **and** in another **it is written:** "And they shall put on the fringe of the corner a sky-blue **thread**" (Numbers 15:38), it teaches that the ritual fringes may be composed entirely of **either twisted cords,** i.e., the windings, **or** loose threads or **strings.**

וְרַב סָבַר: לְעוֹלָם פְּתִיל בָּעֵינַן, וְהַהִיא ״גְּדִילִים״ לְמִנְיָינָא הוּא דַּאֲתָא, ״גְּדִיל״ – שְׁנַיִם, ״גְּדִילִים״ – אַרְבָּעָה, עֲשֵׂה גָּדִיל וּפוֹתְלֵיהוּ מִתּוֹכוֹ.

And Rav holds that **actually, we** also **require** loose **strings** in addition to the windings, **and** when **that** term **"twisted cords"** appears in the verse, **it comes for** the purpose of teaching the **number** of strings that are required. If the verse would have employed the singular term **twisted cord,** it would still indicate that **two** strings are required, as twisted means that two strings are wound around each other. Once the verse uses the plural term **"twisted cords,"** it thereby indicates that **four** strings are required. By using the terms "twisted cords" and "thread," the verses indicates: **Form twisted cords** with the four strings that one attaches to each corner, **and let** the strings **hang loose from them.**[N]

אָמַר שְׁמוּאֵל מִשְּׁמֵיהּ דְּלֵוִי: חוּטֵי צֶמֶר פּוֹטְרִין בְּשֶׁל פִּשְׁתָּן.

§ **Shmuel says in the name of Levi: Wool strings exempt** a garment made **of linen,**[NH] i.e., one fulfills the mitzva by affixing wool strings to a linen garment.

אִיבַּעְיָא לְהוּ: שֶׁל פִּשְׁתָּן מַהוּ שֶׁיִּפְטְרוּ בְּשֶׁל צֶמֶר? צֶמֶר בְּשֶׁל פִּשְׁתִּים הוּא דְּפָטַר, דְּכֵיוָן דִּתְכֵלֶת פָּטְרָה – לָבָן נַמִי פָּטַר, אֲבָל פִּשְׁתִּים בְּצֶמֶר לָא.

A dilemma was raised before the Sages: **What is** the *halakha* with regard to whether strings made **of linen exempt** a garment made **of wool?** One can say that **it is** only **wool** strings **that exempt** a garment **of linen, as since the sky-blue** string, which must be wool, **exempts** a linen garment, **white** strings of wool **also exempt** the garment. **But** if one affixes **linen** strings **to a wool** garment, he does **not** fulfill his obligation.

אוֹ דִלְמָא, כֵּיוָן דִּכְתִיב: ״לֹא תִלְבַּשׁ שַׁעַטְנֵז צֶמֶר וּפִשְׁתִּים יַחְדָּו גְּדִלִים תַּעֲשֶׂה לָּךְ״ – לָא שְׁנָא צֶמֶר בְּפִשְׁתִּים וְלָא שְׁנָא פִּשְׁתִּים בְּצֶמֶר?

Or perhaps, since it is written: "You shall not wear diverse kinds, wool and linen together. You shall prepare yourself twisted cords upon the four corners of your covering" (Deuteronomy 22:11–12), which indicates that one may wear wool and linen together in order to fulfill the mitzva of ritual fringes, there **is no difference** whether one affixes **wool** strings **to** a garment of **linen, and** there **is no difference** whether one affixes **linen** strings **to** a garment of **wool.**

תָּא שְׁמַע, דְּאָמַר רַחֲבָה אָמַר רַב יְהוּדָה: חוּטֵי צֶמֶר פּוֹטְרִין בְּשֶׁל פִּשְׁתָּן וְשֶׁל פִּשְׁתָּן פּוֹטְרִין בְּשֶׁל צֶמֶר; חוּטֵי צֶמֶר וּפִשְׁתִּים פּוֹטְרִין בְּכָל מָקוֹם, וַאֲפִילּוּ בְּשִׁירָאִין.

The Gemara suggests: **Come** and **hear** a resolution to this dilemma, **as Raḥava says** that **Rav Yehuda says: Wool strings exempt** a garment made **of linen,** strings **of linen exempt** a garment made **of wool,** and **strings of wool and linen exempt** a garment **in any case,** i.e., all garments, **and even** garments made **from silks** [***beshira'in***].[L]

NOTES

Composed entirely of windings – **גְּדִילָא מִיגְדִיל**: Rashi explains that this individual's ritual fringes consisted only of windings without any portion of the strings hanging loose. *Tosafot* note that based on other sources it is difficult to understand how Rabba bar bar Ḥana could have considered such ritual fringes fit.

Some commentaries hold that even according to Rabba bar bar Ḥana the ritual fringes are required to contain both windings and loose hanging strings, but he holds that since these two components are derived from different passages of the Torah, absence of one component does not prevent fulfillment of the mitzva with the other (*Tosafot Ḥitzoniyyot*).

Some later commentaries explain that the entire discussion of the Gemara addresses only the sky-blue fringe. The Gemara is discussing whether the sky-blue strings need to also hang loose after the windings, or whether it is only the white strings that need to hang loose (Re'em Horowitz; *Ha'amek She'ala* 127:11). Others suggest a completely different understanding, based on the Rambam: Rabba bar bar Ḥana required that the strings hang loose but allowed the portion that was not loose to be either wound or plaited (*Mishkenot Ya'akov, Oraḥ Ḥayyim* 13).

And let the strings hang loose [*ufoteleihu*] from them – **וּפוֹתְלֵיהוּ מִתּוֹכוֹ**: Rashi explains the term *ufoteleihu* to mean that the string that is wound around the others is counted as one of the eight strings. Alternatively, it means that the strings hang loose from the section of the windings. *Tosafot* explain it to mean that the original four strings must be folded over to form eight strings, like a wick [*petila*] (see Ra'avan, *Shabbat* 343).

Wool strings exempt a garment made of linen – **חוּטֵי צֶמֶר פּוֹטְרִין בְּשֶׁל פִּשְׁתָּן**: When the Torah refers to sky-blue [*tekhelet*], it is referring specifically to wool that is dyed sky-blue. Consequently, it is obvious that the sky-blue strings on a linen garment must be wool. The point here is that even the white strings may be wool. Although the verse indicates that the strings should be the same type as the corner of the garment, which could have been understood to indicate that the white strings on a linen garment must be made from linen, the *halakha* is that one fulfills the mitzva with wool strings.

LANGUAGE

Silks [*shira'in*] – **שִׁירָאִין**: From the Greek σηρικόν, *sērikon*, which refers to silk.

HALAKHA

Wool strings exempt a garment made of linen – **חוּטֵי צֶמֶר פּוֹטְרִין בְּשֶׁל פִּשְׁתָּן**: It is permitted to attach white strings made of wool to a linen garment, or white strings made of linen to a wool garment. In the absence of sky-blue dye, one should not do so, because in that case fulfilling the mitzva to wear ritual fringes does not necessitate overriding the general prohibition against wearing a garment of wool and linen. The Rema cites the opinion of the *Smak* that nowadays, one should not affix linen strings to any garment, even if it is not wool; the Rema writes that this is the accepted practice (Rambam *Sefer Ahava, Hilkhot Tzitzit* 3:5–6; *Shulḥan Arukh, Oraḥ Ḥayyim* 9:2).

וּפְלִיגָא דְּרַב נַחְמָן, דְּאָמַר רַב נַחְמָן: הַשִּׁירָאִין פְּטוּרִין מִן הַצִּיצִית. אֵיתִיבֵיהּ רָבָא לְרַב נַחְמָן: הַשִּׁירָאִין, וְהַכָּלָךְ, וְהַסְּרִיקִין – כּוּלָּן חַיָּיבִין בְּצִיצִית! מִדְּרַבָּנַן.

The Gemara notes: **And** this last point **disagrees** with a ruling **of Rav Naḥman, as Rav Naḥman says:** ***Shira'in*** **are** entirely **exempt from** the obligation of **ritual fringes. Rava raised an objection to** the opinion of **Rav Naḥman** from the following *baraita*: Garments made from types of silks known as ***shira'in, kalakh,***[L] **and** ***serikin***[L] **all require ritual fringes.**[H] The Gemara answers: The *baraita* means that there is an obligation **by rabbinic law,** whereas Rav Naḥman meant they are exempt by Torah law.

אִי הָכִי, אֵימָא סֵיפָא: וְכוּלָּן, צֶמֶר וּפִשְׁתִּים פּוֹטְרִין בָּהֶן; אִי אָמְרַתְּ בִּשְׁלָמָא דְּאוֹרָיְיתָא – הַיְינוּ דְּמִישְׁתְּרוּ בְּהוּ כִּלְאַיִם, אֶלָּא אִי אָמְרַתְּ דְּרַבָּנַן, הֵיכִי מִישְׁתְּרֵי בְּהוּ כִּלְאַיִם? אֵימָא: אוֹ צֶמֶר אוֹ פִשְׁתִּים.

The Gemara challenges this suggestion: **If that is so,** then **say the latter clause** of the *baraita*: **And** with regard to **all of these** garments, strings of **wool and linen exempt them.** This indicates that one may affix wool sky-blue strings and white linen strings. **Granted, if you say** that the obligation of ritual fringes for silk garments is **by Torah law, that is** why **diverse kinds are permitted for them. But if you say** that the obligation is **by rabbinic law, how could diverse kinds be permitted for them?** The Gemara answers: **Say** instead: **Either wool or linen** strings exempt silk garments, but one may not affix both wool and linen strings to the same silk garment.

הָכִי נַמִי מִסְתַּבְּרָא, דְּקָתָנֵי סֵיפָא: הֵן בְּמִינָן פּוֹטְרִין, שֶׁלֹּא בְּמִינָן אֵין פּוֹטְרִין; אִי אָמְרַתְּ בִּשְׁלָמָא דְּרַבָּנַן – הַיְינוּ דְּמִיפַּטְרוּ בְּמִינָן, אֶלָּא אִי אָמְרַתְּ דְּאוֹרָיְיתָא, צֶמֶר וּפִשְׁתִּים הוּא דְּפָטַר!

The Gemara comments: **So too, it is reasonable** to assume that this is the correct interpretation of the *baraita*, **as** the *baraita* **teaches** in **the latter clause:** Strings made from **these** silk fabrics **exempt** a garment **of their type** but **do not exempt** a garment **that is not of their type. Granted, if you say** that the obligation to attach ritual fringes to these garments is **by rabbinic law, that is** why **they are exempted** if one affixes strings **of their type. But if you say** that the obligation is **by Torah law,** then **it** should be only **wool or linen that exempt** these garments.[N]

אִי מִשּׁוּם הָא לָא אִירְיָא, כִּדְרָבָא. דְּרָבָא רָמֵי, כְּתִיב: "הַכָּנָף" – מִין כָּנָף, וּכְתִיב: "צֶמֶר וּפִשְׁתִּים",

The Gemara rejects this: **If** it is **due to that** reason, **there is no** conclusive **argument,** because one can maintain that other fabrics also fulfill the obligation of ritual fringes by Torah law, **in accordance with** the opinion **of Rava. As Rava raises a contradiction: It is written** in one verse: "And they shall put on the fringe of the corner a sky-blue thread" (Numbers 15:38). The term **"the corner"** indicates that the fringe must be from the same **type** of fabric as the **corner. And** yet **it is written: "Wool and linen"** (Deuteronomy 22:11), immediately before the verse states: "You shall prepare yourself twisted cords upon the four corners of your covering" (Deuteronomy 22:12), indicating that ritual fringes must be from either wool or linen.

הָא כֵּיצַד? צֶמֶר וּפִשְׁתִּים פּוֹטְרִין בֵּין בְּמִינָן בֵּין שֶׁלֹּא בְּמִינָן; שְׁאָר מִינִין, בְּמִינָן – פּוֹטְרִין, שֶׁלֹּא בְּמִינָן – אֵין פּוֹטְרִין.

How so? Strings made of **wool or linen exempt** any garment, **whether** the garment is made **of their type** of fabric, or **whether** it is **not of their type** of fabric. Strings made of all **other types** of fabric **exempt** garments made **of their type** of fabric, e.g., silk strings exempt a silk garment, but **they do not exempt** a garment made from a fabric **that is not their type,**[H] i.e., a garment made from a different fabric.

וְרַב נַחְמָן כִּדְתַנָא דְּבֵי רַבִּי יִשְׁמָעֵאל,

The Gemara notes: **And Rav Naḥman,** who holds that silk garments do not require ritual fringes by Torah law, holds **in accordance with** the ruling stated by **a** ***tanna*** **of the school of Rabbi Yishmael.**

LANGUAGE

Kalakh – כָּלָךְ: It appears that the word is related to the Persian *kulk*, meaning fine, soft wool. The conventional wisdom is that it is a sort of inferior silk, made from the waste of the silk tubers or the leftovers of the silk. Others maintain that it refers to the plant known as ferula, which belongs to the family of Apiaceous plants.

Ferula plant

Serikin **– סְרִיקִין:** Apparently also from the Greek σηρικόν, *sērikon*, meaning silk or a silk garment.

Silk scarves

NOTES

It should be only wool or linen that exempt these garments – צֶמֶר וּפִשְׁתִּים הוּא דְּפָטַר: Rashi explains that this is derived from the fact that the verse mentions wool and linen, and then in the very next verse states: "You shall prepare yourself twisted cords upon the four corners of your covering" (Deuteronomy 22:12). This juxtaposition indicates that ritual fringes must be from either wool or linen.

HALAKHA

Silks known as *shira'in*, *kalakh*, and *serikin* all require ritual fringes – הַשִּׁירָאִין וְהַכָּלָךְ וְהַסְּרִיקִין כּוּלָּן חַיָּיבִין בְּצִיצִית: Only garments that are made of wool or linen are required to have ritual fringes by Torah law. Garments made of other fabrics are obligated by rabbinic law. This is in accordance with the opinion of Rav Naḥman. Others hold that all garments are obligated by Torah law (*Tosafot*; Rosh). This is in accordance with the opinion of Rava, as the *halakha* is generally in accordance with the *amora* who lived later, and Rava lived after Rav Naḥman. Additionally, this was also the opinion of Rav Yehuda (Rambam *Sefer Ahava, Hilkhot Tzitzit* 3:2; *Shulḥan Arukh, Oraḥ Ḥayyim* 9:1, and in the comment of Rema).

They do not exempt a garment made from a fabric that is not their type – שֶׁלֹּא בְּמִינָן אֵין פּוֹטְרִין: Ritual fringes made from wool or linen are fit for use with garments of all fabrics. Strings of another fabric are fit for use only with garments of that same fabric. This is in accordance with the opinion of Rava (Rambam, *Sefer Ahava, Hilkhot Tzitzit* 3:5; *Shulḥan Arukh, Oraḥ Ḥayyim* 9:2–3).

דתנא דבי רבי ישמעאל: הואיל ונאמרו בגדים בתורה סתם, ופרט לך הכתוב באחד מהן צמר ופשתים – אף כל צמר ופשתים.

As a *tanna* **of the school of Rabbi Yishmael taught: Since** the word **garments is** usually **stated in the Torah without specification** as to the material from which the garments are made, **and the verse specified in one of** its references to garments that it is referring to garments made from **wool or linen,** as it states: "And the garment in which there will be the mark of leprosy, whether it be a woolen garment or a linen garment" (Leviticus 13:47), it may be derived that **so too, all** garments mentioned in the Torah are those made from **wool or linen.** Other fabrics are not classified as garments by Torah law. Consequently, when the Torah requires strings on the corners of garments (see Numbers 15:38), it is referring specifically to garments made of wool or linen.

אמר אביי: והאי תנא דבי רבי ישמעאל מפקא מאידך תנא דבי רבי ישמעאל, דתנא דבי רבי ישמעאל: "בגד" – אין לי אלא בגד צמר, מנין לרבות צמר גמלים וצמר ארנבים ונוצה של עזים, והכלך והסריקין והשיראין, מנין? תלמוד לומר: "או בגד".

Abaye said: This statement by **a** ***tanna*** **of the school of Rabbi Yishmael diverges from another** statement by **a** ***tanna*** **of the school of Rabbi Yishmael,** who holds that all fabrics are considered garments. **As a** ***tanna*** **of the school of Rabbi Yishmael taught:** From the fact that the verse states: "A woolen **garment**" (Leviticus 13:47), **I have** derived **only** that **a garment of wool** can become ritually impure.[N] **From where** is it derived that garments made of **camels' hair, rabbits' wool, goats' hair, or** the types of silk ***kalakh, serikin,*** **and** ***shirayin,*** are also **included** in this *halakha*? **The** same **verse states: "Or** a linen **garment."** The word "or" serves as an amplification to include all types of fabric.

NOTES

I have derived only that a garment of wool can become impure – אין לי אלא בגד צמר: This is based on the premise that when the verse refers to wool without specifying its source, it means sheep's wool, whereas a verse that is referring to the wool of a different animal would specify which animal is the source of the wool (Jerusalem Talmud, *Kilayim* 9:1).

Perek **IV**
Daf **40** Amud **a**

תנו רבנן: סדין בציצית – בית שמאי פוטרין, ובית הלל מחייבין, והלכה כדברי בית הלל.

The Sages taught in a *baraita*: With regard to **ritual fringes** on a linen **cloak,**[H] **Beit Shammai deem** the cloak **exempt**[N] from ritual fringes due to the fact that the sky-blue strings must be made from wool, and there is a Torah prohibition against wearing a mixture of wool and linen. **And Beit Hillel deem** a linen cloak **obligated** in the mitzva of ritual fringes. **And the** ***halakha*** **is in accordance with the statement of Beit Hillel.**

אמר רבי אליעזר בן רבי צדוק: והלא כל המטיל תכלת בירושלים אינו אלא מן המתמיהין!

Rabbi Eliezer ben Rabbi Tzadok[P] **says: But is it not** the case that **anyone who affixes sky-blue** strings to a linen cloak **in Jerusalem is** considered **nothing other than one of those who causes** others **to be astonished**[N] at their behavior, as it appears that he is violating the prohibition against wearing a garment containing wool and linen?

NOTES

Beit Shammai deem it exempt – בית שמאי פוטרין: In the *Sifrei*, the ruling of Beit Shammai is derived from the fact that the verse requires placing ritual fringes on "your covering [*kesut*]" (Deuteronomy 22:12), which is a term that does not apply to linen. Rashi here explains that according to Beit Shammai the mitzva of ritual fringes does not override the prohibition against wearing a garment containing wool and linen because they understood the juxtaposition of two verses differently from Beit Hillel. When the verse states: "You shall not wear diverse kinds, wool and linen together" (Deuteronomy 22:11) and then: "You shall prepare for yourself twisted cords upon the four corners of your covering" (Deuteronomy 22:12), the juxtaposition does not teach, as Beit Hillel maintain, that the mitzva of ritual fringes overrides the prohibition of wool and linen. Rather, the juxtaposition indicates that the prohibition takes precedence over the mitzva, and the principle that a positive mitzva overrides a prohibition does not apply (*Milḥamot HaShem* on tractate *Shabbat*). Similarly, in the *Midrash Tanna'im*, the reason cited for the opinion of Beit Shammai is that the Torah first presents the prohibition against wearing a garment of wool and linen and only then mentions the mitzva of ritual fringes.

Nothing other than one of those who causes others to be astonished – אינו אלא מן המתמיהין: Rabbi Eliezer is ostensibly challenging the opinion of Beit Hillel, who hold that a linen cloak requires ritual fringes, based on the common practice in Jerusalem. If their opinion is accepted, why are people astonished at those who follow it? In Rashi's second interpretation of this Gemara, he explains that this is actually a challenge to the opinion of Beit Shammai, who prohibit attaching ritual fringes to a linen garment. The implication of Rabbi Eliezer's statement is that one who wears ritual fringes on a linen garment causes others to be astonished but does not actually violate a prohibition, as claimed by Beit Shammai.

PERSONALITIES

Rabbi Eliezer ben Rabbi Tzadok – רבי אליעזר בן רבי צדוק: There were at least two Sages named Rabbi Eliezer, or Elazar, ben Rabbi Tzadok. One lived in Jerusalem prior to the destruction of the Temple and testified with regard to various aspects of the Temple service and the customary halakhic practice in Jerusalem.

Some hold that there were actually two different Sages by this name who lived during the Temple era. The first was a disciple of the disciples of Shammai the Elder. He was a storekeeper by profession and lived in Jerusalem his entire life. The second lived in the period immediately preceding the destruction of the Temple and immediately afterward, and was one of the Sages of Yavne. He was the son of the famous scholar Rabbi Tzadok, who was saved by Rabbi Yoḥanan ben Zakkai at the time of the destruction (see *Gittin* 56b).

There was another Sage by this name, possibly a descendant of one of those mentioned above, who lived three generations later. He was a student of Rabbi Meir and a colleague of Rabbi Yehuda HaNasi.

HALAKHA

Ritual fringes on a linen cloak – סדין בציצית: If one has a linen garment he should not attach sky-blue strings to it, due to the fact that these strings must be wool. Instead, he should attach only white strings made from linen. Although the mitzva of ritual fringes overrides the prohibition against wearing a garment that contains wool and linen, there is a rabbinic decree prohibiting attaching the sky-blue strings, due to a concern that one will wear the garment at night, when he does not fulfill the mitzva of ritual fringes. This is in accordance with the opinion of Beit Hillel and the interpretation of Rabbi Zeira (40b). Although in principle it should be permitted to attach white strings made from wool to a linen garment, since it possible to attach white strings made from linen, one must use linen strings.

Some say that one should not wear a four-cornered linen garment at all. This is because one should not attach even strings made from linen to the garment, due to a concern that one might instead attach sky-blue strings made from wool. This opinion accepts the ruling of Beit Shammai that a linen garment is entirely exempt from ritual fringes (*Ge'onim*; Rabbeinu Tam). The *Shulḥan Arukh* comments that a God-fearing individual should wear a four-cornered garment made from wool, which is definitely required to have ritual fringes by Torah law. The Rema adds that if one's only option is a linen garment, it is preferable that he wear it with white strings that are also linen rather than not fulfill the mitzva at all (Rambam *Sefer Ahava, Hilkhot Tzitzit* 3:6–7; *Shulḥan Arukh, Oraḥ Ḥayyim* 9:2, 6).

אָמַר רַבִּי: אִם כֵּן, לָמָּה אֲסָרוּהָ? לְפִי שֶׁאֵין בְּקִיאִין.

The *baraita* concludes: **Rabbi** Yehuda HaNasi **says: If so,** that the *halakha* is in accordance with Beit Hillel and a linen cloak is required to have ritual fringes, **why did** the Sages **prohibit**[N] attaching ritual fringes to linen garments in Jerusalem? It is **because** people **are not well versed** in the *halakha* and might ultimately wear garments of wool and linen even when it is not necessary for the mitzva of ritual fringes.

אֲמַר לֵיהּ רָבָא בַּר רַב חָנָא לְרָבָא: וְלִרְמוּ בֵּי עַשְׂרָה וְנִפְקוּ לְשׁוּקָא וּמְפַרְסְמָא לְמִילְּתָא! כָּל שֶׁכֵּן דְּמִתְמְהוּ עִילָּוָן.

Rava bar Rav Ḥana said to Rava: If that is the concern, then **let ten** people **take** linen cloaks with ritual fringes **and go out to the marketplace and** thereby **publicize the matter,** i.e., that it is permitted to affix wool strings to a linen garment due to the mitzva. Rava answered: **All the more so** people **would be astonished at us** for acting in such an unconventional manner.

וְלִידְרְשָׁא בְּפִירְקָא! גְּזֵירָה מִשּׁוּם קָלָא אִילָן.

The Gemara suggests: **Let** the Rabbis **teach during** their public **lecture** that affixing wool strings to a linen garment is permitted for the mitzva of ritual fringes. The Gemara answers: Wearing strings on a linen garment is prohibited because of a rabbinic **decree due to** the concern that people might use strings that were dyed blue with **indigo** [***kala ilan***],[BLN] instead of with *tekhelet*, the sky-blue dye produced from the *ḥilazon* (see 44b), in which case they would not fulfill the mitzva of ritual fringes and would violate the prohibition against wearing garments containing wool and linen.

וְלֹא יְהֵא אֶלָּא לָבָן! כֵּיוָן דְּאֶפְשָׁר בְּמִינָן – לָא;

The Gemara suggests: Even if one's blue strings are not dyed with *tekhelet* as required for the mitzva, **let them be** considered **merely** as **white** strings. In the absence of *tekhelet* one fulfills the mitzva with white strings, and therefore it should be permitted to affix white woolen strings to a linen garment. The Gemara explains: **Since it is possible** to affix white strings that are **the same type** of material as the garment,[N] i.e., linen, and thereby fulfill the mitzva without overriding the prohibition against wearing a garment made from wool and linen, one may **not** affix white wool strings to a linen garment.

כִּדְרֵישׁ לָקִישׁ, דְּאָמַר רֵישׁ לָקִישׁ: כָּל מָקוֹם שֶׁאַתָּה מוֹצֵא עֲשֵׂה וְלֹא תַעֲשֶׂה, אִם אַתָּה יָכוֹל לְקַיֵּים אֶת שְׁנֵיהֶם – מוּטָב, וְאִם לָאו – יָבוֹא עֲשֵׂה וְיִדְחֶה אֶת לֹא תַעֲשֶׂה.

The Gemara notes: This is **in accordance with** the opinion **of Reish Lakish. As Reish Lakish says: Any place where you find a positive mitzva and a prohibition** that clash with one another, **if you are able to fulfill both of them,** that is **preferable; and if** that is **not** possible, **the positive mitzva shall come and override the prohibition.** In this case, the clash is between the mitzva of ritual fringes and the prohibition against wearing a garment that contains wool and linen. One can fulfill both of them by using white strings that are linen instead of wool if the garment is made from linen.

NOTES

Why did the Sages prohibit – לָמָּה אֲסָרוּהָ: The commentaries differ as to the meaning of this question and the Gemara's answer to it. Rashi's first explanation is that Rabbi Yehuda HaNasi is asking why, being that the *halakha* is in accordance with the opinion of Beit Hillel, did the Sages prohibit affixing ritual fringes to a linen garment in Jerusalem? Alternatively, it is a general inquiry as to the reason for this prohibition (*Tosafot*). Rashi's second explanation is that Rabbi Yehuda HaNasi is asking about the opinion of Beit Shammai: Since even Beit Shammai concede that the prohibition against wearing ritual fringes on a linen garment is by rabbinic decree, what is the reason for that decree?

Rabbinic decree due to the concern that people might use indigo – גְּזֵירָה מִשּׁוּם קָלָא אִילָן: According to this, the phrase: Because people are not well-versed, should be interpreted to mean that people are not expert in discerning the difference between *tekhelet* and indigo (Responsa attributed to the Rashba).

Since it is possible to affix white strings that are the same type of material as the garment – כֵּיוָן דְּאֶפְשָׁר בְּמִינָן: The prohibition of diverse kinds is overridden only in order to attach sky-blue strings to the garment, as fulfilling this aspect of the mitzva necessitates the use of wool. There is no need to use white strings made from wool, as they can just as well be made from linen.

BACKGROUND

Indigo [*kala ilan*] – קָלָא אִילָן: Indigo, *Indigofera tinctora* L., is a plant from the Fabaceae family. Its flowers can be red, pink, or white, and the indigo dye is produced from its leaves. This plant, which was for a long time the most important source of the blue dye for cloth, was grown principally in India, but also in other locales, including in the Middle East. It is only in modern times that use of indigo has decreased, due to the availability of a synthetic substitute. Apparently, the plant-based indigo dye is very similar to the *tekhelet* dye produced from the *ḥilazon*, but it was substantially cheaper. It was possible to detect that blue wool was dyed with indigo rather than *tekhelet* only via a complex examination.

Interestingly, blue dye derived from the *Murex trunculus*, the snail that has been identified by many contemporary researchers as the talmudic *ḥilazon* from which the sky-blue dye was made, is chemically identical to indigo derived from this plant.

Indigo plant

Cakes of indigo dye

LANGUAGE

Indigo [*kala ilan*] – קָלָא אִילָן: This term derives from the Greek Κελαινός, *kelainos*, meaning dark. Some maintain that it derives from *kala* in Sanskrit, where it also means dark blue. If so, the Hebrew term *ilan*, meaning tree, is added to indicate that it comes from a plant.

וְלִיבְדְּקוּהָ! אֶלָּא גְּזֵירָה מִשּׁוּם טְעִימָה.

The Gemara suggests: **And let them test** the strings[N] to ascertain whether they are dyed with indigo or with *tekhelet*, as explained by the Gemara (42b). The Gemara responds: **Rather,** the prohibition against affixing ritual fringes to a linen garment is a rabbinic **decree due to** the concern that perhaps the sky-blue strings were colored with *tekhelet* dye that had been used for **testing**[N] the color of the dye in the vat and therefore became unfit (see 42b). In such a case, there would be no fulfillment of the mitzva of sky-blue ritual fringes to override the prohibition against wearing a garment of wool and linen.

וְלִיכְתְּבָה אַדִּיסְקֵי! אַדִּיסְקֵי לֵיקוּם וְלִיסְמוֹךְ? אֲמַר רָבָא: הָשְׁתָּא

The Gemara suggests: **Let** the Sages **write letters**[N] informing dye producers that *tekhelet* that was used for testing the color of the dye in the vat is unfit for ritual fringes. The Gemara explains: **Shall we go and rely on letters,** assuming that dye producers will follow the instructions they contain? **Rava** responded to this and **said: Now,**

NOTES

And let them test the strings – **וְלִיבְדְּקוּהָ**: Rashi's second explanation of this, which conforms to the standard version of the text, is that the Sages should instruct people to test the blue wool that they buy in order to ensure that it is dyed with *tekhelet* and not indigo. For this purpose, they should also teach people how to conduct this test (Rabbeinu Gershom Meor HaGola). It would then be unnecessary to issue a decree prohibiting people from fulfilling this mitzva.

Testing – **טְעִימָה**: According to the standard version of the text, this sentence is introduced with the word: Rather, indicating that the Gemara has now rejected the claim that the prohibition against wearing ritual fringes with a linen garment is due to the concern that one will use strings dyed with indigo. The Gemara is presenting a different reason for this prohibition, which is that perhaps the wool was dyed as a test and not with the intent that it would be used for ritual fringes, and therefore it is unfit for the mitzva.

Conversely, some editions of the Talmud did not contain the word: Rather. Accordingly, Rashi explains that the Gemara had asked why there is a concern that the strings were dyed with indigo; let people test the vats of dye to ensure that they contain real *tekhelet*. The Gemara answers that this process itself can lead to problems, as people may remove some of the dye to test it and then pour it back into the vat, which would disqualify all the dye in the vat from being used for ritual fringes. Consequently, the concern remains that the strings may have been dyed with disqualified dye. *Tosafot* mention both interpretations according to this latter version of the text (see *Sefer HaIttur*).

Let the Sages write letters – **וְלִיכְתְּבָה אַדִּיסְקֵי**: This means that the Sages should send letters all over informing people that wool that was colored with the dye used for testing is unfit for the mitzva of ritual fringes, or that dye that was removed from the vat as a sample cannot be poured back into the vat (Rashi). The Gemara's response is that it is not possible to assume that everyone would receive the letter and follow its instructions.

Some explain that the Gemara means to suggest that dyed wool should require letters of certification that it was dyed with real *tekhelet*. The Gemara responds that this cannot be relied upon because people might forge the letters or take them from one batch of wool and reuse them with another (*Sefer HaEshkol*).

Perek **IV**
Daf **40** Amud **b**

חָמֵץ בְּפֶסַח וְיוֹם הַכִּפּוּרִים דְּכָרֵת – סָמְכִינַן אַדִּיסְקֵי, הָכָא דַּעֲשֵׂה בְּעָלְמָא לֹא כׇּל שֶׁכֵּן?

with regard to the prohibitions against eating **leavened bread on Passover and** eating on **Yom Kippur, which** are punishable by ***karet*, we rely on letters** sent from the rabbinical court in Eretz Yisrael publicizing whether the year was declared a leap year and when they have declared the New Moon; **here,** with regard to the mitzva of ritual fringes, **which is merely a positive mitzva,** is it **not all the more so** correct that letters can be relied on?

אֶלָּא אֲמַר רָבָא: הָא מִילְּתָא אֲמַרִי, וְאִיתְּמַר בְּמַעְרְבָא מִשְּׁמֵיהּ דְּרַבִּי זֵירָא כְּוָותִי: שֶׁמָּא יִקָּרַע סְדִינוֹ בְּתוֹךְ שָׁלֹשׁ וְיִתְפְּרֶנּוּ,

Rather, Rava said: This is a statement that **I said, and it was stated in the West,** Eretz Yisrael, **in the name of Rabbi Zeira in accordance with my** opinion: The reason for the rabbinic decree is **lest** one's **cloak rip within three** fingerbreadths of the edge of the corner of the garment, which is where the ritual fringes are placed, **and he sew it**[N] with linen string and then use the excess string for ritual fringes.

וְהַתּוֹרָה אָמְרָה: ״תַּעֲשֶׂה״ – וְלֹא מִן הֶעָשׂוּי.

And in such a case the ritual fringes would be unfit because **the Torah states:** "You shall prepare yourself twisted cords" (Deuteronomy 22:12), which teaches: **Prepare it, and not from what has already been prepared.** Consequently, the strings must be attached to the garment for the sake of the mitzva of ritual fringes. When the individual places the linen string there in order to stitch the garment and then decides to use it for the mitzva of ritual fringes and adds sky-blue wool strings, he does not fulfill the mitzva of ritual fringes and violates the prohibition against wearing a garment of wool and linen.

NOTES

Lest one's cloak rip within three fingerbreadths and he sew it – **שֶׁמָּא יִקָּרַע סְדִינוֹ בְּתוֹךְ שָׁלֹשׁ וְיִתְפְּרֶנּוּ**: Rashi explains that the concern applies only to a case where the tear occurred within three fingerbreadths of the corner because that is where the ritual fringes are attached to the garment. The concern is that perhaps he will attach a linen string to sew the garment and then decide to use it for the mitzva of ritual fringes. Other early commentaries explain that the concern is that the corner will tear after the ritual fringes have already been affixed. When he then reattaches that corner to the garment, the ritual fringes on that corner are unfit. This is because the principle: Prepare it, and not from what has already been prepared, requires that the strings be affixed to the garment directly and for the sake of the mitzva, whereas in this case they were affixed to the garment through the sewing of the corner to the rest of the garment (Rav Amram Gaon; *Tosafot*; see 41a).

שְׁרָא רַבִּי זֵירָא לִסְדִינֵיהּ. רַב זֵירָא אֲמַר: גְּזֵירָה נַמִי מִשּׁוּם כְּסוּת לַיְלָה.

Because of this rabbinic decree, **Rabbi Zeira untied** the ritual fringes and removed them from **his** linen **cloak. Rav Zeira said:** The rabbinic **decree** prohibiting ritual fringes on a linen garment is **also due to** the concern that one might affix ritual fringes to **a nighttime garment.**[N] Since the mitzva of ritual fringes does not apply in that case, if one wears the garment he would not fulfill the mitzva and would violate the prohibition against wearing a garment with wool and linen.

וַאֲמַר רָבָא: הָא מִילְּתָא אֲמַרִי, וְאִיתְּמַר בְּמַעֲרָבָא מִשְּׁמֵיהּ דְּרַבִּי זֵירָא כְּוָותִי: הִיא שֶׁל בֶּגֶד וּכְנָפֶיהָ שֶׁל עוֹר – חַיֶּיבֶת, הִיא שֶׁל עוֹר וּכְנָפֶיהָ שֶׁל בֶּגֶד – פְּטוּרָה, מַאי טַעְמָא? עִיקַּר בֶּגֶד בָּעֵינַן.

And Rava said: This is a statement that **I said, and it was stated in the West,** Eretz Yisrael, **in the name of Rabbi Zeira in accordance with my** opinion: If a garment is made **from cloth and its corners** are made **from leather,**[H] it is **required** to have ritual fringes. Conversely, if a cloak is made **from leather**[N] **and its corners** are made **from cloth,** it is **exempt** from the mitzva of ritual fringes. **What is the reason** for this? **We require** that **the main** part of the **garment** be obligated, and a leather garment is not required to have ritual fringes.

רַב אַחַאי אָזֵיל בָּתַר כָּנָף.

The Gemara notes: **Rav Aḥai** would **follow the corner** in determining whether the garment is required to have ritual fringes or not, because the Torah states: "On the corners of their garments" (Numbers 15:38).

אָמַר רָבָא אָמַר רַב סְחוֹרָה אָמַר רַב הוּנָא: הִטִּיל לְבַעֲלַת שָׁלֹשׁ וְהִשְׁלִימָהּ לְאַרְבַּע – פְּסוּלָה, ״תַּעֲשֶׂה״ – וְלֹא מִן הֶעָשׂוּי.

§ **Rava says** that **Rav Seḥora says** that **Rav Huna says:** In a case where one **affixed** ritual fringes **to** a garment **possessing** only **three** corners,[H] which is not required to have ritual fringes, **and** then **completed** its **fourth** corner by sewing on additional material or cutting away some of the material, the ritual fringes he attached to the original three corners are **unfit.** This is due to the principle: **Prepare** it, **and not from what has already been prepared.** Once the garment is required to have ritual fringes one may attach the ritual fringes; the strings that were attached before the garment was required to have them are not fit.

מֵיתִיבֵי: חֲסִידִים הָרִאשׁוֹנִים, כֵּיוָן שֶׁאָרְגוּ בָּהּ שָׁלֹשׁ הָיוּ מַטִּילִין לָהּ תְּכֵלֶת! אֵימָא: כֵּיוָן שֶׁפָּצְעוּ בָּהּ שָׁלֹשׁ הָיוּ מַטִּילִין לָהּ תְּכֵלֶת.

The Gemara **raises an objection** from a *baraita*: It is told of **the early** generations of **pious** men that **once they weaved three** fingerbreadths of the length of the garment, **they would affix** the white and **sky-blue** strings **to** the first two corners, even though the garment was not yet long enough to be obligated to have ritual fringes. The Gemara answers: **Say** that the *baraita* should read as follows: **Once they completed [*shepatzu*]**[LN] the garment until there were only **three** fingerbreadths left to weave, **they would affix** the white and **sky-blue** strings **to** the first two corners.

HALAKHA

If a garment is made from cloth and its corners are made from leather – הִיא שֶׁל בֶּגֶד וּכְנָפֶיהָ שֶׁל עוֹר: If a garment is made from cloth and its corners are made from leather, it is required to have ritual fringes. If the garment is made from leather and the corners are from cloth, it is exempt. The determining factor is the main body of the garment, not the corners. This is in accordance with the opinion of Rava and Rabbi Zeira (Rambam *Sefer Ahava, Hilkhot Tzitzit* 3:4; *Shulḥan Arukh, Oraḥ Ḥayyim* 10:4).

One affixed ritual fringes to a garment possessing only three corners – הִטִּיל לְבַעֲלַת שָׁלֹשׁ: If one affixed ritual fringes to a garment that had three corners and then added a fourth corner and attached ritual fringes to that corner, the strings on the first three corners are unfit because of the principle: Prepare it, and not from what has already been prepared (Rambam *Sefer Ahava, Hilkhot Tzitzit* 1:16; *Shulḥan Arukh, Oraḥ Ḥayyim* 10:5).

LANGUAGE

Completed [*patzu*] – פָּצְעוּ: The correct version of the text appears to be *batzu* rather than *patzu*; alternatively, the word *patzu* means *batzu*, with the *peh* replacing a *beit*, which is a common phenomenon. This term means completed. The root *beit, tzadi, ayin* appears in the sense of completion in the verse: "The hands of Zerubbabel have laid the foundation of this house; his hands shall also finish it [*tevatzana*]" (Zechariah 4:9).

Others explain this term to mean undoing [*potzea*] or unraveling the garment, and refers to the practice of leaving unraveled threads at the end of a garment (Rashash).

NOTES

Nighttime garment – כְּסוּת לַיְלָה: The Gemara states (43a) that the verse: "That you may look on it" (Numbers 15:39), stated with regard to ritual fringes, excludes nighttime, which is not conducive for seeing. Rashi explains here that the concern is that one might wear the garment at night and thereby violate the prohibition of diverse kinds when the mitzva of ritual fringes is not in force. This would be also be prohibited if it was a daytime garment, since the obligation is determined by the time when he wears the garment.

By contrast, Rabbeinu Tam holds that the mitzva of ritual fringes applies to a garment that is generally worn by day, even when one wears that garment at night, and the mitzva does not apply to a nighttime garment, even when one wears it during the day. Consequently, the concern here is that if one attaches wools strings to a linen daytime garment, he might also attach wool strings to a linen nighttime garment. In that case, since the mitzva of ritual fringes does not apply, he would violate the prohibition against wearing a garment containing wool and linen (see Rosh 4:1; *Sha'agat Arye* 30).

From leather – שֶׁל עוֹר: A leather article of clothing is not required to have ritual fringes. This is based on the fact that the verse requires "strings on the corners of their garments" (Numbers 15:38). Leather is not classified as a garment, as indicated in the verse: "Or a garment, or leather" (Leviticus 11:32), pertaining to ritual impurity (*Arukh HaShulḥan*).

Once they completed [*shepatzu*] – כֵּיוָן שֶׁפָּצְעוּ: Rashi explains that at this point the garment is basically completed, since the location where the strings would be attached to the final two corners has been created. Consequently, the ritual fringes can already be attached to all four corners of the garment.

Rabbeinu Gershom Meor HaGola explains that the Gemara means that even the final three fingerbreadths have been completed. According to this understanding, the point is that the pious men would attach the ritual fringes to all four corners immediately upon completion of the garment. Along these lines, *Sefer HaIttur* notes that there is a version of the Gemara that reads: Once they dyed [*shetzavu*] three fingerbreadths of the garment, meaning that they affixed the ritual fringes even before the garment was fully processed and ready to be worn.

HALAKHA

One affixed ritual fringes to a garment that already had ritual fringes affixed to it – הִטִּיל לְמוּטֶּלֶת: If one affixed ritual fringes to a garment that already had ritual fringes affixed to it and he had intended to nullify the first set, then he may remove the first set and the remaining ritual fringes are fit. But if he had intended to add to the first set, the ritual fringes are unfit even if he later removes the first set. This is due to the fact that when he added the second set he rendered all the strings unfit. Then when he removed the first set, the second set remained unfit because of the principle: Prepare it, and not from what has already been prepared, as when he placed the second set initially, it was not fit. The Rema writes that there are those who deem the second set fit even in the case where he intended to add (Rosh), and this is the accepted opinion. In any case, it is noted in *Beit Yosef* that all the ritual fringes are certainly unfit while both sets are attached (Rambam *Sefer Ahava*, *Hilkhot Tzitzit* 1:15; *Shulḥan Arukh*, *Oraḥ Ḥayyim* 10:6).

A cloak that is large enough for a minor to cover, etc. – טַלִּית שֶׁהַקָּטָן מִתְכַּסֶּה וכו׳: If a garment is large enough to cover the head and body of a minor who is old enough to walk around in the marketplace by himself, one is required to attach ritual fringes to it. The Rema adds that this applies only if an adult would occasionally go out in public wearing that garment (Rambam *Sefer Ahava*, *Hilkhot Tzitzit* 3:1; *Shulḥan Arukh*, *Oraḥ Ḥayyim* 16:1).

וּמִי אָמְרִינַן תַּעֲשֶׂה וְלֹא מִן הֶעָשׂוּי? (אִינִי) וְהָאָמַר רַבִּי זֵירָא: הִטִּיל לְמוּטֶּלֶת – כְּשֵׁרָה!

The Gemara asks: **And do we say: Prepare** it, **and not from what has already been prepared? Is that so** that this principle disqualifies ritual fringes that one affixed to a garment before he was required to do so? **But doesn't Rabbi Zeira say:** If one **affixed** ritual fringes **to** a garment that already had ritual fringes **affixed** to it[HN] and then removed the original strings, it is **fit,** despite the fact that when he attached the second set they were superfluous? This indicates that even if one attaches ritual fringes to a garment when there is no obligation to attach them, the ritual fringes are fit.

אֲמַר רָבָא: הַשְׁתָּא בְּבַל תּוֹסִיף קָאֵי, מַעֲשֶׂה לָא הָוֵי.

Rava said: This does not present a difficulty, because **now** that he adds a second, unnecessary set of ritual fringes and **is** liable **for** violating the **prohibition of adding** to a mitzva (see Deuteronomy 13:1), **is it not** considered **an action?**[N]

מַתְקִיף לַהּ רַב פָּפָּא: מִמַּאי דְּגַבְרָא לְאוֹסוֹפֵי קָא מִיכַּוֵּין? דִּלְמָא לְבַטּוֹלֵי קָא מִיכַּוֵּין, וּבַל תּוֹסִיף לֵיכָּא, מַעֲשֶׂה אִיכָּא!

Rav Pappa objects to this:[N] **From where** is it known **that** Rabbi Zeira is discussing a case where the **person intended to add** to the original set of ritual fringes? **Perhaps** Rabbi Zeira is discussing a case where **he intended to nullify** the original strings, **and** therefore **there is no prohibition of adding** to a mitzva, and **there is an action.**

אָמַר רַבִּי זֵירָא אָמַר רַב מַתָּנָא אָמַר שְׁמוּאֵל: תְּכֵלֶת אֵין בָּהּ מִשּׁוּם כִּלְאַיִם, וַאֲפִילּוּ בְּטַלִּית פְּטוּרָה.

With regard to the issue of affixing ritual fringes to a garment that already has ritual fringes, the Gemara relates: **Rabbi Zeira says** that **Rav Mattana says** that **Shmuel says:** White and **sky-blue** strings **are not subject to** the prohibition of **diverse kinds,**[N] **and** this is the *halakha* **even** if they are affixed **to a cloak** that is **exempt** from ritual fringes.

מַאי טַלִּית פְּטוּרָה? אִילֵּימָא דְּלֵית בָּהּ שִׁיעוּרָא, וְהָתַנְיָא: טַלִּית שֶׁהַקָּטָן מִתְכַּסֶּה בּוֹ רֹאשׁוֹ וְרוּבּוֹ,

The Gemara asks: **What** is meant by: **A cloak** that is **exempt** from ritual fringes? **If we say** that it is referring to a cloak **that is not of the size** necessary to require the affixing of ritual fringes, that is difficult: **But isn't it taught** in a *baraita*: With regard to **a cloak that** is large enough for **a minor** to **cover**[H] **his head and most of his** body **with** it,

NOTES

One affixed ritual fringes to a garment that already had ritual fringes affixed to it – הִטִּיל לְמוּטֶּלֶת: Rashi explains that once the first set of ritual fringes are removed, the second set is fit. Some explain that while both sets are attached to the garment, the prohibition against adding to a mitzva nullifies the entire mitzva, and both sets of ritual fringes are unfit (see *Beit Yosef*). Rabbeinu Gershom Meor HaGola explains that the Gemara is referring to a linen garment, and Rabbi Zeira's point is that even though the second set of ritual fringes contains wool and is unnecessary, one does not violate the prohibition against wearing a garment containing wool and linen. This understanding is apparently based on the Gemara on 41a.

Is it not considered an action – מַעֲשֶׂה לָא הָוֵי: There are different versions of the text, with corresponding differences in interpretation. The standard version includes the word: Now, which usually introduces a rhetorical question. This is missing in other versions of the text. All interpretations rely on the idea that the principle: Prepare it, and not from what has already been prepared, indicates that ritual fringes must be appropriately affixed to the garment via an action performed at a time when the garment is required to have ritual fringes.

The version of the text known to Rashi apparently did not have the word: Now, and he therefore explains this line as a statement: Because attaching the second set of ritual fringes violates the prohibition against adding to a mitzva, it is not deemed an action. Removing the first set is therefore viewed as the act that gives the second set of ritual fringes their status as such. Consequently, the second set of ritual fringes is considered to have been attached to a garment that required ritual fringes, because at the time when the relevant act occurred, i.e., the removal of the first set, the garment became required to have ritual fringes. Consequently, this meets the requirement of the principle: Prepare it, and not from what has already been prepared, and the second set of strings is fit. Similarly, Rabbeinu Gershom Meor HaGola explains that the act of attaching the second set of strings cannot be considered an action, since this garment already had ritual fringes attached.

According to the standard version of the text, this sentence is a rhetorical question and therefore must be understood in the opposite sense of the previous explanation: The fact that one is liable for violating the prohibition against adding to a mitzva means that affixing the second set of ritual fringes must be viewed as a significant action. Consequently, the strings are considered to have been given their status via an action, and they are fit. Conversely, in the case where one placed ritual fringes on a garment that had only three corners, the strings became attached to a four-cornered garment via an action that one performed on the garment rather than an action one performed on the strings, and therefore the strings are unfit (*Kesef Mishne*, in explanation of the Rambam; *Sefat Emet*).

By contrast, the *Taz* and the Gra explain that Rava is challenging the opinion of Rabbi Zeira and asking why the ritual fringes are fit if one placed them on a garment that already has ritual fringes. Since he violates the prohibition against adding to a mitzva, his initial placement of the ritual fringes is certainly considered an action. Since the second set becomes valid when the first set is removed, the second set is not becoming fit through an action. It is therefore unfit due to the principle: Prepare it, and not from what has already been prepared.

Rav Pappa objects to this – מַתְקִיף לַהּ רַב פָּפָּא: The interpretation of Rav Pappa's objection depends upon the interpretations of the statement of Rava. According to the interpretation of Rashi and Rabbeinu Gershom Meor HaGola, Rav Pappa is rejecting the reasoning of Rava by asserting that placing the second set of ritual fringes is considered an action. Therefore, the original objection from the statement of Rabbi Zeira remains.

The *Kesef Mishne* explains that according to the interpretation of the Rambam, Rav Pappa accepts Rava's basic assertion that affixing ritual fringes to a garment that already has ritual fringes is considered an action, and therefore they are not disqualified on the basis of the principle: Prepare it, and not from what has already been prepared. Yet, Rav Pappa limits this to where he intended to nullify the first set of ritual fringes. Where he intended to add to the original set, all of the ritual fringes are unfit (see *Taz*, Gra and *Sefat Emet*, who explain that Rav Pappa is defending Rabbi Zeira's opinion, and see *Keren Ora*).

White and sky-blue strings are not subject to the prohibition of diverse kinds – תְּכֵלֶת אֵין בָּהּ מִשּׁוּם כִּלְאַיִם: This refers to a case where one attached wool ritual fringes to a linen garment, or where the ritual fringes themselves included both wool and linen (*Shita Mekubbetzet*, citing Rashi). *Tosafot* note that the fact that the following phrase is introduced with the word: And, indicates that there is significance to Shmuel's statement even where the cloak is required to have ritual fringes. They explain that this applies in the case of one who wears the strings with diverse kinds at night, when he does not fulfill the mitzva of ritual fringes. Similarly, although the priestly vestments contain wool and linen, one does not violate the prohibition of diverse kinds by wearing priestly garments, even if he wears them at a time when he is not performing the Temple service.

וְהַגָּדוֹל יוֹצֵא בָּהּ דֶּרֶךְ עֲרַאי – חַיֶּיבֶת בְּצִיצִית. אֵין הַקָּטָן מִתְכַּסֶּה בּוֹ רֹאשׁוֹ וְרוּבּוֹ, אַף עַל פִּי שֶׁהַגָּדוֹל יוֹצֵא בָּהּ עֲרַאי – פְּטוּרָה, וְכֵן לְעִנְיַן כִּלְאַיִם;

and an adult goes out in public **on occasion** while wearing **it,**[N] it is **required** to have **ritual fringes.** But if it is **not** large enough for **a minor to cover his head and most of his** body **with** it, then **even if an adult goes out** in public **on occasion** while wearing **it,** it is **exempt** from ritual fringes. **And so too with regard to diverse kinds,** i.e., the prohibition against wearing wool and linen together.

וְהָוֵינַן בָּהּ, מַאי ״וְכֵן לְעִנְיַן כִּלְאַיִם״? אִילֵימָא וְכֵן לְעִנְיַן אִיסּוּרָא דְּכִלְאַיִם – וְהָא אֲנַן תְּנַן: אֵין עֲרַאי בְּכִלְאַיִם;

And we discussed it: What is meant by: **And so too with regard to diverse kinds? If we say** that it means: **And so too with regard to the prohibition of diverse kinds,** that if a minor could not cover the majority of his head and body with it, the prohibition of diverse kinds does not apply, that is difficult: **But didn't we learn** in a mishna (*Kilayim* 9:2): **There is no** exemption **with regard to** the prohibition of **diverse kinds** for clothing that an adult would not wear even **occasionally**[NH] in public?

וְאָמַר רַב נַחְמָן בַּר יִצְחָק: וְכֵן לְעִנְיַן סָדִין בְּצִיצִית!

And Rav Naḥman bar Yitzḥak says in explanation: Rather, the *baraita* means: **And so too with regard to** whether a linen **cloak** is required **to** have **ritual fringes.** If the cloak is large enough for a minor to cover his head and most of his body with it, then it requires ritual fringes, and wearing the garment with the ritual fringes is not a violation of the prohibition of diverse kinds. But if the garment is smaller than that, it is prohibited to place ritual fringes on it, due to the prohibition of diverse kinds. Therefore, one cannot explain Shmuel's statement to mean that a cloak that is exempt from ritual fringes because it is too small is not subject to the prohibition of diverse kinds.

אֶלָּא מַאי פְּטוּרָה – הִטִּיל לְמוּטֶּלֶת.

Rather, what is meant by the statement that a cloak that is **exempt** from ritual fringes is not subject to the prohibition of diverse kinds? It is referring to where one **affixed** ritual fringes **to** a garment that already had ritual fringes **affixed** to it. Even though the second set of ritual fringes is superfluous, nevertheless there is no violation of the prohibition of diverse kinds.

וְהָא אֲמַרַהּ רַבִּי זֵירָא חֲדָא זִימְנָא! חֲדָא מִכְּלַל דַּחֲבֵירְתָּהּ אִיתְּמַר.

The Gemara asks: **But didn't Rabbi Zeira** already **say this one time** when he stated that if one attached ritual fringes to a garment that already had ritual fringes attached to it and he then removed the first set of strings, the garment is fit? The Gemara answers: **One was stated from the other by inference,**[N] and Rabbi Zeira did not state both statements.

תָּנוּ רַבָּנַן: טַלִּית כְּפוּלָה חַיֶּיבֶת בְּצִיצִית, וְרַבִּי שִׁמְעוֹן פּוֹטֵר; וְשָׁוִין, שֶׁאִם כְּפָלָהּ וּתְפָרָהּ שֶׁחַיֶּיבֶת.

§ **The Sages taught** in a *baraita*: A very long **cloak that is folded**[NH] in half is **required** to have **ritual fringes** at the fold. **And Rabbi Shimon deems** it **exempt** it from ritual fringes at the fold because that is not where the corners of the garment are located. **And** Rabbi Shimon and the Rabbis **agree that if he folded it and sewed it,** it is **required** to have ritual fringes at the fold.

תְּפָרָהּ, פְּשִׁיטָא! לָא צְרִיכָא, דְּנַקְטָהּ בְּסִיכֵי.

The Gemara challenges: If one **sewed it,** it is **obvious** that it is required to have ritual fringes at the fold. The Gemara explains: **No,** it is **necessary** to state this *halakha* because it is referring to a case **where he fastened it with pins** rather than sewing it in the conventional manner.

רַבָּה בַּר הוּנָא אִיקְּלַע לְבֵי רָבָא בַּר רַב נַחְמָן, חַזְיֵיהּ דַּהֲוָה מִיכַּסֵּי טַלִּית כְּפוּלָה וְרָמֵי לֵיהּ חוּטֵי עִילָּוֵי כְּפֵילָא, אִיפְּשִׁיטָא וַאֲתָא חוּטָא וְקָם לַהֲדֵי רֵישֵׁיהּ.

The Gemara relates that **Rabba bar Huna arrived at the house of Rava bar Rav Naḥman,** and **he saw that** Rava bar Rav Naḥman **was wearing a cloak that was folded and** that he had **affixed strings to it on** the corners of **the fold.** The cloak **unfolded, and the string** that had been on the corner of the fold now **came and settled near his head,** i.e., in the middle of the cloak, as the two sides of the cloak were in the front and back of Rava bar Rav Naḥman.

NOTES

And an adult goes out in public on occasion while wearing it – וְהַגָּדוֹל יוֹצֵא בָּהּ דֶּרֶךְ עֲרַאי: Some commentaries understand this as an additional criterion. According to this explanation, only a garment that meets both of these criteria is required to have ritual fringes (*Baḥ*, citing *Tur*). Others hold that the only criterion is that the garment is large enough to cover most of the child's body and head, and the Gemara here means that if the garment meets that criterion, an adult must place ritual fringes on it even if he wears it only on occasion (*Beit Yosef*).

There is no exemption with regard to diverse kinds for clothing that an adult would not wear even occasionally – אֵין עֲרַאי בְּכִלְאַיִם: The prohibition of diverse kinds is the very act of wearing a garment containing wool and linen, regardless of whether or not this garment is normally worn by people (see *Haggahot Rav Shmuel Taubes*).

One was stated from the other by inference – חֲדָא מִכְּלַל דַּחֲבֵירְתָּהּ אִיתְּמַר: Rashi explains that Rabbi Zeira stated explicitly that the ritual fringes are fit for the mitzva, and it was inferred from this that wearing the garment with the ritual fringes is not a violation of the prohibition of diverse kinds. *Tosafot* maintain that it is more reasonable to assume the opposite, that Rabbi Zeira explicitly stated that there is no prohibition of diverse kinds, as he cited that ruling in the name of Rav Mattana in the name of Shmuel; it was then inferred that the ritual fringes are fit for the mitzva (see *Shita Mekubbetzet*).

A very long cloak that is folded – טַלִּית כְּפוּלָה: According to the Rabbis, one is obligated to place ritual fringes on the corners of the fold, as that is the edge of the garment in terms of how it is currently being worn. Rabbi Shimon deems one exempt from placing ritual fringes there, since when the cloak is opened up the strings will then be in the middle of the garment and not on its corners (Rashi). Others maintain that the reason for the exemption is that the cloak is oversized and not suitable for wearing (*Nimmukei Yosef*). Some note that according to the first explanation, Rabbi Shimon holds that one is exempt from placing ritual fringes on the corners of the fold but must place them on the actual corners of the cloak. By contrast, according to the second explanation, the cloak is completely exempt (*Taz*).

HALAKHA

There is no exemption with regard to diverse kinds for clothing that an adult would not wear even occasionally – אֵין עֲרַאי בְּכִלְאַיִם: It is prohibited to wear any garment that contains wool and linen, even if it is the garment of a child and an adult would not wear it in public (Rambam *Sefer Zera'im, Hilkhot Kilayim* 10:18; *Shulḥan Arukh, Yoreh De'a* 301:4).

A very long cloak that is folded – טַלִּית כְּפוּלָה: If a cloak is folded in half, ritual fringes are attached to the original corners of the garment and not to the corners of the fold. If it was folded and sewn, even on one side, then the ritual fringes are attached to the corners of the garment in its folded form. This is in accordance with the opinion of Rabbi Shimon, which is accepted by Rabba bar Rav Huna. The Rema writes that there are those who rule in accordance with the opinion of the Rabbis and require the ritual fringes to be attached to the corners of the garment in its folded form even if the garment is not sewn (Rosh). Therefore, it is preferable to attach ritual fringes to the corners of the garment in its folded form but to avoid reciting the blessing on the mitzva of *tzitzit*. The *Mishna Berura* and *Sha'ar HaTziyyun* state that one should ideally not fold a four-cornered garment without sewing it in that position, but if one does so, the *halakha* is in accordance with the *Shulḥan Arukh* rather than the Rema (Rambam *Sefer Ahava, Hilkhot Tzitzit* 1:17; *Shulḥan Arukh, Oraḥ Ḥayyim* 10:6).

HALAKHA

An obligation incumbent upon the man – חוֹבַת גַּבְרָא: If a man has a garment to which the mitzva of ritual fringes applies, he must attach the ritual fringes to the garment before putting it on. If he wears the garment without ritual fringes attached, he has violated the mitzva. He is not required to attach strings to a garment that he is not wearing, as the mitzva of ritual fringes pertains to the individual rather than to the garment (Rambam *Sefer Ahava*, *Hilkhot Tzitzit* 3:10).

LANGUAGE

Coat [*sarbela*] – סַרְבְּלָא: This word is mentioned in Daniel 3:21. There, as well as here, its meaning is unclear. It appears from context to refer to a coat or cloak, and is related to the Arabic سربال, *sirbāl*.

אֲמַר לֵיהּ: לָאו הַיְינוּ כָּנָף דִּכְתַב רַחֲמָנָא בְּאוֹרַיְיתָא! אֲתָא שַׁדְיֵיהּ אִיכַּסֵּי גְּלִימָא אַחֲרִיתִי.

Rabba bar Huna **said to** Rava bar Rav Naḥman: **This is not** the **corner** of the garment **that the Merciful One writes** about **in the Torah.** Rava bar Rav Naḥman **went** and **threw it off,** and **he covered himself** with **a different cloak.**

אֲמַר לֵיהּ: מִי סָבְרַתְּ חוֹבַת גַּבְרָא הוּא? חוֹבַת טַלִּית הוּא, זִיל רְמֵי לַהּ.

Rabba bar Huna **said to** Rava bar Rav Naḥman: **Do you hold** that ritual fringes are **an obligation** incumbent upon **the man?**[HN] That is not so. Rather, **it is an obligation** that pertains to every **cloak** that one owns. Therefore, **go** and **affix** ritual fringes **to it** properly.

לֵימָא מְסַיַּיע לֵיהּ: חֲסִידִים הָרִאשׁוֹנִים, כֵּיוָן שֶׁאָרְגוּ בָּהּ שָׁלֹשׁ הָיוּ מַטִּילִין בָּהּ תְּכֵלֶת! שָׁאנֵי חֲסִידִים, דְּמַחְמְרִי אַנַּפְשַׁיְיהוּ.

The Gemara suggests: **Let us say** that a *baraita* **supports** the opinion of Rabba bar Huna: It is told of **the early** generations of **pious** men that **once they weaved three** fingerbreadths **of** the length of the garment,[N] **they would affix** the white and **sky-blue** strings **to** the first two corners, even though the garment was not yet ready to be worn. This seems to prove that there is an obligation to affix ritual fringes to all the cloaks in one's possession, even if he is not currently wearing them. The Gemara rejects this proof: The **pious** men were **different,** **as they would act stringently with themselves.**[N] Therefore, one cannot adduce the actual requirement from their behavior.

וּפְלִיגָא דְּמַלְאָכָא, דְּמַלְאָכָא אַשְׁכְּחֵיהּ לְרַב קְטִינָא דְּמִיכַּסֵּי סְדִינָא, אֲמַר לֵיהּ: קְטִינָא, קְטִינָא! סְדִינָא בְּקַיְיטָא וְסַרְבְּלָא בְּסִיתְוָא, צִיצִית שֶׁל תְּכֵלֶת מַה תְּהֵא עָלֶיהָ?

The Gemara notes that this **disagrees with** what **an angel** said. **As an angel found Rav Ketina when he was wearing** a linen **cloak,** which is exempt from ritual fringes. The angel **said to him: Ketina, Ketina,** if you wear a linen **cloak in the summer and a coat** [*sarbela*],[L] which has only two corners and is therefore also exempt from ritual fringes, **in the winter, what will become of** the **ritual fringes of sky-blue wool?** As a result, you will never fulfill the mitzva.

אֲמַר לֵיהּ: עָנְשִׁיתוּ אַעֲשֵׂה? אֲמַר לֵיהּ: בִּזְמָן דְּאִיכָּא רִיתְחָא עָנְשִׁינַן;

Rav Ketina **said to him: Do you punish** us even **for** failing to fulfill **a positive mitzva?** The angel **said to him: At a time when there is** divine **anger** and judgment, **we punish** even for the failure to fulfill a positive mitzva.

אִי אָמְרַתְּ בִּשְׁלָמָא חוֹבַת גַּבְרָא הוּא – הַיְינוּ דְּמִחַיַּיב, דְּלָא קָא רָמֵי, אֶלָּא אִי אָמְרַתְּ חוֹבַת טַלִּית הוּא – הָא לָא מִיחַיְּיבָא!

The Gemara attempts to draw conclusions from the statement of the angel: **Granted, if you say** that the mitzva of ritual fringes **is an obligation** incumbent upon the **man,**[N] **that is** why Rav Ketina would be **deemed liable** at a time of divine anger, **as he did not affix** ritual fringes to his cloak and thereby neglected the obligation incumbent upon him. **But if you say** that it **is an obligation** to attach them to every **cloak** that one owns, since Rav Ketina's cloaks were not required to have ritual fringes, **he was not obligated** to attach ritual fringes to them. Why should he be punished in a time of divine anger?

NOTES

Do you hold that ritual fringes are an obligation incumbent upon the man – מִי סָבְרַתְּ חוֹבַת גַּבְרָא הוּא: This means: Do you hold that one is required to wear a garment with ritual fringes, and as long as he is wearing such a garment he is exempt from attaching ritual fringes to his other garments? Rabba bar Ḥuna then said that it is an obligation that pertains to the garment, meaning that one is obligated to attach ritual fringes to all of his garments that are earmarked for wearing, just as one who lives in multiple houses is obligated to affix a *mezuza* to the doorpost of every house (*Sefer HaIttur*).

Once they weaved three fingerbreadths of the length of the garment – כֵּיוָן שֶׁאָרְגוּ בָּהּ שָׁלֹשׁ: According to the conclusion of the Gemara on 40b, the text here should actually read: Once they completed the garment until there were only three fingerbreadths left to weave, they would attach the white and sky-blue strings. In fact, this is the version of the text found in many manuscripts and early commentaries.

In any event, the point is that these pious individuals would attach the ritual fringes before the garment was completed (Rashi), or after it was completed but while it was still on the loom and therefore not yet fit to be worn (Rabbeinu Gershom Meor HaGola). This proves that even unworn garments must have ritual fringes.

The pious men were different as they would act stringently with themselves – שָׁאנֵי חֲסִידִים דְּמַחְמְרִי אַנַּפְשַׁיְיהוּ: Consequently, even if the mitzva of ritual fringes is incumbent upon the man, the pious men might have acted stringently and attached the strings even before the garment was ready to be worn, lest they forget later and wear the cloak without ritual fringes (*Sefat Emet*).

Granted, if you say that the mitzva of ritual fringes is an obligation incumbent upon the man – אִי אָמְרַתְּ בִּשְׁלָמָא חוֹבַת גַּבְרָא: According to this suggestion, understanding the mitzva to be incumbent upon the man would entail both a leniency and a stringency. On the one hand, as long as the man is wearing a garment with ritual fringes, there is no obligation for his other garments to have ritual fringes attached. On the other hand, he would be required to ensure that he is wearing a four-cornered garment with ritual fringes attached in order to fulfill the mitzva, just as he is obligated to don phylacteries or to take a *lulav* on *Sukkot* (*Sefer HaIttur*).

אֶלָּא מַאי, חוֹבַת גַּבְרָא הוּא? נְהִי דְּחַיְּיבֵיהּ רַחֲמָנָא כִּי מִיכַּסֵּי טַלִּית דְּבַת חִיּוּבָא, כִּי מִיכַּסֵּי טַלִּית דְּלָאו בַּת חִיּוּבָא הִיא, מִי חַיְּיבֵיהּ רַחֲמָנָא?

The Gemara responds: **Rather, what** should one assume, that **it is an obligation** incumbent upon the **man? Even so, granted that the Merciful One rendered him obligated when he is wearing a cloak that** has four corners and is therefore **subject to the obligation** of ritual fringes, but **when he is wearing a cloak that is not subject to the obligation** of ritual fringes, **did the Merciful One deem him obligated?**

אֶלָּא הָכִי קָאָמַר לֵיהּ: טַצְדְּקֵי לְמִיפְטַר נַפְשָׁךְ מִצִּיצִית?

Rather, this is what the angel **is saying to** Rav Ketina:[N] Are you seeking **ploys** [*tatzdeki*][L] **to exempt yourself from** performing the mitzva of **ritual fringes?**[H]

אָמַר רַב טוֹבִי בַּר קִיסְנָא אָמַר שְׁמוּאֵל: כְּלֵי קוּפְסָא חַיָּיבִין בְּצִיצִית. וּמוֹדֶה שְׁמוּאֵל בְּזָקֵן שֶׁעֲשָׂאָהּ לִכְבוֹדוֹ שֶׁפְּטוּרָה, מַאי טַעְמָא? ״אֲשֶׁר תְּכַסֶּה בָּהּ״ אָמַר רַחֲמָנָא, הַאי לָאו לְאִיכַּסּוּיֵי עֲבִידָא.

Rav Tovi bar Kisna says that **Shmuel says: Garments** that are not being worn but are stored in **a box are required** to have **ritual fringes,** because the mitzva pertains to the garment, not the man. **But Shmuel concedes in** the case of **an old man, where** the garment **was made** as a shroud **in his honor,**[H] **that** the shroud is **exempt. What is the reason** for this? **The Merciful One states** in the Torah that one must place ritual fringes on the corners of garments **"with which you cover yourself"** (Deuteronomy 22:12). **This** shroud **is not made for** the purpose of **covering** oneself.

בְּהַהִיא שַׁעְתָּא וַדַּאי רָמֵינַן לֵיהּ, מִשּׁוּם ״לֹעֵג לָרָשׁ חֵרֵף עֹשֵׂהוּ״.

The Gemara comments: **At that time,**[H] i.e., a person's burial, **we certainly affix** ritual fringes **to** the shroud, **because** otherwise it would be a violation of: **"Whoever mocks the poor blasphemes his Maker"** (Proverbs 17:5). If we did not place them, it would be mocking the deceased, as if to taunt him that now he is no longer obligated in mitzvot.

אָמַר רַחֲבָה אָמַר רַבִּי יְהוּדָה: טַלִּית שֶׁנִּקְרְעָה, חוּץ לְשָׁלֹשׁ – יִתְפּוֹר, תּוֹךְ שָׁלֹשׁ – לֹא יִתְפּוֹר.

§ **Raḥava says** that **Rabbi Yehuda says:** In the case of **a cloak that became torn** at one of its corners,[H] if it was torn **beyond three** fingerbreadths from the edge of the garment, one **may sew it.**[N] But if it was torn **within three** fingerbreadths of the edge of the garment, then one **may not sew** it. There is a concern that he might use the thread with which he sewed the garment for the ritual fringes, in which case the strings would be unfit due to the principle: Prepare it, and not from what has already been prepared.

תַּנְיָא נָמֵי הָכִי: טַלִּית שֶׁנִּקְרְעָה, חוּץ לְשָׁלֹשׁ – יִתְפּוֹר. תּוֹךְ שָׁלֹשׁ – רַבִּי מֵאִיר אוֹמֵר: לֹא יִתְפּוֹר, וַחֲכָמִים אוֹמְרִים: יִתְפּוֹר;

The Gemara comments: **This** *halakha* **is also taught** in a *baraita*: In the case of **a cloak that became torn** at one of its corners, if it was torn **beyond three** fingerbreadths from the edge of the garment, one **may sew it.** But if it was torn **within three** fingerbreadths of the edge of the garment, **Rabbi Meir says:** One **may not sew** it. **And the Rabbis say:** One **may sew** it.

LANGUAGE

Ploys [*tatzdeki*] – טַצְדְּקֵי: The correct reading is *tatzreki*, similar to the Zoroastrian Middle Persian word čārag, which can have the technical sense of: A legal way out. It has a similar usage in Arabic, where it means a trick or ploy.

HALAKHA

Ploys to exempt yourself from the mitzva of ritual fringes – טַצְדְּקֵי לְמִיפְטַר נַפְשָׁךְ מִצִּיצִית: One is not required to wear a four-cornered garment in order to be obligated to fulfill the mitzva of ritual fringes. Nevertheless, it is proper for one to wear such a garment in order to fulfill the mitzva and to be reminded of all of the mitzvot at all times. At the very least, one should be sure to wear ritual fringes while praying (Rambam *Sefer Ahava*, *Hilkhot Tzitzit* 3:11; *Shulḥan Arukh*, *Oraḥ Ḥayyim* 24:1).

An old man, where the garment was made as a shroud in his honor – זָקֵן שֶׁעֲשָׂאָהּ לִכְבוֹדוֹ: If a garment was made as a shroud it is exempt from ritual fringes, even if a living person occasionally wears it. Later commentaries, cited by the *Mishna Berura*, claim that according to the Rambam, who holds that a nighttime garment is required to have ritual fringes when worn during the daytime, one is required to attach ritual fringes to a shroud that one decides to wear. Consequently, one should attach ritual fringes but should not recite a blessing (*Shulḥan Arukh*, *Oraḥ Ḥayyim* 19:2).

At that time – בְּהַהִיא שַׁעְתָּא: A corpse should be buried in a cloak with ritual fringes. The Rema cites opinions that there is no need to attach ritual fringes, and adds that it is customary to bury people in a cloak with ritual fringes but to first render the ritual fringes unfit or to tie up one of the corners. The *Baḥ* writes that one should not render them unfit; rather, one should tie the strings together or cover them up by tucking them into the corners (*Shakh*). The custom in Eretz Yisrael, as cited in *Gesher HaḤayyim*, is not to bury people in cloaks with ritual fringes (*Shulḥan Arukh*, *Yoreh De'a* 351:2).

Cloak that became torn at one of its corners – טַלִּית שֶׁנִּקְרְעָה: If the corner of a cloak became detached more than three fingerbreadths from its edge, according to Rav Amram Gaon one may sew the corner back on together with the ritual fringes that it contains. If it became torn within three fingerbreadths of the edge, Rashi holds that one may not use wool string to sew it back on, lest he include that string in the ritual fringes. It is permitted to sew it on with another type of string. According to Rav Amram Gaon, if the corner was completely severed from the garment within three fingerbreadths of the edge and one sewed it back on, the ritual fringes on that corner are unfit. Some maintain that according to Rav Amram Gaon only the ritual fringes that were there before it ripped are rendered unfit, due to the principle: Prepare it, and not from what has already been prepared. But if one placed new ritual fringes after sewing the corner back on, then it is fit. One who is God fearing should attempt to satisfy all of the opinions to the extent possible (Rambam *Sefer Ahava*, *Hilkhot Tzitzit* 1:18; *Shulḥan Arukh*, *Oraḥ Ḥayyim* 15:4, and see *Mishna Berura* there).

NOTES

Rather, this is what the angel is saying to Rav Ketina – אֶלָּא הָכִי קָאָמַר לֵיהּ: That is to say, one cannot reach any conclusion from this incident as to the nature of the mitzva of ritual fringes, because the angel was not admonishing Rav Ketina for failing to fulfill an obligation but rather for going out of his way to avoid becoming obligated in the first place. Some versions of the text omit the word: Rather. According to these versions, the Gemara is stating that the angel was admonishing Rav Ketina because the mitzva of ritual fringes is incumbent upon the man (*Tosafot*).

If it was torn beyond three fingerbreadths from the edge, one may sew it – חוּץ לְשָׁלֹשׁ יִתְפּוֹר: The reason for this is that since one does not attach ritual fringes that far from the edge of the garment (see 41b), there is no concern that he will use the threads with which he sewed the garment as ritual fringes (Rashi). Others explain that the case is that the corner was completely severed from the garment. The Gemara is saying that if the part that was severed is at least three square fingerbreadths, it retains its status as the corner of the garment, and one may simply reattach it to the garment without untying and retying the ritual fringes. But if the part of the garment that was severed is less than three square fingerbreadths, it does not retain its status, and therefore it is not sufficient to merely sew it back on. The ritual fringes attached to the severed corner must be untied, reinserted into the garment, and retied, as otherwise they are unfit due to the principle: Prepare it, and not from what has already been prepared (*Shita Mekubbetzet*, citing Rabbeinu Yitzḥak and Rid; *Nimmukei Yosef*, citing Rav Amram Gaon). Others cite Rav Amram Gaon as stating that if the severed corner is three by three fingerbreadths, which is the minimum size of a garment, it is deemed significant, and the ritual fringes may be attached to it. If it is smaller than this size, it is not significant, and ritual fringes may not be attached to it even after it is sewn back onto the garment (Rosh).

HALAKHA

That one may not bring a piece of cloth, even if it is a square cubit in size, etc. – שֶׁלֹּא יָבִיא אֲפִילּוּ אַמָּה עַל אַמָּה וכו׳: One may not take a piece of fabric that already contains ritual fringes and sew it on to the corner of a garment. This is due to the fact that the verse requires "that they prepare for themselves strings on the corners of their garments" (Numbers 15:38), which indicates that the strings must be attached to the garment itself and not to a piece of fabric that is later sewn onto a garment (*Shulḥan Arukh, Oraḥ Ḥayyim* 15:2).

וְשָׁוִין, שֶׁלֹּא יָבִיא אֲפִילּוּ אַמָּה עַל אַמָּה מִמָּקוֹם אַחֵר וּבָהּ תְּכֵלֶת וְתוֹלֶה בָּהּ; וְשָׁוִין, שֶׁמֵּבִיא תְּכֵלֶת מִמָּקוֹם אַחֵר וְתוֹלֶה בָּהּ,

And Rabbi Meir and the Rabbis **agree that one may not bring a** piece of cloth, **even** if it is **a square cubit** in size,[H] **from elsewhere, containing** white and **sky-blue** strings, **and attach it to** a cloak. This is because one must attach the ritual fringes directly to the corner of the garment, rather than attaching them to a piece of cloth and then attaching that cloth to the garment. **And** Rabbi Meir and the Rabbis also **agree that one may bring** white or **sky-blue** strings **from elsewhere and attach** them **to** the garment,[N] i.e., one may remove strings from one garment in order to attach them to another garment.

NOTES

That one may bring white or sky-blue strings from elsewhere and attach them to the garment – שֶׁמֵּבִיא תְּכֵלֶת מִמָּקוֹם אַחֵר וְתוֹלֶה בָּהּ: Rashi explains that there is no problem of: Prepare it, and not from what has already been prepared, as one will have to wind and tie the strings after inserting them into the hole in the corner of the garment. Conversely, the Rid holds that it is permitted even to transfer the ritual fringes to the second garment when they are already wound and tied (see 42a). This is acceptable, as the essential obligation is attaching the ritual fringes to the garment, not tying them onto it. The later commentaries discuss this explanation and its implications at length (see *Rav Pe'alim* 3:1).

וּבִלְבַד שֶׁלֹּא תְּהֵא מוּפְסֶקֶת. שָׁמְעַתְּ מִינַּהּ: מַתִּירִין מִבֶּגֶד לְבֶגֶד? דִּילְמָא דְּאִי בְּלַאי.

This is permitted **provided that** the strings **are not broken.**[N] The Gemara asks: Should one **conclude from** this *baraita* that it is always permitted to **untie** ritual fringes **from** one **garment** in order to affix them **to** another **garment?** The Gemara rejects this inference: **Perhaps** the ruling of this *baraita* applies only **if** the first garment was **worn out** and no longer wearable.

תָּנוּ רַבָּנַן: טַלִּית שֶׁכּוּלָּהּ תְּכֵלֶת – כׇּל מִינֵי צִבְעוֹנִין פּוֹטְרִין בָּהּ, חוּץ מִקָּלָא אִילָן.

The Sages taught in a *baraita*: In the case of **a cloak that** is made **entirely** of **sky-blue wool,** strings of **every type of color exempt it,**[N] i.e., the ritual fringes that are not *tekhelet* may be any color **except for indigo,**[N] a color that is indistinguishable from *tekhelet*. This indicates that if one attached strings dyed with indigo alongside the strings dyed with *tekhelet*, the ritual fringes are unfit.

NOTES

Provided that the strings are not broken – וּבִלְבַד שֶׁלֹּא תְּהֵא מוּפְסֶקֶת: The point is that this is viewed as attaching the strings to the garment initially, in which case there is a minimum length the strings must have, as discussed subsequently on 41b, which is longer than the minimum length for strings that were attached to the garment and were later shortened (see 38b and *Shita Mekubbetzet*). The Rid records a different version of the Gemara text: Provided that the strings were broken. This means that the strings must be differentiated when they are initially attached to the garment; one may not attach one long string that is folded over and then cut it on the folds in order to create separate strings once it is already attached to the garment. Rabbeinu Gershom Meor HaGola explains the standard version of the Gemara text along similar lines.

Strings of every type of color exempt it – כׇּל מִינֵי צִבְעוֹנִין פּוֹטְרִין בָּהּ: The verse states: "And they shall put on the fringe of the corner a sky-blue thread" (Numbers 15:38). The phrase "the fringe of the corner" indicates that some of the strings should be the same color as the garment itself, which is generally assumed to be white, while others must be sky-blue. According to the Ra'avad, the strings that are the color of the garment must be attached to the garment before the sky-blue strings are attached. Rashi explains that in the case here, it is impossible for the strings that are not sky-blue to be the same color as the garment, because the garment itself is sky-blue. Consequently, the strings that are not sky-blue may be any color other than sky-blue and indigo.

Except for indigo – חוּץ מִקָּלָא אִילָן: Rashi suggests two possibilities with regard to why these ritual fringes are unfit. His second and primary explanation is that the ritual fringes must contain two different colors, and indigo is the same color as the sky-blue color *tekhelet* required by the Torah. According to this explanation, if one does use strings dyed with indigo in addition to the strings dyed with *tekhelet*, the ritual fringes are inherently unfit. Rashi's first explanation is that the ritual fringes are unfit due to a rabbinic decree. The concern is that one might take strings that are dyed with indigo and attach them to another garment thinking that they are *tekhelet*. This could lead to violating the prohibition against wearing a garment containing wool and linen where it is not necessary to fulfill the mitzva of ritual fringes.

מֵיתִיבֵי: טַלִּית אֵין פּוֹטֵר בָּהּ אֶלָּא מִינָהּ. טַלִּית שֶׁכּוּלָּהּ תְּכֵלֶת – מֵבִיא תְּכֵלֶת וְדָבָר אַחֵר וְתוֹלֶה בָּהּ; וְקָלָא אִילָן לֹא יָבִיא, וְאִם הֵבִיא – כָּשֵׁר!

The Gemara **raises an objection** from a *baraita*: **A cloak is exempted only by** strings **of its own type.**[NH] In the case of **a cloak that** is made **entirely of sky-blue wool,**[H] one **brings sky-blue [*tekhelet*]** strings **and something else,** i.e., strings of a different color, **and attaches** them **to the** cloak. **And he may not bring** strings dyed with **indigo** along with the strings dyed with *tekhelet*. **But if he brought** strings dyed with indigo together with the strings dyed with *tekhelet*, the ritual fringes are **fit.**

אָמַר רַב נַחְמָן בַּר יִצְחָק, לָא קַשְׁיָא: כָּאן בְּטַלִּית בַּת אַרְבָּעָה חוּטִין, כָּאן בְּטַלִּית בַּת שְׁמוֹנָה חוּטִין.

Rav Naḥman bar Yitzḥak said: This is **not difficult,** because **here,** in the *baraita* that holds that the ritual fringes are fit after the fact, it is referring **to a cloak that has** only **four strings,**[N] two of *tekhelet* and two of indigo. **There,** in the *baraita* that holds that the ritual fringes are unfit after the fact, it is referring **to a cloak that has eight strings,** four of *tekhelet* and four of indigo. In this case, the Sages were concerned that one would take the four indigo strings from this garment and use them in another garment, thinking that they were *tekhelet*.

שָׁמְעַתְּ מִינַּהּ: מַתִּירִין מִבֶּגֶד לְבֶגֶד? דִּלְמָא דְּאִי עָבֵד.

The Gemara asks: Should **you conclude from** the fact that the Sages were concerned lest one take the indigo strings from this garment for use in another garment that in general **one may untie** ritual fringes **from** one **garment** in order **to** affix them to another **garment?** The Gemara responds: **Perhaps** their concern was **that if** one **did** transfer the strings, he might mistake indigo for *tekhelet*, but it is not permitted to transfer the strings *ab initio*.

אִיתְּמַר, רַב אָמַר: אֵין מַתִּירִין מִבֶּגֶד לְבֶגֶד, וּשְׁמוּאֵל אָמַר: מַתִּירִין מִבֶּגֶד לְבֶגֶד.

It was stated that there is a dispute between *amora'im* with regard to this *halakha*. **Rav says: One may not untie** ritual fringes **from** one **garment** in order **to** affix them to another **garment.**[N] **And Shmuel says: One may untie**[N] them **from** one **garment** and affix them **to** another **garment.**[H]

רַב אָמַר: אֵין מַדְלִיקִין מִנֵּר לְנֵר, וּשְׁמוּאֵל אָמַר: מַדְלִיקִין מִנֵּר לְנֵר.

The Gemara cites additional disputes between Rav and Shmuel: **Rav says: One may not light from** one Hanukkah **lamp to** another Hanukkah **lamp. And Shmuel says: One may light from** one Hanukkah **lamp to** another Hanukkah **lamp.**[H]

NOTES

Exempted only by strings of its own type – אֵין פּוֹטֵר בָּהּ אֶלָּא מִינָהּ: Rashi explains that this means strings of the same color as the garment, e.g., if the garment is red, the strings that are not sky-blue should be red. This is apparently the understanding of the Rambam as well. *Tosafot* disagree and hold, based on the statement of Rava (38b), that the type refers to the material from which the garment is made and not to its color. Others maintain that the *baraita* here defines the type as referring to the color, but the mishna (38a) disagrees and defines it as the type of material, and Rava follows the opinion of the mishna (Responsa of the Rashba 3:280).

It is referring to a cloak that has only four strings, etc. – בְּטַלִּית בַּת אַרְבָּעָה חוּטִין וכו׳: According to Rashi's second explanation, there is an inherent need for strings that are not sky-blue in addition to the strings that are sky-blue, and indigo cannot be used for either of these types of strings. Consequently, if there are only four strings and two of them are *tekhelet* and two are indigo, the ritual fringes are unfit even after the fact. If there are already four strings of *tekhelet* and another color and now one wants to add an additional four strings, the Sages decreed that he should not add strings dyed with indigo, lest one later transfer them to a different garment under the assumption that they are *tekhelet*. But if one did add these strings, the ritual fringes remain fit due to the original four strings.

According to Rashi's first explanation, the only reason that strings dyed with indigo are unfit is due to the concern that one might transfer them to another garment under the assumption that they are *tekhelet*. If there are only four strings on the garment and two are *tekhelet* and two are indigo, the ritual fringes are fit after the fact. This is because it is unlikely that one will transfer any of the strings to a different garment, because one may not have fewer than four strings on the original garment (*Shita Mekubbetzet*). But if there are eight strings on this garment, four of which are *tekhelet* and four of which are indigo, there is a much greater concern that one will transfer some of the indigo strings to a different garment and use them as *tekhelet*. Consequently, the Sages declared the ritual fringes on this garment to be unfit even after the fact.

One may not untie ritual fringes from one garment in order to affix them to another garment – אֵין מַתִּירִין מִבֶּגֶד לְבֶגֶד: This is due to the fact that when the strings are detached from the first garment they are not being used for a mitzva, and this is considered a sign of disrespect to the ritual fringes (*She'iltot deRav Aḥai Gaon* 126). Rashi explains that the concern is for the denigration of the garment, as untying its strings indicates that the garment is no longer fit for ritual fringes.

One may untie – מַתִּירִין: Shmuel's reasoning is that since one is detaching the strings in order to attach them to a different garment, this does not constitute disrespectful behavior toward the ritual fringes. Shmuel himself holds (see 41a) that the mitzva of ritual fringes pertains to the garment and therefore one must have ritual fringes on all four-cornered garments he owns, even if he is not wearing them. The case here must be where one has only one set of ritual fringes, in which case it is better that he attach the ritual fringes to the garment he is wearing than have them attached to a garment he is not wearing (*Tosafot*).

The early commentaries add that one may not remove ritual fringes from a garment if he has no intention of attaching them to another garment. Some hold that it is prohibited to remove the strings only if one intends to continue wearing the garment. If he does not intend to continue using this garment, there is no concern at all (Ramban; for a lengthy discussion of this topic, see *Birkei Yosef, Oraḥ Ḥayyim* 15:2).

HALAKHA

Exempted only by strings of its own type – אֵין פּוֹטֵר בָּהּ אֶלָּא מִינָהּ: There are authorities who hold that the ritual fringes must be the same color as the garment. Those who are meticulous about their observance of mitzvot follow this practice. This is in accordance with the *baraita* and the interpretation of Rashi (Gra). Some explain that this is in order to show honor for the mitzva by performing it in a beautiful manner (*Beit Yosef*, citing *Tosafot*).

The Rema writes that the practice of Ashkenazic Jews is to use white strings regardless of the color of the garment, and that one should not deviate from this practice. The later commentaries (cited in *Mishna Berura*) therefore recommend wearing a garment that is white, or that at least has white corners, so that one can wear white strings that are the same color as the garment (Rambam *Sefer Ahava, Hilkhot Tzitzit* 2:8; *Shulḥan Arukh, Oraḥ Ḥayyim* 9:5).

A cloak that is made entirely of sky-blue wool – טַלִּית שֶׁכּוּלָּהּ תְּכֵלֶת: If one has a cloak that is made entirely of sky-blue wool, he may attach strings of any color, as long as they are not sky-blue (*Kesef Mishne*) or a color dark enough to be confused with sky-blue. He should include a single string of sky-blue, as usual, which he should use to wind around the other strings (Rambam *Sefer Ahava, Hilkhot Tzitzit* 2:8).

One may untie them from one garment and affix them to another garment – מַתִּירִין מִבֶּגֶד לְבֶגֶד: It is permitted to untie ritual fringes from one garment to tie them onto another. This is the *halakha* in the case of both the white strings and the sky-blue ones. It is prohibited to untie the ritual fringes if one does not intend to attach them to another garment. This is in accordance with the opinion of Shmuel. Nevertheless, it is permitted to detach the ritual fringes in order to replace them with nicer ones, or because one of the strings broke and he wants to replace it with a full string (*Mishna Berura*), as this is a beautification of the mitzva (Rambam *Sefer Ahava, Hilkhot Tzitzit* 1:13; *Shulḥan Arukh, Oraḥ Ḥayyim* 15:1).

One may light from one Hanukkah lamp to another Hanukkah lamp – מַדְלִיקִין מִנֵּר לְנֵר: Lighting one Hanukkah lamp directly from another is permitted. But one may not use a Hanukkah lamp to light a lamp that will not be used for the mitzva, even if he intends to use that lamp to light another Hanukkah lamp. This is in accordance with the opinion of Rav, as the later *amora'im* (see *Shabbat* 22a) analyze his opinion and therefore seem to accept it (*Tosafot* on *Shabbat* 22b). The Rema writes that it is customary to be stringent with Hanukkah lights and to refrain from lighting one lamp from another, even directly. The *Mishna Berura*, citing *Darkhei Moshe*, adds that one is permitted to light from one lamp used for a mitzva to another in the case of other lights lit for a mitzva, e.g., those of Shabbat and the synagogue (Rambam *Sefer Zemanim, Hilkhot Megilla VaḤanukka* 4:9; *Shulḥan Arukh, Oraḥ Ḥayyim* 674:1).

רַב אָמַר: אֵין הֲלָכָה כְּרַבִּי שִׁמְעוֹן בִּגְרִירָה, וּשְׁמוּאֵל אָמַר: הֲלָכָה כְּרַבִּי שִׁמְעוֹן בִּגְרִירָה.

Rabbi Shimon rules that it is permitted to drag items on Shabbat despite the possibility that one might thereby create a furrow in the ground. Creating a furrow is a labor prohibited on Shabbat, but since he does not intend to create the furrow, and it is not certain that a furrow will be created, dragging the item is permitted. **Rav says:** The *halakha* **is not in accordance with** the opinion of **Rabbi Shimon with regard to dragging** items on Shabbat. **And Shmuel says** that the *halakha* **is in accordance with** the opinion of **Rabbi Shimon with regard to dragging** items on Shabbat.

אֲמַר אַבָּיֵי: כָּל מִילֵּי דְּמָר עָבֵיד כְּרַב, לְבַר מֵהָנֵי תְּלָת דְּעָבֵיד כִּשְׁמוּאֵל: מַתִּירִין מִבֶּגֶד לְבֶגֶד, וּמַדְלִיקִין מִנֵּר לְנֵר, וַהֲלָכָה כְּרַבִּי שִׁמְעוֹן בִּגְרִירָה;

Abaye said: In **all** halakhic **matters of the Master,** Rabba, **he conducted himself in accordance with** the opinion of **Rav, except these three where he conducted himself in accordance with** the opinion of **Shmuel.** He ruled that **one may untie** ritual fringes **from** one **garment** in order to affix them **to** another **garment, and one may light from** one Hanukkah **lamp to** another Hanukkah **lamp, and the** *halakha* **is in accordance with** the opinion of **Rabbi Shimon with regard to dragging** items on Shabbat.

דְּתַנְיָא, רַבִּי שִׁמְעוֹן אוֹמֵר: גּוֹרֵר אָדָם מִטָּה, כִּסֵּא וְסַפְסָל, וּבִלְבַד שֶׁלֹּא יִתְכַּוֵּין לַעֲשׂוֹת חָרִיץ.

As it is taught in a *baraita* that **Rabbi Shimon says: A person may drag a bed, chair, or bench**[H] on the ground on Shabbat, **provided that he does not intend to make a furrow** in the ground. Even if a furrow is formed inadvertently, one does not need to be concerned.

רַב יְהוּדָה מָסַר לֵיהּ לְקַצְרָא. רַב חֲנִינָא עָבֵיד לְהוּ סִיסָא. רָבִינָא חָיֵיט לְהוּ מֵיחָט.

The Gemara relates that **Rav Yehuda** would **give** his garments containing ritual fringes **to a laundryman** and was not concerned that the strings dyed with *tekhelet* might become detached and that the laundryman would replace them with strings dyed with indigo. **Rav Ḥanina** would **form a bundle**[N] with his ritual fringes so that they would not become detached while they were being laundered. **Ravina** would tuck **them** into a pocket he formed on the garment and **sew** the cover of the pocket in order to protect the ritual fringes.

תָּנוּ רַבָּנַן: כַּמָּה חוּטִין הוּא נוֹתֵן? בֵּית שַׁמַּאי אוֹמְרִים: אַרְבָּעָה, וּבֵית הִלֵּל אוֹמְרִים: שְׁלֹשָׁה.

§ **The Sages taught** in a *baraita*: **How many strings does one place** on a garment?[H] **Beit Shammai say: Four** strings[N] are inserted into the hole in the garment, so that there are eight strings hanging down altogether, **and Beit Hillel say: Three** strings are inserted into the garment.

וְכַמָּה תְּהֵא מְשׁוּלֶּשֶׁת? בֵּית שַׁמַּאי אוֹמְרִים: אַרְבַּע, וּבֵית הִלֵּל אוֹמְרִים: שָׁלֹשׁ; וְשָׁלֹשׁ שֶׁבֵּית הִלֵּל אוֹמְרִים – אַחַת מֵאַרְבַּע בְּטֶפַח שֶׁל כָּל אָדָם. אָמַר רַב פַּפָּא: טֶפַח דְּאוֹרָיְיתָא – אַרְבַּע בְּגוּדָל, שֵׁית בִּקְטַנָּה, חָמֵשׁ בִּתְלִיתָא.

And how much should be hanging [*meshulleshet*][HN] beyond the knots and windings? **Beit Shammai say: Four** fingerbreadths, **and Beit Hillel say: Three** fingerbreadths. **And the three** fingerbreadths **that Beit Hillel say** should be hanging are each **one-fourth of a handbreadth** [*tefaḥ*][B] **of any** average **person.** The Gemara notes that **Rav Pappa said:** The **handbreadth of the Torah is four** fingerbreadths if measured **by the thumb; six** fingerbreadths if measured **by the smallest** finger; and **five** if measured **by the third,** i.e., the middle, finger.

NOTES

Rav Ḥanina would form a bundle – רַב חֲנִינָא עָבֵיד לְהוּ סִיסָא: Some explain that according to both Rav Ḥanina and Rava it is prohibited to remove ritual fringes from a garment even in order to attach them to a different garment. Therefore, they attempted to make it difficult to remove the strings (*Sefer HaIttur*). Rashi explains that they were trying to ensure that the strings would not be severed inadvertently. Rabbeinu Gershom Meor HaGola holds that Rav Ḥanina wrapped the ritual fringes inside other strings in order to protect the hue of the sky-blue strings.

Beit Shammai say four strings – בֵּית שַׁמַּאי אוֹמְרִים אַרְבָּעָה: Of these four strings, two are sky-blue and two are white (*Tosafot*). The Ra'avad holds that three are white and one is sky-blue. The Rambam holds that half of one string is dyed sky-blue. Therefore, once the strings are inserted into the garment and allowed to hang down on both sides of the hole, there are seven white strings and one sky-blue string. The sky-blue string is then used to wind around the other seven strings.

And how much should be hanging [*meshulleshet*] – וְכַמָּה תְּהֵא מְשׁוּלֶּשֶׁת: Rashi understands that the word *meshulleshet* is the same as *meshulshelet*, meaning hanging. It refers to the length of the loose strings that hang down from the wrapped portion of the ritual fringes. Others explain that, on the contrary, it refers to the wrapped portion, which resembles a chain [*shalshelet*] (second explanation of Rashi on *Bekhorot* 39b; Rabbeinu Tam). According to this explanation, there must then be a portion of loose strings that is twice as long as the wrapped portion. This is based on the fact that the Gemara (39a) states that the portion of the strings that contains the knots and windings should be one-third of the total length of the strings (see *Shita Mekubbetzet*, citing Rabbeinu Gershom Meor HaGola). Other commentaries understand the Gemara as referring to the total length of the ritual fringes (Rabbeinu Gershom Meor HaGola and Rid, citing Rav Amram Gaon). It would appear that the Rambam understood *meshulleshet* to mean divided equally, referring to the lengths of the two sides of each string after the string is inserted into the hole in the garment.

HALAKHA

A person may drag a bed, chair, or bench – גּוֹרֵר אָדָם מִטָּה כִּסֵּא וְסַפְסָל: A person may drag a bed, chair, or bench on Shabbat, provided that he does not intend to dig a furrow. This is in accordance with the opinion of Rabbi Shimon, who holds that it is permitted to perform an act that may cause a prohibited labor to occur, as long as one does not intend to perform the prohibited labor. The *Magen Avraham* notes that if the object is so heavy that dragging it will certainly create a furrow, then it is prohibited to drag it (Rambam *Sefer Zemanim*, *Hilkhot Shabbat* 1:5; *Shulḥan Arukh*, *Oraḥ Ḥayyim* 337:1).

How many strings does one place on a garment – כַּמָּה חוּטִין הוּא נוֹתֵן: One must attach four strings to each corner of the garment. This is in accordance with the opinion of Beit Shammai, which is accepted by Rav Pappa. Once the strings are inserted into the hole in the corner and allowed to hang down on each side, there are eight strings hanging down. If one attaches additional strings, the ritual fringes are unfit. Some hold that it is permitted to add extra strings (see *Mishna Berura*).

Rashi and *Tosafot* hold that two of the strings are white and two are sky-blue [*tekhelet*]. The Ra'avad holds that three strings are white and one is sky-blue. The Rambam holds that only one half of a string is sky-blue, so that when it is inserted into the garment, one of the eight strings hanging down is sky-blue. When *tekhelet* is not available, one attaches four white strings (Rambam *Sefer Ahava*, *Hilkhot Tzitzit* 1:6; *Shulḥan Arukh*, *Oraḥ Ḥayyim* 11:12).

And how much should be hanging – וְכַמָּה תְּהֵא מְשׁוּלֶּשֶׁת: The minimum length for ritual fringes is four fingerbreadths, which equals one handbreadth (Rambam; Rosh). Some hold that the knots and windings must be four fingerbreadths and the strings must hang down an additional eight fingerbreadths beyond that (Rabbeinu Tam). This is the accepted practice.

These measurements refer to the length of the strings after the first knot and do not include the portion of the strings that rests on the garment (*Beit Yosef*). The string that one winds around the others must be longer than the others.

According to the *Ḥazon Ish*, one fingerbreadth is 2.4 cm, while Rabbi Ḥayyim Na'e holds that it is 2 cm (Rambam *Sefer Ahava*, *Hilkhot Tzitzit* 1:6; *Shulḥan Arukh*, *Oraḥ Ḥayyim* 11:4).

BACKGROUND

Handbreadth [*tefaḥ*] – טֶפַח: The handbreadth is a measurement that is mentioned in the Torah (Exodus 25:25). It refers to the width of the four fingers when they are side by side. By contrast, an expansive handbreadth is measured with the fingers spread apart. There are those who understand the term to relate to the palm of one's hand. Consequently, the Radak explains that the term *metapeḥin*, which in rabbinic literature means clapping, reflects the fact that one strikes his two palms together.

Calculations for the measurement of the handbreadth range between 8 cm (Rabbi Ḥayyim Na'e) and 9.6 cm (*Ḥazon Ish*).

אָמַר רַב הוּנָא: אַרְבָּעָה בְּתוֹךְ אַרְבַּע וּמְשׁוּלֶּשֶׁת אַרְבַּע, וְרַב יְהוּדָה אָמַר: שְׁלֹשָׁה בְּתוֹךְ שָׁלֹשׁ מְשׁוּלֶּשֶׁת שָׁלֹשׁ.

Rav Huna says that the *halakha* is: One must attach **four** strings **within four** fingerbreadths of the edge of the garment, **and** they should **hang** down **four** fingerbreadths beyond the knots and windings. **And Rav Yehuda says:** One must attach **three** strings **within three**[H] fingerbreadths of the edge of the garment, and they should **hang** down **three** fingerbreadths beyond the knots and windings.

אָמַר רַב פַּפָּא, הִלְכְתָא: אַרְבָּעָה בְּתוֹךְ שָׁלֹשׁ מְשׁוּלֶּשֶׁת אַרְבַּע.

Rav Pappa says that **the** ***halakha*** is that one must attach **four** strings **within three** fingerbreadths of the edge of the garment, and they should **hang** down **four** fingerbreadths beyond the knots and windings.

לְמֵימְרָא, דְּאִית לְהוּ שִׁיעוּרָא; וּרְמִינְהוּ: "צִיצִית" – אֵין צִיצִית אֶלָּא יוֹצֵא, וְאֵין צִיצִית אֶלָּא מַשֶּׁהוּ. וּכְבָר עָלוּ זִקְנֵי בֵית שַׁמַּאי וְזִקְנֵי בֵית הִלֵּל לַעֲלִיַּית יוֹחָנָן בֶּן בְּתֵירָא, וְאָמְרוּ: צִיצִית אֵין לָהּ שִׁיעוּר. כַּיּוֹצֵא בּוֹ, לוּלָב אֵין בּוֹ שִׁיעוּר;

The Gemara asks: **Is this to say that** ritual fringes **have** a required **measure? And** the Gemara **raises a contradiction** to this from a *baraita*: The verse states: "That they prepare for themselves **strings**" (Numbers 15:38). **Strings** are **nothing other than** what **emerges** from the corner of the garment, **and** the term **strings** indicates **only** that there must be strings of **any length. And** it **already** occurred that **the elders of Beit Shammai and the elders of Beit Hillel ascended to the attic of Yoḥanan ben Beteira, and** they discussed the matter and **said: Ritual fringes have no measure. Similarly, a** ***lulav*** **has no measure.**

מַאי לָאו אֵין לָהּ שִׁיעוּר כְּלָל? לָא,

What, does this **not** mean that ritual fringes **have no** required **measure at all?** The Gemara answers: **No,**

HALAKHA

Within three – בְּתוֹךְ שָׁלֹשׁ: The ritual fringes should be inserted into the garment through a hole, or two holes, not more than three fingerbreadths from the edge of the garment, as beyond that is no longer considered the corner of the garment. Some hold that the measure is three thumbbreadths, and some hold that it is the width of the third, fourth, and fifth fingers together. This is in accordance with the opinion of Rav Pappa (Rambam *Sefer Ahava, Hilkhot Tzitzit* 1:6; *Shulḥan Arukh, Oraḥ Ḥayyim* 11:9).

אֵין לָהּ שִׁיעוּר לְמַעְלָה, אֲבָל יֵשׁ לָהּ שִׁיעוּר לְמַטָּה. דְּאִי לָא תֵּימָא הָכִי, כַּיּוֹצֵא בּוֹ לוּלָב אֵין לוֹ שִׁיעוּר, הָכִי נָמֵי דְּאֵין לוֹ שִׁיעוּר כְּלָל?

the *baraita* means that ritual fringes **do not have a maximum measure,**[HN] i.e., the strings can be as long as one wants; **however, they do have a minimum measure,**[N] and if the strings are shorter than this measure they are not fit. **As, if you do not say so,** in a case **similar to it,** where it is taught that **a** ***lulav***[H] **has no measure,** is it possible **that it also has no measure whatsoever?**

וְהָתְנַן: לוּלָב שֶׁיֵּשׁ בּוֹ שְׁלֹשָׁה טְפָחִים כְּדֵי לְנַעְנֵעַ בּוֹ – כָּשֵׁר! אֶלָּא, אֵין לוֹ שִׁיעוּר לְמַעְלָה, אֲבָל יֵשׁ לוֹ שִׁיעוּר לְמַטָּה; הָכִי נָמֵי אֵין לוֹ שִׁיעוּר לְמַעְלָה, אֲבָל יֵשׁ לוֹ שִׁיעוּר לְמַטָּה.

But didn't we learn in a mishna (*Sukka* 29b): **A** ***lulav*** **that has three handbreadths** in length, **sufficient** to enable one **to wave with it,** is **fit** for use in fulfilling the mitzva? This indicates that if the *lulav* is less than the measure, it is not fit. **Rather,** it must be that a *lulav* **has no maximum measure, but it does have a minimum measure. So too,** ritual fringes **have no maximum measure, but they have a minimum measure.**

HALAKHA

Ritual fringes do not have a maximum measure – אֵין לָהּ שִׁיעוּר לְמַעְלָה: Ritual fringes do not have a maximum measure, and they are fit even if they are a cubit or two long (Rambam *Sefer Ahava, Hilkhot Tzitzit* 1:6; *Shulḥan Arukh, Oraḥ Ḥayyim* 11:4).

***Lulav* – לוּלָב:** The spine of a *lulav* must be at least four handbreadths long (see *Sukka* 32b), but there is no maximum length (Rambam *Sefer Zemanim, Hilkhot Shofar VeSukka VeLulav* 7:8 and *Maggid Mishne* there; *Shulḥan Arukh, Oraḥ Ḥayyim* 650:2).

NOTES

Ritual fringes do not have a maximum measure – אֵין לָהּ שִׁיעוּר לְמַעְלָה: Some hold that this refers not only to the length of the strings but to the number of strings. According to this interpretation, if one adds extra strings, as mentioned in the Gemara (41b), one does not violate the prohibition against adding to a mitzva (*Sefer HaIttur*).

They do have a minimum measure – יֵשׁ לָהּ שִׁיעוּר לְמַטָּה: Accordingly, when the *baraita* states that the ritual fringes may be any length (41b), it is referring to a case where the strings were initially the appropriate length and were later severed, as discussed on 38b (Rashi; see *Keren Ora*).

תָּנוּ רַבָּנַן: "צִיצִת" – אֵין צִיצִית אֶלָּא עָנָף, וְכֵן הוּא אוֹמֵר: "וַיִּקָּחֵנִי בְּצִיצִת רֹאשִׁי". וְאָמַר אַבַּיֵי: וְצָרִיךְ לְפָרוֹדָה כִּי צוּצִיתָא דְּאַרְמָאֵי.

§ **The Sages taught** in a *baraita*: The verse states: "That they prepare for themselves **strings**" (Numbers 15:38). The term **strings** [***tzitzit***] means **nothing other than strings that hang down** [***anaf***],[N] **and so it states** in the verse: **"I was taken by a lock** [***betzitzit***] **of my head"** (Ezekiel 8:3). **And Abaye says:** And one is **required to separate** the ritual fringes[H] **like a gentile's lock** of hair,[N] part of which is braided and the rest of which is allowed to hang loose.

תָּנוּ רַבָּנַן: הִטִּיל עַל הַקֶּרֶן אוֹ עַל הַגָּדִיל – כְּשֵׁירָה, רַבִּי אֱלִיעֶזֶר בֶּן יַעֲקֹב (אוֹמֵר) פּוֹסֵל בִּשְׁתֵּיהֶן.

The Sages taught in a *baraita*: If one **affixed** the ritual fringes **to the** tip of **the corner or to the border** [***gadil***],[HN] they are **fit. Rabbi Eliezer ben Ya'akov disqualifies** them **in both** cases.[N]

כְּמַאן אָזְלָא הָא דְּאָמַר רַב גִּידֵּל אָמַר רַב: צִיצִית צְרִיכָה שֶׁתְּהֵא נוֹטֶפֶת עַל הַקֶּרֶן, שֶׁנֶּאֱמַר: "עַל כַּנְפֵי בִגְדֵיהֶם", כְּמַאן? כְּרַבִּי אֱלִיעֶזֶר בֶּן יַעֲקֹב.

The Gemara asks: **In accordance with whose** opinion **is that which Rav Giddel says** that **Rav says: Ritual fringes must** be inserted into a hole above the corner and **hang down onto the corner**[HN] of the garment, **as it is stated: "On the corners of their garments"** (Numbers 15:38)? **In accordance with whose** opinion is this? The Gemara answers: It is **in accordance with** the opinion of **Rabbi Eliezer ben Ya'akov.**

HALAKHA

One is required to separate the ritual fringes – צָרִיךְ לְפָרוֹדָה: According to the *Beur Halakha*, there is a requirement to separate the strings before reciting the blessing on the garment. According to the *Ḥazon Ish*, this is a way to beautify the mitzva, but one fulfills the mitzva even if he does not separate the strings from each other (*Shulḥan Arukh*, *Oraḥ Ḥayyim* 8:7).

Or to the border [*gadil*] – אוֹ עַל הַגָּדִיל: One may not attach the ritual fringes to the *gadil*, i.e., the warp strings at the edge of the garment, in accordance with Rashi's second interpretation (Gra; see *Mishna Berura*). This is the *halakha* even if the area of the warp strings is wider than the length of a full thumb joint. If the ritual fringes are attached to that area, they are unfit. This is due to the fact that the ritual fringes must be placed "on the corners of their garments" (Numbers 15:38), and this segment is not deemed part of the garment (*Shulḥan Arukh*, *Oraḥ Ḥayyim* 11:11).

Hang down onto the corner – שֶׁתְּהֵא נוֹטֶפֶת עַל הַקֶּרֶן: Some say that one should take care to affix the ritual fringes such that they extend from the hole toward the side of the garment and hang from there down over the corner, rather than tying them so that they hang directly downward. If one did not take care to do so, the ritual fringes are nevertheless fit. The *Mishna Berura* notes that one should be very careful that the strings do not go diagonally to the tip of the corner, which was the practice of the Karaites (*Shulḥan Arukh*, *Oraḥ Ḥayyim* 11:15).

NOTES

The term strings means nothing other than strings that hang down [*anaf*] – אֵין צִיצִית אֶלָּא עָנָף: It would appear from the *ge'onim* and early commentaries that the point is that ritual fringes must include two components: The first is the section of knots and windings, which is derived from the verse: "You shall prepare for yourself twisted cords" (Deuteronomy 22:12). The second is a section of loose strings [*anaf*], which is derived from the verse: "That they prepare for themselves strings" (Numbers 15:38).

It appears that the Rambam understood *anaf* as referring to that which comes out of the garment. This relates to the statement on the previous *amud*: Strings are nothing other than what emerges from the corner of the garment. According to this understanding, *anaf* includes the entirety of the ritual fringes, both the portion with the windings and the portion with the loose strings.

One is required to separate the ritual fringes like a gentile's lock of hair – צָרִיךְ לְפָרוֹדָה כִּי צוּצִיתָא דְּאַרְמָאֵי: The Romans had long locks of hair that they would braid on the top and leave loose on the bottom (Rid). According to this understanding, Abaye was echoing the statement of the *baraita* that in addition to the portion of the ritual fringes that has windings, there also needs to be a section of loose strings (*Sefer HaEshkol*). *Sefer Yere'im* (401) interprets Abaye's statement as adding that one must separate the loose strings from each other.

To the tip of the corner [*keren*] or to the border [*gadil*] – עַל הַקֶּרֶן אוֹ עַל הַגָּדִיל: The translation here follows the interpretation of a number of early commentaries who explain that *keren* refers to the edge of the corner. Others understand it as referring to the bottom edge of the garment. It would appear that Rashi understands it this way.

With regard to the term *gadil*, Rashi offers two explanations: The first is that it refers to a very thick woof string that is woven into the edges of the garment in order to protect it from ripping. The second interpretation is that it refers to strings of the warp on the edges of the width of the garment (see the textual variant cited in *Shita Mekubbetzet*).

Others explain that it refers to an unwoven section that is left at the beginning and the end of the garment (*Sefer Halttur*, citing *Sifrei*; *Taz*, citing Rashi and Rashba on *Bava Kamma* 119b).

The reason that Rabbi Eliezer ben Ya'akov disqualifies ritual fringes when they are attached to the *gadil* is that the *gadil* is not considered part of the garment (see *Beit Yosef*).

Rabbi Eliezer ben Ya'akov disqualifies them in both cases – רַבִּי אֱלִיעֶזֶר בֶּן יַעֲקֹב אוֹמֵר פּוֹסֵל בִּשְׁתֵּיהֶן: This literally translates to: Rabbi Eliezer ben Ya'akov says disqualifies them in both cases. The *Shita Mekubbetzet* notes that the word: Says, appears to have been added in error in this sentence, which is why it appears in parentheses in the standard version of the text.

Hang down onto the corner – שֶׁתְּהֵא נוֹטֶפֶת עַל הַקֶּרֶן: Rashi explains that this means one should place the ritual fringes above the edge of the garment, such that they hang down onto the corner. Some commentaries cite another version of Rashi, which explains that the ritual fringes are to be tied from the side, causing them to hang down onto the edge of the garment (*Nimmukei Yosef*; *Sefer Yere'im*). *She'iltot deRav Aḥai Gaon* (127) explains that it should be tied loosely, and not tightly in such a way that the ritual fringes stick out sideways (*Sefer HaManhig*; see *Ha'amek She'ala*). *Sefer Halttur* writes that one should form two holes in the garment and insert the strings through one hole and then back through the other, so that they hang down on only one side of the garment (see *Magen Avraham* 11:24).

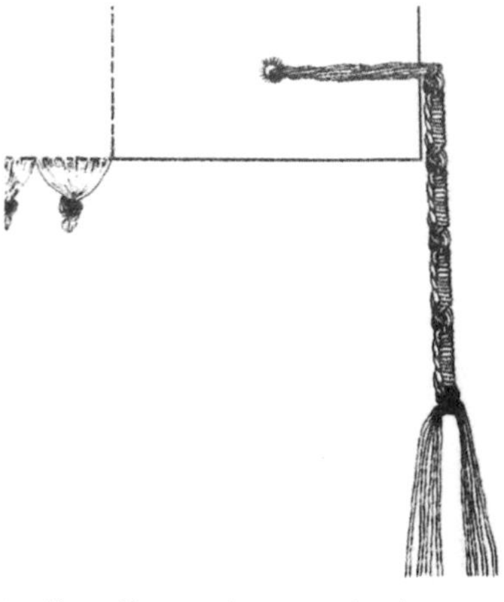

Position of the ritual fringes according to most early authorities

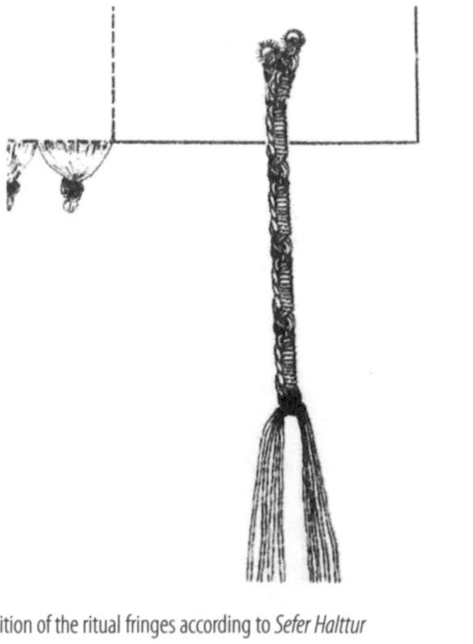

Position of the ritual fringes according to *Sefer Halttur*

אָמַר רַבִּי יַעֲקֹב אָמַר רַבִּי יוֹחָנָן: וְצָרִיךְ שֶׁיַּרְחִיק מְלֹא קֶשֶׁר גּוּדָל.

Rabbi Ya'akov says that Rabbi Yoḥanan says: And one **must distance** the hole through which the ritual fringes are inserted into the garment the length of **a full thumb joint**[N] from the edge of the garment.[H]

וְאִיצְטְרִיךְ דְּרַב פַּפָּא, וְאִיצְטְרִיךְ דְּרַבִּי יַעֲקֹב; דְּאִי מִדְּרַב פַּפָּא, הֲוָה אָמִינָא: תּוֹךְ שָׁלֹשׁ – דְּלָא לִירַחֵיק טְפֵי, וְכַמָּה דְּמִקָּרַב מְעַלֵּי, אִיצְטְרִיךְ דְּרַבִּי יַעֲקֹב;

The Gemara notes: **And it was necessary** to state the ruling **of Rav Pappa** (41b)[N] that the ritual fringes must be inserted into a hole within three fingerbreadths of the edge of the garment, **and it was** also **necessary** to state the ruling **of Rabbi Ya'akov.** This is **because if** the location of the hole was taught only **from** the statement **of Rav Pappa, I would say** that his ruling that the hole must be **within three** fingerbreadths of the edge of the garment was to teach **that one may not distance** the hole from the edge of the garment by **more** than this amount, **but the closer** the hole is to the edge of the garment, **the better.** Consequently, **it was necessary** to include the statement **of Rabbi Ya'akov.**

וְאִי מִדְּרַבִּי יַעֲקֹב, הֲוָה אָמִינָא: מְלֹא קֶשֶׁר גּוּדָל – דְּלָא לִיקָּרַב טְפֵי, וְכַמָּה דְּרַחֵיק מְעַלֵּי, צְרִיכָא.

And if the location of the hole was taught only **from** the statement **of Rabbi Ya'akov, I would say** that his ruling that it must be **a full thumb joint** away from the edge of the garment was to teach **that one may not** situate the hole **closer** than that to the edge of the garment, **but the further** he places it, **the better.** Therefore, both statements were **necessary.**

רָבִינָא וְרַב סַמָּא הָווּ יָתְבִי קַמֵּיהּ דְּרַב אַשִׁי, חַזְיֵיהּ רַב סַמָּא לְקַרְנֵיהּ דִּגְלִימֵיהּ דְּרָבִינָא דְּסָתַר וּבָצַר מִמְּלֹא קֶשֶׁר גּוּדָל, אֲמַר לֵיהּ: לָא סָבַר לָהּ מָר לְהָא דְּרַבִּי יַעֲקֹב? אֲמַר לֵיהּ: בִּשְׁעַת עֲשִׂיָּיה אִיתְּמַר.

The Gemara relates that **Ravina and Rav Samma were sitting before Rav Ashi. Rav Samma saw that the corner of Ravina's cloak was torn and** therefore the hole through which the ritual fringes were inserted was **less than** the **full** length of **a thumb joint** from the edge of the garment.[N] Rav Samma **said to** Ravina: **Doesn't the Master hold in accordance with that** statement **of Rabbi Ya'akov** that the hole must be at least the length of a thumb joint from the edge of the garment? Ravina **said to** Rav Samma: It **was stated** that this distance is required **at the time** when the ritual fringes are **made.**[HN] If the corner tears later, causing the hole to be closer to the edge of the garment, the ritual fringes remain fit.

אִיכְסִיף. אֲמַר לֵיהּ רַב אַשִׁי: לָא תִּתְקִיף לָךְ, חַד מִינַּיְיהוּ כִּתְרֵי מִינַּן.

Rav Samma **became embarrassed** because he had asked his question based on a mistaken assumption. **Rav Ashi said to** Rav Samma: **Do not be upset** that Ravina is a greater scholar than you are; **one of them,** i.e., the Sages of Eretz Yisrael, **is like two of us,**[N] i.e., the Sages of Babylonia.

HALAKHA

One must distance the hole the length of a full thumb joint from the edge of the garment – צָרִיךְ שֶׁיַּרְחִיק מְלֹא קֶשֶׁר גּוּדָל: The hole through which the ritual fringes are inserted into a garment should be no less than the length of a full thumb joint from the edge of the garment. This distance is measured in a straight line from the bottom of the garment, not diagonally from the tip of the corner. Some hold that this distance must also be measured across from the side of the garment, and the *halakha* is in accordance with this opinion (Rambam *Sefer Ahava, Hilkhot Tzitzit* 1:6; *Shulḥan Arukh, Oraḥ Ḥayyim* 11:9–10).

It was stated that this distance is required at the time when the ritual fringes are made – בִּשְׁעַת עֲשִׂיָּיה אִיתְּמַר: If the ritual fringes were inserted into a hole that was the length of a full thumb joint from the edge of the garment, and then the garment unraveled or the hole expanded and now the hole is no longer the requisite distance from the edge of the garment, the ritual fringes remain fit. Nevertheless, the Rema notes that it is customary to reinforce the hole and the edges of the garment to prevent such an occurrence (Rambam *Sefer Ahava, Hilkhot Tzitzit* 1:18; *Shulḥan Arukh, Oraḥ Ḥayyim* 11:10).

NOTES

One must distance the hole the length of a full thumb joint – צָרִיךְ שֶׁיַּרְחִיק מְלֹא קֶשֶׁר גּוּדָל: Rashi explains that this refers to the length from the tip of the thumb to the first joint. If so, this measure is smaller than that of three fingerbreadths. Others hold that this refers to the entire length of the thumb, from its tip until the second joint, in which case it is equivalent to three fingerbreadths. According to this opinion, the strings must be inserted through a hole exactly this distance from the corner of the garment (Rabbeinu Gershom Meor HaGola; Rid; see Rashi on *Bekhorot* 39b). They interpret the continuation of the Gemara's discussion accordingly.

It was necessary to state the ruling of Rav Pappa, etc. – אִיצְטְרִיךְ דְּרַב פַּפָּא וכו׳: The reason that the strings must be inserted into the garment in this area is because the verse specifies that the strings be attached to the corner of the garment (see Numbers 15:38). More than three fingerbreadths from the corner is no longer considered the corner, and less than the length of one thumb joint from the corner is considered the tip rather than the corner (*Beit Yosef*, citing *Smag*).

And was less than the full length of a thumb joint from the edge of the garment – וּבָצַר מִמְּלֹא קֶשֶׁר גּוּדָל: The hole had ripped and thereby spread toward the edge of the garment, or the garment had unraveled at its edge (Rashi).

It was stated that this distance is required at the time when the ritual fringes are made – בִּשְׁעַת עֲשִׂיָּיה אִיתְּמַר: This is based on the fact that the verse states: "Speak unto the children of Israel and command them that they prepare for themselves throughout their generations strings on the corners of their garments" (Numbers 15:38). Since the verse that discusses the placement of the strings on the corner refers to when "they prepare for themselves…strings," the precise location of the hole is significant specifically when the strings are affixed, but not afterward.

One of them is like two of us – חַד מִינַּיְיהוּ כִּתְרֵי מִינַּן: Rashi explains that Ravina was from Eretz Yisrael. Rabbeinu Gershom Meor HaGola adds that the Sages of Eretz Yisrael were greater because the atmosphere of Eretz Yisrael makes one wise (see *Bava Batra* 158b). Conversely, the Rid claims that Ravina was from Pumbedita, a Babylonian city whose Sages were known for their sharp intellects, whereas Rav Ashi and Rav Samma were from Mata Meḥasya. Rav Ashi was saying that a Sage from Pumbedita could be expected to be twice as sharp as one from Mata Meḥasya.

NOTES

In order that there be twisted cord and twisted cords – כִּי הֵיכִי דְּלֶיהֱוֵי גְּדִיל גְּדִילִים: This is based on the interpretation cited in the Gemara on 39b that the singular term twisted cord would have indicated two strings, and therefore the plural term "twisted cords," which appears in the verse, indicates four strings. Rav Aḥa understood that the term twisted also indicates that the strings are folded, and since the verse states: "Twisted cords you shall prepare for yourself," Rav Aḥa understood that the four strings must be doubled over at the time that "you shall prepare for yourself" the strings by affixing them to the garment. Rav Yirmeya of Difti accepted Rav Aḥa's derivation and applied it equally to the white and sky-blue strings, thereby doubling the required number of strings (see *Tosafot* here and on 38a).

רַב אַחָא בַּר יַעֲקֹב רָמֵי אַרְבַּע, וְעָיֵיף לְהוּ מֵיעָף, וּמְעַיֵּיל לְהוּ בִּגְלִימָא וְאָבֵיק לְהוּ מֵיבָק; קָסָבַר: בָּעֵינַן תְּמַנְיָא בִּגְלִימָא, כִּי הֵיכִי דְּלֶיהֱוֵי "גְּדִיל" "גְּדִילִים" בִּמְקוֹם פְּתִיל.

§ With regard to attaching ritual fringes to a garment, the Gemara relates that **Rav Aḥa bar Ya'akov would affix four** strings[H] to the garment, **and he would** first **fold them** in half **and** then **insert them** at the point of the folds **into** the hole of **the garment,** so that on one side there were eight strings and on the other side there were four loops. He would then take the eight strings **and loop them** through the four loops and pull them tight, thereby attaching them to the garment. The Gemara explains that **he held** that **we require eight** strings when they are initially placed **in the garment, in order that there be twisted cord** and **"twisted cords"** (Deuteronomy 22:12),[N] i.e., four doubled strings, **at the place,** i.e., the time, when he creates the **loose hanging string.**

רַב יִרְמְיָה מִדִּפְתִּי רָמֵי תְּמַנְיָא דְּאִינְהוּ שִׁיתְסַר, וְלָא אָבֵיק לְהוּ. מָר בְּרֵיהּ דְּרָבִינָא עָבֵיד כְּדִידַן.

Rav Yirmeya of Difti would affix eight strings **that are sixteen** strings after they are placed in the hole of the garment and half of each string hangs down on each side, **and he would not loop them** as Rav Aha bar Ya'akov did. **Mar, son of Ravina, would prepare** ritual fringes **like ours,** placing four strings through the hole and allowing both ends of each string to hang down, thereby forming eight.

רַב נַחְמָן אַשְׁכַּחֵיהּ לְרַב אַדָּא בַּר אַהֲבָה רָמֵי חוּטֵי וְקָא מְבָרֵךְ: "לַעֲשׂוֹת צִיצִית", אֲמַר לֵיהּ: מַאי צִיצִי שָׁמַעְנָא? הָכִי אָמַר רַב: צִיצִית אֵין צְרִיכָה בְּרָכָה!

§ The Gemara relates that **Rav Naḥman found Rav Adda bar Ahava affixing strings** to a garment **and reciting the blessing** that concludes: **To prepare ritual fringes** [*tzitzit*]. Rav Naḥman **said to** Rav Adda bar Ahava: **What** is this *tzitzi* sound that **I hear? This is what Rav says: Ritual fringes do not require a blessing**[H] when one attaches them to the garment.

כִּי נָח נַפְשֵׁיהּ דְּרַב הוּנָא, עַל רַב חִסְדָּא לְמִירְמָא דְּרַב אַדְּרַב: וּמִי אָמַר רַב צִיצִית אֵין צָרִיךְ בְּרָכָה? וְהָא אָמַר רַב יְהוּדָה אָמַר רַב: מִנַּיִן לְצִיצִית בְּגוֹי שֶׁהִיא פְּסוּלָה? שֶׁנֶּאֱמַר: "דַּבֵּר אֶל בְּנֵי יִשְׂרָאֵל... וְעָשׂוּ לָהֶם צִיצִת" – בְּנֵי יִשְׂרָאֵל יַעֲשׂוּ, וְלֹא הַגּוֹיִם יַעֲשׂוּ!

With regard to this statement of Rav, the Gemara relates that **when Rav Huna died, Rav Ḥisda went into** the study hall **to raise a contradiction** from one statement **of Rav to** another statement **of Rav,** as follows: **Did Rav** actually **say** that **ritual fringes do not require a blessing** when one attaches them to the garment? **But doesn't Rav Yehuda say** that **Rav says: From where** is it derived that **ritual fringes** attached **by a gentile**[H] are **unfit?** It is derived from a verse, **as it is stated: "Speak unto the children of Israel** and command them **that they prepare for themselves strings"** (Numbers 15:38). The Sages derive from here that **the children of Israel shall prepare** ritual fringes, **but the gentiles shall not prepare** ritual fringes.

וְהָא מַאי רוּמְיָא? אֲמַר רַב יוֹסֵף, קָסָבַר רַב חִסְדָּא: כָּל מִצְוָה שֶׁכְּשֵׁירָה בְּגוֹי – בְּיִשְׂרָאֵל אֵין צָרִיךְ לְבָרֵךְ, כָּל מִצְוָה שֶׁפְּסוּלָה בְּגוֹי – בְּיִשְׂרָאֵל צָרִיךְ לְבָרֵךְ.

The Gemara asks: **But what** is the **contradiction** between these two statements of Rav? **Rav Yosef said: Rav Ḥisda held** that in the case of **any mitzva** for **which** the necessary item is **fit** when produced **by a gentile,** if it is produced **by a Jew, he does not need to recite a blessing.** Conversely, **any mitzva** for **which** the necessary item is **unfit** when produced **by a gentile,** if it is produced **by a Jew, he needs to recite a blessing** when he produces the item.

HALAKHA

Would affix four strings – רָמֵי אַרְבַּע: The required quantity for ritual fringes in each corner of the garment is four strings, which become eight once they are inserted into the garment and doubled over. If one attached additional strings, the ritual fringes are unfit. It is proper that the four strings be separate from each other at the time they are placed in the hole of the garment, i.e., one should not insert one string and then take the edge and insert it through the hole again, and then cut it so that it is two separate strings. It is essential that they be separate at least from the time they are wound, because if even one set of windings is formed before the strings are separated, the ritual fringes are unfit due to the principle: Prepare it, and not from what has already been prepared, in accordance with the Gemara in *Sukka* 11a–b (Rambam *Sefer Ahava, Hilkhot Tzitzit* 1:6; *Shulḥan Arukh, Oraḥ Ḥayyim* 11:12–13).

Ritual fringes do not require a blessing – צִיצִית אֵין צְרִיכָה בְּרָכָה: One does not recite a blessing when he attaches ritual fringes to a garment, because one fulfills the mitzva only when he wears it, and there is a principle that one does not recite a blessing on a mitzva when there is a further stage of fulfillment (Rambam). Others explain that it is because the obligation is incumbent upon the man and not the garment, and therefore the mitzva applies only when one actually wears the garment (*Tur*; *Shulḥan Arukh*). This is in accordance with the opinion of Rav as interpreted by the Gemara on 42b (Rambam *Sefer Ahava, Hilkhot Tzitzit* 3:8; *Shulḥan Arukh, Oraḥ Ḥayyim* 19:1).

Ritual fringes attached by a gentile – צִיצִית בְּגוֹי: If a gentile attached ritual fringes to a garment, the ritual fringes are unfit. This is in accordance with the opinion of Rav cited by Rav Yehuda (Rambam *Sefer Ahava, Hilkhot Tzitzit* 1:12; *Shulḥan Arukh, Oraḥ Ḥayyim* 14:1).

וּכְלָלָא הוּא? וַהֲרֵי מִילָה דִּכְשֵׁירָה בְּגוֹי, דְּתַנְיָא: עִיר שֶׁאֵין בָּהּ רוֹפֵא יִשְׂרָאֵל וְיֵשׁ בָּהּ רוֹפֵא אֲרַמַּאי וְרוֹפֵא כּוּתִי – יָמוּל אֲרַמַּאי וְאַל יָמוּל כּוּתִי, דִּבְרֵי רַבִּי מֵאִיר, רַבִּי יְהוּדָה אוֹמֵר: כּוּתִי וְלֹא אֲרַמַּאי;

The Gemara asks: **And is this an established principle? But** what about **circumcision, which is valid** if performed **by a gentile,**[N] **as it is taught** in a *baraita*: In **a city in which there is no Jewish physician, and in which there is an Aramean,** i.e., a gentile, **physician and a Samaritan physician,** it is preferable that the **Aramean circumcise** the Jewish boys of the city **and the Samaritan not circumcise** them; this is **the statement of Rabbi Meir. Rabbi Yehuda says:** It is preferable that the **Samaritan** circumcise the boys **and the Aramean not** circumcise them. Nevertheless, all agree that a circumcision performed by a gentile is valid.

וּבְיִשְׂרָאֵל צָרִיךְ לְבָרֵךְ, דְּאָמַר מָר: הַמָּל אוֹמֵר: ״בָּרוּךְ אֲשֶׁר קִדְּשָׁנוּ בְּמִצְוֹתָיו וְצִוָּנוּ עַל הַמִּילָה״!

And despite the fact that circumcision performed by a gentile is valid, when it is performed **by a Jew, he must recite a blessing, as the Master said: The one who circumcises** a child **says:**[H] **Blessed** are You, Lord our God, King of the universe, **Who has sanctified us through His mitzvot and has commanded us concerning circumcision.**

מִידֵי הוּא טַעְמָא אֶלָּא לְרַב, רַב מִיפְסַל פָּסֵיל, דְּאִיתְּמַר: מִנַּיִן לְמִילָה בְּגוֹי שֶׁפְּסוּלָה? דָּרוּ בַּר פַּפָּא מִשְּׁמֵיהּ דְּרַב אָמַר: ״וְאַתָּה אֶת בְּרִיתִי תִשְׁמֹר״,

The Gemara answers: **Is there reason** to resolve the contradiction **according to** anyone **but Rav? Rav** himself **invalidates** circumcision performed by a gentile, **as it was stated: From where** is it derived **that circumcision** performed **by a gentile**[H] **is not valid? Daru bar Pappa says in the name of Rav:** This is derived from the verse: "And God said unto Abraham: **And as for you, you shall keep My covenant,** you, and your seed after you throughout their generations" (Genesis 17:9). The verse indicates that only the descendants of Abraham may perform circumcision.

רַבִּי יוֹחָנָן אָמַר: ״הִמּוֹל יִמּוֹל״ – הַמָּל יָמוּל.

Rabbi Yoḥanan says that this *halakha* is derived from the doubled verb in the verse: **"Must be circumcised [*himmol yimmol*]"** (Genesis 17:13), which he interprets to mean: Only **one who is circumcised** [***hammal***] **may circumcise** [***yamul***] others.

סוּכָּה מְסַיֵּיעַ לֵיהּ, תְּפִילִּין הָוֵי תְּיוּבְתֵּיהּ.

The Gemara notes that the *halakha* with regard to **a *sukka* supports** the opinion of Rav Ḥisda, who holds that when an item used for a mitzva can be created by a gentile, a Jew who creates it does not recite a blessing. And the *halakha* with regard to **phylacteries is a conclusive refutation of his** opinion.

הֲרֵי סוּכָּה דִּכְשֵׁירָה בְּגוֹי, דְּתַנְיָא: סוּכַּת גּוֹיִם, סוּכַּת נָשִׁים, סוּכַּת בְּהֵמָה, סוּכַּת כּוּתִיִּים, סוּכָּה מִכׇּל מָקוֹם – כְּשֵׁירָה, וּבִלְבַד שֶׁתְּהֵא מְסוּכֶּכֶת כְּהִילְכָתָא;

The Gemara explains: **A *sukka* is fit** even if it was built **by a gentile, as it is taught** in a *baraita*: With regard to **a booth** built by **gentiles,**[H] **a booth** built by **women, a booth for domesticated animals, a booth** built by **Samaritans, a booth of any sort,** each **is fit** for use as a *sukka*, **provided that it is roofed in accordance with the *halakha*.**

NOTES

But what about circumcision, which is valid if performed by a gentile – וַהֲרֵי מִילָה דִּכְשֵׁירָה בְּגוֹי: The Gemara (*Avoda Zara* 26b) clarifies that according to both Rabbi Meir and Rabbi Yehuda, a circumcision performed by a gentile is not inherently invalid. The reason that Rabbi Yehuda, or, according to the Gemara in *Avoda Zara*, Rabbi Meir, holds that one should not allow a gentile to circumcise a Jewish child is due to concern that the gentile will try to harm the child. By contrast, the reason Rabbi Meir, or, according to the Gemara in *Avoda Zara*, Rabbi Yehuda, holds that one should not allow a Samaritan to circumcise a Jewish child is due to a concern that the Samaritan will intend to perform the circumcision as an idolatrous rite. This was a concern specifically with regard to Samaritans, who would circumcise themselves as an idolatrous rite. Gentiles would not perform circumcisions as idolatrous rites. Consequently, if a gentile were to circumcise a Jew, he would presumably do so with proper intentions (see *Tosafot*). The Gemara here responds that Rav does not hold in accordance with Rabbi Meir or Rabbi Yehuda; he holds in accordance with the opinion of Rabbi Yehuda HaNasi (see *Avoda Zara* 26b), who holds that a circumcision performed by a gentile is inherently invalid by Torah edict.

HALAKHA

The one who circumcises a child says – הַמָּל אוֹמֵר: Before circumcising a child, one recites a blessing that concludes: Who has sanctified us through His mitzvot and has commanded us concerning circumcision (Rambam *Sefer Ahava*, *Hilkhot Mila* 3:1; *Shulḥan Arukh*, *Yoreh De'a* 265:1).

Circumcision performed by a gentile – מִילָה בְּגוֹי: A gentile may not perform a circumcision even if he himself is circumcised. If he did perform the circumcision, it is valid after the fact and nothing further needs to be done to the child. This is in accordance with the *amora'im* who disagree with Rav (*Kesef Mishne*). Some explain that it is valid because circumcision does not need to be performed for the sake of the mitzva (Rabbeinu Manoaḥ). The Rema adds that some hold that the circumcision is invalid even after the fact, and one must therefore draw blood from the location of the circumcision (Rambam *Sefer Ahava*, *Hilkhot Mila* 2:1; *Shulḥan Arukh*, *Yoreh De'a* 264:1, and see *Pitḥei Teshuva* there).

A booth built by gentiles, etc. – סוּכַּת גּוֹיִם וכו׳: A booth that was not built for the purpose of fulfilling the mitzva of *sukka* is nevertheless fit, as long as it was constructed for the purpose of providing shade. Therefore, a booth built by gentiles or women, who are not commanded to fulfill the mitzva of *sukka*, one that was constructed in order to provide shade for animals, and the booth of a Samaritan are all fit (Rambam *Sefer Zemanim*, *Hilkhot Shofar VeSukka VeLulav* 5:9; *Shulḥan Arukh*, *Oraḥ Ḥayyim* 635:1).

ובישראל אין צריך לברך, דתניא: העושה סוכה לעצמו, אומר: "ברוך אתה ה׳ אלהינו מלך העולם שהחיינו וקימנו והגיענו לזמן הזה", בא לישב בה, אומר: "ברוך אתה ה׳ אלהינו מלך העולם אשר קדשנו במצותיו וצונו לישב בסוכה", ואילו "לעשות סוכה" לא מברך.

And if a *sukka* was built **by a Jew, he is not required to recite a blessing** upon its construction, **as it is taught** in a *baraita*: **One who constructs a *sukka*[H] for himself recites: Blessed are You, Lord our God, King of the universe, Who has given us life,[N] sustained us, and brought us to this time. When he comes to sit in the** *sukka*, **he recites: Blessed are You, Lord our God, King of the universe, Who has sanctified us through His mitzvot and commanded us to reside in the *sukka*.** The Gemara notes that the *baraita* indicates that he recites a blessing at the time of construction, **whereas he does not recite a blessing** including the words: **To construct a *sukka*,** which confirms the opinion of Rav Ḥisda.

תפילין תיובתיה; והרי תפילין דפסולות בגוי, דתני רב חיננא בריה דרבא

By contrast, the *halakha* with regard to **phylacteries is a conclusive refutation of** Rav Ḥisda's opinion. **Phylacteries are unfit** when written **by a gentile, as it is taught by Rav Ḥinnana, son of Rava,**

HALAKHA

One who constructs a *sukka* – העושה סוכה: There is no blessing that was formulated specifically for constructing a *sukka*. When constructing a *sukka* for oneself it would be fitting to recite the blessing that concludes: Who has given us life, sustained us, and brought us to this time; but it is customary to instead rely on the recital of that blessing when reciting *kiddush* on the first night of the Festival (Rambam *Sefer Ahava, Hilkhot Berakhot* 11:8–9; *Shulḥan Arukh, Oraḥ Ḥayyim* 641:1).

NOTES

Who has given us life – שהחיינו: Blessings over mitzvot were instituted to be recited when the mitzva is fulfilled, which in the case of *sukka* is when the individual sits in his *sukka* on *Sukkot*. By contrast, the blessing: Who has given us life, was instituted as an expression of the joy that one experiences over something new. Therefore, it is appropriate to recite it at the beginning of one's involvement with the mitzva, when he builds the *sukka* (see Rabbi David Luria).

Perek **IV**
Daf **42** Amud **b**

מפשרוניא: ספר תורה, תפילין ומזוזות שכתבן מין, כותי, גוי, עבד, אשה, וקטן, וישראל משומד – פסולין, שנאמר: "וקשרתם...וכתבתם", כל שישנו בקשירה – ישנו בכתיבה, כל שאינו בקשירה – אינו בכתיבה;

of Pashronya: A Torah scroll, phylacteries, or *mezuzot* that were written by a heretic,[N] a Samaritan, a gentile, a Canaanite **slave, a woman, a minor, or a Jewish apostate** [*meshummad*][L] **are unfit, as it is stated: "And you shall bind them** for a sign on your arm … **and you shall write them** on the doorposts of your house" (Deuteronomy 6:8–9). From this juxtaposition, one can derive the following: **Anyone who is** included **in** the mitzva of **binding**[H] the phylacteries, i.e., one who is both obligated and performs the mitzva, **is** included **in** the class of people who may **write** Torah scrolls, phylacteries, and *mezuzot*; and **anyone who is not** included **in** the mitzva of **binding is not** included **in** the class of people who may **write**[N] sacred texts.

LANGUAGE

Apostate [*meshummad*] – משומד: Although it is clear that this term refers to one who converted from Judaism to another religion, its etymology remains uncertain. Some *ge'onim* explain that this is a slightly abridged version of the term *meshuamad*, whose root *ayin, mem, dalet* connotes baptism in Aramaic and is also a pejorative reference to a chamber pot. It seems that gentile scholars concurred with this understanding, because censored editions of the Talmud replace this word with the term transgressor [*mumar*].

Others explain that the root of *meshummad* is *shin, mem, dalet*, which means a curse or excommunication in Aramaic. Accordingly, *meshummad* literally means: One who is cursed or excommunicated. Still others hold that it is from the Mandaic dialect of Aramaic and means to go astray by adopting heretical practices.

HALAKHA

Anyone who is included in the mitzva of binding, etc. – כל שישנו בקשירה וכו׳: A Torah scroll, phylacteries, or *mezuza* that was written by a heretic must be burned. If it was written by a gentile, a Jewish apostate, an informer, a Canaanite slave, a woman or a minor, it is unfit. This is due to the fact that the verse states: "And you shall bind them for a sign on your arm…and you shall write them" (Deuteronomy 6:8–9). The Sages derive from this verse that anyone who is not obligated in the mitzva, or does not believe in it, is not eligible to write Torah scrolls, phylacteries, or *mezuzot* (Rambam *Sefer Ahava, Hilkhot Tefillin UMezuza VeSefer Torah* 1:13; *Shulḥan Arukh, Oraḥ Ḥayyim* 39:1 and *Yoreh De'a* 281:1).

NOTES

That were written by a heretic – שכתבן מין: It appears that Rashi's version of the text referred to priests, and from other sources it is clear that this means Christian priests (see *Shita Mekubbetzet*). Although the same *halakha* would apply to all gentiles, Christian priests are mentioned because they studied the Bible and were generally literate. According to the standard version of the text, the reference here is to a Jewish idol worshipper, or according to the Rambam, a Jew who denies fundamental Jewish beliefs.

Anyone who is not included in the mitzva of binding is not included in the class of people who may write – כל שאינו בקשירה אינו בכתיבה: The verse refers to phylacteries and *mezuzot*, but the *halakha* certainly applies to Torah scrolls as well, which have an even higher level of sanctity (Ritva on *Gittin* 45b). The groups enumerated here are not involved in these mitzvot for the following reasons: Samaritans are excluded in accordance with the opinion that they are not true converts and therefore have the status of gentiles. Women and Canaanite slaves are excluded because donning phylacteries is a positive, time-bound mitzva, from which they are exempt. Minors are excluded because they are exempt from mitzvot. Rashi (*Gittin* 45b) explains that heretics and apostates are excluded because they have rejected their subservience to mitzvot. According to this explanation, it would appear that they are disqualified by Torah law. Some hold that this is the Rambam's opinion. Other early commentaries maintain that they are disqualified by rabbinic law (see Ritva on *Gittin* 45b citing his teacher, the Ra'ah; and see Ran on *Gittin* 45b).

וּבְיִשְׂרָאֵל אֵין צָרִיךְ לְבָרֵךְ, דִּשְׁלַח רַב חִיָּיא בְּרֵיהּ דְּרַב הוּנָא מִשְּׁמֵיהּ דְּרַבִּי יוֹחָנָן: עַל תְּפִילִּין שֶׁל יָד, אוֹמֵר: "בָּרוּךְ אֲשֶׁר קִדְּשָׁנוּ בְּמִצְוֹתָיו וְצִוָּנוּ לְהָנִיחַ תְּפִילִּין", עַל תְּפִילִּין שֶׁל רֹאשׁ, אוֹמֵר: "בָּרוּךְ אֲשֶׁר קִדְּשָׁנוּ בְּמִצְוֹתָיו וְצִוָּנוּ עַל מִצְוַת תְּפִילִּין", וְאִילּוּ "לַעֲשׂוֹת תְּפִילִּין" לָא מְבָרֵךְ!

And despite the fact that phylacteries written by a gentile are unfit, **a Jew** who writes them **does not have to recite a blessing. As Rav Ḥiyya, son of Rav Huna, sent** a ruling **in the name of Rabbi Yoḥanan: On phylacteries of the arm** one **says** the blessing: **Blessed** are You, Lord our God, King of the universe, **Who has sanctified us through His mitzvot and commanded us to don phylacteries. On phylacteries of the head** one **says** the blessing: **Blessed** are You, Lord our God, King of the universe, **Who has sanctified us through His mitzvot and commanded us concerning the mitzva of phylacteries.** The implication of this is that one recites blessings only when he dons the phylacteries, **whereas** when he writes the phylacteries he **does not recite a blessing: To prepare phylacteries.**[N]

אֶלָּא לָאו הַיְינוּ טַעְמָא: כׇּל מִצְוָה דַּעֲשִׂיָּיתָהּ גְּמַר מִצְוָה, כְּגוֹן מִילָה, אַף עַל גַּב דִּכְשֵׁירָה בְּגוֹי – בְּיִשְׂרָאֵל צָרִיךְ לְבָרֵךְ, וְכׇל מִצְוָה דַּעֲשִׂיָּיתָהּ לָאו גְּמַר מִצְוָה, כְּגוֹן תְּפִילִּין, אַף עַל גַּב דִּפְסוּלוֹת בְּגוֹי – בְּיִשְׂרָאֵל אֵינוֹ צָרִיךְ לְבָרֵךְ;

Rather, isn't this the reason[N] for the distinction between different mitzvot: For **any mitzva whose performance is the completion of** the **mitzva,**[H] **such as circumcision, even though it is valid** when performed **by a gentile,** when it is performed **by a Jew he must recite a blessing. But** for **any mitzva where the performance of** a particular act **is not the completion of** the **mitzva, such as** writing **phylacteries,** where one does not complete the mitzva until he dons them, **even though it is not valid** when performed **by a gentile,** when it is performed **by a Jew he does not need to recite a blessing.**

וּבְצִיצִית בְּהָא קָמִיפַּלְגִי, מָר סָבַר: חוֹבַת טַלִּית הוּא, וּמָר סָבַר: חוֹבַת גַּבְרָא הוּא.

And with regard to reciting a blessing when one attaches **ritual fringes** to a garment, the Sages **disagree about this:**[N] One **Sage,** Rav Adda bar Ahava, **holds** that **it is an obligation** pertaining to the **cloak.** Therefore, when one attaches the ritual fringes he is completing the mitzva, and he should recite a blessing: To prepare ritual fringes. **And** one **Sage,** Rav Naḥman, citing Rav, **holds** that **it is an obligation** incumbent upon **the man.** Consequently, the mitzva is not complete until he wears the garment; and he should not recite a blessing when he attaches the ritual fringes to the garment.

אֲמַר לֵיהּ רַב מָרְדֳּכַי לְרַב אָשֵׁי: אַתּוּן הָכִי מַתְנִיתוּ לַהּ,

Rav Mordekhai[P] **said to Rav Ashi: You teach this** *halakha* about gentiles attaching ritual fringes to a garment **in this manner,** citing Rav Yehuda in the name of Rav that the ritual fringes are invalid. Consequently, Rav Ḥisda raises a contradiction between this ruling and another ruling of Rav.

אֲנַן הָכִי מַתְנִינַן לַהּ, אָמַר רַב יְהוּדָה אָמַר רַב: מִנַּיִן לְצִיצִית בְּגוֹי שֶׁכְּשֵׁירָה? שֶׁנֶּאֱמַר: "דַּבֵּר אֶל בְּנֵי יִשְׂרָאֵל...וְעָשׂוּ לָהֶם צִיצִת" – יַעֲשׂוּ לָהֶם אֲחֵרִים.

We teach it in this way, according to which there is no contradiction: **Rav Yehuda says** that **Rav says: From where** is it derived that if **ritual fringes** are attached to a garment **by a gentile** they are **valid?** It is derived from **that** which **is stated: "Speak unto the children of Israel** and command them **that they prepare for themselves** [*lahem*] **strings"** (Numbers 15:38). From the fact that the verse does not merely state: That they prepare [*ve'asu*], but rather states "*ve'asu lahem,*" which can be translated as: That they prepare for them, the indication is that even **others,** i.e., gentiles, **shall prepare** ritual fringes **for them.**

HALAKHA

Whose performance is the completion of the mitzva – דַּעֲשִׂיָּיתָהּ גְּמַר מִצְוָה: One recites a blessing over a mitzva only upon completing the mitzva. Consequently, when building a *sukka*, preparing a *lulav* or a *shofar*, attaching ritual fringes to a garment, or writing phylacteries or a *mezuza*, one does not recite a blessing over the mitzva; the blessing is recited only upon sitting in the *sukka* or picking up the *lulav* on *Sukkot*, hearing the *shofar* blast on Rosh HaShana, wearing the garment with its ritual fringes, donning the phylacteries, or affixing the *mezuza* to one's doorway. One who builds a fence around his roof recites the blessing: Who has sanctified us with His mitzvot and has commanded us to construct a fence. The blessing is recited at the time of the construction because that is the completion of the mitzva, as nothing further must be done (Rambam *Sefer Ahava, Hilkhot Berakhot* 11:8).

PERSONALITIES

Rav Mordekhai – רַב מָרְדֳּכַי: Rav Mordekhai was a sixth- and seventh-generation Babylonian *amora* and a student of Rav Ashi. There was also an *amora* named Rav Mordekhai who was a student of Rava, but these two Sages are presumably not the same individual. Although Rav Mordekhai studied under Rav Ashi, it appears that Rav Ashi was not his primary teacher. Rather, he received traditions from other Sages, perhaps from his hometown of Hagronya. There are several instances in which Rav Mordekhai is cited as reporting these traditions to Rav Ashi. At times, as in the Gemara here, when Rav Ashi had difficulty resolving a tradition he had received, Rav Mordekhai would report to him traditions he had received that were somewhat different from those received by Rav Ashi. Rav Mordekhai outlived Rav Ashi, and when the Sages of the next generation would have a halakhic question and would inquire of Rav Mordekhai, he would report to them what he had heard from Rav Ashi.

NOTES

Whereas when he writes the phylacteries he does not recite a blessing: To prepare phylacteries – וְאִילּוּ לַעֲשׂוֹת תְּפִילִּין לָא מְבָרֵךְ: It appears from *Tosafot* that this phrase is part of Rav Ḥiyya's quote of what Rabbi Yoḥanan said, and that he clarified both which blessings one does recite and what one does not recite. Alternatively, this was not stated explicitly by Rabbi Yoḥanan, but since Rabbi Yoḥanan mentioned which blessings to recite and did not mention a blessing that one recites upon writing phylacteries, the implication is that one does not recite a blessing at that time (see Jerusalem Talmud, *Berakhot* 9:3).

Rather, isn't this the reason – אֶלָּא לָאו הַיְינוּ טַעְמָא: This can be understood as a rejection of the opinion of Rav Ḥisda (42a), who maintains that since Rav holds that ritual fringes are unfit if they are attached to a garment by a gentile, he must also hold that a Jew must recite a blessing when he attaches them to a garment.

Rashi explains that this is an alternative to Rav Yosef's interpretation of Rav Ḥisda's opinion. According to this interpretation, it does not follow directly from Rav's ruling about ritual fringes attached by a gentile that if they are attached by a Jew, he must recite a blessing. Rather, Rav Ḥisda's point is as follows: From the fact that Rav rules that ritual fringes attached by a gentile are unfit, it can be deduced that he holds that the mitzva pertains to the garment, and therefore attaching the ritual fringes is the completion of the mitzva. Consequently, one must recite a blessing upon attaching ritual fringes to a garment (see commentary attributed to Rashba).

And with regard to ritual fringes, the Sages disagree about this – וּבְצִיצִית בְּהָא קָמִיפַּלְגִי: Some explain that this is referring to the disagreement between Rav Adda bar Ahava, who recited a blessing when he attached ritual fringes to a garment, and Rav Naḥman, who admonished him for doing so (*Keren Ora*, citing Rif; see Rabbeinu Gershom Meor HaGola). Rashi explains that this is referring to the disagreement between Rav Naḥman and Rav Ḥisda about the opinion of Rav (see commentary attributed to Rashba).

אָמַר רַב יְהוּדָה אָמַר רַב: עֲשָׂאָן מִן הַקּוֹצִים וּמִן הַנִּימִין וּמִן הַגְּרָדִין – פְּסוּלָה, מִן הַסִּיסִין – כְּשֵׁירָה;

§ **Rav Yehuda says** that **Rav says: If one prepared** ritual fringes **from** threads that protrude from the fabric like **thorns** [*kotzim*],[HN] **or** if he prepared them **from threads** [*nimin*] that were used to sew the garment and remain attached to it, **or from the strings** [*geradin*] that hang from the bottom of a garment, the ritual fringes are **unfit**, as one must attach ritual fringes to a garment for the sake of the mitzva. But if he prepared ritual fringes **from swatches** of wool that were not spun for the sake of the mitzva, they are **fit.**

כִּי אֲמַרִיתָהּ קַמֵּיהּ דִּשְׁמוּאֵל, אָמַר: אַף מִן הַסִּיסִין פְּסוּלָה, בָּעֵינַן טְוִיָּיה לִשְׁמָהּ.

Rav Yehuda continues: **When I stated this** *halakha* in the name of Rav **before Shmuel,** he **said** to me: **Even** ritual fringes tied **from swatches** of wool that were not spun for the sake of the mitzva are **unfit,** as **we require the spinning** of the string to be **for the sake of** the mitzva.[H]

כְּתַנָּאֵי: צִיפָּן זָהָב, אוֹ שֶׁטָּלָה עֲלֵיהֶן עוֹר בְּהֵמָה טְמֵאָה – פְּסוּלוֹת; עוֹר בְּהֵמָה טְהוֹרָה – כְּשֵׁירוֹת, וְאַף עַל פִּי שֶׁלֹּא עִיבְּדָן לִשְׁמָן. רַבָּן שִׁמְעוֹן בֶּן גַּמְלִיאֵל אוֹמֵר: אַף עוֹר בְּהֵמָה טְהוֹרָה – פְּסוּלוֹת, עַד שֶׁיְּעַבְּדָן לִשְׁמָן.

The Gemara notes that this dispute **is like** a dispute between *tanna'im*, as it is taught in a *baraita*: If one took phylacteries and **coated them** with **gold or patched them** with the **skin of a non-kosher animal,**[HN] then **they are unfit.** But if one patched them with the **skin of a kosher animal,** then **they are fit, and** this is so **even though he did not prepare** the skin **for their sake,** i.e., for the sake of its use in a mitzva. **Rabban Shimon ben Gamliel says: Even** if he patched them with the **skin of a kosher animal they are unfit, until he prepares them for their sake.**[H]

אֲמַר לֵיהּ אַבָּיֵי לְרַב שְׁמוּאֵל בַּר רַב יְהוּדָה: הָא תְּכֵילְתָּא הֵיכִי צָבְעִיתוּ לָהּ? אֲמַר לֵיהּ: מַיְיתִינַן דַּם חִלָּזוֹן וְסַמָּנִין וְרָמֵינַן לְהוּ בְּיוֹרָה, וְשַׁקְלִינָא פּוּרְתָּא בְּבֵיעֲתָא וְטַעְמִינַן לְהוּ בְּאוּדְרָא, וְשָׁדֵינַן לֵיהּ לְהַהוּא בֵּיעֲתָא וְקָלֵינַן לֵיהּ לְאוּדְרָא.

§ **Abaye said to Rav Shmuel bar Rav Yehuda:**[P] **How do you dye this sky-blue wool**[H] to be used for ritual fringes? Rav Shmuel bar Rav Yehuda **said to** Abaye: **We bring blood of a *ḥilazon* and** various **herbs**[N] **and put them in a pot** and boil them. **And then we take a bit** of the resulting dye **in an egg** shell **and test it by** using it to dye **a wad** of wool to see if it has attained the desired hue. **And then we throw** away **that egg** shell and its contents **and burn the wad** of wool.

NOTES

If one prepared ritual fringes from threads that protrude like thorns [*kotzim*] – עֲשָׂאָן מִן הַקּוֹצִים: According to Rashi, this is referring to leftover strings at the bottom of the garment. In his commentary on *Sukka* 9a he explains that it refers to warp strings that came loose and were then tied back onto the garment. They are called *kotzim* because one cuts [*kotzetzim*] them, or because they look like thorns [*kotzim*] (according to the text cited in *Haggahot Tzon Kodashim*; see also Ritva on *Sukka* 9a).

Rashi explains that the various threads mentioned here are unfit because they were not attached to the garment for the sake of ritual fringes. *Tosafot* quote Rashi as stating that this is problematic due to the principle: Prepare it, and not from what has already been prepared. According to this interpretation, if one cut these strings off of the garment and then reattached them, they would then be fit for use as ritual fringes. Others explain that the reason they are unfit is that they were already used for another purpose (*Sefer HaIttur*).

The *ge'onim* offer a different interpretation, which is adopted by the Rambam. They explain that the term *kotzim* is referring to wool that one collects from thorns after sheep have passed by and some of their wool has caught on the thorns. *Nimin* are thick strands of wool that are separated from the finer strands. *Geradin* are threads that form bumps in the weave and are cut off by the weaver in order to smooth out the cloth. According to the explanation of the *ge'onim*, it is prohibited to use these scraps as ritual fringes because they are not of high enough quality to use for making a garment (Ba'al HaMaor on *Sukka* 9a; see Meiri), or because it is disrespectful to use threads of inferior quality for the mitzva of ritual fringes (*Kesef Mishne*).

Coated them with gold or patched them with the skin of a non-kosher animal – צִיפָּן זָהָב אוֹ שֶׁטָּלָה עֲלֵיהֶן עוֹר בְּהֵמָה טְמֵאָה: It appears that Rashi and the Rambam explain this to mean that he made the boxes of the phylacteries, in which the parchments are placed, from gold or from leather from a non-kosher animal. These boxes are unfit because the boxes must be made from the hide of a kosher animal.

In his commentary on *Sanhedrin* 48b, Rashi explains that the case is where one had valid boxes for phylacteries and covered them with gold or with leather from a non-kosher animal (see *Noda BiYehuda*, *Oraḥ Ḥayyim* 1, and the comment of the *Netziv* there).

Blood of a *ḥilazon* and various herbs – דַּם חִלָּזוֹן וְסַמָּנִין: According to Rashi the sky-blue dye [*tekhelet*] of the Torah refers to the blood of a certain sea creature known as the *ḥilazon* (see 44a). The herbs are added to facilitate the wool's absorption of the dye. According to *Tosafot tekhelet* is defined as a dye that is derived from the blood of a *ḥilazon* and various herbs.

HALAKHA

Ritual fringes from threads that protrude like thorns, etc. – מִן הַקּוֹצִים וכו׳: One may not use wool that was detached from the animal when it became caught on thorns, or hairs that animals shed, or leftover warp strings for ritual fringes, because this would be a degradation of the mitzva. This is in accordance with the *baraita* (Rambam *Sefer Ahava*, *Hilkhot Tzitzit* 1:11; *Shulḥan Arukh*, *Oraḥ Ḥayyim* 11:5 and *Magen Avraham* there).

We require the spinning of the string to be for the sake of the mitzva – בָּעֵינַן טְוִיָּיה לִשְׁמָהּ: The ritual fringes must be spun for the sake of the mitzva. This is the *halakha* concerning both the white strings and the sky-blue ones. Consequently, one may not take ready-made strings and use them as ritual fringes, as they were presumably not spun for the sake of the mitzva. Although the *halakha* is usually in accordance with the opinion of Rav in cases of ritual law, in this case the *halakha* is in accordance with the opinion of Shmuel, because he rules in accordance with the opinion of Rabban Shimon ben Gamliel. In addition, the Gemara (*Sukka* 9a) rejects Rav's reasoning (Rambam *Sefer Ahava*, *Hilkhot Tzitzit* 1:11; *Shulḥan Arukh*, *Oraḥ Ḥayyim* 11:1).

Coated them with gold or patched them with the skin of a non-kosher animal – צִיפָּן זָהָב אוֹ שֶׁטָּלָה עֲלֵיהֶן עוֹר בְּהֵמָה טְמֵאָה: If one plated his phylacteries with gold, or covered them with the hide of a non-kosher animal, the phylacteries are unfit (Rambam *Sefer Ahava*, *Hilkhot Tefillin UMezuza VeSefer Torah* 3:15; *Shulḥan Arukh*, *Oraḥ Ḥayyim* 32:48).

Until he prepares them for their sake – עַד שֶׁיְּעַבְּדָן לִשְׁמָן: The hide used for the boxes of the phylacteries must be prepared for the sake of the mitzva. This is in accordance with the opinion of Rabban Shimon ben Gamliel. The Rambam holds in accordance with the opinion of the first *tanna*. One may rely on his opinion in exigent circumstances, and therefore if one does not have access to another pair of phylacteries, he may use a pair made from a hide that was not prepared for the sake of the mitzva. Authorities disagree as to whether or not one recites a blessing under such circumstances (Rambam *Sefer Ahava*, *Hilkhot Tefillin UMezuza VeSefer Torah* 3:15; *Shulḥan Arukh*, *Oraḥ Ḥayyim* 32:37, and see *Mishna Berura* there).

How do you dye this sky-blue wool – הָא תְּכֵילְתָּא הֵיכִי צָבְעִיתוּ לָהּ: One dyes sky-blue wool in the following manner: One takes wool and soaks it in lime and then washes it until it is clean. He then boils it in aloe or the like, as dyers do, so that the wool will absorb the dye. He then he takes the blood of a *ḥilazon*, a sea creature that has black blood and that is commonly found in the Mediterranean Sea. The blood is placed in a pot with various herbs and boiled. The wool is placed in the dye until it turns the color of the heavens (Rambam *Sefer Ahava*, *Hilkhot Tzitzit* 2:2).

PERSONALITIES

Rav Shmuel bar Rav Yehuda – רַב שְׁמוּאֵל בַּר רַב יְהוּדָה: Rav Shmuel bar Rav Yehuda was a second- and third-generation Babylonian *amora*. He was a member of a family of converts; apparently both he and his father converted. Some suggest that his father was Rav Yehuda Hindua. Rav Shmuel bar Rav Yehuda's primary teacher was apparently Rav Yehuda, with whom he was very close. Rav Yehuda valued Rav Shmuel's great integrity. Rav Shmuel bar Rav Yehuda also apparently spent a significant period of time in Eretz Yisrael. He studied under the Sages there and transmitted to them what he had received from the Babylonian *amora'im*. Later he returned to Babylonia and, like Ulla and Ravin, he is considered one of the emissaries who conveyed the Torah of Eretz Yisrael to Babylonia. This Gemara tells of his describing to Abaye the process by which sky-blue dye was prepared in Eretz Yisrael.

שְׁמַע מִינַּהּ תְּלָת: שְׁמַע מִינָּהּ טְעִימָה פְּסוּלָה, וּשְׁמַע מִינָּהּ דְּבָעֵינַן צְבִיעָה לִשְׁמָהּ, וּשְׁמַע מִינָּהּ טְעִימָה פָּסְלָה.

The Gemara comments: **Learn from** this statement **three** *halakhot*: **Learn from it** that wool that was dyed for the purpose of **testing** the dye and not for use as ritual fringes is **unfit** for ritual fringes. Consequently, one burns the wad of wool so that no one will use it for ritual fringes. **And learn from it that we require dyeing for the sake of** the mitzva. **And learn from it** that using dye for **testing renders** all the dye in that vessel **unfit.**[N] Therefore, some of the dye is removed from the pot before it is tested.

הַיְינוּ טְעִימָה פְּסוּלָה, הַיְינוּ צְבִיעָה לִשְׁמָהּ! אֲמַר רַב אַשִׁי: מַה טַּעַם קָאָמַר, מַה טַּעַם טְעִימָה פְּסוּלָה – מִשּׁוּם דְּבָעֵינַן צְבִיעָה לִשְׁמָהּ.

The Gemara challenges: The *halakha* that wool dyed for the purpose of **testing** the dye is **unfit is** the same as the requirement of **dyeing for the sake of** the mitzva. It is only because the sky-blue strings must be dyed for the sake of the mitzva that wool dyed as a test is unfit for use as ritual fringes, so why are these stated as two *halakhot*? **Rav Ashi said:** The statement about learning three *halakhot* **employs** the style known as: **What is the reason,**[N] and it means: **What is the reason** that wool that was dyed for the purpose of **testing** is **unfit?** It is **because we require dyeing for the sake of** the mitzva.[H]

כְּתַנָּאֵי: טְעִימָה פְּסוּלָה, מִשּׁוּם שֶׁנֶּאֱמַר: "כְּלִיל תְּכֵלֶת", דִּבְרֵי רַבִּי חֲנִינָא בֶּן גַּמְלִיאֵל.

The Gemara notes that the *halakha* that using the dye for testing renders all the dye in the pot unfit is **subject to** a dispute between *tanna'im*, as it is taught in a *baraita*: *Tekhelet* dye that was used for **testing** is **unfit, as it is stated** concerning the priestly vestments: "And you shall make the robe of the ephod **entirely of blue** [***kelil tekhelet***]" (Exodus 28:31),[N] which indicates that the dye must be used exclusively for this purpose, i.e., this must be the first item it is being used to dye. This is **the statement of Rabbi Ḥanina ben Gamliel.**

רַבִּי יוֹחָנָן בֶּן דְּהַבַאי אוֹמֵר: אֲפִילּוּ מַרְאֶה שֵׁנִי שֶׁבָּהּ כָּשֵׁר, מִשּׁוּם שֶׁנֶּאֱמַר: "וּשְׁנִי תוֹלַעַת".

Rabbi Yoḥanan ben Dahavai says: Even a second appearance caused by the dye **is fit,** meaning even if it is the second time that the dye is being used, it is still fit. **As it is stated** in the verse: **"And scarlet wool [*ushni tola'at*]"** (Leviticus 14:4),[N] which is interpreted to mean that this may be the second [*sheni*] usage of the dye.

תָּנוּ רַבָּנַן: תְּכֵלֶת אֵין לָהּ בְּדִיקָה, וְאֵין נִקַּחַת אֶלָּא מִן הַמּוּמְחֶה; תְּפִילִּין יֵשׁ לָהֶם בְּדִיקָה, וְאֵין נִיקָּחִין אֶלָּא מִן הַמּוּמְחֶה; סְפָרִים וּמְזוּזוֹת יֵשׁ לָהֶן בְּדִיקָה, וְנִיקָּחִין מִכׇּל אָדָם.

The Sages taught in a *baraita*: **There is no** reliable method of **testing sky-blue wool,**[N] **and** therefore **it may be purchased only from an expert.**[H] **There is** a method of **testing phylacteries** to ensure they were written properly, **but** nevertheless **they may be purchased only from an expert. There is** a method of **testing Torah scrolls and *mezuzot*,**[HN] **and they may be purchased from anyone.**

HALAKHA

We require dyeing for the sake of the mitzva – בָּעֵינַן צְבִיעָה לִשְׁמָהּ: The sky-blue wool of ritual fringes must be dyed for the sake of the mitzva, otherwise it is not fit. If one dyed a bit of wool to test a batch of dye, all of the dye in that container is rendered unfit. Therefore, one should place a small amount of the dye in a small vessel and use that for testing. He should then burn the wool that was used for testing, as it is unfit because it was dyed for the purpose of testing. He should also discard the dye in the small vessel, since using the dye for testing renders the entire contents of the vessel unfit (Rambam *Sefer Ahava, Hilkhot Tzitzit* 2:3).

From an expert – מִן הַמּוּמְחֶה: One should acquire sky-blue wool for ritual fringes only from an expert, so as to be sure that it was dyed for the sake of the mitzva (Rambam *Sefer Ahava, Hilkhot Tzitzit* 2:4).

Phylacteries…Torah scrolls and *mezuzot* – תְּפִילִּין...סְפָרִים וּמְזוּזוֹת: One should purchase phylacteries only from a scribe who is an expert in the details of how to write phylacteries. Although one can inspect the writing to ensure that it was written properly, there is concern that one might not expend the effort to open the boxes and perform the examination. One may purchase *mezuzot* or the parchments of phylacteries before they are inserted into the boxes from anyone, provided that one inspects them (Rambam *Sefer Ahava, Hilkhot Tefillin UMezuza VeSefer Torah* 2:10; *Shulḥan Arukh, Oraḥ Ḥayyim* 39:8, and see 39:9).

NOTES

And learn from it that using dye for testing renders all the dye in that vessel unfit – וּשְׁמַע מִינָּהּ טְעִימָה פָּסְלָה: Rashi adds that not only would all the dye in the vat become disqualified if the wool were dyed for testing in the vat itself, but even if the testing were done from the dye in the eggshell, if the rest of that dye were poured back into the vat, the entire vat would be disqualified.

Employs the style known as: What is the reason – מַה טַּעַם קָאָמַר: According to this, there are actually only two conclusions to be drawn, and not three as initially stated (*Tosafot*). Alternatively, since one point is the consequence of the other, it is possible to view these as two distinct points, and there are still a total of three conclusions (commentary attributed to Rashba).

And you shall make the robe of the ephod entirely of blue [*kelil tekhelet*] – כְּלִיל תְּכֵלֶת: This phrase appears in the context of the priestly vestments. Nevertheless, it sets the standard for *tekhelet* required for any mitzva (*Tosafot*).

Rashi explains that the point is that the dye may be used only once because the first dyeing absorbs the essence of the pigment and the second dyeing will not be as effective. For this reason, if some of the dye is removed and used for testing, the rest of the dye may still be used (commentary attributed to Rashba). *Tosafot* disagree with Rashi's opinion that a batch of dye may be used only once. They understand the phrase *kelil tekhelet* to mean that the dye in the vat must be used exclusively to dye wool that is fit for the mitzva of ritual fringes. Alternatively, *Keren Ora* suggests that *kelil tekhelet* is interpreted to mean perfectly sky-blue, i.e., dye whose color is so pure that it does not require any testing.

And scarlet wool [*ushni tola'at*] – וּשְׁנִי תוֹלַעַת: The plain sense of the term *shni tola'at* is wool that is dyed scarlet, but Rabbi Yoḥanan ben Dahavai interprets it homiletically, as though the word were pronounced *sheni*, i.e., second. He then extrapolates that just as the scarlet dye may be used more than once, the same is true of sky-blue dye, which is often mentioned in the Torah together with scarlet (see, e.g., Exodus 28:6).

There is no reliable method of testing sky-blue wool – תְּכֵלֶת אֵין לָהּ בְּדִיקָה: Rashi explains that the Gemara initially assumes that this means that it is impossible to test whether wool has been dyed with real *tekhelet* or with indigo. Rabbeinu Gershom Meor HaGola explains that Gemara initially assumes that this means that there is no need to test whether it is *tekhelet* or indigo.

Phylacteries…Torah scrolls and *mezuzot* – תְּפִילִּין...סְפָרִים וּמְזוּזוֹת: Rashi explains that it is possible to check whether the Torah portions contained in these items have been written accurately. Nevertheless, phylacteries must be purchased from an expert because they must be written on parchment that was prepared for the purpose of being used for phylacteries. This *tanna* holds that Torah scrolls and *mezuzot* do not have this requirement, and therefore they may be purchased from anyone.

Tosafot contend that even the parchment used in Torah scrolls and *mezuzot* must be prepared for the sake of the mitzva. Nevertheless, one may purchase these items from anyone, because everyone is aware of and careful about this requirement. The reason one must purchase phylacteries only from an expert is due to the concern that the phylacteries may not have been written properly. Although the writing can be checked, checking them requires opening up the boxes, which is a denigration of the phylacteries. Alternatively, since opening the boxes requires effort, there is concern that one will not take the trouble to check the phylacteries (Rosh).

וּתְכֵלֶת אֵין לָהּ בְּדִיקָה? וְהָא רַב יִצְחָק בְּרֵיהּ דְּרַב יְהוּדָה בָּדֵיק לֵיהּ (סִימָן: בגש״ם), מַיְיתֵי מְגַבְיָא גִּילָא, וּמַיָּא דְּשַׁבְלִילְתָּא, וּמֵימֵי רַגְלַיִם

The Gemara asks: **And is there no** method for **testing sky-blue wool? But didn't Rav Yitzhak, son of Rav Yehuda, test it** to ensure it was dyed with *tekhelet*? The Gemara provides **a mnemonic** for the test, which was carried out **with** items whose names contain the letters *gimmel, shin,* or *mem.* He would **bring alum clay** [*megavya gila*],[L] **and water of fenugreek** [*shavlilta*],[B] **and urine** [*meimei raglayim*]

LANGUAGE

Alum clay [*megavya gila*] – מְגַבְיָא גִּילָא: *Megavya* is an ancient Akkadian word for alum. Alum was used in talmudic times for various purposes, including gluing together shards of earthenware vessels, as an ingredient in medical potions, and as a binding agent in the dyeing process. It appears from this Gemara that it was also used to remove certain stains from fabric. *Gila* apparently refers to clay or earth. The Rambam holds that *megavya gila* refers to straw, which is how the word *gila* is used in *Targum Onkelos* (see, e.g., Exodus 5:12).

BACKGROUND

Fenugreek [*shavlilta*] – שַׁבְלִילְתָּא: Usually called *tiltan* by the Sages, fenugreek is a legume from the Fabaceae family, *Trigonella foenum-graecum*. It grows to less than 1 m in height, has furry, hollow stalks, and sprouts triangular, light-green leaves and white flowers. The fruit grows in thin pods up to 15 cm in size, and contains flat seeds roughly 5 mm in size. Fenugreek is usually cultivated for its seeds, which are eaten and utilized in the preparation of many seasonings. Its young stalks are also used as seasoning. In various countries fenugreek is used as fodder as well as fertilizer. Water of fenugreek would appear to be water in which fenugreek had been soaked. The Rambam, apparently following Rav Shmuel ben Hofni Gaon, understands it as the mucilage of the fenugreek plant.

Fenugreek

Perek **IV**
Daf **43** Amud **a**

בֶּן אַרְבָּעִים יוֹם, וְתָרֵי לָהּ בְּגַוַּויְיהוּ מֵאוּרְתָּא וְעַד לְצַפְרָא, אִיפַּרַד חָזוּתֵיהּ – פְּסוּלָה, לָא אִיפַּרַד חָזוּתֵיהּ – כְּשֵׁרָה.

that was **forty days old.**[N] He would **soak** the sky-blue wool **in** this solution **from night until morning. If its color would fade** [*ipparad hazutei*],[B] the sky-blue wool was determined to be **unfit,** as it was not dyed with *tekhelet* derived from a *hilazon.* **If its color would not fade,** the sky-blue wool was determined to be **fit.**

וְרַב אַדָּא קַמֵּיהּ דְּרָבָא מִשְּׁמֵיהּ דְּרַב עֵוִירָא אֲמַר: מַיְיתֵי חֲמִירָא אַרְכְּסָא דְּשַׂעֲרֵי וְאָפְיָא לָהּ בְּגַוֵּיהּ, אִישְׁתַּנַּאי לְמַעַלְיוּתָא – כְּשֵׁרָה, לִגְרִיעוּתָא – פְּסוּלָה, וְסִימָנֵיךְ: שִׁינּוּי שֶׁקֶר, שִׁינּוּי אֱמֶת!

And Rav Adda said before Rava in the name of Rav Avira: One brings hard [*arkesa*][L] **leavened barley** dough **and bakes** the sky-blue wool **in it.** If the color of the sky-blue wool **changes for the better,** meaning that the process intensifies the color of the sky-blue wool, then it is **fit.** If the color of the sky-blue wool changes for the **worse,** i.e., it fades, then it is **unfit. And your mnemonic** is: **Change** reveals **falsehood** and **change** reveals **truth.** All of this indicates that it is possible to test whether sky-blue wool has been dyed with real *tekhelet,* contrary to the *baraita.*

מַאי אֵין לָהּ בְּדִיקָה נַמִי דְּקָאָמַר? אַטְעִימָה.

The Gemara explains the *baraita:* **What does it mean when it says: There is no** reliable method of **testing** sky-blue wool? It means that there is no way to test whether it was dyed for the sake of the mitzva or **for** the purpose of **testing** the dye.[N]

מָר מִמַּשְׁכֵי אַיְיתֵי תְּכֵלְתָּא בִּשְׁנֵי רַב אַחַאי, בַּדְקוּהָ בִּדְרַב יִצְחָק בְּרֵיהּ דְּרַב יְהוּדָה וְאִיפַּרַד חָזוּתֵיהּ, בִּדְרַב אַדָּא – וְאִישְׁתַּנַּאי לְמַעַלְיוּתָא;

The Gemara relates that **Mar,** a Sage **from Mashkhei, brought sky-blue** wool **in the years** when **Rav Ahai** was a preeminent Sage. **They tested it in** the manner described by **Rav Yitzhak, son of Rav Yehuda, and its color faded.** They then tested it **in** the manner described by **Rav Adda and** the color **changed for the better.**

BACKGROUND

Its color would fade [*ippārad hazutei*] – אִיפַּרַד חָזוּתֵיהּ: *Ipparad* means separated or detached, and therefore the expression *ipparad hazutei* may mean that the color became detached from the fabric, or that there are now different hues that are distinct and separate from one another, indicating that the dye cannot withstand the laundering agents. It should be noted that attempts to replicate these methods of testing in modern times in order to identify the authentic sky-blue dye have been inconclusive.

LANGUAGE

Hard [*arkesa*] – אַרְכְּסָא: This word, which does not appear anywhere else in the Gemara, is understood by the early commentaries to mean strong or sharp. Some suggest that it is a corruption of a Greek word of the same meaning. According to the version of the text that is recorded in some early commentaries (see, e.g., Rif), the word is *harsena* or *harsanya*, which can refer to shelled or ground barley. It appears that the Rambam's version of the text had the word *harsena*, which means a small fish, as he explains that the reference is to dough prepared for a sharp food that included fish, brine, and either flour or fermented dough.

NOTES

Forty days old – בֶּן אַרְבָּעִים יוֹם: Rashi explains that this refers to urine from a baby that is forty days old. Alternatively, it refers to urine that left a person's body forty days earlier. The Rambam interprets the Gemara in accordance with this second explanation.

To test whether it was dyed for the purpose of testing the dye – אַטְעִימָה: For this reason, the *baraita* requires that one purchase sky-blue wool from an expert, who is aware that wool that was dyed for testing is unfit for the mitzva of ritual fringes. Nevertheless, it is still necessary to test whether the wool was dyed with *tekhelet* or indigo, as some sellers are not knowledgeable with regard to this issue (*Tosafot*; see *Birkat HaZevah* and *Tzon Kodashim*, which cite differing interpretations as to the precise intent of *Tosafot*). The Rambam infers from the Gemara here that although one is not obligated to test sky-blue wool purchased from an expert, if one does perform the tests described in the Gemara and the wool does not pass, it is unfit for ritual fringes (Rambam *Sefer Ahava*, *Hilkhot Tzitzit* 2:4, and see *Kesef Mishne* there).

סָבַר לְמִיפְסְלָהּ, אֲמַר לְהוּ רַב אַחַאי: אֶלָּא הָא לָא תְּכֵילְתָּא הִיא וְלָא קָלָא אִילַן הִיא! אֶלָּא שְׁמַע מִינַּהּ שְׁמוּעָתָא אַהֲדָדֵי אִיתְּמַר;

The Sages **thought** that the sky-blue wool should be **deemed unfit** because it did not pass the first test. **Rav Aḥai said to them: But** how could it be that **this** wool **is not *tekhelet*,** as it failed one of the tests, **and is** also **not indigo,** as it passed the other? This is impossible, because it must be one or the other. **Rather, conclude from it that these *halakhot* were stated together.**[H]

הֵיכָא דִּבְדַקְנָא בִּדְרַב יִצְחָק בְּרֵיהּ דְּרַב יְהוּדָה, לָא אִיפְּרַד חֲזוּתֵיהּ – כְּשֵׁרָה, אִיפְּרַד חֲזוּתֵיהּ – בָּדְקִינַן לַהּ בִּדְרַב אַדָּא בַּחֲמִירָא אַרְכְּסָא; אִישְׁתַּנֵּי לְמַעַלְיוּתָא – כְּשֵׁרָה, לִגְרִיעוּתָא – פְּסוּלָה. שְׁלַחוּ מִתָּם: שְׁמוּעָתָא אַהֲדָדֵי אִיתְּמַר.

He explains: In a case **where we tested** the wool **in** the manner described **by Rav Yitzḥak, son of Rav Yehuda,** and **its color did not fade,** it is **fit** and requires no further testing. If **its color faded,** then **we test it in** the manner described **by Rav Adda, with hard leavened** barley dough. If the color **changed for the better** it is **fit;** if the color changed **for the worse** it is **unfit.** The Gemara adds: **They sent** a message **from there,** i.e., Eretz Yisrael: These ***halakhot*** **were** in fact **stated together,** as explained by Rav Aḥai.

רַבִּי מָנִי דָּיֵיק וְזָבֵין כְּחוּמְרֵי מַתְנִיתָא, אֲמַר לֵיהּ הַהוּא סָבָא: הָכִי עֲבוּד קַמָּאֵי דְּקַמָּךְ וְאַצְלַח עִיסְקַיְיהוּ.

The Gemara relates that **Rabbi Mani was exacting and purchased** sky-blue wool **in accordance with the stringencies of the *baraita***[N] cited earlier, i.e., that wool dyed as a test is unfit for ritual fringes, and that therefore one should purchase sky-blue wool for ritual fringes only from an expert. **A certain elder said to him: This is what your early predecessors did, and their businesses were successful.**[N]

תָּנוּ רַבָּנַן: הַלּוֹקֵחַ טַלִּית מְצוּיֶּיצֶת מִן הַשּׁוּק מִיִּשְׂרָאֵל – הֲרֵי הִיא בְּחֶזְקָתָהּ. מִן הַגּוֹי: מִן הַתַּגָּר – כְּשֵׁרָה, מִן הַהֶדְיוֹט – פְּסוּלָה,

The Sages taught in a *baraita*: In the case of **one who purchases a cloak with ritual fringes from the marketplace,**[H] if he purchased it **from a Jew it retains its presumptive status**[N] that it is fit for the mitzva. If he purchased it **from a gentile,** then if he purchased it **from a merchant** it is presumed to be **fit,**[N] as the merchant would want to maintain his credibility and would therefore purchase the sky-blue strings only from a reliable source. But if he purchased it **from** a gentile who is **an ordinary** person rather than a professional merchant, the sky-blue strings are **unfit,** as the seller presumably dyed them himself.

וְאַף עַל פִּי שֶׁאָמְרוּ: אֵין אָדָם רַשַּׁאי לִמְכּוֹר טַלִּית מְצוּיֶּיצֶת לְגוֹי עַד שֶׁיַּתִּיר צִיצִיּוֹתֶיהָ.

And even though the Sages **said: A person is not permitted to sell**[H] **a cloak with ritual fringes to a gentile until he unties** and removes **its ritual fringes,** it is permitted to purchase such a cloak from a gentile merchant, as it is assumed that the merchant acquired the cloak from a Jew who ignored this *halakha*.

מַאי טַעְמָא? הָכָא תַּרְגִּימוּ: מִשּׁוּם זוֹנָה. רַב יְהוּדָה אָמַר: שֶׁמָּא יִתְלַוֶּה עִמּוֹ בַּדֶּרֶךְ וְיַהַרְגֶנּוּ.

The Gemara asks: **What is the reason** for the prohibition against selling a cloak with ritual fringes to a gentile? The Gemara answers: **Here they interpreted** that it is prohibited **because** of the concern that the gentile will visit **a prostitute**[N] and observers will think that he is a Jew. Alternatively, **Rav Yehuda said:** It is prohibited **lest** a Jew mistake the gentile for a Jew and **accompany him on a journey** thinking that he is also Jewish, due to his ritual fringes, **and** the gentile might then **kill him.**

NOTES

Rabbi Mani was exacting and purchased sky-blue wool in accordance with the stringencies of the *baraita* – רַבִּי מָנִי דָּיֵיק וְזָבֵין כְּחוּמְרֵי מַתְנִיתָא: Rabbi Mani purchased sky-blue dye in order to sell it to others. Rabbeinu Gershom Meor HaGola explains that Rabbi Mani would follow all possible stringencies by purchasing exclusively from experts and then performing both tests. Others explain that his stringency consisted of not relying on testing and therefore purchasing only from experts (*Nimmukei Yosef*).

And their businesses were successful – וְאַצְלַח עִיסְקַיְיהוּ: This is in accordance with the Gemara in *Pesaḥim* (50b) that those who sell sky-blue dye or otherwise engage in the work of Heaven for a profit do not see a sign of blessing from their labor, but if they engage in these activities for the sake of Heaven, they do see blessing from their labor (*Keren Ora*).

From a Jew it retains its presumptive status – מִיִּשְׂרָאֵל הֲרֵי הִיא בְּחֶזְקָתָהּ: There is a presumptive status that the ritual fringes were prepared properly, because most of those who involve themselves with the preparation of ritual fringes are experts (*Nimmukei Yosef*; *Olat Shlomo*). The *Baḥ* (*Oraḥ Ḥayyim* 20) infers from the fact that the Gemara does not simply state that the ritual fringes are fit that it depends on whether the seller is a reliable individual.

If he purchased it from a merchant it is presumed to be fit – מִן הַתַּגָּר כְּשֵׁרָה: The assumption is that the gentile merchant purchased the cloak and ritual fringes from a Jew who is an expert and knows that the sky-blue wool must be dyed for the sake of the mitzva in order to be fit for use as ritual fringes, and knows that wool that was colored in order to test the dye is considered unfit. The merchant would not lie, as he does not want to ruin his professional reputation. This is not the case if he is a private individual rather than a professional merchant (Rashi). There are those who explain that this refers to an established merchant who routinely does business with Jews (*Nimmukei Yosef*). Rabbeinu Gershom Meor HaGola explains that whereas there might be circumstances under which a Jew would sell sky-blue wool to a gentile merchant, a Jew would never sell it to a gentile who is a private individual.

Because of the concern that the gentile will visit a prostitute – מִשּׁוּם זוֹנָה: Rashi offers two interpretations: One is that this refers to a Jewish prostitute, and the concern is that she will engage in intercourse with this gentile because she believes him to be a Jew. Consequently, the prostitute will violate the prohibition: "Neither shall you make marriages with them" (Deuteronomy 7:3). Some commentaries claim that this interpretation is difficult because the prohibition does not apply to intercourse that occurs outside of the context of marriage (*Karnei Re'em*).

Rashi's second interpretation, which is also the explanation of Rabbeinu Gershom Meor HaGola, is that the gentile will visit a gentile prostitute and give her the cloak with the ritual fringes as payment for her services. She will then claim that the cloak was given to her by a particular Jew, thereby unfairly sullying his reputation.

HALAKHA

These *halakhot* were stated together – שְׁמוּעָתָא אַהֲדָדֵי אִיתְּמַר: How does one test sky-blue wool to determine whether it was dyed properly or not? One soaks it for a twenty-four hour period in a solution of straw, water of fenugreek, and urine that fermented for forty days. If the color does not fade, it is deemed fit. If it does fade, one takes barley dough that has been fermented for use with fish and brine, and he bakes the wool in that dough. He then inspects the wool. If it faded further it is unfit. If the color became darker and more intense, then it is fit (Rambam *Sefer Ahava*, *Hilkhot Tzitzit* 2:5).

One who purchases a cloak with ritual fringes from the marketplace – הַלּוֹקֵחַ טַלִּית מְצוּיֶּיצֶת מִן הַשּׁוּק: If one purchases a cloak with ritual fringes from a Jew, or from a gentile merchant who claims to have purchased it from a Jew, it is fit. The *Mishna Berura* discusses whether it is permitted to purchase ritual fringes that are not attached to a cloak from a gentile merchant. But if he purchased them from a gentile who is not a merchant, the ritual fringes are presumed to be unfit (Rambam *Sefer Ahava*, *Hilkhot Tzitzit* 2:7; *Shulḥan Arukh*, *Oraḥ Ḥayyim* 20:1).

A person is not permitted to sell, etc. – אֵין אָדָם רַשַּׁאי לִמְכּוֹר וכו׳: One may not sell a cloak with ritual fringes to a gentile, due to the concern lest a Jew think that the buyer is Jewish and accompany him on a journey, in which case the gentile might kill him. There are those who say that even in a situation where this concern does not apply, it remains prohibited to sell a cloak with ritual fringes to a gentile due to the concern that he may visit a prostitute and observers will assume he is a Jew (*Ḥayyei Adam*). It is prohibited even to give him a cloak with ritual fringes as collateral or a deposit, unless it is for a very short period of time (Rambam *Sefer Ahava*, *Hilkhot Tzitzit* 3:9; *Shulḥan Arukh*, *Oraḥ Ḥayyim* 20:2).

§ Rav Yehuda would affix white and sky-blue strings to the garment [*pirzuma*][L] of his wife. And every morning he would recite the blessing:[H] To wrap ourselves in garments with ritual fringes.

רַב יְהוּדָה רָמֵי תְּכֵילְתָּא לְפִרְזוּמָא דְּאֵינָשֵׁי בֵּיתֵיהּ, וּמְבָרֵךְ כׇּל צַפְרָא: ״לְהִתְעַטֵּף בְּצִיצִית״.

The Gemara asks: From the fact that he would affix ritual fringes to his wife's garments, it is apparent that he holds that the obligation of ritual fringes is a positive mitzva that is not time-bound, and therefore women are also obligated in it. But if that is his opinion, why did he recite the blessing on ritual fringes each and every morning?[N] In order for the mitzva to not be time-bound, it must apply at night, in which case a new blessing should not be recited in the morning.

מִדְּרָמֵי – קָסָבַר: מִצְוַת עֲשֵׂה שֶׁלֹּא הַזְּמַן גְּרָמָא הוּא, אַמַּאי מְבָרֵךְ כׇּל צַפְרָא וְצַפְרָא?

The Gemara answers: Rav Yehuda was acting in accordance with the opinion of Rabbi Yehuda HaNasi, as it is taught in a *baraita*: With regard to phylacteries, every time one dons them[H] he recites the blessing over them, even several times in one day; this is the statement of Rabbi Yehuda HaNasi.

כְּרַבִּי, דְּתַנְיָא: תְּפִילִּין, כׇּל זְמַן שֶׁמַּנִּיחָן מְבָרֵךְ עֲלֵיהֶן, דִּבְרֵי רַבִּי.

The Gemara asks: If so, he should have also recited a blessing every time that he took the cloak off and put it back on, and not merely once a day in the morning. The Gemara answers: Rav Yehuda was a modest man and he did not remove his cloak the entire day. The Gemara asks: In what way is it different from the morning, i.e., why did he recite a blessing in the morning? The Gemara answers: He recited the blessing in the morning when he changed from a nighttime garment to a daytime garment.[N]

אִי הָכִי, כׇּל שַׁעְתָּא נָמֵי! רַב יְהוּדָה אִינִישׁ צְנִיעָא הֲוָה, וְלָא שָׁרֵי לֵיהּ לִגְלִימֵיהּ כּוּלֵּיהּ יוֹמָא. וּמַאי שְׁנָא מִצַּפְרָא? כִּי מְשַׁנֵּי מִכְּסוּת לַיְלָה לִכְסוּת יוֹם.

§ The Sages taught in a *baraita*: Everyone is obligated in the mitzva of ritual fringes, including priests, Levites, Israelites, converts, women, and Canaanite slaves. Rabbi Shimon deems women exempt,[H] because the mitzva of ritual fringes is a positive, time-bound mitzva,[B] and women are exempt from every positive, time-bound mitzva.

תָּנוּ רַבָּנַן: הַכֹּל חַיָּיבִין בְּצִיצִית, כֹּהֲנִים, לְוִיִּם וְיִשְׂרְאֵלִים, גֵּרִים, נָשִׁים וַעֲבָדִים. רַבִּי שִׁמְעוֹן פּוֹטֵר בְּנָשִׁים, מִפְּנֵי שֶׁמִּצְוַת עֲשֵׂה שֶׁהַזְּמַן גְּרָמָא הוּא, וְכׇל מִצְוַת עֲשֵׂה שֶׁהַזְּמַן גְּרָמָא נָשִׁים פְּטוּרוֹת.

The Gemara analyzes the *baraita*. The Master said in the *baraita*: Everyone is obligated in the mitzva of ritual fringes, including priests, Levites, and Israelites. The Gemara asks: Isn't that obvious? As, if priests, Levites, and Israelites were exempt from the mitzva, who then is to be obligated?

אָמַר מָר: הַכֹּל חַיָּיבִין בְּצִיצִית, כֹּהֲנִים, לְוִיִּם וְיִשְׂרְאֵלִים. פְּשִׁיטָא, דְּאִי כֹּהֲנִים לְוִיִּם וְיִשְׂרְאֵלִים פְּטִירִי, מַאן לִיחַיַּיב?

LANGUAGE

Garment [*pirzuma*] – פִּרְזוּמָא: From the Greek περίζωμα, *perizoma*, meaning loincloth or smock.

HALAKHA

Every morning he would recite the blessing – וּמְבָרֵךְ כׇּל צַפְרָא: One must recite a blessing on his ritual fringes in the morning, even if he wore his daytime garment throughout the entire night. This is in accordance with the opinion of Rabbi Shimon, who holds that the obligation of ritual fringes does not apply at night. He must recite a blessing in the morning even according to the opinion that a daytime garment is required to have ritual fringes if worn during the night, because since the night exempts a garment that is generally worn at night, it serves as an interruption between the daytime preceding it and the daytime following it (*Beit Yosef*). It is proper to touch the ritual fringes when reciting the blessing. There are those who say that he should not recite a blessing if he wore a daytime garment all night long, since there has not been an interruption in the mitzva with regard to the specific garment he is wearing (*Baḥ*). The *Magen Avraham* concludes that it is advisable not to recite a blessing on the garment, and the blessing he recites on his prayer shawl will apply to the garment as well (*Shulḥan Arukh, Oraḥ Ḥayyim* 8:16).

Every time one dons them – כׇּל זְמַן שֶׁמַּנִּיחָן: One recites a blessing on his phylacteries every time he dons them, even if he removes them and dons them again several times in one day. The same applies to ritual fringes. Some hold that if he removed them with the intention of putting them back on a short time later, he does not recite a new blessing (Rambam *Sefer Ahava, Hilkhot Tefillin UMezuza VeSefer Torah* 4:7; *Shulḥan Arukh, Oraḥ Ḥayyim* 8:14, 25:12).

Deems women exempt – פּוֹטֵר בְּנָשִׁים: Women and Canaanite slaves are not obligated in the mitzva of ritual fringes, as it is a positive, time-bound mitzva. This is in accordance with the opinion of Rabbi Shimon, whose opinion is expressed in unattributed *mishnayot* and accepted by the Gemara in several places (Rambam *Sefer Ahava, Hilkhot Tzitzit* 3:8; *Shulḥan Arukh, Oraḥ Ḥayyim* 17:2, and see *Beur HaGra* there).

NOTES

Why did he recite the blessing on ritual fringes each and every morning – אַמַּאי מְבָרֵךְ כׇּל צַפְרָא וְצַפְרָא: Since this mitzva is not limited to the daytime, one should recite the blessing only the first time he puts on his cloak. The days and nights that follow are considered like one long time period, as there is no interruption in the obligation (Rashi).

When he changed from a nighttime garment to a daytime garment – כִּי מְשַׁנֵּי מִכְּסוּת לַיְלָה לִכְסוּת יוֹם: The Gemara's question assumes that the Sages would arise before daybreak in order to study Torah. Therefore, the Gemara asks why Rav Yehuda did not recite the blessing when he awoke, rather than waiting until the morning. It answers that he wore one cloak at night and in the morning he would put on a nicer cloak, which he would wear in public. He recited the blessing when he put on the daytime cloak (Rabbeinu Gershom Meor HaGola; Rashi).

BACKGROUND

Positive time-bound mitzva – מִצְוַת עֲשֵׂה שֶׁהַזְּמַן גְּרָמָא: Neither the mishna nor the Gemara explains why women are exempt from mitzvot that must be performed at specific times. Jewish thinkers through the ages have tried to explain this legal distinction between the sexes. The fourteenth-century halakhic work *Kolbo* by Rabbi Aaron HaKohen, and the commentary to the prayer book known as Abudirham from the same century, both claim that a woman is subservient to her husband and must be prepared at all times to do his bidding. Were a woman obligated to perform a mitzva at a set time, conflicts might arise between serving her husband and fulfilling her legal requirements. A quandary of this kind will not occur when a woman can postpone a mitzva such as charity, which does not need to be performed at a particular time. An extension of this opinion is that for a woman with children, time is not her own. A mother cannot be expected to perform mitzvot at fixed times during the day when she must tend to her young ones. This theory apparently does not take into account the fact that many females have long periods in their lives when they are not married or do not have children requiring constant attention. Still, there are *halakhot* that are imposed universally despite being applicable in only some situations.

A different explanation is that women are on a higher spiritual plane than men and therefore do not require time-bound mitzvot to deepen their relationship with God. One proponent of this theory is the nineteenth-century scholar Rabbi Samson Raphael Hirsch, who wrote in his commentary to Leviticus 23:43 that a man's loyalty to Torah is constantly being tested, which is why he must be periodically guided by mitzvot reminding him of his religion. Women are tempted less by their environment because their inherent spirituality naturally draws them to God.

It should be noted that the category of time-bound mitzvot from which women are exempt is relatively small compared to the number of positive mitzvot that women must perform. The mitzvot from which women are exempt include reciting *Shema* twice daily, wearing ritual fringes, donning phylacteries, taking the four species on the festival of *Sukkot*, sitting in the *sukka*, and hearing the shofar on Rosh HaShana. Many women nevertheless do observe the majority of these mitzvot. There is an additional list of positive, time-bound mitzvot that women are obligated to observe. This list includes reciting *kiddush* on Shabbat and eating *matza* on the first night of Passover.

כֹּהֲנִים אִיצְטְרִיכָא לֵיהּ, סָלְקָא דַּעְתָּךְ אָמִינָא, הוֹאִיל וּכְתִיב: ״לֹא תִלְבַּשׁ שַׁעַטְנֵז צֶמֶר וּפִשְׁתִּים יַחְדָּו, גְּדִילִים תַּעֲשֶׂה לָּךְ״, מַאן דְּלָא אִישְׁתְּרֵי כִּלְאַיִם לְגַבֵּיהּ בִּלְבִישָׁה – הוּא דְּמִיחַיַּיב בְּצִיצִית, הָנֵי כֹּהֲנִים הוֹאִיל וְאִישְׁתְּרֵי כִּלְאַיִם לְגַבַּיְיהוּ – לָא לִיחַיְּיבוּ,

The Gemara answers: **It was necessary for** the *baraita* to mention that **priests** are obligated to fulfill the mitzva, as **it may enter your mind to say** as follows: **Since it is written: "You shall not wear diverse kinds, wool and linen together. You shall prepare yourself twisted cords** upon the four corners of your covering" (Deuteronomy 22:11–12), only **one who is not permitted to wear diverse kinds is obligated in** the mitzva of **ritual fringes.** With regard to **these priests, since diverse kinds are permitted for them** when they perform the Temple service, as the belt of the priestly vestments contains diverse kinds, **they should not be obligated** in the mitzva of ritual fringes.

קָא מַשְׁמַע לָן, נְהִי דְּאִישְׁתְּרֵי בְּעִידַּן עֲבוֹדָה, בְּלָא עִידַּן עֲבוֹדָה לָא אִישְׁתְּרֵי.

Therefore, the *baraita* **teaches us** that **although** the prohibition of diverse kinds is **permitted** for them **at the time** when they perform the Temple **service, when** it is **not the time of** the Temple **service** it is **not permitted,**[H] and therefore priests are obligated in the mitzva of ritual fringes.

רַבִּי שִׁמְעוֹן פּוֹטֵר בְּנָשִׁים. מַאי טַעְמָא דְּרַבִּי שִׁמְעוֹן? דְּתַנְיָא: ״וּרְאִיתֶם אוֹתוֹ״ – פְּרָט לִכְסוּת לַיְלָה.

The *baraita* states that **Rabbi Shimon deems women exempt.** The Gemara asks: **What is the reasoning of Rabbi Shimon?** The Gemara answers: **As it is taught** in a *baraita* that with regard to ritual fringes it is stated: "And it shall be unto you for a fringe, **that you may look upon it** and remember all the commandments of the Lord" (Numbers 15:39). The term "that you may look" **excludes a nighttime garment,**[N] as it is dark at night and it is therefore difficult to see.

אַתָּה אוֹמֵר: פְּרָט לִכְסוּת לַיְלָה, אוֹ אֵינוֹ אֶלָּא פְּרָט לִכְסוּת סוּמָא? כְּשֶׁהוּא אוֹמֵר: ״אֲשֶׁר תְּכַסֶּה בָּהּ״ – הֲרֵי כְּסוּת סוּמָא אָמוּר, הָא מָה אֲנִי מְקַיֵּים ״וּרְאִיתֶם אוֹתוֹ״ – פְּרָט לִכְסוּת לַיְלָה.

The *baraita* continues: One may ask: **Do you say** that the verse serves to **exclude a nighttime garment? Or is it** to **exclude only the garment of a blind person,** who is also unable to see his ritual fringes? The *tanna* explains: **When** the verse **states:** "Of your covering, **with which you cover yourself"** (Deuteronomy 22:12), the **garment of a blind person is mentioned** as being included, as the verse already stated: "Of your covering," and did not need to state: "With which you cover yourself." If so, **how do I realize** the meaning of the exclusion: **"That you may look upon it"?** It must **exclude a nighttime garment.**

וּמָה רָאִיתָ לְרַבּוֹת כְּסוּת סוּמָא וּלְהוֹצִיא כְּסוּת לַיְלָה? מְרַבֶּה אֲנִי כְּסוּת סוּמָא שֶׁיֶּשְׁנָהּ בִּרְאִיָּה אֵצֶל אֲחֵרִים, וּמוֹצִיא אֲנִי כְּסוּת לַיְלָה שֶׁאֵינָהּ בִּרְאִיָּה אֵצֶל אֲחֵרִים.

The Gemara asks: **What did you see** that led you **to include the garment of a blind person** from the phrase: "With which you cover yourself," **and to exclude a nighttime garment** from the phrase: "That you may look upon it," rather than including a nighttime garment in the obligation and excluding the garment of a blind person? The Gemara answers: **I include the garment of a blind person,**[NH] **which is visible to others,** even though the blind person himself cannot see it, **and I exclude a nighttime garment,**[H] **which is not visible** even **to others.**

וְרַבָּנַן

The Gemara asks: **And the Rabbis** who disagree with Rabbi Shimon,

NOTES

Excludes a nighttime garment – **פְּרָט לִכְסוּת לַיְלָה:** There is a dispute among the early commentaries as to the precise meaning of this statement. Rabbeinu Tam holds that a nighttime garment is exempt from ritual fringes even when it is occasionally worn during the day, whereas a daytime garment is obligated even when it is worn at night. Conversely, Rashi and the Rambam hold that any garment is exempt from ritual fringes if it is worn at night, and any garment is obligated to have ritual fringes if it is worn during the day (see Rosh, *Hilkhot Tzitzit* 1; *Sha'agat Arye* 30).

I include the garment of a blind person, etc. – **מְרַבֶּה אֲנִי כְּסוּת סוּמָא וכו׳:** The midrash offers another explanation: After the verse states: "That you may look upon it and remember" (Numbers 15:39), it states: "That you may remember" (Numbers 15:40). The Torah thereby refers to both sight and remembrance, indicating that the mitzva is limited to times of the day when people can see, whereas individuals who cannot see are included in the mitzva as long as they can remember it (*Bemidbar Rabba* 17:5).

HALAKHA

When it is not the time of the Temple service it is not permitted – **בְּלָא עִידַּן עֲבוֹדָה לָא אִישְׁתְּרֵי:** If a priest wears his priestly vestments when he is not performing the Temple service, he is flogged, because the belt contains both wool and linen. He is permitted to wear it only when he is performing the Temple service, when wearing the belt is a positive mitzva, like that of ritual fringes. The Ra'avad holds that priests are permitted to wear their vestments as long as they are in the Temple (Rambam *Sefer Zera'im, Hilkhot Kilayim* 10:32 and *Sefer Avoda, Hilkhot Kelei HaMikdash* 8:11, and see *Kesef Mishne* and Radbaz there).

I include the garment of a blind person – **מְרַבֶּה אֲנִי כְּסוּת סוּמָא:** Although the verse states: "That you may look upon it" (Numbers 15:39), a blind man is obligated in the mitzva of ritual fringes. This is due to the fact that although he cannot see his ritual fringes, others can see them. This is in accordance with the opinion of Rabbi Shimon and the explanation of the *baraita* (Rambam *Sefer Ahava, Hilkhot Tzitzit* 3:7; *Shulḥan Arukh, Oraḥ Ḥayyim* 17:1).

And I exclude a nighttime garment – **וּמוֹצִיא אֲנִי כְּסוּת לַיְלָה:** The obligation of ritual fringes is limited to the daytime, as the verse states: "That you may look upon it" (Numbers 15:39); this limits the mitzva to the daytime, which is the time for seeing. This is in accordance with the opinion of Rabbi Shimon and the explanation of the *baraita*. The Rambam holds that any garment that one wears during the day, even if its primary designation is for nighttime use, requires ritual fringes. Conversely, a garment that is worn at night is exempt from the obligation of ritual fringes even if its primary designation is for daytime use.

According to the Rosh, any garment whose primary designation is for nighttime use is exempt from ritual fringes even if it is worn during the day, and a garment whose primary designation is for daytime use requires ritual fringes even if it is worn at night. The Rema writes that since the principle is to be lenient in a case of uncertainty as to whether or not to recite a blessing, one should recite a blessing only if he is wearing a daytime garment and it is currently daytime (Rambam *Sefer Ahava, Hilkhot Tzitzit* 3:7; *Shulḥan Arukh, Oraḥ Ḥayyim* 18:1).

הַאי ״אֲשֶׁר תְּכַסֶּה בָּהּ״ מַאי עָבְדִי לֵיהּ? מִיבָּעֵי לְהוּ לְכִדְתַנְיָא: ״עַל אַרְבַּע כַּנְפוֹת כְּסוּתְךָ״, אַרְבַּע – וְלֹא שָׁלֹשׁ.

what do they do with,[N] i.e., how do they interpret, **this** verse: **"With which you cover yourself"** (Deuteronomy 22:12)? The Gemara answers that the Rabbis **require it for that which is taught** in a *baraita*: The phrase **"on the four corners of your garment"** (Deuteronomy 22:12) indicates that one is required to attach ritual fringes to a garment that has **four** corners, **but not** to one that has **three** corners.[H]

אַתָּה אוֹמֵר: אַרְבַּע וְלֹא שָׁלֹשׁ, אוֹ אֵינוֹ אֶלָּא אַרְבַּע וְלֹא חָמֵשׁ? כְּשֶׁהוּא אוֹמֵר: ״אֲשֶׁר תְּכַסֶּה בָּהּ״ – הֲרֵי בַּעֲלַת חָמֵשׁ אָמוּר, וּמָה אֲנִי מְקַיֵּים עַל אַרְבַּע? אַרְבַּע וְלֹא שָׁלֹשׁ.

The *baraita* continues: **Do you say** that a garment with **four** corners is obligated **but not** a garment with **three** corners? **Or is it** teaching **only** that a garment with **four** corners is obligated **but not** a garment that has **five** corners? **When** the verse **states: "With which you cover yourself,"** a garment **with five** corners **is thereby mentioned** in the verse as being obligated. Then **how do I realize** the meaning of: **"On the four** corners of your garment"? It teaches that this obligation is limited to a garment that has **four** corners, **but not** to one that has **three** corners.

וּמָה רָאִיתָ לְרַבּוֹת בַּעֲלַת חָמֵשׁ וּלְהוֹצִיא בַּעֲלַת שָׁלֹשׁ? מְרַבֶּה אֲנִי בַּעֲלַת חָמֵשׁ – שֶׁיֵּשׁ בִּכְלַל חָמֵשׁ אַרְבַּע, וּמוֹצִיא אֲנִי בַּעֲלַת שָׁלֹשׁ – שֶׁאֵין בִּכְלַל שָׁלֹשׁ אַרְבַּע.

The Gemara asks: **But what did you see** that led you **to include** a garment **with five** corners **and to exclude** a garment **with three** corners, rather than including a garment with three corners and excluding a garment with five corners? The Gemara answers: **I include** a garment **with five** corners, **as five includes four,**[N] **and I exclude** a garment **with three** corners, **as three does not include four.**

וְרַבִּי שִׁמְעוֹן? מֵ״אֲשֶׁר״ נָפְקָא. וְרַבָּנַן? ״אֲשֶׁר״ לָא מַשְׁמַע לְהוּ.

The Gemara asks: **And** how does **Rabbi Shimon** derive the *halakha* that a five-cornered garment is required to have ritual fringes? The Gemara answers: He **derives** it **from** the seemingly extraneous word: "With **which** [*asher*] you cover yourself" (Deuteronomy 22:12). The Gemara asks: **And** what do **the Rabbis** derive from this word? The Gemara answers: **They do not learn** any new *halakhot* from the word **"which [*asher*]."**

וְרַבָּנַן, הַאי ״וּרְאִיתֶם אֹתוֹ״ מַאי עָבְדִי לֵיהּ? מִיבָּעֵי לְהוּ לְכִדְתַנְיָא: ״וּרְאִיתֶם אֹתוֹ וּזְכַרְתֶּם״ – רְאֵה מִצְוָה זוֹ וּזְכוֹר מִצְוָה אַחֶרֶת הַתְּלוּיָה בּוֹ, וְאֵיזוֹ זוֹ? זוֹ קְרִיַּת שְׁמַע, דִּתְנַן: מֵאֵימָתַי קוֹרִין אֶת שְׁמַע בְּשַׁחֲרִית? מִשֶּׁיַּכִּיר בֵּין תְּכֵלֶת לְלָבָן.

The Gemara asks: **And** as for **the Rabbis, what do they do with this** phrase: **"That you may look upon it"** (Numbers 15:39), from which Rabbi Shimon derives that a nighttime garment is exempt? The Gemara answers: **They require it for that which is taught** in a *baraita*: The verse: **"That you may look upon it and remember"** (Numbers 15:39), teaches that one should **see this mitzva** of ritual fringes **and remember another mitzva that is contingent on it. And which** mitzva **is that? It is** the mitzva of **the recitation of** ***Shema*****. As we learned** in a mishna (*Berakhot* 9b): **From when may one recite** ***Shema*** **in the morning? From when** one **can distinguish between** the **sky-blue** strings **and** the **white** strings of his ritual fringes.

וְתַנְיָא אִידָךְ: ״וּרְאִיתֶם אוֹתוֹ וּזְכַרְתֶּם״ – רְאֵה מִצְוָה זוֹ וּזְכוֹר מִצְוָה אַחֶרֶת הַסְּמוּכָה לָהּ, וְאֵיזוֹ זוֹ? זוֹ מִצְוַת כִּלְאַיִם, דִּכְתִיב: ״לֹא תִלְבַּשׁ שַׁעַטְנֵז צֶמֶר וּפִשְׁתִּים יַחְדָּו. גְּדִילִים תַּעֲשֶׂה לָּךְ״.

And it **is taught** in **another** *baraita*: The phrase **"that you may look upon it and remember"** teaches that one should **see this mitzva** of ritual fringes **and remember another mitzva that is adjacent to it** in the Torah. **And which** mitzva **is that? It is the mitzva of** diverse kinds of wool and linen, **as it is written: "You shall not wear diverse kinds, wool and linen together. You shall prepare yourself twisted cords"** (Deuteronomy 22:11–12).

תַּנְיָא אִידָךְ: ״וּרְאִיתֶם אֹתוֹ וּזְכַרְתֶּם אֶת כׇּל מִצְוֹת ה׳״, כֵּיוָן שֶׁנִּתְחַיֵּיב אָדָם בְּמִצְוָה זוֹ – נִתְחַיֵּיב בְּכׇל מִצְוֹת כּוּלָּן; וְרַבִּי שִׁמְעוֹן הִיא, דְּאָמַר: מִצְוַת עֲשֵׂה שֶׁהַזְּמַן גְּרָמָא הִיא.

It **is taught** in **another** *baraita*: The verse states: **"That you may look upon it and remember all the commandments of the Lord"** (Numbers 15:39). This indicates that **once a person is obligated in this mitzva** of ritual fringes, **he is obligated in all of the mitzvot.**[N] The Gemara comments: **And this is** in accordance with the opinion of **Rabbi Shimon, who says** that ritual fringes are **a positive, time-bound mitzva,** and women are exempt from it. Only men are obligated in all mitzvot, including positive, time-bound mitzvot, just as they are obligated in the mitzva of ritual fringes.

NOTES

What do they do with – מַאי עָבְדִי לֵיהּ: Rashi explains that the explanation suggested previously, that this phrase includes the garment of a blind man, is not feasible according to the Rabbis: Since they hold that even a nighttime garment requires ritual fringes, it is obvious that the garment of a blind man, which can be seen by others, requires ritual fringes (Rashi).

As five includes four – שֶׁיֵּשׁ בִּכְלַל חָמֵשׁ אַרְבַּע: A five-cornered garment is obligated because it is essentially a four-cornered garment with one additional corner. Consequently, ritual fringes are attached to only four of the corners. The *halakha* is the same for a garment with more than five corners (Rambam *Sefer Ahava*, *Hilkhot Tzitzit* 3:3).

Once a person is obligated in this mitzva of ritual fringes he is obligated in all of the mitzvot – כֵּיוָן שֶׁנִּתְחַיֵּיב אָדָם בְּמִצְוָה זוֹ נִתְחַיֵּיב בְּכׇל מִצְוֹת כּוּלָּן: Rashi explains this to mean that once morning arrives and one becomes obligated in the mitzva of ritual fringes, he becomes obligated in all mitzvot, because many mitzvot apply specifically during the daytime. This is in accordance with the opinion of Rabbi Shimon, who holds that the mitzva of ritual fringes does not apply at night. Alternatively, Rashi explains that once an individual becomes obligated in this mitzva when he reaches the age of majority, he becomes obligated in all of the mitzvot (see Maharsha and *Sefat Emet*).

HALAKHA

A garment that has four corners but not one that has three corners – אַרְבַּע וְלֹא שָׁלֹשׁ: A garment that does not have four corners is exempt from ritual fringes. If a garment has more than four corners, it is obligated to have ritual fringes, and these are attached to the four corners that are farthest apart from each other (Rambam *Sefer Ahava*, *Hilkhot Tzitzit* 3:3; *Shulhan Arukh*, *Orah Hayyim* 10:1).

תניא אידך: "וראיתם אתו וזכרתם את כל מצות ה'" – שקולה מצוה זו כנגד כל המצות כולן.

It is taught in another *baraita*: The verse states: **"That you may look upon it and remember all the commandments of the Lord"**; this teaches that **this mitzva** of ritual fringes **is equivalent to all the mitzvot**[N] of the Torah.

ותניא אידך: "וראיתם אתו וזכרתם...ועשיתם" – ראיה מביאה לידי זכירה, זכירה מביאה לידי עשיה. ורבי שמעון בר יוחאי אומר: כל הזריז במצוה זו – זוכה ומקבל פני שכינה, כתיב הכא: "וראיתם אתו", וכתיב התם: "את ה' אלהיך תירא ואתו תעבד".

And it is taught in **another** *baraita*: The verse states: **"That you may look upon it and remember** all the commandments of the Lord **and do them."** This teaches that **looking** at the ritual fringes **leads to remembering** the mitzvot, and **remembering** them **leads to doing** them. **And Rabbi Shimon bar Yoḥai says: Anyone who is diligent in this mitzva** of ritual fringes **merits receiving the Divine Presence.**[H] It **is written here: "That you may look upon it** [*oto*]" (Numbers 15:39), **and it is written there: "You shall fear the Lord your God; and Him** [*oto*] **shall you serve"** (Deuteronomy 6:13).[N] Just as *oto* in that verse is referring to the Divine Presence, so too in this verse it is referring to the Divine Presence.

תנו רבנן: חביבין ישראל שסיבבן הקדוש ברוך הוא במצות, תפילין בראשיהן ותפילין בזרועותיהן וציצית בבגדיהן ומזוזה לפתחיהן, ועליהן אמר דוד: "שבע ביום הללתיך על משפטי צדקך".

The Sages taught in a *baraita*: **The Jewish people are beloved,** as **the Holy One, Blessed be He, surrounded them with mitzvot:** They have **phylacteries on their heads, and phylacteries on their arms, and ritual fringes on their garments, and a *mezuza* for their doorways. Concerning them David said: "Seven times a day I praise You, because of Your righteous ordinances"** (Psalms 119:164). This alludes to the two phylacteries, the four ritual fringes, and the *mezuza*, which total seven.

ובשעה שנכנס דוד לבית המרחץ וראה עצמו עומד ערום, אמר: אוי לי שאעמוד ערום בלא מצוה! וכיון שנזכר במילה שבבשרו נתיישבה דעתו; לאחר שיצא, אמר עליה שירה, שנאמר: "למנצח על השמינית מזמור לדוד" – על מילה שניתנה בשמיני.

And when David entered the bathhouse and saw himself standing naked, he said: Woe to me that that I stand naked without any **mitzva. But once he remembered the** mitzva of **circumcision that was in his flesh his mind was put at ease,** as he realized he was still accompanied by this mitzva. **After he left** the bathhouse, **he recited a song about** the mitzva of circumcision, **as it is stated** in the verse: **"For the leader, on the *Sheminith*: A Psalm of David"** (Psalms 12:1). This is interpreted as a psalm **about circumcision, which was given** to be performed **on the eighth** [***bashemini***] day of the baby's life.

רבי אליעזר בן יעקב אומר: כל שיש לו תפילין בראשו ותפילין בזרועו וציצית בבגדו ומזוזה בפתחו – הכל בחיזוק שלא יחטא, שנאמר: "והחוט המשלש לא במהרה ינתק", ואומר: "חנה מלאך ה' סביב ליראיו ויחלצם".

Rabbi Eliezer ben Ya'akov says: Anyone who has phylacteries on his head,[H] **phylacteries on his arm, ritual fringes on his garment, and a *mezuza* on his doorway is strengthened** from **all** sides **so that he will not sin, as it is stated** in the verse: **"And a threefold cord is not quickly broken"** (Ecclesiastes 4:12).[N] This is interpreted as an allusion to the three mitzvot of phylacteries, ritual fringes, and *mezuza*. **And the verse states: "The angel of the Lord encamps round about them that fear Him, and delivers them"** (Psalms 34:8). This is interpreted to mean that the angel of the Lord surrounds those who fulfill the mitzvot and saves them from sin.

HALAKHA

Merits receiving the Divine Presence – זוכה ומקבל פני שכינה: One should be very diligent to fulfill the mitzva of ritual fringes, as the Torah equates it to all the mitzvot and states that it is a reminder for all the mitzvot, as the verse states: "That you may look upon it and remember all the commandments of the Lord" (Numbers 15:39). One who is diligent in performing this mitzva merits receiving the Divine Presence (Rambam *Sefer Ahava, Hilkhot Tzitzit* 3:12; *Shulḥan Arukh, Oraḥ Ḥayyim* 24:6).

Anyone who has phylacteries on his head – כל שיש לו תפילין בראשו: The early Sages said: Anyone who has phylacteries on his head and arm, ritual fringes on his garment, and a *mezuza* on his doorway is protected from sin by these mitzvot, which remind him of his responsibilities. These mitzvot are referred to as angels that protect him from sin, as the verse states (Psalms 34:8): "The angel of the Lord encamps round about them that fear Him, and delivers them" (Rambam *Sefer Ahava, Hilkhot Tefillin UMezuza VeSefer Torah* 6:13).

NOTES

This mitzva of ritual fringes is equivalent to all the mitzvot – שקולה מצוה זו כנגד כל המצות כולן: This is because the mitzva of ritual fringes reminds one to fulfill all of the mitzvot (*Iyyun Ya'akov*; see *Sifrei*).

You shall fear [*tira*] the Lord your God; and Him [*oto*] shall you serve – את ה' אלהיך תירא ואתו תעבד: Rabbeinu Gershom Meor HaGola explains that the inference is from the term "you shall fear [*tira*]," which is being interpreted as though it referred to seeing [*re'iya*]. It would appear that this also alludes to the statement that sky-blue resembles the Throne of Glory, which is derived from the verse: "And they saw [*vayyiru*] the God of Israel, and there was under His feet the like of a paved work of sapphire stone, and the like of the very heaven for clearness" (Exodus 24:10). In this verse the term *vayyiru* is understood as a reference to receiving the Divine Presence.

And a threefold cord is not quickly broken – והחוט המשלש לא במהרה ינתק: This verse deals with protection from one's enemy, as the beginning of the verse states: "And if a man prevail against him that is alone, two shall withstand him" (Ecclesiastes 4:12).

תַּנְיָא, הָיָה רַבִּי מֵאִיר אוֹמֵר: מַה נִּשְׁתַּנָּה תְּכֵלֶת מִכׇּל מִינֵי צִבְעוֹנִין? מִפְּנֵי שֶׁהַתְּכֵלֶת דּוֹמָה לַיָּם, וְיָם דּוֹמֶה לָרָקִיעַ, וְרָקִיעַ לְכִסֵּא הַכָּבוֹד, שֶׁנֶּאֱמַר: ״וְתַחַת רַגְלָיו כְּמַעֲשֵׂה לִבְנַת הַסַּפִּיר וּכְעֶצֶם הַשָּׁמַיִם לָטֹהַר״, וּכְתִיב: ״כְּמַרְאֵה אֶבֶן סַפִּיר דְּמוּת כִּסֵּא״.

It is taught in a *baraita* that **Rabbi Meir would say: What is different about *tekhelet* from all** other **types of colors** such that it was chosen for the mitzva of ritual fringes? It is **because *tekhelet* is similar** in its color **to the sea,**[BH] **and the sea is similar to the sky, and the sky is similar to the Throne of Glory,**[N] **as it is stated:** "And they saw the God of Israel; **and there was under His feet**[N] **the like of a paved work of sapphire stone, and the like of the very heaven for clearness"** (Exodus 24:10), indicating that the sky is like a sapphire brickwork. **And it is written: "The likeness of a throne, as the appearance of a sapphire stone"** (Ezekiel 1:26).

תַּנְיָא, הָיָה רַבִּי מֵאִיר אוֹמֵר: גָּדוֹל עׇנְשׁוֹ שֶׁל לָבָן יוֹתֵר מֵעׇנְשׁוֹ שֶׁל תְּכֵלֶת; מָשָׁל לְמָה הַדָּבָר דּוֹמֶה? לְמֶלֶךְ בָּשָׂר וָדָם שֶׁאָמַר לִשְׁנֵי עֲבָדָיו, לְאֶחָד אָמַר: הָבֵא לִי חוֹתָם שֶׁל טִיט, וּלְאֶחָד אָמַר: הָבֵא לִי חוֹתָם שֶׁל זָהָב, וּפָשְׁעוּ שְׁנֵיהֶם וְלֹא הֵבִיאוּ, אֵיזֶה מֵהֶן עׇנְשׁוֹ מְרוּבֶּה? הֱוֵי אוֹמֵר: זֶה שֶׁאָמַר לוֹ הָבֵא לִי חוֹתָם שֶׁל טִיט וְלֹא הֵבִיא.

It is taught in a *baraita* that **Rabbi Meir would say:** The **punishment for** not attaching **white** strings **is greater**[H] **than the punishment for** not attaching **sky-blue** strings, despite the fact that the sky-blue strings are more important. Rabbi Meir illustrates this with **a parable: To what is this matter comparable?** It is comparable **to a king of flesh and blood who said to his two subjects** that they must bring him a seal. The king **said to one** of them: **Bring me a seal of clay, and he said to** the other **one: Bring me a seal of gold. And both of them were negligent and did not bring** the seals. **Which of them** will have **a greater punishment? You must say** that it is **this** one **to whom he said: Bring me a seal of clay, and** despite its availability and low cost, he **did not bring** it.

תַּנְיָא, הָיָה רַבִּי מֵאִיר אוֹמֵר: חַיָּיב אָדָם לְבָרֵךְ מֵאָה בְּרָכוֹת בְּכׇל יוֹם, שֶׁנֶּאֱמַר: ״וְעַתָּה יִשְׂרָאֵל מָה ה׳ אֱלֹהֶיךָ שֹׁאֵל מֵעִמָּךְ״.

It is taught in a *baraita* that **Rabbi Meir would say: A person is obligated to recite one hundred blessings every day,**[H] **as it is stated** in the verse: **"And now, Israel, what [*ma*] does the Lord your God require of you"** (Deuteronomy 10:12). Rabbi Meir interprets the verse as though it said one hundred [*me'a*], rather than *ma*.

רַב חִיָּיא בְּרֵיהּ דְּרַב אַוְיָא בְּשַׁבְּתָא וּבְיוֹמֵי טָבֵי טָרַח וּמְמַלֵּי לְהוּ בְּאִיסְפַּרְמָקֵי וּמִגְדֵי.

The Gemara relates that **on Shabbat and Festivals,** when the prayers contain fewer blessings, **Rav Ḥiyya, son of Rav Avya, made an effort to fill** this quota of blessings **with** blessings on **spices [*be'isparmakei*]**[L] **and sweet fruit,** of which he would partake in order to recite extra blessings.

תַּנְיָא, הָיָה רַבִּי מֵאִיר אוֹמֵר: חַיָּיב אָדָם לְבָרֵךְ שָׁלֹשׁ בְּרָכוֹת בְּכׇל יוֹם, אֵלּוּ הֵן: ״שֶׁלֹּא עָשַׂנִי גּוֹי״, ״שֶׁלֹּא עָשַׂנִי אִשָּׁה״, ״שֶׁלֹּא עָשַׂנִי בּוּר״.

It is taught in a *baraita* that **Rabbi Meir would say: A man is obligated to recite three blessings**[H] **every day**[N] praising God for His kindnesses, and **these** blessings **are: Who did not make me a gentile; Who did not make me a woman;** and **Who did not make me an ignoramus.**

BACKGROUND

***Tekhelet* is similar in its color to the sea – תְּכֵלֶת דּוֹמָה לַיָּם:** The precise identification of the color of *tekhelet* is uncertain, as the names used in all languages to refer to various hues have shifted over time. Even the description in the Gemara here is not absolute, as the heavens and the sea have different hues depending on factors such as the time of day and the different seasons. There are several different opinions as to the color of *tekhelet* in the early commentaries. Rav Se'adya Gaon and the Rambam hold that it is the color of a clear sky, namely light blue. Rashi refers to *tekhelet* as a shade of green, possibly a reference to turquoise. Moshe HaDarshan holds that it refers to the color of the sky when it darkens toward the end of the day. According to this opinion, *tekhelet* is closer to purple. A similar range of opinions can be found in the works of modern researchers, who have attempted to identify the *ḥilazon* from which the dye is extracted. Another method of identifying the color of *tekhelet* is to identify *kala ilan*, whose color is indistinguishable from *tekhelet*. If *kala ilan* is indigo, as widely assumed, it would seem that *tekhelet* is a deep, dark blue.

LANGUAGE

Spices [*isparmakei*] – אִיסְפַּרְמָקֵי: This word apparently derives from the Iranian isprahmak, a flower or fragrant herb.

HALAKHA

***Tekhelet* is similar in its color to the sea – תְּכֵלֶת דּוֹמָה לַיָּם:** Whenever the Torah refers to *tekhelet* it is referring to wool dyed with a blue dye that is the hue of a clear sky on a sunny day (Rambam *Sefer Ahava, Hilkhot Tzitzit* 2:1 and *Sefer Avoda, Hilkhot Kelei HaMikdash* 8:13, and Mahari Kurkus there).

The punishment for not attaching white strings is greater – גָּדוֹל עׇנְשׁוֹ שֶׁל לָבָן: The punishment for not attaching white strings to one's garment is greater than the punishment for not attaching sky-blue strings, as white strings are always readily available to all and sky-blue wool is not (Rambam *Sefer Ahava, Hilkhot Tzitzit* 2:9).

A person is obligated to recite one hundred blessings every day – חַיָּיב אָדָם לְבָרֵךְ מֵאָה בְּרָכוֹת: One is obligated to recite a minimum of one hundred blessings every day. On Shabbat, when the prayers contain fewer blessings, one should eat additional fruit and delicacies and smell spices in order to complete the quota of blessings (Rambam *Sefer Ahava, Hilkhot Tefilla UVirkat Kohanim* 7:14; *Shulḥan Arukh, Oraḥ Ḥayyim* 46:3, 190:1).

Three blessings – שָׁלֹשׁ בְּרָכוֹת: A man is obligated to recite the following three blessings every day, which conclude: Who did not make me a gentile, Who did not make me a slave, and Who did not make me a woman. One should not recite a blessing: Who did not make me an ignoramus. This is in accordance with the opinion of Rav Aḥa bar Ya'akov (Rambam *Sefer Ahava, Hilkhot Tefilla UVirkat Kohanim* 7:6; *Shulḥan Arukh, Oraḥ Ḥayyim* 46:4).

NOTES

To the Throne of Glory – לְכִסֵּא הַכָּבוֹד: Consequently, one who sees the sky-blue strings of his ritual fringes is reminded of God, who sits on the Throne of Glory. Additionally, it is a privilege for the Jewish people to have a sign of the Throne of Glory on their garments (Rashi) as an indication of God's affection for them. In his commentary on tractate *Ḥullin* (89a), Rashi explains that when God looks at His Throne of Glory, he is reminded of this mitzva, which is equivalent to all of the mitzvot.

And there was under His feet, etc. – וְתַחַת רַגְלָיו וכו׳: The verse indicates that the sapphire stone has the appearance of the heavens. The following verse teaches that this is the appearance of the Throne of Glory. This indicates that the appearance of the Throne of Glory is like that of the heavens (see also *Tosafot*).

A man is obligated to recite three blessings every day – חַיָּיב אָדָם לְבָרֵךְ שָׁלֹשׁ בְּרָכוֹת בְּכׇל יוֹם: These three are included in the quota of one hundred daily blessings despite the fact that there is no specific catalyst for reciting them, unlike the blessings mentioned in *Berakhot* 60b (Rabbeinu Gershom Meor HaGola).

Some explain that all of these blessings were mentioned here because of the blessing: Who did not make me a woman, which relates to the fact that a woman is not obligated in certain mitzvot, e.g., ritual fringes (see *Ben Yehoyada*).

רַב אַחָא בַּר יַעֲקֹב שַׁמְעֵיהּ לִבְרֵיהּ דַּהֲוָה קָא מְבָרֵךְ "שֶׁלֹּא עֲשָׂאַנִי בּוּר", אֲמַר לֵיהּ: כּוּלֵּי הַאי נַמִּי? אֲמַר לֵיהּ: וְאֶלָּא מַאי מְבָרֵךְ, "שֶׁלֹּא עֲשָׂאַנִי עֶבֶד"? הַיְינוּ אִשָּׁה! עֶבֶד

Rav Aḥa bar Ya'akov heard his son reciting the blessing: Who did not make me an ignoramus. Rav Aḥa bar Ya'akov said to him: Is it **in fact** proper to go **this far** in reciting blessings?[N] Rav Aḥa bar Ya'akov's son **said to him: Rather, what blessing** should one **recite?** If you will say that one should recite: **Who did not make me a slave, that is** the same as **a woman;**[N] why should one recite two blessings about the same matter? Rav Aḥa bar Ya'akov answered: Nevertheless, **a slave**

NOTES

Is it in fact proper to go this far in reciting blessings – כּוּלֵּי הַאי נַמִּי: Rashi's first explanation of this statement is that Rav Aḥa rebuked his son for praising himself for not being an ignoramus, which shows haughtiness (Rid). Rashi's second interpretation is that these blessings were intended as thanks for being obligated in mitzvot, as gentiles are not obligated in most mitzvot and even women are not obligated in some mitzvot. By contrast, an ignoramus is obligated in all mitzvot. Others explain that one should praise God for creating him in ways that pertain to his natural state of existence, whereas one achieves the status of a scholar rather than an ignoramus due to his own dedication to study (*Keren Ora*).

That is the same as a woman – הַיְינוּ אִשָּׁה: Rashi explains that the comparison is in that both women and Canaanite slaves are exempt from positive, time-bound mitzvot.

Perek **IV**
Daf **44** Amud **a**

זִיל טְפֵי.

is **more lowly**[N] than a woman, and therefore it is appropriate to recite an additional blessing on not having been born a slave.

תָּנוּ רַבָּנַן: חִלָּזוֹן זֶהוּ – גּוּפוֹ דּוֹמֶה לַיָּם, וּבְרִיָּיתוֹ דּוֹמָה לְדָג, וְעוֹלֶה אֶחָד לְשִׁבְעִים שָׁנָה, וּבְדָמוֹ צוֹבְעִין תְּכֵלֶת, לְפִיכָךְ דָּמָיו יְקָרִים.

§ **The Sages taught: This *ḥilazon*,**[B] which **is** the source of the sky blue dye used in ritual fringes, has the following characteristics: **Its body resembles the sea,**[N] **its form resembles** that of **a fish, it emerges once in seventy years,**[N] **and with its blood one dyes** wool **sky-blue** for ritual fringes. It is scarce, and **therefore it is expensive.**

תַּנְיָא, אָמַר רַבִּי נָתָן: אֵין לְךָ כָּל מִצְוָה קַלָּה שֶׁכְּתוּבָה בַּתּוֹרָה, שֶׁאֵין מַתַּן שְׂכָרָהּ בָּעוֹלָם הַזֶּה, וְלָעוֹלָם הַבָּא – אֵינִי יוֹדֵעַ כַּמָּה. צֵא וּלְמַד מִמִּצְוַת צִיצִית;

It is **taught** in a *baraita* that **Rabbi Natan says: There is no mitzva,** however **minor,**[N] **that is written in the Torah, for which there is no reward given in this world; and in the World-to-Come I do not know how much** reward is given. **Go and learn from** the following incident concerning **the mitzva of ritual fringes.**

מַעֲשֶׂה בְּאָדָם אֶחָד שֶׁהָיָה זָהִיר בְּמִצְוַת צִיצִית, שָׁמַע שֶׁיֵּשׁ זוֹנָה בִּכְרַכֵּי הַיָּם שֶׁנּוֹטֶלֶת אַרְבַּע מֵאוֹת זְהוּבִים בִּשְׂכָרָהּ, שִׁיגֵּר לָהּ אַרְבַּע מֵאוֹת זְהוּבִים וְקָבַע לָהּ זְמַן. כְּשֶׁהִגִּיעַ זְמַנּוֹ, בָּא וְיָשַׁב עַל הַפֶּתַח.

There was **an incident involving a certain man who was diligent about the mitzva of ritual fringes.**[N] This man **heard that there was a prostitute in** one of **the cities overseas who took four hundred gold coins as her payment. He sent her four hundred gold coins and fixed a time to meet with her. When his time came, he came and sat at the entrance** to her house.

BACKGROUND

***Ḥilazon* – חִלָּזוֹן:** There have been numerous attempts to identify the *ḥilazon* from which *tekhelet* is derived. Aside from the characteristics mentioned in this Gemara, some of which are ambiguous, there are other characteristics mentioned by the Sages elsewhere. Among these are the following: The *ḥilazon* was trapped with nets in the tribal portion of Zebulun, along the coast of Eretz Yisrael from Haifa to Tyre (see *Shabbat* 26a; *Megilla* 6a). The *ḥilazon* has a pouch that grows with it. It would be cracked open while alive, to enhance the clarity of the dye (see *Shabbat* 75a).

In recent generations, there has been a renewed effort to identify the *ḥilazon* utilizing these descriptions found in traditional sources, as well as historical, archeological, and linguistic sources.

The Hasidic leader Rabbi Gershon Chanoch Henech of Radzin reached the conclusion that the *ḥilazon* is the common cuttlefish, *Sepia officinalis*. Those who accepted this conclusion produced dye from the ink sac that the cuttlefish uses for self-defense. The late Chief Rabbi of Israel, Rabbi Isaac Herzog, held that the *ḥilazon* is the *Janthina janthina*, the violet sea snail or common violet snail.

Of the various identifications of the *ḥilazon*, the one that is currently the most widely accepted is that the *ḥilazon* is the *Murex trunculus*, a type of sea snail, which fits most of the Sages' descriptions of the *ḥilazon*. This identification is corroborated by archeological evidence and chemical analysis.

There is a gland in the *ḥilazon* that produces a clear secretion that, when exposed to sunlight, turns dark purple and then, after processing, dark blue.

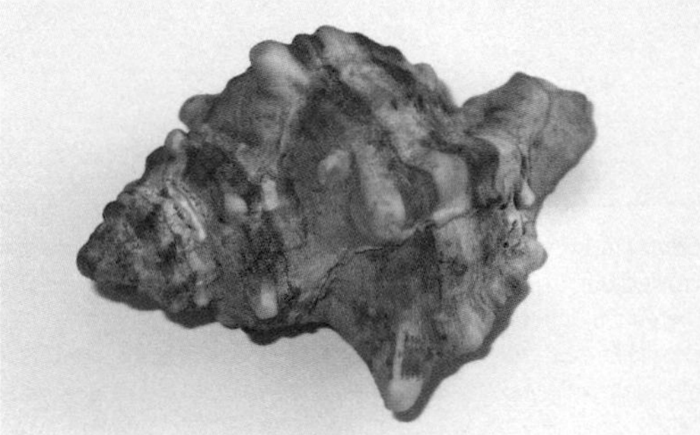

Murex trunculus shell

NOTES

More lowly – זִיל טְפֵי: A Canaanite slave must perform menial tasks for his master, whereas a husband is obligated to honor his wife (*Siddur Izeluta DeAvraham*). Alternatively, although both women and Canaanite slaves are exempt from positive, time-bound mitzvot, Canaanite slaves are of lower stature in that they may not marry Jews.

Its body resembles the sea – גּוּפוֹ דּוֹמֶה לַיָּם: It appears from Rashi that this refers to the appearance of the body of the *ḥilazon* and its color. The Rambam also explains it in this manner (Rambam *Sefer Ahava*, *Hilkhot Tzitzit* 2:2). In tractate *Ḥullin* (89a) Rashi explains that it is the blood of the *ḥilazon*, from which the dye is produced, that resembles the sea, whereas the shape of its body resembles a fish.

It emerges once in seventy years – וְעוֹלֶה אֶחָד לְשִׁבְעִים שָׁנָה: Rashi here explains that the *ḥilazon* emerges from the earth. In his commentary on tractate *Megilla* (6a), he explains that it emerges from the water to the land (see *Gilyon HaShas*).

Mitzva, however minor – מִצְוָה קַלָּה: It is clear from context that ritual fringes are referred to as a minor mitzva. Rashi explains that this is because it is a positive mitzva. This is based on the fact that a mitzva is described as minor or major based on the severity of the punishment for failing to observe it (see *Yoma* 85b).

Diligent about the mitzva of ritual fringes – זָהִיר בְּמִצְוַת צִיצִית: It would seem from context that the Gemara is emphasizing that he was diligent about this mitzva despite the fact that he was not careful about other, more severe transgressions.

HALAKHA

A borrowed cloak – טַלִּית שְׁאוּלָה: If one borrows a four-cornered garment that does not have ritual fringes, he is not required to place ritual fringes on it for the first thirty days, as the verse states that one is obligated to place them on "your garments" (Deuteronomy 22:12), and not on other people's garments that one has in his possession. If he has the garment for thirty consecutive (*Nimmukei Yosef*) days he is obligated by rabbinic law to attach ritual fringes, because the garment is perceived as being his. If he borrowed a cloak that already had ritual fringes, he recites blessing as soon as he dons it (Rambam *Sefer Ahava*, *Hilkhot Tzitzit* 3:4; *Shulḥan Arukh*, *Oraḥ Ḥayyim* 14:3, and see *Mishna Berura* there).

NOTES

In the case of a borrowed cloak, for the first thirty days it is exempt from ritual fringes – טַלִּית שְׁאוּלָה כָּל שְׁלֹשִׁים יוֹם פְּטוּרָה מִן הַצִּיצִית: The reason is that the verse states: "You shall prepare yourself twisted cords upon the four corners of your garment" (Deuteronomy 22:12), which indicates that the mitzva applies only to a garment that one owns. The Sages obligated one to attach ritual fringes to the garment after thirty days, because at that point it is perceived as belonging to him (*Tosafot*).

נִכְנְסָה שִׁפְחָתָהּ וְאָמְרָה לָהּ: אוֹתוֹ אָדָם שֶׁשִּׁיגֵּר לֵיךְ אַרְבַּע מֵאוֹת זְהוּבִים בָּא וְיָשַׁב עַל הַפֶּתַח, אָמְרָה הִיא: יִכָּנֵס, נִכְנַס. הִצִּיעָה לוֹ שֶׁבַע מִטּוֹת, שֵׁשׁ שֶׁל כֶּסֶף וְאַחַת שֶׁל זָהָב, וּבֵין כָּל אַחַת וְאַחַת סוּלָּם שֶׁל כֶּסֶף, וְעֶלְיוֹנָה שֶׁל זָהָב.

The maidservant of that prostitute **entered and said to her: That man who sent you four hundred gold coins came and sat at the entrance. She said: Let him enter. He entered. She arranged seven beds for him, six of silver and one of gold. Between each and every one** of them there was **a ladder** made **of silver, and the top** bed was the one that was made **of gold.**

עָלְתָה וְיָשְׁבָה עַל גַּבֵּי עֶלְיוֹנָה כְּשֶׁהִיא עֲרוּמָּה, וְאַף הוּא עָלָה לֵישֵׁב עָרוֹם כְּנֶגְדָּהּ, בָּאוּ אַרְבַּע צִיצִיּוֹתָיו וְטָפְחוּ לוֹ עַל פָּנָיו, נִשְׁמַט וְיָשַׁב לוֹ עַל גַּבֵּי קַרְקַע, וְאַף הִיא נִשְׁמְטָה וְיָשְׁבָה עַל גַּבֵּי קַרְקַע. אָמְרָה לוֹ: גַּפָּה שֶׁל רוֹמִי, שֶׁאֵינִי מַנִּיחַתְךָ עַד שֶׁתֹּאמַר לִי מַה מּוּם רָאִיתָ בִּי.

She went up and sat naked on the top bed, **and he too went up** in order **to sit naked facing her.** In the meantime, **his four ritual fringes came and slapped him on his face. He dropped down and sat himself on the ground, and she also dropped down and sat on the ground. She said to him:** I take an oath by the ***gappa* of Rome**[L] **that I will not allow you** to go **until you tell me what defect you saw in me.**

אָמַר לָהּ: הָעֲבוֹדָה, שֶׁלֹּא רָאִיתִי אִשָּׁה יָפָה כְּמוֹתֵךְ, אֶלָּא מִצְוָה אַחַת צִוָּנוּ ה׳ אֱלֹהֵינוּ וְצִיצִית שְׁמָהּ, וּכְתִיב בָּהּ ״אֲנִי ה׳ אֱלֹהֵיכֶם״ שְׁתֵּי פְּעָמִים – אֲנִי הוּא שֶׁעָתִיד לִיפָּרַע, וַאֲנִי הוּא שֶׁעָתִיד לְשַׁלֵּם שָׂכָר, עַכְשָׁיו נִדְמוּ עָלַי כְּאַרְבָּעָה עֵדִים.

He said to her: I take an oath by **the Temple** service **that I never saw a woman as beautiful as you. But** there is **one mitzva** that **the Lord, our God, commanded us, and its name is ritual fringes, and in** the passage where **it** is commanded, **it is written twice: "I am the Lord your God"** (Numbers 15:41). The doubling of this phrase indicates: **I am the one who will punish** those who transgress My mitzvot, **and I am the one who will reward** those who fulfill them. **Now,** said the man, the four sets of ritual fringes **appeared to me as** if they were **four witnesses** who will testify against me.

אָמְרָה לוֹ: אֵינִי מַנִּיחֲךָ עַד שֶׁתֹּאמַר לִי מַה שִּׁמְךָ, וּמַה שֵּׁם עִירְךָ, וּמַה שֵּׁם רַבְּךָ, וּמַה שֵּׁם מִדְרָשְׁךָ שֶׁאַתָּה לָמֵד בּוֹ תּוֹרָה. כָּתַב וְנָתַן בְּיָדָהּ.

She said to him: I will not allow you to go **until you tell me: What is your name, and what is the name of your city, and what is the name of your teacher, and what is the name of the study hall in which you studied Torah? He wrote** the information **and placed** it **in her hand.**

עָמְדָה וְחִילְּקָה כָּל נְכָסֶיהָ, שְׁלִישׁ לַמַּלְכוּת וּשְׁלִישׁ לַעֲנִיִּים וּשְׁלִישׁ נָטְלָה בְּיָדָהּ, חוּץ מֵאוֹתָן מַצָּעוֹת.

She arose and divided all of her property, giving **one-third** as a bribe **to the government, one-third to the poor, and she took one-third** with her **in her possession, in addition to those beds** of gold and silver.

וּבָאת לְבֵית מִדְרָשׁוֹ שֶׁל רַבִּי חִיָּיא. אָמְרָה לוֹ: רַבִּי, צַוֵּה עָלַי וְיַעֲשׂוּנִי גִּיּוֹרֶת. אָמַר לָהּ: בִּתִּי, שֶׁמָּא עֵינַיִךְ נָתַתְּ בְּאֶחָד מִן הַתַּלְמִידִים? הוֹצִיאָה כְּתָב מִיָּדָהּ וּנְתָנָה לוֹ, אָמַר לָהּ: לְכִי זְכִי בְּמִקָּחֵךְ.

She came to the study hall of Rabbi Ḥiyya and **said to him: My teacher, instruct** your students **concerning me and** have them **make me a convert.** Rabbi Ḥiyya **said to her: My daughter, perhaps you set your sights on one of the students** and that is why you want to convert? **She took** the **note** the student had given her **from her hand and gave it to** Rabbi Ḥiyya. **He said to her: Go take possession of your purchase.**

אוֹתָן מַצָּעוֹת שֶׁהִצִּיעָה לוֹ בְּאִיסּוּר הִצִּיעָה לוֹ בְּהֶיתֵּר. זֶה מַתַּן שְׂכָרוֹ בָּעוֹלָם הַזֶּה, וְלָעוֹלָם הַבָּא – אֵינִי יוֹדֵעַ כַּמָּה.

Those beds that she had arranged for him in a prohibited fashion, **she** now **arranged for him in a permitted** fashion. The Gemara completes its point about the reward of mitzvot and points out how this story illustrates the concept: **This is the reward given to him in this world, and** with regard **to the World-to-Come, I do not know how much** reward he will be given.

אָמַר רַב יְהוּדָה: טַלִּית שְׁאוּלָה – כָּל שְׁלֹשִׁים יוֹם פְּטוּרָה מִן הַצִּיצִית, מִיכָּן וָאֵילָךְ חַיֶּיבֶת.

§ **Rav Yehuda says:** In the case of **a borrowed cloak,**[H] **for the** first **thirty days it is exempt from ritual fringes;**[N] **from then on** it **is obligated.**

LANGUAGE

***Gappa* of Rome – גַּפָּה שֶׁל רוֹמִי:** Some suggest that *gappa* means citadel, as in: "The highest places [*gappei*] of the city" (Proverbs 9:3). The *gappa* of Rome would therefore refer to the capital city of the Roman Empire. Others explain that it is a derivative of the word *agaf*, meaning wing. According to this, *gappa* refers to a god spreading his wing over the city to protect it. Some assert that the text should be changed from *gappa* to *gadda*, meaning a sign of the zodiac.

Others posited that it is distortion, possibly a deliberate one, of the name of the chief Roman god Jupiter (Rabbi Binyamin Musafya). Others suggest that it is an abbreviation of the Greek ἀγάπη, *agapē*, meaning love. According to this, the prostitute took an oath by the love of Rome. Some hypothesize that it refers to the goddess Isis, who was known by this nickname.

תַּנְיָא נַמִי הָכִי: הַדָּר בְּפוּנְדְּקִי בְּאֶרֶץ יִשְׂרָאֵל, וְהַשּׂוֹכֵר בַּיִת בְּחוּץ לָאָרֶץ – כׇּל שְׁלֹשִׁים יוֹם פָּטוּר מִן הַמְּזוּזָה, מִיכָּן וְאֵילָךְ חַיָּיב; אֲבָל הַשּׂוֹכֵר בַּיִת בְּאֶרֶץ יִשְׂרָאֵל – עוֹשֶׂה מְזוּזָה לְאַלְתַּר, מִשּׁוּם יִישּׁוּב דְּאֶרֶץ יִשְׂרָאֵל.

The Gemara notes: **That** distinction **is also taught** in a *baraita*: In the case of **one who resides in a guesthouse** [*pundaki*][LH] **in Eretz Yisrael, or one who rents a house outside of Eretz Yisrael, for** the first **thirty days** he is **exempt from the** mitzva of *mezuza*; **from then on** he is **obligated. But one who rents a house in Eretz Yisrael** must **affix a** *mezuza* **immediately, due to the settlement of Eretz Yisrael.**[N]

״תְּפִלָּה שֶׁל יָד אֵינָהּ מְעַכֶּבֶת״. אָמַר רַב חִסְדָּא: לֹא שָׁנוּ אֶלָּא שֶׁיֵּשׁ לוֹ, אֲבָל אֵין לוֹ – מְעַכֶּבֶת.

§ The mishna teaches: Absence of the **phylacteries of** the **arm does not prevent** fulfillment of the mitzva of the phylacteries of the head, and absence of the phylacteries of the head does not prevent fulfillment of the mitzva of the phylacteries of the arm. **Rav Ḥisda said: They taught** this **only** in a case **where one has** the other phylacteries, but they are not with him or he is unable to wear them for some reason. **But if he does not have** the other phylacteries at all, then their absence **does prevent** the fulfillment of the mitzva to don the phylacteries that he has.

אָמְרוּ לוֹ: אֲמַרְתְּ? אֲמַר לְהוּ: לָא, אֶלָּא מַאן דְּלֵית לֵיהּ תְּרֵי מִצְוֹת, חַד מִצְוָה נַמִי לָא לִיעֲבֵיד?! וּמֵעִיקָּרָא מַאי סְבַר? גְּזֵירָה שֶׁמָּא יִפְשַׁע.

Later on, the students **said to him:** Do **you** still **say** that? Rav Ḥisda **said to them: No, rather** I would say the opposite: Concerning **one who does not have** the ability to fulfill **two mitzvot,**[H] **should he also not perform** the **one mitzva** that he does have the ability to fulfill? The Gemara asks: **And what did he hold initially** when he said not to don one of the phylacteries in the absence of the other? The Gemara answers: He held that it was due to a rabbinic **decree, lest he be negligent** and not try to acquire the phylacteries that he lacks.

אָמַר רַב שֵׁשֶׁת: כׇּל שֶׁאֵינוֹ מַנִּיחַ תְּפִילִּין – עוֹבֵר בִּשְׁמוֹנָה עֲשֵׂה,

Rav Sheshet says: Anyone who does not don phylacteries violates eight positive mitzvot. This is referring to the mitzva to don phylacteries of the arm and head, each of which is mentioned in four different passages (Exodus 13:9; Exodus 13:16; Deuteronomy 6:8; Deuteronomy 11:18).

וְכׇל שֶׁאֵין לוֹ צִיצִית בְּבִגְדוֹ – עוֹבֵר בַּחֲמִשָּׁה עֲשֵׂה,

And anyone who does not have ritual fringes on his garments violates five positive mitzvot. This is because the mitzva of ritual fringes is stated four times in the primary passage concerning ritual fringes in Numbers: "That they prepare for themselves strings… and they shall put on the fringe of the corner a sky-blue thread. And it shall be to you for a fringe that you may look upon it and remember all the commandments of the Lord" (Numbers 15:38–39). An additional command appears in the verse: "You shall prepare yourself twisted cords" (Deuteronomy 22:12).

וְכׇל כֹּהֵן שֶׁאֵינוֹ עוֹלֶה לַדּוּכָן – עוֹבֵר בִּשְׁלֹשָׁה עֲשֵׂה,

And any priest who does not ascend the platform[H] to recite the Priestly Benediction **violates three positive mitzvot** expressed in the verses: "So you shall bless the children of Israel; you shall say to them" (Numbers 6:23), and: "And they shall put My name upon the children of Israel" (Numbers 6:27).

כׇּל שֶׁאֵין לוֹ מְזוּזָה בְּפִתְחוֹ – עוֹבֵר בִּשְׁנֵי עֲשֵׂה, ״וּכְתַבְתָּם״ ״וּכְתַבְתָּם״.

Anyone who does not have a *mezuza* **in his doorway violates two positive mitzvot,** stated in the verses: **"And you shall write them** on the doorposts of your house" (Deuteronomy 6:9), and: **"And you shall write them** on the doorposts of your house" (Deuteronomy 11:20).

וְאָמַר רֵישׁ לָקִישׁ: כׇּל הַמַּנִּיחַ תְּפִילִּין מַאֲרִיךְ יָמִים, שֶׁנֶּאֱמַר:

And Reish Lakish says: Anyone who dons phylacteries lives a **long life, as it is stated:**

LANGUAGE

Guesthouse [*pundaki*] – פּוּנְדְּקִי: From the Greek πανδοκεῖον, *pandokeion*, meaning guesthouse or hotel. This word also serves as the source for the term for innkeeper, *pundakai*.

NOTES

Due to the settlement of Eretz Yisrael – מִשּׁוּם יִישּׁוּב דְּאֶרֶץ יִשְׂרָאֵל: Rashi explains this based on the Gemara (*Bava Metzia* 102a) that states that it is not permitted to remove the *mezuza* when one moves out of a house. Therefore, if one is required to affix a *mezuza*, he will be hesitant to move out, and even if he does, another Jew is more likely to rent the house, since it already has a *mezuza*. This facilitates the settlement of Eretz Yisrael. The *Sefat Emet* explains that the benefit is that more houses will have *mezuzot*, which protect the inhabitants (see 33b), thereby furthering the settlement of Eretz Yisrael.

HALAKHA

One who resides in a guesthouse – הַדָּר בְּפוּנְדְּקִי: If one rents a house outside of Eretz Yisrael or resides in a guesthouse even in Eretz Yisrael, he is not required to affix a *mezuza* to the doorpost for the first thirty days. One who rents a house in Eretz Yisrael is obligated to affix a *mezuza* immediately (Rambam *Sefer Ahava*, *Hilkhot Tefillin UMezuza VeSefer Torah* 5:10; *Shulḥan Arukh*, *Yoreh De'a* 286:22).

One who does not have the ability to fulfill two mitzvot – מַאן דְּלֵית לֵיהּ תְּרֵי מִצְוֹת: An individual who has only one of the phylacteries dons the one that he has and recites a blessing, as each of the phylacteries is an independent mitzva. The same applies if he has both but is unable to don one of them (Rambam *Sefer Ahava*, *Hilkhot Tefillin UMezuza VeSefer Torah* 4:4; *Shulḥan Arukh*, *Oraḥ Ḥayyim* 26:1).

Who does not ascend the platform – שֶׁאֵינוֹ עוֹלֶה לַדּוּכָן: Although a priest who does not ascend the platform for the Priestly Benediction violates one positive mitzva, it is deemed as though he violated three, as the mitzva to recite the Priestly Benediction is expressed three times in the verses (Numbers 6:23, 27). This applies only when he was in the synagogue when the priests were called to recite the benediction, or if he was asked to ascend the platform or to wash his hands in preparation for the benediction (Rambam *Sefer Ahava*, *Hilkhot Tefilla UVirkat Kohanim* 15:12; *Shulḥan Arukh*, *Oraḥ Ḥayyim* 128:2, and see *Mishna Berura* there).

"ה׳ עֲלֵיהֶם יִחְיוּ וּלְכׇל בָּהֶן חַיֵּי רוּחִי וְתַחֲלִימֵנִי וְהַחֲיֵנִי".

"The Lord is upon them, they will live, and altogether therein is the life of my spirit; and have me recover, and make me to live" (Isaiah 38:16). This is interpreted as referring to those who don phylacteries, which contain the name of the Lord, on their heads; as a result, they will live, be healed and merit long life.

מתני׳ הַסּוֹלֶת וְהַשֶּׁמֶן אֵין מְעַכְּבִין אֶת הַיַּיִן, וְלֹא הַיַּיִן מְעַכְּבָן. הַמַּתָּנוֹת שֶׁעַל הַמִּזְבֵּחַ הַחִיצוֹן אֵין מְעַכְּבוֹת זוֹ אֶת זוֹ.

MISHNA The mishna returns to discussing the *halakhot* of meal offerings, which are the central theme of this tractate. The absence of **the fine flour and the oil** for the meal offering accompanying burnt offerings and peace offerings **does not prevent** libation of **the wine,**[H] **and** the absence of **the wine** for libation **does not prevent** sacrifice of the flour and the oil. Failure to perform some of **the placements**[N] of blood **on the external altar does not prevent**[H] fulfillment of the mitzva with **the other** placements, as even if the priest performed only one placement of blood, the offering effects atonement after the fact.

גמ׳ תָּנוּ רַבָּנַן: "וּמִנְחָתָם וְנִסְכֵּיהֶם" – הָבֵא מִנְחָה, וְאַחַר כָּךְ הָבֵא נְסָכִים. רַבִּי אוֹמֵר: "זֶבַח וּנְסָכִים" – הָבֵא זֶבַח, וְאַחַר כָּךְ הָבֵא נְסָכִים.

GEMARA **The Sages taught** in a *baraita*: The verse concerning the additional offerings sacrificed on *Sukkot* and the Eighth Day of Assembly states: **"And their meal offering and their libations** for the bulls, for the rams and for the lambs" (Numbers 29:18). This indicates that after the animal is sacrificed, one must **bring** the **meal offering and then bring** the **libations. Rabbi** Yehuda HaNasi **says** that since the verse states: "To bring an offering made by fire to the Lord, a burnt offering, and a meal offering, **an animal offering, and libations,** each on its own day" (Leviticus 23:37), one must **bring** the **animal offering and then bring** the **libations,**[N] and only then bring the meal offering.

וְרַבִּי נַמִי הָכְתִיב "וּמִנְחָתָם וְנִסְכֵּיהֶם"! הַהוּא מִיבְּעֵי לְמִנְחָתָם וְנִסְכֵּיהֶם בַּלַּיְלָה, וּמִנְחָתָם וְנִסְכֵּיהֶם אֲפִילּוּ לְמָחָר.

The Gemara asks: **But** according **to Rabbi** Yehuda HaNasi **also, isn't it written: "And their meal offering and their libations,"** indicating that the meal offering precedes the libations? The Gemara answers: **That** verse **is necessary** in order **to** teach that once the animals have been sacrificed during the day, **their meal offering and their libations** may be offered even **at night, and** similarly, **their meal offering and their libations** may be offered even **the next day.**

וְרַבָּנַן נַמִי, הָכְתִיב "זֶבַח וּנְסָכִים"! הַהוּא מִיבְּעֵי לֵיהּ לְכִדְזְעֵירִי, דְּאָמַר זְעֵירִי: אֵין נְסָכִים מִתְקַדְּשִׁין אֶלָּא בִּשְׁחִיטַת הַזֶּבַח.

The Gemara asks: **But** according **to the Rabbis also, isn't it written: "An animal offering, and libations,"** indicating that the libations immediately follow the animal offering and precede the meal offering? The Gemara answers: **That** verse **is necessary to** teach that the *halakha* is **in accordance with** the statement **of Ze'eiri, as Ze'eiri says:** The **libations** that accompany animal offerings **are consecrated only through the slaughter of the animal offering.**[H] This means that once the animal is slaughtered, the libations that were set aside to be brought with that animal offering cannot be diverted to accompany a different animal offering.

וְרַבִּי נַמִי מִיבְּעֵי לֵיהּ לְכִדְזְעֵירִי! וְרַבָּנַן נַמִי מִיבְּעֵי לְהוּ לְמִנְחָתָם וְנִסְכֵּיהֶם בַּלַּיְלָה, וּמִנְחָתָם וְנִסְכֵּיהֶם אֲפִילּוּ לְמָחָר!

The Gemara points out that both opinions remain difficult: **But Rabbi** Yehuda HaNasi should **also require** the phrase "an animal offering, and libations" **to** teach that the *halakha* is **in accordance with** the statement **of Ze'eiri. And the Rabbis** should **also require** the phrase "and their meal offering and their libations" **to** indicate that **their meal offering and their libations** may be offered even **at night, and their meal offering and their libations** may be offered even **the next day.**

אֶלָּא הַיְינוּ טַעְמַיְיהוּ דְּרַבָּנַן, דִּכְתִיב: "עֹלָה וּמִנְחָה". וְרַבִּי נַמִי הָכְתִיב "עֹלָה וּמִנְחָה"!

The Gemara offers a different explanation of the dispute in the *baraita*: **Rather, this is the reasoning of the Rabbis, as it is written** in the verse: "To bring an offering made by fire to the Lord, **a burnt offering, and a meal offering,** an animal offering, and libations, each on its own day." The Rabbis derive from this that the meal offering should be offered immediately following the animal burnt offering. The Gemara asks: **But** according to **Rabbi** Yehuda HaNasi **also, isn't it written: "A burnt offering, and a meal offering"?**

HALAKHA

The absence of the fine flour and the oil does not prevent libation of the wine – הַסּוֹלֶת וְהַשֶּׁמֶן אֵין מְעַכְּבִין אֶת הַיַּיִן: The absence of the fine flour and the oil accompanying offerings does not prevent the libation of the wine, nor does the absence of the wine prevent the sacrifice of the fine flour and oil (Rambam *Sefer Avoda, Hilkhot Ma'aseh HaKorbanot* 2:12).

Failure to perform some of the placements of blood on the external altar does not prevent, etc. – הַמַּתָּנוֹת שֶׁעַל הַמִּזְבֵּחַ הַחִיצוֹן אֵין מְעַכְּבוֹת וכו׳: With regard to offerings whose blood is supposed to be presented on the outer altar, as long as the blood was presented once, the offering is valid and has effected atonement after the fact. Even in the case of a sin offering, whose blood is supposed to be presented four times, only one presentation is absolutely essential (Rambam *Sefer Avoda, Hilkhot Pesulei HaMukdashin* 2:1).

The libations are consecrated only through the slaughter of the animal offering – אֵין נְסָכִים מִתְקַדְּשִׁין אֶלָּא בִּשְׁחִיטַת הַזֶּבַח: The libations that accompany animal offerings are consecrated through the slaughter of the animal. Consequently, if the libations were already in a service vessel when the animal offering was slaughtered, the libations may not be used for any other animal offering (Rambam *Sefer Avoda, Hilkhot Pesulei HaMukdashin* 12:6).

NOTES

The placements – הַמַּתָּנוֹת: This refers to the application of blood to the corners of the outer altar, which stood in the Temple courtyard, as opposed to the inner altar, which was the golden altar that stood in the Sanctuary. The blood of some offerings, e.g., sin offerings, is placed on each of the four corners of the altar. The blood of other offerings, e.g., burnt offerings and guilt offerings, is presented on two corners diagonally opposite from one another, so that the blood actually reaches all four walls of the altar. There are yet other offerings, including firstborn animal offerings, animal tithe offerings, and Paschal offerings, whose blood is poured on the base of the altar rather than being presented upon the altar.

Bring the animal offering and then bring the libations – הָבֵא זֶבַח וְאַחַר כָּךְ הָבֵא נְסָכִים: The later commentaries discuss the meaning of this statement. Some hold that one may bring the libations immediately after slaughtering the animal offering (*Tzafenat Pa'ane'aḥ* on the Torah). Others hold that since the obligation to bring the libations is an extension of the obligation to bring the animal offering, the libations cannot be brought until all the sacrificial rites of the animal offering have been performed (*Keneset HaRishonim*).

אֶלָּא, בְּבָאִים עִם הַזֶּבַח דְּכוּלֵּי עָלְמָא לָא פְּלִיגִי דְּמִנְחָה וְאַחַר כָּךְ נְסָכִים, דְּהָכְתִיב "עֹלָה וּמִנְחָה", כִּי פְּלִיגִי – בְּבָאִין בִּפְנֵי עַצְמָן, רַבָּנַן סָבְרִי: מִדְּבָאִין עִם הַזֶּבַח מִנְחָה וְאַחַר כָּךְ נְסָכִים, בִּפְנֵי עַצְמָן נַמִּי מִנְחָה וְאַחַר כָּךְ נְסָכִים.

Rather, with regard to libations that accompany an animal offering, everyone agrees that the meal offering should be brought and afterward the libations should be brought, as it is written: "A burnt offering, and a meal offering." When they disagree it is with regard to meal offerings and libations that are brought by themselves.[N] The Rabbis hold that from the fact that when meal offerings and libations accompany offerings, the meal offerings are brought and then the libations are brought, it can be derived that when they are brought by themselves also, first the meal offering is brought and then the libations are brought.

וְרַבִּי: הָתָם הוּא דְּאַיְּידֵי דְּאַתְחֵיל בַּאֲכִילָה גָּמַר לָהּ לְכוּלָּא מִילְּתָא דַּאֲכִילָה, אֲבָל בִּפְנֵי עַצְמָן נְסָכִים עֲדִיפִי, הוֹאִיל דְּמִיתְאַמְרָא שִׁירָה עֲלַיְיהוּ.

And Rabbi Yehuda HaNasi holds that it is specifically there, in the case of meal offerings and libations that accompany an animal offering, that the meal offering is burned on the altar before the wine libation is poured on the altar. This is because since the altar has started to eat, i.e., consume, the animal offering, one must first complete the entire matter of the altar's eating, including the meal offering. The pouring of the wine on the altar is likened more to drinking than to eating. But when the meal offering and the libations are brought by themselves, the libations are considered preferable, because the song of the Levites is recited over them.[H] Consequently, the pouring of the libations precedes the burning of the meal offering on the altar.

"הַמַּתָּנוֹת שֶׁעַל מִזְבֵּחַ הַחִיצוֹן אֵין מְעַכְּבוֹת זוֹ אֶת זוֹ".

§ The mishna teaches: Failure to perform some of the placements of blood on the external altar does not prevent fulfillment of the mitzva with the other placements, as even if the priest performed only one placement, the offering effects atonement after the fact.

תָּנוּ רַבָּנַן: מִנַּיִן לְכָל הַנִּיתָּנִין עַל מִזְבֵּחַ הַחִיצוֹן שֶׁנְּתָנָן בְּמַתָּנָה אַחַת, שֶׁכִּיפֵּר? שֶׁנֶּאֱמַר: "וְדַם זְבָחֶיךָ יִשָּׁפֵךְ עַל מִזְבַּח ה׳ אֱלֹהֶיךָ".

Apropos this statement, the Sages taught in a *baraita*: From where is it derived with regard to all offerings whose blood is to be placed on the external altar that if one placed their blood with one act of placement, as opposed to the two or four that are required depending upon the offering, that the offering has nevertheless effected atonement after the fact, i.e., one has fulfilled his obligation to bring the offering? As it is stated: "And the blood of your offerings shall be poured out[N] against the altar of the Lord your God" (Deuteronomy 12:27).

מתני׳ הַפָּרִים וְהָאֵילִים וְהַכְּבָשִׂים וְהַשְּׂעִירִים אֵינָן מְעַכְּבִין זֶה אֶת זֶה. רַבִּי שִׁמְעוֹן אוֹמֵר: אִם הָיוּ לָהֶם פָּרִים מְרוּבִּים וְלֹא הָיוּ לָהֶם נְסָכִים – יָבִיא פַּר אֶחָד וּנְסָכִים, וְלֹא יַקְרִיבוּ כּוּלָּם בְּלֹא נְסָכִים.

MISHNA Failure to sacrifice one of the bulls,[H] the rams, the sheep, or the goats of the additional offerings brought on Festivals does not prevent the sacrifice of the others. Rabbi Shimon says: If the Temple treasurers had sufficient funds for the numerous bulls that are required to be sacrificed on that day but they did not also have sufficient funds for the accompanying libations, they should rather bring one bull and its libations, and they should not sacrifice all of them without libations.

גמ׳ הָנֵי פָּרִים וּכְבָשִׂים דְּהֵיכָא? אִילֵימָא דְּחַג – "כַּמִּשְׁפָּט" "כְּמִשְׁפָּטָם" כְּתִיב בְּהוּ!

GEMARA The Gemara asks: With regard to these bulls, rams, and sheep mentioned in the mishna, on which festival are they offered? If we say that these are the offerings of the festival of *Sukkot*, this is difficult: It is written with regard to those days that their offerings must be brought: "According to the ordinance" (see, e.g., Numbers 29:18), and: "According to their ordinance" (Numbers 29:33). This indicates that no deviation from the Torah's prescription is possible.

אֶלָּא דְּרֹאשׁ חֹדֶשׁ וַעֲצֶרֶת דְּחוּמַּשׁ הַפְּקוּדִים.

Rather, the mishna must be referring to the two bulls, one ram, and seven sheep of the New Moon and *Shavuot*, as mentioned in the book of Numbers (28:11, 27).[B]

NOTES

When they disagree it is with regard to meal offerings and libations that are brought by themselves – כִּי פְּלִיגִי בְּבָאִין בִּפְנֵי עַצְמָן: The early commentaries disagree about the meaning of this statement. Some hold that this is referring to a case where the meal offering and libations had not yet been set aside when the animal offering was slaughtered. Consequently, even if they are brought later that day, they are considered to have been brought independently of the animal offering (Rashi on *Temura* 14a). Others hold that this is referring to a case where they were not brought on the same day as the animal offering, whereas if they were brought on the same day they are considered to have been brought together with the animal offering (Rabbeinu Gershom Meor HaGola).

And the blood of your offerings shall be poured out – וְדַם זְבָחֶיךָ יִשָּׁפֵךְ: Rashi explains that the term "shall be poured out" indicates that the blood is poured out all at once. Consequently, even if the blood of an offering is presented on the altar only once, the offering effects atonement. In his commentary on *Zevaḥim* (52b) Rashi adds that the continuation of the verse: "And you shall eat the flesh," indicates that the offering is accepted and atonement has been achieved.

The Gemara (*Zevaḥim* 52b) derives that just as the presentation of the blood upon the altar is effective even if the priest did not perform the prescribed number of presentations, the offering is likewise valid if the blood was not presented on the right part of the altar, e.g., it was poured out on the base of the altar rather than being presented upon its corners.

HALAKHA

Because the song of the Levites is recited over them – דְּמִיתְאַמְרָא שִׁירָה עֲלַיְיהוּ: When libations are brought independently, the Levites do not sing. The Gemara in *Arakhin* (11b) raises a dilemma about whether the Levites sing in such a case, and it is unresolved. Consequently, it is decided that the Levites do not sing, contrary to the statement of the Gemara here (Rambam *Sefer Avoda, Hilkhot Temidin UMusafin* 6:8).

The bulls – הַפָּרִים: The failure to sacrifice one of the two bulls that are brought as additional offerings or the bull that accompanies the offering of the two loaves on *Shavuot* does not prevent the sacrifice of the others (Rambam *Sefer Avoda, Hilkhot Temidin UMusafin* 8:17).

BACKGROUND

Book of Numbers – חוּמַּשׁ הַפְּקוּדִים: The Sages often referred to the fourth book of the Torah as the book of Numbers (*Yoma* 3a, 68b; *Sota* 36b). This name was adopted by Christian translations as well. It was referred to by this name because of the two censuses that appear in the book, in chapters 1 and 26. It is also called the book of *Vaydabber*, after its opening word (Rashi on *Sota* 36b).

Nevertheless, the most common Hebrew name for this book is *Bemidbar*, meaning: In the wilderness. One reason for this is that it focuses on the mitzvot that the Jewish people were given in the wilderness and the miracles that happened to them there (Ramban, introduction to the book of Numbers). Another reason is that it describes the nation's conduct in the wilderness (Abravanel, introduction to the book of Numbers).

NOTES

A term of being is written about them – **הֲוָיָה כְּתִיב בְּהוּ**: The early commentaries disagree about whether this is limited to the two rams that accompany the two loaves. According to Rashi and *Tosafot*, it applies also to the bull and the sheep that accompany the two loaves, as the mitzva to sacrifice these offerings also appears in the same verse as the phrase: "They shall be a burnt offering to the Lord." Consequently, none of these offerings may be sacrificed unless all of them are being sacrificed. Conversely, others hold that this *halakha* is limited to the rams that accompany the two loaves, and does not apply to the bull and sheep (Rambam *Sefer Avoda*, *Hilkhot Temidin UMusafin* 8:19 and *Kesef Mishne* there; see also Rashi, as explained in *Shita Mekubbetzet*).

HALAKHA

That if one did not find seven lambs he should bring six – **שֶׁאִם לֹא מָצָא שִׁבְעָה יָבִיא שִׁשָּׁה**: It is possible to fulfill the obligation to bring additional offerings by bringing fewer than the prescribed number of burnt offerings. Consequently, although the priests are commanded to sacrifice seven sheep as burnt offerings, if only six could be acquired, they sacrifice six. Even if they could procure only one sheep, they would sacrifice that one sheep (Rambam *Sefer Avoda*, *Hilkhot Temidin UMusafin* 8:20).

אֵילִים דְּהֵיכָא? אִי דְּהָנְהוּ – דְּאַיִל הוּא! אִי דַּעֲצֶרֶת דְּתוֹרַת כֹּהֲנִים – הֲוָיָה כְּתִיב בְּהוּ!

The Gemara asks: The mishna mentioned **rams**, in plural; **on which** festival are multiple rams offered? **If** the mishna is referring to the additional offerings sacrificed **on those** days of the new moon and *Shavuot* as prescribed in the book of Numbers, these offerings include only one **ram** and not two. And **if** it is referring to the two rams **of *Shavuot*** that accompany the two loaves, as prescribed **in Leviticus,** a term of **being is written about them**[N] in the verse: "They shall be a burnt offering to the Lord" (Leviticus 23:18). This term indicates that the offerings must be sacrificed exactly as prescribed in order to be valid. Consequently, one may not sacrifice fewer than two rams.

לְעוֹלָם דַּעֲצֶרֶת דְּתוֹרַת כֹּהֲנִים, וְהָכִי קָאָמַר: לֹא אֵילִים דְּתוֹרַת כֹּהֲנִים מְעַכְּבִי לֵיהּ לְאַיִל דְּחוּמַשׁ הַפְּקוּדִים, וְלֹא אַיִל דְּחוּמַשׁ הַפְּקוּדִים מְעַכֵּב לְהוּ לְאֵילִים דְּתוֹרַת כֹּהֲנִים.

The Gemara answers: **Actually,** it is referring to the two rams **of *Shavuot*** that are prescribed **in Leviticus, and this** is what the mishna **is saying:** Failure to sacrifice the **rams** that accompany the two loaves, as prescribed **in Leviticus, does not prevent** the sacrifice of the **ram** of the additional offering prescribed **in the book of Numbers.** Similarly, failure to sacrifice the **ram** of the additional offering, prescribed **in the book of Numbers, does not prevent** the sacrifice of the **rams** that accompany the two loaves, as prescribed **in Leviticus.**

אֶלָּא פָּרִים דַּאֲפִילּוּ אַהֲדָדֵי לָא מְעַכְּבִי, וְאֵילִים דְּהָכָא וּדְהָכָא הוּא דְּלָא מְעַכְּבִי, אִינְהוּ מְעַכְּבִי?

The Gemara challenges: **But** if that is the explanation, then when the mishna mentions **bulls** and sheep it means **that even** the bulls or sheep of the additional offering prescribed in the book of Numbers **do not prevent each other** from being sacrificed, i.e., the inability to sacrifice one of the bulls or sheep does not prevent one from sacrificing the rest. **But** when the mishna mentions **rams, it is the** rams mentioned **here** in Leviticus **that do not prevent** sacrifice of the rams mentioned **there,** in Numbers, and vice versa; but the failure to sacrifice one of **those** rams in Leviticus **does prevent** sacrifice of the other. Consequently, although the mishna mentions bulls, rams, and sheep together, the *halakha* is not the same with regard to these different animals.

תַּנָּא מִילֵּי מִילֵּי קָתָנֵי.

The Gemara responds: The ***tanna*** of the mishna **teaches each statement** individually, i.e., the *halakha* applies to each of the animals listed in a different manner.

״וּבְיוֹם הַחֹדֶשׁ (תִּקַּח) פַּר בֶּן בָּקָר תְּמִים וְשִׁשָּׁה כְבָשִׂים וָאַיִל תְּמִימִים יִהְיוּ״. ״פַּר״ מַה תַּלְמוּד לוֹמַר?

§ The Gemara cites a *baraita* with regard to the offerings sacrificed on the New Moon: The verse states: **"And on the day of the new moon, a young bull without blemish; and six lambs, and a ram; they shall be without blemish"** (Ezekiel 46:6) The *baraita* asks: **Why** does **the verse state "a bull"** when the verse in the Torah requires two bulls, as it is stated: "And on your New Moons you shall present a burnt offering to the Lord: Two young bulls, and one ram, seven lambs of the first year without blemish" (Numbers 28:11)?

לְפִי שֶׁנֶּאֱמַר בַּתּוֹרָה ״פָּרִים״, וּמִנַּיִן שֶׁאִם לֹא מָצָא שְׁנַיִם מֵבִיא אֶחָד? תַּלְמוּד לוֹמַר: ״פַּר״.

The *baraita* answers: **Since** it **is stated in the Torah** with regard to the offering of the New Moon: "Two young **bulls,**" one might think that it is not acceptable to bring fewer than two bulls under any circumstances. **From where** is it derived **that if** one **did not find two** bulls, **he brings one?** Therefore, **the verse states:** "A young **bull,**" in the singular, to teach that even if one has only one bull it should be sacrificed.

״שִׁשָּׁה כְּבָשִׂים״ מַה תַּלְמוּד לוֹמַר? לְפִי שֶׁכָּתַב בַּתּוֹרָה ״שִׁבְעָה״. וּמִנַּיִן שֶׁאִם לֹא מָצָא שִׁבְעָה יָבִיא שִׁשָּׁה? תַּלְמוּד לוֹמַר: ״שִׁשָּׁה״.

The *baraita* discusses the continuation of the verse in Ezekiel, which mentions **"six lambs." Why** does **the verse state** only six lambs when the verse in the Torah requires seven? The *baraita* answers: **Since it is stated in the Torah** with regard to the offering of the New Moon: **"Seven** lambs," one might think that it is not acceptable to bring fewer than seven lambs under any circumstances. **From where** is it derived **that if** one **did not find seven** lambs, **he should bring six?**[H] **Therefore, the verse** in Ezekiel **states: "Six** lambs," to teach that in the absence of all seven lambs one should sacrifice six.

וּמִנַּיִן שֶׁאִם לֹא מָצָא שִׁשָּׁה יָבִיא חֲמִשָּׁה, חֲמִשָּׁה – יָבִיא אַרְבָּעָה, אַרְבָּעָה – יָבִיא שְׁלֹשָׁה, שְׁלֹשָׁה – יָבִיא שְׁנַיִם, וַאֲפִילּוּ אֶחָד? תַּלְמוּד לוֹמַר ״וְלַכְּבָשִׂים כַּאֲשֶׁר תַּשִּׂיג יָדוֹ״.

And from where is it derived **that if he did not find six** lambs, **he should bring five;** and that if he did not find **five** lambs, **he should bring four;** and that if he did not find **four** lambs, **he should bring three;** and that if he did not find **three** lambs, **he should bring two; and** that if he could not find even two lambs, he should bring **even one** lamb? Therefore, **the** next **verse** in Ezekiel **states: "And for the lambs as his means suffice"** (Ezekiel 46:7), indicating that one should bring however many lambs one is able to bring.

וּמֵאַחַר דִּכְתִיב הָכִי, ״שִׁשָּׁה כְּבָשִׂים״ לָמָּה לִי? דְּכַמָּה דְּאֶפְשָׁר לַהֲדוּרֵי מְהַדְּרִינַן.

The Gemara asks: **But once this is written, why do I** need the previous verse to state **"six lambs,"** indicating that if one does not have seven lambs he should bring six? The Gemara answers: It teaches **that** although the minimal obligation is satisfied with even one lamb, nevertheless, **to the degree that it is possible to seek** more lambs, **we seek** them.

וּמִנַּיִן (לָאֵילִים שֶׁבְּתוֹרַת כֹּהֲנִים) שֶׁמְּעַכְּבִין זֶה אֶת זֶה? תַּלְמוּד לוֹמַר ״יִהְיוּ״.

The Gemara presents another *halakha* derived from these verses: **And from where** is it derived[N] **that** failure to slaughter some of the required two bulls and seven sheep of the additional offering on *Shavuot* **prevents** fulfillment of the mitzva with **the others?**[N] The Gemara answers that **the verse states: "They shall be"** (Numbers 28:31); the term "they shall be" indicates that the offerings must be brought precisely as prescribed.

״כֹּה אָמַר ה׳ אֱלֹהִים בָּרִאשׁוֹן בְּאֶחָד לַחוֹדֶשׁ תִּקַּח פַּר בֶּן בָּקָר תָּמִים וְחִטֵּאתָ אֶת הַמִּקְדָּשׁ״, ״חִטֵּאתָ״? עוֹלָה הִיא! אָמַר רַבִּי יוֹחָנָן: פָּרָשָׁה זוֹ אֵלִיָּהוּ עָתִיד לְדוֹרְשָׁהּ.

§ The Gemara discusses the meaning of another difficult verse in Ezekiel: **"So says the Lord God: In the first month, on the first day of the month, you shall take a young bull without blemish; and you shall purify [*vehitteita*] the Sanctuary"** (Ezekiel 45:18). The Gemara asks: Since this verse speaks of the first of Nisan, which is a New Moon, why does it state **"you shall purify [*hitteita*],"** which indicates the sacrifice of a sin offering [*hatat*], when in fact each of the two the bulls sacrificed on the New Moon **is a burnt offering** (see Numbers 28:11)? **Rabbi Yoḥanan says: This passage** is indeed difficult, and in the **future Elijah** the prophet[P] **will interpret it.**

רַב אַשִׁי אָמַר: מִילּוּאִים הִקְרִיבוּ בִּימֵי עֶזְרָא, כְּדֶרֶךְ שֶׁהִקְרִיבוּ בִּימֵי מֹשֶׁה.

Rav Ashi says: It is possible to explain that this verse is not referring to the additional offerings sacrificed on the New Moon but rather to the offerings of the **inauguration** that **they sacrificed** later **in the days of Ezra,**[NH] **similar to** the offerings **that were sacrificed** during the period of inauguration of the Tabernacle **in the days of Moses.** When the Temple service was restored in the Second Temple, the Jewish people observed eight days of inauguration, initiating the priests in the Temple service, from the twenty-third of Adar through the New Moon of Nisan. During these eight days, they offered a bull for a sin offering in addition to the offerings of the inauguration, just as had been done at the inauguration of the Tabernacle (see Leviticus 9:2).

תַּנְיָא נַמִי הָכִי, רַבִּי יְהוּדָה אוֹמֵר: פָּרָשָׁה זוֹ אֵלִיָּהוּ עָתִיד לְדוֹרְשָׁהּ. אָמַר לוֹ רַבִּי יוֹסֵי: מִלּוּאִים הִקְרִיבוּ בִּימֵי עֶזְרָא, כְּדֶרֶךְ שֶׁהִקְרִיבוּ בִּימֵי מֹשֶׁה. אָמַר לוֹ: תָּנוּחַ דַּעְתְּךָ שֶׁהֵנַחְתָּ דַּעְתִּי.

The Gemara comments that **this** discussion with regard to the interpretation of the verse in Ezekiel **is also taught** in a *baraita*: **Rabbi Yehuda says: This passage** is indeed difficult, but in the **future Elijah** the prophet **will interpret it. Rabbi Yosei said to** Rabbi Yehuda: This verse is referring to the offerings of the **inauguration** that **they sacrificed** later **in the days of Ezra, similar to** the offerings **that were sacrificed** during the period of inauguration **in the days of Moses.** Rabbi Yehuda **said to** Rabbi Yosei: **May your mind be at ease, as you have put my mind at ease** with this interpretation of the verse.

״וְכׇל נְבֵלָה וּטְרֵפָה מִן הָעוֹף וּמִן הַבְּהֵמָה לֹא יֹאכְלוּ הַכֹּהֲנִים״, כֹּהֲנִים הוּא דְּלֹא יֹאכְלוּ, הָא יִשְׂרָאֵל אָכְלִי? אָמַר רַבִּי יוֹחָנָן: פָּרָשָׁה זוֹ אֵלִיָּהוּ עָתִיד לְדוֹרְשָׁהּ.

§ The Gemara discusses the meaning of another difficult verse in Ezekiel: **"The priests shall not eat of anything that dies of itself, or is torn, whether it be fowl or beast"** (Ezekiel 44:31). The Gemara asks: **Is it** only the **priests who may not eat** an unslaughtered animal carcass or an animal that was torn and now has a wound that will cause it to die within twelve months [*tereifa*], **but** an ordinary **Jew may eat** them? In fact, these items are prohibited for consumption by all. **Rabbi Yoḥanan says: This passage** is indeed difficult, but in the **future Elijah** the prophet **will interpret it.**

NOTES

From where is it derived, etc. – וּמִנַּיִן (לָאֵילִים שֶׁבְּתוֹרַת כֹּהֲנִים) וכו׳: Some versions of the text state: From where is it derived that the absence of one of the rams that accompany the two loaves, as prescribed in Leviticus, prevents the sacrifice of the other ram? According to this version of the text, the Gemara's answer is that the verse: "They shall be" (Leviticus 23:18), indicates that the offerings must be brought precisely as commanded in the verse. This is difficult, as this *halakha* and derivation have already been ascertained earlier on this *amud*, and it seems unnecessary to repeat the same discussion. Other versions of the text omit the words that refer to the rams prescribed in Leviticus. According to this version of the text, the question pertains to the two bulls and seven sheep of the additional offering brought on *Shavuot*.

That failure to slaughter some prevents fulfillment of the mitzva with the others – שֶׁמְּעַכְּבִין זֶה אֶת זֶה: The early commentaries struggle to explain this line, as the Gemara has already established that if one does not have two bulls or seven sheep, he may sacrifice fewer than those numbers of animals. Some explain that one may sacrifice fewer than two bulls and seven sheep only if the full number of bulls and sheep is not available. But if the full number is available and one sacrifices fewer, one has not fulfilled the mitzva and even the offerings one has sacrificed are deemed unfit (Rashi; *Hazon Ish*). Others explain that the question here pertains to the derivation for the *halakha* that if there is enough money to purchase all the animal offerings but not enough to purchase all of the libations that accompany them, one should still sacrifice all the animal offerings. This is in contrast to the opinion of Rabbi Shimon cited in the mishna that one should not sacrifice animal offerings for which one does not have libations (*Tosafot*). Others explain that this teaches that if the sheep were all slaughtered and then one was lost, the others are rendered unfit and are not burned on the altar (*Birkat HaZevah*, interpreting Rambam *Sefer Avoda*, *Hilkhot Temidin UMusafin* 8:19).

The offerings of the inauguration that they sacrificed later in the days of Ezra – מִילּוּאִים הִקְרִיבוּ בִּימֵי עֶזְרָא: Some commentaries explain that Ezekiel was prophesying about the bull that would be sacrificed as a sin offering on the first of Nisan during the inauguration of the Second Temple in the time of Ezra (Rashi). Others hold that all of Ezekiel's prophecies refer to the future Third Temple. According to this explanation, Ezekiel meant that just as there were offerings of inauguration for the Tabernacle and the Second Temple, these offerings will also be sacrificed at the inauguration of the Third Temple. At that time, they will sacrifice a bull as a sin offering (Rabbeinu Gershom Meor HaGola; commentary attributed to Rashba). Some explain that in fact there were no offerings of inauguration that were sacrificed at the time of the Second Temple; the Gemara means to say that were the Jewish people to have merited it, they would have had such a celebration just as they did in the days of Moses (*Shita Mekubbetzet*, citing *Tosafot Hitzoniyyot*).

PERSONALITIES

Elijah the prophet – אֵלִיָּהוּ: In many places in the Talmud and the Midrash, Elijah the prophet appears to people, especially to Sages, and resolves their dilemmas. As it is stated in the Prophets (II Kings 2:11), Elijah never died, and he continues to serve as an emissary of God.

HALAKHA

The offerings of the inauguration that they sacrificed later in the days of Ezra – מִילּוּאִים הִקְרִיבוּ בִּימֵי עֶזְרָא: The offerings that were sacrificed by those who returned to Eretz Yisrael from the exile were offerings of the inauguration and are not offerings brought throughout the generations. This is in accordance with the opinion of Rav Ashi (Rambam *Sefer Avoda*, *Hilkhot Ma'aseh HaKorbanot* 2:15).

BACKGROUND

Unwitting communal sin – **הֶעְלֵם דָּבָר שֶׁל צִיבּוּר**: This is a communal sin offering brought due to an active unwitting transgression committed by the Jewish people, as a result of an erroneous halakhic ruling handed down by the Great Sanhedrin (see Leviticus 4:13–21). Members of the Sanhedrin would perform the ritual of placing their hands on the head of the offering. As in the case of the bull of the High Priest, the blood of this offering is sprinkled against the Curtain dividing the Sanctuary from the Holy of Holies and on the Temple's golden altar. The sacrificial portions are burned on the altar, and the rest of the flesh and the hide are burned outside Jerusalem in the place of the ashes.

PERSONALITIES

Ḥanina ben Ḥizkiyya – **חֲנִינָא בֶּן חִזְקִיָּה**: Ḥanina ben Ḥizkiyya ben Garon was one of the most prominent Sages of the generation following Shammai and Hillel. He was also sometimes known as Ḥananya, and in some sources his grandfather's name appears as Guryon. The upper story of his house served as a meeting place for the scholars of the generation, and many important decisions were made there. One of his important projects was the composition of *Megillat Ta'anit*, the first written book of Oral Law, which lists and details festive days established in commemoration of various historical events. His son Rabbi Eliezer, who is mentioned several times in rabbinic literature, assisted him in authoring *Megillat Ta'anit* and may have even composed most of it himself.

As explained here, Ḥanina ben Ḥizkiyya also went to great lengths to ensure that the book of Ezekiel would not be suppressed, and to that end he homiletically interpreted the verses that appear to contradict what is stated in the Torah.

LANGUAGE

Jugs [*garbei*] – **גַּרְבֵּי**: The Hebrew word *garbei*, or the singular *garav*, refers to containers used for liquids such as wine and oil. It has this meaning in Aramaic as well. The *garav* was generally made of earthenware in the form of a large pitcher or barrel (see *Terumot* 10:8).

רָבִינָא אָמַר: כֹּהֲנִים אִיצְטְרִיךְ לֵיהּ, סָלְקָא דַּעְתָּךְ אָמִינָא: הוֹאִיל וְאִשְׁתְּרֵי מְלִיקָה לְגַבַּיְיהוּ תִּשְׁתְּרֵי נַמִי נְבֵלָה וּטְרֵפָה, קָא מַשְׁמַע לַן.

Ravina said that it **was necessary for** the verse to emphasize that these prohibitions apply to **priests** for the following reason: It might **enter your mind to say** that **since pinching is permitted with regard to** priests, therefore an animal **carcass or a** ***tereifa*** **should also be permitted** for them. A bird sin offering is killed by a priest pinching the nape of its neck. This is not a valid method of slaughter and would generally render a bird or animal an unslaughtered carcass, yet the priests are permitted to partake of the bird sin offering. Consequently, one might think that the prohibitions against eating an animal carcass or a *tereifa* in general do not apply to priests. Therefore, the verse **teaches us** that these prohibitions apply to priests as well.

"וְכֵן תַּעֲשֶׂה בְּשִׁבְעָה בַחֹדֶשׁ מֵאִישׁ שֹׁגֶה וּמִפֶּתִי וְכִפַּרְתֶּם אֶת הַבָּיִת". "שִׁבְעָה",

§ The Gemara discusses the meaning of another difficult verse in Ezekiel: **"And so shall you do on the seventh of the month for every one that errs, and for him that is simple; so shall you make atonement for the house"** (Ezekiel 45:20). The Gemara asks: What is the meaning of the expression "on the **seventh** of the month"? There are no special offerings that are sacrificed on the seventh day of any month.

אָמַר רַבִּי יוֹחָנָן: אֵלּוּ שִׁבְעָה שְׁבָטִים שֶׁחָטְאוּ, וְאַף עַל פִּי שֶׁאֵין רוּבָּהּ שֶׁל קָהָל.

Rabbi Yoḥanan says: The verse must be reinterpreted as referring to the bull for an unwitting communal sin,[B] which is brought when the majority of the Jewish people have sinned as a result of following a mistaken ruling of the Sanhedrin. **These** seven alluded to in the verse are **seven tribes who sinned.**[H] In such a case, a bull for an unwitting communal sin is brought **even though** the number of individuals who sinned **are not the majority of the congregation.** Because the majority of the individuals in the majority of the tribes have sinned, it is considered a sin of the congregation and not sins of many individuals.

"חֹדֶשׁ" – אִם חִדְּשׁוּ וְאָמְרוּ: חֵלֶב מוּתָּר. "מֵאִישׁ שֹׁגֶה וּמִפֶּתִי" – מְלַמֵּד שֶׁאֵין חַיָּיבִין אֶלָּא עַל הֶעְלֵם דָּבָר עִם שִׁגְגַת מַעֲשֶׂה.

Similarly, the word **"month [*ḥodesh*]"** is to be interpreted as meaning that a bull for an unwitting communal sin is brought **if** the court **innovated [*ḥiddeshu*]** a new *halakha* contradicting the Torah, e.g., if **they said** that eating forbidden **fat** is **permitted.** The continuation of the verse: **"For every one that errs, and for him that is simple,"** **teaches that** the Sanhedrin is **liable** to sacrifice the bull for unwitting communal sin **only for a matter** that was **hidden** from the Sanhedrin, i.e., about which the Sanhedrin issued a mistaken ruling, and **accompanied by unwitting action** by the majority of the community, who relied on the mistaken ruling.

אָמַר רַב יְהוּדָה, אָמַר רַב: זָכוּר אוֹתוֹ הָאִישׁ לְטוֹב, וַחֲנִינָא בֶּן חִזְקִיָּה שְׁמוֹ, שֶׁאִלְמָלֵא הוּא נִגְנַז סֵפֶר יְחֶזְקֵאל, שֶׁהָיוּ דְּבָרָיו סוֹתְרִין דִּבְרֵי תוֹרָה. מָה עָשָׂה? הֶעֱלָה שְׁלֹשׁ מֵאוֹת גַּרְבֵּי שֶׁמֶן, וְיָשַׁב בַּעֲלִיָּיה וּדְרָשׁוֹ.

The Gemara concludes the discussion of specific difficult verses in Ezekiel with the following general statement: **Rav Yehuda says** that **Rav says: That man is remembered for good, and Ḥanina ben Ḥizkiyya**[P] **is his name. As were it not for him, the book of Ezekiel would have been suppressed** and not included in the biblical canon, **because** various details of **its contents** appear to **contradict statements of the Torah. What did** Ḥanina ben Ḥizkiyya **do? He brought up** to his upper story **three hundred jugs [*garbei*]**[L] **of oil** for light so that he could study even at night, **and he sat** isolated **in the upper story and** did not move from there until **he homiletically interpreted** all of those verses in the book of Ezekiel that seemed to contradict verses in the Torah.

"אָמַר רַבִּי שִׁמְעוֹן אִם הָיוּ לָהֶם פָּרִים מְרוּבִּין" [וכו'].

§ The mishna teaches that **Rabbi Shimon says: If** the Temple treasurers **had** sufficient funds for the **numerous bulls** that are required to be sacrificed on that day but they did not also have sufficient funds for the accompanying libations, they should rather bring one bull and its libations, and they should not sacrifice all of them without libations.

HALAKHA

Seven tribes who sinned – **שִׁבְעָה שְׁבָטִים שֶׁחָטְאוּ**: If the Sanhedrin issued a mistaken ruling permitting an item or action that is in fact prohibited and for which one is liable to bring a sin offering, and the people of Eretz Yisrael relied on that ruling and then the Sanhedrin realized its error, the Sanhedrin is obligated to bring a sin offering. This sin offering is sacrificed even if the judges themselves did not act on their own ruling, as long as the majority of the Jews of Eretz Yisrael acted on it. The definition of the majority of the Jewish people is that the majority of the individuals acted upon the ruling, or that seven of the twelve tribes acted upon the ruling, even if they do not constitute a majority of the individuals. This is in accordance with the opinion of Rabbi Yoḥanan (Rambam *Sefer Korbanot*, *Hilkhot Shegagot* 12:1, 13:2).

תָּנוּ רַבָּנַן: ״וְאֵיפָה לַפָּר וְאֵיפָה לָאַיִל יַעֲשֶׂה מִנְחָה וְלַכְּבָשִׂים כַּאֲשֶׁר תַּשִּׂיג יָדוֹ וְשֶׁמֶן הִין לָאֵיפָה״. אָמַר רַבִּי שִׁמְעוֹן: וְכִי מִדַּת פָּרִים וְאֵילִים אַחַת הִיא?

Concerning this, **the Sages taught** in a *baraita*: The verse states: **"And he shall prepare a meal offering, an ephah for the bull, and an ephah for the ram, and for the lambs as his means suffice, and a *hin* of oil to an ephah"** (Ezekiel 46:7). **Rabbi Shimon says: Is the measure of** the meal offering accompanying **bulls and rams the same,** as stated in this verse that it is an ephah for each? In fact, this is not the *halakha*, as the meal offering accompanying a bull is three-tenths of an ephah of fine flour (see Numbers 15:9), whereas the meal offering accompanying a ram is only two-tenths of an ephah (see Numbers 15:6).

אֶלָּא, שֶׁאִם הָיוּ לָהֶם פָּרִים מְרוּבִּין וְלֹא הָיוּ נְסָכִים – יָבִיאוּ פַּר אֶחָד וּנְסָכָיו, וְאַל יִקְרְבוּ כּוּלָּן בְּלֹא נְסָכִים. וְאִם הָיוּ לָהֶם

Rather, the verse teaches **that if** the Temple treasurers **had** sufficient funds for the **numerous bulls** that are required to be sacrificed on that day **but they did not** also **have** sufficient funds for the accompanying **libations, they should bring one bull and its libations, and they should not sacrifice all of them without libations. And** similarly, **if** the Temple treasurers **had** sufficient funds for

אֵילִים מְרוּבִּין, וְלֹא הָיָה לָהֶן אֵיפָתָן – יָבִיאוּ אַיִל אֶחָד וְאֵיפָתוֹ, וְלֹא יִקְרְבוּ כּוּלָּם בְּלֹא אֵיפוֹת.

the **numerous rams** that are required to be sacrificed on that day **and they did not** also **have** sufficient funds for the **ephah,** i.e., the prescribed measure, of flour **for** all of the rams, **they should bring one ram and its ephah** of flour, **and they should not sacrifice all of them without their ephahs** of flour.

מתני׳ הַפָּר וְהָאֵילִים וְהַכְּבָשִׂים וְהַשָּׂעִיר אֵין מְעַכְּבִין אֶת הַלֶּחֶם, וְלֹא הַלֶּחֶם מְעַכְּבָן.

MISHNA On *Shavuot* there is an obligation to sacrifice burnt offerings, a sin offering, and peace offerings together with the offering of the two loaves. The burnt offerings consists of a bull, two rams, and seven sheep. A goat is brought for the sin offering. Two sheep are brought as peace offerings and waved together with the two loaves. Failure to sacrifice **the bull, the rams, and the sheep,**[NH] which are all brought as burnt offerings, **and the goat** that is brought as a sin offering, **does not prevent** the bringing of **the** two **loaves,** and they are sacrificed nevertheless. Failure to bring **the** two **loaves does not prevent** sacrifice of the accompanying animal offerings.

הַלֶּחֶם מְעַכֵּב אֶת הַכְּבָשִׂים, וְאֵין הַכְּבָשִׂים מְעַכְּבִין אֶת הַלֶּחֶם, דִּבְרֵי רַבִּי עֲקִיבָא.

Failure to bring **the** two **loaves prevents** sacrifice of **the** accompanying peace offering of two **sheep,**[H] **but** failure to sacrifice **the** two **sheep does not prevent** the bringing of **the** two **loaves;** this is **the statement of Rabbi Akiva.**

אָמַר רַבִּי שִׁמְעוֹן בֶּן נַנָּס: לֹא כִּי, אֶלָּא הַכְּבָשִׂים מְעַכְּבִין אֶת הַלֶּחֶם, וְהַלֶּחֶם אֵינוֹ מְעַכֵּב הַכְּבָשִׂים. שֶׁכֵּן מָצִינוּ כְּשֶׁהָיוּ יִשְׂרָאֵל בַּמִּדְבָּר אַרְבָּעִים שָׁנָה קָרְבוּ כְּבָשִׂים בְּלֹא לֶחֶם, אַף כָּאן יִקְרְבוּ כְּבָשִׂים בְּלֹא לֶחֶם.

Rabbi Shimon ben Nannas[P] **says: No, rather** the opposite is true. Failure to sacrifice **the** peace offering of two **sheep prevents** the bringing of **the** two **loaves, but** failure to bring **the** two **loaves does not prevent** sacrifice of **the** accompanying peace offering of two **sheep. As we found that when the Jewish people were in the wilderness** for **forty years** after the exodus from Egypt, **they sacrificed** the two **sheep** as a peace offering on *Shavuot* **without** the two **loaves,** as the two loaves may be brought only from wheat grown in Eretz Yisrael after the Jewish people entered the land. **Here too,** whenever wheat is unavailable, **they** should **sacrifice** the two **sheep** without the two **loaves.** However, the two loaves are not sacrificed without the peace offering of two sheep.

אָמַר רַבִּי שִׁמְעוֹן: הֲלָכָה כְּדִבְרֵי בֶּן נַנָּס, אֲבָל אֵין הַטַּעַם כִּדְבָרָיו,

Rabbi Shimon says: The ***halakha*** **is in accordance with the statement** of Rabbi Shimon **ben Nannas** that failure to sacrifice the two sheep prevents the bringing of the two loaves but failure to bring the two loaves does not prevent sacrifice of the accompanying peace offering of two sheep, **but the reason** for that ruling **is not in accordance with his statement.**

NOTES

The bull, the rams, and the sheep – הַפָּר וְהָאֵילִים וְהַכְּבָשִׂים: These offerings, mentioned in Leviticus (23:18–19), accompany the two loaves of *Shavuot*. In addition, there were also additional offerings that were sacrificed, as on other Festivals: Two bulls, a ram, and seven sheep were sacrificed as burnt offerings, and a goat was sacrificed as a sin offering.

HALAKHA

Failure to sacrifice the bull, the rams, and the sheep – הַפָּר וְהָאֵילִים וְהַכְּבָשִׂים וְהַשָּׂעִיר: Failure to sacrifice the bull, the rams, and the sheep, which are brought as a burnt offering along with the two loaves, and the goat that is brought as a sin offering, does not prevent the bringing of the two loaves, and they are brought nevertheless. Failure to bring the two loaves does not prevent sacrifice of the accompanying animal offerings (Rambam *Sefer Avoda, Hilkhot Temidin UMusafin* 8:17).

Failure to bring the two loaves prevents sacrifice of the accompanying peace offering of two sheep – הַלֶּחֶם מְעַכֵּב אֶת הַכְּבָשִׂים: The Rambam holds that failure to bring the two loaves prevents sacrifice of the accompanying peace offering of two sheep, but failure to sacrifice the two sheep does not prevent the bringing of the two loaves. The Ra'avad disagrees and rules that failure to sacrifice the sheep prevents the bringing of the loaves, but not the reverse. This is in accordance with the opinion of Rabbi Shimon ben Nannas and Rabbi Shimon (Rambam *Sefer Avoda, Hilkhot Temidin UMusafin* 8:15).

PERSONALITIES

Rabbi Shimon ben Nannas – רַבִּי שִׁמְעוֹן בֶּן נַנָּס: Rabbi Shimon ben Nannas, sometimes referred to simply as ben Nannas, was a third-generation *tanna*. He was a colleague of Rabbi Akiva and Rabbi Yishmael, with whom he engaged in halakhic discourse. He was particularly expert in matters of monetary law, as evidenced by the fact that Rabbi Yishmael once praised ben Nannas by saying: One who wants to acquire wisdom should occupy himself with monetary law…and one who wants to occupy himself with monetary law should serve Shimon ben Nannas (*Bava Batra* 175b).

שֶׁכָּל הָאָמוּר בְּחוּמַּשׁ הַפְּקוּדִים קָרֵב בַּמִּדְבָּר, וְכָל הָאָמוּר בְּתוֹרַת כֹּהֲנִים אֵין קָרֵב בַּמִּדְבָּר. מִשֶּׁבָּאוּ לָאָרֶץ – קָרְבוּ אֵלּוּ וָאֵלּוּ.

As all the offerings that must be sacrificed on *Shavuot* **that are stated in the book of Numbers** (see 28:27), i.e., two bulls, one ram, and seven sheep as additional offerings and a goat as a sin offering, were **sacrificed** when the Jewish people were **in the wilderness. But all** the offerings **stated in Leviticus** (see 23:18–20), i.e., the offerings accompanying the two loaves, were **not sacrificed** when the Jewish people were **in the wilderness.**[N] Not only were the two loaves not sacrificed, but the accompanying offerings, including the peace offering of the two sheep, were also not sacrificed, because it was only **when they arrived in Eretz** Yisrael that **these** additional offerings **and those** offerings accompanying the two loaves **were sacrificed.** Neither the additional offerings of *Shavuot* nor the two loaves, and the offerings that accompany them, were sacrificed in the wilderness, contrary to the opinion of Rabbi Shimon ben Nannas.

מִפְּנֵי מָה אֲנִי אוֹמֵר יִקְרְבוּ כְּבָשִׂים בְּלֹא לֶחֶם? מִפְּנֵי שֶׁהַכְּבָשִׂים מַתִּירִין אֶת עַצְמָן, וְלֹא הַלֶּחֶם בְּלֹא כְּבָשִׂים? שֶׁאֵין לוֹ מִי יַתִּירֶנּוּ.

Rather, **for what** reason **do I** nevertheless **say that the sheep should be sacrificed without** the **loaves,** in accordance with the opinion of Rabbi Shimon ben Nannas? It is **due to** the fact **that the sheep permit themselves,** as the sprinkling of their blood and the burning of the portions consumed on the altar renders it permitted to partake of their meat. **And** why are **the loaves not** sacrificed **without the sheep?** It is **because there is no** item **to permit** the loaves, as the loaves are permitted only after the sheep are sacrificed.

גמ׳ תָּנוּ רַבָּנַן: "וְהִקְרַבְתֶּם עַל הַלֶּחֶם" – חוֹבָה עַל הַלֶּחֶם, "שִׁבְעַת כְּבָשִׂים תְּמִימִים" – אַף עַל פִּי שֶׁאֵין לֶחֶם,

GEMARA The mishna teaches the *halakhot* of the sacrifices that generally accompany the two loaves on *Shavuot* in a case when the two loaves are not available. The Gemara cites a relevant *baraita*. **The Sages taught:** The verse that mandates these offerings states: "And you shall sacrifice with the bread seven lambs without blemish of the first year, and one young bull, and two rams" (Leviticus 23:18). The phrase **"and you shall sacrifice with the bread"** indicates that it is **obligatory** to sacrifice these burnt offerings **with the loaves** of bread, and if the loaves are not available, then these offerings are not sacrificed. The continuation of the verse: **"Seven lambs without blemish,"** teaches that the lambs are sacrificed **even if there are no loaves** available.

אִם כֵּן מָה תַּלְמוּד לוֹמַר "עַל הַלֶּחֶם"? מְלַמֵּד שֶׁלֹּא נִתְחַיְּיבוּ בִּכְבָשִׂים קוֹדֶם שֶׁנִּתְחַיְּיבוּ בַּלֶּחֶם, דִּבְרֵי רַבִּי טַרְפוֹן.

If so, that the animal offerings may be sacrificed even without loaves, **what** is the meaning when **the verse states "with the bread"?** It **teaches that they were not obligated to** sacrifice **the sheep before they were obligated to** sacrifice **loaves,** i.e., they became obligated to sacrifice all of these offerings only when they entered Eretz Yisrael. This is **the statement of Rabbi Tarfon.**

רַבִּי עֲקִיבָא אוֹמֵר: יָכוֹל הֵן הֵן כְּבָשִׂים הָאֲמוּרִים כָּאן הֵן הֵן כְּבָשִׂים הָאֲמוּרִים בְּחוּמַּשׁ הַפְּקוּדִים? אָמַרְתָּ, כְּשֶׁאַתָּה מַגִּיעַ אֵצֶל פָּרִים וְאֵילִים אֵינָן הֵן, אֶלָּא הַלָּלוּ בָּאִין בִּגְלַל עַצְמָן וְהַלָּלוּ בָּאִין בִּגְלַל לֶחֶם.

Rabbi Akiva says: One **might** have thought that the **sheep mentioned here** in Leviticus, which accompany the two loaves, **are the very same ones mentioned in the book of Numbers** (see 28:27), in the passage prescribing the additional offerings. You must **say when you reach** the **bulls and rams** that are enumerated in the two passages that the offerings mentioned in one **are not those** mentioned in the other, as the number of bulls and rams are not equal. Whereas in Leviticus the verse requires the sacrifice of one bull and two rams, in Numbers the verse requires the sacrifice of two bulls and one ram. **Rather,** the two passages are referring to different offerings. **These** mentioned in Numbers **come** upon the altar **for their own sake, and those** mentioned in Leviticus **come** upon the altar **for the sake of** the two **loaves.**

נִמְצָא מַה שֶּׁאָמוּר בְּחוּמַּשׁ הַפְּקוּדִים – קָרֵב בַּמִּדְבָּר, וּמַה שֶּׁאָמוּר בְּתוֹרַת כֹּהֲנִים – לֹא קָרֵב בַּמִּדְבָּר.

It is therefore **found** that the offerings **that are mentioned in the book of Numbers were sacrificed** even when the Jewish people were **in the wilderness** and could not bring the offering of the two loaves, **but** the offerings **that are mentioned in Leviticus were not sacrificed in the wilderness,** due to the fact that the two loaves could not be sacrificed in the wilderness.

וְדִלְמָא פָּרִים וְאֵילִים לָאו אִינְהוּ, הָא כְּבָשִׂים אִינְהוּ נִינְהוּ! מִדְּהָנֵי אִישְׁתַּנּוּ, הָנֵי נַמִי דְּאַחֲרִינֵי.

The Gemara challenges: **But perhaps the bulls and rams** mentioned in Numbers **are not those** mentioned in Leviticus, **but the sheep** mentioned in Numbers **are** the same as **those** mentioned in Leviticus. The Gemara explains: **From** the fact **that these** bulls and rams **are different,** it is apparent that **those** sheep **are also different** offerings.

NOTES

But all the offerings stated in Leviticus were not sacrificed when the Jewish people were in the wilderness – וְכָל הָאָמוּר בְּתוֹרַת כֹּהֲנִים אֵין קָרֵב בַּמִּדְבָּר: The commentaries explain that this does not mean that none of the offerings mentioned anywhere in Leviticus were sacrificed when the Jewish people were in the wilderness, as the offerings of Yom Kippur, detailed in Leviticus, chapter 16, were sacrificed during this time period (see Leviticus 16:34). Rather, the Gemara is referring specifically to the offerings of *Shavuot*. They adduce proof to this explanation from the fact that in the passage describing the additional offerings of Yom Kippur, it states: "Beside the sin offering of atonement" (Numbers 29:11), whereas the passage describing the additional offerings of *Shavuot* (Numbers 28:26–31) does not mention the offering of the two loaves and the offerings that accompanied it (*Sefat Emet*).

וּפָרִים וְאֵילִים מִמַּאי דְּאִישְׁתַּנּוּ? דִּלְמָא הָכִי קָאָמַר רַחֲמָנָא: אִי בָּעֵי פַּר וּשְׁנֵי אֵילִים – לִיקְרַב, אִי בָּעֵי שְׁנֵי פָּרִים וְאַיִל אֶחָד – לִיקְרַב! מִדְּאִישְׁתַּנִּי סִדְרָן, שְׁמַע מִינָּהּ אַחֲרִינֵי נִינְהוּ.

The Gemara asks: **But from where** is it proven **that** the **bulls and rams** in Numbers **are different** offerings than the bulls and rams mentioned in Leviticus? **Perhaps** they are actually the same offerings, and **this** is what **the Merciful One is saying: If** you **want, sacrifice a bull and two rams,** as the verse states in Leviticus; and **if** you **want, sacrifice two bulls and one ram,** as the verse states in Numbers. The Gemara answers: **From** the fact **that the order of** the offerings **is different** in the two passages, as the verse in Leviticus mentions the sheep, then the bull, and then the rams, whereas the verse in Numbers mentions the bulls, then the ram, and then the sheep, one may **conclude from it** that **they are different** offerings.

״הַלֶּחֶם מְעַכֵּב אֶת הַכְּבָשִׂים״. מַאי טַעְמָא דְּרַבִּי עֲקִיבָא?

§ The mishna teaches: Failure to bring **the** two **loaves prevents** sacrifice of **the** accompanying peace offering of two **sheep,** but failure to sacrifice the two sheep does not prevent the bringing of the two loaves; this is the statement of Rabbi Akiva. The Gemara asks: **What is the reasoning of Rabbi Akiva?**

גָּמַר ״יִהְיוּ״ מִ״תִּהְיֶינָה״,

The Gemara answers: **He derived** the *halakha* based upon a verbal analogy[B] between two verses. One verse states: "And the priest shall wave them with the bread of the first fruits for a wave offering before the Lord, with the two lambs; **they shall be** [*yihyu*] holy to the Lord for the priest" (Leviticus 23:20). The term "they shall be" indicates that it is essential that the offering be brought precisely as commanded, but it is unclear whether this is referring to the loaves or to the sheep brought as peace offerings. This is clarified by means of a verbal analogy **from** the verse: "You shall bring out of your dwellings two loaves of waving of two tenth parts of an ephah; **they shall be** [*tihyena*] of fine flour" (Leviticus 23:17).

מָה לְהַלָּן לֶחֶם, אַף כָּאן לֶחֶם.

The verbal analogy teaches that **just as there** the requirement that it be done as prescribed is referring to the **loaves** rather than the sheep, **so too here** it is referring to the **loaves** rather than the sheep. Consequently, failure to bring the loaves prevents sacrifice of the sheep, but failure to sacrifice the sheep does not prevent the bringing of the loaves.

וּבֶן נַנָּס? גָּמַר ״יִהְיוּ״ ״יִהְיוּ״, מָה לְהַלָּן כְּבָשִׂים, אַף כָּאן כְּבָשִׂים.

The Gemara asks: **And** how did Rabbi Shimon **ben Nannas,** who holds that failure to sacrifice the sheep prevents the bringing of the loaves but failure to bring the loaves does not prevent sacrifice of the sheep, derive his ruling? **He derived** the *halakha* through a verbal analogy between the verse: **"They shall be** [*yihyu*] holy to the Lord for the priest," and the verse that states, concerning the seven sheep brought as burnt offerings: **"They shall be** [*yihyu*] a burnt offering to the Lord" (Leviticus 23:18). **Just as there** the requirement that it be done as prescribed is referring to the **sheep, so too here** it is referring to **sheep** rather than loaves.

וּבֶן נַנָּס נַמִּי נֵילַף מִ״תִּהְיֶינָה״, מָה לְהַלָּן לֶחֶם, אַף כָּאן לֶחֶם! דָּנִין ״יִהְיוּ״ מִ״יִּהְיוּ״, וְאֵין דָּנִין ״יִהְיוּ״ מִ״תִּהְיֶינָה״.

The Gemara challenges: **And** according to Rabbi Shimon **ben Nannas also, we should derive** the *halakha* based upon a verbal analogy **from** the word ***tihyena*** as Rabbi Akiva does, and conclude that **just as there** it is referring to the **loaves, so too here** it is referring to the **loaves.** The Gemara responds: It is preferable to **derive** the meaning of the term ***yihyu*** **from** a verbal analogy using the identical form ***yihyu,*** **and** one should **not derive** the meaning of the term ***yihyu*** **from** a verbal analogy using the term ***tihyena.***

מַאי נָפְקָא מִינָּהּ? הָתָנָא דְּבֵי רַבִּי יִשְׁמָעֵאל: ״וְשָׁב הַכֹּהֵן״ ״וּבָא הַכֹּהֵן״, זֶהוּ שִׁיבָה, זֶהוּ בִּיאָה!

The Gemara asks: **What difference is** there whether or not the words are identical? **Didn't the school of Rabbi Yishmael teach** a verbal analogy with regard to leprosy of houses? The verse states: **"And the priest shall return** [*veshav*] on the seventh day" (Leviticus 14:39), and another verse with regard to the priest's visit seven days later states: **"And the priest shall come** [*uva*][N] and look" (Leviticus 14:44). **This returning** and **this coming** have the same meaning, and one can therefore derive by verbal analogy that the *halakha* which applies if the leprosy had spread at the conclusion of the first week likewise applies if it had spread again by the end of the following week. Certainly, if the *halakha* can be derived via a verbal analogy with the words *veshav* and *uva,* the even slighter difference in form between *yihyu* and *tihyena* should not prevent the application of a verbal analogy.

BACKGROUND

Verbal analogy – גְּזֵרָה שָׁוָה: The verbal analogy is a fundamental talmudic principle of biblical exegesis, appearing in all the standard lists of hermeneutical principles. If the same word or phrase appears in two places in the Torah, and a specific halakha is explicitly stated in one of these places, then on the basis of verbal analogy it is inferred that the same halakha applies to the other case as well. Certain restrictions were placed on this principle to prevent unfounded derivations, most significantly, that one may not infer a verbal analogy on his own, i.e., only a verbal analogy received through tradition is valid.

NOTES

And the priest shall return [*veshav*], and the priest shall come [*uva*] – וְשָׁב הַכֹּהֵן וּבָא הַכֹּהֵן: If a priest confirms that there are signs of leprosy on a house, the house is left uninhabited for one week. After that time the priest reexamines the house, as described in Leviticus 14:39. If the leprosy has spread, he orders the affected parts of the house removed and replaced with other building materials. If the leprosy has not spread, the priest then reexamines the house after another week passes (see Leviticus 14:44). The following verse states that if the leprosy has spread, the priest orders the house destroyed. Based on the verbal analogy between verses 39 and 44, the *halakha* is that the affected areas of the house are removed and replaced with other building material, and the priest reexamines the house once more a week later. Only if the leprosy is again found to have spread does the priest order the house destroyed (Rashi on *Eiruvin* 51a).

הָנֵי מִילֵּי הֵיכָא דְּלֵיכָּא דְּדָמֵי לֵיהּ, אֲבָל הֵיכָא דְּאִיכָּא דְּדָמֵי לֵיהּ – מִדְּדָמֵי לֵיהּ יָלְפִינַן.

The Gemara answers: **This matter** applies only **when there are no** terms that are **identical to it. But where there are** terms that are **identical to it, we derive** the verbal analogy **from** terms **identical to it** rather than from the terms that are not precisely identical. Consequently, it is preferable to derive the meaning of the term *yihyu* from the identical term rather than from *tihyena*.

וְרַבִּי עֲקִיבָא נַמִּי לֵילַף "יִהְיוּ" מִ"יִּהְיוּ"! דָּנִין דָּבָר שֶׁמַּתָּנָה לַכֹּהֵן מִדָּבָר שֶׁמַּתָּנָה לַכֹּהֵן, לְאַפּוּקֵי הָנֵי, דְּעוֹלוֹת נִינְהוּ.

The Gemara challenges: **And let Rabbi Akiva also derive** the meaning of the term ***yihyu* from** a verbal analogy to the identical term ***yihyu***, as Rabbi Shimon ben Nannas does. The Gemara responds: Rabbi Akiva holds that it is preferable to **derive** the *halakha* concerning **an item that** is given as **a gift to the priest,** such as the loaves or the sheep brought as peace offerings, which are the subject of Leviticus 23:20, **from** the *halakha* concerning **an item that** is also **a gift to the priest,** i.e., the two loaves, which are the subject of Leviticus 23:17. This is **to the exclusion of these** seven sheep that are mentioned in Leviticus 23:18, **which are burnt offerings** and wholly consumed by the altar, and are not a gift to the priest. Consequently, it is preferable to derive the meaning of the term *yihyu* in verse 20 from the term *tihyena* in verse 17, rather than from the term *yihyu* in verse 18.

וְאִיבָּעֵית אֵימָא: בִּקְרָא גּוּפֵיהּ קָא מִיפַּלְגִי, "קֹדֶשׁ יִהְיוּ לַה' לַכֹּהֵן" – רַבִּי עֲקִיבָא סָבַר: אֵי זֶהוּ דָּבָר שֶׁכּוּלּוֹ לַכֹּהֵן? הֱוֵי אוֹמֵר: זֶה לֶחֶם.

The Gemara presents an alternative explanation for the basis of their divergent opinions: **And if you wish, say** instead that they **disagree about the** interpretation of the **verse itself: "They shall be** [*yihyu*] **holy to the Lord for the priest"** (Leviticus 23:20). **Rabbi Akiva holds: Which item is entirely** given **to the priest? You must say** that **it is** the loaves of **bread.** Therefore he concludes that the word *yihyu* is referring to the loaves of bread, and if they are not sacrificed, the two sheep cannot be sacrificed as peace offerings.

וּבֶן נַנָּס? מִי כְּתִיב "קֹדֶשׁ יִהְיוּ לַכֹּהֵן"?! "קֹדֶשׁ יִהְיוּ לַה' לַכֹּהֵן" כְּתִיב, אֵיזֶהוּ דָּבָר שֶׁמִּקְצָתוֹ לַה' וּמִקְצָתוֹ לַכֹּהֵן? הֱוֵי אוֹמֵר: אֵלּוּ כְּבָשִׂים.

The Gemara asks: **And** how would Rabbi Shimon **ben Nannas** respond to this? He would say: **Is it** in fact **written: They shall be** [*yihyu*] **holy for the priest,** in which case one should interpret it as Rabbi Akiva does? **It is written** in the verse: **"They shall be** [*yihyu*] **holy to the Lord for the priest."** Therefore, it should be understood in the following manner: **Which item is partially** given **to the Lord and partially** given **to the priest? You must say** that **it is** the **sheep,** which are sacrificed as a peace offering, part of which is burned on the altar and part of which is consumed by the priests. Consequently, the word *yihyu* should be understood as referring to the sheep, and if they are not sacrificed, the two loaves cannot be sacrificed either.

וְרַבִּי עֲקִיבָא? מִי כְּתִיב "קֹדֶשׁ יִהְיוּ לַה' וְלַכֹּהֵן"?! "לַה' לַכֹּהֵן" כְּתִיב, כִּדְרַב הוּנָא, דְּאָמַר רַב הוּנָא: קְנָאוֹ הַשֵּׁם וּנְתָנוֹ לַכֹּהֵן.

The Gemara asks: **And** how would **Rabbi Akiva** respond to this? He would say: **Is it** in fact **written: They shall be** [*yihyu*] **holy for the Lord and for the priest? It is written** in the verse: "They shall be [*yihyu*] holy **to the Lord for the priest."** Therefore, it should be understood to mean that it is given to the Lord, and it is then given by Him entirely to the priests, **in accordance with** the statement of **Rav Huna,**[N] **as Rav Huna says: The Lord acquired it** initially **and** then **gave it to the priest.**

אָמַר רַבִּי יוֹחָנָן: הַכֹּל מוֹדִים

§ With regard to the dispute in the mishna about whether failure to sacrifice the two sheep as peace offerings prevents the bringing of the two loaves or vice versa, **Rabbi Yoḥanan says: Everyone concedes**

NOTES

In accordance with the statement of Rav Huna – כִּדְרַב הוּנָא: According to Rashi, the Gemara is applying Rav Huna's statement from another context to the current discussion. He explains that the context in which Rav Huna made his statement is a case where one robs a convert, takes an oath that he is innocent, and then admits his guilt after the convert has passed away. If the convert has no Jewish heirs, payment is made to the priests (see *Bava Kamma* 109b). By contrast, *Tosafot* hold that Rav Huna made his statement in the context of the Gemara's discussion here.

שֶׁאִם הוּזְקְקוּ זֶה לָזֶה – שֶׁמְּעַכְּבִין זֶה אֶת זֶה, וְאֵיזֶה הוּא זִיקָה שֶׁלָּהֶן? שְׁחִיטָה.

that if **they became bound to each other**[HN] and then one of them became lost, **that** the lost item **prevents** fulfillment of the mitzva with **the other,**[N] i.e., the remaining item is unfit and must be burned. Rabbi Yoḥanan clarifies: **And what is** it that establishes **their bond?** It is the **slaughter**[N] of the sheep. If the loaves existed at the time of the slaughter, then the loaves and sheep are sanctified as one unit. Consequently, if one of them is lost, the other is unfit and must be burned.

אֲמַר עוּלָּא, בָּעוּ בְּמַעֲרָבָא: תְּנוּפָה עוֹשָׂה זִיקָה אוֹ אֵינוֹ עוֹשָׂה זִיקָה?

With regard to the establishment of the bond between the loaves and the sheep, **Ulla said** that the Sages **in the West,** Eretz Yisrael, **raise a dilemma:** Does **waving**[N] of the sheep and loaves before the sheep are slaughtered **establish a bond** between the sheep and the loaves, such that if one is lost the other becomes unfit, **or does it not establish a bond** between them?

פְּשׁוֹט לֵיהּ מִדְּרַבִּי יוֹחָנָן, דְּאָמַר רַבִּי יוֹחָנָן: שְׁחִיטָה עוֹשָׂה זִיקָה, מִכְּלָל דִּתְנוּפָה אֵינוֹ עוֹשָׂה זִיקָה!

The Gemara asks: Why is there a dilemma about this issue? **Resolve it from** the statement **of Rabbi Yoḥanan, as Rabbi Yoḥanan says** that **slaughter** of the sheep **establishes a bond** between sheep and the loaves. On can conclude **by inference** that **waving,** which precedes the slaughter, **does not establish a bond** between them.

HALAKHA

That if they became bound to each other – שֶׁאִם הוּזְקְקוּ זֶה לָזֶה: Failure to sacrifice the two sheep brought as peace offerings does not prevent one from bringing the two loaves of *Shavuot*. But once the sheep and loaves have been waved together, they become bound to each other, and if the sheep are lost the loaves cannot be brought (Rambam *Sefer Avoda, Hilkhot Temidin UMusafin* 8:15).

NOTES

That if they became bound to each other – שֶׁאִם הוּזְקְקוּ זֶה לָזֶה: Rabbi Yoḥanan does not specify which Sages concede this point, nor does he clarify which offering he is referring to, and commentaries disagree as to the interpretation of his statement. Rashi explains that he is referring to the dispute between Rabbi Akiva and Rabbi Shimon ben Nannas concerning the two loaves and the accompanying two sheep brought as peace offerings on *Shavuot*. If so, Rabbi Yoḥanan is limiting their dispute to a case where a bond was not yet established between them by means of slaughtering. Some explain that Rabbi Yoḥanan is also referring to the other offerings sacrificed with the two loaves on *Shavuot* as well as the additional offerings of the day, and he is qualifying the first clause of the mishna on 45b (see Rambam *Sefer Avoda, Hilkhot Temidin UMusafin* 8:17–19, and *Kesef Mishne* and *Leḥem Mishne* there).

That the lost item prevents fulfillment of the mitzva with the other – שֶׁמְּעַכְּבִין זֶה אֶת זֶה: Rashi explains that this refers to a case where one of them is lost, and therefore the other becomes unfit and must be burned. Later commentaries derive from here that perhaps this *halakha* applies only if one of them is lost. But in a case where the sheep were slaughtered and then one wanted to bring the loaves with other, better-quality sheep, perhaps the loaves may still be used for that purpose (see *Mikdash David, Kodashim* 29).

And what is it that establishes their bond? It is the slaughter – וְאֵיזֶה הוּא זִיקָה שֶׁלָּהֶן שְׁחִיטָה: *Tosafot* note that according to the Gemara on 47a, Rabbi Yehuda HaNasi holds that the slaughter of a thanks offering sanctifies the accompanying loaves, whereas Rabbi Elazar, son of Rabbi Shimon, holds that it is the sprinkling of the blood that sanctifies them. Ostensibly, Rabbi Yoḥanan's statement is in accordance with the opinion of Rabbi Yehuda HaNasi. *Tosafot* conclude that even Rabbi Elazar, son of Rabbi Shimon, agrees that the slaughter establishes a bond between the sheep and the loaves such that if one is lost the other becomes unfit. Later commentaries add that despite the fact that Rashi (72b) apparently holds that according to Rabbi Elazar, son of Rabbi Shimon, the slaughter does not preclude bringing the loaves with other sheep, nevertheless it does establish a bond so that if one of the items is lost the other becomes unfit (Griz).

Waving – תְּנוּפָה: The source of the obligation to wave the two loaves together with the accompanying sheep that are brought as peace offerings on *Shavuot* is from the verse: "And the priest shall wave them with the bread of the first fruits for a wave offering before the Lord, with the two lambs" (Leviticus 23:20). The waving was performed in the following fashion: The priest would first wave the live sheep before slaughtering them. After slaughter, he would take the breast and the thigh of the sheep and place them beside the two loaves and wave them. In both cases, he would extend his hands back and forth in each of the four directions and then raise them upward and lower them. The waving was performed to the east of the altar (Rambam *Sefer Avoda, Hilkhot Temidin UMusafin*, 8:11 and *Hilkhot Ma'aseh HaKorbanot* 9:6). Others hold that it may even be performed there, but it may certainly be performed to the west of the altar, which is closer to the Sanctuary (Rashi on 61a).

Waving the breast, thigh, and two loaves

דְּרַבִּי יוֹחָנָן גּוּפָא קָא מִיבַּעְיָא לֵיהּ: מִיפְשַׁט פְּשִׁיטָא לֵיהּ לְרַבִּי יוֹחָנָן דִּשְׁחִיטָה עוֹשָׂה זִיקָה וּתְנוּפָה אֵינוֹ עוֹשָׂה זִיקָה, אוֹ דִּלְמָא שְׁחִיטָה פְּשִׁיטָא לֵיהּ וּתְנוּפָה מְסַפְּקָא לֵיהּ? תֵּיקוּ.

The Gemara answers: It is with regard to the statement **of Rabbi Yoḥanan itself** that Ulla **raises the dilemma:** Is it **obvious to Rabbi Yoḥanan that slaughter establishes a bond** between them **but waving does not establish a bond** between them? **Or perhaps it is obvious to him** that **slaughter** establishes a bond between them, **but he is uncertain** as to whether or not **waving** establishes a bond between them. According to the second possibility, the reason that he mentioned slaughter is that he was certain about it. The Gemara notes that the question **shall stand** unresolved.

אֲמַר לֵיהּ רַבִּי יְהוּדָה בַּר חֲנִינָא לְרַב הוּנָא בְּרֵיהּ דְּרַב יְהוֹשֻׁעַ: וְהָא כִּי כְּתִיב ״קֹדֶשׁ יִהְיוּ לַה׳ לַכֹּהֵן״, בָּתַר תְּנוּפָה כְּתִיב, וּפְלִיגִי בֶּן נַנָּס וְרַבִּי עֲקִיבָא!

Rabbi Yehuda bar Ḥanina said to Rav Huna, son of Rav Yehoshua: But when it is written: "They shall be holy to the Lord for the priest" (Leviticus 23:20), it is **written** immediately **after** the verse mentions **waving, and** nevertheless Rabbi Shimon **ben Nannas and Rabbi Akiva disagree,** based on this phrase, about whether the loaves can be brought without the sheep or the sheep can be sacrificed without the loaves. This indicates that the waving does not establish a bond between these two items.

וְלִיטַעְמֵיךְ, בָּתַר תְּנוּפָה וְלָא בָּתַר שְׁחִיטָה?!

Rav Huna, son of Rav Yehoshua, replied to Rabbi Yehuda bar Ḥanina: **And according to your reasoning** that one can infer the *halakha* based upon the placement of the phrase: "They shall be holy to the Lord for the priest," is this phrase referring to the time **after waving but not after** the **slaughter** of the sheep? After all, the verse speaks of giving them to the priest, which is done after the sheep have been slaughtered. How then did Rabbi Shimon ben Nannas and Rabbi Akiva disagree concerning this verse?

אֶלָּא מַאי אִית לָךְ לְמֵימְרָא? מֵעִיקָּרָא קָאֵי, וּמַאי ״קֹדֶשׁ יִהְיוּ לַה׳ לַכֹּהֵן״ – דָּבָר שֶׁסּוֹפוֹ לַכֹּהֵן, הָכָא נַמִי – דָּבָר שֶׁסּוֹפוֹ לַכֹּהֵן.

Rather, what do you have to say concerning this verse? It must be **referring** to a time **before** the slaughter, **and what** is meant by: **"They shall be holy to the Lord for the priest"?** It means **an item that is ultimately** given **to the priest. Here too,** one can explain that the verse is referring to a time before the waving, and it means **an item that is ultimately** given **to the priest.** The issue of whether or not waving establishes a bond between the sheep and loaves therefore remains an open question.

וּשְׁחִיטָה עוֹשָׂה זִיקָה? וּרְמִינְהִי: עַד שֶׁלֹּא שְׁחָטָהּ נִפְרַס לַחְמָהּ – יָבִיא לֶחֶם אַחֵר וְשׁוֹחֵט.

The Gemara asks: **But** is it so that **slaughter establishes a bond** between them? **And** the Gemara **raises a contradiction** to this from a *baraita* concerning a thanks offering, which consists of an animal offering accompanied by forty loaves. The *baraita* states: If one of **its** accompanying **loaves broke before he slaughtered** the thanks offering,[H] **he should bring another loaf and slaughter** the thanks offering.

מִשֶּׁשְּׁחָטָהּ נִפְרַס לַחְמָהּ – הַדָּם יִזָּרֵק, וְהַבָּשָׂר יֵאָכֵל, וִידֵי נִדְרוֹ לֹא יָצָא, וְהַלֶּחֶם פָּסוּל.

But if one of **its** accompanying **loaves broke**[N] **once he slaughtered** the thanks offering, it is not possible to bring another loaf because the loaves of a thanks offering are sanctified through the slaughter of the animal, which has already taken place. Consequently, **the blood** should **be sprinkled**[N] on the altar **and the meat** should **be eaten, but he has not fulfilled his vow** to bring a thanks offering, **and the loaves are** all **unfit.**

נִזְרַק הַדָּם – תּוֹרֵם מִן הַשָּׁלֵם עַל הַפָּרוּס.

If one of its accompanying loaves broke after **the blood was sprinkled** on the altar, the loaves are not deemed unfit and the individual has fulfilled his vow to bring a thanks offering. **He separates** the four loaves for the priest **from the whole** loaves **for the broken** loaf.[N] The priest receives whole loaves and not the broken one.

NOTES

If one of its accompanying loaves broke – נִפְרַס לַחְמָהּ: Rashi notes that it is evident from this passage that if one of the loaves breaks, all of the loaves are deemed unfit, but the source of this *halakha* is not clear. He suggests that it is derived from the *halakha* of the shewbread, which is comparable to the loaves of the thanks offering. With regard to the shewbread, the Gemara (12b) states that if one is broken they all become unfit. *Shita Mekubbetzet* cites *Tosafot Ḥitzoniyyot*, who suggest based on Rashi that the reason they become unfit is that all of the loaves must be fit to give to the priest. A broken loaf is not fit to give to the priest because the verse states that the priest is given "one loaf of each offering" (Leviticus 7:14), and not a piece of a loaf.

The blood should be sprinkled – הַדָּם יִזָּרֵק: Rashi explains that the blood is not sprinkled for the sake of a thanks offering, as the individual bringing the offering does not fulfill his vow to bring a thanks offering in any event. Rather, the blood is sprinkled for the sake of a peace offering, as the thanks offering is also referred to as a peace offering, as the Gemara will soon note. *Tosafot* indicate that even if the blood was sprinkled for the sake of a thanks offering the meat may still be eaten.

He separates from the whole loaves for the broken loaf – תּוֹרֵם מִן הַשָּׁלֵם עַל הַפָּרוּס: The thanks offering includes ten loaves each of four different types, for a total of forty loaves. One loaf from each type is given to the priests, and the remaining loaves are given to the individual who brought the offering. In a case where some of the loaves become broken before the individual gives loaves to the priest, he must give the priest whole loaves rather than broken ones.

HALAKHA

If one of its accompanying loaves broke before he slaughtered the thanks offering – עַד שֶׁלֹּא שְׁחָטָהּ נִפְרַס לַחְמָהּ: If one of the loaves that accompany a thanks offering broke before the offering was slaughtered, one must bring another loaf and slaughter the offering. If it broke after the offering was slaughtered, the blood should be sprinkled on the altar and the meat of the offering should be eaten. Nevertheless, all of the loaves are considered unfit, and the individual who brought the offering has not fulfilled his vow and must bring another offering. If a loaf broke after the blood was sprinkled, the loaves remain fit and the individual has fulfilled his vow. The loaves he gives to a priest must be unbroken (Rambam *Sefer Avoda*, *Hilkhot Pesulei HaMukdashin* 12:14, and see Ra'avad there).

עַד שֶׁלֹּא שְׁחָטָהּ יָצָא לַחְמָהּ – מַכְנִיסָהּ וְשׁוֹחֵט.

The *baraita* continues: If one of **its accompanying loaves left**[H] the confines of the walls of Jerusalem **before he slaughtered** the thanks offering, it is not unfit because the loaves were not yet sanctified by the slaughter. Therefore, **he brings it** back **into** the city **and slaughters** the thanks offering.[N]

מִשֶּׁשְּׁחָטָהּ יָצָא לַחְמָהּ – הַדָּם יִזָּרֵק, וְהַבָּשָׂר יֵאָכֵל, וִידֵי נִדְרוֹ לֹא יָצָא, וְהַלֶּחֶם פָּסוּל. נִזְרַק הַדָּם – תּוֹרֵם מִמַּה שֶּׁבִּפְנִים עַל שֶׁבַּחוּץ.

If one of **its accompanying loaves left** the confines of the walls of Jerusalem **once he slaughtered** the thanks offering, the loaves are rendered unfit. Consequently, **the blood** should **be sprinkled** on the altar **and the meat** should **be eaten, but he has not fulfilled his vow** to bring a thanks offering **and the loaves are** all **unfit.** If one of the loaves left the confines of the walls of Jerusalem after **the blood was sprinkled** on the altar, the remainder of the offering is fit, and **he separates** the four loaves for the priest **from the** ones **that** remained **inside** the city **for the loaf that** went **outside** the walls of the city.

עַד שֶׁלֹּא שְׁחָטָהּ נִטְמָא לַחְמָהּ – מֵבִיא לֶחֶם אַחֵר וְשׁוֹחֵט. מִשֶּׁשְּׁחָטָהּ נִטְמָא לַחְמָהּ – הַדָּם יִזָּרֵק, וְהַבָּשָׂר יֵאָכֵל, וִידֵי נִדְרוֹ יָצָא, שֶׁהַצִּיץ מְרַצֶּה עַל הַטָּמֵא, וְהַלֶּחֶם פָּסוּל.

The *baraita* continues: If one of **its accompanying loaves became impure**[H] **before he slaughtered** the thanks offering, **he brings another loaf and slaughters** the thanks offering. But if one of **its** accompanying **loaves became impure once he slaughtered** the thanks offering, then **the blood** should **be sprinkled** on the altar **and the meat** should **be eaten, and he has fulfilled his vow** to bring a thanks offering. This is due to the fact **that the frontplate effects acceptance of** offerings that are **impure.**[N] Nevertheless, **the loaf** that became impure **is unfit**, as the frontplate effects acceptance of the offering but does not render impure items pure.

נִזְרַק הַדָּם – תּוֹרֵם מִן הַטָּהוֹר עַל הַטָּמֵא.

The *baraita* concludes: If one of its accompanying loaves became impure after **the blood was sprinkled** on the altar, **he separates** the four loaves that are given to the priest **from the** loaves that remained **pure for the impure** loaf.

וְאִי סָלְקָא דַּעְתָּךְ שְׁחִיטָה עוֹשָׂה זִיקָה, כֵּיוָן דְּהוּזְקְקוּ זֶה לָזֶה בִּשְׁחִיטָה אִיפְּסִיל לֵיהּ לֶחֶם, תִּיפָּסֵל נָמֵי תּוֹדָה!

The Gemara comes to its question: **If it enters your mind** to say that **slaughter establishes a bond** between the sheep and the two loaves of *Shavuot*, and similarly between the animal offering and the loaves of a thanks offering, then in the cases where a loaf became unfit after the animal was slaughtered but before the blood was sprinkled, **since** the animal and the loaves **bonded with each other through the slaughtering**, once the **loaf became unfit, the thanks offering should also become unfit.** Consequently, the blood of the offering should not be sprinkled on the altar and the meat should not be eaten, contrary to what is stated in the *baraita*.

שָׁאנֵי תּוֹדָה, דְּרַחֲמָנָא קַרְיֵיהּ שְׁלָמִים, מָה שְׁלָמִים קְרֵבִים בְּלֹא לֶחֶם, אַף תּוֹדָה קְרֵבָה בְּלֹא לֶחֶם.

The Gemara answers: The **thanks offering is different, as the Merciful One called it a peace offering,**[N] as the verse states: "The sacrifice of his peace offerings for thanksgiving" (Leviticus 7:13). Consequently, **just as a peace offering is sacrificed without loaves, so too a thanks offering** can be **sacrificed without loaves.**

אָמַר רַבִּי יִרְמְיָה, אִם תִּמְצָא לוֹמַר: תְּנוּפָה עוֹשָׂה זִיקָה, אָבַד הַלֶּחֶם

§ **Rabbi Yirmeya says: If you say** that **waving establishes a bond** between the loaves and the sheep, then in a case where **the loaves were lost** after the waving,

NOTES

He brings it back into the city and slaughters the thanks offering – מַכְנִיסָהּ וְשׁוֹחֵט: The case of the loaf being taken out before the slaughter of the offering is different from the other cases mentioned in the *baraita* of a loaf breaking or becoming impure. In the other cases one must bring another loaf, whereas in this case he merely brings the loaf back inside. Rashi explains that the loaf is not rendered unfit because it has not yet been sanctified through the slaughter of the offering.

That the frontplate effects acceptance of offerings that are impure, etc. – שֶׁהַצִּיץ מְרַצֶּה עַל הַטָּמֵא וכו׳: Some commentaries explain that the individual has fulfilled his vow because the frontplate effects acceptance of impure offerings, but it does not allow one to eat the loaves of bread, one of which has become impure. Since one of the loaves has become unfit, none of the loaves may be eaten (*Tosafot*; commentary attributed to Rashba). Others hold that the frontplate allows one to eat the loaves that did not become impure, and it is only the impure loaf that may not be eaten (Rabbeinu Gershom Meor HaGola; Rashi).

The thanks offering is different as the Merciful One called it a peace offering – שָׁאנֵי תּוֹדָה דְּרַחֲמָנָא קַרְיֵיהּ שְׁלָמִים: The Torah refers to the thanks offering as both a thanks offering and a peace offering, as the verse states: "The sacrifice of his peace offerings for thanksgiving" (Leviticus 7:13). Therefore, although it is initially a thanks offering when accompanied by its loaves, when lacking them it reverts to the status of a peace offering. Therefore, it is fit without its loaves if its blood is sprinkled for the sake of a peace offering. This is not the *halakha* in the case of the sheep that accompany the two loaves of *Shavuot*. Once a bond is established between them by means of slaughter, if the loaves become unfit then the sheep too are rendered unfit (Rabbeinu Gershom Meor HaGola; Rashi).

HALAKHA

If one of its accompanying loaves left – יָצָא לַחְמָהּ: If one of the loaves of the thanks offering was brought outside of the Temple courtyard before the slaughter of the offering, one must replace it with another loaf and then slaughter the offering. If it was brought outside the Temple courtyard after the offering was slaughtered, then the blood is sprinkled and the meat is eaten, but all of the loaves are unfit and the individual has not fulfilled his vow. If the loaf was brought out after the blood was sprinkled, then he has fulfilled his vow. The loaves he separates for the priest must be ones that were not taken out of the courtyard (Rambam *Sefer Avoda*, *Hilkhot Pesulei HaMukdashin* 12:14).

If its accompanying loaves became impure – נִטְמָא לַחְמָהּ: If one of the loaves of the thanks offering became impure before the offering was slaughtered, one must replace it with another loaf and then slaughter the offering. If it became impure after the offering was slaughtered, then the blood is sprinkled and the meat is eaten, but all of the loaves are unfit and the individual has not fulfilled his vow. If it became impure after the blood was sprinkled, he has fulfilled his vow. The loaves he separates for the priest must be ones that did not become impure (Rambam *Sefer Avoda*, *Hilkhot Pesulei HaMukdashin* 12:14).

HALAKHA

If the sheep are lost – אָבְדוּ כְּבָשִׂים: The Rambam holds that if the sheep of the thanks offering are lost after they have been waved with the bread, the accompanying loaves are disqualified as well, and new sheep and loaves must be brought. The Ra'avad holds that it is uncertain whether the loaves become disqualified (Rambam *Sefer Avoda, Hilkhot Temidin UMusafin* 8:15).

אָבְדוּ כְּבָשִׂים, אָבְדוּ כְּבָשִׂים – אָבַד הַלֶּחֶם.

the **sheep are lost** as well, i.e., they cannot be sacrificed, and one must bring different loaves and sheep. Similarly, if the **sheep are lost**[H] after the waving, **the loaves are** thereby **lost** as well, since a bond was established between them by means of the waving.

וְאִם תִּמְצָא לוֹמַר: תְּנוּפָה אֵינָהּ עוֹשָׂה זִיקָה, הֵבִיא לֶחֶם וּכְבָשִׂים וְהוּנְפוּ, וְאָבַד הַלֶּחֶם וְהֵבִיא לֶחֶם אַחֵר – אוֹתוֹ הַלֶּחֶם טְעוּן תְּנוּפָה אוֹ אֵינוֹ טָעוּן תְּנוּפָה?

And if you say that **waving does not establish a bond** between the loaves and the sheep, then one can raise the following dilemma: If one **brought loaves and sheep and they were waved, and** then **the loaves were lost and** he **brought other loaves** to replace the original loaves, does **that** second set of **loaves require waving** with the sheep, as it has not yet been waved? **Or does it not require waving,** as the accompanying sheep have already been waved with the original loaves, and the sheep are the subject in the verse that serves as the source of the requirement of waving (see Leviticus 23:20)?

אָבְדוּ כְּבָשִׂים לָא תִּיבָּעֵי לָךְ – דְּוַדַּאי בָּעֵי תְּנוּפָה. כִּי תִּיבָּעֵי לָךְ – אָבַד הַלֶּחֶם.

Rabbi Yirmeya clarifies the dilemma: In a case where the **sheep were lost** after the waving, **do not raise the dilemma, as** in this case **they certainly require waving,**[N] because the primary obligation of waving is mentioned with respect to the sheep, and these sheep have not yet been waved. **When should you raise the dilemma?** You should raise it in a case where **the loaves were lost** after the waving.

וְאַלִּיבָּא דְּבֶן נַנָּס לָא תִּיבָּעֵי לָךְ, דְּאָמַר: כְּבָשִׂים עִיקָּר. כִּי תִּיבָּעֵי לָךְ – אַלִּיבָּא דְּרַבִּי עֲקִיבָא דְּאָמַר: לֶחֶם עִיקָּר, מַאי?

And according to the opinion **of** Rabbi Shimon **ben Nannas,** who holds that failure to sacrifice the sheep prevents one from sacrificing the loaves, **do not raise the dilemma,**[N] **as he says** that the **sheep are primary.** Consequently, since the sheep have been waved, there is no need to repeat the waving. **When should you raise the dilemma?** Raise it **according to** the opinion **of Rabbi Akiva,** who holds that failure to bring the loaves prevents one from sacrificing the sheep, **as he says** that the **loaves are primary.** According to his opinion, **what** is the *halakha* concerning the loaves that are brought as replacements?

כֵּיוָן דְּלֶחֶם עִיקָּר – בָּעֵי תְּנוּפָה, אוֹ דִּלְמָא כֵּיוָן דְּמַתִּירִין דִּידֵיהּ כְּבָשִׂים נִינְהוּ – לָא צָרִיךְ תְּנוּפָה? תֵּיקוּ.

On the one hand, one might say that **since the loaves are primary** and this set of loaves has not yet been waved, **it requires waving. Or** on the other hand, **perhaps** one should say that **since its permitting factors are** the **sheep,** and they were already waved, the new set of loaves **does not require waving.** The Gemara concludes that the question **shall stand** unresolved.

אֲמַר לֵיהּ אַבַּיֵּי לְרָבָא: מַאי שְׁנָא שְׁנֵי כְּבָשִׂים דִּמְקַדְּשִׁי לֶחֶם וּמְעַכְּבִי, וּמַאי שְׁנָא שִׁבְעָה כְּבָשִׂים וּפַר וְאֵילִים דְּלָא מְקַדְּשִׁי לֶחֶם וְלָא מְעַכְּבִי?

§ **Abaye said to Rava: What is different** about the **two sheep** brought as peace offerings together with the two loaves of *Shavuot*, such **that their** slaughter **sanctifies the loaves** (see 47a), **and** according to Rabbi Yoḥanan failure to sacrifice them once they have been slaughtered **prevents** the bringing of the loaves; **and what is different** about the **seven sheep, the bull, and** the two **rams** brought on *Shavuot* as an additional offering, such **that their** slaughter **does not sanctify** the **loaves, and** failure to sacrifice them **does not prevent** the bringing of the loaves?

NOTES

As in this case they certainly require waving – דְּוַדַּאי בָּעֵי תְּנוּפָה: Rashi explains that only the replacement sheep need to be waved, but the loaves, which have already been waved, do not need to be waved again. The replacement sheep need to be waved because their sacrifice renders the loaves permitted to be eaten, and because the sheep are the subject in the verse that serves as the source of the requirement of waving (see Leviticus 23:20). *Tosafot* explain that the loaves must be waved together with the replacement sheep.

And according to the opinion of Rabbi Shimon ben Nannas do not raise the dilemma – וְאַלִּיבָּא דְּבֶן נַנָּס לָא תִּיבָּעֵי לָךְ: The later commentaries note that one might have claimed that since the loaves were lost, it is as though they were never brought and the sheep had not been waved with loaves, and therefore the sheep must be waved with the replacement loaves. Nevertheless, according to Rabbi Shimon ben Nannas, who holds that the sheep are the primary element of the waving, since the sheep have been waved with loaves it does not matter that those loaves have been lost, and no further waving must be performed (*Keren Ora*).

אֲמַר לֵיהּ: הוֹאִיל וְהוּזְקְקוּ זֶה לָזֶה בִּתְנוּפָה. וַהֲרֵי תּוֹדָה דְּלֹא הוּזְקְקוּ זֶה לָזֶה בִּתְנוּפָה, וּמְקַדְּשָׁא וּמְעַכְּבָא!

Rava **said to** Abaye: The reason for the distinction is **because** the two sheep and the loaves brought as peace offerings **are bound to each other through the waving.** This is not so with regard to the additional offerings, which are not waved with the loaves. The Gemara challenges: **But** in the case of **a thanks offering** and its loaves, which are not waved together, **they are not bound to each other through waving,**[N] **and** nevertheless the slaughter of the animal offering **sanctifies** the loaves **and** failure to sacrifice the animal offering **prevents** the bringing of the loaves. This indicates that the waving is not the critical factor.

אֶלָּא כְּתוֹדָה, מַה תּוֹדָה – שְׁלָמִים, אַף הָכָא נַמִי – שְׁלָמִים.

Rather, the reason for the distinction is that the two sheep brought as peace offerings are **comparable to a thanks offering. Just as a thanks offering is a peace offering, so too** the two sheep are **also a peace offering.** Consequently, just as the slaughter of the thanks offering sanctifies the accompanying loaves, and failure to sacrifice the animal prevents one from bringing the loaves, the same applies with regard to the sheep peace offerings and loaves of *Shavuot*.

מִי דָּמֵי? הָתָם לֵיכָּא זְבָחִים אַחֲרִינֵי בַּהֲדֵיהּ, הָכָא דְּאִיכָּא זְבָחִים אַחֲרִינֵי בַּהֲדֵיהּ, לִיקַדְּשׁוּ הָנֵי וְהָנֵי!

The Gemara responds: **Are** the two sheep of *Shavuot* and the thanks offering really **comparable? There,** in the case of the thanks offering, **there are no other animal offerings** brought **with it.** But **here,** in the case of the offerings brought on *Shavuot*, **where there are other animal offerings** brought **with it, let these** peace offerings **and those** additional offerings **sanctify** the loaves. Why is it only the sheep brought as peace offerings that sanctify the loaves?

אֶלָּא כְּאֵיל נָזִיר, מָה אֵיל נָזִיר אַף עַל גַּב דְּאִיכָּא זְבָחִים אַחֲרִינֵי – שְׁלָמִים הוּא דִּמְקַדְּשִׁי, מִידֵּי אַחֲרִינָא – לָא, הָכָא נַמִי לָא שְׁנָא.

Rather, the reason for the distinction is that the two sheep brought as peace offerings are **comparable to a nazirite's ram,** which is sacrificed as a peace offering when he completes his term of naziriteship, in addition to a lamb that he sacrifices as a burnt offering, a female lamb that he brings then as a sin offering, and the nazirite loaves (see Numbers 6:14–15). **Just as** in the case of a **nazirite's ram, even though there are other offerings** brought with it, nevertheless **it is** the slaughter of the **peace offering that sanctifies** the nazirite loaves and **not** the slaughter of **anything else, here too,** the *halakha* **is no different,** and it is specifically the slaughter of the peace offerings that sanctifies the loaves.

וְהָתָם מְנָלַן? דְּתַנְיָא: "וְאֶת הָאַיִל יַעֲשֶׂה זֶבַח שְׁלָמִים לַה׳ עַל סַל הַמַּצּוֹת" – מְלַמֵּד שֶׁהַסַּל בָּא חוֹבָה לָאַיִל וּשְׁחִיטַת אַיִל מְקַדַּשְׁתּוֹ, לְפִיכָךְ שְׁחָטוֹ שֶׁלֹּא לִשְׁמוֹ – לֹא קָדְשׁוּ הַלֶּחֶם.

The Gemara asks: **And there,** in the case of the offerings of the nazirite, **from where do we** derive that it is specifically the slaughter of the peace offering that sanctifies the loaves? The Gemara answers: This is **as it is taught** in a *baraita* concerning a verse stated with regard to the offerings of the nazirite: **"And he shall offer the ram for a sacrifice of peace offerings to the Lord, with the basket of unleavened bread"** (Numbers 6:17). This verse, which connects the ram and the loaves, **teaches that the basket** of the nazirite loaves **comes as an obligation for the ram,** which is a peace offering, **and the slaughter of the ram sanctifies** the loaves. **Therefore,** if the slaughter was unfit, e.g., in a case where **he slaughtered** the ram **not for the sake of** a peace offering,[H] **the loaves were not sanctified.**

תָּנוּ רַבָּנַן: שְׁתֵּי הַלֶּחֶם הַבָּאוֹת בִּפְנֵי עַצְמָן – יוּנְפוּ, וּתְעוּבַּר צוּרָתָן, וְיֵצְאוּ לְבֵית הַשְּׂרֵיפָה.

§ The mishna teaches that according to Rabbi Akiva failure to sacrifice the two sheep brought as peace offerings does not prevent sacrifice of the loaves. Consequently, if there are no sheep, the loaves are sacrificed by themselves. Concerning this **the Sages taught** in a *baraita*: In a case where **the two loaves** are **brought by themselves,**[NH] **they should be waved.** They should then be left overnight so that **their form decays,** i.e., they become disqualified, **and they are** then **brought out to the place of burning,**[B] like any disqualified offering.

מַה נַּפְשָׁךְ? אִי לַאֲכִילָה אָתְיָין – לֵיכְלִינְהוּ! אִי לִשְׂרֵיפָה אָתְיָין – לִשְׂרְפִינְהוּ לְאַלְתַּר, לָמָּה לְהוּ עִיבּוּר צוּרָה?

The Gemara challenges: **Whichever way you** look at it, this is difficult: **If** the loaves are **brought** and waved in order **to be eaten, let** the priests **eat them** rather than burn them. **If** they are **brought** only **to be burned, let** the priests **burn them immediately. Why are they** left overnight so that they undergo **a decay of form,** i.e., become disqualified?

NOTES

In the case of a thanks offering and its loaves, they are not bound to each other through waving – **תּוֹדָה דְּלֹא הוּזְקְקוּ זֶה לָזֶה בִּתְנוּפָה:** The straightforward reading of this Gemara is that the animal sacrificed as a thanks offering is not waved together with the accompanying loaves. This is also how Rashi explains the Gemara. The Rambam rules that the loaves of the thanks offering must be waved together with the breast, the thigh, and the portions of the offering that are to be consumed on the altar (Rambam *Sefer Avoda, Hilkhot Ma'aseh HaKorbanot* 9:7). The later commentaries explain that according to the Rambam, the Gemara here means that the offering is not waved with the loaves while it is alive, in contrast to the peace offerings and the two loaves brought on *Shavuot*. After the thanks offering is slaughtered it does need to be waved with the loaves. Proof of this can be adduced from the Gemara (62a) that states that whenever there are loaves brought with an offering, the waving is performed with the loaves on top of the offering. This indicates that waving of the offering with the loaves is performed whenever an offering is brought with loaves (Rashash).

The two loaves are brought by themselves – **שְׁתֵּי הַלֶּחֶם הַבָּאוֹת בִּפְנֵי עַצְמָן:** Rashi (74b) offers two suggestions as to the circumstances under which the loaves would be brought by themselves. One scenario is that the community did not have two sheep for the *Shavuot* offering. The second is that an individual volunteered to bring the two loaves without sheep. Some of the later commentaries omit the second suggestion, as the Gemara (58a) states that an individual cannot volunteer to bring the two loaves (*Tzon Kodashim*).

HALAKHA

Slaughtered the ram not for the sake of a peace offering – **שְׁחָטוֹ שֶׁלֹּא לִשְׁמוֹ:** If one slaughtered the peace offering of a nazirite with the intention that it is a different offering, the accompanying loaves are not sanctified (Rambam *Sefer Avoda, Hilkhot Pesulei HaMukdashin* 12:18).

The two loaves are brought by themselves – **שְׁתֵּי הַלֶּחֶם הַבָּאוֹת בִּפְנֵי עַצְמָן:** When the two loaves are brought by themselves without sheep, they are waved and then left overnight, after which they are brought to the place designated for burning. They may not be eaten due to a rabbinic decree, lest there be sheep available the next year and the nation nevertheless bring the loaves without sheep because they remembered doing so the previous year. This is in accordance with the *baraita*, as interpreted by Rabba (Rambam *Sefer Avoda, Hilkhot Temidin UMusafin* 8:16).

BACKGROUND

The place of burning – **בֵּית הַשְּׂרֵיפָה:** This term is used in the Talmud to refer to three different places. One was in the Temple courtyard, where offerings disqualified within the Temple would be burned. The second was outside the Temple, on the Temple Mount, where sacrificial bulls and goats that had become disqualified due to leaving the Temple courtyard were burned. The third was outside Jerusalem, where the priests would burn those sacrificial bulls and goats whose proper procedure entailed burning them outside the Temple.

LANGUAGE

Last year [*eshtakad*] – אֶשְׁתָּקַד: This word is a contraction of the Aramaic words *shata kadma'a*, the previous year, or *sha'ata kadma'a*, a previous time.

BACKGROUND

Yavne – יַבְנֶה: Yavne is an ancient city mentioned in the Bible. Apparently, it is the city Yavne'el, located in the territory of Judah (see Joshua 15:11), far from the modern town named Yavne'el. It was a Philistine city for many years and is listed as one of the cities whose walls were breached by King Uzziah.

Yavne was conquered by Vespasian during the Roman campaign to quash the Great Revolt. Apparently, several Sages who did not support the revolt settled there. When Rabban Yoḥanan ben Zakkai joined them, Yavne became the spiritual center of Eretz Yisrael and the seat of the Sanhedrin for many years, apparently until the bar Kokheva rebellion. The main academy, known as the vineyard in Yavne, was located there, as was the residence of the *Nasi*. One of the activities that took place there was the gathering of Sages' testimonies as to the practices in the Temple, including ben Bukhri's testimony in this Gemara.

HALAKHA

Any priest who does not contribute his half-shekel – כֹּהֵן שֶׁאֵינוֹ שׁוֹקֵל: Priests are obligated to contribute the half-shekel. This is in accordance with the opinion of Rabban Yoḥanan ben Zakkai (Rambam *Sefer Zemanim*, *Hilkhot Shekalim* 1:7).

Is that to say that priests cannot volunteer to bring a thanks offering and its loaves and eat them – אַטּוּ תּוֹדָה וְלַחְמָהּ מִי לָא מְנַדְּבִי כֹּהֲנִים וְאָכְלִי לְהוּ: If the owner of a thanks offering was a priest, he eats the loaves that are normally eaten by the owners, just as an ordinary Israelite would (Rambam *Sefer Avoda*, *Hilkhot Ma'aseh HaKorbanot* 9:14).

NOTES

The two loaves of *Shavuot* are called a meal offering – שְׁתֵּי הַלֶּחֶם אִיקְּרוּ מִנְחָה: The priests also mentioned the shewbread, despite the fact that the shewbread is not explicitly referred to as a meal offering. Nevertheless, since the shewbread is brought by itself without an accompanying animal offering and is made of fine flour, it is included in the category of meal offerings. This is not true of the loaves of the thanks offering, which accompany an animal offering and are therefore not considered a meal offering. One might have said the same of the two loaves of *Shavuot*, which accompany the two sheep brought as peace offerings, if not for the fact that the verse refers to them as a meal offering (*Yosef Da'at*).

אֲמַר רַבָּה: לְעוֹלָם לַאֲכִילָה אָתְיָין, גְּזֵירָה שֶׁמָּא יִזְדַּמְּנוּ לָהֶן כְּבָשִׂים לַשָּׁנָה הַבָּאָה, וְיֹאמְרוּ: אֶשְׁתָּקַד לֹא אָכַלְנוּ לֶחֶם בְּלֹא כְּבָשִׂים? עַכְשָׁיו נַמִּי נֵיכוּל.

Rabba said: Actually, the loaves are **brought** and waved in order **to be eaten.** Nevertheless, the Sages instituted a rabbinic **decree** that they not be eaten out of concern **lest sheep become available to** the nation **the following year, and they** might **say: Didn't we eat the loaves without** any accompanying **sheep last year** [*eshtakad*]?[L] **Now too, we will eat** the loaves without sacrificing sheep.

וְאִינְהוּ לָא יָדְעִי דְּאֶשְׁתָּקַד לָא הָווּ כְּבָשִׂים – אִינְהוּ שָׁרְיָין נַפְשַׁיְיהוּ, הָשְׁתָּא דְּאִיכָּא כְּבָשִׂים – כְּבָשִׂים הוּא דְּשָׁרוּ לְהוּ.

And they will not know that the reason they were permitted to eat the loaves without sacrificing sheep **last year** is that **there were no sheep,** and therefore the two loaves **permitted themselves** to be eaten, i.e., they could be eaten without the sacrifice of the sheep. But **now that there are sheep, it is** the sacrifice of **the sheep that permits** the loaves to be eaten. Since loaves brought without sheep are fit by Torah law and may not be eaten due to rabbinic decree, they may not be burned until they become disqualified by remaining overnight.

אֲמַר רַבָּה: מְנָא אָמִינָא לַהּ? דִּתְנַן: אָמַר רַבִּי יְהוּדָה, הֵעִיד בֶּן בּוּכְרִי בְּיַבְנֶה: כָּל כֹּהֵן שֶׁשּׁוֹקֵל – אֵינוֹ חוֹטֵא.

Rabba said: From where do I say this, i.e., what is the source for my statement? It is **as we learned** in a mishna (*Shekalim* 1:4): **Rabbi Yehuda said** that **ben Bukhri testified** before the Sages **in Yavne:**[B] **Any priest who contributes his** half-**shekel is not** considered **a sinner,** despite the fact that he is not obligated to do so.

אָמַר לוֹ רַבָּן יוֹחָנָן בֶּן זַכַּאי: לֹא כִּי, אֶלָּא כָּל כֹּהֵן שֶׁאֵינוֹ שׁוֹקֵל – חוֹטֵא. אֶלָּא שֶׁהַכֹּהֲנִים דּוֹרְשִׁין מִקְרָא זֶה לְעַצְמָן.

Rabbi Yehuda added that **Rabban Yoḥanan ben Zakkai said to** ben Bukhri: **That is not** the case, **rather, any priest who does not contribute his** half-**shekel**[H] is considered **a sinner,** as they are obligated in this mitzva like all other Jews. **But the priests** who do not contribute the half-shekel **interpret this** following **verse to their own** advantage in order to excuse themselves from the mitzva.

״וְכָל מִנְחַת כֹּהֵן כָּלִיל תִּהְיֶה לֹא תֵאָכֵל״. הוֹאִיל וְעוֹמֶר וּשְׁתֵּי הַלֶּחֶם וְלֶחֶם הַפָּנִים שֶׁלָּנוּ הֵן, הֵיאָךְ נֶאֱכָלִין?

The verse states: **"And every meal offering of the priest shall be wholly made to smoke; it shall not be eaten"** (Leviticus 6:16). Those priests claim as follows: **Since the** ***omer*** offering **and the two loaves,** i.e., the public offering of two loaves from the new wheat, brought on the festival of *Shavuot*, **and the shewbread** placed on the Table in the Sanctuary each Shabbat, which are all meal offerings, **are ours,** then if we contribute half-shekels we will have partial ownership of these communal offerings, as they are purchased with the half-shekels. **How,** then, **can they be eaten?** They would then be regarded as priests' meal offerings, which must be wholly burned.

הָנֵי שְׁתֵּי הַלֶּחֶם הֵיכִי דָּמֵי? אִילֵימָא בְּבָאוֹת עִם הַזֶּבַח – אַטּוּ תּוֹדָה וְלַחְמָהּ מִי לָא מְנַדְּבִי כֹּהֲנִים וְאָכְלִי לְהוּ?

Rabba discusses this mishna: **What are the circumstances of these two loaves? If we say** that the mishna is referring **to** a case **where** they are **brought with the animal offering,** i.e., the two sheep brought as peace offerings, why shouldn't the loaves be eaten? **Is that to say** that **priests cannot volunteer** to bring **a thanks offering and its loaves and eat them?**[H] Just as the loaves that accompany a thanks offering may be eaten, even if brought by a priest, the same *halakha* should apply to the two loaves when they accompany sheep brought as peace offerings.

אֶלָּא לָאו בְּבָאוֹת בִּפְנֵי עַצְמָן, וְקָתָנֵי ״הֵיאָךְ הֵן נֶאֱכָלִין״, אַלְמָא לַאֲכִילָה אָתְיָין.

Rather, is it **not** referring to a case **where** the two loaves are **brought by themselves,** and the mishna **teaches** that the priests claimed: **How can they be eaten? Apparently,** in principle the loaves **come to be eaten,** but due to rabbinic decree they are not eaten and are left overnight until their form decays.

אֲמַר לֵיהּ אַבַּיֵי: לְעוֹלָם בְּבָאוֹת עִם הַזֶּבַח, וּדְקָא קַשְׁיָא לָךְ מִתּוֹדָה וְלַחְמָהּ – לַחְמֵי תוֹדָה לָא אִיקְּרוּ ״מִנְחָה״, שְׁתֵּי הַלֶּחֶם אִיקְּרוּ ״מִנְחָה״, שֶׁנֶּאֱמַר ״בְּהַקְרִיבְכֶם מִנְחָה חֲדָשָׁה לַה׳״.

Abaye said to Rabba in response: **Actually,** the mishna can be interpreted as referring **to** loaves **brought with the animal offering,** and therefore it does not prove that when the two loaves are brought by themselves they may be eaten. **And as for that which** is **difficult for you** based **on** the case of **a thanks offering and its loaves,** the resolution is that the **loaves of a thanks offering are not called a meal offering,** and therefore even when a priest brings a thanks offering, the loaves may be eaten. By contrast, **the two loaves** of *Shavuot* **are called a meal offering,**[N] **as it is stated** with regard to the two loaves: "Also in the day of the first fruits, **when you bring a new meal offering to the Lord"** (Numbers 28:26). Therefore, the priests held that if they would donate half-shekels, the two loaves would not be permitted to be eaten.

רַב יוֹסֵף אָמַר: לְעוֹלָם לִשְׂרֵיפָה אָתְיָין, וְהַיְינוּ טַעְמָא דְּלָא שָׂרְפִינַן – לְפִי שֶׁאֵין שׂוֹרְפִין קָדָשִׁים בְּיוֹם טוֹב.

Rav Yosef said a different response to Rabba's proof: **Actually,** when the two loaves of *Shavuot* are brought by themselves **they come to be burned,** i.e., they may not be eaten. **And this is the reason that we do not burn them** until the following day: It is **because one may not burn consecrated** items **on a Festival.**[H]

אֲמַר לֵיהּ אַבָּיֵי: מִי דָּמֵי? הָתָם – לָאו מִצְוָתָן בְּכָךְ, הָכָא דְּמִצְוָתָן בְּכָךְ – לִישְׂרְפִינְהוּ, מִידֵּי דַּהֲוָה אַפַּר וְשָׂעִיר שֶׁל יוֹם הַכִּיפּוּרִים!

Abaye said to Rav Yosef: **Is** the burning of the two loaves **comparable** to the burning of other consecrated items, such that the loaves may not be burned right away for this reason? **There,** in the case of other consecrated items, **this is not their mitzva,** i.e., they are supposed to be eaten, but if they become disqualified they must be burned. Conversely, **here,** in the case of the two loaves of *Shavuot* that are brought by themselves, **where this is their mitzva,** i.e., they are supposed to be burned, **let** the priests **burn them** on the Festival, **just as is** the *halakha* in the case **of the bull and the goat of Yom Kippur,** which are burned on Yom Kippur despite the fact that it is a Festival.

אֶלָּא אֲמַר רַב יוֹסֵף: גְּזֵירָה שֶׁמָּא יִזְדַּמְּנוּ לָהֶם כְּבָשִׂים לְאַחַר מִכָּאן. אֲמַר לֵיהּ אַבָּיֵי: תֵּינַח כׇּל זְמַן הַקְרָבָתָם, לְבָתַר הָכִי – לִשְׂרְפִינְהוּ! מַאי ״תְּעוּבַּר צוּרָתָן״ נַמִּי דְּקָתָנֵי? צוּרַת הַקְרָבָתָם.

Rather, Rav Yosef said: The reason the loaves are left overnight is due to a rabbinic **decree** not to burn them immediately, **lest sheep become available to** the nation **afterward,** i.e., later in the day, in which case the loaves could be waved with them and then eaten. **Abaye said to** Rav Yosef: That **works out well** for the **entire time** period when **they** may be **sacrificed,** i.e., until the afternoon daily offering is sacrificed. But **after that, let them burn** the loaves immediately and not wait until the next day. Rav Yosef replied: **What** is the meaning of the phrase in the *baraita* **that teaches** that the loaves must be left until **their form decays?** It means that they must be left until **the form of their sacrifice** has passed, i.e., until after the time when the sheep could be sacrificed.

רָבָא אָמַר: לַאֲכִילָה אָתְיָין, וּגְזֵירָה מִשּׁוּם דְּרַבָּה, וְלָאו מִטַּעְמֵיהּ אֶלָּא מִקְּרָא.

Rava said that there is a different response to Rabba's proof: When the two loaves of *Shavuot* are brought by themselves, by Torah law **they come to be eaten, but** due to rabbinic **decree** they are not eaten and are left overnight until they are disqualified. The reason for the decree is **due to** that **which Rabba** said, i.e., due to the concern that the following year sheep will be available and nevertheless the nation will bring the two loaves without sheep. **But** the proof that by Torah law the loaves may be eaten is **not from** Rabba's line of **reasoning,** i.e., from the mishna in *Shekalim*; **rather,** it is **from a verse.**

וַאֲמַר רָבָא: מְנָא אָמִינָא לַהּ? דִּכְתִיב ״מִמּוֹשְׁבֹתֵיכֶם תָּבִיאוּ לֶחֶם תְּנוּפָה וגו׳ בִּכּוּרִים לַה׳״, מַה בִּכּוּרִים – בִּפְנֵי עַצְמָן, אַף שְׁתֵּי הַלֶּחֶם – בִּפְנֵי עַצְמָן. וּמִינַּהּ, מַה בִּכּוּרִים – לַאֲכִילָה, אַף שְׁתֵּי הַלֶּחֶם – נַמִּי לַאֲכִילָה.

And Rava said by way of explanation: **From where do I state** this *halakha*? From the fact **that it is written** with regard to the two loaves: **"You shall bring out of your dwellings** two **loaves of waving** of two tenth parts of an ephah; they shall be of fine flour, they shall be baked with leaven, **for first fruits to the Lord"** (Leviticus 23:17). **Just as first fruits**[B] are brought **by themselves,** without an accompanying animal offering, **so too the two loaves** are brought **by themselves** when there are no sheep available. **And** learn **from this** comparison to first fruits that **just as first fruits** are brought **to be eaten, so too the two loaves** are **also** brought **to be eaten,** even in the absence of the sheep brought as peace offerings.

HALAKHA

One may not burn consecrated items on a Festival – אֵין שׂוֹרְפִין קָדָשִׁים בְּיוֹם טוֹב: The burning of disqualified offerings, *notar*, and *piggul* is not performed on Shabbat or a Festival (Rambam *Sefer Avoda*, *Hilkhot Pesulei HaMukdashin* 19:5).

BACKGROUND

First fruits – בִּכּוּרִים: The obligation to bring first fruits to the Temple is stated in the Torah (see Deuteronomy 26:1–11) and is discussed in great detail in tractate *Bikkurim* and in the Jerusalem Talmud. This mitzva involves the bringing of a small amount of first fruits, one-sixtieth of the harvest, separated before *teruma* is separated from the crop. The first fruits must be brought from the seven types of fruit for which Eretz Yisrael is praised: Wheat, barley, grapes, figs, pomegranates, olives, and dates; these are brought to the Temple in Jerusalem. A festive ceremony accompanied the procession of the first fruits to the city. The owner of the fruit would bring his basket up to the altar, where he would wave it and recite prayers of praise and thanksgiving, whose texts appear in the Torah. At this stage of the ritual, the status of the first fruits becomes like that of *teruma*, and they belong to the priest.

תָּנוּ רַבָּנַן: כִּבְשֵׂי עֲצֶרֶת אֵין מְקַדְּשִׁין אֶת הַלֶּחֶם אֶלָּא בִּשְׁחִיטָה.

§ The Gemara cites further discussion of the two sheep and the two loaves of *Shavuot*: **The Sages taught** in a *baraita*: **The** two **sheep** of ***Shavuot*** **consecrate the** two **loaves** that accompany them **only by** means of their **slaughter.**[H]

כֵּיצַד? שְׁחָטָן לִשְׁמָן וְזָרַק דָּמָן לִשְׁמָן – קָדַשׁ הַלֶּחֶם, שְׁחָטָן שֶׁלֹּא לִשְׁמָן וְזָרַק דָּמָן שֶׁלֹּא לִשְׁמָן – לֹא קָדַשׁ הַלֶּחֶם. שְׁחָטָן לִשְׁמָן וְזָרַק דָּמָן שֶׁלֹּא לִשְׁמָן – הַלֶּחֶם קָדוֹשׁ וְאֵינוֹ קָדוֹשׁ, דִּבְרֵי רַבִּי. רַבִּי אֶלְעָזָר בְּרַבִּי שִׁמְעוֹן אוֹמֵר: לְעוֹלָם אֵינוֹ קָדוֹשׁ, עַד שֶׁיִּשְׁחוֹט לִשְׁמָן וְיִזְרוֹק דָּמָן לִשְׁמָן.

How so? If **one slaughtered** the sheep **for their** own **sake,** as the peace offerings that are supposed to be sacrificed on *Shavuot*, **and** then the priest **sprinkled their blood** on the altar **for their** own **sake,** then **the loaves are consecrated.**[N] But if **one slaughtered them not for their** own **sake, and** the priest **sprinkled their blood not for their** own **sake,**[N] **the loaves are not consecrated. If one slaughtered them for their** own **sake and he sprinkled their blood not for their** own **sake, the loaves are** partially **consecrated, but they are not** fully **consecrated.** This is **the statement of Rabbi** Yehuda HaNasi. **Rabbi Elazar, son of Rabbi Shimon, says:** The loaves are **never consecrated** at all **until one slaughters** the offerings **for their** own **sake and sprinkles their blood for their** own **sake.**

מַאי טַעְמָא דְּרַבִּי?

The Gemara asks: **What is the reasoning of Rabbi** Yehuda HaNasi, who holds that the slaughtering of the sheep partially consecrates the loaves even without the sprinkling of the blood?

דִּכְתִיב ״וְאֶת הָאַיִל יַעֲשֶׂה זֶבַח שְׁלָמִים לַה׳ עַל סַל הַמַּצּוֹת״ – לְמֵימְרָא דִּשְׁחִיטָה מְקַדְּשָׁא.

The Gemara answers: It is based on the fact **that it is written** concerning the ram brought by the nazirite when he completes his naziriteship: **"And he shall offer the ram for a sacrifice [*zevaḥ*] of peace offerings to the Lord, with the basket of unleavened bread"** (Numbers 6:17). Since the verse uses the word *zevaḥ*, which also means slaughter, and the verse then makes reference to the loaves, **that is to say that** it is specifically the **slaughter** that **consecrates** the loaves that accompany the offering. Similarly, the slaughter of the sheep brought as peace offerings on *Shavuot* consecrates the accompanying two loaves, as the *halakha* of the loaves of *Shavuot* is derived from that of the loaves of the nazirite.

וְרַבִּי אֶלְעָזָר בְּרַבִּי שִׁמְעוֹן? ״יַעֲשֶׂה״ – עַד שֶׁיַּעֲשֶׂה כׇּל עֲשִׂיּוֹתָיו.

The Gemara asks: **And** what is the reasoning of **Rabbi Elazar, son of Rabbi Shimon,** who holds that the slaughtering and sprinkling of the blood together consecrate the loaves? The Gemara answers: He derives it from the term: **"He shall offer,"** which he understands to mean that the loaves are not consecrated **until** the priest **performs all of the actions** included in the sacrificial rites of that offering, including the sprinkling of the blood.

וְרַבִּי נַמִי הָכְתִיב ״יַעֲשֶׂה״? אִי כְּתִיב ״זֶבַח יַעֲשֶׂה״ – כִּדְקָאָמְרַתְּ, הָשְׁתָּא דִּכְתִיב ״יַעֲשֶׂה זֶבַח״ – בַּמֶּה יַעֲשֶׂה? בִּזְבִיחָה.

The Gemara asks: **And** according to **Rabbi** Yehuda HaNasi **also, isn't it written: "He shall offer,"** which indicates that the loaves are consecrated only once the blood has been sprinkled on the altar? The Gemara answers: **If** it were **written: A sacrifice [*zevaḥ*] he shall offer,** it would be **as you are saying** that he should slaughter it and then perform a further action, i.e., sprinkling the blood, in order to consecrate the loaves. **Now that it is written: "He shall offer** the ram for **a sacrifice [*zevaḥ*],"** it should be understood as: **By what** means **should he offer** the ram in order to consecrate the loaves? **By** means **of slaughtering [*zeviḥa*].**

HALAKHA

The two sheep of *Shavuot* consecrate the two loaves that accompany them only by means of their slaughter – כִּבְשֵׂי עֲצֶרֶת אֵין מְקַדְּשִׁין אֶת הַלֶּחֶם אֶלָּא בִּשְׁחִיטָה: The two sheep of *Shavuot* consecrate the two loaves that accompany them only by means of their slaughter. How so? If they were slaughtered or their blood was sprinkled with the intent that the sheep are actually a different offering, the loaves are not consecrated. If they were slaughtered for their own sake but their blood was sprinkled not for their sake, the loaves are partially consecrated. If they were slaughtered not for their sake, even if the blood was sprinkled for their sake, the loaves are not consecrated. This is in accordance with the opinion of Rabbi Yehuda HaNasi. His opinion is accepted due to the principle that the *halakha* is in accordance with Rabbi Yehuda HaNasi when he disagrees with a single colleague. In addition, Rav Sheshet establishes that his opinion is in agreement with those of Rabbi Akiva and Rabbi Eliezer (Rambam *Sefer Avoda, Hilkhot Pesulei HaMukdashin* 17:18).

NOTES

The loaves are consecrated – קָדַשׁ הַלֶּחֶם: The loaves are actually consecrated even before the slaughter of the peace offerings and therefore may not be used for mundane purposes. The Gemara here means to say that the loaves are elevated from being the property of the Temple treasury and are now endowed with inherent sanctity as an offering. Consequently, after the blood of the sheep is sprinkled on the altar, the loaves may be eaten.

If one slaughtered them not for their own sake and the priest sprinkled their blood not for their own sake – שְׁחָטָן שֶׁלֹּא לִשְׁמָן וְזָרַק דָּמָן שֶׁלֹּא לִשְׁמָן: The early commentaries point out that whether or not the blood was sprinkled with the right intent is irrelevant; once the animal is slaughtered with the wrong intent, the loaves are disqualified. The *baraita* mentions the priest's intent during the sprinkling of the blood only because the sprinkling of the blood is important in the previous case and in the following case of the *baraita*, and therefore the *baraita* mentions it here (*Tosafot* on *Pesaḥim* 13b). This is in accordance with the Gemara in *Yevamot* (104b) and the Rambam (*Sefer Avoda, Hilkhot Pesulei HaMukdashin* 17:18).

וְרַבִּי אֶלְעָזָר בְּרַבִּי שִׁמְעוֹן הָכְתִיב ״זֶבַח״? הַהוּא מִיבָּעֵי לֵיהּ לְכִדְרַבִּי יוֹחָנָן, דְּאָמַר רַבִּי יוֹחָנָן: הַכֹּל מוֹדִים שֶׁצָּרִיךְ שֶׁיְּהֵא לֶחֶם בִּשְׁעַת שְׁחִיטָה.

The Gemara asks: **And** according to **Rabbi Elazar, son of Rabbi Shimon, isn't it written: "A sacrifice** [*zevaḥ*]," indicating that slaughtering alone consecrates the loaves? The Gemara answers: **He requires that** expression **for that which Rabbi Yoḥanan** says, **as Rabbi Yoḥanan says** that **everyone,** including Rabbi Elazar, son of Rabbi Shimon, **concedes that the loaves must be** in existence **at the time of the slaughter.**

מַאי ״קָדוֹשׁ וְאֵינוֹ קָדוֹשׁ״? אַבָּיֵי אָמַר: קָדוֹשׁ וְאֵינוֹ גָּמוּר, רָבָא אָמַר: קָדוֹשׁ וְאֵינוֹ נִיתָּר.

§ The Gemara asks: **What** is meant by Rabbi Yehuda HaNasi's statement in the *baraita* that if one slaughtered the sheep for their own sake and sprinkled their blood not for their own sake, then the loaves are partially **consecrated, but they are not** fully **consecrated? Abaye says:** The loaves are **consecrated** by means of the slaughtering, **but** their consecration is **not complete. Rava says:** The loaves are fully **consecrated** by means of the slaughtering, **but** they are **not** thereby **permitted** to be eaten.

מַאי בֵּינַיְיהוּ? אִיכָּא בֵּינַיְיהוּ לְמִיתְפַּס פִּדְיוֹנוֹ. לְאַבָּיֵי – לָא תָּפֵיס פִּדְיוֹנוֹ, לְרָבָא – תָּפֵיס פִּדְיוֹנוֹ.

The Gemara asks: **What is** the practical difference **between them?** Everyone concedes that the loaves may not be eaten as a result of this slaughtering. The Gemara answers: The practical difference **between them** is the ability **to transfer** sanctity to **their redemption** money. **According to Abaye,**[N] who holds that the loaves are not completely consecrated, they **do not transfer** sanctity to **their redemption** money if one tries to redeem them for money. **According to Rava,** who holds that the loaves are completely consecrated, they **transfer** sanctity to **their redemption** money.

בִּשְׁלָמָא לְרָבָא, הַיְינוּ דְּאִיכָּא בֵּין רַבִּי לְרַבִּי אֶלְעָזָר בְּרַבִּי שִׁמְעוֹן, אֶלָּא לְאַבָּיֵי מַאי אִיכָּא בֵּין רַבִּי לְרַבִּי אֶלְעָזָר בְּרַבִּי שִׁמְעוֹן?

The Gemara asks: **Granted, according to Rava,** who holds that according to Rabbi Yehuda HaNasi the loaves are completely sanctified, **that is** the difference **between** the opinions of **Rabbi** Yehuda HaNasi and **Rabbi Elazar, son of Rabbi Shimon.** But **according to Abaye, what** difference **is there between** the opinions of **Rabbi** Yehuda HaNasi and **Rabbi Elazar, son of Rabbi Shimon?**

אִיכָּא [בֵּינַיְיהוּ] לְאִיפְּסוּלֵי בְּיוֹצֵא.

The Gemara answers: The practical difference **between them** is **with regard to** whether the loaves are **rendered unfit by** means of **leaving** the Temple courtyard after the slaughtering of the offering. According to Rabbi Yehuda HaNasi, the loaves are rendered unfit if they leave the courtyard. According to Rabbi Elazar, son of Rabbi Shimon, who holds that the loaves are not consecrated, they are not rendered unfit if they leave the courtyard.

בְּעָא מִינֵּיהּ רַבִּי שְׁמוּאֵל בַּר רַב יִצְחָק מֵרַבִּי חִיָּיא בַּר אַבָּא: כִּבְשֵׂי עֲצֶרֶת שֶׁשְּׁחָטָן לִשְׁמָן וְזָרַק דָּמָן שֶׁלֹּא לִשְׁמָן, אוֹתוֹ הַלֶּחֶם מַהוּ בַּאֲכִילָה?

§ The Gemara continues the discussion of the dispute between Rabbi Yehuda HaNasi and Rabbi Elazar, son of Rabbi Shimon, concerning the consecration of the two loaves by means of the slaughter and sprinkling of the blood of the sheep of *Shavuot*. **Rabbi Shmuel bar Rav Yitzḥak raised a dilemma before Rabbi Ḥiyya bar Abba:** In the case of a communal peace offering of two **sheep** that accompany the two loaves on ***Shavuot*** **that one slaughtered for their sake but** the priest **sprinkled their blood not for their sake,** concerning **those** accompanying **loaves, what is** the *halakha* **with regard to eating** them?

NOTES

According to Abaye – **לְאַבָּיֵי**: Other versions of the Gemara text state that according to Abaye it does transfer sanctity to its redemption money and according to Rava it does not. Rashi had both versions of the text and initially offered the following interpretation of the standard version: According to Abaye, since the loaves have not been fully sanctified, their sanctity is not transferred to the money of their redemption, meaning that although the money does become sanctified, it can be used for other communal offerings. According to Rava, since the loaves have been fully sanctified, their sanctity is transferred to the money of their redemption. Rashi rejected this interpretation as being an outright error, as according to Rava, since the loaves have been fully sanctified they possess inherent sanctity and cannot be redeemed. Rashi therefore prefers the other version of the text.

אַלִּיבָּא דְּמַאן? אִי אַלִּיבָּא דְּרַבִּי אֶלְעָזָר בְּרַבִּי שִׁמְעוֹן – הָאָמַר: זְרִיקָה הִיא דִּמְקַדְּשָׁא! אִי אַלִּיבָּא דְּרַבִּי – בֵּין לְאַבָּיֵי בֵּין לְרָבָא קָדוֹשׁ וְאֵינוֹ נִיתָּר הוּא!

The Gemara asks: **In accordance with whose** opinion was this dilemma raised? **If** it was raised **in accordance with** the opinion **of Rabbi Elazar, son of Rabbi Shimon, doesn't he say** that **it is** the **sprinkling** of the blood **that consecrates the loaves?** Consequently, if the blood was not properly sprinkled, it is clear that the loves are unfit and may not be eaten. And **if** it was raised **in accordance with** the opinion **of Rabbi** Yehuda HaNasi, **both according to** the opinion **of Abaye and according to** that **of Rava,** Rabbi Yehuda HaNasi holds that the loaves **are consecrated but are not permitted** to be eaten.

אֶלָּא אַלִּיבָּא דְּהַאי תַּנָּא, דְּתָנֵי אֲבוּהּ דְּרַבִּי יִרְמְיָה בַּר אַבָּא: שְׁתֵּי הַלֶּחֶם שֶׁיָּצְאוּ בֵּין שְׁחִיטָה לִזְרִיקָה, וְזָרַק דָּמָן שֶׁל כְּבָשִׂים חוּץ לִזְמַנָּן – רַבִּי אֱלִיעֶזֶר אוֹמֵר: אֵין בַּלֶּחֶם מִשּׁוּם פִּיגּוּל, רַבִּי עֲקִיבָא אוֹמֵר: יֵשׁ בַּלֶּחֶם מִשּׁוּם פִּיגּוּל.

The Gemara responds: **Rather,** one must say that the question was asked **in accordance with** the opinion **of this** following *tanna***. As the father of Rabbi Yirmeya bar Abba**[N] **teaches** in a *baraita*: In a case where **the two loaves left** the Temple courtyard **between the slaughtering** of the offering **and** the **sprinkling** of its blood, **and** then the priest **sprinkled the blood of** the **sheep** with the intent that their meat would be eaten **beyond their** designated **time,** the sheep are rendered *piggul*. With regard to the loaves, **Rabbi Eliezer says: The loaves do not** become prohibited **due to** the prohibition of ***piggul*.**[B] **Rabbi Akiva says: The loaves do** become prohibited **due to** the prohibition of ***piggul*.**[H]

אָמַר רַב שֵׁשֶׁת: הָנֵי תַּנָּאֵי כְּרַבִּי סְבִירָא לְהוּ, דְּאָמַר: שְׁחִיטָה מְקַדְּשָׁא,

Rav Sheshet said: These *tanna'im*, Rabbi Eliezer and Rabbi Akiva, both **hold in accordance with** the opinion of **Rabbi** Yehuda HaNasi,[N] **who said:** The **slaughtering consecrates** the loaves by itself. Consequently, if the loaves are taken out of the Temple courtyard after the sheep are slaughtered, the loaves become disqualified.

מִיהוּ רַבִּי אֱלִיעֶזֶר לְטַעְמֵיהּ, דְּאָמַר: אֵין זְרִיקָה מוֹעֶלֶת לְיוֹצֵא, וְרַבִּי עֲקִיבָא לְטַעְמֵיהּ, דְּאָמַר: זְרִיקָה מוֹעֶלֶת לְיוֹצֵא.

But they disagree as to the following: **Rabbi Eliezer** conforms **to his** line of **reasoning, as** Rabbi Eliezer **says** that **sprinkling** the blood **is not effective with regard to** offerings that **left** the Temple courtyard. Since the loaves left the courtyard before the sprinkling of the blood, the intent of the priest while sprinkling the blood that the offering be eaten outside of its designated time does not render the loaves *piggul*. **And Rabbi Akiva** conforms **to his** line of **reasoning, as Rabbi Akiva says** that **sprinkling** the blood **is effective with regard to** offerings that **left** the Temple courtyard. Therefore, the intent of the priest while sprinkling the blood that the offering be eaten outside of its designated time renders the loaves *piggul*, even though they left the courtyard.

NOTES

The father of Rabbi Yirmeya bar Abba – אֲבוּהּ דְּרַבִּי יִרְמְיָה בַּר אַבָּא: This refers to Rabbi Abba. He is referred to in this roundabout way because his son was better known than he was (see Rashi on *Ḥullin* 38a). Alternatively, he is referred to in this way in order to distinguish him from another Sage of the same name.

Both hold in accordance with the opinion of Rabbi Yehuda HaNasi – הָנֵי תַּנָּאֵי כְּרַבִּי סְבִירָא לְהוּ: According to the understanding of Rav Sheshet, it follows that Rabbi Yehuda HaNasi holds that in a case where the sheep were slaughtered for their own sake and their blood was sprinkled not for its sake, the loaves are permitted to be eaten. Rav Sheshet understands Rabbi Yehuda HaNasi's opinion to be that the loaves are fully consecrated once the sheep are slaughtered, but if the blood is sprinkled with the wrong intent, the consecration was not performed in the optimum manner. This is different from the interpretations of Abaye and Rava, who hold that according to Rabbi Yehuda HaNasi the loaves may not be eaten (*Sefat Emet*).

BACKGROUND

***Piggul* – פִּיגּוּל:** The *halakha* of *piggul* is based on the verse: "And if any of the flesh of the sacrifice of his peace offerings be at all eaten on the third day, it shall not be accepted, neither shall it be imputed to him that offers it; it shall be *piggul*" (Leviticus 7:18). The Rabbis interpreted the verse as referring to one who had the intent during the performance of the sacrificial rites in the Temple to eat from the offering after its appointed time. That disqualifies the offering, and one who eats it is liable to receive *karet*. Some rabbis hold that it is *piggul* only when one expresses that intent aloud.

HALAKHA

The loaves do become prohibited due to the prohibition of *piggul* – יֵשׁ בַּלֶּחֶם מִשּׁוּם פִּיגּוּל: If the two loaves were brought out of the Temple courtyard between the slaughter of the two sheep and the sprinkling of their blood, and then the priest sprinkled the blood with the intent that the offering be eaten beyond its designated time, the loaves are rendered *piggul* even though they are outside of the courtyard. This is due to the fact that *piggul* is effective with regard to that which was brought outside of the Temple courtyard, even if it is still outside. This is in accordance with the opinion of Rabbi Akiva (Rambam *Sefer Avoda*, *Hilkhot Pesulei HaMukdashin* 17:19).

דִּתְנַן: אֵימוּרֵי קָדָשִׁים קַלִּים שֶׁיָּצְאוּ לִפְנֵי זְרִיקַת דָּמִים – רַבִּי אֱלִיעֶזֶר אוֹמֵר: אֵין מוֹעֲלִין בָּהֶן, וְאֵין חַיָּיבִין עֲלֵיהֶן מִשּׁוּם פִּיגּוּל וְנוֹתָר וְטָמֵא.

As we learned in a mishna (*Me'ila* 6b): In the case of **sacrificial portions of offerings of lesser sanctity**[HB] **that left** the Temple courtyard **before the sprinkling of the blood, Rabbi Eliezer says:** The sprinkling of the blood is completely ineffective with regard to these portions, and therefore one is **not** liable for **misusing them. And** if **one** eats **them, he is not liable due to** the prohibitions of ***piggul, notar,***[B] **or** of partaking of sacrificial meat while one is **ritually impure.**

רַבִּי עֲקִיבָא אוֹמֵר: מוֹעֲלִין בָּהֶן, וְחַיָּיבִין עֲלֵיהֶן מִשּׁוּם פִּיגּוּל וְנוֹתָר וְטָמֵא.

Rabbi Akiva says: The sprinkling is effective and therefore, one is liable for **misusing them. And** if **one** eats **them he is liable due to** the prohibitions of ***piggul, notar,* or** of partaking of sacrificial meat while one is **ritually impure.**

מַאי?

The Gemara now concludes the dilemma that Rabbi Shmuel bar Rav Yitzḥak raised before Rabbi Ḥiyya bar Abba: According to the opinion of Rabbi Akiva, **what** is the *halakha* with regard to eating the loaves when the sheep were slaughtered for their own sake, but their blood was sprinkled not for their sake?

מִדִּזְרִיקַת פִּיגּוּל קָבְעָה לַלֶּחֶם בְּפִיגּוּל בְּיוֹצֵא כְּבָשָׂר, זְרִיקָה שֶׁלֹּא לִשְׁמָהּ נַמִּי שָׁרְיָא לֵיהּ לַלֶּחֶם. אוֹ דִּלְמָא, לְחוּמְרָא – אָמְרִינַן, לְקוּלָּא – לָא אָמְרִינַן?

The Gemara clarifies the two sides of the dilemma: Should one say that **from** the fact **that sprinkling** the blood of the sheep in a manner that renders it ***piggul***[H] **renders** the loaves ***piggul,* like the meat** of the offering, despite the fact that the loaves were disqualified **by leaving** the courtyard of the Temple, it can be derived that **sprinkling** the blood **not for its own sake also permits the loaves** to be eaten, just as it permits the meat of the sheep to be eaten? **Or perhaps** it is only **to be stringent** that **we say** that sprinkling the blood is effective with regard to loaves that have left the Temple courtyard, but **we do not say** this in order **to be lenient,** e.g., to render the loaves permitted to be eaten.

מַתְקִיף לַהּ רַב פָּפָּא: וּמִמַּאי דְּכִי אִיתְנְהוּ אַבָּרָאֵי פְּלִיגִי?

Rav Pappa objects to this understanding of the dispute between Rabbi Akiva and Rabbi Eliezer. **From where** do we know that **they disagree** in a case **where** the loaves **are outside** the courtyard at the time of the sprinkling?

דִּילְמָא בְּדְאִיתְנְהוּ אַבָּרָאֵי – דְּכוּלֵּי עָלְמָא לָא פְּלִיגִי דְּאֵין זְרִיקָה מוֹעֶלֶת לְיוֹצֵא. וּבַהֲדַר עַיְּילִינְהוּ פְּלִיגִי, דְּרַבִּי אֱלִיעֶזֶר סָבַר לַהּ כְּרַבִּי, דְּאָמַר: שְׁחִיטָה מְקַדְּשָׁא, וְאִיפַּסְלוּ לְהוּ בְּיוֹצֵא.

Perhaps in a case **where** the loaves **are** still **outside** the courtyard **everyone agrees that sprinkling** the blood **is not effective with regard to** offerings that **left** the Temple courtyard, **and they disagree in** a case **where** the loaves left the courtyard and **one then brought them** back into the courtyard before the sprinkling. **As Rabbi Eliezer holds in accordance with** the opinion of **Rabbi** Yehuda HaNasi, **who said:** The **slaughter** of the sheep **consecrates** the loaves, **and** therefore the loaves **became disqualified by leaving** the courtyard after the sheep were slaughtered. Consequently, even if they were brought back into the courtyard before the sprinkling of the blood they cannot become *piggul* because they have already been disqualified for a different reason.

וְרַבִּי עֲקִיבָא כְּרַבִּי אֶלְעָזָר בְּרַבִּי שִׁמְעוֹן, דְּאָמַר: שְׁחִיטָה לָא מְקַדְּשָׁא, וְלָא מִיפַּסְלִי בְּיוֹצֵא!

And Rabbi Akiva holds **in accordance with** the opinion of **Rabbi Elazar, son of Rabbi Shimon, who said:** The **slaughter** of the sheep **does not consecrate** the loaves at all before the sprinkling of the blood. Since the loaves were not yet consecrated, **they do not become disqualified by leaving** the Temple courtyard.[N]

HALAKHA

Sacrificial portions of offerings of lesser sanctity, etc. – 'אֵימוּרֵי קָדָשִׁים קַלִּים וכו: In a case of sacrificial portions of offerings of lesser sanctity that were removed from the Temple courtyard before the offering's blood was sprinkled, and the blood was sprinkled while they were still outside of the courtyard, the offering is not disqualified. If the portions are brought back in, the Rambam holds that they are burned on the altar. The Ra'avad holds that they are not burned on the altar. Even if these portions remain outside the courtyard, the prohibitions of *piggul*, *notar*, and of partaking of sacrificial meat while one is ritually impure apply to them. This is in accordance with the opinion of Rabbi Akiva, as interpreted by Rav Pappa (Rambam *Sefer Avoda, Hilkhot Pesulei HaMukdashin* 1:33, and see *Kesef Mishne* and *Leḥem Mishne* there).

Sprinkling the blood in a manner that renders it *piggul* – זְרִיקַת פִּיגּוּל: If an offering of lesser sanctity was rendered *piggul*, its sacrificial portions are not subject to the prohibition against misuse of consecrated property even though the blood was sprinkled. This is in accordance with the opinion of Rav Giddel in the name of Rav (Rambam *Sefer Avoda, Hilkhot Me'ila* 3:3).

NOTES

They do not become disqualified by leaving the Temple courtyard – לָא מִיפַּסְלִי בְּיוֹצֵא: Consequently, if they are brought back into the courtyard and the priest sprinkles the blood of the sheep with the intent that the offering will be consumed beyond the proper time, even the loaves become *piggul*. Nevertheless, even Rabbi Akiva would agree that an improper sprinkling is not effective with regard to the loaves, e.g., if the blood of the sheep is sprinkled while the loaves are outside the courtyard they do not become *piggul*. Similarly, if the blood is sprinkled for the sake of a different offering, although the meat of the sheep is permitted to be eaten, the loaves are not permitted to be eaten.

BACKGROUND

Offerings of lesser sanctity – קָדָשִׁים קַלִּים: In this category are the various types of individual peace offerings, the thanksgiving offering, the nazirite's ram, the male firstborn of a kosher animal, the animal tithes, and the Paschal offering. These offerings may be slaughtered anywhere in the Temple courtyard. With the exception of the thanksgiving offering, the nazirite's ram, and the Paschal offering, they may be eaten during a period of two days and the intervening night from the time they were sacrificed. They may be eaten by the people bringing the offering and any ritually pure, circumcised individual whom they invite, except for the firstborn offering, which may be eaten only by the priests and their wives, children, and slaves. There is no need to consume them within the Temple, but they must be eaten within the walls of Jerusalem. The prohibition against misuse of consecrated property applies only to those portions of offerings consumed on the altar and only after the blood has been sprinkled on the altar.

***Notar* – נוֹתָר:** This refers to parts of an offering left over after the time when it is permitted to be eaten. One who eats *notar* is liable to receive *karet*. The Sages decreed that the leftover portion be considered ritually impure so that the priests would be prompt and meticulous in its removal.

NOTES

Wasn't that which Rav Giddel says that Rav says conclusively refuted – לָאו אִיתּוֹתַב דְּרַב גִּידֵּל אָמַר רַב: This Gemara here does not explain the basis for his opinion being rejected. The Gemara in *Me'ila* (3b) adds that Rav Pappa asked Abaye concerning this *halakha* based on the mishna (*Menaḥot* 78b) that states that if one slaughters the thanks offering with the intent to eat the meat or to sacrifice its portions outside of its designated time or place, the loaves are nevertheless consecrated to the extent that they are subject to the prohibition against misuse. Since the thanks offering is an offering of lesser sanctity, this contradicts Rav's assertion that sprinkling with the intent of *piggul* does not subject such offerings to the prohibition against misuse. The Gemara there records that Abaye was unable to defend Rav's statement against this question.

HALAKHA

And the loaves were then lost – וְאָבַד הַלֶּחֶם: In a case where the two sheep of *Shavuot* were slaughtered for their own sake and then the accompanying loaves were lost, if the blood was sprinkled for its own sake, the sheep are disqualified. If the blood was sprinkled with the intent to eat the meat after the designated time, then there is an uncertainty as to whether or not the meat has been rendered permitted to be eaten (Rambam *Sefer Avoda, Hilkhot Pesulei HaMukdashin* 17:20, and see Mahari Kurkus and *Kesef Mishne* there).

Paschal offering before midday – פֶּסַח קוֹדֶם חֲצוֹת: If the Paschal offering was slaughtered for the sake of a different offering or as a non-sacred animal, it is disqualified. This is the *halakha* only when it was slaughtered on the fourteenth of Nisan, even if it was slaughtered in the morning, before the Paschal offering is allowed to be slaughtered. If it was slaughtered on a different day as a different offering, it is valid. This is in accordance with the mishna on *Zevaḥim* 2a and the opinion of ben Beteira cited on *Zevaḥim* 11b (Rambam *Sefer Avoda, Hilkhot Pesulei HaMukdashin* 15:11).

הַאי מַאי? אִי אָמְרַתְּ בִּשְׁלָמָא רַבִּי עֲקִיבָא כְּרַבִּי סְבִירָא לֵיהּ, דְּאָמַר: שְׁחִיטָה מְקַדְּשָׁא לְהוּ – הַיְינוּ דְּקָאָמַר רַבִּי עֲקִיבָא דְּקָדְשִׁי לְהוּ בִּשְׁחִיטָה, וְאָתְיָא זְרִיקָה קָבְעָה לְהוּ בְּפִיגּוּל.

The Gemara asks: **What is this** interpretation of the dispute between Rabbi Akiva and Rabbi Eliezer? It does not fit what they say. **Granted, if you say** that **Rabbi Akiva holds in accordance with** the opinion of **Rabbi** Yehuda HaNasi, **who said:** The **slaughter** of the sheep **consecrates** the loaves, **that is what Rabbi Akiva** means when he **says that** the loaves **are consecrated by** the **slaughter** of the sheep **and** then the **sprinkling** that was done with the intent to consume the offering after its appointed time **comes and renders** the loaves ***piggul.***

אֶלָּא אִי אָמְרַתְּ כְּרַבִּי אֶלְעָזָר בְּרַבִּי שִׁמְעוֹן סְבִירָא לֵיהּ, דְּאָמַר: זְבִיחָה לָא מְקַדְּשָׁא, זְרִיקַת פִּיגּוּל מִי מְקַדְּשָׁא?

But if you say that Rabbi Akiva holds **in accordance with** the opinion of **Rabbi Elazar, son of Rabbi Shimon, who said:** The **slaughter** of the sheep **does not consecrate** the loaves without the sprinkling of the blood, **does sprinkling** with an intent that renders the sheep ***piggul*** actually **consecrate** the loaves?

וְהָאָמַר רַב גִּידֵּל, אָמַר רַב: זְרִיקַת פִּיגּוּל אֵינָהּ מְבִיאָה לִידֵי מְעִילָה וְאֵינָהּ מוֹצִיאָה מִידֵי מְעִילָה.

But doesn't Rav Giddel say that **Rav says: Sprinkling** with an intent that renders an offering ***piggul*** **does not cause** items **to** become subject to the prohibition against **misuse** of consecrated property, **and it does not remove** items **from** being subject to the prohibition against **misuse** of consecrated property?

אֵינָהּ מְבִיאָה לִידֵי מְעִילָה – בְּאֵימוּרֵי קָדָשִׁים קַלִּים,

Rav explains: The *halakha* that it **does not cause** items **to** become subject to the prohibition against **misuse** of consecrated property applies **with regard to sacrificial portions of offerings of lesser sanctity.** The prohibition against misusing consecrated property applies to: "The sacred items of the Lord" (Leviticus 5:15). Consequently, it does not apply to offerings of lesser sanctity, as the meat is the property of those who brought the offering, and the sacrificial portions are disqualified by the sprinkling performed with improper intent.

וְאֵינָהּ מוֹצִיאָה מִידֵי מְעִילָה – בִּבְשַׂר קָדְשֵׁי קָדָשִׁים!

And the *halakha* that **it does not remove** items **from** being subject to the prohibition against **misuse** of consecrated property applies **with regard to meat of offerings of the most sacred order,** such as a sin offering, a guilt offering, or a communal peace offering. Since the sprinkling of the blood was not valid, the meat, which would have become permitted for the priests to eat, retains the status of "the sacred items of the Lord," and the prohibition against misuse of consecrated property still applies.

לָאו אִיתּוֹתַב דְּרַב גִּידֵּל אָמַר רַב?!

The Gemara rejects this explanation: **Wasn't that which Rav Giddel says that Rav says conclusively refuted?**[N] Consequently, one cannot ask a question based on this statement.

בְּעָא מִינֵּיהּ רַבִּי יִרְמְיָה מֵרַבִּי זֵירָא: כִּבְשֵׂי עֲצֶרֶת שֶׁשְּׁחָטָן לִשְׁמָן וְאָבַד הַלֶּחֶם, מַהוּ שֶׁיִּזְרוֹק דָּמָן שֶׁלֹּא לִשְׁמָן לְהַתִּיר בָּשָׂר בַּאֲכִילָה?

§ The Gemara cites another dilemma concerning the sheep and loaves of *Shavuot.* **Rabbi Yirmeya raised a dilemma before Rabbi Zeira:** In a case of the two **sheep of *Shavuot* that one slaughtered for their own sake,** thereby establishing a bond between the sheep and the loaves, **and the loaves were** then **lost,**[H] if the blood of the sheep would be sprinkled for their sake, the meat would not be permitted to be eaten because the loaves were lost. That said, **what is** the *halakha* with regard to whether the priest may **sprinkle their blood not for their own sake** but rather for the sake of a peace offering in order **to permit** the **meat** of the sheep **to be eaten?**

אֲמַר לֵיהּ: יֵשׁ לְךָ דָּבָר שֶׁאֵינוֹ כָּשֵׁר לִשְׁמוֹ, וְכָשֵׁר שֶׁלֹּא לִשְׁמוֹ?! וְלָא? וַהֲרֵי פֶּסַח קוֹדֶם חֲצוֹת, דְּאֵינוֹ כָּשֵׁר לִשְׁמוֹ וְכָשֵׁר שֶׁלֹּא לִשְׁמוֹ!

Rabbi Zeira **said to** Rabbi Yirmeya: **Do you have anything that is not fit** if the sacrificial rites are performed **for its own sake, and** yet it is **fit** if the sacrificial rites are performed **not for its own sake?** This is certainly not a logical option. Rabbi Yirmeya responded: **And is** there **no** precedent for this? **But there is** the **Paschal offering before midday**[H] on the fourteenth of Nisan, **which is not fit** if it is slaughtered **for its own sake,** as it is before the proper time for the Paschal offering, **and** yet it is **fit** if it is slaughtered **not for its own sake** but rather for the sake of a peace offering.

הָכִי קָא אָמֵינָא: יֵשׁ לָךְ דָּבָר שֶׁנִּרְאֶה לִשְׁמוֹ וְנִדְחֶה מִלִּשְׁמוֹ, וְאֵינוֹ כָּשֵׁר לִשְׁמוֹ וְכָשֵׁר שֶׁלֹּא לִשְׁמוֹ?

Rabbi Zeira replied: **This is what I** was **saying: Do you have anything that was fit** to be sacrificed **for its own sake,** like these sheep of *Shavuot* that were slaughtered before the loaves were lost, **and was** then **rejected from** being sacrificed **for its own sake,** like these sheep when the loaves were lost, **and is not fit** if it is sacrificed **for its own sake, and** yet it is **fit** if it is sacrificed **not for its own sake?**

וְלָא? וַהֲרֵי פֶּסַח אַחַר זְמַנּוֹ בִּשְׁאָר יְמוֹת הַשָּׁנָה קוֹדֶם חֲצוֹת!

Rabbi Yirmeya responded: **And** is there **no** precedent for this? **But there is** the **Paschal offering,** which was fit to be sacrificed for its own sake during its designated time, and **after its** designated **time, during** the **rest of the days of the year before midday,**[N] it is not fit to be sacrificed as a Paschal offering but it is fit to be sacrificed as a peace offering.

הָכִי קָאָמֵינָא: יֵשׁ לָךְ דָּבָר שֶׁנִּרְאֶה לִשְׁמוֹ וְנִשְׁחַט לִשְׁמוֹ וְנִדְחֶה מִלִּשְׁמוֹ, וְאֵינוֹ כָּשֵׁר לִשְׁמוֹ וְכָשֵׁר שֶׁלֹּא לִשְׁמוֹ?

Rabbi Zeira replied: **This is what I** was **saying: Do you have anything that was fit** to be sacrificed **for its own sake,** like the two sheep of *Shavuot* that were slaughtered before the loaves were lost, **and it was slaughtered for its own sake, and was** then **rejected from** being sacrificed **for its own sake,** like the two sheep when the loaves were lost, **and it is not fit** if it is sacrificed **for its own sake, and** yet it is **fit** if it is sacrificed **not for its own sake?**

וְלָא? וַהֲרֵי תּוֹדָה!

Rabbi Yirmeya responded: **And** is there **no** precedent for this? **But there is** the **thanks offering,** as the Gemara (46a) states that if the thanks offering was slaughtered and then its accompanying loaves broke into pieces and thereby became disqualified, the blood should be sprinkled for the sake of a peace offering rather than a thanks offering, and then the meat may be eaten. Yet, if the blood was sprinkled for the sake of a thanks offering, the meat would not be permitted to be eaten.

שָׁאנֵי תּוֹדָה, דְּרַחֲמָנָא קַרְיֵיהּ "שְׁלָמִים".

Rabbi Zeira answered: The **thanks offering is different, as the Merciful One called it a peace offering** (see Leviticus 7:13). Just as a peace offering is sacrificed without loaves, so too a thanks offering may sometimes be sacrificed without loaves. Therefore, the loss of the loaves does not render the thanks offering disqualified, and this case is not comparable to the case of the two sheep and two loaves of *Shavuot*.

תָּנוּ רַבָּנַן: שָׁחַט שְׁנֵי כְבָשִׂים עַל אַרְבַּע חַלּוֹת – מוֹשֵׁךְ שְׁתַּיִם מֵהֶן וּמְנִיפָן,

§ The Gemara cites another discussion concerning the sheep and loaves of *Shavuot*. **The Sages taught** in a *baraita*: If one **slaughtered** the **two sheep** as required but they were accompanied **by four loaves**[H] rather than the requisite two loaves, **he draws two of** the loaves from the four **and waves them** together with the sheep,

Perek **IV**
Daf **48** Amud **a**

וְהַשְּׁאָר נֶאֱכָלוֹת בְּפִדְיוֹן. אֲמַרוּהָ רַבָּנַן קַמֵּיהּ דְּרַב חִסְדָּא: הָא – דְּלָא כְּרַבִּי.

and the rest of the loaves **are** permitted to be **eaten through redemption. The Sages said** the following **before Rav Ḥisda: This** *baraita* **is not in accordance with** the opinion of **Rabbi** Yehuda HaNasi,[N] who holds that the slaughter of the sheep grants the loaves inherent sanctity, and in this case two of the loaves have inherent sanctity but it is not known which ones.

דְּאִי רַבִּי – כֵּיוָן דְּאָמַר: שְׁחִיטָה מְקַדְּשָׁא, דְּפָרֵיק לְהוּ הֵיכָא?

As, if the *baraita* **is** in accordance with the opinion of **Rabbi** Yehuda HaNasi, **since he says** that the **slaughter** of the sheep **consecrates** the loaves with inherent sanctity, when the *baraita* states **that he redeems** the loaves, **where** does he redeem them?

NOTES

During the rest of the days of the year before midday – בִּשְׁאָר יְמוֹת הַשָּׁנָה קוֹדֶם חֲצוֹת: The standard version of the text includes the words: Before midday, at the end of this sentence. It is not clear what this clause would mean in context, as there is no difference whether one sacrifices the animal before or after midday.

This *baraita* is not in accordance with the opinion of Rabbi Yehuda HaNasi – הָא דְּלָא כְּרַבִּי: Rashi explains that the *baraita* is understood according to the opinion of Rabbi Elazar, son of Rabbi Shimon, who holds that slaughtering the sheep does not invest the loaves with inherent sanctity. Consequently, two of the loaves can be waved with the sheep before the blood of the sheep is sprinkled, and the other two can be taken outside the Temple courtyard and redeemed there.

HALAKHA

If one slaughtered the two sheep but they were accompanied by four loaves – שָׁחַט שְׁנֵי כְבָשִׂים עַל אַרְבַּע חַלּוֹת: In a case where one slaughtered the two sheep but they were accompanied by four loaves, if he stipulated that two of them should be consecrated, he should wave two of the loaves together with the offering. He should then redeem the other two in the Temple courtyard, after which they may be brought out of the Temple courtyard and eaten as non-sacred food. If he did not stipulate that only two of them should be consecrated, then none of the loaves are consecrated. This is in accordance with the *baraita* and the opinion of Rabbi Yoḥanan (Rambam *Sefer Avoda, Hilkhot Temidin UMusafin* 8:12).

אִי דְּפָרֵיק לְהוּ מֵאַבְּרָאֵי – כֵּיוָן דִּכְתִיב "לִפְנֵי ה׳", אִיפְּסִיל לְהוּ בְּיוֹצֵא! אִי גַּוַּואי – הָא מְעַיֵּיל חוּלִּין לַעֲזָרָה!

The process of redemption would be to place all four loaves in front of him and state that whichever two of the loaves do not have inherent sanctity are redeemed for money. **If he redeems them outside** of the Temple courtyard, **since it is written:** "And the priest shall wave them with the bread of the first fruits for a wave offering **before the Lord,** with the two lambs" (Leviticus 23:20), **he disqualifies** the two loaves that possess inherent sanctity **by** causing them to **leave** the courtyard, at which point they are no longer "before the Lord." Conversely, **if** he redeems them **inside** the courtyard, once the two loaves that do not possess inherent sanctity are redeemed, he violates the prohibition against **bringing non-sacred** items **into the** Temple **courtyard.**

אֲמַר לְהוּ רַב חִסְדָּא: לְעוֹלָם כְּרַבִּי, וּפָרֵיק לְהוּ גַּוַּואי, וְחוּלִּין מִמֵּילָא קָא הָוְיָין.

Rav Ḥisda said to them: **Actually** the *baraita* is **in accordance with** the opinion of **Rabbi** Yehuda HaNasi, **and** one **redeems** the loaves **inside**[N] the courtyard. Nevertheless, it is not considered to be a violation of the prohibition against bringing non-sacred items into the courtyard because the **non-sacred** loaves **came** into the courtyard **by themselves,** i.e., they were already there when they became non-sacred and were not actively brought into the courtyard in their non-sacred state.

אֲמַר לֵיהּ רָבִינָא לְרַב אַשִׁי, וְהָתַנְיָא: כְּשֶׁהוּא פּוֹדָן, אֵין פּוֹדָן אֶלָּא בַּחוּץ!

Ravina said to Rav Ashi: But isn't it taught in a *baraita* with regard to this very case: **When he redeems** the loaves, **he** may **redeem them only outside** of the courtyard? This contradicts Rav Ḥisda's claim that according to Rabbi Yehuda HaNasi one redeems the loaves inside the courtyard.

הָא וַדַּאי רַבִּי אֶלְעָזָר בְּרַבִּי שִׁמְעוֹן הִיא, דְּאִי רַבִּי – הָא אִיפְּסְלוּ לְהוּ בְּיוֹצֵא.

Rav Ashi answered: **This** *baraita* **is certainly** in accordance with the opinion of **Rabbi Elazar, son of Rabbi Shimon,**[N] **because if** it were in accordance with the opinion of **Rabbi** Yehuda HaNasi, when he brings the loaves outside the courtyard **he thereby disqualifies them by** causing them to **leave** the courtyard.

אֲמַר לֵיהּ רַב אַחָא בְּרֵיהּ דְּרָבָא לְרַב אַשִׁי: לֵימָא, תֶּיהֱוֵי תְּיוּבְתֵּיהּ דְּרַבִּי יוֹחָנָן, מֵיהָא דְּאִיתְּמַר: תּוֹדָה שֶׁשְּׁחָטָהּ עַל שְׁמוֹנִים חַלּוֹת – חִזְקִיָּה אָמַר: קָדְשׁוּ אַרְבָּעִים מִתּוֹךְ שְׁמוֹנִים, וְרַבִּי יוֹחָנָן אָמַר: לֹא קָדְשׁוּ אַרְבָּעִים מִתּוֹךְ שְׁמוֹנִים!

§ **Rav Aḥa, son of Rava, said to Rav Ashi: Let us say** that the *baraita,* which states that if the sheep of *Shavuot* are slaughtered with four loaves instead of two, two of the four are invested with inherent sanctity, **is a conclusive refutation** of the opinion **of Rabbi Yoḥanan that was stated** with regard to **a thanks offering that one slaughtered** accompanied **by eighty loaves**[H] rather than the required forty. In that case, **Ḥizkiyya says: Forty of the eighty** loaves **are consecrated, and Rabbi Yoḥanan says: Not** even **forty of** the **eighty** loaves **are consecrated.**

וְלָאו מִי אִיתְּמַר עֲלַהּ, אָמַר רַבִּי זֵירָא: הַכֹּל מוֹדִים הֵיכָא דְּאָמַר "לִיקַדְּשׁוּ אַרְבָּעִים מִתּוֹךְ שְׁמוֹנִים" דְּקָדְשָׁה? הָכָא נַמִי דְּאָמַר "לִיקַדְּשׁוּ תַּרְתֵּי מִתּוֹךְ אַרְבַּע".

The Gemara answers: **Wasn't it stated with regard to this** dispute that **Rabbi Zeira says: Everyone,** even Rabbi Yoḥanan, **concedes** that in a case **where** the individual bringing the offering **said: Let forty of** the **eighty** loaves **be consecrated,**[H] **that** forty **are consecrated? Here too,** one can say that the *baraita* is referring to a case **where one said: Let two of the four** loaves **be consecrated.**

תָּנֵי רַבִּי חֲנִינָא טִירָתָא קַמֵּיהּ דְּרַבִּי יוֹחָנָן: שָׁחַט אַרְבָּעָה כְּבָשִׂים עַל שְׁתֵּי חַלּוֹת – מוֹשֵׁךְ שְׁנַיִם מֵהֶן, וְזוֹרֵק דָּמָן שֶׁלֹּא לִשְׁמָן.

§ The Gemara cites another discussion concerning the sheep and loaves of *Shavuot.* **Rabbi Ḥanina Tirata taught** a *baraita* **before Rabbi Yoḥanan: If one slaughtered four sheep** for *Shavuot*, rather than the required two, accompanied **by two loaves,**[H] he **draws two of** the sheep out of the four **and sprinkles their blood not for the sake** of the sheep of *Shavuot.* He then sprinkles the blood of the other sheep for the sake of the sheep of *Shavuot.*

שֶׁאִם אִי אַתָּה אוֹמֵר כָּךְ, הִפְסַדְתָּ אֶת הָאַחֲרוֹנִים.

As, if you do not say to do **this,** but rather require him to first sprinkle the blood of two of the sheep for their own sake, then **you have caused the loss of the latter** two sheep. Since they were previously fit to have their blood sprinkled on the altar for the sake of the sheep of *Shavuot,* and were disqualified from this status when the blood of the other two sheep was sprinkled for that purpose, they are no longer fit to have their blood sprinkled even for the sake of a different offering.

NOTES

And one redeems the loaves inside – וּפָרֵיק לְהוּ גַּוַּואי: After the loaves are redeemed they are eaten inside the courtyard, as it is not known which loaves have inherent sanctity and which have been redeemed.

This *baraita* is certainly in accordance with the opinion of Rabbi Elazar son of Rabbi Shimon – הָא וַדַּאי רַבִּי אֶלְעָזָר בְּרַבִּי שִׁמְעוֹן הִיא: This seems to indicate that whereas this *baraita* is certainly in accordance with the opinion of Rabbi Elazar, son of Rabbi Shimon, the previous *baraita* can be understood in accordance with the opinion of Rabbi Yehuda HaNasi. Rashi holds that the first *baraita* is also in accordance with the opinion of Rabbi Elazar, son of Rabbi Shimon. By contrast, the Rambam rules in accordance with the first *baraita* and also rules that the redemption must be performed inside the courtyard. This indicates that he holds in accordance with the opinion of Rabbi Yehuda HaNasi and accepts the reasoning that there is no prohibition against redeeming items and thereby rendering them non-sacred in the Temple courtyard (Mahari Kurkus; *Ḥok Natan*).

HALAKHA

A thanks offering that one slaughtered accompanied by eighty loaves – תּוֹדָה שֶׁשְּׁחָטָהּ עַל שְׁמוֹנִים חַלּוֹת: If a thanks offering was slaughtered with eighty loaves, not even forty of them become consecrated. This is in accordance with the opinion of Rabbi Yoḥanan (Rambam *Sefer Avoda, Hilkhot Pesulei HaMukdashin* 12:15).

Let forty of the eighty loaves be consecrated – לִיקַדְּשׁוּ אַרְבָּעִים מִתּוֹךְ שְׁמוֹנִים: If a thanks offering was slaughtered with eighty loaves, and the owner of the offering had stipulated that forty of the eighty loaves should be consecrated, he selects forty out of the eighty loaves. These loaves must comprise four different types of loaves, and one of each type is set aside for the priests. The forty loaves that were not selected are redeemed and rendered non-sacred. This is in accordance with the opinion of Rabbi Yoḥanan as interpreted by Rabbi Zeira. The *Kesef Mishne* discusses why the Rambam did not decide the *halakha* in accordance with Ḥizkiyya, who was Rabbi Yoḥanan's teacher (Rambam *Sefer Avoda, Hilkhot Pesulei HaMukdashin* 12:15).

If one slaughtered four sheep for *Shavuot* accompanied by two loaves – שָׁחַט אַרְבָּעָה כְּבָשִׂים עַל שְׁתֵּי חַלּוֹת: If one slaughtered four sheep accompanied by the two loaves, he selects two of them and sprinkles the blood of those sheep not for their own sake, and waves the remaining two sheep together with the two loaves. This is in accordance with the opinion of Rabbi Ḥanina Tirata (Rambam *Sefer Avoda, Hilkhot Temidin UMusafin* 8:13).

אָמַר לוֹ רַבִּי יוֹחָנָן: וְכִי אוֹמֵר לוֹ לְאָדָם ״עֲמוֹד וַחֲטָא בִּשְׁבִיל שֶׁתִּזְכֶּה״?!

Rabbi Yoḥanan said to Rabbi Ḥanina Tirata: **And does** the court **say to a person: Arise and sin in order that you may gain?** Is it proper for the priest to sprinkle the blood of the first pair not for their own sake so that the second pair will remain fit?

וְהָתְנַן: אֵבְרֵי חַטָּאת שֶׁנִּתְעָרְבוּ בְּאֵבְרֵי עוֹלָה – רַבִּי אֱלִיעֶזֶר אוֹמֵר: יִתְּנוּ לְמַעְלָה, וְרוֹאֶה אֲנִי אֶת בְּשַׂר חַטָּאת לְמַעְלָה כְּאִילּוּ הִיא עֵצִים. וַחֲכָמִים אוֹמְרִים: תְּעוּבַּר צוּרָתָן וְיֵצְאוּ לְבֵית הַשְּׂרֵיפָה.

But didn't we learn in a mishna (*Zevaḥim* 77a) that *tanna'im* disagree concerning this matter? The mishna teaches: In the case of **the limbs of a sin offering,** whose flesh is eaten by priests and may not be burned on the altar, **that were intermingled with the limbs of a burnt offering,**[H] which are burned on the altar, **Rabbi Eliezer says:** The priest **shall place** all the limbs **above,** on the altar, **and I view the flesh** of the limbs **of the sin offering above** on the altar **as though they are** pieces of **wood** burned on the altar, not an offering. **And the Rabbis say:** One should wait until **the form of** all the intermingled limbs **decays and they will** all **go out to the place of burning** in the Temple courtyard, where all disqualified offerings of the most sacred order are burned.

אַמַּאי? לֵימָא ״עֲמוֹד וַחֲטָא בִּשְׁבִיל שֶׁתִּזְכֶּה״!

Rabbi Yoḥanan continued: According to your opinion, **why** do the Rabbis say that the mixture is burned? **Let** the court **say** to the priest instead: **Arise and sin** by burning all the limbs on the altar, including the limbs of the sin offering, **in order that you may gain** by performing the mitzva of sacrificing the limbs of the burnt offering.

״עֲמוֹד וַחֲטָא בְּחַטָּאת בִּשְׁבִיל שֶׁתִּזְכֶּה בְּחַטָּאת״ – אָמְרִינַן, ״עֲמוֹד וַחֲטָא בְּחַטָּאת בִּשְׁבִיל שֶׁתִּזְכֶּה בְּעוֹלָה״ – לָא אָמְרִינַן.

Rabbi Ḥanina Tirata answered Rabbi Yoḥanan: **We do say: Arise and sin with a sin offering in order that you may gain with regard to a sin offering,** since it is the same type of offering. Similarly, one may sin with regard to the sheep of *Shavuot* in order to gain with regard to the other sheep brought for the same offering. **We do not say: Arise and sin with a sin offering in order that you may gain with regard to a burnt offering.** Therefore, the Rabbis prohibit burning the limbs of the sin offering on the altar in order to allow for the burning of the limbs of the burnt offering.

וּבַחֲדָא מִילְּתָא מִי אֲמַר? וְהָא תַּנְיָא: כִּבְשֵׂי עֲצֶרֶת שֶׁשְּׁחָטָן שֶׁלֹּא לִשְׁמָן, אוֹ שֶׁשְּׁחָטָן בֵּין לִפְנֵי זְמַנָּן בֵּין לְאַחַר זְמַנָּן – הַדָּם יִזָּרֵק וְהַבָּשָׂר יֵאָכֵל.

Rabbi Yoḥanan asked Rabbi Ḥanina Tirata: **And does** the court actually **say:** Arise and sin in order that you may gain in a case where the sin and the gain are **with regard to one matter? But isn't it taught** in a *baraita* concerning a case of the two **sheep of *Shavuot* where one slaughtered them not for their** own **sake,**[H] **or where he slaughtered them either before their time,** i.e., before *Shavuot*, **or after their time,** that **the blood shall be sprinkled,** although it shall be sprinkled for the sake of a peace offering, **and the meat shall be eaten.**

וְאִם הָיְתָה שַׁבָּת – לֹא יִזְרוֹק, וְאִם זָרַק – הוּרְצָה לְהַקְטִיר אֵימוּרִין לָעֶרֶב.

Rabbi Yoḥanan continued: **And if** the Festival **was on Shabbat, one may not sprinkle** the blood, the sacrificial portions may not be burned on the altar, and the meat may not be eaten. This is because the improper slaughter of the sheep disqualified them as communal offerings, whereas individual offerings may not be sacrificed on Shabbat. **But if** the priest nevertheless **sprinkled** the blood of these sheep on Shabbat, the offering **is accepted** in that it is permitted **to burn** its sacrificial **portions** on the altar **in the evening,** after the conclusion of Shabbat, and then the meat may be eaten.

HALAKHA

Limbs of a sin offering that were intermingled with the limbs of a burnt offering – אֵבְרֵי חַטָּאת שֶׁנִּתְעָרְבוּ בְּאֵבְרֵי עוֹלָה: If the limbs of a sin offering were intermingled with the limbs of a burnt offering, the intermingled limbs should all be left overnight, and then they are burned in the place in the Temple courtyard designated for burning disqualified sacrificial offerings. This is in accordance with the opinion of the Rabbis (Rambam *Sefer Avoda*, *Hilkhot Pesulei HaMukdashin* 6:20).

The two sheep of *Shavuot* where one slaughtered them not for their own sake – כִּבְשֵׂי עֲצֶרֶת שֶׁשְּׁחָטָן שֶׁלֹּא לִשְׁמָן: If the sheep of *Shavuot* were slaughtered not for their own sake, or not at the appropriate time, the blood is sprinkled and the meat is eaten, but the community has not fulfilled its obligation. If this occurred on Shabbat, they may not sprinkle the blood. If they did so, the offering is accepted in that its sacrificial parts may be burned on the altar after Shabbat, and its meat may be eaten (Rambam *Sefer Avoda*, *Hilkhot Pesulei HaMukdashin* 15:19).

BACKGROUND

The upper section of a winepress – גַּת הָעֶלְיוֹנָה: In the talmudic era winepresses were typically carved into a rock into which grapes were placed and trampled on. Between the upper press, where the grapes were pressed, and the lower press, where the wine was collected, there was a small pipe through which the liquid flowed.

Upper and lower presses

Quarter-*log* – רְבִיעִית: This is a unit of liquid volume that serves as the standard unit of measurement for certain purposes. For example, a quarter-*log* is the minimum amount of wine over which *kiddush* may be recited, the amount of wine that a nazirite is flogged for drinking, and the minimum amount of certain foods for whose transfer from one domain to another one is liable on Shabbat. In addition, a quarter-*log* of blood from a corpse imparts ritual impurity. In contemporary terms, the exact volume of a quarter-*log* is subject to dispute among authorities, with opinions ranging from 60 to 120 cc.

וְאַמַּאי? לֵימָא ״עֲמוֹד חֲטָא בִּשְׁבִיל שֶׁתִּזְכֶּה״!

Rabbi Yoḥanan concluded his proof: **But** according to your opinion, **why** is it not permitted to sprinkle the blood on Shabbat? **Let** the court **say: Arise** and **sin** by sprinkling the blood of these offerings **in order that you may gain** by being able to burn their sacrificial portions in the evening and then eat their meat.

״עֲמוֹד חֲטָא בְּשַׁבָּת כְּדֵי שֶׁתִּזְכֶּה בְּשַׁבָּת״ – אָמְרִינַן, ״עֲמוֹד חֲטָא בְּשַׁבָּת כְּדֵי שֶׁתִּזְכֶּה בְּחוֹל״ – לָא אָמְרִינַן.

Rabbi Ḥanina Tirata answered: **We do say: Arise and sin on Shabbat in order that you may gain on Shabbat. We do not say: Arise and sin on Shabbat in order that you may gain on a weekday.**

וּבְתַרְתֵּי מִילֵּי לָא אֲמַר? וְהָתְנַן: חָבִית שֶׁל תְּרוּמָה שֶׁנִּשְׁבְּרָה בַּגַּת הָעֶלְיוֹנָה וּבַתַּחְתּוֹנָה חוּלִּין טְמֵאִין, מוֹדֶה רַבִּי אֱלִיעֶזֶר וְרַבִּי יְהוֹשֻׁעַ שֶׁאִם יָכוֹל לְהַצִּיל מִמֶּנָּה רְבִיעִית בְּטׇהֳרָה – יַצִּיל.

The Gemara asks: **And** is it so that **with regard to two** separate **matters** the court does **not say** that one should sin with regard to one in order to gain with regard to other? **But didn't we learn** in a mishna (*Terumot* 8:9): In the case of **a barrel of** wine that is ***teruma*** **that broke in the upper** section of a **winepress,**[B] **and in the lower** section of the winepress there is **non-sacred, impure** wine, and the wine that is *teruma* will flow into the lower press and become impure, **Rabbi Eliezer and Rabbi Yehoshua** both **concede that if one is able to rescue** even a **quarter-*log***[B] of the wine that is *teruma* in a pure vessel so that it retains its **ritual purity, he** should **rescue** it, even if, in the process, the rest of the wine that is *teruma* will mix with the non-sacred wine. This will cause the owner a financial loss, because the wine that is *teruma* will become impure, causing the entire mixture to become prohibited for consumption.

וְאִם לָאו – רַבִּי אֱלִיעֶזֶר אוֹמֵר:

But if not, i.e., one cannot save any of the wine that is *teruma*, e.g., if one does not have any pure vessels in which to collect it, **Rabbi Eliezer says:**

Perek **IV**
Daf **48** Amud **b**

תֵּרֵד וְתִטַּמֵּא, וְאַל יְטַמְּאֶנָּה בַּיָּד. וְרַבִּי יְהוֹשֻׁעַ אוֹמֵר: אַף יְטַמְּאֶנָּה בַּיָּד!

The *teruma* wine should be allowed to **descend and become impure** on its own, ruining the non-sacred wine in the lower press, **but one** should **not render it impure through** his direct **action** by catching it in an impure vessel, even though catching it would prevent the wine that is *teruma* from mixing with his impure, non-sacred wine. **And Rabbi Yehoshua says:** Since the wine that is *teruma* will become impure in any event, **one** may **even render it impure through** his direct **action**[N] in order to save his non-sacred wine. This indicates that according to Rabbi Yehoshua it is permitted to sin with regard to one matter, i.e., the wine that is *teruma*, in order to gain with regard to another matter, i.e., the non-sacred wine.

שָׁאנֵי הָתָם, דִּלְטוּמְאָה קָא אָזְלָא.

The Gemara responds: It **is different there,** in the case of the wine, **because** the wine that is *teruma* **is going to** become **impure**[N] in any event. Consequently, his action is not considered a sin, and this is not a case of sinning with regard to one matter in order to gain in another.

NOTES

Render it impure through his direct action [*bayyad*] – יְטַמְּאֶנָּה בַּיָּד: Some early commentaries translate *bayyad* literally, to mean: With his hand. They explain that it is permitted to render the *teruma* impure specifically by touching it with one's hands because one's hands are impure by rabbinic law but not by Torah law. One may not render the *teruma* impure through contact with an impure vessel, which is impure by Torah law (Rambam *Sefer Zera'im, Hilkhot Terumot* 12:4). Others understand it to mean that he may render it impure actively and directly, even with impure vessels (Rashi).

It is different there because the wine that is *teruma* is going to become impure – שָׁאנֵי הָתָם דִּלְטוּמְאָה קָא אָזְלָא: The commentaries explain that Rabbi Eliezer disagrees even though the wine that is *teruma* will become impure in any event, despite the fact that he allows one to bring the mixture of limbs up to the altar. The reason for the distinction is that in the latter case one fulfills the mitzva of burning the limbs of the burnt offering on the altar, whereas in the case of *teruma*, although there is a financial loss involved, there is no mitzva that one fulfills through rendering the *teruma* impure (*Tohorat HaKodesh*).

כִּי אֲתָא רַב יִצְחָק תָּנֵי: כִּבְשֵׂי עֲצֶרֶת שֶׁשְּׁחָטָן שֶׁלֹּא כְּמִצְוָתָן – פְּסוּלִין, וּתְעוּבַּר צוּרָתָן וְיֵצְאוּ לְבֵית הַשְּׂרֵיפָה.

§ The Gemara continues its discussion of the sheep of *Shavuot*. **When Rav Yitzḥak came** from Eretz Yisrael to Babylonia he reported traditions that he learned in Eretz Yisrael, and **he taught** a *baraita*: With regard to a case of the two **sheep** of ***Shavuot* where one slaughtered them not in accordance with their mitzva,**[N] e.g., he slaughtered them for the sake of a different offering, they are **disqualified; and** they should be left overnight until **their form decays**[N] and they attain the status of leftover sacrificial meat, **and** then **they are brought out to the place** designated **for burning.**[N]

אֲמַר רַב נַחְמָן: מָר דְּמַקִּישׁ לְהוּ לְחַטָּאת – תָּנֵי ״פְּסוּלִין״, תַּנָּא דְּבֵי לֵוִי דְּגָמַר שַׁלְמֵי חוֹבָה מִשַּׁלְמֵי נְדָבָה – תָּנֵי ״כְּשֵׁרִים״.

Rav Naḥman said to Rav Yitzḥak: The **Master,** i.e., Rav Yitzḥak, **who compares** the sheep of *Shavuot* **to a sin offering** because they are juxtaposed in a verse (see Leviticus 23:19), **teaches:** The sheep are **disqualified,** like a sin offering that was slaughtered not for its own sake. By contrast, the ***tanna* of the school of Levi,**[B] **who derives** the *halakha* with regard to **an obligatory peace offering,** e.g., the two sheep of *Shavuot*, **from** the *halakha* concerning **a voluntary peace offering, teaches** that the two sheep remain **valid** offerings, just as a voluntary peace offering remains valid even if it is slaughtered for the sake of a different offering.

דְּתָנֵי לֵוִי: וּשְׁאָר שַׁלְמֵי נָזִיר שֶׁשְּׁחָטָן שֶׁלֹּא כְּמִצְוָתָן – כְּשֵׁרִין, וְלֹא עָלוּ לַבְּעָלִים לְשֵׁם חוֹבָה, וְנֶאֱכָלִין לְיוֹם וָלַיְלָה, וְאֵין טְעוּנִין לֹא לֶחֶם וְלֹא זְרוֹעַ.

As Levi teaches: And with regard to the **other peace offerings of a nazirite that one slaughtered not in accordance with their mitzva,**[H] they are **valid** offerings like voluntary peace offerings, **but they do not satisfy the obligation of the owner** to bring the required nazirite peace offerings. **And** these offerings **are eaten for** only **one day and one night,**[N] in accordance with the *halakha* concerning the peace offerings of nazirite, and not for two days and one night like voluntary peace offerings. They **require neither bread nor the foreleg,**[N] unlike the required peace offering of a nazirite.

מֵיתִיבִי: אָשָׁם בֶּן שָׁנָה וְהֵבִיא בֶּן שְׁתַּיִם, בֶּן שְׁתַּיִם וְהֵבִיא בֶּן שָׁנָה – פְּסוּלִין, וּתְעוּבַּר צוּרָתָן וְיֵצְאוּ לְבֵית הַשְּׂרֵפָה.

The Gemara **raises an objection** to the opinion of Rav Yitzḥak from that which was taught in a *baraita*: In a case where one is obligated to sacrifice as **a guilt offering** an animal **in its** first **year,** which the Torah calls a lamb, **and** instead he **brought** an animal **in its second** year,[H] which is considered a ram; or if he is obligated to sacrifice as a guilt offering an animal **in its second** year **and he brought** an animal **in its first year;** the offerings are **disqualified.** They are to be left overnight until **their form decays, and are brought out to the place** designated for **burning.**

NOTES

The two sheep of *Shavuot* where one slaughtered them not in accordance with their mitzva – כִּבְשֵׂי עֲצֶרֶת שֶׁשְּׁחָטָן שֶׁלֹּא כְּמִצְוָתָן: Rashi interprets this phrase to mean that they were slaughtered not for their own sake. Rashi also cites an additional interpretation in the name of the *ge'onim*, which is that the sheep are in their second year rather than being in their first year. Rashi rejects this interpretation because the disqualification in such a case is not a function of how they were slaughtered, and the formulation should have been: The two sheep of *Shavuot* that one brought not in accordance with their mitzva. Rabbeinu Gershom Meor HaGola and *Tosafot* accept the interpretation of the *ge'onim* and explain that the *tanna* mentioned the slaughtering rather than stating only that they were brought not in accordance with their mitzva in order to include other cases, e.g., when the offering is sacrificed at the wrong time. *Tosafot* also note that in the *Tosefta*, this *halakha* is actually formulated as: If the two sheep of *Shavuot* were brought not in accordance with their mitzva.

And they should be left overnight until their form decays – וּתְעוּבַּר צוּרָתָן: This translation is in accordance with Rashi, who explains that when the Gemara states that an offering should be left until its form decays, it means that it should be left overnight so that it becomes disqualified as leftover sacrificial meat, which must be burned. The reason the offering is not burned right away is that it would be considered degrading to the offering. Once it is left over, since all leftover sacrificial meat is burned, it is no longer degrading to burn it. Leaving the offering overnight is referred to as letting its form decay because the meat starts to decay when it is left overnight (*Mikdash David*). Others understand the phrase literally and hold that this means that the offering is left for several days until the meat actually spoils and changes form (Rabbeinu Ḥananel on *Pesahim* 34a and 73b; Rambam's Commentary on the Mishna on tractate *Pesaḥim*).

And then they are brought out to the place designated for burning – וְיֵצְאוּ לְבֵית הַשְּׂרֵיפָה: Rashi notes that there is a distinction between two categories of disqualifications: In a case where the disqualification pertains to the status of the offering itself, e.g., where the offering was rendered *piggul* or impure, the offering is burned immediately. In a case where the disqualification is external, e.g., where the offering was disqualified because it was slaughtered not for its own sake, it must be left overnight before it is burned.

And these offerings are eaten for only one day and one night – וְנֶאֱכָלִין לְיוֹם וָלַיְלָה: Although they have the status of voluntary peace offerings, they are not eaten for two days and one night like other peace offerings. Rather, they are eaten for the same amount of time as the meat of a peace offering of a nazirite.

And they require neither bread nor the foreleg – וְאֵין טְעוּנִין לֹא לֶחֶם וְלֹא זְרוֹעַ: Some understand this to mean that there is no need for bread or for the waving of the foreleg that is generally performed when a nazirite offers his nazirite's ram as a peace offering. Although the ram that was slaughtered not for its own sake is still treated according to the stringency of a peace offering of a nazirite, in that it may be eaten only for one day and one night, the *halakhot* concerning the bread and foreleg do not apply because this offering does not free the nazirite from the restrictions of naziriteship (Rashi). Some derive this *halakha* from the verse: "And the priest shall take the shoulder…and one unleavened cake…and one unleavened wafer, and shall put them upon the hands of the nazirite" (Numbers 6:19). This teaches that they are brought only when the nazirite waves them by hand upon the conclusion of his naziriteship (*Tosafot* on *Nazir* 24a). Others hold that the bread is brought but not waved as it usually is, and the foreleg is given to the priest but is not waved (Rosh, citing Rabbeinu Yitzḥak). Rabbeinu Tam explains this to mean that the foreleg does not have the status of the cooked foreleg of the nazirite ram. Normally, although the foreleg may be eaten only by priests, it may be cooked together with the rest of the meat of the ram, which is eaten by the nazirite even if he is not a priest. In the case of this ram, the foreleg may not be cooked together with the rest of the meat of the ram (Meiri).

BACKGROUND

***Tanna* of the school of Levi – תַּנָּא דְּבֵי לֵוִי:** Even when the Sages permitted writing the Oral Torah, most of it was not recorded until later. In fact, some say that the Mishna itself was not written at the time of its redaction. Therefore, many rabbinic statements, such as the *Tosefta* and the *baraitot*, were preserved and transmitted orally. Each Sage was expected to commit the entire Mishna as well as a significant number of other tannaitic statements to memory. Yet, complete mastery of all of these sources was the province of amoraic Sages called *tanna'im*, experts who memorized massive amounts of material and were capable of reciting it on demand. Often, the most prominent of these *tanna'im* were affiliated with the specific study hall of one of the Sages, where they served as living anthologies of this material. One such study hall was that of Levi ben Sisi, one of the Sages in Eretz Yisrael in the transitional generation between the *tanna'im* and the *amora'im*. He was one of the preeminent disciples of Rabbi Yehuda HaNasi.

HALAKHA

Peace offerings of a nazirite that one slaughtered not in accordance with their mitzva – שַׁלְמֵי נָזִיר שֶׁשְּׁחָטָן שֶׁלֹּא כְּמִצְוָתָן: Peace offerings of a nazirite that one slaughtered not for their own sake do not satisfy the obligation of their owners, but they are eaten for one day and one night. They do not require bread. This is in accordance with the opinion of Levi (Rambam *Sefer Avoda, Hilkhot Pesulei HaMukdashin* 15:20).

And instead he brought an animal in its second year – וְהֵבִיא בֶּן שְׁתַּיִם: If one is obligated to sacrifice as a guilt offering an animal in its first year, and instead he brought one that was in its second year, or vice versa, it is disqualified. It should be left overnight and then it is brought out to the place of burning (Rambam *Sefer Avoda, Hilkhot Pesulei HaMukdashin* 4:26).

HALAKHA

The animals were in their second year – שֶׁהָיוּ בְּנֵי שְׁתֵּי שָׁנִים: If one slaughtered a ram that was twelve months and one day old for the burnt offering of a nazirite, a woman after childbirth, or a leper, it is valid and requires libations. The *Kesef Mishne* adds that it does not satisfy the obligation of its owners and they must bring another burnt offering (Rambam *Sefer Avoda, Hilkhot Pesulei HaMukdashin* 4:27).

That one slaughtered not for their sake – שֶׁשְּׁחָטָן שֶׁלֹּא לִשְׁמָן: The guilt offering of a nazirite or the guilt offering of a leper that was slaughtered not for its own sake does not satisfy the obligation of its owner, but it may be eaten. This is in accordance with the opinion of Levi (Rambam *Sefer Avoda, Hilkhot Pesulei HaMukdashin* 15:20).

אֲבָל עוֹלַת נָזִיר וְעוֹלַת יוֹלֶדֶת וְעוֹלַת מְצוֹרָע שֶׁהָיוּ בְּנֵי שְׁתֵּי שָׁנִים וּשְׁחָטָן – כְּשֵׁרִין.

But in the case of **the burnt offering of a nazirite,** i.e., the lamb that is sacrificed when he completes his naziriteship; **or the burnt offering of a woman after childbirth,** i.e., the lamb she sacrifices on the forty-first day after giving birth to a son or on the eighty-first day after giving birth to a daughter; **or the burnt offering of a leper,** i.e., the lamb that is sacrificed after he is purified; in all of these cases if the animals **were in their second year**[H] instead, **and one slaughtered them,** the offerings are **valid.**

כְּלָלוֹ שֶׁל דָּבָר: כָּל הַכָּשֵׁר בְּעוֹלַת נְדָבָה – כָּשֵׁר בְּעוֹלַת חוֹבָה, וְכָל הַפָּסוּל בְּחַטָּאת – פָּסוּל בְּאָשָׁם, חוּץ מִשֶּׁלֹּא לִשְׁמוֹ!

The *baraita* concludes: **The principle of the matter is: Any** animal **that is valid as a voluntary burnt offering is** also **valid as an obligatory burnt offering, and any** animal **that is disqualified as a sin offering is** also **disqualified as a guilt offering, except for** an offering that was sacrificed **not for its own sake,** which is disqualified in the case of a sin offering but not a guilt offering. This demonstrates that the *halakhot* of obligatory burnt offerings are derived from those of voluntary burnt offerings, despite the fact that the burnt offering of a nazirite is juxtaposed to the sin offering of a nazirite (see Numbers 6:14) and the burnt offering of a leper is juxtaposed to the sin offering of a leper (see Leviticus 14:19). Similarly, the *halakha* pertaining to the sheep of *Shavuot*, which are obligatory peace offerings, should be derived from the *halakha* pertaining to voluntary peace offerings, and not from the *halakha* pertaining to a sin offering as Rav Yitzḥak holds.

הַאי תַּנָּא, תַּנָּא דְּבֵי לֵוִי הוּא.

The Gemara answers: **This *tanna*,** who taught this *baraita*, **is the *tanna* of the school of Levi** cited earlier, who holds that if one slaughters a sheep of *Shavuot* not for its own sake, it is nevertheless valid.

תָּא שְׁמַע, דְּתָנֵי לֵוִי: אֲשַׁם נָזִיר וַאֲשַׁם מְצוֹרָע שֶׁשְּׁחָטָן שֶׁלֹּא לִשְׁמָן – כְּשֵׁרִים, וְלֹא עָלוּ לַבְּעָלִים לְשׁוּם חוֹבָה.

The Gemara discusses the opinion of Rav Naḥman, who maintains that the *tanna* of the school of Levi holds that a sheep of *Shavuot* slaughtered not for its own sake is valid because he derives its *halakha* from that of a voluntary peace offering. **Come and hear** what Levi teaches to the contrary, **as Levi teaches: The guilt offering of a nazirite,** i.e., the lamb he brings on the eighth day after becoming impure through contact with a corpse, **and the guilt offering of a leper,** i.e., the lamb he brings at the completion of his purification, **that one slaughtered not for their sake**[H] **are valid, but they did not satisfy the obligation of the owner.**

שְׁחָטָן מְחוּסַּר זְמַן בִּבְעָלִים, אוֹ שֶׁהָיוּ בְּנֵי שְׁתֵּי שָׁנִים וּשְׁחָטָן – פְּסוּלִין.

If **one slaughtered them** when the **time had not yet** arrived **for** their **owners** to sacrifice these offerings, **or they were in their second year** instead of their first year **and one slaughtered them,** they are **disqualified.**

וְאִם אִיתָא, לִיגְמַר מִשְּׁלָמִים! שְׁלָמִים מִשְּׁלָמִים – גָּמַר, אָשָׁם מִשְּׁלָמִים – לָא גָּמַר.

The Gemara comments: **But if it is so** that Levi derives the *halakhot* of an obligatory offering from those of a voluntary one, **let him derive** the *halakha* of the guilt offering **from** that of the **peace offering,** in which case the guilt offerings should be valid even if they were in their second year. The Gemara answers: Levi **derives** the *halakha* concerning an obligatory **peace offering from** the *halakha* concerning a voluntary **peace offering,** but **he does not derive** the *halakha* concerning **a guilt offering from** the *halakha* concerning **a peace offering.**

וְאִי גָּמַר שְׁלָמִים מִשְּׁלָמִים, לִיגְמַר נַמִי אָשָׁם מֵאָשָׁם, אֲשַׁם נָזִיר וַאֲשַׁם מְצוֹרָע מֵאֲשַׁם גְּזֵילוֹת וַאֲשַׁם מְעִילוֹת, אוֹ אֲשַׁם גְּזֵילוֹת וַאֲשַׁם מְעִילוֹת מֵאֲשַׁם נָזִיר וַאֲשַׁם מְצוֹרָע!

The Gemara further challenges the statement of Rav Naḥman: **But if** Levi **derives** the *halakha* of an obligatory **peace offering from** that of a voluntary **peace offering, let him** similarly **derive** the *halakha* of one **guilt offering from** that of another **guilt offering.** He should derive that **the guilt offering of a nazirite and the guilt offering of a leper** are valid even if the animal is in its second year **from** the *halakha* concerning **a guilt offering for robbery and a guilt offering for misuse** of consecrated property, which are supposed to be a ram in its second year. **Or,** if one brought a lamb in its first year as **a guilt offering for robbery or a guilt offering for misuse** of consecrated property, Levi should derive that it is valid **from** the *halakha* concerning the **guilt offering of a nazirite and the guilt offering of a leper,** which are lambs in their first year.

אֲמַר רַב שִׁימִי בַּר אַשִׁי: דָּנִין דָּבָר שֶׁלֹּא בְּהֶכְשֵׁירוֹ מִדָּבָר שֶׁלֹּא בְּהֶכְשֵׁירוֹ, וְאֵין דָּנִין דָּבָר שֶׁלֹּא בְּהֶכְשֵׁירוֹ מִדָּבָר שֶׁבְּהֶכְשֵׁירוֹ.

Rav Shimi bar Ashi said: One can derive the *halakha* with regard to **an item that is** prepared **not in its valid manner,** e.g., the sheep of *Shavuot* that were slaughtered not for their own sake, **from** the *halakha* with regard to another **item that is** prepared **not in its valid manner,** e.g., a voluntary peace offering slaughtered not for its own sake. **But one cannot derive** the *halakha* with regard to **an item that is** prepared **not in its valid manner,** e.g., the guilt offering of a nazirite or a leper that is sacrificed when it is in its second year, **from** the *halakha* with regard to **an item that is** prepared **in its valid manner,** e.g., a guilt offering for robbery or for misuse of consecrated property that is sacrificed when it is in its second year.

וְלָא? וְהָא תַּנְיָא: מִנַּיִן לַיּוֹצֵא שֶׁאִם עָלָה, לֹא יֵרֵד? שֶׁהֲרֵי יוֹצֵא כָּשֵׁר בְּבָמָה!

The Gemara asks: **And** can one **not** derive the *halakha* with regard to disqualified offerings from the *halakha* with regard to fit offerings? **But isn't it taught** in a *baraita*: **From where** is it derived **with regard to** an item that **left** the Temple courtyard and was thereby disqualified **that if** it nevertheless **ascended** upon the altar **it shall not descend?** It is derived from the fact **that** an item that **left is valid** for sacrifice **on** a private **altar.** Here, the *baraita* derives the *halakha* with regard to an disqualified offering from the *halakha* with regard to a fit offering.

Perek **IV**
Daf **49** Amud **a**

תָּנָא אַ״זֹאת תּוֹרַת הָעֹלָה״ רִיבָּה סָמֵיךְ לֵיהּ.

The Gemara answers: The ***tanna*** of that *baraita* **relies on** the phrase: **"This is the law of the burnt offering [*ha'ola*]:** It is that which goes up on its firewood upon the altar all night unto the morning" (Leviticus 6:2), a seemingly superfluous general phrase which is interpreted homiletically to **include**[N] the *halakha* that any item that ascends [*ola*] upon the altar shall not descend from it, even if it was disqualified. The verse is the actual source for the *halakha* of the *baraita,* whereas the case of a private altar is cited merely in support of this ruling. Accordingly, the *baraita* does not contradict the opinion of Rav Shimi bar Ashi.

תָּנֵי רַבָּה בַּר בַּר חָנָה קַמֵּיהּ דְּרַב: כִּבְשֵׂי עֲצֶרֶת שֶׁשְּׁחָטָן לְשׁוּם אֵילִים – כְּשֵׁרִין, וְלֹא עָלוּ לַבְּעָלִים לְשׁוּם חוֹבָה. אֲמַר לֵיהּ רַב: עָלוּ וְעָלוּ.

§ The Gemara cites another discussion concerning the sheep of *Shavuot.* **Rabba bar bar Ḥana taught** a *baraita* **before Rav:** In a case of **the two sheep of *Shavuot* where one slaughtered them for the sake of rams**[H] and not for their own sake, **they are valid** offerings, **but they do not satisfy the obligation of the owner,** i.e., the community, to sacrifice these offerings. **Rav said to** Rabba bar bar Ḥana: That is not so; rather, the sheep **certainly satisfy** the obligation of the community.

HALAKHA

The two sheep of *Shavuot* where one slaughtered them for the sake of rams – כִּבְשֵׂי עֲצֶרֶת שֶׁשְּׁחָטָן לְשׁוּם אֵילִים: If one slaughtered the two sheep of *Shavuot* for the sake of rams they do not satisfy the obligation of the community, in accordance with the opinion of Rabba bar bar Ḥana (Rambam *Sefer Avoda, Hilkhot Pesulei HaMukdashin* 15:16).

NOTES

Include – רִיבָּה: The Sages (see *Nidda* 40a–b) disagree as to the interpretation of the verse cited in the Gemara. Rabbi Yehuda interprets three of the terms in the verse, "this," "the," and "it," as restricting the *halakha* that an offering brought onto the altar is not taken off. Consequently, he rules that this *halakha* does not apply to a burnt offering that is disqualified because it was slaughtered at night, a burnt offering whose blood was spilled before it could be sprinkled on the altar, and a burnt offering that left the Temple courtyard.

Conversely, Rabbi Shimon holds that the intention of this verse is to extend the applicability of this *halakha* to the three aforementioned cases as well as others, including a burnt offering that was left overnight off of the altar, one that become ritually impure, one that was slaughtered with the intent to perform sacrificial rites beyond the designated time or outside the designated area, and an offering whose blood was collected or sprinkled on the altar by individuals unfit to perform the Temple service.

Even Rabbi Shimon concedes that the verse contains a limitation, and therefore certain types of disqualified burnt offerings are brought down from the altar. This category includes an animal with which a person engaged in intercourse, an animal that was worshipped as a deity or that was designated for idolatrous worship, an animal that was given as payment to a prostitute, an animal that was used to purchase a dog, an animal born of a forbidden mixture of diverse kinds, an animal that is a *tereifa*, an animal born by caesarean section, and an animal that has a blemish.

NOTES

The statement of Rav is reasonable, etc. – מִסְתַּבְּרָא מִילְּתֵיהּ דְּרַב וכו׳: Later commentaries explain that Rav Ḥisda holds that the *baraita* cited by Rabba bar bar Ḥana before Rav is referring to a case where the priest misidentified the animal. If it was a simple case where the priest sacrificed the animals for the sake of a different offering, the *baraita* would have stated explicitly that the sheep of *Shavuot* were slaughtered not for their own sake. The reason the offering remains valid is that the lambs were actually sacrificed for the sake of lambs. But if the priest had thought they were rams and sacrificed them for the sake of rams, the offering would be disqualified, because even the erroneous uprooting of the identity of an offering takes effect. Conversely, Rabba, who holds that the erroneous uprooting of the identity of an offering does not take effect, understands the *baraita* as referring to a case where the priest misidentified the animals as rams and therefore slaughtered them for the sake of rams, and holds in accordance with the opinion of Rav (*Ḥazon Ish; Tohorat HaKodesh*).

Others suggest that Rav himself holds that the offering would satisfy the community's obligation even if the priest knew that they were lambs and knowingly slaughtered them for the sake of rams. The *halakha* is not in accordance with Rav in this regard, as Rav Ḥisda and Rabba disagree, and the *baraita* contradicts him, as Rabba bar bar Ḥana points out (Rashash on *Yevamot* 14a).

Rava said – אָמַר רָבָא: Some versions of the text cite Rabba instead of Rava wherever Rava's name appears in this passage.

BACKGROUND

Rams – אֵילִים: The Torah uses the word lambs in reference to the sheep of *Shavuot*. In fact, the only difference between an animal considered in *halakha* to be a lamb and one considered to be a ram is age. In the first year of the animal's life it is called a lamb, and once it is a year and thirty-one days old it is called a ram. Between these times it is defined as a *palges*, which is no longer called a lamb but is not yet called a ram, and is therefore not fit for any offering.

אָמַר רַב חִסְדָּא: מִסְתַּבְּרָא מִילְּתֵיהּ דְּרַב בִּכְסָבוּר אֵילִים וּשְׁחָטָן לְשׁוּם כְּבָשִׂים, שֶׁהֲרֵי כְּבָשִׂים לְשׁוּם כְּבָשִׂים נִשְׁחֲטוּ.

Rav Ḥisda said: The statement of Rav is reasonable[N] **in** a case where **one thought** that they were **rams**[B] when he slaughtered them, **and** nevertheless **slaughtered them for the sake of lambs.** In such a case, it makes sense that they satisfy the community's obligation **since the lambs were slaughtered for the sake of lambs.**

אֲבָל כִּסְבוּר אֵילִים וּשְׁחָטָן לְשׁוּם אֵילִים – לֹא, עֲקִירָה בִּטְעוּת הָוְיָא עֲקִירָה. וְרַבָּה אָמַר: עֲקִירָה בִּטְעוּת לָא הָוְיָא עֲקִירָה.

But in a case where **he thought** that they were **rams** when he slaughtered them, **and** therefore **slaughtered them for the sake of rams,**[H] they do **not** satisfy the community's obligation, even though they were actually lambs. This is due to the fact that the **erroneous uprooting** of the status of an offering **constitutes uprooting,** despite the fact that it was done in error. **But Rabba said:** The **erroneous uprooting** of the status of an offering **does not constitute uprooting.**

אָמַר רָבָא, וּמוֹתְבִינַן אַשְׁמַעְתִּין: הַכֹּהֲנִים שֶׁפִּיגְּלוּ בַּמִּקְדָּשׁ, מְזִידִין – חַיָּיבִין, הָא שׁוֹגְגִין – פְּטוּרִין, וְתָנֵי עֲלָהּ: פִּיגּוּלָן פִּיגּוּל.

Rava said:[N] **We raise an objection to our** own ruling concerning this *halakha* from that which was taught in a mishna (*Gittin* 54a): In a case of **priests who disqualified** an offering **through improper intention in the Temple,**[H] by expressing, while sacrificing the offering, the intention to eat it after the appropriate time, if they did so **intentionally, they are liable** to pay the value of the offering to its owner, who must now bring another offering. It follows, **therefore,** that if the priests did so **unintentionally they are exempt. And** it is **taught concerning this** case in a *baraita*: Even though they slaughtered it with improper intent unintentionally, **their** act of **improper intention** renders the offering ***piggul,*** despite the fact that they are exempt from paying damages.

הֵיכִי דָּמֵי? אִילֵימָא דְּיָדַע דְּחַטָּאת הִיא וְקָא מְחַשֵּׁב בָּהּ לְשׁוּם שְׁלָמִים – הַאי שׁוֹגְגִין? מְזִידִין הָווּ!

What are the circumstances in which this is the *halakha*? **If we say** that it is referring to a case where the priest **knew that** the offering **was a sin offering,** which is eaten for only one day and one night, **and** nevertheless **he intended** the offering to be **for the sake of a peace offering,** which is eaten for two days and one night, and thereby his intention was that it be eaten after its appropriate time, is **this** considered **an unintentional** act by the priests? Certainly **they were** acting **intentionally.**

אֶלָּא לָאו דִּכְסָבוּר שְׁלָמִים הוּא, וְקָא מְחַשֵּׁב בָּהּ לְשׁוּם שְׁלָמִים, וְקָתָנֵי: פִּיגּוּלָן פִּיגּוּל, אַלְמָא עֲקִירָה בִּטְעוּת הָוְיָא עֲקִירָה!

Rather, is it not referring to a case where the offering was a sin offering, which is eaten for only one day and one night, and the priest **thought that it was a peace offering and** therefore **he intended** the offering to be **for the sake of a peace offering,** which is eaten for two days and one night, and thereby his intention was that it be eaten after its appropriate time? **And** with regard to this case the *tanna* **taught: Their** act of **improper intention** renders the offering ***piggul.* Apparently,** this proves that the **erroneous uprooting** of the status of an offering **constitutes uprooting,** contrary to the ruling of Rabba.

אָמַר לֵיהּ אַבָּיֵי: לְעוֹלָם דְּיָדַע דְּחַטָּאת הִיא, וְקָא מְחַשֵּׁב בָּהּ לְשׁוּם שְׁלָמִים, וּבְאוֹמֵר מוּתָּר.

Abaye said to Rava: There is no objection from this *baraita,* because **actually** it is referring to a case **where** the priest **knew that it** was **a sin offering and** nevertheless **he intended** the offering to be **for the sake of a peace offering,** and his uprooting was done intentionally. Nevertheless, the *baraita* refers to the priests as acting unintentionally because it is referring to circumstances **where** the priest **says,** i.e., he mistakenly thinks, that it is **permitted** to sacrifice the offering with this intent.

HALAKHA

He thought that they were rams and slaughtered them for the sake of rams – כִּסְבוּר אֵילִים וּשְׁחָטָן לְשׁוּם אֵילִים: If one thought that the two sheep of *Shavuot* were rams and slaughtered them for the sake of rams, the obligation of the community to sacrifice the offerings has been fulfilled. This is due to the fact that the status of the offering was uprooted in error, and the erroneous uprooting of the status of an offering is insignificant. This is in accordance with the opinions of Rav and Rabba (Rambam *Sefer Avoda, Hilkhot Pesulei HaMukdashin* 15:16).

Priests who disqualified an offering through improper intention in the Temple – הַכֹּהֲנִים שֶׁפִּיגְּלוּ בַּמִּקְדָּשׁ: The Rambam holds that if priests intentionally disqualified an offering with an improper intention, they are required to reimburse the owner, but if they did so unintentionally, they are exempt. The Ra'avad holds that even if they disqualified an offering with an improper intention intentionally they are exempt, in accordance with the opinion that maintains that one is not liable for damage that is not externally evident. The *Kesef Mishne* notes that this is also the opinion of the Ramban (Rambam *Sefer Nezikin, Hilkhot Ḥovel UMazik* 7:4, and see *Leḥem Mishne* there).

מְתִיב רַבִּי זֵירָא, רַבִּי שִׁמְעוֹן אוֹמֵר: כׇּל מְנָחוֹת שֶׁנִּקְמְצוּ שֶׁלֹּא לִשְׁמָן – כְּשֵׁירוֹת, וְעָלוּ לַבְּעָלִים לְשׁוּם חוֹבָה,

Rabbi Zeira raises an objection to Rabba's opinion that erroneous uprooting of the status of an offering does not constitute uprooting. A *baraita* teaches that **Rabbi Shimon says: All meal offerings** from which **the handful was removed not for their sake are** entirely **valid, and have** even **satisfied the obligation of the owner,** unlike animal offerings slaughtered not for their sake, which do not satisfy the obligation of the owner.

שֶׁאֵין הַמְּנָחוֹת דּוֹמוֹת לַזְּבָחִים, שֶׁהַקּוֹמֵץ מַחֲבַת לְשׁוּם מַרְחֶשֶׁת – מַעֲשֶׂיהָ מוֹכִיחִין עָלֶיהָ שֶׁהִיא מַחֲבַת, חֲרֵבָה לְשׁוּם בְּלוּלָה – מַעֲשֶׂיהָ מוֹכִיחִין עָלֶיהָ שֶׁהִיא חֲרֵבָה.

This is **because meal offerings are not similar to animal offerings. As,** in the case of **one who removes a handful** from a meal offering prepared in a shallow **pan for the sake of** a meal offering prepared in **a deep pan, its mode of preparation proves** that **it** is a shallow-**pan** meal offering and not a deep-pan meal offering. Since a meal offering prepared in a shallow pan is hard and one prepared in a deep pan is soft, his intention is plainly false. Similarly, if one removes a handful from **a dry** meal offering, the meal offering of a sinner, which has no oil, **for the sake of** a meal offering **mixed** with oil, his intention is plainly false, as **its mode of preparation proves** that **it is a dry** meal offering.

אֲבָל בִּזְבָחִים אֵינוֹ כֵּן, שְׁחִיטָה אַחַת לְכוּלָּן, קַבָּלָה אַחַת לְכוּלָּן, זְרִיקָה אַחַת לְכוּלָּן.

But with regard to animal offerings this **is not so.** There is **one** mode of **slaughter for all of** the offerings, **one** mode of **collection** of the blood **for all of them,** and **one** mode of **sprinkling for all of them.** Since the only factor that distinguishes between one type of offering and another is the intention of the individuals involved in its sacrifice, their intention is significant. Consequently, if one of the sacrificial rites is performed for the sake of the wrong type of offering, the offering does not satisfy its owner's obligation.

הֵיכִי דָּמֵי? אִילֵימָא דְּיָדַע דְּמַחֲבַת הִיא, וְקָא קָמֵיץ לַהּ לְשׁוּם מַרְחֶשֶׁת – כִּי מַעֲשֶׂיהָ מוֹכִיחִין מַאי הָוֵי? הָא מִיעְקַר קָא עָקַר לַהּ!

The Gemara clarifies: **What are the circumstances** to which Rabbi Shimon is referring? **If we say** that he is referring to a case **where** the priest **knew that** the meal offering **was** prepared in a shallow **pan, and** nevertheless **he removed a handful** from it **for the sake of** a meal offering prepared in **a deep pan,** then although **its mode of preparation proves** that it was prepared in a shallow pan, **what of it?** In any case **he is** consciously **uprooting** its status as a shallow-pan meal offering, changing it to a deep-pan meal offering by means of his intention when he removes the handful.

אֶלָּא לָאו דִּכְסָבוּר מַרְחֶשֶׁת הִיא, וְקָא קָמֵיץ לַהּ לְשׁוּם מַרְחֶשֶׁת וְטָעָה, דְּהָכָא הוּא דְּמַעֲשֶׂיהָ מוֹכִיחִין עָלֶיהָ, הָא בְּעָלְמָא – עֲקִירָה בְּטָעוּת הָוְיָא עֲקִירָה!

Rather, is it not referring to a case **where** the priest **thought it was** a meal offering prepared in **a deep pan and** therefore **removed a handful for the sake of** a meal offering prepared in **a deep pan, but he was mistaken,** as it was actually a meal offering prepared in a shallow pan? **It is** specifically **here,** in this case, that Rabbi Shimon rules that the offering remains valid, **since its mode of preparation proves** that **it** is a shallow-pan meal offering, which indicates **that in general, erroneous uprooting** of the status of an offering **constitutes uprooting,** contrary the ruling of Rabba.

אֲמַר לֵיהּ אַבָּיֵי: לְעוֹלָם דְּיָדַע דְּמַחֲבַת הִיא, וְקָא קָמֵיץ לַהּ לְשׁוּם מַרְחֶשֶׁת,

Abaye said to Rabbi Zeira, in response to his objection: This objection to Rabba's opinion is inconclusive, because one can explain that the *baraita* is **actually** referring to a case **where** the priest **knew that** the meal offering **was** prepared in a shallow **pan, and** nevertheless **he removed a handful for the sake of** a meal offering prepared in **a deep pan.**

וּדְקָא אָמְרַתְּ: כִּי מַעֲשֶׂיהָ מוֹכִיחִין עָלֶיהָ מַאי הָוֵי? רָבָא לְטַעְמֵיהּ, דְּאָמַר רָבָא: מַחֲשָׁבָה דְּלָא מִינַּכְּרָא – פְּסַל רַחֲמָנָא, מַחֲשָׁבָה דְּמִינַּכְּרָא – לָא פְּסַל רַחֲמָנָא.

And with regard to **that which you said** in your question: Although **its mode of preparation proves** that **it** is prepared in a shallow pan, **what of it,** i.e., since he is consciously uprooting its identity, how can it satisfy its owner's obligation? Abaye answers that **Rava** conforms **to his** line of **reasoning, as Rava says: The Merciful One disqualifies** an offering due to improper **intent that is not recognizably** false, i.e., when the physical properties of the offering itself do not prove that the intent is mistaken. **The Merciful One does not disqualify** an offering due to improper **intent that is recognizably** false. Consequently, if one removes a handful from a shallow-pan meal offering for the sake of a deep-pan meal offering, even if he did so consciously, the offering remains valid and satisfies the owner's obligation.

מתני׳ הַתְּמִידִין אֵין מְעַכְּבִין אֶת הַמּוּסָפִין, וְלֹא הַמּוּסָפִין מְעַכְּבִין אֶת הַתְּמִידִין, וְלֹא הַמּוּסָפִין מְעַכְּבִין זֶה אֶת זֶה. לֹא הִקְרִיבוּ כֶּבֶשׂ בַּבּוֹקֶר – יַקְרִיבוּ בֵּין הָעַרְבַּיִם.

MISHNA Failure to sacrifice **the daily offerings does not prevent** sacrifice of **the additional offerings,**[H] and likewise, failure to sacrifice **the additional offerings does not prevent** sacrifice of **the daily offerings. And** failure to sacrifice some of **the additional offerings** on a day when more than one is sacrificed, e.g., if it was both Shabbat and the New Moon, **does not prevent** sacrifice of the **other** additional offerings. If the priests **did not sacrifice a lamb in the morning**[H] as the daily offering, nevertheless, **they should sacrifice** a lamb **in the afternoon** as the daily offering, as failure to sacrifice one daily offering does not prevent sacrifice of the other. In all of these cases, if they failed to sacrifice one offering, they should still sacrifice the other.

אָמַר רַבִּי שִׁמְעוֹן: אֵימָתַי? בִּזְמַן שֶׁהָיוּ אֲנוּסִין אוֹ שׁוֹגְגִין, אֲבָל אִם הָיוּ מְזִידִין וְלֹא הִקְרִיבוּ כֶּבֶשׂ בַּבּוֹקֶר – לֹא יַקְרִיבוּ בֵּין הָעַרְבַּיִם.

Rabbi Shimon said: When does this *halakha* apply? It applies **at a time when** the failure to sacrifice the daily morning offering was because **they were** prevented from sacrificing it due to **circumstances beyond their control or** they failed to sacrifice it **unwittingly. But if** the priests acted **intentionally and did not sacrifice a lamb in the morning** as the daily offering, **they should not sacrifice** a lamb **in the afternoon** as the daily offering.

לֹא הִקְטִירוּ קְטוֹרֶת בַּבּוֹקֶר – יַקְטִירוּ בֵּין הָעַרְבַּיִם.

Incense was burned twice a day, half a measure in the morning and half a measure in the afternoon. If **they did not burn** the half-measure of **incense in the morning,**[H] **they should burn** the half-measure **in the afternoon.**

אָמַר רַבִּי שִׁמְעוֹן: וְכוּלָּהּ הָיְתָה קְרֵיבָה בֵּין הָעַרְבַּיִם, שֶׁאֵין מְחַנְּכִין אֶת מִזְבַּח הַזָּהָב אֶלָּא בִּקְטוֹרֶת הַסַּמִּים, וְלֹא מִזְבַּח הָעוֹלָה אֶלָּא בְּתָמִיד שֶׁל שַׁחַר, וְלֹא אֶת הַשּׁוּלְחָן אֶלָּא בְּלֶחֶם הַפָּנִים בְּשַׁבָּת, וְלֹא אֶת הַמְּנוֹרָה אֶלָּא בְּשִׁבְעָה נֵרוֹתֶיהָ בֵּין הָעַרְבַּיִם.

Rabbi Shimon said: And in such a case, **the entire** measure **was sacrificed in the afternoon.** The reason for the difference between the daily offerings and the incense is **that** the daily service on a new **golden altar is initiated only with** the burning of **the incense of the spices**[HN] in the afternoon, at which time they would burn a full measure. **And the** daily service on a new **altar of the burnt offering,** on which the daily offerings were sacrificed, is initiated **only with the daily morning offering. And** use of a new **Table** was initiated **only with** the arrangement of **the shewbread on Shabbat,**[H] **and** use of a new **Candelabrum** was initiated **only with** the kindling **of its seven lamps in the afternoon.**[H]

גמ׳ בְּעָא מִינֵּיהּ רַבִּי חִיָּיא בַּר אָבִין מֵרַב חִסְדָּא: צִיבּוּר שֶׁאֵין לָהֶן תְּמִידִין וּמוּסָפִין, אֵי זֶה מֵהֶן קוֹדֵם?

GEMARA The mishna teaches that the daily offerings and the additional offerings each do not prevent fulfillment of the mitzva with the other. Concerning this, **Rabbi Ḥiyya bar Avin raised a dilemma before Rav Ḥisda:** In the case of **a community that did not have** the resources to sacrifice both **the daily offerings and the additional offerings, which of them takes precedence** over the other?

הֵיכִי דָּמֵי? אִילֵימָא תְּמִידִין דְּיוֹמֵיהּ וּמוּסָפִין דְּיוֹמֵיהּ – פְּשִׁיטָא, תְּמִידִין עֲדִיפִי, דְּהָווּ לְהוּ תָּדִיר וּמְקוּדָּשׁ!

The Gemara clarifies: **What are the circumstances** to which Rabbi Ḥiyya bar Avin is referring? **If we say** that he is referring to a case where the choice is between **the daily offerings of that day and the additional offerings of that** same **day,** it is **obvious** that **the daily offerings are given preference, as** the sacrifice of the daily offerings **is** more **frequent** than the sacrifice of the additional offerings, which are sacrificed only on special occasions, **and** the daily offerings are also **sanctified.**[N]

HALAKHA

Failure to sacrifice the daily offerings does not prevent sacrifice of the additional offerings – הַתְּמִידִין אֵין מְעַכְּבִין אֶת הַמּוּסָפִין: Failure to sacrifice the daily offerings does not prevent sacrifice of the additional offerings. Similarly, failure to sacrifice the additional offerings does not prevent sacrifice of the daily offerings, and failure to sacrifice some of the additional offerings does not prevent sacrifice of the other additional offerings (Rambam *Sefer Avoda, Hilkhot Temidin UMusafin* 8:20).

If the priests did not sacrifice a lamb in the morning – לֹא הִקְרִיבוּ כֶּבֶשׂ בַּבּוֹקֶר: If the community did not sacrifice the daily offering of the morning, they should nevertheless sacrifice the daily offering of the afternoon. This is the *halakha* whether the omission was unwitting or deliberate. This applies only if the service of the altar had already been initiated. If the altar had never been used for a sacrifice they may not sacrifice the afternoon offering, as the service of a new altar may be initiated only by means of the morning offering (Rambam *Sefer Avoda, Hilkhot Temidin UMusafin* 1:12).

If they did not burn the half-measure of incense in the morning – לֹא הִקְטִירוּ קְטוֹרֶת בַּבּוֹקֶר: If the community did not burn the half-measure of incense in the morning, they should nevertheless sacrifice incense in the afternoon, even if the omission was deliberate. This is in accordance with the first *tanna*. According to the *Leḥem Mishne*, only a half-measure of incense should be burned (Rambam *Sefer Avoda, Hilkhot Temidin UMusafin* 3:1).

That the daily service on a golden altar is initiated only with the burning of the incense of the spices – שֶׁאֵין מְחַנְּכִין אֶת מִזְבַּח הַזָּהָב אֶלָּא בִּקְטוֹרֶת הַסַּמִּים: The daily service on a new golden altar is initiated only with the burning of the incense of the spice in the afternoon. This is in accordance with the *tanna* of the mishna and the ruling of Abaye on 50b, and not in accordance with the *baraita* cited on 50a (Rambam *Sefer Avoda, Hilkhot Temidin UMusafin* 3:1).

And use of a Table was initiated only with the arrangement of the shewbread on Shabbat – וְלֹא אֶת הַשּׁוּלְחָן אֶלָּא בְּלֶחֶם הַפָּנִים בְּשַׁבָּת: Use of a new Table is initiated only with the arrangement of the shewbread on Shabbat (Rambam *Sefer Avoda, Hilkhot Temidin UMusafin* 5:3).

And use of a new Candelabrum was initiated only with the kindling of its seven lamps in the afternoon – וְלֹא אֶת הַמְּנוֹרָה אֶלָּא בְּשִׁבְעָה נֵרוֹתֶיהָ בֵּין הָעַרְבַּיִם: Use of a new Candelabrum is initiated only with the kindling of its seven lamps in the afternoon (Rambam *Sefer Avoda, Hilkhot Temidin UMusafin* 3:11).

NOTES

The golden altar is initiated only with the burning of the incense of the spices – אֵין מְחַנְּכִין אֶת מִזְבַּח הַזָּהָב אֶלָּא בִּקְטוֹרֶת הַסַּמִּים: The language indicates that this is intended to be an explanation, but it is not clear which opinion it is explaining. Some hold that it is presented as an explanation for the opinion of Rabbi Shimon, who maintains that the full measure of incense is sacrificed in the afternoon if the first half was not sacrificed in the morning (Rashi, cited by *Tosafot* on 50a; Rabbeinu Gershom Meor HaGola).

Others hold that it is presented as an explanation for the opinion of the Rabbis, and there is a lacuna in the mishna. Accordingly, the mishna should include a comment clarifying that the Rabbis are referring only to daily offerings, but they concede in the case of the initiations of the services mentioned in the end of the mishna. The initiations of the service for the two altars differ from each other, because the service of the altar of the burnt offering is initiated in the morning, whereas the service of a new golden incense altar is initiated in the afternoon (*Tosafot* on 50a; commentary attributed to Rashba).

Frequent and sanctified – תָּדִיר וּמְקוּדָּשׁ: Rashi mentions two explanations of this statement. One is that when the Gemara refers to the offerings as sanctified, it means that the sanctity of the day of Shabbat or a Festival elevates the sanctity of all the offerings that are sacrificed on that day. According to this explanation, both the daily offering and the additional offering that are sacrificed on a Shabbat or a Festival are equally sanctified. The Gemara's point here is that whereas the daily offering is more frequent than the additional offering and is sanctified due to the day, the additional offering has only one of those two factors, which is that it is sanctified due to the day. Consequently, the daily offering takes precedence. Rashi's second explanation is that the fact that the daily offering is sacrificed before the additional offering indicates that it has greater sanctity than the additional offering. Consequently, the Gemara's point is that since the daily offering is both more frequent and more sanctified than the additional offering, it takes precedence.

אֶלָּא תְּמִידִין דִּלְמָחָר וּמוּסָפִין דְּהָאִידָּנָא: תְּמִידִין עֲדִיפִי – שֶׁכֵּן תָּדִיר, אוֹ דִּלְמָא מוּסָפִין עֲדִיפִי – דְּהָווּ לְהוּ מְקוּדָּשׁ?

Rather, Rabbi Ḥiyya bar Avin must be referring to a case where they have enough animals for the daily offerings of today and also for either **the daily offerings for tomorrow**[N] **or the additional offerings for today.** In such a case, are **the daily offerings given preference since** their sacrifice is more **frequent? Or perhaps the additional offerings are given preference because they are** considered more **sanctified** because they are sacrificed on a holy day.

אֲמַר לֵיהּ, תְּנִיתוּהָ: הַתְּמִידִין אֵין מְעַכְּבִין אֶת הַמּוּסָפִין, וְלֹא הַמּוּסָפִין מְעַכְּבִין אֶת הַתְּמִידִין, וְלֹא (אֶת) הַמּוּסָפִין מְעַכְּבִין זֶה אֶת זֶה.

Rav Ḥisda **said to** Rabbi Ḥiyya bar Avin: The resolution to this dilemma can be derived from that which **you learned** in the mishna: Failure to sacrifice **the daily offerings does not prevent** sacrifice of **the additional offerings, and** likewise, failure to sacrifice **the additional offerings does not prevent** sacrifice of **the daily offerings. And** failure to sacrifice some of **the additional offerings does not prevent** sacrifice of the **other** additional offerings.

הֵיכִי דָּמֵי? אִילֵּימָא דְּאִית לֵיהּ, וּלְקַדֵּם – וְהָתַנְיָא: מִנַּיִן שֶׁלֹּא יְהֵא דָּבָר קוֹדֵם לְתָמִיד שֶׁל שַׁחַר? תַּלְמוּד לוֹמַר "וְעָרַךְ עָלֶיהָ הָעֹלָה",

What are the circumstances to which the mishna is referring? **If we say** that it is referring to a case where the Temple treasury **has** all of the animals necessary for both offerings, **and** the only question is **in** terms of sacrificing one **before** the other, **isn't it taught** in a *baraita*: **From where** is it derived **that no** sacrifice **should precede** the sacrifice of the **daily offering of morning?**[H] The *baraita* continues: It is derived from that which **the verse states:** "And the fire upon the altar shall be kept burning thereby, it shall not go out; and the priest shall kindle wood on it every morning; **and he shall lay the burnt offering in order on it,** and shall cause the fats of the peace offering to go up in smoke upon it" (Leviticus 6:5).

וְאָמַר רָבָא: "הָעֹלָה" – עוֹלָה רִאשׁוֹנָה!

And Rava says in explanation of this derivation in the *baraita* that the term **"the burnt offering,"** with the definite article, is referring to **the first burnt offering** of the day, which is the daily offering. Consequently, one may not sacrifice the additional offerings before the daily offering.

Perek **IV**
Daf **49** Amud **b**

אֶלָּא פְּשִׁיטָא דְּלֵית לֵיהּ, וְאִי דְּיוֹמֵיהּ אַמַּאי? תָּדִיר וּמְקוּדָּשׁ – תָּדִיר עָדִיף!

Rather, it is **obvious** that the mishna is referring to a case **where he does not have** a sufficient number of animals for both offerings. **And if** it is referring to the offerings **of that day, why** does the mishna say that failure to sacrifice one does not prevent sacrifice of the other? Since the daily offering is more **frequent** and it is sanctified, **and** the additional offerings are **sanctified** but are less frequent than the daily offering, the **frequent** offering **are given preference.** Consequently, failure to sacrifice the daily offering should prevent the sacrifice of the additional offerings.

אֶלָּא לָאו דִּלְמָחָר, וְקָתָנֵי: אֵין מְעַכְּבִין זֶה אֶת זֶה – אַלְמָא כִּי הֲדָדֵי נִינְהוּ!

Rather, is it not referring to a case where the Temple treasury does not have enough animals for both the additional offerings of today and the daily offering **of tomorrow, and** yet the mishna **teaches** that failure to sacrifice one does **not prevent** one from sacrificing **the other? Evidently, they are equal** and he may sacrifice whichever offering he chooses. This would resolve Rabbi Ḥiyya bar Avin's dilemma.

אֲמַר לֵיהּ אַבַּיֵי: לְעוֹלָם דְּאִית לְהוּ, וּלְקַדֵּם. וּדְקָא קַשְׁיָא לָךְ שֶׁלֹּא יְהֵא דָּבָר קוֹדֵם – מִצְוָה בְּעָלְמָא הוּא.

Abaye said to Rav Ḥisda: That is not a valid resolution of the dilemma, as one can claim that **actually,** the mishna is referring to a case **where they have** enough animals for all the offerings, **and** the mishna is referring to the issue of sacrificing one **before** the other. **And** with regard to **that which** poses **a difficulty for you** based upon the *baraita* that states that **no** sacrifice **should precede** the sacrifice of the daily offering of the morning, that *baraita* **is merely** stating **the mitzva** *ab initio*.

NOTES

The daily offerings for tomorrow – תְּמִידִין דִּלְמָחָר: The Re'em Horowitz on *Sukka* 25b comments that this is a dilemma only because there is an obligation to inspect, for four days, an animal that is to be sacrificed as the daily offering, to ensure that it does not develop a blemish. Therefore, it can be claimed that the mitzva concerning the next day's daily offering begins even before the day upon which it is sacrificed. But generally, when one has a choice between performing a mitzva on that day or a different mitzva on a later date, he would be obligated to perform the mitzva on that day.

HALAKHA

That no sacrifice should precede the sacrifice of the daily offering of morning – שֶׁלֹּא יְהֵא דָּבָר קוֹדֵם לְתָמִיד שֶׁל שַׁחַר: It is prohibited to sacrifice any offering before the daily morning offering, in accordance with the *baraita* (Rambam *Sefer Avoda*, *Hilkhot Temidin UMusafin* 1:3).

תָּא שְׁמַע: אֵין פּוֹחֲתִין מִשִּׁשָּׁה טְלָאִים הַמְבוּקָּרִין בְּלִשְׁכַּת הַטְּלָאִים כְּדֵי לְשַׁבָּת וְלִשְׁנֵי יָמִים טוֹבִים שֶׁל רֹאשׁ הַשָּׁנָה.

The Gemara suggests: **Come** and **hear** a resolution to Rabbi Ḥiyya bar Avin's dilemma based upon a mishna (*Arakhin* 13a): One maintains **no fewer than six lambs that** have been **inspected**[H] and found to be unblemished **in the Chamber of the Lambs,**[B] **sufficient for Shabbat and for the two festival days of Rosh HaShana** that in some years occur adjacent to it.

הֵיכִי דָּמֵי? אִילֵּימָא דְּאִית לֵיהּ – תְּמִידִין וּמוּסָפִין טוּבָא הָווּ!

The Gemara clarifies: **What are the circumstances** of this case? **If we say that** it is referring to a case where the Temple treasury **has** enough animals for all of the offerings that should be brought, six lambs are not enough, as **there are many** lambs sacrificed for **daily offerings and additional offerings** on those three days. In total, twenty-two lambs are required: Two each day for the daily offerings, two for the additional offering of Shabbat, seven for the additional offering of Rosh HaShana, and seven for the additional offering of the New Moon.

אֶלָּא לָאו דְּלֵית לֵיהּ – וּשְׁמַע מִינָּהּ: תְּמִידִין עֲדִיפִי!

Rather, is it not that the mishna is referring to a case where the Temple treasury **does not have** enough animals for all of the offerings, and it is teaching that the animals that he does have are utilized for the daily offerings of all three days rather than for the additional offering of Shabbat on the first of the three days? Consequently, one may **conclude from it** that the **daily offerings** of tomorrow **are given preference** over the additional offerings of today.

לָא, לְעוֹלָם דְּאִית לֵיהּ, וְהָכִי קָא אָמַר: אֵין פּוֹחֲתִין מִשִּׁשָּׁה טְלָאִים הַמְבוּקָּרִין בְּלִשְׁכַּת הַטְּלָאִים אַרְבָּעָה יָמִים קוֹדֶם שְׁחִיטָה, וּמַנִּי? בֶּן בַּג בַּג הִיא.

The Gemara replies: **No,** this is not a valid proof, as one can claim that **actually,** the mishna is referring to a case **where** the Temple treasury **has** enough animals for all of the offerings of the three days, **and this is what** the mishna **is saying** when it mentions six lambs: One maintains for use as daily offerings **no fewer than six lambs that** have been **inspected** and found to be unblemished **in the Chamber of the Lambs four days prior to** their **slaughter.** Lambs sacrificed as other offerings do not have to be inspected four days prior to being slaughtered. **And** in accordance with **whose** opinion is this mishna? **It is** in accordance with the opinion of **ben Bag Bag.**[P]

דְּתַנְיָא, בֶּן בַּג בַּג אוֹמֵר: מִנַּיִן לְתָמִיד שֶׁטָּעוּן בִּיקּוּר אַרְבָּעָה יָמִים קוֹדֶם שְׁחִיטָה? תַּלְמוּד לוֹמַר ״תִּשְׁמְרוּ לְהַקְרִיב לִי בְּמוֹעֲדוֹ״, וּלְהַלָּן הוּא אוֹמֵר: ״וְהָיָה לָכֶם לְמִשְׁמֶרֶת עַד אַרְבָּעָה עָשָׂר יוֹם״,

As it is taught in a *baraita* that **ben Bag Bag says: From where** is it derived that **the daily offering requires inspection four days prior to** its **slaughter? The verse states** with regard to the daily offering: **"You shall observe [*tishmeru*] to sacrifice to Me in its due season"** (Numbers 28:2), **and elsewhere,** with regard to the Paschal offering, the verse **states:** "On the tenth day of this month they shall take for them every man a lamb… **and you shall keep it [*mishmeret*] until the fourteenth day** of this month" (Exodus 12:3–6).

מַה לְּהַלָּן – טָעוּן בִּיקּוּר אַרְבָּעָה יָמִים קוֹדֶם שְׁחִיטָה, אַף כָּאן – טָעוּן בִּיקּוּר אַרְבָּעָה יָמִים קוֹדֶם שְׁחִיטָה.

Consequently, it is derived by means of a verbal analogy that **just as** in the verse **there,** the Paschal offering **requires inspection four days prior to** its **slaughter,** from the tenth of the month to the fourteenth, **so too here,** the daily offering **requires inspection four days prior to** its **slaughter.** This is not a requirement that pertains to all offerings; it is stated specifically with regard to the Paschal offering and extended by means of a verbal analogy to the daily offering.

אֲמַר לֵיהּ רָבִינָא לְרַב אַשִׁי: הָנֵי שִׁשָּׁה – שִׁבְעָה הָווּ, דְּהָא אִיכָּא דְּצַפְרָא דִּתְלָתָא בְּשַׁבְּתָא!

§ The Gemara cites a discussion pertaining to the mishna cited earlier. **Ravina said to Rav Ashi:** With regard to **these six** inspected lambs that must always be kept in the Chamber of Lambs, there ought to **be seven, as there is** a need for another lamb for the daily offering **of the morning of the third** day **of the week,** since it cannot be inspected on Shabbat or the subsequent festival days of Rosh HaShana, and therefore should be inspected and kept beforehand.

וּלְטַעֲמִיךְ, תְּמַנְיָא הָווּ, דְּהָאִיכָּא דְּפַנְיָא דְּמַעֲלֵי שַׁבְּתָא!

Rav Ashi responded to Ravina: **According to your reasoning** the correct number is not seven, but rather **it is eight; as there is** also the daily offering **of the afternoon of Shabbat eve** that should also be counted.

הָא לָא קַשְׁיָא, דִּלְבָתַר דְּאַקְרִיב קָאָמַר.

Ravina replied: **That** is **not difficult,** because the mishna **is saying that after he sacrificed** the daily offering of the afternoon there must be six inspected lambs.

HALAKHA

One maintains no fewer than six lambs that have been inspected – אֵין פּוֹחֲתִין מִשִּׁשָּׁה טְלָאִים הַמְבוּקָּרִין: One must keep no fewer than six lambs that have already been inspected in the Chamber of Lambs. They must be inspected four days before they are sacrificed (Rambam *Sefer Avoda, Hilkhot Temidin UMusafin* 1:9).

BACKGROUND

Chamber of the Lambs – לִשְׁכַּת הַטְּלָאִים: The Chamber of the Lambs was the chamber used for inspecting the animals to be brought as offerings in order to determine that they were free of blemishes. Every day in the early morning, the appointed priest would instruct the other priests to bring a lamb from this chamber for the daily offering of the morning. It was located in the northwest corner of the Hall of the Hearth in the Temple courtyard (*Tamid* 3:3).

Chamber of the Lambs

PERSONALITIES

Ben Bag Bag – בֶּן בַּג בַּג: The full name of this early Sage was Rabbi Yoḥanan ben Bag Bag. He is cited occasionally in the Mishna and Talmud and is referred to simply as ben Bag Bag. He lived during the time of the Second Temple and after its destruction. The Rambam maintains that he was a contemporary of Hillel and Shammai, who lived several generations earlier. If so, he must have been a very young student of Hillel's and lived to a very old age. *Tosafot* claim that he was a convert or a descendent of converts.

מִכָּל מָקוֹם שִׁבְעָה הָווּ! אֶלָּא תַּנָּא בְּעָלְמָא קָאֵי, וּמַאי ״כְּדֵי לְשַׁבָּת וּשְׁנֵי יָמִים טוֹבִים שֶׁל רֹאשׁ הַשָּׁנָה״? סִימָנָא בְּעָלְמָא.

The Gemara asks: **In any case,** the question stands: Why does the mishna say six lambs when, in fact the number required **is seven?** The Gemara answers: **Rather, the** ***tanna*** **is speaking generally,** referring to how many inspected lambs are required throughout the year. **And what** did he mean by his statement: **Sufficient for Shabbat and for the two festival days of Rosh HaShana?** It is **merely** intended as **a mnemonic,** to help one remember that there must be enough lambs for the daily offering of three days.

דַּיְקָא נַמִי, דְּקָתָנֵי ״כְּדֵי לְשַׁבָּת״, וְלָא קָתָנֵי ״לְשַׁבָּת וְלִשְׁנֵי יָמִים טוֹבִים שֶׁל רֹאשׁ הַשָּׁנָה״, שְׁמַע מִינַּהּ.

According to this the language of the mishna **is also precise,** as it **teaches: Sufficient for Shabbat** and for the two festival days of Rosh HaShana, **and it does not teach** that there must be six lambs **for Shabbat and for the two festival days of Rosh HaShana,** which would have indicated that these lambs are meant to actually be sacrificed on those days. The Gemara concludes that in fact one can **learn from** the language of the mishna that this is the correct interpretation.

״לֹא הִקְרִיבוּ כֶּבֶשׂ בַּבּוֹקֶר וכו׳. אָמַר רַבִּי שִׁמְעוֹן: וְכוּלָּהּ הָיְתָה קְרֵיבָה בֵּין הָעַרְבַּיִם, שֶׁאֵין מְחַנְּכִין אֶת מִזְבַּח הַזָּהָב אֶלָּא בִּקְטֹרֶת הַסַּמִּים״. חִינּוּךְ מַאן דְּכַר שְׁמֵיהּ?

§ The mishna teaches: If the priests **did not sacrifice a lamb in the morning** as the daily offering, nevertheless, they should sacrifice a lamb in the afternoon as the daily offering. If they did not burn the half-measure of incense in the morning, they should burn the half-measure in the afternoon. **Rabbi Shimon said: And** in such a case, **the entire** measure **was sacrificed in the afternoon, as** the daily service on a new **golden altar is initiated only with** the burning of **the incense of the spices** in the afternoon, at which time they would burn a full measure. The Gemara asks: **Who mentioned anything about** the **initiation** of the Temple vessels, i.e., what is its relevance to the mishna?

חַסּוּרֵי מִיחַסְּרָא, וְהָכִי קָתָנֵי: ״לֹא הִקְרִיבוּ כֶּבֶשׂ בַּבֹּקֶר – לֹא יַקְרִיבוּ בֵּין הָעַרְבַּיִם. בַּמֶּה דְּבָרִים אֲמוּרִים? שֶׁלֹּא נִתְחַנֵּךְ הַמִּזְבֵּחַ, אֲבָל נִתְחַנֵּךְ הַמִּזְבֵּחַ – יַקְרִיבוּ בֵּין הָעַרְבַּיִם.

The Gemara answers that the mishna **is incomplete, and this is what it is teaching:**[B] **If they did not sacrifice a lamb** for the daily offering **in the morning, they should not sacrifice** a lamb in **the afternoon. In what** case **is this statement said?** It is said in a case **where** the service of a new **altar had not** yet **been initiated,**[H] since it must first be initiated with the daily offering of the morning. **But** if the service of **the altar had** already **been initiated,** then **they should sacrifice** the lamb of the daily offering in **the afternoon** even though they did not sacrifice the lamb of the morning offering.

אָמַר רַבִּי שִׁמְעוֹן: אֵימָתַי? בִּזְמַן שֶׁהָיוּ אֲנוּסִין אוֹ שׁוֹגְגִין, אֲבָל אִם הָיוּ מְזִידִין, לֹא הִקְרִיבוּ כֶּבֶשׂ בַּבֹּקֶר – לֹא יַקְרִיבוּ בֵּין הָעַרְבַּיִם. לֹא הִקְטִירוּ קְטֹרֶת בַּבֹּקֶר – יַקְטִירוּ בֵּין הָעַרְבַּיִם״.

Rabbi Shimon said: When does this *halakha* apply? It applies **at a time when** the failure to sacrifice the daily morning offering was because **they were** prevented from sacrificing it due to **circumstances beyond their control or** they failed to sacrifice it **unwittingly. But if** the priests acted **intentionally and did not sacrifice a lamb in the morning** as the daily offering, **they should not sacrifice** a lamb **in the afternoon** as the daily offering. By contrast, if **they did not burn** the half-measure of **incense in the morning, they should burn** the half-measure **in the afternoon** regardless of the circumstances.

מְנָא הָנֵי מִילֵּי? דְּתָנוּ רַבָּנַן: ״וְאֵת הַכֶּבֶשׂ הַשֵּׁנִי תַּעֲשֶׂה בֵּין הָעַרְבָּיִם״ – שֵׁנִי בֵּין הָעַרְבַּיִם, וְלֹא רִאשׁוֹן בֵּין הָעַרְבַּיִם.

The Gemara asks: **From where are these matters** derived, that if the lamb of the daily offering of the morning was not sacrificed and the service of a new altar had not yet been initiated, then the lamb of the afternoon is also not sacrificed? The Gemara explains that it is derived **as the Sages taught** in a *baraita*: "The one lamb you shall offer in the morning; **and the second lamb you shall offer in the afternoon**" (Exodus 29:39). This verse teaches that **the second** lamb of the daily offering is sacrificed **in the afternoon, but** if it is **the first** one to be sacrificed, it may **not** be sacrificed **in the afternoon.**[N]

BACKGROUND

The mishna is incomplete and this is what it is teaching – חַסּוּרֵי מִיחַסְּרָא וְהָכִי קָתָנֵי: This method of explanation is often found in the Gemara. The addition introduced by the Gemara is an elaboration upon that which is written in the mishna, based on various difficulties raised in the Gemara that render the mishna in its original form incoherent or inconsistent with another authoritative source. The addition provides the necessary clarification.

HALAKHA

In a case where the altar had not yet been initiated – שֶׁלֹּא נִתְחַנֵּךְ הַמִּזְבֵּחַ: If they did not sacrifice a lamb for the daily offering in the morning, whether unwittingly or deliberately, they should nevertheless sacrifice a lamb for the daily offering in the afternoon. This is the *halakha* only in a case where the service of the altar was already initiated. If the altar is new and no sacrifice had ever been brought on it, then the afternoon offering should not be sacrificed on it, as the service of a new altar may be initiated only through the daily offering of the morning (Rambam *Sefer Avoda*, *Hilkhot Temidin UMusafin* 1:12).

NOTES

But if it is the first one to be sacrificed, it may not be sacrificed in the afternoon – וְלֹא רִאשׁוֹן בֵּין הָעַרְבַּיִם: Since the verse refers to the afternoon daily offering as the second lamb, it cannot be sacrificed if no other offering preceded it. Alternatively, Rashi explains that the second half of the verse is conditional upon the first half, so that the verse states that if "the one lamb you shall offer in the morning," then "the second lamb you shall offer in the afternoon."

בַּמֶּה דְּבָרִים אֲמוּרִים – שֶׁלֹּא נִתְחַנֵּךְ הַמִּזְבֵּחַ, אֲבָל נִתְחַנֵּךְ הַמִּזְבֵּחַ – אֲפִילּוּ רִאשׁוֹן בֵּין הָעַרְבַּיִם.

In what case **is this statement said?** It is said in a case **where the** service of a new **altar had not** yet **been initiated,**[N] since it must first be initiated with the offering of the morning. When the verse refers to the first or second offering, it means the first or second offering ever sacrificed on the altar. **But** if the service of **the altar had** already **been initiated,** then **even** if it is **the first** to be sacrificed that day, it should be sacrificed **in the afternoon.**

אָמַר רַבִּי שִׁמְעוֹן: אֵימָתַי? בִּזְמַן שֶׁהָיוּ אֲנוּסִין אוֹ שׁוֹגְגִין, אֲבָל אִם הָיוּ מְזִידִין, לֹא הִקְרִיבוּ כֶּבֶשׂ בַּבֹּקֶר – לֹא יַקְרִיבוּ בֵּין הָעַרְבַּיִם, לֹא הִקְטִירוּ קְטֹרֶת בַּבּוֹקֶר – יַקְטִירוּ בֵּין הָעַרְבַּיִם.

Rabbi Shimon said: When does this *halakha* apply? It applies **at a time when** the failure to sacrifice the daily morning offering was because **they were** prevented from sacrificing it due to **circumstances beyond their control or** they failed to sacrifice it **unwittingly. But if** the priests acted **intentionally and did not sacrifice a lamb in the morning** as the daily offering, **they should not sacrifice** a lamb **in the afternoon** as the daily offering. By contrast, if **they did not burn** the half-measure of **incense in the morning, they should burn** the half-measure **in the afternoon** regardless of the circumstances.

וְכִי כֹּהֲנִים חָטְאוּ, מִזְבֵּחַ בָּטֵל?! אָמַר רָבָא, הָכִי קָאָמַר: לֹא יַקְרִיבוּ הֵן, אֲבָל אֲחֵרִים – יַקְרִיבוּ.

The Gemara asks: Does it make sense that **because the priests sinned** by intentionally failing to sacrifice the morning daily offering, **the altar** should be entirely **idle? Rava said** that **this** is what Rabbi Shimon **is saying: They,** the priests who deliberately failed to sacrifice the morning daily offering, **should not sacrifice** the afternoon daily offering; **but other** priests **should sacrifice** it.[N]

״לֹא הִקְטִירוּ קְטֹרֶת בַּבֹּקֶר – יַקְטִירוּ בֵּין הָעַרְבַּיִם״. דְּכֵיוָן דְּלָא שְׁכִיחָא וּמְעַתְּרָא – חֲבִיבָא לְהוּ, וְלָא פָּשְׁעִי.

By contrast, if the priests acted intentionally and **did not burn** the **incense in the morning,** even those same priests **may burn** it in the **afternoon.** The reason for this is **that since** burning the incense **is uncommon**[N] **and causes** those who do so to become **wealthy,** it is **dear to the** priests, **and they will not be negligent** in the performance of this rite.

״אָמַר רַבִּי שִׁמְעוֹן: וְכוּלָּהּ הָיְתָה קְרֵיבָה בֵּין הָעַרְבַּיִם שֶׁאֵין מְחַנְּכִין אֶת מִזְבַּח הַזָּהָב אֶלָּא בִּקְטֹרֶת הַסַּמִּים שֶׁל בֵּין הָעַרְבַּיִם״ וכו׳. וְהָתַנְיָא: בִּקְטֹרֶת הַסַּמִּים שֶׁל שַׁחַר! תַּנָּאֵי הִיא.

§ The mishna teaches that if they did not burn the half-measure of incense in the morning, they should burn the half-measure in the afternoon. **Rabbi Shimon said: And** in such a case, **the entire** measure **was sacrificed in the afternoon.** The reason for the difference between the daily offerings and the incense is **that** the daily service on a new **golden altar is initiated only with** the burning of **the incense of the spices of the afternoon,**[H] at which time they would burn a full measure. The Gemara asks: **But isn't it taught** in a *baraita*: The service of a new golden altar is initiated **with** the burning **of the incense of the spices of the morning?** The Gemara answers: The question of whether the incense of the morning or the afternoon initiates the service of a new golden altar **is** a dispute between ***tanna'im*.**

אָמַר אַבָּיֵי: מִסְתַּבְּרָא כְּמַאן דְּאָמַר בִּקְטֹרֶת הַסַּמִּים שֶׁל בֵּין הָעַרְבַּיִם, דִּכְתִיב: ״בַּבֹּקֶר בַּבֹּקֶר בְּהֵיטִיבוֹ אֶת הַנֵּרוֹת יַקְטִירֶנָּה״

Abaye said: It **stands to reason** that the *halakha* should be **in accordance with the one who says** that it was initiated **with the incense of the spices of the afternoon, as it is written** with regard to the golden altar: "And Aaron shall burn thereon incense of sweet spices; **every morning, when he dresses the lamps, he shall burn it.** And when Aaron lights the lamps at dusk, he shall burn it, a perpetual incense before the Lord throughout your generations" (Exodus 30:7–8).

HALAKHA

With the burning of the incense of the spices of the afternoon – בִּקְטֹרֶת הַסַּמִּים שֶׁל בֵּין הָעַרְבַּיִם: The service of a new golden altar must be initiated with the burning of the incense of the spices of the afternoon. This is in accordance with the unattributed opinion in the mishna (49a) and the ruling of Abaye, and not in accordance with the *baraita* here (Rambam *Sefer Avoda, Hilkhot Temidin UMusafin* 3:1).

NOTES

In a case where the altar had not yet been initiated – שֶׁלֹּא נִתְחַנֵּךְ הַמִּזְבֵּחַ: Rashi explains that the verse is interpreted as referring to the first or second offering ever sacrificed on the altar, because the previous verse is referring to the inauguration of the altar, as it states: "Now this is that which you shall offer upon the altar" (Exodus 29:38).

But other priests should sacrifice it – אֲבָל אֲחֵרִים יַקְרִיבוּ: The Gemara does not clarify who these others are. It is unclear whether this penalty applies only to the specific priests who were designated to sacrifice the morning offering and refrained from doing so, or whether it applies even to their entire patrilineal family or to the entire priestly watch (commentary attributed to Rashba).

Burning the incense is uncommon – לָא שְׁכִיחָא: Rashi offers two suggestions as to why the incense is considered uncommon in comparison to the daily offering, despite the fact that they are both sacrificed twice a day. His first explanation is that the daily offering is a type of burnt offering, and burnt offerings may be sacrificed many times per day. His second explanation is that it is not that the offering of the incense itself is uncommon, but that it is uncommon for any one particular priest to burn it, as each priest was granted the opportunity to burn the incense only once in his lifetime (*Yoma* 26a).

אִי לָאו דַּעֲבַד הַדְלָקָה מֵאוּרְתָּא, הֲטָבָה בְּצַפְרָא מֵהֵיכָא?

The fact that ashes are removed from the lamps of the Candelabrum in the morning indicates that the lamps had been lit previously, since **if** the priest had **not performed the lighting** of the lamps the previous **evening, from where** would the ashes be **removed in the morning?** This proves that the Candelabrum must have been lit for the first time in the evening. Since the verse states: "When Aaron lights the lamps at dusk, he shall burn it, a perpetual incense before the Lord," it must be that the incense was burned for the first time in the evening.

וּלְמַאן דְּאָמַר בִּקְטֹרֶת הַסַּמִּים שֶׁל שַׁחַר – גָּמַר מִמִּזְבַּח הָעוֹלָה, מָה לְהַלָּן בְּתָמִיד שֶׁל שַׁחַר, אַף כָּאן בִּקְטֹרֶת הַסַּמִּים שֶׁל שַׁחַר.

The Gemara asks: **And according to the one who says** that the service of a new golden altar is initiated **with** the burning of **the incense of the spices of the morning,** from where is this *halakha* derived? The Gemara answers: He **derives it from** the initiation of **the altar of the burnt offering. Just as there,** the service of a new altar of the burnt offering is initiated **by** means of the **daily offering of the morning** rather than the afternoon, **so too here,** the service of a new golden altar is initiated **by** means of the burning of **the incense of the spices of the morning.**

"וְלֹא אֶת הַשֻּׁלְחָן אֶלָּא בְּלֶחֶם הַפָּנִים בְּשַׁבָּת". אֶלָּא בְּחוֹל אִיחֲנוּכֵי הוּא דְּלָא מִחֲנַךְ, הָא קַדּוֹשֵׁי מִיקְדִּישׁ?

§The mishna teaches: **And** use of a new **Table** was initiated **only with** the arrangement of **the shewbread on Shabbat.** The Gemara asks: **But** does the mishna mean to indicate that if the shewbread was placed on the Table **on a weekday it is** merely that the use of a new Table **is not initiated, but** the shewbread **is sanctified?** The *halakha* is that the shewbread is sanctified only when it is placed on the Table on Shabbat.

הִיא גּוּפָהּ קָא מַשְׁמַע לַן, דְּחִינּוּךְ וְקִידּוּשׁ דְּשֻׁלְחָן בְּשַׁבָּת הוּא. כִּדְקָתָנֵי סֵיפָא: וְלֹא אֶת הַמְּנוֹרָה אֶלָּא בְּשִׁבְעָה נֵרוֹתֶיהָ בֵּין הָעַרְבַּיִם.

The Gemara answers: The mishna **teaches us this** *halakha* **itself, that the initiation** of the use of a new Table **and the sanctification of** the shewbread when it is placed on **the Table** occur only **on Shabbat.**[H] This is **as** the mishna **teaches in the latter clause**[N] with regard to the initiation of the use of a new Candelabrum: **And** use of a new **Candelabrum** was initiated **only with** the kindling **of its seven lamps in the afternoon.**

תָּנוּ רַבָּנַן: זֶהוּ קְטֹרֶת שֶׁעָלְתָה לְיָחִיד עַל מִזְבֵּחַ הַחִיצוֹן, וְהוֹרָאַת שָׁעָה הָיְתָה. הֵיכָא? אָמַר רַב פָּפָּא: בַּנְּשִׂיאִים.

§The Gemara cites another *halakha* relating to the burning of incense. **The Sages taught** in a *baraita*: **This is incense that was offered for an individual** rather than the community **on the external altar,** and not on the golden altar as usual; **and this was a provisional edict,** permitted temporarily for that time only. The Gemara clarifies: To **what** case is the *baraita* referring? **Rav Pappa said:** It is referring to the incense brought **by the** tribal **princes** at the inauguration of the Tabernacle (see Numbers, chapter 7).

אֶלָּא יָחִיד עַל מִזְבֵּחַ הַחִיצוֹן הוּא דְּלָא, הָא עַל מִזְבֵּחַ הַפְּנִימִי – מַקְרִיב? וְתוּ, עַל מִזְבֵּחַ הַחִיצוֹן יָחִיד הוּא דְּלָא, הָא צִיבּוּר – מַקְרְבוּ?

The Gemara asks: **But** with regard to the incense of **an individual, is it** only **on the external altar that** it is **not** generally permitted to be burned, **but** an individual **may sacrifice** incense **on the inner altar,** as indicated by the *baraita*? **And furthermore, on the external altar, is it** only an **individual who may not** sacrifice incense, **but the community may sacrifice** incense on the external altar?

וְהָתַנְיָא: יָכוֹל יְהֵא יָחִיד מִתְנַדֵּב וּמֵבִיא כַּיּוֹצֵא בָּהּ נְדָבָה, וְקוֹרֵא אֲנִי בָּהּ "מוֹצָא שְׂפָתֶיךָ תִּשְׁמֹר וְעָשִׂיתָ"? תַּלְמוּד לוֹמַר "לֹא תַעֲלוּ עָלָיו קְטֹרֶת זָרָה".

But isn't it taught in a *baraita* contrary to those two inferences: One **might** have thought that **an individual may voluntarily donate and bring** incense[H] **similar to** the incense brought by the tribal princes to the Temple as **a gift** offering, **and I will read with regard to** this incense, as in the case of other gift offerings: **"That which has gone out of your lips you shall observe and do"** (Deuteronomy 23:24). Therefore, **the verse states** concerning the inner altar: **"You shall bring no strange incense thereon"** (Exodus 30:9). This indicates that an individual may not sacrifice incense even on the inner altar.

יָכוֹל לֹא יְהֵא יָחִיד מֵבִיא – שֶׁאֵין מֵבִיא חוֹבָתוֹ כַּיּוֹצֵא בָּהּ,

One **might** have thought that only **an individual may not bring** a gift of incense on the inner altar, **as** an individual **does not bring his obligatory** offering **similar to this** gift of incense, i.e., since an individual is never obligated to sacrifice incense, he may not voluntarily sacrifice incense either;

HALAKHA

The initiation of a new Table and the sanctification of the shewbread when it is placed on the Table occur only on Shabbat – דְּחִינּוּךְ וְקִידּוּשׁ דְּשֻׁלְחָן בְּשַׁבָּת הוּא: The use of a new Table must be initiated by placing the shewbread on it on Shabbat, in accordance with the mishna (49a) and the Gemara here. Additionally, the shewbread is sanctified on the Table only on Shabbat (Rambam *Sefer Avoda, Hilkhot Temidin UMusafin* 5:3, 12–13).

One might have thought that an individual may voluntarily donate and bring incense – יָכוֹל יְהֵא יָחִיד מִתְנַדֵּב וּמֵבִיא: One may not burn incense offered by an individual on the golden altar unless he has transferred its ownership to the community (Rambam *Sefer Avoda, Hilkhot Kelei HaMikdash* 2:11 and *Kesef Mishne* there).

NOTES

This is as the mishna teaches in the latter clause – כִּדְקָתָנֵי סֵיפָא: It is not clear how the latter clause of the mishna relates to the case of the Table and shewbread, as the Table sanctifies the shewbread whereas the Candelabrum does not sanctify the oil burned in it, which is sanctified in a service vessel before it is placed in the Candelabrum. Rashi explains that just as everything that is accomplished with the Candelabrum, i.e., its initiation and the mitzva to light it, is accomplished in the evening, so too everything that is accomplished on the Table, including the sanctification of the shewbread, is accomplished on Shabbat (Rashi).

Rabbeinu Gershom Meor HaGola explains that just as both the initiation and sanctification of the Candelabrum took place on a weekday rather than Shabbat, so too, the initiation and the sanctification of the Table were on Shabbat and not on a weekday. Later commentaries explain that this is consistent with Rabbeinu Gershom Meor HaGola's opinion that the Candelabrum does sanctify the oil (*Eizehu Mekoman*). Some inquire as to the source for his assumption that the Candelabrum was initiated on a weekday (*Mikdash David*).

אֲבָל צִבּוּר יְהֵא מֵבִיא, שֶׁמֵּבִיא חוֹבָה כַּיּוֹצֵא בָּהּ? תַּלְמוּד לוֹמַר ״לֹא תַעֲלוּ״.

but a community may bring incense as a gift offering, as the community **does bring its obligatory** offering **similar to this,** i.e., since the community is obligated to sacrifice incense it can also voluntarily sacrifice incense. Therefore, **the verse states: You shall not bring** [***lo ta'alu***] strange incense thereon" (Exodus 30:9). The fact that the verse formulates the prohibition with the plural word *ta'alu* indicates that even the community may not sacrifice incense as a voluntary gift offering.

יָכוֹל לֹא יַעֲלוּ עַל מִזְבֵּחַ הַפְּנִימִי, אֲבָל יַעֲלוּ עַל מִזְבֵּחַ הַחִיצוֹן? תַּלְמוּד לוֹמַר ״אֵת שֶׁמֶן הַמִּשְׁחָה וְאֶת קְטֹרֶת הַסַּמִּים לַקֹּדֶשׁ כְּכֹל אֲשֶׁר צִוִּיתִךָ יַעֲשׂוּ״ – אֵין לְךָ אֶלָּא מַה שֶּׁאָמוּר בָּעִנְיָן!

The *baraita* continues: One **might** have thought that the community **may not bring** a gift offering of incense **on the inner altar, but** it **may bring** incense **on the external altar.** Therefore, **the verse states: "And the anointing oil, and the incense of sweet spices for the sacred place; according to all that I have commanded you shall they do"** (Exodus 31:11). This teaches that one **has** the right to do **only that which is stated with regard to the matter,** without deviation. Consequently, incense may sacrificed only by the community, only when there is an obligation to sacrifice it, and it must be burned only on the inner altar. This contradicts the implication of the previously cited *baraita* that it is permitted to burn the incense of an individual on the golden altar or the incense of a community on the outer altar.

אָמַר רַב פַּפָּא: לָא מִיבַּעְיָא קָאָמַר, לָא מִיבַּעְיָא צִיבּוּר עַל מִזְבֵּחַ הַחִיצוֹן – דְּלָא אַשְׁכְּחַן, וְלָא מִיבַּעְיָא יָחִיד עַל מִזְבֵּחַ הַפְּנִימִי – דְּלָא אַשְׁכְּחַן, אֶלָּא אֲפִילּוּ יָחִיד עַל מִזְבֵּחַ הַחִיצוֹן, דְּאַשְׁכְּחַן בַּנְּשִׂיאִים – הוֹרָאַת שָׁעָה הָיְתָה.

Rav Pappa said: This is not problematic. The *baraita* **is speaking** utilizing the style of: **It is not necessary,** as follows. **It is not necessary** to state that **the community** may not sacrifice incense **on the external altar, as we have not found** a precedent for it. And similarly, **it is not necessary** to state that **an individual** may not sacrifice incense **on the inner altar, as we have not found** a precedent for it. **But** it is necessary to state that it is **even** prohibited for **an individual** to sacrifice incense **on the external altar,** despite the fact **that we have** ostensibly **found** a precedent for it **in** the case of **the** tribal **princes;** as that **was a provisional edict**[B] and therefore cannot serve as a precedent.

מתני׳ חֲבִיתֵּי כֹּהֵן גָּדוֹל לֹא הָיוּ בָּאִין חֲצָאִין, אֶלָּא מֵבִיא עִשָּׂרוֹן שָׁלֵם וְחוֹצֵהוּ, מַקְרִיב מֶחֱצָה בַּבֹּקֶר וּמֶחֱצָה בֵּין הָעַרְבַּיִם.

MISHNA The twelve loaves of *matza* prepared from a tenth of an ephah of flour of the **griddle-cake** offering **of the High Priest**[N] **did not come** from the house of the High Priest **in halves. Rather,** the High Priest **brings** from his house **a complete tenth** of an ephah of flour (see Leviticus 6:13) **and divides it**[N] in half, and he **sacrifices half in the morning and half in the afternoon.**[N]

כֹּהֵן שֶׁמֵּבִיא מֶחֱצָה שַׁחֲרִית, וּמֵת, וּמִינּוּ כֹּהֵן אַחֵר תַּחְתָּיו – לֹא יָבִיא חֲצִי עִשָּׂרוֹן מִבֵּיתוֹ וַחֲצִי עִשְׂרוֹנוֹ שֶׁל רִאשׁוֹן, אֶלָּא מֵבִיא עִשָּׂרוֹן שָׁלֵם (מֶחֱצָה) וְחוֹצֵהוּ, מַקְרִיב מֶחֱצָה, וּמֶחֱצָה אָבֵד. נִמְצְאוּ שְׁנֵי חֲצָאִין קְרֵבִין, וּשְׁנֵי חֲצָאִין אוֹבְדִין.

In the case of a High **Priest who brings** and sacrifices **half in the morning and dies,**[H] **and they appointed another** High **Priest in his stead,** the replacement High Priest **should neither bring half of a tenth** of an ephah of flour **from his house nor** sacrifice the remaining **half of the tenth of an ephah of** his **predecessor. Rather, he brings** from his house **an entire tenth** of an ephah **and divides it** in half, **sacrifices half, and** the other **half** is not sacrificed and **is lost. Consequently, two halves** of a tenth of an ephah **are sacrificed,** one-half of what was brought by each priest, **and** the other **two halves are lost.**

NOTES

The griddle-cake offering of the High Priest – חֲבִיתֵּי כֹּהֵן גָּדוֹל: The definition of a High Priest with regard to the obligation of the griddle-cake offering includes both one who was sanctified by means of the anointing oil and one sanctified by means of wearing the vestments of the High Priest, as was the procedure in the period of the second Temple. Rashi on *Makkot* 11a explains that the anointing oil was sequestered in the time of King Josiah, and thereafter the High Priests were sanctified exclusively by means of the priestly vestments (*Minḥat Ḥinnukh*).

The High Priest brings a complete tenth of an ephah of flour and divides it – מֵבִיא עִשָּׂרוֹן שָׁלֵם וְחוֹצֵהוּ: Some understand that this is referring to dividing the loaves. The Rambam holds that the preparation of the High Priest's griddle-cake offering was performed in the following manner: Each half of a tenth of an ephah would be kneaded into six loaves and baked, after which each of the twelve loaves would be divided in half. Twelve halves of loaves would then be sacrificed in the morning and twelve in the afternoon (Rambam *Sefer Avoda, Hilkhot Ma'aseh HaKorbanot* 13:4). The commentaries on the Rambam explain that he derives his opinion from the Gemara on 87b (*Kesef Mishne*; Radbaz; Mahari Kurkus).

Others reject the Rambam's explanation, claiming that nowhere is it suggested that each loaf was divided in half. Rather, the mishna means that the tenth of an ephah of flour would be divided into two halves. Each half would be baked into six loaves, and the six loaves of one half would be sacrificed in the morning while the other six loaves would be sacrificed in the afternoon (Ra'avad).

He sacrifices half in the morning and half in the afternoon – מַקְרִיב מֶחֱצָה בַּבֹּקֶר וּמֶחֱצָה בֵּין הָעַרְבַּיִם: The High Priest's griddle-cake offering is similar to the daily offering, inasmuch as they are both sacrificed twice daily, in the morning and in the afternoon. Nevertheless, early commentaries note that they are viewed differently in terms of the enumeration of the mitzvot. There are those who hold that the morning daily offering and the afternoon daily offering are counted as two separate mitzvot (Ramban's Commentary on *Sefer HaMitzvot*, end of the Ninth Principle). All agree that the High Priest's griddle-cake offering is counted as only one mitzva comprising two components (*Sefer HaḤinnukh* 136).

HALAKHA

A High Priest who brings and sacrifices half in the morning and dies – כֹּהֵן שֶׁמֵּבִיא מֶחֱצָה שַׁחֲרִית וּמֵת: If a High Priest sacrifices the morning half of the griddle-cake offering of the High Priest and then dies, and then another High Priest is appointed in his stead, the new High Priest must bring an entire tenth of an ephah of flour. He then divides it in half and sacrifices one of the halves. The remaining half of a tenth of an ephah from each of the two High Priests are left overnight and are then brought to the place designated for burning (Rambam *Sefer Avoda, Hilkhot Temidin UMusafin* 3:20–21).

BACKGROUND

Provisional edict – הוֹרָאַת שָׁעָה: This concept explains several incidents described in the Bible that do not conform to permanent halakhic guidelines, some of which occurred when the pertinent *halakha* had not yet been given to the Jewish people. In these instances, a specific mitzva was given as a temporary measure and the Jewish people acted on it, but practical *halakha* cannot be derived from it. There are also some examples of provisional edicts instituted by the Sages, when the unique needs of the time required acting more leniently or more strictly than the *halakha* generally allows or requires. The principle derived from the verse: "It is time to act for the Lord; they have made void Your law" (Psalms 119:126), dictates that at times even Torah law may be violated in order to uphold the Torah.

גמ׳ תנו רבנן: אילו נאמר ״מנחה מחצית״ – הייתי אומר: מביא חצי עשרון מביתו שחרית ומקריב, חצי עשרון מביתו ערבית ומקריב.

GEMARA The Gemara cites that which **the Sages taught** in a *baraita*, commenting on the verse: "This is the offering of Aaron and of his sons, which they shall offer to the Lord on the day when he is anointed: The tenth part of an ephah of fine flour for a meal offering perpetually, half of it in the morning, and half of it in the evening" (Leviticus 6:13). **If the verse** had **stated: A meal offering** perpetually, **half** in the morning and half in the evening; **I would have said** that the High Priest **brings half of a tenth** of an ephah **in the morning and sacrifices** it, and then he brings **half of a tenth** of an ephah **in the afternoon and sacrifices** it.

תלמוד לומר ״מחציתה בבקר ומחציתה בערב״ – מחצה משלם הוא מקריב, הא כיצד? מביא עשרון שלם וחוצהו, ומקריב מחצה בבקר ומחצה בין הערבים.

Since **the verse states: "Half of it in the morning, and half of it in the evening"** (Leviticus 6:13),[N] it teaches that **he sacrifices half of a complete** tenth of an ephah. **How so?** The High Priest **brings** from his house **a complete tenth** of an ephah of fine flour, **and divides it** in half, **and sacrifices half in the morning and half in the afternoon.**

נטמא מחצה של בין הערבים או שאבד, יכול יביא חצי עשרון מביתו ערבית ויקריב? תלמוד לומר ״מחציתה בבקר ומחציתה בערב״ – מחצה משלם הוא מביא,

In a case where the **half of** a tenth of an ephah that was supposed to be offered in **the afternoon became impure or was lost** after the High Priest sacrificed the first half in the morning, one **might** have thought that **he should bring half of a tenth** of an ephah **from his house and sacrifice** it. Therefore, **the verse states: "Half of it in the morning, and half of it in the evening,"** which teaches that **he brings half of a complete** tenth of an ephah.

הא כיצד? מביא עשרון שלם [מביתו] וחוצהו, ומקריב מחצה ומחצה אבד, נמצאו שני חצאין קריבין ושני חצאין אובדין.

How so? The High Priest **brings a complete tenth** of an ephah of fine flour **from his house and divides it** in half, **and he sacrifices half, and** the other **half** is not sacrificed and **is lost. Consequently, two halves** of a tenth of an ephah **are sacrificed,** the half that was sacrificed in the morning from the original tenth of an ephah, and half of the replacement tenth of an ephah, **and** the other **two halves are lost.**

כהן גדול שהקריב מחצה שחרית ומת, ומינו אחר תחתיו, יכול יביא חצי עשרון מביתו או חצי עשרונו של ראשון? תלמוד לומר ״ומחציתה בערב״ – מחצה משלם הוא מביא ומקריב,

In the case of a High **Priest who sacrificed half in the morning and died, and they appointed another** High **Priest in his stead,** one **might** have thought that the second High Priest **should bring half of a tenth** of an ephah **from his house** and sacrifice it, **or** that he should sacrifice the remaining **half of a tenth** of an ephah **of the first** High Priest. Therefore, **the verse states: "And half of it in the evening,"** which teaches that he **brings and sacrifices half of a complete** tenth of an ephah.

הא כיצד? מביא עשרון שלם וחוצהו ומקריב, ומחצה אבד. נמצאו שני חצאין אובדין, ושני חצאין קריבין.

How so? The replacement High Priest **brings a complete tenth** of an ephah of fine flour **from his house and divides it** in half, **and he sacrifices** half, **and half** is not sacrificed and **is lost. Consequently, two halves** of a tenth of an ephah **are lost,** half of the tenth of an ephah brought by each priest, **and** the other **two halves are sacrificed.**

תני תנא קמיה דרב נחמן: מחצה ראשון ומחצה שני – תעובר צורתן ויצאו לבית השריפה.

§ With regard to the two halves of a tenth of an ephah that are lost, **a *tanna*,** i.e., a Sage who recited *baraitot*, **taught** a *baraita* **before Rav Naḥman:** With regard to **the half** that was not sacrificed by the **first** High Priest, who died, **and the half** brought but not sacrificed by the **second** High Priest who replaced him, **their form should decay,** i.e., they should be left overnight so they become disqualified, **and** then they should be **brought out to the place** designated **for burning.**

אמר ליה רב נחמן: בשלמא ראשון – איחזי להקרבה, אלא שני – למה ליה עיבור צורה? מעיקרא לאיבוד קא אתי!

Rav Naḥman said to the *tanna*: **Granted,** the half that was not sacrificed by the **first** High Priest should be left overnight before it is burned, because it was initially **fit for sacrifice** before the first High Priest died. **But** with regard to the half that was not sacrificed by the **second** High Priest, **why** must **it** be left overnight so that its **form decays?** It was **brought to be lost from the outset,** i.e., when the full tenth of an ephah was brought it was known that only half would be sacrificed and half would be lost. Consequently, it is unnecessary to leave it overnight before burning it.

NOTES

Since the verse states: Half of it in the morning and half of it in the evening – **תלמוד לומר מחציתה בבקר ומחציתה בערב**: This exposition is cited three times in this Gemara to teach three *halakhot*: The basic *halakha* that both halves are initially brought together as a complete tenth of an ephah, the *halakha* in a case where the first half was sacrificed and then the second half was lost or became impure, and the *halakha* in a case where the High Priest died after sacrificing the first half. Rashi and the commentary attributed to Rashba note that the first two *halakhot* are derived from the two instances of the term "half of it," and the third *halakha* is derived from the extra "and" between the two usages of that expression.

דְּאָמַר לָךְ מַנִּי? תַּנָּא דְּבֵי רַבָּה בַּר אֲבוּהּ הוּא, דְּאָמַר: אֲפִילּוּ פִּיגּוּל טָעוּן עִיבּוּר צוּרָה.

Rav Naḥman continued: **Who is the one who said this** *baraita* **to you? It was the** ***tanna*** **of the school of Rabba bar Avuh, who says:** All disqualified offerings, **even** ***piggul,*** which is disqualified by Torah law, **require decay of form** before they are burned.

רַב אַשִׁי אָמַר: אֲפִילּוּ תֵּימָא רַבָּנַן, כֵּיוָן דִּבְעִידָּנָא דְּפָלְגִי בְּהוּ, אִי בָּעֵי הַאי מַקְרִיב וְאִי בָּעֵי הַאי מַקְרִיב – מִיחְזָא חֲזוּ.

Rav Ashi said: The *baraita* can be understood **even** if **you say** it is in accordance with the opinion of **the Rabbis** who disagree with Rabba bar Avuh and hold that *piggul* does not require decay of form. Nevertheless, **since at the time when** the second High Priest **divides the** two halves, **if he wants** he can **sacrifice this** half, **and if he wants** he can **sacrifice that** other half, both halves are considered **fit** to be sacrificed and may not be burned until they are left overnight.

אִיתְּמַר: חֲבִיתֵּי כֹּהֵן גָּדוֹל כֵּיצַד עוֹשִׂין אוֹתָן? רַבִּי חִיָּיא בַּר אַבָּא אָמַר רַבִּי יוֹחָנָן: אוֹפָהּ, וְאַחַר כָּךְ מְטַגְּנָהּ. רַבִּי אַסִּי אָמַר רַבִּי חֲנִינָא: מְטַגְּנָהּ, וְאַחַר כָּךְ אוֹפָהּ.

§ The Gemara cites that which **was stated** further about the griddle-cake offering: **How are the griddle-cake** offerings of **the High Priest prepared?** The verse seems to prescribe a variety of methods of preparation: "On a griddle it shall be made with oil; when it is soaked, you shall bring it in; and baked pieces [*tufinei*] of the meal offering shall you sacrifice for a pleasing aroma to the Lord" (Leviticus 6:14). **Rabbi Ḥiyya bar Abba** says that **Rabbi Yoḥanan says** that it is prepared in the following manner: The individual preparing it **bakes it** in an oven **and afterward he fries it** in a pan. **Rabbi Asi** says that **Rabbi Ḥanina says** that it is prepared in the following manner: The individual preparing it **fries it** in a pan **and afterward he bakes** it in an oven.

אָמַר רַבִּי חִיָּיא בַּר אַבָּא: כְּוָותֵיהּ דִּידִי מִסְתַּבְּרָא, "תֻּפִינֵי" – תֵּאָפֵינָה נָאָה. רַבִּי אַסִּי אָמַר: כְּוָותֵיהּ דִּידִי מִסְתַּבְּרָא, "תֻּפִינֵי" – תֵּאָפֵינָה נָא.

Rabbi Ḥiyya bar Abba said: It stands to reason in accordance with my opinion because the verse states: "And baked pieces [*tufinei*] of the meal offering." The word for **baked pieces** [*tufinei*] should be understood as meaning that **they shall be baked** when they are still **beautiful** [*te'afena na'a*], i.e., before being fried. **Rabbi Asi said: It stands to reason in accordance with my** opinion because the word *tufinei* should be understood as meaning that **they shall be baked** when they are already **partially cooked** [***te'afena na***], i.e., after being fried.

כְּתַנָּאֵי: "תֻּפִינֵי" – תֵּאָפֵינָה נָא. רַבִּי אוֹמֵר: תֵּאָפֵינָה נָאָה. רַבִּי יוֹסֵי אוֹמֵר: תֵּאָפֵינָה רַבָּה, אִית לֵיהּ נָא, וְאִית לֵיהּ נָאָה.

This dispute between the *amora'im* is **parallel to** a dispute between *tanna'im* in a *baraita*: The word for baked pieces [*tufinei*] should be understood as meaning that **they shall be baked** when they are already **partially cooked** [***te'afena na***]. **Rabbi** Yehuda HaNasi **says:** It should be understood as meaning that **they shall be baked** when they are still **beautiful** [***te'afena na'a***]. **Rabbi Yosei says:** The word *tufinei* is plural, indicating that the pieces **should be baked extensively,**[NH] i.e., more than once. Consequently, Rabbi Yosei **accepts** the opinion that the pieces should be baked when they are already **partially cooked, and he** also **accepts** the opinion that they should be baked when they are **beautiful.** Therefore the offering should first be baked, then fried, then baked again.

תְּנַן הָתָם: חֲבִיתֵּי כֹּהֵן גָּדוֹל – לִישָׁתָן וַעֲרִיכָתָן וַאֲפִיָּיתָן בִּפְנִים, וְדוֹחוֹת אֶת הַשַּׁבָּת.

§ **We learned** in a mishna **elsewhere** (96a): Concerning the twelve loaves of **the High Priest's griddle-cake** offering, of which six are sacrificed in the morning and six in the evening, **their kneading, and forming of their** loaves, **and their baking are** performed **inside** the Temple courtyard, **and** all labors involved in those actions **override Shabbat.**[H]

מְנָא הָנֵי מִילֵּי? אָמַר רַב הוּנָא: "תֻּפִינֵי" – תֵּאָפֵינָה נָאָה, וְאִי אָפֵי לָהּ מֵאֶתְמוֹל – אִינְשְׁפָה לָהּ. מַתְקִיף לָהּ רַב יוֹסֵף: אֵימָא, דְּכָבֵישׁ לֵיהּ בְּיַרְקָא!

The Gemara asks: **From where is this matter,** i.e., that these actions override Shabbat, derived? **Rav Huna said:** The verse says ***tufinei,*** meaning that when it is already **baked it must** still **be beautiful** [***te'afena na'a***]. **And if** one would **bake it yesterday,** on the eve of Shabbat, **it** would become **swollen** [***inshefa***][L] and no longer beautiful. **Rav Yosef objects to this:** If the purpose of baking them on Shabbat is to ensure they remain fresh, **say that** the loaves should be baked before Shabbat and **covered with greens** to preserve them.

NOTES

Should be baked extensively [*rabba*] – תֵּאָפֵינָה רַבָּה: Rashi cites three interpretations of this exposition and the opinion of Rabbi Yosei: One interpretation is that the offering must be baked multiple times. Rabbi Yosei accepts the opinion that interprets the verse as *te'afena na'a* and therefore requires that it be baked before it is fried, and he also accepts the opinion that interprets the verse as *te'afena na* and therefore requires that it be baked after it is fried as well.

A second interpretation is that the offering must be baked in a manner that causes it to be large [*rabba*] and thin. In order to facilitate this, it should be fried before it is baked, thereby fulfilling *te'afena na*. The loaves will end up being beautiful, which is a fulfillment of *te'afena na'a*.

The third interpretation is based on a version of the text that states that the offering should be baked so that it is soft [*rakka*], rather than *rabba*. According to this, the point is that it must be softened by being fried in a large quantity of oil. Since it is first fried one fulfills the requirement of *te'afena na*, and because the loaves end up soft and beautiful, one fulfills the requirement of *te'afena na'a*.

HALAKHA

Should be baked extensively – תֵּאָפֵינָה רַבָּה: The High Priest would partially bake each of the loaves of his griddle-cake offering and then fry it in a shallow pan with the remainder of its quarter-*log* of oil. According to the Rambam the loaves would not be baked extensively. He interprets the opinion of Rabbi Yosei as meaning that the loaves should first be lightly baked and then fried. The Rambam rules in accordance with the opinion of Rabbi Yosei because the *halakha* is generally in accordance with his opinion and because his reasoning is compelling (Rambam *Sefer Avoda*, *Hilkhot Ma'aseh HaKorbanot* 13:3, and see *Kesef Mishne* there).

And they override Shabbat – וְדוֹחוֹת אֶת הַשַּׁבָּת: The kneading and baking of the High Priest's griddle-cake offering override the prohibitions against performing these labors on Shabbat. This is due to the fact that the verse refers to the loaves as *tufinei*, which means that they must be beautiful, and they would not be beautiful if they were baked the previous afternoon. This is in accordance with the mishna and the interpretation of Rav Huna in the Gemara. See *Leḥem Mishne*, which addresses the question of why the Rambam quotes this reasoning despite the fact that it is rejected in the Gemara (Rambam *Sefer Avoda*, *Hilkhot Temidin UMusafin* 3:18).

LANGUAGE

Swollen [*inshefa*] – אִינְשְׁפָה: Both the exact reading of this Aramaic word and its meaning are uncertain. Rashi explains that it means that it becomes swollen due to exposure to air, and that it is similar to the Hebrew term in the verse: "You blew [*nashafta*] with your wind" (Exodus 15:10). As a result, its form has changed and it is not considered beautiful (*Arukh*).

דְּבֵי רַבִּי יִשְׁמָעֵאל תָּנָא: "תֵּעָשֶׂה" – וַאֲפִילּוּ בְּשַׁבָּת, "תֵּעָשֶׂה" – וַאֲפִילּוּ בְּטוּמְאָה.

The Gemara cites another explanation of why the preparation of these loaves overrides Shabbat. A Sage from **the school of Rabbi Yishmael taught:** The verse states: "On a griddle it **shall be made** with oil" (Leviticus 6:14), which teaches that it shall be made under all circumstances, **even on Shabbat.** Similarly, this phrase **"shall be made"** teaches that it should be made **even in** a state of **ritual impurity.**

אַבַּיֵי אָמַר, אָמַר קְרָא: "סֹלֶת מִנְחָה תָּמִיד",

Abaye said that there is a different explanation: The **verse states: "Fine flour for a meal offering perpetually"** (Leviticus 6:13);

Perek **IV**
Daf **51** Amud **a**

הֲרֵי הִיא כְּמִנְחַת תְּמִידִין.

this teaches that the *halakha* of the griddle-cake offering of the High Priest **is like** that of **the meal offering** that is a component **of the daily offerings.** The daily offerings override Shabbat, as the verse says: "This is the burnt offering of every Shabbat, beside the continual burnt offering, and the drink offering thereof" (Numbers 28:10). Therefore, preparing the griddle-cake offering of the High Priest likewise overrides Shabbat.

רָבָא אָמַר: "עַל מַחֲבַת" – מְלַמֵּד שֶׁטְּעוּנָה כְּלִי, וְאִי אָפֵי לַהּ מֵאֶתְמוֹל – אִיפְּסִיל לֵיהּ בְּלִינָה. תַּנְיָא כְּוָותֵיהּ דְּרָבָא: "עַל מַחֲבַת" – מְלַמֵּד שֶׁטְּעוּנָה כְּלִי.

Rava said that the basis for it overriding Shabbat is the fact that the verse states: **"On a griddle"** (Leviticus 6:14), which **teaches that** the griddle-cake offering of the High Priest **requires a vessel.** Therefore, **if he had baked it the previous day** rather than on Shabbat, it would be **disqualified by** being **left overnight,** since the loaves had already been consecrated in a service vessel. It **is taught** in a *baraita* **in accordance with** the opinion **of Rava:**[N] **"On a griddle" teaches that** the griddle-cake offering of the High Priest **requires a vessel.**

"בַּשֶּׁמֶן" – לְהוֹסִיף לָהּ שֶׁמֶן וְאֵינִי יוֹדֵעַ כַּמָּה.

The *baraita* continues: The continuation of the verse states: "It shall be made **with the oil."** The fact that the verse makes reference to "the oil" rather than just oil indicates that one is supposed **to add** extra **oil to it,** but **I do not know how much** oil to add.

הֲרֵינִי דָּן: נֶאֱמַר כָּאן "שֶׁמֶן", וְנֶאֱמַר לְהַלָּן בְּמִנְחַת נְסָכִים "שֶׁמֶן". מָה לְהַלָּן – שְׁלֹשֶׁת לוּגִּין לְעִשָּׂרוֹן, אַף כָּאן – שְׁלֹשֶׁת לוּגִּין לְעִשָּׂרוֹן.

Therefore **I** must **deduce** as follows: **It is stated here,** concerning the griddle-cake offering of the High Priest: **"Oil," and it is stated there, with regard to the meal offering** brought with the **libations** that accompany animal offerings: "A tenth part of an ephah of fine flour mingled with the fourth part of a *hin* of beaten **oil"** (Exodus 29:40). **Just as there,** with regard to the meal offering brought with the libations, the amount of oil required is **three *log* per tenth** of an ephah of flour; **so too here,** in the case of the griddle-cake offering of the High Priest, one brings **three *log*** of oil **per tenth** of an ephah of flour.[H]

HALAKHA

Three *log* of oil per tenth of an ephah of flour – שְׁלֹשֶׁת לוּגִּין לְעִשָּׂרוֹן: The High Priest brings three *log* of oil together with a tenth of an ephah of fine flour for his griddle-cake offering (Rambam *Sefer Avoda*, *Hilkhot Ma'aseh HaKorbanot* 13:2).

NOTES

It is taught in a *baraita* in accordance with the opinion of Rava – תַּנְיָא כְּוָותֵיהּ דְּרָבָא: *Tosafot* note that although the *baraita* is adduced as support for Rava's opinion, it also lends support to the opinion of Abaye, because it cites the opinion of Rabbi Yishmael, son of Rabbi Yoḥanan ben Beroka, who equates the *halakha* of the griddle-cake offering of the High Priest and the meal offering of the daily offerings by means of the verse: "Fine flour for a meal offering perpetually [*tamid*]."

The reason that the *baraita* is cited in support of Rava is that Rava actually agrees with Abaye (*Tosafot*). Rava's point is merely that in order to derive the *halakha* that one may prepare the griddle-cake offering of the High Priest on Shabbat there is no need to resort to the verse: "Fine flour for a meal offering perpetually [*tamid*]." According to this explanation, Rabbi Yishmael, son of Rabbi Yoḥanan ben Beroka, utilizes this verse to teach about the quantity of oil, not about preparing the offering on Shabbat.

אוֹ כְּלֵךְ לְדֶרֶךְ זוֹ: נֶאֱמַר כָּאן ״שֶׁמֶן״, וְנֶאֱמַר בְּמִנְחַת נְדָבָה ״שֶׁמֶן״. מָה לְהַלָּן – לוֹג אֶחָד, אַף כָּאן – לוֹג אֶחָד?

Or perhaps, **go this way: It is stated here,** concerning the griddle-cake offering of the High Priest: **"Oil," and it is stated with regard to** the **voluntary meal offering:** "And when anyone brings a meal offering to the Lord, his offering shall be of fine flour; and he shall pour **oil** upon it" (Leviticus 2:1). **Just as there,** with regard to the voluntary meal offering, one brings **one *log*** of oil for each tenth of an ephah of flour (see 88a); **so too here,** one brings **one *log*** of oil for each tenth of an ephah of flour.

נִרְאֶה לְמִי דּוֹמֶה, דָּנִין תבש״ט מִתבש״ט, תָּדִיר, בָּאָה חוֹבָה, דּוֹחָה שַׁבָּת, דּוֹחָה טוּמְאָה,

The *baraita* analyzes these two possibilities: **Let us see to which** case **it is** more **similar,** i.e., which is a better comparison to the griddle-cake offering of the High Priest. Perhaps **we** should **derive** the *halakha* with regard to the griddle-cake offering of the High Priest, which has characteristics represented by the letters ***tav, beit, shin, tet,* from** the *halakha* with regard to a meal offering brought with libations, which also has the characteristics represented by the letters ***tav, beit, shin, tet.*** These characteristics are that they are **frequent** [***tadir***], as these offerings are sacrificed twice daily; they are **brought** [***ba'ah***] **as an obligation;** they **override Shabbat;** and they **override impurity** [***tuma***].

וְאֵין דָּנִין תבש״ט מִשֶּׁאֵינוֹ תבש״ט.

And we should not derive the *halakha* with regard to the griddle-cake offering of the High Priest, which has the characteristics represented by the letters ***tav, beit, shin, tet,* from** the voluntary meal offering, which **does not** have the characteristics represented by the letters ***tav, beit, shin, tet.***

אוֹ כְּלֵךְ לְדֶרֶךְ זוֹ: דָּנִין יגי״ל מִיגי״ל, יָחִיד, בִּגְלַל עַצְמָהּ, יַיִן, לְבוֹנָה,

Or perhaps, **go this way: We** should **derive** the *halakha* with regard to the griddle-cake offering of the High Priest, which has the characteristics represented by the letters ***yod, gimmel, yod, lamed,* from** the voluntary meal offering, which also has the characteristics represented by the letters ***yod, gimmel, yod, lamed,*** which stand for the following *halakhot*: Each of these offerings may be brought by **an individual** [***yaḥid***]; each is **brought for** [***biglal***] **its own sake,** rather than accompanying another offering; they are not accompanied by **wine** [***yayin***] for a libation; and they require **frankincense** [***levona***].

וְאֵין דָּנִין יגי״ל מִשֶּׁאֵינוֹ יגי״ל.

And we should not derive the *halakha* with regard to the griddle-cake offering of the High Priest, which has the characteristics represented by the letters ***yod, gimmel, yod, lamed,* from** the *halakha* with regard to the meal offering brought with libations, **which does not** have the characteristics represented by the letters ***yod, gimmel, yod, lamed.*** Consequently, the comparisons in both directions are equally compelling.

רַבִּי יִשְׁמָעֵאל בְּנוֹ שֶׁל רַבִּי יוֹחָנָן בֶּן בְּרוֹקָה אוֹמֵר: ״סֹלֶת מִנְחָה תָּמִיד״ – הֲרֵי הִיא לְךָ כְּמִנְחַת תְּמִידִין, מָה מִנְחַת תְּמִידִין – שְׁלֹשָׁה לוּגִּין לְעִשָּׂרוֹן, אַף זוֹ – שְׁלֹשָׁה לוּגִּין לְעִשָּׂרוֹן.

The *baraita* continues its determination of how much oil is brought with the griddle-cake offering of the High Priest. **Rabbi Yishmael, son of Rabbi Yoḥanan ben Beroka, says:** "This is the offering of Aaron… the tenth part of an ephah of **fine flour for a meal offering perpetually** [***tamid***], half of it in the morning, and half of it in the evening" (Leviticus 6:13). The fact that the verse makes reference to the griddle-cake offering of the High Priest as *tamid* teaches that **it is in** the same category as **the meal offering** component **of the daily offerings** [***temidin***]. **Just as the meal offering** component **of the daily offerings** requires **three *log*** of oil **for** each **tenth** of an ephah of flour, **so too this** griddle-cake offering of the High Priest requires **three *log*** of oil **for** each **tenth** of an ephah of flour.

רַבִּי שִׁמְעוֹן אוֹמֵר: רִיבָּה כָּאן שֶׁמֶן, וְרִיבָּה בְּמִנְחַת כְּבָשִׂים שֶׁמֶן. מָה לְהַלָּן – שְׁלֹשֶׁת לוּגִּין לְעִשָּׂרוֹן, אַף כָּאן – שְׁלֹשֶׁת לוּגִּין לְעִשָּׂרוֹן.

Rabbi Shimon says: The verse **adds** to the amount of **oil** that is required **here,** with regard to the griddle-cake offering of the High Priest, **and** it similarly **adds** to the amount of **oil** that is required **there,** in the case of the **meal offering** that accompanies the sacrifice of **sheep. Just as there,** in the case of the meal offering that accompanies the sacrifice of sheep, **three *log*** of oil are required **for** each **tenth** of an ephah of flour, **so too here,** in the case of the griddle-cake offering of the High Priest, **three *log*** of oil are required **for** each **tenth** of an ephah of flour.

אוֹ כַּלֵּךְ לְדֶרֶךְ זוֹ: רִיבָּה כָּאן שֶׁמֶן, וְרִיבָּה בְּמִנְחַת פָּרִים וְאֵילִים שֶׁמֶן. מַה לְּהַלָּן – שְׁנֵי לוּגִּין לְעִשָּׂרוֹן, אַף כָּאן – שְׁנֵי לוּגִּין לְעִשָּׂרוֹן?

Or perhaps, **go this way:** The verse **adds** to the amount of **oil** that is required **here,** and it similarly **adds** to the amount of **oil** that is required in the case of **the meal offering** that accompanies the sacrifice of **bulls and rams. Just as there,** in the case of the meal offering that accompanies the sacrifice of bulls and rams, **two** ***log*** of oil are required **for each tenth** of an ephah of flour,[N] **so too here,** in the case of the griddle-cake offering of the High Priest, **two** ***log*** of oil are required **for** each **tenth** of an ephah of flour.

נִרְאֶה לְמִי דּוֹמֶה, דָּנִין מִנְחָה הַבָּאָה עִשָּׂרוֹן מִמִּנְחָה הַבָּאָה בְּעִשָּׂרוֹן, וְאֵין דָּנִין מִנְחָה הַבָּאָה עִשָּׂרוֹן מִמִּנְחָה הַבָּאָה שְׁנַיִם וּשְׁלֹשָׁה עֶשְׂרוֹנִים.

With regard to these two possibilities, **let us see to which** case **it is** more **similar,** i.e., which is a better comparison to the griddle-cake offering of the High Priest. Perhaps **we** should **derive** the *halakha* with regard to the griddle-cake offering of the High Priest, which is **a meal offering that comes** in the amount of **a tenth** of an ephah of flour, **from** the meal offering that accompanies the sacrifice of sheep, which is also **a meal offering that comes** in the amount of **a tenth** of an ephah of flour. **And we should not derive** the *halakha* with regard to **a meal offering that comes** in the amount of **a tenth** of an ephah of flour **from** the *halakha* in the case of **a meal offering that comes** in the amount of **two or three tenths** of an ephah of flour, such as the meal offerings that accompany the sacrifice of bulls and rams.

הָא גּוּפָא קַשְׁיָא, אָמְרַתְּ: ״בַּשֶּׁמֶן״ – לְהוֹסִיף לָהּ שֶׁמֶן, וַהֲדַר תָּנֵי: נֶאֱמַר כָּאן ״שֶׁמֶן״, וְנֶאֱמַר בְּמִנְחַת נְדָבָה ״שֶׁמֶן״!

The Gemara asks a question with regard to the beginning of the *baraita*: **This** *baraita* **itself** is **difficult,** as it contains an internal contradiction. First **you said** that the expression **"with the oil"** stated in the verse concerning the griddle-cake offering of the High Priest serves **to add** extra **oil,** which indicates that more than the basic amount of one *log* of oil is required. **And then it teaches: It is stated here,** concerning the griddle-cake offering of the High Priest: **"Oil," and it is stated with regard to** the **voluntary meal offering** that it must be brought with **"oil."** The *baraita* suggests that just as one *log* of oil is brought with the voluntary meal offering, so too one *log* is brought with the griddle-cake offering of the High Priest.

אֲמַר אַבַּיֵי: מַאן תָּנָא ״בַּשֶּׁמֶן״ לְהוֹסִיף? רַבִּי שִׁמְעוֹן הִיא, וְ״אִילּוּ לֹא נֶאֱמַר״ קָאָמַר. וּבְדִינָא מַאן קָא מְהַדַּר? רַבִּי יִשְׁמָעֵאל.

In answer to this question, **Abaye said: Who is the** *tanna* who **taught** that the term **"with the oil"** with regard to the griddle-cake offering of the High Priest serves **to add** extra oil? **It is Rabbi Shimon,** who holds that three *log* of oil are required, as derived from the meal offering that accompanies the sacrifice of sheep. **And** Rabbi Shimon **is speaking** utilizing the style of: **If it were not stated.** If the verse had not indicated by the term "with the oil" that extra oil is required, it would have been possible to derive from the voluntary meal offering that only one *log* is required. **And who** is the *tanna* who **responds** to Rabbi Shimon's **derivation** and suggests that in fact the amount of oil can be derived from the case of the voluntary meal offering? It is **Rabbi Yishmael.**

רַב הוּנָא בְּרֵיהּ דְּרַב יְהוֹשֻׁעַ אֲמַר: כּוּלָּהּ רַבִּי יִשְׁמָעֵאל בְּנוֹ שֶׁל רַבִּי יוֹחָנָן בֶּן בְּרוֹקָה הִיא,

Rav Huna, son of Rav Yehoshua, said that the *baraita* should be understood differently: The **entire** *baraita* **is** in accordance with the opinion of **Rabbi Yishmael, son of Rabbi Yoḥanan ben Beroka,** who derives that three *log* of oil are required in the griddle-cake offering based upon the amount required in the meal offering component of the daily offerings.

וְהָכִי קָאָמַר: ״בַּשֶּׁמֶן״ – לְהוֹסִיף לָהּ שֶׁמֶן, דְּאִי לִקְבּוֹעַ שֶׁמֶן – לָא צְרִיךְ, כֵּיוָן דִּכְתִיב בָּהּ ״עַל מַחֲבַת״ – כְּמִנְחַת מַחֲבַת דָּמְיָא.

And with regard to the possibility of deriving that only one *log* is required, as in the voluntary meal offering, **this** is what **he is saying:** The term **"with the oil"** stated with regard to the griddle-cake offering of the High Priest comes **to add** more **oil to it** than the single *log* required for the voluntary meal offering. **As,** if the purpose of that term were merely **to establish** the basic fact that the offering must include **oil,** a verse is **not needed** to teach that. **Since it is written with** respect to the griddle-cake offering of the High Priest: **"On a griddle [*maḥavat*]"** (Leviticus 6:14), it is **comparable to a pan [*maḥavat*] meal offering,** which requires oil.

אוֹ אֵינוֹ אֶלָּא לִקְבּוֹעַ לָהּ שֶׁמֶן, דְּאִי לָא כָּתַב רַחֲמָנָא ״בַּשֶּׁמֶן״ – הֲוָה אָמֵינָא: תֶּיהֱוֵי כְּמִנְחַת חוֹטֵא?

Or perhaps the purpose of the verse is **to establish only** that the offering must include **oil,** and it is necessary to teach that **because if the Merciful One had not stated: "With the oil," I would say: Let it be like** the **meal offering of a sinner,**[N] which does not include oil.

NOTES

Two *log* of oil are required for each tenth of an ephah of flour – שְׁנֵי לוּגִּין לְעִשָּׂרוֹן: The verse states: "Or for a ram, you shall prepare for a meal offering two tenth-parts of an ephah of fine flour mingled with the third-part of a *hin* of oil" (Numbers 15:6). Another verse states: "Then shall there be presented with the bull a meal offering of three tenth-parts of an ephah of fine flour mingled with half a *hin* of oil" (Numbers 15:9). Since one-third of a *hin* is four *log* and half a *hin* is six *log*, the ratio for both a ram and a bull is the same: Two *log* of oil per tenth of an ephah of flour.

I would say let it be like the meal offering of a sinner – הֲוָה אָמֵינָא תֶּיהֱוֵי כְּמִנְחַת חוֹטֵא: The early commentaries struggle to understand this suggestion, as the Gemara (*Sota* 15a) explains that the reason the meal offering of a sinner has no oil is so that it will not be of superior quality. One would think the griddle-cake offering of the High Priest should be of particularly superior quality. They answer that this suggestion is in accordance with the opinion of Rabbi Yishmael, son of Rabbi Yoḥanan ben Beroka, whereas it is Rabbi Shimon who explains that the reason for the lack of oil in the meal offering of a sinner is so that it will not be of superior quality, and the two *tanna'im* need not agree. Another suggestion, assuming that they agree, is that the High Priest should also bring an offering which is not of superior quality so that he will not become haughty (commentary attributed to Rashba).

הֲדַר אֲמַר: תִּיהְוֵי נַמִּי לִקְבּוֹעַ לָהּ שֶׁמֶן, תֵּיתֵי מִדִּינָא. וְדָן דִּינָא, וְלָא אָתְיָא לֵיהּ, וְאִצְטְרִכָא קְרָא "סֹלֶת מִנְחָה תָּמִיד", כִּדְמְסַיֵּים רַבִּי יִשְׁמָעֵאל מִילְּתֵיהּ.

Rabbi Yishmael, son of Rabbi Yoḥanan ben Beroka, **then said: Let it even be** that the purpose of the verse is **to establish only** that **it** requires **oil,** and even so one can **arrive** at the conclusion that three *log* are required due to the **derivation** based upon the verbal analogy from the meal offering brought with the libations that accompany animal offerings. **But** although Rabbi Yishmael, son of Rabbi Yoḥanan ben Beroka, attempts to **employ** this **derivation he is unsuccessful,** as there is a counter-indication from another verbal analogy to the voluntary meal offering. Therefore, Rabbi Yishmael, son of Rabbi Yoḥanan ben Beroka, **needed** to derive the *halakha* from the **verse: "Fine flour for a meal offering perpetually** [*tamid*]" (Leviticus 6:13), **as Rabbi Yishmael,** son of Rabbi Yoḥanan ben Beroka, **concluded his statement** in the *baraita*.

רַבָּה אֲמַר: כּוּלָּהּ רַבִּי שִׁמְעוֹן, [וְ"אִילּוּ לֹא נֶאֱמַר" קָאָמַר],

Rabba said that the *baraita* should be understood differently: The **entire** *baraita* **is** in accordance with the opinion of **Rabbi Shimon, and** Rabbi Shimon **is speaking** utilizing the style of: **If it were not stated.**

וְהָכִי קָאָמַר: "בַּשֶּׁמֶן" – לְהוֹסִיף לָהּ שֶׁמֶן, דְּאִי לִקְבּוֹעַ לָהּ שֶׁמֶן – לָא צְרִיךְ, כֵּיוָן דִּכְתִיב בָּהּ "עַל מַחֲבַת" – כְּמַחֲבַת דָּמְיָא, וְעַד שֶׁלֹּא יֹאמַר "בַּשֶּׁמֶן" יֵשׁ לִי בַּדִּין.

And this is what Rabbi Shimon **is saying:** The term **"with the oil"** serves **to add** extra **oil to it. As, if** the purpose of that term were merely **to establish** that the offering must include **oil,** a verse is **not needed** to teach that. **Since it is written with** respect to the griddle-cake offering of the High Priest: **"On a griddle** [*maḥavat*]" (Leviticus 6:14), it is **comparable to a pan** [*maḥavat*] meal offering, which requires oil. **And** even **if** the verse **had not stated: "With the oil," I have** a manner of **derivation** for the fact that more than one *log* of oil is required, based upon a verbal analogy.

וְדָן דִּינָא, לָא אָתְיָא לֵיהּ, וְאִצְטְרִכָא "בַּשֶּׁמֶן". הֲדַר אֲמַר: תֶּיהֱוֵי כְּמִנְחַת פָּרִים וְאֵילִים.

But although Rabbi Shimon attempts to **employ** this **derivation he is unsuccessful,** as there is a counter-indication from another verbal analogy, **and** therefore the term **"with the oil" is needed** to teach that more than one *log* of oil is required. Nevertheless, this teaches only that more oil than usual is required, but the specific amount still must be clarified. Rabbi Shimon **then said: Let** the griddle-cake offering of the High Priest **be like the meal offering** that accompanies the sacrifice of **bulls and rams,** which require two *log* of oil per ephah of flour.

הֲדַר אֲמַר: דָּנִין מִנְחָה הַבָּאָה עִשָּׂרוֹן וכו׳.

Rabbi Shimon **then said:** We should **derive** the *halakha* with regard to the griddle-cake offering of the High Priest, which is **a meal offering that comes** in the amount of **a tenth** of an ephah of flour, from the meal offering that accompanies the sacrifice of sheep, which is also a meal offering that comes in the amount of a tenth of an ephah of flour, and not from a meal offering that is brought in the amount of two or three tenths of an ephah of flour.

Perek **IV**
Daf **51** Amud **b**

מתני׳ לֹא מִינּוּ כֹּהֵן אַחֵר תַּחְתָּיו, מִשֶּׁל מִי הָיְתָה קְרֵיבָה? רַבִּי שִׁמְעוֹן אוֹמֵר: מִשֶּׁל צִיבּוּר, רַבִּי יְהוּדָה אוֹמֵר: מִשֶּׁל יוֹרְשִׁין. וּשְׁלֵימָה הָיְתָה קְרֵיבָה.

MISHNA If they did not appoint another High **Priest in his stead,**[H] **from whose** property **was** the griddle-cake offering brought and **sacrificed? Rabbi Shimon says:** It is brought and sacrificed **from** the property **of the community. Rabbi Yehuda says:** It is brought and sacrificed **from** the property **of the heirs** of the High Priest. **And** for the duration of the period until a new High Priest was appointed, the griddle-cake offering **was sacrificed** as **a complete** tenth of an ephah of fine flour.

HALAKHA

If they did not appoint another High Priest in his stead – לֹא מִינּוּ כֹּהֵן אַחֵר תַּחְתָּיו: If the High Priest died after sacrificing the morning half of his griddle-cake offering, and no High Priest was yet appointed in his stead, his heirs bring an entire tenth of an ephah of fine flour and it is made into griddle cakes. The entirety of the tenth of an ephah is sacrificed, not half of it. This is in accordance with the opinion of Rabbi Yehuda in the mishna and *baraita* (Rambam *Sefer Avoda, Hilkhot Temidin UMusafin* 3:22).

גמ׳ תָּנוּ רַבָּנַן: כֹּהֵן גָּדוֹל שֶׁמֵּת, וְלֹא מִינּוּ כֹּהֵן אַחֵר תַּחְתָּיו, מִנַּיִן שֶׁתְּהֵא מִנְחָתוֹ קְרֵיבָה מִשֶּׁל יוֹרְשִׁין? תַּלְמוּד לוֹמַר ״וְהַכֹּהֵן הַמָּשִׁיחַ תַּחְתָּיו מִבָּנָיו יַעֲשֶׂה אֹתָהּ״.

GEMARA **The Sages taught** in a *baraita*: In a case where the **High Priest died and they did not appoint another** High Priest **in his stead, from where** is it derived **that his** griddle-cake **meal offering should be sacrificed from** the property **of the heirs** of the High Priest? **The verse states** in reference to the griddle-cake offering: **"And the anointed priest that shall be in his stead from among his sons shall offer it"** (Leviticus 6:15).

יָכוֹל יַקְרִיבֶנָּה חֲצָאִין? תַּלְמוּד לוֹמַר ״אֹתָהּ״ – כּוּלָּהּ וְלֹא חֶצְיָהּ, דִּבְרֵי רַבִּי יְהוּדָה.

One **might** have thought that the heirs should **sacrifice it in halves** as the High Priest does. Therefore **the verse states "it,"** teaching that they should sacrifice **all of** the tenth of an ephah **and not half of it;** this is **the statement of Rabbi Yehuda.**

רַבִּי שִׁמְעוֹן אוֹמֵר: ״חָק עוֹלָם״ – מִשֶּׁל עוֹלָם, ״כָּלִיל תָּקְטָר״ – שֶׁתְּהֵא כּוּלָּהּ בְּהַקְטָרָה.

Rabbi Shimon says: The continuation of the verse: **"It is a statute forever** [*olam*] to the Lord," teaches that in this case of a High Priest who has died and has not yet been replaced, the offering is brought **from** the property **of the world** [*olam*], i.e., the community. The end of the verse: **"It shall be wholly made to smoke** to the Lord," teaches **that** although it is brought by the community and not by a priest, **the entire** tenth of an ephah **should be sacrificed** and not eaten.

וְהַאי ״הַכֹּהֵן הַמָּשִׁיחַ״ לְהָכִי הוּא דְּאָתָא?

The Gemara asks: **And did that** verse: **"And the anointed priest** that shall be in his stead from among his sons shall offer it," **come to** teach **this** *halakha* that Rabbi Yehuda derived from it?

הַאי מִיבְּעֵי לֵיהּ לְכִדְתַנְיָא: ״זֶה קָרְבַּן אַהֲרֹן וּבָנָיו אֲשֶׁר יַקְרִיבוּ לַה׳ בְּיוֹם הִמָּשַׁח אֹתוֹ״ – יָכוֹל יְהוּ אַהֲרֹן וּבָנָיו מַקְרִיבִין קָרְבָּן אֶחָד? תַּלְמוּד לוֹמַר ״אֲשֶׁר יַקְרִיבוּ לַה׳״ – אַהֲרֹן בִּפְנֵי עַצְמוֹ, וּבָנָיו בִּפְנֵי עַצְמָן. ״בָּנָיו״ – אֵלּוּ כֹּהֲנִים הֶדְיוֹטוֹת.

That verse **is needed for that which is taught** in a *baraita*: **"This is the offering of Aaron and of his sons, which they shall offer to the Lord in the day when he is anointed"** (Leviticus 6:13). One **might** have thought that since the verse speaks of the offering in the singular, it means that **Aaron and his sons should sacrifice one offering.** Therefore **the verse states: "Which they shall offer to the Lord,"** in plural, teaching that **Aaron** sacrifices an offering **by himself**[N] as the High Priest, **and his sons** sacrifice offerings **by themselves** as ordinary priests. When the verse refers to **"his sons," these are the ordinary priests.** Each priest must bring a griddle-cake offering as an offering of initiation when he begins his service.

אַתָּה אוֹמֵר: כֹּהֲנִים הֶדְיוֹטוֹת, אוֹ אֵינוֹ אֶלָּא כֹּהֲנִים גְּדוֹלִים? כְּשֶׁהוּא אוֹמֵר ״וְהַכֹּהֵן הַמָּשִׁיחַ תַּחְתָּיו מִבָּנָיו״ – הֲרֵי כֹּהֵן גָּדוֹל אָמוּר, הָא מָה אֲנִי מְקַיֵּים ״בָּנָיו״? אֵלּוּ כֹּהֲנִים הֶדְיוֹטוֹת!

Do you say that this is referring to the offering of initiation of **ordinary priests, or is it** referring **only** to the griddle-cake offering of the **High Priests? When** the verse **states** in the continuation of that passage: **"And the anointed priest that shall be in his stead from among his sons** shall offer it; it is a statute forever to the Lord; it shall be wholly made to smoke to the Lord" (Leviticus 6:15), the griddle-cake offering of the **High Priest is thereby mentioned. How do I realize** the meaning of the term **"his sons"** in Leviticus 6:13? **These are the ordinary priests,** and the verse is referring to their offering of initiation. Consequently, verse 15 is referring to the basic obligation of the High Priest to bring the griddle-cake offering, rather than referring to a case of a High Priest who died.

NOTES

Aaron sacrifices an offering by himself – אַהֲרֹן בִּפְנֵי עַצְמוֹ: The requirement for the High Priest to bring a griddle-cake offering is distinct from the requirement for an ordinary priest to bring a griddle-cake offering upon his initiation to the Temple service, in that the initiation offering is brought only once in the priest's lifetime, whereas the High Priest brings his offering twice daily. Rabbeinu Yitzḥak Abravanel offers ten reasons why the High Priest is unique in this regard.

אִם כֵּן, לִכְתּוֹב קְרָא ״הַכֹּהֵן הַמָּשִׁיחַ תַּחְתָּיו בָּנָיו יַעֲשֶׂה״, מַאי ״מִבָּנָיו״? שְׁמַעַת מִינָּהּ תַּרְתֵּי.

The Gemara answers: The verse teaches both the basic obligation of the High Priest to bring the griddle-cake offering daily and the fact that when he dies his heirs must bring the offering until a new High Priest is appointed. **If** it were **so** that the verse is teaching only that the heirs of a High Priest who died must bring the griddle-cake offering until a new High Priest is appointed, **let the verse** merely **write: The anointed priest that shall be in his stead, his sons shall offer. What** is the need to say: **"From among** his sons"? **Learn from** the fact that verse uses this term that **two** *halakhot* are derived from the verse.

וְרַבִּי שִׁמְעוֹן, הַאי ״אֹתָהּ״ מַאי עָבֵיד לֵיהּ? מִיבְּעֵי לֵיהּ לְכֹהֵן גָּדוֹל שֶׁמֵּת וּמִינּוּ אַחֵר תַּחְתָּיו, שֶׁלֹּא יָבִיא חֲצִי עִשָּׂרוֹן מִבֵּיתוֹ וְלֹא חֲצִי עִשָּׂרוֹן שֶׁל רִאשׁוֹן.

The Gemara asks: **And what does Rabbi Shimon,** who derives the *halakha* that it should be entirely sacrificed from the phrase: "It shall be wholly made to smoke," **do with that** word **"it,"** from which Rabbi Yehuda derives this *halakha*? The Gemara answers: **He requires** it **to** teach that in the case of **a High Priest who died** after bringing the first half of his griddle-cake offering, **and** then **they appointed another** High Priest **in his stead,** the replacement High Priest **should neither bring half of a tenth** of an ephah of flour **from his house nor** sacrifice the remaining **half of the tenth of an ephah of the first** High Priest, i.e., his predecessor.

וְתֵיפּוֹק לֵיהּ מִן ״וּמַחֲצִיתָהּ״! וי״ו לָא דָּרֵישׁ.

The Gemara asks: **Let him derive** this *halakha* **from** the expression: **"And half of it"** (Leviticus 6:13), as discussed on 50b; the word "and," which is added by the letter *vav* at the beginning of the word, is expounded to mean that the replacement High Priest must bring a complete tenth of an ephah of fine flour. The Gemara answers: He did not derive the *halakha* from there because **he does not expound** the extra letter ***vav*** in that word, as he holds that its addition is not significant.

וְרַבִּי יְהוּדָה, הַאי ״חָק עוֹלָם״ מַאי עָבֵיד לֵיהּ? חוּקָּה לְעוֹלָם תְּהֵא.

The Gemara asks: **And what does Rabbi Yehuda,** who holds that if the High Priest dies and a new one has not yet been appointed the griddle-cake offering is brought by the previous High Priest's heirs, **do with that** phrase: **"It is a statute forever** to the Lord," from which Rabbi Shimon derives that it is brought from communal resources? The Gemara answers: It teaches that the **statute** requiring the High Priest to sacrifice the griddle-cake offering **is to** apply **forever.**

״כָּלִיל תָּקְטָר״ לָמָּה לִי? מִיבְּעֵי לֵיהּ לְכִדְתַנְיָא: אֵין לִי אֶלָּא עֶלְיוֹנָה מִנְחַת כֹּהֵן גָּדוֹל בְּ״כָלִיל תָּקְטָר״, וְתַחְתּוֹנָה מִנְחַת כֹּהֵן הֶדְיוֹט בְּ״לֹא תֵאָכֵל״.

The Gemara asks: According to Rabbi Yehuda, **why do I** need the phrase: **"It shall be wholly made to smoke"?** The Gemara answers: **He requires it for that which is taught** in a *baraita*: **I have** derived **only** that the griddle-cake **meal offering of the High Priest** mentioned **above is** included **in** the mandate: **"It shall be wholly made to smoke"** (Leviticus 6:15), **and** that the voluntary **meal offering** of the **ordinary priest** mentioned **below is** included **in** the prohibition: **"It shall not be eaten"** (Leviticus 6:16).

מִנַּיִן לִיתֵּן אֶת הָאָמוּר שֶׁל זֶה בְּזֶה וְאֶת הָאָמוּר שֶׁל זֶה בְּזֶה? תַּלְמוּד לוֹמַר ״כָּלִיל״ ״כָּלִיל״ לִגְזֵירָה שָׁוָה: נֶאֱמַר כָּאן ״כָּלִיל״ וְנֶאֱמַר לְהַלָּן ״כָּלִיל״,

From where is it derived that one is mandated **to apply what is said about that** verse **to this** one, **and** what is said **about this** verse **to that** one? **The verse states** with regard to the griddle-cake offering: **"Wholly,"** and the verse uses the word **"wholly"** with regard to the voluntary meal offering of a priest, in order **to** teach **a verbal analogy: It is stated here,** with regard to the griddle-cake meal offering of the High Priest: **"Wholly"** (Leviticus 6:15), **and it is stated there,** with regard to the voluntary meal offering of the ordinary priest: **"Wholly"** (Leviticus 6:16).

מַה כָּאן – בְּ״כָלִיל תָּקְטָר״, אַף לְהַלָּן – בְּ״כָלִיל תָּקְטָר״. וּמַה לְהַלָּן – לִיתֵּן לֹא תַעֲשֶׂה עַל אֲכִילָתוֹ, אַף כָּאן – לִיתֵּן לֹא תַעֲשֶׂה עַל אֲכִילָתָהּ.

Just as here, with regard to the griddle-cake meal offering, it is included **in** the mandate: **"It shall be wholly made to smoke," so too there,** the voluntary meal offering of the ordinary priest is included **in** the mandate: **It shall be wholly made to smoke. And just as there,** with regard to the voluntary meal offering of the ordinary priest, the verse comes **to place a prohibition on its consumption, so too here,** with regard to the griddle-cake meal offering of the High Priest, the verse comes **to place a prohibition on its consumption.**

וְסָבַר רַבִּי שִׁמְעוֹן: מִשֶּׁל צִיבּוּר דְּאוֹרַיְיתָא?

The Gemara asks: **And does Rabbi Shimon hold** that in a case where the High Priest died and a new one has not been appointed, the requirement that the griddle offering be brought **from** the property **of the community is by Torah law,** as indicated by the fact that he derives this *halakha* from a verse?

וְהָתְנַן, אָמַר רַבִּי שִׁמְעוֹן: שִׁבְעָה דְּבָרִים הִתְקִינוּ בֵּית דִּין, וְזֶה אֶחָד מֵהֶן. גּוֹי שֶׁשָּׁלַח עוֹלָתוֹ מִמְּדִינַת הַיָּם, שָׁלַח עִמָּהּ נְסָכִים – קְרֵיבָה מִשֶּׁלּוֹ, וְאִם לָאו – קְרֵיבִין מִשֶּׁל צִיבּוּר.

But didn't we learn in a mishna (*Shekalim* 7:6) that **Rabbi Shimon said: The court instituted seven ordinances** with regard to the financial aspects of offerings and consecrations; **and this** ordinance, namely, that the cost of the libations accompanying the sacrifice of a found animal is borne by the public, **is one of them.** These are the other ordinances: In the case of **a gentile who sent his burnt offering from a country overseas,**[NH] and **he sent with it** money for the purchase of the **libations** that must accompany it, the libations **are sacrificed at his** expense. **And if** the gentile did **not** cover the cost of the libations, it is a condition of the court that the libations are **sacrificed at the public's** expense, with funds taken from the Temple treasury.

וְכֵן גֵּר שֶׁמֵּת וְהִנִּיחַ זְבָחִים. יֵשׁ לוֹ נְסָכִים – קְרֵיבִין מִשֶּׁלּוֹ, וְאִם לָאו – קְרֵיבִין מִשֶּׁל צִיבּוּר.

And similarly, in the case of **a convert who died** without heirs **and left** animals that he had designated as **offerings,**[H] **if he has the libations,** i.e., if he also had set aside libations or money for that purpose, the libations **are sacrificed from his** estate. **And if** he did **not** do so, the libations **are sacrificed from public** funds.

וּתְנַאי בֵּית דִּין הוּא, כֹּהֵן גָּדוֹל שֶׁמֵּת וְלֹא מִינּוּ כֹּהֵן אַחֵר תַּחְתָּיו – שֶׁתְּהֵא מִנְחָתוֹ קְרֵיבָה מִשֶּׁל צִיבּוּר!

And another ordinance: **It is a stipulation of the court** with regard to **a High Priest who died, and they did not** yet **appoint another High Priest in his stead,**[H] **that his** griddle-cake **meal offering** would be **sacrificed from public** funds. Rabbi Shimon then enumerates three additional ordinances. In any case, it is clear from this mishna that Rabbi Shimon holds that this *halakha* concerning the offering of a High Priest who died is a rabbinic ordinance, rather than Torah law.

אָמַר רַבִּי אַבָּהוּ: שְׁנֵי תַקָּנוֹת הֲווּ,

Rabbi Abbahu[P] **said** in response: In fact, Rabbi Shimon holds that this *halakha* is by Torah law. But in fact, there **were two ordinances** that were enacted concerning this matter.

דְּאוֹרַיְיתָא – מִדְּצִיבּוּר. כֵּיוָן דַּחֲזוּ דְּקָא מִידַּחְקָא לִישְׁכָּה – תַּקִּינוּ דְּלִגְבֵּי מִיּוֹרְשִׁים. כֵּיוָן דַּחֲזוּ דְּקָא פָּשְׁעִי בַּהּ – אוֹקְמוּהָ אַדְּאוֹרַיְיתָא.

Initially, they acted in accordance with that which is prescribed **by Torah law,** and if a High Priest died and a new High Priest had not yet been appointed in his stead, his griddle-cake meal offering would be sacrificed **from public** funds. **Once they saw that the** funds in the **chamber** of the Temple treasury were being **depleted,** the Sages **instituted** an ordinance **that** the payment for the offering **should be collected from the** previous High Priest's **heirs. Once they saw that** the heirs **were negligent in** the matter and did not bring the offering, **they** revoked the previous ordinance and **established it in accordance with the** *halakha* as it is **by Torah law,** that it is brought from public funds.

"וְעַל פָּרָה, שֶׁלֹּא יְהֵא מוֹעֲלִין בְּאֶפְרָהּ". דְּאוֹרַיְיתָא הִיא! דְּתַנְיָא: "חַטָּאת הִיא" – מְלַמֵּד שֶׁמּוֹעֲלִין בָּהּ, "הִיא" – בָּהּ מוֹעֲלִין,

§ The Gemara cites the continuation of the mishna in *Shekalim* (7:7): **And** the court enacted an ordinance **with regard to the** red **heifer that one is not** liable to bring an offering **for misusing** consecrated property if he derives benefit **from its ashes.**[H] The Gemara asks: Why does the *baraita* state that this is an ordinance of the court, when in fact **it is by Torah law? As it is taught** in a *baraita*: The verse states with regard to a red heifer: **"It is a sin offering"** (Numbers 19:9), which **teaches** that a red heifer is treated like a sin offering in that **one** is liable for **misusing it.** The fact that it states: **"It is a sin offering"** indicates that if one derives benefit from **it,** the animal itself, he is liable for **misusing** consecrated property,

NOTES

A gentile who sent his burnt offering from a country overseas – גּוֹי שֶׁשָּׁלַח עוֹלָתוֹ מִמְּדִינַת הַיָּם: Some explain that the reason Rabbi Shimon discussed a case where the gentile sent the offering from overseas as opposed to from somewhere in Eretz Yisrael is that the Sages tend to discuss prevalent cases, and at the time of the Temple, there were not many gentiles living in Eretz Yisrael. The Rambam writes: If a gentile sent his burnt offering from another province, indicating that this *halakha* applies only in that case (Rambam *Sefer Zemanim*, *Hilkhot Shekalim* 4:3). He may have understood that if the gentile lives nearby, he is instructed to provide the libations (*Tosefot Yom Tov* on *Shekalim* 7:6).

HALAKHA

A gentile who sent his burnt offering from a country overseas – גּוֹי שֶׁשָּׁלַח עוֹלָתוֹ מִמְּדִינַת הַיָּם: If a gentile sent his burnt offering from another province but failed to send money for the required libations along with it, the libations are sacrificed at the public's expense with funds taken from the Temple treasury, in accordance with the opinion of Rabbi Shimon (Rambam *Sefer Zemanim*, *Hilkhot Shekalim* 4:3).

A convert who died without heirs and left animals that he had designated as offerings – גֵּר שֶׁמֵּת וְהִנִּיחַ זְבָחִים: If a convert died without heirs and left animals designated as offerings, and he also left wine or money for their libations, the libations are sacrificed from that which he had designated. If he did not leave the libations or the money for their purchase, they are purchased with public funds taken from the Temple treasury, in accordance with the statement of Rabbi Shimon (Rambam *Sefer Zemanim*, *Hilkhot Shekalim* 4:4).

And they did not yet appoint another High Priest in his stead – וְלֹא מִינּוּ כֹּהֵן אַחֵר תַּחְתָּיו: If the High Priest died and no High Priest was yet appointed in his stead, the griddle-cake offering is brought from the Temple treasury. This is in accordance with the opinion of Rabbi Shimon (Rambam *Sefer Zemanim*, *Hilkhot Shekalim* 4:4, and see *Kesef Mishne* 4:3 there).

One is not liable for misusing consecrated property if he derives benefit from its ashes – לֹא יְהֵא מוֹעֲלִין בְּאֶפְרָהּ: One who derives benefit from a red heifer from the time of its consecration until it is burned to ashes is liable for the prohibition against misusing consecrated property. Once it has turned to ashes, this prohibition no longer applies (Rambam *Sefer Avoda*, *Hilkhot Me'ila* 2:5).

PERSONALITIES

Rabbi Abbahu – רַבִּי אַבָּהוּ: Rabbi Abbahu was an *amora* in Eretz Yisrael during the third generation of *amora'im*. He was the preeminent disciple of Rabbi Yoḥanan, whom he cites hundreds of times throughout the Talmud. Rabbi Abbahu also cites contemporaries of Rabbi Yoḥanan, including Reish Lakish and Rabbi Elazar. He in turn is quoted often by his student Rabbi Zeira. Rabbi Abbahu eventually became head of the academy at Caesarea. Much is related in the Talmud about this Sage's generosity, righteousness, wisdom, modesty, and reverence. Rabbi Abbahu would say: The world endures only due to the merit of those who humble themselves (*Ḥullin* 89a). Rabbi Abbahu was most famous for his homilies, and many people would flock to hear his sermons. He was also skilled in mathematics and fluent in Greek. In addition to all these abilities, Rabbi Abbahu was known for his handsome looks, physical strength, and his wealth.

בְּאֶפְרָהּ אֵין מוֹעֲלִין!

but if one derives benefit **from its ashes, one is not** liable for **misusing** consecrated property. It is clear from the *baraita* that by Torah law one is not liable for misuse of consecrated property if he derives benefit from the ashes of a red heifer.

אֲמַר רַב אַשִׁי: שְׁתֵּי תַּקָּנוֹת הֲוַאי, דְּאוֹרַיְיתָא – בָּהּ מוֹעֲלִין, בְּאֶפְרָהּ אֵין מוֹעֲלִין. כֵּיוָן דְּחָזוּ דְּקָא מְזַלְזְלִי בָּהּ, וְקָא עָבְדִי מִינַּהּ לְמַכָּתָן – גָּזְרוּ בֵּיהּ מְעִילָה.

Rav Ashi said in response: In fact, this *halakha* is by Torah law, but **there were two ordinances** that were enacted concerning this matter. **By Torah law,** if one derives benefit from **it,** the animal itself, he is liable for **misusing** consecrated property,[N] but if he derives benefit **from its ashes** he is not liable for **misusing** consecrated property. **Once** the Sages **saw that** people **were treating** the ashes of the heifer **disrespectfully, and making** salves **for their wounds from it,**[B] **they decreed** that it is subject to the *halakhot* of **misuse** of consecrated property[NB] and one may not derive benefit from it.

כֵּיוָן דְּחָזוּ דְּקָא פָּרְשִׁי מִסְּפֵק הַזָּאוֹת – אוֹקְמוּהָ אַדְּאוֹרַיְיתָא.

Once they saw that as a result of this decree people **were refraining from** sprinkling it in cases where there was **uncertainty** as to whether or not an individual was impure and required **sprinkling, they** revoked the decree and **established it in accordance with** the *halakha* as it is **by Torah law,**[N] that one is not liable for misusing the ashes of a red heifer.

תָּנוּ רַבָּנַן: פַּר הֶעְלֵם דָּבָר שֶׁל צִיבּוּר וּשְׂעִירֵי עֲבוֹדָה זָרָה – בַּתְּחִילָּה מַגְבִּין לָהֶן, דִּבְרֵי רַבִּי יְהוּדָה. רַבִּי שִׁמְעוֹן אוֹמֵר: מִתְּרוּמַת הַלִּשְׁכָּה הֵן בָּאִין.

§ The Gemara cites a dispute between Rabbi Shimon and Rabbi Yehuda that is similar to the one cited earlier. **The Sages taught** in a *baraita*: If there is a need to sacrifice the **bull for an unwitting communal sin,** brought if the Sanhedrin issues an erroneous halakhic ruling concerning a prohibition for which one is liable to receive *karet* and the majority of the community acts upon it, **or the goats** brought if the Sanhedrin issues an erroneous ruling permitting **idol worship** and the majority of the community acts on it, **a new collection** of funds is organized **for them.**[H] The funds are not taken from the collection of the Temple treasury chamber, unlike other communal offerings. This is **the statement of Rabbi Yehuda. Rabbi Shimon says:** The funds for these sacrifices **come from the collection of the chamber.**

וְהָתַנְיָא אִיפְּכָא! הֵי מִינַּיְיהוּ אַחֲרִיתָא?

The Gemara challenges: **But isn't it taught** in a *baraita* **the opposite,** i.e., that the first opinion cited above is that of Rabbi Shimon and the second is that of Rabbi Yehuda? **Which of** the two *baraitot* is **the later** one and therefore the more accurate and authoritative version of their opinions?

אֲמָרוּהָ רַבָּנַן קַמֵּיהּ דְּרַב אַשִׁי: לֵימָא קַמַּיְיתָא – אַחֲרִיתָא, דְּשָׁמְעִינַן לֵיהּ לְרַבִּי שִׁמְעוֹן דְּחָיֵישׁ לִפְשִׁיעָה.

The Sages said the following **before Rav Ashi: Let us say** that **the first** *baraita* cited above **is the later** one, **as we have heard that Rabbi Shimon is concerned about** the possibility of **negligence.** Just as Rabbi Shimon was concerned above that the heirs of the High Priest would not provide the funds for the griddle-cake offering, it is reasonable to assume that he would be concerned that people would not contribute to a new collection, and therefore the funds are taken from the collection of the chamber.

NOTES

By Torah law if one derives benefit from it he is liable for misusing consecrated property – דְּאוֹרַיְיתָא בָּהּ מוֹעֲלִין: *Tosafot* (51b) note that it is not necessary to derive that the prohibition against deriving benefit applies with regard to a red heifer, as it applies with regard to any consecrated item. Rather, the derivation here teaches that even after one has violated this prohibition, the prohibition remains in force. This is different from the general *halakha*, which is that once one has derived benefit from consecrated property, the prohibition no longer applies to that property. Some later commentaries maintain that it is necessary to derive that the prohibition against misusing consecrated property applies at all to a red heifer, because otherwise one might have thought that the red heifer is not even considered to be in the category of items consecrated for Temple maintenance. One might have thought that the red heifer is like communal ritual baths, which do not have the sanctity of the Temple maintenance (*Sefat Emet*; Griz; *Keren Ora*; *Hazon Ish*).

They decreed that it is subject to the *halakhot* of misuse of consecrated property – גָּזְרוּ בֵּיהּ מְעִילָה: One interpretation of this is that the Sages decreed that the ashes be subject to the *halakhot* of misuse, even though they are not subject to these *halakhot* by Torah law (Rashi). Another understanding is that the Sages decreed that the ashes are consecrated with sanctity that inheres in their value. Once this consecration is in effect, one who derives benefit from the ashes is liable by Torah law for misuse of consecrated property (*Shita Mekubbetzet* on 51b, citing Rashi).

They established it in accordance with the *halakha* as it is by Torah law – אוֹקְמוּהָ אַדְּאוֹרַיְיתָא: The result of their ordinance was that people refrained not only from using the ashes for their wounds, but they also ceased sprinkling it on people in cases where it was uncertain whether they required sprinkling. Since the ordinance was too effective in preventing people from using the ashes, it was necessary to revert to the *halakha* by Torah law that the ashes are not subject to the *halakhot* of misuse (Rambam's Commentary on the Mishna, *Shekalim* 7:7).

HALAKHA

A new collection of funds is organized for them – בַּתְּחִילָּה מַגְבִּין לָהֶן: If there is a need to sacrifice a bull for an unwitting communal sin or to sacrifice a goat due to communal idol worship, the funds are not taken from the Temple treasury. Rather, a separate collection is undertaken to raise the funds (Rambam *Sefer Zemanim*, *Hilkhot Shekalim* 4:2).

BACKGROUND

Making salves for their wounds from it – עָבְדִי מִינַּהּ לְמַכָּתָן: It was very common to use ashes in order to treat topical wounds and skin irritation or infection. Placing ashes on a wound stopped the bleeding and constricted the spread of an infection, although it could leave a scar. It is possible that people specifically used the ashes of the red heifer because they ascribed supernatural curative powers to them due to their sanctity.

Misuse of consecrated property – מְעִילָה: The *halakhot* of misuse of consecrated property are stated in the Torah (see Leviticus 5:14–16) and discussed at length in tractate *Me'ila*. The basic principle is that anyone who derives benefit from consecrated property unwittingly, i.e., without the knowledge that it was consecrated property, violates this prohibition. One who does so is obligated to bring a guilt offering and to pay to the Temple the value of the item from which he derived benefit. In addition, he pays an additional one-fifth of the value as a fine. In most cases, after that item is misused it loses its consecrated status, and the sanctity is transferred to the money that he pays to the Temple. The Torah does not discuss the case of one who derives benefit intentionally. Atonement for intentional misuse cannot be attained by sacrifice of a guilt offering or by payment of a fine of one-fifth of the value of the misused item.

אֲמַר לְהוּ רַב אַשִׁי: אֲפִילּוּ תֵּימָא בַּתְרַיְיתָא – אַחֲרֵיתָא, כִּי קָא חָיֵישׁ רַבִּי שִׁמְעוֹן לִפְשִׁיעָה מִילְּתָא דְּלֵית בְּהוּ כַּפָּרָה בְּגַוֵּוהּ, בְּמִילְּתָא דְּאִית לְהוּ כַּפָּרָה בְּגַוֵּוהּ – לָא חָיֵישׁ רַבִּי שִׁמְעוֹן לִפְשִׁיעָה.

Rav Ashi said to the Sages: You may **even say** that **the latter** *baraita* cited above **is the later** and more authoritative one. **When Rabbi Shimon** expressed that he **is concerned about** the possibility of people acting with **negligence,** that was only with regard to **a matter that does not provide them with atonement,** e.g., the griddle-cake offering of the deceased High Priest. But **Rabbi Shimon is not concerned about** the possibility of **negligence with regard to a matter that does provide them with atonement,** e.g., these sin offerings.

מַאי הָוֵי עֲלַהּ?

The Gemara asks, in light of the fact that the discussion above was inconclusive: **What** conclusion **was** reached **about it;** which *baraita* is later and more authoritative?

אֲמַר לֵיהּ רַבָּה זוּטִי לְרַב אַשִׁי: תָּא שְׁמַע, דְּתַנְיָא: "אֶת קָרְבָּנִי לַחְמִי לְאִשַּׁי רֵיחַ נִיחֹחִי תִּשְׁמְרוּ לְהַקְרִיב לִי בְּמוֹעֲדוֹ" – לְרַבּוֹת פַּר הֶעְלֵם דָּבָר שֶׁל צִיבּוּר וּשְׂעִירֵי עֲבוֹדָה זָרָה, שֶׁבָּאִין מִתְּרוּמַת הַלִּשְׁכָּה, דִּבְרֵי רַבִּי שִׁמְעוֹן.

Rabba Zuti[P] **said to Rav Ashi: Come** and **hear** a resolution, **as it is taught** in a *baraita*: The verse concerning the daily sacrifice: "Command the children of Israel, and say to them: **My food that is presented to Me for offerings made by fire, of a pleasing aroma to Me, you shall observe to sacrifice to Me in its due season**" (Numbers 28:2), serves **to include** the **bull for an unwitting communal sin and the goats of idol worship.** This teaches **that** the funds for these offerings **come from the collection of the chamber;** this is **the statement of Rabbi Shimon.** This proves that it is Rabbi Shimon who holds that these sacrifices are brought from the collection of the chamber.

"וּשְׁלֵימָה הָיְתָה קְרֵיבָה" וכו׳. אָמַר רַבִּי חִיָּיא בַּר אַבָּא, בָּעֵי רַבִּי יוֹחָנָן: שְׁלֵימָה שַׁחֲרִית וּשְׁלֵימָה בֵּין הָעַרְבַּיִם, אוֹ דִּילְמָא שְׁלֵימָה שַׁחֲרִית וּבְטֵילָה בֵּין הָעַרְבַּיִם?

§ The mishna teaches: **And** for the duration of the period until a new High Priest is appointed, the griddle-cake offering **was sacrificed** as **a complete** tenth of an ephah of fine flour. **Rabbi Ḥiyya bar Abba says** that **Rabbi Yoḥanan raises a dilemma:** Does the mishna mean that **a complete** tenth of an ephah is offered in the **morning and** another **complete** tenth of an ephah is offered **in the afternoon,** because this offering is sacrificed twice a day and is not divided in half when it is not brought by the High Priest himself? **Or** does it **perhaps** mean that **a complete** tenth of an ephah is sacrificed in the **morning and** the offering is **canceled in the afternoon?**

אֲמַר רָבָא, תָּא שְׁמַע: "שְׁמִינִי – בַּחֲבִיתִּים". וְאִם אִיתָא דִּבְטֵילָה בֵּין הָעַרְבַּיִם – הָא זִמְנִין דְּלָא מַשְׁכַּח לֵיהּ שְׁמִינִי בַּחֲבִיתִּים, הֵיכִי דָּמֵי? דְּמֵת כֹּהֵן גָּדוֹל וְלֹא מִינּוּ אַחֵר תַּחְתָּיו.

Rava said: Come and **hear** the resolution to this dilemma from that which is taught in a mishna (*Tamid* 31b) describing the order of the nine priests who brought the limbs of the daily offering up to the ramp of the altar, both in the morning and in the afternoon: The **eighth** priest carries **the griddle-cake** offering of the High Priest. **And if it were so that** the offering is **canceled in the afternoon,** then **sometimes** one would **not find the eighth** priest carrying **the griddle-cake** offering. **What are the circumstances** when there would be no eighth priest? In a case **where the High Priest died** after he brought his griddle-cake offering in the morning **and they did not** yet **appoint another** High Priest **in his stead.** Therefore, it must be that a complete tenth of an ephah was also brought for the afternoon offering.

אַמְרוּהָ רַבָּנַן קַמֵּיהּ דְּרַבִּי יִרְמְיָה, אֲמַר: בַּבְלָאֵי טַפְשָׁאֵי, מִשּׁוּם דְּיָתְבוּ בְּאַתְרָא דַּחֲשׁוֹכָא, אָמְרִי שְׁמַעְתְּתָא דִּמְחַשְּׁכָן.

The Sages stated this proof **before Rabbi Yirmeya.** Rabbi Yirmeya rejected it and **said:** Those **foolish Babylonians, because they dwell in** a low-lying and therefore **dark land, they state** ***halakhot*** **that are dark,** i.e., erroneous.

אֶלָּא דְּקָתָנֵי "שְׁבִיעִי – בְּסֹלֶת, תְּשִׁיעִי – בְּיַיִן", הָכִי נָמֵי דְּלָא בָּטְלִי?

Rather, with regard to **that** which the same mishna **teaches:** The **seventh** priest carries **the fine flour** for the meal offering component of the daily offering and **the ninth** priest carries **the wine** for the libations that accompany the daily offering, is it **also** the case **that they are never canceled?**

"מִנְחָתָם וְנִסְכֵּיהֶם" בַּלַּיְלָה, "מִנְחָתָם וְנִסְכֵּיהֶם" אֲפִילּוּ לְמָחָר!

That is not correct, as it is derived from the verse "**Their meal offering and their libations**" (Numbers 29:18) that these items may be sacrificed even **at night,** despite the fact that the daily offering they accompany must be sacrificed during the day. Similarly, the phrase "**their meal offering and their libations**" indicates that these items may be sacrificed even **the next day** (see 44b). Under those circumstances there would not have been fine flour and wine brought by the seventh and nine priests at the time of the daily offering.

PERSONALITIES

Rabba Zuti – רַבָּה זוּטִי: Rabba Zuti, who is sometimes referred to as Rava Zuti, was a sixth-generation Babylonian *amora*. He was a colleague of Ravina and Rav Ashi, and he worked together with them to clarify traditions of the Sages. He was known by this name, meaning Rabba the Small, to distinguish him from the great third-generation *amora* Rabba bar Naḥmani.

אֶלָּא "דְּאִי" לָא קָתָנֵי, הָכִי נַמִי "דְּאִי" לָא קָתָנֵי.

Rather, one must explain that the *tanna* **does not teach** cases of **what if,** and is speaking only about the typical case. **So too** with regard to Rava's proof from the mishna, it is not compelling because the *tanna* **does not teach** cases of **what if** the High Priest dies and a successor has not yet been appointed.

אַהַדְרוּהָ קַמֵּיהּ דְּרָבָא, אֲמַר: מִבִּישׁוּתִין – אָמְרִי קַמַּיְיהוּ, מִטִּיבוּתִין – לָא אָמְרִי קַמַּיְיהוּ.

The Sages then **brought** Rabbi Yirmeya's analysis **before Rava.** Rava initially **said** to them: **You state our inferior** statements, which can be refuted, **before** the Sages of Eretz Yisrael, but **you do not state our superior** statements **before them?**

וַהֲדַר אֲמַר רָבָא: הָנֵי נַמִי טִיבוּתִין הִיא, אָמַר קְרָא: "סֹלֶת מִנְחָה תָּמִיד" – הֲרֵי הִיא לָךְ כְּמִנְחַת תְּמִידִין.

And Rava then said to them: **This** statement, that the griddle-cake offering is sacrificed twice a day even if there is no High Priest, is **also** one of **our superior** statements, as **the verse states** concerning the griddle-cake offering of the High Priest: **"Fine flour for a meal offering perpetually** [*tamid*], half of it in the morning, and half of it in the evening" (Leviticus 6:13). This teaches that the griddle-cake offering of the High Priest **is like the meal offering** component of the **daily offerings** [*temidin*] and must be sacrificed in the morning and the afternoon, even if the High Priest died and was not yet replaced.

מַאי הֲוֵי עֲלַהּ? אָמַר רַב נַחְמָן בַּר יִצְחָק: תָּא שְׁמַע, דְּתַנְיָא: שְׁלֵימָה שַׁחֲרִית וּשְׁלֵימָה בֵּין הָעַרְבַּיִם.

The Gemara asks: **What** halakhic conclusion **was** reached **about** this matter? **Rav Naḥman bar Yitzḥak said: Come** and **hear** a resolution to Rabbi Yoḥanan's dilemma, **as it is taught** explicitly in a *baraita*: If the High Priest died and was not yet replaced, **a complete** tenth of an ephah is sacrificed in the **morning and** another **complete** tenth of an ephah is sacrificed **in the afternoon.**

אָמַר רַבִּי יוֹחָנָן: פְּלִיגִי בָּהּ אַבָּא יוֹסֵי בֶּן דּוֹסְתַּאי וְרַבָּנַן.

§ **Rabbi Yoḥanan says: Abba Yosei ben Dostai and the Rabbis disagree** as to the amount of frankincense brought with the griddle-cake offering of the High Priest.

אַבָּא יוֹסֵי בֶּן דּוֹסְתַּאי אוֹמֵר: מַפְרִישׁ לָהּ שְׁנֵי קְמָצִים שֶׁל לְבוֹנָה, קוֹמֶץ – שַׁחֲרִית, וְקוֹמֶץ – בֵּין הָעַרְבַּיִם. וְרַבָּנַן אָמְרִי: מַפְרִישׁ לָהּ קוֹמֶץ אֶחָד, חֲצִי קוֹמֶץ – שַׁחֲרִית, וַחֲצִי קוֹמֶץ – בֵּין הָעַרְבַּיִם.

Abba Yosei ben Dostai says: The High Priest **separates two handfuls of frankincense for** his griddle-cake offering each day; one **handful** for his **morning** offering **and** one **handful** for his **afternoon** offering. **And the Rabbis say:** The High Priest **separates one handful** of frankincense each day **for** his griddle-cake offering. He divides it in half and brings **half a handful** for his **morning** offering **and half a handful** for his **afternoon** offering.[H]

בְּמַאי קָמִיפַּלְגִי? אַבָּא יוֹסֵי בֶּן דּוֹסְתַּאי סָבַר: לָא אַשְׁכְּחַן חֲצִי קוֹמֶץ דְּקָרֵיב, וְרַבָּנַן סָבְרִי: לָא אַשְׁכְּחַן עִשָּׂרוֹן דְּבָעֵי שְׁנֵי קְמָצִים.

The Gemara clarifies: **With regard to what** principle **do they disagree? Abba Yosei ben Dostai holds** that since **one does not find** a case where the Torah explicitly states that **half a handful is sacrificed,** he brings a complete handful for each offering. **And the Rabbis hold that** since **one does not find** a case where **a tenth** of an ephah **requires two handfuls** of frankincense, he brings only one handful and divides it between the two offerings.

בָּעֵי רַבִּי יוֹחָנָן: כֹּהֵן גָּדוֹל שֶׁמֵּת, וְלֹא מִינּוּ אַחֵר תַּחְתָּיו,

Having discussed the quantity of frankincense that is generally brought with the griddle-cake offering, the Gemara now addresses a case where the High Priest died. **Rabbi Yoḥanan raises a dilemma:** In the case of **a High Priest who died and they did not** yet **appoint another in his stead,**

HALAKHA

Half a handful for his morning offering and half a handful for his afternoon offering – חֲצִי קוֹמֶץ שַׁחֲרִית וַחֲצִי קוֹמֶץ בֵּין הָעַרְבַּיִם: If the High Priest died and another was not yet appointed, a complete tenth of an ephah of fine flour is sacrificed in the morning and another complete tenth of an ephah is sacrificed in the afternoon for the griddle-cake offering. The amount of oil and frankincense is not doubled, despite the fact that the amount of fine flour is doubled. The normal amount of three *log* of oil and one handful of frankincense is brought, and they are each divided in half. Half a handful of frankincense and one and a half *log* of oil are used for the morning offering, and the same amounts are used for the afternoon offering. This is in accordance with the opinion of the Rabbis (Rambam *Sefer Avoda*, *Hilkhot Temidin UMusafin* 3:22).

לְרַבָּנַן הוּכְפְּלָה לְבוֹנָתוֹ אוֹ לֹא? מִי אָמְרִינַן, מִתּוֹךְ שֶׁהוּכְפְּלָה סׇלְתּוֹ – הוּכְפְּלָה לְבוֹנָתוֹ, אוֹ דִילְמָא מַאי דְּגַלֵּי – גַּלֵּי, מַאי דְּלָא גַּלֵּי – לָא גַּלֵּי?

according to the Rabbis,[N] who hold that generally one handful of frankincense is divided between the morning and afternoon offerings, **is the** amount of **frankincense doubled or not? Do we say** that **since** in this case **its fine flour is doubled,** as a complete tenth of an ephah of fine flour is sacrificed in both the morning and evening, **its frankincense** is also **doubled? Or perhaps that which** the verse **reveals,** i.e., that a complete tenth of an ephah is sacrificed in the morning and afternoon, **it reveals,** and **that which** it **does not reveal,** it **does not reveal;** and therefore, since the verse does not indicate that the amount of frankincense is doubled, only one handful is brought.

וְשֶׁמֶן בֵּין לְאַבָּא יוֹסֵי בֶּן דּוֹסְתַּאי וּבֵין לְרַבָּנַן, מַהוּ?

And furthermore, **what is** the *halakha* concerning the **oil** of the griddle-cake offering in a case where the High Priest died and was not yet replaced, **both** according **to Abba Yosei ben Dostai and** according **to the Rabbis?** Is the required amount three *log*, as it is when the High Priest brings the griddle-cake offering, or is the amount of oil doubled just as the amount of fine flour is doubled?

אֲמַר רָבָא, תָּא שְׁמַע: ״חֲמִשָּׁה קְמָצִין הֵן״, וְאִם אִיתָא – זִימְנִין דְּמַשְׁכַּחַתְּ לַהּ שִׁבְעָה!

Rava said: Come and **hear** a resolution to the dilemma concerning the quantity of frankincense that is brought in this case, based upon a mishna (106b): **There are five** *halakhot* pertaining to **a handful.** The *halakha* of the frankincense sacrificed with the griddle-cake offering of the High Priest is not included in this number, because only half a handful of frankincense is sacrificed at one time. **And if it is so** that when there is no High Priest a complete handful is brought in the morning and in the afternoon, then **sometimes you find** that there are **seven**[N] *halakhot* pertaining to a handful.

״דְּאִי״ – לָא קָתָנֵי. יָתֵיב רַב פָּפָּא וְקָאָמַר לַהּ לְהָא שְׁמַעְתָּא. אֲמַר לֵיהּ רַב יוֹסֵף בַּר שְׁמַעְיָה לְרַב פָּפָּא: וְהָא ״מַעֲלֶה קוֹמֶץ בַּחוּץ״, ״דְּאִי״ הָוֵה, וְקָתָנֵי!

The Gemara rejects this proof: The *tanna* **does not teach** cases of **what if** the High Priest died, and is speaking only about a typical case. The Gemara relates that **Rav Pappa was sitting and teaching this** *halakha.* **Rav Yosef bar Shemaya said to Rav Pappa: But** the mishna does list the case of **one who** intentionally **offers up** the **handful** from a meal offering **outside** the Temple courtyard, who is liable to receive *karet*. This **is** not a standard case but rather a case of **what if, and** nevertheless it **is taught** in the mishna. Accordingly, Rava's proof is valid.

מַאי הָוֵי עֲלַהּ? אֲמַר רַב נַחְמָן בַּר יִצְחָק: תָּא שְׁמַע, דְּתַנְיָא: כֹּהֵן גָּדוֹל שֶׁמֵּת וְלֹא מִינּוּ אַחֵר תַּחְתָּיו – שְׁלֵימָה שַׁחֲרִית וּשְׁלֵימָה בֵּין הָעַרְבַּיִם. וּמַפְרִישׁ לַהּ שְׁנֵי קְמָצִין – קוֹמֶץ שַׁחֲרִית וְקוֹמֶץ בֵּין הָעַרְבַּיִם. וּמַפְרִישׁ לַהּ שְׁלֹשֶׁת לוּגִּין – לוֹג וּמֶחֱצָה שַׁחֲרִית לוֹג וּמֶחֱצָה בֵּין הָעַרְבַּיִם.

The Gemara asks: **What** conclusion **was** reached **about** this matter? **Rav Naḥman bar Yitzḥak said: Come** and **hear** a resolution, **as it is taught** in a *baraita*: In the case of a **High Priest who died and they did not** yet **appoint another in his stead, a complete** tenth of an ephah of fine flour is brought for the griddle-cake offering in the **morning and** another **complete** tenth of an ephah is brought **in the afternoon. And one separates two handfuls** of frankincense **for it,** and sacrifices one **handful** with the **morning** offering **and** one **handful** with the **afternoon** offering. **And** one **separates three** *log* of oil **for it,** and brings **a** *log* **and a half** with the **morning** offering **and a** *log* **and a half** with the **afternoon** offering.

מַנִּי? אִילֵימָא רַבָּנַן – מַאי שְׁנָא לְבוֹנָתָהּ דְּהוּכְפְּלָה, וּמַאי שְׁנָא שַׁמְנָהּ דְּלָא הוּכְפְּלָה?

The Gemara asks: In accordance with **whose** opinion is this *baraita*? **If we say** that it is in accordance with the opinion of **the Rabbis, what is different** about **its frankincense** such **that it is doubled** in the case where the High Priest died, **and what is different** about **its oil** such **that it is not doubled?**

אֶלָּא אַבָּא יוֹסֵי בֶּן דּוֹסְתַּאי הִיא, דַּאֲמַר: חֲבִיתֵּי כֹּהֵן גָּדוֹל בְּעָלְמָא שְׁנֵי קְמָצִין בָּעְיָא, וּלְבוֹנָה לֹא הוּכְפְּלָה וְשֶׁמֶן לֹא הוּכְפַּל.

Rather, the *baraita* **is** in accordance with the opinion of **Abba Yosei ben Dostai, who said:** The **griddle-cake** offering of the **High Priest generally requires two handfuls. And** therefore when the *baraita* requires two handfuls of frankincense in the case where the High Priest died and another has not yet been appointed, the **frankincense is not** being **doubled and the oil is** also **not doubled.** Therefore, three *log* of oil are required, as usual.

NOTES

According to the Rabbis – לְרַבָּנַן: Rashi explains that this dilemma is relevant only with regard to the opinion of the Rabbis but not with regard to the opinion of Abba Yosei ben Dostai, who holds that a full handful of frankincense is always brought with the griddle-cake offering in both the morning and the evening. The reason for this is that there is no precedent for burning two handfuls of frankincense as a single offering.

Sometimes you find that there are seven – זִימְנִין דְּמַשְׁכַּחַתְּ לַהּ שִׁבְעָה: Rashi explains that although the two handfuls are both brought with the griddle-cake offering, and the sacrifice of the griddle-cake offering in the morning and afternoon comprises two components of the same mitzva, the handfuls of frankincense would have been counted separately in the mishna's list. There is precedent for this in this mishna, which counts the two bowls of frankincense that accompanied the shewbread separately, despite the fact that they are actually components of one mitzva.

וּמִדְּשֶׁמֶן לְאַבָּא יוֹסֵי בֶּן דּוֹסְתַּאי לֹא הוּכְפְּלָה, לְבוֹנָתָהּ וְשַׁמְנָהּ לְרַבָּנַן נַמִי לֹא הוּכְפְּלוּ.

And from the fact **that** according **to Abba Yosei ben Dostai** the requisite **oil is not doubled,** one can conclude that **also** according **to the Rabbis its frankincense and its oil are not doubled.**

אָמַר רַבִּי יוֹחָנָן: הֲלָכָה כְּאַבָּא יוֹסֵי בֶּן דּוֹסְתַּאי. וּמִי אֲמַר רַבִּי יוֹחָנָן הָכִי? וְהָא אָמַר רַבִּי יוֹחָנָן: הֲלָכָה כִּסְתַם מִשְׁנָה, וּתְנַן: חֲמִשָּׁה קְמָצִין הֵן!

This discussion in the Gemara began with Rabbi Yoḥanan presenting the dispute between Abba Yosei ben Dostai and the Rabbis, and it concludes with his ruling concerning their dispute. **Rabbi Yoḥanan says:** The ***halakha*** is **in accordance with** the opinion of **Abba Yosei ben Dostai.** The Gemara asks: **And did Rabbi Yoḥanan** actually **say this? But doesn't Rabbi Yoḥanan state** a principle that the ***halakha*** is **in accordance with** the ruling of **an unattributed mishna,** and **we learned** in the unattributed mishna cited earlier: **There are** only **five** *halakhot* pertaining to **a handful.** Since the mishna does not list the fact that a handful of frankincense is offered twice daily with the griddle-cake offering, how can Rabbi Yoḥanan accept that opinion?

אֲמוֹרָאֵי נִינְהוּ, וְאַלִּיבָּא דְּרַבִּי יוֹחָנָן.

The Gemara answers: **They are** different ***amora'im,*** **and** they disagree **with regard to** the opinion **of Rabbi Yoḥanan.** One said that Rabbi Yoḥanan rules in accordance with Abba Yosei ben Dostai, and one said that according to Rabbi Yoḥanan the *halakha* is always in accordance with an unattributed mishna.

הדרן עלך התכלת

Summary of **Perek IV**

This chapter discussed mitzvot and offerings with regard to which the failure to fulfill one component does not prevent one from fulfilling another component. The beginning of the chapter dealt with the white and sky-blue strings of ritual fringes. The mishna explains that each of these two components can be fulfilled independently, and if one does not have sky-blue strings he can still fulfill the mitzva of wearing white strings.

The Gemara then expanded the discussion to address in depth the topic of sky-blue wool. This discussion included clarification of how the sky-blue dye is produced and how the sky-blue strings are tied onto a garment. The Gemara also engaged in a more general discussion concerning ritual fringes, including the relationship between the corners of the garment and the strings, as well as the size and other characteristics that determine whether a garment is required to have ritual fringes. The Gemara also cited homiletical expositions emphasizing the importance of the mitzva and its meaning. This chapter contains the primary discussion of the mitzva of ritual fringes in the Talmud, and serves as the source for most of the *halakhot* of ritual fringes.

The chapter then discussed various offerings that are interconnected, and clarified when the lack of one prevents the sacrifice of the other and when it does not. In many instances, one may sacrifice an offering even though one is not able to sacrifice a related offering. This is true not only of different offerings brought on the same day, e.g., the daily offerings and the additional offerings, but even of components of the same offering. It is possible to sacrifice one of the animals required for the additional offering if the others are not available. There are some additional offerings where each individual component prevents the fulfillment of the mitzva with the others. This is true of the additional offerings of *Sukkot* and the offerings of *Shavuot* mentioned in Leviticus, chapter 23.

This chapter also contained an extensive discussion of the two loaves of *Shavuot* and the communal peace offering of two sheep that accompanies them. The Gemara explores the question of their interdependence and the nature of their relationship.

The daily offering, the incense, and the griddle-cake offering of the High Priest are all sacrificed in two halves, half in the morning and half in the afternoon. In all these cases, if the morning offering was not sacrificed, the afternoon offering may still be sacrificed. An exception to this is the case where the service of a new altar had not yet been initiated, as it must be initiated by means of the daily offering of the morning.

There is a unique requirement in the case of the griddle-cake offering of the High Priest, which is that he must bring the entire offering at one time and then divide it in half. Therefore, if the High Priest sacrificed the morning component of his griddle-cake offering, and he then died and a replacement was appointed, the new High Priest must bring another complete offering in the afternoon and sacrifice half of it. The Gemara tangentially delved into the topic of this unusual offering, which, on the one hand, is an offering incumbent on an individual, the High Priest, and on the other hand is part of the fixed communal Temple service.

These were the main topics discussed in this chapter. Other topics that were discussed tangentially include the apparent contradictions between the verses in Ezekiel and the Torah concerning the Temple service; whether the court instructs people to sin in order to achieve a greater religious gain; and priorities among offerings depending on their relative sanctity and frequency.

Common **Acronyms**

Since the publication of the first volume of the *Koren Talmud Bavli* we have employed some transliterated acronyms, such as Rambam, to give the translation a more authentic flavor. These acronyms are used throughout this volume where they are well known and where the acronym helps readers easily identify the author in question. The following chart provides the full name of each author or work alongside its common acronym.

Acronym	Full Name
HaAri	Rabbi Yitzḥak Luria
Ba'al HaMaor	Rabbi Zeraḥya HaLevi
Baḥ	*Bayit Ḥadash*
Beur HaGra	Commentary of Rabbi Eliyahu of Vilna on the *Shulḥan Arukh*
Derashot Mahari Mintz	Homilies of Rabbi Yehuda Mintz
Derashot Ra'anaḥ	Homilies of Rabbi Eliyahu ben Ḥayyim
Geranat	Rabbi Naftali Trop
Gilyon Maharsha	Marginalia of Rabbi Shlomo Eiger
Gra	Rabbi Eliyahu of Vilna, the Vilna Gaon
Graḥ	Rabbi Ḥayyim Soloveitchik
Grib	Rabbi Yehuda Bakhrakh
Griz	Rabbi Yitzḥak Ze'ev Soloveitchik
Haggahot HaGra	Comments of Rabbi Eliyahu of Vilna on the Talmud
Haggahot Maharsha	Comments of Rabbi Shmuel Eliezer Eidels
Hassagot HaRa'avad	Comments of Rabbi Avraham ben David on the Rambam's *Mishne Torah*
Ḥida	Rabbi Ḥayyim David Azulai
Ḥiddushei Aggadot LaMaharal	*Ḥiddushei Aggadot* by Rabbi Yehuda Loew of Prague
Ḥiddushei Aggadot LaRashba	*Ḥiddushei Aggadot* by Rabbi Shlomo ben Adderet
Ḥiddushei HaGeranat	*Ḥiddushei* Rabbi Naftali Trop
Ḥiddushei HaGriz	*Ḥiddushei* Rabbi Yitzḥak Ze'ev Soloveitchik
Ḥiddushei HaRim	*Ḥiddushei* Rabbi Yitzḥak Meir of Gur
Ḥiddushei Ri Ḥaver	*Ḥiddushei* Rabbi Yitzḥak Isaac Ḥaver
Kitzur Piskei HaRosh	Abridged Halakhic Rulings of Rabbeinu Asher ben Rabbi Yeḥiel
Mabit	Rabbi Moshe ben Yosef di Trani

Acronym	Full Name
Maharal	Rabbi Yehuda Loew of Prague
Maharam Alashkar	Rabbi Moshe Alashkar
Maharam Brisk	Rabbi Mordekhai Brisk
Maharam Ḥalawa	Rabbi Moshe Ḥalawa
Maharam Lublin	Rabbi Meir of Lublin
Maharam Mintz	Rabbi Moshe Mintz
Maharam of Rothenburg	Rabbi Meir of Rothenburg
Maharam Padua	Rabbi Meir of Padua
Maharam Schick	Rabbi Moshe Schick
Maharam Schiff	Rabbi Meir Schiff
Maharatz Ḥayyut	Rabbi Tzvi Hirsch Chajes
Mahari Abuhav	Rabbi Yitzḥak Abuhav
Mahari Bassan	Rabbi Yeḥiel Bassan
Mahari Beirav	Rabbi Ya'akov Beirav
Mahari ben Lev	Rabbi Yosef ben Lev
Mahari ben Malkitzedek	Rabbi Yitzḥak ben Malkitzedek
Mahari Berona	Rabbi Yisrael Berona
Mahari Kurkus	Rabbi Yosef Kurkus
Mahari Mintz	Rabbi Yehuda Mintz
Mahari Weil	Rabbi Ya'akov Weil
Mahariḥ	Rabbi Yeḥezkia ben Ya'akov of Magdeburg
Maharik	Rabbi Yosef Colon
Maharikash	Rabbi Ya'akov Castro
Maharil	Rabbi Ya'akov HaLevi Molin
Maharit	Rabbi Yosef di Trani
Maharit Algazi	Rabbi Yom Tov Algazi
Maharsha	Rabbi Shmuel Eliezer Eidels
Maharshal	Rabbi Shlomo Luria
Malbim	Rabbi Meir Leibush ben Yeḥiel Michel Wisser
Netziv	Rabbi Naftali Tzvi Yehuda Berlin
Nimmukei HaGrib	Comments of Rabbi Yehuda Bakhrakh on the Maharsha
Piskei HaRid	Halakhic Rulings of Rabbi Yeshaya di Trani the Elder
Piskei Riaz	Halakhic Rulings of Rabbi Yeshaya di Trani the Younger
Ra'ah	Rabbi Aharon HaLevi
Ra'anaḥ	Rabbi Eliyahu ben Ḥayyim
Ra'avad	Rabbi Avraham ben David
Ra'avan	Rabbi Eliezer ben Natan
Ra'avya	Rabbi Eliezer ben Yoel HaLevi
Rabbi Avraham ben HaRambam	Rabbi Avraham, son of the Rambam

Acronym	Full Name
Rabbi Shlomo ben Rashbatz	Rabbi Shlomo, son of Rabbi Shimon ben Tzemaḥ Duran
Radak	Rabbi David Kimḥi
Radbaz	Rabbi David ben Zimra
Ralbag	Rabbi Levi ben Gershon
Ramah	Rabbi Meir HaLevi
Rambam	Rabbi Moshe ben Maimon
Ramban	Rabbi Moshe ben Naḥman
Ran	Rabbeinu Nissim ben Reuven of Gerona
Rashash	Rabbi Shmuel Strashun
Rashba	Rabbi Shlomo ben Adderet
Rashbam	Rabbi Shmuel ben Meir
Rashbatz	Rabbi Shimon ben Tzemaḥ Duran
Rashi	Rabbi Shlomo Yitzḥaki
Re'em Horowitz	Rabbi Elazar Moshe Horowitz
Rema	Rabbi Moshe Isserles
Ri HaLavan	Rabbeinu Yitzḥak ben Ya'akov of Prague
Ri Ḥaver	Rabbi Yitzḥak Isaac Ḥaver
Ri Migash	Rabbi Yosef Migash
Riaf	Rabbi Yoshiya Pinto
Riaz	Rabbi Yeshaya di Trani the Younger
Rid	Rabbi Yeshaya di Trani the Elder
Ridvaz	Rabbi Ya'akov David ben Ze'ev Wilovsky
Rif	Rabbi Yitzḥak Alfasi
Rim	Rabbi Yitzḥak Meir of Gur
Ritva	Rabbi Yom Tov ben Avraham Asevilli (of Seville)
Riva	Rabbeinu Yitzḥak ben Asher
Rivam	Rabbi Yitzḥak ben Meir
Rivan	Rabbi Yehuda bar Natan
Rivash	Rabbi Yitzḥak ben Sheshet
Rosh	Rabbeinu Asher ben Rabbi Yeḥiel
Shakh	*Siftei Kohen* by Rabbi Shabtai Cohen Rappaport
Shas	The Six Orders of the Mishna
She'elat Ya'avetz	Responsa of Rabbi Ya'akov Emden
Shela	*Shenei Luḥot HaBerit* by Rabbi Yeshaya HaLevi Horowitz
Siddur Rashi	Siddur compiled by Rashi's students
Sma	*Sefer Meirat Einayim* by Rabbi Yehoshua Falk
Smag	*Sefer Mitzvot Gadol* by Rabbi Moshe of Coucy
Smak	*Sefer Mitzvot Katan* by Rabbi Yitzḥak ben Yosef of Corbeil
Talmid HaRa'ah	A student of Rabbi Aharon HaLevi

Acronym	Full Name
Talmid HaRashba	A student of Rabbi Shlomo ben Adderet
Tashbetz	Responsa of Rabbi Shimon ben Tzemaḥ Duran
Taz	*Turei Zahav* by Rabbi David HaLevi
Tosefot HaRosh	*Tosefot* of Rabbeinu Asher ben Rabbi Yeḥiel
Tosefot Ri HaLavan	*Tosefot* of Rabbeinu Yitzḥak ben Ya'akov of Prague
Tosefot Rid	*Tosefot* of Rabbi Yeshaya di Trani the Elder
Tur	*Sefer HaTurim* by Rabbi Ya'akov ben Asher
Tzlaḥ	*Tziyyun LeNefesh Ḥayya* by Rabbi Yeḥezkel Landau
Ya'avetz	Rabbi Ya'akov Emden

Index of **Background**

Index of **Background**

Index of Language

Index of **Personalities**

Image **Credits**

p14 © Filip Maljkovic; **p24** © Jay Garfinkel 2015; **p36** © Mauro Raffaelli; **p43** © courtesy of the Temple Institute; **p50** © courtesy of the Temple Institute; **p52** © Ariely; **p74** © courtesy of the Temple Institute; **p91** top image © courtesy of the Temple Institute; **p91** bottom image © courtesy of the Temple Institute; **p95** top image © Brian Stalter; **p95** bottom image © Eitan f; **p133** top image © Sylvia Steinberg; **p133** bottom image © Wilson44691; **p134** © HaRav Menachem Makover, courtesy of *Harenu Bevinyano*; **p138** top image © Tamorlan; **p146** © Wolfgang Thanner; **p149** © Wolfgang Sauber; **p171** © HaRav Menachem Makover, courtesy of *Harenu Bevinyano*; **p181** © Rama; **p191** © Moumou82; **p194** © Sebastià Giralt; **p195** top image © The International Institute of Tropical Agriculture in Nigeria (IITA); **p195** center image © The International Institute of Tropical Agriculture in Nigeria (IITA); **p195** bottom image © Larry Milligan; **p203** © courtesy of Hebrew Stam Forum, www.hebrewstam.blogspot.co.il; **p204** top image © Olan, www.shutterstock.com; **p204** bottom image © Hanay; **p206** bottom image © Thomas Steiner; **p208** lower right image © Jerry-Rainey, www.shutterstock.com; **p209** top image © Sara Goldsmith; **p210** top image © High Contrast; **p215** © courtesy of Moreshet Avot Institute; **p229** bottom image © Johann Dréo; **p239** © Sputnikcccp; **p245** © Petil Tekhelet; **p247** top image © Jean-Pol GRANDMONT; **p247** bottom image © Annie Spratt; **p249** top image © Francis; **p249** bottom image © David Stroe; **p275** © H. Zell; **p287** © courtesy of the Temple Institute; **p302** © ש.י.; **p310** © courtesy of the Temple Institute

לְרַבָּנַן הוּכְפְּלָה לְבוֹנָתוֹ אוֹ לֹא? מִי אָמְרִינַן, מִתּוֹךְ שֶׁהוּכְפְּלָה סָלְתּוֹ – הוּכְפְּלָה לְבוֹנָתוֹ, אוֹ דִילְמָא מַאי *דְּגַלֵּי – גַּלֵּי, מַאי דְּלָא גַּלֵּי – לָא גַּלֵּי? וְשֶׁמֶן בֵּין (א)לְאַבָּא יוֹסֵי בֶּן דּוֹסְתַּאי וּבֵין לְרַבָּנַן, מַהוּ? אָמַר רָבָא, ת"ש: *"ה' קְמָצִין הֵן", וְאִם אִיתָא – זִימְנִין דְּמַשְׁכַּחַתְּ לָהּ ז'! "דְּאִי" – לָא קָתָנֵי. יָתֵיב רַב פַּפָּא וְקָאָמַר לָהּ לְהָא שְׁמַעְתָּא. אֲמַר לֵיהּ רַב יוֹסֵף בַּר שְׁמַעְיָה לְרַב פַּפָּא: וְהָא "מַעֲלֶה קוֹמֶץ בַּחוּץ", ד"אִי הֲוָה", וְקָתָנֵי! מַאי הֲוֵי עֲלַהּ? אָמַר ר"נ בַּר יִצְחָק: ת"ש, דְּתַנְיָא: א] כ"ג שֶׁמֵּת וְלֹא מִינּוּ אַחֵר תַּחְתָּיו – שְׁלֵימָה שַׁחֲרִית וּשְׁלֵימָה בֵּין הָעַרְבַּיִם. וּמַפְרִישׁ לָהּ ב' קְמָצִין – קוֹמֶץ שַׁחֲרִית וְקוֹמֶץ בֵּין הָעַרְבַּיִם. וּמַפְרִישׁ לָהּ שְׁלֹשֶׁת לוּגִּין – לוֹג וּמֶחֱצָה שַׁחֲרִית לוֹג וּמֶחֱצָה בֵּין הָעַרְבַּיִם. מַנִּי? אִילֵימָא רַבָּנַן – מַאי שְׁנָא לְבוֹנָתָהּ דְּהוּכְפְּלָה, וּמַאי שְׁנָא שַׁמְנָהּ דְּלָא הוּכְפְּלָה? אֶלָּא אַבָּא יוֹסֵי בֶּן דּוֹסְתַּאי הִיא, דְּאָמַר: חֲבִיתֵּי כ"ג בְּעָלְמָא שְׁנֵי קְמָצִין בָּעֲיָא, וּלְבוֹנָה לֹא הוּכְפְּלָה וְשֶׁמֶן לֹא הוּכְפַּל. וּמִדְּשֶׁמֶן לְאַבָּא יוֹסֵי בֶּן דּוֹסְתַּאי לֹא הוּכְפְּלָה, אלְבוֹנָתָהּ וְשַׁמְנָהּ לְרַבָּנַן נַמִי לֹא הוּכְפְּלוּ. א"ר יוֹחָנָן: הֲלָכָה כְּאַבָּא יוֹסֵי בֶּן דּוֹסְתַּאי. וּמִי א"ר יוֹחָנָן הָכִי? וְהָא *א"ר יוֹחָנָן: הֲלָכָה כִּסְתַם מִשְׁנָה, וּתְנַן: חֲמִשָּׁה קְמָצִין הֵן! *אֲמוֹרָאֵי נִינְהוּ, וְאַלִּיבָּא דְּרַבִּי יוֹחָנָן.§

הדרן עלך התכלת

כָּל בהַמְּנָחוֹת בָּאוֹת מַצָּה, גחוּץ מֵחָמֵץ שֶׁבַּתּוֹדָה דוּשְׁתֵּי הַלֶּחֶם, שֶׁהֵן בָּאוֹת חָמֵץ. ר"מ אוֹמֵר: ב] הַשְּׂאוֹר בּוֹדֶה לָהֶן מִתּוֹכָן וּמְחַמְּצָן. ר' יְהוּדָה אוֹמֵר: אַף הִיא אֵינָהּ מִן הַמּוּבְחָר, אֶלָּא הַמֵּבִיא אֶת הַשְּׂאוֹר, וְנוֹתְנוֹ לְתוֹךְ הַמִּדָּה וּמְמַלֵּא אֶת הַמִּדָּה. אָמְרוּ לוֹ: אַף הִיא הָיְתָה חֲסֵרָה אוֹ יְתֵרָה.§ גמ' בְּעָא מִינֵּיהּ רַבִּי פְּרִידָא מֵרַבִּי אַמִי: מִנַּיִן לְכָל הַמְּנָחוֹת שֶׁהֵן בָּאוֹת מַצָּה? מְנָלַן? דִּכְתִיב בָּהּ – כְּתִיב בָּהּ, דְּלָא כְּתִיב בָּהּ – כְּתִיב בָּהּ

זאת

ולא מינו אחר. דקריבה שלימה*. לרבנן הוכפלה לבונתו. שייביא קומץ שחרית וקומץ בערב. דבשלמא לאבא יוסי לא מבעיא ליה דלא הוכפל שיביא שני קמצים לכל הקטרה, דלא מצינו ב' קמצים בהקטרה אחת. מאי דגלי גלי. סלת גלי קרא בהוספה, כדאמרינן לעיל (דף נא:): לרבי יהודה מ"אותה", ולר"ש מ"כליל תקטר". ושמן. מבעיא ליה אליבא דכולהו, אם צריך להביא ג' לוגין לכל עשרון. דעד שלא ימות היה מביא ג' לוגין, ג] *וחוצן: לוג ומחצה לחצי עשרון דשחר, ולוג ומחצה לבין הערבים. השתא מאי. ה' קמצין הן. בפרק "האומר הרי עלי עשרון" (לקמן דף קו:) חשיב, ד] והאי קומץ לבונה של חביתין – לא חשיב התם, משום דלחצאין קרב, ובשלימה קמיירי ולא בחצאין. ואם איתא דכי מת כ"ג ה] קרבו שלם בכל הקטרות – זימנין דמשכחת ו] [שבעה] כגון ב' קמצים של חביתין. דהא התם קא חשיב ב' קמצים של בזיכי לחם הפנים, אע"ג דחד קרבן נינהו, וה"נ ליחשוב. ומשני: לעולם אימא לך דהוכפל, והאי דלא חשיב להו – משום "דאי מת כהן" לא קתני, אלא בקריבים כדרכן קא מיירי. להא שמעתא. ד"אי" לא קתני. והא מעלה קומץ בחוץ. דקתני ליה התם גבי ה' קמצין, דאי עבר והעלהו בחוץ – *חייב, וקתני ליה ז] נמי, ש"מ דאם איתא דהוכפל – ליתנינהו, ואפילו ד"אי". מאי הוי עלה. דהא לא תנינן ליה בהדיא? אלא אבא יוסי. דאמר: חביתין דעלמא נמי בחיי כהן בעי ב' קמצין, הילכך הא נמי ב' קמצין, וקתני "לוג ומחצה שחרית" כו' – אלמא שמן לא הוכפל, ואיפשיטא בעיא דשמן לאבא יוסי. ומדשמן לאבא יוסי לא הוכפל – דמאי דלא גלי לא גלי, לרבנן נמי – לבונה ושמן לא הוכפלו, דמאי דלא גלי לא גלי. דאינהו לא פליגי אלא בלבונה מחיים, אבל בלאחר מיתה אי הוכפל אי לא הוכפל – לא פליגי. הילכתא כאבא יוסי. דאמר: בחיי כהן מקריב קומץ לבונה שחרית וקומץ ערבית. ותנן ה' קמצין הן. ולא חשיב ליה לקומץ דחביתין – משום דלחצאין קרב. ואם איתא דקרב שלם – ליתני "ז' קמצים הן". אמוראי נינהו. מר אמר: כסתם משנה אמר רבי יוחנן, ומר אמר: הלכה כאבא יוסי אמר רבי יוחנן.

הדרן עלך התכלת

כל המנחות. חוץ מחמץ שבתודה. דכתיב "על חלות לחם חמץ" וגו' (ויקרא ז), ושתי הלחם – דכתיב "חמץ תאפינה" (שם כג). שאור בודה להן מתוכו. מתוך עשרון דתודה ושתי הלחם היה מוציא שאור, *שהוא לש מן הסלת מעט לאחר שנמדד וטומנו בסלת ומתחמץ מאליו, וממנו מחמץ את השאר ח]. אף היא אינה מן המובחר. שאינה מחמלת יפה, לפי שאין לה שאור מחומץ יפה. אלא מביא שאור. המחומץ יפה מתוך ביתו, ונותן לתוך העשרון, ומוסיף וממלא סלת. אף היא היתה יתרה או חסרה. כגון אם השאור עבה ומגובל בקושי במעט מים, אינו מחזיק נפח גדול כאילו היה קמח – ונמצא העשרון יתר, לפי שאם לא היה שאור מגובל, היה נפחו גדול מעכשיו. ואם אינו מגובל יפה, שנתן בו מים הרבה, נמצא נפחו גדול מאילו היה קמח – ונמצא העשרון חסר, שאם לא בשביל המים, לא היה מלא. גמ' דכתיבא כתיבא. אותה מנחה שכתוב בה "מצה", כגון מנחת מאפה ומנחת מחבת – הרי כתיב בה, ודלא כתיבא – אתא מהאי קרא דכייל לכל המנחות,

כלו

לרבנן הוכפלה לבונתו. אבל לאבא יוסי בן דוסתאי, כיון דצריך קומץ בבוקר וקומץ בערב – לא שייך לאיכפולי טפי מסיעור שלם. *דלרבנן הוא דבעי אי בעינן שלם בלבונה, כי היכי דבעינן שלם בעשרון. אבל משמן בעי *(טפי) לאבא יוסי בן דוסתאי נמי – דבכל יום לא היה רק לוג ומחצה בבוקר, וכן בערב והשתא נמי. או דילמא, לכל עשרון היו ג' לוגין, וזו היא בלילתן. הלכה כאבא יוסי בן דוסתאי. תימה: הילכתא למשיחא?*

הדרן עלך התכלת

כל המנחות באות מצה חוץ מחמץ שבתודה ושתי הלחם. שתי הלחם ניחא דכייל בהדי שאר מנחות, דאיקרי "מנחה", ט] כדאמר בפרק "התכלת" (לעיל דף מז:). אבל לחמי תודה, *לא אשכחן. י] ומ"מ ניחא לאשמועינן דינא. בודה. בדל"ת גרסינן בערוך, ופי': לשון הוצאה, כמו: (מלכים א יב) "בחודש אשר בדא מלבו", (נחמיה ו) "כי מלבך אתה בודאם". חסרה או יתרה. מכאן פי' הרב רבינו חיים דכשמודדין במדה בפסח או לצורך חלה, אין להכביד יא] על הסלת, דא"כ נמצאת יתרה כמו לענין מנחות. ועוד אמרינן לקמן (דף פז.): "גודשא תילתא". מנין לכל המנחות שהן באות מצה כו'. תימה: מתני' היא (לקמן דף נה.), דתנן: כל המנחות נילושות בפושרים, ומשמרם שלא יחמיצו כו', שנאמר: "כל המנחה יב] *בל תאפה חמץ". וה"נ דרשי' לקמן בגמ' (שם): שאר מנחות מנין? – ת"ל "כל המנחה". ועוד: משמע דשייך לרבויי טפי מההוא קרא ד"כל מנחה" ממאי דמרבה מהאי קרא ד"זאת תורת המנחה" דמייתי הכא. דמההוא לא שייך לרבויי אלא מנחות שיש בהם דין הכתוב בפרשה, הגשה קמיצה ולבונה, כגון מנחת סלת ומחבת ומרחשת. אבל מ"כל המנחה" איתרבו אפילו מנחת העומר ומנחת קנאות ומנחת כהן ומנחת [נסכים] ולחם הפנים! ונראה לפרש: דרבי אמי לא רצה להביא לן הא דדרשינן מייתורא דקראי, יג] (אלא) לפי שהיה סבור דאפילו למצוה קא מיבעיא ליה היכא דלא כתיבא מצה, הביא לו מקראות פשוטות ותמה על שאלתו. והשיב לו: דכתיבא – כתיבא, כגון מחבת ומאפה. דלא כתיבא, כגון מנחת סלת ומרחשת – כתיב "זאת תורת", וה"ה דאכתי מהנך קראי לא ידעינן כולהו שאר מנחות. *עוד משמע דמנחת סלת נמי כתיבא, דאותה פרשה ד"זאת תורת" דכתיב בה "מצות תאכל" פשטיה דקרא במנחת סלת [כתיב], דכתיב "מסלת המנחה ומשמנה", ומ"זאת תורת" מרבי מרחשת. ומהשתא מצינו למימר דנתרבו כל מנחות, אפילו אותם דאין בהם הגשה קמיצה ולבונה, כי היכי דמרבינן מרחשת אע"ג דלא איירי בה קרא. אבל קשיא: א"כ, "כל המנחה" – לרבות שאר מנחות, למה לי? דאם נאמר: ללאו – א"כ, היכי מייתי לעכב מ"לא תאפה" דלקמן דריש ליה על הכלל! ור"ת מפרש, דמיבעיא ליה לרבי פרידא – מנלן דבאות מצה ולא שיאור וחלוט, דאי מ"לא תעשה חמץ" דמתני', הוה אמינא שיאור וחלוט שרי. א"ל: דכתיבא כתיבא, אלמא מצות בעינן, ושיאור וחלוט לאו מצה היא. א"ל: לעכב קא מיבעיא לן מנלן דמיפסלא, אם הביא שיאור וחלוט. א"ל: דכתיב "לא תאפה חמץ", דמשמע: אלא מצה, דכתיב "מצה" באותה פרשה. יד] ורב חסדא פריך: דילמא *מ"לא תאפה חמץ" אלא שיאור. אע"ג דכבר כתיב "לא תעשה", איצטריך טובא, לכדדרשינן לקמן. ופי' זה דחוק ומגומגם.

כי

קנז א מיי' פ"ג מהל' תמידים ומוספים הלכה כב:
ולרבנן. נ"ק
נ"ק מ"ז
א ב מיי' פי"ב מהל' מעה"ק הלי"ד:
ב ג מיי' פ"ט מהל' מעה"ק הלי"ז:
[מ"ק ז: זבחים ז: יד:]
[ע' תוס' זבחים דף מה. ד"ה הלכתא וכו' וגם במה שכתבתי שם על הגליון]
ג ד מיי' פ"ח מהל' תמידין ומוספין הל"ט ופי"ב מהל' מעה"ק הל"ג:
ד ה מיי' פ"ח שם ופ"ט מהל' מעה"ק הלי"ח:
[כלומר כדלעיל מז: פסיק אביי לחמי תודה לא איקרי מנחה]
[שבת מו. וש"נ]
וגו' לא תעשה חמץ וה"נ נ"ק
נ"ק מ"ז
ועוד דמשמע. נ"ק
נ"ק
לא. נ"ק

ע"כ שייך לע"א
נ"ל והוציא
[לקמן קו:]
[פסחים קה. יבמות י.]
נ"ק
חייב הס"ד אח"כ ד"ה וקתני ליה ש"מ אפילו דאי קתני ואם איתא דהוכפל ליתנינהו הס"ד נ"ק
[יבמות טז: גיטין פא: חולין מג. נדה נז:]
שהיה נ"ק

הגהות הב"ח
(א) גמ' אבא יוסף בן דוסתאי כצ"ל וכן בכל העמוד:

שיטה מקובצת

א] תיבות כ"ג שמת ולא מנו אחר תחתיו נמחק: ב] אומר שאור אות ה' נמחק: ג] לוגין. וחוצה: ד] חשיב. להו: ה] כ"ג. קרב: ו] הקטרות זימנין דמשכחת לה שבעה: ז] ליה. והכי נמי אם איתא: ח] השאר. דממקום אחר לא היה יכול להביא שאור שלא תהא מנחה יתירה הס"ד: ט] מנחה. ס"א כדכתיב וביום הבכורים בהקריבכם מנחה חדשה: י] אשכחן. עיין ברש"י דף מז ע"א: יא] להכביד וצריך להניח הקמח בנחת. תו"ח: יב] המנחה. לא תעשנה חמץ: יג] תיבת אלא נמחק: יד] באותה פרשה. אבל קרא דלא תעשה דלקמן לא כתיב מצות באותה פרשה:

רבינו גרשום

בערבית אף הא נמי. פליגי בה במנחת חביתין דעלמא היכא דלא מת כ"ג. מפריש לה ב' קמצין של לבונה. כ"ג שמת ולא מינו כהן אחר ואמר לרבנן דאמרי בעלמא משום דליכא אלא עשרון אחד ולא בעינן ב' קמצין הכא דאיכא עשרונות כדאמרי' שלימה שחרית ושלימה בין הערבים מי אמרי' ב' קמצין אי לא או דילמא מאי דגלי כדכתיב אותה שלימה גלי. אליבא דאבא יוסף לא תיבעי לך דהשתא בעלמא דליכא אלא עשרון אחד בעי ב' קמצין כ"ש הכא. ושמן מיבעיא לי אפילו לאבא יוסי אי אמרינן דהוכפל דמפריש ג' לוגין שחרית וג' לוגין בין הערבים. ת"ש ה' קמצין הן כדאמרי' בפירקין בתרא האומר הרי עלי לבונה לא יפחות מקומץ וכו'. ואם איתא דסבירא להו לרבנן דהיכא דמת כ"ג בעינן ב' קמצין א"כ משכחת לה ז' אלא לעולם לרבנן לא הוי אלא קומץ א' לשחרית ולבין הערבים. ואי אמרת א"כ ליתני ו' קמצין הן והאי קומץ דחביתין להוי ששי. הא לא קשיא כיון דהאי קומץ דחביתין לא קריב שלם אלא חציו בבקר וחציו בערב לא קתני ליה והא מעלה קומץ בחוץ דאי הוא דלא הוי לכתחילה אלא דאי עבד. אילימא רבנן דלא בעו בעלמא אלא קומץ אחד מאי שנא לבונתה דהוכפל דקתני מפריש לה ב' קמצין ומדשמן לאבא יוסי לא הוכפל אלא כחביתין דעלמא היכא דלא מת *) ולא לבונה נמי לרבנן לבונתה ושמנה לא הוכפלו. ותיפשוט מיהא הא דקא בעי ר' יוחנן דלבונה לרבנן ושמן בין לאבא יוסי ובין לרבנן דלא הוכפל. הלכה כאבא יוסי בן דוסתאי דמפריש לה ב' קומצי לבונה לכל חביתין אפילו לעלמא: הדרן עלך התכלת

כל המנחות דכתיבא בהדיא. מצה כתיבא:

זאת

*) נ"ל לבונתה ושמנה לרבנן נמי לא הוכפלו וכו'.

[שם בתמורה וכן בפסחים כז:]

קנה א מיי' פ"ד מהל' שקלים הלכה ב:

קנו ב ג מיי' פ"ג מהל' תמידין ומוספין הלכה כב:

באפרה אין מועלין! אמר רב אשי: שתי תקנות הואי, דאורייתא — בה מועלין, באפרה אין מועלין. כיון דחזו דקא מזלזלי בה, וקא עבדי מיניה למכתן — גזרו ביה מעילה. כיון דחזו דקא פרשי מספק הזאות — אוקמוה אדאורייתא.§ ת"ר: *פר [א]העלם דבר של ציבור ושעירי עבודה זרה — בתחילה מגבין להן, דברי ר' יהודה. ר"ש אומר: מתרומת הלשכה הן באין. והתניא איפכא! *הי מינייהו א] אחריתא? אמרוה רבנן קמיה דרב אשי: לימא קמייתא — אחריתא, דשמעינן ליה לר"ש דחייש לפשיעה. אמר להו רב אשי: אפי' תימא בתרייתא — אחריתא, כי קא חייש ר"ש לפשיעה במילתא דלית בהו כפרה בגווה, במילתא דאית להו כפרה בגווה — לא חייש ר"ש לפשיעה. מאי הוי עלה? א"ל רבה זוטי לרב אשי: ת"ש, דתניא: °"את קרבני לחמי לאשי ריח ניחוחי (במדבר כח) תשמרו להקריב לי במועדו" — לרבות פר העלם דבר של ציבור ושעירי עבודה זרה, שבאין מתרומת הלשכה, דברי ר"ש.§ "ושלימה היתה קריבה" וכו'.§ א"ר חייא בר אבא, בעי רבי יוחנן: שלימה שחרית ושלימה בין הערבים, או דילמא שלימה שחרית ובטילה בין הערבים? אמר רבא, ת"ש: "שמיני — בחביתים". ואם איתא דבטילה בין הערבים — הא זמנין דלא משכח ליה שמיני בחביתים, ה"ד? דמת כ"ג ולא מינו אחר תחתיו. אמרוה רבנן קמיה דרבי ירמיה, אמר: *בבלאי טפשאי, משום דיתבו באתרא דחשוכא, אמרי שמעתתא דמחשכן. אלא דקתני "שביעי — בסלת, תשיעי — ביין", ה"נ דלא בטלי? °"מנחתם (שם כט) ונסכיהם" *בלילה, "מנחתם ונסכיהם" אפילו למחר! אלא "דאי לא" קתני, ה"נ "דאי לא" קתני. אהדרוה קמיה דרבא, אמר: מבישותין — אמרי קמייהו, מטיבותין — לא אמרי קמייהו. ב] (א) והדר אמר רבא: הני נמי טיבותין היא, *אמר קרא: °"סלת מנחה תמיד" — הרי היא (ויקרא ו) לך כמנחת ג] תמידין. מאי הוי עלה? אמר ר"נ בר יצחק: ת"ש, דתניא: שלימה [ב]שחרית ושלימה בין הערבים. א"ר יוחנן: פליגי בה אבא (ג) יוסי בן דוסתאי ורבנן. אבא יוסי בן דוסתאי אומר: מפריש לה שני קמצים של לבונה, קומץ — שחרית, וקומץ — בין הערבים. ורבנן [ג]אמרי: מפריש לה קומץ אחד, חצי קומץ — שחרית, וחצי קומץ — בין הערבים. במאי קמיפלגי? אבא יוסי בן דוסתאי סבר: לא אשכחן חצי קומץ דקריב, ורבנן סברי: לא אשכחן עשרון דבעי שני קמצים. בעי רבי יוחנן: כהן גדול שמת, ולא מינו אחר תחתיו, לרבנן

רש"י

הי מינייהו ד] אחריתי. איזו נאמר באחרונה שנסמוך עליה, ה] דשמא הדר ביה מחידך, משום דקי"ל (עירובין דף מו:): ר' יהודה ור' שמעון — הלכה כרבי יהודה. קמייתא. דקתני לר"ש שבאין מן הלשכה ו]. דלית בהו כפרה. מנחת כהן — ליתא ליורשים כפרה בגוה, אבל פר העלם דבר — כפרה לציבור היא. תורה אור

קרבני לחמי לאשי. ריבה הכתוב קרבנות הרבה, דכל הני — לשון קרבן נינהו. לרבות פר העלם ז]. דבאין מתרומת הלשכה כתמיד, דבתמיד משתעי. ואע"ג דלאו אדעתא דהכי הביאו שקליהם, שהרי לא היו יודעים שיחטא, אפ"ה מרבה להו קרא. דברי ר"ש. וכיון דמקרא יליף — עיקר הוא, *ח] הך היא (ג) דאחריתא. שמיני בחביתין. במסכת תמיד (דף לא:) מני (ד) לכהנים י"ג העסוקים בתמיד, בין בבקר בין בערב, זה בכך וזה בכך. באתרא דחשוכא. דבבל עמוקה היא, דכתיב: "האומר לצולה חרבי" (ישעיה מד). שביעי. מקריב הסלת דמנחת נסכי תמיד. תשיעי ביין ה"נ דלא בטלי. לעולם? והא קיימא לן: מנחתם ונסכיהם בלילה כו' — דאם לא הקריבו היום נסכים, יקריבום למחר. וכגון שלא קדשו בכלי, דלא נפסלו בלינה, אלמא זימנין דקרב תמיד בלא נסכים! אלא דאי. לא הוו נסכים — לא קתני, ה"נ גבי חביתין "דאי מת כ"ג" — לא קתני, ולעולם אם מת — בטילה כל בין הערבים, עד שיעמוד כהן אחר. אהדרוה לקמיה דרבא. הא דקאמר רבי ירמיה "בבלאי טפשאי". מבישותין אמרי קמייהו. כשאנו אומרים שום טעם שאינו יפה — אומרים אותו השומעין לפני בני ארץ ישראל. מטיבותין. כי אמרי' מילי מעלייתא — לא אמרי להו קמייהו. הא נמי. דאמרן דאינה בטילה — מטיבותין היא, דיפה אמרתי ט] (דאי לא), דנפקא לי מקרא דכתיב בחביתין (ויקרא ו) "סלת מנחה תמיד" — מה תמיד אינו בטל, אף היא אינה *בטלה. מאי הוי עלה. כרבא או כרבי ירמיה? פליגי בה. בחביתי כ"ג שלא מת. מפריש לה שני קמצין של לבונה. כשהיה מביא עשרון שלם מביתו — מביא עמו שני קמצים לבונה, ומקריב האחד לחצי עשרון של שחרית, והאחד לחצי של בין הערבים. ולא

תוספתא דשקלים פ"ב [הוריות ג:]

נ"ל והך קמייתא היא לאחריתא

[תמיד לא:]

פסחים לד: יומא נז. זבחים ס: [בכורות כה: כתובות עה.]

[תמיד לא:]

ס"א נ"ג וגי' רש"ק דאי קתני [פסחים קה. יבמות י.]

[פסחים קה. יבמות י.]

בטלה ודאי לא קתני הס"ד. נ"ק

[לעיל נ: ע"ש]

הגהות הב"ח

(א) גמ' הדר אמר רבא הא נמי: (ב) שם יוסף וכן בכל העמוד: (ג) רש"י ד"ה דברי ר"ש וכיון דמקרא יליף עיקר הוא הך היא לאחרונה לאחריתא היא כצ"ל ונ"ב ושם ס"ל לר' יהודה דמן תרומת הלשכה באין וקי"ל כר' יהודה כו' דכן ילפינן מקרא וק"ל: (ד) ד"ה שמיני וכו' מני לי"ג כהנים העסוקים:

תוספות

ואין מועלין באפרה. תימה: תיפוק ליה דאפר הקדש — מותר, כדאי' בסוף תמורה (דף לד.). ולמאן דמוקי *הא דתניא "אסור", בנפלה דליקה מאליה, דלא הוי אינש דלמעול — ניחא. אלא למאן דמוקי לה בתרומת הדשן, [התם] ובפ' "כל שעה" (פסחים דף כו:) קשיא! וי"ל: דשאני הכא, דכל מצותה לשריפה עומד. ועוד נראה: דטעם דהתם — משום דאין לך דבר שנעשית מצותו ומועלין בו, אבל הכא — אכתי לא איתעביד.

דקא עבדי למכתן. רב אשי לטעמיה דאמר במסכת מכות (דף כא.) דאפר מקלה מותר להניח על מכתו, משום דמכתו מוכחת עליו. גזרו ביה מעילה. משמע הכא דאיכא מעילה מדרבנן, וה"נ אמרינן פרק "הוציאו לו" (יומא דף נט. ושם:), ובפרק "ולד חטאת" (תמורה ד' יא:) מועלין בדמים, דברי ר"מ ור"ש. וחכ"א: אין מועלין. ועד כאן לא פליגי אלא דרבנן, אבל דאורייתא — אין מועלין. ואית דגרסי פרק "ולד חטאת": "מ"ט דמ"ד אין מועלין", ושיבוש הוא. אלא ה"ג: "מ"ט דלכולהו אין מועלין מדאורייתא". והתם נמי תנן, ר"ש אומר: הדם קל בתחילתו וחמור בסופו כו' — אלמא דמדרבנן הוא. ותימה דבסוף פרק בתרא דתמורה (דף לג:*) בעי גבי "מקדיש עולה לבדק הבית — אסור לשוחטה עד שתיפדה, ומועלין בה שתי מעילות", ופריך: ואי דרבנן, מי איכא מעילה דרבנן? וי"ל: דכיון דאיכא מעילה דאורייתא — לא שייך לתקן מעילה אחר דרבנן. ומיהו תימה: דריש מעילה (דף ב.) תנן: קדשי קדשים ששחטן בדרום — מועלין בהן דרבנן. ומאי איכא בין מעילה דאורייתא ומעילה דרבנן? דאורייתא — משלם חומש, דרבנן — לא משלם חומש, וכ"ש קרבן. ופריך: מי איכא מעילה דרבנן? אין, דאמר עולא: קדשים שמתו — יצאו מידי מעילה דבר תורה, הא דרבנן — איכא מעילה. ואמאי לא מייתי מתני' דאיכא מעילה בדמים? וי"ל: משום דדמיא טפי לקדשי קדשים ששחטן בדרום, *וכמאן דתנקינהו דמי. *(והרב ר' חיים, וכן פי' בקונטרס כאן): דדם — אקדשוה רבנן, והשתא איכא שפיר מעילה דאורייתא. אבל קדשים שמתו — לא נחתא להו קדושת דמים, הילכך מייתי טפי שפיר. י] *ואפר פרה נמי איכא קדושה מדרבנן. וקשה לפירושו: דבפרק "ולד חטאת" (תמורה דף יב.) גבי "קדשים שמתו", דפריך: מי איכא מידי דמעיקרא לית ביה מעילה, יא] דפסקת ואמרת אפי' בקדשים קלים, ולבסוף אית ביה מעילה? ולא, והרי דם! ומאי פריך, לפירושו טובא איכא לפלוגי! *לכך נראה כמו שפירשתי. ומיהו תימה קצת: אמאי לא מייתי מתני' דמייתי מינה סייעתא לעולא "הנהנה מן החטאת, כשהיא חיה — לא מעל עד שיפגום. כשהיא מתה — כיון שנהנה כל שהוא, מעל"? ושמא להכי לא מייתי לה, דדילמא היינו דוקא חטאת — הואיל ולכפרה אתיא, לא בדילי מינה. ותקנו רבנן מעילה טפי, כדקאמר בתר הכי דמחטאת לא שמעינן *העולה. ואית ספרים דגרסי "הואיל ולכפרה אתיא — בדילי מינה", ואין הסוגיא מוכחת כן. ושמא ה"ק: מתני' אשמעינן דאפילו חטאת דבדילי — איכא מעילה. ועולא אשמעינן: אילו היכא דלא בדילי — איכא מעילה.

פר העלם דבר ושעירי עבודה זרה. יש לדקדק: אמאי נקט גבי פר לשון יחיד, וגבי שעירי לשון רבים, והוי מצי למינקט פרי עבודה זרה"?* דשמעינן ליה לר"ש דחייש לפשיעה. קצת קשיא: דרבי יהודה נמי חייש לפשיעה, דלא אשכחן דניפלוג אתקנות, ולעיל ס"ל משל יורשים? דאי לא קתני. כלומר, דבר שאינו רגיל אלא באקראי בעלמא. לרבנן

[שם בתמורה וכן בפסחים כז:]

[יבמות סד: חולין פו:]

[ע"ש היטב]

[לעיל מד: וש"נ]

דכמאן נ"ק

נ"ל וכן פי' בקונטר' התם והרב רבינו חיים תירץ דדם אקדשוה בית דין והשתא כו'. נ"ק

עי' נ"ק

ועוד אמאי לא מייתי מאפר פרה דאיכא נמי מעילה מדרבנן לכך כו' נ"ק

[נ"ל הא דעולה. נ"ק]

[ויקשה על זה עיין תוס' יומא נ. ד"ה פר]

רבינו גרשום

כיון דקא פרשי מספק הזאות. כשהיה ספיקא לאדם אם נטמא אם לא לא היה רוצה שיהו מזין עליו שהיה חושב בדעתו שמא לא נטמאתי והייתי מועל. אוקמוה אדאורייתא שאין מועלין באפרה. בתחילה מגבין להן כלומר שלא היו לוקחין אותה מתרומת הלשכה אלא גובין עכשיו מכל אחד ואחד פרוטה וקונין מהן: הי מינייהו באחריתא. כלומר צריכין אנו לידע אי זו נשנית באחרונה מאלו הברייתות שחזר בה ר' שמעון ואמר כר' יהודה דקיימא לן ר' שמעון ור' יהודה הלכה כר' יהודה: לימא קמייתא היא אחריתא שחזר בו מההיא דאמר בה בתחלה הן באין ואמר מתרומת הלשכה הן באין דחייש לפשיעותא כדאמרינן לעיל כיון דחזו דקא פשעי בה אוקמוה אדאורייתא דניתו מלשכה: במלתא דלית להו כפרה בגוה. כגון כ"ג שמת דאם היו היורשים מביאין בעבורו היו מביאין ולא בעבור עצמן משום הכי פשעי. במילתא דאית להו כפרה בגוה כגון פר העלם דבר של צבור ושעירי ע"ז ניחא להו דליכפר ולא פשע ויהיב ובתחילה מגבין להן: לרבות פר העלם דבר של צבור ושעירי ע"ז דהיינו נמי לאישי דנשרפין הן ודינן כתמידין: ת"ש שמיני בחביתין במס' תמיד חשיב כמה כהנים זוכים בתמיד. והשמיני בחביתין: באתרא דחשוכא. דבבל עמוקה וחשוכה: זמנין א) ומנחתם ונסכיהם בלילה או למחר והשתא בטלו שנים אלא דאי לא קתני שאם לא הביא נסכים היום [מביא] בלילה או למחר אבל בתר רוב הימים אזיל ורוב ימים באין נסכין עמו הכא נמי דאם מת כהן לא קתני הילכך קאמר שמיני בחביתין. ומהא ליכא למשמע מינה. אהדרוה קמי דרבא הא דקאמר ר' ירמיה בבלאי טפשאי אמר מבישתן כלומר מה שאין אנו מתרצין יפה שיש בו קושיא אומרין לפני בני ארץ ישראל כדי שילעיגו עלינו. ומטיבותן כלומר ומה שאנו מתרצין יפה אין אומרין לפניהן. הרי היא לך כמנחת תמידין שאינה בטלה לא בשחרית לא בערבית

א) נראה דצ"ל ה"נ דלא בטלי הא זימנין דקרבי מנחה ונסכים בלילה או כו':

שיטה מקובצת

א] מינייהו דאחריתא: ב] קמייהו. הדר אמר רבא הא נמי מטבותן: ג] כמנחת תמיד: ד] מינייהו דאחריתא: ה] עליה דנימא הדר: ו] מן הלשכה. נאמרה באחרונה דשמעינן לר"ש דאמר לעיל משל צבור תהא מנחת כהן שמת ולא מיורשין שמא יפשעו וה"נ גזר דילמא דלא גבו להו הילכך באין מן הלשכה: ז] העלם דבר: ח] והך היא: ט] אמרתי. דאי לא נפקא לי*) מקרא. מתמיד נפקא: י] ואפר פרה. עיין תוס' יומא דף מו ע"ב: יא] דפסק ותני אפי':

תיבות

*) אולי צ"ל אמרתי דאי לא נפקא לי ממתני' מקרא דתמיד נפקא דכתיב וכו':

מִנְחָה הַבָּאָה עִשָּׂרוֹן וכו'.§ א] **מתני'** לֹא מִינּוּ כֹּהֵן אַחֵר תַּחְתָּיו, מִשֶּׁל מִי הָיְתָה קְרֵיבָה? ר"ש אוֹמֵר: מִשֶּׁל צִיבּוּר, ר' יְהוּדָה אוֹמֵר: אמִשֶּׁל יוֹרְשִׁין. וּשְׁלֵימָה הָיְתָה קְרֵיבָה.§ **גמ'** *ת"ר: כ"ג שֶׁמֵּת, וְלֹא מִינּוּ כֹּהֵן אַחֵר תַּחְתָּיו, מִנַּיִן שֶׁתְּהֵא מִנְחָתוֹ קְרֵיבָה מִשֶּׁל יוֹרְשִׁין? ת"ל: °"וְהַכֹּהֵן הַמָּשִׁיחַ תַּחְתָּיו מִבָּנָיו יַעֲשֶׂה אוֹתָהּ". יָכוֹל יַקְרִיבֶנָּה חֲצָאִין? ת"ל "אוֹתָהּ" – בכּוּלָּהּ וְלֹא חֶצְיָהּ, דִּבְרֵי רַבִּי יְהוּדָה. ר"ש אוֹמֵר: °"חָק עוֹלָם" – מִשֶּׁל עוֹלָם, °"כָּלִיל תָּקְטָר" – שֶׁתְּהֵא כּוּלָּהּ בְּהַקְטָרָה. וְהַאי "הַכֹּהֵן הַמָּשִׁיחַ" לְהָכִי הוּא דַּאֲתָא? הַאי מִיבְּעֵי לֵיהּ לִכְדְתַנְיָא: °"זֶה קָרְבַּן אַהֲרֹן וּבָנָיו אֲשֶׁר יַקְרִיבוּ לַה' בְּיוֹם הִמָּשַׁח אוֹתוֹ" – יָכוֹל יְהוּ אַהֲרֹן וּבָנָיו מַקְרִיבִין קָרְבָּן אֶחָד? ת"ל: "אֲשֶׁר יַקְרִיבוּ לַה'" – גאַהֲרֹן בִּפְנֵי עַצְמוֹ, וּבָנָיו בִּפְנֵי עַצְמָן. "בָּנָיו" – אֵלּוּ כֹּהֲנִים הֶדְיוֹטוֹת. אַתָּה אוֹמֵר: כֹּהֲנִים הֶדְיוֹטוֹת, אוֹ אֵינוֹ אֶלָּא כֹּהֲנִים גְּדוֹלִים? כְּשֶׁהוּא אוֹמֵר "וְהַכֹּהֵן הַמָּשִׁיחַ תַּחְתָּיו מִבָּנָיו" – הֲרֵי כ"ג אָמוּר, הָא מָה אֲנִי מְקַיֵּים "בָּנָיו"? אֵלּוּ כֹּהֲנִים הֶדְיוֹטוֹת! א"כ, לִכְתּוֹב קְרָא "הַכֹּהֵן הַמָּשִׁיחַ תַּחְתָּיו בָּנָיו יַעֲשֶׂה", מַאי "מִבָּנָיו"? שָׁמְעַתְּ מִינַּהּ תַּרְתֵּי. וְר"ש, הַאי "אוֹתָהּ" מַאי עָבֵיד לֵיהּ? מִיבְּעֵי לֵיהּ לְכ"ג שֶׁמֵּת וּמִינּוּ אַחֵר תַּחְתָּיו, שֶׁלֹּא יָבִיא חֲצִי עִשָּׂרוֹן מִבֵּיתוֹ וְלֹא חֲצִי עִשָּׂרוֹן שֶׁל רִאשׁוֹן. וְתֵיפּוֹק לֵיהּ מִן "וּמַחֲצִיתָהּ"! *וָי"ו לָא דָּרֵישׁ. וְרַבִּי יְהוּדָה, הַאי "חָק עוֹלָם" מַאי עָבֵיד לֵיהּ? חוּקָּה לְעוֹלָם תְּהֵא. "כָּלִיל תָּקְטָר" לָמָּה לִי? מִיבְּעֵי לֵיהּ לִכְדְתַנְיָא: אֵין לִי אֶלָּא עֶלְיוֹנָה ב] מִנְחַת כ"ג בְּ"כָלִיל תָּקְטָר", וְתַחְתּוֹנָה מִנְחַת כֹּהֵן הֶדְיוֹט בְּ"לֹא תֵאָכֵל". מִנַּיִן לִיתֵּן אֶת הָאָמוּר שֶׁל זֶה בָּזֶה וְאֶת הָאָמוּר שֶׁל זֶה בָּזֶה? ת"ל "כָּלִיל" "כָּלִיל" לִגְזֵירָה שָׁוָה: נֶאֱמַר כָּאן "כָּלִיל" וְנֶאֱמַר לְהַלָּן "כָּלִיל", מָה כָּאן – בְּ"כָלִיל תָּקְטָר", אַף לְהַלָּן – בְּ"כָלִיל תָּקְטָר". וּמָה לְהַלָּן – לִיתֵּן ג] לֹא תַעֲשֶׂה עַל אֲכִילָתוֹ, אַף כָּאן – לִיתֵּן לֹא תַעֲשֶׂה עַל אֲכִילָתָהּ. וְסָבַר ר"ש: מִשֶּׁל צִיבּוּר דְּאוֹרַיְיתָא? *וְהָתְנַן, אר"ש: שִׁבְעָה *דְבָרִים הִתְקִינוּ ב"ד, וְזֶה אֶחָד מֵהֶן – גּוֹי שֶׁשָּׁלַח דעוֹלָתוֹ מִמְּדִינַת הַיָּם. שָׁלַח עִמָּהּ נְסָכִים – קְרֵיבָה מִשֶּׁלּוֹ, וְאִם לָאו – קְרֵיבִין מִשֶּׁל צִיבּוּר. וְכֵן גֵּר שֶׁמֵּת הוְהִנִּיחַ זְבָחִים. יֵשׁ לוֹ נְסָכִים – קְרֵיבִין מִשֶּׁלּוֹ, וְאִם לָאו – קְרֵיבִין מִשֶּׁל צִיבּוּר. וּתְנַאי ב"ד הוּא, כ"ג שֶׁמֵּת וְלֹא מִינּוּ כֹּהֵן אַחֵר תַּחְתָּיו – ושֶׁתְּהֵא מִנְחָתוֹ קְרֵיבָה מִשֶּׁל צִיבּוּר! א"ר אַבָּהוּ: שְׁנֵי ד] תַקָּנוֹת הָווּ, דְּאוֹרַיְיתָא – מִדְּצִיבּוּר. כֵּיוָן דְּחָזוּ דְּקָא מִידַּחְקָא לִישְׁכָּה – תַּקִּינוּ דְּלִגְבֵי מִיּוֹרְשִׁים. כֵּיוָן דְּחָזוּ דְּקָא פָּשְׁעִי בָּהּ – אוֹקְמוּהָ אַדְּאוֹרַיְיתָא. ז"וְעַל פָּרָה, שֶׁלֹּא יְהֵא מוֹעֲלִין בְּאֶפְרָהּ". דְּאוֹרַיְיתָא הִיא! דְּתַנְיָא: °ח"חַטָּאת הִיא" – מְלַמֵּד שֶׁמּוֹעֲלִין בָּהּ, "הִיא" – בָּהּ מוֹעֲלִין, בְּאֶפְרָהּ

מִנְחָה הַבָּאָה עִשָּׂרוֹן מִמִּנְחָה הַבָּאָה עִשָּׂרוֹן כו'. ה] **מתני'** וּשְׁלֵימָה. עִשָּׂרוֹן שָׁלֵם בַּבּוֹקֶר, וְעִשָּׂרוֹן בֵּין הָעַרְבַּיִם, כָּל זְמַן שֶׁהִיא קְרֵיבָה מִשֶּׁל לִיבּוּר. **גמ'** הַכֹּהֵן ו] הַמָּשִׁיחַ תַּחְתָּיו אֶחָד מִבָּנָיו יַעֲשֶׂה אוֹתָהּ. דְּמִשֶּׁל יוֹרְשִׁים קְרֵיבָה, עַד יַעֲמוֹד אַחֵר. יָכוֹל יַקְרִיבוּ יוֹרְשִׁין לַחֲצָאִין. כְּמוֹ שֶׁהָיָה אֲבִיהֶן עוֹשֶׂה? מִשֶּׁל עוֹלָם. מִשֶּׁל לִיבּוּר, מִתְּרוּמַת הַלִּשְׁכָּה. שֶׁתְּהֵא כּוּלָּהּ בְּהַקְטָרָה. שֶׁלֹּא יַעֲשֶׂה מִמֶּנָּה שִׁירַיִים לַאֲכִילָה. לִישָּׁנָא אַחֲרִינָא: שֶׁיַּקְטִירוּ שְׁלֵימָה, וְלֹא לַחֲלָאִין, כָּל זְמַן שֶׁהִיא קְרֵיבָה מִשֶּׁל לִיבּוּר. דִּבִשְׁלֵימָה לָא פְּלִיגִי ר' יְהוּדָה וְר"ש. מִפִּי הַמּוֹרֶה. יָכוֹל יְהוּ אַהֲרֹן וּבָנָיו מַקְרִיבִין קָרְבָּן אֶחָד. בְּיוֹם הִמָּשְׁחָם. וּבָנָיו בִּפְנֵי עַצְמָן. ז] לְשֵׁם הַחִינּוּךְ, וּמֵאוֹתוֹ יוֹם וְאֵילָךְ – לֹא. אֲבָל כ"ג – בְּכָל יוֹם, דִּכְתִיב "תָּמִיד"? כֹּהֲנִים הֶדְיוֹטוֹת. דִּכְשֶׁכֹּהֵן הֶדְיוֹט נִתְחַנֵּךְ לַעֲבוֹדָה, בְּאוֹתוֹ יוֹם הָיָה מַקְרִיב עִשָּׂרוֹן. ל"א: בְּיוֹם הַמִּלּוּאִים הָיָה כָּךְ, אֲבָל לְדוֹרוֹת – לֹא נוֹהֵג. וְלֹא מִפִּי הַמּוֹרֶה. אוֹ אֵינוֹ אֶלָּא כֹּהֲנִים גְּדוֹלִים. דְּה"ק: קָרְבָּן זֶה יַקְרִיבוּ בְּנֵי אַהֲרֹן לְדוֹרוֹת, כָּל כ"ג שֶׁיַּעֲמוֹד ח]. הֲרֵי כ"ג אָמוּר. דְּה"ק קְרָא: הַכֹּהֵן הַמָּשִׁיחַ שֶׁיַּעֲמוֹד מִבְּנֵי אַהֲרֹן תַּחְתָּיו לְאַחַר מוֹתוֹ יַעֲשֶׂה אוֹתָהּ. א"כ. דְּכוּלֵּיהּ לְיוֹרְשִׁין אָתֵי, שֶׁיַּקְרִיבוּ הַחֲבִיתִּים כָּל זְמַן שֶׁלֹּא מִנּוּ כֹּהֵן אַחֵר תַּחְתָּיו. לִכְתּוֹב הַכֹּהֵן הַמָּשִׁיחַ תַּחְתָּיו בָּנָיו יַעֲשֶׂה אוֹתָהּ. כְּשֶׁיָּמוּת הוּא. מַאי מִבָּנָיו. דְּמַשְׁמַע: אֶחָד מִבָּנָיו שֶׁיַּעֲמוֹד תַּחְתָּיו לְכ"ג (א), דְּמַשְׁמַע תַּרְתֵּי. אוֹתָהּ מַאי עָבֵיד לֵיהּ. כֵּיוָן דְּנָפְקָא לֵיהּ שְׁלֵימָה מִ"כָּלִיל תָּקְטָר". דְּבִשְׁלָמָא "הַכֹּהֵן הַמָּשִׁיחַ" – מוֹקֵי לְהָךְ דְּרָשָׁא דְּאָמְרִינַן לְעֵיל, הֲרֵי כ"ג אָמוּר, אֶלָּא "אוֹתָהּ" מַאי עָבֵיד לֵיהּ? וּמִינּוּ כֹּהֵן אַחֵר תַּחְתָּיו. בּוֹ בַּיּוֹם. וְתֵיפּוֹק לֵיהּ מִן וּמַחֲצִיתָהּ בָּעֶרֶב. כִּדְאָמְרַן לְעֵיל? חוּקָּה לְעוֹלָם תְּהֵא. שֶׁתְּהֵא מִצְוָה זוֹ נוֹהֶגֶת לְדוֹרוֹת. עֶלְיוֹנָה. חֲבִיתִּין, ט] דִּכְתִיב בִּקְרָא בְּרֵישָׁא, בְּ"זֶה קָרְבַּן אַהֲרֹן", וּכְתִיב בָּהּ "כָּלִיל תָּקְטָר". וַהֲדַר "כָּל מִנְחַת כֹּהֵן כָּלִיל תִּהְיֶה" – דְּמִשְׁתָּעֵי בְּמִנְחַת נִדְבָתוֹ, וּכְתִיב בָּהּ "לֹא תֵאָכֵל". מִנַּיִן לִיתֵּן הָאָמוּר כו'. שֶׁיְּהוּ שְׁנֵיהֶם כָּלִיל בְּהַקְטָרָה, וְהָאוֹכֵל מִשְּׁיָרֵי שְׁתֵּיהֶם יַעֲבוֹר בְּלָאו? ת"ל כָּלִיל כָּלִיל. "כָּלִיל תָּקְטָר", "כָּלִיל תִּהְיֶה לֹא תֵאָכֵל". ז' דְּבָרִים. בְּמַסֶּכֶת שְׁקָלִים בְּפֶרֶק "מָעוֹת שֶׁנִּמְצְאוּ". וְזֶה אֶחָד מֵהֶם. הָתָם קָאֵי. דְּקָתָנֵי לְעֵיל: בְּהֵמָה שֶׁנִּמְצֵאת מִירוּשָׁלַיִם לְמִגְדַּל עֵדֶר וּכְמִדָּתָהּ לְכָל רוּחַ. זְכָרִים – עוֹלוֹת, נְקֵבוֹת – שְׁלָמִים. בָּרִאשׁוֹנָה י] מְמַשְׁכְּנִין אֶת מוֹצְאָהּ לְהָבִיא נְסָכֶיהָ, עַד שֶׁהָיוּ מַנִּיחִין אוֹתָהּ וּבוֹרְחִין. הִתְקִינוּ ב"ד שֶׁיְּהוּ נְסָכֶיהָ קְרֵיבִין מִשֶּׁל לִיבּוּר. וְקָאָמַר ר"ש: ז' דְּבָרִים הִתְקִינוּ ב"ד, וְזֶה שֶׁאָמַרְנוּ אֶחָד מֵהֶם. וַהֲדַר מְפָרֵשׁ לְאִינָךְ שֵׁשׁ: גּוֹי שֶׁשָּׁלַח כו', דְּגוֹי מְשַׁלֵּחַ קָרְבְּנוֹתָיו, כִּדְאָמַר בְּפֶרֶק "אֵלּוּ מְנָחוֹת" (לקמן דף עג:): "אִישׁ" – מַה ת"ל "אִישׁ" "אִישׁ"? לְרַבּוֹת אֶת הַגּוֹיִם שֶׁנּוֹדְרִים יא] נְדָבוֹת כְּיִשְׂרָאֵל. שָׁלַח עִמָּהּ נְסָכִים. דְּמֵי נְסָכֶיהָ. וְכֵן גֵּר. לְהָכִי נָקַט גֵּר – דְּאֵין לוֹ יוֹרְשִׁים. דְּאִי יִשְׂרָאֵל – הָווּ מַקְרְבֵי יוֹרְשִׁים נְסָכָיו. מִשֶּׁל לִיבּוּר. אַלְמָא, תְּנַאי ב"ד הוּא, וְלָאו דְּאוֹרַיְיתָא! דְּאוֹרַיְיתָא מִדְּצִבּוּר. כִּדְכְתִיב (ויקרא ו): "חָק עוֹלָם" – מִשֶּׁל עוֹלָם. דְּקָא מִדַּחְקָא לִשְׁכָּה. שֶׁהָיוּ פּוֹחֲתִין הַשְּׁקָלִים שֶׁבַּלִּשְׁכָּה, לְפִי שֶׁבְּכָל שָׁנָה הָיוּ צְרִיכִין כָּךְ, כִּדְאָמְרִינַן בְּפ"ק דְּמַסֶּכֶת יוֹמָא (דף ט.): "וּשְׁנוֹת רְשָׁעִים תִּקְצוֹרְנָה" – זֶה מִקְדָּשׁ שֵׁנִי, שֶׁעָמְדוּ יוֹתֵר מִג' מֵאוֹת כֹּהֲנִים גְּדוֹלִים, דְּכָל אֶחָד לֹא הוֹצִיא שְׁנָתוֹ, תַּקִּינוּ (ב) מִיּוֹרְשִׁין. דְּקָפָשְׁעֵי. וְאֵין מְבִיאִין אוֹתָהּ. יב] דְּהַיְינוּ שְׁתֵּי תַקָּנוֹת: דְּמֵעִיקָּרָא תַּקְּנוּהָ מִיּוֹרְשִׁין, וַהֲדַר תַּקְּנוּהָ לְהַדּוּרָהּ אַדְּאוֹרַיְיתָא יג] כְּמֵעִיקָּרָא. וְעַל פָּרָה. הַיְינוּ מֵאוֹתָן ז' דְּבָרִים. שֶׁלֹּא יְהֵא מוֹעֲלִין בְּאֶפְרָהּ. הַנֶּהֱנֶה מֵאֶפְרָהּ – לֹא יִתְחַיֵּיב קָרְבַּן מְעִילָה. חַטָּאת הִיא. כַּפָּרָה כְּתִיב, מְלַמֵּד שֶׁמּוֹעֲלִין בָּהּ כִּשְׁאָר חַטָּאוֹת, עַד שֶׁלֹּא הָיְתָה לָהֶן שְׁעַת הֶיתֵּר לַכֹּהֲנִים. *)לְמַכָּתָן. אֵפֶר מְרַפֵּא מַכָּה. פָּרְשֵׁי מִסְּפֵק הַזָּאוֹת. מִשּׁוּם יד] מְעִילָה. בִּשְׁמַעְתָּא קַמַּיְיתָא דִּמְעִילָה (דף ג:) מְפָרֵשׁ מַאי אִיכָּא בֵּין מְעִילָה דְּרַבָּנַן לִמְעִילָה דְּאוֹרַיְיתָא. סְפֵק הַזָּאוֹת. כְּגוֹן שֶׁנִּטְמָא בִּסְפֵק טְמֵא מֵת, כְּגוֹן סְכָכוֹת וּפְרָעוֹת. בַּתְּחִילָּה מְגַבִּין לָהֶן. כְּלוֹמַר, עַכְשָׁיו כְּשֶׁמְּבִיאִין אוֹתָן – גּוֹבִין אֶת הַמָּעוֹת מִכָּל אֶחָד וְאֶחָד, וְאֵין בָּאִין מִתְּרוּמַת הַלִּשְׁכָּה כִּשְׁאָר קָרְבְּנוֹת לִיבּוּר.

הֵי

*) שייך לדף שאח"ז

והכהן המשיח תחתיו מבניו יעשה אותה. *מהכא דרשינן פ"ק דכריתות (דף ה:) דכ"ג בן כ"ג טעון משיחה, והיינו הא נמי דמצריך בתמורה (דף יא) ההוא קרא לכהנים גדולים.

שתהא כולה בהקטרה. פי' בקונטרס: שלא יעשה לה טו] שיריים. והא דבעי לקמן: ורבי יהודה האי "כליל תקטר" מאי עביד ליה? כיון דההוא מנחת כהנים – פשיטא דכולה כליל, ולא איצטריך אלא לר"ש דקסבר: משל עולם תהא. עוד פי' ל"א: שאינה קריבה לחצאין. **וי"ו לא דריש.** הכא לא דריש ר"ש וי"ו, וכן פ"ק דסנהדרין (דף יד.) גבי "זקניך ושופטיך" ובפ"ק דסוטה (דף ו:). אבל "וי"ו מוסיף על ענין ראשון" [בפרק "הקומץ רבה"*] – דריש, טז] וכן "וי"ו הדר ערביה" – דריש "מרובה" (ב"ק דף סה:) ופרק ב' דע"ז (דף כד.). וקשה דבפרק "כל האסורין" (תמורה דף כח:) דריש ליה, גבי "אם נאמר נוגח, למה נאמר רובע", ומוי"ו הוא דדרשינן הכי! ויש לומר: דמשום דאיכא "מן" – מוכח ד"ומן" למדרש אתא. מיהו הך קושיא דריש "ד' מיתות" (סנהדרין דף נא:) גבי "בת כהן, אחת ארוסה ואחת נשואה – בשריפה" דריש "בת" "ובת" כר' עקיבא, ובריתא דריש פירקין* מוכח כר"ש. ובמעילה פרק "קדשי מזבח" (דף יז.*) דריש ר"ש דם שרץ דטמא, מדכתיב "וזה", ומוכח *בבראשית רבה דמוי"ו קדריש! ותו: דרבי יהודה דריש הכא וי"ו, ובפרק "אלו מציאות" (ב"מ דף כז.) גבי "ומצאתה", וסוף פ"ק דסנהדרין (דף יד.) גבי "ושופטיך" – דריש וי"ו. ובריש תמורה (דף ב:) גבי "ואם המר ימיר" – אמרינן: וי"ו לא דריש. ופ' "טרף בקלפי" (יומא דף מה.): "איברים ופדרים שנתעכלו מבערב", ופ"ב דסנהדרין (דף כא.) גבי מלך, דלא שרו רבי יהודה ור"ש אלא י"ח נשים, ומאן דדריש וי"ו – דריש טפי! ושמא: להני דרשי הוא דלא דרשי ליה, וטובא אשכחן כי ה"ג*.

חק זו לעולם תהא. דה"א: אהרן מקריב חביתין בכל יום, ובניו – בשעה שנעשו כהנים גדולים, אע"פ שכבר נתחנכו בכהונת הדיוט. ורבי שמעון לית ליה האי סברא.

אף כאן לא תעשה על אכילתו. אבל איסורא נפקא לן מ"כליל תקטר". וקצת קשיא: אמאי לא דרשינן לאו נמי, מדכתיב "לאמר" – לאו אמור, כדדרשינן פרק "כל שעה" (פסחים דף מג.)?

יש לו נסכים. שהפרישן בחייו, דלאחר מיתה הוי הכל הפקר.

דקא מדחקא לישכא. שבבית שני, שהיו כהנים שלא הוציאו שנתן.

חטאת מלמד שמועלין בה. תימה: יז] תיפוק לי דקדשי בדק הבית היא! ויש לומר: דאיצטריך למועל אחר מועל, *דאינו אלא בבהמה וכלי שרת בלבד.

ואין

גירסת הב"ח תימה מהכא כו' משיחה וי"ל דהתם דריש מדכתיב המשיח והיינו הא נמי דמצריך הא בתמורה כו' ותיבת קרא לקמן כו' נמחק דלא מצינו בתמורה ההוא דרשה

קמט א מיי' פ"ג מהל' תמידין ומוספין הלכה כב:

קנ ב מיי' שם ופי"ג מהל' מעה"ק הל"ד:

קנא ג מיי' פ"ה מהל' כלי מקדש הלט"ז:

קנב ד מיי' פ"ג מהל' מעה"ק הל"ה ופ"ד מהל' שקלים הל"ג:

קנג ה מיי' פ"ד מהל' שקלים הל"ד:

לעיל יט.

קנד ו ז מיי' פ"ב מהל' מעילה הל"ה:

[דף נ:]

[וע"ע היטב בתוס' ד"ה דכתיב]

[סדר רש"י פ"ה וע"ש דר"ש מפיק מדכתיב הטמאה ולא כתיב בטמאה ובע"כ שטומאה אחרת היה לפני תוס' בכ"ר]

[וע"ע תוס' מ"ק ח. ד"ה מאי וביום ותוס' סנהדרין יז. ד"ה ור"ש]

שקלים יח.

[יומא מה. וש"נ]

לקמן עג: שקלים יח: פ"ז מ"ו

הגהות הב"ח

(א) רש"י ד"ה מאי וכו' לכ"ג משמע כצ"ל ואות ד' נמחק: (ב) ד"ה דקא וכו' תקינו לגבי מיורשין:

שיטה מקובצת

א] מתיבות מתני' לא מינו כו' עד היתה קריבה גמ' נמחק ומקומו לעיל נ ע"ב בסוף מתני': ב] תיבות מנחת כ"ג מנחת כהן הדיוט נמחק: כליל. תימה תקטר למה לי כיון דכתיב כליל כליל: ג] תיבת ליתן נמחק: ד] תקנות. כתובות דף יב ע"א: ה] מתיבות מתני' ושלימה עד משל צבור גמ' נמחק ומקומו לעיל נ ע"ב אחר ד"ה לא יביא: ו] המשיח. דהכי משמע הכהן המשיח שמת תחתיו: ז] עצמן ליום: ח] שיעמוד מהן הס"ד: ט] כתיב בקרא: י] בראשונה. היו: יא] שנודרים. נדרים ונדבות: יב] אותה. והיינו: יג] אדאורייתא. כדמעיקרא: יד] מעילה. ס"י דקרבן מעילה ממש תקין רבנן וא"ת שהוא מביא חולין לעזרה י"ל דכיון שהתנו ב"ד שתקדש קדושת דמים האפר ממילא אית בה מעילה וכן מועלין בדמים משיצאו לנחל קדרון כדתנן במס' יומא ואמרי' דהך מעילה מדרבנן משום האי טעמא נמי ב"ד מתנו שיקדשו לדמיו משיצאו מידי מעילתו ראשונה חוזרת קדושה לחול עליו בתנאי ב"ד: טו] שיריים. ולא נהירא דא"כ מאי קא קשיא ליה בסמוך ור"ש האי אותה מאי עביד ליה הא מבעיא ליה לדרשה דאותה ולא חציה עכ"ל תו"ח וי"ל כיון דרישא דקרא לר"ש לא אתי לכהן שמת ולא מינו אף אותה דסיפא דקרא לא אתי למימר אותה ולא חציה. דברי תלמיד: טז] דריש עיין תום' לעיל דף יט ע"א: יז] תימה. בין למ"ד קדשי בדק הבית היא ובין למ"ד קדשי מזבח היא בתרוייהו אית בהו מעילה וי"ל דאשמועינן קרא דמועלין בה בקדשי מזבח דיש בה מועל אחר מועל. תום' אחרות:

רבינו גרשום

ושלימה היתה קריבה בין לר' שמעון בין לר' יהודה. שלא היו מקריבין אותה לחצאין אלא שלימה. חק עולם משל עולם. כלומר משל רבים דהיינו צבור. שתהא כולה בהקטרה כלומר שלימה. אהרן בפני עצמו חביתין שלו: ובניו בפני עצמן כשמתמנין אחד מבניו לכ"ג מקריב תחילה עשירית האיפה: אם כן לדהדרא דרשא אתי ולא לכתוב בניו. ור' שמעון דנפקא ליה דשלימה היתה קריבה מכליל תקטר אותה מאי עביד ליה: לכ"ג שמת בחצי היום. חוקה לעולם תהא שבכל יום יקריבנה. עליונה חביתים ותחתונה שאר מנחת כהן. בלא תאכל. שלוקה אם אכלה. והתנן א"ר שמעון ז' דברים התקנו במס' שקלים וזה אחד מהן אותה שנאמר למעלה בראשונה היו ממשכנין את מוצאה וכו'. ועובד כוכבים ששלח עולתו וכו' כיון דחזו דקא מידחקו לישכה שהיו מתין בכל שנה כדאמרי' במס' יומא ושנות רשעים תקצורנה. ואילו היו מביאין מן הלשכה היתה מתרוששת: כיון דחזו דקא פשעי ביה שפעמים

הֲרֵי הִיא א] כְּמִנְחַת תְּמִידִין. רָבָא אָמַר: °"עַל מַחֲבַת" – מְלַמֵּד ב] אשֶׁטְּעוּנָה כְּלִי, וְאִי אָפֵי לָהּ מֵאֶתְמוֹל – ג] אִיפְּסִיל לֵיהּ בְּלִינָה. תַּנְיָא כְּוָותֵיהּ דְּרָבָא: "עַל מַחֲבַת" – מְלַמֵּד שֶׁטְּעוּנָה כְּלִי. "בַּשֶּׁמֶן" – לְהוֹסִיף לָהּ שֶׁמֶן. וְאֵינִי יוֹדֵעַ כַּמָּה. הֲרֵינִי דָּן: נֶאֱמַר כָּאן "שֶׁמֶן", וְנֶאֱמַר לְהַלָּן בְּמִנְחַת נְסָכִים "שֶׁמֶן". מַה לְּהַלָּן – שְׁלֹשֶׁת לוּגִּין לְעִשָּׂרוֹן, אַף בכָּאן – שְׁלֹשֶׁת לוּגִּין לְעִשָּׂרוֹן. אוֹ כַּלֵּךְ לְדֶרֶךְ זוֹ: נֶאֱמַר כָּאן "שֶׁמֶן", וְנֶאֱמַר בְּמִנְחַת נְדָבָה "שֶׁמֶן". מַה לְּהַלָּן – לוֹג אֶחָד, אַף כָּאן – לוֹג אֶחָד? נִרְאֶה לְמִי דּוֹמֶה, דָּנִין *תבש"ט מִתבש"ט, תָּדִיר, (בָּאָה חוֹבָה,) דּוֹחָה שַׁבָּת, דּוֹחָה טוּמְאָה, וְאֵין דָּנִין תבש"ט מִשֶּׁאֵינוֹ תבש"ט. אוֹ כַּלֵּךְ לְדֶרֶךְ זוֹ: ד] דָּנִין יגי"ל מִיגי"ל, יָחִיד, בִּגְלַל עַצְמָהּ, ה] (יַיִן,) לְבוֹנָה, וְאֵין דָּנִין יגי"ל מִשֶּׁאֵינוֹ יגי"ל. רַבִּי יִשְׁמָעֵאל בְּנוֹ שֶׁל רַבִּי יוֹחָנָן בֶּן בְּרוֹקָה אוֹמֵר: °"סֹלֶת מִנְחָה תָּמִיד" – הֲרֵי הִיא לְךָ כְּמִנְחַת ו] תְּמִידִין, מַה מִּנְחַת תְּמִידִין – ג' לוּגִּין לְעִשָּׂרוֹן, אַף זוֹ – ג' לוּגִּין לְעִשָּׂרוֹן. ר"ש אוֹמֵר: רִיבָּה כָּאן שֶׁמֶן, וְרִיבָּה בְּמִנְחַת כְּבָשִׂים שֶׁמֶן. מַה לְּהַלָּן – שְׁלֹשֶׁת לוּגִּין לְעִשָּׂרוֹן, אַף כָּאן – שְׁלֹשֶׁת לוּגִּין לְעִשָּׂרוֹן. אוֹ כַּלֵּךְ לְדֶרֶךְ זוֹ: רִיבָּה כָּאן שֶׁמֶן, וְרִיבָּה בְּמִנְחַת פָּרִים וְאֵילִים שֶׁמֶן. מַה לְּהַלָּן – שְׁנֵי לוּגִּין לְעִשָּׂרוֹן, אַף כָּאן – שְׁנֵי לוּגִּין לְעִשָּׂרוֹן? נִרְאֶה לְמִי דּוֹמֶה, דָּנִין מִנְחָה הַבָּאָה עִשָּׂרוֹן מִמִּנְחָה הַבָּאָה בְּעִשָּׂרוֹן, וְאֵין דָּנִין מִנְחָה הַבָּאָה עִשָּׂרוֹן מִמִּנְחָה הַבָּאָה ב' וְג' עֶשְׂרוֹנִים. הָא גּוּפָא קַשְׁיָא, אָמַרְתְּ: "בַּשֶּׁמֶן" – לְהוֹסִיף לָהּ שֶׁמֶן, וַהֲדַר תָּנֵי: נֶאֱמַר כָּאן "שֶׁמֶן", וְנֶאֱמַר בְּמִנְחַת נְדָבָה "שֶׁמֶן"! אָמַר אַבַּיֵי: מַאן תַּנָּא "בַּשֶּׁמֶן" לְהוֹסִיף? ר"ש הִיא, ז] (וְ"אִילּוּ לֹא נֶאֱמַר" קָאָמַר) וּבְדִינָא מַאן קָא מְהַדַּר? ח] רַבִּי יִשְׁמָעֵאל. *רַב הוּנָא בְּרֵיהּ דְּרַב יְהוֹשֻׁעַ אָמַר: כּוּלָּהּ ר' יִשְׁמָעֵאל בְּנוֹ שֶׁל ר' יוֹחָנָן בֶּן בְּרוֹקָה הִיא, וְהָכִי קָאָמַר: "בַּשֶּׁמֶן" – גלְהוֹסִיף לָהּ שֶׁמֶן, דְּאִי לִקְבּוֹעַ ט] שֶׁמֶן – לָא צְרִיךְ, כֵּיוָן דִּכְתִיב בָּהּ °"עַל מַחֲבַת" – כְּמִנְחַת מַחֲבַת דָּמְיָא. י] אוֹ אֵינוֹ אֶלָּא לִקְבּוֹעַ לָהּ שֶׁמֶן, דְּאִי לָא כָּתַב רַחֲמָנָא "בַּשֶּׁמֶן" – ה"א: תֶּיהֱוֵי כְּמִנְחַת חוֹטֵא? הֲדַר אֲמַר: תֶּיהֱוֵי נַמִּי לִקְבּוֹעַ לָהּ שֶׁמֶן, תֵּיתֵי מִדִּינָא. וְדָן דִּינָא, וְלָא אָתְיָא לֵיהּ, וְאִצְטְרִיכָא קְרָא יא] "סוֹלֶת מִנְחָה תָּמִיד", כִּדְמְסַיֵּים רַבִּי יִשְׁמָעֵאל מִילְּתֵיהּ. רַבָּה יב] אָמַר: כּוּלָּהּ ר"ש, [וְ"אִילּוּ לֹא נֶאֱמַר" קָאָמַר], וְה"ק: "בַּשֶּׁמֶן" – לְהוֹסִיף לָהּ שֶׁמֶן, דְּאִי לִקְבּוֹעַ לָהּ שֶׁמֶן – לָא צְרִיךְ, כֵּיוָן דִּכְתִיב בָּהּ "עַל מַחֲבַת" – יג] כְּמַחֲבַת דָּמְיָא, וְעַד שֶׁלֹּא יֹאמַר "בַּשֶּׁמֶן" יֵשׁ לִי בַּדִּין. וְדָן דִּינָא, לָא אַתְיָא לֵיהּ, וְאִצְטְרִיכָא "בַּשֶּׁמֶן". הֲדַר אֲמַר: תֶּיהֱוֵי כְּמִנְחַת פָּרִים יד] וְאֵילִים. הֲדַר אֲמַר: דָּנִין מִנְחָה

והכהן

רש"י

רבא אמר. "על מחבת" – מלמד שטעונה כלי שרת הוא. טו] [ואי אפי לה מאתמול איפסל ליה בלינה]. דאפי' מנחות, משקדשו בכלי – נפסלו בלינה, במסכת מעילה (דף ט.). ה"ג: ונאמר במנחת כבשים שמן. (שמות כט), "ועשרון סלת בלול בשמן כתית רובע ההין", ובמנחת יז] נסכי תמיד כתיב. לישנא אחרינא: ונאמר במנחת נסכים "שמן", והיינו הך. ג' לוגין לעשרון. ד"רובע ההין" – יח] ג' לוגין, דהין – י"ב לוגין. במנחת נדבה. נאמר (ויקרא ב) "ויצק עליה שמן", מה להלן – לוג אחד, כדאמר לקמן (דף פח.): "למנחה ולוג שמן". ולקמן פריך: והיכי מצי למידייניה ממנחת נדבה, הא הכא כתיב "בשמן" להוסיף, והוא "שמן" דהתם לאו להוסיף הוא יט] (ב)? דחביתין באין תמיד. בבקר ובערב, ומנחת נסכים באין תמיד עם התמיד. מנחת נדבה לא דחיא שבת וטומאה, דכל קרבן שאין כ] לה זמן קבוע – אינה דוחה שבת וטומאה. חביתין מנחת יחיד היא. ובאה בגלל עצמה, שאין באה עם הזבח. מנחת נסכים אינה טעונה לבונה. בפ' "כל המנחות באות" כא] (לקמן ד' נט.). כב] תדיר חובה, טומאה, שבת, כג] יחיד, גלל עצמה, לבונה. רבי ישמעאל אומר. הואיל ולא אתיא מדינא, תיתי מקרא "סלת מנחה תמיד" דכתיב בחביתין. ריבה כאן. כדאמרן לעיל: "בשמן" – להוסיף לה שמן, וריבה במנחת נסכים שמן – ג' לוגין לעשרון, דהיינו ריבוי, דבמנחת נדבה ליכא אלא לוג. במנחת נסכי פרים ואילים. ב' לוגין לעשרון, דכתיב בפרשת "שלח לך": "והקריב על בן הבקר כד] (ג) סלת שלשה עשרונים בלול בשמן חצי ההין" – דהיינו ו' לוגין, שתים לעשרון. ובאיל כתיב: "לאיל תעשה מנחה סלת שני עשרונים בלול בשמן שלישית ההין" – דהיינו ד' לוגין, שנים לעשרון. והדר תני נאמר כאן שמן ונאמר במנחת נדבה שמן (ד) [א]. והיכי מצי למיפרך, כה] והא שמן דנדבה – לאו להוסיף הוא, אלא לקבוע לה שמן. והאי "בשמן" – להוסיף הוא, דלקבוע לא צריך, כדמפרש לקמן א). [מאן תנא בשמן להוסיף ר"ש היא. דקאמר בסיפא: ריבה כאן שמן כו', כו] וילפינן לטעמיה מדינא דריבה כאן שמן. ולר' שמעון ליכא למיפרך "ניליף ממנחת נדבה" – משום דהאי להוסיף, ונדבה לקבוע. והא דלא סיימא ברישא – משום דרבי ישמעאל אפסקיה ממאי דאמר להוסיף הוא. ובדינא דמנחת נדבה מאן [ב] קמהדר. דהא ר' שמעון נפקא ליה שפיר מדינא בתרא? ר' ישמעאל. ואיהו קאמר "או כלך". דלרבי ישמעאל איכא למיפרך שפיר "ניליף ממנחת נדבה" – דהא לדידיה תרוייהו לקבוע ולא להוסיף, ואילטריך קרא. *(כולה רישא. ר"י אמר, והכי קאמר רישא: "בשמן" להוסיף לה שמן, ור"י קאמר ליה. דאי לקבוע לה לוג שמן. כשאר מנחות – לא צריך, דכיון דכתיב "על מחבת" – ממילא ידענא דצריכה שמן כמנחת מחבת). תהא כמנחת חוטא. והאי דכתיב "מחבת" – שיביאנה באותו כלי. הדר אמר ר"י וליהוי נמי לקבוע. כדאמרת, הכי נפקא ליה מדינא: נאמר כאן שמן כו'. ודן דינא ולא אתיא ליה. משום דפרכינן "כלך לדרך זו: דנין יג"ל מיג"ל" [ג] כו'. ואצרכא קרא סלת מנחה תמיד. ואתא ר"ש למימר דל"ל קרא, כיון דמוקמת לה להוסיף. כולה. רישא עד "רבי ישמעאל אמר", ואצרכא קרא "סלת מנחה תמיד", אתא רבי שמעון למימר: ודאי להוסיף הוא, ולא לקבוע, ואיני יודע כמה יוסיף. הדר אמר: קרא נמי לא צריך, דמדינא בתרא נפקא. וה"ק רישא בשמן להוסיף לה שמן ג). ור' שמעון קאמר לה. דאי לקבוע לה לוג שמן כשאר מנחות – לא צריך, דכיון דכתיב "על מחבת" – ממילא ידעינן דצריכה שמן כמנחת מחבת]. הדר אמר ג) רבי שמעון תהא כמנחת פרים ואילים. דאף על גב דלהוסיף הוא, לא הויין אלא שני לוגין לעשרון ד). הדר אמר: האי דפרכת תיהוי כמנחת פרים ואילים – דנין

כ"ה גי' ל"ק עד מחבת

תוספות

הרי היא לך כמנחת תמידין. דכתיב גבי שבת (במדבר כח): "על עולת התמיד", ופסח נמי גמרינן "מועדו" "מועדו" מתמיד. תימה: כז] דלמד מן הלמד הוא! ונראה דגלויי מילתא בעלמא הוא. אפי לה מאתמול איפסלה בלינה. תימה: דבסוף "רבי ישמעאל" (לקמן דף עב:) מרבינן שתי הלחם, מדכתיב: "מועדי ה'" – הכתוב קבע מועד אחד לכולן. ומסיק: שתי הלחם לאפייה, וקסבר: תנור מקדש, ואי אפי לה מאתמול – איפסלה בלינה, ואפ"ה בעי קרא! וי"ל: דה"א, דאפי לה בתנור חול. אבל הכא כתיב "מחבת" – על כרחו צריך לעשות במחבת כלי שרת. ותימה: דה"נ לא בעי אלא אפייה, אבל הקטרה – פשיטא ליה דדחי, ובכל קרבנות בעינן קרא, כדפי' לעיל לשחיטתן ולהקטרה. ובמה הצד לא ילפינן אפילו מעומר ושתי הלחם, שכן באים עמהם מיני דמים! וי"ל: [ד] דכי קטרה פשיטא להו דבעינן, או מ"תעשה – אפי' בשבת", כתנא דבי רבי ישמעאל, או מ"הרי היא לך כמנחת תמידין" דדריש אביי, דשלהי האי פירקא (דף נב.) דריש ליה רבא גופיה. ותימה: היכי מוכח דאי אפי לה מאתמול איפסלה בלינה? הא כלי שרת אין מקדשין *אלא בזמנן! וי"ל: כדפי' לעיל, כיון דכתיב בקרא "על מחבת" – על כרחין בעי קידוש כלי. מיהו קשיא לקמן (דף צה:) גבי שתי הלחם, דהא לא כתיב "תנור" בקרא, והיכי מוכח דאפייתן דוחה שבת? ויש לומר: כיון דלא דחו שבת, אם כן מאתמול נמי הוי זמנן. וא"ת: בסוף "לולב וערבה" (סוכה דף מט:) גבי "כמעשהו בחול כך מעשהו בשבת", ופריך בגמרא: ונייתי במקודשת! אמר זעירי: אין שיעור למים, ואי שדי לה במקודשת – איפסלה לה בלינה. ואמאי איפסל, כיון דאין זמנה מאתמול? כח] וי"ל: דהתם שאיבת מים בלילה – לאו מחוסר זמן הוא, [ה] וכי האי גוונא כט] בסוף "שתי הלחם" (לקמן דף צה:) דבחול אשכחינהו דקאפו, אמר להו: דרך חול קאפיתו? "אף כי היום יקדש" – בלינה איפסיל ליה. לפי דבריהם היה אומר שהיו סבורים דזמנו בחול, וגם אופין אותו בכלי שרת. א"נ: לאחר אפייה נותנין אותו בקערות זהב, כפירוש הקונטרס, והיה שם בלילה, ומיפסלא בלינה, דלילה אין מחוסר זמן. ולמ"ד (לקמן דף צה:): תנור אינו מקדש, נראה לי שגם הקערות לא התקדשו. [illegible] **תניא** כוותיה דרבא – [illegible] נמי לא פליג עליה, אלא דלא צריך.

תלמוד לומר סולת למנחה תמיד. תימה: דא"כ, "בשמן" למה לי? ויש לומר: דאי לא "בשמן" – לא הוה מסתבר לאקושי לגבי שמן.

רבינו גרשום

כמנחת תמידין שדוחה את השבת דכתיב בה במועדו. מלמד שטעונה כלי שרת דהיינו מחבת ואי אפי לה מאתמול איפסילה בלינה דכל דבר שקדש בכלי נפסל בלינה חוץ מלחם הפנים: בשמן להוסיף לה שמן יותר ממנחת נדבה וקאמר לקמן היכי משמע האי בשמן להוסיף: במנחת כבשים שלשת לוגין לעשרון דכתיב ביה רביעית ההין דהיינו ג' לוגין. מנחת כבשים היינו תמידים: מנחת נדבה. כגון מנחת מחבת ומרחשת. שהיא באה [יחיד] בגלל עצמה בלא זבח וטעונה לבונה כדאמרי' לקמן מנחת כבשים של תמיד אין תמיד בא משל יחיד: הרי היא לך כמנחת תמידין שצריכה ג' לוגין. תבש"ט סימן תמיד וחובה. ודוחה שבת וטומאה. יג"ל סימן. יחיד בגלל עצמה ולבונה: וריבה במנחת כבשים שמן יותר ממנחת נדבה א) והכי קאמר בשמן להוסיף לה שמן אליביה דר' שמעון [היא] דקתני ר"ש אומר ריבה כאן שמן ב) והיכי משמע דריבה דהא לקבוע לא צריך. ובדינא מאן קא מהדר ר' ישמעאל הילכך ליכא (למימר) [למקשי] והדר תני נאמר כאן שמן וכו' דהאי ר' ישמעאל הוא דקא מהדר ולא ר' שמעון. (וי"א היינו ר' ישמעאל) דאם לא כתב שמן הוה אמינא תיהוי חביתין כמנחת חוטא בלא שמן אע"ג דכתיב בה מחבת להכי איצטריך בשמן לקבוע לה שמן ולא להוסיף: הדר א"ר ישמעאל וליהוי נמי דלקבוע אתא ואפי' הכי להוסיף תיתי מדינא ולא אתיא ואצרכא קרא דקתני ר' ישמעאל אומר מנחת תמיד הרי היא כמנחת תמידין. רבא אמר בשמן להוסיף לה שמן ודינא קא מהדר כולה (ר' ישמעאל) [ר"ש היא] ועד שלא יאמר בשמן כלומר שאפי' לא נאמר בשמן יש לי בדין דלהוסיף לה שמן ודן דינא וכו':

קמז א מיי' פ"ג מהל' תמידים ומוספים הלכה יח:

קמח ב ג מיי' פי"ג מהל' מעה"ק הל' ב:

שיטה מקובצת

א] הרי היא לו: ב] שטעונה כלי. עיין תוס' דף סג ע"א: ג] עי' בהשמטות בסוף המסכת: ד] דנין יג"ל מיג"ל השני יודין האחרונים נמחק: ה] תיבת יין נמחק: ו] כמנחת תמיד. ותיבות מה מנחת תמידין ג' לוגין לעשרון אף זו ג' לוגין לעשרון נמחק: ז] תיבות ואילו לא נאמר קאמר נמחק: ח] מהדר אמר רב הונא בריה דרב יהושע ר' ישמעאל בנו של ריב"ב היא: ט] לקבוע לה שמן: י] ויש אומרים לקבוע ותיבות או אינו אלא נמחק: יא] תיבות סולת מנחת תמיד כדמסיים ר' ישמעאל מילתא רבה נמחק: יב] רבא אמר כולה ר' ישמעאל בנו של ר' יוחנן בן ברוקא היא: יג] מחבת: כמחבת דמיא.

שיטה מקובצת

ואח"כ מה"ד חביתין: כ] שאין זמן קבוע לו: כא] באות מצה: כב] תבש"ט. תמיד באה חובה שבת טומאה תיבת תדיר ל"ש: כג] יג"ל יחיד: כד] הבקר. מנחת סולת: כה] למיפרך הכי: כו] בכאן צ"ל ד"ה וה"ק רישא בשמן להוסיף לה שמן ור' שמעון קאמר ליה: דאי לקבוע לה שמן. כשאר מנחות: לא צריך. קרא דכיון דכתיב על מחבת ממילא ידענא דצריכה שמן כמנחת מחבת: ויש אומרים. כו' ישמעאל: תהא כמנחת חוטא. והאי דכתיב מחבת שיביאנה באותו כלי: הדר אמר. ר' ישמעאל וליהוי נמי לקבוע כדאמרינא אכתי נפקא ליה מדינא נאמר כאן שמן כו': ודן דינא ולא אתיא ליה משום דפרכינן כלך לדרך זו דנין יג"ל מיג"ל כו' דלר' ישמעאל איכא למיפרך שפיר ממנחת נדבה דהא לדידיה תרוייהו לקבוע ולא להוסיף: ואצטריכה קרא. וילפיה ולא ילפיה לטעמיה מדינא דריבה כאן שמן ולר' שמעון ליכא למיפרך ממנחת נדבה משום דהאי להוסיף ונדבה לקבוע והא דלא סיימא ברישא משום דר' ישמעאל אפסקיה ממאי דאמר דלהוסיף הוא: כולה ר' ישמעאל היא. כולה רישא עד ר' שמעון אומר תיבת ישמעאל נמחק: ואצרכה קרא סולת מנחת תמיד ואתא ר' שמעון למימר ודאי להוסיף ולא לקבוע ואיני יודע כמה יוסף וקרא נמי לא צריך דמדינא בתרא נפקא: הדר אמר תהא כמנחת פרים ואילים דאע"ג דלהוסיף הוא לא הוין אלא שני לוגין לעשרון ואצטרכא קרא סולת מנחת תמיד ואתא ר' שמעון למימר דלא צריך קרא כיון דמוקמת לה להוסיף והאי תיהוי כמנחת פרים ואילים דנין מנחה: כז] דלמד מן הלמד. פי' דתמיד יליף מפסח לענין טומאה במס' פסחים ד' סו ע"ב: כט] מאתמול היאך מקדש ליפסל

[illegible]

הגהות הב"ח [illegible]

גליון הש"ס גמ' מחבת מלמד שטעונה כלי. ע' לקמן דף סג ע"א תוספות ד"ה וכשירות.

הגהות צ"ק [illegible]

מסורת הש"ס / תורה אור

אֲבָל צִבּוּר יְהֵא מֵבִיא, שֶׁמֵּבִיא חוֹבָה כַּיּוֹצֵא בָּהּ? ת"ל: °"לֹא תַעֲלוּ". יָכוֹל לֹא יַעֲלוּ עַל מִזְבֵּחַ הַפְּנִימִי, אֲבָל יַעֲלוּ עַל מִזְבֵּחַ הַחִיצוֹן? ת"ל: °"אֶת שֶׁמֶן הַמִּשְׁחָה וְאֶת קְטֹרֶת הַסַּמִּים לַקֹּדֶשׁ כְּכֹל אֲשֶׁר צִוִּיתִךָ יַעֲשׂוּ" — אֵין לְךָ אֶלָּא מַה שֶּׁאָמוּר בָּעִנְיָן! אָמַר רַב פָּפָּא: לָא מִיבָּעְיָא קָאָמַר, לָא מִיבָּעְיָא צִיבּוּר עַל מִזְבֵּחַ הַחִיצוֹן — דְּלָא אַשְׁכַּחַן, וְלָא מִיבָּעְיָא יָחִיד עַל מִזְבֵּחַ הַפְּנִימִי — דְּלָא אַשְׁכַּחַן, אֶלָּא אֲפִילּוּ יָחִיד עַל מִזְבֵּחַ הַחִיצוֹן, דְּאַשְׁכַּחַן בִּנְשִׂיאִים — הוֹרָאַת שָׁעָה הָיְתָה.§

מתני' *חֲבִיתֵּי כ"ג לֹא [א]הָיוּ בָּאִין חֲצָאִין, אֶלָּא מֵבִיא עִשָּׂרוֹן שָׁלֵם וְחוֹצֵהוּ, א] מַקְרִיב מֶחֱצָה בַּבֹּקֶר וּמֶחֱצָה בֵּין הָעַרְבַּיִם. ב] כֹּהֵן [ב]שֶׁמֵּבִיא מֶחֱצָה שַׁחֲרִית, וּמֵת, וּמִינּוּ כֹּהֵן אַחֵר תַּחְתָּיו — לֹא יָבִיא חֲצִי עִשָּׂרוֹן מִבֵּיתוֹ ג] (א) וַחֲצִי עֶשְׂרוֹנוֹ שֶׁל רִאשׁוֹן, אֶלָּא מֵבִיא עִשָּׂרוֹן שָׁלֵם (מֶחֱצָה) ד] וְחוֹצֵהוּ, מַקְרִיב מֶחֱצָה, וּמֶחֱצָה אָבֵד. [ג]נִמְצְאוּ שְׁנֵי חֲצָאִין קְרֵיבִין, וּשְׁנֵי חֲצָאִין אוֹבְדִין. ה] §

גמ' ת"ר: אִילּוּ נֶאֱמַר "מִנְחָה מַחֲצִית" — הָיִיתִי אוֹמֵר: מֵבִיא חֲצִי עִשָּׂרוֹן מִבֵּיתוֹ שַׁחֲרִית וּמַקְרִיב, חֲצִי עִשָּׂרוֹן מִבֵּיתוֹ עַרְבִית וּמַקְרִיב. ת"ל: °"מַחֲצִיתָהּ בַּבֹּקֶר ו] וּמַחֲצִיתָהּ בָּעֶרֶב" — מֶחֱצָה מִשָּׁלֵם הוּא ז] מַקְרִיב, הָא כֵּיצַד? מֵבִיא עִשָּׂרוֹן שָׁלֵם וְחוֹצֵהוּ, וּמַקְרִיב מֶחֱצָה בַּבֹּקֶר וּמֶחֱצָה בֵּין הָעַרְבַּיִם. נִטְמָא מֶחֱצָה שֶׁל בֵּין הָעַרְבַּיִם אוֹ שֶׁאָבַד, יָכוֹל יָבִיא חֲצִי עִשָּׂרוֹן מִבֵּיתוֹ עַרְבִית וְיַקְרִיב? ת"ל: ח] "מַחֲצִיתָהּ בַּבֹּקֶר וּמַחֲצִיתָהּ בָּעֶרֶב" — מֶחֱצָה מִשָּׁלֵם הוּא מֵבִיא, הָא כֵּיצַד? מֵבִיא עִשָּׂרוֹן שָׁלֵם ט] [מִבֵּיתוֹ] וְחוֹצֵהוּ, וּמַקְרִיב מֶחֱצָה וּמֶחֱצָה אָבֵד, נִמְצְאוּ שְׁנֵי חֲצָאִין קְרֵיבִין וּשְׁנֵי חֲצָאִין אוֹבְדִין. כ"ג שֶׁהִקְרִיב מֶחֱצָה שַׁחֲרִית וּמֵת, וּמִינּוּ י] אַחֵר תַּחְתָּיו, יָכוֹל יָבִיא חֲצִי עִשָּׂרוֹן מִבֵּיתוֹ אוֹ חֲצִי עֶשְׂרוֹנוֹ שֶׁל רִאשׁוֹן? ת"ל: "וּמַחֲצִיתָהּ בָּעֶרֶב" — מֶחֱצָה מִשָּׁלֵם הוּא מֵבִיא וּמַקְרִיב, הָא כֵּיצַד? מֵבִיא עִשָּׂרוֹן שָׁלֵם וְחוֹצֵהוּ יא] וּמַקְרִיב, (ג) וּמֶחֱצָה אָבֵד. נִמְצְאוּ שְׁנֵי חֲצָאִין אוֹבְדִין, וּשְׁנֵי חֲצָאִין קְרֵיבִין.§ תָּנֵי תַּנָּא קַמֵּיהּ דְּר"נ: [ד]מֶחֱצָה רִאשׁוֹן וּמֶחֱצָה שֵׁנִי — תְּעוּבַּר צוּרָתָן וְיֵצְאוּ לְבֵית הַשְּׂרֵיפָה. א"ל ר"נ: בִּשְׁלָמָא רִאשׁוֹן — אִיחֲזֵי לְהַקְרָבָה, אֶלָּא שֵׁנִי — לָמָּה לֵיהּ עִיבּוּר צוּרָה? מֵעִיקָּרָא לְאִיבּוּד קָא אָתֵי! דְּאָמַר לָךְ מַנִּי? תַּנָּא דְּבֵי רַבָּה בַּר אֲבוּהּ הוּא, דְּאָמַר: אֲפִילּוּ *פִּיגּוּל טָעוּן עִיבּוּר צוּרָה. רַב אַשִׁי אָמַר: אֲפִילּוּ תֵּימָא רַבָּנַן, כֵּיוָן דִּבְעִידָּנָא *יב] דְּפָלְגִי בְּהוּ, אִי בָּעֵי הַאי מַקְרִיב וְאִי בָּעֵי הַאי מַקְרִיב — מִיחֲזָא חֲזוּ.§ אִיתְּמַר: חֲבִיתֵּי כֹּהֵן גָּדוֹל כֵּיצַד עוֹשִׂין אוֹתָן? רַבִּי חִיָּיא בַּר אַבָּא א"ר יג] יוֹחָנָן: אוֹפָהּ, וְאַחַר כָּךְ מְטַגְּנָהּ. רַבִּי אַסִּי א"ר חֲנִינָא: מְטַגְּנָהּ, וְאח"כ אוֹפָהּ. א"ר חִיָּיא בַּר אַבָּא: כְּוָותֵיהּ דִּידִי מִסְתַּבְּרָא, "תּוּפִינֵי" — תֵּאָפֶינָה נָאָה. רַבִּי אַסִּי אָמַר: כְּוָותֵיהּ דִּידִי מִסְתַּבְּרָא, "תּוּפִינֵי" — תֵּאָפֶינָה נָא. כְּתַנָּאֵי: °"תּוּפִינֵי" — תֵּאָפֶינָה נָא. רַבִּי אוֹמֵר: תֵּאָפֶינָה נָאָה. רַבִּי יד] יוֹסֵי אוֹמֵר: תֵּאָפֶינָה רַבָּה, אִית לֵיהּ [ה]נָא, וְאִית לֵיהּ נָאָה. *תְּנַן הָתָם: [ו]חֲבִיתֵּי כ"ג — לִישָׁתָן וַעֲרִיכָתָן וַאֲפִיָּיתָן בִּפְנִים, [ז]וְדוֹחוֹת אֶת הַשַּׁבָּת. מְנָא ה"מ? אָמַר רַב הוּנָא: [ח]"תּוּפִינֵי" — תֵּאָפֶינָה נָאָה, וְאִי אָפֵי לָהּ מֵאֶתְמוֹל — אִינְשְׁפָה לָהּ. מַתְקִיף לָהּ רַב יוֹסֵף: אֵימָא, דְּכָבֵישׁ לֵיהּ בְּיַרְקָא! דְּבֵי ר' יִשְׁמָעֵאל תָּנָא: "תֵּעָשֶׂה" — וַאֲפִילּוּ בְּשַׁבָּת, "תֵּעָשֶׂה" — וַאֲפִילּוּ בְּטוּמְאָה. אַבַּיֵּי אָמַר, אָמַר *קְרָא °"סֹלֶת מִנְחָה תָּמִיד", הֲרֵי

(שמות ל; שם לא; ויקרא ו; שם)

רש"י

אֲבָל צִיבּוּר יְבִיאוּהָ. נְדָבָה, שֶׁהֲרֵי מְבִיאִין חוֹבָה כַּיּוֹצֵא בָּהּ פַּעֲמַיִם בְּכָל יוֹם. לֹא תַעֲלוּ. מַשְׁמַע לְרַבִּים קָאָמַר. לֹא מִיבָּעְיָא יָחִיד עַל הַמִּזְבֵּחַ הַפְּנִימִי. דְּלָא יָבִיא, דְּהָא לָא אַשְׁכְּחַן לָהּ. טו] **מתני'** חֲבִיתֵּי. הַיְינוּ [מִנְחַת] מַחֲבַת כ"ג שֶׁמֵּבִיא בְּכָל יוֹם, כְּדִכְתִיב "צַו אֶת אַהֲרֹן": "מַחֲצִיתָהּ בַּבֹּקֶר". עַל שֵׁם מַחֲבַת קָרוּ טז] לְהוּ "חֲבִיתִּים", דִּכְתִיב (ויקרא ו): "עַל מַחֲבַת בַּשֶּׁמֶן תֵּעָשֶׂה". לֹא הָיוּ בָּאִין חֲצָאִין. שֶׁלֹּא יָבִיא חֲצִי עִשָּׂרוֹן בַּבֹּקֶר מִבֵּיתוֹ, וַחֲצִי עִשָּׂרוֹן בָּעֶרֶב. וְאַע"פ שֶׁקְּרֵיבָה לַחֲצָאִין, כְּדִכְתִיב: "מַחֲצִיתָהּ בַּבֹּקֶר" — "מַחֲצִיתָהּ" מַשְׁמַע: מַחֲצִיתָהּ שֶׁל שְׁלֵימָה יז] (מֶחֱצָה מִשְּׁלֵמָה), מֶחֱצָה מִתּוֹךְ שָׁלֵם הוּא מֵבִיא, שֶׁמֵּבִיא עִשָּׂרוֹן שָׁלֵם וְחוֹצֵהוּ. וּמִינּוּ אַחֵר תַּחְתָּיו. קוֹדֶם תָּמִיד שֶׁל בֵּין הָעַרְבַּיִם. "לֹא יָבִיא חֲצִי עִשָּׂרוֹן מִבֵּיתוֹ וְלֹא חֲצִי עֶשְׂרוֹנוֹ שֶׁל רִאשׁוֹן" גָּרַס. יח] **גמ'** ת"ל וּמַחֲצִיתָהּ. מְרִיבּוּיָא דְּוָי"ו מַשְׁמַע: אֲפִי' כֹּהֵן הָעוֹמֵד בֵּין הָעַרְבַּיִם, אע"ג דְּאִיכָּא יט] חֲצִי עִשָּׂרוֹן דְּרִאשׁוֹן (ג). מֶחֱצָה רִאשׁוֹן. שֶׁנִּשְׁאַר מִכֹּהֵן רִאשׁוֹן כ], [וּמֶחֱצָה שֵׁנִי שֶׁנִּשְׁאַר מִכֹּהֵן שֵׁנִי]. תְּעוּבַּר צוּרָתָהּ = יִפְסוֹל בְּלִינָה. כא] חֲזִי לְהַקְרָבָה (ד). כִּי אַפְרְשֵׁיהּ, הֲוָה חֲזִי לְהַקְרָבָה, הִילְכָּךְ בָּעֵי עִיבּוּר צוּרָה. לְאִיבּוּד אָתֵי. וְלִשְׂרֵפָה לְאַלְתַּר. אֲפִילּוּ פִּיגּוּל. דִּפְסוּל חָמוּר הוּא, וּפְסוּל דְּאוֹרַיְיתָא הוּא, טָעוּן צוּרָה כב]. חֲבִיתֵּי כ"ג. דִּכְתִיב "מַחֲבַת" וּכְתִיב "מוּרְבֶּכֶת". אוֹפָה. בְּתַנּוּר תְּחִלָּה, וְאח"כ מְטַגְּנָהּ בְּמַחֲבַת. תֵּאָפֶינָה נָאָה. בִּשְׁעַת אֲפִיָּיתָהּ בְּתַנּוּר תְּהֵא נָאָה, וְאִם מְטַגְּנָהּ תְּחִלָּה — הֲרֵי הִיא שְׁחוֹרָה מִן הַשֶּׁמֶן וּמִן הַמַּחֲבַת. תֵּאָפֶינָה נָא. בִּשְׁעַת אֲפִיָּיתָהּ בַּתַּנּוּר תְּהֵא נָא, כְּמוֹ (שמות יב) "אַל תֹּאכְלוּ מִמֶּנּוּ נָא" — כְּלוֹמַר, כג] *בְּכָךְ תְּהֵא מְבוּשֶּׁלֶת קְצָתוֹ, וְאֵינָהּ מְבוּשֶּׁלֶת כָּל צָרְכָּהּ, וְהַיְינוּ טִיגּוּן. דְּהָא מוֹדוּ כ"ע דְּתַרְוַיְיהוּ בָּעֵינַן, כְּדִכְתִיב: "עַל מַחֲבַת בַּשֶּׁמֶן" וּכְתִיב "תּוּפִינֵי". תֵּאָפֶינָה רַבָּה. אֲפִיּוֹת הַרְבֵּה אוֹפָהּ, וּמְטַגְּנָהּ וְאוֹפָהּ. אִית לֵיהּ נָא. מש"ה, אוֹפָהּ אַחַר טִיגּוּן. וְאִית לֵיהּ נָאָה, מש"ה אוֹפָהּ תְּחִלָּה. לִישָּׁנָא אַחֲרִינָא: כד] "רַבָּה" — גְּדוֹלָה וּמְרוּקַּעַת וְדַקָּה, וְזֶהוּ נוֹיָיהּ. וְאִית לֵיהּ מְטַגְּנָהּ תְּחִלָּה, וְאח"כ אוֹפָהּ. כה] וְאִיכָּא [א] טִיגּוּן נָא, וְנָאָה וּגְדוֹלָה הִיא. ל"א [ב] "תֵּאָפֶה רַבָּה" — שֶׁיְּרַכְּכֶנָּה בַּשֶּׁמֶן כו] (קְרֵיבָה נָאָה) [הַרְבֵּה] וְזֶהוּ נוֹיָיהּ. תְּחִלָּה מְטַגְּנָהּ, וְאח"כ אוֹפָהּ, וְאִיכָּא נָא וְנָאֶה. שְׁלָשְׁתָּן שָׁמַעְתִּי. עֲרִיכָתָן. תִּקּוּן הַחַלּוֹת, שֶׁקּוֹרִין כז] אטינו"ר וּבִלְשׁוֹן צָרְפַת סוני"ר. בִּפְנִים. בָּעֲזָרָה. דְּתַנּוּר שֶׁל מַתֶּכֶת הָיָה בָּעֲזָרָה (ה), וְלִישָׁה וַעֲרִיכָה, וְאַע"ג דְּקוֹדֶם מַתַּן שֶׁמֶן הִיא. וְהַאי תַּנָּא אִית לֵיהּ: מִדַּת יָבֵשׁ לֹא נִתְקַדְּשָׁה, מִדְּלָא מַצְרִיךְ לִישַׁת שְׁאָר מְנָחוֹת בִּפְנִים. כח] הָא *בָּעֵינַן פְּנִים, דְּקָסָבַר חֲצִי עִשָּׂרוֹן שֶׁבּוֹ הָיָה חוֹלֵק חֲבִיתֵּי כ"ג נִמְשַׁח. וְהַאי דְּלָא מָשְׁחוּ אֶת הָעִשָּׂרוֹן הַשָּׁלֵם — מִפְּנֵי שֶׁכָּל אָדָם מוֹדֵד בּוֹ מִנְחָתוֹ, וּפְעָמִים כט] שֶׁמּוֹצִיאוֹ לַחוּץ, אֲבָל זֶה אֵינוֹ מָסוּר אֶלָּא ל] לַכֹּהֲנִים. מְנָא הָנֵי מִילֵּי. דְּדוֹחוֹת שַׁבָּת? אִינְשְׁפָא. נְפוּחָה בָּרוּחַ, כְּמוֹ (שמות טו) "נָשַׁפְתָּ בְרוּחֲךָ". דְּכָבֵישׁ לֵיהּ בְּיַרְקָא. טוֹמְנִין בְּיַרָקוֹת, כְּדֵי שֶׁלֹּא יִשְׁלוֹט בָּהּ רוּחַ. תֵּעָשֶׂה. "עַל מַחֲבַת בַּשֶּׁמֶן תֵּעָשֶׂה" (ויקרא ו). כְּמִנְחַת תְּמִידִין. דְּדוֹחוֹת שַׁבָּת.

רָבָא

תוספות

תלמוד לומר [כו'] ככל אשר צויתיך יעשו. תימה: לא] למה לי קרא ד"לא תעלו עליו קטרת זרה", ותיפוק ליה לב] מהכא? ואומר רבי: דה"א דלצבור הוא דמפקדי שלא ישנו, אבל יחיד כעין לצבור — מביא. ותימה: דא"כ, "לא תעלו" בלשון רבים למה לי? דמיניה דרשינן לעיל לצבור ויחיד מקטרת זרה! וי"ל: לג] [דהוי אמינא, לצבור שרי לגבי קטרת נדבה על מזבח הפנימי, והוי] שפיר בכלל "כאשר צויתיך", לד] כיון דמייתו חובה *(או) מייתו נדבה. ונראה דלא מהדר אלא אקטרת סמים, דשייך למזבח הקטרת בההיא פרשתא, אבל אמאי דלא כתיב קודש — לא מהדר [וה"א דעל מזבח החיצון מביא].

ומחצה אבד. קשיא: לר' אלעזר דאמר (לעיל דף ח.): קדוש לחצאין, ו"מחציתה" דאמר קרא — מחצה משלם (להבאה) הוא, וא"כ אמאי אבד? דהא אכתי לא איקדיש קדושת הגוף, וא"כ בר פדיון הוא! ואע"ג דמשמע במסכת שקלים לה] (דף ד.): "אבודין *מליקרב", מ"מ לו] מה בין זה לסולת אחר, כיון דנפדה. מיהו מש"ה קרי ליה "אבד". **אפי'** פיגול טעון עיבור צורה. דיליף "עון" "עון" מנותר אף לענין הא: מדהתם — איכא [עיבור] צורה, הכא — ה"נ, כדדרשינן פרק קמא (דפסחים דף ג.) ובפרק "איזהו מקומן" (זבחים דף נו:): ביום אתה שורפו, ואי אתה שורפו בלילה.

תעשה אפילו בשבת תעשה אפילו בטומאה. הא דמפקינן הכא מחד קרא שבת *וטומאה — היינו משום דגלי רחמנא גבי פסח דדרשינן מ"במועדו" — לז] אפילו בשבת, ואיצטריך קרא אחרינא גבי טומאה: איש נדחה, ואין צבור נדחין! ונראה: דהי מינייהו מפקת? דשקולין הם, ולא דמו לפסח*.

הרי

רבינו גרשום

אבל ציבור יהא מתנדב ומביא שכן מביא חובתו כיוצא בה בכל יום דקטרת משל צבור היתה באה: אין לך אלא מה שאמור בענין ככל אשר צויתיך יעשו: חביתי כהן גדול. מנחתו שהיה מקריב בכל יום קרויה חביתין משום דכתיב בה על מחבת בשמן: תלמוד לומר ומחציתה מוי"ו דומחציתה קא מרבה: מחצה של ראשון ושל שני שאובדין תעובר צורתן לעביד להו לינה ושורפן. בשל ראשון משום הכי בעי צורה. דאיחזי ליה להקרבה דבשעת הפרשה שניהם היו ראוים להקריב אחד בבקר ואחד בין הערבים: אפי' פיגול טעון צורה דיליף עון עון מנותר ונותר הרי [עיבור] צורה: אופה בתנור תחילה ואח"כ מטגנה בשמן: תופיני תאפינה כשהיא נאה. כלומר בלא שמן שאם היה מטגנה תחלה ואח"כ אופה היתה שחורה מחמת השמן ולא היתה נאה: תאפינה נא. האי נא אפוי ולא אפוי כל צרכו והיינו כשהוא מטגנה אינה אפויה כל צורכה וכשהוא מכניסה לתנור היא נא היינו תאפינה נא: תאפינה רבה. כלומר תאפינה הרבה אפיות. אית ליה לר' דוסא נא ואית ליה נאה. הילכך תאפינה לכתחילה נאה בלא שמן ולא כל צרכה והדר מטגנה ועדיין היא נא והדר חוזר ואופה כל צרכה. ואית דאמרי תאפינה רבה כלומר שיעשה חלה דקה ורחבה הרבה. אית ליה נא שמטגנה תחלה והויא נא והדר אופה ואית ליה נאה. היינו נאה שהיתה רחבה. מורבכת אמר לן ר' היינו שאחר אפייתה היה חולטה ברותחין. פתים היינו שכופלה לשנים ושנים לארבעה ופותת ואח"כ היה מקריבה: אינשפא לה. כלומר שניא צורתה השתא ולא הויא נאה: אימא דכביש לה בירקא. כלומר שיכסנה בירק מפני החמה או מפני הרוח ולא תשתנה צורתה ולא תדחה שבת:

עין משפט נר מצוה

קמב א מיי' פי"ג מהל' מעה"ק הלכה ב:

קמג ב מיי' פ"ג מהל' תמידין ומוספין הל' כ:

קמד ג ד מיי' שם הלכה כא:

קמה ה מיי' פי"ג מהל' מעה"ק הלכה ג:

קמו ו ז ח מיי' פ"ג מהל' תמידין ומוספין הל' יח:

גליון / הגהות בשוליים

נ"ק — אי מייתו נדבה יעשו כמו בחובה ועוד נראה נ"ק

נ"א למנוה

ממש מה בין כו' נ"ק

נ"ק

דטומאה וגבי פסח דרשינן מבמועדו נ"ק

[וע' תוספות פסחים סו. ד"ה מה מועדו כו' ותו' לקמן עב: ד"ה שנאמר]

לקמן נו.

נ"ל בעי. חלופי גרסאות

[לקמן נב. ע"ש]

שיטה מקובצת

א] וחוצהו ומקריב: ב] הערבים וכהן: ג] מביתו. ולא חצי. ד] שלם וחוצהו ומקריב: ה] אובדין לא מינו כהן הגדול אחר משל מי היתה קריבה ר' שמעון אומר משל צבור ר' יהודה אומר משל יורשין ושלימה היתה קריבה: ו] תיבות ומחציתה בערב נמחק: ז] הוא מביא: ח] תיבות מחציתה בבקר נמחק: ט] שלם וחוצהו: י] ומינו כהן גדול אחר: יא] ומקריב מחצה ומחצה אבד נמצאו שני חצאין קריבין ושני חצאין אובדין: יב] דבעידנא דפלגינהו: יג] אבא א"ר חנינא: יד] ר' דוסא אומר תאפנה רבה ס"א רכה: טו] אשכחן לה הס"ד ואח"כ מה"ד אין לך אלא מה שאמור בענין. בפרשה החובה ועל מזבח הפנימי ודצבור דכתיב והקריב עליו אהרן בבקר: טז] לה חביתין: יז] מחצה משלמה נמחק: יח] גרס הס"ד ואח"כ מה"ד ושלימה. עשרון שלם בבקר ועשרון בין הערבים כל זמן שהיא קריבה משל צבור הס"ד ואח"כ מה"ד גמ' ומינו אחר תחתיו. קודם תמיד של בין הערבים: יט] דאיכא. חצי: כ] מכהן ראשון. ומחצה שני שנשאר מכהן שני: כא] מחזי: כב] טעון צורה. כדילפי' עון עון מנותר בפ' כיצד צולין הס"ד: כג] תיבת בכך נמחק: כד] ל"א גרסי' תאפינה רבה: כה] אופה והטיגון הוא נא: כו] בשמן הרבה. תיבות קריבה נאה נמחק: כז] אנטישטיר ובלשון צרפת טוניר: כח] בפנים. והא בעינן בפנים: כט] שמוציאו לחוץ ואע"ג דאמרינן כלי שרת לא קדיש ליפסל ביוצא מיהו גנאי הוא להוציא לחוץ לאחר שנתקדש בכלי וא"ת מ"מ היתה בה שמן וכלי הלח נתקדש וי"ל דלא היה מודד בלוג של כלי שרת. תו"ח: ל] לכהנים. ולא נראה לר"י דאין זה טעם ברור לחלק בין עשרון לחצי עשרון כיון דתרוייהו מדת יבש היא ואומר ר"י דלהכי נקט חביתי כהן גדול כי אם משום דדוחות את השבת ואינו כשאר מנחות דאינן דוחות את השבת אבל לישתה ועריכתה בפנים לאו לאפוקי שאר מנחות אתא דה"ה שאר מנחות כן וכן משמע לקמן בפ' שתי הלחם דקתני אחר בבא זו דמייתי הכא כל המנחות יש בהן מעשה כלי בפנים פי' כגון לישה ועריכה ואפיה אלמא דשאר מנחות נמי לישתן ועריכתן בפנים. תוס' אחרות: לא] למה לי קרא. ושמא לעבור עליו בלאו כתבינהו רחמנא תוס' אחרות: לב] מהכא. וי"ל דלא שמעינן מהאי קרא [אלא] שלא ישנה מקומות שלא יקריב קטורת (של) [על] מזבח החיצון לפי שהכתוב מדבר על מזבח הפנימי ובכל כליה וכן במזבח העולה וכליה ועל זה קאי כאשר צויתיך כו' תו"ח: לג] וי"ל דהוי שפיר בכלל: לד] צויתיך. בין: לה] שקלים. גליון בירושלמי במס' שקלים פ"ז משמע דמותר מעות דעשירית האיפה של כה"ג אבודין דילכו לים המלח: גליון אחר. י"ל אפי' דקדושת דמים אבוד כדמוכח בפרק בתרא דאפי' מותר מעות אבודין: לו] מ"מ עיין פסחים דף מ"ו ע"א: לז] מבמועדו. עיין פסחים דף ס"ו ולקמן בתוס' דף ע"ב ע"ב:

הרי

הגהות צ"ק [א] נא טיגון ונאה דגדולה היא: [ב] ל"א רכה שירככנה בשמן הרבה:

הגהות הב"ח (א) במשנה חצי עשרון מביתו ולא חצי עשרונו: (ב) גמ' ומקריב מחצה ומחצה אבד: (ג) רש"י ד"ה ת"ל ומחציתה וכו' דראשון יביא מביתו הס"ד: (ד) ד"ה חזי להקרבה כשאפרשי' הוה: (ה) ד"ה בפנים וכו' בעזרה ואע"ג דקודם כצ"ל ותיבות ולישה ועריכה נמחק:

מ"מ שבעה הוו! אלא *תנא בעלמא קאי, ומאי "כדי לשבת וב' ימים טובים של ר"ה"? סימנא בעלמא. דיקא נמי, דקתני "כדי לשבת", ולא קתני "לשבת ולב' ימים טובים של ר"ה", ש"מ.§ "לא הקריבו כבש בבוקר וכו'. אמר ר"ש: וכולה היתה קריבה בין הערבים, שאין מחנכין את מזבח הזהב אלא בקטרת הסמים".§ חינוך מאן דכר שמיה? חסורי מיחסרא, והכי קתני: "לא הקריבו כבש בבקר — לא יקריבו בין הערבים. א] במה דברים אמורים? אשלא נתחנך המזבח, אבל נתחנך המזבח — יקריבו בין הערבים. אר"ש: אימתי? בזמן שהיו אנוסין או שוגגין, אבל אם היו מזידין, לא הקריבו כבש בבקר — לא יקריבו בין הערבים. לא הקטירו קטרת בבקר — יקטירו בין הערבים". מנא הני מילי? דת"ר: °"ואת הכבש השני תעשה בין הערבים" — שני בין הערבים, ולא ראשון בין הערבים. במד"א — שלא נתחנך המזבח, אבל נתחנך המזבח — אפילו ראשון בין הערבים. אמר ר"ש: אימתי? בזמן שהיו אנוסין או שוגגין, אבל אם היו מזידין, (א) לא הקריבו כבש בבקר — לא יקריבו בין הערבים, לא הקטירו קטרת בבוקר — יקטירו בין הערבים. וכי כהנים חטאו, מזבח בטל?! אמר רבא, ה"ק: לא יקריבו הן, אבל אחרים — יקריבו. "לא הקטירו קטרת בבקר — יקטירו בין הערבים". דכיון ב] דלא שכיחא ומעתרא — חביבא להו, ולא פשעי.§ "אמר ר"ש: וכולה היתה קריבה בין הערבים שאין מחנכין את מזבח הזהב אלא בקטרת הסמים של ג] בין הערבים" וכו'.§ והתניא: בקטרת הסמים של שחר! תנאי היא. אמר אביי: במסתברא כמ"ד בקטרת הסמים של בין הערבים, דכתיב: °"בבקר בבקר בהיטיבו את הנרות יקטירנה" — אי לאו דעבד הדלקה מאורתא, הטבה בצפרא מהיכא? ולמ"ד בקטרת הסמים של שחר — גמר ממזבח העולה, מה להלן בתמיד של שחר, אף כאן בקטרת הסמים של שחר.§ "ולא את השלחן אלא בלחם הפנים בשבת".§ אלא בחול איחנוכי הוא דלא מחנך, הא קדושי מיקדיש? היא גופה קמ"ל, דחינוך גוקידוש דשלחן בשבת הוא. כדקתני סיפא: ולא את המנורה אלא בשבעה נרותיה בין הערבים.§ ת"ר: ד] זהו קטרת שעלתה ליחיד על מזבח החיצון, והוראת שעה היתה. היכא? אמר רב פפא: בנשיאים. אלא יחיד על מזבח החיצון הוא דלא, הא על מזבח הפנימי — מקריב? ותו, על מזבח החיצון יחיד הוא דלא, הא ציבור — מקרבו? והתניא: *)יכול יהא יחיד המתנדב ומביא כיוצא בה נדבה, וקורא אני ה] בה °"מוצא שפתיך תשמור ועשית"? ת"ל °"לא תעלו עליו קטרת זרה". יכול לא יהא יחיד מביא — שאין מביא חובתו כיוצא בה, אבל

*) [לקמן נח.]

שמות כט | שמות ל | דברים כג | שמות ל

(י"ב) תורה אור

רש"י

*ה"ג: תנא בעלמא קאי. "סימנא בעלמא נקט". כלומר, האי דנקט "ששה" — לאו לשבת וב' ימים ו] דוקא קאמר, אלא אפי' כל ימות החול ז] בעי' בלשכה ו' טלאים, כולן ח] מבוקרין ד' ימים קודם שחיטה, לבד יום השחיטה. שהיו שם בכל יום ששה ראויין ליטול אחד שנים מהן שירצה. כגון דביום חינוך הוה בה (י"ב) ט] (ב) ששה מבוקרים ד' ימים קודם. ונטלו ב' ביום ראשון, ובקרו שנים י] והכניסן תחתיהן. ליום ב' נטלו ב' מן הראשונים, ובקרו ב' יא] מן השוק ונתנו שנים תחתיהן. לשלישי נטלו ב' מן הראשונים, ובקרו שנים יב] (ג) תחתיהם אחרים והכניסו תחתיהן — נשארו שם *ששה מן הראשונים. ליום רביעי *יטלו עוד ב' מן הראשונים, והשנים שנתבקרו בראשון יהיו [א] ראוין יג] שנים של ראשון ושנים של שני ושנים של שלישי, וכן יד] כולם. לעולם יהיו שם ששה ראויין לישחט. ולא פי' טעם הדבר. ולי נראה דקבעו חכמים מנין קבוע לדבר, טו] דאי מתרמין (לא) משכחי טלאים מבוקרין זה ד' ימים. סימנא בעלמא. שלא תטעה בגירסא אם טז] ו' או ה' או ד'. כדי לשבת ולב' ימים. משמע: סימן. כלומר, שראוי לג' ימים. ולא תני לשבת ולב' ימים טובים. דליהוי משמע: לצורך שבת וב' ימים טובים של ר"ה. ולא ראשון בין הערבים. שאם לא הקריבו בבקר — לא יקריבו בין הערבים. דהכי מידריש קרא: אם את הכבש יז] האחד תעשה בבקר — הוכשר שני ליקרב בין הערבים, ואי לא — לא. במה דברים אמורים שלא נתחנך המזבח. דהאי קרא — בחינוך כתיב, דכתיב לעיל מיניה "וזה אשר תעשה על המזבח", בפרשת "ואתה תצוה". אבל נתחנך המזבח אפילו ראשון בין הערבים. דכתיב בפרשת "פינחס": "ואת הכבש השני תעשה בין הערבים כמנחת הבקר" כו'. ובההוא קרא לא כתיב "את הכבש אחד תעשה בבקר" א). ותניא בספרי: האי קרא למה נאמר? והלא כבר נאמר למעלה בפרשה "את הכבש אחד תעשה בבקר יח] ואת הכבש" וגו' — [ב] שנים הוא ב) מקריב, ולא ארבעה. יקטירו בין הערבים. כדתנא טעמא: דלא שכיחי דפשעו בה, הילכך לא קנסי בה להו (ד). ומזבח בטל יט] כו'. דקאמר "לא יקריבו בין הערבים". דלא שכיח [ג]. *דתמיד — עולה הוא, ואע"ג דלא קרבה אלא תרי זימני ביומא, איכא עולות אחריני דמקרבי כל יומא טובא. הילכך לא חביב להו, ופשעי — הילכך קנסו להו. אבל קטרת — לעולם ליתא אלא תרי זימני ביומא. לישנא אחרינא: לא שכיחא כחד גברא, כדאמרי' במסכת יומא (דף כו.): מעולם לא שנה אדם בה. מעתרא. מעשרת, כדכתיב "ישימו קטורה" וכתיב בתריה "ברך ה' חילו" (דברים לג) ג). ולא מזבח העולה אלא בתמיד של שחר. כדאמרינן לעיל: ולא ראשון בין [ד] הערבים, כ] דכתיב: "בבקר בבקר בהיטיבו את הנרות" וגו', כשמדשן את המנורה מן האפר שיש שם מן הנרות. אי לאו דעבד (ה) מאורתא הדלקה. מאי בעי לתקן כא] לצפרא? אלמא חינוך מנורה בין הערבים. וכיון דמנורה נתחנכה בערב — קטרת נמי תחילתה בערב, דכתיב (שמות ל): "ובהעלות אהרן את הנרות בין הערבים יקטירנה". הא קדושי מקדש. לאחם אם יסדירוהו עליו בחול? בתמיה. דהא קיימא לן בפרק "שתי הלחם" (לקמן דף ק.) דלא מקדש לחם אלא בשבת...

תוספות

הלא יזרוק היטב אחר התמיד! לכך נראה: דמדרבנן מיפסיל, אפילו הקטיר ועשה הכל, ולא העמידו דבריהם היכא דלא אפשר.

*אית דגרסי "הא איכא לפרא דתלתא בשבתא", ואלו שני ימים טובים של ר"ה אחר השבת! ופריך: וליטעמיך, תמניא הוו, דהאיכא דפניא דמעלי שבתא! וכסבור היה שבאמצע היום היה מדבר. ואית דגרסי "הא איכא לפרא דחד בשבתא", ומונה הב' ימים טובים לפני השבת. ובתר הכי נגרוס "דפניא דמעלי יומא טבא". מכל מקום ז' הוו. דבשלמא [בין הערבים] דראשון, אע"פ שצריך ביקור ד' ימים — יטרח וימלא מבוקרין. שהמבקרין היו מבקרין אותן, כדי למוכרן. אבל בצפרא — לא יכול בלילה לטרוח ולבקש מבקרין. דיקא נמי דקתני כדי לשבת. אף ע"ג דלעיל (דף לט.) תניא "כדי שיכרוך וישנה וישלש" — ליכא למיטעי התם.

שאין מחנכין. [ו] פירש בקונטרס: דטעמיה דר"ש קאמר, ומ"מ פריך שפיר "חינוך מאן דכר שמיה" מעולת התמיד. ולא יתכן: חדא, כיון דההוא הוה טעמא — אידך נקט אידי. ותו, דבחסורי מיחסרא משמע דמהדר אדרבנן — (ותו) אלמא דרבנן מודו בחינוך. ותו, מנלן דשלם הוה?

במה ד"א שלא נתחנך. והא קאי "שאין מחנכין" [ז] דמתני', אבל נתחנך — יקריבו כבש אחד דוקא, ולא שנים, מדלא קתני "וב' היו קריבים" לר"ש. אע"ג דגבי קטורת קרב כולה — לא דמי כלל, דהתם חדא מילתא היא.

דלא שכיחא ומעתרא. עיקר הטעם: משום דלא שכיחא. דבפ"ב דיומא (דף כו.) מוכח מקרא דכתיב "וכליל על מזבחך ברך ה' חילו", *דעולה נמי מעתרא [ח].

יכול יהא יחיד מתנדב ומביא. והא דאמרינן במעילה פרק "חטאת העוף" (דף ט:): הנהנה מבשר קדשי קדשים קודם זריקה וכו' — יביא קטורת שכולה למזבח", היינו למוסרה לצבור.

ב"ח ל"ג | צ"ק

שיטה מקובצת

א] בר"א שלא נתחנך המזבח. ובהכי קאמר דלא יקריבו בין הערבים תחילה לפי שצריך לחנכו בתמיד של שחר: ב] דלא שכיחא. ללישנא (קמא) [אחרינא] דפ"ה קשה דמשמע דכ"ש אם הקטירו אותה בבקר שיקטירו בין הערבים וקשה הא אמרי' מעולם לא שנה בה אדם והוכיח הרב ר' יוסף ביומא דאפי' מבקר ועד ערב לא שנה בה: תו"ח (אא"ה עיין תו"י יומא דף כ"ו ע"א שם כתבו בשם הרב ר' יוסף איפכא דכהן הזוכה בה שחרית היה זוכה בה ערבית עכ"ה): [ואכן מכאן] משמע שאותם כהנים עצמן שהיה [להם] להקטיר בבקר ולא הקטירו הן עצמן יכולין להקטיר בין הערבים ומכאן יש להוכיח דאע"ג דחדשים מפיסין על הקטרת ולא ישנים מפני שמעשרת מיהו בקטרת של בין הערבים אין צריך חדשים אלא אפי' ישנים שהפיסו בשחרית מפיסין ובמס' יומא מספקא לן בהכי [אא"ה בתוס' שלנו ובתו"י שם לא נמצא שום ספק עכ"ה]: ג] בין הערבים. ולא מזבח העולה אלא בתמיד של שחר והתניא בקטרת סמים של שחר ובמתני' משמע שמחנכין אותו בקטרת של ערב כדתנן לא הקריבו בבקר לא יקריבו בין הערבים ואוקימנא שלא נתחנך וקתני לא הקטירו בבקר יקטירו בין הערבים אלמא דבשל ערב מחנך ליה: ד] ת"ר זו היא: ה] אני בו: ו] וב' ימים דר"ה: ז] החול נמי בעינן: ח] מבוקרין [כיצד מהרה יבנה בית המקדש אם ראוי המזבח להתחנך ברביעי בשבת צריך שיתחיל לבקר התמידין של יום החינוך מיום השבת שלפניו דהיינו ד' ימים לפני הקרבתו לבד מיום שחיטה וביום אחד בשבת יקח שנים אחרים לצורך יום ה' ובשני בשבת שנים אחרים לצורך יום ו' ובשלישי בשבת שנים אחרים ליום השבת נמצא...

רבינו גרשום

מכל מקום שבעה הוו דהא איכא ההוא דשחרית דמוצאי י"ט. תנא בעלמא קאי אפי' בימות החול דעלמא בכל שבוע ושבוע בכל יום לא יפחתו בלשכה משמשה טלאים והאי דקאמר לשבת ולב' י"ט לאו לצורך ממש קאמר אלא לסימנא בעלמא. ואשמועינן דליהוו לעולם ששה כדי שיעור של שבת וב' י"ט. ואמאי הוו ששה כדי שיבואו לכל ימי השבוע שני כבשים שיהו מבוקרין ד' ימים קודם שחיטה. הא כיצד היו לו ביום א' ששה מבוקרין שחט ב' מהן ביום א' והביא ב' תחתיהן נשתיירו ד' מבוקרין וב' שאינן מבוקרין הרי ו' ביום ב' ישחט ב' מן המבוקרין ויביא ב' תחתיהן וביום הג' ישחט ב' המבוקרין ויביא ב' תחתיהן. אותו שהביא ביום א' תחת אותו ששחט יהיו ראוין להקריב ליום ד' שהרי הן מבוקרין ד' ימים דמקצת יום ד' הוי ככולו ואותן שהביא ביום ב' יהיו ראוין ליום ה'. ושל יום ג' ליום ו'. ושל יום ד' ליום שבת ושל יום ה' ליום א'. וכך חוזרין חלילה [ונמצא] דבכל יום הוי ב' שמבוקרין ד' ימים הילכך אין פוחתין בלשכה משמשה טלאים. דיקא נמי דקתני כדי לשבת דהוי סימן בעלמא ולא קתני לשבת דהוי משמע דלצורך שבת וי"ט קאמר ש"מ דלסימנא בעלמא הוא: בד"א בשלא הקריבו כבש בבקר לא יקריבו בין הערבים. כשלא נתחנך המזבח שאין מחנכין אותו בתמיד של ערב. אבל נתחנך כבר ולא הקריבו בבקר יקריבו בין הערבים. מנא הני מילי שאין מחנכין...

[ערכין יג.]

שנים מן ל"ק

נ"ל יטלו עוד ב' מן הראשונים ובקרו שנים והכניסו תחתיהן והשנים שנתבקרו בראשון יהיו ראוין למחר ליום ה' וכן אח"כ היו ראוין ושנים של שני

עיין ל"ק גורסים גירסא אחרת כרש"י כמו שנרשם פה בסמוך

עין משפט נר מצוה

קלח א מיי' פ"א מהל' תמידין ומוספין הל' יב:
שייך לדף מט:
קלט ב מיי' שם פ"ג הלכה ה:
קם ג מיי' שם פ"ג הלכה יב:
קמא ד מיי' פ"ב מהלכות כלי מקדש הל' יא:

דדרשינן ממלבד איפכא דעולת הבקר קדמה לכך נראה כו' נ"ק

קלו א מיי' פ"ח מהל' תמידין ומוספין הלכה כ:

קלז ב ג מיי' שם פ"א הלכה ט:

מלבד כתיב כדכתיב נ"ק

גי' רש"ק בדיעבד וגי' נ"ק בכך ניחא

מהעולה שאין נ"ק

בהקטרה נ"ק

היינו ופר שני תקח לחטאת דלא כהרש"ק

ניחא

נ"ק

תורה אור

אֶלָּא פְּשִׁיטָא דְּלֵית לֵיהּ, וְאִי דְּיוֹמֵיהּ אַמַּאי? תָּדִיר וּמְקוּדָּשׁ — תָּדִיר עָדִיף! אֶלָּא לָאו דִּלְמָחָר, וְקָתָנֵי: אֵין מְעַכְּבִין זֶה אֶת זֶה — אאַלְמָא כִּי הֲדָדֵי נִינְהוּ! אֲמַר לֵיהּ אַבָּיֵי: לְעוֹלָם דְּאִית לְהוּ, וּלְקַדֵּם. וּדְקָא קַשְׁיָא לָךְ שֶׁלֹּא יְהֵא דָּבָר קוֹדֵם — מִצְוָה בְּעָלְמָא הוּא. ת"ש: *אֵין פּוֹחֲתִין במִשִּׁשָּׁה טְלָאִים הַמְבוּקָּרִין בְּלִשְׁכַּת הַטְּלָאִים כְּדֵי לְשַׁבָּת וְלִשְׁנֵי יָמִים טוֹבִים שֶׁל רֹאשׁ הַשָּׁנָה. הֵיכִי דָּמֵי? אִילֵימָא דְּאִית לֵיהּ — תְּמִידִין וּמוּסָפִין א] טוּבָא הָווּ! אֶלָּא לָאו דְּלֵית לֵיהּ — וּשְׁמַע מִינַּהּ: תְּמִידִין עֲדִיפִי! לָא, לְעוֹלָם דְּאִית לֵיהּ, וְהָכִי קָא אָמַר: גאֵין פּוֹחֲתִין מִשִּׁשָּׁה טְלָאִים הַמְבוּקָּרִין בְּלִשְׁכַּת הַטְּלָאִים ד' יָמִים קוֹדֶם שְׁחִיטָה, וּמַנִּי? בֶּן בַּג בַּג הִיא. *דְּתַנְיָא, בֶּן בַּג בַּג אוֹמֵר: מִנַּיִן לְתָמִיד שֶׁטָּעוּן בִּיקּוּר ד' יָמִים קוֹדֶם שְׁחִיטָה? תַּלְמוּד לוֹמַר: °"תִּשְׁמְרוּ לְהַקְרִיב לִי בְּמוֹעֲדוֹ" (במדבר כח), וּלְהַלָּן הוּא אוֹמֵר: °"וְהָיָה לָכֶם לְמִשְׁמֶרֶת עַד אַרְבָּעָה עָשָׂר יוֹם" (שמות יב), מַה לְּהַלָּן — טָעוּן בִּיקּוּר אַרְבָּעָה יָמִים קוֹדֶם שְׁחִיטָה, אַף כָּאן — טָעוּן בִּיקּוּר אַרְבָּעָה יָמִים קוֹדֶם שְׁחִיטָה. אֲמַר לֵיהּ רָבִינָא לְרַב אַשִׁי: הָנֵי שִׁשָּׁה — שִׁבְעָה הָווּ, דְּהָא אִיכָּא ב] דְּצַפְרָא *דִּתְלָתָא בְּשַׁבְּתָא! וּלְטַעְמִיךְ, תְּמַנְיָא הָווּ, דְּהָאִיכָּא דְּפַנְיָא דְּמַעֲלֵי שַׁבְּתָא! הָא לָא קַשְׁיָא, דִּלְבָתַר דְּאַקְרִיב קָאָמַר.

מ"מ

אלא פשיטא דלית ליה. אלא או לתמידין או למוספין. **מבוקרים**. בלא מום, שצריך לבודקן שלא יהא בהן מום ארבעה ימים קודם לשחיטה. ולהכי צריכין ששה — שמא יארעו שני ימים טובים של ראש השנה בחמישי בשבת, ויצטרכו בכל יום שנים. כדי לשבת ולשני ימים טובים של ראש השנה. אם אירעו ביחד, שיהא כדי להקריב שני תמידין ליום. **אילימא** דאית להו. כבשים הרבה. תמידין ומוספין **טובא** הוו. ועשרים ותרתי טלאים בעינן [ותיהוי ששה — לתמידין, ושש עשרה — למוספין]. **ושמע** מינה תמידין עדיפי. דלא אמרינן: יקריב הארבעה בשבת — לתמידין ולמוספין, ויבטל תמידין ג] יום טוב שני של ראש השנה. אלמא, תמידין דיום שני עדיפי ממוספי שבת, ואע"פ שמוספי שבת מקודש, הן (א) ושבת קדוש מיום טוב. **לעולם** דאית ליה. לתמידין ומוספין. והאי דלא נקט אלא תמידין — משום ד] דבמבוקרין ארבעה ימים קודם שחיטה קאמר, לתמידין הוא דבעינן ביקור ארבעה ימים, אבל מוספין — לא. **שמירה** שמירה לגזירה שוה. מה פסח — מבוקר ד' ימים, דמקחו מבעשור, ושחיטתו בי"ד. אף תמיד — טעון ביקור ד' ימים. **דהאיכא צפרא** דחד **בשבתא**. דבשלמא דבין הערבים, ודיום שני ושלישי — איכא למימר שיחזור ביום ראשון אחר טלאים מבוקרים ארבעה ימים קודם. אלא במוצאי שבת — לא יכול לחזור, ומה יקריב לבוקר? והא דנקט חד בשבת — היינו כי הוי ראש השנה חמישי וששי, והוא הדין נמי אי הוי ראש השנה בראשון ושני מאי למיפרך: **והאיכא** נפרא דשלישי בשבת? **דפניא** דמעלי **שבתא**. דקא סלקא דעתך: דקודם שהקריב תמיד של בין הערבים — של ערב שבת קאמר, דליהוו ששה. והוא הדין דמצי למיפרך: דפניא דמעלי יומא טבא, היכי דהוי ראש השנה חמישי וששי. דלבתר דמקריב. תמיד של בין הערבים קאמרינן דליהוו שש.

ה"ג

העולה". והשתא ליפרוך ממתניתין ה] *דדרשא מהא איפכא, דעולת הבקר קדמה ברישא! לכך נראה לפרש: דמהכא לא נפקא לן אלא הקטרה, דכולי קרא — בהקטרה איירי. ומהתם נפקא לן עבודת דם, דכתיב "תעשו" — משמע: עשיית הדם. ופ' "הגוזל [קמא]" (ב"ק קיא.) איצטריך לאיתויי האי קרא. דהא לא כתיב אלא הקטרה אשה ריח ניחוח קמי תמיד, ולמאי הקטרת מוסף קדמה? ועשיות בתר* ו] הכי (מלבד איכתיבו) — כדכתיב (במדבר כח) "מלבד עולת *התמיד תעשו את אלה". [הבוקר אשר לעולת] תימה: למה לי קרא דתמיד קודם למוסף? תיפוק לי' דתדיר קודם, דאע"ג דקדמי בקרא, אמרינן בזבחים (ד' פט.) דמוספי חודש קדמי למוספי ראש השנה, אע"ג דכתי' "מלבד עולת החדש" לבסוף. ואי מיפסיל *ביוצא — ניחא, ובסמוך נפקא דלא מיפסיל! וי"ל: דהיא גופא שמעינן, *מה עולה — שאין לאחר, אף על גב דכתיב "מלבד" לבסוף. והא דאמרינן בריש "כל התדיר" (זבחים דף פט:): יכול יהא חטאת קודמת למעשה עולה, משום דכתיב "ועשה את האחד חטאת ואת האחד עולה"? ת"ל: "ופר שני בן בקר תקח לחטאת". יכול תהא עולה קודמת לכל מעשיה? ת"ל: "ועשה" וגו'. הא כיצד? דם חטאת — קודם לדם עולה, מפני שמרצים. אברי עולה קודמין לחטאת — מפני שכולה כליל. אלמא בעי לאקדומי אפי' *מהקטרה, אע"ג דכתיב "ועשה" דלא משמע אלא עשיית הדם — לאו מילתא היא. דכיון דגלי גבי תמידין, הוא הדין נמי התם. אי נמי: מ"והקריב את אשר לחטאת ראשונה" הוה קא דריש, דמיניה דרשינן (זבחים דף ז.): זה בנה אב: כל החטאות קודמות לעולה. אי נמי: אי לאו *קרא, ה"א: מאי דבעי בהקטרה — מקדים ברישא. ותימה: למה לי קרא ד"העולה"? בלא האי קרא נמי תיפוק לי מיוקדם דבר שנאמר בו "בבקר" מדבר שלא נאמר בו אלא "ביום" — דמשמע בעילומו של יום. דמיניה שמעינן בפרק "תמיד נשחט" (פסחים נח.) דמוספין קרבי עד שש. והכי אמרינן פרק "אמר להם הממונה" (יומא דף לג:): קטורת קודם לאברים — יוקדם דבר שנאמר בו "בבקר בבקר" לדבר שלא נאמר בו אלא "בבקר"? וי"ל: אהא לא קשיא מידי, דאי לאו "העולה" — הוה דרשינן "מלבד" כדבעי למדרשי' ב"הגוזל קמא" (ב"ק דף קיא.). אלא אי קשיא — לישתוק מ"מלבד", ואי מיפסיל בכך — *נראה שפיר דמההוא לא שמעינן פסול. אי נמי: מ"יוקדם" לא שמעי' אלא שמצוה להקדים, אבל אם הקדים ושחט — יגמור. ומהכא שמעינן — דלא. ותימה: הא דאמרינן ריש ערובין (דף ב.): שלמים ששחטן קודם פתיחת דלתות ההיכל — פסולין. ותיפוק לי דא"כ, אקדמינהו קודם תמיד. דפשטא דמילתא משמע: קודם שנפתחו באותו יום. וכן נמי לקמן פרק "שתי מדות" (דף פט:): עולת תמיד ששחטה שלא לשמה — כשרה. ואמאי? הא קודם תמיד איתעביד! מיהו מהתם לא קשיא מידי — דשחיטה, לאו עבודה היא, דלא הויא בכלל עשיה. מיהו תימה: דאמרינן פ' "אמר להן הממונה" (יומא דף כט.) ופרק "שתי הלחם" (לקמן דף ק.): לא זו בלבד אמרו, אלא אפי' עולת העוף שנמלקה ומנחה שנקמצה — תצא לבית השריפה. וא"לילה" קאי. ותיפוק לי' דקמי תמיד עבדינהו, אבל משום קודם פתיחת דלתות ההיכל — לא מיפסלי, דלא כתיב בהו "פתח"! ושמא, כיון דהכתי לא מטא זמן תמיד — קרא לא איירי בהכי. אי נמי: לא מיפסיל בשביל כך, כדמסקינן הכא: למצוה בעלמא. וכן משמע פ' תמיד נשחט (פסחים דף נט:) דעשה דפסח ועשה דאכילת קדשים דחי לעשה דהשלמה דדרשינן "עליה השלם כל הקרבנות כולם", ואי הוה מיפסל לא שייך ביה דחייה, ו"עליה השלם" מהאי קרא (ויקרא ו) ד"וערך עליה העולה" הוא דדרשינן וכיון דהתם לא מיפסל הוא הדין הכא. וכן משמע נמי שלהי "מי שהיה טמא" ז] (שם דף לח.): בכור שנתערב בפסח, אם חבורת כהנים — יאכלו. ונתערבו מחיים קאמר, מדפריך בגמ': והא אין מביאין קדשים לבית הפסול [ופי' רש"י:] והוה ליה למימר ירעו עד שיסתאבו, וזמן שחיטת פסח אחר תמיד הוא, ואפי' הכי לא מיפסיל הבכור. וכן משמע נמי ב"האשה" (שם דף פח:): חמשה שנתערבו עורות פסחיהן [זה בזה], ונמצאת יבלת באחד מהן [כו'], ופטורין מלעשות (פסח ראשון ו) פסח שני. ופריך טובא: ונייתי פסח שני, וניתני במותר פסח! ח] ודחיק טובא לשנויי. והשתא, אי מפסיל, מאי קשיא ליה? הא פסח שני זמנו נמי אחר תמיד, דלא חשיב ליה בין דברים שבין פסח ראשון לפסח שני. ואם כן, אי שלמים הוי, דמותר הפסח קרב שלמים — הא מיפסלי! ואין לומר: דעשה דפסח דחי לעשה דהשלמה, דהא לא הוי אלא ספיקא בעלמא. ומיהו קשיא בהכי: כיון דאיכא איסורא דאורייתא, היכי מקריבין לכתחלה? ואין לומר: דמשום ספיקת פסח דחי ליה איסורא דאורייתא. ועו, דמסקינן התם דמשום סמיכה שבקינן ליה, דליכא נמי אלא מצוה בעלמא, וגבי בכור ט] דוחה נמי ([א] דבמותר הפסח איירי). לכך נראה: דודאי בתמיד של שחר, דכתיב "תעשו" — הוא דמעכבי עשיות דדם, אבל בתמיד של ערב — לא מעכבא אלא הקטרה. דכולי קרא בהקטרה איירי. וכן משמע בריש "תמיד נשחט" (שם דף נט.), דמוקי לה בחטאת העוף, שאין למזבח אלא דמה. אי נמי: בבהמה, ומעלה ומלינה בראשו של מזבח. ואי קרא לא איירי אלא בהקטרה — ניחא דלא מעכבא אלא הקטרה, ד"עליה השלם כל ההקטרות כולן" משמע. אבל אי מ"תעשו" נפיק, דמסתבר לאשווי תמיד של שחר לתמיד של ערב, מאי טעמא לא מעכבא נמי עשייה? והשתא ניחא דהני איירי בשלא הקטיר התמיד, דהקטרת אימורים — כל הלילה, כדדרשי' לעיל (דף כו:). [ב] והההוא דריש "תמיד נשחט" דמוקי לה בחטאת העוף, לא בעי לאוקומה כי האי גוונא — דאם כן, מאי דחייה איכא? אבל השתא, איכא דחייה מדרבנן מיהא, גזירה אטו הקטרה. מיהו בשמעתין מוכח דלא הוי אלא למצוה. ותימה: דבפ' "אלו דברים" (פסחים עג.) אמרינן: שחטו, ונודע שמשכו ידיהם קודם או שנטמאו — ישרף מיד. ופריך: ואי אמרת לא בעי עקירה — פסולו מחמת מאי הוי? ששחטו אחר תמיד של בין הערבים. אלמא, בהכי מיפסיל! וי"ל: דהאי דנשרף — לפי שלכתחילה אסור להקטירו, וממילא יפסל. והא דלאין מעלה ומלינה — דקסבר: לינה מועלת בראשו של מזבח. ואע"ג דהקטרת אימורים לא מעכב, כי אבדו כשר באכילה — הני מילי כי איתזו להקטרה, אבל הכא — הא לא איחזו. אי נמי: מדרבנן אסור י] ליזרק. ולפירוש זה לא קשיא מידי מה שמביא ריב"א, דתניא יא] בתוספתא דפסחים: כל הקדשים שהקריבן קודם תמיד של שחר, או שעיכבן אחר תמיד הערב — פסולין. והשתא, אי אמרת דמדרבנן פסילי שלא ליזרק — ניחא. מיהו "הקריבו" משמע שהקריב כולו, ואדרבה אי בשחטן איירי — קשיא קודם תמיד של שחר *)אפי' אסרינן ליזרק, אמאי פסלינן ליה?

*) נ"א אפילו מדרבנן אמאי אסורין ליזרק ופסלינן להו

הלא

ל"ק

ערכין יג.

ג"ז שם: פסחים נו. מגילה תענית פרק א

הגהות הב"ח

(א) רש"י ד"ה ושמע מינה וכו' דשבת קדוש:

רבינו גרשום

דאין מעכבין ואי זה שירצה יכול להקדים: אין פוחתין לעולם משישה טלאים המבוקרין ממום כשיעור שצריך לשבת ולב' ימים טובים של ראש השנה שחל להיות אחר השבת לצורך תמידין: היכי דמי דקאמר ששה ולא טפי אילימא דאית ליה כלומר שיכול למצוא כמה טלאים שהוא צורך א"כ אמאי קאמר ששה טלאים מבוקרין לשבת ולב' יו"ט טובא הוו כלומר הרבה יותר משישה מבוקרין היה צריך לצורך תמידיה ומוספיהן אלא לאו דליה ליה אלא לצורך התמידין וש"מ דתמידי דלמחר עדיפי ממוספי דהאידנא דהא שבקינן להו לצורך תמידי דלמחר ולא עבדינן מינייהו מוספין דשבת: לא לעולם דאית ליה כל צרכו והכי קאמר אין פוחתין משישה טלאים מבוקרין לעולם ואפילו בחול שאין בהן מוסף לצורך ימי השבוע ולא לצורך שבת וב' ימים טובים דווקא: ומני בן בג בג היא וכו'. מה פסח טעון ביקור ד' ימים דכתיב דברו אל כל עדת בני ישראל לאמר בעשור וגו' וכתיב והיה לכם למשמרת עד ארבעה עשר: א"ל רבינא לרב אשי ולמאי דאמרינן מעיקרא כדי לצורך שבת ושני ימים טובים הני ששה טלאים שבעה הוו צריכי דהא איכא תמיד דצפרא דחד בשבא [השתא קא מיירי בב' יו"ט שהן לפני שבת] לפי שבלילה אינו יכול לחזור אחר תמיד: ולטעמיך תמניא הוו צריך למיהוי ביחד דהא איכא דפניא דמעלי שבתא שהוא לפני ראש השנה וצפרא דתלתא בשבא הא לא קשיא דלבתר דאקריב ההוא דפניא דמעלי שבתא קאמר שצריך להיות ששה:

שיטה מקובצת

א] טובא הוו. פ"ה ששה לתמידים ושש עשרה למוספין. ולא נהירא שלעולם אין מוספין של ר"ה קריבין שני ימים שאם באו עדים קודם מנחה למחר חול ואם באו עדים לאחר המנחה אותו היום לא הקריבו (מנחתם) [מוספין] ונראה דלא דק דלא הוי אלא ארבע עשר. תו"ח [א"ה לא הבנתי דבריהם כי לפענ"ד דברי רש"י מכוונים ומדויקים דודאי ליכא אלא יום אחד ר"ה וז' כבשים דר"ח וח' כבשים משום ר"ה הרי י"ד ועיין רמב"ם ה' תו"מ פ"ט וב' כבשים למוסף דשבת הרי ט"ז. עכ"ה]: ב] דהא איכא צפרא דחד בשבתא: ג] ויבטל תמידין דיום טוב: ד] משום דמבוקרין: ה] ממתניתין דכל התדיר ו] בתר הכי דבתר מלבד: ז] טמא (דף לא ע"א) פסח שנתערב בבכורות: ח] במותר פסח ודחי דחוייא טובא: ט] וגבי בכור יש לדחות נמי דבמותר הפסח איירי: י] אסור ליזרוק: יא] בתוספתא דפסחים עיין תו"י יומא (דף כט ע"א):

הגהות צ"ק [א] דבמותר הפסח דמי: [ב] והא דמוקי לה בחטאת כו':

תַּנָּא אַ"זֹאת תּוֹרַת הָעוֹלָה" רִיבָּה סָמֵיךְ לֵיהּ. תָּנֵי רַבָּה בַּר בַּר חָנָה קַמֵּיהּ דְּרַב: אכִּבְשֵׂי עֲצֶרֶת שֶׁשְּׁחָטָן לְשׁוּם אֵילִים — כְּשֵׁרִין, וְלֹא עָלוּ לַבְּעָלִים לְשׁוּם חוֹבָה. אֲמַר לֵיהּ רַב: עָלוּ וְעָלוּ. אָמַר רַב חִסְדָּא: מִסְתַּבְּרָא מִילְּתֵיהּ דְּרַב בִּכְסָבוּר אֵילִים וּשְׁחָטָן לְשׁוּם כְּבָשִׂים, שֶׁהֲרֵי כְּבָשִׂים לְשׁוּם כְּבָשִׂים נִשְׁחֲטוּ. אֲבָל כְּסָבוּר באֵילִים וּשְׁחָטָן לְשׁוּם אֵילִים — לֹא, עֲקִירָה בְּטָעוּת הָוְיָא עֲקִירָה. *וְרַבָּה אָמַר: עֲקִירָה בְּטָעוּת לָא הָוְיָא עֲקִירָה. אָמַר רָבָא, (א) *וּמוֹתְבִינַן אַשְּׁמַעְתִּין: *הַכֹּהֲנִים שֶׁפִּיגְּלוּ בַּמִּקְדָּשׁ, גמְזִידִין — חַיָּיבִין, הָא שׁוֹגְגִין — פְּטוּרִין, וְתָנֵי עֲלָהּ: פִּיגּוּלָן פִּיגּוּל. הֵיכִי דָּמֵי? אִילֵימָא דְּיָדַע דְּחַטָּאת הִיא וְקָא מְחַשֵּׁב בָּהּ לְשׁוּם שְׁלָמִים — הַאי שׁוֹגְגִין? מְזִידִין הָווּ! אֶלָּא לָאו דִּכְסָבוּר שְׁלָמִים הוּא, וְקָא מְחַשֵּׁב בָּהּ לְשׁוּם שְׁלָמִים, וְקָתָנֵי: פִּיגּוּלָן פִּיגּוּל, אַלְמָא עֲקִירָה בְּטָעוּת הָוְיָא עֲקִירָה! אֲמַר לֵיהּ אַבַּיֵּי: לְעוֹלָם דְּיָדַע דְּחַטָּאת הִיא, וְקָא מְחַשֵּׁב בָּהּ לְשׁוּם שְׁלָמִים, וּבְאוֹמֵר מוּתָּר. מְתִיב ר' זֵירָא, *ר' שִׁמְעוֹן אוֹמֵר: כָּל מְנָחוֹת שֶׁנִּקְמְצוּ שֶׁלֹּא לִשְׁמָן — כְּשֵׁרוֹת, וְעָלוּ לַבְּעָלִים לְשׁוּם חוֹבָה, שֶׁאֵין הַמְּנָחוֹת דּוֹמוֹת לִזְבָחִים, שֶׁהַקּוֹמֵץ מַחֲבַת לְשׁוּם מַרְחֶשֶׁת — מַעֲשֶׂיהָ מוֹכִיחִין עָלֶיהָ שֶׁהִיא מַחֲבַת, חֲרֵבָה לְשׁוּם בְּלוּלָה — מַעֲשֶׂיהָ מוֹכִיחִין עָלֶיהָ שֶׁהִיא חֲרֵבָה. אֲבָל בִּזְבָחִים אֵינוֹ כֵּן, שְׁחִיטָה אַחַת לְכוּלָּן, קַבָּלָה אַחַת לְכוּלָּן, זְרִיקָה אַחַת לְכוּלָּן. הֵיכִי דָּמֵי? אִילֵימָא דְּיָדַע דְּמַחֲבַת הִיא, וְקָא קָמֵיץ לָהּ לְשׁוּם מַרְחֶשֶׁת — כִּי מַעֲשֶׂיהָ [א] מוֹכִיחִין מַאי הָוֵי? הָא מִיעֲקַר קָא עָקִיר לָהּ! אֶלָּא לָאו דִּכְסָבוּר מַרְחֶשֶׁת הִיא, וְקָא קָמֵיץ לָהּ לְשׁוּם מַרְחֶשֶׁת וְטָעָה, דְּהָכָא הוּא דְּמַעֲשֶׂיהָ מוֹכִיחִין עָלֶיהָ, הָא בְּעָלְמָא — עֲקִירָה בְּטָעוּת הָוְיָא עֲקִירָה! אֲמַר לֵיהּ אַבַּיֵּי: לְעוֹלָם דְּיָדַע דְּמַחֲבַת הִיא, וְקָא קָמֵיץ לָהּ לְשׁוּם מַרְחֶשֶׁת, וּדְקָא אָמְרַתְּ: כִּי מַעֲשֶׂיהָ מוֹכִיחִין עָלֶיהָ מַאי הָוֵי? רָבָא לְטַעְמֵיהּ, דְּאָמַר רָבָא: *מַחֲשָׁבָה דְּלָא מִינְכְּרָא — פְּסַל רַחֲמָנָא, מַחֲשָׁבָה דְּמִינְכְּרָא — לָא פְּסַל רַחֲמָנָא.§

מתני' הַתְּמִידִין דאֵין מְעַכְּבִין אֶת הַמּוּסָפִין, וְלֹא הַמּוּסָפִין מְעַכְּבִין אֶת הַתְּמִידִין, וְלֹא הַמּוּסָפִין מְעַכְּבִין זֶה אֶת זֶה. הלֹא הִקְרִיבוּ כֶּבֶשׂ בַּבּוֹקֶר — יַקְרִיבוּ בֵּין הָעַרְבַּיִם. אָמַר ר' שִׁמְעוֹן: אֵימָתַי? בִּזְמַן שֶׁהָיוּ אֲנוּסִין אוֹ שׁוֹגְגִין, אֲבָל אִם הָיוּ מְזִידִין וְלֹא הִקְרִיבוּ כֶּבֶשׂ בַּבּוֹקֶר — לֹא יַקְרִיבוּ בֵּין הָעַרְבַּיִם. ולֹא הִקְטִירוּ קְטוֹרֶת בַּבּוֹקֶר — יַקְטִירוּ בֵּין הָעַרְבַּיִם. אָמַר רַבִּי שִׁמְעוֹן: וְכוּלָּהּ הָיְתָה קְרֵיבָה בֵּין הָעַרְבַּיִם, שֶׁאֵין זמְחַנְּכִין אֶת מִזְבַּח הַזָּהָב אֶלָּא בִּקְטוֹרֶת הַסַּמִּים, [א] חוְלֹא מִזְבַּח הָעוֹלָה אֶלָּא בְּתָמִיד שֶׁל שַׁחַר, וְלֹא אֶת הַשּׁוּלְחָן טאֶלָּא בְּלֶחֶם הַפָּנִים בְּשַׁבָּת, יוְלֹא אֶת הַמְּנוֹרָה אֶלָּא בְּשִׁבְעָה נֵרוֹתֶיהָ בֵּין הָעַרְבַּיִם.§ **גמ'** בְּעָא מִינֵּיהּ ר' חִיָּיא בַּר אָבִין מֵרַב חִסְדָּא: *צִיבּוּר שֶׁאֵין לָהֶן תְּמִידִין וּמוּסָפִין, אֵי זֶה מֵהֶן קוֹדֵם? הֵיכִי דָּמֵי? אִילֵימָא תְּמִידִין דְּיוֹמֵיהּ וּמוּסָפִין דְּיוֹמֵיהּ — פְּשִׁיטָא, תְּמִידִין עֲדִיפִי, דַּהֲווּ לְהוּ [ב] תָּדִיר וּמְקוּדָּשׁ! אֶלָּא תְּמִידִין דִּלְמָחָר וּמוּסָפִין דְּהָאִידָּנָא: ג] תְּמִידִין עֲדִיפִי — שֶׁכֵּן תָּדִיר, אוֹ דִלְמָא מוּסָפִין עֲדִיפִי — דַּהֲווּ לְהוּ מְקוּדָּשׁ? אֲמַר לֵיהּ, תְּנִיתוּהָ: הַתְּמִידִין אֵין מְעַכְּבִין אֶת הַמּוּסָפִין, וְלֹא הַמּוּסָפִין מְעַכְּבִין אֶת הַתְּמִידִין, וְלֹא ד] (אֶת) הַמּוּסָפִין מְעַכְּבִין זֶה אֶת זֶה. הֵיכִי דָּמֵי? אִילֵימָא דְּאִית לֵיהּ, וּלְקַדֵּם — וְהָתַנְיָא: *)מִנַּיִן שֶׁלֹּא כיְהֵא דָּבָר קוֹדֵם לְתָמִיד שֶׁל שַׁחַר? ת"ל: °"וְעָרַךְ עָלֶיהָ הָעוֹלָה", וְאָמַר **)רָבָא: "הָעוֹלָה" — עוֹלָה רִאשׁוֹנָה! אֶלָּא

[נדרים לו.] גיטין נד:
זבחים ל: פ"ע

*) ב"ק קיא. תמיד כח: פסחים נח: יומא לג:
°ויקרא ו
**) [זבחים קג. ב"מ נה. כתובות קו:]

רש"י

תַּנָּא אַזֹּאת תּוֹרַת הָעוֹלָה ה] קָאֵי. תּוֹרָה אַחַת לְכָל הָעוֹלִים, שֶׁאִם עָלוּ — לֹא יֵרְדוּ. בְּמַסֶּכֶת נִדָּה בְּפֶרֶק "יוֹצֵא דּוֹפֶן" (דף מ.). וְהַאי דְּנָקַט בָּמָה — ו] אַסְמַכְתָּא וְסִימָנָא בְּעָלְמָא. לְשׁוּם אֵילִים. דְּאָמַר: "הֲרֵינִי שׁוֹחֲטָן לְשׁוּם אֵילִים". לַבְּעָלִים. לַצִּבּוּר. עֲקִירָה בְּטָעוּת. כְּגוֹן הַאי, דְּאִי הֲוָה יָדַע דִּכְבָשִׂים נִינְהוּ — הֲוָה שָׁחֵיט לְהוּ לְשֵׁם כְּבָשִׂים. וּמוֹתְבִינַן אַשְּׁמַעְתִּין. אַדִּידֵיהּ גּוּפֵיהּ קָא מוֹתִיב. מְזִידִין חַיָּיבִין. לְשַׁלֵּם לַבְּעָלִים דְּמֵי קָרְבָּן. פִּיגּוּלָן פִּיגּוּל (ב). דְּשׁוֹגְגִין, וְאֵין צָרִיךְ לוֹמַר דִּמְזִידִין. וּמְחַשֵּׁב בְּהוּ לְשׁוּם שְׁלָמִים. לְאוֹכְלָן שְׁנֵי יָמִים וְלַיְלָה אֶחָד, דְּהַשְׁתָּא חִישֵּׁב לֶאֱכוֹל חַטָּאת חוּץ לִזְמַנּוֹ, דְּפִיגּוּל הוּא, דְּדִין חַטָּאת יוֹם וְלַיְלָה. וּבְאוֹמֵר מוּתָּר. לְשַׁנּוֹת, דְּהַיְינוּ שׁוֹגְגִין. שֶׁנִּקְמְצוּ ז]. מַחֲבַת וּמַרְחֶשֶׁת — שְׁנֵי כֵּלִים הֵם: מַחֲבַת — ח] [ב] עָבָה וּמַעֲשֶׂיהָ קָשִׁין, וּמַרְחֶשֶׁת — עֲמוּקָּה וּמַעֲשֶׂיהָ רַכִּין. חֲרֵבָה. מִנְחַת חוֹטֵא, דִּכְתִיב (ויקרא ה): "לֹא יִתֵּן עָלֶיהָ שֶׁמֶן". וְרָבָא לְטַעְמֵיהּ. דְּאָמַר בְּפֶרֶק קַמָּא. מַחֲשָׁבָה דְּלָא מִינְכְּרָא. אִם הוּא מְכַזֵּב אִם לָאו — פָּסַל רַחֲמָנָא. מַחֲשָׁבָה דְּמִינְכְּרָא. שֶׁהוּא מְכַזֵּב — לָא פָּסַל רַחֲמָנָא. **מתני'** הַתְּמִידִין אֵין מְעַכְּבִין הַמּוּסָפִין. מְפָרֵשׁ בַּגְּמָרָא. וְכוּלָּהּ הָיְתָה קְרֵיבָה. כָּל [ג] ט] הַמִּנְחָה כּוּלָּהּ. שֶׁאֵין מְחַנְּכִין. בַּגְּמָ' מְפָרֵשׁ י] מַאן דְּבַר שְׁמֵיהּ. אֶלָּא בִּקְטוֹרֶת הַסַּמִּים [ד]. שְׁלֵימָה שֶׁל מָנֶה, וּבֵין הָעַרְבַּיִם. וּבַגְּמָ' מְפָרֵשׁ מְנָלַן. **גמ'** תָּדִיר וּמְקוּדָּשׁ. תָּדִיר — בְּכָל יוֹם, וּמְקוּדָּשׁ — שֶׁהַיּוֹם יוֹם טוֹב הוּא, דְּאִי לָאו יוֹם טוֹב — לֵיכָּא מוּסָף. וּמוּסָפִין לָא הָווּ אֶלָּא מְקוּדָּשׁ. לָשׁוֹן אַחֵר: תְּמִידִין מְקוּדָּשִׁים — קוֹדֶם מוּסָפִים, דִּתְמִידִין קָרְבֵי בְּרֵישָׁא. תְּמִידִין דִּלְמָחָר וּמוּסָפִין דְּהָאִידָּנָא. כְּגוֹן דְּיֵשׁ לָהֶם בְּשַׁבָּת שְׁנֵי כְבָשִׂים לְבַד הַתְּמִידִין, וְקָא מִיבַּעְיָא לֵיהּ: אִם יַקְרִיבֵם הַיּוֹם לְמוּסָפִין וְלֹא יְהוּ לוֹ יא] תָּמִיד לְמָחָר, אוֹ יַנִּיחֵם לְצוֹרֶךְ תָּמִיד מָחָר. מוּסָפִין דְּהָאִידָּנָא מְקוּדָּשׁ נִינְהוּ. דְּהַיּוֹם שַׁבָּת קוֹדֶשׁ, וּתְמִידִין דִּלְמָחָר — לָא הָווּ לְהוּ מְקוּדָּשׁ, דִּלְמָחָר — חוֹל. ל"א: מוּסָפִין הָווּ מְקוּדָּשׁ — קוֹדֶם תְּמִידִין, דְּמוּסָפִין יִקְרְבוּ הַיּוֹם, וּתְמִידִין לֹא יִקְרְבוּ הַיּוֹם עַד לְמָחָר. אִילֵימָא דְּאִית לֵיהּ. תְּמִידִין וּמוּסָפִין. וְלִיקְדַּם. קָאָמַר, דְּאֵין מְעַכְּבִין זֶה אֶת זֶה, דְּאִי בָּעֵי — תְּמִידִין קָרֵיב בְּרֵישָׁא, וְאִי בָּעֵי — מוּסָפִין מַקְרִיב בְּרֵישָׁא יב]. הָעוֹלָה. מַשְׁמַע: הָעוֹלָה תְּהֵא רִאשׁוֹנָה לְכָל הַקָּרְבָּנוֹת.

ר' רש"ק בכל הסוגיא רבה [קדושין כ: וש"נ]
[תוספתא' בפ"א זבחים ט:] לעיל ב:
לעיל ב:

תוספות

עקירה בטעות הויא עקירה. ל"ע: הא דתניא בתוספתא בפרק קמא דזבחים, כבשי ציבור ששחטן לשם כבשים, ונמלאו אילים – עלו לציבור לשם אילים. אילים של ציבור ששחטן לשם אילים, ונמלאו כבשים – עלו לשם כבשים. אלמא, עקירה בטעות – לא הויא עקירה! ושמא משום שלמי נדבה קאמר, ותנא הוא דלא מפרש יג].

וקא [ה] מפרש בה לשלמים. כלומר, לאוכלן שני ימים. וכפירוש הקונטרס.

מתיב ר' זירא ר' שמעון אומר. נראה דר' זירא לית ליה לא כרבה ולא כרב אשי דריש מכילתין (דף ב.), אלא טעמא דנפשיה קאמר כדמשמע. ולא מסיק אדעתא קושיא דר"ש אדר"ש. וצריך עיון.

תדיר ומקודש. לשון א' פירש הקונט': ביום קדוש. וכן משמע בסוף "כל התדיר" (זבחים דף צא.): אטו שבת למוסף אהני, לתמיד לא אהני?! וקלת קשה: דהתם לא מייתי הא, והכא לא מייתי ההיא דהתם! ולשון אחר פירש בקונטר': אותו שזמנו עכשיו מיקרי "מקודש". והא דנקט תמידין דלמחר ומוספין דהאידנא, דמשמע דתמיד של בין הערבים קודם למוסף, והא לא מקודש הוא! התם מטעמא אחרינא, דהכי קאמר רחמנא: כל היכא דאיכא אחד בבוקר – עשה שני בין הערבים.

תלמוד לומר וערך עליה העולה. תימה: דבפרק "כל התדיר" (שם דף פט.) נפקא ליה מדכתיב "מלבד עולת הבוקר תעשו את אלה" – מכלל דתמיד קרב ברישא! וי"ל: דקרא דהכא איצטריך למנחת חביתין, דאע"ג דתדיר. וכן משמע בפרק "אמר להם הממונה" (יומא דף לד.): איברין קודמין למנחה, דכתיב "וערך עליה העולה", ועל כרחך מנחת חביתין קאמר, דמנחת נסכים נפקא לן מדכתיב "עולה ומנחה", כדאיתא לעיל בפירקין (דף מד:). ופר' קמא דתמיד (דף כח:) נמי אמרינן: למימרא דחביתין קדמי, והתניא: "וערך" וכו', ומהכא גמרינן לכל מיני דמים דקדמי [ו] לחביתין, דתנן בפ' "כל התדיר" (זבחים ד' פט.): העופות קודמין למנחות, שהללו מיני דמים. ואי לא מהכא, מנא ליה הא? ומיהו קשיא: הכא אמאי לא מייתי מתניתין יד] [ז] דלענין מוספין איירי? דאין לומר: דהכא מיירי דאית ליה ולקדם, והתם איירי דלית ליה – דהתם נמי איירי דאית ליה, דומיא דדם חטאת קודם לדם עולה דתנן התם! וי"ל: משום דלא יהא דבר קודם משמע טפי עיכובא, אייתיה. מיהו תימה: דב"הגוזל קמא" (ב"ק דף קיא.) תנן: הביא [ח] אשמו עד שלא הביא גזילו – לא יצא. ומפרש בגמרא: משום דכתיב "מלבד איל הכפורים" – מכלל דכסף ברישא. ופריך: אלא מעתה, "מלבד עולת הבוקר" – הכי נמי דמוספין קרבי ברישא?! והתניא: "וערך עליה העולה"

עין משפט נר מצוה

קכז א ב מיי' פט"ו מהלכות פסולי המוקדשין הלכה טז [עקירה בטעות לא הוי עקירה וכתב הכ"מ משום דרבא דהוא בתרא ס"ל הכי ע"ש ריש פט"ו דין א' וכן דין טז בכ"מ]:
קכח ג מיי' פ"ז מהל' חובל ומזי' הל' ד:
קכט ד מיי' פ"ח מהל' תמידין ומוספין הלכה כ:
קל ה מיי' שם פ"א הלכה יב:
קלא ו ז מיי' פ"ג מהל' תמידין ומוספין הלכה א:
קלב ח מיי' שם פ"א הלכה יב:
קלג ט מיי' שם פ"ה הלכה ג:
קלד י מיי' שם פ"ג הלכה יא:
קלה כ מיי' שם פ"א הלכה ג:

הגהות הב"ח

א) גמ' אמר רבא שמעתי' זו ומותבינן שמעתיה הכהנים: ב) רש"י ד"ה פיגולן פיגול שוגגין וכו' במזידין הס"ד ואח"כ מ"ה וקא מחשב:

שיטה מקובצת

א] מוכיחין מאי הוי. קס"ד השתא דאין זה עיקר הטעם ומסיק דעיקר טעמא משום הכי הוא ורבה לטעמיה כו': ב] תדיר ומקודש. פ"ה ב' לשונות וקשה ללישנא (קמא) [בתרא] מאי בעי הא הוי פשיטא ליה דתדיר גרידא עדיף ממקודש ושמא דתדיר דלמחר לא אלים כתדיר דהיום. ומיהו לאו דוקא עדיף דהא כי פשיט בעיא לא פשיט אלא אלמא כי הדדי נינהו וא"כ הוא פשיט מאי דלא בעי מיניה דהוא בעי מיניה איזה מהן עדיף והוא פשיט כי הדדי נינהו אלא ודאי ה"ק או דלמא מוספין עדיפא דיש בהם כח לפי שהן מקודשין ולכל הפחות [צריכין] להיות שוין. תו"ח: ג] דהאידנא מאי: ד] תיבת את נמחק: ה] העולה סמיך תיבת קאי נמחק: ו] במה ס"א אין זה אלא גילוי מילתא בעלמא ליתן טעם דיש פסולין דאם עלו לא ירדו ויש דאפילו אם עלו נמי ירדו אבל עיקר הטעם אקרא סמיך: ז] שנקמצו כו': ח] מחבת צפה: ט] המנחה ס"א המנה: י] מפרש חנוך מאן: יא] יהו לו לתמיד: יב] ברישא. וא"ת התינח בתמידין אין מעכבין את המוספין דדין התמיד להקריבו תחלה ואם לא הקריבו אינו מעכב המוספין אלא מוספין אין מעכבין את התמידין היכא משכחת לה וי"ל דמשכחת לה בתמיד הערב דדין מוספין ליקרב תחלה ואם הקדים תמיד הערב למוספין אינו מעכב המוספין: יג] דלא מפרש וה"פ דמאי דאמרינן עלו לשם אילים היינו לשם שלמי נדבה ולא יצאו מידי חובתו והוה ליה כאילו אמר התנא כשרים ולא עלו אלא דלא פריש: יד] מתניתין דכל התדיר: טובא

רבינו גרשום

מרינן למזבח מינה ע"ג דלא הוי הכשירו אם עלה לא ירד: תנא הוא לא יליף מבמה לא אתורת העולה מיך שריבה לכל עולין שלא ירדו: ששחטן לשם אילים. סבור שהן בני שתים. לא עלו לבעלים לצבור: רבא אמר עקירה טעות לא הויא עקירה עלו לבעלים: מזידין ייבין לשלם דמי קרבן בעלים. הא שוגגין טורין מלשלם ותני לה אפילו שוגגין פיגולן] פיגול ובאומר ותר שסבור שמותר וא והיינו שוגג ועקירה דעת היא: ודקאמרת י מעשיה מוכיחין עליה אי הוי הא מעקר קא קר לה רבה לטעמיה דאמר מחשבה דמינכרא דלא הוי כדאמר הוא. לא פסל רחמנא משום הכי עלו לבעלים אבל בעלמא עקירה בטעות אכתי לא ידענא אי הויא עקירה אי לא הויא עקירה: התמידין אין מעכבין את המוספין שאם לא היה להם תמידין אלא מוספין אין מעכבין את המוספין אבל בתמידין ליכא מימר אין מעכבין זה את זה דלא קרבי תרי ביחד אלא אחד בבקר ואחד בערב: אמר רבי שמעון משום הכי לא הקטיר בבקר יקטיר בין הערבים דכולה היתה קריבה בין הערבים אפילו של שחר. כלומר עיקר תחילת הקטרה על המזבח בין הערבים היה שאין מחנכין וכו': תמידין הוה להו תדיר בכל יום. ומקודש דמיקדשו תמידין מקמי דליקדשו מוספין שהקרבת תמידין הוא קודם: אילימא דאית ליה לצורך תרויהו וליקדם כלו' דאין

הגהות צ"ק [א] נ"א של בין הערבים: [ב] נ"ל צפה: [ג] נ"א הקטורת וגי' הצ"ק המנה: [ד] של מנה שלימה: [ה] נ"ל מחשב: [ו] למנחות דתנן: [ז] דהתם דלענין: [ח] גזילו עד שלא הביא אשמו יצא:

עין משפט נר מצוה

קכג א מיי' פי"ב מהל' תרומות הלכה ז:
קכד ב מיי' פט"ו מהל' פסה"מ הלכה כ:

הך ר' יהושע ליתא בהך משנה דתרומות ועיין ר"ש בתרומות פ"ח משנה יא

קכה ג ד מיי' פ"ד מהל' פסה"מ הלכה כו:
קכו ה מיי' פט"ו מהל' פסה"מ הלכה כ:

גמרא

תֵּרֵד וְתִטַּמֵּא, וְאַל יְטַמְּאֶנָּה בַּיָּד. *וְר' יְהוֹשֻׁעַ אוֹמֵר: אאַף יְטַמְּאֶנָּה בַּיָּד! שָׁאנֵי הָתָם, דִּלְטוּמְאָה קָא אָזְלָא. כִּי אֲתָא רַב יִצְחָק תָּנֵי: כִּבְשֵׂי עֲצֶרֶת שֶׁשְּׁחָטָן שֶׁלֹּא כְּמִצְוָתָן — פְּסוּלִין, א] וּתְעוּבַּר צוּרָתָן וְיֵצְאוּ לְבֵית הַשְּׂרֵיפָה. אָמַר ב] רַב נַחְמָן: מָר דְּמַקִּישׁ לְהוּ לְחַטָּאת — תָּנֵי "פְּסוּלִין", תַּנָּא דְּבֵי לֵוִי דְּגָמַר שַׁלְמֵי חוֹבָה מִשַּׁלְמֵי נְדָבָה — תָּנֵי "כְּשֵׁרִים". *דְּתָנֵי לֵוִי: וּשְׁאָר בשַׁלְמֵי נָזִיר שֶׁשְּׁחָטָן שֶׁלֹּא כְּמִצְוָתָן — (כְּשֵׁרִין, וְלֹא עָלוּ לַבְּעָלִים לְשֵׁם חוֹבָה, ו)נֶאֱכָלִין לְיוֹם וְלַיְלָה, וְאֵין טְעוּנִין לֹא לֶחֶם וְלֹא זְרוֹעַ. מֵיתִיבֵי: *גאָשָׁם בֶּן שָׁנָה וְהֵבִיא בֶּן שְׁתַּיִם, בֶּן שְׁתַּיִם וְהֵבִיא בֶּן שָׁנָה — פְּסוּלִין, וּתְעוּבַּר צוּרָתָן וְיֵצְאוּ לְבֵית הַשְּׂרֵפָה. אֲבָל דעוֹלַת נָזִיר וְעוֹלַת יוֹלֶדֶת וְעוֹלַת מְצוֹרָע שֶׁהָיוּ בְּנֵי שְׁתֵּי שָׁנִים וּשְׁחָטָן — כְּשֵׁרִין. כְּלָלוֹ שֶׁל דָּבָר: כָּל הַכָּשֵׁר בְּעוֹלַת נְדָבָה — כָּשֵׁר בְּעוֹלַת חוֹבָה, וְכָל הַפָּסוּל בְּחַטָּאת — פָּסוּל בְּאָשָׁם, חוּץ מִשֶּׁלֹּא לִשְׁמוֹ! הַאי תַּנָּא, תַּנָּא דְּבֵי לֵוִי הוּא. תָּא שְׁמַע, *דְּתָנֵי לֵוִי: האֲשַׁם נָזִיר וַאֲשַׁם מְצוֹרָע שֶׁשְּׁחָטָן שֶׁלֹּא לִשְׁמָן — כְּשֵׁרִים, וְלֹא עָלוּ לַבְּעָלִים לְשׁוּם חוֹבָה. שְׁחָטָן מְחוּסַּר זְמַן בִּבְעָלִים, אוֹ שֶׁהָיוּ בְּנֵי שְׁתֵּי שָׁנִים וּשְׁחָטָן — פְּסוּלִין. ג] וְאִם אִיתָא, לִיגְמַר מִשְּׁלָמִים! שְׁלָמִים מִשְּׁלָמִים — גְּמַר, אָשָׁם מִשְּׁלָמִים — לָא גְּמַר. וְאִי גְּמַר שְׁלָמִים מִשְּׁלָמִים, לִיגְמַר נַמִּי אָשָׁם מֵאָשָׁם, אֲשַׁם נָזִיר וַאֲשַׁם מְצוֹרָע מֵאֲשַׁם גְּזֵילוֹת וַאֲשַׁם מְעִילוֹת, ד] אוֹ אֲשַׁם גְּזֵילוֹת וַאֲשַׁם מְעִילוֹת מֵאֲשַׁם נָזִיר וַאֲשַׁם מְצוֹרָע! אָמַר רַב שִׁימִי בַּר אַשִׁי: דָּנִין דָּבָר שֶׁלֹּא בְּהֶכְשֵׁירוֹ מִדָּבָר שֶׁלֹּא בְּהֶכְשֵׁירוֹ, וְאֵין דָּנִין דָּבָר שֶׁלֹּא בְּהֶכְשֵׁירוֹ מִדָּבָר שֶׁבְּהֶכְשֵׁירוֹ. וְלָא? וְהָא תַּנְיָא: *)מִנַּיִן לַיּוֹצֵא שֶׁאִם עָלָה, לֹא יֵרֵד? שֶׁהֲרֵי יוֹצֵא כָּשֵׁר בְּבָמָה!

תַּנָּא

*) לעיל ו: זבחים נא. סח: סט: פד:

רש"י

תֵּרֵד וְתִטַּמֵּא. אע"ג דְּמִיפַּסְדָא לְחוּלִּין, דְּעַד הָשְׁתָּא הָווּ חֲזוּ לֵיהּ בִּימֵי ה] טוּמְאָה, וְהָשְׁתָּא לָא חֲזוּ לְמִידֵּי. וְלֹא יְטַמְּאֶנָּה בַּיָּד. לְקַבְּלָהּ בְּכֵלִים טְמֵאִים, כְּדֵי לְהַצִּיל הַחוּלִּין. אַף ו] יְטַמֵּא בַּיָּד. אַלְמָא *"חֲטָא בִּתְרוּמָה, כְּדֵי שֶׁתִּזְכֶּה בְּחוּלִּין". דִּלְטוּמְאָה ז] אָזְלָא. אִם תִּפּוֹל בְּחוּלִּין נַמִּי אֲבוּדָה – ח] לָאו חוֹטֵא הוּא. כִּי אֲתָא רַב יִצְחָק תְּנָא שֶׁלֹּא כְּמִצְוָתָן. שֶׁלֹּא לִשְׁמָן. ל"א: ט] שֶׁדֵּינָן בְּנֵי שָׁנָה, וְהֵבִיא בְּנֵי שְׁתַּיִם. וּמִפִּי הַמּוֹרֶה שְׁמַעְתִּיהוּ, וּמִפִּי רוֹב הַגְּאוֹנִים, וְלָשׁוֹן אַחֲרוֹן אֵינוֹ כְּלוּם – דְּאִם כֵּן, מַאי "שֶׁשְּׁחָטָן"? "שֶׁהֱבִיאָן" מִיבָּעֵי לֵיהּ! וּתְעוּבַּר צוּרָתָן. לְפִי שֶׁאֵין שׂוֹרְפִין קָדָשִׁים עַד שֶׁיִּפָּסְלוּ בְּלִינָה, מִשּׁוּם בִּזְיוֹן קָדָשִׁים. אֶלָּא אִם כֵּן פְּסוּלוֹ בְּגוּפוֹ, כְּגוֹן פִּיגּוּל וְטָמֵא. דְּמַקִּישׁ י] (א) [א]. דִּכְתִיב גַּבֵּי חַטָּאת "וַעֲשִׂיתֶם שְׂעִיר עִזִּים אֶחָד לְחַטָּאת וּשְׁנֵי כְבָשִׂים בְּנֵי שָׁנָה לְזֶבַח שְׁלָמִים". תָּנֵי פְּסוּלִין. כְּחַטָּאת, דִּתְנַן: כָּל הַזְּבָחִים שֶׁנִּזְבְּחוּ שֶׁלֹּא לִשְׁמָן כְּשֵׁרִין, חוּץ מִפֶּסַח וְחַטָּאת. וּלְאִידָךְ לִישָּׁנָא מְדַמֵּי לְהוּ לְחַטָּאת שֶׁעָבְרָה שְׁנָתָהּ דִּפְסוּלָה, כִּדְתְנַן: חָמֵשׁ חַטָּאוֹת מֵתוֹת, בְּמַסֶּכֶת תְּמוּרָה (דף טו.). שַׁלְמֵי חוֹבָה מִשַּׁלְמֵי נְדָבָה. דִּכְשֵׁרִין שֶׁלֹּא לִשְׁמָן, דִּבְכְלַל כָּל הַזְּבָחִים הֵן. וּלְאִידָךְ לִישָּׁנָא: אִם נָדַר טָלֶה לִשְׁלָמִים, וְהֵבִיא אַיִל – כָּשֵׁר, כִּדְאָמְרִינַן בְּפֶ' "הֲרֵי עָלַי [עִשָּׂרוֹן]" (לקמן קז:): "קָטָן", וְהֵבִיא גָּדוֹל – יָצָא. רַבִּי אוֹמֵר: לֹא יָצָא, וַאֲפִי' רַבִּי מוֹדֶה דְּזֶבַח כָּשֵׁר. וּשְׁאָר שַׁלְמֵי נָזִיר (ב) יא] [ב]. דִּלְעֵיל מִינֵּיהּ קָאֵי אַקָּרְבְּנוֹת נָזִיר, בְּתוֹסֶפְתָּא דְּנָזִיר בְּפֶרֶק "נָזִיר שֶׁאָכַל אֶחָד מִכָּל הָאִיסּוּרִין". וְקָתָנֵי: הָרְאוּיִין לָבוֹא בֶּן שָׁנָה, וֶהֱבִיאוּ בֶּן שְׁתַּיִם; יב] שְׁתַּיִם, וֶהֱבִיאוּ בֶּן שָׁנָה – תִּגְלַחְתּוֹ פְּסוּלָה, וּזְבָחָיו לֹא עָלוּ לוֹ. וּשְׁאָר יג] שְׁלָמִים, כְּגוֹן שַׁלְמֵי נָזִיר דְּחוֹבָה הֵן, שֶׁשְּׁחָטָן שֶׁלֹּא כְּמִצְוָתָן, שֶׁלֹּא לִשְׁמָן. וּלְאִידָךְ לִישָּׁנָא: בֶּן שָׁנָה, דְּשַׁלְמֵי נָזִיר "אַיִל" כְּתִיב בְּהוּ, וְאַיִל – בֶּן שְׁתֵּי שָׁנִים. כְּשֵׁרִין. כְּשַׁלְמֵי נְדָבָה, וְנֶאֱכָלִין לְיוֹם וְלַיְלָה כְּחוֹמֶר שַׁלְמֵי נָזִיר, דְּדִינוֹ כְּדִין תּוֹדָה. דְּאָמַר מָר: "שְׁלָמָיו" – לְרַבּוֹת שַׁלְמֵי נָזִיר. וְאֵין טְעוּנִין לֹא לֶחֶם וְלֹא זְרוֹעַ. הוֹאִיל וְאֵין הַנָּזִיר נִיתָּר בָּהֶן. יד] קָתָנֵי מִיהָא "כְּשֵׁרִין", וְאע"ג דְּאִיתְקַשׁ לְחַטָּאת, דִּכְתִיב: "וְכַבְשָׂה אַחַת בַּת שְׁנָתָהּ תְּמִימָה לְחַטָּאת וְאַיִל אֶחָד תָּמִים לִשְׁלָמִים" (במדבר ו) – אַלְמָא, מִגְמַר שְׁלָמִים מִשְּׁלָמִים, חוֹבָה מִנְּדָבָה, עֲדִיף לֵיהּ. אָשָׁם בֶּן שָׁנָה. כְּגוֹן דְּנָזִיר טָמֵא וּמְצוֹרָע, דִּכְתִיב "כֶּבֶשׂ". בֶּן שְׁתַּיִם. כְּגוֹן גְּזֵילוֹת וּמְעִילוֹת, דִּכְתִיב טו] "אַיִל". עוֹלַת נָזִיר וְיוֹלֶדֶת וּמְצוֹרָע. דִּכְתִיב בְּהוּ "כֶּבֶשׂ". בֶּן שְׁתֵּי שָׁנִים כו' כְּשֵׁרִין. דְּגָמְרִינַן מֵעוֹלַת נְדָבָה דְּאִם נָדַר קָטָן, וְהֵבִיא גָּדוֹל – הַזֶּבַח כָּשֵׁר. חוּץ מִשֶּׁלֹּא לִשְׁמוֹ. דְּפָסוּל בְּחַטָּאת וְכָשֵׁר בְּאָשָׁם. וְקַשְׁיָא לְר' יִצְחָק, דְּקָתָנֵי בְּהֶדְיָא דְּגָמַר עוֹלַת חוֹבָה מֵעוֹלַת נְדָבָה. וְאע"ג דְּגַבֵּי חַטָּאת כְּתִיבֵי עוֹלַת מְצוֹרָע וְעוֹלַת נָזִיר – לָא מַקְשֵׁי לָהּ לְחַטָּאת לְמִיפְסְלִינְהוּ בְּנֵי שְׁתֵּי שָׁנִים, דְּמִגְמַר חוֹבָה מִנְּדָבָה עָדִיף. וְרַבִּי יִצְחָק נַמִּי – לִיגְמַר שַׁלְמֵי חוֹבָה מִשַּׁלְמֵי נְדָבָה, בֵּין טז] שֶׁלֹּא לִשְׁמוֹ בֵּין לְב' שָׁנִים! וְאִי קַשְׁיָא: מַאי שְׁנָא אָשָׁם יז] שֶׁלֹּא כְּמִצְוָתוֹ פָּסוּל יוֹתֵר מֵעוֹלָה? תָּרֵיץ: מִשּׁוּם דְּלָא אַשְׁכַּחַן אָשָׁם יח] נְדָבָה לְמִגְמַר מִינֵּיהּ. תַּנָּא דְּבֵי לֵוִי. דְּגָמַר חוֹבָה מִנְּדָבָה, וְלֹא גָּמַר חוֹבָה מֵחוֹבָה. מְחוּסַּר זְמַן בִּבְעָלִים. קוֹדֶם שֶׁיִּכְלוּ שִׁבְעַת יְמֵי סְפִירָתָן, דְּאֵין אָשָׁם אֶלָּא בְּנָזִיר טָמֵא. וְאִי אִיתָא. דְּגָמַר תַּנָּא דְּבֵי לֵוִי חוֹבָה מִנְּדָבָה, לִגְמַר אָשָׁם בֶּן שְׁתֵּי שָׁנִים מִשְּׁלָמִים דִּנְדָבָה בֶּן שְׁתֵּי שָׁנִים יט]! דָּנִין דָּבָר שֶׁלֹּא בְּהֶכְשֵׁירוֹ. כְּגוֹן כ] שַׁלְמֵי נְדָבָה שֶׁבָּאוּ שֶׁלֹּא בְּהֶכְשֵׁרָן, כְּגוֹן שֶׁלֹּא לִשְׁמָן אוֹ קָטָן וְהֵבִיא גָּדוֹל. וְאֵין דָּנִין דָּבָר שֶׁלֹּא בְּהֶכְשֵׁרָן. כְּגוֹן אֲשַׁם נָזִיר בֶּן שְׁתַּיִם, מִדָּבָר שֶׁבְּהֶכְשֵׁרָן – מֵאֲשַׁם גְּזֵילוֹת בֶּן שְׁתַּיִם, שֶׁהֲרֵי הֶכְשֵׁירוֹ בְּכָךְ (ג). יוֹצֵא בְּבָמָה. הֶכְשֵׁירוֹ בְּכָךְ, דְּהָא לֵיכָּא קְלָעִים.

תַּנָּא

תוספות

כבשי עצרת ששחטן שלא כמצותן פסולין. פירש בקונטרס: שלא לשמן. והא דתנן (זבחים דף ב.): כל הזבחים שנזבחו שלא לשמן – כשרין, חוץ מן הפסח והחטאת, ולא מפיק כבשי עצרת – דלא פסיק ליה לאפוקי שלמים. אי נמי: כי קתני – באין בגלל עצמן, באין בגלל אחס – לא קתני.

והא דלא ממעטינן להו מ"אותה לחטאת" כי היכי דממעטינן אשם – כיון דאיתקוש לחטאת, ואתו בהדיה, דכתיב (ויקרא כג): "ועשיתם שעיר עזים אחד לחטאת ושני כבשים". ותימה: מנא ליה דטעמא משום היקישא? דלמא הואיל ובאים להתיר חדש במקדש, ולא התירו, [ג] ואמאי איתותב רב בפ"ק (לעיל ד.)? וי"ל: דא"כ, ליתשוב [נמי] רב כבשי עצרת, והכא נמי ליתשוב מנחת העומר ואשם נזיר ומצורע. אי נמי: הלחם הוא המתיר, וכבשים דמתירין לחם – לא איקרו מתיר. אי נמי: לחם נמי לא מיקרי מתיר (היא), כיון דקודם לשתי הלחם אם הביא – כשר. ומיהו קשה לפי זה: דכי פריך בסמוך, ליפרוך מההיא דאייתינן לעיל, כבשי עצרת ששחטן שלא לשמן – הדם יזרק והבשר יאכל! וכל"א שפירש בקונטרס נראה, "שלא כמצותן" – בן שנה, והביאו בן שתים. כא] והא דלא נקט לשון הבאה דשייכא גבי בן שנה והביא בן שתים – משום דהוי שלא בזמנו ומחוסר זמן בכלל. ובתוספתא דנזיר קתני בהך דבסמוך "שהביאן שלא כמצותן".

תעובר צורתן. האי תנא – *דרבה בר אבוה הוא, כב] דאפי' פיגול בעינן *לורה. דבפ"ק דזבחים (דף ז.) קרינן לשינוי קודש "פסולו בגופו", ואיכא דאמרי: כל שפסולו בגופו – ישרף מיד. **ותנא** דבי לוי. לא מקיש להו לחטאת להא מילתא, אבל כולי עלמא אית להו לענין זכרי כהונה, פ' "איזהו מקומן" (זבחים דף נה.) לגבי כבשי עצרת. אבל לענין הא – לית ליה, דהא שלמי נזיר איתקשו לחטאת, ואפי' הכי סברי דכשרין.

איתיביה אשם בן שנה. הא דלא פריך ממתני' דפ' בתרא דזבחים (דף קיב:), דקתני בה: עולת נזיר ועולת מצורע קודם זמנו ששחטן בחוץ – חייבין. והיינו טעמא: משום דחזיא לעולת נדבה בפנים, וקודם זמנו לא חזי לנזיר ומצורע – לא דמי כלל להכא. דהתם – אינהו גופייהו חזו לעולה, אבל הכא – מייתינן דגמר חובה מנדבה. תימה: דבפ' "אלו קדשים" (תמורה דף יט:) *תנן: אשם בן שנה, והביאו בן שתים; בן שתים, והביאו בן שנה – כשרים, ולא עלו לבעלים לשם חובה. רבי שמעון אומר: כל עצמן אינם קדושים. והשתא, האי דקתני הכא "פסולין" – לא כרבי שמעון ולא כרבנן! ויש לומר: כדמשני פרק בתרא דזבחים (דף קטו.) דפריך מהא דתני לוי: אשם נזיר ואשם מצורע ששחטן מחוסר זמן בבעלים, ששחטן בחוץ – חייב. ומשני: כאן – לשמן, כאן – שלא לשמן. פירוש: שלא לשמן – כשרין, כג] לשמן – פסולין. כד] ומיהו קשה: לרב הונא, דאית ליה התם דליכא מידי דפסול לשמו, וכשר שלא לשמו, ומאי משני מהא? ואין לתרץ: בהפריש שתי אשמות לאחריות, כדמשני [ד] ארב דימי – דמדקתני "לא עלו" משמע דאין מצוה בכך! ותו: אמאי איצטריך למיתני כה] "לא עלו לבעלים לשם חובה" – פשיטא דלא עלו, כיון דשלא לשמן איתעביד! כו] *)

אשם נזיר ואשם מצורע ששחטן שלא לשמן כשרין. מהכא לא מצי לאוכוחי דילפינן אשם משלמים, מדמכשר בהו שלא לשמן – ד"אותה" דגבי חטאת הוא דממעט ליה. ולא דמי לשלמי ציבור – דלא ממעטינן מ"אותה" אלא קרבנות יחיד. והא דלא עלו לבעלים לשם חובה – מסברא הוא, ולא מטעם מילף. ואי "שלא כמצותן" דלעיל לאו היינו שלא לשמן – ניחא טפי. והא דכי אמרי לעיל "האי תנא דבי לוי הוא", לא בעי למיפרך מגופה: אמאי פסולין? דדלמא האי דמכשר עולה – דחזי לנדבה, אבל אשם דלא חזי לנדבה – מיפסל, ותנא אחרינא הוא. אבל מלוי אלוי פריך שפיר – דשלמי נזיר נמי לא חזו לנדבה, דטובא איתפליגו.

*) [וע"ע תוס' תמורה יט: ד"ה אשם בן שנה]

שיטה מקובצת

א] ותעובר צורתן. תימה הא אמרינן [בפסחים דף לד:] כל שפסולו בגופו ישרף מיד. ובן שנה שהביא בן שתים פסול בגופו וכן פסול שלא לשמה הוי פסול בגופו כדאמרינן (פ' כל שעה דף לד ע"ב) [בזבחים דף ז.] וי"מ בן שנה שהביא בן שתים לא חשבינן פסול בגופו והא דחשבינן ליה בזבחים (דף ז.) היינו לענין שינוי בעלים וי"מ דההיא דהכא אתיא כרבה דאפי' פגול טעון [עבור] צורה. לשון תוס' אחרות תימה הא אמרי' (בביצד צולין) [בפרק אלו דברים דף עג] כל שפסולו בגופו ישרף מיד בדם ובבעלים תעובר צורתן כו' וי"ל דפסול שלא לשמן קל הוא דנכשר בכל הזבחים הלכך לא חשבינן ליה פסול בגופו ולאידך לישנא דדינו בן שנה (ודינו) [והביא] בן שתים נמי קל הוא דכשר הוא בכל שלמי נדבה כדאמר לקמן בפ' (המנחות והנסכים) [הרי עלי עשרון] קטן והביא גדול יצא: ב] אמר ליה רב נחמן מר דמקיש. פ"ה דכתיב גבי חטאת כו' וקשה *) דה"מ [בחמש חטאות שעברה שנתה] ושכפר בעליה באחר ופי' הר"מ דמ"מ עברה שנתה פסולה ולא מכח הל"מ אלא משום דכתיב ביה הוא שצריך להביא בן שנה והוא שינה וכל שינוי פסול בו משום דכתיב ביה (הויא) [הוא] והשתא ניחא [מה] דקשיא לן (דריש) [בריש] פ"ק למה לי הוא מאותו נפקא והשתא איצטריך (לפסוק) [לפסול] בן שתי שנים. תו"ח: ג] ואם איתא ליגמר משלמים. וא"ת אמאי לא מותיב כמו כן מברייתא דלעיל דאוקימנא כתנא דבי לוי מרישא לסיפא דבסיפא יליף עולת נדבה מעולת חובה וא"כ אמאי פסול ברישא אשם בן שנה שקרבה בן שתים ליליף אשם משלמים וי"ל דלעיל מיירי ששחטו לשמו דלא דמי כלל לשלמים אבל הכא מיירי ששחטו שלא לשמו דהוי כשלמים. תו"ח: ד] ואשם מעילות וליהדר נמי אשם גזילות ואשם מעילות ליגמר מאשם נזיר ותיבת או נמחק: ה] בימי טומאתו: ו] אף יטמאנה ביד: ז] דלטומאה קאולא: ח] אבודה הלכך לאו: ט] ל"א שלא כדרכן דבעינן בני: י] דמקיש דכתיבא: יא] שלמי נזיר אלעיל מיניה קאי בקרבנות: יב] בן שתים בן שתים: יג] ושאר זבחים: יד] ניתר בהן ולא עלו לשם חובה: טו] דכתיב בהו: טז] בין לשלא לשמו: יז] אשם דשלא: יח] אשם בא: יט] שתי שנים: לגמור נמי אשם מאשם אשם נזיר ממעילה ומעילה מנזיר וליתכשרו כולהו בין בני שנה בין בני שתים: כ] בהכשירו כגון כשבי עצרת הבאים בני שתים שלא בהכשירו או שלא לשמן דלכשרו מדבר שלא בהכשרן כגון שלמי נדבה שלא לשמן או קטן והביא גדול דכשר וה"ה נמי עולת יולדת שלא בהכשרה מעולת נדבה שלא בהכשרה ותיבות שלמי נדבה שבאו שלא בהכשרן נמחק: כא] והא דלא נקט לשון הבאה. גליון כדבסמוך דשמא לשון שלא כמצותן נופל על לשון ששחטן בין לפני זמנם כו' ושמא י"ל דלאחר זמנם אין ר"ל בן שנה שהביא בן שתים או להפך לפי שזה פסול גדול אלא ר"ל קודם עצרת ולאחר עצרת: כב] דרבה בר אבוה הוא. פסחים דף לד ע"ב ודף עג ע"ב ולקמן דף נ ע"ב: כג] שלא לשמן כשרין. דהוי ככל הזבחים שנזבחו שלא לשמן דכשרים: כד] ומיהו קשה וכו' וי"ל דהיינו דווקא שסופו להיות ראוי לשמו אבל בן שנה והביא בן שתים אין סופו להיות בן שנה ובן שתי שנים שהביא בן שנה נהי דסופו להיות כשר לשמו לכשיגדל שמא לא ימתין או אם הפריש אחר. תו"ח. עי"ל דהתם מיירי אחר שניתק לרעייה דסתמא לשם עולה כשר דאשם מותרו עולת נדבה והכא מיירי קודם שניתק לרעייה ומש"ה פסולים כדפי' בפ"ק דמכילתין דגזרינן אחר כפרה אטו לפני כפרה: כה] למיתני בההיא דנזיר: כו] איתעביד אלא אפילו שחטן כדינן נמי כגון בן שנה שנה ובן שתים שתים כיון דשלא לשמן נשחטו לא עלו לבעלים לשם חובה:

רבינו גרשום

רביעית בטהרה בכלים טהורים יציל ואם לאו שאינו יכול להציל בטהרה תרד ותטמא בעצמה בחולין טמאין ותפסיד את החולין א). אלמא אמרינן עמוד וחטא בתרומה כדי שתזכה בחולין: שאני התם דלטומאה קא אזלא ממילא כשתרד בתחתונה משום הכי אף יטמאנה ביד: ששחטן שלא כמצוותן. כגון שהיו יתירין מבני שנה: מר משום הכי פסיל. דמקיש להו לחטאת מה חטאת שעברה שנתה פסולה אף הני נמי: תנא דבי לוי דגמר שלמי חובה היינו שלמי נזיר משלמי נדבה מה שלמי נדבה נדר זבח קטן והביא גדול יצא כדאמרינן בפרק הרי עלי עשרון אף שלמי נזיר וכבשי עצרת דהיינו שלמי חובה ששחטן שלא כמצותן יתירין מבן שנה כשרין ונאכלין ליום ולילה כשלמי נזיר ואינן טעונין לא לחם של המצות ולא זרוע בשלה הואיל ולא עלו לבעלים: אשם בן ב' שנים כגון אשם גזילות ומעילות שקרוי איל. כל הכשר בעולת נדבה דכשר בין ב' שנים בין בן שנה. כל הפסול בחטאת כגון בן ב' שנים פסול באשם חוץ משלא לשמו דפסול בחטאת ולא באשם. ושמעינן מיהא דכי היכא דיליף עולת חובה מעולת נדבה דכשרים הם הכי גמר שלמי חובה כגון כבשים משלמי נדבה דכשירין שלא כמצותן וקשיא לר' יצחק דאמר פסולין: האי תנא דהא ברייתא תנא דבי לוי היא: שחטן מחוסר זמן בבעלים שדרכן לשחט ביום השמיני לטהרתו ושחטן בשביעי: אשם נזיר ואשם מצורע. שהן בן שנה ליגמר מאשם גזילות ואשם מעילות מה הני בני ב' שנה וכשרין אף הני ליתכשרי בן ב' שנים ואשם גזילות מאשם נזיר מה אשם נזיר כשר בן שנה אף בגזלות נמי: דנין דבר שלא בהכשירו. שלמי חובה שלא כמצותן משלמי נדבה שלא כמצותן דכשרין ואין דנין דבר שלא בהכשרו אשם נזיר דאין כשר להביא בן ב' שנים מאשם גזילה דכשר להביא בתחלה בן שתי שנים דקרוי איל. והרי במה דיוצא כשר בה בתחלה וגמרי'

מסורת הש"ס

אמרינן חטא נ"ק

נזיר כד: תוספתא דנזיר פ"ד

תוספתא דזבחים פ"א [תמורה יט:]

זבחים קטו.

עקירה

*) נראה דל"ל דהא הלמ"מ הוא כחמש כו' באחר וכו' ופי' הר"מ ונראה שכוונתו למש"כ רש"י בשבת דף קלב. ד"ה עקיבא דכל י"ג מידות אין דנין מהלכה.

א) נראה דל"ל ור' יהושע אומר אף יטמאנה ביד כדי להציל את החולין אלמא אמרינן וכו'.

הגהות צ"ק [א] לחטאת דכתיב: [ב] אלעיל: [ג] כדאמר רב בפרק כנ"ל: [ד] רב הונא:

הגהות הב"ח (א) רש"י ד"ה דמקיש לחטאת דכתיב: (ב) ד"ה ושאר וכו' אלעיל מיניה וכו' בן שתים בן שתים: (ג) ד"ה ואין דנין וכו' בכך הס"ד ואח"כ מ"ה יוצא כשר בבמה והרי יוצא בבמה:

גליון הש"ס תוס' ד"ה תעובר כו' דרבה בר אבוה הוא. פסחים דף לד ע"ב:

והשאר נאכלות בפדיון. אמרוה רבנן קמיה דרב חסדא: א] הא – דלא כרבי. דאי רבי – כיון דאמר: שחיטה מקדשא, דפריק להו היכא? אי דפריק להו מאבראי – כיון דכתיב "לפני ה'" איפסיל להו ביוצא! אי גוואי – *הא מעייל *חולין לעזרה! אמר להו רב חסדא: לעולם כרבי, ופריק להו גוואי, וחולין ממילא קא הויין. אמר ליה רבינא לרב אשי, והתניא: כשהוא פודן, אין פודן אלא בחוץ! הא ודאי רבי אלעזר בר' שמעון היא, דאי רבי – הא איפסלו להו ביוצא. אמר ליה רב אחא בריה דרבא לרב אשי: לימא, תיהוי תיובתיה דר' יוחנן, (א) מיהא דאיתמר: *תודה ששחטה על שמונים חלות – חזקיה אמר: קדשו ארבעים מתוך שמונים, ור' יוחנן ^א אמר: לא קדשו ארבעים מתוך שמונים! ולאו מי איתמר עלה, אמר רבי זירא: הכל ^ב מודים היכא דאמר "ליקדשו ארבעים מתוך שמונים" דקדשה? הכא נמי דאמר "ליקדשו תרתי מתוך ארבע". תני ר' חנינא טירתא קמיה דר' יוחנן: שחט ארבעה ^ג כבשים על ב' חלות – ב] מושך שנים מהן, וזורק דמן שלא לשמן. שאם אי אתה אומר כך, הפסדת את האחרונים. אמר לו ר' יוחנן: *וכי אומר לו לאדם "עמוד וחטא בשביל שתזכה"?! והתנן: *אברי חטאת שנתערבו באברי עולה – ר' אליעזר אומר: יתנו למעלה, ורואה אני את בשר חטאת למעלה כאילו היא עצים. וחכמים אומרים: ^ד תעובר צורתן ויצאו לבית השריפה. אמאי? לימא "עמוד וחטא בשביל שתזכה"! "עמוד וחטא בחטאת בשביל שתזכה בחטאת" – אמרינן, "עמוד וחטא בחטאת בשביל שתזכה בעולה" – לא אמרינן. ובחדא מילתא מי אמר? והא *תניא: ^ה כבשי עצרת ששחטן שלא לשמן, או ששחטן בין לפני זמנן בין לאחר זמנן – ג] הדם יזרק והבשר יאכל. ואם היתה שבת – לא יזרוק, ואם זרק – הורצה להקטיר אימורין לערב. ואמאי? לימא "עמוד חטא בשביל שתזכה"! "עמוד חטא בשבת כדי שתזכה בשבת" – אמרינן, "עמוד חטא בשבת כדי שתזכה בחול" – לא אמרינן. ובתרתי מילי לא אמר? *)והתנן: חבית (א) ד] של תרומה שנשברה בגת העליונה ה] ובתחתונה חולין טמאין – מודה רבי אליעזר ור' יהושע שאם יכול להציל ממנה רביעית בטהרה – יציל. ואם לאו – ר' אליעזר אומר: תרד

*) פסחים טו. תרומות פ"ח משנה ט

רש"י

והשאר נאכלות בפדיון. כדמפרש ואזיל. הא דלא כרבי. אלא כרבי אלעזר בר' שמעון, דאמר: שחיטה לא מקדשא. לפיכך אפשר להו בתקנה זו קודם זריקה, שעדיין אין להם שום קדושת הגוף, והרי הן כתחלתן. ומושך איזה שנים שירצה, וזורק הדם עליהן ומקדשן, ומתירן. ואלו שנשארו בקדושת דמים שלהן – אסורות עד שיפדו. ופודן ככל קדושת דמים, ואוכל כל ו] מה שירצה. דאי רבי כיון דאמר שחיטה מקדשא. נהי דשתים מהן אין להן אלא קדושת דמים, וישנן בפדיה, דכבשים – מידי דחזו להו קמקדשי, ואינך – קדושת דמים בעלמא עלייהו, ונפקי לחולין. ומביא מעות, ואומר: "בכל מקום שהן השתים שאינן מקודשות – יתחללו על מעות הללו". ובלא פדיה לא מתאכלי, דלא שריא להו זריקת הכבשים. מיהו, היכא פריק להו, והיכי משתרו? והרי אינו מכיר אלו הן שאינן מקודשות! ואי מפיק להו לכולהו אבראי. ופריק להו לתרתי מינייהו. כיון דכתיב. בשתי הלחם. לפני ה'. "והניף הכהן אותם על לחם הבכורים" וגו' (ויקרא כג), שמע מינה פנים נינהו. איפסלו להו. המקודשות ביוצא, ומתוך שאין אתה מכירן – הרי כולם פסולות. ואי דפריק להו גואי. ואוכלן ז] כהן בפנים לארבעתן, השתים חולין והשתים קודש – קמעייל חולין לעזרה! ממילא הויין. דתוך העזרה הן נעשין חולין, והוא לא הכניסן משנעשו חולין. והתניא אין פודן אלא בחוץ. משום חולין לעזרה. הא ודאי. ח] דקתני "פודן בחוץ" – דלא כרבי. ועושה תקנה זו קודם זריקה, ומושך איזו שתים ט] שירצה. והוא הדין דהוה מצי למיפרך ברישא: דאי רבי – י] ארבעתן בעי לאנופי בהדייהו, דהא לא ידע מי הן יא] דקדושות! ומיהו דאלימא מיניה אקשי ליה, עד דאפקיה (ג) מטעמיה. לא קדשו יב] לה כלל. והכא נמי, אמאי קדשו שתי חלות מתוך ארבע? הכל מודים כו'. ואע"ג דלא (ד) פריש הי מינייהו. טוראתא. שם מקום. ד' כבשים. ואין הדין אלא שנים. שאם אי אתה אומר כן. לזרוק את שלא לשמה תחילה, אלא את לשמו תחילה. הפסדת את האחרונים. כדאמר לעיל (דף מז:): אין לך דבר שנראה יג] לשמן, ונדחה מלשמן, כגון הני דמשזרק ראשונים לשמן – תו לא חזו הנך לשמן, וכיון יד] דנדחה מלשמן – אין כשרין שלא לשמן כשאר כל הזבחים טו]. ל"א: שאם אי אתה אומר כן אלא ארבעתן לשמן – הפסדת את הנזרקים באחרונה, דהא לא נריכי, ופסולין. עמוד (ה) חטא. טז] ושלא לשמן – חוטא הוא, דאסור לשנות בזבחים. בשביל שתזכה. לאכול את השנים. אברי חטאת. הנאכלין לכהנים. שנתערבו באברי עולה. העולים [א] למזבח – ינתנו למעלה כולם על המערכה. ואמאי. ילאו לבית השריפה? לימא עמוד חטא. והעלה למזבח חטאת שאינה ראויה לו, בשביל שתזכה שלא להפסיד עולה. חטא בחטאת לזכות בחטאת. כגון לעיל בכבשים, שחוטא בעצמו וזוכה בעצמו אמר. לפני זמנן. קודם עצרת. לאחר זמנן. לאחר עצרת. הדם יזרק. שלא לשמן. ואם היתה שבת. דשלא לשמן קאי, ועצרת שבת. ואם זרק הורצה ע"מ להקטיר אימורין לערב. אבל היום – לא יקטיר אימורין לערב ותאכל יז] בשר. ואמאי אמר "לא יזרוק", ונפסל הדם בשקיעת החמה? כבשים דזוכה יח] בהן בו ביום. חבית של תרומה *)[שנשברה בגת] העליונה. התחתונה שיש שם חולין טמאין. מודה רבי אליעזר ורבי יהושע כו'. אע"ג דקיים [illegible] טהור לקבל, או אפי' רביעית – יציל, ואע"פ שבין כך ובין כך תפול התרומה [illegible]

*) גי' צ"ק

תוספות

כיון דכתיב לפני ה' אפסיל ליה ביוצא. אע"ג דגבי לחמי תודה נמי כתיב "לפני ה'" (ויקרא ז) ונאכלין בכל העיר – הכי קאמר: כיון דכתיב "לפני ה'", אלמא בעינן פנים, ומיפסיל ביוצא מדאיתקש לחטאת, כדאמר ב"איזהו מקומן" (זבחים דף נה.), ופרק "התערובות" (שם עז.) מייתי כה"ג, וגרסינן: "אי אבראי – איפסילו ביוצא". *לעולם כרבי. ואין התנור מקדש – כיון דלא [ב] יט] קדשי כולהו, כ] כדפרישית. אי נמי: כמאן דאמר (לעיל דף ז.): אין כלי שרת מקדשין אלא מדעת. הא דלא כרבי. משמע דלרבי אלעזר ברבי שמעון לא מקדשא שחיטה כלל, אלא זריקה. דאי מקדשא – היאך מושך אחר שחיטה? דילמא הני לא קידשה השחיטה! כא] ונראה שמקדשת הכל, [ג] [ולא] כמו גמר קדושה. אבל לרבי שהוא גמר קדושה – אי אפשר לקדש זה בלא זה. מושך שנים מהן וזורק דמן שלא כב] לשמה. תימה: הא כיון דהוזקקו בשחיטה, אבד הלחם – אבדו הכבשים, אבדו הכבשים – אבד הלחם! וי"ל: דשחיטה דהני כבשים – לא קבעה, כיון דלא נתברר מי הם המוקדשין, וכולהו לא חזו.

חטא בחטאת בשביל שתזכה בחטאת אמרינן. ואפילו היה עובר, דומיא [ד] דעולה דעובר בלאו ד"כל שממנו לאישים הרי הוא בבל תקטירו". [illegible]

או ששחטן בין לפני זמנן בין לאחר זמנן. [illegible] דבי לוי [ה] דסמוך, דלמאן דפסל [illegible]

חטא בשבת בשביל שתזכה בשבת. תימה: יזרוק כדי לאוכלן מי, דכי האי גוונא תנן פרק "שתי הלחם" (לקמן דף צה:)! כד] וי"ל: דאין זה זכות, ואין לחטא בכך. ואין [illegible] כבשי

עין משפט נר מצוה

קיט א ב מיי' פי"ב מהלכות פסה"מ הלכה טו.

קכ ג מיי' פ"ח מהל' תמידין ומוספין הלכה יג.

קכא ד מיי' פ"ו מהל' פסה"מ הלכה כ.

קכב ה מיי' פט"ו מהל' פסה"מ הלכה יט.

[illegible]

מסורת הש"ס

[illegible]

שיטה מקובצת

[illegible]

רבינו גרשום

[illegible]

[illegible]

הגהות צ"ק

[illegible]

הגהות הב"ח

[illegible]

קיג א מיי' פ"ו מהל' מעילה הלכה ה:
קיד ב מיי' פ"ח מהלכות פסה"מ הלכה לג:
קטו ג מיי' פ"ג מהל' מעילה הלכה ג:
קטז ד מיי' פ"ו מהל' פסה"מ הלכה כ:
קיז ה מיי' פט"ו מהל' פסה"מ הל' יח:
קיח ו מיי' פ"ח מהלכות תמידין ומוספין הלכה יג:

מסורת הש"ס

*דְּתְנַן: אֵימוּרֵי קָדָשִׁים קַלִּים שֶׁיָּצְאוּ לִפְנֵי זְרִיקַת דָּמִים — ר' אֱלִיעֶזֶר אוֹמֵר: אֵין מוֹעֲלִין בָּהֶן, וְאֵין חַיָּיבִין עֲלֵיהֶן מִשּׁוּם פִּיגּוּל וְנוֹתָר וְטָמֵא. ר"ע אוֹמֵר: אמוֹעֲלִין בָּהֶן, בוְחַיָּיבִין עֲלֵיהֶן מִשּׁוּם פִּיגּוּל וְנוֹתָר וְטָמֵא. מַאי? מִדִּזְרִיקַת פִּיגּוּל קָבְעָה לַלֶּחֶם בְּפִיגּוּל א] בְּיוֹצֵא כְּבָשָׂר, זְרִיקָה שֶׁלֹּא לִשְׁמָהּ נַמִי שָׁרְיָא לֵיהּ לַלֶּחֶם. אוֹ דִּלְמָא, לְחוּמְרָא — אָמְרִינַן, ב] לְקוּלָּא — לָא אָמְרִי'? מַתְקִיף לָהּ רַב פַּפָּא: *וּמִמַּאי ג] דְּכִי אִיתְנְהוּ אַבְּרַאי פְּלִיגִי? דִּילְמָא בְּדְאִיתְנְהוּ אַבְּרַאי — דְּכ"ע לָא פְּלִיגִי דְּאֵין זְרִיקָה מוֹעֶלֶת לְיוֹצֵא. וּבַהֲדַר עָיְילִינְהוּ פְּלִיגִי, דְּרַבִּי אֱלִיעֶזֶר סָבַר לָהּ כְּרַבִּי, דְּאָמַר: שְׁחִיטָה מְקַדְּשָׁא, וְאִיפַּסְלוּ לְהוּ בְּיוֹצֵא. וְר"ע כְּר' אֶלְעָזָר בְּר' שִׁמְעוֹן, דְּאָמַר: שְׁחִיטָה לָא מְקַדְּשָׁא, וְלָא מִיפַּסְלֵי בְּיוֹצֵא! הַאי מַאי? אִי אָמְרַתְּ בִּשְׁלָמָא ר"ע כְּרַבִּי ס"ל, דְּאָמַר: שְׁחִיטָה מְקַדְּשָׁא לְהוּ — ד] הַיְינוּ דְּקָאָמַר ר' עֲקִיבָא דְּקָדְשִׁי לְהוּ בִּשְׁחִיטָה, וְאָתְיָא זְרִיקָה קָבְעָה לְהוּ בְּפִיגּוּל. אֶלָּא אִי אָמְרַתְּ כְּר' אֶלְעָזָר בְּר' שִׁמְעוֹן ס"ל, דְּאָמַר: זְבִיחָה לָא מְקַדְּשָׁא, זְרִיקַת פִּיגּוּל מִי מְקַדְּשָׁא? *וְהָאָמַר רַב גִּידֵּל, אָמַר רַב: גזְרִיקַת פִּיגּוּל אֵינָהּ מְבִיאָה לִידֵי מְעִילָ' וְאֵינָהּ מוֹצִיאָה מִידֵי מְעִילָ'. אֵינָהּ מְבִיאָה ה] לִידֵי מְעִילָה — בְּאֵימוּרֵי קָדָשִׁים קַלִּים, ו] וְאֵינָהּ מוֹצִיאָה מִידֵי מְעִילָה — בִּבְשַׂר קָדְשֵׁי קֳדָשִׁים! ז] לָאו אִיתּוֹתַב דְּרַב גִּידֵּל אָמַר רַב?! בְּעָא מִינֵּי' ר' יִרְמְיָ' מִר' זֵירָא: דכִּבְשֵׂי עֲצֶרֶת שֶׁשְּׁחָטָן לִשְׁמָן וְאָבַד הַלֶּחֶם, מַהוּ שֶׁיִּזְרוֹק דָּמָן שֶׁלֹּא לִשְׁמָן לְהַתִּיר ח] בָּשָׂר בַּאֲכִילָה? א"ל: *יֵשׁ לְךָ דָּבָר שֶׁאֵינוֹ כָּשֵׁר לִשְׁמוֹ, וְכָשֵׁר שֶׁלֹּא לִשְׁמוֹ?! וְלָא? וַהֲרֵי הפֶּסַח קוֹדֶם חֲצוֹת, דְּאֵינוֹ כָּשֵׁר לִשְׁמוֹ וְכָשֵׁר שֶׁלֹּא לִשְׁמוֹ! הָכִי קָא אָמֵינָא: יֵשׁ לְךָ דָּבָר שֶׁנִּרְאֶה לִשְׁמוֹ וְנִדְחֶה מִלִּשְׁמוֹ, וְאֵינוֹ כָּשֵׁר לִשְׁמוֹ וְכָשֵׁר שֶׁלֹּא לִשְׁמוֹ? וְלָא? וַהֲרֵי פֶּסַח אַחַר ט] זְמַנּוֹ בִּשְׁאָר יְמוֹת הַשָּׁנָה (קוֹדֶם חֲצוֹת!) הָכִי קָאָמֵינָא: יֵשׁ לְךָ דָּבָר שֶׁנִּרְאֶה לִשְׁמוֹ וְנִשְׁחַט לִשְׁמוֹ וְנִדְחֶה מִלִּשְׁמוֹ, וְאֵינוֹ כָּשֵׁר לִשְׁמוֹ וְכָשֵׁר שֶׁלֹּא לִשְׁמוֹ? וְלָא? וַהֲרֵי תוֹדָה! *שָׁאנֵי תוֹדָה, דְּרַחֲמָנָא קַרְיֵיהּ "שְׁלָמִים". ת"ר: ושָׁחַט שְׁנֵי כְבָשִׂים עַל אַרְבַּע חַלּוֹת — מוֹשֵׁךְ שְׁתַּיִם מֵהֶן וּמְנִיפָן, וְהַשְּׁאָר

רש"י

קָדָשִׁים קַלִּים. מָמוֹן בְּעָלִים הֵן, וְאֵין בָּהֶן י] מְעִילָה אֶלָּא בָּאֵימוּרִים, כִּדְאָמְרִינַן בְּפֶ' "כָּל הַבָּשָׂר" בְּסוֹפוֹ (חולין דף קיז.): "כָּל חֵלֶב לַה'" — לְרַבּוֹת אֵימוּרֵי קָדָשִׁים קַלִּים לִמְעִילָה. אֵין מוֹעֲלִין בָּהֶם. דְּלָא יא] מְעַלְּיָא בְּהוּ הַךְ זְרִיקָה לְבָרֵר אוֹתָם לְחֵלֶק גָּבוֹהַּ, דְּאֵין זְרִיקָה מוֹעֶלֶת לְיוֹצֵא. וּפִיגּוּל נַמִי לֵית בְּהוּ — דְּהָא פְּסוּלִין הֵן כְּבָר יב]. מַאי. כְּלוֹמַר, אַלִּיבָּא דְּר"ע מִיבַּעְיָא לֵיהּ לְרַבִּי שְׁמוּאֵל בַּר רַב יִצְחָק: מַאי? מִדִּזְרִיקַת פִּיגּוּל [א] קָבַע לֵי' לַלֶּחֶם בְּפִיגּוּל, וְאע"ג דִּזְרִיקָה פְּסוּלָה הִיא, דְּהָא יוֹצֵא הוּא — קָבְעָה לַלֶּחֶם בְּפִיגּוּל [ב], כִּי יג] בָּשָׂר — כְּבָשָׂר שֶׁלֹּא יָצָא. אַלְמָא לֶחֶם כְּגוּף הַכְּבָשִׂים, דִּכִי הֵיכִי דְּגוּף הַכְּבָשִׂים — מְפוּגָּלִים, לֶחֶם נַמִי — מְפוּגָּל. זְרִיקָה שֶׁלֹּא יד] לִשְׁמָן נַמִי דִּפְסוּלָה הִיא — טו] שָׁרֵי לְהוּ, דְּהָא קיי"ל (זבחים ד' ב.): כָּל הַזְּבָחִים שֶׁנִּזְבְּחוּ שֶׁלֹּא לִשְׁמָן — כְּשֵׁרִים, וְלֶחֶם נַמִי כְּגוּף הַכְּבָשִׂים דָּמוּ, טז] וּמִדִּכְבָשִׂים נֶאֱכָלִין — לֶחֶם נַמִי נֶאֱכָל. אוֹ דִּלְמָא לְחוּמְרָא יז] [ג] אָמְרִי' לְקוּלָּא. לִהְיוֹת לֶחֶם נֶאֱכָל — לָא אָמְרִי' לְעִנְיַן זְרִיקָה שֶׁאֵינָהּ הוֹגֶנֶת כְּגוֹן שֶׁלֹּא לִשְׁמָן דְּלֶיהֱוֵי לֶחֶם כְּגוּף הַכְּבָשִׂים, לִהְיוֹת לֶחֶם נֶאֱכָל כִּכְבָשִׂים [ד]. וּמִמַּאי דְּבְאִיתְנְהוּ. לִשְׁתֵּי הַלֶּחֶם אַבְּרַאי בִּשְׁעַת זְרִיקָה פְּלִיגִי רַבִּי אֱלִיעֶזֶר וְר"ע, דְּתֵימָא: אֲפִי' בִּזְרִיקָה שֶׁאֵינָהּ הוֹגֶנֶת מְדַמֵּי ר"ע לְלֶחֶם כְּגוּף הַכְּבָשִׂים. דִּילְמָא בְּדְאִיתְנְהוּ אַבְּרַאי, דְּהָוְיָא זְרִיקָה שֶׁאֵינָהּ הוֹגֶנֶת — [ה] דְּכ"ע (א) לָא מִקְבַּע לֶחֶם בְּפִיגּוּל, דְּאֵין זְרִיקָה מוֹעֶלֶת לְיוֹצֵא. וְאע"ג דִּפְלִיגֵי בְּאֵימוּרֵי קָדָשִׁים קַלִּים — יח] דְּהָתָם כִּי [ו] גּוּפֵיהּ דְּזֶבַח דָּמוּ, יט] וּמוֹדֶה ר"ע דְּלֶחֶם לָא הָוֵי כְּגוּף שֶׁל כְּבָשִׂים, וּבִזְרִיקָה שֶׁלֹּא כ] לִשְׁמָן — נַמִי [ז] לָא מִשְׁתְּרֵי כא] כְּבָשִׂים לְלֶחֶם. אֶלָּא ר"ע סָבַר כְּרַבִּי אֶלְעָזָר בְּר' שִׁמְעוֹן דְּאָמַר: לָא קַדְּשִׁתִּינְהוּ שְׁחִיטָה, וְלָא אִיפְּסוּל בְּיוֹצֵא. הִלְכָּךְ, הֲוַאי זְרִיקָה הוֹגֶנֶת שֶׁאֵין בָּהּ פְּסוּל אַחֵר, הִלְכָּךְ מִקְבַּע לֶחֶם בְּפִיגּוּל. וְדִכְוָותַהּ הֵיכָא דְּלֵיכָּא כב] פְּסוּל, וְאִיזְרִיק לֵיהּ זְרִיקָה הוֹגֶנֶת, כְּגוֹן לִשְׁמָן — מִשְׁתְּרֵי לֶחֶם כג] כְּמוֹ כְּבָשִׂים, אֲבָל בִּזְרִיקָה שֶׁלֹּא לִשְׁמָן — [ח] לָא. אֶלָּא אִי אָמְרַתְּ כְּר' אֶלְעָזָר וכו'. אַכַּתִּי אִיכָּא לְמִיפְרַךְ כד]. זְרִיקַת פִּיגּוּל מִי מְקַדְּשָׁא. לְמִיקְבַּע בְּפִיגּוּל, אִי לָא קָדוֹשׁ מֵעִיקָּרָא בִּשְׁחִיטָה? כה] דְּאָמַר רַב גִּידֵּל זְרִיקַת פִּיגּוּל אֵינָהּ מְבִיאָה לִידֵי מְעִילָה. בְּאֵימוּרֵי קָדָשִׁים קַלִּים, דְּמָמוֹן בְּעָלִים הוּא, דְּלֵית בְּהוּ מְעִילָה. דְּלָא קָרֵינָא בֵּיהּ "מִקָּדְשֵׁי ה'" עַד לְאַחַר זְרִיקָה, דְּהוּבְרַר בָּשָׂר לְהֶדְיוֹט וְחֵלֶב לַגָּבוֹהַּ, דְּקָרֵינָא בֵּיהּ כו] חֵלֶב "קָדְשֵׁי ה'" [ט], אִם זְרִיקַת פִּיגּוּל לָא מִקְבַּע בִּקְדוּשָּׁה לִמְעוֹל בָּהֶן, דְּלָא זְרִיקָה כְּשֵׁרָה הִיא. וְאֵינָהּ יוֹצְאָה. מִידֵי מְעִילָה [י] בִּבְשַׂר קָדְשֵׁי קָדָשִׁים, דְּמָמוֹן גָּבוֹהַּ הֵם מֵחַיִּים, וְיֵשׁ בָּהֶן מְעִילָה קוֹדֶם זְרִיקַת דָּם. וּזְרִיקַת דָּם הוֹצִיאָה הַבָּשָׂר מִידֵי מְעִילָה, שֶׁהֲרֵי מַתִּירָתוֹ לַכֹּהֲנִים. וְאָמַר בְּמַסֶּכֶת מְעִילָה (דף ב.): כְּלָל אָמַר ר' יְהוֹשֻׁעַ: כָּל שֶׁיֵּשׁ לוֹ שְׁעַת הֶיתֵּר לַכֹּהֲנִים — אֵין מוֹעֲלִין בָּהֶן, וְכָל שֶׁאֵין לוֹ שְׁעַת הֶיתֵּר לַכֹּהֲנִים — מוֹעֲלִין בָּהֶן. הַךְ זְרִיקַת פִּיגּוּל לָא מַפְקַע לְהוּ מִידֵי מְעִילָה — אַלְמָא לָאו זְרִיקָה הִיא. וְהַנֵּי כִּבְשֵׂי עֲצֶרֶת נַמִי, כֵּיוָן דְּלָאו זְרִיקָה הִיא, הֵיכִי מִיקַּדְּשָׁא לְהוּ, וְהֵיכִי מִקְבְּעֵי לְהוּ בְּפִיגּוּל? לָאו אִיתּוֹתַב רַב גִּידֵּל. בִּתְמִיָּה. כז] בְּפ"ק דִּמְעִילָה (דף ג.). מַהוּ שֶׁיִּזְרוֹק דָּמָן שֶׁלֹּא לִשְׁמָן. אֶלָּא לְשֵׁם שְׁלָמִים, לְהַתִּיר בָּשָׂר בַּאֲכִילָה. דְּוַדַּאי לִשְׁמָן — [כ] לָא הָווּ זְרִיקָה, כִּדְאָמְרִי' לְעֵיל (דף מו.): הַכֹּל מוֹדִים שֶׁאִם הוּזְקְקוּ זֶה לָזֶה — מְעַכְּבִין זֶה אֶת זֶה [ל]. פֶּסַח בִּשְׁאָר יְמוֹת הַשָּׁנָה כָּשֵׁר לִשְׁלָמִים. בְּפֶ' "תָּמִיד נִשְׁחָט" (פסחים דף סד.). פֶּסַח קוֹדֶם חֲצוֹת הַיּוֹם. שֶׁל אַרְבָּעָה עָשָׂר — אֵינוֹ כָּשֵׁר לִשְׁמוֹ עַד בֵּין הָעַרְבַּיִם, וְכָשֵׁר לִשְׁלָמִים כח]. שֶׁנִּרְאָה לִשְׁמוֹ. כְּגוֹן הָנָךְ כְּבָשִׂים קוֹדֶם אֲבֵידַת הַלֶּחֶם. וְנִדְחָה מִלִּשְׁמוֹ. לְאַחַר אֲבֵידַת הַלֶּחֶם כט]. פֶּסַח אַחַר חֲצוֹת. נִרְאָה לִשְׁמוֹ, וּכְשֶׁעָבַר הַיּוֹם — נִדְחָה מִלִּשְׁמוֹ, וְכָשֵׁר לִשְׁלָמִים. וַהֲרֵי תוֹדָה. דַּאֲמַרַן בְּהַאי פִּירְקִין (ד' מו.): מִשֶּׁנִּשְׁחֲטָה נִפְרַס לַחְמָהּ — הַדָּם יִזָּרֵק לְשֵׁם שְׁלָמִים, וְהַבָּשָׂר יֵאָכֵל, וִידֵי נִדְרוֹ לֹא יָצָא. הָא הָכָא — שֶׁנִּשְׁחֲטָה לִשְׁמוֹ, וְנִדְחֵית מִלִּשְׁמוֹ, וּכְשֵׁרָה שֶׁלֹּא לִשְׁמוֹ. תּוֹדָה רַחֲמָנָא קַרְיֵיהּ שְׁלָמִים. "תּוֹדַת שְׁלָמָיו", כִּדַאֲמַרַן לְעֵיל (שם): מַה שְּׁלָמִים — קָרְבֵי בְּלֹא לֶחֶם, אַף תּוֹדָה — קְרֵבָה בְּלֹא לֶחֶם, וּמֵעוֹלָם לֹא נִדְחָה מִלִּשְׁמוֹ. וּמְנִיפָן. עִם הַכְּבָשִׂים. דְּכִבְשֵׂי עֲצֶרֶת טְעוּנִין תְּנוּפָה חַיִּים וּשְׁחוּטִין, לְקַמָּן בְּפֶ' "כָּל הַמְּנָחוֹת" (ד' סא.). וְהַשְּׁאָר

תוספות

דתנן אימורי קדשים קלים כו'. תימה: דלא מייתי רישא, דתנן: בשר קדשי קדשים שיצא לפני זריקת דמים רבי אליעזר אומר וכו'. פיגול. מפרש התם: כהרצאת כשר, כך הרצאת פסול. ומה הרצאת כשר – עד שיקרבו כל מתירין וכו'. וטמא הניתר לטהורים – חייבין עליהם משום טומאה, שאינו ניתר – לא. ונותר יליף "חילול" מטמא. קבעה לחם בפיגול. כי בשר, אלמא כגופיה דזיבחא, דמי הכא נמי כיון דזבח ניתר בזריקה שלא לשמן – לחם נמי כיון דכגופי' דזבח דמי. או דלמא: לחומרא – אמרינן, לקולא – לא אמרינן שיהא כי גופיה דזבח. [ג] ובהדר עיילינהו פליגי. אלחם קאי, אבל אאימורין (אפי') כי לא הדר עיילינהו, פליגי. וכן מוכח פ' "התדיר" (זבחים ד' צ.). ואינה מוציאה מידי מעילה. בבשר קדשי קדשים. תימה: דהא תנן פ"א דמעילה (דף ב.): איזו היא שלא היתה לה שעת היתר לכהנים? שנשחטה חוץ לזמנה. משמע: דכי נשחטה בהיתר – לא מלי משכח. ולאו קושיא היא. ולאו איתותב רב גידל. לא] ולא חשיב שינויא דהתם דריש מעילה* – דרב פפא הוא דמקשה לה התם, ולא ס"ל ההוא שינויי'. מיהו תימה: דהתם בסוף שמעתין (גם זה *שם) מייתי ליה סיוע. ואית דגרסי "ולא איתותב רב גידל" בניחותא. לב] ואינו נראה. מהו שיזרוק דמן שלא [מ] לשמן. לר' ירמיה דאמר: תנופה עושה זיקה, אבד הלחם – אבדו הכבשים, דקודם שחיטה – לא צרינן לשנויי. אבל היכא דכבר נשחטה – צרינן לשנויי, כדי לתקוני זבחא. והרי פסח [נ] אחר חצות. מצי לשנויי כדמשני פ' בתרא דזבחים (דף קטו.): שאני פסח דבשאר ימות השנה שלמים הוי. והרי תודה. דאם נפרס הלחם או שאבד ונזרק הדם לשמה – פסולה, דהא אבד הלחם אבדה התודה. דלית ליה סוגיא דלעיל לג] (דף מו:), אלא קסבר דשלא לשמן [בעי למזרק], וכי זריק שלא לשמה – כשר. ומשני: שאני תודה דקרייה רחמנא "שלמים", הלכך לכתחלה יכול לזרוק לשם שלמים כי אבד הלחם. והמקשה היה יכול להקשות, כמו שהקשה למעלה: והא כיון דשחיטה עושה זיקה, איפסיל לחם – תיפסיל נמי תודה. וקשה: מאי שני "שאני תודה, דקרייה רחמנא שלמים", הו"ל: לאו מילתא היא, דלשמו נמי כשר! אלא נראה לפרש: דודאי לשם תודה – פסולה. ופריך שפיר, ומשני דלשם שלמים נמי לשמה מיקרי, והילכך לא מיפסלא בהכי. אבל לשם תודה – פסול, דלא הוי בלא לחם. ואפי' [ס] לד] בפסח דלא בעי עקירה, הכא שאני – דכבר נשחטה [לשם תודה, מש"ה בעי עקירה]. מושך שתים מהן ומניפן. למאי דמוקי לה כרבי, צריך לומר שמניף כולם, דהא לא ידעי' הי אקדיש. ותימה: דכיון דבתנופה שאחר שחיטה איירי, א"כ לימא "וזורק את הדם עליהן", כדמזכיר תנופה דלא צריך! ועוד: דלישנא לא משמע שיניף הד'! ונראה לפרש: נוטל אחת, לה] ומניף השלש אחרות עמהן זו אחר זו. וכן בשניה, וכן בשלישית, וכן ברביעית. והשתא אורי לן שצריך שלא יניף הד' בבת אחת, כדי שיהא ניכר, שלא יזרק הדם רק על השתים.

כיון

רבינו גרשום

אימורי קדשים קלים שיצאו לפני זריקה רבי אליעזר אומר אין מועלין בהן דאכתי ממון בעלים הם קודם זריקה. וכיון שיצאו לפני זריקה אע"פ שזורק אין אותה זריקה מועלת שאין בה היתר למזבח ואין באימורין משום מעילה שאותה זריקה אינה ראויה ואינה מועלת לא לחייבו משום מעילה ולא משום פיגול ונותר וטמא: ור' עקיבא אמר מועלין בהן דסבר דזריקה מועלת לחייבו משום יוצא ומשום מעילה ומשום פיגול: מאי מדזריקה פיגול היכא דזרק דמן על מנת חוץ לזמנן קבעה ללחם בפיגול לר' עקיבא כי כשר כאילו הוה לחם כשר שלא יצא. זריקה שלא לשמה נמי אע"ג דהויא זריקה שאינה ראויה שריא נמי ללחם באכילה כזריקה כשרה או דילמא לחומרא אמרי' דזריקה שאינה ראויה קבעה למיהוי פיגול כזריקה כשרה אבל לקולא דזריקת פסול לישתרי לחם באכילה לא אמרינן: מתקיף לה רב פפא והיכי מצית לאוקמי להני תנאי כרבי ולא כרבי אלעזר ב"ר שמעון כלו' דשחיטה מקדש כרבי וכיון דיצאו הוה בהו איסור יוצא ור' אליעזר לטעמיה דאמר אין זריקה מועלת ליוצא ור' עקיבא אומר מועלת ממאי דבאיתנייהו אבראי שתי הלחם והאימורים פליגי דילמא בדהדר עיילינהו לפנים קודם זריקה. ור' אליעזר דאמר אין זריקה מועלת ליוצא כר' דאמר שחיטה מקדש ור' עקיבא כר' אלעזר בר' שמעון דאמר שחיט' לא מקדשא. וכי הדר עיילינהו לפני זריקה לית בהו יוצא כלל וליכא למימר הכא דזריקה מועלת ליוצא דהכא ליכא יוצא כלל וליכא לאוקמי כרבי עקיבא: האי מאי. כלו' ליכא למימר הכי כדקאמ' דבהדר עיילינהו פליגי דאי אמרת בשלמא רבי עקיבא כרבי כדאמרן מעיקרא. וכיון דקדישי להו בשחיטה אתיא זריקה דחוץ לזמנן קבעא להו בפיגול הלכך קאמר ר' עקיבא מועלין בהן וחייבין עליהן משום פיגול: זריקת פיגול מי מיקדשא דליחייבו עלה משום פיגול. זריקת פיגול. בשחישב בזריקה משום פיגול אינה מביאה לידי מעילה באימורי קדשים קלים דכיון דלא נזרק הדם בכשרות לא מישתרו אימורין לגבי מזבח ואין מועלין בהן: ואין מוציאה מידי מעילה בבשר קדשי קדשים דכיון דלא היתה הזריקה בכשרו' לא מישתרי בשר לכהנים ומועלין בו: ולא איתותב רב גידל התם בפ"ק של מסכת מעילה ואכתי איכ' למימר דבהדר עיילינהו פליגי וליכא למפשט דשריין שתי הלחם באכילה: מהו שיזרוק דמן לשם שלמים אחר: ויש לך דבר שאינו כשר לשמו וכשר שלא לשמו דאבד הלחם. והרי פסח ששחטו קודם חצות היום דאינו כשר לשמו דכתיב בין הערבים ושחטו אותו בין הערבים וכשר שלא לשמו לשם שלמים: והרי

ל"ק מ"ז

(זבחים צ.)

שיטה מקובצת

א] בפיגול כי בשר כמו בשר הזבח ויש"ג כי כשר כלומר כאילו לא היה בו פסול. תוס' אחרות: ב] ע' בהשמטה בסוף המסכת: ג] ע' בהשמטה בסוף המסכת: ד] להו אתי שחיטה מקדשה להו וכיון דקדשי להו שחיטה אתיא זריקה וקבעה להו בפיגול אלא אי אמרת זריקה מקדשא: ה] אינה מביאה לידי (פיגול) [מעילה] בבשר קדשים קלים דקי"ל דאין מעילה בבשר קדשים קלים אבל זריקה מביאה לידי מעילה והאי זריקה (לפיגול) [דפיגול] לא מייתי לידי מעילה: ו] ואינה מוציאה מידי מעילה בבשר קדשי קדשים דקדשי קדשים אית בהו מעילה משקדשו כלי עד שעת זריקה זריקה מפקעא להו מידי מעילה והך זריקה דפיגול לא חשיבה לעבד תרתי לאקבועי בפיגול (ולהביא) [ולהוציא] הבשר (לידי) [מידי] מעילה כדאמרי' בפ"ק דמעילה כלל אמר ר' יהושע כו': ז] ולא איתותב. פי' דבהא מילתא איתותב דהיה רוצה [לדמות] דכי היכא דאין זריקת פיגול לא מביא לידי מעילה בקדשי (קדשים) [קלים] ולא מוציאה מידי מעילה בקדשי (קלים) [קדשים] ה"נ לא מקדשי ללחם בהא מילתא איתותב דמסיק התם (נמי) [נהי] דמעילה לית בהו לחם מיהא קדיש: ח] להתיר הבשר באכילה דאי זריק להו לשמן פשיטא ליה דאין הבשר מותר באכילה כדאמרינן לעיל אבד הלחם אבדו הכבשים אבל כי זריק דמן שלא לשמן הוי להו כשלמי נדבה הבאים בלא לחם: ט] והרי פסח אחר חצות הכי כו' והרי תודה. פי' בשחטה לשמה ונדחה מלשמה שנפרס הלחם או שאבד הלחם או אבד הלחם ואם הי' שוחטו בלא לחם כשרה כדאמרינן גבי כבשי עצרת ששחטן בין לפני זמנן בין לאחר זמנן שכשרים בלא לחם ואפ"ה ששחטן לשמן ואבד הלחם בין שחיטה לזריקה פסולין והא לעיל גבי

תודה שנפרס לחמה לאחר שחיטה הדם יזרוק היינו שלא לשמה והשתא לא ס"ל להאי מקשה הא דאמרן לעיל מה שלמים קרבין בלא לחם אף תודה נמי קרבי בלא לחם אף שהוקבעו הלחם בשחיטה ומשני שאני שלמי תודה דרחמנא קרייה שלמים ואפי' לכתחלה לזרוק לשם שלמים ...

פסח ששחטו אחר חצות שנשתייר אחר זמן שחיטת פסח דנראה ונדחה ואינו כשר לשמו דנראה לשמו דהיינו בין הערבים ואם עבר והפריש אחר תחתיו ושחטו ונמצא הראשון הרי זה וכשר שלא לשמו לשום שלמים. הרי תודה דנשחט לשמו ונדחה מלשמו וכשר שלא לשמו ואינו ראוי לשמו דכיון משנשחטה יצא לשום שלמים מה הדם זורק לשם שלמים והבשר יאכל (שלא לשמו): דרחמנא קרייה שלמים מה שלמים קרבי בלא לחם ולא הוי דחוי מלשמו

הגהות צ"ק [א] כבעה: [ב] כבשר כבשר: ...

הגהות הב"ח (א) רש"י ד"ה וממאי וכו' דכ"ע ס"ל לא מקבע וכו' ...

*ת"ר: כבשי עצרת אאין מקדשין את הלחם אלא בשחיטה. כיצד? שחטן לשמן וזרק דמן לשמן — קדש הלחם, שחטן שלא לשמן וזרק דמן א] שלא לשמן — לא קדש הלחם. שחטן לשמן וזרק דמן שלא לשמן — הלחם קדוש ואינו קדוש, דברי רבי. רבי אלעזר בר' שמעון אומר: לעולם אינו קדוש, עד שישחוט לשמן ויזרוק דמן לשמן. מאי טעמא דרבי? דכתיב: °"ואת האיל יעשה זבח שלמים לה' על סל המצות" — למימרא דשחיטה מקדשא. ור' אלעזר ברבי שמעון? "יעשה" — עד שיעשה כל עשיותיו. ורבי נמי הכתיב "יעשה"? אי כתיב "זבח יעשה" — כדקאמרת, השתא דכתיב "יעשה זבח" — במה יעשה? בזביחה. ורבי אלעזר בר' שמעון הכתיב "זבח"? ההוא מיבעי ליה לכדרבי יוחנן, דאמר ר' יוחנן: הכל מודים שצריך שיהא לחם בשעת שחיטה. מאי "קדוש ואינו קדוש"? אביי אמר: קדוש ואינו גמור, רבא אמר: קדוש ואינו ניתר. ב] מאי בינייהו? איכא בינייהו למיתפס פדיונו. לאביי — לא תפיס פדיונו, לרבא — תפיס פדיונו. בשלמא לרבא, היינו דאיכא בין רבי לר' אלעזר בר"ש, אלא לאביי מאי איכא בין רבי לר' אלעזר בר' שמעון? איכא [בינייהו] ג] לאיפסולי ביוצא. בעא מיניה ר' שמואל בר רב יצחק מר' חייא בר אבא: ד] כבשי עצרת ששחטן לשמן וזרק דמן שלא לשמן, אותו הלחם מהו באכילה? אליבא דמאן? אי אליבא דר' אלעזר בר' שמעון — ה] האמר: זריקה היא דמקדשא! אי אליבא דרבי — בין לאביי בין לרבא ו] קדוש ואינו ניתר הוא! ז] אלא אליבא דהאי תנא, דתני אבוה דר' ירמיה בר אבא: שתי הלחם שיצאו בין שחיטה לזריקה, וזרק דמן של כבשים חוץ לזמנן — ר' אליעזר אומר: אין בלחם משום פיגול, רבי עקיבא אומר: ב יש בלחם משום פיגול. אמר רב ששת: הני תנאי ח] כרבי סבירא להו, דאמר: שחיטה מקדשא, מיהו ר' אליעזר לטעמיה, דאמר: *אין זריקה מועלת ליוצא, ור"ע לטעמי', דאמ': זריקה מועלת ליוצא. דתנן

במדבר ו

מסורת הש"ס: לקמן עג: יבמות קד: פסחים יג: [לעיל יג:]

רש"י

אין מקדשין את הלחם אלא בשחיטה. טעמא מפ' ט] לקמן. קדש את הלחם. מותר באכילה. לא קדש הלחם. ולא תפים פדיונו בקדושת שתי הלחם אלא בקדושת שאר י] קדושת הלשכה. ובת"כ יליף לה מ"קרבנו על זבח יא] תודה" — מגיד שאם נזבח שלא לשם תודה, לא קדש לחמו. וכבשי עצרת דמקדשי לחם, מתודה ואיל נזיר יב] גמרינן. קדוש ואינו קדוש. מפרש יג] לקמן. ואת האיל. איל נזיר. יעשה זבח שלמים לה' על סל המצות. אלמא זביחת איל מקדשא לסל, ומיניה גמרינן לכבשי עצרת. אי כתיב זבח יעשה. משמע: אע"ג דזבח בעי עשייה אחריתי. הכל מודים. אפילו לר' אליעזר דאמר זריקה עיקר, מודי דצריך שיהא לחם בשעת שחיטה, ואי לא הוה בשעת שחיטה — לא מקדשא ליה זריקה. ואינו גמור. מפרש יד] לקמן. ואינו ניתר. לכהנים. מאי בינייהו. כלומר, כיון דאמר אביי אינו גמור — כל שכן דאינו ניתר, דהא ממעות תרומת הלשכה בא, טו] וזריקת דם לא הואי לשמה דתשתרייה (א) באכילה, "ואינו גמור" דאמר אביי, למאי הלכתא? לאביי לא תפים פדיונו. בקדושת שתי הלחם, ואם רצה — משנה המעות לשאר קרבנות צבור. לרבא. דאמר קדוש גמור — תופס פדיונו, ויוצא לחולין. והא דאמר לקמן (דף ק:): מנחות אין להם פדיון — לאחר שקדשו בכלי. אלא לאביי. דאמר לא תפים פדיונו. מאי איכא בין רבי לר' אלעזר. ו"קדוש" דא"ר למאי הלכתא? הא לא תפים פדיונו, ולתרוייהו אסור באכילה. לאיפסולי ביוצא. לרבי דאמר קדוש קצת בשחיטה, אם יצא — נפסל, שאפי' זרקו טז] לשמו נמי אסור באכילה. יז] לרבי אלעזר דאמר שחיטה לא מקדשא — אין נפסל ביוצא, דאינו קדוש יח] אם יצאו בין שחיטה לזריקה, ואם אחר כך זרק לשמן — כשר (ב). יט] שבוש גמור הוא זה, דכל שכן לרבא כיון דקדשתן שחיטה קדושת הגוף גמורה — לא כ] נפיק תו לחולין. ובפ"ק דפסחים (דף יג:) נמי אמר הכי: לרבי דאמר שני דברים המתירים מעלים זה בלא זה — [א] לא כא] נפיק לחולין, ור' אלעזר דאמר אינו קדוש — פריק להו, ונפקי לחולין. וכיון דנפקי לחולין ע"י פדייה — על כרחך פדיונן נתפס. לפיכך נראה לר' דה"ג, ולשון הגון הוא: לאביי — תפים פדיונו, ולרבא — לא תפים פדיונו. לאביי דאמר אינו גמור — עדיין לא חלה עליו קדושת הגוף גמורה, ואכתי שייך ביה פדיון. והכי דקדישתיה שחיטה במקצת, דלא נפיק לחולין, ומיהו אכתי מחוסר גמר קדושה, ושייך ביה קדושת דמים לתפוס פדיונו בקדושה. לרבא דאמר קדוש גמור קדושת הגוף — לא שייך ביה פדיון, ואם התפיס מעות בפדיונו — אינן נתפסין, דכיון דאינו יוצא מקדושה כלל, איזו קדושה תחול בפדיונו? בשלמא לרבא. דאמר: לרבי לאו בני פדיון נינהו דאקדשינהו שחיטתה. היינו דאיכא בין רבי לר' כב] אלעזר. דלר' כג] אלעזר אינו קדוש כלל קדושת הגוף אלא קדושת דמים שניקח מתרומת הלשכה, ונפיק לחולין, ותפים פדיונו ככל קדושת דמים. אלא לאביי. דאמר לרבי נמי תפים פדיונו, וכל שכן לר' כד] אלעזר, מאי איכא בין רבי כה] לר' אלעזר? איכא בינייהו לאיפסולי ביוצא. לרבי — מיפסל ביוצא, אם יצא — לא יהא כשר לשחוט עליו כבשים אחרים. לר' כו] אלעזר — לא מיפסיל ביוצא, שלא ירדה לה קדושת הגוף אלא קדושת דמים, ואין יוצא פוסל בה, וכשרין לשחוט עליה כבשים אחרים. וזה שפירשתי תחילה שבוש גמור (ג) הוא, כדפרישנא לעיל. האמר זריקה מקדשא. והאי, אפילו קדוש לא הוי, כל שכן דאסור באכילה. בין לאביי בין לרבא קדוש ואינו ניתר. דכיון דאמר אביי אינו גמור, כל שכן דאינו ניתר. חוץ לזמנו. כלומר, על מנת לאכול מן הכבשים חוץ לזמנו. הני תנאי. ר' אליעזר ור' עקיבא. שחיטה מקדשא כז]. והאי בהו פסול יוצא. אין זריקה מועלת ליוצא. הלכך לא קבעתיה ללחם בפיגול, דהא כבר פסול הוא, ואמר בפ"ק (לעיל דף יב.): אין פיגול במקום פסול. זריקה מועלת ליוצא כח]. דפסול מחמת דבר אחר הוא, כדמפרש בשילהי פ"ק (שם) כט]. קדשים

תוספות

עד שישחוט לשמן ויזרוק דמן לשמן. תימה: למה לי זריקה, הא פ"ק דפסחים (ד' יג:) מסקינן דר' אלעזר בר' שמעון סבר לה כאבוה, דאמר: כל העומד ליזרק – כזרוק דמי? ותירץ ריב"א: זריקה שלא לשמה גריעה מנשפך דם. וקשה: דלקמן פ' "המנחות והנסכים" (ד' קב.) מוכח דאע"ג דנעשה פסול בזריקה, שזרק על מנת לאכול חוץ לזמנן – אמר: כל העומד ליזרק – כזרוק דמי! והכי איתא בגמ' התם: לא, דפיגל בשחיטה. ומקשה: אבל פיגל בזריקה – מאי? הכי נמי דמטמא טומאת אוכלין כו'. יש לחלק: דשלא לשמה עוקר הקרבן ועושהו קרבן אחר. אי נמי: הכא נמי בעי לד] למימר, ויהיה ראוי לזריקה. *ואת האיל יעשה זבח שלמים. אין לפרש דיליף הכא מדאיתקוש לחמי תודה לשלמי נזיר, כדילפינן פרק "התודה" (לקמן ד' עח.): "שלמיו" – לרבות שלמי נזיר לעשרה קבין ירושלמיות, ושתי הלחם נמי איתקוש ללחמי תודה, כדדריש נמי התם מ"תביאו" – שכל מה שאתה מביא, כזה. הא ליתא, דא"כ הוה ליה למד מן הלמד. ואע"ג דהוה ליה הימנו ודבר אחר – איכא למאן דלא ילפינן, בסוף "איזהו מקומן" (זבחים דף נז.) ופ' "התודה" (לקמן דף עח.). אלא גלויי מילתא בעלמא הוי, וילפינן שפיר. ומיהו קשה: דא"כ, אמאי איצטריך קרא בתודה: לה] "על חלות לחם חמץ יקריב קרבנו על זבח" – מלמד שאין הלחם קדוש אלא בשחיטת הזבח? ותו: ר' אלעזר בר' שמעון דדריש "כל עשיות" – גבי התודה לא כתיב "עשיה", וגבי תודה נמי פליג כדאי' פ"ק דפסחים (דף יג:) ובתוספתא דזבחים! וי"ל: דהוה אמינא מדקרייה רחמנא "שלמים" דלא מקדשי לחם לו] כי שלמים, ונזיר נמי לא סגי בלא קרא כמו גבי תודה, משום דקרייה רחמנא "שלמים". ולר"א בר"ש נמי, כיון דגלי קרא בנזיר דבכל עשיות הקידוש תלוי, הוא הדין בכולהו. במה יעשה בזביחה. תימה: דבפ"ק דזבחים (דף ד:) דריש מכאן שינוי בעלים, ודריש לכל עשיות: נימא דלא כר"א בר"ש? וי"ל: ודאי שמעי' שפיר תרתי. ול"ע לרבי: מנא ליה [ב] שינוי בעלים? ול"ע. שיהא לחם בשעת שחיטה. תימה: הא משעת תנופה בעי לחם. לז] ואע"ג דלא מעכב, ראוי מיהא בעינן! ושמא אפי' ראוי לא בעינן. ועוד: שמא אתא למימר דבשעת שחיטה בעינן שיהא בפנים, לח] אע"ג דכשר ביוצא. בקונטרס גרס וברוב הספרים נמי גרס הכי: "לאביי לא תפיס פדיונו, לרבא תפיס פדיונו". ופי': לאביי לא אלימא קדושתא כולי האי שיהא נפדה. וכה"ג איכא קלא פ"ב דבכורות (דף טו:) גבי ולדות בעלי מומין: כונסן לכיפה. היכי ליעבד? ליקרבינהו – מכח קדושה דחוייה אתיין, ליפרקינהו – לא אלימי למיתפס פדיונן. והשתא בעי לאביי מאי בינייהו, כיון דלרבי לא אלימי קדושתא – כל שכן לר"א בר"ש. וקשה: דלאביי נמי ליבעי אליבא דרבי: מה בין שוחטן לשמן לשוחטן שלא לשמן, דכ"ש דלא אלים למיתפס פדיונו. דהא לר"א בר"ש לא מהני שחיטה מידי, ומש"ה לא תפיס פדיונו! ותו: דבפסחים (דף יג:) משמע איפכא, דלרבי – לא תפיס, ולר"א בר"ש – תפיס. ולקמן (דף מח.) נמי, לר"א בר"ש פודן בחוץ! ושמא ודאי כי אין תנופה, [ג] וקדושת תנור לא קדיש, אלא קדושת פה, ומיפריק. אבל הכא [דאיכא שחיטה ותנופה ותנור] – להכי לא מיפריק, וכדפרישית לעיל. ופי' הקונט' דפי': לאביי – נפדה, ולרבא – אינו נפדה, לט] צ"ע. [ד] דתחילה פי' לרא"ש אינו קדוש כלל ונפיק לחולין לגמרי, ולבסוף פירש: וכ"ש לרא"ש. ולפירושו (ל"ד) לאביי קדוש טפי, דאלים דלא נפיק [לחולין ולרא"ש נפיק לחולין]. ויתכן יותר גירסא אחריתי. ומיהו גירסת הקונטרס נכונה: "לאביי – תפיס, ולרבא – לא תפיס". והשתא איכא בינייהו במקומות אחרים, ודחקינן לאשכוחי הכא מאי בינייהו. דתנן

עין משפט נר מצוה

קיא א מיי' פי"ז מהל' פסה"מ הלכה יח:
קיב ב מיי' שם הל' יט:

רבינו גרשום

דכתיב ואת האיל יעשה זבח שלמים לה' על סל המצות למימר דזביחה מקדשה לסל המצות. והכא נמי גבי כבשי עצרת. קדוש ואינו גמור שאינו ראוי לאכילה. ורבא אמר קדוש וגמור ואינו ניתר באכילה. לאביי דאמר ואינו [גמור] לא חמירא קדושתיה למתפס פדיונו שיהא קדוש כמוהו: בשלמא לרבא היינו דאיכא בין רבי לר"א בר"ש דלרבי דאמר קדוש למתפס פדיונו ואינו קדוש שאינו ניתר באכילה. ורבי אלעזר ב"ר שמעון דאמר אינו קדוש דאפי' פדיונו לא תפים: איכא בינייהו לאיפסולי ביוצא לרבי דאמר שחיטה מקדשא אם יצא הלחם בין שחיטה לזריקה נפסל. לר' אלעזר ב"ר שמעון לא מקדש ולא מפסיל ביוצא דאי אהדריה ועייליה לגואי קדש: וזרק דמן של כבשים על מנת לאוכלן לשתי הלחם ובשר חוץ לזמנן ר' אליעזר דאמר אין בלחם משום פיגול לטעמיה דאמר אין זריקה מועלת לחייבו משום איסור יוצא הואיל ויצא לפני זריקה ולא משום פיגול נמי:

שיטה מקובצת

א] שלא לשמן לא קדש הלחם. וא"ת כבשי עצרת מנ"ל שלא לשמה לא מקדש (וכתיב) [וא"ל] [דילפינן] מאיל נזיר ודרשי' זבח שלמים עד שיהא זביחתו לשם שלמי' כי היכי דדרשי' גבי תודה מלמד שאם שחטה שלא לשמה לא קדש הלחם הא לא מצית אמרת דהא אמרי' ריש פ"ק אם אינו ענין לשינוי קודש תנהו לשינוי בעלים ואם איתא (לשינוי קודש ומאי) [הא] איצטריך לומר דלא קדיש הלחם וי"ל דהדין זה ילפי' מתודה ואע"ג דלא ילפי' שאר דיניו [מתודה] מ"מ בתר דגלי קרא בקדוש לחם ילפי' שפיר שלא לשמו דאין זה רק גילוי מילתא בעלמא. תו"ח: ב] מאי בינייהו. רש"י פי' ב' לשונות וא"ת והיכא קאמר ר"א דאין מיפסל ביוצא הא אמרי' לעיל משנשחטה יצא לחמה כו' הלחם פסול אלמא נפסל ביוצא וי"ל דההוא מוקי לה כשנתקבל הדם בכלי קודם יציאה וסבר לה כאבוה דאמר כל העומד ליזרק כזרוק דמי אבל הכא יצא קודם זריקה ונזרק שלא לשמה וא"ת לאביי היאך תפים פדיונו ונפיק לחולין לרבי הא סבירא ליה לקמן דתנור מקדש וי"ל דהו"א מנחות הבאות בפני עצמן אבל הבאות עם הזבח השחיטה מקדשא להו ולא תנור ולפי מה דפי' רש"י ניחא נהי דתפים פדיונו לא נפיק לחולין תימה למורי הרמ"ר דלאביי הוי איפכא קדוש' דשחיטה מקדושת כלי דשאר מנחות דאילו קדושת כלי דשאר מנחות אין נפסלין ביוצא כדפי' בפ"ק ומהניא להו קדושה דאין להם פדיון ואילו קדושה דשחיטה דהכא מיקדשא להו דנפסלין ביוצא ותפום פדיונו דאין קדושתו גמורה לאביי כדפי' וי"ל דאין לחוש בהא דתפים פדיונו כיון דלא נפיק לחולין כדפי': ג] לאפסולי ביוצא. [דלרבי] דאמר קדוש איפסיל ביוצא וקשה להר"ם [דהסברות] הפוכות שיקדש ליפסל ביוצא ועדיין יקדש לתפוס פדיונו שהרי בתמימים הוי איפכא דאין תופס פדיון כלל ועדיין אינן נפסלין ביוצא וכן במנחות שקדשו בכלי וע"כ צריך לפי' השני של רש"י: ולרבי [אליעזר] לא מיפסל ביוצא תימה הא תניא לעיל נשחטה ויצא לחמה הלחם פסול וי"ל דלעיל כשנתקדש הדם בכוס ונשפך ור' אליעזר סבר כאבוה דאמר כל העומד ליזרק כזרוק דמי: ד] כבשי עצרת ששחטן לשמן כו' אותו הלחם מהו באכילה וא"ת היאך אפשר דתיתסר הלחם באכילה והלא הכבשים מותרים באכילה כדתנן כל הזבחים שנזבחו שלא לשמן כשרים וי"ל דה"מ כבשים דגופא דזביחא נינהו מהניא להו זריקה דשלא לשמו להתיר הבשר באכילה וא"ת מאחר דכבשים לא עלו לשם חובה הוי ליה כאלו אבדו ואמרי' לעיל אבדו הכבשים אבדו הלחם וי"ל דהא דאמרינן אבד הלחם היינו דלא חזי הא לחם להביא עם הכבשים אחרים שצריך לשמה משום דהוקקו זה לזה בשחיטה מיהו מיבעיא ליה אם משתרי הלחם באכילה כמו הכבשים דחשבינן ליה ללחם כגופא דזיבחא וכי היכא דמהניא זריקה שלא לשמה להתיר הבשר באכילה הכא נמי מהניא להתיר הלחם באכילה: [עוד מתו"ח] וא"ת כיון שנזרק שלא לשמה הוי ליה אבד הכבשים שאינן צריכין עוד ללחם וא"כ הוי להו אבד לחם כמו ביוצא [וי"ל] דודאי פשיטא שלא יהא עוד עליהם תורת שתי הלחם ולא יצאו ציבור חובתם אבל מבעיא אם שחיטה שלא לשמה מתרת הלחם לאכילה בעלמא כמו שהיא מתרת הכבשים לאכילה וא"ת ולר"א דאמר אין בלחם משום פיגול משמע אבל כבשים יש בהם משום פיגול ואמאי הא אבד הלחם וא"כ אבדו הכבשים ולא הוי קרבו מתיריו כמצותו וי"ל דודאי יש בבשר משום פיגול אם יזרקנה שלא לשמה מיהו (קשה אז) [דאז] לא יהיה פיגול בלחם ומיהו לא הוי לצדדין דה"ק אין בלחם משום פיגול בשום פנים בין לשמו בין שלא לשמו אבל כבשים יש בהם משום פיגול לכל הפחות בשלא לשמו ור"ע דאמר יש בלחם משום פיגול היינו בלשמו א"נ נהי דהלחם מפסיל משום יוצא מהניא ליה ההקטרה לאקבועי [הבשר] בפיגול כדאמרי סוף פ"ק [גבי] שירים שחסרו בין קמיצה להקטרה (דהוי) [דשאני] חיסרון (דאי) [כיון דאיתא] בפנים מהניא ליה הקטרה [למקבעינהו בפיגול]: ה] הא אמר זריק' היא דמקדשא והכא כיון דנזרק שלא לשמה פשיט' דאין הלחם נאכל: ו] קדוש ואינו ניתר הוא. דאפי' לאביי דאמר קדוש ואינו גמור כ"ש דאינו ניתר: ז] אלא אליבא דהאי תנא כו' אין בלחם משום פיגול. כמו שהולך ומפרש (דרבי) [דר"א] לטעמיה דאמר אין זריקה מועלת ליוצא באימורים שיצאו ה"נ [לא] מהניא ללחם לחייבו בפיגול: ח] כר' ס"ל. עי' בסוף המס' בהשמטות: ט] מפ' לקמיה: י] בקדושת שאר תרומת הלשכה: יא] זבח תודת שלמיו מגיד: יב] נזיר גמרי': יג] מפרש לקמיה: יד] מפרש לקמיה: טו] בא וזריקה לא הואי כשרה ותיבת לשמה נמחק: טז] זרקו אח"כ: יז] באכילה ולר': יח] קדוש ואם [כו' אח"כ]: יט] שבוש בס"א הכל אינו אבל ברש"י של מהר"פ איתא: כ] לא נפקי: כא] נפקי לחולין ולר' אליעזר: כב] לר' אליעזר: כג] אליעזר: כד] לר' אליעזר: כה] לר' אליעזר: כו] לר' אליעזר: כז] מקדשה. לשתי הלחם: כח] ליוצא דלא דמי פסול יוצא לשאר פסולים שפיסולו מחמת. ותיבת דפסול נמחק: כט] פ"ק הילכך אית בהו משום פיגול הס"ד: ל] למימר ויהא ראוי לזריקה וכן כתוב בגליון ויזרוק דהכא ר"ל ויקבל שנראה לזריקה: לא] בתודה לקמן [דף ע"א ע"ב]: לב] כי שלמים וא"ת ולכתוב רחמנא תודה ולא בעי נזיר וי"ל דבאיל נזיר כיון דאיכא זבחים אחרינא בהדי לא הוי ידענא הי מינייהו מקדש אי נמי כולהו צריכי לקדושי איצטריך קרא באיל נזיר למימר דאיל דוקא מקדש תו"ח: לג] לחם ותנופה מחיים הוא דהויא: לד] בפנים כדתנן לקמן בפ' התודה השוחט את התודה לפנים ולחמה חוץ לחומה לא קדש הלחם: עי' בסוף המס' בהשמטות:
בפיגול

הגהות צ"ק [א] ולא: [ב] שאר עבודות כשינוי בעלים וצ"ע הס"ד: [ג] אלא קדושת תנור כו' אבל הכא דאיכא תנופה להכי כו': [ד] דתחילה פי' לאביי דכ"ש שאינו ניתר ולפירושו לאביי קדיש טפי דאלים מלמיתפס ויתכן יותר כו' ודייקינן לאשכוחי:

הגהות הב"ח (א) רש"י ד"ה מאי בינייהו וכו' באכילה הס"ד ואח"כ מ"ה למתפס פדיונו דאינו גמור דאמר אביי למימר דלא תפיס פדיונו בקדושת שתי: (ב) ד"ה לאפסולי וכו' ושבוש גמור הוא גי' זה: (ג) ד"ה איכא בינייהו וכו' שבוש גמור אלא כדפרישנא לעיל:

גליון הש"ס תוס' ד"ה בקונטרס כו' ולבסוף פי' וכ"ש. ק"ל למאי הקשו על לשון רש"י דנקט וכ"ש הא בלא"ה קשה דמאי פרכי מאי איכא בין רבי לראב"ש הא לרבי תפיס פדיונו ואינו יוצא לחולין ולראב"ש יוצא לחולין:

קו א מיי' פ"ח מהלכות תמידין ומוספין הלכה טו:
קז ב מיי' פי"ב מהלכות פסה"מ הלכה יח:
קח ג ד מיי' פ"ח מהל' תמידין ומוספין הל' טז:
קט ה מיי' פ"א מהלכות שקלים הלכה ז: [הה] מיי' פ"ט מהל' מעה"ק דין יד:
קי ו מיי' פי"ט מהל' פסה"מ הל' ה:

מסורת הש"ס | תורה אור

[א]אָבְדוּ כְּבָשִׂים, אָבְדוּ כְּבָשִׂים — אָבַד הַלֶּחֶם. וְאִם תִּמְצָא לוֹמַר: תְּנוּפָה אֵינָהּ עוֹשָׂה זִיקָּה, הֵבִיא לֶחֶם וּכְבָשִׂים וְהוּנְפוּ, וְאָבַד הַלֶּחֶם וְהֵבִיא לֶחֶם אַחֵר — אוֹתוֹ הַלֶּחֶם טָעוּן תְּנוּפָה אוֹ אֵינוֹ טָעוּן תְּנוּפָה? אָבְדוּ כְּבָשִׂים לָא תִּיבָּעֵי לָךְ — דְּוַדַּאי בָּעֵי תְּנוּפָה. כִּי תִּיבָּעֵי לָךְ — אָבַד הַלֶּחֶם. וְאַלִּיבָּא דְּבֶן נַנָּס לָא תִּיבָּעֵי לָךְ, דְּאָמַר: כְּבָשִׂים עִיקָּר. כִּי תִּיבָּעֵי לָךְ — אַלִּיבָּא דְּר"ע דְּאָמַר: לֶחֶם עִיקָּר, מַאי? כֵּיוָן דְּלֶחֶם עִיקָּר — בָּעֵי תְּנוּפָה, אוֹ דִּלְמָא כֵּיוָן דְּמַתִּירִין דִּידֵיהּ כְּבָשִׂים נִינְהוּ — לָא צָרִיךְ תְּנוּפָה? תֵּיקוּ. אֲמַר לֵיהּ אַבָּיֵי לְרָבָא: מַאי שְׁנָא שְׁנֵי כְבָשִׂים דִּמְקַדְּשִׁי לֶחֶם וּמְעַכְּבִי, וּמַאי שְׁנָא שִׁבְעָה כְּבָשִׂים וּפָר וְאֵילִים דְּלָא מְקַדְּשִׁי לֶחֶם א] וְלָא מְעַכְּבִי? אָמַר לֵי': הוֹאִיל וְהוּזְקְקוּ זֶה לָזֶה בִּתְנוּפָה. וַהֲרֵי תּוֹדָה דְּלָא הוּזְקְקוּ זֶה לָזֶה בִּתְנוּפָה, וּמְקַדְּשָׁא וּמְעַכְּבָא! אֶלָּא כְּתוֹדָה, מַה תּוֹדָה — שְׁלָמִים, אַף הָכָא נַמִי — שְׁלָמִים. מִי דָּמֵי? הָתָם לֵיכָּא זְבָחִים אַחֲרִינֵי בַּהֲדֵיהּ, הָכָא דְּאִיכָּא זְבָחִים אַחֲרִינֵי בַּהֲדֵיהּ, לִיקַדְּשׁוּ הָנֵי וְהָנֵי! אֶלָּא כְּאֵיל נָזִיר, מָה אֵיל נָזִיר אע"ג דְּאִיכָּא זְבָחִים אַחֲרִינֵי — שְׁלָמִים הוּא דִּמְקַדְּשִׁי, מִידֵי אַחֲרִינָא — לָא, הָכָא נַמִי לָא שְׁנָא. וְהָתָם מְנָלַן? ב] דְּתַנְיָא: °"וְאֶת הָאַיִל יַעֲשֶׂה זֶבַח שְׁלָמִים לַה' עַל סַל הַמַּצּוֹת" — מְלַמֵּד, שֶׁהַסַּל בָּא חוֹבָה לָאַיִל וּשְׁחִיטַת אַיִל מְקַדְּשָׁן, לְפִיכָךְ [ב]שְׁחָטוֹ שֶׁלֹּא לִשְׁמוֹ — לֹא קָדְשׁוּ הַלֶּחֶם. תָּנוּ רַבָּנַן: *[ג]שְׁתֵּי הַלֶּחֶם הַבָּאוֹת בִּפְנֵי עַצְמָן — יוּנְפוּ, וְתִעוּבַּר צוּרָתָן, °וְיֵצְאוּ לְבֵית הַשְּׂרֵיפָה. מַה נַּפְשָׁךְ? אִי לַאֲכִילָה אָתְיָין — לֵיכְלִינְהוּ! אִי לִשְׂרֵיפָה אָתְיָין — לִשְׂרְפִינְהוּ לְאַלְתַּר, לָמָּה לְהוּ עִיבּוּר צוּרָה? אֲמַר רַבָּה: לְעוֹלָם לַאֲכִילָה אָתְיָין, גְּזֵירָה [ד]שֶׁמָּא יִזְדַּמְּנוּ לָהֶן כְּבָשִׂים לַשָּׁנָה הַבָּאָה, וְיֹאמְרוּ: אֶשְׁתָּקַד לֹא אָכַלְנוּ לֶחֶם בְּלֹא כְּבָשִׂים? עַכְשָׁיו נַמִי נֵיכוּל. וְאִינְהוּ לָא יָדְעִי דְּאֶשְׁתָּקַד לָא הֲווּ כְּבָשִׂים — אִינְהוּ שָׁרְיָין נַפְשַׁיְיהוּ, הַשְׁתָּא דְּאִיכָּא כְּבָשִׂים — כְּבָשִׂים הוּא דְּשָׁרוּ לְהוּ. (א) אֲמַר רַבָּה: מְנָא אָמֵינָא לַהּ? [א]דִּתְנַן: א"ר יְהוּדָה, הֵעִיד בֶּן *בּוּכְרִי בְּיַבְנֶה: כָּל כֹּהֵן שֶׁשּׁוֹקֵל — אֵינוֹ חוֹטֵא. אָמַר לוֹ רַבָּן יוֹחָנָן בֶּן זַכַּאי: לֹא כִּי, אֶלָּא [ה]כָּל כֹּהֵן שֶׁאֵינוֹ שׁוֹקֵל — חוֹטֵא. אֶלָּא שֶׁהַכֹּהֲנִים דּוֹרְשִׁין מִקְרָא זֶה לְעַצְמָן °"וְכָל מִנְחַת כֹּהֵן כָּלִיל תִּהְיֶה לֹא תֵאָכֵל" — הוֹאִיל וְעוֹמֶר וּשְׁתֵּי הַלֶּחֶם וְלֶחֶם הַפָּנִים שֶׁלָּנוּ הֵן, הֵיאַךְ נֶאֱכָלִין? הָנֵי שְׁתֵּי הַלֶּחֶם הֵיכִי דָּמֵי? אִילֵימָא בְּבָאוֹת עִם הַזֶּבַח — אַטּוּ תּוֹדָה וְלַחְמָהּ [הה]מִי לָא מְנַדְּבִי כֹּהֲנִים וְאָכְלִי לְהוּ? אֶלָּא לָאו בְּבָאוֹת בִּפְנֵי עַצְמָן, וְקָתָנֵי "הֵיאַךְ הֵן נֶאֱכָלִין", אַלְמָא לַאֲכִילָה אָתְיָין. אֲמַר לֵיהּ אַבָּיֵי: לְעוֹלָם בְּבָאוֹת עִם הַזֶּבַח, וּדְקָא קַשְׁיָא לָךְ מִתּוֹדָה וְלַחְמָהּ — לַחְמֵי תּוֹדָה לָא אִיקְּרוּ "מִנְחָה", שְׁתֵּי הַלֶּחֶם אִיקְּרוּ "מִנְחָה", שֶׁנֶּאֱ': °"בְּהַקְרִיבְכֶם מִנְחָה חֲדָשָׁה לַה'". רַב יוֹסֵף אֲמַר: לְעוֹלָם לִשְׂרֵיפָה אָתְיָין, וְהַיְינוּ טַעְמָא דְּלָא שָׂרְפִינַן — לְפִי *[ו]שֶׁאֵין שׂוֹרְפִין קָדָשִׁים בְּיו"ט. א"ל אַבָּיֵי: מִי דָּמֵי? הָתָם — לָאו מִצְוָתָן בְּכָךְ, הָכָא דְּמִצְוָתָן בְּכָךְ — לִישְׂרְפִינְהוּ, מִידֵי דַּהֲוָה אַפָּר וְשָׂעִיר שֶׁל יוֹם הַכִּיפּוּרִים! אֶלָּא אֲמַר רַב יוֹסֵף: גְּזֵירָה שֶׁמָּא יִזְדַּמְּנוּ לָהֶם כְּבָשִׂים לְאַחַר מִכָּאן. א"ל אַבָּיֵי: תֵּינַח כָּל זְמַן הַקְרָבָתָם, ג] לְבָתַר הָכִי — לִשְׂרְפִינְהוּ! מַאי "תְּעוּבַּר צוּרָתָן" נַמִי דְּקָתָנֵי? ד] צוּרַת הַקְרָבָתָם. רָבָא אֲמַר: לַאֲכִילָה אָתְיָין, וּגְזֵירָה מִשּׁוּם דְּרַבָּה, וְלָאו מִטַּעֲמֵיהּ ה] אֶלָּא מִקְּרָא. וַאֲמַר רָבָא: מְנָא אָמֵינָא לַהּ? דִּכְתִיב: °"מִמּוֹשְׁבוֹתֵיכֶם תָּבִיאוּ לֶחֶם תְּנוּפָה [וגו'] בִּכּוּרִים לַה'", מַה בִּכּוּרִים — בִּפְנֵי עַצְמָן, אַף שְׁתֵּי הַלֶּחֶם — בִּפְנֵי עַצְמָן. וּמִינַּהּ, מַה בִּכּוּרִים — לַאֲכִילָה, אַף שְׁתֵּי הַלֶּחֶם — נַמִי לַאֲכִילָה. ת"ר

(במדבר ו; [לקמן עד:]; ויקרא ו; במדבר כח; ויקרא כג)

א) שקלים פ"א מ"ד לעיל כא: ערכין ז.

רש"י

בָּעוּ תְּנוּפָה. כְּבָשִׂים הָאֲחֵרִים [בָּעוּ תְּנוּפָה] לְדִבְרֵי הַכֹּל, דְּמַתִּירִין הֵן. וְעוֹד: דִּבְהוּ כְּתִיב תְּנוּפָה — ו] "וְהֵנִיף אוֹתָם הַכֹּהֵן". מַאי שְׁנָא שְׁנֵי כְּבָשִׂים. דִּשְׁלָמִים דִּמְקַדְּשִׁי לֶחֶם, כִּדְתַנְיָא לְקַמָּן בִּשְׁמַעְתָּא (דף מז.), אֵין מְקַדְּשִׁין הַלֶּחֶם אֶלָּא בִּשְׁחִיטָה. וּמְעַכְּבִי. אִם הוּזְקְקוּ זֶה לָזֶה בִּשְׁחִיטָה, כִּדְאָמַר ר' יוֹחָנָן לְעֵיל, וַאֲפִי' לֹא הוּזְקְקוּ — מְעַכְּבִי לְבֶן נַנָּס. ז] הוֹאִיל וְהוּזְקְקוּ. שְׁנֵי כְבָשִׂים וְלֶחֶם. וְהָא תּוֹדָה ח] לֹא הוּזְקְקוּ. הִיא וְלַחְמָהּ לִתְנוּפָה כְּיַחַד. וּמְקַדְּשָׁא. לַלֶּחֶם בִּשְׁחִיטָה? וְהַיְינוּ דְּאָמְרִינַן: "קָרְבָּנוֹ עַל זֶבַח" — מְלַמֵּד שֶׁאֵין הַלֶּחֶם קָדוֹשׁ אֶלָּא בִּשְׁחִיטַת הַזֶּבַח, בְּפֶ' "הַתּוֹדָה" (לקמן ד' עח:). וּמְעַכְּבָא. דְּאִם אֵין תּוֹדָה — אֵין לֶחֶם, דְּהָא אֵינָן קְדוֹשִׁין אֶלָּא בִּשְׁחִיטָה. וּמְשַׁנֵּי: שְׁנֵי כִּבְשֵׂי עֲצֶרֶת ט] שְׁלָמִים. אֲבָל שִׁבְעָה כְּבָשִׂים וּפָרִים וְאֵילִים — עוֹלָה נִינְהוּ (א) [א], כְּמוֹ אֵיל נָזִיר שְׁלָמִים הוּא וּמְקַדֵּשׁ הַלֶּחֶם, כִּדְמְפָרֵשׁ לְקַמֵּיהּ. לְפִיכָךְ. [ב] דִּשְׁחִיטַת אֵיל מְקַדְּשָׁן, שְׁחָטֵיהּ לְאֵיל שֶׁלֹּא לִשְׁמוֹ — לֹא קָדַשׁ הַלֶּחֶם, דִּכְתִיב "זֶבַח שְׁלָמִים (ג) עַל סַל הַמַּצּוֹת": אִי זְבִיחָתוֹ לְשֵׁם שְׁלָמִים — מְקַדֵּשׁ אֶת הַסַּל, וְאִי לָא — לָא. הַבָּאוֹת בִּפְנֵי עַצְמָן. אַלִּיבָּא דְּרַבִּי עֲקִיבָא, דְּאָמַר: כְּבָשִׂים אֵין מְעַכְּבִין אֶת הַלֶּחֶם. תְּעוּבַּר צוּרָתָן. יִפָּסְלוּ בְּלִינָה. אִי לַאֲכִילָה אָתְיָין. י] דְּלָא בָּעוּ מַתִּירִין — לֵיכְלִינְהוּ! וְאִי לִשְׂרֵיפָה אָתְיָין לִשְׂרְפִינְהוּ לְאַלְתַּר. הוֹאִיל וְזוּ הִיא עִיקַּר מִצְוָתָם. הַשְׁתָּא דְּאִיכָּא כְּבָשִׂים כו'. הִלְכָּךְ הוֹאִיל וְקָדָשִׁים מַעַלְיָא נִינְהוּ, וּמִשּׁוּם גְּזֵירָה הוּא דְּשָׂרְפִינַן לְהוּ — לָא מָצֵי לְמִשְׂרְפִינְהוּ עַד דְּלִיפָּסְלוּ בְּלִינָה. מְנָא אָמֵינָא לַהּ. דְּלַאֲכִילָה אָתְיָין, אֲפִי' בָּאִין בִּפְנֵי עַצְמָן? אֵינוֹ חוֹטֵא. וְאע"ג דִּכְתִיב (שמות ל): "כָּל הָעוֹבֵר עַל הַפְּקוּדִים", וְכֹהֲנִים לֹא נִפְקְדוּ — אֵינוֹ חוֹטֵא, כִּדְפָרְשִׁינַן בְּפ"ג (לעיל ד' כא:) דְּמַיְיתוּ וּמָסְרִי לְהוּ לַצִּיבּוּר. שֶׁאֵינוֹ שׁוֹקֵל חוֹטֵא. דְּכָל הָרָאוּי לִיפָּקֵד קָאָמַר, דְּהַיְינוּ מִבֶּן כ' שָׁנָה וָמַעְלָה יא]. לְעַצְמָן. לַהֲנָאָתָן. שֶׁלָּנוּ הֵן. אִם אָנוּ נוֹתְנִים שְׁקָלִים לַלִּשְׁכָּה — נִמְצְאוּ בָּאִין אַף מִשֶּׁלָּנוּ, שֶׁהֲרֵי כָּל הַקָּרְבָּנוֹת מִן הַלִּשְׁכָּה בָּאִין. וְרַבָּן יוֹחָנָן בֶּן זַכַּאי לָא דָּרֵישׁ "וְכָל מִנְחַת כֹּהֵן" אֶלָּא בְּמִנְחָה שֶׁהַכֹּהֵן מֵבִיא יב] בִּפְנֵי עַצְמוֹ, מש"ה יג] — חוֹטֵא. אִילֵימָא בְּבָאִין שְׁתֵּי הַלֶּחֶם עִם הַזֶּבַח. אַמַּאי קָתָנֵי "הֵיאַךְ הֵן נֶאֱכָלִין?" הָא לְלַחְמֵי תוֹדָה דָּמֵי, וְתוֹדָה וְלַחְמָהּ מִי לָא מְנַדְּבִי כֹּהֲנִים וְאָכְלִי? הָתָם. גַּבֵּי קָדָשִׁים הַנִּשְׂרָפִין — לָאו מִצְוָתָן בְּכָךְ, דְּמֵעִיקָּרָא לַאֲכִילָה אָתוּ, אֶלָּא שֶׁאֵירַע בָּהֶן פְּסוּל כְּגוֹן נוֹתָר אוֹ טָמֵא, הִלְכָּךְ שָׁבְקִינְהוּ עַד הַחוֹל וְשָׂרְפִינְהוּ לְהוּ. שֶׁמָּא יִזְדַּמְּנוּ לָהֶם כְּבָשִׂים לְאַחַר מִכָּאן. לְאַחַר שְׂרֵיפַת הַלֶּחֶם. הִילְכָּךְ מַשְׁהֵינַן לְהוּ, שֶׁאִם יָבֹאוּ הַכְּבָשִׂים — יוּנְפוּ עִמָּהֶם יד] וְאוֹכְלוּ. זְמַן הַקְרָבָתָן. עַד תָּמִיד שֶׁל בֵּין הָעַרְבַּיִם. לְבָתַר הָכִי לִשְׂרְפִינְהוּ. אַמַּאי מַשְׁהֵינַן לְהוּ כָּל הַלַּיְלָה? גְּזֵירָה מִשּׁוּם דְּרַבָּה. דְּאָמַר לְעֵיל: גְּזֵירָה שֶׁמָּא יִזְדַּמְּנוּ לָהֶם כְּבָשִׂים לַשָּׁנָה הַבָּאָה. וְלָאו מִטַּעֲמֵיהּ, דְּהוּא אוֹמֵר לְעֵיל: מְנָא אָמֵינָא לַהּ? טו] מִדְּתַנְיָא "הֵעִיד בֶּן בּוּכְרִי" כו'. מִמּוֹשְׁבוֹתֵיכֶם וגו' בִּכּוּרִים לַה'. הִקִּישָׁן לְבִכּוּרִים. אַף שְׁתֵּי הַלֶּחֶם. יְכוֹלִין לָבֹא בִּפְנֵי עַצְמָן. אֵין

תוספות

אבדו כבשים לא תיבעי לך דודאי בעי תנופה. נהדי כבשים אחריני. ולא דמי ל"זו תודה וזו לחמה", דאי אבדה התודה – אינו מביא אחרת. ומאי שנא שבעה כבשים ופרים ואלים דלא מקדשי ולא מעכבי. אגב "מקדשי" נקט "מעכבי", דהא דרשינן לעיל (ד' מה:): "שבעת כבשים" – אע"פ שאין לחם, וה"נ "לחם" – אע"פ שאין שבעה כבשים. ומיהו בקונטרס פי' דמיבעיא ליה בתר דהוזקקו זה לזה בשחיטה. לפיכך שחטן שלא לשמן לא קדש הלחם. טפי הוה ניחא למיתני שחטן לשמן דקדש הלחם, אלא אשמעינן: אע"ג דאחריני לשמן נשחטו – לא קדש הלחם. שתי הלחם הבאות בפני עצמן. כמ"ד: לחם עיקר. טו] לשרפינהו לאלתר. ואפי' למ"ד (פסחים דף לד:): אפי' פיגול טעון *צורה – הכא שאני, דמצותן בכך. לפי שאין שורפין קדשים בי"ט. הוה מצי למיפרך: למוצאי יו"ט לאלתר לשרפינהו, דמנותר לא יליף, מדמסיק צורת הקרבתן. צורת הקרבתן. פירש בקונטרס: עד תמיד של בין הערבים. מיהו בשמעתא ד"נתקלקלו הלוים בשיר" (ר"ה דף ל:) מפרש: דקרבנות ציבור קרבי אחר התמיד, ודחו עשה דהשלמה. לכך נראה לפרש: עד הלילה. מה ביכורים בפני עצמן. ואפילו הכי איצטריך *לרבי עקיבא "יהיו" מ"תהיינה" ללחם דמעכב כבשים. עד

([נ"ל נידון]; [לעיל מה:])

שיטה מקובצת

א] ולא מעכבי. ואע"ג דאפיקנא לעיל [מקרא] דשבעת כבשים לא מעכבין את הלחם דאפי' לר"ע דאמר [השני כבשים] לא מעכבי [ללחם] היכא דהוזקקו זה לזה בשחיטה מקדשי ומעכבי ומאי שנא שני כבשים כו' היכא דהוזקקו זה לזה בשחיטה לקדשיה ולעכביה. תוס' אחרות: ב] והתם מנלן. דכתיב ואת האיל יעשה זבח שלמים לה' וא"ת לקמן בפ' התודה מפיק דלחמי תודה מקדשו מקראי אחריני דכתיבי בתודה עצמה ולמה לי תרי קראי נילף חד מחבריה [דהיכא דאיכא] לחם בהדי זבח שחיטת הזבח מקדשן וי"ל דתודה מאיל נזיר לא אתי דאמינא תודה שלמים נינהו כשאר שלמים דעלמא דלאו לחם אגיד [ביה הכי] נמי לא אגיד לחם זבח כלל להכי צריכי קראי דהתם ואיל נזיר וכבשי עצרת לאו מקראי דתודה גמרינן דהו"א תודה ליכא זיבחא אחריני [בהדייהו אבל] הני דאית בהו זיבחא אחרינא בהדייהו לא לקדש בשחיטת השלמים כדאי' לעיל להכי צריכי תרוייהו וא"ת מהיכא נפקא לן באיל נזיר [וכבשי עצרת] דשלא לשמן לא מקדש לחם בהדייהו ואין לומר משום דכתיב ואת האיל יעשה זבח שלמים על סל המצות דבעינן לשם שלמים על סל [המצות] זה אינו דא"כ הוי צריך האי קרא לגופיה והיכא מפיק מינה בפרק קמא דזבחים דשינוי בעלים לא עלו לבעלים לשם חובה דאמר התם אשכחן שינוי קודש כו' עד שינוי בעלים ואם איתא דאצטריך לגופיה הכא למיגמר דשלא לשמן לא קידש הלחם היכא נפקא שינוי בעלים מינה וצריך לומר דשלא לשמן בכבשי עצרת [ואיל נזיר] דלא קדשי הלחם ילפי' מלחמי תודה דכתיב קרא כדאי' לקמן בפרק התודה וכן פירש"י כאן [בדף מ"ז. בד"ה] לא קידש הלחם ולא תפים פדיונו כו':

ג] לאחר זמן הקרבתן לישרפינהו פי' בקונטרס אחר תמיד בין הערבים דאמר קרא עליה השלם ולא נהירא דהא קרבן צבור דוחה עשה דהשלמה ונראה לפרש בתר זמן הקרבה לאחר שקיעת החמה דאין מקריבין קרבנות באותן חמשת מילין שקודם לילה ועדיין יכול לשרוף דאכתי יום הוא אבל הא לא פריך ולשרפינהו בלילה ממש דאין שורפין קדשים בלילה כן משמע במס' ביצה (דף ה) דאין עשה דהשלמה עומד במקום קרבן צבור גם פעם [אחת] נתקלקלו הלוים בשיר תו"ח תיבת הכי נמחק: ד] דקתני כל זמן הקרבתן רבא אמר לעולם: ה] תיבות אלא מקרא נמחק: ו] תנופה דכתיב: ז] ננס ולר"ע הואיל: ח] תודה דלא: ט] עצרת כתודה מה תודה שלמים ומקדש לחם אף הכא נמי אותה של שלמים מקדשה לחם אבל כו' נינהו הס"ד ואח"כ מה"ד מה איל: י] דלא ס"א דאין להן מתירין: יא] ומעלה תשקלו ודרשי' לריב"ז כל העובר בים וכהנים עברו יתן תרומת ה': יב] מבן עשרים שנה ומעלה: יב] מביא מביתו: יג] מש"ה אמר: יד] ויאכל תיבת ואוכלו נמחק: טו] לה מדתנן תיבת דתניא נמחק: טז] לישרפינהו לאלתר. לאו דוקא דאין שורפין קדשים בי"ט אלא לאלתר רוצה לומר במוצאי יו"ט ולמה לי עבור צורה דהיינו לינה עד עמוד השחר. תוס' אחרות:

רבינו גרשום

ואליבא דבן ננס. דאמ' כבשים עיקר לא תב' לך דכיון דהונפו כבש' סגי: כתודה. כלומ' וממקום שבאתה מ' תודה שלמים ומעכ' לחם. הכא נמי אף ע' דאיכא זבחים אחר' בהדי איל נזיר עו' וחטאת: שתי הלח' הבאים בפני עצמ' בשלא היו להם כבש' יונפו כדי להתיר החד' במקדש: ותעובר צורת' שיעשה להן לינה ויצ' לבית השרפה: א' רבא לעולם לאכי' אתיין. האי לחם ש' בלא כבשים ואמ' תעובר צורתה ויצ' לבית השריפה גזיר' שמא יזדמנו לה' כבשים לשנה הבאה ו' יחושו להביאם ע' הלחם ויאמרו אשתק' וכו': לחמי תודה ל' איקרו מנחה הלכך לי' למימר בהו כל מנח' כליל ושריין. לפי שא' שורפין קדשים ביום טו' דהכי אמרינן במס' שב' תן לו בקר ש' לשריפתו: התם לא' מצותן בכך. דמעיקר' לאו לשריפה אתי' אלא אמר רב יוס' משום הכי לא שרפי' להו לאלתר גזיר' שמא יזדמנו כו': תנ' דליעכבינהו כל ז' הקרבתם בכל היו' שמא יזדמנו: לבתר ה' כיון דלא נזדמ' לישרפינהו בלילה ואמ' צריכי לינה: ולאו מטעמי' דלא מצי למילף ל' מהא דתנן העיד בן בוכ' אלא מהא דכת' ממושבותיכם וגו':

[גיר' הערוך כוברי]

הגהות הב"ח

(א) גמ' ואמר רב[ה] (ב) רש"י ד"ה ומשני וכ'[ו] נינהו הס"ד ואח"כ מ"[ה] מה איל: (ג) ד"ה לפיכ[ך] וכו' שלים לה' על סל:

[שבת כג: וכד:]

גליון הש"ס

גמ' ויצאו לבי[ת] השריפה: עי' לקמן דף ע[ח] ע"ב:

הגהות צ"ק

[א] נינהו הס"ד אח"כ ד"ה מה איל נזיר כו': [ב] הואיל והאיל מקדשן:

שלא

גמרא

שֶׁאִם הוּזְקְקוּ זֶה לָזֶה — שֶׁמְּעַכְּבִין זֶה אֶת זֶה, וְאֵיזֶה הוּא זִיקָה שֶׁלָּהֶן? אשְׁחִיטָה. אֲמַר עוּלָּא, בָּעוּ בְּמַעֲרָבָא: תְּנוּפָה עוֹשָׂה זִיקָה אוֹ אֵינוֹ עוֹשָׂה זִיקָה? פְּשׁוֹט לֵיהּ מִדְּרַבִּי יוֹחָנָן, דְּאָמַר רַבִּי יוֹחָנָן: שְׁחִיטָה עוֹשָׂה זִיקָה, מִכְּלָל דִּתְנוּפָה אֵינוֹ עוֹשָׂה זִיקָה! דְּר' יוֹחָנָן גּוּפָא קָא מִיבַּעְיָא לֵיהּ: מִיפְשַׁט פְּשִׁיטָא לֵיהּ לְרַבִּי יוֹחָנָן דִּשְׁחִיטָה עוֹשָׂה זִיקָה וּתְנוּפָה אֵינוֹ עוֹשָׂה זִיקָה, אוֹ דִּלְמָא שְׁחִיטָה פְּשִׁיטָא לֵיהּ וּתְנוּפָה מְסַפְּקָא לֵיהּ? תֵּיקוּ. א"ל ר' יְהוּדָה בַּר חֲנִינָא לְרַב הוּנָא בְּרֵיהּ דְּרַב יְהוֹשֻׁעַ: וְהָא כִּי כְּתִיב °"קוֹדֶשׁ יִהְיוּ לַה' לַכֹּהֵן", בָּתַר תְּנוּפָה כְּתִיב, וּפְלִיגִי בֶּן נַנָּס וְר' עֲקִיבָא! וְלִיטַעְמֵיךְ, בָּתַר תְּנוּפָה וְלָא בָּתַר שְׁחִיטָה?! אֶלָּא מַאי אִית לָךְ לְמֵימְרָא? מֵעִיקָּרָא קָאֵי, וּמַאי "קֹדֶשׁ יִהְיוּ לַה' לַכֹּהֵן" — דָּבָר שֶׁסּוֹפוֹ לַכֹּהֵן, הָכָא נַמִי — דָּבָר שֶׁסּוֹפוֹ לַכֹּהֵן. וּשְׁחִיטָה עוֹשָׂה זִיקָה? וּרְמִינְהִי: בעַד שֶׁלֹּא שְׁחָטָהּ נִפְרַס לַחְמָהּ — יָבִיא לֶחֶם אַחֵר וְשׁוֹחֵט. מִשֶּׁשְּׁחָטָהּ נִפְרַס לַחְמָהּ — הַדָּם יִזָּרֵק, וְהַבָּשָׂר יֵאָכֵל, וִידֵי נִדְרוֹ לֹא יָצָא, וְהַלֶּחֶם פָּסוּל. נִזְרַק הַדָּם — תּוֹרֵם מִן הַשָּׁלֵם עַל הַפָּרוּס. געַד שֶׁלֹּא שְׁחָטָהּ יָצָא לַחְמָהּ — מַכְנִיסָהּ וְשׁוֹחֵט. מִשֶּׁשְּׁחָטָהּ יָצָא לַחְמָהּ — הַדָּם יִזָּרֵק, וְהַבָּשָׂר יֵאָכֵל, וִידֵי נִדְרוֹ לֹא יָצָא, וְהַלֶּחֶם פָּסוּל. נִזְרַק הַדָּם — תּוֹרֵם מִמָּה שֶׁבִּפְנִים עַל שֶׁבַּחוּץ. עַד שֶׁלֹּא שְׁחָטָהּ נִטְמָא לַחְמָהּ — מֵבִיא לֶחֶם אַחֵר וְשׁוֹחֵט. מִשֶּׁשְּׁחָטָהּ נִטְמָא לַחְמָהּ — הַדָּם יִזָּרֵק, וְהַבָּשָׂר יֵאָכֵל, וִידֵי נִדְרוֹ יָצָא, שֶׁהַצִּיץ מְרַצֶּה עַל הַטָּמֵא, וְהַלֶּחֶם פָּסוּל. נִזְרַק הַדָּם — תּוֹרֵם מִן הַטָּהוֹר עַל הַטָּמֵא. וְאִי ס"ד שְׁחִיטָה עוֹשָׂה זִיקָה, כֵּיוָן דְּהוּזְקְקוּ זֶה לָזֶה בִּשְׁחִיטָה אִיפְּסִיל לֵיהּ א] לֶחֶם, תִּיפָּסֵל נַמִּי תּוֹדָה! *שָׁאנֵי תּוֹדָה, דְּרַחֲמָנָא קַרְיֵיהּ שְׁלָמִים, מַה שְּׁלָמִים קְרֵבִים בְּלֹא לֶחֶם, אַף ב] תּוֹדָה קְרֵבָה בְּלֹא לֶחֶם. א"ר יִרְמְיָה, אִם תִּמְצָא לוֹמַר: תְּנוּפָה עוֹשָׂה זִיקָה, אָבַד הַלֶּחֶם — אָבְדוּ

רש"י

שאם הוזקקו זה לזה. שהיו ביחד, ואח"כ אבד לחם או כבשים – שמעכבין זה לזה, והנותר לפנינו יצא לבית השריפה, דנדחה באבוד חבירו. ואיזו זיקה. שלהן הקובעתן יחד? שחיטה. שאם היה לחם בשעת שחיטה, ואח"כ אבד או לחם או כבשים – אבד הכל. תנופה. ג] כבשים היו מניפין (א) עם הלחם מחיים, בפ' "כל המנחות באות מצה" (לקמן סא.). ופליגי בן ננס ור' עקיבא. וש"מ דאין תנופה עושה זיקה. ולא בתר שחיטה. בתמיה. הא ודאי דלכהן לא הוי אלא לאחר שחיטה. מעיקרא. קודם שחיטה. עד שלא שחטה. לתודה (ב). לחם תודה אין מתקדש אלא בשחיטתה, בפרק "התודה" (לקמן דף עח:), דכתיב: "קרבנו על זבח (התודה)" וגו' (ויקרא ז) – מלמד שאין הלחם קדוש אלא בשחיטת הזבח. נפרס לחמה. לא ידענא מנלן דמיפסל לכולהו משום דנפרסה אחת מהן. ונראה בעיני: דמלחם ד] הפנים גמר, שהיא ה] [א] מנחת תודה, וכתיב בה "היא" ו] (קדש קדשים הוא) (שם כד), שאם נפרסה אחד מחלותיה – [כולן] פסולות. הדם יזרק. לשם שלמים, ולא לשם תודה ז]. נזרק הדם. עד שלא נפרס הלחם. תורם. ח] כדכתיב: "והקריב ממנו אחד מכל קרבן" (שם). דמ' חלות היו, והיה תורם אחד מעשר לכהן, והשאר לבעלים. ברים פרק "התודה" (לקמן דף עז:). מן השלם. ולא מן הפרוס. דתניא ב"התודה" (שם עז:): "אחת" – שלא יטול פרוס. יצא לחמה. חוץ לחומת ירושלים. מכניסה ושוחט. דכל זמן שאינו קדוש בשחיטה, אינו נפסל ביוצא. הדם יזרק. לשם שלמים. תורם ממה שבפנים על שבחוץ. ולא שיאכל אותו שיצא, אלא יחשב במנין להיות תרומתו תרומה ולהכשיר את הפנימיות. כל יוצא דתודה – לאו חוץ לעזרה קאמר, אלא חוץ לעיר, דהא התודה ולחמה נאכלין בכל העיר. משנשחטה נטמא לחמה הדם יזרק. לשם תודה, והבשר יאכל בתורת תודה. וידי נדרו יצא. דהציץ מרצה על אכילתן לענין טומאה ט]. ותיפסל נמי תודה. ולא תזרק אפילו שלא לשמה? רחמנא קרייה שלמים. "תודת שלמיו" – י] משמע: דאע"פ שהיתה תודה בשעת לחמה, חוזרת להיות שלמים בלא לחם. אבל כבשי עצרת עם לחמה *קרוי "שלמים". אבד הלחם. אחר תנופה.

בעו

*כ"א לא

תוספות

ואיזו היא זיקה שלהן זו שחיטה. דאם אבד הלחם – אבדו הכבשים, ואם אבדו הכבשים – אבד הלחם. והיינו כרבי, דאמר לקמן (ד' מז.): כבשי עצרת אין מקדשין הלחם אלא בשחיטה. ולרבי אלעזר בר' שמעון (קשה) נהי דאם אבד הלחם – אבדו הכבשים, כדאמר רבי יוחנן לקמן

מסורת הש"ם

(שם): הכל מודים שצריך שיהא לחם בשעת שחיטה, מכ"מ אבדו כבשים – אמאי אבד הלחם? הא אית ליה פדיון, *[ב] (כדפי' בקונט') בפ"ק דפסחים (ד' יג:) גבי "לחמי תודה ונפרקינהו ונפקינהו לחולין. כמאן? כרבי דאמר" וכו' – משמע דלרבי אלעזר בר"ש נפקי לחולין. ולא מסתבר לחלק דשאני הכא דאיכא תנופה מחיים – דהא מספקא לן אי עושה זיקה, כל שכן דלא מסייעא לקדש! ותו: דאמרינן לקמן (ד' מז:): שחט שני כבשים על ארבעה חלות – מושך שתים מהן [ג] ומניחן, והשאר נאכלות בפדיון, אע"ג דאיכא תנופה [ד] בכולהו. וצ"ע. ומשמע התם דלרבי אלעזר בר' שמעון פודן בחוץ ונאכלין בחוץ. והא דאיפליגו אביי ורבא לקמן (שם.) במילתיה דרבי דאמר "קדוש ואינו קדוש", אביי אמר: קדוש ואינו [ה] ניתר. רבא אמר: קדוש ואינו [ו] נפדה, ואמרי': לאביי – תפיס פדיונו, לרבא – לא תפיס. אלמא לאביי לרבי נמי נפקי לחולין. ואם כן, מאי "אבד הלחם" דהכא? ואין לומר: "אבד מליקרב", דפשיטא, [ז] דאכתי חזו יא] *לדבר אחר, מ"ש מלחם אחר, וש"מ: כיון דנפדו – פקעה קדושת תנור. ורבי דסבירא ליה תנור מקדש, *אי אפי לה בתנור דחול – לא מקדשו. ותימה הוא. וי"ל: דלאביי תפיס פדיונו, ולא נפיק לחולין. והשתא ניחא לשון "תפיס", דהוה ליה למימר "נפדה". ותדע, דהא רבי הוא דאמר תנור מקדש בסוף "רבי ישמעאל" (לקמן עב:), ותנן (לקמן ד' ק:): המנחות והנסכים אין להם פדיון משקדשו בכלי. ושתי הלחם נמי איקרו "מנחה", לקמן (ד' נג:). מיהו יש לחלק בין מנחה דבהדי זבח למנחה לחודה, כדאיתא בפ"ק (לעיל ו.). והא דלא קאמר: איכא בינייהו אליבא דאביי, דלרבי אלעזר ברבי שמעון – יכול לפדות את הלחם, ולרבי – אינו יכול? יב] וי"ל: הא דרבי אלעזר בר' שמעון נמי הכי אית ליה, אי ס"ל דתהנור מקדש, ולאו מטעמיה דהכא [ח] דפליג עליה. אבל למאי דמפרש, איכא בינייהו לאיפסולי ביוצא קדושת כלי, אינו מועיל דבר, כמו שהוכחתי בפ"ק (שם דף ו.). וסוגיא דפסחים (דף יג:) דסברה דלרבי לא נפקי לחולין – כרבא אתיא, דלחמי תודה לית להו תנור. וא"כ, לאביי נפקי לחולין. ותימה: דמשמע הכא דאי תנופה עושה זיקה – [ט] אבד הלחם, אבדו הכבשים. ואמאי? הא מדרבי אלעזר בר' שמעון נשמע דקודם שחיטה לרבי, כקודם זריקה לר"א ברבי שמעון דמי, יג] [י] ואין להם פדיון לכולי עלמא, כדאיתא לקמן (דף מז:) גבי "שוחט כבשים על ד' חלות", דלר"א ברבי שמעון פודן בחוץ! וי"ל: דהכא קסבר תנור מקדש, ולקמן קא סבר אין תנור מקדש. והלכך שמעתין אתיא שפיר אף כר"א בר' שמעון אי קסבר תנור מקדש. ולקמן איירי אי קסבר אין תנור מקדש. אי נמי: התם אפילו אפאם בבת אחת – אין התנור מקדשן, כיון דלא חזו כולהו. כי ההיא דסוף "לולב וערבה" יד] (סוכה דף מט.)[יא] דאין שיעור למים – מגי למלאות בחבית מקודשת, ולא איפסלי בלינה. אי נמי: שאני הכא דאיכא תנופה חשיבא, אבל התם כיון שאינה ראויה אלא לשתי חלות – לא אלימא ההוא תנופה לאקבועי. ואפילו ר"א ברבי שמעון מודה הכא[יב] דשחיטה קבעה. והא דמיבעיא לקמן (דף מז.): כבשי עצרת ששחטן לשמן וזרק דמן שלא לשמן, אותו הלחם מהו באכילה? ופריך: למאן? אי לר"א בר' שמעון – האמר: זריקה היא דמקדשה. כלומר, טו] וכל שכן שאסורין באכילה. [יג] דהא התם הוה תנופה. וכדפרשי'. *)ובקונטרס פירש לקמן (דף מח.) גבי "פודן בחוץ" לר"א בר' שמעון דפריק להו קודם זריקה, [יד]ומיגו דחזו לקרבן דאי בעי מניף, אלימי למיתפס פדיונן. והא דבסוף "רבי ישמעאל" (לקמן דף עב:) משמע דאיפליגו רבי ור"א ברבי שמעון אי הוקבעו בשחיטה אי לא הוקבעו, ופירש בקונטרס: לשנותן לשם זבח אחר – הא ליתא, דאפילו בתנופה הוזקקו זה לזה אם תנופה עושה זיקה. ועוד קשה: דמשמע דלר"א יכול לשנותן לשם זבח אחר – והא ליתא, דלכולי עלמא אינו יכול לשנותן לשם זבח אחר, לפירוש דפירשנו. אלא התם מיירי לאפסולי ביוצא. **נפרס** לחמה. תלת גווני קתני: "נפרס", "יצא", "נטמא". וכולהו צריכי. וצ"ע: שלא יקשה מכאן *לרבא דאמר בפ"ק (לעיל דף יב:) דלמ"ד טז] זריקה מועלת ליוצא, דבחסרות מודה. **משנשחטה** נטמא לחמה הדם יזרק והבשר יאכל וידי נדרו יצא והלחם פסול. הך גירסא איתא בספרים. ותימה: דמדקתני "יצא" – אלמא קסבר: הציץ מרצה על אכילות, והדר קאמר "והלחם פסול" – דלשון "פסול" משמע דאפילו נטמא מקצתו – פסול כולו. יז] ועוד: דהוה ליה למיתני "תורם מן הטהור על הטמא", כדקתני סיפא גבי נזרק הדם! לכך נראה דגרסינן "וידי נדרו לא יצא". ותימה דלעיל (דף כה.) דייק: מאן שמעת ליה דאמר אין זריקה מועלת ליוצא? רבי אליעזר, יח] וקסבר: הציץ מרצה על אכילות. והא הכא קתני "משנשחטה יצא לחמה – ידי נדרו לא יצא", וסברה דאין הציץ מרצה על אכילות. **דרחמנא** קרייה שלמים. אף על גב דכבשי עצרת נמי איקרו "שלמים" – יט] לא דמי. שהרי הם קדשי קדשים, ולא ילפינן מקדשים קלים. אי נמי: לא ילפינן שלמי ציבור משלמי יחיד.

אבדו

*) זהו תירוץ על התימה ועיין רש"ק

רבינו גרשום

שאם הוזקקו זה לזה שאם נשחטו הכבשים א) לשם הלחם: תנופה קודם שחיטה עושה זיקה אי לא: א"ל רב יהודה אמאי מספקא לי' בתנופה אי עושה [זיקה] והכתיב קדש יהיו לה' לכהן בתר תנופה כתיב דרישיה דקרא כתיב והניף אותם. ופליגי בן ננס ור' עקיבא ואי סלקא דעתך דתנופה עושה זיקה אמאי פליגי. אלא מדפליגי ש"מ דפשיטא להו דתנופה אינה עושה זיקה ומשום הכי פליגי: ולטעמיך הא בתר שחיטה נמי כתי' יהיו לה' לכהן שכבר נשחט וראוי לכהן מי נימא נמי דבתר שחיטה פליגי הא"ר יוחנן הכל מודים אלא מאי אית לך למימר מעיקרא קאי כלומר האי קרא לאו בתר שחיטה כתי' אלא קודם שחיטה ומאי קדש לה' לכהן דבר שסופו לכהן לאחר שנשחט: הכא נמי לא תימא דבתר תנופה כתיב אלא קודם תנופה וקודם תנופה פליגי הילכך אכתי מספקא אי תנופה עושה זיקה אי לא: עד שלא שחטה נפרס לחמה של תודה: הדם יזרק שלא לשם תודה אלא לשם שלמים. והבשר יאכל שלא לשם תודה והלחם פסול משום דשחיטת הזבח מקדש הלחם משום הכי אינו מביא לחם אחר מאחר שנשחט אלא הלחם פסול: נזרק הדם ואח"כ נפרס הואיל וזריקה מתרת ובשעת זריקה היה שלם כשר הוא הלחם אבל תורם מן השלם על הפרוס היינו תורם דמארבעים חלות היה תורם ד' אחת מכל מין דכתיב והקריב ממנו אחד שלא יטול פרוס מכל קרבן תרומה לה' יוצא דינו כנפרס: אבל נטמא לחמה יש לו דין אחר: הדם יזרק לשום תודה והבשר יאכל לשום תודה וידי נדרו יצא דציץ מרצה על אכילות ואין מרצה על יוצא: שאני תודה דרחמנא קריה שלמים דכתיב וזאת תורת זבח השלמים וגו' אם על תודה יקריבנו משום הכין הדם יזרק לשם שלמים כי נטמא הלחם. ואי אמרת הואיל וכן הוא כבשי עצרת שהוזקקו עם הלחם בשחיטה אמאי מעכבי הלחם הא איקרו שלמים דכתיב ושני כבשים בני שנה לזבח שלמים ב) הא לא קשיא זבח שלמים איקרו ולא דבר אחר אבל הכא איקרי תודה ואיקרי זבח שלמים:

א) אולי צ"ל שאם נשחטו הכבשים ואח"כ אבד הלחם אבדו הכבשים.
ב) עי' תוס' ד"ה דרחמנא:

[נ"ל לרב הונא]

עין משפט נר מצוה

קד א מיי' פ"ח מהלכות תמידין ומוספין הל' יט ופי"ז מהל' פסה"מ הלכה יח:
קה ב ג מיי' פי"ב מהל' פסה"מ הלכה יז:

הגהות הב"ח

(א) רש"י ד"ה תנופה וכו' מניפין מחיים עם הלחם בפרק: (ב) ד"ה עד שלא שחטה לתודה אין הלחם מתקדש ללחם תודה:

שיטה מקובצת

א] לחם ותיפסל: ב] תודה קרבה בלא לחם. ודוקא שלא לשמה מקריב לה א"נ אפילו לשמה: ג] הכבשים: ד] הפנים גמר. גליון א"נ משום דכתיב אחד מכל קרבן שלא יטול פרוס ובעינן שיהא כולן ראויות לכהן. תו"ח. ועיין תוס' לקמן (דף נג ע"ב): ה] מנחה כלחם תודה: ו] תיבות קדש קדשים הוא נמחק: ז] תודה. עיין תוס' לקמן (דף מז ע"ב): ח] תורם דכתיב: ט] טומאה: והלחם פסול. ולא ידענא אמאי כיון דזריקה כשירה לחם הטהור אמאי פסול ונראה בעיני דגרסי' וידי נדרו לא יצא והאי תנא סבירא ליה אין הציץ מרצה על אכילה וכן מצאתיה בתוספתא ולבי מגמגם: י] תיבת משמע בס"א אינו: יא] חזו לכבשים אחרים דמאי שנא. ועיין תוס' לקמן (דף נ ע"ב): יב] יכול. גליון וי"ל דלא חשיב נפקותא דכיון דלרבי הא דלא נפקי לחולין היינו משום דתנור מקדש ה"נ הו"א לרבי אלעזר אי סבר דתנור מקדש אבל לאפסולי ביוצא (דמשני) [דחשיב שאני] התם הדבר תלוי בשחיטה: יג] דמי ויש: יד] וערבה דאמרי' קסבר דאין שיעור למים ואי מייתי במקודשת איפסלו להו בלינה אבל אי אמרינן דיש שיעור: טו] כלומר אינו ר"ל שיהא לו פדיון: טז] דלמ"ד אין זריקה: יז] פסול כולו. אפי' הטהור: יח] אליעזר וקתני דציץ מרצה על אכילות משמע דשום תנא ליכא אלא ר' אליעזר והא איכא האי תנא דסבר אין זריקה מועלת ליוצא ומש"ה אמר רש"י ולבי מגמגם כך פי' הר"ר אלחנן: עוד שם וי"ל דבקל סותר התם סברא דאיפוך אי נמי מצי למימר דלא כר' אליעזר אלא כרבי עקיבא וקסבר אין הציץ מרצה וע"כ לא קאמר רבי עקיבא זריקה מועלת ליוצא ה"מ לאימורים אבל בלחמי תודה דלאו גופיה דזביחה מודה דאין זריקה מועלת ליוצא לכ"ע והכי משמע פ' כל התדיר (דף לא ע"א) גבי אימורים קדשים קלים כשיצאו ומוקי פלוגתייהו כי הדר עיילינהו בדאיתנהו אבראי כ"ע לא פליגי ומשני ה"מ גבי שתי הלחם דלאו גופיה דזבח יט] שלמים. וי"ל דלא הן כך תירץ הר"מ. תו"ח. וא"כ אפשר דהאי ברייתא אתיא כר"ע ולדידיה אין הציץ מרצה על אכילות אבל ר"א אימא לעולם שפיר אית ליה הציץ מרצה על אכילות כדאיתא בהקומץ רבה: יט] דמי דגבי תודה הוה מקרא דגבי תודה כתיב זאת תורת זבח השלמים אם על תודה יקריבנו וגו' ע"כ תו"ח:

גליון הש"ס

רש"י ד"ה הדם יזרק לשם שלמים. עיין לקמן דף מז ע"ב תוד"ה אי תודה.

הגהות צ"ק

[א] מנחה כתודה: [ב] כלפריך בפ"ק: [ג] נ"ל ומניחן: [ד] בכולהו ומשמע כו' ונאכלין בחוץ ונ"ע הא כו': [ה] גמורף: [ו] ניתר: [ז] דאינו חזי לזבח אחר: [ח] פליג: [ט] נ"ל אבדו הכבשים אבד הלחם: [י] ואית להם: [יא] למ"ד דיש: [יב] נ"א לתנופה: [יג] דהתם הוי תנופה וכדפי' רש"י: [יד] מיגו:

אֵילִים מְרוּבִּין, וְלֹא הָיָה לָהֶן אֵיפָתָן — יָבִיאוּ אַיִל אֶחָד וְאֵיפָתוֹ, וְלֹא יִקְרְבוּ כּוּלָּם בְּלֹא אֵיפוֹת.§ **מתני'** אהַפָּר וְהָאֵילִים וְהַכְּבָשִׂים וְהַשָּׂעִיר אֵין מְעַכְּבִין אֶת הַלֶּחֶם, וְלֹא הַלֶּחֶם מְעַכְּבָן. בהַלֶּחֶם מְעַכֵּב אֶת הַכְּבָשִׂים, וְאֵין הַכְּבָשִׂים מְעַכְּבִין אֶת הַלֶּחֶם, דִּבְרֵי ר"ע. אָמַר ר"ש בֶּן נַנָּס: לֹא כִּי, אֶלָּא הַכְּבָשִׂים מְעַכְּבִין אֶת הַלֶּחֶם, וְהַלֶּחֶם אֵינוֹ מְעַכֵּב הַכְּבָשִׂים. שֶׁכֵּן מָצִינוּ כְּשֶׁהָיוּ יִשְׂרָאֵל בַּמִּדְבָּר מ' שָׁנָה קָרְבוּ כְּבָשִׂים בְּלֹא לֶחֶם, אַף כָּאן יִקְרְבוּ כְּבָשִׂים בְּלֹא לֶחֶם. אָמַר ר"ש: הֲלָכָה כְּדִבְרֵי בֶּן נַנָּס, אֲבָל אֵין הַטַּעַם כִּדְבָרָיו, שֶׁכָּל הָאָמוּר בְּחוּמַּשׁ הַפְּקוּדִים קָרֵב בַּמִּדְבָּר, וְכָל הָאָמוּר בְּתוֹרַת כֹּהֲנִים א] אֵין קָרֵב בַּמִּדְבָּר. מִשֶּׁבָּאוּ לָאָרֶץ — קָרְבוּ אֵלּוּ וְאֵלּוּ. מִפְּנֵי מָה אֲנִי אוֹמֵר יִקְרְבוּ כְּבָשִׂים בְּלֹא לֶחֶם? מִפְּנֵי שֶׁהַכְּבָשִׂים מַתִּירִין אֶת ב] עַצְמָן, וְלֹא הַלֶּחֶם בְּלֹא כְּבָשִׂים? שֶׁאֵין לוֹ מִי יַתִּירֶנּוּ.§ **גמ'** תָּנוּ רַבָּנַן: °"וְהִקְרַבְתֶּם עַל הַלֶּחֶם" — חוֹבָה עַל הַלֶּחֶם, "שִׁבְעַת כְּבָשִׂים תְּמִימִים" — אע"פ שֶׁאֵין לֶחֶם, א"כ מַה ת"ל "עַל הַלֶּחֶם"? מְלַמֵּד שֶׁלֹּא נִתְחַיְּיבוּ בִּכְבָשִׂים קוֹדֶם שֶׁנִּתְחַיְּיבוּ בַּלֶּחֶם, דִּבְרֵי ר' טַרְפוֹן. ג] ר"ע אוֹמֵר: יָכוֹל הֵן הֵן כְּבָשִׂים הָאֲמוּרִים כָּאן הֵן הֵן כְּבָשִׂים הָאֲמוּרִים בְּחוּמַּשׁ הַפְּקוּדִים? אָמַרְתָּ, כְּשֶׁאַתָּה מַגִּיעַ אֵצֶל פָּרִים וְאֵילִים אֵינָן הֵן, אֶלָּא הַלָּלוּ בָּאִין בִּגְלַל עַצְמָן וְהַלָּלוּ בָּאִין בִּגְלַל לֶחֶם. נִמְצָא מַה שֶּׁאָמוּר בְּחוּמַּשׁ הַפְּקוּדִים — קָרֵב בַּמִּדְבָּר, וּמַה שֶּׁאָמוּר בְּתוֹרַת כֹּהֲנִים — לֹא קָרֵב בַּמִּדְבָּר. וְדִלְמָא פָּרִים וְאֵילִים לָאו אִינְהוּ, ד] הָא כְּבָשִׂים אִינְהוּ נִינְהוּ! מִדְּהָנֵי אִישְׁתְּנוּ, הָנֵי נַמִי דַּאֲחֵרִינֵי. וּפָרִים וְאֵילִים מִמַּאי דְּאִישְׁתְּנוּ? דִּלְמָא הָכִי קָאָמַר רַחֲמָנָא: אִי בָּעֵי פַּר וּשְׁנֵי אֵילִים — לִיקְרַב, אִי בָּעֵי שְׁנֵי פָּרִים וְאַיִל אֶחָד — לִיקְרַב! ה] מִדְּאִישְׁתְּנִי סִדְרָן, ש"מ אַחֲרִינֵי נִינְהוּ.§ "הַלֶּחֶם מְעַכֵּב אֶת הַכְּבָשִׂים".§ מ"ט דְּר"ע? ו] גָּמַר "יִהְיוּ" מִ"תִּהְיֶינָה", מַה לְּהַלָּן לֶחֶם, אַף כָּאן לֶחֶם. וּבֶן נַנָּס? גָּמַר "יִהְיוּ" ["יִהְיוּ",] מַה לְּהַלָּן כְּבָשִׂים, אַף כָּאן כְּבָשִׂים. ז] וּבֶן נַנָּס נַמִי נֵילַף מִ"תִּהְיֶינָה", ח] מַה לְּהַלָּן לֶחֶם, אַף כָּאן לֶחֶם! דָּנִין "יִהְיוּ" מִ"יִּהְיוּ", וְאֵין דָּנִין "יִהְיוּ" מִ"תִּהְיֶינָה". מַאי נָפְקָא מִינָּהּ? אהָתָנָא דְּבֵי ר' יִשְׁמָעֵאל: °"וְשָׁב הַכֹּהֵן" "וּבָא הַכֹּהֵן", זֶהוּ שִׁיבָה, זֶהוּ בִּיאָה! ה"מ הֵיכָא דְּלֵיכָּא דְּדָמֵי לֵיהּ, אֲבָל הֵיכָא דְּאִיכָּא דְּדָמֵי לֵיהּ — מִדְּדָמֵי לֵיהּ יָלְפִינַן. וְר"ע נַמִי לֵילַף "יִהְיוּ" מִ"יִּהְיוּ"! דָּנִין דָּבָר שֶׁמַּתָּנָה לַכֹּהֵן מִדָּבָר שֶׁמַּתָּנָה לַכֹּהֵן, לְאַפּוֹקֵי הָנֵי, דְּעוֹלוֹת נִינְהוּ. וְאִיבָּעֵית אֵימָא: בִּקְרָא גּוּפֵיהּ קָא מִיפַּלְגִי, °"קֹדֶשׁ יִהְיוּ לַה' לַכֹּהֵן" — ר"ע סָבַר: אֵי זֶהוּ דָּבָר שֶׁכּוּלּוֹ לַכֹּהֵן? הֱוֵי אוֹמֵר: זֶה לֶחֶם. וּבֶן נַנָּס? מִי כְּתִיב "קוֹדֶשׁ יִהְיוּ לַכֹּהֵן"?! "קוֹדֶשׁ יִהְיוּ לַה' לַכֹּהֵן" כְּתִיב, אֵיזֶהוּ דָּבָר שֶׁמִּקְצָתוֹ לַה' וּמִקְצָתוֹ לַכֹּהֵן? הֱוֵי אוֹמֵר: אֵלּוּ כְּבָשִׂים. וְר"ע? מִי כְּתִיב "קֹדֶשׁ יִהְיוּ לַה' וְלַכֹּהֵן"?! "לַה' לַכֹּהֵן" כְּתִיב, כִּדְרַב הוּנָא, דְּאָמַר רַב הוּנָא: בקָנָאוֹ הַשֵּׁם וּנְתָנוֹ לַכֹּהֵן.§ אָמַר ר' יוֹחָנָן: הַכֹּל מוֹדִים שֶׁאִם

א) יומא ב: נזיר ה: מכות יג: חולין פה. לעיל ז. וש"נ ב) [ב"ק קט: ערכין כח:]

תורה אור: °והקרבתם על הלחם (ויקרא כג). °ושב הכהן (שם יד). °קדש יהיו לה' לכהן (שם כג).

רש"י

*שֶׁאִם הָיוּ לָהֶם פָּרִים מְרוּבִּים. כְּלוֹמַר, דָּמִים לִקְנוֹת פָּרִים וְאֵילִים כְּדֵי צָרְכָּן. וְלֹא הָיוּ לָהֶם נְסָכִים. כְּלוֹמַר, אִם יִקְנוּ מִן הַדָּמִים אֵילִים וּפָרִים — לֹא יְהֵא בְּיָדָם דָּמִים לִקְנוֹת נְסָכִים. יָבִיאוּ פַּר אֶחָד וּנְסָכִים כו'. (אֵילִים מְרוּבִּין. בְּלֹא מִנְחָתָם). **מתני'** הַפָּר ט] הָאֵילִ' וְהַכְּבָשִׂ'. דִּכְתִיבִי בְּהַאי קְרָא: "וְהִקְרַבְתֶּם עַל הַלֶּחֶם שִׁבְעַת כְּבָשִׂים תְּמִימִים בְּנֵי שָׁנָה וּפַר בֶּן בָּקָר" וגו' (ויקרא כג). אֶת הַלֶּחֶם. שְׁתֵּי הַלֶּחֶם דַּעֲצֶרֶת. הַלֶּחֶם מְעַכֵּב אֶת הַכְּבָשִׂים. הָנָךְ שְׁנֵי כְבָשִׂים דִּשְׁלָמִים. בַּמִּדְבָּר קָרְבוּ כְּבָשִׂים בְּלֹא לֶחֶם. כְּלוֹמַר, בְּלֹא שְׁתֵּי הַלֶּחֶם הַבָּאִים עִם שְׁנֵי כְבָשִׂים. שֶׁהֲרֵי י] עוֹמֶר וּשְׁתֵּי הַלֶּחֶם אֵינָן בָּאִין אֶלָּא מִן הָאָרֶץ (לקמן דף פג:). הֲלָכָה כְּדִבְרֵי בֶּן נַנָּס. דִּכְבָשִׂים מְעַכְּבֵי לֶחֶם. אֵין הַטַּעַם כִּדְבָרָיו. דְּהוּא אוֹמֵר: בַּמִּדְבָּר קָרְבוּ יא] [א] נְסָכִים וּשְׁלָמִים, וְלֹא הִיא. שֶׁכָּל הָאָמוּר בְּפָרָשַׁת פִּנְחָס. כְּגוֹן הָנָךְ דְּמוּסָף קָרְבוּ בַּמִּדְבָּר. וְהָאָמוּר בְּת"כ. כְּגוֹן הָנָךְ ז' כְּבָשִׂים וּפָר וְאֵילִים [ב] לְעוֹלָה דְּעַל הַלֶּחֶם, וּשְׁנֵי כְבָשִׂים דִּשְׁלָמִים — לֹא קָרְבוּ בַּמִּדְבָּר, כִּדְאָמַר בַּגְּמָ'. **גמ'** חוֹבָה עַל הַלֶּחֶם. דְּמַשְׁמַע: דְּאֵינָן קְרֵיבִין בְּלֹא לֶחֶם וְלֹא לֶחֶם קָרֵב בְּלֹא כְבָשִׂים, וַהֲדַר כְּתִיב "שִׁבְעַת כְּבָשִׂים" — דְּמַשְׁמַע: אע"פ שֶׁאֵין לֶחֶם. א"כ מַה ת"ל עַל הַלֶּחֶם כו' קוֹדֶם שֶׁנִּתְחַיְּיבוּ בַּלֶּחֶם. כָּל זְמַן שֶׁהָיוּ בַּמִּדְבָּר. כְּשֶׁאַתָּה מַגִּיעַ כו'. דְּבְת"כ (ויקרא כג) כְּתִיב פַּר וּשְׁנֵי אֵילִים, וּבְחוּמַּשׁ הַפְּקוּדִים (במדבר כח) כְּתִיב "פָּרִים בְּנֵי בָקָר שְׁנַיִם וְאַיִל אֶחָד". אֶלָּא אֵלּוּ דְּחוּמַּשׁ הַפְּקוּדִים בָּאִין בִּגְלַל עַצְמָן, יב] דְּמוּסָפִין הֵן, וְאֵינָן טְעוּנִין לֶחֶם. וְהָאָמוּר בְּתוֹרַת כֹּהֲנִים לֹא קָרֵב בַּמִּדְבָּר. כִּדְאַמְרַן, שֶׁלֹּא נִתְחַיְּיבוּ בִּכְבָשִׂים קוֹדֶם שֶׁנִּתְחַיְּיבוּ בַּלֶּחֶם. מִדְּהָנֵי אִישְׁתַּנּוּ. פַּר וְאֵילִים (א). דַּאֲחֵרִינֵי יג]. וְאַע"ג דְּשָׁוִין. מִדְּאִשְׁתַּנֵּי סִדְרָן. דְּבְת"כ יד] [ג]: כְּבָשִׂים וּפָר וְאֵילִים, וּבְפִנְחָס: וְהִקְרַבְתֶּם פָּרִים וְאֵילִ' כְּבָשִׂים וגו'. גָּמַר יִהְיוּ מִתִּהְיֶינָה. דִּכְתִיב בְּלֶחֶם (ויקרא כג): "וּשְׁנֵי כְבָשִׂים וְהֵנִיף הַכֹּהֵן אוֹתָם עַל לֶחֶם הַבִּכּוּרִים תְּנוּפָה וגו' יִהְיוּ לַה' לַכֹּהֵן". "יִהְיוּ" — הֲוָיָה. וְלָא יָדְעִינַן אַהַיָּיא קַיְימָא הֲוָיָה: אוֹ אַלֶּחֶם, אוֹ אַכְּבָשִׂים — הִלְכָּךְ גָּמַר "יִהְיוּ" מִ"סֹּלֶת תִּהְיֶינָה" (שם). מַה הָתָם הֲוָיָה — אַלֶּחֶם, אַף הָכָא הֲוָיָה — אַלֶּחֶם. גָּמַר יִהְיוּ מִיִּהְיוּ. דִּכְתִיב גַּבֵּי ז' כְּבָשִׂים (שם) טו] (עוֹלָה) "יִהְיוּ עוֹלָה לַה'" (ב). [ד] לֶחֶם וּכְבָשִׂים דִּשְׁלָמִים. מַתָּנָה לַכֹּהֵן. טז] שֶׁכּוּלּוֹ לַכֹּהֵן. לְאַפּוֹקֵי כְּבָשִׂים, אֵימוּרֵיהֶן — לַמִּזְבֵּחַ. הֱוֵי אוֹמֵר אֵלּוּ כְּבָשִׂים. אַלְמָא "יִהְיוּ" — אַכְּבָשִׂ' יז] כְּתִיב. קָנָאוֹ הַשֵּׁם וּנְתָנוֹ לַכֹּהֵן. דְּמִשּׁוּלְחַן גָּבוֹהַּ קָזָכוּ. וְעִיקַּר מִילְּתֵיהּ דְּרַב הוּנָא אַגֶּזֶל הַגֵּר אִיתְּמַר, בְּפֶ' "הַגּוֹזֵל עֵצִים" בְּב"ק (ד' קט:): יח] הָאָשָׁם (ג) לַה' לַכֹּהֵן.

תוספות

דורש בספרי בפרשת "כי תלא", דא"ר חנינא בן חזקיה בן גרון: וכי מדת פרים אילים וכבשים אחת היא?! והלא כבר נאמר "שלשה עשרונים לפר" וגו'! אלא מלמד שאיפה גדולה ואיפה קטנה קרויה "איפה".

קרבו כבשים בלא לחם. פי' *בקונטרס: שלא היה להם אלא מן. וקשה: דפ"ב דיומא (עה:) מוכח [ה] דאומות העולם היו מביאין להם מיני מאכל. ובפ' שתי הלחם (לקמן צה.) נמי מוכח שהיה עמהם לחם הפנים במדבר, והיו מקריבין מנחת העומר! ואומר ר"ת: דהיינו טעמא, דכתיב "כי תבואו אל הארץ". ור"ע לטעמיה, ד"כי תבואו" — לאו דווקא. אבל ר"ש — כרבי ישמעאל ספ"ק דקדושין (ד' לז:) דביאה לאחר ישיבה. מיהו קשה: דאם כן, אף קרבניהם לא יקריבו! ויש לחלק (ונראה לפרש) משום דשתי הלחם איקרו "ביכורים" כדלקמן (ד' מו:), ומה בכורים בארץ, אף שתי הלחם כן. ועוד דרשינן בהדיא פרק "רבי ישמעאל" (לקמן סט:): "ממושבותיכם" — למעוטי ח"ל.

הלכה כרבי שמעון בן ננס. תימה: הילכתא למשיחא? כדפריך יט] פ' "בית שמאי" (זבחים מה.), ובפ' "ד' מיתות" (סנהדרין נא:), ובפרק "עשרה יוחסין" (קדושין עב.) גבי ממזרים *פירשתי.

שבעת כבשים אע"פ שאין לחם. מדלא כתיב "והקרבתם [ו] על הלחם *שבעת כבשים".

מדאשתני סידרן. משמע: אי לא אשתנו ה"א דחד נינהו. וקשה: דפרק "בא לו" (יומא ע:) מצריך (איל אחד) לאשמועינן "איל" האמור בת"כ זהו האמור בחומש הפקודים, ואיכא דדריש התם מ"אחד" מיוחד! וי"ל: דמדהכא כתיב פרים ושני אילים, והכא כתיב איל ושני פרים — [ז] ש"מ: אי בעי קאמר, מדלא כתיב ג' פרים וג' אילים, והיינו כדרשא דהתם: "א'" — ולא שנים.

גמר יהיו מתהיינה. ואף על גב כ] דקאי אלחם לבד ואכבשים לבד, כדאי' ב"הקומץ [רבה"] (לעיל כז.), מיהו מסתבר ליה דלא ניקום אעיכוב כבשים בלחם. ותימה הוא.

ובן ננס לילף יהיו מתהיינה. דהא דמו אהדדי טפי, דתרוייהו מיירו בענין לחם. ואף על גב דאמר טעמא [ח] במתניתין ["שכן מצינו במדבר מ' שנה" כו'], *ד"יהיו" מ"יהיו" לא דמו להדדי — דהדא ז' כבשים, והדא שני כבשים. ובתר דאסיק ד"יהיו" מ"יהיו" עדיף ליה, פריך לר"ע, כיון דעדיף, אע"ג דלא דמו. ובתוספתא [פ"ו] ובת"כ משמע דאמר ר"ע: [ט] דבר שקול מי מכריע? ואמר בן ננס: אני אכריע. **זו** היא שיבה זו היא ביאה. ל"ע: אי מלינן למילף מתרוייהו, אמאי לא ילפינן?*

דנין דבר שמתנה לכהן. תימה: אדרבה, דנין דבר שממנו קרב למזבח מדבר שממנו קרב למזבח! ויש לומר: דהאי כא] לד מסתבר ליה טפי, כיון דאידי ואידי אלחם קיימי.

דאמר רב הונא קנאו השם ונתנו לכהן. פירש בקונטרס: סוף "הגוזל קמא" (ב"ק דף קט:) קאמר הכי. וליתא, כב] [י] דהתם קאמר בברייתא "קנאו השם ונתנו לכהן שבאותו משמר", והכא לא מצית אמרת הכי — דקרבנות הרגל שוין לכל, כדדרשינן פרק בתרא דסוכה (דף נה:). ותו: דנתינה דהתם הוי לקדש בו את האשה ולכל צרכיו, והכא לא הוי הכי, כדאיתא בקדושין (דף נג.): המקדש בחלקו — לא קידש! אלא נראה לי דמילתא דרב הונא — אהא איתמר*). ואיזו

*) [וע"ע תוספות זבחים מז: ד"ה ואפי']

רבינו גרשום

קודם זה הדיבור נ"ל אילים מרובים בלא מנחתם שבקורה ד' והוא שייך לדיבור דלעיל וכי עלת פרים וכו' ונמחק לקמן ד"ה אילים כו'

לפר ושני עשרונים לאיל ונסכיהם דינן כמנחה ואמר לן ר' האי איפה דהכא או היא הויא כעשרון דאורייתא או דין עשרון להיות לעתיד לבא איפה: ב' פרים ואיל וכבשים ושעיר של מוסף עצרת שבחומש הפקודים ופר ואילים וכבשים ושעיר דתורת כהנים דחובות היום כולן קריבין בעצרת משבאו לארץ ושל מוסף היו קריבין תחלה ואח"כ של חובת היום: הפר והאילים ושבעת הכבשים ושעיר אין מעכבין את הלחם והלחם מעכב את הכבשים אותן שני כבשים של זבח השלמים כשהיו ישראל במדבר קרבו כבשים של זבח שלמים בלא לחם שלא היה להם לחם במדבר ועוד משום דכתיב ממושבותיכם תביאו לחם תנופה משיכנסו לארץ ולא קודם: אף כאן יקרבו וכו' אבל אין הטעם כדבריו שאותן ב' כבשים של שלמים שהיו באין על הלחם לא קרבו כלל במדבר לפי שהן אמורים בת"כ עם הלחם וכל האמור בתורת כהנים לא קרבו במדבר לא פרים ולא אילים ולא כבשים ולא שעיר: אלא מפני מה אני אומר יקרבו כבשים בלא לחם מפני שהכבשי' מתירין את עצמן בשחיטתן: חובה על הלחם. סמוך ללחם (שני כבשים) מה ת"ל על הלחם שלא נתחייבו בכבשים האמורים כאן בתורת כהנים קודם שנתחייבו בלחם דהיינו לאחר כניסתן לארץ: אמרת כשאתה מגיע אצל פרים ואצל אילים של חומש הפקודים אינן הן של תורת כהנים ומה שאמור בתורת כהנים לא קרב במדבר הואיל ובאין בגלל לחם: ודלמא פרים ואילים לאו אינהו נינהו משום דהכא שנים והכא אחד אבל כבשים דהכא ז' והכא ז' נימא דהן הן: מדאישתני סדרן דהכא (אמר) קדים לז' כבשים ברישא דפר וב' אילים והתם ב' פרים ואיל אחד וז' כבשים לבסוף ש"מ כולהו אחריני נינהו: גמרי יהיו מתהיינה דכתיב בלחם הויה דכתי' קדש יהיו לה' לכהן: א) ומנא לן דהאי יהיו דלח' דגמר מסולת תהיינה מה להלן לחם הכא נמי בלחם כתיב הויה ולא אכבשים ובן ננס גמר יהיו מיהיו עולה לה' דכבשים הוו עולה ולא לחם אף האי יהיו אכבשים קאי:

א] נראה דל"ל ומפיק ליה דהאי יהיו אלחם קאי דגמר מסולת וכו'.

עין משפט נר מצוה

קב א מיי' פ"ח מהל' תמידין ומוספין הלכה יז:

ברכ"י דהכלה שלפנינו ד"ה במדבר ליתא הכי אלא פירש כמ"ש תוספו' לקמן בסמוך

קנ ב מיי' שם הל' טו:

נ"ק מ"ז

[לא נמצא שם ועי' תוס' יומא ע. ד"ה הלכה כו' מה שליינתי שם]

נ"א שבעה ובעל קרבן אהרן מפרש מדלא כתיב והקרבתם שבת כבשים על הלחם

נ"ק מ"ז

הגהות הב"ח

(א) רש"י ד"ה מדהני וכו' ואילים דאחריני ואח"כ מ"ה הני נמי דאישתני כבשים ואע"ג דשוים: (ב) ד"ה גמר וכו' לה' הס"ד ואח"כ מ"ה דבר שמתנה לכהן לחם וכו' לכהן הס"ד ואח"כ מ"ה כולו לכהן לכל כבשים: (ג) ד"ה קנאו וכו' האשם המושב לה' לכהן:

פי' אעפ"כ עדיף טפי ללמוד יהיו מתהיינה מללמוד יהיו מיהיו דלא דמי כו' רש"ק

[וע"ע תוס' לעיל ד. ד"ה מאי נ"מ]

שיטה מקובצת

א] כהנים לא תיבת אין נמחק: ב] עצמן בלא לחם ולחם בלא כבשים אין: ג] תיבות ר"ע אומר נמחק: ד] אינהו כבשים אינהו מדהני: ה] מדאישתני סדרן. ומעתה אין אנו צריכין כשאתה מגיע אצל פרים ואילים אינן (הכי) [הן] א"נ אי לאו משום דאשתני פרים ואילים משום סברא דאשתני סדרן גרידא לא הוה אמינא אחריני נינהו. תו"ח: ו] גמר יהיו מתהיינה. משמע דיהיו לא קאי אכבשים והא דאמרינן בפ' הקומץ כבשים מעכבין זה את זה מ"ט הויה כתיב בהו [י"ל] דודאי אין מקרא יוצא מידי פשוטו וקאי אכבשים לענין שיעכבו זה את זה אבל לא שיעכבו את הלחם דמכח הגז"ש אנו אומרים דעיקר קרא אתא ללחם לומר שמעכב לחם דהכי משמע לן דאותו יהיו דאתא לומר דחד מינייהו שמעכב את חבירו מדכתיב גבי תרווייהו. תו"ח: ז] ובן ננס נמי נילף. וא"ת הלא בן ננס פי' טעמו במתניתין וי"ל דבמתני' לאו עיקר הטעם אמר אלא ה"ק לדבריך היה לך להודות לגז"ש דידי משום דאשכחנא במדבר קרבו כבשים בלא לחם. תו"ח: ח] מה להלן לחם כו' משמע דלר"ע לא קאי יהיו אכבשים וקשה האמרינן בהקומץ רבה שני כבשי עצרת מעכבין זה את זה יהיו כתיב בהו וי"ל דאה"נ דקאי יהיו אכבשים [מיהו] לא קאי כל כך אכבשים אלא אלחם דלחם מעכב את הכבשים ואין הכבשים מעכבין את הלחם וה"נ אנו צריכין לומר לבן ננס איפכא דאמר יהיו אכבשים קאי ולא אלחם ובהקומץ רבה תנן דשתי הלחם מעכבין זה את זה יהיו כתיב בהו אלא צ"ל דאע"ג דהאי יהיו [קאי נמי] אלחם לא קאי כל כך כמו אכבשים. תו"ח: ט] הפר. והאילים: י] שהרי נ"א לא היה להם לחם אלא מן: יא] קרבו כבשים: יב] עצמן בלא לחם נמצא מה שאמור בחומש הפקודים קרב במדבר כדאמרת: יג] דאחריני נינהו כבשים נמי אישתני דאחריני נינהו: יד] דבת"כ הקדים כבשים ופר לאילים ובפנחס הקדים פרים ואילים לכבשים: טו] תיבת עולה נמחק: טז] והם כולו לכהן אבל כבשים: יז] אכבשים קאי: יח] בב"ק דכתיב האשם המושב לה': יט] בפרק ב"ש. (דף מה ע"א) תירצו בתוס' קושיא זו ובפ"ד מיתות (דף נא ע"ב) ובפ' עשרה יוחסין לא דברו בתוס' שלנו ממנו כלום: כ] דקאי אלחם לבד. ורש"י ז"ל פי' לעיל דהויה דשתי החלות דמעכבי זו את זו היינו סולת תהיינה ולאו קרא דקדש יהיו עיין לעיל: כא] צד מסתבר. גליון וה"פ דנין יהיו מתהיינה דתרווייהו בלחם מיירי מלמילף יהיו מיהיו ונילף כבשים דבר שיש בו נמי מתנה לכהן מעולה שכולו כליל: כב] דהתם. ברייתא היא ולא רב הונא אמרה ותו דהתם: לחם

הגהות צ"ק

[א] נ"א כבשים דשלמים: [ב] העולה: [ג] כתיב כבשים כו' ובפנחס כתיב פרים שנים ואיל אחד ושבעה כבשים וגו'. [ד] שמתנה לכהן לחם כו': [ה] נ"א דתגרי אומות העולם וכו': [ו] עם הלחם: [ז] ולא כתב ג' פרים ושלשה אילים ש"מ אי בעי קאמר והיינו כדרשא כו': [ח] במתני' מ"מ יהיו מיהיו: [ט] הדבר: [י] התם ותו דהתם:

תורה אור

אֵילִים דְּהֵיכָא? אִי דְּהָנְהוּ — א] דְּאַיִל הוּא! (א) אִי דַּעֲצֶרֶת דְּתוֹרַת כֹּהֲנִים — הֲוָיָה כְּתִיב בְּהוּ! לְעוֹלָם דַּעֲצֶרֶת דְּתוֹרַת כֹּהֲנִים, וְהָכִי קָאָמַר: לֹא אֵילִים דְּתוֹרַת כֹּהֲנִים מְעַכְּבִי לֵיהּ לְאַיִל דְּחוּמַּשׁ הַפְּקוּדִים, וְלֹא אַיִל דְּחוּמַּשׁ הַפְּקוּדִים מְעַכֵּב לְהוּ לְאֵילִים דְּתוֹרַת כֹּהֲנִים. אֶלָּא פָּרִים דַּאֲפִילּוּ אַהֲדָדֵי לָא מְעַכְּבִי, וְאֵילִים דְּהָכָא וּדְהָכָא הוּא דְּלָא מְעַכְּבִי, אִינְהוּ מְעַכְּבִי? תַּנָּא מִילֵּי מִילֵּי קָתָנֵי. °"וּבְיוֹם הַחֹדֶשׁ ב] (תִּקַּח) פַּר בֶּן בָּקָר *תְּמִימִם וְשִׁשָּׁה כְבָשִׂים וָאַיִל תְּמִימִם יִהְיוּ". "פַּר" *מַה ת"ל? לְפִי שֶׁנֶּאֱמַר בַּתּוֹרָה "פָּרִים", וּמִנַּיִן שֶׁאִם לֹא מָצָא שְׁנַיִם מֵבִיא אֶחָד? ת"ל: "פַּר". "שִׁשָּׁה כְבָשִׂים" מַה ת"ל? לְפִי שֶׁכָּתַב בַּתּוֹרָה "שִׁבְעָה". וּמִנַּיִן אשֶׁאִם לֹא מָצָא שִׁבְעָה יָבִיא שִׁשָּׁה? ת"ל: "שִׁשָּׁה". וּמִנַּיִן שֶׁאִם לֹא מָצָא שִׁשָּׁה יָבִיא חֲמִשָּׁה, חֲמִשָּׁה — יָבִיא אַרְבָּעָה, אַרְבָּעָה — יָבִיא שְׁלֹשָׁה, שְׁלֹשָׁה — יָבִיא שְׁנַיִם, בוַאֲפִילּוּ אֶחָד? ת"ל: "וְלַכְּבָשִׂים כַּאֲשֶׁר תַּשִּׂיג יָדוֹ". וּמֵאַחַר דִּכְתִיב הָכִי, "שִׁשָּׁה כְבָשִׂים" לָמָּה לִי? דְּכַמָּה דְּאֶפְשָׁר לְהַדּוּרֵי מְהַדְּרִינַן. וּמִנַּיִן ג] (לָאֵילִים שֶׁבְּת"כ) גשֶׁמְּעַכְּבִין זֶה אֶת זֶה? ת"ל: "יִהְיוּ". °"כֹּה אָמַר ה' אֱלֹהִים בָּרִאשׁוֹן בְּאֶחָד לַחוֹדֶשׁ תִּקַּח פַּר בֶּן בָּקָר תָּמִים וְחִטֵּאתָ אֶת הַמִּקְדָּשׁ", "חַטָּאת"? עוֹלָה הִיא! א"ר יוֹחָנָן: פָּרָשָׁה זוֹ אֵלִיָּהוּ עָתִיד לְדוֹרְשָׁהּ. רַב אַשִׁי אָמַר: ד] דמִילּוּאִים הִקְרִיבוּ בִּימֵי עֶזְרָא, כְּדֶרֶךְ שֶׁהִקְרִיבוּ בִּימֵי מֹשֶׁה. תַּנְיָא נַמִּי הָכִי, רַבִּי יְהוּדָה אוֹמֵר: פָּרָשָׁה זוֹ אֵלִיָּהוּ עָתִיד לְדוֹרְשָׁהּ. אָמַר לוֹ ר' יוֹסֵי: מִלּוּאִים הִקְרִיבוּ בִּימֵי עֶזְרָא, כְּדֶרֶךְ שֶׁהִקְרִיבוּ בִּימֵי מֹשֶׁה. אָמַר לוֹ: אתָּנוּחַ דַּעְתְּךָ שֶׁהֵנַחְתָּ דַּעְתִּי. °"וְכָל נְבֵלָה וּטְרֵפָה מִן הָעוֹף וּמִן הַבְּהֵמָה לֹא יֹאכְלוּ הַכֹּהֲנִים", כֹּהֲנִים הוּא דְּלֹא יֹאכְלוּ, הָא יִשְׂרָאֵל אָכְלִי? א"ר יוֹחָנָן: פָּרָשָׁה זוֹ אֵלִיָּהוּ עָתִיד לְדוֹרְשָׁהּ. רָבִינָא אָמַר: כֹּהֲנִים אִיצְטְרִיךְ לֵיהּ, ס"ד אָמִינָא: הוֹאִיל וְאִשְׁתְּרִי מְלִיקָה לְגַבַּיְיהוּ תִּשְׁתְּרִי נַמִּי נְבֵילָה וּטְרֵפָה, קמ"ל. °"וְכֵן תַּעֲשֶׂה בְּשִׁבְעָה בַחוֹדֶשׁ מֵאִישׁ שֹׁגֶה וּמִפֶּתִי וְכִפַּרְתֶּם אֶת הַבָּיִת". (ב) "שִׁבְעָה" — אָמַר ר' יוֹחָנָן: אֵלּוּ שִׁבְעָה שְׁבָטִים שֶׁחָטְאוּ, ה] הוְאַף עַל פִּי שֶׁאֵין רוּבָּהּ שֶׁל קָהָל. (ג) "חוֹדֶשׁ" — אִם חִדְּשׁוּ וְאָמְרוּ: חֵלֶב מוּתָּר. "מֵאִישׁ שֹׁגֶה וּמִפֶּתִי" — מְלַמֵּד, ושֶׁאֵין חַיָּיבִין אֶלָּא עַל הֶעְלֵם דָּבָר עִם שִׁגְגַת מַעֲשֶׂה. *אָמַר רַב יְהוּדָה, אָמַר רַב: זָכוּר אוֹתוֹ הָאִישׁ לְטוֹב, וַחֲנִינָא בֶּן חִזְקִיָּה שְׁמוֹ, שֶׁאִלְמָלֵא הוּא נִגְנַז סֵפֶר יְחֶזְקֵאל, שֶׁהָיוּ דְּבָרָיו סוֹתְרִין דִּבְרֵי תוֹרָה. מֶה עָשָׂה? הֶעֱלָה ו] שְׁלֹשׁ מֵאוֹת גַּרְבֵּי שֶׁמֶן, וְיָשַׁב בַּעֲלִיָּיה וּדְרָשׁוֹ.§ "א"ר שִׁמְעוֹן אִם הָיוּ לָהֶם פָּרִים מְרוּבִּין" [וכו'].§ ת"ר: °"וְאֵיפָה לַפָּר וְאֵיפָה לָאַיִל יַעֲשֶׂה מִנְחָה וְלַכְּבָשִׂים כַּאֲשֶׁר תַּשִּׂיג יָדוֹ וְשֶׁמֶן הִין לָאֵיפָה" — א"ר שִׁמְעוֹן: וְכִי מִדַּת פָּרִים וְאֵילִים אַחַת הִיא? אֶלָּא, שֶׁאִם הָיוּ לָהֶם פָּרִים מְרוּבִּין וְלֹא הָיוּ בנְסָכִים — יָבִיאוּ פַּר אֶחָד וּנְסָכָיו, וְאַל יִקְרְבוּ כּוּלָּן בְּלֹא נְסָכִים. וְאִם הָיוּ לָהֶם
אֵילִים

א) [שבת קנב: לקמן ק. פסחים לב: יומא סו: סנהדרין לג:] ב) [נ"ל להם]

אֵילִים שְׁנַיִם: "וְהִקְרַבְתֶּם עַל הַלֶּחֶם ז' כְּבָשִׂים ז] וְאֵילִים שְׁנַיִם" וְהָנָךְ דְּת"כ לָאו נִינְהוּ הָנָךְ דְּחוּמַּשׁ הַפְּקוּדִים, ח] כִּדְלְקַמָּן. הֲוָיָה כְּתִיב בְּהוּ. "יִהְיוּ עוֹלָה" (ויקרא כג), וְכָל הֲוָיָה — עִיכּוּבָא. לֹא [א] (ד) ט] דְּת"כ. הַכְּבָשִׂים בִּגְלַל שְׁתֵּי הַלֶּחֶם, שֶׁנֶּאֱמַר: "וְהִקְרַבְתֶּם עַל הַלֶּחֶם". מְעַכְּבִי לְאַיִל דְּחוּמַּשׁ הַפְּקוּדִים. י] הַבָּא בִּגְלַל מוּסָף, וְלָאו [ב] אַאֵיל דְּלֶחֶם קָאֵי. וְקָפָרֵיךְ הַתַּלְמוּד: יא] הֵיכָא פַּלְגָא לְתַנָּא הָכִי, גַּבֵּי אֵילִים — מוֹקְמַתְּ דְּאֵילִים יב] מְעַכְּבִין זֶה אֶת זֶה, וְגַבֵּי פָּרִים וּכְבָשִׂים — אֲפִילּוּ דַּהֲדָדֵי לָא מְעַכְּבִי יג] הָנָךְ דְּחוּמַּשׁ הַפְּקוּדִים יד] זֶה אֶת זֶה? מִילֵּי מִילֵּי. וְכִדְפָרֵישְׁנָא. וּבְיוֹם הַחֹדֶשׁ. פָּסוּק הוּא בִּיחֶזְקֵאל. פַּר מַה ת"ל. כְּלוֹמַר, טו] הֲרֵי כְּתוּבָה בַּתּוֹרָ' לְהָבִיא פָּר בְּרֹאשׁ חֹדֶשׁ? לְפִי שֶׁנֶּאֱמַר בַּתּוֹרָה טז] [ג]. בְּר"ח "כְּבָשִׂים בְּנֵי שָׁנָה שִׁבְעָה" (במדבר כח). וּמִנַּיִן שֶׁמְּעַכְּבִין זֶה אֶת זֶה. אִם יֵשׁ לָהֶם פָּרִים שְׁנַיִם אוֹ כְּבָשִׂים שִׁבְעָה, דְּאֵין יְכוֹלִין לְהַקְרִיב זֶה בְּלֹא זֶה? ת"ל יִהְיוּ. "וְשֵׁשֶׁת כְּבָשִׂים *וְאֵילִים תְּמִימִים יִהְיוּ" (יחזקאל מו). חַטָּאת. בִּתְמִיָּה. אַמַּאי כְּתִיב "וְחִטֵּאתָ", דְּמַשְׁמַע חַטָּאת, הָא עוֹלָה הָווּ פָּרִים דְּר"ח, כִּדְכְתִיב (במדבר כח) "וּבְרָאשֵׁי חָדְשֵׁיכֶם תַּקְרִיבוּ עוֹלָה" וגו'. פָּרָשָׁה זוֹ. דִּיחֶזְקֵאל. אֵלִיָּהוּ עָתִיד לְדוֹרְשָׁהּ. דְּעַד שֶׁיָּבֹא אֵלִיָּהוּ וִיפָרְשֶׁנָּה לָנוּ, אֵין אָנוּ יוֹדְעִים יז] לְדוֹרְשָׁהּ. רַב אַשִׁי אָמַר. אֲנִי אֲפָרְשֶׁנָּה: מִילּוּאִים הִקְרִיבוּ. יח] וְהַךְ נְבוּאָה דִּיחֶזְקֵאל — עַל בַּיִת שֵׁנִי נִתְנַבְּאָה, שֶׁהִקְרִיבוּ מִילּוּאִים. וְכִי הֵיכִי יט] דְּהִקְרִיבוּ מִילּוּאִים כ] דְּמֹשֶׁה בִּשְׁמִינִי דִּידְהוּ, דַּהֲוָה ר"ח, כא] כִּדְאָמְרִי' בְּמַסֶּ' שַׁבָּת (דף פז.): "בָּרִאשׁוֹן כב] בְּאֶחָד לַחֹדֶשׁ", וְתָנָא: אוֹתוֹ הַיּוֹם נָטַל עֶשֶׂר עֲטָרוֹת כו', וְהִקְרִיב עֵגֶל בֶּן בָּקָר לְחַטָּאת. הָכָא נַמִּי הִקְרִיב פָּר בְּר"ח. אֵלּוּ שִׁבְעָה שְׁבָטִים. וְהָכִי מַשְׁמַע "וְכֵן תַּעֲשֶׂה" (ה) כג] [ד] *(וְגַבֵּי פָּר): כִּי הֵיכִי דִּכְתִיב לְעֵיל מִינֵּיהּ "תִּקַּח פַּר בֶּן בָּקָר", "כֵּן תַּעֲשֶׂה בְּשִׁבְעָה" — שְׁבָטִים, פַּר הֶעְלֵם דָּבָר, אִם חִדְּשׁוּ שׁוּם הוֹרָאַת אִיסּוּר וְאָמְרוּ: חֵלֶב מוּתָּר. "מֵאִישׁ שֹׁגֶה" — שֶׁשָּׁגְגוּ עַל פִּיהֶם, וְאָכְלוּ חֵלֶב בְּשׁוֹגֵג, מְבִיאִין פַּר. וְאַעַ"פ שֶׁאֵין. בַּז' שְׁבָטִים הַלָּלוּ רוּבָּן שֶׁל יִשְׂרָאֵל, וְאִיכָּא לְמֵימַר כִּיחִידִים דָּמוּ, וְיָבִיא כָּל אֶחָד כִּשְׂבָּה אוֹ שְׂעִירָה — אפ"ה, הוֹאִיל וְרוֹב שְׁבָטִים הֵם, חֲשִׁיבֵי רוּבָּא, וְיָבִיאוּ פַּר. הֶעְלֵם דָּבָר. שֶׁנֶּעְלַם דָּבָר מִסַּנְהֶדְרִין, הוֹרוּ שֶׁחֵלֶב מוּתָּר. עִם שִׁגְגַת מַעֲשֶׂה. שֶׁאָכְלוּ צִיבּוּר חֵלֶב שׁוֹגֵג עַל פִּיהֶם. דְּבָרָיו סוֹתְרִין דִּבְרֵי תוֹרָה. כְּגוֹן כָּל הָנָךְ דְּאָמְרִי' לְעֵיל, דְּקָרֵי לְפָר דְּר"ח "חַטָּאת", וְכֵן אוֹתָן דִּלְעֵיל. שְׁלֹשׁ מֵאוֹת גַּרְבֵּי שֶׁמֶן. לְנֵרוֹת, לְהַדְלִיק בַּלַּיְלָה וּלְדָרְשׁוֹ. וְכִי מִדַּת פָּרִים וְאֵילִים אַחַת. וַהֲלֹא מִנְחַת פָּרִים שְׁלֹשָׁה עֶשְׂרוֹנִים, וּמִנְחַת אֵילִים שְׁנֵי עֶשְׂרוֹנִים (במדבר טו)? וְלֹא בָּא הַכָּתוּב אֶלָּא לְהוֹדִיעֲךָ שֶׁמּוּטָב לְהָבִיא אַיִל אֶחָד עִם אֵיפָתוֹ, מִדָּה הָרְאוּיָה לוֹ, מִלְּהָבִיא.
שֶׁאִם

אלא פרים דאפי' אהדדי לא מעכבי. והא דלא מוקי ליה בראש השנה ויום הכיפורים ושמיני עצרת – משום דבכל חד ליכא אלא חד פר וחד איל. והא דלא משני: בפרים ואילים דעלמא, כדמשני פ"ק [ה] דיומא (דף ז.) גבי פר דעבודה זרה ואילו של אהרן, וקתני "היה מקריב מנחת פרים ואילים" – לא דמי להכא כלל. **ומנין** שמעכבין זה את זה. פירוש: כשיש להם כל הצורך. (וכי) וכה"ג דריש בספרי שהבאתי לעיל. א"נ: קמ"ל כרבנן דפליגי עליה דר"ש במתני', שיקריב פרים ולא יקנה נסכים מאחד מהן. אי נמי: אם יש לו כבשים ואין לו לתמיד של בין הערבים – מקריב כולן לשם מוסף. ומיהו לקמן (דף מט.) משמע דתמידין דיומיה קודמין למוספין דיומיה, משום דתדיר ומקודש. וצ"ע.

מילואים הקריבו בימי עזרא כדרך שהקריבו בימי משה. ולא דמו הני להני: דשל משה – כד] עגל, וכאן – פר. וגם מתנותיו חלוקות, כמפורש ביחזקאל (מה): "אל מזוזת הבית ואל ארבע פינות העזרה למזבח ועל מזוזת שער החצר הפנימית". ופירש שם רש"י: שהוא פר האמור שם למעלה כה] [ו] "אלה חקות המזבח ביום העשותו", כו] פר בן בקר לחטאת. אבל שם כתיב: "ולקחת מדמו ונתתה על ארבע קרנותיו כז] ועל ארבע פינות העזרה כח] ועל הגבול סביב". וצריך לדחוק המקרא שיהיו שוים. ועוד לפי מה שמפרש "וכן תעשה בשבעה בחדש", דאיירי בשבעה שבטים דאייתו פר בהוראה. וצריך ליישב שיהיו אותן מתנות כאותן הכתובין גבי פר בהוראה ב"ויקרא", ואי אפשר ליישבו. ושמא "וכן תעשה" דקאמר – לענין שמביא פר שנשרף, ולא לענין המתנות. ודבר תימה הוא: מי דחקו להתלמוד להעמיד הפסוק בז' שבטים, כט] ופשיטא דקרא קאי אהא דכתיב לעיל גבי "חקות המזבח ביום העשותו" שמביאין פר בן בקר לחטאת, וביום השני שעיר עזים ופר ואיל, ואח"כ "שבעת ימים תעשה שעיר חטאת ליום ופר בן בקר ואיל מן הצאן תמימים יעשו". לפיכך אומר כאן "וכן תעשה בשבעה בחודש".

הואיל ואישתרי מליקה. אע"ג דלעיל (דף ה:) פרכינן: שכן מצוותו בכך, וכלאים נמי אסרינן להו בלא קרא, *מ"מ אתא לאורויי לך, דלא ניטעי למילף מינה. ולמאן דקאמר דאין שחיטה לעוף [מן התורה] – פירשתי בחולין (דף כ.)*.

בשבעה שבטים שחטאו. השתא דריש: "בחדש" – כמו בדברים שחדשו בית דין, והוא של ז' שבטים, שחלב מותר. ועשו על פיהם, והיינו "מאיש שוגה" – ששגגו בהוראתם. ומפני שהלכו ציבור ועשו פתאום על פיהם. והא דלא כרבי יהודה (הוריות דף ה.) דבעי פר לכל שבט. ונראה דאפי' לר' יהודה ניחא, דמיירי במיעוט שבט. **וכי** מדת פרים ואילים אחת היא. תימה: דליפרוך, וכי יש שם איפה? ורש"י פירש ביחזקאל: דאיפה קמח היה מביא, להוציא סולת עשרון מן הסאה. והאיפה – שלש סאין, והיינו ג' עשרונים לפר. "ואיפה לאיל" [ז] – כמו ששנינו ב"שתי הלחם" (לקמן עו.): שני עשרונים משלש סאין. ושל פרים, ג' מג' סאין, למדך: שאם לא מצא סולת מנופה כל כך, יביא משל עשרון לסאה. "ושמן הין" – ל] [לא שיקריב ההין כולו אלא] לא] שנתות היו בהין. וכי האי גוונא שפרש"י בשמן, יש לפרש באיפה: שהיה שם איפה גדולה וקטנה. ומה שמדקדק, משום דנקט בכולה חד לישנא, משמע שניהם שוין. וכן
דורש

רבינו גרשום

אלא פרים דר"ח ופרים דעצרת דחומש הפקודים דפנחס דהוו ב' פרים: ואי אמרת מ"ט לא אמר פרים דפסח דהוו נמי ב' משום דהויה כתיב בהו ומעכבי זה את זה: אי דהני דר"ח ודעצרת דחומש הפקודים חד איל הוא דאית לכל חד: דעצרת דתורת כהנים דאית ביה ב' אילים דכתיב והקרבתם על הלחם וגו'. הויה כתיב בהו יהיו עולה לה' אלמא דמעכבי: הכי קאמר לא אילים דעצרת דתורת כהנים מעכבי ליה לאיל דחומש הפקודים דהכי אמרינן לקמן דמשבאו לארץ קרבו הב' של תורת כהנים והא' שבחומש הפקודים. ואם (אבל) [אבד] האיל של חומש הפקודים לא מעכב להו לאיל של תורת כהנים ולא אילים דתורת כהנים מעכבי לאיל דחומש הפקודים וכן השעיר והכבשים של תורת כהנים שהן חובת היום אינן מעכבי של חומש הפקודים שהן של מוסף ולא דחומש הפקודים מעכב דתורת כהנים ופרים וכבשים דתנן במתני' בהני דחומש הפקודים קאמר דלא כתב בהו הויה: (אבל) [אלא] פרים וכו'. ומתמה בעל התלמוד פרים דחומש הפקודים אמרת במתני' דאפילו אהדדי לא מעכבי שאם אבד האחד אין מעכב את הב' והדר אוקמת מאי אילים אין מעכבין זה את זה דהכא והכא לא מעכבי כלומר שהב' של תורת כהנים [אינו מעכב] את הא' של חומש הפקודים ולא האחד את השני (והדר אמרת) [אבל] אינהו שני אילים של תורת כהנים עצמן מעכבין זה את זה דהויה כתיב בהו. וכי לצדדין קא מוקמת לה למתני': א"ל אין מילי מילי קתני מתני' כמה דאפשר לאהדורי אחר רוב מהדרינן: ומנין שמעכבין זה את זה אם היו ז' או ו': וְחִטֵּאתָ משמע חטאת עולה היא דכתיב ובראשי חדשיכם תקריבו עולה לה' פרים: פרשה זו אליהו עתיד לדורשה. כלומר שיש בה קושיות: רב אשי אמר מאי קושיא מילואים הקריבו בימי עזרא לחנוכת הבית כדרך שהקריבו בימי משה אף הכא נמי האי פר דיחזקאל לצורך מילואים הוא לעתיד לבא ומשום הכי הוי חטאת כההוא דמשה דכתיב קח לך עגל בן בקר לחטאת וראש חדש נמי הוה: וכן תעשה נמי פר לחטאת לז' שבטים שחטאו: שחידשו שהורו ב"ד ואמרו שחלב מותר: מאיש שוגה. זה שגגת מעשה. ומפתי זה העלם דבר דבעינן תרווייהו בשוגג הוראה ועשיה: שלש מאות גרבי שמן א) לצורך. היינו לצורך מנחה: וכי מדת פרים ואילים אחת הם והכתיב שלשה עשרונים
לפר

א) נראה דלרבינו היה לו גירסא אחרת בגמרא.

שיטה מקובצת

א] דהנהו. חד איל הוא אלא דעצרת: ב] פר בן בקר תמימים וששת כבשים ואיל תמימים יהיו. תיבות תקח תמים וששה נמחק: ג] ומנין שמעכבין זא"ז תימה מאי קאמר האי כבר אמרנו דאין מעכבין ופרש"י דאם יש להם ב' פרים או ז' כבשים דאין מקריבין זה בלא זה וגם זה לא נהיר דהא כבר אמרנו דכמה דאפשר לאהדורי מהדרינן ונראה דהא דקאמר הכא דמעכבין לאפוקי מדר"ש דאמר אם היה להם פרים מרובים כו' וקמ"ל האי תנא דטוב לו להביא כבשים כמו דאפשר ולא ימעט הכבשים בשביל הנסכים: ד] מילואים הקריבו בימי עזרא. לאו דוקא שהרי כל אותן הקרבנות ואותו הבנין על העתיד אלא אם (יזכו) [זכו] ישראל היו מקריבין אותו בימי עזרא. תו"ה: ה] שחטאו. פירוש בהוראת ב"ד דמייתי [פר] העלם דבר של צבור אע"ג שאינו רוב קהל (על) [עם] שגגת מעשה שאכלו חלב ע"פ הוראת ב"ד לאפוקי [שאם] היו סבורים (על) שהוא שומן ואכלו צבור בשוגג שאין מביאין פר אלא כל אחד מביא כשבה או שעירה כדין יחיד שחטא: ו] העלה לו: ז] כבשים וגו': ח] הפקודים כדמפרש לקמן: ט] לא אילים דת"כ דהוי מוסף: י] הוכי פלגת למתני' תיבות פלגא לתנא נמחק: יא] דאילים דהכא ודהכא דת"כ ודחומש הפקודים הוא דלא מעכבי הואיל ולא כתיבי גבי הדדי הא איתנהו הדדי כגון הנך שנים דת"כ מעכבין: יב] לא מעכבי בת"כ דכתיבי גבי הדדי והנך: יג] הפקודים לא מעכבי כו': טו] היכן כתוב: טז] בתורה פרים בני בקר שנים שבר"ח הס"ד ואח"כ מה"ד לפי שנאמר בתורה: יז] יודעים לפורשה: יח] והקריבו כו': יט] והקריבו מילואים: כ] דמילואים:

כא] ר"ח ניסן: כב] תיבות באחד לחדש נמחק: כג] תעשה פר בן בקר כי: כד] ע[...] וכאן פר בן ג' שנים ור' נתנאל תירץ דבת"כ אשכחנא תנא דאית ליה היכא דכתיב עגל שנים ופר הוא נמי בן ב' שנים: כה] למעלה אלה: כו] העשותו וגו': כז] קרנותיו ואל: כח] ופשטיה: ל] תיבות לא שיקריב ההין כולו אלא ל"ש: לא] שנתות שמן לפי הסולת כמשפט הזבח לפר כמשפטו ולאיל כמשפטו עכ"ל ברש"י ביחזקאל:

עין משפט נר מצוה

צז א ב מיי' פ"א מהל' תמידין ומוספין הלכה כ:
צח ג מיי' שם הלכה יט וע"ש בכ"מ:
צט ד מיי' פ"ב מהל' מעה"ק הלכה טו:
ק ה מיי' פי"ב מהלכות שגגות הלכה א ופי"ג הלכה ב:
קא ו מיי' שם פי"ב הל' א:

[בערוך ערך פר ג' גיר' אחרת היה לו עיין שם ותמצא נחת]

הגהות הב"ח

(א) גמ' דאיל הוא אלא דעצרת: (ב) שם בשבעה א"ר יוחנן כו': (ג) שם בחדש אם חדשו: (ד) רש"י ד"ה לא אילים דת"כ הכבשים וכו' על הלחם מעכבי לאיל דחומש הפקודים למוסף ואחיל קאי וקפריך הש"ס היכא כל"ל והס"ד: (ה) ד"ה אלו שבעה וכו' תעשה כמו גבי פר:

תמימים וששת

הגהות צ"ק [א] אילים דת"כ: [ב] אאילים: [ג] בר"ח הס"ד אח"כ ד"ה שבעה כבשים: [ד] תעשה פר כי כו': [ה] דיומא פר דעבודת כוכבים ואילו של אהרן גבי הא דקתני היה: [ו] אלה חוקת: [ז] להוציא ממנה שני עשרונים סלת כמו:

עין משפט נר מצוה

צ א מיי' פ"ב מהל' מעה"ק הלכה יב:
צא ב מיי' פ"ב מהל' פסה"מ הלכה א:
צב ג מיי' שם פי"ב הלכה ו:
צג ד מיי' פ"ז מהל' תמידין ומוספין הלכה ה:
צד ה מיי' שם הלכה ח וע"ש מוכח הלכה כחכמים:
צה ו מיי' פ"ב מהל' פסה"מ הלכה א:
צו ז מיי' פ"ח מהל' תמידין ומוספין הלכה יז:

מסורת הש"ס

°"ה' עֲלֵיהֶם יִחְיוּ וּלְכָל בָּהֶן חַיֵּי רוּחִי וְתַחֲלִימֵנִי וְהַחֲיֵינִי". (ישעיהו לח) § **מתני'** אהַסּוֹלֶת וְהַשֶּׁמֶן אֵין מְעַכְּבִין אֶת הַיַּיִן, וְלֹא הַיַּיִן מְעַכְּבָן. בהַמַּתָּנוֹת שֶׁעַל הַמִּזְבֵּחַ הַחִיצוֹן אֵין מְעַכְּבוֹת זוֹ אֶת זוֹ. § **גמ'** ת"ר: °"וּמִנְחָתָם וְנִסְכֵּיהֶם" (במדבר כט) — הָבֵא מִנְחָה, וְאַחַר כָּךְ הָבֵא נְסָכִים. רַבִּי אוֹמֵר: "זֶבַח וּנְסָכִים" — הָבֵא זֶבַח, וְאַחַר כָּךְ הָבֵא נְסָכִים. וְרַבִּי נַמִי הָכְתִיב "וּמִנְחָתָם וְנִסְכֵּיהֶם"! הַהוּא מִיבָּעֵי *לְמִנְחָתָם וְנִסְכֵּיהֶם בַּלַּיְלָה, וּמִנְחָתָם וְנִסְכֵּיהֶם אֲפִילּוּ לְמָחָר. [לקמן נב. זבחי' ה. פז. תמורה יד.] וְרַבָּנַן נַמִי, הָכְתִיב "זֶבַח וּנְסָכִים"! הַהוּא מִיבָּעֵי לֵיהּ לְכִדְזְעִירִי, *דְּאָמַר זְעִירִי: א] גאֵין נְסָכִים מִתְקַדְּשִׁין אֶלָּא בִּשְׁחִיטַת הַזֶּבַח. [לקמן עט.] [תענית ב:] וְרַבִּי נַמִי מִיבָּעֵי לֵיהּ לְכִדְזְעִירִי! וְרַבָּנַן נַמִי מִיבָּעֵי לְהוּ לְמִנְחָתָם וְנִסְכֵּיהֶם בַּלַּיְלָה, וּמִנְחָתָם וְנִסְכֵּיהֶם אֲפִי' לְמָחָר! אֶלָּא הַיְינוּ טַעֲמַיְיהוּ דְּרַבָּנַן, דִּכְתִיב: °"עוֹלָה וּמִנְחָה" (ויקרא כג). וְרַבִּי נַמִי הָכְתִיב "עוֹלָה וּמִנְחָה"! אֶלָּא, בַּבָּאִים עִם הַזֶּבַח דְּכ"ע לָא פְּלִיגֵי ידְּמִנְחָה וְאַחַר כָּךְ נְסָכִים, דְּהָכְתִיב "עוֹלָה וּמִנְחָה", כִּי פְּלִיגֵי ב] — בַּבָּאִין בִּפְנֵי עַצְמָן, רַבָּנַן סָבְרִי: מִדְּבָאִין עִם הַזֶּבַח מִנְחָה וְאַחַר כָּךְ נְסָכִים, בִּפְנֵי עַצְמָן נַמִי מִנְחָה וְאַחַר כָּךְ נְסָכִים. וְרַבִּי: הָתָם הוּא דְּאַיְידֵי דְּאַתְחֵיל בַּאֲכִילָה גָּמַר לָהּ לְכוּלָּא מִילְּתָא דַּאֲכִילָה, אֲבָל בִּפְנֵי עַצְמָן נְסָכִים עֲדִיפֵי, הוֹאִיל ג] הדְּמִיתַּאַמְרָא שִׁירָה עֲלַיְיהוּ. § "הַמַּתָּנוֹת שֶׁעַל מִזְבֵּחַ הַחִיצוֹן אֵין מְעַכְּבוֹת זוֹ אֶת זוֹ". § *ת"ר: [זבחים לו:] ומִנַּיִן לְכָל הַנִּיתָּנִין עַל מִזְבֵּחַ הַחִיצוֹן שֶׁנְּתָנָן בְּמַתָּנָה אַחַת, שֶׁכִּיפֵּר? שֶׁנֶּאֱמַר: °"וְדַם זְבָחֶיךָ יִשָּׁפֵךְ עַל מִזְבַּח ה' אֱלֹהֶיךָ" (דברים יב). § **מתני'** זהַפָּרִים וְהָאֵילִים וְהַכְּבָשִׂים (וְהַשְּׂעִירִים) אֵינָן מְעַכְּבִין זֶה אֶת זֶה. ד] ר' שִׁמְעוֹן [אוֹמֵר:] אִם הָיוּ לָהֶם פָּרִים מְרוּבִּים וְלֹא הָיוּ לָהֶם נְסָכִים — יָבִיא פַּר אֶחָד ה] וּנְסָכִים, וְלֹא יַקְרִיבוּ כּוּלָּם בְּלֹא נְסָכִים. § **גמ'** הָנֵי פָּרִים וּכְבָשִׂים דְּהֵיכָא? ו] אִילֵימָא דְּחַג — °"כַּמִּשְׁפָּט" "כְּמִשְׁפָּטָם" כְּתִיב בְּהוּ! (במדבר כט) ז] אֶלָּא דְּר"ח וַעֲצֶרֶת דְּחוּמַּשׁ הַפְּקוּדִים. אֵילִים

רש"י

ה' עֲלֵיהֶם. אוֹתָם שֶׁעוֹשִׂין עֲלֵיהֶם שֵׁם ה' בִּתְפִילִּין, יִחְיוּ. **מתני'** הַסּוֹלֶת וְהַשֶּׁמֶן. שֶׁל מִנְחַת נְסָכִים אֵין מְעַכְּבִין אֶת הַיַּיִן, שֶׁאִם הֵבִיא יַיִן בְּלֹא סוֹלֶת וְשֶׁמֶן — ח] מְנַסְּכָן. הַמַּתָּנוֹת כו'. כְּגוֹן ד' מַתָּנוֹת שֶׁל חַטָּאת אֵין מְעַכְּבוֹת זוֹ אֶת זוֹ, שֶׁאִם לֹא נָתַן אֶלָּא אַחַת — כִּיפֵּר. **גמ'** הָבֵא מִנְחָה כו'. דְּמִנְחַת נְסָכִים קְרֵיבִים תְּחִילָּה ט]. וְאַחַר כָּךְ נְסָכִים. אַחַר הָאֵבָרִים מִיָּד, וְאַחַר הַנְּסָכִים — הַמִּנְחָה. מִנְחָתָם וְנִסְכֵּיהֶם בַּלַּיְלָה. דְּמִנְחַת נְסָכִים קְרֵיבִין בַּלַּיְלָה. וְאִי קַשְׁיָא: הָא אָמְרִי' בְּ"הַקּוֹמֵץ [רַבָּה]" (לעיל כו:): דְּבָרִים שֶׁדַּרְכָּן לִיקְרַב בַּיּוֹם, וְקָחָשֵׁיב מִנְחַת נְסָכִים! מְפָרֵשׁ לָהּ בְּפֶ' "יֵשׁ קָרְבָּנוֹת" בְּמַסֶּכֶת תְּמוּרָה (דף יד.) דְּהָא דְּקָתָנֵי "בַּיּוֹם" — בִּנְסָכִים הַבָּאִים עִם הַזֶּבַח, וְהָא דְּקָתָנֵי "בַּלַּיְלָה" — בִּנְסָכִים הַבָּאִין בִּפְנֵי עַצְמָן. כְּגוֹן שֶׁהֵבִיא זֶבַח בְּלֹא נְסָכִים, וּלְאַחַר זְמַן הֵבִיא הַנְּסָכִים בִּפְנֵי עַצְמָן — יָכוֹל לַהֲבִיאָן בַּלַּיְלָה. וַאֲפִילּוּ לְמָחָר. אִם הֵבִיא הַיּוֹם — י] (א) יָכוֹל לְהַקְרִיב נְסָכָיו לְמָחָר, וּבִלְבַד שֶׁלֹּא יִקְדְּשׁוּ בִּכְלִי מֵאֶתְמוֹל, דְּאִי קָדְשִׁי — נִפְסָלִין בְּלִינָה, כִּדְתַנְיָא בְּמַסֶּכֶ' מְעִילָה (דף ט.): קָדְשׁוּ בִּכְלִי — הוּכְשְׁרוּ לִיפָּסֵל בִּטְבוּל יוֹם וּבִמְחוּסַּר כִּפּוּרִים וּבְלִינָה (ב). אֵין הַנְּסָכִים. הַבָּאִין עִם הַזֶּבַח [א]. יא] דְּכָל זְמַן שֶׁלֹּא נִשְׁחַט הַזֶּבַח, אַע"פ שֶׁהִפְרִישָׁן לְשֵׁם זֶבַח זֶה — יָכוֹל לְשַׁנּוֹתָן לְשֵׁם זֶבַח אַחֵר. אֲבָל לְאַחַר שְׁחִיטָה — אֵינוֹ יָכוֹל לְשַׁנּוֹתָן לְשֵׁם זֶבַח אַחֵר. עוֹלָה וּמִנְחָה. מַשְׁמַע: אַחַר הָעוֹלָה מִיָּד יַקְרִיב מִנְחָה (ג) יב]. עַל הַנְּסָכִים אוֹמְרִים שִׁירָה. הַלְוִיִּם, בְּמַסֶּ' עֲרָכִין בְּפֶרֶק "אֵין נֶעֱרָכִין" (דף יא.). יִשָּׁפֵךְ. שְׁפִיכָה אַחַת. כְּמִשְׁפָּטָם. מַשְׁמַע: עִיכּוּבָא (ד) יג]. כָּל הַקָּרְבָּנוֹת הָאֲמוּרִים בְּחוּמַּשׁ הַפְּקוּדִים יד]. *)דְּהָנֵי. דְּר"ח וַעֲצֶרֶת שֶׁכְּתוּבִים בְּחוּמַּשׁ הַפְּקוּדִים [ב]. אֶלָּא דַּעֲלָךְ' גְּרִידָ' קָתָנֵי (ה). טו] מנת"כ, דִּכְתִיב בְּ"אֱמוֹר אֶל הַכֹּהֲנִים" אֵילִים

*) שייך לדף שאח"ז

תוספות

מלמד שחזן הכנסת אומר להם: "אמרו". ובירושלמי אמרינן: ובלבד שיהא החזן ישראל. ו"חזן" לאו היינו ש"ץ, ש"חזן" הוא שמש הכנסת, כדאיתא פ"ק דסנהדרין (דף יז:): וב' חזנים, ופ"ז דבבא מציעא (דף צג:): חזני מתא. אבל ש"ץ הוא הקורא. ואומר ר"ת: שש"ץ הוא פותח ב"ברכנו" ומסיים, ואין הכהנים רשאין להתחיל עד שיכלה הדבור מפי הקורא. ודווקא כשעומד בבית הכנסת ואומר לו [ג] – עובר, אבל אם עומד בחוץ – אינו עובר. דאמרינן בירושלמי: רבי שמעון בן פזי כד הוה תשיש [הוה] קאי אחורי עמודי, ר' אלעזר נפיק לברא.

הסולת והשמן אין מעכבין את היין. משמע: הא סולת ושמן – מעכבין אהדדי, ותימה דהא לא כתיב שום קרא במנחת נסכים? ושמא ילפינן ממנחת נדבה, דכתיב בה עיכובא לעיל (דף כז.). וגלויי מילתא בעלמא הוי, דגבי מיעוטו מעכב את רובו כתיב קרא גם במנחת נסכים, והתם גלי לן קרא.

[ד] **מנחתם** ונסכיהם (אפי') בלילה מנחתם ונסכיהם אפילו למחר. בפ"ב דתמורה (דף יד.) מוכח דלמחר נפקא לן טז] [ה'] "דבר יום ביומו מלבד שבתות ה'". ודרך התלמוד להביא על פסוק הרהוט בשני דרשות, אע"ג דנפקי מקראי אחריני. כי ההיא ד"שבת נעורים לאביה" *)(קדושין דף ג.), וכן מ"והתעלמת" (ב"מ דף ל.), וכן "ספר כורתה, ואין דבר אחר כורתה" (גיטין דף כא:), וכן "מותר הפסח ושלמים הבאין מחמת הפסח" פ"ק דזבחים (דף ט.) ופ"ד דזבחים (דף לז.) ופרק "התודה" (לקמן פג:) ופ' "מי שהיה טמא" (פסחים דף צו:). ופ"ב דבכורות (דף טו.), דדריש "אך" – ולא חלבו, ומסיק רבא ד"אך" – לאותו ואת בנו הוא דאתא, וחלבו מ"דמו" נפקא. וכן בשמעתין דתניא בברייתא "זבח ונסכים", ומסקינן דבסברא פליגי. **מנחתם** ונסכיהם. פי' בקונט' פ"ק דזבחים (דף ח.) ופרק "המזבח מקדש" (שם פד.) ופ"ב דתמורה (דף יד.): ד"מנחתם ונסכיהם" דפרי החג קדריש. וקשה לר"ת: היכי משמע מיניה לילה? ועוד: היכי דרשינן מיניה מנחה ואח"כ נסכים, הא קרא דבתריה כתיב "לפרים ולאילים", ואינם כתובים יז] על הסדר, דפרים ואילים קדמי! ותו: דפריך "ורבנן נמי הא בעי ליה ומנחתם" וכו', ומאי [ו] לריך? הא טובא כתיב. אלא על כרחין כיון שכולם משונים זה מזה כולהו לריכי! לכך נראה לר"ת דדריש מקרא דעצרת פרשת "אמור אל הכהנים": "ואילים שנים יהיו עולה לה' ומנחתם ונסכיהם אשה ריח ניחוח לה'" מדכתב נסכים בין עולה לאשה – ש"מ דבאים בלילה, כי "אשה", דהיינו הקטרה, ולא מייתורא. ונקט מנחה ברישא – דדמי לעולה טפי בהקטרה. והא דפ"ק דזבחים (דף ח.) דריש: [ז] "מנחתו ונסכים" אפי' בלילה, ומשמע התם יח] דמייתורא דווקא קדריש. [ח] והתם גבי נזיר דרש מדכתי': "מנחתו ונסכו", וכתיב נמי: "ומנחתם ונסכיהם". למחר נמי שמעינן, כיון דגלי גבי עצרת – תו אין לחלק. ותימה: והא הני קראי בבאין עם הזבח כתיבי, והנהו לא אתו אלא ביום, כדאיתא בפ"ב דתמורה (דף יד.)? וי"ל: דאם אינו ענין בבאין עם הזבח, תנהו ענין בבאין לאחר הזבח. והא דאמרינן בריש תענית (דף ג:): מה ניסוך המים בלילה, דאמר מר: "ונסכיהם" אפי' בלילה, משמע דמקרא דפרי החג מייתי, שאין ניסוך המים אלא בחג – לאו מילתא היא, דכיון דגלי לן קרא בעצרת דהוי נסכי צבור, ה"ה לכל נסכי צבור. וקרא דאיצטריך בנזיר, דהוי נסכי יחיד. **כיון** דמתאמרא שירה עלייהו. יט] פי': [ט] להביאם עם הזבח, אבל בפני עצמו – בעיא היא פ' "אין נערכין" (ערכין יב.). ומ"מ אף בלאו זבח עדיפי, כיון שהיו ראויין לשירה ולבא עם הזבח.

ודם זבחיך ישפך. פ' "בית שמאי" (זבחים דף לו:) מעיקרא דריש מהאי קרא, ולא קאי לבסוף. **כמשפט** כמשפטם. וביום ראשון דלא כתיב "כמשפט", כתיב ביה "יהיו". **אלא** דר"ח ועצרת דכתיב בחומש הפקודים. ואע"ג דכתיב "יהיו לכם" – לאו עלייהו קאי. והא דלא פריך מפסח כי היכי דפריך מהני, דהא כתיב ביה "יהיו". ורש"י פי' כ] ביחזקאל דהא דכתיב כא] גבי פסח "ז' פרים וז' אילים ליום" – דלז' ימי פסח קאמר פר ואיל ליום. דאם לא מצא שנים בכל יום – מביא אחד. והשתא ניחא שפיר, דהא לא מעכבי אהדדי. ותימה: דהא כתיב ביה "יהיו"? ואין לומר דקאי אכבשים ולא אפרים ואילים – דגבי עצרת לא קאמרינן הכי. והא דנקט בסמוך "אילים דהכא והכא לא מעכבי, הא אינהו מעכבי", ה"נ מצי למינקט כבשים. ולא דמי ל"קודש יהיו" דגבי לחם, דפליגי ר"ע ובן ננס (לקמן דף מה:) כב] אהייא קאי, אי אכבשים אי אלחם, אבל אתרווייהו פשיטא להו דלא קאי, אע"ג דכתיב בחד קרא – היינו כבשים ללחם, אבל כבשים אהדדי – ה"נ דמעכבי. כדתנן ב"הקומץ רבה" (לעיל כז.): ב' כבשי עצרת מעכבין זה את זה, וכן ב' חלות. ולא מסתברא נמי למימר דהוייה דפסח לא קיימא אלא אתמימים – דלהא לא איצטריך קרא, דבעלי מומין פשיטא דפסולין. ונ"ל לשום דרשא אתא, דלא מסתבר לדורשו בעיכוב – כיון דלא מישתמיט התלמוד. ובספרי דורש גבי פסח: הרי שמצא פרים ולא מצא אילים, אילים ולא מצא כבשים, שומע אני שלא יקריב עד שימצא כולן – ת"ל: "שבעת ימים תקריבו אשה", אפילו אחד מהן. יכול אפי' כולן מצויין – ת"ל: "פרים בני בקר שנים ואיל אחד". ומיהו הא דקאמר "שומע אני שלא יקריב עד שימצא כולן" – על כרחין לאו משום דסמיך א"יהיו", דגבי עצרת דריש נמי הכי התם, וכן בחג, אע"ג דכתיב ביה "כמשפט" וכו', ואכל חד מייתי קרא ד"שבעת ימים", ואע"ג דלא כתיב לא בעצרת ולא בחג.
אלא

*) [ועמ"ש בגליון תוס' שבת קכח. ד"ה ונתן]

רבינו גרשום

הסולת והשמן. דמנחת נסכים אין מעכבין את היין שמנסך את היין אע"פ שאינן: הבא זבח ואחר כך הבא נסכים. ואח"כ הבא מנחה: ומנחתם ונסכיהם אפי' למחר. אבל אותן נסכים שמביא עם הזבח נפסלין בלינה מאחר שנשחט עליהן הזבח: דכתיב עולה ומנחה. סמוך לעולה מנחה ואחר כך נסכים: כי פליגי בנסכים הבאין בפני עצמן. שלא הביאן עם הזבח אלא לאחר כמה ימים. ולא תיתני להברייתא כמעיקרא ר' אמר זבח ונסכים דבבאין עם הזבח לא פליגי: ור' סבר התם הוא. בבאין עם הזבח איידי דאתחיל באכילה דזבח גמר לה לאכילה ומייתי מנחה: דאיתאמרא שירה עלייהו דכתיב המשמח אלהים:

שיטה מקובצת

א] דאמר זעירי. בפ' הקומץ זוטא הארכתי: ב] כי פליגי. בנסכים הבאים בפני עצמן דאף על גב דמייתי [קרא] זבח ונסכים משמע דמנחות הבאים עם הזבח פליגי אין זה עיקר דרשה דהא [חזינן] דלמסקנא מוקי ליה (מאי) [האי קרא] להא דזעירי: ג] הואיל דמתאמרא שירה עליהו תימה דבעיא היא בפ' אין נערכין אם אומרים שירה על הנסכים הבאים בפני עצמן וי"ל דה"פ הואיל דמתאמרא שירה עליהו כשבאים עם הזבח: ד] אמר ר' שמעון אם היו להם פרים ואילים: ה] אחד ונסכיו: ו] דהיכא. פ"א מאי עבידתייהו: ז] אלא דר"ח ועצרת. וקשה אמאי לא מוקי לה בכבשים ואילים דפסח וי"ל דהנהו מעכבי להדדי דהא כתיב ביה יהיו ואין זה כפרש"י דפי' ביחזקאל בהפטרה דפרשת חדש דכתיב גבי פסח שבעה פרים ושבעה אילים (חמשה) תמימים ליום לשבעת הימים והלא לשבעה ימים י"ד פרים הוו בהם דכתיב בפר' פנחס פרים בני בקר שנים ופרש"י לומר דלא מעכבי אהדדי כדדרשינן לקמן בשמעתין גבי כבשים דכתיב ביחזקאל ששה כבשים מה ת"ל לפי שכתוב בתורה שבעה כבשים כו' ודריש דלא מעכבא ואם כן הא דכתיב בפסח יהיו דעיכובא הוא דלא דרשינן ליה עיכובא אלא היכא דדריש תלמודא א"נ י"ל יהיו דפסח אתמימים קאי וא"ת אמאי לא מוקי מתניתין באילים דפסח וי"ל משום דבפסח לא כתיב אלא איל אחד ובמתניתין תנן האילים ולהכי מוקי לה בעצרת דכתיב בהו [ואילים] והשתא דאתא לידן נדרוש קראי סתומים דפרשת החדש דכתיב איפה לפר ואיפה לאיל יעשה מנחה ואיפה איכא עשרה עשרונים ובתורה כתיב שלשה עשרונים לפר ושני עשרונים לאיל וצריך לפירוש. וצריך לומר דמאיפה תוציא ג' עשרונים לפר שיהא מנופה יפה ואם יש להם חיטים בריוח מאיפה תוציא ב' עשרונים לאיל. ועוד כתיב התם ושמן הין לאיפה ומאי קאמר והלא כתיב בתורה חצי ההין יהיה לפר ושלישית ההין לאיל וצריך לפרש דהכי קאמר ושמן שבהן לאיפה לפי השנתות שהיו בהין כדאמרינן עד כאן לפר כו'. ועוד כתיב התם מנחה יעשו עליו בבקר בבקר ששית האיפה ומאי קאמר והלא לאיל משישית האיפה תוציא לפר כי לפי השיעור של איפה לפר. ומאי דפרש"י מ"ה דהאי ששית האיפה היינו לעשרון של מנחת תמיד ולחצי עשרון של מחבת שהיה בו עשרון ומחציתו בבקר ומחציתו בערב.

ואין השיעור שוה שהרי עשרון ומחצה זהו ששית [מתשעה] עשרונים ובאיפה יש בה עשרה עשרונים ונ"ל ברור דיש לישב ששית האיפה במנחת חביתין שנפו אותה עד שתבא לחצי עשרון והשתא אתי בכיוון לפי איפה לפר. ועוד כתיב ושמן שלישית ההין לרוס את הסולת פי' לתקן הסולת של מנחה ומאי קאמר והלא לא היו בו כי אם [רביעית ההין למנחת] תמיד השחר ואמר ריב"א דהאי שלישית דכתיב בהאי קרא היינו לעשרון של מנחת התמיד וחצי עשרון של מנחת מחבת הבקר ולעשרון [וחצי צריך ד'] לוגין וחצי שמן דהב' לוגין (דהן) [שהן] שלישית ההין היה לבלול עם הסולת בעודו חי קודם אפיה ולאחר אפיה היה יוצק בהן חצי לוג הנשאר [ועוד יש לפרש] דשלישית ההין קאי אשנתות שבהין וה"ק דשנת שלישית שבהין היה לרוס הסלת של מנחת התמיד והיינו רביעית ההין שנת ראשונה היה לפר והשני לאיל והשלישית לכבש. תו"א. ע"ש [הא] דכתיב נמי ביחזקאל ושמן שלישית ההין לרוס את הסלת. פירוש לתקן הסלת של מנחה. מנחה לה' חקת עולם (להם) תמיד. וקשה באיזה מנחה משתעי קרא אי דמנחת נסכים הבאה עם התמיד אינה כי אם שלשה לוגין ואי דחביתין דסליק מיניה והא כתיב ומנחה תעשה עליו בבקר בבקר ששית האיפה וגו' ופרש"י התם דהיינו חביתין וחביתין לא היה רק לוג ומחצה וי"מ דקא חשיב שמן של שחרית כולו בבת אחת של תמיד ושל חביתין והן ד' לוגין ומחצה וי"מ דקא חשיב שמן של שחרית כולו בבת אחת של תמיד ושל חביתין והן ד' לוגין ומחצה וד' לוגין היינו שלישית ההין וחצי לוג לא חשיב שלא היה באה לסלת אלא לטגן מנחת חביתין עוד פי' הר"ם דשלישית ההין לאו דוקא אלא עד שנת שלישית לפי שהיו ג' שנתות להין לפר ולאיל ולכבש נמצא כשהתחיל למנות משנת עליונה של כלי תמצא תחתון שהוא לכבש השלישי עכ"ל תוס' וכן כתוב בגליון דשלישית ההין ר"ל שנת שלישי כדאמרינן שנתות היו בהין עד כאן לפר וע"כ לאיל כו' נמצא השלישי מחזיק רביעית ההין דהיינו לנסכים: ח] ושמן מנסכן: ט] נסכים קריבה תחלה: ואח"כ. מנסך יין הס"ד ומה"ד זבח ואחר כך נסכים: י] הביא היום זבח: יא] הזבח מתקדש אלא בשחיטת זבח הכל: יב] מנחה הס"ד ואח"כ מה"ד דמתאמרא שירה עליהו על: יג] עיכובא הס"ד ואח"כ מה"ד דחומש הפקודים כו': יד] הפקודים חד איל

כתיב בהו דהיינו בפרשת פנחס והן מוספין דר"ח ועצרת דחומש הפקודים: טו] דת"כ אות מ' נמחק: טז] נפקא לן מדבר: יז] על הסדר דכ"ע דפרים לאילים קודמי דהא מסיים בפ' התדיר דפרים קודמי לאילים ואילים לכבשים וכסדר הכתוב ומאי פריך: יח] דמיתורא דוקא קדריש. עיין תוס' לקמן (דף נא:) פי' וה"נ נדרוש מיתורא ממנחת מנחתם ונסך ונסכיהם ולאו משום דאסמכיה לאשה ותירץ דשאני התם בפ"ק דזבחים גבי נזיר דכתיב ומנחתו ונסכו וכתיב נמי ומנחתם ונסכיהם ולהכי דריש התם ליתורא דוי"ו. ובתוס' חיצונית כתוב מיהו קשה דפ"ק דזבחים פריך מנחת מנחתו נסך נסכו מאי דרשת בהו ההוא מבעיא להו מנחתם ונסכיהם בלילה אלמא דריש לה אע"ג דלא כתיב ביה אשה ושמא מיתורא דוי"ו דריש ליה ודוחק הוא לפירושו והריב"א מיישב הקושיא ואומר דבקרבנות החג יש בהם שתי פעמים ביום אחד ואותו מיותר (דמ"מ) [וממ"ה] דריש. וכמו כן ההוא דהתם גבי נזיר מיותר וא"ת והלא איצטריך הכא תרי לבלילה ולמחר והתם היכי מפיק תרווייהו ממנחתם ונסכהם וי"ל דבתר דגלי הכא דאין חילוק בין לילה ולמחר ה"ה פ"ק דזבחים מפרי החג דריש אפי' למחר וממנחתם ונסכיהם דביום שני שהוא שב לפרים ולאילים ואע"ג דמינה דרשינן ניסוך המים בחג דריש' מיתורא והכא הלכה למשה מסיני הוא ההוא דדרשינן הבא בלילה משום דכתיב והקטיר המשמש דומיא דהקטרה שהוא עליהו (פשוט כדאיתא) (פירוש בראתן) קרא ביחזקאל ותיבות דהא כתיב נמחק: כא] גבי פסח. ושבעת ימי החג יעשה עולה לה': כב] אהיכא קאי: דהנהו

הגהות צ"ק [א] הזבח הס"ד ואח"כ ד"ה בשחיטת הזבח לכל זמן: [ב] לא לעצרת: [ג] עלה אבל: [ד] למנחתם: [ה] מדבר: [ו] פריך: [ז] נ"ל מנחתם ונסכיהם: [ח] דהתם: [ט] להביאם:

הגהות הב"ח

(א) רש"י ד"ה ואפי' וכו' היום הזבח יכול להקריב וכו': (ב) שם בסה"ד ובלינה הס"ד ואח"כ מ"ה שחיטת זבח אין הנסכים נפסלין עם הזבח מקדשן אלא בשחיטת הזבח לכל זמן שלא: (ג) ד"ה עולה וכו' מנחה הס"ד ואח"כ מ"ה שירה עליהו על הנסכים אומרים הלוים שירה במסכת: (ד) ד"ה במשפטן משמע עיכובא הס"ד ואח"כ מ"ה לחומש הפקודים כל הקרבנות וכו' הפקודים בכלי שרת: (ה) ד"ה אלא דעלך וכו' קתני אלו הס"ד ואח"כ מ"ה דר"ח:

גמרא

זיל טפי. ת"ר: חלזון זהו – גופו דומה לים, ובריתו אדומה לדג, ועולה אחד לשבעים שנה, ובדמו צובעין תכלת, לפיכך דמיו יקרים. תניא, א"ר נתן: אין לך כל מצוה קלה שכתובה בתורה, שאין מתן שכרה בעה"ז,* ולעה"ב – א] איני יודע כמה. צא ולמד ממצות ציצית; מעשה באדם אחד שהיה זהיר במצות ציצית, שמע שיש זונה בכרכי הים שנוטלת ד' מאות זהובים בשכרה, שיגר לה ארבע מאות זהובים וקבע לה זמן. כשהגיע זמנו, בא וישב על הפתח. נכנסה שפחתה ואמרה לה: אותו אדם ששיגר ליך ד' מאות זהובים בא וישב על הפתח, אמרה היא: יכנס, נכנס. הציעה לו ז' מטות, שש של כסף ואחת של זהב, ובין כל אחת ואחת סולם של כסף, ועליונה של זהב. עלתה וישבה על גבי עליונה כשהיא ערומה, ואף הוא עלה לישב ערום כנגדה, באו ד' ציציותיו וטפחו לו על פניו, נשמט וישב לו ע"ג קרקע, ואף היא נשמטה וישבה ע"ג קרקע. אמרה לו: גפה של רומי, שאיני מניחתך עד שתאמר לי מה מום ראית בי. אמר לה: העבודה, שלא ראיתי אשה יפה כמותך, אלא מצוה אחת צונו ה' אלהינו וציצית שמה, וכתיב בה °"אני ה' אלהיכם" (במדבר טו) שתי פעמים – אני הוא שעתיד ליפרע, ואני הוא שעתיד לשלם שכר, עכשיו נדמו עלי כד' עדים. אמרה לו: איני מניחך עד שתאמר לי מה שמך, ומה שם עירך, ומה שם רבך, ומה שם מדרשך שאתה למד בו תורה. כתב ונתן בידה. עמדה וחילקה כל נכסיה, שליש למלכות ושליש לעניים ושליש נטלה בידה, חוץ מאותן מצעות, ובאת לבית מדרשו של ר' ב] חייא. אמרה לו: רבי, °צוה עלי ויעשוני גיורת. אמר לה: בתי, שמא עיניך נתת באחד מן התלמידים? הוציאה כתב מידה ונתנה לו, אמר לה: לכי זכי במקחך. אותן מצעות שהציעה לו באיסור הציעה לו בהיתר. זה מתן שכרו בעה"ז, ולעה"ב – איני יודע כמה. אמר רב יהודה: *טלית שאולה – יג] גכל שלשים יום פטורה מן הציצית, מיכן ואילך חייבת. תניא נמי הכי: דהדר בפונדקי בא"י, והשוכר בית בח"ל – כל שלשים יום פטור מן המזוזה, מיכן ואילך חייב; אבל השוכר בית בא"י – עושה מזוזה לאלתר, משום ישוב דא"י. § "תפלה של יד אינה מעכבת" ד]. § אמר רב חסדא: לא שנו אלא שיש לו, אבל אין לו – מעכבת. אמרו לו: אמרת? אמר להו: לא, דאלא מאן דלית ליה תרי מצות, חד מצוה נמי לא ליעביד?! ומעיקרא מאי סבר? גזירה שמא יפשע. אמר רב ששת: הכל שאינו מניח תפילין – עובר בשמונה עשה, וכל שאין לו ציצית בבגדו – עובר בחמשה עשה, *ה] וכל כהן שאינו עולה לדוכן – עובר בג' עשה, כל שאין לו מזוזה בפתחו – עובר בשני עשה, "וכתבתם" "וכתבתם". ואמר ר"ל: כל המניח תפילין מאריך ימים, שנאמר:

[חולין קי. קלו.] [סוטה לח: ע"ש] [ג"ל ובעה"ב אבל איני כו'] [ועי' תו' ברכות לד. ד"ה לא יענה וכו']

רש"י

זיל טפי. ו] אפ"ה מזולזל העבד יותר מן האשה. ל"א: זיל טפי – כלומר, זיל והוסיף וברך "שלא עשאני עבד" כדי להשלים. גופו. מראה גופו ז]. תבנית דיוקנו. ועולה. מן הארץ. לפיכך. שאינו עולה אלא אחת לע' שנה, דמיו יקרין. ציצית. מצוה קלה, עשה בעלמא. גפה של רומי. נשבעה בחיי המלך שהוא שרה של רומי. ל"א: ע"ז (א). בפסוק אחרון של פרשה (במדבר טו) כתי' ב' פעמים "אני ה' אלהיכם", אחד בראשו ואחד בסופו. שליש למלכות. שניתנה להתגייר. ח] אותן מצעות. לא מכרה, והביאתן, ט] והוא היה מתן שכרו בעה"ז. הוציאה כתב מידה. וספרה לו כל המאורע, שלשם שמים היא מתגיירת, לפי ששמעה נס גדול של חומר מצות, שטפחו לו ד' ציציות על פניו. פונדק. שלנים בו עוברים ושבים. והשוכר בית כו'. פטור, שמא יחזור בו. משום יישוב א"י. דלאחר שקבעה שוב אינו נוטלה משם אפי' יוצא ממנו, כדאמר בפ' "השואל" בב"מ (דף קב.), הלכך בקושי יצא ממנה מפני טורח מזוזה אחרת, ואפי' יוצא ממנה – ישכרנה אחר מהרה כשימצאנה מזומנת במזוזה, ונמצאת א"י מיושבת. אלא שיש לו שתיהן. ואם אינו מניח אלא אחת, אותה מצוה מיהא קיים. חדא מצוה נמי לא ליעביד. בתמיה. ומעיקרא. דאמר מעכבת. מאי סבר שמא יפשע. אי אמרי' דאינה מעכבת, יפשע ולא יקנה האחרת. בשמונה עשה. ד' פרשיות יש בהן, ואכל חדא קיימי תרי עשה, "וקשרתם לאות" "והיו לטוטפות" (דברים יא). ל"א (ב): ב"והיה כי יביאך" (שמות יג) כתיב: י] "והיה [א] כי יביאך לאות וגו' ושמרת את החוקה" וגו', ובסוף הפרשה כתיב: "והיה לאות" וגו' – הרי ג', ובק"ש (דברים ו) "וקשרתם לאות והיו לטוטפות", וכן ב"והיה אם שמוע" (שם יא) תרי – הרי ז'. "ושמתם את דברי אלה" דדרשינן בפ' "הקומץ [רבה]" (לעיל דף לז:) דבתפילין קמישתעי, שתהא שימה כנגד הלב – הרי ח'. יא] בציצית ה'. "ועשו", "ונתנו", "והיה", "וראיתם", "גדילים תעשה לך" יב].

תוספות

זיל טפי. אבל אגור לא מברכינן, דאינו מצוי, דהוי כל שאינו לא במקרא ולא במשנה ולא בדרך ארץ. ונראה יותר שמברך אעבד ואשה שאינן [ב] יג] מצויין כמותו. לבית מדרשו של רבי [ג] יד] חייא. אינו רבי חייא. שר' נתן שהיה חשוב מרבי, כדאמרינן (ב"ב קלא.): ילדות היתה בי והעזתי פני בנתן הבבלי, לא היה מביא ראיה מרבי חייא. ובתוספתא גרסינן: לבית מדרשו של רבי מאיר.

טלית שאולה טו] כל ל' יום. אין לדקדק מכאן דסתם שאלה ל' יום, כמו הלואה בפ"ק דמכות (דף ג:). אלא – דדילמא שאלה דטלית דוקא. [ד] ועוד, *הכא לא מיפטר אלא דעד ל' יום סברי אינשי דשאולה היא, דאין דרך שאלה יותר, דמדאורייתא פטורה לעולם, כדדרשינן (חולין דף קלה.): "ראשית גז צאנך" – ולא של אחרים, הכי נמי "כסותך" – ולא של אחרים. אע"ג דבמזוזה חייב השוכר, כדמסיק התם (שם:) ד"ביתך" לא אתא לאפוקי בית אחרים, אלא לכדרבא דאמר: דרך ביאתך (לעיל דף לד.). ופ"ק דיומא (דף יא:) נמי איכא הכי. וה"ט, דלא מסתבר קרא למעוטי בית אחרים, דכיון דלשימור עביד ל"ש. מיהו, כל ל' יום פטור, דלאו בית דירה דידיה הוא, [ה] כדאמרינן פ"ק דבבא בתרא (דף ח.) גבי נשתהה שם ל' יום הרי הוא כאנשי העיר. והא דמייתי הכא טז] סיוע לרב יהודה להא דטלית שאולה, דמסתבר ליה לדמות טלית מדרבנן למזוזה דאורייתא. ול"ע אי מצינן למימר דלענין לפטור עד ל' יום הוא דמייתי. ומיהו י"ל דמזוזה נמי מדרבנן, דתרי "ביתך" כתיבי. והא דבעי בסוף "השואל" (ב"מ קא:): מזוזה על מי? ופריך: הא אמר רב משרשיא חובת הדר היא – לאו לחיובי שוכר מייתי לה, אלא ה"ק: פשיטא שהמשכיר אינו חייב כיון שאינו דר שם. וכן פ"ק דמסכת ע"ז (דף כא. ושם) דפריך: בית נמי מפקע ליה ממזוזה! ומשני: חובת הדר היא, פי': שאם ירצה לא ידור בו, אלא ישתמש בו לתבן וקש, ולא מיחייב. והא דאמרינן ריש "ר"א דמילה" (שבת קלא:): לא לכל אמר ר"א מכשירי מצוה דוחין את השבת, דמודה ר"א שאם לייץ טליתו ועשה מזוזה לפתחו חייב הואיל ובידו להפקירן, ה"מ למימר: הואיל ובידו [ו] שלא להניחה, אלא הטעם השוה בכל לכ"ע, ולמ"ד חובת טלית בלא לבישה חייב.

כל כהן שאינו עולה לדוכן וכו'. דוקא כשאומר לו עלה, כדאיתא [ז] בסוטה (דף לט.): צריך שיאמר להם חזן הכנסת: "שאו ידיכם קודש". ובתרגום בבלי נמי מתרגמינן ["אמור להם"] – כד תימרון להון. ואע"ג דדרשי' מיניה עשה, [ח] מפיק ליה פ' "ואלו נאמרין" (סוטה לח.): שנים נקראו כהנים ולא כהן אחד, [ט] ותרתי שמעינן מינה. ומ"מ אומר ר"ת, שאפי' כהן אחד עולה לכל הפחות מדרבנן. ודייק מלישנא, דלא קאמר "שני כהנים עולים ולא אחד", משמע אפי' אחד. *ועוד פי' שש"צ אין לו להקרות לפי שהוא מפסיק, ואין להפסיק אפי' ל"יהא שמיה רבה" ואפי' נחש כרוך על עקיבו. וכן פר"ת, דש"צ המפסיק עבירה היא בידו. ותניא בספרי: "אמור להם" –

מלמד

עין משפט נר מצוה

פג א מיי' פ"ב מהל' ציצית הלכה ב סמג עשין ג:

פד ב מיי' פ"ג מהל' ציצית הלכה ד סמג עשין כו טוש"ע א"ח סימן יד סעיף ג:

פה ג מיי' פ"ה מהל' תפילין הל' י סמג עשין כג טוש"ע י"ד סי' רפו סעיף כב:

פו ד מיי' פ"ד מהל' תפילין הלכה ד סמג עשין כב טוש"ע א"ח סי' כו סעיף א:

[וע"ע תוס' שבת קמח. ד"ה שואל]

פז ה מיי' שם הל' כו:

פח ו מיי' פט"ו מהל' תפלה הלכה יב טוש"ע א"ח סימן קכח סעיף ב:

פט ז מיי' פ"ד מהל' תפילין הלכה כו סמג עשין כב טוש"ע א"ח סימן לז סעיף א:

רבינו גרשום

זול טפי. כלומר אע"ג דהיינו אשה לך והוסיף לברך פעם שניה ומה בכך: גופו דומה לים. מראה גופו: ובריתו. צורתו: שליש למלכות. כדי שיניחנה להתגייר: כל שלשים יום פטורה מן הציצית דלא הויא דידיה דסתם שאלה ל' יום: משום ישוב ארץ ישראל. דאי הוה נפיק למהר עייל ביה אחרינא משום דמשכח לה מזומנת דהאי דנפיק לא שקיל מזוזתיה בהדיה כדאמרינן בבבא מציעא [דף קב ע"ב]: אלא שיש לו ואע"פ שאין מניחה אינה מעכבת: חד מצוה נמי לא ליעביד. אלא אין מעכבין: גזירה שמא יפשע אי אמרת כי לית ליה לא מעכבא פשע ולא זבין אלא חדא: עובר בח' עשה דכתיב והיה לך לאות על ידכה. ולזכרון בין עיניך. היינו תרי חד דידך חד דבין עיניך וכתיב והיה לאות על ידך. ולטוטפות בין עיניך. הוו נמי תרי ד' עשה. ותרי וקשרתם לאות על ידך. והיו לטוטפת בין עיניך. הא שית וקשרתם אותם לאות על ידכם. והיו לטוטפת בין עיניכם הא תמני: ציצית עובר בה' עשה. גדילים תעשה לך. ועשו להם ציצית. ונתנו על ציצית. והיה לכם לציצית. וראיתם אותו: לדוכן בג' כה תברכו אמור להם: ושמו את שמי: דכתיב ה' עליהם היינו תפילין דכתיב כי שם ה' נקרא עליך:

שיטה מקובצת

א] איני יודע מסכת ע"ז דף יז: ב] ר' אחייא: ג] טלית שאולה. מזוזה כל שלשים יום פטור מכאן ואילך חייבת. [מן התורה והא] דכתיב ביתך [הא אמרי' בפ'] ראשית הגז דרך ביאתך והכי איתא התם [ציצית אע"ג] דכתיב כסותך דמשמע ולא של שותפות הא [כתיב] בגדיהם ואפי' דשותפות וכסותך ולא של [אחרים מזוזה] אע"ג דכתיב ביתך [דמשמע] ולא של שותפות הא כתיב למען ירבו ימיכם [ואפי'] דשותפות וביתך דרך ביאתך (ולא) [ומדלא] קאמר ולא של אחרים ש"מ דמן התורה שאולה חייבת: ד] אינה מעכבת. של ראש: ה] וכל כהן שאינו עולה לדוכן. כ' רבינו חיים כהן דבשעת דוכן אין לומר אלהינו ואלהי אבותינו ברכנו וכו' אלא מיד שחתם ברכת הודאה קורא כהנים ומביא ראיה ממס' סוטה דאמרינן אין הקורא רשאי לקרות כהנים עד [שיכלה] אמן מפי הצבור והיינו ע"כ אמן דברכת הודאה דהרי אין כאן אמן אחר ואי הוי אמר אלהינו ואלהי אבותינו וכו' מאי קאמר אין הקורא כו' הלא יש כאן הפסקה גדולה בין אמן דצבור לקריאת כהנים אלא ש"מ דמיד אחר חתימה דברכת הודאה הקורא קורא כהנים ועוד מביא ראיה דאמרינן התם לשנים קורא כהנים לאחד אינו קורא ואי הוי אומר שליח צבור אלהינו ואלהי אבותינו כו' בין לאחד ובין לשנים קורא כהנים וקאמר נמי התם אין העובר לפני התיבה רשאי לקרות לכהנים יברכך אלא אם כן יודע בו שיודע לחזור לתפלה שלא תטרף דעתו עליו וכן היה מנהג של מורי הרמ"ר [שהוא היה] מקרא לכהנים ולא הניח השליח צבור לקרות אבל מנהג רבינו פרץ אינו כן אלא הש"ץ מקרא: ו] תיבות אפ"ה נמחק: ז] מראה גופו: ובריתו תבנית כו': ח] חוץ מאותן: ט] והביאתן עמה: י] והיה לך לאות וכן בתר קדש כתיב ושמרת וגו' ותיבות כי יביאך נמחק: יא] ציצית: יב] לך הס"ד ואח"כ מה"ד כהן שאינו עולה לדוכן עובר בשלש. כה תברכו אמור להם ושמו את שמי הרי שנים הרי שלשה: יג] שאינן מצויין: יד] של ר' אחייא: טו] שאולה. עיין בתוספות בפרק השואל ובהר"ן שם: טז] הכא ממזוזה סיוע:

דאמר

הגהות צ"ק

[א] לאות והיו לטוטפות ובסוף הפרשה דקדש כתיב והיה כו': [ב] מצוין: [ג] אחייה ואינו: [ד] נ"ל ועוד הכא דלא מיפטר אלא עד ל' יום משום דעד ל' יום סברי אינשי דשאול הוא אבל אחר ל' יום נראית כשלו הוא דאין דרך שאלה יותר אבל מדאורייתא פטורה כו': [ה] ומשום הא לא מייתי בפ"ק דב"ב הא דמזוזה גבי נשתהה שם ל' יום ה"ה כאנשי העיר והכא דסייע לר"י דמסתבר ליה כו': [ו] להניחן אלא: [ז] כדאי' בספרי צריך כו' וגי' שלפנינו אינו בסוטה ועיין בר"ן מסכת מגילה פ"ד: [ח] ומפיק ליה בפ' כו': [ט] תרתי שמעינן מיניה:

הגהות הב"ח

(א) רש"י ד"ה גפה וכו' ע"ז הס"ד ואח"כ מ"ה שתי פעמים בפסוק וכו' אני ה' אלהיכם: (ב) ד"ה בשמונה וכו' לשון אחר בפ' קדש כתיב והיה כי יביאך וגו' לאות וגו' וכן בוהיה כי יביאך וגו' בסוף הפרשה כתיב והיה לאות וגו' ולטוטפות וגו' הרי ג' ובק"ש וקשרתם כצ"ל:

גליון הש"ס

גמ' צוה עלי ויעשוני גיורת. עיין יבמות דף כד ע"ב תוספות ד"ה לא בימי: רש"י ד"ה ועולה מן הארץ. עיין רש"י במגילה דף ו ע"א ד"ה על ידי חלזון ובסנהדרין דף קא ע"א ברש"י ד"ה חלזון ועיין שבת דף עה ע"א ושם דף עג ע"ב תוספות ד"ה מפרק:

הַאי "אֲשֶׁר תְּכַסֶּה בָּהּ" מַאי עָבְדִי לֵיהּ? מִיבָּעֵי לְהוּ *לְכִדְתַנְיָא: (דברים כב) °"עַל אַרְבַּע כַּנְפוֹת כְּסוּתְךָ", אַרְבַּע – אוְלֹא שָׁלֹשׁ. אַתָּה אוֹמֵר: אַרְבַּע וְלֹא שָׁלֹשׁ, אוֹ אֵינוֹ אֶלָּא אַרְבַּע וְלֹא חָמֵשׁ? כְּשֶׁהוּא אוֹמֵר: "אֲשֶׁר תְּכַסֶּה בָּהּ" – הֲרֵי בַּעֲלַת חָמֵשׁ אָמוּר, וּמָה אֲנִי מְקַיֵּים עַל אַרְבַּע? אַרְבַּע וְלֹא שָׁלֹשׁ. וּמָה רָאִיתָ לְרַבּוֹת בַּעֲלַת חָמֵשׁ וּלְהוֹצִיא בַּעֲלַת שָׁלֹשׁ? מְרַבֶּה אֲנִי בַּעֲלַת חָמֵשׁ – שֶׁיֵּשׁ בִּכְלַל חָמֵשׁ אַרְבַּע, וּמוֹצִיא אֲנִי בַּעֲלַת שָׁלֹשׁ – שֶׁאֵין בִּכְלַל שָׁלֹשׁ אַרְבַּע. וְר"ש? מֵ"אֲשֶׁר" נָפְקָא. וְרַבָּנַן? "אֲשֶׁר" לָא מַשְׁמַע לְהוּ. וְרַבָּנַן, הַאי (במדבר טו) °"וּרְאִיתֶם אוֹתוֹ" מַאי עָבְדִי לֵיהּ? מִיבָּעֵי לְהוּ לְכִדְתַנְיָא: "וּרְאִיתֶם אוֹתוֹ וּזְכַרְתֶּם" – רְאֵה מִצְוָה זוֹ וּזְכוֹר מִצְוָה אַחֶרֶת הַתְּלוּיָה בּוֹ, וְאֵיזוֹ זוֹ? זוֹ קְרִיַּת שְׁמַע, *דִּתְנַן: מֵאֵימָתַי קוֹרִין אֶת שְׁמַע בְּשַׁחֲרִית? מִשֶּׁיַּכִּיר בֵּין תְּכֵלֶת לְלָבָן. וְתַנְיָא אִידָךְ: "וּרְאִיתֶם אוֹתוֹ וּזְכַרְתֶּם" – רְאֵה מִצְוָה זוֹ וּזְכוֹר מִצְוָה אַחֶרֶת הַסְּמוּכָה לָהּ, וְאֵיזוֹ זוֹ? זוֹ מִצְוַת כִּלְאַיִם, דִּכְתִיב: (דברים כב) °"לֹא תִלְבַּשׁ שַׁעַטְנֵז צֶמֶר וּפִשְׁתִּים יַחְדָּו. גְּדִילִים תַּעֲשֶׂה לָּךְ". תַּנְיָא אִידָךְ: "וּרְאִיתֶם אוֹתוֹ וּזְכַרְתֶּם אֶת כָּל מִצְוֹת ה'", כֵּיוָן שֶׁנִּתְחַיֵּיב אָדָם בְּמִצְוָה זוֹ – נִתְחַיֵּיב בְּכָל מִצְוֹת כּוּלָּן; וְר"ש הִיא, דְּאָמַר: מִצְוַת עֲשֵׂה שֶׁהַזְּמַן גְּרָמָא הִיא. תַּנְיָא אִידָךְ: "וּרְאִיתֶם אוֹתוֹ וּזְכַרְתֶּם אֶת כָּל מִצְוֹת ה'" – *בשְׁקוּלָה מִצְוָה זוֹ כְּנֶגֶד כָּל הַמִּצְוֹת כּוּלָּן. וְתַנְיָא אִידָךְ: "וּרְאִיתֶם אוֹתוֹ וּזְכַרְתֶּם וַעֲשִׂיתֶם" – רְאִיָּה מְבִיאָה לִידֵי זְכִירָה, זְכִירָה מְבִיאָה לִידֵי עֲשִׂיָּה. וְרשב"י אוֹמֵר: גכָּל הַזָּרִיז בְּמִצְוָה זוֹ – זוֹכֶה וּמְקַבֵּל פְּנֵי שְׁכִינָה, כְּתִיב הָכָא: "וּרְאִיתֶם אוֹתוֹ", וּכְתִיב הָתָם: (דברים ו) °"אֶת ה' אֱלֹהֶיךָ תִּירָא וְאוֹתוֹ תַעֲבוֹד". ת"ר: *חֲבִיבִין יִשְׂרָאֵל שֶׁסִּיבְּבָן הקב"ה בְּמִצְוֹת, תְּפִילִּין בְּרָאשֵׁיהֶן וּתְפִילִּין בִּזְרוֹעוֹתֵיהֶן וְצִיצִית בְּבִגְדֵיהֶן א] וּמְזוּזָה לְפִתְחֵיהֶן, וַעֲלֵיהֶן אָמַר דָּוִד: (תהלים קיט) °"שֶׁבַע בַּיּוֹם הִלַּלְתִּיךָ עַל מִשְׁפְּטֵי צִדְקֶךָ". וּבְשָׁעָה שֶׁנִּכְנַס דָּוִד לְבֵית הַמֶּרְחָץ וְרָאָה עַצְמוֹ עוֹמֵד עָרוֹם, אָמַר: אוֹי לִי שֶׁאֶעֱמוֹד עָרוֹם בְּלֹא מִצְוָה! וְכֵיוָן שֶׁנִּזְכַּר בְּמִילָה שֶׁבִּבְשָׂרוֹ נִתְיַישְּׁבָה דַּעְתּוֹ; לְאַחַר שֶׁיָּצָא, אָמַר עָלֶיהָ שִׁירָה, שֶׁנֶּאֱמַר: (שם יב) °"לַמְנַצֵּחַ עַל הַשְּׁמִינִית מִזְמוֹר לְדָוִד" – עַל מִילָה שֶׁנִּיתְּנָה בַּשְּׁמִינִי. רַבִּי אֱלִיעֶזֶר בֶּן יַעֲקֹב אוֹמֵר: דכָּל שֶׁיֵּשׁ לוֹ תְּפִילִּין בְּרֹאשׁוֹ וּתְפִילִּין בִּזְרוֹעוֹ וְצִיצִית בְּבִגְדוֹ וּמְזוּזָה בְּפִתְחוֹ – הַכֹּל בְּחִיזּוּק שֶׁלֹּא יֶחְטָא, שֶׁנֶּאֱמַר: (קהלת ד) °"וְהַחוּט הַמְשׁוּלָּשׁ לֹא בִמְהֵרָה יִנָּתֵק", וְאוֹמֵר: (תהלים לד) °"חוֹנֶה מַלְאַךְ ה' סָבִיב לִירֵאָיו וַיְחַלְּצֵם". תַּנְיָא, הָיָה ר' מֵאִיר *אוֹמֵר: מָה נִּשְׁתַּנָּה תְּכֵלֶת מִכָּל מִינֵי צִבְעוֹנִין? מִפְּנֵי השֶׁהַתְּכֵלֶת דּוֹמֶה לַיָּם, וְיָם דּוֹמֶה לָרָקִיעַ, וְרָקִיעַ לְכִסֵּא הַכָּבוֹד, שֶׁנֶּאֱמַר: (שמות כד) °"וְתַחַת רַגְלָיו כְּמַעֲשֵׂה לִבְנַת הַסַּפִּיר וּכְעֶצֶם הַשָּׁמַיִם לָטֹהַר", וּכְתִיב: (יחזקאל א) °"כְּמַרְאֵה אֶבֶן סַפִּיר דְּמוּת כִּסֵּא". תַּנְיָא, הָיָה רַבִּי מֵאִיר אוֹמֵר: וגָּדוֹל עוֹנְשׁוֹ שֶׁל לָבָן יוֹתֵר מֵעוֹנְשׁוֹ שֶׁל תְּכֵלֶת; מָשָׁל לְמָה הַדָּבָר דּוֹמֶה? לְמֶלֶךְ בָּשָׂר וָדָם שֶׁאָמַר לִשְׁנֵי עֲבָדָיו, לְאֶחָד אָמַר: הָבֵא לִי חוֹתָם שֶׁל טִיט, וּלְאֶחָד אָמַר: הָבֵא לִי חוֹתָם שֶׁל זָהָב, וּפָשְׁעוּ שְׁנֵיהֶם וְלֹא הֵבִיאוּ, אֵיזֶה מֵהֶן עוֹנְשׁוֹ מְרוּבֶּה? הֱוֵי אוֹמֵר: זֶה שֶׁאָמַר לוֹ הָבֵא לִי חוֹתָם שֶׁל טִיט וְלֹא הֵבִיא. תַּנְיָא, הָיָה רַבִּי מֵאִיר אוֹמֵר: חַיָּיב אָדָם לְבָרֵךְ זמֵאָה בְּרָכוֹת בְּכָל יוֹם, שֶׁנֶּאֱמַר: °)"וְעַתָּה יִשְׂרָאֵל מָה ה' אֱלֹהֶיךָ שׁוֹאֵל מֵעִמָּךְ". רַב חִיָּיא בְּרֵיהּ דְּרַב אָוְיָא חבְּשַׁבְּתָא וּבְיוֹמֵי טָבֵי טָרַח וּמְמַלֵּי לְהוּ בְּאִיסְפַּרְמָקֵי וּמִגְדֵי. תַּנְיָא, הָיָה *)ר"מ אוֹמֵר: טחַיָּיב אָדָם לְבָרֵךְ שָׁלֹשׁ בְּרָכוֹת בְּכָל יוֹם, אֵלּוּ הֵן: **)"שֶׁלֹּא עָשַׂנִי גּוֹי", "שֶׁלֹּא עָשַׂנִי אִשָּׁה", "שֶׁלֹּא עָשַׂנִי בּוּר". רַב אַחָא בַּר יַעֲקֹב שַׁמְעֵיהּ לִבְרֵיהּ דַּהֲוָה קָא מְבָרֵךְ "שֶׁלֹּא עָשַׂנִי בּוּר", אֲמַר לֵיהּ: כּוּלֵּי הַאי נָמֵי? אֲמַר לֵיהּ: וְאֶלָּא מַאי מְבָרֵךְ, "שֶׁלֹּא עָשַׂנִי עֶבֶד"? הַיְינוּ אִשָּׁה! עֶבֶד

זיל

° דברים י *) [צ"ל רבי יהודה וכן איתא בתוספתא דברכות פ"ו וכ"ה ברי"ף ורא"ש סוף פ"ט דברכות] **) [בתוספתא אי' שלא עשני גוי וכן העתיקו הרי"ף והרא"ש]

רש"י

האי אשר תכסה בה מאי עבדי ליה. לרבות כסות סומא לא איצטריך, דהשתא ומה כסות לילה מיחייבי – כ"ש כסות סומא, דישנה בראייה אצל אחרים. ולא ג'. דטלית בעלת ג' פטורה. מאשר. ב] ריבויא. זו קריאת שמע. דכשמכיר ג] *מנין של לילית קרא את ק"ש. כיון דנתחייב במצוה זו. שהגיע היום – נתחייב בכל המצות, דרוב מצות נוהגות ביום, ור"ש היא. ל"א: כיון שנתחייב אדם – שהגיע לכלל מצוה, דהיינו י"ג שנה – נתחייב בכל המצות, ד] ולהכי אתא עיקר מילתא. ור"ש היא. דפוטר בנשים, דאי רבנן – הא איכא נשים ה] חייבות בה, ופטורות מכמה מצות. שקולה מצוה זו. מדכתיב: "את כל מצות". ועוד, *ד"ציצית" בגימטריא ת"ר, וה' קשרים וח' חוטין – הרי תרי"ג. ראיה. ציצית מביאה לידי זכירת מצות. כתיב הכא "וראיתם אותו" וכתיב התם ו] (דברים ו) "ואותו תעבוד". מה להלן שכינה אף כאן שכינה. שבע ביום. תפילין בראש ובזרוע – הרי שתים, וארבע ציציות ומזוזה – הרי שבע. הכל בחיזוק. מכל וכל עומד בחזקה שלא יחטא. המשולש. תפילין וציצית ומזוזה. סביב ליראיו. העושים מצות, ויחלצם מחטא [את הצדיקים]. מה נשתנה תכלת. שייחדו הקב"ה למצוה זו. דומה לים. שנעשו בו נסים לישראל. ורקיע לכסא הכבוד (א). ז] ומכח התכלת מזכיר היושב על כסא. ועוד, נאה לישראל שיהא ח] כסאו עליהם. שנאמר ותחת רגליו וגו' דהיינו רקיע. וכתיב ספיר. ובכסא כתיב ספיר, אלמא רקיע ט] כדמתחזה כסא. ותכלת לים וים לרקיע, י] ואנן קחזינן. גדול עונשו של לבן יא]. למי שאינו מטיל ציצית יב] *ותכלת. חותם. היו עושים לבהמה ולעבד כשקונין אותן לשם סימן עבדות. זה שאמר לו המלך הבא חותם של טיט. שמצוי הוא ולא הביא, עונשו מרובה. מה ה' אלהיך וגו'. קרי ביה "מאה". בשבתות וימים טובים. דלא מצלו י"ח. טרח וממלא להו. למאה ברכות. באספרמקי ומגדי. אספרמקי = בשמים, ומגדי = מיני מגדים, שטעונים ברכה. כולי האי נמי. דמשבחת נפשך דאיך עם הארץ. ל"א: כולי האי נמי – בשלמא גוי ואשה, הואיל ולא בני מצוה נינהו – שפיר מברכת, אלא בור בר מצות הוא! אלא מאי מברך. להשלים ג' ברכות דר"מ. היינו אשה. דאשה נמי שפחה לבעלה כעבד לרבו. ל"א: היינו אשה – דלענין מצות אשה ועבד שוין, דגמרינן "לה" "לה" יג] (חגיגה דף ד.).

זיל

תוספות

ורבי שמעון מאשר [נפקא]. יד] ר"ת לא גריס ליה, דא"כ כולהו מרבו בעלת חמש. ופ"ב דזבחים (דף יח:) תניא: "ארבע" ולא שלש, "ארבע" ולא חמש, ומוקי לה כר"ש. ומיהו, על כרחין צ"ל דתלת תנאי הוו, ואליבא דר"ש פליגי התם, דהא קיימא לן הלכה כר"ש טו] בכסות לילה כמו שהוכחתי למעלה (דף מ:), וקיימא לן נמי דבעלת חמש חייבת, לעיל (דף לז:) גבי האי מאן *דחייטיה לגלימיה לא עבד כלום דשויה בעלת חמש, ואנן כמאן? אלא על כרחין גירסא נכונה היא. והא דפ' "בית שמאי" (זבחים דף מ.) לא דריש ר"ש "אשר" – היינו לההיא דרשא, וכי האי גוונא הוי טובא.

ואיזו זו קרית שמע. אסמכתא בעלמא, דקרית שמע דרבנן.*

בין תכלת ללבן. בברכות (דף ט:) אמרינן: בין תכלת [שבה] ללבן שבה, פירש בקונטרס: בין צמר שקלט צבע תכלת לצמר שלא קלט. וליתא, דא"כ מאי ראיה זו? ובערוך פי': בין חוליא של תכלת לחוליא של לבן. ופ"ק דברכות ירושלמי, *כיני מתניתין: בין תכלת שבציצית ללבן שבה. "וראיתם אותו" – מן הסמוך. ר"א דאמר כדי שיכיר בין תכלת לכרתי, "וראיתם אותו" – שיהא ניכר בין הצבועים.

ה"ג: רקיע דומה לספיר. דהכי כתיב קרא. וה"נ גרסי' פרק "כסוי הדם" (חולין דף פט.), ולא כספרים דגרסי: רקיע דומה לכסא הכבוד.

חותם של טיט. מה שמדמה חותם של טיט לציצית – שכן עושין לעבדים, והציצית מעיד על ישראל שהם עבדי הקב"ה, כדאיתא פרק "במה אשה" (שבת דף נז:): כבלא דעבדא תנן.

שואל מעמך. פי' ר"ת: דהוי טז] מלא, ויש מאה אותיות בפסוק. וי"מ ד"מה" עולה בא"ת ב"ש מאה. ובקונטרס פירש: אל תקרי "מה" אלא "מאה", *)כלומר שחייב ק' ברכות. וי"מ: כדי להשלים מאה באותיותיה, וכי קרית "מאה" הרי כולן.

*) [וכ"כ בערוך ערך מאה א' ע"ש] זיל

עין משפט נר מצוה

עד א מיי' פ"ג מהל' ציצית הל' ג טוש"ע א"ח סימן י סעיף א:
עה ב מיי' שם הל' יב:
עו ג טוש"ע א"ח סי' כד סעיף ו:

נ"ל דבלריה

עז ד מיי' פ"ו מהלכות תפילין הלכה יג:
עח ה מיי' פ"ב מהל' ציצית הלכה א סמג עשין כו:

[ע' תוס' ברכות כח. ד"ה הכי גרסינן ותוס' סוטה לב: ד"ה ורבי]

עט ו מיי' שם הל' ט:
פ ז מיי' פ"ז מהלכות תפלה הלכה יד סמג עשין יט טוש"ע א"ח סי' מו סעיף ג:

בעי מתניתא בין כו' ללבן שבה ומ"ע דרבנן וראיתם אותו מן הסמוך לו ומ"ע דר"א כו' נ"ק

פא ח טוש"ע א"ח סי' רל סעיף א:
פב ט מיי' שם הלכה ו טוש"ע א"ח סימן מו סעיף ד:

מסורת הש"ס

ג"א לבע של. נ"ק
זבחים יח:
[עמ"ש תוספות לעיל לט ד"ה לא יפחות]
[זבחים יח: מ.]
ברכות ט:
[וכ"ה ברש"י ברי"ף]
[נדרים כה. שבועות כט.]
מתכלת נ"ק
תוספתא דברכות פ"ו
[סוטה יז. חולין פט.]

גליון הש"ס

גמ' וים דומה לרקיע. בסוכה דף לא ע"ב תוס' ד"ה ירוק הביאו ירושלמי דאיתא מים דומה לעשבים ועשבים לרקיע:

הגהות הב"ח

(א) רש"י ד"ה ורקיע לכסא הכבוד ומכיר ע"י התכלת היושב:

שיטה מקובצת

א] ומזוזות בפתחיהן: ב] מאשר ריבויא ורבנן האי וראיתם מאי עבדי ליה דלדידהו הוי זמן [ציצי'] בלילה הואיל והא אמרי נשים חייבות: ג] דכשתכיר גוונין של: ד] המצות. ואגב ריהטא משמע דמי שחייב בההוא חייב בכל המצות: ה] נשים דחייבות: ו] התם. את ה' אלהיך תירא: ז] ומתוך כך יוכר היושב על הכסא: ח] שיהא דמות: ט] רקיע כמראה כסא דכתיב כמראה אבן ספיר דמות כסא: י] לרקיע. אנן: יא] לבן שהוא מצוי: יב] יותר משל תכלת שאינו מצוי הס"ד: יג] לה לה מאשה: יד] ר"ת לא גרים וכו' ואור"י דאין למחוק הספר ותדע דא"כ דר"ש שפטר מבעלת חמש קשיא הלכתא אהלכתא דקי"ל כר"ש דלילה לאו זמן ציצית כדפי' לעיל גבי גזירה משום כסות לילה וקי"ל דבעלת חמש חייבת כדאיתא בסוף הקומץ (דנהי) דמאן דבצריה לגלימא לא עביד כלום שויא בעלת חמש לכך נראה דגרסי' שפיר ולר"ש מאשר [נפקא] והאי תנא דפ"ב דזבחים פליגי אהני. תוס' אחרות: טו] כר"ש ודוחק לומר תלתא תנאי הוו: טז] דהוי שואל:

רבינו גרשום

מברך עליהן אלא שחרית סבירא א) לה דהזמן גרמא: ורבנן דפליגי עליה דר' שמעון דאמרי לאו הזמן גרמא אשר תכסה בה מאי עבדי ליה לרבויי כסות סומא לא איצטריך דאיכא למימר השתא כסות לילה שאינו בראיה אצל אחרים מיחייבא כסות סומא שישנה בראיה אצל אחרים לא כ"ש: ור שמעון מאשר מרב בעלת ה': כיון שנתחייב אדם במצוה זו כשהוא בן י"ג שנה ויום אחד נתחייב בכל המצות לאפוקי נשים שאינן חייבות בכל המצות ור' שמעון היא: זו מצות כלאים שאם היה כלאים בבגדו חייב להסירו: את ה' אלהיך תירא האי תירא עביד לשון ראיה: שבע ביום. שתי תפילין וד' ציציות ומזוזה היינו שבע: חונה מלאך ה' סביב ליראיו המסובן במצות ויחלצם מחטא: שנאמר כמעשה לבנת הספיר וכעצם השמים וכתיב כמראה אבן ספיר דמות כסא להכי הוי צריכי קראי לאשמועינן מה שאנו יכולין לראות היינו רקיע דומא לכסא הכבוד: מה [ה' אלהיך] שואל מעמך. כלומר מאה שואל: בשבתא וביומי טבי. שאין מתפלל י"ח ברכות (חסרו ד'): אספרמקי. מיני בשמים: חייב אדם לברך ג' ברכות משום הכי אמר חייב שהשאר ברכות מברכן על צורך דבר מעשה ואלו אינן לצורך מעשה וגם הם מכלל המאה: כולי האי. נמי אתה מוסיף לברך

א) נראה דר"ל דס"ל דלילה לאו זמן תפילין ומשו"ה צריך לברך עליהן בשחרית.

בֶּן אַרְבָּעִים יוֹם, וְתָרֵי לָהּ בְּגַוַּיְיהוּ מֵאוּרְתָא וְעַד א] לְצַפְרָא, אִיפַּרַד חֲזוּתֵיהּ — פְּסוּלָה, לָא אִיפַּרַד חֲזוּתֵיהּ — כְּשֵׁרָה. וְרַב ב] אַדָּא קַמֵּיהּ דְּרָבָא מִשְּׁמֵיהּ דְּרַב עֲוִירָא אֲמַר: מַיְיתֵי אחֲמִירָא אַרְכְּסָא דְּשַׂעֲרֵי וְאָפְיָא לָהּ בְּגַוֵּויהּ, אִישְׁתַּנַּאי לְמַעַלְיוּתָא — כְּשֵׁרָה, לִגְרִיעוּתָא — פְּסוּלָה, וְסִימָנֵיךְ: שִׁינּוּי שֶׁקֶר, שִׁינּוּי אֱמֶת! מַאי אֵין לָהּ בְּדִיקָה נַמִי דְּקָאָמַר? אַטְעִימָה. מָר מִמַּשְׁכֵי אַיְיתֵי תְּכֶלְתָּא בִּשְׁנֵי רַב אַחַאי, בַּדְקוּהָ בִּדְרַב יִצְחָק בְּרֵיהּ דְּרַב יְהוּדָה וְאִיפַּרַד חֲזוּתֵיהּ, בִּדְרַב ג] אַדָּא — וְאִישְׁתַּנַּאי לְמַעַלְיוּתָא; סָבַר לְמִיפְסְלָהּ, אֲמַר לְהוּ רַב אַחַאי: אֶלָּא הָא לָא תְּכֵילְתָּא הִיא וְלָא קָלָא אִילָן הִיא! אֶלָּא שְׁמַע מִינָּהּ שְׁמוּעָתָא אַהֲדָדֵי אִיתְּמַר; הֵיכָא דִּבְדַקְנָא בִּדְרַב יִצְחָק בְּרֵיהּ דְּרַב יְהוּדָה, לָא אִיפַּרַד חֲזוּתֵיהּ — כְּשֵׁרָה, אִיפַּרַד חֲזוּתֵיהּ — בָּדְקִינַן לָהּ בִּדְרַב ד] אַדָּא בַּחֲמִירָא אַרְכְּסָא; אִישְׁתַּנֵּי לְמַעַלְיוּתָא — כְּשֵׁרָה, לִגְרִיעוּתָא — פְּסוּלָה. שָׁלְחוּ מִתָּם: בשְׁמוּעָתָא אַהֲדָדֵי אִיתְּמַר. רַבִּי מָנִי דָּיֵיק וְזָבִין כְּחוּמְרֵי מַתְנִיתָא, א"ל הַהוּא סָבָא: הָכִי עֲבוּד קַמָּאֵי דְּקַמָּךְ וְאַצְלַח עִיסְקַיְיהוּ. ת"ר: גהַלּוֹקֵחַ טַלִּית מְצוּיֶּיצֶת מִן הַשּׁוּק מִיִּשְׂרָאֵל — הֲרֵי הִיא בְּחֶזְקָתָהּ. מִן הַגּוֹי; מִן הַתַּגָּר — כְּשֵׁרָה, מִן הַהֶדְיוֹט — פְּסוּלָה, וְאע"פ שֶׁאָמְרוּ: אֵין אָדָם דרַשַּׁאי לִמְכּוֹר טַלִּית מְצוּיֶּיצֶת לְגוֹי עַד שֶׁיַּתִּיר צִיצִיּוֹתֶיהָ. מַאי טַעְמָא? הָכָא תַּרְגִּימוּ: מִשּׁוּם זוֹנָה. רַב יְהוּדָה אָמַר: שֶׁמָּא יִתְלַוֶּה עִמּוֹ בַּדֶּרֶךְ הוְיַהַרְגֶנּוּ. רַב יְהוּדָה *רָמֵי תְּכֵילְתָּא °לְפִרְזוּמָא דְּאֱינָשֵׁי בֵּיתֵיהּ, וּמְבָרֵךְ וכָּל צַפְרָא: "לְהִתְעַטֵּף בְּצִיצִית". מִדְּרָמֵי — קָסָבַר: מִצְוַת עֲשֵׂה שֶׁלֹּא הַזְּמַן גְּרָמָא הוּא, אַמַּאי מְבָרֵךְ כָּל צַפְרָא וְצַפְרָא? כְּרַבִּי, *דְּתַנְיָא: תְּפִילִּין, כָּל זְמַן זשֶׁמַּנִּיחָן מְבָרֵךְ עֲלֵיהֶן, דִּבְרֵי רַבִּי. אִי הָכִי, כָּל שַׁעְתָּא נַמִי! רַב יְהוּדָה אִינִישׁ צְנִיעָא הֲוָה, וְלָא שָׁרֵי לֵיהּ לִגְלִימֵיהּ כּוּלֵּיהּ יוֹמָא. וּמַאי שְׁנָא מִצַּפְרָא? כִּי מְשַׁנֵּי מִכְּסוּת לַיְלָה לִכְסוּת יוֹם. ת"ר: *הַכֹּל חַיָּיבִין בְּצִיצִית, כֹּהֲנִים, לְוִיִּם וְיִשְׂרְאֵלִים, גֵּרִים, נָשִׁים וַעֲבָדִים. ר"ש חפּוֹטֵר בְּנָשִׁים, מִפְּנֵי *שֶׁמִּצְוַת עֲשֵׂה שֶׁהַזְּמַן גְּרָמָא הוּא, *וְכָל מִצְוַת עֲשֵׂה שֶׁהַזְּמַן גְּרָמָא נָשִׁים פְּטוּרוֹת. [קידושין לג: לד.] אָמַר מָר: הַכֹּל חַיָּיבִין בְּצִיצִית, כֹּהֲנִים, לְוִיִּם וְיִשְׂרְאֵלִים. פְּשִׁיטָא, דְּאִי כֹּהֲנִים לְוִיִּם וְיִשְׂרְאֵלִים פְּטִירִי, מַאן לִיחַיֵּיב? כֹּהֲנִים אִיצְטְרִיכָא לֵיהּ, ס"ד אָמֵינָא, הוֹאִיל וּכְתִיב: °"לֹא תִלְבַּשׁ שַׁעַטְנֵז צֶמֶר וּפִשְׁתִּים יַחְדָּיו, גְּדִילִים תַּעֲשֶׂה לָּךְ", מַאן דְּלָא אִישְׁתְּרֵי כִּלְאַיִם לְגַבֵּיהּ בִּלְבִישָׁה — הוּא דְּמִיחַיֵּיב בְּצִיצִית, הָנֵי כֹּהֲנִים הוֹאִיל וְאִישְׁתְּרֵי כִּלְאַיִם לְגַבַּיְיהוּ — לָא לִיחַיְּיבוּ, קמ"ל, *)נְהִי דְּאִישְׁתְּרֵי בְּעִידַּן עֲבוֹדָה, בְּלָא טעִידַּן עֲבוֹדָה לָא אִישְׁתְּרֵי. ר"ש פּוֹטֵר בְּנָשִׁים. מַאי טַעְמָא דר"ש? **)דְּתַנְיָא: °"וּרְאִיתֶם אוֹתוֹ" — פְּרָט לִכְסוּת לַיְלָה. אַתָּה אוֹמֵר: פְּרָט לִכְסוּת לַיְלָה, אוֹ אֵינוֹ אֶלָּא פְּרָט לִכְסוּת סוּמָא? כְּשֶׁהוּא אוֹמֵר: °"אֲשֶׁר תְּכַסֶּה בָּהּ" — הֲרֵי כְּסוּת סוּמָא אָמוּר, הָא מָה אֲנִי מְקַיֵּים "וּרְאִיתֶם אוֹתוֹ" — פְּרָט לִכְסוּת לַיְלָה. וּמָה רָאִיתָ לְרַבּוֹת כְּסוּת סוּמָא וּלְהוֹצִיא כְּסוּת לַיְלָה? ימְרַבֶּה אֲנִי כְּסוּת סוּמָא שֶׁיֶּשְׁנָהּ בִּרְאִיָּה אֵצֶל אֲחֵרִים, וּמוֹצִיא אֲנִי כּכְּסוּת לַיְלָה שֶׁאֵינָהּ בִּרְאִיָּה אֵצֶל אֲחֵרִים. וְרַבָּנַן הַאי

תורה אור: דברים כב | במדבר טו | דברים כב

*) [ע' תוס' לעיל מא. בתוך ד"ה תכלת] **) שבת כז. זבחים יח:

רש"י

בֶּן אַרְבָּעִים. יוֹם. מִתִּינוֹק בֶּן אַרְבָּעִים. ה] ל"א: שֶׁעָבְרוּ מ' יוֹם מִשֶּׁנַּעֲשָׂאוֹ מִגּוּף הָאָדָם [א] (נִתְקַלְקֵל). וְנִפְרַד חֲזוּתָא. נִתְקַלְקֵל הַמַּרְאֶה פְּסוּלָה, דְּקָלָא אִילָן הוּא. חֲמִירָא אַרְכְּסָא. שְׂאוֹר קָשֶׁה. וְסִימָנֵיךְ. אֵיזֶה שִׁינּוּי כָּשֵׁר וְאֵיזֶה שִׁינּוּי פָּסוּל, שִׁינּוּי שֶׁקֶר – הַמְשַׁנֶּה דְּבָרוֹ לְרָעָה הַכֹּל יוֹדְעִין שֶׁרַע הוּא ו] [ב], [שִׁינּוּי אֱמֶת – הַמְשַׁנֶּה דְּבָרוֹ לְהוֹסִיף עָלָיו וּלְקַיְּימוֹ הַכֹּל יוֹדְעִין שֶׁטּוֹב הוּא]. מַאי אֵין לָהּ בְּדִיקָה דְּקָאָמַר נַמִי אַטְעִימָה. אֵין אָדָם יָכוֹל לִבְדּוֹק הַצֶּמֶר אִם לְשֵׁם תְּכֵלֶת נִצְבַּע אִם לִטְעִימָה לְשֵׁם נִסָּיוֹן, וְאָמְרוּ לְעֵיל דִּטְעִימָה פְּסוּלָה. ל"א: אַטְּעִימָה – וְה"ק: אֵין בּוֹדְקִין יוֹרָה שֶׁל תְּכֵלֶת בִּטְעִימָה, שֶׁלֹּא יִפָּסֵל כָּל הַיּוֹרָה, אֶלָּא שָׁקֵיל בְּבֵיעֲתָא כִּדְמְפָרֵשׁ לְעֵיל. מָר. שֵׁם חָכָם. מִמַּשְׁכֵי. שֵׁם מָקוֹם. לָאו תְּכֵלֶת הוּא. דְּהָא אִיפָּרַד חֲזוּתָא בִּדְרַב יִצְחָק, וְלָאו קָלָא אִילָן – דְּהָא אִישְׁתַּנֵּי לְמַעַלְיוּתָא כִּדְר"א ז]. שְׁמוּעֲתָא. דְּרַב יִצְחָק וּדְרַב ח] חֲדָא אַהֲדָדֵי אִיתְּמַר. כְּלוֹמַר, בִּשְׁתֵּיהֶן יַחַד בָּדְקִינַן, וְלָא פְּלִיגֵי, אֶלָּא הֵיכָא דְּבָדַקְנָא כו', ט] וְהָא דְּרַב חֲדָא מוּסֶפֶת עַל דְּרַב יִצְחָק וּמְפָרֵשׁ אוֹתָהּ. דָּיֵיק וְזָבִין. מִן הַמּוּמְחֶה. כְּחוּמְרֵי מַתְנִיתָא. דִּלְעֵיל, דְּקָתָנֵי: טְעִימָה פְּסוּלָה, הִלְכָּךְ בָּעֵי מוּמְחֶה. מִן הַגּוֹי. אִם תַּגָּר הוּא כְּשֵׁרָה, דְּלָא מְרַע נַפְשֵׁיהּ, וְזַבֵּין לָהּ מִיִּשְׂרָאֵל וּכְשֵׁרָה. פְּסוּלָה. דְּשֶׁמָּא הוּא לְבָעָהּ, וְשֶׁלֹּא לִשְׁמָהּ נַעֲשֵׂית. וְאע"פ שֶׁאָמְרוּ כו'. אַפ"ה אָמְרִינַן: (גַּבֵּי) תַּגָּר יִשְׂרָאֵל מְכָרָהּ לוֹ. מַאי טַעְמָא. אֵין מוֹכְרִין י] מְצוּיֶּיצֶת לְגוֹי. מִשּׁוּם זוֹנָה. דִּלְמָא הָוְיָא לֵיהּ זוֹנָה יִשְׂרְאֵלִית, וּסְבוּרָה יא] יִשְׂרָאֵל הוּא וְתִבָּעֵל לֵיהּ, יב] וְעָבְרִין מִשּׁוּם "לֹא תִתְחַתֵּן בָּם" (דברים ז). ל"א: מִשּׁוּם זוֹנָה גּוֹיָה, דִּלְמָא יָהֵיב לָהּ הַהוּא גּוֹי יג] בְּאֶתְנַנָּהּ, וְאָמְרָה כִּי יִשְׂרָאֵל יד] נְתָנָהּ לִי, וְאָתֵי לְמִחְשְׁדֵיהּ. שֶׁמָּא יִתְלַוֶּה. יִשְׂרָאֵל עִם הַגּוֹי זֶה, וְסָבוּר: יִשְׂרָאֵל הוּא, דְּהָא יֵשׁ לוֹ צִיצִית, וְיַהַרְגֶנּוּ. רַב יְהוּדָה רָמֵי לֵיהּ תְּכֵילְתָּא לְפוּרְזִימָא דְּאִינְשֵׁי בֵּיתֵיהּ. הָיָה מַטִּיל צִיצִית לְבֶגֶד שֶׁמִּתְכַּסָּה בּוֹ אִשְׁתּוֹ. וּמְבָרֵךְ כָּל צַפְרָא. וְעוֹד עוֹשֶׂה דָּבָר זֶה, כְּשֶׁמִּתְעַטֵּף בְּטַלִּיתוֹ בְּכָל בּוֹקֶר וּבוֹקֶר הָיָה מְבָרֵךְ. מִדְּרָמֵי. תְּכֵילְתָּא לִכְסוּת אִשְׁתּוֹ, קָסָבַר נָשִׁים חַיָּיבוֹת בָּהּ – אַלְמָא קָסָבַר מִצְוַת עֲשֵׂה שֶׁלֹּא הַזְּמַן גְּרָמָא הִיא, דִּזְמַנָּהּ בֵּין בַּיּוֹם וּבֵין בַּלַּיְלָה, דְּאִי זְמַן גְּרָמָא – נָשִׁים פְּטוּרוֹת. אִם כֵּן דְּלַיְלָה טו] זְמַנָּהּ אַמַּאי מְבָרֵךְ [ג] (א). אֶלָּא פַּעַם רִאשׁוֹן כְּשֶׁנִּתְעַטֵּף טז] כְּשֶׁהָיְתָה חֲדָשָׁה ה"ל לְבָרֵךְ, הָא מִכָּאן וְאֵילָךְ יז] [ד] יוֹמָא אֲרִיכָא דָּמֵי, דְּהָא אֵין לַיְלָה מַפְסִיקוֹ. וְלָא הֲוָה שָׁרֵי לָהּ יח] כָּל יוֹמָא. אֶלָּא בַּלַּיְלָה, וְהִלְכָּךְ לֹא מְבָרֵךְ אֶלָּא בְּצַפְרָא, וּלְעוֹלָם כְּרַבִּי. וּמַאי שְׁנָא מִצַּפְרָא. יט] לִבְרִיךְ כְּשֶׁהוּא עוֹמֵד וּמִתְעַטֵּף בָּהּ בָּאַשְׁמוֹרֶת קוֹדֶם הַיּוֹם כ] לְגִירְסֵיהּ! וּמְשַׁנֵּי: כִּי מְשַׁנֵּי מִכְּסוּת לַיְלָה לִכְסוּת יוֹם. כא] שְׁנֵי טַלִּיתוֹת מְצוּיָּיצוֹת הָיוּ, אַחַת לַיּוֹם וְאַחַת לַלַּיְלָה (ב). שֶׁהַזְּמַן גְּרָמָא הִיא. דְּלַיְלָה לְר"ש לָאו זְמַן צִיצִית, וְהָוֵי יוֹם זְמַנָּהּ. כֹּהֲנִים אִישְׁתְּרַאי כִּלְאַיִם לְגַבַּיְיהוּ. אַבְנֵט, דִּכְתִיב בֵּיהּ (שמות לט): "שֵׁשׁ וּתְכֵלֶת". כְּסוּת סוּמָא (ג). דְּחַיָּיב. וְרַבָּנַן. דְּאִית לְהוּ לַיְלָה זְמַן צִיצִית, וְהָוְיָא מִצְוַת [עֲשֵׂה] שֶׁלֹּא הַזְּמַן גְּרָמָא, וְנָשִׁים חַיָּיבוֹת. הַאי

תוספות

תורה [ה] בעי עיבוד! כב] ושמא הכא בשאר ספרים איירי. ונראה לפרש: תפילין יש להם בדיקה – בחסירות ויתירות, ואפ"ה אין ניקחין – כג] שבגאי לסותרן. אבל לעיבוד לשמה לא חיישינן, שהכל בקיאין בו. והא דתניא ב"המוצא תפילין" (עירובין דף צז.*): הלוקח תפילין [ו] מן השוק בודקה אחת אחת – בדיעבד איירי. (ולפי' הקונטרס נראה לי לפרש דבדיעבד לא חיישינן) והכי תניא בתוספתא דמסכת ע"ז: אין לוקחין תפילין אלא מן המומחה, ואם לקח ממי שאינו מומחה ומצא בידו שנים או שלשה למדים – בודק ממנו תפילין אחד של יד או של ראש בגמיד הראשון, וכן שני וכן שלישי. והא דתנן (שם דף צה.): המוצא תפילין מכניסן זוג זוג אע"פ שלא בדקן – התם משום כבוד דתפילין לא חיישינן. א"נ, מוצא שאני, דרוב מצויין אצל תפילין מומחין הן. ובמכילתא איתא: נאמר כאן "ימימה" ונאמר להלן (ויקרא כה) "ימים תהיה גאולתו", מה להלן י"ב חדש – אף כאן, מגיד שצריך לבדוק תפילין [ז] אחת לי"ב חדש, דברי ב"ה. ב"ש אומרים: אין צריך בדיקה. *שמאי אומר: אלו תפילין של אבי אימא. ופרק "המוצא תפילין" ירושלמי נמי תניא: תפילין צריך [בדיקה] אחת לי"ב חדש, דברי רבי. רשב"ג אומר: אין צריך. וכל הני דמצרכי בדיקה סבירא להו בחזקת תפילין הכתוב מדבר, ולא קי"ל הכי. מיהו בשימושא רבה איכא שמצריך לבדקן פעמיים בשבוע. והני בדיקות לא הוו משום חסירות ויתירות, אלא שמא בלו ונתקלקלו. ובמזוזה אשכחן [ח] בדיקה, דאמרינן במס' יומא (דף יא.) שנבדקת פעמיים בשבוע, ויש לחלק.

בן ארבעים. פירשתי פרק "האשה" בנדה (דף סג.). **מאי** אין לה בדיקה נמי דקאמר אטעימה. ובדיקה דרב יצחק ורב כד] אדא אהני בלוקח מן המומחה שיודע דטעימה כה] פסולה, [ט] אבל לא ידע מקלא אילן, דאיהו גופיה לא ידע. **ור"ש** פוטר בנשים. אף על גב דאמרינן ברכות (דף כ:) גבי קידוש דנשים חייבות, דכל שישנו בשמירה ישנו בזכירה וזכור ושמור בדבור אחד נאמרו, ואמרינן נמי במכילתין ובירושלמי ד"גדילים" ו"לא תלבש" בדיבור אחד נאמרו – לאו מילתא היא, דהתם לא איתמר בדבור אחד אלא לאשמועינן הא, אבל הכא איתמר כי היכי דלא [י] ניסתרו אהדדי. והכי נמי אין להקשות דנידרוש כי היכי דמרבינן (פסחים מג:) גבי אכילת מצה, דהתם שאני, דכתיבי בחד קרא*).

*) [וע' תוס' פסחים מג: סד"ה סד"א ובמה שציינתי שם על גליו]

סה א ב מיי' פ"ב מהל' ציצית הל' ה: [וכס וע"ש דליתא הכי לפנינו רס"ק מ"ז]

סו ג מיי' פ"ג מהל' ציצית הל' ז טוש"ע א"ח סימן ט סעיף ד:

סז ד ה מיי' שם פ"ג הלכה ט [עי' טוש"ע א"ח סימן כא סעיף ד בהג"ה]:

סח ו מיי' פ"ג מהלכות ציצית הלכה ח וע"ש סמג עשין כו טוש"ע א"ח סימן כ סעיף ב:

סט ז מיי' פ"ד מהלכות תפילין הל' ז סמג עשין כב טוש"ע א"ח סי' לט סעיף ח:

ע ח מיי' פ"ג מהל' ציצית הלכה ח ועי' בהשגות ובכ"מ סמג עשין כו טוש"ע א"ח סי' יז סעיף ב:

עא ט מיי' פ"ח מהל' כלי מקדש הלכה יא ופ"י מהלכות כלאים הל' לב:

ע' הגירסא ברב אלפס וברא"ש הלכות קטנות

עב י מיי' פרק ג' מהל' ציצית הל' ט טוש"ע א"ח סי' יז סעיף ג:

עג כ מיי' שם הל' ז טוש"ע שם:

שיטה מקובצת

א] צפרא אי איפרד: ב] ורב אויא: ג] בדרב אויא ואשתני: ד] בדרב אויא: ה] ארבעים יום לא שעברו עליהם מ': ו] הוא שינוי אמת המשנה דבריו להוסיף עליו ולקיימו הכל יודעין שטוב הוא: ז] כדרב אויא: אלא ש"מ מדבהאי נסין הוא תכלת ובהאי קלא אילן: שמועתא: ח] ודרב אויא: ט] כו' דהא דרב אויא: י] מוכרין טלית: יא] ובסבורה דישראל ליה ועברה: יב] גוי לזונה גויה הטלית: יד] ישראל פלוני: טו] וזמנה: טז] כשנתעטף בה: יז] ואילך כחד: יח] כוליה: יט] מצפרא ליברך: כ] היום הם"ד ואח"כ מה"ד כי משני מכסות: כא] יום דשני: כב] עיבוד לשמה ואפ"ה נקחים: כג] ניקחין. לפי שיש תורה לנתק [הפרשיות] ולחזור ולתפור ואתי למסמך ולא בדיק ושמא אינם מדוקדקות בחסירות ויתירות אבל ספרים ומזוזות אין בהן תורה לבודקן ולא סמך עליהו ובודקן. מהר"פ: כד] ורב אויא: כה] פסולה ס"א ובדיקה משום חששא דקלא אילן:

הגהות הב"ח

(א) רש"י ד"ה א"כ דלילה וכו' אמאי מברך הא א"ל לברך אלא פעם: (ב) ד"ה ומשני כו' וכו' ואחת בלילה לילה לר"ש כל' והד"א: (ג) ד"ה כסות סומא אמור דחייב:

גליון הש"ס

גמ' לפרזומא דאינשי ביתיה. עיין תוס' יו"ט ריש סוטה ד"ה ר"מ: תד"ה ור"ש וכו' דהתם שאני דכתיבי בחד קרא. עיין יבמות דף ד ע"א תד"ה דכתיב:

מסורת הש"ס

[סוכה יא.] [שם מו.] ערכין ג: [חולין ב:] [ע' תוס' ברכות יד: ד"ה ואמר]

רבינו גרשום

איפרד חזותא. אם נפסל מראהו: ארכבא קשה שהחמיץ ביותר: שינוי שקר. היינו לגריעותא ופסול: ושינוי אמת. היינו למעליותא וכשרה: אטעימה קאמר. כלומר כיון דצבעי נמי לשום טעימה משום הכי אין לה בדיקה דאין אדם יכול להבחין אם נצבעה לשום טעימה או לשם תכלת לציצית: ממשכי. שם מקום: הא לא תכלתא היא. דאיפרד חזותא ולא קלא אילן דאישתני למעליותא: דאיק וזבין כחומרי מתניתא. דלא זבין תכלת אלא מן המומחה שצבעו לשם תכלת ובדיק לה בתרייהו: מן הגוי מן התגר. אם לקחה מגוי תגר כשרה דישראל יהביה ניהליה לזבוני: מן הגוי הדיוט פסול. דליכא למימר דישראל היא דלהדיוט לא יהיב איניש מידי לזבוני אלא עשאה להטעות עצמו: הכא תרגימו משום זונה. שמא גוי היה נותן לה אותו טלית באתננה ותוציא לעז על שום בר ישראל ותאמר פלוני נתן לה טליתו מצויצת בשכר ומשום הכי אין ראשן למכור: שמא. יתעטף בו הגוי ויראהו ישראל ויחשוב שיהודי הוא ויבא להתלוות עמו בדרך ויהרגנו הגוי. ואעפ"כ מן הגוי מן התגר כשרה: לפרזומא דאינשי ביתיה. לבגד שאשתו מתכסה בו והוא נמי היה מתעטף בה: מדרמי. לבגד אשתו קסבר ציצית לאו זמן גרמא דסבר דלילה נמי זמן ציצית ונשים חייבות וטליתה חייבת: ומאחר דלאו זמן גרמא אמאי מברך מצפרא (ותו לא): רב יהודה איניש צניעא הוה. מאחר שהיה מתעטף טליתו לא היה מסירה ממנו כל היום ולא הוצרך לברך אלא פעם אחת: ומאי שנא דבצפרא מברך ליברך עלה בלילה קודם היום משעה שהיה עומד לשנות ולא יהא צריך לברך בשחרית: כי משני מכסות לילה לכסות יום. [illegible]

הגהות צ"ק [א] נ"ק מ"ז: [ב] וכן הוא כרש"י כרי"ף: [ג] כל נפלח פעמים: [ד] כיומא: [ה] בעי עבוד לשמה [illegible]

מפשרניא: *ספר תורה, אתפילין ומזוזות שכתבן א] *מין, כותי, גוי, עבד, אשה, וקטן, וישראל משומד – פסולין, שנאמר: "וקשרתם וכתבתם", כל שישנו בקשירה – ישנו בכתיבה, כל שאינו בקשירה – אינו בכתיבה; ובישראל א"צ לברך, דשלח *רב חייא בריה דרב הונא משמיה דר' יוחנן: *בעל תפילין של יד, אומר: "ברוך אשר קדשנו במצותיו וצונו להניח תפילין", על תפילין של ב] ראש, אומר: "ברוך אשר קדשנו במצותיו וצונו על מצות תפילין", ואילו "לעשות תפילין" לא מברך! אלא לאו היינו טעמא: כל מצוה גדעשייתה גמר מצוה, כגון מילה, אע"ג דכשירה בגוי – בישראל צריך לברך, וכל מצוה דעשייתה לאו גמר מצוה, כגון תפילין, אע"ג דפסולות בגוי – בישראל אינו צריך לברך; ובציצית בהא קמיפלגי, מר *סבר: חובת טלית הוא, ומר סבר: חובת גברא הוא. א"ל רב מרדכי לרב אשי: אתון הכי מתניתו לה, אנן הכי מתנינן לה, א"ר יהודה אמר רב: מנין לציצית בגוי שפסולה? שנאמר: °"דבר אל בני ישראל ועשו להם ציצית" – ישראל יעשו ולא אחרים. *אמר רב יהודה אמר רב: דעשאן מן הקוצים ומן הנימין ומן הגרדין – פסולה, מן הסיסין – כשירה; כי אמריתה קמיה דשמואל, אמר: אף מן הסיסין פסולה, הבעינן טויה לשמה. כתנאי: *וציפן זהב, או שטלה עליהן עור בהמה טמאה – פסולות; עור בהמה טהורה – כשירות, ואע"פ שלא עיבדן לשמן. רבן שמעון בן גמליאל אומר: זאף עור בהמה טהורה – פסולות, עד שיעבדן לשמן. אמר ליה אביי לרב שמואל בר רב יהודה: הא תכילתא היכי צבעיתו לה? אמר ליה: חמייתינן דם ג] חלזון וסמנין ורמינן להו ביורה, [ומרתחינן ליה] ושקלינא פורתא בביעתא וטעמינן להו באודרא, ושדינן ליה להוא ד] ביעתא וקלינן ליה לאודרא. שמע מינה תלת: שמע מינה טעימה טפסולה, ושמע מינה ידבעינן צביעה לשמה, ושמע מינה [א] טעימה פסלה. היינו טעימה פסולה, היינו צביעה לשמה! אמר רב אשי: מה טעם קאמר, מה טעם טעימה פסולה – משום דבעינן צביעה לשמה. כתנאי: טעימה פסולה, משום שנאמר: °"כליל תכלת", דברי ר' חנינא בן גמליאל. רבי יוחנן בן דהבאי אומר: אפילו מראה שני שבה כשר, משום שנאמר: °"ושני תולעת". ת"ר: תכלת אין לה בדיקה, ואין נקחית כאלא מן המומחה; °תפילין יש להם בדיקה, לואין ניקחין אלא מן המומחה; ספרים ומזוזות יש להן בדיקה, מוניקחין מכל אדם. ותכלת אין לה בדיקה? והא רב יצחק בריה דרב יהודה בדיק ליה (סי' בגשם), מייתי נמגביא גילא, ה] ומיא דשבלילתא, ומימי רגלים בן בן

במדבר טו · שמות כח · ויקרא יד · תורה אור

מפשרניא. שם מקום. ו] צדוקי גוי. להכי נקט, דסתמיה בקי בכתיבה (א). תפילין עשייתן לא זו היא גמר מצותם עד שיקשרם. בהא פליגי. רב נחמן ורב חסדא אליבא דרב: רב חסדא סבר ציצית חובת טלית, הילכך עשייתן היא גמר מצותן. ורב נחמן סבר חובת גברא היא, ועטיפתה זוהי מצותה. הכי מתניתו לה. להא דאמר רב יהודה אמר רב לעיל, משום הכי קשיא להו לעיל דרב אדרב. עשאה לציצית מן הקוצים. הנקנלים, היינו חוטין ז] התלויין בכל היריעה, שקורין פרוקי"ש, וקוצצין אותם מן הבגד. ל"א: להכי קרי להו [ב] הוצין – שיוצאין מן הבגד [ג] כהוצין. נימין. היינו אותן שיוצאין מן הבגד בתפירה. גרדין. פריינ"ש. פסולה. כל זמן שמחוברין לבגד, דבעינן עשייה לשמה ח]. ציפן זהב. לתפילין. פסולות ט]. בתים, דתיק של עור בעינן, דאפילו קשירתן אינן אלא י] רצועות במינן, כדאמרינן ב"הקומץ". או שטלה עליהן. שעשה בתים של עור בהמה טמאה – פסולות, כדאמרינן בפרק "שמונה שרצים" (שבת דף קח.): "למען תהיה תורת ה' בפיך" – מן המותר בפיך. וסממנים [ד]. דרך הצובעים לשרות בגדים בצריף שקורין דייל"א. וטעמ' ליה באודרא. אודרא = מוך, וצובעין אותה בתוך אותה קליפה לידע אם תכלת יפה. שמע מינה. מדקלינן יא] לאודרא, בעינן צביעה לשם ציצית [ה]. ושמע מינה. מדשדינן ביעתא לברא, ולא שדינן ליה ביורה. [ו] טעימה פסולה. אם עירה צבע נסיון ביורה – פוסל את כל היורה. משום שנאמר כליל תכלת. כל תכלת בעינן [ז] (כליל), שיהא כל עיקר מראה החלזון בצמר, שלא יהא דבר אחר צבוע בה מתחילתה. אפילו מראה שני שבה. שכבר נצבע בה צמר אחר, וזה השני – כשר. ושני תולעת. משמע שני, דאפילו מראה שני של זהורית קרוי תולעת, וה"ה לתכלת דכתיב נמי בההוא קרא. אין לה בדיקה. קס"ד: אין אדם יכול לבודקו אם תכלת הוא אם קלא אילן הוא. ואינה נקחת אלא מן המומחה. דהואיל ואין לה בדיקה – אין לוקחין אותה אלא מן המומחה, שיודע שקלא אילן אסור. תפילין יש להן בדיקה. אדם יכול לבודקן אם דקדק בהן בחסרות ויתרות אם לאו. ואעפ"כ אין נקחין אלא מן המומחה, היודע שצריכין עיבוד לשמם. ונקחין מכל האדם. דליכא בהן עיבוד לשמן. מגביא גילא = בייס"א, ובלשון צרפת אלו"ם. מיא דשבלילתא. מים היוצאין מן התלתן שקורין פנגרי"א.

ואילו לעשות תפילין לא מברך. ויודע היה [שלא לברך "לעשות תפילין"] ששאלו כל ענייני ברכות. ופ' "הרואה" ירושלמי מצריך לברך אעשיית ציצית סוכה ותפילין, ובערוך הביאו בערך "לך" ג', וחולק על התלמוד שלנו. ובתוספתא דברכות (פ"ו) תני: העושה ציצית לעצמו מברך "שהחיינו", יב] ובפ' "הרואה" (ברכות דף נד.) נמי אמר דאכלים חדשים מברך שהחיינו, וכ"כ רב שרירא גאון*. הקוצים כו'. פירש בקונטרס: משום "תעשה ולא מן העשוי". ולי נראה, דמה דעביד אחר כך היינו העשייה, דאמר רב גופיה: תלאן ואחר כך פסק ראשי חוטין שלהן כשר, דזו היא עשייתן. וכן פרק קמא דסוכה (דף יא.) גבי הדלה עליה את הגפן ואת הדלעת, דקיצתן זו היא עשייתן. אלא טעמא – משום דבעינן תלייה לשמה. והא דתנן פרק קמא דסוכה (דף ט.): סוכה הישנה בית הלל מכשירין, ופריך בגמ': ובית הלל לית להו דרב יהודה אמר רב: עשאה מן הקוצים וכו'? כי אמריתה קמיה דשמואל אמר: אף מן הסיסין פסולה, אלמא בעינן טוייה לשמה, הכא נמי בעינן עשייה לשמה! לפי אותה גירסא [ח] אדשמואל פריך ולא מרב, ומרב נמי מצי למפרך. כתנאי ציפן זהב. תימה: דילמא ציצית שאני, דפ"ק דסוכה (דף ט.) דריש: "גדילים תעשה לך" – לשם חובך. ואי משום דכתיב "לך לאות", הא דרשינן ליה לעיל (דף לז:): לך לאות ולא לאחרים! והתם גבי סוכה פריך כי האי גוונא מ"חג הסוכות תעשה לך", [ומשני] דאיצטריך למעוטי גזולה, ולא דרשי תו מיניה לשם חובך. ואי משום דתפילין איתקוש למזוזה, ומזוזה וספר תורה יליף (לעיל דף לד.) כתיבה כתיבה מגט – הא בגט גופיה לא בעינן עשייה לשמו! עד שיעבדן לשמן. אומר ר"ת: דהילכתא כרשב"ג, דאע"ג דהילכתא כרב באיסורי, דסוגיין ד"הניזקין" (גיטין דף נד:) דגוילין שלו לא עיבדתים לשמן כוותיה אזלא. והא דפרק "נגמר הדין" (סנהדרין דף מח:) דאיפליגו אביי ורבא בהזמנה אי מילתא היא אי לא, ומייתי הני תנאי, ופי' בקונטרס דרבא כרבנן דלא בעו עיבוד, יג] דהזמנה לאו מילתא היא. מיהו ר"ת ור"ח פירשו דרבא כרשב"ג, דכיון דבעי עיבוד לשמו, א"כ הזמנה לאו מילתא היא, דאי מילתא היא – אפשר באיתוך העור, ובתיקונים קטנים סגי לשויי לשמה. והא דבעא אביי מרב שמואל בר' יהודה בסמוך: היכי צבעיתו ליה, ואהדר כרשב"ג – לא קיבלה מיניה. וי"מ דההיא ד"הניזקין" אפילו כרבנן, דלא פליגי אלא בעור תפילין דתשמיש מצוה. וליתא, דהא איכא שי"ן של תפילין, ועיקר קדושה יש בה, כדמוכח פ' "במה מדליקין" (שבת דף כח:) ופ' "במה אשה" (שם דף סב.)*). וסממנים. דבר תימה הוא: היאך מערב שום דבר בהדי תכלת? ושמא עם הסממנין נקרא תכלת. ובקונטרס פי': לשרות בהן, כדרך הצובעין ששורין אותו בצריף. מה טעם טעימה פסולה. ואפילו לשם ציצית, מ"מ לשם נסיון נמי עבידא, והוי כמנחה שקמצה לשמה ושלא לשמה. והשתא הנך תלת, תרי נינהו. משום שנאמר כליל תכלת. פי' בקונטרס: שלא יהא דבר אחר צבוע בה מתחילה ואפילו צמר, והוא [ט] שקרוי מראה שני שבה. משמע דאם צבע בה שני פעמים זה אחר זה – פסול אפילו לשמו. ולעיל משמע דלא פסלי' אלא [י] טעימה משום דהויא שלא לשמה, ומשמע דלא מייתי תנאי אלא מטעמה פסלה, אבל לכ"ע [כ] הטעימה כדלעיל, א"כ לא אתיא כחד תנא מילתא דהקונטרס! לכך נ"ל: דאפילו מאה פעמים לשמו יד] משמע דכשר, דהא "כליל תכלת" קרינן ביה, אבל כשטעם – הרי יש צבע שאינו ראוי לתכלת, ולכך קרוי "מראה שני". ואע"ג דהאי קרא בבגדי כהונה כתיב, ילפינן תכלת מבגדי כהונה. ופ' "בא לו" (יומא דף עב.) דריש ליה לדרשא אחרינא. ואין ניקחים אלא מן המומחה. שיש ריעותא, שמא הוא צבעו ואינו בקי. אבל אם נמצאו בשוק – רוב מצויין אצל תכלת מומחין הן, ולכך מכשירין המוצא חוטי תכלת פ' "המוצא תפילין" (עירובין צו:). וכה"ג אמר בחולין גבי שחיטה טו] (דף יב.). תפילין יש להן בדיקה. פי' בקונט': בחסירות ויתרות. ואפי' הכי אין נקחין אלא מן המומחה [ל] לעבדן לשמן. אבל ספרים ומזוזות לא בעי עיבוד לשמן. וכן פי' ה"ר משה בר מיימון דמזוזה לא בעיא לשמה, ולא פירש מנא ליה, ושמא מהכא. וקשה: דפ' "הניזקין" (גיטין דף נד:) משמע דספר תורה

*) [וע"ע תוס' סנהדרין מח: ד"ה אע"פ ותוס' גיטין מה: ד"ה עד]

גיטין מה: ע"ש · [לעיל מו.] · [ברכות מ:] · [לעיל מא.] · סוכה ט. · סנהדרין מח: גיטין מה:

גליון הש"ס

גמ' תפילין יש להם בדיקה. גי' הרי"ף ספרים יש להם בדיקה ואין ניקחין אלא מן המומחה ותפילין ומזוזות אין להם בדיקה וניקחין מכל אדם. ועיין ברמב"ן במלחמות פ"ק דסוכה.

רבינו גרשום

בציצית בהא פליגי. רב אדא בר אהבה דקא מברך לעשות ציצית סבר חובת טלית היא ולאו חובת גברא ועשיית ציצית זו היא גמר מצוה. ורב חסדא סבר ציצית אינה צריכה ברכה דחובת גברא היא. ועשייתה לאו גמר מצוה עד דמעטף לה: עשאה. לציצית מן הקוצין מאותן חוטין שיוצאין מן הבגד הארוג וקוצצין אותו להשוותו: מן הנימין. א) מן נימין חוטין שמצא: מן הגרדין. שקורין פרנש: פסולין. שכל אלו לא נחתכו לשמן: מן הסיסין כשירה. עדיין לא היה לשום צורך דבר ואיכא חתיכה לשמה: ציפן זהב. לתפילין: פורתא בביעתא. בקליפה של ביצה: אודרא. צמר רך: ש"מ טעימה פסול מדקלינן לאודרא: ומדלא טעמינן ביורה ש"מ טעמה פסלה משום שנאמר כליל תכלת. כלומר כל הצמר שביורה בעינן שיהא לשם תכלת: אפילו מראה שניה שצובעין פעם שניה מן התכלת כשר משום תכלת שנ' תכלת וארגמן ותולעת שני. קרי ביה שני. וקא משמע האי שני [קאי] נמי אתכל' דמכשר אפילו מראה שניה: תכלת אין לה בדיקה קא משמע השתא דאינה צריכה בדיקה: ואין ניקחין אלא מן המומחה. שיודע שקלא אילן אסור: תפילין יש להן בדיקה בחסידות ויתירות או אם עשויין כהלכתן: ואין ניקחין אלא מן המומחה שעשאם לשמן: מגביא גילא. מין צבע וקשולטר בלע"ז: שבליליתא. תלתן. ומי רגלים של קטן שעבר עליהן ארבעים יום:

א) אולי צ"ל מן החוטין שיוצאין מהתפירה וכמו שפרש"י.

נב א מיי' פ"א מהל' תפילין הלכה יג טוש"ע א"ח סימן לט סעיף א וטוש"ע י"ד סי' רפא סעיף א:
נג ב מיי' שם פ"ד הל' ד טוש"ע א"ח סימן כה סעיף ה:
[ועי' היטב תוס' סוכה מו. סד"ה העושה וכו' כתב רב שרירא וכו' אמנם לפי הנוסחא שהיה לפני המהרש"א דהכא ע"ש אתי שפיר]
נד ג מיי' פי"א מהל' ברכות הלכה ח:
נה ד מיי' פ"א מהלכות ציצית הלכה יא סמג עשין כו טוש"ע א"ח סי' יא סעיף ה:
נו ה מיי' שם טוש"ע שם סעיף א:
נז ו מיי' פ"ג מהל' תפילין הלכה טו טוש"ע א"ח סימן לב סעיף מח:
נח ז מיי' שם טוש"ע שם סעיף לז:
נט ח ט מיי' פ"ב מהלכות ציצית הל' ב ג סמג עשין כו:
ס י מיי' וסמג שם:
סא כ מיי' שם הל' ז:
סב ל מיי' שם פ"ב הלכה י טוש"ע א"ח סימן לט סעיף ח:
סג מ מיי' פ"א מהל' תפילין הלכה יא והל' יג סמג עשין כה:
סד נ מיי' פ"ב מהלכות ציצית הלכה ה:

שיטה מקובצת

א] משומד מסור גוי: ב] ראש. היינו כשאין לו אלא אחת או שסח בין תפילה לתפילה תו"א: ג] חלזון. וסממנין ורמינן להו ביורה ומרתחינן להו: ד] לההוא. דביעתא: ה] מיא דשבלילתא: ו] מין גוי כומר להכי נקט כומר: ז] התלויין. בסוף: ח] לשמה. והאי תלוי ועומד בה: מן הסיסין למשיל: כשירה דאיכא תליה לשמה: כתנאי אי בעינן טויה לשמה: ט] פסולות. הבתים דבתים של עור. ותיבות בתים דתיק נמחק: י] ברצועות במינן: יא] לאודרא. שלא יעשנו ממנה ציצית: טעימה פסולה. אותו צמר שצובעין לשם נסיון פסולה לציצית: יב] שהחיינו. ורב שרירא גאון כתב דלא סמכינן עלה ואין מברכין שהחיינו רק מדבר הבא מזמן לזמן: יג] עבוד. לשמה דהזמנה: יד] לשמו כשר. תיבת משמע נמחק: טו] שחיטה. א"נ (לא) שאני בין התחלה להכא דמצאן דכיון שבא ליקח אל יקח אלא מן המומחה אבל להפסיד מציאתו הוי כמו בדיעבד שלא יפסיד מציאתו. מהר"פ:

הגהות הב"ח

(א) רש"י ד"ה צדוקי וכו' בכתיבה הס"ד ואח"כ מ"ה לאו גמר מצוה תפילין:

הגהות צ"ק [א] טעמה פסלה: [ב] נ"ל קולין: [ג] כקולין: [ד] לשרות בהן כדרך הצובעין לשרות בצריף: [ה] עיין נ"ק: [ו] טעמה פסלה אם צבע נסיון: [ז] נ"ק מ"ז: [ח] משמואל: [ט] קרוי: [י] משום טעמא דהוה: [כ] הטעם כדלעיל א"כ לא אתיא כחד תנא סוגיא דהכא לחי' הקונטרס: [ל] שמא לא עיבדין:

אאין לה שיעור למעלה, אבל יש לה שיעור למטה. דאי לא תימא הכי, כיוצא בו לולב אין לו שיעור, הכי נמי דאין לו שיעור כלל? והתנן: *לולב שיש בו ג' טפחים כדי לנענע בו — כשר! באלא, אין לו שיעור למעלה, אבל יש לו שיעור למטה; ה"נ אין לו שיעור למעלה, אבל יש לו שיעור למטה. ת"ר: "ציצית" — אין ציצית אלא ענף, וכן הוא אומר: א] °"ויקחני בציצית ראשי". ואמר אביי: גוצריך ב] לפרודה כי צוציתא דארמאי. ת"ר: הטיל על הקרן או ג] על הגדיל — כשירה, רבי אליעזר בן יעקב ד] (אומר) פוסל בשתיהן. כמאן אזלא הא דאמר רב גידל אמר רב: דציצית צריכה ה] שתהא נוטפת על הקרן, שנאמר: °"על כנפי בגדיהם", כמאן? כרבי אליעזר בן יעקב. אמר ר' יעקב אמר רבי יוחנן: הוצריך שירחיק מלא קשר גודל. ואיצטריך דרב פפא, ואיצטריך דר' יעקב; דאי מדרב פפא, הוה אמינא: תוך ג' — דלא לירחיק טפי, וכמה דמקרב מעלי, איצטריך דר' יעקב; ואי מדרבי יעקב, הוה אמינא: מלא קשר גודל — דלא ליקרב טפי, וכמה דרחיק מעלי, צריכא. רבינא ורב סמא הוו יתבי קמיה דרב אשי, חזייה רב סמא לקרניה דגלימיה דרבינא דסתר ובצר ממלא קשר גודל, אמר ליה: לא סבר לה מר להא דר' יעקב? אמר ליה: ובשעת עשייה איתמר. איכסיף. אמר ליה רב אשי: לא תתקיף לך, *חד מינייהו כתרי מינן. רב אחא בר יעקב זרמי ארבע, ועייף להו מיעף, ומעייל להו בגלימא ואביק להו מיבק; קסבר: בעינן תמניא בגלימא, כי היכי דליהוי "גדיל" "גדילים" במקום פתיל. רב ירמיה מדפתי רמי תמניא דאינהו שיתסר, ולא אביק להו. *מר בריה דרבינא עביד כדידן. רב נחמן אשכחיה לרב אדא בר אהבה רמי חוטי וקא מברך: "לעשות ציצית", א"ל: מאי ציצי ו] שמענא? הכי אמר רב: חציצית אין צריכה ברכה! כי נח נפשיה דרב הונא, על רב חסדא למירמא דרב אדרב: ומי אמר רב ציצית אין צריך ברכה? והא אמר רב יהודה אמר רב: מנין טלציצית בגוי שהיא פסולה? שנאמר: °"דבר אל בני ישראל ועשו להם ציצית" — בני ישראל יעשו, ולא הגוים יעשו! והא מאי רומיא? אמר רב יוסף, קסבר רב חסדא: כל מצוה שכשירה בגוי — בישראל אין צריך לברך, כל מצוה שפסולה בגוי — בישראל צריך לברך. וכללא הוא? והרי מילה דכשירה בגוי, דתניא: *עיר שאין בה רופא ישראל ויש בה רופא ארמאי ורופא כותי — ימול ארמאי ז] ואל ימול כותי, דברי רבי מאיר, רבי יהודה אומר: יכותי ולא ארמאי; ובישראל צריך לברך, דאמר מר: *המל אומר: כ"ברוך אשר קדשנו במצותיו וצונו על המילה"! מידי הוא טעמא אלא לרב, רב ח] מיפסיל פסיל, דאיתמר: מנין למילה בגוי שפסולה? דרו בר פפא משמיה דרב אמר: °"ואתה את בריתי תשמור", ר' יוחנן אמר: ט] °"המול ימול" — המל ימול. סוכה מסייע ליה, תפילין הוי תיובתיה. הרי סוכה דכשירה בגוי, *דתניא: לסוכת גוים, סוכת נשים, סוכת בהמה, סוכת כותיים, סוכה מכל מקום — כשירה, ובלבד שתהא מסוככת כהילכתא; ובישראל אין צריך לברך, דתניא: *העושה סוכה לעצמו, אומר: מ"ברוך אתה ה' אלהינו מלך העולם שהחיינו וקימנו והגיענו לזמן הזה", י] בא לישב בה, אומר: "ברוך אתה ה' אלהינו מלך העולם אשר קדשנו במצותיו וצונו לישב בסוכה", ואילו "לעשות סוכה" לא מברך. תפילין תיובתיה; והרי תפילין דפסולות בגוי, דתני *רב חיננא בריה דרבא מפשרניא

תורה אור: יחזקאל ח | במדבר טו | שם | בראשית יז | שם

מסורת הש"ס: סוכה לז: | [לקמן לט: ע"ש] | [חולין קיב: עבודה זרה כו.] | [לעיל לח:] | ע"ז כו: | שבת קלז: תוספתא ברכות פ"ו | סוכה ח: | סוכה מו. פסחים ז: תוספתא ברכות פ"ו | גיטין מה: ע"ש

רש"י

אין לה שיעור למעלה. דכמה דבעי ליהוי ארוך. ויש לה שיעור למטה. דמשולשת ד' בעינן, אבל בציר מהכי לא. יח] והדקתני "מעשהו" – דמעשהו נמי מתכשרי יב] גרדומי. וצריך לפרודה כי צוציתא דארמאי. כבלורית של גוים, דדבוקות מלמטה ופרודות מלמעלה. על הקרן. על שפת חודה של קרן. גדיל. חוט עבה וחזק יג] בבגד תחילה כדי שלא יהא נוח ליקרע. ל"א: גדיל – אלו הן חוטין יד] שבשפתי שני הצדדים, וקורין אוריל"ש. שתהא נוטפת על הקרן. שתהא תולה ומכה על הקרן. כלומר טו] [א], כשיגביהנה למעלה מן השפה, כדי שתהא תולה ונוגעת התלויה בקרן. שירחיק מלא קשר גודל. צריך שיגביהנה מן השפה מלא קשר גודל, שיעור הציפורן עם טז] בשר עד פרק ראשון. ואיצטריך דרב פפא. דאמר לעיל: ארבעה בתוך שלשה, דמשמע שלא יגביהנה יותר מג' אצבעות. וכמה דקריב לשפה טפי מעלי. ואפילו בחודה של שפה ליתכשר. דסתר ובצר ממלא קשר גודל. דנסתר יז] [ב] ונרחב [הנקב], וירד [הגדיל] למטה עד יח] שעמד בציר ממלא קשר. אי נמי, נסתר יט] הבגד מלמטה שקורין אנפיליי"ר, עד שנפחת מן השפה עד הנקב ממלא קשר גודל. בשעת כ] עשייה [ג] [איתמר]. [הא] דרבי יעקב. ואנא נמי בשעת כא] [ד] עשייה [הוה] מלא קשר גודל. איכסף. רב סמא. א"ל. כב] לרב סמא. חד מינייהו. מבני ארץ ישראל, ורבינא מא"י הוה. ועייף כג] להו. כופל לה [ה] קודם שיתלם בטלית. ומעייל להו בגלימא. מכניס הכפל בנקב הטלית. ואביק להו מיבק. עונבן, שחוזר ומכניס כד] [ו] שתים הראשים בתוך הכפל, ותלויין בעניבה כה] בטלית. דהכי דריש: "גדיל" — שנים, כו] "גדילים" — תרתי משמע, שהן ד' חוטין, כז] ואחר כך כופלן לשמנה. רמי ח'. חוטין, כח] דכתיב "גדילים" — לרבות עוד כט] שנים גדילים, דהוו תמניא חוטין. כך ל] קבלה מרבינו יעקב הזקן לא] דמסכת יבמות. דאינהו שיתסר. לאחר שהכניסן בטלית כופלן והן שיתסר. כדידן. מכניס ד' חוטין ואחר כך כופלן לשמונה. רמי חוטין. היה מטיל ציצית לטליתו. ציצי. לב] ליגלג. אין צריכה ברכה. בשעת עשייה. מאי רומיא. מאי קושיא. כל מצוה שכשירה בגוי בישראל אינו צריך ברכה. דאין יכול לומר "אשר קדשנו", דהא גוי נמי כשר בה. מפי המורה. רופא = מוהל. ואל ימול כותי. לפי שמל לשם הר גריזים, כדמפרש התם במסכת ע"ז (דף כז.). מידי הוא טעמא. דמקשי רב חסדא. אלא לרב רב מיפסל פסיל. מילה בגוי. הלכך איכא למימר דרב חסדא לא לג] קשיא אלא לרב. ואתה את בריתי תשמור. לד] לנימול כמותך אני מוסרו. המול ימול. קרי ביה: המל ימול. סוכה מסייע ליה. לרב חסדא. סוכה מכל מקום. מפרש בפ"ק דמסכת סוכה. מפשרניא

תוספות

ואביק להו מיבק. נ"ל שלא היה מעביר דרך נקב האבק אלא שבעה חוטין לכל היותר, והשמיני מניח וקושר בו. דאל"כ היה יכול להעביר הציצית מן הטלית דרך האבק אחר עשייתן, ולא משכחת כלאים בציצית. תמניא בגלימא. דריש "גדילים" ארבעה, וכן מתכלת, שבשעת נתינתן בטלית יהו שמונה. ורבי ירמיה מדפתי סובר כן, ואם כן הוו להו שיתסר, דלית ליה אבק. מנין לציצית בגוי שהיא פסולה. משמע: הא אשה כשירה. ולא אמר: כל שאינו בלבישה אינו בעשייה, דהא לא כתיב בגופה לבישה אלא בכלאים, ומילתא אחריתי היא. וגבי תפילין [ז] דרשי כי האי גוונא. בישראל אינו צריך לברך. דמשמע "לונו" — ולא לאחרים. ואל ימול כותי. לאחר שהמיר דתו, דסתמייהו לשם הר גריזים, אע"ג דגירי אמת הן. וגוי, אע"ג דבפ' "המביא תניין" (גיטין דף כג.) [ח] קא אמר גבי גט: גוי אדעתא דנפשיה עביד — שאני התם דסתם אשה לאו לגירושין קיימא, אבל סתם מילה לשמה קיימא. והכי משני גבי זבחים (דף ג:). ומתוך כך ניחא בסמוך דמכשר ציצית בגוי מדכתיב "ועשו להם", דמשמע: אחרים יעשו להם, ובתר הכי מכשר רב טוייה שלא לשמה, ומייתי תנאי מתפילין, משמע דציצית נמי בעי לשמה אע"ג דגוי כשר. ותימה: כיון דסתמא לשמו קאי, אמאי איצטריך לרבות גוי? וי"ל: כי היכי דלא נימעטי מ"בני ישראל". ותימה: וגבי ספרים ותפילין ומזוזות, למה לי למעוטי גוי מ"וקשרתם וכתבתם"? תיפוק לי דסתמא לאו לשמו קאי! דבפרק "הניזקין" (גיטין דף נד:) פסל אזכרות שלא כתב לשמן, דאמרינן התם: "ס"ת שכתבתי, אזכרות שבה לא כתבתי לשמן", משמע: אלא סתמן כתבן, דאיבעי למימר "שכתבתי שלא לשמן"! וי"ל: [ט] דאיצטריך משום עבד ואשה מין ומסור ומשומד אע"ג דתני גוי, הכי נמי תני כותי אע"ג דסתמיה לשם הר גריזים ולא איצטריך ליה קרא. אי נמי: לא דק, ובעי למימר: "שלא לשמן". דפ' "כל הגט" (שם דף כד.) תנן: כל הגט שנכתב שלא לשם אשה פסול, ואע"ג דסתמא נמי פסול, אלמא לא דייק. אי נמי, נראה דאזכרות לבד בעינן כולי האי, ואיצטריך למעוטי אי כתב בלא אזכרה. ואילו

רבינו גרשום

אבל יש לה שיעור למטה. שפחות מד' אצבעות לא יעשה: וצריך לפרודה. הפתילין היוצאין מן הגדיל: כי צוציתא דארמאה. כקווצות שיער של בלורי' שדבוקה מלמעלה ופרודה מלמטה א): הטיל על הקרן. לסוף הקרן שלא הרחיק שלשה אצבעות: או על הגדיל. על אותו חוט גס שבתחילת הבגד. ואית דאמרי על הגדיל שהטיל הציצית בכנף לרוחב הבגד. שכשאורגין הבגד לרוחבו אורגין אותו וגדל משם: שתהא נוטפת על הקרן. כלומר תהא מרוחקת מן הקרן ותהא יותר ארוך מן הקרן: מלא קשר גודל. היינו קשר השני של גודל דהיינו כאורך אצבע הגודל והיינו בתוך ג' אצבעות דקאמר רב פפא ואידי ואידי הוי חד שיעורא: דלא לירחק טפי מן הקרן. וכמה דמקרב לגבי הקרן טפי מעלי: איצטריך. דר' יעקב דאמר צריך להרחיק מלא קשר גודל: וכמה דרחיק טפי מעלי קמ"ל דרב פפא דבתוך שלש: דסתר. שהיה מסותר הכנף: ובצר ממלא הקשר גודל עד הציצית: בשעת עשיה איתמר. שצריך שירחיק כמלא [קשר] גודל. אבל אי הדר בצר ממלא קשר גודל לית לן בה: חד מיניהו. מבני א"י עדיף כתרי מינן דאוירא דא"י מחכים. משום ב) הוא רבינא: ועייף להו מיעף. דליהוו תמניא והדר מעייל להו בגלימא: ואביק להו מיבק. והיה עונבן סמוך לכנף: קסבר בעינן דליהוו תמניא חוטין בגלימא עצמה כי היכי דבעינן תמניא במקום פתיל: ולא אביק להו. אלא היה כורך על גבי חמיסר: כי דידן. ארבעה וכופלן: רופא קרי אומן שמל ומרפא: סוכה מסייעא ליה. לרב חסדא:

א) וברש"י ז"ל כתוב להיפך שדבוקות מלמטה ונראה שניהם כוונו לדבר אחד דלגבי הראש הוא דבוק וסוף השער הוא פרוד.
ב) אולי צ"ל משום דרבינא מא"י הוה.

עין משפט נר מצוה

לט א מיי' פ"א מהלכות ציצית הל' ו טוש"ע א"ח סי' יא סעיף ד:
מ ב מיי' פ"ז מהל' לולב הל' ח סמג עשין מד טוש"ע א"ח סימן תרנ סעיף ב:
מא ג מיי' פ"א מהלכות ציצית הלכה א סמג עשין כו טוש"ע א"ח סי' ח סעיף ז:
מב ד מיי' שם הלכה ו טוש"ע א"ח סי' יא סעיף טו:
מג ה מיי' שם טוש"ע שם סעיף ט:
מד ו מיי' שם הל' יח טוש"ע שם סעיף י:
מה ז מיי' שם הלכה ו טוש"ע שם סעיף יג:
מו ח מיי' שם פ"ג ה"ח טוש"ע א"ח סימן יט סעיף א:
מז ט מיי' פ"א מהלכות ציצית הל' יב סמג עשין כו טוש"ע א"ח סי' יד סעיף א:
מח י מיי' פ"ב מהל' מילה הל' א סמג עשין כח טוש"ע י"ד סימן רסד סעיף א:
מט כ מיי' פ"ג מהל' מילה ה"א סמג שם טוש"ע י"ד סימן רסה סעיף א:
נ ל מיי' פ"ה מהלכות סוכה הל' ט טוש"ע א"ח סימן תרלה:
נא מ מיי' פי"א מהל' ברכות הל' ח ופ"ו מהל' סוכה הל' יב סמג עשין מד טוש"ע א"ח סימן תרמא וסימן תרלט סעיף ח:

שיטה מקובצת

א] אומר. וישלח תבנית יד ויקחני בציצית ראשי אמר אות ו' נמחק: ב] לפורדה: ג] על הגדיל. פי' רש"י ב' לשונות ונראה דצריך להקפיד על החוטין שבסוף הטלית מכאן ומכאן שאין בהם ערב כמו בשאר טלית [שלא יהא תוך] ג' אצבעות שצריך להרחיק מחודו של כנף וכן מסקנא דשמעתין שלא ירחיק יותר מג' אצבעות ולא יפחות להרחיק ממלא קשר גודל [לפיכך טוב] שלא ירחיק מן הכנף יותר מדאי: ד] תיבת אומר נמחק: ה] שתהא נוטפת על הקרן. שיהא תולה ומכה על הקרן ולפיכך לא יקשור הציצית למטה ממש שאם כן לא יהא [נוטפת על הקרן] אלא קושר בצד העליון ויהא נוטפת על הקרן וצריך להרחיק כשיעור המפורש משני צידי הכנף: ו] ציצי. דקא שמענא: ז] ואל ימול כותי דברי ר' מאיר. ואע"ג דסבר ר"מ דכותים גירי אמת הן צריך לומר דלאחר מכאן נתקלקלו: הלכה דאין צריך לברך לא לעשות סוכה ולא לעשות ציצית מיהו העושה סוכה מברך שהחיינו ומנהג העולם לסודרו על הכוס: ח] רב. מיפסל: ט] המול ימול. סוכה: י] הזה. נכנס לישב: יא] לא. והא דקתני: יב] מתכשרי. בגרדומי': יג] וחזק. שאורגין בבגד: יד] חוטין. שבשפתי: טו] שיגביהנה: טז] עם. הבשר: יז] ונרחב. הנקב וירד למטה: יח] עד. שניפחת מן הנקב עד השפה ממלא קשר גודל תיבות שעמד בציר נמחק*): יט] נסתר. אריגת הבגד: כ] עשייה. איתמר דר': כא] עשייה הרחבתי: כב] א"ל. רב אשי לרב: כג] להו. היה כופל לשמנה קודם שיתלם בכנף ומעייל: כד] ומכנים. שני הראשין: כה] בטלית. אביק לשון נקב שמכניסים בנקב של כפל כדאמרינן בהקומץ רבה [דף לג ע"א] הכר ציר אבקתא: בעינא תמניא בנקב הטלית דהכי דריש: כו] שנים. גדילים משמע. גדילים ד' גדילים שמנה. מרש"י של מהר"פ: כז] תיבות ואח"כ כופלן לשמנה נמחק: כח] וכתב גדילים. ותיבות רמי ח' חוטין דכתיב נמחק: כט] עוד. שני ואות מ' נמחק: ל] כך קבלתי: לא] במסכת ואות ד' נמחק: לב] ציצי. לשון: לג] חסדא לא. מצי לאקשוי ותיבת אלא נמחק: לד] להומל כמותך:

*) נראה דהא"כ שכתב רש"י שייך אחר תיבת קשר גודל.

הגהות צ"ק [א] שיגביהנה: [ב] ונרקב הנקב וירד למטה כו' קשר א"נ הד"א: [ג] נ"ק: [ד] עשייה היה לו מלא: [ה] לשמונה קודם: [ו] שתי: [ז] דרשינן: [ח] קאמרינן גבי גט: [ט] לאגב דתני עבד ואשה כו' ומומר תני נמי עובד כוכבים דהכי נמי כו':

עין משפט נר מצוה

לב א מיי' פ"ב מהלכות ציצית הלכה ח:

לג ב מיי' פ"א מהלכות ציצית הלכה יג טוש"ע א"ח סי' טו סעיף א: רש"ק

לד ג מיי' פ"ד מהלכות חנוכה הלכה ט טוש"ע א"ח סימן תרעד סעיף א:

לה ד מיי' פ"א מהלכות שבת הלכה ה טוש"ע א"ח סי' שלז סעיף א:

לו ה טוש"ע שם סימן כא סעיף ג בהג"ה:

לז ו מיי' פ"א מהלכות ציצית הלכה ו סמג עשין כו טוש"ע א"ח סי' יא ס"ד:

לח ז מיי' שם טוש"ע שם סעיף ט:

א] וּבִלְבַד שֶׁלֹּא תְּהֵא מוּפְסֶקֶת. שָׁמְעַתְּ מִינָּהּ: *מַתִּירִין מִבֶּגֶד לְבֶגֶד? דִּילְמָא דְּאִי בְּלַאי. ת"ר: ב] טַלִּית שֶׁכּוּלָּהּ תְּכֵלֶת – אכָּל מִינֵי צִבְעוֹנִין פּוֹטְרִין בָּהּ, חוּץ מִקָּלָא אִילָן. מֵיתִיבִי: טַלִּית אֵין פּוֹטֵר בָּהּ אֶלָּא מִינָהּ. טַלִּית שֶׁכּוּלָּהּ תְּכֵלֶת – מֵבִיא תְּכֵלֶת וד"א וְתוֹלֶה בָּהּ; וְקָלָא אִילָן לֹא יָבִיא, וְאִם הֵבִיא – כָּשֵׁר! אָמַר רַב נַחְמָן בַּר יִצְחָק, לָא קַשְׁיָא: כָּאן בְּטַלִּית בַּת אַרְבָּעָה חוּטִין, כָּאן בְּטַלִּית בַּת שְׁמוֹנָה חוּטִין. שָׁמְעַתְּ מִינָּהּ: מַתִּירִין מִבֶּגֶד לְבֶגֶד? דִּלְמָא דְּאִי עֲבַד. *אִיתְּמַר, רַב אָמַר: אֵין מַתִּירִין מִבֶּגֶד לְבֶגֶד, וּשְׁמוּאֵל אָמַר: במַתִּירִין מִבֶּגֶד לְבֶגֶד. רַב אָמַר: אֵין מַדְלִיקִין מִנֵּר לְנֵר, וּשְׁמוּאֵל אָמַר: מַדְלִיקִין גמִנֵּר לְנֵר. רַב אָמַר: אֵין הֲלָכָה כְּרַבִּי שִׁמְעוֹן בִּגְרִירָה, וּשְׁמוּאֵל אָמַר: הֲלָכָה כְּר' שִׁמְעוֹן בִּגְרִירָה. אָמַר *אַבַּיֵי: כָּל מִילֵּי דְּמָר עָבֵיד כְּרַב, לְבַר מֵהָנֵי תְּלָת דְּעָבֵיד כִּשְׁמוּאֵל: מַתִּירִין מִבֶּגֶד לְבֶגֶד, וּמַדְלִיקִין מִנֵּר לְנֵר, וַהֲלָכָה כְּרַבִּי שִׁמְעוֹן בִּגְרִירָה; דְּתַנְיָא, *רַבִּי שִׁמְעוֹן אוֹמֵר: גּוֹרֵר דאָדָם מִטָּה, כִּסֵּא וְסַפְסָל, וּבִלְבַד שֶׁלֹּא יִתְכַּוֵּין לַעֲשׂוֹת חָרִיץ. רַב יְהוּדָה מָסַר לֵיהּ הלְקַצְרָא. רַב חֲנִינָא עָבֵיד לָהּ סִיסָא. רָבִינָא חַיֵּיט לְהוּ מִיחָט. *ת"ר: כַּמָּה חוּטִין הוּא נוֹתֵן? ב"ש אוֹמְרִים: ד', וּב"ה אוֹמְרִים: ג'. ג] וְכַמָּה תְּהֵא מְשׁוּלֶּשֶׁת? ב"ש אוֹמְרִים: ד', וּב"ה אוֹמְרִים: ד] ג'; וְג' שֶׁבֵּית הִלֵּל אוֹמְרִים – אַחַת מֵאַרְבַּע בְּטֶפַח שֶׁל כָּל אָדָם. אָמַר רַב פַּפָּא: טֶפַח דְּאוֹרָיְיתָא – ד' ובְּגוּדָל, שִׁית בִּקְטַנָּה, חָמֵשׁ ה] בְּתִילְתָּא. אָמַר רַב הוּנָא: ד' בְּתוֹךְ ד' וּמְשׁוּלֶּשֶׁת ד', וְרַב יְהוּדָה אָמַר: ג' בְּתוֹךְ ג' מְשׁוּלֶּשֶׁת ג'. אָמַר רַב פַּפָּא, הִלְכְתָא: ד' זבְּתוֹךְ שָׁלֹשׁ מְשׁוּלֶּשֶׁת אַרְבַּע. לְמֵימְרָא, דְּאִית לְהוּ שִׁיעוּרָא; וּרְמִינְהוּ: "צִיצִית" – אֵין צִיצִית אֶלָּא יוֹצֵא, וְאֵין צִיצִית אֶלָּא מַשֶּׁהוּ. וּכְבָר עָלוּ זִקְנֵי ב"ש וְזִקְנֵי ב"ה לַעֲלִיַּית ו] יוֹחָנָן בֶּן בְּתֵירָא, וְאָמְרוּ: צִיצִית אֵין לָהּ שִׁיעוּר. כַּיּוֹצֵא בּוֹ, לוּלָב אֵין בּוֹ שִׁיעוּר; מַאי לָאו אֵין לָהּ שִׁיעוּר כְּלָל? לָא, אֵין

רש"י

ובלבד שלא תהא מופסקת ז]. שיהא כל חוטיה שלימין. שמע מינה. מתירים מבגד לבגד ח]. דילמא אי בלאי. הא דקתני: שמביא תכלת ממקום אחר ותולה בה, ולא חיישינן לבזיון דמבזה לה, לטלית ראשונה ט] [א] דנתבלה דאין ראויה לציצית קאמר דמתיר ממנה הציצית. כל מיני צבעים פוטרין בה. לשום לבן. דכיון דמין כנף ליכא לקיומי בה – אין לך לחזור אחר לבן, אלא שיהו בה שני מינין. חוץ מקלא אילן. דדמי לתכלת י], וזימנין דמזבן לה לאיניש אחרינא וסבר דכל חוטיה תכלת, וכי מצריך לטלית אחריתי – שקיל תרי חוטים מהכא יא] ונותן שם עם לבן, ותחת אלו יתן לבן. ונמצאת אחת מהן נפטר בקלא אילן לשום תכלת, ושדי קלא אילן עם לבן בציצית, והוי כלאים בלא מצוה. מיתיבי טלית אין פוטרין בה לשם לבן אלא מינה. אם אדומה היא – יטיל בה שני חוטין אדומים ושני חוטין תכלת, וכן שאר גוונים. מביא תכלת. שני חוטין לשם תכלת, ודבר אחר לשם לבן. ואע"ג דהאי תכלת הוי מין כנף, אפילו הכי שני מינים בעינן, דאזלינן בתר רוב טליתות. ואם הביא כשר. אלמא קלא אילן נמי פוטר בה. בטלית בת ד' חוטין. שנים תכלת ושנים קלא אילן – כשר יב]. בטלית בת שמנה חוטין. ארבע תכלת והטיל בה ארבע קלא אילן לקיים מצות שני מינים – יג] פסולין. דהואיל ולבר קלא אילן איכא חוטין כל צורכה, חיישינן דלמא יד] מצריך לטלית אחריתי, ושקיל הנך דתכלת מהכא ותלי להו התם, וליכא הכא אלא קלא אילן. אי נמי, שקיל הנך דקלא אילן ותלי בה. ל"א ועיקר: חוץ מקלא אילן – דהא אשני מראות טו] שבה קפדינן, ואלו מראיהן שוין. מיתיבי כו' טז] אם הביא כשר. טלית בת שמנה חוטין, ד' של תכלת ומין אחר, וביקש להטיל עוד ארבעה אחרים – לא יטיל קלא אילן, שמא ימכרנו לאיש אחר ויהא סבור שהם תכלת, ויתירם מכאן ויתן בטלית אחרת במקום תכלת עם לבן. ואם הביא כשר – דהא נפטרה בארבע חוטין של תכלת ודבר אחר. שמע מינה. מדפסל יז] בה משום הך חששא, דמתירין מבגד לבגד. דלמא דאי עבד. אם עבר והתירן אז נפקא חורבה [ג], (דסבר) דמשתרא ציצית מקלא אילן לחודיה יח]. מנר לנר. אותן דחנוכה. מסר. טליתו עם הציצית. לקצרא. לכובס, ולא חייש דילמא מינתקא תכלת ורמי בה קלא אילן. עביד להו סיסא. כשנותנה לכובס מקפל יט] הציצית כמין פקעת שקורים למוסי"ל, כדי שלא ינתק. חייט להו מיחט. עושה לטלית כמין שפה, ומחביא החוטין בתוכה, ותופר השפה. ארבעה. חוטין נתן בחור הטלית, וכופלן לשמונה. משולשת. תלויה הענף [לבד] מן הגדיל. ארבע. אצבעות. ושלש כ] שב"ה אומרים. שתהא כל אצבע אחת מארבע בטפח של כל אדם, דהיינו מדת גודל, ושית בקטנה (א) כא]. כב] בתילתא. אצבע. וכולן מדה אחת. ארבע. חוטין בתוך ארבע אצבעות, שלא ירחיק מן השפה יותר מארבע אצבעות. אין [ג] שם ציצית אלא יוצא. תלוי ויוצא מן הכנף משהו. אין

תוספות

ובלבד שלא תהא מופסקת. ל"ע מאי פי' ומאי *אשמעינן.

אין פוטר בה אלא מינה. פי' בקונט': אם אדומה היא יטיל בה שני חוטים אדומים. ותימה: מידי ליבעא קגריס? ושמא מדרבנן, משום "זה אלי [ד] ואנוהו" (סוכה דף יא:) הוי. [ועוד נראה דאיירי בשאר מינים כגון שיראין וכלך וסיריקין, דאין פוטר אלא במינם מדאורייתא] ומה דפי' בשיראים לאו דוקא, דהא אמרי' דצמר ופשתים פוטרין בהם.

ואם הביא כשר. לאי דפירש בקונטרס, דקלא אילן במקום לבן פסול משום שדומה לתכלת ואין כאן שני מינים, קשה: מאי פריך? דלמא האי ברייתא כרבנן דריש פירקין, דאמרי: אין הלבן מעכבת את התכלת!

כאן בטלית בת שמנה חוטין. פירשתי ריש פירקין.

רב אמר אין מתירין. כג] ואפי' למ"ד חובת גברא, סבר רב דאין לבטל מצות הטלית, כדאשכחן במזוזה בסוף "השואל" (ב"מ קב.) שנענש אותו שנטל המזוזה, ואע"ג דחובת הדר היא. ושמואל דאמר מתירין, אע"ג דקסבר חובת טלית היא, דהא שמואל מחייב לעיל כלי קופסא, כיון דאין לו אלא כדי טלית אחת – טוב שיתן באותה שהוא חפץ להתעטף בה, ולא דמי למזוזה. כד]*.

כל מילי דמר עביד כרב. והא דסוף "כירה" (שבת דף מו.) שרי רבה שרגא דנפטא, ופלוגתא דרב ושמואל במוקצה מחמת מיאוס שילהי שבת (דף קנז.) – דלמא דמתכת איירי. ותו, דהתם איכא פלוגתא דרברבתא טובא. ול"ע.

בית שמאי אומרים ארבע. טעמא דבית שמאי ניחא, כדדרשינן לעיל (דף לט:): "גדיל" – שנים, "גדילים" – ד'. אבל טעמא דבית הלל קשה, דדוחק לומר דלית להו אלא גדילים שנים ופתיל תכלת – הרי תלתא! כה] [ה] ושמע מינה הא דדרשינן "גדילים" ד' – היינו בכפילה. ואלבן קאי. והשתא סברי ב"ש דהוא הדין תכלת, ד"פתיל" לאו דוקא, וסברא הוא להשוותם, והיינו ד' חוטין בלא כפילה, ובית הלל סברי ד"פתיל" דווקא. והא כו] דביומא (דף עב.) דריש מ"פתיל" – כז] [ו] התם *)(הוה ראשונים) דכתיב ברישא (תרי) מהדר, דמיירי בכפול. כח] ור"ת פי' ד"מגדיל" נפקא להו לבית הלל, ד"עבות" מתורגם "עובד גדילו". ונראה לפי' זה דבית הלל דרשי "גדילים" הרי ששה, וכשנכפלו י"ב. ויתכן יותר [ז] דלא דריש "גדילים". וכן משמע בספרי: "ועשו להם" – שומע אני יעשה אותן אחד בפני עצמו? תלמוד לומר "גדילים", מכמה [ח] גדיל אחד נעשית – אין פחות משלשה, דברי ב"ה. ב"ש אומרים: ד' של תכלת ד' של צמר. (אכן) כי דייקת בה משמע דב"ה דרשי "גדילים", ואכל גדיל קיימי, והשתא הויא דומיא דבית שמאי דאיירי בתכלת ולבן. ומיהו בספרי איכא דאמרי: שנים של לבן ואחד של תכלת. [וע"ע תוס' בכורות לט: ד"ה כמה].

בית שמאי אומרים ארבע. פירש בקונטרס: הפתיל יהא ארבע, נמצא הגדיל שנים. ורבינו תם פירש דאגדיל קאי, והענף שמנה – הרי שנים עשר. וכן אנו נוהגין, וכן משמע בספרי בפרשת "כי תצא": גדילים למה נאמר? לפי שנאמר "ועשו להם ציצית" שומע אני יעשה חוט א' בפני עצמו? ת"ל "גדילים", [ט] כמה גדיל נעשית – אין פחות משלשה חוטין כדברי בית הלל, ובית שמאי אומרים: מארבע חוטין של תכלת וארבעה של לבן, [י] על ארבע ארבע אצבעות. משמע דאגדיל קאי. והקונטרס נמי פירש כן בל"א פרק "על אלו מומין" (בכורות דף לט:), וכן יסד רבי שלמה ספרדי: **) "המשולש יהא נכפל כדי אצבעות ארבע". קורא הגדיל, כמו: ***) "מפשילין חבלים לתוכן" פרק "אלו הן הגולין" (מכות דף י.), וכמו "אין מפשילין חבלים לתוכן" דכפ' "בני העיר" (מגילה דף כח.).

ארבעה בגודל. במסכת זבחים בפ' "קדשי קדשים" (דף סג.) [קתני] דכבש של מזבח היה שלש אמות ומחצה ואצבע ושליש אצבע בזכרותו. ואית דמפרשי התם דקשר האצבע קמא כט) [כ] הזכרות, ואית דגרסי "בזכרונו" היינו ראשונות. והכא דלא מפרש מידי ל"ע.

*) נ"א הוקבץ דכתיב כו' ועי' תוס' לעיל ריש פירקין רש"ק. **) בפיוט פ' שלח. ***) נ"ל אין מפשילין.

הגהות הב"ח

(א) רש"י ד"ה ושלש שב"ה וכו' בקטנה זרת הס"ד:

רבינו גרשום

שיטה מקובצת

גמרא

תורה אור | מסורת הש"ם

וְהַגָּדוֹל יוֹצֵא בָּהּ דֶּרֶךְ [א]עֲרַאי – חַיֶּיבֶת בְּצִיצִית. אֵין הַקָּטָן מִתְכַּסֶּה בּוֹ רֹאשׁוֹ וְרוּבּוֹ, אע"פ שֶׁהַגָּדוֹל יוֹצֵא בָּהּ עֲרַאי – פְּטוּרָה, וְכֵן לְעִנְיַן כִּלְאַיִם; וְהָוֵינַן בָּהּ, מַאי "וְכֵן לְעִנְיַן כִּלְאַיִם"? אִילֵימָא וְכֵן לְעִנְיַן אִיסּוּרָא דְּכִלְאַיִם – וְהָא אֲנַן תְּנַן: *[ב]אֵין עֲרַאי בְּכִלְאַיִם (כלאים פ"ט משנה ב); וְאָמַר רַב נַחְמָן בַּר יִצְחָק: וְכֵן לְעִנְיַן סָדִין בְּצִיצִית! אֶלָּא מַאי פְּטוּרָה – הִטִּיל לְמוּטֶּלֶת. א] וְהָא אֲמָרָהּ רַבִּי זֵירָא חֲדָא זִימְנָא! ב] *חֲדָא מִכְּלַל דַּחֲבֶירְתָּהּ אִיתְּמַר (מגילה כט: וש"נ). ת"ר: טַלִּית כְּפוּלָה חַיֶּיבֶת בְּצִיצִית, וְרַבִּי שִׁמְעוֹן [ג]פּוֹטֵר; וְשָׁוִין, שֶׁאִם כְּפָלָהּ וּתְפָרָהּ [ד]שֶׁחַיֶּיבֶת. תְּפָרָהּ, פְּשִׁיטָא! לָא צְרִיכָא, דְּנַקְטָהּ בְּסִיכֵי. רַבָּה בַּר הוּנָא אִיקְּלַע לְבֵי ג] רָבָא בַּר רַב נַחְמָן, חַזְיֵיהּ דַּהֲוָה מִיכַּסֵּי ד] טַלִּית כְּפוּלָה וְרָמֵי לֵיהּ חוּטֵי עִילָּוֵי כְּפֵילָא, אִיפְּשִׁיטָא וַאֲתָא חוּטָא וְקָם לַהֲדֵי רֵישֵׁיהּ. אֲמַר לֵיהּ: לָאו הַיְינוּ כָּנָף דִּכְתַב רַחֲמָנָא בְּאוֹרָיְיתָא! אֲתָא שַׁדְיֵיהּ אִיכַּסֵּי גְּלִימָא אַחְרִיתִי (לקמן מג:). אֲמַר לֵיהּ: מִי סָבְרַתְּ *חוֹבַת גַּבְרָא הוּא? *)חוֹבַת טַלִּית הוּא, זִיל רְמֵי לַהּ. לֵימָא מְסַיֵּיעַ לֵיהּ: חֲסִידִים הָרִאשׁוֹנִים, כֵּיוָן שֶׁאָרְגוּ בָּהּ שָׁלֹשׁ הָיוּ מַטִּילִין בָּהּ תְּכֵלֶת! שָׁאנֵי חֲסִידִים, דְּמַחְמְרִי אַנַּפְשַׁיְיהוּ. וּפְלִיגָא דְּמַלְאָכָא, דְּמַלְאָכָא אַשְׁכְּחֵיהּ לְרַב קְטִינָא דְּמִיכַּסֵּי סְדִינָא, אֲמַר לֵיהּ: קְטִינָא, קְטִינָא! סְדִינָא בְּקַיְיטָא וְסַרְבָּלָא בְּסִיתְוָא, צִיצִית ה] **)שֶׁל תְּכֵלֶת מַה תְּהֵא עָלֶיהָ? אֲמַר לֵיהּ: ו] עֲנַשְׁתִּיתוּ אַעֲשֵׂה? אֲמַר לֵיהּ: בִּזְמַן דְּאִיכָּא רִיתְחָא עָנְשִׁינַן; אִי אָמְרַתְּ בִּשְׁלָמָא חוֹבַת גַּבְרָא הוּא – הַיְינוּ דְּמִחַיַּיב, דְּלָא קָא רָמֵי, אֶלָּא אִי אָמְרַתְּ חוֹבַת טַלִּית הוּא – הָא לָא מִיחַיְּיבָא! אֶלָּא מַאי, חוֹבַת גַּבְרָא הוּא? נְהִי דְּחַיְּיבֵיהּ רַחֲמָנָא כִּי מִיכַּסֵּי טַלִּית דְּבַת חִיּוּבָא, ז] כִּי מִיכַּסֵּי טַלִּית דְּלָאו בַּת חִיּוּבָא הִיא, מִי חַיְּיבֵיהּ רַחֲמָנָא? אֶלָּא הָכִי קָאָמַר לֵיהּ: ח] [ה]טַצְדְּקִי לְמִיפְטַר נַפְשָׁךְ מִצִּיצִית? אָמַר רַב טוֹבִי בַּר ט] קִיסְנָא אָמַר שְׁמוּאֵל: כְּלֵי קוּפְסָא חַיָּיבִין בְּצִיצִית. וּמוֹדֶה שְׁמוּאֵל *בְּזָקֵן [ו]שֶׁעֲשָׂאָהּ לִכְבוֹדוֹ שֶׁפְּטוּרָה, מ"ט? °"אֲשֶׁר תְּכַסֶּה בָּהּ" (דברים כב) אָמַר רַחֲמָנָא, הַאי לָאו לְאִיכַּסּוּיֵי עֲבִידָא. בְּהַהִיא שַׁעְתָּא [ז]וַדַּאי רָמֵינַן לֵיהּ, מִשּׁוּם °"לוֹעֵג לָרָשׁ חֵרֵף י] עוֹשֵׂהוּ" (משלי יז). אָמַר רַחֲבָה אָמַר ר' יְהוּדָה: טַלִּית [ח]שֶׁנִּקְרְעָה, יא] חוּץ לְשָׁלֹשׁ – יִתְפּוֹר, תּוֹךְ שָׁלֹשׁ – לֹא יִתְפּוֹר. תַּנְיָא נַמִי הָכִי: טַלִּית שֶׁנִּקְרְעָה, חוּץ לְשָׁלֹשׁ – יִתְפּוֹר. תּוֹךְ שָׁלֹשׁ – רַבִּי מֵאִיר אוֹמֵר: לֹא יִתְפּוֹר, וַחֲכ"א: יִתְפּוֹר; וְשָׁוִין, שֶׁלֹּא יָבִיא אֲפִילּוּ אַמָּה עַל אַמָּה מִמָּקוֹם אַחֵר וּבָהּ תְּכֵלֶת וְתוֹלֶה בָּהּ; [ט]וְשָׁוִין, שֶׁמֵּבִיא תְּכֵלֶת מִמָּקוֹם אַחֵר וְתוֹלֶה בָּהּ, וּבִלְבַד

*) [עי' תוס' ברכות יז: ד"ה ויאמר]
**) [עי' תוס' לעיל מ. ד"ה סדין כו']

רש"י

וְהַגָּדוֹל יוֹצֵא בָּהּ עֲרַאי. שֶׁאֵינוֹ בּוֹשׁ לָצֵאת בָּהּ יב] לַשּׁוּק. אִילֵימָא וְכֵן לְעִנְיַן אִיסּוּרָא דְּכִלְאַיִם. דְּאִי אֵין קָטָן מִתְכַּסֶּה בָּהּ – אֵין בָּהּ מִשּׁוּם כִּלְאַיִם אִם נֶאֱרַג בָּהּ כִּלְאַיִם. וְהָתְנַן אֵין עֲרַאי בְּכִלְאַיִם. כְּלוֹמַר, אֵין דִּין עֲרַאי בְּכִלְאַיִם, שֶׁאַע"פ שֶׁאֵין הַגָּדוֹל יוֹצֵא בָּהּ עֲרַאי – יֵשׁ בָּהּ מִשּׁוּם כִּלְאַיִם אִם נֶאֱרַג בָּהּ כִּלְאַיִם. וְאָמַר רַב נַחְמָן. מַאי "וְכֵן לְעִנְיַן כִּלְאַיִם" – וְכֵן לְעִנְיַן סָדִין בְּצִיצִית. יג] אַלְמָא, צִיצִית בְּטַלִּית שֶׁאֵין בָּהּ שִׁיעוּר – יֵשׁ בָּהּ מִשּׁוּם כִּלְאַיִם! אֶלָּא מַאי פְּטוּרָה. דְּקָאָמַר לְעֵיל: וַאֲפִילּוּ בְּטַלִּית פְּטוּרָה – כְּגוֹן הִטִּיל לְמוּטֶּלֶת יד], דְּכִי שַׁרְיָא רַחֲמָנָא כִּלְאַיִם בְּצִיצִית – לְגַמְרֵי אִישְׁתְּרוּ טו]. חֲדָא זִימְנָא. לְעֵיל: הִטִּיל לְמוּטֶּלֶת כְּשֵׁרָה. וְכֵיוָן דְּמִתַּכְשְׁרָא בְּהָנָךְ בָּתְרָאֵי, וְכָל שֶׁכֵּן בְּקַמָּאֵי אִי הֲוָה פָּסִיק לְבָתְרָאֵי – פְּשִׁיטָא דְּאֵין בָּהּ מִשּׁוּם כִּלְאַיִם, דְּהָא כּוּלָּהּ צִיצִית מִיקְרוּ! חֲדָא מִכְּלַל חֲבֶרְתָּהּ אִיתְּמַר. מִכְּלָל דְּהִטִּיל לְמוּטֶּלֶת כְּשֵׁרָה אִיתְּמַר הָךְ דְּכִלְאַיִם. טַלִּית כְּפוּלָה. שֶׁהָיְתָה אֲרוּכָּה כִּשְׁתַּיִם וּכְפָלָהּ. וְרַבִּי שִׁמְעוֹן פּוֹטֵר. שֶׁאִם תִּפָּשֵׁט נִמְצֵאת צִיצִיּוֹת בְּאֶמְצָעִיתָהּ. שֶׁאִם (א) תְּפָרָהּ חַיֶּיבֶת. דְּלָא תִּפָּשֵׁט. דְּנַקְטָהּ בְּסִיכֵי. ברוק"ש. ל"א: תְּפִירָה רְחָבָה, בשטי"ר. וְקַשְׁיָא לִי הָא דְּאָמַר בְּסוֹף "הַקּוֹמֵץ" (לעיל לז: ע"ש): הַאי מַאן דְּחַיְּיטֵיהּ לִגְלִימָא כו'. אִיפְּשִׁיט. הַטַּלִּית, הָיוּ טז] צִיצִית בְּאֶמְצָעִיתָהּ. שֶׁהָיְתָה יז] [א] רְחָבָה כִּפְלַיִם בְּקוֹמָתוֹ וְהָיְתָה כְּפוּלָה, וְהַכֶּפֶל מוּטָּל עַל רֹאשׁוֹ, וּשְׁנֵי הָרָאשִׁין שֶׁל טַלִּית לְמַטָּה מֵאֲחוֹרָיו, וּשְׁתֵּי צִיצִיּוֹת הָיוּ [ב] בַּקֶּרֶן הָאֶחָד, וּשְׁנַיִם בִּשְׁנֵי רָאשֵׁי הַכֶּפֶל מָקוֹם שֶׁאָרְכּוֹ כָּלֶה, יח] וּכְשֶׁנִּפְשְׁטָה הָיָה (ב) תָּחוּב כּוּלּוֹ בָּהּ, וְנִמְצְאוּ שְׁתֵּי צִיצִיּוֹת שֶׁל כֶּפֶל בְּאֶמְצַע הַטַּלִּית כְּנֶגֶד רֹאשׁוֹ שֶׁל רַבָּה. לָאו הַיְינוּ כָּנָף. דְּהָא בְּאֶמְצָעִיתָהּ עוֹמְדִין. מִי סָבְרַתְּ חוֹבַת גַּבְרָא הוּא. לְקַיֵּים מִצְוַת צִיצִית בְּאַחַת מֵהֶן, דְּתִיפָּטֵר בְּהָךְ אַחְרִיתֵי? חוֹבַת טַלִּית הוּא. וַאֲפִילּוּ יט] עֶשֶׂר יֵשׁ לְךָ, טְעוּנוֹת צִיצִית כ]. מְסַיֵּיעַ לֵיהּ. דְּחוֹבַת טַלִּית הוּא. [ג] הָרִאשׁוֹנִים כו'. וְאִי חוֹבַת גַּבְרָא הוּא, לָמָּה לָהּ צִיצִית עַד שֶׁיִּתְכַּסֶּה בָּהּ? וּפְלִיגָא דְּמַלְאָכָא כא] [ד]. דְּרַבָּה בַּר רַב הוּנָא, דְּהַמַּלְאָךְ אוֹמֵר דְּחוֹבַת גַּבְרָא הִיא. דְּמִיכַּסֵּי סְדִינָא. דְּלָא הֲוָה לֵיהּ צִיצִית, כִּדְאָמְרִינַן לְעֵיל מִשּׁוּם כְּסוּת לַיְלָה. סַרְבָּלָא. כְּגוֹן אוֹתָן שֶׁלָּנוּ שֶׁהֵן עֲגוּלִין, וְאֵין לָהּ אֶלָּא שְׁנֵי כְּנָפַיִם [לְמַטָּה], דִּפְטוּרָה מִצִּיצִית. [סַרְבָּלָא. מנט"ל בְּלַעַ"ז]. הָא לָא מִיחַיְּיבָא. הֵן טַלִּית דְּסָדִין וְדְסַרְבָּלָא, וּמַאי אִיכְפַּת לֵיהּ? נְהִי דְּחַיְּיבֵיהּ רַחֲמָנָא כב]. כִּי מִיכַּסֵּי טַלִּית בַּת חִיּוּבָא, הָרָאוּי [ה] לְצִיצִית, כג] חַיְּיבֵיהּ רַחֲמָנָא (ג) לְגַבְרָא. לְאַהֲדוּרֵי בָּתַר טַלִּית כד] דְּחִיּוּבָא וּלְאַכְסוּיֵי בָּהּ מִי [חַיְּיבֵיהּ]? אֶלָּא הָכִי קָאָמַר לֵיהּ טַצְדְּקֵי לְמִיפְטַר עַצְמְךָ מִצִּיצִית. תְּבַקֵּשׁ תַּחְבּוּלוֹת לִפְטוֹר עַצְמְךָ מִצִּיצִית. טַצְדְּקֵי = תַּחְבּוּלוֹת, וַחֲבֵירוֹ בְּבָבָא קַמָּא בְּפֶרֶק "הַכּוֹנֵס" (דף נו.): כָּל טַצְדְּקֵי דְּאִית לָהּ לְמֶיעֱבַד עָבְדָה. כְּלֵי קוּפְסָא. טַלִּיתוֹת הָרְאוּיִין לְצִיצִית, אַף עַל פִּי שֶׁמְּקוּפֶּלֶת וּמוּנַּחַת בְּקוּפְסָא – חַיֶּיבֶת בְּצִיצִית, דְּהוֹאִיל וְעוֹמֶדֶת הִיא לְהִתְכַּסּוֹת בָּהּ – "אֲשֶׁר תְּכַסֶּה בָּהּ" קָרֵינָא בֵּיהּ. לִכְבוֹדוֹ. לְתַכְרִיכִין. כה] בְּהַהִיא שַׁעְתָּא. כְּשֶׁלּוֹבְשִׁין אוֹתוֹ לַמֵּת. וַדַּאי רָמֵינַן לֵיהּ. מַטִּילִין בֵּיהּ צִיצִית, דְּאִי לָא רָמֵינָא דָּמֵי כְּלִיעוּג, כְּלוֹמַר: אִיפְּטַר לֵיהּ מִמִּצְוֹת. חוּץ לְשָׁלֹשׁ. לְמַעְלָה מִשָּׁלֹשׁ אֶצְבָּעוֹת מִשְּׂפַת הַכָּנָף. יִתְפּוֹר. וְלָא חָיְישִׁינַן דִּילְמָא פָּיֵישׁ מִידֵי מִן חוּט כו] הַתְּפִירָה, וְיַנִּיחֵם וְיוֹסִיף עָלָיו עַד ד' חוּטִים לְשֵׁם צִיצִית, וְאִיכָּא "תַּעֲשֶׂה וְלֹא מִן הֶעָשׂוּי". דְּהָא חוּץ לְג' לָא חֲזוּ לִתְלוֹת צִיצִית, כִּדְאָמְרִינַן לְקַמָּן. בְּתוֹךְ שָׁלֹשׁ. הָרָאוּי לְהַנִּיחַ שָׁם צִיצִית. לֹא יִתְפּוֹר. דְּהָכָא חָיְישִׁינַן לְהָכִי כִּדְפָרִישְׁנָא. מִמָּקוֹם אַחֵר. מִטַּלִּית אַחֶרֶת, וְיֵשׁ בָּהּ תְּכֵלֶת וְתוֹלֶה בָּהּ. מִשּׁוּם דְּ"עַל כַּנְפֵי בִגְדֵיהֶם" בָּעֵינַן, וְכָנָף זֶה לֹא הָיָה מִבֶּגֶד זֶה בִּשְׁעַת עֲשִׂיָּיה. וְשָׁוִין שֶׁמֵּבִיא תְּכֵלֶת. מַתִּיר צִיצִית מִטַּלִּית אַחֶרֶת וְתוֹלֶה בָּהּ. דְּהָכָא לֵיכָּא "וְלֹא מִן הֶעָשׂוּי", דְּהָא צָרִיךְ לַחֲזוֹר וּלְכוֹרְכָהּ וּלְתַקְּנָהּ כָּאן כְּבַתְּחִילָּה. וּבִלְבַד

תוספות

דאמרינן לקמן (דף מד.): טלית שאולה כל ל' יום פטורה מן הציצית, מכאן ואילך חייבת ואפי' של כלאים, ואע"ג דפטור מדאורייתא. דאין לחלק, כיון *דלגבי גברא דהוי דידיה ליכא כלאים, וכן לנשים. והא דאמרינן (לקמן מג.) גבי הכהנים: נהי דבעידן עבודה אישתראי, שלא בעידן עבודה לא – לא דמי כלל, דהא כתיב (דברים כב): "לא תלבש שעטנז גדילים תעשה לך", לומר שבמקום גדילים תלבש שעטנז, משמע דכל לבישה שרא רחמנא. כו] ועוד, דבטלית שעשוי להנאתו חייב הכתוב כלאים, אבל בגדי כהונה לא לביש אלא בעידן עבודה. ועוד אומר ר"ת: דבגדי כהונה נמי שלא בעידן עבודה שרו. והכי קאמר: נהי דבעידן עבודה אישתראי – כלומר, המיוחדים לעבודה, שלא בעידן עבודה – כלומר, אותם שאינם מיוחדים לעבודה, לא אישתראי. וכן מוכח בתוספתא דכלאים, דתניא: בגדי כהונה ובגדי כהן גדול אין בהם משום כלאים. בגדי כ"ג שילא במדינה – חייב, במקדש בין לשרת בין שלא לשרת – פטור. וצ"ע אי לילה דומה למדינה דחייב. וי"ל: דחייב מדרבנן. וההוא עובדא דשמעון הצדיק פרק "בא לו" (יומא דף סט.) ד"עת לעשות לה' הפרו תורתך" – בדרבנן נמי שייך הפרה. מיהו לא משמע הכי, אלא נראה טפי דחייב מדאורייתא, ואין לדמות *[ו] מקומות למדינה, דבמדינה ליכא שום היתר. ותדע, דהתם לא מפליג בין שעה הראויה לשרת לשעה שאינה ראויה לשרת. והא דאמרינן פרק "בא לו" (גם זה שם) גבי בגדי כהונה שמקפלין אותן תחת ראשיהן, דלאו דווקא כח] [תחת ראשיהן, אלא [ז] שלא כנגד ראשיהן] משום כלאים – היינו בהנאה, דלא דמי ללבישה דשרא רחמנא. אבל גבי ציצית אין לחלק בין הנאה ללבישה. ובספרי תניא: כסות המיוחד ליום ולילה חייב בציצית, רבי יהודה בן בבא אומר: ביחוד בטלו חכמים את כסות של אשה מן הציצית, ולא חייבו בטלית אלא מפני שבעלה מתכסה בו. לכך נראה דכלאים בציצית שרי, בין ביום בין בלילה בין לאשה. כט].

חדא מכלל דחבירתה איתמר. פירש בקונט': בתרייתא מכלל דקמייתא. ואיפכא נראה, דבתרייתא משמיה דשמואל קאמר לה.

ענשיתו [אעשה. כי האי] [שאין אדם חייב] לקנות טלית המחוייב אם אין לו. *)אבל עשה גמור – אפילו בית דין שלמטה היו מכין אותו עד שתצא נפשו.

הכי קאמר ליה טצדקי למפטר נפשך מציצית. ומ"מ, אי לאו חובת גברא לא שייך למיענש עליה, כיון דלית ליה. ובקונטרס גרס "אלא", ומשמע דלא מוכח מידי.

רמינן ליה. פירשתי בפרק בתרא דנדה (דף סא:)**).

ובלבד

*) דרב קטינא סבר חובת טלית הוא עיין רש"א
**) [וע"ע תוס' ברכות יח. ד"ה למחר וכו' ומ"ש שם על צידו]

עין משפט נר מצוה

כד א מיי' פ"ג מהלכות ציצית הלכה א וע"ש בכ"מ טוש"ע א"ח סימן טז בהג"ה:
כה ב מיי' פ"י מהלכות כלאים הלכה יח טוש"ע י"ד סימן שא סעיף ז:
כו ג מיי' פ"א מהלכות ציצית הלכה יז טוש"ע א"ח סימן י סעיף ו:
כז ד מיי' שם טוש"ע שם:
כח ה מיי' פ"ג מהלכות ציצית הלכה יא סמג עשין כ:
כט ו מיי' שם הלכה י ועיין בכ"מ טוש"ע א"ח סימן יט סעיף ב:
ל ז טוש"ע י"ד סימן שנא סעיף ב וע"ש בהג"ה:
לא ח מיי' פ"א מהלכות ציצית הלכה יח טוש"ע א"ח סימן טו סעיף ז:
[ט מיי' שם]:

רבינו גרשום

(וכן לענין איסורין דכלא' דאי אין הקטן כדי להתכסות) וכן לענין איסורין דכלאים דכי אין הקטן מתכסה בה ראשו ורובו אף על פי שהגדול יצא בה עראי אין בה משום כלאים: והתנן אין עראי פוטר מאיסור כלאים. אלא חייב על עראי כעל קבע אפי' בטלית קטנה: וכן לענין סדין בציצית אם אין הקטן מתכסה בה ראשו ורובו חייבת משום כלאים והיכי אומר אפי' בטלית פטורה אין בה משום כלאים: אלא מאי אפי' בטלית פטורה דקאמר שאם הטיל ציצית לסדין שכבר מוטלת לה ציצית בתחלה: והאמר ר' זירא חדא זימנא הטיל למוטלת כשרה. ההיא מכלל דהא איתמר: טלית כפולה שהיתה גדולה כשתים וכפלה חייבת בציצית ור' שמעון פוטר דאי רמי ליה כשהיא כפולה זימנין דמפשטא ולא קאי חוטא להדי כנף: בסוכי אסולי' בלע"ז. (חייבת) חובת טלית היא ואף על גב דלא מיכסית בה אסור להניחה בלא ציצית: כיון שבצעו בה ג' לאלתר כשנארגה כולה קודם שהסירוה מן העץ היו מטילין לה ציצית קודם שתהא ראויה להתכסות אלמא דסברי דחובת טלית היא. הא דקאמר דחובת טלית היא היינו פליגא דמלאכא. מלאך ממש. סרבלא מקטורן שאין לו ד' כנפים: סדינא. לפי שאסרו תכלת בסדין לא הוה רמי: ענשיתו אעשה אם אין אדם מקיים מצות עשה כגון ציצית: א"ל בזמן ריתחא ענשינן אפי' אעשה: הא לא מיחייבא. סדינא וסרבלא בציצית: ודאי לאיכסויי טלית דבת חיובא לא חייביה רחמנא: אלא הכי קאמר ליה טצדקי כלומר הערמה קא עבדת לפטור נפשך דלא בעית למיכסי טלית דבת חיובא: כלי קופסא בגדים שמיוחדין לטליות ומונחין בקופסא בארגז: בזקן שעשאה לכבודו שעשאה למיתתו שיעטפוהו בה כשימות. בההיא שעתא ודאי לכי מיית ומיעטף בה רמינן לה ציצית משום לועג לרש כלומר שלא יהא חלישות הדעת למת שמחשבין אותו פטור מן המצות. חוץ לג' אצבעות סמוך לכנף יתפור: נקרעה תוך ג' מקום שראוי להניח בו ציצית לא יתפור שמא ישתייר מחוט של תפירה והיה ד' חוטין ומצטרף עמו ויעשה ציצית והוי תעשה ולא מן העשוי אלא יביא טלית אחרת. ושוין שלא יביא כנף אחר ממקום אחר אפי' משל אמה על אמה ובו תכלת ציצית דהיינו תעשה ולא מן העשוי משום הכי אמר אפי' אמה על אמה אע"ג דהתפר יבוא חוץ לג': ושוין שמביא תכלת ציצית. ממקום אחר מטלית אחרת

שיטה מקובצת

א] והא אמרה ר' זירא כו'. ליכא למימר דפריך לשמואל מהא דהא לא שמעינן מידי מהא דלעיל דהו"א הטיל למוטלת כשרה כשפסק הראשון אבל כל זמן שלא פסק (אפילו) [אפשר] ציצית שלא במקום מצוה הוי אלא לשתוק מההיא דלעיל ואנא ידענא כיון דאינו חייב משום כלאים [הרי] דלא הוי ציצית שלא במקום מצוה משום דאי בעי בהאי מתכשר ואי בעי בהאי מתכשר א"כ פשיטא דהטיל למוטלת וחתך לראשון כשרה כך נראה להר"ם. תו"ח: ב] חדא מכלל חברתה כו'. פ"ה (ההיא) [הך דהכא] אתיא מכלל ההיא דלעיל ולא נהירא דבההיא ליכא אמר שמואל וא"כ איך בא מכלל איידך אם שמענו לו כשרה מנא לך הא דהכא [אלא נראה איפכא דההיא דלעיל מהא דהכא] דכיון דשמע למה דקאמר ליה משמיה דשמואל רביה א"כ ס"ל כך מסתמא וגם קשה לפ"ה מה שפי' הר"ם דודאי מההיא דלעיל לא שמענו הך דהכא. תו"ח: ג] לבי רבה: ד] מיכסי בטלית: ה] תיבות של תכלת נמחק: ו] ענשיתו אעשה אע"ג דאמרינן [כתובות (דף פו ע"א) עשה סוכה ואינו עושה כו' מכין אותו] עד שתצא נפשו [התם במצוה] הקבועה [אבל] ציצית אין זמנו [קבוע לא] ענשי אעשה כי האי: ז] לאכסויי מי חייביה ותיבות כי מיכסי טלית דלאו בת חיובא היא נמחק: ח] טצדקי למפטר כו'. פ"ה והשתא שפיר ענשינן [אי] חובת גברא אי חובת טלית. ומיהו משמע דבחובת גברא דוקא איכא עונש דלא הוה עביד וכולהו אחרים עבדי ליה דאי חובת טלית למה היה גוער בו ממה שהיה לבוש סדין והלא היה יכול לחייב נפשיה במצות ציצית בטלית אחד שהיה מונח בקופסא ואין זה טצדקי דשמא היה לו טלית מצוייצת בבית וכ"ת המלאך היה יודע שלא היה לו טלית אחר מ"מ היה לו לומר קנה לך טלית החייבת ולבוש מה שתרצה ולא היה לו לגעור בו על הלבשה. תו"ח: טצדקי כו' משמע דקאי בין אחובת גברא בין אחובת טלית וי"מ דלא קאי אלא אחובת גברא אבל אחובת טלית לא קאי (דאי אפשר שלא) [דאפשר שיש] לו כלי בקופסא שהיו בהן ציצית ולעולם פליגי אדמלאכא ובהלכות גדולות פסק הלכה דחובת גברא מדרבנן להתעטף בציצית כדאיתא בפרק במה מדליקין דמוכח דההדלקה עושה מצוה מדבריך להדליק נר של חנוכה: ט] בר ביסנא: י] עושהו. עי' ברכות (דף יח ע"א) בתוס' ונדה (דף סא) בתוס': יא] חוץ לשלש יתפור פ"ה דלא חיישינן שמא ישלים חוט התפירה עם הציצית דאין זה מקום ציצית תוך ג' לא יתפור שמא ישלים כו' ולא נהירא דאם כן תקשי ברייתא לרב הונא דקאמר ד' בתוך ד' ועוד דאמרי' בסמוך שלא יביא אמה על אמה ממקום אחר ותולה ומה ענין ושוין לזה של מעלה ועוד הא דאמר ר' זירא שמא יקרע סדינו בתוך שלש ויתפרנו נימא דלא כר"מ אמרה למילתא דאי ר' מאיר הא אמר לא יתפור ופי' הר"י טלית שנקרע פי' הכנף נקרע ונפל מן הטלית מכל וכל חוץ לג' יתפור שלא נתבטל הכנף מתורתו הואיל ונשאר ג' על ג' דהוא שיעור חשוב וכשהוא תופרו חוזר לקדמותו אבל תוך ג' לא יתפור שנתבטל מתורת כנף והרי הוא כאלו נפל הציצית לבד ותפרם דבטלים שאינה תחובה בכנף כלל. וחכמים אומרים יתפור דלא נתבטל הכנף ושוין שלא יביא אמה על אמה ממקום אחר [ס"א פי' אם נקרע חצי טליתו ולא נשאר בה רק שתי ציצית לא יביא חצי טלית ממקום אחר שיש בה ב' ציציות ויתפרנו עם זה דהוי ליה תעשה ולא מן העשוי והשתא לא דמי לההיא דרבי זירא דמיירי שאין בו ציצית וחיישינן שמא יקרע כו' וישאר חוט התפירה ויסמוך עליו לציצית והכא מיירי שיש בה ציצית ולא דמי להא דרב הונא דלקמן דאיירי שיש בה ציצית והשתא ניחא נמי ושוין וכו' דאפי' למ"ד (חוץ לשלש לא) [תוך שלש] יתפור לפי שלא נתבטל להכנף הכא מודה] דלאו מן אותו טלית הוא ולא פוטר ליה דהוי מן העשוי לצורך טלית [זה] ואין פוטר כנף זה והשתא ניחא דאמרינן לעיל גזירה שמא יקרע סדינו תוך ג' כו' אלמא גזרינן שמא יקרע והשתא אמרינן דאפי' לכתחלה תופר ולא חיישינן שמא ישלים אלא ודאי לעיל מיירי שמא יקרע קודם עשיית ציצית והכא לאחר שנעשו הציצית ואז אין לו לחוש ואמנם יש ליישבו אפי' לפי הקונטרס (דלעיל) [דהכא] ודאי מיירי בסדין הרגיל לקרוע אבל שאר בגדים אף כי נקרע מילתא דלא שכיחא היא ולא גזרו ביה רבנן. תו"ח: יב] לצאת בה עראי לשוק: יג] בציצית דאם הגדול יוצא בסדין עראי מותר להטיל בה ציצית ואם אין הקטן מתכסה בה אסור להטיל בה ציצית: יד] למוטלת. ס"א ולהכי קרי ליה פטור משום דפטור מציצית בהני קמאי וכי שרא רחמנא כלאים בציצית אשתרי למצוה דציציות כשרים הוו הנך אחרונות: טו] אישתרי: טז] היו הציצית: יז] שהיתה ארכו: יח] כלה וכשנתפשטה: יט] ואפי' יש לך עשר: כ] ציצית הס"ד ואח"כ מה"ד זיל רמי לה הסר אותן ציצית שהיה בכפול והטיל בה אחרים כמצותן: מסייע לי' כו' הוא הס"ד ואח"כ מה"ד חסידים הראשונים: כא] דמלאכא הך דרבה: כב] רחמנא לגברא: כג] לציצית למירמי ביה [חייביה רחמנא] תיבת לגברא נמחק: כד] טלית בת חיובא אות ד' נמחק: כה] בההיא שעתא דמכסינן ליה ביה לאחר מיתה ודאי רמינן ליה חוטין משום לועג לרש כו': כו] התפירה ושיניחם ויוסיף עליו חוטים לשם: כז] רחמנא עוד י"מ נהי דאשתרי בעידן עבודה כלומר בבית המקדש מקום הראוי לעבודה שלא במקום עבודה מי שרייה רחמנא כמו בגבולין אבל במקדש לעולם מותרין וכמו כן טלית כיון שחייב בכל מקום מותר בלילה כמו ביום כו'. תו"ח: כח] דלאו דוקא תחת ראשיהן משום: כט] אר"ת הא דאמר תכלת אין בה משום

הגהות צ"ק [א] ארוכה כפלים: [ב] בקרנות האחד: [ג] חסידים הראשונים: [ד] אדרבה: [ה] לציצית הס"ד אח"כ ד"ה מי חייביה כו' בה הס"ד והשאר יש למחוק: [ו] מקדש למדינה: [ז] דוקא תחת ראשיהן אלא כנגד ראשיהן משום:

הגהות הב"ח (א) רש"י ד"ה שאם כפלה ותפרה שחייבת דלא תפשט: (ב) ד"ה איפשיט וכו' וכשנפשטה היה תחוב כולו: (ג) ד"ה נהי וכו' רחמנא אבל מי חייביה רחמנא לגברא לאהדורי:

גליון הש"ס גמ' טלדקי. עיין ערכין דף ב ע"ב תוס' ד"ה הכל חייבין: **תוס'** ד"ה ענשיתו וכו' שאין אדם חייב. עיין פסחים קיג ע"ב תוס' ד"ה ואין לו:

עין משפט נר מצוה

יח א מיי' פ"ד מהלכות קדוש החודש הלכ' יז:
יט ב מיי' פ"ג מהלכות ציצית הלכה ג:
כ ג מיי' שם הלכה ד טוש"ע א"ח סימן י סעיף ה:
כא ד מיי' שם פ"א הלכה טוש"ע שם סעיף ב:
כב ה מיי' שם הלכה טו טוש"ע שם סעיף ו:
כג ו מיי' שם פ"ג הלכה טוש"ע א"ח סימן טז סעיף א:

גמרא

מסורת הש"ס

חָמֵץ בְּפֶסַח וְיוה"כ דְּכָרֵת – סָמְכִינַן [א]אַדִּיסְקֵי, הָכָא דַּעֲשֵׂה בְּעָלְמָא לֹא כָּל שֶׁכֵּן? אֶלָּא אָמַר רָבָא: הָא מִילְּתָא אֲמַרִי, וְאִיתְּמַר בְּמַעֲרָבָא מִשּׁוּם דְּרַבִּי זֵירָא כְּוָותִי: שֶׁמָּא יִקָּרַע סְדִינוֹ בְּתוֹךְ ג' וְיִתְפְּרֶנּוּ, וְהַתּוֹרָה אָמְרָה: "תַּעֲשֶׂה" – וְלֹא מִן הֶעָשׂוּי. שְׁרָא רַבִּי זֵירָא לִסְדִינֵיהּ. רַב זֵירָא אָמַר: גְּזֵירָה א] נַמִּי מִשּׁוּם [ב]כְּסוּת לַיְלָה. וְאָמַר רָבָא: הָא *מִילְּתָא אֲמַרִי, וְאִיתְּמַר בְּמַעֲרָבָא (ברכות מה:) מִשְּׁמֵיהּ דְּר' זֵירָא כְּוָותִי: [ג]הִיא שֶׁל בֶּגֶד וּכְנָפֶיהָ שֶׁל עוֹר – חַיֶּיבֶת, הִיא שֶׁל עוֹר וּכְנָפֶיהָ שֶׁל בֶּגֶד – פְּטוּרָה, מַאי טַעְמָא? עִיקַּר בֶּגֶד בָּעֵינַן. ב] רַב אַחַאי אָזֵיל בָּתַר כָּנָף. אָמַר רָבָא אָמַר רַב סְחוֹרָה אָמַר רַב הוּנָא: [ד]הִטִּיל לְבַעֲלַת שָׁלֹשׁ וְהִשְׁלִימָהּ לְאַרְבַּע – פְּסוּלָה, [מִשּׁוּם] "תַּעֲשֶׂה" – וְלֹא מִן הֶעָשׂוּי. ג] מֵיתִיבֵי: חֲסִידִים *הָרִאשׁוֹנִים, (לקמן מא.) כֵּיוָן שֶׁאָרְגוּ בָּהּ ג' הָיוּ מַטִּילִין לָהּ תְּכֵלֶת! אֵימָא: כֵּיוָן ד] שֶׁפָּצְעוּ בָּהּ ג' הָיוּ מַטִּילִין לָהּ תְּכֵלֶת. וּמִי אָמְרִינַן תַּעֲשֶׂה וְלֹא מִן הֶעָשׂוּי? (אִינִי) ה] וְהָאָמַר ר' זֵירָא: הִטִּיל לִמְוּטֶּלֶת – כְּשֵׁרָה! אָמַר רָבָא: ו] הַשְׁתָּא בְּבַל תּוֹסִיף קָאֵי, מַעֲשֶׂה לָא הָוֵי. מַתְקִיף לָהּ רַב פַּפָּא: ז] מִמַּאי דְּגַבְרָא לְאוֹסוֹפֵי קָא מִיכַּוֵּין? דִּלְמָא לְבַטּוֹלֵי [ה]קָא מִיכַּוֵּין, וּבַל תּוֹסִיף לֵיכָּא, מַעֲשֶׂה אִיכָּא! אָמַר ר' זֵירָא אָמַר רַב מַתָּנָא אָמַר שְׁמוּאֵל: תְּכֵלֶת אֵין בָּהּ מִשּׁוּם כִּלְאַיִם, וַאֲפִי' בְּטַלִּית פְּטוּרָה. מַאי טַלִּית פְּטוּרָה? אִילֵימָא דְּלֵית בָּהּ שִׁיעוּרָא, וְהָתַנְיָא: [ו]טַלִּית שֶׁהַקָּטָן מִתְכַּסֶּה בּוֹ רֹאשׁוֹ וְרוּבּוֹ,

וְהַגָּדוֹל

רש"י

חָמֵץ בְּפֶסַח כו'. כְּשֶׁהָיוּ מְעַבְּרִים שָׁנָה הָיוּ שׁוֹלְחִין אִגְּרוֹת לַגּוֹלָה לַעֲשׂוֹת ב' אֲדָרִים, כִּדְאָמְרִינַן בְּפ' קַמָּא דְּסַנְהֶדְרִין (דף יא.): "מוֹדָעִין אֲנַחְנָא לְכוֹן" כו'. הָא מִילְּתָא אֲמַרִי. אֲנָא הָכָא, ח] וְאָמְרִי בְּמַעֲרָבָא מִשּׁוּם רַבִּי זֵירָא כְּוָותִי, דְּמִשּׁוּם הָכִי אָסְרוּ צִיצִית בִּסְדִין. גְּזֵירָה ט] מִשּׁוּם שֶׁמָּא יִקָּרַע סָדִין. קוֹדֶם לָכֵן בְּתוֹךְ ג' אֶצְבָּעוֹת י] לִשְׂפַת הַכָּנָף, דְּהַיְינוּ מְקוֹם הַצִּיצִית. וְיִתְפְּרֶנּוּ. בְּחוּטֵי פִּשְׁתָּן, וְיַנִּיחַ סוֹף הַחוּטִין הַתְּלוּיִין שָׁם, וְאַחַר כָּךְ יִתֵּן בָּהּ שְׁנֵי חוּטֵי תְכֵלֶת, וִיצָרֵף אוֹתָן שְׁנַיִם שֶׁל לָבָן עִמָּהֶם. וְהַתּוֹרָה אָמְרָה תַּעֲשֶׂה וְלֹא מִן הֶעָשׂוּי. וְנִמְצֵאת צִיצִית פְּסוּלָה, וְהָווּ כִּלְאַיִם שֶׁלֹּא בִּמְקוֹם מִצְוָה. תַּעֲשֶׂה וְלֹא מִן הֶעָשׂוּי. דְּפָסוּל. הַיְינוּ שֶׁעוֹשֶׂה מִתְּחִילָּה שֶׁלֹּא לְשֵׁם צִיצִית וְלֹא נַעֲשָׂה כְּמִצְוָתוֹ, וְאַחַר כָּךְ תִּקְּנוֹ – קָרֵינַן בֵּיהּ יב] "וְלֹא מִן הֶעָשׂוּי", וְנִמְצָא צִיצִית פְּסוּלָה. שְׁרָא ר' זֵירָא לִסְדִינֵיהּ. הִתִּיר צִיצִיּוֹתָיו מִסְּדִינוֹ שֶׁהָיָה שֶׁל פִּשְׁתָּן, וּנְטָלָן, מִשּׁוּם שֶׁמָּא יִקָּרַע. וְהַיְינוּ דְּאָמַר רָבָא: אִיתְּמַר בְּמַעֲרָבָא מִשְּׁמֵיהּ דְּרַבִּי זֵירָא כְּוָותִי. ה"ג: ר' זֵירָא אָמַר גְּזֵירָה מִשּׁוּם כְּסוּת לַיְלָה. שֶׁמָּא יִתְכַּסֶּה בּוֹ בַּלַּיְלָה דְּפָטוּר מִצִּיצִית, שֶׁנֶּאֱמַר: "וּרְאִיתֶם אוֹתוֹ וּזְכַרְתֶּם" – פְּרָט לִכְסוּת לַיְלָה, וְנִמְצָא נֶהֱנֶה מִכִּלְאַיִם שֶׁלֹּא בִּשְׁעַת מִצְוָה. וּכְנָפֶיהָ שֶׁל עוֹר. שֶׁנֶּחְתְּכוּ קַרְנֶיהָ וְתָלָה בָּהֶן עוֹר. אָזֵיל בָּתַר כָּנָף. וְעָבֵיד אִיפְּכָא. הִטִּיל. ג' צִיצִית לְבַעֲלַת ג' כְּנָפַיִם, וְאַחַר כָּךְ תָּלָה בָּהֶן קֶרֶן ד' וְעָשָׂה בּוֹ צִיצִית – פְּסוּלָה, דְּג' רִאשׁוֹנוֹת עֲשׂוּיִין מִתְּחִילָּה שֶׁלֹּא כְּמִצְוָתָהּ, וְכִי הָדַר מְתַקְּנָהּ אִיכָּא "תַּעֲשֶׂה וְלֹא מִן הֶעָשׂוּי". חֲסִידִים = זְרִיזִין בְּמִצְוֹת. כֵּיוָן שֶׁאָרְגוּ. בְּטַלִּית ג' אֶצְבָּעוֹת, יג] דְּמִיקְרֵי בֶּגֶד, כִּדְאָמְרִינַן לְגַבֵּי טוּמְאָה. הָיוּ מַטִּילִין בָּהּ תְּכֵלֶת. בִּשְׁנֵי קַרְנֶיהָ, וּלְכִי גָּמְרֵי לָהּ הָיוּ מַטִּילִין לִשְׁנַיִם אֲחֵרִים, וְלֹא אָמְרִינַן "תַּעֲשֶׂה וְלֹא מִן הֶעָשׂוּי", יד] וְאַע"ג דְּלָא הֲוָה מְחַיְּיבִין בְּצִיצִית עַד שֶׁתְּהֵא כְּדֵי שֶׁיִּתְכַּסֶּה בָּהּ קָטָן רֹאשׁוֹ וְרוּבּוֹ כִּדְלְקַמָּן (א) [א]. שֶׁכָּל צִיצִית שֶׁלֹּא נַעֲשֵׂית מִתְּחִילָּתָהּ לְשֵׁם צִיצִית, אַע"פ כְּשֶׁנַּעֲשֵׂית שֶׁלֹּא לְצוֹרֶךְ – אִיכָּא "מִן הֶעָשׂוּי", דְּהָא הָכָא שֶׁלֹּא לְצוֹרֶךְ נַעֲשֵׂית, דְּלֹא הָיוּ לָהּ אֶלָּא ב' קְרָנוֹת, דְּאִלּוּ קַרְנוֹתֶיהָ הָאֲחֵרִים אֵינָן רְאוּיִין לְצִיצִית, שֶׁהֲרֵי סוֹפוֹ לְהוֹסִיף עָלֶיהָ הַרְבֵּה, וְהָוְיָא לָהּ צִיצִית לְמַעְלָה מִג', וְתַנְיָא תּוֹךְ שְׁלֹשָׁה בָּעֵינַן. כֵּיוָן טו] שֶׁפָּצְעוּ בָּהּ ג'. כֵּיוָן שֶׁהִגִּיעוּ לְג' אֶצְבָּעוֹת הָאַחֲרוֹנִים – מַטִּילִין לָהּ תְּכֵלֶת מִיָּד, וְלֹא מַשְׁהוּ לָהּ מִידֵי. דְּהַשְׁתָּא לֵיכָּא לְמֵימַר "תַּעֲשֶׂה וְלֹא מִן הֶעָשׂוּי", דְּהָא מִכֵּיוָן שֶׁהִגִּיעוּ לְתוֹךְ ג' הָאַחֲרוֹנִים הָווּ לְהוּ אוֹתָן שְׁתֵּי קְרָנוֹת נַמִּי רְאוּיִין לְצִיצִית, שֶׁכְּשֶׁתִּגָּמֵר נִמְצֵאת צִיצִית בְּתוֹךְ ג'. הִטִּיל לִמְוּטֶּלֶת. שֶׁהָיָה בָּהּ ד' צִיצִית וְהִטִּיל לָהּ ד' אֲחֵרִים – טז] כְּשֵׁרָה בְּהָנֵי בַּתְרָאֵי, וְאַע"ג דַּהֲדַר פַּסְקִינְהוּ לְקַמָּאֵי. וְהָא הָכָא דְּשֶׁלֹּא לְצוֹרֶךְ עֲבַדִינְהוּ בִּשְׁעַת עֲשִׂיָּיה, וּמַכְשְׁרָא בְּהוּ! אָמַר רָבָא. לְעוֹלָם שֶׁלֹּא לְצוֹרֶךְ – "מִן הֶעָשׂוּי" קָרֵינַן בֵּיהּ. וְהָכָא לְהָכִי מַכְשְׁרָא בְּבַתְרָאֵי – דְּקָאֵי בְּבַל תּוֹסִיף כִּי עֲבַדִינְהוּ, וְלָא הָווּ מַעֲשֶׂה, דְּכֵיוָן דְּעוֹבֵר עַל דִּבְרֵי תוֹרָה לָא מִיקְרֵי מַעֲשֶׂה, הִלְכָּךְ כִּי פָּסֵיק לְקַמָּאֵי הִיא הָוְיָא עֲשִׂיָּיתָן דְּבַתְרָאֵי (עֲשִׂיָּיה) אֲבָל שֶׁלֹּא לְצוֹרֶךְ דְּבַעֲלַת ג', שֶׁאֵינוֹ עוֹבֵר עֲלֵיהֶן – הָוֵי מַעֲשֶׂה לְאַקְרוּיֵי צִיצִית הָעֲשׂוּיָה בְּפָסוּל, וְאִיכָּא כְּשֶׁגּוֹמְרָהּ "תַּעֲשֶׂה וְלֹא מִן הֶעָשׂוּי" יז]. מַעֲשֶׂה אִיכָּא. וְהָדַר קוּשְׁיָא לְדוּכְתָּהּ. תְּכֵלֶת אֵין [בָּהּ] מִשּׁוּם כִּלְאַיִם. קס"ד דְּהָכִי קָאָמַר: צִיצִית יח] אֵין בָּהֶם מִשּׁוּם כִּלְאַיִם, וַאֲפִילּוּ כו'.

וְהַגָּדוֹל

תוספות

שמא יקרע סדינו בתוך ג'. פי' בקונטרס: בתוך שלש לכנף, וכשיתפרנו בחוטי פשתן יניח סוף החוטין תלויין שם לציצית, והוה ליה "תעשה ולא מן העשוי". ואפי' לרבנן דאמרי (לעיל דף לח.) דתכלת אינה מעכבת את הלבן – היינו כשיש ד' חוטין, אבל הכא דליכא אלא ב' – לא. מיהו הוה ליה למינקט משום דבעינן טוויה או תלייה לשמה, אבל "תעשה ולא מן העשוי" ליכא, לפי מה שאפרש לקמן גבי עשאה מן הקוצים ומן הגרדין וכו'. והא דתניא לקמן (דף מא.): טלית שנקרעה חוץ לשלש יתפור, תוך ג' רבי מאיר אומר: לא יתפור, וחכ"א: יתפור – אפי' [ב] לרבנן גזרינן שמא יתפור ויהא בו איסור כלאים. ומיהו קשה מההוא דרב הונא דאמר לקמן (דף מא:): רחוק מן הכנף ד' הוי מצות ציצית. אבל מברייתא דחסידי ליכא לאקשויי, דהא מפרשינן בסמוך: כיון שפצעו שלש. לכך צריך לפרש: תוך שלש – היינו שנקרע הכנף שהציצית תלוי בה, ולא נשתייר ג', והוי כאילו נפסק לגמרי, אבל אם נשתייר בו ג' – לדברי הכל חיבור מעליא הוי. והשתא שמעתין כר' מאיר אתיא. והא דלא גזרינן שמא יקרע כולה – דהא לא טעו. והא דמשמע פ' "דם חטאת" (זבחים דף צד:) גבי בגד שילא חוץ לקלעים, דאפילו נשתייר בו ג' אלא שאין בו כדי מעפורת לא חשיב חיבור, ובפרק "העור והרוטב" (חולין דף קכג.) מוכח דכדי מעפורת הוי טפי מג' – שאני התם, דכל הבגד נקרע, אבל הכא שאינו נקרע רק חתיכה – לא הוי יט] בפסול.

כ] **ר'** זירא אמר. משמע דרב זירא לאו היינו רבי זירא, ולא כפירוש הקונטרס בכתובות (דף מג:).

משום כסות לילה. ר"ת פי' דכן עיקר, כדאיתא פ' "במה מדליקין" (שבת דף כה:): ואינהו סבור משום כסות לילה. מתוך כך יש להוכיח מכאן דהלכה כר' שמעון, *דלילה לאו זמן ציצית היא. ועוד אמרינן פ' "במה מדליקין" (דף כז.): "אשר תכסה בה" למה לי – לאתויי כסות סומא. והיינו כר"ש, דלרבנן דרבי שמעון מוקמי ליה לרבות בעלת חמש, אלמא סתם התלמוד כר"ש אתא. ועוד בפ' ב' דברכות (דף יד:) אמרינן שלא היו אומרים במערבא פרשת ציצית בלילה, [ורב יוסף אמר עלה] כמה מעליא האי שמעתא. וסתם ברייתא נמי פ"ק דזבחים (דף יח:) כר' שמעון מוקי. ורב יהודה דרמי תכלתא לפרזומא דאינשי ביתיה לקמן (דף מג.) ובפ"ק דסוכה (דף יא.) – ר"י לבד היה עושה כן. ובפ"ק דברכות (דף יג.) אמר ר' יהושע בן קרחה: למה נסמכה פרשה וכו' לומר שזו נוהגת בין ביום בין בלילה, וזו אינה נוהגת אלא ביום. ואור"ת: אע"ג דכסות יום חייב אפי' בלילה, וכסות לילה פטור אפי' ביום, מכל מקום מיקרי שפיר זמן גרמא, שהיום גורם לחייב המלבוש. מיהו, בירושלמי דקדושין ובתוספתא גרסינן: איזו היא מצות עשה שלא הזמן גרמא – כגון אבידה ושילוח הקן ומעקה וציצית, ורבי שמעון פוטר את הנשים מן הציצית. אמר להם רבי שמעון: אי אתם מודים לי שהיא מצות עשה שהזמן גרמא, שהרי כסות לילה פטור! אמר ר' אילא: טעמא דרבנן, שאם היתה טלית המיוחדת ליום וללילה – חייבת. ובספרי נמי תניא: "על כנפי בגדיהם" – שומע אני אף בעלת ג' וכו', שומע אני אף כסות לילה במשמע? ת"ל: "וראיתם אותו" – ביום ולא בלילה, ואם היתה טלית מיוחדת ליום ולילה חייבת בציצית. וצ"ע.

והאמר ר' זירא הטיל למוטלת כשירה. תימה: היכי ס"ד דרבי זירא לית ליה "תעשה ולא מן העשוי"? הא כא] ר' זירא גופיה אית ליה לעיל! וי"ל, דס"ד: כיון דתחילת הנחתן לשם מצוה – לא שייך ביה "תעשה ולא מן העשוי", אבל לעיל כי חתך – נתבטלה הנחתו.

בבל תוסיף קאי מעשה לא הוי. דכיון דעביד איסורא לא חשיב עשייה, ובשעת קצילת הראשונים זו היא עשייתן. ולא דמי להאיא דפ' קמא דסוכה (דף יא.) דלא אמרינן: קצילתן זו היא עשייתן. וצ"ע.

ממאי דגברא לאוסופי קמיכוין. [ג] אפילו למאן דאמר בפ' בתרא דעירובין (דף ק.) דלעבור משום בל תוסיף לא בעי כוונה, ומשמע נמי בההוא פירקא דלרבי יהושע לא בעי כוונה, מ"מ הכא מודה דליכא בל תוסיף, כיון דלבטולי קמיכוין.

תכלת אין בה משום כלאים ואפילו בטלית פטורה. מדקאמר "ואפילו" ולא קאמר "אפי'" בלא וי"ו, משמע דלאשמועינן דתכלת אין בה משום כלאים. וכי האי גוונא דייק פ' "טרף בקלפי" (יומא מו.) אומר היה ר"מ: אברי עולת חול שניתותרו – עושה להן מערכה וסודרן ואפי' בשבת, ומוכחא [ד] סוגיא דהתם דתרתי מילי אשמעינן. כב] ואור"ת: דהכא נמי אשמעינן דאין בה משום כלאים, אף על גב דלאו זמן ציצית היא, דלגמרי התיר הכתוב כלאים של ציצית. והא דגזרינן לעיל משום כסות לילה – היינו כסות שאינו מיוחד רק [ה] ללילה (ור"ת סותר פירוש שלמעלה) דכסות יום חייב אפילו בלילה, וכן פרק קמא דקדושין (דף לד.). ותדע,

דאמרינן

רבינו גרשום

אחמץ בפסח ויוה"כ דאיסור כרת סמכינן אדיסקא ששולחין לגולה כשמעברין אדר או אלול: הכא דעשה בעלמא הוא דכתיב ועשו להם ציצית לשמן לא כ"ש דסמכינן: אלא מה טעם אסורה גזירה שמא יקרע סדינו בתוך ג' אצבעות סמוך לכנף מקום שראוי להטיל ציצית ויתפרנו להקרע בחוט של צמר או של פשתים ופעמים שמשתייר מן החוט של תפר ויעשנו ציצית עם חוטין אחרים והתורה אמרה תעשה ולא מן העשוי ולא הוי ציצית ועובר משום כלאים. מאי טעמא. האי דכתיב על כנפי בגדיהם בעינן עיקר טלית רובו שיהא של בגד: אמר רב סחורא הטיל ציצית לבעלת שלש כנפים והשלימה לד' שעשה לה כנף רביעי והניח בו ציצית רביעי פסולה מאי טעמא דכי הטיל לבעלת ג' לא הוי ציצית דלאו בת חיובא היא ההיא שעתא דעל ארבע כנפות כסותך אמר רחמנא ולא על ג' וכי משלים לה ד' לאו כלום הוי דהני תלת מיחזי כמו שלא נעשו לשום ציצית ולא מצי למיחשבינהו השתא דתעשה אמר רחמנא בעידן חיובא ולא מן העשוי כבר שלא בזמן חיובא: חסידים הראשוני' כיון שארגו בה בטלית ג' אצבעות היו מטילין לה תכלת לאותן שתי כנפים מפני שהיו זריזין במצות וכי משלמי לה לטלית כולה רמו לה ב' ציצית האחרים אלמא לא אמרי' תעשה ולא מן העשוי כבר: אימא כיון שבצעו בה שלשה כלומר כיון שגמרו ג' אצבעות האחרונים לא הוו משהו לה אלא לאלתר רמו לה תכילתא וכל הכנפים ביחד: והאמר ר' זירא הטיל למוטלת. היינו שהטיל ציציות אחרים לסדין שכבר היתה מוטלת לה ציציות כשרה ואין בה חיוב כלאים דחשבינן להו כמי שהטילן כולן ביחד דמי ולא אמרינן כי רמי הני בתראי לאו בת חיובא הואי דכבר היו לה ציציות הכא נמי שהטיל לבעלת ג' כי חזר והטיל הרביעי ליחשוב כהטיל עכשיו כולן ביחד הוו ולא תפסל: אמר רבא מהא לא קשיא דהאי הטיל למוטלת משום הכי כשרה דבבל תוסיף (בעל) קאי אבל מעשה לא הוי הנך בתראי לצורך תיקון הטלית שכבר היא מתוקנת והוי כמאן דליתנהו משום הכי כשרה. אבל הכא בהטיל לבעלת ג' מעשה קא עביד דהשתא הוא דמיתקנא כד משוי ביה האי ציצית רביעי. וכיון דהנך ג' קמאי לאו בכשרות עבדינהו קרינא ביה תעשה ולא מן העשוי הלכך פסולה: מתקיף לה רב פפא לאו תירוץ הוא דממאי דהאי גברא דהטיל למוטלת לאוסופי קא מיכוין ולא לבטל כך קאמרת דלמא לבטולי

שיטה מקובצת

א] גזירה משום כסות לילה האי טעמא הוא עיקר ומינה שמעינן דלילה לאו זמן ציצית הוא ולפיכך אין להטיל ציצית בכסות לילה ואפילו מינה וקי"ל דבהא כב"ש דסדין בציצית פטור ופר"ת דאפילו במינה פטור וכסות המיוחד ביום אי לביש ליה בלילה נמי מברך עליו וכן משמע בירושלמי [illegible]

[illegible]

הגהות הב"ח (א) רש"י ד"ה היו מטילין וכו' כדלקמן אלמא לכל ציצית שנעשית מתחלתה אע"פ שנעשית שלא לצורך ליכא מן העשוי.

א] תָּנוּ רַבָּנַן: *סָדִין בְּצִיצִית — ב"ש פּוֹטְרִין, וּב"ה מְחַיְּיבִין, אוַהֲלָכָה כְּדִבְרֵי ב"ה. א"ר אֱלִיעֶזֶר ב"ר צָדוֹק: וַהֲלֹא כָּל הַמַּטִּיל תְּכֵלֶת ב] בִּירוּשָׁלַיִם אֵינוֹ אֶלָּא מִן הַמַּתְמִיהִין! אָמַר רַבִּי: א"כ, לָמָּה אֲסָרוּהָ? לְפִי שֶׁאֵין בְּקִיאִין. אֲמַר לֵיהּ רָבָא בַּר רַב חָנָא לְרָבָא: ג] וְלִרְמוֹ בֵּי עֲשָׂרָה וְנִפְקוּ לְשׁוּקָא וּמְפַרְסְמָא לְמִילְּתָא! כָּל שֶׁכֵּן דְּמַתְמְהוּ עִילָּוֵן. וְלִידְרְשָׁא בְּפִירְקָא! גְּזֵירָה מִשּׁוּם קָלָא אִילָן. וְלֹא יְהֵא אֶלָּא לָבָן! כֵּיוָן דְּאֶפְשָׁר בְּמִינָן — לָא; כִּדְרֵישׁ לָקִישׁ, *דְּאָמַר רֵישׁ לָקִישׁ: כָּל מָקוֹם שֶׁאַתָּה מוֹצֵא עֲשֵׂה וְלֹא תַעֲשֶׂה, אִם אַתָּה יָכוֹל לְקַיֵּים אֶת שְׁנֵיהֶם — מוּטָב, וְאִם לָאו — יָבוֹא עֲשֵׂה וְיִדְחֶה אֶת לֹא תַעֲשֶׂה. ד] וְלִיבְדְּקוּהָ! אֶלָּא גְּזֵירָה מִשּׁוּם טְעִימָה. וְלִיכְתְּבָהּ אַדִּיסְקֵי! אַדִּיסְקֵי לֵיקוּם וְלִיסְמוֹךְ? אָמַר רָבָא: הַשְׁתָּא חָמֵץ

רש"י

סָדִין. ה] פִּשְׁתָּן. ב"ש פּוֹטְרִין. מִן הַצִּיצִית, דְּלָא דָּרְשִׁינַן סְמוּכִין לְמִישְׁרֵי כִּלְאַיִם בְּצִיצִית. הַאי דְּנָקַט לְשׁוֹן פְּטוּר וְחִיּוּב וְלָא נָקַט לְשׁוֹן אוֹסְרִין וּמַתִּירִין — מִשּׁוּם דְּצִיצִית חוֹבָה הוּא לַבֶּגֶד, וַאֲפִילּוּ אֵינוֹ לוֹבְשׁוֹ. וְאִיסּוּר וְהֶיתֵּר נַמִּי בְּהָא תַּלְיָא, ו] וְכֵיוָן דְּלְב"ש פָּטוּר — הָוֵי לְהוּ כִּלְאַיִם שֶׁלֹּא בִּמְקוֹם מִצְוָה, וְעוֹבֵר עֲלֵיהֶם מִשּׁוּם כִּלְאַיִם. וּלְב"ה דִּמְחַיְּיבִי לֵיהּ בְּצִיצִית — ז] דְּדָרְשִׁינַן (יבמות ד.) סְמוּכִין, וְאֵין כָּאן מִשּׁוּם כִּלְאַיִם, וּמוּתָּר לְלוֹבְשָׁן. וּבְטַלִּית שֶׁל צֶמֶר נַמִּי, לְב"ש אָסוּר לַעֲשׂוֹת בָּהּ לָבָן שֶׁל פִּשְׁתָּן וּתְכֵלֶת שֶׁל צֶמֶר, אֶלָּא הַלָּבָן וְהַתְּכֵלֶת שֶׁל צֶמֶר, וּלְב"ה מוּתָּר. וְהַאי דְּנָקַט פְּלוּגְתַּיְיהוּ בְּסָדִין — מִשּׁוּם דִּפְסִיקָא לֵיהּ מִילְּתֵיהּ, דְּאֵין בּוֹ צִיצִית בְּלֹא כִּלְאַיִם, שֶׁעִיקַּר מִצְוַת צִיצִית תְּכֵלֶת כְּתִיבָא בֵּיהּ, וּתְכֵלֶת עַמְרָא הוּא. אֵינוֹ אֶלָּא מִן הַמַּתְמִיהִין. מַתְמִיהַּ אֶת כָּל הָרוֹאִין, שֶׁאוֹמֵר: כִּלְאַיִם הוּא לָבוּשׁ! אַדְּבֵית הִלֵּל פָּלֵיג רַבִּי אֱלִיעֶזֶר. אָמַר רַבִּי אִם כֵּן. דַּהֲלָכָה כְּבֵ"ה, לָמָּה אֲסָרוּהָ בִּירוּשָׁלַיִם? לְפִי שֶׁאֵין בְּקִיאִין. לִדְרוֹשׁ סְמוּכִין דְּכִלְאַיִם בְּצִיצִית מוּתָּר, וְאָתוּ לְמִישְׁרֵי כִּלְאַיִם בְּכָל מָקוֹם. וְאִי קַשְׁיָא: כֵּיוָן דְּמִדְּאוֹרַיְיתָא חַיָּיב, הֵיכִי מָצוּ רַבָּנַן לַעֲקוֹר דָּבָר מִן הַתּוֹרָה וּלְמִיפְטְרֵיהּ מִצִּיצִית מִשּׁוּם גְּזֵירָה? ח] (הִיא) הָא אוֹתִיבְנָא בִּיבָמוֹת בְּפֶרֶק "הָאִשָּׁה רַבָּה" (דף צ:), וּמְשַׁנֵּינַן דְּכָל דָּבָר שֶׁאָמְרוּ לְךָ בֵּית דִּין: שֵׁב וְלֹא תַעֲשֶׂה מִצְוַת עֲשֵׂה זוֹ שֶׁבַּתּוֹרָה, וְרָאוּ טַעַם לְדִבְרֵיהֶם — אֵין זֶה עוֹקֵר דָּבָר מִן הַתּוֹרָה, דְּמִמֵּילָא מִיעֲקַר וְלָא אִיהוּ עָקַר לָהּ בְּיָדַיִם. ל"א: רַבִּי אֱלִיעֶזֶר אַדְּב"ש פָּלֵיג, דְּאָמְרִי סָדִין פָּטוּר, אַלְמָא דְּאִי רָמֵי ט] צִיצִית הָוֵה כִּלְאַיִם. וַהֲלֹא הַמַּטִּיל כו' — תֵּימָה הוּא דְּאִיכָּא, אֲבָל אִיסּוּרָא לֵיכָּא! אָמַר רַבִּי: א"כ דְּלֵיכָּא אִיסּוּרָא, מִפְּנֵי מָה אֲסָרוּהָ ב"ש? לְפִי שֶׁאֵין בְּנֵי אָדָם בְּקִיאִין דְּכִלְאַיִם בְּצִיצִית מוּתָּר, וְאָתֵי לְמִישְׁרֵי כִּלְאַיִם שֶׁלֹּא בִּמְקוֹם מִצְוָה. וּנְפַרְסְמָה לְמִילְּתֵיהּ. דְּכִלְאַיִם בְּצִיצִית מוּתָּר. כָּל שֶׁכֵּן דְּמַתְמְהִי עִלָּוַן. דְּאָמְרִי: אֲנָשִׁים הַגּוּנִים כָּאֵלּוּ לוֹבְשִׁים כִּלְאַיִם! גְּזֵירָה מִשּׁוּם קָלָא אִילָן. צֶבַע הִיא שֶׁדּוֹמָה לִתְכֵלֶת, וְאִי שָׁרֵית שֶׁל תְּכֵלֶת בְּסָדִין — אָתֵי לְמִירְמֵי צֶמֶר צָבוּעַ בְּקָלָא אִילָן, וְהָוֵי כִּלְאַיִם שֶׁלֹּא בִּמְקוֹם מִצְוָה. וְקָפְרֵיךְ: מַאי אִיכְפַּת לָן אִי רָמֵי קָלָא אִילָן? לֹא יְהֵא הַאי קָלָא אִילָן אֶלָּא לָבָן בְּעָלְמָא, כְּלוֹמַר צֶמֶר לָבָן, י] הָאֲמַרַן לְעֵיל: אֵין לוֹ תְּכֵלֶת — מַטִּיל לָבָן! וּמְשַׁנֵּי: כֵּיוָן דְּאֶפְשָׁר בְּמִינוֹ, *כֵּיוָן יא] דְּלָאֵס לָבָן (אִי) אֶפְשָׁר לָתֵת חוּטֵי פִּשְׁתָּן, לָא רָמֵינַן לָבָן דְּצֶמֶר בְּסָדִין. כִּדְרֵישׁ לָקִישׁ. כְּלוֹמַר (א), יב] *הֲרֵי לָבָן גָּמוּר לָא מָצֵי יג] לְהַטִּילָן לְשׁוּם צִיצִית, מִשּׁוּם דְּהָוֵי כִּלְאַיִם בְּצִיצִית, הוֹאִיל וְאֶפְשָׁר יד] לְהַטִּילָן בְּמִינוֹ. אֲבָל תְּכֵלֶת דְּצֶמֶר דְּאִי אֶפְשָׁר בְּמִינוֹ, דְּכָל תְּכֵלֶת צֶמֶר הוּא — (ב) רָמֵינַן, אִי לָאו מִשּׁוּם גְּזֵירָה דְּקָלָא אִילָן. לְקַיֵּים אֶת שְׁנֵיהֶן. כְּגוֹן לָבָן דְּפִשְׁתָּן בְּסָדִין. מְקַיֵּים (ג) עֲשֵׂה דְּצִיצִית, טו] *)וְיִדְחֶה לָאו דְּכִלְאַיִם. וְלִיבְדְּקֵיהּ. לְכָל הַיּוֹרוֹת שֶׁצּוֹבְעִין בָּהֶן צִיצִית, טז] אוֹ אוֹתָן מוֹכְרֵי תְּכֵלֶת, דְּלָא יז] לֶיהֱוֵי קָלָא אִילָן! גְּזֵירָה מִשּׁוּם טְעִימָה. אִי מַצְרְכִינַן לְכָל הַקּוֹנִים לִבְדּוֹק הַיּוֹרוֹת — אָתֵי לִשְׁפּוֹךְ הַנִּסָּיוֹן יח] בְּכָל הַיּוֹרוֹת, וְאָמְרִי' לְקַמָּן (דף מג:) בְּשְׁמַעְתִּין: יט] אִם שָׂם הַנִּסָּיוֹן בַּיּוֹרָה — פְּסָלָהּ לְכָל הַיּוֹרָה. טְעִימָה = נִסָּיוֹן. וְלִיכְתְּבֵיהּ אַדִּיסְקֵי. יִכְתְּבוּ אִיגֶּרֶת וְיִשְׁלְחוּ לַגּוֹלָה הִלְכוֹת טְעִימָה, כִּדְמְפָרֵשׁ לְקַמֵּיהּ: לִיטּוֹל מְלֹא קְלִיפַּת בֵּיצָה בַּיּוֹרָה, וְיִבְלַע הַנִּסָּיוֹן בְּתוֹךְ הַקְּלִיפָּה! וְאַדִּיסְקֵי לֵיקוּם וְלִיסְמוֹךְ. כְּלוֹמַר, דְּלָא חֲשִׁיבָא לְהוּ לֶאֱינָשֵׁי הָנָךְ אִגְּרוֹת, וְעָבְדֵי עֲלַיְיהוּ. ל"א. וְלִיבְדְּקֵיהּ — נִיתְקַן רַבָּנַן שֶׁלֹּא יִקַּח אָדָם תְּכֵלֶת אֶלָּא אִם כֵּן בְּדָקָהּ, דְּהָא אֶפְשָׁר דְּלִיבְדְּקֵיהּ כִּדְלְקַמָּן (שם), שֶׁמֵּבִיא גִּילָא וְשַׁבְּלִילְתָּא! ה"ג: אֶלָּא כ] מִשּׁוּם טְעִימָה. פְּעָמִים שֶׁיִּמְכְּרוּ כא] לִתְכֵלֶת שֶׁל נִסָּיוֹן שֶׁנִּצְבַּע לְנַסּוֹת בּוֹ אֶת הַיּוֹרָה, וְאָמְרִי' לְקַמָּן (שם): טְעָמָהּ — פְּסוּלָה. וְהָא מִילְּתָא לֵיכָּא לְמֵיקַם בִּבְדִיקָה, וַהֲוָה לֵיהּ כִּלְאַיִם שֶׁלֹּא בִּמְקוֹם מִצְוָה. וְנִיכְתְּבֵיהּ כב] (הָא) אַדִּיסְקָא [א]. לִשְׁלוֹחַ בְּאוֹתָן הַמְּקוֹמוֹת שֶׁצּוֹבְעִין בָּהֶן תְּכֵלֶת: הֱווּ יוֹדְעִין שֶׁהַטְּעִימָה פְּסוּלָה. וּמֵאַחַר שֶׁיְּהוּ הַצּוֹבְעִין יוֹדְעִין בַּדָּבָר נִסְמוֹךְ עֲלֵיהֶן! וְהָכָא לֵיכָּא לְמֵימַר לִידְרְשֵׁיהּ בְּפִרְקָא, לְפִי שֶׁצּוֹבְעִין תְּכֵלֶת הַרְבֵּה בִּכְרַכִּין וּבִכְפָרִים שֶׁאֵין שׁוֹמְעִין דְּרָשָׁה שֶׁלָּנוּ, וְגַם בִּמְקוֹמוֹת רְחוֹקִים. חָמֵץ

תוספות

סדין בציצית בית שמאי פוטרין. פירש בקונטרס: דלא דרשינן סמוכין, ולא איסתרי כלל כלאים בציצית. והא דנקט לשון פטור וחיוב, ויתכן יותר לשון איסור והיתר — משום דקסבר חובת טלית ואיסור והיתר נמי בהא תליא. וה"ה נמי בטלית של צמר שלא יפטרו בו חוטי פשתן, ומילתא דפסיקא נקט, דכל סדין מפשתן ואי אפשר בו בלא כלאים, שעיקר מצות ציצית תכלת, ותכלת עמרא הוא. משמע מתוך פירוש הקונטרס דציצית [ב] כלאים הוא דאסרינן, וכן פירש בתשובה, וכן [כתב] רבינו יצחק ברבי יהודה. וקשה, דהא אמרינן בריש יבמות (דף ד.): אפילו מאן דלא דריש סמוכין בעלמא, במשנה תורה דריש! וי"ל: דאיכא חד תנא בנזיר (דף נח.) דמפיק מ"ראשו" דעשה דוחה לא תעשה, ו"צמר ופשתים" לכדרבא, ובית שמאי סבירא להו כההוא תנא, וסבירא להו כרבי יהודה דלא דריש סמוכין אלא היכא דמוכח או מופנה. ואע"ג דעשה דוחה לא תעשה — לא שרי ציצית כלאים, דהא אפשר לקיים שניהם, ועיקר מצות תכלת לא יהא אלא בצמר. אי נמי, לאשמעינן קשר, [ג] דלעיל לא ידעינן אלא מדאישתרי כלאים בציצית.

ומיהו לא יתכן למימר כג] לפי מה [ד] שפירש למעלה גבי קשר העליון. מיהו גם אההוא תנא דנזיר פר"ת דסמיך א"גדילים", דמ"ראשו" לא מצי מפיק כדאיתא ביבמות. ותו דבסדר רב עמרם פסיק כב"ש בהא, ואנן *פשיטא דלפירוש הקונטרס קיס לן כב"ה, כדמוכח בכל דוכתי. ולפי' הקונטרס צ"ל דאין הלכה אלא כתנאי דבסמוך, וכדמפרש ומשום גזירה, וציצית ממינו שרי לכולי עלמא. וצריך לדחוק: הא דשרא רבי זירא לסדיניה — היינו ציצית תכלת. ומלאכא נמי (לקמן דף מא.) דאמר לרב קטינא: סדינא בקייטא ציצית מה תהא עליה — מציצית מן המובחר קא מקפיד. ותו קשה לפירוש הקונטרס, דפלוגתא דאמוראי הוא* אי ציצית חובת גברא או חובת טלית. כד] ועוד, דקי"ל (שם *דף מג) חובת גברא מדמברכינן "להתעטף", ומדב"ש נשמע לב"ה דחובת טלית הוי! לכך פי' ר"ת: דמדאורייתא ב"ש נמי חיובי מחייבי, ולא פטרי אלא משום הני טעמי דמפרש בשמעתין. ואפילו ממינו נמי פטרי ליה, דלמא אתי למיעבד תכלת, והלכך שייך שפיר לשון "פטור". ועוד יש לומר לפי' הקונט', דב"ש אף במינן פטרי, דסברי לה כרבי דאמר (לעיל דף לח.): התכלת מעכבת הלבן. והשתא ניחא הא *דנקט סדין דווקא. ומיהו תימה: *)דהשתא כיון דלא איפשר, נדחי עשה ללא תעשה!

אמר רבי אליעזר ברבי צדוק. בקונטרס פי' שני לשונות. [ה] ולשון שני שפי', דקאי אב"ש דפטרי — "והלא" אין בו רק תמיה. ורבי נמי קאי אב"ש — אם כן למה אסרוה ב"ש? וזהו כפי' ר"ת שלמעלה, דטעמא דב"ש משום גזירה היא. אבל לפי' הקונט' שלמעלה לא יתכן דניקו אב"ש. והיה יכול לפרש: א"כ למה אסרו העולם? וטעמא דנפשיה קאמר, ולא קים ליה כב"ש. ועוד פי' דרבי אליעזר אב"ה מהדר, דמחייבי ליה: והלא בני ירושלים יתמהו עליו! ואמר רבי: א"כ למה אסרוה? דפשיטא כב"ש לא קי"ל, ולמה [ו] מתמיהין? והלכה כדברי ב"ה. י"ס גורסין: אי איכא ציצית של צמר ביום מיכסי ביה ופטור, וכי שקעה חמה אי מלביש ליה חייב. ומחקו ר"ת, כמו שאפרש לקמן. לא יהא אלא לבן. אע"ג דאליבא דרבי קיימי, דס"ל (לעיל דף לח.) התכלת מעכבת את הלבן, מיהו רבי לאו טעמא דנפשיה קאמר, אלא מהדר אבני ירושלים כדפרישית. כיון דאפשר במינן. לעיל (דף לט:) כה] דמסיקנא דחוטי פשתן פוטרין בשל צמר — היינו בהדי תכלת, דמיגו דתכלת [ז] פטר בשל פשתן — לבן נמי פטר, ואע"ג דאפשר במינו. והאי דפשיטא ליה טפי דחוטי צמר פוטרין בשל פשתן, היינו משום דבלאו הכי איכא כלאים. אי נמי, מדאורייתא (דרחמנא) שרייה, ורבנן הוא דגזור, דכיון דאפשר לקיים שניהם. אבל מדאורייתא שרי, דכלאים ממש הותר אצל ציצית, ולאו משום דחיה. והא דמסקינן לעיל דפוטר — היינו מדאורייתא. אי נמי, מסקנא לא קיימא הכי.

וליבדקיה. פי' בקונטרס שתי לשונות. לשון אחד: לידבוק כל יורות הצובעים, ומשני: משום טעימה, דהוי שלא לשמו. והכי נמי הוה מצי למימר: שמא שלא לשמו עבד כוליה. ל"א ועיקר: וליבדקיה — כדאיתא לקמן, דמייתי גילתא ושבלילתא ובדקינן ליה לציצית אי תכלת הוא או קלא אילן. ומשני: משום טעימה — שמא ציצית זה נעשה מן הצמר שטעם בו, וזה אי אפשר בבדיקה. שמא

*) ר"ל בזמן הזה דאין לנו תכלת עי' רש"ק

עין משפט נר מצוה

יז א מיי' פ"ג מהלכות ציצית הלכה ו סמג עשין כו טוש"ע א"ח סי' ט סעיף ו:

מסורת הש"ס

שבת נה: עדיות פ"ד מ"י

נזיר מא. נח. שבת קלג. יבמות כ:

ל"ק מ"ז

לב"ש דלעס רש"א

נ"א הא לבן דלמר

[ועי' תוספות סוכה ג. ד"ה לאמר]

[לקמן מב:]

[דבר זה ליתא לקמן ולא בשום מקום בש"ס ודע דתוס' בשבת כה: ד"ה סדין כתבו דבר זה בשם בעל ה"ג וחובת גברא הוא מדמברכינן להתעטף בציצית וכ"כ תוס' עוד ביבמו' ד: סד"ה כולהו נמי]

נ"א דנקט סדין בציצית ולא תכלת בסדין

*) [נ"א בלבן דפשתים ולא ידחה לאו דכלאים וכ"א מקיים שניהם וכל"ל והס"ד ואח"כ מה"ד עשה לציצית כגון לבן דפשתן וידחה לאו דכלאים וכל"ל]

הגהות הב"ח

(א) רש"י ד"ה כדריש לקיש כלומר לבן וכו': (ב) בא"ד צמר הוא הוה שרי אי לאו משום: (ג) ד"ה לקיים וכו' מקיים הס"ד ואח"כ מ"ה עשה לציצית כגון צמר לבן בפשתן וידחה לאו:

שיטה מקובצת

א] ת"ר. (שבת כה) וע"ש בתוס': ב] תכלת בסדינו בירושלים: ג] לרבא ולירמו: ד] תעשה וליבדקה: ה] סדין של פשתן: ו] תליא דכיון דלב"ש: ז] בציצית דדרשי: ח] תיבת היא נמחק: ט] רמי ביה ציצית: י] צמר לבן הא אמרינן: יא] כיון דלשל לבן אפשר: יב] כלומר אפי' הוי לבן: יג] להטילו: יד] להטיל במינו אבל תכלת דצמר דאי אפשר בסדין: טו] דציצית ולאו דכלאים הס"ד ומה"ד ואם לאו כגון תכלת דאי אפשר בשל פשתן יבא עשה דציצית וידחה: טז] תיבות או אותן נמחק: יז] דלא להוי: יח] הנסיון בתוך היורה: יט] בשמעתין טעימה אם: כ] אלא גזירה משום: כא] שימכרו לו תכלת: כב] תיבת הא נמחק: כג] למימר *) כמו תיבת לפי נמחק: כד] טלית ולפירושו משמע דהך ברייתא סבירא לה דכלי קופסא חייבת בציצית וא"כ תקשי מינה למ"ד כלי קופסא פטורין ועוד דבסדר רב עמרם פסק כב"ש היאך אפשר לפסוק כמאן דלא דריש סמוכין הא איכא כמה גופי תורה דמסמוכין אתי ועוד פרש"י בתשובה דאע"ג דב"ש פוטרין סדין בציצית היינו דוקא תכלת דהוי כלאים אבל מינו מיהו צריך למשדי ביה ותימה אמאי דאמר לקמן דמלאכא כו' ואי כתשובת רש"י אמאי קאמר ציצית מה תהא עליה הא נוכל לקיים במינה וי"ל דעיקר ציצית של תכלת היא ועיקר מצוה מן המובחר קפיד וכן ההיא דפ' במה מדליקין דף כ"ה ע"ב דאמר כך היה מנהגו של רבי יהודה בר אלעאי כו' עד היו מחבין ממנו כנפי כסותן ואם היה להם ציצית של מינם למה היו מחבאין אלא לפי שלא היה להם תכלת דעיקר מצות ציצית בכך ור"ת פירש סדין בציצית ב"ש פוטרין מדרבנן ומשום הני טעמא דמפרש לקמן גזירה משום קלא אילן כו' ותנא פוטרים ולא אוסרין לפי שאפי' הטיל בהן מינן פוטרים ור"א אב"ש פליגי דהלא כל המטיל כו' תמיהא הוא דאיכא הא איסורא ליכא וכל הך סוגיא אליבא דב"ש קאי. תו"ח: כה] דמסיקנא דחוטי צמר פוטרין בשל פשתן ושל פשתן:

רבינו גרשום

סדין של פשתים בציצית בית שמאי פוטרין. לפי שתכלת צמר הוא והוי כלאים: וב"ה מחייבין. דרחמנא שריה ומשו"ה נקט לשון פטור וחיוב דכל בגד שיש לו ד' כנפים חייב בציצית: א"ר אלעזר ב"ר צדוק האיך בית שמאי פוטרין והלא כל המטיל תכלת לסדינו בירושלים אינו אלא מן המתמיהין (אבל) שתמיהין עליו בני אדם אותן שאין יודעין שמותר. תמיהא איכא איסורא ליכא: אמר ר' א"כ שאינה אסורה בציצית למה אסרוה חכמים לפי שאין בקיאין. מפני בני אדם שאינן בקיאין בהלכות ציצית ולא ידעי דשרי להכי אסרו בירושלים משום דהוה רוב עם ולא בקיאי לישנא אחרינא אמאי מחייבי ב"ה והלא כל המטיל אינו אלא מן המתמיהין שתמיהין עליו בני אדם מפני מה הטיל והלא אינו חייב בציצית. אמר ר' (יוסי) א"כ הואיל וב"ה מחייבין למה אסרוה חכמים והלשון הראשון הוא עיקר: ולרמו בי עשרה תכלת לסדינין וליפקו לשוקא וניפרסמא למילתא לאותן שאינן בקיאין דמותר כ"ש דמתמהי כי חזו בי עשרה בסדיניהון ומשום הכי אסורה: ולדרוש בפרקא בדרשא בבית הכנסת דשרי לשוויי תכלת בסדין ולא ליתמהו: גזירה דלמא אתו למירמא קלא אילן צמר שצבוע בקלא אילן שדומה לתכלת וההוא לא הוי מצוה וחייב משום כלאים הילכך אסרוה: ואמאי אסרוה מפני כך לא יהיה אותו קלא אילן אלא כלבן כלומר אם אינו חשיב כתכלת נדוננו כלבן ולימא דשרי: כיון דאפשר מינן כלומר א) כיון שמטיל הכנף והוא עיקר מצותן של ציצית הילכך לא נדוננו כלבן של צמר הקלא אילן להתירה דאפי' לבן של צמר אין עיקר מצותה: אם אתה יכול לקיים את שניהם עשה דציצית ולאו דלא תלבש שעטנז כגון הכא דמצי לקיים שניהם דיכול למירמי ביה חוטי פשתן והלכך אסרוה גזירה משום קלא אילן: ואמאי אסרוה משום קלא אילן וליבדקה. כלומר נידרש להו בפירקא היאך אדם יכול לבדוק אם הוא תכלת או קלא אילן וידעי למיבדקיה ואכתי לישתרי. אע"ג דידעי למיבדקיה להכי אסרוה גזירה משום טעימה דתכלת. ניסיון שמנסין את הצבע של תכלת שלוקחין מעט צמר ומטבילין בצבע לידע אם יהיה לו מראה יפה של תכלת וזו היא טעימה ואותה טעימה פסולה שלא נצבעה לשום ציצית. ושמא יטלנו בסדין ואותו אי אפשר לבדוק והוו כלאים הלכך אסורה: ואכתי מפני מה אסרוה בשביל טעימה: ולכתבה אדיסקי כלומר יכתבו ספרים ולשדרן לגולה דטעימה פסולה לציצית ולא אתו למירמי בסדין ואנן אדיסקא ליקום וליסמוך למישריה שמא איכא מאן דלא חזי לדיסקא ואתו למירמי טעימה אמר רבא השתא

*) אולי צ"ל למימר כן כמו שפירשתי למעלה וכו' ותיבות לפי מה נמחק.

הגהות צ"ק [א] ולשלוח: [ב] דכלאים הוא דאסירי: [ג] עליון דלא ידעינן: [ד] שפירשת: [ה] וללשון שני פירש דקאי: [ו] מתמיהין דהלכה כב"ה וי"ס גורסין אי עשה ציצית כצ"ל והלא: [ז] פטר לבן של פשתן נמי פטר:

יג א מיי' פ"ג מהלכות ציצית הלכה ה סמג עשין כו טוש"ע או"ח סי' יא סעיף ב:
יד ב מיי' שם הלכה ב ועיין בהשגות ובכ"מ טוש"ע שם סעיף ח:
טו ג מיי' שם הלכה ה טוש"ע שם סעיף ג:
טז ד מיי' שם הלכה א טוש"ע שם סעיף א:

תורה אור

וגדילא מיגדל, אמר רב: יאי גלימא ולא יאי תכלתא, רבה בר בר חנה אמר: יאי גלימא ויאי תכלתא. במאי קא מיפלגי? רבה בר בר חנה סבר: כתיב °"גדיל" וכתיב °"פתיל", או גדיל או פתיל; ורב סבר: לעולם פתיל בעינן, והההיא "גדילים" למניינא הוא דאתא, "גדיל" — שנים, "גדילים" — ארבעה, *עשה גדיל א] ופותליהו מתוכו. אמר שמואל משמיה דלוי: חוטי צמר פוטרין בשל פשתן. איבעיא להו: של פשתן מהו שיפטרו בשל צמר? צמר בשל פשתים הוא דפטר, דכיון דתכלת פטרה — לבן נמי פטר, אבל פשתים בצמר לא. או דלמא, כיון דכתיב: °"לא תלבש שעטנז צמר ופשתים יחדו גדילים תעשה לך" — לא שנא צמר בפשתים ולא שנא פשתים בצמר? ת"ש, דאמר רחבה אמר רב יהודה: אחוטי צמר פוטרין בשל פשתן ושל פשתן פוטרין בשל צמר; חוטי צמר ופשתים פוטרין בכל מקום, ואפילו בשיראין. ופליגא דרב נחמן, דאמר רב נחמן: השיראין פטורין מן הציצית. איתיביה רבא לרב נחמן: *השיראין, בוהכלך, והסריקין — כולן חייבין בציצית! מדרבנן. אי הכי, אימא סיפא: וכולן, צמר ופשתים פוטרין בהן; אי אמרת בשלמא דאורייתא — היינו דמישתרו בהו כלאים, אלא אי אמרת דרבנן, היכי מישתרי בהו כלאים? ב] אימא: או צמר או פשתים. הכי נמי מסתברא, דקתני סיפא: הן ג] במינן פוטרין, שלא במינן אין פוטרין; אי אמרת בשלמא דרבנן — היינו דמיפטרו במינן, אלא אי אמרת דאורייתא, צמר ופשתים הוא דפטר! אי משום הא לא איריא, כדרבא. *דרבא רמי, כתיב: "הכנף" — מין כנף, וכתיב: "צמר ופשתים", הא כיצד? גצמר ופשתים פוטרין בין במינן בין שלא במינן; שאר מינין, במינן — פוטרין, שלא במינן — אין פוטרין. ורב נחמן ד] כדתנא דבי רבי ישמעאל, *דתנא דבי רבי ישמעאל: הואיל ונאמרו בגדים בתורה סתם, ופרט לך הכתוב באחד מהן צמר ופשתים — דאף כל צמר ופשתים. *אמר אביי: והאי תנא דבי רבי ישמעאל ה] מפקא מאידך תנא דבי רבי ישמעאל, דתנא דבי ר' ישמעאל: ו] "בגד" — אין לי אלא בגד צמר, מנין לרבות צמר גמלים וצמר ארנבים ונוצה של עזים, והכלך והסריקין והשיראין, מנין? ת"ל: "או בגד".§
תנו

במדבר טו | דברים כב | דברים כב | [שבת כו: שבת כז: יבמות ד:]

וגדילא מיגדל. כל הציצית היתה גדיל, ולא שייר בה ענף כלל. ולא יאי תכלתא. משום דאין בה ענף. גדיל שנים. כלומר, אי הוה כתיב "גדיל תעשה לך" — ז] משמע ב' חוטין, דאין גדיל פחות משנים. השתא דכתיב "גדילים" משמע ארבעה. עשה גדיל. מד' חוטין, שיניח ד' חוטין בחור הטלית, ולכשיכפלם ויעשה מהן *גדיל יהו שמונה ח]. ופותליהו מתוכו. אותו חוט שכורך בו יהא מן המנין. ל"א: ופותליהו מתוכו — תנה פתיל ענף למטה. חוטי צמר פוטרין בשל פשתן. אותם שני חוטין של לבן, אם של צמר הן — פוטרין בסדין של פשתן עם התכלת, ט] ואע"ג דליכא השתא מין כנף, דהוי של צמר. כיון דתכלת י] שנים חוטין הן, *דתכלת עמרא נינהו ופוטר בשל פשתן, דהא תכלת כתב רחמנא בהדיא — לבן דצמר נמי פוטר בשל פשתן משום לבן. חוטי צמר ופשתים. לבן של פשתים, ושל *צמר תכלת. פוטרין בכל מקום. בכל מיני בגד, ואפי' בשיראים. דמהו דתימא: שיראין פטורין, והוו כלאים שלא במקום מצוה, קמ"ל דחייבין. השיראין = מעיל של משי. והכלך = מעיל שעושין מאותן יא] דגים [הוא בית התולעת] שמלויים *במינוי שקורין פלוצי"ל. סריקין. מעיל עשוי מנעורת של משי. צמר ופשתים פוטרין בהן. קא ס"ד שני חוטין צמר ושני חוטין לבן של פשתים. הן. עצמן, כלך וסריקין — במינן פוטרין, דאם עשה (א) ציצית יב] בטלית שהוא מינו יצא. אלא אי אמרת מדאורייתא. מחייבין שיראין בציצית, היכי פטרה בהו ציצית *דכלך? הא מדאורייתא ציצית דצמר ופשתים הוא (ב) דפוטרין, כדאמרינן לעיל: "צמר ופשתים יחדו גדילים תעשה לך"! ורב נחמן. דאמר לעיל: שיראין מדרבנן הוא דחייבין, דאי מדאורייתא לא פטר בהו מינו. כדתנא דבי ר' ישמעאל. יג] דאומר: אין מחייבין בציצית אלא בגד צמר או בגד פשתים. בגדים בתורה סתם. "על כנפי בגדיהם". ופרט לך. יד] בכלאים (דברים כב), ובגבי נגעים (ויקרא יג): "בבגד צמר או בבגד פשתים". מפיק מאידך תנא כו'. דהא אידך טו] מרבה כל הבגדים. צמר ארנבים ונוצה. צמר של עזים קרי נוצה, לפי שאין רך כשאר צמר. מנין. שמטמאין בנגעים. תלמוד לומר או בגד. "בגד צמר או טז] בגד פשתים" (שם).
סדין

גדילים יהיו ל"ק | [יבמות ה: וע"ש וברש"י ובתוספות] | פתיל עשה ל"ק | ותכלת ל"ק | תכלת לצמר ל"ק | נ"א כמינין | שבת כ: | דמינס הא ל"ק

או גדיל או פתיל. למאי דפרישית לעיל דמ"פתיל" שמעינן דבעי ב' חוטין תכלת, קשיא, דהכא דרשינן ליה ל"או גדיל או פתיל"! וי"ל: דהא נמי שמעת מינה, כיון דבחד פרשה כתיב "גדיל" ובאידך כתיב "פתיל". ומיהו קשה, דפתיל מ"ציצית" נפקא, דדרשינן לקמן (דף מב.): אין ציצית אלא ענף! ויש לומר: דאיצטריך "ציצית" לאשמועינן דלאחר עשייתן צריך לפרוד, כדאיתא לקמן. ובספרי דריש: "ועשו להם ציצית" — שומע אני יעשה כולה גדילים? ת"ל "ציצית", הא כיצד? כדי שתהא גדיל יוצאת מן הכנף, וציצית מן הגדיל. והא ברייתא קשיא לרבה בר בר חנה. וקשה נמי לרב, דדריש ליה הכא מ"פתיל", והתם דריש ליה מ"ציצית".

יז] והוא גדילים למניינא. תימה: מאי דוחקיה דרב למימר "גדילים" למניינא? נימא דקרא בא לומר תרווייהו בעי, גדיל ופתיל! ויש לדחוק ולפרש, דטעם דרבה בר בר חנה משום דדריש "גדילים" כמו מיעוט אחר מיעוט, משום דכתיב בלשון רבים, ואע"ג דליכא *גדיל כלל. וכי תימא: אם כן, "פתיל" דכתב רחמנא למה לי? איצטריך, דאי לא "פתיל" הוה פסלינן פתיל וגדיל בהדי הדדי, קמשמע לן: "פתיל". ורב סבר למניינא, ולא למעט *גדילים. ותימה: רבה בר בר חנה מניינא מנא ליה?

ופותליהו מתוכו. פירש בקונט': שחוט של כרך מן המניין. ובלשון אחר פי' שיהא הפתיל, דהיינו הענף, משולשל למטה ויוצא מן הגדיל. ותימה: דהא נפקא לן מ"ציצית" לקמן (דף מב.)! ובמתניתין פירשתי בע"א — שכפלו כעין פתילה, והיינו "עייף להו מיעף" דלקמן (שם).

לבן נמי פטר. פירש בקונטרס: אע"ג דלא מינא דכנף הוא. ולא יתכן לפי מה שפירשתי לעיל, דכולהו בר מתכלת איקרו "מין לבן". אלא הכי פירושא: אע"ג דכלאים נינהו.

ופליגא דרב נחמן. הוה מצי למימר דמדרבנן הוא, אלא משום שהאמוראים יש להם לבאר דבריהם יותר. אי נמי, לא מסתבר ליה, כמו שנבאר בסמוך. ורב נחמן דאמר כתנא דבי רבי ישמעאל. תימה, הא שפיר שני: מדרבנן! ויש לומר: דלא מסתבר ליה למימר הכי אלא מכח "הכי נמי מסתברא", וכי דחי ליה צריך למצוא תנא. אי נמי, לא מסתבר ליה לפלוגי אדרשא ד"מינה" אי לא משכח ליה (א) תנא. ונראה דמכולהו תנאי מוכח דאית ליה "הכנף" מין כנף, ולא מייתי דתנא דבי רבי ישמעאל אלא לומר דבגדיהם צמר ופשתים, (ב) דאי לאו האי טעמא לא מפיק ליה מ"הכנף" מין הכנף. יח] ור"ת ורש"י פסקו כרבא, משום דהוא בתרא. אף כל צמר ופשתים. תימה: מנא ליה דפליג? דלמא שאני הכא דאיכא ייתורא ד"הכנף" מין כנף. דהכי נמי דריש פרק "במה מדליקין" (שבת דף כז.) מ"או בגד" שאר בגדים לתנא דבי רבי ישמעאל! ויש לומר: דלא דמי, דהתם לא מפקינן בגד דקרא ממשמעותיה, דלעולם בגד דקרא צמר ופשתים הוא, אלא דמרבינן אף שאר יט] מינין. אבל הכא, אי דרשת מיניה בשאר מינין, א"כ בגד דכתיב ברישא הוי נמי שאר מינין, וא"כ מפקת בגד ממשמעותא. אי נמי י"ל: דרבא לא דריש מייתורא מידי, אלא משום דסבר "בגדיהם" — כל בגדיהם משמע, ועלה כתיב "הכנף" מין כנף, שמדבר מן הציצית. ולפירוש זה, על כרחיך תנא דבי רבי ישמעאל לית ליה דרבא. אמר אביי האי תנא דבי רבי ישמעאל. פרק "במה מדליקין" (גם זה שם) איתא להא מילתא, ודחי ליה רבא התם. בגד אין לי אלא בגד צמר. פי' בקונטרס: בנגעים כתיב. וקשה: חדא, דא"כ צריך לגרוס: "או בבגד", דהכי כתיב כ] גבי נגעים. ועוד, ג) דפ' "במה מדליקין" (גם זה שם) דרשינן ליה למילתא אחריתי. ד) ועוד, היכי ילפינן מנגעים, לרבא דמתרץ לה התם דלא מפקא מאידך תנא דבי רבי ישמעאל? הא גבי נגעים מרבה שאר בגדים! ועוד, ה) דהתם משמע בפירוש הכי. ו) ועוד תנן בהדיא דשאר מינין לא מיטמו בנגעים, נימא דלא כתנא דבי רבי ישמעאל? לכך צריך לפרש: דבשרצים הוא דכתיב (ויקרא יא). ותימה: דא"כ, אמאי איצטריך לאתויי נוצה של עזים? הא שק כתיב בהדיא! וי"ל: ז) דאיכא בגד מן הדק שבנוצה של עזים. וכן מוכח פרק "ראשית הגז" (חולין קלו.) דממעט גיזה של שור מ"מתן לו" ולא לשקו. ופריך: אלא מעתה נוצה של עזים ליחייב! אלמא לאו מכלל שק הוי. והשתא ניחא הא דמרבה לאביי מהכא ג' על ג' בשאר בגדים, ודין שק הוי ד' על ד'.
סדין

גדיל כלל ל"ק | פתילים ל"ק

הגהות הב"ח
(א) רש"י ד"ה הן כו' עשה אותן ציצית: נ"ב ד"ה אלא כו' לפער:

רבינו גרשום
תכילתא. ופסול: חוטי צמר פוטרין בטלית של פשתן: דכיון דתכלת מעמרא הוא דפטר של פשתים: כולן. השיראין והכלך והסריקין חוטי צמר ופשתים פוטרין בהן ביחד: בעצמן פוטרין השיראין: במינן פוטרין. אם הציצית הוא של מינן פוטרין: אלא אי אמרת דאורייתא ציצית דצמר ופשתי' הוא דפטרי ולאו ציצית דשאר מינין: כדרבא דסבר דמדאורי' נמי ציצית דשאר מינין פוטרין במינו כדרבא דרמי כתיב כו': ורב נחמן דאמר שיראים פטורין מן הציצית מדאורייתא אמר כדתנא דבי ר' ישמעאל הואיל ונאמרו בגדים בתורה סתם כנפי בגדיהם וכגון גבי שרצים וכל כלי עץ או בגד ופרט לך הכתוב באחד מהן צמר ופשתים דכתיב גבי נגעים או בבגד פשתים:

שיטה מקובצת
א] ופותליהו מתוכו. פ"ה בלשון שני תנה פתיל ענף למטה. ואף על גב דאמרינן לקמן מציצית [אין ציצית] אלא פתיל מיהו לא ידעינן מיניה אם הפתיל למעלה או למטה לכך הוצרך לומר ופותליהו מתוכו שיהא הפתיל למטה ועוד י"מ ופותליהו מתוכו לאחר שיתחוב הד' חוטין בכנף כופלו כמין פתיל ויהא ח' חוטין: ב] אימא או צמר או פשתים. וא"ת לעיל נמי אמאי קאמר ופליגא דרב נחמן לימא כי קאמר רב יהודה או צמר או פשתים וי"ל שהאמורא הי' לו לפרש דבריו כי היכא דלא תיפוק חורבה. תוה"ח: ג] הן עצמן במינן: ד] ורב נחמן דאמר כדתנא דבי ר' ישמעאל: ה] ר' ישמעאל מפיק מאידך: ו] בגד. שבת דף כו ויבמות דף ד': ז] לך דף הוה משמע: ח] יהו שמונה חוטין הס"ד: ט] והתכלת דבעינן מין כנף שיהא תכלת עמרא הוא ובהדיא כתב רחמנא דפוטר ושל לבן נמי אם של צמר הם פוטר הס"ד ומה"ד של פשתן אותם חוטין של לבן אם הם של פשתן מהו שיפטרו לבגד דצמר עם התכלת ואע"ג כיון דתכלת. שני חוטין ותכלת דעמרא ניהו: יא] מאותן הדגים הוא בית התולעת שמצוי מהן בשמש: יב] ציצית במין בטלית: יג] ר' ישמעאל דאמר אין חייבין בציצית: יד] ופרט לך הכתוב גבי נגעים: [illegible]

א) תנא דמכולהו מתני' מוכחא דלית כו' ל"ק. ב) אבל מאי טעמא לא מפיק מהכנף ל"ק. ג) דבפרק במה אשה יוצאה דרשינן ל"ק. ד) וי"ל דהאי או בגד לא כתיב בנגעים עיין שם בתוס' ד"ה נפקא ליה מאו בגד. ה) דהתם לא משמע הכי דתנן בהדיא לשאר ל"ק. ו) עיין רש"ק. ז) דשקין בגדים מן הדק ל"ק.

ט] איזה תנא מרבה: טו] או בבגד: יז] והוא גדילים למניינא הוא דאתא. תימה מאי א) דחקו כו' גדיל או פתיל לימא רב גדיל ופתיל בעינן וי"ל דאה"נ דטעמיה דרבה בר בר חנה הוא משום דכתיב בפרשה אחת כתיב גדיל ולא כתיב פתיל ובפרשה אחרת כתיב פתיל ולא כתיב גדיל אלמא אין זה מעכב בזה ואשמעינן רב דע"כ ילפינן זה מזה ומה שאמר בזה צריך בזה [illegible]

א) אולי צ"ל מאי דוחקיה דרב למימר דגדילים למניינא ולא למדרש דלאו גדיל או פתיל לימא וכו'.

דלמא דאיקטר. ואמר *רבה, א] שמע מינה: קשר עליון דאורייתא, דאי ס"ד דרבנן, מאי איצטריך למישרי סדין בציצית? פשיטא, אהתוכף *תכיפה אחת אינו חיבור! אלא שמע מינה: דאורייתא. אמר רבה בר רב אדא אמר רב אדא אמר רב: אם נפסק החוט מעיקרו — פסולה. יתיב רב נחמן וקא אמר להא שמעתא. איתיביה רבא לרב נחמן: בבמה דברים אמורים — בתחילתו, אבל ב] סופו — שיריו וגרדומיו כל שהוא; מאי שיריו ומאי גרדומיו? מאי לאו שיריו — דאיפסיק מינייהו ואישתייר מינייהו, גרדומיו — דאיגרדום איגרדומי! לא, חדא קתני, שיורי גרדומיו כל שהוא. וליפמא גרדומיו, שיריו למה לי? הא קמ"ל, דבעינן שיורא לגרדומיו כדי לענבן. יתיב רבה וקאמר משמיה דרב: גחוט של כרך עולה מן המנין. אמר ליה רב יוסף: שמואל אמרה ולא רב. איתמר נמי: אמר רבה בר בר חנה, סח לי רבי יאשיה דמן אושא: *חוט של כרך עולה לה מן המנין. יתיב *רבא וקא אמר משמיה דשמואל: תכלת שכרך רובה כשרה. אמר ליה רב יוסף: רב אמרה ולא שמואל. איתמר נמי, אמר רב הונא בר יהודה אמר רב ששת אמר רב ירמיה בר אבא אמר רב: תכלת שכרך רובה — כשרה. רב חייא בריה דרב נתן מתני הכי, אמר רב הונא אמר רב ששת אמר רב ירמיה בר אבא אמר רב: דתכלת שכרך רובה — כשרה, האפילו לא כרך בה אלא חוליא אחת — כשרה. ונויי תכלת — שליש גדיל ושני שלישי ענף. וכמה שיעור חוליא? תניא, רבי אומר: כדי *שיכרוך וישנה וישלש. תאנא: זהפוחת לא יפחות משבע, והמוסיף לא יוסיף על שלש עשרה; הפוחת לא יפחות משבע — כנגד שבעה רקיעים, והמוסיף לא יוסיף על שלש עשרה — כנגד שבעה רקיעין וששה אוירין שביניהם. תנא: חכשהוא מתחיל — מתחיל בלבן, "הכנף" — מין כנף, וכשהוא מסיים — מסיים בלבן, (א) *)מעלין בקודש ולא מורידין. רב ורבה בר בר חנה הוו יתבי, הוה קא חליף ואזיל ההוא גברא דמיכסי גלימא דכולה תכלתא, ורמי ליה תכלתא, וגדילא

*) לקמן לט. וש"נ

רש"י

דלמא דאיקטר. כלומר, ממאי דצריך להקשר בכל חוליא? דלמא הא דאמרי *דבי רבי חייא, ה"ק: אם קשר על כל חוליא וחוליא הוו גרדומין כשרין. אבל ברוב ציציות לא קא מכשרי גרדומין, דרוב ציציות אין נקשרים על כל חוליא וחוליא. קשר עליון. היינו נמי ההוא קשר ג] *למטה, *הלכה למשה מסיני. כלומר, [נ"ל דאורייתא] קשר אחד בציצית מיהא דאורייתא. ולהכי נקט עליון, משום ד] דאי לא עביד אלא חד קשר — בסופו עביד ליה, שמקיים את הגדיל כולו. דאורייתא. ואפי' יכול לכרוך יפה ולהתקיים בלא קשר יום או יומים פסולה. דאי מדרבנן למה לי למישרי סדין בציצית. דכתיב: "לא תלבש שעטנז", וסמיך ליה: "גדילים תעשה לך" (דברים כב)? פשיטא דמותר! ה] התוכף תכיפה. תופר תכיפה אחת אינו חיבור. משום הכי תכיפה שתוחב החוטין בטלית אינו חיבור ו]. מעיקרו. היינו ראש המחובר לטלית. במה דברים אמורים. דבעינן שיעור לציצית, כדאמרינן לקמן (דף מא:): כמה תהא משולשלת כו'. בתחלתו. בשעת עשייה. אבל בסופו — כגון אם נפסק לאחר זמן. מאי לאו שיריו. דאיפסיק מינייהו קצת מחוטיו, ונשאר *קצת גרדומין. דאיגרדם איגרדומי. ולגמרי נפסק ז] עד העיקר. וקשיא למאן דאמר: נפסק החוט מעיקרו פסולה! שירי גרדומין. דנשאר קצת ונפסק קצת. הא קמשמע לן. מדקתני שיריים בגרדומין משמע דלהוי בגרדומים שיורא קצת ח] שיהיו נקרא שיריים, כדי לעונבן כדפרישית לעיל, והאי "כל שהוא" דקתני — כדי עניבה. חוט של כרך. אותו שכורך סביב ועושה ממנו הגדיל, עולה ממנין שמונה חוטין, דשמונה חוטין בעינן כדמפרש לקמן (מב.). תכלת. זהו שם כל הציצית. שכרך רובה. שעשה שני שלישי גדיל ושליש ענף — כשרה, ואע"ג דמצותה שליש גדיל ושני שלישי ענף, כדאמרינן לקמן. אלא חוליא אחת. הקפה ג' פעמים. ונויי תכלת. עיקר מצות ציצית, שליש גדיל ושני שלישי ענף. לא יפחות משבע. חוליות. ששה אוירים. שבין שבעה רקיעים. ועל שם שהתכלת דומה לים וים דומה לרקיע כדלקמן (דף מג:) מדמי סידורא לסידור הרקיעים, כדי *לזכרנו לטובה (ב), שאף צבעה ט] כמו כן נזקק לציצית. כשהוא מתחיל לכרוך מתחיל בלבן. שמניח שני חוטין ארוכין לעשות מהן הגדיל, ומתחיל לכרוך בלבן, ובאמצע כורך של תכלת, וחוזר ומסיים בלבן. מין כנף. תחילה, ואח"כ פתיל תכלת. והאידנא דעבדינן חמשה קשרים, היינו דאמרינן (שם): שקולה מצות ציצית ככל התורה כולה, י] הלכך (ג) עבדינן שני קשרים מלמעלה ושלשה מלמטה. משום מעלין בקדש ואין מורידין — וכיון דאקדמה קרא למין כנף שמע מינה חשוב הוא, הלכך אי מסיים בתכלת הוה ליה מוריד סוף הציצית מתחילתה. דכוליה תכלתא. כל הטלית. ורמי ליה תכלתא. ציצית. וגדילא

תוספות

קשר העליון. בקונטרס פירש שני פירושים: אחד — אחר הגדיל, ונקרא עליון כמו (נדה דף יג.) "למעלה מן העטרה". וזה אינו מוכח אלא דמיהא בעינן קשר. *ול"א פירש: סמוך לכנף. אבל קשר שאחר הגדיל, כיון שרחוק מן הטלית – משום ההוא לא הוי כלאים. ותימה: להאי דמוכח, היכי מסיק ביבמות (דף ד:) למאן דלא דריש סמוכים אלא היכא *דמוכח, ד"למר ופשתים" למה ליה? דכלאים *מתנא דבי רבי ישמעאל שמעינן, דבגדיהם למר ופשתים וכו'. והשתא קשר העליון לא שמעינן, *וא"כ לא הוי כלאים, ואיצטריך שפיר לאיתויי למר ופשתים, לומר שיהא צריך לעשותם בענין שיהא בהם כלאים! וי"ל: דהכא לא מפיק מקרא ד"למר ופשתים", אלא מ"גדיל", ומוכח *דכלאים דדרשה דגדיל דרשה נכונה היא, דבעינן גדיל טוב. אי נמי, סוגיא דהתם אתיא כמאן דאמר גדיל דווקא. ושמא דהתם אתיא כמאן דאמר או גדיל או פתיל, ופלוגתא דאמוראי הוא בסמוך. והכי נמי תימה, דבפרק "המוצא תפילין" (עירובין צו:) משמע דבעינן שזורין, ור"ת נמי פירש דאינו חייב על כלאים עד שיהא משזר, ואם כן איצטריך טובא קרא דכלאים בציצית! ויש לומר: דבעלמא יליף ליה *מתכלת דבגדי כהונה, וכיון דתכלת שזור – הוא הדין לבן.

דאיגרדום איגרדומי. פירש בקונטרס: שנפסקו לגמרי. וקשה: דהא "כל שהוא" קתני! וצריך לומר דלגרדין קתני, ולא קאי אלא אשיריו. ונראה לפרש: מאי לאו שיריו דאיפסיק מינייהו, כלומר: שיש מן החוטים שנפסקו מעיקרם, ואישתייר מן השלימין נמי. וגרדומיו – דאיגרדמו כולם. והשתא לא קאי "כל שהוא" אלא אגרדומיו. והא ד"איפסיק מינייהו" הוי השתא כמו "נפסק החוט מעיקרו" דלעיל. וכי האי גוונא קרי "שיריו" פרק קמא דסוכה (דף יג.) גבי אזוב תחילתו שלשה וסופו שנים. וצ"ע.

שירי גרדומיו כל שהוא. פרק "מי שמת" (ב"ב דף קנ.) הוה מצי לאיתויי הך, גבי הך דפריך: וכל היכא דתני "כל שהוא" לית ליה שיעורא.

לא יפחות משבע כנגד שבעה רקיעים. לפי *שתכלת דומה לים וים דומה לרקיע. ואנן דלית לן תכלת לא קפדינן בהא. והא נמי דאמרינן: צריך לקשור על כל חוליא וחוליא — היינו כדי שיהא ניכר התכלת. ומה שאנו נוהגים חמשה קשרים, פירש בקונטרס יא] (א) גבי ב) ציצית שקולה כנגד כל המצות: לפי שציצית עולה ת"ר, וח' חוטין וחמשה קשרים עולה יב] תרי"ג. ומיהו, כל "ציצית" האמורים בפרשה חסירים יו"ד. ויש לומר שיש פסוק "והיה לכם לציצית", וג' ציצית כתובים בפרשה, ולמ"ד זו משלימתן. וכן נוהג רבינו תם לעשות אותן ה' קשרים, ב' בסמוך לטלית וג' סמוך לפתיל משום מעלין בקדש ולא יג] מורידין, כדאמרינן שמסיים בלבן, ועל כל קשר שני קשרים כדי שיהא קשר של קיימא. מיהו, לא מצינו שום סמך בהתלמוד מפורש מה' קשרים. ויש לומר, דהא דאמרינן: צריך לקשור על כל חוליא וחוליא — היינו אחת של לבן ואחת של תכלת, שהן שתים. והשתא, כשאין פוחת משבע עושה ה' קשרים: סמוך לטלית קשר אחד, ואחר כך שתי חוליות אחת של תכלת ואחת של לבן *קשר אחד, עד שמסיים שש חוליות — הרי ארבעה קשרים, ואחר כך עושה חוליא שביעית של לבן כדי שיהא מסיים בלבן, ואחר כך קושר אחד — הרי ה' קשרים. ויש מפרשים: לא יפחות משבע כריכות בין כל קשר וקשר. או

א) [לקמן מג: ד"ה שקולה] ב) הא דאמרינן לציצית שקולה כו' נ"ק

עין משפט נר מצוה

ז א מיי' פ"י מהל' כלאים הלכה כד טוש"ע י"ד סי' ש סעיף ב:

ח ב מיי' פ"א מהלכות ציצית הלכה יח סמג עשין כו טוש"ע א"ח סי' יב סעיף א:

ט ג ד ה מיי' שם הלכה ז ועיין בהשגות ובכ"מ טוש"ע שם סי' יא סעיף יד:

י ו מיי' שם הלכה ח טוש"ע שם בהג"ה:

יא ז מיי' שם טוש"ע שם:

יב ח מיי' שם הלכה ז:

לא נמצא בפ"ה שלפנינו ועיין רש"ק

דמופנה דלמר נ"ק

בציצית מתנא נ"ק

אלא משום דא"כ נ"ק

מכלאים נ"ק

תכלת בציצית מתכלת דבגדי כהונה דבעינן שזורים וכיון נ"ק

מסורת הש"ס

נ"ל בני

שלמטה הלכה נ"א

נ"א רבא

כלאים פ"ט מ"י [שבת נז. יבמות ה:]

קצת הס"ד אח"כ ד"ה גרדומיו לאיגרדם כו' נפסק מעיקרו וקשיא נ"ק

[עי' תוס' לקמן נ. ד"ה דיקא נמי]

[לעיל לח.]

לזכור להקב"ה שאף כו' נ"ק

וקשר נ"ק

הגהות הב"ח

(א) גמ' מסיים בלבן משום מעלין: (ב) רש"י ד"ה לא יפחות וכו' לטובה וזה בזמנם שאף צבע תכלת נזקק לציצית: (ג) ד"ה מין כנף וכו' הלכך ציצית עולה ת"ר וח' חוטין וה' קשרים הרי תרי"ג ועבדינן שני קשרים:

שיטה מקובצת

א] ש"מ קשר עליון דאורייתא לפום רהיטא משמע מדאצטריך סמוכין למשרי סדין בציצית וקשה מפ"ק דיבמות א) לא שרי סדין בציצית דקאמר תלמודא הא למה לי סמוכין מתנא דבי ר' ישמעאל נפקא דאמר ר' ישמעאל כל מקום שנאמר בגדים כו' ואמר רחמנא עביד תכלת ותכלת עמרא הוא ומאי קאמר לעולם אימא לך דאי לאו סמוכים הוי אמינא אין ציצית דוחה כלאים והא דאמר רחמנא עביד תכלת היינו בלא (דמיה) [קשירה] ע"י תכיפה אחת דאינו חיבור להכי איצטריך סמוכין למימר דבעינן קשר ואעפ"כ שריא רחמנא ותירץ הר"ר יוסף קלצון איש ירשלים דהכי פריך התם לתנא דבי רבי ישמעאל כדפי' שם בתוס' מיהו קשה למורי הר"י שי' מאי פריך הכא למאי איצטריך סמוכין הא רבא עצמו אמר לקמן דאתא למימר צמר ופשתים פוטרים בין במינן בין שלא במינן ותירץ הר"ם המדקדק בפי' הקושיא ימצא הכל ב) מכוון דה"ק ש"מ קשר העליון הלכה למשה מסיני מדאצטריך למשרי סדין בציצית אינו ר"ל מדאיצטריך סמוכין אלא מדאיצטריך בכמה מקומות ברייתות לומר דציצית דוחה כלאים כההיא סדין בציצית ב"ה מחייבין ואי קשר העליון לאו דאורייתא פשיטא דסדין חייב דתכיפה אחת אינו חיבור וכשיטה זו אשכחנא ריש בבא מציעא ש"מ הילך חייב דאי ס"ד הילך פטור למה אצטריך למפטר קרקעות משבועה כל קרקעות הילך הוא ואין רוצה לומר למה לי קרא דהא ליכא קרא למפטר קרקעות משבועה אלא ר"ל למה לי מתני' דאמר אין נשבעין על הקרקעות ופטור דשבועות קרקעות גמרינן מכפל אבל בקרקעות גופיה ליכא קרא לפטור. תו"ח: ב] אבל בסופו: ג] דלמטה דאורייתא הלכה: ד] משום דמאן דלא עביד: ה] (מה"ד דהא) התוכף תכיפה אחת תופר: ו] חיבור ל"א דאי קשר עליון היינו הך דסמיכי לטלית מדרבנן למה לי למישרי סדין בציצית דאי משום ההיא תחיבה דתחב חוטין בסדין לאו תכיפה היא דתוכף תכיפה אחת אינה חיבור ואי משום קשר התחתון לאו תכיפה היא דמרוחק מן הטלית: ז] נפסק עד העיקר: ח] קצת שיהיה: ט] צבעה כך לכך נזקק: י] כולה דמנין ציצית בגימטריא ת"ר ושמונה חוטין וחמשה קשרים דהיינו תרי"ג כנגד כל המצות: יא] בקונטרס דהא ציצית שקולה: יב] תרי"ג מכאן סמך לפי' הקונטרס במתני' דאין למעט מנין החוטין אם אין תכלת וצריך לעולם ח' חוטין תוס' אחרות: יג] מורידין ואמר ריב"א שראה ציצית של ר"ת עשוי כך ורוב העולם נהגו לעשות הקשרים בין החוליות וראיה מהא דאמרינן לעיל צריך לקשור על כל חוליא וחוליא ומסתמא היינו אחר כריכות של לבן וכן של תכלת וקאמר הפוחת לא יפחות מז' היינו ג' חוליות של לבן וג' של תכלת ואחת שמסיים בלבן נמצא קשר סמוך לכנף ואח"כ כורך ג' של לבן וג' של תכלת ואח"כ קושר הרי שני קשרים וחוזר וכורך ג' של לבן וג' של תכלת וקושר הרי ג' וחוזר וכורך ג' של לבן וג' של תכלת וקושר הרי ד' ומסיים בלבן ג' כריכות של לבן בלא תכלת וקושר הרי ה' קשרים ואורך הציצית מפורש לקמן ולדידן שאין לנו תכלת אין להקפיד לעשות חוליות אלא לכרוך סביב בלא חוליא ומנהג ר"ת שהיה קושר חוט שכורך בו כנגד ז' חוטין ואין מנהג העולם כן ג) אלא חולקין החוטין ד' מכאן וד' מכאן תוס' אחרות:

א) נראה דצ"ל דאמר שם דסמוכין אתא למשרי סדין בציצית דקאמר תלמודא וכו'. ב) אולי צ"ל ימצא הכל מבואר דהא דקאמר ש"מ. ג) ועי' ברא"ש הלכות ציצית בהלק"ט סי' טו.

ד א מיי' פ"א מהלכות ציצית הלכה ד:
ה ב ג מיי' פ"א מהלכות ציצית הלכה יח סמג עשין כו טוש"ע א"ח סי' יב ס"א:
ו ד טוש"ע שם סעיף ב:

אִילֵימָא חִיסֵּר מִצְוָה דְּלָבָן, וְקִיֵּים מִצְוָה דִּתְכֵלֶת – א] לְרַבִּי עַכּוּבֵי מְעַכֵּב אַהֲדָדֵי! אָמַר רַב יְהוּדָה אָמַר רַב: שֶׁחִיסֵּר מִצְוָה וְעָשָׂה מִצְוָה, וּמַאי חִיסֵּר מִצְוָה? דְּלָא עֲבַד מִצְוָה מִן הַמּוּבְחָר. הָתֵינַח לָבָן דְּאֵינוֹ מְעַכֵּב אֶת הַתְּכֵלֶת, תְּכֵלֶת דְּאֵינָהּ מְעַכֶּבֶת אֶת הַלָּבָן מַאי הִיא? ב] אָמַר רָמִי בַּר חָמָא: לָא נִצְרְכָא אֶלָּא לְטַלִּית שֶׁכּוּלָּהּ תְּכֵלֶת. אִיתְּמַר נַמִּי, אֲמַר לֵיהּ לֵוִי לִשְׁמוּאֵל: אַרְיוֹךְ, *לָא תֵּיתִיב *אַכַּרְעָךְ עַד דִּמְפָרְשַׁתְּ לִי לְהָא מִילְּתָא: הַתְּכֵלֶת אֵינָהּ מְעַכֶּבֶת אֶת הַלָּבָן, וְהַלָּבָן אֵינוֹ מְעַכֵּב אֶת הַתְּכֵלֶת, מַאי הִיא? אֲמַר לֵיהּ: לָא נִצְרְכָא אֶלָּא ג] לְסָדִין בְּצִיצִית, דְּמִצְוָה לְאַקְדּוּמֵי לָבָן בְּרֵישָׁא, מ"ט? "הַכָּנָף" – מִין כָּנָף, וְאִי אַקְדֵּים תְּכֵלֶת לַלָּבָן לֵית לָן בָּהּ. תֵּינַח לָבָן דְּאֵינוֹ מְעַכֵּב אֶת הַתְּכֵלֶת, תְּכֵלֶת דְּאֵינָהּ מְעַכֶּבֶת אֶת הַלָּבָן מַאי הִיא? אֲמַר ד] לֵיהּ רָמִי בַּר חָמָא: לָא נִצְרְכָא אֶלָּא לְטַלִּית שֶׁכּוּלָּהּ תְּכֵלֶת, דְּמִצְוָה לְאַקְדּוּמֵי תְּכֵלֶת בְּרֵישָׁא, דְּ"הַכָּנָף" – מִין כָּנָף, וְאִי אַקְדֵּים לָבָן בְּרֵישָׁא לֵית לָן בָּהּ. אָמַר רָבָא: ה] מִידֵי צִיבְעָא קָא גָּרֵים? אֶלָּא אָמַר רָבָא: לָא נִצְרְכָא אֶלָּא לְגַרְדּוּמִין, דְּאִי אִיגַּרְדַּם תְּכֵלֶת וְקָאֵי לָבָן, וְאִי אִיגַּרְדַּם לָבָן וְקָאֵי תְּכֵלֶת – לֵית לָן בָּהּ, *דְּאָמְרִי בְּנֵי ר' חִיָּיא: גַּרְדּוּמֵי תְּכֵלֶת כְּשֵׁרִין, [א]וְגַרְדּוּמֵי אֵזוֹב כְּשֵׁרִין. וְכַמָּה שִׁיעוּר גַּרְדּוּמִין? אָמַר בַּר הַמְּדוּרִי אָמַר שְׁמוּאֵל: *[ב]כְּדֵי לְעָנְבָן. אִיבַּעְיָא לְהוּ: כְּדֵי לְעָנְבָן – לְעָנְבָן כּוּלְּהוּ בַּהֲדָדֵי, אוֹ דִּלְמָא כָּל חַד וְחַד לְחוּדֵיהּ? [ג]תֵּיקוּ. בָּעֵי רַב אַשִׁי: אַלִּימֵי דְּלָא מִיעַנְּבִי וְאִי הָווּ קְטִינֵי מִיעַנְּבִי, מַאי? אֲמַר לֵיהּ רַב אַחָא בְּרֵיהּ דְּרָבָא לְרַב אַשִׁי: [ד]כָּל שֶׁכֵּן דְּמִינַּכְּרָא מִצְוָתַיְיהוּ. וּמַאן תַּנָּא דְּפָלֵיג עֲלֵיהּ דְּרַבִּי? הַאי תַּנָּא הוּא, דְּתַנְיָא: רַבִּי יִצְחָק אוֹמֵר מִשּׁוּם ר' נָתָן, שֶׁאָמַר מִשּׁוּם רַבִּי יוֹסֵי הַגְּלִילִי, שֶׁאָמַר מִשּׁוּם רַבִּי יוֹחָנָן בֶּן נוּרִי: אֵין לוֹ תְּכֵלֶת – מַטִּיל לָבָן. אָמַר רָבָא, שְׁמַע מִינָּהּ: ו] צָרִיךְ לִקְשׁוֹר עַל כָּל חוּלְיָא וְחוּלְיָא, דְּאִי ס"ד לָא צָרִיךְ, הָא דְּאָמְרִי בְּנֵי רַבִּי חִיָּיא: גַּרְדּוּמֵי תְּכֵלֶת כְּשֵׁרִין וְגַרְדּוּמֵי אֵזוֹב כְּשֵׁרִין, כֵּיוָן דְּאִישְׁתְּרֵי לֵיהּ עִילָּאֵי – אִישְׁתְּרֵי לֵיהּ כּוּלָּהּ!
דִּלְמָא

אִילֵימָא חִיסֵּר מִצְוָה. דְּלָבָן, וַהֲוֵי כְּאִילּוּ לֹא נְתָנוֹ לְגַמְרֵי, אַמַּאי יָצָא? הָא לְרַבִּי עִיכּוּבֵי מְעַכְּבָא, וּמַתְנִי' כְּרַבִּי אוֹקְמָא לָהּ! חִיסֵּר מִצְוָה. מִצְוַת הַקְּדָמָה. וְעָשָׂה מִצְוָה. דְּהָאִיכָּא לָבָן וּתְכֵלֶת. תְּכֵלֶת דְּאֵין מְעַכֶּבֶת לָבָן מַאי הִיא. דְּמַשְׁמַע: אִם הִקְדִּים לָבָן, ז] וּמַאי עִיכּוּב אִיכָּא לְמֵימַר? אִיתְּמַר נַמִּי. ח] *מַתְנִי' דְּקָתָנֵי [תְּכֵלֶת וכו' אַיְּירֵי לְהַקְדִּים], *וְאִיבַּעְיָא לֵיהּ נַמִּי, תְּכֵלֶת דְּאֵין מְעַכֵּב לָבָן מַאי הִיא. אַרְיוֹךְ. לְשׁוֹן מֶלֶךְ, כְּמוֹ (בראשית מט): "גּוּר אַרְיֵה יְהוּדָה". לְהָכִי קָרֵי לִשְׁמוּאֵל "אַרְיוֹךְ" – דְּקַיְימָא לָן (בכורות מט:): הֲלָכָה כִּשְׁמוּאֵל בְּדִינֵי כִּי הֵיכִי דְּדִינָא דְּמַלְכוּתָא דִּינָא (א). *לְהָכִי נָקֵיט סָדִין – מִשּׁוּם דְּלָבָן הוּא. מִידֵי צִבְעָא גָּרֵים. אֲפִי' כּוּלָּהּ תְּכֵלֶת נַמִּי מִצְוָה לְהַקְדִּים לָבָן ט] לִתְכֵלֶת. הוֹאִיל וְרוֹב טַלִּיתוֹת לְבָנוֹת הֵן, לָבָן קָא גָּרֵים. וּלְהָכִי כְּתִיב תְּכֵלֶת אַחַר הַכָּנָף, דִּלְעוֹלָם יְהֵא הַמְאוּחָר. אִיגַּרְדַּם. נִפְסְקוּ י] הַחוּטִין שֶׁל צִיצִית. גַּרְדּוּמִין. הַיְינוּ שְׁיָרֶיהָ שֶׁנִּשְׁתַּיְּירוּ לְאַחַר שֶׁנִּפְסְקוּ. כְּדֵי יא] לַעֲנוֹב כָּל הַחוּטִין אַהֲדָדֵי. דְּהַיְינוּ שִׁיעוּר גָּדוֹל. אַלִּימֵי. עָבִים. דְּאִי הָווּ קְטִינֵי. דַּקִּים, הָווּ מִיעַנְּבֵי. דַּאֲרוּכִּין הֵן כ"כ, אֲבָל מִפְּנֵי עוֹבְיָין הָווּ יב] קְטַנִּים לַעֲנוֹב. כָּל שֶׁכֵּן. דִּכְשֵׁרִין. דְּהוֹאִיל וְאִילּוּ הָווּ דַּקִּים יג] כָּל כָּךְ כְּשֵׁרִים, דְּהָא אֲרוּכִּין הֵן כְּדֵי עֲנִיבָה – כָּל שֶׁכֵּן כְּשֶׁהֵם עָבִים, דְּמִינַּכְּרָא יד] מִצְוֹתֵיהֶן טְפֵי. וּמַאן תַּנָּא דְּפָלֵיג עֲלֵיהּ דְּרַבִּי. הָנָךְ חֲכָמִים דְּאָמְרִי לְעֵיל: אֵין מְעַכְּבִין זֶה אֶת זֶה. מַטִּיל לָבָן. כָּל הַד' חוּטִין. ש"מ. מִדְּאָמְרִי בְּנֵי רַבִּי חִיָּיא גַּרְדּוּמֵי תְּכֵלֶת טו] כְּשֵׁרִים, אַמַּאי? הָא כֵּיוָן דְּנִפְסַק *קְצָת טז] הַגְּדִיל מִשְׁתְּרֵי הַהוּא קֶשֶׁר שֶׁבְּסוֹף הַגְּדִיל, וְכֵיוָן דְּמִשְׁתְּרֵי הַהוּא קֶשֶׁר – מִשְׁתְּרֵי יז] הַגְּדִיל, וְאֵין שָׁם גְּדִיל כְּלָל! אֶלָּא ש"מ יֵשׁ קֶשֶׁר בְּכָל חוּלְיָא, הִלְכָּךְ כִּי מִשְׁתְּרֵי הַהוּא קֶשֶׁר מִתְקַיֵּים הַגְּדִיל בִּשְׁאָר קְשָׁרִים. עִילָּאֵי. הַיְינוּ הַהוּא קֶשֶׁר תַּחְתּוֹן, דְּמִלְּמַטָּה לְמַעְלָה קָחָשֵׁיב. וְעוֹד, דִּבְגַרְדּוּמִין קָא מַיְירֵי בִּשְׁמַעְתִּין, וּבְגַרְדּוּמִין יח] *מוּקָפִין הָווּ אִיהוּ עֶלְיוֹן.
של מוקפין נ"ק
דִּילְמָא

אילימא חיסר מצוה דלבן וקיים מצוה דתכלת. תימה: דאיפכא הוה ליה למימר, דמצות לבן עבד, אבל מצות תכלת הנעשית שלא כהלכה חיסר! וי"ל: דמשום מתניתין נקט הכי הלבן אינו מעכב התכלת, פירוש: אינו מעכב כלל התכלת שקידם.

לרבי עכובי מעכב. פירש בקונטרס: וכדרבי בעינן לאוקמה. ותימה: דמשמע דלרבנן ניחא, ואם כן למסקנא לא נצטרך לתירוץ רב יהודה, ולא מיסתבר הכי! מיהו, למסקנא נמי מצינו למימר דבעי לאוקומי מתניתא כרבי. אי נמי י"ל, דכל שכן לרבנן דקשה טפי: אמאי חיסר מצוה? הא לא מעכבי אהדדי!

לא נצרכא אלא לסדין בציצית. תימה: אמאי נקט הכי? לינקוט טלית צמר בציצית! יט] ויש מפרשים: דווקא תכלת לא הוי מין דסדין, משום דהוו כלאים גביה, אבל צמר ותכלת הוי מינו. ולבן נמי דתניא לעיל, מפשתן הוי. וקשה, דאם כן, מאי קשיא ליה: תינח לבן אינו מעכב התכלת, אלא תכלת אינה מעכבת את הלבן מאי ניהו? ומאי פירכא? הא נמי משכחת לה, דהא תכלת וצמר חד מינא הוי ואינה מעכבת חוטי לבן. אי נמי חוטי פשתן, למאי דפשטינן לקמן (דף לט:) חוטי פשתן פוטרין בשל צמר! לכך נראה כפי' הקונטרס, דלהכי נקט סדין – דפשיטא דהוי לבן, *ולבן של צמר הוה *מצטרף לפשתן טפי.

מידי ציבעא קא גרים. משמע שרוצה בקונטרס לפרש: משום דקרא ברוב טליתות איירי, שהן לבנות ואינן צבועות תכלת, וכיון דכתיב "הכנף" מין כנף, הוי כאילו כתב בהדיא: תן שני חוטי לבן תחילה ואח"כ פתיל תכלת. וצריך לומר דסתם טליתות שלהם היו גם משאר מינים, דרבא הוא דדריש לקמן מדכתיב "הכנף" מין כנף דשאר מינים במינם פוטרין. ומיהו תימה: אם היו רגילים בטלית של צמר, נהי דלא איירי קרא באותו שהוא צבוע תכלת, מכל מקום איירי בצבוע בצבע אחר, כי היכי דדרשינן כלך ושיראין וסיריקין, וחוטי תכלת הוי טפי מינא דידיה מחוטי פשתן. וא"כ ליפשי הכי, דכי מקדים לבן של פשתן בטלית צמר לית לן בה! ויש לומר: כיון דקרא על כרחין לא איירי בצבוע תכלת, דהא כתיב מין כנף וכתיב פתיל תכלת – אלמא תכלת לאו מין דכנף הוי. ואע"ג דמ"מ הוי מינו טפי – לא חשיב מידי, דהא לא הוי בכלל מין כנף דקרא. ועוד יש לפרש: דצביעה דלאו מצוה לאו מידי היא. ותו, דתניא לקמן (דף מא:): טלית שכולה תכלת – כל מיני צבעונין פוטרין בה חוץ מקלא אילן, ופירש בקונטרס: פוטרין בה לשם לבן, דכיון דמין כנף [ליכא] לקיומי אין לך לחזור אחר לבן אלא שיהיו בה שני מינין, משמע דטלית לבנה בעי לבן. ובאידך ברייתא (שם) דתניא: טלית אין פוטר בה אלא מינה, פירש בקונטרס: אם אדומה יטיל בה חוטין אדומין ושני חוטין תכלת, אלמא ציבעא גריס! ולפי תירוץ ראשון ניחא, דציבעא הוי חד מינא בר מתכלת. וי"ל: דמדרבנן הוי. אי נמי יש לומר שם בע"א.

אלא לגרדומין וכו'. משמע כ] דאי אגרדום כולהו מיפסלי. ואור"ת: דעכשיו שנותנין ד' חוטין ב' משום לבן וב' משום תכלת וכופלן לשמונה, צריך ליזהר דאם נפסקו שלשה מן החוטין – כא] שמא הם משלשה חוטין, ונמצא שלא נשארו ב' חוטין שלימין. ויש לדקדק קצת, דסוגיא זו כרבי אתיא דהשתא הוי מצוה אחת, והלכה כרבי מחבירו אבל לא מחביריו (עירובין דף מו:), וכ"ש מרבו, ורבי יוסי הגלילי רבו היה, ואהא סומכין שאין לנו תכלת [ומטילין לבן] ולרבנן אפי' בחד מיפסיל, דהא תרי מצות נינהו ולא תועיל האחת לחבירתה, דהוי כאילו איגרדם תכלת ומקלא לבן. ומיהו נראה, למאי דבעינן בלבן נמי ד' חוטין – א"כ חד מצוה נינהו, ואי לא בעינן אלא ב' – כ"ש דלא מעכבי, וכמאן דליתנהו הוו. ומיהו, לא מיסתבר דסוגיין לא הוי כרבנן, דהא דאמרי בני ר' חייא הוי דלא כהלכתא. *ועוד י"ל: דאי איגרדם תכלת וקם אלבן, היינו דנפסק החוט כב] מעיקרו ולא נשתייר אלא כל שהוא (מן הלבן) – דקרינן כה"ג גרדומיו בכל שהוא, ולא הוי כאילו נפסקו שניהם לגמרי, (ל"ה וכל זה) [דהואיל מצוה אחת היא – מועיל השלם לחבירו. אבל לרבנן נפסק חוט א' מעיקרו פסול, אלא אם נשאר כדי עניבה. והא דאמרי בני ר' חייא: גרדומי תכלת וכו' משמע דאיגרדום כל ארבעתן, כי קראו לכל הציצית "תכלת", ובנשאר כדי עניבה]:

כדי לענבם. מתוך פי' הקונטרס דבסמוך, גבי הא דמוכח רבא דצריך לקשור על כל חוליא וכו' וכיון דמישתרי עילאי מישתרי כולהו, ופי': לית ליה הא דאמרן לעיל כדי שיעור עניבה, משמע דסבירא ליה דעניבה חוץ לקשר אחרון שבציצית. ויתכן יותר לפרש דשיעור עניבה סמוך לכנף קאמר, והשתא לא פליג אלעיל. וכן משמע קצת בספרי בפרשת "גדילים": בד"א – בתחילה, אבל בשירים גרדומים כל שהוא. משמע דאגדילים קאי. וכן נראה להוכיח משם שהקשר הוא מן הד' אל הד'. דאי מחוט הכריכה ואחד מן החוטין, כמו שהיה נוהג ר"ת כשהיה נפסק אחד מן החוטין הנכרכין, ולא מחוט הכורך – היכי מישתרי הקשר בכך? דבשלמא אי מן הד' לד', כשנפסק האחד מד' ואינו מקשר סותר הקשר! וי"ל: דהכי קאמר: דמסתמא *(כשיעור דאי מד') אכתי קיימא (תלתא) אבל אחד תו לא קאי.

כיון דאישתרי חד אישתרו כולהו. ואין כאן גדיל. ואפילו *)למ"ד או גדיל או פתיל מוכח שפיר, דאפי' פתיל ליכא, דהא סופו ליפול. ולא מוכח מידי אלא דבעי קשרא אחרינא, אבל מהא לא מוכח דצריך לקשור על כל חוליא. ונראה **)שמביא כן דבמקום אחר לא אשכחן אתרא דמסתבר טפי, אי לא בין חוליא לחוליא, כדי להפסיק.
קשר

*) [לקמן לט:] **) נ"ל שמוכיח כן כו' נ"ק

שיטה מקובצת

א] לרבי עכובי מעכבי אהדדי [כלומר] כיון דאמרת חיסר מצוה דלבן והוי לבן כמאן דליתא גם התכלת לרבי לאו כלום היא משמע הא לרבנן ניחא ולפרש"י דמתני' דכי לית ליה תכלת צריך לעשות ד' חוטין של לבן ואין למעט מנין החוטין לרבנן נמי תיקשי דכיון דלבן כמאן דליתיה (דאיכא) [דמי] חוטין דתכלת לאו כלום נינהו: ב] תיבות אמר רמב"ח כו' שכולה תכלת נמחק: ג] לסדין בציצית לאו דוקא וה"ה בשאר טליתות לבנים והכי נמי מסתברא דבסמוך לא מצי לאוקמא רישא דמתני' דתכלת אינה מעכבת את הלבן אלא בטלית שכולה תכלת אלמא בשאר טליתות מצוה לאקדומי לבן ברישא כמו שמפרש הכנף מין כנף וסתם טליתות לבנים הי': ד] תיבת ליה נמחק: ה] מידי ציבעא גרים. תימה מאי קאמר אר"י דציבעא גרים דהא לקמן קאמר טלית אינו פוטר בה אלא מינה ופרש"י אינו פוטר לשם לבן אלא אם אדומה היא יטיל בה שני חוטין אדומין ושני חוטין תכלת וכן בשאר גוונים אלמא בציבעא תליא מילתא וי"ל דה"פ מידי ציבעא גרים אפי' כולה תכלת נמי מצוה להקדים לבן מדקתני בברייתא לעיל מצוה להקדים לבן לתכלת ורוב טליתות לבנות הן וכן

הגהות הב"ח

(א) רש"י ד"ה אריוך וכו' דינא הס"ד ואח"כ מ"ה לסדין בציצית להכי:

[עי' תוספות נזיר כד: ד"ה אמר שמואל כו' פירוש על זה]
ותכלת אע"ג דשל צמר הוי מצוה להקדים לפשתן טפי הס"ד נ"ק
נ"א מקדים
דהאי מתני' כו'
ואיבעיא נמי נ"ק
לסדין בציצית להכי כו' נ"ק
קדושין לו: וש"נ
תוס' דפרה פי"א לעיל לה:
עד הגדיל נ"ק
[לקמן לט.]
נ"ל מקלמן וכו"א מופסקין מעיקרא הוו וגו' רש"ח ובמשמעות גרדומים מקלמן הוה איהו עליון
נ"ק
נ"ק
וי"מ דאי נ"ק
עי' בהרא"ש
כי איפשרי תלתא אכתי קיימי תלתא אבל אחד תו לא קאי וגירסת רש"ק כשיש עוד כו'

ה) ונפקא מינה במה שפרש"י לקמן אינו פוטר אלא מינה דהשתא שאין לנו תכלת מ"מ צריך לצבוע הציצית מצבע הטלית ור"י מפרש פי' אחר לקמן טלית אינו פוטר אלא מינה כדאמר רבא לקמן כתיב הכנף מין כנף וכתוב צמר ופשתים הא כיצד צמר ופשתן כו': מידי ציבעא גרים וכו' פי' הצבע של תכלת שבטלית גרים להקדים תכלת ללבן כיון דאיירי ברוב טליתות שהן לבנות ומין כנף שהוא לבן קודם לתכלת לעולם יש לנו לומר שהתכלת מאוחר ואין לפרש מידי ציבעא גרים להיות נקרא מין כנף וירצה לומר דאפי' בטלית של תכלת נקרא לבן מין כנף לפי שהקדים הכתוב הא ליכא למימר דהא אמרינן לקמן טלית אין פוטר בה אלא מינה ופי' מין צבע טלית אי ירוק לירוק ואדום לאדום. תו"ח: ו] צריך לקשור על כל חוליא לאו דוקא אלא מלבד קשר העליון לפי שאדם מגביה ידו עם ציציותיו וצריך קשר אחר סמוך לטלית ובתוס' אחרות לאו דוקא על כל חוליא דמהכא לא שמעינן זה אלא כלומר צריך לקשור קשר אחר מלבד הקשר שלאחר הגדיל דדרך הוא לקשור אחר הגדיל ומדאמרי בני רבי חייא שמעינן דמלבד אותו קשר סמוך לגדיל צריך קשר אחר סמוך לכנף דאי ס"ד לא צריך כו' שהרי עתיד להתיר וליפול והוי הקשר כמאן דליתיה ובעינן קשר כדמוכח רבא בסמוך ש"מ קשר עליון דאורייתא: ז] הקדים לבן אין תכלת מעכבתו ואין צריך לפסוק אלא יתן התכלת אחריו והא פשיטא דהא דינא הכי להקדים לבן ומאי: ח] גמי דמתני' הקדים קתני: ט] לבן כדקתני ברישא דלעיל ומצוה להקדים לבן לתכלת כו' טליתות לבנות הן ומין כנף הס"ד והשאר נמחק: י] נפסקו הפתילין של ציצית: יא] כדי לענבן כל שמונה: יב] עוביין הוו קשים למיענבי הס"ד: יג] דקים הוי כשרים: יד] דמינכרא מצותייהו טפי: טו] תכלת כשר צריך לקשור על כל חוליא וחוליא מפרש לקמן כמה שיעור של גדיל שלש פעמים צריך לעשות קשרים דאי ס"ד אין צריך לעשות קשר אלא למטה לסוף הגדיל הא דאמרי בני רבי חייא גרדומי תכלת כשרין (בהדי) אמאי: טז] קצת מן הפתיל הסמוכים לגדיל משתרי מן הגדיל ואין שם גדיל כלל ואמאי כשרים: יח] ובגרדומין דוקפי הוו איהו עליון ורבא לית ליה הא דפרשה לעיל דבעי גרדום שיעור עניבה: יט] בציצית גליון וי"מ ולכך נקט סדין ולא בטלית צמר לבנה דגם בלבן כו' לפי שתכלת הוי שפיר מינה לטלית צמר דאמו ציבעא גרים לה כדפריך לקמן וקשה דעדיין לא ידע הך פרכא ועוד דלקמן ניחא דרוב טליתות לבנים וזה צבוע פריך שפיר אטו ציבעא גרים אבל הכא לא שייך ציבעא גרים לכך נראה דנקט סדין דמסתמא הוא לבן ואי נקט שאר טליתות היה לנו לפרש לבנה. תו"ח: כ] משמע דמ"מ בעינן ששארו או התכלת או הלבן שלימים ואי: כא] שמא פי' דשמא הן שלשתן מצד אחד ובצרי להו ששה דלדידהו ודאי איכא היכרא שהיו משני צבעים וידוע שאחד מן הצבעים קיים אם כן אינם מצד אחד. תו"ח: כב] מעיקרו. עיין הרא"ש הלכות ציצית:

בלאו דלא תסור. כגון טלטול ד] איסור מדרבנן, ואבנים מקורזלות מותר להכניס לבית הכסא משום כבוד הבריות, אבל לשאת משא דכתיב בהדיא לא דחי כבוד הבריות. איכא דאמרי מהתם אמר ליה. ה] רבינא: איפסיק קרנא דחוטא. כרמלית. מותר לטלטל בתוכה מן התורה. ו] ל"א ועיקר: האי מאן דגרייה לגלימיה – קרנות טליתו כפל *קשר, ודומה כאילו קיפלן ואין לה כנפות, כדי להפקיעה מתורת ציצית. לא עשה כלום. לפוטרה מציצית. מ"ט כמאן דשדי דמי? וכל ד' כנפים שסופה לחזור לתחילתה. אמר רב דימי האי מאן דחייטיה לגלימיה. כפל כנפותיה כאילו הן מקוצעות, ותפר הכפלים שלא ישובו, אפ"ה לא עשה ולא כלום להפקיעה מן הציצית. דכל כמה דלא פסק ליה ש"מ מיבעי ליה, ועדיין הן מן הטלית. וללשון ראשון קשיא דתניא בפרק "התכלת" (לקמן מא.) שאם כפלה ותפרה שחייבת.

(דברים יז) בלאו °ד"לא תסור". ואיכא דאמרי: מהתם א"ל, וא"ל: מאי דעתיך, [אא] א] למישדייה? והאמר מר: גדול כבוד הבריות שדוחה את לא תעשה שבתורה! והא תרגומה רב בר שבא קמיה דרב כהנא: בלאו ד"לא תסור"! הכא נמי כרמלית דרבנן היא.§

הדרן עלך הקומץ

התכלת [א]אינה מעכבת את הלבן, והלבן אינו מעכב את התכלת. *[ב]תפלה *של יד אינה מעכבת את של ראש, ושל ראש אינה מעכבת את של יד.§ **גמ'** לימא מתני' דלא כרבי; דתניא: (במדבר טו) °"וראיתם אותו" – מלמד שמעכבין זה את זה, דברי רבי, וחכ"א: אין מעכבין. מ"ט דרבי? דכתיב: °"הכנף" – *מין כנף, וכתיב: "פתיל תכלת", ואמר רחמנא: "וראיתם אותו" – עד דאיכא תרוייהו בחד. ורבנן? "וראיתם אותו", כל חד לחודיה משמע. לימא דלא כרבי? אמר רב יהודה אמר רב: אפי' תימא רבי, לא נצרכא אלא ב] לקדם; דתניא: ג] [ג]מצוה להקדים לבן לתכלת, ואם הקדים תכלת ללבן – יצא, אלא שחיסר מצוה. מאי חיסר מצוה? אילימא

הדרן עלך הקומץ את המנחה

התכלת אינה מעכבת את הלבן. ואע"ג דמצוה לתת תכלת ב' חוטין ז] בציצית כדמפרש לקמן, אפ"ה אין זה מעכב את זה, ואי עביד ארבעתן תכלת או ארבעתן לבן יצא. **גמ'** מין כנף. היינו לבן, דרוב טליתות של פשתים הן ולבנות. תכלת. צמר צבוע, כדאמרינן (יבמות דף ד:): מקשש כיתנא – תכלת עמרא. ח] לא נצרכא. מתניתין דקתני: אין מעכבין זה את זה. אלא להקדים. שאם הקדים המאוחר, דהיינו תכלת, דלבן כתיב ברישא. הכנף מין כנף. ואם הקדים התכלת ט] את הלבן אינה מעכבת, ואין צריך לפסוק התכלת, אלא יתן הלבן אחריו. אילימא

התכלת אינה מעכבת את הלבן. מצוה לתת ב' חוטין תכלת וב' חוטין לבן בציצית. ומשמע לכאורה דאין זה מעכב את זה – שאם הטיל שני חוטין מן האחד יצא, כי *הנך דקתני: תפלה של יד אינה מעכבת את של ראש כו'. אבל בקונטרס פירש: אי עבד ארבעתן תכלת או ארבעתן לבן יצא. וכן אנו י] נוהגין. ובגמרא *מוכיח כן: והלא כל המטיל תכלת בסדינו בירושלים אינו אלא מן המתמיהין, ומפרש דאסוריה גזירה משום קלא אילן. ופריך: לא יהא אלא לבן! משמע דאי הוי לבן אין כאן איסורא, אע"ג דבלא הני דקלא אילן איכא שני חוטי לבן. ומיהו יש לדחות, דאע"ג דבשני חוטי לבן איכא מצוה, כי רמי טפי ליכא איסור כלאים, דאין זה מוסיף על המצוה, ד"גדיל" – שנים, "גדילים" – ארבעה, דדרשינן מיניה שנים לבן ושנים תכלת – לאו למעוטי טפי קאתי, כדאשכחן גבי ערבי נחל דדרשינן (סוכה דף לד:): "ערבי" – שתים, ונוהגים להשים הרבה בלולב. ולקמן גבי טלית שכולה תכלת כו' דאמרינן: בטלית בת שמונה חוטין, פירש בקונטרס שאין כאן איסור בל תוסיף כיון שכל השמונה בכרך אחד, ולא דמי להטיל למוטלת. והיינו טעמא, דבהטיל למוטלת לבד שייך בל תוסיף, משום דציצית אחד על כנף אחד אמר רחמנא. ומהתם נמי יש ראיה דכי ליכא אלא לבן או תכלת בעינן לעולם ד' חוטין, דמשמע דבטלית בת ד' חוטין לא חיישינן שמא יסיר ב' מהן ויניח בטלית *אחר, דארבעתן מצוה. מיהו, בסוף "אלו הן הנחנקין" (סנהדרין דף פח:) משמע דאם הוסיף חוטין בכרך אחד פסול, גבי זקן ממרא, דא"ר אלעזר: אינו חייב אלא על דבר שעיקרו מדברי תורה ופירושו מדברי סופרים, ויש בו להוסיף ואם הוסיף גורע, ואנו אין לנו אלא תפילין. ופריך: והאיכא ציצית! ומשני: אי קשר העליון לאו דאורייתא – האי לחודיה קאי והאי לחודיה קאי, ואי קשר העליון דאורייתא – גרוע ועומד הוא. והאי דלא מוקי לה התם בהטיל למוטלת – משום דדילמא לא מיפסלא בכך, אע"ג דעובר על בל תוסיף אם נתכוין להוסיף, ואם לא נתכוין להוסיף שרי. ומאן דמפליג לקמן (דף מא:) בין טלית בת ארבעה לטלית בת שמונה, ה"פ: בטלית בת ארבעה – דהיינו שנים חוטין, שהן ארבעה כשהן כפולין. שלא היה לו תכלת, ונותן אלו שצבוען קלא אילן במקום לבן. וטלית בת ח' היינו בת ד' שהן כפולין, שיסבור *כולם תכלת ויקח מהן לפטור טלית אחרת. ומיהו קשה לפי' זה, דבת ד' נמי יסבור שהוא תכלת ויוסיף עליהן לבן של פשתן! ועוד, דההיא ברייתא דמוקי בבת ד', קתני: מביא תכלת ודבר אחר ותולה בה, וקלא אילן לא יביא ואם הביא כשר – אלמא משמע דמיירי בתולה קלא אילן עם התכלת, ועל כרחיך ארבעה ושמונה דוקא קאמר, בלא כפולות! ושמא כל מה שמוסיף חוטין מד' עד ח' לאו מוסיף הוא ולא מיפסיל בכך, כדאשכחן אמוראי לקמן (דף מב.) דרב אחא בר יעקב רמי ד' ורב אחא מדפתי רמי ח'. והשתא לא פליגי כולי האי, אלא דמר עביד הפחות ומר עביד היתר, ובסנהדרין מיירי דמוסיף טפי מתמניא. וצריך טעם מנלן, דבשלמא *אי פליגי בהא, דמאן דרמי ד' סבר כדדרשינן: "גדיל" – שנים, "גדילים" – ארבעה, ומאן דרמי תמניא סבר ד"גדילים" דקאמר רחמנא אכל מין ומין קאי, גדילים מלבן וגדילים מתכלת, דהיינו צמר ופשתים, דעלייהו קאי. אבל אי לא פליגי, מה סברא היא זו דלאי בעי עביד הכי ואי בעי עביד הכי? וי"ל דכל זה יש במשמעות "גדילים", דאי עביד תכלת ולבן בין שניהם ד' חוטין – "גדילים" קרינא ביה, ואי עביד מכל חד וחד גדילים, כגון ד' חוטין לבן וד' חוטין תכלת – "גדילים" נמי קרינא ביה, ולאו מוסיף הוא, אבל אי רמי טפי מוסיף הוא וגרוע ועומד הוא. ועוד צריך טעם, מנלן דכי לית ליה אלא או לבן או תכלת, דלא מיפטר בתרי חוטי לחודייהו עד דרמי ד'? ושמא משום דדרשינן: "גדיל" – שנים, "גדילים" – ד', בין יש בו מין אחד בין יש בו שני מינין. וקצת קשה הא דאמרי' בגמרא: אם הקדים תכלת ללבן יצא אלא שחיסר מצוה, מאי חיסר מצוה? [אילימא חיסר מצוה] דלבן וקיים מצוה דתכלת, לרבי עכובי מעכבי אהדדי! דמשמע דאי לא מעכבי ניחא, אלמא אע"ג דחיסר מצוה דלבן – קיים מצוה דתכלת בב' חוטין! ויש לומר: להכשיר תכלת מיהא מהני לבן, דקרינא ביה גדילים ד'. וא"ת: ומנלן דבעינן ב' חוטין לבן וב' חוטין דתכלת? דילמא אגדילים קפיד קרא, אפילו חד מהאי וג' מהאי! ויש לומר: כיון דתרי מיני בעי רחמנא, סברא הוא שיהיו שוין. ועוד, "פתיל תכלת" כתיב, ו"פתיל" משמע תרי, כדדרשינן פרק "בא לו" (יומא עב.): "וקילך פתילים", "פתיל" – שנים, "פתילים" – ד'. ולבן נמי לא פחות מתרי, דקדיש טפי, כדאמרינן בגמרא דמתחיל בלבן ומסיים בלבן, דמעלין בקודש ולא מורידין. ומיהו, טעם זה ד"פתיל" לא יתכן, דבפרק "בא לו" משמע "וקילך" דמקלך אחד לשנים, והכא על כרחין לא משמע תרי, כדמוכח בספרי בפרשת ["שלח] לך" ובפרשת "כי תצא": "ועשו להם ציצית" – שומע אני חוט אחד בפני עצמו? ת"ל: "גדילים", כמה גדילים נעשין? אין [גדיל] פחות משלשה חוטין כדברי בית הילל. משמע דמ"פתיל" לא הוה שמעינן אלא חד. ועוד, דאי "פתיל" משמע תרי, ו"הכנף" מין כנף לכל הפחות חד, א"כ בלא "גדילים" נמי תיפוק ליה תלתא! וצריך לומר שחולק על התלמוד שלנו, דמשמע דחד מתכלת מהני. ומה שאנו כופלים הד' לח', סמכינן אהא דאמרינן לקמן (דף מב.): רב אחא בר יעקב רמי ד' ועייף להו מיעף ומעייל להו בגלימא ואדיק להו כו' עד: מר בריה דרבנא עביד כי דידן, ופירש בקונטרס דלא אדיק להו. ועוד תניא בספרי, ב"ש אומרים: ד' של צמר וד' של תכלת. ואם תאמר: היא גופה מנלן שצריך לכופלן? ואי הוה מפרשינן עשה גדיל ופותליהו מתוכו, היינו שצריך לפותלו כעין פתילה שהיא כפולה – ניחא, אבל בקונט' לא פירש כן. וגם אפרש.

כתיב הכנף מין הכנף. ואפילו לתנא דבי ר"י פ"ק דיבמות (דף ד:) דפליג ארבא דדריש הכי, לא פליג אלא אהא דמרבה שאר מינים, אבל "הכנף" מין כנף דריש שפיר. **ואם** הקדים תכלת ללבן יצא. תימה: כיון דמקרא הוא דדרשינן דלבן ברישא – נימא דמעכב, דהא לא בעינן שנה הכתוב לעכב אלא בקדשים! ויש לומר: דלית לן למימר דאסדר לבד יקפיד הכתוב לעכב, כמו גבי חליצה (יבמות דף קה.): הקדים רקיקה לחליצה מה שעשה עשוי. ואע"ג דכתיב "ככה" עיכובא לא קאי אלא אחסרון מעשה. אילימא

עין משפט נר מצוה:
הא דקתני נ"ק
א א מיי' פ"א מהלכות ציצית הלכה ד סמג עשין כו:
[לקמן מ.]
ב ב מיי' פ"ד מהלכות תפילין הלכה ד סמג עשין כב טור וש"ע א"ח סימן כו ס"א:
ג ג מיי' פ"א מהלכות ציצית הלכה ז סמג עשין כו:
[ערכין ג:]
אחר נ"ק

מסורת הש"ס:
וקשר נ"ק
[עי' תוספות ערכין ג: ד"ה של יד]
[לקמן לט.]
שכולם נ"ק
נ"א פליגי היכא למימר בהא פליגי דמאן כו' נ"ק
נ"ק
נ"ק
נ"ק

שיטה מקובצת

א] דעתיך אשדייה גדול כבוד הבריות: ב] אלא להקדים: ג] מצוה להקדים לבן לתכלת. פ"ה לתחוב הלבן בכנף תחילה ולא נהירא דבהא מאי חביבותא דמצוה איכא וי"ל דמצוה להקדים חוליות של לבן לחוליא של תכלת כדאמרינן לקמן מתחיל בשל לבן ומסיים בשל לבן. תו"ח: ובתוס' אחרות כתבו מצוה להקדים פרש"י מתני' דקתני אין מעכבין זה לזה להקדים המאוחר מתוך פי' משמע דמיירי לענין תחיבת החוטין בכנף דמצוה להקדים לבן ואם הקדים תכלת ללבן לא מעכב ולא נהירא דמאי שייך לומר הקדמה בדבר שאינו ניכר שהרי אחר שנתחבו שניהם אין ניכר מי הקדים לתחיבות לכך נראה לפרש דמיירי בבריכות החוטין דמצוה להקדים חוליא של לבן תחלה כדאמר לקמן מתחיל בשל לבן ומסיים בשל לבן וקאמר שאם הקדים חוליא של תכלת לשל לבן אין מעכב וה"פ דמתני' הלבן שראוי להקדים תחילה אינו מעכב התכלת אם הקדימו תחילה ללבן ולקמן מפרש התינח

התכלת אינו מעכב את הלבן הלבן אינו מעכב את התכלת מאי היא ע"כ: ד] טלטול אבנים איסור: ה] אמר ליה היכא דאפסיק אמר ליה: ו] מן ל"א עד סוף הפרק נמחק: ז] חוטין ולבן שני חוטין בציצית: ח] עמרא וס"ד ומה"ד תרוייהו בחד לבן ותכלת ביחד ולא כמתני': ט] התכלת אין הלבן מעכב וא"צ: י] נוהגין [והא] דפריך לא יהא אלא לבן היינו מפרשים דהיכא דליכא תפילת בב' חוטי לבן סגי ולא רצה לפרש דבב' חוטין תכלת או בב' חוטי לבן יצא והויא דומיא דתפלה של יד אינו מעכב של ראש ושל ראש אינו מעכב של יד דא"כ הוי קשיא הא דאמר לקמן ולא יהא אלא לבן כו' מאי קא פריך מ"מ הוו להו חוטין יותר מדאי ודוי להו אותן נוספין כלאים שלא במקום מצוה ולפרש"י ניחא. ויש לדחות דאפילו תימא דסגי לן בב' חוטי לבן אם אין לו תכלת לא קשיא לן הא דאמר לא יהא אלא לבן שהרי אין זו בל תוסיף בתוספת חוטין כדאיתא לקמן רב רמיה מדפתי כו' ואע"ג דבסנהדרין קאמר גבי זקן ממרא דאינו חייב אלא שישנו בבל תוסיף ויש בו לגרוע ואין לנו אלא תפילין ופריך והאיכא מצות ציצית כו' משמע דשייך בל תוסיף בציצית וי"ל דמשכחת שפיר בל תוסיף כגון שהוסיף מין אחר שאינו לא צמר ולא פשתן. תוס' אחרות:

קצח א ב מיי' פ"ד מהל' תפילין הלכה א ב טוש"ע א"ח סימן כז סעיף א ט:

קצט ג מיי' פי"ט מהל' שבת הלכה כ סמג עשין כו טוש"ע א"ח סי' יג סעיף א וסימן שא סעיף לח:

ר ד מיי' פ"ג מהלכות ציצית הלכה ג טוש"ע א"ח סי' י סעיף ב:

רא ה טוש"ע שם סעיף ג:

רב ו מיי' פכ"ד מהלכות כלים הלכה יא:

רג ז מיי' פ"א מהלכות ציצית הלכה יז טוש"ע א"ח סי' י סעיף ג:

גירסת רש"א ר"י שאל את נ"א וכ"ג צ"ק

[וע"ע תוס' ב"ק יא: ד"ה בכור]

[עיין מה שכיינתי על לדו של תוס' ב"מ סא. ד"ה אלא לאו]

תורה אור

°*"אַךְ" חִלֵּק! שָׁאנֵי הָכָא, דִּבְגוּלְגּוֹלֶת תָּלָא רַחֲמָנָא. אָמַר מָר: "יָדְךָ" – זוֹ קִיבּוֹרֶת. מְנָלַן? דְּת"ר: °"עַל יָדְךָ" – זוֹ גּוֹבַהּ שֶׁבַּיָּד; אַתָּה אוֹמֵר: זוֹ גּוֹבַהּ שֶׁבַּיָּד, אוֹ אֵינוֹ אֶלָּא עַל יָדְךָ מַמָּשׁ? אָמְרָה תּוֹרָה: הַנַּח תְּפִילִּין בַּיָּד וְהַנַּח תְּפִילִּין בָּרֹאשׁ, מַה לְּהַלָּן בְּגוֹבַהּ שֶׁבָּרֹאשׁ – אַף כָּאן בְּגוֹבַהּ שֶׁבַּיָּד. רַבִּי אֱלִיעֶזֶר אוֹמֵר: אֵינוֹ צָרִיךְ, הֲרֵי הוּא אוֹמֵר: °"וְהָיָה לְךָ לְאוֹת" – א] לְךָ לְאוֹת, וְלֹא לַאֲחֵרִים לְאוֹת. ר' יִצְחָק *אוֹמֵר: אֵינוֹ צָרִיךְ, הֲרֵי הוּא אוֹמֵר: °"וְשַׂמְתֶּם אֶת דְּבָרַי אֵלֶּה עַל לְבַבְכֶם וּקְשַׁרְתֶּם" – שֶׁתְּהֵא אשִׂימָה כְּנֶגֶד הַלֵּב. ר' חִיָּיא ב] וְרַב אַחָא בְּרֵיהּ דְּרַב אָוְיָא מְכַוֵּין וּמַנַּח לֵיהּ לַהֲדֵי לִיבֵּיהּ. רַב אַשִׁי הֲוָה יָתֵיב קַמֵּיהּ דְּאַמֵּימָר, הֲוָה צִירְיָא בִּידֵיהּ וְקָא מִתַּחְזְיָין תְּפִילִּין, אֲמַר לֵיהּ, לָא סָבַר לָהּ מָר: לְךָ לְאוֹת – וְלֹא לַאֲחֵרִים לְאוֹת? אֲמַר לֵיהּ: בִּמְקוֹם לְךָ לְאוֹת אִיתְּמַר. בגּוֹבַהּ שֶׁבָּרֹאשׁ מְנָלַן? דְּת"ר: "בֵּין עֵינֶיךָ" – זוֹ גּוֹבַהּ שֶׁבָּרֹאשׁ; אַתָּה אוֹמֵר: זוֹ גּוֹבַהּ שֶׁבָּרֹאשׁ, אוֹ אֵינוֹ אֶלָּא בֵּין עֵינֶיךָ מַמָּשׁ? נֶאֱמַר כָּאן "בֵּין עֵינֶיךָ", וְנֶאֱמַר לְהַלָּן °"לֹא תָשִׂימוּ קׇרְחָה בֵּין עֵינֵיכֶם לָמֵת", מַה *לְּהַלָּן בְּגוֹבַהּ שֶׁבָּרֹאשׁ, מָקוֹם שֶׁעוֹשֶׂה קׇרְחָה – אַף כָּאן בְּגוֹבַהּ שֶׁל רֹאשׁ, מָקוֹם שֶׁעוֹשֶׂה קׇרְחָה. ר' יְהוּדָה אוֹמֵר: אֵינוֹ צָרִיךְ, אָמְרָה תּוֹרָה: הַנַּח תְּפִילִּין בַּיָּד הַנַּח תְּפִילִּין בָּרֹאשׁ, מַה לְּהַלָּן בְּמָקוֹם הָרָאוּי לִיטַּמֵּא בְּנֶגַע אֶחָד – אַף כָּאן בְּמָקוֹם הָרָאוּי לִיטַּמֵּא בְּנֶגַע אֶחָד; לְאַפּוֹקֵי "בֵּין עֵינֶיךָ", דְּאִיכָּא בָּשָׂר ג] וְשֵׂעָר, דְּאִיכָּא שֵׂעָר לָבָן וְאִיכָּא נַמִּי שֵׂעָר צָהוֹב.§ "אַרְבַּע צִיצִיּוֹת מְעַכְּבוֹת זוֹ אֶת זוֹ, שֶׁאַרְבַּעְתָּן מִצְוָה אַחַת".§ מַאי בֵּינַיְיהוּ? אָמַר רַב יוֹסֵף: סָדִין בְּצִיצִית אִיכָּא בֵּינַיְיהוּ. רָבָא בַּר אָהִינָא אָמַר: טַלִּית בַּעֲלַת חָמֵשׁ אִיכָּא ד] בֵּינַיְיהוּ. רָבִינָא אָמַר: דְּרַב הוּנָא אִיכָּא בֵּינַיְיהוּ, *דְּאָמַר רַב הוּנָא: גהַיּוֹצֵא בְּטַלִּית שֶׁאֵינָהּ מְצוּיֶּיצֶת כְּהִלְכָתָהּ בְּשַׁבָּת – חַיָּיב חַטָּאת. אָמַר רַב שֵׁישָׁא בְּרֵיהּ דְּרַב אִידִי: דהַאי מַאן דְּבַצְרֵיהּ לִגְלִימֵיהּ – לָא עֲבֵיד וְלָא כְּלוּם, שַׁוְויֵהּ טַלִּית בַּעֲלַת חָמֵשׁ. אָמַר רַב מְשַׁרְשְׁיָא: ההַאי מַאן דְּצַיְּירֵיהּ לִגְלִימֵיהּ – לָא עֲבַד וְלָא כְּלוּם; מַאי טַעְמָא? דִּכְמַאן דְּשַׁרְיֵיהּ דָּמֵי, *ותְנַן נַמִּי: כׇּל חֲמָתוֹת הַצְּרוּרוֹת טְהוֹרוֹת, חוּץ מִשֶּׁל עַרְבִיִּים. אָמַר רַב דִּימִי מִנְּהַרְדְּעָא: זהַאי מַאן דְּחַיְיטֵיהּ לִגְלִימֵיהּ – לָא עֲבַד וְלָא כְּלוּם, אִם אִיתָא דְּלָא מִיבָּעֵי לֵיהּ, לִיפְסוֹק וְלִישַׁדְיֵיהּ.§ "רַבִּי יִשְׁמָעֵאל אוֹמֵר: אַרְבַּעְתָּן אַרְבַּע מִצְוֹת".§ אָמַר רַב יְהוּדָה אָמַר שְׁמוּאֵל: הֲלָכָה כְּרַבִּי יִשְׁמָעֵאל. ה] וְלֵית הִלְכְתָא כְּוָתֵיהּ. רָבִינָא הֲוָה קָא אָזֵיל אַבַּתְרֵיהּ דְּמָר בַּר רַב אַשִׁי בְּשַׁבְּתָא דְּרִיגְלָא, אִיפְסִיק קַרְנָא דְּחוּטֵיהּ וְלָא אֲמַר לֵיהּ וְלָא מִידֵּי; כַּד מְטָא לְבֵיתֵיהּ, אֲמַר לֵיהּ: מֵהָתָם אִיפְּסִיק. א"ל: אִי אֲמַרְתְּ לִי, מֵהָתָם שְׁדִיתֵיהּ. וְהָא אָמַר מָר: *גָּדוֹל כְּבוֹד הַבְּרִיּוֹת שֶׁדּוֹחֶה אֶת לֹא תַעֲשֶׂה שֶׁבַּתּוֹרָה! תַּרְגּוּמַהּ רַב בַּר שַׁבָּא קַמֵּיהּ דְּרַב כָּהֲנָא: בְּלָאו

במדבר יח | שמות יג | שם | דברים יא | שם יד

אַךְ חִלֵּק. "אַךְ פָּדֹה תִפְדֶּה" (במדבר יח). וְהָאִי נַמִּי כִּנְטְרַף דָּמֵי, שֶׁהֲרֵי לֹא יִחְיֶה! בְּגוּלְגּוֹלֶת תָּלָא רַחֲמָנָא. לְפִדְיוֹן בְּכוֹר, דִּכְתִיב (שם ג): "חֲמֵשֶׁת שְׁקָלִים לַגּוּלְגּוֹלֶת", וְהָאִי אִית לֵיהּ תְּרֵי. וְאִי מִשּׁוּם "אַךְ חִלֵּק" – הַשְׁתָּא מִיהָא לָא מִית. גּוֹבַהּ. קִיבּוֹרֶת, דְּהוּא אֵצֶל הַכָּתֵף. יָדְךָ מַמָּשׁ. כַּף. מַה לְּהַלָּן בְּגוֹבַהּ שֶׁבָּרֹאשׁ. כִּדְיָלְפִינַן לְקַמָּן מִקְּרָאֵי. וְלֹא לַאֲחֵרִים לְאוֹת. שֶׁלֹּא יִרְאוּ הַחוּלָה. וְאִי בְּכַף, מִיתְחֲזֵי (א) לְכ"ע. קִיבּוֹרֶת כְּנֶגֶד הַלֵּב הִיא. הֲוָה צִירְיָא בִּידֵיהּ. מַכָּה הָיְתָה לוֹ אֵצֶל הַקִּיבּוֹרֶת, וְנִקְרַע חֲלוּקוֹ שָׁם כְּדֵי שֶׁלֹּא תִּדָּחֵק הַמַּכָּה, וְהָיוּ נִרְאִין הַתְּפִילִּין דֶּרֶךְ הַקְּרִיעָה. בִּמְקוֹם לְךָ לְאוֹת אִיתְּמַר. מָקוֹם שֶׁרוֹב בְּנֵי אָדָם אֵין נִרְאֶה לַאֲחֵרִים, דְּהַיְינוּ קִבּוֹרֶת, וּלְעוֹלָם אִם נִקְרַע שָׁרֵי. בֵּין עֵינֶיךָ ו] מַמָּשׁ. *בְּגוֹבַהּ עֵינָיו. שֶׁעוֹשֶׂה קׇרְחָה. ז] [שֶׁיֵּשׁ בּוֹ] שֵׂעָר, וְאִם מוֹרְטוֹ עוֹשֶׂה קׇרְחָה. יָד בְּנֶגַע א' – שֵׂעָר לָבָן, וְרֹאשׁ *בְּנֶגַע א' – שֵׂעָר צָהוֹב, דִּכְתִיב בְּפָרָשַׁת נְגָעִים גַּבֵּי ח] רֹאשׁ וְזָקָן *בָּעֵי שֵׂעָר צָהוֹב לְטַמְּאוֹ, אַלְמָא מְקוֹם שֵׂעָר מְטַמֵּא (בְּשֵׂעָר צָהוֹב). לְאַפּוֹקֵי בֵּין עֵינֶיךָ. דְּאִיכָּא שֵׂעָר דְּגַבּוֹת עֵינַיִם וְאִיכָּא בָּשָׂר, וּבָעֵי תַּרְתֵּי: שֵׂעָר לָבָן בְּבָשָׂר, וְשֵׂעָר צָהוֹב בִּמְקוֹם שֵׂעָר. מַאי בֵּינַיְיהוּ. מ"מ בֵּין לְמָר וּבֵין לְמָר בָּעֵינַן ד' צִיצִית, כִּדְכְתִיב (דברים כב): "עַל אַרְבַּע כַּנְפוֹת כְּסוּתְךָ"! סָדִין. דְּפִשְׁתָּן, בְּצִיצִית *בִּתְכֵלֶת דְּעַמְרָא הוּא, אִיכָּא בֵּינַיְיהוּ. לְת"ק דְּאָמַר מִצְוָה אַחַת הֵן, הִלְכָּךְ אִי חָסֵר סָדִין צִיצִית אֶחָד לֵיכָּא מִצְוָה, וַהֲווּ לְהוּ אִינָךְ כִּלְאַיִם. וּלְרַבִּי ט] יִשְׁמָעֵאל לָא הָווּ כִּלְאַיִם, דְּהַשָּׁלֹשׁ שֶׁנִּשְׁאֲרוּ שְׁלֹשָׁה מִצְוֹת הֵן. בַּעֲלַת חָמֵשׁ. שֶׁחָתַךְ מִקֶּרֶן הָא' בְּאַלַּכְסוֹן וַהֲווּ בֵּהּ שְׁנֵי קְרָנַיִם, וְתַנְיָא לְקַמָּן בְּ"הַתְּכֵלֶת" (דף מג.): טַלִּית בַּעֲלַת חָמֵשׁ חַיֶּיבֶת בְּצִיצִית, וְיָלֵיף מֵרִיבּוּיָא דַּ"אֲשֶׁר תְּכַסֶּה בָּהּ". לְת"ק דְּאָמַר מִצְוָה אַחַת הֵן, סָבַר: אַרְבָּעָה דַּוְקָא לְמִצְוָה אַחַת, וְכִי רַבִּי רַחֲמָנָא בַּעֲלַת חָמֵשׁ – לְהַטִּיל י] אַרְבַּע כַּנְפוֹתֶיהָ רַבְּיֵיהּ, וְלֹא לְהַטִּיל לְכָנָף חֲמִישִׁי, וּמִצְוַת צִיצִית בְּד' כְּנָפוֹת. וּלְר' יִשְׁמָעֵאל דְּאָמַר: אַרְבַּעְתָּן [אַרְבַּע] מִצְוֹת, כִּי רַבִּי רַחֲמָנָא בַּעֲלַת חָמֵשׁ נַמִּי, לְהַטִּיל (ב) לְכוּלְּהוּ רַבְּיָיהּ, דְּהָא כׇּל חַד מִצְוָה בְּאַנְפֵּי נַפְשָׁהּ יא]. דְּרַב הוּנָא אִיכָּא בֵּינַיְיהוּ כו'. וְכ"ע אִית לְהוּ דְּרַב הוּנָא. מִיהוּ הִטִּיל לְשָׁלֹשׁ וְלֹא לְד', לְת"ק הָוְיָא מְצוּיֶּיצֶת שֶׁלֹּא כְּהִלְכָתָהּ וְחַיָּיב חַטָּאת, דְּהָווּ לְהוּ צִיצִית מַשּׂוֹי. וּלְרַבִּי יִשְׁמָעֵאל יב] (נְהִי ד') הָוְיָא מְצוּיֶּיצֶת כְּהִלְכָתָהּ, דְּג' מִצְוֹת יג] (מִיהָא) אִיכָּא וְאֵינוֹ פָּסוּל, וּדְרַב הוּנָא בַּעֲשׂוּיָה בְּפָסוּל (ג) (דְּהָאִיכָּא שְׁלֹשָׁה מִצְוֹת). דְּבַצְרֵיהּ לִגְלִימָא. שֶׁחָתַךְ יד] אֶחָד מִן הַקְּרָנוֹת חֲתִיכָה כְּגוֹן פְּגִימָה, דְּנִרְאִין כִּשְׁנֵי קְרָנַיִם. לָא עֲבַד כְּלוּם. לְפוֹטְרָהּ מִן הַצִּיצִית. שַׁוְויֵהּ טַלִּית בַּעֲלַת ה'. וְחַיֶּיבֶת. הָאִי מַאן דְּצַיְּירֵיהּ לִגְלִימֵיהּ. שֶׁהָיְתָה טַלִּיתוֹ אֲרוּכָּה וּכְפָלָהּ, וְתָלָה הַצִּיצִית בְּקַרְנוֹת הַכֶּפֶל, אַף עַל גַּב שֶׁצְּרָרָהּ וּדְיבְּקָהּ שֶׁלֹּא תַּחֲזוֹר לְאֵיתָנָהּ – לָא עָבַד כְּלוּם. דְּסוֹפוֹ לְהַתִּיר וְלַחֲזוֹר לְאֵיתָנָהּ וְנִמְצְאוּ צִיצִית בְּאֶמְצָעִיתָהּ, וַאֲנַן כְּנָפוֹת בָּעֵינַן, הִלְכָּךְ מֵהַשְׁתָּא כְּמַאן דִּשְׁרְיָיהּ דָּמְיָא טו]. כׇּל חֲמָתוֹת. נוֹדוֹת הַצְּרוּרוֹת, שֶׁאֵין שׁוּלֵיהֶן תְּפוּרִין אֶלָּא צְרוּרִין – טְהוֹרִין, דְּאֵין מְקַבְּלִין טוּמְאָה, דְּרוֹאִין כְּאִילּוּ נִיתַּר הַקֶּשֶׁר וְלֵיכָּא בֵּית קִיבּוּל, וַהֲוֵי כִּכְלֵי הַנָּקוּב בְּמוֹצִיא רִימּוֹן. חוּץ מִשֶּׁל עַרְבִיִּים. דְּדַרְכָּן בְּכָךְ. הָאִי מַאן דְּחַיְיטֵיהּ לִגְלִימֵיהּ. שֶׁכָּפַל לְטַלִּיתוֹ כִּדְפָרִישִׁית, וּתְפָרָהּ שֶׁלֹּא תָּשׁוּב לְאֵיתָנָהּ, וְאַפ"ה לֹא עָשָׂה כְּלוּם, דִּכְמַאן טז] *דְּשַׁיְירֵיהּ דָּמְיָא. אִם אִיתָא דְּלָא מִיבַּעְיָא לֵיהּ. אִם אֲרוּכָּה הִיא לוֹ, וְאֵינָהּ צְרִיכָה לוֹ אֲרוּכָּה כׇּל כָּךְ – יז] לִפְסוֹק אוֹתוֹ כֶּפֶל וְלִישַׁדְיֵיהּ, וְאַחַר כָּךְ יִתְלֶה הַצִּיצִית*. הֲלָכָה כְּרַבִּי יִשְׁמָעֵאל. וְכִי הָנָךְ שִׁינּוּיֵי דַּאֲמַרַן לְעֵיל מַאי בֵּינַיְיהוּ. שַׁבְּתָא דְּרִגְלָא. שַׁבָּת יח] שֶׁדּוֹרְשִׁין בְּהִילְכוֹת הָרֶגֶל, כִּדְקַיְ"ל (פסחים דף ו.): שׁוֹאֲלִין בְּהִלְכוֹת הַפֶּסַח קוֹדֶם הַפֶּסַח ל' יוֹם. אִיפְסִיק קַרְנָא דְּחוּטֵי יט]. צִיצִית דְּמָר בַּר רַב אַשִׁי. מֵהָתָם. דְּאִיפְּסִיקָא. שְׁדִיתֵיהּ. הָיִיתִי מַשְׁלִיכָהּ מֵעָלַי, דְּלֵית הִלְכְתָא כְּרַבִּי יִשְׁמָעֵאל אֶלָּא כְּתַנָּא קַמָּא, וְכֵיוָן דְּחָסְרוּ – אֵין בָּהּ מִצְוָה, וְהָוְיָא כְּמַשּׂוֹי. בְּלָאו

ומיהו הוה אמינא לשנויי דנהרג איצטריכא ליה, דהוה אמינא דווקא מת מעצמו, דמוכח מילתא דנפל הוא. וכן פירש שם בקונטרס, דמת מעצמו לא איצטריכא ליה דאין פודין, דהא כתיב (במדבר יח): "ופדויו מבן חדש תפדה", אבל נהרג איצטריכא ליה לאשמועינן דלא אמרינן דאי לא קטליה הוי חיי, ולאו נפל הוא ולפרקיה. וקשה לפירושו, ד"ופדויו מבן חודש" גזירת הכתוב הוא, ולא לאפוקיה מתורת נפל, אלא אפילו קים ליה בגויה שכלו לו חדשיו. אע"ג דמהכא נפקא דכל ששהה ל' יום באדם אינו נפל. מידי דהוה אבן שמנה ימים דבהמה, דילפינן מינה דאינו נפל, אע"ג דגזירת הכתוב, כי קים לן בגוויה שכלו לו חדשיו, כדמוכח בפ"ק דראש השנה (דף ו:) דאין מונין לו אלא משעת הרצאה. כ] ועוד אמרי' בפרק "יש בכור" (בכורות דף מט.) גבי פודה את בנו בתוך שלשים יום ונתאכלו המעות בתוך ל' יום – אין בנו פדוי. עוד אמרי' בירושלמי בפ"ק דקדושין, גמרא: "בהמה גסה ניקנית במסירה", *רבי יהודה אמר שאל רבי אלעזר: בכור שנטרף בתוך ל' יום, א"ל: דומה לו כמי שמת ופטור מחמש סלעים של בן. ואי בנהרג – מאי שייך למימר כמי שמת? ומפרש ר"ת דנטרף כא] היינו דנעשה טריפה אע"פ שחיה יותר מל' יום, וכיון שיש לו שני ראשים היינו טריפה, דכל יתר כנטול דמי. מ"ר*.

מה להלן במקום הראוי ליטמא בנגע אחד כו'. וא"ת: אי מה להלן במקום בשר אף כאן במקום בשר, כגון פדחתו! מ"ר*.

האי מאן דחייטיה לגלימיה לא עבד כלום דכמאן דשריה [דמי]. פירש בקונטרס בלשון *אחר: שנכפל טליתו ותפרה שלא תשוב לאיתנה, אפ"ה לא עבד כלום. ולא כב] היה לו לפרש כן, דלקמן בפ' "התכלת" (דף מא.) תניא: טלית כפולה חייבת בציצית, ורבי שמעון פוטר, ושוין שאם כפלה ותפרה שחייבת. אלמא שחייבת במקום הכפילות להטיל שם ציצית, ולא אמרינן כמאן דשרייה דמי ויועילה ציצית שבקרנותיה.

הדרן עלך הקומץ את המנחה

[פסחים ה. וש"נ]

[ברכות יג:]
בין גבות עיניו צ"ק

מטמא בנגע צ"ק

דבעי צ"ק

צ"ק מ"ז

דתכלת צ"ק

[קידושין לו.]

הגהות הב"ח

(א) רש"י ד"ה ולא לאחרים וכו' לכ"ע הס"ד ואח"כ מ"ה נגד הלב קיבורת: (ב) ד"ה בעלת חמש וכו' להטיל לכנפיה רבייה דהא כל חד: (ג) ד"ה דרב הונא וכו' בפסול דליכא שלשה מצות:

צ"ק
שבת קלט. ע"ש

כלים פכ"ו מ"ד

רש"א מ"ז

רש"א מ"ז

צ"ק מ"ז

ברכות יט: [שבת פא: לד:
עירובין מא: מגילה ג:]

צ"ל דשרייה

בכאן שייך צ"ל ועיקר שבכף שאחר זה

שיטה מקובצת

א] לך לאות ולא לאחרים לאות ומפיק יד ממש שאינו מכוסה ועדיין אינו ידעינן מהכא אם הוא קיבורת למעלה מן המרפק או למטה מן המרפק שגם הוא מכוסה בבגדים אלא אדרבי יצחק סמיך דאמר שתהא שימה כנגד הלב: ב] רבי חייא בריה דרב אויא: ג] בשר ואיכא שיער: ד] בינייהו. ס"א למ"ד מצוה אחת אי איפסקא חדא הנך הוו להו כלאים ולמ"ד ד' מצות לא (רב ארא) [רבא בר אהינא] אמר כו' למ"ד מצוה אחת כיון דרמא ליה ארבעתן לא צריך למ"ד ארבע מצות הן צריך רבינא אמר כו' מ"ד ארבע מצות לית ליה דרב הונא ומ"ד מצוה אחת אית ליה דרב הונא ורש"י לא פי' כן: ה] ולית הלכתא כר"י ונפקא מינה לכל הני נפקותא דאמרן לעיל ואם נפסק בשבת אחת מן הציצית אע"ג דבחול אסור ללובשו בשבת מותר ללובשו שהרי כבוד הבריות הוא להיות מעוטף בטליתו דבחול דוקא אמר רחמנא גדילים תעשה לך על ארבע כנפות כסותך בזמן שהוא בר עשייה אבל בשבת שאינו בר עשייה אינו מוזהר ואין לומר דמוזהר הוא שלא ללבוש ד' כנפות בלא ציצית דע"כ אינו מוזהר על הלבישה אלא מצווה על העשייה וראיה לדבר מפרק האשה רבה דפריך גבי סדין בציצית דפטור מדרבנן גזירה משום קלא אילן וכי יש כח ביד חכמים לעקור דבר מן התורה ומשני שב ואל תעשה משום גזירה דקלא אילן ואם היה מוזהר שלא ללבוש טלית של ד' כנפות בלא ציצית הוי קום עשה: ו] עיניך ואשמועינן בגובה ותיבת ממש נמחק: ז] קרחה שיער ותיבות שיש בו ל"ש: ח] גבי נתקי ראש: ט] ישמעאל דאמר כל אחד ואחד מצוה בפני עצמה לא הוו כלאים דמ"מ דהשלש שנשארו שלשה מצות הן ואינן כלאים: י] להטיל לד': יא] נפשה היא: יב] תיבות נהי ד' ל"ש: יג] מצות מיהא איכא ואינו משוי ורב הונא מיירי בעשויה בפסול הס"ד והשאר נמחק: יד] שחתך. באחד מן הקרנות חתיכה כמין פגימה נ"א באלכסון דנראין תיבת כגון נמחק: טו] דמיא ל"א ועיקר האי מאן דצייריה לגלימיה קרנות טליתו כפל וקשר ודומה כאלו קצצן ואין לה כנפות להפקיעה מתורת ציצית לא עביד כלום לפוטרה מן הציצית וכמאן דשייריה דמי ובת [ד'] כנפים היא שהרי סופיה לחזור לתחלתה: טז] דכמאן דשרי דמיא: יז] לפסוק לאותו כפל ולישדייה ואח"כ יתלה הציצית ל"א ועיקר האי מאן דחייטיה לגלימא כפל הכנפות כאלו הם מקוצצות ותפר הכפלים של שניהן אפ"ה לא עביד ולא כלום להפקיעה מן הציצית דכל כמה דלא פסק להו חשובין הן מן הטלית ובעלת כנפים היא דאם איתא דלא מבעיא ליה לצורך לפסוק ולשדייה אבל השתא מדלא פסק להו שמא מבעיא ליה ועדיין מן הטלית הן וללישנא קמא קשה דתניא בפרק התכלת ושוין שאם כפלה ותפרה שחייבת: יח] שבת שהיו דורשין: יט] דחוטים. דמר בר רב אשי עם הציצית ולא ידע ולא אמר ליה רבינא ולא מידי הס"ד ומה"ד מהתם איפסוק בר"ה הס"ד ומה"ד אי אמרת לי מהתם דאיפסק הס"ד: כ] ועוד מאי רבותא אתא לאשמועינן דאם הוא נהרג תוך שלשים דאינו נפדה פשיטא דאפי' חי הרבה ופדאו תוך שלשים אינו פדוי דהא תום' אחרות: כא] היינו דנולד בו סימנים והיינו דומה בדומה ותיבת דנעשה נמחק: כב] היה לו לפרש ויש לחלק בין האי דחייטיה לגלימא להיא דלקמן מיירי כגון טלית כפולה לשנים ואין עתיד להתירה כלל אבל הכא לא כפל כי אם הקרנות ועתיד להתירן דאם איתא דלא מבעיא ליה לשדייה תום' אחרות:

רַבִּי יוֹסֵי א] הַחוֹרֵם אוֹמֵר: מָצִינוּ יָמִין שֶׁנִּקְרָא יָד, שֶׁנֶּאֱמַר: °"וַיַּרְא יוֹסֵף כִּי יָשִׁית אָבִיו יַד יְמִינוֹ". (בראשית מח) וְאִידָךְ? יַד יְמִינוֹ אִיקְּרִי, יָד סְתָמָא לָא אִיקְּרִי. ר' נָתָן אוֹמֵר: אֵינוֹ צָרִיךְ, הֲרֵי הוּא אוֹמֵר: °"וּקְשַׁרְתָּם וּכְתַבְתָּם", (דברים ו) מַה כְּתִיבָה בְּיָמִין – אַף קְשִׁירָה בְּיָמִין, וְכֵיוָן דִּקְשִׁירָה בְּיָמִין – הַנָּחָה בִּשְׂמֹאל הִיא. וְר' יוֹסֵי ב] הַחוֹרֵם, הַנָּחָה דְּבִשְׂמֹאל מְנָא לֵיהּ? נָפְקָא לֵיהּ מֵהֵיכָא דְּנָפְקָא לֵיהּ לְר' נָתָן. רַב אַשִׁי אָמַר: מִ"יָּדְכָה" ג] כְּתִיב בְּהֵ"י – כֵּהָה. א"ל ר' אַבָּא לְרַב אַשִׁי, וְאֵימָא: יָדְךָ שֶׁבְּכֹחַ! א"ל: מִי כְּתִיב בְּחֵי"ת? כְּתַנָּאֵי: "יָדְכָה" בְּהֵ"י – זוֹ שְׂמֹאל; אֲחֵרִים אוֹמְרִים: "יָדְךָ" – לְרַבּוֹת אֶת הַגִּידֵּם. תַּנְיָא אִידָךְ: אֵין לוֹ זְרוֹעַ – פָּטוּר מִן הַתְּפִילִּין; אֲחֵרִים אוֹמְרִים: "יָדְכָה" – לְרַבּוֹת אֶת הַגִּידֵּם. ת"ר: [א]אִטֵּר מַנִּיחַ תְּפִילִּין בִּימִינוֹ שֶׁהוּא שְׂמֹאלוֹ. וְהָתַנְיָא: מַנִּיחַ בִּשְׂמֹאלוֹ שֶׁהוּא שְׂמֹאלוֹ שֶׁל כָּל אָדָם! אָמַר אַבַּיֵּי: כִּי תַּנְיָא הַהִיא – [ב]בְּשׁוֹלֵט בִּשְׁתֵּי יָדָיו. תָּנָא *דְּבֵי מְנַשֶּׁה: "עַל יָדְךָ" – [ג]זוֹ קִיבּוֹרֶת, "בֵּין עֵינֶיךָ" – זוֹ קׇדְקֹד. הֵיכָא? אָמְרִי דְּבֵי רַבִּי יַנַּאי: מָקוֹם [ד]שֶׁמּוֹחוֹ שֶׁל תִּינוֹק רוֹפֵס. °בְּעָא מִינֵּיהּ פְּלֵימוֹ מֵרַבִּי: מִי שֶׁיֵּשׁ לוֹ שְׁנֵי רָאשִׁים, בְּאֵיזֶה מֵהֶן מַנִּיחַ תְּפִילִּין? א"ל: אוֹ קוּם גְּלֵי אוֹ קַבֵּל עֲלָךְ שַׁמְתָּא. אַדְּהָכִי אֲתָא הַהוּא גַּבְרָא, א"ל: אִתְיְלִיד לִי יָנוֹקָא דְּאִית לֵיהּ תְּרֵי רֵישֵׁי, כַּמָּה בָּעֵינַן לְמֵיתַב לְכֹהֵן? אֲתָא הַהוּא סָבָא תְּנָא לֵיהּ: חַיָּיב לִיתֵּן לוֹ י' סְלָעִים. אִינִי? וְהָתָנֵי *רָמִי בַּר חָמָא: מִתּוֹךְ שֶׁנֶּאֱמַר °"פָּדֹה תִפְדֶּה אֵת בְּכוֹר הָאָדָם", (במדבר יח) שׁוֹמֵעַ אֲנִי אֲפִילּוּ נִטְרַף בְּתוֹךְ ל'? [ה]ת"ל: אַךְ

רש"י

ר' יוֹסֵי ד] הַחוֹרֵם. חוֹטְמוֹ מְשׁוּקָּע, כִּדְאָמְרִי' בִּבְכוֹרוֹת (דף מג:): חָרוּם – זֶה שֶׁחוֹטְמוֹ מְשׁוּקָּע. מָצִינוּ יָמִין שֶׁנִּקְרָא יָד. וְלָא ה] יָלְפִינַן מֵהָכָא. מַה ו] (מְזוּזָה) כְּתִיבָה בְּיָמִין. כְּשֶׁכּוֹתְבִין הַמְּזוּזָה בְּיָמִין, דְּרוֹב בְּנֵי אָדָם כּוֹתְבִין בְּיָמִין – אַף קְשִׁירָה נַמִי עֲבַד קֶשֶׁר בְּיָמִין, וּמִדְּקָשַׁר בְּיָמִין – מִכְּלָל הַנָּחָה בִּשְׂמֹאל, דְּאִי הַנָּחָה ז] עַל יָמִין שׁוּב אֵינוֹ יָכוֹל לְקוֹשְׁרָהּ בְּיָמִין. מִיָּדְכָה בְּה'. מִדִּכְתִיב *בְּהֵ"י, ח] כֵּהָה מַשְׁמַע, לְשׁוֹן נְקֵיבָה – שְׁמַע מִינָּהּ בִּשְׂמֹאל קָאָמַר, דְּאֵין בָּהּ כֹּחַ כִּנְקֵיבָה. ל"א: "יָדְכָה" יָד כֵּהָה – עַמְיָא, בְּלָא כֹּחַ. כְּתַנָּאֵי. דְּאִיכָּא תַּנָּא דְּיָלֵיף שְׂמֹאל מִ"יָּדְכָה" כְּרַב אַשִׁי, וְאִיכָּא דְּלָא יָלֵיף. לְרַבּוֹת אֶת הַגִּידֵּם. שֶׁאֵין לוֹ יָד, ט] דְּ"יָדְכָה" דְּמַשְׁמַע יָד רְצוּצָה וּמְקוּלְקֶלֶת. אֵין לוֹ זְרוֹעַ. שְׂמֹאל. (א) יָמִין שֶׁל אִטֵּר הָוְיָא שְׂמֹאל לְדִידֵיהּ, הוֹאִיל וְרוֹב כֹּחוֹ בִּשְׂמֹאלוֹ. בְּשׁוֹלֵט בִּשְׁתֵּי יָדָיו. שֶׁשְּׁתֵּיהֶן שָׁווֹת לוֹ בְּכֹחַ, דְּכֵיוָן דְּאַף בְּיָמִין נַמִי שׁוֹלֵט – הִלְכָּךְ מַנִּיחָהּ בִּשְׂמֹאלוֹ, לְפִי שֶׁהִיא שְׂמֹאל לְכָל אָדָם, וְאַע"ג דִּלְדִידֵיהּ הָוְיָא י] יָמִין. קִבּוֹרֶת. בדרו"ן. הֵיכָא. אַקׇּדְקוֹד קָאֵי. רוֹפֵס. רַךְ, כְּשֶׁהוּא קָטָן בֶּן שָׁנָה. אוֹ קוּם גְּלֵי. אוֹ עֲמוֹד וְלֵךְ בְּגָלוּת, אוֹ קַבֵּל עָלֶיךָ שַׁמְתָּא, דְּאַחוּכֵי חַיְּיכַתְּ בִּי. עֶשֶׂר סְלָעִים. דְּחַד בְּכוֹר הוּא וְאִית לֵיהּ תְּרֵי רֵישֵׁי, וְחָשֵׁיב כִּתְרֵין. וְאַע"ג דְּיוֹלֶדֶת תְּאוֹמִים לָא יָהֵיב אֶלָּא ה' סְלָעִים, כִּדְאָמְרִינַן בְּפֶ' "יֵשׁ בְּכוֹר לְנַחֲלָה" (בכורות מח.), אפ"ה, הָתָם הוּא מִשּׁוּם דְּאִי אֶפְשָׁר לְצַמְצֵם, אֲבָל הָכָא חַד הוּא, וְאֶפְשָׁר לְצַמְצֵם שֶׁיָּצְאוּ כְּאֶחָד, וְהָוֵי שְׁנֵיהֶם פֶּטֶר רֶחֶם. שׁוֹמֵעַ אֲנִי אֲפִי' נִטְרַף. נֶהֱרַג בְּתוֹךְ ל' יוֹם נַמִי חַיָּיב. דְּאַף עַל גַּב דִּכְתִיב (במדבר יח) "וּפְדוּיָו מִבֶּן חֹדֶשׁ תִּפְדֶּה", אפ"ה הָכָא אִיכָּא לְמֵימַר: אִם לֹא נֶהֱרַג הָוֵי חַי ל', וּבְכוֹר מַעַלְיָא הוּא יא]. אַךְ

תוספות

רבי יוסי החורם. פי' בקונטרס: חוטמו היה שקוע, כעין "חרוס" דבכורות (דף מג:). ותימה הוא לומר שכינהו בלשון גנאי. אלא על שם מקומו נקרא כן. מ"ר. יד ימינו איקרי. ומדכתיב (בראשית מח) "ויתמוך יד אביו" לא קשיא מידי, °כיון שכבר פירש "יד ימינו". ונראה דר' יוסי נמי אההוא קא סמיך, ומשום הכי לא מייתי מ"ידו הימנית" דמצורע. מ"ר*.

מה כתיבה בימין אף קשירה בימין. בסמוך אמרי' דאיטר מניח תפילין בימינו שהיא שמאלו. והשתא אדם הכותב בימינו ושאר רוב מעשיו בשמאלו, יש להסתפק באיזה מהן יב] מניח תפילין. ושמא יש לדמותו כשולט בשתי ידיו. יג] מ"ר.

אין לו זרוע פטור מן התפילין אחרים אומרים ידכה כו'. מר אמר חדא ומר אמר חדא ולא פליגי. יד] *מ"ר.

קיבורת. פירש בקונטרס: בדרו"ן. וקיבורת הוא לשון קבולת בשר, כמו (ב"ב דף ה.) "קיבורא דאהיני". ואור"ת דהוא גובה הבשר טו] שבזרוע שבין בית השחי למרפק שקורין קודא. טז] (ואור"ת) לא כדברי המפרשים גובה בשר שבאותו עצם שבין היד למרפק, דהא משמע בכל דוכתי דמצות תפילין בזרוע, כדאמרינן לקמן (דף מג:): חביבין ישראל שסיבבן הקב"ה במצות, תפילין בראשיהן ובזרועותיהן. ובפ' בתרא דעירובין (דף צה:): וקושר בזרועו במקום תפילין. ואמרינן נמי: אין לו זרוע – פטור מן התפילין. ואותו עצם שבין יד לקודא אינו קרוי זרוע אלא קנה, כדתנן במס' אהלות (פ"א מ"ח) דקחשיב רמ"ח איברים, ל' בפיסת יד [ו' בכל אצבע] שנים בקנה, שנים במרפק, אחד בזרוע וד' בכתף. ומשמע בהדיא דההוא דסמוך לכתף הוא זרוע שבין הכתף למרפק, ומרפק הוא קודא, כדמשמע במסכת ערכין (דף יט:) בפ' "האומר משקלי", דקתני: מכנים ביד עד האציל וברגל עד הארכובה, *קרי לאציל מרפק במתני'. וכתיב נמי: "על כל אצילי ידי" ומתרגם: מרפיקי ידי, ומשמע דמרפק ביד כנגד ארכובה ברגל. וגם בכל דוכתי משמע דאציל הוא קודא, ולא כפירוש הקונטרס דפירש *גבי אוב וידעוני: אייסיל. ובמסכת סופרים (פ"ג) תניא: לא ישים שני אציליו על הספר, וזהו הקודא, שדרך להשען עליו. עוד אמרי' בפ"ב דזבחים (דף יח.): "ולא יחגרו ביזע" שאין חוגרין במקום שמזיעין ולא למטה ממתניהן ולא למעלה מאציליהן, אלא כנגד אצילי ידיהן, והיינו כנגד הקודא, ששם דרך לחגור, ולא כנגד אייסיל, דאדרבה שם מקום זיעה יותר. ובפרק "המפלת" (נדה דף ל:) *דאמרינן גבי ולד במעי אמו: ושני אציליו על ברכיו. ומהא דכתיב בירמיה (לח): "שים נא בלויי הסחבות תחת אצילי ידיך" לא קשיא מידי, *ולפי שהיה אוחז בחבלים בידיו ומשים תחת הקודא בלויי הסחבים שלא יזיקו לו. והא דתנן גבי שבת:* המוציא בפיו ובמרפיקו – אפשר שיתן אדם גרוגרת כנגד אותו פרק של קודא מבפנים, וכופף ידו על כתיפו שלא תפול הגרוגרת ויוציאנה. והא דתנן בפ' "ד' מיתות" (סנהדרין דף סה.): בעל אוב זה פיתום המדבר בשחיו, ובגמ' תניא: בעל אוב זה המדבר בין הפרקים ובין אצילי ידיו, משמע דאציל הוא בית השחי, צריך לומר דמאי דשייר במתני' פירש בברייתא, וכמו שהוסיפו בין הפרקים היינו פירקי אצבעות – כך הוסיפו אצילי ידיו שהוא מרפק, קודא בלע"ז כדפרישית. ומדקדק ר"ת מהא דערכין (דף יט:) דמשמע התם דמדאורייתא "ידך" זו קיבורת, אבל בנדרים הלך אחר לשון בני אדם, ועד מרפיקו הוא דמיקריא יד, משום דקיבורת לא הוי בכלל. ועוד, מדאמרינן בשמעתין שתהא שימה כנגד הלב, והיינו כנגד הדדים, כדאמרינן במועד קטן (דף כז:): הספד על הלב כדכתיב "על שדים סופדים". ומההיא דערכין קשה לדברי המפרשים בפ' "כל הבשר" (חולין דף קו:): לחולין עד הפרק, הוא פרק שלישי של האצבעות עד חיבורן לפיסת ידים. ולתרומה כל היד, ולקידוש ידים ורגלים עד הפרק, דהיינו קודא, והכי איתא בספר הזהיר. ולא יתכן, כדמוכח ההיא דערכין (דף יט:) דקודא היינו שיעורא דנדרים. עוד ראיה מדתנן בפ' "הזרוע" (חולין דף קלד.): איזהו זרוע? מן הפרק של ארכובה עד הכף של יד, והוא של נזיר, וכנגדו ברגל שוק האמור בשלמים יז] מן הארכובה – *הפרק של הארכובה, עד סובך של רגל, והוא עצם האמצעי המחובר לקולית, ולאותו פרק קרי סובך של רגל, כך פירש שם בקונטרס. ומיהו, אין ראיה מזרוע דבהמה לזרוע דאדם, דהא שוק דאדם נמי לא הוי כשוק דבהמות, דתנן באהלות: ב' בשוק, חמשה בארכובה, וא' בירך – אלמא קרי שוק עצם המחובר לרגל. ויתכן לר' יהודה נמי היינו שוק דבהמה. *ויש מפרשים דסובך של רגל דקאמר ר' יהודה היינו פרק הסמוך לרגל, דהיינו איסתוירא, קביל"א בלע"ז, וכן משמע בתוספתא דמסכת ידים דקתני: שיעור שבקידוש ידים עד הפרק, וברגלים עד הסובך. והיינו עד הפרק, דקאמר במסכת ערכין. ובירושלמי ד"מצות חליצה" נמי מוכיח כן, דקאמר גבי חליצה: כיני מתני' בקשור מן הארכובה ולמטה כשירה, אבל מן הארכובה ולמעלה פסולה. ופריך: והכתיב (שמות ל) "ורחצו בני אהרן את ידיהם ואת רגליהם", ותנן עלה: ביד עד הפרק וברגל עד הסובך, והיכי אמר כך? שנייה, דכתיב (דברים כה) "מעל רגלו". מעתה אפילו מן הארכובה ולמעלה תהא כשירה! שנייה (היא) דכתיב "מעל רגלו" ולא מעל דמעל רגלו. משמע דקרי סובך לפרק הסמוך לרגל. מ"ר*.

מקום שמוחו של תינוק רופס. הוא הדין הסמוך למטה, כדמוכח לקמן: מקום הראוי לטמא בנגע א', ואמרינן בעירובין (דף צה:): מקום יש בראש שראוי להניח שם שני תפילין. מ"ר.

או קום גלי כו'. בעולם הזה ליכא, אבל יש במדרש: אשמדאי הוציא מתחת קרקע אדם א' שיש לו שני ראשים לפני שלמה המלך, ונשא אשה והוליד בנים כיוצא בו בשני ראשים, וכיוצא באשתו בראש אחד, וכשבאו לחלוק בנכסי אביהם מי שיש לו שני ראשים שאל שני חלקים ובאו לדין לפני שלמה. יח] מ"ר.

שומע אני אפי' נטרף בתוך ל' יום. פירש בקונטרס: נטרף – נהרג. יט] וקשה לר"ת, דממתני' הוה ליה לאקשויי, דתנן בבכורות (דף מט.): מת הבן בתוך ל' יום – האב פטור מחמש סלעים! ועוד קשה, דבפ"ק דבבא קמא (דף יא:) דאמר עולא א"ר אלעזר: בכור שנטרף בתוך ל' יום אין פודין אותו, מאי קמ"ל? מתני' היא! ומיהו

ג] ... דפליגי דאמר לרבות את הגידם שמניח בימינו וכן אמרי' בהדיא ב) במכילתא דפליגי: טו] שבזרוע שהוא למעלה מן המרפק שקורין קודא אבל אי אפשר לומר שהוא במקום קבוצת בשר למטה מן המרפק דהא משמע כו' וזרוע הוא העצם שבין מרפק לשחי כדתנן בפ"ק דאהלות כו' תוס' אחרות: טז] תיבת ואור"ת נמחק: יז] בשלמים (ומיהו בעצמות) מן הפרק של הארכובה עד בוקא דאטמא דהיינו כל הירך שני עצמות: יח] שלמה. נ"א שלמה בחכמתו הרתיח מים וכסה אחד מן הראשים ושפך הרותחים על ראש השני מחמת צער הרותחים צעק בשני ראשים אמר שלמה ש"מ דתולדה אחת לשתי הראשים ואין נידון אלא כאיש אחד: יט] וקשה לר"ת הדא דהל"ל נהרג בהדיא ולמה שינה את לשונו לומר נטרף ועוד דמה ענין זה למי שיש לו שני ראשים. תוס' אחרות:

א) נ"ל נפקא כדילפת. ב) עי' בשו"ת שבות יעקב ח"א סימן ג' שכתב דאינו מוכרח כלל מהמכילתא דפליגי ע"ש:

עין משפט נר מצוה

קצה א ב מיי' פ"ד מהלכות תפילין הלכ' ג טוש"ע או"ח סי' כז סעיף ו:

קצו ג ד מיי' שם הלכה א ב טוש"ע שם סעיף א ט:

[וע"ע תוס' עירובין ב: ד"ה בין לרבנן]

קצז ה מיי' פי"א מהל' ביכורים הלכה יז סמג עשין קמד טוש"ע י"ד סי' שה סעיף יב:

[עיין מג"א סי' כז סק"ג ובתשובת שבות יעקב ח"א סי' ג]

נ"ק נ"ז

נ"ק

[יחזקאל יג]

[לב. ושם]

מסורת הש"ס

בה"י משמע כו' נ"ק

נ"ל ידכה

עירובין צה: ערכין יט:

ב"ק יא:

וקרי נ"ק

[סנהדרין סה.]

אמרינן נמי גבי נ"ק

נ"ל לפי

מן הפרק נ"ק

ויסיט כל הירך והוי שני עצמות עצם האמצעי נ"ק

ויש נ"ק

נ"ק מ"ז

[ועי' עוד שבת צב. ד"ה במרפקו וכו' ומה שליינתי שם על הגליון]

הגהות הב"ח

(א) רש"י ד"ה אין לו זרוע שמאל הס"ד ואח"כ מ"ה בימינו ימין של איטר:

גליון הש"ס

גמ' בעא מיניה פלימו. עיין בכתבות אור להגאון בעל פנים מאירות פ' במדבר: תוס' ד"ה יד ימינו כו' כיון שכבר פירש כו'. עי' עירובין דף ב ע"ב תוס' ד"ה בין לרבנן:

שיטה מקובצת

א] ר' יוסי החרום ובתוס' חיצונית גרים ההרס על שם מקום כמו עיר ההרס [ישעיה י"ט] או חרס כמו תמנת חרס [שופטים ב]: ב] ור' יוסי החרום: ג] מידכה. בה"י יד כהה א"ל ר"א לרב אשי ואימא יד שבכח א"ל: ד] ר' יוסי החרום: ה] ולא מהכא נפקא א) כדי ליפנא ותיבת ילפינן ל"ש: ו] מה מזוזה: ז] הנחה הוי על קיבורת ימין: ח] תיבת כהה נמחק: ט] דידך כהה דמשמע יד רעועה ומקולקלת: י] הויא כימין: יא] מעליא הוא נ"א שנטרף שנולדו לו סימני טריפה כגון ניקב קרום של מוח: יב] מניח תפילין. אי אזלינן בתר כתיבה הואיל דכתיב וקשרתם וכתבתם אי לא. יג] ידיו ולא כתב כן בעל התרומות: יד] פליגי ...

והא רב חסדא ורבה בר רב הונא מצלו בהו באורתא! ההוא פליגא. ומי אמר רבה בר רב הונא הכי? והא אמר רבה בר רב הונא: ספק חשיכה ספק לא חשיכה — לא חולץ ולא מניח; הא ודאי חשיכה — חולץ! התם בערב שבת איתמר. מאי קסבר? אי קסבר: *לילה זמן תפילין — שבת נמי זמן תפילין! אי קסבר: שבת לאו זמן תפילין — לילה נמי לאו זמן תפילין, דמהיכא דממעטא שבת מהתם ממעטי לילות! *דתניא: °"ושמרת את החוקה הזאת למועדה מימים ימימה", "ימים" — ולא לילות, "מימים" — ולא כל ימים, פרט לשבתות וימים טובים, דברי רבי יוסי הגלילי; ר"ע אומר: לא נאמר חוקה זו אלא לפסח בלבד! נפקא ליה מהיכא דנפקא ליה לר' עקיבא; *דתניא, ר' עקיבא אומר: איכול יניח אדם תפילין בשבתות ובימים טובים? ת"ל: °"והיה *לאות על ידך ולטוטפת בין עיניך" — מי שצריכין אות, יצאו שבתות וימים טובים שהן גופן אות. אמר ר' אלעזר: כל *המניח תפילין אחר שקיעת החמה — עובר בעשה, ור' יוחנן אמר: בעובר בלאו. לימא, בר' אבין אמר ר' אילעא קא מיפלגי, *דאמר ר' אבין אמר ר' אילעא: כל מקום שנאמר "השמר" "פן" ו"אל" — אינו אלא לא תעשה, דמר אית ליה דר' אבין, ומר לית ליה דר' אבין? לא, דכולי עלמא אית להו דרבי אבין אמר ר' אילעא, והכא בהא קא מיפלגי, מר סבר: "השמר" דלאו — לאו, ו"השמר" דעשה — עשה, ומר סבר: "השמר" דעשה נמי לאו. ואמר רבי אלעזר: א] גואם לשמרן — מותר. ואמר רבינא: הוה יתיבנא קמיה דרב אשי וחשך ב] והניח תפילין, ואמרי ליה: לשמרן קא בעי להו מר? ואמר לי: אין, וחזיתיה לדעתיה דלאו לשמרן הוא ג] בעי, קסבר: דהלכה ואין מורין כן. *אמר רבה בר רב הונא: החייב אדם ד] למשמש בתפילין בכל שעה, ה] קל וחומר מציץ: ומה ציץ שאין בו אלא אזכרה אחת — אמרה תורה: "והיה על מצחו תמיד" שלא תסיח דעתו ממנו, תפילין שיש בהן אזכרות הרבה, על אחת כמה וכמה! ת"ר: "ידך" — זו ישמאל; אתה אומר: שמאל, או אינו אלא ימין? תלמוד לומר: °"אף ידי יסדה ארץ וימיני טפחה שמים", ואומר: °"ידה ליתד תשלחנה וימינה להלמות עמלים", ואומר: *°"למה תשיב ידך וימינך מקרב חיקך כלה".

רבי

רש"י

ה"ג: מימים ולא כל ימים כו'. אלא לפסח בלבד. וה"ק: עשה פסח משנה לשנה. נפקא ליה. כלומר, לעולם קסבר לילה זמן תפילין הוא, ושבת מימעיט ליה מהיכא דנפקא ליה לר' עקיבא. שהן עצמן אות. בין הקב"ה לישראל, דכתיב (שמות לא): "כי אות היא" וגו'. ו] עובר בלאו. דכתיב: "ושמרת", וכל "השמר" לא תעשה הוא. השמר דלאו לאו. רבי אלעזר סבר: "השמר" דכתיב במילתא דמזהר רחמנא לא תעשה — הוי לאו גמור ללקות, כגון (דברים כד): "השמר בנגע צרעת", דמשמע שלא יקוץ בהרתו, וכן (שמות לד): "השמר לך פן תכרות ברית" וגו', אבל "השמר" דעשה כגון האי, דמשמע ז] לעשות תפילין — עשה הוא. ואם לשומרן. שלא יאבדו, מותר להניחן אפילו לאחר שקיעת החמה. קסבר הלכה. דלילה זמן תפילין הוא. ואין מורין כן. שמא ישכחם ח] ויישן בהן, מדקאמר ליה "לשומרן קבעינא". ידי יסדה ארץ וימיני וגו'. מדכתיב "ידי" וימין — ש"מ יד היינו שמאל.

רבי

תוספות

והא רב חסדא ורבה בר רב הונא מצלו בהו באורתא. פשיטא ליה דהא דקאמר רב נחמן: אין הלכה כרבי יעקב — לאו משום שיהא הלכה כחכמים, דאם כן לימא: הלכה כחכמים. אלא למימר דהלכה כתנא קמא. והא דלא אמר: הלכה כת"ק — לפי שהדבר שנוי סתם, ולא נזכר בה לשון רבים ולא לשון יחיד*. מ"ר. אי קסבר לילה זמן תפילין. וא"ת: מכל מקום חולץ, כדאמרינן בפ' "במה אשה" (שבת דף סא.) גמרא ולא בתפילין, דאפי' למאן דאמר שבת זמן תפילין — לא יצא, דלמא מיפסקן ואתי לאיתויינהו ארבע אמות ברשות הרבים! ומיהו, לרבי ענני בר ששון, דאמר בפרק "במה אשה יוצאה" (שם דף סד:): *בכבול לא אסרו אלא ברה"ר, אבל בחצר שרי — ניחא, דהכא בחצר. ור"ת פוסק כרבי ענני. אבל לרב דאמר: כל שאסרו חכמים לצאת לרה"ר אסרו לצאת לחצר, קשה! ואין לומר דמודה רב בבית דשרי, דהא אמרינן ט] בריש "כירה" (שם מו.): השירים והנזמים והטבעות הרי הן ככל הכלים הניטלים בחצר, ואמר עולא: מה טעם? הואיל ואיכא תורת כלי עליהם. ואם היו ראוין להתקשט — לא היה לומר טעם (דמשמע) דשרי לטלטל משום תורת כלי, אע"ג דלא חזי בשבת, דמדמי ליה התם לשרגא דנפטא! וי"ל: דמודה רב דתפילין דשרי בחצר, דלא אסירי אלא ברה"ר. דלא דמי לשאר תכשיטין דגזר רב בחצר דלמא מישתלי ואתי לאפוקי לרה"ר, אבל תפילין כיון דעשויין למשמש בתפילין מידכר דכיר ליה. כדאמר בפ"ק דשבת (דף יב.) גמרא לא יצא החייט במחטו, דאמר *שמואל: יוצא אדם בתפילין עם חשיכה, מ"ט? כיון דאמר רבה בר אבוה חייב אדם למשמש בתפילין כל שעה ושעה, הלכך מידכר דכיר להו. וא"ת: אם כן, כי אמר רב (שבת דף סד:): כל שאסרו חכמים לצאת לר"ה אסור לצאת לחצר, חוץ מכבול ופאה נכרית, הוה ליה למימר נמי חוץ מתפילין! וי"ל: דלא מיירי רב אלא בתכשיטין. ועוד, משום דלמאן דאמר שבת לאו זמן תפילין *הוא לא שייך למימר חוץ מתפילין. ואם תאמר: דהכא אמרינן ספק חשיכה לא חולץ ולא מניח, ובפ"ק דשבת (דף יב.) קאמר: יוצא אדם בתפילין ע"ש עם חשיכה, משמע: הא ספק חשיכה לא! וי"ל: התם ברשות הרבים והכא בחצר. מ"ר. ושמרת את החוקה הזאת למועדה כו'. בפרק "בא סימן" (נדה נא:) ובסוף "כילד מברכין" (ברכות דף מד:) דאמרינן דבני מערבא מברכי בתר דמסלקי תפלייהו: "לשמור חוקיו", מפרש רבינו תם דלאחר שמסלק את טליתו ליכא מאן דמברך, דלא שייכא ברכה ד"לשמור חוקיו" אלא מתפילין דווקא, דכתיב בהו "חוקה", ודווקא כשמסלקן סמוך לשקיעת החמה, דדרשינן: "ימים" ולא לילות, ומחויב לסלקן, כדאמרינן בסמוך: הניח תפילין אחר שקיעת החמה עובר בעשה. ובירושלמי דברכות פרק "היה קורא" אמרינן נמי על מילתא דבני מערבא דמברכי: "לשמור חוקיו" — כמאן דאמר: בחוקת תפילין הכתוב מדבר, אבל למאן דאמר דבחוקת הפסח הכתוב מדבר — לא, א"כ כל שכן דלאחר ציצית לא מברך. ובפרק "בא סימן" (נדה נא:) גבי יש טעון ברכה לפניו ואין טעון ברכה לאחריו, דקאמר: לאיתויי מצות, ופריך: לבני מערבא דמברכי לבתר דמסלקי תפלייהו לאיתויי מאי? הוה מצי למימר *ציצית. והאידנא לא מברכי "לשמור חוקיו" אפי' לאחר תפילין, דבסמוך פסקינן דלילה זמן תפילין, דקאמר: הלכה ואין מורין כן, ומדרבנן הוא דאסור דחיישינן שלא יישן בהם, וקרא ד"ושמרת את החוקה" בחוקת הפסח הכתוב מדבר*. מ"ר. יצאו שבתות וימים טובים שהן עצמן קרויין אות. לא משום דאסירי בעשיית מלאכה, דאפי' חולו של מועד דשרי בעשיית מלאכה איכא אות, בפסח דאסור באכילת חמץ, ובסוכות י] דחייב בסוכה. ובפרק בתרא דמועד קטן (דף יט. ושם) משמע דחולו של מועד חייב, דאמר התם: כותב תפילין לעצמו ולאחרים בטובה, דברי ר"מ, ר' יהודה אומר: מערים ומוכר כדי פרנסתו את שלו וכותב לעצמו כו'. אורי ליה רבה בר בר חנה לרב חננאל, וכן אורי ליה רב: הלכה כותב ומוכר כדי פרנסתו. משמע דמניח במועד, דאי משום לאחר המועד — מה לי לעצמו מה לי לאחרים? למה מותר לכתוב לעצמו, שאין זה צורך פרנסתו! מיהו לאו ראיה, אפשר דרבי מאיר ור' יהודה לטעמייהו, דאית להו שבת זמן תפילין, בפרק בתרא דעירובין (דף צו:). עוד ראיה מירושלמי פרק בתרא דמועד קטן: חד בר נש איבד תפילוי במועדא, אתא לגבי רב חננאל, יא] שלח לגבי רבה בר בר חנה, אמר ליה: *יהיב יב] תפילוי ואזיל כתוב לך. אמר ליה רב: זיל כתוב ליה, פירוש: בלא הערמה. מתני' פליגא על רב: כותב הוא אדם תפילין ומזוזה לעצמו, הא לאחר אסור! רב פתר לה בכותב להניח. *)ומסתמא רב **)(גרסינן כו') הוה סבירא ליה כהלכתא דשבתות וימים טובים לאו זמן תפילין, אפילו הכי שרי לכתוב ולמכור תפילין בלא הערמה, ולרבה בר בר חנה ע"י הערמה, דכולהו אמוראי סבירא להו שבת לאו זמן תפילין, רב חסדא ורבה בר רב הונא, ואע"ג דסבירא להו לילה זמן תפילין. ומיהו בזה חולק התלמוד שלנו, דרבה בר בר חנה סבר כרב, והתם פליגי. מ"ר. ידך זו שמאל. ואם תאמר: לעיל בספ"ק (דף י.) דאייתר ליה "יד" דמצורע לאגמורי א"יד" דקמיצה, ד"וימלא כפו" היינו נמי בימין — אדרבה, הוה לן לאגמורי א"יד" דתפילין דהוי בימין ודמי ליה, דילפינן "יד" מ"יד", והתם ילפינן "כפו" מ"יד"! ויש לפרש: דניחא ליה לאגמורי התם עבודה מעבודה. מיהו קשה, דאתרוייהו נילף! ושמא משום דלא דמי להדדי, דהתם יד ממש, והכא קיבורת בזרוע. מ"ר.

רבי

*) נ"א ומסתמא רב ס"ל כהלכתא דשבתות וי"ט לאו זמן תפילין דכולהו אמוראי ס"ל שבת לאו זמן תפלין ר"ח ורבה בר רב הונא ואע"ג דס"ל לילה זמן תפילין ואפילו הכי שרי לכתוב ולמכור תפילין בלא הערמה ולרבה בר בר חנה ע"י הערמה ומיהו בזה חולק כו' נ"ק **) רש"א מ"ז ועיין רש"ק

עין משפט נר מצוה

קצ א מיי' פ"ד מהל' תפילין הלכה י טוש"ע א"ח סימן לא סעיף א:
קצא ב מיי' שם הלכה יא:
[ועי' היטב תוס' ביצה יז. ד"ה אין]
במה אשה ולא בתפילין וקאמר עלה בגמרא דאפי' כו' נ"ק
קצב ג ד מיי' שם טוש"ע א"ח סי' ל ס"ב:
הכל ככבול דלא אסרו נ"ק
קצג ה מיי' שם הלכה יד סמג שם טוש"ע א"ח סי' כח ס"א:
קצד ו מיי' שם הלכה ב סמג שם טוש"ע א"ח סי' כז ס"א:
[בעירובין צו. איתא והיה לך לאות על ידך מי שצריכין אות כו' והיינו קרא המוקדם שמות יג פ"ט]
[לעניננו שם איתא גנבא רבי ישמעאל]
[בהרי"ף והרא"ש ליתא להך ואומר למה וכו' וכן בשאלתות פ' בא סי' מה ליתא]

מסורת הש"ס

[שבת סא. עירובין לה: זבחים יט.]
עירובין צו.
גס זה שם
שם
[עי' תוס' לעיל כ: ד"ה נפסל]
שבועות ד. לו. מכות יג: סוטה ה. זבחים קו. לקמן לט: ע"ז נא: עירובין צו.
[שבת יב. יומא ז:]
ישעיה מח
שופטים ה
תהלים עד
גירסת רש"א לא הוה שייך כו'
לאתויי ציצית נ"ק
[וע"ע תוס' ברכות מד: ותוס' נדה נא: ד"ה ולבני מערבא ותוס' סוכה לט. ד"ה אבל לפניו]
זיל הב ליה תפילך ואת כתוב לך אתא לקמיה דרב א"ל כתוב כו' נ"ק

שיטה מקובצת

א] ואם לשמרן מותר וא"ת וכי בשביל לשמרן יעבור על לאו וי"ל דלקיים קאמר אם כבר הם מונחים בראשו אבל להניחן לכתחילה לא קאמר וכן משמע בסמוך דקאמר קסבר הלכה ואין מורין כן וא"ת נהי נמי דלילה זמן תפילין הא לעיל [אמר] דאם חלצן אינו חוזר ומניחן ולפי מאי דפרישית דהכא מיירי לקיימן ניחא וא"ת הא אמרינן לעיל אם היה משכים לדרך ומתירא שמא יאבדו מניחן לכתחילה והיאך יעבור על לאו וצ"ל דלעיל מיירי אחר עמוד השחר ומיהו לאו זמן תפילין הוא עדיין לברך כדאיתא בברכות [דף ט' ע"ב] (לכתחילה) [לתפילין] כאחרי' דאמרי כדי שיראה חבירו ברחוק ד' אמות ויכירהו: ב] וחשך והוה מניח תפילי ולא סליק תפילי ואמרי: ג] הוא אלא קסבר ותיבת בעי נמחק: ד] למשמש. והא דאמרי' במס' סוכה רבנן דבי רב אשי אימתי דהויא ממשמשי בתפילייהו הוי מברכין וכי תעלה על דעתך דמברכי כל שעה ושעה דאמרינן הכא חייב למשמש כל שעה ושעה. משמוש דהתם לאו כמשמוש דהכא דהתם מיירי במשמש לתקנם ולהניחן במקומם אם נהפכו לצדדין: ה] קו"ח מציץ כו'. גליון והקשה הר"ר שמחה כיון דתפילין בעו כוונה איך יכול להתפלל או לקרוא ק"ש בהם דהא אינהו נמי בעי כוונה ותירץ דהעוסק במצוה פטור מן המצוה כיון דאי אפשר לו לקיים שניהם ביחד ועוד הקשה ר"י הואיל ועוסק במצוה פטור מן המצוה מי (שמניח) [שמונח] טלית ותפילין עליו יהא פטור מללמוד וכן כל תרי"ג מצות דליכא למימר דמיירי דאינו יכול לעשות שניהם בבת אחת דא"כ פשיטא. דפטורים דאיך יעשה זאת ויניח זאת דאין אתה יודע מתן שכרן של מצות אלא ע"כ מיירי אפילו יכול לעשות שניהם בבת אחת אפ"ה פטור עיין תוס' ב"ק דף נ"ו ע"ב ד"ה בההיא: ו] עובר בעשה דכתיב ושמרת את החוקה וגו' מימים ימימה ולא לילות לאו הבא מכלל עשה הס"ד ומה"ד עובר: ז] דמשמע שמור לעשות: ח] ישכחם בראשו ויישן בהן כו' לשומרן קא בעינא הס"ד: ט] אמרי' בסוף: י] דחייב בסוכה. ולפי זה לאו זמן תפילין הוא ולפי הירושלמי לא משמע כן דבעי התם מהו לכתוב תפילין לעצמו אמר ליה שרי ובעי נמי מהו לכתוב ולמכור לאדם שאין לו יציאה לצורך המועד ואמר ליה זבין דידך וכתוב לעצמך משמע דזמן תפילין הוא בחול המועד ויש לדחות דהני ס"ל דשבת ויו"ט זמן תפילין הוא אבל מ"מ דוחק הוא זה לומר דס"ל כל הני אמוראי דהתם דלא כהלכתא. תו"א: יא] חננאל שלחיה: יב] יהיב ליה תפילוי וזיל:

תורה אור

אָמַר א] רַב חִסְדָּא: סָח בֵּין תְּפִילָּה לִתְפִילָּה — חוֹזֵר וּמְבָרֵךְ. סָח — אִין, לֹא סָח — לָא? וְהָא שְׁלַח *רַב חִיָּיא בְּרֵיהּ דְּרַב הוּנָא מִשְּׁמֵיהּ דְּר׳ יוֹחָנָן: עַל תְּפִילָּה שֶׁל יָד אאוֹמֵר: ״בָּרוּךְ אֲשֶׁר קִדְּשָׁנוּ בְּמִצְוֹתָיו וְצִוָּנוּ לְהָנִיחַ תְּפִילִּין״, עַל תְּפִילִּין שֶׁל רֹאשׁ אוֹמֵר: ״בָּרוּךְ אֲשֶׁר קִדְּשָׁנוּ בְּמִצְוֹתָיו וְצִוָּנוּ עַל מִצְוַת תְּפִילִּין״! אַבַּיֵי וְרָבָא בדְּאָמְרִי תַּרְוַיְיהוּ: לֹא סָח — מְבָרֵךְ אַחַת, סָח — מְבָרֵךְ שְׁתַּיִם. תָּנָא: *סָח בֵּין תְּפִילָּה לִתְפִילָּה — געֲבֵירָה הִיא בְּיָדוֹ, (ג) וְחוֹזֵר עָלֶיהָ מֵעֶרְכֵי הַמִּלְחָמָה. תָּנָא: דכְּשֶׁהוּא מַנִּיחַ — מַנִּיחַ שֶׁל יָד וְאַחַר כָּךְ מַנִּיחַ שֶׁל רֹאשׁ, הוּכְשֶׁהוּא חוֹלֵץ — חוֹלֵץ שֶׁל רֹאשׁ וְאַחַר כָּךְ חוֹלֵץ שֶׁל יָד. בִּשְׁלָמָא כְּשֶׁהוּא מַנִּיחַ, מַנִּיחַ שֶׁל יָד וְאח״כ מַנִּיחַ שֶׁל רֹאשׁ — דִּכְתִיב: °״וּקְשַׁרְתָּם לְאוֹת עַל יָדֶךָ״ וַהֲדַר: ״וְהָיוּ לְטוֹטָפֹת בֵּין עֵינֶיךָ״, אֶלָּא כְּשֶׁהוּא חוֹלֵץ, חוֹלֵץ שֶׁל רֹאשׁ וְאח״כ חוֹלֵץ שֶׁל יָד, מְנָלַן? אָמַר רַבָּה: רַב ב] הוּנָא אַסְבְּרָא לִי, אָמַר קְרָא: ״וְהָיוּ לְטוֹטָפֹת בֵּין עֵינֶיךָ״, כָּל *זְמַן שֶׁבֵּין עֵינֶיךָ יְהוּ שְׁתַּיִם. ת״ר: תְּפִילִּין מֵאֵימָתַי מְבָרֵךְ עֲלֵיהֶן? מִשְּׁעַת הֲנָחָתָן. כֵּיצַד? הָיָה ומַשְׁכִּים לָצֵאת לַדֶּרֶךְ וּמִתְיָרֵא שֶׁמָּא יֹאבְדוּ — מַנִּיחָן, וּכְשֶׁיַּגִּיעַ זְמַנָּן מְמַשְׁמֵשׁ בָּהֶן וּמְבָרֵךְ עֲלֵיהֶן. וְעַד מָתַי מַנִּיחָן? עַד זשֶׁתִּשְׁקַע הַחַמָּה, רַבִּי יַעֲקֹב אוֹמֵר: עַד שֶׁתִּכְלֶה רֶגֶל מִן הַשּׁוּק, וַחֲכָמִים אוֹמְרִים: עַד זְמַן שֵׁינָה; וּמוֹדִים חֲכָמִים ג] *לְר׳ יַעֲקֹב, שֶׁאִם חֲלָצָן לָצֵאת לְבֵית הַכִּסֵּא אוֹ לִיכָּנֵס לְבֵית הַמֶּרְחָץ וְשָׁקְעָה חַמָּה, שׁוּב אֵינוֹ חוֹזֵר ד] וּמַנִּיחָן. אָמַר רַב נַחְמָן: הֲלָכָה כְּרַבִּי יַעֲקֹב. ה] רַב חִסְדָּא וְרַבָּה בַּר רַב הוּנָא מְצַלּוּ בְּהוּ בְּאוֹרְתָא. אִיכָּא דְּאָמְרִי: ו] *אֵין הֲלָכָה כְּר׳ יַעֲקֹב. וְהָא

דברים ו

בֵּין תְּפִילָּה לִתְפִילָּה. בֵּין שֶׁל יָד לְשֶׁל רֹאשׁ, דְּסִיפֵּר קוֹדֶם ז] שֶׁיַּנִּיחַ אוֹתָן עַל הָרֹאשׁ. לְהַנִּיחַ. דִּבְשֶׁל יָד מַתְחִיל לְהַנִּיחַ. מִצְוַת תְּפִילִּין. דְּעַכְשָׁיו גּוֹמֵר אֶת הַמִּצְוָה. לֹא סָח. אֵין מְבָרֵךְ אֶלָּא עַל שֶׁל יָד בִּלְבַד. סָח מְבָרֵךְ שְׁתַּיִם. כִּדְשָׁלַח רַב חִיָּיא. סָח בֵּין תְּפִילָּה לִתְפִילָּה. וְלֹא בֵּירֵךְ עַל שֶׁל רֹאשׁ, אֶלָּא סָמַךְ עַל בְּרָכָה רִאשׁוֹנָה. עֲבֵירָה הִיא בְּיָדוֹ וְחוֹזֵר עָלֶיהָ מֵעֶרְכֵי הַמִּלְחָמָה. כִּדְאָמְרִינַן בְּפֶרֶק ״מְשׁוּחַ מִלְחָמָה״ (סוטה מד:): הַיָּרֵא וְרַךְ הַלֵּבָב מֵעֲבֵירוֹת שֶׁבְּיָדוֹ. וְהָיוּ. מַשְׁמַע שְׁתַּיִם. כָּל זְמַן שֶׁיְּהוּ בֵּין עֵינֶיךָ יְהוּ שְׁתַּיִם, כָּל זְמַן שֶׁאוֹתָן שֶׁל רֹאשׁ מוּנָּחִים — ח] אוֹתָן שֶׁל יָד נַמִי מוּנָּחִין, אַלְמָא דְּרֹאשׁ ט] חָלֵיץ בְּרֵישָׁא. תְּפִילִּין. שֶׁהִנִּיחָן קוֹדֶם עַמּוּד הַשַּׁחַר מְבָרֵךְ עֲלֵיהֶן מִשְּׁעַת הֲנָחָתָן — מִשְּׁעַת זְמַן הֲנָחָתָן, דְּאָמַר בְּפֶרֶק קַמָּא דִּבְרָכוֹת (דף ט:) בִּק״ש, אֲחֵרִים אוֹמְרִים: מִשֶּׁיִּרְאֶה חֲבֵירוֹ י] מֵרָחוֹק ד׳ אַמּוֹת, וְאָמְרִינַן הָתָם: לִתְפִילִּין כַּאֲחֵרִים, כְּלוֹמַר, לַהֲנָחַת תְּפִילִּין יא] כַּאֲחֵרִים. שֶׁמָּא יֹאבְדוּ. אִם יַשְּׂאֵם בְּיָדוֹ. מַנִּיחָם. בְּרֹאשׁוֹ. מְמַשְׁמֵשׁ בְּהוּ. דַּהֲוֵי כְּאִילּוּ מַנִּיחָן. שֶׁתִּכְלֶה רֶגֶל מִן הַשּׁוּק. לְאַחַר שֶׁחָשְׁכָה. מוֹדִים חֲכָמִים יב] לְרַבִּי יַעֲקֹב שֶׁאִם חֲלָצָן כו׳ אֵין חוֹזֵר וּמַנִּיחָן. יג] דְּלַיְלָה לָאו זְמַן תְּפִילִּין הוּא, כִּדְאָמְרִינַן לְקַמָּן. מְצַלּוּ בְּהוּ בְּאוֹרְתָא. תְּפִלַּת עַרְבִית, כְּר׳ יַעֲקֹב. *לֹא יד] חוֹלְצִין. אִם מוּנָּחִין, וְלֹא מַנִּיחַ אִם חֲלוּצִין.

ה״ג

של תפילין קשר של קיימא, ואם היה צריך להתיר ולקשור בכל יום אם כן לא הוי של קיימא. ו״משעת הנחה עד קשירה״ דהכא, מפרש ר״ת דהך קשירה היינו ההדוק שמהדקו ומלמלמו בראשו, כמו ״שליא קשורה בולד״ דנדה (דף כו:) – לאו קשורה ממש היא, וכמו ״קשורה בו ככלב״. ולפירוש רבינו אליהו הוה ליה למימר: משעת קשירה ועד שעת הנחה, ויש ספרים שכתוב כן. ומסתברא כדברי ר״ת בתפילין של ראש, וכדברי רבינו אליהו בתפילין של יד, דכתיב בשל יד: ״וקשרתם לאות על ידך״, דמשמע דכל שעה שמניח צריך לקשירה. *תדע, דלקמן (דף לז.) דריש ר׳ נתן הנחה בשמאל מדכתיב: ״וקשרתם וכתבתם״ מה כתיבה בימין אף קשירה בימין, וכיון דקשירה בימין הנחה בשמאל היא, ואם היה קושר תחילה ואח״כ היה מכניס בזרוע, אם כן היכי דייק מינה דהנחה בשמאל? ועוד אמרינן בפרק ״אין מעמידין״ (ע״ז לט.): מעשה באשה אחת שהיתה נישאת לחבר והיתה קושרת לו תפילין *בזרועו, משמע דתמיד היתה עושה כן ואפילו לספרים שכתוב בהם ״קומעת״ מכל מקום רוצה לומר שהיתה קושרת לו כעין קמיע, ולפי שאין נוח לקשור ביד אחת היתה מסייעת לו. תדע, דלא קאמר שהיתה מסייעה לתפילין של ראש, דתפילין של ראש ודאי אין צריך לקשור בכל יום, דלא צוותה תורה לקשור כל שעה, וקשר שלה הלכה למשה מסיני, והכי גמירי דליהוי קשורין תמיד. והשתא קשירה דשמעתין קשירה ממש, *דבשל יד מתחיל לברך. חוזרני לומר דתפילין של יד נמי לא בעו קשירה בכל יום. דבפרק בתרא דמקוואות (מ״ג) קתני קשרים דאין צריכין שיבואו בהן המים: תפילין של ראש בזמן שהיא חולה, ושל זרוע בזמן שאינה עולה ויורדת. פירוש ״חולה״ – כמו ״אולא״ דטבעות ידיו דתוספתא דמקואות, דהקשר מיהדק שפיר. ״בזמן שאינה עולה ויורדת״ דיד היינו לפי שיש קושרים ראש הרצועה באמצע זו בזו שאינה יכולה להרחיב ולעלות ולירד, ויש *מסבבים טו] הרצועה שמסובבת בקשר העשוי בראשה שהרצועה *נתחבר בקשר, ועולה ויורדת. ומדקאמר כשאינה עולה לא חייץ וא״צ להתירו בשעת טבילה – ש״מ קשר של קיימא הוא. **סח** בין תפילה לתפילה חוזר ומברך. מ״ר. מכאן מדקדקים כשאדם שוחט עופות או בהמות הרבה וסח בין עוף לעוף, שחוזר ומברך. ומ״מ עבירה היא בידו, כדאמרינן הכא שחוזר עליהם מערכי המלחמה. ושאני תפילין שמצוה אחת הן, אבל התם שאם ירצה ישחוט ואם ירצה לא ישחוט. ומיהו מסתברא דכיון דיכול לפטור בברכה אחת אין לו לדבר כדי שיהא זקוק לברכה שניה, כדמוכח בפרק ״בא לו״ (יומא דף ע.) וב״אלו נאמרין״ (סוטה מ:), דתנן: נוטל ספר תורה וקורא ב״אחרי מות״ ו״אך בעשור״, וב״עשור״ שבחומש הפקודים קורא על פה. ופריך בגמרא: *ונייתי ספר תורה וניקרי ביה! ומשני ר׳ שמעון בן לקיש: משום ברכה שאינה צריכה. אלמא, כיון דיכול לפטור עצמו מברכה שניה קרי לה ברכה שאינה צריכה. ושמא סח בין עוף לעוף כסח באמצע סעודתו. וזה דבר פשוט שאם שואל עוף לשחוט לא חשוב הפסק, מידי דהוה *א״טול ברוך״, ומידי דהוי נמי אברכת כסוי הדם, דאמרינן בפרק ״כסוי הדם״ (חולין דף פו:) אמר רב יהודה: שחט חיה יכסנה, ואח״כ ישחוט עוף, ומשמע התם דאין צריך לחזור ולברך. וכן כשאדם מברך יקנה״ז אין הברכות האחרת הפסק בין ברכת היין לשתיה. ומיהו, אם היה זקוק לחזור ולברך כשסח בין עוף לעוף כמו כן היה זקוק לכסות, דהא *זימנין *)אפילו במקום שזקוק לכסוי אמרינן בפרק ״כסוי הדם״ (גם זה שם) דנפטר בברכה אחת. מ״ר. **לא** סח מברך אחת סח מברך שתים. פירש בקונטרס: לא סח – מברך אחת בין של יד בין של ראש, סח – מברך שתים: ״להניח תפילין״ בשל יד, ו״על מצות תפילין״ טז] בשל ראש. °ור״ת פירש: לא סח מברך אחת – *לשל ראש מברך ״על מצות תפילין״, שזו היא ברכתו. סח מברך ב׳ – יז] לשל ראש ״להניח״ ו״על מצות״. וכן [כתב] בשימושא רבא דתפילין. *מ״ר. **עבירה** היא בידו וחוזר עליה מערכי המלחמה. מתוך פירוש הקונטרס משמע דאם סח ובירך – שרי, וליכא איסורא, אלא אדרבה מצוה ושכר ברכה. וזה לשונו: סח בין תפילה לתפילה ולא בירך על של ראש יח] ״על מצות״, אלא סמך על ברכה ראשונה, עבירה היא בידו. מ״ר. **וקשרתם** לאות על ידך והדר והיו לטוטפת בין עיניך. מכאן קשה לפירוש הקונטרס דפרק ״אמר להם הממונה״ (יומא לג: ושם) גבי אין מעבירין על המצות, דאמר: שמע מינה עבורי דרעא אטוטפתא אסור, כשפוגע בתפילין של יד תחילה – אסור להעביר ולהניח של ראש, דאין מעבירין על המצות. והשתא, מאי איריא משום דאין מעבירין על המצות? תיפוק לי משום דכך מצותו, דמניח של יד ואח״כ מניח של ראש! ומפרש ר״ת משום ר׳ חננאל בשם רב האי גאון, דאיירי בשעה שחולץ תפילין ומניחן בתיק, שלא יעביר אותן של יד ויתננה בתיק תחילה ואח״כ של ראש למעלה, דא״כ כשבא להניח תפילין היה פוגע בשל ראש תחילה, והיה צריך להעביר על המצות משום דשל יד מניח תחילה ואח״כ של ראש. לפיכך צריך להניח בתוך התיק של ראש תחילה ואח״כ של יד למעלה. ורבינו אליהו מפרש לענין משמוש איירי, דאמרינן לקמן שאדם חייב למשמש בתפילין בכל שעה ושעה, קל וחומר מציץ, והשתא קאמר דבשל יד ממשמש תחילה, משום דפגע בהו ברישא ואין מעבירין על המצות. מ״ר. **אמר** רבה רב הונא אסברא לי. ״רבה״ גרסינן ולא ״רבא״, דרבא לא ראה רב הונא מעולם, דהא אמרינן בפרק בתרא דקדושין (דף עב:) דביום שמת רב יהודה נולד רבא, ורב הונא שכיב קודם רב יהודה, כדמוכח במועד קטן (דף יז.) דכי נח נפשיה דרב יהודה קאמר התם: גברא רבה כרב יהודה ליכא הכא, ורב הונא *היה גדול בחכמה ובמנין מכל תלמידים דרב, כדמשמע בפרק בתרא דכתובות (דף קו.). מ״ר. **וכשיגיע** זמנן ממשמש בהן ומברך. מכאן נראה כשאדם משכים קודם היום ומתעטף בציצית, כשיאור היום – אין צריך להסיר טליתו כדי לחזור וללבוש ולהתעטף ולברך, דכיון שממשמש בו יכול לברך. אף על פי שיש לחלק בין תפילין לציצית, שהמשמוש מצוה כדלקמן – אין נראה לחלק, דבפרק ״התכלת״ (לקמן דף מג.) מדמי תפילין לציצית לענין מישמוש ולברך. מ״ר. **רבי** יעקב אומר עד שתכלה רגל מן השוק וחכמים אומרים עד זמן שינה. רבי יעקב וחכמים סבירא להו דלילה זמן תפילין, אלא חיישינן לשמא ישן בהן, ועביד רבי יעקב הרחקה טפי מדרבנן. מ״ר. והא

*) נ״א אפילו במקום שנפטר בברכה אחת זקוק לכסוי וכו׳

עין משפט נר מצוה

קפג א מיי׳ פ״ד מהלכות תפילין הלכה ד טוש״ע או״ח סימן כה סעיף ה וע״ש:

קפד ב ג מיי׳ שם הלכה ו טוש״ע שם סעי׳ ט וע״ש בכ״מ:

קפה (ג מיי׳ פ״ז מהל׳ מלכים הלכה ז וע״ש בכ״מ):

קפו ד מיי׳ פ״ד מהל׳ תפילין הלכה ה סמג עשין כב טוש״ע א״ח סימן כה סעיף ה:

קפז ה מיי׳ שם טוש״ע א״ח סי׳ כח ס״ב:

קפח ו (מיי׳) וסמג שם טוש״ע א״ח סי׳ ל סעיף ג:

קפט ז מיי׳ שם הלכה י טוש״ע שם סעי׳ ב:

[סוטה ג:]

[ועיין במי״ט הל״ק סי׳ ג׳]

[נ״ל על ידו]

ובשל יד מתחיל לברך משעת קשירה עד שעת הנחה חוזרני כו׳ נ״ק

[אמר רב נחמן כנ״ל וכ״א בהלק״ט וברמ״ע שם]

מכניסים הרצועה נ״ק

מסורת הש״ס

[לקמן מב:]

תוספתא דברכות [פ״ו ע״ש ברכות ס:]

סוטה מד:

[עי׳ תוס׳ ערכין ג. ד״ה ושל יד]

[ור׳ יעקב כן ראוי להיות וכן בהלק״ט להרא״ש נדפס על צידו ורבי יעקב וכן מצאתי בתוספת רמ״ע מפאנו סימן קח ע״ש שהאריך ליישב גם הגי׳ ס״א לרבי יעקב]

נ״ל נתחבת

[שם מח.]

[ברכות מ.]

זקוק לכסות אפילו אם נפטר בברכה אחת הס״ד נ״ק

על של ראש על מצות נ״ק

[עיין תוס׳ ברכות ס: ד״ה אשר וכו׳ מ״ש באריכות]

[עי׳ תוס׳ בכורות יז. ד״ה רב אשי]

גליון הש״ס

תום׳ ד״ה לא כו׳ ור״ת פי׳ וכו׳. הראה לי חכם אחד שכן מפורש בהדיא במדרש תנחומא בפרשת בא:

שיטה מקובצת

א] אמר רבה בר שילא אמר רב חסדא: ב] רב המנונא אסברא לי: ג] חכמים ורבי יעקב: ד] ומניחן עיין תוס׳ חולין דף פ״ח ע״א: ה] דהא רב חסדא: ו] דאמרי אמר רב נחמן אין: ז] שיניח אותו של הראש: ח] מונחים יהו של יד ותיבת אותן נמחק: ט] דראש אותו חליץ: י] חבירו ברחוק: יא] תפילין הלכה כאחרים: יב] חכמים ורבי יעקב לת״ק שאם: יג] דלילה. כתוב בגליון פרש״י דלילה לאו זמן תפילין הוא כדאמרינן לקמן ולא נהירא דא״כ מאי קאמר למר עד שתכלה רגל מן השוק ולמר עד זמן שינה ואי לילה לאו זמן תפילין הוא לא היה לו להניחם כלל אחר שקיעת החמה לכך נראה דכולהו ס״ל דלילה זמן תפילין ואפ״ה אין מניחן למר כדאית ליה ולמר כדאית ליה ואם חלצן אינו חוזר ומניחן דחיישינן שמא ירדם. ע״כ: יד] לא חולץ אם: טו] ויש מסבבים אל הרצועה כו׳ ומדקאמר כשאינה עולה דלא חייץ: טז] בשל ראש. ואין נראה כן במסכת ברכות [דף ס׳ ע״ב] שהולך ומפרש סדר מאה ברכות שאדם חייב לברך בכל יום כי משי ידיה מברך על נטילת ידים כי מנח תפילין של יד מברך להניח תפילין ואשל ראש על מצות תפילין ולכן נראה לא סח מברך כו׳ ויש לדחות דהיא דברכות דמיירי דאין לו אלא אחת מהן של יד לבד או של ראש לבד (ובהכי) [ולהכי] קאמר של יד מברך להניח בשאין לו של ראש ועל של ראש מברך על מצות אם [אין] לו של יד אבל אם יש לו שתים אינו מברך אלא אחת בלא סח: יז] סח מברך שתים על של ראש: יח] תיבות על מצות נמחק:

תורה אור

ואי"נ, כל היכי דכי מיתלי ביה במתנא אתייה אבתריה – חדתתא, ואידך עתיקתא. א] אביי הוה יתיב קמיה דרב יוסף, איפסיק ליה רצועה דתפילי, א"ל: מהו למיקטריה? א"ל: "וקשרתם" כתיב, שתהא קשירה ‎אתמה. א"ל רב אחא בריה דרב יוסף לרב אשי: מהו למיתפריה ועייליה לתפירה לגאו? אמר: ב] *בפוק חזי מה עמא דבר. אמר רב פפא: גרדומי רצועות כשירות. ולאו מילתא היא, מדאמרי בני רבי חייא: *גרדומי תכלת וגרדומי *)אזוב גכשירין – התם הוא דתשמישי מצוה נינהו, אבל הכא דתשמישי קדושה נינהו – לא. מכלל דאית להו שיעורא, וכמה שיעורייהו? אמר רמי בר חמא אמר ר"ל: דעד אצבע צרדה. רב כהנא מחוי כפוף. רב אשי מחוי פשוט. רבה קטר להו ופשיט ושדי להו. רב אחא בר יעקב קטר להו ומתלית להו. *מר בריה דרבנא עביד כדידן. *אמר רב יהודה בריה דרב שמואל בר שילת משמיה דרב: הקשר של תפילין – הלכה למשה מסיני. אמר ר"נ: ונוייהן לבר. רב אשי הוה יתיב קמיה דמר זוטרא, איתהפכא ליה רצועה דתפילין, א"ל: לא סבר לה מר ונוייהן לבר? א"ל: *לאו אדעתאי. °"וראו כל עמי הארץ כי שם ה' נקרא עליך ויראו ממך" – *תניא, ר"א הגדול אומר: אלו תפילין שבראש. °"והסרותי את כפי וראית את אחורי" – אמר רב *חנא בר ביזנא אמר ר"ש חסידא: מלמד שהראה לו הקב"ה למשה קשר של תפילין. אמר רב יהודה: וקשר של תפילין צריך שיהא למעלה, כדי שיהו ישראל למעלה ולא למטה; וצריך שיהא כלפי פנים, כדי שיהו ישראל לפנים ולא לאחור. אמר רב שמואל בר בידרי אמר רב, ואמרי לה אמר ר' אחא אריכא אמר רב הונא, ואמרי לה אמר רב מנשיא אמר שמואל: תפילין מאימתי מברך עליהן? משעת הנחתן. איני? והא *אמר רב יהודה אמר שמואל: כל המצות כולן מברך עליהן עובר לעשייתן! אביי ורבא דאמרי תרוייהו: משעת חהנחה ועד שעת קשירה.

אמר

[לקמן לח:] [לקמן מג:] דברים כח שמות לג לפי גי' רש"ק ל"ל שיר שירים וע"ש

א"נ כל היכי דמתלי במתנא. כשאוחז אדם ברצועה התלויה בהן ואתו תפילין אבתריה ואינן נתקין – חדתא, ואידך שנתקין – עתיקא. ל"א: אתיא אבתריה – שמתפשט העור הויא ג] חדתתא. **קשירה תמה.** שתהא הקשירה נאה, ואם יש ד] קשר אחר ברצועה לבד מקשר שקושרין בראש – תו לא הויא קשירה יפה. לשון אחר: קשירה תמה – רצועה שלימה, ולא קשורה. **ועייליה לתפירה לגאו.** שלא יראה, ויהא כשלימה. **מה עמא דבר.** וכיון דאין נוהגין כן לא תעשה. **גרדומי רצועות.** מה שתולה מן הרצועות לאחר שנתקשרו בראש, אם נפסק מאותן שירים ונשתיירו גרדומין – כשירין. גרדומין היינו *שירים. **שיעור תכלת.** מפרש בפרק "התכלת" (לקמן דף לח.), ושיעור אזוב מפרש בפ"ק *דסוכה (דף יג.). **גרדומים.** *(שירי) שיריהן. **מכלל דאית להו שיעורא.** לתליית הרצועות *לבר הקשר, מדמני ה] להו שירים לגרדומין. **מחוי כפוף.** ו] [אורך הרצועה תהא עודפת על הקשר] כמה שיכול לפשוט מאצבע עד אמה. **פשוט.** כמה שיכול לפשוט מגודל ועד אצבע, דלגבי ז] *(פשיטת) אצבע וגודל הויא בפשיטה, ולגבי אמה ואצבע בכפיפה, לפי שמאצבע לגודל מתפשט יותר הרבה מבין אצבע לאמה. **צרדה** – לשון "צרתא דדא", צרה של אגודל, והיינו אצבע הסמוך לגודל. **רבה.** ח] כשמניח תפילין קטר ליה ברישיה, ושירי הרצועות פשיט ושדי להו, ותולין ט] על כתיפו מאחריו. **ומתלית להו.** לרצועות התלויות היה גודלן י] ומשלשלן טורני"ס בלע"ז. **כדידן.** כמנהג שלנו יא] [ותולין לפניו]. **קשר של תפילין.** שעושים הרצועות על ראשו יב] *[בעינן] שיהא דל"ת, כדי שיהא "שדי" נראה עליהן, דשי"ן נראה בקמט בית חיצונה שכפל הקלף כעין שי"ן, ודל"ת נראה בקשר, ויו"ד נראה באותו של יד, כמין רצועה קטנה וראשה כפוף מעט כמין יו"ד. **ונוייהן לבר.** השם יהא נראה מבחוץ. לשון אחר: נוייהן של רצועות, שהן חלוקות מצד א' וצבועות שחורות והוא נוייהן (א). וראיה לדבר מדאמרינן: איתהפיכא ליה רצועה דתפילין, *א"ל: ולא סבר לה מר ונוייהן לבר? והכי אמרינן לעיל: מבפנים מאי גנאי ודבר אחר איכא? זימנין דמתהפכין, יג] אלמא כה"ג הוי מתהפכין – שנהפך לד הרצועה התחתון למעלה ונראה. **איתהפכא ליה.** שלא היתה הדל"ת ניכרת מבחוץ. **לאו אדעתאי.** שוגג הייתי. **שם ה' נקרא עליך אלו תפילין של ראש.** שכתוב יד] בו רוב השם, שי"ן ודל"ת. **קשר של תפילין.** מאחורי העורף. והקב"ה מניח תפילין, טו] *כדאמר לעיל דמשום תפילין ש"ר יראו הגוים כדכתיב: "ויראו ממך". **למעלה.** בגובה הראש, ולא למטה בצואר. **כלפי פנים.** ממול עורף ולא בצידי הראש. ל"א: *כלפי פנים – שיהא הקשר מבפנים והנוי של דל"ת מבחוץ, כדאמרן: טז] ונוייהן לבר. **בידרי.** שם. **מאימתי מברך עליהן משעת הנחתן.** משמע לאחר שהניחן. **אביי ורבא דאמרי תרוייהו.** מאי משעת הנחתן דקאמר – משעת הנחה ועד שעת קשירה, דכיון דעדיין לא קשרן עובר לעשייתן הוא.

בין

פוק חזי מה עמא דבר. פי' בקונטרס: להחמיר. ור"ת מפרש: להקל, כי ההיא דפ"ק דעירובין (דף יד:) גבי הילמי ולחיים. וכן בפרק "שלשה שאכלו" (ברכות דף מה.). מ"ר. **וכמה** שיעורייהו. *לכאורה בתפילין של ראש איירי, דמר פשיט שדי להו על כתפיו לאחוריו ומר מתלית להו. אבל הערוך פי' בערך "צרדה" דכתב בילמדנו בסוף "בא אל פרעה": ושיעור רצועה של יד עד אצבע צרדה, ומאי צרדה – אמצעי, פי': היא אצבע ארוכה. ועוד הביא בערוך דתניא בתוספתא: *איזוהי אצבע צרדה – זו אצבע גדולה של ימין. ובקונט' פי' דהיא אצבע הסמוכה לגודל. ור"א קליר יסד כפי' הערוך בסילוק של פרשת שקלים: "גיא וכל עפרה בצרדה הכילו", פי': משום דכתיב (ישעיה מ) "וכל בשליש עפר הארץ", והיינו אצבע אמצעי שהוא שלישי. ובפ"ק דיומא (דף יט:) דאמרינן גבי כ"ג שמכין לפניו באצבע צרדה, הדבר ידוע שא"א להשמיע קול אלא כשמכה באמצעי. ולפי' זה, *דחזי פשוט היינו מגודל עד אמה, וכפוף – מאצבע עד אמה. ובערוך פי' בערך "כף" דכפוף היינו מעיקר גודל עד ראש אצבע כשהן דבוקות זו בזו, ופשוט – מראש אצבע עד ראש גודל כשהן פשוטות. וי"מ: עד אצבע צרדה – שצריך לעשות הרצועות ארוכות ממקום הנחתן עד אצבע צרדה, וכפוף היינו שכופף את אצבעו ומשער הרצועה עד שם, ופשוטה היינו שמשער הרצועה ממקום הנחה עד ראש אצבע פשוטה. ובתפילין של ראש משערין הרצועות שתגיע ראש האחד עד טיבורו, וראש השני עד הלב. ושמא שום מדרש יש, וגבי תפילין של יד הוא דאמרינן בפ' שני דברכות (דף יג:): "ושמתם את דברי אלה על לבבכם" – שתהא שימה כנגד הלב. ובשימושא רבה דתפילין יש: דליפשו רצועי עד דלימטי לחדא כנגד מילה מימינא, ולחדא כנגד הלב משמאלא. עוד יש אומר דמצות שיעור רוחב הרצועות יותר מכשעורה ופחות מכשעורה, ואם יותר כשר. מ"ר. **עביד** כי דידן. דפשיט ושדי להו על כתיפיו מלפניו. מ"ר. **ונוייהן** לבר. הכא מוכח דארצועות קאי, ולא כמו שפירש בקונטרס במסכת שבת (דף כח:) דקאי *אקציצה. מ"ר. **אלו** תפילין שבראש. פי' בקונטרס: שכתוב עליהן רוב השם שי"ן ודלי"ת. ונראה דדלי"ת ויו"ד שברצועות לאו אותיות גמורות הן, ולא חשיבי מן השם של "שדי", מדחשיב להו לעיל ובריש פ' בתרא דמגילה (דף כו: ושם) תשמישי קדושה, ולא הן עצמן קדושין, ובשום דוכתא לא קרי להו כי אם "קשר של תפילין". עוד אמרינן בפ' "במה מדליקין" (שבת דף כח:): לא הוכשרו למלאכת שמים אלא עור בהמה טהורה בלבד. למאי הילכתא? אילימא כו' אלא לעורות. והאמר אביי: שי"ן של תפילין הלכה למשה מסיני, פירוש: ופשיטא דצריך בהמה טהורה! ומסיק: אלא לרצועות. משמע דד' ויו"ד לא חשיבי אותיות. וה"ר יעקב דאורלינ"ש מסופק °אם צריך לחלוץ תפילין של יד כשנכנס לבית הכסא, דשמא כיון דמחופות עור לא צריך, דלא אסרו אלא תפילין של ראש שכתוב שי"ן בעור. ויש עוד לפרש, דלכך קאמר: אלו תפילין שבראש משום דנראין יותר משל יד, דעל של יד אמרינן לקמן: לך לאות ולא לאחרים לאות*. מ"ר. **משעת** הנחה ועד שעת קשירה. מכאן היה מדקדק רבינו אליהו שצריך אדם לקשר תפילין בכל יום. ור"ת מפרש דאין צריך, ומביא ראיה מהא דאמרינן בפ"ק דחולין (דף ט. ושם) דצריך אדם שילמוד ג' דברים: כתב שחיטה ומילה, ורב יהודה אמר: אף קשר של תפילין וברכת חתנים וציצית. ואידך, הני שכיחן, פי': יז] וצריך ללומדן, לפי שתמיד צריך להן. ואי בעי למקשר קשר של תפילין בכל יום איכא דשכיחא טפי! ומיהו בקונטרס פי' שם איפכא: הני שכיחן – קשר של תפילין וברכת חתנים וציצית, ואין צריכין ללמוד, שמנעוריו בקי בהן. וכמו שפירשתי נראה, דאדרבה כתב ושחיטה שכיחי טפי מכולהו. ועוד מדקדק ר"ת דהך קשירה לאו ממש היא, מהא דחשיב בריש פ' בתרא דעירובין (דף לז. ושם): קשר של

עין משפט נר מצוה

לכאורה משמע מפירש"י דבתפילין של ראש איירי דפי' דמר פשיט ושדי כו' מתלית להו לרצועות התלויות בו אבל כו' כצ"ל ל"ק

קעז א ב מיי' פ"ג מהל' תפילין הלכה יט סמג עשין כב טוש"ע או"ח סי' לג סעי' ה: [פ"א דיומא]

קעח ג מיי' פי"א מהל' פרה אדומה הל"ד:

קעט ד מיי' פ"ג מהל' תפילין הל' יב טוש"ע או"ח סי' כז סעי' ח:

*) [ע' תוס' סוכה יג' ד"ה וגרדומיו]

דמחוי לפשוט ל"ק

קפ ה ו מיי' שם הלכה יג יד טוש"ע שם סעי' י וסי' לב סעיף נב:

קפא ז מיי' שם פ"ד הל"א טוש"ע שם סי' כז סעי' י:

קפב ח מיי' פ"ד מהל' תפילין הל' ז טוש"ע או"ח סי' כה סעי' ח:

גליון הש"ס

תוס' ד"ה אלו כו' אם צריך לחלוץ תפילין של יד. עיין שבת דף סא ע"א תוס' ד"ה דלמא:

[וע' היטב תוס' עירובין לז. ד"ה ונוייהן ועי' פירש"י שם וברש"י דהכא]

שיטה מקובצת

א] אביי. כתב הרשב"א סי' תתשכ"ז איתא בירושל'. [פ"א דמס' מגילה] רבי זירא איפסיק ליה גידא דרצועתא פי' שנפסקה ותפרה (א) בגידין מהו למיתפריה ושרי הדר ואפסקא תניינית ושרייה ולא מן אולפנה פי' ולא מן הקבלה דלא הו"ל למשרי בשניה דאין זה אלי ואנוהו: ב] אמר ליה פוק: ג] חדתתא. אע"ג דהדר חלים חלים לשון חיבור שמתחבר וחוזר הקמט למקומו: ד] ואם יש שם קשר: ה] מדמני בהו שירים אגרדומין הס"ד: ו] תיבות אורך כו' עד על הקשר ל"ש: ז] דלגבי. ב) פשיטת אצבע לגודל הויא פשיטת אמה לאצבע ככפיפה לפי: ח] רבה. כשהיה מניח תפילין קטר ליה: ט] ותולין. לו על כתפיו מאחו[ריו] י] גודלן. ומשלשלן: יא] תיבות ותולין לפניו ל"ש: יב] ראשו. כעין דלת כדי: יג] דמתהפכין. ליה: יד] שכתוב. בהם: טו] כדאמר. בפ"ק דברכות נשבע ה' בימינו ובזרוע עוזו ואין עוז אלא תפילין וכדאמר ל[עיל] דמשום תפילין של ראש הקב"ה מטיל יראתו על הגוים ותיבת יראו נמחק: טז] כדאמרן. לעיל: יז] פי' ואידך אמאי לא חשיב הנך דרב יהודה הני שכיחן כתב שחיטה ומילה וצריך ללומדן לפי שת[מיד] צריך להן ואי בעי למעבד קשר של תפילין דשכיחא טפי מכולהו:

א) ברא"ש הלכות תפילין סימן י"א איתא שנפסקה הרצועה ותפרה בגידין ונפסק הגיד והתיר לו לחזור ולקשור הגיד איפסיק לה תניינא. ב) נראה דצ"ל דלגבי פשיטת אצבע לגודל קרי ליה פשיטה ולגבי פשיטת אמה מאצבע קרי ליה כפיפה לפי.

מסורת הש"ס

[ברכות מה. עירובין פסחים נד.]

דסוכה הס"ד אח"כ מכלל והשאר יש לג[רוס] ל"ק

לבד כו' שירים וגרד[ומין] הס"ד ל"ק

פשיטות אצבע מגודל פשיטות לגבי אמה מא[צבע] כפיפות לפי כו' ל"ק

[ברכות כו. וש"נ]

ברכות ו. נז. סוטה חולין פט. [מגילה טז:]

כעין דל"ת ל"ק

הגהות הב"ח

(א) רש"י ד"ה ונוייהן נוייהן לבר וראיה לד[בר]

פסחים ז: קיט: מגילה סוכה לט. נדה סג. ל"ק וא"ל ל"ק

כדאמרינן בברכות ואמרינן לעיל ל"ק רש"י בע"י *מבפנים שיהא ל"ק

[וע' תוס' ברכות ו. ד"ה אלו ומה שליינתי שם]

אֶלָּא גַּוַּיְיתָא לְבָרַיְיתָא וּבָרַיְיתָא לְגַוַּיְיתָא, אֲבָל גַּוַּיְיתָא לְגַוַּיְיתָא וּבָרַיְיתָא לְבָרַיְיתָא — לֵית לָן בָּהּ. א"ל רָבָא: מַאי שְׁנָא גַּוַּיְיתָא לְבָרַיְיתָא וּבָרַיְיתָא לְגַוַּיְיתָא דְּלָא — דְּהָךְ דְּבָעֵי לְמֶיחֱזֵי אֲוִירָא לָא קָא חָזְיָא, וְהָא דְּלָא א]קָא בָּעֵי לְמֶיחֱזֵי אֲוִירָא קָא חָזְיָא; בָּרַיְיתָא לְבָרַיְיתָא וְגַוַּיְיתָא לְגַוַּיְיתָא נַמִי — הָךְ דְּבָעֲיָא לְמֶיחֱזֵי אֲוִירָא דְּיָמִין קָא חָזְיָא אֲוִירָא דִּשְׂמֹאל, וְדִשְׂמֹאל קָא חָזְיָא אֲוִירָא דְּיָמִין! אֶלָּא ל"ש. וְאָמַר רַב חֲנַנְאֵל אָמַר רַב: אתִּיתוֹרָא דִּתְפִילִּין — הֲלָכָה לְמֹשֶׁה מִסִּינַי. אָמַר אַבָּיֵי: במַעְבַּרְתָּא דִּתְפִילִּין — הֲלָכָה לְמֹשֶׁה מִסִּינַי. *וְאָמַר אַבָּיֵי: גשִׁי"ן שֶׁל תְּפִילִּין — הֲלָכָה לְמֹשֶׁה מִסִּינַי, דוְצָרִיךְ שֶׁיַּגִּיעַ חָרִיץ לִמְקוֹם הַתֶּפֶר; רַב דִּימִי מִנְּהַרְדְּעָא אָמַר: כֵּיוָן דְּמִנְכַּר לָא צְרִיךְ. וְאָמַר אַבָּיֵי: הַאי קִילְפָא דִּתְפִילִּין צָרִיךְ לְמִיבְדְּקֵיהּ, דִּדִילְמָא אִית בָּהּ רֵיעוּתָא, וּבָעֵינָא כְּתִיבָה תַּמָּה וְלֵיכָּא. רַב דִּימִי מִנְּהַרְדְּעָא אָמַר: לָא צְרִיךְ, קוּלְמוּסָא בָּדֵיק לָהּ. א"ר יִצְחָק: *רְצוּעוֹת השְׁחוֹרוֹת — הֲלָכָה לְמֹשֶׁה מִסִּינַי. מֵיתִיבֵי: תְּפִילִּין אֵין קוֹשְׁרִין אוֹתָן אֶלָּא בְּמִינָן, בֵּין יְרוּקוֹת בֵּין שְׁחוֹרוֹת בֵּין לְבָנוֹת; אֲדוּמּוֹת לֹא יַעֲשֶׂה, מִפְּנֵי גְּנַאי וְדָבָר אַחֵר. א"ר יְהוּדָה: מַעֲשֶׂה בְּתַלְמִידוֹ שֶׁל ר"ע שֶׁהָיָה קוֹשֵׁר תְּפִילָּיו בִּלְשׁוֹנוֹת שֶׁל תְּכֵלֶת וְלֹא אָמַר לוֹ דָּבָר, אֶפְשָׁר אוֹתוֹ צַדִּיק רָאָה תַּלְמִידוֹ וְלֹא מִיחָה בּוֹ? אָמַר לוֹ: הֵן! לֹא רָאָה אוֹתוֹ, וְאִם רָאָה אוֹתוֹ — לֹא הָיָה מַנִּיחוֹ. מַעֲשֶׂה בְּהוּרְקָנוֹס בְּנוֹ שֶׁל ר' אֱלִיעֶזֶר בֶּן הוּרְקָנוֹס שֶׁהָיָה קוֹשֵׁר תְּפִילָּיו בִּלְשׁוֹנוֹת שֶׁל אַרְגָּמָן וְלֹא אָמַר לוֹ דָּבָר, אֶפְשָׁר אוֹתוֹ צַדִּיק רָאָה בְּנוֹ וְלֹא מִיחָה בּוֹ? אָמְרוּ לוֹ: הֵן, לֹא רָאָה אוֹתוֹ, וְאִם רָאָה אוֹתוֹ — לֹא הָיָה מַנִּיחוֹ. קָתָנֵי מִיהָא: בֵּין יְרוּקוֹת בֵּין שְׁחוֹרוֹת וּבֵין לְבָנוֹת! לָא קַשְׁיָא: כָּאן מִבִּפְנִים, וכָּאן מִבַּחוּץ. אִי מִבִּפְנִים, מַאי גְּנַאי וְדָבָר אַחֵר אִיכָּא? זִימְנִין דְּמִתְהַפְּכִין לֵיהּ. *תָּנָא: ב] תְּפִילִּין זמְרוּבָּעוֹת — הֲלָכָה לְמֹשֶׁה מִסִּינַי. אָמַר *רַב פַּפָּא: בְּתִפְרָן חוּבַאֲלַכְסוֹנָן. לֵימָא מְסַיֵּיעַ לֵיהּ: הָעוֹשֶׂה טתְּפִלָּתוֹ עֲגוּלָּה — סַכָּנָה וְאֵין בָּהּ מִצְוָה! אָמַר רַב פַּפָּא: מַתְנִי' — דַּעֲבִידָא כִּי אַמְגּוּזָא. אָמַר רַב הוּנָא: תְּפִילִּין, כָּל זְמַן שֶׁפְּנֵי טַבְלָא קַיֶּימֶת — כְּשֵׁירוֹת. רַב חִסְדָּא אָמַר: ינִפְסְקוּ שְׁתַּיִם — כְּשֵׁירוֹת, שָׁלֹשׁ — פְּסוּלוֹת. אָמַר רָבָא: הָא דְּאָמַרְתְּ שְׁתַּיִם כְּשֵׁירוֹת, לָא אֲמָרָן אֶלָּא כזֶה שֶׁלֹּא כְּנֶגֶד זֶה, אֲבָל זֶה כְּנֶגֶד זֶה — פְּסוּלוֹת; וְזֶה כְּנֶגֶד זֶה נַמִי לָא אֲמָרָן אֶלָּא בְּחַדְתָּתָא, לאֲבָל בְּעַתִּיקָתָא לֵית לָן בָּהּ. אֲמַר לֵיהּ אַבָּיֵי לְרַב יוֹסֵף: הֵיכִי דָּמְיָין חַדְתָּתָא, וְהֵיכִי דָּמְיָין עַתִּיקָתָא? אֲמַר לֵיהּ: כָּל הֵיכָא ג] כִּי ממִיתְלֵי בֵּיהּ בְּשִׁלְחָא וַהֲדַר ד] חָלֵים — עַתִּיקָתָא, וְאִידָּךְ חַדְתָּתָא;

וא"נ

רש"י

גַּוַּיְיתָא לְבָרַיְיתָא (א). שֶׁכָּתַב "וְהָיָה כִּי יְבִיאֲךָ" קוֹדֶם לְ"קַדֶּשׁ", דְּנַעֲשֵׂית פְּנִימִית חִיצוֹנָה ה]. אֲבָל גַּוַּיְיתָא לְגַוַּיְיתָא. כְּגוֹן אִם הִקְדִּים "שְׁמַע" לְ"וְהָיָה כִּי יְבִיאֲךָ". אוֹ בָּרַיְיתָא לְבָרַיְיתָא. כְּגוֹן "וְהָיָה אִם שָׁמוֹעַ" ו] בִּשְׂמֹאל, "קַדֶּשׁ" בְּיָמִין שֶׁל מַנִּיחַ. תִּיתוֹרָא = גֶּשֶׁר. לְאַחַר שֶׁנָּתַן הָאִגְּרוֹת בַּבָּתִּים *דֶּרֶךְ הַפֶּה הָרָחָב, שֶׁהַבָּתִּים עֲשׂוּיִין כְּעֵין בָּתֵּי יָדַיִם שֶׁקּוֹרִין גוט"ן, וּמַכְנִיס הָאִגְּרוֹת דֶּרֶךְ הַפֶּה וְנוֹתְנָם בְּבָתֵּי הָאֶצְבָּעוֹת, וְחוֹתֵךְ מִג' הַדְּפָנוֹת מִכָּל אַחַת מְעַט, וְהַד' נִשְׁאֶרֶת אֲרוּכָּה. וְכוֹפְלָהּ לְאוֹתוֹ אוֹרֶךְ, וּמַטִּילָהּ עַל חוֹדָן שֶׁל ג' הַדְּפָנוֹת, וְתוֹפֵר חוֹדָן שֶׁל ג' *דְּפָנוֹת עַל רָחְבּוֹ שֶׁל זֶה, וְהוּא בֵּית מוֹשָׁבוֹ שֶׁל תְּפִילִּין, וְנִרְאֶה כְּעֵין דַּף שֶׁל גֶּשֶׁר. מַעְבַּרְתָּא. כְּשֶׁנּוֹתֵן הָרְצוּעָה שֶׁל תְּפִילִּין סָבִיב אוֹתוֹ תִּיתוֹרָא יַכְפִּיל הַקָּלָף סָבִיב הָרְצוּעָה, כְּעֵין שֶׁעוֹשִׂים לְפִי הַמִּכְנָסַיִם שֶׁלֹּא תְּהֵא הָרְצוּעָה קְבוּעָה, אֶלָּא כְּשֶׁהוּא רוֹצֶה מוֹשְׁכָהּ אֵילָךְ וְאֵילָךְ, וּמַאֲרִיךְ רֹאשׁ זֶה וּמְקַצֵּר רֹאשׁ זֶה. וְלָשׁוֹן "מַעְבַּרְתָּא" — שֶׁמַּעֲבִירָהּ וּמוֹשְׁכָהּ לְכָל צַד שֶׁיִּרְצֶה. שִׁי"ן שֶׁל תְּפִילִּין. לְבַיִת ז] חִיצוֹנָה עוֹשִׂין כְּמִין קְמָטִים דַּקִּים בַּקָּלָף וְנִרְאִין בּוֹ כְּעֵין שִׁי"ן. וְצָרִיךְ שֶׁיַּגִּיעַ חָרִיץ. שֶׁבֵּין בַּיִת לְבַיִת עַד מְקוֹם הַתֶּפֶר לְמַטָּה, כְּלוֹמַר עַד בֵּית מוֹשָׁבוֹ, דְּהַיְינוּ תִּיתוֹרָא ח]. כֵּיוָן דְּמִינְכַּר. חָרִיץ לְמַעְלָה קְצָת, אֵין צָרִיךְ לְהַגִּיעַ לִמְקוֹם הַתֶּפֶר. קִילְפָא = קָלָף. רֵיעוּתָא = נֶקֶב. אֶלָּא בְּמִינָן. שֶׁל עוֹר, וְלֹא שֶׁל מֶשִׁי וּפִשְׁתָּן. אֲדוּמּוֹת לֹא יַעֲשֶׂה. מִפְּנֵי גְּנַאי, שֶׁמָּא יֹאמְרוּ: גַּרְדָּן הוּא, וּמִדַּם חֲטָטָיו נִצְבְּעוּ וְהֶאְדִּימוּ הָרְצוּעוֹת. וְדָבָר אַחֵר. שֶׁמָּא יֹאמְרוּ: אִשְׁתּוֹ נִדָּה בָּעַל, וְנִצְבְּעוּ בְּדָם. שֶׁל תְּכֵלֶת. דְּלָאו ט] מִינָן הוּא. מִבִּפְנִים. אֲפִילוּ לְבָנוֹת, וּדְא"ר יִצְחָק שְׁחוֹרוֹת — מִבַּחוּץ. דְּמִתְהַפְּכִין לֵיהּ. מַה שֶּׁבִּפְנִים (ב) בַּחוּץ וְנִרְאֶה הָאוֹדֶם. תְּפִילִּין מְרוּבָּעוֹת י] בְּתוֹפְרָן. בִּתְפִירָתָן יִשְׁמוֹר אֶת רִיבּוּעָן, שֶׁלֹּא יִמְשׁוֹךְ חוּט הַתְּפִירָה יוֹתֵר מִדַּאי, שֶׁלֹּא יִכָּוְוצוּ וְיִקְצַר רָחְבּוֹ, שֶׁקּוֹרִין דגרזלי"ר. וּבַאֲלַכְסוֹנָן. שֶׁיְּהֵא רִיבּוּעָן מְכוּוָּן אָרְכּוֹ כְּרָחְבּוֹ, כְּדֵי שֶׁיְּהֵא לָהֶם אוֹתוֹ אֲלַכְסוֹן שֶׁאָמְרוּ חֲכָמִים (סוכה דף ח.): כָּל אַמְּתָא בְּרִיבּוּעָא — אַמְּתָא וּתְרֵי חוּמְשֵׁי בַּאֲלַכְסוֹנָא, וְלֹא יְהֵא אָרְכּוֹ יָתֵר עַל רָחְבּוֹ, שֶׁאֲפִי' יֵשׁ לְהוּ זָוִיּוֹת – פְּסוּלִין. תְּפִלָּתוֹ עֲגוּלָּה. בֵּית מוֹשַׁב תְּפִילִּין עָגוֹל, שֶׁאֵין לָהֶם בֵּית מוֹשָׁב, אֶלָּא יא] כְּמִין דּוֹפֶן בֵּיצָה. סַכָּנָה. יב] שֶׁכְּשֶׁיִּכָּנֵס בַּפֶּתַח וְיַכֶּה רֹאשׁוֹ בָּאִיסְקוּפָה שֶׁלֹּא יִכָּנְסוּ הַתְּפִילִּין בְּרֹאשׁוֹ. וְאֵין בָּהּ מִצְוָה. דִּמְרוּבָּעוֹת הֲלָכָה לְמֹשֶׁה מִסִּינַי. כְּאַמְגּוּזָא. שֶׁעוֹר בֵּית מוֹשָׁבָם חָדוּד בְּיוֹתֵר. אֲבָל עָגוֹל כְּעָגִיל וּכְטַבַּעַת – אֵימָא דִּכְשֵׁירָה, שֶׁהֲרֵי יֵשׁ לָהֶם [*בֵּית מוֹשָׁב. טַבְלָא. זֶהוּ עוֹר שֶׁל בָּתִּים יג] . שְׁתַּיִם. שְׁנֵי דְּפָנוֹת בִּשְׁנֵי בָּתִּים. זֶה שֶׁלֹּא כְּנֶגֶד זֶה. כְּגוֹן שֶׁנִּפְסַק בַּיִת רִאשׁוֹן וּבַיִת ג' וְאֶחָד שָׁלֵם בֵּינֵיהֶם. זֶה כְּנֶגֶד זֶה — יד] *[בָּתִּים הַסְּמוּכוֹת] ל"א: זֶה כְּנֶגֶד זֶה — בְּתוֹךְ אֲוִיר חָרִיץ אֶחָד נִפְסַק דּוֹפֶן בַּיִת זֶה וְדוֹפֶן בַּיִת שֶׁכְּנֶגְדּוֹ. זֶה שֶׁלֹּא כְּנֶגֶד זֶה – שֶׁנִּפְסַק זֶה בַּאֲוִיר אֶחָד וְזֶה בַּאֲוִיר אַחֵר, שֶׁאֵין קֶרַע רוֹאֶה אֶת חֲבֵירוֹ, שֶׁהַבַּיִת מַפְסִיק בֵּינֵיהֶן (ג). טו] לָא אֲמָרָן. ב' בָּתִּים הַסְּמוּכִים דִּפְסוּלִים. בַּחֲדַתָּתָא. וְנִפְסְקוּ, וַדַּאי עוֹר מְקוּלְקָל הוּא טז] . דְּמִתְלֵי יז] בְּשִׁילְחָא. כְּשֶׁאוֹחֵז בָּעוֹר וּמְפַשֵּׁט. וַהֲדַר חָלֵים. כְּשֶׁמַּנִּיחָן חוֹזֵר וְכוֹוֵץ יח]. שִׁילְחָא = עוֹר, כְּמוֹ (ויקרא א) "וְהִפְשִׁיט" – *וַיְשַׁלַּח. יט] (אַף ע"ג דַּהֲדַר) חָלֵים. לְשׁוֹן חִיבּוּר, שֶׁמִּתְחַבֵּר הַקֶּמֶט לִמְקוֹמוֹ.

א"נ

תוספות

תיתורא דתפילין הלכה למשה מסיני. הוא העור הנכפל למטה שמכסה פי הבתים, והוא בית מושבו של תפילין, ונראה כעין דף של גשר. ומשמע מתוך פירוש הקונטרס שהבתים והתיתורא הכל מעור אחד, כ] ואין נוהגין כן. מ"ר.

מעברתא דתפילין. הוא העור הנעשה מכפילות העור שהוכפל למטה לכסות פי הבתים, ומכניסים בו הרצועות, ונקראת "מעברתא" על שם שצריך שלא יהו הרצועות קבועות, אלא מעבירן ומושכן לכל צד שירצה, מאריך ראש זה כא] ומקצר ראש זה. ובערוך ערך "מעבר" פי': מעברתא כב] *הוא תיתורא, וכן גשרים נקראין מעברתא. *ותיתורא הוא מקום שמכניסין בו הרצועה, ונקראת מעברתא דתפילין. ונראה דלא פירש הערוך כן בשביל שיהא מעברתא דתפילין ותיתורא דתפילין הכל א', כג] דבגמ' חשיב ליה בתרתי, אלא משום דמחברי אהדדי חשיב להו כחדא. וי"מ: מעברתא – רצועה קטנה שמעבירין למעלה על בית תפילין של יד. ואין נראה לפסול משום שאינו רואה כל הבית את האויר, חדא – דלא שייך אינו רואה האויר בכי האי גוונא, אלא כי חבר ביתא אחרינא תמן. ועוד, דשמא דבית החיצון שאינו רואה האויר פסול לא שייך אלא בתפילין של ראש ולא בשל יד, כמו שיש בתשובות הגאונים. ועוד, כי הרצועה שנותנים על בית הזרוע אינו מכסה כל הבית, אלא הבית עצמה מגולה ימין ושמאל, א"כ הבית רואה שפיר את האויר לצד המעברתא כד] ולצד *שכנגדו. מ"ר.

דשי"ן של תפילין הלכה למשה מסיני. בשל ראש איירי, והנותנה *)אם אין דינו להיות פוסלת, דנמלא דאין בית רואה את האויר. דלא דמי לטוטה תפלה של ראש ועושה אותה של יד. מ"ר.

שי"ן של תפילין הלכה למשה מסיני. כתב בשימושא רבה דתפילין: צורה דשי"ן כה] דימינא ג' רישי, ודשמאלא ד' רישי, ואי אפיך לית לן בה. עוד כתוב *בו שמניחין על קלף הפרשיות קלף תלק אחד וכורכו בו. ושמא בשל יד קאמר, אם כתבו בד' עורות, כדאמרינן לעיל: וצריך לדבק. עוד כתוב שם, אמר אביי: כתבינהו אגויל שפיר דמי, וכן הלכה. וזה א"א, דבהדיא אמרינן בפ' "המוציא יין" (שבת דף עט:): תפילין אגויל מי כתבינן? עוד כתוב בתקון תפילין שעושה אותם רחבים ב' אצבעות, ואי עבדינהו טפי שפיר דמי, ואי פחית לא מיפסיל בהכי. ובריש "המוצא תפילין" (עירובין דף נה:) פירשתי טעם, דומיא דלין. מ"ר.

קולמוסא בדיק ליה. וכן הלכה, וה"נ אמרינן ב"העור והרוטב" (חולין דף קיט:): כל נקב שהדיו עובר עליו אינו נקב. מ"ר.

רצועות שחורות. יש שעושין בתים של תפילין מקלף לבן, דלא בעי' שחורות אלא רצועות. מ"ר.

תפילין מרובעות. יש שאין מרבעין אלא במקום מושבן. ושמא לריך הבתים מרובעין של ראש כשמרבעתן דבוקות, וכן בית של יד. וקלת היה נראה דלא בעי כו] מרובעות אלא בתופרן ובאלכסונן, כמו שמפרש רב פפא. מ"ר.

*) על שי"ן דינו כו' דאין שי"ן רואה. ל"ק

פוק

עין משפט נר מצוה

קע א ב מיי' פ"ג מהלכות תפילין הל"א סמג עשין כה טוש"ע או"ח סי' לב סעי' מז:

קעא ג מיי' שם טוש"ע שם סעי' מב:

קעב ד מיי' שם הלכה יא טוש"ע שם סעי' מג:

קעג ה ו מיי' פ"ג מהל' תפילין הלכה יד סמג שם טוש"ע או"ח סי' לג סעי' ג:

קעד ז ח מיי' פ"ג מהל' תפילין הלכה א טוש"ע או"ח סי' לב סעי' לט:

קעה ט מיי' פ"ד שם הלכה ג:

נ"א ונקראין תיתורא רש"א

קעו י כ ל מ מיי' פ"ג מהל' תפילין הלכה יח סמג עשין כב טוש"ע או"ח סי' לג סעי' א:

הגהות הב"ח

(א) רש"י ד"ה גוויתא לברייתא שנתן והיה כי: (ב) ד"ה דמתהפכין וכו' לחוץ ונראה האודם הס"ד ואח"כ מ"ה בתופרן ותיבות תפילין מרובעות נמחק: (ג) ד"ה זה שלא כנגד וכו' מפסיק ביניהן הס"ד ואח"כ מ"ה בחדתתא:

שכנגדו לקיין כו' הד"א ל"ק. רש"ק הגיה של"ל הכל דיבור א' וכל"ל שכנגדו ואין להוכיח מדקאמ' מעברתא דתפילין סתם דמשמע נמי בשל ראש דהא סתמא קאמר שין של תפילין הל"מ דבשל ראש איירי כו' ולפי דעת הרש"א הם שני דיבורים

שם שמניחים ל"ק

שיטה מקובצת

א] תיבת קא נמחק: ב] תפילין מרובעות. פ"ה הבתים מרובעים והולך לטעמו א) שפי' דהתיתורא מעור אחד של הבתים עצמן ועוד נראה לפרש שצריך שיהיה גם התפירה מרובעת ויהיה בה דין אלכסון כל אמתא בריבוע כו'. גליון: ג] היכא דמיתלי. ותיבת כי נמחק: ד] חלים עתיקתא. נ"א חלים חדתא ואינך עתיקא: ה] פנימית חיצונה. אי נמי הקדים והיה אם שמוע לשמע דנעשית פנימית חיצונה וחיצונה פנימית: ו] אם שמוע משמאל קדש מימין: ז] לבית החיצונה עושין כו' ונראין בו כמין שין: ח] תיתורא. וי"מ חריץ של קמטין של שין שאין נראה דמסתמא אי אפשר בלאו הכי. תוס': ט] דלאו מינו הוא: י] תפילין מרובעות. הבתים מרובעים הס"ד ומה"ד בתופרן: יא] אלא כעין ביצה הס"ד: יב] שכשיכנוס פתאום בפתח: יג] בתים: קיימת. שלא יהיה בה נקב: יד] כנגד זה. שני בתים: טו] תיבות לא אמרן כו' דפסולין נמחק: טז] מקולקל הוא. ל"א מגונה קריעה בחדש יותר מבישן: יז] דמיתלי בשלחא: יח] וכווין במקומו: יט] תיבות אע"ג דהדר כו' למקומו נמחק: כ] ואין נוהגין כן. ור"י מפרש תיתורא זה עור אחר כפול ואינו מעור הבתים אלא עור אחר הוא וחציו העליון נקוב הוא להוציא הבתים דרך אותו הנקב וחציו השני הוא למטה וחופה פי הבתים מלמטה לפיכך נקרא תיתורא לפי שהוא כעין דף של גשר למטה מהבתים וכן נהגו העולם: כא] ומקצר ראש זה. וי"מ זהו רצועה הנתונה על הבית של יד ומכסה ראש הבית מבחוץ וגם צד ימין וצד שמאל של בית מכוסה בו באותו עור קטן. תוס' אחרות: כב] [מעברתא] דתפילין הוא תיתורא כו' מעברתא. ונקראין תיתורא ובתפילין מקום שמכניסין בו הרצועה נקראת מעברתא: כג] תיבות דבגמ' כו' חשיב להו כחדא ל"ש: כד] ולצד שכנגדו. ואין להוכיח מדקאמר תפילין סתם דמשמע נמי בשל ראש בשין דהא סתמא קאמר שין של תפילין הל"מ ד' אויר כמו שין של לוחות. תו"ה: כו] מרובעות. נהגו העולם שין דארבע רישי צד קדש ותלתא צד שמע ומאי טעמא כו' והעולם רגילים לעשות הכל מרובעים ואפי' גוף התפילין למעלה מן הבתים. תו"ה:

מסורת הש"ס

טפה הרחב שלכן שהבתים ל"ק

הדפנות ל"ק

שבת כח: סב.

[שבת כח:]

מגילה כד.

שם איתא רבא

גי' רש"ק ורש"א הגיה טוב

שני בתים הסמוכות ל"ק

ויקלח הס"ד אח"כ מ"ה דהדר חלים ל"ק

א) אולי חסר כאן איזה תיבות וצ"ע

קסז א ב מיי' פ"ב מהל' תפילין הל"א סמג עשין כב טוש"ע או"ח סי' לב סעי' ב:

סנהדרין ד: זבחים לז:

קסח ג ד ה מיי' שם פ"ג הלי"ז סמג שם טוש"ע או"ח סימן מב סעי' א:

קסט ו מיי' שם הל' ה סמג שם טוש"ע או"ח סי' לד סעי' א:

דאי שקלת לוי"ו דויסף ושדית ליה לחמשיתו הוי ליה חמשיותו והשתא מוקמינן ליה באמצע תיבה ומוקמית ליה אגב יו"ד וקשה לפירושו דקאמר בתר הכי גבי הקדש נמי דכ' ויסף חמישית אע"ג דכי כו' נ"ק

[וע' היטב תוס' זבחים לז: תוס' סנהדרין דף ד"ה לטוטפת וכו' מ"ש בשם ר"ת]

ת"ר: "לְטֹטָפֹת" "לְטֹטָפֹת" "לְטוֹטָפֹת" — הֲרֵי כָּאן ד', דִּבְרֵי רַבִּי יִשְׁמָעֵאל. ר"ע אוֹמֵר: אֵינוֹ צָרִיךְ, "טַט" בְּכַתְפֵּי שְׁתַּיִם, א] "פַּת" בְּאַפְרִיקִי שְׁתַּיִם. ת"ר: יָכוֹל יִכְתְּבֵם עַל ד' עוֹרוֹת, וְיַנִּיחֵם בְּד' בָּתִּים בְּד' עוֹרוֹת? ת"ל: °"וּלְזִכָּרוֹן בֵּין עֵינֶיךָ" (שמות יג) — זִכָּרוֹן אֶחָד אָמַרְתִּי לְךָ, וְלֹא ב' וג' זִכְרוֹנוֹת, הָא אכֵּיצַד? ב] כּוֹתְבָן עַל ד' עוֹרוֹת, וּמַנִּיחָן בְּד' בָּתִּים בְּעוֹר אֶחָד. ג] וְאִם כְּתָבָן בְּעוֹר אֶחָד וְהִנִּיחָן בְּד' בָּתִּים — יָצָא. וְצָרִיךְ שֶׁיְּהֵא רֶיוַח בֵּינֵיהֶן, דִּבְרֵי רַבִּי, וַחכ"א: אֵינוֹ צָרִיךְ; ד] וְשָׁוִין, שֶׁנּוֹתֵן חוּט אוֹ מְשִׁיחָה בֵּין כָּל אַחַת וְאַחַת. ה] וְאִם אֵין חָרִיצָן נִיכָּר — פְּסוּלוֹת. תָּנוּ רַבָּנַן: בכֵּיצַד כּוֹתְבָן? תְּפִלָּה שֶׁל יָד — כּוֹתְבָהּ עַל עוֹר אֶחָד, וְאִם כְּתָבָהּ בְּאַרְבַּע עוֹרוֹת וְהִנִּיחָהּ בְּבַיִת אֶחָד — יָצָא. וְצָרִיךְ לְדַבֵּק, שֶׁנֶּאֱמַר: °"וְהָיָה לְךָ לְאוֹת עַל יָדְךָ" (שם), כְּשֵׁם שֶׁאוֹת אַחַת מִבַּחוּץ — כָּךְ אוֹת אַחַת מִבִּפְנִים, דִּבְרֵי ר' יְהוּדָה. ר' יוֹסֵי אוֹמֵר: אֵינוֹ צָרִיךְ. א"ר יוֹסֵי: וּמוֹדֶה לִי ר' יְהוּדָה בְּרַבִּי, שֶׁאִם אֵין לוֹ תְּפִילִּין שֶׁל יָד וְיֵשׁ לוֹ גשְׁתֵּי תְפִילִּין שֶׁל רֹאשׁ, שֶׁטּוֹלֶה עוֹר עַל אַחַת מֵהֶן וּמַנִּיחָהּ. מוֹדֶה? הַיְינוּ פְּלוּגְתַּיְיהוּ! אָמַר רָבָא: מִדְּבָרָיו שֶׁל ר' יוֹסֵי, חָזַר בּוֹ ר' יְהוּדָה. אִינִי? וְהָא שָׁלַח רַב חֲנַנְיָה מִשְּׁמֵיהּ דר' יוֹחָנָן: דתְּפִלָּה שֶׁל יָד עוֹשִׂין אוֹתָהּ שֶׁל רֹאשׁ, וְשֶׁל רֹאשׁ אֵין עוֹשִׂין אוֹתָהּ שֶׁל יָד, לְפִי שֶׁאֵין מוֹרִידִין מִקְּדוּשָּׁה חֲמוּרָ' לִקְדוּשָּׁה קַלָּה! ל"ק: ההָא בְּעַתִּיקְתָא, הָא בְּחַדְתְּתָא. וּלְמ"ד הַזְמָנָה *מִילְּתָא הִיא — דְּאַתְנֵי עֲלַיְיהוּ מֵעִיקָּרָא. ת"ר: ו] וכֵּיצַד סִדְרָן? "קַדֶּשׁ לִי" "וְהָיָ' כִּי יְבִיאֲךָ" מִיָּמִין, "שְׁמַע" "וְהָיָ' אִם שָׁמוֹעַ" מִשְּׂמֹאל. (ל"ק מ"ז) וְהָתַנְיָא אִיפְּכָא! אָמַר אַבַּיֵי, ל"ק: כָּאן מִימִינוֹ שֶׁל קוֹרֵא, כָּאן מִימִינוֹ שֶׁל מַנִּיחַ, וְהַקּוֹרֵא קוֹרֵא כְּסִדְרָן.§ אָמַר רַב חֲנַנְאֵל אָמַר רַב: הֶחֱלִיף פָּרָשִׁיּוֹתֶיהָ — פְּסוּלוֹת. אָמַר אַבַּיֵי: לָא אֲמַרַן אֶלָּא

לְטֹטָפֹת לְטֹטָפֹת ז] לְטוֹטָפֹת הֲרֵי כָּאן ד'. מִכָּאן ח] שֶׁכּוֹתֵב ד' פָּרָשִׁיּוֹת בְּד' בָּתִּים. טַט בְּכַתְפֵּי שְׁתַּיִם. כְּאוֹתוֹ מָקוֹם קוֹרִין לִשְׁתַּיִם "טַט". עַל ד' עוֹרוֹת ט]. ד' חֲתִיכוֹת קְלָף, וְיַנִּיחֶנָּה בְּד' בָּתִּים שֶׁל ד' חֲתִיכוֹת קְלָף. בְּד' בָּתִּים בְּעוֹר אֶחָד. שֶׁמַּפְשִׁיטִין עֵגֶל קָטָן *[וְלוֹקְחִים חֲתִיכַת עוֹר] וּמַנִּיחִין אוֹתוֹ בִּדְפוּס שֶׁיֵּשׁ בּוֹ כְּמִין י] [*ד'] אֶצְבָּעוֹת, וּמַנִּיחִין אוֹתוֹ לְיַיבֵּשׁ עַל הַדְּפוּס, וְנוֹטְלִין אֶת הַדְּפוּס וְנַעֲשִׂים בָּתִּים מֵאֲלֵיהֶן. וְאִם כְּתָבָן בְּעוֹר אֶחָד. שֶׁעָשָׂה עוֹר אֶחָד וְכָתַב בּוֹ ד' פָּרָשִׁיּוֹת, וְהִנִּיחָן בְּד' בָּתִּים שֶׁל עוֹר אֶחָד כְּמָה שֶׁפֵּירַשְׁנוּ. וְצָרִיךְ שֶׁיְּהֵא רֶיוַח בֵּין הַפָּרָשִׁיּוֹת. כְּשֶׁיִּכְתְּבֵם (א), יא] שֶׁלְּאַחַר שֶׁכְּתָבָן בְּעוֹר אֶחָד יַחְתּוֹךְ מִלְמַעְלָה הָעוֹר כְּמִין *ד' אֶצְבָּעוֹת וְיַנִּיחֵן בְּד' בָּתִּים *וְיִהְיֶה מְדוּבָּק לְמַטָּה עוֹר אֶחָד, כְּדֵי שֶׁתְּהֵא פָּרָשָׁה אַחַת בְּבַיִת אֶחָד. בֵּינֵיהֶם. בְּתוֹךְ הַד' בָּתִּים שֶׁל עוֹר הָאֶחָד. שֶׁנּוֹתֵן חוּט אוֹ מְשִׁיחָה. בֵּין כָּל בַּיִת וּבַיִת. וְאִם אֵין חֲרִיצָן. הֶחָרִיץ שֶׁבֵּין כָּל בַּיִת וּבַיִת, יב] אִם אֵינוֹ נִיכָּר מִבַּחוּץ – פְּסוּלָה, כְּגוֹן אִם עָשָׂה מְחִיצּוֹת הַבָּתִּים מִבִּפְנִים וְאֵין חָרִיץ נִיכָּר מִבַּחוּץ. כּוֹתְבָהּ עַל עוֹר אֶחָד. כָּל הָאַרְבַּע פָּרָשִׁיּוֹת. בְּד' עוֹרוֹת. בְּד' אִגְּרוֹת. וְצָרִיךְ לְדַבֵּק. אֶת הַד' אִגְּרוֹת בְּיַחַד, בִּתְפִירָה, אוֹ בְּדֶבֶק שֶׁקּוֹרִין גלו"ד. אוֹת. סִימָן. וְהָיָה לְךָ לְאוֹת. אֲפִי' לְךָ לֹא יְהֵא אֶלָּא אוֹת אַחַת. דְּכִי הָווּ בִּפְנִים ד' אִגְּרוֹת שֶׁאֵינָם דְּבוּקוֹת וּנְתוּנוֹת בְּבַיִת אֶחָד, לַאֲחֵרִים שֶׁאֵין רוֹאִין אֶלָּא *חִיצוֹן יג] חָשׁוּב אוֹת אַחַת, אֲבָל לְךָ הַמְשַׁמֵּשׁ בָּהֶן, וְנִיכָּר (ב) מַמָּשָׁן שֶׁל ד' אִגְּרוֹת כָּל אַחַת לְבַדָּהּ – הָווּ ב' אוֹתוֹת. אֵינוֹ צָרִיךְ. לְדַבֵּק. יְהוּדָה בְּרַבִּי. יְהוּדָה הֶחָכָם. וְיֵשׁ לוֹ ב' (ג). (זוּגוֹת) תְּפִילִּין שֶׁל רֹאשׁ הָעֲשׂוּיִין בְּד' בָּתִּים. שֶׁטּוֹלֶה עוֹר עַל אַחַת מֵהֶן. עַל הַד' בָּתִּים תְּכַסֶּה עוֹר אֶחָד, וְנִרְאִין כְּבַיִת אֶחָד. וּמַנִּיחָהּ. בְּיָדוֹ, אע"פ שֶׁאֵין מְדוּבָּקוֹת בִּפְנִים. מִתּוֹךְ דְּבָרָיו שֶׁל רַבִּי יוֹסֵי נִשְׁמַע שֶׁחָזַר בּוֹ רַבִּי יְהוּדָה. וְאֵין צָרִיךְ לְדַבֵּק (ד). תְּפִילִּין שֶׁל רֹאשׁ חֲמוּרָה קְדוּשָּׁתָהּ. שֶׁרוּבּוֹ שֶׁל "שַׁדַּי" *נַעֲשֶׂה (בְּקֶשֶׁר) בְּשֶׁל רֹאשׁ – שִׁי"ן דָּלֶ"ת, אֲבָל בְּשֶׁל זְרוֹעַ אֵין יד] אֶלָּא יו"ד, שֶׁיֵּשׁ שָׁם רְצוּעָה קְטַנָּה כְּשִׁיעוּר רֹחַב אֶצְבַּע *וּבְסוֹף רֹאשָׁהּ מְעַט כְּמִין יו"ד. וְעוֹד כְּתִיב: "וְרָאוּ כָּל עַמֵּי" וגו', וְתַנְיָא ר"א הַגָּדוֹל אוֹמֵר: אֵלּוּ תְּפִילִּין שֶׁבְּרֹאשׁ טו] (לקמן לה:). עַתִּיקְתָא. שֶׁכְּבָר נִקְשְׁרוּ בָּרֹאשׁ, אָסוּר לְהוֹרִידָן וְלַעֲשׂוֹת שֶׁל יָד. וּלְמַאן דְּאָמַר. בְּסַנְהֶדְרִין בְּפֶרֶק "נִגְמַר הַדִּין" (דף מז:). הַזְמָנָה מִילְּתָא הִיא. וּמִשֶּׁזִּימְּנָהּ לְעוֹרֶךְ הָרֹאשׁ אֵין רַשַּׁאי לְשַׁנּוֹתָהּ לְשֶׁל יָד טז]. כְּגוֹן דְּאַתְנֵי עֲלֶיהָ. מֵעִיקָּרָא *לְשֶׁל יָד אִי צָרִיךְ לָהֶם. כֵּיצַד סִדְרָן. סֵדֶר הֲנָחָתָן. כָּאן מִיָּמִין שֶׁל קוֹרֵא כָּאן מִימִינוֹ שֶׁל מַנִּיחַ. כְּשֶׁהַקּוֹרֵא עוֹמֵד כְּנֶגֶד מַנִּיחַ הָוֵי יְמִינוֹ שֶׁל זֶה לִשְׂמֹאל שֶׁל זֶה. וְהַקּוֹרֵא קוֹרֵא כְּסִדְרָן. כְּסֵדֶר שֶׁהֵן כְּתוּבִין בַּתּוֹרָה, מוּקְדָּם מוּקְדָּם וּמְאוּחָר מְאוּחָר. הִילְכָּךְ, הָא דְּקָתָנֵי לְעֵיל: "קַדֵּשׁ" "וְהָיָה כִּי יְבִיאֲךָ" מִיָּמִין – מִימִינוֹ שֶׁל קוֹרֵא קָאָמַר, דְּהַשְׁתָּא כְּשֶׁהוּא קוֹרֵא כְּדַרְכּוֹ מִימִינוֹ יז] לִשְׂמֹאלוֹ וְנִמְצָא קוֹרְאָן כְּסִדְרָן. וְהָא דְּתַנְיָא אִיפְּכָא, דְּמַשְׁמַע "קַדֵּשׁ" "וְהָיָה כִּי יְבִיאֲךָ" מִשְּׂמֹאל – אַמַּנִּיחַ קָאָמַר, דְּהוּא יָמִין שֶׁל קוֹרֵא. הֶחֱלִיף. יח] כִּדְמְפָרֵשׁ.

גּוּיְיתָא

לטטפת לטוטפת. ב"שמע" "והיה אם שמוע" כתיב: "לטטפת", ב"והיה כי יביאך" כתיב: "ולטוטפת" בספרים מדויקים, אבל בין פ"א לתי"ו לא כתיב וי"ו. ותימה: היכי משמע תרי? ואי הוה אמרינן גורעין ומוסיפין ודורשין ניחא, אבל לא אשכחן אלא בתחילת תיבה וסוף תיבה, כפ' שני דזבחים (דף כה. וע"ש) גבי "ולקח מדם הפר", דדרשינן: דם מהפר יקבלנו. וכן "ונתתם את נחלתו לשארו" דדרשינן בפרק "י"נ" (ב"ב דף קיא:): ונתתם נחלת שארו לו! ומפרש ר"ת: דוי"ו קמא ד"ולטוטפת" מוקמינן בסוף, כאילו כתיב "לטוטפות". כדאשכחן בפ' "הזהב" (ב"מ דף נד:): *שקליה לוי"ו ד"ויסף" ה"ל "חמישיתו", והשתא מוקמינן ליה באמצע תיבה והוה ליה "חמישיותו", ומוקמינן ליה במקום יו"ד באמצע תיבה. וק' לפי', דפריך בתר הכי: א"ה גבי הקדש נמי דכתב "ויסף חמישית" כו'! ומשני: דכי שקלת לוי"ו ד"ויסף" ה"ל "חמישיתו". והשתא, לוקמיה באמצע תיבה דליהוי "חמישיות". הילכך נראה דבשום פעם לא מוקמינן ליה אלא בסוף תיבה, ככל הני שהבאתי*. מ"ר.

לטוטפת. נראה *דלשון טוטפת הוא הראש אבל המלת, כמו "טוטפת וסרביטים" דפרק "במה אשה" (שבת דף נז.), דהיינו כלילא שמקפת כל המלת. א"נ, נקראו טוטפות על שם שהם בראש בין העינים, לשון הבטה, כמו (מגילה דף יד:): שפיל ואזיל בר אווזא ועינוהי מטייפין. וכן ניך לשון הבטה, על שם שהוא למעלה מבין שתי ריסי עיניו. ותפילין נראה לשון ויכוח, כמו (סנהדרין דף מד.): "ויפלל" – שעשה פלילות עם קונו, על שם שהם עדות והוכחה שהשם נקרא עליו ויראים ממנו, יט] כגון דאמרינן לקמן (דף לה:): "וראו כל עמי הארץ כי שם ה' נקרא עליך" וגו' – אלו תפילין שבראש. מ"ר.

טט בכתפי שתים. להאי תנא לא אמרינן דליבעי י"ב בתים, כ] דמסתבר ליה שכתוב הכל *בפסוק אחד, דלא אשכחן בתורה שלא הוזכרו תפילין אלא בד' פרשיות. יש גורסין "טוט", ומפרשין כי האי דאמרינן במו"ק (דף טז.): "טוט אסר טוט שרי" גבי שמתא, היינו שני ת"ח אוסרין וב' אחרים יכולין להתיר. ואין נראה, דתרי לאו ב"ד ניהו. אלא בתקיעת שופר איירי, כדאמר התם: בארבעה מאה שיפורי שמתיה ברק למרוז, אפיק שיפורא ושמתיה. *מ"ר. **ושוין** שנותן חוט או משיחה בין כל אחת. היינו דוקא בכתובות בעור אחד, אבל בד' עורות לא. ויש נוהגין אפי' בד' עורות. מ"ר. **והקורא** קורא כסדרן. פירש בקונטרס: כסדר שהן כתובין בתורה, מוקדם מוקדם מאוחר מאוחר. הילכך, הא דקתני לעיל: "קדש" "והיה כי יביאך" מימין – מימינו של קורא קאמר, והשתא כשהוא קורא כדרכו מימינו לשמאלו נמצא קורא קורא כסידרן. וקשה לר"ת: דמאי פלגינהו, שקורא *שתיהן הראשונות מימין וכל האחרונות משמאל? היה לו לומר: ראשונה מימין וכל אחרות משמאל, או איפכא, דג' ראשונות מימין ורביעית משמאל. כמו גבי נר מערבי דפרק "שתי הלחם" (לקמן דף צח:) דיליף דנרות של מנורה מזרח ומערב מונחים, מדכתיב בנר מערבי "לפני ה'" – מכלל דכולהו לאו לפני ה', ולא אמרינן: חצי הנרות לפני ה' וחצי האחר לאו לפני ה'! כא] ומפרש ר"ת: "קדש" "והיה כי יביאך" מימין של קורא, ומשמאל של קורא הוי "שמע" מבחוץ, ואחריה "והיה אם שמוע" מבפנים. וניחא השתא מה שחלקו. וכן פירש רבינו חננאל *בסנהדרין (דף פט.): כל בית החיצון שאינו רואה את האויר פסול – *כגון "קדש" ו"שמע", וכן רב האי גאון. והיה מניח סימן – הויות להדדי, פי': "והיה כי יביאך" "והיה אם שמוע" פנימיות זו אצל זו. וכן בתשובת הגאונים שכתב ה"ר יוסף טוב עלם. והאי דקאמר: הקורא קורא כסדרן – לאו כמו שפירש בקונטרס, כסדר שכתובות בתורה, אלא מפרש ר"ת דהוא סיום הברייתא ד"כילד סדרן", וקאמר שקורא כסדר שמונחין בתפילין מימינו לשמאלו, דהיינו: "קדש" "והיה כי יביאך" "והיה אם שמוע" "שמע". ואפילו לא יהא מן ברייתא אין קשה כלום. ובמכילתא משמע כפירוש הקונטרס, בפרשת "והיה כי יביאך", דקתני התם: בד' מקומות מזכיר פרשת תפילין – "קדש" "והיה כי יביאך" "שמע" "והיה אם שמוע", מכאן אמרו: מצות תפילין ארבע פרשיות כו', והדר קתני: כותבן כסדרן, ואם כתבן שלא כסידרן יגנזו, משמע: כסדר שנאמן ברישא. ויש לדחות: דבכתיבת הסופר קאמר, אבל אין קובעין בתפילין כסדר זה. ואין נראה כלל. (ה) ובשימושא רבא *תיקון התפילין משמע כפירוש הקונטרס, וז"ל: ומשוי פרשתא ד"קדש" מימין בביתא קמא, ופרשתא דבסמוך ליה *בביתא תניינא "והיה כי יביאך", ופרשתא ד"שמע" בשלישית, ופרשה ד"והיה" אם שמוע" ברביעית. מ"ר.

תיתורא

[וכ"ה ברש"י ברי"ף]

גי' רש"א

ד' פרשיות נ"ק

נ"ל ויהא מדובק למטה בעור אחד כדי שתהא כל פרשה בבית אחד בפני עצמה בתוך הד' בתים של עור האחד נ"ק. וכן הוא ברש"י ברי"ף

הגהות הב"ח

(א) רש"י ד"ה וצריך וכו' כשיכתבם בעור אחד שלאחר שכתבן יחתוך מלמעלה העור כמין ד' פרשיות ומניחן בד' בתים: (ב) ד"ה והיה לך וכו' וניכר משמוש של ד' אגרות: (ג) ד"ה ויש לו ב' תפילין כצ"ל ותיבה זוגות נמחק: (ד) ד"ה מתוך וכו' לדבק הס"ד ואח"כ מ"ה מקודשה חמורה תפילין של ראש: (ה) תוס' ד"ה והקורא וכו' ואין נראה כלל דבשימושא:

ברכות כג: מגילה כו: סנהדרין ח. מז:

נעשה בשל ראש נ"ק

וכפוף ראשה נ"ק

על של ראש לעשות לשל יד נ"ק

בכתיבה אחד בפסוק אחד אי נמי דלא אשכחן בתורה שהוזכרו תפילין כו' נ"ק

(וע"ע תוס' סנהדרין שם ותוס' זבחים שם ד"ה טט)

שתים הראשונות מימין ושתים האחרונות כו' נ"ק

בסנהדרין באלו הן הנחנקין כל כו' נ"ק ופי' ר"ח כגון נ"ק

שהוא תיקון נ"ק

והיה כי יביאך בביתא תניינא ופרשתא נ"ק

שיטה מקובצת

א] פת באפריקי שתים (פי' דחד לטטפת לגופא ונשאר שנים לדרשה עיין תוס' סנהדרין דף ד) דהוו להו באפריקי ד' וטט באפריקי לאו כלום הוא ועי"ל כל מקום שפירש לנו הכתוב במקום אחד מנין ונישנית פעמים או שלש אין לנו להרבות בהכי המנין ככל דבר שנאמרה ונישנית לא נישנית אלא מפני דבר שנתחדש בה: ב] כותבן על ד' עורות ומניחן בד' בתים בעור אחד וכן הלכה: ג] ואם כתבן בעור אחד והניחן בד' בתים. כגון שחלק למטה ומחוברים קצת למעלה והניח מה שנחלק מלמטה בד' בתים: ד] ושוין כו' יש מפרשים על הקלף אחר שנכרך כל פרשה ופרשה לבדה כורך עליה חוט או משיחה ויש מפרשים אחר שנתפרו שמעביר חוט של התפירה בין כל בית ובית: ה] ואם אין חריצן כו' פרש"י כגון אם עשה מחיצת הבתים מבפנים כו' וקשה להבין איך אפשר שנעשו מבפנים המחיצות ואין החריץ ניכר מבחוץ אם לא העביר עור עליהם: ו] כיצד סדרן. סדר רש"י פסול לר"ת וסדר ר"ת פסול לרש"י ויש מניחין שני זוגות כדי לצאת ידי שניהם ויש אומרים לפיכך טוב לברך על של יד ולהניח של ראש בלא ברכה וטעם לדבר דמסתמא בשל יד לא פליגי ורבינו ברוך אמר דכי היכא דפליגי בשל ראש פליגי נמי בשל יד ואע"ג דבכתיבה לא פליגי אפ"ה נראה דלר"ת כותב בתחלה קדש ואח"כ והיה כי יביאך ומניח מקום חלק לכתוב והיה אם שמוע כדי לכתוב תחילה שמע כסדר הכתוב בתורה ואח"כ חוזר וכותב והיה אם שמוע במקום חלק שהניח ונהגו העולם כדברי רש"י: ז] לטוטפת. תלתא קראי כתיבי תרין בק"ש וחד בוהיה כי יביאך תרי חסרים וחד מלא לטטפת לטטפת ולטוטפות תרי הרי. גליון ואינו כן בכל הספרים אלא גורעין ויו של דולטוטפת א): ח] מכאן שכותבין: ט] ד' עורות על: י] כמין ארבע: יא] כשיכתבם ויהיה של עור אחד כדי שתהא פרשה אחת בבית אחת כשיניחם בתוך [הד' בתים] והד"א והשאר נמחק: יב] בית ובית. ניכר ותיבות אם אינו נמחק: יג] חיצון. הוי אות ותיבת חשוב נמחק: יד] זרוע אין שם אלא יו"ד כו' אצבע. וכפוף ראשה מעט: טו] שבראש הס"ד ומה"ד חדתא שלא נקשרו עדיין בראש מותרים לעשות של יד הס"ד ומה"ד עתיקתא: טז] לשל יד. אשכחה לה כגון דאתני עליה מעיקרא. לשם של יד. דאי איצטריך להם הס"ד והד"א: יז] לשמאלו. נמצא: יח] כדפרישית הס"ד: יט] ממנו. כמו דאמרינן: כ] כיון דמסתבר ליה כו' דלא אשכחן בתורה שהוזכרו תפילין: כא] ומפרש ר"ת דרך סדר הנחה קדש יביאך שמוע שמע וה"פ כשבא להתחיל לקרות מימין מוצא קדש יביאך וכל הסדר מימין וכשהוא מתחיל משמאל מוצא שמע תחילה ואח"כ שמוע וכל הסדר יביאך קדש והקורא קורא כסדרן האמור בברייתא ראשונה ולפי שתירץ התלמוד כאן מימינו של מניח ולא פירש איזו נעמיד בקורא ואיזו נעמיד במניח לפיכך פי' הקורא קורא כסדר של ברייתא ראשונה. תו"ח:

א) עי' בתוס' כאן ד"ה לטטפת.

אדעתא דגינה הוא דעבידא. אביי ורבא עבדי כרבה ורב יוסף, ורב אשי עביד כרב ושמואל לחומרא. א] והילכתא אכרב ושמואל לחומרא. איתמר: לול ב] פתוח מן הבית לעלייה, אמר רב הונא: באם יש לו פתח אחד — חייב במזוזה אחת, אם יש לו ב' פתחין — חייב בשתי מזוזות. אמר רב פפא: גשמע מינה מדרב הונא, האי אינדרונא דאית ליה ארבעה באבי — חייב בארבע מזוזות. פשיטא! לא צריכא, אף על גב ג] דרגיל בחד. אמר אמימר: האי פיתחא דאקרנא חייב במזוזה. אמר ליה רב אשי לאמימר: והא לית ד] ליה פצימין! א"ל: עדי פצימי. רב *פפא איקלע לבי מר שמואל, חזא ההוא פיתחא דלא הוה ליה אלא פצים אחד משמאלא ועבידא ליה מזוזה, א"ל: כמאן, כר"מ? אימר דאמר ר"מ — מימין, משמאל מי אמר? מאי היא? דתניא: "ביתך" — ביאתך מן הימין; אתה אומר: מן הימין, או אינו אלא משמאל! ת"ל: "ביתך". מאי תלמודא? אמר רבה: ודרך *ביאתך מן הימין, דכי עקר איניש כרעיה — דימינא עקר. * ה] רב שמואל בר אחא קמיה דרב פפא משמיה דרבא בר עולא אמר, מהכא: °"ויקח יהוידע הכהן ארון אחד ויקב חור בדלתו ויתן אותו אצל המזבח מימין בבוא איש בית ה' ונתנו שמה הכהנים שומרי הסף את כל הכסף המובא בית ה'". מאי ר"מ? דתניא: בית שאין לו אלא פצים אחד — ר"מ מחייב במזוזה, וחכמים פוטרין. ו] מאי טעמא דרבנן? °"מזוזות" כתיב. מ"ט דר' מאיר? דתניא: "מזוזות" — שומע אני מיעוט מזוזות שתים, כשהוא אומר °"מזוזות" בפרשה שניה — שאין תלמוד לומר, הוי ריבוי אחר ריבוי, ואין ריבוי אחר ריבוי אלא למעט, מיעטו הכתוב למזוזה ז] אחת, דברי ר' ישמעאל. ר"ע אומר: אינו צריך, כשהוא אומר: °"על המשקוף ועל שתי המזוזות" — שאין ת"ל "שתי", מה ת"ל "שתי"? זה בנה אב, כל מקום שנאמר "מזוזות" אינו אלא אחת, עד שיפרט לך הכתוב שתים. ת"ר: "וכתבתם" — יכול יכתבנה על האבנים? נאמר כאן כתיבה ונאמר להלן כתיבה, מה להלן על הספר — אף כאן העל הספר. או כלך לדרך זו: נאמר כאן כתיבה ונאמר להלן כתיבה, מה להלן על האבנים — אף כאן על האבנים! נראה למי דומה, דנין כתיבה הנוהגת לדורות מכתיבה הנוהגת לדורות, ואין דנין כתיבה הנוהגת לדורות מכתיבה שאינה נוהגת לדורות, וכמו שנאמר להלן: °"ויאמר להם ברוך מפיו יקרא אלי את הדברים האלה ואני כותב על הספר בדיו". אמר ליה רב אחא בריה דרבא לרב אשי, רחמנא אמר "על מזוזות", ואת אמרת: נילף כתיבה כתיבה?! אמר קרא: °"וכתבתם" — *כתיבה תמה, והדר "על המזוזות". ומאחר דכתיב, ["וכתבתם"] האי גזירה שוה למה לי? אי לאו גזירה שוה, ח] הוה אמינא ליכתבא אאבנא וליקבעה אסיפא, קמ"ל.§ "ארבע פרשיות שבתפילין מעכבות זו את זו, ואפילו כתב אחד מעכבן".§ פשיטא! אמר רב יהודה אמר רב: לא *נצרכא אלא ט] ילקוצו של יו"ד. והא נמי פשיטא! לא נצרכא אלא לאידך דרב יהודה, דאמר רב יהודה אמר רב: *יכל אות שאין גויל מוקף לה מארבע רוחותיה — פסולה.§ ת"ר

רש"י

י] והילכתא כרב ושמואל לחומרא. *ומצריך מזוזה לתרווייהו, דס"ל כרבי יוסי. לול הפתוח מן הבית לעלייה. זהו דרכן: יא] ארובה באמצע העלייה ועולין לה מן הבית במעלות, ועושין ד' מחיצות סביב המעלות למטה כדי שלא ירד אדם מן העלייה לבית כי אם ברשות בעליה, ועושין פתח במחיצות. וכן עושין בני העלייה ד' מחיצות סביב הארובה למעלה ובהן פתח. אם יש לו ב' פתחים. אחד בבית ואחד בעלייה כדפירשתי. אע"ג דרגיל בחד. מינייהו טפי. דהא דאמרן לעיל: הלך אחר הרגיל – ה"מ כגון תרי בבי, ורגיל בחד – בטילה אידך לגביה, אבל תלתא לגבי חד לא בטלי. ל"א מתשובת הגאונים: *הלך אחר הרגיל – יב] שהיה רגיל שבני אדם רגילים לצאת ולבא בו, ולמעוטי פתחא דרבי שאינו עשוי אלא לו לבדו, ולאיתויי פתחא דרב הונא שהיה רגיל אף לאחרים. אבל ד' פתחים או ג' לחדר אחד וכולן נעשו לביאת כל בני הבית שהיו מרובין, ותשמיש (א) אחד *בחדר תדיר והוצרכו לו פתחים הרבה – כולן חייבין במזוזה, ואף על פי יג] שנתמעט *תשמיש ואינן צריכין עכשיו לכולן אלא לאחד מהן. דאקרנא. בקרן זוית של בית. והא אין לה פצימין. מזוזות, אלא ראשי הכתלים. עדי = הרי. כלומר, אלו ראשי הכתלים הן הן פצימין. פצים אחד. שהיה הפתח אצל הזוית, וקיר הפתח הוא הזוית ואין אצלו *כלום, ואין לו פצים אלא סף שסוגר בו. כר"מ. מפרש לקמן, דמחייב מזוזה לבית שאין לו אלא פצים אחד. מאי היא. מנלן דמימין? ביאתך מן הימין. דרך ימין לביאה. דרך ביאתך יד]. לביאה ולא ליציאה. מימין בבוא איש בית ה'. כשהיה אדם נכנס לפתח עזרה מזרחי והולך למערב – ה"ל אותו ארון מימין, שהיה נתון אצל קיר צפוני של (ב) טו] מזבח מימין בבוא אצל המזבח. אלמא דרך ימין הויא ביאה, וכל דבר הנתון דרך ביאה צריך ליתנו מימין. מיעט הכתוב למזוזה (ג). שאם אין בו אלא פצים אחד – חייב. שאין תלמוד לומר שתי. דמיעוט מזוזות שתים. טז] להלן כתיבה. "וכתב לה ספר" (ד) (דברים כד). ולהלן כתיב. *"וכתבת על האבנים". ספר כריתות נוהג לדורות. כתיבת אבנים הוראת שעה היתה. יז] שנאמר להלן כו'. כלומר, וצריך ליכתוב בדיו, בין במזוזות בין בגט, כמו שנאמר: יח] "מפיו יקרא אלי" וגו' כלומר, מהאי קרא נפקא דספר בדיו בעינן. רחמנא אמר על מזוזות. דמשמע יט]: *כתבם על הסף ממש, ולא באגרת. כתיבה תמה. ואין כ] כתיבה תמה על העצים והאבנים, אלא על הספר. והדר. שימה במזוזות. ג"ש. כתיבה כתיבה. ליכתבא אאבנים. יקתקקה בסכין על האבנים, דהויא כתיבה תמה. והדר ליקבעה. לאפוקי אסיפה בצורת הפתח, ולקיים כתיבה תמה והדר על המזוזות.

לטטפת

תוספות

מ"ר כשהוא אומר מזוזות בפרשה שניה שאין ת"ל. משמע קלא דכתיבי "מזוזות" מלא בב' ווי"ן, ולא "מזוזת" חסר, דהא רבי ישמעאל אית ליה יש אם למסורת בריש סנהדרין (דף ד:) גבי "לטטפת". ומיהו אין ראיה מזה, דה"נ אשכחן ר"ע דאית ליה יש אם למקרא בההיא ד"לטטפת", ובפרק "כל שעה" (פסחים דף לו.) אית ליה יש אם למסורת*. נאמר כאן כתיבה ונאמר להלן כתיבה. ופירש בקונטרס: גבי גט, דכתיב "וכתב לה ספר כריתות". וקשיא: דהא תנן (גיטין דף יט.): על עלה של זית ועל קרן של פרה כותבין, כא] ודקאמר ספר — לספירת דברים! ונראה לפרש: דדריש מכתיבה דפרשת סוטה, כב] או מכתיבה דמשנה תורה שהמלך כותב, דכתיב (דברים יז): "וכתב לו את משנה התורה הזאת על ספר", והיינו נוהג לדורות. ואם תאמר: אדרבה, נילף מגט! וי"ל: דמזוזה וס"ת חובת דורות, ומצות. כג] מ"ר. כמה שנאמר להלן כו'. פירש בקונטרס: כלומר, וצריכה ליכתב בדיו, בין מזוזה בין גט, כמה שנאמר להלן. ותימה גדולה פירושו, דהא מכשירין גט בסיקרא ובסם (גיטין דף יט.)! מ"ר. וכתבתם אמר קרא כתיבה תמה והדר על מזוזות. צריך הוא לדרשה דכתיבה תמה. דלא מצינו למימר: אמר קרא "וכתבתם" והדר "על מזוזות", דה"נ *כתיבה דהתם "וכתבת על האבנים", ולא אמרינן "וכתבת" והדר "על האבנים". אלא מכתיבה תמה דריש, כדפירש הקונטר' דכתיבה תמה לא שייכא על האבנים, לפי שאינה מתקיימת. מ"ר.

עין משפט נר מצוה

קם א מיי' פ"ו מהל' מזוזה הל"א טוש"ע יו"ד סימן רפו סעי' ט:

קמא ב מיי' שם הל"י טוש"ע שם סעי' יט:

קמב ג מיי' שם טוש"ע שם סעי' יח:

[וע' היטב תוס' סוכה ו: ד"ה ור"ש ותוס' סנהדרין ד. ד"ה כולהו ותוס' זבחים מ. ד"ה לא נצרכא]

קמג ד מיי' פ"א מהל' תפילין הל"ב סמג עשין כב טוש"ע יו"ד סי' רפט סעי' ב:

קמד ה מיי' פ"א מהל' תפילין הל"ו סמג עשין כב כה טוש"ע יו"ד סי' רפח סעי' ו:

קמה ו מיי' פ"א מהל' תפילין הל"ב סמג עשין כב טוש"ע או"ח סי' לב סעי' ד בהג"ה:

קמו ז מיי' שם הלי"ט סמג שם טוש"ע שם סעי' ד:

שיטה מקובצת

א] תיבות והילכתא כרב ושמואל לחומרא נמחק: ב] לול הפתוח: ג] דרגיל בחד כו' פירש"י כו'.

עין משפט נר מצוה

קנד א מיי' פ"ו מהל' תפילין הלי"ב טוש"ע יו"ד סי' רפה סעי' ב וסי' רפט סעי' ב:
קנה ב מיי' שם פ"ה הלכה ח טוש"ע יו"ד סי' רפט סעי' ד:
קנו ג מיי' שם טוש"ע שם סעי' ה:
קנז ד מיי' פ"ו שם הלכה ה סמג שם טוש"ע יו"ד סי' רפו סעי' יד:
קנח ה ו מיי' שם הל"ג טוש"ע שם סעי' ו:
קנט ז מיי' שם הל' ח טוש"ע שם סעי' ח:

גמרא

תורה אור

ומאי תחילת שליש העליון דקא אמר — להרחיקה, א] שלא להרחיקה מן הקורה של מעלה יותר משליש. אמר רבא: *אמצוה להניחה בטפח הסמוך לרה"ר. מאי טעמא? רבנן אמרי: כדי שיפגע ב] במזוזה מיד, רב חנינא מסורא אומר: כי היכי דתינטריה. אמר רבי חנינא: בוא וראה שלא *כמדת הקב"ה מדת בשר ודם, מדת בשר ודם — מלך יושב מבפנים *ועם משמרין אותו מבחוץ, מדת הקב"ה אינו כן, עבדיו יושבין מבפנים והוא משמרן מבחוץ, שנאמר: °"ה' שומרך ה' צלך על יד ימינך". [תהלים קכא] דרש רב יוסף בריה דרבא משמיה דרבא: בהעמיק לה טפח — פסולה. לימא מסייעא ליה: הניחה בפצין או שטלה עליה מלבן, אם יש שם טפח — צריך מזוזה אחרת, אם לאו — אינו צריך מזוזה אחרת! כי תניא ההיא, ג] בפתח שאחורי הדלת. הא בהדיא קתני לה: פתח שאחורי הדלת, אם יש שם טפח — צריך מזוזה אחרת, ואם לאו — אינו צריך מזוזה אחרת! כיצד קתני. תנא: העמיד לה מלבן של קנים, חותך שפופרת ומניחה. אמר רב אחא בריה דרבא: לא שנו אלא שהעמיד ולבסוף חתך והניחה, גאבל חתך והניח ולבסוף העמיד — פסולה, "תעשה" — ולא מן העשוי. ואמר רבא: הני פיתחי שימאי פטורין מן המזוזה. מאי *פיתחי שימאי? פליגי בה רב ריחומי ואבא יוסי, חד אמר: דדלית להו תקרה, וחד אמר: דלית להו שקופי. אמר רבה בר שילא אמר רב חסדא: האכסדרה פטורה מן המזוזה, לפי שאין לה פצימין. הא יש לה פצימין — חייב? לחיזוק תקרה הוא דעבידי! הכי קאמר: אע"פ שיש לה פצימין — פטורה, שאין עשויין אלא לחיזוק לתקרה. אמר אביי: חזינא להו לאיספלידי דבי מר דאית להו פצימי ולית להו מזוזתא, קסבר: לחיזוק תקרה הוא דעבידי. מיתיבי: בית שער, אכסדרה, ומרפסת — חייבין במזוזה! *ובאכסדרה דבי רב. אכסדרה דבי רב כאינדרונא מעלייתא הוא! באכסדרה רומיתא. אמר רחבה אמר רב יהודה: בי הרזיקי חייב בשתי מזוזות. מאי בי הרזיקי? אמר רב פפא סבא משמיה דרב: בית שער זהפתוח לחצר, ובתים פתוחין לבית שער. ת"ר: בית שער הפתוח לגינה ולקיטונית — רבי יוסי אומר: נידון כקיטונית, וחכ"א: נידון ד] כבית שער. רב ושמואל דאמרי תרוייהו: ה] מגינה לבית כולי עלמא לא פליגי דחייב, מאי טעמא? ביאה דבית היא, כי פליגי — מבית לגינה, מר סבר: ו] קיטונית עיקר, ומר סבר: גינה עיקר. רבה ורב יוסף דאמרי תרוייהו: מבית לגינה דכולי עלמא לא פליגי דפטור, מאי טעמא? פיתחא דגינה הוא, כי פליגי — מגינה לבית, מר סבר: ביאה דבית הוא, ומר סבר: כולה אדעתא

רש"י

דתינטריה. לכל הבית מן המזיקין. על יד ימינך. דמזוזה ליד הימין היא בכניסתו. העמיק. חסר טפח, וקבע בו המזוזה — פסולה. פצים. ז] דהיינו סף מזוזה של צורת הפתח. או שטלה עליה מלבן. לבנה, שלאחר שקבע המזוזה בסף הוסיף מלבן בפתח כנגד ח] *הפתח, אם יש בעומק הפצים או באותו מלבן (שלה) שטלה על המזוזה טפח, דהשתא היא מזוזה תחובה בעומק הכותל טפח — צריך מזוזה אחרת כו'. טלה. לשון טלאי, פלסטר"א. בפתח שאחורי הדלת. כגון שיש ט] במקצוע הבית פצים קבוע, ושני פתחים מחותכין אחד לדרום ואחד למערב, וקבע מזוזה (א) *בפנים בחלל פתח הדרומי, וכשהדלת *סתום הוי פתוח למערב אחורי הדלת, אם יש עובי בפצים המבדילן טפח בין פתח לפתח — צריך מזוזה אחרת לפתח מערבי, הואיל ואין המזוזה י] בחללו, *ואם לאו — אין צריך מזוזה אחרת, שהרי כמונח באותו פתח עצמו. וכן שטלה מלבן לפצים משני צדדים, והמלבן ריבה את עביו *והבדיל את הבדלתו. פי' אחר: שדרך עשירים לעשות פתח אצל שער הגדול, שאין פותחים שער הגדול תמיד.* יא] והכי קאמר: או שטלה עליה מלבן ועשה אצל המלבן פתח אחר, אם יש בין פתח לפתח טפח — הוי שניהם חשובין, וצריך מזוזה אחרת לקטן. הא בהדיא קתני לה. בסיפא דההיא. כיצד קתני. והכי קאמר: הניחה בפצים או שטלה עליה מלבן, אם יש שם טפח כו', כיצד? כגון פתח שאחורי הדלת יב]. מלבן של קנים. שלא מצא מזוזות עץ ועשה צורת פתח של קנים. מלבן *מזוזה סף. חותך. חתיכה מאחד הקנים, שהן חלולים, ויתן המזוזה באותו מקום יג] חתך. אבל חתך בשפופרת. והניח מזוזה בתוכה, ואחר כך *העמיד המלבן יד] בגידה — לא, משום תעשה ולא מן העשוי. פיתחי שימאי. מקולקלין ואשמים, כמו "זקן אשמאי" דאמרינן בקידושין (דף לג:). תקרה. אסקופה עליונה. שקפי. מזוזות. ל"א: תקרה — שאין טו] הבית מקורה, שקפי — אסקופה עליונה טז]. (ב) פצימין = עמודים. אכסדרה. שלשה דפנות סתומות בלא פתח, והרביעית פתוחה לגמרי מפתח, אבל למעלה יש דופן מעט המחזיק את הסכך. הואיל ואין לה יז] פצימין. אוישריא"ש, ואותה פתיחה לא פתח הוא. הא יש לה פצימין חייבין. בתמיה, ואמאי? חיזוק לתקרה הוא דעבידי הפצימין, ולא לשום פתח! אלא יח] לחיזוק תקרה. שלא תפול. אספלידי דבי מר = אכסדראות דבי *רבה. בית שער = בית קטן שעושין בצד שערי חצירות, ויושב שם שומר הפתח. מרפסת = אלוייר"א. יט] חייבת במזוזה. מדרבנן, קשיא לאביי (ג). ההיא דקתני חייבת באכסדרא דבי רב. שיש לה ד' דפנות אלא שאין מגיעות לסכך. אינדרונא = קמבר"א. באכסדרא רומיתא. עשויה (ד) חלונות חלונות, וקורין לויא"י. בית שער הפתוח לחצר כו'. בעי ב' מזוזות, כ] אחת בפתח שמן בית שער לבתים, ואחת בפתח שמן החצר לבית שער. כא] נדון בקיטוניות. וצריך מזוזה. נדון כב] כבית שער. *כאויר, ואין צריך מזוזה. מגינה לבית. באותו פתח שבין הגינה לבית שער — דכ"ע חייב, דביאת בית שער הוי, אותו שער כג] שבו נכנסין *מן הקיטונית [לבית שער כשרוצים ליכנס לגינה, ולהכי קרי ליה מבית לגינה. ולי נראה איפכא מגינה לבית היינו פתח הקיטונית] שהבאים מן הגינה דרך בית שער נכנסין בו לקיטוניות — כ"ע לא פליגי דחייב. כד] כי פליגי מבית לגינה. פתח החיצון שיוצא מבית [שער] לגינה, שהיוצאין מן הבית דרך בית שער יוצאין בו לגינה. מר סבר עיקר בית שער כה] כו'. לשם כניסת קיטונית נעשה, והוי כשאר בית שער דעלמא, שחייבין כל פתחיו במזוזה. כו] ומר סבר עיקר בית שער לגינה נעשה. ליליא מקיטונית לגינה, הילכך נדון כאויר *ולא כבית שער. *) (מר סבר. הפתח לשם קיטונית עבידא וחייב במזוזה, ומר סבר עיקרו לשם גינה עביד ופטורה). ל"א, ועיקר היא: מגינה לבית, אם כשהוא פותח פתח מגינה לבית, *) דהיכר ציר הוי בבית — דכ"ע לא פליגי (ה) דחייבת. קיטונית עיקר. וחייב, ואף על גב דציר סובב בגינה. דכי אמרינן לעיל הלך אחר היכר ציר — הני מילי בפתח דבין תרי בתי, דתרווייהו עיקר, אבל הכא עיקר קיטונית, ולשמה נעשה — חייב. ומר סבר: עיקרו לשם גינה עביד, ופטור.

והילכתא

*) היכר הציר הוי בבית דכ"ע לא פליגי דחייב כי פליגי מבית לגינה דהיכר ציר הוי בגינה מ"ס קיטונית עיקר וחייב ואע"ג כו' גינה עביד ולשומר ופטור הס"ד נ"ק

תוספות

ומאי תחילת שליש העליון דקאמר להרחיקה. שיותר לא ירחיקנה מן התקרה. ובירושלמי משמע בפ"ב דמגילה דכשהפתח גבוה הרבה מניחה כנגד כתפיו. וחולק על התלמוד שלנו. מ"ר.

דלית להו תקרה. פירוש: מקום שהפתח שוקף שם מלמעלה אינו שוה, אלא האבנים מן הכיפה אבן נכנסת ואבן יוצאת. וכענין זה דלית ליה שיקפי — שאין שם מזוזות, אלא האבנים בולטות כגון שיני חומה. וכענין זה [איתא] בפ"ק דעירובין (דף יא.) גבי סוכה. ומה שפי' הקונט' לשון אחר: דלית ליה תיקרה — שאין הבית מקורה, *)קשיא: מי גרע משערי אלירות דחייבין במזוזה, כדאמר פרק קמא דיומא (דף יא.)? מ"ר.

איספלידי דבי מר. סוגיא דשמעתין מוכחא דהיינו אכסדרא, ולא כמו שפי' בקונט' בפ"ק דבבא בתרא (דף ז.) דהיינו טרקלין נאה. ובערוך פירש דהיינו מערה, כדמתרגמינן (תהלים נג) "בברחו מפני שאול במערה" — באיספלידא. וסוגיא דבבא בתרא קשיא לפי' הערוך, דמשמע התם שיש באיספלידא כשורי וליבני, ובמערה ליכא כשורי וליבני! ועוד, דקאמרינן התם: מעיקרא איספלידא והשתא אינדרונא, פירוש: לפי שבנה אשיתא אפומא דאיספלידא. ואי איספלידא היינו מערה — אין לך חדר אפל ממערה! *מ"ר.

אכסדרה ומרפסת חייבין במזוזה. וכן משמע בפ"ק דסוכה (דף ח:) דבית שער חייב במזוזה, גבי שתי סוכות של יוצרים זו לפנים מזו, דפריך: ותיהוי חיצונה בית שער לפנימית ותתחייב במזוזה. ותימה, דבפ"ק דיומא (דף יא.) [illegible] אכסדרה ומרפסת? תלמוד לומר כז] בית כו'! וי"ל: דהתם מדאורייתא והכא מדרבנן. *והר"ר יצחק אלפס תירץ דהכא בפתוחה לבית. מ"ר.

כשהוא

*) וע' בהרא"ש בה"ק שמתרץ קושיא זו

הגהות הב"ח

(א) רש"י ד"ה בפתח וכו' וקבע מזוזה בפנים בחלל: (ב) ד"ה פצימין נ"ל אחר ד"ה הא יש: (ג) ד"ה חייבת וכו' לאביי הס"ד ואח"כ מ"ה באכסדרה דבי רב ההיא דקתני וכו' שיש לה סביב דפנות אלא שמוקפת חלונות הס"ד: (ד) ד"ה באכסדרה רומיתא עשויה דפנות נמוכות שאין מגיעות לתקרה הס"ד וכ"כ קך פרש"י בב"ב דף יא ע"ב: (ה) ד"ה מר סבר הפתח וכו' דחייב הס"ד ואח"כ מ"ה כי פליגי מבית לגינה דהיכר ציר הוי בגינה מר סבר קיטונית עיקר וחייב ואע"ג:

[וע"ע תוס' ב"ב ז. ד"ה איספלידא]

[עירובין יא. ע"ש]

ותוס' במסכת סוכה ח ע"ב דוחה פי' זה דא"כ ה"ל לשנויי הכא דהא דאמר ר"ח אכסדרה פטורה כשאינה פתוחה לבית אבל מלשון פטורה משמע אפילו מדרבנן עכ"ל וע' נ"ק

מסורת הש"ס

המזוזה נ"ק | נ"ק מ"ז | [לעיל לב:] | נ"א בפנים נ"ק | פתוח הוי למערב אחורי הדלת נ"ק | עיין נ"ק שהאריך | והגדיל נ"ק | ופתח הקטן פתוח תמיד וה"ק נ"ק | [ע' פירש"י לעיל בע"א ד"ה תלי דקא בריעה העמיד כו'] | הוא סף המזוזה הס"ד נ"ק | העמיד המלבן בצורת הפתח לא משום דכתיב כו' נ"ק | ב"ב יא. | רב נ"ק | כאויר הגינה ואין נ"ק | לקיטונית שהבאים רש"ק | הגנה ולא נ"ק | *) רש"ק מ"ז

שיטה מקובצת

א] תיבות שלא להרחיקה מן כו' יותר משליש נמחק: ב] שיפגע במצוה מיד: ג] בפתח שאחורי הדלת. רש"י פי' ב' לשונות וללשון ראשון צ"ל שאותו פצים שבמקצוע [העמיד] לשני פתחים [לצד] ימין ביאה לזה ולזה וללשון שני קשה להבין דמה ענין הוא זה לפתח שאחורי הדלת: ז"ל תו"ח בפתח שאחורי הדלת. פ"ה כגון במקצועות הבית כו' ולפירושו קשה אי תרוייהו פתוחות לרה"ר היכא משכחת לה דרך ימין לזה ולזה וצ"ל שאחת פתוחה לרה"ר ואחת פתוחה לחדר ואז הוי דרך ימין לזה ולזה ע"כ: ד] וחכ"א נדון. כאויר. (ותיבות כבית שער נמחק). דנהי דאמרינן לעיל גבי בי הרזקי חייב בשתי מזוזות ואפי' בפתח של צד החצר היינו דוקא חצר אבל קיטונית אינו עשוי כל כך לתשמיש ולא מחייב במזוזה: תו"ח: ה] מגינה לבית. פ"ה בלשון אחר אם כשהוא פותח כו' עד עיקר ואע"ג דאמרי' לעיל הלך אחר היכר ציר ה"מ בפתח שבין גברי לנשי דתרווייהו חייבין וליכא אלא לידע איזה דרך ימין ולדין זה אזלינן בתר היכר ציר אבל לפטור כשהיכר ציר במקום פטור ודאי לא אז... דפטר סבר דאף לפטור אזלינן בתר היכר ציר. תו"ח: ז"ל תוס' מהר"פ מגינה לבית היינו פתח קיטונית שהבאין מן הגינה דרך בית שער נכנסין בו לקיטונית כ"ע לא פליגי דחייב כי פליגי מבית לגינה פתח החי... שער לגינה שהיוצאין מן הבית דרך בית שער יוצאין בו לגינה כך פרש"י בלשון ראשון וצ"ל דלא דמי בית שער הגינה דהכא לבית שער דחצר לעיל דבית שער החצר רגיל יותר מבית שער הגינה ועוד... ועיקר. ע"כ: ו] מ"ם עיקר קיטונית ומ"ם גינה עיקר: ז] פצים. והיינו סף המזוזה: ח] כנגד. המזוזה אם יש כו' או באותו מלבן שטלה על: ט] שיש במקצועות הבית פצים קבוע בו ושני פתחים מחותכין... כו' מזוזה בפצים בחלל פתח הדרומי וכשהדלת פתוח הוי פתח מערב אחורי הדלת אם יש עובי בפצים. עובי הבדל טפח בין פתח לפתח: י] המזוזה. מונחת בחללו ואם לאו כו' שהרי הוא כמונח באותו... צדדיו והמלבן ריבה את עביו והרחיב את הבדלתו פי' כו' לעשות פתח קטן אצל שער הגדול כו': יא] תמיד. ואותו פתח קטן פתוח תדיר וה"ק כו' מלבן כגון טפח ועשה אצל המלבן פתח אחר אם יש... הדלת. העמיד לפתח: יג] מקום החתך: יד] העמיד המלבן בצורת הפתח: טו] שאין בו בית מקורה: טז] עליונה הס"ד ומה"ד אכסדרה: יז] הואיל ואין לה פצימין. עמודין פצימין בלעז אוישרא... התקרה: יט] חייבין: כ] אחד בפתח שבין בית שער לבתים. ואחד מפתח חיצון שבין החצר לבית שער. ולא אמרינן כיון דבתים פתוחים לו לבטיל לגבי בית ולא בעי מזוזה פתח חיצון וכי א... חייב במזוזה היינו בית שער שאין בתים פתוחים לו: כא] נדון בקיטונית: כב] נדון. הבית שער כאויר בגינה: כג] אותו שער. הפתוח הימנו לבית שער אמרי' לעיל דחשיבי בית לענין מזוזה שבו נכנס... לבית שער כשרוצים ליכנס לגינה ולהכי קרי ליה מבית לגינה שהבאים: כד] כי פליגי מבית לגינה. כלומר באותו פתח שבין הקיטונית לבית שער פתח החיצון שיוצא מבית לגינה: כה] עיקר בית שער ותיבת כו' נמחק: כו] מ"ם עיקר. ההוא פתח לשם קיטונית עביד וחייב ומ"ם עיקר לשם גינה עביד ופטור ול"נ איפכא מגינה לבית היינו פתח הקיטונית: כז] בית כו'. בשלמא אכסדרה לא קשיא דיש לחלק בשמעתין אלא בית שער ומרפסת קשיא:

בטפח הסמוך לרשות הרבים, כמה דמרחק מעלי, קמ"ל. ואמר רב יהודה אמר שמואל: כתבה על שני דפין — פסולה. מיתיבי: כתבה על שני דפין והניחה בשני סיפין — פסולה; הא בסף אחד — כשרה! ראויה לשני סיפין קאמר. ואמר רב יהודה אמר שמואל: במזוזה הלך אחר היכר ציר. *מאי היכר ציר? *אמר רב אדא: אבקתא. היכי דמי? כגון פיתחא דבין תרי בתי, בין בי גברי לבי נשי. ריש גלותא בנא ביתא, אמר ליה לרב נחמן: קבע לי מזוזתא, א"ר נחמן: תלי דשי ברישא. אמר רב יהודה אמר רב: עשאה כמין נגר — פסולה. איני? והא כי אתא רב יצחק בר יוסף אמר: כולהו מזוזתא דבי רבי כמין נגר הוו עבידן, והההיא פיתחא דעייל ביה רבי לבי מדרשא לא הוה לה מזוזה! לא קשיא: הא דעבידא כסיכתא, הא דעבידא כאיסתוירא. איני? והא ההוא פיתחא דהוה עייל א] בה רב הונא לבי מדרשא והויא לה מזוזה! ההוא רגיל הוה, דאמר רב יהודה אמר רב: במזוזה הלך אחר הרגיל. א"ר זירא אמר רב מתנא אמר שמואל: מצוה להניחה בתחלת שליש העליון, ורב הונא אמר: מגביה מן הקרקע טפח, ומרחיק מן הקורה טפח, וכל הפתח כולו כשר למזוזה. מיתיבי: מגביה מן הקרקע טפח, ומרחיק מן הקורה טפח, וכל הפתח כולו כשר למזוזה, דברי רבי יהודה; רבי יוסי אומר: "וקשרתם וכתבתם", מה קשירה בגובה — אף כתיבה בגובה. בשלמא לרב הונא — הוא דאמר כר' יהודה, אלא לשמואל דאמר כמאן? לא כר' יהודה ולא כר' יוסי! אמר ר"ה בריה דרב נתן: לעולם כרבי יוסי, ומאי

רש"י

בטפח הסמוך לרשות *הרבים. ב] (כדאמר לקמן דקדים פגע במצוה) אם היה עובי החלל ד' טפחים או ה', כגון חומת אבנים – יניחנה בחלל טפח הסמוך לרה"ר, כדאמר *לקמן דקדים פגע במצוה כי אתי לביתיה. כמה דמרחיק. מן הבית טפי מעלי, ויניחנה מבחוץ, קמ"ל. על שני דפין. אליה בדף זה ואליה בדף זה. בשני סיפין. בשני מזוזות של פתח. ראויה לשני סיפין. שהניח גויל חלק בין דף לדף, וראוין לחלק לשתים, אליה כאן ואליה כאן. אבקתא. אותו חור שבאיסקופה שציר הדלת סובב בו. היכי דמי. האי "הלך אחר היכר ציר" דרב יהודה. כגון פתחא דתרי בתי ג] בי גברי ובי נשי. אדם שחולק ביתו, אליו להילוך אנשים המחזרין בביתו, ואליו לאשתו לעשות מלאכתה בהצנע, ויש פתח בין זו לזו ופתח לכל בית לרה"ר. ואמרי' לקמן (דף לד.): מזוזה דרך ימין לביאה ולא ליציאה, והכא בפתח שבין זו לזו לא ידעינן הי ליחשוב ביאה והי ליחשוב יציאה, אי יציאה מהאי להאי ואי מהאי להאי. אלא הלך אחר חור שבסף שציר הדלת סובב בו, ההוא צד שהחור בו חשיב בית, ודרך ימין ד] כשנכנסין בו נותנין מזוזה. תלי דשי ברישא. העמיד ה] הסיפא בבנין תחלה ואח"כ *קבעינהו המזוזות. דגמרינן מצילית דכתיב בה "תעשה" – ולא מן העשוי, ואי קבענא תחילה המזוזה ו] בסיפא והדר הסיפא בבנין הוה ליה עשוי המזוזה קודם שתבא לידי מצוה. עשאה כמין נגר. שקבעה ותחבה בסף כנגר שתוחבין הנגרין בכותל כזה:*. פסולה. דמזוזה לתתה בארך בסף כזה:* נגר = קביל"א. ההוא פתחא דעייל ביה רבי לבי מדרשא. פתח קטן היה לו לרבי אצל מקומו, ונכנס ויצא בו כדי שלא יטריח תלמידיו לעמוד בפניו אם יעבור לפניהם. איסתוירא. היינו מקום חיבור השוק והרגל, ומעומד הוא כזה – כשירה (א). עבידא כסיכתא. נגר כשל אומנים כזה: פסול. ל"א: איסתוירא – כי היכי דמקום חיבור השוק והרגל הוי השוק זקוף מלמעלה והרגל שוכב כזה:

כך הניחה למזוזה כשירה, הואיל וראשה אחד זקוף. רגיל הוה. רוב הנכנסין לבית המדרש (ב) ז] באותו פתח. הלך אחר הרגיל. אם יש ב' פתחים לחדר א', באותו פתח שרגיל לצאת ולבא יותר יניח המזוזה. בתחילת שליש העליון. ימדוד מלמטה ח] שני שלישי הפתח, ולכשיכנס לתחילת שליש העליון יתן המזוזה. מה קשירת תפילין בגובה הראש. כדאמרי' בהאי פירקא (דף לז.) מקום שמוחו של תינוק רופס. אף נתינת מזוזה בגובה הפתח. ומשמע: סמוך לתקרת הפתח יניחנה, ולא כשמואל דאמר: בתחילת שליש העליון מלמטה למעלה. *להרחיקה. כלומר, יותר משליש לא ירחיקנה מן התקרה, ולעולם כרבי יוסי. מצוה בטפח הסמוך כו'. פירשתי למעלה.

דתינטריה

תוספות

כתבה על שני דפין פסולה. פי' בקונטרס: שהניח גויל חלק בין דף לדף. ולפירושו יש ליישב בדוחק *הניחו בשני סיפין. אלא: על ב' דפין – בשתי חתיכות קאמר, כי ההיא דפ"ב דסוטה (דף יח.) דאמר: בשני דפין פסולה, ספר אחד אמר רחמנא ולא שנים. והיינו בשתי חתיכות, דומיא דגט בפ"ב דגיטין (דף כ:) דבעי רבא: בין שיטה לשיטה בין תיבה לתיבה, מהו? ופריך: תיפוק לי דספר אחד אמר רחמנא ולא שנים וג' ספרים! ומשני: לא צריכא דמעורה. ועל כרחיך לא מיפסיל לגט בשני דפין בחתיכה אחת, דהא אמרינן בפרק בתרא דגיטין (דף פז:): שייר מקצת הגט וכתבו בדף השני כשר, ולא אמרינן דהוי כשני ספרים ופסול. ויש לדחות, משום דגבי גט כתוב "ספר", אבל בסוטה כתוב "בספר", דמשמע: בספר המבורר ומיוחד, למעוטי ב' דפין אפילו בחתיכה אחת. ובירושלמי משמע דבשני עורות פסולה, דפריך, ולמה לא תנינן: שהספרים נכתבין בשני עורות, והתפילין ומזוזות אין נכתבין אלא בעור א'. מ"ר.

תלי דשא ברישא. פי' בקונטרס: העמיד הסיפין תחילה, שאם לא כן ה"ל תעשה ולא מן העשוי. וקשה, דהוה ליה למימר: קבע סיפי ברישא! ועוד, לקמן הוה ליה לאיתנויי, גבי לא שנו אלא שהעמיד ולבסוף חתך כו'! ט] ונראה לפרש דהאי ביתא דבנה ריש גלותא היינו כגון פיתחא בין גברי לבין נשי דסליק מינה, ומשום היכר ציר קאמר ליה תלי דשא ברישא. מ"ר.

הא דעבידא כסיכתא הא דעבידא כאיסתוירא. פי' בקונטרס: דסיכתא פסולה – שתחובה בסף כנגר שתוחבים בכותל. איסתוירא – מקום חיבור השוק והרגל, ומעומד הוא כשירה. והשתא בין מעומד בין מושכב תרווייהו מיקריין "כמין נגר". וקשיא *לר"ת: דמעומד לאו דרך כבוד הוא, וקבורת חמור קרי ליה ב"המוכר פירות" (ב"ב דף קא.). וספר תורה ולוחות שבארון מושכב ולא מעומד, כדמשמע בפ"ק דבבא בתרא (דף יד.) אע"פ שהיו יכולין להניחו מעומד, דארון י] רומו כרחבו. ועוד, אמרינן בסמוך: העמיד לה מלבן של קנים – חותך שפופרת ומניחה, ואי מעומד – יניחנה באחת מן הקנים של מלבן! יא] וע"כ פר"ת: כי סיכתא – מעומד כיתדות המשכן הנועצות בארץ – פסולה, כאיסתוירא הנתון בשוק לרחבה, בלע"ז קביל"א – כשרה. ומיהו, בפרק "מצות חליצה" (יבמות דף קג.) דאמרינן: האי איסתוירא עד ארעא נחית, על כרחין היינו עצם היורד מן השוק עד הרגל, ולא קבילא. ומיהו, הא דאמר *בפ"ב דמגילה ירושלמי: צריך שיהא "שמע" שלה רואה את הפתח, אין ראיה לפי' הקונטרס. דלפירוש ר"ת יש ליישב, כגון דשיטה אחרונה לצד רשות הרבים היא יב] וראשונה לצד פנים, והופך שמע לצד אויר הפתח. וכן פרשיות של תפילין נמי היה אור"ת שמניח מושכב ולא מעומד. ומיהו, הא דאמרינן לקמן (דף לד:): כתב על עור אחת והניח בארבע בתים יצא – לא קשיא מידי, דמעומד נמי יש ליישב. וקשה לפי' ר"ת מהא דתניא בתוספתא דכלים: שפופרת שחתכה ונתן בה את המזוזה ואח"כ נתנה בכותל, אע"פ שלא כדרך קבלתה – טמאה. נתנה בכותל ואח"כ קבע בה המזוזה, כדרך קבלתה – טמאה, שלא כדרך קבלתה – טהורה. משמע שהשפופרת סתומה מצד א', *ולפי' ר"ת דמפרש: כמין נגר פסולה – מעומד, אבל מיושב כשירה, מאי כדרך קבלתה? ויש ליישב: שהשפופרת פתוחה לאורכה, *משני ראשיה סתומה, ושלא כדרך קבלתה היינו דכפאה על פיה. ול"ע האי דקאמר: כולהו מזוזתא דבי רבי כמין נגר עבידן, משמע: אבל שאר מזוזתא דעלמא לא עבידא כמין נגר! הלכך נראה, בין לפי' הקונטרס בין לפי' ר"ת, דכאיסתוירא דכשירה – היינו באלכסון, לא שוכב ולא זקוף. אי נמי, כמין נון, מקצה שוכב ומקצה זקוף. וכן פי' בקונטרס בלשון אחר. אבל שאר מזוזתא דעלמא לאו הכי עבידן, אלא לפר"ת הוין מיושב, ולפי' הקונטרס מעומד. ואומר ר"ת: צא ולמד, דהא מעשה בכל יום כשספר תורה עומד על הבימה הכל עומדין, וכששליח ציבור מושיבו הכל יושבין. יג] מ"ר.

והא ההוא פיתחא דהוה בי רב הונא והויא ליה מזוזה. מתוך הלשון משמע: דווקא פתח הבית שהיה יוצא ממנו לבית המדרש, אבל פתח בית המדרש עצמו לא בעי מזוזה. ובפ' קמא דיומא (דף יא:) איכא פלוגתא, דתניא: יכול יהו בתי כנסיות ובתי מדרשות מטמאין בנגעים? ת"ל "ובא אשר לו הבית" – מי שמיוחד לו בית. ומסיק: הא רבי מאיר הא רבנן, דפליגי לענין מזוזה יד] לבית הכנסת שאין בה דירה לחזן הכנסת. ובמסכת ברכות (דף מז.) נמי משמע דהלכה כמאן דפטר, גבי אביי ורבין דהוו אזלי באורחא וכי מטו לבי כנישתא אמר ליה רבין לאביי: ליעול מר, אמר ליה: עד השתא לאו מר אנא? א"ל: הכי אמר רבי יוחנן אין מכבדין אלא בפתח שיש בו מזוזה, יש בו מזוזה ס"ד? אלא בפתח הראוי למזוזה. משמע דפתח בית הכנסת פטור. ובירושלמי בפרק טו] שני דמגילה משמע דבי מדרשא דרבי חנינא היה בו מזוזה ומונחת כנגד כתיפותיו של אדם.* מ"ר.

ומאי

עין משפט נר מצוה

היאך הניחו נ"ק

קמח א מיי' פ"ה מהל' תפילין הל"א סמג עשין כג כה טוש"ע יו"ד סימן רפח סעי' ב:

קמט ב מיי' פ"ו שם הל' יא סמג שם טוש"ע יו"ד סי' רפט סעי' ג:

קנ ג מיי' שם הל' ה סמג שם טוש"ע שם סעי' ה:

קנא ד מיי' פ"ה שם הל' ח טוש"ע שם סעיף ו:

[גירסת הערוך אמר רב אויא וכ"א בערובין יא:]

קנב ה ו מיי' פ"ו שם הל' יא סמג שם טוש"ע יו"ד סי' רפו סעי' י:

קנג ז מיי' שם הל' יב סמג שם טוש"ע יו"ד סי' רפט סעי' ב:

[ע' תוס' ב"מ קב. ד"ה בגובהא]

בירושלמי בפ"ב דמגילה לריך נ"ק

מסורת הש"ס

הרבים דקדים כו' נ"ק

לקמן שיפגע במזוזה כי אתי לביתיה הס"ד נ"ק

[עירובין יא:]

בס"י קבע בהו

שייך לע"ב

עיין במרדכי

ומשני נ"ק

[וע"ע תוס' יומא יא: ד"ה שאין]

הגהות הב"ח

(א) רש"י ד"ה עבידא כו' סיכתא נ"ל קודם ד"ה איסתוירא: (ב) ד"ה רגיל וכו' לבית המדרש היו באין באותו פתח:

גליון הש"ס

רש"י ד"ה איסתוירא היינו מקום חיבור השוק כו'. ע' יבמות דף קג ע"א:

שיטה מקובצת

א] עייל ביה: ב] תיבות כדאמר לקמן דקדים פגע במצוה נמחק: ג] גבתי בין בי גברא לבי נשי: ד] ימין שנכנסין: ה] הסיפין תיבת הסיפא נמחק: ו] המזוזה. בסיפין והדר הסיפין בבנין: ז] המדרש. נכנסין באותו פתח אבל אותו של בית לא היה רגיל אלא פתח קטן היה שעשה אצל מקומו ונכנס ויוצא לפעמים כדי שלא יטריח את תלמידיו לעמוד בפניו אבל פתח אחר רגיל היה בו לנכנסים ויוצאין ואע"ג דאמרינן בתי כנסיות ובתי מדרשות אינן חייבין במזוזה צריך לומר שהיה נמי (לתמיש) [לתשמיש] ביתו. תוס' אחרות: ח] מלמטה למעלה: ט] חתך כו' דמייתי נמי דין תעשה ולא מן העשוי: י] רומו ברחבו. ועוד אנו רואין מנהג בכל יום שבכל זמן שהס"ת זקוף על הבימה כל העם עומדים וכשהוא שוכב על הבימה הן יושבין אלמא חשבינן לה כל זמן שהוא זקוף שלא כדרך מקומו. תוס' אחרות: יא] מלבן. בשלמא לפר"ת דמצות מזוזה מושכב ולא זקופה לפיכך צריך לחתוך אחד מן הקנים לתחוב בתוכו המזוזה אבל לפרש"י למה לו לחתוך אינו צריך אלא להניחה דרך נקב העליון שהרי הקנה כולו חלול וי"ל דמ"מ צריך לחתוך לפי שהוא סתום בין קשר לקשר. תוס' אחרות: יב] היא. ואחד לצד פנים: יג] יושבין. והעולם נהגו כרש"י. והרוצה לצאת ידי שניהם יקבענה מוטה כזה: יד] מזוזה בבית הכנסת: טו] בפרק שלישי דמגילה:

תיבות

עין משפט נר מצוה

קמב א מיי' פ"א מהל' תפילין וס"ת הל' יב סמג עשין כה טוש"ע או"ח סי' לב סעי' ו:
קמג ב מיי' שם טוש"ע יו"ד סי' רפח סעי' ח:
קמד ג מיי' פ"ה שם הלכה יב:
קמה ד מיי' פ"י שם הל' ו טוש"ע יו"ד סי' רפב סעי' ז:
קמו ה מיי' פ"ה מהל' תפילין ומזוזה וס"ת הל"ח סמג עשין כג טוש"ע יו"ד סי' רפט סעי' ד:
קמז ו מיי' פ"ו שם הל"ב סמג שם טוש"ע שם סעי' ב:

דְּכָתְבִינְהוּ אֲדוּכְסוּסְטוֹס בִּמְקוֹם בָּשָׂר. וְאִיבָּעֵית אֵימָא: שִׁינָּה בָּזֶה וּבָזֶה תַּנָּאֵי הִיא, דְּתַנְיָא: שִׁינָּה בָּזֶה וּבָזֶה — פָּסוּל, ר' א] *[אַחָא מַכְשִׁיר מִשּׁוּם רַבִּי] אַחַאי בְּרַבִּי חֲנִינָא, וְאָמְרִי לָהּ: מִשְּׁמֵיהּ דְּרַבִּי ב] *עֲקִיבָא בְּרַבִּי חֲנִינָא. (א) הָא מוֹרִידִין — עוֹשִׂין? וְהָא בָּעֲיָא שִׂרְטוּט! דְּאָמַר רַב מְנִיּוֹמֵי בַּר חִלְקִיָּה אָמַר רַב חָמָא בַּר גּוּרְיָא אָמַר רַב: כָּל מְזוּזָה שֶׁאֵינָהּ מְשׂוּרְטֶטֶת — פְּסוּלָה, וְרַב מְנְיָמִין בַּר חִלְקִיָּה דִּידֵיהּ אָמַר: שִׂרְטוּט שֶׁל מְזוּזָה — הֲלָכָה לְמֹשֶׁה מִסִּינַי! תַּנָּאֵי הִיא; *דְּתַנְיָא, ר' יִרְמְיָה אוֹמֵר מִשּׁוּם רַבֵּינוּ: תְּפִילִּין וּמְזוּזוֹת נִכְתָּבוֹת שֶׁלֹּא מִן הַכְּתָב, וְאֵין צְרִיכוֹת שִׂירְטוּט. וְהִילְכְתָא: אתְּפִילִּין לָא בָּעֵי שִׂרְטוּט, בוּמְזוּזָה בָּעֲיָא שִׂירְטוּט, גוְאִידִי וְאִידִי נִכְתָּבוֹת שֶׁלֹּא מִן הַכְּתָב; מ"ט? מִיגְרַס גְּרִיסִין. *אָמַר רַב חֶלְבּוֹ: אֲנָא חֲזִיתֵיהּ לְרַב הוּנָא ג] *דַּהֲוָה יָתֵיב אַפּוּרְיָא דְּס"ת עֲלֶיהָ, וְכַף לְכַדָּא אַאַרְעָא וְאַנַּח עֲלֵיהּ ס"ת, וַהֲדַר יָתֵיב בְּמִיטָּה; קָסָבַר: דאָסוּר לֵישֵׁב עַל גַּבֵּי מִיטָּה שֶׁס"ת מוּנָּח עָלֶיהָ. וּפְלִיגָא דְּרַבָּה בַּר בַּר חָנָה, דְּאָמַר רַבָּה בַּר בַּר חָנָה א"ר יוֹחָנָן: מוּתָּר לֵישֵׁב עַל גַּבֵּי מִיטָּה שֶׁסֵּפֶר תּוֹרָה מוּנָּח עָלֶיהָ, וְאִם לְחָשֵׁשׁ אָדָם לוֹמַר: *מַעֲשֶׂה בְּר' אֶלְעָזָר שֶׁהָיָה יוֹשֵׁב עַל הַמִּיטָּה וְנִזְכַּר שֶׁס"ת מוּנָּח עָלֶיהָ, וְנִשְׁמַט וְיָשַׁב ע"ג קַרְקַע, (ב) וְדוֹמֶה כְּמִי שֶׁהִכִּישׁוֹ נָחָשׁ — הָתָם ס"ת עַל גַּבֵּי קַרְקַע הֲוָה. אָמַר רַב יְהוּדָה אָמַר שְׁמוּאֵל: כְּתָבָהּ אִגֶּרֶת — פְּסוּלָה; מ"ט? אָתְיָא כְּתִיבָה כְּתִיבָה מִסֵּפֶר.

וְאָמַר רַב יְהוּדָה אָמַר שְׁמוּאֵל: התְּלָאָהּ בְּמַקֵּל — פְּסוּלָה; ד] מ"ט? "בִּשְׁעָרֶיךָ" בָּעֵינַן. תַּנְיָא נַמִּי הָכִי: *תְּלָאָהּ בְּמַקֵּל אוֹ שֶׁהִנִּיחָהּ אַחַר הַדֶּלֶת — סַכָּנָה וְאֵין בָּהּ מִצְוָה. שֶׁל בֵּית מוֹנְבַּז הַמֶּלֶךְ הָיוּ עוֹשִׂין בְּפוּנְדְּקוֹתֵיהֶן כֵּן, זֵכֶר לִמְזוּזָה. וְאָמַר רַב יְהוּדָה אָמַר שְׁמוּאֵל: ומִצְוָה לְהַנִּיחָהּ בְּתוֹךְ חֲלָלוֹ שֶׁל פֶּתַח. פְּשִׁיטָא, "בִּשְׁעָרֶיךָ" אָמַר רַחֲמָנָא! ס"ד אָמִינָא, הוֹאִיל וְאָמַר רָבָא: *מִצְוָה לְהַנִּיחָהּ בְּטֶפַח

רש"י

דְּאִם כְּתָבָן אֲדוּכְסוּסְטוֹס פָּסוּל, אֲבָל מְזוּזָה אַקְּלָף שַׁפִּיר דָּמֵי? וְהָא בָּעֲיָא שִׂרְטוּט. כִּדְמְפָרֵשׁ לְקַמָּן, וּבִתְפִילִּין לָא אַשְׁכְּחַן דְּבָעֵי שִׂרְטוּט! מִגְרַס גְּרִיסִין. רְהוּטִים הֵם בְּפִי כָּל אָדָם וְאֵין טוֹעִין בָּהֶם, הִילְכָּךְ אֵין צָרִיךְ לְהַעְתִּיקָם מִסֵּפֶר אַחֵר. ה] כַּף *כַּדָּא אַאַרְעָא. כָּפָה כַּד עַל הָאָרֶץ. וְהִנִּיחַ ס"ת עָלָיו. לְפִי שֶׁהָיָה ס"ת מוּנָּח עַל ו] רֹאשָׁהּ, וְהָיָה רוֹצֶה לֵישֵׁב עַל הַמִּיטָּה. וְנִדְמֶה לוֹ. מֵרוֹב לַעַר כְּמִי שֶׁהִכִּישׁוֹ נָחָשׁ. עַל גַּבֵּי קַרְקַע. הָיָה ס"ת מוּשְׁלָךְ, דְּאִיכָּא בִּזְיוֹנָא יְתֵירָא, לְכָךְ נִצְטַעֵר. כְּתָבָהּ אִיגֶּרֶת. בְּלֹא שִׂרְטוּט, וְלֹא דִּקְדֵּק בַּחֲסֵרוֹת וִיתֵרוֹת, כְּאִיגֶּרֶת בְּעָלְמָא. כְּתִיבָה כְּתִיבָה. "וּכְתַבְתָּם עַל מְזוּזוֹת" "וְכָתַב לָהּ סֵפֶר כְּרִיתוּת". אִי נַמִּי, "כְּתוֹב זֹאת זִכָּרוֹן בַּסֵּפֶר", מַה סֵּפֶר בָּעֵי דִּקְדּוּק — אַף מְזוּזָה בָּעֲיָא דִּקְדּוּק. תְּלָאָהּ. לַמְּזוּזָה עַל הַפֶּתַח בְּמַקֵּל. שֶׁהִנִּיחָהּ אֲחוֹרֵי הַדֶּלֶת. שֶׁקְּבָעָהּ בַּכּוֹתֶל אֲחוֹרֵי הַדֶּלֶת. סַכָּנָה. מִן הַמַּזִּיקִים, שֶׁאֵין הַבַּיִת מִשְׁתַּמֵּר בָּהּ עַד שֶׁיִּקְבָּעֶנָּה בְּצוּרַת הַפֶּתַח כְּהִילְכָתָהּ. הָיוּ עוֹשִׂין בְּפוּנְדְּקוֹתֵיהֶן כֵּן. פּוּנְדָּק הַיְינוּ בַּיִת שֶׁלָּנִין בּוֹ עוֹבְרֵי דְרָכִים בַּדֶּרֶךְ, וְאֵין חַיָּיבִין בִּמְזוּזָה, דְּלָאו דִּירַת קֶבַע הוּא, כִּדְתַנְיָא לְקַמָּן בְּ"הַתְּכֵלֶת"*: הַדָּר בְּפוּנְדְּקִי בְּאֶרֶץ יִשְׂרָאֵל כָּל שְׁלֹשִׁים יוֹם פָּטוּר מִן הַמְּזוּזָה. וְשֶׁל בֵּית מוֹנְבַּז הַמֶּלֶךְ, כְּשֶׁהָיוּ מְהַלְּכִים בַּדֶּרֶךְ נוֹשְׂאִין מְזוּזוֹת עִמָּהֶם וְתוֹלִין אוֹתָן בְּפוּנְדָּק בְּמַקֵּל עַד הַבֹּקֶר זֵכֶר לִמְזוּזָה, לְפִי שֶׁלֹּא הָיוּ דָּרִין לְעוֹלָם דִּירַת קֶבַע, אֶלָּא הוֹלֵךְ הָיָה מֵעִיר לְעִיר ז] בְּמַלְכוּתוֹ. בְּתוֹךְ חֲלַל הַפֶּתַח. וְלֹא מִבַּחוּץ. פְּשִׁיטָא בִּשְׁעָרֶיךָ כְּתִיב. דְּהַיְינוּ מְקוֹם סְגִירַת הַשַּׁעַר.

בַּטֶּפַח

תוספות

הא מורידין עושין והא בעיא שרטוט. וא"ת: דילמא במשרטטין! וי"ל: דלא היו רגילין לשרטט ספר תורה ותפילין, כיון דלא בעו שרטוט, כדאמרינן בירושלמי בפ"ק דשבת: כל הפטור מן הדבר ועושהו נקרא הדיוט, ובסדר רב עמרם מביאו. והא דאמרינן בספ"ק דמגילה (דף טז:): "דברי שלום ואמת" — מלמד שצריכה שרטוט כאמיתה של תורה — לא כמו שפירש שם בקונטרס דמיירי בס"ת ממש, אלא במזוזה קאמר, שהיא אמיתה של תורה, שיש בה *מלכות שמים, וכדמוכח הכא דמזוזה בעיא שירטוט. ותדע, דאי בספר תורה כפירוש הקונטרס, היה לו לדרוש מדנקראת ספר, כדדרשינן התם* דרשא אחריתי מדנקראת ספר. ומיהו י"ל, דאי מדנקראת ספר הוה ליה לאשכוחי חד עניינא דלא ליבעי שרטוט, כיון דנקראת כמו כן איגרת, כדאמרינן נמי (מגילה דף יט.) לענין תפירה דלא צריך לתופרה כולה בגידין. ובירושלמי משמע כפירוש הקונטרס, דמספר תורה עצמה יליף, דקאמר התם: נאמר כאן "דברי שלום ואמת" ונאמר להלן "אמת קנה ואל תמכור", מה להלן צריך שרטוט אף כאן צריך שרטוט, משמע דאיירי בכל התורה כולה, דאכל התורה כולה כתיבא קרא. ואמר רבינו תם: דס"ת בעי שרטוט משום (שמות טו) "זה אלי ואנוהו", אבל תפילין דמכוסין בעור לא בעו שרטוט, דלא שייך בהו נוי. וקשה תימה: דבסמוך ילפינן מזוזה מס"ת בג"ש כתיבה כתיבה לענין כתיבת אגרת, ואמאי לא ילפינן מינה ס"ת ממזוזה לענין שירטוט? וכ"ת: לענין כתיבה לא ילפינן — הא לקמן* בעי למילף לענין כתיבה על האבנים! ומהא דאמרינן במסכת סופרים (פ"א): מסרגלין בקנים וכותבין בדיו, עוד נמי אמרינן התם דכל יריעה שאינה מסורגלת פסולה — משם אין ראיה, ח] דדילמא בשרטוט עליון איירי, *דאי אפשר לכתוב שלש תיבות או ארבע בלא שרטוט, כדתניא בפ"ק דגיטין (דף ו:), אבל שרטוט *בין שיטה לשיטה אפשר דלא בעיא. ט] ומהא אמר שנוהגין לכתוב באגרות שלומים ארבע וחמש תיבות מן הפסוק בלא שרטוט — משום דלא אסרו אלא דוקא שכותב הפסוק לדרשא, כי ההוא עובדא דרבי אביתר דגיטין, אבל מה שאדם כותב באגרת מן הפסוק לדבר לחות* שרי בלא שרטוט. ומיהו משמע בירושלמי דאסור בכל ענין, שאפי' באגרת שלומים היו מהפכים הפסוק ולא היו כותבים אותו ככתבו, דקאמרינן בפ"ג דמגילה: מהו *מיכתב תרתין תלת מילין מן הפסוק? מר עוקבא שלח* לריש גלותא דהוה דמיך וקאי: "בזימרי ישראל אל תשמח (ישראל אל) בעמים [אל] גיל". וחולק על התלמוד שלנו דקאמר בגיטין (דף ז.*) דשירטט וכתב ליה. רבי זעירא כתב: "ולא זכר יואש המלך", ולא כתב כדכתיב "המלך יואש". רבי ירמיה שלח כתב לרבי יודן: "לשנוא את אהוביך ולאהוב את שונאיך". שלח רבי אבהו: "אבל תמר תמרורים בתמרוריה היא עומדת ובקשנו למתקה ולשוא לרף לרוף" (ירמיה ו). רבי מנא שלח כתב לרבי אושעיא בר שמאי: "ראשיתך מצער היה ואחריתך מאד תשגיא" (איוב ח). *מ"ר. אסור לישב על גבי מטה שספר תורה מונח עליה. בירושלמי בפרק "מי שמתו" אמרינן: תיבה שהיא מליאה ספרים נותנה לראש המטה ואינו נותנה למרגלות המטה. רבי אבין בשם רב הונא: והוא שתהא מטה גבוהה עשרה טפחים, ולא יהו *רגלי המטה נוגעין בתיבה. עוד קאמר: לא ישב אדם על גבי ספסל שס"ת מונח עליה, ומעשה ברבי אליעזר כו'. אם היה נתון על גבי דבר אחר מותר. עד כמה? רבי אבא בשם רב הונא: טפח, רבי ירמיה בשם רבי זירא: כל שהוא. דאמר רבה בר בר חנה א"ר יוחנן מותר לישב על גבי מטה שס"ת מונח עליה. נראה דהלכה כר' יוחנן לגבי רב הונא, דאפי' לגביה רב רביה הלכה כמותו, כדאמר *(ביצה ד.). ותלמידי דרב הונא לא סברי כוותיה, דבעי לאותובי ס"ת אפורייה בפ' בתרא דמועד קטן (דף כה.). מ"ר.

כתבה אגרת פסולה מ"ט אתיא כתיבה כתיבה מספר. פירש בקונטרס: איגרת — בלא שרטוט. וקשה: דלעיל אמרינן שרטוט של מזוזה הלכה למשה מסיני, י] והכא יליף כתיבה כתיבה! ומפרש ר"ת: אגרת — מקרא ולא מסורת, שלא דקדק בחסירות ויתירות אלא כאגרת בעלמא. והא דיליף כתיבה כתיבה — לא כמו שפירש בקונטרס מ"וכתב לה ספר כריתות", דכמה חסירות ויתירות יש בגט, "דיתיהוויין" "דיתילביין" חמשה חמשה יודין, וגם חסירות כגן "למהך", *ושרטוט נמי אשכחן דבעי בגט. ועוד, מ"ספר" הכתוב בגט לאו למעוטי אגרת, דלספירת דברים הוא דאתא, כדאמרינן בגיטין (דף כא:). ומיהו, בפרק שני דגיטין (דף כ:) דאמרינן ד"ספר" דגט אתא למעוטי שנים וג' ספרים, וה"ה דנמעט נמי כתבו אגרת, כמו בפרק שני דסוטה (דף יז:) דדרשינן תרווייהו מ"ספר". ועוד יש לפרש, דיליף הכא מסוטה, דממעטינן בפרק שני דסוטה כתבה איגרת מדכתיב "בספר". ובפירוש הקונטרס לשון אחר, דיליף מ"כתוב זאת זכרון". וצ"ע, אמאי לא ילפינן ליה גט כתיבה כתיבה דליפסול בהכי *(או) מדכתיב ביה "ספר"! ואין לפרש אגרת ר"ל בעמודים קצרים שאינם רחבים כג' פעמים "למשפחותיכם", כדאמר לעיל (דף ל.): ולא ירבה בדפין שנראה כאגרת, דהא אמרינן לעיל: מזוזה שעשאה שתים שלש ואחת כשירה. ואע"פ שפירשתי שצריך לדקדק בחסירות ויתירות, אין להקשות מהא דתנן בפרק "השואל" (ב"מ דף קא:) דמשכיר חייב בכל דבר שהוא מעשה אומן, ומשמע בגמרא דשוכר חייב במזוזה דחובת הדר היא, דהתם לא מיירי אלא בבנייני הבית. ומקום מזוזה נמי דהוי על השוכר, כדאמר התם משום דלא מעשה אומן הוא דאיפשר בגובתא דקניא, היינו מעשה *שהוא בגוף הבית עצמו. מ"ר. סכנה ואין בה מצוה. פי' בקונטרס: כיון דעשאה שלא כהילכתה אין הבית משתמר מפני המזיקין. וקשה לרבינו תם: דא"כ הו"ל יא] למימר הכי: *אבל העשויה שלא כהילכתה! ונראה: דתלאה במקל נוקף בה ראשו, דלאו אדעתיה. וכן אחורי הדלת, רגילה להיות בולטת ומכה בה ראשו יב] והא דאמר בפ' "השואל" (ב"מ ד' קב.): אפשר בגובתא דקניא, ופירש שם בקונטרס דתלי ליה בגובתא דקניא חלול — לא תלי ממש קאמר. מ"ר.

כתבה

הגהות הב"ח

(א) גמ' ר' אחאי בר' חנינא ואמרי לה משמיה דר' עקיבא בר' חנינא אמר כשר הא מורידין: (ב) שם על גבי קרקע ונדמה כמי שהכישו:

שיטה מקובצת

א] ר' אחאי. מכשיר משום רבי יהודה ברבי חנינא: ב] יעקב תיבת עקיבא נמחק: ג] לרב הונא דכף כדא אארעא ואנח עליה ס"ת קסבר אסור והשאר נמחק: ד] תיבות מ"ט בשעריך בעינן נמחק: ה] דכף כדא: ו] על המטה והיה: ז] לעיר בכל מלכותו: ח] דדילמא. בד' שירטוטין דהיינו עליון ותחתון ומן הצדדין תוס' אחרות: ט] ומה שנוהגין לכתוב באגרות: י] מסיני. וס"ת אמרינן לעיל דלא בעי שרטוט ועוד פי' שלא דקדק בחסירות ויתירות דכתיב וכתבתם כתיבה תמה ויתירות נמי אמרינן לעיל בס"ת אבל ביתירות לית לן בה לכך נראה דלא גרסי' מס"ת אלא ה"ג אתיא כתיבה מספר והיינו מספר דכתיב גבי סוטה וה"נ אמרינן בפ"ב דסוטה גבי מגילת סוטה כתבה אגרת פסולה שנאמר בספר ולענין חסירות ויתירות יליף לה מסוטה. תוס' אחרות: יא] הוה ליה למימר הכי כל העשויה שלא כהלכתה. ומאי שנא הכא דנקט האי לישנא דסכנה טפי מבכל שאר פסולין ותיבת אבל נמחק: יב] ראשו. לפי שאינה קבועה (בסוף) [בתוך] הפסח:

מסורת הש"ס

כרא אארעא כפה כד כו' נ"ק
גי' רש"ק והרש"א לא מוסיף רק תיבת מכשיר קודם תיבת הא מורידין
מגילה יח:
מ"ק כה. (וסם איתא רב תחליפא)
דף מד.
מס' סופרים פרק ג
תוספתא דמגילה פ"ג
[לקמן לג:]
קבלת של מלכות שמים נ"ק
[דף יט.]
דבעי למיתב אפוריה נ"ק
[לד.]
דאסור לכתוב נ"ק
על כל שיטה ושיטה אפשר דלא בעי ומה שנוהגין כו' נ"ק
לשום שרי נ"ק
למיכתב נ"ק
וכ"ה בירושלמי
כתב לריש גלותא דהוה קאי ודמיך בזמרא נ"ק
כך הוא הגי' שם ראשיתך מצער תשגא אחריתך
אבל תמר תמרורים בתמרוריה כו' נ"ק
(ועי' תוס' גיטין ז: ד"ה ר' ילחק ותוס' סוטה יז: ד"ה כתבה)
גרסת רש"א חבלי
בערובין ועוד דאף תלמידי כו' נ"ק
ושרטוט נמי לא אשכחן נ"ק
רש"א מ"ז וכן נ"ק ומהרש"ק תולק
נ"א שהוא
נ"ל כל העשויה כו' רש"א ונ"ק

ועושה ריוח מלמעלה וריוח מלמטה, ועושה פרשיותיה פתוחות. אמרתי לו: *רבי, מה טעם? אמר לי: הואיל ואין סמוכות מן התורה; ואמר רב חננאל אמר רב: הלכה כר"ש בן אלעזר, מאי לאו אפתוחות? לא, אריוח. וכמה ריוח? אמר רב מנשיא בר יעקב, ואמרי לה אמר רב שמואל בר יעקב: כמלא אטבא א] דסיפרי. אמר ליה אביי לרב יוסף: ואת לא תסברא דכי אמר רב אריוח? והא רב אית ליה מנהגא, והאידנא נהוג עלמא ב] בסתומות; *דאמר רבה אמר רב כהנא אמר רב: אם יבא אליהו ויאמר ג] חולצין במנעל – שומעין לו, אין חולצין בסנדל – אין שומעין לו, שכבר נהגו העם בסנדל. ורב יוסף אמר רב כהנא אמר רב: אם יבא אליהו ויאמר אין חולצין במנעל – שומעין לו, אין חולצין בסנדל – אין שומעין לו, שכבר נהגו העם בסנדל; ואמרינן: מאי בינייהו? ד] מנעל לכתחילה איכא בינייהו! אלא לאו שמע מינה אריוח, ש"מ. רב נחמן בר יצחק אמר: [א]מצוה לעשותן סתומות, ואי עבדינהו פתוחות – שפיר דמי, ומאי פתוחות דקאמר רשב"א – אף פתוחות. לימא מסייע ליה: *כיוצא בו, [ב]ספר תורה שבלה ותפילין שבלו אין עושין מהן מזוזה, לפי שאין מורידין מקדושה חמורה לקדושה קלה; הא מורידין – עושין, אמאי? הכא סתומות והכא פתוחות! דלמא ה] להשלים. הא מורידין – עושין? והתניא: *הלכה למשה מסיני – תפילין על הקלף ומזוזה על דוכסוסטוס; קלף במקום בשר, דוכסוסטוס במקום שער! [ג]למצוה. והתניא: שינה – פסול! [ד]בתפילין. והתניא: שינה בין בזה ובין בזה – פסול! ו] אידי ואידי בתפילין, והא דכתבינהו אקלף במקום שער, והא דכתבינהו

רש"י

אמרתי לו רבי מה טעם. אתה עושה אותם פתוחות? והלא בתורה סתומות הן, אותו ריוח שלאחר "ובשעריך" ז] הוא סתום (שמאל של שיטה) והריוח באמצע השיטה! אמר לי הואיל ובתורה אינן סמוכות. הנך שתי פרשיות, שזו כתובה ב"ואתחנן" וזו כתובה ב"והיה עקב", לפיכך ח] אנו עושין פתוחות. מאי לאו אפתוחות. קאמר רב (א) ט] זה דהלכה כר"ש? אטבא י] דסיפרי. גלוע"ן, עץ סדוק הנושק דפי קונטרס שלא יכפלו. אית ליה מנהגא. כדמפרש: אם יבא אליהו כו'. מנעל לכתחילה. למ"ד אם יבא אליהו ויאמר חולצין במנעל שומעין לו, קסבר: מנעל השתא לכתחילה לא, עד שיבא אליהו ויורה יא] כו'. למ"ד אם יבא אליהו ויאמר אין חולצין במנעל שומעין לו, מכלל יב] עד שיבא אליהו ויאמר לא תחלצו במנעל – חולצין כו' (ב). תפילין קדושתן חמורה ממזוזה, שיש בהן ד' פרשיות. הכא סתומות. בס"ת, והכא פתוחות – במזוזה! אלא ש"מ במזוזה נמי סתומות הן. ודילמא להשלים. דילמא הא דדייקינן: הא מורידין *עושין – יג] שאם חסרה, מתפילין מזוזה. קלף כותבין עליו במקום בשר כו'. אלמא תפילין אי אפשר לעשות מזוזה, דהא על הקלף נכתבו! ומשני: למצוה. מצות תפילין על הקלף ומזוזה אדוכסוסטוס, אבל אם שינה אין בכך כלום, הילכך אם מורידין עושין. והתניא יד] שינה פסול. ומשני: בתפילין קמיירי, דאם

תוספות

ועושה ריוח מלמעלה וריוח מלמטה. מן הצדדים לא פירש. ושמא כיון דכורך מ"אחד" כלפי "שמע" צריך טו] לכתחילה כדי לגול בהיקף, כעין ס"ת. מ"ר. והאידנא נהוג עלמא בסתומות. פירש בקונטרס: *דכשיש כתוב בתחילת שיטה ובסוף שיטה והריוח באמצע – זו היא סתומה. ואנו נוהגין להניח חלק מעט בתחילת שיטה ואחר כך מתחיל "והיה אם שמוע", ושמא גם זה קרוי סתומה. ור"ת מפרש: דכשמסיים פסוק באמצע שיטה ומניח עד סוף שיטה כשיעור "למשפחותיכם" – זו היא פתוחה, ואם לא נשתייר בסוף שיטה כשיעור חלק "למשפחותיכם" מניח שיטה שניה ומתחיל וכותב בשלישית, וזו היא פתוחה. וסתומה – כל שכותב בתחילת שיטה וסוף שיטה ומניח חלק באמצע כדי לכתוב בו שם שתי אותיות או יותר, וזו היא סתומה. סדורה – כל שכותב והולך השיטה עד חציה או עד שלישיתה ומניחה, ומתחיל לכתוב בשיטה שתחתיה כנגד הנחה של שיטה העליונה, וזו היא סדורה. זה מצא ר"ת בסידור קדמונים. ובמסכת סופרים מצא: איזו היא פתוחה – כל שלא התחיל בראש השיטה, ואיזו היא סתומה – כל שהניח באמצע שיטה. וכמה יניח בראש שיטה ויהא נקראת פתוחה – כדי לכתוב שם של ג' אותיות. גמר כל הפרשה בסוף הדף *ושייר שיטה אחת מלמעלה, ואם שייר מלמטה כדי לכתוב שם של ג' אותיות מתחיל מלמעלה. ועוד דירושלמי בפ"ק דמגילה קאמר בהדיא דפתוחה מראשה – פתוחה. *מתוך כל הני קשה אמנהג דידן, דשבקינן חלק בראש שיטה ואח"כ מתחילין "והיה אם שמוע", והתלמוד קאמר דהאידנא נהוג עלמא בסתומות! ושמא סמכינן אההיא דירושלמי דפליג אתלמוד דידן, דמסקינן הכא כי אמר רב אריוח ולא אפתוחות, והתם פסיק רב בהדיא כמ"ד פתוחות. והכי איתא התם: מזוזה – אית תנא תני פתוחות ואית תנא תני סתומות. שמואל בר שילת בשם רב: הלכה כדברי מי שאומר פתוחה, שאין זה מקומה. פתוחה מראשה – פתוחה, פתוחה מסופה – פתוחה, פתוחה מכאן ומכאן – סתומה. ודבר תימה הוא, דלפי הירושל' משמע לכאורה דאם מסיים פרשה באמצע שיטה ואחר כך מתחיל לכתוב באמצע שיטה שתחתיה, שזו היא נקראת סתומה, ואיך יתכן זה? מי גרע מפתוחה מראשה לחוד או פתוחה מסופה לחוד? ונראה לפרש: דקאי לפרושי מילתיה דרב, דהא דאמר הלכה כדברי מי שאמר פתוחה – כגון שיעשה פתוחה מראשה, או פתוחה מסופה, או פתוחה באמצע ומכאן ומכאן סתומה. והאי "מכאן ומכאן" דקאמר אסתומה דבתר הכי קאי, ולא אפתוחה דקמיה, דההיא פתוחה באמצע איקרי. ואע"ג דבעלמא מקרי סתומה, כי ה"ג לא חיישינן גבי מזוזה, דכיון דטעם משום דאין זה מקומה. ומתיישב בכך דלא קשיא ההיא דירושלמי אתלמוד שלנו אליבא דרב. מ"ר. **מנעל** לכתחילה איכא בינייהו. אע"ג דקי"ל (ב"ב דף קיד:): רבה ורב יוסף – הלכה כרבה, בר משדה ענין ומחצה, ולרבה אין חולצין במנעל לכתחילה, *עכשיו נוהגין לחלוץ במנעל לפי שאין אנו בקיאין בסנדל. אי נמי, במילתא דקאמרי משמיה דאחריני אפשר דהלכה כרב יוסף*. מ"ר. **דילמא** להשלים. פירש בקונטרס: שאם חסרה מזוזה שיטה אחת, אי לאו דאין מורידין, היו נוטלין שיטה אחת מס"ת ותופרין במזוזה. והא דאמרינן בירושלמי בפ"ק דמגילה, דתפילין ומזוזות אין נכתבין אלא על עור אחד – ההיא בשלא תפר העורות זה בזה. טז] ויש עוד לפרש: להשלים – כגון יז] דפרשת "שמע" א) בסוף עמוד, והוסיף פרשת "והיה אם שמוע" בגליון שלמטה. או פרשת "והיה אם שמוע" ב) בתחלת עמוד, והוסיף "שמע" בגליון שלמעלה. יח] ג) מ"ר. **הא** מורידין עושין. אע"ג דנוהגין בתפילין של יד *ד' שיטין, ובשל ראש ז' שיטין, ובמזוזה כ"ה שיטין, אם שינה לא פסול. מ"ר. ד) **תפילין** על הקלף מזוזה על דוכסוסטוס. ושניהן פסולין אגויל, וס"ת כשירה אגויל, כדמוכח בפרק "המוציא יין" (שבת דף עט:). ותימה: דלא חשיב ליה בהדי "אין בין ספרים לתפילין ומזוזות" בפ"ק דמגילה (דף ח:)! ויש לפרש: דלא איירי בדבר שכותבין בו, כדאשכחן (שם דף ז:) גבי "אין בין שבת ליום הכיפורים" דלא חשיב אכילה, וגבי "אין בין יום טוב לשבת" דלא חשיב סקילה. אי נמי, משום דתפילין ומזוזות לאו מחד טעמא *מיפסלן אגויל. ולא דמו לאשורית דהוי מחד טעמא, משום דכתיב "והיו". מ"ר. **אידי** ואידי בתפילין הא דכתבינהו אקלף במקום שיער והא דכתבינהו אדוכסוסטוס במקום בשר. פירוש: אף במקום בשר, וה"ה במקום שיער, דלא הכשיר תפילין אלא על הקלף. וקשה, דלא משני "אלא אידי ואידי במזוזה", והוי השתא שינה בזה ובזה מענין אחד, דמזוזה כשירה אשניהם, ולא מיפסל כלל אלא מחמת שינוי מקום. דלמאי דמוקי לה אתפילין מיפסלי אדוכסוסטוס מתרי טעמי, חדא – דדינם אקלף, וחדא – דדין דוכסוסטוס אשיער, והוא שינה וכתב במקום בשר. וכענין זה קשה בפרק "המוציא יין" (שבת דף עט:) דמשני התם איפכא: אידי ואידי אמזוזה, גבי הא דאמר *רבא התם: דוכסוסטוס הרי הוא כקלף וכותבין עליו תפילין. והא תניא: תפילין על הקלף ומזוזה על דוכסוסטוס! למצוה. והא תניא: שינה בזה ובזה פסול! אידי ואידי אמזוזה, הא דכתב אקלף במקום שיער, והא דכתב אדוכסוסטוס במקום בשר. והשתא קשיא, דה"ל לשנויי: אידי ואידי אתפילין, דכשירין אשניהם, והוי שינוייא מענין אחד כענין שפירש כאן! ופירש שם הר"ר יוסף, דמדלא תירץ כן נראה דתפילין אם שינה לכתוב בקלף במקום שיער – לא פסל, כמו שלא פסל אם שינה ממלותן וכתב אדוכסוסטוס. ובענין זה נוכל לתרץ בשמעתין, דלכך לא תירץ אידי ואידי אמזוזה, דכיון דכשירה כששינה מלוותה וכתבה אקלף – ה"ה דכשירה כשכתבה אדוכסוסטוס במקום בשר. ועוד יש לתרץ, דלא הוי מצי לשנויי הכא: אידי ואידי אמזוזה, יט] דכל כמה דלא אשמעינן דמזוזה כשירה משניהם לא שייך למיתני: שינה בזה ובזה פסול. אבל כל דין תפילין כבר אשמעינן. ובענין זה יש לתרץ בפרק "המוציא יין" (שם). מ"ר.

הא

א) נ"א בתחילת ב) נ"א בסוף ג) [עי' ט"ז יו"ד סי' רנ ס"ק א' ובנקה"כ] ד) עיין בספר תפארת שמואל דף לא ע"א

עין משפט נר מצוה

קלח א מיי' פ"ה מהל' תפילין הל"ב טוש"ע יו"ד סי' רפח סעי' יג:

קלט ב מיי' פ"ה מהל' תפילין הל"א טוש"ע יו"ד סי' לב:

קמ ג מיי' פ"א מהל' תפילין וס"ת הל' ח ט סמג עשין כה טוש"ע יו"ד סי' רעא סעי' ג:

קמא ד מיי' שם טוש"ע או"ח סי' לב סעי' ז:

מסורת הש"ס

מתוס' ד"ה רשב"א אומר כו' לעיל לא: מוכח דלא היה הגירסא רבי לפניהם]

יבמות קב.

עושין מתפילין מזוזה אם חסרה הס"ד נ"ק

דכשכותבים בתחילת נ"ק

נריך לשייר שיטה נ"ק

שבת עט:

מסופה פתוחה מכל הני נ"ק

ועכשיו נ"ק

[וע' תוס' קדושין ט. ד"ה והלכתא ותו' גיטין עב: ותוס' ב"ב קיד: ותוס' מגילה כ.]

ז' שיטין ובשל ראש ד' שיטין כצ"ל נ"ק

דמיפסלן רש"ק

נ"ל רב

גליון הש"ס

גמ' לא אחריות. כעין זה פסחים דף יג ע"א תענית יח ע"א: **שם** והאידנא נהוג עלמא בסתומות. עיין תשובות מהרי"ק שורש נג:

הגהות הב"ח

(א) רש"י ד"ה קאמר רב וכו' רב דהלכה כצ"ל ותיבת זה נמחק: (ב) ד"ה למ"ד אם וכו' חולצין כו' הס"ד ואח"כ מ"ה מקדושה חמורה תפילין:

שיטה מקובצת

א] אטבא דספרי ואות י' נמחק. פרש"י עץ סדוק כו' וזהו כדי אחיזת גודל ואצבע וזהו למעלה ולמטה אבל מן הצד לא מצינו שיעור הריוח ושמא כיון דכורך מאחד כלפי שמע צריך בראשו כדי לגול היקף ולפי מה שנהגו העולם עתה לכתוב שדי מבחוץ כנגד האויר שלפני והיה ונוקבין הסף לקרותו מבחוץ [נראה שאין צריך] דאי כדי לגול היקף א"כ יהיה מכוסה מאותו היקף ושמא יחתוך הקלף מאותו מקום. תוס' אחרות: ב] בסתומה. פרש"י כתב בתחילת [השיטה] ובסוף שיטה והחלק באמצע וכן מנהג קדמונים והיכא שנזדמן לו שגמר השיטה בסוף הפרשה ולא נשאר מקום בשיטה להניח חלק ולהתחיל פרשה אחרת יגמור כל השיטה באותה פרשה ויניח חלק בתחילת שיטה שתחתיה בצד ימין ויתחיל פרשה אחרת באמצע השיטה ופתוחה זה שמניח חלק בסוף השיטה בצד שמאל ואינו מתחיל פרשה אחרת באותה שיטה אלא מתחיל בראש השיטה ממש ואם נזדמן לו וגמר השיטה בסוף הפרשה יניח שיטה שלימה חלק ויתחיל בראש השיטה שלישית סדורה כו' עד מתחיל מלמעלה [הוא בתוס' ולכן לא העתיק] לפיכך הנהיג ר"ת בפתוחה להניח ריוח בסוף שיטה ובראש שיטה שניה כדי לקיים שניהם ומיהו לפי זה קשה למנהג שלנו שאנו מניחין ריוח במזוזה בסוף שיטה אחר ובשעריך ואין אנו מתחילין והיה בראש שיטה שניה אלא מניחין ריוח קצת ולפי דברי ר"ת קרי פתוחה ואמר הכא דעושין פרשיותיו סתומה לכך נראה דטוב שלא יניח ריוח בסוף שיטה אחר ובשעריך כדי שיעור. ושיעור ריוח אויר פרשה י"א כשיעור לכתוב בו למשפחותיכם כו' וי"א כדי לכתוב ג' אותיות והר"י מאורליינש מצא במסכת סופרים ישן כמו בסדר הקדמונים איזה פתוחה כל שמניח באמצע השיטה. תוס' אחרות: ג] חולצין במנעל. מנעל הוא מעור דק ואיכא למגזר אטו מנעל המרופט שאינו חופה הרגל: ד] מנעל לכתחילה כו' אע"ג דללישנא בתרא מותר לכתחילה לחלוץ במנעל עד שיבא אליהו מ"מ טוב לחזור אחר סנדל מעור עבה. תוס' אחרות: ה] להשלים. כגון שכתב בסוף דף של ס"ת (מקצת) פרשת שמע והוא מסיימה בגליון ועושה פרשה סתומה וכותב והיה אם שמוע תו"ח: ו] אידי ואידי בתפילין והא דכתב אדוכסוסטום במקום בשר. וה"ה במקום שיער אלא רבותא נקט דאע"ג דעיקר מצות כתיבת תפילין הוא אקלף במקום בשר אבל על דוכסוסטום פסול אף במקום בשר וכ"ש במקום שיער דעיקר מצות כתיבת תפילין במקום בשר הוא וא"ת אמאי לא קאמר אמזוזה שינה בזה ובזה פסול אדוכסוסטום במקום בשר ואקלף במקום שיער נמי פסול ומשכחת לה דאם מורידין עושין כגון שנכתבו אקלף ובמקום בשר ואומר הר"ר יוסף דאין זה סברא כיון דפסלינן מזוזה אדוכסוסטום במקום בשר להכשיר אקלף במקום בשר דאדרבה עיקר מצות כתיבת מזוזה במקום שיער ועוד אומר רבינו נתנאל דשינה בזה ובזה פסול משמע בג' מקומות שינה חד בזה תרי בזה [הרי] תלת ובמזוזה לא משכחת להפסיל שלישי תוס' אחרות. ח"ל תו"ח אידי ואידי אתפילין. וא"ת לישני אידי ואידי במזוזה ופי' הר"ר יוסף דכיון דשינוי אחד כשר במזוזה משמע ליה דכל השינוים כשרים בה ע"מ דכיון דמקום המובחר במזוזה כשהיא נכתבת על דוכסוסטום ואמת הוא שאף [על] (כל) הקלף כשר אין לנו לפסול מקום שיער בקלף במזוזה והר"ר נתנאל פי' דשינה בזה ובזה משמע שלשה פסולים וזה לא נמצא אלא בתפילין ולא הבנתי. ע"כ: ז] ובשעריך. סתום צד שמאל של שיטה תיבת הוא ל"ש: ח] לפיכך אני עושה אותן פתוחות: ט] תיבת זה נמחק: י] אטבא דספרי אות י' נמחק: יא] ויורה. כן שחולצין במנעל ותיבת וכו' נמחק: יב] מכלל. דעד שיבא אליהו וכו' חולצין בו הס"ד: יג] עושין. לא לעשות מזוזה כולה מס"ת דלעולם פתוחות בעינן אבל אם חסרה מזוזה שיטה אחת אי לאו דאין מורידין היו נוטלין שיטה אחת מס"ת ותיפרה במזוזה ומשלימין וקא פריך הא מורידין עושין מתפילין מזוזה הס"ד: יד] והתניא. אם שינה: טו] צריך בתחילה: טז] העורות זה בזה. אבל תפר לית לן בה: יז] כגון. אם גמר פרשת שמע בסוף עמוד: יח] בגליון שלמעלה. אם לאו דאין מורידין עושין: יט] אידי ואידי אמזוזה. כל כמה אות ד' נמחק:

מִי קָאָמַר "בְּמִשְׁנָתֵינוּ"? *"כָּל מָקוֹם שֶׁשָּׁנָה" קָאָמַר. אָמַר רַב *זְעֵירָא אָמַר רַב חֲנַנְאֵל אָמַר רַב: קֶרַע הַבָּא אבִּשְׁנֵי שִׁיטִּין — יִתָּפוֹר, בְּשָׁלֹשׁ — אַל יִתָּפוֹר. א"ל רַבָּה זוּטִי לְרַב אַשִׁי, הָכִי אֲמַר רַבִּי יִרְמְיָה מִדִּיפְתִּי מִשְּׁמֵיהּ דְּרָבָא: הָא דְּאָמְרִינַן בְּשָׁלֹשׁ אַל יִתָּפוֹר — לָא אֲמַרַן אֶלָּא בַּעֲתִיקָתָא, אֲבָל בחַדְתָּתָא לֵית לָן בָּהּ; וְלָא עֲתִיקָתָא — עֲתִיקָתָא מַמָּשׁ, וְלָא חַדְתָּתָא — חַדְתָּתָא מַמָּשׁ, אֶלָּא °הָא דְּלָא אֲפִיצָן, הָא גדַּאֲפִיצָן; וְה"מ דבְּגִידִין, אֲבָל בִּגְרָדִין לָא. בָּעֵי רַב יְהוּדָה בַּר אַבָּא: בֵּין דַּף לְדַף, בֵּין שִׁיטָּה לְשִׁיטָּה, מַאי? התֵּיקוּ. אָמַר ר' זְעֵירִי אָמַר רַב חֲנַנְאֵל אָמַר רַב: מְזוּזָה שֶׁכְּתָבָהּ שְׁתַּיִם שְׁתַּיִם — כְּשֵׁרָה. אִיבַּעְיָא לְהוּ: שְׁתַּיִם וְשָׁלֹשׁ וְאַחַת, מַהוּ? אָמַר רַב נַחְמָן בַּר יִצְחָק: כָּל שֶׁכֵּן, שֶׁעֲשָׂאָהּ כְּשִׁירָה. מֵיתִיבֵי: *עֲשָׂאָהּ כְּשִׁירָה, אוֹ שִׁירָה כְּמוֹתָהּ — פְּסוּלָה! כִּי תַּנְיָא הַהִיא ובְּס"ת. אִתְּמַר נַמִּי: אָמַר רַבָּה בַּר בַּר חָנָה אָמַר רַבִּי יוֹחָנָן, וְאָמְרִי לָהּ אָמַר רַב אַחָא בַּר בַּר חָנָה אָמַר רַבִּי יוֹחָנָן: זמְזוּזָה שֶׁעֲשָׂאָהּ שְׁתַּיִם וְשָׁלֹשׁ וְאַחַת — כְּשֵׁרָה, וּבִלְבַד שֶׁלֹּא יַעֲשֶׂנָּה כְּקוּבָּה, וּבִלְבַד שֶׁלֹּא יַעֲשֶׂנָּה כְּזָנָב. אָמַר רַב חִסְדָּא: ח"עַל הָאָרֶץ" — בְּשִׁיטָּה אַחֲרוֹנָה; א"ד: בְּסוֹף שִׁיטָּה, וְאִיכָּא דְּאָמְרִי: טבִּתְחִלַּת שִׁיטָּה. מ"ד בְּסוֹף שִׁיטָּה — °"כִּגְבוֹהַּ שָׁמַיִם עַל הָאָרֶץ" (תהלים קג), ומ"ד בִּתְחִילַּת שִׁיטָּה — כִּי הֵיכִי דְּמִרַחֲקָא שָׁמַיִם מֵאָרֶץ. א"ר חֶלְבּוֹ: חֲזֵינָא לֵיהּ לְרַב הוּנָא יְדְּכָרֵיךְ לָהּ מֵ"אֶחָד" כְּלַפֵּי "שְׁמַע", וְעוֹשֶׂה פָּרְשִׁיּוֹתֶיהָ א] כסְתוּמוֹת. מֵיתִיבֵי, אָמַר רשב"א: ר"מ הָיָה כּוֹתְבָהּ עַל דּוֹכְסוֹסְטוֹס כְּמִין דַּף, וְעוֹשֶׂה

רש"י

מִי קָאָמַר בְּמִשְׁנָתֵינוּ. דְּמַשְׁמַע: מִשְׁנָה וְלֹא בָּרַיְיתָא? קֶרַע הַבָּא בִּשְׁנֵי שִׁיטִּין. אִם נִתְקָרַע גִּלָּיוֹן שֶׁל סֵפֶר תּוֹרָה, וְנִכְנַס הַקֶּרַע בִּשְׁנֵי שִׁיטִּין בְּתוֹךְ הַכְּתָב – יִתָּפוֹר. בְּשָׁלֹשׁ אַל יִתָּפוֹר. אֶלָּא יְסַלֵּק אֶת הַיְרִיעָה. עַתִּיקָא. קְלָף יָשָׁן, מִיגַּנְיָא קְרִיעָה. אֲפִיצָן. הָוֵי שָׁחוֹר כַּעֲתִיקָא. אֲפִיצָן = מְתוּקָּן הַקְּלָף בַּעֲפָצִין שֶׁקּוֹרִין גל"ש. וְהָנֵי מִילֵּי. דְּתוֹפֵר. בְּגִידִין. ב] יִתָּפוֹר, אֲבָל לֹא בִּגְרָדִים = פינדי"ש בְּלַעַ"ז. בֵּין דַּף לְדַף. אִם נִקְרַע עַד כְּנֶגֶד הַכְּתָב, שֶׁאִילּוּ הָיָה בַּכְּתָב הָיָה יוֹתֵר מג' שִׁיטִּין. וּבֵין שִׁיטָּה לְשִׁיטָּה. אִם נִקְרַע, יִתָּפוֹר אוֹ לֹא יִתָּפוֹר. שְׁתַּיִם שְׁתַּיִם. שִׁיטּוֹת קְצָרוֹת, שִׁיטָּה שִׁיטָּה בַּת שְׁתֵּי תֵּיבוֹת. שְׁתַּיִם (א). בְּזוֹ וְג' בְּזוֹ וְא' בְּזוֹ, מַאי? כָּל שֶׁכֵּן. דִּכְשֵׁרָה, שֶׁעֲשָׂאָהּ כְּשִׁירָה דְּ"אָז יָשִׁיר מֹשֶׁה", שֶׁשִּׁיטָּה אַחַת אֲרוּכָּה וְשִׁיטָּה אַחַת קְצָרָה, שֶׁאֵין מְמַלֵּא כָּל הַשִּׁיטָּה. אוֹ שִׁירָה כְּמוֹתָהּ. שֶׁכָּתַב הַשִּׁירָה כִּשְׁאָר ג] הַתֵּיבוֹת אָרִיחַ עַל גַּבֵּי אָרִיחַ. שְׁתַּיִם שָׁלֹשׁ וְאַחַת. הַיְינוּ כְּשִׁירָה ד]. שֶׁלֹּא יַעֲשֶׂנָּה כְּקוּבָּה. כָּזֶה: ה] — — — כְּאֹהֶל רָחָב מִלְּמַטָּה וְקָצָר — — — מִלְמַעְלָה, דְּהַיְינוּ אַחַת שְׁתַּיִם שָׁלֹשׁ. זָנָב. שָׁלֹשׁ שְׁתַּיִם וְאַחַת כָּזֶה: ו] — — — עַל הָאָרֶץ בְּשִׁיטָּה אַחֲרוֹנָה. — כְּלוֹמַר, אֵין בְּשִׁיטָּה אַחֲרוֹנָה אֶלָּא שְׁתֵּי תֵּיבוֹת הַלָּלוּ. בְּסוֹף שִׁיטָּה. הָיוּ מַתְחִילִין לְשִׁיטָּה אַחֲרוֹנָה, כָּזֶה: ז] ———— בִּתְחִילַּת שִׁיטָּה. ———— הָיוּ מַתְחִילִין לְשִׁיטָּה אַחֲרוֹנָה כָּזֶה: ח] ———— מ"ד בְּסוֹף שִׁיטָּה. כְּדֵי ———— שֶׁיְּהוּ שָׁמַיִם עַל הָאָרֶץ, דְּמַשְׁמַע כְּדִכְתִיב: כִּי כִּגְבוֹהַּ שָׁמַיִם עַל הָאָרֶץ – כֵּן יַאֲרִיךְ יְמֵיכֶם. ומ"ד בִּתְחִילַּת שִׁיטָּה. כְּלוֹמַר, בָּעֵי אַרְחוֹקֵי אֶרֶץ מִשָּׁמַיִם, דְּהָכִי מַשְׁמַע: כִּי הֵיכִי דְּמִרַחֲקָא שָׁמַיִם מֵאֶרֶץ – כֵּן יַאֲרִיכוּ יְמֵיכֶם. דְּכָרֵיךְ לָהּ מֵאֶחָד כְּלַפֵּי שְׁמַע. לְאַחַר שֶׁנִּכְתְּבָה כּוֹפְלָהּ מִצַּד שְׂמֹאל לְצַד יָמִין כְּשֶׁהִנִּיחָהּ בַּדֶּלֶת. וְהַיְינוּ מֵ"אֶחָד" כְּלַפֵּי "שְׁמַע", שֶׁרֹאשׁ הַשּׁוּרָה "שְׁמַע יִשְׂרָאֵל" וְסוֹפָהּ "יי' אֶחָד", וְהִתְחִיל לְכוֹפְלָהּ מֵ"אֶחָד" וְקִיפֵּל וּבָא עַד "שְׁמַע" ט]. דּוּכְסוּסְטוּס = קְלָף י] שֶׁלֹּא נִקְלַף. כְּמִין דַּף. כְּמִין עַמּוּד שֶׁבִּסְפָרִים, אֲרוּכָּה וּקְצָרָה. אֲמַרְתִּי

תוספות

מי קאמר במשנתינו כו'. כי האי גוונא דייק בפ' בתרא דכתובות (דף קט.) גבי כל מקום שאמר רבן גמליאל רואה אני את דברי אדמון. ותימה: דבפ' "כירה" (שבת דף לט:) גבי: כל מקום שאתה מוצא שנים חולקים ואחד מכריע – הלכה כדברי המכריע חוץ מקולי מטלניות, וקא פריך: אימא ה"מ במתניתין, אבל בברייתא לא! ויש לומר: כיון דאמר "חוץ מקולי מטלניות" שהיא משנה, הוי כאילו פירש "במשנתינו". *ומיהו קשה: בהני כללות דבפ' "מי שהוליאוהו" (עירובין מו:) דקאמר: רבי מאיר ורבי יהודה – הלכה כר' יהודה, ר' יהודה ור' יוסי – הלכה כר' יוסי, אמרי': *סד"א הני מילי במתני' אבל בברייתא לא, אע"ג דלא קאמר "במשנתינו"! ושמא שאני התם דלא קאמר "כל מקום". מ"ר. **הא** דאפיצן הא דלא אפיצן. משמע דס"ת כשר בלא אפיצן. והקשה ר"ת מהא דאמרי' פרק "המוליא יין" (שבת דף עט: ושם) גבי ס"ת: על הגויל ועל הדוכסוסטוס כשירה, משמע: אבל דיפתרא דמליח וקמיח ולא עפיץ – לא* (מיקרי ספר). ובפ' שני דסוטה (דף יז.) אמרי': אין כותבין פרשת סוטה לא על הלוח ולא על הנייר ולא על הדיפתרא אלא על המגילה, שנא' "בספר", וכ"ש ס"ת דנקרא ספר טפי, *כדאמרי' במס' סופרים: אין כותבין לא על הנייר ולא על הדפתרא! ומיהו "מחוק" לא גרס, דהא בפרק "המוליא יין" (שבת דף עט:) קתני: על הנייר ועל המטלית פסולה, ולא קתני מחוק. ועוד קשה: היאך אנו כותבין ס"ת על הקלפים שלנו? הא אינם מעופלין, וכן גיטין שאנו כותבין בקלפין שלנו, ובפ' [שני] דגטין (דף יט.) משמע דווקא בדאפילן כותבין אבל לא אפילן – לא, דיכול להזדייף! ומפרש ר"ת: דתיקון שלנו חשיב כאפילן. תדע, דהא קמן דאין יכול להזדייף, והא דמשמע בגיטין בדלא אפילן יכול להזדייף – היינו בקלפים שלהם שהיו עושים בהם תיקון של עיפוץ, דקודם עיפוץ יכול להזדייף ונקרא "דיפתרא" ופסול. ותדע שגם בימיהם כותבין שטרות בקלף שאינו מעופץ, כדאמרי' בפ' שני דגיטין (שם): כתבו במי טריא ועפלא – כשר, ומוקי לה בדלא אפילן. ומיהו איכא לאוקומי בנייר של עשבים, דלא מיתקני ליה בעפצים, כמו שפי' שם בקונטרס גבי חיישינן שמא במי מילין כתבו. א"נ, בעדי מסירה ורבי אלעזר. מ"ר. **עשאה** כשירה. מכאן משמע, הא דתניא בפ' "הבונה" (שבת דף קג:): כתבה כשירה, או שכתב השירה כיולא בה, או שכתב שלא בדיו, או שכתב האזכרות בזהב הרי אלו יגנזו – בס"ת איירי, דהא מוקמינא לה הכא בס"ת. ותימה, דבפ' "כל כתבי" (שבת דף קטו:) בתחילתו תניא: אין בין ספרים למגילה אלא שספרים נכתבין בכל לשון, ומגילה עד שתהא כתובה אשורית על הספר ובדיו! ותירץ הרב רבי יוסף: דההיא ד"כל כתבי" בשאר ספרים דלאו ס"ת. ואכתי קשה: דבפ"ק דמגילה (דף ח:) תניא: מקרא שכתבו תרגום, ותרגום שכתבו מקרא, וכתב עברי – אינו מטמא את הידים עד שיכתבנו בכתב אשורית על הספר ובדיו. ומוקי לה רב אשי בשאר ספרים ור' יהודה היא, אלמא שאר ספרים בעי דיו. ולא אשכחן דפליגי עליה דרבי יהודה אלא לגבי הא דשרי בכל לשון, אבל בדיו לא אשכחן דפליגי! ונראה לפרש: דההיא ד"כל כתבי" לענין להציל מפני הדליקה דווקא מיירי, ולא לענין לקרות בהם, ולפי שיש בהן אזכרות מצילין אותן אע"פ שלא נכתבו כהלכתן, אבל מגילה – עד שתהא כתובה כהלכתה. תדע, דבעיא דריש גלותא התם לענין הצלה, אבל הא לא מיבעיא ליה אם ניתנו ליקרות בהם או לא. וא"ת: תיקשי *הך ברייתא לרב הונא דאמר בריש גמרא ד"כל כתבי" (שבת דף קטו.): היו כתובין תרגום ובכל לשון אין מצילין, למ"ד אין ניתנין לקרות בהן! ויש לומר, דהאמר התם: תנאי היא. **שלא** יעשנה כזנב. כעין שפירש בקונטרס כאן יש לפרש הא דאמר בבבא בתרא (דף יד.) גבי כרס: שתים כנגד שתים ואחד יולא זנב, שאחד בשורות שתים, ולא כנגד אויר שבין שתי השורות שתים שתים. מ"ר. **ועושה** פרשיותיה סתומות. קלא קשה דנקט לשון רבים, ואין שם כי אם פרשה אחת. ושמא משום "על הארץ" דבסוף שיטה אע"פ שאין כתוב כלום *אח"כ. מ"ר. **רבי** שמעון בן אלעזר אומר ר"מ היה כותבה על הדוכסוסטוס. משמע דתלמידו של ר"מ היה, שאמר דברים הרבה משמו בשאר מקומות, כדאשכחן נמי לעיל (ל:) דקאמר ר"ש בן אלעזר משום ר"מ: אין כותבין את השם לא על *הנייר ולא על המחק. וכן בפ"ק דקדושין (דף כד.) *גמרא ובלבד שיהא הכסף משל אחרים, דקאמר ר"ש בן אלעזר משום ר"מ: אשה פודה מעשר שני בלא חומש. ותימה, דבפ' "המוליא יין" (שבת דף עט:) כתוב בכל הספרים: אמר רבי שמעון: מאיר היה כותבה על הקלף *מפני שהיתה משתמרת – משמע שהיה חבירו, דקאמר "מאיר" ולא קאמר "ר"מ"! ושמא טעות סופר יש בכל הספרים. ואי הוה אמרי' דתרי רשב"א הוה – ניחא. ומיתרלא בהכי פירכא אחריתי, דהכא קתני אדוכסוסטוס והתם תני אקלף. והיה נראה לומר דתרי תנאי אליבא דר"מ, אבל אי אפשר לומר כן, דבפ' "מרובה" (ב"ק דף עח:) גבי מכרה חוץ מגיזותיה, משני: תרי תנאי אליבא דרשב"א, ולא משני דתרי היו. ומיהו יש לדחוק, משום דהנהו דאיפלגי עליה בחדא איפלגי עליה באידך ברייתא. ויש לתרץ: דעל הדוכסוסטוס דקתני הכא היינו: אף הדוכסוסטוס, כדמפרשינן נמי: אף פתוחות, וכ"ש נמי אקלף דמשתמר. ולפי מה שר"ל בסמוך דוכסוסטוס דווקא ולא קלף הוי תימה, דלמר דוכסוסטוס עדיף למזוזה ולמר קלף עדיף. מ"ר.

ועושה

עין משפט נר מצוה

קלב א ב ג ד ה מיי' פ"ט מהל' תפילין וס"ת הלכה טו טוש"ע י"ד סימן רפ סעיף א:
קלג ו מיי' שם פ"ז הל' יא טוש"ע יו"ד סי' רהע סעיף ג:
קלד ז מיי' פ"ה מהל' תפילין וס"ת הל' א סמג עשין כג טוש"ע י"ד סי' רפח סעי' ט:
קלה ח ט מיי' שם הל"ה טוש"ע שם סעי' י:
קלו י מיי' שם הלכה ו טוש"ע שם סעי' יד:
קלז כ מיי' שם הל' ב טוש"ע שם סעי' יג:

[ועי' תוס' שבת מ. ד"ה דילמא]
[שם מז:]
ועוד דאמרינן במסכת כו' נ"ק
נ"ק

שיטה מקובצת

א] פרשיותיו סתומה:
ב] תיבת יתפור נמחק:
ג] כשאר כתיבות:
ד] רשירה כזה

והיו הדברים האלה אשר אנכי מצוך

ה] כזה

והיו הדברים האלה אשר אנכי מצוך

ו] כזה

והיו הדברים האלה אשר אנכי מצוך

ז] כזה

לתת להם כימי השמים על הארץ

ח] כזה

לתת להם כימי השמים על הארץ

ט] שמע הס"ד ומה"ד סתומה היינו שמניח ריוח באמצע ויש כתב משני צדדין אי נמי מניח חלק בראש השיטה:
י] קלף שהוא נקלף:

מסורת הש"ס

[ברכות יט. וש"נ]
בס"י זעירי
[שבת קג:]
מה"ד נ"ק
ס"א אומר כך ועיין נ"ק שמקיים גירסת אח"כ
[הגרר] *נ"א גבי ובלבד כו' נ"ק
גי' נ"ק מפני שמשתמרת ומוחק תיבת שהיתה

הגהות הב"ח

(א) רש"י ד"ה שתים ושלש כו' ר"ל ב' בזו וג' בזו:

גליון הש"ס

גמ' הא דלא אפיצן בהרי"ף הגי' הא דאפיצן הא דלא אפיצן:

אַשִּׁידָה, *דִּתְנַן: [הַשִּׁידָּה] ב"ש אוֹמְרִים: נִמְדֶּדֶת א] מִבִּפְנִים, וּבֵית הִלֵּל אוֹמְרִים: אמִבַּחוּץ, וּמוֹדִים אֵלּוּ וְאֵלּוּ שֶׁאֵין עוֹבִי הָרַגְלַיִם וְעוֹבִי הַלְּבַזְבָּזִין נִמְדָּד; ב] ר' יוֹסֵי אוֹמֵר: מוֹדִים שֶׁעוֹבִי הָרַגְלַיִם וְעוֹבִי הַלְּבַזְבָּזִין נִמְדָּד, וּבֵינֵיהֶן אֵין נִמְדָּד; ר"ש שְׁזוּרִי אוֹמֵר: באִם הָיוּ רַגְלַיִם גְּבוֹהוֹת טֶפַח – אֵין בֵּינֵיהֶן נִמְדָּד, וְאִם לָאו – בֵּינֵיהֶן נִמְדָּד. רַב נַחְמָן בַּר יִצְחָק אָמַר: אַיַּיִן, *דִּתְנַן, רַבִּי מֵאִיר אוֹמֵר: גשֶׁמֶן תְּחִלָּה לְעוֹלָם, וַחכ"א: אַף דהַדְּבַשׁ, ר"ש שְׁזוּרִי אוֹמֵר: אַף הַיַּיִן. מִכְּלָל דְּת"ק סָבַר: יַיִן לָא? אֵימָא, רַבִּי שִׁמְעוֹן שְׁזוּרִי אוֹמֵר: יַיִן. *תַּנְיָא, אָמַר ג] ר"ש שְׁזוּרִי: פַּעַם אַחַת נִתְעָרֵב לִי טֶבֶל בְּחוּלִּין, וּבָאתִי וְשָׁאַלְתִּי אֶת רַבִּי טַרְפוֹן, וְאָמַר לִי: לֵךְ קַח לְךָ מִן הַשּׁוּק וְעַשֵּׂר עָלָיו; קָסָבַר: ד] *דְּאוֹרָיְיתָא בְּרוּבָּא בָּטֵל, וְרוֹב *עַמֵּי הָאָרֶץ מְעַשְּׂרִים הֵן, וַהֲוָה לֵיהּ כְּתוֹרֵם מִן הַפְּטוּר עַל הַפְּטוּר. וְלֵימָא לֵיהּ: לֵךְ קַח מִן הַגּוֹי! קָסָבַר: *ה] האֵין קִנְיָן לְגוֹי בְּאֶרֶץ יִשְׂרָאֵל לְהַפְקִיעַ מִיַּד מַעֲשֵׂר, וַהֲוָה לֵיהּ מִן הַחִיּוּב עַל הַפְּטוּר. אִיכָּא דְּאָמְרִי, אֲמַר לֵיהּ: לֵךְ קַח מִן הַגּוֹי; קָסָבַר: *יֵשׁ קִנְיָן לְגוֹי בְּאֶרֶץ יִשְׂרָאֵל לְהַפְקִיעַ מִיַּד מַעֲשֵׂר, וַהֲוָה לֵיהּ מִן הַפְּטוּר עַל הַפְּטוּר. וְלֵימָא לֵיהּ: קַח מֵהַשּׁוּק! קָסָבַר: אֵין רוֹב עַמֵּי הָאָרֶץ מְעַשְּׂרִין. שְׁלַח לֵיהּ רַב יֵימַר בַּר שֶׁלֶמְיָא לְרַב פַּפָּא, הָא דַּאֲמַר רָבִין בַּר חִינָּנָא אָמַר עוּלָּא א"ר חֲנִינָא: הֲלָכָה כְּר"ש שְׁזוּרִי, וְלֹא עוֹד, אֶלָּא כָּל מָקוֹם שֶׁשָּׁנָה רַבִּי שִׁמְעוֹן שְׁזוּרִי הֲלָכָה כְּמוֹתוֹ, אַף בְּנִתְעָרֵב לֵיהּ טֶבֶל בְּחוּלִּין? אֲמַר לֵיהּ: אִין. אָמַר רַב אַשִׁי: אֲמַר לִי מָר זוּטְרָא, קָשֵׁי בָּהּ ר' חֲנִינָא מְסוּרָא: פְּשִׁיטָא! מִי

רש"י

נמדדת מבפנים (א). דאמרינן התם: כוורת הקש וכוורת הקנים ובור ספינה אלכסנדרית ושידה תיבה ומגדל, שמחזיקים מ' סאה בלח, שהן כוריים ביבש – יצאו מתורת כלי ו] ואין מקבלין טומאה. השידה נמדדת מבפנים. אם מחזיק חללה כוריים – טהורה. מבחוץ. עובי הנסרים נמדד עמה, דרואין ז] אילו היה חלל מבפנים היה משלים לכוריים. עובי הרגלים. הרגלים עבים יותר מן הנסרים. לבזבז. מסגרת סביב לפיהם. וביניהם. אותו אויר שבין הרגלים מתחת אין נמדד, דלא אמרי' רואין כאילו שולים יורדין עד סוף הרגלים. טפח. מקום חשוב הוא. שמן תחילה לעולם. בין שנטמא באב הטומאה או בראשון או בשני – הוי איהו ראשון, דקי"ל (פסחים דף יד:): כל הפוסל את התרומה – מטמא משקין להיות תחילה, ושמן משקה (ב). יין לא. בתמיה, דיין מי איכא למ"ד ח] לאו משקה הוא? אלא אימא ר"ש שזורי אומר יין. ולא שמן ודבש, דלא הוו משקין. ואהך קא"ר חנינא הלכה כר"ש. נתערב לי טבל. דמאי בחולין, ולא יכול להפריש ממנו מפני חולין המעורבין בו. ואע"ג דדמאי לא מיחייב מדאורייתא במעשר, אפילו הכי, הואיל ומיחייב מדרבנן – הוה ליה מן חולין הפטור על טבל החייב. קח מן השוק. דמאי מעם הארץ, דהוי נמי פטור מדאורייתא על הפטור דאורייתא ט]. ולימא קח מן הגוי. דפטור מדאורייתא וחייב מדרבנן. אין רוב עמי הארץ מעשרין. אלא מספקינן (ג) בהו י] מחצה על מחצה, הילכך איכא למימר: המעורב נתעשר וזה לא נתעשר, אי נמי איפכא. כך שמעתי. וקשיא לי: א"כ כשלוקחה מן הגוי נמי, שמא ע"ה זה שמכר פירות (ד) הללו לא עשרן, והוה ליה מן פטור על החיוב! ונראה בעיני שהטבל הזה טבל גמור היה, וכיון שנתערב בחולין – בטל, דמדאורייתא חד בתרי בטיל, והוה ליה פטור מדאורייתא, ורבנן הוא דאחמור ביה ואמור: טבל אסור במשהו, והצריכו להפריש עליו תרומה. ומיהו, מיניה וביה – לא, דחולין מתוקנין נפטרו לגמרי, ואפי' חיובא דרבנן ליכא. וא"ל: לא וקח מן השוק ועשר עליו לפי חשבון טבל שבו. קסבר: רוב עמי הארץ מעשרין הן, והוה ליה פטור מדאורייתא וחייב מדרבנן כי האי. ולימא ליה קח מן הגוי, דפטור נמי מדאורייתא! דקס"ד יש קנין [לגוי להפקיע] כו' וחייב (ה) מדרבנן. קסבר אין קנין לגוי. א"ד כו' קסבר אין רוב עמי הארץ מעשרין, ושמא זה שמכרו לא עישר, והוה ליה חייב מדאורייתא, וטבל המעורב בה פטור מדאורייתא יא]. קשי. פריך.
מי

תוספות

שידה דתנן בית שמאי אומרים נמדדת בפנים כו'. בפ' "כירה" (שבת דף מד:). ושם פי' בקונטרס דשידה היא מרכבת נשים. וקשה: דא"כ למה לי מדידה? דבמיוחדים למדרס לא בעינן מיטלטל מלא וריקן. דאפי' פשוטי כלי עץ המיוחדים למדרס מיטמא מדרס, כדמוכח בבכורות בפ' "על אלו מומין" (דף לח.) דאמרינן: בהנך דחזו למדרסות דלא איתקוש לשק! ועוד קשה: כיון דמיטמא מדרס – מיטמא טמא מת, כדתניא בפ' "בא סימן" (נדה דף מט.): כל המיטמא מדרס מיטמא טמא מת, אלמה תנן במס' כלים (פי"ח מ"ג) דשידה מצלת באהל המת? ובפ' "כירה" (שבת דף מד:) מייתי לה בגמרא. (ואין ניאותין) וכן מוכח בנזיר בפרק "כהן גדול" (דף נה.) דאינה עשויה למרכבת אדם, דאמרינן: הנכנס לארץ העמים בשידה תיבה ומגדל כו', וקאמר התם: כיון דלא שכיחא לא גזרו ביה רבנן – משמע דלא שכיחא ליכנס בה! ונראה לפרש: דעשויה להניח בה כלים. ומיהו קשה מספינה פרק "ר"ע" במסכת שבת (דף פג:) דתניא, רבי חנינא אומר: נלמדנה משק, מה שק מיטלטל מלא וריקן כו', ואמאי? הא עשויה למדרס, שנכנסים בה בני אדם! וי"ל: דאיירי בספינות גדולות, שעיקרן עשויות לתת לתוכן פרקמטיא, ולא דמיא למדרס. ועוד נראה, דאפי' עיקרו *אתי להעביר בני אדם מעיר לעיר, וכן שידה למרכבת נשים – לא חשיב מדרס, כיון דלא עבידא להיות נשען עליה, אלא ללכת ממקום למקום. מידי דהוה אלוקטמין טהורין. בפ' "במה אשה יוצאה" יב] (שבת דף סו:), פירש: אשקינ"ש בלעז, שהולכים עליהן בימות הגשמים, ולא דמי לעגלה של קטן [בסוף פרק שני] דביצה (דף כג:) דטמאה מדרס. ומיהו ר"ח פירש: אלוקטמים – מקי"נש גדולות שהולכין עליהן הליצנים לחידוש, ואין טמאין מדרס כיון דאין עשויות להנאת מדרס. מידי דהוה אסולם, דממעט בפרשת "ויהי ביום השמיני" סולם וקולב וניחותיה ומנורה, מדכתי' (ויקרא יא): "מכל כלי עץ" ולא כתיב "כל כלי עץ", ומדאינה מטמא במת – אינה מטמא מדרס, דכל המטמא במדרס מטמא טמא מת, כדתנן בפ' "בא סימן" (נדה מט.). והיינו טעמא, משום דאינו עשוי להנאת מדרס אלא לירד בו ולעלות. מ"ר. **אימא** ר"ש שזורי אומר יין. פי': יין דווקא, ולא שמן ודבש. והקשה ר"ת: דהלא פסקינן כר"ש שזורי, ובכל דוכתא משמע סתמא דהתלמוד דשמן חשיב משקה, בפ"ק דשבת (דף יז.) גבי מפני מה בוצרין בטהרה ואין מוסקין בטהרה, ובמסכת מכשירין (פ"ו מ"ד) (ר"ע) דחשיב בשבעה משקין יין ושמן, ובפ' "חבית" (שבת דף קמד:) גבי מוהל השמן, ובפ"ק דפסחים (דף יד: ושם) גבי הוסיף ר"ע: מימיהן של כהנים לא נמנעו מלהדליק שמן שנפסל בטבול יום בנר שנטמא בטמא מת, ומוקי לה בנר של מתכת דהויא אב הטומאה, דחרב הרי הוא כחלל. ודייק: קסבר ר"ע טומאת משקין לטמא אחרים דאורייתא כו', מאי איריא בטמא מת? אפי' בראשון ושני נמי תחילה הוי, דתנן: כל הפוסל את התרומה מטמא משקין להיות תחילה! והשתא מאי קושיא? לימא דר"ע סבר כר"ש שזורי דלא חשיב שמן משקה אלא אוכל! ומיהו, מר"ע אינה קושיא, דשמעינן ליה דחשיב שמן משקה במסכת מכשירין, ומייתי ליה במס' שבת בריש פרק "חבית" (דף קמג:): חלב האשה מטמא לרצון ושלא לרצון כו', וקאמר: סלי זיתים וענבים יוכיחו כו'. אבל מסתמא דהתלמוד קשה כמו שפירשתי! ותירץ ר"ת: דהכא מיירי בקרוש, כדקתני רישא: יג] השמן והחלב של גריסין, בזמן שהם לחים – הרי הן ראשונים, פי': דהוו משקין, קרשו – הרי הן שניים. ויש ספרים שרישא זו כתובה בהן, והדר קתני: ר"מ אומר שמן תחילה לעולם אפי' קרוש. והשתא ניחא הא דנקט "לעולם". וכן דבש דחכמים, ויין דר"ש שזורי – כולה בקרוש איירי. *מ"ר. **קסבר** אין קנין *(מחייב). וא"ת: והא מיפטר משעת מירוח הגוי! ואין לומר דקסבר אינו פוטר, דלא אשכחן תנא דאית ליה תרתי: מירוח הגוי אינו פוטר, ואין קנין. דא"כ "דגנך" במאי מוקים ליה? דר"מ אשכחן דאית ליה מירוח הגוי דאינו פוטר יד] (*וסבר יש קנין לגוי דאינו פוטר) לקמן בפרק "רבי ישמעאל" (דף סו:), אבל קסבר יש קנין בספ"ק דע"ז (דף כא.). ורבי יהודה אית ליה יש קנין בפ' "השואל" (ב"מ דף קא.), ואית ליה נמי מירוח הגוי [אינו] פוטר לקמן בפ' "ר' ישמעאל"! וי"ל: דמ"מ דמי לחיוב, כי היכי דלא א"ל: קח מעציץ שאינו נקוב או מתבואת חוצה לארץ. ועוד, כל לקוח דרבנן הוא, כדדרשינן: "תבואת זרעך" ולא לקוח, בפ' "השוכר את הפועלים" (ב"מ דף פח.). ומיהו הר"ר יצחק בהר"ר מאיר מפרש: הני מילי בשלקחו עד שלא נתמרח. ואפשר שלא היה מצוי. ומיהו ר"ת מפרש לאדרבה, בממורח הוא דמיפטר לקוח. טו] וצריך עיון אי מירוח הגוי פוטר אפילו מדרבנן בתבואה דגוי, דאמרינן בפ"ק דבכורות (דף יא:): הלוקח טבלים ממורחים מן הגוי כו', דמרחינהו מאן? אילימא דמרחינהו גוי כו'. והא דגזרינן משום בעלי כיסין – בגוי שלקח מישראל*. מ"ר.
מי

מסורת הש"ס

כלים פי"ח מ"א
טהרות פ"ג מ"ב
תוספתא דדמאי פרק ה
[שבת יג. וש"נ]
[גיטין מז. ב"מ קא. בכורות יא:]
[גיטין מז. ב"מ קא.]
עיין רש"ק [וע"ע תוס' עירובין עא: ד"ה שמן]
*וסבר יש קנין לנכרי ואינו פוטר לקמן בפ' ר"י ויש קנין בספ"ק ג"א וסבר יש קנין בספ"ק כו'
[ועי' היטב תוספות ב"מ פח. ד"ה תבואת]

הגהות הב"ח

(א) רש"י ד"ה נמדדת וכו' דאמרי' נ"ב ר"פ ט"ו במס' כלים: (ב) ד"ה שמן וכו' משקה הוא הס"ד: (ג) ד"ה אין רוב וכו' מספקינן בה והוה מחלה וכו': (ד) בא"ד פירות הטבל הללו לא וכו': (ה) בא"ד מדרבנן הס"ד ואח"כ מ"ה ומשני קסבר:

גליון הש"ס

גמ' קח לך מן השוק. ע' בב"מ דף נג ע"א תוס' דלמא: **תום'** ד"ה קסבר כו' דמ"מ דמי. עי' מגילה דף יט ע"ב בטורי אבן ד"ה ר"י:

עין משפט נר מצוה

קכט א ב מיי' פ"ג מהל' כלים הלכה ד [ודלא כר"ש שזורי ועי' הטעם בתי"ט]:
קל ג ד מיי' פ"א מהל' טומאת אוכלים הל' יט ופ"ט הל"א ועי' בהשגות ובכ"מ ורש"ק:
קלא ה מיי' פ"א מהל' תרומות הלכה י טוש"ע י"ד סי' שלא סעי' ג:

מ"כ יש מוחקין תיבה זו ע"פ פרש"י ולהרבה זו הגי' נכונה דהשתא הוי שפיר מן הפטור מדאורייתא על הפטור מדאורייתא וע"פ פירוש רש"י הוכח כך בפנים ע"כ
*נ"ל עשוי
נ"ק ס"ז
ומחייב נ"ק

שיטה מקובצת

א] מבפנים את חללה שאם חללה מחזקת מ' סאה [טהורה] מבחוץ משלשלין כל השידה בתוך כלי גדול מלא מים ואם היא מפלת מן המים מ' סאה טהורה ואם לאו [טמאה]: ב] נמדד עמה ר' יוסי אומר אלו ואלו מודין כו'. קשה למורי הר"ר שמואל היאך אפשר דמודה ב"ש דעובי רגלים נמדדין (בהא) [עמה] הא אמר נמדדת מבפנים ומצא בפירושים ישנים במסכת שבת [דלר' יוסי] לא נחלקו ב"ש וב"ה: ג] ר"ש שזורי עיין שו"ת מהר"מ סי' א': ד] קסבר רוב עמי הארץ מעשרין הן והשאר נמחק: ה] קסבר אין קנין כו' וא"ת כיון דס"ל אין קנין אלמא ס"ל דמירוח הגוי פוטר דדריש דיגנך ולא דיגון גוי וא"כ אמאי לא א"ל קח מפירות שמירחו גוי [דפטור] מדאורייתא וחייב מדרבנן כי האי וי"ל דלא דמי להני כל כך כמו אלו מייתי דה"נ המ"ל ולימא ליה קח מפירות שנזרעו בעציץ שאינו נקוב דאינו חייב [אלא] מדרבנן ולא פריך מיניה משום דלא דמי ה"נ אמרינן במירוח הגוי וא"ת אמאי לא א"ל יצביר גורנו לתוכו ולעשר מיניה וביה כדאמרי' לעיל וי"ל [דאה"נ] אלא שלא היה רוצה להפריש עליו אלא כשיעור הטבל שהיה מעורב ואם היה צובר גורנו לתוכו היה צריך להפריש מכל המעורב כאילו היה כולו [טבל גמור] ונמצא מפסיד להרבות בתרומה ליתן לכהן: ו] כלי ואין מטלטלין מלא וריקם כשק ואין: ז] דרואין כאילו היה חלל משלים לכוריים: ח] למ"ד דלאו: ט] מדאורייתא דרוב ע"ה מעשרין והו"ל מן הפטור מדאורייתא הס"ד ואח"כ מה"ד ולימא ליה קח: י] בהו כמחצה: יא] מדאורייתא דקא בטל: יב] יוצאה (דף ס"ג) שהן ותיבת פירש נמחק: יג] רישא הרוטב והחלב והגריסין בזמן שהן משקה טופח הרי הן תחילה פי' דהוו משקה קרשו: יד] תיבות וסבר יש קנין לגוי דאינו פוטר נמחק: טו] וצ"ע אי מירוח עיין ר"ש בסוף פ"ק דפיאה:
פרשיותיו

קכא א מיי' פ"ז מהל' תפילין וס"ת הל' ו טוש"ע י"ד סימן רעג סעיף ד:
קכב ב מיי' פ"א מהל' תפילין וס"ת הל' טז סמג עשין כל טוש"ע י"ד סימן רעו סעיף ז:
קכג ג מיי' שם טוש"ע שם סעיף ו:
קכד ד מיי' שם טוש"ע שם:

ועיין במרדכי שהעתיק ל' הירושלמי בזה הלשון ואני ה' אלהיכם מותר לתלות ומיבעיא ליה מאיזה טעם מותר אי משום שהם ג' תיבות אין גנאי כ"כ לתלות השם או משום דאיכא תיבות חול בהדייהו מאי נ"מ לתלות ג' שמות אל אלהים ה' כו' וע"ש והוא יותר נכון. רש"ק

קכה ה מיי' פ"ה מהל' מאכלות אסורות הלכה יד טוש"ע י"ד סימן יג סעיף ב ומדרבנן:
קכו ו ז ח מיי' פ"ב מהל' גירושין הל' יב סמג עשין כ טוש"ע אה"ע סימן קמא סעיף טז:
קכז ט מיי' פי"ב מהל' מעשר הלכה ד:
קכח י מיי' פ"ה מהל' תרומות הלכה יח:

אֶלָּא שָׁלֹשׁ בְּתוֹךְ הַדַּף וּשְׁתַּיִם חוּץ לַדַּף. אנִזְדַּמְּנָה לוֹ תֵּיבָה בַּת שְׁתֵּי אוֹתִיּוֹת – לֹא יְזָרְקֶנָּה לְבֵין הַדַּפִּין, א] אֶלָּא חוֹזֵר וְכוֹתֵב בִּתְחִילַּת הַשִּׁיטָה. ב] *בהַטּוֹעֶה בַּשֵּׁם – גּוֹרֵר אֶת מַה שֶּׁכָּתַב, וְתוֹלֶה אֶת מַה שֶּׁגָּרַר, וְכוֹתֵב אֶת הַשֵּׁם עַל מְקוֹם הַגְּרָר, דִּבְרֵי רַבִּי יְהוּדָה. רַבִּי יוֹסֵי אוֹמֵר: גאַף תּוֹלִין אֶת הַשֵּׁם. רַבִּי יִצְחָק אוֹמֵר: אַף מוֹחֵק וְכוֹתֵב. ר"ש שְׁזוּרִי אוֹמֵר: דכָּל הַשֵּׁם כּוּלּוֹ תּוֹלִין, מִקְצָתוֹ אֵין תּוֹלִין. ר"ש בֶּן אֶלְעָזָר אוֹמֵר מִשּׁוּם ר"מ: אֵין כּוֹתְבִין אֶת הַשֵּׁם לֹא עַל מְקוֹם הַגְּרָר וְלֹא עַל מְקוֹם הַמְּחָק וְאֵין תּוֹלִין אוֹתוֹ, כֵּיצַד עוֹשֶׂה? מְסַלֵּק אֶת הַיְרִיעָה כּוּלָּהּ וְגוֹנְזָהּ. אִיתְּמַר: רַב חֲנַנְאֵל אָמַר רַב, הֲלָכָה: תּוֹלִין אֶת הַשֵּׁם. רַבָּה בַּר בַּר חָנָה א"ר יִצְחָק בַּר שְׁמוּאֵל, הֲלָכָה: מוֹחֵק וְכוֹתֵב. וְלֵימָא *מָר הֲלָכָה כְּמָר, וּמָר הֲלָכָה כְּמָר! מִשּׁוּם דְּאַפְכִי לְהוּ. אָמַר רָבִין בַּר חִינָּנָא *אָמַר עוּלָּא א"ר חֲנִינָא: הֲלָכָה כְּר"ש שְׁזוּרִי; וְלֹא עוֹד, אֶלָּא כָּל מָקוֹם שֶׁשָּׁנָה ר"ש שְׁזוּרִי – הֲלָכָה כְּמוֹתוֹ. אַהַיָּיא? אִילֵימָא אַהָא, ר"ש שְׁזוּרִי אוֹמֵר: כָּל הַשֵּׁם כּוּלּוֹ תּוֹלִין, מִקְצָתוֹ אֵין תּוֹלִין; וְהָא אִיתְּמַר עֲלָהּ: אָמַר רַב חֲנַנְאֵל אָמַר רַב, הֲלָכָה: תּוֹלִין אֶת הַשֵּׁם, וְרַבָּה בַּר בַּר חָנָה אָמַר רַב יִצְחָק בַּר שְׁמוּאֵל, הֲלָכָה: מוֹחֵק וְכוֹתֵב; וְאִם אִיתָא, הוּא נַמִי לֵימָא! אֶלָּא אַהָא, *ר"ש שְׁזוּרִי אוֹמֵר: אֲפִי' בֶּן ג] חָמֵשׁ שָׁנִים וְחוֹרֵשׁ בַּשָּׂדֶה – שְׁחִיטַת אִמּוֹ מְטַהַרְתּוֹ; הָא אִיתְּמַר עֲלָהּ, ד] זְעִירִי א"ר חֲנִינָא: ההֲלָכָה כְּר"ש שְׁזוּרִי, וְאִם אִיתָא, הוּא נַמִי לֵימָא! אֶלָּא אַהָא, בָּרִאשׁוֹנָה הָיוּ אוֹמְרִים: *והַיּוֹצֵא בְּקוֹלָר וְאָמַר "כִּתְבוּ גֵּט לְאִשְׁתִּי" – הֲרֵי אֵלּוּ יִכְתְּבוּ וְיִתְּנוּ, חָזְרוּ לוֹמַר: זאַף הַמְפָרֵשׁ וְהַיּוֹצֵא בְּשַׁיָּירָא, ר"ש שְׁזוּרִי אוֹמֵר: חאַף הַמְסוּכָּן. אִי נַמִי, אַהָא: *תְּרוּמַת מַעֲשֵׂר שֶׁל דְּמַאי שֶׁחָזְרָה לִמְקוֹמָהּ – ר"ש שְׁזוּרִי אוֹמֵר: אַף טבַּחוֹל שׁוֹאֲלוֹ וְאוֹכְלוֹ עַל פִּיו; וְהָא אִיתְּמַר עֲלָהּ, א"ר *יוֹחָנָן: הֲלָכָה כְּר"ש שְׁזוּרִי בִּמְסוּכָּן וּבִתְרוּמַת מַעֲשֵׂר שֶׁל דְּמַאי, וְאִם אִיתָא, הוּא נַמִי לֵימָא! אֶלָּא אַהָא, רַבִּי יוֹסֵי בֶּן כֵּיפַר אוֹמֵר מִשּׁוּם ר"ש שְׁזוּרִי: *פּוֹל הַמִּצְרִי שֶׁזְּרָעוֹ לְזֶרַע, מִקְצָתוֹ הִשְׁרִישׁ לִפְנֵי ר"ה וּמִקְצָתוֹ אַחַר ר"ה – אֵין תּוֹרְמִין ה] מִזֶּה עַל זֶה, ילְפִי שֶׁאֵין תּוֹרְמִין וּמְעַשְּׂרִין לֹא מִן הֶחָדָשׁ עַל הַיָּשָׁן וְלֹא מִן הַיָּשָׁן עַל הֶחָדָשׁ, כֵּיצַד יַעֲשֶׂה? צוֹבֵר גָּרְנוֹ לְתוֹכוֹ, וְנִמְצָא תּוֹרֵם וּמְעַשֵּׂר מִן הֶחָדָשׁ שֶׁבּוֹ עַל הֶחָדָשׁ שֶׁבּוֹ, וּמִן הַיָּשָׁן שֶׁבּוֹ עַל הַיָּשָׁן שֶׁבּוֹ; הָא אִיתְּמַר עֲלָהּ, אָמַר רַבִּי שְׁמוּאֵל בַּר נַחְמָנִי *אָמַר רַבִּי יוֹחָנָן: הֲלָכָה *)כְּרַבִּי שִׁמְעוֹן שְׁזוּרִי, וְאִם אִיתָא, הוּא נַמִי לֵימָא! אֶלָּא אָמַר רַב פַּפָּא: אַשִּׁידָה, רַב נַחְמָן בַּר יִצְחָק אָמַר: אַיַּין. רַב פַּפָּא אָמַר אַשִּׁידָה

*) [ר"ה יג: ע"ש]

רש"י

לא יזרקנה לבין הדפין. ו] ולא יכתבנה חוץ לשרטוט הגליון של דף. אע"פ שהתירו לכתוב ב' אותיות חוץ לדף מתיבה בת חמש (א), תיבה שלימה לא התירו. תולה. מגיה בין השיטין. מוחק. בעוד שהכתיבה לחה. וכותב. השם על המחק, אע"פ שאינו הדור כ"כ כגורר. כיצד הוא עושה. אם טעה בשם (ב). ולימא. רב חננאל: הלכה כר' יוסי. ולימא. רב יצחק: הלכה כר' יצחק. משום דאיכא תנאי דאפכי. דרבי יוסי כר' יצחק, ור' יצחק כר' יוסי. אהייא. איתמר הא דר' חנינא. ואם איתא. דהא א"ר חנינא, ז] לימא הוא נמי למילתיה בהדי הנך אמוראי. בן חמש שנים. אבן פקועה קאי. הוא נמי נימא. ח] הך מילתא התם בשחיטת חולין בהדי זעירי. בקולר. ליהרג. יכתבו ויתנו. אע"ג דהוא לא אמר "תנו". דמסתמא גלי דעתיה מדאמר "כתבו" – ט] לשם נתינה קאמר, משום דיוצא ליהרג, דלא ניחא ליה דתיפול קמי יבם. המפרש. בים (ג). י] (דמאי, היינו) תרומת מעשר. אחד ממאה, כדמפרש בפ' "עגלה ערופה" (סוטה דף מח.). ה"ג: תרומת מעשר של דמאי שחזרה למקומה ר"ש שזורי אומר אף בחול שואלו ואוכלו על פיו. רישא דהך מתני' הכי איתא במס' דמאי: הלוקח פירות ממי שאינו נאמן על המעשרות ושכח ולא עשרן דמאי – שואלו בשבת ואוכל על פיו, ולמוצאי שבת לא יאכל עד שיעשר. תרומת מעשר של דמאי שחזרה כו'. וה"פ: בשבת – שאין לו מה יאכל, דאינו יכול לתרום בשבת, והקילו חכמים אללו משום עונג שבת. הואיל ודמאי דרבנן, ורוב עמי הארץ מעשרין הן – שואלו לע"ה אם עשרן, ואוכלן על פיו. תרומת מעשר של דמאי שחזרה למקומה, דעכשיו אין לה תקנה, דכיון דנקרא עליה שם תרומה – מדמעת ואוסרת את החולין, בזו אמר ר"ש שזורי דאף בחול סומך על המוכר משום הפסד חולין, ושואלו אם הפריש מעשר קודם שמכרו לו, ואוכל על פיו, דנמצאת שלא חלה ע"ז שם יא] תרומת מעשר, דכבר נפטר. פול המצרי. מין קטנית יב] ושמן פאזול"א. שזרעו לזרע. דאם זרעו לירק הוה אזיל מעשר דידיה בתר לקיטה, כדמפרש בר"ה (דף יג:), אבל מיני קטנית בתר השרשה אזלי. צובר גורנו לתוכו. כלומר, מערבן יפה ויתרום. ונמצא. חדש שבתוך התרומה מתקן את החדש הנשאר, וישן שבתרומה מתקן את הישן הנשאר. נמדדת

תוספות

שלשה בתוך הדף וב' חוץ לדף. אומר ר"ת דשם צריך שיהא כולו בתוך הדף. מ"ר. רבי יוסי אומר אף תולין את השם ר' יצחק אומר אף מוחק וכותב. גורר – היינו לאחר שנתייבשה הכתיבה, ומוחק – היינו בעוד לחה, ואינו הדור כל כך. ומדקתני: ר' יוסי אומר אף תולין, ר' יצחק אומר אף מוחק, משמע לכאורה דגורר עדיף מכולהו, ותולה גרע מיניה, ומוחק גרע מתולה. אבל א"א לומר כן, אלא ר' יצחק אדר' יהודה קאי ולא אדר' יוסי, דתולה גרע ממוחק, כדאמרינן *בירושלמי פ"ק דמגילה דא"ר זעירא בר' חננאל בשם רב, הלכה כמו שהוא אומר: מוחק את החול וכותב את השם ותולה את החול. ומיבעיא ליה התם בג' תיבות שיש בהם שם אי שרי לתלות, דדלמא דוקא כשיש בהן תיבות של חול לא מיחזי כי טפל למה שבפנים, ואיבעיא ליה אפי' בג' תיבות שכולם שם, כגון "אל אלקים יי'" דכתיב בספר תהלים אי שרי לתלות או לא. ור"ת פי' דתולין עדיף מכולהו לר' יוסי, ולא גריס "אף תולין". ומאן דפסיק הלכה תולין קסבר דוקא תולין ולא מוחק וכותב, וכן פוסק ר"ת. אבל א"א לומר כן, כדמוכח בירושלמי דתולין גרע. ומיהו קשה אי גרסי' במילתיה דר' יוסי "אף תולין", דהא ר"י נמי מודה דתולין כדאי' במס' סופרים פ"ב, דקתני: טעה את כל השם – יתלנו בין השיטין, דברי ר"י, ר"מ אומר: מוחק מלפניו וכותב את השם על מה שמחק. והיה נראה לומר דבהא פליגי, דמר סבר תולין עדיף ומר סבר מוחק עדיף. ומיהו אין לחוש אי פליגא ברייתא דמסכת סופרים אהא דשמעתין, דעל כרחין אליבא דר"מ פליגי, דקתני הכא ר"ש בן אלעזר אומר משום ר"מ: אין כותבין את השם לא על מקום הגרר ולא על מקום המחק ואין תולין את השם, כילד עושה? מסלק את היריעה כולה וגונזה. מ"ר.

ולימא מר הלכה כמר. בפרק "כל הגט" (גיטין דף כח.) ובסוף מגילה (דף לא:) בתרי דוכתי, ובקידושין פ' "האומר" (דף נט:) פריך כי האי גוונא. וצריך ליתן טעם בשאר דוכתי דלא פריך. יג] *מ"ר. תרומת מעשר של דמאי שחזרה למקומה כו'. משנה היא במס' דמאי (פ"ד מ"א) וקתני רישא: הלוקח פירות ממי שאינו נאמן על המעשרות ושכח ולא עישרן *(דמאי) שואלו בשבת ואוכלן על פיו, ולמוצאי שבת לא יאכל עד שיעשר. תרומת מעשר של דמאי שחזרה למקומה כו'. ופי' בקונטרס: בשבת הקילו משום כבוד שבת, הואיל ודמאי דרבנן הוא דרוב ע"ה מעשרין הן. וטעם זה הוא בירושלמי במס' דמאי. ועוד מפרש שם טעם אחר: אימת שבת על עם הארץ. וזה לשון הירושלמי, סברייא משמיה דר' חנינא: מפני כבוד השבת התירו. ואם מפני כבוד השבת למה לי שואלו ע"י עילה? רב בידי בשם ר' חנינא: אימת שבת על ע"ה והוא אומר אמת. פי': משום דשבת קובעת למעשר יד] אימת שבת עליו. ופריך, בדא תנינן: חשכה מול"ש לא יאכל עד שיעשר? מפני *אחר שאין שבת עליו באימה. תני: שאלו בחול לא יאכל בשבת, מ"ד אימת שבת עליו – ניחא, מ"ד משום כבוד שבת – אפי' שאלו בחול יאכל בשבת! ומשני: לא אמרו אלא בשוגג ולא במזיד. וטעמא דר"ש שזורי מפרש התם: משום דאימת דימוע עליו והוא אומר אמת, פי': מאחר שהופרשה. מ"ר. הא איתמר עלה א"ר יוחנן הלכה כר"ש שזורי במסוכן ובתרומת מעשר של דמאי. ברוב ספרים גרס "ר' יונתן" ולא "ר' יוחנן", כאן ובפ' "בהמה המקשה" (חולין דף עה:) ובפ' "אע"פ" (כתובות דף נה.), וכן מוכח שם בפ' "אע"פ", דמייתי לה אפלוגתא דרב ור' יונתן לאומדנא. וקשה: דבסמוך גבי ההיא דפול המצרי קא פסיק רבי שמואל בר נחמני א"ר יונתן הלכה כר"ש שזורי, ובפ' "בהמה המקשה" (שם:) מוכח דדוקא במסוכן ובתרומת מעשר של דמאי הוא דקאמר דהלכה כמותו ולא באחריני. גבי ההיא בן פקועה, דרב אדא בר חנן דא"ל רב אשי: זיל שחטיה! ופריך, והא"ר חנינא: הלכה כרבי שמעון שזורי, ולא עוד אלא כל מקום ששנה ר"ש שזורי כו'! ומשני: אנא כי הא סבירא לי דאמר רבי יונתן: הלכה כר"ש שזורי במסוכן ובתרומת מעשר של דמאי, אבל באחריני לא. ויש לדחות. ובספר רבינו גרשום כתיב בההיא דפול המצרי: ר' יצחק בר נחמני אמר שמואל, וכן בספרים ישנים. טו] *מ"ר. שידה

מסורת הש"ס

מס' סופרים פ"ה
[מגילה לב. גיטין כח.]
[חולין עה.]
שם עה:
גיטין יג: סה: ב"ב קמז. חולין עה: [טבול יום פ"ד מ"ה]
דמאי פ"ד משנה א [חולין עה:]
[בכתובות נה. איתא ר' נתן וכחולין עה: אי' ר' יונתן]
ר"ה יג: שביעית פ"ב בתוספתא
לפני ג' התוס' לא גרסו כאן ר' יוחנן
[ועי' תוס' שבת נד. ד"ה רב אמר]
נ"ק מ"ז
אחד נ"ק ובכס"מ ליתא
[ועי' תוספות ר"ה יג. ד"ה אמר רב יצחק]

הגהות הב"ח

(א) רש"י ד"ה לא יזרקנה וכו' בת חמש אבל תיבה: (ב) ד"ה כילד וכו' בשם הס"ד ואח"כ מ"ה לימא מר ולימא רב חננאל: (ג) ד"ה המפרש בים הס"ד ואח"כ מ"ה תרומת מעשר של דמאי היינו אחד ממאה:

שיטה מקובצת

א] אלא חוזר כו' ק"ק לפרש"י מאי חוזר וכותב לא הוי ליה למימר חוזר כיון שלא התחיל בסוף מהשיטה אלא כותב בראש השיטה ופי' הרב"ר אליעזר מגרמיזא כגון שנזדמנה לו תיבה של ה' אותיות כגון אברהם והוא כתב אבר וניתותר הם אף על פי שאמרנו שתי אותיות כותב לחוץ הכא כיון שהם תיבה אחת בפני עצמה לא יזרקנה אלא חוזר וכותב אברהם כולו בראש השיטה.

תו"ח: ב] הטועה בשם בתקון סופרים שלא יכתוב אפי' אות אחת של שם חוץ לשירטוט וכיון שהתחיל לכתוב באותיות השם אפי' המלך שואל בשלומו לא יפסוק עד שיגמור כל השם וצריך לגמור כל השם בטבילה אחת בדיו שלא יפסיק בינתים לטבול הקולמוס בדיו ואם פסק הדיו שבקולמוס השם לא יטבול הקולמוס בדיו שבכלי אלא יטבול באותיות של חול שכתב ואם טעה ודילג לא יגיה בין הדפין לפי שלא יהיה הכתיבה נקראת כהלכתה כסדר דהויין להו שלא כסדרן אלא מוטב שיכתוב בין שיטה לשיטה ויהיו נקראין יותר כסדרן. אם דילג בסוף השיטה ממש אין לחוש להגיה בין דף לדף דהוי להו שפיר נקראין כסדרן ובלבד שלא יגיה בו שיטין זו למעלה מזו ושנינו בירושלמי הטועה בשיטה גורר שיטה וכותב שתים גורר שתים וכותב ארבע שלשה לא יגרור אלא מסלק היריעה כולה וגונזה. ונמצא בתקון סופרים טוב לעשות ע' שיטין בדף כנגד ע' זקנים וי"א מ"ב כנגד מ"ב מסעות שעשאו ישראל ממצרים עד שנכנסו לארץ והם כתובים באלה מסעי ויש נזהרין שלא לכתוב השם בסוף השיטה: ג] אפי' בן ארבעה וחמש שנים וחורש עם אמו בשדה: ד] עלה אמר זעירי: ה] אין תורמין ומעשרין מזה: ו] הדפין לא: ז] חנינא הוא נמי לימא למילתא: ח] להך מילתא: ט] דלשם נתינה: י] תיבות דמאי היינו נמחק: יא] שם תרומה דכבר נפטר: יב] קטנית ושמו: יג] פריך. ושמא לא פריך רק במשניות או ברייתות ידועות ובהא קים ליה דידועות היתה: יד] קובעת למעשר ואם אימת שבת עליו ותיבת ופריך נמחק: טו] ישנים שהרי בפ"ק דר"ה מותיב משמואל דאמר לכל אין בילה חוץ מיין ושמן אשמואל דהכא דאמר הלכה כר"ש שזורי דאמר צובר גורנו לתוכו אלמא ס"ל יש בילה אפי' בשאר פירות:

מבפנים

אבל יתרות לית לן בה. איְדך, דְּאָמַר רַב: הַכּוֹתֵב ס"ת וּבָא לִגְמוֹר, גּוֹמֵר וַאֲפִילּוּ בְּאֶמְצַע הַדַּף. מֵיתִיבֵי: *הַכּוֹתֵב ס"ת, בָּא לוֹ לִגְמוֹר — לֹא יִגְמוֹר בְּאֶמְצַע הַדַּף כְּדֶרֶךְ שֶׁגּוֹמֵר בְּחוּמָּשִׁין, אֶלָּא אמְקַצֵּר וְהוֹלֵךְ עַד סוֹף הַדַּף! כִּי קָא אָמַר רַב — בְּחוּמָּשִׁין. וְהָא ס"ת קָאָמַר! בְּחוּמָּשִׁין שֶׁל ס"ת. אִינִי? וְהָא"ר יְהוֹשֻׁעַ בַּר אַבָּא אָמַר רַב גִּידֵּל אָמַר רַב: "לְעֵינֵי כָּל יִשְׂרָאֵל" בְּאֶמְצַע הַדַּף! הַהִיא בְּאֶמְצַע שִׁיטָּה אִיתְּמַר. רַבָּנַן אָמְרִי: אַף בְּאֶמְצַע שִׁיטָּה. רַב אַשִׁי אָמַר: בְּאֶמְצַע שִׁיטָּה א] דַּוְוקָא. בוְהִלְכְתָא: בְּאֶמְצַע שִׁיטָּה דַּוְוקָא. אָמַר רַבִּי יְהוֹשֻׁעַ בַּר אַבָּא אָמַר רַב גִּידֵּל אָמַר רַב: גשְׁמוֹנָה פְּסוּקִים שֶׁבַּתּוֹרָה, *יָחִיד קוֹרֵא אוֹתָן בְּבהכ"נ. כְּמַאן? דְּלָא כְּר"ש דְּתַנְיָא: °"וַיָּמָת שָׁם מֹשֶׁה עֶבֶד יי'". אֶפְשָׁר מֹשֶׁה *חַי, וְכָתַב: "וַיָּמָת שָׁם מֹשֶׁה"? אֶלָּא עַד כָּאן כָּתַב מֹשֶׁה, מִכָּאן וְאֵילָךְ כָּתַב יְהוֹשֻׁעַ בִּן נוּן, דִּבְרֵי רַבִּי יְהוּדָה, וְאָמְרִי לָהּ רַבִּי נְחֶמְיָה. אָמַר לוֹ ר"ש: אֶפְשָׁר ס"ת חָסֵר אוֹת אַחַת? וּכְתִיב: °"לָקוֹחַ אֵת סֵפֶר הַתּוֹרָה הַזֶּה וְשַׂמְתֶּם אוֹתוֹ" וגו'! אֶלָּא, עַד כָּאן הקב"ה אוֹמֵר וּמֹשֶׁה ב] *כּוֹתֵב וְאוֹמֵר, מִכָּאן וְאֵילָךְ הקב"ה אוֹמֵר וּמֹשֶׁה כּוֹתֵב בְּדֶמַע, כְּמָה שֶׁנֶּאֱמַר לְהַלָּן: °"וַיֹּאמֶר לָהֶם בָּרוּךְ מִפִּיו יִקְרָא אֵלַי אֵת כָּל הַדְּבָרִים הָאֵלֶּה וַאֲנִי כּוֹתֵב עַל הַסֵּפֶר בַּדְּיוֹ"; לֵימָא, דְּלָא כְּר"ש? אֲפִי' תֵּימָא ר"ש, הוֹאִיל וְאִישְׁתַּנֵּי אִישְׁתַּנֵּי. וְא"ר יְהוֹשֻׁעַ בַּר אַבָּא אָמַר רַב גִּידֵּל אָמַר רַב: הַלּוֹקֵחַ ס"ת מִן הַשּׁוּק — כְּחוֹטֵף מִצְוָה מִן הַשּׁוּק; כְּתָבוֹ — דמַעֲלֶה עָלָיו הַכָּתוּב כְּאִילּוּ קִיבְּלוֹ מֵהַר סִינַי. אָמַר רַב שֵׁשֶׁת: אִם הִגִּיהַּ ג] אֲפִי' האוֹת אַחַת — מַעֲלֶה עָלָיו כְּאִילּוּ כְּתָבוֹ. ד] (סִי' סגלם) *ת"ר: עוֹשֶׂה אָדָם יְרִיעָה מִבַּת שָׁלֹשׁ דַּפִּין וְעַד בַּת שְׁמוֹנֶה דַּפִּין, ופָּחוֹת מִיכָּן וְיָתֵר עַל כֵּן לֹא יַעֲשֶׂה. זוְלֹא יַרְבֶּה בְּדַפִּין — מִפְּנֵי שֶׁנִּרְאֶה אִגֶּרֶת, ה] וְלֹא יְמַעֵט בְּדַפִּין — מִפְּנֵי שֶׁעֵינָיו מְשׁוֹטְטוֹת, אֶלָּא כְּגוֹן: "לְמִשְׁפְּחוֹתֵיכֶם (לְמִשְׁפְּחוֹתֵיכֶם לְמִשְׁפְּחוֹתֵיכֶם)" ג' פְּעָמִים. חנִזְדַּמְּנָה לוֹ יְרִיעָה בַּת תֵּשַׁע דַּפִּים — לֹא יַחֲלוֹק שָׁלֹשׁ לְכָאן וְשֵׁשׁ לְכָאן, אֶלָּא אַרְבַּע לְכָאן וְחָמֵשׁ לְכָאן. בד"א — בִּתְחִלַּת הַסֵּפֶר, אֲבָל בְּסוֹף הַסֵּפֶר — ו] אֲפִי' פָּסוּק אֶחָד וַאֲפִי' דַּף אֶחָד. פָּסוּק אֶחָד ס"ד? אֶלָּא אֵימָא: פָּסוּק אֶחָד בְּדַף אֶחָד. טשִׁיעוּר גִּלָּיוֹן: מִלְּמַטָּה — טֶפַח, מִלְמַעְלָה — ג' אֶצְבָּעוֹת, וּבֵין *דַּף לְדַף — כִּמְלֹא רֶיוַח ז] רוֹחַב שְׁתֵּי אֶצְבָּעוֹת; וּבְחוּמָּשִׁין, מִלְּמַטָּה — שָׁלֹשׁ אֶצְבָּעוֹת, מִלְמַעְלָה — שְׁתֵּי אֶצְבָּעוֹת, וּבֵין דַּף לְדַף — כִּמְלֹא רֶיוַח ח] רוֹחַב גּוּדָל; וּבֵין שִׁיטָּה לְשִׁיטָּה — כִּמְלֹא שִׁיטָּה, וּבֵין תֵּיבָה לְתֵיבָה — כִּמְלֹא אוֹת קְטַנָּה, וּבֵין אוֹת לְאוֹת — כִּמְלֹא חוּט הַשַּׂעֲרָה. יאַל יְמַעֵט אָדָם אֶת הַכְּתָב, לֹא מִפְּנֵי רֶיוַח שֶׁל מַטָּה וְלֹא מִפְּנֵי רֶיוַח שֶׁל מַעְלָה, וְלֹא מִפְּנֵי רֶיוַח שֶׁבֵּין שִׁיטָּה לְשִׁיטָּה, וְלֹא מִפְּנֵי רֶיוַח שֶׁבֵּין פָּרָשָׁה לְפָרָשָׁה. כנִזְדַּמְּנָה לוֹ תֵּיבָה בַּת חָמֵשׁ אוֹתִיּוֹת — לֹא יִכְתּוֹב שְׁתַּיִם בְּתוֹךְ הַדַּף וְשָׁלֹשׁ חוּץ לַדַּף, אֶלָּא

תורה אור: דברים לד | שם לא | ירמיהו לו

רש"י

(א) אֲבָל יְתֵרוֹת לֵית לָן בָּהּ. אֶלָּא גּוֹרְרָן. מֶחֱזֵי כִּמְנוּמָּר. *כְּשֶׁכּוֹתֵב וּמַגִּיהַּ בּוֹ הַשִּׁיטִּין אֶת מַה שֶּׁחִיסֵּר. הָוָה לֵיהּ יְתֵירוֹת בְּסִפְרֵיהּ. ד' בְּכָל דַּף*. מְקַצֵּר. הַשִּׁיטִּין וְהוֹלֵךְ עַד שֶׁיִּגְמוֹר לְעֵינֵי כָּל יִשְׂרָאֵל בְּסוֹף הַדַּף כָּזֶה*. כִּי קָאָמַר רַב. יִגְמוֹר בְּאֶמְצַע הַדַּף. בְּחוּמָּשִׁין. קָא ס"ד: בִּשְׁאָר חוּמָּשִׁין שֶׁאֵין עֲשׂוּיִין כִּקְדוּשַּׁת סֵפֶר תּוֹרָה, אֲבָל עֲשׂוּיִין הֵן בְּגִלָּיוֹן כְּס"ת. בְּחוּמָּשִׁין שֶׁל ס"ת. כְּגוֹן (בראשית נ) "וַיִּישֶׂם בָּאָרוֹן בְּמִצְרָיִם", וּכְגוֹן "בְּכָל מַסְעֵיהֶם" (ב) (שמות מ) וּ"בְהַר סִינַי" (ויקרא כז) וְ"יַרְדֵּן יְרֵיחוֹ" (במדבר לו) — יָכוֹל לִכְתּוֹב בְּאֶמְצַע הַדַּף, כְּדֶרֶךְ שֶׁגּוֹמֵר בִּשְׁאָר חוּמָּשִׁין שֶׁאֵינָן שֶׁל ס"ת. אֲבָל "לְעֵינֵי כָּל יִשְׂרָאֵל" מוֹדֵי דִּבְסוֹף הַדַּף. אַף בְּאֶמְצַע שִׁיטָּה. וּבְאֶמְצַע הַדַּף ט]. בְּאֶמְצַע שִׁיטָּה דַּוְוקָא. וְלֹא בְּאֶמְצַע הַדַּף. שְׁמוֹנָה פְּסוּקִים. מִ"וַּיָּמָת י] מֹשֶׁה". יָחִיד קוֹרֵא אוֹתָן. אָדָם אֶחָד קוֹרְאָן, וְאֵין מַפְסִיק בֵּינְתַיִם כְּדֵי לַעֲמוֹד אַחֵר וְלִקְרוֹת. אֶפְשָׁר ס"ת חָסֵר יא]. וּמֹשֶׁה קוֹרֵא לוֹ ס"ת "לָקוֹחַ אֵת סֵפֶר הַתּוֹרָה הַזֶּה"? הקב"ה אוֹמֵר. וּמֹשֶׁה אוֹמֵר אַחֲרָיו כְּדֵי שֶׁלֹּא יִטְעֶה בִּכְתָב, וְכוֹתֵב. מִכָּאן וְאֵילָךְ מֹשֶׁה כּוֹתֵב בְּדֶמַע. יב] וְלֹא הָיָה אוֹמֵר אַחֲרָיו מֵרוֹב צַעֲרוֹ. כְּמוֹ שֶׁנֶּאֱמַר לְהַלָּן מִפִּיו יִקְרָא וגו'. שֶׁלֹּא הָיָה אוֹמֵר אַחֲרָיו, מִשּׁוּם דְּקִינוֹת הָווּ. לֵימָא דְּלָא כְּר"ש. דְּכֵיוָן דְּאָמַר ר"ש מֹשֶׁה יג] כָּתַב — הָווּ לְהוּ כִּשְׁאָר פְּסוּקִים, וְיַפְסִיק בֵּינֵיהֶם וְיִקְרָא אַחֵר. דְּאִישְׁתַּנֵּי. דִּנְכְתַּב בְּדֶמַע, אִישְׁתַּנֵּי מִשְּׁאָר יד] ס"ת. כְּחוֹטֵף מִצְוָה. וּמִצְוָה עָבַד, אֲבָל אִי כָּתַב הֲוָה מִצְוָה יְתֵירָה טְפֵי. פָּחוֹת מִכָּאן אוֹ יָתֵר עַל כֵּן לֹא יַעֲשֶׂה. טו] שֶׁתְּפָרִים שֶׁל חִבּוּרֵי הַיְרִיעוֹת יָפִין בָּהּ כְּשֶׁאֵין בָּהֶן יוֹתֵר מִדַּאי. *הִלְכָּךְ לֹא יַעֲשֶׂה יְרִיעוֹת קְצָרוֹת — שֶׁלֹּא יְהוּ טז] הַתְּפָרִים מְקוֹרָבִין יוֹתֵר מִדַּאי, וְלֹא אֲרוּכּוֹת — שֶׁלֹּא לְהַרְחִיקָן יוֹתֵר מִדַּאי. וְלֹא יַרְבֶּה בְּדַפִּים. לַעֲשׂוֹת שְׁמוֹנָה בִּקְלָף, אִם קְלָף קָטָן הוּא, מִפְּנֵי שֶׁהַדַּפִּין קְצָרִים וְנִרְאִין כְּאִגְּרוֹת. וְלֹא יְמַעֵט בְּדַפִּין. לַעֲשׂוֹת *ג' יז] (בִּירִיעָה) אִם יְרִיעָה גְּדוֹלָה הִיא. מִפְּנֵי שֶׁעֵינָיו מְשׁוֹטְטוֹת. כְּשֶׁהַדַּפִּין רְחָבִים, וְטוֹעֶה בְּרָאשֵׁי הַשִּׁיטוֹת. נִזְדַּמְּנָה לוֹ יְרִיעָה שֶׁיֵּשׁ בָּהּ ט' דַּפִּין. לְמַדַּת (ג) הָאֲחֵרִים, וְצָרִיךְ לְקַצְּרָהּ מִפְּנֵי שֶׁאָמְרוּ: לֹא יָתֵר עַל שְׁמוֹנָה. אֶלָּא ד' לְכָאן וְה' לְכָאן. כְּדֵי שֶׁלֹּא תְּהֵא זוֹ יְתֵירָה עַל זוֹ יוֹתֵר מִדַּאי. בד"א. דְּלֹא יְמַעֵט וְלֹא יַרְבֶּה בְּדַפִּין. בִּתְחִלַּת הַסֵּפֶר. אֲבָל בְּסוֹפוֹ, אֲפִילּוּ אֵין לוֹ לִכְתּוֹב אֶלָּא פָּסוּק אֶחָד — יִכְתְּבֶנּוּ בְּכָל הַיְרִיעָה. וַאֲפִילּוּ דַּף אֶחָד. יַעֲשֶׂה יח] בְּכָל הַיְרִיעָה. אֶלָּא אֵימָא פָּסוּק אֶחָד בְּדַף אֶחָד. אִם רוֹצֶה יַעֲשֶׂה דַּף קָצָר יט] מִן תֵּיבָה אַחַת בְּשִׁיטָּה אַחַת, כְּדֵי שֶׁיִּגְמוֹר בְּסוֹף הַדַּף. שִׁיעוּר גִּלָּיוֹן. דְּס"ת. וּבְחוּמָּשִׁין. שֶׁאֵינָן עֲשׂוּיִין לְס"ת, אֲבָל עֲשׂוּיִין הֵן כְּגִלָּיוֹן דְּס"ת. לֹא יְמַעֵט. לַעֲשׂוֹת אוֹתִיּוֹת קְטַנּוֹת בְּשִׁיטָּה עֶלְיוֹנָה וְתַחְתּוֹנָה מִפְּנֵי רֶיוַח כ] הַגִּלָּיוֹן. מִפְּנֵי רֶיוַח שֶׁבֵּין שִׁיטָּה לְשִׁיטָּה. כְּגוֹן אִם שִׂרְטֵט בְּאֶמְצַע הַדַּף כא] שְׁנֵי שִׁיטִּין שֶׁאֵין רֶיוַח כְּדֵי שִׁיעוּר בֵּינֵיהֶם — לֹא יְמַעֵט הַכְּתָב מִפְּנֵי אוֹתוֹ רֶיוַח. לֹא

*) מהרש"א מגיה כמו

תוספות

אבל יתירות לית לן בה. יש טועים, כשמסופקין בתיבה אם מלאה אם חסירה שעושין אותה מלאה, משום דיתירות לית לן בה. ולאו מילתא היא, דהכא איירי ביתירות שגררן, דלא אמרינן דמיחזי כמנומר. מ"ר. **שמנה** פסוקים שבתורה יחיד קורא אותן. ה"ר משולם היה מפרש: למעוטי שלא יקרא ש"צ עמו. וקשה לר"ת: דבימי החכמים לא היה רגילות שיסייע שליח ציבור לקורא בתורה, כדמוכח בפ' שני דמגילה (דף כא: ושם) דאמרינן: קראוה שנים יצאו, מש"כ בתורה! אלא כן עיקר כמו שפירש בקונטרס: לאפוקי שלא יקראו זה אחר זה אותם ח' פסוקין, כגון זה ד' וזה ד', או זה ה' וזה ג'. ומה שנוהגין עכשיו שמסייע ש"צ לקורא בתורה — כדי שלא לבייש את מי שאינו יודע לקרות, כענין שמצינו במס' ביכורים (פ"ג מ"ז) שהתקינו שמקרין את הכל, וכי ההיא דפ' בתרא דנדה (דף עא.) שהתקינו שמטבילין כלים על גבי כל הנשים. כב] מ"ר. **מכאן** ואילך כתב יהושע. מה שנוהגין לומר צידוק הדין בשבת במנחה, פירש רב שר שלום גאון: °על שנפטר משה רבינו באותה שעה, לפיכך נמנעו מלעסוק בתורה, משום דאמרי':* חכם שמת — כל בתי מדרשות שבעיר בטילין. וקשה: דהא כתיב "בן מאה ועשרים שנה אנכי היום", ודרשינן:* היום מלאו ימי ושנותי ואם בשבת מת א"כ כתב "היום" מערב שבת, ויש לתמוה דכתב על העתיד! ולר"ש לא בעי למימר דהפסוק נאמר על העתיד, מדקשיא ליה מהא דכתיב "לקוח את ספר התורה הזה", שמא על שם שעתיד יהושע כג] להשלימו. ועוד קשה: דבסדר עולם משמע דבשבעה באדר שמת משה בו ערב שבת היה, דקתני: ואחר הפסח בעשרים ושנים סבבו את העיר כל אנשי המלחמה הקף פעם אחת, ויהי ביום השביעי וישכימו בבוקר וגו'. רבי יוסי אומר: יום שבת היה. והשתא משהתחילו לסבב לו בכ"ב בניסן, א"כ יום שביעי שהיה שבת — כ"ח בניסן היה, ומדכ"ח בניסן שבת — שבעה באדר ערב שבת! מ"ר.* : **ומשה** כותב. יש ספרים דגרסי: "ומשה אומר וכותב". וחומרא היא לכותבי ס"ת ומזוזה ותפילין. אע"ג דמייתי ראיה מברוך, שמא גם הוא היה עושה כן. מ"ר. ובקונטרס נמי גרים: "אומר וכותב", ופירש טעם (בברוך) וזה לשונו: הקב"ה היה אומר ומשה אומר כד] (וכותב) אחריו כדי שלא יטעה בכתב וכותב, מכאן ואילך משה כותב בדמע ולא היה אומר אחריו מרוב צערו, כמה שנאמר להלן "מפיו יקרא" וגו', שלא היה אומר אחריו משום דקינות הוו. מ"ר. **אם** הגיה בו אפי' אות אחת. פירוש: בס"ת שלקח מן השוק, לא נחשב עוד כחוטף מצוה. שהיה אצל חבירו בעבירה, שהיה משהה ספר שאינו מוגה, ומעלין על זה כאילו כתבו. מ"ר. **כגון** למשפחותיכם ג"פ. ר"ת פי' בתיקון ס"ת שלו בשם רבינו חננאל, שאמר בשם הגאון: דהיינו כשהכתיבה דקה, אבל כשהכתיבה גסה — הכל לפי הנוי, ויכול לעשות דפין בשיטין ארוכין, דאין עיניו משוטטות כיון שהכתיבה גסה. מ"ר.

פסוק אחד בדף אחד. ואף על גב דליכא ס' שיטין או שיעורין אחריני דמסכת סופרים — ליכא למיחש בדף אחרון, *אף על פי שאי אפשר לו לסיים הדף בפסוק אחד, *)כיון שיש בדפין אחרים ס' שיטין אלא אם כן יעשה בדף אחרון כה] שיטין ארוכות. מ"ר.

שלשה

עין משפט נר מצוה

קיב א ב מיי' פ"ז מהל' תפילין הל' ז טוש"ע י"ד סימן ערב סעיף ד:

קיג ג מיי' פי"ג מהל' תפלה הלכה ו סמג עשין יט טוש"ע א"ח סי' תכח סעיף ז:

קיד ד ה מיי' פ"ז מהל' תפילין וס"ת הל"א סמג עשין כד טוש"ע י"ד סימן ער סעי' א:

קטו ו מיי' פ"ט מהל' תפילין וס"ת הל' ב סמג עשין כה טוש"ע י"ד סימן ערב סעי' ג:

קטז ז מיי' שם פ"ז הל' ד טוש"ע י"ד סי' ערב סעי' ב:

קיז ח מיי' שם פ"ט הל' יב טוש"ע שם סעי' ג:

קיח ט מיי' שם הל"ב טוש"ע י"ד סימן רעג סעי' א:

קיט י מיי' שם פ"ז הל' ה טוש"ע שם סעי' ב:

קכ כ מיי' שם טוש"ע שם סעיף ג:

[מ"ק כב. ע"ש היטב]

[ועי' בהרא"ש כ' ע"ה סימן יג]

נ"ק מ"ז

נ"ק מ"ז

מס' סופרים פ"ב

מסורת הש"ס

רש"א הגיה אלא כשכתב ומגיה בין השיטין

ע"כ שייך לעיל

מס' סופרים פ"ב

ב"ב טו.

[מת כך איתא בב"ב]

ר"ה יא.

[אומר וכותב כצ"ל וכ"ה בב"ב]

נ"א ומיהו

מס' סופרים פ"ב

נ"ל ג' דפין גדולות ורחבות אם כו'

רש"ק מ"ז ונ"ק מקיים הגירסא בשם הרמב"ם

כיון שיש בדפין אחרים ס' שיטין אע"פ שאי אפשר לו לסיים הדף בפסוק אחד יעשה בדף אחרון אותיות ארוכות הס"ד נ"ק

הגהות הב"ח

(א) רש"י ד"ה הוה ליה יתירות נ"ל קודם ד"ה אבל וכו' אלא גוררן דלא אמר מחזי כמנומר אלא כשכותב: (ב) ד"ה מבחומשין וכו' מסיעהם כגון בהר: (ג) ד"ה נזדמנה וכו' למדת השורות וצריך:

גליון הש"ס

תוס' ד"ה מכאן וכו' על שנפטר משה רבינו באותה שעה. עי' סוטה דף יג ע"ב רש"י ד"ה דיו זוגי:

שיטה מקובצת

א] דוקא. ולעולם בסוף ולפיכך אין להקפיד ביריעה אחרונה אם הוא פחות מג' דפין ואע"ג דאמרינן לקמן עושה אדם יריעה של ג' דפין באחרונה אין להקפיד כדי לכוון לעיני כל ישראל באמצע השיטה ובסוף הדף: ב] הקב"ה אומר ומשה אומר וכותב. מכאן שצריך לקרות לאדם כשהוא כותב ס"ת תפילין או

מוזה: ג] הגיה בו אפי': ד] סי' עגלם ואות ס' נמחק: ה] ולא ימעט כגון אם שירטט למטה כל כך שלא השאיר למטה טפח או למעלה ד' אצבעות או שלא הניח בין שיטה לשיטה כמלא שיטה אם אינו ממעט בכתיבתו א] לא ימעט בין פרשה לפרשה כגון אם כתב בשיטה ג' תיבות או ד' והוצרך להניח פרשה סתומה ולהתחיל בסוף אותה שיטה לא ימעט כתיבתו כדי להשלים התיבה של סוף שיטה אלא יצמצם בשיטה שלמעלה הימנה כדי לעשות פרשה סתומה כהלכתה: ו] אפי' פסוק אחד עיין בהרא"ש הס"ת: ז] ריוח שתי ותיבת רוחב נמחק: ח] ריוח גודל ותיבת רוחב נמחק: ט] הדף ובחינם פי' כן אלא נראה לפרש אף באמצע השיטה וה"ה בסוף השיטה ולעולם בסוף הדף. תו"ח: י] מוימת שם משה: יא] חסר אות אחת ומשה קורא לו ס"ת דכתיב לקוח: יב] בדמע או שלא היה אומר: יג] משה כתבו: יד] משאר פסוקי דס"ת: טו] יעשה מפני שתפרים: טז] יהיו התפירות מקורבין: יז] לעשות ג' ביריעה אם יריעה גדולה היא: יח] יעשה מכל היריעה הס"ד ומה"ד פסוק אחד ס"ד הא אמרינן לעיל דצריך לגמור בסוף הדף וא"כ היכא משכחת לה שימלא פסוק אחד כל היריעה: יט] קצר מתיבה: כ] ריוח הגיליונות הס"ד: כא] הדף שהם שני: כב] הנשים ויש מפרשים יחיד קורא אותם שאין צריך לקרות במנין של עשרה דאמרינן אין קורין בתורה פחות מעשרה בני אדם ובהנך ח' פסוקים אין לחוש: כג] להשלימו אבל לרבי יהודה נאמר הפסוק על העתיד: כד] תיבת וכותב נמחק: כה] בדף אחרון תיבות ארוכות מ"ר הס"ד ותיבת שיטין נמחק:

א] נראה דצ"ל וכן לא ימעט מפני רוח שבין פרשה וכו':

אלא

קז א מיי' פ"א מהלכות תפילין הל' כ טוש"ע א"ח סימן לב סעיף טז:
קח ב מיי' שם הל' יט טוש"ע שם סעיף טו:
בטוי"ד סימן רעד לא הביא רק השני פירושים
קט ג מיי' פ"ה מהל' תפילין וס"ת הל' ג סמג עשין כה טוש"ע יו"ד סימן רעד סעיף ו וא"ח סימן לו סעיף ג: בשימושא רבה כתוב דט"ט דלטטפות צריכה ה' ה' זוינין כצ"ל נ"ק
קי ד טוש"ע א"ח סימן לב סעיף כה:
קיא ה ו ז מיי' פ"ז מהל' תפילין הלכה יב יג טוש"ע י"ד סימן רעט סעיף ז:
[היינו שלא לתלות רגל שמאלית]

זיל אייתי ינוקא דלא חכים ולא טפש כו'. מעשה היה נגע שהיה לוי"ו של "כדת משה" קטנה כמעט כמו יו"ד, והביא רבי אליהו ינוקא דלא חכים ולא טיפש וקרא בו "כדת", והכשירו מהך דשמעתין. מ"ר. **ואי** לא יהרג הוא ופסול. יש לדקדק מכאן דכתיב "ויהרג" חסר בלא וי"ו. מ"ר. **שעטנז** גץ. יש מפרשים: ג' זוינים, השנים לצד שמאל אחד מלמעלה ואחד מלמטה והאחד לצד ימין, כזה: שעטנ"ז ג"ץ. *ובפי' שבת כתיבת יד *רבי' ש"י צייר אחד מימין ואחד משמאל ואחד מלמעלה, כזה: עוד פי', שיש שעושין שלשתן למעלה, כזה: מ"ר. *כתיב בשימושא רבה דמשמע טט ד"לטטפות" צריכה ג' ג' זוינין, ור"ת כתב בתיקון ס"ת שלו שהוא שיבוש. מ"ר. [כתב דרבי' לאיר נ"ק]

דחטריה לגגיה דחי"ת. פי' בקונטרס: שהגביה רגל שמאלו של ח' עד למעלה, כזה: *ור"ת פירש: באמצע גגו של חית גבוה מעט, כמו חטרתא דגמלא דבאמצע כזה: ולפי' הקונטרס לא יתיישב כל כך הא דאמרינן בסוף "הבונה" (שבת דף קד:): כגון שנטלו לגגו של חית ועשאו שני זיינין. **ומאי** טעמא אית ליה תגא. פי' בקונטרס: בסוף ה"י כזה: ורבינו תם מפרש: בתחילה, כזה: כמו תגא דד' בעירובין (דף יג.) ובסוטה (דף כ.). וכפירוש הקונטרס נראה, שהכתר לצד פתח התשובה. ותגא דקוף כיולא בו, דאמר בפ' "הבונה" (שבת דף קד.): מ"ט מהדר תגא דקוף לגבי רי"ש? אמר הקב"ה: רשע, אם אתה חוזר בך אני אעשה לך כתר כמותי. מ"ר. **ותניא** תיובתא. בחדא לאו תיובתא גמורה היא, אלא דבדוחק מיתרלא. מ"ר. **תנא** אם יש בו דף אחד כו'. ודוקא מעיקרא, דאי יכול לתקן במה שיחזור ויכתוב דף שלם אמאי יגנז? מ"ר.

אבל

איפסיקא ליה כרעא דה"י דהעם בניקבא, אתא לקמיה דר' אבא, א"ל: אם א] אמשתייר בו כשיעור אות קטנה — כשר, ואם לאו — פסול.§ ראמי בר תמרי, דהוא ב] חמוה דרמי בר דיקולי, איפסיקא ליה כרעא דוי"ו ד"ויהרג" בניקבא, אתא לקמיה דרבי זירא, א"ל: זיל אייתי ינוקא בדלא חכים ולא טפש, אי קרי ליה "ויהרג" — כשר, אי לא — "יהרג" הוא, ופסול. אמר רב יהודה אמר רב: בשעה *שעלה משה למרום, מצאו להקב"ה שיושב וקושר כתרים לאותיות, אמר לפניו: רבש"ע, מי מעכב על ידך? אמר לו: אדם אחד יש שעתיד להיות בסוף כמה דורות ועקיבא בן יוסף שמו, שעתיד לדרוש על כל קוץ וקוץ תילין תילין של הלכות. אמר לפניו: רבש"ע, הראהו לי. אמר לו: חזור לאחורך. הלך וישב בסוף ג] שמונה שורות, ולא היה יודע מה הן אומרים, תשש כחו; כיון שהגיע לדבר ד] אחד, אמרו לו תלמידיו: רבי, מנין לך? אמר להן: הלכה למשה מסיני. נתיישבה דעתו. חזר ה] ובא לפני הקב"ה, אמר לפניו: רבונו של עולם, יש לך אדם כזה ואתה נותן תורה ע"י? אמר לו: שתוק, כך עלה במחשבה לפני. אמר לפניו: רבונו של עולם, הראיתני תורתו, הראני שכרו. אמר לו: חזור. ו] [לאחורך] חזר לאחוריו, ראה ששוקלין בשרו במקולין, אמר לפניו: רבש"ע, *זו תורה וזו שכרה? א"ל: שתוק, כך עלה במחשבה לפני. אמר רבא: גשבעה אותיות צריכות ז] שלשה זיונין, ואלו הן: שעטנ"ז ג"ץ. אמר רב אשי: חזינא להו לספרי דווקני ח] דבי רב, דדחטרי להו לגגיה דחי"ת ותלו ליה לכרעיה דה"י; חטרי להו לגגיה דחי"ת — כלומר: חי הוא ברומו של עולם; ותלו ליה לכרעיה דה"י — כדבעא מיניה רבי יהודה נשיאה מר' אמי: מאי דכתיב °"בטחו בי' עדי עד כי ביה יי' צור עולמים"? אמר ליה: כל התולה בטחונו בהקב"ה — ט] הרי לו מחסה בעולם הזה ולעולם הבא. אמר ליה: אנא הכי קא קשיא לי, מאי שנא דכתיב "ביה" ולא כתיב "יה"? כדדרש ר' יהודה בר ר' אילעאי: *אלו שני עולמות שברא הקב"ה, אחד בה"י ואחד ביו"ד, ואיני יודע אם העולם הבא ביו"ד והעולם הזה בה"י, אם העולם הזה ביו"ד והעולם הבא בה"י; כשהוא אומר: °"אלה תולדות השמים והארץ בהבראם" — אל תקרי "בהבראם" אלא: בה"י בראם. [הוי אומר העולם הזה בה"י? והעולם הבא ביו"ד] ומפני מה נברא העולם הזה בה"י? מפני שדומה לאכסדרה, שכל הרוצה לצאת יצא. ומ"ט תליא כרעיה? דאי הדר בתשובה מעיילי ליה. וליעייל בהך! לא מסתייעא מילתא; כדריש לקיש, *דאמר ריש לקיש, מאי דכתיב: °"אם ללצים הוא יליץ ולענוים יתן חן"? בא לטהר — מסייעין אותו, בא לטמא — פותחין לו. ומ"ט אית ליה תאגא? אמר הקב"ה: אם חוזר [בו] י] אני קושר לו *קשר. מפני מה נברא העולם הבא ביו"ד? מפני שצדיקים שבו מועטים. ומפני מה כפוף ראשו? מפני שצדיקים שבו כפוף ראשיהם, מפני מעשיהן שאינן דומין זה לזה. אמר רב יוסף: הני תרתי מילי אמר רב בספרים, ותניא תיובתיה; חדא, הא דאמר רב: ס"ת שיש בו שתי טעיות בכל דף ודף — יתקן, שלש — יגנז; ותניא תיובתיה: השלש — יתקן, ארבע — יגנז. תנא: אם יש בו דף אחת שלימה — מצלת על כולו.§ א"ר יצחק בר שמואל בר מרתא משמיה דרב: ווהוא דכתיב רוביה דספרא *שפיר. א"ל אביי לרב יוסף: אי אית בההוא דף שלש טעיות, מאי? א"ל: הואיל ואיתיהיב לאיתקוני, מיתקן. וה"מ חסירות, אבל יתירות לית לן בה. חסירות מ"ט לא? אמר רב כהנא: משום דמיחזי כמנומר.§ אגרא חמוה דרבי אבא הוה ליה יתירות בסיפריה, אתא לקמיה דרבי אבא, א"ל: לא אמרן אלא בחסירות, אבל

תורה אור: יחזקאל כו — בטחו; בראשית ב — אלה תולדות; משלי ג — אם ללצים

[יהדות וכן איתא במוס' גיטין סח: ד"ה ולוקמיה]

איפסיקא ליה כרעא דה"י. בתפילין. וי"ו ד"ויהרג". "כל בכור" יא] אירע במקום נקב ונראה כמין יו"ד. דלא חכים. דאי חכים, מבין שמחסר הוא לומר יהרג כלפי מעלה, ואומר "ויהרג". לא טפש. שאם טפש, אינו יודע לקרות אלא אות שלימה. כתרים. כגון התגין דס"ת. מי מעכב על ידך. מה שכתבת, שאתה צריך להוסיף עוד עליהם כתרים? שהגיע לדבר. שצריך טעם. נתיישבה דעתו. של משה, הואיל ומשמו אומר אע"פ שעדיין לא קיבלה. במקולין. יב] מקום הקצבין. שוקלין בשרו — כדאמר בברכות (דף סא:) שסרקו בשרו במסרקות יג] ברזל. שלשה זיונין. ג' תגין קטנים בכל אחת, כשין יד] *רגל השמאלית, וכן כעין בראש הרגל הפנימי, וכן כולם. ואותם ג' תגין אחד נוטה לימין ואחד נוטה לשמאל ואחד טו] למעלה. שעטנז גץ. והוא הדין לבדיק כפופה ולנון פשוטה. דווקני = שמדקדקים לעשות כתב מיושר. חטרי לגגיה דחית. לגגו של חית, עושין למעלה כעין חוטר כזה: [ח] כלומר, הקב"ה חי שוכן ברומו של עולם, חי"ת היינו חי. ותלו כרעיה דה"י. רגל הפנימי של ה"י תלוי באויר ואינו דבוק לגגו. הוה לו מחסה. דהיינו טז] הכי משמע: על שבטחו בי' עדי עד — הוו להם ביה יי' מחסה, צור מעוז לעולמים. אחת בה"י ואחת ביו"ד. חלק את שמו והטיף מכל אות ג' טיפין, ומאותן טיפין נעשו מים ואש יז] ואויר וכל העולם כולו. וכן כתוב בספר יצירה. שדומה לאכסדרה. שפתוח מתחתיו. שכל הרוצה לצאת. ממנו לתרבות רעה, יוצא יח] מעלין ליה. בפתח העליון, בין רגל שבתוכו לגגו. וליעיילו בהך. פתח התחתון דנפיק ביה! לא מסתייעא מילתא. דהבא ליטהר בעי סיוע מפני יצר הרע, הלכך עבדי ליה סיוע *פתח יתירה. הוא *יליץ. יט] (אותו) כלומר, פותח לו להיות לץ. מסייעין אותו. אלמא בעי סיוע. אית ליה תגא. לה"י, כתר קטן בסוף גגו דה"י. מעשיהם אין דומין כו'. וכבודו של זה גדול משל זה, משום הכי ראשיהם כפופים, דמתבייש מחבירו. תרתי מילי אמר רב בספרים. בהלכות ספרי תורה. ולקמן אמרינן אידך מילתא דרב. מצלת על כולן. שאפילו טעיות בכל דף ודף כ] אז מצלת עליהם הך דף שלימה כא] ומתקן. אי בההוא דף שלימה שלשה טעיות מאי. מצלת או אין מצלת? מי אמרינן שלימה בלי טעות, או דלמא שלימה מד' טעיות, אבל שלש לא איכפת לן? הואיל ואתיהב רשות לתקוני. ס"ת שיש ג' טעיות בכל דף — מתקן להך דף בת ג', ומצלת על כולם אף על פי שיש כב] ד' בכל שאר הדפין. וה"מ. דאמרינן ד' יגנז — כגון חסרות, שחסרו ממנו אותיות.

אבל

מהרש"א הגהה בדל ומהרש"ק הגהה בדפני [שבת פט.]
[ברכות סא:]
ילין הקב"ה ילין אות כלומר נ"ק
[עי' תוספות ברכות נו: ד"ה והוכה כו' אל תקרי נור אלא נר]
שבת קד. יומא לח: ע' נ
כתר נ"ק
[עי' בית יוסף יו"ד ס רעט]

שיטה מקובצת

א] אם נשתייר: ב] דהוא רמי בר דיקולי: ג] שמונה. ס"א עשר: ד] תיבת אחד נמחק: ה] תיבת ובא נמחק: ו] חזור לאחורך: ז] שלשה שלשה זוינין: ח] תיבות דבי רב נמחק: ט] בהקב"ה הוה לו ותיב' הרי נמחק: י] חוזר בו אני קושר לו כתר: יא] בכור. בתפילין בפרשת והיה כי יביאך האחרון שבקדש לי כל בכור הס"ד ומה"ד בניקבא. במשך רגלו של וי"ו אירע: יב] במקולין במקום: יג] במסרקות של ברזל: יד] בשין בראש רגל: טו] ואחד נוטה למעלה: טז] דהיינו דהכי: יז] ואויר. נ"א ועפר: יח] יוצא. בברייתא דשמואל מצאתי העולם דומה לאכסדרה שאין לה אלא שלשה זויות והעולם הזה אין לו אלא ג' זויות לפי שמרוח צפונית אין לו זויות הס"ד ומה"ד מעיילי ליה בפתח: יט] יליץ אותו הקב"ה יליץ אותו כלומר: כ] ודף יתקן והוא שכתוב רובא דספרא שפיר שרוב כל דף ודף כתוב בלא טעות שאין יותר משמונה או ששה טעות בכל דף ודף אז: כא] דף שלמה הס"ד ומה"ד אי אית בההוא: כב] אע"פ שיש בכל שאר הדפין הרבה טעויות הס"ד דוקא

ותְמָנֵי סְרֵי דְקָנִים — הָא עֶשְׂרִין וְתַרְתֵּין; כַּפְתּוֹרִין נַמִי אַחַד עָשָׂר: א] כַּפְתּוֹרִין תְּרֵי דִידָהּ, וְשִׁשָּׁה דְקָנִים, וְכַפְתֹּר וְכַפְתֹּר וְכַפְתֹּר — הָא חַד סָר; אֶלָּא פְּרָחִים תִּשְׁעָה מְנָלַן? פְּרָחִים תְּרֵי דִידָהּ וְשִׁשָּׁה דְקָנִים — תְּמַנְיָא הָווּ! אָמַר רַב שַׁלְמָן, כְּתִיב: °"עַד יְרֵכָהּ עַד פִּרְחָהּ מִקְשָׁה הִיא". אָמַר רַב: גּוֹבְהָהּ שֶׁל מְנוֹרָה תִּשְׁעָה טְפָחִים. אֵיתִיבֵיהּ רַב שִׁימִי בַּר חִיָּיא לְרַב: *אֶבֶן הָיְתָה לִפְנֵי ב] מְנוֹרָה אוּבָהּ שָׁלֹשׁ מַעֲלוֹת, שֶׁעָלֶיהָ הַכֹּהֵן עוֹמֵד וּמֵטִיב אֶת הַנֵּרוֹת! א"ל: שִׁימִי, *אַתְּ? כִּי קָאָמִינָא מִשְּׂפַת קָנִים וּלְמַעְלָה. כְּתִיב: °"וְהַפֶּרַח וְהַנֵּרוֹת וְהַמֶּלְקָחַיִם זָהָב הוּא *מִיכְלוֹת זָהָב", מַאי "מִיכְלוֹת זָהָב"? אָמַר רַב אַמִי: שֶׁכִּילַּתּוּ לְכָל זָהָב סָגוּר שֶׁל שְׁלֹמֹה; דא"ר יְהוּדָה אָמַר רַב: עֶשֶׂר מְנוֹרוֹת עָשָׂה שְׁלֹמֹה, וְכָל אַחַת וְאַחַת הֵבִיא לָהּ אֶלֶף כִּכַּר זָהָב, וְהִכְנִיסוּהוּ אֶלֶף פְּעָמִים לַכּוּר וְהֶעֱמִידוּהוּ עַל כִּכָּר. אִינִי? וְהָכְתִיב: ג] °"וְכֹל כְּלֵי מַשְׁקֵה הַמֶּלֶךְ שְׁלֹמֹה זָהָב וְכֹל כְּלֵי בֵּית יַעַר הַלְּבָנוֹן זָהָב סָגוּר אֵין כֶּסֶף נֶחְשָׁב בִּימֵי שְׁלֹמֹה לִמְאוּמָה"! זָהָב סָגוּר קָא אָמְרִינַן. וּמִי *חָסֵר כּוּלֵּי הַאי? וְהָתַנְיָא, ר' יוֹסֵי בְּר' יְהוּדָה אוֹמֵר: מַעֲשֶׂה וְהָיְתָה [מְנוֹרַת] בֵּית הַמִּקְדָּשׁ יְתֵירָה עַל שֶׁל מֹשֶׁה בְּדִינָר זָהָב ד] קוֹרְדִּיקִינִי, וְהִכְנִיסוּהָ פ' פְּעָמִים לַכּוּר וְהֶעֱמִידוּהָ עַל כִּכָּר! כֵּיוָן דְּקָאֵי קָאֵי. א"ר שְׁמוּאֵל בַּר נַחְמָנִי אָמַר ר' יוֹנָתָן, מַאי דִּכְתִיב: °"עַל הַמְּנוֹרָה הַטְּהוֹרָה"? שֶׁיָּרְדוּ מַעֲשֶׂיהָ מִמְּקוֹם טָהֳרָה. אֶלָּא מֵעַתָּה, °"עַל הַשֻּׁלְחָן הַטָּהֹר" — שֶׁיָּרְדוּ מַעֲשָׂיו מִמָּקוֹם טָהוֹר? אֶלָּא, טָהוֹר מִכְּלָל שֶׁהוּא טָמֵא, הָכָא נַמִי — טְהוֹרָה מִכְּלָל שֶׁהִיא טְמֵאָה! בִּשְׁלָמָא הָתָם כִּדְרֵישׁ לָקִישׁ, דְּאָמַר רֵישׁ לָקִישׁ, מַאי דִּכְתִיב: "עַל *הַשּׁוּלְחָן הַטָּהוֹר", מִכְּלָל שֶׁהוּא טָמֵא? כְּלִי עֵץ הֶעָשׂוּי לְנַחַת הוּא, וְכָל כְּלִי עֵץ בהֶעָשׂוּי לְנַחַת אֵינוֹ מְקַבֵּל טוּמְאָה! אֶלָּא, מְלַמֵּד *שֶׁמַּגְבִּיהִין אוֹתוֹ ה] לְעוֹלֵי רְגָלִים וּמַרְאִים לָהֶם לֶחֶם הַפָּנִים, וְאוֹמֵר לָהֶם: רְאוּ חִיבַּתְכֶם לִפְנֵי הַמָּקוֹם. מַאי חִיבַּתְכֶם? כִּדְרִיב"ל, *דא"ר יְהוֹשֻׁעַ בֶּן לֵוִי: נֵס גָּדוֹל נַעֲשָׂה בְּלֶחֶם הַפָּנִים, סִילּוּקוֹ כְּסִידּוּרוֹ, שֶׁנֶּאֱמַר: °"לָשׂוּם לֶחֶם חֹם בְּיוֹם הִלָּקְחוֹ". אֶלָּא הָכָא טְהוֹרָה מִכְּלָל שֶׁהִיא טְמֵאָה — פְּשִׁיטָא, כְּלֵי מַתָּכוֹת נִינְהוּ, וּכְלֵי מַתָּכוֹת ו] מְקַבְּלִין טוּמְאָה! אֶלָּא שֶׁיָּרְדוּ מַעֲשֶׂיהָ מִמְּקוֹם טָהֳרָה. תַּנְיָא, רַבִּי יוֹסֵי בְּרַבִּי יְהוּדָה אוֹמֵר: אָרוֹן שֶׁל אֵשׁ וְשֻׁלְחָן שֶׁל אֵשׁ וּמְנוֹרָה שֶׁל אֵשׁ יָרְדוּ מִן הַשָּׁמַיִם, וְרָאָה מֹשֶׁה וְעָשָׂה כְּמוֹתָם, שֶׁנֶּאֱמַר: °"וּרְאֵה וַעֲשֵׂה בְּתַבְנִיתָם אֲשֶׁר אַתָּה מָרְאֶה בָּהָר". אֶלָּא מֵעַתָּה, °"וַהֲקֵמֹתָ אֶת הַמִּשְׁכָּן כְּמִשְׁפָּטוֹ אֲשֶׁר הָרְאֵיתָ בָּהָר" הָכִי נַמִי? הָכָא כְּתִיב: "כְּמִשְׁפָּטוֹ", הָתָם כְּתִיב: "כְּתַבְנִיתָם". א"ר חִיָּיא בַּר אַבָּא אָמַר ר' יוֹחָנָן: גַּבְרִיאֵל חָגוּר כְּמִין פְּסִיקְיָא הָיָה, וְהֶרְאָה לוֹ לְמֹשֶׁה מַעֲשֵׂה מְנוֹרָה, דִּכְתִיב: "וְזֶה מַעֲשֵׂה הַמְּנוֹרָה". תָּנָא דְּבֵי רַבִּי יִשְׁמָעֵאל: שְׁלֹשָׁה דְּבָרִים הָיוּ קָשִׁין לוֹ לְמֹשֶׁה, עַד שֶׁהֶרְאָה לוֹ הקב"ה בְּאֶצְבָּעוֹ, וְאֵלּוּ הֵן: מְנוֹרָה, וְרֹאשׁ חֹדֶשׁ, וּשְׁרָצִים; מְנוֹרָה — דִּכְתִיב: °"וְזֶה מַעֲשֵׂה הַמְּנוֹרָה"; רֹאשׁ חוֹדֶשׁ — דִּכְתִיב: °"הַחוֹדֶשׁ הַזֶּה לָכֶם רֹאשׁ חֳדָשִׁים"; שְׁרָצִים — דִּכְתִיב: °"וְזֶה לָכֶם הַטָּמֵא"; וְיֵשׁ אוֹמְרִים: אַף הִלְכוֹת שְׁחִיטָה, שֶׁנֶּאֱמַר: °"וְזֶה אֲשֶׁר תַּעֲשֶׂה עַל הַמִּזְבֵּחַ". § "שְׁתֵּי פָרָשִׁיּוֹת שֶׁבַּמְּזוּזָה מְעַכְּבוֹת זוֹ אֶת זוֹ, וַאֲפִילּוּ כְּתָב אֶחָד מְעַכְּבָן". § פְּשִׁיטָא! אָמַר רַב *יְהוּדָה אָמַר רַב: לֹא נִצְרְכָה אֶלָּא לְקוֹצָהּ גשֶׁל יוֹד. וְהָא נַמִי פְּשִׁיטָא! אֶלָּא לְכְאִידָךְ דְּרַב יְהוּדָה אָמַר רַב, דְּאָמַר רַב יְהוּדָה אָמַר רַב: *דכָּל אוֹת שֶׁאֵין גְּוִיל מוּקָּף לָהּ מֵאַרְבַּע רוּחוֹתֶיהָ — פְּסוּלָה. אָמַר ז] אַשְׁיָאן בַּר נַדְבָּךְ מִשְּׁמֵיהּ דְּרַב יְהוּדָה: נִיקַּב תּוֹכוֹ שֶׁל הֵ"י — כָּשֵׁר, יְרֵיכוֹ — פָּסוּל. א"ר זֵירָא: לְדִידִי מְפָרְשָׁה לִי מִינֵּיהּ דְּרַב הוּנָא; וְרַבִּי יַעֲקֹב אָמַר, לְדִידִי מְפָרְשָׁה לִי מִינֵּיהּ דְּרַב יְהוּדָה: נִיקַּב התּוֹכוֹ שֶׁל הֵ"י — כָּשֵׁר; יְרֵיכוֹ, אִם נִשְׁתַּיֵּיר בּוֹ כְּשִׁיעוּר ח] אוֹת קְטַנָּה — כָּשֵׁר, וְאִם לָאו — פָּסוּל. אַגְרָא חֲמוּהּ דְּר' אַבָּא אִיפְּסִיקָא

תורה אור: במדבר ח; דה"ב ד; מ"א י; ויקרא כד; שם; ש"א; שמות כה; שם כו; במדבר ח; שמות יב; ויקרא יא; שמות כט

רש"י

תַּמְנֵי סְרֵי דְקָנִים. דִּכְתִיב: "שְׁלֹשָׁה גְבִיעִים מְשׁוּקָּדִים בַּקָּנֶה הָאֶחָד". כַּפְתּוֹרֶיהָ. *דִּמְנוֹרָה גּוּפָהּ תְּרֵי. וְשִׁית דְקָנִים. דְּיֵשׁ בְּכָל קָנֶה וְקָנֶה כַּפְתּוֹר, ט] כִּדְכְתִיב: "שְׁלֹשָׁה גְבִיעִים מְשׁוּקָּדִים בַּקָּנֶה הָאֶחָד כַּפְתֹּר וָפֶרַח" — הֲרֵי ח', וְכַפְתּוֹר תַּחַת שְׁנֵי קָנִים, וְכֵן לִשְׁנַיִם הָאַחֲרוֹנִים י] כִּדְאֲמַרַן לְעֵיל, וּשְׁנֵי קָנִים יוֹצְאִין מִמֶּנָּה — הָא חַד סַר. [וְשִׁשָּׁה דְקָנִים]. בְּכָל קָנֶה כַּפְתּוֹר וָפֶרַח, כִּדְכְתִיב: "בַּקָּנֶה הָאֶחָד כַּפְתּוֹר וָפֶרַח". עַד פִּרְחָהּ. רִיבָּה לָךְ הַכָּתוּב חַד פֶּרַח. אֶבֶן יא] גְּדוֹלָה כו'. וְאִם אֵינָהּ גְּדוֹלָה אֶלָּא ט' טְפָחִים, לָמָּה לִי אֶבֶן תַּחַת הַכֹּהֵן? יב] שִׁימִי אַתְּ. אַתָּה הוּא הַמַּקְשֶׁה לִי? בִּתְמִיָּה. מִשְּׂפַת קָנִים וּלְמַעְלָה. הָיְתָה ט', וּמִן הָאָרֶץ וְעַד לַקָּנִים ט', כִּדְמְפָרֵשׁ לְעֵיל. הוּא מִיכְלוֹת זָהָב. יג] וּפָסוּק הוּא. זָהָב סָגוּר. שֶׁבְּשָׁעָה שֶׁמּוֹכְרִין אוֹתוֹ נִסְגָּרוֹת כָּל הַחֲנוּיוֹת שֶׁמּוֹכְרִין יד] אֶת הַזָּהָב (יומא מה.). וְהָכְתִי' אֵין כֶּסֶף נֶחְשָׁב. אַלְמָא עָשִׁיר הֲוָה, וְאַתְּ אָמְרַתְּ טו] "כִּלִּיתוֹ". וּמִי חָסֵר כּוּלֵּי הַאי. דְּקָאָמְרַתְּ: אֶלֶף טז] *הַכִּכָּר הִכְנִיסוּ אֶלֶף פְּעָמִים לְכוּר עַד שֶׁיַּעֲמוֹד עַל כִּכָּר, אַלְמָא בְּכָל פַּעַם חָסֵר כִּכָּר. יז] קוֹרְדִּיקִינִי. שֵׁם מַטְבֵּעַ. כֵּיוָן דְּקָאֵי. שֶׁנִּצְרַף יָפֶה בִּימֵי שְׁלֹמֹה, קָאֵי, לְפִיכָךְ לֹא חָסֵר עַכְשָׁיו אֶלָּא דִינָר. מִמְּקוֹם טָהֳרָה. מִן הַשָּׁמַיִם *הֶרְאוּ לְמֹשֶׁה יח] לְנֶגֶד הַמְּנוֹרָה. מִכְּלָל שֶׁהוּא טָמֵא. כְּלוֹמַר, מְקַבֵּל טוּמְאָה. בִּשְׁלָמָא הָתָם. גַּבֵּי שׁוּלְחָן, אִיצְטְרִיךְ לְאַשְׁמוּעִינַן דִּמְקַבֵּל טוּמְאָה, מִשּׁוּם פִּירְכֵיהּ דְּרֵישׁ לָקִישׁ. לְנַחַת. שֶׁאֵינוֹ מִטַּלְטֵל. כְּלִי עֵץ הֶעָשׂוּי לְנַחַת אֵינוֹ מְקַבֵּל טוּמְאָה, דִּכְתִיב גַּבֵּי שְׁרָצִים: "מִכָּל כְּלִי עֵץ אוֹ עוֹר אוֹ שָׂק" (ויקרא יא), מַה שַּׂק מִיטַּלְטֵל מָלֵא וְרֵיקָם יט]. שֶׁמַּגְבִּיהִין אוֹתוֹ. הִלְכָּךְ מִיטַּלְטֵל מָלֵא וְרֵיקָם הוּא. חוֹם בְּיוֹם הִלָּקְחוֹ. מַשְׁמַע: כְּשֶׁמְּסַלְּקִים הָיָה חוֹם. כְּתַבְנִיתָם. אֲרוֹן וְשׁוּלְחָן וּמְנוֹרָה כְּתִיב, וּכְתִיב: "אֲשֶׁר אַתָּה מָרְאֶה בָּהָר", אַלְמָא הֶרְאוּהוּ. הָכִי נַמִי. דְּמִשְׁכָּן שֶׁל אֵשׁ יָרַד מִן הַשָּׁמַיִם? בִּתְמִיָּה. הָכָא כְּתִיב כְּמִשְׁפָּטוֹ. מַשְׁמַע: הִלְכוֹתָיו נֶאֶמְרוּ לוֹ. הָתָם כְּתִיב כְּתַבְנִיתָם. מַשְׁמַע דְּהֶרְאוּהוּ כ] כְּמוֹתָם. חָגוּר כְּמִין פְּסִיקְיָא. אֵזוֹר כא] כָּרוּךְ. אוּמָּנִים שֶׁרוֹצִים לַעֲשׂוֹת מְלָאכָה נָאָה חוֹגְרִין עַצְמָן שֶׁלֹּא יְהוּ נִגְרָרִין בְּבִגְדֵיהֶם. רֹאשׁ חֹדֶשׁ. בִּשְׁעַת מוֹלַד לְבָנָה אֵינָהּ נִרְאֵית כִּי אִם מְעַט וְאֵינָהּ נִיכֶּרֶת, כִּדְאָמְרִינַן בְּרֹאשׁ הַשָּׁנָה (דף כ.): "כָּזֶה רְאִיתֶם אִם כָּזֶה רְאִיתֶם". שְׁרָצִים. לֹא הָיָה מַכִּיר אֵיזֶה טָמֵא וְאֵיזֶה טָהוֹר. הִלְכוֹת שְׁחִיטָה. לֹא הָיָה מֵבִין מֵהֵיכָן הִיא מוּגְרֶמֶת. וְזֶה אֲשֶׁר תַּעֲשֶׂה עַל הַמִּזְבֵּחַ. (א) וַעֲשִׂיָּיה תְּחִילַּת זְבִיחָה [הִיא], וּכְתִיב "וְזֶה", אַלְמָא הֶרְאָהוּ בְּאֶצְבַּע. פְּשִׁיטָא. דְּאוֹת אַחַת מְעַכַּבְתָּן, דִּכְתִיב "וּכְתַבְתָּם" — כְּתִיבָה תַּמָּה (שבת קג:). קוֹצוֹ שֶׁל יוֹד. רֶגֶל יְמִינִי שֶׁל יוֹד. הָא נַמִי פְּשִׁיטָא. כב] הָא לֹא נַעֲשֵׂית הָאוֹת. שֶׁאֵין גְּוִיל מוּקָּף לָהּ. שֶׁמּוּדְבֶּקֶת בְּאוֹת אַחֶרֶת. וְהַיְינוּ דְּקָתָנֵי: כְּתָב אֶחָד מְעַכְּבָן, כְּלוֹמַר הִלְכוֹת מִשְׁפַּט אוֹת אַחַת *מְעַכְּבוֹ לִמְזוּזָה וּתְפִילִּין. תּוֹכוֹ שֶׁל ה'. רֶגֶל שֶׁבְּפָנִים. יְרֵיכוֹ. רֶגֶל הַיְמָנִית. ל"א: תּוֹכוֹ — הַגְּוִיל וְהֶחָלָק שֶׁבְּתוֹכוֹ, וּבִתְפִילִּין קָמַיְירֵי. אִיפְּסִיקָא

תוספות

אבן היתה לפני המנורה. משנה היא במסכת תמיד (פ"ג מ"ט). מ"ר. **סילוקו** כסידורו. ולמ"ד אין כג] תנור מקדש (לקמן דף צה:*) לא היה חם בשעת סידורו, אלא כלומר רך. מ"ר. **הכא** כתיב כמשפטו והתם כתיב כתבניתם. ואם תאמר: גבי משכן נמי כתיב "ככל אשר אני מראה אותך את תבנית המשכן ואת תבנית כל כליו"! וי"ל: דהכא לא כתיב "בהר", והתם כתיב "בהר", דמשמע שמן השמים ירדו למשה על ההר. מ"ר.

שלשה דברים היו קשין לו למשה כו'. ואם תאמר: וליחשוב נמי ההיא ד"אלו טריפות" (חולין דף מב.) דאמר: "וזאת החיה אשר תאכלו" — מלמד שתפס הקב"ה כל מין ומין והראה לו למשה, ואמר לו: זאת אכול וזאת לא תאכל! *ויש לומר: דלא חשיב אלא הך דכתיב "זה". ויש לתמוה דלא חשיב מחצית השקל, דכתיב "זה יתנו", ואמרינן *(שקלים דף ג ומ"ר): כמין מטבע של אש הראהו למשה! ויש לומר: דלא שייך התם נתקשה, אלא משום דלא הוה ידע כד] בשום ענין אם לא היה מראהו. מ"ר.

קוצו של יו"ד. פירש בקונטרס: רגל ימיני. וקשה, *דהא פשיטא דאין זה אות! כה] ומפרש ר"ת: דהוא ראשו כפוף, כדאמרינן בסמוך: מפני מה כפוף ראשו. ואם תאמר, דאמרינן בהגדת "חלק" (סנהדרין דף נה:): "ונער יכתבם" דהיינו יו"ד, שאם השליך נער אבן בקיר ועושה רושם עושה יו"ד! ויש לומר: דכעין יו"ד קאמר, ולא יו"ד ממש.
זיל

עין משפט נר מצוה

קב א מיי' פ"ג מהלכות בית הבחירה הל' יא:

[שהיא נאפית מע"ש וכ"כ תוס' בחגיגה כו':]

קג ב מיי' פ"ג מהלכות כלים הלכה א:

קד ג מיי' פ"א מהלכות תפילין וס"ת הל' כ סמג עשין כח טוש"ע י"ד סי' רעד סעיף ו וא"ח סי' לב סעיף ד בהג"ה:

קה ד מיי' פ"ה מהלכות תפילין וס"ת הלכה יט סמג עשין כה טוש"ע י"ד סי' רעד סעיף ד:

[ועי' תוספות חולין שם בד"ה זאת]

במדרש כמין נ"ק

קו ה מיי' שם הלכה כ סמג שם טוש"ע א"ח סימן לב סעיף טו:

[עי' בפנים מאירות שאלה סו]

מסורת הש"ס

מנורה גופה תרי ושיתא קנים ויש בכל קנה וקנה כפתור ופרח כדכתיב כצ"ל והר"א נ"ק

תמיד ל:

[לקמן קו. ע"ש פירש"י נדה כו. וע"ש פירש"י בכורות מג: ע"ש פירש"י]

מכלות נ"ק

ככר נ"ק

הראוהו למשה מנורה ועשה כנגדה נ"ק

גירסת הערוך חסוך וכן איתא ברש"י בתענית יח. [ד"ה חסוכי בנים וכו']

[לקמן לו:]

גם זה שם חגיגה כו:

גם זה שם [יומא כא.]

נ"ק

לקמן לז.

לקמן לז.

[בנמק"י העתיק הדבוקה לחברתה כו']

הגהות הב"ח

(א) רש"י ד"ה וזה אשר וכו' ותחלת עשייה זביחה וכתב:

שיטה מקובצת

א] עשר כפתוריה: ב] לפני המנורה: ג] מתיבת וכל עד תיבת זהב סגור נמחק: ד] זהב קורדינקי: ה] שמגביהין אותו ומראין עליה לחם לחם הפנים: ו] וכלי מתכות קבולי מקבלי טומאה: ז] פסולה אמר רב אשיאן: ח] כשיעור. פי' למעלה אצל הגג אבל בירכות אינו כלום. תו"ח: ט] כפתור דכתיב: י] האחרים כדאמרינן: יא] תיבת גדולה נמחק: יב] שימי את ס"א לפי שהיה חביב בעיניו זה המקשה היה רגיל לומר כן וי"א לפי שרב עניו היה ולא היה מסתכל חוץ לד' אמות ולא היה רואהו היה רגיל לומר לו כן ולא נהירא דמאי לשימי יותר מכל שאר תלמידים: יג] הוא מכלות זהב. פסוק הוא בדברי הימים: יד] שמוכרין שם הזהב הס"ד: טו] אמרת כילתו: טז] ככר ואות ה' נמחק: יז] קורדיניקי: יח] למשה מנורה ועשה כנגד זה: יט] וריקם אף כל מטלטל מלא וריקם אבל בכלי מתכות לא כתיב שק לפיכך אף פשוטיהן מקבלין טומאה הס"ד: כ] דהראהו דמותם הס"ד: כא] אזור כדרך אומנים: כב] פשיטא דהא: כג] תנור מקדש. פי' למ"ד אין תנור מקדש לא היה דוחה שבת והיה נאפה מע"ש אבל למ"ד תנור מקדש היה דוחה שבת דאילו מע"ש הוה מפסל בלינה כיון דתנור מקדש. תו"ח: כד] ידע ס"א איזה מטבע יביאו אם לא כו' א"נ התם לא נתקשה רק בהא דבר מועט יכפר על עון העגל: כה] דאין זה אות עיין בהרא"ש בה' ס"ת. ומפרש ר"ת אותו שלצד שמאל דהוא אותו דאמרינן בסמוך מפני מה ראשו כפוף. תו"ח:
אם

תורה אור

שֶׁעָשָׂה מֹשֶׁה – כְּשֵׁרִים לוֹ וּכְשֵׁרִים לְדוֹרוֹת, חֲצוֹצְרוֹת – כְּשֵׁרוֹת לוֹ וּפְסוּלוֹת לְדוֹרוֹת. חֲצוֹצְרוֹת מ"ט? אִילֵימָא דְּאָמַר קְרָא: °"עֲשֵׂה לְךָ" – לְךָ וְלֹא לְדוֹרוֹת, אֶלָּא מֵעַתָּה, °"וְעָשִׂיתָ לְּךָ אֲרוֹן עֵץ", הָכִי נַמִי דִּלְךָ – וְלֹא לְדוֹרוֹת?! אֶלָּא, אִי *לְמַאן דְּאָמַר: "לְךָ" – מִשֶּׁלְּךָ, אִי לְמ"ד: כִּבְיָכוֹל, בְּשֶׁלְּךָ אֲנִי רוֹצֶה יוֹתֵר מִשֶּׁלָּהֶם; הַאי נַמִי מִיבְּעֵי לֵיהּ לְהָכִי! שָׁאנֵי הָתָם, דְּאָמַר קְרָא "לְךָ" "לְךָ" תְּרֵי זִימְנֵי: "עֲשֵׂה לְךָ" "וְהָיוּ לְךָ". תָּנֵי רַב פַּפָּא בְּרֵיהּ דְּרַב חָנִין קַמֵּיהּ דְּרַב יוֹסֵף: א] אמְנוֹרָה הָיְתָה בָּאָה מִן הֶעָשֶׁת מִן הַזָּהָב, עֲשָׂאָהּ שֶׁל כֶּסֶף – כְּשֵׁרָה; שֶׁל בַּעַץ וְשֶׁל אֵבֶר וְשֶׁל גִּיסְטְרוֹן – רַבִּי בפּוֹסֵל, וְר' יוֹסֵי בְּרַבִּי יְהוּדָה מַכְשִׁיר; שֶׁל עֵץ וְשֶׁל עֶצֶם וְשֶׁל זְכוּכִית – דִּבְרֵי הַכֹּל גפְּסוּלָה. א"ל: מַאי דַּעְתָּךְ? א"ל: בֵּין מָר וּבֵין מָר כְּלָלֵי וּפְרָטֵי דָּרְשִׁי, מִיהוּ מָר סָבַר: מַה הַפְּרָט מְפוֹרָשׁ – שֶׁל מַתֶּכֶת, אַף כֹּל – שֶׁל מַתֶּכֶת, וּמָר סָבַר: מַה הַפְּרָט מְפוֹרָשׁ – דָּבָר חָשׁוּב, אַף כֹּל – דָּבָר חָשׁוּב. אֲמַר לֵיהּ: סְמֵי דִּידָךְ מִקַּמֵּי דִּידִי, *דְּתַנְיָא: דכְּלֵי שָׁרֵת שֶׁעֲשָׂאָן שֶׁל עֵץ – רַבִּי פּוֹסֵל, וְרַבִּי יוֹסֵי בְּרַבִּי יְהוּדָה מַכְשִׁיר. בְּמַאי קָא מִיפַּלְגִי? רַבִּי דָּרֵישׁ כְּלָלֵי וּפְרָטֵי, *וְרַבִּי יוֹסֵי בַּר' יְהוּדָה דָּרֵישׁ רִיבּוּיֵי וּמִיעוּטֵי; רַבִּי דָּרֵישׁ כְּלָלֵי וּפְרָטֵי: °"וְעָשִׂיתָ מְנוֹרַת" – כְּלָל, "זָהָב טָהוֹר" – פְּרָט, "מִקְשָׁה תֵּיעָשֶׂה הַמְּנוֹרָה" – חָזַר וְכָלַל; כְּלָל וּפְרָט וּכְלָל – אִי אַתָּה דָּן אֶלָּא כְּעֵין הַפְּרָט, מַה הַפְּרָט מְפוֹרָשׁ שֶׁל מַתֶּכֶת, אַף כֹּל – שֶׁל מַתֶּכֶת. ר' יוֹסֵי בַּר' יְהוּדָה דָּרֵישׁ רִיבּוּיֵי וּמִיעוּטֵי: "וְעָשִׂיתָ מְנוֹרַת" – רִיבָּה, "זָהָב טָהוֹר" – מִיעֵט, "מִקְשָׁה תֵּיעָשֶׂה הַמְּנוֹרָה" – חָזַר וְרִיבָּה; רִיבָּה וּמִיעֵט וְרִיבָּה – רִיבָּה הַכֹּל, וּמַאי רַבֵּי? רַבֵּי כָּל מִילֵּי, וּמַאי מִיעֵט? מִיעֵט שֶׁל חֶרֶס. אַדְּרַבָּה, סְמֵי דִּידָךְ מִקַּמֵּי דִּידִי! לָא ס"ד, דְּתַנְיָא: אֵין לוֹ זָהָב – מֵבִיא אַף שֶׁל כֶּסֶף, שֶׁל נְחֹשֶׁת, שֶׁל בַּרְזֶל, וְשֶׁל בְּדִיל, וְשֶׁל עוֹפֶרֶת; רַבִּי יוֹסֵי בְּרַבִּי יְהוּדָה מַכְשִׁיר אַף בְּשֶׁל עֵץ. *וְתַנְיָא אִידָךְ: הלֹא יַעֲשֶׂה אָדָם בַּיִת תַּבְנִית הֵיכָל, ב] אַכְסַדְרָה כְּנֶגֶד אוּלָם, חָצֵר כְּנֶגֶד עֲזָרָה, שֻׁלְחָן כְּנֶגֶד שֻׁלְחָן, מְנוֹרָה כְּנֶגֶד מְנוֹרָה, אֲבָל עוֹשֶׂה הוּא שֶׁל חֲמִשָּׁה וְשֶׁל שִׁשָּׁה וְשֶׁל שְׁמֹנָה; וְשֶׁל שִׁבְעָה לֹא יַעֲשֶׂה וַאֲפִילּוּ מִשְּׁאָר מִינֵי מַתָּכוֹת. ר' יוֹסֵי בַּר רַבִּי יְהוּדָה אוֹמֵר: אַף שֶׁל עֵץ לֹא יַעֲשֶׂה, כְּדֶרֶךְ שֶׁעָשׂוּ מַלְכֵי בֵּית חַשְׁמוֹנַאי. אָמְרוּ לוֹ: *מִשָּׁם רְאָיָה? שַׁפּוּדִים שֶׁל בַּרְזֶל הָיוּ וְחִיפּוּם בְּבַעַץ, זהֶעֱשִׁירוּ – עֲשָׂאוּם שֶׁל כֶּסֶף, חָזְרוּ וְהֶעֱשִׁירוּ – עֲשָׂאוּם שֶׁל זָהָב. אָמַר שְׁמוּאֵל מִשְּׁמֵיהּ דְּסָבָא: חגּוֹבְהָהּ שֶׁל מְנוֹרָה שְׁמֹנָה עָשָׂר טְפָחִים; הָרַגְלַיִם וְהַפֶּרַח ג' טְפָחִים, וּטְפָחַיִים חָלָק, וְטֶפַח שֶׁבּוֹ גָּבִיעַ וְכַפְתּוֹר וָפֶרַח, וּטְפָחַיִים חָלָק, וְטֶפַח כַּפְתּוֹר, וּשְׁנֵי קָנִים יוֹצְאִין מִמֶּנּוּ אֶחָד אֵילָךְ וְאֶחָד אֵילָךְ וְנִמְשָׁכִין וְעוֹלִין כְּנֶגֶד גּוֹבְהָהּ שֶׁל מְנוֹרָה, וְטֶפַח חָלָק, וְטֶפַח כַּפְתּוֹר, וּשְׁנֵי קָנִים יוֹצְאִין מִמֶּנּוּ אֶחָד אֵילָךְ וְאֶחָד אֵילָךְ נִמְשָׁכִין וְעוֹלִין כְּנֶגֶד גּוֹבְהָהּ שֶׁל מְנוֹרָה, וְטֶפַח חָלָק, וְטֶפַח כַּפְתּוֹר, וּשְׁנֵי קָנִים יוֹצְאִין מִמֶּנּוּ אֶחָד אֵילָךְ וְאֶחָד אֵילָךְ וְנִמְשָׁכִין וְעוֹלִין כְּנֶגֶד גּוֹבְהָהּ שֶׁל מְנוֹרָה, וּטְפָחַיִים חָלָק, נִשְׁתַּיְּירוּ שָׁם ג' טְפָחִים שֶׁבָּהֶן ג' גְּבִיעִין וְכַפְתּוֹר וָפֶרַח. וּגְבִיעִין טלְמָה הֵן דּוֹמִין? כְּמִין כּוֹסוֹת אַלֶּכְסַנְדְּרִיִּים, כַּפְתּוֹרִים לְמָה הֵן דּוֹמִין? *כְּמִין תַּפּוּחֵי הַכְּרֵתִיִּים, פְּרָחִים לְמָה הֵן דּוֹמִין? כְּמִין פִּרְחֵי הָעַמּוּדִין. וְנִמְצְאוּ גְּבִיעִין – עֶשְׂרִים וּשְׁנַיִם, כַּפְתּוֹרִים – אַחַד עָשָׂר, פְּרָחִים – יתִּשְׁעָה. גְּבִיעִים מְעַכְּבִין זֶה אֶת זֶה, כַּפְתּוֹרִים מְעַכְּבִין זֶה אֶת זֶה, פְּרָחִים מְעַכְּבִין זֶה אֶת זֶה, גְּבִיעִים כַּפְתּוֹרִים וּפְרָחִים – מְעַכְּבִין זֶה אֶת זֶה. בִּשְׁלָמָא גְּבִיעִים עֶשְׂרִים וּשְׁנַיִם – דִּכְתִיב: °"וּבַמְּנוֹרָה אַרְבָּעָה גְבִעִים" וגו', וּכְתִיב: °"שְׁלֹשָׁה גְבִעִים מְשֻׁקָּדִים בַּקָּנֶה הָאֶחָד כַּפְתֹּר וָפֶרַח" וגו', אַרְבָּעָה דִּידָהּ וּתְמָנֵי

אֶלָּא. ג] אָתֵי הַאי "לְךָ", אִי לְמ"ד בִּשְׁמַעְתָּא קַמַּיְיתָא דְּמַס' יוֹמָא: לְךָ – מִשֶּׁלְּךָ, אִי לְמ"ד: ד] כִּבְיָכוֹל אִם הָיָה אֶפְשָׁר לְהִיפָּטֵר לָבוֹר בְּשֶׁל יָחִיד, בְּשֶׁלְּךָ הָיִיתִי רוֹצֶה יוֹתֵר מִשֶּׁלָּהֶם ה]. שָׁאנֵי הָתָם. גַּבֵּי חֲצוֹצְרוֹת, דְּאָמַר קְרָא "לְךָ" תְּרֵי זִימְנֵי. בַּעַץ = בְּדִיל, דְּמְתַרְגְּמִינַן "אֲבָצָא". גִּסְטְרוֹן = ו] לייטו"ן. לע"ז: מיט"ל. מַאי דַּעְתָּךְ. דְּקָאָמְרַתְּ דְּרַבִּי יוֹסֵי בְּרַבִּי יְהוּדָה מַכְשִׁיר בְּשֶׁל ז] בַּעַץ וּפָסַל בְּשֶׁל עֵץ. א"ל. רַב פַּפָּא לְרַב יוֹסֵף: בֵּין ח] לְמָר וּבֵין לְמָר, רַבִּי וְרַבִּי יוֹסֵי בְּר"י, כְּלָלֵי וּפְרָטֵי דָּרְשִׁי, כִּדְאָמְרִינַן לְקַמָּן: "וְעָשִׂיתָ מְנוֹרַת" – כְּלָל, "זָהָב טָהוֹר" – פְּרָט, "מִקְשָׁה תֵּיעָשֶׂה" מִכָּל מָקוֹם – חָזַר וְכָלַל. מָה הַפְּרָט מְפוֹרָשׁ. זָהָב [שֶׁהוּא חָשׁוּב] – אַף כָּל דָּבָר חָשׁוּב כְּגוֹן כֶּסֶף, אֲבָל אֵבָר וּבַעַץ לֹא. א"ל. רַב יוֹסֵף לְרַב פַּפָּא: סְמֵי דִּידָךְ, הָסֵר מִשְׁנָתְךָ שֶׁאַתָּה שׁוֹנֶה דְּר' יוֹסֵי *פּוֹסֵל בְּשֶׁל עֵץ, וְרַבִּי (א) ט] נַמִי מַכְשִׁיר בְּשֶׁל אֵבָר וּבַעַץ. וְעָשִׂיתָ מְנוֹרַת כְּלָל. דְּמַשְׁמַע מִכָּל דָּבָר. שֶׁל חֶרֶס. שֶׁהוּא פָּחוּת מִכָּל הַכֵּלִים, וְאֵינוֹ רָאוּי אֲפִילּוּ לְמֶלֶךְ בָּשָׂר וָדָם. לָא ס"ד. י] דְּהָוֵי דִּידָךְ מִתָּרְצָא, דְּאָמַר ר' יוֹסֵי פּוֹסֵל בְּשֶׁל עֵץ. אֵין לוֹ זָהָב. לַמְּנוֹרָה. תַּבְנִית הֵיכָל. לְמִדַּת אוֹרֶךְ וְרוֹחַב וְקוֹמָה, שֶׁתְּהֵא דּוֹמָה לוֹ בִּשְׁלָשְׁתָּן. אַכְסַדְרָה. אֵין לָהּ מְחִיצָּה רְבִיעִית, וְכֵן אוּלָם. כְּנֶגֶד אוּלָם. יא] שֶׁהָיָה רוֹחְבּוֹ [עֶשְׂרִים וְגוֹבְהוֹ אַרְבָּעִים], כִּדְאָמְרִינַן בִּשְׁמַעְתָּא קַמַּיְיתָא דְּעֵירוּבִין (דף ב.). אֲבָל עוֹשֶׂה. יב] הַמְּנוֹרָה שֶׁל חֲמִשָּׁה אוֹ שֶׁל שִׁשָּׁה קָנִים אוֹ שֶׁל שְׁמֹנָה, יג] דְּאֵינוֹ דּוֹמֶה לִמְנוֹרַת מִקְדָּשׁ שֶׁשָּׁם הָיָה שִׁבְעָה קָנִים. וְשֶׁל שִׁבְעָה קָנִים לֹא יַעֲשֶׂה וַאֲפִילּוּ שֶׁל שְׁאָר מִינֵי מַתָּכוֹת. שֶׁאֵינוֹ יד] זָהָב, מִשּׁוּם דְּדוֹמֶה לְשֶׁל מִקְדָּשׁ, שֶׁאַף הוּא כָּשֵׁר בִּשְׁאָר מִינֵי מַתָּכוֹת. אַף שֶׁל עֵץ לֹא יַעֲשֶׂה. שֶׁהֲרֵי הוּא כְּדֶרֶךְ שֶׁעָשׂוּ מַלְכֵי בֵּית חַשְׁמוֹנַאי טו]. בְּבַעַץ = בְּדִיל, אשטיי"ן. מִשְּׁמֵיהּ דְּסָבָא. מִשּׁוּם זָקֵן אֶחָד. הָרַגְלַיִם טז] וְהַפֶּרַח. מִתַּחַת שְׁלֹשָׁה טְפָחִים. פֶּרַח = לִיוּרִין שֶׁחוֹקְקִים הַצּוֹרְפִים זָהָב בָּעוֹמֶק בִּמְנוֹרוֹת וּבְכֵלִים. וּטְפָחַיִים חָלָק. בְּלֹא שׁוּם צוּרָה, הֲרֵי ה'. וְטֶפַח שֶׁבּוֹ. מִצַּד אֶחָד שֶׁל מְנוֹרָה גָּבִיעַ, וּמִצַּד שֵׁנִי כַּפְתּוֹר = פומ"ל, וּמִצַּד יז] *שֵׁנִי פֶּרַח. וְזֶהוּ אֶחָד מִן הַגָּבִיעַ וְכַפְתּוֹרִים וּפְרָחִים שֶׁבְּגוּף אֶמְצַע שֶׁל מְנוֹרָה, דִּכְתִיב: "וּבַמְּנוֹרָה אַרְבָּעָה גְבִיעִים מְשֻׁקָּדִים כַּפְתּוֹרֶיהָ וּפְרָחֶיהָ", וְדָרְשִׁינַן לְקַמָּן: "כַּפְתּוֹרֶיהָ" – תְּרֵי, "וּפְרָחֶיהָ" – תְּרֵי, לְבַד אוֹתָן (ד') שֶׁבְּכָל קָנֶה וְקָנֶה. וּטְפָחַיִים חָלָק – הֲרֵי ח', וְטֶפַח כַּפְתּוֹר – הֲרֵי ט'. וּשְׁנֵי קָנִים יוֹצְאִים. מִן הַכַּפְתּוֹר, אֶחָד אֵילָךְ כו'. שֶׁבָּהֶן יח] שָׁלֹשׁ גְּבִיעִים *כַּפְתּוֹר וָפֶרַח. שֶׁלֹּא הָיוּ בְּגוּף הַמְּנוֹרָה אֶלָּא תְּרֵי כַּפְתּוֹרִים וּתְרֵי פְּרָחִים, כִּדְכְתִיב: "כַּפְתּוֹרֶיהָ וּפְרָחֶיהָ", יט] *וְחַד (חַד) פֶּרַח אוֹקִימְנָא בְּטֶפַח הַסָּמוּךְ לִטְפָחַיִים חָלָק הָרִאשׁוֹנִים. אַלֶּכְסַנְדְּרִים. שֶׁנַּעֲשָׂה בְּאַלֶּכְסַנְדְּרִיָּא שֶׁל מִצְרַיִם. וַאֲרוּכִּין וְצָרִים הֵן, וּקְרוּיִים מדרנ"ש. תַּפּוּחַ הַכְּרֵתִיִּים. מָקוֹס. פִּרְחֵי הָעַמּוּדִים. לִיוּרִין שֶׁמְּצַיְּירִין בָּעַמּוּדִים. וְנִמְצְאוּ גְּבִיעִים כו'. מְפָרֵשׁ לְקַמָּן.

תְּמָנֵי

אכסדרה תבנית אולם. אף על גב דאולם היה בו ד' מחיצות, כדתנן במסכת מדות (פ"ד מ"ו), וכריש גמרא דעירובין (דף ב.) מייתי לה: פתחו של אולם גובהו מ' אמה ורחבו עשרים אמה, וחמש אמלתראות של *מילא היו על גביו. ואכסדרה אין לה אלא ג' דפנות, כדמוכח בסמוך: מפני מה נברא העולם בה' – מפני שדומה לאכסדרה, ועוד אמרינן בפ' "לא יחפור" (ב"ב כה.): עולם לאכסדרה הוא דומה ורוח צפונית אינה מסובבת, מ"מ מחמת שפתח אולם רחב וגבוה מאד ולא היו לו דלתות – דומה לאכסדרה, שנראה כפרוץ בצד אחד. מ"ר.

שפודים של ברזל. קרי להו שפודים מפני שלא היו בה גביעים כפתורים ופרחים, כדאמרי' לעיל: באה זהב – באה גביעים כפתורים ופרחים. מ"ר. גובהה של מנורה י"ח טפחים. יש אומרים בשם ר"ת דנפקא ליה לסבא מסניפין שאצל השולחן לצורך לחם הפנים, שהיו גובהן י"ח טפחים, והמנורה היתה להאיר על השולחן. ונראה דלא אמר ר"ת דבר זה מעולם, דהא סניפים כנגד לחם הפנים, ולקמן בפ' "שתי הלחם" (דף צו.) אמרינן דלר' מאיר מקדש שולחן י"ב טפחים למעלה, ולר' יהודה ט"ו לבד (מרגלי) השולחן אמה וחצי. מ"ר.

וטפח שבו היה גביע כפתור ופרח. יש תימה: למה היה משונה משאר גביעים כפתורים ופרחים שהיה לכל אחד טפח, ולג' אלו לא היה כי אם טפח? מ"ר.

אבן

צו א ב ג ד מיי' פ"א מהלכות בית הבחירה הלכה יח:

נ"א מילת

צז ה ו מיי' שם פ"ז הלכה י:

צח ז מיי' שם פ"א הלכה יט:

צט ח מיי' שם פ"ג הלכה י:

ק ט מיי' שם הל' ט:

קא י מיי' שם הל' ז:

[פי' שרחבן יתר על עביין ערוך ערך תפוח וגורס למה הן דומין לתפוחי הכרתיים ועי' לקמן סג. על הגליון מש"ש]

במדבר י

דברים י

שמות כה

שם

שם

יומא ג:

נ"א מכשיר

סוכה נ: סוטה יד:

[סוכה שם]

ר"ה כד. ע"ז מג.

[שבת כט: וש"נ]

שליש נ"ק

והיו בגוף המנורה ד' גביעים ותרי כפתורים ותרי פרחים כו' כצ"ל נ"י

נ"ל וחד כפתור וחד פרח וחד גביע אוקימנא נ"ק

הגהות הב"ח

(א) רש"י ד"ה א"ל רב יוסף וכו' ורבי לפי משנה נמי מכשיר:

שיטה מקובצת

א] יוסף ואמרי לה רב פפא בריה דרב יוסף קמיה דרב יוסף: ב] אכסדרה כנגד אולם. מתוך פרש"י משמע דמחיצות היה באולם ואינו כן אלא י"א אמות היה לפני ההיכל במזרח שלא היה בהן שום דבר ולפנים היה חומה גבוה מאה אמה וארכה מאה אמה מצפון לדרום והיה עוברת אותה חומה ט"ו אמה לדרום וט"ו לצפון יותר על רוחב ההיכל והתאים והמסיבות והן בית החליפות מקום לגנוז שם הסכינים ובאמצע היה פתח גובהו ארבעים אמה ורוחבו כ' אמות כדאיתא בשמעתא קמייתא דמסכת עירובין: ג] אלא דאתי להכי [האי לך] הס"ד ומה"ד אי למ"ד: ד] למ"ד כביכול משלך אני רוצה אם: ה] משלהם והאי פלוגתא בריש מס' יומא: ו] גיסטרון לימפרון ל"א מיט"ל ותיבת לייטין נמחק: ז] בשל אבר ופסל: ח] בין מר ובין מר: ט] ורבי פוסל בשל אבר מקמי דידי מפני משנתי שאני שונה דרבי יוסי מכשיר בשל עץ ורבי מכשיר נמי בשל: י] דתהוי דידך מתרצא דאמרת דרבי יוסי: יא] כנגד אולם שיהא דומה לו בשלשתן: יב] עושה הוא מנורה: יג] שמנה שהר אינו: יד] שאינו של זהב: טו] חשמונאי למקדש הס"ד: טז] הרגלים מתחת והפרח עליהן שלשה טפחים: יז] שלישי פרח: יח] שבהן גביעים באותן שלשה טפחים היו ג' גביעים מהנך ארבע דכתיב ובמנורה ארבעה גביעים וכפתור אחד ופרח אחד ולא היה בגוף והשאר נמחק: יט] ופרחיה וחד כפתור וחד פרח אוקימנא:

הא דקאי מזרח ומערב ואדי. הא דקאי צפון ודרום ואדי. אמר מר: ושבפנים ושבמצורע, שלא לשמן — פסולות, שלא מכוונות — כשרות. והתניא: בין שלא לשמן בין שלא מכוונות — כשרות! אמר רב יוסף, לא קשיא: הא רבי אליעזר והא רבנן, רבי אליעזר *דמקיש אשם לחטאת — מקיש נמי לוג לאשם, רבנן לא מקשי. ולרבי אליעזר, וכי *דבר הלמד בהיקש חוזר ומלמד בהיקש? אלא אמר רבא: הא והא רבנן, כאן — להכשיר (הקרבן,) כאן — להרצות, (שלא עלו לבעלים לשום חובה.)§ **מתני'** אשבעה קני מנורה מעכבין זה את זה. שבעה נרותיה מעכבין זה את זה. שתי פרשיות שבמזוזה מעכבות זו את זו, באפילו כתב אחד מעכבן. גד' פרשיות שבתפילין מעכבין זו את זו, דאפילו כתב אחד מעכבן. הד' ציציות מעכבות זו את זו, שארבעתן מצוה אחת; רבי ישמעאל אומר: ארבעתן ארבע מצות.§ **גמ'** מ"ט? הויה כתיב בהו. *תנו רבנן: מנורה היתה באה מן העשת ומן הזהב; ועשאה מן הגרוטאות — פסולה, משאר מיני מתכות — כשרה. מאי שנא מן הגרוטאות פסולה — דכתיב °מקשה והויה, שאר מיני מתכות נמי — זהב והויה! אמר קרא: "תיעשה" — לרבות שאר מיני מתכות. ואימא: לרבות גרוטאות! לא ס"ד, דאמקשה כתיבה הויה. "תיעשה" נמי אמקשה כתיב! "מקשה" "מקשה" לעכב. "זהב" "זהב" נמי לעכב! האי מאי? אי אמרת בשלמא: מן הגרוטאות פסולה, משאר מיני מתכות כשרה — היינו "זהב" "זהב" "מקשה" "מקשה" לדרשא; אלא אי אמרת: מן הגרוטאות כשרה, משאר מיני מתכות פסולה — "זהב" "זהב" "מקשה" "מקשה" מאי דרשת ביה! מאי דרשא? דתניא: °"ככר זהב טהור יעשה אותה את כל הכלים האלה", זבאה זהב — באה ככר, אינה באה זהב — אינה באה ככר; א] °"גביעיה כפתוריה ופרחיה", חבאה זהב — באה גביעים כפתורים ופרחים, אינה באה זהב — אינה באה גביעים כפתורים ופרחים. ואימא נמי: באה זהב — באה קנים, אינה באה זהב — אינה באה קנים! ההוא פמוט מיקרי. °"וזה מעשה המנורה מקשה זהב", באה זהב — באה מקשה, אינה באה זהב — אינה באה מקשה. "מקשה" דסיפא למאי אתא? למעוטי חצוצרות, *טדתניא: חצוצרות היו באים מן העשת מן הכסף; עשאם מן הגרוטאות — כשרים, משאר מיני מתכות — פסולים. ומאי שנא משאר מיני מתכות פסולים — דכתיב כסף והויה, מן הגרוטאות נמי — מקשה והויה! מיעט רחמנא גבי מנורה: "מקשה היא", היא — ולא חצוצרות. תנו רבנן: כל הכלים שעשה

שעשה

רש"י

הא דקאי כהן מזרח ומערב ואדי. ואם עמד כהן פניו למערב ואחוריו למזרח והזה, שכך מלותו, אפילו אינם מכוונות כנגד הפתח – כשרות. והא דתני פסולות – דקאי צפון ודרום שלא כמלותו, ואדי ב]. והתניא בין שלא לשמן כו' כשרות. אדמצורע קאי. ר' אליעזר דמקיש אשם לחטאת ג]. ואפילו אשם דמצורע פסול שלא לשמה. תורה אור וכי. אשם הלמד בהיקש מחטאת דליהוי פסול שלא לשמו, חוזר ומלמד בהיקש על הלוג דליהוי פסול שלא לשמו? והא קיימא לן בפ' "איזהו מקומן" (זבחים דף מט:) דאין למידין למד מן הלמד בקדשים! היקש. דחטאת ואשם – דכתיב (בחטאת) (ויקרא ז): "כחטאת כאשם תורה אחת להם", וקא יליף ר' אליעזר: מה חטאת שלא לשמה פסולה, דאפילו רבנן מודו – אף אשם נמי פסול. היקש. דאשם מצורע ולוגו – דכתיב (שם יד): "כבש ד] אשם לתנופה" וגו', סיפיה דקרא: "ולוג שמן". לרצות. ה] *להיות לעלות לשם חובה ולהתיר מצורע *בקהל – פסול שלא ו] לשמן. והא דתני כשרות – להכשיר, דהזאותיו כשרות להכשיר שירי הלוג באכילה. ז] דשירי לוג מצורע נאכלין, כדאמרינן בפ' "אלו מנחות" (לקמן דף עג.): "וזה יהיה לך מקדש הקדשים מן האש לכל קרבנם" (במדבר יח) – לרבות לוג שמן של מצורע, וכתיב בתריה: "בקדש הקדשים תאכלנו", בפרשת "ויקח קרח". **מתני'** שבעה קני מנורה. כדכתיב: "וששה קנים יוצאים מצדיה" (שמות כה), והמנורה עצמה שבאמצע היא השביעית כזה*. שבעה נרותיה. בראש של קנה וקנה היה ח] נר אחד כעין בזך, ושם נותנין השמן והפתילות. שתי פרשיות שבמזוזה. "שמע" "והיה אם שמוע". כתב אחד. אות אחת, ט] מעכבין *זו את זו, דכתיב (דברים ו): "וכתבתם" – כתיבה תמה ושלימה. י] ובתפילין כתיב הויה (שם): "והיו לטוטפות". ד' פרשיות שבתפילין. "שמע" (שם), "והיה אם שמוע" (שם יא), "קדש לי כל בכור" (שמות יג), "והיה כי יביאך" (שם) שבגלילה, דבכולהו כתיב: "ולטוטפות" או: "ולזכרון בין עיניך" יא]. **גמ'** הויה כתיב בהו. "כפתוריהם וקנותם ממנה יהיו" (שם כה). מן העשת. יב] עשייתה חתיכה שלמה, ומכה בקורנס עד שיוצאו ממנה כל כליה. מן הגרוטאות. זהב שבור. מקשה. משמע חתיכה אחת, כדמתרגמינן: "נגיד" – משוך, שנמשך הכל מחתיכה אחת. "מקשה" משמע דבר יג] המוכה ונהלם, כדכתיב (דניאל ה): "וארכבתיה דא לדא נקשן". משאר מתכות נמי תיפסל. דהא כתיב "זהב טהור", וכתיב הויה לעכב! אמר קרא תיעשה. המנורה, משמע: תיעשה מ"מ, לרבות שאר מתכות. ואימא לרבות גרוטאות. דכתיב "מקשה", והדר "תיעשה" מ"מ. אמקשה כתיבה הויה. הויה סמוכה ל"מקשה" יותר מל"זהב" יד]. ומשני: מקשה מקשה כתיב. תרי זימני ב"ויקחו לי תרומה" לעכב. וקפריך: זהב זהב נמי תרי זימני כתיב. ואימא לעכב! ומשני: האי מאי אי אמרת בשלמא גרוטאות פסולות ושאר מתכות כשרות. דאמרינן: "מקשה" "מקשה" ד"ויקחו לי תרומה" לעכב. היינו. דאילטריך "זהב זהב" "מקשה" ד"בהעלותך" לדרשה אחריתי, דשמעינן מינה נמי דמשאר מיני מתכות נמי כשירה, כדדרשינן טו] *לקמן. באה זהב באה ככר שאינה באה זהב. שהביאה משאר מיני מתכות – אינה צריכה לבא ככר, אלא או פחות או יותר. אלמא, משאר מיני מתכות שמעינן דכשרה. יז] אלא לדידך, "זהב" "זהב" "מקשה מקשה" למה לי? אינה באה גביעין. אינה צריכה לבא גביעים כפתורים ופרחים. פמוט. מנורה קטנה. וזה מעשה המנורה. ד"בהעלותך". מקשה. דסיפא: "עד ירכה ועד פרחה מקשה היא". כסף והויה. "שתי חצוצרות כסף מקשה תעשה אותם והיו לך" וגו' (במדבר י). אלא

תוספות

שבעה קני מנורה. תימה: דלא חשיב גביעים פרחים וכפתורים דמעכבין זה את זה, כדאמרינן בגמ'! ושמא משום דליתנהו בשאר מיני מתכות. מ"ר. **דתניא** ככר זהב טהור. חמשה "זהב" כתיבי, ד' בפרשת "ויקחו" וחד בפרשת "בהעלותך", והכא לא דריש אלא שלשה. ושמא אינך תרי, חד – לגופיה דמלוה בזהב, וחד – לכלל ופרט דבסמוך, וצ"ע. *והשתא קרא קמא "ועשית מנורת זהב" אתי לכלל ופרט *כדבסמוך. יח] וכדכתב: "כולה מקשה אחת זהב טהור" דרשינן: באה זהב – באה כפתורים גביעים ופרחים, ד"כולה" משמע כל המנורה. ולהכי פריך נמי: ואימא באה זהב באה קנים. וה"ה דהוה מצי למפרך: באה זהב באה ירכה, והוה מצי לשנויי דלא איקרי מנורה בלא ירך. והדר כתיב: "מלקחיה ומחתותיה זהב טהור". ושמא האי אתא לגופיה, דמלוה בזהב. והדר כתיב: "ככר זהב טהור", דדרשינן: באה זהב – באה ככר. ובפרשת "בהעלותך" כתיב: "וזה מעשה המנורה מקשה זהב", דרשינן: באה זהב – באה מקשה. וכסדר זה שפיר כתיבי, אבל בברייתא אין דורש כסדר. מ"ר.

מקשה דסיפא למאי אתא כו'. והשתא צריכי כולהו: חד – למצוה, וחד – לעיכובא לפסול גרוטאות, וחד – באה זהב באה מקשה, וחד – למעוטי חצוצרות. מ"ר.

חצוצרות היו באים מן העשת מן הכסף יט]. תימה: דבפ' "כל הצלמים" (ע"ז דף מז.) משמע דאות שלא מן הכסף. דבעי רמי בר חמא: המשתחוה לבהמה, קרניה מהו לחצוצרות? ותנן נמי במסכת קינין (פ"ג מ"ו): זה הוא שאמרו כשהוא חי קולו אחד וכשהוא מת קולו שבעה, קרניו לחצוצרות. ומהך שמעתין אין קשה כל כך, דהכא בשל משה שלא היו כשרות לדורות, כדבסמוך. אבל קשה, דבמסכת תמיד (דף לג:) תנן: ושתי חצוצרות של כסף בידם, משמע דאף לדורות של כסף! ותירץ ר"ת: דשתי חצוצרות היו, לכהנים – בשל כסף, והלוים – של קרני בהמה לכלי שיר. ועוד, דחצוצרות דקינים ודע"ז היינו שופר, כדאמרינן בסוף "במה מדליקין" (שבת דף לו.) וב"לולב הגזול" (סוכה דף לד.) דאישתני שמייהו, חצוצרתא – שיפורא, שיפורא – חצוצרתא. ובסוף "במה מדליקין" איכא ברייתא כ] דקרא לחצוצרות שופר. ומיהו קשה, דבמסכת ע"ז (דף מז.) מיירי במכשירי קרבן, כדקאמר התם: ועל הקרבן לא היו תוקעים בשופר אלא בחצוצרות, כדכתיב (במדבר י): "ותקעתם בחצוצרות על עולותיכם" וגו'. מ"ר.

אכסדרה

עין משפט נר מצוה

צ א מיי' פ"ג מהלכות בית הבחירה הל' ז:
צא ב מיי' פ"א מהלכות תפילין ומזוזה הל' טוש"ע י"ד סימן רפט סעיף ג:
צב ג ד מיי' שם הל' א [טוש"ע א"ח סימן לב סעיף ד]:
צג ה מיי' פ"א מהלכות ציצית הל' ה [טוש"ע א"ח סימן יג סעיף א]:
צד ו ז ח מיי' פ"ג מהל' בית הבחירה הלכה ד ה:
צה ט מיי' פ"ג מהל' כלי המקדש הל' ה:

והשתא ל"ק
כדבסמוך והדר כתיב כולה ל"ק

שיטה מקובצת

א] ה"ג ברוב הספרים גביעיה כפתוריה ופרחיה באה זהב באה גביעיה כפתוריה ופרחיה וקשה לר"י דהתם לא כתיב זהב אלא הראשון דכתיב ועשית מנורת זהב טהור מקשה תעשה המנורה ירכה וקנה גביעיה כפתוריה ופרחיה ממנה יהיו וההוא איצטריך לכלל ופרט וכלל ונ"ל דה"ג כפתוריהם וקנותם ממנה יהיו כולה מקשה אחת זהב טהור באה זהב באה גביעיה וכפתוריה ופרחיה ואע"ג דלא כתיב בהאי קרא לא גביעיה ולא פרחיה אפ"ה כיון דכתיב כפתורי' מסתמא דרשינן באה זהב באה גביעיה כפתוריה ופרחיה והכי מידרשי כולהו קראי ועשית מנורת זהב טהור לכלל ופרט וכלל כדלקמן. שני. ככר זהב טהור יעשה אותה באה זהב באה ככר. שלישי. כפתוריהם וקנותם ממנה יהיו כולה מקשה אחת זהב טהור לומר באה זהב באה גביעיה כפתוריה ופרחיה ואע"ג דגביעיה ופרחיה לא כתיב בהאי קרא כדפי'. רביעי. מלקוחיה ומחתותיה זהב טהור לאשמועינן דאף הכלים האלו שלא היו מן העשת של מנורה היו זהב טהור. חמישי. בפרשת בהעלותך וזה מעשה המנורה מקשה זהב לומר באה זהב באה מקשה וד' מקשה כתיבי ב' בפרשת תרומה וב' בפרשת בהעלותך והכי מדרשי חד למצוה כו': ב] ואדי והזה: ג] לחטאת. בפ"ק דזבחים (דף י ע"א וכ') דאמר אשם שלא לשמו פסול ה"נ הזאות דלוג שמן דמצורע שלא לשמן פסול דמקיש לוגו של מצורע לאשמו. והא דקתני כשרות לרבנן דלא מקשינן אשם לחטאת ואפילו אשם מצורע שלא לשמו כשר וכ"ש הזאת לוגו הס"ד ומה"ד ולר"א א"נ הוי אשמו פסול שלא לשמו הזאות אמאי פסול שלא

לשמו וכו' והד"א: ד] כבש אחד אשם לתנופה וגו' וסיפא דקרא ולוג אחד שמן: ה] לרצות להיות [עולות]: ו] לשמו: ז] דשירי הלוג דמצורע: ח] היה עשוי נר: ט] מעכבות זו את זו: י] ושלימה ולהכי מעכבות ובתפילין כו' והיו לטוטפות ובאותן פרשיות כתיב וכתבתם על מזוזות לפיכך הם נכתבות במזוזות: יא] עיניך לפיכך ארבעתם נכתבות בתפילין הס"ד ומה"ד גמ' מאי טעמא אמנורה קאי: יב] העשת חתיכה נטל ככר אחת ותיבות עשייתה חתיכה נמחק: יג] דבר המנבח תיבת מוכה ל"ש: יד] יותר מלזהב דכתיב זהב טהור תעשה המנורה ירכה כו' ממנה יהיו כו' הס"ד ומה"ד תעשה נמי א) משמע מ"מ אמקשה כתיב תעשה סמיך למקשה יותר מאל זהב הס"ד ומה"ד ומשני מקשה מקשה דויקחו: טו] ומקשה דבהעלותך ותיבת מקשה נמחק: טז] לקמן נ"א וארבעה מקשה כתיבי (וארבעה) [וחמשה] זהב כתיבי (שלשה) [שנים] בויקחו לי תרומה (ואחד) [ושנים] בפ' בהעלותך וכי אמרינן דמן הגרוטאות פסולות הוי תרי מקשה חד למצוה וחד לעכב ואידך תרי לדרשא דלקמן וכי אמרינן נמי דמשאר מתכות כשרה הוה חד זהב לגופא ואידך לדרשא דלקמן: יז] תיבות אלא לדידך [זהב זהב] מקשה מקשה למה לי נמחק: אינה באה זהב שהביאה משאר מיני מתכות [אינה צריכה] תיבות אינה באה גביעים ל"ש: יח] כדבסמוך וכדכתיב: יט] הכסף משמע דחצוצרות של כסף היה ואפילו עיכובא כתיב בהו כדאיתא לעיל ותימה: כ] ברייתא דקרי תיבת דקרא נמחק:

א] נראה דצ"ל תעשה דמשמע מ"מ נמי אמקשה כתיב. תעשה סמיך וכו'.

שֶׁאִם חִיסֵּר אַחַת מִן הַמַּתָּנוֹת — לֹא עָשָׂה כְלוּם.§ ת"ר: א] *שֶׁבַע הַזָּאוֹת אשֶׁבַּפָּרָה שֶׁעֲשָׂאָן, בֵּין שֶׁלֹּא לִשְׁמָן, בֵּין שֶׁלֹּא מְכוּוָּנוֹת ב] (אֶל נֹכַח פְּנֵי אוֹהֶל מוֹעֵד) — פְּסוּלוֹת; בוְשֶׁבִּפְנִים גוְשֶׁבַּמְצוֹרָע, שֶׁלֹּא לִשְׁמָן — פְּסוּלוֹת, ג] שֶׁלֹּא מְכוּוָּנוֹת — כְּשֵׁרוֹת. וְהָתַנְיָא גַּבֵּי פָרָה: שֶׁלֹּא לִשְׁמָן — פְּסוּלוֹת, שֶׁלֹּא מְכוּוָּנוֹת — כְּשֵׁרוֹת! אָמַר רַב חִסְדָּא, ל"ק: ד] הָא רַבִּי יְהוּדָה, הָא רַבָּנַן. דְּתַנְיָא: דמְחוּסְּרֵי כַפָּרָה שֶׁנִּכְנְסוּ לָעֲזָרָה בְּשׁוֹגֵג — חַיָּיב חַטָּאת, בְּמֵזִיד — ה] עָנוּשׁ כָּרֵת, וְאֵין צ"ל טְבוּל יוֹם וּשְׁאָר כָּל הַטְּמֵאִים. ו] *הוּטְהוֹרִים שֶׁנִּכְנְסוּ לִפְנִים מִמְּחִיצָתָן, לַהֵיכָל כּוּלּוֹ — בְּאַרְבָּעִים, מִבֵּית לַפָּרֹכֶת אֶל פְּנֵי הַכַּפֹּרֶת — ובְּמִיתָה. רַבִּי יְהוּדָה אוֹמֵר: כָּל הֵיכָל כּוּלּוֹ וּמִבֵּית לַפָּרֹכֶת — בְּאַרְבָּעִים, וְאֶל פְּנֵי הַכַּפֹּרֶת — בְּמִיתָה. בְּמַאי קָא מִיפַּלְגִי? בְּהַאי קְרָא: °"וַיֹּאמֶר יי' אֶל מֹשֶׁה דַּבֵּר אֶל אַהֲרֹן אָחִיךָ וְאַל יָבוֹא בְכָל עֵת אֶל הַקּוֹדֶשׁ מִבֵּית לַפָּרוֹכֶת אֶל פְּנֵי הַכַּפּוֹרֶת אֲשֶׁר עַל הָאָרוֹן וְלֹא יָמוּת", רַבָּנַן סָבְרִי: אֶל הַקּוֹדֶשׁ — בְּלֹא יָבֹא, מִבֵּית לַפָּרֹכֶת וְאֶל פְּנֵי הַכַּפֹּרֶת — בְּלֹא יָמוּת; וְר' יְהוּדָה סָבַר: אֶל הַקּוֹדֶשׁ וּמִבֵּית לַפָּרֹכֶת — בְּלֹא יָבֹא, וְאֶל פְּנֵי הַכַּפֹּרֶת — בְּלֹא יָמוּת. מ"ט דְּרַבָּנַן? אִי ס"ד כִּדְקָאָמַר ר' יְהוּדָה — לִכְתּוֹב רַחֲמָנָא אֶל הַקּוֹדֶשׁ וְאֶל פְּנֵי הַכַּפֹּרֶת, וְלָא בָּעֵי מִבֵּית לַפָּרֹכֶת, וַאֲנָא ז] אָמֵינָא: הֵיכָל מִיחַיַּיב, מִבֵּית לַפָּרֹכֶת מִבַּעְיָא?! מִבֵּית הַפָּרֹכֶת דִּכְתַב רַחֲמָנָא לָמָּה לִי? ש"מ בְּמִיתָה. וְר' יְהוּדָה: אִי כָּתַב רַחֲמָנָא אֶל הַקּוֹדֶשׁ וְלָא כָּתַב מִבֵּית לַפָּרֹכֶת, הֲוָה אָמֵינָא: מַאי קוֹדֶשׁ — מִבֵּית לַפָּרֹכֶת, אֲבָל הֵיכָל — לָאו נַמִי לָא.

וְרַבָּנַן: הַהוּא לָא מָצֵית אָמְרַתְּ, דְּהֵיכָל כּוּלּוֹ אִיקְרֵי "קוֹדֶשׁ", שֶׁנֶּאֱמַר: °"וְהִבְדִּילָה הַפָּרֹכֶת לָכֶם בֵּין הַקּוֹדֶשׁ וּבֵין קֹדֶשׁ הַקֳּדָשִׁים". וְרַבִּי יְהוּדָה מ"ט? אִי ס"ד כִּדְקָא אָמְרִי רַבָּנַן — לִכְתּוֹב רַחֲמָנָא אֶל הַקּוֹדֶשׁ וּמִבֵּית לַפָּרֹכֶת, וְלָא בָּעֵי אֶל פְּנֵי הַכַּפֹּרֶת, וַאֲנָא אָמֵינָא: מִבֵּית לַפָּרוֹכֶת בְּמִיתָה, אֶל פְּנֵי הַכַּפֹּרֶת מִיבַּעְיָא?! אֶל פְּנֵי הַכַּפֹּרֶת דִּכְתַב רַחֲמָנָא לָמָּה לִי? ש"מ: אֶל פְּנֵי הַכַּפֹּרֶת — בְּמִיתָה, מִבֵּית לַפָּרֹכֶת — בְּאַזְהָרָה. וְרַבָּנַן: ה"נ דְּלָא צְרִיךְ, וְהַאי דִּכְתַב רַחֲמָנָא אֶל פְּנֵי הַכַּפֹּרֶת — לְמַעוּטֵי ח] דֶּרֶךְ מְשׁוּפָּשׁ, *כִּדְתָנָא דְּבֵי ר"א בֶּן יַעֲקֹב: "אֶל פְּנֵי הַכַּפֹּרֶת קֵדְמָה" — זֶה בָּנָה אָב, כָּל מָקוֹם שֶׁנֶּאֱמַר "פְּנֵי" אֵינוֹ אֶלָּא פְּנֵי קָדִים. וְרַבִּי יְהוּדָה: לֵימָא קְרָא: "פְּנֵי", מַאי "אֶל"? ש"מ: "אֶל" דַּוְקָא. וְרַבָּנַן: "אֶל" לָאו דַּוְקָא. *וְרַבִּי יְהוּדָה דְּאָמַר: "אֶל פְּנֵי הַכַּפֹּרֶת" דַּוְקָא — °"וְהִזָּה אֶל נֹכַח" נַמִי דַּוְקָא. *וְרַבָּנַן, מִדְּהָתָם לָאו דַּוְקָא — ה"נ לָאו דַּוְקָא. מַתְקִיף לָהּ רַב יוֹסֵף: לְרַבִּי יְהוּדָה מִדְּ"אֶל" דַּוְקָא — *)("אֶל נֹכַח") נַמִי דַּוְקָא; אֶלָּא דְּמִקְדָּשׁ שֵׁנִי דְּלָא הֲוֵו אָרוֹן וְכַפּוֹרֶת, ה"נ דְּלָא עָבֵיד הַזָּאוֹת? אָמַר רַבָּה בַּר עוּלָּא, אָמַר קְרָא: °"וְכִפֶּר אֶת מִקְדַּשׁ הַקּוֹדֶשׁ" — מָקוֹם הַמְקוּדָּשׁ לַקּוֹדֶשׁ. רָבָא אָמַר: הָא וְהָא רַבָּנַן, הָא

*) על נמי דוקא נ"ק

רש"י

שֶׁאִם חִיסֵּר ט] [אַחַת] מֵהֶן לֹא עָשָׂה כְּלוּם. *אֵין לִי אֶלָּא מַתַּן שִׁבְעָה י] דְּפָרֹכֶת הוּא דְּעִיכְּבוּ, שֶׁהֵן מַתַּן שֶׁבַע מְעַכְּבִין בְּכָל מָקוֹם, כְּגוֹן פָּרָה אֲדוּמָּה וְהַזָּאָה דִּמְצוֹרָע, וְהָכִי מְפָ' לָהּ בִּזְבָחִים בְּפֶ' "ב"ש" (דף לט.). יא] מִנַּיִן לְרַבּוֹת יב] בְּמִזְבַּח הַזָּהָב שֶׁאִם חִיסֵּר פָּסַל, אע"ג דִּשְׁאָר ד' מַתָּנוֹת דְּמִזְבֵּחַ הַחִיצוֹן לֹא מְעַכְּבִין, כִּדְאָמְרִי' בְּמַתְנִיתָא קַמַּיְיתָא דְּסַנְהֶדְרִין (ד' ד:): "וְכִפֵּר" "וְכִפֵּר" "וְכִפֵּר" — אֲפִי' ג' מַתָּנוֹת וַאֲפִי' ב' וַאֲפִי' אַחַת? יג] ת"ל: "כֵּן יַעֲשֶׂה", *מְרַבִּינַן כָּל עֲשִׂיּוֹתָיו שֶׁיְּעַכְּבוּ. מֵרֵישֵׁיהּ דִּקְרָא "וְעָשָׂה לַפָּר" (וְעָשָׂה הָא) דָּרְשִׁינַן (אֶלָּא) "לַפָּר" — לְרַבּוֹת פַּר יה"כ. וּבִשְׁחִיטַת קָדָשִׁים בְּפֶרֶק "ב"ש" פָּרֵיךְ: לְמַאי הִילְכְתָא? אִי נֵימָא לְעַכֵּב — פְּשִׁיטָא, חוּקָּה כְּתִיב בֵּיהּ! וּמְשַׁנֵּי לָהּ הָתָם: לִשְׁפִיכַת שִׁירַיִם דְּלָא כְּתִיבִי בְּפַר יה"כ, וְעוֹד מִילֵּי אַחֲרָנְיָיתָא. יד] "כַּאֲשֶׁר עָשָׂה לַפָּר" — לְרַבּוֹת פַּר כֹּהֵן מָשִׁיחַ, שֶׁאִם חִיסֵּר אַחַת מִמַּתְּנוֹתָיו פָּסַל. "הַחַטָּאת" — לְרַבּוֹת שְׂעִירֵי עֲבוֹדָה זָרָה שֶׁל צִיבּוּר, כִּדְכְתִיב בְּפָרָשַׁת "שְׁלַח לְךָ": "וְכִי תִשְׁגּוּ" וגו' טו] בַּעֲבוֹדָה זָרָה מְדַבֵּר, וְאוֹתָן שְׂעִירִים טְעוּנִין הַזָּיָיה עַל הַפָּרֹכֶת וְעַל מִזְבַּח הַזָּהָב, דְּדָרְשִׁי' בְּת"כ דְּהַאי "חַטָּאת" לְרַבּוֹת שְׂעִירֵי עֲבוֹדָה זָרָה. טז] הַזָּאוֹת דְּפָרָה. שֶׁלֹּא לִשְׁמָן פְּסוּלוֹת, דִּכְתִיב בֵּיהּ "חַטָּאת הִיא" יז]. שֶׁלֹּא מְכוּוָּנוֹת. שֶׁלֹּא כִּוֵּון כְּנֶגֶד פִּתְחוֹ שֶׁל הֵיכָל יח] פְּסוּלוֹת, דִּכְתִיב בָּהּ "חוּקָּה" וְ"אֶל נֹכַח". וְשֶׁבִּפְנִים. כְּגוֹן דְּיה"כ וּפַר כֹּהֵן מָשִׁיחַ וּפַר הֶעְלֵם דָּבָר וּשְׂעִירֵי עֲבוֹדָה זָרָה. וְשֶׁבַּמְצוֹרָע. בְּשַׁעַר נִקָּנוֹר (א) מִשֶּׁמֶן שֶׁל מְצוֹרָע יט]. שֶׁלֹּא לִשְׁמָן פְּסוּלוֹת. שֶׁבִּפְנִים חַטָּאת נִינְהוּ. כ] שֶׁל מְצוֹרָע לְקַמֵּיהּ מוֹקֵי' לָהּ (ב) לְהַתִּיר, שֶׁלֹּא עָלוּ לוֹ לְשֵׁם חוֹבָה לְהַכְשִׁירוֹ בְּקָדָשִׁים. שֶׁלֹּא מְכוּוָּנוֹת כא]. בֵּין מִזְרָח לְמַעֲרָב כְּשֵׁרוֹת (ג), דְּלָא כְּתִיב בְּהוּ "אֶל נֹכַח". הָא רַבִּי יְהוּדָה הָא רַבָּנַן. בְּסֵיפָא דְּמִילְּתָא מְפָרֵשׁ לָהּ. עָנוּשׁ כָּרֵת. דְּכָל זְמַן שֶׁלֹּא הֵבִיא כַּפָּרָתוֹ לֹא יָצָא מִידֵי טוּמְאָתוֹ. כב] נָפְקָא לַן מִקְּרָאֵי, דְּתַנְיָא: *"אִישׁ (אִישׁ) אֲשֶׁר יִטְמָא וְלֹא יִתְחַטָּא" (במדבר יט) — בְּדָמִים, כְּלוֹמַר, אִם מֵאוֹתָן טְמֵאִים הוּא שֶׁצְּרִיכִין כג] דָּמִים וְלֹא הֱבִיאָם, וְנִכְנַס לַמִּקְדָּשׁ — "וְנִכְרְתָה". אַתָּה אוֹמֵר בְּדָמִים, אוֹ כד] לֹא נִתְחַטָּא בְּמֵי נִדָּה? כְּשֶׁהוּא אוֹמֵר: "מֵי נִדָּה לֹא זוֹרַק עָלָיו" — הֲרֵי מַיִם אֲמוּרִין, הָא מַה כה] ת"ל "וְלֹא יִתְחַטָּא" — בְּדָמִים, כו] לְהָבִיא *אֶת הַמְחוּסָּר כַּפָּרָה. וְאֵין צ"ל טְבוּל יוֹם, דְּנָפְקָא לַן כז] הָתָם מֵ"עוֹד טוּמְאָתוֹ בוֹ", וּשְׁאָר כָּל הַטְּמֵאִין שֶׁחַיָּיבִין. וּטְהוֹרִין שֶׁנִּכְנְסוּ לִפְנִים מִמְּחִיצָתָן. י"א אַמָּה מְקוֹם דְּרִיסַת רַגְלֵי יִשְׂרָאֵל. לַהֵיכָל כח] כו'. אִם נִכְנְסוּ שָׁם. בְּאַרְבָּעִים. מַכּוֹת, מִשּׁוּם דִּכְתִיב: "וְאַל יָבֹא בְכָל עֵת אֶל הַקֹּדֶשׁ" וגו' (ויקרא טז). מִבֵּית לַפָּרֹכֶת. לִפְנַי וְלִפְנִים שֶׁשָּׁם כט] אָרוֹן. "וְאֶל פְּנֵי הַכַּפֹּרֶת" נַמִי הַיְינוּ מִבֵּית לַפָּרֹכֶת, אֶלָּא שֶׁהָלַךְ עַד לִפְנֵי הָאָרוֹן (ד). ל] בְּאַרְבָּעִים. אֶל פְּנֵי הַכַּפּוֹרֶת. שֶׁהָלַךְ עַד לִפְנֵי הָאָרוֹן — בְּמִיתָה לא]. מִבַּעְיָא. הָא הֵיכָל בִּכְלַל מִבֵּית לַפָּרֹכֶת, דְּלֹא נִכְנַס לְשָׁם אֶלָּא דֶּרֶךְ הֵיכָל, וּמִשְּׁעַת בִּיאַת הֵיכָל קָם לֵיהּ בְּמַלְקוֹת! לָאו נַמִי לָא. אֲפִילּוּ לָאו נַמִי לֵיכָּא. בֵּין הַקֹּדֶשׁ. הַיְינוּ לב] הֵיכָל. אֶל פְּנֵי הַכַּפֹּרֶת מִבַּעְיָא. דְּמִיחַיַּיב מִיתָה? הָא מִשָּׁעָה שֶׁנִּכְנַס מִבֵּית לַפָּרֹכֶת מִיחַיַּיב מִיתָה, וְיֵשׁ בִּכְלָל מִבֵּית לַפָּרֹכֶת פְּנֵי הַכַּפֹּרֶת! לְמַעוּטֵי דֶּרֶךְ מְשׁוּפָּשׁ. כְּגוֹן לג] "מְשׁוּפָּשׁ", שֶׁסָּתַר הַחוֹמָה שֶׁל לִפְנַי וְלִפְנִים וְעָשָׂה פֶּתַח בַּדָּרוֹם אוֹ בַּצָּפוֹן וְנִכְנַס, וְלֹא נִכְנַס בַּפֶּתַח שֶׁבַּמִּזְרָח שֶׁיְּהֵא פָּנָיו לַמַּעֲרָב. א"נ, נִכְנַס בַּפֶּתַח לד] וְלָיֵיד בַּאֲלַכְסוֹן וְהָלַךְ לִצְדָדִין — לָא מִיחַיַּיב, דְּ"אֶל פְּנֵי" בָּעֵינַן שֶׁיְּהוּ לה] פָּנִים אֶל פָּנִים מִזְרָחִי שֶׁל כַּפֹּרֶת. "מְשׁוּפָּשׁ" — כְּמוֹ "מְשׁוּבָּשׁ", דְּפֵי"א וּבֵי"ת מִתְחַלְּפִין, דִּכְתִיב (ישעיהו יג *) "נִשְׁפֶּה" וּכְתִיב (ישעיהו מ): "נָשְׁבָה בוֹ". זֶה בָּנָה אָב. לו] הִקִּישָׁהּ אָב וּמְלַמֵּד לְכָל "פְּנֵי" שֶׁבַּתּוֹרָה דְּקָדִים הֵן, כִּי הֵיכִי דִּבְהַאי "פְּנֵי" כְּתִיב "קֵדְמָה". וְהַשְׁתָּא מְפָרֵשׁ לְהַאי דַּאֲמַרַן לְעֵיל: הָא ר"י הָא רַבָּנַן. לְרַבִּי יְהוּדָה דְּאָמַר אֶל פְּנֵי הַכַּפֹּרֶת דַּוְקָא. דִּבְמִיתָה, וּמִבֵּית לַפָּרֹכֶת לָאו דַּוְקָא — ה"נ "אֶל נוֹכַח" דַּוְקָא, הִלְכָּךְ שֶׁלֹּא מְכוּוָּנוֹת פְּסוּלוֹת. וּלְרַבָּנַן, מִדְּ"אֶל פְּנֵי" לָאו דַּוְקָא — ה"נ "אֶל נֹכַח" לָאו דַּוְקָא, הִלְכָּךְ כְּשֵׁרוֹת. עַל נַמִי דַּוְקָא. בִּתְמִיָּה. כְּלוֹמַר, "עַל פְּנֵי הַכַּפֹּרֶת" דְּיה"כ מִי הָוֵי דַּוְקָא? דְּאִי דַּוְקָא הוּא, מִקְדָּשׁ שֵׁנִי דְּלָא הָוֵי אָרוֹן וְכַפֹּרֶת, דְּאָמְרִינַן בְּמַסֶּכֶת יוֹמָא (דף נג:) דְּיֹאשִׁיָּהוּ גְּנָזוֹ, ה"נ דְּלֹא מַזֶּה? וְהָא אָמְרִינַן בְּמַסֶּכֶת יוֹמָא (שם) דְּמַזֶּה! מָקוֹם הַמְקוּדָּשׁ לַקֹּדֶשׁ. אָרוֹן. עַל מְקוֹם הָאָרוֹן מַזֶּה, אֲפִילּוּ לֵיכָּא אָרוֹן. הָא

*) [נ"ל נשפת שמות טו]

תוספות

להיכל כולו בארבעים. הקשה ה"ר י"ט מלפנלו, מהא דתנן בפרק בתרא דתמיד (דף לג:): בזמן שכ"ג נכנס *להשתחוות לשם [שלשה] אוחזין בו, א' מימינו וא' משמאלו ואחד באבנים טובות כו', הגביה לו הפרוכת נכנס והשתחווה ויצא, נכנסו אחיו הכהנים והשתחוו ויצאו. אלמא (לבית קדשי הקדשים) שרו! ותירץ ר"ת, דהשתחוואה לורך עבודה היא. מ"ר.

למעוטי דרך משופש. וא"ת: לז] תיפוק ליה מדכתיב "ואל יבא", דמשמע דרך ביאה, כדממעטינן בפ"ב דשבועות (דף יז:) טמא שנכנס דרך גגין להיכל! וי"ל: התם לח] כשפיחת התקרה איירי. אבל הכא, לשנכנס דרך לול שהיה בעליית בית קדשי הקדשי' שבו היו משלשלין את האומנים בתיבות — דרך ביאה הוא, דלכך נעשה. א"נ, כמו שפירש בקונטרס כאן: שסתר את החומה שלפני ולפנים ועשה פתח בדרום או בצפון ונכנס, ולא נכנס בפתח שבמזרח שיהיו פניו למערב. ועוד פי' בקונטרס: א"נ, נכנס בפתח מזרח ולדד באלכסון והלך בצדדין לא מיחייב, ד"לפני" בעינן, שיהו פניו אל פני מזרחיים של כפורת. אבל בזבחים בפרק "התערובות" (דף פב:) *מפרש (התוספות) דרך משופש כגון דרך לול שהיה אחורי בית הכפרת, כדאמרי' בסוף "איזהו מקומן" (שם נה:): שנים לפרבר. וה"ר יעקב מאורלינ"ש הקשה מהיא דס"פ "התערובת" (שם פב: ושם ד"ה לא) גבי דם שנכנס לפנים, דאמרי': יאמר "אל הקדש" ואל יאמר "פנימית"! ומשני: לא נצרכה אלא לדרך משופש. ופריך: והא הבאה כתיב ביה, אלמא ממעטינן דרך משופש מדכתיב ביה הבאה! ויש לחלק בין הבאת דם להבאת גוף אדם. מ"ר.

פירשתי נ"ק
נ"ל פנימה

עין משפט נר מצוה

פד א מיי' פ"ד מהל' פרה הל' ג' והל' ה:
להשתחוות שלשה אוחזין נ"ק
גיר' רש"ק וג"ק להיכל
פה ב מיי' פ"ה מהל' מעשה"ק הלכה יב:
פו ג מיי' פ"ד מהלכות מחוסרי כפרה הלכה ב:
פז ד מיי' שם ופ"ג מהל' ביאת המקדש הל' יח ופ"ד מהלכות ביאת מקדש הלכה יב:
פח ה מיי' פ"ב מהלכות ביאת מקדש הל' ד:
פט ו מיי' שם (פ"ג הלכה יט):

מסורת הש"ס

כלום וכוי כו' כ"ש אין לי כו' שכן מתן שבע בו' למצורע מנין לרבות כו' נ"ק
תורה אור
תוספתא דזבחים פ"א
ומרבינן נ"ק
לפר לפר לרבות נ"ק
תוספתא דכלים פ"א:
רש"ק מ"ז
(ספרי פרשה חקת)
יומא נה.
נ"ל לרבי יהודה
נ"ל ולרבנן
[ועיין היטב במכות יח. ובנזיר מה:]

הגהות הב"ח

(א) רש"י ד"ה ושבמצורע וכו' משמן של: (ב) ד"ה שלא לשמן וכו' מוקים לה לפסולות להתיר: (ג) ד"ה שלא מכוונות וכו' כשרות אע"ג דכתיב בהו: (ד) ד"ה מבית לפרוכת וכו' הארון הס"ד ואח"כ מ"ה מבית לפרוכת בארבעים ואל פני וכו' במיתה הס"ד ואח"כ מ"ה מבית לפרוכת מבעיא דהא:

גליון הש"ס

גמ' ושבפנים ושבמצורע. עיין לקמן דף עד ע"ב תוספות ד"ה איכא:

שיטה מקובצת

א] שבע הזאות שבפרה פרש"י דכתיב חטאת וקשה שהרי בזבחים מצריך קרא לכל החטאות ולא גמר חד מחבריה לכך נראה לומר משום דכתיב היא עיכובא: ב] תיבות אל נכח פני אהל מועד נמחק: ג] שלא מכוונות כשירות אבל למצוה בעינן מכוונות משום דכתיב לפני ה' מיהו עכובא לא אשכחן בפ"ק (מיום כפורים) ולא נהירא דהא הויא (מיום כפורים) שלא לשמה וחטאת קריה רחמנא אע"ג שאינו חטאת א"נ [גבי יוה"כ] כתיב בה היא חוקה וי"ל מדכתיב בפרה אל נוכח והכא לא כתיב נוכח ש"מ דמכוונות לא מעכבי: תו"ח: ד] הא רבי יהודה הא רבנן פ"ה לר"י דאמר אל פני הכפורת דוקא בבמיתה ומבית לפרוכת לאו דוקא ה"נ אל נכח דוקא ולרבנן לאו דוקא הלכך כשרות וקשה מה ענין זה לזה דר"י דאל פני הכפורת דוקא במיתה דכתיב במפורש בלא ימות כדקאמר רבנן לכתוב רחמנא אל הקודש ומבית לפרוכת אבל אל נוכח אין כאן יתור להשמיענו דבעינן מכוונות ועוד מה ענין (מענות) [מכוונות] למשמע אל נכח דוקא אל לפני

וי"ל ללשון ראשון כגון שהיה בדרום או בצפון פתח קבוע ונכנס דרך שם דהיינו שפיר דרך ביאה ואשמועינן אל פני הכפורת דלא מחייב בה: ט] חיסר מתן אחת לא עשה כלום ופירש [אין] לי אלא ליתא שם: י] דפרוכת הוא דמעכבת שהן מתן כו' כגון הזאות פרה אדומה והזאות דמצורע והכי מפרש לה בפרק ב"ש הס"ד: יא] גליון בכאן לא כתוב בכל הספרים

הכפורת אל קאי [עליה] ולא ימות ולא קאי אל הקדש מבית לפרוכת ועוד דאדרבה אנו רואין היפך הדברים דרבנן אית להו אל פני דוקא דמאל פני ממעטי דרך משופש דסבירא להו הא דרבי אליעזר בן יעקב ור"י לית להו דאי הוה טעמא דמוקי אל פני הכפורת למידרשה בלא ימות ולא אל הקודש אמבית לפרוכת לכך נראה לי דרבי יהודה נמי אית ליה הא דראב"י ומשמע ליה לרבי יהודה דלא אצטריך ליתורא להכי דממשמעות דאל פני נפקא והשתא ניחא דקא תלי לר' יהודה מדאל פני הכפורת דוקא דמשמע ליה לכפורת אל הכפורת אל נכח פני אהל מועד שכמו שמיעט דרך משופש ממשמעות פני כך ימעט שלא (מענות) [מכוונות] ממשמעות פני אבל לרבנן דאצטריך להו ייתורא להכי לית להו פני דוקא כמו כן אל נכח לאו דוקא. נ"ל ברוך: ה] ענוש כרת פרש"י דנפקא לן בספרי כו' ור"ש בר שמשון מפרש שאין אנו צריכין לזה שהרי בתלמוד שלנו דריש ליה מטמא יהיה לרבות טבול יום עוד טומאתו בו לרבות מחוסרי כפורים: ו] וטהורים שנכנסו לפנים כו' פ"ה מקום דריסת רגלי ישראל דהיינו י"א אמה ולא נהירא דהוא הא אלא מעלה מדרבנן שהרי בשחיטת הפסח נתמלאת כל העזרה כלה אנשים וכן זקני ירושלים סובבים את המזבח ולולביהם בידיהם וכן לקמן מגביהין את השולחן ואומר להם ראו כו' ואמר ר' שמשון מקומי דפרושי קא מפרש טהורים שנכנסו לפנים ממחיצתם דהיינו ההיכל. תו"ח: ז] עיין בהשמטות בסוף המסכת: ח] דרך משופש ללשון ראשון שבקונטרס קשה מפ"ב דשבועות [דף יז ע"ב] וללשון שני ניחא א"נ י"ל

א) אולי יש כאן איזה חסרון תיבות וצ"ע:

והיא בתורת כהנים: יב] לרבות מתן ארבע במזבח: יג] ואפילו אחת הס"ד ומה"ד ת"ל כן יעשה מרבינן דקרא מרבינן כל עשיותיו שיעכבו הס"ד ומה"ד ועשה לפר הא דרשינן אלא: יד] אחרינייתא כדמפרש התם כאשר: טו] וגו' ובעבודת: טז] שבע הזאות: יז] חטאת היא וחטאת ששינה שלא לשמה פסולה: יח] של היכל שהיה עומד בהר המשחה ומתכוון כנגד פתח ההיכל פסולות דכתיב בה חוקה ואל נכח פני אהל מועד הס"ד ומה"ד ושבפנים כגון פר ושעיר דיוה"כ: יט] מצורע מזה ז' הזאות בבית קדשי הקדשים וכן מצותה מדכתיב והזה מן השמן באצבעו לפני ה' בת"כ: כ] נינהו לענין קדשים ובפרתה: כא] מכוונות נ"א כנגד בית קדשי הקדשים כשרות משום דלא כתיב בהו: כב] טומאתו בו ונפקא לן מקראי בספרי: כג] שצריכין כפרה דמים: כד] או אינו אלא: כה] מה אני מקיים ולא יתחטא הס"ד ומה"ד להביא: כז] לן נמי התם: כח] להיכל כולו ותיבת כו' נמחק: כט] ששם הארון במיתה דכתיב ולא ימות כי בענן אראה וגו' הס"ד ומה"ד מבית לפרוכת אם נכנס שם ולא הלך עד פני הכפורת בארבעים: לא] במיתה מבית לפרוכת מבעיא הא: לב] היינו נמי היכל: לג] נמחק: לד] בפתח מזרח וצידד: לה] שיהו פניו אל פני: לו] אב. זה בנה הקדוש ברוך הוא [אב] ותיבת הקישה נמחק: לז] וא"ת למה לי טעמא דאל פני הכפורת תיפוק: לח] התם מיירי כשפחת התקרה אבל הכא מיירי לכשנכנס:

א] ד"על העצים" כתיב, כי תיבעי לך — אליבא דמ"ד: *"על" — בסמוך, מאי? ה"נ "על" — בסמוך, או דלמא: "על העצים" דומיא ד"על המזבח", מה התם "על" — ממש, אף ה"נ "על" — ממש? תיקו.§

מתני' אהקומץ, מיעוטו מעכב את רובו. ב] בעשרון, מיעוטו מעכב את רובו. גהיין, מיעוטו מעכב את רובו. דהשמן, מיעוטו מעכב את רובו. ההסולת והשמן מעכבין זה את זה. והקומץ והלבונה מעכבין זה את זה.§

גמ' מ"ט? אמר קרא: °"מלא קומצו" תרי זימני. עשרון מיעוטו מעכב את רובו, מאי טעמא? אמר קרא: °"מסלתה" — שאם *חסרה כל שהוא פסולה. היין מיעוטו מעכב את רובו — "ככה". השמן מיעוטו מעכב את רובו; דמנחת נסכים — "ככה", ג] ומנחת נדבה — אמר קרא °"ומשמנה" — שאם חסר כל שהוא — פסולה. השמן והסולת מעכבין זה את זה — "מסלתה ומשמנה", "מגרשה ומשמנה". הקומץ והלבונה מעכבין זה את זה — °"על כל לבונתה", °"ואת כל הלבונה אשר על המנחה".§

מתני' שני שעירי יה"כ מעכבין זה את זה. ושני כבשי עצרת מעכבין זה את זה. חב' חלות מעכבות זו את זו. טשני סדרין מעכבין זה את זה. שני בזיכין מעכבין זה את זה. הסדרין יוהבזיכין מעכבין זה את זה. כב' מינים שבנזיר, ג' שבפרה, וד' שבתודה, לוד' שבלולב, מוארבע שבמצורע — מעכבין זה את זה. נשבעה הזאות שבפרה מעכבות זו את זו. סז' הזיות שעל בין הבדים, שעל הפרכת, שעל מזבח הזהב — מעכבות זו את זו.§

גמ' שני שעירי יה"כ מעכבין זה את זה — חוקה. שני כבשי עצרת מעכבין זה את זה — הויה. שתי חלות — הויה. שני סדרין — חוקה. שני בזיכין — חוקה. הסדרין והבזיכין — חוקה. שני מינים שבנזיר — דכתיב: "כן יעשה". ג' שבפרה — חוקה. ארבעה שבתודה — דאיתקש לנזיר, דכתיב: °"על זבח תודת שלמיו", *ואמר מר: "שלמיו" — לרבות שלמי נזיר. וארבעה שבמצורע — דכתי': °"זאת תהיה תורת המצורע". וד' שבלולב — °"ולקחתם" — לקיחה תמה. אמר רב חנן בר רבא: ל"ש אלא שאין לו, אבל יש לו — אין מעכבין. מיתיבי: ד' מינין שבלולב, ב' מהן עושין פירות וב' מהם אין עושין פירות; העושין פירות יהיו זקוקין לשאין עושין, ד] ושאין עושין פירות יהיו זקוקין לעושין פירות, ואין אדם יוצא ידי חובתו בהן עד שיהו כולן באגודה אחת; וכן *ישראל בהרצאה — עד שיהו כולן באגודה אחת, שנאמר: °"הבונה בשמים מעלותיו ואגודתו על ארץ יסדה"! תנאי היא, דתניא: *לולב בין אגוד בין שאינו אגוד — כשר; ר' יהודה אומר: אגוד — כשר, שאינו אגוד — פסול. מאי טעמא דר' יהודה? גמר קיחה קיחה מאגודת אזוב, מה להלן באגודה — אף כאן באגודה. ורבנן? לא גמרי קיחה קיחה. כמאן אזלא הא *דתניא: עלולב מצוה לאוגדו, ואם לא אגדו — כשר, כמאן? אי כרבי יהודה, לא אגדו אמאי כשר? אי רבנן, מאי מצוה? לעולם רבנן, ומאי מצוה? משום °"זה אלי ואנוהו".§ שבע הזאות שבפרה מעכבות זו את זו — חוקה. שבע הזאות שעל בין הבדים ושעל מזבח הזהב ושעל הפרוכת מעכבות זו את זו; דיה"כ — כתיב חוקה, דפר כהן משוח ודפר העלם דבר של ציבור ודשעירי עבודה זרה — כדתניא: °) *ה] "ועשה לפר כאשר עשה לפר" מה ת"ל? לכפול בהזאות, שאם

°) ויקרא ד

רש"י

אגל העצים על המזבח. אליבא דמ"ד ו] (על העצים) על בסמוך. בפ' "שתי הלחם" (לקמן דף צו.) במשנה פליגי, ה"נ דכתיב "על העצים" "על" — בסמוך ז]. **מתני'** מיעוטו מעכב את רובו. שאם חיסר כל שהוא — פסול. היין. שלישית ההין של איל, ורביעית ההין לכבש, וחצי ההין לפר. וכן השמן, בין דמנחת נסכים *כשיעור ח] ההין, בין בלוג דמנחת נדבה. **גמ'** מלא קומצו תרי זימני. ב"ויקרא", חד במנחת נדבה: "וקמץ משם מלא קומצו", וחד במנחת חוטא: *"וקמץ הכהן ממנה מלא קומצו", חד למצוה וחד לעכב. שאם חסר כל שהוא פסולה. ט] *ד"סלתה" מריבויא דה"א י] [דריש]. ככה. בנסכים יא] (א): "ככה יעשה לשור האחד" בפרשת "שלח לך". מסלתה ומשמנה. יב] ומשמע שיהו שניהן, והדר כתיב נמי "מגרשה ומשמנה" שיהו שניהן, שנה הכתוב לעכב. יג] גרש וסולת חד הוא, אלא שגרש במנחת *ביכורים וסלת בשאר מנחות. על כל לבונתה ואת כל הלבונה. שנה הכתוב לעכב. יד] **מתני'** *במעשה יה"כ כתיב חוקה ב"אחרי מות": "והיתה זאת טו] לחוקת עולם" וגו', וחוקה עיכובא. הוייה. "סלת תהיינה". בלחם הפנים. כתיב: "מאשי ה' חק עולם", ואכולהו קאי, אסדרים ואבזיכין.

מתני' שתי חלות. טז] *עצרת. שני סדרים. דלחם הפנים. שני מינין שבנזיר. חלות ורקיקין בפרשת "נשא". ג' שבפרה אדומה. עץ ארז ואזוב ושני תולעת, יז] ולפורין במצורע*. שבע הזאות שבפרה. "והזה אל נכח פני אהל מועד" וגו'. שעל בין הבדים. ביה"כ, כדאמרינן במס' יומא (דף נג:). שעל הפרכת ומזבח הזהב. בין דיה"כ, בין דפר העלם דבר, יח] בין דפר כהן משיח, ב"ויקרא". *גמ' כן יעשה. "על תורת נזרו" (במדבר ו) עיכובא. חוקה. "זאת חוקת התורה". תהיה. הויא עיכובא. לקיחה תמה. ארבעתן כאחד (ב). יט] *שלמי נזיר. ליו"ד קבין ירושלמיות סלת, ולרביעית שמן כ] כתודה בפ' "התודה" (לקמן עח.). שאין לו. ד' מינין דלולב, מעכבין. אבל יש לו אין מעכבין. אפילו לא אגדן כאחד. שנים מהן עושין פירות. דאתרוג ותמרים. יהו זקוקים. כלומר, כולן יהו כאחד. בהרצאה. כשהן מתענין, אין נענין עד שיהו כולן באגודה אחת *לדיקים ורשעים, דומיא דעושין ואין עושים פירות. על הארץ יסדה. בזמן שאגודתו ביחד אז יסדה. ועשה לפר כאשר עשה לפר חטאת. בפר העלם דבר כתיב, שיעשו לו כאשר עשה לפר כהן משיח שלמעלה הימנו. מה ת"ל. והלא כל מה שפירש לפר כהן משיח פירש לפר העלם דבר! לכפול בהזיות. לשנות באזהרת הזאת כא] הדם עליו. שאם

(בשוליים: צ"ל לרבות שלמי נזיר. פי')

תוספות

מסלתה ומשמנה מגרשה ומשמנה. לגבי עיכובא דנפשיה — לא בעי שנה הכתוב, אבל למעכבין זה את זה בעי שנה הכתוב, כדפרישית לעיל (דף יט.). מ"ר.

ארבעה שבמצורע. עץ ארז ואזוב ושני תולעת [ולפורין] אבל מים חיים לא חשיב, לפי שהיה מערב בהם הדם, כדכתיב (ויקרא יד) "וטבל אותם בדם". תימה: דלא חשיב הזאות דמצורע דמעכבות זו את זו! וי"ל: דתנא ושייר. דהא לא חשיב נמי דפרים ואילים דחג, דכתיב בהו (במדבר כט) "כמשפט" לעכב, ואיכא טובא. מ"ר.

ולקחתם לקיחה תמה. י"מ דביום ב' סגי בחד מד' מינים, ומברך "על נטילת לולב", כמו אתרוג דשרי חסר, ולא בעינן תמות אלא ביום ראשון. כב] ולדבריהם ביום שני תיסגי שיטול האחד בשביל כולם. וליתא, דבסוף "לולב הגזול" (סוכה מא:) ובריש "לולב וערבה" (שם מג.) דרשינן מ"ולקחתם" — לקיחה לכל אחד ואחד, מדכתיב "ולקחתם" לשון רבים, ולא כתיב "ולקחת". כג] אלא כי היכי דעיקר לקיחה קיימא אכולהו יומי — הוא הדין לקיחה תמה, כד] דבעי לקיחת ד' מינים אכולהו יומי, ולקיחת כל אחד ואחד. אבל תמות של עצמן, וכן "לכם" למעוטי שאול וגזול — לא בעי אלא ביום ראשון. מ"ר.

לא שנו אלא שאין לו אבל יש לו אין מעכבין. פי' בהלכות גדולות בהלכות לולב: יש לו אין מעכבין — דלא תימא עד דמגבה להו בהדי הדדי לא נפיק, אלא אי מגבה חד חד לאודיה שפיר דמי, דקי"ל לולב אין צריך אגודה. מ"ר. ור"ת הגיה בספרו: *ל"ש, פירוש: דמעכב' משום תמה — אלא שאין לו, אבל יש לו — תמה הוא, אף על פי שלא חיברו באגודה, כדאמרי' לקמן דלא דרשי רבנן קיחה קיחה. ולר' יהודה דדריש ליה קיחה קיחה, דלא הויא תמה אלא א"כ אגדו. *וכולהו פי' דגמ', אפי' לפי' הלכות גדולות, נראה דצריך לאוגדו, כדמסיק עליה: "זה אלי ואנוהו". מ"ר*.

לא גמרי קיחה קיחה. אע"ג דגמרי קיחה קיחה משדה עפרון בריש קידושין (דף ב.), שמא הך דהכא אינה מופנה. א"נ, קיחה קיחה גמרי, לקיחה לקיחה לא גמרי. מ"ר.

ועשה כאשר עשה כו'. ברייתא זו מיתנייא בפרק "ב"ש" כה] (זבחים לט.), והתם מפרש לה שפיר. מ"ר.

להיכל

עין משפט נר מצוה

עב א מיי' פי"ג מהל' מעה"ק הלכה יז:
עג ב מיי' שם הלכה ה:
עד ג מיי' פ"ב שם הלכה ה:
עה ד ה ו מיי' שם פי"ג הלכה יז:
עו ז ח מיי' פ"ח מהל' תמידין ומוספין הלכה יז:
עז ט י מיי' שם פ"ה הלכה ג:
עח כ מיי' פ"ט מהל' מעשה הקרבנות הלכה כב:
עט ל מיי' פ"ז מהל' לולב הלכה ה טור ש"ע א"ח סימן תרנא סעיף יב:
פ מ מיי' פי"א מהלכות מצורע הלכה א:
פא נ מיי' פ"ד מהל' פרה הלכה ז:
פב ס מיי' פ"ב מהלכות פסה"מ הלכה ג:
פג ע מיי' פ"ז מהל' לולב הלכה ו טוש"ע א"ח סי' תרנא סעיף א:

הגהות הב"ח

(א) רש"י ד"ה ככה בנסכים כתיב ככה: (ב) ד"ה שלמי נ"ל קודם ד"ה תהיה:

(גליון: ל"ק; [לעיל ט:]; ל"ש למעכבים משום ל"ק; נ"א ולכולהו; [וע"ע תוספות סוכה לד: ד"ה שתהא]; לקמן עח. לעיל יט.)

שיטה מקובצת

א] תיבות דעל העצים כתיב נמחק: ב] רובו העשרון: ג] ככה דמנחת: ד] עושין פירות ושאין: ה] ועשה כאשר עשה וכיפר: ו] אליבא דמ"ד על העצים ס"א דמ"ד על בסמוך כדכתיב ועליו מטה מנשה ופלוגתא היא בפרק שתי הלחם גבי בזיכי לבונה אם מסדרן על המערכה של לחם הפנים ממש או בסמוך: ז] בסמוך נ"א אבל על המזבח לא קאמר שכשאתה אומר על העצים אתה מקיים על המזבח כשאתה אומר על המזבח אתה מבטל על העצים ותפים אותו שמקיים את עצמו ומקיים חבירו: ח] כשיעור היין בין לוג: ט] פסולה מסלתה: י] תיבת דריש ליתא שם: יא] בנסכים כתיב ככה: יב] משמע: יג] מתיבות גרש עד תיבות מנחות ס"א אינו: יד] תיבות מתני' במעשה כו' אסדרים ואבזיכין נמחק מכאן ושייך לקמן אחר תיבת גמ' קודם ד"ה כן יעשה: טו] זאת להם לחוקת: טז] חלות של עצרת: יז] תולעת הס"ד ומה"ד ארבע שבתודה חמץ וחלות ורקיקן ורבוכה בפרק התודה הס"ד ומה"ד ארבע שבמצורע עץ ארז ואזוב ושני תולעת וצפרים הס"ד ומה"ד שבע: יח] דבר של צבור בין דפר כהן משיח כדמפורש בויקרא: יט] לרבות שלמי: כ] שמן שבתודה: כא] באזהרת הזאות בפר העלם דבר הס"ד: כב] ראשון ולא נהירא דלדבריהם: כג] ולקחת ואינו בו דהתם לא מחלקינן בין יו"ט ראשון לשאר ימים: כד] תמה עיין בתוס' ר"פ לולב הגזול: כה] ב"ש (דף מא):

מסורת הש"ס

ל"ק מ"ז; פסחים סג: לקמן סב. נח. סוטה לז. סנהד' יג:; שטות כשיעור היין ל"ק; מסלתה כו'; ל"ק; ל"ג עומר; ע"א נהפך הוא מן במעשה יה"כ עד שתי חלות וצ"ל אחר המתני' ושם צריך לבוא גמרא; עצרת הס"ד אח"כ מה"ד ב' שבפרה כו' תולעת הס"ד ואח"כ מה"ד וד' שבמצורע מוסיף ליפריס במצורע הס"ד וכו"ל ל"ק; צ"ל במצורע איכא לפריס מוסיף על ג' שבפרה; גמ' ד"ה חוקה במעשה יה"כ אח"כ מ"ה הויה בלחם הפנים כו' ואכולהו קאי כו' אח"כ ד"ה כן עשה עיכובא אח"כ ד"ה חוקה כו' אח"כ ד"ה תהיה הויה עיכובא אח"כ ד"ה לקיחה כו' אח"כ ד"ה שלמי כו' אח"כ ד"ה שאין לו כו' ל"ק

גליון הש"ס

מתני' הסולת והשמן מעכבין. עיין לקמן דף מד ע"ב תוספות ד"ה הסולת.

[כריתות ו:]; עיין הגירסא בילקוט פרשה אמור]; סוכה יא: לג.; שם יא:; שמות טו; [זבחים לט.]

ויקרא ב; שם; שם; שם; שם ו; ויקרא ז; שם יד; שם כג; עמוס ט

א] וחישב עליה, בין חוץ למקומו בין חוץ לזמנו – פסול ואין בו כרת. ב] (*ל"א:) חישב עליה חוץ למקומו – פסול ואין בו כרת, חוץ לזמנו – פיגול וחייבין עליו כרת, דברי ר' אלעזר ור"ש. וחכ"א: כיון אשנתנו לשמאל – פסלתו מתנתו; מ"ט? משום דבעי ג] קדושה בכלי, וכיון שנתנו לשמאל – נעשה כדם שנשפך מצואר בהמה על הרצפה בואספו, שפסול; מכלל דר"א ור"ש לא בעו מתן כלי, תיובתא דרב נחמן! תיובתא. לרבי יהודה בריה דרבי חייא מסייעא ליה, לרבי ינאי לימא תיהוי תיובתא? אמר לך רבי ינאי: אנא דאמרי כתנא דהקטר, ולאו לצדדים קתני.§ "הקטיר קומצה פעמים – כשרה".§ אמר רבי יהושע בן לוי: פעמים – ולא פעמי פעמים, ור' יוחנן אמר: גפעמים – ואפילו פעמי פעמים. מאי בינייהו? א"ר זירא: *יש קומץ פחות משני זיתים *ויש הקטרה פחותה מכזית איכא בינייהו; ריב"ל סבר: דאין קומץ פחות משני זיתים, הואין הקטרה פחותה מכזית; ורבי יוחנן סבר: יש קומץ פחות משני זיתים, ויש הקטרה ד] פחותה מכזית.§ איתמר: *קומץ מאימתי מתיר שירים באכילה? רבי חנינא אומר: משמשלה בו את האור, רבי יוחנן אמר: ומשתצית בו את האור ברובו. אמר ליה רב יהודה לרבה בר רב ה] יצחק: אסברה לך טעמא דר' יוחנן, אמר קרא: °"והנה עלה קיטור הארץ כקיטור הכבשן", אין כבשן מעלה קיטור עד שתצית האור ברובו. אמר ליה רבין בר רב אדא לרבא: אמרי תלמידך אמר רב עמרם, *תניא: אין לי אלא זדברים שדרכן ליקרב בלילה, כגון אברים ופדרים – שמעלן ומקטירן מבוא השמש ומתעכלין והולכין כל הלילה כולה; חדברים שדרכן ליקרב ביום, כגון הקומץ והלבונה והקטרת, ומנחת כהנים ומנחת כהן משוח טומנחת נסכים, שמעלן ומקטירן מבוא השמש. והא אמרת: דרכן ליקרב ביום! אלא: עם בא השמש, *שמתעכלין והולכין כל הלילה מנין? ת"ל: °"זאת תורת העולה" – ריבה; והא עם בא השמש לא משכחת לה שתצית האור ברובו! לא קשיא: כאן לקלוט, כאן להתיר. רבי אלעזר מתני לה "מבוא השמש", ומוקים לה בפוקעין. וכן כי אתא רב דימי אמר רבי ינאי: בפוקעין. ומי אמר רבי ינאי הכי? והא א"ר ינאי: יקטרת שפקעה מעל גבי המזבח, אפילו קרטין שבה אין מחזירין אותן; *ותני רב חנינא בר מניומי ו] בדבי ר"א בן יעקב: °"אשר תאכל האש את העולה על המזבח" – עיכולי עולה אתה מחזיר, ואי אתה מחזיר עיכולי קטרת! סמי ז] מיכן קטרת. א"ר אסי: כי פשיט רבי אלעזר במנחות בעי הכי, ח] (בעי ר' אלעזר:) קומץ שסידרו וסידר עליו את המערכה, מהו? דרך הקטרה בכך, או אין דרך הקטרה בכך? כתיקו.§ בעי חזקיה: אברין שסידרן וסידר עליהן את המערכה, מהו? "על העצים" אמר רחמנא – דוקא על העצים. או דלמא, כיון דכתיב קרא אחרינא: "אשר תאכל האש את העולה על המזבח" – אי בעי הכי עביד, אי בעי הכי עביד? לתיקו.§ בעי רבי יצחק נפחא: מאברין שסידרן בצידי המערכה, מהו? אליבא דמ"ד: "על" ממש – לא תיבעי לך, ד"על

רש"י:

וחישב. כלומר, אם חישב עליה כל זמן שהוא בשמאלו – לאו מחשבה היא, ולא מחייבי כרת האוכלו. שאין מחשבה פוסלת אלא במי שראוי לעבודה, ושמאל בלא כלי לר"ש אינו כשרה, כדאמרינן לעיל: בא לעבודה ביד עובדה בימין. פסלתו מתנתו. מה שניתן בשמאלו, ושוב אין לו תקנה בחזרה. מ"ט משום דבעי לקדושיה בכלי כו' ואספו שפסול. עוד להקדישן בכלי. דאי לא הוי בעי עוד האי קומץ קידוש כלי – לא הוה מפסיל, דהוה כדם שנשפך מן הכלי על הרצפה ואספו שכשר, כדאמרינן במס' יומא בפ' "הוציאו לו" (דף מח.): נשפך מן הכלי על הרצפה ואספו – כשר. לא בעו מתן כלי. דאי י] בעי, לית ליה תקנתא בחזרה כדפרישית, דהוה ליה כנשפך על הרצפה מן הצואר שפסול, דנפקא לן *מ"ולקח מדם הפר" – דם מהפר יקבלנו. וקידוש קומץ במקום קבלת דם, ושמאל בלא כלי הרי היא כרצפה, דכי אכשר רבי שמעון שמאל בקבלה לא הכשיר אלא בכלי. לרבי יהודה מסייע ליה. דאמר: כשעובדה ביד בעינן ימין, והכא נמי קתני: יחזיר לימינו. לרבי ינאי לימא תיהוי תיובתא. דאמר: אפילו בהמיינו, וכל שכן בשמאל, והכא קתני: יחזיר לימינו! דאמר כתנא דהקטר. דקתני לעיל: הקטר חלבים ואברים כו', ומכשר עבודת קומץ בשמאל ואפילו ביד. ולאו לצדדין קתני. כדתרלה רבי יהודה בריה דרבי חייא לעיל. פעמים. חציו בראשונה וחציו בשניה, ולא פעמי פעמים יא]. משני זיתים. הלכך, האי דנקיט מתניתין "פעמים" דוקא נקט, שתהא בכל הקטרה כזית ולא פחות, דאין הקטרה בפחות מכזית. ורבי יוחנן אמר יש קומץ בפחות משני זיתים. ואפילו הכי קתני מתניתין: פעמים כשרה יב]. מאימתי מתיר *כו'. דכתיב: "קדש קדשים מאשי ה'" – אין להן חלק אלא לאחר אשי ה', בת"כ. משמשלה. במקצתה. אין כבשן מעלה קיטור כו'. ובקומץ נמי כתיב והקטיר הלכך בעינן קיטור. אמרי תלמידך. תלמידך אומרים משמיה דרב עמרם. אין לי. אעל יג] מזבח כל הלילה קאי. מבוא השמש. אחר יד] *שבא השמש. קומץ. ולבונה וכל הקרבנות *דרכן ליקרב ביום דנפקא לן מ"ביום צוותו" בת"כ, ולא יצא מאותו כלל אלא אברי עולה שהתירן הכתוב בלילה דכתיב (ויקרא ו): על מוקדה וגו'. אברים ופדרים. דדרכן ליקרב בלילה, מהאי קרא גופיה נפקא בתורת כהנים. עם בא השמש. קודם ביאת השמש. ואי קשיא, הא קיימא לן: מנחתם ונסכיהם בלילה, והכא תני: ומנחת נסכים ביום! תריץ: הא מותיב לה בפ"ב דמסכת תמורה (דף יד:), ומשני: כאן בנסכים הבאין עם הזבח, כאן בנסכים הבאין בפני עצמן. והא (א) טו] עם בא השמש לא משכחת דיצית האור ברובו. קודם שקיעת החמה. ואי לא חשיב הקטרה עד שתצית האור ברובו, איפסלו להו בשקיעת החמה! לקלוט. שתהא מזבח קולטו שלא יפסל בלינה, הויא משמשלה בו האור. להתיר. טז] שיריה, לא הוי הקטרה עד שתצית בו האור ברובו. ר' אלעזר מתני לה. כדקתני לעיל דקומץ ולבונה, שמעלן מבוא השמש יז]. בפוקעין. דקומץ ולבונה הקופצין מתוך האור ונופלים, מעלין אותן כל הלילה. אפי' קרטין. שלמים וחשובין שבה. אין מחזירין. ולעיל קתני קטרת, ומוקי לה איהו בפוקעין! תאכל. קרי ביה "תעוכל". עיכולי. *)פוקעין. יח] כי פשיט. כשהיה שונה. על המזבח. יט] תחת העצים. בצידי המערכה. אצל

*) שפוקעין נ"ק

תוספות:

אין הקטרה פחותה מכזית. בפ' "כל המנחות באות מצה" (לקמן דף נח.) פליגי אביי ורבא, וקיימא רבא כרבי יהושע בן לוי דהכא, ואביי כרבי יוחנן. ול"ע בפ' "אלו עוברין" (פסחים דף מג:) דאמר רבי יוחנן: כל איסורין שבתורה אין היתר מצטרף לאיסור, חוץ מאיסורי נזיר שאמרה תורה "משרת" "וכל משרת". זעירי אמר: אף שאור בבל תקטירו. כמאן כר' אליעזר דדריש "כל"? אי הכי אפילו חמץ בפסח נמי! אין הכי נמי, ולאפוקי דאביי. והשתא מרבי יוחנן מיהא תקשי, דכרבי אליעזר הוי. ולא מ"ל דלאפוקי מדאביי, דהא ר"י קאי כאביי! *וי"ל: כ] (דאביי) אפילו מ"ד דלא דריש "כל" – "וכל" דריש. וצריך עיון, דמ"משרת" דריש, מדפריך לקמיה: והא "משרת" להכי הוא דאתא! מ"ר.

יש הקטרה בפחות מכזית. בהקטר שומשום בסוף "הקומץ זוטא" (לעיל טז:) מודה דאין דרך הקטרה בכך. והא דמשמע בכל דוכתי דאין הקטרה בפחות מכזית, כדאמר לעיל דאם לא נשתייר כזית חלב אין זורק את הדם, הכא היינו טעמא – משום דיש קומץ פחות משני זיתים, ואלי קומץ מרבין בפרק "כל המנחות באות מצה" (לקמן נח.) ובריש "אלו עוברין" (פסחים מג:) מדכתיב "כל שאור". מ"ר.

תורת העולה ריבה. אכתי דרשינן מינה בפ' "יוצא דופן" (נדה מ:): תורה אחת לכל העולין שאם עלו לא ירדו. מ"ר.

קומץ מאימתי מתיר את השירים לאכילה. הוה מצי למינקט אימורים, דכמה דלא (פסחים נט:) מיקטרי אימורים לא מישתרי בשר באכילה. אלא משום דכי נטמאו או שאבדו מישתרי בשר – לא פסיקא ליה, אבל קומץ פסיקא ליה. מ"ר.

אלא עם בא השמש כו'. מקומץ ולבונה לא קשה היאך הם קריבין אחר התמיד. כא] דשמא כיון שנקמצו קודם – הוי כאברים שנתותרו, שהתירתן הקמיצה. ומנחת כהנים וכהן משיח, אף על פי שאין בהם קמיצה – יש בהם קידוש כלי, כדאמרינן (זבחים דף מה:) דכל דבר שאין לו מתירין – משקידש בכלי חשיב כב] כמתירין. מ"ר.

ואי אתה מחזיר עיכולי קטורת. מ"העולה" לא ממעט עיכולי קומץ ולבונה, כיון דאיתנהו על מזבח החיצון. אבל קטורת על מזבח הפנימי. מ"ר.

מסלתה

עין משפט נר מצוה:

סא א מיי' פי"א מהל' פסה"מ הלכה ב:
סב ב מיי' פי"א שם הלכה כה:
סג ג מיי' פי"א מהל' פסה"מ הלכה טו ע"ש במיימוני ובכ"מ תמלא שפסק כריב"ל:
סד ד מיי' פי"ג מהל' מעה"ק הלכה יד:
סה ה מיי' פי"א מהל' פסה"מ הלכה טו:
סו ו מיי' פי"ב מהלכות מעה"ק הלכה יג:
סז ז מיי' פ"ד מהל' מעה"ק הלכה ב:
סח ח מיי' שם הל' ד:
סט ט מיי' שם הל' ה:
ע י מיי' פ"ג מהלכות תמידין ומוספין הלכה ג:
עא כ ל מיי' פ"ב מהלכות פסה"מ הלכה כו:

וגי' נ"ק וי"ל דר"י דריש וכל דאפילו למ"ד דלא כו' ול"ע דאי מוכל משרת דריש מאי פריך לקמיה והא משרת כו' וכן הוא בתוספות פסחים שם ובנזיר דף לו ע"א ולקמן דף נח ע"א וע"ש בנ"ק

מסורת הש"ס:

גי' רש"י בימינו ל"ק מוחק מכאן עד וחייבין עליו כרת בשם ס"מ

יומא מח.

לקמן נח.

[שם: פסחים מג. נזיר לו:]

סוטה טו.

שיריים דקדש קדשים מאשי ה' כתיב אין כו' ל"ק

ביאת ל"ק

שדרכן ל"ק

ל"ק מ"ה

בראשית יט

תמורה יד. ע"ש

ויקרא ו

ומתעכלין נ"ק

שם

יומא מה. ע"ש זבחים פג.

הגהות הב"ח

(א) רש"י ד"ה והא אם תמצא עם בא השמש:

שיטה מקובצת

א] וחישב עליה. פ"ה כלומר אם חישב עליה כל זמן שהוא בשמאלו משמע דקאי אהא דקאמר קמץ בימינו ונתן בשמאלו א"כ ע"כ הא דפסיל היינו מטעם מחשבה דאילו מטעם שמאל ר"ש מכשיר שלא בהילוך וקשיא אמאי פסול כיון דאינו נתפש בפיגול הא אמרינן לעיל בפ"ק [דף ה ע"א] מנחת העומר שקמצה שלא לשמה כשרה דאין מחשבה פוסלת אלא בדבר הראוי לעבודה ועוד במאי מחשב אי בהולכה בשמאל הא תנן בפ"ק דזבחים [דף יג ע"א] ור"ש מכשיר בהילוך לכך נראה לפרש בשמאל וחישב עליו פסול ואין בו כרת האוכלו פירוש קמץ בשמאלו דבשמאלו קאי אקומץ דלא תפיס ביה פיגול כיון דיש בו פסול אחר דבעינן שיהא קרב כל המתיר כמצותו בלא שום פסול אחר כדתנן בשלהי פ"ק ומיהו פסול הוי משום דעביד בשמאל. תו"ח: לשון תוס' אחרות בשמאל וחישב עליו כו' פ"ה דאין מחשבה פוסלת אלא במי שראוי לעבודה ומיהו מהניא מחשבה לפסול ולא נהירא דהא אמרינן לעיל גבי מנחת העומר דכשירה לפי שאין מחשבה אלא בדבר הראוי לעבודה ואפילו כשרה נמי הוי ונראה לפרש דפסולה מפני שעשה הקטרה בשמאל. תו"ח: ב] כרת. בימינו [חישב עליה וכו'] ותיבות ל"א נמחק: ג] דבעי לקדושיה: ד] פחותה מכזית וא"ת לדבריו אמאי אמרינן אם חישב להקטיר פחות מכזית בחוץ [אינו] חייב כיון דיש הקטרה פחות מכזית וי"ל דגלי ביה קרא כדאיתא בריש פרקין [דף יז ע"ב] מה אכילה בכזית אף הקטרה בכזית מיהו תימה הא דתנן ומייתי לה שלהי פ"ק [דף יג ע"ב] קומץ ולבונה וקטורת כו' שאם הקריב מאחד מהן כזית בחוץ חייב ואמאי בעינן כזית ואפילו פחות מכזית לחייב עליה בחוץ כיון דיש הקטרה פחותה מכזית וי"ל דהא נמי מפיק ליה מקרא

שיטה מקובצת

בפרק השוחט והמעלה לעשות אותו כשהוא שלם דהיינו כזית ולא כשהוא חסר. תוס' (זבחים דף קז ע"ב): ה] נחמן תיבת יצחק נמחק: ו] מניומי ברבי: ז] סמי מכאן תיבת מיכן נמחק: ח] בעי הכי בעי ר' אלעזר: ט] היא לחיובה כרת האוכלו כו' שראוי לעבודה ובשמאל בלא כלי כו' כשירה לעבודת קומץ כדאמרינן לעיל בא לעבודה ביד עובדה בימין כחטאת הס"ד: י] הוי בעי מתן כלי לית: יא] פעמים שלשה או ארבעה פעמים הס"ד ומה"ד מאי בינייהו במאי פליגי ומאי טעמיה הס"ד ומה"ד רבי יהושע סבר אין קומץ פחות משני זיתים ואין הקטרה פחות מכזית כו' הס"ד ומה"ד משני זיתים: יב] כשירה אלמא יש הקטרה בפחות מכזית הלכך אפילו ג' וד' נמי הס"ד ומה"ד קומץ מאימתי מתיר שירים דהא כתיב והנותרת וגו' קדש קדשים מאשי ה': יג] אין לי אעל המזבח: יד] אחר שיבא: טו] הא כמשמען עם: טז] להתיר השירים: יז] השמש ודקשיא לך הא אמרת דרכן ליקרב ביום מוקי לה להא דתני מעלה מבא השמש בפוקעין: יח] פוקעין הס"ד ומה"ד סמי מכאן מההיא דקתני מעלן ומקטיר מבא השמש לא קתני בהדייהו קטורת: יט] המזבח משמע סמוך למזבח: כ] וי"ל דסבר ר' יוחנן דאפי' מאן דלא: כא] התמיד הא אמרינן עליה השלם כל הקרבנות כולן מכאן שאין מקטירין [שום] דבר אחר תמיד של בין הערבים דבשלמא אברים ופדרים לא קשיא כדמוקי לה בפסח שני באברים ופדרים שניתותרו כלומר שנשחט הזבח ונזרק הדם קודם התמיד דבהא לא הזהיר הכתוב שלא להקטיר: כב] כמתירין וכיון שקידש בכלי קודם התמיד הוי כקמיצה דשאר מנחות:

תָּא שְׁמַע דָּם שֶׁנִּטְמָא וְזָרְקוֹ כו'. קַשְׁיָא לְרַב שֵׁילָא, דְּקָתָנֵי: אִם זְרָקוֹ בְּמֵזִיד לֹא הוּרְצָה. **מתני'** כְּמִדַּת רַבִּי אֱלִיעֶזֶר. דְּאָמַר בְּפֶרֶק "כֵּיצַד צוֹלִין" (פסחים דף עז.): דָּם אע"פ שֶׁאֵין בָּשָׂר – ה"נ קוֹמֶץ אע"פ שֶׁאֵין שִׁירַיִים י] (בְּשִׁירֶיהָ) כְּשֵׁרָה לְהַקְטִיר הַקּוֹמֶץ. כְּמִדַּת רַבִּי יְהוֹשֻׁעַ. דְּאָמַר (שם): אִם אֵין בָּשָׂר אֵין דָּם, יא] אִם אֵין דָּם אֵין בָּשָׂר. **גמ'** וְהוּא שֶׁנִּטְמְאוּ כָּל שִׁירֶיהָ. *הוּא יב] דְּאָמַר רַבִּי יְהוֹשֻׁעַ דְּפָסוּל לְהַקְטִיר הַקּוֹמֶץ. קס"ד נִטְמָא אִין. כְּלוֹמַר, כְּנִטְמְאוּ שִׁירֶיהָ הוּא דְּאָמְרִינַן: אִם נִשְׁתַּיֵּיר **מִקְצָת שֶׁלֹּא נִטְמָא כְּשֵׁרָה אֲפִי' לְרַבִּי יְהוֹשֻׁעַ יג], אֲבָל אָבְדוּ קְצָת שִׁירֶיהָ אוֹ נִשְׂרְפוּ אָמַר רַבִּי יְהוֹשֻׁעַ דִּפְסוּלָה, הוֹאִיל וְכוּלָּהּ בָּעֵינַן קַיָּים. מִדְּקָא נָקֵיט רַב לְשׁוֹן טוּמְאָה וְלָא נָקַט נַמִי לִשְׂרוֹף וְאָבוּד דְּמַתְנִי'. מַאי קָסָבַר. רַב, אִי קָסָבַר שִׁיּוּרָא מִילְּתָא כו'. רֵישַׁיְיהוּ. דְּנִטְמְאוּ קָתָנֵי בְּמַתְנִי' בְּרֵישָׁא. כִּדְתַנְיָא. יד] רַבִּי יְהוֹשֻׁעַ נַמִי מַכְשֵׁר הֵיכָא דְּאִיכָּא שִׁיּוּר, אֲפִי' בְּאָבוּד וְשָׂרוּף. זוֹרֵק *הַדָּם. דְּקָרֵינָא בֵּיהּ "הַבָּשָׂר וְהַדָּם". כַּחֲצִי זַיִת בָּשָׂר וְכַחֲצִי זַיִת חֵלֶב אֵין זוֹרֵק. שֶׁאֵין אֲכִילָה וְהַקְטָרָה מִצְטָרְפִין. מִנְחָה מַאי עֲבִידְתֵּיהּ. מַאי זְרִיקָה אִיתָא בְּמִנְחָה? כְּגוּפָא דְּזִבְחָא דָּמְיָא. טו] דְּתֶיהֱוֵי בִּמְקוֹם בָּשָׂר כְּאִילּוּ נִשְׁתַּיֵּיר בָּשָׂר, קמ"ל דְּלָא. מְנָהָנֵי מִילֵּי. דְּאִם לֹא נִשְׁתַּיֵּיר בָּשָׂר אֶלָּא חֵלֶב, זוֹרֵק אֶת הַדָּם? דִּכְתִיב וְהִקְטִיר הַחֵלֶב וגו'. רֵישֵׁיהּ דִּקְרָא הָכִי: טז] "וְזָרַק הַכֹּהֵן אֶת הַדָּם עַל מִזְבַּח ה' לִפְנֵי אֹהֶל מוֹעֵד וְהִקְטִיר הַחֵלֶב" וגו', אַלְמָא דְּמִשּׁוּם חֵלֶב זָרֵיק לֵיהּ לַדָּם. יוֹתֶרֶת וּשְׁתֵּי הַכְּלָיוֹת מְנָלַן. דְּאִם לֹא נִשְׁתַּיְּירוּ אֶלָּא הֵן, זוֹרֵק אֶת הַדָּם? דַּחֲזֵינַן לְעֵיל דְּהָכִי הוּא, דְּקָתָנֵי: וּבְמִנְחָה אֲפִילּוּ *כּוּלָּהּ יז] (כָּלִיל) [קַיָּים] כו'. לְרֵיחַ נִיחוֹחַ. "וְהִקְטִיר הַחֵלֶב לְרֵיחַ נִיחוֹחַ". כָּתַב רַחֲמָנָא חֵלֶב. דְּמַשְׁמַע דְּרֵיחַ נִיחוֹחַ לָא מְרַבֵּי אֶלָּא דּוּמְיָא דְּחֵלֶב, דִּמְגוּפֵיהּ דְּזֶבַח הוּא. **מתני'** שֶׁלֹּא בִּכְלֵי שָׁרֵת. שֶׁלֹּא קִדֵּשׁ קוֹמֶץ בִּכְלֵי שָׁרֵת. דִּבְתְחִילַּת מִנְחָה וַדַּאי לָא פְּלִיגִי דְּבָעֵינַן כְּלִי, כִּדְאָמְרִינַן בְּפֶרֶק "שְׁתֵּי הַלֶּחֶם" (לקמן צו.): שָׁאֲלוּ אֶת רַבִּי זוֹ מִנַּיִן כו'. **גמ'** בָּא לַעֲבוֹדָה בַּיָּד. הַקְטָרַת קוֹמֶץ, שֶׁהִיא בִּמְקוֹם זְרִיקָה בַּיָּד, שֶׁלֹּא קִדְּשׁוֹ בִּכְלִי. עֲבוֹדָה בְּיָמִין כַּחַטָּאת. יח] שֶׁהוּא עוֹמֵד נַמִי זְרִיקָתָהּ בְּאֶצְבַּע יט] וּבְיָמִין, דִּכְתִיב בֵּיהּ: "וְלָקַח הַכֹּהֵן מִדָּמָהּ בְּאֶצְבָּעוֹ", וְאָמְרִי' (זבחים כד:): כ"מ שֶׁנֶּאֱמַר אֶצְבַּע וּכְהוּנָּה אֵינָהּ אֶלָּא יָמִין. אַלְמָא, מִדְּאַקְשָׁהּ לְחַטָּאת – ש"מ דְּלָא בָּעְיָא כְּלִי, וּבִלְבַד שֶׁיַּעַבְדֶנּוּ בְּיָמִין. בִּשְׂמֹאל כְּאָשָׁם. שֶׁזְּרִיקָתוֹ בִּכְלִי וְלֹא בַּיָּד, דְּאֵין לָךְ טָעוּן מַתְּנַת אֶצְבַּע אֶלָּא חַטָּאת בִּלְבַד. דְּהָכִי אָמְרִינַן בִּזְבָחִים (דף כד:) כ] דְּלְר' שִׁמְעוֹן זְרִיקָה כְּשֵׁרָה, *דְּתַנְיָא: זָרַק בִּשְׂמֹאל פָּסוּל, וְר' שִׁמְעוֹן מַכְשִׁיר. מִשּׁוּם דִּבְשָׂר זְרִיקַת הַקָּרְבָּנוֹת לָא כְּתִיב אֶצְבַּע אֶלָּא כְּהוּנָּה, וּלְר' שִׁמְעוֹן כְּהוּנָּה בָּעְיָא אֶצְבַּע כא]. בְּהֶמְיָינוֹ. אַבְנֵט. מְקֵידָה. כְּלִי חֶרֶס. הַכֹּל מוֹדִים בְּקוֹמֶץ שֶׁטָּעוּן קִידּוּשׁ. וְכִי מַכְשֵׁר ר' שִׁמְעוֹן – בְּהֶקְטֵר, שֶׁאִם נְטָלוֹ מִתּוֹךְ כְּלִי שָׁרֵת לְאַחַר שֶׁקִּדְּשׁוֹ בּוֹ, וְהֶעֱלָהוּ בְּיָדוֹ וְהִקְטִירוֹ – כָּשֵׁר. וְעֵצִים. עֲצֵי מַעֲרָכָה. תְּיוּבְתָּא כב] דְּרַבִּי יְהוּדָה. דְּאָמַר: בַּיָּד עוֹבְדָהּ בְּיָמִין, דְּהָא הָכָא קָתָנֵי אֲפִי' בַּיָּד בִּשְׂמֹאל בְּלָא כְּלִי. וְהָא וַדַּאי ר' שִׁמְעוֹן הִיא, דְּהָא מַכְשֵׁר שֶׁלֹּא בִּכְלִי (א) שָׁרֵת. קְמָצוֹ כג] שֶׁלֹּא מִכְּלֵי שָׁרֵת. שֶׁנִּתְקַדְּשָׁה בּוֹ הַמִּנְחָה. מַכְשִׁירִין בְּמַתַּן כְּלִי. אֲפִי' שֶׁלֹּא בִּכְלֵי שָׁרֵת. תְּיוּבְתָּא דְּרַב נַחְמָן דְּאָמַר: הַכֹּל מוֹדִים כו'! מִמַּתַּן כְּלִי וְאֵילָךְ. הוֹלָכָה וְהַקְטָרָה לָא כד] בָּעֵינַן כְּלִי שָׁרֵת. תָּא שְׁמַע. לְרַב נַחְמָן. וְנָתַן בִּשְׂמֹאלוֹ. בְּלָא כְּלִי, כה] יַחֲזִיר *לִימִינוֹ. [כִּדְאָמְרִינַן לְעֵיל: בָּא לַעֲבוֹדָה בַּיָּד – עֲבוֹדָה בְּיָמִין. בִּשְׂמֹאלוֹ

וְחִישֵׁב

תורה אור

ת"ש: דָּם שֶׁנִּטְמָא וּזְרָקוֹ, בְּשׁוֹגֵג – הוּרְצָה, בְּמֵזִיד – לֹא הוּרְצָה! הָכִי קָאָמַר: דָּם שֶׁנִּטְמָא וּזְרָקוֹ א] בֵּין בְּשׁוֹגֵג בֵּין בְּמֵזִיד, נִטְמָא בְּשׁוֹגֵג – הוּרְצָה, בְּמֵזִיד – לֹא הוּרְצָה.§ **מתני'** *נִטְמְאוּ שְׁיָרֶיהָ, נִשְׂרְפוּ שְׁיָרֶיהָ, אָבְדוּ שְׁיָרֶיהָ – כְּמִדַּת ר' אֱלִיעֶזֶר [א]כְּשֵׁרָה, וּכְמִדַּת רַבִּי יְהוֹשֻׁעַ פְּסוּלָה.§ **גמ'** אָמַר רַב: וְהוּא [ב]שֶׁנִּטְמְאוּ כָּל שְׁיָרֶיהָ, אֲבָל מִקְצָת שְׁיָרֶיהָ – לֹא. קָא סָלְקָא ב] דַּעְתָּךְ: נִטְמָא – אִין, אָבוּד וְשָׂרוּף – לָא. מַאי קָסָבַר? אִי קָסָבַר: שִׁיּוּרָא מִילְּתָא הִיא, אֲפִילּוּ אָבוּד וְשָׂרוּף נַמִי! אִי קָסָבַר: שִׁיּוּרָא לָאו מִילְּתָא הִיא, ג] וְנִטְמָא מַאי טַעְמָא – דִּמְרַצֶּה צִיץ, אִי הָכִי, כָּל שְׁיָרֶיהָ נַמִי! לְעוֹלָם קָסָבַר: שִׁיּוּרָא מִילְּתָא הִיא, וְנִטְמָא – [ג]וְהוּא הַדִּין לְאָבוּד וְשָׂרוּף, וְהַאי דְּקָאָמַר נִטְמָא – רֵישַׁיְיהוּ נָקַט. *כִּדְתַנְיָ', רַבִּי יְהוֹשֻׁעַ אוֹמֵר: [ד]כָּל הַזְּבָחִים שֶׁבַּתּוֹרָה שֶׁנִּשְׁתַּיֵּיר מֵהֶן כַּזַּיִת בָּשָׂר אוֹ כַּזַּיִת חֵלֶב – זוֹרֵק אֶת הַדָּם, כַּחֲצִי זַיִת בָּשָׂר וְכַחֲצִי זַיִת חֵלֶב – אֵינוֹ זוֹרֵק אֶת הַדָּם. [ה]וּבְעוֹלָה אֲפִי' כַּחֲצִי זַיִת בָּשָׂר וְכַחֲצִי זַיִת חֵלֶב – זוֹרֵק אֶת הַדָּם, מִפְּנֵי שֶׁכּוּלָּהּ כָּלִיל. וּבְמִנְחָה אֲפִי' כּוּלָּהּ קַיֶּימֶת – לֹא יִזְרוֹק. מִנְחָה מַאי עֲבִידְתָּהּ? אָמַר רַב פָּפָּא: מִנְחַת נְסָכִים, ד] ס"ד: הוֹאִיל וּבַהֲדֵי זֶבַח קָא אָתְיָא – כְּגוּפֵיהּ דְּזִיבְחָא דָּמְיָא, קמ"ל. מְנָהָנֵי מִילֵּי? אָמַר רַבִּי יוֹחָנָן מִשּׁוּם רַבִּי יִשְׁמָעֵאל, וּמָטוּ בָּהּ מִשּׁוּם רַבִּי יְהוֹשֻׁעַ בֶּן חֲנַנְיָא, אָמַר קְרָא: °"וְהִקְטִיר הַחֵלֶב לְרֵיחַ נִיחוֹחַ לַה'", חֵלֶב – וְאע"פ שֶׁאֵין בָּשָׂר. וְאַשְׁכְּחַן חֵלֶב, יוֹתֶרֶת וּשְׁתֵּי כְּלָיוֹת מְנָלַן? דְּקָתָנֵי: וּבְמִנְחָה אֲפִילּוּ כּוּלָּהּ קַיֶּימֶת – לֹא יִזְרוֹק; מִנְחָה הוּא דְּלֹא יִזְרוֹק, הָא יוֹתֶרֶת וּשְׁתֵּי כְּלָיוֹת – יִזְרוֹק. מְנָלַן? רַבִּי יוֹחָנָן דִּידֵיהּ אָמַר: "לְרֵיחַ נִיחוֹחַ" – כָּל שֶׁאַתָּה מַעֲלֶה לְרֵיחַ נִיחוֹחַ. וְאִיצְטְרִיךְ לְמִכְתַּב "חֵלֶב" וְאִיצְטְרִיךְ לְמִיכְתַּב "לְרֵיחַ נִיחוֹחַ", דְּאִי כְּתַב "חֵלֶב", הֲוָה אָמִינָא: חֵלֶב – אִין, יוֹתֶרֶת וּשְׁתֵּי כְּלָיוֹת – לָא, כְּתַב רַחֲמָנָא: "רֵיחַ נִיחוֹחַ"; וְאִי כָּתַב רַחֲמָנָא "לְרֵיחַ נִיחוֹחַ", הֲוָה אָמִינָא: אֲפִילּוּ מִנְחָה, כְּתַב רַחֲמָנָא: "חֵלֶב".§ **מתני'** *[ו]שֶׁלֹּא בִּכְלֵי שָׁרֵת – פָּסוּל, וְרַבִּי שִׁמְעוֹן מַכְשִׁיר. הִקְטִיר קוּמְצָהּ פַּעֲמַיִם – כְּשֵׁרָה.§ **גמ'** *אָמַר ה] רַבִּי יְהוּדָה בְּרֵיהּ דְּרַבִּי חִיָּיא: מַאי טַעְמָא דְּר' שִׁמְעוֹן? אָמַר קְרָא: °"קֹדֶשׁ קָדָשִׁים הִיא כַּחַטָּאת וְכָאָשָׁם", בָּא לַעֲבוֹדָה בַּיָּד ו] (כַּחַטָּאת) – עוֹבְדָהּ בְּיָמִין כַּחַטָּאת, בִּכְלִי – עוֹבְדָהּ בִּשְׂמֹאל כָּאָשָׁם. וְרַבִּי יַנַּאי אָמַר: כֵּיוָן שֶׁקְּמָצוֹ מִכְּלִי שָׁרֵת, מַעֲלֵהוּ וּמַקְטִירוֹ אֲפִילּוּ בְּהֶמְיָינוֹ, וַאֲפִילּוּ בִּמְקֵידָה שֶׁל חֶרֶשׂ. °רַב נַחְמָן בַּר יִצְחָק אָמַר: הַכֹּל מוֹדִים בְּקוֹמֶץ שֶׁטָּעוּן קִידּוּשׁ. מֵיתִיבֵי: *[ז]הֶקְטֵר חֲלָבִים וְאֵבָרִים וְעֵצִים שֶׁהֶעֱלָן בֵּין בַּיָּד בֵּין בִּכְלִי, בֵּין בְּיָמִין וּבֵין בִּשְׂמֹאל – כְּשֵׁרִין; [ח]הַקּוֹמֶץ וְהַקְּטוֹרֶת וְהַלְּבוֹנָה שֶׁהֶעֱלָן בֵּין בַּיָּד בֵּין בִּכְלִי, בֵּין בְּיָמִין בֵּין בִּשְׂמֹאל – כְּשֵׁרִין; תְּיוּבְתָּא ז] דְּרַבִּי יְהוּדָה בְּרֵיהּ דְּרַבִּי חִיָּיא! אָמַר לָךְ רַבִּי יְהוּדָה בְּרֵיהּ דְּרַבִּי חִיָּיא: לְצַדְדִין קָתָנֵי, בַּיָּד – בְּיָמִין, בִּכְלִי – בֵּין בְּיָמִין בֵּין בִּשְׂמֹאל.§ תָּא שְׁמַע: קְמָצוֹ ח] שֶׁלֹּא מִכְּלִי שָׁרֵת, וְקִידְּשׁוֹ שֶׁלֹּא בִּכְלִי שָׁרֵת, וְהֶעֱלוּ וְהִקְטִירוֹ שֶׁלֹּא בִּכְלִי שָׁרֵת – פָּסוּל; רַבִּי אֶלְעָזָר וְרַבִּי שִׁמְעוֹן מַכְשִׁירִין בְּמַתַּן כְּלִי! אֵימָא: מִמַּתַּן כְּלִי וָאֵילָךְ. תָּא שְׁמַע, וַחֲכָמִים אוֹמְרִים: קוֹמֶץ טָעוּן כְּלִי שָׁרֵת, כֵּיצַד? קוֹמְצוֹ מִכְּלִי שָׁרֵת, וּמְקַדְּשׁוֹ בִּכְלִי שָׁרֵת, וּמַעֲלוֹ וּמַקְטִירוֹ בִּכְלִי שָׁרֵת. ר' שִׁמְעוֹן אוֹמֵר: כֵּיוָן שֶׁקְּמָצוֹ מִכְּלִי שָׁרֵת, מַעֲלוֹ וּמַקְטִירוֹ ט] שֶׁלֹּא בִּכְלִי שָׁרֵת וְדַיּוֹ! אֵימָא: [ט]כֵּיוָן שֶׁקְּמָצוֹ וְקִדְּשׁוֹ בִּכְלִי שָׁרֵת, מַעֲלוֹ וּמַקְטִירוֹ וְדַיּוֹ. תָּא שְׁמַע: קָמַץ בִּימִינוֹ וְנָתַן בִּשְׂמֹאלוֹ – יַחֲזִיר לִימִינוֹ; בִּשְׂמֹאלוֹ

וְחִישֵׁב

אשכחן חלב כו'. ובשר נפקא לן מקרא בפרק "כילד צולין" (פסחים דף פ.). מ"ר.

ורבי ינאי אמר כיון שקמצו מכלי שרת כו'. קמילה בימין נפקא לן בפ' קמא בסופו (לעיל דף י:) אליבא דרבי שמעון מרבי יהודה בריה דרבי חייא. ורבי ינאי דלית ליה, נפקא ליה שפיר בג"ש ד"יד" "יד", כדמוכח לעיל בסוף פ"ק (ג"ז שם). מ"ר.

הקטר חלבים ואברים בין בימין בין בשמאל כשירה. מצי למימר דאתיא כר"ש, כמו דסיפא דקומץ, אבל לרבנן בעי ימין. אי נמי, אפילו לרבנן איכא לאכשורי הקטר חלבים בשמאל, כמו הולכת איברים לכבש דלעיל בסוף פ"ק (ג"ז שם.). מ"ר.

הקומץ והקטורת ולבונה כו'. האי דלא ערבינהו, דלמא תלת תלת שמעינהו. *מ"ר.

אין

נו א ב ג מיי' פי"א מהלכות פסה"מ הל' כ:

נז ד ה מיי' פ"א מהל' פסה"מ הלכה ל:

נח ו מיי' פ"א מהלכות פסה"מ הלכה ו:

נט ז ח מיי' שם פ"ב הל' ל:

ס ט מיי' שם:

לעיל ע. פסחים עז:

[כה"ג משני הש"ס בקדושין ו.]

כ"א קומץ · ויקרא יז · שם ז · תוספתא דזבחים פ"ט

שיטה מקובצת

א] שנטמא וזרקו זרקו בין: ב] קא סלקא דעתיה: ג] היא נטמא מ"ט דמרצה ציץ על אכילות: ד] נסכים סד"א: ה] אמר יהודה ותיבת רבי נמחק: ו] ביד עובדה: ז] תיובתא דיהודה בריה דר"ח א"ל אמר לך יהודה: ח] קמצו מכלי ותיבת שלא נמחק: ט] ומקטירו [ודיו] תיבות שלא בכלי שרת נמחק: י] תיבת בשיריה נמחק: יא] אין דם ס"א ה"נ אם אין שירים אין קומץ: יב] דאומר: יג] לרבי יהושע הואיל וכולה בעינא קיימא אבל אבדו קצת כו' דפסולה מדקא נקיט רב כו': יד] כדתניא דרבי יהושע: טו] דמיא דהא הוי במקום בשר וכאילו נשתייר: טז] הכי הוא זורק: יז] כולה קיימת: יח] בימין כחטאת ס"א דכתיב ולקח הכהן וגו' ואמרי' כל מקום כו': יט] באצבעו ממש ובימין דכתיב ביה ולקח הכהן מדם החטאת באצבעו: כ] בזבחים ולרבי שמעון זריקתה כשרה בשמאל דתניא בהקומץ א) זוטא זרק: כא] בעיא אצבע ובאשם מצורע כתיב ביה על כף הכהן השמאלית וכדין שמן דין דם האשם ועוד שלא מצינו בשום אשם אצבע וכהונה לא בשחיטה ולא בזריקה הס"ד ומה"ד בהמיינו: כב] תיובתא דיהודה דאמר בא לעובדה ביד: כג] קמצו מכלי שרת שנתקדשה ותיבת שלא נמחק: כד] לא בעינא: כה] יחזיר לימינו בדיהודה בריה דרבי חייא בא לעובדה ביד כו':

א) בהקומץ זוטא ליתא לברייתא זו כלל רק הוא בזבחים דף כד ולעיל בפ"ק דף י ע"ב:

ל"ק מ"ז

הא דלאמר כמדת ר"י דפסול כו' נ"ק

הקומץ שלא כו' לר"י הואיל וכולה בעין קיימא אבל אבדו כו' דפסולה מדקא נקט כצ"ל נ"ק

גליון הש"ס

גמ' רנב"י אמר הכל מודים בקומץ שטעון קידוש. עיין לעיל דף ב ע"ב תוספות ד"ה שחיטה:

את הדם נ"ק

זבחים כה: קט. מעילה טו: פסחים עט. לעיל ט. תוספתא דזבחים פ"ד [תוספתא פסחים פ"ו בכורות לט:]

הגהות הב"ח

(א) רש"י ד"ה תיובתא וכו' בכלי שרת הס"ד ואח"כ מ"ה במתן כלי כו' אלמא היכא דקמצו מכלי שנתקדשה בו המנחה מכשירין כלי אפילו:

זבחים יח. כולה כו' הס"ד נ"ק

ל"ק מ"ז

רבינו גרשום

ת"ש כו' וקתני וזורקו בשוגג הורצה ובמזיד לא הורצה אלמא בזורקו בשוגג הורצה במזיד לא הורצה אבל טומאתו שנטמא משמע בין בשוגג בין במזיד ותיובתא דרב שילא דאמר דכי בין במזיד לא הורצה הכי קאמר דם שנטמא וזרקו כו' זרקו בין בשוגג בין במזיד אם נטמא בשוגג הורצה במזיד לא הורצה והיינו כרבי שילא דאמר טומאה בשוגג הורצה כו':

בשמאל דתניא נ"ק

לימינו דביד כו' נ"ק

לֹא הוּרְצָה. וּרְמִינְהִי: א] *אעַל מַה הַצִּיץ מְרַצֶּה? עַל הַדָּם ב] וְעַל הַבָּשָׂר וְעַל הַחֵלֶב שֶׁנִּטְמָא, בֵּין בְּשׁוֹגֵג בֵּין בְּמֵזִיד, בֵּין בְּאוֹנֶס בֵּין בְּרָצוֹן, בֵּין בְּיָחִיד בֵּין בְּצִיבּוּר! אָמַר רַב יוֹסֵף, לָא קַשְׁיָא: הָא ר' יוֹסֵי, הָא רַבָּנַן; *דְּתַנְיָא: *באֵין תּוֹרְמִין מִן הַטָּמֵא עַל הַטָּהוֹר, וְאִם תָּרַם, בְּשׁוֹגֵג – תְּרוּמָתוֹ תְּרוּמָה, בְּמֵזִיד – אֵין תְּרוּמָתוֹ תְּרוּמָה. ר' יוֹסֵי אוֹמֵר: בֵּין בְּשׁוֹגֵג בֵּין בְּמֵזִיד – תְּרוּמָתוֹ תְּרוּמָה. אֵימַר דְּשָׁמְעַתְּ לֵיהּ לְר' יוֹסֵי – דְּלָא קָנֵיס, דִּמְרַצֶּה צִיץ עַל אֲכִילוֹת מִי שָׁמְעַתְּ לֵיהּ? *וְהָתַנְיָא, ר' אֱלִיעֶזֶר אוֹמֵר: הַצִּיץ מְרַצֶּה עַל אֲכִילוֹת, רַבִּי יוֹסֵי אוֹמֵר: גאֵין הַצִּיץ מְרַצֶּה עַל אֲכִילוֹת! אֵיפוּךְ, רַבִּי אֱלִיעֶזֶר אוֹמֵר: אֵין הַצִּיץ מְרַצֶּה עַל אֲכִילוֹת, רַבִּי יוֹסֵי אוֹמֵר: הַצִּיץ מְרַצֶּה עַל אֲכִילוֹת. מַתְקִיף לָהּ רַב שֵׁשֶׁת: וּמִי מָצֵית אָפְכַתְּ לָהּ? *וְהָתַנְיָא: יָכוֹל בָּשָׂר שֶׁנִּטְמָא לִפְנֵי זְרִיקַת דָּמִים יְהוּ חַיָּיבִין ג] עֲלֵיהֶן מִשּׁוּם טוּמְאָה? ת"ל: °"כָּל טָהוֹר יֹאכַל בָּשָׂר וְהַנֶּפֶשׁ אֲשֶׁר תֹּאכַל בָּשָׂר מִזֶּבַח הַשְּׁלָמִים אֲשֶׁר לַיי' וְטוּמְאָתוֹ עָלָיו וְנִכְרְתָה" – *הַנִּיתָּר לַטְּהוֹרִין חַיָּיבִין עָלָיו מִשּׁוּם טוּמְאָה, וְשֶׁאֵינוֹ נִיתָּר לַטְּהוֹרִין דאֵין חַיָּיבִין עָלָיו מִשּׁוּם טוּמְאָה. אוֹ אֵינוֹ, אֶלָּא: נֶאֱכָל לַטְּהוֹרִין חַיָּיבִין עָלָיו מִשּׁוּם טוּמְאָה, וְשֶׁאֵינוֹ נֶאֱכָל לַטְּהוֹרִין אֵין חַיָּיבִין עָלָיו מִשּׁוּם טוּמְאָה; אוֹצִיא אֲנִי אֶת הַלָּן וְאֶת הַיּוֹצֵא שֶׁאֵינָן נֶאֱכָלִין לַטְּהוֹרִים! ת"ל: "אֲשֶׁר לַיי'" – רִיבָּה. יָכוֹל שֶׁאֲנִי מְרַבֶּה אֶת הַפִּיגּוּלִין וְאֶת הַנּוֹתָרוֹת? נוֹתָרוֹת הַיְינוּ לָן! אֶלָּא: ד] אַף הַפִּיגּוּלִין כַּנּוֹתָרוֹת? ת"ל: °"מִזֶּבַח הַשְּׁלָמִים" – מִיעֵט. וּמָה רָאִיתָ לְרַבּוֹת אֶת אֵלּוּ וּלְהוֹצִיא אֶת אֵלּוּ? אַחַר שֶׁרִיבָּה הַכָּתוּב וּמִיעֵט, אָמַרְתָּ: מְרַבֶּה אֲנִי אֶת אֵלּוּ שֶׁהָיְתָה לָהֶן שְׁעַת הַכּוֹשֶׁר, וּמוֹצִיא אֲנִי אֶת אֵלּוּ שֶׁלֹּא הָיְתָה לָהֶן שְׁעַת הַכּוֹשֶׁר; וְא"ת: בָּשָׂר שֶׁנִּטְמָא לִפְנֵי זְרִיקַת דָּמִים וַאֲכָלוֹ לְאַחַר זְרִיקַת דָּמִים, מִפְּנֵי מָה חַיָּיבִין עָלָיו מִשּׁוּם טוּמְאָה? מִפְּנֵי שֶׁהַצִּיץ מְרַצֶּה. נִטְמָא – אִין, יוֹצֵא – לָא; ה] מַאן שָׁמְעַתְּ לֵיהּ דְּאָמַר: אֵין *זְרִיקָה מוֹעֶלֶת לַיּוֹצֵא – רַבִּי אֱלִיעֶזֶר, וְקָתָנֵי דִּמְרַצֶּה צִיץ עַל אֲכִילוֹת! אֶלָּא אָמַר רַב חִסְדָּא, לָא קַשְׁיָא: הָא רַבִּי אֱלִיעֶזֶר, הָא רַבָּנַן. אֵימַר דְּשָׁמְעַתְּ לֵיהּ לְר' אֱלִיעֶזֶר – דִּמְרַצֶּה צִיץ עַל אֲכִילוֹת, דְּלָא קָנֵיס מִי שָׁמְעַתְּ לֵיהּ? אִין, כִּי הֵיכִי דְּשָׁמְעַתְּ לֵיהּ לְר' יוֹסֵי – שָׁמְעַתְּ לֵיהּ לְרַבִּי אֱלִיעֶזֶר; דְּתַנְיָא, רַבִּי אֱלִיעֶזֶר אוֹמֵר: בֵּין בְּשׁוֹגֵג בֵּין בְּמֵזִיד – תְּרוּמָתוֹ תְּרוּמָה. אֵימַר דְּשָׁמְעַתְּ לֵיהּ לְרַבִּי אֱלִיעֶזֶר – בִּתְרוּמָה דְּקִילָּא, בְּקָדָשִׁים דַּחֲמִירֵי מִי שָׁמְעַתְּ לֵיהּ? א"כ, הָא אַמַּאן תִּרְמְיֵיהּ? ו] רָבִינָא *אָמַר: טוּמְאָתוֹ, בֵּין בְּשׁוֹגֵג בֵּין בְּמֵזִיד – הוּרְצָה; זְרִיקָתוֹ, בְּשׁוֹגֵג – הוּרְצָה, בְּמֵזִיד – לֹא הוּרְצָה. וְרַב שֵׁילָא אָמַר: זְרִיקָתוֹ, בֵּין בְּשׁוֹגֵג בֵּין בְּמֵזִיד – הוּרְצָה; טוּמְאָתוֹ, בְּשׁוֹגֵג – הוּרְצָה, בְּמֵזִיד – לֹא הוּרְצָה. וּלְרַב שֵׁילָא, ז] *[הָא] דְּקָתָנֵי: שֶׁנִּטְמָא בֵּין בְּשׁוֹגֵג בֵּין בְּמֵזִיד! ה"ק: נִטְמָא בְּשׁוֹגֵג, וּזְרָקוֹ בֵּין בְּשׁוֹגֵג בֵּין בְּמֵזִיד.

ת"ש

רש"י

שׁוֹגֵג. *ח] קָסָבַר אֵין קָרְבָּנוֹת מְקַבְּלִין טוּמְאָה. אוֹנֶס – שֶׁנִּטְמָא בְּעַל כָּרְחוֹ. אֲבָל מֵזִיד וְרָצוֹן חֲדָא מִילְּתָא הִיא, אֶלָּא אַיְּידֵי דְּתָנָא אוֹנֶס תָּנָא רָצוֹן. לֹא הוּרְצָה. דִּכְתִיב: "וְהָיָה עַל מִצְחוֹ תָּמִיד לְרָצוֹן לָהֶם" (שמות כח), וְלֹא לְגוֹיִם. וּרְמִינְהוּ כו'. אַלְמָא לֵיךְ מְרַצֶּה אַמֵּזִיד דְּיָחִיד! בְּשׁוֹגֵג תְּרוּמָתוֹ תְּרוּמָה. דְּאָמְרִינַן בְּבַמָּה דּוֹכְתֵּי (ב"מ דף נו.): "וְלֹא תִשְׂאוּ עָלָיו חֵטְא" (א), אִם אֵינוֹ קָדוֹשׁ – נְשִׂיאוּת חֵטְא לָמָּה? מִכָּאן לַתּוֹרֵם מִן הָרָעָה עַל הַיָּפָה שֶׁתְּרוּמָתוֹ תְּרוּמָה. בְּמֵזִיד אֵין תְּרוּמָתוֹ תְּרוּמָה. דְּרַבָּנַן קְנָסוּהוּ מִשּׁוּם דְּהֵזִיד. וּפְלִיגִי בָּהּ אֲמוֹרָאֵי בִּיבָמוֹת בְּפֶרֶק "הָאִשָּׁה", אִיכָּא לְמ"ד אֵין תְּרוּמָתוֹ תְּרוּמָה – ט] לְתַקֵּן אֶת הַשִּׁירַיִם, אֲבָל תְּרוּמָה הָוֵי. י] דִּמְרַצֶּה צִיץ עַל אֲכִילוֹת מִי שָׁמְעַתְּ לֵיהּ. דְּמוֹקַמְתְּ לְהַךְ בָּרַיְיתָא בַּתְרַיְיתָא (ב) אַלִּיבֵּיהּ, *דְּקָתָנֵי בָּהּ: הַצִּיץ מְרַצֶּה עַל אֲכִילַת טוּמְאַת בָּשָׂר, דְּהַיְינוּ אֲכִילוֹת. לְהָכִי נָקַט אֲכִילוֹת, דְּאַעוֹלִין כ"ע מוֹדוּ דְּלֵיךְ מְרַצֶּה, דְּקָתָנֵי בְּרֵישׁ ת"כ: "וְנִרְצָה לוֹ לְכַפֵּר עָלָיו" – בְּדָם, דִּכְתִיב (ויקרא יז): "כִּי הַדָּם הוּא בַּנֶּפֶשׁ יְכַפֵּר", אֵין לִי אֶלָּא דָּם טָהוֹר, טָמֵא מִנַּיִן? ת"ל (שמות כח): "וְנָשָׂא אַהֲרֹן" וגו'. וְהוּא בְּדָם קָמַיְירֵי, דִּכְתִיב (שם) "לְרָצוֹן לָהֶם", יא] וְהָכָא כְּתִיב: "וְנִרְצָה", מַה הָכָא דָּם – אַף הָתָם דָּם. וְאֵין לִי אֶלָּא דָּם, מִנַּיִן לְרַבּוֹת כָּל הָעוֹלִים? ת"ל: "לְכָל מַתְּנוֹת קָדְשֵׁיהֶם" וגו' (שם). יָכוֹל בָּשָׂר שֶׁנִּטְמָא לִפְנֵי זְרִיקַת דָּמִים. וַאֲכָלוֹ לִפְנֵי זְרִיקָה בְּטוּמְאַת הַגּוּף, יְהוּ חַיָּיבִין עָלָיו כָּרֵת? וּבְתוֹרַת כֹּהֲנִים מָצָאתִי לָשׁוֹן יב] נְקִיָּה: יָכוֹל יְהוּ חַיָּיבִין מִשּׁוּם טוּמְאַת הַגּוּף לִפְנֵי זְרִיקָה? וּבְבָשָׂר טָהוֹר קָמַיְירֵי. וְשֶׁאֵינוֹ נִיתָּר לַטְּהוֹרִין. כְּגוֹן אִם אָכַל אֲפִילּוּ בָּשָׂר טָהוֹר יג] בְּטוּמְאַת הַגּוּף, קוֹדֶם זְרִיקַת דָּם, עֲדַיִין לֹא הָיְתָה נִיתֶּרֶת לִטְהוֹרִים, דִּזְרִיקָה הִיא הַמַּתֶּרֶת. אוֹ אֵינוֹ אֶלָּא. הָכִי דָּרְשִׁינַן: שֶׁאֵינוֹ נֶאֱכָל לַטְּהוֹרִין אֵין חַיָּיבִין יד] מִשּׁוּם טוּמְאַת הַגּוּף, אַף שֶׁנִּיתָּר לַטְּהוֹרִין. וְאוֹצִיא אֶת הַלָּן וְאֶת הַיּוֹצֵא. לְאַחַר זְרִיקָה. שֶׁאע"פ שֶׁנִּיתָּר בִּזְרִיקָה, הוֹאִיל וְעַכְשָׁיו אֵירַע בּוֹ פְּסוּל – לֹא יְהוּ חַיָּיבִין עָלָיו הָאוֹכְלוֹ בְּטוּמְאָה. הַיְינוּ לָן. *וְאָמַרְתְּ לְעֵיל דְּחַיָּיבִין עָלָיו מִשּׁוּם טוּמְאָה. "מִזְבֵּחַ" – וְלֹא כָּל הַזְּבָחִים. אַחַר שֶׁרִיבָּה הַכָּתוּב וּמִיעֵט. כְּלוֹמַר, הוֹאִיל וּמָלֵינוּ רִיבּוּי וּמִיעוּט. אָמַרְתְּ מְרַבֶּה אֲנִי לָן וְיוֹצֵא. שֶׁהָיְתָה לָהֶן שְׁעַת הַכּוֹשֶׁר, טו] שֶׁהֲרֵי הָיְתָה זְרִיקָתוֹ כְּשֵׁירָה. וְא"ת בָּשָׂר שֶׁנִּטְמָא לִפְנֵי זְרִיקָה וַאֲכָלוֹ בְּטוּמְאַת הַגּוּף לְאַחַר זְרִיקָה מִפְּנֵי מָה חַיָּיבִין עָלָיו. הָא לֹא הָיְתָה לוֹ שְׁעַת הַכּוֹשֶׁר! טז] וַאֲנַן פִּיגּוּל הוּא דְּמַעֲטִינַן דְּאֵין חַיָּיבִין, אֲבָל נִטְמָא אֲפִילּוּ קוֹדֶם זְרִיקָה, וְאַחַר זְרִיקָה אֲכָלוֹ – חַיָּיב! שֶׁהַצִּיץ מְרַצֶּה. לְמֶיהֱוֵי זְרִיקָה מַעַלְיָיתָא, וְנִיתָּר לִטְהוֹרִים קָרֵינָא בֵּיהּ, וְאע"פ שֶׁלֹּא נֶאֱכַל (ג). נִטְמָא. לִפְנֵי זְרִיקָה, הוּא דְּחַיָּיב עָלָיו הָאוֹכְלוֹ לְאַחַר זְרִיקָה בְּטוּמְאַת הַגּוּף יז]. יוֹצֵא לֹא. מִשּׁוּם דְּלָא הָוְיָא זְרִיקָה מַעַלְיָיתָא, דְּאֵין הַצִּיץ מְרַצֶּה עַל הַיּוֹצֵא, דְּלֹא הָיְתָה לוֹ שְׁעַת הַכּוֹשֶׁר. מַאן שָׁמְעַתְּ לֵיהּ דְּאָמַר אֵין זְרִיקָה מוֹעֶלֶת יח] בַּיּוֹצֵא. לְמֶיהֱוֵי קָרְבָּן כָּשֵׁר – רַבִּי אֱלִיעֶזֶר הִיא בְּפ"ק דִּמְעִילָה (דף ו:), דְּקָתָנֵי: בְּשַׂר קָדְשֵׁי קָדָשִׁים שֶׁיָּצָא לִפְנֵי זְרִיקַת דָּמִים, ר' אֱלִיעֶזֶר אוֹמֵר: מוֹעֲלִין בּוֹ וַאֲפִי' לְאַחַר זְרִיקָה, מִשּׁוּם דְּאֵין זְרִיקָה מוֹעֶלֶת לוֹ לְהוֹצִיאוֹ מִידֵי מְעִילָה. אֶלָּא אָמַר רַב חִסְדָּא לָא קַשְׁיָא. הָנָךְ מַתְנִיתָא דִּלְעֵיל. הָא דְּקָתָנֵי בְּמַתְנִיתָא בְּמֵזִיד הוּרְצָה נַמִּי בְּיָחִיד – ר"א, מִדְּקָתָנֵי דְּלֵיךְ מְרַצֶּה עַל אֲכִילוֹת. וְהָא דְּקָתָנֵי לֹא הוּרְצָה – רַבָּנַן. דְּלָא קָנֵיס. הֵיכָא דְּזָרִיק דָּם טָמֵא בְּמֵזִיד, מִי שָׁמְעַתְּ לֵיהּ? א"כ אַמַּאן תִּרְמְיֵיהּ. לְהָא דְּקָתָנֵי הוּרְצָה. טוּמְאָתוֹ בֵּין בְּשׁוֹגֵג. בֵּין שֶׁנִּטְמָא בְּשׁוֹגֵג בֵּין שֶׁנִּטְמָא יט] *) בְּמֵזִיד – הוּרְצָה אִם זְרָקוֹ בְּשׁוֹגֵג. וְהָא דְּתָנֵי לֹא הוּרְצָה – אַמֵּזִיד דִּזְרִיקָה קָאֵי.

*) במזיד הורצה הס"ד ואח"כ מה"ד זריקתו בשוגג אם כנ"ל

קָא

תוספות

בשוגג תרומתו תרומה. שהיתה לו שעת הכושר איירי, שלא ניטמא בתחילת תלישתו. שאם תלשו אדם טמא ועדיין משקה טופח עליו – אין תרומתו תרומה, כדמוכח בפ' "כל שעה" (פסחים דף לג.). **במזיד** אין תרומתו תרומה. אע"ג דתורם מן הרעה על היפה תרומתו תרומה, כדאמרינן ב"האשה רבה" (יבמות דף פט:) וכדתנן במס' תרומות (פרק שני מ"ו) – התם חזי קצת, הכא לא חזי כלל.

דמרצה ציץ על אכילות מי שמעת ליה. פי' בקונטרס: להכי נקט אכילות, דאעולין כ"ע מודו דליך מרצה, כדקתני בריש תורת כהנים: "ונרצה לו לכפר עליו" בדם כו'. ולא דק בקונטרס, דבעולין נמי אשכחן פלוגתא בפרק "כיצד צולין" (פסחים דף עז:). **ת"ל** אשר ליי'. הכא מוקמינא ליה לרבות לן ויוצא. ותימה: דבסוף "דם שחיטה" (כריתות דף כג: ושם) דריש ליה לרבות אימורים, דאיסור טומאה חייל אאיסור חלב! וי"ל: דשקולים הן. אבל קשה אההיא דכריתות *בסוף פ"ב דמעילה (דף י:) דריש אימורים מ"אשר יקרב אל הקדשים", דדבר שאין לו מתירין – משיקדש בכלי! וי"ל: דהתם לא מיירי אלא בעולה ושאר קדשים. אבל שלמים לא הייתי מרבה, כיון דילאו מן הכלל. מ"ר. **ורב** שילא אמר כו'. וא"ת: מאי דוחקייהו דרבינא ורב שילא לשנויי כלל? הא מוכח בהדיא ב"האשה רבה" (יבמות דף צ. ושם) דחדא מדאורייתא וחדא מדרבנן, מדקאמר: והא הכא דמדאורייתא ארצויי מרצה, דתנן: על מה הציץ מרצה כו'! וי"ל: דלעולם משמע ליה נמי ביבמות דאפילו מדרבנן נמי קתני: על מה הציץ מרצה כו', למר כדאית ליה ולמר כדאית ליה, אזריקה או אטומאה, אלא דפשיטא ליה דמדאורייתא אין חילוק בין טומאה לזריקה. והכי פירושו: והא מדאורייתא ארצויי מרצה בכל ענין, בין מטומאה בין מזריקה. מ"ר. **זריקתו** בין בשוגג בין במזיד הורצה. אע"פ שצריך לדחוק הלשון אליביה, ניחא ליה לשנויי הכי ולא כרבינא, כדאמר בפרק "הנזקין" (גיטין דף נד.): גברא לכפורי קא בעי, ואנן ניקום וניקנסיה?: אשכחן

מסורת הש"ס

[נ"ל כסבור]

פסחים עז: ועט. וש"נ

תרומות פ"ב משנה ב יבמות פט. פסחים לג.

פסחים עז.

דר"י דקתני הציץ מרצה על טומאת בשר נ"ק

(פסחים מו)

[פסחים לה: ע"ש]

ואמרינן כו' טומאה הס"ד נ"ק

[זבחים ל.]

[פסחים פ:]

הא קתני נ"ק

דבסוף נ"ק

עין משפט נר מצוה

נב א מיי' פ"ח מהל' פסה"מ הל' לד ובפ"ד מהל' ביאת מקדש הלכה ז:

נג ב מיי' פ"ה מהל' תרומות הל' ב:

נד ג מיי' פ"ד מהל' ביאת מקדש הל"ז:

נה ד מיי' פ"ח מהל' פסה"מ הל"ג:

[פלוגתא דר"י ליתא במשנה דתרומות ולכך שפיר גרסינן דתניא]

גליון הש"ס

גמ' לטהורין חייבין. ע' זבחים דף מו ע"ב תוס' ד"ה אחד לכלל: שם מזבח השלמים מיעט. ע' לקמן דף מו ע"ב תוס' ד"ה משקשטה:

הגהות הב"ח

(א) רש"י ד"ה בשוגג וכו' ולא תשאו עליו חטא בהרימכם את חלבו אם אינו: (ב) ד"ה דמרצה וכו' אליבא דר' יוסי דקתני בה: (ג) ד"ה שהציץ מרצה וכו' שלא נאכל הס"ד ואח"כ מ"ה נטמא אין נטמא לפני:

רבינו גרשום

רבינא אמר לא איצטריך לאוקומי להני מתנייתא כתנאי דטומאתו דקתני בברייתא קמא היינו בין בשוגג בין במזיד דהכי משמע (תנו רבנן) [לישנא] דם שניטמא משמע דניטמא בין בשוגג בין במזיד וזרקו בשוגג. דעביד זריקה בשוגג הורצה. במזיד אי עביד זריקה במזיד לא הורצה דקנסינן ליה היינו זריקתו בשוגג הורצה במזיד לא הורצה והילכך לא קשיין הני מתנייתא אהדדי דהכי נמי תניא אידך דקתני על מה הציץ מרצה על הדם ועל הבשר ועל החלב שנטמא בין בשוגג בין במזיד כלומר דטומאה הוי בין בשוגג בין במזיד הורצה ולעולם נמי אמרינן שניטמא היינו בין ניטמא בשוגג בין ניטמא במזיד: זריקתו בין בשוגג בין במזיד דברייתא קמא אתוקמא כד הוה סליקא אדעתין מעיקרא דהכי קאמר ת"ר דם שניטמא וזרקו בשוגג דהאי בשוגג אניטמא קאי. והכי קאמר דם שניטמא בשוגג וזרקו בין שזרקו בשוגג בין שזרקו במזיד הורצה הואיל דאיטמא בשוגג אבל דאיטמא במזיד לא הורצה אפי' זרקו בשוגג והיינו דאמר רב שילא זריקה בין בשוגג וכו': ולרב שילא הא קתני אידך ברייתא שנטמא בין בשוגג בין במזיד דאלמא בשוגג ומזיד בתר טומאה אזיל ותיובתא אאידך ברייתא דתני דכי נטמא במזיד לא הורצה. הכי קאמר דהכי תני לה להא ברייתא דעל מה הציץ מרצה כו'. דהיינו כי הך ברייתא קמא דאזריקה קאי בין בשוגג בין במזיד:

שניטמא

שיטה מקובצת

א] על מה הציץ מרצה. אלמא מהני ריצוי ציץ דאע"ג דנטמא או זריק ליה כשר: ב] ועל הבשר. וא"ת למאי מהני ליה ריצוי ציץ לאוכלה טמאה אי אפשר דהא כתיב והבשר אשר יגע בכל טמא לא יאכל וי"ל דלר"י דאמר אם אין בשר אין דם ניחא דמהני ליה ריצוי ציץ לאחשובי בשר כמאן דאיתיה וליזרוק הדם עליה ולא חשבינן ליה כמאן דליתיה ואפי' לר"א דאמר יש דם אע"פ שאין בשר אפ"ה מהני ליה ריצוי ציץ א) לאקבועי בפיגול [ולהוציאו] מידי מעילה: שנטמא עיין בתוס' יבמות דף צ ע"א: ג] חייבין עליו: ד] אף הפיגולין כנותרות. וא"ת והלא פיגול אין ניתר לטהורים וי"ל כיון דאין פיגול נקבע עד שיקבעו כל מתיריו ובאים בבת אחת אכילה ופיגול הוי שפיר ניתר לטהורים. תו"ח: ה] מאן שמעת ליה. עי' תוס' לקמן דף מו ע"א: ו] רבינא אמר כו' ובריית קמייתא דבשוגג הורצה כו' קיימא אזריקה ובריית דבין בשוגג ובין במזיד הורצה קיימא אטומאה ותימה דבמסכת יבמות [דף צ ע"א] דייק עלה דההיא דבמזיד לא הורצה דהיינו מדרבנן מדקתני באידך ברייתא בין בשוגג בין במזיד הורצה והיינו דין תורה ודייק עלה דיש כח ביד חכמים לעקור דבר מן התורה ומאי קאמר והא אמרינן דבחדא מיירי בטומאה וחדא מיירי בזריקה וי"ל דמשמע ליה דכל הני שינויי דהכא נמי דבמזיד לא הורצה היינו מדרבנן וא"ת הכא אמאי לא משני הא מדאורייתא הא דרבנן כדאמרינן ביבמות וי"ל דניחא ליה לשנויי אפי' נאמר בין בשוגג בין במזיד הורצה אפי' מדרבנן: ז] שילא הא קתני ח] שוגג. קסבור אין קרבנות מקבלין טומאה באונס שנטמא: ט] תרומה. לגמרי וקסבר בית דין מתנין לעקור דבר מן התורה ושויוה חולין ואיכא למ"ד אין תרומתו תרומה לתקן: י] תרומה הוי. הס"ד ומה"ד רבי יוסי אומר דלא קנים לגביה (טומאה) [תרומה] א"כ הא דקתני יחיד במזיד לא הורצה רבנן היא והא דתני הורצה רבי יוסי היא הס"ד ומה"ד דמרצה: יא] לרצון להם. ב) ובבשר כתיב ונרצה להם מה הכא: יב] לשון. אחר נקיה: יג] טהור. שלא בטומאת: יד] חייבין עליו משום טומאת הגוף. ואע"פ שניתר לטהורין: טו] שעת הכושר משעת זריקה עד שעת לינה ויצאה הס"ד ומה"ד ואוציא אני פיגול שלא היה לו שעת הכושר שהרי היתה זריקתו פסולה וא"ת: טז] ואנן. ס"א אמרינן בפרק גיד הנשה דחייבין עליו משום טומאה אם אכלו בטומאת הגוף ולעיל נמי פיגול כו': יז] בטומאת הגוף. הא יצא לפני זריקה לא מחייב עליה האוכלו לאחר זריקה בטומאת הגוף משום והד"א: יח] זריקה מועלת. ליוצא: יט] במזיד הורצה והס"ד ואח"כ מה"ד ג) טומאתו בין בשוגג בין שנטמא במזיד הורצה אם זרקו:

א) וכן אמרינן בפסחים דף ע"ח ע"ש. ב) נראה דטס"ה וצ"ל והכא כתיב ונרצה לו לכפר מה הכא כו'. ג) נראה דצ"ל זריקתו כו' וטומאתו היה בין בשוגג ובין במזיד הורצה אם כו'.

מתני' נטמא אהקומץ והקריבו – הציץ מרצה, יצא והקריבו – אין הציץ מרצה, שהציץ מרצה על הטמא ואינו מרצה על היוצא.§ גמ' *תנו רבנן: °"ונשא אהרן את עון הקדשים" (שמות כח) – א] וכי איזה עון הוא נושא? אם תאמר: ב] עון פיגול – הרי כבר נאמר "לא יחשב"! א"ת: עון נותר – הרי כבר נאמר "לא ירצה"! ג] הא אינו נושא אלא עון טומאה, שהותרה מכללה בציבור. מתקיף לה רבי זירא, אימא: עון יוצא, ד] שהותר מכללו בבמה! אמר ליה אביי, אמר קרא: °"לרצון להם לפני ה'" (שם), עון דלפני ה' – אין, עון דיוצא – לא. מתקיף לה רבי אילעא, אימא: עון שמאל, שהותר מכללו ביום הכפורים! אמר ליה אביי, אמר קרא: "עון" – עון שהיה בו ודחיתיו, לאפוקי יוה"כ דהכשירו בשמאל הוא. רב אשי אמר: "עון הקדשים" – ולא עון המקדישין. אמר ליה רב סימא בריה דרב אידי לרב אשי, ואמרי לה רב סימא בריה דרב אשי לרב אשי: ואימא עון בעל מום, שהותר מכללו בעופות, דאמר מר: *בתמות וזכרות בבהמה, ואין תמות וזכרות בעופות! אמר ליה, עליך אמר קרא: "לא ירצה", ה] °"כי לא לרצון יהיה לכם" (ויקרא כב).§ תנו רבנן: *גדם שנטמא וזרקו, בשוגג – הורצה, במזיד – לא הורצה; במה דברים אמורים – ביחיד, אבל בציבור, בין בשוגג בין במזיד – הורצה; *ובגוי, בין בשוגג בין במזיד, בין באונס בין ברצון – לא

רש"י

מתני' הציץ מרצה. והמנחה כשירה והשירים נאכלין. גמ' ו] הא אינו נושא אלא עון טומאה. הואיל ויש בה צד קל. שהותרה מכללה בצבור. דכתיב בתמיד (במדבר כח): "במועדו" – אפילו בטומאה. מכללו בבמה. מכללו שנאסר יוצא במשכן – הותר בבמות נוב וגבעון, דאין שם קלעים. ויוצא דנאסר במשכן, מפרש ב"כיצד צולין" (פסחים דף פב) ז] [מקרא]: "מדוע לא אכלתם את ח] [החטאת] במקום הקדש". ואימא עון שמאל. דלכתחילה בעינן ימין, כדאמרינן בפרק ראשון (לעיל דף י.): כ"מ שנאמר אצבע כו'. ביום הכפורים. "נטל את המחתה בימינו ואת הכף בשמאלו". אמר קרא עון. "ונשא אהרן את עון", משמע שיש בו עון לכתחילה בכל מקום, ודחיתי לעון בצבור מפני כבוד צבור, ביחיד הציץ מרצה. לאפוקי שמאל. דאין בה שום עון, דהכי הוא הכשר מצותו. רב אשי אמר. לא מצית אמרת ציץ מרצה על עון שמאל. דאמר קרא עון הקדשים ולא ט] מקדישים. עון התלוי בכהנים, שחייבין לעבוד ולקדש קומץ בימין ועבדו בשמאל, אינו נושא. לא ירצה. ב"שור ושה שרוע וקלוט" וגו' (ויקרא כב). לא לרצון. "כל אשר בו מום לא תקריבו" וכו' (א). והאי שוגג ומזיד. מפרש לקמן אהייא קאי, אי אזריקה אי י] אטמאה. ובגוי. גוי ששילח קרבנו ונטמא הדם, דאמרינן בפרק "אלו מנחות" (לקמן דף עג:): "איש איש מבית ישראל אשר יקריב קרבנו", מה ת"ל יא] (קרבנו) "איש איש" – לרבות את הגוים שנודרין נדרים ונדבות כישראל.

תוספות

קיימא שניה, שניה נמי הא מיתקנא ראשונה! ומשני: פנים חדשות באו. (ב) והשתא, אימת אתא ליה? אי קודם שנפסקה ראשונה, אם כן כמו שטיהר מן המדרס – יטהר ממגע, *) דהא שבע ליה טומאה! *ויש לומר: דכשתיקן אוזן ראשונה – חל על אוזן מגע ומדרס בבת אחת, ובבת אחת לא אמרינן שבע ליה טומאה, כדמסקינן. ומגו דחייל מגע אאוזן – חייל נמי אכוליה סנדל, כיון דהכל כלי א'. והר"ש מפרש: דלא שייך שבע ליה טומאה בטומאה הבאה מעצמו, כגון ההיא דסנדל, דהישב עליו ואחר כך חתכו, (ג) ומדרס מגע דת"ק דר' יוסי דבאה מעצמו, שנוגע בעצמו. אבל סדינים המקופלים – טמא על מה שנגע *בחבירו. בשני סדינים המקופלים כו'. בשניתלה למעלה (ד) מזה ויש אויר קצת ביניהם איירי. דאי בזה על גב זה ממש, אי כשישב הכביד עליהם שניהם בבת אחת – א"כ עליון ליטמא מגע כמו תחתון, ואם הכביד על העליון תחילה – א"כ *קודם לתחתון מגע למדרס כשנגע בעליון, וטומאת מדרס לא מטמא תחתון עד שיכביד עליו. אבל כשיש אויר ביניהם, כי אתי זב ויתיב בעליון – מיד כשנוגע עליון בתחתון אתי לתחתון מדרס ומגע בבת אחת, ולעליון קדם לה מדרס למגע. וא"ת: אמאי איצטריך לשנויי שיש חילוק בין בת אחת לזה אחר זה? לימא דקא איירי במקופלים זה על גב זה, דקדם התחתון מגע למדרס! ושמא קסבר דמכביד על שניהם בבת אחת. ועוד, א"כ מאי מודה? היינו שאם נגע בהם הזב, דאוקימנא מקמי מדרס. וא"ת: ותיקשי ליה לאביי היא גופא, מאי שנא תחתון מעליון? שאין אביי מחלק בבת אחת, וא"כ עליון נמי ליטמא מדרס ומגע, דהא קנגע בתחתון! וי"ל: דיודע היה אביי שיש חילוק, אלא לרבא הוה מקשה, משום דלית ליה שבע טומאה אפי' היכי דמהני מגעו לטמא החצי עשרון אחר, דא"כ אפילו בבת אחת נמי נימא שבע ליה טומאה, ולא ליחול עליה טומאת מגע! אי נמי, משוה בת אחת לזה אחר זה דלעיל, דהוי קלה על קלה. **ונשא** אהרן את עון הקדשים כו'. פי' הקונטרס בפ"ק דפסחים (דף טז:) יב] גרסינן: אם עון נותר הרי כבר נאמר "לא יחשב", ואם עון פיגול הרי כבר נאמר "לא ירצה". ופי' דהכי איתא בפ"ב דזבחים (דף כח:) דאיסורא רבה חוץ לזמנו שהוא בכרת – מקרא רבה ופרשה רבה בפרשת "צו", ואיסורא זוטא דחוץ למקומו דליכא כרת – מקרא זוטא ופרשה זוטא בפרשת "קדושים". והביא ראיה דהכי איתא בת"כ. ור"ת גרים איפכא: בפיגול "לא יחשב" ובנותר "לא ירצה", משום דמסקינן בפ"ב דזבחים: *ותרוייהו מקרא אריכא נפקי, דכתב ביה "לא ירצה" ו"לא יחשב". ומה יג] שנזכר פיגול קודם לנותר, אע"ג דבמקרא כתיב ברישא חוץ לזמנו – משום דלשון פיגול כתב במקרא בהדיא. **אם** עון נותר כו'. לאו נותר ממש קאמר, כדאמר בזבחים*: לאחר שהוכשר יחזור ויפסל? אלא מחשבת נותר דהיינו מחשב לאוכלו חוץ לזמנו. **הא** אינו נושא אלא עון טומאה שהותרה מכללה בציבור. וא"ת: יד] תיפוק ליה דלא משכחת לה מידי דמתוקם ביה קרא אלא בטומאה! ואומר ר"ת: משום דכתיב "לרצון להם", משמע: דבר שהוא לרצון במקום אחר, ולהכי דחיק לאשכוחי הותר מכללו בכל הני דפריך. וא"ת: ונותר ופיגול היכן הותרו מכללן, דאיצטריך ליה "לא ירצה" "ולא יחשב"? ואומר ר"ת: דפיגול הותר מכללו בבמה, דלא שייך שם מחשבת חוץ למקומו. ונותר כדי נסבה, ואגב פיגול נקט נותר, הואיל ואשכח ביה קרא אע"ג דלא צריך. אי נמי, הותר מכללו בראשו של מזבח, דאיכא למ"ד אין לינה מועלת *שם, בריש "תמיד נשחט" (פסחים דף נט.) ובפרק "המזבח מקדש" (זבחים דף פז:). ומיהו פלוגתא דאמוראי היא, וקשיא למ"ד לינה מועלת שם טו] בראשו מהך ברייתא! ונראה דנותר יש ללמדו "עון" "עון" *מרילוי ציץ, ופיגול נמי מצי למילף הכי. ועוד יש לפרש, דנותר טז] הותר מכללו במנחת כהנים ומנחת כהן משיח וקומץ וכל דבר שאין לו מתירין, דאין חייבין עליו משום פיגול, כדתנן בזבחים בפרק "בית שמאי" (דף מג.). ואפי' פסולא נמי נראה דליכא, כדאמרינן בסוף פ"ק דזבחים (דף יד.): מודה רבי שמעון בהולכת חטאות הפנימיות, ופריך: והאמר רבי יז] *(ישמעאל) כל שאינו על מזבח החיצון כשלמים אין חייבין עליו משום פיגול! ושני: מודה ר"ש לפסול מקל וחומר, ומה שלא יח] לשמן הכשר בשלמים פסול בחטאת, חוץ לזמנו הפסול בשלמים אינו דין שפסול בחטאת? משמע דאי לאו קל וחומר הוה אמינא דאפי' פסולא ליכא. א"כ במנחת כהנים ומנחת נסכים דליכא קל וחומר, דלא איפסלי שלא לשמן – ליכא פסול כלל. אלמא אשכחן נותר דהותר מכללו לגמרי. **אימא** עון יוצא כו'. יט] מעון דזרות שהותר מכללו בבמה הוה מצי לאקשויי, ולשנויי: כ] כגון מעון יוצא. **ואימא** עון שמאל שהותר מכללו ביוה"כ. הא דלא קאמר: בהולכת אברים לכבש, כדאמר בסוף פ"ק דזבחים (דף יד.*): הרגל של ימין בשמאלו – משום דאין זו עבודה המעכבת כפרה. ומהאי טעמא נמי לא פריך מעון לינה שהותר לאיברים ופדרים.

עון קדשים ולא עון המקדישים. תימה: הא למ"ד טומאה דחויה היא בצבור ובעיא ציץ לרצויי, דאמרינן בפ"ק דיומא (דף ז:) דמרצה על הכהנים העושים בטומאה! ולעיל ב"הקומץ זוטא"* פירשתי. **ואימא** עון בעל מום שהותר מכללו בעופות. וא"ת: ואמאי לא פריך מעון טריפה שהותר במליקה? דהא חשיב הותר מכללו בפרק קמא (לעיל דף ו.), דאמר: טריפה שהותרה מכללה מאי היא, אילימא בעולת העוף כו', ובטריפה לא כתיב "לא ירצה"! ולאביי דמשני: עון שהיה בו ודחיתיו – ניחא, דלאפוקי טריפת מליקה שהוכשרה בכך. אבל לרב אשי קשיא! ויש לומר, דאמרינן: עון קדשים – ולא עון חולין, לאפוקי טריפות דשייך בחולין. וא"ת:* כא] עון אונן שהותר מכללו אצל כהן גדול! ולרב אשי דמשני לעיל: עון קדשים ולא עון מקדישין – ניחא, אלא לאביי קשיא! ושמא כב] אית להו דהדדי. וא"ת: ואימא עון דמחוסר זמן, כגון תוך ח' שהותר מכללו בעופות, כדאמר בפ"ק דחולין (דף כב:) דבני יונה כשירין משיעלעו דם! ויש לומר: דכתיב ביה "לא ירצה", דהא כג] "מיום השמיני והלאה ירצה" כתיב, הא קודם לא ירצה. ומיהו קשה מעון אותו ואת בנו, דהותר מכללו בעופות! ולפי מה שפי': עון קדשים ולא עון חולין, ניחא. ועוד אמרינן בפ' "אותו ואת בנו" (שם דף פ:) דכל הפסולין שבשור ושה הרי הם בלא ירצה. **אבל** בצבור בין בשוגג בין במזיד הורצה. תימה: דב"האשה רבה" (יבמות דף צ.) מייתי רישא דהך ברייתא, ודייק עלה: והא הכא כד] דרצויי מרצי ציץ, דתניא: על מה הציץ מרצה כו'. והשתא, מסיפא גופא הוה ליה לאיתויי, כדקתני בסיפא הכא דבצבור בין בשוגג בין במזיד הורצה, ומשמע: הוא הדין יחיד, אי לא משום דביחיד קנסינן מזיד! ויש לומר: דאי מסיפא הוה אמינא דטעמא לאו משום ציץ, אלא משום דטומאה הותרה בצבור, אף על גב דלשון "הורצה" משמע ציץ.

בשוגג

מסורת הש"ס

*) אלא ע"כ אחר שניטלה הראשונה וניתקנה בא לו מגע מדרס הא שבע כו' נ"ק

פסחים עז: יומא ז. זבחים כג.

לעיל י. חולין כג. זבחים קטז. קדושין נז. תמורה יז.

פסחים עז: פ: יומא ז. יבמות ל. זבחים מה. גיטין כג:

זבחים טו: מה:

ותרוייהו נ"ק

[דף כט.]

בראשו של מזבח שם כו' נ"ק מגין

שמעון

[בפרק שני דזבחים כו:]

[דף טו. ד"ה והכא]

ואימא

הגהות הב"ח

(א) רש"י ד"ה לא לרצון וכו' תקריבו כו' הס"ד ואח"כ מ"ה בשוגג כו' האי שוגג וכו' אי אנטמאה הס"ד: (ב) תוס' ד"ה (בכף הקודש) כי נגע וכו' הלכות כלו לכלן והשתא: (ג) בא"ד ואח"כ התכו ומגע מדרס דת"ק דר' יוסי וכו' לבייל מה שנגע בחבירו: (ד) ד"ה בשני וכו' למעלה זה מזה:

עין משפט נר מצוה

עיין משנה למלך הלכות שאר אבות הטומאה פי"ב הלכה י' ד"ה ודע

מט א מיי' פ"א מהל' פסה"מ הל"ט ופ"ב מהל' מעילה הל"ט:

נ ב מיי' פ"ג מהל' איסורי מזבח הל"ח:

נא ג מיי' פ"א מהל' פסה"מ הל' לג ופ"ב מהל' ביאת מקדש הל"ז:

בחבירו ובגניתלה למעלה מזה ויש אויר קלת ביניהם איירי כנ"ל והל"ח נ"ק

קדם לתחתון מגע למדרס דמגע כשנגע נ"ק

שיטה מקובצת

א] וכי איזה עון הוא נושא. עי' תוס' זבחים [דף כג ע"ב ופסחים דף] טז ע"ב: ב] עון פגול ה"ג א"ת עון פגול הרי נאמר לא ירצה אם עון נותר כתיב לא יחשב וה"פ תרי קראי כתיבי חד בפרשת צו את אהרן אם האכל יאכל מבשר זבח שלמיו ביום השלישי [לא ירצה המקריב אותו] לא יחשב לו פגול יהיה (המקריב אותו לא ירצה) והיינו קרא אריכא כדאיתא בזבחים [דף כח ע"א] ודרשינן במחשב לאכול ביום השלישי [הכתוב מדבר] דאי באוכל בשלישי אחר שהוכשר יחזור ויפסול [בתמיהה] וכרת כתיב ביה ואידך קרא בפרשת קדושים ואם האכל יאכל ביום השלישי פגול הוא לא ירצה והאי קרא זוטא מוקי לה בזבחים [שם] במחשב לאכול חוץ למקומו באם אינו ענין וממעיט ליה מכרת התם. ואם עון פגול פי' חוץ למקומו הרי כבר נאמר לא ירצה בקרא זוטא ואם עון נותר כלומר מחשבת נותר דהיינו חוץ לזמנו הרי כבר נאמר לא יחשב בקרא אריכא: ג] הא אינו נושא כו' [שהותר מכללו בצבור] דדרשינן (בזבחים) במועדו אפי' בטומאה וא"ת מאי פריך מפיגול ונותר והרי לא הותר מכללן וי"ל דאשכחן הותר מכללו בנותר כגון שלן בראשו של מזבח דתו לא שייך ביה פסול לינה ופיגול דחוץ (לזמנו) [למקומו] אע"ג דלא שייך ביה הותר מכללו מ"מ גמרינן לה עון עון מחוץ לזמנו. ועוד י"ל דהותר מכללו דפיגול ונותר הותר מכללו במנחת כהנים כו'

כדתנן במס' מעילה [דף י' ע"א] דאין חייבין עליהן משום פיגול (ונותר וטמא) דגמרינן משלמים שיש להן מתירין והני לית להו מתיר אחר: ד] שהותר מכללו בבמה. עי' תוס' זבחים דף טז ע"ב: ה] כי לא לרצון יהיה לכם. תימה אמאי לא פריך ואימא עון אונן כו' ולשינויי דרב אשי ניחא ועוד אמר מורי דמשום הכי לא פריך מאונן משום דגלי קרא דמחלל עבודה כדמוכח בזבחים בפרק שני [דף טז ע"א] וא"ת א"כ משמאל לא הוי ליה למיפרך דהא גלי ביה קרא דמחלל עבודה ושמא דפריך משמאל דנהי דבשר פסול מ"מ מרצי ליה ציץ לענין דלכפריה ביה בעלים כדאמרי' בפ"ב דזבחים [דף כו ע"ב] גבי ניתנין למעלה שנתנן למטה כו' דבשר פסול ובעלים מתכפרים. ותימה דבאונן נמי נימא הכי: ו] גמ'. מה"ד ונשא אהרן אציץ קאי הס"ד ומה"ד הא: ז] תיבת מקרא ל"ש: ח] את החטאת: ט] ולא עון המקדישים: י] אזריקה אי אטומאה הס"ד: יא] מה ת"ל איש וכו' ותיבת קרבנו נמחק: יב] דפסחים. הכי גרסינן: יג] שנזכר פגול. גיליון וקשה להר"ם דהכי לא דריש בזבחים אלא מפיק חוץ לזמנו מביום השלישי וחוץ למקומו מפיק מפיגול יהיה ולא ירצה לדרשה אחרינא כהרצאת כשר כך הרצאת פסול ולא יחשב שלא יערב בו מחשבות אחרות. ע"כ תו"ח: יד] וא"ת למה לי האי טעמא תיפוק: טו] תיבת בראשו נמחק: טז] הותר מכללו גליון והר"ם מפרש דחוץ לזמנו דתודה וחטאת יש להם הכשר בשלמים וחוץ למקומו דחטאת הוכשרו בקדשים קלים הנאכלים בכל העיר: יז] רבי. שמעון כל: יח] שלא לשמו: יט] אימא עון יוצא. תימה אמאי לא פריך מעון זר שהותר בבמה וי"ל דכי היכא דדרשינן עון דלפני השם מרצה כמו כן [illegible] כ] [illegible] כא] [illegible] כב] אית להו להדדי וי"ל דשאני אונן דגלי קרא [illegible] למימר קרבן מפסיל ובעלים מתכפרים [illegible] כתיב מיום: כד] והא הכא. דמדאורייתא מרצה ציץ:

מו א מיי' פכ"ג מהל' כלים הל"י:
מז ב מיי' פי"א מהל' פסה"מ הל' כו:
מח ג ד מיי' שם הל' כז:

א] מִדְרָס אוַעֲשָׂאוֹ וִילוֹן – טָהוֹר מִן הַמִּדְרָס, אֲבָל טָמֵא מַגַּע מִדְרָס. ב] א"ר יוֹסֵי: (א) בְּאֵיזֶה מִדְרָס נָגַע זֶה? אֶלָּא, שֶׁאִם נָגַע בּוֹ הַזָּב – טָמֵא מַגַּע הַזָּב. כִּי נָגַע בּוֹ הַזָּב מִיהָא טָמֵא, וַאֲפִי' לְבַסּוֹף, (ב)(כְּטָמֵא מִדְרָס וְאח"כ מַגַּע הַזָּב.) רש"ק מ"ז (ג) אַמַּאי? לֵימָא: שָׁבַע לֵיהּ טוּמְאָה! א"ל: וּמִמַּאי דְּהַאי "שֶׁאִם נָגַע בּוֹ הַזָּב" לְבָתַר מִדְרָס? דִּילְמָא מִקַּמֵּי מִדְרָס, דְּהָוְיָא טוּמְאָה חֲמוּרָה עַל טוּמְאָה קַלָּה, אֲבָל הָכָא דְּאִידֵי וְאִידֵי טוּמְאָה קַלָּה – לָא! אֶלָּא מִסֵּיפָא: מוֹדֶה רַבִּי יוֹסֵי ג] בִּשְׁנֵי סְדִינִין הַמְקוּפָּלִין וּמוּנָּחִין זֶה עַל זֶה, וְיָשַׁב זָב עֲלֵיהֶן – שֶׁהָעֶלְיוֹן טָמֵא מִדְרָס, וְהַתַּחְתּוֹן טָמֵא מִדְרָס וּמַגַּע מִדְרָס; ד] וְאַמַּאי? לֵימָא: שָׁבַע לֵיהּ טוּמְאָה! הָתָם בְּבַת אַחַת, הָכָא בָּזֶה אַחַר זֶה. °אָמַר רָבָא: עִשָּׂרוֹן בשֶׁחִלְּקוֹ, וְאָבַד אֶחָד מֵהֶן וְהִפְרִישׁ אַחֵר תַּחְתָּיו, וְנִמְצָא הָרִאשׁוֹן, וַהֲרֵי שְׁלָשְׁתָּן מוּנָּחִין בְּבִיסָא; נִטְמָא אָבוּד – אָבוּד וְרִאשׁוֹן מִצְטָרְפִין, מוּפְרָשׁ אֵין מִצְטָרֵף; נִטְמָא מוּפְרָשׁ – מוּפְרָשׁ וְרִאשׁוֹן מִצְטָרְפִין, אָבוּד אֵין מִצְטָרֵף; נִטְמָא רִאשׁוֹן – שְׁנֵיהֶם מִצְטָרְפִין. אַבַּיֵי אָמַר: אֲפִילּוּ נִטְמָא אֶחָד מֵהֶן נַמִּי – שְׁנֵיהֶם מִצְטָרְפִין, מ"ט? כּוּלְּהוּ בְּנֵי בִיקְתָא דַּהֲדָדֵי נִינְהוּ. גוְכֵן לְעִנְיַן קְמִיצָה, קָמַץ מִן הָאָבוּד – שְׁיָרָיו וְרִאשׁוֹן נֶאֱכָלִין, מוּפְרָשׁ אֵינוֹ נֶאֱכָל; קָמַץ מִן הַמּוּפְרָשׁ – שְׁיָרָיו וְרִאשׁוֹן נֶאֱכָלִין, אָבוּד אֵינוֹ נֶאֱכָל; קָמַץ מִן רִאשׁוֹן – שְׁנֵיהֶם אֵינָן נֶאֱכָלִין. אַבַּיֵי אָמַר: אֲפִילּוּ קָמַץ מֵאֶחָד מֵהֶן – שְׁנֵיהֶן אֵינָן נֶאֱכָלִין, מ"ט? כּוּלְּהוּ נַמִּי בְּנֵי בִיקְתָא דַּהֲדָדֵי נִינְהוּ. מַתְקִיף לָהּ רַב פַּפָּא: וְשִׁירַיִם דִּידֵיהּ מִיהָא נֶאֱכָלִין? ה] הָא אִיכָּא דַּנְקָא דְּקוֹמֶץ דְּלָא קָרֵיב! [illegible] רַב יִצְחָק בְּרֵיהּ דְּרַב מְשַׁרְשְׁיָא: וְקוֹמֶץ גּוּפֵיהּ הֵיכִי קָרֵיב? הָא אִיכָּא תִּלְתָּא חוּלִּין! * (ד) רַב אַשִׁי דאָמַר: קוֹמֶץ ו] בְּדַעְתָּא דְּכֹהֵן תַּלְיָא מִילְּתָא, וְכֹהֵן כִּי קָמֵיץ – אַעִשָּׂרוֹן קָא קָמֵיץ.§ מתני'

ועשאו וילון טהור מן המדרס. וכגון דעבד ביה שינוי מעשה, כדאמר בפרק "במה אשה" (שבת ד' נח:) דאין עולין מטומאתן אלא בשינוי מעשה. ובמסכת כלים בפרק "הכרים" (מ"ו) מפרש איזו היא שינוי מעשה, דתנן: סדין שהוא טמא מדרס, עשאה וילון – טהור מן המדרס אבל טמאה טמא מת. מאימתי טהרתה? ב"ש אומרים: משיתפר, וב"ה אומרים: משיקשר, ר"ע אומר: משיקבע. (ט) וכי באיזה מדרס נגע זה. לפי מה שהוא ר"ל דלא אמרינן שבע ליה טומאה, צ"ל דאיירי בבגד שלא נקפל משדרס עליו הזב. ועוד צ"ל דלא מיירי בשדרס עליו ברגלו ערום או נעול, או בדבר שמטמא מדרס, דא"כ אתיא ליה מדרס ומגע בבת אחת, ובבת אחת לא אמרינן שבע ליה טומאה, כדמסקי'. אלא כגון שיש פשוטי כלי עץ מפסיקין, או דברים שאין מטמאין מדרס. כי נגע בו הזב מיהא טמא ואפילו לבסוף כו'. לפי מה דס"ל לאביי שאין חילוק בין בת אחת לזה אחר זה, כדמוכח בסמוך כשבא לדקדק מסיפא, יש לתמוה: דמתנא קמא היה לו לדקדק דלא אמרינן שבע ליה טומאה, דקאמר: אבל טמא מגע מדרס, ופירושו: בבת אחת באתה לו טומאת מדרס וטומאת מגע, לפי שנוגע בעצמו. דת"ק דרבי יוסי הוא ר"מ דקסבר: טומאת בית הסתרים מטמא, כדאשכחן בפ' "בהמה המקשה" (חולין דף עג:) דפליגי כי האי גוונא בשלשה על שלשה שנחלק! וי"ל: דלכך דייק מר' יוסי, שלא תאמר: הא דפליג עליה ר' יוסי וקאמר (י) "באיזה מדרס נגע זה" – היינו משום דס"ל דאמרינן שבע ליה טומאה. וא"ת: בס"פ "העור והרוטב" (שם דף קכח:) גבי *(חתיכת כזית אבר) מן החי, דאמר: חישב עליו ואח"כ חתכו – טמא, לפי שירד עליו תורת טומאת אוכלין כשחישב עליו. ואמאי? נימא שבע ליה טומאה, שהוא טמא טומאת אבר מן החי החמורה! וי"ל: דאיכא נמי חומרא בטומאת אוכלין, שמועיל לטמא טומאה בפחות מכביצה אוכלין וזה משלימו לכביצה. *ואין לתרץ דהאי דחישב עליו ואח"כ חתכו טמא – משום דטומאת בית הסתרים טז] [לא] מטמיא, [דהתם אמרי' דמטמיא] דמוקי לה כר"מ. ומיהו היא גופא תימה: ואמאי לא אתיא כרבי יוסי, ונימא דטמא משום דמקבל טומאה משעת פרישתו, כדאמרינן בפרק "בהמה המקשה" (שם דף עג:) בשלש על שלש יז] (הבגד) הבאות מבגד גדול, דבשעת פרישתן מאביהן מקבלות טומאה מאביהן! וי"ל: ד"בהעור והרוטב" (שם דף קכח:) מיירי אפילו אין נשאר באבר כדי להעלות ארוכה כשחותכו, דלא מטמיא. ומיהו קשה בסוף "כיצד צולין" (פסחים דף פה:) גבי יוצא גזרו ביה טומאה או לא גזרו, דקאמר: ת"ש, אבר שיצא מקצתו חותך כו', ואי אמרת גזרו ביה רבנן טומאה, כי חתיך ליה מאי הוי? הא קא מטמא ליה! ומשני: טומאת בית הסתרים היא ולא מטמא. ואכתי, הא קא מטמא בשעת פרישתו! ואין לומר דליכא כשיעור במה שבחוץ, דא"כ לא הוה צריך לטעמא דבית הסתרים, ואליבא דרבינא הוא דמשני הכי אחר כך. ויש לומר: דמיירי בפסחים (דף פה.) וב"העור והרוטב" (חולין דף קכח:) יח] בניתזים (כ) בעל כרחו, דהא בכריתות בפרק "אמרו לו" (דף טו:) מוכח דלא מקבל טומאה בשעת פרישתו, גבי אבר המדולדל באדם. ומיהו לא מסתברא דמיתוקם ההיא *)דפסחים בניתזין בעל כרחו, דהא קתני: חותך עד שמגיע לעצם וקולף עד שמגיע לפרק וחותך. ושמא כשחותך בסכין לא מקבל טומאה בשעת פרישתו, לפי שהסכין מפריש בין זה לזה. א"נ, מחתך בסכין מעט ומשליך וחוזר ומחתך מעט [ומשליך] עד שמחתך את כולו, שאינו נוגע עכשיו בבת אחת. וכן מפרש בהדיא בירושלמי, במחתך כל שהוא ומשליך. ואם תאמר: אמאי איצטריך לשנויי ב"העור והרוטב" (שם דף קכט.) דאתיא כר"מ? לימא דחיבורי אוכלין כמאן דמיפרתי דמו, כדקאמר רבינא בפרק "בהמה המקשה" (חולין דף עג:) ובפרק "כיצד צולין" (פסחים דף פה.)! ויש לומר: דההיא סוגיא דלא כרבינא. א"נ, לא אמרינן חיבורי אוכלין כמאן דמיפרתי דמו אלא בדבר העומד ליחתך, כי יט] ההיא (ל) דבשר שילא והוליא עובר את ידו, ודומיא דידות הכלים שעתיד לקצצן. ואם תאמר: בפרק "ואלו קשרים" (שבת דף קיב:) ובפרק ב' דעירובין (דף כד.) דאמרינן: סנדל שנפסקה אחת מאזניו ותיקנה – טמא מדרס, נפסקה שניה ותיקנה – טהור מן המדרס אבל טמא מגע מדרס. ופריך: מאי שנא ראשונה – דהא קיימא

*) דפסחים בניתזין בכל כחו רש"ק ול"ק

מִדְרָס. שֶׁשָּׁכַב עָלָיו זָב. וַעֲשָׂאוֹ וִילוֹן. פְּרָשׂוֹ לִפְנֵי הַפֶּתַח וּקְבָעוֹ שָׁם. טָהוֹר מִן הַמִּדְרָס. וְלֹא יְטַמֵּא עוֹד אָדָם, ז] שֶׁהֲרֵי אֵין עָשׂוּי לְמִדְרָס, וְכָל שֶׁאֵינוֹ רָאוּי לְמִדְרָס – אֵינוֹ טָמֵא מִדְרָס, דְּאָמְרִינַן בְּמַסֶּכֶת חֲגִיגָה (דף כג:): מִי שֶׁמְּיוּחָד לִישִׁיבָה, יָצָא זֶה שֶׁאוֹמֵר לוֹ עֲמוֹד וְנַעֲשֶׂה מְלַאכְתֵּנוּ. אֲבָל טָמֵא מַגַּע מִדְרָס לְטַמֵּא אוֹכָלִים וּמַשְׁקִים *כְּמִי שֶׁנָּגַע בְּמִדְרָס. אֶלָּא. לְהָכִי מְהַנֵּי לֵיהּ וִילוֹן, שֶׁאִם נָגַע בּוֹ זָב קוֹדֶם שֶׁעֲשָׂאוֹ וִילוֹן, וְהָיוּ עָלָיו שְׁתֵּי טוּמְאוֹת, מִדְרָס וּמַגָּע – עַכְשָׁיו טָהוֹר מִן הַמִּדְרָס מִלְּטַמֵּא אָדָם אוֹ כֵּלִים, וְנִשְׁאֲרָה עָלָיו ח] תּוֹרַת מַגָּע לְאוֹכָלִין וּמַשְׁקִין. כִּי נָגַע בּוֹ זָב מִיהָא טָמֵא. נַמִּי טוּמְאַת מַגָּע (ה). אֲפִי' לְבַסּוֹף, לְאַחַר שֶׁנִּטְמָא מִדְרָס, חָלָה ט] טוּמְאַת מַגָּע לְהַאי עִנְיָנָא, שֶׁכְּשֶׁיַּעֲשֶׂנּוּ וִילוֹן וְיִטַּהֵר מִן הַמִּדְרָס – תָּחוּל עָלָיו טוּמְאַת מַגָּע. וְאַמַּאי נֵימָא הָא שָׁבַע לֵיהּ. טוּמְאַת מִדְרָס. דִּילְמָא מְקַמֵּי מִדְרָס. נָגַע בּוֹ, וְאַחַ"כ דָּרַס עָלָיו. דְּהָכָא לֵיכָּא לְמִיפְרַךְ: הָא שָׁבַע לֵיהּ י] (ו), מִשּׁוּם דְּטוּמְאָה *אַחֲרִינָא חֲמוּרָה מִן הָרִאשׁוֹנָה וְחָלָה עָלֶיהָ. אֲבָל הָכָא גַּבֵּי עֶשְׂרוֹנוֹת, דְּאִידֵי וְאִידֵי רִאשׁוֹנָה וּשְׁנִיָּה קַלָּה הִיא, דְּבֵין זוֹ וּבֵין זוֹ טוּמְאַת אוֹכָלִין הִיא, וְלָא חָיְילָא שְׁנִיָּה כְּלָל. אֶלָּא מִסֵּיפָא. נָפְקָא דְּלָא אָמַר שָׁבַע לָהּ טוּמְאָה. תַּחְתּוֹן *טוּמְאַת מִדְרָס. שֶׁאֲפִילּוּ י' מַפָּעוֹת תַּחְתָּיו – כּוּלָּן *מְטַמְּאוֹת מִדְרָס. (ז) מַגַּע מִדְרָס. מִשּׁוּם דְּנָגַע בָּעֶלְיוֹן. וְנָפְקָא מִינַּהּ, שֶׁכְּשֶׁיַּעֲשֶׂנּוּ לַתַּחְתּוֹן וִילוֹן וְיִטַּהֵר מִן הַמִּדְרָס – עֲדַיִין יְהֵא טָמֵא טוּמְאַת מַגָּע. לֵימָא שָׁבַע לֵיהּ. טוּמְאַת מִדְרָס. הָכָא בָּזֶה אַחַר זֶה. גַּבֵּי חֲצִי עֶשְׂרוֹנִים. אָבוּד וְרִאשׁוֹן מִצְטָרְפִין. וְנִטְמָא הָרִאשׁוֹן מֵחֲמַת זֶה בְּצֵירוּף כְּלִי. מוּפְרָשׁ. שֶׁהִפְרִישׁ תַּחַת זֶה – אֵינוֹ מִצְטָרֵף לִפְסוֹל עִמּוֹ, שֶׁהֲרֵי לֹא הוּפְרַשׁ ע"מ לְהִצְטָרֵף עִמּוֹ יא] *הָאָבוּד, שֶׁהֲרֵי שְׁנֵיהֶם יב] אֲבוּדִים. בְּנֵי בִּיקְתָא דַּהֲדָדֵי. בְּנֵי בַּיִת אֶחָד הֵן, שֶׁכּוּלָּן מִכֹּחַ מִנְחָה יג] *אֶחָד בָּאוּ. בִּיקְתָא = בֵּי עַקְתָּא, *בַּיִת נֵר. קָמַץ מִן הָרִאשׁוֹן שְׁנֵיהֶם הָאֲחֵרִים אֵין נֶאֱכָלִין. שֶׁהֲרֵי שְׁנֵיהֶם נִזְקָקִין לְקוּמְצוֹ שֶׁל רִאשׁוֹן, וְקוֹמֶץ אֵינוֹ מַתִּיר אֶלָּא עִשָּׂרוֹן אוֹתוֹ רש"ק חֲצִי שֶׁהוּפְרַשׁ מִמֶּנּוּ וְאֶחָד מִן הַחֲצָאִין הַלָּלוּ, וְכֵיוָן דְּלֹא יָדַע אֵיזֶהוּ – יד] לֹא נֶאֱכָל לֹא זֶה וְלֹא זֶה. וְשִׁירַיִ' דִּידֵיהּ. דְּאוֹתוֹ חֲצִי עִשָּׂרוֹן רִאשׁוֹן שֶׁהוּפְרַשׁ מִמֶּנּוּ הַקּוֹמֶץ. וְהָא אִיכָּא דַּנְקָא דְּקוֹמֶץ דְּלָא קָרֵיב. דְּהָא תִּילְתָּא דְּהַאי קוֹמְצָא אֵינוֹ טו] חָשׁוּב (ח), מֵחֲמַת חֲצִי עִשָּׂרוֹן הַשְּׁלִישִׁי הוּא, שֶׁהֲרֵי שְׁלָשְׁתָּן הוּזְקְקוּ לְקוֹמֶץ זֶה. הִילְכָּךְ הָוֵי הַאי קוֹמֶץ חָסֵר תִּילְתָּא, דְּמָטֵי דַּנְקָא לְכָל חַד מִשְּׁנֵי חֲצָאֵי עֶשְׂרוֹנִים הַמַּכְשִׁירִים אֶת הַמִּנְחָה. דַּנְקָא = שְׁתוּת. דַּנְקָא קוֹמֶץ לְכָל חֲצִי עִשָּׂרוֹן מִן הַשְּׁנַיִם שֶׁהַמִּנְחָה נִכְשֶׁרֶת בָּהֶן. אָמַר רַב אַשִׁי. הָנָךְ תַּרְתֵּי פִּירְכֵי לָאו פִּירְכֵי, דְּכֵיוָן דְּלֹא קָמַץ אֶלָּא מִן הָאֶחָד, קְמִיצַת הַמִּנְחָה בְּדַעְתָּא דְּכֹהֵן תַּלְיָא, וְכֹהֵן כִּי קָמַץ – אַדַּעְתָּא דְּעִשָּׂרוֹן חַד הוּא דְּקָמַץ. הִילְכָּךְ קוֹמֶץ קָרֵב, שְׁיָרֵי רִאשׁוֹן נֶאֱכָלִין, וְהַשְּׁנַיִם אֵינָן נֶאֱכָלִין, מִשּׁוּם דְּאֵין לַעֲמוֹד עַל סוֹפוֹ אֵיזֶה מֵהֶן נִצְטָרֵף עִם הָרִאשׁוֹן בְּדַעַת הַכֹּהֵן לִהְיוֹת נִיתַּר בַּקּוֹמֶץ. מתני'

כמו נ"ק
נ"ל אחרונה
נ"ל טמא
טמאות מדרס ומגע מדרס והד"א נ"ק
האבוד הס"ד והשאר יש למחוק נ"ק
אחת נ"ק
[שבת עז:]

[החותך כזית בשר מאבר]
[יתכן להיות אמר רב אשי וכ"ה ברש"י על נכון]
ואפשר עוד לתרץ כו' הסתרים מטמיא דמוקי כו' נ"ק
רש"ק
נ"ק מ"ז

גליון הש"ס

גמ' אמר רבא עשרון שחלקו ואבד א' מהן. עי' לקמן דף פ' ע"ב תוס' ד"ה כולהו:

הגהות הב"ח

(א) גמ' א"ר יוסי וכי באיזה מדרס: (ב) שם בטמא מדרס ואח"כ נ"ב ר"ל באופן זה נטמא: (ג) שם ואמאי לימא: (ד) שם אמר רב אשי קומץ: (ה) רש"י ד"ה כי נגע וכו' ואפילו וכו' חלה עליו טומאת מגע: (ו) ד"ה דילמא וכו' הא שבע ליה טומאה משום: (ז) ד"ה ומגע מדרס וכו' מגע מדרס הס"ד: (ח) ד"ה והא איכא וכו' דמחמת: (ט) תום' ד"ה ועשאו וכו' משיקבע הס"ד ואח"כ מ"ה וכי באיזה וכו' שמטמא מדרס דאם לא כן אתיא ליה: (י) ד"ה כי נגע וכו' וקאמר וכי באיזה: (כ) בא"ד בניתזין בכל כחו דהא: (ל) בא"ד בדבר העומד ליחתך כי ההיא דאבר שילא מקלו והוליא עובר:

שיטה מקובצת

א] מדרס ועשאו וילון טהור מן המדרס. אליבא דרבי (יהודה) [מאיר] אבל טמא מגע מדרס משום דנוגעת כל נימא ונימא שהיא טמאה מדרס בחברתה והוה ליה מגע מדרס לטמא אוכלין ומשקין ואע"ג דסלקא מיניה טומאת מדרס שלא יטמא טומאה חמורה לטמא אדם וכלים הואיל ואינו מיוחד למדרס: ב] א"ר יוסי. וכי באיזה מדרס וכו' ואי משום שנוגעת כל נימא ונימא בחברתה טומאת בית הסתרים אינו מטמא: ג] בשני סדינין המקופלין כו'. וצ"ל דמיירי כשיש אויר מפסיק בין עליון לתחתון דאי במקופלין זה ע"ג זה בלא הפסק אויר נמצא שהכביד עצמו על שניהם יחד וא"כ העליון נמי היה לו ליטמא מגע מדרס בבת אחת כמו בתחתון אבל כשיש אויר מפסיק ביניהם נמצא דנחת מדרס על העליון קודם שיגע בתחתון ותו לא חלה ביה מגע מדרס דהוי ליה טומאה קלה על החמורה: ד] ואמאי נימא שבע ליה טומאה חמורה על התחתון ולא יחות עליה תו טומאת מגע מדרס וא"ת לפי סברת המקשה דלא מחלק בין בבאין בבת אחת לבאין בזה אחר זה תיקשי ליה היא גופיה העליון אמאי אינו טמא מגע מדרס משום דנוגע בתחתון וי"ל שלעולם היה יודע המקשה שיש לנו לחלק בין בת אחת לזה אחר זה לגבי דלא ירד בזה אחר זה קלה על החמורה והכא היה מקשה כיון דלא אמרינן שבע ליה טומאה בקלה וחמורה בבת אחת הכי נמי לא הל"ל שבע ליה טומאה בקלה על קלה אפי' בזה אחר זה ומשני דאין לדמות כלל בת אחת לזה אחר זה דנהי דלא אמרינן שבע ליה טומאה בבת אחת בזה אחר זה יש לנו לומר שבע ליה טומאה וא"ת לעיל דמקשה לימא שבע ליה טומאה אפי' בזה אחר זה ב) לגבי כי נגע ביה הזב לבסוף תיקשי ליה מסיפא עליון אמאי אינו טמא נמי מגע מדרס לפי שנוגע בתחתון וי"ל דאה"נ דמצי לאקשויי מיניה וא"ת אדמקשה ליה מסיפא דלא אמרינן שבע ליה טומאה תיקשי ליה מרישא גופיה ממילתיה דת"ק דאמר אבל טמא מגע מדרס אלמא לא אמרינן שבע ליה טומאה ותירץ ר' שמעון מייזילא דפשיטא ליה דטומאה דאתיא מגופיה כגון במילתא דת"ק לא אמרינן דשבע ליה טומאה: ה] הא איכא תילתא דקומץ דלא קריב שהרי מחמת חצי העשרון הוא שהרי שלשתן הוזקקו לקומץ זה הילכך הוי האי קומץ חסר תילתא ל"א הא איכא דנקא והיא היא דהיינו דנקא לכל אחד ואחד משני חצאי עשרון הצריכין למנחה והיינו תילתא לשניהן יחד: ו] בדעתא דכהן. עי' תוס' לקמן דף עו ע"ב: וכהן כי קמיץ אעשרון קא קמיץ. וא"ת א"כ היכי מפסלא מנחה משום יתר ג) משום דדילמא קמיץ מעשרון שלא הופרש עמו ואומר הר"ל דהכא שאני שחצאי העשרונים מבוררין ואינן נוגעין דיכול הכהן להתכוין מה שהוא רואה אבל בנתערב כיון דאינו יכול לבררם זה מזה דעתו אינו מועיל כלום והשתא ניחא נמי הא דאמרינן באלו מנחות [דף עו ע"ב] ריבה במדת עשרונו פסולה ולא אמרינן בדעתו דכהן תליא מילתא דכיון דלא בריר עשרון דידיה מעולם לאו בדעתא דכהן תליא מילתא: ז] אדם וכלים שהרי: ח] עליו טומאת מגע: ט] חלה עליו טומאת: י] שבע ליה טומאה משום דטומאה אחרונה חמורה: יא] עם האבוד. למנחה הס"ד ומה"ד מופרש וראשון מצטרפים שהרי חבירים היו הס"ד ומה"ד נטמא הראשון שניהם האחרים מצטרפין: יב] שהרי שניהם חביריו הס"ד: יג] מנחה אחת באים הס"ד: יד] איזהו אינו נאכל תיבת לא ל"ש: טו] חשוב שהרי מחמת: טז] דטומאת בית הסתרים מטמיא דמוקי: יז] בשלש על שלש הבאות ותיבת הבגד נמחק: יח] בניתזין בכל כחו: יט] כי ההיא דאבר שיצא מקצתו:

א) ר"ל לאביי דמוכיח דלא אמרינן שבע ליה טומאה אפי' בזה אחר זה תקשה ליה מסיפא וכו'. ב) ר"ל והתם נמי נימא דלא קמיץ רק על העשרון שהופרש למנחה זו ולא על התערובת.

והניחו בביסא, ונגע טבול יום באחד מהן, מהו? כי *תנן אכלי מצרף מה שבתוכו לקדש – ה"מ היכא דנגעי בהדדי, אבל היכא דלא נגעי בהדדי לא, או דילמא ל"ש? אמר להו איהו: מי תנן "כלי מחבר"? "כלי מצרף" תנן, בכל דהו. הושיט אחד לביניהן, מהו? א"ל: *גצריך לכלי – כלי מצרפו, אין צריך לכלי – אין כלי מצרפו. הושיט טבול יום את אצבעו ביניהן, מהו? אמר להו: דאין לך דבר שמטמא מאוירו אלא כלי חרס בלבד. הדר איהו בעא מינייהו: מהו הלקמוץ מזה על זה? א] צירוף דאורייתא או דרבנן? אמרו לו: זו לא שמענו, כיוצא בו שמענו, דתנן: שני מנחות שלא נקמצו ונתערבו זו בזו, אם יכול לקמוץ מזו בפני עצמה ומזו בפני עצמה – כשירות, ואם לאו – פסולות; כי יכול לקמוץ מיהא כשירות, ב] אמאי? הך דמערב הא לא נגע! אמר רבא: דלמא *בגושין המחולקין העשויין כמסרק. מאי הוי עלה? אמר רבא: ת"ש, דתניא: °"והרים ממנו" – מן המחובר, °שלא יביא עשרון בשני כלים ויקמוץ; הא בכלי אחד דומיא דשני כלים – קמיץ. א"ל אביי: דילמא שני כלים ה"ד? כגון קפיזא בקבא, דאע"ג דעריבי מעילאי, כיון דמיפסק מחיצתא דקפיזא ג] מתתא; *הא כלי אחד דומיא דב' כלים ה"ד? כגון עריבתה ד] של תרנגולין, ואע"ג דמיפסקן מחיצתא – הא נגיע; אבל הכא דלא נגיע כלל תיבעי לך! בעי רבי ירמיה: ה] צירוף כלי וחיבור מים, מהו? כי תנן כלי מצרף מה שבתוכו לקדש – ה"מ דגואי, אבל דבראי – לא, או דילמא כיון דמחבר מחבר? ואם תימצי לומר יכיון דמחבר מחבר, חיבור מים וצירוף כלי ו] ונגע טבול יום מבחוץ, מהו? כי תנן כלי מצרף – ה"מ דנגע מגואי, אבל מבראי – לא, או דילמא לא שנא? זתיקו. § בעי רבא: חעשרון שחלקו, ונטמא אחד מהן והניחו בביסא, וחזר טבול יום ונגע באותו טמא, מהו? °מי אמרינן שבע (א)לו טומאה, או לא? אמר ליה אביי: ומי אמרינן שבע ליה טומאה? והתנן: *סדין טמא מדרס

רש"י

והניחו בביסא. ואלו שני החלאין אין נוגעין זה ז] לזה. מהו. מי נטמא חבירו או לא? כי תנן. בפרק "חומר בקודש" (חגיגה דף כ:): הכלי מצרף מה שבתוכו לקדש, שאם נגע טבול יום במקצתו פסל את כולו. ה"מ דנגעי אהדדי כו'. להכי נקט טבול יום, משום דאין טומאתו חמורה לעשות ראשון ושני. דאי טומאה אחרת, ל"ל צירוף? הא מטמא אותו הטמא את הכלי, והכלי מטמא את השאר. מי תנן כלי מחבר (ב). הוה משמע דנגעי אהדדי, והכלי מחברם כאילו הוי חד, ואם נטמא זה נטמא זה. "מצרף" משמע דאין נוגעין, וזה מצרפן ח] להיות אחד. הושיט. חצי עשרון אחד לבין הנך ט] חצי עשרון. מהו. אם נגע טבול יום בזה, מהו שיטמא אותן י] שניים? אין צריך לכלי. כגון האי חצי עשרון שלישי, דאין צריך לכלי, דהא אינו מצטרף עם אלו למנחה אחת – אין הכלי מצרפו, וטהורים הראשונים. הושיט טבול יום כו'. באוירן, ולא נגע לא בהן ולא בכלי. צירוף כלי דאורייתא. יא] דאמרינן (חגיגה דף כג:): "כף אחת" – הכתוב עשאו לכל מה שבכף אחת, לא שנא לחומרא כגון טומאה, ול"ש לקולא כגון קמיצה, דהוי כאילו נוגעין וקמיצה מעלייתא היא. או דרבנן. ולחומרא ולא לקולא. מזו בפני עצמה. משמע שעומד מזו בצד הכלי כדי קומץ שאינו מעורב, וכן יב] בזו. הך דמערב הא לא נגע. בקומץ, וקתני: כשרות, אלמא צירוף דאורייתא. אמר רבא דילמא. לאו דקאי קומץ בפני עצמו יג]. *בגושין המחולקין העשויין כמסרק. גופי המנחה מחולקין מראש האחד, מזו כדי קומץ ומזו כדי קומץ, אבל בראש האחד נוגעין, כמסרק זה שמצד אחד מחובר ומצד אחד שיניו מפוזרות. מאי הוי עלה. דשני חלאים מחולקים, מהו לקמוץ מזה על זה משום צירוף כלי? והרים ממנו. בקומצו. דומיא דב' כלים. כגון דאין נוגעין זה בזה. כגון קפיזא בקבא. שחקק מדה קטנה בתוך מדה גדולה, ונותן בפנימי חצי עשרון וחציו בחיצון. דאע"ג דעריבי שני החלאין מעילאי בגודש הכלי. כיון דמפסקי מחיצתא מתתאי. דאין עירוב הגודש עירוב, הואיל ואינו יד] באויר הכלי. ובהא דייקינן: הא כלי אחד דומיא דהאי שהוא בשני כלים כשר. כגון עריבת. טו] *ארובה של תרנגולין, ומחיצה נמוכה באמצעית כדי לחלוק בין מים למורסן, ואותה מחיצה נמוכה ואינה מגעת לשפת העריבה. הילכך לאו הפסק הוא, טז] דנגעי למעלה מן המחיצה שני החלאין באויר הכלי. אבל הכא גבי ביסא דחלוקין הן לגמרי – לא. צירוף כלי וחיבור מים מהו. כלומר, חצי עשרון שנטמא בצירוף כלי, מהו שיטמא אחר בחיבור מים. כגון אם יש שני חצאי עשרון בכלי ואין נוגעין, וחצי עשרון יש חוץ לכלי, וחיבור מים כגון נצוק או צנור מחבר את של חוץ לכלי יז] ומה שבתוך הכלי. ונגע טומאה בזה שבכלי שאינו נוגע במים, ונטמא חבירו משום צירוף כלי. מהו. שיטמא את יח] של זה בחיבור מים. ה"מ דגואי. לאותו שבכלי מהני, ולא לשל חוץ. מחבר. וטמא החיצון. חיבור מים וצירוף כלי. כגון אם נטמא החיצון, ונטמא זה שבכלי בחיבור מים. מהו. שיטמא זה את האחר משום צירוף כלי? מי אמרינן דלא מהני צירוף אלא לטומאה שאירעה בתוך הכלי, או לא אמרינן? ונטמא אחד מהן. ואח"כ הניחם לשניהם בביסא ואין נוגעין, דלהכיא ודאי לא מהני צירוף שיחזור זה ויטמא את זה, שהרי לא היה הכלי בשעת טומאה. יט] *(אלא אם כן) חזר טבול יום ונגע בטמא, מהו שיקבל טומאה זו כדי לפסול חבירו? הא שבע ליה טומאה ראשונה, ולא יקבל עוד טומאה אחרת.

תוספות

קדשי קדשים" (דף נט.): כי סליק רב כהנא אשכחיה לר"ש ברבי דיתיב וקאמר משמיה דר' ישמעאל בר' יוסי: מזבח שנפגם כולו. אבל ודאי הא דשאל לו רבי יוחנן ספיקותיו היה בסוף ימיו, כשהיה ר' יוחנן ראש ישיבה, כדמוכח בסוף ב"ק (דף קיז:). ור"ת פי' ההיא דגיטין (דף פד:) רבי יוחנן לתלמידיו שמבבל היה אומר, כמו שמפרש "הא לן והא להו" בקידושין (דף כט:).

שאין צריך לכלי אין כלי מצרפו. בפרק בתרא דחגיגה (דף כג:) בגמרא: הכלי מצרף כן] מדכתיב "כף אחת", ומותיב רב כהנא מההיא דמוסיף ר"ע, ודייק מינה שהוא מדרבנן. ומשני ר"ש בן לקיש משום בר קפרא: לא נצרכא *לשירי מנחה דאורייתא, את שצריך לכלי הכלי מצרפו, ושאין צריך לכלי אין הכלי מצרפו, ואתו רבנן וגזור אפי' אין צריך לכלי כלי מצרפו. וזהו תימה, שפשוט לרב כהנא כל כך דאין כלי מצרף מה שאין צריך לכלי, *דלא משמע דפליג אההיא שינויא! ושמא סבר לה כההיא שינויא דרבה בר אבוה, דמשני התם: כשנצברו ע"ג קטבליא. א"נ, דוקא בשירי מנחה, שהיה כבר צריך לכלי – מצרף כלי מדרבנן, שלא יצא מקדושתו דקודש קמיצה. ולא דמי להכא, °דלא היה מעולם צריך לכלי.

צירוף דאורייתא או דרבנן. וא"ת: והא רב כהנא גופיה מדקדק בפרק בתרא דחגיגה (ג"ז שם) שהוא דרבנן, מההיא דהוסיף ר"ע! ויש לומר: דשמא מספקא ליה משום שינויא דהתם.

צירוף כלי וחיבור מים מהו. פי' בקונטרס: כלומר, חצי עשרון שנטמא בצירוף כלי, מהו שיטמא כא] בחיבור מים. כגון אם יש שני חצאי עשרון בכלי ואין נוגעין, וחצי עשרון יש חוץ לכלי, וחיבור מים כגון נצוק או צינור מחבר את אשר חוץ לכלי למה שבתוך הכלי, ונגע טומאה בזה שבכלי שאינו נוגע במים, ונטמא חבירו משום צירוף כלי, מהו שיטמא את זה שבחוץ בחיבור מים? ודבר תימה הוא לומר שמשקין מחברין אוכלין לקבל טומאה ולטמא אחרים! ועוד, שפירש שמתחברין ע"י נצוק. והלא אפי' למים עצמן קיימא לן במכשירין (פ"ה מ"ט) דאין נצוק חיבור לטומאה? וכעין פי' הקונטרס יש משנה אחת במסכת טהרות פרק שמיני (מ"ח): עריבה שהיה קטפרס (*ונצוק) מלמעלן, ומשקה טופח מלמטן וג' חתיכות כבילה אינן מצטרפות, ושתים מצטרפות. ור' יוסי אומר: אפי' שתים אינם מצטרפות, אא"כ היו רוללות משקה. ואם היה משקה עומד, אפי' כעין החרדל מצטרף. ר' דוסא אומר: האוכל פרור אינו מצטרף. ובתוספתא א) תניא: אתרוג שנפרך ותחבו בכוש או בקיסם – הרי זה אין חיבור, שאין חיבורי אדם חיבור. כב] עיסה שלשה במי פירות – טהורה, שאין לך דבר שמחבר את האוכלין אלא שבעה משקין. ודבר תימה הוא אם כג] לישת מי פירות אינה מועלת לחבר את הקמח! ושמא לשה לאו דוקא, אלא אורחא דמילתא נקט, כד] דבר שאדם לש במי פירות פעמים שמי פירות מחברין ב' חצאי זיתים עיסה כה] במשקין הבאין מזה לזה ב). ועשאו

א) פ"א דעוקצין ב) וע' תו' זבחים קה: ד"ה חיבור

עין משפט נר מצוה

מ א ג מיי' פי"ב מהל' אבות הטומאה הל"ז:
מא ג מיי' שם הל"ח:
מב ד מיי' פי"ג מהל' כלים הל"א:
מג ה מיי' פי"א מהל' פסה"מ הל' כג:
מד ו ז מיי' פי"ב מהל' אבות הטומאה הל"ט:
מה ח מיי' שם הל"י:

מסורת הש"ס

פסחים יט. חגיגה כ:
[חגיגה כז.]
בגופין נ"ק
ויקרא ו
לא נ"ק
בגופין נ"ק
כלים פכ"ז מ"ט [ופ"כ מ"ו]
נ"א עריבה
נ"א ואח"כ וגו' נ"ק אלא אח"כ וחזר
שם איתא אלא לשירי כו'
ולא נ"ק
[והכלק]

הגהות הב"ח

(א) גמ' שבע ליה טומאה או לא: (ב) רש"י ד"ה מי תנן כלי מחבר אי תנא כלי מחבר הוה משמע וכו' נטמא זה אבל מצרף משמע:

גליון הש"ס

גמ' שלא יביא עשרון בשני כלים. עי' לקמן דף ק ע"ב תוס' ד"ה אפשר: שם מי אמרי' שבע ליה טומאה. עיין שבת דף לא ע"ב תוס' ד"ה פתות: תוס' ד"ה שאין כו' דלא היה מעולם צריך לכלי. ע' בהר"ש פ"א דטהרות משנה ט:

שיטה מקובצת

א] צירוף עיין בתוס' לקמן דף עז ע"ב: ב] אמאי הא דמערב הא לא נגע. דס"ד שהן מעורבין כל כך מצד אחד שיהא הסולת של זו חולק מקצת חבירו ומכסהו שלא יהא כל העשרון של זו חולק מקצת חבירו ומכסהו שלא יהא כל העשרון של זו מחובר לעצמו והו"ל כגושין המחולקין בזה: ג] מתחתא: עשרון לא כלי אחד ותיבת כלי ליתא שם: ד] עריבת תרגולין

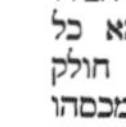

תיבות של ל"ש: ה] צירוף כלי וחיבור מים. כגון עשרון שנחלק לג' חלקים השני חלקים הן בביסא אחד ולא נגעי אהדדי אלא שהכלי מצרפן לטומאה וחלק שלישי הוא חוץ לביסא ומים של נצוק או משקה טופח מחבר החיצון לאחד מן החלקים שבתוך הביסא ונגע טבול יום בחלק הפנימי שאינו מחובר לחיצון ונטמא חבירו שבתוך הביסא כמותו מחמת צירוף הכלי ומבעיא ליה אם טמא האחר החיצון מפני חיבור המים והדר מבעיא ליה אם נגע טבול יום בחלק החיצון ונטמא הפנימי המחובר לו מהו שיטמא האחר שאינו מחובר לחיצון מפני צירוף הכלי: ו] וצירוף כלי [מאי] תיקו והשאר נמחק: ז] אין נוגעין זה בזה: ח] מצרפן כאילו הם אחד: ט] חצאי עשרון. ונתנו בינהם: י] אותן. השנים: יא] דאורייתא. דכתיב כף ותיבת כף נמחק: יב] וכן. מזו תיבת בזו נמחק: יג] בפני עצמו. אלא בגושין, והד"א: יד] ואינו. מערב באויר: טו] עריבה. תרנגולין ארוכה של: טז] הוא. דקא נגעי למעלה: יז] חוץ לכלי לאחר שבתוך תיבת וחוץ נמחק: יח] שיטמא זה את זה של חוץ: יט] בשעת טומאה אלא אם. עיין ברש"י בסמ"ש: כ] מצרף. יליף מדכתיב: כא] שיטמא. אחר בחבור: כב] עסה שלשה: כג] הוא אם. אין לישת מי פירות מועלת: כד] נקט. דכשאדם לש: כה] זיתים עיסה הבאין מזה ומזה במשקין:

לט א מיי' פי"ב מהל' מעה"ק הלכה יז ועי"ש ומיי' פ"ה מהלכות מצה הלכה כ טוש"ע א"ח סימן תנה סעיף ו:

רַבִּי יְהוּדָה בָּתַר חֲזוּתָא אָזֵיל, וְאִידִי וְאִידִי מִין בְּמִינוֹ הוּא! אֶלָּא אַלִּיבָּא דְּרַבִּי חִיָּיא, *דְּתָנֵי רַבִּי חִיָּיא: נְבֵילָה וּשְׁחוּטָה בְּטֵילוֹת זוֹ בָּזוֹ. רַבִּי חִיָּיא אַלִּיבָּא דְּמַאן? אִי אַלִּיבָּא דְּרַבָּנַן — הָא אָמְרִי: עוֹלִין הוּא דְּלָא מְבַטְּלִי אַהֲדָדֵי, הָא מִין בְּמִינוֹ בָּטֵיל! וְאִי אַלִּיבָּא דְּר' יְהוּדָה — *כָּל מִין בְּמִינוֹ לְר' יְהוּדָה לָא בָּטֵיל! א] לְעוֹלָם אַלִּיבָּא דְּר' יְהוּדָה, וְכִי קָא אָמַר ר' יְהוּדָה מִין בְּמִינוֹ לָא בָּטֵל — ה"מ הֵיכָא דְּאֶפְשָׁר לֵיהּ לְמֶיהֱוֵי כְּוָותֵיהּ, אֲבָל הֵיכָא דְּלָא אֶפְשָׁר לֵיהּ לְמֶיהֱוֵי כְּוָותֵיהּ — בָּטֵל; וּבְהָא קָא מִיפַּלְגִי, דְּרַב חִסְדָּא סָבַר: בָּתַר מְבַטֵּל אָזְלִינַן, וְר' חֲנִינָא סָבַר: בָּתַר בָּטֵל אָזְלִינַן. תְּנַן: שְׁתֵּי מְנָחוֹת שֶׁלֹּא נִקְמְצוּ וְנִתְעָרְבוּ זוֹ בְּזוֹ, אִם יָכוֹל לִקְמוֹץ מִזּוֹ בִּפְנֵי עַצְמָהּ וּמִזּוֹ בִּפְנֵי עַצְמָהּ — כְּשֵׁרוֹת, וְאִם לָאו — פְּסוּלוֹת. ב] וְהָא הָכָא, כֵּיוָן דְּקָמֵיץ לֵיהּ מֵחֲדָא — אִידָךְ הֲוָה לֵיהּ שִׁירַיִם, וְלָא קָא מְבַטְּלִי שִׁירַיִם לְטִיבְלָא; מַנִּי? אִי רַבָּנַן — הָא אָמְרִי: עוֹלִין הוּא דְּלָא מְבַטְּלִי הֲדָדֵי, הָא מִין בְּמִינוֹ בָּטֵל! אֶלָּא פְּשִׁיטָא רַבִּי יְהוּדָה; בִּשְׁלָמָא לְמ"ד: בָּתַר בָּטֵל אָזְלִינַן — בָּטֵל הָוֵי כִּמְבַטֵּל, דִּלְכִי קָמֵיץ מֵאִידָךְ — הָווּ לְהוּ שִׁירַיִם כִּי הָנֵי. ג] אֶלָּא לְמ"ד: בָּתַר מְבַטֵּל אָזְלִינַן, שִׁירַיִם מִי קָא הָווּ טִיבְלָא? ד] לֵימָא (אַלִּיבָּא דְּרַב חִסְדָּא) דְּלָא כְּרַבִּי חִיָּיא? הָתָם כִּדְר' זֵירָא, דְּא"ר זֵירָא: נֶאֶמְרָה *הַקְטָרָה בְּקוֹמֶץ ה] וְנֶאֶמְרָה הַקְטָרָה בְּשִׁירַיִם, מַה הַקְטָרָה הָאֲמוּרָה בְּקוֹמֶץ — אֵין הַקּוֹמֶץ מְבַטֵּל אֶת חֲבֵירוֹ, אַף הַקְטָרָה הָאֲמוּרָה בְּשִׁירַיִם — אֵין שִׁירַיִם מְבַטְּלִין אֶת הַקּוֹמֶץ. ת"ש: הַקּוֹמֶץ שֶׁנִּתְעָרֵב בְּמִנְחָה שֶׁלֹּא נִקְמְצָה — לֹא יַקְטִיר, וְאִם הִקְטִיר — זוֹ שֶׁנִּקְמְצָה עָלְתָה לַבְּעָלִים, וְזוֹ שֶׁלֹּא נִקְמְצָה לֹא עָלְתָה לַבְּעָלִים, וְלָא קָא מְבַטֵּיל לֵיהּ טִיבְלָא לְקוֹמֶץ; מַנִּי? אִי רַבָּנַן — הָא אָמְרִי: עוֹלִין הוּא דְּלָא מְבַטְּלִי הֲדָדֵי, הָא מִין בְּמִינוֹ בָּטֵיל! אֶלָּא פְּשִׁיטָא ר' יְהוּדָה; ו] בִּשְׁלָמָא לְמ"ד: בָּתַר מְבַטֵּל אָזְלִינַן — מְבַטֵּל הָוֵי כְּבָטֵל, דְּכָל פּוּרְתָּא חֲזֵי לְמִקְמַץ מִינֵּיהּ, ז] וְהָוֵי לֵיהּ מִין וּמִינוֹ, וּמִין בְּמִינוֹ לֹא בָּטֵל; אֶלָּא לְמ"ד: בָּתַר בָּטֵל אָזְלִינַן, קוֹמֶץ מִי קָא הָוֵי טִיבְלָא? ח] לֵימָא, דְּלָא כְּרַבִּי חִיָּיא? הָא נַמִי כִּדְרַבִּי זֵירָא. ת"ש: נִתְעָרֵב קוּמְצָהּ ט] בְּשִׁירַיִם שֶׁל חֲבֶרְתָּהּ — לֹא יַקְטִיר, וְאִם הִקְטִיר — עָלְתָה לַבְּעָלִים; וְהָא הָכָא דְּלָא הָוֵי מְבַטֵּל כְּבָטֵיל, *וְלָא קָא מְבַטְּלִי לֵיהּ שִׁירַיִם לְקוֹמֶץ, י] מַנִּי? אִי רַבָּנַן וכו'! יא] א"ר זֵירָא: נֶאֶמְרָה הַקְטָרָה בְּקוֹמֶץ וְנֶאֶמְרָה הַקְטָרָה בְּשִׁירַיִם, מַה הַקְטָרָה הָאֲמוּרָה בְּקוֹמֶץ — אֵין קוֹמֶץ מְבַטֵּל אֶת חֲבֵירוֹ, אַף הַקְטָרָה הָאֲמוּרָה בְּשִׁירַיִם — יב] אֵין שִׁירַיִם מְבַטְּלִין אֶת הַקּוֹמֶץ. ת"ש: אתִּיבְּלָהּ בְּקֶצַח, בְּשׁוּמְשְׁמִין, וּבְכָל מִינֵי תַבְלִין — כְּשֵׁרָה, מַצָּה הִיא אֶלָּא שֶׁנִּקְרֵאת מַצָּה מְתוּבֶּלֶת. קָא סָלְקָא דַּעְתָּךְ דְּאַפֵּישׁ לָהּ תַּבְלִין טְפֵי מִמַּצָּה; בִּשְׁלָמָא לְמַאן דְּאָמַר: בָּתַר בָּטֵל אָזְלִינַן — בָּטֵיל הָוֵי כִּמְבַטֵּל, דִּלְכִי מְעַפְּשָׁא — הָוֵי לָהּ כְּתַבְלִין; אֶלָּא לְמַאן דְּאָמַר: בָּתַר מְבַטֵּל אָזְלִינַן, יג] תַּבְלִין מִי קָא הָווּ מַצָּה? הָכָא בְּמַאי עָסְקִינַן — דְּלָא אַפֵּישׁ לָהּ תַּבְלִין, דְּרוּבָּהּ מַצָּה הִיא וְלָא בָּטְלָה. דַּיְקָא נַמִי, דְּקָתָנֵי: מַצָּה הִיא אֶלָּא שֶׁנִּקְרֵאת מַצָּה מְתוּבֶּלֶת, ש"מ. כִּי סָלֵיק רַב כָּהֲנָא, אַשְׁכְּחִינְהוּ לִבְנֵי רַבִּי חִיָּיא דְּיָתְבִי וְקָאָמְרִי: עִשָּׂרוֹן שֶׁחִלְּקוֹ

וְהִנִּיחוֹ

בָּתַר חֲזוּתָא אָזֵיל. יד] *דְּקָאָמְרִי' לְעֵיל: אֵין דָּם מְבַטֵּל דָּם, וְאע"ג שֶׁאִ"א לָהּ לִהְיוֹת *כָּזֶה. ה"נ אָזֵיל בָּתַר חֲזוּתָא, וְהוֹאִיל וּשְׁנֵיהֶם מִין טו] (*כָּשֵׁר) אֵין בְּטֵלִים זֶה בָּזֶה. בְּטֵלוֹת זוֹ בָּזוֹ. וְרַבִּי חֲנִינָא וְרַב חִסְדָּא מְפָרְשֵׁי טַעְמָא דְּרַבִּי חִיָּיא. וּבְהָא פְּלִיגִי, דְּרַב חִסְדָּא סָבַר: נְבֵילָה בִּשְׁחוּטָה א"ר חִיָּיא, וְלֹא שְׁחוּטָה בִּנְבֵילָה, וְרַבִּי חֲנִינָא מְפָרֵשׁ אִיפְּכָא. לְעוֹלָם אַלִּיבָּא דְּרַבִּי יְהוּדָה כו'. וְאִי קַשְׁיָא: גַּבֵּי דָּמִים דְּא"ר יְהוּדָה לְעֵיל: אֵין דַּם חוּלִּין מְבַטֵּל דַּם קָדָשִׁים! בִּשְׁלָמָא לְרַבִּי חֲנִינָא — הָכָא אֶפְשָׁר לְקָדָשִׁים *לִהְיוֹת (א) כִּמְבַטְּלִין כְּחוּלִּין, שֶׁכְּשֶׁיָּלִין לַיְלָה אֶחָד יֵצֵא מִקְּדוּשָּׁתוֹ כְּחוּלִּין. אֶלָּא לְרַב חִסְדָּא — *לִיבָּטֵל, דְּהָא אִי אֶפְשָׁר לְחוּלִּין לִהְיוֹת כְּקָדָשִׁים, וַה"ל מִין בְּשֶׁאֵינוֹ מִינוֹ טז] לְרַב חִסְדָּא, וְהָוֵי דְּלָא כְּר' חִיָּיא! הֲוָה לֵיהּ שִׁירַיִם. מַה שֶּׁנִּשְׁתַּיֵּיר מִמִּנְחָה זוֹ, וְלָא מְבַטְּלֵי שִׁירַיִם דְּהַךְ מִנְחָה לְטִיבְלָא דְּאִידָךְ מִנְחָה, מַה שֶּׁנִּתְעָרֵב שֶׁאֵין נִיכָּר, דְּלֶהֱוֵי לֵיהּ כְּמִנְחָה שֶׁחָסְרָה קוֹדֶם קְמִיצָה יז] *אֶלָּא תֶּיהֱוֵי קְמִיצָה לְאִידָךְ. עוֹלִין הוּא דְּלָא מְבַטְּלִין. וְשִׁירַיִם לָאו עוֹלִין נִינְהוּ. (ב) לֵימָא דְּלָא כְּרַבִּי חִיָּיא. דְּקָאָמַר: לָא אָמַר ר' יְהוּדָה דְּאֵין בָּטֵל יח] אִם לֹא הֵיכָא דְּאֶפְשָׁר לְמֵיהֱוֵי כְּוָותֵיהּ. יט] *וְאַמַּאי דְּלָא מְבַטֵּל לֵיהּ טִיבְלָא לַשִּׁירַיִם דְּתֶיהֱוֵי כ] כְּרִיבָּה סָלְתָּהּ — לָא מָצֵי לְמִפְרַךְ לְרַבִּי חֲנִינָא, דְּנֵימָא מֵהָכָא דְּבָתַר מְבַטֵּל אָזְלִינַן, דְּאִי בָּתַר בָּטֵל אָזְלִינַן שִׁירַיִם מִי הָווּ טִיבְלָא. דְּאִי נַמִי בָּתַר בָּטֵל אָזְלִינַן, וְטִיבְלָא מְבַטֵּל לַשִּׁירַיִם — לָא הֲוָה רִיבָּה סָלְתָּהּ, דְּבָטֵל כְּמַאן דְּלֵיתֵיהּ דָּמֵי, וְלָא אִייַתַּר לֵיהּ. הַקְטָרָה בְּשִׁירַיִם. "כִּי כָל שְׂאוֹר וְכָל דְּבַשׁ לֹא תַקְטִירוּ מִמֶּנּוּ אִשֶּׁה לַה'" (ויקרא ב), וְאָמְרִינַן: כָּל שֶׁמִּמֶּנּוּ לָאִשִּׁים, דְּהַיְינוּ שִׁירַיִם — הֲרֵי הוּא בְּבַל תַּקְטִירוּ. אַלְמָא אִיכָּא הַקְטָרָה בַּשִּׁירַיִם. אֵין הַקּוֹמֶץ מְבַטֵּל אֶת חֲבֵירוֹ. *דְּהָא אֲפִי' כא] רַבִּי יְהוּדָה מוֹדֶה, דְּלָא פָּלֵיג רַבִּי יְהוּדָה בְּמַתְנִי' אַנִּתְעָרֵב קוּמְצָהּ בְּקוֹמֶץ חֲבֵירְתָּהּ. הַקּוֹמֶץ שֶׁנִּתְעָרֵב. מַתְנִי' הִיא, וּכְבָר פֵּירַשְׁתִּיהָ לְמַעְלָה. דְּכָל פּוּרְתָּא וּפוּרְתָּא חֲזֵי לְמִקְמַץ מִינֵּיהּ. אִי לָא נִתְעָרֵב. לֹא יַקְטִיר. דְּאֵין מִצְוַת הַקְטָרָה אֶלָּא בְּקוֹמֶץ. תִּיבְּלָהּ בְּקֶצַח. לְעִיסַּת פֶּסַח. הָווּ לֵיהּ כְּתַבְלִין. כְּלוֹמַר, יָצְאָה מִתּוֹרַת מַצָּה בְּתַבְלִין. דַּיְקָא נַמִי דְּקָתָנֵי מַצָּה הִיא. אַלְמָא רוּבָּהּ מַצָּה. *בִּיסָא. כְּלִי שֶׁשָּׁם בּוֹלְלִין מִנְחָה.

וְהִנִּיחוֹ

ולא מבטלי שירים לטיבלא. השתא ניחא ליה האי דטיבלא לא מבטלא לשיריים דליהוי כריבה סולתה, ובקונטרס פירש טעמא. אבל עדיין קשה, דליהוי כשירים שחסרו בין קמיצה להקטרה! וי"ל: דקיימא לן כרבי יוחנן דאמר בפ"ק (לעיל ט.): מקטיר קומץ עליהם, ור' שמעון בן לקיש חזר בו.

לימא דלא כרבי חייא. משמע מתוך הלשון דפשיטא ליה *דאיכא דמפליג על רבי חייא. ולעיל *פירש טובא דלא כוותיה.

התם כר' זירא. בסמוך אנתערב קומצה בשיריה אמרה רבי זירא לעיקר מילתיה, משום דלא מיתרץ כלל בענין אחר. ועוד בפרק "השוחט והמעלה" (זבחים קי.) על הא דתנן: קמצה ואחר כך חזר קומצה לתוכה והקריבה בחוץ חייב, פריך: ונבטלו שיריים לקומץ! ומשני *רבי זירא: נאמרה הקטרה כו', ולא משני "כדרבי זירא". *אלא אהנך תרתי איתמר עיקר מילתיה. תיבלה כב] בקצח כו'. (כדתניא) לענין מצה מיתניא, כדקתני: מצה היא אלא שנקראת מצה מתובלת. ובתוספתא דפסחים (פ"ג) תני כה"ג: יוצאין במצה מתובלת. אבל ברייתא זו לא אשכחן לא במנחות ולא בפסחים. קסלקא דעתך דאפיש לה תבלין טפי ממצה. אע"פ שאין דרך לעשות כן, פעמים שנאספין תבלין במקום אחד, ואכל מאותו צד שיש בו רוב תבלין.

אלא למ"ד בתר מבטל אזלינן תבלין מי קא הוו מצה. יש לתמוה, דמדמי ההיא דלעיל שהטעם שוה, להך דהכא שאין הטעם שוה, דכיון שיש בתבלין טעם מצה — ראוי לצאת ידי חובתו, כדאמרינן בפ' "התערובות" (זבחים עח. ושם): עשה עיסה מן חטים ומן אורז (ומן שעורים ואורז) אם יש בו טעם דגן — חייב בחלה ואדם יוצא בו ידי חובתו בפסח! וי"ל, דהך שמעתא פליגא אההיא דהתם. ואין להקשות אההיא ד"תערובות" מהא דאמרינן ב"ערבי פסחים" (פסחים קטו.): לא ליכרוך איניש מצה ומרור בהדי הדדי דלמא אתי מרור דרבנן ומבטל למצה דאורייתא. דהתם חוזק המרירות הוא דמבטל טעם המצה, אבל אורז לא מבטל טעם דגן. ועוד יש לפרש: דהתם — כשאוכל כזית מצה, דכי מבטל ליה מרור — ליכא טעם כזית מצה. אבל אם אוכל הרבה שרי. כי סליק רב כהנא אשכחינהו לבני רבי חייא. מכאן יש סייעתא לפי' הקונטרס, שפירש בפרק בתרא דגיטין (דף פד:) דבימי רבי חייא עלה רב כהנא מבבל, גבי כילד יעשה יטלנו ממנה כו', דקאמר: מאן תנא? אמר חזקיה: ר"ש בן אלעזר היא, ורבי יוחנן אמר: דילכון אמר הואיל וקנאתו ליפסל בו. ופי' שם בקונטרס דלחזקיה רבו היה אומר, שרב כהנא עלה מבבל כמו בנו של רבי חייא שהיה מבבל, ורבי יוחנן שאל הרבה ספיקות לרב כהנא, כדאיתא בפ' בתרא דב"ק (דף קיז:). והיו מקשים לפי' הקונטרס: דמשמע שכבר שכיב כג] רבי חייא כשעלה רב כהנא מבבל. דחזקיה רבו של רבי יוחנן היה כדמוכח בפרק "אלו קשרים" (שבת קיב:), וכשעלה רב כהנא היה רבי יוחנן זקן ויושב בישיבה, דמסרחי ליה גביניה, והתלמידים יושבים לפניו שורות שורות ורבי שמעון בן לקיש לומד לפניו! והשתא אינה קושיא, דעל כרחך בימי חזקיה עלה, כדמוכח כאן. ושמא כמה פעמים עלה, דאשכחן עדיין שעלה בימי רבי שמעון בר רבי שהיה חבירו של רבי חייא, דאמרינן בזבחים בפרק "קדשי

רש"ק דליכא וכ"ג נ"ק | פירשתי דאיכא טובא נ"ק | יבמות פב. זבחים עט: חולין לח: לט: ק. לעיל כב: | א"ר זירא נ"ק | דלא נ"ק | נ"ק מ"ז | רש"ק מ"ז

נ"ל דקאמר | זה כזה נ"ק | *כשר נ"ק | בכורות כג. | להיות כחולין נ"ק | ליבטל תריץ אפשר לחולין כו' וה"ל מין במינו לר"ח והס"ד כנ"ל וכאשר הוא בפנים הוא גי' רש"ק | ולא תהני נ"ק | ומהאי נ"ק | דלא כרב חסדא ודלא כרבי חייא נ"ק | [זבחים קי.] | בהא נ"ק | שייך לדף כד. | ולא בטיל כמבטל ולא קא נ"ק

הגהות הב"ח

(א) רש"י ד"ה לעולם וכו' לקדשים להיות כחולין כנ"ל ותיבת כמבטלין נמחק: (ב) ד"ה לימא אליביה דרב חסדא דלא כרבי חייא וכו' דאין בטל אלא היכא דאפשר למיהוי כוותיה ומ"ה לא מבטל ליה וכו' שיריים מי הוו נ"ב ואם כן הוה כמו ריבוי סולת לאידך מנחה:

שיטה מקובצת

א] לעולם אליבא דרבי יהודה כו'. פ"ה ואי קשיא כו' תריץ דרבי יהודה לא אמר דאין דם מבטל דם אלא כשהדם קדשים רוב על דם החולין והכי קאמר לא מבטל ליה דאפשר למבטל להיות כבטל ולא הוי זריקה דדם חיה לא בטיל ולא נהירא דנהי דלא בטיל מ"מ יש בילה וראוי [לזריקה] דלא גרע מדם שנתערב במים ואומר ר"י דלרב חסדא ודאי נאמר [ר' חייא] תנא הוא ור' חייא פליג אתנא דזבחים ואומר דלעולם לא אמר ר' יהודה דאין דם מבטל דם ולא תלי בחזותא אלא במבטל כבטל. תו"ח: ב] והא הכא כיון דקמיץ [ליה] מחד אידך מה שנשתייר ממנחה זו הו"ל שירים ומנחה אחרת שלא נקמצה הו"ל טיבלא ולא קא מבטל להו שירים לטיבלא ואע"ג דטיבלא רוב על השירים מיהו אי אפשר שלא ירבה שתי פרידות מסולת של שירים על פרידה אחת של סולת דטיבלא דכה"ג אמרינן במס' נדה (דף כז ע"א) אי אפשר שלא ירבו שתי פרידות של עפר הבית על פרידה אחת של רקב ומבטל ליה ואפ"ה לא מבטל ליה הכא שירים לטיבלא: ג] אלא למ"ד בתר מבטל אזלי' שירים כו' הקשה בקונט' ולמ"ד בתר בטל אזלינן מי ניחא אמאי לא אמרי' שיבטל הקומץ לשירים ותירץ אי לפסול שירים הא אמרינן שירים שחסרו בין קמיצה להקטרה מקטיר קומץ עליהן ואי משום יתר דטבלא (מבלול) [מבטל] אין כאן יתר ולא נהירא כדהקשה בתוס' לעיל אלא ודאי שייך שפיר פסול יתר והא דלא קאמר ונבטלי טבל לשירים משום דפסול יתר לא למדנו אלא לקמן שילהי פרק ואלו מנחות דקאמר ת"ר כל המנחות שריבה במדת עשרונה כו' ומפרש הקונטרס לשם ב' טעמים חד משום דאם ריבה העשרון שמא קמץ בו מן הריבוי קצת ולא קמץ הכל מן העשרון והוי קומץ חסר ולהך פי' דהתם ניחא הכא דהתם דוקא פסול משום דמעורב הכל אבל האי דיכול לקמוץ מזה בפני עצמו לא פסול משום יתור וגם לפי' השני דפ"ה [לא קשה] דטעמא דפסול משום דכתיב עשרון לעכב מצינו למימר דאינו מעכב רק היכא שעירבן בכלי אחד ואינו יכול לקמוץ אלא בתערובת אבל הכא דיכול לקמוץ מכל חד בפני עצמו לא מיפסל כלל. כך נראה להר"ם ז"ל: ד] לימא מתניתין דלא כרבי חייא. מכאן ראיה לפי' ר"י דלא פריך אלא לרבי חייא אבל לתנא דזבחים דפ' התערובת ניחא דאמר אין דם מבטל דם ואזיל בתר חזותא והני תרי מנחות תואר אחד להם דאי ס"ד דר' חייא לא פליג אתנא דהתם לימא מתני' דלא כמאן. תו"ח. תיבות אליבא דרב חסדא נמחק: ה] ונאמרה הקטרה בשירים כו' אין שירים מבטלין [את] הקומץ ומש"ה לא בטלי שירים לטבל דבטבל יש שירים וקומץ שירים אינם יכולין לבטל דאין שירים מבטלין שירים כמו דאין קומץ מבטל קומץ ואין מבטלין הקומץ דאין השירים מבטלין הקומץ: ו] עי' בהשמטות בסוף המסכת: ז] תיבות והוי ליה כו' לא בטל נמחק:

תיבות

שיטה מקובצת

ח] תיבות לימא דלא כרבי חייא נמחק: ט] בשיריה או בשירה של חברתה: י] עיין בהשמטות בסוף המס': יא] אמר רבי זירא נאמר הקטרה כו' הכא הוא עיקר מילתיה דר' זירא משום דקשיא בין למ"ד דאזלי' בתר מבטל ובין למ"ד דאזלינן בתר בטל אבל לעיל לא קשה אלא למ"ד דאזלינן בתר מבטל לא חש ר' זירא לתרץ אותו. תו"ח: ה"ג אמר ר' זירא ול"ג כדאמר רבי זירא דהכא אמר ר' זירא לעיקר מילתיה משום דפריך בין לרב חסדא בין לרבי חנינא: יב] אין שירים מבטלין את הקומץ לפיכך לא מבטלי שירים לטיבלא שהרי בטיבלא שירים וקומץ הוא דאית ביה ושירים לא מבטלי קומץ כדיליף בגז"ש דהקטרה ושירים נמי לא מבטלי שירים משום דמין במינו לא בטיל ופירש רש"י דהא אפילו ר"י כו' ואף על גב דפליג היכא דנתערב הקומץ במנחת כהנים ובמנחת כהן משוח כו' ואף על גב דבכולהו כתיב בהו הקטרה ואפילו הכי בטלי אהדדי לאו פירכא היא כדפי' לעיל דהתם משום דאין בלילתן שוות ובלע עבה מרכה: יג] עיין בהשמטות בסוף המסכת: יד] אזיל דקאמר: טו] מין בשר: טז] לרב חסדא תריץ הכי רב חסדא משמע מתניתין דדם קדשים רבה על של חולין והכי קאמר רואין אותו כאילו הוא מים וכשר של קדשים הואיל ואין המים ניכרים רבי יהודה אומר אין דם קדשים מבטל דם חולין הואיל ואפשר לו להיות כמוהו ותיבות והוי דלא כרבי חייא ליתא שמה: יז] קמיצה שלא תיהוי: יח] אלא היכי ותיבות אם לא נמחק: יט] וממאי דלא: כ] דתיהוי ריבה אות כ' נמחק: כא] ר' יהודה. ס"א רבנן מודו דאין עולין מבטלין זה את זה: כב] בקצה כו' הא דתניא: כג] שכיב חזקיה כשעלה:

אָמַר רָבָא, קָסָבַר רַבִּי יְהוּדָה: כָּל *שֶׁהוּא מִין בְּמִינוֹ וְדָבָר אַחֵר – סַלֵּק אֶת מִינוֹ כְּמִי שֶׁאֵינוֹ, וְשֶׁאֵינוֹ מִינוֹ רָבָה עָלָיו וּמְבַטְּלוֹ.§ אִיתְּמַר: קוֹמֶץ דְּמִנְחַת חוֹטֵא שֶׁשְּׁמְּנוֹ – רַבִּי יוֹחָנָן אוֹמֵר: אפָּסוּל, וְרֵישׁ לָקִישׁ אָמַר: א] הוּא עַצְמוֹ מְשַׁכְשְׁכוֹ בְּשְׁיָרֵי הַלּוֹג וּמַעֲלֵהוּ. וְהָכְתִיב: °"לֹא יָשִׂים עָלֶיהָ שֶׁמֶן וְלֹא יִתֵּן עָלֶיהָ לְבוֹנָה"! הַהוּא שֶׁלֹּא יִקְבַּע לָהּ שֶׁמֶן כַּחֲבֶרוֹתֶיהָ. אֵיתִיבֵיהּ ר' יוֹחָנָן לְרֵישׁ לָקִישׁ: חָרֵב שֶׁנִּתְעָרֵב בְּבָלוּל – יַקְרִיב, רַבִּי יְהוּדָה אוֹמֵר: לֹא יַקְרִיב; מַאי לָאו קוֹמֶץ דְּמִנְחַת חוֹטֵא דְּאִיעֲרַב בְּקוֹמֶץ דְּמִנְחַת נְדָבָה? לָא, מִנְחַת פָּרִים וְאֵילִים בְּמִנְחַת כְּבָשִׂים. וְהָא בְּהֶדְיָא קָתָנֵי לָהּ: במִנְחַת פָּרִים וְאֵילִים בְּמִנְחַת כְּבָשִׂים, וְחָרֵב שֶׁנִּתְעָרֵב בְּבָלוּל – יִקְרַב, רַבִּי יְהוּדָה אוֹמֵר: לֹא יִקְרַב! פֵּירוּשֵׁי קָמְפָרֵשׁ לָהּ. בָּעֵי רָבָא: ב] גקוֹמֶץ שֶׁמִּיצָּה שַׁמְנוֹ עַל גַּבֵּי עֵצִים, מַהוּ? ג] חִיבּוּרֵי עוֹלִין כְּעוֹלִין דָּמוּ, אוֹ לָאו כְּעוֹלִין דָּמוּ? אֲמַר לֵיהּ רָבִינָא לְרַב אַשִׁי: לָאו הַיְינוּ דְּרַבִּי יוֹחָנָן וְרֵישׁ לָקִישׁ? דְּאִיתְּמַר: *הַמַּעֲלֶה אֵבֶר שֶׁאֵין בּוֹ כַּזַּיִת וְעֶצֶם מַשְׁלִימוֹ לְכַזַּיִת – רַבִּי יוֹחָנָן אָמַר: דחַיָּיב, רֵישׁ לָקִישׁ אָמַר: פָּטוּר; רַבִּי יוֹחָנָן אָמַר חַיָּיב – חִיבּוּרֵי עוֹלִין כְּעוֹלִין דָּמוּ, וְר"ל אָמַר פָּטוּר – חִיבּוּרֵי עוֹלִין לָאו כְּעוֹלִין דָּמוּ? תִּיבָּעֵי לְר' יוֹחָנָן, וְתִיבָּעֵי לְרֵישׁ לָקִישׁ; תִּיבָּעֵי לְר' יוֹחָנָן, עַד כָּאן לָא קָא אָמַר ר' יוֹחָנָן הָתָם אֶלָּא בְּעֶצֶם, דְּמִינָא דְּבָשָׂר הוּא, אֲבָל ד] הַאי דְּלָאו דְּמִינָא דְּקוֹמֶץ הוּא – לָא. אוֹ דִּלְמָא אֲפִי' ה] לְרֵישׁ לָקִישׁ, לָא קָא אָמַר אֶלָּא בְּעֶצֶם, דָּבָר מְפוֹרָשׁ הוּא, וְאִי פָּרֵישׁ – לָאו מִצְוָה לְאַהֲדוּרֵי, ו] אֲבָל שֶׁמֶן דְּלָאו בַּר מִפְרָשׁ הוּא – לָא. אוֹ דִּלְמָא לָא שְׁנָא? תֵּיקוּ.§

מתני' שְׁתֵּי המְּנָחוֹת שֶׁלֹּא נִקְמְצוּ וְנִתְעָרְבוּ זוֹ בָּזוֹ, אִם יָכוֹל לִקְמוֹץ מִזּוֹ בִּפְנֵי עַצְמָהּ וּמִזּוֹ בִּפְנֵי עַצְמָהּ – כְּשֵׁירוֹת, וְאִם לָאו – פְּסוּלוֹת. ז] וקוֹמֶץ שֶׁנִּתְעָרֵב בְּמִנְחָה שֶׁלֹּא נִקְמְצָה – לֹא יַקְטִיר, וְאִם הִקְטִיר – זוֹ שֶׁנִּקְמְצָה ח] עוֹלָה לַבְּעָלִים, וְזוֹ שֶׁלֹּא נִקְמְצָה לֹא עוֹלָה לַבְּעָלִים. זנִתְעָרֵב קוּמְצָהּ בְּשִׁירֶיהָ אוֹ °בְּשִׁירֶיהָ שֶׁל חֲבֶירְתָּהּ – לֹא יַקְטִיר, וְאִם הִקְטִיר – עוֹלָה לַבְּעָלִים.§ **גמ'** *אָמַר רַב חִסְדָּא: חנְבֵילָה בְּטֵילָה בִּשְׁחוּטָה, שֶׁאִי אֶפְשָׁר לִשְׁחוּטָה שֶׁתֵּעָשֶׂה נְבֵילָה; ט] וּשְׁחוּטָה אֵינָהּ בְּטֵילָה בִּנְבֵילָה, שֶׁאֶפְשָׁר לִנְבֵילָה שֶׁתֵּעָשֶׂה שְׁחוּטָה, דְּלְכִי מַסְרְחָה פָּרְחָה טוּמְאָתָהּ. וְרַבִּי חֲנִינָא אָמַר: כָּל שֶׁאֶפְשָׁר לוֹ לִהְיוֹת כָּמוֹהוּ – אֵינוֹ בָּטֵל, וְכָל שֶׁאִי אֶפְשָׁר לוֹ לִהְיוֹת כָּמוֹהוּ – בָּטֵל. אַלִּיבָּא דְּמַאן? אִי אַלִּיבָּא דְּרַבָּנַן – הָא אָמְרִי: *עוֹלִין הוּא דְּלָא מְבַטְּלִי אַהֲדָדֵי, אֲבָל מִין בְּמִינוֹ בָּטֵל! אִי אַלִּיבָּא דְּרַבִּי יְהוּדָה – וְהָא רַבִּי

תורה אור: ויקרא ה

חולין ק: קח.

רש"י: מִין בְּמִינוֹ. שֶׁמֶן וְשֶׁמֶן. וְדָבָר אַחֵר. סוֹלֶת. סַלֵּק אֶת מִינוֹ. שֶׁמֶן י] דְּקוֹמֶץ מִשּׁוּם נְדָבָה – כְּמִי שֶׁאֵינוֹ, וְנִמְצָא סוֹלְתּוֹ שֶׁל קוֹמֶץ רָבָה עַל שֶׁמֶן הַנִּבְלָע בּוֹ, וּמְבַטְּלָהּ. שֶׁשְּׁמְּנוֹ. שֶׁנָּתַן עָלָיו שֶׁמֶן לְאַחַר שֶׁקְּמָצוֹ. הוּא עַצְמוֹ. כְּלוֹמַר, תְּחִילַּת יא] מִצְוָה שֶׁיְּשַׁפְשְׁפֶנּוּ לַקּוֹמֶץ בִּשְׁיָרֵי מִנְחָה אֶחָד מִן הַלּוּגִּין, וְכָל שֶׁכֵּן דְּאִם שְׁמָּנוֹ כָּשֵׁר. שֶׁלֹּא יִקְבַּע לָהּ שֶׁמֶן. בְּעוֹד שֶׁלֹּא נִקְמְצָה, אֲבָל לְאַחַר קְמִיצָה אִם שְׁמָנָהּ קָלֶת – כָּשֵׁר. יַקְרִיב. דְּרַבָּנַן לְטַעְמַיְיהוּ, דְּעוֹלִין אֵין מְבַטְּלִין זֶה אֶת זֶה. רַבִּי יְהוּדָה אוֹמֵר לֹא יַקְרִיב. וַאֲפִי' רַבָּנַן לָא אָמְרִי יִקְרַב אֶלָּא מִשּׁוּם דְּעוֹלִין אֵין מְבַטְּלִין זֶה אֶת זֶה, יב] וְהֵיכָא דְּאִיתֵיהּ – אַמִּנְחַת נְדָבָה שֶׁדָּיְינַן לֵיהּ. אֲבָל אִם נָפַל שֶׁמֶן בַּקּוֹמֶץ דְּחוֹטֵא – אֲפִילּוּ לְרַבָּנַן לֹא (א) יִקְרַב! מִנְחַת נְסָכִים שֶׁל פָּרִים וְאֵילִים. חֲרֵיבָה לְגַבֵּי מִנְחַת נִסְכֵי יג] כֶּבֶשׂ, דְּכֶבֶשׂ הָוֵי שְׁלֹשָׁה לוּגִּין לְעִשָּׂרוֹן, דִּכְתִיב בְּפָרָשַׁת "שְׁלַח לְךָ": "סֹלֶת עִשָּׂרוֹן בָּלוּל בִּרְבִיעִית הַהִין שֶׁמֶן", וְהִין שְׁנֵים עָשָׂר לוּגִּין. וְשֶׁל פָּרִים וְאֵילִים שְׁנֵי לוּגִּין לְעִשָּׂרוֹן, דִּכְתִיב בְּפַר: "בָּלוּל בַּשֶּׁמֶן חֲצִי הַהִין", דְּהַיְינוּ שִׁשָּׁה לוּגִּין וּשְׁלֹשָׁה עֶשְׂרוֹנִים סֹלֶת. וּבְאֵילִים: "סֹלֶת שְׁנֵי עֶשְׂרוֹנִים בָּלוּל בַּשֶּׁמֶן שְׁלִישִׁית הַהִין". וְהֵיכָא דְּנִתְעָרְבָה מִנְחַת פָּרִים יד] בְּמִנְחַת כְּבָשִׂים – הָתָם וַדַּאי לֹא יִקְרַב, מִשּׁוּם דְּנִמְלֵאת הֶעָבָה רַכָּה. אֲבָל קוֹמֶץ דְּמִנְחַת חוֹטֵא דְּאִיעֲרַב בְּקוֹמֶץ דְּמִנְחַת נְדָבָה – יִקְרַב. פֵּירוּשֵׁי קָמְפָרֵשׁ. וְהָכִי קָאָמַר: מִנְחַת פָּרִים בְּשֶׁל כְּבָשִׂים, דְּהַיְינוּ חָרֵב שֶׁנִּתְעָרֵב בְּבָלוּל, טו] דִּבְלוּעִין זֶה מִזֶּה – אֲפִי' הָכִי לְרַבָּנַן יִקְרַב, דְּאֵין עוֹלִין מְבַטְּלִין זֶה אֶת זֶה. רַבִּי יְהוּדָה אוֹמֵר לֹא יִקְרַב. דְּשֶׁאֵינוֹ מִינוֹ רָבֶה עָלָיו וּמְבַטְּלוֹ. עַל גַּבֵּי עֵצִים. וְהִנִּיחַ הַקּוֹמֶץ עָלָיו. מַהוּ. מִי הָוֵי חָסֵר קוֹמֶץ אוֹ לָא? מִי אָמְרִינַן חִבּוּרֵי עוֹלִין, מַה שֶּׁהוּא מְחַבֵּר הַשֶּׁמֶן לַקּוֹמֶץ, שֶׁחוֹזֵר וְנוֹתֵן הַקּוֹמֶץ עַל הָעֵצִים. כְּעוֹלִין דָּמוּ. כְּאִילּוּ הָוֵי הַשֶּׁמֶן מוּבְלָע בַּקּוֹמֶץ וְכָשֵׁר, אוֹ לָאו כְּעוֹלִין וּפָסוּל? הַמַּעֲלֶה. בַּחוּץ. עוֹלִין. בָּשָׂר, חִבּוּרֵי עוֹלִין – (ב) עֶצֶם. שֶׁמֶן. לָאו מִין סֹלֶת הִיא. עֶצֶם אִי פָּרֵישׁ. כְּגוֹן פּוֹקְעִין, לָאו מִצְוָה לְאַהֲדוּרֵי, בְּפֶרֶק "גִּיד הַנָּשֶׁה" (חולין צ.), הִלְכָּךְ לָאו כְּעוֹלִין דָּמוּ. לָשׁוֹן אַחֵר: קוֹמֶץ שֶׁמִּיצָּה שַׁמְנוֹ עַל גַּבֵּי עֵצִים, מַהוּ? מִי בָּעֵיָא לְהַקְטִיר עֵצִים עִם טז] קוֹמֶץ אוֹ לָא? חִבּוּרֵי עוֹלִין – שֶׁמֶן שֶׁמְּחַבֵּר לַקּוֹמֶץ כְּעוֹלִין דָּמוּ, וְאִם אֵינוֹ מַקְטִירוֹ הָוֵי כְּקוֹמֶץ חָסֵר, אוֹ לָא כְּעוֹלִין וְלָא אִיכְפַּת לָן. יז] מתני' שְׁתֵּי מְנָחוֹת כו'. כְּבָר פֵּירַשְׁתִּי לְמַעְלָה (דף כב.). גמ' נְבֵילָה בְּטֵלָה בִּשְׁחוּטָה. אִם יֵשׁ שְׁתֵּי חֲתִיכוֹת יח] (אַחַת) שְׁחוּטָה וְאַחַת נְבֵילָה, וְאֵין יָדוּעַ אֵיזוֹהִי – בְּטֵלָה יט] בָּהֶן, שֶׁאִם נָגַע בְּאַחַת מֵחֲתִיכוֹת – אֵינוֹ טָמֵא, דְּאָמְרִינַן: שְׁחוּטָה הִיא. שֶׁאִי אֶפְשָׁר לִשְׁחוּטָה שֶׁתֵּעָשֶׂה נְבֵילָה. וַהֲוָה לֵיהּ מִין בְּשֶׁאֵינוֹ מִינוֹ, וּבָטֵל לְדִבְרֵי הַכֹּל. וּשְׁחוּטָה אֵינָהּ בְּטֵלָה בִּנְבֵילָה. אִם יֵשׁ שְׁתֵּי חֲתִיכוֹת נְבֵילָה וְאַחַת שְׁחוּטָה בֵּינֵיהֶן – אֵינָהּ בְּטֵילָה, וְאִם נָגְעָה אַחַת מֵהֶן בִּתְרוּמָה אֵינָהּ נִשְׂרֶפֶת עָלֶיהָ, אֶלָּא חוּלִין, דְּשֶׁמָּא זוֹ הִיא הַשְּׁחוּטָה. שֶׁאֶפְשָׁר לִנְבֵילָה שֶׁתֵּיעָשֶׂה שְׁחוּטָה כ]. לְקַמֵּיהּ מְפָרֵשׁ טַעְמָא דְּרַב חִסְדָּא, דְּאָזֵיל בָּתַר מְבַטֵּל, וְהוֹאִיל וְאִי אֶפְשָׁר לָרוֹב לִהְיוֹת כַּמּוּעָט – הָוֵי כְּמִין בְּשֶׁאֵינוֹ מִינוֹ. וְלָא אָזְלִינַן בָּתַר בָּטֵיל, דְּאַף עַל גַּב דְּאֶפְשָׁר לַמּוּעָט לִהְיוֹת כַּמְרוּבֶּה – הָוֵי כְּמִין בְּשֶׁאֵינוֹ מִינוֹ. פָּרְחָה טוּמְאָה. דִּכְתִיב (דברים יד): "לַגֵּר אֲשֶׁר בִּשְׁעָרֶיךָ תִּתְּנֶנָּה", כא] וְאָמְרִינַן בִּבְכוֹרוֹת (דף כג:). קְרָאָהּ לְגֵר קְרוּיָה נְבֵילָה כב]. כָּל שֶׁאֶפְשָׁר לוֹ. לְבַטֵּל, דְּהַיְינוּ מוּעָט, לִהְיוֹת כָּמוֹהוּ שֶׁל מְבַטֵּל – אֵינוֹ בָּטֵל, הִלְכָּךְ, נְבֵילָה אֵינָהּ בְּטֵלָה בִּשְׁחוּטָה. אֲבָל שְׁחוּטָה בְּטֵילָה בִּנְבֵילָה, דְּאִי אֶפְשָׁר לִשְׁחוּטָה שֶׁתֵּיעָשֶׂה נְבֵילָה, וְאִם נָגְעָה אַחַת מִן הַחֲתִיכוֹת בִּתְרוּמָה – נִשְׂרֶפֶת עָלֶיהָ, דְּרַבִּי חֲנִינָא אָזֵיל בָּתַר בָּטֵיל. הָא מִין בְּמִינוֹ בָּטֵל. הִלְכָּךְ, בֵּין נְבֵילָה בִּשְׁחוּטָה בֵּין שְׁחוּטָה בִּנְבֵילָה, בְּטֵלִין. בָּתַר

תוספות: אמר רבא קסבר רבי יהודה כו'. הא דאמר בפ' "כל הבשר" (חולין קח.) בשמעתא דטיפת חלב, דאמר רבא: קסבר רבי יהודה כל שהוא מין ומינו כו' – היינו הכא בשמעתין, שהוא עיקר מילתיה דרבא. ולא כמו שפי' שם בקונטרס, דהיינו רבא דפרק "גיד הנשה" (שם ק: ושם) שאמר: אפילו לא קדם וסלקו הוי מין ומינו ודבר אחר כו'. דהתם לא קאמר בהאי לישנא: קסבר רבי יהודה כו'*. **הוא** עצמו משכשכו בשירי הלוג. פירוש: לוג של מנחות שניתותר. וא"ת, הא תנן בפירקין (דף כז.) השמן מיעוטו מעכב את רובו! כג] וי"ל: שלא ניתנה תורה למלאכי השרת, ואי אפשר שלא ישאר בלוג מן השמן. **חרב** שנתערב בבלול כו'. יש תימה: מאי קא פריך? דלעולם מודה רבי שמעון בן לקיש דאם היו עולין מבטלין ואפי' לרבנן לא יקרב. ולא משום חרב שנשתמן, אלא משום בלול שנחסר, דהוה ליה חיסר שמנה, דהא נתערב שמנו בחרב ובטל, וה"ל כד] ככשר ופסול שנתערבו זה בזה, וצריך עיון אם הוה אמרינן יקרב אם לאו! וי"ל: דלא חשיב חיסר שמנה. דאע"ג דמספקי' ליה לרבא בסמוך גבי קומץ שמיצה שמנו על גבי עצים אי חיבורי עולין כעולין, הכא פשיטא דכעולין דמיא כשמיצה שמנו בחרב, כיון דשניהן נקטרים. ולפי זה לא מיפסלו כה] לעולם משום חיסר שמנה, אלא משום ריבה שמנה. **קומץ** שמיצה שמנו ע"ג עצים. פי': קצת נבלע מן השמן בעצים, ומקצתו בעין על גבי עצים עם הקומץ. ומבעיא ליה אי חשיב הנבלע כאילו הוא בעין ע"ג עצים, הואיל ומחובר למה שבחוץ, מחמת דחיבורי עולין כעולין דמו, או לא. ובקונט' פירש ב' לשונות, וכמו שפירש' נראה. **נבילה** בטילה בשחוטה. היינו מלטמא במגע, אבל במשא מטמא, כדאמרי' בפרק שלישי דבכורות (דף כג.). **שחוטה** אינה בטילה בנבילה. והיכא *דקבעי ברשות הרבים ואינו יודע באיזו מהן נגע – ספיקו טהור, דכל קבוע כמחצה על מחצה *דמי, היכא דאפשר למיהוי כוותיה. ודם הפר ודם השעיר, כיון שהיה מעורב בו כאחת ונתן מהן מתנה – חשיב דאפשר להיות זה כזה. ולא

[ועי' תוס' חולין קח. ד"ה דאמר]

זבחים קז:

דקעבר. יעב"ץ

דמי הס"ד ומה"ד כל היכא ל"ק ושייך לקמן

ביצה לח: [בכורות כג. ע"ש]

עין משפט נר מצוה

לא א מיי' פי"א מהל' פסה"מ הלכה ו:
לב ב מיי' שם הל' כט:
לג ג מיי' פ"ג מהלכות פסה"מ הלכה יז:
לד ד מיי' פי"ט מהל' מעה"ק הלכה ו:
לה ה מיי' פי"א מהל' פסה"מ הלכה כט:
לו ו מיי' שם הלכה ל:
לז ז מיי' שם הלכה לא:
לח ח מיי' פי"ט מהל' אבות הטומאה הלכה יז:

גליון הש"ס

מתני' בשיריה של חבירתה כו'. עיין לקמן מח ע"א תוס' ד"ה בחטאת:

הגהות הב"ח

(א) רש"י ד"ה ר' יהודה וכו' לרבנן לא יקרב הס"ד ואח"כ מ"ה מנחת פרים ואילים כו' מנחת נסכים וכו' נסכים דכבש: (ב) ד"ה עולין וכו' עצם הס"ד ואח"כ מ"ה לאו מינה כו' פירש לאו וכו' היה הס"ד ואח"כ מ"ה ואי פריש עצם אי:

שיטה מקובצת

א] הוא עצמו משכשכו בשירי הלוג. וא"ת כי נשתייר בלוג מן השמן אמאי לא הוי כחסר מנחה מאותה מנחה שמדד השמן באותו הלוג דהא תנן בפרקין השמן מיעוטו מעכב את רובו וי"ל דלא נתנה תורה למלאכי השרת דאי אפשר למצות הלוג כל כך שלא ישאר בו קצת מן השמן: [illegible]

שיטה מקובצת

אינה בטילה בנבלה. פ"ה אם נגעה אחת מהם בתרומה תולין [illegible]

[illegible]

לעולם

מכאן לעולין שאין מבטלין זה את זה. וא"ת: תיפוק ליה משום דאין מצות מבטלות זו את זו, כדאמרינן ב"ערבי פסחים" (דף קטו.) גבי הלל שהיה כורך פסח ומצה ומרור. וכן בפ' התערובות (זבחים עט.) פליג ר' אלעזר אר' שמעון בן לקיש בההיא דפיגול ונותר וטמא שבללן, וקאמר שאין מבטלין זה את זה, ומייתי ראייה מדהלל! ושמא לגבי אכילה שאני. ורבי יהודה סבר מכאן למין במינו שאינו בטל. וא"ת: היכי מסיק רבי יוחנן דטעמא דרבי יהודה מהא קרא? הא מסקינן בפרק "אותו ואת בנו" (חולין עט.) דרבי יהודה ספוקי מספקא ליה אי חוששין לזרע האב או לא, ומאן דאמר חוששין לזרע האב *לא בעי "אותו" לחלק, דמסקינן התם: לחנניא דלא מייתר ליה "אותו" קסבר דלחלק לא צריך קרא, דסבר לה כרבי יונתן! וביומא פרק "הוציאו לו" (דף נז:) אמרינן: רבי יאשיה ורבי יונתן, חד אמר מערבין וחד אמר אין מערבין, ואמרינן: תסתיים דר' יאשיה דאמר מערבין, דאע"ג דלא כתיב "יחדו" כמאן דכתיב דמי. ואע"ג דדחינן: אפי' תימא רבי יונתן דאמר מערבין, שאני הכא דכתיב "אחת", הא מסקינן התם: תניא דלא כשינויין! וי"ל: דנהי דרבי יונתן סבר "ולקח מדם הפר ומדם השעיר" זה בפני עצמו וזה בפני עצמו, ולא דריש "אחת" – ר' יהודה "אחת בשנה" דריש, וקסבר דמערבין. וא"ת: ור' יונתן, נהי דלא דריש "אחת", הוה לן למימר: כיון דכתיב "ומדם" כמאן דכתיב "יחדו" דמי, כדאשכחן בפ' "שתי מדות" (לקמן צ:) דדריש ר' יונתן "או מן הצאן" לומר: רצה אחד מביא, רצה שנים מביא, משום דכתיב באידך קרא "ומן הצאן" כמאן דכתיב "יחדו" דמי! ה] *(ויש לומר) דהתם פירש בקונט' דדריש מדשני קרא בדיבוריה, דכתיב "מן הבקר ומן הצאן". ומיהו, ו] אין זה כל כך שינוי, דלא הוה מצי למכתב "ומן הבקר", דתרוייהו לפרושי מן הבהמה קאתי, ודמיא "מן הבקר ומן הצאן" "לדם הפר ולדם השעיר", האי דכתיב וי"ו לאוסופי – הכא נמי וי"ו לאוסופי. וא"ת: ומאן דאמר אין מערבין, מנא ליה עולין ומין במינו? וי"ל: דנפקא להו מדכתיב "דם" "דם", כדאיתא בזבחים בפ' "התערובות" (דף פא. וע"ש תו' ד"ה תנאי). וא"ת: בפרק "הניזקין" (גיטין נד:) גבי ערלה וכלאי הכרם קאמר רבי יהודה: נפלו אגוזי פרך ונתפלעו – *בשוגג יעלו, במזיד לא יעלו. והתם מין במינו הוא, ומשמע התם מדאורייתא ברובא בטיל, אלא משום דקנים כדאמרינן התם. וכל תרומה נמי מודה ר' יהודה דעולה באחד ומאה, כדמוכח בפרק "נוטל" (שבת קמב.) דקאמר ר' יהודה: מעלין את המדומע באחד ומאה! וי"ל: דדבר לח המתערב יפה – בכל שהוא, אבל דבר יבש בטיל שפיר. ולא גרסינן בגיטין (דף נד:) "נפלו לגת ונתפלעו", דלא איירי בלח אלא ביבש. והא דקאמר בחולין (דף ק.) דחתיכה אחת אוסרת כל החתיכות שהן מינה – טעם המתערב כלח דמי. ובסוף מסכת נילה (דף לח:) דאמרי': חיטין בחיטין נמי, נהי דלרבי יהודה לא בטיל לרבנן מבטיל בטיל – בקמח איירי, שמתערב יפה וכלח דמי, אבל חיטין בחיטין עצמן בטלי. תדע, דהא דאמר ז] חיטין ושעורין בקמח איירי שמתערב, דאי כברייתם כיון דמינכרי לא בטלי. וכענין זה מפרש ר"ת דהא דאמר ר' יוחנן בסוף מסכת ע"ז (דף עג:): *שתי כוסות אחד של חולין ואחד של תרומה שמזגן ונתערבו זה בזה – סלק את מינו כמי שאינו, ושאינו מינו רבה עליו ומבטלו. דקשיא ליה: כיון דתרומה עולה בק"א, אם כן *מין במינו נמי יסייע לשאינו מינו לבטל התרומה! אלא שמע מינה דמינו במשהו. והא דאמר רבי יוחנן התם דכל איסורים שבתורה במינן בנותן טעם חוץ מטבל ויין נסך, ולא חשיב תרומה – משום דבכלל טבל הוא, וחד טעמא לתרוייהו, דמפרש התם טעמא דטבל דכהיתירו כך איסורו, דחיטה אחת פוטרת את הכרי – והוא הדין תרומה כעלייתה כך איסורה. ובכל דוכתי דתרומה עולה באחד ומאה – בדבר יבש. ומתניתין דשתי מנחות שלא נקמצו, דלא מבטלי ליה שירייס לטיבלא, דמוקמי לקמן כר' יהודה – במנחת סולת איירי, שמתערב לגמרי *בדבר לח, ולא במאפה תנור ומחבת ומרחשת. וההיא דלקמן דנבילה בשחוטה – בשנימוחה. והרב רבינו יוסף טוב עלם מפלנ"ו הקשה לרבינו תם מההיא דפסחים (דף כ:) דחבית של תרומה שנשברה בגת העליונה ותחתיה חולין טמאין, דאמרינן התם (דף כא.) דאם נפלה למאה חולין – דברי הכל תרד ותטמא. אלמא, אפי' דבר לח עולה באחד ומאה! ונראה שכמו כן היה יכול להקשות מההיא *של שאור של חולין ושל תרומה שנפלו בעיסה, דאין לח *ומתערב יתר ממנו. ועוד ח] *במס' תרומות פרק "סאה תרומה" בתוספתא: לוג יין צלול שנפל לתוך מאה לוגין עכורין – יעלה. וחזר בו ר"ת, דודאי אין חילוק בין לח ליבש. ותירץ, דהא דתרומה עולה באחד ומאה – בנפלה לתוך חולין מתוקנין, דאי אפשר למבטל דהיינו החולין, ליעשות כבטל דהיינו התרומה. וההיא דשני כוסות אחד של תרומה ואחד של חולין – בחולין שאינם מתוקנין, דאפשר להו ליעשות תרומה, וסבר לה ר' יוחנן כמ"ד לקמן: בתר מבטל *אזלי רבנן, והוה ליה מין במינו. וההיא דפסחים (גם זה שם) לא קשיא אף למ"ד בתר בטל אזלינן, דמשקים לכי מסרחי אין שם משקה עליהן, ולא אפשר לה לתרומה שתיעשה חולין. וא"ת: וטבל במינו במשהו היכי משכחת לה? הא אי אפשר למבטל דהיינו החולין שיעשו טבל! וי"ל: שנפל טבל טבול לתרומה בטבל שאינו טבול לתרומה, דהוי מין במינו כיון דשם טבל על שניהם. אי נמי, טבל שראה פני הבית בטבל שלא ראה פני הבית. אי נמי, אפילו נפל לחולין מתוקנין – ובעודה לתרומה ביד בעלים, דאפשר לאיתשולי עלה. והשתא דאתינן להכי, איכא לאוקומי אותה דשני כוסות בחולין מתוקנין – כגון דתרומה ביד בעלים, וההיא דפסחים – בתרומה ביד כהן. ועוד יש ליישב *תי' ראשון דר"ת וההיא דפסחים כר' חייא דלקמן, דאית ליה לר' יהודה נבילה ושחוטה בטילות זו את זו, ולהכי חשיב התם מין בשאינו מינו ט] *במשהו ואע"פ שחשובין מין ומינו לענין אחד ומאה, דלא סגי להו בששים. אבל רבי יוחנן דלא כרבי חייא, דהכי נמי מוכח לקמן דלאו כולי עלמא אית להו דר' חייא. והך משנה דאין דם מבטל דם, פירש בקונטרס לקמן דלרב חסדא דאזיל בתר מבטל הויא דלא כרבי חייא. ואפי' לר' חנינא דאזיל בתר בטל, נראה דאיכא טובא, דההיא דאין רוק מבטל רוק ואין מי רגלים מבטל מי רגלים, וגבי דם כיסוי (חולין דף פז:) שנתערב בדם בהמה, דא"ר יהודה: אין דם מבטל דם – כולהו אי אפשר לזה להיות כזה אפי' לר' חנינא. דלא דמי לדם קדשים דאיפשר להיות כחולין, כמו שפי' הקונטרס לקמן (דף כג:) דכשילין לילה אחד יצאו מקדושתן כחולין. וכל סתמא דהתלמוד לרב חסדא דלא כר' חייא. דאמר בפרק "גיד הנשה" (שם ק.): חתיכה עצמה נעשית נבילה ואוסרת כל החתיכות לר' יהודה, וגבי זרוע בשילה דקאמר: לא נצרכה *לרבי יהודה דקאמר מין במינו לא בטיל. וגבי ליר דקא"ר יהודה שיעורה במאתים, ופריך דהא אמר ר' יהודה מין במינו לא בטיל, ומשני כו'. וההיא דבילה דמין במינו י] לרבי יהודה, ודם תבוסה דאמר בנדה (דף עא.) דאמר אין דם מבטל דם לרבי יהודה. ואפי' לר' חנינא צ"ע, דנראה שיש מהנך שהבאתי דלא כרבי חייא. ועוד יש ליישב תירוץ ר"ת שמחלק בין לח ליבש, ולא קשה *ההיא דפסחים (דף כא.) לרבי יוחנן, דלאו אליבא דכ"ע קאמר טבל ויין נסך במשהו, דמודה רבי יוחנן לרבנן (דרבי יהודה) בנותן טעם. אלא רבי יוחנן סבר כרבנן בשאר איסורי, וכרבי יהודה בטבל ויין נסך. וכן ברייתא דתניא כוותיה. יא] והשתא ההיא דפסחים (ג"ז שם) כרבנן, דמין במינו בטיל בכל מקום. והשתא איכא שלשה מחלוקת של תנאים בדבר. דהא תניא כוותיה דרבי יוחנן. והדתניא בפ' "הנודר מן הירק" (נדרים נח. ע"ש) כלל אמר ר"ש: כל דבר שיש לו מתירין כו', אמרו לו: הרי שביעית שאין לה מתירין, ותנן: השביעית אוסרת כל שהוא במינה, אמר להם: לא אמרו שביעית במינה אלא לביעור, אבל לאכילה לא – לא מצי למיפרך מטבל ויין נסך, דהתם סבירא יב] כרבנן דכל איסורין בטלין אפי' מין במינו. והשתא ניחא הא דתניא בתוספתא: יין נסך שנפל על גבי ענבים – ידיחם, על גבי יין – יקלף את היין והשאר מותר, אע"פ שאי אפשר שלא ישאר שם משהו יין. אבל קשיא מההיא דתניא בתוס' דטבול יום גבי חבית שניקבה בין מפיה בין משוליה טמאה, רבי יהודה אומר: מפיה ומשוליה טמאה, מפיה – מפני שמשקה מתמיך לתוך ידו, משוליה – מפני שהמשקה גרוד על גבי ידו, מן הצדדין – יעלה באחד ומאה! והרב רבינו יצחק תירץ: הא דידיה הא דרביה, בפרק "התערובות" (זבחים עט.) אמר רבי יהודה משום רבן גמליאל: אין דם מבטל דם, וההיא דהניזקין (גיטין נד:) *ראיה. והכי משני אביי בפ' "התערובות" (שם דף עח:). אבל קשיא, דרבא פליג התם עליה! ויש עוד לפרש, דההיא דשני כוסות של היין של חולין צריך מאה של חולין, וכאן אין *(צריך) מאה כנגד תרומה בין יין של חולין ומים, *שבכוס של תרומה שלשה חלקים מים, ובכוס של חולין חמשים ושבעה חלקים מים כנגד התרומה, יג] *ושליש מהיין שבכוס של חולין י"ט מאותן חלקים, הרי בין כל המים והיין של חולין אין עולין אלא לשבעים ותשעה חלקים כנגד התרומה. וגם אם יהיה מזוג שני חלקים מים ואחד יין – אין בין יין של חולין והמים מאה חלקים כנגד התרומה, לכן אין יכול היין של חולין להצטרף עם המים. כי ביטול אינו אלא במאה, והרי אין מאה בין הכל, כי מזג כוס התרומה שני חלקים, ומי הכוס של חולין חמשים ושמנה חלקים, ואם כן היין של חולין עשרים ותשעה חלקים – הרי כאן שמונים *ותשעה חלקים ולא יותר. ואפילו יש מאה בין הכל, יש לומר דשמא לא יצטרפו המים למאה והיין לששים. אמר

[לקמן כג. זבחים פא. תמורה ה:]

א] מִכָּאן *לָעוֹלִין שֶׁאֵין מְבַטְּלִין זֶה אֶת זֶה, וְרַבִּי יְהוּדָה סָבַר: מִכָּאן לְמִין *)בְּמִינוֹ שֶׁאֵינוֹ בָּטֵל. רַבָּנַן סָבְרִי: מִכָּאן לָעוֹלִין שֶׁאֵין מְבַטְּלִין זֶה אֶת זֶה. וְדִלְמָא מִשּׁוּם דְּמִין בְּמִינוֹ הוּא! אִי אַשְׁמְעִינַן מִין בְּמִינוֹ וְלָא אַשְׁמְעִינַן עוֹלִין – כִּדְקָא אָמְרַתְּ; הַשְׁתָּא דְּאַשְׁמְעִינַן עוֹלִין – מִשּׁוּם דְּעוֹלִין. וְדִלְמָא עַד דְּאִיכָּא מִין בְּמִינוֹ וְעוֹלִין! קַשְׁיָא. וְר' יְהוּדָה סָבַר: מִכָּאן לְמִין בְּמִינוֹ שֶׁאֵינוֹ בָּטֵל. וְדִלְמָא מִשּׁוּם דְּעוֹלִין הוּא! אִי אַשְׁמְעִינַן עוֹלִין מִין בְּשֶׁאֵינוֹ מִינוֹ – כִּדְקָאָמְרַתְּ; הַשְׁתָּא דְּאַשְׁמְעִינַן מִין בְּמִינוֹ – מִשּׁוּם דְּמִין בְּמִינוֹ הוּא. וְדִילְמָא עַד דְּאִיכָּא מִין בְּמִינוֹ וְעוֹלִין! קַשְׁיָא.§ תְּנַן, רַבִּי יְהוּדָה אוֹמֵר: ב] (בְּמִנְחַת כֹּהֲנִים) בְּמִנְחַת כֹּהֵן מָשִׁיחַ וּבְמִנְחַת נְסָכִים – פְּסוּלָה, שֶׁזּוֹ בְּלִילָתָהּ עָבָה וְזוֹ בְּלִילָתָהּ רַכָּה, וְהֵן בּוֹלְעוֹת זוֹ מִזּוֹ. וְכִי בּוֹלְעוֹת זוֹ מִזּוֹ ג] מַה הָוֵי? מִין בְּמִינוֹ הוּא! אָמַר

*) [לקמן כג: וש"נ]

מִכָּאן לָעוֹלִין כו'. וְהָנֵי דָּמִים דְּמַתְנִי' דִּזְבָחֵי *ד] עוֹלִין נִינְהוּ, וְלָא מְבַטְּלֵי אַהֲדָדֵי. מִין

הא"נ היינו חנניא ולחנניא לא בעי או לחלק דמסקי' התם כו' נ"ק

דמי והתם נ"ק

אחד שוגג ואחד מזיד לא יעלו נ"ק

מתערב נ"ק

נ"א לאו עולין נינהו ומבטלי אהדדי וגיר' נ"ק חולין נינהו ומבטלי

נ"ק מ"ז

למדם הפר ומדם השעיר דהאי מדכתיב וי"ו כו' והתי' חסר כאן ועי' יומא דף נז ע"ב תוס' ד"ה תניא כו' דמתרצו שם

[וע"ש תוס' ד"ה שני]

מינו נמי נ"ק

והוי כדבר לח נ"ק

דשאור של חולין נ"ק

תניא במסכת נ"ק

אזלינן והוה נ"ק

לתירוץ ראשון דר"ת דהתיר נ"ק

לענין משהו נ"ק

אלא לר"י נ"ק

מההיא נ"ק

נ"ק מ"ז

דידיה והכי נ"ק

נ"ק מ"ז *שאם שבכוס נ"ק

ורביעית נ"ק

ושמונה נ"ק

שיטה מקובצת

א] מכאן לעולין. עי' (תוס' זבחים דף עז ע"ב): ב] תיבות במנחת כהנים נמחק: ג] מאי הוי מין במינו הוא. שמן עבה ושמן רכה המתערב עמו ולא בטיל וא"ת מה בכך מ"מ איכא נמי סולת העבה דהוי שאינו מינו הוא בולע משמן רכה ומתבטל הוא בתוכו וי"ל דס"ד דמקשה כיון דאיירי דאיכא סולת ושמן הסולת מתערב עם הסולת והשמן עם השמן ואמאי בטל מין במינו הוא ומשני קסבר רבי יהודה כו' ומיהו אכתי קשה למה ליה לשנויי קסבר ר' יהודה כו' לישני הכי מי סברת סולת בלע מסולת דוקא ושמן משמן דוקא לא שמן בלע נמי סולת וסולת בלע נמי שמן וע"ק דלישנא דמתניתין נמי משמע הכי דקתני והן בולעות זו מזו משמע שהן בולעות בתערובות שמן מסולת נמי לכך נראה להר"מ דלעולם ידע המקשה דסולת עבה בלע נמי שמן הרכה ומ"מ השיב ליה מין במינו לפי שאין כל פורתא ופורתא מסולת העבה דלא בלע משמנה והלכך אותו שמן של בלילות העבה מציל על יתרון שמן הרכה המתערב בעבה לבלתי התבטל משום דלגבי אותו שמן הוי מין במינו ואי משום הסולת העבה מ"מ אינו מתבטל מתוכו כיון שאינו לבדו וליכא פורתא ופורתא ממנה דלא בלע משמן הבלילה ואידי ואידי סולת בלול הוא ומשני דאדרבה סילק מינו שזהו שמן העבה כמי שאינו וחשוב כאילו נשאר סולת העבה לבדו הלכך אותו סולת דהוי שאינו מינו רבה על יתרון השמן הרכה הנבלע בו ומבטלו. תו"ח: ד] דזבחים לאו עולין נינהו דהא חד מיניה חולין (ונתערב) [אבל נתערב] קומץ נדבה במנחת נסכים דקומץ נדבה נמי עולין נינהו ולא: ה] דמי וי"ל דהתם: ו] ומיהו. עי' תוס' (יומא דף נז ע"ב): ז] תדע דהא דאמר התם חיטין ושעורין בטלי דוקא בקמח: ח] ועוד תניא: ט] מין בשאינו מינו לענין משהו: י] והיא דביצה דמין במינו לא בטיל לר' יהודה ודם תבוסה דאמר בנדה דאין: יא] כוותיה דר' יוחנן: יב] דהתם סבירא להו כרבנן: יג] התרומה ורביעי מהיין שבכוס של חולין תשעה ושבעים חלקים הרי:

תורה אור

כִּי זָכֵי לְהוּ רַחֲמָנָא — לְיִשְׂרָאֵל, דְּאִית לְהוּ לִשְׁכָּה, לַכֹּהֲנִים דְּלֵית לְהוּ לִשְׁכָּה — לָא זָכֵי לְהוּ רַחֲמָנָא, קמ"ל. וְעֵצִים דִּפְשִׁיטָא לֵיהּ לְתַנָּא דְּמִשֶּׁל צִיבּוּר, מְנָלַן? דְּתַנְיָא: יָכוֹל הָאוֹמֵר "הֲרֵי עָלַי עוֹלָה" יָבִיא עֵצִים מִתּוֹךְ בֵּיתוֹ, כְּדֶרֶךְ שֶׁמֵּבִיא נְסָכִים מִתּוֹךְ בֵּיתוֹ? ת"ל: °"עַל הָעֵצִים אֲשֶׁר עַל הָאֵשׁ אֲשֶׁר עַל הַמִּזְבֵּחַ" (ויקרא ח), מַה מִּזְבֵּחַ מִשֶּׁל צִיבּוּר — אַף עֵצִים וְאֵשׁ מִשֶּׁל צִיבּוּר, דִּבְרֵי רַבִּי אֶלְעָזָר בַּר ר"ש; רַבִּי אֶלְעָזָר בֶּן שַׁמּוּעַ אוֹמֵר: *מַה מִּזְבֵּחַ שֶׁלֹּא נִשְׁתַּמֵּשׁ בּוֹ הֶדְיוֹט — אַף [א]עֵצִים וְאֵשׁ שֶׁלֹּא נִשְׁתַּמֵּשׁ בָּהֶן הֶדְיוֹט. מַאי בֵּינַיְיהוּ? אִיכָּא בֵּינַיְיהוּ: חֲדָתֵי. וְעַתִּיקֵי לָא? וְהָכְתִיב: °"וַיֹּאמֶר אֲרַוְנָה אֶל דָּוִד יִקַּח וְיַעַל אֲדוֹנִי הַמֶּלֶךְ הַטּוֹב בְּעֵינָיו רְאֵה הַבָּקָר לָעוֹלָה וְהַמּוֹרִיגִים וּכְלֵי הַבָּקָר לָעֵצִים" (שמואל ב כד)! הָכָא נַמִי בַּחֲדָתֵי. מַאי "מוֹרִיגִים"? אָמַר עוּלָּא: מִטָּה שֶׁל טַרְבָּל. מַאי מִטָּה שֶׁל טַרְבָּל? אָמַר רַב יְהוּדָה: עִיזָּא דְּקוּרְקְסָא א] דְּדָשׁוּ בָּהּ דִּשְׁתָּאֵי. אָמַר רַב יוֹסֵף: מַאי קְרָאָה? °"הִנֵּה שַׂמְתִּיךְ לְמוֹרַג חָרוּץ חָדָשׁ בַּעַל פִּיפִיּוֹת תָּדוּשׁ הָרִים" (ישעיהו מא).§ **מתני'** [ב]נִתְעָרֵב קוּמְצָהּ בְּקוֹמֶץ חֲבֵירְתָהּ, בְּמִנְחַת כֹּהֲנִים, בְּמִנְחַת כֹּהֵן מָשִׁיחַ, בְּמִנְחַת נְסָכִים — כְּשֵׁרָה. רַבִּי יְהוּדָה אוֹמֵר: בְּמִנְחַת כֹּהֵן מָשִׁיחַ, ב] בְּמִנְחַת נְסָכִים — פְּסוּלָה, שֶׁזּוֹ בְּלִילָתָהּ עָבָה וְזוֹ בְּלִילָתָהּ רַכָּה, ג] וְהֵן בּוֹלְעוֹת זוֹ מִזּוֹ.§ **גמ'** תְּנַן הָתָם: *[ג]דָּם שֶׁנִּתְעָרֵב בְּמַיִם, אִם יֵשׁ בּוֹ מַרְאִית דָּם — כָּשֵׁר. נִתְעָרֵב בְּיַיִן — רוֹאִין אוֹתוֹ כְּאִילּוּ הוּא מַיִם. ד] [ד]נִתְעָרֵב בְּדַם בְּהֵמָה ה] אוֹ בְּדַם חַיָּה — רוֹאִין אוֹתוֹ כְּאִילּוּ הוּא מַיִם. *רַבִּי יְהוּדָה אוֹמֵר: אֵין דָּם מְבַטֵּל דָּם. א"ר יוֹחָנָן, וּשְׁנֵיהֶם מִקְרָא אֶחָד דָּרְשׁוּ: °"וְלָקַח מִדַּם הַפָּר וּמִדַּם הַשָּׂעִיר" (ויקרא טז) — הַדָּבָר יָדוּעַ שֶׁדָּמוֹ שֶׁל פָּר מְרוּבֶּה מִדָּמוֹ שֶׁל שָׂעִיר; רַבָּנַן סָבְרִי:
מִכָּאן

רש"י

כִּי זָכֵי לְהוּ רַחֲמָנָא. לִשְׁכָּה לִמְלוֹחַ קָרְבָּנָם מִשֶּׁל הֶקְדֵּשׁ, לְיִשְׂרָאֵל הוּא דְּזָכֵי לְהוּ מִשּׁוּם דְּאִית לְהוּ לִשְׁכָּה, כְּלוֹמַר, שֶׁהֵם נָתְנוּ הַשְּׁקָלִים בַּלִּשְׁכָּה שֶׁמֵּהֶן נִקְנֶה הַמֶּלַח. אֲבָל כֹּהֲנִים שֶׁאֵין חַיָּיבִין לִשְׁקוֹל – לֹא, לְהָכִי אִיצְטְרִיךְ תַּנָּאָה. חֲדָתֵי. לְר' אֶלְעָזָר בֶּן שַׁמּוּעַ בָּעֵינַן חֲדָתֵי. הָכָא נַמִי בַּחֲדָתֵי. שֶׁעֲדַיִין לֹא נִשְׁתַּמֵּשׁ בָּהֶן אֲרַוְנָה. עִיזָּא = עֵז שֶׁל בַּרְזֶל נוֹתְנִין עָלָיו לְהַכְבִּידוֹ. עִיזָּא דְּקוּרְקְסָא. קוּרְקְסָא = נֶסֶר גָּדוֹל מָלֵא יְתֵידוֹת. דְּדַיְישֵׁי ו] דַּיְשָׁא. שֶׁנּוֹתְנִין אוֹתוֹ עַל הַתְּבוּאָה וְקוֹשְׁרִין בּוֹ שְׁוָורִים וּמוֹשְׁכִין אוֹתוֹ, וְנִידּוֹשֶׁת הַתְּבוּאָה. מַאי קְרָא. מוֹרִיגִים לְנוֹרֶג דַּיְשָׁה, דִּכְתִיב "מוֹרַג" וּכְתִיב "תָּדוּשׁ". חָרוּץ = יָפֶה ז] וּמַלְמִיד. **מתני'** בְּמִנְחַת כֹּהֲנִים ח] כְּשֵׁרָה. שֶׁהֲרֵי כּוּלּוֹ כָּלִיל כְּמוֹתוֹ. ר' יְהוּדָה אוֹמֵר אִם נִתְעָרֵב הַקּוֹמֶץ בְּמִנְחַת נְסָכִים ט] וּמִנְחַת כֹּהֵן מָשִׁיחַ פְּסוּלָה. לְפִי שֶׁהַקּוֹמֶץ דְּמִנְחַת נִדְבַת יִשְׂרָאֵל בְּלִילָתוֹ עָבָה, לוֹג לְעִשָּׂרוֹן. וּמִנְחַת כֹּהֵן מָשִׁיחַ וּמִנְחַת נְסָכִים בְּלִילָתָן רַכָּה, שְׁלֹשָׁה לוּגִּין לְעִשָּׂרוֹן. דִּכְתִיב בְּמִנְחַת נְסָכִים: "בָּלוּל בִּרְבִיעִית הַהִין שֶׁמֶן", י] וְיָלֵיף חֲבִיתִּין מִינַּהּ שְׁלֹשָׁה לוּגִּין לְעִשָּׂרוֹן בְּפֶ' "הַתְּכֵלֶת" (לקמן נא.). וְהֵן בּוֹלְעוֹת זוֹ מִזּוֹ. הַקּוֹמֶץ בּוֹלֵעַ מִמִּנְחַת נְסָכִים, וַהֲוָה לֵיהּ רִיבָּה שַׁמְנָהּ. וּמִנְחַת נְסָכִים נַמִי פְּסוּלָה, דַּהֲוָה לֵיהּ חִיסֵּר שַׁמְנָהּ. וְהַאי דְּקָתָנֵי "פְּסוּלָה" וְלָא קָתָנֵי "פְּסוּלוֹת" – מִשּׁוּם דְּכוּלָּהּ מַתְנִיתִין בְּלִישָּׁנָא דַּחֲדָא מִנְחָה אַיְירֵי, וְרֵישָׁא נַמִי הָכִי תָּנָא: נִתְעָרֵב קוּמְצָהּ בְּקוֹמֶץ חֲבֵירְתָּהּ כְּשֵׁרָה, וַהֲוָה לֵיהּ לְמִיתְנֵי "כְּשֵׁרוֹת". יא] *אִם יָכוֹל לִקְמוֹץ מִזּוֹ בִּפְנֵי עַצְמָהּ. שֶׁנָּפְלָה יב] זוֹ בְּצַד זוֹ, וְנִשְׁאַר מִזּוֹ כְּדֵי קוֹמֶץ שֶׁלֹּא נִתְעָרֵב – כְּשֵׁרוֹת, וְאִם לָאו פְּסוּלוֹת, דְּאָמַר בְּתוֹרַת כֹּהֲנִים: "מִסָּלְתָּהּ" – וְלֹא מִסֹּלֶת חֲבֵירְתָּהּ. לֹא יַקְטִיר. אֲפִי' כָּל הַמְעוֹרֶבֶת, דְּאֵין הַקְטָרָה מִצְוָה אֶלָּא בַּקּוֹמֶץ. וּמִקְמַץ נַמִי לָא מָצֵי קָמֵיץ שְׁנֵי קוֹמָצִים, דְּדִלְמָא בְּכָל קוֹמֶץ וְקוֹמֶץ יֵשׁ מִזֶּה שֶׁנִּתְעָרֵב, וְלֵיכָּא קוֹמֶץ שָׁלֵם [א] (א) מֵחֲמַת מִנְחָה. וְאִם הִקְטִיר. כָּל הַמְעוֹרֶבֶת, הִיא לֹא עָלְתָה לַבְּעָלִים, דְּהָא לֹא נִקְמְצָה, וְאֵין מִנְחַת נְדָבָה נִתֶּרֶת בְּלֹא קְמִיצָה. נִתְעָרֵב קוּמְצָהּ בְּשִׁירֶיהָ. לֹא יַקְטִיר אֶת כּוּלָּהּ, מִשּׁוּם דְּשִׁירַיִם אֲסוּרִין לְהַקְטִיר, דִּכְתִיב: "לֹא תַקְטִירוּ מִמֶּנּוּ אִשֶּׁה לַה'" (ויקרא ב), כָּל שֶׁמִּמֶּנּוּ לָאִשִּׁים הֲרֵי הוּא בְּ"בַל תַּקְטִירוּ". **גמ'** דָּם. דְּקָדָשִׁים. כָּשֵׁר. לִזְרִיקָה. נִתְעָרֵב בְּיַיִן. שֶׁהוּא אָדוֹם. רוֹאִין יג] אוֹתוֹ כְּאִילּוּ הוּא מַיִם. וְאִם הָיָה מַיִם וְהָיָה מַרְאִית הַדָּם נִיכָּר בֵּינֵיהֶם – כָּשֵׁר. בְּדַם הַבְּהֵמָה. שֶׁל חוּלִּין. רוֹאִין אוֹתוֹ. אֶת שֶׁל חוּלִּין. אֵין דָּם מְבַטֵּל דָּם. וְכָשֵׁר. הַדָּבָר יָדוּעַ כו'. אֲפִילּוּ הָכִי קָרֵי לֵיהּ אַחְתֵּי נַמִי דַּם שָׂעִיר, וְאַף עַל פִּי שֶׁנִּתְעָרֵב בּוֹ דַּם הַפָּר, כִּדְאָמְרִינַן בְּמַסֶּכֶת יוֹמָא (דף נג:): עֵירָה דַּם הַפָּר לְתוֹךְ דַּם הַשָּׂעִיר.
מִכָּאן

תוספות

ועצים דפשיטא ליה לתנא משל צבור מנלן. וא"ת: ולילף ממלח כדלעיל, דאין להשיב מלבונה! ושמא יש לד אחד.

שזו בלילתה עבה. מנחת נדבה יד] [ב] ולוג לעשרון, כדדרשי' בפ' "שתי מדות" (לקמן פט.), טו] כדכתיב במצורע עני: "ועשרון סלת בלול בשמן למנחה ולוג שמן" [ג] טז] דמייתא ליה למנחה ולוג שמן, למתנדב מנחה לא יפחות מדבר הטעון לוג, ומאי ניהו עשרון. ומנחת הנסכים וכהן משיח שלשה לוגין לעשרון, כדמפרש בקונט'.

שזו בלילתה עבה וזו בלילתה רכה והן בולעות זו מזו. אע"ג דקתני "פסולה", דמשמע האחת, נראה דשתיהן פסולות, העבה והרכה, מדקתני: "והן בולעות זו מזו". ומיהו בבליעה חדא מיפסלי תרווייהו, דכי בלע קומץ ממנחת נסכים מיפסיל קומץ – דהוה ליה ריבה שמנה, ומיפסלא מנחת נסכים – דהוה ליה חיסר שמנה. והא דקתני "פסולה" ולא קתני "פסולות" – משום דכולה מתניתין בלישנא דחדא מנחה איירי. ורישא נמי הכי תנן: נתערב קומצה בקומץ של חבירתה – כשרה, והוה ליה למיתני "כשרות". וכששתיהן בלילתן עבה או רכה, אף על פי שבולעות זו מזו – לא חשיב לא ריבה שמנה ולא חיסר שמנה, ולא [ד] מפסלא. **והן** בולעות זו מזו. פי' בקונטרס: הקומץ בולע מן מנחת נסכים, והוה ליה יז] ריבה שמנה. ובגמ' גבי הא דפריך לרב חסדא דאמר בתר מבטל אזלינן, ממתניתין דשתי מנחות שלא נקמצו, דאם יכול לקמוץ מזו בפני עצמה ומזו בפני עצמה כשרה: והא כיון דקמיץ ליה מחדא – אידך הוה ליה שירייס, ולא מבטל ליה שירייס לטיבלא! ופי' בקונטרס [ה] שטיבלא דלא מבטל להו לשירייס דניהוו כריבה סולתה – לא מצי למיפרך לרבי חנינא, דנימא מהכא דבתר מבטל אזלינן, דאי בתר בטל אזלינן שירייס מי הוי טיבלא. דאי נמי בתר בטל אזלינן, וטיבלא מבטל לשירייס – לא הוי ריבה סולתה, דבטילי וכמאן דליתיה דמי, ולא מייתר ליה. ופירוש זה סותר מה שפירש במשנה, דמהאי טעמא לא יחשוב [ו] כמו ריבה שמנה. ואין לפרש דמה דמיפסלן הכא לאו משום ריבה שמנה, אלא משום חיסר שמנה. דאדרבה, לפי מה שמפרש בגמ' גבי חרב שנתערב בבלול, לא מיפסלן אלא משום [ז] ריבה שמנה. **והן** בולעות זו מזו. מין בשאינו מינו חשיב ליה בגמרא, משום דאמרי': סלק את מינו כמי שאינו, ושאינו מינו רבה עליו ומבטלו. שהסולת של קומץ רבה על השמן של מנחת נסכים ומבטלו. ותימה: דמהאי טעמא נמי ליפסול לרבי יהודה נתערב קומצה בקומץ חבירתה. וזה הוא תימה לומר משום דבלילתן שוות אין זו בולעת מזו! ועוד, נתערב קומצה בשיריה, דקתני סיפא דאם הקטיר עלתה לבעלים, ופריך מינה בגמרא דליבטלו שירייס לקומץ, ומשני ר' זירא: נאמרה הקטרה בקומץ כו'. למה לן האי שינויא? הא אמרינן דבלילתן שוות ואין בולעות זו מזו, יח] ומאי אין קומץ מבטל קומץ שייך כאן! ועוד תימה: [ח] דבגזירה שוה דר' זירא אליבא דרבי יהודה נמי מסקי לה, ומשמע דאין הקומץ מבטל חבירו, אפי' קומץ דמנחת חוטא וקומץ דמנחת נדבה, אף על פי שזה חרב וזה בלול! ומה שכתוב בספרים בגמ' גבי חרב שנתערב עם בלול: מאי לאו קומץ דמנחת חוטא דאיערב בקומץ דמנחת נדבה לא גרסינן הכי, אלא כספרים דגרסי: דאיערב במנחת נסכים. אבל שום קומץ אין מבטל חבירו, אפי' לרבי יהודה, דאי משכחת חד קומץ דמבטל לא תתקיים גזירה שוה. והשתא, מנלן לרבי יהודה דלא יבטלו זה את זה קומץ דמנחת חוטא וקומץ דמנחת נדבה? [ט] הא בלעי מהדדי! ועוד תימה: למאי דמסקינן מגזירה שוה דר' זירא אליבא דר' יהודה, א"כ מנחת נסכים וקומץ נמי לא ליבטלו זה את זה! ומיהו הא לאו פירכא היא, דדוקא בקומץ ושירייס איכא גזירה שוה דהקטרה הקטרה, אבל מנחת נסכים כולה כליל, ואין כאן קומץ ושירייס. **אם** יש בו מראית דם כשר. לא באדמומית מעט מתכשר, אלא מראית דם גמור קאמר, למעוטי היכא דדיהה מראיתו. דהא דדם הפר מרובה על דמו של שעיר, משמע דאי לאו משום עולין או משום מין במינו – היה בטל, אע"פ שאם היה דמו של פר מים היה בו מראית דם שעיר קצת. **הדבר** ידוע שדמו של פר מרובה על דמו של שעיר. פי': והיה לו לדמו של שעיר להיות בטל. תימה: דאיפכא הוה ליה למידק, דאמרינן ביומא (דף נג:) [י] שעירב דם הפר בדם השעיר. והיא דדם שנתערב במים אמרי' בפ' "התערובות" (זבחים עח.) ובפרק "כיסוי הדם" (חולין פז:): לא שנו אלא שנפלו מים לתוך דם, אבל דם לתוך מים – ראשון ראשון בטל. והילכך, האי דם הפר היה לו להבטל ראשון ראשון בדם השעיר! ואפי' מאן דלית ליה ראשון ראשון בטל בפ' בתרא דמסכת ע"ז (דף עג.) הכא מודה, משום דהוה ליה נראה ונדחה! וי"ל: דלא אמרינן ראשון ראשון בטל כשמערה בשפע הרבה ביחד, כמו שמחלק בפרק בתרא דמסכת ע"ז (שם) בין חבית דנפיש עמודיה לצרצור קטן דלא נפיש עמודיה. ואפילו מאן דאית ליה ראשון ראשון בטל בחבית, ביותר מפי חבית היה מודה דלא בטל*.
מכאן

עין משפט נר מצוה

כח א מיי' פ"ו מהל' איסורי מזבח הלכה ב ופ"ו הלכה ג:
כט ב מיי' פ"ו מהל' פסה"מ הלכה כח:
ל ג ד מיי' פ"כ מהלכות פסה"מ הלכה כב:

שיטה מקובצת

א] דקורקסא דדיישא דשתאי: ב] במנחת נסכים פסולה פי' הקומץ של מנחת ישראל לפי שבלע הקומץ ממנחת נסכים ורבה שמן דמנחת נסכים על הקומץ ומבטלו והוי מנחה שלא נקטרו קומצה ופסולה אבל מנחת נסכים כשרה דלא הוי כריבה שמנה כיון דשלא מדעת ערבו בטל וכמאן דליתא ע"כ בגירסא של רש"י כת"י: ג] והן בולעות כו' פי' רש"י הקומץ כו' ובגמ' פי' שיטה אחרת דבטל הוא לעולם כמאן דליתא וא"כ לא יפסל הקומץ דלא הוי ליה ריבה שמנה כיון דהשמן אשר יש בו ממנחת נסכים הוא בטל והוי כמאן דליתא ולפי זה לא יפסול כי אם מנחת נסכים לבד ולא הקומץ וניחא לפי זה הא דתני פסולה ולא פסולות ובספרים אחרים מצאתי וזה לשונו והן בולעות זו מזו הקומץ בולע ממנחת נסכים ורבה שמן דמנחת נסכים על הקומץ ומבטל ליה והוי ליה כמנחה שלא הקטיר קומצה ופסולה הנקמצת אבל מנחת נסכים כשרה ולא הוי כריבה שמנה כיון דשלא מדעת ערבן בטל לגביה וכמאן דליתא וא"ת משמע דבמנחת כהנים ובקומץ חברתה מודה ר"י דכשרות לפי שהן שוות בבלילתן ולא מבטל זו את זו ותימה מאי שנא מהא דאמר' בגמרא גבי הא דמייתי תנן שתי מנחות כו' ופריך כו' וי"ל כו' [עיין לקמן בתו"ח] מין במינו וכו' ור"י סבר מין במינו לא בטיל כדיליף מדם הפר ומדם השעיר: ד] נתערב בדם בהמה. וא"ת כ"ש בדם חיה (ולמה ליה למיתני או בדם חיה] וי"ל דלהודיעך כחו דר"י תניא: ה] או בדם חיה. חיה ממש. וי"א בדם בהמה שיצא ממנה בחייה כגון בדם הקזה: ו] דשתאי ותיבת דישא נמחק: ז] יפה ומצוייר הס"ד: ח] במנחת כהנים כו' ותיבת כשרה נמחק: ט] נסכים ובמנחת: י] שמן והביתי כהן גדול נמי שלשה ותיבות ויליף חביתין מינה ליתא שמה: יא] אם יכול. שייך למתניתין שאחרי זאת: יב] זו בצד זו של כלי וזו בצד זו ונשאר מזו כדי קומץ שלא נתערב ומזו כדי קומץ כשרות ואם: יג] רואין את היין כאילו: יד] נדבה לוג: טו] מדות מדכתיב ואות כ' נמחק: טז] שמן דמייתר: יז] ריבה שמנה וקשה דאמרינן בגמרא גבי שתי מנחות שלא נקמצו כו' קא פריך כיון דקמיץ (ליה) [להו] מחדא אידך הוו (להו) [ליה] שירים ולא מבטלי שירים למטבלא והתם הוי בלילתן שוה ואינם יכולים לבלוע זו מזו וא"כ אמאי (ה"ל) [הו"א] שיבטלו זו את זו והלא אמרינן הכא דאם בלילתן שוה לא מבטלי אהדדי ויש לומר דשאני התם משום דשיריים ובטל הוי מין בשאינו מינו ומשום הכי מבטלין זה את זה אבל הכא דהוו מין במינו אם בלילתו שוה לא מבטלי זה את זה אבל היכא דאינם שוות דזו בלילתן עבה וזו בלילתן רכה הוי מין בשאינו מינו ובולע הקומץ מן המנחה וחסרה שהרי בטל את שמנה קומץ העבה דלא הוי מינו כדפי' וא"ת כיון שהוא מתבטל בקומץ העבה א"כ העבה [אמאי] פסולה משום קומץ [יתר] ומשמע דעיקר פסולה משום קומץ תני לה מדקתני נתערב קומצה וכן פ"ה והא בטיל ליה ופי' הר"מ דודאי נהי דבטיל היינו דוקא לחסר את הרכה ממה שנפלט ממנה שהרי [בלע] העבה ובטלי הרכה אבל ודאי אינו בטל למיהוי כמאן דליתא כלל אלא כאשר הוא שדינן ליה והוי קומץ יתר והקונטרס בגמרא לא פירש כן כמו שכתוב בתוס' לקמן. תו"ח: יח] ומאי אין קומץ מבטל קומץ. גליון ואומר ר"י דודאי לא בלעי מיהו בטלי אהדדי אי לאו טעמא דר' זירא והקשה הר"מ לדברי ר' זירא רכה בעבה אמאי בטלה נאמר הקטרה בקומץ ונאמר הקטרה במנחת כהנים כליל תקטר (ומהאי) [וי"ל דמהאי] טעמא לא בטלי ומיהו מבלע בלעי ופסלה:
מכאן

מסורת הש"ס

זבחים קטז:
ג"ז שם: ע"ש ע"ז כד: ע"ש
שייך לדף כג ע"א
זבחים עז: חולין פז:
[זבחים לה. וש"נ]
[ועי' תוס' יומא נז: ד"ה עירה ותוס' זבחים עז: ד"ה רואין]

הגהות הב"ח

(א) רש"י ד"ה לא יקטיר וכו' קומץ שלם ממנחה אחת הס"ד ואח"כ מ"ה ואח"כ מ"ה המעורבת הס"ד ואח"כ מ"ה לא עלתה ותיבת היא נמחק:

הגהות צ"ק

[א] נ"א מכל וגי' צ"ק מחלה: [ב] לוג: [ג] דמייתר: [ד] מיפסלא ותימה דהכא פי' בקונטרס כו' והד"א וכ"ה בס"י: [ה] מהא שטיבלא: [ו] נמי ריבה: [ז] ריבה שמנה ובגמרא חשיב ליה מין בשאינו מינו ומשום דאמרינן כו' הד"א וכ"ה בס"י: [ח] דגזירה: [ט] דהא: [י] שעירה דס הפר לתוך דס השעיר:

עין משפט נר מצוה

כא א מיי' פ"ח מהלכות מעילה הלכה ז:
כב ב מיי' שם הל' ו:
כג ג מיי' פ"ה מהל' איסורי מזבח הלכה יג:
כד ד מיי' פ"ו מהל' מעשה"ק הלכה יא:
כה ה מיי' פ"ח מהל' מעילה הלכה ו:
כו ו מיי' פ"ה מהל' איסורי מזבח הל' יג:
כז ז מיי' פ"א מהלכות שקלים הלכה ז:

גמרא

תורה אור

*תָּנוּ רַבָּנַן: אמֶלַח שֶׁעַל גַּבֵּי הָאֵבָר — מוֹעֲלִין בּוֹ, שֶׁעַ"ג הַכֶּבֶשׁ וְשֶׁבְּרֹאשׁוֹ שֶׁל מִזְבֵּחַ — אֵין מוֹעֲלִין בּוֹ. א] וְאָמַר רַב מַתָּנָה: מַאי קְרָאָה? °"וְהִקְרַבְתָּם לִפְנֵי ה' וְהִשְׁלִיכוּ הַכֹּהֲנִים עֲלֵיהֶם מֶלַח וְהֶעֱלוּ אוֹתָם עוֹלָה לַה'". § *תְּנַן הָתָם: בעַל הַמֶּלַח וְעַל הָעֵצִים, שֶׁיְּהוּ הַכֹּהֲנִים נֵאוֹתִין בָּהֶן. אָמַר שְׁמוּאֵל: לֹא שָׁנוּ אֶלָּא לְקָרְבָּנָם, אֲבָל לַאֲכִילָה — לֹא. קָא ס"ד: מַאי "לְקָרְבָּנָם" — לִמְלוֹחַ קָרְבָּנָם, ב] "לֶאֱכוֹל" — אֲכִילַת קָדָשִׁים; הַשְׁתָּא לִמְלוֹחַ עוֹרוֹת קָדָשִׁים יָהֲבִינַן, לַאֲכִילַת קָדָשִׁים לָא יָהֲבִינַן? *דְּתַנְיָא: נִמְצֵאתָ אַתָּה אוֹמֵר, גבִּשְׁלֹשָׁה מְקוֹמוֹת הַמֶּלַח נְתוּנָה: בְּלִשְׁכַּת הַמֶּלַח, וְעַל גַּבֵּי הַכֶּבֶשׁ, וּבְרֹאשׁוֹ שֶׁל מִזְבֵּחַ; בְּלִשְׁכַּת הַמֶּלַח — *שֶׁשָּׁם מוֹלְחִין עוֹרוֹת קָדָשִׁים, עַל גַּבֵּי הַכֶּבֶשׁ — שֶׁשָּׁם מוֹלְחִים אֶת הָאֵבָרִים, בְּרֹאשׁוֹ שֶׁל מִזְבֵּחַ — שֶׁשָּׁם מוֹלְחִין הַקּוֹמֶץ וְהַלְּבוֹנָה, וְהַקְּטוֹרֶת, וּמִנְחַת כֹּהֲנִים, וּמִנְחַת כֹּהֵן מָשִׁיחַ, וּמִנְחַת נְסָכִים, וְעוֹלַת הָעוֹף! אֶלָּא מַאי "לְקָרְבָּנָם" — לַאֲכִילַת קָרְבָּנָם, וּמַאי "לַאֲכִילָה" — אֲכִילָה דְּחוּלִּין. ג] חוּלִּין, פְּשִׁיטָא! מַאי בָּעוּ הָתָם? אע"ג דְּאָמַר מָר: "יֹאכְלוּ" — דשֶׁיֹּאכְלוּ עִמָּהּ חוּלִּין וּתְרוּמָה כְּדֵי שֶׁתְּהֵא נֶאֱכֶלֶת עַל הַשּׂוֹבַע, אֲפִילּוּ הָכִי המֶלַח דְּקָדָשִׁים לָא יָהֲבִינַן לְהוּ. אֲמַר לֵיהּ רָבִינָא לְרַב אַשִׁי: ה"נ מִסְתַּבְּרָא, דְּאִי סָלְקָא דַעְתָּךְ מַאי "לְקָרְבָּנָם" — לִמְלוֹחַ, טַעְמָא דְּאַתְנֵי בֵּית דִּין, הָא לָא אַתְנֵי בֵּית דִּין — לָא; הַשְׁתָּא לְיִשְׂרָאֵל יָהֲבִינַן, לְכֹהֲנִים לָא יָהֲבִינַן? דְּתַנְיָא: יָכוֹל הָאוֹמֵר "הֲרֵי עָלַי מִנְחָה" יָבִיא מֶלַח מִתּוֹךְ בֵּיתוֹ, כְּדֶרֶךְ שֶׁמֵּבִיא לְבוֹנָה מִתּוֹךְ בֵּיתוֹ? וְדִין הוּא: נֶאֱמַר הָבֵיא מִנְחָה וְהָבֵיא מֶלַח, וְנֶאֱמַר הָבֵיא מִנְחָה וְהָבֵיא לְבוֹנָה, מַה לְּבוֹנָה מִתּוֹךְ בֵּיתוֹ — אַף מֶלַח מִתּוֹךְ בֵּיתוֹ. אוֹ כְּלָךְ לְדֶרֶךְ זוֹ: נֶאֱמַר הָבֵיא מִנְחָה וְהָבֵיא מֶלַח, וְנֶאֱמַר הָבֵיא מִנְחָה וְהָבֵיא עֵצִים, °מָה עֵצִים מִשֶּׁל צִיבּוּר — אַף ומֶלַח מִשֶּׁל צִיבּוּר? נִרְאֶה לְמִי דּוֹמֶה, דָּנִין דָּבָר הַנּוֹהֵג בְּכָל הַזְּבָחִים מִדָּבָר הַנּוֹהֵג בְּכָל הַזְּבָחִים, וְאַל תּוֹכִיחַ לְבוֹנָה שֶׁאֵינָהּ נוֹהֶגֶת בְּכָל הַזְּבָחִים. אוֹ כְּלָךְ לְדֶרֶךְ זוֹ: דָּנִין דָּבָר הַבָּא עִמָּהּ בִּכְלִי אֶחָד מִדָּבָר הַבָּא עִמָּהּ בִּכְלִי אֶחָד, וְאַל יוֹכִיחוּ עֵצִים שֶׁאֵינָן בָּאִין עִמָּהּ בִּכְלִי אֶחָד? ת"ל: °"בְּרִית מֶלַח עוֹלָם הוּא", וּלְהַלָּן הוּא אוֹמֵר: °"מֵאֵת בְּנֵי יִשְׂרָאֵל בְּרִית עוֹלָם", מַה לְּהַלָּן מִשֶּׁל צִיבּוּר — אַף כָּאן מִשֶּׁל צִיבּוּר! אֲמַר לֵיהּ רַב מָרְדֳּכַי לְרַב אַשִׁי, ד] הָכִי קָאָמַר רַב שֵׁישָׁא בְּרֵיהּ דְּרַב אִידִי: לָא נִצְרְכָא אֶלָּא לְבֶן בּוּכְרִי, דִּתְנַן: *אָמַר רַבִּי יְהוּדָה, הֵעִיד בֶּן *בּוּכְרִי בְּיַבְנֶה: כָּל כֹּהֵן שֶׁשּׁוֹקֵל אֵינוֹ חוֹטֵא; אָמַר לוֹ רַבָּן יוֹחָנָן בֶּן זַכַּאי: לֹא כִּי, אֶלָּא זכָּל כֹּהֵן שֶׁאֵינוֹ שׁוֹקֵל חוֹטֵא, אֶלָּא ה] שֶׁהַכֹּהֲנִים דּוֹרְשִׁין מִקְרָא זֶה לְעַצְמָן: °"וְכָל מִנְחַת ו] כֹּהֵן כָּלִיל תִּהְיֶה לֹא תֵאָכֵל", הוֹאִיל וְעוֹמֶר וּשְׁתֵּי הַלֶּחֶם וְלֶחֶם הַפָּנִים שֶׁלָּנוּ הִיא, הֵיאַךְ נֶאֱכָלִין? וּלְבֶן בּוּכְרִי, כֵּיוָן דִּלְכַתְּחִילָּה לָא מִיחַיַּיב לְאֵיתוּיֵי, כִּי מַיְיתֵי נַמִי — חוֹטֵא הוּא, דְּקָא מְעַיֵּיל חוּלִּין לַעֲזָרָה! *דְּמַיְיתֵי וּמָסַר לְהוּן לַצִּיבּוּר. סָלְקָא דַעְתָּךְ אָמִינָא, כִּי

יחזקאל מג
במדבר יח
ויקרא כד
שקלים פ"א מ"ד [לק' מו: ערכין ד. [בערוך גורס כוכרי]
ויקרא ו
[וע' תוס' יומא לה: ד"ה ניחוח]

רש"י

*וְכֵן לִקְדֵרָה. אֵין צָרִיךְ לְמוֹלְחָהּ יוֹתֵר. שֶׁעַל הַכֶּבֶשׁ כו'. שֶׁנּוֹפֵל שָׁם כְּשֶׁמּוֹלְחִין (אֶת הַקּוֹמֶץ) ז] אֶת הָאֵבָרִים, כִּדְאַמְרִינַן לְקַמָּן: בִּשְׁלֹשָׁה מְקוֹמוֹת נְתוּנָה. אֵין מוֹעֲלִין בּוֹ. דְּשׁוּב אֵינוֹ רָאוּי. מַאי ח] קְרָאָה. דְּשֶׁעַל גַּבֵּי הָאֵבָר מוֹעֲלִין? דִּכְתִיב: "וְהִשְׁלִיכוּ עֲלֵיהֶם הַכֹּהֲנִים מֶלַח וְהֶעֱלוּ אוֹתָם עוֹלָה", אַלְמָא דְּאֵבָר עִם מִלְחוֹ שְׁנֵיהֶם קְרוּיִין עוֹלָה. תְּנַן הָתָם. בְּמַסֶּכֶת שְׁקָלִים: עַל שִׁבְעָה דְּבָרִים הִתְנוּ ב"ד, וְאֵלּוּ שְׁנַיִם מֵהֶם: עַל הַמֶּלַח וְעַל הָעֵצִים שֶׁל קֹדֶשׁ. שֶׁהַכֹּהֲנִים נֵיאוֹתִין בָּהֶן. נֶהֱנִין מֵהֶן. לִמְלוֹחַ קָרְבָּנָם. עוֹלוֹתָם וּמִנְחָתָם שֶׁהֵן מְבִיאִין. לַאֲכִילַת קָרְבָּנָם. כְּלוֹמַר, לַאֲכִילָה הַמַּגִּיעַ לְחֶלְקָם, כְּגוֹן חָזֶה וְשׁוֹק חַטָּאוֹת וַאֲשָׁמוֹת שֶׁהַיָּחִיד מֵבִיא וְהֵן אוֹכְלִין. מַאי בָּעוּ הָתָם. חוּלִּין בָּעֲזָרָה. הָכִי גָּרְסִינַן: יֹאכְלוּ שֶׁיֹּאכְלוּ עִמָּהּ. ט] כּוּלָּהּ בְּתוֹרַת כֹּהֲנִים קָא דָּרֵישׁ י] (עִמָּהּ כו') הַאי קְרָא "וְהַנּוֹתֶרֶת מִמֶּנָּה" וגו', דִּכְתִיב בְּרֵישֵׁיהּ דִּקְרָא: "יֹאכְלוּ אַהֲרֹן וּבָנָיו" וּבְסֵיפֵיהּ כְּתִיב: "יֹאכְלוּהָ", וְדָרֵישׁ הָתָם: "יֹאכְלוּ" — שֶׁיֹּאכְלוּ עִמָּהּ חוּלִּין וּתְרוּמָה בִּזְמַן שֶׁהִיא מְעוּטָה, "יֹאכְלוּהָ" דְּסֵיפָא — שֶׁלֹּא יֹאכְלוּ עִמָּהּ חוּלִּין וּתְרוּמָה בִּזְמַן שֶׁהִיא מְרוּבָּה. לְבוֹנָה מִתּוֹךְ בֵּיתוֹ. דִּכְתִיב (ויקרא ב): "וְנָתַן עָלֶיהָ לְבוֹנָה" וַהֲדַר "וֶהֱבִיאָהּ אֶל בְּנֵי אַהֲרֹן". וְהֵבִיא עֵצִים. דִּכְתִיב: "עַל הָעֵצִים אֲשֶׁר עַל הָאֵשׁ". עֵצִים מִשֶּׁל צִיבּוּר. מְפָרֵשׁ לְקַמָּן (א). עֵצִים וּמֶלַח נוֹהֲגִים בְּכָל הַזְּבָחִים. מֶלַח בָּא עִם הַקּוֹמֶץ בִּכְלִי. בְּרִית עוֹלָם. בְּלֶחֶם הַפָּנִים כְּתִיב. מַה לְּהַלָּן מִשֶּׁל צִיבּוּר. דִּכְתִיב: "מֵאֵת בְּנֵי יִשְׂרָאֵל". לָא נִצְרְכָא. לְהַתְנוֹת לְבֵית דִּין שֶׁיְּהוּ כֹּהֲנִים מוֹלְחִין קָרְבָּנָם מִשֶּׁל הֶקְדֵּשׁ. אֶלָּא לְבֶן בּוּכְרִי. הָאוֹמֵר: אֵין כֹּהֲנִים חַיָּיבִים (ב) בִּשְׁקָלִים. כָּל כֹּהֵן שֶׁשּׁוֹקֵל. שֶׁמֵּבִיא שִׁקְלוֹ לַלִּשְׁכָּה בַּאֲדָר. אֵינוֹ חוֹטֵא. מִדְּקָאָמַר אֵינוֹ חוֹטֵא, מִכְּלָל דִּלְכַתְּחִילָּה לָא מִיחַיַּיב. וְטַעְמָא מְפָרֵשׁ בְּמַסֶּ' שְׁקָלִים — דִּכְתִיב: "כָּל הָעוֹבֵר עַל הַפְּקוּדִים", וְשֵׁבֶט לֵוִי לֹא נִפְקָד. וְאַע"ג דְּאִיכָּא לְמֵימַר: הָא מַיְיתֵי חוּלִּין לָעֲזָרָה, אֲפִילּוּ הָכִי אֵינוֹ חוֹטֵא כִּדְמְפָרֵשׁ לְקַמָּן. כָּל כֹּהֵן שֶׁאֵינוֹ שׁוֹקֵל חוֹטֵא. בִּשְׁקָלִים מְפָרֵשׁ טַעְמָא, דִּכְתִיב: "זֶה יִתְּנוּ" — "זֶה" בְּגִימַטְרִיָּא שְׁנֵים עָשָׂר שְׁבָטִים, וְהַיְינוּ (ג) שֵׁבֶט לֵוִי. וְ"כָל הָעוֹבֵר" מְפָרֵשׁ הָתָם: כָּל הָעוֹבֵר בַּיָּם סוּף. לְעַצְמָן. לַהֲנָאָתָן. וְקָא פָּרֵיךְ: וּלְבֶן בּוּכְרִי כו'. סד"א וכו'. וְהַשְׁתָּא מְפָרֵשׁ "לָא נִצְרְכָא" דִּלְעֵיל.

תוספות

בלשכת המלח ששם מולחין עורות קדשים. תימה: דבמסכת מדות (פ"ה מ"ג) דחשיב שם לשכות שבעזרה, קתני: לשכת המלח – ששם היו נותנין מלח לקרבן, לשכת הפרוה – ששם היו מולחים עורות יא] קדשים! וי"ל: דהא דקאמר הכא ששם מולחין עורות קדשים – יב] לאו דוקא, אלא כלומר: משם היו נוטלין מלח למלוח עורות קדשים בלשכת הפרוה. והמלח לא היה נתון בלשכת המלח למלוח, כי אם להצניעו שם. והא דקתני עלה במסכת מדות (גם זה שם) ששם היו נותנין מלח לקרבן – היינו כלומר הצניעו לצורך קרבנות, כגון למלוח עורות וכל דבר. וקשיא לפירוש זה, דא"כ היתה מלח בד' מקומות, והכא לא חשיב אלא שלשה! **והקטרת**. ואם תאמר: למה מולחין את הקטורת בראשו של מזבח יותר יג] מעל הכבש? והלא במזבח הפנימי היה קרבו! וי"ל: לפי שעל הכבש היה מתלכלך בדם האברים, אבל על המזבח היו מולחין דבר יבש – קומץ ולבונה ומנחת כהנים ומנחת כהן משיח. ואע"פ שהיו מולחין שם עולת העוף, היה יד] מועט.

חולין פשיטא מאי בעו התם. פי' בקונטרס: משום דמכניס חולין לעזרה. ומשני: אע"ג דאמר מר "יאכלו" שיאכלו עמה חולין ותרומה, ופי' *בקונטרס: כלומר, חוץ לעזרה יאכלו חולין ותרומה, ויכניסו ויאכלוה על השובע. ותימה: הואיל והני חולין לורך אכילת קדשים הן, ליתיב להו מלח *לקדש! ומיהו אפילו בעזרה מכניסים תבלי חולין, דתנן בפ' "כל התדיר" (זבחים דף צ:): וכולן רשאין הכהנים לתת לתוכן תבלי חולין ותרומה, ונפקא ליה בגמ' מדכתיב "למשחה" – לגדולה. ושמא באותן תבלין פשיטא שיכול ליתן מלח של קודש, כמו בקדשים עצמן.

ת"ל ברית מלח עולם הוא. ר"ת גורס: "מלח ברית" כדפרישית לעיל (דף יט:). **כל** כהן ששוקל אינו חוטא. לבן בוכרי אפילו לוים פטורים כמו כהנים, כדפריש טעמא במסכת שקלים: "כל העובר על הפקודים", ושבט לוי לא נפקד. אבל רבן יוחנן בן זכאי דריש: "כל העובר" – עובר בים סוף. אף על גב דכתיב בפרשת "אלה פקודי" מאת ככר ואלף טו] ותשעה – היינו לתרומת האדנים. דשלש תרומות היו כדמפרש בקונטרס בפרשת "כי תשא", ובאותה של האדנים לא היה שבט לוי, אבל באותה של צורך קרבנות היו. והשתא ניחא טפי הא דכתיב "כל העובר" – בים סוף טז] [משמע] (על הפקודים יז] דהא) [והא] דכתיב "על הפקודים" – משום תרומת אדנים. ומיהו בלא"ה יש לפרש "כל העובר על הפקודים" – שנפקדו, בין לבדם בין עם ישראל. **שהכהנים** דורשין מקרא זה לעצמן. משמע דרבן יוחנן בן זכאי לא *)היה כהן. והא דתניא בסיפרי גבי פרה שאמר רבן יוחנן בן זכאי לתלמידיו: מה שעשו ושרתו ידי שכחתי – לאו דהוא עצמו קאמר, אלא כלומר: ע"פ הוראתו. והא דמסקינן התם: ויש אומרים הילל היה, אלא שלא היה יכול לומר "מה שעשו ושרתו ידי" היינו טעמא – לפי שלא שרפו פרה בימיו.

*) [וע' רש"י שבת לד. ד"ה תורמסי תרומה]

ועלים

[וע"ע תוס' תמורה כג: ד"ה אוכלין עמה ובתוס' פסחים סו: ד"ה מביאה ובתוס' לקמן פ: ד"ה וכי ובתוס' ב"ב פא: ד"ה ודלמא ובתוס' חולין קל: ד"ה אי ותוס' זבחים עז. ד"ה וחולין]

מסורת הש"ם

ד"ז שייך לעיל
תוספתא פ"ו דמנחות
שקלים פ"ז מ"ז
תוספתא פ"ו ע"ש
ל"ק מ"ז
יומא יט.
תמורה כג.

הגהות הב"ח

(א) רש"י ד"ה עצים ו... לקמן הס"ד ואח"כ מ... בכל הזבחים עצים ומ... וכו'. הזבחים הס"ד ואח... מ"ה בכלי אחד מלח ו... בכלי אחד הס"ד: (ב) ד... אלא וכו' בשקלים. כ... א"כ אין להם חלק במ... וה"א שגרועים מישר... כדמסיים בסוף הש... (ג) ד"ה כל כהן וכו' והי... גם שבט לוי:

גליון הש"ס

גמ' מה עצים משל צבור. ע' זבחים דף ק ע"א תו' ד"ה לא:

שיטה מקובצת

א] בו אמר רב מתנה אמר קרא: ב] קרבנם לאכילה לאכילת קדשים: ג] חולין פשיטא מאי בעו התם. פ"ה משום דמכנים חולין לעזרה ולא נהירא דלא שייך לאסור כי אם בהקרבה ועוד דבפרק התערובות אמרינן דרשאין הכהנים לתת לתוכו תבלין חולין כו' א) א"כ משמע דלא שייך חולין בעזרה כי אם בביתם תו"ח: ד] הכי אמר. ערכין (דף ד ע"א): ה] אלא הכהנים. גליון ומוטעים הם שאינו ר"ל אלא אותה שבאה מכהנים לבדם עיין רש"י לקמן (דף מו ע"ב): ו] כהן. עי' תוס' לקמן (דף נז ע"א): ז] את הקומץ תיבות את האברים ליתא שם: ח] מאי קרא אות ה' נמחק: ט] עמה כו' ותיבת כולה נמחק: י] בתורת כהנים קא דריש עמה כו': יא] קדשים וי"ל דהא דהכא ר"ל שנוטלין המלח למלוח עורות קדשים ולעולם בלשכת בית הפרוה היו מולחין אותו שנוטלין מהתם והא דאמר הכא ששם היו מולחין עורות קדשים לאו דוקא אלא ר"ל משם היו מולחין כלומר ממלח שהיה בלשכת המלח היו נוטלין וי"מ איפכא נוטלין ממלח שהיה בלשכת הפרוה ומולחין העורות בלשכת המלח ולא נהירא דא"כ הוה ליה למתני בד' מקומות המלח נתונה. מהר"... יב] לאו דוקא ועי"ל דלשכת בית הפרוה דהתם קרי הכא לשכת בית המלח דהתם אוצר המלח שמשם נוטלים כל הצורך ונראה לומר דלכך נקרא בית הפרוה בית המלח לפי שהיה שם רוב מליחות יותר מן הכבש ומרא... של מזבח. תו"ח: יג] מעל הכבש ולמולחו על הכבש שהיה קרוב להוליכו לפנים. תו"ח: יד] מעט אות ו' נמחק וא"ת אמאי לא היו מולחין הקטורת אצל המזבח וי"ל דאיכא טירחא יתירא משום שהמלח לא היה ש... תו"ח: טו] ואלף ות"ש ע"ה: טז] העובר בים סוף עובר על הפקודים תיבת משמע ליתא שם: יז] דהא כתיב על הפקודים ובתו"ח תירצו דעל הפקודים ר"ל עם הפקודים ועל ר"ל אצל כמו ועליו מטה מנש...

א) נראה דל"ל א"כ משמע למותר להכניס חולין בעזרה ולכן נראה לפרש פשיטא מאי בעי התם משום דלא שכיח חולין בעזרה כי אם בביתם:

אַפֵּיק עֵצִים וְעַיֵּיל נְסָכִים, דְּתַנְיָא: אאֲבָל הַיַּיִן וְהַדָּם, וְהָעֵצִים וְהַקְּטֹרֶת — אֵין טְעוּנִין מֶלַח. מַנִּי? אִי רַבִּי — קַשְׁיָא עֵצִים, אִי רַבָּנַן — קַשְׁיָא קְטֹרֶת! הַאי תַּנָּא הוּא, דְּתַנְיָא, רַבִּי יִשְׁמָעֵאל בְּנוֹ שֶׁל ר' יוֹחָנָן בֶּן בְּרוֹקָה אוֹמֵר: מַה הַפְּרָט מְפוֹרָשׁ — דָּבָר שֶׁמְּקַבֵּל טוּמְאָה וְעוֹלֶה לָאִשִּׁים וְיֶשְׁנוֹ עַל מִזְבֵּחַ הַחִיצוֹן, אַף כָּל דָּבָר הַמְקַבֵּל טוּמְאָה וְעוֹלֶה לָאִשִּׁים וְיֶשְׁנוֹ עַל מִזְבֵּחַ הַחִיצוֹן; יָצְאוּ עֵצִים — שֶׁאֵין מְקַבְּלִין טוּמְאָה, יָצְאוּ דָּם וְיַיִן — שֶׁאֵין עוֹלִים לָאִשִּׁים, יָצְאָה קְטֹרֶת — שֶׁאֵינָהּ עַל מִזְבֵּחַ הַחִיצוֹן. אֶלָּא טַעְמָא דְּמַעֲטֵיהּ קְרָא לְדָם, הָא לָאו הָכִי — הֲוָה אָמֵינָא: דָּם לִיבְעֵי מֶלַח? כֵּיוָן דְּמַלְחֵיהּ נָפֵיק לֵיהּ מִתּוֹרַת דָּם! דְּאָמַר זְעִירִי א"ר חֲנִינָא: דָּם שֶׁבִּישְּׁלוֹ — אֵינוֹ עוֹבֵר עָלָיו, וְרַב יְהוּדָה אָמַר זְעִירִי: דָּם שֶׁמְּלָחוֹ — אֵינוֹ עוֹבֵר עָלָיו, *וְרַב יְהוּדָה דִּידֵיהּ אָמַר: באֵבָרִים שֶׁצְּלָאָן וְהֶעֱלָן — אֵין בָּהֶם מִשּׁוּם לְרֵיחַ נִיחוֹחַ! מַהוּ דְּתֵימָא, מִישְׁדָא בָּהּ מַשֶּׁהוּ לְמִצְוָה בְּעָלְמָא, קמ"ל. § גּוּפָא, אָמַר זְעִירִי א"ר חֲנִינָא: דָּם שֶׁבִּישְּׁלוֹ אֵינוֹ עוֹבֵר עָלָיו. יָתֵיב רָבָא וְקָא אָמַר לָהּ לְהָא שְׁמַעְתָּא. אֵיתִיבֵיהּ אַבָּיֵי: *הִקְפָּה אֶת הַדָּם וַאֲכָלוֹ, אוֹ *גשֶׁהִמְחָה אֶת הַחֵלֶב וּגְמָעוֹ — חַיָּיב! לָא קַשְׁיָא: כָּאן שֶׁהִקְפָּה בָּאוּר, כָּאן א] שֶׁהִקְפָּה בַּחַמָּה; בָּאוּר — לָא הָדַר, בַּחַמָּה — הָדַר. בַּחַמָּה נַמִי, לֵימָא: הוֹאִיל וְאִידְּחֵי אִידְּחֵי, דְּהָא בְּעָא מִינֵּיהּ רַבִּי מָנִי מֵר' יוֹחָנָן: דָּם שֶׁקָּרַשׁ וַאֲכָלוֹ, מַהוּ? אֲמַר לֵיהּ: הוֹאִיל וְנִדְחָה יִדָּחֶה! אִישְׁתִּיק. אֲמַר לֵיהּ: דִּלְמָא (א) וַדַּאי כָּאן בְּחַטָּאוֹת הַחִיצוֹנִיּוֹת ב] (הַחִיצוֹנוֹת,) כָּאן בְּחַטָּאוֹת הַפְּנִימִיּוֹת! אֲמַר: אַדְכַּרְתַּן מִילְּתָא, דְּאָמַר ג] *רַב חִסְדָּא: דָּם שֶׁקָּרַשׁ *בְּחַטָּאוֹת ד] וַאֲכָלוֹ — חַיָּיב, °"וְלָקַח וְנָתַן" אָמַר רַחֲמָנָא, ה] [וְהַאי] בַּר לְקִיחָה וּנְתִינָה הוּא; בְּחַטָּאוֹת הַפְּנִימִיּוֹת וַאֲכָלוֹ — פָּטוּר, "וְטָבַל וְהִזָּה" אָמַר רַחֲמָנָא, וְהַאי לָאו בַּר טְבִילָה וְהַזָּאָה הוּא. *וְרָבָא דִּידֵיהּ אָמַר: אֲפִילּוּ בְּחַטָּאוֹת הַפְּנִימִיּוֹת וַאֲכָלוֹ — חַיָּיב, הוֹאִיל וּכְנֶגְדּוֹ רָאוּי בְּחַטָּאוֹת הַחִיצוֹנוֹת. אָמַר רַב פַּפָּא: הִלְכָּךְ, ו] דַּם חֲמוֹר שֶׁקָּרַשׁ וַאֲכָלוֹ — חַיָּיב, הוֹאִיל וּכְנֶגְדּוֹ רָאוּי בְּחַטָּאוֹת הַחִיצוֹנוֹת. אָמַר רַב גִּידֵּל אָמַר זְעִירִי: דָּם, בֵּין לַח בֵּין יָבֵשׁ — ז] חוֹצֵץ. מֵיתִיבֵי: *הַדָּם וְהַדְּיוֹ, דוְהַדְּבַשׁ וְהֶחָלָב — יְבֵשִׁין חוֹצְצִין, לַחִין אֵינָן חוֹצְצִין! לָא קַשְׁיָא: הָא דִּסְרִיךְ, הָא דְּלָא סְרִיךְ. § "תִּמְלָח" לְמַאי אֲתָא? לְכִדְתַנְיָא: "בַּמֶּלַח" — יָכוֹל תְּבוּנֵהוּ? ת"ל: "תִּמְלָח"; אִי "תִּמְלָח", יָכוֹל בְּמֵי מֶלַח? ת"ל: "בַּמֶּלַח". °"וְלֹא תַשְׁבִּית מֶלַח" — הָבֵא מֶלַח *שֶׁאֵינָהּ שׁוֹבֶתֶת, וְאֵיזוֹ? זוֹ מֶלַח סְדוֹמִית. וּמִנַּיִן שֶׁאִם לֹא מָצָא מֶלַח ח] סְדוֹמִית שֶׁמֵּבִיא מֶלַח אִיסְתְּרוֹקָנִית? ת"ל: "תַּקְרִיב" — תַּקְרִיב כָּל שֶׁהוּא, תַּקְרִיב מִכָּל מָקוֹם, תַּקְרִיב ט] וַאֲפִילּוּ בְּשַׁבָּת, תַּקְרִיב וַאֲפִילּוּ בְּטוּמְאָה. מַאי "תְּבוּנֵהוּ"? אָמַר רַבָּה בַּר עוּלָּא, הָכִי קָאָמַר: יָכוֹל י] יִתְבּוֹנְנוּ כְּתֶבֶן בְּטִיט. אֲמַר לֵיהּ אַבָּיֵי: אִי הָכִי, יא] "יִתְבּוֹנְנוּ" מִיבָּעֵי לֵיהּ! אֶלָּא אָמַר אַבָּיֵי: יָכוֹל יַעֲשֶׂנּוּ כְּבִנְיָן. אֲמַר לֵיהּ רָבָא: אִי הָכִי, יב] "יִבְנֶנּוּ" מִיבָּעֵי לֵיהּ! אֶלָּא אָמַר רָבָא: יָכוֹל יג] תְּבוּנֵהוּ. מַאי "תְּבוּנֵהוּ"? אָמַר רַב אַשִׁי: יָכוֹל יִתֵּן בּוֹ טַעַם *כְּבִינָה? תַּלְמוּד לוֹמַר: "תִּמְלָח", כֵּיצַד הוּא העוֹשֶׂה? מֵבִיא הָאֵבָר וְהוֹפְכוֹ וְנוֹתֵן עָלָיו מֶלַח וּמַעֲלֵהוּ. אָמַר *אַבָּיֵי: וְכֵן לִקְדֵירָה.
תָּנוּ

רש"י

דְּתַנְיָא. דְּיַיִן אֵין טָעוּן מֶלַח. וְקָפְרֵיךְ הַתַּלְמוּד מַנִּי. הַךְ בָּרַיְיתָא. קַשְׁיָא קְטֹרֶת. דְּהָא (ג) רַבִּינַן לְעֵיל (דף כ.) כָּל שֶׁאֲחֵרִים בָּאִין לוֹ חוֹבָה, וּקְטֹרֶת נַמִי דְּבָעֵי עֵצִים בָּעֵי מֶלַח. וּלְקַמָּן נַמִי אָמְרִינַן: בְּרֹאשׁוֹ שֶׁל מִזְבֵּחַ, שֶׁשָּׁם מוֹלְחִין הַקְּטֹרֶת וְהַקּוֹמֶץ. הַפְּרָט. "מִנְחָתְךָ". עֵצִים אֵין מְקַבְּלִין טוּמְאָה. וְאַע"ג דַּעֲצֵי מַעֲרָכָה מְקַבְּלִין טוּמְאָה, כִּדְאָמְרִינַן בְּפֶרֶק שֵׁנִי דִּפְסָחִים (דף לה.): "וְהַבָּשָׂר" — לְרַבּוֹת עֵצִים וּלְבוֹנָה, הַהִיא מִדְּרַבָּנַן הוּא מִשּׁוּם חִיבַּת הַקֹּדֶשׁ, וּקְרָא אַסְמַכְתָּא בְּעָלְמָא, דְּהָא עֵצִים בְּעָלְמָא לָא מְקַבְּלֵי טוּמְאָה. דָּם שֶׁבִּשְּׁלוֹ. בֵּין דְּחוּלִּין בֵּין דְּקָדָשִׁים, וַאֲכָלוֹ — אֵינוֹ עוֹבֵר עָלָיו, דְּהָא לָא חִיְּיבָה תּוֹרָה אֶלָּא עַל הַדָּם הָרָאוּי לְכַפָּרָה, וְדַם קָדָשִׁים מִשֶּׁבִּישְּׁלוֹ לָא חֲזֵי לְמִילְּתֵיהּ וּנְפַק מִתּוֹרַת דָּם, יד] וּמָלִיחַ הֲרֵי הוּא כְּרוֹתֵחַ. מַהוּ דְּתֵימָא מִישְׁדָא בָּהּ מַשֶּׁהוּ טו] לְמִצְוָה בְּעָלְמָא. וּמִשּׁוּם הַהוּא מַשֶּׁהוּ לָא נָפֵיק מִתּוֹרַת דָּם. הִקְפָּה. כְּמוֹ (שמות טו) "קָפְאוּ (ג) תְהוֹמֹת" טז]. (קָפָה בָּאוּר). וַאֲכָלוֹ, חַיָּיב מִשּׁוּם דָּם אוֹ חֵלֶב. בַּחַמָּה. הָדְרָא לִכְמוֹת שֶׁהָיְתָה נְלוּלָה, לְכָךְ חַיָּיב. דָּם שֶׁקָּרַשׁ. קָא סָלְקָא דַּעְתָּךְ: וַאֲפִילּוּ דְּחוּלִּין. כָּאן בְּחַטָּאוֹת הַחִיצוֹנוֹת. הָא דְּקָתָנֵי: הִקְפָּה אֶת הַדָּם בַּחַמָּה וַאֲכָלוֹ חַיָּיב. וְהוּא הַדִּין לְשֶׁל חוּלִּין, הוֹאִיל וְרָאוּי לְכַפָּרָה בְּקָדָשִׁים. וְהָא דְּאָמַר זְעִירִי אֵינוֹ עוֹבֵר עָלָיו בְּחַטָּאוֹת הַפְּנִימִיּוֹת. כְּגוֹן פָּרִים וּשְׂעִירִים הַנִּשְׂרָפִים. וְטַעְמָא מְפָרֵשׁ לְקַמָּן. הִלְכָּךְ. יז] דְּאָמְרַתְּ: אָמְרִינַן הוֹאִיל וּכְנֶגְדּוֹ רָאוּי. דַּם חֲמוֹר. אַע"פ שֶׁאֵינוֹ רָאוּי לְקָרְבָּן, וְאִיכָּא לְמֵימַר דְּלָא חִיְּיבָה יח] תּוֹרָה כָּרֵת אֶלָּא עַל דָּם הָרָאוּי לְקָרְבָּן. *אֶלָּא אֲפִילּוּ חֲמוֹר, דְּאֵין קָרְבָּן בִּטְמֵאִין, אֲפִילּוּ הָכִי חַיָּיב. חוֹצֵץ. לְעִנְיַן טְבִילָה. סְרִיךְ. שֶׁמַּתְחִיל לְהִתְיַיבֵּשׁ וּלְהִדָּבֵק קְצָת, חוֹצֵץ. לָא סְרִיךְ. יט] שֶׁכְּשֶׁתּוֹלִין בּוֹ אֶצְבַּע נִמְשָׁךְ וְהוֹלֵךְ חוּט מִמֶּנּוּ (ד) (וּפוֹסֵק הַדָּם). תְּבוּנֵהוּ. מְפָרֵשׁ לְקַמָּן. מֵי מֶלַח. כ] מוֹרִים. שֶׁאֵינָהּ שׁוֹבֶתֶת. שֶׁמְּצוּיָה בַּקַּיִץ *וּבַחוֹרֶף, וּמֶלַח סְדוֹמִית כא] הַיָּם מַשְׁלִיכָהּ לָאֲגַפֶּיהָ. אִיסְתְּרוֹקָנִית. מִן הַקַּרְקַע נַעֲשֵׂית, וּבִידֵי אָדָם. *מִכָּל שֶׁהוּא. בֵּין סְדוֹמִית בֵּין *אִסְתְּרוֹקָנִית. מִכָּל מָקוֹם. וַאֲפִילּוּ מִחוּץ לָאָרֶץ. סְדוֹמִית. דַּקָּה, אִסְתְּרוֹקָנִית גַּסָּה. (ה) יָכוֹל יִתְבּוֹנְנוּ. יִתֵּן מֶלַח הַרְבֵּה כְּתֶבֶן בְּטִיט. כְּבִנְיָן. מֶלַח הַרְבֵּה, שׁוּרָה עַל שׁוּרָה. נוֹתֶנֶת טַעַם [כְּבִינָה]. כָּאָדָם. תַּקְרִיב בְּשַׁבָּת וּבְטוּמְאָה. אִם קָרְבַּן לִיבּוּר הוּא. וְאַשְׁמוֹעִינַן דִּמְלִיחָתָן עֲבוֹדָה הִיא, וְדָחֵי שַׁבָּת וְטוּמְאָה כִּשְׁאָר עֲבוֹדוֹת.
וְכֵן

תוספות

אפיק עצים ועייל נסכים. ונמעט נסכים ב"מה מנחה מיוחדת" כו', ודם מ"ועל מנחתך". וא"ת: אימא איפכא! וי"ל: דלא שייך לומר איפכא כלל, דהא כדי שלא נאמר (משום) לד של מתיר הוא דאיצטריכא למיכתב "מעל מנחתך" למעוטי דם דמתרבי מההוא לד, ואילו נסכים ממעטי מיניה.

יצאו עצים שאין מקבלין טומאה. פי' בקונטרס, דהא דאמר בפ' "כל שעה" (פסחים דף לה.): "והבשר" לרבות עצים ולבונה, אסמכתא בעלמא. ואי אפשר לומר כן, דבהדיא אמרינן בפ' שני דחולין (דף לו:) דחיבת הקדש דאורייתא מהיא קרא ד"והבשר"! וכן מוכח בפ' "כל הפסולין" (זבחים דף לד.) גבי אוכל בשר לפני זריקת דמה, דאמרינן: אבל טומאת בשר – דברי הכל לוקה, דאמר מר: "והבשר" לרבות עצים ולבונה כו'! והאי דקרי ליה בפרק "בית שמאי" (שם דף מו:) פסולא בעלמא – לאו מדרבנן קאמר אלא מדאורייתא, ו"פסולא בעלמא" קאמר – דלית ליה מלקות. ועוד, דהיא גופא משמע דלרבנן הוי דאורייתא, דלר' כב] ישמעאל דאמר פסולא בעלמא. והיא דקרי לה "מעלה" בפ' "כל שעה" (פסחים דף לה.) – הכי נמי קאמר גבי מעלות: הערב שמשו אוכל בתרומה, דנפקא לן מקרא בפרק "הערל" (יבמות דף עד:), אלמא מעלה דאורייתא קאמר. והא דקאמר הכא: יצאו עצים שאין מקבלין טומאה – בעצי כג] *עצים קאמר, ולא בעצי המערכה. וא"ת: מנין לנו לרבות עצים לטומאה מ"והבשר", מאחר דיש להו פדיון מן התורה אפילו בתר דשפינהו לגיזרי, כדמשמע בריש "המנחות והנסכים" (לקמן דף*) לרבנן דפליגי עליה דרבי? דלרבי ודאי ניחא, דחשיב להו קרבן גמור. וי"ל: דההיא דמרבי עצים בכל מקום – היינו לרבי. וקצת קשיא: מאחר דחייבים על העצים משום טומאה, אמאי לא תני להו בפרק שני דמעילה (דף י.), דתנן: הקומץ והלבונה והקטורת – כולם הוכשרו ליפסל בטבול יום, וחייבין עליהם משום נותר וטמא, ופיגול אין בהם? וי"ל: בין לרבי בין לרבנן לא מצי תני, דלרבנן לא מיחייב אעצים, ולרבי יש בעצים משום פיגול לאחר שנקמצו, ככל דבר שיש לו מתירין לאדם או למזבח, כאיברי עולה שדם מתירן.*:

*[**כאן** בחטאות החיצונות וכאן בחטאות הפנימיות. פרש"י, דבחטאות הפנימיות אינו עובר עליו, וטעמא כמו שמפרש לקמן. ולא נהירא, דא"כ בחטאות הפנימיות נמי. משמע לפי שיטת רש"י שאם בשלו ללול, הואיל וראוי לטבילה והזאה – יהא חייב עלה אם יאכלנו. ואין הסוגיא מוכיח הכי, דאמרינן לעיל: כיון דמלחיה נפיק ליה מתורת דם ולא יתחייב עליו! ועוד, דרבא דידיה אמר: אפילו בחטאות הפנימיות ואכלו חייב, ומשמע לפי' רש"י דרבא לית ליה דזעירי. ולעיל קאמר: יתיב רבא וקאמר להא שמעתא, משמע דסבירא לרבא כזעירי! לכן נ"ל, דבזעירי (היינו בבשלו באור) כ"ע לא פליגי דאינו עובר עליו. והא דמחלק הכא בין חטאות הפנימיות לחיצוניות, קאי אהקפאו בחמה]: דם שבישלו אינו עובר עליו כד]. [והיינו] הא דתנן בפ' "כל הבשר" (חולין דף קט. ושם): הלב קורעו ומוציא את דמו, לא קרעו אינו עובר *)עליו, כה] [דמיירי אחר בישולו] מדמייתי הנך תרי מילי בהדי הדדי, דם שבישלו ודם שמלחו – משמע דתרווייהו חד טעמא, כדפי' בקונטרס דלא חייבה תורה אלא דבר הראוי לכפרה, וכיון דבישלו או מלחו נפקא ליה מתורת דם. ומשמע הכא דסתם מליחה דקדשים היינו דמליח כרותח – היינו דאין נאכל מחמת מלחו, כדפרישית בפ' "כל הבשר" (שם דף קיב.), ואפסס מליחה דקדשים הוא דדייק הכא: הא לאו הכי הוה אמינא דם ליבעי מלח? כיון דמלחיה נפקא ליה מתורת דם, דאמר זעירי דם שמלחו וכו'. ובסמוך אמרינן: וכן לקדירה. לפיכך מדקדק ר"ת מכאן דמליחה לקדרה באין נאכל מחמת מלחו סגי, ולא כמו שמפרשים: כמו שאדם מולח להצניע, וכמליח לצורך עיכוד, או כדבעי ליה לאלתר. ובפרק "כל הבשר" (שם זה שם) *פירשתי גבי אינו נאכל מחמת מלחו. יתן בו טעם כבינה. היינו דלא חזי לאכילה בלא הדחה, כמו שהבינה מתקנת אותם. וכן לקדירה גרסי'. ובספר רבינו גרשם כתוב: [וכן ללאי] וכן פי' רבינו חננאל בפ"ק דחולין (דף יד.) גבי אסורה **)בהנאה ליומא.
בלשכת

*) עלוו הס"ד אח"כ ד"ה דם שמלחו אינו עובר עליו מדמייתי כו' נ"ק **) נ"ל באכילה

עין משפט נר מצוה

טו א מיי' פ"ה מהל' איסורי מזבח הל' יא:
טז ב מיי' פ"ו מהל' מעשה"ק הלכה ד:
יז ג מיי' פ"ו מהלכות מאכלות אסורות הלכה יא:
יח ד מיי' פ"ב מהל' מקוואות הל' כ:
יט ה מיי' פ"ה מהל' איסורי מזבח הל' יא:
כ ו מיי' פ"ו מהלכות מאכלות אסורות הל' י טוש"ע י"ד סימן סט סעיף ד:

גליון הש"ס

רש"י ד"ה דם חמור וכו' דאין קרבן בטמאין. נראה להדיא דלאו דוקא נקרט דהא בלא נקרב הוא נמי הך חיובו לאף לאין קרבן בטמאים ובודאי הכי הוא דאם בלא נקרב פשוט דחייב משום דם והוי כדם בהמה דעלמא מה"ת לא לחייב בקרוב דמ"ש מבהמת חולין דחייב בקרוב אתמנא תמוה לי דא"כ מאי חידש ר"פ הא מתניתין ערוכה היא ריש פרק דם שחיטה דבין טמאים בין טהורים חייבים על דמו:

שיטה מקובצת

א] שהקפהו בחמה באור לא הדר בחמה הדר. לאו דוקא דלאו בהכי תליא מילתא אלא כלומר באור לא חזיא למילתא בחמה (לא) חזיא למילתא: ב] בחטאות החיצונות תיבת החיצונות השני נמחק: ג] דאמר רבא אמר רב חסדא: ד] בחטאות החיצונות ואכלו: ה] רחמנא דבר לקיחה תיבת והאי ליתא שם: ו] דם חמור שקרש כו'. משום רבותא דחמור נקט לה דאע"פ דאין ראוי לקרבן לפי שאין קרבן בטמאים אפ"ה חייב עליו [כך פ"ה] ולא נהירא שהרי איכא קרא בפ' בקונטרס שחיטה לרבות דם חיה ודם בהמה טמאה לחייב עליו כרת לכך נראה לפרש דהכא הרבותא משום דקרש דסד"א דהא דקרש חייב ה"מ בדם טהורה שכנגדו ראוי לחטאות החיצונות אבל דם חמור שקרש דאין דם בהמה טמאה ראויה אפילו צלול לחטאות

הגהות הב"ח

(א) גמ' אמר ליה דלמא כאן כצ"ל ותיבת ודאי נמחק: (ב) רש"י ד"ה קשיא וכו' דהא רבינן לעיל אמרי כל שאחרים: (ג) ד"ה הקפה וכו' תהומות הס"ד ואח"כ מ"ה הקפאה בחור ואכלו חייב: (ד) ד"ה לא סריך שכשתולין וכו' ופוסק הדם הס"ד ואח"כ מ"ה תבונהו הס"ד: (ה) ד"ה יכול יתבוננו:

אַדְרַבָּה, דָּם הֲוָה לֵיהּ לְרַבּוּיֵי, שֶׁכֵּן מַתִּיר כְּמוֹתָהּ, *נִפְסָל בִּשְׁקִיעַת הַחַמָּה כְּמוֹתָהּ! הָנָךְ נְפִישָׁן. אָמַר מָר: שׁוֹמֵעַ אֲנִי אֲפִילּוּ עֵצִים וְדָם שֶׁנִּקְרָאוּ קָרְבָּן. א] מַאן שָׁמְעַתְּ לֵיהּ דְּאָמַר: עֵצִים אִיקְּרִי קָרְבָּן — ב] רַבִּי, לְרַבִּי מִבָּעֲיָא ג] בָּעוּ מֶלַח! *דְּתַנְיָא: "קָרְבַּן (מִנְחָה") — מְלַמֵּד אשֶׁמִּתְנַדְּבִין עֵצִים, וְכַמָּה? שְׁנֵי גְּזָרִין, וְכֵן הוּא אוֹמֵר: °"וְהַגּוֹרָלוֹת הִפַּלְנוּ עַל קֻרְבַּן הָעֵצִים". *רַבִּי ד] אָמַר: עֵצִים קָרְבַּן מִנְחָה הֵן, וּטְעוּנִין מֶלַח וּטְעוּנִין הַגָּשָׁה. *וְאָמַר רָבָא: לְדִבְרֵי רַבִּי — עֵצִים טְעוּנִין קְמִיצָה; וְא"ר פַּפָּא: לְדִבְרֵי רַבִּי — עֵצִים צְרִיכִין עֵצִים! סְמֵי מִיכָּן עֵצִים. וְאֶלָּא קְרָא לְמַעוּטֵי מַאי? אִי לְמַעוּטֵי דָּם, מֵ"עַל מִנְחָתֶךָ" נָפְקָא! אַפֵּיק

נחמיה י

תורה אור

דָּם נִפְסָל בִּשְׁקִיעַת הַחַמָּה. דְּאֵינוֹ רָאוּי לִזְרוֹק בַּלַּיְלָה, דִּכְתִיב: "בְּיוֹם צַוֺּתוֹ אֶת בְּנֵי יִשְׂרָאֵל לְהַקְרִיב" וגו' (ויקרא ז), ה] *וְדָם לְמָחָר נִפְסָל בְּלִינָה, כִּדְאָמְרִינַן בְּמַסֶּ' זְבָחִים בְּפֶרֶק "אֵיזֶהוּ מְקוֹמָן" (דף נו.): מִנַּיִן לְדָם שֶׁנִּפְסָל בִּשְׁקִיעַת הַחַמָּה — תַּלְמוּד לוֹמַר: "בְּיוֹם הַקְרִיבוֹ אֶת זִבְחוֹ" וגו', וְהָתָם יָלֵיף לָהּ שַׁפִּיר. וְכֵן קוֹמֶץ דִּלְעֵיל מִ"בְּיוֹם צַוֺּתוֹ", ו] כְּתַב: "זֹאת הַתּוֹרָה לָעוֹלָה וְלַמִּנְחָה" וגו'. אֲבָל אֵבְרֵי עוֹלָה הוּתְּרוּ לְהַקְרִיב כָּל הַלַּיְלָה, כִּדְאָמְרִינַן בְּהַאי פִּירְקִין (דף כו:): *מְנָלַן מִבָּא הַשֶּׁמֶשׁ, כְּלוֹמַר לְאַחַר בֹּא הַשֶּׁמֶשׁ, וּמַקְטִירָן כָּל הַלַּיְלָה. קָרְבָּן. "נֶפֶשׁ כִּי תַקְרִיב קָרְבַּן מִנְחָה" וגו'. שְׁנֵי גְּזָרִין. שְׁנֵי בְּקָעִיּוֹת גְּדוֹלוֹת. וְכֵן הוּא אוֹמֵר. דְּעֵצִים קָרְבָּן מִקְרוּ. וּלְהָכִי נְקַט שְׁנֵי גְּזָרִין, ז] כִּדְיָלְפִינַן מִקְּרָאֵי פֶּרֶק שְׁלִישִׁי דְּמַסֶּכֶת יוֹמָא (דף לג.) ח]. לְדִבְרֵי רַבִּי. דְּמַקִּישׁ עֵצִים ט] *לְמְלִיחָה וּלְהַצְרִיךְ הַגָּשָׁה כַּמִּנְחָה — טְעוּנִין קְמִיצָה כַּמִּנְחָה, וְהַמִּתְנַדֵּב שְׁנֵי גְּזָרִין יָבִיא עֵצִים אֲחֵרִים לְהַסִּיקָן. דָּם מֵעַל מִנְחָתֶךָ נָפְקָא. וּתְרֵי מִיעוּטֵי לָמָּה לִי? נֵימָא: "קָרְבָּן" — כְּלָל, "מֵעַל מִנְחָתֶךָ" — פְּרָט, "כָּל קָרְבָּנְךָ" חָזַר וְכָלַל — י] אַף כָּל שֶׁאֲחֵרִים בָּאִין לוֹ חוֹבָה, וְלֹא דָּם דְּאֵין אֲחֵרִים בָּאִין לוֹ חוֹבָה. דְּהַשְׁתָּא לֵיכָּא לְמִיפְרַךְ: אִי מַה יא] מִנְחָה שֶׁמַּתֶּרֶת אַף כָּל כו', דְּאִם כֵּן (א), דְּמִדְּרַבֵּית בְּצַד דַּאֲחֵרִים בָּאִין חוֹבָה לָהּ כָּל הָנָךְ, וּבְצַד דְּמַתִּיר מְרַבֵּית דָּם, "אַף כָּל" לְמַעוּטֵי מַאי? בִּשְׁלָמָא לְמַאי דַּהֲוָה סָלֵיק אַדַּעְתִּין מֵעִיקָּרָא יב] *(וְאַע"ג) דְּ"אַף כָּל" הֲוָה מְמַעֵט נַמִּי עֵצִים, יג] הֲוָה מָצֵי לְמִיפְרַךְ *דְּנִרַבֵּי בְּצַד אֲחֵרִים בָּאִין חוֹבָה כָּל הָנָךְ, וּבְצַד דְּמַתִּיר מְרַבֵּית לְדָם (וּנְרַבֵּי דָּם בְּצַד דְּמַתִּיר), וְ"אַף כָּל" לְמַעוּטֵי עֵצִים, שֶׁאֵין אֲחֵרִים בָּאִין לָהֶם חוֹבָה וְאֵינָן מַתִּירִין, וּלְהָכִי אִיצְטְרִיךְ "מֵעַל מִנְחָתֶךָ" יְתֵירָא לְמַעוּטֵי דָּם. אֲבָל הַשְׁתָּא דְּאָמְרַתְּ עֵצִים אֲחֵרִים בָּאִין חוֹבָה לָהֶם, אִי מְרַבֵּי דָּם בְּצַד דְּמַתִּיר, "אַף כָּל" לְמַעוּטֵי מַאי? יד] (קְרָאֵי לְמַאי אֲתָא — "מִנְחָה") דְּדָרְשִׁינַן מִינֵּיהּ לְעֵיל: אַף כָּל שֶׁאֲחֵרִים בָּאִין לָהֶם חוֹבָה, אֲבָל מִידֵּי אַחֲרִינָא לָא, מַאי אֲתָא לְמַעוּטֵי? נְסָכִים. טו] אֵין אֲחֵרִים בָּאִין לוֹ חוֹבָה. דְּתַנְיָא

אדרבה דם הוה ליה לרבויי כו'. ותימה: דלא חשיב פיגול, דדם וקומץ לא מיחייב עלייהו משום פיגול, כדאמרינן ב"הקומץ זוטא" (לעיל דף יד.) דאינהו גופייהו מתירין נינהו, אבל אברים חייבים עלייהו משום פיגול!

נפסל בשקיעת החמה כמותה. בריש "מי שהיה טמא" (פסחים ד' נג.) דאמרינן: דמשקיעת החמה עד צאת הכוכבים ד' מילין לר' יהודה, הקשה ר"ת: דבסוף "במה מדליקין" (שבת דף לה.) משמע טז] דלרבי יהודה משתשקע החמה עד *הלילה שני חלקי מיל! ותירץ ר"ת: ד"משתשקע החמה" משמע סוף שקיעת החמה, שכבר שקעה החמה, אבל "משקיעת החמה" משמע מתחילת שקיעה. תדע, מדאמרי' (שבת דף כא:) גבי נר חנוכה: מצותה משתשקע החמה, ואי בתחילת שקיעה — עדיין הוא יום גדול, והוה שרגא בטיהרא. ולפיכך "שקיעת החמה" נמי דהכא גבי דם — בתחילת שקיעה איירי. וניחא טפי, משום דאמרינן בסוף "איזהו מקומן" (זבחים דף נו.): מנין לדם שנפסל בשקיעת החמה? שנאמר: "ביום הקריבו את זבחו" — ביום שאתה זובח אתה מקריב. ואי בסוף שקיעה קאמר, למה לי קרא? פשיטא דנפסל בלילה, דאין יכול לזורקו, דכתיב "ביום צותו". ועמוד השחר פשיטא דפוסלת בו דומיא דאימורים! ופי' שם בקונטרס דנ"מ אם עלה לגבי מזבח, משום דאין לינה מועלת בראשו של מזבח. וקשיא: למ"ד מועלת מאי איכא למימר? ואין לומר דאיצטריך משום דקי"ל גבי דם אם עלה לא ירד הואיל ולן כשר באימורים, ואם מעלהו לגבי מזבח הוה אמינא דיכול לזרוק. יז] משום דהא פלוגתא היא דרבן גמליאל ור' יהושע, דר' יהושע אמר ירד ולרבן גמליאל לא ירד. וכי תימא דאיצטריך משום דס"ד דלא מיפסיל בלינה כי היכי דאין חייבין עליו משום פיגול ונותר, כדאיתא בסוף "כל הבשר" (חולין דף קיז.), הרי עצים ולבונה דאין חייבין עליהן משום נותר לרבי שמעון, ואפילו הכי מיפסלי בלינה כשקדשו בכלי שרת! וכי תימא משום דילפינן מדם, דלמא שאני דם דמתיר! ולפי מה שמפרש רבינו תם דמיירי בתחילת שקיעה, ניחא. וכן משמע בפ' "מי שהיה טמא" (פסחים דף נג:) דשחיטה אסורה מתחילת שקיעה, גבי מי שהיה בדרך רחוקה, דקאמר התם: איזוהי דרך רחוקה — מן המודיעים לירושלים חמשה עשר מילין. ומוכח התם דהיינו חמשה עשר מילין מפלגא דיומא עד שקיעת החמה, ולא חשיב *ד' מילין דמשקיעת החמה עד צאת הכוכבים. ואי לא מיפסלא דם עד צאת הכוכבים, אם כן הוי שעת שחיטה. ומיהו קשיא: אי בתחילת שקיעה קאמר, היכי ממעט לה מ"ביום הקריבו"? הא עד צאת הכוכבים יום הוא, דכתיב (נחמיה ד): "והיה לנו הלילה למשמר והיום מלאכה"! ואשכחן נמי "שקיעת החמה" דאיירי בסוף שקיעה, כגון צאת הכוכבים, כדאמרינן בפרק "הריני נזיר מן הגרוגרת" (נזיר דף טו.): כגון דחזאי תלתא יומי סמוך לשקיעת החמה, והיינו בבין השמשות, כדאמר עלה בפרק "כיצד צולין" (פסחים דף פא.): ברואה בין השמשות. וגם בפירקין (לקמן דף לו:): כל המניח תפילין אחר שקיעת החמה עובר בעשה. והיינו בלילה, מדקאמר רבה בר רב הונא: ספק חשיכה ספק אינה חשיכה לא חולץ ולא מניח. ועוד אמרינן במס' תענית (דף יב.): כל תענית שלא שקעה עליו חמה לא שמיה תענית, *ומנהג אבותינו תורה היא שהכל נוהגין עד צאת הכוכבים! ויש לומר: דלעולם נפקא ליה שפיר תחילת שקיעה מ"ביום", דאם אינו ענין לסוף שקיעה דנפקא מ"ביום צותו" — תנהו ענין לתחילת שקיעה. ויש מפרשים דמן התורה אינו נפסל עד צאת הכוכבים, אלא רבנן עבוד הרחקה ופסלוהו מתחילת שקיעה, והעמידו דבריהם במקום כרת לענין דרך רחוקה, כדי שיהו זריזין למהר לבא. וקשיא: דא"כ ליחשביה *(בסוף) פסחים בסוף "האשה" (דף נב.) בהדי הנך שהעמידו דבריהם במקום כרת! ויש לומר: דלא חשיב אלא מידי (דלא) דהוו חידוש, אבל זה אינו חידוש אם תקנו כדי שימהרו לבא, דהכי נמי לא חשיב חתיכת יבלתו והבאתו מחוץ לתחום והרכבתו. ובאונן גופיה יש לחלק בין מת לו מת קודם חצות למת לו אחר חצות, כדמשמע בפרק "מי שהיה טמא" (פסחים דף נח.), ואפילו הכי לא חשיב לה. והשתא הא דאמרינן בפ' "המנחות והנסכים" (לקמן דף קא:) ובריש מעילה (דף ו.): לפני זריקה מועלין בו, ומוקי לה דקבליה סמוך לשקיעת החמה דלא הוה שהות למזרקיה — ההוא מעילה דרבנן, דעד צאת הכוכבים יש שהות לזורקו. ומיהו קשיא, מדאמרינן בסוף "איזהו מקומן" (זבחים דף נו:): קדשים הנאכלים ליום אחד — מחשבין בדמן משתשקע החמה, דאי חישב לזורקו לאחר שקיעה — מיד הוי פיגול, דהוי מחשב חוץ לזמנו! ואין לומר פיגול דרבנן, דהא דומיא דאימורים ובשר קדשים איירי, דהוי פיגול דאורייתא. ולא קתני בשר קדשי קדשים מחצות ואילך, דזמן אכילתו מדרבנן! וי"ל: דההיא שקיעה — בסוף שקיעה, דהיינו צאת הכוכבים, כמו שמפרש ר"ת ד"משתשקע" משמע סוף שקיעה*.

מלמד שמתנדבים עצים כו'. הא דפליגי הכא רבי ורבנן, לרבנן נדבה ולרבי קרבן גמור — היינו כשאמר "הרי עלי שני גזירי עצים אלו למזבח". כדתניא בתוספתא דשקלים (פ"ג): האומר "הרי עלי עצים" — מביא דמי שני גיזרי עצים ונותן לשופר, *ולוקחין כהנים בהן עצים ומקריבין אותן על גבי המזבח, וניאותים מהן ואין מועלין בהן, ואם הקריבן בחוץ — פטור. ואם אמר "הרי עלי שני גיזרי עצים אלו למזבח" — כהן מקבלן הימנו ומקריבן לגבי מזבח, ואין ניאותין בהם *אבל מועלין בהם, ואם הקריבן בחוץ — חייב, דברי רבי. וחכמים אומרים: אם הקריבן בחוץ — פטור. ואלו ואלו נופלין בלשכת דיר העצים. ואם תאמר, אמאי קאמר: מאן שמעת ליה דאמר עצים קרבן, רבי היא? והא לרבנן נמי איקרו קרבן, ולא בעו מליחה! וי"ל: דמדקאמר "עצים ודם" משמע ליה דחשיבי קרבן גמור כדם, והיינו כרבי. **לדברי** רבי עצים טעונין קמיצה. ואם תאמר: יח] מ"ש דרבי מקיש עצים למנחה יותר מלשאר קרבנות? ויש לומר: דהאי "קרבן" דמרבי מינה עצים, מ"קרבן" דגבי מנחה דריש לה בתורת כהנים. וא"ת: מנלן דמקשינן למנחה דנקמצת? האיכא מנחות טובא יט] דאינן נקמצות! ויש לומר: דלגבי מנחה הנקמצת כתיב (ויקרא ב): "ונפש כי תקריב קרבן מנחה". ואם תאמר: ומה קמיצה שייך בעצים? הא אין בהם שיריים, וכולן נשרפין! ויש לומר: דאשכחן כי האי גוונא בריש "ואלו מנחות" (דף עב:) לר' שמעון דמנחת חוטא של כהנים נקמצת, הקומץ קרב לעצמו והשירים קריבין לעצמן, והוא הדין כ]כאן עצים. **עצים** טעונין קמיצה. והוא הדין ימין וקידוש כלי. אפיק

ולמחר נפסל נ"ק

[נ"ל מעלן]

לקמן קו:

שם

למליחה ולהגשה כמ[נחה] צריך קמילה כמנחה [...] אח"כ ד"ה צריכין [...] המתנדב כו' נ"ק

דאע"ג כו' דמרבי אחרים נ"ק

ס"א דמרבי הנך נ"ק מ"ז

וקראי למאי כו' נ"ק

[וע"ע תוס' ע"ז לד. מתענין]

[נ"ל במסכת]

[וע"ע תוס' זבחים נו: מנין וכל מה שליינתי על לידו]

וכהנים לוקחין בהן נ"[ק]

ומועלים בהם נ"ק

יד א מיי' פט"ז מהל' מעה"ק הלכה יג:

[זבחים נו.]

הלילה תלתא ריבעי מיל נ"ק

רש"ק מ"ז

מעילה יט: ע"ש כי מילתא דרבא ורב פפא מהופך

ה' מילין נ"ק

הגהות הב"ח

(א) רש"י ד"ה דם מעל וכו' דאם כן דמדמרבית בלד וכו' ובלד דמתיר מרבית להם ג"כ ונרבי דם וכו' למעוטי מאי א"כ קראי למאי:

שיטה מקובצת

א] מאן שמעת ליה כו' (כדקתני) [דתניא] קרבן מלמד שמתנדבין עצים רבי כו' ויש לה קדושת הגוף דאילו רבנן אין לה קדושת הגוף ויכול לפדותה אבל לרבי הוי קדושת הגוף ממש כמו מנחה. גליון: ב] רבי עיין תוס' לקמן (דף פ"ה ע"ב): ג] מבעא בעיא: ד] רבי אומר עצים קרבן הן ותיבת מנחה נמחק: ה] וגומר וגם תיבת ודם נמחק: ו] כתיב: ז] גזרין משום דחשיבי שראויין למזבח למערכה דלאחר שהיתה המערכה סדורה הי' נותנים עליה ב' גזרי עצים: ח] יומא הס"ד ומה"ד טעונים הגשה כמנחה: ט] דמקיש עצים למנחה הס"ד ואח"כ מה"ד קמיצה המתנדב שני גיזרין מבקע מלא קומצו קסמים דקים ונותן על המערכה ואח"כ נותן האחרים הס"ד ומה"ד עצים טעונים עצים והמתנדב: י] וכלל מה הפרט שאחרים באים לה חובה אף: יא] מנחה מיוחדת שמתרת: יב] תיבות ואף על גב נמחק: יג] עצים דהוה מצי למיפרך דנרבי הנך בצד אחרים באים ח[ובה] להן ותיבות כל הנך ובצד דמתיר מרבית לדם נמחק: יד] מאי הס"ד ומה"ד קרא למאי אתא מנחה: טו] נסכים נסכי יין אין: טז] דלרבי יהודה. עי' בתוס' זבחים (דף נ"ו ע"א): יז] משום. (תוס') זבחים (דף ע"א [דף פג.]): יח] וא"ת מנ"ל לרבא דרבי ותיבות מאי שנא ליתא שם: יט] דאינן נקמצות וי"ל דאין לך מנחת נדבה של ישראל שאינה נקמצת. מהר"פ: כ] וה"ה כמו כן נימא בעצים לרבי ותיבות כאן עצים נמ[חק]

יא א ב מיי׳ פ״ה מהל׳ איסורי מזבח הלכה יא:
יב ג מיי׳ שם הלכה יב ופי״ג מהל׳ פסה״מ הלכה טז:
יג ד מיי׳ פט״ז מהל׳ מעשה״ק הלכה יד:

בְּרִית אֲמוּרָה בְּמֶלַח, דִּבְרֵי ר׳ יְהוּדָה. ר׳ שִׁמְעוֹן אוֹמֵר: נֶאֱמַר כָּאן ״בְּרִית מֶלַח עוֹלָם הוּא״, וְנֶאֱמַר לְהַלָּן °״בְּרִית כְּהוּנַּת עוֹלָם״, כְּשֵׁם שֶׁאִי אֶפְשָׁר לַקָּרְבָּנוֹת בְּלֹא כְּהוּנָּה — כָּךְ אִי אֶפְשָׁר לַקָּרְבָּנוֹת בְּלֹא מֶלַח! אָמַר רַב יוֹסֵף: רַב כְּתַנָּא דִּידַן ס״ל, דְּאָמַר: לֹא מָלַח — כָּשֵׁר. אֲמַר לֵיהּ אַבַּיֵי: אִי הָכִי, לֹא יָצַק נַמִי — לֹא יָצַק כְּלָל? אֶלָּא, *לֹא יָצַק כֹּהֵן אֶלָּא זָר; הָכָא נַמִי — לֹא מָלַח כֹּהֵן אֶלָּא זָר! אֲמַר לֵיהּ: א] וְכִי תַּעֲלֶה עַל דַּעְתְּךָ שֶׁזָּר קָרֵב לְגַבֵּי מִזְבֵּחַ? וְאִי בָּעֵית אֵימָא: כֵּיוָן דִּכְתִיבָא בֵּיהּ בְּרִית, כְּמַאן דִּתְנָא בֵּיהּ קְרָא דָּמְיָא. וְלָא תְּנָא בֵּיהּ קְרָא? וְהָכְתִיב: °״וְכָל קָרְבַּן מִנְחָתְךָ בַּמֶּלַח תִּמְלָח״! הַהוּא מִיבָּעֵי לֵיהּ לִכְדְתַנְיָא: אִילּוּ נֶאֱמַר ב] קָרְבָּן בְּמֶלַח, שׁוֹמֵעַ אֲנִי אֲפִילּוּ עֵצִים וָדָם שֶׁנִּקְרָאוּ קָרְבָּן? ת״ל: מִנְחָה, מַה מִּנְחָה מְיוּחֶדֶת שֶׁאֲחֵרִים בָּאִין ג] חוֹבָה לָהּ — אַף כָּל שֶׁאֲחֵרִים בָּאִין ד] חוֹבָה לָהּ. אִי מַה מִּנְחָה מְיוּחֶדֶת שֶׁמַּתֶּרֶת — אַף כָּל שֶׁמַּתִּיר, אָבִיא דָּם שֶׁמַּתִּיר! ת״ל: ״מֵעַל מִנְחָתֶךָ״, וְלֹא מֵעַל דָּמְךָ. ה] יָכוֹל תְּהֵא מִנְחָה כּוּלָּהּ טְעוּנָה מֶלַח? ת״ל: ״קָרְבָּן״ — קָרְבָּן טָעוּן מֶלַח, וְאֵין מִנְחָה כּוּלָּהּ טְעוּנָה מֶלַח. וְאֵין לִי אֶלָּא קוֹמֶץ (מִנְחָה,) מִנַּיִן לְרַבּוֹת אֶת הַלְּבוֹנָה? מְרַבֶּה אֲנִי אֶת הַלְּבוֹנָה שֶׁכֵּן בָּאָה עִמָּהּ בִּכְלִי אֶחָד, מִנַּיִן לְרַבּוֹת אֶת הַלְּבוֹנָה הַבָּאָה בִּפְנֵי עַצְמָהּ, וּלְבוֹנָה הַבָּאָה בְּבָזִיכִין, וְהַקְּטֹרֶת, ו] מִנְחַת כֹּהֲנִים, וּמִנְחַת כֹּהֵן מָשִׁיחַ, וּמִנְחַת נְסָכִים, אֵימוּרֵי חַטָּאת, וְאֵימוּרֵי אָשָׁם, וְאֵימוּרֵי קָדְשֵׁי קָדָשִׁים, וְאֵימוּרֵי קָדָשִׁים קַלִּים, וְאֵבְרֵי עוֹלָה, וְעוֹלַת הָעוֹף, ז] מִנַּיִן? תַּלְמוּד לוֹמַר: °״עַל כָּל קָרְבָּנְךָ תַּקְרִיב מֶלַח״. אָמַר מָר: אֵין לִי אֶלָּא קוֹמֶץ (מִנְחָה,) מִנַּיִן לְרַבּוֹת אֶת הַלְּבוֹנָה? מְרַבֶּה אֲנִי אֶת הַלְּבוֹנָה שֶׁכֵּן בָּאָה עִמָּהּ בִּכְלִי אֶחָד. וְהָא אֲמַרְתְּ: מַה מִּנְחָה מְיוּחֶדֶת שֶׁאֲחֵרִים בָּאִין חוֹבָה לָהּ! הָכִי קָאָמַר, אֵימָא: קָרְבָּן — כְּלָל, וּמִנְחָה — פְּרָט; כְּלָל וּפְרָט — אֵין בִּכְלָל אֶלָּא מַה שֶּׁבִּפְרָט, מִנְחָה — אִין, מִידֵּי אַחֲרִינָא — לָא! ח] הֲדַר אָמַר: ״עַל כָּל קָרְבָּנְךָ״ — חָזַר וְכָלַל; כְּלָל וּפְרָט וּכְלָל — אִי אַתָּה דָּן אֶלָּא כְּעֵין הַפְּרָט, מַה הַפְּרָט מְפוֹרָשׁ שֶׁאֲחֵרִים בָּאִין חוֹבָה לָהּ, אַף כָּל שֶׁאֲחֵרִים בָּאִין חוֹבָה לָהּ. אֲחֵרִים דְּבָאִין חוֹבָה לָהּ מַאי נִיהוּ? עֵצִים, אַף כָּל — עֵצִים. אֵימָא: ט] *)(אֲחֵרִים דְּבָאִין חוֹבָה לָהּ נִיהוּ) — לְבוֹנָה, י] וְאַיְיתֵי דָּם, דְּאִיכָּא נְסָכִים! יא] נְסָכִים בַּהֲדֵי אֵימוּרִין הוּא דְּאָתוּ, מ״ט? אֲכִילָה וּשְׁתִיָּה. אַדְּרַבָּה, כַּפָּרָה וְשִׂמְחָה! אֶלָּא לְבוֹנָה בָּאָה עִמָּהּ בִּכְלִי אֶחָד, [נְסָכִים אֵין בָּאִין בִּכְלִי אֶחָד] אֲבָל עֵצִים, כִּי הֵיכִי דְּמִתְכַּשְׁרָא בְּהוּ מִנְחָה — הָכִי מִתְכַּשְׁרָא בְּהוּ כּוּלְּהוּ קָרְבָּנוֹת. וְאֵימָא: יב] מַה הַפְּרָט מְפוֹרָשׁ שֶׁאֲחֵרִים בָּאִין חוֹבָה לָהּ וּמַתֶּרֶת, אַף כָּל שֶׁאֲחֵרִים בָּאִין חוֹבָה לָהּ וּמַתֶּרֶת, וּמַאי נִיהוּ? לְבוֹנָה הַבָּאָה בְּבָזִיכִין, דְּשַׁרְיָא לֶחֶם, יג] אֲבָל מִידֵּי אַחֲרִינָא לָא! מִדְּאִיצְטְרִיךְ ״מֵעַל מִנְחָתֶךָ״ — וְלֹא מֵעַל דָּמְךָ, מִכְּלָל דְּהָנָךְ כּוּלְּהוּ אָתוּ בְּחַד צַד. אָמַר מָר: ״מֵעַל מִנְחָתֶךָ״ — וְלֹא מֵעַל דָּמְךָ. וְאֵימָא: ״מֵעַל מִנְחָתֶךָ״ — וְלֹא מֵעַל אֵיבָרֶיךָ! מִסְתַּבְּרָא אֵבָרִים הֲוָה לֵיהּ לְרַבּוּיֵי, שֶׁכֵּן יד] (אשב״נ טמ״א סימן) אֲחֵרִים בָּאִין חוֹבָה לָהּ כְּמוֹתָהּ, אִישִּׁים כְּמוֹתָהּ, בַּחוּץ כְּמוֹתָהּ, נוֹתָר כְּמוֹתָהּ, טוּמְאָה כְּמוֹתָהּ, מְעִילָה כְּמוֹתָהּ. אַדְּרַבָּה

*) רש״ק מ״ז והצ״ק מקיים הגירסא וגרס מאי ניהו

רש״י

בְּרִית אֲמוּרָה בְּמֶלַח. שֶׁלֹּא תִּפְסוֹק מִקָּרְבָּנוֹת. בֵּין לְרַבִּי יְהוּדָה בֵּין לְר׳ שִׁמְעוֹן לֵיכָּא מִידֵּי אֶלָּא מַשְׁמָעוּת דּוֹרְשִׁין. רַב. דְּאָמַר טו] [א]: הֶחֱזִירָהּ אֵין לֹא הֶחֱזִירָהּ לֹא, כְּתַנָּא דִּידַן ס״ל, דְּאָמַר: לֹא מָלַח הַקּוֹמֶץ — כָּשֵׁר. שֶׁזָּר קָרֵב לְגַבֵּי מִזְבֵּחַ. דִּמְלִיחַת קוֹמֶץ בְּרֹאשׁוֹ שֶׁל מִזְבֵּחַ הִיא, כִּדְאָמַר בִּשְׁמַעְתָּא: בְּרֹאשׁוֹ שֶׁל מִזְבֵּחַ, שֶׁשָּׁם מוֹלְחִים אֶת הַקּוֹמֶץ. עֵצִים. נִקְרְאוּ קָרְבָּן, שֶׁנֶּאֱמַר: ״וְהַגּוֹרָלוֹת הִפַּלְנוּ עַל קֻרְבַּן הָעֵצִים״ (נחמיה י), וְדָם אִיקְרֵי קָרְבָּן, שֶׁהוּא עִיקַּר כָּל הַזֶּבַח. אֲחֵרִים בָּאִין לָהּ חוֹבָה. שֶׁצְּרִיכָה עֵצִים לְהַקְטָרָה. אַף כָּל. שֶׁצְּרִיכִין עֵצִים טְעוּנִין מֶלַח, יָצְאוּ עֵצִים וְדָם (א) [ב]. קוֹמֶץ דְּמִנְחָה מַתִּיר שִׁירַיִים, וְדָם מַתִּיר אֵימוּרִין לַמִּזְבֵּחַ וּבָשָׂר לַכֹּהֲנִים. טז] אִי מַה מִּנְחָה מְיוּחֶדֶת שֶׁמַּתֶּרֶת. הָכִי פָּרֵיךְ: יז] אוֹ אֵימָא, כִּי הֵיכִי דִּמְרַבֵּינַן כָּל דְּדָמֵי לֵיהּ בְּהַאי צַד שֶׁאֲחֵרִים בָּאִין חוֹבָה יח] לָהֶן — תְּרַבֵּי נַמִי דָּם דְּדָמֵי לָהּ לְאִידָךְ גִּיסָא בְּחַד צַד דְּמַתִּיר כְּמוֹתָהּ (ב א), וְ״אַף כָּל״ לְמַעוּטֵי עֵצִים הוּא דַּאֲתָא, דְּלָא דָּמֵי לָהּ בְּמִידֵּי! ת״ל יט] בְּמִיעוּטָא אַחֲרִינָא לְמַעוּטֵי צַד דְּמַתִּיר כְּמוֹתָהּ, וּלְרַבּוּיֵי [ג] דַּאֲחֵרִים בָּאִין חוֹבָה לְהוּ אֲתָא. דְּלֵיכָּא לְפָרוּשֵׁי (אִיפְכָא): אָבִיא דָּם שֶׁמַּתִּיר וְאוֹצִיא אֶת אֵלּוּ שֶׁאֵין מַתִּירִין, דְּא״כ לָמָּה לִי לְמֵימַר ״מֵעַל מִנְחָתֶךָ״? נֵימָא כ] (אִי נַמִי) כִּדְאָמְרִינַן לְקַמָּן: מִסְתַּבְּרָא הָנֵי הֲוָה לֵיהּ לְמֵילַף שֶׁכֵּן אשב״נ טמ״א סִימָן. הִלְכָּךְ, עַל כָּרְחָךְ ב) כּוּלְּהוּ הֲוָה בָּעֵי לְרַבּוּיֵי הָנֵי בְּחַד צַד, כא] לְהָכִי אִיצְטְרִיךְ מִיעוּט לְמַעוּטֵי חַד מִינַּיְיהוּ. כּוּלָּהּ. גַּם הַשִּׁירַיִים. ת״ל קָרְבָּן (ג) כב] [ד]. קוֹמֶץ, ״וְכָל קָרְבַּן מִנְחָתְךָ״ (ויקרא ב). בִּפְנֵי עַצְמָהּ. כְּגוֹן הָאוֹמֵר ״הֲרֵי עָלַי לְבוֹנָה״, דְּאָמַר בְּפֶ׳ ״הֲרֵי עָלַי עִשָּׂרוֹן״ (לקמן קו:): כג] לֹא יִפְחוֹת מִן הַקּוֹמֶץ. מִנְחַת כֹּהֲנִים. מִנְחַת כד] נִדְבוֹתֵיהֶם, דְּכָלִיל הוּא. כֹּהֵן מָשִׁיחַ. חֲבִיתִּין. קָדְשֵׁי קָדָשִׁים. זִבְחֵי שַׁלְמֵי צִבּוּר, דְּהַיְינוּ כִּבְשֵׂי עֲצֶרֶת. דְּקָדְשֵׁי קָדָשִׁים נִינְהוּ, וְאַע״ג דִּשְׁלָמִים הֵן, דְּהָא אֵין נֶאֱכָלִין אֶלָּא יוֹם וְלַיְלָה, כִּדְאָמְרִינַן בְּ״אֵיזֶהוּ מְקוֹמָן״ (זבחים דף נד:): זִבְחֵי שַׁלְמֵי צִבּוּר וַאֲשָׁמוֹת כו׳. וְהָא אָמַרְתְּ כה] (לֵיהּ) מַה מִּנְחָה מְיוּחֶדֶת שֶׁאֲחֵרִים בָּאִין כו׳. וּמֵהָתָם אִירַבְּיָא לְבוֹנָה וְכוּלְּהוּ הָנָךְ דִּצְרִיכִין עֵצִים, וְ״עַל כָּל קָרְבָּנְךָ״ אַמַּאי לָמָּה לִי? הָכִי קָאָמַר. הַאי דְּפָרֵיךְ: אֵין לִי אֶלָּא קוֹמֶץ, הָכִי קָא פָּרֵיךְ: אֵימָא לָא דָּרְשִׁי כִּדְדָרַשְׁתְּ ״מַה מִּנְחָה מְיוּחֶדֶת״, אֶלָּא בִּכְלָל וּפְרָט דָּרְשִׁינַן: ״קָרְבָּן״ רִאשׁוֹן — כְּלָל, ״מִנְחָתְךָ״ — פְּרָט. מִנְחָה אִין מִידֵּי אַחֲרִינָא לָא. וְהַיְינוּ דְּפָרֵיךְ: אֵין לִי אֶלָּא קוֹמֶץ, מִנַּיִן כּוּלְּהוּ אַחֲרִינֵי? הֲדַר אָמַר עַל כָּל קָרְבָּנְךָ תַּקְרִיב מֶלַח. דְּאִי נַמִי דָּרְשִׁי כְּלָל וּפְרָט — [ה] אִיתְרַבּוּ כּוּלְּהוּ, דְּ״עַל כָּל קָרְבָּנְךָ״ חָזַר וְכָלַל, כְּלָל וּפְרָט וּכְלָל אִי אַתָּה דָּן אֶלָּא כְּעֵין הַפְּרָט, וְעַל כָּרְחָךְ הָדְרִינַן לְמִילְּתָא קַמַּיְיתָא, לְ״כָל (ד) שֶׁאֲחֵרִים בָּאִין״ וְאִיתְרַבּוּ לְהוּ כָּל הָנֵי. אַף כָּל עֵצִים. אַף כָּל הַצְּרִיכִים עֵצִים טְעוּנִין מֶלַח כו]. וְאַיְיתֵי דָם דְּאִיכָּא נְסָכִים. יַיִן וְשֶׁמֶן בָּאִין לָהּ... אֲכִילָה. אֵימוּרִים. וּשְׁתִיָּה. יַיִן. אַדְּרַבָּה. לְצוֹרֶךְ דָּם אָתוּ, דְּהָכִי אוֹרְחָא: לְאַחַר כַּפָּרַת דָּם שֶׁכִּיפֵּר עַל הַחֵטְא, בָּא הַיַּיִן... וַאֲנָשִׁים, דָּמֵי שֶׁנִּתְכַּפֵּר חֶטְאוֹ שָׂמֵחַ. אֶלָּא. לְהָכִי לָא אִיתְרַבֵּי דָּם, אַף עַל גַּב דִּנְסָכִים בָּאִין לוֹ חוֹבָה — לָא דָּמוּ לִלְבוֹנָה הַבָּאָה לְמִנְחָה, דִּלְבוֹנָה בָּאָה עִם הַמִּנְחָה בִּכְלִי אֶחָד, וּנְסָכִים אֵין בָּאִין עִם הַדָּם בִּכְלִי אֶחָד. מִדְּאִיצְטְרִיךְ מֵעַל מִנְחָתֶךָ. לְמַעוּטֵי דָּם, ... מַעֲטֵיהּ קְרָא — הֲוָה אָמִינָא דְּטָעוּן מֶלַח, מִשּׁוּם דְּדָמֵי לְמִנְחָה בְּחַד צַד שֶׁמַּתִּיר כַּמִּנְחָה. מִכְּלָל דְּהָנָךְ כּוּלְּהוּ דְּלָא מַעֲטִינְהוּ קְרָא — (ה) מֵחַד צַד דָּמוּ בְּחַד צַד דַּאֲחֵרִים בָּאִין לָהּ חוֹבָה — אָמְרִינַן דִּטְעוּנִין מֶלַח. אִישִּׁים. עַל הָאֵשׁ נִשְׂרֶפֶת, לְמַעוּטֵי דָּם שֶׁאֵינוֹ נִשְׂרָף. בַּחוּץ כְּמוֹתָהּ...

תוספות

אימא מה הפרט מפורש שאחרים באים חובה לה וגם מתרת. פירוש: ונימא כללא קמא דוקא. אי נמי, אפילו למ״ד כללא בתרא דוקא – בעינן שני צדדין, כדמוכח בריש ״בכל מערבין״ (ערובין דף כח.). וצריך עיון בפרק ״שלשה מינין״ (נזיר דף לה:). ושמא יש מקומות לג] שניש מסורת הש״ס ושלשה [ו] מקומות לא חשיבי ליה להתלמוד אלא בחד צד.

מדאיצטריך מעל מנחתך מכלל דהנך כולהו לג] מייתו בחד צד. פי׳: כמו דם, דלית ליה אלא חד צד. ובסמוך מוגה לצדדין הרבה, בדם לא חשיבי ליה הנך לצדדין. והא דקתני בברייתא: אביא דם, דמשמע לישנא דאי לא כתיב ״מעל מנחתך״ הייתי מרבה דם, ואדרבה הייתי מצריך שני לצדדין כדמשמע הכא – התנא נקט האמת שכך היה ראוי לדרוש, והתלמוד טועה כאן להקשות דנבעי שני לצדדין, והמתרץ מוכיח לו מתוך הפסוק דממה נפשך סגי בחד צד. **ואימא** מעל מנחתך ולא מעל אבריך. פי׳: באברים ליכא אלא חד צד – שאחרים באים חובה, ובדם חד צד – שמתיר כמותה, ומה ראית [ז] לרבות אברים ולמעט דם? אימא איפכא! **שכן** אחרים באין חובה לה כו׳. כתוב בספרים סימן ״אשב״נ טמ״א״ ואין התלמוד מפרש אלף אחרונה. ומפרש רבינו תם: לד] אוכל כמותה, שרגילות למלוח אוכלין. ולפי שאין זה קולא וחומרא, לא חש התלמוד לפרש. אדרבה

תורה אור

*גרש ושמן מעכבין, ואין דבר אחר מעכב. גופא, אמר רב: *כל מקום שהחזיר לך הכתוב בתורה מנחה אינו אלא לעכב. ושמואל אמר: גרש ושמן מעכבין, ואין דבר אחר מעכב. ולשמואל, אע"ג דתנא ביה קרא לא מעכבא א] ליה?! אלא, כל היכא *דתנא ביה קרא ודאי מעכבא, והכא ב"מלא קומצו" "בקומצו" קא מיפלגי. דתניא: "מלא קומצו" "בקומצו" – שלא יעשה מדה לקומץ; רב סבר: הא נמי תנא ביה קרא, דכתיב: °"ויקרב את המנחה וימלא כפו ממנה", (ויקרא ט) ושמואל: ב] *דורות משעה לא ילפינן. ולא יליף שמואל דורות משעה? *והתנן: כלי הלח מקדשין את הלח, ומדות ג] יבש מקדשין את היבש, ואין כלי הלח מקדשין את היבש, ולא מדות יבש מקדשין את הלח; ואמר שמואל: *ל"ש אלא מדות, אבל מזרקות מקדשין, דכתיב: °"שניהם מלאים סלת"! (במדבר ז) שאני התם, דתנא בה קרא תריסר זימנין. א"ל רב כהנא ורב אסי לרב: והרי הגשה דתנא בה קרא, ולא מעכבא! ד] מאן תנא ביה? דכתיב: °"זאת (ויקרא ו) תורת המנחה הקרב אותה ה] בני אהרן לפני ה'"! ההוא לקבוע לה מקום הוא דאתא. דתניא: "לפני ה'" – *יכול במערב? ת"ל: "אל פני המזבח"; אי אל פני המזבח, יכול בדרום? ת"ל: "לפני ה'"; הא כיצד? מגישה בקרן דרומית מערבית כנגד חודה של קרן ודיו. רבי אליעזר אומר: יכול יגישנה למערבה של קרן ו] (או) לדרומה של קרן? אמרת: *כל מקום שאתה מוצא שתי מקראות, אחד מקיים עצמו ומקיים חבירו, ואחד מקיים עצמו ומבטל את חבירו – מניחין את שמקיים עצמו ומבטל חבירו, ותופשין את שמקיים עצמו ומקיים חבירו; שכשאתה אומר "לפני ה'" במערב – בטלתה "אל פני המזבח" בדרום, וכשאתה אומר "אל פני המזבח" בדרום – קיימתה "לפני ה'". והיכא קיימתה? אמר רב אשי: ז] *)קסבר האי תנא כוליה מזבח בצפון קאי. מתקיף לה ח] רב הונא: הרי מלח דלא תנא ביה קרא, ומעכבא ט] ביה! דתניא: °"ברית מלח עולם הוא" (במדבר יח) – שתהא
ברית

*) זבחים נג. נח. סג: סוטה יד:

גרש ושמן. הוא דהחזיר בהן הכתוב ומעכבא. ואין דבר אחר מעכב. ואע"פ שהחזיר בו הכתוב י]. ואע"ג דתנא ביה קרא כו'. בתמיה. מלא קומצו. יא] כתיב בחד דוכתא. הדר שני בדבוריה וכתיב "בקומצו" למידרש מיניה: בידו (א) יקמוץ, לא יעשה כלי למדת קומצו. כפו. ולא כלי. הילכך, אם קמץ בכלי פסל. יב] דורות משעה לא ילפינן. ה"ק: חזרה דגרש ושמן הוא דאתאי לעיכובא, וכן דוגמתה, שהוחזרו בתורה מנחת דורות, אבל "וימלא כפו" לא חזרה היא. לא שנו. יג] דאין *מקדיש יבש, אלא במדת לח כגון הין ולוג, דכל מדה לא חזיא ליה אלא למילתיה למדות, והין ולוג במדת יבש ליכא. אבל מזרקות. שהן כלי דם, מקדשין סלת יבש, ויליף טעמא מנשיאים. אלמא גמר דורות משעה! יד] מאן תנא בה. כלומר, איזה מקרא שנה בה – "הקרב אותה טו] בני אהרן לפני ה'". יכול במערב. בקיר מערבי של מזבח, טז] היינו "לפני ה'" – כנגד פתח ההיכל, דהיכל במערב. ת"ל אל פני המזבח. ופני המזבח זה דרום, שהכבש בדרום.

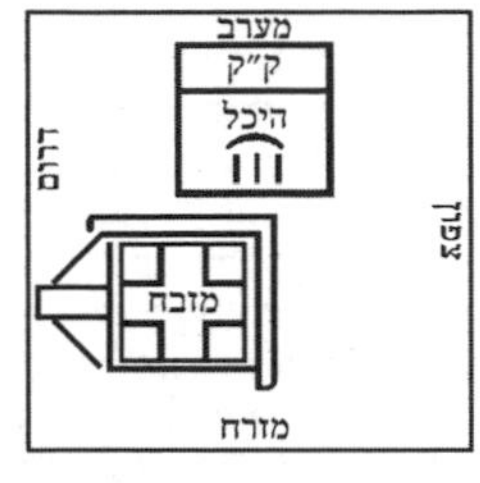

כנגד חודה של קרן. בפ"ב דסוטה (דף יד:) פריך, מאי יז] "דיו". למערבה לדרומה. כאן וכאן. כוליה מזבח בצפון עזרה קאי. ופתח היכל באמצע עזרה. וכיון דכל המזבח בחלי עזרה עומד יח] בו בצפון, אישתכח דקיר דרומית של מזבח כלה לפני פתח יט] (אהל) ההיכל, ונקרא דרומו של מזבח "לפני ה'".
ברית

ושמן מעכבי' ואין דבר אחר מעכב, משמע דבריו סותרים זה את זה, דתלי טעמא בחזרה ולא בה"א יתירא! וע"ק: אמאי לא מייתי קרא ד"מסלתה", דדרשי' מיניה בפ"ק (לעיל ד' ט:) שאם חיסר כל שהוא *פסולה, כ] [שמע מינה] דה"נ מטעם שינה הכתוב כא] קאמר! ונראה, דהכא מיירי לענין שיעכבו זה את זה דבעי דשנה עליו הכתוב, וסמיך א"מסלתה ומשמנה", דגבי מנחת העומר כתיב (ויקרא ב) "מגרשה ומשמנה", ובשאר מנחות כתיב "מסלתה ומשמנה", ו"גרשה" ו"סלתה" הכל סולת. ולקמן בפירקין (דף כז.) גבי סולת ושמן מעכבין זה את זה מייתי "מגרשה ומשמנה" ו"מסלתה ומשמנה". אבל לגבי דמיעוטן מעכב את רובן מייתי "מסלתה ומשמנה". וכן גבי עיכובא דנפשיה לא בעי שנה לעכב, אבל לגבי מעכבין זה את זה בעי שנה לעכב.

בקומצו שלא יעשה מדה לקומץ. בפ"ק (לעיל ד' יא.) דרשי': "מלא קומצו" – יכול מבורץ? ת"ל "בקומצו". תרתי שמעת מינה.

ושמואל אמר דורות משעה לא ילפינן. הא דבעי רבי זירא למילף בפ"ק (לעיל דף ט:) מ"וימלא כפו ממנה" דכל מקום שנא' "כפו" אינו אלא ימין – לא מתוקמא מילתיה במסקנא. והא דמסיק רבא: "יד" "יד" לקמיצה, דיליף "וימלא כפו" מיד דמצורע לענין קמיצה ולדורות – שמא כיון דשאר גזירות שוות דאזן ורגל לדורות עבדינן נמי הך. והא דא"ר אלעזר בזבחים בפרק "קדשי קדשים" (דף ס.): מזבח שנפגם אין אוכלין בגינו שירי מנחה, שנא' "ואכלוה אצל המזבח", וכי אצל המזבח אכלוה כו' – שאני התם דאשכחן כיוצא בה קדשי דורות, דדריש התם לעיל: מזבח שנפגם, כל קדשים שנשחטו שם פסולין, שנאמר "וזבחת עליו" כו'. אבל אין לפרש, דלא יליף הכא דורות משעה משום דנתחנך אהרן כל ז' ימי המלואים ועשה קמיצה בכפו, דא"כ מאי קפריך מהא דאמר *שמואל: אבל מזרקות מקדשים דכתיב "שניהם מלאים סולת"? ועוד, אמרינן בזבחים בפרק "טבול יום" (דף קא.) גבי אניות, שאמר לו אהרן למשה: אם שמעת בקדשי שעה שהותרה אניות, לא שמעת בקדשי דורות. ומיהו, שמא התם כך נאמר לו בפירוש, דאי לאו הכי קשיא ליה לרב דיליף *שעה מדורות. והא דבעי קרא בפרק "נגמר הדין" (סנהדרין דף מה. ושם) דלדורות יריה וסקילה, ולא יליף מסיני – לא דמי להכא, דדילמא אעבירה דסיני מיחייב תרתי ולא בשאר עבירות. והא דבעי בפ"ק דסנהדרין (דף טו:): שור סיני בכמה? ילפינן שעה מדורות או לא – התם גלוי מילתא בעלמא. תדע, דלבסוף יליף לה מדכתיב "אם בהמה אם איש" כו', ומנלן דאיש סיני בכ"ג אי לאו דיליף מדורות! והא דילפינן לקמן בסוף "התודה" (דף פב:) פסח דורות מפסח מצרים, ואפילו מאן דפליג לא פליג אלא משום דאין דנין אפשר משאי אפשר – שאני התם, דפסח מפסח שייך למילף טפי. וצריך לדקדק, לשמואל דקסבר הכא: מדה לקומץ לא פסל משום דלא יליף דורות משעה, הא תנא בפ"ק (לעיל דף ו.): קמץ ועלה בידו גרגיר מלח או קורט של לבונה פסל, מפני שאמרו הקומץ החסר והיתר פסול. ומהאי קרא גופיה דריש ליה התם בגמרא, מדכתיב "מלא קומצו" "בקומצו", ולא מצינו ששנה, אי לאו מ"וימלא כפו"! ואי בלא שנה הכתוב מסתבר לן שעיכב, א"כ גם לענין מדה לקומץ נמי מעכב, כיון דתרוייהו מהאי קרא נפקי!

כלי הלח מקדשין את הלח. פירשתי בפ"ק (לעיל דף ח:).

דתנא ביה קרא תריסר זימני. אין להקשות: אדרבה, ליהוו שני כתובין הבאין כאחד ואין מלמדין.

ההוא לקבוע לה מקום. וא"ת: קביעות מקום שמעי' מקרא ד"הקריב", ואייתר ליה "והגישה" לומר דשנה הכתוב לעכב! וי"ל: אי מ"הקריב" הוה אמינא על הכבש סמוך למזבח, ולא על המזבח ממש, כדאשכחן "והקריב הכהן את הכל המזבחה" דאמרינן בפ"ק (לעיל דף י.): זו הולכת איברים לכבש.

כנגד חודו של קרן ודיו. בפ"ב דסוטה (דף יד:) דייק: מאי "ודיו"? ומשני: ס"ד תיבעי הגשה *כמנחה גופה, פי': שיסירנה מן הכלי ויגיש הסולת עצמו למזבח. ובריש נדה (דף ג.) גבי כל הנשים דיין שעתן, אין מדקדק: מאי "דיין". וי"ל: דהתם שייך שפיר למיתני "דיין" לאפוקי מהלל וחכמים.

למערבה של קרן לדרומה של קרן. פי' בקונטרס: כאן וכאן. וקשיא: א"כ מאי מקיים עצמו ומבטל חבירו? והלא מגישה כאן וכאן! ובזבחים פ' "קדשי קדשים" (דף סג:) גרסי' בספרים: או לדרומה של קרן, פירוש: לאיזה רוח שירצה. והשתא ניחא, דתופסין את שמקיים עצמו וחבירו, ואם מגישה ברוח מערבית סמוך לקרן – נמצא מבטל פני המזבח דהיינו דרום, כדאמרינן בזבחים (דף סב:): "על ירך המזבח צפונה" – כאדם שוכב דיריכו בצפון וראשו בדרום. ואם מגישה ברוח דרום סמוך לקרן מערבית – נמצא מקיים שניהם, שגם זה "לפני ה'", דכוליה מזבח בצפון, והיכל ממוצע באמצע עזרה, ונמצא י' אמות פתחו של היכל ה' בצפון וה' בדרום, ונמצא דרומו של מזבח לפני הפתח. ואינו יכול להתרחק מהקרן, דלא קרינא ביה "לפני ה'", כיון דיש קרוב ממנו. וסימן לדבר קני מנורה, דמזרח ומערב מונחים, ולא קרינא "לפני ה'" אלא בנר הסמוך, אע"ג דכולן סדורות ברוח אחת זו אחר זו. ומיהו, נר שני של ב' נרות מזרחיות קרי "נר מערבי", כמו שאפרש לקמן בפרק "כל קרבנות" (דף פו:).

הרי מלח דלא תנא ביה קרא. במסקנא משני: כיון דכתיב ביה ברית – כמאן דתנא ביה קרא דמי. והשתא ס"ד דמדקאמר אמר רב: כל מקום שהחזיר – משמע שלא מצא עיכוב *אחר אלא במנחות. דתניא ברית מלח עולם הוא. ר"ת גריס: "מלח ברית", והוא קרא דכתיב בפרשת "ויקרא": "לא תשבית מלח ברית אלהיך מעל מנחתך". אבל "ברית מלח עולם הוא" לא כתיב גבי קרבנות אלא גבי כב] מתנות כהונה (במדבר יח) ואם תמצי לומר דדרשינן מדאפקיה רחמנא בלשון מלח, א"כ אשכחן דשנה הכתוב במלח לעכב. וכן לקמן בברייתא (דף כא:) ד"האומר הרי עלי מנחה" שכתוב בסיפרא: תלמוד לומר "ברית מלח עולם הוא", ולהלן הוא אומר "מאת בני ישראל ברית עולם" – גריס נמי ר"ת "מלח ברית", דקרא ד"ולא תשבית" דריש לה בת"כ.
אימא

פסולה ונראה דהכא נמי כו' קאמר והכא מיירי ל"ק

ט א מיי' פ"ה מהל' איסורי מזבח הלי"ב ופי"ג מהל' פסה"מ הלכה

י ב מיי' פי"ב מהל' מעשה"ק הל' ו:

[פסחים סה. עת. יומא לב: נח. יבמות מ. שבועות יז. זבחים כג.]

הגהות הב"ח

(א) רש"י ד"ה מלא וכו' בידו קומץ אבל לא יעשה:

נ"א שמואל הס"ד ומה"ד אבל מזרקות כו' מלאים סולת והא דאמרינן כו' דורות מיהו כו' כל"ל. וג"ע' זה הדיבור בפ' גמר הדין דף מה.

נ"א דורות משעה ל"ק

מנחה גופה. ל"ק

נ"א עיכוב אחר במנחות אלא משום שהחזיר והס"ד ומה"ד דתניא ברית כו' מנחה שכתוב בספרים ת"ל כו' כל"ל. ל"ק

ל"ק מוחק מן גרש עד מעכב וכל"ל מגרשה ומשמנה גופה וכ"ה בס"י

כלי הלח מקדש יבש כו' למילותיה למדוד ל"ק

[לקמן נו. נט. סנהדרין טו: ע"ש] לעיל ח: זבחים פח.

ג"ז סס

[לקמן סא. סוטה יד: זבחים סג:]

סוטה יד: זבחים סג:

שיטה מקובצת

א] תיבת ליה נמחק: ב] ושמואל לא יליף דורות משעה. ומצי למיעבד לשמואל מדה לקומץ ולרב נמי אי לאו דתנא ביה קרא הוי אמינא דמצי למיעבד מדה לקומץ ותימה מאי שנא מהא דאמרינן בפ"ק [דף יא ע"א] אי (בקומצו) [מלא קומצו] יכול אפי' מבורץ ופשוט דאפי' פסול הוי ולא בעינא תנא ביה קרא וצריך לומר דיש סברא לפסול מבורץ בקומץ טפי ממדה לקומץ דהכא: ג] ומדת היבש מקדשין כו' ולא מדת היבש מקדשין: ד] מעכבת מאי תנא בה: ה] אותה. וגו' ותנן לא הגיש כשר ותיבות בני אהרן לפני ה' נמחק: ו] תיבת או נמחק: ז] קא סבר האי תנא. רבי אליעזר כולו מזבח בצפון קאי ומתחיל דרומו של מזבח כנגד החמש אמות צפונית של פתח ההיכל והוי שפיר בדרום נמי לפני ה' לפי שהיה כל רוח הדרומי כנגד אמצעו של פתח היכל ומיהו כדי לקיים לפני ה' ממש היה מגישו לסוף קרן דרומית מערבית ומסיים בת"כ מילתי' דר"א הא כיצד מגישו לקרן דרומית מערבית וא"ת למה לי לפני ה' להכי תיפוק לי משום דכתיב כחטאת וכאשם מה חטאת ואשם טעונה יסוד אף הגשת מנחה טעונה יסוד ורוח דרומית לא היה בו יסוד אלא אמה הסמוכה למערבית וצריך לומר דמ"מ אצטריך לפני ה' לאשמועינן שהיה צריך להגישו ממש סמוך להקרן כדי לקיים לפני ה' בכל מה שיוכל ולהקריבו לקרן דרומית מערבית ממש אבל ת"ק סבר דמזבח ממוצע היה וקאי ל"ב אמות כנגד (מ') [ל"ב] אמות של חלל ההיכל וכתליו א"כ לא היה הדרומי כלל לפני ה' לפיכך היה צריך לת"ק להגישו ממש כנגד חודו של קרן והיינו שפיר לפני ה' שהרי מקום זה היה נידון כמו מערבית ממש: ח] רבי אויא הרי: ט] תיבת ביה נמחק: י] הכתוב. כדמפרש לקמן במלא קומצו בקומצו קא מפלגי דשמואל דורות משעה לא ילפינן והכי קאמר חזרה דגרש ושמן הוא דאתאי לעיכובא וכן דוגמתה שהוחזרו בתורה מנחת דורות אבל וימלא כפו לא חזרה היא. הס"ד ומה"ד ואע"ג: יא] מלא קומצו. בקומצו. תרי קראי כתיבי מלא קומצו כתיב: יב] ד"ה דורות משעה נמחק מכאן ושייך לעיל (ועמ"ש באות י): יג] לא שנו דכלי לח אין מקדשין יבש אלא במדת כו' לא חזיא אלא למלתיה והין ולוג וכו': יד] מה"ד מאי תנא: טו] אותה. היינו הגשה ולא מעכב כדתנן במתניתין לא הגיש כשירה הס"ד ומה"ד הקרב אותה בני: טז] דהיינו: יז] מאי. ודיו: יח] עומד מצד צפון אשתכח: יט] לפני פתח היכל. היינו דרומו של מזבח לפני ה': כ] תיבות שמע מינה ליתא: כא] קאמר. גליון ואין לומר דה"נ הוי טעמא משום דשנה בהו קרא וסמיך אמסולתה ומשמנה דגבי מנחת העומר כתיב מגרשה ומשמנה וגרש וסולת הכל אחד ולא נהירא דלקמן בפרקין גבי סולת דמיעוטו מעכב את רובו לא מייתי אלא קרא דמסולתה כו' לכן נראה דגבי עיכובא דנפשיה לא בעי שנה לעכב אבל לגבי מעכבין זה את זה בעי שנה לעכב ונראה דהכא מיירי לענין שיעכבו זה את זה וסמיך אמסולתה ומשמנה: תו"ח: כב] מתנות כהונה. גליון לומר שברית מתנות כהונה קיים לעולם כמלח ולא קאי ברית אמלח כלל. תו"ח:

במקרא נדרש לפניו ולאחריו קא מיפלגי. וא"ת: מנלן דבהכי פליגי? דילמא טעמא דרבנן כדאסיקנא בפ"ק (לעיל דף י.) ופרק שני דזבחים (דף כד:) דכל מקום שנאמר אצבע או כהונה אינו אלא ימין, ור"ש בעי תרתי! וי"ל: דלשון הברייתא משמע משום דקאי עליה "באצבעו", כדקתני: באצבע ולקח. והא דלא מפרשי רבנן טעמייהו מדכתיב "הכהן", משום דאיצטריך הכהן בכיהונו. ואע"ג דבפ' שני דזבחים (דף כד.) קאמר אליבא דר"ש: ואלא "הכהן" ל"ל? ומשני: הכהן בכיהונו – הוא הדין דלרבנן איצטריך נמי, אלא נטר עד לבסוף דמקשי' לר"ש ומשני ליה, והוא הדין לרבנן. וא"ת: דבפ' "השואל" (ב"מ דף לה. ושם) פליגי תנאי במקרא נדרש לפני פניו, ופריך: תנן השואל את הפרה כו', *והא שומר חנם דלפני פניו לא קתני! וליטעמיך שומר שכר דלפניו מי קתני? מאי קושיא? לימא דההיא משנה ר"ש היא, דקסבר הכא ובפ' ב' דזבחים (דף כד:) דמקרא נדרש לאחריו ולא לפניו! וי"ל: דהתם [טעמא] דר"ש משום דוי"ו מוסיף על ענין ראשון, כדאמרינן הכא גבי "והביאה". וא"ת: ואמאי לא אמרינן הכא דקאי אתרוייהו, כמו "תתננה ואכלה ומכור" בפ' "כל שעה" (פסחים דף כא:) ובפ' "כל הבשר" (חולין ד' קיד.) ובפ"ק דמסכת ע"ז (ד' כ.), וגבי "נשך ומרבית" בפ' "איזהו נשך" (ב"מ דף סא.)? כא] *דלא דמי ל"תקום והדרת" בפ"ק דקדושין (דף לג:). ומיהו לא דמי ל"תתננה ואכלה", דתרי מילי נינהו, אבל הכא חדא מילתא, ד"באצבעו" *חדא קאי, דכי האי גונא מחלקין *אה' מקראות דאין להם הכרע ש"את" "מחר" "משוקדים" "ארור" "וקם". וכי תימא: "באצבעו" נמי לא יהיה לו הכרע! ויש לחלק: *משום דאשכחן "ונתת על קרנות המזבח באצבעך", כדאמרינן בפ' ב' דזבחים (ד' כד:). וצריך עיון במסכת תענית (ד' טו.*) דכתיב: "אור זרוע לצדיק ולישרי לב שמחה", דאמרינן: לצדיקים לאורה וישרים לשמחה, ולא אמרינן דקיימי אתרוייהו כמו "תתננה ואכלה". אלא ה"ט דר"ש והביאה וי"ו מוסיף על ענין ראשון. אפילו לא ידרוש ר"ש כב] לפניו ולאחריו, וי"ו מוסיף דריש. וגבי "ולקח ונתן" לא אמרינן וי"ו מוסיף למילף קבלה מנתינה בימין, כדפי' בקונטרס, ד"באצבעו" מפסיק בין "ולקח" ל"ונתן", דה"ל למכתב "ולקח הכהן ונתן מן הדם באצבעו". וא"ת: בפ' ב' דזבחים (ד' כד:) דא"ר אלעזר בן שמוע: כל מקום שנאמר אצבע בנתינה, שינה בנתינה – פסול, בקבלה – כשר, והיכן נאמרה אצבע בנתינה – דכתיב: "ולקחת מדם הפר ונתת על קרנות המזבח באצבעך", וקסבר מקרא נדרש לפניו ולא לפני פניו ולאחריו. לימא: וי"ו מוסיף על ענין ראשון! ושמא ר"א בר ר"ש לית ליה וי"ו מוסיף על ענין ראשון. א"נ, לא דריש וי"ו מוסיף כדי לדרוש המקרא לפני פניו. גלי רחמנא גבי פרו של אהרן כו'. משמע הכא דלר"ש שחיטת פרו בזר פסולה. ואף ע"ג דמסקינן בפרק קמא דזבחים (דף יד.) לר"ש שחיטה לאו עבודה היא – ל"ק מידי, כדפי' בפ"ק (לעיל ד' ה.). ואמר רב תנופה מעכבא בנזיר. כג] ממתני' הוה מצי לאקשויי, דתנן (לקמן ד' כז.): ג' מינין שבנזיר מעכבין זה את זה. אלא ניחא ליה לאקשויי דרב אדרב. א"נ, משום דאפילו תנופה, שהיא שירי מצוה *בשאר קרבנות, מעכבת בנזיר. ואמר מר שלמיו לרבות שלמי נזיר. לקמן איתא בפ' "התודה" (ד' עח.). תורה בעיא חוקה וחוקה לא בעיא תורה. אומר ר"ת, דכל מקום דאמרי' חוקה עיכובא – לא ממשמעותא, אלא מג"ש ילפינן לה בריש פרק ב' דזבחים (ד' יח. ושם). דאמרי': אשכחן מחוסר בגדים, פירוש: דאם עבד חילל, שתויי יין מנלן? אתיא חוקה חוקה ממחוסר בגדים, דמעכב כדיליף התם לעיל – אף שתויי יין לעכב. ואם ממשמעותא הוא, ל"ל למילף ג"ש? ומיהו, מעיקרא ודאי הוה בעי למימר בשמעתין ממשמעותא, דהוה בעי תורה וחוקה. חוקה לא בעיא תורה. וא"ת: ותורה למאי אתא? דכה"ג פריך בפ"ק (לעיל ד' י.) גבי אצבע לא בעיא כהונה, דפריך: אלא כהן ל"ל! וי"ל: דתורה אתא לשום דרשה. ושאני התם דאמר קרא מגרשה ומשמנה. פירש בקונטרס: דמאי למיכתב "מגרש ומשמן" וכתב "מגרשה ומשמנה" – שמע מינה הכי אמר רחמנא: מגרשה שלה, משמנה שלה, שאם חיסר כל שהוא פסול. ובסמוך דאמר שמואל: גרש ושמן

מִקְרָא. ו] "הַכֹּהֵן", נִדְרָשׁ לְפָנָיו – לְ"וְלָקַח". וּלְאַחֲרָיו. "וְקָמַץ מִשָּׁם ז] *בְּאֶצְבָּעוֹ". וְלָקַח. "וְלָקַח (קִבֵּלַת) הַכֹּהֵן מִדַּם הַחַטָּאת בְּאֶצְבָּעוֹ וְנָתַן עַל קַרְנוֹת" וגו'. אֶלָּא בְּיָמִין. דְּכָל מָקוֹם שֶׁנֶּאֱמַר אֶצְבַּע וּכְהוּנָּה אֵינָהּ אֶלָּא יָמִין. (ב) נְתִינָה. מַתְּנַת הַקֶּרֶן דְּמִזְבֵּחַ. וְכִי נֶאֶמְרָה יָד*). כְּלוֹמַר, וְכִי נֶאֶמְרָה אֶצְבַּע בְּ"וְלָקַח"? וַהֲלֹא בְּ"וְנָתַן" הוּא אָמוּר (ג) ח]! וָי"ו דְּ"וְהֵבִיאָהּ" מוֹסִיף עַל עִנְיָן רִאשׁוֹן (ד) ט]. [וכ"ת: וָי"ו דְּ"וְנָתַן" נַמִּי יְהֵא] מְלַמֵּד קַבָּלָה מִנְּתִינָה! פָּרֵיךְ: לֵיכָּא לְמֵימַר הָכִי, דְּאִי י] כְּתִיב "וְנָתַן בְּאֶצְבָּעוֹ" – הָוֵי גְּמִירָא "וְלָקַח" מִ"וְנָתַן" בְּוָי"ו מוֹסִיף עַל עִנְיָן רִאשׁוֹן, אֲבָל הָשְׁתָּא "בְּאֶצְבָּעוֹ" הִפְסִיק הָעִנְיָן. וְאִי יא] מַה סְּמִיכָה* (ה). לְר"ש פָּרֵיךְ: "וְסָמַךְ יָדוֹ עַל רֹאשׁ קָרְבָּנוֹ" – אַלְמָא סְמִיכָה בִּבְעָלִים, אַף שְׁחִיטָה בִּבְעָלִים וְלֹא בְּאַחֵר! זְרִיקָה לָא בָּעֵינַן בִּבְעָלִים, דְּכֹהֵן זוֹרֵק יב]. אֶפְשָׁר. שְׁחִיטָה יג]. לֹא אֶפְשָׁר. זְרִיקָה בִּבְעָלִים, דִּכְתִיב: "וְזָרְקוּ בְּנֵי אַהֲרֹן". נָזִיר. כְּתִיב בֵּיהּ: "זֹאת תּוֹרַת הַנָּזִיר אֲשֶׁר יִדּוֹר" (במדבר ו). תְּנוּפָה בְּנָזִיר. דִּכְתִיב: "וְנָתַן עַל כַּפֵּי הַנָּזִיר" – יד] לְעַכֵּב, מִשּׁוּם דִּכְתִיב "תּוֹרַת". וְאע"ג דְּלָא מְעַכְּבָא בְּעָלְמָא, כִּדְאָמְרִינַן (ו) בִּשְׁמַעְתָּא קַמַּיְיתָא טו] דְּמַסֶּ' יוֹמָא (ד' ה.): שֶׁאִם עֲשָׂאָהּ לִתְנוּפָה שִׁירֵי מִצְוָה מַעֲלֶה עָלָיו הַכָּתוּב כְּאִילּוּ לֹא כִּיפֵּר, וְכִפֵּר. כֵּן יַעֲשֶׂה. עַל תּוֹרַת נִזְרוֹ. תּוֹדָה. כְּתִיב בָּהּ: "וְזֹאת תּוֹרַת זֶבַח הַשְּׁלָמִים וגו' אִם עַל תּוֹדָה יַקְרִיבֶנּוּ" וגו' (ויקרא ז). ד' מִינִין. חָמֵץ חַלּוֹת *וּרְקִיקִים וּרְבוּכָה, בְּפֶרֶק "הַתּוֹדָה" (לקמן דף עו.). שְׁלָמָיו. "עַל זֶבַח תּוֹדַת שְׁלָמָיו" – לְרַבּוֹת שַׁלְמֵי נָזִיר לַעֲשָׂרָה קַבִּין יְרוּשַׁלְמִיּוֹת וְלִרְבִיעִית שֶׁמֶן טז] *בְּתוֹדָה (בְּפֶ' "הַתּוֹדָה"). אַרְבָּעָה שֶׁבִּמְצוֹרָע. עֵץ אֶרֶז וּשְׁנִי תּוֹלַעַת וְאֵזוֹב וְצִפֳּרִים. תִּהְיֶה. מַשְׁמַע עִיכּוּבָא. יוה"כ. כְּתִיב: "וְהָיְתָה לָכֶם לְחֻקַּת עוֹלָם בַּחֹדֶשׁ הַשְּׁבִיעִי" וגו' בְּ"אַחֲרֵי מוֹת". שְׁאָר קָרְבָּנוֹת כְּתִיב בְּהוּ תּוֹרָה. "זֹאת הַתּוֹרָה לָעֹלָה וְלַמִּנְחָה" וגו' (ויקרא ז). וְלָא מְעַכְּבֵי. יז] דְּאָמַר בְּפ"ק (לעיל ד, ד.) בְּאָשָׁם: הוּא עַצְמוֹ שֶׁלֹּא הוּקְטְרוּ אֵימוּרָיו כָּשֵׁר. וּבְמִנְחָה יח] כְּתִיב: "וְזֹאת תּוֹרַת הַמִּנְחָה הַקְרֵב" וגו' (ויקרא ו) דְּהַיְינוּ הַגָּשָׁה, וּתְנַן: לֹא הִגִּישׁ כָּשֵׁר. הָא תּוֹרָה וְחוּקָּה קָאָמַר. יט] מַשְׁמַע תַּרְוַיְיהוּ כִּי הֲדָדֵי שְׁקוּלִין. מִנְחָה כְּתִיבָא חוּקָּה. "כָּל זָכָר בִּבְנֵי אַהֲרֹן [א] יֹאכְלֶנָּה חָק עוֹלָם" (וגו') (שם). שֶׁהֶחֱזִיר הַכָּתוּב. בְּ"צַו אֶת אַהֲרֹן" מַה שֶּׁכְּבָר אָמוּר בְּ"וַיִּקְרָא", אֵינוֹ אֶלָּא לְעַכֵּב. אֲכִילָה כְּתִיבָא. הִילְכָּךְ לָאו לְעִיכּוּבָא אָתָא. לֶחֶם הַפָּנִים. "וַאֲכָלוּהוּ בְּמָקוֹם קָדוֹשׁ כִּי קֹדֶשׁ קָדָשִׁים הוּא לוֹ מֵאִשֵּׁי ה' חָק עוֹלָם" וגו' (שם כד). וְשָׁאנֵי הָתָם. גַּבֵּי מִנְחָה, לְהָכִי לָא הָוְיָא חוּקָּה דִּידָהּ עִיכּוּבָא – מִשּׁוּם דִּכְתִיב: "מִגִּרְשָׂהּ וּמִשַּׁמְנָהּ". מִדְּמָלֵי לְמִכְתַּב "מִגֶּרֶשׂ וּמִשֶּׁמֶן" וּכְתִיב "מִגִּרְשָׂהּ וּמִשַּׁמְנָהּ" – שְׁמַע מִינָּהּ ה"ק: גִּרְשָׂהּ שָׁלֵם וְשַׁמְנָהּ שָׁלֵם, שֶׁאִם חִסֵּר כָּל שֶׁהוּא פָּסוּל. וּמִדְּאִיצְטְרִיךְ לְמִיכְתַּב לְהָכִי, שְׁמַע מִינָּהּ "חוּקָּה" דִּידָהּ לָאו כ] [ב] חוּקָּה.

[א] יאכלנה ל"ק. [ב] חוקה הס"ד ל"ק

תורה אור

הַכֹּהֲנִים" – *מִקְרָא נִדְרָשׁ לְפָנָיו וּלְאַחֲרָיו. וְסָבַר ר"ש מִקְרָא נִדְרָשׁ לְפָנָיו וּלְאַחֲרָיו? וְהָתַנְיָא: א] °"וְלָקַח הַכֹּהֵן מִדַּם הַחַטָּאת בְּאֶצְבָּעוֹ וְנָתַן עַל קַרְנוֹת הַמִּזְבֵּחַ", "בְּאֶצְבָּעוֹ וְלָקַח" – *מְלַמֵּד שֶׁלֹּא תְהֵא קַבָּלָה אֶלָּא בְּיָמִין, "בְּאֶצְבָּעוֹ וְנָתַן" – מְלַמֵּד שֶׁלֹּא תְהֵא נְתִינָה אֶלָּא בְּיָמִין. אר"ש: וְכִי ב] *נֶאֱמַר יָד בְּקַבָּלָה? הוֹאִיל וְלֹא נֶאֱמַר יָד בְּקַבָּלָה, קִיבֵּל בִּשְׂמֹאל – כָּשֵׁר; וְאָמַר *אַבָּיֵי: בְּמִקְרָא נִדְרָשׁ לְפָנָיו וּלְאַחֲרָיו קָא מִיפַּלְגִי, ג] (וְר"ש סָבַר: לְאַחֲרָיו נִדְרָשׁ וּלְפָנָיו אֵין נִדְרָשׁ!) אֶלָּא ה"ט דְּר"ש: "וְהֵבִיאָהּ" – וָי"ו מוֹסִיף עַל עִנְיָן רִאשׁוֹן. וְסָבַר ר"ש וָי"ו מוֹסִיף עַל עִנְיָן רִאשׁוֹן? ד] אֶלָּא מֵעַתָּה, דִּכְתִיב: °"וְשָׁחַט אֶת בֶּן הַבָּקָר וְהִקְרִיבוּ בְּנֵי אַהֲרֹן הַכֹּהֲנִים אֶת הַדָּם וְזָרְקוּ אֶת הַדָּם" – *מִקַּבָּלָה וְאֵילָךְ מִצְוַת כְּהוּנָּה, מְלַמֵּד עַל שְׁחִיטָה שֶׁכְּשֵׁרָה בְּזָר; אִי לְר"ש וָי"ו מוֹסִיף עַל עִנְיָן רִאשׁוֹן, שְׁחִיטָה ה"נ בְּזָר תְּהֵא פְּסוּלָה! שָׁאנֵי הָתָם, דְּאָמַר קְרָא: "וְסָמַךְ וְשָׁחַט", מַה סְּמִיכָה בְּזָרִים – אַף שְׁחִיטָה בְּזָרִים. אִי מַה סְּמִיכָה בִּבְעָלִים, °אַף שְׁחִיטָה בִּבְעָלִים! הַהוּא לָא מָצֵית אָמְרַתְּ, ק"ו: וּמַה זְּרִיקָה דְּעִיקַּר כַּפָּרָה לָא בָּעֲיָא בְּעָלִים, שְׁחִיטָה דְּלָאו עִיקַּר כַּפָּרָה לֹא כ"ש? וְכִי תֵּימָא, א) אֵין דָּנִין אֶפְשָׁר מִשֶּׁאִי אֶפְשָׁר – גַּלֵּי רַחֲמָנָא בְּיוה"כ: °"וְשָׁחַט אֶת פַּר הַחַטָּאת אֲשֶׁר לוֹ" – מִכְּלָל דִּשְׁחִיטָה בְּעָלְמָא לָא בָּעֵינַן בְּעָלִים. אָמַר רַב: כָּל מָקוֹם שֶׁנֶּאֱמַר תּוֹרָה וְחוּקָּה – אֵינוֹ אֶלָּא לְעַכֵּב. קָא ס"ד תַּרְתֵּי בָּעֲיָא, כִּדְכְתִיב: °"זֹאת חֻקַּת הַתּוֹרָה"; (סִימָן: נת"ץ יקמ"ל) וַהֲרֵי נָזִיר דְּלָא כְּתִיבָא בֵּיהּ אֶלָּא תּוֹרָה, וְאָמַר רַב: ב) *תְּנוּפָה בְּנָזִיר מְעַכְּבָא! שָׁאנֵי הָתָם, כֵּיוָן דִּכְתִיב: "כֵּן יַעֲשֶׂה" כְּמַאן דִּכְתִיבָא בְּהוּ חוּקָּה דָּמֵי. הֲרֵי תּוֹדָה דְּלָא כְּתִיבָא בֵּיהּ אֶלָּא תּוֹרָה, וּתְנַן: *אַרְבָּעָה (א) שֶׁבַּתּוֹדָה מְעַכְּבִין זֶה אֶת זֶה! שָׁאנֵי תּוֹדָה דְּאִיתְקַשׁ לְנָזִיר, דִּכְתִיב: °"עַל זֶבַח תּוֹדַת שְׁלָמָיו", *וְאָמַר מָר: "שְׁלָמָיו" – לְרַבּוֹת שַׁלְמֵי נָזִיר. וַהֲרֵי מְצוֹרָע דְּלָא כְּתִיב בֵּיהּ אֶלָּא תּוֹרָה, וּתְנַן: *אַרְבָּעָה מִינִין שֶׁבִּמְצוֹרָע מְעַכְּבִין זֶה אֶת זֶה! שָׁאנֵי הָתָם, כֵּיוָן דִּכְתִיב: °"זֹאת תִּהְיֶה תּוֹרַת הַמְּצוֹרָע" כְּמַאן דִּכְתִיב בֵּיהּ חוּקָּה דָּמֵי. וַהֲרֵי יוה"כ דְּלָא כְּתִיב בֵּיהּ אֶלָּא חוּקָּה, וּתְנַן: *שְׁנֵי שְׂעִירֵי יוה"כ מְעַכְּבִין זֶה אֶת זֶה! אֶלָּא אוֹ תּוֹרָה אוֹ חוּקָּה. וַהֲרֵי שְׁאָר קָרְבָּנוֹת דִּכְתִיב בְּהוּ תּוֹרָה, וְלָא מְעַכְּבִי! תּוֹרָה בָּעֲיָא חוּקָּה, וְחוּקָּה לָא בָּעֲיָא תּוֹרָה. וְהָא תּוֹרָה וְחוּקָּה קָא אָמַר! ה"ק: אַף עַל גַּב דִּכְתִיב תּוֹרָה, אִי כְּתִיבָא חוּקָּה – אִין, וְאִי לָא – לָא. וַהֲרֵי מִנְחָה דִּכְתִיב בָּהּ חוּקָּה, וְאָמַר רַב: כָּל מָקוֹם שֶׁהֶחֱזִיר הַכָּתוּב בְּתוֹרַת מִנְחָה אֵינוֹ אֶלָּא לְעַכֵּב; הֶחֱזִיר – אִין, לֹא הֶחֱזִיר – לָא! שָׁאנֵי הָתָם, דְּכִי כְּתִיבָא חוּקָּה – אֲכִילָה כְּתִיבָא. וַהֲרֵי לֶחֶם הַפָּנִים, דְּכִי כְּתִיבָא חוּקָּה אֲכִילָה כְּתִיבָא, ג) וּתְנַן: שְׁנֵי סְדָרִים מְעַכְּבִין זֶה אֶת זֶה, שְׁנֵי בָּזִיכִין מְעַכְּבִין זֶה אֶת זֶה, הַסְּדָרִין וְהַבָּזִיכִין מְעַכְּבִין זֶה אֶת זֶה! אֶלָּא, כָּל הֵיכָא דִּכְתִיבָא אֲכִילָה – אַכּוּלָּא מִילְּתָא כְּתִיבָא; שָׁאנֵי הָתָם, ה) דְּאָמַר קְרָא: °"מִגִּרְשָׂהּ וּמִשַּׁמְנָהּ" – גֶּרֶשׂ

א) לקמן פב. סוכה נ: יבמות מו. סא: הוריות ו: זבחים לח. תמורה עז: יח: נדה לז:
ב) נזיר מו. ג) לקמן כז:

נחק: יח] ובמנחה נמי כתיב: יט] קאמר דמשמע: כ] לאו דוקא הס"ד: כא] נשך הא לא דמי: כב] ר"ש וא"ו וא"ו מוסיף כו' ותיבות לפניו ולאחריו ליתא. עי' תוס' [ד"ה וי"ו לא דריש] לקמן [דף נא ע"ב]: כג] מעכבא בנזיר. לשון מהר"פ וה"ה דמצי לאתויי הא דתנן בסוף נגעים [פי"ד מ"י] שירי מצוה [הן בין שנתן ובין שלא נתן כפר] ומעלה עליו הכתוב כאילו לא כפר וכפר וכן ממתניתין דלקמן בפרקין ב' מינין וכו'.

א) נראה דצ"ל דנזיר וגו' והגיה הס"ד וא"כ מה"ד מעכבא. משום

תורה אור

וְהָתְנַן: *שִׁשִּׁים אנִבְלָלִין, שִׁשִּׁים וְא' אֵין נִבְלָלִין; וְהָוֵינַן בָּהּ: כִּי אֵינָם נִבְלָלִין מַאי הָוֵי? וְהָתְנַן: לֹא בָּלַל – כְּשֵׁרָה! *וְאָמַר ר' זֵירָא: כָּל הָרָאוּי לְבִילָּה – אֵין בִּילָּה מְעַכֶּבֶת בּוֹ, וְכָל שֶׁאֵינוֹ רָאוּי לְבִילָּה – בִּילָּה מְעַכֶּבֶת בּוֹ! מִידֵי אִירְיָא? הָא כִּדְאִיתָא וְהָא כִּדְאִיתָא, לֹא יָצַק – לֹא יָצַק כֹּהֵן אֶלָּא זָר, לֹא בָּלַל – לֹא בָּלַל כְּלָל.§ "אוֹ שֶׁפְּתָתָ' פִּתִּים מְרוּבּוֹת – כְּשֵׁרָה".§ הַשְׁתָּא לֹא פָּתַת כְּלָל כְּשֵׁרָה, פִּתִּין מְרוּבּוֹת מִיבַּעְיָא? מַאי "פִּתִּין מְרוּבּוֹת" – שֶׁרִיבָּה בִּפְתִיתִין. וְאִיבָּעֵית אֵימָא: לְעוֹלָם פִּתִּים מְרוּבּוֹת מַמָּשׁ, וּמַהוּ דְּתֵימָא: הָתָם הוּא דְּאִיכָּא תּוֹרַת חַלּוֹת עֲלֵיהֶן, אֲבָל הָכָא, דְּלָא תּוֹרַת חַלּוֹת אִיכָּא, וְלָא תּוֹרַת פְּתִיתִין אִיכָּא, קמ"ל. לֵימָא, א] מַתְנִיתִין דְּלָא כְּרַבִּי שִׁמְעוֹן; *דְּתַנְיָא, רַבִּי שִׁמְעוֹן אוֹמֵר: בכָּל כֹּהֵן שֶׁאֵינוֹ מוֹדֶה בַּעֲבוֹדָה – אֵין לוֹ חֵלֶק בַּכְּהוּנָּה, שֶׁנֶּאֱמַר: °"הַמַּקְרִיב אֶת דַּם הַשְּׁלָמִים וְאֶת הַחֵלֶב מִבְּנֵי אַהֲרֹן לוֹ תִהְיֶה שׁוֹק הַיָּמִין לְמָנָה", מוֹדֶה בַּעֲבוֹדָה – יֵשׁ לוֹ חֵלֶק בַּכְּהוּנָּה, שֶׁאֵינוֹ מוֹדֶה בַּעֲבוֹדָה – אֵין לוֹ חֵלֶק בַּכְּהוּנָּה. וְאֵין לִי אֶלָּא זוֹ בִּלְבָד, מִנַּיִן לְרַבּוֹת ט"ו עֲבוֹדוֹת: *הַיְּצִיקוֹת, וְהַבְּלִילוֹת, וְהַפְּתִיתוֹת, וְהַמְּלִיחוֹת, וְהַתְּנוּפוֹת, וְהַהַגָּשׁוֹת, וְהַקְּמִיצוֹת, וְהַקְטָרוֹת, וְהַמְּלִיקוֹת, ב] וְהַקַּבָּלוֹת, וְהַהַזָּאוֹת, וְהַשְׁקָאַת סוֹטָה, וַעֲרִיפַת עֶגְלָה, וְטָהֳרַת מְצוֹרָע, וּנְשִׂיאוּת כַּפַּיִם בֵּין מִבִּפְנִים בֵּין מִבַּחוּץ, מִנַּיִן? ת"ל: "מִבְּנֵי אַהֲרֹן", עֲבוֹדָה הַמְסוּרָה לִבְנֵי אַהֲרֹן, כָּל *כֹּהֵן שֶׁאֵינוֹ מוֹדֶה בָּהּ – אֵין לוֹ חֵלֶק בַּכְּהוּנָּה! אָמַר רַב נַחְמָן, לָא קַשְׁיָא: כָּאן ג] בְּמִנְחַת כֹּהֲנִים, כָּאן בְּמִנְחַת יִשְׂרָאֵל; מִנְחַת יִשְׂרָאֵל דְּבַת קְמִיצָה הִיא – *מִקְּמִיצָה וְאֵילָךְ מִצְוַת כְּהוּנָּה, לִימֵּד עַל יְצִיקָה וּבְלִילָה שֶׁכְּשֵׁירָה בְּזָר; מִנְחַת כֹּהֲנִים דְּלָאו בַּת קְמִיצָה הִיא – מֵעִיקָּרָא בָּעְיָא כְּהוּנָּה. אָמַר לֵיהּ רָבָא: מִכְּדִי מִנְחַת כֹּהֲנִים מֵהֵיכָא אִיתְרַבֵּי לִיצִיקָה? מִמִּנְחַת יִשְׂרָאֵל, מַה הָתָם כְּשֵׁירָה בְּזָר – אַף הָכָא נַמִּי כְּשֵׁירָה בְּזָר! אִיכָּא דְּאָמְרִי: אָמַר רַב נַחְמָן, לָא קַשְׁיָא: כָּאן בְּנִקְמָצוֹת, כָּאן בְּשֶׁאֵין נִקְמָצוֹת. אָמַר לֵיהּ רָבָא: מִכְּדִי שֶׁאֵין נִקְמָצוֹת מֵהֵיכָא אִיתְרַבֵּי לִיצִיקָה? מִנִּקְמָצוֹת; כְּנִקְמָצוֹת, מַה הָתָם כְּשֵׁירָה בְּזָר – אַף הָכָא נַמִּי כְּשֵׁירָה בְּזָר! אֶלָּא מְחַוַּורְתָּא, מַתְנִיתִין דְּלָא כְּר' שִׁמְעוֹן. מ"ט דְּרַבָּנַן? אָמַר קְרָא: °"וְיָצַק עָלֶיהָ שֶׁמֶן וְנָתַן עָלֶיהָ לְבוֹנָה וֶהֱבִיאָהּ אֶל בְּנֵי אַהֲרֹן *הַכֹּהֵן וְקָמַץ", גמִקְּמִיצָה וָאֵילָךְ מִצְוַת כְּהוּנָּה, לִימֵּד עַל יְצִיקָה וּבְלִילָה שֶׁכְּשֵׁירָה בְּזָר. וְרַבִּי שִׁמְעוֹן? "בְּנֵי אַהֲרֹן

הַכֹּהֲנִים

רש"י

וְהָתְנַן. בְּפֶרֶק "הַמְּנָחוֹת וְהַנְּסָכִים" (לקמן דף קג:). שִׁשִּׁים. עֶשְׂרוֹנִים נִבְלָלִין בְּלוֹג אֶחָד. שִׁשִּׁים וְאֶחָד אֵין נִבְלָלִין. בְּלוֹג אֶחָד. הִילְכָּךְ לֹא יָבִיא ס"א עֶשְׂרוֹנִים בִּכְלִי אֶחָד, לְפִי שֶׁאֵין רַשַּׁאי לָתֵת שָׁם שְׁנֵי לוּגִּין, וּכְר' אֱלִיעֶזֶר בֶּן יַעֲקֹב דְּאָמַר בְּפֶרֶק "שְׁתֵּי מִדּוֹת" (לקמן דף פח.): אֲפִילּוּ לְמִנְחָה שֶׁל שִׁשִּׁים עִשָּׂרוֹן אֵין לָהּ אֶלָּא לוּגָּהּ. וְלִי נִרְאֶה, דַּאֲפִילּוּ לְרַבָּנַן דְּאָמְרִי שִׁשִּׁים לוֹג – קִים לְהוּ דְּאֵין נִבְלָלִים יָפֶה בִּכְלִי אֶחָד. כָּל הָרָאוּי לְבִילָּה. שִׁשִּׁים עֶשְׂרוֹנִים שֶׁרְאוּיִין לְבָלֵל בְּלוֹג. אֵין בִּילָּה מְעַכֶּבֶת בּוֹ. שְׁמַע מִינָּהּ דְּאִי נַמִּי לֹא בָּלַל כָּשֵׁר. וְשֶׁאֵין רָאוּי לְבִילָּה. שִׁשִּׁים וְאֶחָד, מְעַכֵּב בּוֹ מִצְוַת בִּילָּה וּפְסוּלָה. אַלְמָא, מִדְּשַׁנֵּי לָהּ: אֵין בִּילָּה מְעַכֶּבֶת בּוֹ, שְׁמַע מִינָּהּ "לֹא בָּלַל" דְּמַתְנִיתִין – לֹא בָּלַל כְּלָל מַשְׁמַע, וְה"ה דְּלֹא יָצַק! שֶׁרִיבָּה בִּפְתִיתִין. שֶׁפְּתָתָהּ יוֹתֵר מִדַּאי. וּמַהוּ דְּתֵימָא הָתָם. כִּי לֹא פָּתַת כְּלָל הוּא דִּכְשֵׁרָה, *דְּאִיכָּא תּוֹרַת חַלּוֹת עֲלֵיהֶן. אֲבָל. פָּתַת פִּתִּים מְרוּבּוֹת, אֵימָא תִּיפָּסֵל. מַתְנִיתִין. דְּמַכְשִׁיר יְלִיקָה בְּזָר, דְּלֹא כְּר' שִׁמְעוֹן. חֲמֵשׁ עֶשְׂרֵה עֲבוֹדוֹת. נְשִׂיאַת כַּפַּיִם דִּבְפְנִים וּבַחוּץ חֲדָא חָשִׁיב לֵיהּ. הַקַּבָּלוֹת. קַבָּלַת דָּם. בִּפְנִים. בַּעֲזָרָה, כִּדְכְתִיב: "וַיִּשָּׂא אַהֲרֹן אֶת יָדָיו" (ויקרא ט) וגו'. בַּחוּץ. בְּכָל עִיר וָעִיר. כָּל כֹּהֵן כו'. אַלְמָא, מִדַּחֲשִׁיב יְלִיקָה בִּכְלַל עֲבוֹדָה הַמְסוּרָה לִבְנֵי אַהֲרֹן, שְׁמַע מִינָּהּ אֲסוּרָה בְּזָר. מִקְּמִיצָה וְאֵילָךְ כו'. כִּדְכְתִיב: ד] "וְיָלַק* הַכֹּהֵן" וגו', דְּלֶיהֱוֵי מַשְׁמַע: מִקְּמִיצָה וְאֵילָךְ מִצְוַת כְּהוּנָּה. מִמִּנְחַת יִשְׂרָאֵל. דִּילִיקָה בְּמִנְחַת יִשְׂרָאֵל כְּתִיב, וְגָמְרִי' מִינָּהּ שְׁאָר מְנָחוֹת בְּפֶרֶק "אֵלּוּ מְנָחוֹת" (לקמן דף עה.), דְּדָרְשִׁינַן: "וְיָצַקְתָּ עָלֶיהָ שֶׁמֶן מִנְחָה" – לְרַבּוֹת כָּל הַמְּנָחוֹת לִקְמִיצָה וְלִילִיקָה. כָּאן בְּשֶׁאֵין נִקְמָצוֹת. ה] הַהִיא לִישָּׁנָא בַּתְרָא דְּרַב נַחְמָן אֲתָא לְרַבּוּיֵי מִנְחַת נְסָכִים ו] כְּמִנְחַת כֹּהֲנִים, דִּילִיקָה פְּסוּלָה בְּזָר.

מִקְרָא

תוספות

כי אין נבללים מאי הוי הא תנן לא בלל כשר. ואם תאמר: מכל מקום, כיון דלכתחילה מצוה לבלול, צריך להביא מנחה שיכולה להיבלל! ז]וי"ל: כיון דהאי גברא לקרבן גדול מיכוון – היה לו להביא בכלי אחד, משום דתנן בפרק "המנחות והנסכים" (לקמן דף קג:) שאם נדר בכלי אחד לא יביא בשני כלים, ואם הביא פסול. הילכך, אי לא הוה בילה מעכבא היה לו להביא בכלי אחד ח]. ואמר ר' זירא כל הראוי לבילה כו'. וא"ת: מנא ליה לר' זירא הא? לימא: לא בלל כהן אלא זר, כמו בלא יצק! ושמא קים ליה דלא כתיבא עיכובא בבלילה. ואם תאמר: והא *תנא בה קרא, דכתיבא בלילה במנחת מחבת ומרחשת ומאפה תנור (ויקרא ו) ובנשיאים (במדבר ז) תריסר זימני! ויש לומר: דלא מישתמיט קרא דליכתוב בשום דוכתא "ובללת בשמן" בלשון צווי. *וכל שאינו ראוי לבילה בילה מעכבת בו. וא"ת: מנליה דליבעי ראוי לבילה, מאחר דבילה לא מעכבא? וי"ל: סברא בעלמא הוא, כיון דכתב רחמנא בילה, דנבעי לכל הפחות ראוי לבילה. וכן לגבי קריאה דחליצה דפ' "מצות חליצה" (יבמות דף קד:), וגם קריאה דביכורים בפרק "המוכר את הספינה" (ב"ב דף פא:) ובמכות (דף יח:), דבכל הנהו מייתי דרבי זירא. אבל בפרק קמא דקידושין (דף כה.) קשיא טפי, דבעי כל בשרו ראוי לביאת מים אפילו בית הסתרים, מנלן? הא כיון דכתיב "בשרו" דמה בשרו מאבראי, וא"כ אפילו ראוי לא ניבעי! וי"ל: משום דכתיב "כל בשרו" *[מ"מ] אהני למימר דבעינן ראוי. וא"ת: א"כ, לכתחילה ניבעי רחיצה, כמו בבילה וקריאה! וי"ל: שאני הכא דכתיב "בשרו" דמשמע מאבראי, וכאילו כתב בהדיא: ורחץ מאבראי. וא"ת: בפ' "נגמר הדין" (סנהדרין ד' מה:) דאמר שמואל: נקטעה יד העדים פטור, דבעיא קרא כדכתיב, ומסיק: תנאי היא, ואיכא למ"ד חייב, נימא: הראוי לבילה כו'! וי"ל: דהתם אין סברא לפוטרו בשביל כך. ואם תאמר: בנדרים בפרק "נערה המאורסה" (דף עג.) דבעי: חרש מהו שיפר לאשתו כו', ומספקינן ליה אי בעיא ראוי לשמיעה כדרבי זירא אי לא, אמאי מספקינא ליה? וי"ל: משום דדילמא הא דכתב רחמנא "ושמע" אורחא דמילתא נקט, שאין ראוי להפר אלא ע"י שמיעה. **שריבה** בפתיתין. סבר לה כמ"ד בפרק "אלו מנחות" (לקמן דף עה:) שקופל אחד לשנים ושנים לארבעה, ולא כמ"ד מחזיר *לסולתן שנאמר "המקריב אותו" כו'. **מודה** בעבודה יש לו חלק. הכא נקט "מודה בעבודה", משמע: אפילו ת"ח, אלא שהוא רשע. ובפרק "הזרוע והלחיים" (חולין דף קל.) אמרינן דאין נותנין מתנה לכהן עם הארץ, שנאמר: "לתת מנת למחזיקים בתורת ה'", ולא קאמר: לכהן שאינו מודה מדכתיב "מחזיקים"! ושמא יש לחלק, דהתם בתרומות ומעשרות, שאדם נותן לכל כהן שירצה. והכא בקרבן המתחלק לכל בית אב של אותו היום, וסלקא דעתך שכולן שוין משום "לכל בני אהרן תהיה איש כאחיו", קמ"ל קרא דבעינן מודה בעבודה. **מנין** לרבות ט"ו עבודות. הכא לא חשיב הולכה, דרבי שמעון לטעמיה דלא חשיב לה עבודה, בסוף פרק קמא דזבחים (דף יד:) משום דאיפשר לבטלה. ומיהו קשה, דאיכא קטרת הפנימית דאי אפשר לבטלה, כדקאמר התם רבי שמעון בן לקיש! ונראה דבכלל קבלה היא, כדאמר התם דאפקה לקבלה בלשון הולכה. ומיהו קשה, דאכתי איכא עבודות טובא, כגון תרומת הדשן וסידור מערכה ושני גיזרי עצים ודישון מזבח הפנימי והמנורה ולחם הפנים ובזיכי לבונה! ויש לומר: דתנא ושייר, אע"ג דתנא מניינא. דאע"ג דפריך בפרק קמא דקידושין (דף טז:) גבי ד' מעניקים להן: תנא תני ארבעה, ואת אמרת תנא ושייר – התם אסיפא סמיך, דקתני: ואי אתה יכול לומר ארבעה באחד מהן. וגבי חורש תלם אחד בפרק בתרא דמכות (דף כא:) דפריך: תנא תני שמנה, ואת אמרת תנא ושייר – שאני התם דמשמע דאתא לטפויי לאוי. ובגיטין אשכחן בפרק קמא (דף ח.) דתנא מניינא ושייר, גבי א) שלש דברים בסוריא, ובסוטה בפרק "היה מביא" (דף טז.) גבי בשלשה מקומות הלכה עוקבת את המקרא. ומכל מקום צריך ליתן טעם מניינא למעוטי מאי. ושמא תנא מניינא למעוטי שחיטה והפשט וניתוח, שהיא עבודה שאינה מסורה לבני אהרן, ולא חיישינן אם אינו מודה*.

כאן במנחת כהנים כאן במנחת ישראל. ואם תאמר, אכתי לימא מתניתין דלא כרבי יהודה ור' שמעון. דתנן: לא מלח כשר, ולקמן בברייתא מוכח דמליחה מעכבא לר' יהודה ור"ש, וא"א לפרש מתני' לא מלח כהן אלא זר, כדמוכח לקמן!

מקמיצה ואילך מצות כהונה. פירשתי בפרק קמא (לעיל דף ט.). **ורבי** שמעון בני אהרן נדרש לפניו ולאחריו. ואם תאמר: ומי פליג רבי שמעון א"לא בלל כשר"? ויש לומר: דבלל זר גרע, דמיחל עבודה. ומהאי טעמא ניחא בלל מחוץ לחומת העזרה, דבפרק קמא (לעיל דף ט.) דפסול אע"ג דלא בלל כשר. אי נמי, מכולה מתניתין דייקינן דלא כר"ש, מלא יצק ומלא בלל, דלרבי שמעון כיון דבעי כהן אי לא עביד פסול. ומיהו קשה ממליחה, דבעי רבי שמעון קרא ב) לקמן מנלן דמעכבא, ולמה לי קרא? תיפוק ליה דבעינן כהן כדאמרינן: וכי תעלה על דעתך שזר קרב אצל מזבח! ט] ובלאו האי טעמא בעי דמקמיצה ואילך מצות כהונה, ומליחה אחר קמיצה.

במקרא

א) שלשה דברים שותה סוריא לא"י ובסוטה. נ"ק ב) לקמן דמעכבא כו' האי טעמא בעי כהן נ"ק

עין משפט נר מצוה

ה א מיי' פי"ז מהל' מעה"ק הל"ו:
ו ב מיי' פ"א מהל' בכורים הל"א:
ז ג מיי' פי"ב מהל' מעה"ק הל' כג ופי"א מהל' פסה"מ הל"ז:

שנה בה נ"ק

וא"ת דקאמר וכל שאינו כו' כבו מנליה נ"ק וכ"ה בס"י

תוספתא דדמאי פ"ב ע"ש [חולין קלב: ע"ש]

דמרבה אפילו בית הסתרים משום הכי אהני נ"ק

לסולתן הס"ד אח"כ ד"ה שנאמר המקריב אותו כו' מודה כו' הכא נקט שאינו מודה בעבודה נ"ק

[ועי' תוס' יבמות ג: ד"ה למעוטי ותו' קדושין טז: ד"ה הלא ותו' סוטה טז. ד"ה תנא ותוספות נא: ד"ה תמקק ותוספות גיטין ב: ד"ה אין מוליכין]

מסורת הש"ס

לקמן קג.

ג"ז שם ב"ב פא: חולין פג: קדושין כה. יבמות קד: נדה סו: מכות יח: נדרים עג.

דכשרה דהורת נ"ק

חולין קלב: [תוספתא דדמאי פ"ב ע"ש]

ויקרא ז

רש"ק

הכהן וקמץ דמשמע מקמיצה נ"ק

בכורות ל:

לעיל ט. פסחים לו.

ויקרא ב

[הכהנים]

שיטה מקובצת

א] מתניתין דלא כר"ש דתניא. חולין דף קלב. וא"ת וכי תיסק אדעתין דר' שמעון בעי כל הני בכהן וכי אפי' דיעבד והא בלילות דאם לא בלל כשר וכי עביד ליה זר אמאי מפסיל אלא ע"כ ר"ש לא בעי אלא לכתחילה למצוה וא"כ מאי קאמר מתניתין דלא כר"ש דילמא מתניתין דמכשיר בדיעבד קאמר וי"ל דמתניתין משמע לתלמודא אפי' לכתחילה ותדע דסבר הכי דאמרי' מקמיצה ואילך מצות כהונה אבל קודם לכן זר כשר. תו"ח. עוד אמר מהר"פ אע"ג דבלילה ר"ל לכתחילה ביציקה פסול אפי' בדיעבד כיון דעיכובא כתיב ביה וכי עביד לה זר הוי כאילו חסרה: ב] והקבלות. וא"ת והלא זו א) עצמה קבלה היא דאמרי' בזבחים והקריב זו קבלת הדם וי"ל דבעי אשאר קבלות דלאו דשלמים דקרא דהמקריב לא מיירי אלא בשלמים וא"ת א"כ אמאי לא תני זריקות משום שאר זבחים וי"ל ב) דהו"א בכל הזאות. תו"ח: ג] במנחת כו' וא"ת אכתי קשה ממליחות דמתניתין משמע לא מלח כהן אלא זר ובמילתא דר"ש מליחות בעי כהן דא"ל כאן במנחת כהנים שהרי מליחה אחר קמיצה היא ובדבר שהוא אחר קמיצה אין חילוק בין מנחת כהנים ובין מנחת ישראל וי"ל דבמתניתין ע"כ הוי ליה לא מלח כלל אבל בזר פסולה דהא מליחה בראשו של מזבח ואי אפשר לזר לעלות על גבי המזבח. תו"ח: כאן במנחת כהנים. וא"ת היכי מצי לאוקמי במנחת כהנים והלא תני הקמיצות ומנחת כהנים אינה נקמצת וי"ל דמילי מילי קתני ולא קאי קמיצות אמנחת כהנים אלא אשאר מנחות וא"ת מ"מ מתניתין דלא כר"ש דקתני לא פתת כהן אלא זר והכא קאמר דפתיתות צריכות כהן ואין לומר (דהכי) [דהכא] מיירי במנחת כהנים דהא אמר לקמן בפ' אלו מנחות מנחת כהנים כיון שאין בה קמיצה אין בה פתיתה וי"ל כדאמרינן לעיל כי לא פתת כלל והכא מ"ט מצריך כהן למצוה בלבד א"נ הא דאמרינן לקמן דאין בהם פתיתה ר"ל פתיתה הראויה דהיינו אחת לשנים ושנים לארבע אבל מ"מ פתיתה איכא דכתיב פתות אותה פתים אבל במנחת כהנים לא כתיב כי אם תופיני מנחת פתים וא"כ מוקמינן הא במנחת כהנים. תו"ח: ד] כדכתיב וקמץ: ה] נקמצות. נפקא מינה דהאי לישנא: ו] תיבות כמנחת כהנים נמחק: ז] ס"א וי"ל דפריך שפיר דכיון דכשר בדיעבד כי לא בלל והאי גברא: ח] אחד. לשון מהר"פ ועי"ל דאי איתא דכשירים בדיעבד בלא בלילה הכא היה לו להביא כולו בכלי אחד וסגי ליה בלוג שמן דאי עביד להו בשני כלים יצטרך לה ב' לוג שמן ודמי לריבה שמנה: ט] טעמא תיפוק לי דמקמיצה:

א) ר"ל דבהך קרא דהמקריב את דם השלמים גם קבלה בכלל דהא אמרינן בזבחים והקריב וכו'. ב) נראה לנ"ל וי"ל דהוא בכלל והזאות וראיה לדבריו במשנה דמגילה דף כ' דתני שם והזיה ולא תני זריקה וע"כ דזריקה בכלל הזאה.

ור' יהודה סבר: בהנך פליגי, להניח — דברי הכל פסול, מאי טעמא? גזירה מקצת דמו אטו כל דמו; וכל דמו פסולא דאורייתא, דתניא, *אמר להם רבי יהודה: אי אתם מודים לי שאם הניחו למחר שפסול? חישב להניחו למחר נמי פסול. ואתא ר' אליעזר למימר: אף בזו ר' אליעזר פוסל וחכמים מכשירין. וסבר ר' יהודה: להניח מדמו למחר דברי הכל פסול? והתניא, אמר רבי: כשהלכתי א] למצות מדותי אצל ר' אלעזר בן שמוע, ואמרי לה: למצות מדותיו של ר' אלעזר בן שמוע, מצאתי יוסף *הבבלי יושב לפניו, והיה חביב לו ביותר עד ב] לאחת, אמר לו: רבי, השוחט את הזבח להניח מדמו למחר, מהו? *אמר לו: כשר; ערבית — אמר לו: כשר; שחרית — אמר לו: כשר; צהרים — אמר לו: כשר; מנחה — אמר לו: כשר, אלא שר' אליעזר פוסל. צהבו פניו של יוסף הבבלי. אמר לו: יוסף, כמדומה אני שלא כיוונו שמועתינו עד עתה! אמר לו: ג] רבי, הן! אלא שר' יהודה פסול שנה לי, וחזרתי על כל תלמידיו ובקשתי לי חבר ולא מצאתי, עכשיו ששנית לי פסול החזרת לי אבידתי. זלגו עיניו דמעות של רבי אלעזר בן שמוע, אמר: אשריכם תלמידי חכמים שדברי תורה חביבין עליכם ביותר! קרא עליו המקרא הזה: °"מה אהבתי תורתך כל היום היא שיחתי" וגו', הא מפני שר' יהודה בנו של ר' אלעאי ורבי אלעאי תלמידו של ר' אליעזר, ד] לפיכך שנה לך משנת רבי אליעזר. ואי סלקא דעתך דברי הכל פסול אתנייה, מאי "החזרת לי ה] אבידתי"? איהו פלוגתא קאמר ליה! אלא מאי? כשר, ור' אליעזר (א) פסול פוסל אתנייה? אי הכי, מאי "הא מפני" ו] *(פלוגתא?) אנן נמי פלוגתא קא מתנינן! אלא, לעולם דברי הכל פסול אתנייה, ומאי "החזרת לי אבידתי" — ז] דהדר ליה מיהא שום *פסלות בעולם.§

מתני' לא יצק, לא בלל, ולא פתת, ולא מלח, ולא הניף, לא הגיש, או ח] שפתתן פתים מרובות ולא משחן — כשירה.§

גמ' מאי לא יצק? אילימא לא יצק כלל — עיכובא ט] כתב בה! אלא, לא יצק *כהן אלא זר; אי הכי, לא בלל נמי — לא בלל כהן אלא זר, הא לא בלל כלל — פסולה. והתנן

ור' יהודה סבר. בשחיטה הוא דפליגי רבנן, משום דחישב במידי דלאו אורחיה, אבל בלהניח דברי הכל פסולה. גזירה. דמחשב להניח מקצת דמו אטו כל דמו. וכל דמו פסולא דאורייתא הוא, כדמפרש במסכת זבחים בפ' "כל הפסולין" (דף לו.): תרי קראי כתיבי בנותר כו'. למצות מדותי. לידע מילוי תלמודי ולשאול ספיקותי. למצות מדותיו. ללמוד ולמצות מה שר' אלעזר חכם ממני. והיה חביב. יוסף לרבי אלעזר, *וספרו בהלכות עד שהגיעו להלכה אחת של זבחים. לשון אחר: והיה חביב ליוסף כל מה שרבי אלעזר מלמדו, עד שהגיעו להלכה אחת. צהבו פניו. מחמת שמחה. שלא כיוונו שמועתינו. כלומר, דלא סליק לך הלכה דהילכתא כל דקאמרי לך עד השתא. י] רבי הן. כוונת וכוונה, אלא משום הכי צהבו פני השתא, שר' יהודה פסול שנה לי. ולא מצאתי. וקיימי מתירא שמא שכחתי. הא מפני. "הא" משמע לשון טעם, כלומר: הרי מפני שרבי יהודה בנו של רבי אלעאי, ורבי אלעאי תלמידו של רבי אליעזר, כדאמרי' במסכת סוכה בפרק "הישן" (דף כז:): מעשה ברבי אלעאי שהלך להקביל פני ר' אליעזר כו'. שנה לך משנת רבי אליעזר. ולא שהלכה כן, אלא חביבה היתה עליו ושנאה לך. ואי סלקא דעתך רבי יהודה דברי הכל יא] פסולה אתנייה. לרבי יוסף הבבלי, מאי "החזרת לי אבידה"? הא לא אמר ר' אלעזר בן שמוע כר' יהודה! וקשיא למאן דאמר לעיל: ר' יהודה סבר להניח דברי הכל פסול יב]. אלא מאי, אתנייה ר' יהודה, כשר לרבנן ור' אליעזר פוסל? א"כ מאי "הא מפני", דמשמע מפני חביבה עליו שנאה, ולא שהלכה כן היא! הא אנן נמי יג] דברי ר"א בן שמוע פלוגתא מתנינן לר' יהודה (זבחים דף לו.). **מתני'** לא יצק. היינו יציקה אחרונה, דבתחילה נותן שמן בכלי ואח"כ סולת, יד] ובולל, וחוזר ויוצק שמן. והכי מפרש בפ' "אלו מנחות נקמצות" (דף עד:). טו] (לא יצק) לא בלל *כשר. וכגון שנתן כל הלוג בנתינה הראשון שהוא קודם לעשייתה. *דאי חיסר שמנה, אמרו בפ' קמא (לעיל דף יא.): פסולה. לא פתת. *שנאמר: "פתות אותה פתים". ואע"ג דבמנחת מחבת הוא דכתיב – ה"ה לכל המנחות הנאפות תחילה, כגון מחבת ומרחשת ומאפה, שכולן באות עשר עשר, ומלוה לפותתן כזיתים ואח"כ קומץ. וזה אם לא פתת אלא כדי קמיצה — כשר, כדאמרינן ב"אלו מנחות" (לקמן דף עה:). לא הניף. במנחת (*סוטה) וקנאות דטעונות תנופה, בפרק "כל המנחות" (שם דף סא.). לא הגיש. בקרן דרומית מערבית, כדמפרש במשנתנו (ג). טז] פתתה. לאחר אפייתן פותתן וקומץ, כדמפרש ב"אלו מנחות" (שם דף עה.). ופתתן יז] מרובות גדולות יותר מדינן המפורש ב"אלו מנחות נקמצות" (שם דף עה.): מנחת ישראל כופל אחד לשנים ושנים לד'. ולא משחן. אותן הטעונות משיחה כדכתיב: "ורקיקי מצות משוחים בשמן" (ויקרא ז). **גמ'** עיכובא כתיב בה. דהא יח] נאמר יציקה במנחת סולת, ונשנית במנחת מחבת, ואמרינן לקמן (דף יט:): כל מקום יט] שחזר ושנה הכתוב בתורת מנחה — אינו אלא לעכב. אי נמי, דכתיב (ויקרא ב): "ויצקת עליה שמן מנחה היא" – היא מנחה, ולא שלא יצק מנחה, דכל "היא" עיכובא. ואף על גב דדרשינן ליה ב"אלו מנחות" (לקמן דף עה:) למעוטי מנחת מאפה מיציקה, שמעינן נמי עיכובא מיניה. והתנן

גזירה מקצת דמו כו'. תימה: בלשתות מדמו נמי נגזר אטו כל דמו! וי"ל: לשתות כל דמו נמי לא משמע שלא יעשה זריקה כלל, אלא אחר זריקתה ישתה. וא"ת: *לאכול אמאי מודים? ליגזור אטו כל אימורים דהוי פסולא דאורייתא! וי"ל: דהכא נמי אפשר לאכילה לאחר שהעלן ומשלה בהן האור, שאינם אלא לצויין בעלמא. ולא דמי להניח, דמשמע שלא יעשה זריקה כלל. ועוד, באימורים לא מיפסל זיבחא אם לא הוקטרו. ומיהו, בעל מנת להניח אימורין למחר או להוציאם לחוץ היה פוסל ר' יהודה, כדתנן בזבחים בפרק "כל הפסולין" (דף לה:). ושמא טעמא משום דגזר להניח כל האימורים אטו להניח כל דמו. **עד** אחת. במגילת סתרים דרבינו נסים גרים "עד לאחת", פירוש: עד מאד, כדמתרגמינן "מאד" – לחדא. וי"מ: עד אחת – עד הנפש שנקראת "יחידה". והשתא משמע הכא שרבי למד הרבה מרבי אלעזר בן שמוע. וקשה, דבסוף "הערל" (יבמות ד' פד.) אמר רבי: כשהלכתי ללמוד תורה אצל רבי אלעזר בן שמוע, חברו עלי תלמידיו כתרנגולין של בית בוקיא, ולא הניחו לי ללמוד אלא דבר אחד במשנתנו! ושמא מעשה זה היה אח"כ. תדע, דהתם קאמר "ללמוד תורה", והכא קאמר "למצות מדותיו". **אלא** לעולם דברי הכל פסול אתנייה. לפי מסקנא זו לא נוכל להוכיח לנוס תנא פיגול *כר' אליעזר. ותימה, דבפ"ב דזבחים (דף כז:) תנן: השוחט את הזבח לאכול כזית מעור שתחת האליה למחר – פיגול וחייבין עליו כרת. וקאמרינן בגמרא: סברוה דעור האליה כאליה דמי, *דקא מחשב מאכילת מזבח לאדם. אמר שמואל: הא מני – רבי אליעזר היא דאמר: מחשבין *מאכילת אדם כו'! וכמו כן קשיא מרבי יוחנן לעיל, דמפרש טעמא דרבי אליעזר מקרא! ושמא לית להו מסקנא דהכא. ועוד יש לתרץ, דקסבר *שמואל דלכולהו תנאי הוי פיגול, והשלשה מחלוקות – בלהניח, אבל בהנך הוי פיגול, בין לתנא קמא בין לרבי אליעזר. אבל לרבי יוחנן לא נוכל לומר כן, דהא בהדיא מילתא קאמר ר"י דמודה רבי אליעזר שאין ענוש כרת, ואין שני דבריו של רבי יוחנן יכולים להתקיים, שצריך לגמור שני תנאים אליבא דרבי אליעזר, דחד פסל וחד מפגל, ולמאי דאסיקנא: "דברי הכל פסול" אתנייה, לא משכח להו. כ] **לא** מלח ולא הניף ולא הגיש. לא דקדק בסדר, דתנופה קודמת למליחה, כדתניא *סוטה (דף יט.): והניף והגיש קמץ ומלח והקטיר. ועוד אמרינן בגמרא לקמן (דף כ.) דלאין לומר: לא מלח כהן אלא זר, וכי תעלה על דעתך שזר קרב אצל מזבח? והיינו משום שהיתה המליחה אחר תנופה והגשה.

כי

ד א מיי' פי"ג מהל' מעשה"ק הל' י"ח.

לאכול מאימורים לגזור נ"ק

[זבחים לו.]

לרבי נ"ק

והא קא מחשב כו' נ"ק

מאכילת מזבח לאכילת אדם כו' נ"ק

נמי שמואל נ"ק

פסול בס"י

[לקמן כ.]

[לפנינו שם לא נזכר ומלח אלא רק לאחת שם הניף והגיש קמץ ומלח והקטיר גם בגמרא שם שמפרש המשנה גם בסוגיא שבמשנתנו אם כנ"ל בפ"ג דין טו מהל' סוטה אשר העתיק המשנה והגמרא לא נזכר מדין מליחה ולהיות שגם בסנהדרין פב: ד"ה המולח וכו' העתיקו תוס' הגיש והניף קמץ ומלח והקטיר עי"ש בגליון הש"ס ע"ש א"כ נראה לגרסתם היה כך בסדר המשנה דסוטה יט. וגם בגמ' דכס]

נ"א וספרו

תוספתא דזבחים פ"ב

[חרית אמר לו כשר צהרים כו' מנחה כו' ערבית א"ל כשר אלא כ"א כל"ל וכ"ה בתוספתא]

תהלים קיט

הגהות הב"ח

(א) גמ' ור' אליעזר פוסל אתנייה כצ"ל ותיבת פסול נמחק: (ב) רש"י ד"ה לא יצק וכו' ובמשנתנו הס"ד ואח"כ מ"ה פתים מרובות פתיתה לאחר:

אי הא מפני הא אנן. נ"ק

בשמן וכגון נ"ק

נ"א ובילתה

לאחר אפייתן פותתן קומץ שנאמר כו' כגון מרחשת ומאפה כו' נ"ק

[העומר]

שיטה מקובצת

א] למצות מדותי כו' מצות מדותיו: ב] עד אחת: ג] הן ר' הן: ד] לפיכך שנה לך משנת: ה] אבידתי איהו נמי פלוגתא: ו] מפני פלוגתא: ז] אבידתי אהדר: ח] שפתת'.

פירש"י דלאחר אפייתן כו' משמע מתוך פי' דאין פתיתה במנחת סולת כי אם במנחות הנאפות כמו מחבת או מרחשת וכן פי' בחומש ולקמן משמע דכולן באות חלות אלא שהמנחת סולת היתה נקמצת קודם אפיה ומ"מ בכולן היתה פתיתה: ט] עיכובא כתיב: י] הן ר' הן: יא] דברי הכל פסול אתנייה ליוסף הבבלי מאי החזרת לי אבידתי הא. אות ה' ותיבת לר' נמחק: יב] פסול: איהו נמי. ר' אלעזר בן שמוע: פלוגתא קאמר ליה. כשאר התלמידים שלא הודו ליוסף הבבלי דדברי הכל פסול: יג] נמי לדברי: יד] סולת. וחוזר ויוצק שמן ובולל: טו] לא יצק לא: טז] מה"ד שפתתה: יז] ופתתן פתים מרובות: יח] דהא נאמרה יציקה בויקרא במנחת: יט] מקום שחזר שנה במנחה אינו אלא לעכב ל"א דכתיב והשאר נמחק: כ] יחידה. ופי' זה לא נהירא לרבינו ניסים דא"כ הוה ליה למימר כאחת ולא עד אחת והוא גרים עד לאחת פי' עד מאד וחבירו בזבחים בפרק השוחט והפסח בתוספתא אמר רבי פעם אחת היינו [ושבים] לפני ר' אלעזר והיה יושב לפניו אסי הבבלי והיה חביב לו עד לאחת. קצרתי: כא] לא יצק לא בלל. ג' מתנות שמן היו שם אחד מתן שמן קודם הסולת ואח"כ נותן שמן ובלל וזהו בלילה ואח"כ נתינת שמן שלישית ושמה יציקה ולא דקדק לשנות כסדר שהרי בלילה קודם יציקה וכן לא מלח:

מתניתין

ג א מיי' פי"ד מהלכות פסה"מ הלכה ח:

דְּלָא שְׁנָא כִּי מְחַשֵּׁב בִּלְשׁוֹן אֲכִילָה לְמִזְבֵּחַ וְל"ש כִּי מְחַשֵּׁב בִּלְשׁוֹן הַקְטָרָה לְמִזְבֵּחַ; א"נ, מָה אֲכִילָה בִּכְזַיִת אַף הַקְטָרָה בִּכְזַיִת; וּלְעוֹלָם אֲכִילָה דְּאוֹרְחָא מַשְׁמַע. וְר"א? א"כ, לִכְתּוֹב רַחֲמָנָא: "אִם הֵאָכֹל הֵאָכֵל", א"נ "אִם יֵאָכֵל יֵאָכֵל", מַאי "הֵאָכֹל יֵאָכֵל"? א] שָׁמְעַתְּ מִינָּהּ תַּרְתֵּי. אֲמַר לֵיהּ רַבִּי זֵירָא לְרַב אַסִי: וְאִי טַעְמָא דְּר"א מִשּׁוּם הָכִי הוּא, כָּרֵת נַמִּי לִיחַיַּיב! וְכִי תֵּימָא ה"נ, וְהָא אַתְּ הוּא דַּאֲמַרְתְּ מִשְּׁמֵיהּ דְּרַבִּי יוֹחָנָן: מוֹדֶה ר"א שֶׁאֵין עָנוּשׁ כָּרֵת! א"ל: תַּנָּאֵי הִיא אַלִּיבָּא דְּר"א, אִיכָּא לְמ"ד: פְּסוּלָה דְּאוֹרַיְיתָא, וְאִיכָּא לְמ"ד: פְּסוּלָה דְּרַבָּנַן. דְּתַנְיָא: *אהַשּׁוֹחֵט אֶת הַזֶּבַח לִשְׁתּוֹת מִדָּמוֹ לְמָחָר, לְהַקְטִיר מִבְּשָׂרוֹ לְמָחָר, לֶאֱכוֹל מֵאֵימוּרָיו לְמָחָר — כָּשֵׁר, וְר"א פּוֹסֵל. לְהַנִּיחַ מִדָּמוֹ לְמָחָר — רַבִּי יְהוּדָה פּוֹסֵל. אָמַר ר"א: אַף בָּזוֹ ר"א פּוֹסֵל וַחֲכָמִים מַכְשִׁירִין. רַבִּי יְהוּדָה אַלִּיבָּא דְּמַאן? אִילֵימָא אַלִּיבָּא דְּרַבָּנַן, הַשְׁתָּא וּמַה הָתָם דְּקָא מְחַשֵּׁב בִּלְשׁוֹן אֲכִילָה מַכְשְׁרִי רַבָּנַן, הָכָא לֹא כָּל שֶׁכֵּן? אֶלָּא אַלִּיבָּא דְּר"א; וְאָמַר ר' אֶלְעָזָר: אַף בָּזוֹ ר"א פּוֹסֵל וַחֲכָמִים מַכְשִׁירִין; ר' אֶלְעָזָר הַיְינוּ ר' יְהוּדָה! אֶלָּא לָאו כָּרֵת אִיכָּא בֵּינַיְיהוּ, ב] (א) דְּר' יְהוּדָה *(דְּת"ק) סָבַר: לְהַנִּיחַ — פְּסוּלָא בְּעָלְמָא, בְּהָנָךְ — כָּרֵת נַמִּי מִיחַיַּיב, וַאֲתָא ר' אֶלְעָזָר לְמֵימַר: אִידִי וְאִידִי פָּסוּל וְאֵין בּוֹ כָּרֵת! לָא, דְּכוּלֵּי עָלְמָא כָּרֵת לֵיכָּא, ג] וְהָכָא *ג' מַחֲלוֹקֶת בַּדָּבָר, ת"ק סָבַר: בְּהָנָךְ פְּלִיגִי, לְהַנִּיחַ — דִּבְרֵי הַכֹּל כָּשֵׁר; וְר'

מַחֲשֶׁבֶת אֲכִילַת אָדָם, כְּגוֹן שִׁירַיִם אִם חִישֵּׁב עֲלֵיהֶן לַמִּזְבֵּחַ לְהַקְטִירָן לְמָחָר. *מִדְּאַפְּקִינְהוּ רַחֲמָנָא לְתַרְוַויְהוּ בִּלְשׁוֹן אֲכִילָה. ש"מ כִּי הֲדָדֵי נִינְהוּ וּמְחַשְּׁבִין מִזּוֹ לְזוֹ. בִּלְשׁוֹן אֲכִילָה לַמִּזְבֵּחַ. כְּגוֹן: "הֲרֵינִי קוֹמֵץ עַל מְנָת לְהַאֲכִיל קוֹמֶץ לַמִּזְבֵּחַ לְמָחָר". א"נ. לְהָכִי אַפֵּיק רַחֲמָנָא לְהַקְטָרָה בִּלְשׁוֹן אֲכִילָה. מָה אֲכִילָה בִּכְזַיִת אַף מַחֲשֶׁבֶת הַקְטָרָה בִּכְזַיִת. אִם חִישֵּׁב בַּקְּמִיצָה לְהַקְטִיר כַּזַּיִת קוֹמֶץ לְמָחָר – פִּיגּוּל. לְעוֹלָם אֲכִילָה דְּאוֹרְחָא מַשְׁמַע. קוֹמֶץ לַמִּזְבֵּחַ, וְשִׁירַיִם לָאָדָם. מַאי הֵאָכֹל יֵאָכֵל. מִדְּשַׁנֵּי קְרָא בְּדִיבּוּרָא. שָׁמְעַתְּ מִינָּהּ תַּרְתֵּי. לְמַחֲשֶׁבֶת ד] הַקְטָרָה בִּכְזַיִת, וּמְחַשְּׁבִין מֵאֲכִילָה לַאֲכִילָה. אִיכָּא לְמ"ד. ר' אֱלִיעֶזֶר פָּסַל מִדְּאוֹרַיְיתָא, וּמֵהַאי קְרָא דְּפָרְשִׁינַן, וְאִית לֵיהּ כָּרֵת. לִשְׁתּוֹת מִדָּמוֹ לְמָחָר. אֲכִילַת מִזְבֵּחַ לָאָדָם. לְהַקְטִיר מִבְּשָׂרוֹ לְמָחָר. אֲכִילַת אָדָם לַמִּזְבֵּחַ. לְהַנִּיחַ מִדָּמוֹ. לֹא לְשׁוּם זְרִיקָה וְלֹא ה] לִשְׁתִיָּה. אַלִּיבָּא דְּמַאן. כְּלוֹמַר, בָּתַר טַעְמָא דְּמַאן אֲמָרָהּ לְמִילְּתֵיהּ, וּכְמַאן ס"ל בְּ"לִשְׁתּוֹת מִדָּמוֹ לְמָחָר"? ו] *(ת"ק) רַבִּי יְהוּדָה דְּאָמַר ז] פָּסוּל, סָבַר: הַאי הוּא דְּפָסוּל לְר' אֱלִיעֶזֶר, אֲבָל לִשְׁתּוֹת – אֲפִי' כָּרֵת אִיכָּא. וְר"א דְּאָמַר: אַף בָּזוֹ ח], כְּלוֹמַר שְׁתֵּיהֶן דִּין אֶחָד לָהֶם, מָה כָּאן לֵיכָּא כָּרֵת – אַף בִּלְשְׁתּוֹת אֵין בּוֹ כָּרֵת. *דְּכוּלֵּי עָלְמָא כָּרֵת לֵיכָּא. וְטַעְמָא דְּרַבִּי אֱלִיעֶזֶר לָאו מִדְּאוֹרַיְיתָא, אֲפִילּוּ לְרַבִּי יְהוּדָה. וְהָכָא ג' מַחֲלוֹקֶת בַּדָּבָר ת"ק סָבַר בְּהָנָךְ פְּלִיגִי. דְּרַבִּי אֱלִיעֶזֶר גָּזַר אַטּוּ מַחֲשָׁבָה כְּדַרְכּוֹ דְּהָוֵי פִּיגּוּל, הִילְכָּךְ גָּזַר בְּשֶׁלֹּא כְּדַרְכּוֹ ט] דְּהָוֵי פָּסוּל. אֲבָל לְהַנִּיחַ – דִּבְרֵי הַכֹּל כְּשֵׁרָה, דְּלֹא אָסְרָה תּוֹרָה אֶלָּא מַחֲשֶׁבֶת אֲכִילָה, וּשְׁתִיָּה דְּבִכְלַל אֲכִילָה הוּא. וּמִקְלַט דָּמוֹ אַטּוּ כָּל דָּמוֹ לָא גָּזְרִינַן. וְרַבִּי

דלא שנא כי מחשב בלשון אכילה כו'. תימה: ל"ל קרא להכי? תיפוק ליה מדאיקרי אכילת אש אכילה, כמו חישב שיאכלוהו כלבים למחר, שתאכלהו אש למחר, דמסקינן בסוף פרק ב' דזבחים (דף לא.) דהוי פיגול משום דכתיב: "ואת איזבל יאכלו הכלבים", וכתיב: "תאכלהו אש לא נופח". ומסיק התם דהא דתנן: לאכול כחצי זית ולהקטיר כחצי זית כשר שאין אכילה והקטרה מצטרפין, אי חישב בלשון אכילה – מצטרפין, משום דאיקרי אכילת אש אכילה כדכתיב: "תאכלהו אש לא נופח"! וי"ל: דאיצטריך לרבויי הכא שיאכלהו מזבח למחר אע"פ שלא הזכיר אש, דמקרא ד"תאכלהו אש" לא נפיק אא"כ הזכיר אש. ועוד נראה, דהתם איירי בבשר, דמחשב לאכול דבר שדרכו לאכול. והכא מיירי באימורים, ואי לא דרבי קרא הכא – ה"א דמחשב באימורים שתאכלם אש למחר הוי כמחשב לאכול דבר שדרכו להקטיר, דלא הוי פיגול. דאפי' השתא נמי דרבי קרא מחשב בלשון אכילה, אי חישב באימורים שתאכלם אש של הדיוט למחר – לא הוי פיגול, אע"ג *דבשר הוי פיגול, דמחשב לאכול דבר שדרכו להקטיר. דדוקא אש של מזבח י] דמרבינן בלשון אכילה, דהוי מחשב בלשון מזבח למזבח. והא דקאמר התם דמצטרפין בלשון אכילה, אי לאו דרבי הכא מחשב בלשון אכילה – לא הוי פיגול באימורים, אע"ג דאיקרי אכילה. וקצת קשיא, מאי קא פריך התם: אלא מעתה חישב שתאכלהו אש כו'? וכי תימא ה"נ, והא תנן: לאכול כחצי זית ולהקטיר כחצי זית כשר שאין אכילה והקטרה מצטרפין! מאי קושיא? דלמא חצי זית בשר וחצי זית אימורים לא מצטרפין, שזה לאדם וזה למזבח, אבל חצי זית בשר לאדם וחצי זית בשר למזבח מצטרפין, משום דכתיב אכילה גבי אש! ויותר קשה הא דמשני: אי דאפקיה בלשון אכילה ה"נ, דמשמע דמצטרפין. ואמאי מצטרפין? כיון דאין מחשבין מאכילת אדם למזבח וממזבח לאכילת אדם! וצ"ל שכך היא סברא דמצטרפין, כיון דאיקרי אכילה, ואיתרבי הכא בלשון אכילה באימורים. וקצת תימה, דהתם *דאייתי ראיה דכתיב אכילה באש מדכתיב: "תאכלהו אש לא נופח", דה"ל לאיתויי קרא דכתיב: (ויקרא ו) "אשר תאכל האש את העולה", וכתיב (שם ט): "ותאכל (האש) את העולה ואת החלבים"! ושמא ניחא ליה לאיתויי קרא דאש של הדיוט. ומיהו גבי אש דהדיוט נמי כתיב (שמות כב): "ונאכל גדיש", *וכי מייתי התם קרא: "ואת איזבל יאכלו הכלבים" הוה מצי לאיתויי: "ולבהמתך ולחיה אשר בארצך תהיה כל תבואתה לאכול" (ויקרא כה) ושמא משום דלא כתיב התם אכילה על בשר.

לכתוב קרא האכל האכל או יאכל יאכל. כי האי גוונא בפרק "החובל" (ב"ק דף פה:) גבי "ורפא ירפא". אבל בסנהדרין בריש "היו בודקין" (דף מ:) משמע דאי הוה כתיב "דרש תדרש *וחקרת" לא הוה מצי למדרש טפי מידי, ולא אמרינן: מדלא כתיב "דרש דרש" או "תדרש תדרש"*. מאי האכל יאכל ש"מ תרתי. משמע דלית ליה לר"א דברה תורה כלשון בני אדם. ותימה: דבריש "הערל" (יבמות דף עא.) גבי "איש איש" יא] (לא דרש וס"ל דדברה כו') וכן רבי יוסי, פרק "אין מעמידין" (ע"ז דף כז.) דריש "המול ימול", ובסוטה פרק "ארוסה ושומרת יבם" (דף כו.) דריש "איש איש" לרבות אשת חרש ואשת שוטה, ובזבחים פרק "השוחט המעלה" (ד' קח:) לא דריש "איש איש", אלמא קסבר דברה תורה כלשון בני אדם! ועוד, בעלמא לא אשכחן תנא דפליג אהא דדרשינן (חולין יג.): "איש איש" לרבות את הגוים שנודרין נדרים ונדבות כישראל! ועוד קשה: דב"השוחט והמעלה" (שם) דריש ר"ש "איש איש", ובפ"ק דקידושין (דף כ:) דריש ר"ש "אם גאול יגאל" שלוה וגואל לחצאין, וכן בפסחים בפרק "מי שהיה טמא" (ד' צג.): "איש איש" לחייב זבין ומצורעין ובועלי נדות בפסח שני, ומוקי לה כרבי יהודה ור"ש דפטרי נשים מפסח שני, ולהכי לא תני זבות ומצורעות. ובפרק "אלו מציאות" (ב"מ ד' לא:) ובכתובות (ד' סז.) גבי "העבט תעביטנו" קאמר ר"ש דברה תורה כלשון בני אדם! ועוד קשיא מר' יהודה, דדריש "איש איש" בההיא דפסחים, וכן בריש "בנות כותים" (נדה ד' לב:) דריש ר' יהודה "איש איש" גבי תינוק בן יומו שמטמא בזיבה, וגבי "המול ימול" (ע"ז כז.) סבר רבי יהודה דברה תורה כלשון בני אדם! ועוד, בסוף "אלו מציאות" משמע דדריש ר"ש "הקם תקים" ו"השב תשיבנו", ובפ"ק דר"ה (דף ח.) "עשר תעשר" – בשתי מעשרות! ועוד קשיא מר"ע בפ' "אין עומדין" (ברכות ד' לא:) גבי הני דדריש ר' ישמעאל "אם ראה תראה", ור"ע קאמר דברה תורה כלשון בני אדם. ובסנהדרין בפרק "ד' מיתות" (דף סד:) *איפכא גבי "הכרת תכרת", וכן בסוף פרק שני דכריתות (ד' יא.) גבי "והפדה לא נפדתה"! ועוד קשיא מדאחרים דהיינו ר"מ (גבי איש איש) דאית ליה התם בכריתות דברה תורה כלשון בני אדם, ובפ' "ד' מיתות" (סנהדרין ד' נז.) משמע דדריש ר"מ "איש איש" גבי ברכת השם! ונראה לפרש, דמאן דאית ליה דברה תורה כלשון בני אדם – לאו בכל דוכתי אית ליה, אלא *שום הוכחה יש לו במקום שאינו דורש הכפילות. מדאמר אביי בסוף "אלו הן הגולין" (מכות ד' יב.) גבי "ואם יצא יצא": מסתברא כמ"ד דברה תורה כלשון בני אדם, שלא יהא סופו חמור מתחילתו, משמע דלא בא אביי להביא ראיה אלא שם, ולא שנאמר כן בכל המקומות, דהא לא מייתי דאביי גבי שאר פלוגתייהו. ואם תאמר: א"כ, מאי קא פריך בפרק "השואל" (ב"מ ד' לד:) גבי "אם גנוב יגנב מעמו": הניחא למאן דלית ליה דברה תורה, וכן בריש נדרים (דף ג.): הניחא למ"ד דברה תורה? והא לאו בכל דוכתי פליגי! ועוד, למ"ד דברה תורה נמי מי ניחא? מה טעם יש שם שלא לדרוש "לנדור נדר" לרבות ידות נדרים, כמו גבי נזירות דכתיב "נזיר להזיר"!* אמר ליה תנאי היא. משמע לרבי יוחנן, הא דפסיל ר"א במתני' – היינו מדאורייתא, ואפי' כרת איכא, מדפריש טעמיה דקרא. תימה, דלא הל"ל: ר"א פוסל, אלא "מפגל" מיבעי ליה, דהכי דייק בסוף פ"ק דזבחים (ד' יג.)! וי"ל: דשאני הכא דאיירי נמי בחוץ למקומו. דת"ק סבר להניח פסולא בעלמא בהנך כרת נמי מיחייב. האי ת"ק היינו ר"י, וקרי ליה ת"ק משום דכולה רישא ר"י, דליכא אלא ב' מחלוקת, מדקאמרינן בתר הכי: ג' מחלוקות בדבר, מכלל דעד השתא סבירא לן דליכא אלא ב' מחלוקות.

גזירה

שיטה מקובצת

א] שמעת מינה תרתי. ואין לומר דחד אתא לאשמועינן כי מחשב בלשון אכילה וחד לאכילה כזית דחדא מילתא היא דכיון דלשון אכילה מהני להקטרה מסברא יש לנו לומר שהאכילה הוא כזית. תו"ח: ב] תיבות דרבי יהודה נמחק וכצ"ל בינייהו דת"ק: ג] והכא ג' מחלוקת בדבר וא"ת מי דחקו לומר ג' מחלוקת בדבר לימא ר' יהודה היינו ת"ק ור"י סבר בהנך פליגי ולהניח דברי הכל פסול ואתא ר' אלעזר לומר דאף בלהניח פליגי ואמר הר"מ ז"ל דכיון דנחית לאשכוחי תנא דסבר דברי הכל כשר כתנא דיוסף הבבלי כדלקמן דקאמר ליה כשר בשחרית ובצהרים אבל מעיקרא היה סבור דלא פליגי כלל בלהניח דכ"ע סברי דלהניח פסול. תו"ח. ובתוס' מהר"פ. וא"ת מי דחקו לומר ג' מחלוקת הוי מצי למימר דר"י מפרש מילתיה דת"ק כמו דקאמר מעיקרא וי"ל דניחא ליה למימר דאיכא מאן דאכשיר בלהניח דמו משום. דאשכחן לקמן תנא דמכשר בלהניח ומשום הכי ניחא ליה למצוא אותו תנא במתניתין אבל מעיקרא לא נחית להכי דלא נחית אלא למצוא תנא דאית ליה לר"א כרת בדבר שאין דרכו לאכול ואין דרכו להקטיר וא"ת ומאי שנא לר"י דלא גזרינן נמי לשתות מדמו אטו כל דמו כדגזרינן להניח מדמו אטו כל דמו וי"ל דלא דמי דלשתות מדמו משמע דלאחר זריקה ישתה מן הנשאר ובהא לא שייך גזירה אטו כל דמו אבל להניח מדמו משמע דאמר הכי קודם זריקה ומשום הכי שייך למגזר אטו כל דמו וא"ת להניח מאימוריו למחר אמאי לא אמרינן נמי דלפסול אטו כל אימוריו שהרי בפרק כל הפסולין (דף לה:) אמרינן דאם אמר להניח כל אימוריו למחר שהוא פסול וא"כ לגזור מאימוריו אטו כל אימוריו ועוד תימה התם למה פסול והרי הוא עצמו שלא הוקטרו אימוריו כשר שאין הקטרת אימורין מעכבת כלום גם לא לאכול את הבשר וי"ל דהא דפסיל התם בלהניח כל אימוריו (משום) היינו משום גזירה אטו כל דמי והשתא נמי ניחא דלא גזרינן הכא מאימוריו אטו כל אימוריו משום דהוי גזירה לגזירה ועוד י"ל ליישב הקושיא דהתם דהיכא קאמר דלהניח כל אימוריו פסול והלא הוא עצמו שלא הוקטרו אימוריו כשר לאו קושיא היא דהני מילי כי ליתנהו כגון שאבדו או נטמאו דהוי כמאן דליתנהו אבל כל זמן דאיתנהו אסור לאכול מן הבשר עד לאחר הקטרת האימורים ומשום הכי קאמר דלהניח כל אימוריו פסול ומיהו קושיא דהכא לא יתיישב אמאי לא גזרינן מאימוריו אטו כל אימוריו כמו בדם: ד] למחשבת דהקטרה: ה] זריקה ולא לשום שתיה: ו] למחר ת"ק: ז] דאמר לעיל פסול: ח] בזו פסול כלומר: ט] כדרכו להוי: י] הוא דמרבינן: יא] איש איש אית ליה ותיבות לא דרש וס"ל דדברה כו' ליתא שם:

דבכשר הוי פיגול כדאמרי' התם דמצטרפין בלשון אכילה מ"מ באימורין לא הוי פיגול דמחשב לאכול כו' מרבינן בלשון כו' בלשון אכילה למזבח ואי לאו דרבי נ"ק

שייך לעיל

הגהות הב"ח

(א) גמ' כרת איכא בינייהו דת"ק סבר כצ"ל ותיבות דר' יהודה נמחק:

תוספתא דזבחים פ"ב

רש"ק גורס איכא בינייהו

לא דכ"ע כרת לא טעמא כו' נ"ק

לגירסת רש"י דר"י לגי' תוספות דת"ק רש"ק

[עירובין עה. וש"נ]

דמייתי נ"ק

ועוד דכי מייתי נ"ק

או תקור תתקור לא נ"ק

[וע"ע תוס' פסחים מח: ד"ה א"כ ותוס' ב"ק סה. ד"ה לכתוב ותוס' כתובות לט. ד"ה אין]

גליון הש"ס

תום' ד"ה לכתוב וכו' ורפא ירפא. וכן בפסחים דף ח ע"א עיין בב"ק דף סה ע"א תענית ד' ג ע"א:

דריש איפכא נ"ק

דמשום הוכחה נ"ק

[וע"ע מה שהאריכו תוס' בסוטה כד. ד"ה ור"י כו' ויש על זה והא דכתבו תוס' הכא וא"ת בלתי שום תירוץ עמ"ש בס"ד על הגליון תוס' ב"מ סא. ד"ה אלא לאו כו']

חריפי דפומבדיתא: הקטרה מפגלת הקטרה. ואפילו לרבנן דאמרי: אין מפגלין בחצי מתיר – ה"מ היכא דחישב א] ביה בשירים, ולבונה במילתא קיימא, אבל הכא דחישב לה בלבונה – כמה דחישב ביה בכוליה מתיר דמי. אמר רבא: ב] אף אנן נמי תנינא, *זה הכלל: כל הקומץ ונותן בכלי, והמוליך והמקטיר, לאכול דבר שדרכו לאכול ולהקטיר דבר שדרכו להקטיר, חוץ למקומו – פסול ואין בו כרת, חוץ לזמנו – פגול וחייבין עליו כרת; מאי לאו הקטרה דומיא דהנך? מה הנך – בין לאכול בין להקטיר, ג] אף הקטרה – בין לאכול בין להקטיר? לא, הנך – בין לאכול בין להקטיר; הקטרה, לאכול – אין, להקטיר – לא. יתיב רב מנשיא בר גדא קמיה דאביי, ויתיב וקא אמר משמיה דרב חסדא: [א]אין הקטרה מפגלת הקטרה. ואפילו *לר"מ דאמר: מפגלין בחצי מתיר – ה"מ היכא דחישב בהו בשירים, דקומץ מתיר דידהו, אבל הכא דקומץ לאו מתיר דלבונה הוא – לא מצי מפגל ביה. א"ל אביי: *עני מרי, משמיה דרב? א"ל: אין. איתמר נמי, אמר רב חסדא אמר רב: אין הקטרה מפגלת הקטרה. אמר רב יעקב בר ד] אידי משמיה דאביי, אף אנן נמי תנינא: שחט אחד מן הכבשים לאכול ממנו למחר – הוא פיגול וחבירו כשר, לאכול מחבירו למחר – שניהם כשרין; מ"ט? לאו משום דכיון דלאו מתיר דידיה הוא, לא מצי מפגל ביה? לא, התם הוא דלא איקבע בחד מנא, ה] אבל הכא דאיקבע בחד מנא – כי חד דמו. אמר רב המנונא: *הא מילתא אבלע לי רבי חנינא, ותקילא לי ו] ככוליה תלמודאי: הקטיר [ב]קומץ להקטיר לבונה, ז] (ולבונה) לאכול שירים למחר – פגול. מאי קמ"ל? אי הקטרה מפגלת הקטרה קמ"ל – לימא: הקטיר קומץ להקטיר לבונה! אי מפגלין בחצי מתיר קמ"ל – לימא: הקטיר קומץ לאכול שירים למחר! אי תרווייהו ח] (אתא) קמ"ל – לימא: הקטיר קומץ להקטיר לבונה ולאכול שירים למחר! אמר רב אדא בר אהבה: לעולם קסבר אין הקטרה מפגלת הקטרה, ואין מפגלין בחצי מתיר, ושאני הכא, ט] [ג]דפשטא ליה מחשבה בכולה מנחה. תני תנא קמיה דרב יצחק בר אבא: הקטיר קומץ לאכול שירים – לדברי הכל פגול. והא מיפלג פליגי! אלא אימא: [ד]לדברי הכל פסול. ולימא: ה"ז פגול, ור"מ היא! תנא "דברי הכל" אתניוה, "פיגול" ב"פסול" מיחלף ליה, "הרי זה" ב"דברי הכל" לא מיחלף ליה.§

הדרן עלך הקומץ את המנחה

*הקומץ [ה]את המנחה, לאכול דבר שאין דרכו לאכול ולהקטיר דבר שאין דרכו להקטיר – כשר, ר"א פוסל. לאכול [ו]דבר שדרכו לאכול ולהקטיר דבר שדרכו להקטיר פחות מכזית – כשר. י] *לאכול [ז]כחצי זית ולהקטיר כחצי זית – כשר, שאין אכילה והקטרה מצטרפין.§ גמ' א"ר אסי א"ר יוחנן: מ"ט דר"א? אמר קרא: °"ואם האכל יאכל מבשר זבח שלמיו" – *בשתי אכילות הכתוב מדבר, אחד אכילת אדם ואחד אכילת מזבח, לומר לך: כשם שמחשבין באכילת אדם – כך מחשבין באכילת מזבח, וכשם שמחשבין מאכילת אדם לאכילת אדם ומאכילת מזבח לאכילת מזבח – כך מחשבין מאכילת אדם יא] למזבח ומאכילת מזבח לאדם; מ"ט? מדאפקינהו רחמנא יב] להקטרה בלשון אכילה. ורבנן? האי דאפקינהו רחמנא בלשון אכילה – דלא

תורה אור: ויקרא ז

רש"י

חריפי דפומבדיתא. מפרש בפ"ק דסנהדרין (דף יז:): עיפה ואבימי בני רחבה דפומבדיתא. הקטרה מפגלת הקטרה. הקטיר קומץ ע"מ להקטיר לבונה יג] *לאחר זמן – פיגול, ואע"ג דאין מתיר מפגל את המתיר. ולא דמי לשוחט את הכבש לאכול מחבירו למחר, כדמפרש לקמן, דהתם לא איקבעו בחד מנא, הכא איקבעו בחד מנא. מאי לאו הקטרה דומיא. דקומץ ונותן בכלי. מה הנך. בין חישב לאכול שירים למחר, בין חישב להקטיר לבונה, פיגל יד]. קומץ לאו מתיר דלבונה הוא. טו] דאמרן לעיל (דף יג:) דאינה בעיכוב מנחה. א"ל אביי. לרב מנשיא. עני מרי. עניני אדוני. משמיה דרב. כלומר, אמרה רב חסדא להא מילתא משמיה דרב. מ"ט. שניהם כשרין. כחד דמו. *מפגל להקטרה דלבונה טז] דמי. וה"מ לר"מ ולרבנן, אבל לר' יוסי יז] דבריש פירקין – אין מתיר מפגל את המתיר, ולא מפגלא הקטרת קומץ להקטרת לבונה. אבלע לי. הטעימני ולמדני. ותקילא לי. ושקולה לי, כלומר חביבה עלי. ה"ג: הקטיר קומץ להקטיר לבונה לאכול שירים. ולא גרסי' "ולאכול". יח] וזה פירושו: הקטיר קומץ על מנת להקטיר לבונה למחר וע"מ לאכול שירים למחר. מאי קמ"ל. קא ס"ד דמשום חדא מהנך מחשבות מפגלא, יט] וחד מינייהו אשמעינן. ופיגול משום מחשבת להקטיר לבונה למחר הוא, ולא משום לאכול שירים, דאין מפגלין בחצי מתיר. לימא הקטיר קומץ להקטיר לבונ'. ולא לימא "לאכול שירים". כיון דההיא מחשבה לא מהניא, למה לי *מחשבה (א) בהדי קמייתא? ואי פיגול משום לאכול שירים הוא, דמפגלין בחצי מתיר, אבל להקטיר לבונה לא מהניא, למה לי *לגרפה כ] בחדא? ואי תרוייהו קמ"ל. כא] *ואי לאכול קאמר, שלא חישב אלא באחת מהן. לימא להקטיר לבונה ולאכול שירים. דמשמע תרתי מילי: הקטיר קומץ להקטיר לבונה או לאכול שירים למחר! כב] דפשטא לה מחשבה בכולה מנחה. ואע"ג דלא מפגל בחדא מינייהו, השתא דחשיב בתרוייהו מפגלא. הא מיפלג פליגי. דלרבנן אין מפגלין בחצי מתיר. ולימא. ליה רב יצחק לתנא דלא לשנייה, ולוקמא כדקתני "פיגול". ור"מ היא. ואמאי שני מילתיה ותירץ ליה "פסול"? תנא דברי הכל אתניוה. הלכך איכא למימר ד"פסול" אתנייה, והא דתנא "פיגול" – משום דאיחלף ליה "פיגול" ב"פסול". ה"ז בדברי הכל לא מיחלף ליה. הלכך אי הוה אתנייה "ה"ז" ולא הוה אמר "דברי הכל".

הדרן עלך הקומץ זוטא

הקומץ רבה. לאכול דבר שאין דרכו לאכול כג] וכו' דבר שדרכו לאכול פחות מכזית כשר. הא משנה יתירה, דהא תנן בפ"ק (לעיל יג.): לאכול כחצי זית ולהקטיר חצי זית כשר. אלא לר"א איצטריך, דאע"ג דפסל ר' אליעזר במחשבה שלא כדרכו, דגזר אטו כדרכו ופסל מדרבנן, הכא לא גזר פחות מכזית אטו כזית. גמ' כשם שמחשבין מאכילת אדם לאדם ומאכילת מזבח למזבח. כשם שפוסלת מחשבה בדבר אכילת אדם, כד] כגון שירים אם חישב עליהן לאדם למחר. מאכילת מזבח. כגון קומץ, אם חישב עליו לאדם למחר *)למזבח פוסלת, כך פוסלת

מחשבת

*) למזבח הס"ד אח"כ ד"ה כך פוסלת מחשבת והד"א נ"ק

תוספות

הקומץ את המנחה כו'. משום דבעי למתני' "ר"א פוסל" איצטריך, דלגופיה לא איצטריך דממתני' דפ"ק (לעיל יב.) שמעינן, דקתני: לאכול דבר שדרכו לאכול ולהקטיר דבר שדרכו להקטיר – חוץ למקומו פסול, חוץ לזמנו פיגול, הא לאכול דבר שאין דרכו לאכול ולהקטיר דבר שאין דרכו להקטיר – כשר. דליכא למימר: מדיוקא לא שמעינן כשר, אלא דלא הוי פיגול, אבל פסול הוי. דבסוף פ"ק (יג:) משמע דאפילו כשר שמעינן מינה, גבי האי דדייק: טעמא דלאכול ולהקטיר כו', ועל כרחך מדיוקא דחוץ למקומו שמעינן דכשר.

שאין אכילה והקטרה מצטרפין. בסוף פ"ק (יג שם:) מוקי לה ר' ירמיה כר"א, ואביי מוקי לה כרבנן.

מדאפקינהו רחמנא בלשון אכילה. תימה: תינח *דאכילת מזבח לאדם, אבל כה] (אכילת) אדם לאכילת מזבח מנלן? דדומיא דהכי אמר ב"הקומץ זוטא" (לעיל דף טו.): לחם איקרי תודה לא איקרי לחם! ויש לומר כו] דבפשטי' דקרא קיימי ב' האכילות אבשר זבח תודת שלמיו. וקלא קשה, דמזה לא משנו רבנן מידי.

דלא

עין משפט נר מצוה

כז א ב ג ד מיי' פט"ז מהל' פסה"מ הל"א:
א ה מיי' פ"ד שם הלכה ח:
ב ו ז מיי' שם הלכה ז:

מסורת הש"ס

למחר פיגול נ"ק
לעיל יב.
למפגל להקטרה דלבונה ה"מ כו' דאין כו' המתיר לא מפגלא נ"ק
[פסחים סג. וש"נ]
[לקמן פא. סנהדרין כו: ב"ק מט:]
לגרפה ההיא מחשבה נ"ק
לגרפה בהדי הס"ד נ"ק
נ"ל ואו
[לעיל יב:]
זבחים כט: לה. סה. לעיל יב:
[זבחים יג: כח: חולין פא:]
ברכות כד:
נ"ק מ"ז
מאכילת מזבח לאדם אבל מאכילת אדם כו' נ"ק

הגהות הב"ח

(א) רש"י ד"ה לימא וכו' מחשבה זו בהדי:

שיטה מקובצת

א] דחישב בהו: ב] אף אנן נמי תנינא. לא הוי ממש כמו ההיא דלעיל דע"כ הקטרה לאכול לא מתוקם אלא כר"מ דאמר מפגלין בחצי מתיר ולא מייתי תנינא אלא לאפוקי מהני דלקמיה דאמרי דאפי' לר"מ אין הקטרה מפגלת הקטרה. תו"ח: ג] אף הקטרה בין לאכול בין להקטיר. ע"כ לא אתיא כר' יוסי דלר' יוסי אין מתיר מפגל את המתיר. תו"ח: ד] יעקב בר אבא: ה] אבל הכא דאיקבע בחד מנא כו' משמע דלרבנן דאמרי אין הקטרה מפגלת הקטרה לא סבירא להו האי טעמא ותימה דלעיל קאמר רבנן דפליגי הכי [illegible]

לדברי יוסי בריש פרקין [דף יג ע"ב] [illegible] תו"ח: ו] ותקילא לי בכולי: ז] תיבת ולבונה נמחק: ח] תיבת אתא נמחק: ט] דפשטה אות א' נמחק: י] לאכול כחצי זית ולהקטיר כחצי זית. [illegible] תו"ח: יא] מאכילת אדם לאדם ומאכילת מזבח למזבח: יב] להקטרה בלשון אכילה: יג] לאחר זמן [illegible]: יד] [illegible]: טו] [illegible]: טז] [illegible]: יז] [illegible]: יח] [illegible]: יט] [illegible]: כ] [illegible]: כא] [illegible]: כב] [illegible]: כג] [illegible]: כד] [illegible]: כה] [illegible]: כו] [illegible]

שמעת

א) נראה דנ"ל שבעת הקמיצה חישב להקטיר הלבונה למחר ועדיין הוי בכלי אחד קודם קמילה.

נ"א בקבלה ושחיט' כו' דכי חשיב בשחיטה או בקבלה איפסל כו' נ"ק

כו א מיי' פי"ז מהל' פסה"מ הלכה ט:

הגהות הב"ח

(א) גמ' הקטיר שומשום לאכול למחר עד וכו' כולו מהו רב חסדא: (ב) רש"י ד"ה אף הרצאת פסול: (ג) ד"ה בד' פרים וכו' קרבו כל מתירין: (ד) ד"ה חשובה וכו' לעכב הס"ד ואח"כ מ"ה שאינה מתרת שחיטתה אינה: (ה) ד"ה ה"ג בא לו:

כמו מתחלת עבודה לגמר עבודה דמהני גזירת נ"ק

זבחים מג. והא "בין" "בין" קתני! קשיא.§ אמר מר, *ר"מ אומר: פגול וחייבין עליו כרת. מכדי כרת לא מיחייב עד שיקרבו כל המתירין, *דאמר מר: "ירצה" — כהרצאת כשר כך הרצאת פסול, מה הרצאת כשר עד שיקרבו כל המתירין — אף הרצאת פסול עד שיקרבו כל המתירין; והאי כיון דחשיב בה בפנים — פסליה, כי מדי בהיכל — א] מיא בעלמא הוא דקא מדי! אמר רבה: משכחת לה ב] בארבעה פרים וארבעה שעירים. רבא אמר: אפילו תימא פר אחד ושעיר אחד, לפגולי מרצי. "ארבעים ושלש". והתניא: ארבעים ושבע! לא קשיא: הא כמ"ד *מערבין לקרנות, והא כמ"ד אין מערבין. והתניא: ארבעים ושמונה! לא קשיא: הא כמ"ד *שירים מעכבין, הא כמ"ד ג] שירים לא מעכבין.§ איבעיא להו: פיגל בהולכה, מהו? אמר ר' יוחנן: הולכה כקמיצה, וריש לקיש אמר: הולכה כהקטרה. בשלמא לריש לקיש — איכא נמי הולכה דלבונה, אלא לרבי יוחנן מ"ט? אמר רבא, קסבר רבי יוחנן: ד] כל עבודה שאינה מתרת, עבודה חשובה היא לפגל עליה בפני עצמה. א"ל אביי: הרי שחיטת אחד מן הכבשים, דעבודה שאינה ה] מתירתה, ופליגי! דתנן: שחט אחד מן הכבשים לאכול שתי חלות למחר, הקטיר אחד מן הבזיכין לאכול שני סדרים למחר — ר"מ אומר: פגול וחייבין עליו כרת, וחכ"א: אין בו כרת עד שיפגל בכל המתיר! א"ל: מי סברת לחם בתנור קדוש? שחיטת כבשים מקדשא ליה, והבא לקדש — כבא להתיר דמי. מתיב רב שימי בר אשי, *אחרים אומרים: הקדים מולים לערלים — כשר, הקדים ערלים למולים — פסול; וקיי"ל דבחצי *מתיר פליגי! א"ל: מי סברת דם בצואר בהמה קדוש? דם — סכין מקדשא ליה, והבא לקדש — כבא להתיר דמי. תא שמע: בד"א — בקמיצה ובמתן כלי ובהילוך; מאי לאו הילוך דהקטרה? לא, הילוך דמתן כלי. אי הכי, במתן כלי ובהילוך — בהילוך ובמתן כלי מיבעי ליה! הא לא קשיא, תני הכי. בא לו להקטרה — בא לו להולכה מיבעי ליה! הא לא קשיא, כיון דהולכה צורך דהקטרה היא, קרי לה הקטרה. אלא, נתן ו] את הקומץ בשתיקה — הוליך מיבעי ליה! קשיא.§ הקטיר שומשום (א) לאכול שומשום, עד שכלה קומץ כולו — רב חסדא ורב המנונא ורב ששת, חד אמר: פיגול, וחד אמר: אפסול, וחד אמר: כשר. לימא, ז] מ"ד פיגול — כר"מ, ומ"ד פסול — כרבנן, ומ"ד כשר — *כרבי? ממאי? דלמא עד כאן לא קאמר ר' מאיר התם אלא ח] דחישב בשיעורו, אבל הכא דלא חישב בשיעורו — לא! ועד כאן לא קא אמרי רבנן התם אלא דלא חישב ביה בכוליה מתיר, אבל הכא דחישב ביה בכוליה מתיר — ה"נ דפגיל! ועד כאן לא קא אמר רבי התם אלא דלא הדר מלייה מאותה עבודה, אבל הכא דהדר מלייה מאותה עבודה — הכי נמי דפסיל! אלא מ"ד פיגול — דברי הכל, מאן דאמר פסול — דברי הכל, מאן דאמר כשר — דברי הכל; מאן דאמר פיגול דברי הכל — קסבר: דרך אכילה בכך ודרך הקטרה בכך; ומ"ד פסול דברי הכל — קסבר: (אין) דרך אכילה בכך [רש"ק מ"ז] ואין דרך הקטרה בכך, והואי לה כמנחה שלא הוקטרה; ומאן דאמר כשר דברי הכל — קסבר: דרך הקטרה בכך ואין דרך אכילה בכך.§ אמרי
חריפי

כי מדי בהיכל מיא בעלמא קא מדי. הקשה בקונטרס: *בקומץ ושוחט נמי נימא דלא מיפגל, דכי חשיב בקבלה איפסיל, וכי זרק — מיא זריק! כח] ותירץ בפ' "בית שמאי" (זבחים דף מג: ושם) דהתם גזירת הכתוב הוא. אבל כאן תירץ דהתם אותה עבודה שפיגל בה נעשית כולה בקדושה, אבל הנך הזאות כולהו חדא עבודה, ולא קרבו כל מתירי אותה עבודה בקדושתה. וקשה: דאם כן, פיגל בקומץ ולא בלבונה, לר"מ אמאי הוי פיגול בחצי מתיר? הא חד עבודה לא נעשית בקדושתה, וכי מקטיר ללבונה — עפרא בעלמא מקטרי! וכי תימא משום דהוו ב' מינין, אכתי קשה משני בזיכין! אם לא נחלק, דכיון דבעו שני כלים הוו כשני מינין. ור"ת מפרש דבחד מקום פשיטא ליה דלא אמרי' מיא בעלמא הוא דקא מדי, *תחילת עבודה כגמר עבודה, והכא גזירת הכתוב. אבל בשני מקומות — בהכי לא איירי קרא, ומיא בעלמא קא מדי.

משכחת לה בד' פרים. פי' בקונטרס: פר ושעיר פנים וחישב עליו, ונשפך הדם לאחר הזאות פנים.

הדרן עלך הקומץ זוטא

והא בין בין קתני. דמשמע באחת ולא בשתים. ירצה. "פיגול הוא לא ירצה" (ויקרא יט), וכתיב בכשר: "ירצה לקרבן אשה" (שם כב). אף (ב) פסול עד שיקרבו כל מתירין ט]. לא מחייבין כרת על אכילת פסול עד שיקרבו כל מתירין *באותה עבודה שהוא מתפגל בה. והאי כיון דחשיב כו'. ואי קשיא: *בקומץ ושוחט נמי לימא דלא מפגל, דכי חשיב י] (*בקבלה) איפסול, כי זריק — מיא בעלמא זריק! לאו פירכא היא, דהתם אותה עבודה שפיגל בה נעשית כולה בקדושתה, אבל הנך הזאות יא] חדא עבודה היא. משכחת לה. דמפגלי כולהו. בד' פרים וד' שעירים. פר ושעיר פנים וחישב עליו, ונשפך הדם לאחר הזאות פנים, והביא פר ושעיר א' להיכל יב] וא' למזבח לשבע הזאותיו, וכן לקרנות. דבכל א' קרבו (ג) מתירין, דהא כולם כשרים, וא"צ לחזור ולהזות מן השני בפנים, יג] ובמקום שפוסק הוא מתחיל, כדאמרינן במסכת יומא בפרק "הוציאו לו" (דף סא.). לפיגול מרצה. לענין כן הן חשובות, שלא יצא מידי פיגול. מערבין לקרנות. פלוגתא היא בפרק "הוציאו לו" (שם דף נז:). הא דקתני מ"ג כמ"ד מערבין. דם פר ושעיר בשעת יד] ארבע מתנות דקרנות דמזבח הפנימי. והא דקתני מ"ז כמ"ד טו]. מכל אחד נותן ד' מתנות, ואייתר להו ד'. שירים. של כל ההזאות מעכבי, אם לא שפכן על יסוד מזבח החיצון, והוו להו מ"ח. והא דקתני מ"ז כמ"ד שירים לא מעכבי. ופלוגתא היא בפרק "הוציאו לו" (שם דף ס:). פיגל *בהולכת קומץ מאי. מי הויא חלי עבודה, ופליגי רבנן עד שיפגל בכל המתיר, כלומר אף בהולכת לבונה, או לא פליגי? כקמיצה. דהויא עבודה שלימה, דאין קמילה בלבונה. כהקטרה טז]. ופליגי. כל עבודה שאינה מתרת. כגון הולכה, דלא מיעכבא, דאפשר להושיט יז] זה לזה. חשובה לפגל עליה בפני עצמה. דליכא למימר עד שיפגל בכל המתיר, דהא לאו מתיר הוא, ואין כח לאחרת לעכב (ד). שחיטתה אינה מתרת לא בשר ולא אימורין, דזריקה מתירתן. כבא להתיר דמי. ובעינן עד שיפגל בכל המתיר. הקדים מולים לערלים. בשחיטת פסח מיירי, דשחט סימן ראשון למולים סימן שני לערלים. וקיימא לן. בפ' "תמיד נשחט" במס' פסחים (דף סג.). יח] אלמא בעבודה שאינה מתרת ולא מקדשת, כגון הכא דליכא לחם יט] דמתקדיש ליה שחיטה, פליגי נמי רבנן! בד"א. דמפגלין בעבודת הקומץ. והיינו ההיא ברייתא דמותיב רב אחא בר רב הונא לעיל. מאי לאו בהילוך דהקטרה. וקתני דלא פליגי רבנן, ותיובתא דריש לקיש! הילוך דמתן כלי. כשמוליכו לתתו בכלי, דההיא עבודה שלימה היא, דאין מתן כלי בעבודת לבונה. תני הכי. בהילוך ובמתן כלי (ה). בא לו להולכה מיבעי ליה כ]. הקטיר כדי שומשום. כא] כשיעור שומשום, וכן עשה עד שהקטיר כל הקומץ וכן בלבונה, [מהו], פיגל או לא? כרבי מאיר. דאמר: מפגלים בחצי מתיר, והכא נמי כל שומשום ושומשום כב] חשיב ליה כחצי מתיר. כרבנן. דאמרי: אין בו כרת, אבל פסול הוא. כרבי. דאמר לעיל (דף יד.): אומר אני שזה כשר, דאין חצאין מצטרפין. דחישב בשיעורו. שחישב כשיעור הקטרה שלימה כאחד. הכא כג] חישב בכל המתיר. בקומץ ובלבונה, חשיב כה"ג כל המתיר. דלא הדר מלייה. לשיעור אכילה מאותה עבודה, שחישב בכבש האחד ובחלה האחרת כד] השלמה זית, ולא חישב לא באותו כבש ולא באותה חלה. מאן דאמר פיגול קסבר דרך כה] הקטרה בכך. והוה ליה מחשב בעבודה כשרה, והוי כמקטיר כזית על מנת לאכול זית שירים למחר. ומאן דאמר פסול כו] קסבר אין דרך הקטרה בכך. *)ולא פסל מחשבתו. אבל דרך הקטרה בכך. והקטרה מעלייתא היא כז].

*) ומ"ד כשר קסבר אין דרך אכילה בכך נ"ק

חריפי

כאותה נ"ק
נ"א בקבלה ושחיטה כו' בשחיטה או בקבלה איפסל כו' נ"ק
זבחים כח: מב:
[יומא נז: זבחים מב: פא:]
[יומא ס: זבחים מב: נב: קיא.]
בהולכה דקומץ נ"ק
[פסחים סב:]
[שם סג.]
[לעיל יז.]

שיטה מקובצת

א] מיא בעלמא קא מדי. ואין זה קרבו כל מתיריו בשלמא לרבנן דאמרי אין מפגלין בחצי מתיר אם כן צריך שיחשוב בכל ההזאות והוי שפיר קרבו כל מתיריו דאין שם פסול אחר רק מחשבה שלא בזמנו ואינו נגמר עד שיפגל בכולן אלא לר"מ דאית ליה מפגלין בחצי מתיר א"כ כי פיגל בראשונה גמר פיגולו בכך מכאן ואילך כי מדי מיא בעלמא כו': ב] עי' בהשמטות בסוף המסכת: ג] שירים לא מעכבי. אע"ג דהך סוגיא אתיא כמ"ד דמעכבי מ"מ לא נחית למיחשבה בהדי מנין הזאות: ד] כל עבודה שאינה מתרת. פ"ה משו' דאפשר כו' וקשה דמאי פריך לקמן ומה שחיטה דעבודה שאינה מתרת והוי ליה למימר שחיטה אי אפשר לבטלה [אלא נ"ל] דה"פ שאינה מתרת שאינה מועלת לשום דבר שזריקה מתרת לבשר וקבלה מועלת לזריקה אבל הולכה אינה מועלת לשום דבר והשתא פריך כמו כן שחיטה דאינה מתרת לשום דבר. תו"ח. ז"ל תוס' אחרות עבודה חשובה לפגל עלי' בפני עצמה פ"ה דליכא למימר עד שיפגל כל המתיר דהא לאו מתיר הוא ואין לאחרת כח לעכב ורוצה לומר כיון דגריעא כל כך דאינה מתרת א) כי מחשב בחברתה עבודה חשובה היא והוי כמחשב במתיר שלם שאין באחרת כח לעכבה מיהו הא דפרש"י דאינה מתרת משום דאפשר לבטלה לא נהירא שהרי כי פריך והרי שחיטה דאינה מתרת לא מצינו לפרושי הכי דאפשר לבטלה אלא ה"פ אינה מתרת ממש ולא [דמי] לקבלה שמתרת הזריקה וזריקה מתרת האימורים להקטיר והבשר לאכול אבל הולכה אינה מתרת כלל והשתא פריך שפיר דס"ד [דשחיטה] אינה מתרת ומסיק דשחיטה מתרת הדם: ה] מתרת היא ופליגי: ו] תיבות את הקומץ בשתיקה נמחק: ז] מ"ד פיגול כר"מ ה"ה דהוי מצי למימר אימר דשמעת [illegible] ואכילה שלימה חצי מתיר וחצי אכילה מי שמעת ליה אלא בלאו הכי פריך שפיר: ומ"ד [illegible] למימר דהיינו רבנן דרבי דאמר איהו אומר אני שזה כשר מכלל דפליגי רבנן עליה דאי [illegible] מילי בחצי מתיר ואכילה שלימה דגזר קומץ אטו קומץ דמנחת חוטא כדאמרינן לעיל. [illegible] בשיעורו. פ"ה דחשיב שיעור הקטרה דהקומץ הוי הקטרה שלימה וא"ת לעיל דקאמר [illegible] ומוקמא התם סימן אחד למולים וסימן אחד לערלים אמאי פסל ר' מאיר הא לא הוי [illegible] וי"ל דמ"מ לא הוי שומשום דבר מסויים כמו סימן אחד של שחיטה דאין דרך הקטרה [illegible] דאמר לקמן יש הקטרה בפחות מכזית הני מילי חצי זית אבל שומשום לא הוי דרך הקטרה. [illegible] דלא מחייבי כרת על אכילתו עד שיקרבו בהכשר כו': י] בקבלה איפסול וכי זריק: [illegible]: יב] א' להיכל וכן למזבח: יג] בפנים דבמקום: יד] בשעת מתן ארבע ותיבת מתנות [illegible] דאמר אין מערבין אלא מכל: טז] כהקטרה היא ופליגי: יז] דאפשר להושיט להו זה לזה [illegible] רש"י כגון ששחט בצד המזבח וזריק ליה כדאמרינן פ"ק דזבחים: יח] פסחים דבחצי [illegible] אחד ששני סימנין מתירין הבשר לאכילה אלמא: יט] לחם דתקדיש: כ] מבעי ליה כיון דלא [illegible] דהקטרה הס"ד ומה"ד אלא נתן דקתני נתן את הקומץ בשתיקה הוליך מיבעי ליה: כא] כשיעור [illegible] ע"מ לאכול כדי שומשום מן השירים למחר והקטיר שומשום לאכול שומשום כמו שפרשתי

שיטה מקובצת

וכן עשה עד הקטיר כל הקומץ מהו וכן הלבונה: כב] שומשום ושומשום חצי מתיר ותיבות חשיב ליה בחצי נמחק: כג] הכא חשיב: כד] האחרת השלים הוית תיבות השלמה זית נמחק: כה] קסבר דרך נ"א אכילה בכך והוי חל עליה שם פיגול והוי מחשבה גמורה דרך הקטרה בכך והוי ליה מחשב בעבודה כשרה והוי ליה כמקטיר כו' ומ"ד פסול קא סבר אין דרך אכילה בכך ולא הוי חל עליה שם פיגול ואין דרך הקטרה בכך והוי ליה מנחה שלא נקטרה ופסולה: כו] ומאן דאמר פסול קסבר דרך אכילה בכך ואין דרך הקטרה בכך והוי ליה מנחה שלא הוקטרה ומאן דאמר כשר קסבר אין דרך אכילה בכך: כז] מעלייתא היא למשרי שירים באכילה הס"ד: כח] ותירץ בפ' ב"ש וקשה לתירוץ הקונטרס (דפ"ק) [דבסוף פ"ב] דזבחים [דף כט ע"ב] ופ"ק דמעילה [דף ד ע"א] אמר אילפא גבי פלוגתא דר"י ורבנן (דלעיל) דאמר רבי יהודה אם מחשבת הזמן קדמה כו' מחלוקת בעבודה אחת כעין שתי עבודות כגון דשחט סימן אחד במחשבת חוץ לזמנו דר"י סבר פיגול ואמאי כי קא שחיט השני עפרא בעלמא קא שחיט וע"כ (כר"ל) [כר"מ] דאי כרבנן הא בעיא (ר"ל) [כל] המתיר (וחצי סימן) [וסימן אחד] לאו מתיר שלם הוא ואפילו הכי קאמר דאפילו בעבודה אחת לא אמרינן מיא בעלמא ובהזאות נמי עבודה אחת כעין שתי עבודות ופי' הר"מ דסבר אילפא דלפיגולו מרצה כדמפרש רבא ור"ת מפרש דבחד מקום כו' וקשה להשר מאיוורא דלעיל [דף יד] אמרינן היה עומד בפנים ואמר הריני שוחט ע"מ לשפוך שירים למחר דהיינו בחוץ שהשירים נשפכים על מזבח החיצון פיגל ואמאי לא אמרינן מכי חשיב בפנים פסליה כי הדר שופך השירים בחוץ מיא בעלמא קא זריק. תו"ח. ולא הבנתי דבריו דלעיל [לא] אמרינן הכי כלל אלא שהמחשבה שבפנים בדבר הנעשה בחוץ לא פיגל ב) ושמא ס"ל דה"מ במחשבה בפנים בדבר השייך בפנים כגון הזאה אבל שחיטה דעבודת חוץ היא אפילו עומד בפנים קרי ליה מחשב בחוץ בדבר הנעשה בחוץ וצ"ע [עוד] לפ"ה דהכא קשה הא (דפ"ק) [דבסוף פ"ב] דזבחים מחלוקת כו' ופרש"י התם כגון ששחט כו' דהתם חד עבודה היא אמאי לא אמרינן כיון דשחיט סימן איפסל ליה כי הדר שחיט ליה לשני עפרא בעלמא הוא דקא מחתך ואין זה קרבו כל מתיריו ופר"י דכל היכא דנגמרה העבודה באותו מקום שפיגל בו גמר העבודה הוא אין זה עפרא בעלמא אבל הני הזאות דהכא דשינוי מקום להם לפני ולפנים ובהיכל ובמזבח בהא אמרינן דכי פיגל בחד מקום כשמשנה מקומו מיא בעלמא כו':

א) אולי צ"ל דאינה מתרת עבודה חשובה היא אף שאינו מחשב בחבירתה והוי כמחשב וכו': ב) לולא דבריו ז"ל י"ל דהש"ס מקשה מדרבנן דפליגי עליה וס"ל דלאף דמתחשב בפנים על דבר הנעשה בחוץ פיגל ודו"ק:

מתני' *פיגל בקומץ ולא בלבונה, בלבונה ולא בקומץ — ר' מאיר אומר: פיגול וחייבין עליו כרת, וחכמים אומרים: אאין בו כרת עד שיפגל בכל המתיר. ומודים בחכמים לר' מאיר במנחת חוטא ובמנחת קנאות, שאם פיגל בקומץ — שהוא פיגול וחייבין עליו כרת, שהקומץ הוא המתיר. שחט אחד מן הכבשים לאכול ב' חלות למחר, הקטיר אחד מן הבזיכין לאכול ב' סדרים למחר — ר"מ אומר: פיגול וחייבין עליו כרת, וחכמים אומרים: גאין בו כרת עד שיפגל בכל המתיר. דשחט אחד מן הכבשים לאכול ממנו למחר — הוא פיגול וחבירו כשר, הלאכול מחבירו למחר — שניהם כשרים.§ גמ' אמר רב: מחלוקת — שנתן את הקומץ בשתיקה ואת הלבונה במחשבה, אבל נתן הקומץ במחשבה ואת הלבונה בשתיקה — דברי הכל פיגול, שכל העושה — על דעת ראשונה הוא עושה. ושמואל אמר: עדיין הוא מחלוקת. א] יתיב רבא וקאמר לה להא שמעתא. איתיביה רב אחא בר רב הונא לרבא: *בד"א — בקמיצה ובמתן כלי ובהילוך; [אבל] בא לו להקטרה, נתן את הקומץ בשתיקה ואת הלבונה במחשבה, ב] את הקומץ במחשבה ואת הלבונה בשתיקה — ר"מ אומר: פיגול וחייבין עליו כרת, וחכמים אומרים: ואין בו כרת עד שיפגל בכל המתיר. קתני מיהא: נתן את הקומץ במחשבה ואת הלבונה בשתיקה, ופליגי! אימא: וכבר נתן את הלבונה בשתיקה מעיקרא. שתי תשובות בדבר: ג] חדא, דהיינו קמייתא. ועוד, התניא: אח"כ! תרגמא רב חנינא: בב' דיעות. *ת"ש: זבד"א — בדמים הניתנין על מזבח החיצון, אבל דמים הניתנין על מזבח הפנימי, כגון מ"ג של יום הכיפורים, ואחת עשרה של פר כהן משוח, ואחת עשרה של פר העלם דבר של ציבור, פיגל בין בראשונה בין בשניה ובין בשלישית — ר"מ אומר: פיגול וחייבין עליו כרת, וחכ"א: חאין בו כרת עד שיפגל בכל המתיר. קתני מיהא: פיגל בין בראשונה בין בשניה ובין בשלישית, ופליגי! וכי תימא: ה"נ בשתי דעות — הניחא *למאן דאמר: "בפר" ואפי' בדמו של פר, אלא למ"ד: "בפר" ולא בדמו של פר, מאי איכא למימר? *אמר רבא: הכא במאי עסקי' — כגון שפיגל *בראשונה ושתק בשניה ופיגל בשלישית, דאמרי': אי ס"ד כל העושה על דעת ראשונה הוא עושה, מיהדר פיגולי בשלישית למה לי? מתקיף לה רב אשי: מידי שתק קתני? אלא אמר רב אשי: הכא במאי עסקי' — כגון שפיגל בראשונה ובשניה ד] *ובשלישית, דאמרי': אי ס"ד כל העושה על דעת ראשונה הוא עושה, מיהדר פגולי בשניה ה] (ובשלישית) למה לי? והא

*מתירו לבהונות. כדכתיב (ויקרא יד): "על דם האשם", דכל זמן שלא נתן מן הדם מעכב השמן, כדאמרי' בפ"ק (לעיל ה.). מתני' פיגל בקומץ. בהקטרת קומץ חישב על השירים. עד שיפגל בכל המתיר. והקטרת אחד מהן חלי מתיר הוא, דאיכא נמי הקטרת חבירו. גמ' שנתן הקומץ כו'. כלומר, הקטרה ראשונה הקטיר בשתיקה ושניה במחשבה. אבל חישב בראשונה ושתק בשניה — פיגול לדברי הכל. להא שמעתא. דרב. בד"א. דמחשבת עבודה הקומץ מפגל ו], בברייתא דמנחות. בקמיצה כו'. דבהנך ג' עבודות אין דומה להן בלבונה, הילכך כולו מתיר הוא. הולכה מפרש בגמ' לקמן בשמעתין, דהא איכא ז] בלבונה. קתני מיהא כו' ופליגי. ותיובתא דרב. בשתי דעות. דאחד הקטיר קומץ במחשבה, ואח"כ הקטיר חבירו לבונה בשתיקה. דמשו"ה פליגי רבנן — דליכא למימר על דעת ראשונה עשה. בד"א. דבמתנה אחת פיגל ח] בדמים הניתנין כו', בברייתא דזבחים (דף מב.). מ"ג דיום הכיפורים. ח' הזאות דפר ט] בין הבדים, אחת למעלה ושבע למטה, וח' דשעיר — הרי ט"ז, וכנגדו בהיכל כדאמרי' במס' יומא (דף נג:) — הרי ל"ב, וד' י] קרנות המזבח הפנימי — הרי ל"ו, וז' על טהרו של אותו מזבח כשהדם הפר והשעיר מעורבין ביחד — הרי מ"ג יא]. י"א של פר כהן משיח. ז' הזאות על הפרוכת וד' מתנות דמזבח, כדכתיב ב"ויקרא", וכן פר העלם דבר. בראשונה. בין הבדים, בשניה — על הפרוכת, בג' — על מזבח הזהב. וחייבים עליו כרת. האוכל מבשר הפר. ופליגי. אפי' פיגל בראשונה פליגי רבנן, אלמא לא אמרי': שניה ושלישית על דעת ראשונה עושה! בשתי דעות. שמת כהן גדול או אירע לו קרי לאחר הזאות דבין הבדים, ושמש אחר תחתיו והזה בהיכל, דליכא למימר על דעת ראשונה עושה. הניחא למ"ד. במס' יומא בפ' "הוציאו לו" (ד' מט:). *פר ואפי' יב] דמו של פר. [שנאמר] "בזאת יבא אהרן [וגו'] בפר" — ואפי' בדמו של פר, שאם שחטו הראשון ואירע בו פסול — יבא אהרן בדמו אל הקדש, וא"צ להביא ולשחוט פר אחר, לדידיה יג] הוה [מצי] לאוקמיה בב' דעות. אלא למ"ד ולא בדמו של פר. לא מצי לאוקומי בשתי דיעות. אלא אמר רב אשי כגון שפיגל בראשונה ובשניה. ושתק בשלישית, דאכתי הוה חלי מתיר. והא

אחר שהיה יד] (זבח) זובח באותה שעה, וגם משום דלב ב"ד מתנה עליהן, כמו שמעמידה בסוף, הא לאו הכי לא קרבי, דמשקדשו בכלי הוקבעו אפי' קודם שחיטה. והא דקרבי עם הזבח אחר הזובח באותה שעה, היינו משום דלב ב"ד מתנה כדמפרש התם. ולפי מה שסובר השתא, לית ליה *דאמרינן הכא לר"מ דשחיטה קובעת ולא כלי קובעת. עוד יש לפרש ההיא התם ד"התודה" אפי' כרבנן, דכי פליגי רבי מאיר ורבנן — בשחיטת פיגול. דבפגול איירי ברישא, וקאי אמתניתין דהזבח מפגל את הנסכים, וקסבר רבי מאיר דהוקבעו בשחיטת פיגול כלחמי תודה, דתנן בפ' "התודה" (לקמן ד' עח:): שחט חוץ לזמנו וחוץ למקומו — קדש הלחם, אבל שחיטה כשרה קובעת אפי' לרבנן. ולזעירי דאמר: נסכים מתקדשים בשחיטה — היינו למר כדאית ליה ולמר כדאית ליה. ופריך ממתני' דזבח פסול, דאלמא שחיטה פסולה מקדשא, וקשיא לרבנן. ואפי' רבי מאיר לא אמר אלא בפיגול טו] *במתנות ולא בשאר פסולי שחיטה. ודווקא דאיכא זבח אחר, משום תנאי ב"ד, הא ליכא זבח אחר — לא. ומיהו קשה לפירוש זה, דא"כ משכחת לרבנן דנסכי בהמה חייבין עליהם משום פיגול, שנעשית השחיטה בהכשר ופיגול בשאר עבודות. *הוקבעו בשחיטה. כרבי דאמר: שני דברים המתירים מעלין זה בלא זה. טז] ולר' אלעזר בר' שמעון דאמר: אין מעלין, הוה ליה למינקט שחיטה וזריקה, או שנתקבל הדם בכוס ונשפך, וכאבוה דאמר: כל העומד לזרוק כזרוק דמי כדקאמרינן בפרק "התודה" (לקמן דף עט:). ופלוגתייהו בפ' "התכלת" (לקמן דף מז.) ובסוף "ר' ישמעאל" לקמן (דף עב:). חדא דהיינו קמייתא. פי': דנתן את הקומץ בשתיקה כו', *לכך שוות זה כזה. ובפ' "בית שמאי" (זבחים מב:) מביא ברייתא זו איפכא, דקתני ברישא: נתן את הקומץ במחשבה. בין בראשונה בין בשניה בין בשלישית. ראשונה — כל הזאות דבין הבדים, שניה — דפרוכת, שלישית — דמזבח הזהב, כך פי' בקונטרס. וכן מוכח בסמוך יז] כל דבין הבדים חשיב חדא, דקאמר: דחשיב בפנים פוסל, כי מדי בהיכל מיא בעלמא קא מדי. ובאלי הזאות דפנים קא מודי ר' מאיר דלא הוי פיגול, מידי דהוה אלי קומץ דלא הוי פיגול, כדאמר בסוף פ' שני דזבחים (דף ל.) דבעינן קומץ שלם, דקאמר: הרי קמילה, דכי לאלות דמי ופליגי. וצ"ע בההיא דלקמן דהקטיר שומשום לאכול שומשום עד שכלה הקומץ. קתני מיהא פיגל בראשון וכו' ופליגי. הוי מצי לשנויי שפי' בהדיא שאינו עושה על דעת ראשונה. כגון שפיגל בראשונה ובשניה ובשלישית. בפ' "ב"ש" (זבחים דף מב. ושם) פי' בקונטרס: וברביעית לא פיגל. וקשה, דרביעית מאן דכר שמה! ובכאן פירש בקונטרס: שפיגל בראשונה ובשניה, ושתק בשלישית. ואם תאמר, א"כ קשיא: מידי שתק קתני, כדאקשינן לעיל! ושמא לעיל דשתק באמצעית הוה ליה לפרושי טפי, כיון דראשונה ושלישית במחשבה ושניה בשתיקה. ולהאי פי' חשיב כל הזאות *דמזבח הזהב באחת, שבע דטיהרו וד' דקרנות. וכן משמע בפרק "הוציאו לו" (יומא דף סא.), דתניא: "וכפר את הקדש" — זה לפני ולפנים, "ואת אהל מועד" — זה היכל, "ואת המזבח" — כמשמעו, משמע דחשיב מזבח כפרה אחת. *עוד קאמר התם: מכאן אמרו כו' עד: גמר מתנות שבהיכל ונשפך הדם — יביא אחר ויתחיל במתנות המזבח, נתן מקצת מתנות המזבח ונשפך הדם — יביא אחר ויתחיל בתחילה. אבל לא קתני: גמר ד' קרנות ונשפך הדם — יביא אחר ויתחיל יח] בטהרו, *דכולהו חשיבי כאחת. וקשה, דלקמן קאמר (ג"כ): משכחת לה בד' פרים וד' שעירים, פירוש: חד אהזאות דבין הבדים, וחד אהזאות דפרוכת, וחד אהזאות דקרנות, וחד אטיהרו. אלמא לא חשיבי כחד הזאות דקרנות ודטיהרו! ושמא סבירא ליה שירייס מעכבין, הוי חד בשביל שירייס. ולפי זה נוכל לגרוס כאן: שפיגל בראשונה ובשניה ושלישית. וכן כתוב בספר רבינו גרשם ובפרק "בית שמאי" (זבחים דף מב.), וחשיב חלי מתיר משום דאיכא עדיין שירייס דמעכבי. ואם תאמר: הא בעל כרחיה האי תנא סבר שירייס לא מעכבי, מדלא חשיב אלא מ"ג, דההוא דסבר שירייס מעכבי חשיב חדא טפי, כדמוכח בסמוך! ויש לומר: דאף על גב דשירייס מעכבי, יט] לא חשיב האי תנא אלא הזאות. כי

שייך לעיל

זבחים מג: לעיל יד:

זבחים מב: [תוספתא פ"ה]

נ"ק

תוספתא דזבחים פ"ד [זבחים מח:]

כפר ואפי' בדמו של פר נ"ק

יומא מט:

[זבחים מב. כל הענין]

בראשונה ובשניה דאמרינן אי ס"ד כל העושה הוא עושה ע"ד ראשונה מיהדר פיגל בשניה למה לי נ"ק וכ"ה בס"י

דמזבח שבע דטיהרו וד' קרנות כאחת נ"ק *ועוד דקאמר התם נ"ק

נ"א משמע דכולהו כו' נ"ק

נ"ק מ"ז

יט א מיי' פט"ז מהל' פסה"מ הלכה ז [ועי' רש"ק שהאריך]:

הא דאמרינן נ"ק

כ ב מיי' שם הל' י:

כא ג מיי' פי"ז מהל' פסה"מ הלכה יד:

כב ד מיי' שם הל' טז:

כג ה מיי' שם הל' יז:

כד ו מיי' שם פט"ז הלכה ח:

כה ז ח מיי' שם פי"ז הלכה א ב:

נ"א במתניתין אבל לא כו' נ"ק

שייך לעיל

נ"א ולמנין כך שוות נ"ק

[נ"ל ושתק בשלישית לפי גי' רש"י]

והקומץ במחשבה. תו"ח: ד] תיבת ובשלישית נמחק: ה] תיבת ובשלישית נמחק: ו] מפגל הס"ד ומה"ד בקמיצה כו' בברייתא דמנחות דבהנך ג' עבודות כו' להן הלבונה הלכך: ז] איכא הולכה: ח] פיגל אפי' לרבנן בדמים הניתנים כו' בברייתא דזבחים במזבח החיצון לפי שכל דמים הניתנים במזבח החיצון שנתן מתנה אחת כיפר לפיכך הוי כל אחד ואחד מתיר שלם אבל דמים הניתנין על מזבח הפנימי שכולן מעכבי אהדדי כגון מ"ג והד"א: ט] דבין הבדים: י] וד' דקרנות: יא] מ"ג וקסבר מערבין דם פר ושעיר קודם מתן קרנות: יב] ואפי' בדמו של פר בזאת יבא אהרן אל הקדש ותיבת שנאמר ותיבת וגו' נמחק: יג] לדידיה איכא ותיבות הוה מצי נמחק: יד] שהיה א) תיבות באותה ותיבות זבח זבוח נמחק: טו] בפיגול ומתניתין אפי' בשאר ותיבות במתנות ולא נמחק: טז] בלא זה ניחא דסגי בשחיטה: יז] בסמוך דכל הזאות דבין הבדים כו' דקאמר כיון דחשיב בפנים: יח] ויתחיל בטיהרו דכולהו חשובי כו' קאמר משכחת לה ותיבות ג"כ ליתא: יט] לא חשיב ואע"ג דצריך לחזור וליתן מתנה אחת על טיהרו כדי שיהיו שירים וא"כ אותה מתנה לא היתה כמצותה וי"ל דאינה באה אלא לקיים בדם ב) ושירים דודאי כמצותה נעשית. תו"ח. לשון תוס' אחרות וקשה דלא קרב המתיר כמצותה וצריך להתחיל ולגמור הכל וי"ל כיון שהתחיל במתנות קרינן ביה קרב המתיר כמצותה:

א) לכאורה נראה דצ"ל שהיה זבוח באותו שעה ותיבת זבח נמחק וכמו שהגיה הצ"ק: ב) אולי צ"ל לקיים בדם מצות שירים והשירים בוודאי כמצותה נעשית:

שיטה מקובצת

א] מחלוקת וכן אמר ר' יוחנן עדיין היא מחלוקת יתיב רבה וקאמר כו' רב הונא לרבה בד"א: ב] במחשבה או שנתן את: ג] חדא דהיינו קמייתא פי' נתן את הקומץ בשתיקה כו' ולמה שינה לשונו היה לו לומר [או] שנתן הלבונה [בשתיקה]

מיא

טו א מיי' פי"ז מהל' פסולי המוקדשין הלכה ח:
טז ב מיי' שם הל' יז:
יז ג מיי' פ"ב מהלכות מעה"ק הלכה יב:
יח ד מיי' פ"ח מהל' ... הלכה ח ופ"ה מהלכות מחוסרי כפרה הלכה ד:

שֶׁזָּרַע כַּרְמוֹ שֶׁל חֲבֵירוֹ א] סְמָדַר, וּבָא מַעֲשֶׂה לִפְנֵי חֲכָמִים, וְאָסְרוּ אֶת הַזְּרָעִים וְהִתִּירוּ אֶת הַגְּפָנִים; וְאַמַּאי? לֵימָא קַל וָחוֹמֶר הוּא: וּמַה הָאוֹסֵר אֵינוֹ נֶאֱסָר, הַבָּא לֶאֱסוֹר וְלֹא אָסַר אֵינוֹ דִּין שֶׁלֹּא יִתְאַסֵּר! הָכִי הַשְׁתָּא? הָתָם ב] קַנַּבּוֹס וְלוּף אָסְרָה תּוֹרָה, ג] (*דִּתְנַן: °הָיְתָה שָׂדֵהוּ זְרוּעָה קַנַּבּוֹס וְלוּף — לֹא יְהֵא זוֹרֵעַ עַל גַּבֵּיהֶם, [א] שֶׁהֵן עוֹשׂוֹת לְשָׁלֹשׁ שָׁנִים;) ד] שְׁאָר זְרָעִים מִדְּרַבָּנַן הוּא דַּאֲסִירִי, הַאי ה] דְּעָבֵיד אִיסּוּרָא קַנְסוּהּ רַבָּנַן, הַאי דְּלָא עָבֵיד אִיסּוּרָא לָא קַנְסוּהּ רַבָּנַן, אֲבָל הָכָא לֵימָא ק"ו! וְאִיכָּא דְּמַתְנֵי לָהּ אַכְּבָשִׂים. בְּעָא מִינֵּיהּ רַבִּי אֶלְעָזָר מֵרַב: הַשּׁוֹחֵט אֶת הַכְּבָשִׂים לֶאֱכוֹל כַּזַּיִת מֵהֶן וּמִלַּחְמָן, מַהוּ? לְאִיפַּגּוּלֵי כְּבָשִׂים לָא קָא מִיבַּעְיָא לִי, הַשְׁתָּא כּוּלּוֹ מִלֶּחֶם לָא מְפַגְּלִי, מֵהֶן וּמִלַּחְמָן מִיבַּעְיָא? כִּי קָא מִיבַּעְיָא לִי — לְאִיפַּגּוּלֵי לֶחֶם, מִי מִצְטָרְפִי כְּבָשִׂים לְאִיפַּגּוּלֵי לַלֶּחֶם אוֹ לָא? א"ל: אַף ^אבָזוֹ, הַלֶּחֶם מְפוּגָּל וְהַכְּבָשִׂים אֵינָן מְפוּגָּלִין. וְאַמַּאי? לֵימָא ק"ו: וּמַה הַמְפַגֵּל אֵינוֹ מִתְפַּגֵּל, הַבָּא לְפַגֵּל וְלֹא פִּיגֵּל — אֵינוֹ דִּין שֶׁלֹּא יִתְפַּגֵּל! וּמִי אָמְרִינַן ק"ו כִּי הַאי גַּוְונָא? וְהָתַנְיָא: מַעֲשֶׂה בְּאֶחָד שֶׁזָּרַע כַּרְמוֹ שֶׁל חֲבֵירוֹ סְמָדַר וכו', וְאַמַּאי? לֵימָא ק"ו: מַה הָאוֹסֵר אֵינוֹ נֶאֱסָר, הַבָּא לֶאֱסוֹר וְלֹא אָסַר אֵינוֹ דִּין שֶׁלֹּא יִתְאַסֵּר! הָכִי הַשְׁתָּא? הָתָם קַנַּבּוֹס וְלוּף אָסְרָה תּוֹרָה, שְׁאָר זְרָעִים מִדְּרַבָּנַן הוּא דַּאֲסִירִי, הַאי דַּעֲבַד אִיסּוּרָא קַנְסוּהּ רַבָּנַן, דְּלָא עֲבַד אִיסּוּרָא לָא קַנְסוּהּ רַבָּנַן; ו] אֲבָל הָכָא לֵימָא ק"ו! מַאן דְּמַתְנֵי לָהּ אַתּוֹדָה — כָּל שֶׁכֵּן אַכְּבָשִׂים, וּמַאן דְּמַתְנֵי לָהּ אַכְּבָשִׂים — כְּבָשִׂים הוּא דְּהוּזְקְקוּ זֶה לָזֶה לִתְנוּפָה, אֲבָל תּוֹדָה דְּלֹא הוּזְקְקָה זֶה לָזֶה בִּתְנוּפָה — לָא. ז] רַבִּי אַבָּא זוּטִי בָּעֵי לָהּ הָכִי, בְּעָא מִינֵּיהּ ר' אֶלְעָזָר מֵרַב: הַשּׁוֹחֵט אֶת הַכֶּבֶשׂ לֶאֱכוֹל כַּזַּיִת מֵחֲבֵירוֹ לְמָחָר, מַהוּ? "חֲבֵירוֹ" כֶּבֶשׂ מַשְׁמַע וְלָא מְפַגֵּל, ח] אוֹ דִּלְמָא לֶחֶם מַשְׁמַע וּמְפַגֵּל לֵיהּ? אֲמַר לֵיהּ, תְּנִיתוּהָ: ט] שָׁחַט אֶחָד מִן הַכְּבָשִׂים לֶאֱכוֹל מִמֶּנּוּ לְמָחָר — הוּא פִּיגּוּל וַחֲבֵירוֹ כָּשֵׁר, לֶאֱכוֹל מֵחֲבֵירוֹ לְמָחָר — שְׁנֵיהֶם כְּשֵׁרִים; י] אַלְמָא ^ב"חֲבֵירוֹ" כֶּבֶשׂ מַשְׁמַע! דִּלְמָא דְּפָרֵישׁ וְאָמַר: "חֲבֵירוֹ כֶּבֶשׂ".§ **מתני'** יא] הַזֶּבַח מְפַגֵּל אֶת הַנְּסָכִים מִשֶּׁקָּדְשׁוּ בִּכְלִי, דִּבְרֵי ר"מ. יב] הַנְּסָכִים אֵינָן מְפַגְּלִים אֶת הַזֶּבַח. כֵּיצַד? הַשּׁוֹחֵט אֶת הַזֶּבַח לֶאֱכוֹל מִמֶּנּוּ לְמָחָר — הוּא וּנְסָכָיו מְפוּגָּלִין, לְהַקְרִיב נְסָכָיו לְמָחָר — הַנְּסָכִים מְפוּגָּלִין, הַזֶּבַח אֵינוֹ מְפוּגָּל.§ **גמ'** *ת"ר: נִסְכֵּי בְהֵמָה חַיָּיבִין עֲלֵיהֶן מִשּׁוּם פִּיגּוּל, מִפְּנֵי שֶׁדַּם הַזֶּבַח מַתִּירָן לִקְרֵב, דִּבְרֵי ר"מ. אָמְרוּ לוֹ לר"מ: וַהֲלֹא ^גאָדָם מֵבִיא זִבְחוֹ הַיּוֹם וּנְסָכָיו יג] *עַד י' יָמִים! אָמַר לָהֶן: אַף אֲנִי לֹא אָמַרְתִּי אֶלָּא בַּבָּאִין עִם הַזֶּבַח. יד] א"ל: אֶפְשָׁר לְשַׁנּוֹתוֹ לְזֶבַח אַחֵר. אָמַר רָבָא, קָסָבַר ר"מ: הוּקְבְּעוּ בִּשְׁחִיטָה, כְּלַחְמֵי תוֹדָה. ת"ר: *לוֹג שֶׁמֶן שֶׁל מְצוֹרָע חַיָּיבִין עָלָיו מִשּׁוּם פִּיגּוּל, מִפְּנֵי שֶׁדַּם אָשָׁם טו] מַתִּירוֹ לִבְהוֹנוֹת, דִּבְרֵי רַבִּי מֵאִיר. אָמְרוּ לוֹ לְרַבִּי מֵאִיר: ^דוַהֲלֹא אָדָם מֵבִיא אֲשָׁמוֹ הַיּוֹם וְלוּגּוֹ מִיכָּן וְעַד י' יָמִים! אָמַר לָהֶן: אַף אֲנִי לֹא אָמַרְתִּי אֶלָּא בַּבָּא עִם הָאָשָׁם. טז] [א"ל:] אֶפְשָׁר לְשַׁנּוֹתוֹ לְאָשָׁם יז] אַחֵר. אָמַר רָבָא, קָסָבַר רַבִּי מֵאִיר: הוּקְבְּעוּ בִּשְׁחִיטָה, כְּלַחְמֵי תוֹדָה.יח] § מתני'

רש"י

שֶׁזָּרַע. מִשֶּׁלּוֹ. סְמָדַר. כְּבָר חָנְטוּ יט] עֲנָבִים, וְכֵן הָיָה מַעֲשֶׂה וְאָסְרוּ אֶת הַזְּרָעִים. טַעְמָא מְפָרֵשׁ לְקַמָּן. הָאוֹסֵר. גְּפָנִים הָאוֹסְרִים אֶת הַזְּרָעִים. הַבָּא לֶאֱסוֹר. זְרָעִים. קַנַּבּוֹס = קַנְבָּא. לוּף = מִינֵי קִיטְנִית. אָסְרָה תּוֹרָה. בְּכֶרֶם [ב], אֵין זַרְעָם כָּלֶה, שֶׁיֵּשׁ לָהֶם שֹׁרֶשׁ. ל"א: קַנַּבּוֹס וְלוּף אָסְרָה תּוֹרָה — (א) דִּכְתִיב (דברים כב): "כַּרְמְךָ כִּלְאָיִם" — זְרָעִים הַדּוֹמִין לְכֶרֶם, וְהָנָךְ תּוֹלִין אֶשְׁכּוֹלוֹת כְּעֵין עֲנָבִים. [ג] בַּעַל הַכֶּרֶם לָא עֲבַד אִיסּוּרָא אֶלָּא הָכָא חַבְּתֵי אִיכָּא לְמִיפְרַךְ: לֵימָא קַל וָחוֹמֶר. כ"ש אַכְּבָשִׂים כ] [ד]. מִצְטָרְפִין הֵן וְהַלֶּחֶם לְפַגֵּל הַלֶּחֶם. אֲבָל תּוֹדָה לָא (ב). כא] פְּשִׁיט לֵיהּ דְּלָא פַּגֵּיל לֶחֶם. בָּעֵי רַבִּי אַבָּא זוּטֵי כו' מֵחֲבֵירוֹ. וְלָא פֵּירֵשׁ כֶּבֶשׂ. וְלָא מִיפַּגֵּל. כִּדְקָתָנֵי בְּמַתְנִי' בְּסֵיפָא: שָׁחַט א' מִן הַכְּבָשִׂים לֶאֱכוֹל מֵחֲבֵירוֹ לְמָחָר שְׁנֵיהֶם כְּשֵׁרִים, דְּאֵין מַתִּיר מְפַגֵּל אֶת הַמַּתִּיר. אוֹ דִּלְמָא: "חֲבֵירוֹ" — לֶחֶם מַשְׁמַע וּמְפַגֵּל לֶחֶם. **מתני'** מְפַגֵּל אֶת הַנְּסָכִים. שֶׁהַשּׁוֹתֶה מֵהֶם חַיָּיב כָּרֵת מִשּׁוּם [ה] פִּיגּוּל. מִשֶּׁקָּדְשׁוּ בִּכְלִי שׁוּב אֵין לָהֶן פִּדְיוֹן, וּקְדוּשָּׁתָן קְדוּשָּׁה. **גמ'** שֶׁדַּם הַזֶּבַח מַתִּירָן לִיקְרַב. וַהֲוֵי דָּבָר שֶׁיֵּשׁ לוֹ מַתִּירִין לַמִּזְבֵּחַ, וְנוֹהֵג בָּהֶן פִּיגּוּל, דְּכָל דָּבָר שֶׁיֵּשׁ לוֹ מַתִּירִין יֵשׁ בּוֹ פִּיגּוּל כב], בְּמַסֶּ' יוֹמָא בְּפֶ' "הוֹצִיאוּ לוֹ" (דף ס.). וּנְסָכָיו מִכָּאן וְעַד י' יָמִים. דְּאָמַר מָר לְקַמָּן (דף מד:): "מִנְחָתָם וְנִסְכֵּיהֶם" — כג] אֲפִילּוּ לְמָחָר, אַלְמָא לָאו *מִזְּבִיחָה נִינְהוּ. אַף אֲנִי לֹא אָמַרְתִּי. אִם פִּיגֵּל בַּזֶּבַח שֶׁיִּהוּ הַנְּסָכִים שֶׁיָּבִיא לְסוֹף י' יָמִים מְפוּגָּלִים, אֶלָּא בַּבָּאִים עִם הַזֶּבַח. אָמְרוּ לוֹ אֶפְשָׁר לְשַׁנּוֹתוֹ לְזֶבַח אַחֵר. הִלְכָּךְ לָא מִיפַּגְּלֵי. בִּשְׁחִיטָה. דְּהָאֵיךְ הוּקְבְּעוּ לְזֶבַח זֶה, וְאֵין רַשָּׁאִין לְשַׁנּוֹתָם לְאַחֵר. כְּלַחְמֵי תוֹדָה. שֶׁהַשְּׁחִיטָה קוֹבַעְתּוֹ, כִּדְאָמְרִי' בְּ"הַתּוֹדָה" כִּדְפְרִישִׁית לְעֵיל. לוֹג שֶׁמֶן כו'. אִם פִּיגֵּל בִּשְׁחִיטַת הָאָשָׁם. מַתִּירוֹ

תוספות

דין שלא יצטרף להתפגל לעצמו? וכי האי גוונא הוי האי דבסמוך: ומה אוסר אינו נאסר – הגפן שאוסר אינו נאסר, הבא לאסור – דהיינו זרעים שבאין לאסור הגפן על ידי צירופם שנעשין כלאים, ולא אסר, אינו דין שלא יאסר ע"י צירוף של גפן? ומהאי טעמא נמי ניחא במתניתין דשוחט את התודה לאכול הלחם, שהלחם מפוגל והתודה אינה מפוגלת, ולא אמרינן קל וחומר. **שזרע** כרמו של חבירו סמדר. הא דנקט סמדר – לאשמועינן דהגפנים התירו, מטעם דאין אדם אוסר דבר שאינו שלו. דלא תימא: מה שהתירו את הגפנים – משום דנגמרו ולא הוסיפו מאתים, ולא משום דאין אדם אוסר. **ואסרו** את הזרעים. היינו דלא כרבי יאשיה דאמר: עד שיזרע חטה ושעורה וחרצן במפולת יד. וכמה סתם משניות דלא כוותיה, אע"ג דקיימא לן כוותיה, כדאיתא בברכות (דף כב.) ובחולין בפרק "ראשית הגז" (דף קלו:): נהוג עלמא כתלתא סבי, כרבי יאשיה בכלאים. ואמרינן בפ"ק דקדושין (דף לט.) גבי ההוא דזרע חיטי ושערי בי גופני: ליתי מר נישמתיה! אמר ליה: לא נהריתו בה, לא קי"ל כרבי יאשיה? פירוש: בתמיה. **והתירו** הגפנים. היינו כרבי יוסי ורבי שמעון דמסכך גפנו על גבי תבואתו של חבירו, דאמר בסוף "הערל" (יבמות פג:): אין אדם אוסר דבר שאינו שלו. וצריך לומר דתבואה דהתם לאו בסתם תבואה של ה' מינין, דאם כן הוי דאורייתא כמו קנבוס ולוף דמסקינן הכא דאסור, [ו] והיכי מסיק רבי יוסי דשרי? אלא דרב פוסק התם *כרבנן. **אפשר** לשנותן לזבח אחר. בתוספתא דזבחים* אין הלשון כן. וגרס התם, אמר: אף אני לא אמרתי אלא כשקדשו בכלי, אמרו לו: אע"פ שנתקדשו אפשר לשנותן לזבח אחר. "וקדשו בכלי" דתוספתא היינו "באים עם הזבח" דהכא. וא"ת: דהשתא משמע דלרבנן דאפשר לשנותן לזבח אחר אפי' לאחר שחיטה. ולקמן בפ' "התודה" (דף עט.) תנן: הנסכים שקדשו בכלי ונמצא זבח פסול, אם יש זבח אחר יקרבו עמו. ופריך בגמ' (שם:), והאמר רב חסדא: שמן שהפרישו לשם מנחה זו – פסול לשם מנחה אחרת! ומשני: לב בית דין מתנה עליהם, אם הוצרכו הוצרכו, ואם לאו יהו לזבח אחר. אלמא דאסור לשנותן אם לא משום תנאי בית דין! ואין לומר דהא דאמרו רבנן נמי הכא אפשר לשנותן – היינו משום תנאי ב"ד. חדא, מי לא עסקינן בקרבן יחיד דלא שייך ביה לב בית דין? ועוד, לוג שמן דאשם מצורע לא משכחת אלא ביחיד! ועוד, דאין לב ב"ד מתנה אלא היכא דלא הוצרכו, אבל אם הוצרכו אי אפשר לשנותו! ונראה לפרש, דסוגיא [ז] דהתם כרבי מאיר. ואם תאמר: והלא רב חסדא סתמא ככולי עלמא, *)כדמפרש טעמא התם – משום דשמן גופא דמנחה הוא, ומאי קשיא ליה מרב חסדא ממתני' דהתם? תיקשי ליה הא דרבנן דהכא! ושמא כמו כן היה יכול להקשות, אלא מקשה אסתם מתניתין, דאפי' לרבי מאיר אפשר לשנותו. והא דלא פריך מסתם מתניתין דהתם, מדר"מ גופיה אדרבי מאיר דהכא – משום דלא נזכר שם רבי מאיר בהדיא. וכן מילתא דזעירי דהתם נמי אליבא דרבי מאיר אתיא, דקאמר התם (דף עט.): אין הנסכים מתקדשין אלא בשחיטת הזבח, פירוש: לענין שלא לשנותן כד](לענין) לזבח אחר. ולא כמו שפירש שם בקונטרס לענין ליפסל בלינה, דלענין לינה ודאי מיפסלי משקדשו בכלי, דאמר בסוף "רבי ישמעאל" (לקמן עב:) גבי שתי הלחם דאי תנור מקדש מיפסלי בלינה. ועוד, בסוף "לולב וערבה" כה](סוכה נ.) קאמר זעירי גופיה דאי מייתי במקודשת איפסלו להו בלינה, ומשנה שלמה שנינו בפ"ב דמעילה (דף י.) גבי נסכים: קדשו בכלי הוכשרו ליפסל בלינה. מיהו הסיא יש לדחות, דדוקא בנסכים הבאים כו] בפני עצמן, וכמו שפירשתי [ח]דאיירי לענין שלא לשנותן לזבח אחר. והא דפריך התם ממתניתין דקתני: אם יש זבח אחר יקרבו עמו, מאי לאו דאיפסול בשחיטה – הכי פריך: דמכשר דווקא משום דאיכא זבח אחר

*) ס"א וי"ל

ס"א אינו

[וע"ע תוספות יבמות פג. ד"ה ר' יוסי ופ"ה ע"ש]

הגהות הב"ח

(א) רש"י ד"ה אסרה וכו' דכתיב לא תזרע כרמך וכו' ענבים הס"ד ואח"כ מ"ה האי דלא עביד איסורא בעל הכרם: (ב) ד"ה אבל וכו' דפשיטא ליה:

גליון הש"ס

גמ' דקנסו רבנן ... שקדהו. עיין תוי"ט פ"ה מ"ח דכלאים:

מסורת הש"ס

כלאים פרק ב משנה ה
נ"ל מזבחה
זבחים מד. תוספתא לזבחים רפ"ה
[עי' תוס' ר"ה ל. ד"ה ונתקלקלו]
תוספתא דזבחים שם זבחים מד.

שיטה מקובצת

א] סמדר. פרש"י כך היה המעשה ואומר ר"י דאלמי ראיתו תני [הכי] שלא תאמר מה שלא נאסר הכרם לפי שלא הוסיף במאתים מש"ה נקט דהוסיף במאתים ואפ"ה לא נאסר הכרם לפי שאין אדם אוסר דבר שאינו שלו: ובא מעשה וכו' וגבי אין אדם אוסר דבר שאינו שלו מייתי לה דתני לעיל מיניה המסכך גפנו ע"ג תבואתו של חבירו כו' זה היה מעשה כו': ב] קנבוס ולוף. מפרש הר"ר חיים כהן בלשון בתמיה כלומ' וכי קנבוס ולוף הוא מדאורייתא ושאר זרעים דרבנן בעלמא כולהו נמי מדאורייתא ניתנו היכא הכרם והזרע שלו אלא הכא משום דאין אדם אוסר דבר שאינו שלו לא אסרו הכרם ומקו"ח נמי היה לנו להתיר הזרעים אלא קנסא הוא וקנסו רבנן להאי דעבר איסורא ורבינו שמשון מפרש שהיה לנו הקו"ח להחמיר והוא המפגל כו' אינו דין שלא יאסר ואפ"ה קאמר דהלחם מתפגל וא"כ יש לנו לפגל התודה מקו"ח ומה הבא לפגל ולא פיגל מתפגל הוא הלחם המתפגל התודה שמפגלת הלחם אינו דין שתתפגל והכ"ג אמרינן גבי קו"ח דכלאים דמן הדין היה לנו להתיר אף הזרעים ומדקאסרת להו היה לך לאסור הכרם מקו"ח מה הבא לאסור וכו' ומשני התורה כי אם מדרבנן משום קנסא והאי דעבד כו' וא"ת והיכא מייתי ראייה מהכא דאין ... שאינו שלו להמסכך גפנו שהוא מן התורה וצריך לומר דתבואה לאו דוקא אלא על גבי ... א"נ שהיה מסכך בזה הענין שאינו אסור אלא דרבנן כגון ברחוק ד' אמות. תום' מהר"פ: ... שאר זרעים כו' והשאר נמחק: ד] שאר זרעים מדרבנן כו'. וא"ת ומה תיקן ומפני שהם ... להחמיר ופי' השר מקוצי ז"ל כל הסוגיא דהקו"ח בא לאסור ולא להתיר וה"פ לעיל ומה ... מתפגל אינו דין (שיתפגל) [שלא יתפגל] ומ"מ הלחם מפגל ואע"ג דאיכא קו"ח א"כ היה לנו לומר מקו"ח שתהא תודה מפוגלת ומה לחם שאינו מפגל מתפגל תודה דהוי עיקר המפגל אינו דין שיתפגל וכה"ג לימא הכא ומה האוסר אינו נאסר כו' ומ"מ אסרו הזרעים אע"ג דאיכא קו"ח וא"כ אמאי התירו הגפנים נימא קו"ח ומה הבא לאסור ולא אסר נאסר דהיינו הזרעים האוסר בעצמו לא כ"ש וע"ז משני דלא אסורים רק מדרבנן ומש"ה התירו הגפנים דמאי דלא עבד איסורא לא קנסו רבנן כך נראה להשר וקצת קשה למורי שיחי' דכיון דלא בעי אלא מאי טעמא התירו הגפנים אמאי לא משני ליה דהגפנים מותרים דאין אדם אוסר דבר שאינו שלו והר"ר חיים כהן פי' בתמיה קנבוס ולוף ולא זרעים אחרים

ומפגל. וא"ת הא אין מפגלין בחצי מתיר וי"ל דסבר כר"מ דאמר מפגלין א"נ אפי' כרבנן ומפגל ... ר"ל מפסל דאפילו למ"ד אין מפגלין בחצי מתיר פסול מיהא הוי. תו"ח: ט] שחט כו' ... מהכא דלמא סבר אין מפגלין בחצי מתיר וי"ל כיון דר"מ תני ברישא אתיא הך סיפא כותיה א... ניחא דמ"מ תפסול ואיך קאמר שניהם כשרים ממש דאי אתיא אפי' כמ"ד אין מפגלין ... י] לשון תוס' אחרות אלמא חבירו כו' מדקתני שניהם כשרים ולא פליג ר"מ כמו בהנך בב... אתיא כרבנן מוכח שפיר דחבירו כבש משמע ומש"ה כשרים דאי הוי משמע לחם פסול ... כשר ממש ע"כ: יא] הזבח. עי' תוס' דזבחים (דף קיט ע"א): יב] והנסכים אינן: יג] ונסכיו מ... א"ל נמחק: טו] מתירו לבהונות ה"ה דהוי מצי למימר למתן שבע. תו"ח: טז] ת... יז] לאשם מצורע אחר: יח] הוקבעו בשחיטה כלחמי תודה. עי' תוס' (לקמן דף לז ע"א): ... כ] דמצטרפין הן: כא] לא פשיטא לרב ותיבת ליה נמחק: כב] פגול דגמרינן ... כג] ונסכיהם בלילה מנחתם ונסכיהם אפילו: כד] לשנותן לענין זבח אחר ואין לומר ל... דאין הסוגיא משמע כן: כה] וערבה א) אמר ר"י ובשבת בצלוחית של זהב שאינה מקודשת ... כו] בפני עצמן מיהו ההיא דלולב וערבה משמע דאין חילוק:

שיטה מקובצת

הא ודאי הכל יודעים דאורייתא ומיהו אין אדם אוסר דבר שאינו שלו מן התורה משום דכתיב (כרמי) [כרמך] שלו ולא של חבירו ולא הוי איסור אלא קנסא בעלמא. תו"ח: ה] האי דעבד איסורא כו' דלא עבד איסורא כו' אלא הכא לימא כו': ו] רבנן אלא הכא לימא: ז] רבה זוטי בעי תיבות ר' אבא נמחק: ח] או דלמא לחם משמע

א) אולי צ"ל על הא דתנן שם ובשבת בצלוחית כו' מקודשת קאמר זעירא גופיה כו'.

הגהות צ"ק [א] הג"ק הגיה דצ"ל שאינן עושין אלא לשלש שנים ועי' כמו שהגיה כך איתא במשנה ה פ"ב דכלאים: [ב] דאין: [ג] דלא עביד איסורא בעל הכרם הס"ד אח"כ ד"ה אלא כו': [ד] דמצטרפין הן כו': [ה] פיגול הס"ד ואח"כ מ"ה משקדשו בכלי דשוב כו': [ו] והתם מסיק: [ז] נ"א דהתם כר"מ ורב חסדא סתמא ככולי עלמא וכדמפרש טעמא כו' הוא וא"ת מאי כו' ליה אדרבנן דהכא כו': [ח] נ"א נראה דאיירי כו':

רַבָּנַן סָבְרִי: *הַצִּיץ מְרַצֶּה עַל אֲכִילוֹת, וְרַבִּי יְהוּדָה סָבַר: א] אֵין הַצִּיץ מְרַצֶּה עַל אֲכִילוֹת. א"ל רַב הוּנָא בְּרֵיהּ דְּרַב נָתָן לְרַב פַּפָּא: וְהָא עוֹלִין, דְּהַצִּיץ מְרַצֶּה עַל הָעוֹלִין, וּפְלִיגִי! דְּתַנְיָא: נִטְמָא אֶחָד מִן הַבָּזִיכִין — רַבִּי יְהוּדָה אוֹמֵר: ב] שְׁנֵיהֶם יֵעָשׂוּ בְּטוּמְאָה, לְפִי שֶׁאֵין קָרְבַּן צִיבּוּר חָלוּק; וַחֲכָמִים אוֹמְרִים: הַטָּמֵא בְּטוּמְאָתוֹ וְהַטָּהוֹר בְּטׇהֳרָתוֹ! וְעוֹד אָמַר רַב אַשִׁי: ת"ש, *ר' יְהוּדָה אוֹמֵר: ג] אֲפִילּוּ שֵׁבֶט אֶחָד טָמֵא וְכׇל הַשְּׁבָטִים טְהוֹרִין — יֵעָשׂוּ בְּטוּמְאָה, לְפִי שֶׁאֵין ד] קׇרְבְּנוֹת צִיבּוּר חָלוּק; ה] וְהָכָא מַאי הַצִּיץ מְרַצֶּה אִיכָּא? וְעוֹד הָאָמַר רָבִינָא: ת"ש, נִטְמֵאת אַחַת מִן הַחַלּוֹת אוֹ אַחַת מִן הַסְּדָרִין — רַבִּי יְהוּדָה אוֹמֵר: שְׁנֵיהֶם יֵצְאוּ לְבֵית הַשְּׂרֵיפָה, לְפִי שֶׁאֵין קׇרְבַּן צִיבּוּר חָלוּק, וַחֲכָמִים אוֹמְרִים: הַטָּמֵא בְּטוּמְאָתוֹ וְהַטָּהוֹר יֵאָכֵל; וְאִם אִיתָא, "לְפִי שֶׁאֵין הַצִּיץ מְרַצֶּה עַל אֲכִילוֹת" מִיבָּעֵי לֵיהּ! אֶלָּא א"ר יוֹחָנָן: ו] תַּלְמוּד עָרוּךְ הוּא בְּפִיו שֶׁל רַבִּי יְהוּדָה, שֶׁאֵין קׇרְבַּן צִיבּוּר חָלוּק.§ **מתני'** הַתּוֹדָה [א]מְפַגֶּלֶת אֶת הַלֶּחֶם, וְהַלֶּחֶם אֵינוֹ מְפַגֵּל אֶת הַתּוֹדָה. כֵּיצַד? שָׁחַט אֶת הַתּוֹדָה לֶאֱכוֹל מִמֶּנָּה לְמָחָר — הִיא וְהַלֶּחֶם מְפוּגָּלִין; לֶאֱכוֹל מִן הַלֶּחֶם לְמָחָר — הַלֶּחֶם מְפוּגָּל וְהַתּוֹדָה אֵינָהּ מְפוּגֶּלֶת. [ב]הַכְּבָשִׂים מְפַגְּלִין אֶת הַלֶּחֶם, וְהַלֶּחֶם אֵינוֹ מְפַגֵּל אֶת הַכְּבָשִׂים. כֵּיצַד? הַשּׁוֹחֵט אֶת הַכְּבָשִׂים לֶאֱכוֹל מֵהֶן לְמָחָר — הֵם וְהַלֶּחֶם מְפוּגָּלִין, לֶאֱכוֹל אֶת הַלֶּחֶם לְמָחָר — הַלֶּחֶם מְפוּגָּל וְהַכְּבָשִׂים אֵינָן מְפוּגָּלִין.§ **גמ'** מ"ט? אִילֵימָא מִשּׁוּם דְּרַב כָּהֲנָא, *דְּאָמַר רַב כָּהֲנָא: מִנַּיִן לְלַחְמֵי תוֹדָה שֶׁנִּקְרְאוּ תּוֹדָה? שֶׁנֶּאֱמַר: °"וְהִקְרִיב עַל זֶבַח הַתּוֹדָה חַלּוֹת", אִי הָכִי אִיפְּכָא נַמִי! הָא לָא קַשְׁיָא, לֶחֶם אִיקְּרֵי תּוֹדָה,(א) תּוֹדָה לָא אִיקְּרֵי לֶחֶם. אֶלָּא הָא דְּקָתָנֵי: הַכְּבָשִׂים מְפַגְּלִין אֶת הַלֶּחֶם וְהַלֶּחֶם אֵינוֹ מְפַגֵּל אֶת הַכְּבָשִׂים, לֶחֶם הֵיכָא אַשְׁכַּחַן דְּאִיקְּרֵי כְּבָשִׂים? אֶלָּא (לָאו) הַיְינוּ טַעְמָא: לֶחֶם גְּלָל תּוֹדָה וְאֵין תּוֹדָה גְּלָל ז] דְּלֶחֶם, לֶחֶם גְּלָל ח] דִּכְבָשִׂים וְאֵין כְּבָשִׂים גְּלָל דְּלֶחֶם. וּצְרִיכִי, דְּאִי אַשְׁמְעִינַן תּוֹדָה — הָתָם הוּא דְּכִי מְפַגֵּל בְּלֶחֶם לָא מִפַּגְּלָא תּוֹדָה, מִשּׁוּם דְּלָא הוּזְקְקוּ זֶה לָזֶה בִּתְנוּפָה, אֲבָל כְּבָשִׂים דְּהוּזְקְקוּ זֶה לָזֶה בִּתְנוּפָה, אֵימָא כִּי מְפַגֵּל בַּלֶּחֶם לִיפַּגְּלִי נַמִי כְּבָשִׂים, צְרִיכָא.§ בְּעָא מִינֵּיהּ ר"א מֵרַב: הַשּׁוֹחֵט אֶת הַתּוֹדָה לֶאֱכוֹל כְּזַיִת מִמֶּנָּה וּמִלַּחְמָהּ לְמָחָר, מַהוּ? לְאִיפַּגּוּלֵי תּוֹדָה לָא מִיבַּעְיָא לִי; הַשְׁתָּא כּוּלּוֹ מִלַּחְמָהּ לָא מִיפַּגְּלָא, ט] מִמֶּנָּה וּמִלַּחְמָהּ מִיבַּעְיָא? כִּי קָא מִיבַּעְיָא לִי — לְאִיפַּגּוּלֵי לֶחֶם, מִי מִצְטָרְפָה תּוֹדָה לְאִיפַּגּוּלֵי לַלֶּחֶם אוֹ לָא? אֲמַר לֵיהּ: אַף בְּזוֹ, הַלֶּחֶם מְפוּגָּל וְהַתּוֹדָה אֵינָהּ מְפוּגֶּלֶת. וְאַמַּאי? לֵימָא קַל וָחוֹמֶר: וּמָה י] (תּוֹדָה) הַמְפַגֵּל — אֵין מִתְפַּגֵּל, הַבָּא לְפַגֵּל וְלֹא פִּיגֵּל — אֵינוֹ דִּין שֶׁלֹּא יִתְפַּגֵּל? וּמִי אָמְרִינַן קַל וָחוֹמֶר כִּי הַאי גַּוְונָא? וְהָתַנְיָא: מַעֲשֶׂה בְּאֶחָד שֶׁזָּרַע

רש"י

רַבָּנַן סָבְרִי הַצִּיץ מְרַצֶּה. עַל טוּמְאַת אֲכִילַת כֹּהֲנִים, לְמֶיהֱוֵי זְרִיקָה שֶׁנִּזְרְקָה יא] עֲלֵיהֶן זְרִיקָה מַעַלְיָיתָא. וּמִיהוּ, כִּי מְרַצֶּה צִיץ — לְמֶיהֱוֵי קׇרְבָּן מְעַלְּיָא, אֲבָל טָמֵא לָא מִישְׁתְּרֵי בַּאֲכִילָה, דְּעָבַר יב] לֵיהּ בְּלָאו מִ"וְהַבָּשָׂר אֲשֶׁר יִגַּע בְּכׇל טָמֵא לֹא יֵאָכֵל" (ויקרא ז). וְר' יְהוּדָה סָבַר אֵין הַצִּיץ מְרַצֶּה. יג] בְּטוּמְאָה שֶׁנָּגְעָה בְּדָבָר הַנֶּאֱכָל לַכֹּהֲנִים. הִלְכָּךְ לָא הָוֵי זְרִיקָה מַעַלְּיָא, וְלָא מִישְׁתְּרֵי טָהוֹר. וְהָא עוֹלִין. דְּדִ"ה צִיץ מְרַצֶּה עַל טוּמְאָה שֶׁנָּגַע בָּעוֹלִין לַמִּזְבֵּחַ. בָּזִיכִין. הָווּ עוֹלִין. יֵעָשׂוּ בַּמִּזְבֵּחַ בְּטוּמְאָה. יד] יַגִּיעַם זֶה לָזֶה אִם יִרְצֶה. שֶׁאֵין קׇרְבַּן צִיבּוּר חָלוּק. וַאֲפִי' טו] *אִי מַגִּיעוּ בִּשְׁנֵיהֶם — טְמֵאִים, וְקׇרְבַּן לְצִבּוּר דּוֹחֶה טוּמְאָה בְּפֶרֶק "כֵּיצַד צוֹלִין" (פסחים פ.). וְאַמַּאי לָא הָוֵי טָהוֹר בְּטׇהֳרָתוֹ? הָא צִיץ מְרַצֶּה עַל הָעוֹלִין, וְהָוְיָא הַקְטָרָה מַעַלְיָיתָא, וְאָסוּר לְטַמֵּא אֶת הַטָּהוֹר! שֵׁבֶט אֶחָד טָמֵא. בְּי"ד בְּנִיסָן. וּס"ל לְרַבִּי יְהוּדָה: שֵׁבֶט אֶחָד אִיקְּרֵי קָהָל, הִלְכָּךְ דּוֹחֶה טוּמְאָה, וְיַעֲשׂוּ כּוּלָּן בְּטוּמְאָה עִמּוֹ. לְפִי שֶׁאֵין קׇרְבַּן צִיבּוּר חָלוּק. וּלְדִבְרֵי חֲכָמִים, טְהוֹרִים עוֹשִׂים הָרִאשׁוֹן, וְהַשֵּׁבֶט עוֹשִׂין פֶּסַח שֵׁנִי טז]. רַבִּי יְהוּדָה לָמוּד עָרוּךְ. שֶׁשְּׁנָאָהּ מֵרַבּוֹתָיו. **מתני'** וְהַתּוֹדָה אֵינָהּ מְפוּגֶּלֶת. וְהָאוֹכְלָהּ אֵין עָנוּשׁ כָּרֵת. **גמ'** מ"ט. הַתּוֹדָה מְפַגֶּלֶת (ב) *לֶחֶם? מִדַּהֲוָה לֵיהּ לְמִיכְתַּב "וְהִקְרִיב חַלּוֹת עַל זֶבַח הַתּוֹדָה", וּכְתִיב: "וְהִקְרִיב עַל זֶבַח הַתּוֹדָה חַלּוֹת" יז] (תּוֹדַת שְׁלָמָיו) דְּמַשְׁמַע: תּוֹדָה הֵם הַחַלּוֹת, הִלְכָּךְ כִּי אָמַר "עַל מְנָת לֶאֱכוֹל תּוֹדָה לְמָחָר" — הָוֵי לֶחֶם בִּכְלָל. אֲבָל תּוֹדָה. הַבְּהֵמָה לָא אִיקְּרֵי לֶחֶם, הִלְכָּךְ כִּי מְפַגֵּל לֶחֶם — לָא הָוְיָא יח] בְּהֵמָה בִּכְלָל. הַכְּבָשִׂים. שֶׁל עֲצֶרֶת. לֶחֶם גְּלָל תּוֹדָה. תּוֹדָה עִיקָּר וְלֶחֶם טָפֵל, דִּשְׁחִיטַת תּוֹדָה יט] מְקַדְּשָׁה לַלֶּחֶם, כִּדְאָמְרִינַן בְּפֶ' "הַתּוֹדָה" (לקמן עח:): כ] "יַקְרִיב קׇרְבָּנוֹ" — מְלַמֵּד שֶׁאֵין הַלֶּחֶם קָדוֹשׁ אֶלָּא בִּשְׁחִיטַת הַזֶּבַח. וְכֵן לֶחֶם גְּלָל כְּבָשִׂים, דִּשְׁחִיטַת כְּבָשִׂים מְקַדְּשִׁים לַלֶּחֶם בְּפֶ' "הַתְּכֵלֶת" (לקמן מו.). כא] תּוֹדָה אֵין מְנִיפִין אוֹתָהּ עִם הַחַלּוֹת, אֲבָל כְּבָשִׂים מְנִיפִין אוֹתָם עִם הַחַלּוֹת, דִּכְתִיב (ויקרא כג): "וְהֵנִיף כב] אוֹתָם", וּכְתִיב: "עַל לֶחֶם" וגו'. זֶה לָזֶה. כְּבָשִׂים עִם לֶחֶם. אֵימָא כו'. וְהוּא הַדִּין אִי תָּנָא כְּבָשִׂים הֲוָה אָמֵינָא: הָתָם כִּי מְפַגְּלִי כְּבָשִׂים כג] מְפַגְּלִי חַלּוֹת, *צְרִיכָא. מִמֶּנָּה וּמִלַּחְמָהּ. כַּחֲצִי זַיִת מִזֶּה וְכֵן מִזֶּה. הַשְׁתָּא זַיִת כּוּלּוֹ מִלֶּחֶם. דְּהָוְיָא מַחֲשָׁבָה כד] חֲמוּרָה דְּלָא בָּעְיָא צֵירוּף, אָמְרִינַן בְּמַתְנִיתִין דְּלָא מִיפַּגֵּל *תּוֹדָה, מִמֶּנָּה וּמִלַּחְמָהּ דְּבָעֵי לְצָרוּפֵי מִיבַּעְיָא? כה] אוֹ לָא. פַּגְּלֵי לֶחֶם, *דְּשַׁיֵּיר בְּמַחֲשָׁבָה. תּוֹדָה הַמְפַגֵּל. תּוֹדָה שֶׁסִּיְּיעָה לְפַגֵּל לֶחֶם — אֵין מִתְפַּגֵּל, כִּדְקָאָמְרִינַן: הַתּוֹדָה אֵינָהּ מְפוּגֶּלֶת. הַבָּא לְפַגֵּל. חֲצִי זַיִת שֶׁל לֶחֶם, הַבָּא לְפַגֵּל כו] גַּם אֶת הַתּוֹדָה וְלֹא פִּגְּלָהּוּ, אֵינוֹ דִּין שֶׁלֹּא יִתְפַּגֵּל? שֶׁזָּרַע

תוספות

רבנן סברי הציץ מרצה על אכילות. לא למישרייה לטמא באכילה, כז] אלא לענין דלא הוי האי טמא כאבוד ושרוף, אלא חשוב כטהור לענין דשריא זריקה לאידך דטהור גמור. **ורבי** יהודה סבר אין הציץ מרצה. והוה ליה האי טמא כאבוד ושרוף, ולא מהניא זריקה כח] לטהור. אע"ג דרבי יהודה ס"ל בפ' "כיצד צולין" (פסחים עז.): טומאה הותרה בציבור, ולא מיבעי ציץ לרצוי. *דמאי דהתר הוא בציבור לא מהניא להאי טמא למישרייה באכילה – הוא הדין נמי דלא מהניא למישרייה לטהור, *דלענין היתר אכילה לא מהניא, ולא הויא כרילוי ציץ. ולמ"ד מרצה – מהניא לטהור ולא מהניא לטמא. **והא** עולין דציץ מרצה כו'. ואפי' למ"ד בפ' "כיצד צולין" (שם עז:): אין הציץ מרצה על העולים – הנ"מ ביחיד, אבל בציבור מודה דציץ מרצה על העולין. **ופליגי**. כט] משמע דאי משכח *תנאי דציץ מרצה על העולין הוה ניחא ליה. ולכאורה כ"ש דהוה קשה טפי, דרבי יהודה דאמר שניהם יעשו בטומאה קסבר דציץ מרצה על העולין, ומתניתין קסבר אין הציץ מרצה על אכילות. ורבנן דאמרי טמא בטומאתו וטהור בטהרתו קסברי אין הציץ מרצה על העולין, ובמתניתין קסברי הציץ מרצה על אכילות! **רבי** יהודה **אומר אפי'** שבט אחד טמא כו' שאין קרבן ציבור חלוק. אף על גב דרבי יהודה ס"ל בפ"ק דיומא (דף ז:) דטומאה הותרה בציבור, מ"מ איצטריך ליה טעמא דאין קרבן ציבור חלוק בפסח, כיון דיש ביה אכילה, כדמוכח התם. **והכא** מאי ציץ מרצה איכא. פי': הא אין הציץ מרצה על טומאת הגוף, כדפי' בקונט', ודריש לקמן ב"הקומץ רבה" (דף כה.): עון הקדשים הוא נושא ולא עון המקדישי'. ובפרק שני דזבחים (דף כג.) נמי אמרינן בהדיא דאין הציץ מרצה על טומאת הגוף. והא דאמר בפ' "כיצד צולין" (פסחים עז.) דלמ"ד טומאה דחויה בעיא ציץ לרצויי – היינו לטומאת בשר דמהני ציץ, אבל לטומאת הגוף דלא מהני ציץ – אפי' בלא ציץ. **מנין** ללחמי תודה כו'. לקמן בפ' "התודה" (דף פ.) עיקר מילתא. **לחם** איקרי תודה תודה לא איקרי לחם. מהאי טעמא מיתרצא מה שמקשים *בפ' "הערל" (יבמות עג:) דיש במעשר וביכורי' מש"כ בתרומה: מ"ט דלא ילפינן (*ביכורים מתרומה) אע"ג דאיתקוש, דדרשינן (פסחים לו:): "ותרומת ידך" אלו הביכורים. דביכורים איקרו תרומה, תרומה לא איקריא ביכורים. והא דמקיש להו בפרק "העור והרוטב" (חולין קכ:), התם אסמכתא בעלמא אמר*). **המפגל** אין מתפגל כו'. פירוש: אותו שאתה ר"ל שהוא מפגל אתה מודה שאין מתפגל. ובריש מכות (דף ב.) רוצה לומר ק"ו כי האי גוונא גבי "מעידין אנו באיש פלוני שהוא בן גרושה" ונמצאו זוממין, דאין אומרים: יעשה זה בן גרושה תחתיו, משום דאמרינן ק"ו: ומה המחלל אין מתחלל, בא לחלל ולא חילל – אינו דין שלא יתחלל? ופריך רבינא: א"כ ביטלת תורת עדים זוממין, ומה הסוקל אינו נסקל, הבא לסקול ולא סקל – אינו דין שלא יסקל? ואע"ג דהכא מתקיים הק"ו, לענין עדים זוממין שאני, משום טעמא דא"כ ביטלת תורת עדים זוממין. ומה הסוקל כו' פי': משום דקים לן הרגו אין נהרגין, משום דדרשינן: "כאשר זמם" ולא כאשר עשה. כך פי' בקונט'. וקשה: א"כ אמאי נקט סקילה יותר משאר מיתות? ומפרש ר"ת: ומה הסוקל אינו נסקל – דרוצה לעולם בסייף, אפי' הרג את חבירו באבן. ועוד נראה דק"ו דהכא לא דמי להתם, (*) דהא לפגל הכא היינו לחם, שבא לפגל חצי זית של תודה ע"י שיצטרף לפוסלה, ולא פיגל – שאינו מצטרף לפוסלה, אינו דין

*) [ועי' תוס' יבמות עג: ד"ה טעונין]

(*) ק"ו דהכא ל"ק

עין משפט נר מצוה

יג א מיי' פ"ז מהלכות פסה"מ הלכה ז:

יד ב מיי' שם הלכה ח:

מסורת הש"ס

[פסחים עז.]

נ"א אין מגיעו בשני שניהם טמאים ל"ק

[שם פ. הוריות ה.]

לקמן פ:

ל"ק מ"ז

ויקרא ז

נ"א דסייע

דמאי דהותרה בצבור ל"ק

וכיון דלענין כו' מהני לא הויא כו' ל"ק

תנא דאין הציץ כו' ל"ק

ל"ק

ל"ק בפרק א' דמנחות

ל"ק ביכורים מתרומה

ס"א אינו

[משום דהוזקקו זה עם זה בתנופה אבל תודה דלא הוזקקו אימא כי מפגל בתודה לא מפגל בחלות צריכא]

[תודה הס"ד ואח"כ מה"ד ממנה כו' מיבעיא הס"ד ואח"כ מה"ד לאיפגולי ללחם דשייך במחשבת תודה והס"ד כנ"ל ל"ק]

הגהות הב"ח

(א) גמ' לחם איקרי תודה ולאכל תודה: (ב) רש"י ד"ה מ"ט וכו' לחם הס"ד ואח"כ מ"ה והקריב וגו' מלחוה ליה:

שיטה מקובצת

איכא פ"ה שהרי אין הציץ מרצה על טומאת גברא וא"ת אפי' יהיה הציץ מרצה מאי פריך ואמאי יעשו הטהורים בטומאה וכי מותר לטמא הטהור אלא נ"ל דהכי פריך מאי ציץ מרצה שייך כאן שהרי פסח אינו מרצה בריצוי ציץ וא"כ ע"כ טעמא דר"י לאו משום דציץ מרצה אלא משום דאין קרבן צבור חלוק כדמפרש ואזיל ר' יוחנן. תו"ח: ו] תלמוד ערוך: ז] גלל לחם: ח] לחם גלל כבשים ואין כבשים גלל לחם: ט] ממנה ומלחמה מבעיא. קצת קשה דאין זה קו"ח דלמא ממנה ומלחמה עדיף מכולו לחם כדאשכחן לעיל גבי שתי יריכות דאין בו כרת עד שיתפגל בשתיהן בכזית וכולו מאחת לא נתפגלה. תו"ח: י] ומה המפגל אין מתפגל כו'. תימה אמאי לא מקשה כמו כן במתניתין דתודה מפגל את הלחם כו' ומה תודה המפגל אינו מתפגל הבא לפגל ולא פגל דהיינו לחם אינו דין שלא יתפגל וי"ל דלפ"ה ניחא דפי' ומה המתפגל שבא לסייע לפגל אבל בתודה דמתניתין אין הלחם מסייע ליה שהרי היא עצמה לבד מתפגל עכ"ל תו"ח. ובתוס' אחרות תירצו בלשון זה וי"ל דהכי פריך אינו דין שלא יתפגל בצירוף המפגל אחרי שלא נתפגל אבל במתניתין אין התודה צריכה לצירוף הלחם ואין לומר מקו"ח עכ"ל עוד כתוב ומה המפגל אינו מתפגל וא"ת סוף הקו"ח סותר את תחלתו דאם אינו מתפגל הלחם מה הזבח מפגל וי"ל דפריך למסקנא כלומר לדבריך שאתה אומר הלחם מפוגל וכיוצא בו לעיל גבי טרפה. תו"ח: יא] שנזרקה עליה: יב] דעבר עליה בלאו והבשר: יג] על טומאה שנגעה: יד] בטומאה יגיעם זה: טו] ואפילו אין מגיען בשניהן: טז] פסח שני הס"ד ומה"ד הכא מאי ריצוי ציץ איכא הא אין

שיטה מקובצת

א] אין הציץ מרצה. הקשה ה"ר שמואל מאייורא ז"ל דא"כ איך הכבשים מותרים באכילה דהא אמרינן לקמן דאם אבד מן החלות אבדו הכבשים והכא משמע דהכבשים מותר באכילה דהא לא פליגי אלא בחלות אבל בכבשים מודו דנאכלים וצריך עיון ע"כ: ב] שניהם יעשו בטומאה. וה"ה אפילו אין ציץ מרצה הוה מצי פריך שהרי בלי ריצוי ציץ טומאה הותרה בצבור ויהודה ...

והוה הקטרה מעליא אלא ה"ק כלומר הכא לא שייך למימר טעמא דר' יהודה משום ... ציץ מרצה על טומאת הגוף כגון הך טומאה דשבט הס"ד ומה"ד תלמוד ערוך ותיבות ר' יהודה נמחק: ... כי מפגל לחם תפגל תודה הס"ד ומה"ד לחם איקרי תודה ... [illegible]

א) נראה דצ"ל לאפגולי לחם דשייך במחשבת תודה קא מבעיא כו'.

י א מיי' פי"ז מהלכות פסה"מ הלכה יב:
יא ב ג מיי' פי"ד מהל' פסה"מ הלכה י:
יב ד מיי' פ"ה מהלכות תמידין ומוספין הל' טז:

מיפגלי. בשר. הכא. פיגל בירך ימין, דחשיב בבשר גופיה. ד] כ"ש. דמיפגלא אף של שמאל. *לאיפגולי מאי. כלומר, מי יתפגל במחשבה זו שיהיו חייבין כרת באכילתו? אלא א"ר יוחנן. ליתא לרב הונא, ואם פיגל בימין – פיגל בשמאל, דהא חזינן אפי' לא חישב אלא בדם נתפגל בשר. וגבי חלות ה"ט דרבי יוסי, דאמר במתניתין ה] דתרי גופי נינהו, ואם פיגל בזו לא נתפגלה זו, ולעיל קתני: בשתיהן בכזית, דמשמע מדמצטרפות דחד גופא נינהו. הכתוב עשאן גוף אחד והכתוב עשאן ב' גופין. הכתוב עשאן גוף אחד דמעכבי אהדדי, דאין זו כשרה בלא זו, דכתיב (ויקרא כג): "שתים שני עשרונים" דמשמע: שתים ולא אחת, וכתיב (שם): "סלת תהיינה", וכל הויה עיכובא. ואותו כתוב עצמו עשאן שני גופים, מדכתיב "שתים", דמשמע דכל אחת לישתה ועריכתה בפני עצמה. הלכך, ערבינהו – דאמר כזית בין שתיהן – מתערבין ומצטרפין, דהכתוב עשאן גוף אחד. פלגינהו. דאמר: ע"מ לאכול מן האחת, ולא עירב חבירתה עמה. מפלגי. ואין חבירתה פיגול, ו] דהרי הכתוב עשאן שני גופים. יש לשונות אחרים בהלכה זו, אבל זו עיקר. פיגל בלחמי תודה. שהן ארבעה מינים, ופיגל באחד מן המינים, מי פליגי רבי יוסי ורבנן בהא אם נתפגלו האחרים או לא? מי אמרינן: כיון דזבח אחד מתירן – כחד דמיין, או דלמא: כיון דלאו חד מינא הוא, פליג רבי יוסי? במנחת מאפה. שיש בה שני מינין, ה' חלות וה' רקיקין, כדאמר בפרק ז] *"התודה" (לקמן דף מז), ואליבא דר"ש קנסיב ח] להו, מהו? מי אמר: הואיל וקומץ אחד לשניהם – לא פליג רבי יוסי, ואם פיגל בחלות נתפגלו רקיקין, או דלמא: כיון דשני מינין ט] פליג? וכן אתה אומר. דהכא נמי פליג. בשעת שחיטה כו'. אפתם זבח *קאי. שחיטה וזריקה מתירין נינהו, י] שחיטה קדשה לדם, כדאמר בשילהי פירקין (דף טז:), ואמר התם: הבא לקדש כבא להתיר דמי, וזריקה מתרת הבשר. קבלה והולכה. דלאו מתירין נינהו לא מצטרפין, דקבלה אינה מתרת, דאינה אלא לצורך (א) זריקה. שחיטה וזריקה מרחקי אהדדי ומצטרפין, וכ"ש קבלה והולכה דמקרבן. אין מצטרפין. שתים מהן כיחד, אם חישב בזו על חצי זית ובזו על חצי זית. הא רבי הא רבנן. הא דתני: אין מצטרפות – רבי היא. חצי מתיר וחצי אכילה. כגון כבש הוי חצי מתיר, ולא חישב עליו אלא בחצי אכילה. כולו מתיר וחצי אכילה. כגון שחיטה דכולו מתיר בדם, וזריקה דכולו מתיר בבשר. מי שמעת ליה. דאם חישב בזו בחצי זית ובזו בחצי זית דאין מצטרפין? ואי אית ליה לרבי כולו מתיר וחצי אכילה. מצטרפין לפיגול. ליגזר חצי מתיר וחצי אכילה. דליפסול, אטו כולו מתיר וחצי אכילה, דכרת הוא! דהא רבי יוסי גזר. במתני' (לעיל דף יג.) בהקומץ את המנחה ע"מ להקטיר לבונתה למחר, ואמר: פסול, ואע"ג דאין בו פיגול, דגזר ליה אטו פיגול. ורבנן. נמי במתניתין דקתני: פיגל בהקטרת קומץ ע"מ לאכול שיריים למחר, ולא פיגל בהקטרת לבונה. ר"מ אומר פיגול. הן השיריים, דאית ליה מפגלין בשעת עבודת חצי מתיר. וחכ"א אין בו כרת כו'. כרת הוא דליכא, אבל פסול הוא מלאכול, דגזרינן אטו כרת. ורבי אומר לעיל (עמוד א) בהדיא כשר! קומץ דלבונה אטו הקטרת קומץ דמנחה. דדמו להדדי, ובקומץ ע"מ להקטיר קומצה למחר מודה רבי יוסי דפיגול הוא. ורבנן נמי יא] דגזרי. דתפסול מנחה במחשב בשיריים בשעת הקטרת קומץ יב]. דמנחת חוטא. דהתם עבודה שלימה היא ומפגלת. לבונה. נמי מחשב אשירים בשעת הקטרת לבונה, יג]ה"ט דפסלי רבנן למנחה – גזרה אטו מחשב בהקטרת לבונה בבזיכין, דהתם פיגול גמור הוא, שאין הקטרה אלא היא. כבש יד]. דאמרי רבנן במתני': שחט אחד מן הכבשים לאכול ב' חלות למחר, או הקטיר אחד מן הבזיכין לאכול שני סדרים למחר, דקאמרי רבנן אין בו כרת, הא פסול איכא, דגזרי חד כבש אטו כבש חבירו, שלא ישחוט שניהם במחשבה, דהתם פיגל בכל המתיר. וכן בבזיכין. כולהו הנך גזירות טו] דאיכא בעלמא דדמי להו הוי פיגול. אבל הכא. בחצי מתיר וחצי אכילה דרבי, מי איכא חצי מתיר וחצי אכילה בעלמא פיגול, דנגזור הכא אטו התם? מש"ה הוא. דמשכחי פיגול דדמי להו. דקתני סיפא. דמתני' דפיגל בקומץ ולא בלבונה: מודים חכמים כו' שאם טז] חישב בקומץ או בהקטרת קומץ – פיגל בשירים. הא קא משמע לן. דטעמא דפסלי רבנן במחשב בשעת הקטרת קומץ דמנחת נדבה משום הכי הוא, דאיכא יז] דמנחת חוטא דדמי ליה, שהם מודים שהוא פיגול. מתני' שאין קרבן ציבור חלוק. הכי מסקנא דגמרא: תלמוד ערוך יח] בפיו של רבי יהודה שמנחה מרבותיו, שאין קרבן ליבור חלוק, ואם נפסל חצי נפסל כולו. יט] גמ' לפני זריקה. נטמאת אחת מן החלות של עצרת, ובלחם הפנים לפני הקטרת בזיכין. כ] אבל לאחר זריקה. דזריקה מעלייתא הוא (הואי) דברי הכל כו'. רבנן

מיפגלי, הכא דחשיב בהו בזביחה גופה לא כ"ש? אלא א"ר יוחנן, ה"ט דרבי יוסי: הכתוב עשאן גוף אחד והכתוב עשאן שני גופין, גוף אחד — דמעכבי אהדדי, שני גופין — דאמר רחמנא: הא לחודה עבידא והא לחודה עבידא; ערבינהו — מתערבין, דהכתוב עשאן גוף אחד, פלגינהו — מיפלגי, דהכתוב עשאן שני גופין. בעי רבי יוחנן: פיגל בלחמי תודה, מהו? א] במנחת מאפה, מהו? תנא ליה רב תחליפא ב] ממערבא: אוכן אתה אומר בלחמי תודה, וכן אתה אומר במנחת מאפה. ת"ר: *בבשעת שחיטה חישב לאכול חצי זית ובשעת זריקה חישב לאכול חצי זית — פיגול, מפני ששחיטה וזריקה מצטרפין. איכא דאמרי: שחיטה וזריקה דתרוייהו מתירין — אין, קבלה והולכה — לא; ואיכא דאמרי: הנך דמרחקן, וכ"ש גהני דמקרבן. איני? והא תני לוי, ארבע עבודות אין מצטרפות לפיגול: שחיטה וזריקה, קבלה והולכה! אמר רבא, ל"ק: הא רבי, הא רבנן; דתניא: השוחט את הכבש לאכול חצי זית מחלה זו, וכן חבירו לאכול חצי זית מחלה זו — רבי אומר: אני אומר שזה כשר. א"ל אביי: אימר דשמעת ליה לרבי חצי מתיר וחצי אכילה, כולו מתיר וחצי אכילה מי שמעת ליה? א"ל רבא בר רב חנן לאביי: ואי אית ליה לרבי כולו מתיר וחצי אכילה, לגזור חצי מתיר וחצי אכילה אטו כולו מתיר וחצי אכילה, דהא רבי יוסי גזר ורבנן גזרי; ר' יוסי גזר, דתנן: להקטיר לבונתה למחר — רבי יוסי אומר: פסול ואין בו כרת, וחכ"א: פיגול וחייבין עליה כרת; ורבנן נמי גזרי, *דתנן: פיגל בקומץ ולא בלבונה, בלבונה ולא בקומץ — ר"מ אומר: פיגול וחייבין עליו כרת, וחכ"א: אין בו כרת עד שיפגל בכל המתיר! א"ל: הכי השתא? בשלמא התם גזר רבי יוסי קומץ דלבונה — אטו קומץ דמנחה, רבנן גזרי קומץ — אטו קומץ דמנחת חוטא, ולבונה — אטו לבונה הבאה בבזיכין, ג] כבשים נמי — כבש אטו כבש חבירו, בזך — אטו בזך חבירו. אלא הכא, מי איכא חצי מתיר וחצי אכילה בעלמא, דליקום וליגזר? הכי נמי מסתברא דטעמא דרבנן מש"ה הוא, דקתני סיפא: מודים חכמים לר"מ במנחת חוטא ומנחת קנאות, שאם פיגל בקומץ — שפיגול וחייבין עליה כרת, שהקומץ הוא המתיר; הא למה לי למיתנא כלל? פשיטא, מי איכא מתיר אחרינא? אלא לאו הא קמ"ל, דטעמא דקומץ — משום דאיכא קומץ דמנחת חוטא דדמי ליה.§ **מתני'** *נטמאת אחת מן החלות או אחד מן הסדרים — רבי יהודה אומר: שניהם יצאו לבית השריפה, שאין קרבן ציבור חלוק. וחכמים אומרים: דהטמא בטומאתו, והטהור יאכל.§ **גמ'** א"ר אלעזר: מחלוקת לפני זריקה, אבל לאחר זריקה — דברי הכל הטמא בטומאתו והטהור יאכל. ולפני זריקה במאי פליגי? אמר רב פפא: בציץ מרצה על אכילות קא מיפלגי, רבנן

הכתוב עשאן גוף אחד. דכתיב (ויקרא כג): "תביאו לחם תנופה", והכתוב עשאן שני גופין – דכתיב (שם): "שתים שני עשרונים". וסדרים דלחם הפנים ילפינן משתי הלחם, אפי' למאן דלא יליף *מלתא ממלתא, דהכא דמו אהדדי טפי כא]. **פיגל** בלחמי תודה מהו. הוא הדין דהוה מצי למבעי ברקיקי נזיר שיש שני מינין. **שחיטה** וזריקה תרווייהו מתירין הן. פירש בקונטרס: שהשחיטה מקדשת את הדם, ואמרינן בסוף פירקין דבא לקדש כבא להתיר דמי. וא"ת: קבלה נמי מקדשת את הדם בכלי שרת! לאו פירכא היא, דדם סכין מקדשא ליה, כדאמרינן בסוף פירקין.

רבנן

שיטה מקובצת
א] במנחת מאפה מהו. גליון במנחת מאפה שהיה עושה מהם פתיתין ואח"כ קומצן מידו מי אמרינן כיון דקומץ לשניהם כחד דמי ומודה ר' יוסי או דלמא כיון דיש בה שני מינים רקיקין ורבוכה פליג ר' יוסי דאותה החלה שחישב עליה פיגול אם היא ניכרת ואם אינה ניכרת ספק כרת בכולן. תו"ח: ב] בר מערבא אות מ' נמחק: ג] בבזיכין כבש נמי אטו כבש חבירו: ד] מה"ד לא כ"ש: ה] במתניתין תרי גופי נינהו כו' לא נתפגל זו ולעיל קתני כו' דמצטרפות דחד גופא נינהו: ו] פיגול דהכתוב עשאן: ז] בפ' כל המנחות באות מצה. ס"א דכל המנחות באות עשר ומחבת ומרחשת עשר חלות ממין אחד וזו מנחת מאפה משני מינין אתו כו': ח] קנסיב לה דאמר מביא מחצה חלות ומחצה רקיקין: ט] מינין הויא פליג: י] דשחיטה מקדשה: יא] דגזרי דתפסל ואות ו' נמחק: יב] קומץ גזירה אטו מחשב בשעת הקטרת קומץ דמנחת: יג] לבונה וה"ט דפסלי כו' בהקטרת לבונה דבזיכין: יד] כבש נמי דאמרי: טו] משום דאיכא: טז] שאם פיגל בקומץ בהקטרת קומץ חישב בשירים ותיבות חישב בקומץ או בהקטרת קומץ פיגל בשירים נמחק: יז] דאיכא קומץ דמנחת: יח] ערוך הוא: יט] תיבות גמרא לפני זריקה נמחק: כ] מה"ד גמ' אבל כו': כא] טפי. ורש"י לא פירש כן:

הגהות הב"ח
(א) רש"י ד"ה קבלה וכו' זריקה הס"ד ואח"כ מ"ה הנך למרחקין שחיטה:

גליון הש"ס
תוס' ד"ה הכתוב וכו' מלתא ממלתא. לעיל דף ח ע"א:

מסורת הש"ס
שייך לע"א
תוספתא דזבחים פ"
(זבחים לא)
[כל המנחות דף סג.]
קאי הס"ד ל"ק
[לקמן טז.]
פסחים עט.
ל"ק מ"

אֶלָּא אִי אָמְרַתְּ תְּרֵי גוּפֵי נִינְהוּ, מִי מִיצְטָרְפִי? הָא מַנִּי? רַבִּי הִיא, דְּתַנְיָא: אהַשּׁוֹחֵט אֶת הַכֶּבֶשׂ לֶאֱכוֹל חֲצִי זַיִת מֵחַלָּה זוֹ וְכֵן חֲבֵירוֹ לֶאֱכוֹל חֲצִי זַיִת מֵחַלָּה זוֹ, *רַבִּי אוֹמֵר: אוֹמֵר אֲנִי שֶׁזֶּה כָּשֵׁר; טַעְמָא דְּאָמַר חֲצִי חֲצִי, אֲבָל אָמַר כְּזַיִת מִשְּׁתֵּיהֶן — מִצְטָרֵף. וְרַבִּי אַלִּיבָּא דְּמַאן? אִי אַלִּיבָּא דְּרַבָּנַן, אֲפִי' בְּאַחַת מֵהֶן נַמִי! (א) אִי אַלִּיבָּא דְּר' יוֹסֵי, הֲדָרָא קוּשְׁיַין לְדוּכְתֵּיהּ! לְעוֹלָם אַלִּיבָּא דְּרַבָּנַן, וְלָא תֵּימָא: עַד שֶׁיְּפַגֵּל בִּשְׁתֵּיהֶן, אֶלָּא: א] [אֵימָא עַד שֶׁיְּפַגֵּל] בִּשְׁנֵיהֶן, וַאֲפִילּוּ בְּאַחַת מֵהֶן; וּלְאַפּוֹקֵי מִדְּר' מֵאִיר *דְּאָמַר: מְפַגְּלִין בַּחֲצִי מַתִּיר, קמ"ל דְּלָא. אִי הָכִי, מַאי "לְעוֹלָם"? אִי אָמְרַתְּ בִּשְׁלָמָא בִּשְׁתֵּיהֶן וּבִשְׁנֵיהֶן וְרַבִּי יוֹסֵי הִיא, וּלְאַפּוֹקֵי מִדְּר"מ וּמִדְּרַבָּנַן קָאָתֵי — הַיְינוּ דְּקָאָמַר "לְעוֹלָם"; אֶלָּא אִי אָמְרַתְּ רַבָּנַן וּלְאַפּוֹקֵי מִדְּר"מ, ב] מַאי "לְעוֹלָם"? וְעוֹד, הָא אָמַר רַב אַשִׁי: ת"ש, *רַבִּי ג] אוֹמֵר מִשּׁוּם רַבִּי יוֹסֵי: ד] בפִּיגֵּל בְּדָבָר הַנַּעֲשֶׂה בַּחוּץ — פִּיגֵּל, גבְּדָבָר הַנַּעֲשֶׂה בִּפְנִים — לֹא פִּיגֵּל, כֵּיצַד? הָיָה עוֹמֵד בַּחוּץ, וְאָמַר: "הֲרֵינִי שׁוֹחֵט ע"מ לְהַזּוֹת מִדָּמוֹ לְמָחָר" — לֹא פִּיגֵּל, שֶׁמַּחֲשָׁבָה בַּחוּץ בְּדָבָר הַנַּעֲשֶׂה בִּפְנִים; הָיָה עוֹמֵד בִּפְנִים, וְאָמַר: "הֲרֵינִי מַזֶּה ע"מ לְהַקְטִיר אֵימוּרִין לְמָחָר וְלִשְׁפּוֹךְ שִׁירַיִים לְמָחָר" — לֹא פִּיגֵּל, שֶׁמַּחֲשָׁבָה בִּפְנִים בְּדָבָר הַנַּעֲשֶׂה בַּחוּץ; הָיָה עוֹמֵד בַּחוּץ, וְאָמַר: "הֲרֵינִי שׁוֹחֵט ע"מ לִשְׁפּוֹךְ שִׁירַיִים לְמָחָר וּלְהַקְטִיר אֵימוּרִין לְמָחָר" — פִּיגֵּל, שֶׁמַּחֲשָׁבָה בַּחוּץ בְּדָבָר הַנַּעֲשֶׂה בַּחוּץ. לִשְׁפּוֹךְ שִׁירַיִים לְאִיפַּגּוּלֵי מַאי? אִילֵימָא לְאִיפַּגּוּלֵי דָּם, דָּם מִי מִיפַּגַּל? וְהָתְנַן, *דאֵלּוּ דְּבָרִים שֶׁאֵין חַיָּיבִין עֲלֵיהֶן מִשּׁוּם פִּיגּוּל: הַקּוֹמֶץ, וְהַלְּבוֹנָה, וְהַקְּטוֹרֶת, וּמִנְחַת כֹּהֲנִים, וּמִנְחַת נְסָכִים, וּמִנְחַת כֹּהֵן מָשִׁיחַ, וְהַדָּם! אֶלָּא פְּשִׁיטָא, לְאִפַּגּוּלֵי בָּשָׂר. הַשְׁתָּא, וּמַה הָתָם דְּלָא חָשֵׁיב בֵּיהּ בְּבָשָׂר גּוּפֵיהּ, א"ר יוֹסֵי: מִיפַּגַּל, הָכָא דְּחָשֵׁיב בֵּיהּ ה] בְּזֶבַח גּוּפֵיהּ, לֹא כ"שׁ ו] דְּפִיגֵּל בְּיָרֵךְ יָמִין פִּיגֵּל בְּיָרֵךְ שְׂמֹאל? וְעוֹד, הָאָמַר רָבִינָא: תָּא שְׁמַע, הַקּוֹמֵץ אֶת הַמִּנְחָה לֶאֱכוֹל שְׁיָרֶיהָ אוֹ לְהַקְטִיר קוּמְצָהּ לְמָחָר, מוֹדֶה רַבִּי יוֹסֵי בָּזוֹ שֶׁפִּיגֵּל וְחַיָּיבִין עָלָיו כָּרֵת; לְהַקְטִיר קוּמְצָהּ לְאִיפַּגּוּלֵי מַאי? אִילֵימָא לְאִיפַּגּוּלֵי קוֹמֶץ, קוֹמֶץ מִי מִיפַּגַּל? וְהָתְנַן, ז] אֵלּוּ דְּבָרִים שֶׁאֵין חַיָּיבִין עֲלֵיהֶן מִשּׁוּם פִּיגּוּל: הַקּוֹמֶץ כו'! אֶלָּא פְּשִׁיטָא, לְאִיפַּגּוּלֵי שִׁירַיִים. הַשְׁתָּא, וּמַה הָתָם דְּלָא חָשֵׁיב בְּהוּ בְּשִׁירַיִים גּוּפֵיהּ — מִיפַּגְּלִי

אֶלָּא אִי אָמְרַתְּ. גַּבֵּי יְרֵיכוֹת דְּמֵחַד גּוּפָא קָאָתוּ, תְּרֵי גוּפֵי נִינְהוּ, וְאִם פִּיגֵּל ח] זוֹ בְּלֹא זוֹ לֹא נִתְפַּגְּלָה זוֹ, גַּבֵּי חַלּוֹת כִּי עָרְבָן לֶאֱכוֹל כְּזַיִת מִשְּׁתֵּיהֶן ט] מִי מִיצְטָרְפִי? מִי מְהַוְּיָא עֵירוּב מַחְשַׁבְתּוֹ לְמֶיהֱוֵי חַד גּוּפָא טְפֵי מֵחִיבּוּר זֶבַח דְּלָא מְהַנֵּי *לְהוּ לִירָכוֹת? רַבִּי הִיא. וְר' יוֹסֵי לָא אַיְירֵי בְּהוּ, וְלָא תִּקְשֵׁי לְרַב הוּנָא. לֶאֱכוֹל חֲצִי זַיִת מֵחַלָּה זוֹ. לְמָחָר. שֶׁזֶּה כָּשֵׁר. לְהַקְטִיר אֵימוּרָיו וְלֶאֱכוֹל בָּשָׂר, דְּהָא לֹא חִישֵּׁב אֶלָּא חֲצִי אֲכִילָה בַּחֲצִי מַתִּיר. אֲבָל אָמַר כְּזַיִת מִשְּׁתֵּיהֶן. דְּעָרְבָן לַחַלּוֹת בְּמַחֲשַׁבְתּוֹ, וְאָמַר בְּכָל אֶחָד וְאֶחָד מִן הַכְּבָשִׂים "הֲרֵינִי שׁוֹחֵט ע"מ לֶאֱכוֹל כְּזַיִת מִשְּׁתֵּיהֶן [לְמָחָר]" — מִצְטָרְפִי. וְרַבִּי אַלִּיבָּא דְּמַאן אֲמָרָהּ. לְהָא מַתְנִיתִין דְּקָתָנֵי לְעֵיל: לְעוֹלָם אֵינוֹ חַיָּיב עַד שֶׁיְּפַגֵּל בִּשְׁתֵּיהֶן כְּכַזַּיִת, בִּשְׁתֵּיהֶן אִין, בְּאֶחָד מֵהֶן לָא. אֶלָּא אַלִּיבָּא דְּרַבִּי יוֹסֵי אֲמָרָהּ. וְקָתָנֵי דְּמִצְטָרְפוֹת הַחַלּוֹת. וְהַדְרָא קוּשְׁיַין לְדוּכְתָּא. דְּאִי אָמְרַתְּ בִּשְׁלָמָא יְרֵיכוֹת חַד גּוּפָא הוּא כו', כִּדְאָמְרִינַן לְעֵיל (דף יג:)! לְעוֹלָם אַלִּיבָּא דְּרַבָּנַן. וּדְקַשְׁיָא לָךְ: אֲפִי' בְּאַחַת מֵהֶן נַמִי! לָא תֵּימָא בִּשְׁתֵּיהֶן, י] דְּהָא וַדַּאי אֲפִילּוּ בְּאַחַת מֵהֶן נַמִי. אֶלָּא אֵימָא עַד שֶׁיְּפַגֵּל בִּשְׁנֵיהֶם יא]. הַכְּבָשִׂים, וַאֲפִילּוּ בְּכַזַּיִת, דְּשָׁחַט ב' כְּבָשִׂים ע"מ לֶאֱכוֹל כַּזַּיִת מֵחַלָּה אַחַת אוֹ מִבּ' חַלּוֹת. אֲבָל אִם חִישֵּׁב בְּכֶבֶשׂ אֶחָד לֶאֱכוֹל כַּזַּיִת אֶחָד מִן הַחַלּוֹת, וּבִשְׁחִיטַת הָאַחֵר לֹא חִישֵּׁב — לָא הָוֵי פִּיגּוּל, דְּאֵין מְפַגְּלִין בַּעֲבוֹדַת חֲצִי מַתִּיר. וּלְאַפּוֹקֵי מִדְּר"מ. דְּאָמַר בְּסוֹף מַתְנִי': *מְפַגְּלִין בַּעֲבוֹדַת חֲצִי מַתִּיר, דְּקָתָנֵי: שָׁחַט אֶחָד מִן הַכְּבָשִׂים לֶאֱכוֹל שְׁתֵּי חַלּוֹת לְמָחָר, ר"מ אוֹמֵר: פִּיגּוּל וְחַיָּיבִין עָלָיו כָּרֵת. וְאִי קַשְׁיָא: הַקּוֹמֵץ אֶת הַמִּנְחָה אַמַּאי פּוֹסֵל בְּמַחֲשַׁבְתּוֹ? הָא עֲבוֹדַת חֲצִי מַתִּיר הוּא, דְּהָאִיכָּא נַמִּי יב] לְבוֹנָה! תָּרֵיץ: בִּקְמִיצָה וַדַּאי עֲבוֹדָה שְׁלֵימָה הִיא, דְּהָא לֵיכָּא קְמִיצָה בִּלְבוֹנָה. תֵּדַע, דְּהָא בְּהַקְטָרַת קוֹמֶץ אִם חִישֵּׁב לֶאֱכוֹל שִׁירַיִם לְמָחָר פְּלִיגִי רַבָּנַן וְאָמְרִי: יג] כֵּיוָן דְּאִיכָּא נַמִּי הַקְטָרַת לְבוֹנָה — לָא חֲשִׁיבָא הַקְטָרַת קוֹמֶץ לְפַגֵּל, דְּקָתָנֵי מַתְנִיתִין: פִּיגֵּל בְּהַקְטָרַת קוֹמֶץ וְלֹא בִּלְבוֹנָה כו' (דף יג.), וַחכ"א: אֵין פִּיגּוּל עַד שֶׁיְּפַגֵּל בְּכָל הַמַּתִּיר. וְאִי קַשְׁיָא: הָא אוֹקִימְנָא בְּרֵישׁ פִּירְקִין (שם) לְכ"ע יד] מְפַגְּלִין בַּחֲצִי מַתִּיר, דְּקָתָנֵי: הַקּוֹמֵץ ע"מ לְהַקְטִיר קוּמְצָהּ לְמָחָר מוֹדֶה ר' יוֹסֵי כו', וַהֲרֵי לֹא חִישֵּׁב אֶלָּא עַל חֲצִי מַתִּיר עַל הַקְטָרַת קוֹמֶץ! לָאו פִּירְכָא הִיא, דְּלָא דָּמֵי לְהַאי דְּהָכָא, דְּהָתָם חִישֵּׁב עַל חֲצִי מַתִּיר בִּשְׁעַת עֲבוֹדָה שְׁלֵימָה, וְהַאי חִישֵּׁב בִּשְׁעַת חֲצִי עֲבוֹדָה, כְּגוֹן שְׁחִיטַת אֶחָד מִן הַכְּבָשִׂים טו] (ב). לְעוֹלָם. מַשְׁמַע דְּמַפֵּיק מִמִּילְּתָא טוּבָא. וְרַבִּי יוֹסֵי הִיא. דְּאָמַר בְּמַתְנִיתִין: בִּשְׁתֵּיהֶן אִין, אֲבָל בְּאַחַת טז] לָא מְפַגְּלָה חֲבֵירְתָּהּ. וּלְאַפּוֹקֵי מִדְּר"מ. דְּאָמַר מְפַגְּלִין בַּעֲבוֹדַת חֲצִי מַתִּיר, *מִדְּקָאָמַר הָכָא יז] "וּבִשְׁנֵיהֶן" — הַיְינוּ דְּקָאָמַר "וּלְעוֹלָם", דְּמַשְׁמַע אֲפִילּוּ פִּיגֵּל אַף בִּשְׁתֵּיהֶן. וּלְאַפּוֹקֵי נַמִּי מִדְּרַבָּנַן. דְּאָמְרִי בְּמַתְנִיתִין: פִּיגֵּל בְּאַחַת נִתְפַּגְּלָה חֲבֵירְתָּהּ (מִדְּקָתָנֵי הָכָא וּבִשְׁתֵּיהֶן) — הַיְינוּ דְּקָאָמַר "לְעוֹלָם", דְּמַשְׁמַע: לְעוֹלָם, אֲפִי' פִּיגֵּל בִּשְׁנֵיהֶן, אֵין פִּיגּוּל עַד שֶׁיְּפַגֵּל אַף בִּשְׁתֵּיהֶן. פִּיגֵּל בְּדָבָר הַנַּעֲשֶׂה בַּחוּץ כו'. גַּבֵּי פָּרִים הַנִּשְׂרָפִים וּשְׂעִירִים הַנִּשְׂרָפִים כְּתִיבִי בְּתוֹרַת כֹּהֲנִים בְּפָרָשַׁת פִּיגּוּל בְּ"צַו אֶת *אַהֲרֹן". לְהַזּוֹת מִדָּמוֹ — עַל הַפָּרוֹכֶת, יח] הַקְטָרַת אֵימוּרִין — עַל מִזְבֵּחַ הַחִיצוֹן. לִשְׁפּוֹךְ שִׁירַיִם. שְׁיָרֵי הַדָּם הָיָה שׁוֹפֵךְ עַל יְסוֹד מַעֲרָבִי שֶׁל מִזְבֵּחַ הַחִיצוֹן. לְאִיפַּגּוּלֵי מַאי. מַה יֹּאכַל מֵאוֹתוֹ פַּר שֶׁיִּתְחַיֵּיב כָּרֵת מִשּׁוּם פִּיגּוּל? לְאִיפַּגּוּלֵי דָּם. כְּלוֹמַר, דְּהַאי דְּקָתָנֵי פִּיגֵּל — בְּדָם קָאָמַר, שֶׁאִם יֹּאכַל מִן הַדָּם בְּשׁוֹגֵג יִתְחַיֵּיב ב' חַטָּאוֹת, אַחַת מִשּׁוּם כָּרֵת יט] דָּם וְאַחַת מִשּׁוּם כָּרֵת דְּפִיגּוּל. הַקּוֹמֶץ וְהַלְּבוֹנָה. דְּמִנְחַת יִשְׂרָאֵל, וְהַקְּטֹרֶת כו'. דְּכָל הָנֵךְ אֵין לָהֶם מַתִּירִין, שֶׁהֵם מַתִּירִין אֲחֵרִים, וְקַיְימָא לָן (לקמן דף יז.) דְּאֵין פִּיגּוּל אֶלָּא בְּדָבָר שֶׁיֵּשׁ לוֹ מַתִּירִין, אוֹ לְאָדָם — כְּגוֹן שְׁיָרֵי מִנְחָה שֶׁהַקּוֹמֶץ כ] מַתִּירָן, אוֹ לַמִּזְבֵּחַ — כְּגוֹן אֵימוּרֵי בְהֵמָה שֶׁדָּם מַתִּירָן לִיקְרַב. דְּגָמְרִינַן מִשְּׁלָמִים, דִּכְתִיב בְּהוּ עִיקַּר פִּיגּוּל: מַה שְּׁלָמִים דָּבָר שֶׁיֵּשׁ מַתִּירִין לְאָדָם וְלַמִּזְבֵּחַ, שֶׁזְּרִיקַת דָּם מַתִּיר הָאֵימוּרִין לִיקְרַב וְהַבָּשָׂר לֵיאָכֵל — אַף כָּל דָּבָר שֶׁיֵּשׁ לוֹ מַתִּירִין אוֹ לָאָדָם אוֹ לַמִּזְבֵּחַ, לְאַפּוֹקֵי הָנֵךְ דְּאֵין אַחֵר מַתִּירָן. וְאִי קַשְׁיָא: פְּשִׁיטָא דְּקוֹמֶץ לָא מִיחַיְּיבִי עֲלֵיהּ כָּרֵת מִשּׁוּם פִּיגּוּל, דְּהָא כִּי אָכֵיל מִינֵּיהּ פָּקַע לֵיהּ פִּיגּוּלֵיהּ, שֶׁהֲרֵי לֹא קָרַב הַמַּתִּיר! כא] תָּרֵיץ: כְּגוֹן שֶׁהוּצַּת הָאוּר בְּרוּבּוֹ, דַּחֲשִׁיב כְּמַאן דְּקָרֵב, כִּדְאָמְרִינַן לְקַמָּן (דף כו:): קוֹמֶץ מֵאֵימָתַי מַתִּיר שִׁירַיִים בַּאֲכִילָה — מִשֶּׁהוּצַּת הָאוּר בְּרוּבּוֹ, דְּלָא חָשֵׁיב כְּבָשָׂר אֶלָּא כִּשְׁיָרֵי הַדָּם. מִיפַּגְּלִי

פיגל בדבר הנעשה בפנים לא פיגל. הא דא"ר יוסי גופיה בפרק "הנזקין" (גיטין נד: ושם): כה"ג ביוה"כ יוכיח, דכי אמר פיגול מהימן – לאו דוקא, אלא פסול. וכי האי גוונא בפ"ק דזבחים (דף יד. ושם) *גמרא ר"ש מכשר בהילוך, דאמר ר"ש בן לקיש: מודה ר"ש בהולכת חטאות הפנימיות כו', ופריך: והאמר ר"ש כל שאינו על מזבח החיצון כו'! ומשני: מודה היה ר"ש לפסול מק"ו כו'.

הקומץ והלבונה. הקשה בקונט': פשיטא דקומץ לא מיחייב עליה כרת משום פיגול, דהא אי אכיל מיניה פקע ליה פיגוליה, שהרי לא קרב המתיר! ותירץ: כגון שהוצת האור ברובו, כב] דחשיב כמאן דקרב, כדאמר לקמן (דף כו:): מאימתי מתיר שיריים באכילה – משהוצת האור ברובו. וקשה לפי', דאי הוצת האור ברובו – פקע פיגול ממנו, ואפי' פלגיה מחית אארעא ופלגא אסקי' למערכה ומשלה בו האור – מסקינן ליה לכתחלה, כדאמר בסוף פרק "ב"ש" כג] (זבחים דף מג:)*.

והלבונה. בפרק "ב"ש" (גם זה שם.) מפרש: משום דאין להם מתירין לאדם ולא למזבח. וא"ת: והרי קומץ מתירה. ואע"פ שיכול להקטירה קודם קומץ כדמוכח לעיל (דף יג:), קודם הקמילה מיהא אין להקטירה! וי"ל: דמ"מ לא הויא לבונה דומיא דשלמים, דלבונה היא גופה מתיר, שמתרת שירים באכילה, ועיקר פיגול ילפינן משלמים. ואע"ג דשייך פיגול באימורים, *דכמה דלא מקטרי אימורים כהנים בשר לא מצו אכלי, מ"מ לא חשיבי מתיר, כיון דאם נטמאו או נאבדו שרי בשר באכילה. ועי"ל: דלבונה אין לה מתיר בעבודת מזבח. ולא הויא דומיא דשלמים שעבודת מזבח מתירן, כגון זריקת דם.*

מנחת נסכים. בפ' "ב"ש" (ג"ז שם.) פי' הקונטרס דלא גרס מנחת נסכים, משום דפליגי בה בסיפא דהך משנה כד] (דבשר והדם) קתני: והנסכים הבאים בפני עצמן, דברי ר"מ, וחכ"א: אף בבאין עם הבהמה. ו"בפני עצמן" דקאמר היינו בין במתנדב נסכים, כדאמרינן: מתנדב אדם מנחת נסכים בכל יום, בין בבאין עם הבהמה, כגון שהביא זבחו היום ונסכיו מכאן עד י' ימים. ומיהו יש ליישב הגירסא, דמנחת נסכים מיירי במתנדב מנחת נסכים בכל יום, ונסכין הבאין כה] בפני עצמן מיירי במביא זבחו היום ונסכיו מכאן עד י' ימים. אבל קשה, שלא היה לו להפסיק בדם, והכי ה"ל למיתני: והדם, ומנחת נסכים, ונסכים הבאין בפני עצמן! ושמא איידי דתנא מנחת כהנים ומנחת כהן משיח תנא מיד מנחת נסכים.

הכתוב

ו א מיי' פי"ז מהלכות פסה"מ הלכה טו:
ז ב מיי' שם הלכה ה:
גבי ר"ש נ"ק
ח ג מיי' שם הלכה ד:
ט ד מיי' שם פי"ח הלכה ח:

[ועי' תוס' כריתות יד. ד"ה פקע ובתוס' זבחים מב: ד"ה הקומץ]
וכמה נ"ק
[וע"ע תוספות זבחים מג. ד"ה והלבונה]
נ"ק מ"ז וכל"ל הכך משנה דקתני והנסכים כו'
נ"ק מ"ז

להו להצטרף הס"ד נ"ק
[נזכר לקמן טז:]
[פסחים סג. וש"נ]
תוספתא דזבחים פ"ה זבחים מז: ע"ש
[לקמן טז. ע"ש]
זבחים מב:

הגהות הב"ח
(א) גמ' באחת מהן נמי אלא אליבא דר' יוסי: (ב) רש"י ד"ה מאי לעולם לעולם משמע:

ומדקאמר הכא ובשתיהן דמשמע אף בשתיהן הס"ד נ"ק
אהרן הס"ד אח"כ מ"ה להזות כו' הפרוכת הס"ד אח"כ מ"ה להקטיר אימורין דהקטרת אימורין כו' כצ"ל נ"ק

שיטה מקובצת
א] שיפגל בשתיהן אלא אימא עד שיפגל בשניהן ב] מדר' מאיר קא אתי ותו לא מאי: ג] ת"ש ר' אלעזר אומר: ד] פיגל. (זבחים דף מד ע"ב): ה] ביה בזביחה: ו] תיבות דפיגל בירך ימין פיגל בירך שמאל נמחק: ז] והתנן. [שם דף מג ע"ב]: ח] פיגל בזו בלא:

ט] משתיהן היכי מצטרפי: י] בשתיהן דמשמע דקאי אחלות: יא] בשניהן. וקאי אכבשים ואפילו כו': יב] נמי עבודת לבונה: יג] ואמרי דכיון: יד] דמפגלין בחצי: טו] הכבשים הס"ד ומה"ד מאי לעולם דמשמע: טז] באחת מהן לא: יז] מדקאמר הכא עד שיפגל בשניהן הס"ד והשאר נמחק: יח] הפרכת ולהקטיר הקטרת: יט] כרת דדם: כ] שהקומץ הוא המתירן או למזבח כגון אימורי בהמה שדם הוא המתירן: כא] המתיר כמצותו תריץ: כב] ברובו. עיין תוספות (זבחים דף מג ע"ב) וקשה דאמרינן בפרק ב"ש פיגול שהעלוהו על גבי מזבח פקע פיגולו ממנו לענין דאם ירדו יעלו וא"כ בלא שלמים נמי ידעינן דאין בהן פיגול ואמר ר"י דאצטריך שפיר למגמר משלמים דס"ד אמינא מיד שנתקדש הקומץ בכלי הוי כאילו קרב המתיר כמצותו דכך לי קדוש כלי לקומץ כהקרבת קומץ לשירים לענין נותר וטמא שהרי לא יתחייב כלום על השירים בנותר וטמא עד שיקרב הקומץ ועל הקומץ הוא חייב בנותר וטמא מיד שנתקדש בכלי כדתנן במעילה (פ"ב) ואי לאו דגמרינן משלמים הוה אמינא דמשום פיגול נמי יתחייב מיד שנתקדש בכלי להכי אצטריך למגמר דאין הקומץ חייב כרת משום פיגול כלל. מהר"פ: כג] ע' תום' (זבחים מ"ב ע"ב): כד] משנה דבתר והדם קתני: כה] בפני עצמן. גליון ולא נהירא דהא לקמן לא מצי לאשכוחי סיועא למילתא דרבא לא ממשנה ולא מברייתא ואי גרסינן ליה לייתיה מיניה סיועא עכ"ל התו"ח:

א] קמ"ל דִּבְהָא מוֹדֶה.§ "לְהַקְטִיר לְבוֹנָתָהּ לְמָחָר — רַבִּי יוֹסֵי אוֹמֵר: פָּסוּל וְאֵין בּוֹ כָּרֵת".§ אָמַר ר"ל, אוֹמֵר הָיָה ר' יוֹסֵי: אֵין מַתִּיר מְפַגֵּל אֶת הַמַּתִּיר, וְכֵן אַתָּה אוֹמֵר ב] בִּשְׁנֵי בָזִיכֵי לְבוֹנָה שֶׁל לֶחֶם הַפָּנִים, שֶׁאֵין מַתִּיר מְפַגֵּל אֶת הַמַּתִּיר. מַאי "וְכֵן אַתָּה אוֹמֵר"? מַהוּ דְּתֵימָא, טַעְמָא דְּרַבִּי יוֹסֵי בִּלְבוֹנָה — מִשּׁוּם דְּלָאו מִינָהּ דְּמִנְחָה הִיא, אֲבָל בִּשְׁנֵי בָזִיכֵי לְבוֹנָה דְּמִינָהּ דַּהֲדָדֵי נִינְהוּ — אֵימָא מְפַגְּלִי אַהֲדָדֵי, קמ"ל. וּמִי מָצֵית אָמְרַתְּ טַעְמָא דר' יוֹסֵי בִּלְבוֹנָה לָאו מִשּׁוּם דְּלָאו מִינָהּ דְּמִנְחָה הִיא? וְהָא קָתָנֵי סֵיפָא, אָמְרוּ לוֹ: מַה ג] שִּׁינְּתָה מִן הַזֶּבַח? אָמַר לָהֶן: הַזֶּבַח דָּמוֹ וּבְשָׂרוֹ וְאֵימוּרָיו אֶחָד, ד] וּלְבוֹנָה אֵינָהּ מִן הַמִּנְחָה! מַאי "אֵינָהּ מִן הַמִּנְחָה" — אֵינָהּ בְּעִיכּוּב מִנְחָה, דְּלָאו כִּי הֵיכִי דִּמְעַכֵּב לְהוּ קוֹמֶץ לַשִּׁירַיִם, דְּכַמָּה דְּלָאו אִמִּתְקַטַּר קוֹמֶץ לָא מִיתְאַכְלִי שִׁירַיִם — ה"נ מְעַכֵּב לָהּ לַלְּבוֹנָה; אֶלָּא אִי בָּעֵי הַאי מַקְטַר בְּרֵישָׁא, וְאִי בָּעֵי הַאי מַקְטַר בְּרֵישָׁא. וְרַבָּנַן? כִּי אָמְרִינַן אֵין מַתִּיר מְפַגֵּל אֶת הַמַּתִּיר, ה] (גַּבֵּי שָׁחַט אֶחָד מִן הַכְּבָשִׂים לֶאֱכוֹל מֵחֲבֵירוֹ לְמָחָר, דְּאָמְרַתְּ שְׁנֵיהֶם כְּשֵׁרִים) — ו] ה"מ הֵיכָא דְּלָא אִיקְּבַעוּ בְּחַד מָנָא, אֲבָל הֵיכָא דְּאִיקְּבַעוּ בְּחַד מָנָא — כְּחַד דָּמֵי. א"ר יַנַּאי: לִיקּוּט ב לְבוֹנָה בְּזָר — פָּסוּל. מ"ט? א"ר יִרְמְיָה: מִשּׁוּם הוֹלָכָה נָגְעוּ בָהּ; ז] קָסָבַר: *הוֹלָכָה שֶׁלֹּא [זבחים יד:] בָּרֶגֶל שְׁמָהּ הוֹלָכָה, ח] וְהוֹלָכָה בְּזָר — פְּסוּלָה. אָמַר רַב מָרִי: אַף אֲנַן נַמִי תְּנֵינָא, זֶה *הַכְּלָל: כָּל הַקּוֹמֵץ וְנוֹתֵן בִּכְלִי וְהַמּוֹלִיךְ וְהַמַּקְטִיר; בִּשְׁלָמָא ט] קוֹמֵץ — הַיְינוּ שׁוֹחֵט, מוֹלִיךְ נַמִי — הַיְינוּ מוֹלִיךְ, מַקְטִיר — הַיְינוּ זוֹרֵק, אֶלָּא נוֹתֵן בִּכְלִי מַאי קָא עָבֵיד? אִילֵימָא מִשּׁוּם דְּדָמֵי לְקַבָּלָה, מִי דָּמֵי? הָתָם מִמֵּילָא, הָכָא קָא שָׁקֵיל וְרָמֵי! אֶלָּא מִשּׁוּם דְּכֵיוָן דְּלָא סַגְיָא לֵיהּ דְּלָא עָבַד לָהּ — עֲבוֹדָה חֲשׁוּבָה הִיא, עַל כָּרְחֵיךְ מְשַׁוֵּי לָהּ כְּקַבָּלָה; ה"נ, כֵּיוָן דְּלָא סַגְיָא לָהּ דְּלָא עָבַד לָהּ — עֲבוֹדָה חֲשׁוּבָה הִיא, עַל כָּרְחֵיךְ מְשַׁוֵּי לָהּ כִּי הוֹלָכָה! לָא, לְעוֹלָם דְּדָמֵי לְקַבָּלָה. וּדְקָא קַשְׁיָא לָךְ: הָתָם מִמֵּילָא, הָכָא קָא שָׁקֵיל וְרָמֵי! מִכְּדֵי תַּרְוַיְיהוּ קְדוּשַּׁת כְּלִי הוּא, מַה לִּי מִמֵּילָא, מַה לִּי קָא שָׁקֵיל וְרָמֵי.§ **מתני'** שָׁחַט שְׁנֵי כְבָשִׂים לֶאֱכוֹל אַחַת מִן הַחַלּוֹת לְמָחָר, הִקְטִיר שְׁנֵי בָזִיכִין לֶאֱכוֹל אֶחָד מִן הַסְּדָרִים י] לְמָחָר, רַבִּי יוֹסֵי אוֹמֵר: אוֹתוֹ הַחַלָּה וְאוֹתוֹ הַסֵּדֶר שֶׁחִישֵּׁב עָלָיו — פִּיגּוּל וְחַיָּיבִין עָלָיו כָּרֵת, וְהַשֵּׁנִי פָּסוּל וְאֵין בּוֹ כָּרֵת; וַחֲכָמִים אוֹמְרִים: ג זֶה וָזֶה פִּיגּוּל וְחַיָּיבִין עָלָיו כָּרֵת.§ **גמ'** אָמַר רַב הוּנָא, אוֹמֵר הָיָה רַבִּי יוֹסֵי: פִּיגֵּל בְּיָרֵךְ שֶׁל יָמִין — לֹא נִתְפַּגֵּל הַיָּרֵךְ שֶׁל שְׂמֹאל; מַאי טַעְמָא? *אִיבָּעֵית אֵימָא: סְבָרָא, וְאִיבָּעֵית אֵימָא: קְרָא. אִיבָּעֵית אֵימָא סְבָרָא: לָא עֲדִיפָא מַחֲשָׁבָה מִמַּעֲשֵׂה הַטּוּמְאָה, אִילּוּ אִיטַּמֵּי חַד אֵבֶר, מִי אִיטַּמֵּי לֵיהּ כּוּלֵּיהּ? וְאִיבָּעֵית אֵימָא קְרָא: °"וְהַנֶּפֶשׁ הָאוֹכֶלֶת מִמֶּנּוּ עֲוֹנָהּ תִּשָּׂא", מִמֶּנּוּ — וְלֹא מֵחֲבֵירוֹ. [ויקרא ז] אֵיתִיבֵיהּ רַב נַחְמָן לְרַב הוּנָא: (וַחֲכָמִים אוֹמְרִים:) לְעוֹלָם אֵין בּוֹ כָּרֵת עַד שֶׁיְּפַגֵּל בִּשְׁתֵּיהֶן בִּכְזַיִת; בִּשְׁתֵּיהֶן — אִין, בְּאַחַת מֵהֶן — לָא. מַנִּי? אִילֵימָא רַבָּנַן, אֲפִילּוּ בְּאַחַת מֵהֶן נַמִי! אֶלָּא פְּשִׁיטָא רַבִּי יוֹסֵי; יא] אִי אָמְרַתְּ בִּשְׁלָמָא חַד גּוּפָא הוּא — מש"ה מִצְטָרֵף, אֶלָּא

קמ"ל דִּבְהָא מוֹדֶה. דְּטַעְמָא לָאו מִשּׁוּם הָכִי הוּא, אֶלָּא מִשּׁוּם דִּמְפָרֵשׁ לְקַמָּן: אֵין מַתִּיר מְפַגֵּל יב] מַתִּיר. אוֹמֵר הָיָה ר' יוֹסֵי. כְּלוֹמַר, ה"ט דְּר' יוֹסֵי. אֵין מַתִּיר מְפַגֵּל אֶת הַמַּתִּיר. אֵין עֲבוֹדַת מַתִּיר זֶה כְּגוֹן קוֹמֶץ, מוֹעֶלֶת לְפַגֵּל יג] מַתִּיר הָאַחֵר הַלְּבוֹנָה, בְּמַחֲשָׁבָה שֶׁהוּא מְחַשֵּׁב עַל הַלְּבוֹנָה בַּעֲבוֹדַת הַקּוֹמֶץ. וְכֵן אַתָּה אוֹמֵר בְּבָזִיכֵי לְבוֹנָה. שֶׁאִם הִקְטִיר הָאֶחָד מִבָּזִיכֵי לֶחֶם הַפָּנִים ע"מ לְהַקְטִיר הָאַחֵר לְמָחָר — אֵינָהּ מַחֲשָׁבָה לְפַגֵּל. מַאי וְכֵן. פְּשִׁיטָא דְּכָל הֵיכָא דְּאִיכָּא שְׁנֵי מַתִּירִין פָּלֵיג ר' יוֹסֵי! לָאו מִינָהּ דְּמִנְחָה הִיא. דְּזוֹ סוֹלֶת וְזוֹ לְבוֹנָה. אֵינָהּ בְּעִיכּוּב מִנְחָה. כְּלוֹמַר, לְעוֹלָם טַעְמָא מִשּׁוּם דְּאֵין מַתִּיר מְפַגֵּל אֶת הַמַּתִּיר. וְה"ק לְהוּ: הַזֶּבַח כּוּלּוֹ אֶחָד, וְהַדָּם הוּא יד] מַתִּיר אֶת הָאֵימוּרִים, הִלְכָּךְ, כִּי חִישֵּׁב עַל הָאֵימוּרִים חוּץ לִזְמַנּוֹ בִּשְׁעַת עֲבוֹדַת דָּם — לָאו שְׁנֵי מַתִּירִין נִינְהוּ. אֲבָל לְבוֹנָה אֵינָהּ מְעַכֶּבֶת מִנְחָה — אֵינָהּ בִּכְלַל עִכּוּב שִׁירַיִם, *וְאֵין הַקּוֹמֶץ מְעַכֵּב הַלְּבוֹנָה מֵהַקְטִיר כִּי הֵיכִי דִּמְעַכֵּב שִׁירַיִם, הִלְכָּךְ הָוְיָא לְבוֹנָה מַתִּיר בִּפְנֵי *עַצְמוֹ, וְאָמַר אֵין מַתִּיר מְפַגֵּל אֶת הַמַּתִּיר. הֵיכָא דְּלָא אִיקְּבְעוּ בְּחַד מָנָא. כְּגוֹן גַּבֵּי כִּבְשֵׂי עֲצֶרֶת, דְּמוֹדוּ רַבָּנַן בְּסֵיפָא דְּמַתְנִי': שָׁחַט אֶחָד מִן הַכְּבָשִׂים לֶאֱכוֹל מֵחֲבֵירוֹ לְמָחָר שְׁנֵיהֶם כְּשֵׁרִים, דִּשְׁנֵיהֶם מַתִּירִין אֶת הַלֶּחֶם — טו] הָתָם וַדַּאי אָמַר אֵין מַתִּיר מְפַגֵּל אֶת הַמַּתִּיר. לִיקּוּט לְבוֹנָה. דִּלְאַחַר הַקְטָרַת הַקּוֹמֶץ הָיָה מְלַקֵּט הַלְּבוֹנָה מֵעַל הַסֹּלֶת וּמַקְטִירוֹ. מִשּׁוּם הוֹלָכָה נָגְעוּ בָּהּ. *שֶׁזֶּה שֶׁלִּיקְּטָהּ וּנְתָנָהּ לַכֹּהֵן מִיעֵט בְּהִילּוּךְ הַכֹּהֵן. וְהוֹלָכָה אַחַת מִן הָעֲבוֹדוֹ', דִּגְמְרִי' מִזְּבָחִים דִּכְתִיב בְּהוּ הוֹלָכָה, טז] דִּכְתִיב: "וְהִקְרִיבוּ בְּנֵי אַהֲרֹן". וְאע"ג דְּאָמַר מָר (זבחים דף ד.): זוֹ קַבָּלַת הַדָּם, אפ"ה לְשׁוֹן הוֹלָכָה הוּא, כִּדְאָמְרִינַן בְּסוֹף "הַכֹּל חַיָּיבִין בִּרְאִיָּיה" (חגיגה יא.). שֶׁלֹּא בָּרֶגֶל. כְּגוֹן *זָר שֶׁלֹּא זָז מִמְּקוֹמוֹ, אֶלָּא לִיקֵּט וְהוֹשִׁיטָהּ לַכֹּהֵן. תָּנֵינָא. דְּלִיקּוּט לְבוֹנָה עֲבוֹדָה הִיא. זֶה הַכְּלָל. בְּפ"ק, *וְקָחָשֵׁיב לְהָנָךְ ד' עֲבוֹדוֹת חֲשׁוּבוֹת. קוֹמֵץ דָּמֵי לְשׁוֹחֵט, דְּזֶה נוֹטֵל וּמַפְרִישׁ חֵלֶק יז] לַגָּבוֹהַּ מֵחֵלֶק כֹּהֲנִים, וְכֵן זֶה. הָתָם מִמֵּילָא. נוֹפֵל הַדָּם בַּמִּזְרָק, הָכָא שָׁקֵיל קוֹמֶץ וְרָמֵי בִּכְלִי. יח] ה"נ. בְּלִיקּוּט לְבוֹנָה. קְדוּשַּׁת כְּלִי הוּא. יט] *דִּמְקַדֵּשׁ מְקַבֵּל דָּם בִּכְלִי, וְהַנּוֹתֵן בִּכְלִי מְקַדֵּשׁ ה"נ קוֹמֵץ בִּכְלִי, וּבְדָבָר זֶה דּוֹמִין. אֲבָל לִיקּוּט לְבוֹנָה דְּלָא דָּמֵי לַחֲדָא מֵהָנָךְ, לָאו עֲבוֹדָה הִיא. **מתני'** שְׁנֵי כְבָשִׂים. כִּבְשֵׂי עֲצֶרֶת, דִּכְתִיב: "וּשְׁנֵי כְבָשִׂים בְּנֵי שָׁנָה לְזֶבַח שְׁלָמִים" (ויקרא כג), וְאוֹתָם כְּבָשִׂים מַתִּירִין וּמְקַדְּשִׁין לִשְׁתֵּי הַלֶּחֶם. וְאע"ג דְּז' כְּבָשִׂים וּפַר וְאֵילִים שְׁנַיִם וּשְׂעִיר עִזִּים כְּתִיבֵי הָתָם, כ] מְפָרֵשׁ בְּפֶרֶק "הַתְּכֵלֶת" (לקמן מו.) שֶׁאֵין הַלֶּחֶם קָדוֹשׁ אֶלָּא בִּשְׁחִיטַת שְׁנֵי כְבָשִׂים שְׁלָמִים, הוֹאִיל וְהוּזְקְקוּ עִמּוֹ בִּתְנוּפָה. אוֹתוֹ הַחַלָּה אוֹ אוֹתוֹ הַסֵּדֶר כו'. וְטַעְמָא דְּרַבִּי יוֹסֵי מְפָרֵשׁ בַּגְּמָ'. **גמ'** יָמִין וּשְׂמֹאל. לָאו דַּוְקָא. לֹא נִתְפַּגֵּל יָרֵךְ שְׂמֹאל. וְהָאוֹכְלָהּ אֵין חַיָּיב כָּרֵת. אִילּוּ אִיטַּמֵּי חַד אֵבֶר. לְאַחַר שֶׁהוּפְרַשׁ מִן הַבָּשָׂר. לְעוֹלָם אֵין בּוֹ כָּרֵת. בַּלֶּחֶם הָאַחֵר שֶׁלֹּא חִישֵּׁב עָלָיו. עַד שֶׁיְּפַגֵּל כא] בִּשְׁתֵּיהֶן *)הַחַלּוֹת בִּכְזַיִת. כְּלוֹמַר, אֲפִילּוּ לֹא פִּיגֵּל אֶלָּא כִּכְזַיִת בֵּין שְׁתֵּיהֶן, הָוֵי כּוּלְּהוּ פִּיגּוּל. בְּאַחַת מֵהֶן. לֹא נִתְפַּגְּלָה חֲבֵירְתָּהּ. אֲפִילּוּ בְּאַחַת מֵהֶן נַמִי. דְּהָא אָמַר בְּמַתְנִי': זֶה וָזֶה פִּיגּוּל. אִי אָמְרַתְּ בִּשְׁלָמָא. גַּבֵּי יְרֵיכוֹת, כב] דְּמִזְּבֵּחַ אֶחָד אָתוּ: חַד גּוּפָא נִינְהוּ, וְאִי פִּיגֵּל בְּזוֹ נִתְפַּגְּלָה זוֹ — מִשּׁוּם הָכִי מִצְטָרְפוֹת חַלּוֹת חֲצִי זַיִת מִזּוֹ וַחֲצִי זַיִת מִזּוֹ כִּי עָרְבִינְהוּ, דְּחִישֵּׁב עַל מְנָת לֶאֱכוֹל כַּזַּיִת לְמָחָר בֵּין שְׁתֵּיהֶן, דְּמְהַנֵּי לְהוּ מַה שֶּׁעֵירְבוֹ זֶה (א) בְּמַחֲשַׁבְתּוֹ כְּאִילּוּ בָּאוּ שְׁתֵּיהֶן מִגּוּף אֶחָד, דְּאָמְרִינַן לְקַמָּן (דף יד:) דְּעֵירֵב מַחֲשַׁבְתּוֹ מְהַנֵּי לְצָרְפָן. וְגַבֵּי חַלּוֹת כג] ה"ט דִּבְאַחַת מֵהֶן לֹא נִתְפַּגְּלָה חֲבֵירְתָּהּ — מִשּׁוּם דְּלָא מֵחַד גּוּפָא אָתוּ, וּבְמַחֲשַׁבְתּוֹ נַמִי לֹא עֵירְבָן. אֶלָּא

*) החלות ס"ד אח"כ ד"ה בכזית כו' פיגול הס"ד

משום הולכה נגעו בה קסבר הולכה שלא ברגל כו'. בסוף פ"ק דזבחים (דף יג:): שמעתי שטבילת אלבע מפגלת. וחד טעמא הוא, דמסיק עלה: אף אנן נמי תנינא, כי הכא, ואפ"ה לא קאמר עלה: קסבר הולכה שלא ברגל כד] הוא. **לאכול** אחד מן הסדרים. הוא הדין חלה אחת מן הסדרים, שאותו הסדר פיגול. כה] מדבעי רבי יוחנן בגמ': בלחמי תודה מהו? במנחת מאפה תנור מהו? משמע דמיבעיא ליה משום דהוו שני מינים, אבל אותו מין פשיטא דנתפגל. והא דקאמרינן בגמרא: אילו איטמא חד אבר מי איטמא כוליה, אע"ג דשייך האי טעמא בחלה אחת, שאם נטמאה אחת לא נטמא כל הסדר, מ"מ לענין פיגול נתפגל, הואיל והוקבעו בסדר אחד, וחשיב כחד לענין פיגול טפי מפיגל בירך של ימין דלא נתפגל ירך שמאל. ושמא גם לענין טומאה, אם נטמאה אחת — נטמא כל הסדר. והא דנקט הכא ובסיפא אחד מן הסדרים, ולא נקט חלה אחת מאחד מן הסדרים — *משום רבותא דר"י, ובסיפא — משום רבותא דחכמים, דאע"פ שחישב על כל הסדר, אפ"ה אותו סדר דוקא פיגול וטמא, והשני אינו פיגול וטהור. **אי** אמרת בשלמא חד גופא. נראה דהשתא נמי ס"ל דהא דמלטרפין כי ערבינהו, היינו מטעם דדרשינן לקמן (דף יד:): הכתוב עשאן גוף אחד והכתוב עשאן שני גופין. ומש"ה פריך: אי אמרת בשלמא דשתי ירכות חשיבי חד גופא, דאם פיגל בזו נתפגלה זו — מש"ה מלטרף כו] *כמו כשמערב, דהכתוב עשאן גוף אחד. אלא אי אמרת דשתי ירכות נמי חשיבי תרי גופי, מה מועיל מה שעשאן הכתוב גוף אחד? דאפשר *נמי דלמאי דקסבר רב הונא, אם חישב בשתי הירכות בכזית לא הוי פיגול, *אם איתא דחשיבא לאחר שהובדלו זו מזו. וצ"ע. ובקונטרס פירש בע"א.

ג א מיי' פי"ח מהלכות פסה"מ הלכה ז:
ד ב מיי' פי"ח מהלכות פסה"מ הלכה ח:
ה ג מיי' פי"ז הלכות פסה"מ הלכה י יא:

הגהות הב"ח

(א) רש"י ד"ה אי אמרת וכו' זה כזה במחשבתו:

הכא משום נ"ק

נ"ל נמי

נמי דקסבר נ"ק

נ"א אם איתא דחשיב כתרי גופי לאחר כו' נ"ק

דלאין כו' מלהקטיר כו' לשיריים הלכך כו' נ"ק

עלמו הס"ד אח"כ מה"ד כי אמר אין מתיר מפגל את המתיר אלא היכא דלא כו' והד"א נ"ק

רש"ק מ"ז

שזר נ"ק

[לעיל יב.]

זה נ"ק

קחשיב נ"ק

דמקבל מקדש הדם בכלי והנותן מקדש הקומץ בכלי ובדבר זה כו' נ"ק

[כריתות ז: וש"נ]

רש"ק מ"ז

שיטה מקובצת

א] קמ"ל דבהא מודה ר"י וטעמיה לאו משום דאין מפגלין בחצי מתיר אלא משום דאין מתיר מפגל מתיר אבל קומץ ע"מ להקטיר קומצה למחר אין זה מתיר [אחר] אלא במתיר עצמו שהוא עובד מחשב לעוותו משמע לפי המסקנא דהכא דס"ל שפיר לר"י דמפגלין בחצי מתיר ותימה דאמרינן לקמן בפירקין פיגל בקומץ ולא בלבונה ר"מ אומר פיגול וחייבין עליו כרת וחכמים אומרים אין בו כרת עד שיפגל בכל המתיר אלמא פליגי במפגלין בחצי מתיר והכא מסקינן דלכ"ע מפגלין בחצי מתירו"ל א) דהכא מיירי במחשב בקמיצה לעוות הלבונה שהיא חצי מתיר אבל לקמן מיירי דמחשב בשעת הקטרת הקומץ ולא חישב בשעת הקטרת הלבונה והיינו מחשב בעסק חצי מתיר ובהא פליגי אבל הכא מיירי במחשב בעסק מתיר שלם כגון מחשב בשעה שהוא עוסק בקמיצה ואין שם קמיצה אחרת שאין הלבונה נקמצת: ב] ע' בהשמטות בסוף המסכת: ג] מה שנא זו מן ותיבת שינתה נמחק: ד] ולבונה אינה מן המנחה. אלמא במינה דהדדי תליא מילתא ומשני אינה בעיכוב מנחה כו'. ואלאו דרישא דמילתא קאי כמו שהולך ומפרש דאי בעי כו'. דלאו כי היכי דמעכב כו' מן הדין היה [לו] לומר נמי כי היכי דמעכבב) דם אימורים אימורים מעכבין הבשר נהי דאם הוקטרו אימוריו כשר מיהו אי אתנהו מעכבי (נמחק ונ"ל שכצ"ל [דכן] היה לו לומר שהרי היה מפרש מתניתין דקתני דמו ובשרו ואימוריו אחד והיא [היא] כלומר כמו דקומץ מפגל לשירים משום דמעכב להו ה"נ דמו מפגל אימוריו משום דמעכב להו אבל הקטרת הקומץ לא [מצי] מעכב ללבונה ולא מצי מפגל ליה. תו"ח: ה] מן תיבת גבי עד תיבת כשרים נמחק: ו] ע' בהשמטות בסוף המסכת: ז] קסבר הולכה שלא ברגל כו' (נמחק בזה הדבור כמה תיבות ונ"ל שכצ"ל) [משמע] דאי לא שמה הולכה כשרה בזר ותימה דבסוף [פ"ק] דזבחים פליגי אמוראי מחשבת פסול אם חישב בהולכה שלא ברגל אי פסל [אי] לא וקאמר אפילו למ"ד הולכה שלא ברגל לא שמה הולכה [פסולה בזר] שמיעט בהולכת כהן [וי"ל] הכא בליקוט לבונה ג) [אי לא] שמה הולכה איכא למילף מזבחים ואי משום דחסרה הולכה ליכא שהרי כהן מוליכה ולא עשה [זר אלא] ליקוט והליקוט אינו [עבודה]. גי' תו"ח: ח] והולכה בזר פסולה בשילהי [פרק קמא] דזבחים קאמר הוליכו זר והחזירו כהן וחזר והוליכו פליגי בה בני ר' חייא ור' ינאי חד אמר כשר וחד אמר פסול מר סבר [אפשר] לתקונה ומר סבר [לא] אפשר לתקונה ותימה אמאי לא קאמר

שיטה מקובצת

קאמר תסתיים דר' ינאי הוא דקאמר לא אפשר לתקוניה מדקאמר הכא לקוט לבונה בזר פסולה וצ"ע. תו"ח: ט] קומץ. (זבחים דף יג ע"ב): י] לאכול אחד מן הסדרים של לחם הפנים. וה"ה דהוה מצי למימר אחת מן השנים עשר חלות: יא] אי אמרת בשלמא חד גופא פי' מסתמא שאם פיגל בירך [זו] נתפגל חבירו וכן בחלות משום הכי כי ערבינהו [לחלות] מתערב וטעמא דר' יוסי במתני' דאמר פיגל בחלה זו לא נתפגל חברתה כדאמרינן בסוף שמעתין דמפיק ליה מקרא אי פלגינהו דמיפלגי אבל ירך דליכא קרא מפגלין לירך שניה בסתם. תו"ח: יב] מפגל את המתיר: יג] לפגל המתיר האחר כגון הלבונה: יד] הוא המתיר את האימורים להקטיר הלכך כי חישב על האימורים להקטיר חוץ לזמנו בשעת עבודת הדם מפגל דלאו שני מתירין כו' אינה בעיכוב מנחה כלומר אינה בכלל עיכוב השירים ואין הקומץ כו' דמעכבב השירים: טו] הלחם הלכך התם ודאי אמר דאין: טז] הולכה כדכתיב: יז] חלק גבוה: יח] בכלי הס"ד ומה"ד דכיון דלא סגי דלא עביד קידוש בקומץ דאמרינן בפ"ב דסוטה (דף יד ע"ב) מידי דהוי אדם אף על גב דקדישתיה הסכין בצואר הדר מקדש ליה בכלי שרת הכי נמי אף על גב דקדיש למנחה כולה הדר בעי קדושי לקומץ: יט] הוא דהמקבל מקדש לדם בכלי והנותן בכלי מקדש קומץ בכלי ותיבות הכי נמי נמחק: כ] התם תריץ הנך דמוספין נינהו דקא הדר וכתבי לה גבי מוספים בפרשת מוסף. רש"י כת"י: כא] בשתי החלות ותיבת בשתיהן נמחק: כב] ירכות דמשום דמזבח: כג] חלות נמי ה"ט: כד] ברגל כו' ותיבת הוא נמחק: כה] פיגול. גליון מדאמרינן דטעמא דר"י משום דפלגינהו מפלגי וכל חלה חלוקה לגוף אחת דכתיב ד) שתים החלות. תו"ח: כו] כאן כשמערב ותיבת כמו נמחק:

שיפגל

א) נראה דל"ל וי"ל דלא דמי להתם כלל דלקמן מיירי במחשב בשעת הקטרת וכו'. ב) אולי צ"ל המעכב להו אימורים לבשר דנהי דאם הוקטרו וכו'. ג) נראה דל"ל בליקוט לבונה אי שמה הולכה איכא למילף מהולכה דאברים דפסולה בזר אבל אי לא שמה הולכה ליכא למילף מזבחים לאו משום דחסרה וכו'. ד) נראה דל"ל דכתיב שני עשרונים יהיה החלה האחת כל"ל וקצת נראה דהך גליון תוס' פליג על התוס' שלנו וס"ל דלא נתפגל החלות האחרות שבאותו הסדר וצ"ע.

א א מיי' פי"ג מהלכות פסה"מ הלכה א:
ב ב מיי' שם פט"ו הלכה ח:

דאין מצטרפין נ"ק

לָמָּה לִי אִי לְמֵידַק מִינָּהּ הָא לֶאֱכוֹל וְלֶאֱכוֹל דָּבָר שֶׁאֵין דַּרְכּוֹ לֶאֱכוֹל. כְּגוֹן לֶאֱכוֹל חֲצִי זַיִת שִׁירַיִם וְלֶאֱכוֹל חֲצִי זַיִת קוֹמֶץ *דְּמִצְטָרְפִין. הָא מֵרֵישָׁא שָׁמְעַתְּ מִינָּהּ. דְּלָא מִצְטָרְפִין, דְּקָתָנֵי רֵישָׁא: דָּבָר שֶׁדַּרְכּוֹ לֶאֱכוֹל – אִין, שֶׁאֵין דַּרְכּוֹ לֶאֱכוֹל – לָא. אִי לֶאֱכוֹל וּלְהַקְטִיר. כְּלוֹמַר, דְּהִיא גּוּפֵיהּ אָתָא לְאַשְׁמוּעִינַן, דְּאֵין אֲכִילָה וְהַקְטָרָה מִצְטָרְפִין. הָא מְדוּקְיָא דְּרֵישָׁא שָׁמְעַתְּ מִינָּהּ. ה] מְדַיְּיקִינַן מֵרֵישָׁא: דָּבָר שֶׁאֵין דַּרְכּוֹ לֶאֱכוֹל, אִם חִישֵּׁב לֶאֱכוֹל חֲצִי זַיִת שִׁירַיִם וַחֲצִי זַיִת קוֹמֶץ לְמָחָר לָא הָוְיָא מַחֲשָׁבָה – כָּל שֶׁכֵּן ו] דְּלֶאֱכוֹל חֲצִי זַיִת שִׁירַיִם וּלְהַקְטִיר חֲצִי זַיִת קוֹמֶץ דְּאֵין מִצְטָרְפִין. דְּהַשְׁתָּא וּמָה אֲכִילוֹת לֹא מִצְטָרְפוֹת. הוֹאִיל וַחֲדָא חֲצִי אֲכִילָה הָוְיָא בְּקוֹמֶץ, אֲכִילָה וְהַקְטָרָה מִיבַּעְיָא דְּאֵין מִצְטָרְפִין? אִיצְטְרִיךְ. לְאַשְׁמוּעִינַן דְּאֵין אֲכִילָה וְהַקְטָרָה מִצְטָרְפִין. דְּסד"א הָתָם. הֵיכָא דְּחִישֵּׁב לֶאֱכוֹל חֲצִי זַיִת שִׁירַיִם וַחֲצִי זַיִת קוֹמֶץ לֹא מִצְטָרְפִין, מִשּׁוּם דְּלָאו כְּבִי אוֹרְחֵיהּ חִישֵּׁב בַּקּוֹמֶץ. אֲבָל לֶאֱכוֹל וּלְהַקְטִיר, דִּבְשִׁירַיִים *כִּי אוֹרְחֵיהּ חִישֵּׁב – ז] אֵימָא לִיצְטָרֵף, קָא מַשְׁמַע לָן.

פי' לפגל והגי' מקובצת כאן ועיין בזבחים לא:
ובקומץ נ"ק

הדרן עלך כל המנחות

דקדוק שפירשו ה"ר מאיר וה"ר שמואל בנו זלה"ה.

*הָא תוּ לָמָּה לִי? אִי לֶאֱכוֹל וְלֶאֱכוֹל דָּבָר שֶׁאֵין דַּרְכּוֹ לֶאֱכוֹל קמ"ל *דְּמִצְטָרֵף – מֵרֵישָׁא א] (דְּסֵיפָא) שָׁמְעַתְּ מִינָּהּ, (דְּקָתָנֵי: כַּחֲצִי זַיִת בַּחוּץ כַּחֲצִי זַיִת לְמָחָר – פָּסוּל, הָא כַּחֲצִי זַיִת לְמָחָר וְכַחֲצִי זַיִת לְמָחָר – פִּיגּוּל)! אִי לֶאֱכוֹל וּלְהַקְטִיר, (דְּהִיא גּוּפָא קמ"ל) – מִדִּיּוּקָא דְּרֵישָׁא שָׁמְעַתְּ מִינָּהּ, דְּהַשְׁתָּא מַה לֶאֱכוֹל וְלֶאֱכוֹל דָּבָר שֶׁאֵין דַּרְכּוֹ לֶאֱכוֹל, אָמְרַתְּ: לֹא מִצְטָרֵף, לֶאֱכוֹל וּלְהַקְטִיר מִיבַּעְיָא? אִין, לֶאֱכוֹל וּלְהַקְטִיר אִיצְטְרִיכָא לֵיהּ; ס"ד אָמִינָא: הָתָם הוּא דְּלָא כִּי אוֹרְחֵיהּ קָמְחַשֵּׁב, אֲבָל הָכָא דְּבְהַאי כִּי אוֹרְחֵיהּ קָמְחַשֵּׁב, וּבְהַאי כִּי אוֹרְחֵיהּ קָא מְחַשֵּׁב אֵימָא לִיצְטָרֵף, קמ"ל.§

מהרב"ק ה

הקומץ את המנחה. לעיל בסוף פרק קמא (דף יב.) דייק מדרבי חייא דלא תני "או כזית", דלא מצי למידק מהכא, דהכא לא איצטריך למיתני "או כזית" כיון דתנא בפ' קמא. קמ"ל דבהאי מודה. והא דבעי למימר בסמוך דר' יוסי דלא כר"מ דאמר מפגלין בחצי מתיר – לא דמי, דהכא קומץ המנחה חשיב עבודה שלמה, כיון שאין כיוצא בה בלבונה, כדמוכח בכוליה פירקין לקמן. וכן פירש בקונטרס בסמוך.

נ"א הא תו למה לי אי לאכול ולאכול דבר שאין דרכו לאכול מרישא ש"מ אי לאכול ולאכול דבר שדרכו לאכול קמ"ל דמצטרף מסיפא ש"מ דקתני כחצי זית כו' נ"ק

הדרן עלך כל המנחות

הַקּוֹמֵץ אֶת הַמִּנְחָה לֶאֱכוֹל שְׁיָרֶיהָ אוֹ לְהַקְטִיר קוּמְצָהּ לְמָחָר – ב] אמוֹדֶה רַבִּי יוֹסֵי בָּזֶה שֶׁהוּא פִּיגּוּל וְחַיָּיבִין עָלָיו כָּרֵת. לְהַקְטִיר לְבוֹנָתָהּ לְמָחָר – ג] רַבִּי יוֹסֵי אוֹמֵר: בפָּסוּל וְאֵין בּוֹ כָּרֵת, וַחכ"א: פִּיגּוּל וְחַיָּיבִין עָלָיו כָּרֵת. אָמְרוּ לוֹ: ד] מַה שִּׁינָּה זֶה מִן הַזֶּבַח? אָמַר לָהֶן: שֶׁהַזֶּבַח דָּמוֹ וּבְשָׂרוֹ וְאֵימוּרָיו אֶחָד, וּלְבוֹנָה אֵינָהּ מִן הַמִּנְחָה.§ **גמ'** לָמָּה לִי לְמִיתְנָא: מוֹדֶה רַבִּי יוֹסֵי בָּזוֹ? מִשּׁוּם דְּקָא בָּעֵי לְמִיתְנָא סֵיפָא: לְהַקְטִיר לְבוֹנָתָהּ לְמָחָר – ר' יוֹסֵי אוֹמֵר: פָּסוּל וְאֵין בּוֹ כָּרֵת; מַהוּ דְּתֵימָא, טַעְמָא דְּר' יוֹסֵי מִשּׁוּם דְּקָסָבַר: *אֵין מְפַגְּלִין בַּחֲצִי מַתִּיר, וַאֲפִי' רֵישָׁא נַמִי, קמ"ל

שייך לדף יב ע"א והוא פי' מן איבעיא להו ואילך נ"ק

ח] *וְקַיְימָא לָן דְּאוֹתָן שִׁירַיִם אֲסוּרִין בַּאֲכִילָה. וְאִי הָווּ מוּתָּרִים – הָוֵי קוֹמֶץ מְפַגֵּל. וְאִי הָווּ פְּסוּלִים לְגַמְרֵי, כְּגוֹן דְּנִטְמְאוּ אוֹ חִישֵּׁב עֲלֵיהֶם לְאָכְלָן חוּץ לִמְקוֹמָן – תּוּ לָא מָצֵי ט] *לְמֵידַק בָּעְיָא בְּפִיגּוּל, דְּהָא לֹא קָרַב הַמַּתִּיר כְּמִצְוָתוֹ. אֲבָל הֵיכָא דְּחָסְרֵי, מִי אָמְרִינַן: הוֹאִיל וְאִיתְנְהוּ קְצָת לָא חֲשִׁיב פָּסוּל, וּכְמוֹ שֶׁקָּרַב י] מַתִּיר כְּמִצְוָתוֹ דָּמֵי, וְיָכוֹל לְקוֹבְעוֹ בְּפִיגּוּל בְּהַקְטָרַת קוֹמֶץ, שֶׁאִם חִישֵּׁב בִּשְׁעַת הַקְטָרָה לֶאֱכוֹל שִׁירַיִים לְמָחָר אִית בְּהוּ פִּיגּוּל בַּשִּׁירַיִים. אוֹ דִּלְמָא, הוֹאִיל יא] *וַאֲבוּדִין בַּאֲכִילָה הָוֵי כִּמְחַשֵּׁב לֶאֱכוֹל דָּבָר שֶׁאֵין דַּרְכּוֹ לֶאֱכוֹל. *וּלְאַפְקוּעִינְהוּ מִידֵי מְעִילָה. דְּאִילּוּ קָדְשֵׁי קָדָשִׁים מוֹעֲלִין בְּכָל הַזֶּבַח קוֹדֶם זְרִיקָה. אֲבָל מִשֶּׁנִּזְרַק הַדָּם – יב] אֵימוּרִים לַגָּבוֹהַּ וְהַבָּשָׂר לַכֹּהֲנִים, וְאֵין מְעִילָה אֶלָּא בְּאֵימוּרִין שֶׁהֵן חֵלֶק הַמִּזְבֵּחַ, וְהַבָּשָׂר אֵין בּוֹ מְעִילָה. וְגַבֵּי מִנְחָה נַמִי, קוֹדֶם הַקְטָרָה יֵשׁ יג] מְעִילָה אֲפִי' בַּשִּׁירַיִם, וּלְאַחַר הַקְטָרָה אֵין מְעִילָה בַּשִּׁירַיִם, כִּדְתְנַן בְּפֶרֶק "חַטַּאת הָעוֹף" (מעילה דף ט.): הַמְּנָחוֹת מוֹעֲלִין בָּהֶן מִשֶּׁהוּקְדְּשׁוּ, קָרַב הַקּוֹמֶץ חַיָּיבִין עֲלֵיהֶם מִשּׁוּם פִּיגּוּל וְנוֹתָר וְטָמֵא, וְאֵין מוֹעֲלִים בַּשִּׁירַיִם. וְקָא מִיבַּעְיָא לְהוּ: מַהוּ דְּתֶיהֱוֵי הַךְ הַקְטָרָה יד] דּוֹמָה *לִשְׁאָר הַקְטָרוֹת לְמַפְקַע שִׁירַיִם מִידֵי מְעִילָה? אֲפִי' לְר' עֲקִיבָא דְּאָמַר זְרִיקָה מוֹעֶלֶת. דִּתְנַן (שם דף ו:): בְּשַׂר קָדְשֵׁי קָדָשִׁים וכו' ר"ע אוֹמֵר: אֵין מוֹעֲלִין בּוֹ, וְחַיָּיבִין עָלָיו מִשּׁוּם פִּיגּוּל וְנוֹתָר וְטָמֵא. דִּזְרִיקַת דָּם מוֹעֶלֶת לֵיהּ לִקְבּוֹעַ בְּפִיגּוּל וּלְהוֹצִיאוֹ מִידֵי מְעִילָה, אע"פ שֶׁאֵינָהּ מַתִּירָתוֹ בַּאֲכִילָה. מֵחֲמַת דָּבָר אַחֵר. שֶׁיָּצָא, דְּבְאֵימוּרִין גּוּפַיְיהוּ לֵיכָּא שׁוּם פְּסוּל. אֲפִי' לְר' אֱלִיעֶזֶר. דְּפָלֵיג אַדְּרַבִּי עֲקִיבָא. מְנָא אָמִינָא לָהּ דִּתְנַן הַקּוֹמֵץ כו' זֶה הַכְּלָל כו' עַד פִּיגּוּל וְחַיָּיבִים עָלָיו כָּרֵת. דְּאִם חִישֵּׁב בְּאַחַת מִן הָעֲבוֹדוֹת לְהַקְטִיר קוּמְצָהּ לְמָחָר אוֹ כַּזַּיִת מִקּוּמְצָהּ לְמָחָר, אוֹ לֶאֱכוֹל שְׁיָרֶיהָ לְמָחָר אוֹ כַּזַּיִת מִשְּׁיָרֶיהָ לְמָחָר – פִּיגּוּל וְחַיָּיבִין עָלָיו כָּרֵת. וְתָנֵי ר' חִיָּיא בְּמַתְנִיתֵיהּ: הַקּוֹמֵץ אֶת הַמִּנְחָה לֶאֱכוֹל שְׁיָרֶיהָ לְמָחָר – פִּיגּוּל. אֲבָל *לֶאֱכוֹל כַּזַּיִת מִשְּׁיָרֶיהָ לְמָחָר פִּיגּוּל לָא קָתָנֵי. מ"ט לָא תָּנֵי "כַּזַּיִת מִשְּׁיָרֶיהָ", דְּהָא אַכַּתִּי לָא חָסְרוּ שִׁירַיִם עַד לְאַחַר קְמִיצָה, דְּאִי חָסְרוּ קוֹדֶם קְמִיצָה הָוְיָא לָהּ מִנְחָה פְּסוּלָה וְאֵינָהּ נִקְמֶצֶת כְּלָל, וּמַאי טַעְמָא לָא תָּנֵי: "אוֹ כַּזַּיִת מִשְּׁיָרֶיהָ לְמָחָר"? לָאו כְּגוֹן דְּאִיתְרַמֵּי מִילְּתָא דְּחָסְרוּ שִׁירַיִים אַחַר קְמִיצָה. וְקָמוּ לְהוּ אַכַּזַּיִת? וְכֵיוָן דִּבְמַתַּן כְּלִי וּבְהִילּוּךְ וְהַקְטָרָה לָא מִיתְנֵי "אוֹ כַּזַּיִת מִשְּׁיָרֶיהָ לְמָחָר", דְּהָא כְּבָר חָסְרוּ לְהוּ, וְלָא הָוֵי מָצֵי לְמִיתְנֵי "הֲרֵינִי מוֹלִיךְ אוֹ מַקְטִיר לֶאֱכוֹל שְׁיָרֶיהָ לְמָחָר", דְּהָא שִׁירַיִם וְכַזַּיִת מִשִּׁירַיִם חֲדָא מִילְּתָא הִיא, וְלָא אִיתְרַמֵּי לֵיהּ *כַּזַּיִת, דְּהָא חָסְרוּ לְהוּ אַחַר קְמִיצָה וְקָמוּ לְהוּ אַכַּזַּיִת – הִלְכָּךְ בִּקְמִיצָה נַמִי לָא תָּנֵי "אוֹ כַּזַּיִת". הָכִי גָּרְסִינַן: בִּקְמִיצָה נַמִי לָא תָּנֵי "אוֹ כַּזַּיִת", וְל"ג "בִּשְׁיָרֶיהָ". הָא מַנִּי ר' אֱלִיעֶזֶר הִיא וכו'. ה"ג: וְכֵיוָן דִּבְקוֹמֶץ לָא מַתְנֵי לֵיהּ "אוֹ כַּזַּיִת" בִּשְׁיָרַיִם נַמִי לָא תָּנֵי "אוֹ כַּזַּיִת". כְּלוֹמַר, כֵּיוָן דְּלָא מָצֵי לְמִיתְנֵי "לְהַקְטִיר קוּמְצָהּ לְמָחָר אוֹ כַּזַּיִת מִקּוּמְצָהּ לְמָחָר", דְּמַחֲשָׁבָה דְּכַזַּיִת קוֹמֶץ לָאו כְּלוּם הוּא וְלָא מְפַגְּלִין – טו] הִלְכָּךְ בְּשִׁירַיִם נַמִי לָא תָּנֵי "אוֹ כַּזַּיִת" בְּאַחַת מִכָּל ד' הָעֲבוֹדוֹת, וְלָא מִשּׁוּם טז] *דְּאִיסּוּר שִׁירַיִם, דְּהָא לָא מַיְירֵי רַבִּי חִיָּיא *בְּאִיסּוּר שִׁירַיִם. וַהֲוָה לֵיהּ לְמִיתְנָא בִּקְמִיצָה וּבְמַתַּן כְּלִי וּבְהִילּוּךְ וּבְהַקְטָרָה "עַל מְנַת לֶאֱכוֹל שְׁיָרֶיהָ לְמָחָר אוֹ כַּזַּיִת מִשְּׁיָרֶיהָ לְמָחָר", אֶלָּא מִשּׁוּם דְּלָא מִיתְנֵי לֵיהּ גַּבֵּי קוֹמֶץ "אוֹ כַּזַּיִת מִקּוּמְצוֹ לְמָחָר", הִלְכָּךְ בְּשִׁירַיִם נַמִי לָא תָּנֵי "אוֹ כַּזַּיִת". אָמַר לֵיהּ אַבַּיֵי. הָא דְּלָא תָּנֵי רַבִּי חִיָּיא "אוֹ כַּזַּיִת" – לָאו כִּדְאָמְרַתְּ, כְּגוֹן דְּחָסְרוּ שִׁירַיִם. אֶלָּא שִׁירַיִם אִיתְנְהוּ בְּעֵינַיְיהוּ, וְהַאי דְּלָא קָתָנֵי כַּזַּיִת רַבִּי חִיָּיא בְּשִׁירַיִם – מִשּׁוּם דְּקָסָבַר כְּר"א דְּאָמַר: עַד שֶׁיַּקְרִיב אֶת כּוּלּוֹ, הָכָא נַמִי כְּשֶׁחִישֵּׁב אַכַּזַּיִת לָא הָוֵי פִּיגּוּל עַד שֶׁיְּהֵא מְחַשֵּׁב אַכּוּלֵּיהּ קוֹמֶץ. וְכֵיוָן דִּבְקוֹמֶץ לָא מִיתְנֵי לֵיהּ "אוֹ כַּזַּיִת" – בְּשִׁירַיִם נַמִי לָא תָּנֵי. וּלְעוֹלָם לָא חָסְרוּ הַשִּׁירַיִם, וּמִשּׁוּם הָכִי תָּנָא סֵיפָא: פִּיגּוּל וְחַיָּיבִין עָלָיו כָּרֵת – הוֹאִיל וְלָא חָסְרוּ הַשִּׁירַיִם, אֲבָל הֵיכָא דְּחָסְרוּ אֵימָא לָךְ דְּלָא מְהַנְּיָא לְהוּ הַקְטָרָה לְמִיקְבְּעִינְהוּ בְּפִיגּוּל. וְר' אֱלִיעֶזֶר אוֹמֵר עַד שֶׁיַּקְרִיב אֶת כּוּלּוֹ. דְּהוֹאִיל וְכוּלּוֹ כָּלִיל – בָּעֵינַן שֶׁיְּהֵא הַכֹּל קָרֵב. הָכָא נַמִי סָבַר: לָא הָוֵי פִּיגּוּל עַד שֶׁיְּהֵא מְחַשֵּׁב לְהַקְטִיר כָּל הַקּוֹמֶץ, דְּאִי אָמַר: הֲרֵינִי קוֹמֵץ ע"מ לְהַקְטִיר כַּזַּיִת מִן הַקּוֹמֶץ אוֹ ע"מ לֶאֱכוֹל כַּזַּיִת מִשְּׁיָרֶיהָ לְמָחָר – לָא הָוֵי פִּיגּוּל. אִי ר' אֱלִיעֶזֶר הוּא. הַךְ בָּרַיְיתָא דְּר' חִיָּיא, אַמַּאי קָתָנֵי בַּהּ: לְהַקְטִיר קוּמְצָהּ לְמָחָר פִּיגּוּל? יז] הִיא. דִּכְתִיב בְּמִילּוּאִים *"אִשֶּׁה הוּא", דְּמַשְׁמַע שָׁלֵם. הָנֵךְ דְּאִיכָּא גַּוָּואֵי. דְּלָא יָצְאוּ. וְהָכִי נַמִי הָנֵי דְּלָא נִטְמְאוּ כְּשֵׁירוֹת, דִּמְהַנְּיָא לְהוּ זְרִיקָה שֶׁבְּדַם הַזֶּבַח (דְּמִלּוּאִים). מַאן שָׁמְעַתְּ לֵיהּ דְּאָמַר זְרִיקָה מוֹעֶלֶת לַיּוֹצֵא. דַּהֲוֵי כְּזֶבַח מַעֲלְיָיא לְכָל עִנְיָינִים, דְּמַה שֶּׁנִּשְׁתַּיֵּיר לִפְנִים כָּשֵׁר לֶאֱכוֹל וְנוֹהֵג בּוֹ נַמִי פִּיגּוּל, דְּקָתָנֵי הָכָא: הָנֵךְ דְּאִיכָּא גַּוָּואֵי כְּשֵׁרוֹת, דִּזְרִיקָה מְהַנְּיָא לַיּוֹצֵא יח]. וְקָאָמַר נִפְרְסָה לֹא. דְּהַיְינוּ חָסְרוּ שִׁירַיִם. יט] אַלְמָא כְּרַב הוּנָא דְּאָמַר: כִּי חָסְרוּ שִׁירַיִם אֲפִילּוּ ר"ע מוֹדֶה דְּלָא מְהַנְּיָא הַקְטָרָה, לָא לְהַתִּיר וְלָא לְמִיקְבַּע בְּפִיגּוּל, וְכ"ש רַבִּי אֱלִיעֶזֶר. ע"א: "הוּא" בְּלֶחֶם הַפָּנִים כְּתִיב. *אֲבָל כ] *)לְרַבָּנַן לָא אַתְיָא הָכִי, מִשּׁוּם דְּקָאָמַר: מַאן שָׁמְעַתְּ לֵיהּ דְּאָמַר זְרִיקָה מוֹעֶלֶת לַיּוֹצֵא וכו', וּבְלֶחֶם הַפָּנִים לֵיכָּא זְרִיקַת דָּם. מִי קָתָנֵי בְּהֶדְיָא: הָא יָצְאת – הָנֵךְ דְּאִיכָּא גַּוָּואֵי כְּשֵׁרוֹת, לְמֵידַק דר"ע הִיא כא]? אֲבָל יָצָאת לָא אָמְרִינַן: הָנֵךְ דְּאִיכָּא גַּוָּואֵי כְּשֵׁרוֹת, אֶלָּא כּוּלָּן פְּסוּלוֹת, וְר' אֱלִיעֶזֶר הוּא. וּבְדִין הוּא דְּאִיבָּעֵי לֵיהּ לְמִיתְנֵי יָצָאת וְלָא כב] *נִפְרַס, וְהָא דְּקָתָנֵי נִפְרַס וכו'. וּלְעוֹלָם לָאו כְּרַב הוּנָא, אֶלָּא כִּדְרַבָּה דְּאָמַר: הַקְטָרָה מְהַנְּיָא נַמִי לְחִיסָּרוֹן, וְאַלִּיבָּא דְּר"ע לְחוּד. עַד כָּאן הַדִּקְדּוּק שֶׁפֵּירֵשׁ ה"ר שְׁמוּאֵל וְאָבִיו ה"ר מֵאִיר.

הַקּוֹמֵץ. רַבִּי יוֹסֵי אוֹמֵר כו'. טַעְמָא מְפָרֵשׁ בַּגְּמָ'. מַה כג] שִּׁינָּה זֶה מִן הַזֶּבַח. שֶׁשּׁוֹחֲטוֹ ע"מ לְהַקְטִיר אֵימוּרָיו לְמָחָר פִּיגּוּל? אֵינָהּ מִן הַמִּנְחָה. מְפָרֵשׁ בַּגְּמָ'. **גמ'** אֵין מְפַגְּלִין בַּחֲצִי מַתִּיר. שֶׁאִם חִישֵּׁב *לַעֲבוֹד לְמָחָר עֲבוֹדַת חֲצִי מַתִּיר, כד] הוּא דְּפָלֵיג ר' יוֹסֵי. קמ"ל

*) לרבה לא נ"ק

ולאפוקי מידי נ"ק
כשאר הקטרות נ"ק
או כזית נ"ק

למקבעיה בפיגול נ"ק
פסחים סג. לקמן יז.
ואסורין באכילה נ"ק
אלא כזית נ"ק
דחסר שירים כו' נ"ק
בחיסור שירים נ"ק
רש"ק קדש קדשים היא
זהו שסותר רשב"ס הע"א
למיתני נפרס לחוד והא נ"ק
להקטיר למחר עבודת חצי מתיר הוא ופליג ר"י נמי ארישא הס"ד נ"ק

שיטה מקובצת

ה"נ מצטרפי [לפיגול] אם תרוייהו חוץ לזמנו אלא שלא הקפיד להאריך כל כך כי התם אלא מ"מ מוכח שפיר דמצטרפי וגרסא דהכא נמי ודאית: א] דמצטרף מרישא שמעת מינה אי לאכול ולהקטיר מדיוקא דרישא שמעת מינה השתא מה כו' והשאר נמחק: ב] מודה ר"י כלומר אף ר"י דפליג בסיפא בהא מודה ובגמרא מפרש טעמא: ג] ר"י אומר פסול ואין בו כרת מפורש בגמרא טעמא דר"י משום דאין מתיר מפגל את המתיר קומץ ולבונה שניהן מתירין השירים לאכול לכהנים אחרי שנקטרו שניהן אבל בהקטרת זה בלא זה לא מתאכלי השירים: וחכמים אומרים כו'. ה) דסבירא להו דמפגל מתיר מפגל ומתניתין דפרק קמא דקתני הקומץ את המנחה כו' או להקטיר לבונתה סתמא כרבנן: ד] מאי שנא זו מן הזבח שאם זרק את הדם על מנת להקטיר אימורין למחר הוי פיגול אע"ג דשניהם מתירין הבשר דלכל כמה דלא מקטרי אימורין לא מתאכלי הבשר: שהזבח כו' שזה אגד בזה דלכל כמה דלא מזדריק הדם לא הוי מקטרי האימורין ומעכב זה את זה: ולבונה אינה מן המנחה כלומר אין אגד זה בזה שאין זה מעכב את זה דאי בעי מקטיר קומץ ברישא ואי בעי מקטיר לבונה ברישא והכי מפרש לה בגמרא: ה] שמעת מינה נמי ודדייקינן: ו] כ"ש לאכול: ז] ישב ובקומץ כי אורחיה חישב אימא: ח] שייך לדף שלפני זה: ט] לא מצי למיקבעי בפיגול ותיבות למידק בעיא נמחק: י] שקרב המתיר: יא] הואיל ואסורין באכילה: יב] הדם האימורין: יג] יש בה מעילה: יד] הקטרה כשאר הקטרות לאפוקינהו שירים מידי: טו] מפגלין ביה: טז] משום דחיסור שירים כו' ר' חייא בחיסור שירים: יז] הוא דכתיב במלואים: יח] מהניא ליוצא רבי עקיבא: יט] שירים ש"מ כרב הונא דאמר: כ] אבל הלשון לא משמע הכי ותיבות לרבנן לא אתיא נמחק: כא] דר"ע היא לעולם אבל יצאת והד"א: כב] ולא לתני נפרס והא דקתני נפרס וכו' ולעולם דלא כרב הונא כך נ"ל להגיה זה הדקדוק כי אינו ברש"י כת"י: כג] מה שנא זו מן הזבח שהשוחטן למחר פיגול: כד] חצי מתיר לא פיגול והך דלבונה חצי מתיר הוא דבין הקטרת קומץ ולבונה מתירין השירים: ואפי' רישא נמי. בחישב בהקטרת קומץ עבודת חצי מתיר הוא ופליג ר"י: קמ"ל
א) נראה דל"ל דס"ל דמתיר מפגל את המתיר ומתני' וכו'.

פא א מיי' פי"ט מהל' מעה"ק הלכה ח:
פב ב מיי' שם הל' יד:
פג ג מיי' פי"ב מהלכות פסה"מ הלכה יד ופ"ה מהלכות תמידין ומוספין הלכה טו:
פד ד מיי' פי"ד מהל' פסולי המוקדשים הלכה י:

"אוֹ כַּזַּיִת" א] אַשִּׁירַיִם – בִּקְמִיצָה נַמִי לֶאֱכוֹל שִׁירַיִם לָא תָּנֵי "אוֹ כַּזַּיִת"; וְקָתָנֵי סֵיפָא: פִּיגּוּל וְחַיָּיבִין עָלָיו כָּרֵת, אַלְמָא מְהַנְיָא לְהוּ הַקְטָרָה. א"ל אַבַּיֵי: (א) לָא, הָא מַנִּי? ר"א הִיא, דִּתְנַן: *הַקּוֹמֶץ, וְהַלְּבוֹנָה, וְהַקְּטֹרֶת, וּמִנְחַת כֹּהֲנִים, וּמִנְחַת כֹּהֵן מָשִׁיחַ, וּמִנְחַת נְסָכִים, שֶׁהִקְרִיב מֵאַחַת מֵהֶן כְּזַיִת אבַּחוּץ – חַיָּיב, וְרַבִּי אֱלְעָזָר פּוֹטֵר עַד (ב) שֶׁיַּקְרִיב אֶת כּוּלּוֹ; ב] כֵּיוָן דִּבְהַקְטָרַת קְמִיצָה לָא מִתְנֵי לֵיהּ "אוֹ כַּזַּיִת מִקּוּמְצָהּ בַּחוּץ" – בְּשִׁירַיִם נַמִי לָא מִתְנֵי לֵיהּ "אוֹ כַּזַּיִת". אִי רַבִּי אֱלְעָזָר, הַאי "לְהַקְטִיר קוּמְצָהּ", "לְהַקְטִיר קוּמְצָהּ וּלְבוֹנָתָהּ" מִיבָּעֵי לֵיהּ! דִּתְנַן: *הַקּוֹמֶץ בוְהַלְּבוֹנָה שֶׁהִקְרִיב אֶת אֶחָד מֵהֶן בַּחוּץ – חַיָּיב, וְרַבִּי אֱלְעָזָר פּוֹטֵר עַד שֶׁיַּקְרִיב אֶת שְׁנֵיהֶם! ג] לָא נִצְרְכָא אֶלָּא לְקוֹמֶץ דְּמִנְחַת חוֹטֵא. וְאִיכְפַּל תַּנָּא לְאַשְׁמוּעִינַן קוֹמֶץ דְּמִנְחַת חוֹטֵא? אִין. וְכֵן כִּי אֲתָא רַב דִּימִי א"ר אֶלְעָזָר: קוֹמֶץ דְּמִנְחַת חוֹטֵא הוּא, וְרַבִּי אֶלְעָזָר הִיא. הֲדַר *אָמַר רָבָא: לָאו מִילְּתָא הִיא דַּאֲמַרִי, דְּתַנְיָא: ד] °"קֹדֶשׁ קָדָשִׁים הוּא", שֶׁאִם נִפְרְסָה גאַחַת ה] [א] מֵהֶן – חַלּוֹתֶיהָ כּוּלָּן פְּסוּלוֹת; הָא יָצָאת – ו] הָנֵי דְּאִיכָּא גַּוָּואֵי כְּשֵׁרוֹת. מַאן שָׁמְעַתְּ לֵיהּ דְּאָמַר: זְרִיקָה מוֹעֶלֶת לַיּוֹצֵא? ר"ע הִיא, וְקָאָמַר: נִפְרְסָה – לָא. ז] א"ל אַבַּיֵי: מִי קָתָנֵי "הָא יָצָאת"? דִּלְמָא, הָא נִטְמֵאת – הָנָךְ כְּשֵׁרוֹת, מ"ט? דִּמְרַצֶּה צִיץ, אֲבָל יָצָאת – לָא, וְר' אֱלִיעֶזֶר הִיא, דְּאָמַר: אֵין זְרִיקָה מוֹעֶלֶת לַיּוֹצֵא; וּבְדִין הוּא דְּאִיבָּעֵי לֵיהּ לְמִיתְנֵי נַמִי יָצָאת, וְהַאי דְּקָתָנֵי נִפְרְסָה – הָא קמ"ל, דַּאֲפִי' נִפְרְסָה, דְּאִיתֵיהּ בִּפְנִים – לָא מְהַנְיָא לֵיהּ הַקְטָרָה. אֲבָל לְר"ע דְּאָמַר: זְרִיקָה מוֹעֶלֶת לַיּוֹצֵא, אֲפִי' חִסָּרוֹן נַמִי מְהַנְיָא לֵיהּ הַקְטָרָה.§ **מתני'** *לֶאֱכוֹל כַּחֲצִי דזַיִת וּלְהַקְטִיר כַּחֲצִי זַיִת – כָּשֵׁר, שֶׁאֵין אֲכִילָה וְהַקְטָרָה מִצְטָרְפִין.§ **גמ'** *טַעְמָא דְּלֶאֱכוֹל וּלְהַקְטִיר, הָא לֶאֱכוֹל וְלֶאֱכוֹל דָּבָר שֶׁאֵין דַּרְכּוֹ לֶאֱכוֹל – מִצְטָרֵף. וְהָקָתָנֵי רֵישָׁא: לֶאֱכוֹל דָּבָר שֶׁדַּרְכּוֹ לֶאֱכוֹל וּלְהַקְטִיר דָּבָר שֶׁדַּרְכּוֹ לְהַקְטִיר; דָּבָר שֶׁדַּרְכּוֹ לֶאֱכוֹל – אִין, שֶׁאֵין דַּרְכּוֹ לֶאֱכוֹל – לָא! מַאן תַּנָּא? א"ר יִרְמְיָה: הָא מַנִּי? ר"א הִיא, דְּאָמַר: מְחַשְּׁבִין מֵאֲכִילַת אָדָם [לַאֲכִילַת] מִזְבֵּחַ וּמֵאֲכִילַת מִזְבֵּחַ [לַאֲכִילַת] אָדָם, דִּתְנַן: *הַקּוֹמֵץ אֶת הַמִּנְחָה לֶאֱכוֹל דָּבָר שֶׁאֵין דַּרְכּוֹ לֶאֱכוֹל וּלְהַקְטִיר דָּבָר שֶׁאֵין דַּרְכּוֹ לְהַקְטִיר – כָּשֵׁר, וְר"א פּוֹסֵל. אַבַּיֵי אָמַר: אֲפִי' תֵּימָא רַבָּנַן, לָא תֵּימָא: הָא לֶאֱכוֹל וְלֶאֱכוֹל דָּבָר שֶׁאֵין דַּרְכּוֹ לֶאֱכוֹל, אֶלָּא אֵימָא: הָא לֶאֱכוֹל וְלֶאֱכוֹל דָּבָר שֶׁדַּרְכּוֹ לֶאֱכוֹל. וּמַאי קמ"ל? הָא בְּהֶדְיָא קָתָנֵי לָהּ: לֶאֱכוֹל כַּזַּיִת בַּחוּץ וְכַזַּיִת לְמָחָר, כְּזַיִת לְמָחָר וּכְזַיִת בַּחוּץ, כַּחֲצִי זַיִת בַּחוּץ וְכַחֲצִי זַיִת לְמָחָר, כַּחֲצִי זַיִת לְמָחָר וְכַחֲצִי זַיִת בַּחוּץ – פָּסוּל וְאֵין בּוֹ כָּרֵת; הָא

הדרן עלך כל המנחות

כז] מש"ה לא תני רבי חייא "או כזית" ברישא, משום דבסיפא במתן כלי והילוך והקטרה לא מיתני ליה "או כזית בקומצה או כזית בשיריה", פירוש: אפי' בשירים לא מיתני ליה "או כזית", משום דלא מיתני אקומץ – לא תני ליה "כזית" ברישא. ומה שכתוב בספרים "בשירים נמי" לא גרס "נמי". אבל תנא דמתני' לא חייש, ותני ליה ברישא אע"ג דבסיפא לא הוי [ז] בשיריה. **הוא** שאם נפרסה אחת כו'. פי' בקונטרס: בלחם הפנים, כח] דכתיב "כי קדש קדשים הוא לו". ונראה דע"כ כשנפרסה משפירקה איירי, או משראויה לפרק. דאי עד שלא פירקה, מאי קשיא ליה לרבא מהכא? הא כי אמר רבא דמהניא כט] ביה הקטרה הני מילי בשחסרו בין קמילה להקטרה, והכא ה"ל כמנחה שחסרה קודם קמילה, דפסולה היא ואין מקטיר עליה את הקומץ, כדאמר לעיל (דף ח.): עד שלא פירקה נפרס לחמה – הלחם פסול ואין מקטיר עליו את הבזיכין! ועוד, דדייק מינה: הא יצאת או נטמאת, והיינו לאחר שפירקה, ודומיא דהכי מיירי נפרסה אחת מחלותיה לאחר שפירקה, דמקטיר עליו את הבזיכין כדאמרינן לעיל. ותימה: היכי דייק מהכא דלא מהניא הקטרה למיקבעיה בפיגול ולאפוקי מידי מעילה? ודוחק לומר דמדקתני לשון "פסולות" דייק, דהוה ליה למימר "אין [ח] נאכלות". ועוד, אם כן לידוק נמי מההיא דלעיל דקתני: הלחם פסול ומקטיר עליו את הבזיכין! ושמא ל] [ט] הכא איכא לדחויי, דהא מני – רבי אליעזר היא דאמר אין זריקה מועלת ליוצא. אבל מהך דייק ואפילו לרבי עקיבא. ואם תאמר: למה לי למידק רבי עקיבא היא, משום דמשמע: הא יצאת הנך דאיכא גוואי כשרה? הוה ליה למידק: הא יצאת אין שום פסול עליהם, ומהניא להו הקטרה לפיגול ומעילה, אלמא רבי עקיבא היא. וכי האי גוונא הוי מצי למידק מההיא דלעיל דרבי עקיבא היא! ושמא לא משמע ליה למידק הא יצאת מלשון "פסולות" כמו [י] אהא דקתני "כולן" כו'. ועוד נראה לפרש, דדייק הכל מדדרש ליה קרא מדכתיב "הוא", שמע מינה לא מהניא להו הקטרה כלל. אי נמי, דייק מדאחמיר כולי האי, דכי נפרסה האחת כולן פסולות, שמע מינה דלא מהניא ליה הקטרה לפיגול ומעילה.

שאם נפרסה אחת מחלותיה כולן פסולות. למאי דמסיק דאתיא כרבי אליעזר, אבל לרבי עקיבא האחרות כולן כשרות, יש לתמוה: לא] דמאן דיליף מילתא ממילתא, י' חלות שבמנחה של מחבת או של מרחשת, כשחסרה אחת אמאי כולן פסולות, כדדרשינן לעיל (דף ט:): פרט למנחה שחסרה? נילף מהכא דכשרות! ושמא התם חשיבי כולהו טפי כחלה אחת.

אלא אימא הא לאכול ולאכול דבר שדרכו לאכול. מכאן ואילך כתובה בספרים בשיבוש, וצריך להגיה כאן כמו שהיא כתובה בסוף לב] פ"ב דזבחים (דף לא:).

"אוֹ כַּזַּיִת", דְּכֵיוָן דְּמַחֲשֶׁבֶת ג' עֲבוֹדוֹת הַלָּלוּ מוּקְמִינַן בְּשֶׁכְּבָר חָסְרוּ הַשִּׁירַיִם וְעָמְדוּ עַל כַּזַּיִת, הִילְכָּךְ לָא מָצֵי לְמִיתְנֵי "אוֹ כַּזַּיִת מִקּוּמְצוֹ לְמָחָר" דּוּמְיָא דְּשִׁירַיִם, דְּאִם חִיסֵּר קוֹמֶץ בִּשְׁעַת מַחֲשָׁבָה – כְּבָר פְּסוּלָה, וְלָא מִיפַּגֵּל מִנְחָה בְּהַהִיא מַחֲשָׁבָה. הִילְכָּךְ, כֵּיוָן דְּלָא מִיתְנֵי לֵיהּ "אוֹ כַּזַּיִת מִקּוּמְצָהּ" – לָא תָּנָא "כַּזַּיִת" ח] בְּשִׁירַיִם. וְרֵישָׁא כִּי חָשֵׁיב בִּקְמִיצָה, דְּמִיתְנֵי לֵיהּ "אוֹ כַּזַּיִת" אַף בְּקוֹמֶץ, דְּהַהִיא וַדַּאי בְּשֶׁלֹּא חָסְרָה עֲדַיִין מִתּוֹקְמָא, אפ"ה, כֵּיוָן דְּסֵיפָא לָא מִיתְנֵי לֵיהּ אַקּוֹמֶץ – לָא תָּנֵי לֵיהּ בְּרֵישָׁא אֲפִילּוּ אַשִּׁירַיִם. ט] **א"ל אַבַּיֵי.** לְרָבָא: לְעוֹלָם מִדְּרַבִּי חִיָּיא לָא מַשְׁמַע דְּמַתְנִי' מַיְירֵי בְּחִסָּרוֹן. דְּה"ט דְּלָא תָּנֵי רַבִּי חִיָּיא "אוֹ כַּזַּיִת" בְּבָרַיְיתָא דִּידֵיהּ – י] דְּרַבִּי חִיָּיא ר"א הִיא, דְּלָא חָשֵׁיב הַקְטָרָה עַד שֶׁיַּקְטִיר כּוּלּוֹ. דִּתְנַן הַקּוֹמֶץ. דְּמִנְחַת יִשְׂרָאֵל. וְהַלְּבוֹנָה. שֶׁל מִנְחָה. וְהַקְּטֹרֶת. שֶׁבְּכָל יוֹם. (*וּמִנְחַת כֹּהֲנִים. מִנְחָה שֶׁהִתְנַדֵּב כֹּהֵן, דְּאֵינָהּ נִקְמֶצֶת אֶלָּא יא] כָּלִיל, דִּכְתִיב: "וְכָל מִנְחַת כֹּהֵן כָּלִיל תִּהְיֶה") (ויקרא ו). וּמִנְחַת כֹּהֵן מָשִׁיחַ. חֲבִיתֵּי כ"ג יב] נַמִי (ג) כְּתִיב בָּהּ (ויקרא ו) "כָּלִיל תָּקְטָר". וּמִנְחַת נְסָכִים. נַמִי כָּלִיל הִיא. עַד שֶׁיַּקְטִיר [אֶת] כּוּלּוֹ. אַלְמָא לָא חָשֵׁיב הַקְטָרָה בְּכַזַּיִת. הִלְכָּךְ לָא תָּנֵי ר' חִיָּיא "אוֹ כַּזַּיִת" בְּמַתְנִי' אֲפִי' בְּשִׁירַיִם, כֵּיוָן דִּבְקְמִיצָה לָא מִיתְנֵי לֵיהּ "אוֹ כַּזַּיִת". כְּלוֹמַר, בְּהַקְטָרַת קְמִיצָה – לָא מָצֵי לְמִיתְנֵי יג] מַתְנִי': "הַקּוֹמֵץ ע"מ לְהַקְטִיר כַּזַּיִת מִקּוּמְצָהּ לְמָחָר", דְּהָא לָא מְפַגֵּל בְּהָכִי, דְּלָא חָשֵׁיב יד] כְּהַקְטָרָה גְּמוּרָה, הִילְכָּךְ לָאו מַחֲשָׁבָה הִיא [ג]. וְאִי קַשְׁיָא: תַּנָּא דִּידַן אַמַּאי תָּנָא: טו] "לְהַקְטִיר מִקּוּמְצָהּ לְמָחָר"? הָא לְר"א לָא הָוְיָא הַקְטָרָה עַד שֶׁיַּקְטִיר גַּם הַלְּבוֹנָה, וְאִשְׁתַּכַּח (ד) טז] דְּלֵית בְּהַקְטָרָה מַחֲשָׁבָה שְׁלֵמָה! וּמְשַׁנֵּי: מַתְנִי' יז] בְּהַקְטָרַת קוֹמֶץ לְחוּדֵיהּ בְּמִנְחַת **חוֹטֵא** קָמַיְירֵי. דְּאֵין בָּהּ לְבוֹנָה, וְ"ע"מ לְהַקְטִיר לְבוֹנָתָהּ" דְּתָנֵי בְּמַתְנִי' דְּהָוֵי פִּיגּוּל – מוֹקִים לָהּ בְּלֶחֶם הַפָּנִים, דְּאֵין בָּהּ אֶלָּא הַקְטָרַת לְבוֹנָה. **אִיכְפַּל** = טָרַח. **לָאו מִילְּתָא הִיא** דַּאֲמַרִי. דְּוַדַּאי לָא מְהַנְיָא לְהוּ הַקְטָרָה לְשִׁירַיִם שֶׁחָסְרוּ. **הוּא.** בְּלֶחֶם הַפָּנִים כְּתִיב (שם כד) "כִּי קֹדֶשׁ קָדָשִׁים הוּא לוֹ". **פְּסוּלוֹת.** וְיִשָּׂרְפוּ. **הָנָךְ דְּגַוָּואֵי** כְּשֵׁרוֹת. אַף עַל גַּב דְּלָא הָוְיָא הַקְטָרַת בָּזִיכִין כְּשֵׁרָה עַד שֶׁתְּהֵא כָּל הַמִּנְחָה שְׁלֵמָה יח], י"ב חַלּוֹת שֶׁל לֶחֶם הַפָּנִים. אַלְמָא, הַךְ חַלָּה יט] דִּילֵיהּ מְהַנְיָא לְהוּ לְמֶיהֱוֵי י"ב חַלּוֹת, וּלְאַכְשׁוּרֵי לַבָּזִיכִין, וּלְאִישְׁתְּרוּיֵי הָנָךְ (ה) [ג] בַּאֲכִילָה. אַלְמָא זְרִיקָה, כְּגוֹן הַקְטָרַת בָּזִיכִין שֶׁהוּא בִּמְקוֹם דַּם זְבָחִים, מוֹעֶלֶת לַיּוֹצֵא, מִדְּחָשֵׁיב לֵיהּ בִּכְלַל י"ב חַלּוֹת. אַלְמָא מְהַנְיָא הַקְטָרָה לְאַחְשׁוּבֵי בַּהֲדֵי הָנָךְ, אַף ע"ג דַּאֲסוּרָה בַּאֲכִילָה. וְקָאָמַר נִפְרְסָה כּוּלָּן פְּסוּלוֹת. אַלְמָא, אֲפִי' לְר' עֲקִיבָא דְּאָמַר: מְהַנְיָא הַקְטָרָה לַיּוֹצֵא כ] מִידֵי חִסָּרוֹן – לָא מְהַנְיָא הַקְטָרָה! מִי קָתָנֵי יָצָאת. כְּשֵׁרָה, דְּתֵימָא ר"ע הִיא? **דִּלְמָא.** הָכִי דּוּק מִינֵּיהּ: הָא נִטְמְאָה אַחַת – [ד] חַבְרוֹתֶיהָ כְּשֵׁרוֹת, דְּהָא כא] טוּמְאָה הַצִּיץ מְרַצֶּה. **אֲבָל יָצָאת.** דְּאֵין צִיץ מְרַצֶּה עַל הַיּוֹצֵא – לָא מִיתַּכְשְׁרִי הָנָךְ דְּגַוָּאֵי, מִשּׁוּם דְּלֵיכָּא הַקְטָרָה עַל י"ב חַלּוֹת, דְּהָא חָסְרוּ לְהוּ. וְרַבִּי אֱלִיעֶזֶר הִיא דְּאָמַר. לְעֵיל: אֵין זְרִיקָה מוֹעֶלֶת בַּיּוֹצֵא. וּבְדִין. דְּאִיבָּעֵי כב] לְהוּ לְמִיתְנֵי נַמִי: שֶׁאִם יָצְאת אַחַת מֵהֶן כּוּלָּן פְּסוּלוֹת.

מתני' לֶאֱכוֹל כַּחֲצִי זַיִת וּלְהַקְטִיר חֲצִי זַיִת. לְמָחָר כָּשֵׁר. **גמ'** הָא לֶאֱכוֹל. חֲצִי זַיִת שִׁירַיִם, כג] [ה] לֶאֱכוֹל חֲצִי זַיִת קוֹמֶץ, דְּהַיְינוּ דָּבָר שֶׁאֵין דַּרְכּוֹ לֶאֱכוֹל – מִצְטָרְפִין לִפְסוֹל. כד] שֶׁאֵין דַּרְכּוֹ לֶאֱכוֹל [ו]. לָא הָוְיָא מַחֲשָׁבָה אִם חִישֵּׁב לְאוֹכְלוֹ לְמָחָר, וְכֵיוָן דְּלָא הָוְיָא מַחֲשָׁבָה – לָא מִצְטָרְפִין לִפְסוֹל. מַאן תַּנָּא. לְהַךְ כה] *(רֵישָׁא) דְּמַתְנִיתִין, דְּדַיְיקִינַן מִינַּהּ דְּאִם חִישֵּׁב לֶאֱכוֹל קוֹמֶץ לְמָחָר הָוְיָא מַחֲשָׁבָה? **אָמַר רַבִּי יִרְמְיָה ר"א הִיא דְּאָמַר מְחַשְּׁבִין** מֵאֲכִילַת אָדָם לַמִּזְבֵּחַ. שֶׁאִם חִישֵּׁב לְהַקְטִיר שִׁירַיִים לְמָחָר הָוֵי מַחֲשָׁבָה. וּמֵאֲכִילַת מִזְבֵּחַ לְאָדָם. שֶׁאִם חִישֵּׁב עַל מְנָת לֶאֱכוֹל קוֹמֶץ לְמָחָר כו]. שֶׁאֵין דַּרְכּוֹ לְהַקְטִיר. שִׁירַיִם. פּוֹסֵל. וְאֵין חַיָּיבִים עָלָיו כָּרֵת. וְטַעְמָא מְפָרֵשׁ בְּרֵישׁ פ"ג. **אֶלָּא אֵימָא הָא לֶאֱכוֹל וְלֶאֱכוֹל דָּבָר שֶׁדַּרְכּוֹ לֶאֱכוֹל.** כְּגוֹן כַּחֲצִי זַיִת בַּחוּץ כַּחֲצִי זַיִת לְמָחָר – מִצְטָרְפִין לִפְסוֹל. הָא בְּהֶדְיָא קָתָנֵי לָהּ כו'. וְהַךְ סֵיפָא דְּקָתָנֵי: שֶׁאֵין אֲכִילָה וְהַקְטָרָה מִצְטָרְפִין, לָמָּה

*) נ"א סיפא

תורה אור: ויקרא כד; קמן י.

גי' נ"ק או כזית בקמיצה בשירים נמי לא תני

זבחים קטו:

עיין רש"ק שמוחק כל ד"ז עד כליל תהיה זבחים קי.

נ"ק

[שבת סג: וש"נ]

[זבחים כט: לה. פה. לקמן יז.]

[זבחים לא:]

הגהות הב"ח

(א) גמ' א"ל אביי לעולם לא מהניא תני ר' אלעזר:
(ב) שם ור' אלעזר פוטר עד שיקטיר את כולו וכיון דבקמילה כצ"ל ותיבת דבהקטרת נמחק:
(ג) רש"י ד"ה ומנחת כהן וכו' נמי כליל דכתיב בה:
(ד) ד"ה עד שיקטיר וכו' ואישתכח דלא בהקטרה שלימה מחשב הס"ד:
(ה) ד"ה הנך דגואי וכו' ולאישתרויי הנך דבגואי באכילה:

שיטה מקובצת

א] או כזית בשירים נמי לא תני והשאר נמחק: ב] כולו וכיון דבקמיצה לא מתני ליה או כזית בשירים נמי לא מתני ליה והשאר נמחק: ג] את שניהם בקומץ דמנחת והשאר נמחק: ד] תיבות קדש קדשים נמחק: ה] אחת מחלותיה: ו] יצאת הא נטמאת: ז] א"ל אביי לעולם מצית למימר כדקאמרת מעיקרא דפסול חסרון אינו פסול כל כך כמו פסול דיוצא והך ברייתא דר' חייא ר"א היא דפסול א) ביוצא דלא מהני ליה הקטרה ליוצא (נמחק וצ"ל שכך צ"ל) [ה"ה נמי] פסול דחסרון וכ"ש פסול דיוצא שהוא רב ואין זה ממש כמו דפי' רבא מעיקרא שהרי הוה ס"ד דרבא למימר מעיקרא דבחסרון מהניא הקטרה אף לר"א ובזה אין מעמיד דברי רבא [רק] דא"ל אביי לא תהדר בך מאי דקאמרת מעיקרא דפסול יוצא מרובה מפסול חסרון ודקדק מורי הרב למה היה רבא סותר דבריו הראשונים משום ברייתא [שניה] ומי היה מזקיקו למידק הא יצאת כשרות אלא תנא פסול חסרון וכ"ש פסול דיוצא כדס"ד מעיקרא דחסרון מהניא ליה הקטרה מה שאין כן לפסול דיוצא ונראה לו שהיה סברתו להעמיד ברייתא מסתמא כר"ע דאמר מועלת ליוצא וה"נ מהניא ליה הקטרה אלמא דייקינן הא יצאת כשרות א"ל אבי ר"א היא ולא למידק הא יצאת כשירות מתניא אלא תנא פסול דחסרון וכ"ש פסול דיוצא וא"ת אמאי לא מוכח דפסול חסרון מרובה מפסול יוצא מהא דאמרן שירים שחסרו בין קמיצה להקטרה לכ"ע שירים אסורים באכילה מקרא דוהנותרת ומקרא דמהמנחה ואילו לר"ע יצאו מקצת שיריה מהני הקטרה והנך דאיתנהו גוואי מתאכלי אלמא דפסול חסרון מרובה מפסול יוצא וי"ל דשאני התם דגלי קרא נותרת ולא הנותרת מן הנותרת ודין [הוא] דלא מתאכלי מיהו אפשר דמהניא להו הקטרה לענין למקבעינהו בפיגול או לאפוקינהו ממעילה אבל הכא [ליכא] למימר דגלי קרא למיפסלינהו והכא מצי להעמיד [קרא] דהוא לפסול חלה הנפרסת לבד וכל אינך דשלימות כשירות אלא מדפסלינהו לכולהו ש"מ אפילו הני רשלימות דגוואי אלמא משתמע ליה דפסול דחסרון מרובה: ח] כזית משירים אות ב' נמחק: ט] א"ל אביי לא. ספרים אחרים הא דלא תני ר' חייא או כזית לאו טעמא כדקאמרת אלא משום דס"ל כר"א דפוטר כזית בחוץ מן הקומץ עד שיקריבנו כולו וה"נ לא מפגל במחשבה עד שיחשוב להקטיר כל הקומץ למחר וכיון דבקמיצה לא מצי לאתויי כזית בשירים נמי [לא תני] או כזית אבל תנא דידן דתני או כזית אפילו בקמיצה ס"ל דמתני' רבנן היא דמחייב במקריב כזית מן הקומץ בחוץ ה"ה דמפגל במחשבה דכזית: להקטיר קומצה (או) ולבונתה מיבעיא ליה דלא מפגלי לר"א (כשחישב) [עד שחישב] בשתיהן למחר כמו דס"ל דלא מחייב במקטיר בחוץ עד שיקטיר שתיהן דתנן כו' ומשני הא אף לר"א במחשבת קומץ לבד בלא לבונה דאיירי בקומץ מנחת חוטא דלא היה בה לבונה וע"מ להקטיר לבונתה דהוי פיגול מדקי ליה בבזיכי של לבונה של לחם הפנים שהיה בהן לבונה בלא קומץ והיכא דקמיץ ע"מ ולעשות שאר עבודות למחר לא מצי לאוקמי בהכי פיגול דאם קמץ ע"מ שאם יחסר הקומץ שיעמוד על כזית ויקטירנו למחר לא מפגל דבקומץ פסול קא מחשב דלאחר שיחסר יפסול ושוב אין פגול בדבר פסול הלכך

לא תני בשירים או כזית ושמעינן מהא מדלא תני ר' חייא ש"מ בחסר מיירי במתני' ואפ"ה קתני במתניתין דאם הקטיר לאכול אותו כזית למחר פיגול אלמא מהניא [מחשבה] לשירים שחסרו [בין קמיצה] להקטרה (לכולן) ואי קשיא תנא דידן אמאי תנא או כזית למחר פיגול כיון דבחסר מיירי הא מחשב בקומץ פסול תריץ תנא דידן תרתי גווני קתני דלגבי שירים מיירי בשחסרו ולגבי הקטרת קומץ מיירי בחשב להקטיר כזית מקומץ שלם למחר. כך נמצא ברש"י ישן של כת"י: י] דידיה דברייתא דידיה ר"א היא: יא] אלא כולה כליל: יב] תיבת נמי נמחק: יג] תיבת מתני' נמחק: יד] חשיב מחשבה גמורה: טו] תנא או כזית מקומצה למחר תריץ תנא דידן לית ליה דמתניתין ר' אלעזר היא ואית ליה דמפגל בהכי הס"ד ומה"ד אי רבי אלעזר אמאי תני רבי חייא להקטיר קומצה למחר הא: טז] דלאו בהקטרה שלמה מחשב הס"ד: יז] מתניתין דחשיבא הקטרה קומץ לחודיה בקומץ דמנחת חוטא: יח] שלמה שתים מערכות ותיבות י"ב חלות של לחם הפנים נמחק: יט] דיצאת מהני להני למיהוי י"ב חלות כו'. הנך י"א דגוואי באכילה אלמא כו' שהוא במקום זריקת דם מועלת ליוצא: כ] מודה דבחסרון לא: כא] בטומאה אי חשבת בהדי אינך למיהוי י"ב חלות ולאכשורי ההקטרה משום דמרצה ציץ על הטומאה הס"ד ואח"כ מה"ד אבל יצאה: כב] דאיבעי ליה: כג] שירים ולאכול: כד] דבר שאין: כה] להך סיפא: כו] קומץ למחר הוי מחשבה הס"ד ואח"כ מה"ד לאכול דבר שאין דרכו לאכול קומץ שאין: כז] מיירי בחסרו שירים ועמדו על כזית מש"ה: כח] כתיב: כט] דמהניא בהו: ל] ושמא ההיא הכי איכא: לא] לתמוה למאן: לב] בסוף נראה למורי דאין צריך להגיה אלא בזבחים גרים הא תו למה לי אי לאכול דבר שדרכו לאכול דמצטרף מרישא שמעת מינה דמצטרפי כחצי זית למחר וכחצי זית בחוץ פסול ואין בו כרת הא תרוייהו למחר הוי פיגול דרוצה למידק דמצטרפי לפיגול ולחייב כרת והכא מוכח דמצטרפי לפסול בחוץ למקומו ומדמצטרפי לפסול חוץ למקומו ה"נ

א) נראה דצ"ל ר"א היה דלפסול יוצא לא מהני ליה הקטרה ותני פסול דחסרון וכ"ש פסול יוצא שהוא מרובה.

הגהות צ"ק [א] מחלותיה כולן: [ב] נ"ל ואיקשי וי"ג מחשבה היא הס"ד ומה"ד ואי ר"א קשיא תנא וגי' נ"ק ואי קשיא תנא דידן אמאי תאני או כזית מקומצה למחר הא לר"א לא הוי הקטרה תנא דידן כת"ק דר"א ס"ל הס"ד אח"כ ד"ה עד שיקטיר הלבונה ואשתכח דלא בהקטרה שלמה מחשב הס"ד וכצ"ל: [ג] דגואי באכילה: [ד] מתכרותיה כשרות הנך דלא נטמא דהא: [ה] ולאכול: [ו] לא דלא הויא: [ז] תני בשירייס הס"ד: [ח] נאכלות דא"כ לידוק: [ט] הא לעיל איכא: [י] מהא דקתני

פיגול וחייבין עליו כרת. *זה הכלל: אכל הקומץ, א] [או] נותן בכלי, המוליך, המקטיר, לאכול דבר שדרכו לאכול ולהקטיר דבר שדרכו להקטיר, חוץ למקומו — פסול ואין בו כרת, חוץ לזמנו — פיגול וחייבין עליו כרת, ובלבד שיקריב המתיר כמצותו. כיצד קרב בהמתיר כמצותו? קמץ בשתיקה, נתן בכלי ב] והוליך והקטיר חוץ לזמנו; או שקמץ חוץ לזמנו, נתן בכלי והוליך והקטיר בשתיקה; או שקמץ ונתן בכלי והוליך והקטיר חוץ לזמנו — זהו שקרב המתיר כמצותו. גכיצד לא קרב המתיר כמצותו? קמץ חוץ למקומו, נתן בכלי והוליך והקטיר חוץ לזמנו; או שקמץ חוץ לזמנו, נתן בכלי והוליך והקטיר חוץ למקומו; או שקמץ ג] נתן בכלי והוליך והקטיר חוץ למקומו — ד] זהו שלא קרב המתיר כמצותו. דמנחת חוטא ומנחת קנאות שקמצן שלא לשמן, נתן בכלי והוליך והקטיר חוץ לזמנו; או שקמץ חוץ לזמנו, נתן בכלי והוליך והקטיר שלא לשמן; או שקמץ ונתן בכלי והוליך והקטיר שלא לשמן — *זהו שלא קרב המתיר כמצותו. לאכול כזית הבחוץ ה] כזית למחר, כזית למחר כזית בחוץ, כחצי זית בחוץ כחצי זית למחר, כחצי זית למחר כחצי זית בחוץ — פסול ואין בו כרת. ו] א"ר יהודה, זה הכלל: אם מחשבת הזמן קדמה למחשבת המקום — פיגול וחייבין עליו כרת, אם מחשבת המקום קדמה למחשבת הזמן — פסול ואין בו כרת. וחכמי' אומרים: וזה וזה פסול ואין בו כרת.§ **גמ'** *איבעיא להו: זלדברי האומר שירים שחסרו בין קמיצה להקטרה — מקטיר קומץ עליהן, *וקיימא לן דאותן שירים אסורים באכילה, ז] מהו דתיהני להו הקטרה למיקבעינהו בפיגול חולאפקינהו מידי מעילה? אמר רב הונא, אפילו לר"ע *דאמר: זריקה מועלת ליוצא — ה"מ יוצא, דאיתיה בעיניה ופסול מחמת דבר אחר הוא, אבל חסרון, דפסולא דגופיה הוא — לא מהני ליה הקטרה. אמר ליה רבא: אדרבה, אפי' לר"א *דאמר: אין זריקה מועלת ליוצא — ה"מ יוצא, דליתיה בפנים, °אבל חסרון דאיתיה בפנים — ח] מהניא ליה הקטרה. אמר רבא: מנא אמינא לה? דתנן: ט] הקומץ את המנחה לאכול שיריה בחוץ או כזית משיריה בחוץ, ותני רבי חייא: הקומץ את המנחה, ולא תני "או כזית"; י] מ"ט לא תני "או כזית", לאו כגון שחסרו שירים וקמו להו אכזית? וכיון דבמתן כלי יא] בהילוך ובהקטרה לא מתני ליה
או

רש"י

פיגול וחייבים עליו כרת. האוכל משירי מנחה, דכתיב בחוץ לזמנו (ויקרא ז): "עונה תשא", וכתיב בנותר: "ואוכליו עונו ישא" (שם יט), מה להלן כתיב: "ונכרתה" — אף כאן האוכלו בכרת. והך ג"ש בפ"ק דכריתות (דף ה.). כל הקומץ או נותן. קומץ, יב] או מוליך או מקטיר, ע"מ לאכול דבר שדרכו לאכול — כגון שיריים, או להקטיר דבר שדרכו להקטיר — כגון קומץ חוץ לזמנו כו'. אבל אם חישב להקטיר שיריים למחר או לאכול קומץ למחר — כשר, דבטלה דעתו אצל כל אדם. בד' עבודות הללו מפגלין במנחה, דגמרינן מזבחים בהקישא כדאמר בריש פירקין (דף ב:) דאיתקש מנחה לחטאת, יג] [א] ומה היא היקישא גמרי' מחשבה דפוסלת במנחה, ומינה: מה זבח נפגל בד' עבודות, שחיטה וקבלה הולכה וזריקה, כדאמרינן בת"כ — אף מנחה בד' עבודות, קמילה כנגד שחיטה, יד] [ב] קבלה כנגד מתן כלי, והולכה כנגד הולכה, והקטרה כנגד זריקה. ובלבד טו] שיהא קרב [ג] המתיר כמצותו. כאילו היה כשר, שלא יהא טז] שום פסול אלא הפיגול. אבל אם יש שם פסול אחר — תו לא פגיל, ואין בו כרת, כדאמר בפ"ב (לקמן טז:): "ירצה" כתיב בפיגול, וכתיב בכשר "ירצה", כהרצאת כשר — כך הרצאת פיגול, שלא יהא בו שום פסול אחר. בשתיקה. שלא [ד] חישב. או שקומץ ונתן בכלי יז] והוליך והקטיר. כל אלה חוץ לזמנו, זהו שקרב המתיר כמצותו, דלא היה בו שום פסול אחר. או שקמץ ונתן בכלי יח] והוליך והקטיר כל אלה חוץ למקומו. כלומר, "או" קתני, אם עשה אחת מאלה על מנת לאכול שיריים חוץ למקומו, וכל הג' חוץ לזמנו — לא קרב הקומץ כמצותו. מנחת חוטא יט] וקנאות. יש בהן עוד פסול אחר המוציאן מידי פיגול, כגון שלא לשמן, דאמרינן בריש פירקין (דף ב) כ] דפסולה, אם קומצו שלא [ה] לשמן — לא קרב המתיר כמצותו, ואין בשיריים כרת. כזית בחוץ כא] וכזית למחר. חישב באחת העבודות ב' מחשבות, חוץ לזמנו וחוץ למקומו. ועד השתא איירי בשתי עבודות, שחישב באחת חוץ לזמנו ובאחת חוץ למקומו, והשתא מיירי כב] שחישב [ו] בשתיהן בעבודה אחת. ולרבי יהודה הוא דאיצטריך, דלא תימא שחישב שתיהן בשתי עבודות הוא דפליג ר' יהודה, דבתר קמייתא אזלינן, אבל כג] (בההיא) [בחדא] עבודה מודה, קמ"ל. והכי מפרש בזבחים בפ' שני (דף ל.) [ז]. כזית למחר כזית בחוץ. אע"פ שחישב כד] תחילה חוץ לזמנו — הוציאתו שניה מידי כרת. רבי יהודה פליג את"ק בין בעבודה אחת בין בשתי עבודות. **גמ'** מהו דתהני להו הקטרה למיקבעינהו בפיגול. כגון כה] אם הקטיר הקומץ ע"מ לאכול הני שירים חוץ כו] לזמנו — מקבעי בפיגול בהך הקטרה כבהקטרה מעלייתא, הואיל וברשות מקטיר. או דלמא, כיון דאין שיריים נאכלים — ה"ל כמחשב לאכול למחר דבר שאין דרכו לאכול, כז] כדאמר לקמן (דף יז.) דלא מהניא מחשבתו? אי נמי לאפוקינהו כח] ממעילה. אם הקטירו כדרכו בשתיקה, מי אמרינן: כיון דניתן רשות להקטירו — הויא הקטרה מעלייתא, ומפקא לשיריים מידי מעילה כהקטרה מעלייתא, דאמר במס' מעילה בפ' "חטאת העוף" (דף ט.): המנחות מועלין בהן משהוקדשו, קרב הקומץ — חייבין עליהן משום פיגול נותר וטמא, ואין מעילה בשיריים כו', דה"ל שעת היתר לכהנים, וכל שיש לו שעת היתר לכהנים אין בו מעילה, בפ"ק דמעילה. או דלמא, כיון דסוף סוף אין שיריים נאכלין — הוו להו דבר שאין לו כט] היתר לכהנים, ולא נפקי ממעילה? אפילו ר"ע. דאמר בפ"ק דמעילה (דף ז.): זריקה מועלת ליוצא ל] חוץ לקלעים, למיהוי כדבר שיש לו היתר לכהנים ולמיפק מידי אשם מעילות,*) [ח] (ר"ע אומר: אין מועלין בו,) דזריקתו הוציאתו מידי מעילה. אע"פ שאינה לא] מתרת באכילה, אעפ"כ מועלת לו להוציאו מידי מעילה. מחמת דבר אחר. אויר ירושלים פוסלו, שיצא לב] מן הקלעים. ולא נפקא לג] ממעילה [ט]. ר"א ס"ל דפסול יוצא חמור לד] מחסרון. מנא אמינא לה. דמהניא להו הקטרה לפיגול וליציאת לה] מעילה. ותני רבי חייא [י]. למתני', ולא תני "או כזית" לא בקומץ ולא בשירים, לא בפגול ולא בפסול. מ"ט לא תני או כזית. משירים למחר. לאו. משום דמאן דקתני "או כזית" משמע ליה דהכי הדר תני: הנותן בכלי והמוליך והמקטיר לאכול דבר לו] כו' או להקטיר קומצה או כזית מקומצה למחר. כגון שחסרו שירים. ועמדו על כזית, לז] ואמר "הריני נותן בכלי ומוליך ומקטיר ע"מ לאכול כזית של לח] שירים למחר". ואע"ג דמחשבת קמילה ליכא למימר שכבר חסרו, דא"כ ה"ל מנחה שחסרה קודם קמילה, ופסולה ותו לא מקבעה בפיגול, אפילו הכי מחשבת מתן כלי והילוך והקטרה, הואיל ואפילו חסרו לט] מותר להקטיר הקומץ — מוקי לה בשכבר חסרו לאחר קמילה, אפילו הכי הן מ] פיגול. והאי דלא תני ליה רבי חייא, לאו [משום] דלא סבירא ליה [הכי], דלא פליג עליה מא] דרבי, דסתמא דמתניתין רבי היא, אלא משום דלא מצי לאוקומי לכולה מתניתין [יא] בכה"ג. דבמתן כלי ובהילוך ובהקטרה לא מתני ליה
או

*) [נ"ל מעילות דר' עקיבא]

תוספות

יתירה ופסולה. והשתא, כיון דבלא אבד פסולה — אמאי נקט אבד? על מב] כן נראה דבלא אבד כשרה, דתרווייהו חזו לה, ואבד לאחר קמילה [יב]. **וחכ"א** אחד זה ואחד זה פסול ואין בו כרת. וא"ת: היינו ת"ק! וי"ל: דאתא למעוטי כוותיה, דכי האי גוונא משני בפ' "המפלת" (נדה ל:).

ה"מ יוצא דאיתיה בעיניה כו'. הוה מצי למימר: ה"מ יוצא מקצתו, אבל יוצא כולו לא, כדאמרינן בפ"ק דמעילה (דף ו:), והכא כיצא כולו דמי, כיון דאסורין באכילה. ומיהו פלוגתא היא התם. וא"ת: למ"ד יצא כולו לא, הא דתניא פרק [יג]"כל שעה" (פסחים לד:): נטמא בשר או נפסל או שיצא חוץ לקלעי', ר"א אומר: יזרוק, פי': דיש דם אע"פ שאין בשר. ר' יהושע אומר: לא יזרוק, פי': דאם אין בשר אין דם. ומודה ר' יהושע דאם זרק הורצה — על כרחך ביצא כולו, דאי נשתייר כזית — זורק לכתחילה. ומדקאמר: אם זרק הורצה, ש"מ דזריקה מועלת ליצא כולו! ושמא דרבי יהושע עדיפא מדר"ע. א"נ, לענין הרצאה שאני לרבי יהושע בין לכתחילה בין לדיעבד אפי' ביצא כולו, [יד] כדאמר בפ' "כילד צולין" (שם עז:). אבל לעולם לא מיקבע בפיגול ולא נפיק מידי מעילה היכא דיצא כולו, מידי דהוה אחסרון לרב הונא. **ותני** רבי חייא כו'. ולא תני "או כזית". רבי חייא תני בברייתא דידיה בשיטת משנתינו, אלא דלא תני "או כזית". והכי תני: הקומץ את המנחה לאכול שיריה כו' זה הכלל כל הקומץ ונותן בכלי והמוליך והמקטיר כו'. ועל כרחין, הא דמשמע ליה לרבי חייא "או כזית" מיירי בשחסרו שיריים ועמדו על כך — לאו היינו "או כזית" משירים דרישא, כדפי' בקונטרס, דא"כ הוה ליה מנחה שחסרה קודם קמילה ופסולה בקומץ, ותו לא מיקבע בפיגול. אלא משום ד"זה הכלל" דסיפא קאי אכל מה דתנא ברישא, וברישא תנא "או כזית", א"כ נותן בכלי ומוליך ומקטיר — עליה נמי קאי. ובכזית משירים מיתוקם שפיר בשחסרו שיריים, דהא מקטיר קומץ עליהן. אבל [טו]כזית מקטיר קומצה — לא מיתוקם כשחסר קומץ ועמד על כזית, דאי חסר קומץ בשעת מחשבה — כבר נפסלה המנחה ותו לא מיפגלא. ומשמע ליה לרבי חייא דמאי דמיתוקם מג] "כזית [טז] משיריה" מיירי בחסר ועמד על כזית,
מס"ה

עין משפט נר מצוה

עה א מיי' פי"ג מהל' פסה"מ הלכה ו:
עו ב ג מיי' שם פט"ו הלכה ג:
עז ד מיי' שם פט"ו הלכה ג:
עח ה ו מיי' שם פ"ח הלכה ב:
עט ז מיי' פט"ו מהל' פסה"מ הלכה יא:
פ ח מיי' פ"ג מהלכות מעילה הלכה ז:

מסורת הש"ס

זבחים יג. [לעיל ז.] לקמן יג: יז.
זבחים כעוף סה.
לעיל ט.
[לקמן יג. בפרש"י בסוף הפרק הלזה נדפס ביאור רחב בשם הר"מ והר"ש כנו על סוגיא זו]
[מעילה ז. לקמן מז.]
נ"ק מ"ז

גליון הש"ס

גמ' אבל חסרון דאיתא בפנים. עיין לקמן דף מו ע"א תוספות ד"ה נפרס:

שיטה מקובצת

ב' מחשבות: כן תיבות שחישב שתיהן נמחק: כג] אבל בחד עבודה מודה: כד] שחישב בתחלה: כה] אם הקטיר הקומץ. ותימה תינח אם הקטיר הקומץ לאכול שירים למחר אבל אם חישב להקטיר הקומץ למחר לא שייך למימר הכי לכן נראה דמשום הכי מבעיא ליה אי מקבע בפגול בהאי הקטרה משום דכיון דאין השירים נאכלין הוי כאילו לא קרב המתיר כמצותו: כו] חוץ לזמנו מי מקבעי: כז] מידי מעילה: דאמר: כח] מידי מעילה: כט] שאין לו שעת היתר: ל] ליוצא דתנן בשר קדשי קדשים שיצא לפני זריקת דמים רבי אליעזר אומר מועלין בו כאילו לא נזרק הדם דאין זריקה מועלת ליוצא חוץ לקלעים למיהוי כדבר שיש לו שעת היתר לכהנים ולמיפק מידי אשם מעילות ר"ע אומר אין מועלין בו דזריקתו מוציאתו מידי מעילה: לא] שאינה מתירתו באכילה אפילו הכי מועלת: לב] חוץ מן הקלעים: לג] נפקא מידי מעילה: לד] חמור מפסול חסרון: לה] לפיגול וליציאת מידי מעילה: לו] לאכול דבר שדרכו לאכול ולהקטיר דבר שדרכו להקטיר קאי נמי מה דתנא בהדיא או כזית לאכול שירים או כזית משירים או: לז] או כזית אחר הקמיצה ומחשב בהני ג' עבודות ואמר: לח] שירים למחר. ספרים אחרים ומש"ה לא תני ר' חייא או כזית משום דהוי לצדדין שהרי במחשב להקטיר הקומץ או כזית מן הקומץ למחר לא מצינו לפרושי ביה כגון שחסר הקומץ ועמד על כזית וחישב להקטיר אותו כזית המשוייר למחר דבהכי לא מהניא ביה מחשבה אי חסר הקומץ ולא מיפגלא המנחה בההוא מחשבה וכיון דלא מצי לפרושי או כזית דהקטיר קומץ במחשבה דהני ג' עבודות כשחסר הקומץ ועמד על כזית וחישב על כזית המשוייר לאכול למחר ומשום דלא מצי לפרושי לתרווייהו בחד גוונא לא תני ר' חייא או כזית כלל ואף על גב במחשב עבודת קמיצה הוה מצי למיתני או כזית משיריה ולא ג) במחשב להקטיר קומצה או כזית מקומצה כגון שחסרו ועמדו על כזית שהרי לא מהניא מחשבה בהכי לפגל משום דהוי ליה מנחה שחסרה קודם קמיצה דפסולה להקטיר וא"כ לא מיפגלא במחשבה אפ"ה כיון דבמחשבה דמתן כלי והילוך והקטרה לא מצי למיתני או כזית דהוי לצדדין כדפירשתי במחשב בעבודת קמיצה נמי לא תני או כזית אע"ג דהכא לא הוי לצדדין כדפי' אבל תנא דידן דתני או כזית לא מקפיד [אי] הפי' דאו כזית [הוי] לצדדין ומפרשינן כגון שחסרו ועמדו על כזית היכא דמצינא לפרושי ליה כגון במחשב באחת מג' עבודות לאכול כזית משיריה למחר דהקטרה מהניא היכא שחסרו שיריה אחר הקמיצה כך נמצא ברש"י ישן של כתיבת יד: לט] ואפי' חסרו (נותן) [מותר] להקטיר את הקומץ מוקי לה כו' אפ"ה הוי: מ] פיגול דהכי חשיב בהן הריני קומץ ע"מ שאם יחסרו השירים ויעמדו על כזית למחר ובמוליך ונותן בכלי ומקטיר נמי כגון שחסרו שיריה ועמדו על כזית ואמר הריני נותן בכלי ומוליך ומקטיר ע"מ לאכול כזית שירים למחר ותיבת הכי נמחק: מא] דרבי דסתמה למתניתין דהא רבי הוה ותיבות דמתני' דרבי הוא נמחק: מב] כן נראה בלשון שני שהפריש לה שני קמצים כשרה. מהר"פ: מג] רמאי דמיתוקם בשחסר ועמד על כזית והשאר נמחק:

שיטה מקובצת

א] והנותן בכלי והמוליך והמקטיר לאכול: ב] בכלי והיה הולך והקטיר חוץ לזמנו והקטיר: ג] שקמץ ונתן בכלי והוליך והקטיר: ד] זהו שלא קרב המתיר כמצותו נמחק: ה] כזית למחר. ע' (זבחים יב.) ברש"י: ו] אמר ר' יהודה (שם דף כט:) מהו דתהני (ע"ש דף כז בתוס'): ח] מהניא ליה הקטרה. וא"ת מאי שנא דאין השירים נאכלים היה מהניא ליה הקטרה לפגולי מאי שנא מהא דאמרינן (פסחים סג.) דזריקה מפגלא בבשר לא וי"ל דלא דמי דהכא מיירי כשהקטרה היא תיקונה אלא שהרעותא היא בחסרון השירים אבל התם מיירי שלא היה הזריקה כתיקונה ועי' קלקול הזריקה אין הבשר נאכלת כגון חישב בשחיטה ע"מ לזרוק למחר מה שצריך למעלה למטה או איפכא א"נ זרק דמים הניתנים למטה למעלה או איפכא וכוון באותו זריקה לאכול ... למחר או להקטיר מן האימורים למחר בהא קאמר דלא מיפגלא כך פרש"י בזבחים ג): ט] תיבות את המנחה נמחק: י] עי' בהשמטות בסוף המסכת: יא] כלי ובהילוך: יב] נותן קומץ בכלי: יג] ... ומהיא היקישא: יד] שחיטה ומתן כלי כנגד קבלה: טו] ובלבד שיקריב המתיר הקומץ שיהא קרב נמחק: טז] שם פסול אחר אלא הפיגול כו' תו לא מפגל ואין בו כרת: יז] והילך והקטיר ... אחרינא וחישב באחד מהם לאכול שירים חוץ לזמנו: יח] בכלי והילך והקטיר: יט] חוטא ומנחת כ] דפסולות אם קומצו שלא לשמן ושלשת שאר העבודות חוץ לזמנו או או אפילו הראשון חוץ לזמנו שלא לשמן הוציאו מידי פיגול הס"ד ומה"ד או שקמץ או נתן בכלי או הלך או הקטיר שלא לשמן ע"מ לאכול שירים חוץ לזמנו זהו שלא קרב המתיר: כא] בחוץ כזית למחר חישב באחת מן העבודות

א) ... מ"ש הכא גבי שירים דס"ד דאף דאין השירים נאכלים כו'. ב) אולי נ"ל כך פירשו התוס' בזבחים דף כז ד"ה יצא. ג) אולי נ"ל או כזית משיריה או במחשב להקטיר קומצה או כזית מקומצה שהרי התם ע"כ לא מיירי מחסרון כלל דאם חסר מקומץ ... קודם קמילה לא מהני וכו':

הגהות צ"ק [א] ומהאי הקישא: [ב] מתן כלי כנגד קבלה והולכה כו': [ג] קומץ המתיר: [ד] חישב או שקומץ ונתן הד"א: [ה] לשון הס"ד ואח"כ ד"ה שלא קרב: [ו] שתיהן: [ז] דר' יהודה פליג את"ק בין בעבודה אחת בין בשתי עבודות הס"ד אח"כ ד"ה כזית למחר כו' הוציאתו שניה מידי כרת הס"ד כנ"ל: [ח] דתנן בשר קדשי קדשים שיצא לפני זריקת דמים רע"א כו': [ט] אמר ליה רבא דרבא ס"ל דפסול יוצא כו': [י] למתני' הס"ד אח"כ ד"ה לאו משום דקתני או כזית משמע ליה כגון שירים ועמדו על כזית וכי הדר ותני הנותן בכלי המוליך המקטיר לאכול דבר שדרכו לאכול הייטו לאמר הריני נותן בכלי ומוליך ומקטיר ע"מ לאכול כזית של שירים למחר כו' כנ"ל: [יא] בכה"ג הס"ד ואח"כ מה"ד דבמתן: [יב] פסולה: [יג] כילד צולין דף עז נטמאה: [יד] כדאמרינן התם אבל: [טו] כזית מקומצה לא כו': [טז] משירים שחסרו מיירי:

תורה אור

וְהָתַנְיָא, א](ר' שִׁמְעוֹן אוֹמֵר:) קוֹמֶץ וּלְבוֹנָה שֶׁחָסַר כָּל שֶׁהוּא — פָּסוּל! תְּנֵי: קוֹרֶט לְבוֹנָה שֶׁחָסַר כָּל שֶׁהוּא — פָּסוּל. וְאִיבָּעֵית אֵימָא: כָּאן בִּלְבוֹנָה הַבָּאָה עִם הַמִּנְחָה, כָּאן בִּלְבוֹנָה הַבָּאָה בִּפְנֵי עַצְמָהּ. א"ר יִצְחָק בַּר יוֹסֵף א"ר יוֹחָנָן: *ג' מַחֲלוֹקֶת בַּדָּבָר, ר"מ סָבַר: קוֹמֶץ בַּתְּחִילָּה וְקוֹמֶץ בַּסּוֹף, וְרַבִּי יְהוּדָה סָבַר: קוֹמֶץ בַּתְּחִילָּה וּשְׁנֵי קְרָטִין בַּסּוֹף, וְר"ש סָבַר: קוֹמֶץ בַּתְּחִילָּה וְקוֹרֶט אֶחָד בַּסּוֹף. וּשְׁלָשְׁתָּן מִקְרָא אֶחָד דָּרְשׁוּ: °"וְאֵת כָּל הַלְּבוֹנָה אֲשֶׁר עַל הַמִּנְחָה", ב] ר"מ סָבַר: עַד דְּאִיתָא לַלְּבוֹנָה דְּאִיקַּבְעָה בַּהֲדֵי מִנְחָה מֵעִיקָּרָא; וְרַבִּי יְהוּדָה סָבַר: "כָּל" — וַאֲפִי' חַד קוֹרֶט, "אֵת" — לְרַבּוֹת קוֹרֶט אַחֵר; וְר"ש "אֵת" לָא דָּרֵישׁ. וְא"ר יִצְחָק בַּר יוֹסֵף א"ר יוֹחָנָן: מַחֲלוֹקֶת בִּלְבוֹנָה הַבָּאָה עִם הַמִּנְחָה, אֲבָל בִּלְבוֹנָה הַבָּאָה בִּפְנֵי עַצְמָהּ — ד"ה אקוֹמֶץ בַּתְּחִילָּה וְקוֹמֶץ בַּסּוֹף; לְהָכִי אִיצְטְרִיךְ "אֲשֶׁר עַל הַמִּנְחָה", דְּבַהֲדֵי מִנְחָה — אִין, בִּפְנֵי עַצְמָהּ — לָא. וְא"ר יִצְחָק בַּר יוֹסֵף א"ר יוֹחָנָן: מַחֲלוֹקֶת בִּלְבוֹנָה הַבָּאָה עִם הַמִּנְחָה, אֲבָל בִּלְבוֹנָה הַבָּאָה בְּבָזִיכִין — בדִּבְרֵי הַכֹּל שְׁנֵי קְמָצִין בַּתְּחִילָּה וּשְׁנֵי קְמָצִין בַּסּוֹף. פְּשִׁיטָא! מַהוּ דְּתֵימָא כֵּיוָן דְּבַהֲדֵי לֶחֶם אָתְיָא, כַּ"אֲשֶׁר עַל הַמִּנְחָה" דָּמְיָא, קמ"ל. פְּלִיגִי בָּהּ רַבִּי אַמִּי וְרַבִּי יִצְחָק נַפָּחָא, חַד אָמַר: מַחֲלוֹקֶת בִּלְבוֹנָה הַבָּאָה עִם הַמִּנְחָה, אֲבָל בִּלְבוֹנָה הַבָּאָה בִּפְנֵי עַצְמָהּ — דִּבְרֵי הַכֹּל קוֹמֶץ בַּתְּחִילָּה וְקוֹמֶץ בַּסּוֹף; וְחַד אָמַר: כְּמַחֲלוֹקֶת בַּזּוֹ כָּךְ מַחֲלוֹקֶת בַּזּוֹ. § "חִיסַּר לְבוֹנָתָהּ". [פְּסוּלָה!] § הָא יָתֵיר — כְּשֵׁרָה; וְהָתַנְיָא: יָתֵיר — פְּסוּלָה! אָמַר רָמִי בַּר חָמָא: כְּגוֹן גשֶׁהִפְרִישׁ לָהּ שְׁנֵי קְמָצִין. וְאָמַר רָמִי בַּר חָמָא: דהִפְרִישׁ לָהּ שְׁנֵי קְמָצִין וְאָבַד אֶחָד מֵהֶן, קוֹדֶם קְמִיצָה — לֹא הוּקְבְּעוּ, אַחַר קְמִיצָה — הוּקְבְּעוּ. וְאָמַר רָמִי בַּר חָמָא: ההִפְרִישׁ אַרְבָּעָה קְמָצִין לִשְׁנֵי בָזִיכִין וְאָבְדוּ שְׁנַיִם מֵהֶן, קוֹדֶם סִילּוּק בָּזִיכִין — לֹא הוּקְבְּעוּ, לְאַחַר סִילּוּק בָּזִיכִין — הוּקְבְּעוּ. הָא תּוּ לָמָּה לִי? הַיְינוּ הָךְ! מַהוּ דְּתֵימָא: כֵּיוָן דִּבְרִיר קוֹמֶץ דִּידָהּ, כֵּיוָן שֶׁהִגִּיעַ זְמַנָּהּ לְפוֹרְקָהּ — כְּמַאן דִּפְרִיקָה דָּמְיָא, קמ"ל. § מתני' הַקּוֹמֵץ ואֶת הַמִּנְחָה לֶאֱכוֹל שְׁיָרֶיהָ בַּחוּץ אוֹ כְּזַיִת מִשְּׁיָרֶיהָ בַּחוּץ, לְהַקְטִיר קוּמְצָהּ בַּחוּץ אוֹ כְּזַיִת ג] קוּמְצָהּ בַּחוּץ, אוֹ לְהַקְטִיר לְבוֹנָתָהּ בַּחוּץ — פָּסוּל ד] וְאֵין בּוֹ כָּרֵת. זלֶאֱכוֹל שְׁיָרֶיהָ לְמָחָר אוֹ כְּזַיִת מִשְּׁיָרֶיהָ לְמָחָר, לְהַקְטִיר קוּמְצָהּ לְמָחָר אוֹ כְּזַיִת מִקּוּמְצָהּ לְמָחָר, אוֹ לְהַקְטִיר לְבוֹנָה לְמָחָר — פִּיגּוּל

(ויקרא ו)

רש"י

וְהָתַנְיָא ה] הַקּוֹמֵץ אֶת הַלְּבוֹנָה כו'. כִּמְדוּמֶּה לִי דְּהַיְירֵי בָּהּ ר' שִׁמְעוֹן כו' קָפָרֵיךְ מִינָּהּ לְרַבִּי שִׁמְעוֹן. לְבוֹנָה הַבָּאָה עִם הַמִּנְחָה. אִם חָסְרָה בִּשְׁעַת הַקְטָרָה כְּשֵׁרָה לְר"ש, כִּדְיָלֵיף לְקַמֵּיהּ (סְמוּכָה בְּסוּגְיָ' זוֹ) מִ"כָּל הַלְּבוֹנָה אֲשֶׁר עַל הַמִּנְחָה". וְהַאי דְּקָתָנֵי: חָסֵר כָּל שֶׁהוּא פָּסוּל – בִּלְבוֹנָה הַבָּאָה בִּפְנֵי עַצְמָהּ, כְּגוֹן הָאוֹמֵר "הֲרֵי עָלַי לְבוֹנָה" יָבִיא מְלֹא קוֹמֶץ לְבוֹנָה עַל הַמִּזְבֵּחַ, בְּפֶ' "הָאוֹמֵר הֲרֵי עָלַי עִשָּׂרוֹן" ו] (לְקַמָּן קו:), דְּהָתָם וַדַּאי חָסֵר ז] פָּסוּל, דְּלָא כְּתִיב בֵּיהּ "וְאֶת כָּל הַלְּבוֹנָה" דְּיָלְפִינַן מִינָּהּ לְקַמָּן: "כָּל" – אֲפִילּוּ כָּל שֶׁהוּא. רַבִּי מֵאִיר. סְתָם מַתְנִיתִין דְּקָתָנֵי: חִיסֵּר לְבוֹנָתָהּ פְּסוּלָה. קוֹמֵץ בַּתְּחִלָּה. בִּשְׁעַת קְמִיצָה בָּעֵינַן שֶׁיְּהֵא בַּכְּלִי מְלֹא קוֹמֶץ לְבוֹנָה. וּבְהָא כּוּלְּהוּ מוֹדוּ דְּמִתְּחִילָּה בָּעֵי קוֹמֶץ, וְכִדְיָלְפִינַן מִג"ש בְּפֶ' "הָאוֹמֵר הֲרֵי עָלַי עִשָּׂרוֹן" ח] (שם דף קו:). וְקוֹמֵץ בַּסּוֹף. בִּשְׁעַת הַקְטָרַת לְבוֹנָה, שֶׁלֹּא תֶּחְסַר. רַבִּי יְהוּדָה סָבַר. *אִי הֲוָה כָּתַב "כֹּל" מַשְׁמַע דַּאֲפִי' קוֹרֶט אֶחָד, דְּ"כֹל" מַשְׁמַע כָּל שֶׁהוּא, כְּמוֹ "אֵין לְשִׁפְחָתְךָ ט] כֹּל" (מלכים ב ד). אֵת לְרַבּוֹת קוֹרֶט אַחֵר. הֲרֵי י] הוּא שְׁנַיִם. אֵת לָא דָּרֵישׁ. וְ"כֹל" מַשְׁמַע לֵיהּ כָּל דְּהוּ כְּר' יְהוּדָה. בָּזִיכִין. מְפָרֵשׁ בְּפֶרֶק "הָאוֹמֵר הֲרֵי עָלַי עִשָּׂרוֹן" (שם דף קו:) דְּבָעֵי חַד קוֹמֶץ בְּכָל בָּזָךְ וּבָזָךְ יא]. פְּשִׁיטָא. דְּהָא לָא כְּתִיב בָּהּ "כֹּל" דְּלִישְׁתַּמַּע כָּל שֶׁהוּא. כַּאֲשֶׁר עַל הַמִּנְחָה דָּמְיָא. וְלֵימָא נַמִי דְּהַאי "כָּל הַלְּבוֹנָה אֲשֶׁר עַל הַמִּנְחָה" קָאֵי נַמִי אַלְּבוֹנָה דְּבָזִיכִין, וְלִדְרוֹשׁ בָּהּ כָּל דְּהוּ, קמ"ל. שֶׁהִפְרִישׁ לָהּ שְׁנֵי קְמָצִים. פְּסוּלָה, דְּיוֹתֵר מִדַּאי רִיבָּה. קוֹדֶם קְמִיצָה. יב] נֶאֱבַד, לֹא הוּקְבְּעוּ עִם הַמִּנְחָה, וּכְשֵׁרָה. הוּקְבְּעוּ. וְהָוֵי כְּיָתֵר, וּפְסוּלָה. הַיְינוּ הַךְ. דְּהָא פְּשִׁיטָא לָן דְּסִילּוּק בָּזִיכִין כְּקוֹמֶץ דְּמִנְחָה יג]. שֶׁהִגִּיעַ זְמַנָּהּ. דְּקָרְבַּן מוּסָפִין. כְּמַאן דִּפְרִיקָה דָּמְיָא. וְאִם אָבַד לְאַחַר הַמּוּסָפִין אֵימָא הוּקְבְּעוּ כְּבָר יד] וּפְסָלָהּ. קמ"ל (א) כ"ש. ל"א, טו] וְלָא שְׁמַעְתִּי: כְּגוֹן שֶׁהִפְרִישׁ לָהּ שְׁנֵי קְמָצִין – כְּשֵׁרָה, דְּאָמְרִינַן: זִיל לְגַבֵּיהּ דְּהַאי חֲזֵי לֵיהּ, זִיל לְגַבֵּיהּ דְּהַאי חֲזֵי לֵיהּ. לֹא (ב) הוּקְבְּעוּ – וּכְשֵׁרָה, דְּלָא קָרֵינָא בֵּיהּ "פְּרָט לְשֶׁחָסְרָה" אֲפִי' לְר"מ דְּפָסֵיל בְּחִיסּוּר לְבוֹנָה. הוּקְבְּעוּ – וְהָוֵי חִיסּוּר לְבוֹנָתָהּ בִּשְׁעַת הַקְטָרָה, וּפָסוּל לְר' מֵאִיר. מתני' לֶאֱכוֹל שְׁיָרֶיהָ בַּחוּץ. חוּץ לָעֲזָרָה. אוֹ לְהַקְטִיר קוּמְצָהּ בַּחוּץ. דְּמַחֲשָׁבָה פּוֹסֶלֶת בֵּין שֶׁחִישֵּׁב טז] לַאֲכִילַת אָדָם בֵּין שֶׁחִישֵּׁב עַל אֲכִילַת מִזְבֵּחַ כְּגוֹן הַקְטָרָה, דִּכְתִיב יז] בֵּיהּ גַּבֵּי מַחֲשָׁבָה (ויקרא ז): "וְאִם הֵאָכֹל יֵאָכֵל מִבְּשַׂר זֶבַח שְׁלָמָיו בַּיּוֹם הַשְּׁלִישִׁי" כו', וְאָמַר בְּתוֹרַת כֹּהֲנִים: *יָכוֹל כְּמַשְׁמָעוֹ, שֶׁאִם אָכַל מִמֶּנּוּ בַּיּוֹם שְׁלִישִׁי יְהֵא נִפְגָּל? ת"ל "הַמַּקְרִיב אוֹתוֹ" – בִּשְׁעַת הַקְרָבָה נִפְגָּל וְאֵינוֹ נִפְגָּל בַּשְּׁלִישִׁי. אַלְמָא בְּמַחֲשָׁבָה מַיְירֵי, שֶׁחִישֵּׁב לֶאֱכוֹל מִמֶּנּוּ בַּשְּׁלִישִׁי. וּכְתִיב "אִם הֵאָכֹל יֵאָכֵל" – בִּשְׁתֵּי אֲכִילוֹת הַכָּתוּב מְדַבֵּר, בַּאֲכִילַת אָדָם וַאֲכִילַת מִזְבֵּחַ. פָּסוּל. דְּמַחֲשֶׁבֶת חוּץ לִמְקוֹמוֹ פּוֹסֶלֶת, דְּאָמַר בְּת"כ: *יָכוֹל לֹא יח] תִּפְסַל מַחֲשֶׁבֶת חוּץ לִמְקוֹמוֹ? כְּשֶׁהוּא אוֹמֵר בְּפָרָשַׁת "קְדוֹשִׁים תִּהְיוּ": "אִם הֵאָכֹל יֵאָכֵל בַּיּוֹם הַשְּׁלִישִׁי", אִם אֵינוֹ עִנְיָן לְחוּץ לִזְמַנּוֹ, דְּהָא יט] כְּתָבֵיהּ בְּ"צַו אֶת אַהֲרֹן": "הָאוֹכֶלֶת מִמֶּנּוּ עֲוֹנָהּ תִּשָּׂא" – תְּנֵהוּ עִנְיָן לְחוּץ *לִמְקוֹמוֹ, חוּץ לִזְמַנּוֹ בְּהִכָּרֵת וְאֵין חוּץ לִמְקוֹמוֹ כ] כָּרֵת. וְאִי קַשְׁיָא, הָא כָּתַב גַּבֵּי חוּץ לִמְקוֹמוֹ בִּ"קְדוֹשִׁים תִּהְיוּ": "וְאוֹכְלָיו עֲוֹנוֹ יִשָּׂא וְנִכְרְתָה" וגו'! הַהוּא מוֹקְמִינַן לֵהּ בִּכְרֵיתוֹת בְּפ"ק (דף ה.) לְכָרֵת דְּנוֹתָר, בִּגְזֵירָה שָׁוָה דְּ"קוֹדֶשׁ" "קוֹדֶשׁ". כא] וְאִי קַשְׁיָא: אַמַּאי לָא תְּנָא נַמִי כַּזַּיִת מִלְּבוֹנָתָהּ? תָּרֵיץ: הַךְ סְתָמָא *כְּרַבָּנַן דְּאָמְרִי לְעֵיל דִּלְבוֹנָה כְּשֵׁרָה בְּקוֹרֶט אֶחָד, הִלְכָּךְ לָא תָּנָא כַּזַּיִת. לְמָחָר. דְּהַיְינוּ חוּץ לִזְמַנּוֹ, דְּמִנְחָה אֵינָהּ נֶאֱכֶלֶת אֶלָּא לְיוֹם וָלַיְלָה.* כב] וְאִיתְקַשׁ לְחַטָּאת וְאָשָׁם, וּבְחַטָּאת וְאָשָׁם אָמַר בְּת"כ גַּבֵּי תּוֹדָה: מִנַּיִן לְרַבּוֹת חַטָּאת וְאָשָׁם דְּיֵאָכֵל בְּיוֹם קָרְבָּנוֹ? תַּלְמוּד לוֹמַר "זֶבַח", "וּבְשַׂר זֶבַח תּוֹדַת שְׁלָמָיו" וגו' (ויקרא ו).

פִּיגּוּל

תוספות

קומץ ולבונה שחסר כו'. בכל דוכתי משמע דשיעור לבונה כקומץ. ולקמן בפרק בתרא (דף קו:) גמר דלבונה לא יפחות מן הקומץ, דכתיב: "והרים ממנו בקומצו מסלת המנחה ומשמנה ואת כל הלבונה", מקיש לבונה להרמה דמנחה, מה הרמה דמנחה קומץ – אף לבונה קומץ. ולבונה באה בבזיכין שני קמצים יליף לה בת"כ בג"ש, דנאמר כאן "אזכרתה" וגבי קומץ "אזכרתה", מה להלן מלא הקומץ אף כאן מלא הקומץ. והיינו שני קמצים, מלא הקומץ לסדר זה ומלא הקומץ לסדר זה. **ר'** יהודה סבר כל ואפי' חד קורט. משמע הכא דרבי יהודה סבר ד"הלבונה" – כולה לבונה משמע. וה"נ אית ליה בפ"ק דבכורות (דף ג.): "בכור" – כוליה בכור משמע, כתב רחמנא "כל" דאפי' כל שהוא. ותימה: דבפרק "כסוי הדם" (חולין פח.) שמעינן ליה לר' יהודה: "דמו" – מקצת דמו משמע! ושמא משום דכתיב "דמו" בוי"ו דריש, ד"דם" כל דם משמע – כתב רחמנא "דמו" דאפי' מקצת דמו. ולפי סברא זו לא יתכן מה שפוסק ר"ת כרבי יהודה דאמר: אם יש שם דם שלא הוא – פטור מלכסות, דהא אמר בבכורות (דף ג:): לית דחש לה להא דר' יהודה דאמר: שותפות גוי חייבת בבכורה! ושמא יש לחלק בין דם לבכור. וכמו כן צריך לחלק דלא תקשי הסיא דבכורות אהא דאמר פרק "אלמנה ניזונית" (כתובות נז:): לית דחש לה להא דר"ש דאמר: *מקצת כסף ככל כסף, ובשמעתין משמע דאית ליה לר"ש "הלבונה" – כולה לבונה. והא דדריש רבי יהודה הכא כולה לבונה, וכן לקמן בפ' "כל המנחות באות מצה" (דף נו:) דריש "כל מוס", ובריש "אלו עוברין" (פסחים מג.) לא דריש "כל", לקמן אפרש בפרק "כל המנחות באות מצה" (דף נו:) בע"ה*. **ורבי** שמעון את לא דריש. פי': לא דריש להא דרשא, אבל דלא דריש כלל לא קאמר, דשמעינן דדריש "את" בפ"ק דבכורות (דף ו:) גבי "את הגמל", דדריש ליה לאסור את חלבו, ולקמן בפרק "כל המנחות באות מצה" (דף ס:) דדריש ר"ש "את המנחה" לרבות שאר מנחות להגשה. ומש"ה לא מייתי הכא ההיא דשמעון העמסוני כדמייתי לה התם בבכורות על רבנן. וכן יש לתרץ מרבי יהודה דדריש הכא "את", ובפ"ב דסוטה (דף יז.) *דריש רבי יהודה צוואות וקבלות מ"האלות" כר"מ, ואליבא דר"מ מסיק התם ד"את" לא דריש, וע"כ כמו כן יאמר לרבי יהודה. אלא ודאי לא דריש להאי דרשא קאמר. ומיהו י"ל, דר' יהודה "את" לא דריש, "ואת" דריש, והכא כתב "ואת כל הלבונה". ועוד קשה, דר' יוסי הגלילי דריש בפרק "שור שנגח ד' וה'" (ב"ק מג.): נקי מדמי ולדות, אלמא דריש הנאת עורו מ"את בשרו" כדמשמע התם. ובפרק "בהמה המקשה" (חולין דף ע:) משמע דלא דריש "את" בגמרא *בהמה שמת עוברה כו', דקאמר על מילתיה דר"י הגלילי: קלוט במעי קלוטה ליטמא, משמע דסבר כרבנן דר"ש, דשרו פרק קמא דבכורות (דף ו:) קלוט (במעי קלוטה) ולא דריש אתין. ומיהו יש לפרש, דפריך בחולין (שם) מקלוט במעי קלוטה שראשו ורובו דומה לאמו, דשרי לכ"ע. **כגון** שהפריש לה שני קמצים. וא"ת: והיאך קדשי? אי בבת אחת – האמרינן בפרק "התודה" (לקמן עח:): תודה ששחטה על שמונים חלות לא קדשו לר' יוחנן, ואי בזה אחר זה – האמרי' בקדושין בפ"ב (דף נ:) דכל שאינו בזה אחר זה אפי' בבת אחת אינו. והכא כיון דליתיה בבת אחת – כל שכן בזה אחר זה! וי"ל, כגון דאמר: יקדש קומץ אחד מתוך שני קמצים, כדאמר בפרק "התודה" (שם): הכל מודים היכא דאמר ליקדשו ארבעים מתוך שמונים דקדישי.

כגון שהפריש לה שני קמצין. בלשון כג] אחד פי' בקונטרס: דההיא דקתני פסולה – שהפריש לה שני קמצין. ואי אפשר לומר כן, דלעיל משמע דבהפריש לה שני לוגין יש לי להכשיר יותר, הואיל והאי חזי ליה והאי חזי ליה, וה"ה הכא שיש להכשיר יותר בהפריש לה שני קמצים מבקומץ וחצי. ועוד, דקאמר בסמוך: הפריש שני קמצים ואבד אחד מהן קודם קמיצה – לא הוקבעו, פירוש: וכשרה. אבד לאחר קמיצה – הוקבעו, והויא יתירה

עא א ב מיי' פי"א מהלכות פסה"מ הלכה יז:

עב ג מיי' שם הלכה ט:

עג ד ה מיי' שם הלכה יח:

עד ו ז מיי' פי"ג מהל' פסה"מ הלכה א ופט"ו הלכה א:

לא אמרינן מקלת נ"ק

[ועי' תוס' בכורות ג. ד"ה ור' יהודה ובחולין פח. ד"ה ורבי יהודה]

שיטה מקובצת

א] תיבות ר' שמעון אומר נמחק: ב] ר"מ סבר לפ"ה משמע דפליגי במשמעות דהלבונה דלר"מ הלבונה קצת לבונה משמע וכל אתא לרבות דבעיא כולה לבונה ולר' יהודה לבונה משמע כולה וכל אתא לגרוע אקורט ודוחק ונ"ל דלכ"ע משמע לבונה רוב לבונה ור"מ סבר כל לאסופי אתא ור' יהודה סבר כל לגרוע אתא לשון כל דהו ולאוקמא אקורט וכיוצא בזה יש בריש בכורות גבי כל בכור. תו"ח: ג] מקומצה בחוץ: ד] ואין בו כרת. פ"ה ואי קשיא אמאי לא תנא כזית מלבונה תריץ הך סתמא כרבנן ולא נהירא דא"כ ליתני להקטיר קורט אחד מלבונה ועוד הא אוקימנא מתניתין כר"מ דאמר חסר לבונתה פסולה ונראה לפרש דטעמא דמתירין כזית להקטרת קומץ דילפינן אכילת מזבח מאכילת אדם דכתיב אם האכל יאכל בשתי אכילות הכתוב מדבר ומה אכילת אדם בכזית אף אכילת מזבח בכזית ודוקא במידי דבר אכילה אבל במידי דלאו בר אכילה לא ילפינן אכילת מזבח מאכילת אדם ולבונה לאו בר אכילה ומיהו לא נהירא דהא בהדיא תנא בגמרא הקומץ והלבונה שהקריב מהם כזית בחוץ אלמא גבי הקטרת חוץ יליף אכילת מזבח מאכילת אדם

רש"ק מ"ו

[עירובין עה. וש"נ]

דכל משמע אפילו קורט ל"ק

[פסחים כב: וש"נ]

וכן בזבחים כט.

[ועיין זבחים כח:]

למקומו הס"ד אח"כ ד"ה ואין בו כרת ואי כו' כצ"ל וכ"ה בס"י ל"ק

כר"ש דאמר לעיל

[ועי' רש"י זבחים כט. ד"ה ליום ולילה וכו' ע"ש]

הגהות הב"ח

(א) רש"י ד"ה כמאן דפריקה וכו' קמ"ל ל"א ולא כצ"ל ותיבות כ"ש נמחק: (ב) בא"ד לא הוקבעו כצ"ל ב"ב פירוש זה הוא על הא דאמר רמי בר חמא על פי לשון אחר שפרש"י כאן:

אלא נראה לומר דסמך אכולהו כזית דלעיל ולא חש להאריך והוא הדין ללבונה. תו"ח: ה] והתניא קומץ לבונה כו' וגרס' בתוספתא ר"ש אומר קומץ לבונה שחסר הלכך קא פריך מינה דר' שמעון הס"ד ואח"כ מה"ד לבונה הבאה כו' והשאר נמחק: ו] עשרון ובת"כ נפקא לן קרבן מנחה מלמד שהיחיד מתנדב לבונה: ז] חסר פסל דלא: ח] עשרון ופלוגתא היא [בירושלמי שקלים פ"ו ה"ח] אי קומץ בעלים בעינן או קומץ כהן: ט] כל בבית: י] הרי שנים הס"ד: יא] ובזך ובת"כ יליף לה בגז"ש ר"ש אומר נאמר כאן אזכרה ונאמר להלן אזכרה מה להלן מלא קומץ אף כאן מלא קומץ מלמד שהוא שני קומצין מלא הקומץ לסדר זה ומלא קומץ לסדר זה: אחר ד"ה בזיכין מה"ד בתחלה תחילת סדור והס"ד ומה"ד בסוף ההקטרה והס"ד: יב] קמיצה סבר לא ותיבת נאבד נמחק: יג] דמנחה הס"ד ומה"ד בריר קומץ דידיה שאינו מעורב עם המנחה דהא עומד בבזיכין ומה"ד שהגיע: יד] כבר ופסולה: טו] ל"א כגון שהפריש כו' דאמרינן זיל לגבי האי חזי ליה זיל לגבי האי חזי ליה: טז] שחושב על אכילת: יז] תיבת ביה נמחק: יח] תפסיל במחשבת: יט] כתבה בצו את אהרן כדפרש' לעיל תנהו ענין לחוץ למקומו הס"ד ומה"ד ואין בו כרת. האוכל משירי המנחה אין חייב כרת דהכי אמרינן בת"כ יכול יהא חייב על חוץ למקומו כרת ת"ל בחוץ לזמנו האוכלת [ממנו עונה תשא כו'] ותיבות תנהו ענין לחוץ למקומו נמחק: כ] למקומו בהכרת ואי קשיא הא כתיב: כא] קודש אבל בחוץ למקומו יש כרת דילפינן עון עון מנותר: כב] דאיתקש לחטאת ואשם ו' נמחק: כג] בלשון ראשון ותיבת אחד נמחק:

או קורט לבונה – פסול". § כל הני למה לי? צריכא, דאי תנא צרור – משום דלאו בת הקרבה היא, אבל מלח דבת הקרבה היא – אימא תתכשר; ואי תנא מלח – דלא איקבע בהדי מנחה מעיקרא, א] (שאינו מולח אלא הקומץ בלבד,) אבל לבונה דאיקבע בהדי מנחה מעיקרא – אימא תתכשר, קמ"ל. § "מפני שאמרו: הקומץ החסר או היתר – פסול". § מאי איריא משום חסר ויתר? ב] ותיפוק ליה משום חציצה! א"ר ירמיה: מן הצד. אמר ליה אביי לרבא: כיצד קומצין? אמר ליה: כדקמצי אינשי. איתיביה: *זו זרת, זו קמיצה, זו אמה, זו אצבע, זו גודל! ג] אלא להשוות. (כלומר, קומץ מלא היד כדי שלא יהא חסר, ואחר כך מוחק באצבע קטנה מלמטה.) היכי עביד? אמר רב זוטרא בר טוביה אמר רב: חופה [א]שלש אצבעותיו עד שמגיע על פס ידו וקומץ. תניא נמי הכי: "מלא קומצו" – יכול (א) מבורץ? ת"ל: "בקומצו"; אי "בקומצו", יכול בראשי אצבעותיו? ת"ל: "מלא קומצו"; הא כיצד? חופה שלש אצבעותיו על פס ידו וקומץ; במחבת ובמרחשת מוחק בגודלו מלמעלה ובאצבעו קטנה מלמטה, *וזו היא עבודה קשה ד] שבמקדש. זהו ותו לא? והאיכא מליקה, והאיכא חפינה! אלא, *זו היא אחת מעבודות קשות שבמקדש. א"ר פפא: [ב]פשיטא לי, "מלא קומצו" – כדקמצי אינשי. בעי רב פפא: קמץ בראשי אצבעותיו, ה] מאי? מן הצדדין, מאי? ממטה למעלה, מאי? [ג]תיקו. אמר *רב פפא: פשיטא לי, "מלא חפניו" – [ד]כדחפני אינשי. בעי רב פפא: חפן בראשי אצבעותיו, מהו? מן הצדדין, מהו? ו] חפן בזו ובזו וקרבן זו אצל זו, מהו? תיקו. בעי *רב פפא: דבקיה לקומץ בדפניה דמנא, מאי? תוך כלי בעינן והאיכא, או דלמא הנחה בתוכו בעינן וליכא? [ה]תיקו. בעי מר בר רב אשי: הפכיה למנא ודבקיה לקומץ בארעיתא דמנא, מאי? הנחה בתוכו בעינן והאיכא, או דלמא כתיקנו בעינן וליכא? [ו]תיקו. §

מתני' ז] כיצד הוא עושה? פושט את אצבעותיו על פס ידו. ריבה שמנה, חסר שמנה, חיסר לבונתה – פסולה. §

גמ' היכי דמי ריבה שמנה? א"ר ח] *אליעזר: *)[ז]כגון שהפריש לה שני לוגין. ולוקמה כגון דעריב בה שמן דחולין ושמן דחבירתה! וכי תימא, שמן דחולין ושמן דחבירתה לא פסל, ט] מתקיף לה רב זוטרא בר טוביה: אלא מעתה, מנחת חוטא דפסל בה שמן היכי משכחת לה? אי דידה – הא לית לה, אי דחולין ודחבירת' – הא אמרת: לא פסל! י] (ואי אמרת דאפריש לה שמן, כיון דלית לה שמן כלל – חולין נינהו!) ור' יא] *אליעזר: לא מיבעיא קאמר; לא מיבעיא [ח]דחולין ודחבירתה דפסיל, אבל הפריש לה שני לוגין, הואיל והאי חזי לי' והאי חזי לי' – אימא לא ליפסיל, קמ"ל. ומנא ליה לר' *אליעזר הא? אמר רבא: מתני' קשיתיה, מאי איריא דתני "ריבה שמנה"? ליתני: ריבה לה שמן! אלא הא קמ"ל, דאע"ג דהפריש לה שני לוגין. § "חיסר לבונתה". [ט]ת"ר: חסרה ועמדה על קורט אחד – פסולה, על שני קרטין – כשרה, דברי רבי יהודה. רבי שמעון אומר: על קורט אחד – כשרה, פחות מכאן – פסולה. והתניא

*) [עיין תוספות זבחים ל. ד"ה דבריו]

רש"י

או קורט לבונה פסול. מפני יב] שהקומץ חסר כדי מקום הקורט. וא"ת: כיצד קומץ? והלא לבונה על המנחה היא, דכתיב (ויקרא ו): "כל הלבונה אשר על המנחה"! תשובה לדבר: כשקומץ מסלק הלבונה כולה לצד אחד, וקומץ הסולת מאמצע הכלי יג]. **מלח בת הקרבה היא.** דלאחר שהיה הקומץ על המזבח היה מולחו יד] כדפרישית, דהכי אמר בפ"ג (לקמן כ.): יכול תהא מנחה כולה טעונה מלח? ת"ל: "על כל קרבנך" – טו] קרבן טעון מלח, ואין כל המנחה טעונה מלח. ואי קשיא: ולישמעינן לבונה, וכל שכן צרור ומלח! תריץ: אי תנא לבונה ברישא, הכי נמי דלא מיבעיא ליה למיתני צרור ומלח, אלא הואיל ונקט צרור ברישא – תנא לבונה ומלח טז]. **מאי איריא** משום קומץ חסר תיפוק ליה דצרור פסול משום חציצה. דחוצץ בין ידו לקמח, וחציצה פוסלת בקדשים כדמפ' בזבחים (דף כד.). אי נמי, חוצץ בין קמח לקמח, כגון *באמצע הקומץ, וחולק את הקומץ ונראה כשני חצאי קמצים. **מן הצד.** למעלה אצל גודל, או למטה אצל קמיצה, דליכא חציצה. דהיינו מן הצד, דלאחר שקמץ הופך גב ידו למטה כדי שלא יפול מן הקומץ כלום, והוי יז] גודל וקמיצה מן הצד. והשתא ליכא חציצה, שאצל הקמח מוטל הצרור, אבל חסרון איכא. **כדקמצי אינשי.** משמע בכל האצבעות. יח] **זרת.** אצבע קטנה, ממנה מתחיל הזרת, וכ"מ למדת חשן זרת ארכה. **זו קמיצה.** ממנה מתחיל הקומץ, מאותו אצבע שאצל הקטנה. **זו אמה.** ממנה מודדין כל אמות הבנין והכלים, לפי שהיא ארוכה מכולן. ושתי *אמות היו בשושן הבירה – שתי מקלות שהן אמה, ובהן מודדין אמות הבנין, ואותן מקלות נמדדו באותו אצבע יט] שהוא ארוך. **זו אצבע.** לטבל הכהן אצבעו בדם. **זו גודל.** לבהונות דמצורע. אלמא כ] קמיצה בקומץ ולא זרת! ומשני: כי אמרינן דכולהו אצבעות בעינן לקמיצה. **להשוות.** דאם יוצא קמח למטה מן הקומץ – מוחקו ומשויהו באצבע קטנה שלא יהא מבורץ, וכן מלמעלה בגודל. **היכי עביד.** אמתני' מהדר דקתני: זו קמיצה, דממנה מתחיל הקומץ (ג). **ת"ל בקומצו.** "והרים ממנו בקומצו" (ויקרא ו). **בראשי אצבעותיו.** מעט, כא] שלא יגיע עד פס ידו. **במחבת ומרחשת.** דמעשיהן אפויין, כב] דאמר לקמן בפרק "אלו מנחות נקמצות" (דף עה:) דלאחר שהן אפויין פותתן וקומץ, הלכך אי אפשר לפותתן דקות כל כך, וכשהוא קומץ יוצאות חוץ כג] למקומו, הלכך מוחק בגודלו מלמעלה ובאצבעו קטנה מלמטה. כד] **וזו היא עבודה קשה שבמקדש.** שבקושי גדול הוא משוה שלא יהא לא חסר ולא יותר. **מליקה.** אמרינן בפ' "קדשי קדשים" (זבחים סד:): זו היא עבודה קשה. **ובחפינה.** נמי אמרי' בפ' "הוציאו לו" במסכת יומא (דף מט:): אוחז כה] את הכף בראשי אצבעותיו ומעלה בגודלו כו', וזו היא עבודה קשה. **כדקמצי אינשי.** מכניס לידי אצבעותיו ודוחק בקמח, והקמח נכנס בתוך ידו. **בראשי אצבעותיו.** שהכניס ראשי אצבעותיו בקמח ופס ידו כלפי כו] קמח, וקומץ מלא קומצו עד פס ידו כתקנו, מהו? **מן הצדדין.** שנתן גב ידו על הקמח והוליך ידו עד שנכנס הקמח דרך צידו לתוך ידו. ל"א: מן הצדדין – מצדי הכלי, שלא קמץ באמצע הכלי. **מלמטה למעלה.** שהכניס כז] *אצבעותיו בקמח וגב היד כנגד הקמח וקומץ. **מלא חפניו.** דיום הכיפורים, קטרת סמים דקה. **כדחפני אינשי.** שמכניסין לידי ידיהם וחופנים. **מן הצדדים.** שהכניס קטרת בחפניו דרך בין גודל לאצבע. ל"א: מן הצדדים של כלי. **דבקיה לקומץ.** בשעת קידושו כח] לכלי בדפנו דמנא מבפנים. **בארעיתא דמנא.** כגון שהיה לכלי בית קיבול מאחוריו כמו שיש בקערות כט]. **מתני' ריבה שמנה.** דדינה לוג, כדאמר בפ' "שתי מדות" (לקמן פח.) מהאי קרא: "למנחה ולוג שמן". **חיסר שמנה.** פסולה, כדאמרן לעיל (ט:): "משמנה" – שאם חיסר כל שהוא פסול. **חיסר לבונתה.** דשיעור לבונה מלא הקומץ. בפ' "הרי עלי עשרון" (לקמן קו:) מפרש לה בג"ש, נאמר ל] הרמה כו'. ואי קשיא: ליתני ריבה לבונתה! הא מפרש לה בגמ'. **גמ' שהפריש לה.** לשם מנחה זו (הפריש לה). **ב' לוגין.** לא] ועירבו עמה, דנראית *כשתי הלחם. אבל בלוג ומחצה קס"ד דלא מיפסלא. **ולוקמה כגון דעריב בה.** פורתא שמן לב] דחול, או שמן דחבירתה. **דפסיל בה שמן.** דאמר בפרק "כל המנחות" (לקמן נט:): לא ישים עליה שמן, ואם שם פסול. **אי דידה.** שהפרישו לשמה. **הא לית לה.** וכיון דלא חזי לה – לא מקדיש לג] שמופרש שמן לה. **והאי חזי לה.** כלומר, זיל לגביה דהאי – חזי ליה, וזיל לגביה דהאי – חזי ליה. **ומנא ליה לרבי אליעזר הא.** דאפילו הפרישן לד] לשמן פסול, אם עירבו עמה? **שמנה.** משמע דהופרש לה] לשמה. והתניא

תוספות

וזו היא עבודה קשה שבמקדש. למ"ד בפרק "אלו מנחות" (לקמן עה:) שמחזירן לסולתן, אינה קשה יותר ממנחת סולת. אלא סבר לה כמ"ד שהיה מחלקה לשנים ושנים לארבעה. **והא איכא חפינה.** כשהיה נכנס לפני ולפנים, ולא כשהיה חופן בלשכת בית אבטינס. ועבודה קשה היא מאד כדמוכח ביומא (דף מט:). **מלמטה למעלה.** פירש בקונטרס: שהכניס ראשי אצבעותיו בקמח וגב ידו כנגד הקמח וקמץ. ואין זה כראשי אצבעותיו דלעיל, דהתם פס ידו כנגד הקמח, ומכניס ראשי אצבעותיו וקומץ מלא קומצו עד פס ידו. והשתא לפי' הקונטרס קורא ראשי אצבעותיו למטה. וכן מפרש ר"ת במסכת שבת (דף לד:) גבי ציצין הפורשין למעלה – פירוש: לצד פיסת היד. ומביא ראיה מהא דאמר בפ' "כל היד" (נדה יג.): מן העטרה ולמעלה, דלצד הגוף קורא למעלה. ואינה ראייה כל כך, דלגבי מילה שהיא תלוייה שייך לקרות ראש המילה למטה, אבל אצבעות שאדם זוקף אצבעותיו למעלה שייך לקרות למעלה ראשי האצבעות. ו"מלמטה למעלה" יש לפרש: שמכניס ידו בקמח דרך פס היד עד שמגיע לראשי אצבעותיו*).

*) [וע' תוס' שבת לד: ד"ה והוא] קומץ

עין משפט נר מצוה

סו א ב ג מיי' פי"ג מהלכות מעה"ק הל' יב סמג לאוין שב:
סז ד מיי' פ"ד מהלכות יוה"כ הלכה א:
סח ה ו מיי' פי"א מהל' פסה"מ הלכה כה:
סט ז מיי' שם הלכה ע:
ע ח ט מיי' שם הל' ח:

גליון הש"ס

גמרא זו היא אחת מעבודות קשות. עיין לקמן דף נד ע"א תוספות ד"ה אין לך:

שיטה מקובצת

א] תיבות שאינו מולח אלא הקומץ בלבד נמחק: ב] תיפוק לי' אות ו' נמחק: ג] זו גודל להשוות היכי עביד והשאר נמחק: ד] שבמקדש עיין תוס' (לקמן דף נד ע"א): ה] אצבעותיו מהו מן הצדדין מהו ממטה למעלה מהו: ו] הצדדין מהו ממטה למעלה מהו חפן: ז] תיבות כיצד הוא עושה פושט את אצבעותיו על פס ידוי נמחק: ח] רבי אלעזר: ט] תיבות מתקיף לה רב זוטרא בר טוביא אלא מעתה נמחק: י] תיבות ואי אמרת דאפריש לה שמן כיון דלית לה שמן כלל חולין נינהו נמחק: יא] ר' אלעזר: יב] מפני שחסר הקומץ: יג] הכלי. כן מפורש בפ"ב דסוטה: יד] היה מולחו ממלח של צבור דאמרי' בפ"ג והשאר נמחק: טו] קרבנך קומץ שהוא קרבן: טז] ומלח הס"ד ומה"ד דלא איקבע בהדי מנחה בכלי אחד דהא לאחר שהקטירו לקומץ היה מולחו הס"ד ומה"ד קומץ החסר פסול בהקומץ רבה ילפי לה מדכתיב מלא קומצו תרי זימני: יז] והוי להו גודל: יח] מה"ד זו זרת אצבע קטנה כו' למדת החשן: יט] אצבע ארוכה הס"ד ואח"כ מה"ד זו אצבע דטבל הכהן את אצבעו: כ] אלמא בקמיצה קומץ ולא בזרת: כא] עד שלא יגיע: כב] אפויין ואמר: כג] חוץ לקומץ הלכך מוחק בגודל מלמעלה: כד] מה"ד וזו היא: כה] אוחז בכף בראשי אצבעותיו: כו] כלפי הקמח: כז] שהכניס ראשי אצבעותיו בקמח וגב ידו כנגד: כח] קידושו בכלי: כט] בקערות. רש"י כת"י ולי נראה מארעיתא דמנא שהפך הכלי ודבקיה לקומץ בארעית דמנא מתוכו ע"כ נראה לפרש שהפך הכלי וזרק ונדחק הקומץ מלמטה למעלה: ל] נאמר כאן בגמרא: לא] שני לוגין ועירבן עמה דנראה כשתי מנחות: לב] שמן דחולין ותיבת דחול נמחק. רש"י של מהר"פ דחולין ולוקמה כגון דעריב בה שמן דחולין אפי' לא הפרישו לשמה ואפילו אין בה ב' לוגין שלימים או שעירב בה שמן מחברתה ממנחה אחרת ע"כ: לג] מקדיש שמן המופרש: לד] הפרישן לשמה: לה] דהופרש כולה לשמה.

מסורת הש"ס

רש"ק מ"ז
כתובות ה:
ס"א מוטל באמצע הקומץ חולק את נ"ק
יומא מז: ע"ש
[ס מז: מנ: זבחים סד:]
[יומא מז:]
[לקמן לח.]
[יומא מח.]
נ"ל אלעזר
נ"ל אלעזר
נ"ל אלעזר
ראשי אצבעותיו נ"ק
נ"ק מ"ז
נ"ל כשתי קומצין אבל כו' גירסת נ"ק כשתי מנחות]

הגהות הב"ח

(א) גמ' יכול קמצו מבורץ נ"ל: (ב) רש"י ד"ה אחר ד"ה היכי עביד נ"ל ד"ה קומצו מבורץ גדוש ולישנא אחרינא שיש קמח בין ראשי אצבעותיו לפס ידו:

תורה אור

א] וַהֲרֵי זְרִיקָה דְּלָא כָּתַב בֵּיהּ אֶלָּא כְּהוּנָּה, וּתְנַן: זָרַק בִּשְׂמֹאל – פָּסוּל, וְלָא פָּלֵיג ר' שִׁמְעוֹן! אָמַר *אַבַּיֵי: פָּלֵיג בִּבְרַיְיתָא, דְּתַנְיָא: ב] קִבֵּל בִּשְׂמֹאל – פָּסוּל, וְר"ש מַכְשִׁיר; זָרַק בִּשְׂמֹאל – פָּסוּל, וְרַבִּי שִׁמְעוֹן מַכְשִׁיר. וְאֶלָּא הָא דְּאָמַר רָבָא: "יָד" "יָד" לִקְמִיצָה, לָמָּה לִי? מִכְּהוּנָּה נָפְקָא! חַד לְקוֹמֶץ, ג] וְחַד לְקִידּוּשׁ קוֹמֶץ. *לְרַבִּי שִׁמְעוֹן דְּלָא בָּעֵי קִידּוּשׁ קוֹמֶץ, וּלְמַאן דְּאָמַר נַמִי דְּבָעֵי קִידּוּשׁ קוֹמֶץ ד] לְר' שִׁמְעוֹן, *וּבִשְׂמֹאל אַכְשׁוּרֵי מַכְשַׁר, "יָד" "יָד" דְּרָבָא לָמָּה לִי? אִי לִקְמִיצָה גּוּפָהּ אַלִּיבָּא דְּר' שִׁמְעוֹן – מִדְּר' יְהוּדָה בְּרֵיהּ דְּר' חִיָּיא נָפְקָא, *דְּאָמַר ה] ר' יְהוּדָה בְּרֵיהּ דְּר' חִיָּיא: מַאי טַעְמָא דְּר"ש? דְּאָמַר קְרָא: °"קֹדֶשׁ קָדָשִׁים הִיא כַּחַטָּאת וְכָאָשָׁם" (ויקרא ו), בָּא לְעוֹבְדָהּ בַּיָּד – עוֹבְדָהּ בְּיָמִין כַּחַטָּאת, בָּא לְעוֹבְדָהּ בִּכְלִי – עוֹבְדָהּ בִּשְׂמֹאל כָּאָשָׁם! לָא נִצְרְכָא אֶלָּא לְקוֹמֶץ דְּמִנְחַת חוֹטֵא, סָלְקָא דַּעְתָּךְ אָמִינָא: הוֹאִיל וְאָמַר רַבִּי שִׁמְעוֹן שֶׁלֹּא *יְהֵא קָרְבָּנוֹ מְהוּדָּר, כִּי קָמֵיץ לָהּ נַמִי בִּשְׂמֹאל תִּתְכְּשַׁר, קָמַשְׁמַע לָן. § "קָמַץ וְעָלָה בְּיָדוֹ צְרוֹר אוֹ גַּרְגֵּר מֶלַח אוֹ

פָּלֵיג בִּבְרַיְיתָא. וְה"ה ו] לְמַתְנִיתִין. וְאִי קַשְׁיָא: לֵיתִיב מִקְּמִילָה, דְּלָא כְּתִיב אֶלָּא כְּהוּנָּה, וּתְנַן (לעיל דף ו.): קָמַץ בִּשְׂמֹאל פָּסוּל, וְלָא פָּלֵיג רַבִּי שִׁמְעוֹן! תָּרֵיץ: הַיְינוּ טַעְמָא דְּלָא פָּלֵיג בְּמִנְחָה, כִּדְאָמְרִינַן לְקַמָּן – דְּנָפְקָא לֵיהּ דִּשְׂמֹאל ז] פָּסוּל מִ"קֹּדֶשׁ קָדָשִׁים הִיא (כַּמִּנְחָה) כַּחַטָּאת וְכָאָשָׁם". מִכְּהוּנָּה נָפְקָא. דְּהָא כְּתִיב בָּהּ "וְקָמַץ הַכֹּהֵן", וְאָמַר רָבָא לְעֵיל לְרַבָּנַן, דְּהֵיכָא דִּכְתִיב אֶצְבַּע אוֹ כְּהוּנָּה אֵינוֹ אֶלָּא יָמִין, "יָד" "יָד" לָמָּה לִי? לְקִידּוּשׁ קוֹמֶץ (א). דְּכִי מְקַדֵּשׁ לְקוֹמֶץ בִּכְלִי יִתְּנֵהוּ בִּימִינוֹ לְתוֹךְ הַכְּלִי. וּלְרַבִּי שִׁמְעוֹן דְּלָא בָּעֵי קִידּוּשׁ קוֹמֶץ. בְּפ"ג (לקמן כו.), דְּקָתָנֵי: שֶׁלֹּא בִּכְלִי שָׁרֵת פְּסוּלָה וְרַבִּי שִׁמְעוֹן מַכְשִׁיר, ח] וּפְלִיגִי תְּרֵי אֲמוֹרָאֵי לְקַמָּן בַּגְּמָ', ר' יַנַּאי וְר' נַחְמָן בַּר יִצְחָק, חַד אָמַר: טַעְמָא דְּרַבִּי שִׁמְעוֹן – דְּלָא בָּעֵי מַתַּן כְּלִי, ט] דְּכֵיוָן דְּקָמַץ מִכְּלִי שָׁרֵת מַעֲלֵהוּ וּמַקְטִירוֹ אֲפִי' בְּמַקֵּידָה שֶׁל חֶרֶס. וְחַד אָמַר: הַכֹּל מוֹדִים בְּקוֹמֶץ שֶׁטָּעוּן קִידּוּשׁ, וְהָא דְּמַכְשַׁר ר' שִׁמְעוֹן שֶׁלֹּא בִּכְלֵי שָׁרֵת – י] בְּהַקְטָרַת *הַמִּנְחָה קָאָמַר. וְהַיְינוּ דְּקָפָרֵיךְ: וּלְרַבִּי שִׁמְעוֹן דְּלָא בָּעֵי קִידּוּשׁ קוֹמֶץ – כִּדְמְפָרֵשׁ רַבִּי יַנַּאי, וּלְרַב נַחְמָן יא] דְּאָמַר נַמִי ר' שִׁמְעוֹן בָּעֵי קִידּוּשׁ קוֹמֶץ, בִּשְׂמֹאל שָׁמְעִינַן לֵיהּ דְּמַכְשִׁיר ר' שִׁמְעוֹן לְקִידּוּשׁ קוֹמֶץ, כִּדְאָמְרִינַן לְקַמָּן: בָּא לְעוֹבְדָהּ בִּכְלִי – עוֹבְדָהּ בִּשְׂמֹאל כְּאָשָׁם. יָד יָד דְּרָבָא לָמָּה לִי אִי לִקְמִיצָה גּוּפָהּ. דְּתֶיהֱוֵי בְּיָמִין, דִּלְרַבִּי שִׁמְעוֹן לָא נָפְקָא לֵיהּ מִכְּהוּנָּה, כִּדְאָמְרִינַן לְעֵיל: לְרַבִּי שִׁמְעוֹן כְּהוּנָּה בָּעְיָא אֶצְבַּע. מַאי טַעְמָא דְּרַבִּי שִׁמְעוֹן. דְּאָמַר: שֶׁלֹּא בִּכְלִי שָׁרֵת יב] עוֹבְדָהּ – כְּשֵׁרָה, בְּפ"ג (שם.). יג] קָדְשֵׁי קָדָשִׁים וגו'. בְּמִנְחָה כְּתִיב. בָּא לְעוֹבְדָהּ בַּיָּד. שֶׁלֹּא קִידֵּשׁ קוֹמֶץ בִּכְלִי, אֶלָּא קָמַץ וְהוֹלִיךְ וְהִקְטִיר בְּיָדוֹ – עוֹבְדָהּ בְּיָמִין יד] *כַּחַטָּאת, [דְּחַטָּאת] לְבַד בְּיָמִין הִיא, דִּכְתִיב בָּהּ אֶצְבַּע וּכְהוּנָּה: "וְלָקַח הַכֹּהֵן מִדַּם הַחַטָּאת בְּאֶצְבָּעוֹ" (ויקרא ד). לְעוֹבְדָהּ בִּכְלִי. שֶׁקִּידֵּשׁ קוֹמֶץ בִּכְלִי – עוֹבְדָהּ לְקִידּוּשׁ קוֹמֶץ בִּשְׂמֹאל, כְּאָשָׁם מְצוֹרָע דִּכְתִיב בֵּיהּ שְׂמֹאל. אַלְמָא, מִדְּאַקְשֵׁי לְחַטָּאת מֵהָכָא נָפְקָא דְּכָל עֲבוֹדוֹת מִנְחָה הַנַּעֲשׂוֹת בְּיַד יָמִין בָּעֵינַן, וְ"יָד" "יָד" לָמָּה לִי? לְקוֹמֶץ דְּמִנְחַת חוֹטֵא. אִיצְטְרִיךְ "יָד" "יָד". או

והרי זריקה כו' ותנן זרק בשמאל פסול ולא פליג רבי שמעון **אמר אביי פליג בברייתא.** תימה: דאין זה טו] בא במשנה בשום מקום! ועוד הקשה ה"ר יעקב מאורלינ"ש: אמאי טז] פליג רבי שמעון? נהי דלא כתב בה אלא כהונה, מ"מ אתיא מהיקשא ד"זאת התורה" דאמר לקמן בסוף "התודה" (דף פג.) ובזבחים פרק "דם חטאת" (דף לח.): מה חטאת אינה באה אלא מן החולין וביום ובידו הימנית, אף כל כו'. ופריך: ידו הימנית מדרבה בר בר חנה נפקא, דכל מקום שנאמר אצבע וכהונה אינו אלא ימין! ומשני: כדי נסבה. אי נמי, סבר לה כרבי שמעון דכהונה בעיא אצבע. משמע בהדיא דר' שמעון יליף שאר קרבנות מחטאת! והשיב לו ר"ת, דגרסינן הכא: "והרי מליקה כו' ותנן מלק בשמאל פסולה", ומשנה היא בזבחים בפרק "חטאת העוף" (דף סח.), הכי תנן לה התם: כל הפסולים שמלקו מליקתן פסולה ואינה מטמאה בגדים אבית הבליעה, מלק בשמאל או בלילה כו'. והתלמוד הביאה בקוצר, שכן דרך התלמוד לקצר כמה משניות, והסופרים טעו כאן וכתבו במקום מליקה זריקה. ועוד אמר ר"ת, דאפי' גרסינן זריקה, מצינן למימר דהאי תנא סבר כרבי שמעון, אבל ר' שמעון לא סבר לה כוותיה, דלא יליף ימין בזריקה בשאר קרבנות מחטאת. וקשה לפר"ת, דאפילו גרסי' יז] *)דמלק, על כרחין אמת הוא דמכשר ר' שמעון זריקה בשמאל, כדמוכח בסמוך ומייתי לה בפרק קמא דזבחים (דף יא.) ופרק שני (דף כה.): מאי טעמא דרבי שמעון? בא לעובדה בכלי – עובדה בשמאל כאשם, והיינו בזריקת אשם שהוא בשמאל. דבקבלה לא מיירי, דאפי' חטאת נמי לא בעי ימין בקבלה לרבי שמעון, כדמוכח בפ"ב דזבחים (דף כד.), דאמר ר' שמעון: וכי נאמר יד בקבלה כו'! וצרך לתרץ, דהאי תנא סבר לה כר' שמעון, אבל ר' שמעון לא סבר לה כוותיה. ואם תאמר: לפר"ת, יח] אי נמי גרים "מלק" מליקה נפקא לן בפ"ק דחולין יט] (דף כא.) מדכתיב: "ואת השני יעשה עולה כמשפט" דדרשינן: כמשפט חטאת בהמה, מה חטאת בהמה אינה באה אלא מן החולין וביום ובידו הימנית. והתם נמי פריך: ימנית מדרבה בר בר חנה נפקא! ומשני, כ] *דכהונה בעי אלבע. ומהיקשא נמי ד"זאת התורה" נפקי עופות למאן דאית ליה היקשא כמו שפירשתי בריש פירקין! ויש לומר: דמליקה שהיא כנגד שחיטה לא נפקא, ובהזאה מיירי דבעיא ימין. אי נמי, ההוא תנא סבר לה כההוא תנא דפליג בפ"ב דזבחים (דף כד.) על ר' שמעון, ופוסל קבלה בשמאל משום דקסבר מקרא נדרש לפניו ולאחריו, ומוקי אלבע דכתיב גבי חטאת גם על קבלה. ולדידהו ילפינן שפיר מליקה בימין מחטאת, דקבלה לא *שייך למילתא דליתא בעוף, וילפינן מליקה. אבל ר' שמעון דקאמר קבל בשמאל כשר, ולית ליה ימין בחטאת בהמה אלא בהזאה לחודה – בעולת העוף נמי לא הוה בעי ימין במליקה, אלא בהזאה דוקא. ואם תאמר: כיון דר"ש פליג במליקה, א"כ מתניתין דזבחים פרק "חטאת העוף" (דף סח.) דמלק בשמאל כו' לא אתיא כרבי שמעון. הא ע"כ כר"ש אתיא, מדקתני סיפא: או בלילה אינו מטמא בגדים אבית הבליעה, ומפרש טעמא: משום דכל שפסולו בקודש אינו מטמא בגדים כו', ומפרש בגמ' דכיון דהך שחיטה מתרת את האיסור, פירוש: שאם עלה לא ירד. והיינו כר' שמעון, דלר' יהודה נשחטה בלילה תרד, דממעט לה מ"זאת היא העולה" בפ"ב דזבחים (דף כז:)! ויש לומר: דההוא תנא סבר לה כר' שמעון בחדא כא] ופליג עליה בחדא. אי נמי, אפילו ר' יהודה היה מודה בעופות דלא ירדו משום לילה, כיון דהוה פסולו בקודש, דלא כתיבי מיעוטי אלא בבהמה. ואם תאמר: דבריש "המזבח מקדש" (שם פג:) מפקי ר' עקיבא ור' יוסי הגלילי מעולה וכבשים דמזבח מקדש את הראוי לו, ומאן דדריש מכבשים פוסל הרבה בעוף יותר מבהמה! וי"ל: דר' יהודה סבר כמאן דדריש מעולה ולא כבשים, או משאר דרשות דהתם. ורבינו שמואל מיישב גירסת הספרים, ומפרש: והרי זריקה דלא כתיבא בה אלא כהונה, ותנן: זרק בשמאל פסול – כב] ומכיון דתנא כל הזבחים שקיבל בשמאל פסול כל שכן זריקה שהיא עיקר כפרה, ולא פליג רבי שמעון אלא אקבלה. ואי הוה פליג אזריקה – הוה ליה לאשמועינן כח דהיתירא, דמכשר ר' שמעון בזריקה כג] וכל שכן בקבלה. וא"ת: וכיון דילפינן אלבע דחטאת מג"ש כד] מאלבע מצורע דהוי בימין, היכי ילפינן ימין בשאר קרבנות מחטאת בהיקשא ד"זאת התורה"? הא פלוגתא דאמוראי היא בריש "איזהו מקומן" (זבחים נ.) אי דבר הלמד בג"ש חוזר ומלמד בהיקשא או לא! ונרא' מתוך כך דכל שכן דניחא הכי טפי, דהכי פריך: והרי זריקה דלא כתיבא ביה אלבע ולא פליג ר' שמעון, ואע"ג דדרשינן ימין מהיקשא דחטאת! הניחא למ"ד דבר הלמד מג"ש חוזר ומלמד בהיקשא, אלא למ"ד אין חוזר ומלמד בהיקשא אמאי לא פליג ר' שמעון? והשתא, הא דמשני בחולין (דף כב.): סבר לה כר' שמעון דכהונה בעיא אלבע – היינו כמ"ד חוזר ומלמד בהיקשא, ואידך שנויא דמשני בפרק "התודה" (לקמן פג.): כדי נסבה, הוי כמ"ד אין חוזר ומלמד בהיקשא. ומיהו בפרק קמא דחולין (דף כב.) ליתא שינויא דכדי נסבה, אבל בסוף "דם חטאת" (לקמן לח.) משני תרווייהו. ומיהו, אפשר דהכא מודו כולי עלמא דחוזר ומלמד בהיקשא, כיון דמצורע חול דהוא מלמד ראשון. ולתירוץ זה אנו צריכין בסמוך, דדריש: בא לעובדה ביד עובדה בימין כחטאת – **)דהיינו כה] חטאת, והיקשא גופיה מג"ש ילפינן לה. **פליג** בברייתא. הקשה בקונטרס: כו] ליתי מקמילה דלא כתיב בה אלא כהונה, ותנן: קמץ בשמאל פסל, ולא פליג רבי שמעון! ותירץ: דהיינו טעמא דלא פליג ר' שמעון, דנפיק ליה דשמאל פסול מ"קדשי קדשים היא כחטאת וכאשם". וקשה: דאי ידע לברייתא דבסמוך, מאי קשיא ליה מזריקה? הא בהדיא פליג, דמכשר זריקה בשמאל, כדקתני: לעובדה בכלי – עובדה בשמאל כאשם, דהיינו כזריקת אשם! ונראה דהוה משני: מ"יד" "יד" נפקא. **ולמאן** דאמר נמי בעי קידוש קומץ. היינו רב נחמן בר' יצחק. ואיתותב לקמן ב"הקומץ רבה" (דף כו.), ומכל מקום ניחא כז] לפרושי מילתיה לר' שמעון ככולי עלמא. **בשמאל** אכשורי מכשר. פירש בקונטרס: כדאמרינן לקמן, בא לעובדה בכלי – עובדה בשמאל כאשם. וקשה: דהתם מיירי במעלה הקומץ בכלי להקטיר, אבל כשנותן הקומץ בכלי שרת לקדשו – לעולם אימא לך דבעי נתינה בימין, כמו שהקמילה בימין! ובזבחים (דף כה.) פירש בקונטרס: דמכשר בשמאל – משום דלא עדיף מקבלה דמכשר רבי שמעון בשמאל. וגם זה קשה, דלעולם אימא לך דעדיף משום דכתיב בה קרא "יד" "יד" דרבא! ושמא לא מסתבר ליה למדרש דעדיף מקבלה. ואם תאמר: מאן דבעי קידוש קומץ, היינו רב נחמן לקמן ב"הקומץ רבה" (דף כו.), ***)פליג איהודה בריה דרבי חייא! ויש לומר: דהוה מפרש בא לעובדה ביד – בקמילה גופה כדמשמע הכא, או בהעלאה ביד להקטיר לאחר שנתקדש בכלי. **לקומץ** דמנחת חוטא. אף על גב ד"וימלא כפו ממנה" לא כתיב במנחת חוטא, ומיניה כח] ילפינן לעיל "יד" "יד" לקמילה. **קמץ** ועלה בידו צרור. ואם תאמר: מאי איריא עלה? אפי' נשאר בשיריים נמי, דהויא לה מנחה שחסרה קודם קמילה, ופסולה כדאמרן לעיל! ויש לומר: שאין רגילות לגמגם העשרון שלא יהא בו מעט יותר. ואם תאמר: ולרבי יהודה בן בתירא נימא דיחזור ויקמוץ! ושמא סתם לן תנא דלא כוותיה. אי נמי, יש לחלק בין קמילה פסולה לקמילה הנעשית מפסולין. וזו

*) נ"ל מליקה **) דהיינו היקשא חטאת גופיה מג"ש נ"ק ***) ורב נחמן פליג נ"ק

ג"ק מ"ז
[עירובין כ:]
ולר"ש ג"ק
בשמאל ג"ק
לקמן כו. זבחים יח. כה.
נ"א הקומץ קאמר כו' נ"ק
[לעיל ו. וש"נ]
סוטה יד:
כחטאת דבימין היא נ"ק

הגהות הב"ח
(א) רש"י ד"ה לקידוש קומץ היכא דמקדש:

כר"ש דכהונה נ"ק
שייך למילתא דליתא נ"ק

שיטה מקובצת

א] והרי זריקה דלא כתיב בה. (זבחים דף כד) כל הסוגיא: ב] דתניא זרק בשמאל והשאר נמחק: ג] וחד לקידוש קומץ ולר"ש כו' פרש"י בפ"ג דקתני כו'. עד א) קבל בשמאל פסול ור"ש מכשיר. וא"ת מאי קאמר בשמאל מכשיר ר"ש אין לומר אחר שקמצו בימינו נתנו בשמאל ומניחו בכלי שרת דבהא לא מכשיר ר"ש כדאיתא בפ' הקומץ רבה קבל בימינו ונתן לשמאלו יחזיר לימינו דברי ר"א ור"ש והכ"א כיון שנתנו לשמאל פוסלתו ומפרש מ"ט משום דבעי לאקדושי בכלי וכיון שנתן לשמאל נעשה כדם שנשפך מן הצואר לרצפה ואספו שהוא פסול מכלל דר"א ור"ש לא בעו קדוש אלמא מאן דבעי קידוש כלי מיד שנתנו לשמאל פסלו ואם כן היכי קאמר הכא דבשמאל מכשיר אפילו מאן דבעי קידוש לכך נראה דלא מיירי הכא אלא באחיזת הכלי ולא בנתינת הקומץ. מהר"פ: ד] קומץ בשמאל אכשורי מכשר יד יד כו' לקמיצה גופה מדיהודה בריה דר' חייא נפקא [והשאר נמחק]. לפירוש הר"ר אלחנן דתירץ קושית הר"ר יעקב דאורליניש דהך סוגיא דהכא סבירא לה דדבר הלמד בגז"ש אינו חוזר ומלמד בהיקש דפליגי בה מר זוטרא ורב פפא בפ' איזהו מקומן וגרסי' שפיר והרי זריקה ואין לומר דהיינו מהיקשא דזאת התורה [illegible] ימין בחטאת [illegible] דאצבע אצבע אתיא ותו לא ילפינן שאר קדשים מחטאת מהיקשא דזאת התורה א"כ תימה מאי קאמר מדיהודה כו' הא הוא סבר דבר הלמד בגז"ש חוזר ומלמד בהיקש [illegible]

שיטה מקובצת

דוריקתן בכלי אבל חטאת דמתנתה באצבע מודה וה"נ אמרינן בברייתא בפ"ב דזבחים באצבעו ונתן מלמד שלא תהא מתנתו אלא בימין: בא לעובדה להקטירה בכלי דבכלי עצמו נותנה ע"ג האישים עובדה בשמאל כזריקת אשם שהוא בכלי ולא באצבע דמכשיר רבי שמעון [זריקה] בשמאל משום דלא כתיב אצבע כדאמר לעיל זרק בשמאל פסול ור"ש מכשיר והקטרת קומץ במנחה כנגד זריקת דם במזבח ואשם לאו דוקא אלא לישנא דקרא נקיט והשתא נפקא לן קמיצה בימין ומהכא נפקא לכל עבודות מנחה הנעשות ביד ימין בעי יד יד למה לי ע"כ: טו] דאין זה משנה בשום מקום: טז] מאורליינ"ש [מאי פריך] אמאי לא פליג (מאי פריך) דלמא הא דלא פליג ר"ש בזריקה לאו משום דכהונה אלא מהיקשא דזאת התורה כו'. מהר"פ: יז] דאפי' גרס' מליקה: יח] תיבות אי נמי גרים מלק נמחק: יט] דחולין [illegible] לר"ש [illegible] כר"ש [illegible] כמו [illegible]

ט] כלי כיון דקמצו מכלי: י] שרת בהעלאה ע"ג המזבח וקאמר: יא] ולרב נחמן נמי דאמר כו' קדוש [קומץ] שמעינן ליה דמכשיר בשמאל דהא קידוש קומץ במנחה כקבלה בדם ותנא קבל בשמאל פסול ור"ש מכשיר [גירסת] רש"י של מהר"פ וכת"י: יב] תיבת עובדה נמחק: יג] קדש קדשים ואות י' נמחק: יד] כחטאת דביד ימין [ב]חטאת לבד בימין נמחק נ"א עובדה בימין ומקטירה כמתנות דם דחטאת שהוא בידו ממש ובעיא [י]מין דכתיב ביה ונתן ב) אצבעו וכהונה ולקח הכהן מדם החטאת באצבעו ונתן ומודה ר"ש דבימין הוא דאמר [ר' ש]מעון כל מקום שנאמר אצבע אינו אלא ימין וכי אמר ר' שמעון זרק בשמאל כשר בשאר קרבנות קאמר דוריקתן

פירקין וי"ל הא דבעינא ימין בעוף היינו להזאה ומיצוי דהם במקום זריקה דבהמה אבל מליקה דהוי במקום שחיטה ושחיטה לא בעי ימין מליקה נמי לא בעי ימין. מהר"פ: כא] כר"ש בחדא דיליף שלא מהכשירו ופליג עליה בחדא דמלק בשמאל: כב] פסול כיון: כג] וכ"ש בקבלה א"נ לישמעינן פלוגתייהו בתרוייהו וריב"א פי' דהיינו הא דתנן בזבחים קבל בימינו ונתן לשמאלו יחזיר לימינו ולא פליג ר"ש וע"כ משום דזריקה בעי ימין קאמר יחזיר לימינו דאל"כ אמאי יחזיר לימינו. מהר"פ: כד] מגז"ש דאצבע: כה] דהיינו היקשא וחטאת גופיה: כו] בקונטרס לותיב: כז] ניחא ליה לפרושי: כח] ומיניה הוא ילפינן: תיבות

א) בכ"י שלפנינו ליתא לשון זה אך כן הוא הגירסא בכ"י כת"י וכמ"ש רבינו בלשון יח. ב) נראה דצ"ל דכתיב ביה אצבע וכהונה ולקח הכהן כו'.

סד א מיי' פ"ו מהל' מעשה"ק הלכה יח:
סה ב מיי' פ"ה מהל' ביאת מקדש הל' יח:

(דהא כתב: "על דם האשם"!) חד להכשיר צדדין, וחד לפסול צידי צדדין. °"על דם האשם", "על מקום דם האשם" למאי אתו? הני צריכי, אי כתב רחמנא "על דם האשם", הוה אמינא: איתיה – אין, נתקנח – לא, כתב רחמנא: "על מקום"; ואי כתב רחמנא "על מקום", הוה אמינא: דוקא נתקנח, אבל איתיה – אימא הוי חציצה, קמ"ל: "על דם האשם". § אמר רבא: מאחר דכתיב "על דם האשם" ו"על מקום [דם] האשם", וכתיבא ימנית בדם, "על בהן ידו הימנית ועל בהן רגלו הימנית", *וכתיבי בשמן דמצורע עשיר ועני, למה לי? אלא אמר *רבא: °"יד" "יד" לקמיצה, "רגל" "רגל" לחליצה, "אוזן" "אוזן" לרציעה. שמאלית (*העני) למאי אתא? אמר רב שישא בריה דרב אידי: ליפסול ימין דכהן במצורע, שלא תאמר: ומה במקום שלא נתרבתה שמאל – נתרבתה ימין, במקום שנתרבתה שמאל – אינו דין שנתרבתה ימין? ואידך שמאלית, ויד ורגל ימנית דעני, למאי אתא? *לכדתנא דבי ר' ישמעאל: כל פרשה שנאמרה ונשנית, לא נשנית אלא בשביל דבר שנתחדש בה. *אמר רבה בר בר חנה אמר ר' שמעון בן לקיש: כל מקום שנאמרה אצבע וכהונה – אינה אלא ימין. קס"ד: אצבע וכהונה בעינן, כדכתיב: °"ולקח הכהן מדם החטאת באצבעו", וגמר ממצורע, דכתיב: °"וטבל הכהן את אצבעו הימנית"; הרי קמיצה דלא כתיבא בה אלא כהונה, ותנן: *קמץ בשמאל פסול! אמר רבא: או אצבע או כהונה. אמר ליה אביי: הרי הולכת אברים לכבש דכתיב בהו כהונה, דכתיב: °"והקריב הכהן את הכל *המזבחה", ואמר *מר: זו הולכת אברים לכבש; *ותנן: "הרגל של ימין בשמאל ובית עורה לחוץ! כי אמרי' או אצבע או כהונה – בדבר המעכב כפרה. והרי קבלה דבר המעכב כפרה הוא, וכתב בה כהונה, דכתיב: °"והקריבו בני אהרן הכהנים את הדם" – זו קבלת הדם; *ותנן: "קבל בשמאל – פסל, ורבי שמעון מכשיר! לר' שמעון קאמרת? ר"ש תרתי בעי. ומי בעי רבי שמעון תרתי? והתניא, *ר"ש אומר: כל מקום שנאמרה יד – אינה אלא ימין, אצבע – אינה אלא ימין! אצבע לא בעיא כהונה, כהונ' בעי' אצבע. אלא כהן למה לי? בכהונו.

והרי

[רש"י] דהא כתב כהן יד ורגל בדם האשם לעיל מיניה! חד. "על כהן", בין דיד בין דרגל. להכשיר צדדין. של כהן, דדרשינן לקמן (דף נו.): "על" – בסמוך, כדכתיב: "ועליו מטה מנשה". וחד על. כהן, בין דיד בין דרגל – לפסול לידי לדדין, בשר התחתון שכנגד הכף, דעל אמרינן ולא תחת. על דם האשם. דעשיר, ו"על מקום דם האשם" דעני. למה לי. כלומר, תרי קראי למה לי? בשלמא חד כתביה לאשמועינן דיתן שמן על הדם ולא אצלו, אלא יא] "מקום דם" למה לי? הוה אמינא איתיה אין. איתיה לדם יתן השמן, אבל נתקנח הדם לא יתן השמן. יב] הויא חציצה. בין שמן לבהן, וליפסל, דרחמנא אמר "על בהן" – להכי אילטריך "על דם". אמר רבא כו' יג] וכתב ימנית בדם. למה לי למיהדר ולמכתב ימנית בשמן? יד] לא לכתוב לא בעני ולא בעשיר! נהי ד"על בהן" יתירי אילטריכו דעני ודעשיר להכשיר לדדין ולפסול לידי לדדין, אלא ימנית למה לי? אלא אמר רבא. ליתא למאי דאפק' קמילה דשמאל פסול מדרשת דארבעה שמאלית, דאם כן ימנית טו] דבין שמן דעשיר בין שמן דעני למה לי? אלא ימנית דשמן דעשיר להיא דרשה אתיא. יד יד לקמיצה. כתיב במלורע עשיר ידו הימנית דלא אילטריך, וכתיב בקמילה יד: "וימלא *כפו" (ויקרא ט), מה יד מלורע ימנית – אף דקמילה ימנית. רגל. טז] שמן דמלורע עשיר, למידרש חלילה בגזירה שוה ד"רגל" "רגל", דכתיב נמי בחלילה "וחללה נעלו מעל רגלו" (דברים כה), מה רגל דמלורע ימנית – אף חלילה ימנית. ואוזן. דשמן עשיר דלא אילטריך, אתי למדרש "אזן" "אזן" דרליעה, דכתיב: "ורלע אדניו את אזנו" (שמות כא), מה דמלורע ימנית – אף דרליעה ימנית. וכף גזירה שוה מפורשת בפ"ק דקדושין (ד' טו.). ודעני לא דריש להו רבא, כדלקמן: כל פרשה שנאמרה ונשנית לא נשנית כו'. שמאלית יז] למאי אתא. דעשיר לא אילטריך, למאי אתא? בשלמא קמא לגופיה – שמאלית ולא ימנית, אלא תניינא למאי? במקום יח] שנתרבתה שמאל. כגון הכא דכתיב לעיל שמאלית – כל שכן שנתרבתה ימין! להכי אתא שמאלית אחרינא בעשיר גופיה, דשינה עליו הכתוב לעכב, שמאלית ולא ימנית. ואי קשיא: הוי מיעוט אחר מיעוט! לאו פירכא היא, דשמאלית קמא לאו מיעוט הוא, דכיון דקיימא לן ג"ש ד"יד" "יד" לקמילה, הוה אמינא נמי נדרוש ג"ש יט] האי כף דתיהוי ימנית, ואילטריך למיכתב שמאל לאכשורי שמאל, ולעולם כל שכן ימין – להכי כתב רחמנא שמאלית אחרינא, למעוטי ימין. ואידך שמאלית דעני. כ] מיותר, למאי אתא? שנתחדש בה. כא] ופרשת עני נתחדש קרבן עולה ויורד. קס"ד אצבע וכהונה בעינן. דלא אמרינן ימין אלא אם כן [כתיב] אצבע וכהונה, כגון חטאת דכתיב ביה: "ולקח הכהן מדם החטאת באצבעו" (ויקרא ד) – ההיא ודאי ימנית הוא, דגמר כב] ממלורע עשיר דכתיב ביה: "וטבל הכהן את אצבעו הימנית" (ויקרא יד), מה אצבע וכהונה דהכא ימין – אף דעלמא נמי ימין. כג] ותנן. במסכת תמיד (דף לא:) בהולכת אברים: הרגל של ימין היה מוליך בשמאל, משום דאמרינן במסכת יומא (דף כה.): סדר אברים, הראש והרגל היה נושא בכת אחת. והאי רגל מדחזיל בהדי רישא – ודאי רגל כד] ימין הוא דחשיב. הלכך הראש שהוא כבד וחשוב היה מוליך בימין, והירך בשמאל, ואע"ג דכתב בהו כהן! ומשני: לעולם או אצבע או כהונה. וכי אמרינן אינה אלא ימין – בדבר המעכב כפרה, דומיא דהזאות דמלורע. לאפוקי הולכה דלא מעכבא, דאפשר כה] לפשוט ולנתח אצל הכבש. אי נמי, אם יש כהנים הרבה יושיטו זה לזה. והא קבלה דמעכבא כפרה. דאי אפשר שלא יתקבל הדם בכלי, וכתב בה כהונה: "והקריבו בני אהרן את הדם" (ויקרא א), ואמרינן בתורת כהנים: "והקריבו" זו קבלת הדם, ותנן: רבי שמעון מכשיר קבלה בשמאל! לרבי שמעון קאמרת. כלומר, מדרבי שמעון פרכת? בתמיה. תרתי בעי. אצבע וכהונה. וכי קאמר ריש לקיש או אצבע או כהונה, לרבנן כו] קא אמר דפסול. יד אינה אלא ימין. דגמר מידו הימנית דמלורע כז] [עשיר]. ומשני: אצבע לא בעיא כהונה. דהיכא דכתב אצבע, אע"ג דלא כתב כהן – אינו אלא ימין. ומשכחת לה ב"אחרי מות": "ולקח מדם הפר והזה באצבעו", הרי אצבע בלא כהונה. כהונה בעיא אצבע. לרבי שמעון, אף על גב דכתיב כהונה לא אמרינן ימין אלא אם כן כתב אצבע, כח] משום הכי מכשיר בקבלה. בכהונו. בבגדי כהונה.

פליג

[תוספות] על דם האשם ועל מקום דם האשם למאי אתו. פירוש: דלכתוב או אידי ואידי "על מקום", או אידי כט] ואידי "על דם". אמר רבא מאחר דכתב על דם כו' וכתיבא ימנית בדם על בהן ידו הימנית כו' למה לי. דנהי דעל בהן דעני ודעשיר צריכין לצדדין ולצידי צדדין, מ"מ ימנית למאי אתא? אלא אמר רבא: "יד" "יד" לקמיצה – יד ימנית דשמן דמצורע עשיר אתא לג"ש דקמיצה, ודמצורע עני לפרשה שנאמרה לשנות, כך פירוש הסוגיא ל] לפירוש הקונטרס. וקשה: דמשמע לרבא דימנית דדם איצטריך בין בעני בין בעשיר, ואמאי לא ילפי מהדדי כמו (נמי) בצדדין ובצידי צדדין, והוה לן למימר דימנית דדם דעני הוי לפרשה שנאמרה ונשנית, כמו ימנית דשמן דעני! ושמא לענין ימנית *לא הוו ילפי אי לאו דהוו כתיבי בהדיא, כיון דחלוקין בקרבנותיהם, אע"ג דילפי מהדדי לצדדין ולצידי צדדין. עוד קשה: דמשמע שבא רבי ירמיה להקשות לרבי זירא, ולפירוש הקונטר' לא מקשי מידי! ועוד קשה, הא דלא נקט ר' ירמיה נמי תנוך אוזן! ועוד, כיון דר' ירמיה לא בעי: "על בהן" למה לי, אלא מכח דכתיב "על דם האשם" ו"על מקום דם האשם", אם כן הוה ליה למימר: מאחר דכתיב "על דם האשם" ו"על מקום דם האשם", "על בהן" למה לי, כדקאמר רבא! ונראה לפרש: דפריך משום דדריש רבי זירא מ"כפו" דכל מקום שנאמר כף אינו אלא ימין, אם כן ב"על בהן ידו" דהוי דומיא דכף לא הוה צריך למכתב ימין. ולפי הספרים דגרסינן "במלורע עשיר למה לי" – לאו דוקא, והוא הדין דהוה פריך מלורע עני, אלא נקט עשיר משום דאפילו בעשיר קשיא ליה אמאי איצטריך חד להכשיר לדדין וחד לפסול לידי לדדין, פירוש: ימנית דעשיר וימנית דעני. ואע"ג דימנית לא משמע לא לדדין ולא לידי לדדין, מייתורא בעלמא דריש. ובמילתיה דרבא גרסינן: מאחר דכתיב "על דם האשם" ו"על מקום דם האשם", וכתב ימנית בדם של מלורע עשיר, ימנית דכתב בשמן דמלורע *עני למה לי? ואיני יכול ליישבו יפה. ולריך לדקדק בו. שמאל למאי אתא. משמאל שני דעשיר קא בעי, דקמא אתא לגופיה להכשיר שמאל. ומשני, דאתא למעט ימין. ולמיעוט אחר מיעוט דגרבי ימין אין לדרוש, דא"כ לא לכתוב אלא חד, והדר בעי: ואידך שמאל למאי אתא, היינו דעני.

והרי

[גליון הש"ס] גמ' יד יד לקמיצה. ע' לקמן דף יט ע"ב תוספות ד"ה ידך:

[מסורת הש"ס ושאר הגהות בגליון] ויקרא יד | ס"א ל"ג | נ"ל למיהדר | [זבחים כד.] | נ"ל דעשיר | ויש גורסים ומלא את ידו דכתיב בפרשת אחרי וקאי אכהן שנתחנך וחינוך של כהן הוא במנחה | ויקרא ד | שם יד | לעיל ו. [זבחים כד:] | שם א | [פסחים סה. זבחים ד. יד: כד. לה. עירובין קד: חגיגה יא. יומא כז.] | שם | זבחים טו: כד. | [שם כד.] | בדם לא הוו ילפינן מהדדי אי נ"ק | שבועות יט. ב"ק סד: [סוטה ג. בכורות מג:] | זבחים כד. ע"ש [לקמן פ"ב: מנחות פג.] חולין כב. | והקטיר | זבחים כד: תמיד לא: [יומא מח:] | עשיר נ"ק

שיטה מקובצת

א] תיבות דהא כתב על דם האשם נמחק: ב] ועל מקום דם האשם למאי אתו הנהו צריכי: ג] תיבות על דם האשם נמחק: ד] מקום דם: ה] הימנית דכתיבי בשמן דמצורע ל"ל: ו] תיבת העני נמחק: ז] שמאלית למאי אתא והשאר נמחק: ח] וטבל נ"א והזה הכהן באצבעו הימנית: ט] בשמאל פסול. תימה מאי פריך היינו גז"ש דיד יד לקמיצה ושמא י"ל דפריך מקדוש קומץ: י] קבלה דדבר המעכב כפרה הוא ותנן קבל כו' והשאר נמחק: יא] אלא אידך למה לי והס"ד: יב] מה"ד אימא הוי: יג] וכתיבא ימנית: יד] תיבות לא לכתוב נמחק: טו] ימנית דשמן בין דעשיר בין דעני למה לי ותיבת דבין נמחק: טז] רגל דמצורע עשיר כו' דכתיב בחליצה והלצה וגו' אף רגל דחליצה ימנית הס"ד ומה"ד אזן דמצורע דשמן: יז] שמאלית דעשיר: יח] כגון א) שלא נתרבתה שמאל בכל שאר קרבנות נתרבתה ימין כדאמרינן לקמן כ"מ שנאמר אצבע או כהונה אינו אלא ימין הס"ד ומה"ד מקום שנתרבה שמאל כגון: יט] דהאי (אכף) [כף]: כ] דעני דמייתר: כא] ובפרשת עני: כב] ממצורע עשיר. נ"א עני דכתיב ביה והזה הכהן באצבעו הימנית מה אצבע וכהונה דהכא ימין אף דעלמא נמי ימין ואע"ג דבעשיר נמי כתיב וטבל הכהן את אצבעו הימנית מההיא לא גמרינן דלגופיה איצטרך אבל דעני לא אצטריך דכיון דכל דרך הזאתו כעשיר הא נמי כעשיר הלכך מינה גמרינן: כג] מה"ד והרי קמיצה בקמיצה כתיב כהונה וקמץ הכהן הס"ד ומה"ד ותנן במס' תמיד גבי הולכת: כד] ודאי רגל של ימין הוא דחשיב הלכך הראש שהוא דבר חשוב היה מוליך בימין והירך בשמאלו הס"ד ומה"ד ובית עורו לחוץ מקום החתך היה כנגד האיש כדי שלא יראה מבחוץ שניוול הוא קתני מיהא הולכה בשמאל אע"ג דכתב כו': כה] דאפשר לשחוט ולנתח: כו] לרבנן דאמרי פסול: כז] עני ותיבת עשיר נמחק: כח] אצבע בהדיה משום: כט] ואידי על דם או ואידי על מקום. ולפרש"י קשה דאי לא הוי כתיב אלא חד על הוי דרשינן להכשיר צדדין ולפסול צידי צדדין: ל] לפירוש הקונטרס. לשיטת הקונטרס קשה טובא חדא [דא"כ הא] דא"ל לרבי זירא אלא אידך למה לי ... ולא משמע כן אלא משמע דקאי משום דרבי זירא דדריש שמאלית כו' ... על בהן ידו כו' למה לי כיון דכתיב על דם האשם אם כן הו"ל לפרש לתלמודא מתחלה מאחר דכתחלה מקום דם האשם כו' כמו שמפורש בסוף. ועוד דפי' ימנית דעני נשנית משום דבר שנתחדש

שיטה מקובצת

בה א"כ הו"ל לפרושי בהדיא כמו שמפרש בשמאלית. ועוד כי היכא דקשיא ליה על בהן ידו למה לי ה"נ הו"ל למיפרך על אזן תנוך למה לי שהוא ראשון בפסוק. לכך פי' ר"י דכולהו הני פירכא קיימי אהא דדריש רבי זירא שמאלית לומר הא כל מקום כו' וה"פ כיון דדרשת כ"מ כו' אם כן כולהו הני ימנית דכתיב במצורע למה לי דכיון דכתיב יד ידענא בהו דימין הם מדרשא דשמאלית דר' זירא דבשלמא אי לאו דרשא דר' זירא לא הוי קשיא ליה דאצטרכו כולהו לגופיה ימנית ולא שמאלית אבל מאחר דדרשת שמאלית לגלויי דכל מקום שנאמר כף אינו אלא ימין כולהו הני ימנית דמצורע למאי אתי והאי דנקט בשמן מצורע לאו דוקא ה"ה נמי דקשיא ליה מאותם דכתיב בדם ומשני חד להכשיר כו' על דם האשם ועל מקום דם האשם למה לי אדרבי זירא פריך דבשלמא אי לאו דדרשינן שמאלית לגלויי דכל מקום שנאמר כו' לא הוה פריך מידי דאז הוה אמינא דימנית דדם האשם דעשיר צריכי לגופיהו ועל מקום דם האשם דשמן אצטריך ליה ימנית דשמן בין דעני בין דעשיר חד להכשיר צדדין וחד ליפסול צידי צדדין אבל השתא דאמרת שמאלית לגלויי כל מקום שנאמר כו' ומייתי ימנית ימנית דשמן להכשיר צדדין וליפסול צידי צדדין אם כן על דם האשם למה לי ומשני מצרך צריכי ואם תאמר לשתוק קרא מינייהו וממילא שמעינן בין איתיה ובין נתקנח דמהיכי ממעטינן להו וי"ל דלא סגי דלא כתיב על דם דלא תימא חציצה היא ומאחר דלא סגי דלא כתיב על דם אצטריך נמי למכתב על מקום כמו שהולך ומפרש. אמר רבא כו' הא נמי אדרשה דרבי זירא דבשלמא אי לאו דדריש שמאלית לגלויי בעלמא ימין לא קשיא לך דאז הוה אמינא דימנית דדם בין דעני ובין דעשיר לגופייהו ועל דם האשם ועל מקום דם האשם דכתיבי בשמן צריכי לייתורי דימנית דשמן בין דעני בין דעשיר חד להכשיר צדדין וחד ליפסול צידי צדדין אבל השתא דדריש שמאלית לגלויי דבעלמא ימין ואצטרכו ימנית [דדם] בין דעני בין דעשיר להכשיר צדדין וליפסול צידי צדדין ואצטרכו נמי על דם ועל מקום לומר בין איתיה בין נתקנח ימנית דשמן בין דעני בין דעשיר למאי אתיא ומשני רבא יד לקמיצה כו' ופי' רבינו שמשון דהשתא צריכי כולהו קמא לגופיה לומר ימנית שני לגז"ש יד לקמיצה ושלישי ורביעי חד להכשיר צדדין וחד לפסול צידי צדדין שמאלית למאי אתיא תנינא קא בעי דאילו קמא צריכי לגופיה והני בשביל דבר שנתחדש בו כמו שהולך ומפרש. לשון תוספות מהר"ם:

והרי

א) נראה דצ"ל שלא נתרבתה שמאל כגון בכל שאר קרבנות וכו'.

מנחה מאי עבידתה? אמר רב פפא: מנחת נסכים; ס"ד אמינא: הואיל ובהדי זבח אתיא — כי גופיה דזבח דמיא, קמ"ל. ומאן (א) דפסל? שאני הכא, דאמר קרא: א] °"והרים הכהן מן המנחה את אזכרתה והקטיר המזבחה", "המנחה" — עד ב] דאיתא לכולה *מנחה לא יקטיר. ואידך? "מן המנחה" — ג] מנחה שהיתה כבר (שלימה בשעת קמיצה יקטיר, אע"ג דהשתא אינה שלימה.) ד] איתיביה ר' יוחנן לריש לקיש: *עד שלא פרקה נפרס ה] [לחמה] הלחם — פסול, ואין מקטיר עליו את הבזיכין, ו] ואם משפרקה נפרס לחמה — הלחם פסול ומקטיר עליו את הבזיכין; ז] ואמר רבי אלעזר: לא פרקה ממש, אלא כיון שהגיע זמנה לפרק ואע"פ שלא פירקה! א"ל: הא מני? רבי אליעזר היא. א"ל: אנא אמינא לך משנה שלימה, ואמרת לי את רבי אליעזר? ח] אי ר' אליעזר, מאי איריא נפרס? אפי' שרוף ואבוד נמי מכשר! אישתיק. ואמאי שתק? לימא ליה: צבור שאני, הואיל ואישתרי טומאה לגבייהו, אישתרי נמי חסרות! אמר רב אדא בר אהבה, זאת אומרת: החסרון כבעל מום דמי, ואין בעל (בעל) מום בצבור.§ יתיב רב פפא וקאמר ט] להא שמעתא. א"ל רב יוסף י] בר שמעיה לרב פפא: מי לא עסקינן *דרבי יוחנן וריש לקיש במנחת העומר דציבור היא? ופליגי. אמר רב מלכיו, תנא חדא: *°"מסלתה" — שאם חסרה כל שהוא פסולה, °"משמנה" — שאם *חסרה כל שהוא פסול; ותניא אידך: יא] "והנותרת מן המנחה" — פרט למנחה שחסרה היא ושחסר קומצה ושלא הקטיר מלבונתה כלום; תרי קראי בחסרות למה לי? לאו חד למנחה שחסרה קודם קמיצה, וחד לשירים שחסרו בין קמיצה להקטרה? ותיובתא דר' יוחנן בתרוייהו! לא, חד למנחה שחסרה קודם קמיצה, דאי מביא מביתו וממלאה — אין, ואי לא — לא; וחד לשירים שחסרו בין קמיצה להקטרה, דאע"ג דמקטיר קומץ עליהן, *אותן שירים אסורים יב] לאכילה. דאיבעי' להו: לדברי האומר שירים שחסרו בין קמיצה להקטרה מקטיר קומץ עליהן, אותן שירים מה הן באכילה? אמר זעירי, אמר קרא: "והנותרת" — יג] ולא הנותרת מן הנותרת; ורבי ינאי אמר: יד] "מהמנחה" — מנחה שהיתה כבר.§ "קמץ בשמאל". [וכו']§ מנא הני מילי? אמר רבי זירא, דאמר קרא: °"ויקרב את המנחה וימלא כפו ממנה", כף זה איני יודע מהו, כשהוא אומר: °"ולקח הכהן מלוג השמן ויצק על כף הכהן השמאלית" — כאן שמאלית, הא כל מקום שנאמר כף אינו אלא ימין. והא מיבעי ליה לגופיה! שמאלית אחרינא כתיב. ואימא: אין *מיעוט אחר מיעוט אלא לרבות! שמאלית אחרינא כתיב, כאן שמאלית ואין אחר שמאלית. ואימא: אדרבה, מה כאן שמאלית — אף בעלמא נמי שמאלית! ארבעה שמאלית כתיבי, תרי בעני ותרי בעשיר. אמר ליה ר' ירמיה לרבי זירא: "על בהן ידו הימנית ועל בהן רגלו הימנית" דכתיב *(בשמן דמצורע עשיר) למה לי? דהא

תורה אור: ויקרא ו | שם ב | שם | שם ט | שם יד

רש"י

מנחה מאי עבידתה. מאי *טו] זריקה יש במנחה. במנחת נסכים. הבאים עם הזבח. אם אבד חלב ובשר של זבח ומנחה קיימת — לא יזרוק הדם (ב). *מן המנחה. והרים הכהן מן המנחה את אזכרתה והקטיר המזבחה. עד דאיתא לכולה טז] *קיימת, ואי לא — לא יקטיר (את אזכרתה). שהיתה כבר. שהיתה כבר שלימה בשעת הקומץ, אע"ג דהשתא אינה שלימה, יקטיר. יז] ומקטיר בזיכין. *אלמא שירים שחסרו בין (סילוק) קמילה להקטרה מקטירים עלייהו הקומץ. ואמר ר"א כו'. לא איצטריך, אלא איידי דתנא לעיל תנא הכא. משנה שלימה. סתם משנה. מישתרי טומאה לגבייהו. דכתיב בתמיד (במדבר כח): "במועדו", ומשמע אפילו בשבת יח] וטומאה. זאת אומרת. מדלא שני הכי, שמע מינה חסרון כבעל מום דמי, ואין בעל מום שרי בצבור טפי מביחיד. הלכך, חסרון דבין קמילה להקטרה, אי הוי פסול ביחיד — הוה פסול נמי בצבור. הלכך אישתיק. להא שמעתא יט]. דאישתיק, ולא שני ליה: צבור שאני. מי לא* כ] עסקינן. (דמשום) פלוגתא דלעיל (ג), דהכי נמי קאמר ר"ל אין מקטירין קומץ עליהם — במנחת צבור נמי אמר, כגון בזיכים דלחם הפנים. *סלת כא] עשרון. בעי לוג שמן, דאמר בפ' "שתי מדות" (לקמן פח.): "למנחה ולוג שמן". (מן המנחה) והנותרת מן המנחה פרט לשחסרה היא. דמנחה שלימה משמע. ושחסר קומצה. דשירי מנחה העשויה כהלכתה משמע. וקומץ החסר נפקא לן ב"הקומץ רבה" (לקמן דף כו.) דפסול מדכתיב "מלא כב] קומצו" תרי זימני. ושלא הקטיר מלבונתה כלום. כג] נפקא ב"הקומץ [רבה]" (לקמן דף כו.) דהקטרת לבונה וקומץ כד] *(מעכבות זו את זו). מלבונתה כלום. אבל אם הקטיר קצת נאכלים השירים, כדאמר לקמן בהאי פירקא (דף יב.) דאם חסרה כה] בשעת הקטרה כשרה. תרי קראי. כו] "מסולת" ו"מן המנחה". אבל "משמנה" לא חשיב, דהאי לגופיה אתא לקודם קמילה, אבל בסולת למה לי תרי קראי? לאו כז] לקודם קמיצה. דלא ידיא מתוך ביתו וימלאנה. כח] לשירים שחסרו. דאין מקטירין קומץ עליהם. אסורים באכילה. דהאי קרא ד"מן המנחה" לא משתעי אלא בשירים. כט] נותרת מן הנותרת. (כגון) דמתחילה היו כל השירים נותרות מן הקומץ, וכשחסרו שירים היו הנותרים שירי שירים. שהיתה כבר. בשעת הקומץ היתה שלימה, אע"פ שחסרה בין קמילה להקטרה, קרינא ביה "והנותרת מן המנחה". ופליג ר' ינאי אדזעירי. ל"א: שהיתה כבר בשעת הקטרה. והכי משמע: והנותרת מן המנחה שהיתה שלימה כבר בשעה שנעשו אלו שירים — יאכלו אהרן ובניו, אבל לא יאכלו אותם שירים שנעשו שירים ממנחה חסירה. והיינו דזעירי, ומשמעות דורשין איכא בינייהו (ד) ל] א). (בן בתירא אומר קומץ לתוך הכלי ויחזור ויקמוץ בימין). לגופיה. שמאלית ולא ימנית. שמאלית אחרינא כתיב. נמי (ה) לעשיר. ואימא. להכי אתא שמאל אחרינא — למיעוט אחר מיעוט, לא] דמתרווייהו שמעינן: ימנית לא, ואין מיעוט אחר מיעוט אלא לרבות, דאפי' ימין דכהן כשרה בשמן דמצורע! שמאלית אחרינא כתיב. בעני, לב] ואי משמע מיעוט אחר מיעוט, תלתא למה לי? ארבע שמאלית כתיבי. לג] חד לגופיה *וחד לגלויי עלייהו דהנך תרתי דלאו למיעוט אחר מיעוט אתו, וחד שלא תאמר: האי דקמיה להכי אתא: מה כאן שמאלית אף בעלמא שמאלית, דא"כ האי בתרא למה לי. אלא מדכתיב האי בתרא הוי להו שני כתובים הבאין כאחד ואין מלמדין. לשון אחר: לד] שמאלית תרי לגופייהו, חד בעני וחד לעשיר, שלא תאמר: הואיל ואשתני בעניות אישתני בימין. ותרי לאשמועי': כאן שמאלית ולא אחר. דהוו להו שני כתובין, דאי כתיב חד הוה אמינא: מה כאן שמאלית אף בעלמא יד שמאלית. ואין מיעוט אחר מיעוט נמי ליכא לאקשויי, דהא (ו) מכולהו שמעינן מינה ימנית לא, וא"כ כל הני למה לי. לה] הני לישני לא נהירא, דכל שני כתובין הבאין כאחד שבתלמוד אין דומין לאלו, דכי אמרינן אין מלמדין — הני מילי כשגילה שני כתובין בשני דברים, דאמרי' דאי ניחא למילף מינייהו — נכתוב חד ונילף אידך מיניה. אבל הכא, דבחדא מילתא כתיבי — אינן שני דברים הבאין כאחד, אלא קראי יתירי נינהו. ונראה בעיני: דמדכתיב כל הנך יתירא ילפינן לה: כאן גילה לך שמאלית, אבל בעלמא כל כף הוה ימין. דאי למילף: מה כאן שמאלית אף בעלמא שמאלית, מכדי דאם אינו ענין כאן תנהו ענין לכל המקומות הוא, ואם כן בחדא יתירא סגי ונכתוב תלתא ונשתוק. חד לגופיה, וחד מה כאן שמאלית וכו', וחד שלא תאמר מיעוט אחר מיעוט הוא. אמר ליה ר' ירמיה. לר' זירא: כיון דדרשת לו] ג) (כל השנוי בפרשת מצורע עני לדרשה) כל שמאלית *דמצורע, דריש נמי "על בהן ידו הימנית ועל בהן רגלו הימנית", בין בשמן מצורע עשיר בין בעני. למה לי. כיון דכתיב על דם האשם יתן את השמן, אנא ידענא דעל לז] ידו הימנית היא, דהא

א) רש"ק מ"ז ב) נ"ק מ"ז

תוספות

אותן שירים אסורין באכילה. וא"ת: כיון דאסירי הרי הוא כאילו לא נשתייר כלום, והיאך מקטיר קומץ עליהם? הא בכל זבחים קא"ר יהושע דהיכא דלא נשתייר כלום דאין זורק לח] הדם! וי"ל: כיון דילפינן מנחה מזבח לט] תהא כזבח, דכיון דלא אבדו הוי כאילו הן בעין. וצריך לחלק בין זה לנטמא, דכיון דאין זבח נפסל ע"י חסרון, אע"ג דשיריים נפסלין — עבדינן ליה כזבח להקטיר קומץ עליהם. אותן שיריים מה הן באכילה. הוה מצי למיפשטה מהא דאם משנפרקה נפרס לחמה הלחם פסול. אין מיעוט מ] אחר מיעוט אלא לרבות. ואם תאמר: ולשתוק מתרוייהו! וכי האי גוונא מצי להקשות בכל מיעוט אחר מיעוט*. על בהן ידו הימנית כו'. בין דעני בין דעשיר קא בעי, דכיון דכתיב "על דם האשם" ו"על מקום דם האשם" ממילא ידעינן בשמן. וה"ה דמצי למיבעי מתנוך אוזן, ולפי שהתחיל לדרוש "כף" דמצורע קא מסיק על בהן. מאי דרשת ביה בין דעני בין דעשיר.

על

עין משפט נר מצוה

סג א מיי' פי"א מהל' פסה"מ הלכה כ:

נ"ל מנחה יקטיר ואי לא לא יקטיר נ"ק

[וכן הקשו תוס' ב"ק פו: ד"ה ואין ועי' תוס' יומא ס. ד"ה תרי כו' תירוץ על זה]

דפלוגתא דר' יוחנן נ"ק

[לקמן כז.]

[לקמן כז:]

מסורת הש"ס

זריקת דם יש כו' נ"ק

מקום נ"ק

יקטיר את אזכרתה המזבחה ואי לא יקטיר את אזכרתה כצ"ל נ"ק

אע"ג דלאחר סילוק נפרס אלמא כו' בין קמילה כצ"ל נ"ק

רש"ק מ"ז

לעיל ח.

עסקינן דפלוגתא דלעיל דקאמר ר"ל נ"ק

מסלתה סלת בעי עשרון: משמנה. דמנחה בעי לוג שמן דאמר בפרק כו' שמן: מן המנחה פרט למנחה שחסרה הוא דמנחה כו' כצ"ל נ"ק

[נ"ל מעכבות זו את זו ודוקא שלא הקטיר מלבונתה כלום אבל אם הקטיר סקטיר וכו' וסד"ה]

[יומא מג. וש"נ]

לפי ר' התום' דלקמן נ"ב בגמ' בשמן דמצורע עשיר מהרש"ק

ופליג נ"ק

בינייהו הס"ד בן בתירא אומר יחזיר קומץ לתוך הכלי כצ"ל נ"ק

נ"א וחד לגלויי דכל מקום שנאמר כף אינו אלא ימין

דשנוי בפרשת מצורע דריש כו' נ"ק

שיטה מקובצת

א] דאמר קרא מן המנחה עד דאיתה כו' והשאר נמחק: ב] ע' בהשמטות בסוף המסכת: ג] המנחה שהיתה כבר איתיביה ר"י לר"ל והשאר נמחק: ד] איתיבי' ר"י וא"ת ומאי פריך ר"י [דילמא] ר"ל לא יליף מילתא ממילתא וא"כ לא ילפינן מנחה מבזיכין דהא לעיל לא מצי למפרך מהא דהכא אם לא על הא דקאמר ומנחה ממנחה יליף וי"ל בשלמא לעיל אי לא גמרי מילתא ממילתא ליכא למפרך מלחם הפנים דבלחם הפנים גופיה ליכא קרא דלא הוי אלא סברא בעלמא ליפסול אחר קמיצה כמו קודם וסברא בעלמא לא סברי להו אבל לר"ל דמייתי קרא לפסול במנחה אם איתא דקרא להכי אתא ע"כ יליף לחם הפנים ממנחות דאיכא גז"ש אזכרה אזכרה. עי"ל דר"י הקשה פה אל פה ואם איתא דר"ל לא יליף מילתא ממילתא הי' משיב לו דלא יליף. תו"ח: ה] נפרס לחמה: ו] תיבת ואם נמחק: ז] ואמר ר' אלעזר. מגופיה דמתני' ה"מ לאקשויי אר"ל אלא איידי דאייתי לעיל לאקשויי ר"א אדר"א מייתי נמי הכא. תו"ח: ח] אליעזר היא אי: ט] להא שמעתא. פ"ה להא דאמר רב אדא בר אהבה זאת אומרת כו' וקשיא להר"מ דמ"מ נפשוט חסרון דבעל מום שהרי ר"ל פסל לעיל דקאמר אין מקטיר קומץ עליהם ואי פליגי אפי' במנחת צבור א"כ אין חסרון בצבור לכך נראה להר"מ לפרש להא שמעתא דצבור שאני וע"ז קאמר רב יוסף לרב פפא מי לא עסקינן דפליגי במנחת צבור וא"כ אינו יכול לומר צבור שאני אבל לעולם הא דקאמר רב אדא בר אהבה זאת אומרת קאי שפיר. תו"ח: י] א"ל רב יוסף מי לא עסקינן ר"י ור"ל במנחת צבור הוא דפליגי אמר רב מלכיא תניא והשאר נמחק: יא] תיבת והנותרת נמחק: יב] אסורים באכילה אות ל' נמחק: יג] הנותרת מן המנחה ולא: יד] ע' בהשמטות בסוף המסכת: טו] מאי זריקת דם יש: טז] דאיתא לכולה מנחה קיימת ואי לא לא יקטיר את אזכרתה: יז] יקטיר הס"ד ומה"ד ואמר רבי אלעזר כו' לא כו' ואח"כ מה"ד ומקטיר עליו את הבזיכין אלמא שירים שחסרו בין סילוק בזיכין דהוי כמו בין קמיצה: יח] בשבת ובטומאה: יט] שמעתא דרב אדא בר אהבה: כ] עסקינן כלומר מהכא לא משמע דחסרון כבעל מום דמי משום דפלוגתא נמי דקאמר ר"ל והשאר נמחק: כא] סלת בעי עשרון (שמא) ובעי לוג [שמן] דאמר בפ' כו' שמן הס"ד ומה"ד מן המנחה: כב] קומץ תרי: כג] כלום דנפקא לן: כד] וקומץ מעכבות זו את זו בזמן שלא הקטיר מלבונתה והד"א: כה] חסרה לבונה בשעת: כו] קראי מסולתה ומן המנחה כו' לא חשיב דההוא לגופיה: כז] לאו חד: כח] מה"ד וחד לשירים: כט] מה"ד והנותרת מן הנותרת כגון הנך דמתחלה: ל] תיבות בן בתירא עד תיבת בימין נמחק ומה"ד כאן שמאלית מדאצטריך הכא למשרי שמאלית מכלל דכל הני דעלמא ימנית הס"ד ומה"ד לגופיה שמאלית ולא ימנית ובעלמא בין שמאלית בין ימנית הס"ד ומה"ד שמאלית אחרינא כתיב בה בעשיר הס"ד: לא] אחר מיעוט דתרווייהו שמעינן: לב] בעני ואי משום מיעוט: לג] ארבע שמאלית כתיבי תרי בעני ותרי בעשיר חד לגופיה שמאלית ולא ימנית וחד לכאן שמאלית ולא אחר מדאצטריך למשרי הכא וחד לגלויי עלייהו כו' שלא תאמר האי דקמא להכי אתא כו' אלא מדכתב רחמנא האי בתרא: לד] לשון אחר ארבע שמאלית תרי כו' וחד בעשיר שלא תאמר כו' אישתני נמי בימין ותרי כו' שני כתובין הבאין כאחד דאי כתב חד הוא כו' אף בעלמא נמי שמאלית ואין כו' דהא מכלהו שמעינן ימנית לא: לה] הני לישני לא כו' כאחד שבתלמוד אין דומין לאלו כו' דאי הוה ניחא למילף מינייהו כו' כתיבי אינם שני כתובין הבאים כאחד אלא כו' כל הנך יתירא ילפינן כאן גילה לך כף שמאלית אבל כו' דאי למילף מהכא שמאלית: לו] דדרשת כל שמאלית השנוי בפרשת מצורע דרוש נמי על בהן ידו והשאר נמחק: לז] ידענא דעל בהן ידו: לח] הדם ואומר ר"י כיון דלא ידעינן במנחות אלא דגמרי' מזבחים דיו לבא מן הדין להיות כנדון וכי היכי דמהני שיור בזבחים ה"ה במנחות להקטיר קומץ עליהם אבל באכילה כמו בזבחים לא דלקמן איכא קרא לאסור שירים עוד פי' הר"ר חיים נ"ע דיתור קרא דמנחה שהיתה כבר מגלה לנו לומר כן דאל"כ לשתוק מיניה וממילא ידענא דפסול דהוי כמו נטמאו. תו"ח: לט] תהא כזבח ס"א ובזבח אם נשתייר כזית בשר זורק את הדם ה"נ במנחות היכא דנשתייר מקטיר הקומץ עליו: מ] ע' בהשמטות בסוף המסכת:

הגהות הב"ח

(א) גמ' ומאן דפסל נ"ב אלא מנחה שחסרה בין קמילה להקטרה: (ב) רש"י ד"ה במנחת נסכים וכו' לא יזרוק הדם הס"ד: (ג) ד"ה מי לא עסקינן פלוגתא דלעיל נמי בעומר ודאמר ר"ל אין מקטירין וכו' הפנים הס"ד ואח"כ מ"ה מסלתה סלת עשרון בעי: (ד) ד"ה שהיתה כבר וכו' איכא בינייהו הס"ד ואח"כ מ"ה בשמאל כו' בן בתירא אומר יחזיר קומץ לתוך הכלי: (ה) ד"ה שמאלית וכו' נמי אלא עשיר: (ו) ד"ה אלא מדכתיב וכו' ליכא לאקשויי דהא מדכתיב כולהו שמעינן מינה ימנית לא דאם לא כן כל הני:

גמרא

"בקדש הקדשים תאכלנו". והא למה לי קרא? לימא: "בחצר אהל מועד יאכלוה", ולא יהא טפל חמור מן העיקר! עבודה, דאדם עובד במקום רבו – אמרינן שלא יהא טפל חמור מן העיקר; אכילה, שאין אדם אוכל במקום רבו, טעמא דכתב קרא, הא לא כתב קרא – לא יהא טפל חמור מן העיקר לא אמרי'. איתמר: בללה חוץ לחומת עזרה – ר' יוחנן אמר: פסולה, ר"ל אמר: כשרה. ר"ל אמר כשרה – דכתיב: "ויצק עליה שמן ונתן עליה לבונה", והדר: "והביאה אל בני אהרן הכהנים וקמץ" – *מקמיצה ואילך מצות כהונה, לימד על יציקה ובלילה שכשרין בזר; ומדכהונה לא בעיא, פנים נמי לא בעיא. ורבי יוחנן אמר: פסולה, כיון דעשייתה בכלי הוא, נהי דכהונה לא בעיא, פנים מיהת בעיא. תניא כוותיה דר' יוחנן: בללה זר – כשרה, חוץ לחומת העזרה – פסולה.§ איתמר: מנחה שחסרה קודם קמיצה – ר' יוחנן אמר: יביא מתוך ביתו וימלאנה, ריש לקיש אמר: לא יביא מתוך ביתו וימלאנה. ר' יוחנן אמר מביא מתוך ביתו וימלאנה – קמיצה קבעה ליה; ריש לקיש אמר לא יביא מתוך ביתו וימלאנה – קדושת כלי קבעה ליה. איתיביה ר' יוחנן לרשב"ל: *חסר הלוג, אם עד שלא יצק – ימלאנו! תיובתא.§ איתמר: *שירים שחסרו בין קמיצה להקטרה – רבי יוחנן אמר: המקטיר קומץ עליהן, וריש לקיש אמר: אין מקטיר קומץ עליהן. אליבא דר' אליעזר כ"ע לא פליגי, כי פליגי – אליבא דר' יהושע. *דתנן: נטמאו שיריה, נשרפו שיריה, אבדו שיריה – כמדת ר' אליעזר כשרה, כמדת רבי יהושע פסולה; מאן דפסל – כר' יהושע, ומאן דמכשר – עד כאן לא אמר רבי יהושע התם אלא דלא אישתייר, אבל היכא דאישתייר – אפי' ר' יהושע מודה ליה. *)דתניא, ר' יהושע אומר: כל הזבחים שבתורה שנשתייר מהם כזית בשר או כזית חלב – זורק הדם, כחצי זית בשר כחצי זית חלב – אינו זורק את הדם. ובעולה, אפי' כחצי זית בשר וכחצי זית חלב – זורק את הדם, מפני שבעולה כולה כליל. ובמנחה, אף על פי שכולה קיימת – לא יזרוק.

מנחה

*) זבחים כה: קט. לקמן כו. תוספתא דזבחים פ"ד פסחים עט. בכורות לט: מעילה טו: תוספתא פסחים פ"ו

רש"י

בקדש הקדשים וגו'. בפרשת "ויקח קרח", ולעיל מיניה כתיב: "לכל חטאתם ולכל אשמם וגו' בקדש הקדשים", דמשמע היכל, דאי עזרה – בהדיא כתיב (ויקרא ו): "בחצר אהל מועד". ז] ואם איתא דילפינן מהאי טעמא דלא יהא טפל חמור מעיקר. הא למה לי קרא. לכן בתירא, ליליף מאידך קרא (שם): ח] "בחצר אהל מועד יאכלוה" וכל שכן היכל, והאי "בקדש הקדשים" למה לי דכתיב רחמנא? ומשני: האי דאיצטריך "בקדש הקדשים" לאו לאשמועינן דלא מיפסלי קדשים בכניסת ט] היכל, אלא למישרי אכילה בהיכל, דלא נפקא מההוא דלא יהא טפל חמור מעיקר. דעבודה (א) היא. דדרך ארץ היא לעבוד י] בפני רבו, אמרי': לא יהא טפל וכו'. אבל אכילה, אין דרך ארץ לאכול במקום רבו – (ב) לא אמרי' דכיון דעיקר הוא כ"ש דמצי אכיל בגוויה, אי לא אשמעינן קרא. קמיצה קבעה לה. דכל כמה דלא קמיץ לא מיקריא מנחה, ולא קרינא ביה "מן המנחה" – פרט לשחסרה, כדמפרש לקמן. כל לשון קביעות דאמור במנחות כלומר: זקוק זה לזה, ואין אתה יכול לשנות קצת ממנו להביא אחר תחתיו, לפי שהוקבעו יחד. קדושת כלי קבעה לה יא]. בשם, וקרינא בה "מן המנחה" פרט לכשחסרה. חסר הלוג. שמן של מצורע, עד שלא יצק על כפו השמאלית – יב] ימלאנה, ולא אמרי' דקבעה להו לוג שהוא כלי שרת. כ"ע לא פליגי. יג] דמה היכא דאבדו שירים או נשרפו קמכשר ר' אליעזר לקמן להקטיר קומץ – כ"ש חסרו, דאיכא שיור יד] במקצתה. כמדת ר' אליעזר. דאמר בפ' "כיצד צולין" (פסחים עז.): "ועשית עולותיך הבשר והדם" – טו] דם אע"פ שאין בשר (בשר אע"פ שאין דם). כשרה. להקטיר הקומץ, דקומץ בלא שירים דומיא דדם בלא בשר. כמדת ר' יהושע. דאמר: טז] אם אין בשר אין דם, אם אין דם אין בשר, פסול להקטיר הקומץ. כזית בשר או כזית חלב. בפסחים נפקא לן ב"כיצד צולין" (דף עט.) דמשום חלב נמי זריק, דכתיב (ויקרא יז): "וזרק הכהן את הדם וגו' והקטיר החלב", אלמא: חלב אע"פ שאין בשר יז]. כחצי זית חלב אין זורק. שאין אכילת *בשר ואכילת מזבח מצטרפין. זריקת דם אינה אלא להתיר אימורים למזבח ובשר לאדם, וכיון דאבדו שניהם זריקה למה. ובעולה. דבין בשר בין חלב כולהו למזבח סלקי, מצטרפים.

מנחה

תוספות

רבי יוחנן אמר פסולה. אע"ג דלא בלל כשרה, בלל חוץ לחומת העזרה גרע. ולא דמי להאיא דזבחים בפ' "קדשי קדשים" (דף סג.) דתלינן טעמא מילה דמה בכל מקום במזבח כשרה – שאם היזה ולא מילה כשרה, יח] דהתם בפנים והכא בחוץ. ריש לקיש אמר כשרה. הכא משמע דאע"ג יט] *דקדושה היא לא מיפסלא ביוצא. ואפילו רבי יוחנן לא פליג אלא משום דעשה הבלילה בחוץ, אבל משום יוצא לא. וכן משמע בפרק "התכלת" כ] (לקמן דף מז.) דאמר רב ששת: הני תנאי כרבי סבירא להו, דאמר: שחיטה מקדשא כא] (היא) איפסילא ביוצא. ובסוף שמעתא (שם מח.) קאמר: הא דלא כרבי, כיון דאמר שחיטה מקדשא, דפריך להו היכא? אי אבראי – כב] איפסילו להו ביוצא. משמע משום דשחיטה מקדשא הוא דאיפסיל ביוצא, הא לאו הכי – לא, דאע"ג דאית ליה תנור מקדש בפרק "רבי ישמעאל" (לקמן דף עב:). ומיהו יש לדחות, דבאין עם הזבח שאני, דהא נסכים הבאין עם הזבח לא מיפסלו בלינה אלא בשחיטת זבח, כדאמר זעירי לקמן בפרק "התודה" (דף עט.), ואילו בפני עצמן תנן: קדשו בכלי – נפסלין בלינה. ויש עוד ראיה מהא דתנן בפ' שני דמעילה (דף ט.) גבי מנחות ושתי הלחם: קרמו בתנור – הוכשרו ליפסל בטבול יום ובמחוסר כיפורים ובלינה, אבל יוצא לא קתני. ואע"ג דגבי עופות וזבחים הוה מצי למיתני כג] *(אגב אחרינא) לא תני אגב שתי הלחם ולחם הפנים ומנחות. והא דאמר בפרק "כל שעה" (פסחים דף לו.) גבי לישה דמנחות: נהי דבזריזין ליתא, במקום זריזין איתא – אורחא דמילתא נקט, שדרך לעשותה במקום זריזין. והא דאמרינן בפרק "המזבח מקדש" (זבחים פח.): כד] אין מקדשין ליקרב אבל מקדשין ליפסל – היינו בטבול יום ובמחוסר כיפורים ובלינה, אבל לא ביוצא. ובקונטרס פי' לקמן בריש "שתי מדות" (דף פז:) גבי שולחן: אבל מקדשין ליפסל בלינה וביוצא. ובפרק "המזבח מקדש" (זבחים פח.) פי' בקונטרס: אבל מקדשין ליפסל ביוצא אם יצא חוץ לקלעים או נגע בו טבול יום, ולא יתכן. ומה שפירש *רבינו שלמה כה] בפרק שני דזבחים (דף כ:) גבי יציאה מהו שתועיל בקידוש ידים ורגלים, כדרך כל הקדשים שקדשו בכלי הנפסלים ביוצא – אין הטעם תלוי בכך כלל, *(ועוד) דהא קאמר התם: כיון דפריש אסוחי מסח דעתיה. והא דדייק בפ' "שתי הלחם" (לקמן נה: ושם.): אמרת לישתן ועריכתן בחוץ – אלמא מדת יבש כו] לא נתקדשה, וכן בסוף "כל המנחות באות מצה" (שם סג.) דדריש ר' שמעון "תנור" "תנור" שתי פעמים – שתהא אפייתן בתנור ושתהא הקדישן בתנור. ופריך, והתנן ר' שמעון אומר: לעולם הוי רגיל לומר שתי הלחם ולחם הפנים כשרות בעזרה וכשרות אבי פאגי – לאו משום כז] *דנתקדשה הוי מיפסיל ביוצא, אלא משום דדבר מכוער הוא להוציא לחוץ לאחר שנתקדשה. וא"ת: וכיון דבקדושת כלי לא מיפסלא ביוצא, מנחת כהנים וחביתי כהן גדול דלית בה קמילה *אימא מיפסל ביוצא? ושמא באותם מועיל קידוש כלי, כדאמרי' כח] (זבחים דף מה:): שאין להם מתירין – משיקדש בכלי*. מקמיצה ואילך מצות כהונה. הגשה ותנופה נמי בעו כהונה, שאין זר קרב אצל המזבח. *אלא הכא בד' עבודות שבמנחה איירי, שמתחילין משעת קמילה. ומיהו בלאו הכי ניחא, דליכא תנופה אלא במנחת עומר וקנאות, כדתנן בפ' "כל המנחות באות מצה" (לקמן סא.). ובמנחות קנאות אין יציקה ובלילה, דלית בה שמן. ובמנחת העומר, אע"ג דטעונה שמן לא כתיב בה "וקמץ הכהן". ומדכהונה לא בעיא פנים נמי לא בעיא. וא"ת: הרי שחיטה דלא בעיא כהונה ובעיא פנים, דכתיב (ויקרא א): "ושחט את בן הבקר לפני ה'" כדדרשינן בפ' "כל הפסולין" (זבחים דף לב:) דבעינן שיהא בן הבקר לפנים! וי"ל: דשאני התם משום קבלה. כט] אי נמי, שכן מיני דמים. חסר הלוג עד שלא יצק ימלאנו. משנה היא במס' נגעים (פי"ד מ"י), ותימה שלא היה יודע ר' שמעון בן לקיש. וכה"ג [קשה] בפ' "במה טומנין" (שבת נ:) דפריך ממתניתין דהטומן לפת ולנונות *. עד שלא יצק ימלאנו. משמע: הא משיצק לא ימלאנו. ותימה, דלעיל (דף ה.) תניא: הקדיש מתן שמן למתן דם ימלאנו שמן כו', והיינו לאחר יציקה! וי"ל: דההיא כר' שמעון דפליג במס' נגעים ל] (פי"ד מ"י) ומייתי לה במס' יומא, שאם חסר עד שלא נתן – שימלאנו, ואפי' לא] לאחר יציקה. ואע"פ שכבר נתן קודם מתן דם, הואיל *דבפסול נעשית – לא שמה מתנה, ומהאי טעם אתיא נמי כתנא קמא, דיליקה הנעשית בפסול לא שמה יליקה. מאן דפסיל כרבי יהושע. הא דא"ר יוסי בפ' "כילד צולין" (פסחים עח. ושם) דמסתברא כי היכי דפליגי רבי אליעזר ורבי יהושע בזבחים הכי פליגי לב] במנחות – לאו דוקא לר' שמעון בן לקיש. אלא כי היכי דפליגי בזבחים בלא נשתייר – פליגי במנחות בחסרו שיריים. וא"ת: הא דקאמר התם דעיקר קראי כי כתיבי בזבחים כתיבי, והא במנחות נמי איכא קראי דדריש בסמוך, "המנחה"! ויש לומר: דהתם לרבי יוחנן קאמר, דלדידיה ליכא קראי היכא דחסרו שירים עד כזית, דמקטיר קומץ עליהם.

אותן

שיטה מקובצת

א] לחומת עזרה. עי' תום' זבחים (דף כ ע"ב) ותום' סוכה (דף נ ע"א): ב] כיון דקדושת כלי היא נהי: ג] קבעה לה ר"ל אמר כו' קדושת כלי קבעה לה: ד] תיבת אם נמחק: ה] יהושע מודה דתניא: ו] זורק את הדם: ז] מועד יאכלוה: ח] קרא דבחצר: ט] בכניסת ההיכל אלא למשרי כו' מההוא טעמא דלא יהא: י] לעבוד עבודת רבו בפני: יא] לה לשם מנחה וקרינא: יב] השמאלית ימלאנו ולא אמרינן דקבעה לה לוג: יג] פליגי דהשתא מה אבדו שיריים: יד] דאיכא שיור הס"ד: טו] והדם יש דם בשר בשר א) [אע"פ שאין] אף על פי שאין דם: טז] דאמר התם אם: יז] בשר כחצי זית בשר וכחצי זית חלב אין זורק שאין אכילת אדם ואכילת מזבח והד"א: יח] כשרה וי"ל דשאני התם דמ"מ במזבח קעביד אבל בחוץ מגרע גרע טפי מלא בלל כלל. תו"ח ובתום' אחרות כתוב שאני התם שלא שינה רק במקום המזבח ממקום למקום ושינה מקום זוטא כי האי לא גרע מלא מיצה כלל אבל הכא שהוציא הבלילה מחוץ כל העזרה ודאי גרע מאילו לא בלל כלום עכ"ל תו"ח: יט] דקדושת כלי הוא: כ] התכלת גבי שתי הלחם דאמר: כא] מקדשא ואיפסילא ביוצא ותיבת היא נמחק: כב] אבראי הא איפסילו להו: כג] אגב אחריני: כד] מקדש כלי שרת אין: כה] שלמה שיחיה. עיין תום' זבחים (דף י ע"ב): כו] לא נתקדשה. לשון מהר"פ וא"ת א"כ מאי קאמר לקמן בפ' שתי הלחם הא גופא קשיא אמרת לישתן ועריכתן בחוץ אלמא מדת יבש לא נתקדשה ואפייתן בפנים אלמא מדת יבש נתקדשה והיכא מוכח מלישתן ועריכתן בחוץ דלא נתקדשה דלמא לעולם אימא לך דנתקדשה ואפ"ה לא נפסלו ביוצא כדפי' וי"ל דאין זו קושיא דאע"ג דלא תיפסל ביוצא בדיעבד מ"מ אם נתקדשה גנאי היה לעשות בחוץ לכתחילה: כז] עי' בהשמטות בסוף המסכת: כח] כדאמרינן בפ"ב דמעילה כל דבר שיש לו מתירין משקרבו מתירין ובזבחים (דף מה ע"ב) ושאין: כט] קבלה ולא גרסי' לה דאם כן תסגי בצואר בהמה לפנים והא קי"ל כולה בחוץ וצוארה בפנים פסולה כדלקמן בפ' השוחט והמעלה. תו"ח: ל] נגעים אר' (יעקב) [עקיבא]: לא] לאחר יציקה וא"ת הרי נתן וי"ל דההיא נתינה שלא כמצותה היא שהרי לא נתן בכשרות אלא בפסול אבל ביציקה על כפו כמצותה היא לפיכך צריך למימר תנאי היא. תו"ח: לב] פליגי נמי במנחות לאו לרשב"ל:

דאמר

א) זה תמוה דהא אין כפרה אלא בדם ואולי צ"ל אם אין דם אין בשר:

הגהות הב"ח

(א) רש"י ד"ה דעבודה דדרך כו' ותיבת היא נמחק: (ב) בא"ד לאכול במקום רבו דאמרינן דכיון דעיקר הוא כ"ש דלא מני אכיל:

מסורת הש"ס (שוליים)

פסחים לו. לקמן יח:

נגעים פי"ד משנה י זבחים עו: יומא מז: לעיל ח. לקמן יב. קו.

פסחים עז. לקמן כו.

אדם ואכילת מזבח מצטרפין דזריקת ל"ק

דאי נתקדשה הוי ל"ק

אימתי ל"ק

[וע"ע תוספות סוכה נ. ד"ה ואי] [לקמן כ. ועי' תוספות מגילה כ: ד"ה לקמיצה] ל"ק

[וע"ע תוספות חולין לט. ד"ה הא מקמיה]

דבפסול נעשית לאו ל"ק

עין משפט נר מצוה

נז א מיי' פי"א מהל' פסה"מ הלכה ו:

נח ב מיי' שם הל' ז:

נ"א דקדושת כלי וגירסת ל"ק דנתקדשה בכלי לא מיפסלא

נט ג מיי' שם הל' טז:

ס ד מיי' פ"ה מהלכות מחוסרי כפרה הל' ד:

סא ה ו מיי' פי"א מהל' פסה"מ הלכה כח:

סב ז מיי' שם פי"א הלכה ל לג:

יוצא אגב אחרינא ל"ק

הוא רש"י

נה א מיי' פי"ג מהל' מעה"ק הל' יג:

בס"י ר' יונתן

נו ב ג מיי' פ"ג מהל' פסה"מ הלכה יט:

מסורת הש"ס · תורה אור

א] לא זו אקדושה בלא זו, ולא זו קדושה בלא זו. ב] ולר' חנינא, עשרון למה נמשח? (והלא אינו עשוי אלא למדידת קמח בלבד, והקמח אינו קדוש בלא שמן!) ג] למנחת חוטא. ולוג למה נמשח? ללוג ד] של מצורע. ואף שמואל סבר לה להא דרב, דתנן: *כלי הלח מקדשין את הלח, ומדות היבש מקדשין את היבש, בואין כלי הלח מקדשין את היבש, ולא מדות היבש מקדשין את הלח; ואמר שמואל: ל"ש אלא מדות, אבל גמזרקות ה] (של דם) מקדשות את היבש, שנא': °"שניהם מלאים סלת בלולה בשמן למנחה". א"ל רב אחא מדפתי לרבינא: ו] מנחה לחה היא! א"ל: לא נצרכא אלא ליבש שבה, ז] (דהיינו לבונה. ואי ס"ד קסבר שמואל אין מנחה קדושה עד שיהו כולן, יבש שבה היכי משכחת לה? והלא כולן לחים הן, מפני השמן! אלא ש"מ: קסבר שמואל האי בלא האי.) ח] ואיבעית אימא: מנחה לגבי דם כיבש דמיא. גופא, ט] א"ר אלעזר: מנחה שקמצה בהיכל — כשרה, שכן מצינו בסילוק בזיכין. מתיב ר' ירמיה: "וקמץ משם" — ממקום שרגלי הזר עומדות; בן בתירא אומר: מנין שאם קמץ בשמאל שיחזיר י] ויקמוץ בימין? ת"ל: "וקמץ משם" — ממקום שקמץ כבר! איכא דאמרי: הוא מותיב לה והוא מפרק לה; איכא דאמרי, א"ל ר' יעקב לר' ירמיה בר תחליפא: אסברא לך, לא נצרכא אלא להכשיר את כל עזרה כולה, שלא תאמר: הואיל ועולה קדשי קדשים ומנחה קדשי קדשים, מה עולה טעונה צפון — אף מנחה טעונה צפון. מה לעולה שכן כליל! מחטאת. מה לחטאת שכן מכפרת על חייבי כריתות! מאשם. מה לאשם שכן מיני דמים! מכולהו נמי, שכן מיני דמים! אלא איצטריך, ס"ד אמינא, הואיל וכתיב: °"והקריבה אל הכהן והגישה אל המזבח וקמץ", מה הגשה בקרן דרומית מערבית — אף קמיצה נמי בקרן דרומית מערבית, קמ"ל. גופא, *א"ר יוחנן: שלמים ששחטן בהיכל — כשרין, שנאמר: "ושחטו פתח אהל מועד", ולא יהא טפל חמור מן העיקר. מיתיבי, *ר' יהודה בן בתירא אומר: יא] מנין שאם הקיפו גוים את העזרה, שהכהנים נכנסין להיכל ואוכלין בקדשי קדשים ושירי מנחות? ת"ל: בקדש

רש"י

לא זו קדושה בלא זו. בכל המנחות הטעונות שמן ולבונה, אין כלי שרת מקדש אחד מהם, אלא א"כ שלשתן יב] ביחד בכלי. ולרבי חנינא עשרון. שהיתה במקדש לצורך מנחות, כדאמר בפ' "שתי מדות" (לקמן פז.). למה נמשח. בשמן המשחה כדי לקדש את הנתון בתוכו? הלא אינו יג] מתקדש כלום לר' חנינא, דאין מחזיק לא שמן ולא לבונה עם העשרון של סולת! ומשני: לצורך מנחת חוטא. נמשח, דסולת גרידתא הוא. להא דרב. דכלי שרת מקדש סולת גרידתא, אע"ג דלא חזי להקטיר בלא שמן. דתנן. במס' זבחים בפ' "המזבח מקדש הראוי לו". מדות של יבש. שתים היו, עשרון וחצי עשרון, בפ' "שתי מדות" (לקמן פז.). ל"ש. דאין כלי הלח מקדשין יבש, אלא [א] במדות לח – יד] הין וחצי הין כו' בפ' "שתי מדות" (שם פז.). דכל מדה לא חזיא אלא למילתא [ב] למדוד, הלכך (לח) לא מיקדשין, טו] דמדת לח לא חזיא למדוד יבש, דאין בלח עשרון וחצי עשרון. אבל מזרקות (של דם). שהן כלי לח, מקדשין יבש. שניהם מלאים סלת. ובמנחת נסכים קמשתעי דטעונה שמן, וקאמר דמזרק וקערה קדשו סלת, אלמא אית ליה לשמואל דכלי שרת מקדשין סלת בלי שמן. ואם תאמר: לר' חנינא קשיא מתני' דקתני: מדות יבש מקדשין יבש! איהו מוקי לה בעשרון דמנחת חוטא. טז] מנחה לחה היא. דבלולה בשמן, ומהאי קרא לא תיפוק דמזרקין מקדשין יבש! לא נצרכא אלא ליבש שבה. מנחה בלולה א"א בלא קרטין סלת יבש שלא יגיע בהן השמן, ואפי' הכי מתקדשין במזרקין. וכי היכי דאותו יבש מתקדש, מסתברא נמי דסלת יבש נמי בלא יז] (סלת) שמן מיקדשין. ואיבעית אימא מנחה לגבי דם כיבש דמיא. דדם יח] הוא צלול ומנחה הויא כעיסה, ואפ"ה מקדש לה מזרק שהוא כלי דם, הלכך יבשה גמורה נמי מקדש. רגלי הזר עומדות. אחת עשרה אמה בכניסת העזרה במזרח, מקום דריסת יט] ישראל. אלמא עזרה בעינן! בן בתירא. לאו דווקא נקט, אלא סיומא דברייתא היא. לא נצרכא. האי "וקמץ משם" אלא להכשיר כל העזרה, ולאו למידק מיניה: עזרה ולאו היכל, דלגופיה אילטריך (א) קרא. בעולה ומנחה. כ] [נאמר] קדשי קדשים, ובעולה כתיב צפון, שנאמר (ויקרא א): "ושחט אותו על ירך המזבח צפונה". כא] עולה [כולה] כליל. לגבוה, שנאמר: "וערכו בני אהרן את הנתחים וגו'" (שם). מחטאת. הוי גמרינן דמנחה טעונה צפון, להכי אילטריך "וקמץ" להכשיר כל העזרה. על חייבי כריתות. שוגגין. מאשם. [דאשם] אינו בא על כרת, אלא על שבועת שקר ומעילות ושפחה חרופה, וטעון צפון, דכתיב: "במקום אשר ישחטו את העולה ישחטו את האשם" (שם ז). מיני דמים. תמורה כפרתן, דעיקר כפרה כב] בדם כתיב: "כי הדם הוא בנפש יכפר" (שם יז), אבל תאמר במנחה שאינה מין כג] הדם. אלא איצטריך. "וקמץ". הגשה. שמגיש כל המנחה קודם קמיצה, ומגיע הכלי בחודה של קרן דרומית מערבית בפ"ג (לקמן יט:). קמ"ל. דאם רצה מחזירה אחר הגשה לכל מקום שירצה בעזרה וקומץ. הקיפו גוים. למלחמה, ואין כד] כהנים יכולים לאכול בעזרה מפני רמחים וקשתות. נכנסין להיכל. ולא אמרינן דליפסלו קדשים בהך יציאה דיצאו מעזרה להיכל. בקדש

תוספות

ובמחוק היו מודדין לחביתי כ"ג, ועשרון המחוק כה] [ג] (לא) נמשח לרבי חנינא דאין מנחה קדושה בלא שמן! וי"ל: פן יבא לטעות בשום פעם ולמדוד במחוק למנחת חוטא. אבל אין לתרץ דר"מ סבר כר' *יוחנן דאמר בפ' "כל המנחות באות מצה" [ד] (לקמן דף נז:) גמרינן דחייב על לישתה, דמדת יבש לא נתקדשו. בפ' "שתי מדות" (לקמן דף ל.) משמע דסבר ר"מ דנתקדשו, גבי הא דתנן התם: כל מדות שבמקדש היו גדושות, ומוקי לה כר"מ. ואפי' עשרון גדוש אפשר דמקדש, דהא דאמר לעיל שהחזירן לכיסא גדושה, ומיבעיא לן נמי בפ' "שתי מדות" (שם פז:) גבי שולחן אי מקדשי בגדוש או לא, משמע דשאר כלים לא מקדשי ההוא גדוש לא צריך, אבל גדוש זה שהוא מדתו של כלי מקדש. וזה אין להקשות, לרבי אלעזר דאמר לעיל: מנחת חביתין קדושה לחצאין, עשרון מחוק לר"מ למה נמשח? דבלאו טעמא דפרישית שלא יבא לטעות – מצוה לקדש שלימה. ולאו מקרא ד"מחציתה", דההוא אוקימנא לעיל להביא חביתו שלם ולעכב משום דחוקה כתיבא ביה. וא"ת: לר"ש דאמר לקמן בפ' "שתי מדות" (דף פז:) דמדה יתירה היתה שם של לוג ומחצה שבה היה מודד לחביתי כ"ג, לוג ומחצה בבוקר ולוג ומחצה בערב, למה נמשח? כיון דאין שמן קדוש בפני עצמו כו] לר' חנינא! וי"ל: דתחילה מניחין שלשה לוגין שמן עם הסלת בכיסא, וכדפרישית לעיל, שהיה גנאי להוציא מכלי שרת לכלי חול. **כלי** הלח מקדשין את הלח ומדות היבש כו'. מה שדקדק התנא, דקרי לשל לח "כלי" ולשל יבש "מדות" – משום דבשל יבש היו מדקדקין לעשות כענין זה שיהא גדוש תילתא, כדרך כל שאר מדות. מ"מ גם על של לח שם מדה עליו, כדקאמר שמואל: ל"ש אלא מדות אבל מזרקות מקדשין, ובשל לח איירי. ובפ' "שתי מדות" (שם פז:) תנן: ז' מדות היו במקדש, וקא חשיב דלח. ובפ' "המזבח מקדש" (זבחים פח. ושם) פירש הקונטרס דכמה כלים היו מיוחדים ללח שאינם מדות, כגון מזרקות וקערות לדם ליין ולשמן, אבל ליבש לא היו מיוחדין אלא שתי מדות של יבש שהיו במקדש, עשרון וחצי עשרון. דכלים שנותנין בו [ה] מנחה – כלי לח כז] היו, שמזרקות וקערות ראויין לכך.

אבל מזרקות מקדשין כח] [כו'] שנאמר שניהם מלאים סולת. פירש בקונטרס: כט] (דדייק) דאלמא מזרקות וקערות קידשו בלא שמן. וזהו תימה, דהכתיב "בלולה בשמן", ומנא ליה דמנחה קדושה ל] בלא שמן? ופירש ר' שמואל: דדייק מדסבר [ו] לא] (רישא) דמזרקות מקדשין שאינו ראוי לה, כמו מנחה, הואיל וראויה להתקדש בכלי אחר דהיינו כיסא – אף מנחת סלת מתקדשת בלא שמן ולבונה אע"פ שאינה ראויה לכלי זה, הואיל ומתקדשת בכלי אחר, כגון מנחת חוטא. ומלשון המשנה דקדק ר' שמואל, דקתני פרק "המזבח מקדש" (זבחים פו.): כשם שהמזבח והכבש מקדשין את הראוי להם כך כלים מקדשים. ומדלא קתני [ז] "כלי שרת מקדשין את הראוי להם" ש"מ דמקדשין אע"פ שאינו ראוי להם, כגון מזרקות של דם שמקדשין את המנחה. ועל חנם הוצרך רבי שמואל לדיוק זה. והא דלא ילפי' מינה מדות – משום דלא נראו מעולם אלא זו למדידת לח וזו למדידת יבש. ועוד יש לפרש, דדייק התלמוד מדאמר שמואל: אבל מזרקות מקדשין, ולא קאמר "מקדשין מנחות ונסכים" דכתיב בההוא קרא – ש"מ דאפי' מנחת חוטא קאמר. דילפינן מלתא ממילתא, ומדמקדשין מזרק וקערה מה שאין ראוי להם, הואיל וראוי [ח] לכל אחד – כ"ש זה הכלי שמקדש מה שראוי להיות בתוכו. עוד יש לפרש, דדייק מדיליף שמואל דורות משעה מנשיאים, כ"ש דילפינן מילתא ממילתא כרב דמנחה קדושה בלא שמן, כמו שמצינו במנחת חוטא. ואע"ג דמוכח לקמן ב"הקומץ רבה" (ד' יט:) דלא יליף שמואל דורות משעה אלא משום דתנא ביה קרא תריסר זימני, מ"מ לב]כיון דיליף דורות משעה בכל ענין שילמדו – הוא הדין מילתא ממילתא.

רבי

שיטה מקובצת

א] לא זו קדושה בלא זו אלא עד שיניחם בביסא ביחד. הרגמ"ה. משמע דלא ילפינן לר' חנינא מנחה מלחם הפנים ותימה דאמרינן לעיל קומצין מכלי שעל גבי קרקע שכן מצינו בסילוק בזיכין אלמא ילפינן מנחה מלחם הפנים וי"מ דאתיא דלא כר' חנינא (נראה שחסר כאן כמה תיבות וכך צ"ל [ולא נהירא וי"ל] דהכא ודאי לא יליף מלחם הפנים ליקדש זה בלא זה דאפשר משאי אפשר הוא אבל למילף שקומצין מכלי שעל גבי קרקע שפיר ילפינן מסילוק בזיכין דאי איתא דבקמיצה הוה צריך הגבהה לכלי ה"נ הוה צריך להגביה את השלחן בשעת סילוק בזיכין: ב] ולרבי חנינא א"כ עשרון למה נמשח בשמן המשחה הואיל ואינו יכול לקדש המנחה עד שיניחנה בביסא ויבללנה. הרגמ"ה. ותיבות והלא כו' בלא שמן נמחק: ג] למנחת חוטא דאין בה לא שמן ולא לבונה היה מקדש העשרון מיד וכן לוג לקדש שמן של מצורע דהא לא הוי בו מנחה. הרגמ"ה: ד] ללוג שמן של: ה] אבל מזרקות של דם מקדשות אפי' היבש שנאמר. הרגמ"ה: ו] מנחה לחה היא דכתיב בלולה בשמן: ז] לא נצרכא אלא ליבש שבמנחה שאם יש בה יבש שלא נבלל בשמן היה מקדש המזרק כמו הלח וכמו שהיה מקדש היבש המנחה כך היו מקדשין המנחה אף אם לא היה בו שמן כלל והיינו דרב דאמר דמנחה קדושה בלא שמן. הרגמ"ה: ז] מתיבת דהיינו כו' עד תיבת ואיבעית נמחק: ח] ואיבעית אימא לא תימא ביבש שבה אלא אפי' אותו שבלול בשמן הוי יבש לגבי דם דדם הוא לח הרבה כמשקה והמנחה הוא כעיסה והויא כמו יבשה לגבי לחות של דם וכי היכי דמקדשי מנחה בלולה דהויא יבשה לגבי דם ה"נ מקדש יבש גמור בלא שמן ולהכי הוי דרב. הרגמ"ה: ט] אמר רבי אלעזר זבחים (דף סג ע"א): י] שיחזור ויקמוץ: יא] מנין תוס' זבחים (דף סג ע"א) ובזבחים (דף כ ע"א): יב] שלשתן בכלי ביחד: יג] מקדש כלום: יד] מדת לח כגון הין: טו] מדת לח לא מקדשה יבש דהא מדת יבש לא חזיא למדוד דאין: טז] דמנחת חוטא דאינה צריכה לא שמן אלא סולת גרידתא היא הס"ד: יז] תיבת סלת נמחק: יח] הוי צלול ומנחה הויא כעיסה בלולה: יט] דריסת רגלי ישראל: כ] ומנחה כתיב קדש קדשים: כא] כליל. עולה כולה לגבוה: כב] כפרה הוא בדם דכתיב כי: כג] שאינה מין דם לא: כד] ואין הכהנים: כה] המחוק למה נמשח: כו] לר' חנינא וה"ר שמואל תירץ דאמרינן לקמן כל המדידות היו מודדין בלוג ולוג היה נמשח וגנאי הוא לערות מכלי קודש לכלי חול. תו"ח. לשון מהר"פ וא"ת לר"ש כו' וי"ל שהיו מניחין הכל בביסא תחילת הסולת והלבונה כדאמרי' לעיל שלם הי' מביאהו ואחר כך חוצהו וכיון שהיה מונח בתחלה בכלי קודש גנאי אח"כ ליתנו בכלי שלא נמשח והיה צריך ליזהר שלא יתערב השמן בסולת כשהיה נתון בתחילה בביסא דאם לא כן לא היה יכול לחצותה מחציתה בבוקר ומחציתה בערב וא"ת לעיל דאמר מביא מנחה ואח"כ חוצהו משמע שהיה מביא עשרון שלם מביתו כדי שתהא כולה קדושה ביחד ומהתם מוכיח ר' יוחנן דאינה קדושה לחצאין וכשהביאה שלם מה תיקן והלא אין הסולת קדוש בלא שמן ולבונה ואין לומר שהיה בולל מיד השמן הא אמר התם לוג ומחצה בערב וי"ל שהיה בביסא ג' גומות אחת לשמן ואחת ללבונה ואחת לסולת והיה נותן הכל בבוקר כל אחד בגומה לבדה ואח"כ חוצה ע"כ: כז] כלי לח הוא: כח] מקדשין שנאמר ותיבת כו' נמחק: כט] בקונטרס דדייק: ל] בלא שמן וי"ל דהכי מוכיח מדקאמר שמואל המזרק מקדש יבש א"כ שמן דבהדי מנחה אינו גורם הקדושה ובלא שמן מקדשין. והר"מ תירץ דהכי מוכח דקיי"ל דמנח' נחשון נאכלת כדכתי' קחו את המנחה הנותרת מאשי ה' ואכלוה מצות לרבות מנחת נחשון וכיון שנאכלת נקמצת וכו' (חסר וצ"ל שכך צ"ל) [כמו שאר] מנחה נקמצת ונאכלת בלא (חסר שתי תיבות וצ"ל שכך צ"ל) [לבונה כמו] מנחת חוטא ואפ"ה נתקדשו (חסר שתי תיבות) [השמן והסולת] בלא לבונה אלמא זה קדוש בלא זה ת"ח. ובתוס' אחרות כתוב והר"מ תירץ דודאי האי קרא כתיב גבי מנחת נחשון ולא כפ"ה גבי נסכים. ומנחת נחשון היתה נאכלת ונקמצת והויא כמנחת שמיני למילואים דאמרינן התם והנותרת מן המנחה זו מנחת שמיני למילואים א) ללבונה וכיון דנפקא לן תרוייהו מקרא חדא מנחת נחשון ומנחת שמיני למילואים א"כ שוות הן בשתיהן ללבונה ומ"מ המזרקות מקדשות השמן והסולת בלא לבונה א"כ היינו כרב דאמר זו קדושה בלא זו ולא כר' חנינא דמצריך שיהיו הכל ביחד. עוד בתוס' אחרות ואמר מורי דבמנחת נחשון איירי קרא דלא כפרש"י ומנחת נחשון היתה נקמצת ונאכלת כדתניא בת"כ קחו את המנחה הנותרת זו מנחת נחשון ומנחת שמיני היתה נקמצת כדכתיב וימלא כפו ממנה והי' בה לבונה כדאיתא בפרק (אלו מנחות) [כל המנחות] (דף נט ע"א) המנחה לרבות מנחת שמיני ללבונה גם מנחת נחשון כן והשתא ניחא דמייתי שפיר דמקדשי המזרק והקערות להסולת והשמן שבתוכן ואע"ג דלא היה בהן לבונה והי' עתיד להיות לבונה אלמא קדשה זה בלא זה: לא] מדסבר שמואל: לב] כיון ס"א שמצינו דא"ל לשמואל בשום מקום דילפי' דורות משעה כ"ש דא"ל למילף מילתא ממילתא:

א) נראה דחסר כאן וצ"ל והיה בה לבונה כדאיתא בפ' כל המנחות דף נט המנחה לרבות מנחת שמיני ללבונה כיון דנפקא לן וכו':

הגהות הב"ח (א) רש"י ד"ה לא נצרכא וכו' קרא הס"ד ואח"כ מ"ה ומנחה קדשי קדשים שנאמר קדשי קדשים וכעולה:

הגהות צ"ק [א] במדות לח ז' מדות שהיה שם הין כו': [ב] נ"א למדוד לח הילכך לא כו': [ג] נ"א למה: [ד] מלה דמדת יבש לא נתקדשו דבפ' שתי כו' כל"ל: [ה] מנחות: [ו] מדסבר שמואל דמזרקות: [ז] כך הכלים מקדשין: [ח] לכלי אחד:

ואם איתא, לילף מדם! וכי תימא, רבי אלעזר מילתא ממילתא לא גמר, והא אמר *ר' אלעזר: אמנחה שקמצה בהיכל — כשרה, שכן מצינו בסילוק בזיכין! מנחה ממנחה יליף, מנחה מדם לא יליף. ומנחה ממנחה מי יליף? והתניא: א] *בעד שלא פרקה נפרס לחמה — הלחם פסול ואין מקטיר עליו את הבזיכין, ב] משפרקה נפרס לחמה — הלחם פסול ומקטיר עליו את הבזיכין; ואמר ר' אלעזר: גלא פרקה ממש, אלא כיון שהגיע זמנה לפרק, אע"פ שלא פרקה — כמי שפרקה דמיא; ואמאי? ג] תיהוי כמנחה שחסרה קודם קמיצה! ד] הא לא קשיא, מנחה לא בריר הברירה קומץ דידיה, והא בריר ברירה קומץ דידיה, וכיון שהגיע זמנה לפרק — כמאן דפרקה דמיא. אלא ו] מעתה, תיהוי כשירים שחסרו בין קמיצה להקטרה, דאין מקטירין קומץ עליהן! ז] לאו פלוגתא נינהו? רבי אלעזר סבר לה כמ"ד: *דשירים שחסרו בין קמיצה להקטרה, מקטיר קומץ עליהן. גופא: חביתי כהן גדול — רבי יוחנן אמר: ח] אינה קדושה לחצאין, ור' אלעזר אמר: מתוך שקרבה לחצאין קדושה לחצאין. א"ר אחא: מאי טעמא דרבי יוחנן? אמר קרא: °"מנחה מחציתה" — ט] הביא מנחה ואח"כ חוציהו. מיתיבי: חביתי כהן גדול לא היו באות חצאין, אלא המביא עשרון שלם וחוצהו; ותניא: אילו נאמר "מנחה מחצית" הייתי אומר: מביא חצי עשרון מביתו שחרית ומקריב, חצי עשרון מביתו ערבית ומקריב — ת"ל: "מחציתה בבקר", מחצה משלם הוא מביא! למצוה. אמר ליה רב גביהא מבי כתיל לרב אשי: י] והא חוקה כתיב בה! אמר ליה: לא נצרכא אלא להביאה שלם מביתו. ומי א"ר יוחנן הכי? והא איתמר: יא] הפריש חצי עשרון יב] ודעתו להוסיף — רב אמר: אינו קדוש, ור' יוחנן אמר: קדוש; יג] ואם איתא, לילף מחביתין! וכי תימא, ר' יוחנן מילתא ממילתא לא יליף, יד] *והאמר רבי יוחנן: ישלמים ששחטן בהיכל — כשירין, דכתיב: °"ושחטו פתח אהל מועד", טו] שלא יהא טפל חמור מעיקר! דעתו להוסיף שאני, *דתניא: °"מלאים" — אין טז] מלאים אלא שלמים, *)(כלומר, שאינו קדוש עד שיהא עשרון שלם;) ואמר רבי יוסי: אימתי? בזמן שאין דעתו להוסיף, אבל בזמן שדעתו להוסיף — ראשון ראשון קדוש. ורב בחביתין כמאן ס"ל? אי כר' אלעזר, לילף מחביתין! וכי תימא, רב מילתא ממילתא לא יליף, והאמר רב: יז] מנחה קדושה בלא שמן[א] *(ובלא לבונה) — שכן מצינו בלחם הפנים; בלא לבונה — שכן מצינו במנחת נסכים; בלא שמן ובלא לבונה — שכן מצינו במנחת חוטא! על כרחיך רב כר' יוחנן ס"ל. גופא, אמר רב: מנחה קדושה בלא שמן, יח] (ואין דינה כעשרון חסר) — שכן מצינו בלחם הפנים, בלא לבונה — שכן מצינו במנחת נסכים, בלא שמן ובלא לבונה שכן מצינו במנחת חוטא. ושמן ולבונה יט] קדשי האי בלא האי והאי בלא האי; שמן — שכן מצינו בלוג שמן של מצורע, לבונה — שכן מצינו בלבונה הבאה בבזיכין. ורבי חנינא אמר:

*) רש"ק מ"ז ועיין נ"ק שמוחק ר' תיבת כלומר והשאר נ"ל כן וכן משמע ברש"י דזבחים דף פח ע"א ד"ה ואין מקדשין ע"ש:

רש"י

ואם איתא. דהם לא קידש לחצאין, לילף מנחה מדם! שקמצה בהיכל כשרה. ואע"ג דדינה בעזרה כשאר קרבנות. שכן מצינו בסילוק בזיכין. כ] דהיא בהיכל. אלמא דאיכא קמילה בהיכל, דסילוק היינו קמילה. **עד שלא פרקה.** למערכת לחם הפנים בשבת. הלחם פסול. דהויא לה מנחה שחסרה קודם קמילה, ואמרינן לקמן (דף ט.): "מן המנחה" — פרט לשחסרה. ובלחם הפנים [ב] גופיה אמר לקמן (דף יג:): "[קדש קדשים] היא", שאם נפרסה אחת מחלותיה — כולן פסולות. משפרקה נפרס לחמה הלחם פסול. אף ע"ג דלאחר סילוק כא] (א) (מצה) נפרס — פסולה, דהוי שירים שחסרו בין קמילה להקטרה, ואמרינן לקמן (דף ט:) דאע"ג דמקטירין קומץ עלייהו — שיריים אסורים באכילה. ומקטיר עליו כב] בזיכין. [דלא] גמרינן ממנחה. כג] הגיע זמנה לפרק. שעברו שש שעות, כדאמר בפרק "תמיד נשחט" (פסחים נח.): מוספין בשש, בזיכין בשבע [ג]. קודם קמיצה. דהא עדיין לא פירקה, ומיפסל, דהא אמר לקמן: "מן המנחה" — פרט כד] [ד] לכשחסרה מכשיעור. אלמא לא יליף מנחה (ב) ממנחה! לעולם מנחה ממנחה יליף ולא דמי לחם הפנים לשאר מנחות, דמנחה לא בריר קומץ דידה, שהכל ביחד, הלכך קודם קמילה ליכא למימר כמאן דקמלה דמיא, דהא מחוסר מעשה. אבל לחם הפנים בריר קומץ דידהו. דקאי כה] בבזיכין באפי נפשיה. הלכך, משהגיע זמנה לפרוק — כמאן דקמלה דמיא. כו] **ולא פלוגתא היא.** לקמן בשמעתין. מנחה מחציתה. "מנחה תמיד מחליתה בבקר" [ה] וגומר — כז] הביא מנחה שלימה של עשרון, דאין מנחה פחותה מעשרון, ואח"כ כח] [ו] חוליהו. מחציתה. משמע מחליתה של שלימה זו (ג) שלפניו. ומשני: כי מצריך קרא להביא שלם — למצוה בעלמא. ולעולם אם קדשה לחצאין — כט] מקודש, ואינה יוצאה שוב לחולין. **והא** חוקה כתיב בה. "חק עולם לה'" וגו' (ויקרא ו) ל] [ז], דמשמע: מתוך שלם! **אלא** להביא עשרון שלם לא] מביתו. אבל לענין קידוש בכלי שרת, אם רצה מקדש לחצאין. ודעתו להוסיף. להשלים עשרון, כדאמרינן לקמן בפרק "המנחות והנסכים" (דף קג.) דאין מנחה פחותה מעשרון, דהאומר "הרי עלי חצי עשרון" — מביא עשרון שלם. **ואם איתא.** דגבי חביתין אינו קדוש. **ושחטו.** בשלמים [ח] כתיב. **פתח אהל מועד.** בעזרה. וכיון שעזרה כשרה — כל שכן דהיכל לב] (שלם) כשר, דלא תהא עזרה שהיא טפל, חמורה מן העיקר. אלמא יליף היכל מעזרה! **מלאים.** "שניהם מלאים סלת". **אין מלאים.** שהיו מלאים לג] ממש המזרקים סלת, אלא מלאים — כל העשרונות שקדשו בתוכו שלמים היו. **ורב.** דאמר במפריש לד] חצי עשרון שאינו קדוש. מחביתין. ולקדוש. **מילתא ממילתא לא יליף.** הילכך שאר מנחות לה] דליהוו כחביתין, דבחביתין דין הוא דלקדשו לחצאין, אבל שאר מנחה לא. מנחה קדושה בלא שמן. אם נתן עשרון סולת בכלי שרת לו] אע"פ שאין שם שמן [י]. ולא יצא לחולין, וצריך להביא שמן ולהקריבה. שכן מצינו בלחם הפנים. שהיא מנחה ואין בה שמן, אבל לבונה יש בה כגון בזיכין. לז] הבאין עם כל הזבח. מנחת נסכים. כדכתיב בתמיד (במדבר כח): "עשירית האיפה סלת למנחה בלולה בשמן" וגו', ואין בה לבונה. על כרחך כרבי יוחנן ס"ל. בחביתין דלא קדשה, הלכך גמר שאר מנחות מחביתין. **האי בלא האי.** שמן בלא סלת ובלא לבונה, ולבונה בלא שמן וסלת — לח] שכן מצינו בבזיכין שמקדשין את הלבונה בלא שמן וסלת. ואי קשיא: הא אתי לחם הפנים בהדייהו! לאו פירכא היא, שהרי אינו מתקדש עם הלבונה בבזיכין, ומיהו אשכחן דכלי שרת מקדשין לבונה שבתוכן בלא שמן וסולת.

לא

תוספות

מנחה שנקמצה בהיכל כשרה שכן מצינו בסילוק בזיכין. ואם תאמר, אמאי לא קאמר: כדי שלא יהא טפל חמור מן העיקר, כדאמר בסמוך גבי שלמים ששחטן בהיכל, וגבי כהנים נכנסין בהיכל ואוכלים קדשי קדשים ושירי מנחות? וי"ל: דהתם כתיב (ויקרא ג) "פתח אהל מועד" (שם ו), בחצר אהל מועד שייך למימר שלא יהא טפל חמור מן העיקר, *לפי שתלה הכתוב באהל מועד.

מקטיר עליו את הבזיכין. פירש בקונטרס: דלא גמרינן ממנחה. ולא היה לו לפרש כן, דלקמן (דף ט:) פריך מינה למ"ד שיריים שחסרו בין קמילה להקטרה אין מקטיר קומץ עליהן, ומשני: רבי אלעזר [יא] היא. גם שמועה זו אי אפשר ליישב.

מאי טעמא דרבי יוחנן. וא"ת: לימא לט] משום דיליף מדם! ושמא קבלה היה בידו טעם זה. אי נמי כדפרישית לעיל, דלאפוקי דרבי יוחנן מפרש ר' אלעזר טעמא [יב] ד"מתוך".

מ] *(ראשון ראשון קדוש — ולית ליה דרבי יוסי). **ולרבי** חנינא עשרון למה נמשח למנחת חוטא. תימה: אכתי חצי עשרון למה נמשח לרבי חנינא? דלקמן בפ' "שתי מדות" (דף פז.) מוכח דנמשח למנחת חביתין, ומנחת חביתין טעונה שמן ולבונה! וי"ל: משום דמתחילה היו מקדשין המנחה של חביתין בביסא עם השמן, והיה גנאי בדבר מא] להוליא לכלי חול אחר שנתקדשה, ולכך נמשח חצי עשרון. מב] וטעם זה אנו צריכין נמי לרבי יוחנן דאמר לעיל דאינה קדושה לחצאין, דאחר שנתקדשה שלימה היה גנאי להוליאה מכלי שרת לכלי חול. וצריך לומר השתא לרבי חנינא שלא היו מערבין בביסא המנחה עם השמן, אלא בתוך הביסא עצמה היה זה לצד אחד וזה לצד אחר. שאם היה הכל מעורב לא היו יכולין אחרי כן לחלק בחצי עשרון, מפני לוג ומחצה שמן שהיא עודף על החצי עשרון. ולכ"ע נמי צ"ל כן, דמתניתין ד"שתי מדות" (שם) מוכח שהיו מחלקין הסולת בחצי עשרון, והשמן במדה שהיא מחזקת לוג ומחצה. ואם תאמר: לר' מאיר, דאמר לקמן בפ' "שתי מדות" (שם) דשני עשרונות היו במקדש, אחד גדוש ואחד מחוק, וכמחוק

כב] עליו את הבזיכין דלא: כג] שהגיע זמנה: כד] פרט לשחסרה אפ"ה מכשר אלמא: כה] דקאי בזיכין באפי: כו] ולאו פלוגתא: כז] וגומר הבא: כח] ואח"כ חוצה דמחציתה משמע והד"א: כט] נמי קידש ואינה: ל] דמשמע עיכובא שאם שינה בה והביאה לחצאין לא קדשה הס"ד ומה"ד לא נצרכא קרא דכתיב מחציתה דמשמע מתוך: לא] עשרון שלם ביחד מביתו: לב] תיבת שלם נמחק: לג] מלאים המזרקים

מ] דמתוך הס"ד ומה"ד ראשון ראשון קדוש ורב לית ליה דר' יוסי. גליון דרב תנא הוא ופליג א"נ לא שמיע ליה. תו"ח: מא] להוציאה בכלי חול: מב] עשרון א"נ משום שהיו מודדין אותו בעשרון והעשרון היה מקודש משום מנחת חוטא וגנאי הוא להניחו אח"כ בכלי שאינו מקודש ובזה ניחא למה נמשח חצי לוג משום שהי' קודם לכן בלוג שהיה קדוש משום לוג שמן של מצורע. תו"ח:

א) אולי צ"ל דכן עדיף לן טעמא דמתוך דבחביתין איכו קדוש לחצאין כמו טעמא דדעתו להוסיף:

הגהות צ"ק [א] בלא שמן ובלא לבונה בלא שמן שכן מצינו כו': [ב] גופא אמרינן לקמן היא שאם: [ג] ס"א שייך כאן דבור הקודם המתחיל ומקטיר והד"א: [ד] לכשחסרה ואפ"ה מכשיר אלמא כו' כצ"ל: [ה] וגמרינן: [ו] חוליהו מחליתה הד"א: [ז] דמשמע דוקא שלם כו': [ח] כתיב פתח הד"א: [ט] לא גמיר מחביתין לחביתין דין כו': [י] קדוש ולא כו': [יא] היא ולפי שמועה זו כו': [יב] דמתוך הס"ד ומה"ד ראשון ראשון קדוש ור"י נ"ל דר' יוסי פי' דר' יוחנן אמר הפרש חצי עשרון ודעתו להוסיף משמע דוקא חצי עשרון כיון דאשכחן קלת בחביתי כה"ג דקרב לחצאין אע"ג דלא ס"ל לר"י מ"מ כיון דדעתו להוסיף דהוה תרתי למעליותא אמר קדוש אבל פחות מחצי עשרון לא אמר הקדוש אבל ר"י ס"ל ראשון ראשון אפילו במיעוט קמא קמא דמטו קדיש א"כ ר"י אית ליה דרבי יוחנן ורבי יוחנן נ"ל דרבי יוסי:

הגהות הב"ח (א) רש"י ד"ה משפרקה וכו' דלאחר סילוק המלה נפרס: (ב) ד"ה קודם קמילה וכו' ממנחה הס"ד ואח"כ מ"ה מנחה לא בריר לעולם מנחה: (ג) ד"ה מחליתה וכו' שלפניו הס"ד ואח"כ מ"ה למלוה ומשני כי:

מ א ב מיי' פ"ב מהל' מעה"ק הלכה יג:
מא ג מיי' שם פ"ג הלכה יב:
מב ד מיי' פ"ט מהל' פרה אדומה ה"ג:
מג ה מיי' פ"ה מהל' מעה"ק הלכה ט:
מד ו מיי' שם הל' ח:
מה ז מיי' שם פ"ח הלכה ח:
מו ח מיי' פ"ג מהלכות פרה אדומה הל' ג וע"ש:
מז ט מיי' פ"ה מהל' מעה"ק הלכה ח:
מח י מיי' פי"ג שם הלכה ב:

וְאִילּוּ מַגְבִּיהַּ א] אֶת הַשּׁוּלְחָן לָא קָתָנֵי! לָאו אָמְרַתְּ הָתָם: סֵדֶר עֲבוֹדוֹת נָקֵט? ה"נ סֵדֶר עֲבוֹדוֹת נָקֵט. מִי דָּמֵי? הָתָם לָא נָחֵית לְמִנְיָינָא דְּכֹהֲנִים, הָכָא נָחֵית לְמִנְיָינָא דְּכֹהֲנִים, אִם אִיתָא — לִיתְנֵי מַגְבִּיהַּ! אֶלָּא שְׁמַע מִינַּהּ: קוֹמְצִין מִכְּלִי שֶׁעַל גַּבֵּי קַרְקַע, ש"מ. אָמַר רָבָא: פְּשִׁיטָא לִי, ב] קוֹמֵץ מִכְּלִי שֶׁעַל גַּבֵּי קַרְקַע — שֶׁכֵּן מָצִינוּ בְּסִילּוּק בָּזִיכִין, אמְקַדְּשִׁין מִנְחָה בִּכְלִי שֶׁעַל גַּבֵּי קַרְקַע — שֶׁכֵּן מָצִינוּ בְּסִידּוּר בָּזִיכִין. בָּעֵי רָבָא: קִידּוּשׁ קוֹמֶץ מַאי? מִמִּנְחָה יָלְפִינַן לַהּ, אוֹ ג] מִדָּם יָלְפִינַן לַהּ? הֲדַר פַּשְׁטַהּ: במִדָּם יָלְפִינַן לַהּ. וּמִי אָמַר רָבָא הָכִי? וְהָא אִתְּמַר: קוֹמֶץ שֶׁחִלְּקוֹ בִּשְׁנֵי כֵלִים — רַב נַחְמָן אָמַר: גאֵינוֹ קָדוֹשׁ, וְרָבָא אָמַר: קָדוֹשׁ; ד] וְאִם אִיתָא, לֵילַף מִדָּם! הֲדַר בֵּיהּ רָבָא מֵהַהִיא. וְדָם מְנָלַן דְּלָא קָדוֹשׁ לַחֲצָאִין? *דְּתָנֵי ה] רַב תַּחְלִיפָא בֶּן שָׁאוּל: דקִידֵּשׁ פָּחוֹת מִכְּדֵי הַזָּאָה בִּכְלִי זֶה, וּפָחוֹת מִכְּדֵי הַזָּאָה בִּכְלִי זֶה — לֹא קִידֵּשׁ. וְאִיבַּעְיָא לְהוּ: בְּדָם מַאי? הִלְכְתָא הִיא, ו] וּמֵהִלְכְתָא לָא יָלְפִינַן; אוֹ דִּלְמָא הָתָם מַאי טַעְמָא — דִּכְתִיב: °"וְטָבַל בַּמַּיִם", ז] הָכָא נַמִי הָכְתִיב: °"וְטָבַל בַּדָּם"? וְאִיתְּמַר, א"ר זְרִיקָא אָמַר רַבִּי אֶלְעָזָר: אַף בְּדָם לֹא קִידֵּשׁ. ח] אָמַר רָבָא, תַּנְיָא נַמִי הָכִי (בִּפְנֵי כֹּהֵן מַנִּיחַ:) "וְטָבַל" — וְלֹא הּמְסַפֵּג, "בַּדָּם" — ט] שֶׁיְּהֵא בַּדָּם שִׁיעוּר טְבִילָה מֵעִיקָּרוֹ, "מִן הַדָּם" — י] מִן הַדָּם שֶׁבָּעִנְיָן. וְאִיצְטְרִיךְ לְמִכְתַּב "וְטָבַל" וְאִיצְטְרִיךְ לְמִכְתַּב "בַּדָּם", דְּאִי כָּתַב רַחֲמָנָא "וְטָבַל", הֲוָה אָמִינָא אע"ג דְּלָא קִיבֵּל שִׁיעוּר יא] טְבִילוֹת, (דְּהַיְינוּ הַזָּאָה ז' פְּעָמִים,) מֵעִיקָּרוֹ — כְּתַב רַחֲמָנָא "בַּדָּם"; וְאִי כָּתַב רַחֲמָנָא "בַּדָּם", הֲוָה אָמִינָא יב] אֲפִילּוּ מְסַפֵּג, כְּתַב רַחֲמָנָא "וְטָבַל". "מִן הַדָּם שֶׁבָּעִנְיָן" לְמַעוּטֵי מַאי? אָמַר רָבָא: לְמַעוּטֵי שִׁירַיִם שֶׁבָּאֶצְבַּע. מְסַיַּיע לֵיהּ לר"א, דְּאָמַר: ושִׁירַיִם שֶׁבָּאֶצְבַּע — פְּסוּלִין. א"ל רָבִין בַּר רַב אַדָּא לְרָבָא: אָמְרִי תַּלְמִידָךְ אָמַר רַב עַמְרָם, תַּנְיָא: הָיָה מַזֶּה וְנִתְּזָה הַזָּאָה מִיָּדוֹ, יג] אִם עַד שֶׁלֹּא הִזָּה — טָעוּן כִּיבּוּס, מִשֶּׁהִזָּה — אֵין טָעוּן כִּיבּוּס; מַאי לָאו עַד שֶׁלֹּא גָּמַר יד] הַזָּאָתוֹ וּמִשֶּׁגָּמַר הַזָּאָתוֹ? ש"מ דְּשִׁירַיִם שֶׁבָּאֶצְבַּע — כְּשֵׁרִים! לָא, עַד שֶׁלֹּא יָצְתָה מִיָּדוֹ הַזָּאָה — טָעוּן כִּיבּוּס, זוּמִשֶּׁיָּצְתָה הַזָּאָה מִיָּדוֹ וְנִתְּזָה מִמַּה שֶּׁנִּשְׁאַר — אֵין טָעוּן כִּיבּוּס. אֵיתִיבֵיהּ אַבַּיֵי: א) גָּמַר מִלְּהַזּוֹת, מְקַנֵּחַ יָדוֹ בְּגוּפָהּ שֶׁל פָּרָה; גָּמַר — אִין, טו] לֹא גָּמַר — לָא! א"ל: חגָּמַר — מְקַנֵּחַ יָדוֹ, לֹא גָּמַר — מְקַנֵּחַ אֶצְבָּעוֹ. בִּשְׁלָמָא גָּמַר מְקַנֵּחַ יָדוֹ בְּגוּפָהּ שֶׁל פָּרָה — דִּכְתִיב: °"וְשָׂרַף אֶת הַפָּרָה לְעֵינָיו", אֶלָּא לֹא גָּמַר מְקַנֵּחַ אֶצְבָּעוֹ, טז] בְּמַאי מְקַנֵּחַ? ב) (דְּאִי אָמְרַתְּ בְּגוּפָהּ שֶׁל פָּרָה, אִיבְּעִי לֵיהּ לְמִיתְנֵי: מְקַנֵּחַ יָדוֹ וְאֶצְבָּעוֹ בְּגוּפָהּ שֶׁל פָּרָה; מִדְּלָא קָתָנֵי הָכִי, ש"מ דְּלָא בָּעֵי קִינּוּחַ.) אָמַר אַבַּיֵי: ג) טבִּשְׂפַת מִזְרָק, כִּדְכְתִיב: °"כְּפוֹרֵי זָהָב" וגו'. וּמִי אָמַר רַבִּי אֶלְעָזָר הָכִי? וְהָא אִיתְּמַר: חֲבִיתֵּי כֹּהֵן גָּדוֹל — רַבִּי יוֹחָנָן אָמַר: יאֵינָהּ קְדוֹשָׁה לַחֲצָאִין, רַבִּי אֶלְעָזָר אָמַר: מִתּוֹךְ שֶׁקְּרֵבָה לַחֲצָאִין — קְדוֹשָׁה לַחֲצָאִין;

וְאִם

א) פרה פ"ג משנה ט זבחים לג: ב) רש"ק מ"ז ג) [זבחים כה. ולג:]

רש"י

ואילו מגביה לא קתני. שיהא [א] אחר מגביה השולחן בשעת סילוק הבזיכין, אלמא יז) מכלי שעל קרקע היו סילוק בזיכין. ובזיכין מתירין את הלחם כקומץ שמתיר את המנחה, דקומץ מיקרי אזכרה ובזיכין נמי מיקרי אזכרה, דכתיב (ויקרא כד): "והיתה ללחם לאזכרה", יח) וקומץ מתיר שירים לאכול דכתיב (שם ב): "והנותרת מן המנחה וגו' מאשי ה'" יט). **סדר עבודות נקט.** והגבהה לאו מן העבודות חשובות היא. **מקדשין מנחה.** כשמביאה מביתו כ) נותנה בכלי שעל גבי קרקע. **שכן מצינו בסידור בזיכין.** שמסדר כא) (על) הלחם שהוא שירים, ובזיכין שהן קומץ, על השולחן שעל גבי קרקע. דהיינו דומיא דמנחה כשמביאה מביתו, דמעורבין יחד הקומץ והשירים. **קידוש קומץ מאי.** דלא אשכחן בבזיכין כשהוא מסלקן, דהיינו כב) קמיצה, שיהא נותנו לשום כלי, אלא מיד מקטירו. הלכך ליכא למפשט קידוש קומץ מהתם. כג) **מדם** [ב]. מקבלת [דם] דכתיב (שם א): "והקריבו בני אהרן", ואמרינן בתורת כהנים: *"והקריבו" – זו קבלת הדם. וקידוש קומץ כנגד כד) ארבע עבודות של דם, קמיצה כנגד שחיטה, וקידוש קומץ כנגד קבלה, והולכה כי הולכה, והקטרה כנגד כה) (ד' עבודות של דם קמיצה כנגד שחיטה וקידוש כנגד) זריקה. **ומי אמר רבא הכי.** דמדם ילפינן. **לילף מדם.** ודם לא כו) קידש לחצאין. אם קיבל שיעור הזאות דדם אשם מצורע, או דם פרים כז) ושעירים הנשרפין, בשני כלים – לא עשה כלום, כדאמרינן לקמן. **מההיא.** דודאי אינו כח) קידוש, דמדם ילפינן. **קידש.** מי חטאת. **כדי הזאה.** כדי שיטבול ראשי גבעולין ויזה. **לא קידש.** ואע"פ שחזר ועירבו לאחר קידוש כט), נתינת מים על האפר. **בדם מאי.** אם קיבל מדם שעירים ופרים הנשרפים שטעונין הזייה, וקיבל שיעור ג' הזאות בכלי זה ושיעור ד' הזאות בכלי זה, מהו? ל) **אמר רבא תניא.** דבדם לא קידש. **וטבל בדם** לא) **ולא מספג.** מקנח לב) [ג] אצבעו בדופני הכלי. **בדם.** משמע [שיהא שיעור] דם מעיקרא. **והזה מן הדם** לג) **שבענין.** לקמן מפרש מאי היא. **הוה אמינא אע"ג דלא קבל שיעור** לד) **טבילות.** כל הזאות מעיקרו, ובלבד שיהא בשעת כל טבילה וטבילה כדי שיעור לה). **כתב רחמנא בדם.** דמשמע לו) [שיהא שיעור] דם מעיקרא. **למעוטי שירים שבאצבע.** שצריך לז) [ד] לטבול באצבעו בין כל הזאה והזאה. דהכי משמע: והזה מן הדם האמור בענין למעלה – "וטבל הכהן [ה] באצבעו בדם", מאותו דם שבכלי שטובל – בו יזה כל לח) הזאות, ולא שבאצבע. **היה מזה** לט). מדם חטאת, כגון פרים ושעירים הנשרפין. **עד שלא הזה.** דאכתי חזי ההוא דם שנפל על הבגד להזאת פנים, חשיב דם. **וטעון הבגד כבוס.** כדכתיב: "ואשר יזה מדמה על הבגד" וגו' (ויקרא ו), ואם משהזה נפל לא חשיב דם. **מאי לאו עד שלא גמר.** כל ז' הזאות, מ) קתני דטעון כיבוס, ואפילו לא נפל אלא מן השירים שבאצבע? אלמא כשרין להזאה. **עד שלא יצתה הזאה מידו.** על הפרוכת נפל על הבגד טעון כיבוס, דעיקר מא) הזאה נפל עליו. אבל משיצתה הזאה מידו נפל על הבגד, דהיינו משיריים שבאצבע – אין טעון כיבוס. **גמר מלהזות.** מב) הזאת דם פרה אדומה בהר המשחה אל נכח פני אהל מועד. **לא גמר לא.** אלמא שיריים שבאצבע כשרים, ולא מג) [ו] צריך קינוח! ומשני: גמר מקנח כל ידו לא גמר מקנח אצבעו. בין כל הזאה והזאה. **בשלמא גמר מקנח** מד) **כל ידו בגופה של פרה.** שהרי פרה לפניו נשרפת לאחר שיורד מן ההר, דכתיב (במדבר יט): "ושרף את הפרה לעיניו". **אלא אצבעו.** בין כל הזאה והזאה. **במאי מקנח.** וכי בין כל הזאה והזאה יורד מהר המשחה לקנח בגוף הפרה? **בשפת מזרק.** והיינו דקרי למזרקין "כפורי זהב" בספר עזרא, על שם שמקנח ידו בו, כדאמרינן במס' גיטין (דף נו.) גבי מה) (*נבוזר אדן): וכפר ידיה בההוא גברא. **ומי א"ר אלעזר הכי.** אף בדם לא קידש לחצאין?

תוספות

מדם ילפינן לה. דקידוש קומץ כנגדו קבלת דם. **הדר** ביה רבא. מהך סברא, דהא רבא בשיטתא דרב נחמן רביה. **גמר** מלהזות. משנה היא במסכת פרה*. **מקנח** ידו בגופה של פרה. שהרי פרה לפניו נשרפת לאחר שיורד מן ההר, דכתיב: "ושרף את הפרה לעיניו", כך פי' רבינו שלמה. *ונראה דלא מייתי קרא אלא משום דכתיב בסיפיה "ואת דמה ישרוף" – אלמא דמה טעון שריפה, ולפיכך מקנח ידו בגוף הפרה. ופי' הקונטר' מגומגם. **אלא** אצבעו במאי מקנח. כאן פי' הקונטרס: לפי שהיה מזה מדמה בהר המשחה אל פני אהל מועד, ופרה לפניו נשרפת לאחר שיורד מן ההר, מח) והיאך היה יורד בין כל הזאה והזאה מהר המשחה לקנח בגוף הפרה? ובזבחים בפ' "דם חטאת" (דף צג:) פירש: שלא היה יכול לקנח אצבעו בגוף הפרה, שלא יתלכלך אצבעו בנימין, דהכי נמי חיישינן בנימין בפ' "כל כתבי" (שבת קטז:) גבי מפשיט את הפסח עד החזה. *ולפי' הקונטרס דהכא אין להקשות מהא דאמרינן בפרק בתרא דזבחים (דף קיג.) דשחיטה והזאה כנגד פתחו של היכל. דבשביל כך לא היו במקום אחד, אלא שתיהן היו מכוונות כנגד פתחו של היכל. *ואם איתא לילף מדם. וא"ת: והא בדם ליכא "מתוך", והכא איכא "מתוך". ובשאר מנחות משמע דמודה רבי אלעזר דאין קדושה לחצאין כיון דלא קרבין לחצאין! ומיהו יש לפרש דדם נמי קרב לחצאין, נ) שיש ד' מתנות וז' הזאות דפרה שכל אחת עבודה בפני עצמה. ושיעור טבילה לעיל לאו למעוטי חצי הזאה, אלא שיהא בכלי שיעור ז' הזאות. והא דאמרינן (בסמוך) גבי הפריש חצי עשרון ודעתו להוסיף, דאמר רב אינו קדוש, (ופריך) ואי כרבי אלעזר ס"ל ליליף מחביתין – מגינו לפרש דחשיב ליה דעתו להוסיף, כמו טעמא ד"מתוך" וקדוש לחצאין. ועוד, דאפילו ליכא "מתוך" בשאר מנחות, מ"מ כיון דקדשי חביתין לחצאין מאיזה טעם שיהיה ילפינן שאר מנחות מינייהו. אי נמי, הא דנקט רבי אלעזר טעמא ד"מתוך" – משום דרבי יוחנן נקטיה, דאפילו פלגינהו בשאר מנחות, בחביתין אודו לי מיהת מטעם "מתוך".

מנחה

גליון הש"ס

תום' ד"ה הדר וכו' דר"נ רביה. עי' חולין קד ע"א תוס' ד"ה בלבון:

שיטה מקובצת

א] וְכִי מְהַדַּר לֵיהּ לַקּוֹמֶץ לְדוּכְתֵּיהּ תִּקְדּוֹשׁ וְלִפְסוֹל! ב] אָמַר ר' יוֹחָנָן, זֹאת אוֹמֶרֶת: *כְּלֵי שָׁרֵת אאֵין מְקַדְּשִׁין אֶלָּא מִדַּעַת. הָא מִדַּעַת מְקַדְּשִׁין? ג] וְהָא *בְּעָא מִינֵּיהּ רֵישׁ לָקִישׁ מֵר' יוֹחָנָן: ד] כְּלֵי *שָׁרֵת מַהוּ שֶׁיְּקַדְּשׁוּ פְּסוּלִין לְכַתְּחִילָּה לִיקָּרֵב? וְאָמַר לֵיהּ: אֵין מְקַדְּשִׁין! ה] אָמַר לֵיהּ: באֵין מְקַדְּשִׁין לִיקָּרֵב, ו] אֲבָל מְקַדְּשִׁין לִיפָּסֵל. רַב עַמְרָם אָמַר: כְּגוֹן שֶׁהֶחֱזִירוֹ ז] לְבִיסָא גְּדוּשָׁה. וּמִקְמָץ הֵיכִי קָמֵיץ? אֶלָּא, כְּגוֹן שֶׁהֶחֱזִירוֹ לְבִיסָא ח] טְפוּפָה. וְכֵיוָן דְּקָמֵיץ לֵיהּ עָבֵד לֵיהּ גּוּמָא, כִּי מְהַדַּר – לְגַוֵּיהּ דְּמָנָא קָא מְהַדַּר לֵיהּ! ט] מִכִּי מְהַדַּר לֵיהּ מַנַּח לֵיהּ אַדַּפְנָא דְּמָנָא, י] וּמְנִיד לֵיהּ וְנָפֵל מִמֵּילָא, *דְּנַעֲשָׂה כְּמִי שֶׁהֶחֱזִירוֹ הַקּוֹף. א"ל רַבִּי יִרְמְיָה לְר' זֵירָא: וְלוֹקְמָה כְּגוֹן שֶׁהֶחֱזִירוֹ לִכְלִי הַמּוּנָּח עַל גַּבֵּי קַרְקַע! יא] אֶלָּא ש"מ: גקוֹמְצִין מִכְּלִי שֶׁעַל גַּבֵּי קַרְקַע? (א"ל:) קָא נָגַעַתְּ בְּבָעֲיָא דְּאִיבַּעֲיָא לָן, יב] דְּרַבִּי אֲבִימִי תָּנֵי מְנָחוֹת בֵּי רַב חִסְדָּא. וַאֲבִימִי בֵּי רַב חִסְדָּא תָּנֵי? *וְהָאָמַר רַב חִסְדָּא, *קוּלְפֵי טָאבֵי בָּלְעִי מֵאֲבִימִי עֲלָהּ דְּהָא שְׁמַעְתְּ': בָּא לְהַכְרִיז רְצוּפִין – ל' יוֹם, שֵׁנִי וַחֲמִישִׁי יג] (וְשֵׁנִי) – ס' יוֹמֵי! אֲבִימִי מַסֶּכְתָּא אִיתְעַקְרָא אִיתְעֲקַר לֵיהּ, וַאֲתָא קַמֵּיהּ דְּרַב חִסְדָּא לְאַדְכּוּרֵי גְּמָרֵיהּ. וְלִישְׁלַח לֵיהּ וְלֵיתֵי לְגַבֵּיהּ! סָבַר: הָכִי מִסְתַּיְּיעָא מִילְּתָא טְפֵי. פְּגַע בֵּיהּ רַב נַחְמָן, אֲמַר לֵיהּ: כֵּיצַד קוֹמְצִין? א"ל: מִכְּלִי זֶה. אֲמַר לֵיהּ: וְכִי קוֹמְצִין מִכְּלִי שֶׁעַל גַּבֵּי קַרְקַע? יד] א"ל: דְּמַגְבַּהּ לֵיהּ כֹּהֵן. כֵּיצַד מְקַדְּשִׁין אֶת טו] [א] הַמְּנָחוֹת? אֲמַר לֵיהּ: נוֹתְנָהּ לִכְלִי זֶה. דוְכִי מְקַדְּשִׁין בִּכְלִי שֶׁעַל גַּבֵּי קַרְקַע? א"ל: דְּמַגְבַּהּ לֵיהּ כֹּהֵן. אֲמַר לֵיהּ: א"כ, הוּצְרַכְתָּה טז] ג' כֹּהֲנִים! אֲמַר לֵיהּ: וּתְהֵא צְרִיכָה י"ג, כְּתָמִיד. אִיתְבֵיהּ, יז] *זֶה הַכְּלָל: כָּל הַקּוֹמֵץ וְנוֹתֵן בִּכְלִי, הַמּוֹלִיךְ וְהַמַּקְטִיר לֶאֱכוֹל דָּבָר שֶׁדַּרְכּוֹ לֶאֱכוֹל וְכוּ', וְאִילּוּ מַגְבִּיהַּ לָא קָתָנֵי! תַּנָּא יח] סֵדֶר עֲבוֹדוֹת נָקֵיט, יט] וְלָא סֵדֶר כֹּהֲנִים. בָּעוּ מִינֵּיהּ מִדְּרַב שֵׁשֶׁת: מַהוּ לִקְמוֹץ מִכְּלִי שֶׁעַל גַּבֵּי קַרְקַע? אֲמַר לֵיהּ, פּוּק חֲזִי מָה עָבְדִין לְגָאו: *האַרְבָּעָה כֹּהֲנִים נִכְנָסִין, שְׁנַיִם בְּיָדָם ב' סְדָרִים וּשְׁנַיִם בְּיָדָם שְׁנֵי בָּזִיכִין, וְאַרְבָּעָה מַקְדִּימִין לִפְנֵיהֶם, שְׁנַיִם לִיטּוֹל שְׁנֵי סְדָרִים וּב' לִיטּוֹל ב' בָּזִיכִין; וְאִילּוּ

וְקָא פָּרֵיךְ: כִּי מְהַדַּר לֵיהּ לַקּוֹמֶץ לְדוּכְתֵּיהּ לִיקְדּוֹשׁ וְלִיפְסוֹל. דְּהָא עֲבַד מַתַּן כְּלִי, דְּמַה לִּי כְּלִי שָׁרֵת זֶה וּמַה לִּי כְּלִי שָׁרֵת אַחֵר! אֶלָּא מִדַּעַת. וְהָא לָא יָהֵיב לֵיהּ לְהָתָם אַדַּעְתָּא דְּלִיקְדֵּשׁ. שֶׁיְּקַדְּשׁוּ פְּסוּלִין. כְּגוֹן אִם קָמַץ זָר כ] וְנוֹתֵן לִכְלִי, מַהוּ שֶׁיְּקַדְּשֶׁנּוּ כְּלִי לְהַקְטִירוֹ? לִיפָּסֵל. דְּקָבְעָה הַהוּא כְּלִי בִּקְדוּשָּׁה כא] כִּי יְהָבֵיהּ אַדַּעְתֵּיהּ לְקָדוּשֵׁי, וְלָא מָצֵי לְאַהֲדוּרֵיהּ תּוּ לְתוֹךְ הַשִּׁירַיִם, דְּהָא [ב] פָּסוּל כב] זֶה גָּמַר לְכוּלָּהּ עֲבוֹדָה. רַב עַמְרָם אָמַר. אֲפִילּוּ תֵּימָא שֶׁלֹּא מִדַּעַת נַמִי מְקַדְּשִׁין. וְהָכָא לָא קָדֵישׁ, כג] שֶׁמַּחֲזִירִין לְבִיסָא גְּדוּשָׁה, שֶׁאֵין מַחֲזִירָהּ לְתוֹךְ אֲוִיר הַכְּלִי וְאֵין הַכְּלִי מְקַדְּשׁוֹ. בִּיסָא. כְּלִי שָׁרֵת שֶׁבּוֹ בּוֹלְלִין מִנְחָה. וּמְקַמֵּץ הֵיכִי קָמֵיץ. תְּחִילָּה כד] כְּשֶׁקּוֹמֵץ מִכְּלִי זֶה? וַהֲלֹא גָּדוּשׁ הוּא, וּקְמִילָה מִתּוֹךְ כה] הַכְּלִי בָּעֵינַן, דְּכָל דָּבָר הַטָּעוּן כְּלִי אֵין חָשׁוּב כְּלִי אֶלָּא תּוֹכוֹ. טְפוּפָה. פישל"א, שֶׁאֵינָהּ גְּדוּשָׁה, כו] וּכְשֶׁקּוֹמֵץ מִתּוֹךְ כְּלִי קָמַץ בְּאֶמְצָעִיתוֹ, וּכְשֶׁמַּחֲזִיר הֲרֵי קוֹמֵץ בְּגוֹדֶשֶׁת כְּלִי כִּדְמְפָרֵשׁ בְּסָמוּךְ. וְקָפָרֵיךְ: דְּהָא כִּי קָמֵץ עֲבַד גּוּמָא. וְכִי מְהַדַּר לַקּוֹמֶץ בְּגוּמָא הֲוָה לֵיהּ תּוֹךְ כְּלִי! וּמְשַׁנֵּי: כִּי מְהַדַּר לֵיהּ אַדּוּפְנִיתָא דְּמָנָא. בְּצִדֵּי הַכְּלִי אֵצֶל כז] גּוּמָא הֶחֱזִירוֹ, וְהָוֵי כְּגוֹדֶשׁ הַכְּלִי, וְנָיֵיד לְמָנָא, וְנָפֵיל קוֹמֶץ מִמֵּילָא לַגּוּמָא, כְּדֵי שֶׁיְּהֵא רָאוּי לִקְמִילַת כֹּהֵן, וְכֵיוָן דְּמִמֵּילָא נָפַל לְמָנָא – נַעֲשָׂה כְּמִי שֶׁהֶחֱזִירוֹ הַקּוֹף וְלָא מְקַדֵּשׁ לֵיהּ כְּלִי. וְאע"ג דִּכְלֵי שָׁרֵת מְקַדְּשִׁין שֶׁלֹּא מִדַּעַת, הָנֵי מִילֵּי כִּי מְהַדַּר לֵיהּ אִיהוּ מַמָּשׁ אַדַּעְתָּא דְּלָא לִיקְדּוֹשׁ – מְקַדֵּשׁ לֵיהּ כח]. (הָאי) [ג] לִכְלִי שֶׁמַּחֲזִירוֹ בָּהֶן שֶׁמּוּנָּח עַל גַּבֵּי קַרְקַע. קוֹמְצִין. קוֹמֵץ מִכְּלִי שֶׁעַל גַּבֵּי קַרְקַע. וְה"ג *(מְקַדְּשִׁין) קוֹמֶץ א) מֵהַכְּלוּל שֶׁעַל גַּבֵּי קַרְקַע. דְּאִיבַּעֲיָא לָן. כְּלוֹמַר, לַחֲבֵרֵינוּ אִיבַּעְיָא הַךְ בַּעְיָא, דְּרַב נַחְמָן בָּעֵי מֵאֲבִימִי וְכִדְמְפָרֵשׁ. קוּלְפֵי טָבֵי. הַכָּאוֹת טוֹבוֹת. בָּלְעֵי מֵאֲבִימִי. בָּלַעְתִּי מֵאֲבִימִי, כְּלוֹמַר, שֶׁהָיָה כט] ב) מְנַדֶּה אוֹתוֹ. עֲלָהּ דְּהָא שְׁמַעְתָּא. בְּמַסֶּ' עֲרָכִין, ל] דְּתַנְיָא חֲדָא: שׁוּם הַיְּתוֹמִים ל' יוֹם, וְתַנְיָא אִידָךְ: שִׁשִּׁים. וּמְתָרֵץ לָהּ אֲבִימִי: בָּא לְהַכְרִיז רְצוּפִין כָּל יְמוֹת הַשַּׁבָּת – מַכְרִיז ל' יוֹם. בָּא לְהַכְרִיז שֵׁנִי וַחֲמִישִׁי. מַכְרִיז עַד ס' יוֹם מִיּוֹם שֶׁמַּתְחִיל עַד יוֹם שֶׁפּוֹסֵק, דְּהַיְינוּ י"ח יְמֵי הַכְרָזָה בְּס' יוֹם, וּמַכְרִיז מִי יִקְנֶה נִכְסֵי יְתוֹמִים הַלָּלוּ, כְּדֵי שֶׁיִּמָּכְרוּ בְּיוֹקֶר. וְהָיָה רַב חִסְדָּא לא] [ד] מְשַׁבֵּחַ הַתֵּירוּץ, וּמַכֵּה אֲבִימִי, אַלְמָא רַב חִסְדָּא תַּלְמִיד דַּאֲבִימִי הֲוָה! אֲבִימִי מַסֶּכְתָּא דִּמְנָחוֹת לב] אִיעֲקַר לֵיהּ. נִשְׁתַּכְּחָה הֵימֶנּוּ. וְלִישְׁלַח לֵיהּ. לְרַב חִסְדָּא דְּלֵיתֵי לְגַבֵּיהּ. מִסְתַּיֵּיעַ מִילְּתָא. מִשּׁוּם "יָגַעְתִּי וּמָצָאתִי" (מגילה דף ו:). פָּגַע בֵּיהּ רַב נַחְמָן. בַּאֲבִימִי. מִכְּלִי זֶה. רָאָה כְּלִי מוּנָּח עַל גַּבֵּי קַרְקַע, וְקָאָמַר: כְּלִי זֶה, אִם שֶׁל קוֹדֶשׁ לג] (זֶה) הָיָה רָאוּי לִקְמִילָה. וְכֵיצַד מְקַדְּשִׁין אֶת הַקּוֹמֶץ. לְאַחַר קְמִילָה. הוּצְרַכְתָּה ג' כֹּהֲנִים. שְׁנַיִם לְהַגְבִּיהַּ שְׁנֵי כֵלִים, אֶחָד שֶׁקּוֹמְצִין הֵימֶנּוּ וְאֶחָד לד] שֶׁנּוֹתֵן לְתוֹכוֹ, וּשְׁלִישִׁי קוֹמֵץ. וְכֹהֵן אֶחָד אֵינוֹ יָכוֹל לְהַגְבִּיהַּ שְׁנֵי הַכֵּלִים, דְּאֵין עֲבוֹדָה בִּשְׂמֹאל. תָּמִיד. י"ג כֹּהֲנִים זוֹכִין בּוֹ, בְּמַסֶּכֶת יוֹמָא בְּפ"ב (דף כה.). זֶה הַכְּלָל. מַתְנִי' הִיא. סֵדֶר עֲבוֹדוֹת נָקֵט. אוֹתוֹ שֶׁכֹּהֵן אֶחָד עוֹשֶׂה זוֹ אַחַר זוֹ, אֲבָל לְמִנְיָינָא דְּכֹהֲנִים לָא קָתָנֵי. מָה עָבְדִין לְגָאו. בַּהֵיכָל. נִכְנָסִין. בְּיוֹם הַשַּׁבָּת. שֶׁל לֶחֶם הַפָּנִים, שְׁתֵּי הַמַּעֲרָכוֹת שֵׁשׁ הַמַּעֲרֶכֶת. וְאִילּוּ

א) נ"א לכלי ב) נ"ל מבזה או מכה. רש"ק

וכי מהדר ליה לקומץ לדוכתיה ליקדוש. ואע"פ ששירים מפסיקין בין קומץ לכלי, מין במינו אינו חוצץ. א"ר יוחנן זאת אומרת כלי שרת אין מקדשין אלא מדעת. והא דפליגי חזקיה ורבי יוחנן לקמן בפרק "התודה" (דף עח.) [גבי תודה] ששחטה על שמונים חלות, וקאמר לה] *רבא דכולי עלמא כלי שרת מקדשין שלא מדעת – שאני התם, דמתוך שמקדש מדעת – מקדש נמי שלא מדעת. והא דמשמע בסוף "לולב וערבה" (סוכה דף נ.) דחזקיה סבר כלי שרת אין מקדשין שלא מדעת, גבי הא דתנן: כמעשהו בחול כך מעשהו בשבת, ופריך בגמרא: ונייתי במקודשת! התם אין כל המים ראוין להתקדש, אבל ב"התודה" כיון דראוין לקדש – מקדש שלא מדעת. וצ"ע, דכיון דאין שיעור למים – הרי כולם ראוין להתקדש! ונראה, דכיון דשלא בזמנו הוא, אע"ג דכלי שרת מקדשין שלא בזמנו כדמסקינן בסוף "שתי הלחם" (לקמן דף ק.), שלא מדעת מיהא אין מקדשין, ואע"ג דלילה אין מחוסר זמן [ה]. **אין** מקדשים ליקרב. הקשה ה"ר פטר: דלפי' הקונטרס בזבחים פרק "המזבח מקדש" (דף פז:) משמע שהשיבו ר' יוחנן דמקדשין לכתחילה ליקרב. דקאמר התם, בעי מיניה ר"ש בן לקיש מר' יוחנן: מהו שיקדשו את הפסולין? ופי' שם בקונטרס דלענין פדיון קא בעי, דאי מקדש הכלי אין להם פדיון. א"ל תניתוה: כשם שמזבח והכבש מקדשין את הראוי להם כך כלי שרת מקדשין את הראוי להם. ואע"ג דמזבח וכבש איירי לענין דאם עלו לא ירדו, אייתי מינה ראיה לענין פדיון. א"ל: לכתחילה ליקרב קא מיבעיא לי. הא נמי תנינא: שקיבלו פסולין וזרקו את דמן, מאי לאו קבלו פסולין וזרקו פסולין? פי': הא זרקו כשרין – אף לכתחילה יעלו האברים. אלמא לו] מקדשי לכתחילה ליקרב! ועוד קשה מהא דתנן התם; ואלו אם עלו לא ירדו: הלן והיוצא והטמא והנשחט חוץ לזמנו וחוץ למקומו. וכולהו איירי בשנזרק הדם כדמוכח בגמ', דקאמר עולא: אימורי קדשים קלים שהעלן לפני זריקת דמים – לא ירדו, נעשו לחמו של מזבח. אמר ר' זירא, אף אנן נמי תנינא: שנשפך דמה ושילא דמה חוץ לקלעים. ומה התם דאם בא לזרוק אינו זורק אמרת אם עלו לא ירדו, הכא כו'. ומדלא מייתי מכל הני ש"מ דאחר זריקה מיירי, ואפ"ה לכתחילה לא יעלו, אלמא אין מקדשין לכתחילה ליקרב האברים! ומיהו יש לדחות, דאכולהו קאי "וזרקו לז] את דמם". ועוד קשה, דבכמה דוכתי (פסחים דף טז:) אמרינן: נטמא הדם לא יזרוק, ואם זרק הורצה. ולמה לא יזרוק? הא כלי שרת מקדשין לכתחילה ליקרב! ובפ' "שני שעירי" (יומא דף סב.) אמרינן: נשפך הדם ימות המשתלח, מת המשתלח ישפך הדם. למה ישפך? וכן בדם פסולין ישפך למה. ובפ' "המנחות" (לקמן ק:) תנן: נטמאו משהוקדשו בכלי אין להם פדיון, דמשמע: הא מיקרב לא קרבי! ויש לדחות: כל הני בשעירה אחר כך לכלי חול. והא דשמעתין נמי יש ליישב לפי' הקונטרס, דהא דמשמע שהשיב לו אין מקדשין – היינו לפי שדוחה שם: לא, שקיבלו פסולים, א"נ לח] *וזורקן פסולין. ועוד קשה לפי' הקונטרס, דמדקאמר: לכתחלה ליקרב קא מיבעיא ליה, משמע שגם רבי יוחנן היה יודע דליקרב קמיבעיא ליה, אלא שהיה סבור דמבעיא ליה בדיעבד ולא איירי כלל לענין פדיון! ולפר"ת, דמבעיא ליה אם מקדשין הפסולין לענין דאם עלו לא ירדו. דאע"ג דאי לאו כלי היה מזבח מקדשם, השתא דאיכא כלי – גרע שמפסיק בין הפסול למזבח. ומסיק דלכתחילה ליקרב מיבעיא ליה אם קידשו הקומץ פסול בכלי אם מעליהו, דדילמא כשם שהמזבח מקדש דלא ירד – כך כלי מקדש דיעלה. ופריך, דהא נמי תנינא: שקיבלו פסולים וזרקו, דמשמע זרקו – דיעבד, אבל לכתחילה לא יזרוקו. והא דקאמר: מאי לאו קיבלו פסולין וזרקו פסולין – לאו מלשון פסולין דייק, אלא המשנה קא מסיים, ופירושא דמתני' כך הוא. תדע דהא ר"ש בן לקיש דדחי בפסולין נמי מוקי לה, מכלל שלא דקדק רבי יוחנן בפסולין. **אמר** ליה מכלי זה. למאי דמסיק דמגבה ליה כהן, יש לתמוה: מאי חידוש השיבו "מכלי זה"? ושמא אשמעינן אע"פ שלא נמשח, שעבודתו לט] מחנכת. א"נ, של עץ היה, כרבי יוסי ברבי יהודה דאמר בפרק "החליל" (סוכה דף נ:) דעושין כלי שרת של עץ. *)**שכן** מצינו בסילוק בזיכין. הא מילתא דלא כרבי חנינא דאמר לקמן (דף ח.): לא זו מ] קדושה בלא זו, דאיהו לא יליף מילתא ממילתא.

*) שייך למע"ל

מדס

לו א מיי' פ"ג מהלכות פסה"מ הלכה כ:

נ"ק

נ"ל רב פפא וכן איתא לקמן

לז ב מיי' שם הל' יח:

לח ג ד מיי' פי"ב מהל' מעה"ק הלכה יג:

לט ה מיי' פ"ה מהל' תמידין ומוספין ה"ד:

[לקמן עח: ל.] סוכה נ. סוטה יד:

זבחים פז.

[עי' תוס' כריתות כז: ד"ה קסבר]

ערכין כב.

[פי' שבט שמכין בו בני אדם וראשו עב. ערוך ערך קלפא ז']

גליון הש"ס

גמ' דנעשה כמי שהחזירו הקוף. לקמן דף ק ע"ב:

שיטה מקובצת

א] וכי מהדר ליה לקומץ כו' ואמאי לא גמר עבודה עד דעביד לה מתן כלי אחר שנותן הקומץ בכלי שרת אפילו לא נתנו בכלי אחר כי מהדר ליה לקומץ לדוכתיה בביסא לקדשה כלי ולפסול ואמאי יחזור ויקמוץ. הרגמ"ה: ב] אמר ר' יוחנן מדאמר יחזור ויקמוץ ולא פסלה ש"מ כלי שרת אין מקדשין אלא מדעת לרצון המניח בהם והאי כיון דאהדריה קומץ לדוכתיה לא אהדריה אדעתא לקדושי לשם קומץ ולא אקדש. הרגמ"ה: ג] והא בעא כו' אכולה מילתא פריך אף אמקמץ וקידש: ד] כלי שרת מהו שיקדשו בהן הפסולין לעבודה שום דבר אפילו לדעת כדי שיהיה כשר להקריבו לכתחלה לקרבן וא"ל אין מקדשין הכלים והאי קומץ דקמציה פסול ופסולה בכלי שרת לשום קומץ לא קדש. הרגמ"ה: ה] אין מקדשין אין ותיבות אמר ליה נמחק: ו] אבל מקדשין ליפסל כשמניח על דעת שיהיו קדושין אבל זה לא החזיר הקומץ על דעת להקדישו כלום ומשום הכי יחזור ויקמוץ: רב עמרם אמר אפילו תימא מקדשין הכא שהחזירו כדי לקדש (וקדשי) [ומ"מ לא קדש] כלי שהחזירו לביסא גדושה. הרגמ"ה: ז] ביסא גדושה ביסא כלי שרת שמקמצין בו את המנחה וא"ת היכי מצי למהוי גדושה והיא בלולה בשמן אנן במנחת חוטא איירינן דאין בה שמן. הרגמ"ה: ח] טפופה לא גדושה ולא מחוקה שאין הקומץ (עדיף) [מעודף] עליה. הרגמ"ה:

שיטה מקובצת

וא"ת מה היה סובר אבימי מה היה שואל תחילה כשהשיב לו מכלי זה וי"ל דהיה סובר ששואל אי בעי משיחה לכלי לקדש והשיב לו מכלי זה דלא בעי משיחה דעבודתו מחנכתו כדאי' בסנהדרין [דף ט"ו ע"ב] א"נ היה סובר ששואל לו אי מצי קומץ בשל עץ ולא בענין כלי מתכות והשיב לו אפילו מכלי זה דשל עץ היה כרבי יוסי בר יהודה דאמר בפ' החליל דעושין כלי שרת של עץ: טו] את המנחה: טז] ג' כהנים א' שמקמץ המנחה וא' שמגביה הכלי וא' שקומץ. הרגמ"ה. וז"ל תו"ח ג' כהנים חד להגביה הכלי כשקומצין וחד לקומץ וחד להגביה הכלי שמקדש הקומץ דהקומץ לא היה יכול לקמוץ ולהגביה הכלי שהרי היה קומץ בימין וא"כ לא היה יכול להגביה לאחוז הכלי אלא בשמאל ומסתברא דהכלי נעשה בימין וג' כהנים לאו דוקא דיכול להיות שאותו שמגביה הכלי בשעת קמיצה מגביהו בשעת הקדש בזה אחר זה ולא דק. תו"ח: יז] זה הכלל מתני' היא. הרגמ"ה: יח] סדר עבודות נקט ובהגבהה דלאו עבודה היא לא איירי. הרגמ"ה: יט] סדר עבודות נקט בעו מיניה מרב ששת מהו כו' אמר להו פוק והשאר נמחק: כ] זר ונתן בכלי מהו: כא] בקדושה כי יהביה אדעתיה: כב] פסול והוא דקא גמר זר לכולה: כג] שמחזירו לביסא גדושה שאין הקומץ מונח תוך אויר: כד] תחילה כשקמץ מתוך כלי: כה] וכשקומץ מתוך הכלי קומץ באמצעיתו וכשמחזיר הוי קומץ: כו] אצל הגומא מחזירו והוי כגודש הכלי כו' ממילא בגומא הכלי כי היכי דממילא נפל במנא נעשה: כח] ליה אבל הכא לא הכי ומה"ד ש"מ מדלא משני ליה דמשום הכי לא מקדש ליה האי כלי כשמחזירו

...מר עבודת הפסול שמקדש קמיצתו של פסול: יא] קרקע ש"מ ... בקדוש מנחה איירינן ולא בקמיצה וי"ל לקמן מספקא ליה אי ... כלי דמנחה עדיף ומשום הכי דייק ש"מ קומצין מכלי שע"ג ... משני ליה בהחזירה בכלי שעל גבי קרקע והשתא תפשוט דשוין ... מקדשין וא"כ תקשי ולוקמה כגון שהחזירה לכלי שעל גבי קרקע ... קומצין דאית לן למימר אע"ג דאין מקדשין מ"מ קומצין. תו"ח: ... אבימי מסכת אייקר ליה והשאר נמחק: יד] א"ל דמגבה ליה כהן

כגון שמונח על גבי קרקע דקומצין מכלי שעל גבי קרקע וה"נ מקדשין קומץ בכלי שעל ... כט] שהיה (בידה) [מכה] אותו: ל] ערכין דתני: לא] חסדא משכח התירוץ ומכהו אבימי: ... ליה: לג] קודש הוא: לד] ואחד שנותן לתוכו הקומץ: לה] וקאמר רב פפא: לו] אלמא ... לז] קאי וזרקו את דמו: לח] וזרקו פסולין: לט] מחנכתו: מ] קדושה וה"ר נתנאל תירץ ד... מסילוק בזיכין משום דהוא דבר דלא אפשר שהרי אין בו שמן אבל הכא מידי דאפשר הוא ... היו יכולין לקמוץ מכלי שע"ג קרקע בבזיכין נמי היה צריך להגביה השלחן כיון דאפשר ... קומצין מכלי שעל גבי קרקע ושפיר ס"ל רבי חנינא כרבא. תו"ח:

הגהות צ"ק [א] כיצד מקדשין את הקומץ: [ב] ליפסול וזה גמר: [ג] האי כלי כשמחזירו בכן הס"ד אח"כ ד"ה שעל גבי קרקע וכי היה דקומצין מכלי שעל גבי קרקע ה"נ מקדשין קומץ בכלי שעל גבי קרקע: [ד] נ"א משכח התירוץ ומכה אותו אבימי: [ה] זמן מ"מ לענין זה הוי מחוסר זמן:

עין משפט
נר מצוה

לג א מיי' פ"ד מהל' פרה אדומה הל' ג:
לד ב מיי' פ"ג מהל' פסה"מ הלכה ז:

עיין רש"ק
[ע' תוס' זבחים מח: ד"ה וחטאת ותוס' לקמן קז: ד"ה כבש]

לה ג מיי' שם פי"א הלכה ו:

[ויתר מבואר בע"ז כג: ד"ה אלא מעתה]

טעות הדפוס

יומא מב. ע"ש זבחים יד: סח.
[יומא מב. וש"נ]
נ"ל קדשי בדק הבית בעו עבודה קדשי מזבח מיבעיא

מסורת הש"ס

שלא יהא חוטא נשכר, ומפני מה אינה טעונה? שלא יהא קרבנו מהודר; סד"א, הואיל ואמר ר"ש: שלא יהא קרבנו מהודר, כי קמצי לה פסולין נמי תתכשר, קמ"ל. אי הכי, התם נמי ליתני: א]"אחד חטאת חלב ואחד כל *הזבחים שקבלו דמן זר ואונן", ולימא: לר"ש אצטריך! [זבחים טו:] אלמא, כיון דתנא ליה "כל" ולא קתני "חוץ" – כולהו משמע; ה"נ, כיון דתנא "כל" ולא קתני "חוץ" – כולהו משמע! אצטריך, סד"א: הואיל ואוקימנא לרישא דלא כר"ש – סיפא נמי דלא כר"ש, קמ"ל. אמר רב: זר שקמץ – יחזיר. והא אנן פסל תנן! מאי פסל? פסל עד שיחזיר. אי הכי, היינו בן בתירא! אי דאיתיה לקומץ בעיניה – לא פליגי רבנן עליה דבן בתירא; כי פליגי – דחסר קומץ, רבנן סברי: לא יביא מתוך ביתו וימלאנו, בן בתירא סבר: יביא מתוך ביתו וימלאנו. אי הכי, בן בתירא אומר: יחזיר ויחזור ויקמוץ בימין? בן בתירא אומר: יחזיר ויביא מתוך ביתו וימלאנו ויחזור ויקמוץ בימין, מיבעי ליה! ב] כי קא אמר רב – לבן בתירא. פשיטא! מהו דתימא: עד כאן לא קא מכשר בן בתירא אלא בשמאל, ג] אבל בשאר פסולין לא, קמ"ל. מאי שנא שמאל – ד] דאשכחן לה הכשירא ביום הכפורים, זר נמי – ה] אשכחן לה הכשירא בשחיטה! * ו] שחיטה לאו עבודה היא. ולא? והא"ר זירא אמר רב: *אשחיטת פרה בזר – פסולה, ואמר רב עלה: אלעזר וחוקה כתיב בה! ז] שאני *פרה, דקדשי בדק הבית היא. ולאו כל דכן הוא? *קדשי בדק הבית בעו כהונה, קדשי מזבח לא בעו כהונה? אמר רב ששא בריה דרב אידי: מידי דהוה אמראות נגעים, דלאו עבודה נינהו ובעי כהונה. ונילף מבמה! וכ"ת, מבמה לא ילפינן, * בוהתניא: מנין ליוצא ח] שאם עלה לא ירד – שהרי יוצא כשר בבמה! תנא °א"זאת תורת העולה" סמיך ליה. ט] אלא טעמא דאשמעינן רב, הא לאו הכי, הוה אמינא: בשאר פסולין פסל בן בתירא? והתניא, רבי יוסי ברבי יהודה ורבי אלעזר בר"ש אומרים: מכשיר היה בן בתירא בכל הפסולין כולן. *ותניא: "וקמץ משם" – י] ממקום שרגלי הזר עומדות; בן בתירא אומר: מנין שאם קמץ בשמאל שיחזיר ויחזור ויקמוץ בימין? ת"ל: "וקמץ משם" – ממקום שקמץ כבר; וכיון דקרא סתמא כתיב בה, מה לי שמאל ומה לי שאר הפסולין? אלא הא קמשמע לן רב: יא] קמץ – ואפילו קידש; ולאפוקי מהני תנאי, דתניא, רבי יוסי בן יאסיין ורבי יהודה הנחתום אמרו: יב] בד"א – שקמץ ולא קידש, אבל קידש – פסל. ואיכא דאמרי: קמץ – אין, קידש – לא; כמאן? כהני תנאי, ולאפוקי מתנא קמא. מתקיף לה רב נחמן: מאי קא סברי הני תנאי? אי קמיצת פסולין עבודה היא – אע"ג דלא עביד ליה מתן כלי! אי קמיצת פסולין לאו עבודה היא, כי יג] עבד לה מתן כלי מאי הוה? הדר אמר ר"נ: לעולם עבודה היא, ולא גמרה עבודתה געד דעביד לה מתן כלי. יד] אי הכי, אפילו לא קידש, וכי

ויקרא ו

*) נ"א לא ירדו הואיל דנשפרין ואין פסול נשאר משא"כ בדם רש"ק

תורה אור

אי הכי. במס' זבחים (דף טו:) קתני: כל הזבחים שקיבל דמן זר ואונן וכל הני דמתני' – ליתני נמי כי מתני': אחד חטאת חלב ואחד כל הזבחים כו'! כולהו משמע. ולא פליג ר"ש. אצטריך. אע"ג דבלאו הכי נמי הויא מנחת חוטא בכלל, ולא פליג ר"ש – טו] אפילו הכי אצטריך למיתנייה, דמהו דתימא: מדרישא דקתני דשלא לשמה לא עלו לשם חובה, אוקימנא בריש פירקין (דף ג:) לרבה ולרבא טו] מתני' דלא כר"ש, סיפא נמי דקתני: כל המנחות שקמצן זר כו' דלא כר"ש, דמדפליג ברישא פליג נמי בסיפא, ואמר במנחת חוטא דכי היכי דאין קרבנו מהודר, כי קמצי לה יז] פסולין כשרה. קמ"ל. משנה יתירה "אחד מנחת חוטא" דלא אצטריך למתנייה אלא לר"ש, דר"ש נמי מודה בסיפא. לא יביא מתוך ביתו וימלאנו. סלת לעשרון. דקסברי: קדושת כלי קבעה יח] לשם מנחה, דשוב אין מוסיפין עליה, ומיפסלא בחסרון, כדאמרינן בהאי פירקין (דף ט:): "מן המנחה" – פרט לשחסרה. יביא מתוך ביתו. דקסבר: קמילה קבעה, והא לא קמץ יט] *בהו. וכה"ג פליגי אמוראי לקמן בשמעתין (שם). ומאי שנא שמאל. כלומר, [אמאי] ה"א דבשאר פסולין לא מכשיר לאהדורי כ] אלא בשמאל? ביוה"כ. נטל את המחתה בימינו ואת הכף בשמאלו. בשחיטה. כדאמרינן לקמן בפ"ג (דף יט.): "והקריבו בני אהרן את הדם" – מקבלה ואילך מצות כהונה, לימד על השחיטה שכשרה בזר. ואמר רב עלה. היינו טעמא דפסולה, דכתיב בה אלעזר וכתיב בה "חוקה", ו"חוקה" עיכובא. שאני פרה. דטעמא [א] דשחיטה פסולה בזר – לאו כא] דעבודה היא, דהא קדשי בדק הבית דלא שייכא בהו עבודה. אלא גזירת הכתוב היא דזר פסול בה. ולאו כל דכן הוא. בקדשי בדק הבית חשובה עבודה, בקדשי מזבח לא כל שכן? ואפ"ה זר כשר בשחיטת קדשים, אלמא אשכחן כב] הכשר בעבודה. וגבי קמילה נמי אית ליה תקנתא בחזרה לבן בתירא, ולמה לי דרב? אמר רב ששא. לעולם לאו עבודה כג] [ב]. והאי דבעיא כהן גבי פרה אדומה – גזירת הכתוב היא, מידי דהוה [אמראות] נגעים. ונילף מבמה. כלומר, דרב למה לי? מאי שנא שמאל דמכשיר בן בתירא בחזרה – דאית ליה הכשר ביוה"כ, זר נמי הא ידענא דמכשר נמי בן בתירא, דהא אית ליה הכשר בבמה קודם שנתקדש אהרן, כד] שהעבודה בבכורות! וכי תימא מבמה לא ילפינן. דעדיין לא כה] נגדל אהרן. והתניא מנין ליוצא. מאימורי חטאת ועולה חוץ לקלעים, שאע"פ שהוא פסול, כדאמרינן ב"כיצד צולין" (פסחים דף פב.) מ"הן לא הובא את דמה", אם עלה – לא ירד? שהרי יוצא כשר בבמה. שלא היו שם קלעים. תנא אזאת תורת העולה סמיך. כדאמר במסכת נדה בפרק "יוצא דופן" (דף מ:): תורה אחת לכל העולין שאם עלו לא ירדו. והאי דנקט במה – כו] קלא סמכא בעלמא היא, אבל עיקר טעמא מהתם יליף. וקמץ משם. מלא קומצו. רישיה דקרא כתיב (ויקרא ב): "והביאה אל בני אהרן הכהנים", "וקמץ משם" משמע: כז] ממקום שרגלי הזר עומדים שם קומץ, והיינו מקום דריסת רגלי ישראל אחת עשרה אמה, ובמזרח הם. וקמ"ל דלא בעינן קמילה בצפון כשאר קדשים, אלא כל העזרה כשרה לקומץ. סתמא כתיב. "וקמץ משם" – ממקום שקמץ כבר והחזירו קומצה משום פסלות, כח] *)(אחד) ואחד פסול שמאל ואחד פסול זרות במשמע! אלא כט] קמ"ל רב דבקומץ ואפילו קידש. קומץ במתן כלי, מכשיר בן בתירא. דאי לאו דקידש מיירי רב, לא הוה משמע לן מידי. ל] בד"א. דבן בתירא מכשיר בחזרה. מת"ק. דפליג בברייתא אדר' יוסי בן יאסיין ור' יהודה הנחתום. אי קמיצת פסולין עבודה היא. לפסול אפילו לא נתן קומץ בכלי – לא תתקן בחזרה. ואי לאו עבודה היא. דלא חשיב, הואיל ובפסולין נעשית, כי עבד מתן כלי נמי לא חשיב ואפשר בחזרה! וקא

*) נ"ק מ"ז

שלא יהא חוטא נשכר. תימה: במה נשכר? והלא כיון שיש עמו נסכים בין אין עמו נסכים הוי [ג] כסלע, ותנן לקמן בפ' בתרא (דף קז:): "הרי עלי שור" – יביא הוא ונסכיו במנה, "כבש" – יביא הוא ונסכיו בסלע. ובחטאת של טומאת מקדש נמי בסלע, אף על פי שאין עמה נסכים! *ולאו פירכא *הוא. הואיל לא] ואוקמינן רישא דלא כר"ש. תימה: לרב אשי דריש פירקין, דאתיא כר"ש, מאי איכא למימר? לב]: לג] לא יביא מתוך ביתו וימלאנו. סולת עשרון, דקסבר: קדושת כלי קבעה לשם מנחה, דשוב אין מוסיפין עליה ומיפסלא בחסרון, כדאמרינן בהאי פירקא (דף ט:): "מן המנחה" – פרט לשחסרה, כך פי' בקונטרס. וקשה: דהא ר"ש בן לקיש איתותב לקמן, דאמר: מנחה שחסרה קודם קמילה – לא יביא מתוך ביתו וימלאנה! וע"ק: למה לי קרא לקמן לבן בתירא "וקמץ משם" ויחזור ויקמוץ, מנא תיתי לן דקדושת כלי קבעה? לד] ונראה לפרש: דכולהו [ס"ל] כר' יוחנן דקדושת כלי לא קבעה, אלא בקמילת פסולים פליגי אי קבעה אי לא קבעה, ומצי למימר דהכי ר"ל לה] פירוש הקונטרס. שאני פרה דקדשי בדק הבית היא. משמע דליכא מאן דפליג. ובפ"ק דחולין (דף יא.) ובפ"ק דשבועות (דף יא:) פירשתי*. וכי תימא מבמה לא ילפינן. פירש בקונטרס: קודם שנגדל אהרן. משמע שרוצה לומר דלאחר אהרן לא הותר זר בבמה. וא"א לומר כן, כדמוכח בפ' בתרא דזבחים (דף קיח.) דדריש: "איש" (*איש) להכשיר את הזר, והיינו לאחר שנגדל אהרן. ועוד מצינו (ש"א יג) שאול ושמואל שהקריבו בבמה. לו] שהרי יוצא כשר בבמה. וא"ת: והרי יוצא דדם כשר בבמה, ותנן בפ' "המזבח מקדש" (זבחים דף פד.): ושילא דמה חוץ לקלעים, לרבי יהודה אם עלתה תרד! וי"ל: דהאברין ודאי *)ירדו, אבל הדם אינו מתקנת מכותלי המזבח. אלא טעמא דאשמועינן. בשום מקום לא פריך בענין זה דקשיא ליה הכא, אמאי איצטריך ליה לרב לאשמועינן הא דתניא בברייתא. ושמא שגורה היתה בפי כל לז]. ממקום שרגלי הזר עומדות. לקמן בפירקין מפרש: אצטריך, סד"א הואיל וכתיב "והגישה וקמץ", מה הגשה בקרן מערבית דרומית אף קמילה כו'. ובקונטרס לא פירש כן. וכיון דקרא סתמא כתיב מה לי שמאל כו'. וא"ת: בפרק "המזבח מקדש" (שם) דתנן: שקיבלו פסולין וזרקו את דמן שאם עלה לא ירד, ומוקמינן לה בפסולין דחזו לעבודת צבור, ומרבי לה [ד] (הכא) מ"זאת התורה". ואמאי לא פריך דכיון דקרא סתמא [ה] מה לי חזו ומה לי לא חזו? ויש לומר: משום דדרשינן "זאת היא העולה" – הרי אלו *)מיעוטין.

*) נ"א לא ירדו הואיל דנשפרין ואין פסול נשאר משא"כ בדם רש"ק

שיטה מקובצת

קידש נמחק: טו] ר' שמעון אמנחת חוטא אפילו: טז] ולרבא דלא. תיבת מתני' נמחק: יז] פסולין נמי כשרה: יח] קבעה לה לשם: יט] קמץ כהוגן וכה"ג: כ] לאהדורי כשמאל: כא] בזר לאו משום דעבודה היא כו' הבית היא דלא שייכא: כב] ליה היתר בעבודה ותיבת הכשר נמחק: כג] עבודה היא והאי דבעיא כהן גבי פרה גזרת הכתוב: כד] אהרן שהיתה בבכורות: כה] לא נתקדש אהרן: כו] במה אסמכתא בעלמא: כז] משמע ממקום שרגלי הזר המביא עומדים שם הוא קומץ: כח] משום פסלות ואחד: כט] אלא הא קמ"ל: ל] לא שנו דבן בתירא. תיבות בד"א נמחק: לא] הואיל ואוקימנא: לב] איכא למימר. גליון וי"ל דבלאו הכי נמי צ"ל דרישא לאו כר"ש דהא תנן במתניתין נתן בכלי והוליך ושמעינן ליה לר"ש בפ"ק דזבחים דהולכה לאו עבודה היא ע"כ. וז"ל תו"ח וי"ל דמ"מ ע"כ רישא דלא כר"ש דקא חשיב הוליך שלא לשמו ור"ש מכשיר בהוליך ומיהו לפי סברא זו לא מתוקם שפיר לישנא דתלמודא דקאמר ואוקימנא רישא דלא כר"ש דמשמע דאוקמינא הכי בסוגיין דלעיל וי"ל דודאי התלמוד נסיב הכא לישנא אליבא דרבה ורבא דרובא נינהו ומיהו לרב אשי נאמר הכי דפריך דר"ש מכשיר בהוליך וא"ת אי הכי בזבחים נמי ניתני אחת חטאת חלב ואחת כל הזבחים ונימא דלר"ש איצטריך משום דקתני סיפא התם הוליך שלא לשמו פסול וסד"א מדסיפא לאו כר"ש רישא נמי לאו כר"ש וי"ל דהתם הך רישא וסיפא לאו חדא בבא נינהו כי הכא דהא איכא התם מילי טובא דקא מפסקי בינתים ועי"ל דודאי לא דמו דאילו הכא רישא וסיפא תרוייהו סתמא מתנו ואיכא למימר מדרישא לא סתם לן כר"ש סיפא נמי לא סתם לן כר"ש אבל התם בסיפא פליג ר"ש בהדיא דקתני ר"ש מכשיר בהוליך ואדרבה משמע מדפליג בסיפא מכלל דברישא לא פליג הילכך התם לא אצטריך למתני ברישא אחת חטאת חלב לר"ש וליכא לתרץ קושיין קמייתא דלרב אשי ניחא ליה שפיר דנקטיה לאשמועי' דמתני' כולה ר"ש כרב אשי ולאפוקי דרבה ורבא מדסיפא ר"ש מסתברא רישא נמי ר"ש ולהכי תני אחת מנחת כו' [דהא ע"כ רישא לאו כר"ש מדתני הוליך]: לג] רבנן סברי לא יביא מתוך ביתו. פ"ה משום דכלי שרת קבע כו' עד וכה"ג פליגי אמוראי לקמן וקשה דהא רשב"ל איתותב ועוד קשה דלמה לי קרא לקמן לבן בתירא סברא היא דכלי לא קבע דהא ר"ל איתותב וע"ק דאי פליגי בפלוגתא דאמוראי לקמן אמאי נקט פלוגתייהו בקמיצה בפיסול לינקו' פלוגתייהו בלא נקמצה כלל אלא שחסרה אחר שבאה לתוך הכלי לכך נ"ל דלא הוי כפלוגתייהו דאמוראי דלקמן דכולהו מצי סברי הכא דנקבעה המנחה ולא משום כלי לחוד אלא משום דנקמצה ואף על מכל מקום מהניא למקבעה בפיסול לכ"ע והא דאיתותב ר"ל היינו במתן כלי לבד בביסא אבל הכא דיש קמיצה וקדוש כלי המנחה בביסא בהא ודאי קבע לרבנן דנהי היא מ"מ שם קמיצה הוי ובן בתירא פליג דמ"מ יחזור ויקמוץ מקרא דוקמץ משם ע"כ תו"ח ובתוספות אחרות ונראה לפרש דבהא פליגי דרבנן סברי חסרון פסלי אחרי שיש קמיצה פסולה בהדה ובן בתירא סבר קמיצה פסולה לאו כלום היא דהוי כמו מנחה שחסרה קודם קמיצה דלא פסלא ע"כ: לד] ו הוי אפילו לר"י דהכא קמיצה עם החסרון דהוי תרתי לריעותא. תוס' אחרות: לה] פי' הקונטרס ע' תוס': זבחים (דף ס"ח ע"ב): לו] שהרי יוצא. עיין תוס' זבחים (דף פ"ד ע"ב): לז] בפי כל. מאחר דדרשא דקרא היא:

שיטה מקובצת

א] ליתני אחת חטאת חלב ואחת כל הזבחים: ב] ליה אלא כי: ג] אבל בשאר פסולין לא קמ"ל. והאי דנקט שמאל לרבותא תני ליה דאע"ג דשמאל כשר ביוה"כ ומהו דתימא דעביד שיריים ולא מצי כשר לחזור ולקמוץ דכה"ג אמרינן בזבחים גבי טמא משום דאינו פסול [קמ"ל] דיחזור הכשר ויקמוץ: ד] דאשכחן ליה כו'. פי' אי משום הכי לא פסלא ואית לה תקנה בחזרה ובפ"ק דמעילה הסברות הפוכות דקאמר טמא דאתיא בצבור משוה שיריים פי' דאהנו מעשיו ופוסל השיריים ואין לו תקנה בחזרה ושאר פסולות אינם עושין שיריים לפי שאין להם מתיר בשום מקום אין מעשיהם כלום אלמא משום דיש לו היתר במקום אחר מגרע גרע. תו"ח: ה] אשכחן ליה הכשירה: ו] שחיטה לאו עבודה היא. פרש"י שהרי שחיטה כשרה בזר ותימה דעל זה אנו דנין אלא ה"פ שחיטה לאו עבודה היא. שלא מצינו בשום מקום שהקפיד רחמנא אשחיטה דזר כדאמרינן והקריבו בני אהרן מקבלה ואילך מצות כהונה וכן מוכח הסוגיא דפריך ולא והרי שחיטת פרה שהקפיד בו הכתוב כו'. עיין זבחים (דף י"ד ע"ב) ז] שאני פרה וכו'. לעולם לאו עבודה היא ואמאי בזר פסולה שאני פרה דמדמי קדשי בדק הבית היתה נקנית ולא מדמי מזבח וקמ"ל א) שלא יהו שאר עבודות הפרה חמורות בשחיטתה כמו קדשי מזבח ולעולם לאו עבודה היא אלא גזירת הכתוב היא דבעיא כהונה אבל שאר קדשים לא בעו שחיטה כהונה. הרגמ"ה: ח] שאם עלה לא ירד. ויוצא פסול מדכתיב הן לא הובא את דמה אל הקודש פנימה היתה שלא יצאת חוץ שאם יצאת הי' [מן הדין] לשורפה ושאר זבחים נמי מפקינן להו מדכתיב ובשר בשדה טריפה אזהרה לכל דבר שיצאת חוץ למחיצתה: ט] אלא טעמא כו'. וא"ת ומאי קושיא וכי לא אשמועינן רב מה שהוא ברייתא וי"ל דלפי שהיתה שגורה בפי כל מקשה ממנה: י] משם מלא קומצו ממקום: יא] קמץ ואפילו קדש הקומץ שנתנו בכלי שרת להקטירו יחזיר. הרגמ"ה: יב] אמרו לא שאנו אלא שקמץ. ותיבות במה דברים אמורים נמחק: יג] כי יעביד לה מתן כלי מאי הוי: יד] תיבות אי הכי אפילו לא

א) אולי צ"ל וקמ"ל דמ"מ פסולה בזר שלא וכו'. ב) נראה דצ"ל דהכא מודה ר"י דלא יביא מתוך ביתו דכיון דאיכא קמילה עם חסרון דהוי תרתי לריעותא.

הגהות צ"ק [א] דשחיטתה: [ב] היא: [ג] נ"ל בסלע: [ד] התם: [ה] כתיב:

א] מַה לְּכִלְאַיִם שֶׁמִּצְוָתוֹ בְּכָךְ! רַב שֵׁישָׁא בְּרֵיהּ דְּרַב אִידִי אָמַר: מִשּׁוּם דְּאִיכָּא לְמֵימַר, לִיהֲדַר דִּינָא וְתֵיתֵי בְּמָה הַצַּד: מַה לִּמְלִיקָה שֶׁכֵּן קְדוּשָּׁתָהּ אוֹסַרְתָּהּ — חֵלֶב וָדָם יוֹכִיחוּ; מַה לְּחֵלֶב וָדָם שֶׁכֵּן בָּאִים מִכְּלַל הֵיתֵּר — מְלִיקָה תּוֹכִיחַ; וְחָזַר *הַדִּין, לֹא רְאִי זֶה כִּרְאִי זֶה וְלֹא רְאִי זֶה כִּרְאִי זֶה, ב] הַצַּד הַשָּׁוֶה שֶׁבָּהֶן — שֶׁאֲסוּרִין לְהֶדְיוֹט וּמוּתָּרִין לַגָּבוֹהַּ, אַף אֲנִי אָבִיא טְרֵפָה, אַף עַל פִּי שֶׁאֲסוּרָה לְהֶדְיוֹט תְּהֵא מוּתֶּרֶת לַגָּבוֹהַּ. מַה לְּהַצַּד הַשָּׁוֶה שֶׁבָּהֶן שֶׁכֵּן מִצְוָתָהּ בְּכָךְ! אֶלָּא אָמַר רַב אַשִׁי, מִשּׁוּם דְּאִיכָּא לְמֵימַר: מֵעִיקָּרָא דְּדִינָא פִּרְכָא, מֵהֵיכָא קָא מַיְיתֵית לָהּ? מִבַּעַל מוּם; ג] מַה לְּבַעַל מוּם שֶׁכֵּן עָשָׂה בּוֹ מַקְרִיבִין כִּקְרֵיבִין. אֲמַר לֵיהּ רַב אַחָא ד] סָבָא לְרַב אַשִׁי: יוֹצֵא דוֹפֶן יוֹכִיחַ, שֶׁלֹּא עָשָׂה בּוֹ מַקְרִיבִין כִּקְרֵיבִין, וּמוּתָּר לְהֶדְיוֹט וְאָסוּר לַגָּבוֹהַּ! מַה לְּיוֹצֵא דוֹפֶן שֶׁכֵּן אֵינוֹ קָדוֹשׁ בִּבְכוֹרָה. בַּעַל מוּם יוֹכִיחַ! מַה לְּבַעַל מוּם שֶׁכֵּן עָשָׂה בּוֹ מַקְרִיבִין כִּקְרֵיבִין. יוֹצֵא דוֹפֶן יוֹכִיחַ! וְחָזַר הַדִּין, לֹא רְאִי זֶה כִּרְאִי זֶה וְלֹא רְאִי זֶה כִּרְאִי זֶה, ה] הַצַּד הַשָּׁוֶה שֶׁבָּהֶן — שֶׁמּוּתָּרִים לְהֶדְיוֹט וַאֲסוּרִים לַגָּבוֹהַּ, *וְכ"ש טְרֵפָה שֶׁאֲסוּרָה לְהֶדְיוֹט תְּהֵא אֲסוּרָה לַגָּבוֹהַּ! מַה לְּהַצַּד הַשָּׁוֶה שֶׁבָּהֶן שֶׁכֵּן לֹא הוּתְּרוּ מִכְּלָלָן, תֹּאמַר בִּטְרֵיפָה שֶׁהוּתְּרָה מִכְּלָלָהּ! א"ל רַב אַחָא בְּרֵיהּ דְּרָבָא לְרַב אַשִׁי: טְרֵפָה שֶׁהוּתְּרָה מִכְּלָלָהּ מַאי הִיא? אִילֵימָא מְלִיקָה דְּעוֹלַת הָעוֹף לַגָּבוֹהַּ — בַּעַל מוּם נַמִי בְּעוֹפוֹת אִשְׁתְּרוּיֵי אִשְׁתְּרֵי, *תַּמּוּת וְזַכְרוּת בִּבְהֵמָה וְאֵין תַּמּוּת וְזַכְרוּת בְּעוֹפוֹת! אֶלָּא מְלִיקָה דְּחַטַּאת הָעוֹף לַכֹּהֲנִים — כֹּהֲנִים מִשּׁוּלְחַן גָּבוֹהַּ קָא זָכוּ! וְאֶלָּא פְּרֵיךְ הָכִי: מַה לְּהַצַּד הַשָּׁוֶה שֶׁבָּהֶן שֶׁכֵּן מוּמָן נִיכָּר, תֹּאמַר בִּטְרֵיפָה ו] שֶׁכֵּן אֵין מוּמָהּ נִיכָּר, מש"ה אִיצְטְרִיךְ קְרָא. וּטְרֵיפָה מֵהָכָא נָפְקָא? *מֵהָתָם נָפְקָא: ז] °"מִמַּשְׁקֵה יִשְׂרָאֵל" — מִן הַמּוּתָּר לְיִשְׂרָאֵל; ח] °מִ"כֹּל אֲשֶׁר יַעֲבוֹר תַּחַת הַשָּׁבֶט" נָפְקָא — ט] *פְּרָט לִטְרֵיפָה שֶׁאֵינָהּ עוֹבֶרֶת! צְרִיכִי, דְּאִי מִ"מַּשְׁקֵה יִשְׂרָאֵל" ה"א: לְמַעוּטֵי הֵיכָא דְּלֹא הָיְתָה לָהּ שְׁעַת הַכּוֹשֶׁר, דּוּמְיָא דְּעָרְלָה וְכִלְאֵי הַכֶּרֶם, אֲבָל הָיְתָה לָהּ שְׁעַת הַכּוֹשֶׁר אֵימָא תִּתַּכְשַׁר — כְּתַב רַחֲמָנָא: "כֹּל אֲשֶׁר יַעֲבוֹר"; וְאִי כְּתַב רַחֲמָנָא "כֹּל אֲשֶׁר יַעֲבוֹר" הֲוָה אָמִינָא: לְמַעוּטֵי הֵיכָא דְּנִטְרְפָה וּלְבַסּוֹף הִקְדִּישָׁהּ, דּוּמְיָא דְּמַעֲשֵׂר, אֲבָל הִקְדִּישָׁהּ וּלְבַסּוֹף נִטְרְפָה, דִּבְעִידָּנָא דְּאַקְדְּשָׁהּ הֲוָה חַזְיָא אֵימָא תִּתַּכְשַׁר — י] כְּתַב רַחֲמָנָא: "מִן הַבָּקָר", א) צְרִיכִי.§ **מתני'** יא] אֶחָד מִנְחַת חוֹטֵא וְאֶחָד כָּל [א]הַמְּנָחוֹת שֶׁקְּמָצָן זָר, אוֹנֵן, טְבוּל יוֹם, מְחוּסַּר בְּגָדִים, מְחוּסַּר כִּיפּוּרִים, שֶׁלֹּא רָחַץ יב] יָדָיו וְרַגְלָיו, עָרֵל, טָמֵא, יוֹשֵׁב, עוֹמֵד יג] עַל גַּבֵּי כֵלִים, עַל גַּבֵּי בְהֵמָה, ע"ג רַגְלֵי חֲבֵירוֹ — פָּסוּל. ב) [ב]קָמַץ בִּשְׂמֹאל — פָּסוּל, בֶּן בְּתֵירָא אוֹמֵר: יַחֲזִיר וְיַחֲזוֹר וְיִקְמוֹץ בְּיָמִין. יד] ג) [ג]קָמַץ וְעָלָה בְּיָדוֹ צְרוֹר אוֹ גַּרְגֵּר מֶלַח אוֹ קוֹרֶט שֶׁל לְבוֹנָה — פָּסוּל, מִפְּנֵי שֶׁאָמְרוּ: הַקּוֹמֶץ הַיָּתֵר וְהֶחָסֵר — פָּסוּל. וְאֵיזֶהוּ הַיָּתֵר — [ד]שֶׁקְּמָצוֹ מְבוֹרָץ, וְחָסֵר — טו] שֶׁקְּמָצוֹ בְּרָאשֵׁי אֶצְבְּעוֹתָיו.§ **גמ'** לָמָּה לִי לְמִתְנָא "אֶחָד מִנְחַת חוֹטֵא וְאֶחָד כָּל הַמְּנָחוֹת"? לִיתְנֵי: כָּל הַמְּנָחוֹת שֶׁקְּמָצָן זָר וְאוֹנֵן! לְר"ש אִיצְטְרִיךְ; ד) דְּתַנְיָא, א"ר שִׁמְעוֹן: בְּדִין הוּא שֶׁתְּהֵא מִנְחַת חוֹטֵא טְעוּנָה שֶׁמֶן וּלְבוֹנָה, ה) שֶׁלֹּא יְהֵא חוֹטֵא נִשְׂכָּר, וּמִפְּנֵי מָה אֵינָהּ טְעוּנָה? ו) שֶׁלֹּא יְהֵא קָרְבָּנוֹ טז] מְהוּדָּר; וּבְדִין הוּא שֶׁתְּהֵא חַטַּאת חֵלֶב ז) טְעוּנָה נְסָכִים,

שֶׁלֹּא

א) [מלת צריכי בעי תיקון]: ב) [לקמן י.] זבחים כד: ג) סוטה יד: ד) שם טו. ה) [יבמות לב: וש"נ] ו) [זבחים כה. לקמן י:] ז) [עיין פרש"י בסוטה טו. ותוס' חולין ה: ד"ה מעט]

רש"י

כִּלְאַיִם לַגָּבוֹהַּ. אַבְנֵטוֹ שֶׁל כֹּהֵן יז]. מִצְוָתוֹ בְּכָךְ. גְּזֵירַת הַכָּתוּב שֶׁלֹּא יְהֵא אַבְנֵט אֶלָּא שֶׁל כִּלְאַיִם, דִּכְתִיב (שמות לט): "תְּכֵלֶת וְאַרְגָּמָן" וגו', וְאָמְרִינַן יְבָמוֹת (דף ד:): מִדְּשֵׁשׁ כִּיתָּנָא תְּכֵלֶת עַמְרָא. רַב שֵׁישָׁא בְּרֵיהּ דְּרַב אִידִי אָמַר. לְהָכִי אִיצְטְרִיךְ קְרָא, מִשּׁוּם דְּאִיכָּא לְמֵימַר: נִיהֲדַר דִּינָא וְנֵיתֵי בְּמָה הַצַּד דִּטְרֵיפָה מוּתֶּרֶת לַגָּבוֹהַּ. מַקְרִיבִין כִּקְרֵיבִין. דְּמוּם פָּסוּל בְּכֹהֵן כְּמוֹ בְּזֶבַח. אֲבָל טְרֵיפוּת לָא פָּסֵיל בַּכֹּהֲנִים, דִּתְנַן בִּבְכוֹרוֹת בְּפֶרֶק "מוּמִין אֵלּוּ" (דף מה:): וְאֵלּוּ כְּשֵׁרִין בָּאָדָם וּפְסוּלִין בַּבְּהֵמָה, אוֹתוֹ וְאֶת בְּנוֹ וּטְרֵיפָה וְיוֹצֵא דוֹפֶן. לְהָכִי אִיצְטְרִיךְ קְרָא. אֲמַר לֵיהּ רַב אַחָא [סָבָא] לְרַב אַשִׁי. וְאַכַּתִּי ל"ל קְרָא? הָא אִיכָּא לְמֵימַר. יוֹצֵא דוֹפֶן יוֹכִיחַ. שֶׁכֹּהֵן יוֹצֵא דוֹפֶן כָּשֵׁר לַעֲבוֹדָה, וְקָרְבָּן יוֹצֵא דוֹפֶן פָּסוּל, דְּאָמְרִינַן בְּת"כ: "כִּי יִוָּלֵד" פְּרָט לְיוֹצֵא דוֹפֶן*. מַה לְּיוֹצֵא דוֹפֶן שֶׁאֵינוֹ קָדוֹשׁ בִּבְכוֹרָה. דְּ"פֶטֶר רֶחֶם" כְּתִיב (שמות יג), תֹּאמַר בִּטְרֵיפָה שֶׁקְּדוֹשָׁה בִּבְכוֹרָה אִם נוֹלַד עִם טְרֵיפָתוֹ! הִלְכָּךְ אִיצְטְרִיךְ קְרָא. בַּעַל מוּם יוֹכִיחַ. שֶׁקָּדַשׁ בִּבְכוֹרָה וְאָסוּר לַגָּבוֹהַּ, אַף אֲנִי אָבִיא טְרֵיפָה, וְלָמָּה לִי קְרָא? הַצַּד הַשָּׁוֶה כו'. וְלָמָּה לִי קְרָא? מְלִיקָה. טְרֵיפָה הִיא יח] לְכַתְּחִילָּה, דְּחוֹתֵךְ שִׁדְרָה וּמַפְרֶקֶת, כִּדְאָמְרִי' בְּפ"ק דִּשְׁחִיטַת חוּלִּין (דף כ:). וְהוּתְּרָה לַגָּבוֹהַּ מִכְּלַל אִיסּוּרָהּ לְהֶדְיוֹט יט] אִשְׁתְּרֵי, אַף אֲנִי אָבִיא טְרֵיפָה (*וְלָמָּה לִי קְרָא). מְלִיקָה דְּחַטַּאת הָעוֹף לַכֹּהֲנִים. וּבְבַעַל מוּם וְיוֹצֵא דוֹפֶן לָא אַשְׁכַּחַן הֵיתֵּר לַכֹּהֲנִים מִכְּלַל אִיסּוּר, דְּאֵין בָּהֶן שׁוּם אִיסּוּר לְגַבֵּי כֹּהֲנִים. מִשּׁוּלְחַן גָּבוֹהַּ הוּא דְּזָכוּ. וְגַבֵּי גָּבוֹהַּ אַשְׁכַּחַן בְּבַעַל מוּם בְּעוֹפוֹת הֵיתֵּר מִכְּלַל אִיסּוּר, וְלֵיכָּא כ] מַה לְּהַצַּד כו', וְל"ל קְרָא? בַּעַל מוּם כא] מוּמָן נִיכָּר. שֶׁאֵין מוּמָן פָּסוּל אֶלָּא בְּגָלוּי, כִּדְאָמְרִינַן בִּבְכוֹרוֹת בְּפֶ' "עַל אֵלּוּ מוּמִין" (דף לז.). וְיוֹצֵא דוֹפֶן מוּמוֹ נִיכָּר, דְּאִית לֵיהּ קָלָא וְהַכֹּל יוֹדְעִים. טְרֵיפָה יֵשׁ שֶׁאֵין כב] מוּמָהּ נִיכָּר. כְּגוֹן בִּבְנֵי מֵעַיִים. שֶׁלֹּא הָיְתָה לָהּ שְׁעַת הַכּוֹשֶׁר. דְּנִטְרְפָה מִמְּעֵי אִמָּהּ, דּוּמְיָא דְּעָרְלָה וְכִלְאֵי הַכֶּרֶם דִּכְתִיב בְּהַהוּא קְרָא, דִּכְתִיב בֵּיהּ: כג] "מִן הַצֹּאן מִן הַמָּאתַיִם מִמַּשְׁקֵה יִשְׂרָאֵל", וְאָמְרִינַן בְּפֶרֶק "אֵלּוּ עוֹבְרִין" בְּמַסֶּכֶת פְּסָחִים (דף מח.): "מִן הַמָּאתַיִם" — מִן הַמּוֹתָר ב' מֵאוֹת שֶׁנִּשְׁתַּיְּירוּ בַּבּוֹר, מִכָּאן לְעָרְלָה שֶׁבְּטֵלָה בְּמָאתַיִם. כֹּל אֲשֶׁר יַעֲבוֹר תַּחַת הַשָּׁבֶט. פְּרָט לִטְרֵיפָה שֶׁאֵינָהּ עוֹבֶרֶת, כד] מִשּׁוּם דְּאֵין לָהּ חִיּוּת לָא חָשֵׁיב לָהּ עוֹבֶרֶת. כה] וְהַאי קְרָא כְּתִיב בְּמַעֲשֵׂר וְגָמְרִינַן שְׁאָר קָרְבָּנוֹת מִינֵּיהּ בְּג"ש, נֶאֱמַר כָּאן "תַּחַת אִמּוֹ" וְנֶאֱמַר לְהַלָּן "תַּחַת הַשָּׁבֶט" כו' בְּפ"ט דִּבְכוֹרוֹת (ד' נז.). **מתני'** כו] זָר וְאוֹנֵן. וְכָל הָנֵי כז] מְפָרֵשׁ בִּזְבָחִים (דף טו:) מִקְּרָאֵי דַּעֲבוֹדָתָן פְּסוּלָה. וְאַזְהָרָתָן בְּסַנְהֶדְרִין בְּסוֹף "אֵלּוּ הֵן הַנִּשְׂרָפִין" (דף פג.). עָרֵל. כֹּהֵן עָרֵל, שֶׁמֵּתוּ אֶחָיו מֵחֲמַת מִילָה. יוֹשֵׁב. "לַעֲמוֹד לְשָׁרֵת" כְּתִיב. ע"ג כֵּלִים אוֹ ע"ג בְּהֵמָה אוֹ רֶגֶל חֲבֵירוֹ. בִּזְבָחִים (דף כד.) מְפָרֵשׁ: דְּבָעֵינַן שֶׁלֹּא יְהֵא דָּבָר חוֹצֵץ בֵּין רַגְלָיו כח] לְבֵין הָרִצְפָּה. שְׂמֹאל. מְפָרֵשׁ בַּגְּמָרָא מְנָלַן דְּפָסוּל. בֶּן בְּתֵירָה כט]. אַכּוּלְּהוּ פָּלֵיג, אַזָּר וְאוֹנֵן וְכָל הָנָךְ*). עָלָה בְּיָדוֹ צְרוֹר. נִמְצָא קוֹמֶץ חָסֵר מְקוֹם הַצְּרוֹר, וְכֵן מֶלַח אוֹ לְבוֹנָה. מְבוֹרָץ. גָּדוּשׁ. ל] ל"א: שֶׁנִּרְאֶה קֶמַח חוֹצֵץ בֵּין רָאשֵׁי אֶצְבְּעוֹתָיו לְפַס יָדוֹ. בְּרָאשֵׁי אֶצְבְּעוֹתָיו. מְעַט, שֶׁלֹּא לא] פְּשָׁטוֹ עַל פַּס כָּל הַיָּד. **גמ'** שֶׁלֹּא יְהֵא קָרְבָּנוֹ מְהוּדָּר. שֶׁלֹּא תְּהֵא הַמִּנְחָה נָאָה. חַטַּאת חֵלֶב. לב] (הַיְינוּ חֵלֶב) הַיְינוּ סְתָם חַטָּאת. חַטָּאת אֵינָהּ טְעוּנָה נְסָכִים בְּפֶרֶק שְׁתֵּי מִדּוֹת (לקמן דף צ:).

אִי

*) [בן בתירא אומר יחזיר קומץ לתוך הכלי ויחזור ויקמוץ בימין] כאן שייך ד"ז והוא כתוב בדף ט ע"ב ונמחק שם

תוספות

[א] **מה** לכלאים שכן מצותו בכך. ואע"ג דאפשר לקיים בטלית של צמר, מ"מ בסדין של פשתן שחייב בציצית לא אפשר לקיים בכך. וא"ת, ולימא: גיד הנשה במחובר יוכיח, דאין מצותו בכך ושרי לגבוה, כדאמר בריש ג"ה (חולין צ:). וכי תימא מה לג"ה שכן מחובר — הנך יוכיחו! וי"ל: כיון דאין לו היתר אלא על ידי חיבור, לא שייך למיעבד מיניה "יוכיח".

בעל מום נמי הותר בעופות. וכ"ל דהשתא מצי למילף ממחוסר אבר ויוצא דופן. ולבסוף כשאמר: שכן מומן ניכר, אתי הכל שפיר.

שכן מומן ניכר. ואין לומר דמחוסר זמן ואותו ואת בנו ומוקצה ונעבד ורובע ואתנן ומחיר יוכיחו, דכל הני יש להם לג] קול, יותר מטריפה בבני מעיים שאין יודע כלל, כי היכי דחשיב יוצא דופן מומו ניכר משום דיש לו קול. ומחיה דשריא להדיוט ואסורה לגבוה אין ללמוד טריפה, דמה לחיה שכן אין במינה לגבוה, ושכן מומה ניכר.

דומיא דערלה וכלאי הכרם. וא"ת: °והא אמרינן פ' "כל שעה" (פסחים דף כה.) וב"כל הבשר" (חולין דף קטז.): זאת אומרת כלאי הכרם עיקרן נאסר, הואיל והיתה להם שעת הכושר קודם השרשה! ויש לומר: דכלאים דכתיבי בהאי קרא איירי בענבים שעושין מהם יין לנסכים, כדדרשינן (פסחים דף מח.): "מן המאתים" — ממותר ב' מאות שנשתיירו בבור, הנהו לא היתה להם שעת הכושר, דדוקא דחרצן שנזרע הוא שהיתה לו שעת הכושר קודם השרשה, ומן החרצן אין עושין נסכים. וא"ת: אותם ענבים עצמן היתה להם שעת הכושר קודם שהוסיפו מאתים! וי"ל: דמה שנתוסף באיסור אחר שנעשה כלאים שגדל אחרי כן — לא היה לו מעולם (אחרי כן) שעת הכושר. והאי דמיתסר אף מה שגדל קודם לכן — לפי שא"א להבדיל זה מזה להפריש תערובתם.

כתב רחמנא כל אשר יעבור. אע"ג דמוכח דהיכא שהיתה לו שעת הכושר לא ילפינן מ"משקה ישראל", אפ"ה מייתי ליה בכל דוכתא בפ' "כל האסורין" (תמורה דף כט.) גבי נעבד, משום דע"י תלתא קראי °מסקינן דאין לחלק.

שקמצן זר אונן כו'. והוא הדין [ב] שתויי יין ופרועי ראש במיתה ומחלי עבודה, כדאמרינן בפרק "אלו הן הנשרפין" (סנהדרין דף פג:), ותנא ושייר*).

בן בתירא אומר יחזור ויקמוץ בימין. למאי דמוכח בגמרא דהוא הדין אכולהו פסולי דלעיל, יש לתמוה דלא עריב פסול שמאל בהדי פסולי דלעיל! לד] וי"ל: משום דס"ד דשמאל כיון דאית ליה הכשירה ביום הכיפורים [ג] — קבוע עבודה, ולא תועיל בה חזרה.

חסר שקמצו בראשי אצבעותיו. אגב דמפרש יתר — חוזר ומפרש חסר כיוצא בו, אף על גב דצרור וגרגיר וקורט משום חסר הוא.

*) [ועי' היטב תו' זבחים טו: ד"ה זר]

עין משפט נר מצוה

כט א מיי' פי"א מהל' פסה"מ הלכה א:
ל ב מיי' פ"ה מהלכות ביאת מקדש הל' יח:
לא ג מיי' פי"א מהלכות פסה"מ הלכה ג:
לב ד מיי' פי"ג מהל' מעה"ק הלכה יב:

מסורת הש"ס

[קדושין כא. וש"נ]

[חולין לח:]

[לקמן כה. קדושין כד: זבחים קטז. חולין כג. תמורה יז.]

לעיל ה. תמורה כט. [פסחים מח. חולין:]

[בכורות נז. נח: חולין קלו: תמורה כט.]

תורה אור

יחזקאל מה — ויקרא כז

גליון הש"ס

תום' ד"ה דומיא וכו' וא"ת הא אמרינן פכ"ש. והרמב"ן בחי' לב"ב דף עז ד"ה ה"ג אין אותיות נקנות במסירה כתב דהכא אשגירות ליסנא הוא וכלאי כרם לאו דוקא: **ד"ה** כתב וכו' מסקינן דאין לחלק. עי' חולין דף קמ ע"א תום' ד"ה למעוטי וצ"ע:

נ"ל ולהכי איצטריך קרא

[נ"ל אף אני אביא טריפה]

שיטה מקובצת

א] מה לכלאים שמצותו בכך. וא"ת לפרוך כלאים של ציצית יוכיחו שאסור להדיוט ומותר לגבוה דהא ציצית צורך גבוה הוא וליכא למימר שמצותו בכך שהרי אפשר לקיים מצות ציצית בלא דחיה כגון צמר לצמר וי"ל דמ"מ חשוב מצותו בכך אחרי שיש לו טלית של פשתן והוא חייב בציצית ונראה לי דאיכא למפרך מה לכלאים שכן הותר אצל גבוה בבגדי כהונה. תו"ח: ב] הצד השוה שבהן כו'. אינו כשאר הצד השוה שבאין לקיים הקו"ח וללמוד מן הצד וזה בא לסותרו ולקיים היוכיח כלומר נעשה יוכיח משניהם שהרי שניהם אסורים להדיוט ומותרים לגבוה אף אני אביא טריפה כו'. תו"ח: ג] מה לבעל מום שכן עשה בו מקריבין כו'. תאמר בטריפה שהקריבין אסורין לפי המסקנא [והמקריבין מותרין] וזאת הפרכא לפי המסקנא היא וכיוצא בה בתלמוד וא"ת ונעשה מקריב כקריבין מקו"ח זה ומה בעל מום שמותר להדיוט ואסור לגבוה המקריבין כקריבין טריפה שאסורה להדיוט לא כ"ש וי"ל דאיכא דרשא בהדיא להתיר טריפה לעבודה. תו"ח: שכן עשה מקריבין כקריבין. וא"ת אמאי לא עשינו מקריבין כקריבין מקו"ח דבעל מום ומה בעל מום שמותר להדיוט עשו בו מקריבין כקריבין טריפה שאסורה להדיוט אינו דין שיעשו בו מקריבין כקריבין וכן יוצא דופן נעשו בו מקריבין כקריבין מקו"ח דבעל מום ומה בעל מום שקדוש בבכורה עשו בו מקריבין כקריבין יוצא דופן שאינו קדוש בבכורה אינו דין שנעשו בו מקריבין כקריבין וי"ל דאיכא דרשה בת"כ שור כי יולד ולא אדם כי יולד: ד] אחא בר רבא לרב אשי: ה] הצד השוה שבהם שמותרים להדיוט. אין זה כשאר הצד השוה אלא עושה הוא קו"ח מן הצד השוה מיוצא דופן ובעל מום שמותרים להדיוט ואסורים לגבוה טריפה שאסורה להדיוט לא כל שכן. תו"ח: ו] בטריפה שאין מומה ניכר: ז] ממשקה ישראל. תוס' לקמן (דף ס"ו ע"ב ודף פ"ד ע"א): ח] מן המותר לישראל נפקא אי נמי מכל: ט] תיבות פרט לטריפה שאינה עוברת נמחק: י] תתכשר צריכי. ותיבות כתב רחמנא מן הבקר נמחק: יא] אחת מנחת חוטא ואחת כל: יב] שלא רחץ ידים ורגלים ערל טמא. בבדי נקט טמא דהא תנא טבול יום וכ"ש טמא אלא לפי שרגיל התנא לשנות יחד ערל וטמא הערל וכל הטמאים וכן בקרא לא יוסיף (עוד עבור בך) [יבא בך עוד] ערל וטמא ועי' בתוס' זבחים (דף טו ע"ב) תו"ח: יג] ע"ג כלים כו'. לא זו אף זו קאמר לא מבעיא כלים דחייצי אלא אפילו בהמה דהוי בשר והוי מין במינו חייצי ולא מבעיא בהמה אלא אפילו רגל חבירו שהוא בשר אדם כמותו. תו"ח ועיין תוס' זבחים (דף ק"י ע"א): יד] קמץ ועלה בידו כו'. וא"ת ואיך אפשר בלא מלח הכתיב על כל קרבנך תקריב מלח ולבונה נמי צריכא שתהא בכיסא בשעת קמיצה וי"ל דבשעת הקטרה היה נותן בה את המלח ולא בשעת קמיצה ולבונה נמי היה מצדד לצדדין וקמץ ממקום שלא היה שם לבונה: טו] שקמצו בראשי אצבעותיו שכפף אצבעותיו שלא ע"ג פס ידו: הרגמ"ה. [וכדתנן בסיפא כיצד הוא עושה פושט אצבעותיו על פס ידו: טז] מהודר ממנחה עצמה קאמר דאין בה קרבן אחר. הרגמ"ה: יז] כהן גדול הס"ד ומה"ד מצותו בכך גזירת הכתוב היא: יח] טריפה היא בתחילה: יט] להדיוט הס"ד ומתיבת אשתרי עד תיבת קרא נמחק: כ] וליכא למפרך מה: כא] בעל מום מומו ניכר שאין מום פוסל אלא בגלוי: כב] מומה ניכר: כג] ביה ושה אחת מן הצאן מן המאתים: כד] עוברת כגון שנחתכו רגליה מן הארכובה ולמעלה ל"א מצאתי פרט לטריפה שאינה עוברת משום וכו' עיין רש"י בכורות (דף נ"ז ע"א): כה] עוברת שאינה עוברת בבריאות והאי: כו] מתני' אחת מנחת חוטא בגמ' מפרש אמאי תנא מנחת חוטא והלא בכלל כל המנחות היא: כז] הני מפורשים בזבחים: כח] רגליו להרצפה: כט] בן בתירא אומר יחזיר הקומץ לתוך הכלי ויחזור ויקמוץ בימין בן בתירא אכולהו: ל] גדוש. כמו ברוצי המדו' במס' ביצה. ל"א שנמצא קמח: לא] שלא פשטן על גבי כל פס היד: לב] תיבות היינו חלב נמחק: לג] להם קול. גליון. וא"ת ולימא רובע יוכיח שאין מומו ניכר ובמס' תמורה קרי ליה אין מומו ניכר וי"ל דמ"מ לגבי טריפה קרי ליה מומו ניכר דניכר להו לאותן שראו שרבעו אבל טריפה יש טריפות שאינו ניכר כגון נקבו הדקין. תו"ח: לד] וי"ל. גליון דנקטיה לרבותא דסד"א כיון דשמאל הכשירה ביה"כ אפילו בן בתירא מודה דכיון שהוא קרוב להכשיר (ונפסל) (נמחק ונ"ל שצ"ל) [ומקרי שם] עבודה פסול עלה וכיון שהעבודה נעשית בפסול תו לית ליה [תקנה] והוי כמו נשפך הדם על [הרצפה] דפסול קמ"ל בן בתירא דאפ"ה יחזור ויקמוץ בימין וא"ת והא לקמן קאמר איפכא דאמרינן מ"ש שמאל דאית ליה כו' ומשום הכי מכשיר בן בתירא שיחזור ויקמוץ וי"ל דודאי הסברות הפוכות קאי הכא ומדחי ליה וקאי הכא ומדחי ליה. תו"ח:

ליתני

הגהות צ"ק [א] נ"ל אטו גלית נורך הדיוט מנוה היא ולעו"ג כו' לקיים בכך הס"ד ולח"כ מ"ה מה לכלאים שכן מצותו בכך ול"ט לימא כו': [ב] בעל מום שעויי: [ג] קביעה:

כג א מיי' פ"ו מהל' מאכלות אסורות הל"ח:
כד ב מיי' פ"ב מהל' ביכורים הל"ו ופ"ז מהל' תמידין ומוספין הלכה יז:
כה ג מיי' פ"ד מהל' פסה"מ הל"ב:
כו ד מיי' שם הל"ג:
כז ה מיי' פ"ב מהל' איסורי מזבח הל"י:
כח ו מיי' פ"ד מהל' שמיטה ויובל הל"ח:

אהאיר א] *מזרח מתיר. והא דריש לקיש לאו בפירוש איתמר ב] *אלא מכללא איתמר, *דתנן: באין מביאין ג] *מנחת בכורים ומנחת בהמה קודם לעומר, ד] (דבעינן "ממשקה ישראל",) ואם הביא – פסול; קודם לשתי הלחם לא יביא, ה] (משום דאיקרו בכורים,) ואם הביא – כשר. ואמר רבי יצחק אמר ריש לקיש: לא שנו אלא בארבעה עשר ובחמשה עשר, אבל בששה עשר – אם הביא כשר; ו] (וקשיא לי: ליהוו כמחוסר זמן!) אלמא קסבר: האיר המזרח מתיר. ורבא אמר: גמנחת העומר שקמצה שלא לשמה – כשירה, ושיריה נאכלין, ואינה צריכה מנחת העומר אחרת להתירה; *דשאין מחשבה ז] מועלת אלא במי שראוי לעבודה, ובדבר הראוי לעבודה, ח] ובמקום הראוי לעבודה. ט] במי שראוי לעבודה – לאפוקי כהן בעל מום; ובדבר הראוי לעבודה – לאפוקי מנחת העומר דלא חזיא, דחדוש הוא; ובמקום הראוי לעבודה – לאפוקי נפגם המזבח.§ *ת"ר: כשהוא אומר °"מן הבקר" למטה, שאין ת"ל! האלא להוציא את הטריפה. והלא דין הוא: ומה בעל מום שמותרת להדיוט – אסורה לגבוה, טריפה שאסורה להדיוט – אין דין שאסורה לגבוה? חלב ודם יוכיחו, שאסורין להדיוט ומותרין לגבוה! מה לחלב ודם שכן באין מכלל היתר, תאמר בטריפה שכולה אסורה, י] ולא תהא מותרת לגבוה! מליקה תוכיח, שכולה איסור, ואסורה להדיוט ומותרת לגבוה. מה למליקה שכן קדושתה אוסרתה; (בשעת קדושתה למזבח היא נאסרה להדיוט, דהיינו מליקתה, אבל קודם לכן לא נאסרה להדיוט;) מה שאין כן בטריפה שאין קדושתה אוסרתה! ואם השבתה, כשהוא אומר "מן הבקר" למטה – שאין ת"ל להוציא את הטריפה. יא] מה "אם השבתה"? (סי': רקיח מר אדא לשישי"ה) אמר רב, משום דאיכא למימר: מנחת העומר תוכיח, שאסורה להדיוט ומותרת לגבוה. מה למנחת העומר שכן מתרת חדש! יב] בשביעית. יג] שביעית נמי, שכן מתרת ספיחין בשביעית! כר' עקיבא, *דאמר: ספיחין יאסורים בשביעית. אמר ליה רב אחא בר יד] אבא לרב אשי, לרבי עקיבא נמי לפרוך: מה למנחת העומר שכן מתרת טו] חדש בחוצה לארץ! ואפילו למ"ד: חדש בחו"ל לאו דאורייתא – שכן באה להתיר לאו שבתוכה! א"ל רב אחא מדיפתי לרבינא: טז] א"ה, טריפה נמי תקריב ותתיר לאו שבתוכה! אלא פריך הכי: מה למנחת העומר *שכן יז] מצותה בכך. ריש לקיש אמר, משום דאיכא למימר: מפטם הקטרת יוכיח, שאסור להדיוט ומותר לגבוה. מפטם גברא הוא! אלא, פטום הקטרת יוכיח, שאסור להדיוט ומותר לגבוה. מה לפטום הקטרת שכן מצותו בכך! מר בריה דרבינא אמר, משום דאיכא למימר: שבת תוכיח, שאסורה להדיוט ומותרת לגבוה. מה לשבת שכן הותרה מכללה אצל הדיוט במילה! אטו מילה צורך הדיוט הוא? מילה מצוה היא! אלא, מה לשבת שכן מצותה בכך! רב אדא בר אבא אמר, משום דאיכא למימר: כלאים תוכיח, שאסורין להדיוט ומותרין לגבוה. מה לכלאים שכן הותרו מכללן אצל הדיוט בציצית! אטו ציצית צורך הדיוט היא? מצוה היא! אלא:

מה

האיר מזרח. די"ו בניסן מתיר החדש, דכתיב (ויקרא כג): "עד עצם" ומתרגמינן: עד בכרן, ו"בכרן" היינו מרחית היום, דכתיב (שמות כח): "תרשיש שוהם ישפה" *מתרגמינן: כרום ימא, שמראיתו דומה לים. והאי דאין שיריה נאכלין – דמצוה להמתין עד הבאת העומר. כדפרכינן לריש לקיש בפ' "רבי ישמעאל" (לקמן ד' סח.): והא כתיב "עד הביאכם"! ומשני: למצוה. אין מביאין יח] מנחת ביכורים ומנחת בהמה. היינו מנחת נסכים. קודם יט] לשתי הלחם לא יביא. דאמרינן בתורת כהנים: "קרבן ראשית" – שיהא ראשית לכל המנחות. ומנין אף לביכורים? ת"ל: "בכורי קציר חטים" כ]. ואם הביא כשר. טעמא מפרש בפ' "ר' ישמעאל" (ג"ז שם). כא] במי שראוי לעבודה. למעוטי אחד מן הפסולים. כב] ובדבר הראוי לעבודה. כגון מנחת חטין. אבל מנחת העומר של שעורים כג] אינה ראויה אלא לעבודה זו בלבד, להתיר, ולא משום קרבן אתיא. ואי משום מנחת סוטה – כד] לאו ראויה היא, דמנחת סוטה קמח, ושל עומר גרש. ועוד, דלאו עבודה היא, דלברר עון קאתיא. והאי דפסלה מחשבה במנחת קנאות – משום דרחמנא קרייה חטאת. פגימת המזבח מהיא קרא נפקא: "וזבחת עליו את עולותיך" (שמות כ) – בזמן שהוא שלם כתיב, "עליו" כולו במשמע, במסכת זבחים בפרק "קדשי קדשים" (דף נט.). ואם פיגל בקומץ בשעת פגימת המזבח – לאו פיגול הוא, ואם יתקן המזבח באותו היום יקטירנו. מן הבקר למטה. ד"אם עולה קרבנו מן הבקר". בקרא דלעיל דרשינן: *"מן הבהמה" – להוציא הרובע והנרבע, "מן הבקר" – להוציא הנעבד, ו"מן הצאן" – להוציא את המוקצה. כשהוא אומר "מן הבקר" למטה כו'. והלא דין הוא. דטריפה לא תקרב, ולמה לי קרא? מכלל היתר [א]. שכל שאר כה] הבהמות מותרות להדיוט. שכן קדושתה אוסרתה. בדבר שהוא קדוש לגבוה, דהיינו מליקה – בה נאסרת להדיוט. אבל טריפה אינה קדושה משום טריפות, ואכתי קרא למה לי? כו] מה אם השבתה. הא אינך מוציא מן הדין כז] שהם מותרות! מה למנחת העומר. שכן מרובה מצותה דמתרת חדש, תאמר בטריפה כח]. ספיחין אסורין. כט] קדושת שביעית נוהגת בהו, וחייבין בביעור משנה שעברה, דהא כלה לחיה שבשדה, הילכך אין העומר מתירן ל] [ב] והא נתבערו כולן. ספיחין אסורים. לא] מן הביעור ואילך, דיליף מ"הן לא נזרע ולא נאסוף את תבואתנו", וכי מאחר שאין זורעים מהיכא אוספים? לימד על הספיחים שהן אסורים. וביעור לב] משתרד רביעה שנייה, דהויא לה כלה לחיה שבשדה, כדתניא: עד מתי נהנין ושורפין בתבן וקש של שביעית – משתרד רביעה שנייה, במסכת תענית (דף ו:). הילכך לרבי עקיבא אילטריכא קרא להוציא טריפה. ואפילו למ"ד. במסכת קדושין בסוף פ"ק (דף לז.). חדש בחו"ל לאו דאורייתא. ולא חשיב ליה היתר, אפילו הכי יש בה רבותא, דמתרת לאו שבתוכה – לאו ד"לחם וקלי וכרמל לא תאכלו" שבתוך מנחה עצמה מתרת אפי' לר' עקיבא, שאם נאכלו שירים – לא יעבור האוכלן משום חדש אלא משום שביעית, תאמר בטריפה שאינה מתרת כלום? ולמה לי קרא? א"ל רב אחא כו'. דילמא להכי אילטריך קרא, סד"א: טריפה נמי תקרב כמנחת העומר להתיר לאו שבתוכה, שהאוכלה לא יעבור משום "טריפה לא תאכל". שכן מצותה בכך. שאי אפשר להביא מן הישן, שאין חדש מותר בענין אחר, תאמר בטריפה שאפשר להביא כשירה? גברא הוא. ומאי מותר לגבוה איכא? שבת מותרת לגבוה. להקריב תמידין ומוספין. שכן מצותה בכך. שאי אפשר להקריב תמידין ומוספין אלא בו ביום, אבל טריפה אפשר בכשירה. כלאים

תורה אור

האיר המזרח מתיר. וא"ת: נהי דמתיר הלאו, עשה מיהא איכא, כדמוכח לקמן בפרק "רבי ישמעאל" (דף סח. ושם) ד"ה "עד הביאכם את קרבן אלהיכם" למצוה!* ומיהו קשיא בההיא שמעתא גופא, דפריך מתקנת רבן יוחנן בן זכאי, ואי ס"ד מצוה – משום מצוה ליקו וליגזור? מאי קושיא, אמאי לא נגזור משום עשה? אפילו באיסור הכנה דרבנן אשכחן בפ"ק דביצה (דף ה:) דגזרינן שמא יבנה בית המקדש! לפיכך נראה דאינו אלא מצוה מן המובחר בעלמא, ואפילו עשה ליכא. במי שראוי לעבודה. דאע"פ לג] *שהכהן נפסל, או כשקיבלו פסולין וזרקו את דמו, או שנפגם המזבח – ס"ד דמהניא מחשבה לקובעו בפגול, כדאשכחן גבי יוצא בסוף פירקין. ובדבר הראוי לעבודה. פירש בקונטרס: כגון מנחת *חוטא, לאפוקי מנחת העומר של שעורים, דאינה ראויה אלא לעבודה זו בלבד. וקשיא: דא"כ מנחת קנאות לא תיפסל שלא לשמה! ונראה לפרש: דחשיב מנחת העומר דבר שאין ראוי לעבודה, משום דאפילו לגבוה אסור להקריב חדש קודם העומר. ולפירוש הקונטרס יש קצת לדחוק, דבמנחת העומר דלא שייך ביה שינוי בעלים, דהא דליבור היא, ולא פסול בה (נמי) שינוי קדש כיון דלא הוי ראוי לעבודה. ובקונטרס תירץ דשאני מנחת לד] סוטה דחטאת קרייה רחמנא. וכי תימא: הרי עומר שעורין ראוי לעבודה גבי סוטה! חדא – דהתם קמח והכא גרש, ועוד – אין זה ראוי לעבודה, דלברר עון אתיא. שכן קדושתה אוסרתה. פירוש: שקדושתה גורמת לה להיות *חלוקה, ואינה מותרת בשחיטה כשאר חולין. כרבי עקיבא דאמר ספיחים אסורין. פירש בקונטרס: לה] לאחר הביעור. וקשיא לר"ת, דהא רבנן מודו דכלה לחיה שבשדה כלה לבהמתך שבבית! ועוד, דרבי עקיבא דריש לה בפ' "מקום שנהגו" (פסחים דף נא:) מקרא ד"הן לא נזרע ולא נאסוף", [ג] ואילו לאחר ביעור נפקא לן מ"לבהמתך ולחיה"! ועוד, דבשעת העומר לא היה ביעור, שאדרבה, אז התבואה במילואה ואינה כלה לחיה שבשדה עד שנה א' בימות החורף במרחשון! ובפרק "מקום שנהגו" (ג"ז שם) פירשתי. שכן באה להתיר לאו שבתוכה. פירש בקונטרס: שלא יעבור בה האוכל שירי העומר משום לאו דחדש, לו] אלא משום שביעית. וזהו תימה: אם לא יתיר עומר איסור שביעית איקרי כאן "ממשקה ישראל"! ועוד, מאי קפריך: טריפה נמי תיקרב לז] להתרת לאו שבתוכה שיאכלו הקרבן של טריפה? והלא אינו מתיר איסור שביעית, ולמה יתיר איסור לח] טריפה!.

מה

שיטה מקובצת

שיטה מקובצת

לג] מנחת חוטא גליון ול"נ דלעיל אמרי' בשלמא מנחת חוטא כו'. תו"ח: לה] עיין בהשמטות בסוף המסכת: לו] עיין בהשמטות בסוף המסכת: לז] תיקרב להתיר: לח] טריפה. לכך צריך לפרש דמתרת לאו שבתוכה להתירה לאכול השירים מכל וכל מיהו קשה דהוי ליה למימר לאוין שבתוכה:

א) נ"ל דהשטה כו' מתיר חדש במדינה ושתי הלחם במקדש. ב) היינו לר"י בזבחים דף ט דגם בפסול דשלא לשמו מהני מחשבה מעבודה לעבודה. ג) לכאורה צ"ל משנה שעברה ועולי כוונתו להא דאמרינן בפסחים נ"ג דאוכלין בגרוגרת עד חנוכה ע"ש.

הגהות צ"ק [א] לכל שאר הבהמה: [ב] נ"ל דהא נתבערו כולן וספיחים אסורים כו' והד"א: [ג] ואי:

גליון הש"ס רש"י ד"ה ובדבר הראוי לעבודה כו' מנחת קנאות משום דרחמנא קרייה חטאת. תמוה לי הא מנחת קנאות לא איקרי כלל חטאת (ובתוספות העתיקו דשאני מנחת חוטא)

*דְּאָמַר מָר: גִּילֵּחַ אעַל א' מִשְּׁלָשְׁתָּן — יָצָא. מֵיתִיבֵי: *באָשָׁם מְצוֹרָע שֶׁנִּשְׁחַט שֶׁלֹּא לִשְׁמוֹ, אוֹ שֶׁלֹּא נִיתַּן מִדָּמוֹ ע"ג בְּהוֹנוֹת — ה"ז עוֹלֶה לְגַבֵּי מִזְבֵּחַ, וְטָעוּן נְסָכִים, וְצָרִיךְ אָשָׁם אַחֵר לְהַכְשִׁירוֹ! תְּיוּבְתָּא דְּרַב. א) [א] וְרשב"ל אָמַר: גמִנְחַת הָעוֹמֶר שֶׁקְּמָצָהּ שֶׁלֹּא לִשְׁמָהּ — כְּשֵׁירָה, וּשְׁיָרֶיהָ ב] אֵין נֶאֱכָלִין עַד שֶׁתָּבִיא מִנְחַת הָעוֹמֶר אַחֶרֶת וְתַתִּירֶנָּה. (*שֶׁשְּׁיָרֶיהָ אֵין נֶאֱכָלִין עַד שֶׁתָּבִיא מִנְחַת הָעוֹמֶר אַחֶרֶת,) מִקְּרַב הֵיכִי קָרְבָה? ד] "מִמַּשְׁקֵה יִשְׂרָאֵל" — מִן הַמּוּתָּר לְיִשְׂרָאֵל! אָמַר רַב אַדָּא בַּר אַהֲבָה, קָסָבַר ר"ל: *אֵין מְחוּסַּר זְמַן לְבוֹ בַּיּוֹם. מְתִיב רַב אַדָּא בְּרֵיהּ דְּרַב יִצְחָק: יֵשׁ בָּעוֹפוֹת שֶׁאֵין בַּמְּנָחוֹת, יֵשׁ בַּמְּנָחוֹת שֶׁאֵין בָּעוֹפוֹת; יֵשׁ בָּעוֹפוֹת — שֶׁהָעוֹפוֹת בָּאִין ה] דבִּנְדְבַת שְׁנַיִם, (אֲבָל מְנָחוֹת ה"נֶפֶשׁ" [ב] כְּתִיבָא;) וּמְחוּסְּרֵי כַפָּרָה, (זָב וְזָבָה יוֹלֶדֶת וּמְצוֹרָע;) וְהוּתְּרוּ מִכְּלַל אִיסּוּרָן בַּקּוֹדֶשׁ, משא"כ בַּמְּנָחוֹת. וְיֵשׁ בַּמְּנָחוֹת — שֶׁהַמְּנָחוֹת טְעוּנוֹת וכְּלִי וּתְנוּפָה זוְהַגָּשָׁה, חוְיֶשְׁנָן בְּצִיבּוּר כְּבַיָּחִיד, טמַה שֶּׁאֵין כֵּן בָּעוֹפוֹת; וְאִם אִיתָא, בַּמְּנָחוֹת נַמִי מַשְׁכַּחַתְּ לָהּ דְּהוּתְּרוּ מִכְּלַל אִיסּוּרָן בַּקּוֹדֶשׁ, ו] וּמַאי נִיהוּ? מִנְחַת הָעוֹמֶר! כֵּיוָן דְּאֵין מְחוּסַּר זְמַן לְבוֹ בַּיּוֹם, לָאו אִיסּוּרָא הוּא. מְתִיב רַב שֵׁשֶׁת: יהִקְדִּים מַתַּן שֶׁמֶן לְמַתַּן דָּם — יְמַלְאֶנּוּ שֶׁמֶן וְיַחֲזוֹר וְיִתֵּן ז] שֶׁמֶן אַחַר מַתַּן דָּם, מַתַּן בְּהוֹנוֹת לְמַתַּן שֶׁבַע — *יְמַלְאֶנּוּ שֶׁמֶן ח] וְיַחֲזוֹר וְיִתֵּן מַתַּן בְּהוֹנוֹת אַחַר מַתַּן ז'; וְאִי אָמְרַתְּ אֵין מְחוּסַּר זְמַן לְבוֹ בַּיּוֹם, ט] אַמַּאי יַחֲזוֹר וְיִתֵּן? מַאי דַּעֲבַד עֲבַד! אָמַר רַב פַּפָּא: שָׁאנֵי הִלְכוֹת מְצוֹרָע, דִּכְתִיבָא בְּהוּ הֲוָיָה, דְּאָמַר קְרָא: °"זֹאת תִּהְיֶה תּוֹרַת הַמְּצוֹרָע", "תִּהְיֶה" — בַּהֲוָיָתָהּ תְּהֵא. י] מְתִיב רַב פַּפָּא: *כהִקְדִּים חַטָּאתוֹ לַאֲשָׁמוֹ — לֹא יְהֵא אַחֵר מְמָרֵס בְּדָמָהּ, אֶלָּא תְּעוּבַּר צוּרָתָהּ וְתֵצֵא לְבֵית הַשְּׂרֵיפָה! יא] אַמַּאי קָא מוֹתִיב רַב פַּפָּא? וְהָא רַב פַּפָּא הוּא דְּאָמַר: שָׁאנֵי הִלְכוֹת מְצוֹרָע דִּכְתִיבָא בְּהוּ הֲוָיָה! אֶלָּא רַב פַּפָּא הָכִי קָא קַשְׁיָא לֵיהּ: אֵימָא ה"מ עֲבוֹדָה, יב] *שְׁחִיטָה לָאו עֲבוֹדָה הִיא; וְאִי אֵין מְחוּסַּר זְמַן לְבוֹ בַּיּוֹם — יְהֵא אַחֵר מְמָרֵס בְּדָמָהּ, וְלַקְרִיב אָשָׁם וַהֲדַר לִיקְרַב חַטָּאת! יג] אֶלָּא אָמַר רַב פַּפָּא: הַיְינוּ טַעְמָא דְּר"ל, דְּקָסָבַר: הֵאִיר מִזְרָח מַתִּיר. דְּרַבִּי יוֹחָנָן וְר"ל דְּאָמְרִי תַּרְוַיְיהוּ: אֲפִילּוּ בִּזְמַן שֶׁבֵּית הַמִּקְדָּשׁ קַיָּים, הֵאִיר

ומַכְשִׁירוֹ לְהַתְחִיל נְזִירוּת טָהֳרָה. לְיוֹם אֶחָד. כְּחוֹמֶר שַׁלְמֵי נָזִיר כִּדְאָמְרִינַן בְּ"אֵיזֶהוּ מְקוֹמָן" (זבחים דף נד.). וְאֵין טְעוּנִים לֶחֶם. דְּבָעֵינַן "וְנָתַן עַל כַּפֵּי הַנָּזִיר" וְלֵיכָּא. קָבוּעַ. דְּאֵין בָּא שֵׁם ד"א מַכְשִׁיר הַבְּעָלִים אֶלָּא הוּא*. עַל אַחַת מִשְּׁלָשְׁתָּן. אֲפִילּוּ עַל חַטָּאת, דִּכְתִיב: "וְאַחַר יִשְׁתֶּה הַנָּזִיר יָיִן", וְאָמְרִינַן בְּנָזִיר: יד] אַחַר מַעֲשֶׂה יְחִידִי. וְיָלֵיף הָתָם שַׁפִּיר בְּפֶ' "ג' מִינִין" (דף מו.). וְטָעוּן נְסָכִים. כְּדִין אָשָׁם מְצוֹרָע בְּפֶ' "ב' מִדּוֹת" (לקמן דף נ:). לְהַכְשִׁירוֹ. לִמְצוֹרָע *בַּקָּהָל. תְּיוּבְתָּא דְּרַב. דְּאָמַר לְעֵיל דְּפָסוּל, הוֹאִיל וּבָא לְהַכְשִׁיר וְלֹא הִכְשִׁיר. וּשְׁיָרֶיהָ אֵין נֶאֱכָלִין. מִשּׁוּם אִיסּוּר חָדָשׁ. מִמַּשְׁקֵה יִשְׂרָאֵל. פָּסוּק הוּא בִּיחֶזְקֵאל בְּקָרְבָּנוֹת. מִן הַמּוּתָּר טו]. לְמַשְׁקֵה יִשְׂרָאֵל יָבִיאוּ נְסָכִים, וְלֹא מִן הָאָסוּר. אֵין מְחוּסַּר זְמַן לְבוֹ בַּיּוֹם. הוֹאִיל טז] וְהַיּוֹם תְּהֵא מוּתֶּרֶת לְיִשְׂרָאֵל אַחַר שֶׁתִּקְרַב מִנְחַת הָעוֹמֶר אַחֶרֶת יז], וְלֹא מְחוּסֶּרֶת זְמַן הִיא לַגָּבוֹהַּ. עוֹפוֹת בָּאִין בְּנִדְבַת שְׁנַיִם. בְּפֶרֶק "הַמְּנָחוֹת וְהַנְּסָכִים" (לקמן דף קד:) רַבִּי אוֹמֵר: "לְכָל נִדְרֵיהֶם יח] וְנִדְבוֹתָם אֲשֶׁר יַקְרִיבוּ" — הַכֹּל בָּאִין בְּשׁוּתָּפוּת, חוּץ מִן הַמִּנְחָה מִפְּנֵי שֶׁנֶּאֱמַר בָּהּ "נֶפֶשׁ". יט] וּמְחוּסְּרֵי כַפָּרָה. כּוּלָּן מְבִיאִין עוֹפוֹת לְהַכְשִׁירָן בְּקָדָשִׁים, זָב וְזָבָה וְיוֹלֶדֶת וּמְצוֹרָע. וְהוּתְּרוּ לַקֹּדֶשׁ מִכְּלַל אִיסּוּרָן. לְהֶדְיוֹט, דִּמְלִיקָה אֲסוּרָה בְּחוּלִּין וּכְשֵׁרָה בְּקָדָשִׁים. כ] מְנָחוֹת טְעוּנוֹת כְּלִי. בְּפֶ' "שְׁתֵּי הַלֶּחֶם" (לקמן דף נז.). עוֹפוֹת אֵין טְעוּנִין כְּלִי, שֶׁהֲרֵי מְלִיקָתָן בְּצִיפּוֹרֶן. כא] וְהַגָּשָׁה. בְּפֶ' "כָּל הַמְּנָחוֹת בָּאוֹת מַצָּה" (שם דף ס.). הַגָּשָׁה — מַגִּישָׁהּ בְּקֶרֶן מַעֲרָבִית דְּרוֹמִית שֶׁל מִזְבֵּחַ כְּנֶגֶד חוּדָּהּ שֶׁל קֶרֶן, בְּפֶ' "הַקּוֹמֵץ רַבָּה" (לקמן דף יט:). מִנְחַת הָעוֹמֶר יֶשְׁנָהּ בְּצִיבּוּר כב], עוֹפוֹת אֵין בָּאִין בְּצִיבּוּר, בְּת"כ גַּבֵּי נִדְבַת הָעוֹף: [ג] "קָרְבָּנוֹ" (וְהִקְרִיב) — הַיָּחִיד מֵבִיא עוֹף וְלֹא הַצִּיבּוּר. וְאִם אִיתָא. דַּעֲדַיִין חָדָשׁ אָסוּר, מִנְחַת הָעוֹמֶר נַמִי אִישְׁתַּכַּח דִּקְרֵבָה לַגָּבוֹהַּ, מַה שֶּׁאָסוּר לְהֶדְיוֹט! לָאו אִיסּוּרָא כג] הוּא. דִּכְמַאן דִּקְרֵבָה מִנְחַת הָעוֹמֶר הָאַחֶרֶת דָּמֵי. מַתַּן שֶׁמֶן. דִּמְצוֹרָע. מַתַּן דָּם צָרִיךְ לְהַקְדִּים, כְּמוֹ שֶׁאָמוּר בְּעִנְיָן עַל מְקוֹם דַּם הָאָשָׁם יִתֵּן הַשֶּׁמֶן. יְמַלְאֶנּוּ. לַלּוֹג. לְמַתַּן שֶׁבַע. "וְהִזָּה מִן הַשֶּׁמֶן בְּאֶצְבָּעוֹ שֶׁבַע פְּעָמִים" וגו'. לֹא יְהֵא אַחֵר מְמָרֵס בְּדָם כד]. שֶׁלֹּא יִקְרוֹשׁ כְּשֶׁיַּזֶּה מִדַּם הָאָשָׁם. תְּעוּבַּר צוּרָתָהּ. כה] תַּנִּיחֶנָּה עַד לְמָחָר וְתִיפָּסֵל בְּלִינָה, וּתְעוּבַּר מַרְאֶה לִיחְלוּחִית בְּשַׂר הֵימֶנָּה, מִשּׁוּם בִּזָּיוֹן קָדָשִׁים. דְּכָל זְמַן שֶׁלֹּא נִפְסְלוּ בְּלִינָה אֵין נִשְׂרָפִין, אֶלָּא א"כ פְּסוּלוֹ בְּגוּפוֹ. אַלְמָא, מִדְּקָתָנֵי תֵּצֵא לְבֵית הַשְּׂרֵיפָה — יֵשׁ מְחוּסַּר זְמַן לְבוֹ בַּיּוֹם. ה"מ כו] דִּכְתִיבָא הֲוָיָה. בַּעֲבוֹדָה. אֲבָל שְׁחִיטָה לָאו עֲבוֹדָה הִיא דְּהָא כְּשֵׁרָה בְּזָר. אֶלָּא טַעְמָא דְּר"ל. דְּאָמַר קוּמְצָהּ נִקְטָר. דְּקָסָבַר הֵאִיר

גילח על אחד משלשתן יצא. ואפי' לרבנן דלא שרו לשתות ביין עד שיביא חטאתו בפ' "ג' מינין" (נזיר דף מו.).

תיובתא. הוה מצי למימר: רב תנא הוא ופליג, כדקאמר בכמה דוכתי.

שהמנחות טעונות כלי. וא"ת: אדרבה, זו היא קולא לגבי עופות, דבעו מליקה בעצמו של כהן! כז] וי"ל: דבקדושה איירי, שצריך לקדשו בכלי שרת, מה שאין כן בעופות.

ואם איתא במנחות נמי משכחת לה. פי': ואם איתא שתהא כשרה.

ואי אין מחוסר זמן לבו ביום אמאי יחזור ויתן. לבסוף מסקינן דיש מחוסר זמן לבו ביום. ותימה: דביומא בפ' "הוציאו לו" (דף ס:) מצריך "חוקה" שלא ישנה את הסדר, והיכא דלא כתיבא "חוקה" לא חיישינן אם משנה! כח] וי"ל: דדוקא כט] בהדי מצורע חשיב מחוסר זמן, במה שעדיין לא הגיע זמן טהרתן, אבל סדר עבודת יוה"כ לכפרה – לא חשיב מחוסר זמן.

שחיטה לאו עבודה היא. פי' הקונטרס: מדאכשרה רחמנא בזר. וא"א לומר כן, דאהכשר זר גופיה מייתי לה לקמן בפירקין (דף ו:) ובספ"ק דזבחים (דף יד:). ומיהו יש ליישב פירושו, דכיון דבשום מקום לא בעי כהן בשחיטה – לאו עבודה היא. ולא דמי לשמאל, דיש מקום שצריך ימין, ולהכי פריך עלה ל] [בזבחים] מפרה. והרב רבי יצחק מאורליינ"ש מפרש: לאו עבודה היא – לפי ששוה בחולין ובקדשים, אם כן לא מטעם עבודה לוה המקום שחיטה. ונראה לפרש דלאו עבודה היא מדאכשרינן בפ"ב דזבחים (דף כו.) עמד בדרום והושיט ידו בצפון ושחט בקדשי קדשים, ובמקבל פסול, דדרשינן: אותו בצפון ולא שוחט בצפון, אבל לא] מקבל בצפון. ובשלמים מכשירין עמד בחוץ והושיט ידו לפנים ושחט, ואם קיבל קבלתו פסולה, דדרשינן בפ' "כל הפסולים" (זבחים דף לב:): "בן הבקר לפני ה'" ולא שוחט לפני ה', אבל אם קיבל – קבלתו פסולה משום דכתיב "לעמוד לפני ה' לשרתו" אלמא כל שירות לפני ה'. ש"מ מדאכשרה רחמנא עמד בחוץ והושיט ידו לפנים ושחט – מכלל דשחיטה לאו שירות היא. ועוד, מדאמר בההיא שמעתא בפ"ב (דף כו.) דנתלה ושחט שחיטתו כשירה, שחיטה על ירך אמר רחמנא ולא שוחט על ירך, אלמא שחיטה לאו עבודה היא, דאי עבודה היא – לא היה מכשיר לה רחמנא בכה"ג, דהא נתלה וקיבל אמר דקבלתו פסולה משום דאין לב] שירות בכך. ומיהו, מדפריך לקמן (דף ו:) ובפ"ק דזבחים (ד' יד:) ובפ' "חטאת העוף" (שם ד' סח:) מפרה, דאמר רב: שחיטת פרה בזר פסולה, משמע קצת כפירוש הקונטרס. ומיהו, גם לפי מה [ד] שפירש יש ליישבו. אבל קשיא, לג] דא"כ לשמעון התימני דבעי בפרק "כל הפסולין" (שם דף לב:) שיהו ידיו של השוחט לפנים מן הנשחט, הויא שחיטה עבודה.

שחיטה לאו עבודה היא. לא מצי לשנויי דר"ש בן לקיש סבר דעבודה היא, דבזה לא מצינו שום מחלוקת. דאע"ג דפריך לקמן לד] משחיטת פרה בזר, ומשני דקדשי בדק הבית היא, ומשמע דאי קדשי מזבח היא הוה דייקי מינה דעבודה היא, ובפ' "טרף בקלפי" (יומא דף מב.) איכא למ"ד דשחיטת פרו בזר פסולה, ופרו קדשי מזבח הוא – אין זה דיוק, דמ"מ כיון דאשכחן שחיטת פרה בזר פסולה אע"ג דקדשי בדק הבית היא, א"כ מה שפסלה הכתוב גבי [ה] פרה לאו משום דהוי עבודה, דהא בפרה [ו] אין שחיטה עבודה דפסלה, כדמפרש: מידי דהוה אמראות נגעים דבעי כהונה. תדע, דהא בזבחים (דף יד:) אמרי רבה ורב יוסף: הולכה בזר מחלוקת ר"ש ורבנן, ומסקינן התם: לר"ש שחיטה לאו עבודה היא, ושאני פרה דקדשי בדק הבית היא. ולקמן ב"הקומץ רבה" (דף יט.) משמע דלר"ש שחיטת פרו בזר פסולה, דקאמרינן: מדגלי רחמנא גבי פרו של אהרן "ושחט (אהרן) את פר החטאת אשר לו" – מכלל דבעלמא לא בעינן בעלים. ומיהו קשיא מהא דאמרינן בפרק "טרף בקלפי" (יומא דף מב.): מ"ש פרה דכתיב בה אלעזר וחוקה, פרו נמי הכתיב וכו'! ומשני: שאני פרה דקדשי בדק הבית היא. וכיון דמפרה ידעינן פרו, א"כ מאי קא משני? וקל לתרץ, דה"ק: שאני התם בפרה שהיא קדשי בדק הבית ולא שייך בה עבודה, א"כ יש להעמיד אלעזר וחוקה אשחיטה כמו אשאר דברים שבה. אבל פרו שהוא קדשי מזבח – אין סברא להעמיד אהרן וחוקה אלא אעבודה שבו, ולא אשחיטה, דלאו עבודה היא.

שחיטה לאו עבודה היא. תימה: הא איכא קבלה דעבודה היא, ודילמא משום קבלה הוא דקאמר שלא יהא אחר ממרס בדמה, משום דכתיב בה הוייה! וי"ל: דהוייה לא קאמר אלא אמידי דכתיב באותה פרשה.

אלא א"ר פפא לה] ה"ט דרשב"ל. משמע הכא דסבר רב פפא יש מחוסר זמן לבו ביום. ותימה: דבפ"ק דזבחים (דף יב. ושם) גבי הא דפסיל בן בתירא פסח ששחטו בי"ד בין לשמו בין שלא לשמו, מסיק רב פפא דאי אפרשיה שחרית או בלילה – לאו דחוי מעיקרו הוא, דאין מחוסר זמן לבו ביום! לו] וי"ל: דאין לדמות הפרשה להך דהכא, דאטו בההיא דשמעתין מי לא מודה רב פפא במצורע שיכול להפריש החטאת קודם שיקריב האשם? דדוקא קתני: הקדיש חטאתו לאשמו – ששחטו קודם האשם, כדקתני: לא יהא אחר ממרס בדמה. וההיא דיומא פ' "שני שעירים" (ד' סג:) גבי שעירי יוה"כ ששחטן בחוץ לז] שהגריל עליהן, דמסיק עלה דאין מחוסר זמן לבו ביום וליכא מאן דפליג – אין לדמות כמו כן כאן, דלגבי שחוטי חוץ חשיב ראוי לפתח אהל מועד כיון דחזי בו ביום.

האיר

ה היא הקבלה לאחר שקמץ נותן בכלי הקומץ מה שאין כן בעופות דבעינן עצמו של כהן למליקה. ולא

שחלקתי בין מכשיר למכפר ניחא עוד י"ל דהתם לא איירי אלא בהפרשה. מהר"פ: לז] בחור

א) נראה דצ"ל פ"ה אחר מתן שבע שנתן כבר קודם המילוי ולא נהירא וכו'.

הגהות צ"ק [א] צ"ל תיובתא דרב תיובתא רשב"ל אמר כו': [ב] כתיב בה: [ג] כתיב קרבנו: [ד] שפירשתי: [ה] פרו לאו: [ו] צ"ל לאו משום דשחיטה עבודה הוא פסלה אלא כדמפרש כו':

גליון הש"ס גמ' תיובתא דרב. ע' לקמן דף מח ע"ב תוס' ד"ה פרשי: **שם** ימלאנו שמן. ע' לקמן דף ט ע"א תוס' ד"ה עד שלא:

ט א מיי' פט"ו מהל' פסה"מ הל"א:
י ב מיי' פ"א מהל' מחוסרי כפרה הל"ג:
יא ג ד ה מיי' פ"ד מהל' מעילה הל"ג:

וַאֲשַׁם מְצוֹרָע שֶׁשְּׁחָטָן שֶׁלֹּא לִשְׁמָן — פְּסוּלִין, הוֹאִיל וּבָאוּ לְהַכְשִׁיר וְלֹא הִכְשִׁירוּ. תְּנַן: כָּל הַמְּנָחוֹת שֶׁנִּקְמְצוּ שֶׁלֹּא לִשְׁמָן — כְּשֵׁירוֹת, אֶלָּא שֶׁלֹּא עָלוּ לַבְּעָלִים א] לְשׁוּם חוֹבָה, חוּץ מִמִּנְחַת חוֹטֵא וּמִנְחַת קְנָאוֹת; וְאִם אִיתָא, לִיתְנֵי נַמִּי: חוּץ מִמִּנְחַת הָעוֹמֶר! כִּי קָתָנֵי — בָּאָה יָחִיד, בָּאָה צִבּוּר לָא קָתָנֵי; כִּי ב] תָּנֵי — בָּאָה בִּגְלַל עַצְמָהּ, בָּאָה בִּגְלַל זֶבַח לָא קָתָנֵי; כִּי קָתָנֵי — הָנָךְ שֶׁאֵין קָבוּעַ לָהֶן זְמַן, הָא דִּקְבוּעַ לָהּ זְמַן לָא קָתָנֵי.§ ג] אָמַר מָר: וְכֵן אַתָּה אוֹמֵר בַּאֲשַׁם נָזִיר וַאֲשַׁם מְצוֹרָע שֶׁשְּׁחָטָן שֶׁלֹּא לִשְׁמָן — פְּסוּלִין, הוֹאִיל וּבָאוּ לְהַכְשִׁיר וְלֹא הִכְשִׁירוּ. *תְּנַן: אכָּל הַזְּבָחִים ד] שֶׁשְּׁחָטָן שֶׁלֹּא לִשְׁמָן — כְּשֵׁרִין, אֶלָּא שֶׁלֹּא עָלוּ לַבְּעָלִים לְשׁוּם חוֹבָה, חוּץ מִפֶּסַח וְחַטָּאת; וְאִם אִיתָא, לִיתְנֵי נַמִּי: חוּץ מֵאֲשַׁם נָזִיר וַאֲשַׁם מְצוֹרָע, ה] דְּבָאוּ לְהַכְשִׁיר וְלֹא הִכְשִׁירוּ! כֵּיוָן דְּאִיכָּא אֲשַׁם גְּזֵילוֹת וַאֲשַׁם מְעִילוֹת דִּלְכַפָּרָה אָתוּ, ו] לָא פְּסִיקָא לֵיהּ. מַאי שְׁנָא אֲשַׁם נָזִיר וַאֲשַׁם מְצוֹרָע דְּבָאוּ לְהַכְשִׁיר וְלֹא הִכְשִׁירוּ, הָנֵי נַמִּי בָּאוּ לְכַפָּרָה וְלֹא כִּפְּרוּ! א"ר יִרְמְיָה: מָצִינוּ שֶׁחִלֵּק הַכָּתוּב ז] בֵּין מְכַפְּרִים וּבֵין מַכְשִׁירִין, ח] מְכַפְּרִין — אִית בְּהוּ דְּאָתוּ לְאַחַר מִיתָה, מַכְשִׁירִין — לֵית בְּהוּ דְּאָתוּ לְאַחַר מִיתָה. *דִּתְנַן: בהָאִשָּׁה ט] שֶׁהֵבִיאָה חַטָּאתָהּ וּמֵתָה — יָבִיאוּ יוֹרְשִׁין עוֹלָתָהּ, עוֹלָתָהּ וּמֵתָה — י] לֹא יָבִיאוּ יוֹרְשִׁין חַטָּאתָהּ. מַתְקִיף לָהּ ר' יְהוּדָה בְּרֵיהּ דְּר' שִׁמְעוֹן בֶּן פָּזִי: מַכְשִׁירִין נַמִּי מִי לֵית בְּהוּ דְּאָתוּ לְאַחַר מִיתָה? *וְהָתְנַן: גהַמַּפְרִישׁ מָעוֹת לִנְזִירוּתוֹ — לֹא נֶהֱנִין יא] וְלֹא מוֹעֲלִין, מִפְּנֵי שֶׁרְאוּיִין לָבֹא כּוּלָּן שְׁלָמִים. דמֵת יב] וְהָיוּ לוֹ מָעוֹת סְתוּמִין — יִפְּלוּ לִנְדָבָה. המְפוֹרָשִׁין, דְּמֵי חַטָּאת — יוֹלִיךְ לְיָם הַמֶּלַח, לֹא נֶהֱנִין וְלֹא מוֹעֲלִין; דְּמֵי עוֹלָה — יָבִיא בָּהֶן עוֹלָה וּמוֹעֲלִין בָּהֶן; דְּמֵי שְׁלָמִים — יָבִיא בָּהֶן שְׁלָמִים, וְנֶאֱכָלִין לְיוֹם אֶחָד יג] וְאֵין טְעוּנִין לֶחֶם. וְהָא עוֹלָה וּשְׁלָמִים דְּנָזִיר דְּמַכְשִׁירִים נִינְהוּ, וְקָא אָתוּ לְאַחַר מִיתָה! אָמַר רַב פַּפָּא, הָכִי קָא אָמַר ר' יִרְמְיָה: לֹא מָצִינוּ הֶכְשֵׁר קָבוּעַ דְּבָא לְאַחַר מִיתָה; וּדְנָזִיר הֶכְשֵׁר שֶׁאֵינוֹ קָבוּעַ הוּא, דְּאָמַר

זבחים ב. [ידים פ"ד מ"ב]

קנין פ"ב מ"ה

מסורת הש"ס

אֲשַׁם מְצוֹרָע. בָּא הוּא לְהַכְשִׁירוֹ לָבֹא יד] בַּמַּחֲנֶה. וּלְקַמָּן פָּרֵיךְ: שְׁאָר אֲשָׁמוֹת נַמִּי, בָּאוּ לְכַפֵּר וְלֹא כִּפְּרוּ! בִּגְלַל זֶבַח. עִם הַזֶּבַח. דְּמִנְחַת הָעוֹמֶר בָּאָה עִם הַכֶּבֶשׂ, דִּכְתִיב: "וַעֲשִׂיתֶם בְּיוֹם הֲנִיפְכֶם אֶת הָעוֹמֶר" וגו' (ויקרא כג). דִּקְבוּעַ לוֹ זְמַן. טו] בְּנִיסָן. [מָצִינוּ שֶׁחִילֵּק] [א]. וּבְמַכְשִׁירִים הֶחְמִירוּ. לֹא יָבִיאוּ יוֹרְשִׁין חַטָּאתָהּ. דְּזוֹ אַחַת מֵחָמֵשׁ חַטָּאוֹת הַמֵּתוֹת, חַטָּאת שֶׁמֵּתוּ בְּעָלֶיהָ. וְחַטָּאת יוֹלֶדֶת מַכְשִׁיר הוּא, כִּדְאָמְרִינַן בִּכְרֵיתוֹת בְּפֶ' "דַּם שְׁחִיטָה" (דף כו.): מִפְּנֵי שֶׁמַּכְשַׁרְתָּהּ לֶאֱכוֹל בְּקָדָשִׁים. וּמִדְּחַטָּאתָהּ לְהַכְשִׁיר — עוֹלָתָהּ לְכַפֵּר, כִּדְכְתִיב (ויקרא יב) בְּיוֹלֶדֶת: טז] "אֶחָד לְחַטָּאת וְאֶחָד לְעוֹלָה". אַלְמָא מְכַפְּרִין קָרְבִי מַכְשִׁירִין לָא קָרְבִי, יז] הָכִי נַמִּי מְכַפְּרִין בְּשֶׁלֹּא לִשְׁמָן כְּשֵׁרִין לְהַקְרִיב וְלֹא עָלוּ, וּמַכְשִׁירִין פְּסוּלִין לְגַמְרֵי יח]. לֹא נֶהֱנִין. מִדְּרַבָּנַן, מִפְּנֵי דְּמֵי עוֹלָה שֶׁבָּהֶן. וְלֹא מוֹעֲלִין. מִפְּנֵי שֶׁרְאוּיִין יט] לָבֹא לִשְׁלָמִים, הוֹאִיל וְלֹא הִפְרִישׁ אֵלּוּ לְחַטָּאת וְאֵלּוּ לִשְׁלָמִים. וּשְׁלָמִים אֵין בָּהֶן מְעִילָה, דְּלָאו קָדְשֵׁי ה' נִינְהוּ אֶלָּא מָמוֹן בְּעָלִים, אֶלָּא בָּאֵימוּרִים לְאַחַר זְרִיקַת דָּמִים בְּפ"ק דְּמַסֶּכֶת מְעִילָה (דף ז:). סְתוּמִין. דְּלֹא פֵּירֵשׁ אֵלּוּ לְחַטָּאת וְאֵלּוּ לְעוֹלָה. יִפְּלוּ לִנְדָבָה. לְשׁוֹפָרוֹת, דַּהֲלָכָה הִיא בְּנָזִיר לְמֹשֶׁה מִסִּינַי. וְכֵן מְפָרֵשׁ בְּנָזִיר בְּפֶרֶק "מִי שֶׁאָמַר הֲרֵינִי נָזִיר וְשָׁמַע חֲבֵירוֹ" כו' (דף כד:). יוֹלִיךְ לְיָם הַמֶּלַח. כְּדִין חַטָּאת שֶׁמֵּתוּ בְּעָלֶיהָ דִּלְמִיתָה אָזְלָא. לֹא נֶהֱנִין. מִדְּרַבָּנַן. וְלֹא מוֹעֲלִין. דְּאָמַר בִּשְׁמַעְתָּא קַמַּיְיתָא דִּמְעִילָה (דף ג.): חַטָּאוֹת הַמֵּתוֹת וּמָעוֹת הַהוֹלְכוֹת לְיָם הַמֶּלַח אֵין מוֹעֲלִין בָּהֶן, דִּלְאִיבּוּד קָיְימִי וְלָאו קָדְשֵׁי גָבוֹהַּ נִינְהוּ. דְּמֵי שְׁלָמִים כו'. אֲבָל כ] דְּמֵי אָשָׁם לֵיכָּא, דְּאֵינוֹ בְּנָזִיר טָהוֹר אֶלָּא בְּנָזִיר טָמֵא, וּמַכְשִׁירוֹ

בעליו – ירעה עד שיסתאב וימכר ויביא בדמיו עולה, בדמיו אין אבל הוא גופיה לא, גזירה לאחר כפרה אטו לפני כפרה. הל"ל: משום דגמירי דאשם רועה! ומתוך פי' הקונטרס משמע דלא גמירי אלא ניתק לרעייה בעלמא, ומשמסרו לרועה כשר לעולה משם ואילך אפילו הוא בעצמו, דשוב אין שם אשם עליו. ותימה גדול הוא לומר כן. ועוד, דהוה ליה למימר: גזירה לאחר ניתוק אטו קודם ניתוק. ועוד, דמשמע בהדיא התם בפסחים דניתוק לרעייה דרבנן, מדדייק אמילתיה דרב הונא דהכא דאמר שחטו סתם כשר לעולה – אלמא קסבר לא בעי עקירה, אי הכי כי לא ניתק נמי! ומשני: גזירה לאחר כפרה אטו לפני כפרה! ורבינו שמואל לא גרים התם "כי לא ניתק נמי", אלא הכי גרים: א"ה לכתחילה נמי, פירוש: יכול לשוחטו סתם כיון דלא בעי עקירה, ואמאי נקט "ושחטו" סתם, דמשמע דיעבד? דבשלמא אי הוה אמר "ושחטו לשם עולה" דבעי עקירה – הוה ניחא דנקט דיעבד אפילו לאחר ניתוק, גזירה שמא ישכח לעוקרו! ומשני דכי לא בעי עקירה נמי אסור לכתחילה כמו לפני כפרה. ודוחק הוא שמגיה הספרים. ועוד, דהוה ליה לשנויי: גזירה אטו לפני ניתוק! ור"ת לא גרים כאן ובפ"ק דזבחים (דף ה.) ובנזיר (דף כה:) "ניתק אין לא ניתק לא", ובתמורה אינו ברוב ספרים בפ' "ואלו קדשים" (דף יח.), ובפ"ב דזבחים (דף כח.) אינו בשום ספר, דקרא ד"הוא" בהוייתו יהא – לא לפסול בלא ניתוק קאתי, דרעיי' דרבנן היא, והכי גמירי הלכתא דכל שבחטאת מתה באשם קרב עולה. ומשום דתקון רבנן רעייה גזירה אטו לפני כפרה, נקט התלמוד באשם רועה. וקרא אתא למימר דכשר לעולה בלא עקירה, דבהוייתו – מה שבסופו להיות לאחר עקירה – יהיה בלא עקירה, דהיינו עולה כדגמירי. ואין לחוש אי קאי קרא אהילכתא, דכי האי גוונא אשכחנא בפ' "הלוקח עובר פרתו" (בכורות ד' טז.) דאיצטריך קרא ואיצטריך הילכתא. והשתא ניחא הא דפריך בפסחים (דף עג.): אי הכי כי לא ניתק נמי. ועוד יש לפרש דגרסינן הכא שפיר "ניתק אין לא ניתק לא" דאמר קרא "הוא" – בהוייתו יהא קודם כפרה. והיכא דאבד והפריש אחר ונמצא הראשון והרי שניהם עומדים, דפליגי בפרק "שני שעירי" (יומא דף סד.) דרב אמר מלוה בראשון ור' יוחנן אמר מלוה בשני, לא [ב] אמר שיהא חבירו קרב מיד עולה, דבהויי' אשם יהא קודם כפרה, הילכך ניתק אין לא ניתק לא, משום דגזרינן אטו לפני כפרה. ובפסחים (דף עג.) דפריך: כי לא ניתק נמי – היינו לאחר כפרה, אלא שלא ניתק. [ג] דבשלמא אי בעי עקירה הוה ניחא דבעי ניתוק, כדי שיהא נזכר לעוקרו לשם עולה. וא"ת: ומותר הפסח דקרב שלמים [ד] (לימא) דבעי עקירה – וליבעי ניתוק כדי שיהא נזכר לעוקרו! ועוד, אמאי לא גזרינן ביה אטו לפני כפרה כמו באשם? וי"ל: דשאני פסח שאין זמנו רק ערב הפסח מחצות, ולא שייך למיגזר ביה כלל בשאר ימות השנה. וא"ת: בשלמא אשם שמתו בעליו איכא למיגזר אטו קודם מיתה, ונתכפרו בעליו אטו קודם כפרה, דהוא גופיה לא ליקרב עולה. אלא תמורת אשם וולד תמורת אשם, דתנן בפרק "ואלו קדשים" (דף כ:) ירעו, ובעי למימר בגמרא: קודם כפרה, [ה] דגזרינן שמא הוא עצמו יקרב, ואיתותב התם – מאי גזירה איכא? והלא אף קודם כפרה א) דיש ליקרב עולה, וא"כ הוא עצמו יקרב עולה! וי"ל: דגזרינן אטו אשם גופו לפני כפרה. וקצת קשה לפי' ר"ת מנזיר (דף כה:) דר' ישמעאל דריש: ולד חטאת ותמורת אשם, אי מקריב ליה קאי עליה בעשה מדכתיב "רק". ר"ע אומר: אינו צריך, הרי הוא אומר "אשם הוא" כא] ב) – הוא קריבה ואין תמורתו קריבה. ופריך: למה לי קרא? והא הילכתא גמרינן ליה: כל שבחטאת מתה באשם רועה! ומשני: אין ה"נ, וכי אתא קרא לכדרב הונא כו', משמע ד"הוא" אתא למעוטי מהקרבה ולאו לאכשוריה להקרבה.

מכשירין לית בהו דאתו לאחר מיתה. פי' בקונטרס: כב] חטאת יולדת מכשיר היא, כדאמרינן בפ' "דם שחיטה": מפני שמכשרתה לאכול בקדשים. ותגר ריהטיה לא דק שם, ומשנה היא בפ' "המביא ג) אשם תלוי" כג] (כריתות דף כה:). כד] **ה"ג בת"כ האשה כו'** עולתה ומתה לא יביאו יורשים חטאתה. משמע: אבל היא אם היתה חיה – היתה מביאה חטאתה אחר עולתה, ועלתה לה עולתה לשם חובה. וכן משמע [בת"כ] בפרשת "אשה כי תזריע" שאם הביאה עולתה תחילה – תביא חטאתה ממין עולתה, וכן במסכת קנים (פ"ב מ"ה). ותימה: דבפ' כה] "תמיד נשחט" (פסחים ד' נט.) אמרי': זה בנה אב שכל החטאות קודמות לעולה אפילו חטאת עוף קודם לעולת כו] בהמה. ואפילו דיעבד קאמר, מדמשני: שאני עולת מצורע דרחמנא אמר "והעלה" – שהעלה כבר, והיינו דיעבד, דלכתחילה חטאתה קודמת כדכתיב בקרא בהדיא, ש"מ דבעלמא אפילו דיעבד לא! ותירץ ה"ר חיים: דה"ה בעלמא. והא דבעי קרא במצורע – משום דכתיב ביה הויה "זאת תהיה" – בהוייתו יהא, דמשמע עיכובא כדאמרינן כז] בשמעתין בסוף. אע"ג דמסקינן לקמן יש מחוסר זמן לבו ביום, אין לפסול בעלמא מטעם זה, דלא הוי אלא בסדר מצורע כמו שאפרש לקמן. **לא** יביאו יורשין חטאתה. הגירסא משתבשת בת"כ בפרשת "ויקרא" [בפ'] "אם לא תגיע" [וגו']: "אחד לחטאת ואחד לעולה" – שממין חטאת יביא עולה, שאם הביא חטאתו ומת – יביאו יורשין עולתו. ומנין שאם הביא עולתו ומת שיביאו יורשין חטאתו? ת"ל "אחד לחטאת ואחד לעולה". כח] וכך יש להיות הגירסא: יכול שאם הביא עולתו ומת שיביאו יורשין חטאתו? ת"ל "אחד לחטאת", פי': חטאת קודמת לעולה. כט] ואסמכתא בעלמא היא, דמהילכתא הוא דנפקא לן דחטאת שמתו בעליה למיתה אזלא. **לא** נהנין ולא מועלין. בנזיר בפרק ["מי שאמר הריני נזיר ושמע חבירו ואמר] ואני" (דף כד:) תנן כי האי גוונא. **ואין** טוענין לחם. אע"ג דבסמוך גבי אשם מצורע שלא לשמו קתני דטעון נסכים – יש לחלק בין נסכים, דשייכי בכל הקרבנות, ללחם. ועוד, כדפי' בקונטרס: משום דבעינן "על כפי הנזיר" וליכא. ומיהו קשה: למה הטעינו כאן זרוע בשילה ד) יותר משלא כמצוותו ושלא לשמו בפ' "התכלת" (לקמן דף מח:)? וי"ל: דשלא כמצותו הוי משונה יותר מדאי. ועוד, שלא כמצותו נראה דהיינו בן שנה והביא בן שתים, או מחוסר זמן, דהוי משונה יותר מדאי. וקצת תימה: כיון דאין טעון לחם – יפסול, כדאמר בפ' "שתי מדות" (לקמן דף פט:) גבי אשם מצורע ששחטו שלא לשמו טעון נסכים, שאם אי אתה אומר כן פסלתו. והכא נמי יהא טעון לחם, שאם אי אתה אומר כן – פסלתו! ויש לחלק כמו שפי', דנסכים אלימי מלחם. ובפ' "שתי מדות" אאריך בעזרת האל.

א) נ"א שרי. ב) בהוייתו יהא כ"ה בש"י והכי איתא בגמרא שם ועי' תוס' שם. ג) נ"א אשם תלוי ובת"כ הס"ד ומה"ד א"כ עולתה כו' וכ"ה בש"י. ד) צ"ל יותר משלא במצותו דפירש"י שלא לשמה.

שיטה מקובצת

הני דכתיב חטאת הוא אשם הוא דמשמע בהוייתן אבל הכא דכתיב האשם הוא ה"ק כחטאת יהיה האשם לכהן: א] לשם חובה ב] כי קתני באה: ג] תיבות אמר מר נמחק: ד] הזבחים שנזבחו שלא לשמן כו' לבעלים לשם חובה חוץ מן הפסח והחטאת: ה] תיבות דבאו להכשיר ולא הכשירו נמחק: ו] לא פסיקא ליה. גליון דאי אמר חוץ מפסח ואשם לא ידענא איזה אשם קאמר אי אשם דלהכשיר אי אשם דלכפר. הרגמ"ה: ז] בין מכפרין למכשירין. בין אותם המביאין קרבן לכפרה לאותן המביאין קרבן להכשירם לאכול בזבחים. הרגמ"ה ח] מכפרים אית בהו דאתו כו' יש דבר שקרב עמהם דהוי כמכפר ואתי לאחר מיתה. הרגמ"ה: דאתו לאחר מיתה. וכיון דאשכחן במקום אחר שהן באין (בקל) [לבטלה] ה"נ הכא בשלא לשמו אע"ג דלא מכפרי שהרי לא עלו לבעלים לשם חובה מ"מ כשרים להקטיר אבל מכשיר לית בהו דאתי לאחר מיתה א) אלא אינם בקל ה"נ הכא בשלא לשמו כיון שאינן מכשירין ליפסלו: מכפרים אית בהו דאתו כו' אע"ג דלאו בני כפרה נינהו דאין כפרה למתים וכמו כן כשנקרבו שלא לשמן לא פסלו דמשום דלא כפרו אינם פסולים אלא הוי נדבה. תו"ח: ט] האשה יולדת שהביאה חטאת כו' יביאו יורשין עולתה דעולה דורון הוא וכשרה היא להביאה לאחר מיתה ועולה כיון דאתיא עם מכפר כמכפר דמי. הרגמ"ה: י] לא יביאו יורשים חטאתה. שאין מכפר לאחר מיתה. הרגמ"ה: יא] ולא מועלין. גליון דאמרינן כל מעה ומעה ראויה ליקח בה שלמים ושלמים לפני זריקה ממון בעלים הוא. הרגמ"ה: יב] ע' בהשמטות בסוף המסכת: סתומין יפלו לנדבה כו' גליון במס' נזיר פריך והלא דמי חטאת מעורבין בהן ומשני הלכה היא בנזיר וא"ת מאי פריך והלא הם ראויין לבא כולה עולה כדאמרי' הכא שראויין לבא כולן שלמים ותירץ רבינו יצחק דסיפא איירי שאמר בשעת הפרשה לקרבנות נזירותיו ובכה"ג לא שייך לבא כולן שלמים שהרי פירש שהיה רוצה לעשות מהן קרבנות הרבה ומ"מ כיון שלא פירש זה לחטאת וזה לעולה יפלו לנדבה והא דאמרי' מפני שראויין להביא כולן שלמים היינו היכא דאמר לנזירות סתם וא"ת מנ"ל למקשה דסיפא באומר לקרבנות [נזירותיו] הא קיימינן באומר לנזירתו וי"ל דמשמ' ליה מדאמרי' סתומין דמכדי בסתומין מיירי למה הוצרך למימר סתומין אלא לרבות כל סתומין ואפי' אמר לקרבנות כך פי' הרב ר' מאיר. תו"ח וע"ש בתוס' נזיר: לא נהנין. מדרבנן ולא מועלין דכתיב ומעלה מעל בה' בקדשי ה' ואין אלו קדשי ה' כיון דלמיתה אזלא: יג] אחד. ואינן טוענין: יד] במחנה. גליון וקשה דהא בלא אשם נמי מכי הביא צפורין אתכשר ליכנס במחנה ונראה לפרש להכשיר בקדשים דעד עתה לא היה יכול לאכול בקדשים עד שהביא אשמו. תו"ח ותוס' מהר"פ:

טו] דקבוע לו זמן. בששה עשר בניסן. הס"ד ומה"ד דלכפרה אתו. וכשרין שלא לשמן: הס"ד ומה"ד לא פסיקא ליה. למתני אשם: הס"ד ומה"ד שחילק הכתו'. דבמכפרין הקל ובמכשירין כו': טז] ביולדת אחד לעולה ואחד לחטאת וכפר עליה: יז] קרבי הכא נמי: יח] ע' בהשמטות בסוף המסכת: יט] שראויין להביא כולן שלמים הואיל ולא פירש אלו לחטאת: כ] אבל אשם ליכא דאשם אינו בנזיר: כא] אשם הוא בהוייתו יהא ופריך למה לי והשאר נמחק: כב] חטאת יולדת מכשיר. גליון. כדאמר בכריתות מה לחטאת שכן מכשרת אלמא דחטאת דיולדת בא להכשיר וקשה שהרי לא מצינו זה בכריתות אך נראה שהוא בת"כ דכתיב והקריב אחד לחטאת ואחד לעולה וע"כ ביולדת חטאת מכשיר דהא בכל מקום מצינו כשיש חטאת ועולה החטאת הוי עיקר וחטאת מכפר וכאן ביולדת הכשירה עיקר שהרי לא שייך בה כפרה שהרי לא חטאה וא"כ חטאת מכשירה וא"כ מדחטאת מכשרת עולה מכפרת וקאמר דמכשיר חמור טפי ממכפר עכ"ל תו"ח ובתוס' אחרות כתוב חטאת יולדת מכשיר כדאמרי' בביצד צולין חטאת מכשירתה לאכול בקדשי' ומדחטאת מכשרת עולה מכפרת דבחד מינייהו כתיב וכפר עליה הכהן ע"כ: כג] אשם תלוי. ובת"כ נמי איתא דאמרי' התם כתיב אחד לחטאת ואחד לעולה וכתיב והקריבו לומר דחד לא מעכב ומסתמא החטאת עיקר שבכ"מ החטאת עיקר [illegible] מכשירה שעיקר קרבן יולדת להכשיר הוא בא שהרי אינה צריכה כפרה כל כך: כד] תיבות ה"ג בת"כ האשה כו' נמחק: כה] ותימה דבפ' כל התדיר ובפרק תמיד: כו] בהמה. והיינו יולדת שמביאה חטאת העוף עם עולת בהמה ואפי' דיעבד קאמר וז"ל תו"ח ואין לומר דהיינו למצוה אבל דיעבד קרב חטאת אף אחר העולה זה אינו דהא אמרי' בפ' תמיד נשחט מחוסר כפורים מקריב קרבנו אפי' לאחר תמיד של בין הערבים ואפי' כל השנה כו' עד ומי קרבה כו' משמע דאפי' דיעבד לא קרבה ותירץ רבינו חיים כהן דלעולם הא דאמר זה בנה אב למצוה קאמר וההיא דתמיד נשחט דמשמע אפי' בדיעבד ההיא בקרבנות מצורע קאמר והתם עיכובא דכתיב תהיה בהוייתו תהא ורבינו ברוך תירץ דכיון דמשני התם שאני התם דכתיב והעלה שהעלה כבר כיון דהכי הוא גמרינן מינה גם יולדת דאם העלה כבר כשר ע"כ: כז] כדאמרי' בסוף שמעתין אע"ג דמסקינן. עיין תוס' זבחים דף ה ע"א: כח] וכך יש. גיליון והר"ר יחיאל בר יוסף יישב הגירסא דלא אמרי' חמש חטאות מתות אלא בבהמה אבל בעוף לא ובת"כ בעוף איירי וא"ת והלא הכא בעוף איירינן וקאמר לא יביאו יורשין חטאתה וי"ל דהיינו דוקא הכא משום דחטאת מכשיר גבי יולדת והכשירה עיקר דכפרה לא שייך בה שהרי לא חטאת וקשה להר"ר שמואל מאיוורא שהרי אמרי' [יומא דף מ"א ע"ב] גבי מטמא מקדש הפריש מעות לעולתו וכו' וקאמר כיון דהאי פרידה למיתה אזלא ומאי קאמר והלא בעוף איירי ואנן אמרי' דעוף לא הוי בכלל חטאות המתות וצ"ע תו"ח (ע' שעה"מ הפ"מ בפ' ד' בסופו): כט] קודמת לעולה. לאשמועינן דלא יביא כי הכא: תיובתא

א) אולי צ"ל אלמא דאינן באין לבטלה ה"נ הכא.

הגהות צ"ק [א] במכשירים: [ב] אמרינן: [ג] ופריך דבשלמא: [ד] למ"ד דבעיא עקירה ליבעי: [ה] שהוא עצמו יקרב כו':

מסורת הש"ס

תורה אור

מה לי א"ר שמעון? טעמא דר' שמעון משום מחשבה דמינכרא לא פסלה, והא מחשבה דמינכרא הוא, או דילמא טעמא דר"ש משום דכתיב: °"וזאת תורת המנחה", וזבח לא כתיב? אמר ליה: א] כלום הגענו לסוף דעתו של ר"ש? כרבה לא משני ליה – משום קושיא דאביי; כרבא לא משני ליה – משום ב] קושיא "וזאת תורת החטאת"; כרב אשי לא משני ליה – משום קושיא דרב אחא בריה דרבא. § "חוץ ממנחת חוטא ומנחת קנאות". § בשלמא מנחת חוטא – ג] חטאת קרייה רחמנא: °"לא ישים עליה שמן ולא יתן עליה לבונה כי חטאת היא" וגו', אלא מנחת קנאות מנלן? דתני תנא קמיה דרב נחמן: ד] *אמנחת קנאות מותרה נדבה. א"ל: שפיר קאמרת, ה] °"מזכרת עון" כתיב בה, ובחטאת כתיב: °"ואותה נתן לכם לשאת את עון העדה", מה חטאת מותרה נדבה – אף מנחת קנאות מותרה נדבה; וכחטאת, מה חטאת פסולה שלא לשמה – אף מנחת קנאות פסולה שלא לשמה. אלא מעתה, אשם יהא פסול שלא לשמו, דגמר "עון" "עון" מחטאת! דנין "עון" מ"עון" ואין דנין "עונו" מ"עון". מאי נפקא מינה? והא *תנא דבי ר' ישמעאל: °"ושב הכהן" "ובא הכהן" – זו היא שיבה, זו היא ביאה! ועוד, ליגמר "עונו" "עונו" מעון דשמיעת הקול, דכתיב: °"אם לא יגיד ונשא עונו"! אלא כי ו] גמרי גזירה שוה – למותר נדבה הוא דגמרי. וכי תימא: *אין גזירה שוה למחצה – גלי רחמנא גבי חטאת: ז] °"ושחט אותה לחטאת" – אותה לשמה כשירה, שלא לשמה פסולה, אבל כל קדשים – בין לשמן בין שלא לשמן כשרים. אלא מנחת חוטא ומנחת קנאות דפסולין שלא לשמן, מנלן? חטאת טעמא מאי – משום דכתיב בה "היא", ה"נ – הא כתיב בהו "היא". *אשם נמי, הא כתיב ביה "הוא"! ח] ההוא "הוא" לאחר הקטרת אימורין הוא דכתיב, *כדתניא: אבל אשם לא נאמר בו "הוא" אלא לאחר הקטרת אימורין, הוא עצמו שלא הוקטרו אימוריו – כשר. ואלא "הוא" למה לי? *לכדרב הונא אמר רב: ט] באשם שניתק לרעייה ושחטו סתם – כשר לשום עולה; י] ניתק – אין, לא ניתק – לא, אמר קרא: "הוא" – בהווייתו יהא. § אמר רב: מנחת העומר שקמצה שלא לשמה – פסולה, יא] הואיל ובאת להתיר ולא התירה. וכן אתה אומר באשם נזיר ואשם

רש"י

מה לי שינוי קודש כו'. ושינויא דשני ליה לא מתקבל יב] להו, דכ"ש דמחשבה דמינכרא יג] פסל רחמנא, שלא יאמרו מותר לשנות. חטאת קרייה רחמנא. "לא ישים עליה יד] לבונה כי חטאת היא" (ויקרא ה), מה חטאת פסולה שלא לשמה – טו] אף היא פסולה שלא לשמה. מותרה נדבה. הפריש מעות למנחת סוטה טז] [א], והוו המעות יותר מן השעורים – יפלו לנדבה, דהיינו לשלש עשרה שופרות שהיו במקדש והיו נותנין בהן אותן מעות, וכשהיה מזבח בטל היו קונין מהן כבשים לעולות, הבשר לשם והעורות לכהנים, וקרי להו נדבת ציבור. עון כתיב בה. "מזכרת עון", ובחטאת נמי כתיב: "ואותה נתן לכם לשאת את עון העדה". מה חטאת מותרה נדבה. כדאמר בשילהי "ולד חטאת" במסכת תמורה (דף כג:), זו מדרש דרש יהוידע הכהן: "כסף אשם וכסף חטאות לכהנים יהיו", דבר הבא ממותר חטאת וממותר אשם – *הבשר לשם יז] ועורות לכהנים. באשם כתיב: "ולא ידע ואשם ונשא עונו". זו היא שיבה זו היא ביאה. מפרש בתורת כהנים: מה ביאה חולץ וקוצה וטח ונותן לו שבוע. אלמא גמרינן ג"ש כה"ג, ואע"ג דלא דמו התיבות, הואיל ושניהם לשון ביאת הבית הן. ויש לשונות אחרים אבל זה עיקר. מעונו דשמיעת קול. דשמיעת קול חטאת היא. מנלן. הואיל ולא גמר מחטאת יח]. דכתיב בה [ב]. בחטאת נשיא: "חטאת היא", ולא יט] שבא שלא לשמו. אשם נאמר בו "הוא" לאחר הקטרת אימורין. בפרשת "צו את אהרן": "והקטיר אותם הכהן המזבחה אשה לה' אשם הוא", והילכך אשם לא איפסיל כ] בשלא לשמו, דהא בהקטרה כתיב, כא] והקטרה לאו עיקר הוא. וליכא למיפשק: הוא אשם ולא שנקטרו אימוריו שלא לשמו כב], דהא הוא עצמו שלא הוקטרו אימוריו כשר, כדאמרינן בפ' "תמיד נשחט" במסכת פסחים (דף נט:) דנטמאו אימוריו או שאבדו – לא מעכב כפרה, ונאכל הבשר. אבל פסח וחטאת כתיב "הוא" בשחיטה: "זבח פסח הוא", כג] [ג] בזבח נשיא כתיב: "ושחט אותו במקום אשר ישחט את העולה לפני ה' חטאת הוא". ואלא הוא. דאשם, למה לי? שניתק לרעייה. שנתכפרו בעליו באחר כד], ובחטאת אזלא למיתה, וקיימא לן: כל שבחטאת מתה – באשם רועה, ולכשיסתאב ימכר ויפלו דמיו לנדבה. ואם כבר ניתק לרעייה, שמסרוהו לרועה ושחטו סתם – כשר לעולה, דהא סתמו לעולה ואין שם אשם עליו כה], דשופרות נדבה [לעולה] כדפי' לעיל. לא ניתק. דלא מסרוהו לרועה, ושחטו [ד] (לשם) סתם – לא מתכשר לעולה, דעדיין שם אשם עליו ובעי עקירה דלישחטיה בהדיא לשם עולה, דכל כמה דלא עקר מיניה שם אשם לא מתכשר. דאמר קרא הוא בהווייתו יהא כו] [ה]. פסול הוא. פסולה. מהקטיר, ושיריה אין נאכלין. להתיר. חדש. אשם נזיר. נזיר טמא מביא אשם להכשיר למנין נזירות טהרה, כדכתיב: "והביא כבש בן שנתו לאשם והימים הראשונים יפלו" וגו' (במדבר ו). אשם

תוספות

חטאת קרייה רחמנא. לפי טעם זה לא היה צריך ללמוד בפ"ק דזבחים (דף ח:) כז] דשמיעת הקול במה הצד. ובמסקנא דשמעתין לא קאי, אלא יליף לה מדכתיב "הוא". מאי נפקא מינה הא תנא דבי רבי ישמעאל. ב"כיסוי הדם" (חולין ד' פה.). ופרק "המפלת" כח] (נדה דף כב:) משני: כט] מדדמי ליה ילפינן, לפי שהג"ש מכחישות זו את זו. אבל כאן ובהוריו' בס"פ "הורה כהן" (ד' ח:) דאפש' לדרוש – ל] דרשי' להו [ו] לתרוייהו. והיא דפ' "התכלת" (לקמן ד' מה: ושם) קשיא, גבי כבשים מעכבין את הלחם, לא] וגמר בן ננס "יהיו" מ"יהיו" ולא גמר "יהיו" מ"תהיינה", והתם מלינן למילף תרוייהו דלחם וכבשים מעכבין זה את זה. וכן בפ"ב דיבמות (דף יז:) לא מכחשי אהדדי, דמלי למילף דמן האב ולא מן האם או מן האם ולא מן האב מיקרי אחוה. ליגמר עונו מעונו דשמיעת הקול. אע"ג דשמיעת הקול גופא ילפינן במה הצד בפ"ק דזבחים (ד' ח:), ובעיא היא בפרק "איזהו מקומן" (זבחים דף נא.) אי דבר הלמד בבנין אב חוזר ומלמד בג"ש ולא איפשיטא, מכל מקום פריך שפיר, דלגמר "עונו" מ"עונו" דשמיעת הקול, או נפשט מהכא דבר הלמד בבנין אב אין חוזר ומלמד בג"ש. א) תימה: דבהוריות פרק "הורה כהן" (דף ח:) ב) יליף דלא מייתי אשם תלוי אלא על ספק חטאת קבועה בג"ש, דנאמר "אשם" באשם תלוי ונאמר "ואשמו" בצבור. ואדרבה, נילף "עונו" מ"עונו" דשמיעת הקול דעולה ויורד, דהא דבעי למימר [ז] דמותרה נדבה הוא דגמירי ג) לא קאי, ובפ"ק דשבועות (דף י.) אסכתנא דיליף שעיר דראש חדש לב] מ"עון" "עונו"! חטאת טעמא מאי דכתיב בה היא. בכמה דוכתי משמע דילפינן עיכובא בחטאת דכתיב בה "היא", כאן ובפרק קמא דזבחים (דף י:) בשני מקומות, לג] רבי אליעזר אומר: אף האשם. אמר לו רבי יהושע: חטאת נאמר בה "היא" בשחיטה כו' עד: התם חטאת טעמא מאי דכתיב בה "היא". ותימה, דהתם בההיא פירקא לד] (שם ז:) אמר: חוץ מן הפסח והחטאת לה] יליף מקראי אחריני! ותירץ ה"ר חיים: דחד לחטאת ששחטה לשם עולה, וחד לחטאת לו] ששחטה לשם חטאת נזיר ומצורע. וקשיא לפירושו: א"כ, מאי פריך לעיל דלשם חטאת נזיר ומצורע תהא כשירה ותרלה משום דכתיב "זאת תורת החטאת" תורה אחת לכל חטאות? ויש דוחקים, דהכא דריש "הוא" לעכב – היינו "הוא" דכתיב בשעיר נשיא, משום דקאמר בפ"ק דזבחים (דף ה.) [ח] אינן לז] כשירין למה הן באין, ואמרינן: מלינו בבאין לאחר מיתה שהם כשרין ואינם מרצין, דאשה שהביאה חטאתה ומתה יביאו יורשיה עולתה, ואשם נמי קרב למותרו. והשתא, אי לאו דכתיב "הוא" בשעיר נשיא הוה אמינא: חטאת נקבה, דהיא גופה לא קרבה מותרה אלא לדמים, כגון מפריש שתי חטאות לאחריות – הוא דפסל רחמנא שלא לשמה, אבל שעיר נשיא דהוי זכר והוא גופיה קרב עולה למותרו – ליתכשר שלא לשמו, כתב רחמנא "הוא". וכי תימא: לילפו שאר חטאות מיניה בקל וחומר שמא לא ילפינן יחיד מנשיא. ועוד י"ל: ד"הוא" דחטאת אתא לגלויי א"הוא" דאשם דלא מעכב כ"הוא" דפסח בפ"ק דזבחים (גם זה שם), ושמא אי לא כתב אלא בפסח – לא הוה דרשינן הכי. [ט] א"נ, האי ["הוא"] דחטאת אתא לגלויי אה"הוא" דמנחת חוטא ומנחת קנאות דמעכב כדדריש הכא. ד). לאחר הקטרת אימורים. והא דכתיב לח] "קודש קדשים הוא" דריש בת"כ: הוא קרב ואין תמורתו קריבה, ולמעט תודה ואיל נזיר דאינו נשחט בצפון. ופרק קמא דזבחים (גם זה שם) פירש בקונטרס דלא ילפינן מיניה, משום דלא משמע להו לשמו אלא כשכתב "הוא" עם שם לט] הקרבה, כגון "חטאת הוא" "אשם הוא". ואע"ג דכתב "אשם הוא אשם אשם [לה']" דריש בת"כ למעוטי אשם נזיר ואשם מצורע מכסף שקלים. והא דדריש בספרי בפרשת "זאת תהיה" גבי אשם מצורע: "כי כחטאת [י] כאשם הוא" – פרט לששחטה שלא לשמה, נראה דאסמכתא בעלמא הוא. אלא הוא למה לי לכדרב הונא. משמע ד"הוא" דכתב לאחר הקטרת אימורין קא דריש: "והקטיר אותם הכהן המזבחה אשה לה' אשם הוא" (ויקרא ז), ולא כספרים דגרסי בפרק "ואלו קדשים" (תמורה ד' יז:) במילתיה דרבי עקיבא: "אשם הוא אשם אשם [לה']" – הוא [כ] (הוא) קרב ואין תמורתו קריבה, דלבסוף מוקי ליה לכדרב הונא. ועוד דבת"כ דריש ליה למעוטי אשם נזיר ומצורע מכסף שקלים. אשם שניתק לרעייה ושחטו סתם כשר לעולה. הא תימה: אמאי כשר לעולה? הא אמרינן בתמורה בפרק "אלו קדשים" (גם זה שם דף יח.) דגמירי דכל שבחטאת מתה באשם רועה! וכי תימא: ה"מ לכתחילה, אבל בדיעבד כשר. אכתי הא דתניא בפסחים בסוף "אלו דברים" (דף עג.) ובפרק קמא דשבועות (דף יב.): אשם שמתו בעליו או שנתכפרו ג)

א) עיין רש"ק שהאריך בכוונת התוס' שלכאורה הוא קושיית הש"ס התם ע"ש: ב) המעיין שם יראה דרב שימי בר אשי הקשה קושיא זו לר"פ ומצאתי בבאר שבע דלא היה הגי' בהוריות לפניהם כך: ג) נ"א לה ור"ל אפילו למסקנא דשמעתין קאי: ד) וע' תוס' זבחים ה: ד"ה מיעט:

עין משפט נר מצוה

ז א מיי' פ"ה מהל' פסה"מ הל"ח:
ח ב מיי' פ"ד מהל' פסה"מ הל' טו:

התכלת מה: [לכאורה כך צ"ל משום דבפרק המפלת כב: לא משני כך ע"ש אמנם מדמקשו תוס' בדיבור זה ההיא דפרק התכלת קשה גבי כבשים וכו' א"כ ע"כ גם הגה"ה זו לא הועילו אלא צ"ל דצ"ל ובכמה דוכתי וכן כתבו בלשון זה ביומא ב: ע"ש בד"ה הג"מ וע' תוס' נדה כב: ד"ה זו היא]:

שיטה מקובצת

א] כלום הגענו. כלומר לא הגענו. הרגמ"ה: ב] משום. דקשיא וזאת: ג] ע' בהשמטות בסוף המסכת: חטאת קרייה רחמנא. וא"ת הלא בפ"ק דזבחים מצריך קראי לכל החטאות ולא נפיק חד מאידך משום דחטאת קרייה רחמנא וי"ל דלפי המסקנא ניחא דהאי מילתא דהכא אינה עומדת א"נ אף למאי דס"ד השתא לא קשיא מידי דבשלמא שאר חטאת ששמן חטאת לא ילפינן מהדדי אלא מנחה כו'. תום' אחרות: ד] מנחת קנאות מותרה נדבה. אם הפריש מעות למנחת קנאות ונשתיירו מהן לאחר שקנה המנחה אותו מותר יהא נדבה וניתנין לשופרות המיוחדין למעות נדבת צבור לקנות מהן עולות לקייץ המזבח. הרגמ"ה: ה] קאמרת. עון כתיב וזה כחטאת מה חטאת מותרה נדבה והשאר נמחק: ו] כי גמירי גזירה שוה למותר נדבה הוא דגמירי וכי תימא עיין תום' זבחים דף י ע"ב ד"ה הרי הוא אומר: ז] ושחט אותה לחטאת. עיין זבחים דף ז ע"ב: ח] ההוא לאחר הקטרת אימורין הוא דכתיב. והקשה רש"י בזבחים הא אשכחן הוא באשם שאינו לאחר הקטרת אימורין דכתיב בסוף פרשת ויקרא אשם הוא אשם אשם לה' גבי אשם תלוי וי"ל דאינו מיותר ואצטריך לדרשה כדפרש"י בחומש אשם לרבות אשם גזילות ואשם שפחה חרופה יכול שאני מרבה אשם נזיר ואשם מצורע ת"ל הוא וא"ת לגבי מאי מרבה להו וי"ל לגבי שתי שנים וקשה למה לי קרא לרבות אשם גזילות ואשם שפחה חרופה פשיטא דהא כתיב בהו איל ואיל בן שתי שנים וע"ק דמאי אצטריך למעט אשם נזיר ואשם מצורע משתי שנים פשיטא דהא כתיב בהו כבש בן שנתו לאשם וכבש הוא בן שנה לכך נראה דהא דמרבה והא דממעט היינו לענין כסף שקלים וא"ת אמאי חזית דמרבית אלו וממעט אלו וי"ל דאשם גזילות ואשם שפחה חרופה דמי ליה בשתי שנים מה שאין כן באשם נזיר ואשם מצורע שהן בני שנה א): ט] רב. דאמר רב הונא אמר רב אשם שניתק לרעייה. כגון שנתכפרו בעליו באחר ואח"כ נמצא ואמר הגזבר שיצא לרעייה עד שיסתאב משניתק לרעייה שגזרו עליו שירעוהו ושחטו לשם עולה כשר דלא הוי אשם אבל אם לא ניתק עדיין לרעייה ושחטו לשם ב) עולה פסול דאשם פסול הוי דאמר קרא הוא בהווייתו יהא אע"פ ששינה שמו בהווייתו יהא ואשם פסול הוא ומהאי טעמא אמר ושחטו לשם עולה דאשם כבש ועולה כבש ודוקא הכא דכתיב הוא הא שאר זבחים דלא כתיב בהו ג) הוא בין ניתק ובין לא ניתק כי שחטו לזבח אחר כשר. הרגמ"ה: י] ע' בהשמטות בסוף המסכת: יא] ע' בהשמטות בסוף המסכת: יב] מסתבר ליה: יג] דמנכרא. שהוא מכוב פסל רחמנא שלא יאמרו מותר לשנות בקרבנות: יד] עליה שמן ולא יתן עליה לבונה: טו] שלא לשמה. כדמפרש לקמן אף היא: טז] סוטה. והוזלו שעורים מותר מן המעות

המעות יפלו לנדבה וכל היכא דאמרי' בתלמוד יפלו לנדבה היינו לשלש: יז] אשם. הבשר לשם אל המזבח ועורות לכהנים: יח] מחטאת. דאפי' מנחת חוטא דקרייה רחמנא חטאת לא ילפינן לה מחטאת משום מעוטא דאותה: הס"ד ומה"ד דכתיב בה. היא בחטאת: יט] ולא. שנשחט שלא לשמו ואי קשיא תיפוק לי דחטאת פסולה שלא לשמה מושחט אותה לחטאת תריץ דההוא למצוה: כ] בשלא לשמו. ואי קשיא אשם נמי כתיב ביה הוא קודם שחיטה בצו את אהרן וזאת תורת האשם קדש קדשים הוא לאו פירכא היא דלא חש' אלא היכא דכתיב אשם הוא דמשמע ששחטו לשם אשם. כא] כתיב. הוא והקטרה לאו עיקר הוא וליכא למימר הוא אשם: כב] שלא לשמו. גליון נ"א בס' ישן כת"י אשם נאמר בו הוא אחר הקטרת אימורין בפרשת צו את אהרן והקטיר הכהן המזבחה אשה לה' אשם הוא וליכא למימר הוא אשם ולא שנקטרו אימוריו דהא הוא עצמו שלא הוקטרו אימוריו כשר כדאמר פ' תמיד נשחט: כג] בחטאת נשיא כתיב: כד] באחר. דגבי חטאת: כה] עליו. דנדבה דשופרות עולה: כו] יהא. ואשם פסול הוא: הס"ד ומה"ד פסולה מהקטיר קומצה ושיריה: כז] דזבחים חטאת דשמיעת: כח] ופ' המפלת. נ"ל ט"ס וע"ש בתוס' דף כב ע"ב ותוס' יומא דף ב ע"ב: כט] משני. ה"מ היכא דליכא דדמי ליה אבל איכא דדמי ליה מדדמי ליה ילפינן יש לומר דסמיך אקושיא דועוד א"נ י"ל דהיכא דאין סותרות זו את זו ילפינן אף לא דמי ליה: ל] לדרוש תרוייהו: לא] דגמר בן ננס: לב] מעון עין: לג] מקומות בגמרא דרבי: לד] בההיא פרקא. ד) עי' תוס' זבחים דף ה ע"ב: גמרא דחוץ מן: לה] עי' בהשמטות בסוף המסכת: לו] לחטאת חלב ששחטה: לז] אינן מרצין למה: לח] והא דכתיב וזאת תורת האשם קדש: לט] הקרבן כגון חטאת. גליון וא"ת הא כתיב זאת תורת האשם קדש קדשים הוא וי"ל דלא כתיב במקום עבודה ואז לא דרשינן מינה שום דבר. וקשה להר"ר שמואל מאיוורא דהא במנחת קנאות נמי לא כתיב הוא במקום עבודה ותירץ משה"ח דנהי דלא כתיב במקום עבודה מ"מ מיירי גבי קרבן דכתיב בההוא והביא את קרבנו וגו' וא"ת והא כתיב כי כחטאת האשם הוא וי"ל דלא דרשינן אלא

א) ועי' בכריתות דף י ע"ב. ב) משמע דגרים בגמ' ושחטו לשם עולה ולכאורה צ"ע דא"כ אפילו לא ניתק נמי דהא קיי"ל דאפי' אשם כשר אם שחטו שלא לשמו ואולי דלאחר שנתכפרו בעלים באחר כיון דפסול לשמו פסול נמי שלא לשמו אם לא ניתק. ג) [illegible] ד) נראה דצ"ל בההיא פרקא בגמ' דמן הפסח וכו'. ועי' תוס' זבחים דף ה ע"ב:

הגהות צ"ק [א] והוו השעורים הנותר מן המעות יפלו לנדבה: [ב] הוא כחטאת שעיר נשיא כתיב חטאת כו': [ג] נ"א ובקטיר: [ד] תיבה זו נמחק: [ה] ועדיין אשם הוא ולא חזי לאקרובי לאשם הלכך פסול הוא: [ו] דרשי' להו עי' ביומא דף ב ע"ב שקילו בע"א: [ז] למותר נדבה כו' דבפ"ק דשבועות כו' דר"ח עון עון והס"ד: [ח] צ"ל אם אינן מוליכים למה כו': [ט] ועוד יש לומר דהוא לחטאת כו': [י] לאשם: [כ] תיבה זו נמחק:

ו א מיי' פט"ו מה' פסה"מ הלכה ו:

א] וּמַאי זְבָחִים? רוֹב זְבָחִים. רָבָא אָמַר, ל"ק: כָּאן בְּקוֹמֵץ מִנְחָה ב] לְשׁוּם מִנְחָה, כָּאן בְּקוֹמֵץ מִנְחָה ג] לְשׁוּם זֶבַח. מִנְחָה לְשׁוּם מִנְחָה – °"וְזֹאת תּוֹרַת הַמִּנְחָה", *תּוֹרָה אַחַת לְכָל הַמְּנָחוֹת; מִנְחָה לְשׁוּם זֶבַח – "וְזֹאת תּוֹרַת הַמִּנְחָה וְזֶבַח" לָא כְּתִיב. וְהָא ד] תַּנָּא "מִפְּנֵי שֶׁמַּעֲשֶׂיהָ מוֹכִיחִין עָלֶיהָ" קָאָמַר! הָכִי קָאָמַר: אע"ג דְּמַחֲשָׁבָה דְּלָא מִינְכְּרָא הִיא וְתִיפָּסֵל – "וְזֹאת תּוֹרַת הַמִּנְחָה", תּוֹרָה אַחַת לְכָל הַמְּנָחוֹת. וּמַאי "אֲבָל בִּזְבָחִים אֵינוֹ כֵּן"? אע"ג דִּשְׁחִיטָה אַחַת לְכוּלָּן – ה] "וְזֹאת תּוֹרַת הַמִּנְחָה וְזֶבַח" לָא כְּתִיב. אֶלָּא מֵעַתָּה, ו] חַטַּאת חֵלֶב שֶׁשְּׁחָטָהּ לְשֵׁם חַטַּאת דָּם, לְשׁוּם חַטַּאת עֲבוֹדָה זָרָה, לְשׁוּם חַטַּאת נָזִיר, לְשׁוּם חַטַּאת מְצוֹרָע – תְּהֵא כְּשֵׁירָה וְתִרְצֶה, ז] דְּאָמַר רַחֲמָנָא: °"וְזֹאת תּוֹרַת הַחַטָּאת" – *תּוֹרָה אַחַת לְכָל חַטָּאוֹת! לר"ש [א] ה"נ; *לְרַבָּנַן, ח] הָא *אָמַר: [רָבָא] חַטַּאת חֵלֶב שֶׁשְּׁחָטָהּ לְשֵׁם חַטַּאת דָּם, לְשׁוּם חַטַּאת עֲבוֹדָה זָרָה – כְּשֵׁירָה, לְשֵׁם חַטַּאת נָזִיר, [לְשֵׁם חַטַּאת] מְצוֹרָע – פְּסוּלָה, ט] א) דְּהָנֵי עוֹלוֹת בַּהֲדַיְיהוּ נִינְהוּ. רַב *אַחָא בְּרֵיהּ דְּרָבָא מַתְנֵי לֵיהּ לְכוּלְּהוּ אלִפְסוּלָא: "וְשָׁחַט אוֹתָהּ לְחַטָּאת" – לְשֵׁם אוֹתוֹ חַטָּאת. רַב אַשִׁי אָמַר, ל"ק: כָּאן בְּקוֹמֵץ (מִנְחַת) מַחֲבַת לְשׁוּם מַרְחֶשֶׁת, כָּאן בְּקוֹמֵץ מִנְחַת מַחֲבַת לְשׁוּם מִנְחַת מַרְחֶשֶׁת. (מִנְחַת) מַחֲבַת לְשׁוּם מַרְחֶשֶׁת – י] °בְּמָנָא קָא מְחַשֵּׁב, וּמַחֲשָׁבָה בְּמָנָא לָא פָּסְלָה; מִנְחַת מַחֲבַת לְשׁוּם מִנְחַת מַרְחֶשֶׁת – יא] בְּמִנְחָה דְּפָסְלָה בָּהּ מַחֲשָׁבָה קָא מְחַשֵּׁב. וְהָא תַּנָּא "מִפְּנֵי שֶׁמַּעֲשֶׂיהָ מוֹכִיחִין עָלֶיהָ" קָאָמַר! הָכִי קָאָמַר: אע"ג ב) דְּמַחֲשָׁבָה יב] מִינְכַּר הִיא תִּיפָּסֵל. וּמַאי "אֲבָל בִּזְבָחִים אֵינוֹ כֵּן"? אע"ג דִּשְׁחִיטָה אַחַת לְכוּלָּן, יג] זְרִיקָה אַחַת לְכוּלָּן, קַבָּלָה אַחַת לְכוּלָּן – בִּזְבִיחָה דְּפָסְלָה בֵּיהּ מַחֲשָׁבָה קָא מְחַשֵּׁב. א"ל רַב אַחָא בְּרֵיהּ דְּרָבָא לְרַב אַשִׁי: חֲרֵבָה מִשּׁוּם בְּלוּלָה אַמַּאי אָמַר ר"ש? א"ל: לְשׁוּם יד] בִּילָּה בְּעָלְמָא. אִי הָכִי, לְשׁוּם שְׁלָמִים נַמִי – לְשׁוּם שְׁלָמִים בְּעָלְמָא! הָכִי הַשְׁתָּא? הָתָם זֶבַח גּוּפֵהּ אִיקְּרֵי שְׁלָמִים, דִּכְתִיב: °"הַמַּקְרִיב אֶת דַּם הַשְּׁלָמִים" "הַזּוֹרֵק אֶת דַּם הַשְּׁלָמִים", הָכָא מִנְחָה גּוּפָהּ מִי אִיקְּרֵי בְּלוּלָה? °"וְכָל מִנְחָה בְּלוּלָה בַשֶּׁמֶן" כְּתִיב, "בְּלוּלָה בַשֶּׁמֶן" אִיקְּרֵי, "בְּלוּלָה" סְתָמָא לָא אִיקְּרֵי. כּוּלְּהוּ כְּרַבָּה לָא אָמְרִי – דְּאַדְּרַבָּה, מַחֲשָׁבָה דְּמִנְכְּרָא פָּסַל רַחֲמָנָא; כְּרָבָא לָא אָמְרִי – "וְזֹאת תּוֹרַת" לָא מַשְׁמַע לְהוּ; כְּרַב אַשִׁי לָא אָמְרִי – מִשּׁוּם קוּשְׁיָא דְּרַב אַחָא בְּרֵיהּ דְּרָבָא. מִילְּתָא דִּפְשִׁיטָא לֵיהּ לְרַבָּה לְהַאי גִּיסָא וּלְרָבָא לְהַאי גִּיסָא, מִיבַּעְיָא לֵיהּ לְרַב הוֹשַׁעְיָא; דְּבָעֵי רַב הוֹשַׁעְיָא, וְאָמְרִי לַהּ בְּעָא מִינֵּיהּ רַב הוֹשַׁעְיָא מֵרַבִּי אַסִי: מִנְחָה לְשׁוּם זֶבַח מַה

תורה אור: ויקרא ו; ויקרא ו; ויקרא ז; שם. [זבחים ט:] [זבחים ט:] [זבחים ט:]

א) לפרש"י ולפי' א' הגי' הכא משום דאיכא שוטות וכס"י הגי' עולות נינהו ב) נ"א דמחשבה דלא מינכר תיפסול

מִנְחָה לְשֵׁם מִנְחָה. מַחֲבַת לְשֵׁם מַרְחֶשֶׁת, עָלוּ. וְהָא תַּנָּא טו] מַעֲשֶׂיהָ מוֹכִיחִין עָלֶיהָ קָאָמַר. הִילְכָּךְ מִנְחָה לְשֵׁם זֶבַח נַמִי לִיתַּכְשַׁר! ה"ק. אע"פ שֶׁאֵין הַמְּנָחוֹת דּוֹמוֹת לִזְבָחִים, דְּאע"ג דְּהַקּוֹמֵץ מַחֲבַת לְשֵׁם מַרְחֶשֶׁת – מַחֲשָׁבָה דְּלָא מִינְכְּרָא טז] שֶׁיִּהְיֶה כֵּן הִיא, אֶלָּא וַדַּאי נִיכָּר שֶׁאֵינוֹ כֵּן, דְּהָא מַעֲשֶׂיהָ מוֹכִיחִים אִיכָּא לְמֵימַר דְּתִיפָּסֵל, דְּוַדַּאי סְבִירָא לָן מַחֲשָׁבָה הַגְּלוּיָה לַכֹּל שֶׁהוּא מְכַזֵּב כָּל שֶׁכֵּן שֶׁהִיא פְּסוּלָה – אֲפִילּוּ הָכִי עָלוּ, דִּכְתִיב "זֹאת תּוֹרַת הַמִּנְחָה". יז] הָא "לָא מִינְכְּרָא" לָא דָּמֵי לְהַהוּא דִּלְעֵיל. רָבָא וְרַב אַשִׁי סְבִירָא לְהוּ דְּמַחֲשָׁבָה הַגְּלוּיָה לַכֹּל שֶׁהוּא מְכַזֵּב כָּל שֶׁכֵּן שֶׁפּוֹסֶלֶת, וְהָכִי מְתָרְצֵי לְקַמָּן: אַדְּרַבָּה, מַחֲשָׁבָה דְּמִינְכְּרָא שֶׁהִיא שֶׁקֶר פָּסַל רַחֲמָנָא, שֶׁמָּא יֹאמְרוּ מוּתָּר לְשַׁנּוֹת בְּקָרְבָּנוֹת. וּמַאי אֲבָל בִּזְבָחִים אֵינוֹ כֵּן יח]. דְּמַשְׁמַע: הָתָם דִּין הוּא דְּלָא עָלוּ, מִשּׁוּם דִּשְׁחִיטָה אַחַת לְכוּלָּן? הָא כָּל שֶׁכֵּן דְּדִין הוּא דְּעָלוּ, יט] בְּמַחֲשָׁבָה דְּלָא מִינְכַּר שֶׁהוּא [ב] שֶׁקֶר הִיא! כ] דְּהָא שְׁחִיטָה אַחַת לְכוּלָּן. וְאִיכָּא לְמֵימַר דְּתַעֲלֶה לְשֵׁם תּוֹדָה, דְּהָא לֵיכָּא לְמִיגְזַר שֶׁמָּא יֹאמְרוּ מוּתָּר לְשַׁנּוֹת בִּזְבָחִים – אֲפִילּוּ הָכִי לָא עָלוּ, דְּ"זֹאת תּוֹרַת הַמִּנְחָה וְזֶבַח" לָא כְּתִיב, דְּלֶיהֱוֵי מַשְׁמַע: תּוֹרָה אַחַת לְכָל הַמְּנָחוֹת וְתוֹרָה אַחַת לְכָל הַזְּבָחִים. וְתִרְצֶה. לְשֵׁם תּוֹדָה! אַלְּמָה תְּנַן בִּזְבָחִים (דף ב.): חוּץ מִן הַפֶּסַח וּמִן הַחַטָּאת? (לְרַבָּנַן. דְּלֵית לְהוּ "זֹאת תּוֹרַת") כא]. הָא אָמַר רָבָא חַטַּאת חֵלֶב כו' כְּשֵׁירָה כב] [ג]. וְלָא עָקַר מִינָּהּ שֵׁם חַטָּאת *)(וְלֹא) עָלְתָה לַבְּעָלִים. עוֹלוֹת כג] בַּהֲדַיְיהוּ נִינְהוּ. וְאִיכָּא לְמֵימַר (שֶׁלֹּא יֹאמְרוּ) לְשֵׁם עוֹלַת נָזִיר שָׁחַט, וְנִמְצֵאת חַטָּאת שֶׁלֹּא לִשְׁמָהּ כְּשֵׁירָה לְהַקְרִיב. ל"א: עוֹלוֹת נִינְהוּ – וְאֵין בָּאִין עַל חֵטְא אֶלָּא [ד] לְהַכְשִׁיר, וְלָא חֲשִׁיבֵי כְּמוֹ כְּחַטָּאוֹת. וְיֵשׁ דִּמְפָרְשִׁים: עוֹלוֹת נִינְהוּ – שֶׁטְּעוּנִים נְסָכִים כְּעוֹלָה, מַה שֶּׁאֵין כֵּן בִּשְׁאָר חַטָּאוֹת. וְלָא עִיקָּר הוּא כד], תֵּינַח חַטַּאת מְצוֹרָע כְּדְאָמְרִי' בְּפֶרֶק "שְׁתֵּי מִדּוֹת" (לקמן דף צ:) דִּטְעוּנָה נְסָכִים, אֲבָל חַטַּאת נָזִיר לָא טְעוּנָה נְסָכִים! מַתְנֵי לְהוּ כּוּלְּהוּ לִפְסוּלָא. אֲפִילּוּ חַטַּאת חֵלֶב שֶׁשְּׁחַט לְשֵׁם חַטַּאת דָּם פְּסוּלָה מִלְּהַקְרִיב. ל"ק. דְּר' שִׁמְעוֹן אַדְּר"ש. הָכִי גָּרְסִינַן: מַחֲבַת לְשֵׁם מַרְחֶשֶׁת כה]. וְהָא תַּנָּא כו'. וַאֲפִי' מִנְחַת מַחֲבַת לְשֵׁם מִנְחַת מַרְחֶשֶׁת נַמִי תְּהֵא עוֹלָה לְשֵׁם חוֹבָה, דְּהָא מַעֲשֶׂיהָ מוֹכִיחִין! הָכִי קָאָמַר. כְּלוֹמַר, דְּהָא כו] מַעֲשֶׂיהָ מוֹכִיחִין גְּרִיעוּתָא הִיא, דְּמַחֲשָׁבָה דְּמִינְכְּרָא שֶׁהִיא שֶׁקֶר פָּסַל רַחֲמָנָא, שֶׁמָּא יֹאמְרוּ מוּתָּר לְשַׁנּוֹת. וְהָכִי קָאָמְרִינַן: כז] אע"פ שֶׁהַמִּנְחָה אֵינָהּ דּוֹמָה לִזְבָחִים, דְּבְמִנְחָה אע"ג דְּמַעֲשֶׂיהָ מוֹכִיחִין, וְאִיכָּא לְמֵימַר כח] דְּמִיפַּסְלָא בְּמַחֲשָׁבָה דְּלָא מִינְכְּרָא כְּמוֹת שֶׁהוּא אוֹמֵר הִיא, אֶלָּא וַדַּאי נִיכָּר שֶׁאֵינוֹ כָּךְ – אֲפִילּוּ הָכִי כְּשֵׁירָה הֵיכָא דְּלָא אִידְכַּר שֵׁם מִנְחָה. וּמַאי אֲבָל כו' כִּדְפָרְשִׁינַן לְעֵיל לְטַעְמָא דְּרָבָא. חֲרֵבָה לְשֵׁם בְּלוּלָה. דְּקָתָנֵי דְּעָלוּ. אַמַּאי אָמַר ר"ש. כְּלוֹמַר, מַאי טַעְמָא כט] עָלוּ? [ה] הָא וַדַּאי מַחֲשָׁבָה, דְּהָא לֵיכָּא הָכָא מָנָא! לְשֵׁם בִּילָּה בְּעָלְמָא. כֵּיוָן דְּלָא אִידְכַּר בְּהֶדְיָא מִנְחַת חֲרֵיבָה לְשֵׁם מִנְחַת בְּלוּלָה – דִּבְרֵי רוּחַ בְּעָלְמָא נִינְהוּ, כְּמ"ד "הֲרֵינִי קוֹמֵץ ל] לְשֵׁם ד"א (בָּלוּל)". אִי הָכִי בִּזְבָחִים. דְּמוֹדֶה ר"ש דְּלָא עָלוּ, אַמַּאי מוֹדֶה? כִּי שָׁחֵיט עוֹלָה לְשֵׁם שְׁלָמִים תַּעֲלֶה לְשֵׁם חוֹבָה, דְּהָכִי קָאָמַר: לא] חוֹבָה זוֹ אֲנִי שׁוֹחֵט לְשֵׁם לַעֲשׂוֹת שָׁלוֹם בֵּין קוֹנִי לְבֵינִי! אַדְּרַבָּה מַחֲשָׁבָה דְּמִינְכְּרָא שֶׁהוּא מְכַזֵּב פָּסַל רַחֲמָנָא. שֶׁלֹּא יֹאמְרוּ: מוּתָּר לְשַׁנּוֹת וְלַעֲבוֹר עַל לב] עֲבוֹדַת קָרְבָּנוֹ. וְזֹאת תּוֹרַת לָא מַשְׁמַע לְהוּ. דְּקַשְׁיָא לְהוּ "זֹאת תּוֹרַת הַחַטָּאת" [illegible] דְּרַב אַחָא. [illegible] פְּסָלָה לג] לָהּ, וְלָא הַגְּלוּיָה. וּלְרָבָא לְהַאי גִּיסָא. דְּמַחֲשָׁבָה הַגְּלוּיָה כָּל שֶׁכֵּן דִּפְסוּלָה. [illegible] מִנְחָה לְשֵׁם זֶבַח. מִיבַּעְיָא לְרַבִּי אוֹשַׁעְיָא. **)קוּשְׁיָא. [illegible] מה

*) כצ"ל מותק תיבת ולא **) שייך לדף ז

כאן בקומץ מנחה לשם זבח. בהנס נקט רבא ענין זה, דלא איירי ביה בשום דוכתא. דתירוץ זה עצמו שמחלק משום דכתיב "זאת תורת המנחה" היה יכול לתרץ כמו שתירץ רבה: כאן בשינוי קודש כאן בשינוי בעלים, בשינוי קודש כשר משום דתורה אחת לכל המנחות. ושמא לפיכך שינה לשונו של רבה, דהוה משמע אם היה אומר: כאן בשינוי קודש – דשינוי קודש כשר אפי' במנחה לשם זבח. ועוד יש לומר: דדייק לישנא דברייתא, דמשמע ליה "קמלה שלא לשמה פסולה" בשינוי קודש. ולקמן דקאמר: כולהו כרבה לא אמרי, ולא מפרש לה] טעמא זה [ו] – ניחא לו למימר טעם השוה לכל האמוראים.

אע"ג דמחשבה דלא מינכרא היא ותיפסל. הרבה יש לתמוה: למה שינה לשונו מלישנא דלעיל בריש שמעתא, דמה שקורא לעיל "מינכרא" קורא הכא לו] "לא מינכרא", וחד פירושא לתרוייהו, ד"מינכרא" – היינו שניכר שמחשבתו שקר, ו"לא מינכרא" דהכא – היינו דאין ניכר שיהא כמו שהוא מחשב, אלא אדרבה ניכר שאינו כמו שהוא מחשב! ושמא שינה הלשון לפי שהוא כמו נתינת טעם דתיפסל, לפיכך ניחא ליה למינקט הכא ולעיל על פסול לשון "לא מינכרא". ובסוף שמעתא דקאמר: כולהו כרבה לא אמרי, אדרבה מחשבה דמינכרא פסל רחמנא. משום דקאי ארבה נקט לשון "מינכרא" על פסול. **לר"ש** ה"נ. משמע דרבנן לא דרשי "זאת תורת החטאת". אע"ג לז] דבפ' "דם חטאת" (זבחים ד' צג.) גבי דם חטאת שניתז על הבגד טעון כיבוס, דרשינן: תורה אחת לכל החטאות, וליכא מאן דפליג, במידי דכתיבא בחטאת גופיה דרשי ליה לח] כ"ע, כגון הני דפרק "דם חטאת", אבל שינוי קודש לא כתיב בחטאת. ועוד, דכיבוס בגדים כתיב בההיא פרשתא ד"זאת התורה". וא"ת: דהת"ק דזבחים (ד' ט:) אמר רב משמיה דמבוג: חטאת ששחטה לשם חטאת נחשון כשירה, דתורה אחת לכל החטאות. ופריך רב משרשיא לרבא מברייתא דר"ש, טעמא דמעשיה מוכיחין עליה, הא אין מעשיה מוכיחין עליה – לא, לימא "זאת תורת המנחה"! ומאי קושיא? הא רבא הוא דמפרש הכא טעמא דר"ש מ"זאת תורת"! ואומר ר"ת: דהתם גרים "רבה", ורבה לטעמיה דמשני לעיל: כאן בשינוי קודש כאן בשינוי בעלים. ועוד י"ל: דאפילו גרים התם "רבא" רוצה ליישב דברי רב ככולהו אמוראי דהכא. ולפר"ת קשיא, דנראה דרב משרשיא תלמידו של רבא היה, ולא של רבה! ועוד יש לומר: שרוצה רבא ליישב שם דברי רב משמיה דמבוג אפילו כרבנן דפליגי עליה דר"ש, דלית להו "זאת תורת". ורב משרשיא, כשהקשה לו מר"ש – היה יכול להקשותו ממתני', אלא ניחא ליה לט] לאקשויי מברייתא, דאפילו ר' שמעון דמכשר – לאו מ"זאת תורת" מכשר. וכן משמע שם פירוש הקונטרס. **לשם** חטאת דם לשם חטאת עבודה זרה כשירה. הך מילתא איתא בפ"ק דזבחים (ג"ז שם) בשמעתא דמבוג. ובלאו קרא ד"זאת תורת" מכשר חטאת לשם חטאת, כדקאמר התם רבא [ז] (לעיל) אידך מילתא ד"ושחט אותה לחטאת" אמר רחמנא, והרי חטא' לשם חטאת נשחטה, אבל לשם עולה ודאי פסולה. והוא הדין לשם חטאת נזיר ומצורע, דכעולות דמו כיון דאין באין על חטא. ואע"ג דר"ש הוא דאמר דחטאת נזיר באה לפי שציער עצמו מן היין – אין זה על חטא, כיון [ח] דלצער יין לא מייתי חטאת, אלא דרך נזירות. ועוד דמשום חטא זוטרא כי האי לא מיקרי חטאת. **כאן** בקומץ מחבת לשם מרחשת גרסינן. [illegible]

שיטה מקובצת

[illegible]

גליון הש"ס

גמ' [illegible]

שיטה מקובצת

[illegible]

*) נראה דצ"ל ל"א עולות נינהו לאין באין על חטא וכו'. **) נראה דצ"ל לר' אושעיא [illegible]

הגהות צ"ק [illegible]

אָמְרִי: דִּילְמָא מִיצּוּי דְּבָתַר הַזָּאָה הוּא, דְּאָמַר מָר: מִיצָּה דָּמָהּ בְּכָל מָקוֹם בַּמִּזְבֵּחַ – כְּשֵׁירָה. חַטַּאת הָעוֹף שֶׁהִזָּה דָּמָהּ לְמַטָּה לְשֵׁם עוֹלַת הָעוֹף תֵּרָצֶה; דְּמַעֲשֶׂיהָ מוֹכִיחִין עָלֶיהָ דְּחַטַּאת עוֹף הִיא, דְּאִי עוֹלַת הָעוֹף הִיא – לְמַעְלָה הֲוָה עָבֵיד לָהּ, וּמִיצּוּי הֲוָה עָבֵיד לֵיהּ! ה"נ, *אֶלָּא "לְפִי שֶׁאֵין הַמְּנָחוֹת דּוֹמוֹת לִזְבָחִים" קָאָמַר – לִזְבָחִים, וְלֹא לְעוֹפוֹת.§ קָדְשֵׁי קָדָשִׁים שֶׁשְּׁחָטָן בַּצָּפוֹן לְשֵׁם קָדָשִׁים קַלִּים לֵירָצוּ; מַעֲשֵׂיהֶן מוֹכִיחִין עֲלֵיהֶן דְּקָדְשֵׁי קָדָשִׁים נִינְהוּ, דְּאִי קָדָשִׁים קַלִּים – בַּדָּרוֹם הֲוָה עָבֵיד לְהוּ! אֵימוּר דְּאָמַר רַחֲמָנָא – אַף בַּדָּרוֹם, בַּדָּרוֹם וְלֹא בַצָּפוֹן מִי אָמַר? *דִּתְנַן: אשְׁחִיטָתָן בְּכָל מָקוֹם בָּעֲזָרָה. קָדָשִׁים קַלִּים שֶׁשְּׁחָטָן בַּדָּרוֹם לְשֵׁם קָדְשֵׁי קָדָשִׁים לֵירָצוּ; מַעֲשֵׂיהֶן מוֹכִיחִין עֲלֵיהֶן דְּקָדָשִׁים קַלִּים נִינְהוּ, דְּאִי קָדְשֵׁי קָדָשִׁים – בַּצָּפוֹן הֲוָה עָבֵיד לְהוּ! אָמְרִי: קָדְשֵׁי קָדָשִׁים נִינְהוּ, וּמִיעֲבַר הוּא דַּעֲבַר וְשָׁחַט לְהוּ בַּדָּרוֹם. א] אִי הָכִי, מַחֲבַת לְשֵׁם מַרְחֶשֶׁת נַמִי, *הַאי דְּקָא קָמֵיץ לָהּ לְמַרְחֶשֶׁת – אָמַר: הַאי בְּמַרְחֶשֶׁת נָדַר, וְהָא דְּמַיְיתֵי לָהּ בְּמַחֲבַת – דְּמַרְחֶשֶׁת הִיא, וּמִעֲבַר הוּא דַּעֲבַר וְאַתְיָיהּ בְּמַחֲבַת! הָתָם כִּי נַמִי בְּמַרְחֶשֶׁת נָדַר, כִּי מַיְיתֵי לָהּ בְּמַחֲבַת מַחֲבַת הָוְיָא, כִּדְתְנַן: *בהָאוֹמֵר "הֲרֵי עָלַי בְּמַחֲבַת" וְהֵבִיא בְּמַרְחֶשֶׁת, "בְּמַרְחֶשֶׁת" וְהֵבִיא בְּמַחֲבַת – מַה שֶּׁהֵבִיא הֵבִיא וִידֵי נִדְרוֹ לֹא יָצָא. וְדִילְמָא ב] אָמַר "זוֹ לְהָבִיא בְּמַחֲבַת" וְהֵבִיא בְּמַרְחֶשֶׁת, כִּדְתְנַן: "זוֹ גלְהָבִיא בְּמַחֲבַת" וְהֵבִיא בְּמַרְחֶשֶׁת, "בְּמַרְחֶשֶׁת" וְהֵבִיא בְּמַחֲבַת – הֲרֵי זוֹ פְּסוּלָה! לְרַבָּנַן ה"נ; לר"ש, כֵּיוָן דְּאָמַר ר"ש: אַף יְדֵי נִדְרוֹ יָצָא, אַלְמָא קְבִיעוּתָא דְּמָנָא לָאו כְּלוּם הוּא, וְלָא שְׁנָא אֲמַר "זוֹ" וְלָא שְׁנָא אֲמַר "עָלַי". ג] אֶלָּא מֵעַתָּה, עוֹלָה שֶׁשְּׁחָטָהּ לְשֵׁם חַטָּאת תֵּרָצֶה, ד] דְּהַאי זָכָר וְהַאי נְקֵבָה! *כֵּיוָן דְּאִיכָּא שְׂעִיר נָשִׂיא דְּזָכָר הוּא, לָא יָדִיעַ. אָמַר "לְשֵׁם חַטַּאת יָחִיד" מַאי אִיכָּא לְמֵימַר? וְתוּ, חַטַּאת יָחִיד שֶׁשְּׁחָטָהּ לְשֵׁם עוֹלָה תֵּרָצֶה, דְּחַטָּאת נְקֵבָה וְעוֹלָה זָכָר! מִיכַּסְיָא בְּאַלְיָה. הָתֵינַח הֵיכָא דְּאַיְיתֵי כִּבְשָׂה, אַיְיתֵי שְׂעִירָה מַאי אִיכָּא לְמֵימַר? אֶלָּא, *בֵּין זְכָרִים לִנְקֵבוֹת לָאו אַדַּעְתַּיְיהוּ דֶּאֱינָשֵׁי. ה] פֶּסַח שֶׁשְּׁחָטוֹ לְשֵׁם אָשָׁם לֵירָצֵי, דְּהַאי בֶּן שָׁנָה וְהַאי בֶּן שְׁתַּיִם! כֵּיוָן דְּאִיכָּא אֲשַׁם נָזִיר וַאֲשַׁם מְצוֹרָע, לָא פְּסִיקָא לֵיהּ. אֲמַר "לְשׁוּם אֲשַׁם גְּזֵילוֹת וּלְשׁוּם אֲשַׁם מְעִילוֹת", מַאי אִיכָּא לְמֵימַר? וְתוּ, אֲשַׁם גְּזֵילוֹת וַאֲשַׁם מְעִילוֹת שֶׁשְּׁחָטָן לְשׁוּם פֶּסַח לֵירָצוּ, דְּפֶסַח בֶּן שָׁנָה וְהָנֵי בֶּן שְׁתֵּי שָׁנִים! אֶלָּא, בֵּין בֶּן שָׁנָה לְבֵין בֶּן שְׁתֵּי שָׁנִים לָאו אַדַּעְתַּיְיהוּ דֶּאֱינָשֵׁי, דְּאִיכָּא *בֶּן שָׁנָה דְּמִיחֲזֵי כְּבֶן שְׁתַּיִם, וְאִיכָּא בֶּן שְׁתַּיִם דְּמִיחֲזֵי כְּבֶן שָׁנָה. שָׂעִיר שֶׁשְּׁחָטוֹ לְשׁוּם אָשָׁם לֵירָצֵי, דְּהַאי ו] צֶמֶר וְהַאי שֵׂיעָר! אָמְרִי: דִּיכְרָא אוּכָּמָא הוּא. עֵגֶל וּפָר שֶׁשְּׁחָטָן לְשׁוּם פֶּסַח וְאָשָׁם לֵירָצוּ, דְּעֵגֶל וּפָר בְּפֶסַח וְאָשָׁם לֵיכָּא! אִין הָכִי נַמִי, וּמַאי

רש"י

אָמְרִי. אֱינָשֵׁי: וַדַּאי חַטָּאת הִיא, וְהַךְ מִילּוּי דְּבָתַר הַזָּאָה הוּא. וְהַאי דְּקָעָבֵיד לָהּ לְמַעְלָה – הָא קָאָמַר וכו'. הָכִי נַמִי. דְּוַדַּאי מוֹדֶה ר"ש בָּהּ דִּכְשֵׁירָה. וְלֹא לְעוֹפוֹת. דְּוַדַּאי לְעוֹפוֹת דּוֹמִין, דְּעוֹפוֹת עָלוּ לְשֵׁם חוֹבָה, כְּגוֹן חַטַּאת הָעוֹף שֶׁהִזָּה דָּמָהּ לְמַטָּה לְשֵׁם עוֹלַת הָעוֹף. אֵימַר דְּאָמַר רַחֲמָנָא אַף בַּדָּרוֹם. דְּלָא קָבַע לְהוּ צָפוֹן כִּדְקָבַע לְחַטָּאת וְאָשָׁם וְעוֹלָה, דִּכְתִיב בְּעוֹלָה: "עַל יֶרֶךְ הַמִּזְבֵּחַ צָפוֹנָה" (ויקרא א), וּכְתִיב בְּחַטָּאת: "בִּמְקוֹם אֲשֶׁר תִּשָּׁחֵט הָעוֹלָה תִּשָּׁחֵט הַחַטָּאת" (שם ו), וְכֵן בְּאָשָׁם ז]. *וְהָא דְּקָא קָמֵיץ לָהּ בְּמַרְחֶשֶׁת. כְּלוֹמַר, לְשֵׁם מַרְחֶשֶׁת. מַחֲבַת הָוְיָא. וּמֵידַע יָדְעֵי דְּמַכְזֵב. הָכִי גָּרְסִינַן: וְדִילְמָא זוֹ אָמַר. כְּלוֹמַר, אַכַּתִּי לָא מִינְכְּרָא, דְּסָבְרִי: קוּשְׁטָא קָאָמַר דִּלְשׁוּם מַרְחֶשֶׁת נָדַר, וּמִיעֲבַר עָבַר וְאַתְיֵיהּ בְּמַחֲבַת. וּדְקָא אָמְרַתְּ: כֵּיוָן דְּאַתְיֵיהּ בְּמַחֲבַת מַחֲבַת הָוְיָא – אִיכָּא לְמֵימַר: לָא הִיא, דְּדִילְמָא "מִנְחָה זוֹ אָבִיא בְּמַרְחֶשֶׁת" אָמַר, דְּתוּ לָא מָצֵי לְשַׁנּוּיֵיהּ לְמַחֲבַת. ח] לְרַבָּנַן. דְּאָמְרִי: ט] ה"ז פְּסוּלָה, הָכִי נַמִי דְּאִיכָּא לְמֵימַר וּלְמִיפְרַךְ הָכִי. וַאֲנַן *כְּרַבִּי שִׁמְעוֹן קָמַיְירֵי, ור"ש אוֹמֵר הָתָם: הָאוֹמֵר "הֲרֵי עָלַי בְּמַחֲבַת" וְהֵבִיא בְּמַרְחֶשֶׁת – אַף יְדֵי נִדְרוֹ יָצָא, אַלְמָא קְבִיעוּתָא דְּמָנָא לָאו כְּלוּם הִיא. לָא שְׁנָא אָמַר עָלַי וְלָא שְׁנָא אָמַר ה"ז. הִילְכָּךְ, כִּי אַתְיֵיהּ בְּמַחֲבַת – מַחֲבַת הָוְיָא, וְכִי קָמַץ לָהּ לְשׁוּם מַרְחֶשֶׁת – מַחֲשָׁבָה דְּמִינְכְּרָא הָוְיָא. אֲבָל גַּבֵּי זְבָחִים אִיכָּא לְמֵימַר: מִיעֲבַר עָבַר וְשַׁחְטִינְהוּ בַּדָּרוֹם. וְאִי קַשְׁיָא: גַּבֵּי חַטַּאת הָעוֹף לִישַׁנֵּי לֵיהּ הָכִי, דְּסָבְרִי עוֹלַת הָעוֹף הוּא וּמִיעֲבַר עָבַר! הָא לֵיכָּא לְמִיפְרַךְ, דִּתְרֵי אִיסּוּרֵי לָא מַחְזְקִינַן לֵיהּ, חֲדָא – דְּעָבֵיד לֵיהּ הַזָּאָה, וְעוֹד – דְּקָא עָבֵיד לֵיהּ לְמַטָּה. עוֹלָה זָכָר, וְחַטָּאת נְקֵבָה. אָמַר הֲרֵינִי שׁוֹחֲטָהּ לְשֵׁם יָחִיד מַאי אִיכָּא לְמֵימַר. הָא וַדַּאי יָדְעִינַן דְּחַטַּאת יָחִיד נְקֵבָה הִיא, כִּשְׂבָּה אוֹ שְׂעִירָה! וְתוּ דְּחַטַּאת יָחִיד. נְקֵבָה הִיא, וְהֵבִיא נְקֵבָה לָעֲזָרָה וּשְׁחָטָהּ לְשֵׁם עוֹלָה, מַאי אִיכָּא לְמֵימַר? מִיכַּסְיָא. נְקֵבוֹת דְּרָחֵל בְּאַלְיָה בִּזְנָבָהּ, וְלָא יְדִיעָה. שְׂעִירָה. דְּאֵין לָהּ זָנָב, מַאי אִיכָּא לְמֵימַר? אֲשַׁם גְּזֵילוֹת. דִּכְתִיב בְּ"וַיִּקְרָא": "וְהֵשִׁיב אֶת הַגְּזֵילָה אֲשֶׁר גָּזָל וגו' וְאֶת אֲשָׁמוֹ יָבִיא" וגו' (ויקרא ה), וַאֲשַׁם י] מְעִילוֹת – בְּנֵי ב' שָׁנִים נִינְהוּ, דִּכְתִיב בְּהוּ "אַיִל" (שם). אֲשַׁם נָזִיר וּמְצוֹרָע. כְּתִיב בְּהוּ "כֶּבֶשׂ", וְכָל כֶּבֶשׂ בֶּן שָׁנָה הוּא יא] בְּמַסֶּכֶת פָּרָה (פ"א מ"ג). וְתוּ אֲשַׁם גְּזֵילוֹת וּמְעִילוֹת. דְּאִיתְנְהוּ בְּדִינַיְיהוּ בְּנֵי ב' שָׁנִים, וּשְׁחָטָן לְשֵׁם פֶּסַח לֵירָצוּ! אָשָׁם אֵינוֹ בָּא אֶלָּא מִן הַכְּבָשִׂים יב]. דְּהַאי צֶמֶר. אֲשַׁם כְּבָשִׂים יֵשׁ יג] לוֹ צֶמֶר, וְשָׂעִיר אֵין לוֹ צֶמֶר אֶלָּא שֵׂיעָר בְּעָלְמָא, וְדָבָר גָּלוּי לַכֹּל הוּא. אָמְרִי דִּיכְרָא אוּכָּמָא הוּא. סָבְרִי: אַיִל שָׁחוֹר הוּא. וּלְהָכִי נָקַט אוּכָּמָא, דְּסְתָם שְׂעִירִים שְׁחוֹרִים הֵן. עֵגֶל וּפָר. חַטָּאת, כְּגוֹן פַּר כֹּהֵן מָשִׁיחַ שֶׁשְּׁחָטוֹ לְשֵׁם פֶּסַח וְאָשָׁם, שֶׁאֵין בָּאִין אֶלָּא מִן הַצֹּאן לֵירָצוּ. מִנְחָה

תוספות

מיצה דמה בכל מקום במזבח כשירה. אע"ג דכתיב בה יסוד, כדכתיב (ויקרא ה): "ימלה אל יסוד המזבח", האמרינן בפרק "חטאת העוף" (זבחים דף סה: ושם) דמילוי לא מעכב אפי' לא מילה כלל. ופלוגתא היא בפ"ב דמעילה (דף ח:). חטאת העוף שהזה דמה. לפי שהתחיל להקשות ממילוי והזאה, מקשה כמו כן עתה. אבל כמו כן (עתה) היה יכול להקשות ממליקת חטאת שמלקה למטה לשם עולה, דמליקת עולת העוף למעלה, כדאמרי' בזבחים בפרק "קדשי קדשים" (דף סה. ושם): מה הקטרה בראשו של מזבח – אף מליקה. דאי קדשים קלים בדרום הוה עביד להו. ס"ד: משום דלא ליתי למיטעי ולומר שהם קדשי קדשים.

ומיעבר הוא דעבר ושחטינהו בדרום. הא דלא משני הכי לעיל גבי קושיא דחטאת העוף שהזה דמה למטה לשם עולת העוף, פי' בקונטרס: משום דאיכא תרתי, ולא טעי שיעשה הזאה ולמטה. ולפירושו קשה, דא"כ תקשי לו מחטאת בהמה יד] לשם עולה, דאיכא תרתי שינויי כדפרישנא לעיל! ונראה דהשתא חוזר בו משינויא דלעיל דלזבחים ולא לעופות, דאכולהו איכא לשנויי דאמרי' מיעבר עבר.

טו] אלמא קביעותא דמנא לאו כלום הוא. ובפרק בתרא (לקמן דף קד:) תנן: "פירשתי ואיני יודע מה פירשתי" – יביא חמשתן, ומוקי לה בגמרא כר"ש. והיכי אתיא כוותיה דר"ש? הא לר"ש אפי' פירש מחבת והביא מרחשת יצא! ושמא התם בבא לצאת ידי שמים. אי נמי, כגון דאיכא חדא, *דמייתי וקאמר: אם זו נדרתי – תהא לנדרי, ואם לאו – תהא נדבה. לא שנא אמר עלי ולא שנא אמר זו. הקשה הרב ר' יצחק בן הר"ר מאיר: תינח מחבת לשם מרחשת, אלא חריבה לשם בלולה – אמרי: הא בלולה היא, ומיעבר הוא דעבר ועביד לה חריבה. וכן בלולה לשם חריבה! ויש לומר: דבהא לא טעי אינש, שיעשה חריבה בלולה ובלולה חריבה. ועוד י"ל: טז] דניחא בלאו הכי, בין למ"ד מנחה קדושה בלא שמן, בין למ"ד אין מנחה קדושה בלא שמן לקמן, נ"ע. כיון דאיכא שעיר נשיא. ואם עולה זו איל – אמרי: שעיר נשיא הוא, כדאמרינן בסמוך: אמרי דיכרא אוכמא הוא. אמר לשם אשם גזילות לשם אשם מעילות מאי איכא למימר. וא"ת: אכתי אמרי *דאי עבר עבר ומייתי ליה בן שנה. דהאמר בתמורה בפרק "אלו קדשים" (דף יט:): אשם בן שנה והביאו בן שתים, בן שתים והביאו בן שנה – כשירה, אלא שלא עלו לשם חובה! ויש לומר: דרבי שמעון לטעמיה, דאמר התם: כל עצמה אינה קדושה. דהאי צמר והאי שיער. צמר לבן, כדכתיב (ישעיה א): "אם יאדימו כתולע כצמר יהיו". שיער שחור, כדמשמע בריש "המוציא יין" (שבת דף עז:): מאי טעמא עיזי מסגי ברישא והדר אימרי? כברייתו של עולם, ברישא חשוכא והדר נהורא. והיינו דקאמר הכא: אמרי דיכרא אוכמא הוא. ובקונטרס לא פירש כן. כאן

עין משפט נר מצוה

ד א מיי' פ"ה מהל' מעה"ק הל"ב:
ה ב ג מיי' פ"ז מהל' מעה"ק הל"ב:

מסורת הש"ס

האי דקא קמיץ לה למרחשת. נ"ק
זבחים נה.
כר"ש. נ"ק
לקמן קב:
גם זה שם
[זבחים עה:]

[כס"י הגירסא אמר האי במרחשת נדר כי מייתי לה במחבת והאי דקא קמיץ לה למרחשת דמרחשת היא ומעבר כו']

רבינו גרשום מאור הגולה (מכ"י שיטהמקובצת)

אמרי דילמא. חטאת היא כדקאמר והאי דעבד ליה מיצוי למעלה דכבר עשה לה הזאה למטה כדינה ומיצוי חטאת כשר אפי' למעלה דאמר מר במס' זבחים מיצה דמה בכל מקום במזבח כשרה משום דכתיב והנשאר בדם ימצה אל יסוד המזבח אי איכא שירים בדם אחר שהזה ימצה ואי ליכא לא מעכבי וכי היכי דלא מעכבי כפרה הכי נמי כי איתנהו כשרין בכל מקום הילכך לא מינכרא: ומיצוי הוה עביד לה. כעולה ולא הזאה: הכי נמי. דלר"ש הכא מינכרא מילתא אבל ר"ש לא אמר שאין המנחה דומה לעופות שאין דומה לזבחים קאמר: ומקשי ליה מזבחים קדשי קדשים ששחטן כו': אף בדרום. דכתיב אל פתח אהל מועד דמשמע בכל מקום בעזרה: התינח היכא דאייתי כשבה. לחטאת יחיד ושחט לשם עולה דלא מינכרא מילתא דלכשבה יש לה זנב ארוך ומכסה הנקבות ולא מינכרא מילתא אלא שעירת חטאת יחיד זנבה קצר ואין מכסה הנקבות: לאו אדעתייהו דאינשי. למחזי הי זכר והי נקבה ולא מוכחא מילתא: לא פסיקא ליה. דלשם אשם זקן בן שתי שנים שוחטו אלא לשום אשם סתם ואיכא אשם בן שנה ולא מינכרא מילתא: אמר. בפירוש לשם אשם גזילות א) ומפרש דבן שתי שנים הוא מאי איכא למימר הא מינכרא מילתא: דהאי צמר. דאשם כבש הוא ויש לו צמר ולבן הוא ושעיר צמרו שיער הוא ושחור הוא ומינכר דהאי שחור והאי לבן כדאמר במס' שבת [דף עז] מאי טעמא דעיזא מסגי בריש עדרא כברייתו של עולם וכו' לא מינכרא מילתא דסברי דדכרא אוכמא הוא דחזי לאשם: אין הכי נמי. לטעמא דר"ש לירצי דהא מינכרא מילתא. ע"כ מהרגמ"ה:

א) אולי לכוונתו בזה כדי שלא תקשה לפי זה מה שהקשו התוס' בד"ה אמר.

שיטה מקובצת

א] אי הכי מחבת לשם מרחשת נמי אמר האי במרחשת נדר והאי דקא קמיץ לה לשם מרחשת דמרחשת היא ומעבר הוא דעבר ואתייה במחבת: ב] ודילמא זו אמר כדתנן זו להביא: ג] תיבות אלא מעתה נמחק: ד] דהאי זכר והאי נקבה. לא מצי לשנויי מעבר כו' דבהא לא טעו אינשי: ה] פסח ששחטו לשם אשם כו' וא"ת אמאי לא משני כדלעיל אמרי האי אשם והא דמביא בן שנה מעבר כו' וי"ל דבן שנה לשתי שנים לא טעו אינשי א"נ י"ל דר"ש לטעמיה דאמר בפ"ג דתמורה אשם בן שנה והביא בן שתי שנים או בן שתי שנים והביא בן שנה ר"ש אומר כל עצמה אינה קדושה: ו] צמר והאי שיער. עיין תוס' זבחים דף עה ע"ב ד"ה דהאי צמר והאי שיער: ז] וכן באשם. דכתיב במקום אשר ישחטו את העולה וגו': ח] למחבת. והא דקמיץ לשם מרחשת שפיר קמיץ: ט] דאמרי. בפ' המנחות והנסכים הרי זה: י] ואשם גזילות ואשם מעילות בני: יא] במס' פרה. כבשים בני שנה ואילים בני שתים וכולם מיום ליום: יב] הכבשים. או מן האילים: יג] יש להם צמר: יד] לשם עולה. כמו כן מצינו לאשכוחי *) תרתי שינויי חדא דעשאן בדרום וחדא דעביד למעלה לשם עולה דהא הוה ליה למישחטה בצפון למטה ויש דוחין דהא ליכא תרי שינויים בבת אחת אבל מ"מ קשה ממתן דם גופיה דאיכא תרתי שינויים בבת אחת דחטאת בהמה למעלה ובאצבע וי"ל דאה"נ והשתא חוזר בו משינויי דלעיל והוה כמו אלא והא דלא קאמר אלא דאין דרך התלמוד לומר אלא רק כשיש אמורא בינתים תו"ח: טו] אלמא קביעותא דמנא כו' פירוש מה שאדם קובע מנא בפה אין זה קביעות כי הכלי יקבע כשהמנחה בתוכו הקשה הריב"ם תינח כו' וי"ל כו' [עיין תוס' ד"ה ל"ש] עי"ל (אפי') [דאם] אמר לשם בלולה כי עביד לה נמי חריבה לאו כלום הוא דאמרי' התם השמן והסלת והלבונה אינן קדושות זו בלא זו וא"כ לא אמרי דקא עבר לאתויי חולין בעזרה. מיהו איפכא קשה בלולה לשם חריבה מאי מעשיה מוכיחין איכא הא אמרי' חריבה נדר ומעבר הוא דקא עבר ועביד לה בלולה דההוא לא הוי חולין לכך ניחא טפי כתירוץ ראשון מיהו קשה חריבה לשם חריבה מאי איכא למימר כגון מנחת קנאות לשם מנחת חוטא מאי מעשיה מוכיחין איכא וי"ל דמנחת קנאות קמח ומנחת חוטא סלת וגם מעבר הוא דקא עבר לא שייך כאן דבין קמח לסולת לא טעי אינשי. גליון. גליון אחר ור' טוביה מוינא פי' דאה"נ דחריבה לשם חריבה פסולה לר"ש וכל המנחות רוב המנחות קאמר ודוחק הוא דמדקאמר גבי זבחים מאי זבחים רוב זבחים משמע אבל מנחות דוקא נקט כל המנחות אלא נראה דכל המנחות לא איירי כלל אלא אהנך דמפרש בתר הכי. ע"כ גליון אחר: טז] דניחא בלאו הכי. ס"א דאי עביד חריבה בלולה אין בה קדושה כלל כדאמרינן לקמן:

*) אולי נ"ל תרתי שינויי בקדשים קלים גופייהו ששחטן לשם חטאת לחדא ששחטן בדרום וחדא דעביד למטה דהא הוי ליה למשחטה בצפון ולזרוק הדם למעלה וכו'.

עין משפט נר מצוה

ג א מיי' פ"ז מהל' מעה"ק הלכה ט:

א] וּנְדָבָה מִי שָׁרֵי לְשַׁנּוּיֵי בָּהּ? לֵימָא, מַתְנִי' דְּלָא כְּר' שִׁמְעוֹן? ב] *)דְּתַנְיָא, ר' שִׁמְעוֹן אוֹמֵר: כָּל הַמְּנָחוֹת שֶׁנִּקְמְצוּ שֶׁלֹּא לִשְׁמָן – כְּשֵׁירוֹת וְעָלוּ לַבְּעָלִים לְשֵׁם חוֹבָה. שֶׁאֵין הַמְּנָחוֹת דּוֹמוֹת לַזְּבָחִים, שֶׁהַקּוֹמֵץ מַחֲבַת לְשׁוּם מַרְחֶשֶׁת – מַעֲשֶׂיהָ מוֹכִיחִין עָלֶיהָ לְשׁוּם מַחֲבַת, חֲרֵיבָה לְשׁוּם בְּלוּלָה – מַעֲשֶׂיהָ מוֹכִיחִין עָלֶיהָ *לְשׁוּם חֲרֵיבָה; ג] אֲבָל בִּזְבָחִים אֵינוֹ כֵּן, שְׁחִיטָה אַחַת לְכוּלָּן, ד] וּזְרִיקָה אַחַת לְכוּלָּן, וְקַבָּלָה אַחַת לְכוּלָּן. הָנִיחָא לְרַב אַשִׁי, דְּאָמַר: כָּאן בְּקוֹמֵץ מַחֲבַת לְשׁוּם מַרְחֶשֶׁת, כָּאן בְּקוֹמֵץ מִנְחַת מַחֲבַת לְשׁוּם מִנְחַת מַרְחֶשֶׁת, מַתְנִיתִין – מִנְחָה לְשׁוּם מִנְחָה הִיא. אֶלָּא לְרַבָּה וְרָבָא מַאי אִיכָּא לְמֵימַר? וְכִי תֵּימָא, כִּדְקָא מְשַׁנֵּי רַבָּה: כָּאן בְּשִׁינּוּי קֹדֶשׁ, כָּאן בְּשִׁינּוּי בְּעָלִים; הָא מַתְנִיתִין שִׁינּוּי קוֹדֶשׁ הוּא, דְּקָתָנֵי: כֵּיצַד לִשְׁמָן וְשֶׁלֹּא לִשְׁמָן – לְשׁוּם מִנְחַת חוֹטֵא וּלְשׁוּם מִנְחַת נְדָבָה! וְאִי נַמִּי כִּדְקָא מְשַׁנֵּי רָבָא: כָּאן בְּקוֹמֵץ מִנְחָה לְשׁוּם מִנְחָה, כָּאן בְּקוֹמֵץ מִנְחָה לְשׁוּם זֶבַח; הָא מַתְנִיתִין מִנְחָה לְשׁוּם מִנְחָה הִיא, דְּקָתָנֵי: שֶׁלֹּא לִשְׁמָן וְלִשְׁמָן – לְשֵׁם מִנְחַת נְדָבָה לְשֵׁם מִנְחַת חוֹטֵא! אֶלָּא לְרַבָּה וְרָבָא מְחַוּוְּרְתָּא, מַתְנִי' דְּלָא כְּר"ש. וְרָמֵי דְּר"ש אַדְּר"ש. *דְּתַנְיָא, (זבחים יא.) ר' שִׁמְעוֹן אוֹמֵר: "קֹדֶשׁ קָדָשִׁים הִיא כַּחַטָּאת וְכָאָשָׁם" – ה] יֵשׁ מֵהֶן כַּחַטָּאת וְיֵשׁ מֵהֶן כָּאָשָׁם; מִנְחַת חוֹטֵא הֲרֵי הִיא כַּחַטָּאת, לְפִיכָךְ קְמָצָהּ שֶׁלֹּא לִשְׁמָהּ – פְּסוּלָה כַּחַטָּאת, מִנְחַת נְדָבָה הֲרֵי הִיא כָּאָשָׁם, לְפִיכָךְ קְמָצָהּ שֶׁלֹּא לִשְׁמָהּ – כְּשֵׁירָה; וְכָאָשָׁם, ו] מָה אָשָׁם כָּשֵׁר ז] וְאֵינוֹ מְרַצֶּה – אַף מִנְחַת נְדָבָה כְּשֵׁירָה וְאֵינָהּ מְרַצָּה! אָמַר רַבָּה, לָא קַשְׁיָא: כָּאן בְּשִׁינּוּי קוֹדֶשׁ, כָּאן בְּשִׁינּוּי בְּעָלִים. אָמַר לֵיהּ אַבַּיֵי: מִכְּדֵי מַחֲשָׁבָה[א] דְּפָסַל רַחֲמָנָא הֶקֵּישָׁא הִיא, מַה לִּי שִׁינּוּי קוֹדֶשׁ מ"ל שִׁינּוּי בְּעָלִים? א"ל: "מַעֲשֶׂיהָ מוֹכִיחִין" דְּקָאָמַר ר"ש – סְבָרָא הִיא, [ב] דְּר"ש דָּרֵישׁ ח] *טַעְמָא דִּקְרָא; מַחֲשָׁבָה *דְּלָא מִינְכְּרָא – פָּסַל רַחֲמָנָא, ט] מַחֲשָׁבָה דְּמִינְכְּרָא – לָא פָּסַל רַחֲמָנָא. (סי': עוֹלָה מָלַק וּמִיצָּה חַטַּאת הָעוֹף קָדְשֵׁי קָדָשִׁים קַלִּים). י] אֶלָּא מֵעַתָּה, יא]עוֹלַת הָעוֹף שֶׁמְּלָקָהּ לְמַעְלָה מִשּׁוּם חַטַּאת הָעוֹף תְּרַצֶּה; מַעֲשֶׂיהָ מוֹכִיחִין עָלֶיהָ דְּעוֹלַת הָעוֹף הִיא, דְּאִי חַטַּאת הָעוֹף הִיא – לְמַטָּה הָוֵי עָבֵיד לָהּ! אַטּוּ חַטַּאת הָעוֹף לְמַעְלָה מִי לֵיתָא? *הָאָמַר מָר: יב]אמְלִיקָה בְּכָל מָקוֹם בַּמִּזְבֵּחַ כְּשֵׁרָה! עוֹלַת הָעוֹף שֶׁמִּיצָּה דָּמָהּ לְמַעְלָה לְשֵׁם חַטַּאת הָעוֹף תְּרַצֶּה; מַעֲשֶׂיהָ מוֹכִיחִין עָלֶיהָ דְּעוֹלַת הָעוֹף הִיא, דְּאִי חַטַּאת הָעוֹף הִיא – יג] לְמַטָּה הֲוָה עָבֵיד לָהּ [ג] הַזָּאָה!

אָמְרִי

*) לקמן מט. [זבחים ט:] תוספתא פ"א דמנחות [ע"ש]

ונדבה מי שרי לשנויי בה. והכתיב: "אם זבח שלמים קרבנו" (ויקרא ג) – שתהא זביחה לשם שלמים! יד] רבי שמעון אומר כל המנחות כו'. ואפי' מנחת חוטא. שאין המנחות דומות לזבחים. דבזבחים מודינא דלא עלו. מעשיה מוכיחים. שהוא מכוין, דמרחשת עמוקה ומעשיה רוחשים רכין, מחבת צפה ומעשיה קשין, בפרק "כל המנחות באות מצה" טו] (לקמן דף סג.). אבל בזבחים אינו כן. אין להם מעשה מוכיח, הילכך מהני בהו שינוי דלא עלו לשם חובה. מנחת חריבה. דמנחת חוטא (ויקרא ה) ומנחת קנאות, דכתיב בהו (במדבר ה): "לא ישים עליה שמן". בלולה. שאר מנחות. והשתא פליגא מתניתין עליה דר' שמעון בתרתי: חדא – דמתניתין קתני בכל המנחות דלא עלו, וחדא – דקא פסיל תנא דידן מנחת חוטא לגמרי. הניחא לרב אשי. דמתרץ לקמן, כי רמינן דר' שמעון דקאמר בדוכתא אחריתי [ד] (במתניתין) אדרבי שמעון דהכא, ומתרץ להו רב אשי, דהא דאמר ר' שמעון עלו – באומר: "הריני קומץ מחבת לשם מרחשת", דכיון דלא אדכר שמה דמנחה, אלא שמה דמנא – דברי רוח בעלמא נינהו. והא דקאמר ר' שמעון בעלמא דלא עלו – כגון טז] דאידכר שמה דמנחה. איכא לאוקומה מתני' כר' שמעון, [ה] דמתני' דאידכר שמה דמנח', כדמפר': שלא לשמו ולשמו – לשם מנחת נדבה לשם מנחת חוטא. אלא לרבה ולרבא. דמשנו לה בטעמי אחריני כדמפרש לקמן, מאי איכא למימר? וכי תימא. מתני' יז] מיתוקמא כר' שמעון, כדמשני רבה לקמן [ו] יח] לטעמיה דר' שמעון: כאן בשינוי קדש וכאן בשינוי בעלים; הא דאמר רבי שמעון עלו – בשינוי קדש, כגון מנחת מחבת לשם מנחת מרחשת, דמעשיה מוכיחין שהוא מכוין. והא דאמר לא עלו – בשינוי בעלים, כגון שהביאה ראובן וקמצה כהן לשם שמעון, דליכא מעשה מוכיח אי דראובן היא אי דשמעון. והא מתניתין בשינוי קדש מיירי, וקתני דלא עלו. דקתני: כיצד לשמן ושלא לשמן – כגון שקמץ מנחת חוטא לשם מנחת חוטא ולשם נדבה! ואי נמי כדמשני רבא. לטעמא דר' שמעון יט], דהא דאמר עלו – בקומץ מנחת מחבת לשם מנחת מרחשת, משום דכתיב: "וזאת תורת המנחה" (ויקרא ו) – תורה אחת לכל המנחות. והא דקתני לא עלו – בקומץ [ז] מנחה לשם זבח. ולקמן פריך: כ] בקומץ לשם זבח לתכשר נמי, דהא מעשיה מוכיחין עליה קאמר! ומשני לה לקמן (דף ג.). והא דנקט לאקשויי [ח] במתני' משלא לשמן, ה"ה כא] דמצי לאקשויי לשמן ושלא לשמן כדאקשינן לרבה, אלא כי סידרא דמתני' נקיט ואזיל. קדש קדשים היא וגו'. במנחה כתיב, וקרי לה חטאת ואשם, הא כיצד? מנחת חוטא הרי היא כחטאת, דקי"ל (זבחים דף ב.): כל הזבחים שנזבחו שלא לשמן כשרים אלא שלא עלו לבעלים לשם חובה, חוץ מן פסח וחטאת שפסולין לגמרי. ובפ"ק דזבחים מפרש טעמא [ט] דפסח, ולקמן מפרש טעמא דחטאת. ואינו מרצה. לא עלו לשם חובה, דבזבחים ר"ש מודה כדקתני לעיל. וקשיא דר"ש אדרבי שמעון, בין במנחת חוטא ובין במנחת נדבה! כאן בשינוי קדש. כדפרישית לעיל. מכדי מחשבה דפסל רחמנא במנחה הקישא הוא. דאיתקיש רחמנא מנחה לזבחים, כדכתיב (ויקרא ו): "קדש קדשים היא כחטאת וכאשם", מה זבחים פסלה בה מחשבה כדכתיב (שם ז): "המקריב אותו לא יחשב", אף מנחה נמי כב] מה לי שינוי קדש ומה לי שינוי בעלים? מחשבה דלא מינכרא. אם מכוין ואם לאו, פסיל רחמנא, דחשיב לה מחשבה. אבל מחשבה דמינכרא. לכל שהוא מכוין, לא הוי מחשבה [י]. *) הך מחשבה דקדשים הולכת דיבור בפה הוא, כדאמרי' בבבא מציעא (ד' מד.): "על כל דבר פשע" – לחייב על המחשבה כמעשה, דאי לאו מוציאו בפה – מחשבתו כג] למאי נתחייב לה? עולת העוף. נעשית למעלה מחוט הסיקרא כד], כדתניא בת"כ: "ומלק והקטיר ונמצה", מה הקטרה בראשו של מזבח – אף מליקה בראשו של מזבח, ומיצוי נמי בהאי קרא כתיב. וחטאת העוף למטה, והכי מפרש בשחיטת קדשים בפ' "קדשי קדשים" (דף סה.). [יא]אי הכי. כיון דמחשבה הגלויה לכל לא פסלה, עולת העוף כו'. תרצה. תעלה לשם חובה. אלמה תנן בשחיטת קדשים בפ' "קדשי קדשים" (דף סד:) דלא עלתה? מליקה. לחטאת העוף בכל מקום במזבח כשירה, בפ' "קדשי קדשים" (דף סג.), והויא לה מחשבה דלא מינכרא, משום הכי תנן דלא עלתה. עולת העוף. הכשירה במיצוי, דכתיב (ויקרא א): "ונמצה דמו על קיר המזבח". חטאת העוף כה] הזאה תחילה ואח"כ מיצוי, דכתיב: "והזה מדם החטאת וגו' והנשאר בדם ימצה" וגו' (שם ה). למטה הוה עביד לה. כדכתי' (שם): "על קיר", ומפרש בתורת כהנים: זה קיר התחתון. הזאה. אוחז בגוף העוף ומעלה ומוריד בכח, והדם ניתז מעצמו. מיצוי – סוחט בין אצבעותיו כו] ונצוק הדם הולך למרחוק.

אמרי

*) נ"א כל

שחיטה אחת לכולן. לקמן פריך דחלוקים בשחיטתן, דיש בצפון ויש בדרום. והא דלא קתני "הולכה אחת לכולן" – משום דאיירי הכא אליבא דרבי שמעון דלא חייש בהולכה בפ"ק דזבחים (דף יד:), משום דהויא עבודה שאפשר לבטלה, ורבי שמעון דפליג אהילוך בזבח לא איצטריך לפלוגי בהילוך דמנחות (לקמן דף יב.). אבל תימה קצת: אמאי לא פליג בקבלה דמנחות? דאיפשר נמי לבטלה לר"ש, כדלקמן פרק "הקומץ רבה" (דף כו.): מאי טעמא דרבי שמעון? בא לעובדה ביד – עובדה בימין כחטאת, א"כ לא בעו קבלה! זריקה אחת לכולן. ואע"ג דיש במתנה אחת ויש במתן ארבע, פי' בקונטרס, כז] דתנן: אם ניתנו כולן במתנה אחת – כיפר. ומיהו קשה: כח] דהניתנין במתן ד' שנתן לשם ניתנין במתנה אחת לירצו, דמעשיהן מוכיחין כשיתן השניים! וי"ל: דבשעה שנתן הראשונה שלא לשמו עדיין אין מעשיהן מוכיחין עד שיתן האחרון, ובשניה אין מחשבה פוסלת, כדתנן בפ' "בית שמאי" (זבחים דף לו:) דבמתנה אחת כיפר. אבל קשה מחטאת לשם עולה, דחטאת למעלה בקרנות ובאצבע, ועולה למטה ביסוד ובזריקה מן הכלי! ועוד קשה מקבלה, דאשם קבלתו אף בשמאל, וחטאת בימין, ואף לרבי שמעון [יב]בפ"ב דזבחים (דף כד.) ולקמן בפירקין! (דף י.) ונראה דודאי היה יכול להקשות כן לקמן כט].

מנחת חוטא הרי היא כחטאת. אין זה דבר הלמד בהיקש חוזר ומלמד בהיקש. דאע"ג דחטאת ילפי' למצוה משלמים בפ"ק דזבחים (דף ח.), מכל מקום הא כתיב ביה "היא" ל] [יג] לגופיה לעכב. אבל קשה הא דיליף מנחת נדבה מאשם דאינו מרצה, ואשם גופיה משלמים ילפינן בפ"ק דזבחים (שם). וי"ל: דהך דרשא דהכא אסמכתא בעלמא, כדמפרש בזבחים דעיקר קרא לכדר' יהודה בריה דר' חייא [אתי] וילפינן מנחה משלמים בהיקשא ד"זאת התורה".

מכדי מחשבה דפסל רחמנא לא] הקישא הוא. דאע"ג דהקישא ד"כחטאת וכאשם" לאו עיקר, מ"מ אתיא בהקישא ד"זאת התורה", וכיון דהקישא הוא – מה לי שינוי קודש מה לי שינוי בעלים. וא"ת: מה מקשי אביי לרבה? תיקשי ברייתא גופה דמוכחא שיש חילוק,[יד] מדמפרש טעמא – משום דמעשיה מוכיחין! וי"ל: דיכול ליישב הברייתא כהני אמוראי דלקמן. א"נ, קסבר אביי דכיון דשינוי קודש לא פסול משום דמעשיה מוכיחין – הוא הדין שינוי בעלים. דילפינן משלמים כי ה"ג, דמה שלמים לא חלקת לפסול – אף מנחה לא תחלוק להכשיר. דכי ה"ג דריש תנא דבי חזקיה בפ' "אלו נערות" (כתובות דף לה.) גבי מכה אדם ומכה בהמה. והך סברא דלא חלק אשכחן בפרק קמא דזבחים (דף ז.) גבי שלמים.

עולת העוף שמלקה למעלה. קס"ד: אע"ג דכשירה א) כחטאת, מכל מקום אין דרך לעשות למעלה שלא יפול הדם לארץ קודש שיבא למטה למצוה.

מילה

א) נ"ל בחטאת

שיטה מקובצת

א] ונדבה מי שרי לשנויי בה. פי' הא כתיב לא יחשב קרי ביה לא יחשב. תו"ח: ורש"י פי': בע"א א). מהר"פ: ב] דתניא ר"ש אומר כו'. צ"ע ב) רבנן דפליגי עליה דר"ש ואית להו דמנחה טעונה כלי ולית להו הא דרבי יהודה בריה דרבי חייא א"כ היקשא דכחטאת וכאשם למה לי: ג] אבל בזבחים. דלית בהו היכרא בשחיטה איתא שלא לשמה דשחיטה אחת לכולהו ואין מעשיה מוכיחים הילכך לא עלו לבעלים: ד] וקבלה אחת לכולן וזריקה אחת לכולן. ואע"ג דאיכא דטעון מתנה אחת אפ"ה ליכא הכירא דקי"ל כל הניתנין על מזבח החיצון אם נתן מתנה אחת כיפר הילכך מהני בהם שינוי דלא עלו לשם חובה: ה] כחטאת וכאשם. מנחת חוטא [ותיבות יש מהן כחטאת ויש מהן כאשם נמחק וכן הוא בזבחים דף יא.]: ו] מה אשם כשר. כדדריש פ"ק דזבחים [דף י:] דכתיב בחטאת אותה דממעט כל שאר זבחים דכשרות בשלא לשמן: ז] ואינו מרצה. דילפינן לה מהקישא דזאת התורה דאקשיה רחמנא לשלמים דמה שלמים לא עלו אף אשם כן א"נ ממוצא שפתיך תשמור: ח] דר"ש דריש בכל מקום טעמא דקרא: ט] מחשבה דמינכרא לא פסל רחמנא. וכגון שינוי קודש שאם קמץ מנחת נדבה לשם מנחת חוטא הרי מחשבתו ניכרת מתוך מעשיו דמנחת חוטא אינה טעונה שמן ולבונה והוא נותן בה שמן ולבונה וה"נ מנחת מחבת לשם מנחת מרחשת ניכרת מחשבתו הילכך לא פסל רחמנא אבל מחשבה דלא מינכרא אם מכוין אם לאו כגון שינוי בעלים שהביא חטאת ראובן לשם שמעון ולא קים לב"ע אם מכוין הוא פסל רחמנא: י] אלא מעתה. כיון דאמרת דמחשבה דמינכרא לא פסל רחמנא עולת העוף שמלקה כו' וא"ת תקשי ליה הכי עולת העוף שמלקה לשם חטאת העוף ובדליל תרצה מעשיה מוכיחין עליה דמכוין דאי חטאת העוף היא ג) לא בעי הבדלה וי"ל דבהבדלה לאו אדעתייהו דאינשי פי' אינן מוכיחין [בין] מלק סימן אחד למלק ב' סימנין. תו"ח: יא] עולת העוף שמלקה למעלה וכו'. דעולת העוף למעלה מחוט הסיקרא וחטאת העוף למטה והסימן ע"ן ע"ן עולה למעלה וט"ת ט"ת חטאת למטה עולה למעלה דכתיב ומלק והקטיר מה הקטרה בראשו של מזבח אף מליקה וכו'. מהר"פ: יב] מליקה בכל מקום כו'. תימה ד) תקשי ליה חטאת העוף שמלקה למטה לשם עולת העוף תרצה דמעשיה מוכיחין עליה דחטאת העוף היא דאי עולת העוף למעלה הוה עביד ליה והשתא לא שייך לשנויי מליקה מכל מקום במזבח כשירה דהא עולת העוף פסולה למטה ואחטאת העוף לבד הוא דקאמר מליקה בכל מקום במזבח ולמסקנא ניחא הכל אלא רוב זבחים קאמר: ל] ביה היא בגופיה לעכב: לא] מהיקשא הוא [וכן הגירסא בגמרא]:

כשרה וי"ל דלפי המסקנא דקאמר ה"נ לפי שאין המנחות דומה לזבחים קאמר ולא לעופות ניחא: יג] למטה הוה עביד לה. והזאה הוה עביד לה קודם. כדאמר בפרק קדשי קדשים [דף סד] דבחטאת העוף כתיב [והזה וגומ' על קיר המזבח] והנשאר בדם ימצה אל יסוד המזבח קיר שהשירים שלו מתמצין ליסוד ואיזה זה קיר התחתון: יד] לשם שלמים. ותו דהא אמרי' בת"כ עולה לשם עולה אשם לשם אשם ריח לשם ריח כיצד נשחט שלא לשמי אסור לשנות בו: טו] מצה (דף סג.) והואיל ומעשיה מוכיחין לא מהניא מחשבה זה דהואיל דמינכרא דלא קושטא קאמר כקמיצה לשמה דמי: הס"ד ומה"ד מנחת חריבה. דמנחת חוטא ומנחת קנאות דכתיב בהו לא ישים עליה שמן הס"ד ומה"ד בלולה. שאר מנחות: הס"ד ומה"ד אבל בזבחים אינו כן. אין להם מעשה מוכיח. הילכך מהני בהו שינוי דלא עלו לשם חובה והשתא פליגא כו': טז] דאידכר שמה דמנחה. כגון קומץ מנחת מחבת לשם מנחת מרחשת דבמנחה דפסלה בה מחשבה קא מחשב איכא לאוקמא כו': יז] מתניתין נמי מתוקמא: יח] רבה לקמן. אדר' שמעון: יט] דר"ש לקמן דהא דאמר: כ] ולקמן פריך. והא תנא מפני שמעשיה מוכיחין קאמר ומנחה לשם זבח נמי לתכשר: כא] דמצי לאקשויי מלשמן ושלא לשמן. וז"ל תו"ח ה"נ ה"מ לאתויי רישא שהביא כבר אלא שכן עדיפא ליה לאתויי מה שלא הביא: כב] מה לי שינוי קודש ומה לי שינוי בעלים. הא אשכחנא גבי זבחים בפ"ק דשחיטת קדשים דפסלה בהו מחשבה בין בשינוי קודש בין בשינוי בעלים דכתיב אם האכל יאכל וגומ': כג] למאי נחייב ליה. עיין תוס' זבחים [ד"ה כל הזבחים] דף ב' ע"א: כד] מחוט הסיקרא. החוגר באמצע המזבח כדתניא: כה] חטאת העוף מזה תחילה ואח"כ ממצה דכתיב: כו] סוחט בין אצבעותיו. בית השחיטה ונצוק: כז] פי' בקונטרס. דאפ"ה ליכא היכרא דתנן: כח] קשה. גליון דהא תינח הכא דתנן ניתנין במתנה אחת לשם מתן ארבע דלא מינכר שלא עשה מחשבתו דנוכל לומר ודאי ניתנין לשם מתן ד' והא שלא נתן אלא מתנה אחת ומה בכך הלא כל הניתנין כו' אבל הניתנין מתן ד' לשם מתן אחת ונתן מתן ארבע אמאי לא עלו הלא מעשיו מוכיחין דודאי פסולות דקא עבר על בל תוסיף וי"ל דאמרי' מיד שנתן מתנה אחת אי תעברא מחשבתו ומה שנתן מכאן ואילך מיא בעלמא קא זריק ועי"ל דמ"מ במתנה ראשונה שהוא מחשב בה אין מעשיה מוכיחין דאמרי' לעולם ניתנין במתנה אחת היא ואי משום מתנות דבתר הכי כיון שאינן גורמות פסול המחשבה לא קרינן בה מעשיה מוכיחין כיון דאינן מוכיחין בשעת פיסול המחשבה דהיינו במתנה ראשונה שהיא מעכבת אבל באינך אפי' מחשב בהו לא מידי קא עביד. תו"ה: כט] להקשות כן לקמן.

א) ועי' ברש"י בזבחים דף ב ע"ב דפירש ג"כ דנפק"ל מדכתיב לא יחשב ע"ש. ב) לכאורה לא שייך קושיא זו אלדברי ר"ש דהכא רק לקמן דף כו ע"א במשנה דשלא בכלי שרת פסולה וצ"ע ועי' תוס' כאן ד"ה מנחת ועיל ע"א ד"ה כל. ג) ואף לרא ב"ש בזבחים ד' סה דס"ל דמבדילין בחטאת העוף מ"מ לכתחילה לא בעי הבדלה וכמש"כ שם. ד) עי' בתוס' לקמן בסמוך דף ג ד"ה חטאת העוף.

הגהות צ"ק [א] דפסלה: [ב] ור"ש: [ג] והזאה הוה עביד לה אמרי כו': [ד] כמתני': [ה] דמתני' איירי לאידכר: [ו] אליביה דר"ש: [ז] נ"א מנחת מחבת או מנחת מרחשת לשם: [ח] ממתני' כו' לאקשויי מלשמן כו': [ט] דפסח וחטאת ולקמן מפרש טעמא דמנחה הס"ד:

כל המנחות שֶׁנִּקְמְצוּ שֶׁלֹּא לִשְׁמָן. כְּגוֹן שֶׁהִתְנַדֵּב מִנְחַת מַרְחֶשֶׁת וֶהֱבִיאָהּ, וּקְמָצָהּ הַכֹּהֵן וְאָמַר: "הֲרֵינִי קוֹמֵץ לְשֵׁם מַחֲבַת" ד]. כְּשֵׁרוֹת. וְקוּמְצָן יִקְטַר, וּשְׁיָרֵיהֶן נֶאֱכָלִין. אֶלָּא שֶׁלֹּא עָלוּ לַבְּעָלִים לְשֵׁם חוֹבָה. דְּלֹא יָצָא יְדֵי נִדְרוֹ, וְצָרִיךְ לְהָבִיא אַחֶרֶת לְשֵׁם מַרְחֶשֶׁת. חוּץ מִמִּנְחַת חוֹטֵא. כְּגוֹן הַהִיא דְּמִטַּמֵּא מִקְדָּשׁ דִּכְתִיב בְּ"וַיִּקְרָא": תורה אור (ה) "וְאִם לֹא תַשִּׂיג יָדוֹ לִשְׁתֵּי תוֹרִים" וגו'. וּמִנְחַת קְנָאוֹת. מִנְחַת סוֹטָה, שֶׁאִם קְמָצָן שֶׁלֹּא לִשְׁמָן כְּגוֹן לְשֵׁם נְדָבָה, אוֹ נָתַן בִּכְלִי אֶת הַקּוֹמֶץ שֶׁלֹּא לִשְׁמָן, אוֹ הוֹלִיךְ אוֹ הִקְטִיר שֶׁלֹּא לִשְׁמָן, אוֹ חִישֵּׁב בְּאַחַת מֵעֲבוֹדוֹת הַלָּלוּ: "הֲרֵינִי עוֹבֵד לִשְׁמוֹ וְשֶׁלֹּא לִשְׁמוֹ". אוֹ שֶׁלֹּא לִשְׁמוֹ וְלִשְׁמוֹ. בְּאֵלּוּ שְׁתֵּי מְנָחוֹת פְּסוּלִין וְאֵין שְׁיָרֵיהֶן נֶאֱכָלִין, וְטַעְמָא מְפָרֵשׁ בַּגְּמָ'. וְהָא דִּתְנָא "אוֹ שֶׁלֹּא לִשְׁמוֹ וְלִשְׁמוֹ" – דְּלָא תֵּימָא לִשְׁמוֹ וְשֶׁלֹּא לִשְׁמוֹ הוּא דִּפְסוּלָה, דְּתָפֵיס לָשׁוֹן אַחֲרוֹן, אֲבָל שֶׁלֹּא לִשְׁמוֹ וְלִשְׁמוֹ – לֹא ה], קמ"ל דְּאַף ו] *בִּתְחִלַּת דְּבָרָיו אָדָם נִתְפָּס אִית לָן. גמ' מִדְּקָתָנֵי "אֶלָּא" מַשְׁמַע דְּכָל דִּינָהּ כְּמִנְחָה כְּשֵׁירָה אֶלָּא זֶה בִּלְבַד. וְאָסוּר לְשַׁנּוֹיֵי. בָּהּ שִׁינּוּי אַחֵר, כְּגוֹן אִם עָבַר וּקְמָצָהּ שֶׁלֹּא לִשְׁמָהּ – אָסוּר לָתֵת קוֹמֶץ בִּכְלִי שֶׁלֹּא לִשְׁמָהּ. נְדָבָה. בִּתְמִיָּה, וְהָא נֶדֶר הוּא דִּכְתִיב "כַּאֲשֶׁר נָדַרְתָּ" ז] (דברים כג)! אִם כְּמָה שֶׁנָּדַרְתָּ עָשִׂיתָ. לִשְׁמָהּ – יְהֵא נֶדֶר, כְּלוֹמַר יָצָאתָ יְדֵי נִדְרְךָ. וְאִם לָאו – יְהֵא נְדָבָה, וְיָבִיא אַחֶרֶת לְנִדְרוֹ. וּנְדָבָה

כָּל

א הַמְּנָחוֹת שֶׁנִּקְמְצוּ שֶׁלֹּא לִשְׁמָן – כְּשֵׁירוֹת, אֶלָּא שֶׁלֹּא עָלוּ לַבְּעָלִים לְשֵׁם חוֹבָה, חוּץ ב מִמִּנְחַת חוֹטֵא וּמִנְחַת קְנָאוֹת. א] מִנְחַת חוֹטֵא וּמִנְחַת קְנָאוֹת שֶׁקְּמָצָן שֶׁלֹּא לִשְׁמָן, נָתַן בַּכְּלִי וְהִלֵּךְ וְהִקְטִיר שֶׁלֹּא לִשְׁמָן, אוֹ לִשְׁמָן וְשֶׁלֹּא לִשְׁמָן, אוֹ שֶׁלֹּא לִשְׁמָן וְלִשְׁמָן – פְּסוּלוֹת. כֵּיצַד לִשְׁמָן וְשֶׁלֹּא לִשְׁמָן – לְשֵׁם מִנְחַת חוֹטֵא וּלְשֵׁם מִנְחַת נְדָבָה, שֶׁלֹּא לִשְׁמָן וְלִשְׁמָן – לְשֵׁם מִנְחַת נְדָבָה וּלְשֵׁם מִנְחַת חוֹטֵא.§ גמ' ב] *לָמָּה לִי לְמִיתְנָא "אֶלָּא"? לִיתְנֵי: וְלֹא עָלוּ לַבְּעָלִים לְשֵׁם חוֹבָה! הָא קמ"ל: לַבְּעָלִים הוּא דְּלֹא עָלוּ לְשׁוּם חוֹבָה, הָא מִנְחָה גּוּפָהּ כְּשֵׁרָה ג וְאָסוּר לְשַׁנּוֹיֵי. כִּדְרָבָא, *דְּאָמַר רָבָא: עוֹלָה שֶׁשְּׁחָטָהּ שֶׁלֹּא לִשְׁמָהּ – אָסוּר לִזְרוֹק דָּמָהּ שֶׁלֹּא לִשְׁמָהּ; *אִיבָּעֵית אֵימָא סְבָרָא, וְאִיבָּעֵית אֵימָא קְרָא. אִיבָּעֵית אֵימָא סְבָרָא: מִשּׁוּם דְּמְשַׁנֵּי בָּהּ, כָּל הָנֵי לִישַׁנֵּי בָּהּ וְנֵיזִיל?! וְאִיבָּעֵית אֵימָא קְרָא: °"מוֹצָא שְׂפָתֶיךָ תִּשְׁמוֹר וְעָשִׂיתָ כַּאֲשֶׁר נָדַרְתָּ לַיי' אֱלֹהֶיךָ נְדָבָה"; *נְדָבָה? נֶדֶר הוּא! ג] קָרֵי לֵיהּ נֶדֶר וְקָרֵי לֵיהּ נְדָבָה? אֶלָּא, אִם כְּמָה שֶׁנָּדַרְתָּ עָשִׂיתָ – יְהֵא נֶדֶר, וְאִם לָאו – יְהֵא נְדָבָה; וּנְדָבָה

כל המנחות שנקמצו שלא לשמן כשירות אלא שלא עלו לבעלים כו'. עבודה קמייתא נקט, וה"ה נתינה בכלי והולכה והקטרה כדקתני סיפא. ד' עבודות יש בקומץ כנגד ד' עבודות שיש בדם, כדאמרינן לקמן בפ"ב (ד' טו.) ובפ"ק דזבחים (ד' ד.). ובאותן ד' עבודות פסלה מחשבה שלא לשמן, ומחשבת פיגול דחוץ לזמנו וחוץ למקומו, אבל בתנופה והגשה אין מחשבה פוסלת אע"ג דבעי כהונה. ובפ"ק דזבחים (דף ד:) ילפינן מקראי דמחשבה פוסלת בשלמים בד' עבודות, ושאר זבחים ילפינן משלמים בהיקשא ד"זאת התורה" ומקרא ד"מוצא שפתיך" ומצריך להו. ונראה דלמנחות נמי ילפינן למצוה משלמים מההיא היקשא גופה כמו בזבחים, דמדרשא דר' שמעון דדריש בגמרא בסמוך: "קדש קדשים היא כחטאת וכאשם" – מנחת חוטא הרי היא כחטאת מנחת נדבה הרי היא כאשם, לא מצינן למילף, דלא עיקר דרשא היא, כדאמרינן בפ"ק דזבחים (דף יא.) °דעיקר קרא לכדר' יהודה בריה דרבי חייא: * ח] בא לעבודה ביד – עבודה בימין כחטאת ט] כו'. ולעכב במנחת חוטא מפרש התם – מדכתיב בה "היא" כמו בחטאת. וכן מפרש נמי בפירקין (דף ד.) דגמר מנחת חוטא ומנחת קנאות *דפוסלות שלא לשמן, דכתיב בהו "היא". ואם תאמר: ועופות דבעו לשמן, כדאמרינן בגמרא וכדתנן בזבחים בפ' "חטאת העוף" (דף סו:), מנלן? דאי מהיקשא ד"זאת התורה" – אי אפשר לומר כן, לפירוש הקונט' דפ"ק דחולין (דף כב.) גבי עולת העוף דכתיב: "ואת השני יעשה עולה כמשפט", דדריש התם: כמשפט חטאת בהמה, דאינו בא אלא מן החולין וביום ובידו הימנית. שהקשה שם הקונטרס דמהיקשא ד"זאת התורה" נפקא, דדריש מיניה בסוף "התודה" (לקמן דף פג.): מה חטאת אינו בא אלא מן החולין – אף כל דבר שבחובה אינה באה אלא מן החולין. *ופירש בקונטרס *(דמתוך כך) דעוף לא כתב בההוא קרא, ולא אמרינן אלא בקרבן בהמה! ואין לתרץ דילפינן עופות מזבחים לענין לשמן, דאיכא למיפרך: מה לזבחים שכן טעונין כלים, דכי האי גונא פריך בפ' "איזהו מקומן" (זבחים דף מח:) גבי לפון. ומיהו, לפירוש הקונטרס דחולין קשה: דעל כרחיך עופות כתיבי בקרא ד"זאת התורה", י] דמסיק התם דביום דחטאת העוף מ"ביום צוותו" נפקא דכתיב בתר היקשא ד"זאת התורה". וכן במגילה בפ' "הקורא למפרע" (דף כ:) גבי כל היום כשר למליקה, דדריש בגמרא מ"ביום צוותו". ובפ' קמא דזבחים (דף ז:) גמרא חוץ מן הפסח, דריש פסח לענין לשמן למצוה מדאיתקוש לשלמים, מדכתיב "ביום צוותו להקריב את קרבניהם" – זה בכור מעשר ופסח. א"כ, כיון דעופות נמי מ"ביום צוותו" נפקי שמע מינה דעופות נמי אתיין בהיקשא ד"זאת התורה", והוא הדין לענין שלא לשמן למצוה, מדאיתקוש לשלמים, ולעכב בחטאת העוף דדרשינן בתורת כהנים מדכתיב "היא". והא דאיצטריך לן "כמשפט" בפ' קמא דחולין (דף כב.) יש לפרש אליבא דר' אליעזר דפ' "התודה" (לקמן דף פג:) דלית ליה היקשא ד"זאת התורה". וצ"ע, דההיא דרשא דמייתי בפ"ק דחולין (דף כב.) דמשלו ולא משל ציבור ולא משל מעשר דריש לה בפרק "התודה" (לקמן דף פג.) אליבא דר' עקיבא ולא כר' אליעזר! ועוד, היכי ילפינן עופות מחטאת בהמה? הא חטאת בהמה דקאמר על כרחיך לאו *מפרו של אהרן קאי, דמה ענייני לשם, אלא מחטאת בהמה דלעיל מיניה קאי שמביא בעשירות, שזו באה אליפין לה כדפי' שם בקונטרס. וחטאת בהמה מפרו של אהרן ילפא מדאיקרי חטאת, והיינו למד מן הלמד! ועוד קשה: למה לי למדרש התם דפרו של אהרן: משלו ולא משל מעשר? תיפוק לי' כדאמרינן בסיפרי בפרשת "ראה אנכי" בענין דממעט עולות, משום דכתיב גבי מעשר "ואכלת", ופרו של אהרן לשריפה קאי! ומיהו בזה י"ל: הא דכתיב "אשר לו" עיקר אתא למידרש: משלו ולא משל ציבור. *ונראה לפרש דמיתורא דרשינן כל חטאות, דכתיב בפרו של אהרן "את פר החטאת אשר לו", דהוה מצי למכתב: יא] את הפר אשר לו, וכתיב "החטאת", למימרא דכל חטאות, בין חטאת בהמה בין חטאת העוף – משלו, דהיינו מן החולין ולא משל מעשר. והשתא ניחא דלא הוי היקש. ומיהו, אכתי קשה: למה לי "כמשפט" לענין חולין גבי עולת העוף? תיפוק ליה מדרשא דסיפרי, דהא אינה נאכלת! וי"ל: דס"ד דאתא "והקריבו" לחלק לענין חולין, כדדריש התם דחלק הכתוב בין חטאת העוף לעולת העוף מדכתיב "והקריבו", *מתוך כך ניחא ליה דלא הוה ילפינן לה מהקישא ד"זאת התורה" – משום דכתיב "והקריבו". וא"ת: אם כן, מאי פריך התם: ביום מ"ביום צוותו" נפקא? דילמא הייתי מחלק מ"והקריבו"! וי"ל: ד"ביום צותו" כתיב על "זאת התורה לעולה", דמשמע כל עולות. ולוג שמן של מצורע דבעי לשמן, כדתניא לקמן ב"הקומץ רבה" (דף כז:) *(גמר) שבע הזאות שבפרה (דקתני בברייתא) ושבפנים ושבמצורע שלא לשמן פסולות, פי' להרצות כדמסיק, יש לפרש דנפיק מהקישא ד"זאת התורה", ד"ביום צוותו את בני ישראל להקריב את קרבניהם" (ויקרא ז) איירי נמי בלוג שמן של מצורע דאיקרי קרבן כדדרשינן בפ' "ואלו מנחות" (לקמן ד' עג.): "לכל קרבנם" – לרבות לוג שמן של מצורע. אבל אין לתרץ דהוי בכלל אשם מצורע, דאם כן יפסל שלא לשמו לר' אליעזר כאשם, ולקמן ב"הקומץ רבה" (דף כח.) מסקינן דלא מיפסיל משום דהוי למד בהיקש, ודבר הלמד בהיקש אין חוזר ומלמד בהיקש. ומהא דדריש במגילה (דף כ:) מליקה מ"ביום צוותו", ושחיטה מ"ביום זבחכם", ולא דריש שחיטה מ"ביום צוותו" כמליקה – משום דשחיטה לאו עבודה היא. שלא לשמן. לכאורה משמע דאיירי בשינוי קודש, כדמפרש בסיפא: לשם מנחת חוטא לשם מנחת נדבה, והוא הדין שנוי בעלים כדמוכח בגמרא בפ"ק דזבחים (דף ד.). ושמא פשיטא ליה להתלמוד בכל דוכתי דשנוי בעלים כשנוי קדש, כתירוצו של רבה דמשני בגמרא: כאן בשנוי קדש, כאן בשנוי בעלים. אי נמי, ממתני' דפרק "בית שמאי" (זבחים דף מו:): לשם ששה דברים הזבח נזבח, לשם זבח לשם זובח. לשמן ושלא לשמן. בפ"ק דזבחים (דף ג:) מסקינן דסתמן כלשמן יב]קאמר. קרי ליה נדר וקרי ליה נדבה. משמע מהכא דכל היכא דכתיב "נדר" – נדר דוקא, ונדבה – נדבה דווקא. וכן בפ"ק דר"ה (דף ו.) לענין בל תאחר. ואפילו לר"מ דפ"ק דחולין (דף ב. ושם: ד"ה אבל) דדריש: "טוב אשר לא תדור" – טוב מזה ומזה שאינו *)נודב כל עיקר, אלמא קרי לנדבה נדר – שאני הכא דדריש מדשני קרא בדיבוריה. אי נמי, בחולין דריש, דכיון דחייש קרא לתקלה – לא שנא נדר ולא שנא נדבה, דבתרוייהו איכא למיחש. אי נמי, משום דנדר נפקא לן מ"כי תחדל", שמע מינה ד"טוב אשר לא תדור" לנדבה אתא. ואם לאו יהא נדבה. אע"ג דבפ"ק דראש השנה (דף ו.) דריש ליה לענין בל תאחר דלא שייך לאחר שחיטה, הכא דריש מפשטיה דקרא, דמשמע דקרי ליה לנדר נדבה.

שחיטה

*) נ"א נודר

א ב מיי' פט"ו מהל' פסולי המוקדשים הלכה כ: ב ג מיי' שם הל"ג:

הוא דאתיא. נ"ק

נ"ל לפסלן

דמתוך דעוף לא כתב בהאי קרא לא משמע ליה מההיא היקישא אלא קרבנות בהמה כו' כנ"ל. נ"ק

נ"ל בגמר דבריו ר"ל דאף בגמר וכ"ש בתחלת דיבוריה וכ"ה בכ"ש פסחים סג ע"א ד"ה אלא לאו. נ"ק

זבחים ב.

ג"ז שם

[ברכות ז: וש"נ]

דברים כג

[זבחים ב. ז:]

נ"ל ומתוך כך פי' הקונט'

אפרו כו' אלא מחטאת כו'. נ"ק

נ"ל ונראה לומר דמיתורא כו'

דמתוך כך ניחא לי. נ"ק

גבי. נ"ק

גליון הש"ס

תום' ד"ה כל וכו' לעיקר קרא לכדר' יהודה כו'. ק"ל הא למה לי ק"ל דזרק בשמאל פסול בכל הקדשים ל"ש למדרש לכל הך דרשא דר"י בריה דר"ח אם בא לעבודה בכלי בשמאל דהא גם באשם פסול בשמאל ובזבחים מסקינן ה"נ לר"ש אבל לדידן ע"כ הקרא לענין שלא לשמה דמנחת חוטא כחטאת ומנחת נדבה כאשם וצ"ע:

שיטה מקובצת

א] מנחת חוטא. הכתובה בפרשת ויקרא דהיינו אכילת קודש וכניסת מקדש בטומאה ושמיעת קול וביטוי שפתים דמייתי עשירית האיפה והיא נקראת מנחת חוטא ואין בה לא שמן ולא לבונה: ב] כל המנחות שנקמצו שלא לשמן כשרות. למה לי למתני אלא. פי' דהא אמרינן לעולם ישנה אדם דרך קצרה א"כ למה לי למיתנא אלא דלישנא דאלא משמע דיש בהן כשרות הרבה ואין בהם משום פסול אלא שלא עלו ואיזה כשרות יש אלא שהקומץ נקטר והשירים נאכלין. ומשני דאסור לשנות בהן. תוס' מהר"פ: ג] קרי לה נדר וקרי לה נדבה. ס"א אינו א): אלא אם כמה שנדרת. וה"פ דקרא אם מוצא שפתיך תשמור ועשית מוצא שפתיך אז יהא ממש כמו שנדרת ואם לאו לה' אלהיך נדבה. תוס' חיצונית: ד] לשם מחבת. וה"ה שינוי בעלים כגון מנחת ראובן לשם מנחת שמעון. תוס': ה] ולשמו לא. עיין לקמן רש"י דף ק ע"ב: ו] קמ"ל דאף בגמר דבריו אדם נתפס אית לן הילכך איצטריך למתני הני תרי בבי: ז] נדרת. אלא מדלא כתיב תשמור כאשר נדרת אלא ועשית כאשר נדרת משמע הכי אם כמה שנדרת עשית לשמה יהא נדר כלומר יצאת ידי נדרך ואם לאו יהא נדבה ויביא אחרת לנדרו. אלמא מדמי לנדבה האי שנשחט שלא לשמו וכיון דנדבה היא אסור לשנויי בה: ח] בריה דרבי חייא הוא דאתא בא לעבודה: ט] כחטאת כו'. ועוד דלקמן בפרקין [דף ד.] אמרינן בשלמא מנחת חוטא חטאת קרייה רחמנא אלמא דכחטאת וכאשם אין זה עיקר דרשא. מהר"פ: י] דזאת התורה לעולה ולמנחה ולחטאת וגו' דמיירי בין בהמה בין עוף: יא] את הפר אשר לו. עיין תוס' חולין דף כ"א ע"א [ד"ה כמשפט]: יב] דסתמא כלשמן דמי. הס"ד:

א) וכן בריש זבחים דף ב ליתא לתיבות קרי ליה נדר וקרי ליה נדבה ע"ש.

Please note that the number ranges that appear at the bottom of each daf of the Vilna pages indicate the corresponding pages of the Koren Talmud Bavli translation and commentary.

תלמוד בבלי

הוצאת קוֹרֵן ירושלים

— מהדורת נאה —

מנחות א

COMMENTARY BY

Rabbi Adin Even-Israel Steinsaltz

EDITOR-IN-CHIEF

Rabbi Dr Tzvi Hersh Weinreb

EXECUTIVE EDITOR

Rabbi Joshua Schreier

•

SHEFA FOUNDATION
KOREN PUBLISHERS JERUSALEM

תלמוד בבלי

— מהדורת נאה —

מנחות א

Shefa

ירושלים
KOREN